Current Law

Year Book

2016

VOLUME TWO

Current Law
Year Book

2016

Being a Comprehensive Statement of the Law of 2016

SENIOR EDITOR
JAMES AIDOO-BAIDOE BA (Hons) Law; M.Sc (Wales)

SWEET & MAXWELL EDITORIAL TEAM
CASES DEPARTMENT

SWEET & MAXWELL

THOMSON REUTERS

This volume should be cited as [2016] C.L.Y.

The 2016 Year Book is published in two volumes.

Published in 2017 by Thomson Reuters (Professional) UK Limited, trading as Sweet & Maxwell. Registered in England & Wales, Company No.1679046. Registered Office and address for service: 5 Canada Square, Canary Wharf, London, E14 5AQ.

For further information on our products and services, visit: http://www.sweetandmaxwell.co.uk.

Computerset by Sweet & Maxwell. Printed and bound by CPI Group (UK) Ltd, Croydon, CR0 4YY.

No natural forests were destroyed to make this product: only farmed timber was used and replanted.

A CIP catalogue record for this book is available from the British Library.

The index has been prepared using Sweet & Maxwell's Legal Taxonomy. Please send any suggestions to sweetandmaxwell.taxonomy@tr.com.

Orders to: Orders by email to: TRLUKI.orders@thomsonreuters.com.

Copies of cases from the *Current Law Year Book*, and other articles, cases and related materials, can be obtained from DocDel at Sweet & Maxwell's Yorkshire office. Current rates are: £7.50 + copyright charge + VAT per item for orders by post, DX and email. Fax delivery is guaranteed within 15 minutes of request and is charged at an additional £1.25 per page (£2.35 per page outside the UK). For full details, and how to order, please contact DocDel on Tel: 01422 888 019. Fax: 01422 888 001. Email: trluki.admincentral@thomsonreuters.com. Go to: http://www.sweetandmaxwell.co.uk/our-businesses/docdel.aspx. Please note that all other enquiries should be directed to Customer Support (Email: TRLUKI.cs@thomsonreuters.com; Tel: 0345 600 9355).

ISBN 978-0-414-05975-7

PREFACE

The *Current Law Year Book* 2016 supersedes the issues of the *Current Law Monthly Digest* for 2016 and covers the law from January 1 to December 31 of that year.

Jurisdiction

The text of the *Current Law Year Book* 2016 is divided into three sections respectively: UK, England and Wales and EU, Northern Ireland and Scotland. The European material comprises cases appearing before the Court of First Instance and European Court of Justice, which are published in the reports series and newspapers.

Cases

The *Current Law Year Book* includes digests of cases published in over 90 reports series, journals, *The Times* newspaper, transcripts and ex relatione contributions from barristers and solicitors. A number of reports concerning damages awards in personal injury cases in England and Wales appear under the subject heading PERSONAL INJURY and are collated in tabular form at the beginning of Volume 1.

The editors thank those barristers and solicitors who have submitted case reports, many of which demonstrate developments in county court litigation. Whilst all reasonable care is taken in the preparation of the digests, it is not possible to guarantee the accuracy of each digest, particularly those cases ex relatione which are not taken from an authorised judgment.

An alphabetical Table of Cases digested in the 2016 Year Book appears at the beginning of Volume 1. For more details please refer to the *Current Law Case Citator* series for the years 1947–1976, 1977–1997, 1998–2001, 2002–2004, 2005, 2006, 2007, 2008 2009, 2010, 2011, 2012, 2013, 2014, 2015 and 2016.

Legislation

All public and private Acts of Parliament published in 2016 are abstracted and indexed. All Statutory Instruments, Scottish Statutory Instruments and Statutory Rules of Northern Ireland are abstracted. Cumulative tables of Statutory Instruments, arranged alphabetically, numerically and by subject are published in Volume 1. Cumulative tables of Statutory Rules of Northern Ireland arranged alphabetically, numerically and by subject are also published in Volume 1.

The *Current Law Legislation Citator 2016* appears as a separate bound volume and forms part of the series of bound volumes for the years 1989–1995, 1996–1999 and 2000–2001, 2002–2004, 2005, 2006, 2007, 2008, 2009, 2010, 2011, 2012, 2013, 2014, 2015 and 2016.

Index

The subject matter index is closely associated with the Sweet & Maxwell Legal Taxonomy. The 30-year Index from 1947–1976 may be found in the 1976 *Current Law Year Book.* The Scottish Index for the years 1972–1986 may be found in the *Scottish 1986 Year Book.* Scottish material prior to 1972 can be found in the *Scottish Current Law Year Book Master Volumes*, published in 1956, 1961, 1966 and 1971.

March 2017

CONTENTS

VOLUME 1

VOLUME 2

THE LAW OF 2016 DIGESTED UNDER TITLES:
Note: (NI) denotes the Northern Ireland section and (S) the Scottish section.

VOLUME 1

VOLUME 2

DIGEST HEADINGS IN USE

Accountancy
Administration of justice
Administrative law
Agency
Agriculture
Animals
Arbitration
Armed forces
Arts and culture
Aviation
Banking and finance
Charities
Civil evidence
Civil procedure
Commercial law
Company law
Competition law
Conflict of laws
Constitutional law
Construction law
Consumer law
Contracts
Criminal evidence
Criminal law
Criminal procedure
Customs
Damages
Defamation
Dispute resolution
Ecclesiastical law
Economics
Education
Electoral process
Employment
Energy
Environment
Environmental health
Equity
European Union
Extradition
Family law
Financial regulation
Fisheries
Food
Forestry
Government administration
Health
Health and safety at work
Heritable property
Highways
Hospitality and leisure
Housing
Human rights
Immigration
Industry
Information technology
Insolvency
Insurance
Intellectual property
International law
International trade
Jurisprudence
Landlord and tenant
Legal advice and funding
Legal methodology
Legal profession
Legal systems
Legislation
Libraries
Licensing
Local government
Media and entertainment
Mental health
Mining
Moveable property
Negligence
Nuisance
Partnerships
Peerages and dignities
Penology and criminology
Pensions
Personal injury
Personal property
Planning
Police
Postal services
Prescription
Professions
Public procurement
Rates
Real property
Reparation
Restitution
Rights in security
Road traffic
Sale of goods
Science
Sentencing
Shipping
Social security
Social welfare
Sport
Succession
Tax
Telecommunications
Torts
Transport
Trusts
Unjustified enrichment
Utilities
VAT
Water law

CURRENT LAW
YEAR BOOK 2016

ENGLAND & WALES

INSURANCE

1256 **Business transfer schemes–Payment protection insurance–Inclusion of liability for misselling in transfer**

[Financial Services and Markets Act 2000 (c.8) Pt VII]

The court had to determine whether any mis-selling liabilities of the claimant insurer had been transferred to the first defendant. From 1990 until 2004, the claimant had sold creditor insurance policies. As part of that insurance portfolio, it sold payment protection insurance (PPI) policies through third-party agents. Among them was Next Plc, the clothing retailer. In 2006, the claimant's creditor insurance business was transferred to the first defendant pursuant to a scheme under the Financial Services and Markets Act 2000 Pt VII; that scheme was sanctioned by a court order dated 17 May 2006. Since around 2012, several hundred customers of Next had complained that PPI had been mis-sold to them. New complaints continued to be made. The issue was whether any mis-selling liabilities of the claimant had formed part of the "Transferred Liabilities" under the 2006 scheme and order, such liabilities having been defined as "all liabilities of the Transferor ... under or attaching to the Transferred Policies ... ".

Held: Judgment for defendants. However it arose, it was plain that liability for mis-selling would not arise "under" the contract of insurance; the insurer's primary liability under an insurance policy was its liability to pay claims in the event of an insured loss. As a matter of natural interpretation, a "liability attaching to" a contract would be understood as a reference to a liability that was directly connected with, or emanated from, the contract itself, arising after that contract had come into existence. It would not readily be understood as referring to a liability for an actionable wrong which preceded or gave rise to the contract. In the context of a statutory novation of a book of insurance contracts, the natural interpretation made sense, as it was consistent with the passing of insurance liabilities to the transferee, who was replacing the original insurer as the other contracting party. The natural interpretation made sense in the context of the 2006 scheme, which was primarily concerned with the passing of contractual risks and rewards. It also made commercial sense. It had to be borne in mind that the liabilities in question would already have arisen long before the time of the 2006 scheme, as the claimant had ceased writing PPI insurance two years earlier. Therefore the first defendant would receive no premium income in respect of that business, other than that in respect of renewals of extant policies. Had it taken on historic liabilities, it would face the prospect of having to pay out possibly millions of pounds, most of which had been received by someone else, as well as substantial amounts of interest, for that other person's wrongdoing. It was inherently unlikely to have agreed to have done so, let alone tacitly. One would have expected to see some express provision to that effect in the terms of the scheme or at the very least some clear reference to it in the scheme documentation or in the advertisements about the scheme. An objective reading of the advertisements, as well as of the other scheme documents, would have led to no other assumption than that the contractual rights and liabilities under the policies of insurance were to be transferred to the first defendant. A policyholder would not have gained the impression from reading any of those documents that liabilities for mis-selling PPI policies had transferred to the first defendant. On the contrary, the average lay person would expect liabilities for historic wrongdoing to remain with the wrongdoer unless the converse was expressly spelt out. It would be contrary to business common sense to suppose that the parties to a transfer of insurance business for nil consideration implicitly intended, without referring to it in any document, to pass to the transferee with its consent an open-ended liability for mis-selling PPI, to which conventional limitation would not apply. The natural construction of the definition of "Transferred Liabilities" in the 2006 scheme terms did not produce that result. Accordingly, the "Transferred Liabilities" under the 2006 scheme which were transferred to the first defendant by the court order did not include any liability for the alleged mis-selling of PPI (see paras 29, 33, 37, 39, 54, 57-58 of judgment).

PA(GI) LTD v GICL 2013 LTD, [2015] EWHC 1556 (Ch), [2016] Lloyd's Rep. I.R. 125, Andrews J, Ch D (Companies Ct).

1257 Employers' liability insurance–Directors' liabilities–Employer's failure to insure

[Employers' Liability (Compulsory Insurance) Act 1969 (c.57) s.1, s.1(1), s.5]

The appellant apprentice joiner (C) appealed against a decision (*Campbell v Peter Gordon Joiners Ltd* [2015] CSIH 11, 2015 S.C. 453, [2015] C.L.Y. 3166) that the respondent sole director (G) of a company was not liable to him in damages for personal injuries suffered during the course of his employment. G was responsible for the day-to-day operation of the company. In June 2006, C suffered an injury while working with an electric circular saw. The company's employers' liability insurance excluded claims arising from the use of woodworking machinery powered by electricity. It therefore excluded any claim arising out of C's accident. The company's failure to have in place appropriate insurance was a breach of its obligations under the Employers' Liability (Compulsory Insurance) Act 1969 s.1(1). The company went into liquidation in 2009. C sought to hold G liable in damages for the company's failure to provide adequate insurance cover. The question was whether civil liability attached to G for that failure.

Held: Appeal dismissed. (Lady Hale and Lord Toulson dissenting) Section 5, which was at the heart of the appeal, did not in terms impose a duty to insure on a director or other officer as such, let alone any civil liability for failure to do so. The duty rested on the corporate employer. The veil of incorporation was pierced only where an offence was committed by the company, and then in defined circumstances imposed equivalent criminal responsibility on the director or other officer on the basis that he was "deemed to be guilty" of the offence committed by the company (see paras 5-6 of judgment). As a general rule, where a statute imposed an obligation, and imposed a criminal penalty for failure to comply, there was no civil liability. There was no authority for the proposition that a person could be made indirectly liable for breach of an obligation imposed by statute on someone else. It was no different where the obligation was imposed on a company. Parliament had recognised that a director or officer could bear some responsibility for the failure to insure, but had dealt with it by a specific and closely defined criminal penalty linked to the criminal liability of the company, *Monk v Warbey* [1935] 1 K.B. 75 considered (paras 7, 13-14). The scope of a general common law claim against a director turned entirely on alleged liability under the 1969 Act, which required the court to pay due respect to the language and structure used by Parliament, rather than to preconceptions of what its objectives could or should have been. Other statutory provisions, imposing criminal liability on directors and other officers for offences by their companies, had not been treated as giving rise to civil liability. The language of s.5 was deliberately chosen, and was specifically directed at criminal liability. It was difficult to infer an intention to impose by implication a more general liability of which there was no hint in its actual language (paras 18-19, 22-23).

CAMPBELL v PETER GORDON JOINERS LTD *sub nom.* CAMPBELL v GORDON, [2016] UKSC 38, [2016] 3 W.L.R. 294, Lady Hale DPSC, SC.

1258 Employers' liability insurance–Transfer of assets–Claim for asbestos-related injuries–Transfer of undertaking from subsidiary to parent

[Civil Liability (Contribution) Act 1978 (c.47)]

Where former employees claimed damages for asbestos-induced injuries against a company whose undertaking had been transferred to its parent company, the court was required to determine preliminary issues, which involved construing the relevant sale agreement and ruling upon how it affected an employers' liability insurance policy. The subsidiary had had insurance between 1956 and 1966 and had settled some of the employees' claims under that policy. The Part 20 defendant insurer had succeeded to the policy. The subsidiary's case was that by virtue of the sale agreement entered into with its parent company (P) on 1 January 1964, which purported to transfer the subsidiary's undertaking to P, it had no liability for the claims. In *Chandler v Cape Plc* [2012] EWCA Civ 525, [2012] 1 W.L.R. 3111, [2012] C.L.Y. 2400, the court had held P separately liable to one of the subsidiary's employees. The insurer sought an indemnity from P under the Civil Liability (Contribution) Act 1978. P opposed the relief claimed on the basis of an endorsement to the policy in November 1964, which confirmed the take-over and the insurer's continuing responsibility for existing and future insurance policies. P therefore claimed an indemnity from the insurer. There were 15 preliminary issues concerning the interpretation and effect of the sale agreement and the endorsement.

Held: Preliminary issues determined. (1) Clause 2 of the agreement stated that as consideration for the sale, P assumed "all ... debts, liabilities and obligations ... of the vendor ... subsisting at the time of sale". Those words covered actual or contingent liabilities and obligations, and provided complete protection for the subsidiary, *Bloom v Pensions Regulator* [2013] UKSC 52, [2014] A.C. 209, [2013] C.L.Y. 2138 applied (see paras 44, 48-65, 194(1)). The clause also stated that P "shall adopt, perform and fulfil all contracts and engagements binding on the vendor at the time of sale" and that it would "keep the vendor indemnified against the same". The words "against the same" applied to all P's undertakings, not merely the one concerning contracts and engagements. The words "all contracts and engagements" included binding arrangements between the subsidiary and its employees, so that the subsidiary was entitled to be indemnified in respect of claims concerning such arrangements by calling on P to "adopt and fulfil" those arrangements. However, "all contracts and engagements" did not include tortious obligations (paras 68-76, 194(2) and 194(3)). (2) Clause 4 stated that the balance of the consideration for the sale would be a sum equal to the subsidiary's assets over its liabilities at the time of sale. That did not mean that any liability adopted by P under cl.2 was matched by a countervailing reduction of the consideration for the sale. Clause 4 referred unequivocally to payment by P to the subsidiary not the other way round (paras 77-79, 194(5)). (3) Clause 5 stated that until completion of the sale, the vendor would carry on its business as agent of the purchaser and was entitled to be indemnified accordingly. The subsidiary, as agent, was entitled to be indemnified in respect of its own negligence. The indemnity was not limited to losses not made good by insurance recoveries. P was therefore liable, in principle, to indemnify the subsidiary against its liabilities in the main action. The clause did not entitle P to claim damages from the subsidiary for the latter's breach of duty (paras 82-107, 119-120, 122, 124). (4) The word "completion" in cl.5 referred to steps in later clauses needing to be performed to effect the acquisition. Those steps had not been completed, but "completion" was regarded to have occurred when the subject matter of the sale agreement was transferred to a new purchaser. In any event, cl.2 took effect regardless of whether the sale agreement completed (paras 109-113, 116-117). (5) The 10-year period of insurance amounted to a series of contracts which came into existence on each renewal, not a single contract of insurance (paras 128-129). (6) The effect of the endorsement was that P became an additional insured under the policy. It was not estopped by convention from asserting that it was an insured (paras 135-140, 148, 150-151, 154-157, 194(15)). (7) As the insurance policy indemnified against "liability at law for damages", it extended to P's liability to make a contribution to its subsidiary under the Act and provided a contractual indemnity pursuant to the sale agreement. However, the effect of an exception stating that the policy did not cover "liability which attaches by virtue of an agreement" meant that there was no coverage where liability arose *only* under the sale agreement (paras 161-163,

194(17)). (8) The endorsement operated from 1964 and could not operate retrospectively. P was entitled to an indemnity in respect of claims arising between November 1964 and 1966, but not between 1956 and 1964 (paras 164, 166, 168-169, 194(18)). (9) As the interests of the subsidiary and P under the policy were co-terminous, both being "the insured", the insurer could not maintain a subrogated claim in the name of the subsidiary. It could, however, claim against P in the subsidiary's name in respect of claims when the subsidiary was acting as P's agent, *Mark Rowlands Ltd v Berni Inns Ltd* [1986] Q.B. 211, [1986] C.L.Y. 1787 considered (paras 170, 182-184, 192).

CAPE DISTRIBUTION LTD v CAPE INTERMEDIATE HOLDINGS PLC, [2016] EWHC 1119 (QB), [2016] Lloyd's Rep. I.R. 499, Picken J, QBD.

1259 Exclusion clauses–Non-disclosure–Whether non-disclosure had to involve dishonesty

The court was required to determine the meaning of "deliberate ... non-disclosure" in an exclusion clause in an insurance policy. The claimant company owned and operated an undersea interconnector which provided a link between the electricity systems of Northern Ireland and Scotland. The interconnector was insured by the defendant insurers. In Clause 5 of the policy the insurers acknowledged that they had received adequate information to evaluate the risk of insurance, and in cl.6(a) they agreed that the policy could only be avoided for reasons of non-disclosure where that non-disclosure had been deliberate or fraudulent. In 2011 the company made a claim under the policy. The insurers tried to rely on cl.6(a) by alleging that the company had deliberately failed to disclose that there had been problems with the interconnector's cables. The issue was whether the reference in the policy to "deliberate ... non-disclosure" meant that the contract could be avoided where the company had honestly but mistakenly decided not to disclose a particular document or fact; or whether it meant that avoidance was only available if there had been a deliberate decision not to disclose, such that the non-disclosure involved an element of dishonesty. The insurers argued that fraudulent non-disclosure involved an element of dishonesty, and the presumption against surplusage meant that "deliberate ... non-disclosure" had to be given a separate and distinct meaning.

Held: Judgment for claimant. (1) In light of the Oxford English dictionary definition of "deliberate", the expression "deliberate or fraudulent non-disclosure" suggested a situation where the company intentionally failed to disclose something which it knew it should disclose. There was plenty of authority that the use of "deliberate" in the context of a "breach" or "default" meant an intentional act, and there was no logical distinction between a deliberate breach, on the one hand, and a deliberate non-disclosure on the other, *De Beers UK Ltd (formerly Diamond Trading Co Ltd) v Atos Origin IT Services UK Ltd* [2010] EWHC 3276 (TCC), [2011] B.L.R. 274, [2011] C.L.Y. 540 considered. In each case, the act or omission involved an element of culpability, of doing something which should not be done: it incorporated an element of dishonest wrongdoing. The word "deliberate" meant that the act of non-disclosure was intentional, that the insured acted in a way in which they knew they should not. Furthermore, the presumption against surplusage was not a "hard-edged" rule and the court should guard against giving it too much prominence in circumstances where some surplusage was often found in commercial contracts, *Ener-G Holdings Plc v Hormell* [2012] EWCA Civ 1059, [2013] 1 All E.R. (Comm) 1162, [2013] C.L.Y. 575 considered. In any event, the court was not persuaded that "deliberate" and "fraudulent" meant the same thing. Conduct could be deliberate and dishonest but not fraudulent. For example, a breach of contract could be deliberate and made in the knowledge that it was a breach, but might not be fraudulent. Similarly, a representation might be dishonest but, if there was no intention to deceive or no intention that the misrepresentation be acted upon, then it was not fraudulent. Guidance from the Financial Ombudsman Service also drew that distinction. A sensible and workable distinction between deliberate dishonesty and fraud was readily identifiable. On that basis, both words had utility, but both involved an element of dishonesty. Accordingly, "deliberate or fraudulent non-disclosure" in cl.6(a) meant a deliberate decision not to disclose something which the insured knew should be disclosed, and did not extend to an honest mistake (see paras 25-32, 35-36, 40-43, 45 of judgment). (2) The proviso in cl.6(a) was a carve-out: an acknowledgement that, despite the wide range of remedies which the insurers accepted were not available to them, there was one type of situation which they were not prepared to forego. There was nothing in cl.5 or cl.6(a) which supported the insurers' case for a wide interpretation of the carve out (paras 46-52). (3) A finding that the company would be penalised for dishonesty, but not for an honest mistake accorded with commercial common sense, *HIH Casualty & General Insurance Ltd v Chase Manhattan Bank* [2003] UKHL 6, [2003] 1 All E.R. (Comm) 349, [2003] C.L.Y. 2461 considered (paras 54-55).

MUTUAL ENERGY LTD v STARR UNDERWRITING AGENTS LTD, [2016] EWHC 590 (TCC), [2016] B.L.R. 312, Coulson J, QBD (TCC).

1260 **Insurance brokers–Payment protection insurance–Failure to advise insurer to make block notification**

The claimant companies brought a claim against the defendant broker (O) alleging a breach of contractual/tortious duties by its failure to advise C to make a block notification in relation to PPI policies. The claimants, which sold secured loans and PPI, had retained O as their producing broker, who had in turn retained the second interested party (S) as a placing broker. For the period 2008–2009, the claimants obtained a primary layer policy from one insurer, and an excess layer policy from another. In 2010, the claimants made block notifications to each insurer in relation to the 2009 policy and a 2010 policy; the former paid both claims, but the secondary layer insurer refused, contending that any block notification should have been given in the 2009 policy year according to the policy terms, and that consequential cover was excluded in the following year under the terms of the 2010 policy. The claimants contended in relation to O's failure to advise them to make a block notification in relation to the 2009 policy that it had breached contractual and/or tortious duties. O accepted that a block notification of all PPI sales should have been made in 2009 and that if it had been made, the claimants would have followed the advice and recovered a full indemnity under a 2008/09 excess layer policy. O contended that the main responsibility for failing to recognise and recommend a block notification of sales fell on S which had been in direct contact with the insurers, and that O had relied on S for its specialist advice. S denied breach of duty, asserting that O had not requested the block notification and that S had not received information that would have alerted it to the need for any advice about, or recommendation of, such a notification. S also contended that any information it was given was too late for the necessary steps to be taken to effectively make a block notification.

Held: Judgment accordingly. Both O and S were at fault as they had each failed to grapple with the question of block notification at all in 2009 when they should have done in light of the information they each had, although that information had been different. Had they discussed the matter between them and advised C, legal advice would have been obtained and notification made. As a matter of causation, it was both broker's failure to do what they should have done that led to C's failure to make a block notification and the consequent loss. However, O knew much more than S regarding the widespread nature of the endemic or systemic failures in the sales process and the question of block notification should have been more apparent to it. Apportioning culpability, O was therefore 70% responsible, and S was 30% responsible (see paras 139-140 of judgment).

OCEAN FINANCE & MORTGAGES LTD v OVAL INSURANCE BROKING LTD, [2016] EWHC 160 (Comm), [2016] Lloyd's Rep. I.R. 319, Cooke J, QBD (Comm).

1261 **Insurance claims–Fraudulent claims–False statements–Applicability of fraudulent claim rule where false statement irrelevant to legitimate claim**

A shipowner appealed against a decision that insurers had been entitled to avoid its claim under a marine insurance policy. The ship's engine room had flooded, causing the main engine to be damaged beyond repair. The shipowner made a claim under the policy for €3.2 million. The cause of the flooding was initially unclear and the shipowner recklessly stated that the bilge alarm had sounded but the crew had been unable to deal with the leak because of the rolling of the ship in heavy weather. That was untrue. In fact, the flooding was caused by a combination of the negligence of the crew, who failed to close a sea inlet value on the emergency fire pump; the negligence of earlier contractors in failing to seal the engine room bulkheads properly; and defects in the engine room pumping system. The shipowner's untruth was therefore irrelevant, because the loss was caused by a peril of the seas covered by the policy. However, the High Court and the Court of Appeal concluded that the shipowner's statement amounted to a "fraudulent device" entitling the insurers to avoid the claim.

Held: Appeal allowed. (Lord Mance dissenting) (1) The fraudulent claim rule applied where the whole claim was fabricated and where there was a genuine claim but the amount was dishonestly exaggerated. The insurer would not be liable, even for that part of the claim which was justified, *Britton v Royal Insurance Co* 176 E.R. 843 applied and *Manifest Shipping Co Ltd v Uni-Polaris Insurance Co Ltd (The Star Sea)* [2001] UKHL 1, [2003] 1 A.C. 469, [2001] C.L.Y. 3825 followed. The question was whether the rule applied where the claim was justified but the information given in support of it was dishonestly embellished with a view to obtaining payment faster or improving the prospects of the insurers accepting it. The instant appeal was concerned with embellishments of that kind. They were generally called "fraudulent devices" but a more accurate expression was "collateral lies", as the lie turned out to have no relevance to the insured's right to recover (see paras 1, 49 of judgment). (2) The fraudulent claim rule did not apply to justified claims which were supported by collateral lies. Where a claim was fraudulently exaggerated, the insured's dishonesty was calculated to get him something to which he was not entitled. The reason why the insured could not recover even the honest part of the claim was that the law declined to sever it from the invented part, in order to deter fraud. The position was different where the insured was trying to obtain no more than the law regarded as his entitlement and the lie was irrelevant to the existence or amount of that entitlement. The policy of deterring fraud did not justify the application of the fraudulent claim rule in that situation. The insured gained nothing from the lie to which he was not already entitled, and the underwriter lost nothing if he met a liability that he had anyway, *Royal Boskalis Westminster NV v Mountain* [1999] Q.B. 674, [1997] C.L.Y. 3162 and *K/S Merc-Scandia XXXXII v Lloyd's Underwriters (The Mercandian Continent)* [2001] EWCA Civ 1275, [2001] 2 Lloyd's Rep. 563, [2001] C.L.Y. 3827 considered. (paras 23-26). (3) Difficulties arose from the fact that the fraudulent claim rule did not require the insurer to have relied upon the dishonest information or acted on it in any way. In obiter comments it was suggested by Mance LJ in *Agapitos v Agnew (The Aegeon) (No.1)* [2002] EWCA Civ 247, [2003] Q.B. 556, [2002] C.L.Y. 2732 that the test of materiality would provide the necessary connection between the collateral lie and the claim, *The Aegeon* considered. However, that could not apply to a collateral lie told in the course of making a claim because (a) no impact on the mind of the prudent underwriter was required in that context; (b) the insurer's assessment of a claim was of a different character from his assessment of a risk at the pre-contract stage. When deciding whether to accept a claim under an existing contract, the insurer had no discretion, because he was already bound. Therefore, while the lie might be material to how the insurer dealt with the claim, it could not be material to his liability for it. The extension of the fraudulent claim rule to lies which were found to be irrelevant to the recoverability of the claim was a step too far. It was disproportionately harsh to the insured and went further than any legitimate commercial interest of the insurer could justify (paras 28, 34-36, 42, 91). (4) (Per Lord Mance) The fraudulent claim rule should extend to the use of fraudulent devices, *Lek v Mathews* (1927–28) 29 Ll. L. Rep. 141 considered. Insurance was about the assessment of risk and the settlement of claims. Both processes depended on good faith and fair information. To suggest that a lie which the insured felt was necessary to promote settlement of a claim was immaterial or "collateral", if years later it could be shown that it was after all unnecessary, mistook the nature of the business and the relationship. The threshold test for materiality should be whether the lie, if believed, would significantly improve the insured's prospects at the time of the lie (paras 111-113, 130).

VERSLOOT DREDGING BV v HDI GERLING INDUSTRIE VERSICHERUNG AG, [2016] UKSC 45, [2016] 3 W.L.R. 543, Lord Mance JSC, SC.

1262 **Insurance claims–Insurers' liabilities–Third party rights**

THE THIRD PARTIES (RIGHTS AGAINST INSURERS) REGULATIONS 2016, SI 2016/570; made under the Third Parties (Rights against Insurers) Act 2010 s.19(1)(4)(8)(a)(c)(9). In force: 1 August 2016.

The Third Parties (Rights against Insurers) Act 2010 applies where an insured person incurs a liability to another and is or becomes a "relevant person". In such circumstances, the 2010 Act transfers the rights of the relevant person under the insurance contract to the person to whom the liability is incurred, thus enabling the latter to enforce those rights directly against the insurer, rather than the proceeds of the insurance policy being treated as the assets of the insured for distribution to creditors in the insolvency. The Third Parties (Rights against Insurers) Regulations 2015 amend the 2010 Act to add further circumstances by which a corporate or unincorporated body may become a relevant person and make some related minor amendments to the 2010 Act.

1263 **Insurance policies–Indemnities–Breach of condition precedent–Entitlement to indemnity**

A company (M) appealed against a decision (*Milton Furniture Ltd v Brit Insurance Ltd* [2014] EWHC 965 (QB), [2014] Lloyd's Rep. I.R. 540, [2014] C.L.Y. 1837) that it was not entitled to an indemnity from the respondent insurer in relation to a fire at its premises. M's premises included a warehouse, an area described as "the Link" and a house. The fire had been started deliberately in the early hours of the morning by an unknown person or persons. One of M's owners and an employee had been asleep in the house and the Link. They were awoken by the fire alarm. The burglar alarm had not been set. The insurance policy contained a warranty (PW1) which stated: "It is a condition precedent to the liability of the Underwriters in respect of loss or damage caused by Theft and/or attempted Theft, that the Burglar Alarm shall have been put into full and proper operation whenever the premises [...] are left unattended ... ". General condition 7 (GC7) of the policy also stated: "The whole of the protections including any Burglar Alarm provided for the safety of the premises shall be in use at all times out of business hours or when the Insured's premises are left unattended and such protections shall not be withdrawn or varied to the detriment of the interests of Underwriters without their prior consent". The judge found that GC7 was a condition precedent to B's liability, but that it was qualified by PW1, so that M was only required to set the burglar alarm if the premises were left unattended, which they had not been. However, he concluded that M had breached GC7 because the company responsible for monitoring the burglar alarm had stopped doing so as a result of M failing to pay its invoices. He held that M had been reckless as to the risk that the monitoring service would be cut off. M submitted that (1) GC7 was not a condition precedent; (2) PW1 did not qualify GC7; (3) the building had not been left unattended because people were asleep in parts of it; (4) it had not breached GC7 by causing or permitting the withdrawal of the burglar alarm monitoring service.

Held: Appeal dismissed. (1) GC7 was a condition precedent which applied to the burglar alarm. There was no hierarchy conferring precedence on PW1. Although there was overlap between the two, there was no conflict or inconsistency between them. GC7 simply had a separate commercial purpose and imposed additional obligations on the insured. GC7 applied to all claims, whereas PW1 applied only to claims for theft or attempted theft. M's construction would lead to the commercially unacceptable result that there would be no conditions precedent regarding liability for non-use of the burglar alarm, or associated monitoring, unless the claim was for theft or attempted theft. That cannot have been intended (see paras 22-26 of judgment). (2) PW1 did not reduce or qualify the obligations imposed by GC7. The language of GC7 was plain. It required the whole of the protections provided by the burglar alarm to be in use in two alternative eventualities: at all times out of business hours or when the premises were left unattended. It was impossible to read the words in the conjunctive sense. If the purpose was only to ensure that the burglar alarm was operational whenever the premises were unattended, the policy need only have provided that. The alternative had a sensible commercial purpose, namely to ensure that the alarm was set outside business hours, whether the premises were attended or not. The burglar alarm could be set in the warehouse even if people were present in the house or the Link. GC7 required the alarm to be activated in all parts of the relevant premises save where that was impracticable because of the legitimate presence of persons in certain parts of the premises. That interpretation made commercial sense. M was in breach of that aspect of GC7 (paras 29-42). (3) The judge's conclusion that the premises had not been left unattended did not reflect the reality of the situation. The natural meaning of the word "attended" was that someone was keeping the property under observation and was in a position to observe any attempt to interfere with it, *Starfire Diamond Rings Ltd v Angel* [1962] 2 Lloyd's Rep. 217, [1962] C.L.Y. 1572 applied. The people who were asleep in two small parts of the building could not be said to be attending to the premises (paras 45, 51). (4) It was not necessary to determine the issue about the burglar alarm monitoring service because M had been obliged to set the burglar alarm. However, GC7 imposed a strict obligation on the insured in respect of the monitoring service. If that conclusion was wrong, the test for determining whether M was in breach of GC7 was not a test of recklessness. It was whether M was aware of the facts which gave rise to the withdrawal of the monitoring service, or should have known of those facts, *Melik & Co v Norwich Union Fire Insurance Society* [1980] 1 Lloyd's Rep. 523, [1980] C.L.Y. 1530 applied. The judge did not appear to have addressed the issue of knowledge. However, that made little difference because both tests were satisfied. There was no basis for interfering with the judge's findings that M was in breach of that aspect of GC7 (paras 56-58, 61-72).

MILTON FURNITURE LTD v BRIT INSURANCE LTD, [2015] EWCA Civ 671, [2016] Lloyd's Rep. I.R. 192, Rafferty LJ, CA (Civ Div).

1264 Insurance policies–Rectification–Policy wording not reflecting common intention

[Road Traffic Act 1988 (c.52)]

The court was required to determine whether a contract of insurance between a company (G) and an insurer (E) should be rectified. Another of G's insurers (X) resisted the rectification and sought a contribution from E in respect of a road traffic accident. G had operated an employee car ownership scheme (ECOS) under which employees were required to be insured under a policy arranged by G with E. Employees remained within the scope of the scheme when using temporary vehicles while waiting for their cars to be delivered or repaired. G paid a flat rate premium for each car in the ECOS. G sometimes provided cars for employees outside the scheme and would hire a car from a rental company. Insurance for those cars was arranged with X. An employee (B), who was not a member of the ECOS, drove a car hired by G and hit a motorbike, badly injuring its driver. The injured party's claim was settled by X. E accepted that the wording of its policy had also covered B, but stated, supported by G, that that had never been intended. The intention had been only to cover cars in, and members of, the ECOS. G and E agreed that the contact should be rectified. X contended that B had been doubly insured and that therefore X was entitled to a 50 per cent contribution from E towards what it had paid to the motorcyclist. It was common ground that the wording of the contract between E and G was wide enough to cover any driver authorised by G and that a vehicle described in the certificate would be covered even if it was not a vehicle within the ECOS and that B had been unintentionally covered by E.

Held: Judgment accordingly. (1) Rectification required the parties to objectively show a common continuing intention, which had existed at the time of the contract's execution; an outward expression of accord; and that the contract mistakenly did not reflect the common intention, *Chartbrook Ltd v Persimmon Homes Ltd* [2009] UKHL 38, [2009] 1 A.C. 1101, [2009] C.L.Y. 722 followed (see paras 23-24 of judgment). (2) There was powerful evidence of what had been agreed between E and G in an objective sense. It was inherently probable that G had approached E seeking insurance for vehicles within the ECOS only. Payment of the premium as a fixed sum per vehicle in the ECOS was the strongest possible evidence that the parties intended E to insure only vehicles within it. If wider cover had been intended, E would have wanted information about the number of additional vehicles likely to be affected and the extent of the liability which it was agreeing to accept. If E was insuring all vehicles owned or hired by G when driven by an authorised person, there would have been no point in G paying a premium to X for vehicles hired for the use of employees outside the ECOS (paras 35-37). (3) The heading of the policy strongly indicated its intended subject matter, namely vehicles within the ECOS. The consequence of the agreed wording had not been intended or appreciated by E or G. When G rented cars for employees, different insurance arrangements applied to cars hired for ECOS members and no charge was then payable to X as insurance was already provided separately by E. It had never occurred to G that E's cover extended beyond vehicles in the ECOS and rendered the insurance provided by X for other vehicles redundant. That was convincing proof that there was a prior consensus as to the extent of the cover to be provided. It was a subjective intention which had been outwardly expressed, but the common intention had not been reflected in the written terms of the agreement. The mistake had not been spotted when the contract was renewed (paras 38-43). (4) There was no unfairness in permitting rectification, which gave effect to what the parties had actually agreed and understood to be the position. Refusing rectification would be unfair to E as it would render it liable to contribute to B's liability which it never intended or agreed to insure and for which it had received no premium. It would provide X with a windfall claim in contribution when it was the only insurer to have received a premium for insuring B. Rectification would not affect B or the injured man's rights and would not breach the Road Traffic Act 1988 as B had been insured by X. It would be unjust to refuse rectification. The claim to limit cover to vehicles within the ECOS scheme succeeded and X's claim for contribution was dismissed (paras 47-48).

EQUITY SYNDICATE MANAGEMENT LTD v GLAXOSMITHKLINE PLC; AXA CORPORATE SOLUTIONS ASSURANCE SA v JOSIAH, [2015] EWHC 2163 (Comm), [2016] Lloyd's Rep. I.R. 155, Males J, QBD (Comm).

1265 Legal expenses insurance–Referrals–Solicitors entering into referral agreement with insurance agent in relation to legal expenses insurance policies–Recoverability of monies due under policies from agent

The first defendant applied to strike out certain paragraphs of the claimant solicitors' particulars of claim and sought summary judgment in respect of the claims set out in those paragraphs. The first defendant was an insurance agent with regard to legal expenses insurance policies which were underwritten by insurers. Pursuant to an agreement with the solicitors, the agent referred potential civil claimants to the solicitors in return for referral payments. The terms of the solicitors' client care letter stated that their disbursements and the party costs would be covered by the client's insurance policy, provided that the client had not breached its terms and conditions. Concerns arose as to late payment of referral fees and premiums. The agent refused to make any further referrals. The solicitors issued a claim for lost profits. The first part of the claim was based on the minimum number of monthly referrals which, according to the solicitors, the agent was committed to making under the agreement. The second part of the claim, set out in paragraphs 36 to 48, was for the recovery from the agent, whether contractually or by way of restitution, of monies allegedly due to the solicitors under the policies issued in favour of their clients. Those sums consisted of legal costs and disbursements incurred in handling the referred claims. The agent challenged the solicitors' title to sue as a non-party to the policies and disputed its own liability, as distinct from the liability of the insurers, since it was itself a non-party. The solicitors submitted that they had title to sue because they were appointed by their clients under a contract of appointment to recover sums payable under the policies.

Held: Application granted. (1) The solicitors had no liability of their own because it was their clients, as insured parties, who were liable to pay the relevant costs and disbursements and who were entitled to be indemnified by the insurers. The policies were therefore contracts between the solicitors' clients and the insurers. The terms of the client care letter recognised that arrangement and gave no indication that the solicitors claimed any entitlement in their own right. Since it was their clients who were liable, the solicitors could not claim to have suffered loss. Accordingly, their case had no realistic prospect of success (see paras 40-42, 46 of judgment). (2) Although some of the policies described the insured's solicitors as the legal representative appointed by the insurers, it did not follow that there was any tripartite contract of appointment between the solicitors, the agent and the insurers. That would be fundamentally at odds with the fact that the policies named the clients, not the solicitors, as insureds. Even if there were such a contract, the solicitors would still need to establish the existence of an implied term that the insurers, or the agent on their behalf, would pay the solicitors' disbursements and costs. There was no basis on which to imply such a term, *Marks & Spencer Plc v BNP Paribas Securities Services Trust Co (Jersey) Ltd* [2015] UKSC 72, [2016] A.C. 742, [2016] 1377 followed (paras 50-52). (3) The agent was not an insurance company and was not itself a party to the policies. There was nothing to suggest that it had assumed liability. Its role of administering policies and paying claims on behalf of the insurers did not make it personally and directly liable to make payments under policies, *Temple Legal Protection Ltd v QBE Insurance (Europe) Ltd* [2009] EWCA Civ 453, [2010] 1 All E.R. (Comm) 703, [2009] C.L.Y. 2285 followed. Accordingly, it was appropriate to strike out paragraphs 36 to 48 of the claim and give summary judgment in the agent's favour in respect of the claims set out in those paragraphs (paras 57-59). (4) Even if there was a claim in restitution, the only recoverable sums would be the amounts paid by the solicitors by way of disbursements. The solicitors could not argue that they were liable to pay their own fees; nor could they be liable for adverse costs, since that liability rested with their clients as parties to the proceedings in which the costs orders were made. However, since it was the clients who were liable for the disbursements, the solicitors could not point to any obligation which might found a claim in restitution, *Greene Wood McLean LLP (In Administration) v Templeton Insurance Ltd* [2010] EWHC 2679 (Comm), [2011] 2 Costs L.R. 205, [2011] C.L.Y. 1902 considered (paras 67-70).

PM LAW LTD v MOTORPLUS LTD, [2016] EWHC 193 (QB), [2016] 1 Costs L.R. 143, Picken J, QBD.

1266 Motor insurance–Third party insurance–Whether policy covered damage to property caused during repairs to car

[Road Traffic Act 1988 (c.52) s.145(3), s.145(3)(a); Directive 72/166 on insurance against civil liability in respect of the use of motor vehicles, and to the enforcement of the obligation to insure against such liability 1972 art.3(1)]

The claimant insurer applied for a declaration that the car insurance policy it had issued to the first defendant (D1) did not cover damage he had caused to property belonging to the second defendant (D2) while repairing his car. D1, an employee of D2, had put his car in D2's loading bay to undertake repair work. While welding, he ignited flammable material inside the car, causing substantial damage to D2's premises and adjoining premises. D2's insurer paid D2 and the owner of the adjoining premises. It brought a subrogated claim against D1 for an indemnity. D1's policy with the claimant provided cover for an individual who had an accident "in your vehicle" which killed or injured someone or caused damage to "their property" or "their vehicle". It stated that it provided the minimum cover required under UK and EU law. The claimant contended that its policy did not cover accidents involving the car on private premises or while it was being repaired; the issues were (1) the interpretation of the policy's coverage clause; (2) whether cover was limited to accidents arising from using the car "on a road or other public place", as in the Road Traffic Act 1988 s.145(3); (3) if so, whether that was compatible with the coverage required by Directive 72/166 art.3(1); (4) whether repairs constituted "use" of the car; (5) if so, whether that use caused the accident.

Held: Declaration granted in favour of claimant. (1) The clause was poorly worded; it did not only cover damage to property belonging to someone injured or killed in the accident. It properly covered personal injury or death, or damage to someone's property, or damage to someone's vehicle. The phrase "an accident in your vehicle" was too narrow; the policy covered accidents caused by the vehicle even if the insured person was not in it or driving it at the time. A better wording would be "an accident involving your vehicle". Section 145(3)(a) referred to liability for damage "caused by or arising out of the use of a vehicle" and the coverage clause had to comply with that (see paras 22-23 of judgment). (2) The policy did not expressly limit coverage to roads, suggesting that use of the car elsewhere was covered. It had to comply with the minimum third party cover in the Act, but it could be more generous, *British Waterways v Royal & Sun Alliance Insurance Plc* [2012] EWHC 460 (Comm), [2012] Lloyd's Rep. I.R. 562, [2012] C.L.Y. 1900 applied. The Act contained an explicit limit to roads, which was not repeated in the policy. The policy's certificate excluding coverage of races and track days suggested that other activities not on public roads were not excluded. The policy covered the accident location (paras 27-29, 31). (3) If it had been necessary to decide, *Vnuk v Zavarovalnica Triglav dd (C-162/13)* EU:C:2014:2146, [2016] R.T.R. 10

had not ruled on whether the Directive applied only to public roads, although it implied that cover could extend further than where the accident happened on a road. The key question in *Vnuk* had been whether the use was consistent with the normal function of the vehicle; if it was then cover was required even though private premises were involved. That definition of "use" had to be read into the Act if possible. The Act contained the word "use", but expressly limited the coverage obligation to roads and other public places. The court rejected the submission that the word "including" could be read in before "on a road" in s.145(3)(a); that was a potentially significant addition to the scope of the Act, and while the court should construe primary legislation to be compatible with EU law where possible, it should not cross the line between interpretation and amendment, *Churchill Insurance Co Ltd v Wilkinson (C-442/10)* EU:C:2011:799, [2013] 1 W.L.R. 1776, [2012] C.L.Y. 1901 considered. Section 145(3)(a) was incompatible with art.3(1) of the Directive, *Vnuk* applied (paras 36-39). (4) The definition of "use" suggested some activity performed by the vehicle qua vehicle, *Vnuk* considered. The court considered various Canadian and Australian cases on whether repairing a car constituted "use"; the Canadian cases allowed that approach, but the court found it too broad. Repair of a vehicle did not amount to use, without more. While it was normal and necessary to repair a car from time to time, it was not a normal function of a car to undergo repair. The repair undertaken in the instant case was not "use"; the car was not being operated in any way but was immobile and partly off the ground. The policy did not cover the claim (paras 45, 58, 60, 63, 68). (5) If it had been necessary to decide, what was caused by or arose out of "use" was a question of fact and degree in each case, *Dunthorne v Bentley* [1996] R.T.R. 428, [1996] C.L.Y. 5652 considered. It was artificial to suggest that the fire arose out of D1's use of the car because he had driven it into the loading bay. The fire was caused by the allegedly negligent repairs, namely using grinders and welders without taking precautions regarding flammable materials in the car (paras 65-66).

UK INSURANCE LTD v HOLDEN, [2016] EWHC 264 (QB), [2016] 4 W.L.R. 38, Judge Waksman QC, QBD (Merc).

1267 Motor Insurers' Bureau–Causes of action–Requirement to make request for information–Whether ingredient of cause of action for claim against MIB

[Motor Vehicles (Compulsory Insurance) (Information Centre and Compensation Body) Regulations 2003 (SI 2003/37) reg.13(1)(b), reg.13(2)(b), reg.9(2)]

An English driver claimed against the Motor Insurers' Bureau (MIB) following his injury in a road traffic accident in France with a vehicle which could not be traced. The accident had happened in March 2007. He informed the MIB of the accident later in the year. The MIB handled the driver's claim on behalf of its equivalent French organisation (the FDG). Negotiations between the parties continued for some years, with the driver being medically examined and the FDG making interim payments. In 2014, the FDG refused an interim payment as the amount the driver had already received matched its overall offer to him. The driver issued proceedings in December 2014. The issues were (1) whether the MIB's liability to compensate the driver under the Motor Vehicles (Compulsory Insurance) (Information Centre and Compensation Body) Regulations 2003 was dependent on the FDG being liable to compensate him if he claimed against it. The MIB submitted that the Court of Appeal in *Jacobs v Motor Insurers' Bureau* [2010] EWCA Civ 1208, [2011] 1 W.L.R. 2609, [2011] C.L.Y. 1922 and *Bloy v Motor Insurers' Bureau* [2013] EWCA Civ 1543, [2014] Lloyd's Rep. I.R. 75, [2014] C.L.Y. 2559, which had concerned the provision in reg.13(2)(b) that the compensation body would compensate as if the accident had occurred in Great Britain, had wrongly held that it was not so dependent and that the instant court was not bound by those decisions; (2) if so, whether the driver was statute-barred by a five-year time limit rule from bringing a claim against the FDG; (3) if not, whether the claim against the MIB was statute-barred. The driver submitted that the Regulations modified the Untraced Drivers' Agreement 2003, which applied to accidents in Britain, to make it apply to accidents occurring in EEA states. Alternatively, he had a statutory claim under the Regulations; (4) if the MIB claim was not statute-barred, whether the MIB was precluded from relying on a limitation defence by reason of estoppel by convention or representation. The driver argued that until August 2014, the parties had shared the assumption that no limitation period was applicable to the claim.

Held: Claim dismissed. (1) The instant court was bound by *Jacobs* and *Bloy* as to the effect of the deeming provision in reg.13(2)(b), *Jacobs* and *Bloy* followed, *Marshall v Motor Insurers' Bureau* [2015] EWHC 3421 (QB), [2016] Lloyd's Rep. I.R. 400, [2016] 1628 doubted. The issue in *Jacobs* had been whether English law governed the compensation to be paid, rather than the MIB's liability, but it had been a necessary step in the court's reasoning that the mechanism by which the MIB's obligations compensated those in accidents abroad was to treat the accident as having occurred in Britain. *Bloy* specifically stated that reg.13(2)(b) was a deeming provision, resulting in the assessment of compensation being governed by British law. The MIB's liability did not depend on the FDG being liable (see paras 45-48 of judgment). (2) The question of whether the claim would be statute-barred in France did not arise. However, the court considered the evidence before it regarding French law. The driver would be unable to show that he had been unable to act such as to have the time limit rule lifted. There was a possibility, but not a probability, that a court would find for him on the principle of estoppel. A court would be very likely to reject any suggestion that the FDG had waived the limitation period (paras 53-68). (3) It was possible for statute to modify a non-statutory agreement, but it would be a very substantial leap for the court to uphold such an extensive modification and it was not prepared to do so. Nor could the driver bring a statutory claim under the Regulations. The relevant limitation period was six years from accrual of the cause of action. The driver had sought to argue that, under reg.13(1)(b), accrual had not occurred until he had made a request for information from the MIB under reg.9(2) in November 2014. However, none of the information to be requested under reg.9(2) was relevant to untraced motorists cases. In those cases a reg.13(1)(b) request was meaningless; it was not a necessary ingredient in the cause of action. Accordingly, the claim was statute-barred under English law (paras 73-87). (4) The evidence did not demonstrate a shared assumption that the MIB would not take a limitation defence, nor had there been any reliance or altering of position by the driver on any alleged representation (paras 102-106).

HOWE v MOTOR INSURERS' BUREAU, [2016] EWHC 640 (QB), [2016] 1 W.L.R. 2707, Stewart J, QBD.

1268 Motor Insurers' Bureau–Insolvency–Insurer's insolvency

[Directive 2000/26 on insurance against civil liability in respect of the use of motor vehicles 2000 art.2, art.6; Motor Vehicles (Compulsory Insurance) (Information Centre and Compensation Body) Regulations 2003 (SI 2003/37)]

The court had to determine a preliminary issue concerning the liability of the second defendant Bureau to compensate a person injured in a road traffic accident where the insurer of the vehicle concerned had had its licence revoked by reason of insolvency. The claimant was a passenger in a Greek-registered vehicle driven by the first defendant, who had consumed excessive alcohol. The vehicle, which was rented, was involved in a collision, causing the claimant to suffer serious injuries. The vehicle was insured by a Greek company which had appointed a claims representative in the UK in accordance with Directive 2000/26. In May 2009, the claimant brought a claim for compensation against the Greek insurer through the claims representative but no reply was received within the three-month period after the claim was made. In September 2009, the claims representative reported that the car rental company had brought proceedings in Greece and that it could not comment on the personal injury case at that time. In February 2010, the licence of the Greek insurer was revoked and its insolvency was reported. In October 2010 the claimant brought a claim against the Bureau, which denied liability. It was determined as a preliminary issue that, subject to the liability of the driver being established under Greek law, the Bureau was not liable to compensate the claimant under the Motor Vehicles (Compulsory Insurance) (Information Centre and Compensation Body) Regulations 2003. The court held that neither the Directive nor the Regulations were intended to compensate an injured party in circumstances where the insurer had become insolvent. On appeal, the parties agreed as a revised preliminary issue the question whether, subject to the liability of the driver, the Bureau was liable to compensate the claimant following the failure by the insurer or its UK representative to provide a reasoned reply in time where the insurer's licence had been revoked by reason of its insolvency.

Held: Appeal allowed, preliminary issue determined in favour of appellant. (1) It was not in doubt that, because the Greek insurer's claims representative had not provided a reasoned reply to the claim within three months, the claimant was entitled to notify and subsequently pursue a claim for compensation against the Bureau from the beginning of September 2009. Nor was it in doubt that the Bureau was obliged to respond within two months of receiving that claim (see para.22 of judgment). (2) If the Directive had been intended to compensate claimants in the event of an insurer's insolvency, it was inconceivable that it would not have so provided. Dealing with claims in the insolvency of an insurer was a matter left entirely to domestic legislation. The obligation of the compensation body appointed in accordance with art.6(1) of the Directive to deal with compensation claims for loss or injury resulting from accidents occurring in another Member State than that where the injured party resided arose only in the particular events specified in that provision. It did not follow that, where the obligation of the compensation body was triggered by the occurrence of one of the specified events, it later ceased by reason of the insurer's subsequent insolvency. In the instant case, the claimant's right to notify and pursue a claim against the Bureau arose precisely because the circumstances specified in art.6(1)(a) had occurred, namely that there had been no reasoned reply to the claim made against the Greek insurer's claims representative within three months. The accrual of that right did not arise because of any insolvency on the part of the Greek insurer; indeed, the insolvency had not yet occurred at that time. It was therefore not open to the Bureau to argue that the subsequent insolvency deprived the claimant of her right against it (paras 23, 26-27, 33). (3) The relevant time for considering whether the insurer was an authorised insurance undertaking within the meaning of art.2(a) of the Directive was the time of the accident giving rise to the claim. Insurers might cease to be authorised to carry on new business without becoming insolvent: it would be odd if that were to have the effect of terminating the rights of injured parties under art.6 (paras 38, 40).

WIGLEY-FOSTER v WILSON, [2016] EWCA Civ 454, [2016] 1 W.L.R. 4769, Gloster LJ, CA (Civ Div).

1269 Motor Insurers' Bureau–Qualified one-way costs shifting–Claim against MIB–Whether claim for personal injury for purposes of QOCS regime

[Civil Procedure Rules 1998 r.44.13; Motor Vehicles (Compulsory Insurance) (Information Centre and Compensation Body) Regulations 2003 (SI 2003/37) reg.13]

The court was required to determine whether the claimant's claim for compensation against the defendant (MIB) was a claim for damages for personal injury so as to benefit from the qualified one-way costs shifting regime in CPR r.44.13. The claimant had been rendered paraplegic in a road traffic accident in France by an unidentified driver. His claim for compensation under the Motor Vehicles (Compulsory Insurance) (Information Centre and Compensation Body) Regulations 2003 was dismissed as being time-barred (*Howe v Motor Insurers' Bureau* [2016] EWHC 640 (QB), [2016] 1 W.L.R. 2707, [2016] 1267). The claimant was ordered to pay 85% of the MIB's costs. The issue was whether his claim was for damages for personal injury within the meaning of r.44.13 so as to limit the costs recoverable by the MIB.

Held: Judgment accordingly. The rationale for the qualified one-way costs shifting regime was to protect those who had suffered injuries from the risk of facing adverse costs orders obtained by insured or well-funded parties, which would deter injured persons from making compensation claims, *Wagenaar v Weekend Travel Ltd (t/a Ski Weekend)* [2014] EWCA Civ 1105, [2015] 1 W.L.R. 1968, [2014] C.L.Y. 340 considered. The purpose had to be borne in mind when interpreting the words of r.44.13, *Bloomsbury International Ltd v Sea Fish Industry Authority* [2011] UKSC 25, [2011] 1 W.L.R. 1546, [2011] C.L.Y. 1477 followed. *McGregor on Damages* made it clear that "damages" were simply an award of money for a civil wrong, and that to retain the requirement of a wrong was entirely necessary, that being an essential features of damages; actions claiming money under statute, where the claim was made independently of a wrong, were not actions for damages. As no breach of duty or any other wrong had been alleged against the MIB, a claim based on reg.13 was not a claim for damages for personal injury within the meaning of r.44.13. Regulation 16 was consistent with that analysis; it enabled recourse to the court to recover a sum due under the Regulations as a civil debt, which was recoverable by statute independently of any breach of duty or other wrong by the MIB. On the clear construction of r.44.13, the claimant's claim was not one for damages for personal injury. Whether the non-applicability of the qualified costs regime offended the EU principles of equivalence and effectiveness was not for the instant court to determine. Accordingly, the claimant did not have protection under the qualified costs regime (see paras 11, 14, 16-17, 24-25 of judgment).

HOWE v MOTOR INSURERS' BUREAU, [2016] EWHC 884 (QB), [2016] 1 W.L.R. 2751, Stewart J, QBD.

1270 Professional indemnity insurance–Aggregation–Whether claims against solicitors could be aggregated

The claimant insurer applied for a declaration that claims brought by investors against the first defendant solicitors' firm, giving rise to the firm's insurance claim against the insurer, should be aggregated so as to limit its liability under the policy. The dispute arose from a scheme for investment in two proposed developments of holiday homes in Turkey and Morocco. The developer was advised by the firm, which had designed a scheme under which investors would place their money in an escrow account, with the firm acting as an escrow agent. The investors would then become beneficiaries of a trust, with the trust holding security over the land that was to be purchased for the developments. The investors' money was not to be paid out of the escrow account until adequate checks had been made to ensure that security was in place (the cover test). The funds were released from the escrow accounts even though the mortgage in respect of the Turkish land was defective and the security over the shares in the company which owned the Moroccan land had limited value, because the developer had only acquired a small shareholding in it. The developer failed to complete the land purchases and was later wound up. The investors claimed against the firm and the second to fourth defendants, the firm's partners and an employee, for £10 million, alleging that the cover test had not been properly applied, so that the escrow funds had been released without adequate security. The firm's insurance policy incorporated the aggregation clause in cl.2.5 of the Minimum Terms and Conditions of Professional Indemnity Insurance for Solicitors and Registered European Lawyers in England and Wales (MTC), which provided that claims arising from similar acts or omissions in a series of related matters or transactions would be regarded as one claim. The insurer's case was that the investors' claims were therefore to be regarded as one claim, with the result that its liability was limited to £3 million under the policy. The fifth and sixth defendant trustees, who represented the investors in the underlying claim, opposed the application and submitted that (1) the acts or omissions were not similar as the land purchases had failed for different reasons; (2) the individual investments were not part of a series of related matters or transactions because they were separate and independent of each other.

Held: Application refused. (1) Aggregation clauses permitted two or more claims to be treated as a single claim where they were linked by a unifying factor of some kind. The policy underlying the MTC was to ensure that solicitors were financially able to compensate their clients where claims were made against them, but, the presence of the limit per claim and the aggregation clause meant that the solicitors' ability to compensate might be limited to a sum less than the actual claim. Although the court was entitled to have regard to the policy underlying the MTC, it was too simplistic to adopt the construction which gave the public the greatest level of protection. The court had to construe it in a neutral manner and identify the meaning which it would be reasonably understood to bear in its context (see paras 25, 27 of judgment). (2) The object of cl.2.5 was to permit claims to be aggregated for the purpose of applying the limit of the insurer's liability per claim. The requisite degree of similarity had to be a real or substantial degree of similarity as opposed to a fanciful or insubstantial degree of similarity. In all the claims, the developer could not pay the vendor for the land, and the firm had failed to provide effective security, either over the land or in shares in the company owning the land, which meant that the cover test was not properly applied. After the investors' money had been released, they were exposed to loss in the event of the developments' failure. That was a real and substantial degree of similarity. It therefore followed, in the language of cl.2.5 that all the claims arose out of similar acts or omissions; they were not identical, but they did not have to be (paras 30-31). (3) The phrase "a series of related matters or transactions" served to limit the scope of the aggregation clause, which would otherwise be very wide, by embodying the unifying factor which made it appropriate to aggregate claims. It was unlikely that it had been intended that a "series" of transactions meant transactions which were, on the facts of the case, sufficiently similar and/or connected to one another. That would make the scope of the unifying factor very wide with no clear limit. Whilst it might make sense to aggregate claims as one claim where they all concerned transactions in one development, the wording of the clause, "a series of related matters of transactions", in its context appeared to point to transactions which were, by reason of their terms, dependent on each other rather than independent. It followed that the underlying claims were not aggregated as one claim as, although they arose out of similar acts or omissions, those acts or omissions were not in a series of related transactions because the transactions' terms were not conditional or dependent on each other (paras 32, 38, 41-42).

AIG EUROPE LTD v OC320301 LLP, [2015] EWHC 2398 (Comm), [2016] Lloyd's Rep. I.R. 147, Teare J, QBD (Comm).

1271 Professional indemnity insurance–Cut-off dates–Exclusion of claims before cut-off date–Causation from event occurring before date

To assist in settlement discussions, the court was asked to determine whether the actions of the claimant investment management company were covered by an insurance policy issued by the defendants. The claimant benefitted from a professional indemnity insurance policy, provided in part by the defendants. A company issued proceedings against the claimant for professional negligence following an allegedly negligent investment made on its behalf in 2010 as a result of agreements made in 2008. The company sent the claimant a letter in April 2013, and another in January 2014, following which the claimant notified the defendants that a claim had been made against it. The policy had been renewed before the second letter. The policy had a retroactive date clause excluding coverage of a claim that was "in any way involving any act, error or omission" committed before 5 June 2009. It also contained a clause requiring, as a condition precedent for coverage, that a claim be notified to the insurers as soon as practicable, and another extending cover to claims that should have been notified under the prior year's policy, if the policy had been renewed. The parties were attempting to settle the dispute and asked the court to determine certain issues regarding coverage under the policy. The issues were (1) whether the company's claim against the claimant was excluded from coverage by the retroactive date clause; (2) whether the April 2013 letter constituted a "written demand for monetary damages" and was thus a "claim" within the meaning of the policy; (3) if it was, whether the claimant had breached the condition precedent clause by not notifying the defendants as soon as practicable of the claim, or whether the extension clause applied to the claim.

Held: Judgment accordingly. (1) It would be odd if the words "in any way involving" meant the same as "arising from", if "arising from" meant "proximately caused by", *Coxe v Employers Liability Association Corp Ltd* [1916] 2 K.B. 629 considered. If "in any way involving" was taken to mean "indirectly caused by", the two phrases were given recognisably distinct meaning and the clause hung together as a whole. Accordingly, the clause required a causal connection, either direct or indirect, between a wrongful act committed prior to 5 June 2009 and the claim made in the policy period for which the claimant was liable. Causation was a key element of the exclusion; it was not enough that circumstances arose prior to that date in which a wrongful act took place thereafter. That was merely the historical context. For the exclusion to apply, there had to be an act, error or omission which could give rise to liability, occurring before the retroactive date and which was genuinely part of a chain of causation leading to liability for the claim in question. All complaints about the claimant's acts, errors or omissions related to steps taken or not taken in 2010; the earlier factors in 2008 did not have any causative connection (see paras 36, 39-40, 42-43, 45-46 of judgment). (2) The April 2013 letter was not a demand against the claimant. It was expressly a letter reserving the right to pursue a claim against the claimant, and its principal purpose was to attempt to agree a protocol for the recovery of sums from a third party. In contrast, the January 2014 letter, notified to the defendants two days after receipt, could not be seen as anything but a demand (paras 54-55). (3) Even if the

April 2013 letter had been a demand, the extension clause would apply. The point of the extension clause was to extend cover in circumstances where there had been a breach of the condition precedent of notification in the previous policy year. Such claims were unaffected by the condition precedent clause in the later policy year, and the "as soon as practicable" notification provision did not apply to them. The extension clause was intended to grant coverage to late notified claims, as long as the continuity of cover requirements were satisfied (paras 57, 64-67).

ARC CAPITAL PARTNERS LTD v BRIT SYNDICATES LTD *sub nom.* ARC CAPITAL PARTNERS LTD v BRIT UW LTD, [2016] EWHC 141 (Comm), [2016] 4 W.L.R. 18, Cooke J, QBD (Comm).

1272 Professional indemnity insurance–Exclusion clauses–Exclusion of losses from goods and services–Disbursement funding agreements

A professional indemnity insurer appealed against a decision that it was obliged to indemnify a firm of solicitors in respect of the firm's liability to reimburse loans made to its clients by the respondent finance company. The firm had conducted industrial deafness claims funded by conditional fee agreements. It had arranged for the finance company to provide loans to its clients for payment of disbursements. The firm failed to exercise proper care in selecting cases, thereby misapplying the funds. The disbursements were irrecoverable. Having breached both its duty of care to its clients, and a warranty in its contract with the finance company, the firm went into liquidation. The finance company obtained judgment for damages, being the losses suffered on the loans, and sought indemnification from the professional indemnity insurer. The issue was whether the claim fell within an exclusion clause in the indemnity insurance, which provided that it would not cover loss "arising out of, based upon, or attributable to any...breach...of terms of any contract or arrangement for the supply to...the Insured of goods or services in the course of providing Legal Services". A first instance judge held that the finance company's claim failed because it related to "the supply of goods or services" and therefore fell within the exclusion clause. The Court of Appeal disagreed, finding that the loans were an inherent part of the firm's professional practice and were covered by the policy.

Held: Appeal allowed. (Lord Carnwath dissenting) (1) The general doctrine that exemption clauses should be narrowly construed did not apply in the instant case. That doctrine only applied to clauses excluding or limiting a legal liability arising by operation of law. The exclusion clause in the indemnity insurance was not of that nature. Such policies had to be construed against the regulatory background, which aimed to ensure that solicitors' clients were protected against mistakes. Solicitors did not, as a general rule, owe a duty of care to third parties, but it was widely accepted that indemnity cover extended to protecting third parties to whom solicitors owed duties of care in their performance of legal services, and to whom they had incurred liability in negligence (see paras 7, 16-17, 35 of judgment). (2) In its commercial context, the disbursement funding agreement was an arrangement for the supply of services for four reasons. First, the firm had contracted as principal with the finance company, not as agent for its clients. Second, the firm obtained a benefit from the agreement because it would otherwise have been personally responsible for paying the disbursements, even without funds from its clients. Third, that benefit was not an incidental or collateral benefit derived from a service provided by the firm to its clients, but was part of a wider arrangement enabling the firm to take up claims which their clients might otherwise have been unable to fund, and to earn fees and success fees. Fourth, it was a service for which the firm paid an administration fee and undertook onerous repayment obligations. All in all, the finance company contracted to supply the services in the course of the firm's provision of legal services, and its claim arose out of the firm's breach of that contract. The exclusion clause operated to defeat the finance company's claim unless there was some basis for implying a restriction into the exclusion in order to limit its scope. There was no basis for such implication because the contract had business efficacy without it. The finance company had an independent cause of action. A finding that the action fell within the exclusion clause created no incoherence in that policy, *Marks & Spencer Plc v BNP Paribas Securities Services Trust Co (Jersey) Ltd* [2015] UKSC 72, [2016] A.C. 742, [2016] 1377 followed (paras 18, 29-32). (3) (Per Lord Carnwath) The essential service provided by the disbursement funding agreement was the provision of loans to the firm's clients, not to the firm itself. The benefits to the firm were incidental to that purpose. The facility provided by the finance company was not a service comparable in any way to the supply of goods or services for use in the practice. The finance company should have been entitled to an indemnity under the insurance policy (paras 55-56). (4) (Per Lord Toulson) The clause in issue was a standard form of wording in solicitors' professional liability policies. Relevant to the construction of such policies was the fact that they replicated the minimum terms of the cover that firms were required to maintain under the SRA Solicitors' Indemnity Insurance Rules 2009. The rules did not positively define the scope of solicitors' professional liability, but instead delineated the liability against which they should be required to maintain cover by a process of elimination, which involved combining a very broad insuring clause with a list of exclusions (paras 34, 41, 43, 45).

IMPACT FUNDING SOLUTIONS LTD v BARRINGTON SUPPORT SERVICES LTD (FORMERLY LAWYERS AT WORK LTD) *sub nom.* IMPACT FUNDING SOLUTIONS LTD v AIG EUROPE INSURANCE LTD (FORMERLY CHARTIS INSURANCE UK) LTD), [2016] UKSC 57, [2016] 3 W.L.R. 1422, Lord Mance JSC, SC.

1273 Professional indemnity insurance–Loss–Sums paid into escrow account–Time of loss

The court was required to determine a preliminary issue in relation to disputes arising between the claimant insurer (T) and the defendant reinsurers (R). T provided insurance to a group of companies (B) which operated a global engineering and construction business. B's professional indemnity insurance (PII) programme comprised five layers. R were reinsurers of the top layer, which was a "top and drop" policy. During the policy period, B faced a number of claims. In relation to one particular claim, B reached a settlement with its contracting party (X). Part of the settlement required B to place more than $13 million into escrow on terms set out in an escrow agreement. The issue for determination was whether B suffered a loss for the purposes of its entitlement to an indemnity under its PII programme (a) on the date when B paid the sum into escrow, or (b) as and when X subsequently drew down the money paid into the account in order to pay for remedial works. The court had already dealt with another preliminary issue in the case, namely whether T was entitled to order its claims under the insurances to enable certain claims to fall within the top and drop policy (*Teal Assurance Co Ltd v WR Berkley Insurance (Europe) Ltd* [2011] EWHC 91 (Comm), [2011] Lloyd's Rep. I.R. 285, [2011] C.L.Y. 1909). The judge found for R and held that the contracts of insurance responded to claims "by reference to the order and timing of the establishment and ascertainment of [B's] liability". It was T's case that the "establishment and ascertainment" of liability arose not when payment was made into the escrow account, but only at a later stage, as and when X became entitled to draw down on the escrow account monies. That approach was financially advantageous to T because it meant over $11 million was payable by T to B under the top and drop policy and that R were liable to indemnify T under the contract of reinsurance. However, if R were right, so that the liability was established and ascertained when the money was paid into the escrow account, no payment was due to T. T argued that the payment into escrow was not a payment to X; the money in escrow was subject to conditions which meant that it might never be paid to X; and the amount of B's liability was not ascertained until X submitted certificates which proved the cost of remedial work which had been done. R relied on *Cox v Bankside Members Agency Ltd* [1995] C.L.C. 180, which held that a court order to make an interim payment to a claimant ascertained liability in the amount of, and at the time of, the interim payment for the purpose of a liability policy, and submitted that there was no material difference between the policy wording in the instant case and that which existed in *Cox*, nor between the nature of an interim payment order and the settlement agreement in the instant case.

Held: Preliminary issue determined. (1) The obligation to make an interim payment pursuant to a court order was distinguishable from B's obligation to pay money into escrow in the instant case. The primary ground of the judge's reasoning in *Cox* was that an interim payment order was a legal liability to pay "damages". However, that was true only because a court would only order an interim payment if satisfied that the claimant would obtain judgment for substantial damages from the defendant. An order for an interim payment involved a determination by the court that the defendant was liable to pay damages to the claimant, and of the likely minimum amount of the liability. In contrast, the agreement to pay money into escrow was not an agreement to pay damages to X: the "damages" were payable only as X became entitled to draw down on the fund. Nor did the escrow agreement contain any equivalent assessment of the likely amount of B's liability. Furthermore, it was significant that B had voluntarily undertaken to pay money into escrow, whereas in *Cox*, the interim payment was made pursuant to a court order. The secondary reason for the decision in *Cox* was one of policy, namely that an insured would be liable to be rendered insolvent by an order for an interim payment if it could not call upon its insurers to indemnify it. That point was of no application in the instant case. There was no policy reason why B's PII programme should indemnify it for the payment into escrow which it chose to agree to, rather than the draw downs from the escrow account. The latter, but not the former, were payments to X that B was legally liable to make. The decision in *Cox* did not assist R in the instant case, *Cox* considered (see paras 38-46 of judgment). (2) B had suffered a loss for the purpose of its entitlement to an indemnity under its PII programme in respect of the sum of over $13 million as and when X drew down the money paid into the escrow account (para.53).

TEAL ASSURANCE CO LTD v WR BERKLEY INSURANCE (EUROPE) LTD, [2015] EWHC 1000 (Comm), [2015] 1 C.L.C. 925, Eder J, QBD (Comm).

1274 Professional indemnity insurance–Solicitors–Standard minimum terms and conditions of insurance–Meaning of "a series of related ... transactions"

[Solicitors Act 1974 (c.47)]

The appellant insurance corporation appealed against a judge's interpretation (*AIG Europe Ltd v OC320301 LLP* [2015] EWHC 2398 (Comm), [2016] Lloyd's Rep. I.R. 147, [2016] 1270) of an aggregation clause in a solicitors' indemnity insurance policy. The first respondent law firm had been engaged by a property developer to devise a scheme to help it obtain investment for the construction of holiday properties abroad. The scheme attracted many investors, but hundreds lost their money. The law firm dissolved, but was restored to the Register of Companies for the purposes of meeting claims against it. Before it dissolved, the firm had had professional indemnity insurance with the appellant. Under the terms of that policy, and in accordance with the requirement in the Solicitors Act 1974 for compulsory liability insurance incorporating standard minimum terms and conditions, the appellant provided run-off cover for the claims. Clause 2.5 of the minimum terms and conditions stated that all claims against the insured arising from an act or omission, or "similar acts or omissions in a series of related matters or transactions", would be regarded as "one claim". The appellant sought a declaration that the investors' claims were "one claim" for the purposes of that clause. The judge found that the natural meaning of "a series of related matters or transactions" in the context of a solicitors' insurance policy was a series of matters or transactions that were dependent on each other, or in some way inter-connected. It was common ground that the individual investor transactions were not dependent on each other. The judge therefore refused the declaration. The issue was how the aggregation clause in the minimum terms and conditions of solicitors' compulsory liability insurance, particularly the phrase "a series of related ... transactions", should be construed.

Held: Appeal allowed. The judge had been wrong to say that the transactions had to be "dependent" on each other before aggregation could occur. He had been right to find that there had to be "inter-connection", but there were degrees of connection; it was not the case that any degree of relatedness would do because that was an impossibly wide construction rendering the clause almost meaningless. The connection between the matters or transactions had to be an intrinsic rather than a remote relationship (see paras 15, 17, 19-21, 33 of judgment). Traditional aggregation clauses adopted a particularly wide formulation, whereas the instant clause did not use that formulation and could therefore not have been intended to have the same width. It was important to construe the critical words against the background of knowledge of the availability of wide aggregation clauses as well as narrow ones, *Lloyds TSB General Insurance Holdings Ltd v Lloyds Bank Group Insurance Co Ltd* [2003] UKHL 48, [2003] 4 All E.R. 43, [2003] C.L.Y. 2454 applied. In the instant case, the express language used in the disputed phrase was imprecise and deliberately avoided a wide formulation.

That invited a conclusion that the relationship between the relevant transactions had to be an intrinsic one (paras 22-23, 25-26). Such an interpretation was supported by the published history in the Law Society Gazette, 27 January 2005, of the origin of the clause. That publication was a legitimate construction aid. It supported interpreting the disputed phrase as needing something more than any relation, however loose. There had to be some restriction on the concept of relatedness, and the most satisfactory approach was that the relation must be an intrinsic relationship, not an extrinsic one with a third factor (paras 30, 33).

AIG EUROPE LTD v OC320301 LLP, [2016] EWCA Civ 367, [2016] Lloyd's Rep. I.R. 289, Longmore LJ, CA (Civ Div).

1275 Public liability insurance–Non-disclosure–Insured constructing tunnel under railway–Subsidence–Avoidance of policy

An insurer applied for a declaration that it had validly avoided a public liability policy into which it had entered with the assured. The assured was a sub-contractor which had installed a concrete micro-tunnel under a road and railway level-crossing. It had estimated that after the work, the railway track above the tunnel would settle 2-4mm. However, when the work was completed, the track had settled 11-12mm. The settlement subsequently increased to 15-18mm. A void also appeared in the road. The assured then took out a contractors' combined liability policy with the insurer, which provided cover for employers' liability, public liability and product liability. Shortly afterwards, a freight train derailed when passing over the level-crossing. The cause was severe settlement of the railway track caused by a void in the ground underneath the track. The Rail Accident Investigation Board concluded that the void under the railway and other voids under the adjacent road surface had been caused by excessive ground loss during the construction of the micro-tunnel. The insurer avoided the policy on the grounds that the assured had (i) failed to disclose not only the settlement of the track and the void in the road that had appeared before the policy was taken out, but also that the railway line was active; (ii) misrepresented that it did not carry out tunnelling works on railway lines that were active.

Held: Declaration granted. For an insurer to avoid a policy it had to establish on the balance of probabilities that it was induced to provide cover on the terms agreed as a result of a material non-disclosure or misrepresentation, *Garnat Trading & Shipping (Singapore) Pte Ltd v Baominh Insurance Corp* [2010] EWHC 2578 (Comm), [2011] 1 All E.R. (Comm) 573, [2011] C.L.Y. 1920 applied. An insurer could avoid a contract if, before the contract was concluded, the assured had failed to disclose every material circumstance it had known or ought to have known in the ordinary course of business or had made a material representation which was untrue. A circumstance or representation was material if it would influence the judgment of a prudent insurer in fixing the premium or determining whether he would take the risk. In the instant case, the assured's exposure to a claim by the main contractor for liability for remedial costs and future losses had been plain the moment there was a significant deviation from its predicted 2-4mm of settlement. That deviation would have been important to a prudent underwriter. Equally, the assured's exposure to a claim for liability by the main contractor in respect of the void was plain the moment it appeared in the vicinity of its tunnelling works, absent full investigation ruling out any liability on its part. Accordingly, there had been material non-disclosure on the part of the assured. That non-disclosure had induced the insurer to underwrite the risk on the terms that it did: had proper disclosure been made, it would not have written the risk on those terms. The fact that the assured had tunnelled in and near an active railway line was another material matter that should have been disclosed to the insurer. Furthermore, the assured had falsely represented to the insurer that it had not conducted tunnelling works under or close to an active railway line. The misrepresentation had also induced the insurer to enter into the contract. The insurer had not subsequently affirmed the policy and had validly avoided it for material non-disclosure and misrepresentation (see paras 99-102, 106-107, 143, 146, 149, 155-158, 163, 188-189 of judgment).

BRIT UW LTD v F&B TRENCHLESS SOLUTIONS LTD, [2015] EWHC 2237 (Comm), [2016] Lloyd's Rep. I.R. 69, Carr J, QBD (Comm).

1276 **Reinsurance–Non-disclosure–Non-disclosure of historic loss records–Materiality**

The claimant reinsurer sought to avoid two reinsurance treaties entered into with the defendant reinsured and to recover the sum of about US$5.15 million paid to the defendant under the two treaties. The first treaty was entered into in 1996 by the claimant's predecessor (P). It was a "first loss treaty" covering the first US$500,000 of losses for any one accident or occurrence on the defendant's book of inwards marine energy construction risks attaching from January 1996 to June 1997. There was no aggregate limit. It was "facultative/obligatory" in nature, meaning that the defendant could choose which risks to cede to the treaty. P wrote a 50 per cent line. The claimant sought to avoid the treaty for non-disclosure of loss statistics relating to the defendant's book of inwards marine energy construction risks written from 1989 to 1995, alternatively for misrepresentation, the representation alleged being to the effect that there were no such statistics. It contended that the level of past losses was such that, had it been disclosed, P would not have written the treaty. The second treaty was the 1997 renewal of the 1996 treaty. The claimant sought to avoid it on the same grounds and, in addition, for non-disclosure of three incidents which either had resulted, or were likely to result, in claims under the 1996 treaty. The defendant argued that (1) no representation was made as to the non-existence of loss statistics; (2) disclosure of its historic loss statistics would not have influenced the judgment of a prudent underwriter considering whether to write the 1996 or 1997 treaties, because energy construction risks were unique and because in mid-1991 there had been a change of underwriter and the new underwriter adopted a much more rigorous approach to the selection of risks; (3) the defendant failed to prove that any non-disclosure or misrepresentation induced P's underwriter to write the treaties in question; (4) as to the 1997 renewal, the three incidents separately or together were not material and the claimant had failed to prove its case on inducement.

Held: Judgment for defendant. (1) The misrepresentation claim failed. The defendant's statement that the 1996 treaty was a new treaty for the reassured and as such did not have a corresponding loss record, did not mean that the defendant had no loss statistics for energy construction risks of the kind which would be declared to the 1996 treaty, which would have been untrue. It simply meant that because the treaty was a new treaty, rather than a renewal, there were no records of losses incurred under the treaty in previous years (see paras 124-130 of judgment). (2) The defendant's past loss records in respect of energy construction risks were material and there was therefore a failure to disclose a material circumstance known to the assured. The presentation of the reinsurance risk was not fair. That was so whether a fair presentation would have required disclosure of records going back to 1989 or only to 1991. It would not be consistent with the duty of utmost good faith for the reinsured to conceal from the reinsurer the existence of poor loss records on the grounds that the underwriter or the strategy had changed, even if that were true. The prudent underwriter would wish to be told about such losses. It could then be explained to him that such losses were not properly comparable with the risks that were likely to be ceded to him under the proposed reinsurance because the identity of the underwriter had changed or because a more conservative strategy had been, or was going to be, adopted and he could assess the weight to be given to that explanation for himself and decide what to do. There had been no waiver of disclosure of the loss record *WISE Underwriting Agency Ltd v Grupo Nacional Provincial SA* [2004] EWCA Civ 962, [2004] 2 All E.R. (Comm) 613, [2004] C.L.Y. 2235 considered (see paras 131-149). (3) The claimant failed to show that if there had been a fair presentation of the risk, consisting of the loss record and an explanation of them, it would not have written the treaty on the same terms. The claimant had an existing relationship with the defendant through a quota share reinsurance treaty on which it had offered to write a 35 per cent line. That showed a willingness to follow the fortunes of the defendant's energy underwriting. Also the claimant was not told and never asked about the level of deductibles in the original insurance policies written by the defendant. There was also a cash-flow benefit to P because the defendant had already written a number of risks which were to be ceded to the treaty, thus providing immediate premium. All those matters led to the conclusion that if the loss record had been disclosed and explained the claimant would have written the treaty on the same terms. The non-disclosure had not induced the treaty and the claimant was not entitled to avoid it (paras 151-179). (4) The claimant was not entitled to avoid the 1997 treaty for non-disclosure of the three incidents separately or together (paras 182-192). (5) The defendant's counterclaim in respect of claims made under the treaties succeeded in an amount to be determined if not agreed (paras 211-213).

AXA VERSICHERUNG AG v ARAB INSURANCE GROUP (BSC), [2015] EWHC 1939 (Comm), [2016] Lloyd's Rep. I.R. 1, Males J, QBD (Comm).

1277 Subrogation–Property insurance–Landlord bringing subrogated claim against tenant

[Civil Evidence Act 1995 (c.38) s.4]

The claimant landlord claimed damages as a result of the defendant tenant's alleged negligence and breach of contract which had resulted in water damage to the leased property. The tenant appealed against a master's costs order following the refusal of her application for summary judgment. The landlord leased a cottage property to the tenant under a short-term lease arranged by an estate agent. The lease required the landlord to take out insurance against certain risks including water damage, and required the tenant to leave the heat on when not in the property. The parties added a clause requiring the tenant to compensate the landlord if a claim was made for fire damage. While the tenant was away, the water pipes froze and burst. The tenant alleged that she had left the heat on as required. A plumber's record stated that when he attended the property the heat was turned off. The estate agent's record referenced a telephone call with the tenant's partner, who allegedly stated that they had turned the heat off before leaving. The insurer indemnified the landlord, and then brought proceedings against the tenant through a subrogated claim. The tenant applied for summary judgment; the master refused the application, finding that the claim was sufficiently arguable, and ordered costs against the tenant. The tenant's partner died before the trial. The issues were (1) whether the landlord was entitled to bring a subrogated claim against the tenant; (2) whether, on the balance of probabilities, the tenant had turned off the heat and was therefore liable for the damage; (3) whether the master had erred in finding that the claim was sufficiently arguable.

Held: Judgment accordingly. (1) Where a landlord took out insurance for the benefit of both landlord and tenant, a tenant could be exonerated from liability for negligence that had resulted in the insured risks, and the landlord would only be indemnified by the insurers, *Mark Rowlands Ltd v Berni Inns Ltd* [1986] Q.B. 211, [1986] C.L.Y. 1787 followed. The application of that principle depended on indicators in the tenancy agreement, *Barras v Hamilton* 1994 S.C. 544, [1994] C.L.Y. 5930 considered. A landlord's covenant to provide insurance was part of the mutual obligations in the lease, including the obligation to pay rent. If a landlord was obliged to repair or insure the property, that had a direct effect on the rent payable. The tenant sought to apply the *Rowlands* principle not only to damage resulting from a tenant's negligence, but from a breach of the lease, *Gard Marine & Energy Ltd v China National Chartering Co Ltd* [2015] EWCA Civ 16, [2015] 2 All E.R. (Comm) 894, [2015] C.L.Y. 2325 considered. The clauses in the lease demonstrated a common intention that the insurance policy would benefit both landlord and tenant, even where the tenant was responsible for the damage. The landlord was not entitled to seek damages from the tenant. In particular, the clause which had been added to the standard form obliged the tenant to compensate the landlord if she caused fire damage, despite the insurance coverage. The need to include that clause was consistent with the view that other risks would be compensated by the insurer. The clause requiring the tenant to prevent water damage and keep the heat on did not specify her liability to compensate the landlord. The landlord was therefore not entitled to bring the subrogated claims. For completeness, that conclusion also accorded with reasonableness and public policy, *Rowlands* applied. Parties to short-term leases expected that insured risks would be covered by a landlord's insurance policy and that the landlord would be indemnified by the insurer. If the insurer could pursue a tenant under a subrogated claim, tenants would require their own insurance to cover the same risks. (2) The landlord had the burden of proving on the balance of probabilities that the tenant had turned off the heat when she vacated the property. The plumber and estate agent had not been called to give evidence. The estate agent's record was hearsay evidence to which the Civil Evidence Act 1995 s.4 applied, and although it had been made contemporaneously and the partner could not give evidence, it was significant that no explanation was given as to why the estate agent had not been called. The record conflicted with the tenant's live evidence, which had been consistent and not undermined by cross-examination. The landlord had not discharged the burden of proving that the tenant was responsible for turning off the heat; it remained possible that it had failed after she left the premises. (3) Although the court had come to a firm conclusion on the insurance issue after the trial, the master had not erred in principle in leaving the matter to trial. The master had not found it sufficiently clear on the arguments raised at the application hearing to determine that the claim had no reasonable prospect of success. There was no error and the costs appeal was dismissed.

FRESCA-JUDD v GOLOVINA, [2016] EWHC 497 (QB), [2016] 4 W.L.R. 107, Holgate J, QBD.

1278 Third Parties (Rights against Insurers) Act 2010 (c.10)–Commencement Order 2016

THE THIRD PARTIES (RIGHTS AGAINST INSURERS) ACT 2010 (COMMENCEMENT) ORDER 2016, SI 2016/550; made under the Third Parties (Rights against Insurers) Act 2010 s.21(2). Commencement details: bringing into operation various provisions of the Third Parties (Rights against Insurers) Act 2010 on 1 August 2016.

This Order commences the Third Parties (Rights against Insurers) Act 2010 so far as that Act has not already been commenced. Section 19 of the Act is already in force, having been substituted for the original s.19 by the Insurance Act 2015 s.19, which came into force two months after the passing of the Insurance Act 2015. This Order accordingly commences the rest of the Third Parties (Rights against Insurers) Act 2010, so that the entire Act is now commenced.

1279 War risks–Exclusion clauses–Loss of vessel caused by customs detention

The appellant insurers appealed against a decision that the respondent ship owners were entitled to be indemnified for the constructive total loss of their vessel. The vessel had been in a Venezuelan port when divers inspecting it found 132kg of cocaine strapped to its hull. The vessel was confiscated under Venezuelan anti-drugs laws. The appellants had insured the vessel under a standard war risks contract based on the Institute War and Strike Clauses 1/10/83. Clause 1.5 provided cover for loss caused by perils including "any person acting maliciously". Under clause 4.1.5, liability was excluded for "detainment...by reason of infringement of any customs or trading regulations". The judge found that the concealment of cocaine had been a "malicious act" under clause 1.5, and that while there might have been an infringement of customs regulations, the exclusion of liability would not accord with the policy's spirit. He implied a limitation on the scope of the exclusion in cases of actual malice, so that it did not apply where the only reason for the customs infringement by the vessel was because it was the manifestation of the malicious acts of third parties.

Held: Appeal allowed. (1) To be covered by the policy the owners had to show that the loss had been caused by a peril insured against. The issue was whether the loss was also caused by an excluded matter; that required a search for the proximate cause of the loss. The loss of the vessel was caused both by the malicious act of the drug smugglers and by the vessel's detainment by reason of the customs infringement. The malicious act was rightly found to be a cause, but it would not have caused loss if the detainment had not also occurred. The detainment was itself a proximate cause. Discovery of the drugs was not the inevitable result of concealing them: most smugglers banked on the drugs not being discovered (see paras 22-23, 32 of judgment). (2) The structure of the clauses was that the perils and exclusions together expressed the cover's ambit, and they had to be construed together. One did not have primacy over the other (para.34). (3) Detention of vessels for customs infringement did not always involve smuggling, but smuggling was a paradigm case, *Sunport Shipping Ltd v Tryg Baltica International (UK) Ltd (The Kleovoulos of Rhodes)* [2003] EWCA Civ 12, [2003] 1 All E.R. (Comm) 586, [2004] C.L.Y. 2224 and *Panamanian Oriental Steamship Corp v Wright (The Anita)* [1971] 1 W.L.R. 882, [1971] C.L.Y. 11000 applied. The policy required that six months elapse before a detainment gave rise to constructive total loss; it was likely that some form of smuggling, rather than a less heinous breach of regulation, would give rise to that length of detainment. It would be strange in those circumstances if the one detainment for customs infringement to which clause 4.1.5 did not apply was detention due to smuggling. Clause 4.1.5 intended to exclude any detainment attributable to a breach of customs laws, and in circumstances where the war clauses had traditionally excluded losses caused by smuggling, it was not surprising that smuggling activities by third parties were excluded from cover, *The Anita* applied. There was nothing unbusinesslike in the insurers' position, and there was much to be said for casting the onus of proof on the owners to show circumstances where the war clauses exclusion was inapplicable in respect of claims under those clauses (paras 36-38, 41, 43-45). (4) If the malicious act was concealing drugs on the vessel, and concealing drugs was an infringement of customs regulations, then the vessel was detained by reason of an infringement of customs regulations. The court should be reluctant to "write in" in clauses drafted for use in insurance contracts around the world. There was a difference in function between clauses 1.5 and 4.1.5. The owners were within clause 1.5. The next question was whether the loss arose from detainment by reason of infringement. There was no good reason to interpret that as inapplicable in the case of a malicious act amounting to an infringement. There were many malicious acts which did not involve any infringement of customs regulations. There was no necessity arising from the clause's language or otherwise to imply a limitation. The policy raised two separate questions: what loss was caused by the peril, and whether there was a detainment for customs infringement. The concealment of drugs was the malicious act, and also an infringement of the regulations, carrying the risk of discovery and detention. The smugglers' malice was their reckless indifference to the consequences. The loss was caused by the combination of that concealment, which infringed customs regulations, and the subsequent detention. The second cause was the detention. It was not justifiable to exclude from clause 4.1.5 an infringement consisting of the relevant malicious act; that did not tally with the case law, *John Cory & Sons v Burr* (1883) 8 App. Cas. 393, *The Anita* and *The Kleovoulos of Rhodes* applied (paras 46-47, 50-54, 58, 61).

ATLASNAVIOS NAVEGACAO LDA (FORMERLY BNAVIOS NAVEGACAO LDA) v NAVIGATORS INSURANCE CO LTD, [2016] EWCA Civ 808, [2016] 2 Lloyd's Rep. 351, Laws LJ, CA (Civ Div).

INTELLECTUAL PROPERTY

1280 Co-existence agreements–Infringement–Determination of scope of co-existence agreement between chemical and pharmaceutical businesses in Europe and USA

[Trade Marks Act 1994 (c.26) s.10(1), s.11(2)(b)]

The court was required to determine the scope and operation of a coexistence agreement between the claimant and defendants since the advent of the internet. The parties conducted chemical and pharmaceutical businesses, originating from a family apothecary in Germany in the 17th century, under the Merck name. The defendants were the successors of a Merck business incorporated in the US, and the claimants were the successors of Merck businesses operating in Germany and the rest of the world. A 1955 settlement agreement between them formalised their uses of the Merck name and MERCK trade marks. That agreement was amended in 1970. The key terms were that (i) the defendants would not object to the claimant's corporate use of the Merck name in the US and Canada provided it was geographically identified with Germany; (ii) the claimant would not object to the defendants' corporate use of the Merck name in Germany provided it was geographically identified with the US; (iii) the claimant recognised the defendants' right to use MERCK as a trade mark in the US, and the defendants recognised the claimant's right to use MERCK as a trade mark in Germany and the rest of the world: the parties also agreed that they would not use or attempt to acquire rights in any MERCK trade marks in the others' territory. That agreement, which was governed by German law, remained effective. Issues arose as to how the 1970 agreement currently operated, as the defendant ran a number of globally accessible websites containing the word Merck as a domain name. The claimant complained that that activity was in breach of the 1970 agreement or was otherwise unlawful. The defendants contended that the websites were targeted at US consumers, and that the matters complained of by the claimant were either inevitable accidental references or essentially "overspill" references to their rightful use of Merck.

Held: Judgment accordingly. (1) The 1970 agreement was intended both to settle current disputes and to provide for the unlimited future the uses that might be made of the parties' respective corporate names and of the MERCK mark throughout the world. It covered the use of the word Merck as all or part of a trade name, and as a trade mark (see para.63 of judgment). (2) Under German law the 1970 agreement governed the use of the word Merck as all or part of a trade name or trade mark on the internet (paras 73-78). (3) The 1970 agreement covered use of the word Merck in relation to the provision of services (para.81). (4) Under German law, the use in the UK of the word Merck alone by the defendants as a contraction of the full trade name and without a geographical identifier was a breach of the 1970 agreement, as was the defendants' UK use of MERCK as a trade mark. The defendants' use of the word Merck as branding was plainly deployed to link the Merck brand to the products and services they provided. That amounted to use of Merck as a mark. The defendants' "overspill" argument had to be rejected: their websites were global with some national elements, including a specific UK element. The defendants' deployment of the word Merck in a domain name in a territory in which its use as a company name was forbidden amounted to a prima facie breach of the 1970 agreement (paras 83, 97-100, 110, 116). (5) The German law doctrine of forfeiture, akin to the principle of estoppel, had no application to the defendants' breaches of contract. The defendants had, therefore, breached the 1970 agreement (paras 133-134). (6) The claimant's registered MERCK marks had an extensive reputation in the UK (para.138). (7) The claimant had withdrawn claims for genuine use of its MERCK mark in respect of certain classes, and the defendants had admitted genuine use by the claimant in some cases. Where the claimant's non-use was admitted, there would be a partial revocation of the MERCK mark. Nevertheless, the fact that small revocations might have to be made did not affect the defendants' obligations to stand by their contractual promises; nor did they have any real bearing on what the defendants had been doing and the activities the claimant had complained about (para.146-148). (8) The defendants' US websites were directed at commercial activity in the UK (para.160). (9) The defendants' had used the MERCK mark on its websites and, in relation specifically to the UK, for research and product development, licensing and business development, and in relation to healthcare and pharmaceuticals. There was a clear desire to link use of the MERCK mark to the defendants' various vaccines and drugs for diabetes, cardiovascular conditions and cancer which were otherwise available in the UK under the same product name but with the claimant's branding. That use would create in the mind of the average consumer a link between the defendants' products and the claimant's brand and the MERCK mark which the claimant alone had the right to use as a mark in the UK. The function of the claimant's MERCK mark was adversely affected because a consumer would have difficulty in ascertaining whether the goods and services referred to on the relevant web-pages originated from the claimant, or some economically linked undertaking, which owned the MERCK mark, or from a third party like the defendants (para.165). (10) The defendants' use of the claimant's mark amounted to infringement under the Trade Marks Act 1994 s.10(1), s.10(2) and s.10(3) *Interflora Inc v Marks & Spencer Plc* [2014] EWCA Civ 1403, [2015] Bus. L.R. 492, [2015] C.L.Y. 1531 followed (paras 166, 175, 179). (11) The defendants were unable to avail themselves of the "own name" defence under s.11(2)(b) of the Act; their use of the Merck name as a mark on their websites was not in accordance with honest practices in industrial and commercial matters and was not fair having regard to the claimant's legitimate interests as proprietor of the MERCK mark (paras 183-184). (12) The claimant was entitled to an injunction to restrain the defendants' infringement of its MERCK mark (paras 191-192).

MERCK KGAA v MERCK SHARP AND DOHME CORP, [2016] EWHC 49 (Pat), [2016] E.T.M.R. 19, Norris J, Ch D (Patents Ct).

1281 Confidential information–Breach of confidence–Infringement of privacy–Allegations against publicist–Prospects fo receiving more than nugatory damages

[Limitation Act 1980 (c.58) s.32, s.32(2)]

The defendant publicist applied to strike out a claim for breach of confidence and infringement of privacy, on the basis that it was out of time and an abuse of process. The claimant, a former royal butler, had approached the defendant in 2002 to manage some adverse publicity. He wrote a letter containing details of his relationship with the royal family; it was allegedly given to the defendant in confidence so that the claimant could receive his advice. The defendant had the letter faxed to a tabloid newspaper editor, though the newspaper did not publish any story about it. The defendant contended that the letter had been written to enable negotiations about the sale of the story to the newspaper. In 2003 the claimant published a book containing similar information to the letter's contents. The claimant did not discover that the letter had been faxed until 2011 or 2012 when he obtained disclosure in relation to his action against the newspaper's publishers for phone hacking. He applied to join the defendant to those proceedings, but the action was settled before the joinder application had been decided. The claimant had already incurred over £28,000 in costs in the instant proceedings and estimated his further base costs at £232,000 under a conditional fee agreement. The defendant submitted that the claim should be struck out as (1) the limitation period was not postponed under the Limitation Act 1980 s.32 through the defendant's concealment of the sending of the fax; (2) it was an abuse of process as it presented no real prospect of recovering anything other than meaningless or minor remedies.

Held: Application refused. (1) The circumstances of the transmission of the fax to the newspaper were such that the claimant would not have known about it at the time. It was not apparent at the date of the wrong that there would be a publication, or when it would be. Until that event, the claimant could not have known about the wrongful act. The period between the fax's transmission and the unknown publication was arguably a period which was "for some time" for the purposes of s.32(2). For the defendant to succeed in knocking out a limitation counter-point at the instant stage, the position had to be clear as a matter of fact and law; it was not, and that basis for striking out the claim failed (see paras 10-12 of judgment). (2) None of the factors relied on by the defendant to show an abuse of process under the principles in *Jameel v Dow Jones & Co Inc* [2005] EWCA Civ 75, [2005] Q.B. 946, [2005] C.L.Y. 974 had much weight. The claim was only stale because the wrong had been concealed and the proceedings delayed by the joinder application. While the claimant's own publication could indicate that he did not care about the privacy of the information, which could significantly reduce the damages, he claimed that the circumstances were different; that was a matter for investigation at a trial. The likely costs were very alarming, but without evidence of an improper motivation by the solicitors, that did not make the proceedings an abuse. The main *Jameel* factor was the low level of damages, *Jameel* applied. Those were likely to reflect compensation for the wrong itself and for distress and upset. If the wrong was established, then it was serious, since information transmitted for one purpose had been used for another, which was not likely to result in merely nominal damages. Alarm and distress were likely to be relatively small compared to a situation where there had been widespread publication of the information; they could also be reduced because the claimant had put the private information into the public domain himself. The distress would arise from the premature revelation of private information. Damages might not extend to £25,000, but they were unlikely to be nugatory; there was a real possibility of more than nominal or minimal damages if the claimant established the facts relied on. There was an arguable claim with a real prospect of more than nugatory damages, and it was not an abuse of process (paras 26-30, 32).

BURRELL v CLIFFORD, [2015] EWHC 2001 (Ch), [2015] 6 Costs L.O. 719, Mann J, Ch D.

1282 Copyright–Infringement–Beatles' songs copyright infringement in documentary soundtrack–Lack of synchronisation licence

[Copyright Act (United States) 1976]

The claimants alleged that the defendants had infringed their copyright in songs by "The Beatles". The second defendant had acquired a copy of a recording of The Beatles' first US concert performance. Rights to the tape of the concert video were later transferred to the first defendant. The first claimant owned the worldwide copyrights in eight of the songs performed during the concert, and the second claimant was the exclusive UK licensee of the copyright works. From 2009 to late 2010, the second defendant had negotiated with the claimants for a synchronisation licence, so as to allow it to reproduce the copyright works as part of the soundtrack of a proposed documentary, but no licence was executed. The claimants subsequently discovered that the defendants had made a documentary containing the concert footage, promoted by a website and a trailer. The documentary had been made in the UK but its target market was the US, and the infringement claim concerned the claimants' UK and US copyrights. The action against the second defendant was stayed when it went into liquidation. The first defendant contended that (1) a binding contract had been concluded between the second defendant and the claimants under which the latter became obliged to issue a synchronisation licence; (2) the claimants were estopped from denying the grant of a synchronisation licence since they had represented that a licence would be granted if the documentary met certain conditions, and it had relied on those representations to its detriment by producing the documentary and expending considerable sums of money to that end; (3) under US law, fair use of a copyright was not an infringement.

Held: Judgment for claimants. (1) The defendants had never accepted any offer from the claimants for a synchronisation licence on the terms suggested. In any event, the negotiations were expressly subject to contract, and the claimants had made it clear that they did not intend to be bound unless and until a contract was signed, *RTS Flexible Systems Ltd v Molkerei Alois Muller GmbH & Co KG* [2010] UKSC 14, [2010] 1 W.L.R. 753, [2010] C.L.Y. 631 considered. Furthermore, the claimants had also clearly indicated that they would not grant a synchronisation licence unless and until they had seen and approved the final documentary. There was no question of the claimants having approved the documentary, since at the time of the negotiations it had not yet been produced (see paras 79-82 of judgment). (2) A defence of proprietary estoppel could be advanced in respect of intellectual property rights such as copyrights, *Motivate Publishing FZ LLC v Hello Ltd* [2015] EWHC 1554 (Ch) applied. However, the first defendant could not rely upon the representations in question as founding an estoppel because they were expressed to be subject to contract, *Cobbe v Yeoman's Row Management Ltd* [2008] UKHL 55, [2008] 1 W.L.R. 1752, [2008] C.L.Y. 3081 applied (paras 94-95). (3) Under the Copyright Act 1976 (United States), fair use of a copyrighted work, including its reproduction for purposes such as criticism, comment, news reporting, teaching, scholarship or research, was not an infringement of copyright. In determining whether the use of a particular work was fair, the factors to be considered included (a) the purpose and character of the use, including whether it was of a commercial nature or for non-profit, educational purposes; (b) the nature of the copyrighted work; (c) the amount and substantiality of the portion used in relation to the copyrighted work as a whole; (d) the effect of the use upon the potential market for, or value of, the copyrighted work. The more transformative the new work, the less would be the significance of other factors, like commercialism, that might weigh against a finding of fair use. The first defendant's pleaded case was a bare assertion of fair use, and it had never particularised the facts and matters it relied upon in support of that assertion. Nor had it adduced any factual evidence in support of its defence of fair use. Given that the burden lay upon the first defendant to demonstrate fair use, that point was significant. In respect of the first factor, the documentary amounted to a commercial use of the copyrighted works and was partly, but not wholly, transformative since, although it was a serious, albeit entertaining, study of The Beatles' impact on the US, the performances of the copyright works were presented in their entirety. In relation to the second and third factors, the copyright works were fully expressive works falling within the core of copyright protection, and the documentary reproduced the entirety of each of them. In regard to the fourth factor, it was likely that the documentary would damage the market for, or potential value of, the sale of recordings of the works and the market for synchronisation licences. Accordingly, the inclusion of the copyright works in the documentary did not amount to fair use (paras 96, 99, 102, 110-115, 117-122, 124).

SONY/ATV MUSIC PUBLISHING LLC v WPMC LTD, [2015] EWHC 1853 (Ch), [2015] R.P.C. 28, Arnold J, Ch D.

1283 **Copyright–Infringement–Copyright in television broadcasts of cricket matches–Infringement by allowing uploading, viewing and sharing of clips**

[Copyright, Designs and Patents Act 1988 (c.48) s.30(2); Human Rights Act 1998 (c.42) s.3; European Convention on Human Rights 1950 art.10; Charter of Fundamental Rights of the European Union 2000 art.11]

The claimants alleged copyright infringement by the defendants, and the defendants counterclaimed for a declaration of non-infringement. The first claimant board was the governing body of cricket in England and Wales, and the second claimant was a UK pay-television operator. Together they owned the copyright in television broadcasts of cricket matches staged under the auspices of the board, and in films made during the course of production of the broadcasts, in particular by recording broadcast footage for the purposes of action replays. The defendants operated a website, social media accounts and various mobile applications through which users had uploaded and viewed a considerable number of clips, lasting up to eight seconds, of cricket match broadcasts. The claimants contended that each eight-second clip broadcast by the defendants constituted a substantial part of their copyrighted works, and that that infringement had been flagrant. The defendants relied on the defence of fair dealing for the purposes of reporting current events within the Copyright, Designs and Patents Act 1988 s.30(2).

Held: Judgment for claimants. The expression "reporting current events" was of wide and indefinite scope, and should be interpreted liberally, since the s.30(2) defence was clearly intended to protect the role of the media in informing the public about matters of current concern to the public, *Ashdown v Telegraph Group Ltd* [2001] EWCA Civ 1142, [2002] Ch. 149, [2001] C.L.Y. 3850 applied. The requirement to interpret the expression liberally was reinforced by the requirement of the Human Rights Act 1998 s.3 to construe domestic legislation compatibly with the ECHR art.10, and by the European law requirement to construe legislation compatibly with the Charter of Fundamental Rights of the European Union art.11, *SAS Institute Inc v World Programming Ltd* [2010] EWHC 1829 (Ch), [2010] E.C.D.R. 15, [2011] C.L.Y. 1948 applied. Short excerpts of copyrighted sporting broadcasts could amount to genuine news reports, albeit confined to news of a sporting character, *BBC v British Satellite Broadcasting Ltd* [1992] Ch. 141, [1992] C.L.Y. 575 applied (see paras 77-79, 82 of judgment). It was impossible to lay down any hard-and-fast definition of "fair dealing", which was a matter of fact, degree and impression. In considering whether dealing was fair, it was legitimate to have regard to the user's motive: the most important factor was whether the alleged fair dealing was in fact commercial competition with the proprietor's exploitation of the copyright work, *Ashdown*, *Pro Sieben Media AG v Carlton UK Television Ltd* [1999] 1 W.L.R. 605, [1999] C.L.Y. 3438, *Newspaper Licensing Agency Ltd v Meltwater Holding BV* [2011] EWCA Civ 890, [2012] Bus. L.R. 53, [2011] C.L.Y. 1950 and *Time Warner Entertainments Co LP v Channel Four Television Corp Plc* [1994] E.M.L.R. 1 applied (paras 82-85). Quantitatively, eight seconds was not a large proportion of a broadcast or film lasting two hours or more. Qualitatively, however, it was clear that most of the uploaded clips constituted highlights of the matches: wickets taken, appeals refused, centuries scored and the like. Thus most of clips showed something of interest, and hence value. The majority also involved action replays of that kind. Each clip substantially exploited the claimants' investment in producing the relevant broadcast and/or film and constituted a substantial part of the relevant copyright works (para.99). The clips had been reproduced and communicated to the public by the defendants for the purposes of sharing the clips with other users and facilitating debate amongst them about the sporting events depicted. The clips were not used in order to inform the audience about a current event, but presented for consumption because of their intrinsic interest and value. The defendants' objective had been purely commercial rather than genuinely informatory (paras 128-129). Even if the defendants' use of the claimants' clips had been for the purpose of reporting current events, it did not amount to fair dealing. The use complained of was commercially damaging to the claimants, conflicted with normal exploitation of the copyright works, and its nature and extent was unwarranted and disproportionate (paras 147, 151). The defendants' infringements were not flagrant. Although they had knowingly pushed legal boundaries, they had sought to act lawfully (para.173).

ENGLAND AND WALES CRICKET BOARD LTD v TIXDAQ LTD, [2016] EWHC 575 (Ch), [2016] Bus. L.R. 641, Arnold J, Ch D.

1284 Copyright–Infringement–Jurisdiction of court to order disclosure information identifying third parties who provided goods and services which enabled commission of infringement

[Directive 2004/48 on the enforcement of intellectual property rights 2004 art.8; Senior Courts Act 1981 (c.54) s.37]

The claimant applied for judgment in default of acknowledgement of service against the defendants, and an order requiring them to disclose information identifying third parties who had provided them with goods and/or services enabling them to screen infringing Premier League football matches. The defendants had publicly screened two Premier League matches in their pub without the permission of the claimant, who held the copyright in the graphics associated with Premier League games. The claimant had issued proceedings alleging copyright infringement. The issues were (1) the claimant's entitlement to default judgment; (2) whether the court had jurisdiction to order the defendants to provide details to the claimant of all dealings with any third party who had procured the supply to them of any set-top box, decoded card, IPTV box and/or other goods and/or services which were used to screen the infringing football matches.

Held: Application granted. (1) The claim form had been properly served and the defendants had not filed an acknowledgement of service. The application for judgment in default of acknowledgement of service had also been properly served: the claimant was therefore entitled to judgment in default (see para.3 of judgment). (2) In *Wilko Retail Ltd v Buyology Ltd* [2014] EWHC 2221 (IPEC), [2015] E.T.M.R. 13, [2015] C.L.Y. 1532, the court had decided that it had jurisdiction to grant the type of relief currently sought against a wrongdoer under an extension of the *Norwich Pharmacal* jurisdiction, having regard to Directive 2004/48 art.8 which provided that, in response to a claimant's justified and proportionate request, the competent judicial authorities could order the disclosure of information on the origin and distribution networks of the goods and/or services which infringed an intellectual property right. Whilst art.8 did not have direct effect under English law, the English courts had a duty to interpret the Senior Courts Act 1981 s.37 so as to give effect to the Directive so far as possible, *Cartier International AG v British Sky Broadcasting Ltd* [2014] EWHC 3354 (Ch), [2015] 1 All E.R. 949, [2015] C.L.Y. 1520 applied. That was probably the reason underpinning the decision in *Wilko*, and the court was content to reach a similar conclusion on that basis, *Wilko* explained. The court therefore ordered the defendants to identify the persons who had provided them with the goods and/or services which had enabled them to screen the infringing games (paras 8-11).

FOOTBALL ASSOCIATION PREMIER LEAGUE LTD v WELLS, [2015] EWHC 3910 (Ch), [2016] Bus. L.R. 350, Snowden J, Ch D.

1285 Copyright–Infringement–Substantial copying of design–Whether "entirely innocent" infringment–Whether entitled to account of profits

The claimant alleged copyright infringement by the defendants and sought an account of profits. The claimant manufactured and sold ceramics designed by its sole director and shareholder. In 2002, it had launched its "Red Berry" tableware range at a Paris design show. Copyright in the design was assigned to the claimant. The range was featured in a style magazine and was very successful, becoming the claimant's signature collection. In 2013, an employee of the claimant noticed tableware items on sale at a UK store run by the first defendant bearing a design very similar to Red Berry under the name "Red Blossom". The items had been created in China at the second defendant's order. They were then imported and sold in the UK by the second defendant through stores run by the first defendant. The defendants asserted that its

Red Blossom tableware had been independently designed by an employee (H) of the second defendant. H admitted attending the design show at which Red Berry had been launched and regularly reading the style magazine in which it had featured, but denied having seen or been influenced by Red Berry. The issues were whether (i) Red Blossom was a copy of Red Berry and, if so, whether it was a copy in substantial part; (ii) if the defendants were liable for copyright infringement, the court should exercise its discretion to allow an account of profits; (iii) if so, costs were deductable from the defendants' gross profits in determining the sum due to the claimant.

Held: Judgment for claimant. (1) In the absence of direct evidence of copying, the first step when assessing an allegation of copyright infringement was to consider whether the claimant had established a prima facie inference of copying by reason of similarities between the copyright work and the defendant's work; the stronger the prima facie case of copying, the more compelling the defendant's evidence of independent design had to be to rebut that inference, *John Kaldor Fabricmaker UK Ltd v Lee Ann Fashions Ltd* [2014] EWHC 3779 (IPEC), [2015] E.C.D.R. 2, [2015] C.L.Y. 1479 applied. If copying was established, the claimant had still to show that his design was copied in substantial part, but that conclusion would almost inevitably follow from the finding of copying, *John Kaldor* and *Designers Guild Ltd v Russell Williams (Textiles) Ltd (t/a Washington DC)* [2000] 1 W.L.R. 2416, [2001] C.L.Y. 3859 applied. The similarities between the Red Berry design and the Red Blossom design were very striking indeed. It was almost inconceivable that Red Blossom design should employ exactly the same shade of red as that of Red Berry unless the latter was copied or, alternatively, that there was a very convincing explanation for the coincidence. H had not discharged the burden of explaining away the similarities between her design and Red Berry. Although she had no recollection of being influenced by Red Berry, it was possible that she had forgotten such influence or successfully put it out of her mind. It was likely that Red Berry had played a part in the creation of Red Blossom. The designs appearing on the defendants' tableware were indirect copies of the claimant's copyright work. The design was undoubtedly copied in substantial part. It followed that the defendants had infringed the claimant's copyright by the importation and sale of their Red Blossom range (see paras 32-36, 42-43, 48-50 of judgment). (2) An account of profits made by an infringer was an equitable remedy and the court had a discretion whether to order it; it might be refused if the infringer was entirely innocent, *Hollister Inc v Medik Ostomy Supplies Ltd* [2012] EWCA Civ 1419, [2013] Bus. L.R. 428, [2013] C.L.Y. 1818 applied. The main head of infringement of copyright in the instant case was secondary infringement by reason of importation and sale. That required the claimant to establish that the defendants had known or had reason to believe that the Red Blossom dinnerware bore infringing copies of the claimant's copyright work. "Knowledge" in that sense had been proved, given the finding of copying, and the defendants could not, consequently, be "entirely innocent" infringers. There was no justification for refusing an account of profits (paras 53-54). (3) When assessing the appropriate profits payable by a defendant in an account of profits, a proportion of costs arising from general overheads could be deducted from the defendant's gross profits unless the overheads would have been incurred anyway in the absence of the infringing business and no opportunity cost was incurred by the defendant, *OOO Abbott v Design and Display Ltd* [2014] EWHC 2924 (IPEC) applied. The first defendant's gross profit earned from sales of Red Blossom dinnerware was £2,008.12 from which there were no deductions from overheads since none had been shown to have been increased because of the sales. The second defendant's gross profit from the infringing importation and sales was £33,784.27, from which import duty at 12 per cent was the sole allowable deduction. The defendants were jointly liable for their collective profit of £31,703.01. The claimant was also entitled to interest on that sum (paras 55-57, 59-60).

BODO SPERLEIN LTD v SABICHI LTD, [2015] EWHC 1242 (IPEC), [2016] E.C.D.R. 19, Judge Hacon, IPEC.

1286 Copyright–Musical works–Ownership of copyright in song–Whether agreement unconscionable bargin

The claimants sought declarations concerning the ownership of copyright in a song recorded by the band "The Fall" and released on an album in 1999. The second claimant musician had written the song together with the band's lead singer. They had agreed that the publishing or performing rights in the song should be split 33.34 per cent to the singer and 66.66 per cent to the musician. The singer assigned his rights in the song to the first claimant music publishing company. When the song was recorded for an album, its music and lyrics were changed. The defendant, who had produced the album, claimed to have carried out extensive work on the song. A dispute arose when he applied to register his interest in the album version, but the parties took no active steps to resolve the matter for many years. The musician later corresponded with the producer and they entered into a settlement agreement in September 2011, agreeing that the publishing company, the musician and the producer were each entitled to 33.33 per cent of the rights in the album version of the song and, consequently, the royalties. The publishing company objected and issued proceedings against the producer. The musician was joined to that claim. The main relief claimed was declarations that the copyright in the album version of the song was owned by the publishing company and musician in 33.34 and 66.66 per cent shares respectively, and that the producer owned no part of the copyright. The producer contended that he was entitled to a share in the copyright of the album version on the basis of the settlement agreement and/or his joint authorship. The claimants contended that the settlement agreement was voidable as an unconscionable bargain because the producer had known that the musician was an impecunious single mother and he had unfairly pressed a substantially disadvantageous settlement on her. They argued that the singer had written all the lyrics for the album version and that the producer had made insufficient musical changes to it to be a joint author.

Held: Judgment for defendant. (1) To attract equitable relief on the grounds of an unconscionable bargain, it was not sufficient to prove that a bargain was hard, unreasonable or foolish, that its terms were objectively unreasonable, or that there was unequal bargaining power between the parties. The bargain had to be unconscionable in the sense that one of the parties had imposed the objectionable terms in a morally reprehensible manner, and it was necessary for the party seeking relief to establish such conduct, *Boustany v Pigott* (1995) 69 P. & C.R. 298, [1995] C.L.Y. 3016 applied. At the time the settlement agreement was reached, the producer had been unaware of the full extent of the musician's financial difficulties and so could not have taken advantage of her problems. He had not imposed objectionable terms on her in a morally reprehensible manner and there was no unconscionable conduct on his part. There were no grounds for setting aside the settlement agreement (see paras 25, 35, 37 of judgment). (2) (Obiter) In case that conclusion was wrong, the court considered the producer's claim to be a co-author of the album version. An adaptation of an existing work might attract its own copyright as long as sufficient effort, skill and labour had been expended in producing it, and the changes made to the prior version were not merely trivial and did not slavishly copy the original work, *Redwood Music Ltd v Chappell & Co Ltd* [1982] R.P.C. 109, [1982] C.L.Y. 455, *Sawkins v Hyperion Records Ltd* [2005] EWCA Civ 565, [2005] 1 W.L.R. 3281, [2005] C.L.Y. 2424 and *Bamgboye v Reed* [2002] EWHC 2922 (QB), [2004] E.M.L.R. 5, [2004] C.L.Y. 2252 considered. The singer's evidence that all the lyrics of the album version were written by him was accepted. The producer could not claim to be a joint author of the literary copyright in the album version's lyrics. He had, however, made a small but significant original contribution to the composition of the album version's music by composing and adding string sections to the work. Had the settlement agreement not had effect, his contribution as co-author would have been properly reflected by a 20 per cent share of the copyright in the music of the album version (paras 38, 69-70, 82-83, 90).

MINDER MUSIC LTD v SHARPLES, [2015] EWHC 1454 (IPEC), [2016] F.S.R. 2, Amanda Michaels, IPEC.

1287 Copyright–Songs–Construction of transfer agreement between record companies–Transfer of copyright of musical works

Two record companies (BSI and Cayman) appealed against a decision (*BSI Enterprises Ltd v Blue Mountain Music Ltd* [2014] EWHC 1690 (Ch)) that they were not the owner and licensee respectively of the copyrights in 13 works by the musician Bob Marley. The respondent (Blue Mountain) was a member of the "Island" group of companies, to which Bob Marley had signed in the early 1970s. In 1973, Bob Marley had entered into a publishing contract with Cayman. He wrote the 13 works in question between 1973 and 1976, but did not publicly describe himself as the author. Rather, he misattributed their authorship to various associates because he did not think that he would receive the royalties due to him otherwise (the misattribution ploy). After his death in 1981, the Island group sought to acquire the rights to as many of his works as it could. To that end it entered into agreements with his estate and, in 1992, with Cayman. Blue Mountain claimed that under the 1992 agreement, all the rights owned by Cayman in Bob Marley's output, including the 13 works, passed to the Island group and that, as an Island group company, it was entitled to exploit them. The appellants argued that the copyrights remained with Cayman, which had then sold them to BSI. They argued that the parties to the agreement had agreed, for the limited purposes of that agreement only, that Cayman did not own those 13 works, so they were not transferred. Part of the relevant background was that in 1984, Cayman had brought an action in New York against the administratrix of Bob Marley's estate and another Island group company, seeking to recover money they had obtained as a result of the misattribution ploy. That action was dismissed on limitation grounds, leaving open the possibility of the misattribution ploy being litigated in another forum. In the instant proceedings, the judge found for Blue Mountain, holding that the copyrights in the works had passed to the Island group under the agreement. On appeal, the appellants abandoned the case they had pursued at trial, arguing instead that (1) on its proper interpretation, the agreement imposed no obligation on Cayman to transfer the rights in the 13 works; (2) the judge had erred in directing himself that the language of the agreement had to accommodate the Island group's aim of obtaining as many rights in Bob Marley's works as possible.

Held: Appeal dismissed. (1) Clause 1 of the agreement defined the rights to be acquired as a series of music publishing interests, including "compositions". The language of cl.1.8, which defined the term "composition", clearly signified that all of the works identified in that clause, specifically musical compositions written and recorded by Bob Marley, were compositions for the purposes of the agreement. Had the parties had intended "compositions" in cl.1.1 to mean something different from "compositions" as defined in cl.1.8, they would have used a different term. No limitation on the scope of the term "compositions" could be found elsewhere in the agreement either. Finally, the appellants relied on the preliminary statement in the agreement, which provided that the seller wished to sell "certain of [its] music publishing rights and interests as are hereinafter specified". They argued that that meant that only some of Cayman's assets were to be transferred. However, that attached more weight to the word "certain" than it could bear. It could simply mean that the extent of the assets being sold was to be determined by reference to the terms of the agreement (see paras 59-64 of judgment). (2) The judge had directed himself properly as to the principles governing the interpretation of contracts. He had emphasised that the parties' intentions were to be determined objectively and that the meaning of the agreement was to be determined from the document itself having due regard to the factual matrix. He had then fairly and properly indicated that the factual matrix included the fact that there were likely to be works created by Bob Marley after 1973 which had not been identified, that the Island group was acquiring the estate's interest in Bob Marley's creative output, and that it wanted to obtain as many rights as possible. Finally, he had the importance of the language used by the parties well in mind. Against that background, his reasoning was unimpeachable. He rejected the factual premise underlying the appellants' arguments, finding that it made no sense for the parties to agree not to include the works that were the subject of the misattribution ploy. He properly had regard to the fact that the Island group wanted to buy everything it could, and that Cayman's best opportunity to maximise its potential claim over the misattribution ploy was with the Island group. It was clear that the works were "compositions" within the meaning of the agreement and that the rights in them were transferred to the Island group under the agreement (paras 65-71).

BSI ENTERPRISES LTD v BLUE MOUNTAIN MUSIC LTD, [2015] EWCA Civ 1151, [2016] E.C.C. 11, Arden LJ, CA (Civ Div).

1288 Design right–Infringement–Copyright infringement claim against Swiss company–Jurisdiction

[Regulation 6/2002 2002 art.81, art.82; Community Design Regulations 2005 (SI 2005/2339) reg.2; Lugano Convention on Jurisdiction and the Enforcement of Judgments in Civil and Commercial Matters 2007 art.5(3)]

The defendant applied for a declaration that the court lacked jurisdiction over the claimant's claims for declaratory relief and for an order setting aside the claim form. The claimant was a UK company, and the defendant was a Swiss company with establishments in two Member States, the Netherlands and Croatia. The parties had each launched impact protection cases for iPhones. The defendant's lawyers subsequently wrote to the claimant alleging that its products were nearly identical to the defendant's and gave the same overall impression, and were a clear infringement of the defendant's unregistered Community Design in its phone case. They requested that the claimant sign a cease and desist declaration, stating that "If you do not comply ... our client will reserve its rights to take legal action against you". The claimant issued UK proceedings against the defendant seeking declarations that it had not infringed and would not infringe any Community unregistered design right owned by the defendant within the European Community, nor any UK unregistered design right or other rights subsisting in the iPhone cases' design, and that the defendant had made unjustifiable threats to bring proceedings for infringement of its Community unregistered design right. The issues were whether the court had jurisdiction to (i) hear the claim for a declaration that the claimant's activities did not infringe any Community unregistered design right vesting in the defendant; (ii) hear the claim in respect of the alleged threat; (iii) determine that there was no infringement of any UK unregistered design right which the defendant might have. The defendant contended that under Regulation 6/2002 art.81 and art.82 an action for a declaration of non-infringement of Community designs had to be brought in the Member State in which the defendant was domiciled or had establishments, which was either the Netherlands or Croatia in the instant case. The claimant submitted that, given the defendant's letter, its application for a declaration of non-infringement was purely defensive in nature and it was "the defendant" for the purposes of art.82. It argued that the letter had made a threat to sue in the UK courts which, under the Community Design Regulations 2005 reg.2, was a statutory tort and the Lugano Convention 2007 art.5(3) entitled it, as a person domiciled in the UK, to sue the defendant, as a person domiciled in Switzerland, in the UK since that was where the threat to sue had occurred or might occur.

Held: Application granted in part. (1) A "defendant" within art.82 was clearly the person being sued: the person who was being brought, against his will, to face court proceedings. The person who started proceedings was undoubtedly the claimant, even if the proceedings were defensive in nature, and the person who was required to participate in court proceedings initiated by someone else was undoubtedly the "defendant". Accordingly, the instant court had no jurisdiction to hear the claim for a declaration of non-infringement of any Community design right vesting in the defendant (see para.44 of judgment). (2) The court had to decide, as a fact, whether the letter had contained a threat to bring infringement proceedings in a UK court. Under reg.2, evidence of how a letter was subjectively understood by the recipient was not admissible in deciding if it threatened infringement proceedings, *Best Buy Co Inc v Worldwide Sales Corp Espana SL* [2011] EWCA Civ 618, [2011] Bus. L.R. 1166, [2011] C.L.Y. 2001 followed, *Prince Plc v Prince Sports Group Inc* [1997-98] Info. T.L.R. 329, [1998] C.L.Y. 3528, *Lancecrest Ltd v Asiwaju* [2005] EWCA Civ 117, [2005] L. & T.R. 22, [2005] C.L.Y. 2679 and *Newbold v Coal Authority* [2013] EWCA Civ 584, [2014] 1 W.L.R. 1288, [2013] C.L.Y. 2431 applied. A threat did not have to be explicit: the term "threat" covered any information that would convey to a reasonable man that some person had trademark rights and intended to enforce them against another, *Best Buy* followed. A reasonable reader of the letter in the claimant's position would clearly have understood it to indicate that proceedings in the UK were likely or, at the very least, that there was a realistic possibility of UK proceedings in respect of alleged infringement of the defendant's claimed Community design right, either immediately or in the future. It followed that the court had jurisdiction to hear the claim under reg.2 in respect of the threat made by the letter to bring infringement proceedings in the UK courts (paras 52, 60-65, 81, 124). (3) The court's jurisdiction to make a declaration would only be exercised where there was a real and present dispute between the parties, *Rolls-Royce Plc v Unite the Union* [2009] EWCA Civ 387, [2010] 1 W.L.R. 318, [2009] C.L.Y. 1162 applied. Under art.5(3), if there was a real and present dispute between the parties as to whether the claimant was infringing the defendant's UK unregistered design right by selling its phone cases in the UK, the court would have jurisdiction to make a declaration of non-infringement. However, on the facts, since it was unlikely that the defendant was asserting any UK design right, there was no more than a speculative possibility that there could be such a dispute. The court was therefore unable to hear the claim for a declaration of non-infringement of any UK unregistered design right vested in the defendant (paras 110, 122-124).

TECH 21 UK LTD v LOGITECH EUROPE S.A., [2015] EWHC 2614 (Ch), [2015] Bus. L.R. 1276, Stephen Jourdan QC, Ch D.

1289 **Distinctiveness–Passing off–Trademark infringement claim for London black cabs–Reiteration of principles relating to various issues involved**

[Directive 2008/95 on trade marks 2008 art.3, art.3(1)(b), art.5(1)(b)]

The claimant alleged threatened trade mark infringement and passing off by the defendants, and the defendants sought to revoke the claimant's marks. The claimant was the proprietor of three-dimensional UK and Community trade marks for models of London black taxi-cabs. The second defendant, using parts provided by the first defendant, planned to sell a new model of a London taxi in late 2016. The issues raised included (i) the identity of the "average consumer"; (ii) whether the marks were devoid of inherent distinctive character; (iii) whether the marks had acquired distinctive character; (iv) whether the marks consisted exclusively of a shape which gave substantial value to the goods; (v) genuine use; (vi) the effect of second-hand sales on genuine use; (vii) whether the Community trade mark should be revoked for five years' non-use; (viii) likelihood of confusion; (ix) whether the marks had been infringed; (x) the defence of use in accordance with honest practices; (xi) whether the claimant could establish passing off.

Held: Judgment for defendants. (1) The average consumer of goods or services was deemed to be reasonably well-informed and observant, *Enterprise Holdings Inc v Europcar Group UK Ltd* [2015] EWHC 17 (Ch), [2015] E.T.M.R. 16, [2015] C.L.Y. 1533 applied, *JW Spear & Sons Ltd v Zynga Inc* [2015] EWCA Civ 290, [2016] 1 All E.R. 226, [2015] C.L.Y. 1535 considered. In the instant case, the average consumers were not passengers but taxi drivers, who would be knowledgeable and careful purchasers since taxis were specialised and expensive vehicles (see paras 159-163 of judgment). (2) For a trade mark to possess distinctive character within Directive 2008/95 art.3(1)(b), it had to identify goods and services as originating from a particular undertaking, thus distinguishing them in the perception of the relevant public from those of other undertakings, *Freixenet SA v Office for Harmonisation in the Internal Market (Trade Marks and Designs) (OHIM) (C-344/10 P)* EU:C:2011:680 followed. The claimant's marks would be perceived by taxi drivers merely as a variation of the typical taxi shape without identifying the taxi's origin. They were, accordingly, devoid of inherent distinctive character (paras 165, 174-175). (3) To demonstrate that a trade mark consisting of a product's shape had acquired distinctive character, the trade mark proprietor had to prove that, at the relevant date, a significant proportion of the relevant class of persons perceived the relevant goods or services as originating from a particular undertaking because of the sign or shape, *Societe des Produits Nestle SA v Cadbury UK Ltd* [2016] EWHC 50 (Ch), [2016] Bus. L.R. 354, [2016] 1332 applied. There was no evidence that a substantial proportion of taxi drivers perceived taxis as emanating from the claimant because of their shape; the marks had not acquired distinctive character (paras 178, 190-191). (4) Article 3(1)(e) of the Directive prohibited the registration of a mark for a product's shape where that shape in itself gave the product substantial value, *Hauck GmbH & Co KG v Stokke A/S (C-205/13)* EU:C:2014:2233, [2014] Bus. L.R. 1284 followed, *Julius Samann Ltd v Tetrosyl Ltd* [2006] EWHC 529 (Ch), [2006] E.T.M.R. 75, [2006] C.L.Y. 2598 considered. The shape of the taxis protected by the claimant's marks were iconic, design classics which added substantial value to the vehicles. The marks were therefore declared invalid under art.3(1)(e) (paras 206-209, 213-214). (5) The principles for assessing a trade mark's genuine use included (a) genuine use meant actual use of the trade mark by the proprietor or an authorised third party; (b) use had to be more than merely token use to preserve the mark's registration; (c) use had to be consistent with a mark's purpose in identifying the goods' origin and distinguishing them from others; (d) there had to be real commercial exploitation of the mark, taking into account all relevant facts and circumstances; (e) there need not always be quantitatively significant use of the mark for it to be deemed genuine; (f) not every proven commercial use of the mark would automatically constitute genuine use, *Ansul BV v Ajax Brandbeveiliging BV (C-40/01)* EU:C:2003:145, [2005] Ch. 97, [2004] C.L.Y. 2386, *Sunrider Corp v Office for Harmonisation in the Internal Market (Trade Marks and Designs) (OHIM) (C416/04)* EU:C:2006:310, [2006] E.C.R. I-4237, *Verein Radetzky-Orden v Bundesvereinigung Kameradschaft Feldmarschall Radetzky (C-442/07)* EU:C:2008:696, [2008] E.C.R. I-9223, [2009] C.L.Y. 2448, *Centrotherm Systemtechnik GmbH v OHIM (C-609/11)* EU:C:2013:592, *Leno Merken BV v Hagelkruis Beheer BV (C-149/11)* EU:C:2012:816, [2013] Bus. L.R. 928, *Silberquelle GmbH v Maselli-Strickmode GmbH (C-495/07)* EU:C:2009:10, [2009] E.C.R. I-137, [2009] C.L.Y. 2447, *La Mer Technology Inc v Laboratoires Goemar SA (C-259/02)* EU:C:2004:50, [2004] E.C.R. I-1159, [2004] C.L.Y. 2417 and *Reber Holding GmbH & Co KG v Office for Harmonisation in the Internal Market (Trade Marks and Designs) (OHIM) (C-141/13)* EU:C:2014:2089 followed (paras 217-219). (6) The question whether sales of used vehicles bearing a trade mark by the proprietor constituted genuine use for the purpose of defeating a claim for revocation for non-use was a difficult question of law which would ultimately have to be resolved by the CJEU. Since it was unnecessary to determine that in the instant case, the court simply assumed that such acts did amount to use (para.223). (7) The use of the Community trade mark relied on by the claimant did not constitute genuine use in the Community. The mark should be revoked for lack of genuine use with effect from 2 May 2014 (paras 234-235, 239). (8) The principles relating to likelihood of confusion within art.5(1)(b) of the Directive included (a) the likelihood of confusion had to be appreciated globally, taking account of all relevant factors; (b) the matter had to be judged through the eyes of the average consumer of the goods or services in question, who was deemed to be reasonably well-informed, circumspect and observant; (c) the average consumer normally perceived a mark as a whole without analysing its various details; (d) the marks' visual, aural and conceptual similarities had normally to be assessed by reference to their overall impressions; (e) the overall impression conveyed by a composite trade mark might be dominated by one or more of its components; (f) a lesser degree of similarity between the goods or services might be offset by a greater degree of similarity between the marks, and vice versa; (g) the likelihood of confusion was greater where the earlier mark had a highly distinctive character; (h) mere association, in the sense that the later mark brought the earlier mark to mind, was not sufficient; (i) a likelihood of confusion arose if the association between the marks created a risk that the public might believe that the respective goods or services came from the same or economically-linked undertakings, *Specsavers International Healthcare Ltd v Asda Stores Ltd* [2012] EWCA Civ 24, [2012] E.T.M.R. 17, [2012] C.L.Y. 1915, *JW Spear* and *Maier v ASOS Plc* [2015] EWCA Civ 220, [2016] 2 All E.R. 738, [2015] C.L.Y. 1536 followed. There was no likelihood of confusion on the part of taxi drivers (paras 244, 247). (9) The defendants had not infringed the marks (para.269). (10) In assessing whether a mark had been used in accordance with honest practices in industrial and commercial matters the relevant factors were (a) whether the defendant had known of the mark's existence, and if not, whether it would have been reasonable for it to conduct a search; (b) whether the defendant had used the sign complained of in reliance on competent legal advice based on proper instructions; (c) the nature of the use complained of, in particular the extent to which it was used as a trade mark for the defendant's goods or services; (d) whether the defendant had known that the mark's owner objected to the sign's use or should have appreciated that that was likely; (e) whether the defendant had known or should have appreciated a likelihood of confusion; (f) whether there had been actual confusion; (g) whether the mark had a reputation and the defendant had known or should have appreciated that it would be adversely affected; (h) whether the defendant's use of the sign interfered with the owner's ability to exploit its mark; (i) whether the defendant had a sufficient justification for using the sign; (j) the timing of the trade mark owner's complaint, *Samuel Smith Old Brewery (Tadcaster) v Lee (t/a*

Cropton Brewery) [2011] EWHC 1879 (Ch), [2012] F.S.R. 7, [2012] C.L.Y. 1974 applied. Had it been necessary, the defence of use in accordance with honest practices would have been available to the defendants (paras 272-283). (11) To succeed in an action for passing off, a claimant had to prove (a) goodwill or reputation attached to its goods or services in the mind of the purchasing public by association with the identifying "get-up"; (b) misrepresentation by the defendant to the public, whether or not intentional, leading or likely to lead the public to believe that goods or services offered by it were the claimant's; (c) that it had or was likely to suffer damage by reason of the erroneous belief engendered by the defendant's misrepresentation, *Reckitt & Colman Products Ltd v Borden Inc (No.3)* [1990] 1 W.L.R. 491, [1990] C.L.Y. 3465 applied. As the claimant was unable to establish misrepresentation, its passing off claim failed (paras 284, 296).

LONDON TAXI CORP LTD (T/A LONDON TAXI CO) v FRASER-NASH RESEARCH LTD, [2016] EWHC 52 (Ch), [2016] E.T.M.R. 18, Arnold J, Ch D.

1290 Enterprise and Regulatory Reform Act 2013 (c.24)–Commencement No.10 and Saving Provisions Order

THE ENTERPRISE AND REGULATORY REFORM ACT 2013 (COMMENCEMENT NO.10 AND SAVING PROVISIONS) ORDER 2016, SI 2016/593; made under the Enterprise and Regulatory Reform Act 2013 s.100, s.103(3). Commencement details: bringing into operation various provisions of the Enterprise and Regulatory Reform Act 2013 on 28 July 2016.

This Order brings into force the Enterprise and Regulatory Reform Act 2013 s.74 which repeals the Copyright, Designs and Patents Act 1988 s.52. Section 52 introduced a copyright exception into United Kingdom law relating to the industrial exploitation of artistic works, which limits copyright protection to a period of 25 years from the end of the year in which such articles are first marketed.

1291 EU law–Infringement–Copyright

THE COPYRIGHT (FREE PUBLIC SHOWING OR PLAYING) (AMENDMENT) REGULATIONS 2016, SI 2016/565; made under the European Communities Act 1972 s.2(2). In force: 15 June 2016.

These Regulations amend the Copyright, Designs and Patents Act 1988 to remove s.72(1)(c) (free public showing or playing of a film included in a broadcast). The amendments are being made following a series of decisions in a case brought by the Football Association Premier League Ltd, which found that UK law is incompatible with the requirements of Directive 2001/29.

1292 Infringement–Account of profits–Ability to bring further infringement allegations at inquiry as to damages or account of profits–Applicability of practice from High Court to IPEC

[Civil Procedure Rules 1998 Pt 63, r.63.23(2); European Convention on Human Rights 1950 art.6]

The defendant appealed against a decision (*AP Racing Ltd v Alcon Components Ltd* [2015] EWHC 1371 (IPEC), [2016] F.S.R. 1, [2016] 1313) dismissing its application to strike out parts of the claimant's patent infringement claim. The claimant had brought proceedings for infringement of its patent concerning brake calipers. The Court of Appeal decided that the claimant's patent was valid and that the defendant had infringed it. The claimant wanted to include in the damages inquiry seven calipers that had not been mentioned at trial but which had been manufactured and sold by the defendant before the commencement of the claim. The defendant refused to allow the seven calipers to be included in the inquiry, arguing that it would be an abuse of process to do so, and the claimant therefore restricted the inquiry but lodged a second infringement claim in respect of the seven calipers. The defendant subsequently applied to strike out the claimant's case in respect of the seven calipers on the basis of the principles in *Henderson v Henderson* [1843-60] All E.R. Rep. 378. The judge held that the practice described in *Unilin Beheer BV v Berry Floor NV* [2007] EWCA Civ 364, [2008] 1 All E.R. 156, [2007] C.L.Y. 2606 did not generally apply in the IPEC. In particular, he found that a patentee was not entitled to litigate a broader range of infringements in an inquiry or an account, and that, as a general rule, if the further allegations of infringement required additional evidence, the court would only allow the further allegations at a trial or inquiry in unusual circumstances. He noted that CPR r.63.23(2) allowed parties in IPEC proceedings to submit material other than that permitted at the case management conference only in exceptional circumstances. He refused the defendant's strike out application on the basis that the court would probably have allowed the further alleged infringements to be included in the damages inquiry if the claimant had asked, so that allowing the claimant to litigate in respect of the seven calipers in the second claim would not amount to oppression of the defendant.

Held: Appeal dismissed. (1) The judge was correct that a claimant was under no general duty to exercise reasonable diligence to ascertain whether he had a potential further cause of action against a defendant. A defendant's knowledge as to the likelihood that a subsequent claim might be brought was relevant when considering whether the bringing of such a claim would be oppressive, *Johnson v Gore Wood & Co (No.1)* [2002] 2 A.C. 1, [2001] C.L.Y. 410 followed. A rightholder should not be required to produce evidence of every type of possible infringement in a liability hearing, but just sufficient examples so that a case on infringement could be dealt with in a cost-effective and expeditious way. The practice in *Unilin* of allowing a patentee who had been successful at trial to raise further alleged infringements at a damages inquiry or an account of profits was entirely in accordance with the aims of the IPEC, in particular simplifying trials, shortening proceedings and rendering them cost-effective. The judge was wrong to find that such an approach did not generally apply in the IPEC. If the judge was right, the consequence would be that in the IPEC but not in the High Court, a patentee would be required to come to the first CMC with a complete list of all possible infringements that he had been able to find, and if he had missed any which he could have discovered by reasonable diligence and which required further evidence, he would be debarred from litigating in respect of them. As with all other courts, the IPEC was limited, in respect of allegations of abuse of process, to considering whether oppression had occurred in the sense that the defendant would be harassed unjustly by further allegations of infringement. The practice in *Unilin* therefore did apply to the IPEC, *Unilin* considered. It was clear from CPR Pt 63 that it was anticipated that IPEC proceedings would be split between liability and quantum. It was therefore also clear that there would be a first CMC in relation to liability and a second in relation to damages if liability was established. The damages CMC would necessarily allow for the deployment of additional material to that at the liability trial. It followed that the "exceptional circumstances" rule had to be applied separately in respect of both CMCs. It was a matter for the judge at the quantum CMC to decide which issues should be included and which infringements considered. It could not be the case that, because not all possible infringements had been identified at the first CMC, the court was excluded from considering further infringements at the second CMC. If r.63.23(2) operated so that it was only possible to refer to further infringements if they had been mentioned at the first CMC, the approach in respect of abuse of process would be replaced with a test of exceptional circumstances. That could not be right, as it would mean that absent exceptional circumstances, the patentee would be denied its right of access to the court as guaranteed by ECHR art.6, *Johnson* followed, *Henderson* considered. (2) The judge had been correct to hold that there was no abuse of process in the instant case. The claimant had followed the general cost-effective practice of specifying certain infringements of which it was aware. It had written to the defendant before commencing the first action for information as to other products which might arguably infringe its patent, but the defendant had failed to identify the seven calipers. In such circumstances, it would be misconceived to hold that the defendant would be oppressed if the claimant was permitted to litigate in respect of the seven calipers.

AP RACING LTD v ALCON COMPONENTS LTD, [2016] EWHC 815 (Ch), [2016] Bus. L.R. 838, Henry Carr J, Ch D.

1293 Infringement–Declarations of non-infringement–Declarations sought for various signs for numerous services–Focussing on best case

[Regulation 207/2009 2009 art.9(1)(b), art.9(1)(c)]

The claimant applied for a declaration that its use of the signs SKYSCAPE and SKYSCAPE CLOUD SERVICES did not infringe five of the defendants' trade marks.

The claimant supplied cloud computer services to public sector organisations under a government scheme called G-Cloud. The defendants provided broadcasting and communication services under the mark SKY. They had informed the claimant that they considered it to be infringing five of their marks. The claimant sought a declaration of non-infringement in relation to the signs SKYSCAPE and SKYSCAPE CLOUD SERVICES in numerous fonts, colours and presentations in relation to 10 different types of services and the provision of services enabling transition to each of those services. The claimant submitted that the court should compare all the combinations of signs and services with the defendants' marks and, if not prepared to grant the declaration sought in full, it should grant a narrower one.

Held: Application refused. (1) Applications for a declaration of non-infringement were unusual but could serve a useful purpose. There would be no real difficulty in granting a trade mark declaration of non-infringement if it was sought in relation to all fair and notional use of one or even a number of identified signs. The court would test the application by comparing the trade mark and the signs in relation to goods or services of the alleged infringer which were identical or closest to those for which the trade mark was registered. However, where the applicant sought a qualified and detailed declaration and wanted complete flexibility about the possible outcome, it risked the sort of difficulties facing the claimant in the instant case. For the court to have to consider the large number of combinations of sign and service would contravene the third principle in *Nokia Corp v InterDigital Technology Corp (Application to Set Aside)* [2006] EWHC 802 (Pat), (2006) 29(7) I.P.D. 29053: the issue had to be sufficiently clearly defined to render it properly justiciable, *Nokia* applied. The defendants were entitled to focus on a limited combination of a sign and a service, or even just one, within the scope of each of the orders sought, and argue that it would infringe their marks. If they succeeded, the declaration would be refused. The defendants' best case required the court to compare SKY and SKYSCAPE in relation to email services (see paras 27-28, 38 of judgment). (2) The burden was on the claimant to establish that use of its signs would not infringe the defendants' marks. Likelihood of confusion under Regulation 207/2009 art.9(1)(b), and whether the claimants were taking unfair advantage of or causing a detriment to the defendants' marks under art.9(1)(c), had to be judged through the eyes of the average consumer, *Comic Enterprises Ltd v Twentieth Century Fox Film Corp* [2016] EWCA Civ 41, [2016] E.C.C. 24, [2016] 1330 followed. The average consumer was a consumer of the type of goods or services supplied by the alleged infringer and as a consequence was liable to come across the accused sign. They would have the trade mark alleged to have been infringed, and/or the way in which it was used by the proprietor, imperfectly in mind when seeing it used in its context, across the full range of specified goods and services, and would be aware of any reputation. In the instant case, the average consumer would: carry out a role within a UK public sector body which obtained services through G-cloud or otherwise in compliance with public procurement requirements; be aware of SKY as a trade mark, at the minimum in relation to the core consumer services, such as TV services; have some information technology knowledge equivalent to that of the person in the street, but would also be aware of G-cloud; be aware of email services being provided under the SKY mark, although they would have imperfectly in mind how the SKY mark was used in the context of email services. The average consumer would instinctively split SKYSCAPE into two conceptual parts: "sky" defining a type of "scape" in the sense of a view. The average consumer would be familiar with the use of SKY together with another word as a composite name for a service offered by the defendants, but would have no exact idea of the many ways in which it was used with another word or words. Despite SKYSCAPE being one word, there was a likelihood that a significant proportion of the relevant public and the average consumer, encountering SKYSCAPE used for an email service, would take it to be another service offered by the defendants (paras 62, 66, 68, 77, 81, 84-85, 87). (3) There could be no finding of detriment to the distinctive character of a mark unless the proprietor had established a change in the economic behaviour of the average customer. Arguably, even on an application for a declaration of non-infringement, the burden of proof remained on the proprietor. It was likely that a link between SKY and SKYSCAPE was bound to lead to a dilution, whittling away or blurring of the SKY mark such as to weaken its ability to serve as a badge of origin for email services and thus by inference cause a change in the economic behaviour of the average customer. The claimant had failed to establish that there was no likelihood of detriment to the distinctive character of the SKY mark. The link between SKY and SKYSCAPE in the average customer's mind would enable the claimant to benefit from the defendants' undoubted reputation and goodwill (paras 93, 96).

SKYSCAPE CLOUD SERVICES LTD v SKY PLC, [2016] EWHC 1340 (IPEC), [2016] E.T.M.R. 40, Judge Hacon, IPEC.

1294 Infringement–Standard-essential patents–Whether master sales agreements anti-competitive

[Treaty on the Functioning of the European Union 2008 art.101]

The third and fourth defendant companies (S) in proceedings concerning the infringement of standard-essential telecommunications patents owned by the claimant company appealed against a decision (*Unwired Planet International Ltd v Huawei Technologies Co Ltd* [2015] EWHC 2097 (Pat)) striking out one of its competition law defences. S made and supplied mobile devices and mobile telecommunications network infrastructure equipment. The defence struck out was founded on transactions by which the claimant had acquired five of the patents alleged to have been infringed. S contended that a third party (E) to the claim, one of S's competitors in the network infrastructure equipment market, and three companies in the claimant's group of companies had entered into a master sale agreement and associated agreements and assignments to transfer various patents and applications from E to the claimant without fully transferring an undertaking given by E to the European Telecommunications Standards Institute. The undertaking given was to offer its standard-essential patents, including the five patents in issue, on fair, reasonable and non-discriminatory (FRAND) terms. S contended that the agreements were prohibited by TFEU art.101 and were void. The judge held that there was no prospect of the defence succeeding. S argued that it was a developing area of law, and that its defence depended on factual issues which could not be resolved on a summary application. S further argued that the master sale agreements failed fully to transfer the FRAND undertakings in two respects: first, that the provisions of the agreements were not enforceable by third parties; and second, that the agreements fell short of fully transferring E's FRAND obligation, particularly the non-discrimination aspect of FRAND.

Held: Appeal allowed in part. (1) The Institute had addressed the competition concerns arising from the transfer of standard-essential patents from one company to another by requiring the transferor to include in the relevant transfer documents appropriate provisions to ensure that its FRAND undertaking was binding on the transferee. It had not, however, sought to distinguish between transferees that were members of the Institute and those that were not. Moreover, the European Commission had adopted a practical and realistic approach to any FRAND undertaking that the transferee of a standard-essential patent had given, and had assessed the likelihood of the patent being used significantly to impede legitimate competition despite that undertaking. Nothing had been adduced to suggest that the Commission attached any importance to whether the transferee was a member of the Institute or not. The judge's decision on that issue was therefore unimpeachable. He had properly considered the reality of the case. The claimant companies were required to give FRAND undertakings and had done so shortly after the patents in issue were transferred to them. The claimant was not a member of the Institute, but was just as constrained by the FRAND undertaking it had given as it would be if it were a member, and the judge was right to hold that, as a practical matter, any third party could require the claimant to grant it a licence under the patents on FRAND terms. It was unreasonable to suggest that the claimant companies should have given undertakings before acquiring the patents. Notwithstanding the fact that it was a developing area of law, that argument had no real prospect of success, *Huawei Technologies Co Ltd v ZTE Corp (C-170/13)* EU:C:2015:477, [2015] Bus. L.R. 1261 considered (see paras 25-41 of judgment). (2) Questions posed by the judge in relation to the practical consequences of imposing on the parties to any transfer of standard-essential patents an obligation to ensure that the FRAND undertakings were binding on the transferee provided powerful support for E's position. However, S was right to say that, while the judge's questions were legitimate ones, it could not be said that they were necessarily unanswerable and justified the summary dismissal of S's case. The judge had erred in finding that aspect of S's defence to be unarguable. It was an area of law which was in the course of development and S had a real prospect of persuading a judge at a full trial that art.101 required the effective transfer to the claimant of E's FRAND obligation so that the claimant could not obtain more favourable terms from its licensees than E could have obtained. There was also a degree of inter-relationship between that aspect of the defence and S's other defences, as it was arguable that the matters complained of acted together to allow E to circumvent its own FRAND obligations by increasing licence fees and weakening the competition between E and other users of its patents. It was therefore arguable that, in breach of art.101, the agreements fell short of a full transfer of the non-discrimination aspect of E's FRAND obligation, and that the anti-competitive nature of that breach rendered the agreements as a whole anti-competitive and void (paras 42-51).

UNWIRED PLANET INTERNATIONAL LTD v HUAWEI TECHNOLOGIES CO LTD; SAMSUNG ELECTRONICS CO LTD v TELEFONAKTIEBOLAGET L M ERICSSON *sub nom.* UNWIRED PLANET INC v SAMSUNG ELECTRONICS CO LTD, [2016] EWCA Civ 489, [2016] 5 C.M.L.R. 11, Tomlinson LJ, CA (Civ Div).

1295 Intellectual Property Enterprise Court–Jurisdiction–Intellectual Property Enterprise Court judge seeking to make extended civil restraint order–Whether "judge of the High Court" within meaning of CPR PD 3C para.3.1

[CPR PD 3C (Civil Restraint Orders) 2004 para.3.1, para.3.7; Senior Courts Act 1981 (c.54) s.9(1)]

The court was required to consider whether a judge of the Intellectual Property Enterprise Court had jurisdiction to make an extended civil restraint order under CPR PD 3C para.3.1. Under that provision, "a judge of the High Court" had jurisdiction to make an extended civil restraint order. The issues were whether (i) a judge of the IPEC was sitting as "a judge of the High Court"; (ii) the limitation in para.3.1 turned on the court in which the application was made.

Held: Judgment accordingly. (1) Extended civil restraint orders had previously been granted by deputy High Court judges. The authority of those judges was derived from the Senior Courts Act 1981 s.9(1). To the extent that qualification as "a judge of the High Court" was wholly or partially satisfied if the individual was sitting as a judge nominated under s.9(1), that criterion was satisfied by a judge sitting in the IPEC. A judge of the IPEC therefore had jurisdiction to make extended civil restraint orders (see paras 17-18 of judgment). (2) The IPEC was the successor to the Patents County Court. It was created as a specialist list of the Chancery Division of the High Court and, from 1 October 2013, all proceedings that commenced in the PCC were transferred to it. The IPEC had jurisdiction that was co-extensive with the Chancery Division. Since the meaning of "a judge of the High Court" was not limited to a puisne judge of the High Court, there was no reason why the court's jurisdiction was otherwise limited in relation to extended civil restraint orders (paras 19-22). (3) The term "a judge of the High Court" in para.3.1 and the term "High Court judge" in para.3.7 carried the same meaning within the confines of PD3C (para.24).

PERRY v FH BRUNDLE, [2015] EWHC 2737 (IPEC), [2015] B.P.I.R. 1449, Judge Hacon, IPEC.

1296 Passing off–Summary judgments–Whether website targeted relevant customers–Whether should be assessed in accordance with defendant's subjective intent–Appropriateness of issue for summary judgment

The claimant and defendant each applied for summary judgment on a preliminary issue in a claim for trade mark infringement and passing off. The claimant enjoyed a sizeable reputation in the UK, Ireland and the EU as a retail business using the name and mark ARGOS. Its website had the domain name "argos.co.uk". The defendant was a small US company, supplying computer aided design (CAD) software to the construction industry in North and South America. The claimant alleged that the defendant had infringed its ARGOS mark and committed passing off by operating its website under the domain name "argos.com". There was uncontroverted evidence that sizeable numbers of internet users in the UK and Europe intending to access the claimant's website had been mistakenly accessing the defendant's. The claimant contended that the defendant's website had been targeted at users within the UK and the EU in order to take advantage of those seeking to make contact with the claimant and thereby reap financial benefit from advertising income derived from increased traffic to the defendant's website. The issue whether the defendant's website was targeted to relevant consumers in the UK and the EU was raised as a preliminary issue, on which both parties sought summary judgment. The claimant submitted that the question of targeting should be assessed in accordance with the defendant's subjective intent, and that the evidence disclosed overwhelmingly that the defendant was intending to target the claimant's potential customers in the UK and the EU generally. It argued that the defendant was profiting financially from that targeting, knowing full well that users would come to its website by mistake, and that it was encouraging those mistakes. There was no direct authority on the question whether the website owner's subjective intent was material.

Held: Applications refused. The question of targeting and intention to target was not so straightforward that summary judgment was appropriate. The question of whether a website was targeted to a particular country was a multi-factorial one which depended on all the circumstances, including things which could be inferred from looking at the content on the website itself and elements arising from the inherent nature of the services offered by the website. In the law of passing off, liability was judged objectively. Whilst the test for liability did not depend on actual intentions, a court would readily find that a defendant who intended to misrepresent had accomplished what he set out to do, *Omnibill (Pty) Ltd v Egpsxxx Ltd (In Liquidation)* [2014] EWHC 3762 (IPEC), [2015] E.C.D.R. 1, [2015] C.L.Y. 1483 considered. Where there was evidence of an actual intent to target website viewers in another country, it would be wrong simply to ignore such evidence. An actual intent would nevertheless only be one factor: it could not be definitive. Whilst it was always possible that someone who intended to target a foreign country failed to do so despite his intention, it would be artificial to exclude such evidence of actual intention entirely. Since there was no direct authority, the issue should be decided at a trial in the context of specific findings of fact (see paras 28-29, 35-37 of judgment).

ARGOS LTD v ARGOS SYSTEMS INC, [2015] EWHC 3164 (Ch), [2016] F.S.R. 21, Robert Englehart QC, Ch D.

1297 Passing off–Survey evidence–Permission sought to adduce survey evidence–Assessment of value

The claimant applied for permission to adduce evidence of a pilot survey, to carry out a full survey, and to rely on evidence from both surveys in its passing off claim. The claimant manufactured taxis and had Community trade marks depicting versions of London black cabs. The first defendant carried on research into and testing of transportation solutions, and the second defendant manufactured and sold motor vehicles. They had produced a prototype of a taxi, but had not yet begun commercial sales. The claimant issued proceedings against them, alleging trade mark infringement and passing off arising out of the similarity between the appearance of its and the defendants' proposed vehicles. It complained that the defendants had deliberately adopted a design which resembled its black cab in order to benefit from its extensive goodwill and reputation. The claimant had conducted a pilot survey involving interviews in London with 98 actual or prospective taxi passengers, in which they were shown photographs of the parties' vehicles and asked a number of questions, including whether they thought that there was a connection between the taxis' manufacturers. It proposed a full survey of 500 to 1,000 persons. The claimant contended that the trial judge was likely to be assisted by the evidence from the pilot and a full survey, since he was unlikely to be familiar with how the public, and in particular tourists, perceived the shape of London taxis. The defendants submitted that hailing a London taxi was within a judge's experience and the likelihood of deception of taxi passengers was a question of fact for him. They argued that the costs of a full survey would exceed those allowed for in the parties' costs budgets, and that admitting the survey evidence would have a disproportionate impact on the existing five-day trial.

Held: Application refused. The principles and guidance concerning the admission of surveys and evidence derived from them revolved around the test of "real value": a judge should not admit survey evidence unless satisfied that it would be valuable and that its likely utility justified the costs involved, *Interflora Inc v Marks & Spencer Plc* [2012] EWCA Civ 1501, [2013] 2 All E.R. 663, [2013] C.L.Y. 1830, *Interflora Inc v Marks & Spencer Plc* [2013] EWCA Civ 319, [2013] F.S.R. 26, [2013] C.L.Y. 1828 and *Zee Entertainment Enterprises Ltd v Zeebox Ltd* [2014] EWCA Civ 82, [2014] F.S.R. 26, [2014] C.L.Y. 289 applied. Judges in passing off cases were familiar with taking into account any relevant characteristics of the purchasing public and making allowances for them, *Zee Entertainment* applied. The real issue in passing off cases was deception; accordingly, if a survey went to the question of whether the relevant public had a propensity to make a connection between the parties' goods or services, it was only going to a peripheral or subsidiary issue, which was a reason for degrading its value and not admitting it, *Zee Entertainment* applied. There was nothing that was likely to be unfamiliar or not readily understandable to the trial judge in the instant case so as to suggest that he was likely to need or derive assistance from the admission of the results of the pilot survey, the results of a full survey, or the evidence derived from either of them. Moreover, the question in the survey as to the interviewee's perception of a connection between the parties' vehicles was leading to an unacceptable degree and directed them into a field of speculation upon which they would never have embarked had the question not been put. Furthermore, the cost of the proposed survey would require around 20 per cent of the claimant's litigation budget. Even if the survey satisfied the criterion of being reliable, it was doubtful whether its value would justify the cost. Those costs were significant, whether viewed in absolute or proportionate terms, particularly since, on any view, the survey was relevant to only part of the claimant's case. The factor weighing most heavily against the admission of the survey evidence was, however, the likely impact on the trial hearing. If that evidence was to be admitted, it was likely that the trial estimate would need to be increased, or a disproportionate part of the existing five-day fixture would be spent dealing with it. That would not be worthwhile (see paras 15-16, 18-19, 54, 63, 65, 71-72, 74 of judgment).

LONDON TAXI CORP LTD (T/A LONDON TAXI CO) v FRAZER-NASH RESEARCH LTD, [2015] EWHC 1840 (Ch), [2016] F.S.R. 7, Richard Spearman QC, Ch D.

1298 Patent claims–Claim construction–Running unpleaded argument at trial–Special category–Ability to hear argument of both parties at trial

[Civil Procedure Rules 1998 r.63.20(1)]

The claimant patent proprietors alleged that the defendant had infringed its UK patent, and the defendant counterclaimed for the patent's revocation. The patent concerned a hybrid system for protecting steel rebars in reinforced concrete. Claim 1 of the patent was a method claim describing a two-stage process. In the first phase, anodes were embedded in the concrete and subjected to a high current from a DC source, which arrested corrosion by drawing aggressive chloride ions away from the concrete towards the anode. The second "sacrificial" phase involved using a long-term, low-current on the same anode, causing it to suffer metal dissolution. Claim 12 of the patent was a product claim for an anode suitable for use in that hybrid protection method, such as a zinc anode with a titanium connector. The issues were (i) whether unpleaded arguments on the patent's construction could be raised at trial: (ii) the proper construction of claims 1 and 12; (iii) whether the patent lacked novelty over certain prior art; (iv) whether the patent lacked an inventive step; (v) whether an anode supplied by the defendant infringed the patent. The defendant contended, inter alia, that the patent lacked novelty and was obvious over a UK patent application (Fosroc 1) disclosing a means of protecting rebars by cathodic protection using anodes adapted for embedment in concrete. It acknowledged that if claim 12 of the patent was construed as not requiring connection to a power supply, it had infringed it, but it denied that construction.

Held: Judgment for defendant. (1) A party running an unpleaded argument at trial would ordinarily breach CPR r.63.20(1), but arguments on the construction of a patent claim fell into a special category. The question of construction remained open up to and throughout trial. The court was not limited in its conclusions on construction by the parties' submissions and had to do its best to arrive at the correct construction, *Consafe Engineering (UK) Ltd v Emtunga UK Ltd* [1999] R.P.C. 154, [1999] C.L.Y. 3514 applied. The construction of a claim need not be consistent with the evidence,

Scanvaegt International A/S v Pelcombe Ltd (formerly Portals Engineering Ltd) [1998] F.S.R. 786, [1998] C.L.Y. 3462 applied. It would be unhelpful for arguments on construction during trial to be interrupted by periodic challenges as to whether they fell squarely within the pleaded case. Parties in the IPEC would be well-advised to include all arguments in their pleading, including those on construction, to avoid the risk of having part of their case disregarded. Moreover, deliberately concealing an argument for tactical reasons was liable to be met with a severe sanction. However, provided there had been no deliberate concealment and the opposing party was unable to prove significant prejudice from the failure to plead the argument, the court was unlikely to resist hearing the parties' arguments (see paras 19-21 of judgment). (2) The law on the construction of patent claims was well-established: the starting point was to give the words their ordinary meaning, *Virgin Atlantic Airways Ltd v Premium Aircraft Interiors Group* [2009] EWCA Civ 1062, [2010] R.P.C. 8, [2010] C.L.Y. 1959 considered. On its proper construction, the second phase of claim 1 was limited to the anode's sacrificial metal dissolution, rather than an impressed current treatment. Under claim 12, the connection detail of the anode did not need to be connected to a DC power supply. If claim 12 was found to be valid, it would therefore have been infringed (paras 18, 27-28, 32, 38). (3) The prior art had to both disclose subject-matter which, if performed, would necessarily result in patent infringement and enable the invention in the sense that the skilled person would have been able to perform it, *Synthon BV v SmithKline Beecham Plc (No.2)* [2005] UKHL 59, [2006] 1 All E.R. 685, [2006] C.L.Y. 2525 applied. Fosroc 1 did not disclose a number of elements present in the patent, and claim 12 did not lack novelty over it (paras 40, 57). (4) The structured approach to obviousness had been set out in *Pozzoli SpA v BDMO SA* [2007] EWCA Civ 588, [2007] F.S.R. 37, [2007] C.L.Y. 2634 and guidance had been given in *MedImmune Ltd v Novartis Pharmaceuticals UK Ltd* [2012] EWCA Civ 1234, [2013] R.P.C. 27, *Pozzoli* and *MedImmune* considered. It would have been obvious to the skilled person to use a zinc anode in a Fosroc 1 assembly with a titanium connection. The invention in claim 12 therefore lacked inventive step relative to Fosroc 1 (paras 60-61, 64). (5) On its proper construction, claim 1 of the patent was valid but not infringed; claim 12 was invalid: had it been valid it would have been infringed (para.120).

GLASS v FREYSSINET LTD, [2015] EWHC 2972 (IPEC), [2016] F.S.R. 17, Judge Hacon, IPEC.

1299 Patent claims–Interpretation–Patent claims containing numerical range

A patentee appealed against a declaration (*Smith & Nephew Plc v ConvaTec Technologies Inc* [2013] EWHC 3955 (Pat), [2014] R.P.C. 22, [2014] C.L.Y. 1879) that the respondent (S) had not infringed its European patent by one of its two methods. S cross-appealed against a decision that its other method was infringing. The patent was concerned with a process for the silverisation of gel-forming fibres in wound dressings. It provided a method of making light-stabilised silverised antimicrobial materials. The method comprised three steps, the third of which involved subjecting gel-forming fibres to a binding agent. The claim under consideration provided that the agent had to be present in a concentration of "between 1 per cent and 25 per cent". S produced its own range of wound dressings by following the steps in the patent, save that it used a concentration of binding agent of no more than 0.77 per cent (the modified process). The patentee claimed that the modified process infringed because in a scientific context the standard practice was to express numerical values to a particular degree of accuracy, and that using the standard rounding convention, the number five was always rounded up. Therefore, it claimed that "between 1 per cent and 25 per cent" encompassed all concentrations greater than or equal to 0.5 per cent and less than 25.5 per cent. The judge rejected that argument, finding that the claim included concentrations greater than or equal to 0.95 per cent and less than 25.5 per cent. On that basis he held that while the modified process did not infringe the patent, an earlier process did. The patentee submitted that "between 1 per cent and 25 per cent" encompassed all concentrations greater than or equal to 0.5 per cent and less than 25.5 per cent. S argued that it encompassed all concentrations greater than or equal to precisely 1 per cent, and less than or equal to precisely 25 per cent.

Held: Appeal allowed, cross-appeal dismissed. (1) The approach to be adopted in the interpretation of claims containing a numerical range was the same as that to be adopted in relation to any other patent claim. The exercise was an objective one, and the question was what a skilled person would have understood the patentee to mean. The claims were to be construed purposively and in context, *Kirin-Amgen Inc v Transkaryotic Therapies Inc (No.2)* [2004] UKHL 46, [2005] 1 All E.R. 667, [2005] C.L.Y. 2479 and *Virgin Atlantic Airways Ltd v Premium Aircraft Interiors Group* [2009] EWCA Civ 1062, [2010] R.P.C. 8, [2010] C.L.Y. 1959 followed. The reader came to the specification with the benefit of the common general knowledge, and the patentee was likely to have chosen his words with the benefit of skilled advice. Where a numerical range was being construed, the question was what the skilled person would understand the numerals to mean. The scope of the claim had to be the same whether infringement or validity was being considered; there was no justification for using rounding or approximation to change the disclosure of the prior art or to modify the alleged infringement; and the meaning and scope of the range had to be ascertained in light of the common general knowledge and in the context of the specification as a whole. Whether the skilled person might understand that the patentee had expressed the numerals to a limited degree of precision so as to include all values falling within the claimed range when stated with the same degree of precision would depend on all the circumstances, including the number of decimal places or significant figures to which the numerals were expressed (see paras 16-42 of judgment). (2) There were two questions in the instant case. The first was whether the skilled person would believe that 1 per cent and 25 per cent were exact values, or whether he would understand that the patentee had used a standard number convention to express the limits of the claim to a lesser degree of accuracy. It was common ground that the skilled person could measure concentrations of binding agent to a high degree of accuracy. However, it was clear from the teaching of the specification that the binding agent concentration was not critical, and it was apparent from the body of the specification that the patentee was aware of the possibility of expressing numerical values with a high degree of precision. The skilled person would therefore understand that the patentee had chosen to express the numerical limits of the range to only a limited degree of accuracy. The use of the word "between" did not indicate that the percentages were exact values. It simply denoted the outer limits of the range, saying nothing about the degree of precision with which they were expressed (paras 43-52). The second question was whether the skilled person would understand the numbers to be expressed as whole numbers or in terms of significant figures. There was no logical basis for preferring the significant numbers approach. The patentee was aiming to convey the range of permissible binding agent concentrations and the accuracy with which those concentrations had to be determined. The skilled person would understand the 1 per cent and 25 per cent limits to have been expressed to the nearest whole number. In reaching the opposite conclusion, the judge had erred. He should have found that the skilled reader would understand that the patentee intended the claim to embrace all concentrations of binding agent greater than or equal to 0.5 per cent and less than 25.5 per cent (paras 53-65).

SMITH & NEPHEW PLC v CONVATEC TECHNOLOGIES INC *sub nom.* CONVATEC TECHNOLOGIES INC v SMITH & NEPHEW PLC, [2015] EWCA Civ 607, [2015] R.P.C. 32, Kitchin LJ, CA (Civ Div).

1300 Patent proceedings–Account of profits–Deduction of business overheads

The appellant, which had infringed the respondent's patent, appealed against a judge's determination (*OOO Abbott v Design and Display Ltd* [2014] EWHC 2924 (IPEC)) of the account of profits deriving from the infringement. The court had found in *OOO Abbott v Design and Display Ltd* [2013] EWPCC 27 that shop fittings manufactured and sold by the appellant infringed the respondent's patent for aluminium snap-in inserts used for fixing shelves and brackets to panels or slat walls used by shops to construct displays of merchandise. At that hearing it was held that the invention was a "snap-in insert made from a resilient metal like aluminium". The insert fitted into a horizontal slot on the panel or slat wall. The judge below, when determining the account of profits, considered that the inventive scope of the patent was not just the mere idea of an insert made of resilient metal, but the fact that the insert had a particular shape which engaged with the slot in the panel by snap-in means. He found that the scope of the profit derived from the infringement extended to the profit made from sales of the panels into which the infringing inserts were incorporated. He also found that general overheads could not be offset against the profits. The appellant disputed the judge's characterisation of the invention, maintaining that the panels were part of common general knowledge and not part of the inventive concept. The issues were whether the appellant: (1) was liable for the whole of the profits made on the sale of the panels; (2) was entitled to set off its general overheads against the gross profit for which it was accountable.

Held: Appeal allowed. (1) There was nothing wrong with the judge's identification of the inventive concept. He had not described the panel/slat wall as being part of that concept. His description was much more limited, focusing on the material from which the insert was made, its particular shape and the way in which it interacted with the panels so as to enable it to be snapped in from the front. The judge had then considered causation and had determined that the sale of the inserts and the sale of the panels necessarily went hand-in-hand. However, the question whether an infringement had caused loss was a different question from that of whether the infringer had derived a profit. The judge had asked the wrong question: he had asked whether sales of the insert and the panel would have happened separately instead of asking how much of the profit on the sale was derived from the infringement. In a case in which the infringement did not "drive" the sale, it was wrong in principle to attribute the whole of the profit to the infringement. It did not follow from the fact that customers wanted a slat wall incorporating an insert that they wanted a slat wall incorporating an *infringing* insert. The judge had been wrong to say that because the sales went together, the sale of the inserts drove the sale of the panels. The mere fact that the two went together was not sufficient to establish that the whole of the profit earned on the composite item was derived from the invention. The judge should have apportioned the overall profit. The case was remitted for apportionment, although the judge would not be precluded from finding as a fact that the infringing insert was the "essential ingredient" of the panel / slat wall, *Gerber Garment Technology Inc v Lectra Systems Ltd* [1997] R.P.C. 443, [1997] C.L.Y. 3903, *Meters v Metropolitan Gas Meters* [1911] 28 R.P.C. 157 and *Dart Industries Inc v Decor Corp Pty Ltd* [1994] F.S.R. 567 considered (see paras 13-23, 36-37 of judgment). (2) Set-off of overheads depended on whether the overheads would have been incurred in any event, even if the infringement had not occurred, and whether the sale of infringing products would have been replaced by the sale of non-infringing products. If the infringer established that, but for the infringement, it would have sold other, non-infringing, products, then to the extent that its actual overheads would have been used in sustaining that alternative sale, the overheads could be deducted in computing the profits for which the infringer was required to account, *Dart Industries* and *Woolley v UP Global Sourcing UK Ltd* [2014] EWHC 493 (Ch), [2014] F.S.R. 37, [2014] C.L.Y. 1887 considered. In the instant case, the judge below had found that if the appellant had not been selling the infringing products, it would have used the same overheads in generating profits by selling non-infringing products. His reasoning regarding the overheads did not therefore support the conclusion he had reached. He had thought, incorrectly, that running the business to maximum capacity was a threshold condition which had to have the consequence of displacing the alternative business. His decision on overheads could not stand (paras 42-44, 48, 51).

OOO ABBOTT v DESIGN AND DISPLAY LTD *sub nom.* DESIGN AND DISPLAY LTD v OOO ABBOTT, [2016] EWCA Civ 95, [2016] F.S.R. 27, Sir Terence Etherton C, CA (Civ Div).

1301 Patent proceedings–Case management–Consideration notices of experiments–Need of scientific advisor

[Civil Procedure Rules 1998 r.33.4; CPR PD 63 (Patents and Other Intellectual Property Claims) 2003; Civil Evidence Act 1995 (c.38) s.3]

The court was required to determine various matters in preparation for a patent infringement trial. The claimant patentee claimed that the defendants had infringed its UK patent for a method of finding hydrocarbons by determining the nature of subterranean reservoirs. The defendants counterclaimed for revocation, and a trial had been fixed. A judge had given directions for experiments, including computer modelling, and notices of experiments were given. The claimant sought to rely on a previous witness statement from one of the inventors, given in earlier litigation concerning the patent's validity, as a hearsay statement, and applied for permission to extend its case on infringement. The defendants sought further directions in respect of experiments, raised the possibility of the court sitting with a scientific adviser, and applied for permission to call the inventor for cross-examination. The issues were: (1) the purpose and procedure for notices of experiments; (2) whether a scientific adviser was required; (3) the scope of the inventor's cross-examination; (4) whether, as the defendants contended, it was too late to deal with the issues raised by the amended pleadings, despite them raising an arguable case.

Held: Judgment accordingly. (1) Computer modelling and simulations should generally be subject to the experimental notice regime, *Consafe Engineering (UK) Ltd v Emtunga UK Ltd* [1999] R.P.C. 154, [1999] C.L.Y. 3514 applied. Notices of experiments stated the facts to be admitted and operated as notices to admit facts. The first fact to be admitted in the instant case was that when the experiment was performed, the result provided was produced. Further "interpretative" facts were then set out, but did not make clear overall what role the experiments were to play in the proceedings. The parties appeared to have thought that at the instant stage the court did not need to understand that role in depth; that was incorrect. When the court was being asked to make further directions regarding experiments, it was necessary for the party seeking to rely on them to explain what role the experiments were to play, in context, and with more than a simple reference to an expert's report. CPR PD 63 para.7.1 required a party seeking to establish any fact by experimental proof conducted for the purpose of litigation to serve a notice stating the facts which it sought to establish. That rule allowed the court to understand what the experiment was for and to retain control over the experimental evidence. The requirement that the other party respond to the notice properly was also important. The court gave the defendants permission to rely on the experiments to prove the facts set out in the notices, directed the claimant to respond to the notices and gave it permission to serve a notice in reply (see paras 10, 14, 16, 18, 21-24, 26 of judgment). (2) The court's role was to exercise its judicial function and exclude from consideration extraneous opinions, and a scientific adviser's role was to assist the court in understanding the technical evidence and to help the court evaluate it, *Halliburton Energy Services Inc v Smith International (North Sea) Ltd* [2006] EWCA Civ 1599, [2007] Bus. L.R. 460, [2007] C.L.Y. 2625 followed. Keeping those roles in mind, and since the instant case was technically complex, the right course was for the parties to arrange for the trial judge to have a non-controversial introductory course from a marine controlled source electromagnetic expert. With that assistance the judge would be well-equipped to handle the trial without a scientific advisor sitting in. The parties could see the written materials produced by the adviser after the introductory course had taken place (paras 34-36). (3) The words of the Civil Evidence Act 1995 s.3 were wider than the terms of CPR r.33.4 in terms of whether cross-examination of the maker of a hearsay statement was confined to the contents of the statement. The rule's more limited wording was not an accident. A party cross-examining had in effect got evidence-in-chief in the form of the hearsay statement; if it could cross-examine more widely it could introduce new evidence, effectively in chief, creating confusion for the party serving the hearsay notice as to the scope of its re-examination. Cross-examination under r.33.4 was confined to the contents of the statement, although the court could no doubt permit wider cross-examination in a proper case upon careful consideration of the consequences. Given the previous judge's approach to the inventor's evidence, cross-examination under r.33.4, and not on a wider basis, was appropriate (paras 41, 43-44). (4) As a general principle it was better to resolve the matters raised by the amended pleading in one go, rather than to split them. They could be accommodated at the trial on the basis of the existing disclosures, at the claimant's risk; if further evidence was required for the claimant to prove its amended case, the new issues could be hived off later (paras 48-49).

ELECTROMAGNETIC GEOSERVICES ASA v PETROLEUM GEO-SERVICES ASA, [2016] EWHC 27 (Pat), [2016] 1 W.L.R. 2353, Birss J, Ch D (Patents Ct).

1302 Patent proceedings–Costs–Adjournment of costs assessment in patent infringement proceedings–Meaning of "claim" in r.45.31(1)(a) CPR

[Civil Procedure Rules 1998 r.45.31(1)(a), r.45.42(2)]

The court was required to determine costs issues arising from a patent infringement claim. The claimants had brought claims against the defendants for misrepresentation and unjustified threats of patent infringement proceedings. The first defendant had counterclaimed for royalties due under a licensing agreement. In *Global Flood Defence Systems Ltd v Johann Van Den Noort Beheer BV* [2016] EWHC 99 (IPEC), [2016] F.S.R. 26, [2016] 1305, the court held that the claim for misrepresentation failed, the counterclaim for royalties succeeded, and that the claim in relation to threats should be adjourned. The defendants sought their costs in relation to the misrepresentation and royalties claims, subject to the applicable costs caps. The claimants submitted that the costs assessment should be adjourned until the threats allegation had been resolved, as it was not possible to say which party had won overall and/or whether the court should apply a discount or set-off of that party's costs.

Held: Costs assessment adjourned. At the end of a trial in the instant court, the court would normally decide which party was the overall winner. In appropriate cases, the winner's costs would be subject to a discount or there would be a set-off of costs. Each of the stage costs incurred by the winner would be subjected to summary assessment and then, if appropriate, a discount or set-off would be applied to each of the assessed costs. The total of the assessed stage costs after discount or set-off would be awarded, subject to the £50,000 overall cap, *BOS GmbH & Co KG v Cobra UK Automotive Products Division Ltd (In Administration) (Costs)* [2012] EWPCC 44, [2012] 6 Costs L.R. 1083, [2013] C.L.Y. 325 applied (see para.7 of judgment). The issue of whether to adjourn the costs assessment turned on the correct meaning of the word "claim" in CPR r.45.31(1)(a). It could mean the proceedings as a whole, namely everything in dispute under one claim number, or something less than that. CPR r.45.42(2) expressly required that, where it arose, a set-off had to be applied before the overall cap of £50,000 was to be taken into account. Therefore, if "claim" meant the proceedings as a whole, costs could not be assessed until all issues in the entire proceedings had been decided. The defendants proposed a different construction, relying on *Destra Software Ltd v Comada (UK) LLP* [2012] EWPCC 39, that it meant all of the claims which had been the subject of a final determination by the court. However, that was not a self-evident meaning. It would also have the consequence that there would be separate costs caps for separate parts of a single set of proceedings if a preliminary point was heard, or part of the proceedings adjourned to a separate trial, or if there were an application for summary judgment in respect of part of the proceedings. In other words, the parties would begin the proceedings with the safeguard that, if it all ended badly, their liability in costs to the other side would not rise above £50,000. They would then discover that, because of how the case had developed procedurally, their liability would be twice or more than what they had bargained for. It could even provide parties with an incentive to argue for preliminary points or summary judgment in relation to one or more of the issues in order to put financial pressure on the opposing party. That did not seem to be in accordance with the overall intention of how the instant court should work. The word "claim" therefore referred to a single set of proceedings, and it followed that the court could not assess costs in the instant claim until all the issues, including the threats allegation, had been resolved, *Liversidge v Owen Mumford Ltd* [2012] EWPCC 40, [2012] 6 Costs L.R. 1076, [2013] C.L.Y. 1811 and *Henderson v All Around The World Recordings Ltd (Costs)* [2013] EWPCC 19, [2013] F.S.R. 42, [2014] C.L.Y. 356 applied, *Destra* considered (paras 12-16).

GLOBAL FLOOD DEFENCE SYSTEMS LTD v JOHANN VAN DEN NOORT BEHEER BV, [2016] EWHC 189 (IPEC), [2016] 1 Costs L.R. 137, Judge Hacon, Ch D.

1303 Patent proceedings–Finality–Conditional application to amend claim after trial–Abuse of process

The court was required to determine as a preliminary issue whether an application by the defendant (Warner) to amend its UK patent amounted to an abuse of process. The patent concerned the second medical use of pregabalin for pain relief. Its revocation had been sought in two actions brought by the claimants (Mylan and Actavis). The court had found that certain claims of the patent were invalid for insufficiency. In respect of claim 3 of the patent, providing for "use of pregabalin for the preparation of a pharmaceutical composition for treating neuropathic pain", the judge had held that it was not plausible in the light of the specification and the common general knowledge that pregabalin would be efficacious for the treatment of central neuropathic pain, but it was plausible that it would be efficacious for the treatment of peripheral neuropathic pain. Warner was given permission to appeal against the insufficiency decision and, in case its appeal was unsuccessful, it conditionally applied to amend claim 3 by adding to it the words "caused by injury or infection of peripheral sensory nerves". Mylan and Actavis contended that the application to re-write claim 3 amounted to an abuse of process because it could and should have been made before trial, and a second trial would be required if the amendment was allowed. Warner denied that a second trial would be necessary, but submitted that, even if it was, there was no abuse of process as it was the victim of procedural unfairness by Mylan and Actavis since they had ambushed it by only raising the insufficiency case on which they succeeded at trial during the cross-examination of its witnesses and then in closing submissions.

Held: Preliminary issue determined in favour of Mylan and Actavis. (1) There should be finality in litigation and a party should not be twice-vexed in the same matter; the bringing of a claim or the raising of a defence in later proceedings might, without more, amount to abuse if the court was satisfied (the onus being on the party alleging abuse) that the claim or defence should have been raised in the earlier proceedings, *Johnson v Gore Wood & Co (No.1)* [2002] 2 A.C. 1, [2001] C.L.Y. 410 applied. That principle applied to patent cases, and would be breached where to allow a proposed patent amendment would lead to a second trial on a patent's validity, *Nikken Kosakusho Works v Pioneer Trading Co* [2005] EWCA Civ 906, [2006] F.S.R. 4, [2006] C.L.Y. 2531 followed (see paras 7-8, 14 of judgment). (2) Any objection to the sufficiency of the proposed amended claim 3 could not fairly be determined without giving Mylan and Actavis the opportunity to adduce evidence directed to that issue. If the amendment application was allowed, it would therefore necessitate a second trial in respect of claim 3's validity (paras 131-132). (3) Warner was not the victim of any procedural unfairness. It should have been aware at all material times that there was a distinction between peripheral neuropathic pain and central neuropathic pain. Moreover, Mylan and Actavis had made their case clear in their skeleton arguments exchanged a week before trial, and Warner had raised no complaint during trial that it had been taken by surprise as to the sufficiency of claim 3 (paras 138-143). (4) A key purpose of the patent system, particularly in the pharmaceutical field, was to incentivise research for the public's benefit. However, another key purpose was to ensure that monopolies were properly justified, and in particular that the scope of the patentee's monopoly reflected his technical contribution to the art. Post-trial validating amendments had to be considered on the basis of those competing factors in a way consistent with the courts' general policy on the finality of litigation. The public interest in such finality was another minor factor in favour of Actavis and Mylan's argument on abuse of process (para.147). (5) The application to amend claim 3 was struck out as an abuse of process because it could and should have been made prior to trial. The application amounted to unjust harassment of Mylan and Actavis, and would also be contrary to the interests of other generic suppliers of pregabalin (paras 148-149).

GENERICS (UK) LTD (T/A MYLAN) v WARNER-LAMBERT CO LLC; ACTAVIS GROUP PTC EHFV WARNER-LAMBERT CO LLC; WARNER-LAMBERT CO LLC v ACTAVIS GROUP PTC EHF, [2015] EWHC 3370 (Pat), [2016] R.P.C. 16, Arnold J, Ch D (Patents Ct).

1304 Patent proceedings–Groundless threats–Claiming groundless threats of patent infringement where only pending patent application existing–Ability to try to justify threats when patent granted–Appropriateness of adjournment

[Patents Act 1977 (c.37) s.70, s.70(2A)]

The claimants appealed against the adjournment of the trial of their claim alleging groundless threats of patent infringement proceedings. The second defendant, who owned the first defendant company, had invented a self-closing flood barrier (SCFB). In 2011, they applied for a European patent. Since 2010, the claimants had been licensed by the defendants to make and distribute the SCFB. Their commercial relationship broke down in 2013 and the licence was terminated in early 2014. The claimants stopped selling the SCFB, instead marketing an alternative product. In March 2014, the defendants threatened imminent proceedings for infringement of a granted patent. The claimants issued proceedings against the defendants for groundless threats pursuant to the Patents Act 1977 s.70, and the defendants counterclaimed for royalties due under the licence. The claimants applied for summary judgment on the basis that, as matter of law, the threats could not be justified because they were threats of proceedings for infringement of a granted patent whereas the application had not yet been granted. The judge rejected that argument and the trial was set for December 2015. In October 2015, the defendants' application to adjourn the trial of the threats claim in order to allow time for the patent to be granted was refused. They requested expedition of their patent application, and in November 2015 the EPO gave notice of its decision to grant the patent. At the start of the trial, the judge allowed the defendants' renewed application for an adjournment, permitting them to amend their defence and counterclaim to include any additional defences they might wish to rely on in the light of the fact that the patent was about to be granted. It was granted later that month. The issues were (1) whether, if one person (X) threatened another person (Y) with proceedings for infringement of a granted patent at a time when X only had a pending patent application, it was open to X to attempt to justify that threat once the patent had been granted; (2) the judge had been wrong to adjourn the trial.

Held: Appeal dismissed. (1) The resolution of the first issue depended on the construction of s.70(2A), which provided a defence of justification where the defendant proved that the acts in respect of which proceedings were threatened constituted or would constitute patent infringement. Section 70 created a tort of strict liability which did not require proof of actual damage in order to be actionable. It acted as a restraint on commercial freedom of speech and represented an obstacle to the negotiation and settlement of patent disputes without resorting to infringement proceedings. The court should therefore be slow to conclude that s.70 made a class of threats incapable of justification in the absence of clear wording to that effect. The vice at which s.70 was aimed was the damage which could be caused to a manufacturer or importer of goods by threats of patent infringement proceedings directed at its customers. Nevertheless, it was clear from s.70(2A) that it was lawful to make such threats where they were justified. In considering whether a threat was justified, what mattered was whether the person making the threat was ultimately able to obtain relief in respect of the acts in question. Section 70(2A) required the court to consider whether the acts in respect of which proceedings were threatened constituted an infringement, not whether the terms of the threat were justified. The availability of the justification defence should not depend on the precise manner in which the threat was expressed, and in particular whether the author of the threat took sufficient care to distinguish between the rights presently conferred by a granted patent and the contingent rights conferred by a patent application if and when it was granted. The potential uncertainty if grant of the patent was still awaited at the date of the threat might be undesirable, but it did not greatly alter the position. Accordingly, if a party threatened another with proceedings for infringement of a granted patent at a time when it only had a pending patent application, it was open to the first party to attempt to justify that threat once the patent had been granted (see paras 28, 34-37, 39 of judgment). (2) The judge's decision to adjourn the trial was a case management decision: it contained no error of principle and was well within the ambit of his discretion. Given that the grant of the patent was imminent, an adjournment was fully justified. Otherwise, the consequence would be that the claimants would win the threats claim by default even though the defendants would shortly be in a position to attempt to justify the threats (para.50).

GLOBAL FLOOD DEFENCE SYSTEMS LTD v JOHANN VAN DEN NOORT BEHEER BV, [2016] EWHC 1851 (Pat), [2016] Bus. L.R. 1144, Arnold J, Ch D (Patents Ct).

1305 Patent proceedings–Groundless threats–Trial regarding unjustified threats of patent infringement proceedings by developer–Adjournment after grant of European patent to developer

[Patents Act 1977 (c.37) s.70, s.70(2A)]

The claimants brought a claim for unjustified threats of patent infringement proceedings against the defendants, the first claimant brought a claim for misrepresentation against the defendants, and the first defendant counterclaimed for royalties due under a licensing agreement. The first defendant company had produced a self-closing flood barrier, and the second defendant was its director and shareholder.

The second claimant traded in flood defence products and entered into a licence agreement with the first defendant concerning patent rights and know-how under which the first claimant became the worldwide distributor of the self-closing flood barrier. The claimants alleged that the defendants falsely represented to them prior to the conclusion of the licence agreement that the self-closing flood barrier was protected by a valid European patent for 20 years from January 1996; that just before the end of August 2010 a new patent had been granted for the self-closing flood barrier; and that it was protected by a United States patent. A dispute about royalties arose. The first claimant stopped paying royalties and the first defendant ended the agreement. The first claimant stopped selling the self-closing flood barrier, instead marketing an alternative flood defence product. The defendants alleged that the alternative product infringed their patent and threatened patent infringement proceedings. The claimants brought the instant proceedings, asserting that the defendants' threats were groundless. The defendants had a European patent application in respect of the self-closing flood barrier, but no granted patent. They asserted that the threats were justifiable under the Patents Act 1977 s.70(2A). By the time trial began, the patent had still not been granted. An interim injunction had been made to prevent the defendants from making further threats. The claimants asserted that the defendants had made a further threat after the grant of the injunction. The patent was granted after the trial had begun.

Held: Judgment accordingly. (1) Although *Brain v Ingledew Brown Bennison & Garrett (No.2)* [1997] F.S.R. 271, [1997] C.L.Y. 3916 did not resolve the circumstances in which a stay of threats proceedings concerning a patent application should be granted even though the patent might not yet have been, that did not mean that there were no circumstances in which that might happen, Brain considered. The present circumstances qualified for a stay. Once the notice of grant had been issued, the speculation about what the final claims might be concerned with fell away, Brain considered. The speed with which the defendants prosecuted the patent application was irrelevant to the court's discretion. The delay in the trial was not ideal, but it was as a result of how the proceedings had progressed and, in any event, prejudice to the claimants was limited as they were protected by an interim injunction. The further alleged threat was not actionable under s.70; it could reasonably be interpreted it as being directed at acts outside the UK That did not affect the exercise of the court's discretion on adjourning the issue of threats to allow the defendants an opportunity to defend the threats on the ground that they were justified. The issue was adjourned (see paras 20-29 of judgment). (2) There had been a representation in the recital of the licence agreement that the self-closing flood barrier had been protected by a valid European patent for 20 years from 1996, but it was clear from the operative part of the agreement that the first claimant would not be licensed under any granted European patent. Therefore, the first claimant could not have been induced to enter into the agreement by reason of that combined representation. Clear words in the operative part of an agreement could not be controlled by recitals, *Leggott v Barrett* (1880) 15 Ch. D. 306 applied. An informed reader would have realised that the recital made no sense in the context of the operative terms of the licence and would have realised that the only subsisting patent right owned by the first defendant was the PCT application (paras 66-71). A false representation about the grant of a new patent had not been made. An informed person would have realised that loose language was being used and that the reference to a 'new patent' was in fact a new PCT application and as a result there would be no protection anywhere under any granted patent depending on whether patents were to be granted. Even if there had been a false representation it would have been corrected by the licence agreement. In respect of an alleged US patent, either there was no such misrepresentation or it could not have operated in the mind of the first claimant such as to induce it to enter the agreement (paras 73-75). (3) The claimants' had relied on the alleged misrepresentations as its defence to the counterclaim. However, as its claim for misrepresentation failed and it did not have permission to raise a new defence based on estoppels, the counterclaim for royalties succeeded (paras 77-78).

GLOBAL FLOOD DEFENCE SYSTEMS LTD v JOHANN VAN DEN NOORT BEHEER BV, [2016] EWHC 99 (IPEC), [2016] F.S.R. 26, Judge Hacon, Ch D.

1306 Patent proceedings–Jurisdiction–Claim for infringement relating to German designation of patent–Defence challenging validity–Treatment as single issue–Applicability of rule of jurisdiction in art.24(4) Regulation 1215/2012

[Civil Procedure Rules 1998 r.25.1, r.25.1(1)(c); Regulation 1215/2012 on jurisdiction and the recognition and enforcement of judgments in civil and commercial matters 2012 art.24(2); Civil Jurisdiction and Judgments Act 1982 (c.27) s.25; Senior Courts Act 1981 (c.54) s.37(1)]

A patent proprietor and its licensee applied for declarations in infringement proceedings which they had brought against the defendant in relation to the UK and German designations of the patent. The defendant denied infringement and issued proceedings in the German court, challenging the validity of the patent for lack of novelty and inventive step. It also challenged the jurisdiction of the instant court in the event that the German designation of the patent were found to be invalid. Those proceedings were pending at the date of the instant hearing. The claimants sought an order pursuant to CPR r.25.1(1)(c) and (iv) for the provision by the defendant of samples for independent testing for the purposes of the infringement claims. They also applied to amend their particulars of claim to seek a declaration that, if the German designation were not found to be invalid, the defendant's conduct had infringed it or, alternatively, fell within the scope of the claims of the German designation of the patent. It was common ground that, by virtue of Regulation 1215/2012 art.24(4), the German courts had exclusive jurisdiction over proceedings concerned with the validity of the German designation of the patent. The claimants contended that (1) the proposed amendment was framed so as to exclude any question of the validity of the German designation and to acknowledge the jurisdiction of the German courts over that question; (2) the sampling order was not designed to provide evidence for the purpose of the German infringement proceedings and that, even if the court lacked jurisdiction to make such an order under the Civil Jurisdiction and Judgments Act 1982 s.25, it had power to do so under the Senior Courts Act 1981 s.37(1).

Held: Declaration granted in favour of defendants. (1) The European Court of Justice had held that art.24(4) should be interpreted widely and had implicitly endorsed the reasoning of Laddie J in *Coin Controls Ltd v Suzo International (UK) Ltd* [1999] Ch. 33, [1997] C.L.Y. 896, *Gesellschaft fur Antriebstechnik mbH & Co KG (GAT) v Lamellen und Kupplungsbau Beteiligungs KG (LuK) (C-4/03)* EU:C:2006:457, [2006] E.C.R. I-6509, [2007] C.L.Y. 2617 applied. In *Coin Controls*, it was said that, since the court had to decline jurisdiction in relation to claims which were "principally" concerned with issues relating to the predecessor provision to art.24(4), it followed that jurisdiction over the whole claim had to be declined. It was also said that infringement and validity were so closely interrelated that they should be treated for jurisdiction purposes as one issue or claim, *Coin Controls* applied. Applying those principles to the instant case, the claim advanced was "concerned with" the validity of the German designation of the patent within art.24(4), or at least "principally concerned with" the validity of that designation within art.27. The issue between the parties with respect to the German designation was the single issue of whether the defendant had infringed a valid claim of that patent, notwithstanding the claimants' attempt to split that single issue into the sub-issues of infringement and validity. To allow a court dealing with an infringement action to establish, indirectly, the invalidity of the patent at issue would undermine the binding nature of the rule of jurisdiction laid down in art.24(4) and thus the principle of legal certainty. Accordingly, the instant court lacked jurisdiction over the claim in respect of the German designation of the patent (see paras 18, 20, 23-25, 29 of judgment). (2) The claimants' whole purpose in applying for the order for samples was to obtain evidence to support its infringement claim in Germany. Section 25 of the 1982 Act conferred on the court a power to grant interim relief in relation to matters other than provision for obtaining evidence. It would not be a principled exercise of the court's power to circumvent the limit which Parliament had placed upon s.25. Accordingly, there was no jurisdiction to make an order for the defendant to provide samples (paras 33, 38, 41-42). If the court had had jurisdiction to make the order, however, it would have been expedient to do so on the grounds that (a) the defendant was domiciled within the court's jurisdiction; (b) it was likely that the products of which samples were required would be similar for the claims in both Germany and the UK; and (c) a sampling order in the UK would not interfere with the management of the German proceedings, nor would it be contrary to the policy of the German courts (paras 45, 49).

ANAN KASEI CO LTD v MOLYCORP CHEMICALS & OXIDES (EUROPE) LTD, [2016] EWHC 1722 (Pat), [2016] Bus. L.R. 945, Arnold J, Ch D (Patents Ct).

1307 Patent proceedings–Scientific advisers–Court observations on instructing neutral scientific advisers in patent trials

The court made observations at the conclusion of a patent infringement claim. The patent concerned the use of controlled-source electromagnetism in searching for oil reservoirs under the sea. The trial took 11 days and involved difficult physics and mathematics. Before the trial, the judge had a "teach-in" from a neutral scientific adviser. The adviser was provided with brief instructions, but was not told about the issues in the case. She was asked to prepare materials to educate the court on five topics. The teach-in lasted a single day and took the form of a meeting between the judge and the adviser. The parties were not present. Afterwards, the paper materials were provided to the parties so that they could see what had happened. The adviser did not attend the trial. Before judgment was given, the parties settled the case. However, the court gave the instant judgment in order to comment on the practice of using neutral scientific advisers.

Held: Judgment accordingly. In the instant case, it had been useful to have a neutral scientific adviser to assist the court in understanding the technology, without sitting in court for the whole trial. Without the teach-in, the court would eventually have reached the same level of understanding of the issues, but the judge would have needed much more time to read the case in advance and the trial itself would have had to be conducted more slowly. Time and cost had been saved and the court's comprehension of the issues had been significantly improved. Patent trials inevitably involved the court deciding difficult technical issues on conflicting expert evidence. The judge needed to be able to understand not only the experts' opinions but also the material on which those opinions were based and the reasons for them. That was why the task of educating the judge was of such significance and time spent on it was rarely wasted. In most cases, that result could be achieved by the combined efforts of the legal teams and the expert witnesses. In some cases, however, a further step such as that taken in the instant case was useful and proportionate. The transparency of such an exercise was important. It was helpful for the teach-in to take place in private, to facilitate a candid discussion. However, the adviser did not participate in any way after the teach-in. An appropriate degree of transparency was ensured by having the adviser's instructions settled by the court in advance and then making the written materials available to the parties afterwards, *Halliburton Energy Services Inc v Smith International (North Sea) Ltd* [2006] EWCA Civ 1599, [2007] Bus. L.R. 460, [2007] C.L.Y. 2625 considered. In the instant case, the instructions to the expert did not engage with the issues, but in other cases there might be no reason to avoid the issues.

ELECTROMAGNETIC GEOSERVICES ASA v PETROLEUM GEO-SERVICES ASA, [2016] EWHC 881 (Pat), [2016] Bus. L.R. 503, Birss J, Ch D (Patents Ct).

1308 Patent proceedings–Transfer of proceedings–Transfer of competition elements of cases to Competition Appeal Tribunal–Highlighting of relevant issues

[Treaty on the Functioning of the European Union 2008 art.101, art.102; Enterprise Act 2002 (c.40) s.16; CPR PD 30 (Transfer) 1999; Civil Procedure Rules 1998 Pt 1, r.1.1(2)(e)]

The third and fourth defendants (Samsung) applied to transfer the competition aspects of claims against them to the Competition Appeal Tribunal. The claimant and the ninth and tenth parties (Unwired) held a portfolio of telecommunications patents acquired from the eleventh party (Ericsson). Many of those patents were declared essential to various telecommunications standards. The first and second defendants (Huawei) and Samsung sold mobile devices and infrastructure equipment. Unwired brought proceedings against them complaining of patent infringement and the refusal to take licences on fair, reasonable and non-discriminatory (FRAND) terms. Huawei and Samsung denied the infringement claims, contending that the patents were invalid, not infringed and not essential to the relevant standard. They brought counterclaims for breaches of competition law under TFEU art.101 and art.102, including an allegation that the licence terms offered by Unwired were not FRAND. The relief claimed included injunctive relief restraining Unwired from enforcing the patents until FRAND terms were agreed or settled by the court. The case had been split into five technical trials and a non-technical trial to deal with the competition law issues and FRAND. Samsung's transfer application related to the non-technical trial. Ericsson, supported by Unwired, opposed the transfer, and Huawei adopted a neutral stance. Samsung contended that the CAT offered the dedicated, specialist expertise appropriate for resolving the mixed issues of law and economics that arose in connection with competition law so that it was the appropriate forum for hearing the non-technical trial. Ericsson submitted that a transfer would cause very serious problems because the FRAND issues were not only competition law questions: a key task of the non-technical trial was to decide what FRAND terms were and to deal with the issue of an injunction as a remedy for patent infringement, which could or should not be done by the CAT.

Held: Application refused. (1) The decision to transfer a case to the CAT under the Enterprise Act 2002 s.16 was an exercise of the court's discretion, taking account of all the circumstances, as required by CPR PD 30, and the overriding objective of CPR Pt 1. Saving expense and dealing with a case in a manner proportionate to its value, importance, complexity and the parties' position were all relevant. So too was dealing with the case expeditiously and fairly, and allotting an appropriate share of the court's resources to it. A key practical factor was the extent to which a transfer to the CAT would create delay or an increase in costs. The extent to which dividing the issues between the CAT and the High Court might cause difficulties in the proceedings was also important. No transfer should be made without some positive reason for doing so. That requirement did not impose an unfair burden on the party seeking transfer, but reflected that there should be some reason to disturb the "status quo" of the case proceeding where it was, *Memminger-IRO GmbH v Trip-Lite Ltd* [1992] R.P.C. 210, [1993] C.L.Y. 3039 applied. The parties' wishes should also be taken into account but were not determinative, and the effect on other litigants was also relevant pursuant to CPR r.1.1(2)(e) (see paras 26-29 of judgment). (2) The non-technical trial was likely to be significant for the litigants and, perhaps, generally as something of a test case since FRAND issues and standard-essential patents had caused problems in the telecommunications industry for many years. The competition law issues raised necessarily involved voluminous and complicated economic evidence, but Patents Court judges were used to dealing with complex and lengthy technical evidence, and were capable of handling the sort of economic evidence that would arise. Moreover, it was clear that, whilst it was at the heart of the dispute, FRAND was not the only issue at the non-technical trial. The words of s.16 and PD 30 were not wide enough to transfer for determination a distinct cause of action which did not itself involve art.101 or art.102 infringements; they only empowered transfer to the CAT of that part of proceedings relating to such infringement. The CAT was a specialist tribunal for dealing with infringements of competition law, and the legislator had not intended to broaden the scope of its responsibilities beyond that. To transfer the competition law aspects of non-technical trial to the CAT would therefore leave interrelated claims in the High Court, creating an impractical division in the handling and decision-making process. Transferring competition law FRAND issues but not contractual FRAND issues would be a recipe for confusion (paras 31-32, 38, 44-47).

UNWIRED PLANET INT LTD v HUAWEI TECHNOLOGIES CO LTD, [2016] EWHC 958 (Pat), [2016] Bus. L.R. 796, Birss J, Ch D (Patents Ct).

1309 Patents–Disclosure–Consideration of probative value of disclosure sought

[Civil Procedure Rules 1998 r.31.5(7)]

In a claim for revocation of a patent the court was required to determine whether to order disclosure on the issue of obviousness. The defendant held a patent for robotic lawnmowers. The claimants asserted that the patent was obvious and lacked novelty over a prior international patent. The defendant did not intend to call the inventor of its robotic lawnmower as a witness, and did not seek to rely on internal documents in support of its case on inventive step. The defendant's disclosure report indicated that it would provide disclosure on the issue of validity, but it subsequently refused to do so.

At a case management conference the court was required to determine whether to order disclosure concerning the making of the invention. The claimants relied on *Nichia Corp v Argos Ltd* [2007] EWCA Civ 741, [2007] Bus. L.R. 1753, [2007] C.L.Y. 2622 and submitted that disclosure on obviousness should be given by the defendant patentee. It also argued that the defendant's change of mind on disclosure was suspicious. The defendant argued that disclosure on obviousness would be disproportionate, and the position on disclosure had changed since the amendments to CPR r.31.5(7).

Held: Judgment accordingly. (1) In the IPEC a party had no automatic right to any disclosure from their opponent. Instead it was dealt with at the case management conference on an issue-by-issue basis using a cost/benefit test, which balanced the likely probative value of the documents against the cost or difficulty of the search. In most patent cases secondary evidence, including disclosure from the patentee about what the inventor had done, was a costly distraction, but in a minority of cases it could be important. The amended form of r.31.5(7) did not go as far as introducing a blanket prima facie rule against standard disclosure, but it did have the effect of providing that there was no longer a prima facie rule in favour of standard disclosure. Standard disclosure was one of six options in r.31.5(7). The fact that no disclosure was one of the options did not mean that a party seeking an order for disclosure had a difficult burden to discharge. Whether to order issue-based disclosure on obviousness depended on the overriding objective (see paras 9, 13, 21-25 of judgment) (2) The court took into account the following factors:.. (a) the instant case was not of low value, nor was it at the high end of the cases in the Patents Court. The parties' costs were likely to be in the region of £1 million. Those costs would be unlikely to swamp the value of the dispute; (b) the minimum cost of the disclosure sought would be approximately £90,000, assuming that it did not take up any time at trial. That was not a very substantial proportion of the overall costs of the litigation, nor was it a trivial sum of money; (c) if obviousness was in issue then, without more, cross-examination using the inventor's documents was unlikely to be probative without opening up a further costly and uncertain dispute about the personal qualities of the inventor; (d) the claimants argued that a particular way of thinking from the prior art was what a notional skilled person would do. If that way of thinking was reflected in the inventor's documents, then the claimants contended that it would support the case that the invention was obvious. However, the relevance of the inventor's documents depended on how close to the notional skilled person the inventor actually was, and how close the context in which they were working was the same as the context in which the notional skilled person was to be placed for obviousness; (e) the inference that the defendant's change of heart on disclosure reflected a party who had found "a smoking gun" was unwarranted. In the vast majority of cases in which obviousness disclosure from a patentee was material, it tended to help the patentee. The inference was inherently improbable, and the defendant's concern to keep the cost of the litigation under control was sincere. The change to r.31.5(7) meant that *Nichia* was not a binding authority. The obligation to disclose documents which might be adverse to a party's case could be preserved as a critical aspect of a fair trial within an issue-by-issue-based disclosure regime in which disclosure on some issues, such as obviousness, was not ordered because its likely probative value was not worth the cost. An order for standard disclosure, or an order for issue-based disclosure including the issue of obviousness, would not be in accordance with the overriding objective in the instant case, *Nichia* not applied. The case had no special features which made such disclosure worth the cost (see paras 27-28, 34, 38, 42-43).

POSITEC POWER TOOLS (EUROPE) LTD v HUSQVARNA AB, [2016] EWHC 1061 (Pat), [2016] Bus. L.R. 714, Birss J, Ch D (Patents Ct).

1310 Patents–European patents–Claims in Swiss form directed towards using pregabalin for treating pain–Whether invalid for insufficiency–Invitation to Secretary of State to separate patented and generic markets

[Patents Act 1977 (c.37) s.60(1)(c), s.60(2), s.70(1)]

In joined actions, the court was required to determine the validity of a European patent, whether it had been infringed contrary to the Patents Act 1977 s.60(1)(c) and s.60(2), and whether there had been groundless threats of patent infringement proceedings under s.70(1). Warner-Lambert owned the patent, which was a second medical use patent with claims in Swiss form directed towards using pregabalin for treating pain. Through Pfizer, which held the relevant marketing authorisation, Warner-Lambert marketed pregabalin under the trade mark "Lyrica" for the treatment of epilepsy, generalised anxiety disorder and neuropathic pain. Patent protection for the basic patent for pregabalin itself had expired, and Actavis intended to launch a generic pregabalin product for treating epilepsy and anxiety under the trade mark "Lecaent". Warner-Lambert commenced a patent infringement claim against Actavis, anticipating that Lecaent would wrongly be prescribed for the treatment of pain. Actavis denied infringement and counterclaimed in respect of threats allegedly made by Pfizer. Generics (UK) Ltd, trading as Mylan, and Actavis both commenced claims seeking revocation of the patent, challenging its validity on the grounds of obviousness over a number of items of prior art and insufficiency. An order was made, largely by consent, requiring NHS England to issue guidance to Clinical Commissioning Groups in England and to the NHS Business Services Authority for transmission to NHS pharmacy contractors aimed at preventing Lecaent being prescribed for pain relief. The secretary of state was permitted to intervene in the infringement claim.

Held: Judgment accordingly. (1) The correct test for establishing obviousness was whether Mylan and Actavis could show that it had been obvious to the skilled team that pregabalin would be effective to treat pain, although it was relevant to consider whether the skilled team would have a fair expectation of success if it was to try pregabalin for the treatment of pain, *Hospira UK Ltd v Genentech Inc* [2015] EWHC 1796 (Pat), [2016] R.P.C. 1, [2016] 1311 applied. None of the prior art relied on by Mylan and Actavis disclosed both pregabalin and its use for the treatment of neuropathic pain (or any kind of pain): the patent's claims were not obvious over any of the prior art (see paras 292-293, 338, of judgment). (2) The specification of a patent had to disclose the invention clearly and completely enough for it to be performed over the whole scope of the claim by a person skilled in the art without undue burden, *Eli Lilly & Co v Human Genome Sciences Inc* [2012] EWCA Civ 1185, [2013] R.P.C. 22, [2013] C.L.Y. 1808 followed. The assertion that the invention would work across the scope of the claim had to be plausible or credible; if it was not possible to make such a prediction or if it was shown that the prediction was wrong and the invention did not work with substantially all the products or methods falling within the scope of the claim then the scope of the monopoly would exceed the technical contribution the patentee had made to the art and the claim would be insufficient, *Regeneron Pharmaceuticals Inc v Genentech Inc* [2013] EWCA Civ 93, [2013] R.P.C. 28, [2013] C.L.Y. 1807 followed. It was not plausible that pregabalin would be effective for "all types of pain" within claim 1 of the patent, "central neuropathic pain" within claim 3, "cancer pain" within claim 4, "phantom limb pain" in claim 6, "idiopathic pain" in claim 13, and "fibromyalgia pain" in claim 14. Those claims were invalid on the ground of insufficiency (paras 339, 341, 346-358). (3) A defendant was under a statutory duty not to infringe a patent and it was generally up to the defendant to decide what to do to avoid infringement and to take the necessary steps to achieve that. If infringement of a Swiss claim simply required an intention on the part of Actavis that Lecaent would be used for pregabalin's new therapeutic use, then it was clear that Actavis had not infringed the patent, since it had never intended for Lecaent to be used to treat pain. However, the question to be resolved was whether it was foreseeable to Actavis that, in the five per cent of cases where pregabalin had been prescribed for pain, Lecaent would have been dispensed despite the fact that it was not licensed for pain relief. In considering that, it was relevant that Actavis had notified superintendent pharmacists specifically that Lecaent was not licensed for the treatment of neuropathic pain. In the circumstances, it was not foreseeable to Actavis that Lecaent would be intentionally administered for the treatment of pain save in a small number of exceptional cases that were proper to regard as de minimis. Had the patent been valid, it would not have been infringed. Actavis was entitled to a declaration that neither it, nor wholesalers who dealt in Lecaent, doctors who prescribed generic pregabalin for the treatment of pain, pharmacists who dispensed Lecaent and patients who took Lecaent had infringed the patent (paras 656, 661, 666-667, 671-677, 689). (4) Whether a communication amounted to a threat of infringement proceedings depended on how it would be understood by an ordinary reasonable person in the position of the actual recipient. In order to be aggrieved by a threat, a claimant had to show that its commercial interests had been, or were likely to be, adversely affected in a real, as opposed to a fanciful or minimal, way, *Brain v Ingledew Brown Bennison & Garrett (No.3)* [1997] F.S.R. 511, [1997] C.L.Y. 3917 applied. Where the threat was made against a claimant, that would normally be inferred, *Best Buy Co Inc v Worldwide Sales Corp Espana SL* [2011] EWCA Civ 618, [2011] Bus. L.R. 1166, [2011] C.L.Y. 2001 applied. Pfizer was liable for making some groundless threats of patent infringement proceedings in respect of some, but not all, of the communications Actavis had complained of (paras 693-694, 709-721). (5) (Per curiam) The best solution to the problem of protecting the monopoly conferred by a second medical use patent while allowing lawful generic competition for non-patented indications of the substance in question was to separate the patented market for the substance from the non-patented market by ensuring that prescribers write prescriptions for the patented indication by reference to the patentee's brand name and write prescriptions for non-patented indications by reference to the substance's generic name. Prescribers could not be expected to know when that was required, nor should they be required to take steps to find out. What was needed was for centralised and authoritative guidance to be given to prescribers as to when that practice should be adopted. Such guidance also needed to be conveyed to other relevant stakeholders, and in particular to the software providers. The only body in England which appeared to have the necessary power and authority to issue such centralised and authoritative guidance was NHS England. In Wales, Scotland and Northern Ireland, the devolved governments appeared to have the necessary power and authority. Patentees who wanted their second medical use patents enforced should provide NHS England with all the information and assistance it required to enable it to issue appropriate guidance as and when required. Generic companies who wanted their interests in obtaining untroubled access to lawful markets protected should cooperate with NHS England. A system was needed for dealing with those situations. The secretary of state had accepted the desirability of the proposed solution, and was to be trusted to take steps to ensure that a suitable system was put in place in England, and to liaise with his counterparts in the Welsh, Scottish and Northern Irish administrations to try to ensure that the system operated across the UK (paras 722-726).

GENERICS (UK) LTD (T/A MYLAN) v WARNER-LAMBERT CO LLC *sub nom.* WARNER-LAMBERT CO LLC v GENERICS (UK) LTD (T/A MYLAN); ACTAVIS GROUP PTC EHF v WARNER-LAMBERT CO LLC, [2015] EWHC 2548 (Pat), [2016] R.P.C. 3, Arnold J, Ch D (Patents Ct).

1311 Patents–European patents–Drug for treating breast cancer–Whether invalid for obviousness

The claimant sought the revocation of the defendant's European patent for a drug for treating breast cancer. Taxanes, in particular paclitaxel, were known to be effective chemotherapeutic agents for the treatment of breast cancer. The patent concerned the use of trastuzumab, a humanised anti-HER2 monoclonal antibody, in combination with a taxane for the treatment of HER2-positive breast cancer. The claimant contended that the patent lacked novelty, or alternatively an inventive step, over a piece of prior art (Baselga 97). That was a review article published nine months before the patent's priority date which described, inter alia, a Phase III trial of trastuzumab in combinations with the taxane paclitaxel and other agents, but did not disclose any results from that trial. The claimant submitted that Baselga 97 disclosed the invention within the patent or, alternatively, subject-matter which, if performed, would necessarily infringe it.

Held: Judgment for claimant. (1) For a patent claim to be valid, the claimed process or product had to be novel. For a claim to be deprived of novelty the prior art had to disclose the patented invention itself or an invention which, if performed, would necessarily infringe the patent, *Synthon BV v SmithKline Beecham Plc (No.2)* [2005] UKHL 59, [2006] 1 All E.R. 685, [2006] C.L.Y. 2525 followed. A prior disclosure of the existence of a clinical trial did not anticipate a claim which included a specified therapeutic effect revealed by the undisclosed results of that clinical trial unless the therapeutic effect could be derived directly and unambiguously from the prior disclosure, *PFIZER/Sertraline (T158/96)* [1999] E.P.O.R. 285, *Regeneron Pharmaceuticals Inc v Genentech Inc* [2012] EWHC 657 (Pat), (2012) 109(25) L.S.G. 19 and *Hospira UK Ltd v Genentech Inc* [2014] EWHC 1094 (Pat) applied. The content of Baselga 97 did not enable the clinical benefit claimed in the patent to be directly and unambiguously derived; it did not disclose that the combination of trastuzumab and paclitaxel had increased efficacy in human beings compared to paclitaxel. Following the directions in Baselga 97 would not inevitably result in carrying out the claimed process; the skilled person could not intend to administer the combination of trastuzumab and a taxane to achieve increased efficacy in the treatment of breast cancer compared to the taxane alone unless he knew that that clinical benefit would be obtained. The patent was novel over Baselga 97 (see paras 81, 83-87, 96-98 of judgment). (2) The claimed process or product in a patent could not be obvious. The court had to evaluate all the relevant circumstances in order to answer a single, relatively simple question of fact: whether it was obvious to the skilled but unimaginative addressee to make the product or carry out the process falling within the claim, *Windsurfing International Inc v Tabur Marine (Great Britain) Ltd* [1985] R.P.C. 59, *Pozzoli SpA v BDMO SA* [2007] EWCA Civ 588, [2007] F.S.R. 37, [2007] C.L.Y. 2634 and *MedImmune Ltd v Novartis Pharmaceuticals UK Ltd* [2012] EWCA Civ 1234, [2013] R.P.C. 27 followed, *Regeneron* applied. The key question in the instant case was how the skilled person would interpret Baselga 97, in particular how encouraging he would consider the results from previous studies reported in Baselga 97 to be. The skilled person would be strongly motivated to find a new, effective treatment for HER2-positive breast cancer. A new trial would not be technically burdensome and would not present a risk to patients. The alternative options were limited and none of them detracted from the obviousness of carrying out a Phase III trial or trastuzumab and taxane. Overall, the skilled person would agree with Baselga 97's authors that the results of previous studies were positive and encouraging and justified the decision to move forward to a Phase III trial of the combination of trastuzumab and a taxane, in respect of which the skilled person would have had a fair expectation of success. Accordingly, the claimed invention was obvious and the patent was invalid (paras 105-107, 117-126, 131, 134-135).

HOSPIRA UK LTD v GENENTECH INC, [2015] EWHC 1796 (Pat), [2016] R.P.C. 1, Arnold J, Ch D (Patents Ct).

1312 Patents–European patents–On-board system indicating state of loading of vehicles–Whether invalid for lack of inventive step

The claimant alleged infringement of its European patent for an on-board system for indicating the state of loading of a vehicle; the defendant admitted infringement of the patent if it was valid, but claimed that it was not. The patent described a system for measuring a vehicle's load using a device attached to only the suspension assembly component of the vehicle; the device, described as an inclinometer or accelerometer, exploited the angular deflection of the component when a load was applied to the vehicle. The issues included (i) the meaning of "suspension component" within the patent; (ii) the technical field from which the skilled person was drawn; (iii) the patent's inventive concept; (iv) whether the patent was obvious. The defendant contended that the patent was obvious over three pieces of prior art, in particular a US patent disclosing a system for detecting the loading of a vehicle using an accelerometer. The claimant submitted that if the skilled person found the idea of a system as claimed in the patent technically obvious, but dismissed the idea of making it because it was commercially unattractive, as in the US patent, the claimed invention would not be obvious.

Held: Judgment for defendant. (1) The purpose of a suspension component from the point of view of performing the invention was to be susceptible to variation in its angle relative to the vertical or horizontal when the vehicle was loaded. It could then accommodate an inclinometer or accelerometer which would function as required by the invention. The skilled person would include within the meaning of "suspension component" any component outside the vehicle's chassis, body and drive train which would fulfil that function (see para.22 of judgment). (2) It was generally sufficient to identify the skilled person as one who was likely to have a practical interest in the invention's subject matter, and practical knowledge and experience of the kind of work in which the invention was intended to be used, *Catnic Components Ltd v Hill & Smith Ltd (No.1)* [1981] F.S.R. 60, [1981] C.L.Y. 2042 applied. However, such a characterisation might be inappropriate for the skilled person enrolled to assess inventive step, and care might be needed in identifying the technical field from which the skilled person was drawn for that purpose, *Schlumberger Holdings Ltd v Electromagnetic Geoservices AS* [2010] EWCA Civ 819, [2010] R.P.C. 33, [2011] C.L.Y. 1975 and *Environmental Defence Systems Ltd v Synergy Health Plc* [2014] EWHC 1306 (IPEC), [2015] F.S.R. 6, [2015] C.L.Y. 1517 applied. In the instant case, the skilled person was an individual who designed on-board weighing systems and therefore worked for a supplier to the automotive industry. He would have the usual characteristics of ordinary skill and no inventive capacity (paras 28-29). (3) A patent's inventive concept was not the same thing as its inventive step. The latter could vary according to the prior art under scrutiny, whereas the former had only one identity for each claim. There were differing judicial views as to the importance of identifying the inventive concept: *Brugger v Medicaid Ltd (No.2)* [1996] R.P.C. 635, [1997] C.L.Y. 3905 emphasised that it was important because identifying the inventive concept could reveal the vice of a claim which contained embodiments to which the inventive step did not apply, whereas *Pozzoli SpA v BDMO SA* [2007] EWCA Civ 588, [2007] F.S.R. 37, [2007] C.L.Y. 2634 indicated that coming to a concluded view on the inventive concept was optional, *Brugger* and *Pozzoli* considered. Depending on the facts and how each side presented its case, the court could either define the inventive concept and thereby streamline the assessment of inventive step, or it might leave out any identification of the inventive concept, in which case the prior art would be compared with the claimed invention as a whole. With that in mind, the patent's inventive concept was taken to be the use of an inclinometer or accelerometer mounted on a single suspension component of a vehicle to generate a signal which was used to indicate the state of loading on a display (paras 33-34, 36, 39). (4) The acknowledged difference between the inventive concept of the patent and the US patent was that the latter did not disclose the use of the signal from the accelerometer to indicate the state of loading of the vehicle: the accelerometer's sole function in the US patent was to control the springing and damping behaviour of the vehicle. The patent system was not available to protect mere commercial improvements. The skilled person had to be taken to have in mind all the concerns and prejudices held by those in his field, but only technical ones. The claimant's proposition that commercial prejudices were also to be considered was not supportable, *Hallen Co v Brabantia (UK) Ltd (No.1)* [1991] R.P.C. 195, [1992] C.L.Y. 3318 and *Dyson Appliances Ltd v Hoover Ltd* [2001] EWCA Civ 1440, [2002] E.N.P.R. 5, [2002] C.L.Y. 2845 applied. The skilled person, having read the US patent, would have found it obvious to attach the accelerometer to a suspension component and use the signal from it to indicate to the vehicle's user the vehicle's state of loading. It followed that the patent was invalid for lack of inventive step (paras 50, 56-57, 64, 67).

VPG SYSTEMS UK LTD v AIR-WEIGH EUROPE LTD, [2015] EWHC 1862 (IPEC), [2016] F.S.R. 4, Judge Hacon, IPEC.

1313 Patents–Infringement–Litigation of more infringements than in original claim where awareness came after case management conference–Appropriate way forward

[Civil Procedure Rules 1998 r.63.23(2)]

A defendant applied to strike out a claimant's second claim. The claimant had brought proceedings for infringement of its patent concerning brake calipers. In *AP Racing Ltd v Alcon Components Ltd* [2014] EWCA Civ 40, [2014] R.P.C. 27, [2015] C.L.Y. 1518 the court concluded that the claimant's patent was valid, and the defendant had infringed it. The claimant then sought disclosure prior to election for an account of profits or an inquiry as to damages. The defendant asserted that the disclosure request was too wide, as it covered other products not included in the first claim. The claimant therefore restricted the inquiry as to damages in the first claim, but lodged a second claim against the defendant for infringement. The defendant submitted that the second claim was an abuse of process by reason of the rule in *Henderson v Henderson* [1843-60] All E.R. Rep. 378. The claimant relied on *General Tire & Rubber Co Ltd v Firestone Tyre & Rubber Co Ltd (No.2)* [1974] F.S.R. 122, [1974] C.L.Y. 2782 and argued that a successful patentee could raise further infringements at an inquiry or account, and it could therefore not amount to an abuse of process.

Held: Application refused. (1) A claimant was under no general duty to exercise reasonable diligence to ascertain whether he had a potential further cause of action against the defendant. However, a lack of diligence where the further claim would have been apparent early in the proceedings to a reasonable claimant, exercising reasonable diligence, could tip a claimant's behaviour into an abuse, *Henderson* considered, *Stuart v Goldberg* [2008] EWCA Civ 2, [2008] 1 W.L.R. 823, [2008] C.L.Y. 271, *Aldi Stores Ltd v WSP Group Plc* [2007] EWCA Civ 1260, [2008] 1 W.L.R. 748, [2007] C.L.Y. 346 and *Johnson v Gore Wood & Co (No.1)* [2002] 2 A.C. 1, [2001] C.L.Y. 410 followed. It would depend on other facts which the court had to take into account including: (a) the degree of similarity between the cause of action in the first proceedings and that of the proposed second proceedings; (b) whether the information on which the claimant based his second claim came from the defendant, so that it could be inferred that the defendant had as much information as the claimant; (c) the stage at which the information came, or should have come, to the claimant's notice (see paras 15-17 of judgment). The reforms of civil procedure since the decision in *General Tire*, taken together with the guidance in *Aldi* and *Stuart* regarding the court being informed of a new claim at an appropriately early stage, meant that in the IPEC a patentee was not entitled to free rein to litigate a broader range of infringements in an inquiry or account. As a rule of thumb, if the further allegations required the filing of additional evidence of any sort, the court would only allow the further allegations at a trial or inquiry in unusual circumstances, *General Tire* not applied. CPR r.63.23(2) allowed parties in IPEC proceedings to submit material other than that permitted at the case management conference only in exceptional circumstances. However, r.63.23(2) was not an absolute barrier to the consideration of further infringements at the inquiry or account. This was particularly so where the patentee had no reason to know of the further alleged infringements until after the CMC in the liability stage of the proceedings. The most expeditious, and least costly, way forward might be for the court to consider the further allegations in the inquiry or account where it could be done in reasonably short order, and without additional evidence (paras 23-24). (2) Allowing a successful patentee to add further alleged infringements at the inquiry/account, and the *Henderson* rule on abuse of process did not give rise to the same legal test. When considering whether a patentee should add further allegations into the inquiry or account, the greater the degree of similarity between the infringement allegations already decided and the additional ones sought to be added, the more likely it was that they could be dealt with in the inquiry or account. By contrast, when considering whether a fresh set of proceedings was an abuse of process, it worked the other way around (paras 26-28). (3) A reasonably diligent patentee in the place of the claimant could easily have taken steps to find out more about the precise structure of the calipers complained about in the second claim. The question was whether the claimant's conduct in failing to do so, and in lodging the second claim, was an abuse. The claimant had not brought the possibility of a new claim to the court's attention until after the CMC because it had not given the matter sufficient thought. However, had it asked the court to rule on the further alleged infringements in the inquiry in the first action, the court would probably have permitted further argument, provided it was short and required no evidence. That could still be done at the same time as the inquiry in the first action, and did not amount to unjust oppression or harassment of the defendant. Accordingly, the defendant's strike out application was refused (paras 42-50).

AP RACING LTD v ALCON COMPONENTS LTD, [2015] EWHC 1371 (IPEC), [2016] F.S.R. 1, Judge Hacon, IPEC.

1314 Patents–Infringement–Patent for tubular fabric using fusible yarn

The claimant patentee claimed breach of a settlement agreement by the defendant retailer. The claimant's UK patent concerned a tubular fabric used to encase underwiring in garments such as bras. It proposed a solution to the known problem of underwires protruding from their fabric tubing, during manufacture or use, by including a fusible yarn which, on melting during the dyeing process, strengthened the tubular fabric. Claim 1 of the patent provided that "the fusible yarn is arranged within the fabric tube so that it is capable of forming a penetration barrier". In 2010, the claimant had brought infringement proceedings against the defendant, alleging that bras sold by it fell within the patent. The defendant denied infringement and counterclaimed for revocation. The action was settled in 2011 when the parties entered into a settlement agreement in which the defendant agreed not to deal in any product which fell within any of the patent's claims. In 2013, the claimant issued the instant claim, alleging that the defendant was again selling infringing bras. The defendant denied infringement, and claimed in its defence and counterclaim that the patent was invalid. The defence and counterclaim were struck out on the basis that the settlement agreement precluded the defendant from contesting the patent's validity, and that decision was affirmed on appeal. The remaining issue of whether the defendant had breached the settlement agreement by selling infringing items depended on the correct interpretation of claim 1, in particular whether the defendant's garments contained "a penetration barrier". The claimant contended that a penetration barrier was created by weaving a fusible yarn into the tubular fabric and heating it; the fusible yarn effectively acted as an adhesive which, when melted, spread itself over the surrounding fibres in the fabric to form points of adhesion or bonding between those fibres. The defendant submitted that "points of adhesion" were insufficient as the patent required the fusible yarn to form an identifiable, layer-like barrier or lining, and that its garments did not infringe because they did not contain such a lining. It further argued that, on the claimant's interpretation, the patent would be clearly invalid in the light of common general knowledge as to fusible yarn's well-known purpose of bonding.

Held: Judgment for claimant. (1) Patent claims were to be given a purposive construction: the question was always what the person skilled in the art would have understood the patentee to be using the language of the claim to mean, *Kirin-Amgen Inc v Transkaryotic Therapies Inc (No.2)* [2004] UKHL 46, [2005] 1 All E.R. 667, [2005] C.L.Y. 2479 followed. The object of the patent's invention was to render tubular fabric more resistant to penetration, in order to solve the problem of underwire protrusion, by using fusible, bonding yarn whose function was to fuse other yarns and filaments together. It did not function as a covering or a layer. On melting and cooling it fused the remaining (non-fusible) fibres and yarns together, like mortar bonded the bricks of a brick wall. Like mortar, it was that fusing that gave strength to the structure. No-one would think of creating a barrier of just mortar and by itself it would provide little strength. That was not its function: its function was to bond other materials. When reading the patent, the skilled person would appreciate that that was the function of the fusible yarn in the invention. No skilled person would consider that the patent was referring to a discrete, continuous layer of fused material: that was not required by claim 1's wording (see paras 16, 34, 52-53, 55 of judgment). (2) The settlement agreement precluded the defendant from raising the issue of invalidity or, in its defence, a squeeze between non-infringement and invalidity. The defendant's argument on the basis of common general knowledge was an attempt to introduce that issue, rather than one of real relevance to construction. In any event, the alleged squeeze between non-infringement and obviousness on the basis of common general knowledge would have failed. Whilst fusible yarn was well-known at the priority date, there was no evidence that its use to increase penetration resistance in tubular fabric was common general knowledge at that date; on the contrary, that appeared to be a new use of a known material to solve a long-standing problem (paras 58, 60, 68). (3) The defendant's bras all fell within the patent's claims and their sale breached the settlement agreement (paras 84, 92). (4) (Per curiam) Where a defendant elected to serve a process and/or product description instead of providing disclosure, it was essential that it provided true information, sufficient to enable all issues of infringement to be resolved. The PPD had to be complete in all relevant areas, *Vringo Infrastructure Inc v ZTE (UK) Ltd* [2015] EWHC 818 (Pat) considered (para.77).

STRETCHLINE INTELLECTUAL PROPERTIES LTD v H&M HENNES & MAURITZ UK LTD, [2015] EWHC 3298 (Pat), [2016] R.P.C. 14, Henry Carr J, Ch D (Patents Ct).

1315 Patents–Injunctions–Agreement settling patent proceedings–Appropriateness of injunction to restrain likely future infringement

[Patents Act 1977 (c.37) s.61(1)(d)]

The claimant patentee sought an injunction and account of profits following the court's decision that the defendant had sold infringing products in breach of a settlement agreement. The patent was for a tubular fabric used in making underwired garments such as brassieres. The claimant had brought a claim for infringement of the patent against the defendants, which denied infringement and counterclaimed for revocation.

The proceedings were settled, but the claimant subsequently brought proceedings alleging that the defendant was again selling infringing brassieres. Following a decision of the Court of Appeal that the settlement agreement precluded the defendants from challenging the validity of the patent, the claimant pursued a claim only for breach of the settlement agreement. The court decided that the defendants had been selling products in breach of the settlement agreement. In addition to the remedy of damages, the claimant sought an injunction to restrain further breach and an account of profits.

Held: Applications refused. (1) As the Court of Appeal had held, the parties had intended by the settlement agreement to compromise all issues in dispute between them, including the issue of the validity of the patent, and to substitute for their claims a contractual arrangement which would from that time regulate the defendants' dealings in products falling within the scope of the patent. For so long as the patent remained in force, any dealings by the defendants in products falling within the scope of the patent would amount to an actionable breach of the agreement. That meant that the claimant's remedies were contractual, rather than those which would ordinarily flow in infringement proceedings. It was normal for an injunction to be granted in infringement proceedings, once it had been established that there had been infringement and the infringement had not completely ceased, *Coflexip SA v Stolt Comex Seaway MS Ltd* [2001] 1 All E.R. 952 (Note), [2002] C.L.Y. 2840 followed. The same principles applied where a person established that there had been a breach of contract which prohibited an act akin to infringement of an intellectual property right, *Cantor Gaming Ltd v GameAccount Global Ltd* [2007] EWHC 1914 (Ch), [2007] E.C.C. 24, [2007] C.L.Y. 2520 applied. However, an injunction was a discretionary remedy and would only be granted where it was necessary and appropriate. That meant that a claimant had to show an actual or implied threat that the defendant would again infringe, *Coflexip* followed. The evidence in the instant case showed that the infringements were historic and had reduced over time. It was likely that the claimant had tested for infringing garments and since it did not rely on any the implication was that none had been found. The defendants had told their suppliers not to use any infringing products and none had been found in its stores. There could in the circumstances be no presumption that infringement would recur. The court refused an injunction, but that did not prevent the claimant from returning to court if there was any further infringement and did not mean that the breaches of contract were not serious. An injunction would also be disproportionate because there was only so much that the defendants could do to police their suppliers and it would leave them liable to contempt proceedings in respect of accidental breaches. Such proceedings would also be inconsistent with the terms of the settlement agreement which imposed mandatory mutual obligations on the parties to assist one another in investigating and reporting infringing products. To respect the existence of those provisions any injunction would have had to be more complex than a simple undertaking not to infringe. (2) An account of profits was available in infringement proceedings as a statutory remedy under the Patents Act 1977 s.61(1)(d). It was also available in a breach of contract claim, but only in exceptional circumstances, *Attorney General v Blake* [2001] 1 A.C. 268, [2000] C.L.Y. 797 followed. The instant case was not exceptional and the court declined to order an account of profits or the necessary disclosure.

STRETCHLINE INTELLECTUAL PROPERTIES LTD v H&M HENNES & MAURITZ (UK) LTD, [2016] EWHC 162 (Pat), [2016] R.P.C. 15, Henry Carr J, Ch D (Patents Ct).

1316 Patents–Isle of Man

THE PATENTS (ISLE OF MAN) (AMENDMENT) ORDER 2016, SI 2016/559; made under the Patents Act 1977 s.124(3), s.132(2). In force: 1 June 2016.

This Order amends the Patents (Isle of Man) Order 2013 to make further modifications to the Patents Act 1977 in its application to the Isle of Man.

1317 Patents–Obviousness–New dosage of known drug using known mode of administration–Whether invalid for obviousness

The court was required to determine the validity of a European patent. The patent had a priority date of 21 July 2006. Medac, a privately owned German company, owned the patent which was directed at the use of a formulation of a known drug, methotrexate, with a concentration of about 50 mg/ml for the treatment of pain in individuals with inflammatory autoimmune diseases by subcutaneous injection. Accord claimed that the patent was invalid to clear the way in order to launch its own 50 mg/ml injectable product. It called two experts, a clinician and a formulator, while medac called an expert clinician only. The issues were (i) obviousness, in the light of: the common general knowledge alone; a paper by Jansen dated 1999; a letter by Russo dated 2000; the fact that the patent encompassed embodiments which made no technical contribution; (ii) insufficiency, in that the patent did not render it plausible that the claimed concentration could be safely administered to patients.

Held: Application granted. (1) The patent was plainly addressed to a team in a pharmaceutical manufacturer, consisting of a clinician, who would be a consultant level rheumatologist, and a formulator, who would be someone experienced in developing injectable formulations, working together, *Schlumberger Holdings Ltd v Electromagnetic Geoservices AS* [2010] EWCA Civ 819, [2010] R.P.C. 33, [2011] C.L.Y. 1975 considered. For the purposes of obviousness, such teams existed in reality irrespective of the patent. The invention was the use of a new dosage of a known drug (methotrexate) to treat diseases it was already indicated for using a known mode of administration (subcutaneous). The new dosage form was a formulation of the drug in a solvent at a concentration of 50mg/ml. For the patent to be valid, the invention could not be obvious to such a skilled team. Methotrexate was known to be associated with a wide range of potentially serious side effects which were dose-dependant but were unpredictable. There was a dispute about the common general knowledge relating to pain associated with methotrexate injections, although there was no doubt that they hurt and that the pain could be due to a number of factors including the injection volume and its formulation (see paras 20-21, 24, 26-27, 46, 48 of judgment). Russo's letter was published in a well read journal and read by skilled clinicians at the time, although as a document it was not established to have been common general knowledge. Russo only referred to "parenteral" administration without specifying whether that related to intramuscular and/or subcutaneous administration. The skilled team reading Russo at the priority date would have seen "parenteral" as covering either mode. It would have been entirely obvious to any skilled reader to consider what was disclosed by Russo as applicable to subcutaneous or intramuscular administration or both. On the evidence, a skilled team reading Russo in 2006 would have set about producing a formulation of subcutaneous methotrexate for use as a treatment for inflammatory autoimmune diseases. It was obvious for the formulator to optimise such a putative formulation with respect to pain, and an express reference in Russo was in itself a sufficient impetus to the skilled team to think about pain. Although there were other issues to be addressed when considering pain, it would have been wholly obvious to a skilled formulator to optimise injection volume with that in mind. The court found that it was common general knowledge that larger volumes caused more pain than smaller volumes both in general and in the context of comparing the likely pain caused by 1ml as opposed to 0.5ml. It was obvious to target a small volume like 0.5ml. Thus the invention was obvious over Russo. Accord's case over Jansen was not as strong as its case over Russo and there was no purpose in considering it further. The court was not satisfied that the invention was obvious based on common general knowledge alone. The relevant common general knowledge had to be that in the UK and there the skilled clinician was unaware as a matter of common general knowledge what concentrations were being administered subcutaneously to patients and was unaware of any particular issue of pain arising from the subcutaneous administration. There was therefore nothing to provide an impetus to the skilled team to think about the issue at all, *Generics (UK) Ltd (t/a Mylan) v Warner-Lambert Co LLC* [2015] EWHC 2548 (Pat), [2016] R.P.C. 3, [2016] 1310 applied and *Ratiopharm GmbH v Napp Pharmaceutical Holdings Ltd* [2008] EWHC 3070 (Pat), [2009] R.P.C. 11 considered (paras 67, 69, 99-100, 102, 108, 116-120). On the evidence, it was more likely than not that the reduction in pain caused by reducing injection volume continued to reduce as volume reduced below 0.5ml. No lower limit was established and so there was no basis on which to find that the lower reaches of the claims did not confer a technical benefit (para.125). (2) In the light of the findings on obviousness the insufficiency argument did not arise. However, if the argument about side effects had materially contributed to a finding that the claims involved an inventive step then the claims would have been insufficient because the patent did not make that invention plausible (para.126).

ACCORD HEALTHCARE LTD v MEDAC GESELLSCHAFT FUR KLINISCHE SPEZIALPRAPARATE MBH, [2016] EWHC 24 (Pat), [2016] R.P.C. 17, Birss J, Ch D (Patents Ct).

1318 Patents–Obviousness–Non-aqueous solvent in ointment to treat psoriasis–Difficulty in identifying solvent–Whether invalid for obviousness

The appellant pharmaceutical company (L) appealed against a decision (*Teva UK Ltd v Leo Pharma A/S* [2014] EWHC 3096 (Pat)) that patents it held in respect of an ointment to treat psoriasis were invalid for obviousness. The patents were for an ointment comprising two active ingredients, namely calcipotriol and a corticosteroid, a base, and a non-aqueous solvent called Arlamol E. The key question was whether such an ointment was obvious at the priority date of April 1999. Both active ingredients were well-known and often prescribed together, but in two topical products rather than one, making patient compliance complex. That was because the pHs for stability of the two actives did not overlap. It was known that a non-aqueous solvent would solve the problem as pH was only an issue if water was present. However, not all non-aqueous solvents would be suitable. The judge held that the patents were obvious against the common general knowledge and a US patent published in 1978, finding that the notional formulator would have tested Arlamol E along with a number of other solvents.

Held: Appeal allowed. The judge had missed the real significance of the evidence before him concerning the problem of combining the two actives. That was that to the skilled person, identifying a non-aqueous solvent which would work to produce a stable ointment was not easy. Having the property of being non-aqueous was a necessary, but not a sufficient, condition. Finding one was a research project because there was no sufficient expectation of success. The solution of the patents had been to use Arlamol E. That had been disclosed as a solvent for a corticosteroid in the US patent. That had proposed Arlamol E as a solvent for an anti-inflammatory steroid. Arlamol E had not been significantly used for topical pharmaceuticals; it did not form part of the common general knowledge of a formulator. The judge had accepted that Arlamol E would not have been tried by a real formulator, but held that the notional skilled formulator would not have been as conservative. However, the law of obviousness attributed to the notional person the real prejudices and practices of skilled persons. The judge had held that Arlamol E had the desired characteristics and so there were sufficient grounds to include it in tests. That did not follow: many non-aqueous solvents could have had the desired characteristics, but there was nothing disclosed about Arlamol E that made it different from any other non-aqueous solvent. The judge had effectively said that the idea of including the solvent as part of a research project amounted to obviousness. However, the "obvious to try" standard required a higher expectation of success, *Saint-Gobain Pam SA v Fusion Provida Ltd* [2005] EWCA Civ 177, (2005) 28(6) I.P.D. 28043 followed. The difference between the US patent and the invention was that the US patent was a mono active product using Arlamol E. The invention was a double active product. The US patent would be seen as using one of a large number of possible non-aqueous solvents. Arlamol E might have provided stability for the two actives, just as any of the other solvents might have, but there had been no reasonably optimistic expectation that it would. Finding that it really did was an invention and an advance in human knowledge, *Pozzoli SpA v BDMO SA* [2007] EWCA Civ 588, [2007] F.S.R. 37, [2007] C.L.Y. 2634 followed. The judge had erred in principle (see paras 24-34 of judgment). The judge had dated all his findings about common general knowledge as at the priority date, April 1999. However, all the matters had been known well before then, yet no-one had found a way to put the actives together in an ointment until the invention in the patents. The product was a significant advance in treatment because of much better patient compliance. The case was one where the courts had found invention over the years, a long-felt want, the desired solution and no explanation of why that solution had not been done before. The judge's failure to consider that was another error of principle. The finding of obviousness would be reversed (paras 35-40).

TEVA UK LTD v LEO PHARMA A/S, [2015] EWCA Civ 779, [2016] R.P.C. 5, Kitchin LJ, CA (Civ Div).

1319 Patents–Priority date–Fixing of priority date–Effect on claim of prior art where document said to be prior art available earlier because of time zones

[Patents Act 1977 (c.37) s.2(2)]

The claimant alleged patent infringement by the first to fourth defendants. The claimant had acquired a portfolio of telecommunications patents from another company (Ericsson). The instant UK patent, which claimed a priority date of 8 January, 2008, was concerned with an efficient polling system for a wireless communication network, by which the transmitter of data requested the receiver to send a status report on what information had been received, allowing the transmitter to work out whether the sent data had been received and which data were missing and needed to be re-transmitted. The claimant contended that, on its correct construction, the patent had priority over and covered the Long-term Evolution (LTE) telecommunications standard, so that the defendants' manufacture and sale of equipment operating in accordance with the LTE standard meant that they infringed the patent. The defendants denied that compliance with the standard fell within the claims. They also submitted that the patent was invalid for lack of novelty over a temporary document uploaded by Ericsson to the European Telecommunications Standards Institute's server in Europe on 8 January, 2008, in preparation for an ETSI meeting. They asserted that, because the document had been available to and downloaded by some people in the world for whom, under other time zones, the date was 7 January, 2008, it should form part of the state of the art as at 7 January, 2008, and so represented prior art on the patent's 8 January priority date. The defendants also argued that the patent was obvious over three pieces of prior art.

Held: Judgment for claimant. (1) Patent claims were to be construed in accordance with what the reasonable person would have understood the author to be using the words to mean, having some regard to the patent's purpose, *Kirin-Amgen Inc v Transkaryotic Therapies Inc (No.2)* [2004] UKHL 46, [2005] 1 All E.R. 667, [2005] C.L.Y. 2479 and *Virgin Atlantic Airways Ltd v Premium Aircraft Interiors Group* [2009] EWCA Civ 1062, [2010] R.P.C. 8, [2010] C.L.Y. 1959 followed. On the proper construction of the patent, its claims were clearly and unambiguously derivable from the priority documents, and a telecommunications system compliant with the LTE standard would infringe (see paras 62, 100-102, 137-143 of judgment). (2) A patentable invention had to be new in that it did not form part of the state of the art. Under the Patents Act 1977 s.2(2), the state of the art was held to comprise everything made available to the public before the priority date. At any given moment, the time and date around the world were different. It was therefore meaningless to pretend that a given date had some absolute meaning: it did not. In order to decide if an event took place before it, the priority date had to be based on some frame of reference. The only frame of reference which made sense was the one at the patent office at which the priority document was filed. Using any other approach would mean that an event which happened after the priority document was filed could count as prior art: that would be a very odd result. Knowledge of the filing date was what s.2(2) required. The date on which a priority document was filed and the office in which it was filed were always known facts, and were all that was needed to establish the priority date. A disclosure on the same day as the priority date, albeit earlier in time, was not prior art. Once the priority date was correctly characterised, it fell to be considered whether the putative prior art was available before that date. The defendants' argument on novelty had to be rejected. The patent's priority document had been filed in the US Patents and Trademark Office on 8 January, 2008, under Eastern Standard Time. The temporary document was made available to the public at 02.36 on 8 January, 2008 EST. It was not, therefore, made available to the public before the priority date. The fact that, at that time, it was 7 January, 2008 in some places in the world was irrelevant (paras 144, 157-162, 170-171). (3) The patent was not obvious over the prior art. It was, accordingly, valid and infringed by the defendants' wireless telecommunication networks operating in accordance with the relevant LTE standard (paras 204, 209, 229, 233-234).

UNWIRED PLANET INTERNATIONAL LTD v HUAWEI TECHNOLOGIES CO LTD, [2015] EWHC 3366 (Pat), [2016] Bus. L.R. 435, Birss J, Ch D (Patents Ct).

1320 Patents–Sufficiency–Validity of patent for medical use of atomoxetine–Consideration of standard of "plausibility" required in relation to patent's sufficiency

The claimants sought the revocation of the defendant's UK patent, and the defendant counterclaimed for threatened infringement. The patent disclosed a second medical use of the drug atomoxetine, which was a selective reuptake inhibitor of the neurotransmitter norepinephrine, for treating attention deficit hyperactivity disorder. The claimants challenged its validity in order to clear the way for the second claimant to launch a generic atomoxetine product, which would otherwise infringe the patent. The issues were (i) the state of the common general knowledge at the patent's priority date, in particular the role of neurotransmitters in ADHD; (ii) whether it was obvious to try atomoxetine in the treatment of ADHD from two pieces of prior art: a paper describing a clinical trial of atomoxetine in the treatment of depression, "Chouinard", and a paper explaining that atomoxetine selectively inhibited norepinephrine, "Zerbe"; (iii) the standard of "plausibility" required in relation to a patent's sufficiency; (iv) whether the patent was plausible. In respect of plausibility, the claimants contended that for a patent to provide sufficient disclosure to enable the skilled person to perform it, it had to be possible to reasonably predict that the invention would work.

Held: Judgment for defendant. (1) The underlying causes of ADHD's symptoms were not well understood at the priority date. The existing pharmacological treatments had included tricyclic antidepressants, which the skilled clinician would reasonably have considered effective as a result of their selective inhibition of norepinephrine reuptake. The skilled clinician would, however, have been uncertain as to whether it was desirable to increase or decrease norepinephrine in the treatment of ADHD, and whether other neurotransmitters were also implicated (see paras 36, 43, 77 of judgment). (2) In considering whether the use of atomoxetine for treating ADHD was obvious, the question was whether the skilled team would have been sufficiently optimistic of its success, *Omnipharm Ltd v Merial* [2011] EWHC 3393 (Pat) considered. In the context of pharmaceutical and biotechnology inventions, there were particular policy considerations which might be relevant to the requirement of a fair expectation of success. Those fields were heavily dependent on research, and workers would pursue many possible avenues in the hope that they would find new and useful products: they would not carry out that work if the prospects of success were too low to make them worthwhile, but denying patent protection in all such cases would act as a significant deterrent to research, *MedImmune Ltd v Novartis Pharmaceuticals UK Ltd* [2012] EWCA Civ 1234, [2013] R.P.C. 27 applied. Chouinard did not provide any information relevant to the treatment of ADHD, and the work in Zerbe was not performed on patients with depression, much less patients with ADHD. The patent was not obvious over the prior art. Even if it had been obvious at the priority date, either from Chouinard or Zerbe, to try atomoxetine for the treatment of ADHD, the skilled team would not have had a fair expectation that that drug would be discernibly effective in such treatment given the common general knowledge, in particular that the skilled team would be uncertain as to the role of norepinephrine in the treatment of ADHD (paras 101-104, 124-125, 132, 137, 140). (3) Plausibility did not form a separate ground of objection to a patent's validity and, unlike obviousness, did not require a reasonable expectation that the invention would work. For obviousness, a fair expectation of success was required because many routes might be obvious to try without any real idea of whether they would work. The requirement for the invention of a patent to be plausible was different: it was to exclude speculative patents, based on mere assertion, where there was no real reason to suppose that the assertion was true. The test of plausibility was a threshold test which was satisfied by a "credible", as opposed to a speculative, disclosure. That disclosure might subsequently be confirmed or refuted by further evidence obtained subsequent to the priority date. If it was subsequently shown that the invention did not work with substantially all of the products or methods falling within the scope of the claim then the scope of the monopoly would exceed the technical contribution and the patent would be invalid. A plausible invention might nonetheless be shown to be insufficient. The standard for assessment of plausibility was not the same as the standard for assessment of expectation of success in the context of obviousness (paras 173-178). (4) In contrast to the prior art, the patent disclosed for the first time that atomoxetine was effective in the treatment of ADHD, and that its mechanism of action was as a selective norepinephrine reuptake inhibitor. The skilled team would consider that the patent's invention was plausible, based on the specification and common general knowledge. The patent was valid (paras 179-181, 190).

ACTAVIS GROUP PTC EHF v ELI LILLY & CO, [2015] EWHC 3294 (Pat), [2016] R.P.C. 12, Henry Carr J, Ch D (Patents Ct).

1321 Patents–Supplementary protection certificates–Requirements for compliance with Regulation 469/2009 art.3(a)

[Regulation 469/2009 2009 art.1, art.3(a); Patents Act 1977 (c.37) s.21]

The applicant applied for a supplementary protection certificate. The product for which the SPC was sought was Agalsidase-beta, a glycosylated human a-Galactosidase A enzyme which was the active ingredient in a medicinal product marketed by a third party. The SPC application relied on a basic UK patent containing a single claim to a method for producing secreted human a-Galactosidase A. The third party had filed a number of observations in relation to the application, and the examiner had indicated that he would consider them in preparing his official examination report. The issues were: (i) the propriety of making third party observations and taking them into account in relation to an SPC application; (ii) whether the SPC application complied with Regulation 469/2009 art.3(a) in that the product was protected by a basic patent in force. The applicant contended that art.3(a) was satisfied in the light of *University of Queensland v Comptroller General of Patents, Designs and Trade Marks (C-630/10)* EU:C:2011:780, which required only that the product subject to the SPC application had to be identified in the wording of the basic patent's claims as the product deriving from the process in question. The examiner submitted that *Queensland* required an additional step, namely confirmation that the product for which the SPC was sought was or might be produced by the process as claimed in the basic patent, which the instant application failed to meet.

Held: Application granted. (1) Under the Patents Act 1977 s.21, a third party's observations on patentability could be filed at any time before the grant of an SPC. The observations in relation to the instant SPC application were, consequently, appropriate and had been dealt with properly; the examiner had rightly taken them into account when considering the application (see paras 27-30 of judgment). (2) It was clear from art.1 of the Regulation that a basic patent which protected a process to obtain a product, such as the basic UK patent in the instant case, could be used in support of an SPC application (para.53). In *Queensland*, the CJEU had clarified that if the basic patent related to a process by which a product was obtained, art.3(a) only allowed an SPC to be granted for a product which was identified in the wording of the claims of the patent as the product deriving from the process in question. The grant of an SPC was not conditional on whether it was possible to obtain a product directly as a result of the process by which the product was obtained: that possibility was irrelevant, *Queensland* explained. The applicant's interpretation of *Queensland* was therefore correct (paras 57, 66-67). Although the basic patent did not actually use the words "agalsidase beta", which was the product for which the SPC was sought, that product was identified in the basic patent's single claim; agalsidase-beta clearly shared all of the features of the product which was identified in the claim's wording. The description of the product identified/specified in the patent's claims was also suitable for distinguishing that product from other closely related forms of a-Galactosidase A, such as agalsidase-alpha (paras 77, 80). The definition of the product in the claim of the basic patent was therefore a definition which was suitable for identifying agalsidase-beta. As such, the product for which the SPC was sought was suitably identified in the wording of the patent's claim as the product deriving from the process in question. The application therefore met the requirements of art.3(a) (para.82). The application was remitted to the examiner to grant the SPC (para.90).

ICAHN SCHOOL OF MEDICINE AT MOUNT SINAI'S SPC APPLICATION, [2015] R.P.C. 21, L Cullen, IPO.

1322 Patents–Validity–Anti-PD-1 anti-bodies for treating cancer–Whether branded anti-PD-1 antibody infringing

The claimant (Merck) challenged the validity of a UK patent, and the defendant patentees and exclusive licensee (Ono) counterclaimed alleging patent infringement by Merck. Ono's patent concerned the use of anti-PD-1 antibodies for treating cancer. It claimed a first priority date of July 2002 based on a Japanese filing. The application was filed in July 2003 and the patent was granted in September 2010. Both Ono and Merck had developed a branded anti-PD-1 antibody. Merck acknowledged that, if the patent was valid, it had infringed it. The issues were whether (i) the patent was invalid for added matter; (ii) the patent was entitled to the first claimed priority date in that the claim was supported across its full width by the disclosure; Ono admitted that if priority was lost, the claim was invalid over a Japanese paper published before the patent's second claimed priority date; (iii) the patent was invalid for insufficiency; (iv) the patent was novel in the light of two Patent Cooperation Treaty applications (Dana Farber and Wyeth); (v) the patent was obvious over Dana Farber and three pieces of prior art (the Latchman paper, the Tchekmedyian abstract and the Davis abstract).

Held: Judgment for Ono. (1) The application as filed contained a disclosure of the treatment of cancer with an inhibitory anti-PD-1 antibody. The patent did not contain any wider disclosures and was not invalid for added matter (see paras 119-120 of judgment). (2) Claiming priority for "the same invention" required the skilled person to be able to derive the subject matter of the claim directly and unambiguously using common general knowledge from the priority document as a whole. The approach was not formulaic, but a matter of technical disclosure, explicit or implicit. The important thing was not the consistory clause or claims of the priority document but whether the disclosure as a whole was enabling and effectively gave the skilled person what was in the claim, *MedImmune Ltd v Novartis Pharmaceuticals UK Ltd* [2012] EWCA Civ 1234, [2013] R.P.C. 27 applied. The skilled reader would derive a disclosure of the idea of using an anti-PD-1 inhibitory antibody to treat cancer from the priority document, clearly and unambiguously. The patent's claims were entitled to priority from the first priority document (paras 126, 140, 156). (3) A patent's specification had to disclose the invention clearly and completely enough for it to be performed by a person skilled in the art without undue burden, *Eli Lilly & Co v Human Genome Sciences Inc* [2012] EWCA Civ 1185, [2013] R.P.C. 22, [2013] C.L.Y. 1808 applied. The patent disclosed a therapy of general application using the claimed antibodies to treat substantially all cancers even if they were not hitherto regarded as immunogenic. It was sufficient since it enabled the skilled person to make and use anti-PD-1 antibodies as anti-cancer medicines (paras 128, 154, 165, 168, 243). (4) The general law of novelty was settled in *Synthon BV v SmithKline Beecham Plc (No.2)* [2005] UKHL 59, [2006] 1 All E.R. 685, [2006] C.L.Y. 2525: for anticipation to be established there had to be disclosure of the invention by the prior art, and that disclosure must be enabling, *Synthon* applied. Dana Farber disclosed the idea of manipulating the PD-1 pathway and included the idea of an anti-PD-1 agent as a therapeutic agent to be used to treat a number of diseases including cancer. That agent could be an anti-PD-1 antibody. However, while its disclosure might be enough to support the general idea of using an agent which acted somehow on the PD-1 pathway in medicine, it did not make plausible the specific idea of an anti-PD-1 agent to treat cancer. The same was true for Wyeth. The patent was therefore novel (paras 173-174, 198, 203, 243). (5) To be valid an invention had to involve an inventive step, which meant that it could not be obvious to a skilled person having regard to the state of the art. The structured approach to the assessment of obviousness had been set out in *Pozzoli SpA v BDMO SA* [2007] EWCA Civ 588, [2007] F.S.R. 37, [2007] C.L.Y. 2634, *Pozzoli* applied. The question of obviousness had to be considered on the facts of each case, *Conor Medsystems Inc v Angiotech Pharmaceuticals Inc* [2008] UKHL 49, [2008] 4 All E.R. 621, [2008] C.L.Y. 2325 applied. The patent involved an inventive step over the Latchman paper and Dana Farber because they indicated that a skilled person who conducted a test of PD-1 blockade against a tumour in a mouse would not have a fair expectation of success. The mouse tumour results in the patent were exciting and were not predictable from the prior art. The patent was not obvious. The Tchekmedyian and Davis abstracts did not render the claims obvious either since they were not concerned with the PD-1 pathway at all. The patent was valid (paras 206, 243-244).

MERCK SHARP & DOHME LTD v ONO PHARMACEUTICAL CO LTD; BRISTOL MYERS SQUIBB CO v MERCK AND CO INC, [2015] EWHC 2973 (Pat), [2016] R.P.C. 10, Birss J, Ch D (Patents Ct).

1323 Pharmaceuticals–Supplementary protection certificates–Whether test of usefulness under Directive 93/42 equivalent to test of efficacy under Directive 2001/83

[Regulation 469/2009 2009 art.2, art.3(b); Directive 2001/83 on medicinal products for human use 2001; Directive 93/42 on medical devices 1993]

The applicants applied for supplementary protection certificates (SPCs) for the pharmaceutical product Taxol and a Taxol-eluting stent. The basic patent on which both applications were based concerned a composition including paclitaxel, which was more commonly referred to by its trade mark Taxol, which inhibited the formation of new blood vessels and was used in a method for treating non-tumourigenic, angiogenesis-dependent disease. It described coating a coronary stent with a composition that included Taxol to prevent stenosis recurring in vascular arteries and veins in addition to setting out the general use of Taxol in anti-angiogenic compositions to treat cancer. The examiner considered that that the SPC applications were outwith the scope of Regulation 469/2009 because the marketing authorisations filed in support of them failed to comply with (i) art.2 of the Regulation, since before the applicants' products were placed on the market as medicinal products, they were not subject to an administrative authorisation procedure as laid down in Directive 2001/83; (ii) art.3(b) in that a valid authorisation had not been granted in accordance with those Directives. The applicants contended that the authorisation procedure which had led to the issue of the EC design certificate and declaration of conformity for the medical device under the procedure laid down in Directive 93/42 and filed in support of the SPC applications was equivalent to an authorisation to place the product (for which the SPCs had been applied for) on the market as a medicinal product granted under the administrative procedure laid down in Directive 2001/83. They submitted that the assessment carried out on a medical device to meet the requirements of Directive 93/42 was equivalent to that carried out on a medicinal product to meet the requirements of Directive 2001/83, and that the requirements of the Regulation were therefore met.

Held: Applications refused. (1) It had to be determined whether the test of usefulness under Directive 93/42 was equivalent to the test of efficacy under Directive 2001/83. An assessment of efficacy under Directive 2001/83 would consider the efficacy of the active ingredient alone and would relate to the ability of the active ingredient to exert a pharmacological, immunological or metabolic action with a view to restoring, correcting or modifying physiological functions. The assessment of the stent with the Taxol coating in the instant applications carried out under Directive 93/42 was to determine whether the whole device achieved the performance claimed by its manufacturer and whether it provided a benefit for the person it was being applied to, while taking into account the "the vulnerability of the human body" to the device in operation and "taking account of the potential risks associated with the technical design and manufacture of the device". The assessment in each instance was for a different purpose, which meant that meeting that purpose was judged differently in both situations and was one of degree, where the investigation of the active ingredient under Directive 93/42 would always be in relation to its ancillary role to that of the whole device. The assessment on the basis of Directive 93/42 could not be considered equivalent to an authorisation under Directive 2001/83. Accordingly, Taxol and the Taxol-eluting stent had not been subject to an administrative procedure as laid down in Directive 2001/83. Those products were not, therefore, eligible to be the subject of an SPC certificate under art.2 of the Regulation (see paras 92, 96, 101 of judgment). (2) It followed that the SPC applications did not meet the requirements of art.3 of the Regulation, and had therefore to be rejected (para.102).

ANGIOTECH PHARMACEUTICALS INC'S APPLICATION, RE, [2016] R.P.C. 9, L Cullen, IPO.

1324 Registered Community designs–Infringement–Child's ride-on suitcase–Design infringement–Overall impression–Obiter remarks regarding absence of ornamentation

[Regulation 6/2002 2002 art.10, art.36; Regulation 2245/2002 2002 art.4]

The appellant (M) appealed against a decision (*Magmatic Ltd v PMS International Ltd* [2014] EWCA Civ 181, [2014] E.C.D.R. 20, [2014] C.L.Y. 1908) that the respondent (P) had not infringed its Community registered design (CRD). The CRD was for ride-on suitcases for young children. The design depicted suitcases which resembled animals with horns, with wheels and straps in a contrasting colour. M made and sold the cases under the name "Trunki". P imported and sold similar suitcases under the name "Kiddee Case". They resembled animals or insects, with markings and appendages resembling spots, stripes, ears and antennae. The trial judge found that P had infringed M's CRD. However, the Court of Appeal disagreed, finding that the overall impression created by the Trunki and the Kiddee Case was very different. The CA concluded that the judge had erred by (a) failing to give proper weight to the overall impression of the CRD as an animal with horns, which was significantly different from an insect with antennae or an animal with ears; (b) failing to take into account the effect of the lack of ornamentation on the surface of the CRD; (c) ignoring the colour contrast in the CRD between the body and the wheels.

Held: Appeal dismissed. (1) When determining whether an item infringed a CRD, the issue under Regulation 6/2002 art.10 was whether the accused item produced, on the informed user, a different overall impression from the design. That involved a judgement by the trial judge with which appellate courts should be slow to interfere, *Lucasfilm Ltd v Ainsworth* [2011] UKSC 39, [2012] 1 A.C. 208, [2011] C.L.Y. 1944 considered. The CA had concluded that the judge had gone materially wrong in his approach to that issue, and it therefore reconsidered the matter. M's appeal could only succeed if the CA's criticisms of the judge's approach were wrong (see paras 24-26 of judgment). (2) *Overall impression* - The overall impression given by M's CRD was that of a horned animal. The judge at first instance had not considered the horned animal impression of the CRD as being particularly distinctive, and had wrongly treated the antennae and ears of the Kiddee Case as "horn-like". When a judge gave a full judgment, specifying a significant number of points which weighed with him, an appellate court could properly conclude that his failure to mention a significant point meant that he had overlooked it. That conclusion was particularly valid in the instant case, given that the point in question was more significant than many of those which the judge mentioned, because it went to the overall impression of the image rather than detailed features. The CA's first criticism of the trial judge was justified (paras 37-39). (3) *Decoration* - The point which the CA was making in its second criticism was that the absence of decoration on the CRD reinforced the horned animal impression. It was not raising a free-standing contention that a feature of the CRD was that it contained no decoration (paras 41, 43). (4) *Colour contrast* - If an applicant for a Community registered design elected to submit CADs of an item, whose main body was a uniform grey, but which had a black strip, a black strap and black wheels, the natural inference was that the components shown in black were intended to be in a contrasting colour to that of the main body. The CA was right to conclude that the CRD claimed not merely a specific shape, but a shape in two contrasting colours. The trial judge was wrong to find that the CRD was a claim simply for a shape (paras 52-53). (5) The CA had been entitled to find that the Kiddee Case did not infringe the CRD. While M's concept was original and clever, CRDs were concerned with designs rather than ideas (paras 56-57). (6) *(Obiter)* The court made the following remarks concerning decoration: (a) absence of decoration could be a feature of a registered design; (b) whether absence of ornamentation was a feature of a design right turned on the proper interpretation of the images on the registered design; (c) it could sometimes be hard to decide if absence of ornamentation was a feature of a particular registered design, because Regulation 6/2002 art.36 and Regulation 2245/2002 art.4 precluded any verbal descriptions; (d) if absence of ornamentation was a feature of a registered design, that did not mean that an item with ornamentation could not infringe the registered design: the ornamentation of an allegedly infringing item was a factor which could be taken into account when deciding whether it infringed that design (paras 44-46).

MAGMATIC LTD v PMS INTERNATIONAL LTD *sub nom.* MAGMATIC LTD v PMS INTERNATIONAL GROUP PLC, [2016] UKSC 12, [2016] Bus. L.R. 371, Lord Neuberger PSC, SC.

1325 Trade marks–Blocking injunctions–Orders for website blocking injunctions against internet service providers–Whether principled basis for extending court's jurisdiction

[Senior Courts Act 1981 (c.54) s.37(1); Directive 2004/48 on the enforcement of intellectual property rights 2004 art.11; Charter of Fundamental Rights of the European Union 2000]

Internet service providers appealed against orders requiring them to block customer access to websites advertising and selling counterfeit copies of the respondent trade mark owners' goods. The respondents had contended that the operators of the target websites were infringing those trade marks, using the services of the ISPs. The judge held that he had jurisdiction under the Senior Courts Act 1981 s.37(1) to make the orders sought and that it was appropriate to do so. He held that, in any event, s.37(1) should be construed consistently with the third sentence of Directive 2004/48 art.11, in the light of the Marleasing principle, so as to achieve that result. He identified threshold conditions to be satisfied before a website blocking order was made. First, the ISPs had to be intermediaries within the meaning of art.11; second, either the users or the website operators had to be infringing the trade marks; third, the users or website operators had to use the services of the ISPs; and fourth, the ISPs had to have actual knowledge of that use. He then identified the applicable principles and concluded that the orders were proportionate and struck a fair balance between the respective rights engaged. He also held that the ISPs should bear the costs of implementation of the orders.

Held: Appeals dismissed. (Briggs LJ dissenting on the issue of the costs of implementation of the orders) (1) The ISPs were not guilty of any wrongdoing. They had not infringed the trade marks, nor had they engaged in a common design with the website operators offering counterfeit goods for sale. They did not owe the respondents a common law duty of care to take reasonable care to ensure that their services were not used by the website operators. The question was whether there was a principled basis for making blocking injunctions against the ISPs, who were aware that their services were being used by third parties to infringe registered trade marks and other intellectual property rights. The operators of the target websites needed the ISPs' services to sell their counterfeit goods to UK consumers. The ISPs were therefore essential actors in the infringing activities. There was a further, important, consideration, namely the effect of art.11. Article 11 provided a principled basis for extending the practice of the court in relation to the grant of injunctions to encompass, where appropriate, the services of an intermediary, such as the ISPs, which had been used by a third party to infringe a registered trade mark. It was not disputed that the ISPs were intermediaries within the meaning of art.11. Subject to satisfaction of the threshold conditions, it had to be recognised, pursuant to general equitable principles, that the instant case was one of those new categories of cases in which the court could grant an injunction when it was satisfied that it was just and convenient to do so. The court had jurisdiction to make the orders, *Fourie v Le Roux* [2007] UKHL 1, [2007] 1 W.L.R. 320, [2007] C.L.Y. 453 followed, *Broadmoor Special Hospital Authority v R* [2000] Q.B. 775, [2000] C.L.Y. 4177 and *Samsung Electronics (UK) Ltd v Apple Inc* [2012] EWCA Civ 1339, [2013] E.C.D.R. 2, [2013] C.L.Y. 1813 applied, *Norwich Pharmacal Co v Customs and Excise Commissioners* [1974] A.C. 133, [1973] C.L.Y. 2643 considered (see paras 33-66 of judgment). (2) The orders did not give rise to any illegitimate or otherwise inappropriate limitation on the exercise of the rights and freedoms recognised by the Charter of Fundamental Rights of the European Union (paras 75-79). (3) The judge was right to hold that the threshold conditions were satisfied, *UPC Telekabel Wien GmbH v Constantin Film Verleih GmbH (C-314/12)* EU:C:2014:192, [2014] Bus. L.R. 541 and *L'Oreal SA v eBay International AG (C-324/09)* EU:C:2011:474, [2012] Bus. L.R. 1369 considered. It was not disputed that the ISPs were intermediaries, and the judge was right to find that the website operators were infringing the trade marks. The major dispute was whether the operators had used the ISPs' services to infringe the marks. It was not disputed that if they had, the

ISPs had knowledge of that. The ISPs' services allowed UK consumers to access the target websites. The submission that the infringing activities were complete once the offending materials had been uploaded to the website was rejected. It also did not matter that there was no contractual relationship between the ISPs and the website operators, or that the ISPs did not exercise any control over the services of which the consumers made use (paras 82-99). (4) The judge was entitled to require the ISPs to bear the implementation costs of the orders in issue. He took proper account of the directive and the other parts of the EU legislative scheme, guidance given by the ECJ, the nature of the order sought and the circumstances of the case. He had not erred in principle and there was no basis on which the instant court could interfere with his conclusion, *Twentieth Century Fox Film Corp v British Telecommunications Plc* [2011] EWHC 2714 (Ch), [2012] 1 All E.R. 869, [2012] C.L.Y. 1921 and *L'Oreal SA* considered (paras 132-154). (5) (per Briggs LJ) The specific costs incurred by the ISPs for compliance with a blocking order should, save in exceptional cases, fall on the applicant rightsholder, but not the costs of designing and installing the software necessary to do so. The rightsholder should defray the cost of compliance as the price of obtaining valuable injunctive relief for the better exploitation of its intellectual property (paras 198-212).

CARTIER INTERNATIONAL AG v BRITISH SKY BROADCASTING LTD, [2016] EWCA Civ 658, [2016] E.T.M.R. 43, Jackson LJ, CA (Civ Div).

1326 Trade marks–Blocking injunctions–Websites being used to infringe trade marks

The claimant trade mark owners applied for an injunction requiring the defendant internet service providers (ISPs) to block access to certain websites allegedly being used to infringe the claimants' trade marks. The trade marks were for the advertising and sale of luxury goods. The claimants alleged that while the ISPs were not committing acts of infringement, they provided access to the targeted websites used to infringe the trade marks. The claimants, relying on *Cartier International AG v British Sky Broadcasting Ltd* [2014] EWHC 3354 (Ch), [2015] 1 All E.R. 949, [2015] C.L.Y. 1520 to establish jurisdiction, sought a final injunction, though not summary judgment and not ancillary to any substantive proceedings. The ISPs submitted that (1) the court lacked jurisdiction; (2) in any event, the claimants had not met all of the threshold conditions identified in *Cartier* and that in the absence of full and frank disclosure no relief should be granted as the application was analogous to a *Norwich Pharmacal* or ex parte application; (3) the injunction would be disproportionate with respect to the comparative importance of the rights engaged, the availability of alternative means, efficacy and dissuasiveness, and impact on lawful users.

Held: Application granted. (1) Even though an appeal was pending, the correct way forward was to apply the principles set out in *Cartier*, which had concluded that the court had an unlimited power to grant an injunction against a defendant over whom the court had jurisdiction. *Cartier* set out four threshold requirements to be satisfied before the court would exercise its discretion to grant the website-blocking injunction: the ISPs had to be intermediaries, the websites had to be infringing the trade marks, the websites had to use the ISPs' services, and the ISPs had to have actual knowledge of infringing activity. If those were met, there were six principles to be taken into account in considering whether to grant the injunction: effectiveness, dissuasiveness, costs, avoiding barriers to legitimate trade, proportionality, and safeguards against abuse, *Cartier* applied (see paras 9, 12, 21-22 of judgment). (2) With respect to the threshold requirements at issue, the target websites advertised and offered for sale identical products with identical signs to one or more of the trade marks. Access to the target websites was overwhelmingly likely to be via one or other of the ISPs' broadband services. The evidence showed that it was possible to access the websites via four of the ISPs' services; there was no reason to doubt that it was possible to do so via the second defendant's service even though that had not been tested. It had been sufficient in *Cartier* to show access in order to demonstrate that infringement had occurred via the ISPs' services; that applied in the instant case. They also had actual knowledge of infringement; the claimants had provided evidence of actual use of the ISPs' services and described test purchases, and served that evidence on the ISPs, who had had a reasonable opportunity to investigate the position, *Cartier* applied. That qualified as actual notice, *Twentieth Century Fox Film Corp v British*

Telecommunications Plc [2011] EWHC 1981 (Ch), [2012] 1 All E.R. 806, [2012] C.L.Y. 1922 considered. The duty of full and frank disclosure was not a further threshold requirement; the ISPs were really arguing that notice should have been given to the target website operators. However, the instant application was not completely analogous to a *Norwich Pharmacal* or ex parte application, which required such disclosure. The ISPs had been served with the application and supporting evidence, had had every right to challenge that evidence and present arguments, and could have sought evidence from the target website operators but had not done so (paras 24, 27, 38-39, 41-45). (3) The ISPs' submissions implied that the importance of the claimants' trade mark rights was minimal, and the injunction disproportionate, because some of the targeted websites were insufficiently popular. However, there was evidence showing that a person searching the internet had a significant chance of finding even the less popular websites, and their visibility added to public knowledge of the availability of the fake products; that in itself was liable to damage the trade marks' functions, *L'Oreal SA v Bellure NV (C-487/07)* EU:C:2009:378, [2010] Bus. L.R. 303, [2009] C.L.Y. 2429 considered. Alternative means were not realistic: some website operators were outside the UK, and options such as de-indexing, targeting website hosts, seizing domain names or notifying payment processors were not realistic or efficacious, *Cartier* applied. As for efficacy and dissuasiveness, the claimants were not required to show that blocking access to the target websites was likely to reduce overall infringement of the trade marks, *Cartier* applied. It was possible that the injunction would affect the sale of lawfully marketed goods on the target websites, but the claimants had done their best to warn the operators, who had chosen to continue to put the websites at risk by marketing counterfeit products. Websites that were lawfully marketing legitimate goods, but that shared an IP address with the targeted websites, could be protected by making the order only for domain name system blocking against those targeted websites. The circumstances complied with the criteria for granting a website-blocking order (paras 50, 55, 59-62, 64, 67-68, 72).

CARTIER INTERNATIONAL LTD v BRITISH TELECOMMUNICATIONS PLC, [2016] EWHC 339 (Ch), [2016] E.C.C. 16, Judge Hacon, Ch D.

1327 **Trade marks–Colour–Mark consisting exclusively of one or several colours–Inability to encompass more than one form without contravening art.4 Regulation 207/2009**

[Regulation 207/2009 2009 art.4, art.9]

A defendant in a claim for trade mark infringement applied for the claim to be dismissed and for summary judgment to be entered on its counterclaim for a declaration that the claimants' trade mark was invalid. The claimants' trade mark was registered in respect of inhalers in Class 10. It was visually represented by a colour photograph of an inhaler, and it was described as consisting of the colour dark purple (Pantone code 2587C) applied to a significant proportion of the inhaler, and the colour light purple (Pantone code 2567C) applied to the remainder. The certificate of registration designated the mark with INID Code 558, which covered marks consisting exclusively of one or several colours (colour marks). The defendant's case was that the claimant's mark was invalid because it did not conform to the requirements of Regulation 207/2009 art.4 in that it was not a single sign and was not capable of being represented graphically. The claimants argued that the visual representation of the mark was the starting point, and the single sign being claimed was an abstraction of that visual representation. Alternatively, they argued that if the mark encompassed more than one sign, the variants were fewer than suggested by the defendant and were permitted as a matter of EU trade mark law. The issues were (1) how a trade mark application or registration should be construed where there was no strict congruence between the visual representation and the description, particularly in the context of colour marks; (2) whether a colour mark could encompass more than one form or whether there could be variants without contravening art.4; (3) whether the claimants' mark was invalid.

Held: Application granted. (1) Where there was no strict congruence between the visual representation and the description of the mark, both had to be considered without one having precedence over the other. The weight to be given to each would depend on the circumstances, and interpretation was a matter for the court without reference to what the average consumer might think. Where INID Code 558 indicated that the mark was a colour mark, it had to be construed as consisting exclusively of one or several colours. The court had to do its best to reconcile the visual representation and the description, and questions of clarity, precision and uniformity were particularly important (see paras 39-43 of judgment). (2) A combination of colours could be registered as a trade mark as long as they constituted a sign which was capable of distinguishing the goods or services of one undertaking from those of another, and as long as there was a graphic representation which allowed the mark to be precisely identified, *Heidelberger Bauchemie GmbH's Trade Mark Application (C-49/02)* EU:C:2004:384, [2004] E.C.R. I-6129, [2005] C.L.Y. 2529 and *Libertel Groep BV v Benelux-Merkenbureau (C-104/01)* EU:C:2003:244, [2004] Ch. 83, [2003] C.L.Y. 2599 followed. However, a colour mark could not encompass more than one form without contravening art.4. Relying on *Heidelberger Bauchemie* and *Apple Inc v Deutsches Patent- und Markenamt (C-421/13)* EU:C:2014:2070, [2014] Bus. L.R. 962, the claimants argued that a sign did not have to be delimited with absolute precision and variation was possible in terms of the form it could take. However, there was nothing in either of those cases to support that proposition, *Heidelberger Bauchemie* and *Apple* considered. Pursuant to art.4, an EU trade mark had to be clear, precise, unambiguous and uniform. While minor variations could possibly exist within that narrow ambit, they would be so insignificant as to go unnoticed by the average consumer. One of the criteria for infringement under art.9(2)(a) was that the existing and allegedly infringing marks were identical, and that was incompatible with the idea that a single sign could have a number of variations. There could not be a strict interpretation of identity between mark and sign if a trade mark could exist in various forms (paras 17, 22, 44-56). (3) The claimants' mark did not satisfy art.4. It was not sufficiently precise and uniform, and nor was it sufficiently clear and unambiguous. It was visually represented by a photograph, and while photographs were appropriate for three-dimensional marks claiming a particular form of packaging, they was less appropriate for colour marks that might not be confined to any specific shape of goods. The description was unambiguous with regard to the Pantone shades, but it was not so clear in relation to the respective proportions and the arrangement of dark and light purple. In those respects, the words alone gave something close to complete freedom (paras 39-43, 62-71).

GLAXO WELLCOME UK LTD (T/A ALLEN & HANBURYS) v SANDOZ LTD, [2016] EWHC 1537 (Ch), [2016] F.S.R. 36, Judge Hacon, Ch D.

1328 Trade marks–Compatibility–Whether Trade Marks Act 1994 s.41 compatible with EU law

[Trade Marks Act 1994 (c.26) s.28(1), s.41, s.41(3)(a), s.46; Directive 2008/95 on trade marks 2008 art.2, art.3]

Supplementary to its decision in *Comic Enterprises Ltd v Twentieth Century Fox Film Corp* [2016] EWCA Civ 41, [2016] E.C.C. 24, [2016] 1330, the court ruled upon an outstanding issue in the appeal, namely whether the Trade Marks Act 1994 s.41 was compatible with Directive 2008/95 art.2 and art.3. The High Court had found that the use of the sign "Glee" by the appellant film corporation in its television programme infringed a series of trade marks registered by the respondent comedy club. The instant court had upheld that decision. However, at the outset of the appeal hearing, the appellant had introduced its allegation about s.41. Given its considerable general importance, the issue was reserved to enable the Comptroller-General of Patents, Designs and Trade Marks to be heard. The appellant submitted that the registration of a series of trade marks was essentially a registration of a single trade mark consisting of a number of signs, and that the uncertainty of identifying a "single point of comparison" between all the marks made the exercise contrary to EU law. The Comptroller argued that a series of trade marks was a bundle of individual trade marks, each of which had to comply with the requirements set out in the Directive. He maintained that s.41 of the Act, which entitled certain trade marks to be registered and renewed as a series, was an administrative provision falling outside the scope of the Directive.

Held: Appeal dismissed. (1) The Directive harmonised the trade mark laws of Member States. It was not concerned with the administrative side of applications and registrations, such as the form of the application and the organisation and presentation of the register. Article 2 imposed stringent requirements about the nature of the sign of which a mark must consist. The court had explained, in a series of cases involving applications to register unusual signs as trade marks, how art.2 should be interpreted, and how the graphical representation of a sign had to be self-contained, durable, clear and precise, and easily accessible and intelligible such that the authorities and economic operators would reliably and unambiguously perceive the sign in the same way, *Sieckmann v Deutsches Patent- und Markenamt (C-273/00)* EU:C:2002:748, [2003] Ch. 487, [2003] C.L.Y. 2637, *Libertel Groep BV v Benelux-Merkenbureau (C-104/01)* EU:C:2003:244, [2004] Ch. 83, [2003] C.L.Y. 2599, *Heidelberger Bauchemie GmbH's Trade Mark Application (C-49/02)* EU:C:2004:384, [2004] E.C.R. I-6129, [2005] C.L.Y. 2529 and *Chartered Institute of Patent Attorneys v Registrar of Trade Marks (C-307/10)* EU:C:2012:361, [2013] Bus. L.R. 740, [2013] C.L.Y. 1172 applied (see paras 11, 14, 17-21, 58 of judgment). (2) The structure of the Act and the terms of s.41 suggested that a series of trade marks was a bundle of individual trade marks as contended for by the Comptroller. Under s.1, a trade mark was "any sign" satisfying the statutory criteria. It was not a series of signs. Section 41, which had no counterpart in the Directive, contemplated registration as a series, but only where the trade marks to be registered resembled each other as to their material particulars. It therefore enabled more efficient examination of trade marks (because the registrability decision would normally be the same for each in the series) and a less complicated manner of entering them on the register. As such, it was clearly a supplementary provision intended to facilitate the effective administration of the registration system; it did not purport to create new trade mark rights or a new kind of trade mark. That finding was supported by the wording of s.41(3) (a) and s.28(1), and was not incompatible with s.46. It was also supported by an examination of the application process in previous cases, *Logica Plc's Trade Mark Application, Re*, *Digeo Broadband Inc's Trade Mark Application (No.2230395)* [2004] R.P.C. 32, *Gateway Inc's Trade Mark Application, Re*, *Sony Ericsson Mobile Communications AB's Application Nos.2364422 and 2364423* and *Thomas Pink Ltd v Victoria's Secret UK Ltd* [2014] EWHC 2631 (Ch), [2014] E.T.M.R. 57, [2014] C.L.Y. 1919 considered (paras 22-23, 32, 34-43, 46-51, 54-57, 63-66). (3) Registration of trade marks as a series was not misleading, did not cause material difficulty, and did not contravene EU law (paras 72-73).

COMIC ENTERPRISES LTD v TWENTIETH CENTURY FOX FILM CORP, [2016] EWCA Civ 455, [2016] Bus. L.R. 849, Arden LJ, CA (Civ Div).

1329 Trade marks–Confidentiality orders–Power of hearing officer to review decision to make confidentiality order

[Trade Marks Act 1994 (c.26); Trade Marks Rules 2008 (SI 2008/1797) r.74(1)]

An opponent to the registration of a trade mark appealed against a hearing officer's refusal to allow it to redact its sales figures in a witness statement that it had filed in the opposition proceedings. The hearing officer had originally granted the opponent's request for a confidentiality order in respect of the financial information. However, he later accepted that he had reached his decision without having read the trade mark applicant's objections to the confidentiality order. He therefore reviewed the decision and then reversed it.

Held: Appeal allowed. The hearing officer had issued his second decision in response to a general application by the trade mark applicant for reconsideration of his first decision, to which he acceded as if he were entitled to sit essentially by way of rehearing on appeal from his own decision. However, that was a power of reconsideration which he did not possess. The registrar's statutory power to determine issues arising in registry proceedings was, in principle, a power to decide once and once only. After a registry determination had been duly made and communicated in terms which were not preliminary or provisional, it could only be revoked or modified if the registrar was empowered to do so by the Trade Marks Act 1994 or the Trade Marks Rules 2008, *Andreas Stihl AG & Co's Trade Mark Application* [2001] R.P.C. 12, [2001] C.L.Y. 4042 applied. In the instant case, the hearing officer's first decision had been made and communicated in terms which were not preliminary or provisional. That decision had been the equivalent of a sealed order in civil proceedings in the High Court: the confidentially order was perfected and there was no jurisdiction to change it thereafter unless the registrar had an express power to vary it, but there was no such power under the Act or the Rules. Moreover, his second decision could not be saved from invalidity by deeming it to have been made pursuant to an application under r.74(1) of the 2008 Rules for rectification of a procedural irregularity. While it had been, in principle, open to the trade mark applicant to raise a request for rectification on the ground that the first decision was tainted by an irregularity in procedure, that had not happened and it was not possible to resort to the fiction of deeming the second decision to have been duly made pursuant to an application under r.74(1) (see paras 11-13, 20-22 of judgment).

TWG TEA CO PTE LTD v MARIAGE FRERES SA, [2016] R.P.C. 7, Geoffrey Hobbs QC, App Person.

1330 Trade marks–Confusion–Evidence of "wrong way round" confusion–Admissibility in trade mark infringement claims

[Trade Marks Act 1994 (c.26) s.10(2)(b), s.10(3)]

An entertainment company appealed against a decision (*Comic Enterprises Ltd v Twentieth Century Fox Film Corp* [2014] EWHC 185 (Ch), [2014] E.T.M.R. 46, [2014] C.L.Y. 1928) that its TV series had infringed a trade mark held by the respondent club owner. The club owner cross-appealed against a finding that the entertainment company's activities did not amount to passing off. The club owner operated live entertainment venues in the UK used primarily for stand-up comedy. Its mark, including the words "THE GLEE CLUB" with "GLEE" particularly prominent, was registered in respect of entertainment services. From 2009 the entertainment company broadcast in the UK a successful musical television series entitled "GLEE", with associated concert tours and merchandise, using the sign "GLEE" in similar lettering to the club's mark. The issues were whether there had been (1) infringement under the Trade Marks Act 1994 s.10(2)(b). The entertainment company argued that the judge had erred in finding, having heard witness evidence as to confusion between its sign and the club's mark, that there had been a likelihood of confusion. In particular, he had erred in admitting evidence of "wrong way round" confusion, where a consumer familiar with the accused sign was confused upon seeing the mark, rather than vice versa; (2) infringement under s.10(3); (3) passing off.

Held: Appeal dismissed. (1) The judgment included no analysis of the cause of any confusion of the witnesses, particularly whether it had arisen because of the similarity of the sign to the mark and the similarity of the services covered by the mark and those in relation to which the sign had been used. The court had to review the evidence for itself. Some of the evidence on which the club owner had relied had little probative value, but it was generally supportive of its case. It showed that the similarity between the mark and the sign, and the similarity of the services, had led a significant number of persons to believe that the businesses were connected (see paras 45, 67 of judgment). The judge had not identified the services he considered to be similar, the degree of similarity or how similarity affected the likelihood of confusion. He had also made no reference to the context of use. The absence of reasoning amounted to material deficiencies vitiating the judge's conclusion (paras 70, 74). There was no basis for saying that evidence of "wrong way round" confusion was inadmissible. Whether a particular instance of confusion was right way or wrong way round could be a consequence of nothing more meaningful than the order in which the consumer happened to have seen the mark and the sign. In both cases, the consumer thought that the goods or services came from the same undertaking and they could be equally damaging to the mark (paras 79-80). In the light of the judge's errors, the court had to decide the issue of s.10(2)(b) infringement itself. The mark had a reasonable degree of distinctiveness in its capacity to identify the services for which it was used as originating from a particular undertaking. There was a reasonable degree of similarity between the mark and the sign. The services covered were reasonably similar: there were differences, but comedy shows could be televised, and TV series could give rise to associated activities such as tours and merchandise. As to context of use, it was not unreasonable to suppose that a consumer might think that the TV series' producer was also responsible for or connected with the club. Taking all relevant matters into account, there was a likelihood of confusion (paras 85-106). (2) The mark had had sufficient reputation in 2009 to qualify for protection. On the evidence, there was a possibility that use of the sign would bring the mark to the mind of the average consumer. The evidence of "wrong way round" confusion could not be disregarded. It was inevitable that many consumers would encounter the TV series before the mark, but the evidence of their reaction on doing so demonstrated that the use of the sign was such that average consumers would make a connection. The evidence showed that actual and potential customers made the connection, and the scale of the use of the sign was such as to have a serious impact on the club's business and its ability to use the mark for the purposes of identifying and promoting its venues as its own. There was evidence of a change in economic behaviour of average consumers. The entertainment company had not shown that its use had been with due cause. It had adopted the name in good faith, but there had been a likelihood of confusion and use of the sign had caused significant detriment to the mark (paras 137-148). (3) Although the club had established goodwill in the mark and there had been confusion, that did not establish that the entertainment company had been guilty of actionable misrepresentation. The launch of the series was not a misrepresentation such as to cause significant numbers of consumers to believe that the business behind the clubs was the same as that behind the series (para.158).

COMIC ENTERPRISES LTD v TWENTIETH CENTURY FOX FILM CORP, [2016] EWCA Civ 41, [2016] E.C.C. 24, Arden LJ, CA (Civ Div).

1331 Trade marks–Deletions–Whether mark described was description of two marks–Whether part of description removable

[Trade Marks Act 1994 (c.26) s.41, s.44]

A company appealed against a trade mark hearing officer's refusal of its request under the Trade Mark Rules 2008 r.28(5) to delete a mark from an alleged series of trade marks. The mark was described as consisting "of the colour purple as shown on the form of application, applied to the whole visible surface, or being the predominant colour applied to the whole visible surface, of the packaging of the goods". The company applied to delete "or being the predominant colour applied to the whole visible surface" from the description, thereby limiting the mark to a sign consisting of the colour purple applied to the whole visible surface of the packaging of its goods. The company had sought to argue that the description as registered was in fact a description of two marks, that the two marks were series marks, and that the second of the two could be deleted pursuant to the Trade Marks Act 1994 s.41, thereby leaving a single validly registered mark. The hearing officer held: that the trade mark had not been applied for as a series mark and there had been no such request by the proprietor since registration, therefore the request for deletion could not be entertained; following the Court of Appeal's decision in *Societe des Produits Nestle SA v Cadbury UK Ltd* [2013] EWCA Civ 1174, [2014] 1 All E.R. 1079, [2014] C.L.Y. 1933 the words sought to be deleted did not actually describe a mark and accordingly there was no mark to be deleted pursuant to the provisions for deleting marks; the deletion would involve an alteration of the mark that was contrary to s.44. The company argued that the hearing officer made a material error of principle in failing to recognise that the mark was a series mark, comprising two marks, and that the mark's description was a description of two alternative marks.

Held: Appeal dismissed. The description of the mark as a whole was of an unknown number of signs including not just the colour purple but other colours in which the colour purple predominated. It could not be interpreted as suggesting that the description was of two marks or of a series of marks as that expression was used in the Act. The "alternative" description encompassed a large but unknown number of signs with one characteristic in common, namely that purple was the predominant colour applied to the whole visible surface of the packaging. Moreover, that single common characteristic was patently insufficient to satisfy the s.41 criteria for series trade marks. Purple might, in any particular sign, be the predominant colour in terms of area, but there might be yellow or green spots as well, and it might be that those contributed to the sign's distinctive character. The mark covered a number of marks which were not part of any series. Section 41(2) contained clear safeguards and no sufficient reason had been given for them to be ignored. Section 41 provided the gateway to the rules relating to series marks. It was but one part of the statutory system that had been put in place to ensure that, as far as practical, the only marks which got on the register were those that had a right to be there. Accordingly, the description was not of two marks or a series of marks, there were no identifiable members of any series that might be the subject of a request for deletion, and therefore any such request could not be entertained (see paras 30-34 of judgment).

CADBURY UK LTD v COMPTROLLER GENERAL OF PATENTS DESIGNS AND TRADE MARKS, [2016] EWHC 796 (Ch), [2016] E.T.M.R. 33, John Baldwin QC, Ch D.

1332 Trade marks–Distinctiveness–Requirement for showing mark had acquired distinctive character

[Trade Marks Act 1994 (c.26) s.3(1)(b), s.3(2)(b)]

Following a preliminary ruling from the CJEU, the court was required to determine appeals relating to the appellant's application to register a three-dimensional sign as a UK trade mark for various goods in class 30. The trade mark corresponded to the shape of the appellant's four-finger KIT KAT product, without the KIT KAT logo embossed onto each of the fingers. The respondent had opposed the application on the grounds that the mark lacked distinctive character contrary to the Trade Marks Act 1994 s.3(1)(b) and consisted exclusively of a shape necessary to achieve a technical result within s.3(2)(b). The hearing officer found that the mark was devoid of inherent distinctive character and had not acquired a distinctive character except in relation to cakes and pastries, and that apart from those goods, registration was also precluded under s.3(2)(b). The appellant appealed against the refusal of registration except in relation to cakes and pastries, and the respondent cross-appealed against the registration in respect of those goods. Having found that the hearing officer was incorrect to have found inherent distinctiveness in relation to cakes and pastries, the court stayed proceedings and referred a question for preliminary ruling on acquired distinctiveness and technical result. Following the CJEU's judgment in *Societe des Produits Nestle SA v Cadbury UK Ltd (C-215/14)* EU:C:2015:604, [2015] Bus. L.R. 1034, [2015] C.L.Y. 1522, in which it had reformulated the question referred, the respondent accepted that the mark's registration was not precluded by s.3(2)(b). An issue arose as to the proper interpretation of the CJEU's ruling in respect of acquired distinctiveness.

Held: Appeal dismissed, cross-appeal allowed. (1) It was regrettable that, as often happened, the CJEU had reformulated the question referred to it. Whilst that was occasionally understandable, since questions referred by national courts were often badly worded, in the instant case the question had been worded with precision, and its reformulation meant that the CJEU's answer was unclear. Whilst it was tempting to refer the question again, there was no realistic prospect of a further reference yielding a materially different result. Accordingly, it was necessary for the instant court to try to understand and apply the CJEU's answer as best it could (see paras 45, 48 of judgment). (2) The CJEU's judgment meant that, in order to demonstrate that a sign had acquired distinctive character, it was not sufficient for a trade mark applicant to prove that a significant proportion of the relevant class of persons recognised the sign in question and associated it with the applicant's goods: more was required. The applicant had to prove that, at the relevant date, a significant proportion of the relevant class of persons perceived the goods or services as originating from a particular undertaking because of the sign in question, *Nestle* explained (paras 51-52, 57). (3) The hearing officer had evaluated consumers' perception at the relevant date in a manner consistent with the CJEU's legal test, and his conclusion on acquired distinctiveness was correct. The fact that a majority of consumers shown the mark were able to name KIT KAT did not prove that they perceived the mark as exclusively designating the trade origin of the product (paras 66, 68).

SOCIETE DES PRODUITS NESTLE SA v CADBURY UK LTD, [2016] EWHC 50 (Ch), [2016] Bus. L.R. 354, Arnold J, Ch D.

1333 Trade marks–EU trade marks–Contractual consent to use of trade mark–Whether decisive to refer to implying of consent under English law

[Regulation 207/2009 2009 art.12, art.9, art.9(1)(b), art.9(1)(c)]

The claimant trade mark owner applied for summary judgment against the defendant (D1) for trade mark infringement. The claimant sold high-performance cars under the

EU trade mark "Marussia". Only six had been sold in the EU. D1 was a Formula One (F1) motor racing team. They signed a licensing agreement under which the claimant acquired a majority stake in D1 until 2014. The team was called "Marussia" for the 2011-2014 seasons. F1's commercial rights holder (E) had to agree to any team name changes. D1 earned points in the 2014 season, entitling it to prize money for 2015. A new owner took over D1 under a team purchase agreement with the claimant. E refused to allow D1 to collect the prize money unless it kept the same team name, so D1 competed in the 2015 season under the name "Manor Marussia". The claimant brought the instant claim on the basis that it had not consented to D1 using its trade mark in the 2015 season. D1 advanced the following defences: (1) consent to the trade mark's use under an implied term in the purchase agreement; (2) alternatively, estoppel by acquiescence; (3) no likelihood of confusion for the purpose of the Regulation 207/2009 art.9(1)(b); (4) lack of Community reputation under art.9.1(c); (5) use of the trade mark as an "honest practice" under art.12.

Held: Application granted in part. (1) The Regulation required actual, not deemed consent. An implied contractual term under English law could be effectively imposed on parties, or be one to which they were deemed to have consented, *Marks & Spencer Plc v BNP Paribas Securities Services Trust Co (Jersey) Ltd* [2015] UKSC 72, [2016] A.C. 742, [2016] 1377 followed. It was not decisive under art.9 to refer to whether English law would imply a contractual term, as that might amount to deemed consent only. However, if the need for implication was sufficiently obvious, that might be strong evidence that the proprietor consented. The question was whether the facts and circumstances unequivocally demonstrated a renunciation of rights, *Zino Davidoff SA v A&G Imports Ltd (C-414/99)* EU:C:2001:617, [2002] Ch. 109, [2001] C.L.Y. 4032 followed. In the instant case they did not. When concluding the agreement, the claimant did not know that D1 would need to use the trade mark. It was neither necessary to imply that term, nor so obvious that it went without saying. D1's case was that E was historically reluctant to approve name changes. However, the claimant could reasonably have concluded that D1 had obtained consent or would have asked for permission to use the name. There was no basis for concluding that the claimant was unequivocally renouncing rights when it had no reason to think they would be infringed (see paras 58-59, 63-65, 69-74 of judgment). (2) Estoppel by acquiescence was said to arise because the claimant knew that D1 would likely need to use the "Marussia" name, and a reasonable person in D1's position would have expected to be alerted if the trade mark was going to be asserted against it. The question was whether D1, who had failed to prove consent under the Regulation, could rely on estoppel to achieve a similar result. The Regulation operated as a complete code for an EU trade mark proprietor's rights. If it was precluded from exercising its right because of a national law defence, the system would vary according to the state concerned, *Zino Davidoff* followed. Estoppel by acquiescence operated like deemed consent: a defendant only invoked it when unable to prove actual consent. It was a substantive defence enabling the court to modify the parties' substantive rights, *Jennings v Rice* [2002] EWCA Civ 159, [2003] 1 F.C.R. 501, [2002] C.L.Y. 4319 considered. D1 could not rely on estoppel principles to avoid liability (paras 84, 89-96). (3) The purpose of the licence had been to promote Marussia vehicles to the wider public, who then saw the name "Marussia" used in 2015; those who had followed F1 from 2011-2014 could not be expected to understand D1's new ownership. D1 continued to use the name, previously used under licence, precisely because it was important to E that the 2015 team should be seen by viewers as the same as the previous "Marussia" team, *Specsavers International Healthcare Ltd v Asda Stores Ltd* [2012] EWCA Civ 24, [2012] E.T.M.R. 17, [2012] C.L.Y. 1915 followed. It was highly probable that that led to a likelihood of confusion. That was a question to be determined at trial; it was improbable that the defence would succeed, but it could not be said that there was no real prospect of success (paras 108-110). (4) The conclusion on reputation would depend on the evidence at trial, but it was not an onerous requirement, *Red Bull GmbH v Sun Mark Ltd* [2012] EWHC 1929 (Ch), [2013] E.T.M.R. 53 applied. A reputation did not depend on actual sales. The evidence showed that F1 participation was a valuable marketing aid. It would be surprising if despite its expenditure on sponsorship the claimant had established no relevant reputation. There was a sufficient prospect that D1's case would succeed at trial, but it was improbable (paras 115-117). (5) Summary judgment on art.12 was not appropriate in the instant case, although the factors were similar to those under art.9.1(b) and art.9.1(c). To take a licence permitting use of a trade mark for a limited period, and then claim the right to use the name indefinitely under art.12, did not seem in accordance with honest practices (paras 120-122).

MARUSSIA COMMUNICATIONS IRELAND LTD v MANOR GRAND PRIX RACING LTD, [2016] EWHC 809 (Ch), [2016] Bus. L.R. 808, Males J, Ch D.

1334 Trade marks–Genuine use–Revocation for non-use where limited sales in geographical area–Whether use warranted

The appellant appealed against the revocation of its UK trade mark STRADA for non-use. The trade mark had been registered in respect of spectacles. Its revocation had been sought by the respondent following the appellant's opposition to registration of its international STRADA DEL SOLE mark. The hearing officer had found that the STRADA mark had been applied to spectacles by way of a sticker on dummy lenses in cabinet draws in three opticians stores in Wiltshire, but that just 41 pairs of STRADA spectacles had been bought annually. He held that there had been no use of the STRADA mark on the internet, no sales in other shops or retail outlets, and no real promotion or advertising of the mark. He had invited and received the parties' submissions on *Reber Holding GmbH & Co KG v Office for Harmonisation in the Internal Market (Trade Marks and Designs) (OHIM) (C-141/13)* EU:C:2014:2089, having indicated that whilst that decision had not really changed the law with regard to genuine use, it was a good example of a form of commercial use that was neither sham nor token, but nevertheless was not genuine, and was therefore a clarification of the earlier case-law. He referred to the fact that sales of STRADA spectacles were extremely low when compared to the large size of the UK spectacles market, although they had a certain degree of frequency, and noted that the geographical spread of use was limited to three towns, all in roughly the same geographical area. He concluded that there was insufficient use of the STRADA mark in the UK market to constitute real commercial exploitation and genuine use in any of the relevant periods, so that the mark could not be relied on in the opposition and had to be revoked for non-use. The appellant contended that the hearing officer had erred in (1) overzealously applying *Reber* and wrongly importing a de minimis test into his assessment of genuine use; (2) ignoring material evidence and/or making erroneous factual findings regarding the public display of STRADA spectacles, the use of STRADA on the arms of spectacles, and STRADA promotions.

Held: Appeal dismissed. (1) *Reber* did not mark a departure from prior CJEU law; there had been prior cases where commercial uses were held insufficient to constitute "genuine use" for EU law purposes, *Reber* considered. Neither the commercial success of use nor the economic strategy of an undertaking was necessarily telling, and there was no quantitative threshold for genuine use, even small uses could suffice for genuine use, *TVR Automotive Ltd v Office for Harmonisation in the Internal Market (Trade Marks and Designs) (OHIM) (T-398/13)* EU:T:2015:503 and *La Mer Technology Inc v Laboratoires Goemar SA (C-259/02)* EU:C:2004:50, [2004] E.C.R. I-1159, [2004] C.L.Y. 2417 applied. Genuine use depended on whether the use was warranted in the economic sector concerned to maintain or create a share in the market for the registered goods or services, *Ansul BV v Ajax Brandbeveiliging BV (C-40/01)* EU:C:2003:145, [2005] Ch. 97, [2004] C.L.Y. 2386, *La Mer, Sunrider Corp v Office for Harmonisation in the Internal Market (Trade Marks and Designs) (OHIM) (C416/04)* EU:C:2006:310, [2006] E.C.R. I-4237 and *Reber* applied. Slight use could amount to genuine use, *La Mer* applied. On the other hand, use in a particular locality might not qualify as genuine use, *Reber* applied. The outcome depended on the facts in each case. The hearing officer had not fallen into error in his assessment of genuine use. He had conducted the requisite global assessment of the established use of STRADA and it was open to him to conclude that that use was of mere local significance and did not qualify as genuine use in the relevant periods (see paras 35-37, 40, 45, 52 of judgment). (2) There was no evidence showing the actual display of STRADA spectacles in the shops; simply an undated copy photograph of STRADA spectacles in cabinet drawers. The evidence of display to the public was at best thin. It was entirely a matter for the hearing officer to decide what weight he accorded to the display evidence, and he had done so without error. Moreover, he had accepted at various points in his decision that the STRADA mark had been used on the arms of spectacles. There was no merit in the argument that he had discounted such use. Finally, the appellant's criticism of the hearing officer's finding that there was no real promotion or advertising of the mark merely challenged the weight attributed by the hearing officer to that part of the evidence. No error was identified that justified interference with his decision (paras 57, 62, 66).

MEMORY OPTICIANS LTD v SDS INVESTCORP AG *sub nom.* MEMORY OPTICIANS LTD TRADE MARK APPLICATION (NO.2443998), [2016] E.C.C. 15, Ruth Annand, App Person.

1335 Trade marks–Goodwill–Use of trademark for restaurants–Earlier use by another restaurant–Effect of goodwill

[Trade Marks Act 1994 (c.26) s.5(4)(a)]

The claimants alleged trade mark infringement and passing off by the defendants. The claimants' UK registered marks were a word mark CASPIAN, registered in respect of restaurants and related services in 2005, and a device mark registered in 2010, depicting a chef and the words CASPIAN PIZZA. The claimants contended that the first defendant (D1) had operated a pizza restaurant under an informal franchise agreement with the first claimant company (C1), and that D1's failure to pay royalties whilst using the CASPIAN marks in relation to his business infringed the marks and constituted passing off. The defendants denied that there was ever a franchise agreement and submitted that the goodwill in D1's restaurant had never passed to C1, but remained at all times with D1's business since it had started trading before the alleged agreement was even suggested, and had consequently created its own local goodwill. They further asserted that the word mark was invalid for lack of genuine use in the five-year period following its registration, that both marks should be revoked as having been registered in bad faith, and that the word mark had been registered in contravention of the Trade Marks Act 1994 s.5(4)(a), which prevented the registration of marks giving rise to a passing off action.

Held: Judgment for defendants. (1) The claimants' evidence regarding the date of the franchise agreement and the consequent first trading of D1's restaurant was unreliable, and their allegations in those respects were rejected. Had D1's restaurant really been franchised, there would have been much more compelling documentary evidence of the agreement itself, together with documents establishing regular royalty payments and possibly other matters which flowed from the agreement. D1's restaurant was likely to have generated sufficient local goodwill for the defendants or their successors from 2004 to found an action in passing off to prevent parties other than D1 from conducting a pizza business under the CASPIAN name (see paras 25-26, 31-32 of judgment). (2) The claimants had used the word mark from 2005 to 2014, and the claim for revocation based on lack of use failed (para.59). (3) The highest the defendants could put their case on bad faith on the available evidence was that the claimants knew about D1's restaurant when the application for each of the trade marks was made. That did not go far enough, *Red Bull GmbH v Sun Mark Ltd* [2012] EWHC 1929 (Ch), [2013] E.T.M.R. 53 applied. There remained the likely possibility that at the time of the applications, the second and third claimants had had it in mind to protect their own business and it was only later that they turned their minds to franchise agreements. The allegation of bad faith was rejected (paras 60-62). (4) The defendants or their successors owned goodwill in the business conducted by D1's restaurant under the CASPIAN name from 2004 until the present. When the word mark was applied for in 2005, the defendants or their successors were entitled to prevent another party trading in the sale of pizzas in D1's restaurant's local area under the CASPIAN name. The word mark was, therefore, invalidly registered pursuant to s.5(4)(a) (paras 64, 80). (5) The claimants had not established that their goodwill extended as far as D1's restaurant's local area when that business had started trading, or even that it did now. There was no consequent passing off as a result of trading by D1's restaurant (para.82). (6) In conclusion, the word mark was invalidly registered but the device mark remained valid. Neither of the marks had been infringed by the defendants. The claim for passing off failed (para.83).

CASPIAN PIZZA LTD v SHAH, [2015] EWHC 3567 (IPEC), [2016] F.S.R. 23, Judge Hacon, IPEC.

1336 Trade marks–Infringement–Disclaimers on labels imports of generic medicines–Whether defeating trade mark infringement claims

[Trade Marks Act 1994 (c.26) s.10(1), s.11(2)(b); Treaty on the Functioning of the European Union 2008 art.34, art.36]

The claimant alleged infringement of its "FLYNN" UK and Community trade marks by the defendants. The claimant traded in generic medicines and speciality brands, all of which carried its FLYNN name and logo. The defendants were proposing to import into the UK pharmaceutical products which had been sold in other Member States under the brand name "Epanutin" and affixing to them the name "Phenytoin Sodium Flynn". The claimant contended that the proposed use of Flynn would infringe under the Trade Marks Act 1994 s.10(1) as the use of an identical sign for identical goods. The defendants submitted that their imports would not infringe because they were not using the mark as a trade mark, only as a description of the goods within s.11(2)(b). They relied on a disclaimer on the packaging stating that their products were not manufactured or sold by the claimant, but were equivalent to the claimant's phenytoin sodium products. They further argued that the claimant's reliance on its trade mark rights under domestic legislation to stop the imports constituted a disguised restriction on trade contrary to the free movement provisions of the TFEU.

Held: Judgment for claimant. (1) The defendants' use of "Flynn" did not describe the goods. "Flynn" was not a word associated with medicines or ingredients otherwise denoting the medicine's qualities or characteristics. It would be perceived by consumers as a mark of origin, indicating that the product came from the claimant as the entity responsible for the goods' quality. That was clearly a trade mark use of the sign, *Arsenal Football Club Plc v Reed (C-206/01)* EU:C:2002:651, [2003] Ch. 454, [2002] C.L.Y. 2912 applied. The disclaimer was not sufficient to clarify for the consumer the nature of the relationship between the product and the claimant. The use of a word in naming a product where the word was clearly a brand name was not gainsaid by small print explaining that the product had not been made or marketed by the entity which owned the right to use that name (see paras 36, 40 of judgment). (2) Although art.34 of the TFEU prohibited quantitative restrictions on imports, or equivalent measures, between Member States, art.36 tempered that absolute provision by allowing prohibitions or restrictions on imports where they were justified in protecting industrial or commercial property, provided they did not constitute a disguised restriction on trade. In order to defeat a trade mark owner's infringement claim, a defendant had to show that the product it was seeking to import had been placed in the exporting Member State with the consent of or by the same entity that later tried to prevent its import, *Bristol Myers Squibb Co v Paranova A/S (C-427/93)* EU:C:1996:282, [2003] Ch. 75, [1997] C.L.Y. 4879 and *Speciality European Pharma Ltd v Doncaster Pharmaceuticals Group Ltd* [2015] EWCA Civ 54, [2015] 3 All E.R. 504, [2015] C.L.Y. 1529 considered. The claimant was responsible for placing its phenytoin sodium on the market in the UK, but another company was responsible for placing Epanutin on the market in other Member States. It followed that the claimant's trade mark rights were not exhausted in respect of Epanutin placed on the market in other Member States, and the claimant was entitled to prevent the relabeling of the defendants' parallel imports (paras 41-43, 50, 52, 56, 73, 78, 96-97).

FLYNN PHARMA LTD v DRUGSRUS LTD, [2015] EWHC 2759 (Ch), [2016] E.C.C. 4, Rose J, Ch D.

1337 Trade marks–Infringement–Garage displaying motor vehicle manufacturer's marks

[Regulation 207/2009 2009 art.9]

A motor vehicle manufacturer claimed that an independent garage had infringed three of its trade marks and had passed off repair services as being associated with or approved by the manufacturer. The manufacturer's trade marks were the lettering BMW, a roundel and an M logo. It complained that the garage director had worn a shirt with BMW printed under the garage name and used a Twitter account containing the garage name followed by BMW. Further, the roundel was displayed on signs outside and inside the garage premises and on the garage business cards. Lastly, the garage website contained two signs identical or similar to the M logo. At the instant hearing, the manufacturer stated that only authorised dealers could use the trade marks, and that the garage's usage was likely to lead a substantial proportion of the garage's customers and potential customers to believe that the garage was an approved dealer. The garage stated that usage of the trade marks was not restricted to authorised dealers, as it had been supplied with spare parts kits from such dealers containing packaging and promotional items that displayed the trade marks, to be passed on to customers. The garage argued that its use of the trade marks (1) merely conveyed to the average consumer that it was a specialist in the repair and maintenance of BMW vehicles using genuine BMW spare parts, not an authorised dealer; (2) was not intended to take unfair advantage of their distinctive character or repute.

Held: Judgment for claimant in part. (1) Regarding the roundel, it was likely that the average consumer had come to believe that it would only be displayed on and in the premises of an undertaking that maintained and repaired vehicles if that undertaking was authorised by the manufacturer. That would have been the almost invariable experience of actual consumers. Even if that was not the case, at the least the garage's use of the roundel on and in its premises would cause the average consumer to wonder whether it was an authorised dealer, thereby adversely affecting the trade mark in terms of its function of indicating origin. Further, the average consumer would distinguish between a roundel displayed on the outside of a garage or prominently inside the premises and a similar sign on a promotional item, particularly where the latter was displayed with the wording "Genuine BMW Parts". The former conveyed that the services offered by the garage were authorised; the latter indicated that the spare parts supplied by the garage came from the manufacturer. The same reasoning applied to the use of the M logo on the garage website: the average consumer would take the signs to mean that the garage was an authorised dealer. As to the BMW mark, the position was different. The manufacturer had asserted that the average consumer would not believe that the BMW lettering conveyed any implication of authorised use in general, but that it did when immediately attached to a dealer's name, such as on a shirt or Twitter account. The manufacturer had not supplied sufficient evidence to establish that that was the average consumer's perception of BMW signs. Therefore, the garage had infringed the roundel and the M logo under Regulation 207/2009 art.9(1), but not the BMW mark (see paras 27-33 of judgment). (2) Regarding unfair advantage, it was the objective effect of the use of the trade mark that mattered, not the user's subjective intention, *Enterprise Holdings Inc v Europcar Group UK Ltd* [2015] EWHC 17 (Ch), [2015] E.T.M.R. 16, [2015] C.L.Y. 1533 and *Jack Wills Ltd v House of Fraser (Stores) Ltd* [2014] EWHC 110 (Ch), [2014] E.T.M.R. 28, [2014] C.L.Y. 1921 applied. The use of the roundel conveyed to the average consumer that the garage was an authorised dealer, giving it an enhanced ability to trade and taking unfair advantage of the roundel's distinctive character or repute. However, the use of BMW on the director's shirt and the Twitter account had conveyed nothing more than that the garage traded or specialised in the maintenance and repair of BMW cars. That was insufficient by itself to show that it had taken unfair advantage of the BMW mark (paras 35-38).

BAYERISCHE MOTOREN WERKE AG v TECHNOSPORT LONDON LTD, [2016] EWHC 797 (IPEC), [2016] E.C.C. 20, Judge Hacon, IPEC.

1338 Trade marks–Passing off–Company trading as Intellectual Property Agency Ltd–Liability to UK Intellectual Property Office for passing off and trade mark infringement

The claimant comptroller-general and secretary of state brought proceedings for trade mark infringement and passing off against the first defendant company and the second defendant director and shareholder. The company traded as the "Intellectual Property Agency Ltd" and operated by writing to the proprietors of patents and trade marks reminding them that the right required renewal and requesting a renewal fee. In each case, the company would renew the relevant rights on behalf of the paying rightholder by contacting the UK Intellectual Property Office itself, but would make a profit by charging the rightholder more than just the fee owed to the IPO. The claimants alleged that the defendants were liable for passing off because the rightholders had only agreed to pay because of the misrepresentation that the company was the IPO or otherwise connected with the IPO in an official way. They further contended that the

IPO's trade mark, which used the words INTELLECTUAL PROPERTY OFFICE and included a motif of a crown, had been infringed by the company's use of the sign INTELLECTUAL PROPERTY AGENCY LTD.

Held: Judgment for claimants. (1) A government department or executive agency such as the IPO was entitled to goodwill associated with its name, *Cranford Community College v Cranford College Ltd* [2014] EWHC 2999 (IPEC), [2015] E.T.M.R. 7, [2015] C.L.Y. 1497 applied. The services provided by the IPO undoubtedly generated goodwill (see paras 10-11 of judgment). The logo and overall presentation of the document sent by the company to rightholders suggested a form emanating from an official source. It was unlikely that those who were familiar with the intellectual property system would have thought that the IPO had sent the letter, but those who were unfamiliar with the system might have thought that the form had been sent from the government organisation responsible for intellectual property, the precise name of which they might not have had in mind. There was evidence that confusion had taken place (paras 14-15). For there to have been no misrepresentation on the company's part, the court would have to assume that the rightholder had not believed that the company was the IPO or connected to it, and yet (a) despite never having dealt with the company before, they had trusted the company sufficiently to engage it as an agent and to pay the sums demanded, and (b) they had done so without first checking the IPO's fees. Although it was possible that that was true of some rightholders, it could not be true of most of them. A large proportion of rightholders had accepted the company's misrepresentation that it was the relevant governmental intellectual property body and paid the fee requested because they took on trust that that was the official fee (para.25). Although the IPO had not suffered damage in the usual way, because it had still been paid the appropriate renewal fees, inactivity on the IPO's part in preventing a scam was likely to damage its reputation, Spalding v Gamage (1918) 35 R.P.C. 101 (CA) applied. The claimants had accordingly established all the elements of their passing off claim (paras 28-29). (2) The average consumer would perceive the words INTELLECTUAL PROPERTY OFFICE in the IPO's trade mark as having distinctive significance, separate from the crown device. While there was a relationship between the words and the crown device in that the device was presumably there to indicate that the IPO was a Crown agency, that might not be immediately apparent to the average consumer, and even when it was, that would not alter the meaning given to the words in the mark. The principal impact of the mark was the concept conveyed by those words: they were the dominant part of the mark. The visual, aural and conceptual similarities of the marks were obvious. Since the conceptual impact of the word component of the trade mark was the most important, there would be a significant difference between that and the company's sign only if the concepts of an "Intellectual Property Office" and an "Intellectual Property Agency" would convey significantly different ideas to the average consumer. Government bodies were sometimes called agencies, and therefore it was doubtful that an average consumer would perceive any difference. While it was true that the inclusion of the word "Ltd" in the company's name and sign conveyed the idea of a limited company rather than a government body, that was insufficient to override the inference of a likelihood of confusion. Further, there was actual evidence of confusion, which reinforced the likelihood of confusion in the mind of the construct of the average consumer, *JW Spear & Sons Ltd v Zynga Inc* [2015] EWCA Civ 290, [2016] 1 All E.R. 226, [2015] C.L.Y. 1535 applied. The company had accordingly infringed the IPO's trade mark (paras 33, 35-36). (3) The only conclusion that could be drawn from the facts was that the second defendant was the only individual who had taken steps to institute the company's actions, and therefore he must have intended that those actions would occur. On that basis, the second defendant was jointly liable for the company's acts of passing off and trade mark infringement (para.38). (4) The claimants were awarded the maximum account of profits permitted under the IPEC cap, namely £500,000 (paras 39-41).

COMPTROLLER-GENERAL OF PATENTS DESIGNS AND TRADE MARKS v INTELLECTUAL PROPERTY AGENCY LTD, [2015] EWHC 3256 (IPEC), [2016] F.S.R. 22, Judge Hacon, IPEC.

1339 Trade marks–Passing off–Registration of distinctive domain names–Whether registration itself giving rise to passing off

A number of trade mark owners asked the court to strike out both a claim arising from a domain name dispute and the claimant's defence to the trade mark owners' counterclaim for passing off. The claimant had registered the domain names rbsbank.email, rbs.email, natwest.email and coutts.email for itself through an internet services provider. The trade mark owners, who were the registered proprietors of the marks RBS, RBSBANK, NATWEST and COUTTS, complained that their rights were being infringed. The domain name dispute panel operating under the Internet Corporation for Assigned Names and Numbers Uniform Dispute Resolution Policy of the World Intellectual Property Organisation adopted a decision that the domain names were identical or confusingly similar to the trade marks and that the claimant had registered them with the intention of using them in bad faith. The names were ordered to be transferred to the trade mark owners. The claimant sought to recover the domain names and applied for declaratory relief to the effect that it had been guilty of no wrongdoing. The trade mark owners sought summary judgment on their counterclaim for passing off. The trade mark owners argued that the court lacked jurisdiction to act as a review body from the panel's decision and that the claim should be struck out as giving rise to no reasonably arguable cause of action.

Held: Claim struck out, summary judgment for defendants on counterclaim. (1) The goodwill and reputation of the trade mark owners in the public mind by association with the names RBS, RBSBANK, NATWEST and COUTTS were not in dispute, *Reckitt & Colman Products Ltd v Borden Inc (No.3)* [1990] 1 W.L.R. 491, [1990] C.L.Y. 3465 followed. The mere registration of the distinctive domain names in issue, irrespective of any intended use, represented to persons consulting the register that the claimant was associated with the names registered and was thus the owner of the goodwill in those names. Therefore, such a person would believe the claimant to be connected or associated with the trade mark owners' businesses, *British Telecommunications Plc v One in a Million Ltd* [1999] 1 W.L.R. 903, [1998] C.L.Y. 3520 followed, *Smithkline Beecham Ltd v GSKline Ltd* [2011] EWHC 169 (Ch) and *Vertical Leisure Ltd v Poleplus Ltd* [2014] EWHC 2077 (IPEC) applied. It followed that the claimant's registration of the domain names in issue amounted to passing off. Moreover, there was no need to explore the claimant's proposed business model and intended use of the domain names, as the actionable passing off occurred at the point of registration. Therefore, the claimant had no realistic prospect of defending the counterclaim and the trade mark owners were entitled to summary judgment (see paras 8-9, 13-17, 22 of judgment). (2) The scheme under which the panel operated did not give rise to a separate cause of action in favour of the claimant, nor did it afford any jurisdiction to the instant court to act as an appeal or review body from the panel's decision, *Patel v Allos Therapeutics Inc* [2008] E.T.M.R. 75, [2009] C.L.Y. 2327 applied. There was no practical utility in granting declaratory relief, because the scheme under which the panel had adopted its decision had dealt with the issue between the parties and any declaration made by the instant court could not alter those findings. The declaration sought would have no practical impact on the rights in respect of the domain names. In any event, the effect of the conclusions on the application for summary judgment on the counterclaim rendered the claim itself otiose, *Toth v Emirates* [2012] EWHC 517 (Ch), [2012] 2 All E.R. (Comm) 1302, [2012] C.L.Y. 873 applied. Moreover, there was no compelling reason why the questions of bad faith should be allowed to go to trial, since the panel had found against the claimant in each respect. The claim therefore had to be struck out (paras 31-32).

YOYO.EMAIL LTD v ROYAL BANK OF SCOTLAND GROUP PLC, [2015] EWHC 3509 (Ch), [2016] F.S.R. 18, Judge Dight, Ch D.

1340 Trade marks–Registration–Opposition to "The GapTravel Guide" in respect of services of travel publishing

[Trade Marks Act 1994 (c.26) s.5(2)(b)]

The appellant appealed against the rejection of its opposition to the respondent's application to register a trade mark. The respondent had applied to register "The GapTravel Guide" as a trade mark in respect of the services of magazine publishing in

Class 41. The words "Gap" and "Travel" were conjoined. The appellant, who had already registered the mark "GAP" in respect of a range of services in Class 41 including the publication of electronic books and journals online, opposed the registration under the Trade Marks Act 1994 s.5(2)(b). The hearing officer rejected the opposition, having identified that the average consumer of publishing services were businesses rather than the general public, and having found that the marks shared a low level of visual similarity, a low level of aural similarity and no conceptual similarity. In particular, he found that when combined with "Travel", the presence of the word "Gap" in the respondent's mark was allusive of the concept of a "gap year" in the context of travel guide publishing. The appellant argued that the hearing officer had erred in his identification of the average consumer and in his finding that the marks shared no conceptual similarity. In particular, it argued that if "Gap" in the respondent's mark was allusive of a "gap year" in the context of travel guide publishing, it was similarly so allusive in the appellant's mark when so used, and there was therefore real conceptual similarity between the two marks.

Held: Appeal allowed. (1) The concept of the average consumer was created to strike the right balance between various competing interests including, on the one hand, the need to protect consumers and, on the other hand, the promotion of free trade in an openly competitive market, *Interflora Inc v Marks & Spencer Plc* [2014] EWCA Civ 1403, [2015] Bus. L.R. 492, [2015] C.L.Y. 1531 considered. In the instant case, the respondent was carrying out the service of magazine publishing by producing and distributing magazines. That was the service for which it sought trade mark protection. There was a high degree of correspondence between the carrying out of that service and the magazines which were the end product of that service. A conclusion that a consumer of the product of such a service was not also a consumer of the service was too narrow a perspective and did not accord with practical commerce. Accordingly, the hearing officer was mistaken to conclude that the average consumer would generally be a business (see paras 14-15 of judgment). (2) A necessary corollary of the hearing officer's conclusion was that the allusion which was offered by the respondent's mark was also offered by the appellant's mark, at least when considered in the context of use in respect of those parts of the appellant's services concerned with the publishing of travel guides and bearing in mind that use of mark included use in oral form when the conjoined aspect was unlikely to be noticed (paras 29-30). (3) Looking at the matter afresh, the s.5(2)(b) objection succeeded. Guides and travel guides were common subject matter for magazine publishing services. Taking into account the assumed reputation of the appellant's mark, the presence of the neologism or portmanteau "GapTravel" in the graphic representation of the respondent's mark was not sufficient to remove the likelihood of confusion. The word "Gap" was the differentiating factor between those guides or travel guides and those of some third party, *Reed Executive Plc v Reed Business Information Ltd* [2004] EWCA Civ 159, [2004] E.T.M.R. 56, [2004] C.L.Y. 2402 and *Maier v ASOS Plc* [2015] EWCA Civ 220, [2016] 2 All E.R. 738, [2015] C.L.Y. 1536 applied (paras 4, 6, 33).

GAP (ITM) INC v BRITISH AMERICAN GROUP LTD, [2016] EWHC 599 (Ch), [2016] E.C.C. 14, John Baldwin QC, Ch D.

1341 Trade marks–Visual similarity–Trade marks aurally identical but not visually similar–Likelihood of confusion

The appellant appealed against a decision rejecting its opposition to the registration of the respondent's trade mark. Both the appellant's and respondent's marks comprised the letters "RA" written in capitals. The hearing officer rejected the appellant's opposition, concluding that although the marks were aurally identical and the parties' goods and services were either identical or highly similar, the marks were not visually similar so that there was no likelihood of confusion.

Held: Appeal dismissed. There was no doubt that the officer had proceeded on the basis that the average consumer would understand the letters "RA" to be conveyed by the appellant's mark. Accordingly, when she concluded that there was no visual similarity between the marks, she could not be taken to have forgotten that similarity. Similarly, she could not be taken to have forgotten the fact that both marks comprised the letters "RA" when considering the overall global question whether the average consumer was likely to be confused (see para.11 of judgment). The difference between "no visual similarity" and "a low degree of visual similarity" was not only impossible to define but was subjective. It was hard to imagine a case in which the spread of reasonable opinions about visual similarity could not cover both characterisations. There was no difficulty with the notion that two representations of the same thing might have no visual similarity: two representations of the same thing could have no visual similarity whilst having some limited conceptual similarity (paras 12-13).

ERREA SPORT SPA v ROYAL ACADEMY OF ARTS *sub nom.* ROYAL ACADEMY OF ARTS v ERREA SPORT SPA, [2016] F.S.R. 24, Iain Purvis QC, App Person.

1342 UK Intellectual Property Office–Costs–Ex parte applications to UK Intellectual Property Office–Costs of interveners

The court dealt with costs following its judgment dismissing the appeal of a company (C) against a decision of the respondent Comptroller. The appeal was against the refusal of C's ex parte application to delete a mark from an alleged series of trade marks. C had agreed to pay the respondent's costs, estimated to be about £13,000, but there was a dispute regarding the costs of the intervener (N). N asked for its costs, and its bill was some five times greater than that of the respondent. N argued that the appeal was dismissed, its application to intervene should have been consented to at the outset, and its arguments had been accepted by the court, so it should have its costs in accordance with the usual principles. N also submitted that it had a direct interest in the appeal, the mark having been relied upon in infringement proceedings brought against it, and that that direct interest justified its intervention. C argued that there was no obvious reason why it should pay N's costs since the application was one that it had made ex parte to the respondent to rectify the registration of its own UK trade mark. It submitted that N's intervention had resulted in little more than a substantial increase in the costs of the proceedings, and that in circumstances where the respondent could be relied upon to defend its decisions competently and thoroughly, there was no need for any intervention, and any such should be at the cost and risk of the intervener.

Held: Costs determined. (1) C had drawn attention to the fact that the Competition Appeal Tribunal ordinarily made no order for costs in favour of interveners. In *Ryanair Holdings Plc v Competition and Markets Authority* [2015] CAT 15, [2015] Comp. A.R. 312, [2016] 356, the CAT explained that the rationale for that practice was to strike a balance between not discouraging legitimate interventions and not unduly encouraging interventions which might have implications for the expeditious conduct of proceedings to the detriment of the main parties. It was emphasised that the CAT needed to have a good reason for departing from that general position. Before getting to the stage of considering whether there was good reason to depart from the ordinary position, three elements had to be satisfied: the position of the intervener had to be successful; the intervener's submissions must have added value to the hearing; and the intervener must not have duplicated the submissions of the respondent (see paras 10-11 of judgment). (2) It was desirable to have some certainty in the area of costs in relation to interventions in ex parte applications to the UK Intellectual Property Office. The rationale of the practice in the CAT, as explained in *Ryanair*, was attractive. There were good reasons for adopting that practice in cases such as the instant case, particularly when it was widely recognised that the respondent was usually represented by highly competent counsel with relevant expertise. N had a commercial interest in intervening in C's application, but there was no supervening public interest involved and N was a very well-resourced party. With respect to the three elements referred to in *Ryanair*, the first and third were clearly satisfied, and the second was just about satisfied. However, there was nothing more of substance to go into the balance. There was no suggestion that N would be materially disadvantaged if it did not recover the costs of its intervention. No order should be made with respect to N's costs, *Ryanair* applied (paras 12-13).

CADBURY UK LTD v COMPTROLLER GENERAL OF PATENTS DESIGNS AND TRADE MARKS (COSTS), [2016] EWHC 1609 (Ch), [2016] Bus. L.R. 872, John Baldwin QC, Ch D.

INTERNATIONAL LAW

1343 Antarctica–Recognised assistance dogs–Training

THE ANTARCTIC (RECOGNISED ASSISTANCE DOG) REGULATIONS 2016, SI 2016/697; made under the Antarctic Act 1994 s.8(5), s.32. In force: 23 September 2016.

These Regulations prescribe who may train a "recognised assistance dog" for the purposes of the Antarctic Act 1994 s.8(5) as amended by the Antarctic Act 2013. They revoke and replace The Antarctic (Recognised Assistance Dog) Regulations 2015.

1344 Economic sanctions–British overseas territories–Additional sanctions against North Korea

THE DEMOCRATIC PEOPLE'S REPUBLIC OF KOREA (SANCTIONS) (OVERSEAS TERRITORIES) (AMENDMENT) ORDER 2016, SI 2016/630; made under the United Nations Act 1946 s.1; Saint Helena Act 1833 s.112; British Settlements Act 1945; British Settlements Act 1887. In force: 10 June 2016.

This Order amends the Democratic People's Republic of Korea (Sanctions) (Overseas Territories) Order 2012. This Order gives effect in specified Overseas Territories to the additional sanctions against North Korea adopted by the United Nations Security Council.

1345 EU law–Export controls–Syria

THE EXPORT CONTROL (LIBYA SANCTIONS) ORDER 2016, SI 2016/787; made under the European Communities Act 1972 s.2(2), Sch.2 para.1A(3). In force: 12 August 2016.

This Order provides for the enforcement of trade restrictions against Libya specified in Regulation 2016/44 concerning restrictive measures against Libya.

1346 EU law–Financial sanctions–North Korea

THE DEMOCRATIC PEOPLE'S REPUBLIC OF KOREA (EUROPEAN UNION FINANCIAL SANCTIONS) (AMENDMENT) (NO.2) REGULATIONS 2016, SI 2016/634; made under the European Communities Act 1972 s.2(2). In force: 11 June 2016.

These Regulations make provision relating to the enforcement of Regulation 329/2007 concerning restrictive measures against the Democratic People's Republic of Korea (the DPRK). These measures include the freezing of funds and economic resources of designated persons, ensuring that funds and economic resources are not made available to them, and broader financial sanctions measures. Enforcement of these measures is provided for by the Democratic People's Republic of Korea (European Union Financial Sanctions) Regulations 2013. The Regulation has been amended by Regulation 2016/841 to impose additional financial sanctions measures relating DPRK. These Regulations amend the 2013 Regulations to include these additional financial sanctions measures. Regulations 3 and 4 provide for the imposition of additional financial sanctions measures in relation to investment in DPRK and with DPRK entities, trade and commerce with DPRK entities, and the transfer of funds to and from DPRK.

1347 EU law–Freezing of funds–Iran

THE IRAN (EUROPEAN UNION FINANCIAL SANCTIONS) REGULATIONS 2016, SI 2016/36; made under the European Communities Act 1972 s.2(2), Sch.2 para.1A. In force: 18 January 2016 at 16.00.

These Regulations make provision relating to the enforcement of Regulation 2012/267 concerning restrictive measures against Iran and repealing Regulation 961/2010.

1348 EU law–Freezing of funds–Libya

THE LIBYA (EUROPEAN UNION FINANCIAL SANCTIONS) REGULATIONS 2016, SI 2016/45; made under the European Communities Act 1972 s.2(2), Sch.2 para.1A. In force: 20 January 2016.

1349 EU law–Freezing of funds–North Korea

THE DEMOCRATIC PEOPLE'S REPUBLIC OF KOREA (EUROPEAN UNION FINANCIAL SANCTIONS) (AMENDMENT) REGULATIONS 2016, SI 2016/578; made under the European Communities Act 1972 s.2(2). In force: 13 May 2016.

These Regulations update the Democratic People's Republic of Korea (European Union Financial Sanctions) Regulations 2013 (the 2013 Regulations), which provide for enforcement of the Regulation 329/2007 dated (the Council Regulation). The amendments made by these regulations are necessary to enable enforcement actions to be taken under UK law in respect of some additional financial sanctions measures that were added to the Council Regulation on 4 May 2016.

1350 EU law–Sanctions–Iran

THE EXPORT CONTROL (IRAN SANCTIONS) ORDER 2016, SI 2016/503; made under the European Communities Act 1972 s.2(2), Sch.2 para.1A; Export Control Act 2002 s.1, s.2, s.3, s.4, s.5, s.7. In force: 6 May 2016.

This Order provides for the enforcement of trade restrictions against Iran specified in Regulation 267/2012 concerning restrictive measures against Iran, as last amended by Regulation 2015/1861. The Order also provides for the enforcement of trade restrictions in Regulation 359/2011 concerning restrictive measures directed against certain persons, entities and bodies in view of the situation in Iran. It revokes and replaces the Export Control (Iran Sanctions) Order 2012 and amending instruments, and makes makes a minor amendment to the Export Control (Russia, Crimea and Sevastopol Sanctions) Order 2014 and to the Export Control Order 2008.

1351 Financial sanctions–Freezing of funds–Al-Qaida

THE AL-QAIDA (ASSET-FREEZING) (AMENDMENT) REGULATIONS 2016, SI 2016/937; made under the European Communities Act 1972 s.2(2). In force: 22 September 2016.

Regulation 881/2002 imposes sanctions relating to certain persons and entities associated with the Al-Qaida network. These include restrictive measures freezing the funds and economic resources of persons and entities listed in Annex I. Criminal penalties for the breach of the restrictive measures imposed by the Regulation are imposed in the UK by the Al-Qaida (Asset-Freezing) Regulations 2011. Regulation 363/2016 amended the 2002 Regulation to reflect changes adopted by United Nations Security Council Resolution 2253 (2015), which ensured, amongst other things, that persons or entities supporting ISIL (Da'esh) are eligible for listing by the United Nations. Regulation No 1686/2016 imposes additional restrictive measures against ISIL (Da'esh) and Al-Qaida and natural and legal persons, entities or bodies associated with them. These include restrictive measures freezing the funds and economic resources of persons and entities listed in Annex I. These Regulations amend the 2011 Regulations. These amendments reflect certain amendments made by Regulation 363/2016 to the 2002 Regulation. The amendments also ensure that the enforcement provisions in the 2011 Regulations apply to the enforcement of the 2016 Regulation as well as the 2002 Regulation.

1352 Freezing of funds–Belarus

THE BELARUS (ASSET-FREEZING) (AMENDMENT) REGULATIONS 2016, SI 2016/504; made under the European Communities Act 1972 s.2(2). In force: 6 May 2016.

These Regulations amend the Belarus (Asset-Freezing) Regulations 2013 so that the definition of "designated person" no longer refers to Annex IV, which has been removed from Regulation 765/2006.

1353 International organisations–International Oil Pollution Compensation Fund–Immunity from jurisdiction

[International Oil Pollution Compensation Fund 1992 (Immunities and Privileges) Order 1996 (SI 1996/1295) art.5]

The International Oil Pollution Compensation Fund 1992 applied to set aside a registration order obtained by a Venezuelan trade union registering a Venezuelan judgment in the English courts. The Venezuelan judgment concerned an incident in May 1997 whereby Venezuelan fishing boats and fishermen were affected by an oil spillage. The 1992 Fund was part of an international regime for compensating damage caused by oil spills from tankers. It had been preceded by a 1971 Fund, but the two were separate legal entities. Venezuela had become party to the Fund in July 1999. The Venezuela judgment, which had been secured by the trade union acting on behalf of the fishermen, specifically referred to the 1971 Fund, but not to the 1992 Fund. It did, however, refer often to "the Funds". The issue was whether the 1971 Fund or the 1992 Fund was liable under the judgment. The 1992 Fund had contracted with the UK Government that it was immune from jurisdiction and execution except in certain specified circumstances. The immunities were replicated in the International Oil Pollution Compensation Fund 1992 (Immunities and Privileges) Order 1996 art.5. The 1992 Fund therefore believed it had no liability. The trade union believed that the Venezuelan judgment related to the 1992 Fund because a 1992 Fund Protocol in existence at the time of the spillage had amended the 1971 Fund so that it was no longer the relevant regime at the time. The 1992 Fund submitted that as it was immune from jurisdiction and execution, and that as the Venezuelan judgment was clearly against the 1971 Fund, there was no judgment which fell to be registered against it in the English courts. The trade union argued that the 1992 Fund Protocol had had the effect of replacing the rights and liabilities of the 1971 Fund with those of the 1992 Fund.

Held: Application granted. The trade union's reliance on the 1992 Fund Protocol was misplaced. As was clear from art.28 of the Protocol, if it was to be applicable, Venezuela would not only have had to be a signatory to it before the incident, but it would also have had to ratify, accept, approve and accede to it. Article 30(1), art.30(3) and art.36 supported that conclusion. Venezuela had not done those things until after the oil spillage giving rise to its judgment. The reference in art.36 to the start date being "the date of entry into force of this Convention" meant the start date as far as individual states were concerned, not the entry into force provisions in art.30(1). The transitional provisions in art.36 did not apply retrospectively. Otherwise, a state could recover higher compensation under the 1992 Fund despite having paid contributions under the 1971 Fund which entitled it to recover a lesser amount. They only applied to states which had ratified, accepted, approved or acceded to the 1992 Fund Protocol but had not yet denounced the 1971 Fund. It was clear that the intervention made in the Venezuelan proceedings had been made by the 1971 Fund not the 1992 Fund. The argument that the two funds were to be treated as one and the same was misconceived, nor was there any reason to accept that the Venezuelan judgment was to be regarded as applying to the 1992 Fund when nowhere in the judgment was that fund referred to. The references in the judgment to "the funds" were insufficient to change that conclusion. It had therefore not been open to the trade union to register the Venezuelan judgment against the 1992 Fund (see paras 50-52, 54-59, 62-64 of judgment).

SINDICATO UNICO DE PESCADORES DEL MUNICIPIO MIRANDA DEL ESTADO ZULIA v INTERNATIONAL OIL POLLUTION COMPENSATION FUND, [2015] EWHC 2476 (QB), [2016] 1 Lloyd's Rep. 332, Picken J, QBD.

1354 Sanctions–Iran–British overseas territories

THE IRAN (SANCTIONS) (OVERSEAS TERRITORIES) (AMENDMENT) ORDER 2016, SI 2016/560; made under the United Nations Act 1946 s.1; Saint Helena Act 1833 s.112; British Settlements Act 1945. In force: 1 June 2016.

This Order amends the Iran (Sanctions) (Overseas Territories) Order 2016. Schedule 3 to the principal Order contains provision for obtaining evidence and information for the purpose of enforcing the Order; this Order inserts additional powers into that

Schedule in relation to ships, aircraft or vehicles that are suspected of being used in the commission of certain offences under the principal Order.

1355 **State immunity–Arbitration awards–State's agreement to arbitrate**

[State Immunity Act 1978 (c.33) s.1, s.12(1), s.9; Civil Procedure Rules 1998 r.62.18]

The defendant, the Republic of Venezuela, applied to set aside an ex parte order granting the claimant Canadian company leave to enforce an arbitration award as if it were a judgment. The company had become the indirect owner of a mining project in Venezuela and spent almost US $300 million in developing it. A bilateral investment treaty (BIT) existed between Canada and Venezuela. The company began arbitration proceedings against Venezuela under its purported right as an "investor" under the BIT. An "investor" was defined as an enterprise "who makes the investment in the territory of Venezuela". An "investment" was an "asset owned or controlled by an investor", directly or indirectly, including rights to exploit natural resources. Despite Venezuela's objection, the tribunal found that it had jurisdiction and issued an award in the company's favour. Venezuela submitted that the order should be set aside because (1) it was entitled to immunity under the State Immunity Act 1978 s.1; (2) the arbitration claim form had not been served as required by s.12(1); (3) the company had failed to give full and frank disclosure regarding state immunity by failing to refer to the existence of an ongoing dispute concerning the tribunal's jurisdiction.

Held: Application refused. (1) Venezuela was entitled to state immunity under s.1 unless it had agreed in writing to submit a dispute to arbitration under s.9. Under the BIT, such an agreement arose where the state's consent to arbitrate claims by an investor was regarded as a unilateral offer to investors to arbitrate, which the investor accepted by commencing arbitration, *Ecuador v Occidental Exploration & Production Co* [2005] EWCA Civ 1116, [2006] Q.B. 432, [2005] C.L.Y. 212 applied. The question was whether the company was an "investor" within the meaning of the BIT. Under articles 31 and 32 of the Vienna Convention on the Law of Treaties, the court should look at the ordinary meaning of the words in their context and in light of the BIT's object and purpose, namely promoting and protecting investments in Venezuela by Canadian enterprises. The definition of "investor" referred to "the investment", which had two ordinary meanings: the contribution of resources to acquire an asset, or the asset itself. In the context of the BIT, for someone to "make" an investment, passive ownership of an asset was insufficient. Some action was required. In ordinary language, a person could make an investment in an asset he already owned by expending money in supporting or developing it. Investment in developing an asset could be made by an enterprise which indirectly owned or controlled it, but had not paid for it. That was consistent with the BIT's object and purpose. In developing the project, the company had made an investment in the rights to exploit resources, which were indirectly owned and controlled by it in Venezuela's territory. It was therefore an investor which was entitled to accept Venezuela's offer to arbitrate, and Venezuela was not entitled to state immunity (see paras 13, 17-18, 21-22, 32, 37, 40-42, 46, 49-51 of judgment). (2) Section 12(1) only applied to documents which instituted proceedings that were required to be served. Under CPR r.62.18, the arbitration claim form was not a document that was required to be served. Section 12 made special provision for mode of service, entry of appearance and judgments in default of appearance, but if the proceedings did not involve any of those steps, the special provisions did not apply, *AIC Ltd v Nigeria* [2003] EWHC 1357 (QB), Independent, July 28, 2003 not followed. Section 12(1) had not required that the arbitration claim form be served on Venezuela (paras 57-58, 64, 66). (3) A judge deciding whether to grant permission to enforce an award against a state had to decide whether the state would be likely to claim immunity; if yes, the judge would probably not give permission but instead specify that the claim form be served and hold an inter partes hearing. An applicant therefore had to draw the court's attention to matters suggesting the state was likely to claim immunity. In the instant case, the company knew that Venezuela was likely to continue to claim state immunity, but its witness statement had stated that Venezuela was not entitled to state immunity, and had not summarised the arguments advanced by Venezuela before the tribunal, *Siporex Trade SA v Comdel Commodities Ltd* [1986] 2 Lloyd's Rep. 428, [1987] C.L.Y. 137 applied. It had not mentioned that Venezuela continued to rely on those arguments in other proceedings. If it had given full and frank disclosure, an ex parte order would not have been made. The failure was serious, deliberate, and resulted in judgment being given for a very substantial sum against a sovereign state. There was a powerful case for setting aside the order, *OJSC Ank Yugraneft, Re* [2008] EWHC 2614 (Ch), [2010] B.C.C. 475, [2009] C.L.Y. 2272 applied. However, the instant court had concluded that Venezuela could not rely on state immunity; if the company again sought permission to enforce the award, it would be given. The only consequences of setting aside the order would be extra expense and delay. Setting aside the order would not be wholly disproportionate, but an inter partes hearing had taken place and Venezuela had lost its right to rely on state immunity. In the striking and rare circumstances of the case, it was appropriate to maintain the order and mark the company's failure with an indemnity costs order (paras 70-76, 86-87, 90-91).

GOLD RESERVE INC v VENEZUELA, [2016] EWHC 153 (Comm), [2016] 1 W.L.R. 2829, Teare J, QBD (Comm).

1356 State immunity–Heads of state–Immunity for estate of deceased head of state–Relevance of head of state dying in office or later

[Vienna Convention on Diplomatic Relations 1961 art.39(2); State Immunity Act 1978 (c.33) s.20(1)]

A Saudi Arabian prince appealed against a decision (*Harb v Aziz* [2014] EWHC 1807 (Ch), [2014] 1 W.L.R. 4437, [2014] C.L.Y. 1949) that a claim brought against him by the respondent (H) was not barred by state immunity. H had brought the claim alleging breach of contract. She alleged that she had married the prince's father, the King of Saudi Arabia; she sought proper financial provision after the king stopped providing for her; the prince promised to honour the king's promise to provide for H for the rest of her life; and no such provision was made. The king later died. The prince did not plead a defence but applied to strike out the claim. The judge, and the instant court, proceeded on the following assumptions in determining the application: in making any agreement, the prince had acted as the king's representative, meaning that the prince was entitled to the same immunity from suit as the king had been entitled to then and as the king's estate was still entitled to; and if H's claim had been brought while the king was alive and serving as Saudi head of state, both king and prince would have been able to claim sovereign immunity to defeat her claim. The issue was whether, when the king ceased to be head of state on his death, his immunity continued to cover his private acts while head of state.

Held: Appeal dismissed. (1) There were two stages in the process of divining what immunity applied to a former head of state in respect of a suit regarding a private act done whilst he was head of state. The first was to construe the Vienna Convention on Diplomatic Relations 1961 art.39(2), with the "necessary modifications" required by the State Immunity Act 1978 s.20(1), to see what result it produced. The second was to test that construction against other sources of customary international law or cases commenting on those sources. If art.39(2) was applied to heads of state, when a head of state ceased to be such, his immunity from suit also had to cease, save in respect of official acts performed whilst he was head of state. Article 39(2) did not draw any distinction between a diplomat whose term of office came to an end and one who died in post, suggesting that no distinction should be made, *R. v Bow Street Metropolitan Stipendiary Magistrate Ex p. Pinochet Ugarte (No.3)* [2000] 1 A.C. 147, [1999] C.L.Y. 2292 considered. *Pinochet (No.3)* had concluded that s.20(1) reflected customary international law and no more; to discover the extent of immunity of a living former head of state, the court had to examine customary international law sources. Unless there was some logical or practical reason why the rules for deceased heads of state should be different, the same rules should apply. The provisional conclusion to be drawn from the Convention wording, *Pinochet (No.3)* and other international law sources was that a former head of state had no immunity from suit and that that rule applied whether the person had ceased to be head of state whilst alive or had done so because he had died (see paras 32-39 of judgment). (2) The court rejected the prince's argument that there was immunity for the estate of a head of state who died in office, even if there was no immunity for a former head of state who was still alive. Upon the death of an hereditary monarch, the successor became monarch immediately. The same principle held for heads of state who were elected or appointed otherwise. Upon death, they ceased to be head of state. There was no hint of a penumbra attaching to the deceased head of state that would entitle his estate to immunity from suit for private acts. The estate did not personify the state any longer; nor was it an affront to the state if the estate was sued in respect of private acts. Failure to recognise immunity where a head of state died in office would not frustrate the "functional basis" of the doctrine of state immunity, namely that a head of state should be able to perform his functions without being distracted by litigation, *Aziz v Aziz* [2007] EWCA Civ 712, [2008] 2 All E.R. 501, [2007] C.L.Y. 2699 considered. There was no logic in, for example, immunity attaching to the estate of a head of state who died a day before he was due to quit, but not attaching to the estate of one who died a day after leaving office. Although sovereign immunity was based on broad considerations of public policy, international law and comity, there was no need for it to be extended to create immunity regarding private acts once the head of state had left office. There was no distinction between a head of state who left office and who lived thereafter and one who ceased to be head of state upon dying in office (paras 42-47).

HARB v AZIZ *sub nom.* AZIZ v HARB; HARB v PRINCE FAHD BIN ABDUL AZIZ, [2015] EWCA Civ 481, [2016] Ch. 308, Aikens LJ, CA (Civ Div).

LANDLORD AND TENANT

1357 Assured shorthold tenancies–Notices to quit–Service by sole tenant wife of notice of quit–Whether husband entitled to right of occupation under s.30 Family Law Act 1996

[Family Law Act 1996 (c.27) Sch.7, s.30, s.30(1), s.30(1)(a), s.30(2)(a), s.30(3), s.30(5), s.30(8), s.31(2), s.33(3)(a), s.33(3)(d), s.33(5); Family Procedure Rules 2010 (SI 2010/2955) r.8.31, r.8.32; European Convention on Human Rights 1950 Protocol 1 art.1, art.8]

The occupier (T) of rented accommodation appealed against a decision that he was not entitled to remain in occupation of the former matrimonial home following the service of a valid notice to quit by his wife, the sole tenant, who had left the property. T's wife was the sole tenant of a dwelling house let on an assured shorthold tenancy. It was the matrimonial home and was occupied by her and T. She left the house and gave the landlord a notice to quit which was sufficient under common law to terminate the tenancy. T remained in occupation. The issue was whether he was entitled to remain in occupation in the exercise of "home rights" conferred by the Family Law Act 1996 s.30. T submitted that the 1996 Act regulated the relationship between him and the landlord, who could neither refuse his rent nor recover possession. He argued that once his wife had left, he had become the tenant and therefore his wife no longer had a right to terminate the tenancy.

Held: Appeal dismissed. (1) By virtue of s.30(1)(a), s.30 applied only where a tenant was "entitled" to occupy the dwelling, not where the tenant had once been entitled to occupy but was no longer. As the tenancy had been terminated, there remained nothing for T's home rights to bite on, for the purposes of s.30(1). Further, pursuant to s.30(8) any home rights continued only while the tenant was entitled to occupy the dwelling. T's argument was self-defeating as, if he stepped into her shoes as tenant, then she would no longer be entitled to occupy which would mean that any home rights T had would be terminated. It would be remarkable if a landlord was forced by statute into a tenancy with a tenant he had not selected and without any opportunity to be heard, unlike the position under sch.7 and the Family Procedure Rules 2010 r.8.31 and r.8.32. Although it was true that s.30(3) prescribed the consequences of accepting payment by T, s.30 (5) entitled the landlord to treat a payment by T as having been made by the tenant. That was itself inconsistent with T's argument that he had stepped into the tenant's shoes. The home right given by s.30(2)(a) was a right not to be evicted by the tenant without a court order. It was not a right not to be evicted by the landlord. Similarly, the court's power under s.33(3)(a) was to enforce T's right to remain in occupation as against the tenant, not against the landlord. Although the court did have power under s.33(3)(d) to prohibit, suspend, or restrict a tenant's right to occupy the dwelling, it did not divest her of the right itself. Again, the court had power under s.33(5) to prevent T's home rights being ended by the tenant's death or by the termination of the marriage or civil partnership, but it did not provide that T's rights would survive the termination of the tenant's estate or interest. The home rights charge created by s.31(2) was a charge on the tenant's estate only. If registered, the charge could bind the tenant's successors in title but not a landlord as the holder of a superior title. There was nothing in the Act that restricted a tenant's power to terminate her estate, *Sanctuary Housing Association v Campbell* [1999] 1 W.L.R. 1279, [1999] C.L.Y. 3740 and *Hackney LBC v Snowden* (2001) 33 H.L.R. 49, [2001] C.L.Y. 4189 followed, *Griffiths v Renfree* [1989] F.C.R. 551, [1989] C.L.Y. 2160 distinguished as a protected shorthold tenancy was not terminated by a notice to quit but converted to a statutory tenancy (see paras 4-10 of judgment). (2) The common law rule enabling one of joint tenants to terminate a periodic tenancy by a notice to quit without the consent of the other had been held not to be incompatible with ECHR art.8 or with pcol 1 art.1, *Sims v Dacorum BC* [2014] UKSC 63, [2015] A.C. 1336, [2015] C.L.Y. 1600 followed. So much stronger was the case where there was a termination by a sole tenant without the consent of her spouse (para.11).

DERWENT HOUSING ASSOCIATION LTD v TAYLOR, [2016] EWCA Civ 508, [2016] H.L.R. 25, Longmore LJ, CA (Civ Div).

1358 Business tenancies–Relief against forfeiture–Tenant's wilful breach of lease

A head lessee appealed against a refusal of its application for relief from forfeiture of seven commercial retail units. The head lessee had sub-let a unit to a restaurant in breach of a covenant requiring it to obtain the lessor's consent (the alienation provision). The restaurant caused nuisance and annoyance to surrounding properties and the lessor faced many complaints. The head lessee began the instant proceedings and accepted under cross-examination that breach of the alienation provision had been deliberate. It applied to the Land Registry to have the sub-lease surrendered, but the surrender was not effective until after the judge gave judgment. The judge found that the head lessee had demonstrated a cynical disregard of its obligations, that it therefore faced a "vertiginous" climb to persuade the court to exercise its discretion favourably, and that its case fell far short of what was needed to obtain relief. As the head lease was of high value with a considerable period left to run, the decision meant that the lessor gained a windfall of between £1 million and £2 million. The head lessee reapplied for relief, proposing that it be conditional on there being a period of six months within which to complete the sale and assignment of the lease. The issues were (i) whether the judge had taken the correct approach to the wilfulness of the breach; (ii) if not, how the court should exercise its residual discretion to grant or refuse relief.

Held: Appeal allowed. (1) Relief could still be granted even where a breach had been deliberate. The court should not exercise its discretion to enable a landlord to take advantage of a breach by which he had not been irreparably damaged. The value of the leasehold interest was also relevant, although it was not enough simply to find that the effect of a forfeiture would create a windfall for the lessor *Magnic Ltd v Ul-Hassan* [2015] EWCA Civ 224 applied. The judge had been correct to take account of the wilfulness of the breach; it was not fair to grant relief and restore the parties to their previous contractual position where lessees had acted in continuous disregard of their obligations and where there was no security that the future would be different. A lessee's egregious conduct was a self-standing matter to be considered on its own merits, but the proportionality of forfeiture also fell to be separately examined, and the judge had failed to do that. He had taken the view that the head lessee was reaping what it had sown, which left out of account the advantage which the lessor would gain from forfeiture. He had not considered the possibility of selling the leasehold interest on suitable terms to "square the circle" between the lessor's entitlement to enforce its right of re-entry and the head lessee's right not to be forced into giving the lessor some uncovenanted benefit. The judge had also misdirected himself as to the value of a leasehold interest being nil once relief from forfeiture had been denied, *Khar v Delbounty Ltd* (1998) 75 P. & C.R. 232, [1997] C.L.Y. 3293 considered (see paras 40-45, 47-51 of judgment). (2) Re-exercising the discretion previously vested in the judge, the court granted relief from forfeiture for the purposes of and conditional upon sale of the head lease within six months; the units subject to the head lease were now being properly managed. The lessor was not entitled to control over the marketing and sale of the lease, nor to a right of prior approval of the purchaser (paras 55, 57, 61). (Per Briggs L.J.) The instant decision should not be misinterpreted as conferring *carte blanche* on tenants to disregard their covenants wherever there was value in their leasehold interest. In every case a balance would have to be struck and there might well be cases where even substantial value had to be passed to the landlord if no other way of securing the performance of the tenant's covenants could be found (para.68).

FREIFELD v WEST KENSINGTON COURT LTD, [2015] EWCA Civ 806, [2016] 1 P. & C.R. 5, Arden LJ, CA (Civ Div).

1359 **Business tenancies–Surrender–Tenant vacating premises and handing back keys–Whether landlord accepted surrender by changing locks and marketing property for new lease**

A landlord claimed rent and other moneys from the defendant guarantor. It also claimed specific performance in respect of the defendant's alleged obligation to take a new lease of the property. The landlord, which had a long lease of the property, had assigned it to the defendant's subsidiary company. The defendant guaranteed payment of all moneys due, and covenanted to accept a new lease upon the same terms if the lease were disclaimed or ceased to exist, or if the lessee otherwise ceased to be liable on the covenants. In July 2011 the lessee went into administration. Its assets were sold to another of the defendant's subsidiaries, including the right to occupy the landlord's property under a licence. The licence fee was equivalent to the rent due under the lease. In September 2011, the licensee vacated the property. Shortly afterwards the lessee returned the keys, stating that the security and safety of the property henceforth reverted to the landlord. It also enclosed a cheque for insurance calculated pro rata up until the vacation date, which the landlord did not accept. It sent formal demands to the defendant in respect of the outstanding insurance premium and overdue rent. The empty property became a "hang out" for local youths and there was some damage. The landlord changed some of the locks and installed additional security. During 2012, it briefly put the property on the letting market. In 2013 the lessee went into liquidation and the liquidators disclaimed the lease. The landlord gave notice requiring the defendant to enter into a new lease under the terms of the guarantee. It also demanded payment of outstanding monies under the old lease. The defendant responded that the guaranteed liabilities had ended when the lease was surrendered, and that it had no extant liability. The issue was whether the lease had been surrendered. The defendant submitted that there had been unequivocal acceptance by the landlord of a surrender of the lease on one of four alternative dates: first when the licensee vacated occupation; second when the keys were returned; third when the landlord implemented additional security measures after the property had been vacated; and fourth, when the property was marketed for re-let.

Held: Judgment for claimant. (1) The lease had not been surrendered and the defendant's case was plainly wrong. The departure of the licensee or lessee could not, alone, affect the status of the lease. A tenant could not divest itself of a tenancy simply by walking away. The landlord had made clear that it did not accept vacation of the property as surrender because it had returned the cheque for the pro rata insurance payment and had continued to chase the defendant for outstanding rent. The landlord's changing of the locks and arrangements for additional security were not acts inconsistent with the continuation of the lease, especially as it had acted out of a proper and reasonable desire to protect its own interests and secure a vulnerable property, rather than to exclude the tenant or licensee. On the facts, it had not gone beyond the protection of its interests so as to unequivocally manifest an intention to have possession at the exclusion of rights under the lease, *Relvok Properties v Dixon* (1973) 25 P. & C.R. 1, [1973] C.L.Y. 1931 and *Artworld Financial Corp v Safaryan* [2009] EWCA Civ 303, [2009] L. & T.R. 20, [2009] C.L.Y. 2529 applied. Likewise, the landlord's receipt of the keys was entirely consistent with a concern for the security of the property and was not indicative of a re-taking of possession. It had expressly stated that it did not accept the keys by way of surrender. The marketing of the property for re-let, even with vacant possession, did not mean that the landlord was estopped from denying the termination of the lease. Re-letting would have determined the lease, as the landlord was in a position to take possession whenever it chose. On the facts it chose not to do so, *Oastler v Henderson* (1877) 2 Q.B.D. 575 applied (see paras 9-11, 23, 25, 47-51, 54-55, 57-59 of judgment). (2) There was no reason to deny the landlord its claim for specific performance. The amount due to it for rent, interest, insurance and the cost of preparing a new lease was £4,065,708.19 (paras 60-64).

PADWICK PROPERTIES LTD v PUNJ LLOYD LTD, [2016] EWHC 502 (Ch), [2016] L. & T.R. 18, Judge Keyser QC, Ch D.

1360 Collective enfranchisement–Lease and leaseback–Requirements to be satisfied by freeholder when submitting leaseback proposal in counter-notice

[Leasehold Reform, Housing and Urban Development Act 1993 (c.28) Pt IV, Sch.9 Pt II, Sch.9 Pt III, s.21(3)(a)(ii), s.21(7), s.36, s.36(1), s.91(2)(b)]

The freeholder of a building comprising three flats appealed against a decision of a leasehold valuation tribunal (*Tibber v Buckley* [2014] UKUT 74 (LC)) concerning issues arising out of a leaseback proposal she had made to the respondent tenants. The tenants had long leases of two of the flats. They served a notice to acquire the freehold under the Leasehold Reform, Housing and Urban Development Act 1993. The freeholder served a counter-notice admitting their right to do so, but disputing the price, and proposing a leaseback of the third flat. It was on the top floor and extended up into the roof space. The freeholder wished to convert the flat into two. The tribunal determined the physical extent of the leaseback premises, holding that it was "Flat C as it currently exists" with access over some internal common parts and the front garden, but that it did not include the roof or roof structure. It also decided that the leaseback was to be on the terms set out in Pt IV of the Act because the departures proposed by the freeholder had not been specified in the counter-notice. The Upper Tribunal found that the tribunal had erred in its approach, but dismissed the freeholder's appeal on the basis that she could not now identify the physical limits of Flat C more broadly than she had done in the counter-notice. It noted the mandatory nature of the statutory language in s.21(3)(a)(ii) of the Act, and that there was no provision for amending the counter-notice. The freeholder submitted that neither tribunal had considered her case properly or provided sufficient reasons. She criticised the UT's approach as over-restrictive, maintaining that she was entitled to a leaseback of the true physical extent of Flat C regardless of whether the counter-notice expressly identified the full limit of her claim.

Held: Appeal allowed in part. (1) Neither tribunal had given sufficient reasons for certain aspects of their decisions. The freeholder's case had not received the consideration she might reasonably expect. The lower tribunal had defined the boundaries of Flat C in an inconsistent and unexplained manner; the UT had disposed of the appeal on a very narrow ground, namely that the freeholder was not entitled to ask for anything which she had not asked for in her counter-notice (see paras 55-59 of judgment). (2) Reversioners had to make the identity of the leaseback premises clear in the counter-notice. They should identify its physical limits as precisely as possible. An identifying address would often suffice and if, in the subsequent drafting of the lease, unresolvable differences emerged about the property's precise limits, the tribunal could resolve them under s.91(2)(b) of the Act. Where the counter-notice misdescribed the true extent of the property, the starting point would be s.36 of the Act, which imposed a mandatory obligation on tenants to grant leaseback of premises as were "required to be so granted by virtue of Sch.9 Pt II or Pt III". The reference in s.36(1) to "leases of flats or other units contained in those premises" meant the whole of the relevant flats or units, which suggested that an erroneous misdescription of the relevant flat or unit in the counter-notice should not prohibit reversioners from having a leaseback of the whole flat or unit, *Cawthorne v Hamdan* [2007] EWCA Civ 6, [2007] Ch. 187, [2007] C.L.Y. 3369 considered (paras 61, 68-69). (3) It was not strictly necessary to decide the extent to which the *terms* of any leaseback had to be specified in the counter-notice, particularly terms involving a departure from the provisions in Pt IV, but as it was an issue of some general importance, the court would do so. As long as reversioners identified the leaseback property in the counter-notice in accordance with (2) above, there was no need for them to also spell out their proposed terms of the leaseback. The terms would be negotiated between the tenants and the reversioner, any disputes being resolved by the tribunal. Tenants were not required to identify their terms in their initial notice to acquire the freehold, and there was no reason why reversioners should be under a more extensive duty when completing their counter-notices. There was no reason to interpret the phrase "any additional leaseback proposals" in s.21(3)(a)(ii), as explained in s.21(7), as including proposals as to the leaseback terms. Therefore, there was no logical reason why the UT should have identified a need for the reversioner to spell out in the counter-notice any proposed departures from Pt IV of the Act. It had wrongly construed s.21(3)(a)(ii) (paras 72-77). (4) The court reconsidered the physical extent of the leaseback premises (paras 80-105).

TIBBER v BUCKLEY, [2015] EWCA Civ 1294, [2016] Q.B. 706, Jackson LJ, CA (Civ Div).

1361 **Enfranchisement–Houses–Semi-detached and terraced houses–Applicability of leasehold enfranchisement**

[Leasehold Reform Act 1967 (c.88) Pt I, s.2(1)(a), s.2(1)(b), s.2(2), s.2(5)]

A landlord appealed against a declaration that the respondent tenant was entitled to acquire the freehold of his premises pursuant to the Leasehold Reform Act 1967 Pt I. The house (known as no.3) was a two-storey, terraced mews house. It was joined to its right-hand neighbour (no.1/1A) by a single wall. No.1/1A was several storeys higher than no.3, so the dividing wall rose above the roof level of no.3. It was common ground that up to no.3's roof level, the wall was a party wall. The leases of both houses included one half of the party wall, severed vertically, but the upper part of the wall belonged wholly to no.1/1A. Under the Act, the right to acquire applied to houses but not to flats. Section s.2(2) excluded from enfranchisement houses that were not structurally detached, and of which a material part lay above or below a part of the structure not comprised in the house. The landlord argued that because no.3 extended half-way into the party wall, a material part of no.3 sat below the upper part of the wall, which wholly belonged to no.1/1A. They argued that, pursuant to s.2(2), no.3 was therefore excluded from the right to acquire. The judge held that s.2(2) did not apply and no.3 was not excluded. He found that the upper part of the wall did not overhang no.3, or that if it did, any overhang was de minimis. However, he indicated that if he had found that s.2(2) applied, then he would have gone on to find that the party wall was a material part of the house so as to exclude no.3 from enfranchisement.

Held: Appeal dismissed. (1) The Act was intended to provide for the enfranchisement of houses rather than flats, and s.2(1)(a) excluded buildings that were divided horizontally into flats. Since one of the originating purposes of the Act was to permit the enfranchisement of terraced houses, units in a building that was divided vertically could be separate houses, *Parsons v Viscount Gage (Trustees of Henry Smith's Charity)* [1974] 1 W.L.R. 435, [1974] C.L.Y. 2099 followed. However, to avoid the possibility that a whole terrace might be enfranchised as a single house, s.2(1)(b) provided that where a building was divided vertically, the building as a whole was not a house. Section s.2(2) provided for cases in which the division between houses was partly vertical and partly horizontal, creating a "dog-leg" in the dividing line between them and resulting in an "overhang" and an "underhang". Unless only a trivial or unimportant part of the house was overhanging or underhanging the structure to which it was attached, the house could be excluded from enfranchisement. If the overhanging or underhanging part was immaterial, then the landlord's interests were protected by s.2(5), pursuant to which he could give notice objecting to the severance of parts of the premises, *Malekshad v Howard de Walden Estates Ltd (No.1)* [2002] UKHL 49, [2003] 1 A.C. 1013, [2003] C.L.Y. 2744 followed (see paras 20-23 of judgment). (2) The judge had been right to reject the landlord's argument. There was no "dog-leg" to engage s.2(2); there was simply a single dividing wall, and the fact that it was a party wall made no difference to the physical reality. Section 2(2) was concerned with significant deviations from the vertical division of the building. Even if the thickness of a single brick could be regarded as an overhang or underhand, it was de minimis. It could not be consistent with the purposes of the Act to allow the legal division of a party wall to disqualify a house from enfranchisement (paras 24-27). (3) What formed a material part of the house for the purposes of s.2(2) was a matter of fact and degree. However, the judge was wrong in law and principle to conclude that the party wall was a material part of no.3. His earlier conclusion that the deviation from the vertical was de minimis should have led him to conclude that it was also immaterial. He had erred by focusing on the extent to which the party wall was a supporting wall rather than considering the overall significance of any deviation from the vertical, bearing in mind the purpose of the legislation. He should have approached the question on the basis set out in *Malekshad*, namely that s.2(2) aimed to ensure that the right to enfranchisement was not lost just because a trivial or unimportant part of the house overhung, or was overhung by, the house next door. Assistance was to be found in *Hague on Leasehold Enfranchisement*, which indicated that the term "material" in s.2(2) connoted a substantial part of a room, and that things such as eaves, cupboards, box-rooms and water tanks would not constitute a material part for the purposes of the subsection. In the instant case, the vertical division of the party wall did not make up any part of the floor area of either house and was not a substantial part of a room (paras 28-34). (4) Finally, the party wall was a boundary feature, and s.2(1) and s.2(2) were not concerned with the ownership of boundary features. Section 2(5) was apt to cover the case of a shared party wall, and s.2(2) was not engaged (paras 35-39).

WEST END INVESTMENTS (COWELL GROUP) LTD v BIRCHLEA LTD, [2015] EWHC 3381 (Ch), [2016] 4 W.L.R. 4, Henry Carr J, Ch D.

1362 Extension of leases–Premiums–Valuation–Dismissal of Parthenia model–Guidance for future

[Leasehold Reform, Housing and Urban Development Act 1993 (c.28) Sch.13, s.48, s.56]

Lessees applied under the Leasehold Reform, Housing and Urban Development Act 1993 s.48 for a determination of the amount of the premium payable for extended leases of their flats pursuant to s.56 of and Sch.13 to the Act. In relation to Flat 5, which had been sold for £2,000,000 at around the relevant valuation date, the freehold vacant possession (FHVP) value was agreed at £2,750,000. The FHVP value of Flat 11 was in dispute. Both cases concerned the appropriateness of the Parthenia model for determining the value of the existing leases of each flat relative to its FHVP value, on the assumption that the Act conferred no right to acquire an interest in premises containing the lessee's flat or to acquire a new lease. The Parthenia model had been criticised for tending to exclude price-sensitive characteristics of properties, creating spatial errors which made the co-efficients unreliable. The principal relativity which was relevant in the instant cases was that of the value of the existing lease without rights under the Act to the FHVP value. However, at the time of the instant hearing, the leases of flats for sale on the open market had the benefit of rights under the Act and there was little available market evidence involving the sale of existing leases without such rights. Valuers would typically use a number of leasehold comparables, some of which might involve short or medium term leases, in which case it was necessary to adjust the value revealed by the comparable to reflect the length of the lease and produce an adjusted value appropriate for a freehold interest.

Held: Applications granted. (1) The Parthenia model did not satisfy economic and market logic, as it failed to distinguish between the relativities of longer leases and produced results that were out of line with "real world" transactional evidence and market practice, *Xue v Cherry* [2015] UKUT 651 (LC) applied. Accordingly, it failed the fundamental test of giving results that were observed in practice (see para.165 of judgment and paras 23, 34, 60 of Appendix B). (2) The statutory assumption that the existing lease had no rights under the Act did not change the market in which the existing lease was notionally available. The relevant market was the real market and not a hypothetical market, *Gray v Inland Revenue Commissioners* [1994] S.T.C. 360, [1995] C.L.Y. 534 followed. The statutory assumption did not compel the court to assume a hypothetical market, but rather to assume that a lease without rights under the Act was available for sale in the real market (paras 17-18). (3) The disputed FHVP value of Flat 11 was determined at £581,000, taking into account an actual sale for £495,000 at around the valuation date. In *Earl Cadogan v Sportelli* [2007] 1 E.G.L.R. 153, the Lands Tribunal had indicated that it was not assisted by evidence of market transactions in the "no-Act world". However, it was merely referring to the difference between assets sold in the open market in the real world and hypothetical assets: it was not intending to rule that there was a "no-Act world" in which no lease had rights under the Act and no reversion was encumbered by such rights. In relation to Flat 5, therefore, the instant tribunal was not required to disregard the fact that the existing lease with rights under the Act had sold in the open market for £2,000,000, *Sportelli* considered. Making a 10% deduction from the £2,000,000 market value of the existing lease for the benefit of the Act, the value of the lease for Flat 5, on the assumption that it did not have rights under the Act, was £1,800,000. In relation to Flat 11, the Gerald Eve graph of relativity was used to reach a value of £370,155 for the unexpired term. A 10% deduction was made to take into account onerous ground rent, resulting in the sum of £360,000 for the existing lease without rights under the Act (paras 108, 113, 116-118, 121, 140, 144, 147-160). (4) The Upper Tribunal provided guidance for the future: (a) when negotiating the amount of a premium in accordance with Sch.13, it was necessary to focus on the state of the market at the relevant valuation date and not to replace actual market forces with what might have been more logical or appropriate considerations; (b) any future developments that might affect market behaviour had to be taken into account when assessing market forces; (c) any actual market transaction that took place at around the valuation date in respect of the existing lease with rights under the Act was a useful starting point for determining the value of the existing lease without rights, provided that the price paid for that transaction was a true reflection of market value; and (d) where there was no reliable market transaction concerning the existing lease with rights under the Act at or near the valuation date, valuers would need to consider adopting more than one approach and weigh the relative strengths and weaknesses of each method (paras 166-169).

SLOANE STANLEY ESTATE TRUSTEES v MUNDY, [2016] UKUT 223 (LC), [2016] L. & T.R. 32, Morgan J, UT (Lands).

1363 **Housing (Wales) Act 2014 (anaw 7)–Commencement No.8 Order**

THE HOUSING (WALES) ACT 2014 (COMMENCEMENT NO.8) ORDER 2016, SI 2016/1066; made under the Housing (Wales) Act 2014 s.145(3). Commencement details: bringing into operation various provisions of the Housing (Wales) Act 2014 on 23 November 2016.

This Order revokes the Housing (Wales) Act 2014 (Commencement No.7) Order 2016 and brings into force, on 23 November 2016: ss. 4, 9, 11, 13, 28, 30 to 33, 35, 43 and 44: and ss.5 to 8, 10, 12, 29, 34, 40 to 42 and 46 for all remaining purposes.

1364 **Housing associations–Powers and duties–Refusal to allow mutual exchange of assured tenancies–Amenability of decision to judicial review**

[Housing and Regeneration Act 2008 (c.17) s.69]

The claimant tenant applied for judicial review of the defendant housing association's refusal to approve a mutual exchange of his assured tenancy. In 2009, the claimant had entered an assured tenancy lease agreement for a one bedroom flat in London with the Crown Estate Commissioners (CEC), which was transferred, together with a large number of other properties (the CEC transfer), to the defendant in 2011. The purchase was made with funds raised from a bond issue rather than public funds. The tenancy was an intermediate rent tenancy, which was below market rent but above a social housing rent level; an addendum to the tenancy agreement specified that his rent could not exceed 60% of the market rent for a similar property in the area. That condition applied to those with particular occupations. Having found a suitable exchange with a council housing tenant in Edinburgh, the claimant completed a mutual exchange application form, which was rejected on the basis that the claimant was a non-social housing tenant. The defendant alleged that the refusal was not amenable to judicial review as the claimant could not show that: it had not been required to make the decision it did by reason of its contractual obligations; that it had been exercising a public function when it refused the exchange, and that the decision was not a private law decision.

Held: Application refused. The defendant was not exercising a public function in relation to the claimant's tenancy as it had purchased the CEC transfer using private funds, and it was not clear that the CEC transfer stock was pure social housing where the provision of below market rent for particular workers did not fall under the definition of social housing in the Housing and Regeneration Act 2008 s.69 and the CEC rents were not subject to the same level of statutory regulation as social housing in general, *R. (on the application of Weaver) v London & Quadrant Housing Trust* [2009] EWCA

Civ 587, [2010] 1 W.L.R. 363, [2009] C.L.Y. 2549 followed (see paras 15, 20 of judgment).

R. (ON THE APPLICATION OF MACLEOD) v PEABODY TRUST GOVERNORS, [2016] EWHC 737 (Admin), [2016] H.L.R. 27, William Davis J, QBD (Admin).

1365 Leasehold covenants–Deeds of variation–Application of modify covenants in 999-year lease–Jurisdiction of Upper Tribunal (Lands Chamber)

[Law of Property Act 1925 (c.20) s.84(12)]

The tribunal was asked to determine preliminary issues concerning its jurisdiction under the Law of Property Act 1925 s.84(12) to modify leasehold covenants. The applicant married couple were the leaseholders of the garden flat in a residential property. The husband was also the leaseholder of the hall flat in the same property. The leases had been granted in 1980 for a term of 999 years, and both contained a covenant preventing the lessees from permitting encroachments or easements in relation to the flats. The hall flat lease also contained a covenant that the lessee had to "use and occupy the demised premises solely and exclusively as a self-contained residential flat". The garden flat was extended at some point between 1980 and 1998, and in 1998 a deed of variation was made which gave the lessee a right to park a vehicle in front of the property. A new plan of the garden flat, including the extension, was attached to the deed and was substituted for the original plan. In 2015, the applicants applied for modification of the covenants so that work could be done to combine both flats to create a single larger flat. The objector, who was the leaseholder of another flat in the property, challenged the tribunal's jurisdiction; s.84(12) gave the tribunal jurisdiction to modify leasehold covenants only where the term created by the lease was for more than 40 years and 25 years of that term had expired. He submitted that (1) the deed of variation had altered the demise of the garden flat, which had the effect of surrendering the 1980 lease and bringing into existence a new lease, of which fewer than 25 years had expired; (2) the hall flat covenant positively required that the flat be used and occupied as a self-contained flat, and the tribunal had no jurisdiction to modify or discharge a positive covenant.

Held: Preliminary issues determined in favour of applicants. (1) The variation of an existing lease to add additional land to the demise operated as a surrender of the old lease and a grant of a new lease from the date of the variation. However, the law would give effect to a clear intention not to grant a new lease but to continue an existing lease on varied terms, unless the only way in which the arrangement could be implemented was surrender and re-grant, *Friends Provident Life Office v British Railways Board* [1996] 1 All E.R. 336, [1996] C.L.Y. 3759 applied. Objectively construed, the deed of variation in the instant case indicated no intention to change the boundaries of the premises demised by the 1980 lease. The document was competently drafted and only intended to grant an additional right to park on the land marked "parking" on the plan. The deed was supplemental to the registered lease, which it was the parties' intention to vary, and it was recorded that the covenants and conditions in the registered lease were to continue in full force and effect "in all respects". The substitution of the new plan was therefore only intended to indicate the position of the land over which the new right to park was exercisable. The deed contained no words of demise, and the new plan was not intended to show the boundaries of the demise any more than had the original plan. The parties to the deed had proceeded on the assumption that the existing extensions were already part of the premises comprised in the lease; they had to be understood to have assumed that the lease already included the additions made since the original grant. The deed was capable of achieving its limited purpose without resort to the legal fiction of a surrender and re-grant. Accordingly, the 18 years of the term which had elapsed by the time the deed was executed would not be discounted when considering whether a sufficient period had elapsed for s.84(12) to confer jurisdiction on the tribunal to vary the covenants. More than 25 years of the term had elapsed, and therefore the tribunal had jurisdiction in relation to the covenants in the lease of the garden flat (see paras 20-21, 29-30, 32 of judgment). (2) The hall flat covenant had to be construed in its own context, *Westminster City Council v Duke of Westminster* [1991] 4 All E.R. 136 considered. The obligation in the covenant was not simply to use and occupy the demised premises as a self-contained residential flat, but was to use and occupy it "solely and exclusively" for that purpose. Those words indicated an intention that, if the demised premises were to be used and occupied at all, it had to be as a self-contained flat; if the owner chose not to use and occupy the premises, he was free to leave them vacant. The covenant had the same character as the conventional covenant not to use premises other than for a specified purpose, and the employment of the composite expression "to use and occupy" did not convert that conventional emphatic negative into a positive obligation. It would be most unusual to find a positive obligation in an otherwise unexceptional lease of a residential flat requiring that it be kept occupied and used for the purpose for which it was designed. Such a covenant was so unusual and potentially onerous that much more emphatic and unambiguous language would have to be adopted by the parties intending to impose it (paras 36-40).

STEVENS v ISMAIL, [2016] UKUT 43 (LC), [2016] L. & T.R. 21, Martin Rodger QC, UT (Lands).

1366 **Leasehold covenants–Landlords' duties–Whether landlord under obligation to fit handrail on staircase**

[Defective Premises Act 1972 (c.35) s.4]

A tenant appealed against a decision that the respondent landlord had not acted in breach of the Defective Premises Act 1972 s.4 in connection with an accident she had sustained in the property let to her. At the date of the tenancy agreement, the staircase in the property was steep and there was no handrail or bannister fitted. There were indications that a bannister might have been removed at some stage in the building's history. The tenant slipped and fell as she walked up the stairs. The tenancy agreement required the landlord "to keep in repair the structure and exterior of the premises". It was the tenant's case that without a handrail the stairs were in a dangerous condition, and had there been a handrail the accident would not have happened. Further, the staircase was part of the structure of the premises, the bannister/handrail was part of the staircase and thus was also part of the structure. When the bannister was removed the staircase became unsafe and the absence of a bannister/handrail was a relevant defect which the landlord had a duty to repair under the agreement and under s.4. The claim failed on the basis that there was no obligation on the landlord to fit a handrail so as to make the staircase safe.

Held: Appeal dismissed. The only question to be determined was whether the tenant had established that the premises were in disrepair. Photographs showed a very steep stairway with no railings. There was little doubt that, without a handrail, it was a hazard. However, there was nothing about it that could justify the description of being in disrepair. Furthermore, there had never been a handrail at any relevant time, and to place the landlord under an obligation to fit one would amount to placing him under an obligation to improve the premises or make them safe. That would have been beyond the reach of his obligation, *Alker v Collingwood Housing Association* [2007] EWCA Civ 343, [2007] 1 W.L.R. 2230, [2007] C.L.Y. 2738 considered (see paras 26, 29-30 of judgment).

STERNBAUM v DHESI, [2016] EWCA Civ 155, [2016] H.L.R. 16, Hallett LJ, CA (Civ Div).

1367 **Leases–Assignment–Purported assignment of lease by tenant to its guarantor–Effect of s.25(1)(a) Landlord and Tenant (Covenants) Act 1995**

[Landlord and Tenant (Covenants) Act 1995 (c.30) s.24(2), s.24(2)(b), s.25(1), s.25(1)(a), s.3, s.3(2), s.3(2)(a), s.5(2), s.5(2)(a)]

The claimant, a guarantor of a lease, sought a declaration that the lease had been assigned to it by the tenant and that the tenant's covenants were void by reason of the Landlord and Tenant (Covenants) Act 1995 s.24(2) and s.25(1). When the lease was granted to the tenant, the claimant had undertaken to perform the tenant's obligations to the defendant landlord. The tenant purported to assign the lease to the claimant on terms that the latter covenanted to pay to the landlord all sums due under the lease on the tenant's behalf. According to the claimant, the tenant's covenants were unenforceable as a consequence of the assignment. The defendant did not challenge the validity of the assignment itself, but maintained that the tenant's covenants remained valid and enforceable. Alternatively, the defendant claimed that if the assignment was void and the lease remained vested in the tenant, the claimant remained bound as guarantor of the tenant's obligations and had not been released from those obligations by operation of the Act.

Held: Claim dismissed. (1) The Act implemented the recommendations made by the Law Commission in its report entitled Landlord and Tenant Law: Privity of Contract and Estate (1988) (Law Com No.174). In that report, the Law Commission recommended that, whenever the liability of a tenant would be wholly cancelled by their recommendations, then liabilities which had been undertaken "in parallel" and which were "essentially to the same effect" should also be terminated. The whole thrust of the Act was that a person should not remain liable under a tenancy after the tenant with whose liability he was associated had been released from his liability. On assignment of the tenancy by the tenant to the guarantor, s.5(2)(a) and s.24(2) of the Act operated to release the tenant and the guarantor respectively from the tenant's covenants. Therefore, in practical terms, the guarantor was not released from the covenants. It was that consequence which frustrated the operation of s.24(2)(b), namely to release any other person bound by the tenant's covenants to the same extent as the tenant was released. The assignment was thus rendered void by the wide anti-avoidance provision in s.25(1)(a) and the guarantor was precluded from becoming the assignee, *K/S Victoria Street v House of Fraser (Stores Management) Ltd* [2011] EWCA Civ 904, [2012] Ch. 497, [2011] C.L.Y. 2050 followed (see paras 2, 6, 77-80, 83 of judgment). (2) By operation of s.3(2)(a), an assignee of a tenancy immediately became bound by the tenant's covenants. However, s.3 was not directed to the main thrust of the Act, but was part of the "tidying up" that took place as a result of the reforms recommended in the Law Commission's report. There was nothing in the Act which provided for there to be sequential steps in relation to the release of the guarantor from its liabilities under the tenant's covenants and the re-assumption of those very same liabilities on him as assignee. Rather, s.5(2), s.3(2), and s.24(2) provided that those events should all happen at the same moment, namely "as from" the assignment. There was therefore no moment when a person who was the guarantor, and then became the assignee, was actually released from his liabilities in respect of the tenant's covenants, whereas the need for an actual period of release was clear from *K/S Victoria*. It followed that s.3(2)(a) did not alter the conclusion that the guarantor was absolutely precluded from becoming the tenant's assignee (paras 79, 82-83, 85-86). (3) Since the purported assignment was void under s.25(1)(a), the lease remained vested in the tenant and the claimant remained bound as guarantor of the tenant's obligations (paras 89-91).

EMI GROUP LTD v O & H Q1 LTD, [2016] EWHC 529 (Ch), [2016] Ch. 586, Amanda Tipples QC, Ch D.

1368 Leases–Assignment–Whether transfer fee was enforceable under Consumer Credit Act 1974

[Unfair Terms in Consumer Contracts Regulations 1999 (SI 1999/2083); Consumer Credit Act 1974 (c.39)]

A landlord applied for summary judgment or the striking out of tenants' and former tenants' claims that a fee it charged when they assigned their leases was unfair. The landlord owned the freehold to a retirement village and had granted leases to the tenants. The leases provided for tenants to pay the landlord a fee if they assigned their leases to a third party. Four former tenants had become liable to pay such a fee. Along with four current tenants, they brought proceedings claiming that the fee was unenforceable under the Unfair Terms in Consumer Contracts Regulations 1999 and under the Consumer Credit Act 1974. The landlord applied for summary judgment or the striking out of the claims under the Act, arguing that it had no application as the transfer fee provisions did not amount to a provision of credit.

Held: Application granted. The transfer fee provisions required payment to the landlord of a percentage of the price paid by the assignee. The primary question was whether the percentage which might be paid was an obligation to pay that sum at all and, if so, whether it was an obligation to pay at the outset of the leases, which was then deferred until assignment or termination, followed by sale. Nowhere in the leases was there an obligation upon the tenants to make any payment of the relevant percentage. There was certainly no deferment of the purchase price. The relevant percentage was not part of the purchase price. There was no obligation to assign placed upon the tenants, and there was no obligation to make a payment to the landlord in the event of an assignment. On a plain reading of the leases, there was no deferment of any obligation to pay part of the purchase price, as alleged by the tenants. Furthermore, the relevant percentage was to be paid by an assignee. There was no provision that obliged the tenants to make that payment. In practice, it might be the tenants that made the payment but that was not what the lease provided for. In any event, the point was clear that the tenants were under no obligation pursuant to the leases to make the payment. It followed that there was no provision of credit under the transfer fee provisions. Therefore, the tenants had no real prospect of succeeding on the claim under the Act and there was no other compelling reason why the matter should proceed to trial. There would be summary judgment for the landlord (see paras 21, 41, 44, 46, 57, 61 of judgment).

BURRELL v HELICAL (BRAMSHOTT PLACE) LTD, [2015] EWHC 3727 (Ch), [2016] H.L.R. 18, David Casement QC, Ch D.

1369 **Leases–Forfeiture–Tenant in administration**

[Insolvency Act 1986 (c.45)]

The applicant landlord applied to forfeit a lease it had granted to the fourth respondent tenant. The applicant landlord applied to forfeit a lease it had granted to the fourth respondent tenant. The landlord owned a shopping centre, from which the tenant had run a restaurant. The first to third respondents had been appointed as the tenant's administrators. They applied to assign the lease to a subsidiary of the tenant (STL) in 2014. The landlord refused on the basis that, inter alia, STL was not of sufficient financial standing and that the tenant had not offered an authorised guarantee agreement (AGA) as required under the lease. The respondents applied again for consent to assign the lease to STL. The landlord asked for clarification on a number of issues, but got no response, and refused to consent., The landlord then asked the administrators for confirmation of steps taken to market the lease to entities other than STL but received no response. In response to the instant application, the administrators gave evidence that another company (W) had offered to acquire the leasehold interest for a premium of £250,000 and that such offers demonstrated that the lease had significant value. The landlord said that it would have accepted W as an assignee, but that W had confirmed that the lease was not suitable as it had not been aware that the landlord had terminated an outdoor seating licence. The issues were (i) whether forfeiture would impede the purposes of administration; (ii) if the purpose of the administration was impeded, where the balance lay between the lessor and creditors's interests; (iii) whether forfeiture should be by peaceable re-entry or by way of court proceedings. The landlord submitted that forfeiture would not impede the purposes of the administration, but that if a balancing exercise fell to be performed, the balance came down in favour of granting the relief because otherwise the landlord would suffer financial loss by being denied the opportunity to grant a new lease at a higher rent to a new tenant. The administrators submitted that the administration's purpose would be impeded by forfeiture as the leasehold interest represented a valuable asset which would allow the administrators to achieve a better result for the tenant's creditors. The landlord submitted that forfeiture would not impede the purposes of the administration, but that if a balancing exercise fell to be performed, the balance came down in favour of granting the relief because otherwise the landlord would suffer financial loss by being denied the opportunity to grant a new lease at a higher rent to a new tenant. The administrators submitted that the administration's purpose would be impeded by forfeiture as the leasehold interest represented a valuable asset which would allow the administrators to achieve a better result for the tenant's creditors.

Held: Application granted. (1) The first question was whether forfeiture would impede the purposes of the administration, *Atlantic Computer Systems Plc, Re* [1992] Ch. 505, [1991] C.L.Y. 2127 followed. The higher the lease's value in the administrators' hands, the more likely it was that the purpose of the administration would be impeded by forfeiture. In the instant case, the purpose of the administration would not be impeded by granting the landlord permission to pursue its proprietary rights. There were no grounds to believe that the administrators would be able to achieve a premium by assigning the lease. The lease had some potential premium value, but the administrators were unable to unlock that value due to the landlord's lawful exercise of its rights, including the right to terminate the outdoor seating licence, and to require the provision of an AGA. The purpose of the Insolvency Act 1986 was to provide a moratorium to enable administrators to retain or realise assets on behalf of creditors; that involved postponing the enforcement of substantive rights. However, the law did not go so far as to suggest that a lessor was not entitled to rely on rights which it could invoke without legal process, even if it would further the purpose of administration not to rely on them. If, contrary to those findings, the administrators did obtain a premium, the likely level was modest, and likely to be significantly less than the £250,000 offered by W who had not appreciated that there was no seating licence. The sum would be so small in comparison to the estimated shortfall of £11m that its lack of recoverability would not impede the purpose of administration (see paras 90, 107, 109 of judgment). (2) In any event, the forfeiture's effect on the administration only came into play at the second stage, when balancing the landlord's legitimate interests with those of the creditors. The administrators had taken the risk that their attempts to obtain the landlord's consent to assign to STL would fail, and by the time of the hearing they were not able to demonstrate that other avenues were available. The landlord had never indicated that it had changed its stance towards STL. Fairness did not require that the administrators should be allowed a further opportunity to market the leasehold interest in order to realise the benefit of the lease for creditors. In the meantime, the landlord had lost the opportunity to lease the property to a new tenant on terms which would have been financially advantageous; that comprised a "significant loss" to the landlord, *Atlantic Computers* followed. The guidance in *Atlantic Computers* recognised that administration was intended to be only an interim and temporary regime: by the time the matter came to court they had been appointed for nine months. That did not accord with the guidance, *Atlantic Computers* followed (paras 110, 113-114, 118). (3) The landlord was not restricted to seeking permission to forfeit by way of court proceedings (para.119).

SSRL REALISATIONS LTD (IN ADMINISTRATION), RE *sub nom.* LAZARI INVESTMENTS LTD v SAVILLE, [2015] EWHC 2590 (Ch), [2016] 1 P. & C.R. 2, Richard Spearman QC, Ch D (Companies Ct).

1370 Leases–Grant–Costs recoverable by landlord

[Leasehold Reform, Housing and Urban Development Act 1993 (c.28) s.42, s.60, s.60(1)(a)]

A landlord appealed against a decision of the First-tier Tribunal regarding the costs to which it was entitled under the Leasehold Reform, Housing and Urban Development Act 1993 s.60 from the respondent leaseholders in connection with the grant of new leases. Solicitors acting for the leaseholders of seven flats in a block served notices of claim on the landlord under s.42 of the Act. After arranging a valuation, the landlord's agent served counter-notices. The premium for each flat was agreed, but there was no agreement regarding the legal and valuation fees. The landlord claimed £6,615 for the cost of the work involved in granting the new leases, which was carried out by its in-house solicitor. The breakdown showed four hours and six minutes per claim for the investigation of each tenant's right to a new lease within s.60(1)(a) of the Act, including 12 minutes per flat for considering the valuation report, with an estimated further one-and-a-half hours to be spent in each case for the grant of a new lease under s.60(1)(c). An hourly rate of £275 was claimed. The leaseholders disputed the claimed fees and applied to the tribunal, which directed the landlord to submit evidence of its agent's overheads. A total sum of £1,105 was awarded for all seven transactions, based on an hourly rate of £150. In reaching its decision, the tribunal held that the work done under s.60(1)(a) could have been completed in one-and-a-half-hours for all seven files, with a further four hours to be allowed for the work required under s.60(1)(c). Seeking to distinguish the leading authority of *Eastwood (Deceased), Re* [1975] Ch. 112, [1974] C.L.Y. 2927, the tribunal also held that the charges recoverable by the landlord should not be based on the charging rate of solicitors in private practice but on the tribunal's own assessment of an appropriate in-house rate.

Held: Appeal allowed. (1) The tribunal's reasoning that the overheads of an in-house solicitor were not comparable to those of a private practitioner did not justify adopting a wholly different approach from that taken in *Eastwood* and *Cole v British Telecommunications Plc* [2000] 2 Costs L.R. 310, [2000] C.L.Y. 390. It was nothing to the point that there were expenses of an independent solicitor's practice which would not be incurred by an in-house lawyer. In most cases, particularly those of very modest value, it was necessary to take a pragmatic approach and avoid a detailed inquiry. The tribunal should have given the landlord the benefit of the presumption in *Eastwood* that in-house costs should be determined on the same basis as those of an independent practitioner and should not have directed the filing of evidence as to overheads, which was both irrelevant to the task it was required to undertake and disproportionate to the costs it was required to assess, *Eastwood* and *Cole* followed (see paras 5-7, 29-31 of judgment). (2) The claimed period of 12 minutes to consider and advise on the valuation reports was reasonable; however, given the similarity of the properties concerned, it was not reasonable to spend that amount of time on each report. Accordingly, 20 minutes was allowed for all seven reports (paras 36-38). (3) The tribunal should have made its assessment by reference to the costs of a Band A solicitor in private practice, although not necessarily one based in London. The tribunal's task was to consider whether the landlord would have agreed to pay the bill personally if it could not have been passed on to the leaseholders, since it was only entitled to recoup the costs which it would have incurred if it was personally liable to meet them. Where a landlord's bill was challenged, identifying the ceiling imposed by s.60(2) was likely to be determinative. Assuming a rate of around £230 per hour in the instant case, based on the bottom of the Band A scale, the reasonable cost of the work which the landlord would have considered acceptable would have been £1,400 plus disbursements, giving a total of £1,680 for all seven flats. That figure properly reimbursed the landlord while reflecting the repetitive nature of the work (paras 40-45).

SIDEWALK PROPERTIES LTD v TWINN, [2015] UKUT 122 (LC), [2016] 2 Costs L.R. 253, Martin Rodger QC, UT (Lands).

1371 Leases–Repair covenants–Section of wall including valuable mural–Tenant's entitlement under covenants to remove wall

The claimant applied for summary judgment in its claim against the first defendant tenant for delivery up of a section of wall bearing a mural painting. The claimant company had been assigned the cause of action by the landlord and freehold owner of a building. The tenant ran an amusement arcade in the building under a 20-year lease which demised the building including its structure and exterior to the tenant. A street artist painted a mural on the outside of the building, without the landlord's or tenant's permission. It allegedly had a high value. The tenant caused the section of wall containing the mural to be removed from the building and replaced, without the landlord's permission. It was shipped to the United States and exhibited for sale. The tenant submitted that (1) it had been obliged or entitled to remove the wall in order to comply with its covenants to keep the building in good and substantial repair and condition and to paint the outside every four years; (2) by virtue of an implied term in the lease, once removed from the building the wall became the tenant's property.

Held: Application granted. (1) It was not a breach of the lease for the tenant to cut the walls to the extent necessary to comply with the repair covenant, but that was only engaged if that part of the building was out of repair or condition. The tenant had not suggested that the wall structure had been damaged; its defence was that the mural was a piece of graffiti which would attract other graffiti. The tenant was only required to undertake prudent remedial work. Removing the wall was significantly more invasive than painting over it or removing the mural with chemicals. It might be justified to take a more invasive step if it would prove a more long-term solution, but the onus was on the tenant to show that that was an equally objectively reasonable method. Even if the knowledge that that particular artist's work had been there would attract other graffiti artists, the tenant had not identified why removal would solve or reduce the problem compared to over-painting or cleaning. The tenant had no reasonable prospect of establishing that it had been entitled or obliged to remove the wall (see paras 21-35 of judgment). (2) It was necessary to imply a term into the lease to address what happened to parts of the building replaced or removed by the tenant under its repair covenant. Such parts reverted to the status of chattels once removed. The fact that the mural had substantial aesthetic and economic value was plainly relevant. The authorities, though not directly on point, supported the proposition that a tenant had an implied permission to dispose of parts of land which became chattels of no or de minimis value, but would not acquire title to a chattel of substantial value, *Farrant v Thompson* 106 E.R. 1392, *Elwes v Brigg Gas Co* (1886) 33 Ch. D. 562 and *Herbert v British Railways Board* considered. For four reasons, the term to be implied in the instant lease was that a part of the premises which the tenant justifiably removed under its repair covenant that became a chattel with substantial value was the landlord's property. First, the default position was that every part of the property belonged to the landlord. Second, the mere fact that the tenant was discharging its repair covenant did not imply that it acquired ownership of such a chattel. The covenant only justified an implied term dealing with permission to remove such items and where appropriate dispose of them, not a term transferring ownership of them. Third, even if a term could be implied with respect to ownership of waste or chattels with no more than scrap value, it did not follow that one could be implied for ownership of chattels of substantial value. Such a term would not be necessary, go without saying, or satisfy the officious bystander test, *Attorney General of Belize v Belize Telecom Ltd* [2009] UKPC 10, [2009] 1 W.L.R. 1988 applied. Fourth, it made no difference that the value was attributable to a third party; the landlord had the better right to that windfall. The tenant's defence was unsustainable in law (paras 38, 43, 50, 54-59).

CREATIVE FOUNDATION v DREAMLAND LEISURE LTD, [2015] EWHC 2556 (Ch), [2016] Ch. 253, Arnold J, Ch D.

1372 Lettings agencies–Duty to publicise fees–Enforcement

THE DUTY OF LETTING AGENTS TO PUBLICISE FEES (EXCLUSION) (WALES) REGULATIONS 2016, SI 2016/178; made under the Consumer Rights Act 2015 s.84(3). In force: 15 March 2016.

These Regulations create an exclusion from the Consumer Rights Act 2015 Pt 3 Ch.3 which is applicable to legal professionals in certain circumstances.

1373 Notices–Service–Break notice served on landlord at stipulated address–Landlord no longer at address

[Landlord and Tenant Act 1927 (c.36) s.23(2)]

The landlords claimed for declarations that the defendant tenant's notices purporting to exercise a break clause had not been validly served and that consequently the leases to the tenant subsisted. Four landlords were trustees of a retirement scheme which owned the freehold of a building, three floors of which were let to the tenant on a 10 year lease from 11 July 2010. After three years, the tenant purported to exercise a break clause by serving within the six-month contractual time limit, notices by recorded delivery on each of the individual landlords named in the lease at the business address given therein. Only one named landlord (S) had retained any connection with that address but he had transferred his interest in the leased property in 2011. The tenant's notices were delivered within the time limit and followed up by an email received at the premises by the landlords' property manager. The email was not acknowledged until after the time for service had expired. The landlords disputed service. Just prior to the date on which the leases would end if the break had been effective, the tenant contacted the property manager to arrange for the return of the keys. The manager sent a careful reply accepting the keys without prejudice to the landlords' contention that the notices were ineffective. Subsequently the manager emailed the tenant about service bills for the property, stating that the landlords were responsible from 10 July 2013. On 13 October 2014 the landlords leased the property to another tenant. The tenant argued that the Landlord and Tenant Act 1927 s.23(2), which deemed service on an original landlord's address as good service unless the tenant had been informed of a change, was of general application. The tenant also argued that the landlords had changed their position by the email about utilities and that was sufficient to amount to a surrender by operation of law. Further, the acceptance of the keys, or the subsequent re-letting had terminated the lease. The landlords submitted that the notices were ineffective because the landlords' address in the lease was not the "place of abode or business" of any of the current landlords. Even if that address was S's place of business and the notice had been validly served on him, S had transferred his interest in the reversion to the current landlords so they were not bound. Further, they argued that the notices had not come to their attention by any other means until after the time limit had expired.

Held: Judgment for defendant. There was force in the argument that s.23(2) was needed just as much for service of tenants' notices as for notices for the specific purposes of the 1927 Act. There was a potential for injustice if a tenant had not been informed of any change and had served the person they believed to be their landlord in good faith, only to discover that person had transferred their interest. However, for a number of reasons Parliament could not have intended to make s.23(2) a provision of general effect (see paras 38-40 of judgment). The authorities on service of documents under the CPR contemplated service on a party who had not necessarily agreed to be served and who might have no prior relationship with the person seeking to serve him. Where a contractual relationship existed the court would take note of the agreed details for service. The leases provided that the landlords were to be served at their last known place of abode or business, and also stipulated their address. It was plainly the intention of the Act for "abode" not to be confined to a personal residence but to include a business address. Indeed, in the case of a company, it had to mean something other than a residential address, *National Westminster Bank Ltd v Betchworth Investments* (1975) 234 E.G. 675, [1976] C.L.Y. 1547, *Collier v Williams* [2006] EWCA Civ 20, [2006] 1 W.L.R. 1945, [2006] C.L.Y. 348 and *Price v West London Investment Building Society Ltd* [1964] 1 W.L.R. 616, [1964] C.L.Y. 2103 applied. It was within the landlords' power to inform the tenant of a change of address and, if they failed to do so, they bore the risk of documents not reaching them. The landlords must have assumed, or been content that S would pass on anything addressed to them. The claim was dismissed and the tenant entitled to a declaration that the leases had been terminated at the break point on 10 July 2013 (paras 52-57). In the event that decision was wrong, the court considered the alternative case based on surrender by operation of law. The tenant had made an implied offer to surrender in July 2013 by vacating and returning the keys in case the leases had not been validly terminated by the break clauses. The landlords' acceptance of the keys had been done expressly without prejudice and done to keep the premises secure. Similarly the email regarding the payment of utility bills, though incautiously worded, was intended no more than to confirm that the management company was not responsible. The marketing of the property in 2014 was done to mitigate the landlords' loss. All those acts were equivocal. However, the leasing of the premises was more than an equivocal step and the landlord had retaken possession and terminated the lease by surrender on 13 October 2014, *Artworld Financial Corp v Safaryan* [2009] EWCA Civ 303, [2009] L. & T.R. 20, [2009] C.L.Y. 2529 followed (paras 22, 61-63).

LEVETT-DUNN v NHS PROPERTY SERVICES LTD, [2016] EWHC 943 (Ch), [2016] 3 W.L.R. 773, Judge David Cooke, Ch D (Birmingham).

1374 Possession–Private landlords–Court's ability to consider proportionality of eviction

[Housing Act 1988 (c.50) s.21(4); Human Rights Act 1998 (c.42) s.3(1), s.6(1), s.6(3)(a); European Convention on Human Rights 1950 art.8(2); Protection from Eviction Act 1977 (c.43); Housing Act 1980 (c.51); Housing Act 1996 (c.52) s.127(2), s.143D(2)]

A private sector tenant appealed against a possession order evicting her from the property which she occupied under an assured shorthold tenancy. The tenant was the landlords' daughter. She was in her mid-forties and had suffered since childhood from a personality disorder and psychotic symptoms. She had lost two public sector tenancies owing to her behaviour. The landlords had bought the property for her to occupy. The rent was covered by housing benefit. The landlords fell into arrears with the mortgage repayments and the loan company appointed receivers, who sought possession in the name of the landlords. A judge held that there was no alternative than to make a possession order under the Housing Act 1988 s.21(4). He heard evidence from a medical expert as to the major detrimental effect of eviction on the tenant's mental health, but concluded that the court had no power to consider proportionality under the Human Rights Act 1998 s.6(1) and ECHR art.8(2), given that the person seeking possession was not a public authority. He indicated that if he could have considered proportionality, he would have found that a possession order was disproportionate. The court of appeal agreed that he was not entitled to consider proportionality, but held that if he had been so entitled, he would have been wrong to dismiss the possession claim. The issues were: (1) whether, when hearing a claim for possession by a private sector landlord against a residential occupier, the court should be entitled to consider the proportionality of eviction under s.6(1) of the Act and art.8(2) of the Convention, particularly as, by virtue of s.6(3)(a) of the 1998 Act, "a court" was a "public authority"; (2) if so, whether s.21(4) of the 1988 Act could be read so as to comply with that conclusion; (3) if the answers to (1) and (2) were in the affirmative, whether the judge would have been entitled to find that possession of the property would have been disproportionate.

Held: Appeal dismissed. (1) In the absence of clear and authoritative guidance from the European Court of Human Rights, it was not open to tenants to contend that art.8 of the Convention could justify a different order from that which was mandated by the contractual relationship between them and their landlord. The 1988 Act, the Protection from Eviction Act 1977, and the Housing Act 1980 all reflected the state's assessment of how to balance the art.8 rights of residential tenants and the rights of private sector landlords to the peaceful enjoyment of their possessions when a tenancy ended. To hold otherwise would involve the Convention effectively being directly enforceable as between private citizens so as to alter their contractual rights and obligations, when the purpose of the Convention was to protect citizens from infringement of their rights by the state. Domestic legislature should be allowed to lay down rules of general application with a view to ensuring consistency of application and certainty of outcome. Finding for the tenant in the instant case would involve diluting those rules, *Qazi v Harrow LBC* [2003] UKHL 43, [2004] 1 A.C. 983, [2003] C.L.Y. 2786 applied. There were some ECtHR authorities which supported the notion that art.8 was engaged in the instant case, but there was no support for the proposition that the judge could have been required to consider the proportionality of the order which he would have made under the 1980 and 1988 Acts, *Manchester City Council v Pinnock* [2010] UKSC 45, [2011] 2 A.C. 104, [2011] C.L.Y. 2066, *Zehentner v Austria (20082/02)* (2011) 52 E.H.R.R. 22, *Buckland v United Kingdom (40060/08)* (2013) 56 E.H.R.R. 16, [2013] C.L.Y. 1560 and *Brezec v Croatia (7177/10)* [2014] H.L.R. 3 considered (see paras 40-44, 51, 55 59-60 of judgment). (2) (Obiter) It was not possible to read s.21(4) of the 1988 Act so as to allow the court to assess the proportionality of making otherwise mandatory orders. There were attractive arguments for doing so, based on a comparison of the provisions in the Housing Act 1996 s.143D(2) relating to demoted tenancies, and s.127(2) relating to introductory tenancies, but there were also powerful arguments to the contrary. There was not the same flexibility inherent in the language of s.21(4) and, more importantly, there were substantive limits to what the courts could achieve under s.3(1) of the 1998 Act, *Ghaidan v Godin-Mendoza* [2004] UKHL 30, [2004] 2 A.C. 557, [2004] C.L.Y. 2538 considered (paras 61-70). (3) (Obiter) In rare cases where the court was required to assess the proportionality of making a possession order, it had at least four possible options to consider. The cases in which it would be justifiable to refuse possession had to be very few and far between. They could only be cases in which the landlord's interest in regaining possession was heavily outweighed by the gravity of the interference in the occupier's art.8 rights. It was not easy to imagine circumstances in which the art.8 rights would be so strong as to preclude the making of a possession order, as opposed to granting a short postponement. In the instant case, although the tenant's circumstances were unfortunate, it seemed likely that the best she could have hoped for was a six-week postponement of the order, as there was no justification for postponing indefinitely the lender's right to be paid (paras 72-75).

MCDONALD v MCDONALD, [2016] UKSC 28, [2016] 3 W.L.R. 45, Lord Neuberger PSC, SC.

1375 Property management–Service charges–Residential property

THE APPROVAL OF CODE OF MANAGEMENT PRACTICE (RESIDENTIAL MANAGEMENT) (SERVICE CHARGES) (ENGLAND) ORDER 2016, SI 2016/518; made under the Leasehold Reform, Housing and Urban Development Act 1993 s.87, s.100. In force: 1 June 2016.

By this Order the Secretary of State approves a code of practice relating to the management of residential property by landlords and others who discharge the management function. The approved code is the "Service Charge Residential Management Code" (ISBN 978-1-78321-141-8) by the Royal Institution of Chartered Surveyors (RICS). By this Order the Secretary of State also withdraws approval for "Service Charge Residential Management Code" (ISBN 978-1-84219-168-2) by RICS.

1376 Quiet enjoyment–Noise–Landlord's building works above tenant's art gallery

The claimant tenant, which occupied basement and ground-floor premises in Mayfair for the purpose of carrying on its business as a high-class art gallery, sought relief from the defendant landlord arising from the carrying out of building works above the gallery. The lease entitled the landlord to carry out building works. It also contained a covenant for quiet enjoyment. The building of which the premises formed part consisted of five storeys. In August 2014, contractors began the construction of new apartments from the first floor upwards. The works were expected to be concluded by August 2016. The tenant's case was that, particularly by reason of the noise generated by the works and the encasing of the whole building in scaffolding, the works had substantially interfered with its use and enjoyment of the premises as an art gallery.

Held: Judgment for claimant. In a case like this, the landlord's reservation of a right to build in a way which, but for that reservation, would constitute a breach of the covenant for quiet enjoyment should be construed as entitling the landlord to do the work contemplated by the reservation provided that in doing that work it had taken all reasonable steps to minimise disturbance to the tenant. A relevant consideration was the fact that the landlord was exercising its reserved right to do works entirely for its own purposes, with no benefit being conferred on the tenant. The landlord had not acted reasonably in exercising its right to build and had breached the covenant for quiet enjoyment. The premises were let for use as a high-class art gallery in the centre of Mayfair for a high rent; that required that the right to build should be exercised with particular regard, so far as reasonably possible, to the tenant's need to keep the gallery running and with as little disturbance to it and its customers and staff as possible. The landlord had not done that. Before the scaffolding was erected, the tenant was shown a sketch plan indicating how the scaffolding might be erected in a sympathetic way, preserving the open aspect of the gallery. As it was, the scaffolding caused the gallery to be "enwrapped" in the whole building, giving the impression to outsiders that the gallery had entirely disappeared and was now part of a building site. Further, the main hoist, which was used to bring up materials to the site from ground level, was placed virtually right outside the door of the gallery. As a result of the hoists being placed in the way they were, the front of the gallery was often blocked by lorries delivering building materials. Moreover, the tenant had been experiencing periods of high levels of noise on almost a daily basis. There had been no real liaison with the tenant as to the likely duration of the works, the noise levels likely to be experienced and ways of mitigating the impact of the noise. It was also relevant that the landlord had not offered any discount in the rent. Damages would be assessed at 20% of the rent, payable from August 2014 until the date when the work was completed (see paras 24-25, 59, 82-83, 87, 90, 95, 98, 108, 123, 129 of judgment).

TIMOTHY TAYLOR LTD v MAYFAIR HOUSE CORP, [2016] EWHC 1075 (Ch), [2016] 4 W.L.R. 100, Alan Steinfeld QC, Ch D.

1377 Rent–Repayments–Exercise of break clause–Repayment of rent paid in advance

[Apportionment Act 1870 (c.35) s.2]

A tenant (M) appealed against a decision (*Marks & Spencer Plc v BNP Paribas Securities Services Trust Co (Jersey) Ltd* [2014] EWCA Civ 603, [2014] L. & T.R. 26, [2015] C.L.Y. 1590) that a term concerning repayment of rent could not be implied into a lease. The term of the lease ran until 2 February 2018. Rent was payable quarterly in advance on the usual quarter days. M exercised a right to terminate the lease under a break clause, and the lease terminated on 24 January 2012. Notice given under the break clause would only be effective if there were no arrears of rent and a break premium of one year's rent was paid. M therefore paid the basic rent in full for the quarter starting on 25 December 2011 and ending on 24 March 2012, together with the break premium. Thereafter M demanded repayment of the rent for the period from 25 January to 24 March 2012. The landlord refused to make repayment and M commenced proceedings to recover the rent, a car parking fee, insurance charge and service charge for the post-termination period. The judge at first instance held that a term should be implied into the lease to the effect that M was entitled to those sums. The Court of Appeal disagreed.

Held: Appeal dismissed. (1) *Implied terms generally* - A clear statement of the tests of necessity for business efficacy and obviousness in relation to implying terms appeared in *BP Refinery (Westernport) Pty Ltd v Shire of Hastings* 180 C.L.R. 266, *BP* considered. The instant court made additional observations: (a) the implication of a term was not dependent on proof of an intention of the parties; the court was not concerned with the hypothetical answer of the actual parties, but with that of notional reasonable people in their position; (b) a term should not be implied into a detailed commercial contract merely because it appeared fair or because the parties would have agreed it if it had been suggested to them; (c) business necessity and obviousness could be alternatives, in the sense that only one of them needed to be satisfied; (d) if the officious bystander test was used, it was vital to formulate the question to be posed by him with the utmost care; (e) necessity for business efficacy required a value judgement. A simpler way of putting it was that a term could only be implied if, without the term, the contract would lack commercial or practical coherence, *Philips Electronique Grand Public SA v British Sky Broadcasting Ltd* [1995] E.M.L.R. 472, [1997] C.L.Y. 4845 and *Atkins International HA of Vaduz v Islamic Republic of Iran Shipping Lines (The APJ Priti)* [1987] 2 Lloyd's Rep. 37, [1987] C.L.Y. 3387 applied. The decision in *Attorney General of Belize v Belize Telecom Ltd* [2009] UKPC 10, [2009] 1 W.L.R. 1988 suggested that the process of implying terms into a contract was part of the exercise of construing the contract. However, construing the words used in a contract and implying additional words were different processes governed by different rules. It was only after the process of construing the express words was complete that the issue of an implied term fell to be considered. The observations of Lord Hoffman at paras 17-27 of the *Belize* judgment should be treated as inspired discussion rather than authoritative guidance. *Belize* did not relax the traditional and highly restrictive approach to the implication of terms, *Belize* explained (see paras 18-22, 26, 31, 60, 66, 77 of judgment). (2) *Factors in favour of an implied term* - Each quarter's rent paid in advance was referable to the tenant's use and enjoyment of the premises for that quarter. There was real force in the contention that if the landlord could retain the advance rent it would be unfairly prejudicial to the tenant. Further, the parties had agreed the terms of the break clause not knowing whether the break dates would be after, before or even on a quarter day. That supported the notion that they were unlikely to have intended the apportioned rent be retained by the landlord as part of the compensation for the operation of the break clause (paras 33-34). (3) *Factors against an implied term* - The lease was a very detailed document, entered into between experienced parties and drafted by expert solicitors. The established legal background against which the lease was entered into was also relevant. Rent was not apportionable in time in common law. That position had been remedied to a certain extent by the Apportionment Act 1870 s.2 in relation to rent paid in arrears. However, s.2 did not apply to rent payable in advance, *Ellis v Rowbotham* [1900] 1 Q.B. 740 approved (paras 38, 42-44). (4) *Outcome* - Save in a very clear case, it would be wrong to attribute to a landlord and tenant an intention that the tenant should receive an apportioned part of the rent paid in advance, when the non-apportionability of such rent had been so clearly established for so long. Express words would be needed before it would be right to imply a term to the contrary. The tenant's appeal therefore failed in relation to the advance payments of rent, car parking and insurance (paras 50, 55). (5) *Service charge* - The position in relation to the service charge was different as the lease enabled the service charge to be apportioned (para.55). (6) (Per Lord Carnwath) The judgment in *Belize* had stimulated more than usual academic controversy, but that was not sufficient to question its continuing authority, *Belize* considered (para.74).

MARKS & SPENCER PLC v BNP PARIBAS SECURITIES SERVICES TRUST CO (JERSEY) LTD, [2015] UKSC 72, [2016] A.C. 742, Lord Neuberger PSC, SC.

1378 Rent repayment orders–Supplemental provisions

THE REGULATION OF PRIVATE RENTED HOUSING (RENT REPAYMENT ORDERS) (SUPPLEMENTARY PROVISIONS) (WALES) REGULATIONS 2016, SI 2016/1022; made under the Housing (Wales) Act 2014 s.34(1). In force: 24 November 2016.

These Regulations supplement the provisions of the Housing (Wales) Act 2014 ss.32 and 33. Those sections deal with rent repayment orders. In particular, they deal with the making of rent repayment orders by a residential property tribunal on the application of a licensing authority, a local housing authority or a tenant of a dwelling.

1379 Renting Homes (Wales) Act 2016 (anaw 1)

An Act of the National Assembly for Wales to make provision about tenancies and licences which confer the right to occupy a dwelling as a home, including provision establishing two kinds of contract for the purpose of renting homes; and for connected purposes.

1380 Renting Homes (Wales) Act 2016 (anaw 1)–Commencement No.1 Order

THE RENTING HOMES (WALES) ACT 2016 (COMMENCEMENT NO.1) ORDER 2016, SI 2016/813; made under the Renting Homes (Wales) Act 2016 s.257(2). Commencement details: bringing into operation various provisions of the 2016 Act on 5 August 2016.

This Order is the first commencement order made by the Welsh Ministers under the Renting Homes (Wales) Act 2016 ("the Act"). This Order commences certain provisions of the Act on 5 August 2016 for the purposes of making regulations and issuing guidance.

1381 Repair covenants–Business tenancies–Tenant's right to make internal non-structural alterations–Replacement of carpets

A tenant appealed against decisions made during a claim for breach of repairing covenants brought against it by the respondent landlord. The parties had agreed a substantial programme of fitting out works to be paid for by the tenant, mainly comprising the installation of a lift but including the lifting, cleaning and reinstallation of an existing system of tiled carpeting. The lease provided that the tenant was to repair or replace the landlord's fixtures and fittings as necessary. It also provided that the tenant could make any internal non-structural alterations to the building without the landlord's consent. The fitting out works were carried out. Shortly before the end of the term, the tenant informed the landlord that it would replace the tiled carpets with a strip carpet system. The landlord did not object. After termination of the lease, the landlord claimed that the re-carpeting had not been in compliance with the repairing covenant. The judge held that the tiled carpets had been landlord's fixtures and that the tenant was liable in respect of them. He also awarded damages in respect of other breaches of covenant. He chose the trial date rather than the termination of the lease as the date of the quantification of the landlord's loss, having accepted evidence that, regardless of what proportion of it was required to remedy the tenant's breaches of covenant, the money the landlord intended to spend on the premises before re-letting them would, for cash-flow reasons, only be spent once a new tenant had been found, and no tenant had been found by the time of the trial. The tenant argued that (1) the tiled carpets had been tenant's fixtures, since it had paid for their installation as part of its fitting out works; alternatively, if the tiled carpets had been landlord's fixtures, their replacement was a permitted alteration; (2) since the landlord would be compensated in full for the tenant's breaches of covenant shortly after judgment, the judge had been wrong to impose damages upon the tenant in respect of any void period arising from the landlord's choice to delay the carrying out of the proposed works.

Held: Appeal allowed. (1) The judge had been correct in describing the tiled carpets as landlord's fixtures and fittings, regardless of the fact that they were re-laid at the tenant's cost at the start of the term, and that the lease provided that the tenant's fitting out works were to be disregarded on any rent review. Much the largest part of the fitting out works had consisted of the installation of the lifts, which, on any view, were to become part of the building, so that the provision of payment by the tenant for the fitting out works was of no weight in deciding to whom the carpets had belonged. They had belonged to the landlord before their removal and reinstatement (see para.10 of judgment). However, it did not matter whether the tiles were fixtures or fittings. On the true construction of the tenant's unqualified right to make alterations, that right extended to the tiled carpets whether they were landlord's fixtures or landlord's fittings. The lease contained a heavily qualified right for the tenant to make structural or external alterations to the building, but also an entirely unqualified right to make internal non-structural alterations. It would be a commercial nonsense for the relevant clause to permit alteration by replacement of landlord's fixtures, but make no provision for alteration or replacement of landlord's chattels provided within the building for the tenant's use under the lease. The only sensible interpretation was that it provided a right to the tenant to make alterations affecting any of the landlord's property within, or forming part of the building, save for the structure and exterior. Accordingly, the replacement of the tiled carpets with the strip carpet constituted a permitted alteration (paras 11-13). (2) The tenant's argument was compelling. Nothing in the judge's analysis addressed it. The instant court was entitled to interfere with the judge's conclusion. A conclusion that, once put in funds by payment of damages, further delay by the landlord in carrying out the repairs, including those necessary to remedy the tenant's breach, were not to be imposed as a further recoverable loss upon the tenant, was a matter of legal analysis rather than fact finding (paras 16-18).

SOUTH ESSEX PARTNERSHIP UNIVERSITY NHS FOUNDATION TRUST v LAINDON HOLDINGS LTD, [2016] EWCA Civ 377, [2016] B.L.R. 355, Jackson LJ, CA (Civ Div).

1382 Repair covenants–Footpaths–Flats–Covenant to keep common parts in repair

[Landlord and Tenant Act 1985 (c.70) s.11, s.11(1)(a), s.11(1A), s.11(1A)(a), s.11(3A)]

The headlessee of a flat appealed against a decision that he was liable under a repairing covenant for injury to the subtenant caused by disrepair to a paved area outside the building. The headlessee leased the flat from the building's freeholder. The demise extended to the internal surfaces of the walls, ceiling and floor. It included the right to use the common parts to access the flat. The headlessee granted a subtenancy of the flat. The subtenant was injured by an uneven stone on the paved area. The Court of Appeal held that the headlessee was liable, having failed to keep the paved area from falling into disrepair, thus breaching the repair covenant implied into the subtenancy by the Landlord and Tenant Act 1985 s.11(1)(a). That was on the basis that the area was part of the front hall of the building, in which the headlessee had an "estate or interest" as provided for by s.11(1A). The issues were whether (1) the paved area was part of the exterior of the front hall; (2) the headlessee had an estate or interest in the front hall; (3) the headlessee could be liable despite having had no notice of the disrepair before the subtenant's injury.

Held: Appeal allowed. (1) A path leading to a door opening onto the front hall was not part of the exterior of the front hall. A feature which was not part of the building and lay wholly outside the building could not be part of the exterior of the front hall. Unless the natural meaning of a statutory provision produced a nonsensical result, or a result inconsistent with the legislative intention, its words had to be given their ordinary meaning. One might have expected that s.11(1A)(a) should have a wide effect, on the basis that Parliament would have intended all parts of a building not in an individual demise, but enjoyed by the tenant, to be within the covenant. However, given that the section imposed obligations over and above those contractually agreed, one should not be too ready to give an unnaturally wide meaning to its expressions. Such a wide reading would be very difficult to reconcile with the wording of s.11(1A)(a), *Campden Hill Towers Ltd v Gardner* [1977] Q.B. 823, [1977] C.L.Y. 1765 applied, *Brown v Liverpool Corp* [1969] 3 All E.R. 1345, [1970] C.L.Y. 1524 overruled, *Hopwood v Cannock Chase DC* [1975] 1 W.L.R. 373, [1975] C.L.Y. 1859 approved (see paras 17-21 of judgment). (2) Although there was practical attraction in the headlessee's contention that it was unlikely that Parliament had intended that the headlessee of a single flat, whose interest in the common parts was simply as a means of access, should have an implied liability to his subtenant to repair the common parts, the contention could not be right. There would have to be a powerful reason not to give "interest", appearing in a property statute, its normal meaning in law. If the word was to be given a limited meaning, it was hard to identify a satisfactory way to cut it down. Further, if the headlessee had no such liability, the subtenant would be without any contractual remedy for damage suffered as a result of disrepair to the common parts, whereas if the subtenant had a claim against the headlessee, the headlessee could normally pass on the claim to the freeholder. The headlessee was further protected by s.11(3A) (paras 24-27). (3) A landlord's repair covenant operated as a warranty that the premises would be in repair. An exception to that general principle was the rule that a landlord was not liable under the covenant to repair premises in the possession of the tenant and not of the landlord unless the landlord had notice of the disrepair, *Makin v Watkinson* (1870-71) L.R. 6 Ex. 25 applied. The question arose of whether the applicability of the rule to the structure and exterior of a flat depended on whether the demise was limited to its internal surfaces. The rule would apply, but only to the extent that the structure was included in the demise. If the tenant was not in possession, there was no reason for excluding the general principle. The further question arose of whether the rule applied to property in the possession of neither landlord nor tenant. The rule did not normally apply to premises not in the tenant's possession: the reason for the rule was not only the landlord's inability to know of disrepair, but also the tenant's advantageous position, *Murphy v Hurly* [1922] 1 A.C. 369 and *McCarrick v Liverpool Corp* [1947] A.C. 219, [1947-51] C.L.Y. 4474 applied. It was not normally open to a landlord to invoke the rule against a tenant of one part in relation to another part not in the landlord's possession. The s.11 repairing covenant applied in precisely the same way as a contractual repairing covenant. Under contractual covenants, a landlord was not normally liable for disrepair of property in the tenant's possession; there was no basis for departing from that when it came to s.11 covenants, *O'Brien v Robinson* [1973] A.C. 912, [1973] C.L.Y. 1900 considered. The reasoning on which the rule was based justified the conclusion that any obligation on the headlessee to repair the paved area was only triggered once he had notice of disrepair (paras 29-30, 39-49).

EDWARDS v KUMARASAMY, [2016] UKSC 40, [2016] A.C. 1334, Lord Neuberger PSC, SC.

1383 Repair covenants–Measure of damages–Loss arising from breach of covenant

The appellant residential long leaseholder (M) appealed against a decision rejecting most of his claim against the respondent landlord, for damages arising from a flood in the flat above his own. M owned a flat in a mansion block. The landlord covenanted to maintain and repair the common parts, and to insure and reinstate the building. In 2005 there was a flood which caused serious damage to his flat and those below. Contractors engaged by the landlord's agent undertook repair works to M's flat which were paid for by insurance, and were inadequate. M engaged his own contractors to make good the defects, which were finished by February 2007, and he settled that expenditure with the landlord. At the time of the flood M had not been living in the flat, and he remained living elsewhere until 2008. In 2011 the landlord sold the reversion. M claimed special damages, namely the cost of repairing three outstanding items caused by the flood, general damages for breach of the lessor's obligations in relation to insurance and reinstatement and to repair the common parts from 2001 to 2011. The judge found that M had failed to prove his claim for special damages. She dismissed his claim in respect of the landlord's insurance obligations on the basis that M, for reasons unconnected with the flood damage, had not been living in the flat between the flood and the completion of his repairs. She awarded damages in respect of the common parts for the years when M had been living in the flat. The main issue was whether M could claim for loss arising from a period of disrepair attributable to the landlord's breach if, during that period, and for reasons unconnected with the disrepair, he had chosen to live elsewhere. The underlying issue of principle was whether the loss caused by such a breach, which caused no damage to the capital value of M's flat, lay in the impairment of the amenity value of his proprietary interest, or in the experience of discomfort, inconvenience and distress that he actually suffered because of the disrepair.

Held: Appeal allowed in part. (1) M had proved his case in relation to special damages regarding two of the defects (see para.16 of judgment). (2) The judge's quantification of damages for the landlord's failure to repair the common parts while M was living in the flat was not wrong in principle (paras 17-20). (3) If impairment of a lessee's property right was the correct way of identifying the loss, then in principle it should be irrelevant whether he occupied it continuously or for some of the time, or let others use it, or sub-let it, or left it vacant. By contrast, if the loss for which the lessee sought damage was his own personal inconvenience, discomfort and distress, then what he did with the leasehold property during the period of disrepair was, as the judge found, crucial. Non-use during that period would be fatal to any claim. Use only for weekends or holidays might diminish the claim pro rata (para.22). In the absence of direct authority, the court reached the following conclusions: (i) Although the language of *Calabar Properties Ltd v Stitcher* [1984] 1 W.L.R. 287, [1984] C.L.Y. 1892 and *Wallace v Manchester City Council* (1998) 30 H.L.R. 1111, [1998] C.L.Y. 3678 spoke of discomfort, inconvenience and distress as if they were the very losses caused to the lessee by the lessor's breach, the better view was that the loss consisted in the impairment to the rights of amenity afforded to the lessee by the lease, of which discomfort, inconvenience and distress were only symptoms, *Calabar* and *Wallace* considered, *Earle v Charalambous* [2006] EWCA Civ 1090, [2007] H.L.R. 8, [2007] C.L.Y. 2747 followed. The lessee paid a premium for the assignable right to the enjoyment of occupation of a specific property for a period usually longer than his own lifetime, the quality of which was underpinned by the lessor's repairing and reinstatement obligations and his promise to carry out those obligations diligently and in due time (paras 31, 35). (ii) Therefore it was not a fatal obstacle to a claim for damages for that impairment in the lessee's rights that he might have chosen not to make full, or even any, use of them during part or even all of the relevant period, for reasons unconnected with the disrepair (para.36). (iii) It did not follow that the use or non-use of the lessee's property rights during the period of disrepair was irrelevant for all purposes. It might be relevant to mitigation, for example where a lessee left uninhabitable premises and stayed with parents, *Earle* considered. By contrast, if a lessee had to rent alternative premises then that cost might be the best measure of his loss, *Calabar* considered (paras 37-38). (iv) It would be strange if mitigation was the only principle by reference to which the limited use or non-use of leasehold premises during a period of disrepair was relevant. M had lived elsewhere for reasons unconnected with the disrepair. If his flat had been rendered uninhabitable, it would be strange if he was then entitled to 100% of the flat's rental value during the period of disrepair, whereas a tenant vacating a flat to mitigate his loss, such as in *Earle*, was entitled to only 50% for an equivalent impairment, *Earle* considered. It might be that non-use for reasons unconnected with the disrepair should be regarded as a form of mitigation of loss, even if there was no intention to mitigate, but it would not wholly cancel out the loss constituted by the impairment of amenity, for which a tenant had paid rent, or a lessee a premium, even if he lived elsewhere rent-free (para.39). (v) The court was obliged to temper the rigour of those rules that sought to implement the compensatory principle at the heart of the law of damages, where particular circumstances made it just to do so. That might admit quantification of damages in excess of the current rental value, *English Churches Housing Group v Shine* [2004] EWCA Civ 434, [2004] H.L.R. 42, [2005] C.L.Y. 2683 considered (para.41). The judge had been wrong to treat M's non-occupation of his flat during the period of disrepair as fatal to his claim for compensation for loss of amenity. He had suffered precisely the same loss as a lessee who, in comparable circumstances, had remained in the flat throughout, namely a serious although temporary impairment of the rights conferred on him by the lease, for which he had paid a full premium. The starting point for the valuation of that impairment should be by reference to the rental value during the relevant period, with a very substantial discount to reflect the judge's conclusion that the disrepair was cosmetic. The damages should then be further substantially discounted by reference to the fact that M had chosen not to occupy the flat for most of the relevant period (paras 43-43).

MOORJANI v DURBAN ESTATES LTD, [2015] EWCA Civ 1252, [2016] 1 W.L.R. 2265, Longmore LJ, CA (Civ Div).

1384 Right to manage–Notices of claim–Service at landlord's registered office–Earlier counter-notice containing different address for service–Validity of service

[Commonhold and Leasehold Reform Act 2002 (c.15) s.111(3)(a), s.111(4), s.79, s.79(1); Landlord and Tenant Act 1987 (c.31) s.47, s.48]

A landlord appealed against a decision that the respondent right to manage (RTM) company had properly served a claim notice under the Commonhold and Leasehold Reform Act 2002 s.79. In 2014, the company served a claim notice seeking the right to manage the landlord's building. The landlord's counter-notice stated that any communications about that notice or any further notice had to be sent to its solicitors' office. The company did not pursue the claim. In February 2015, the landlord issued service charge demands to its tenants stating that its registered office was the relevant address for the service of notices; the demands were drafted with the Landlord and Tenant Act 1987 s.47and s.48 in mind. In April 2015, the company served a second claim notice at the landlord's registered office. The landlord disputed the validity of the second claim on the grounds that the notice was sent to the wrong address; it claimed that it should have been sent to its solicitors' office in accordance with the statement in the 2014 counter-notice. The First-tier Tribunal held that the second claim notice was validly given. It found that the statement in the 2014 counter-notice had been "countermanded" by the statement in the service charge demands. The Upper Tribunal had to consider whether s.111(4) of the 2002 Act prohibited service to the landlord's registered office, given the statement in the 2014 counter-notice. If the second claim notice had been served in breach of s.111(4), it also had to consider whether that breach meant that the notice was invalid.

Held: Appeal dismissed. (1) Delivery of the notice to the landlord's office was an effective giving of notice for the purpose of s.79(1). The office had been identified without qualification or restriction as the address for the service of notices in the service charge demands, and reliance on that address was not prohibited by s.111(4) because no different address had been identified by the landlord to the company. The natural meaning of the statement in the 2014 counter-notice was that any further notice in relation to the subject-matter of the first claim notice had to be sent to the solicitors. A reasonable recipient of that notice would read it as referring to communications relating to the first claim; they would not understand it to mean that the solicitors' address had to be used for service of any future claim notice. It was reasonable to assume that if the landlord wished future claim notices to be sent to a specific address it would make that clear in a letter or formal notice. Accordingly, the 2014 counter-notice was not a notification for the purpose of s.111(4) and the company had been free to communicate with the landlord, in reliance on s.111(3)(a) of the 2002 Act, at the address given in the service charge demands (see paras 24, 29-32 of judgment). (2) Although the tribunal rightly concluded that the claim notice had been given at a permissible address, it was wrong to base that decision on the conclusion that the service charge demands "could be said by any reasonable recipient to countermand the notice given" in 2014 by the landlord; that conclusion depended on both documents being intended to communicate information to the same recipient, which they were not. A notification for the purpose of s.111(4) was given for a different purpose and to different recipients from notices under s.47 or s.48. Accordingly, it was not possible to regard a statement made in service charge demands sent to a number of tenants as countermanding or superseding a statement previously made to an RTM company that notices should be served at a specific address (para.28). (3) As the notice had been properly served, it was not necessary to decide whether a claim notice served in breach of the s.111(4) prohibition was a nullity. However, it was noted that Parliament had identified the steps to be taken by RTM companies to acquire the rights and obligations which were the consequence of the landlord's ownership of the property, and it was not for tribunals to confer the same status on those companies by something less than complete compliance with those steps. The proper approach to non-compliance with the procedures under the 2002 Act was considered in *Triplerose Ltd v Mill House RTM Co Ltd* [2016] UKUT 80 (LC), [2016] L. & T.R. 23, [2016] 1386, *Triplerose* applied. If a claim notice was served in breach of s.111(4), the swiftest, cheapest and safest response was to re-serve the notice (paras 33-36).

GATEWAY PROPERTY HOLDINGS LTD v ROSS WHARF RTM CO LTD, [2016] UKUT 97 (LC), [2016] L. & T.R. 15, Martin Rodger QC, UT (Lands).

1385 Right to manage–Notices of claim–Specification of premises–Specification of appurtenant property

[Commonhold and Leasehold Reform Act 2002 (c.15) s.80, s.80(2), s.81(1)]

The appellant landlord appealed against a decision that a claim notice had been validly served on it by the respondent company under the Commonhold and Leasehold Reform Act 2002 s.80. The company had been formed by the leaseholders of a block of flats for the purposes of managing the property themselves. The landlord had replied to the claim notice acknowledging receipt but claimed that the notice was invalid because it included a small yard which did not fall within the statutory definition of "premises" in s.80(2). The notice had been accompanied by the freehold title map, on which the property was edged in red. If the claim notice had been validly served then the company was entitled to the right to manage the property. The tribunal found that if the yard had been included incorrectly that would be an inaccuracy in the particulars required by s.80(2) which would not invalidate the notice and which could be excused under s.81(1) of the Act. The landlord submitted that the claim notice failed to comply with s.80(2) because it had not specified the premises and had been invalidated by the inclusion of the yard, and that that failure could not be excused. The company denied that the claim was made in respect of the whole of the property comprised within the freehold title and contended that the fact that the plan from the title register was referred to in the claim notice did not mean that the company was claiming the right to manage all those premises contained in the title.

Held: Appeal dismissed. If there had been an error of the magnitude alleged by the landlord, it could not be legitimately excused, *Malekshad v Howard de Walden Estates Ltd (No.2)* [2003] EWHC 3106 (Ch), [2004] 1 W.L.R. 862, [2004] C.L.Y. 3226 considered. Section 81(1) could not save a claim notice where the claim wrongly included land which could not be the subject of a right to manage. However it was clear that the claim notice could not be sensibly construed as a claim to manage the whole of the property contained within the area edged red on the plan annexed to the title. The reference made to the title plan was nothing more than a guide to the location of the premises in relation to which the claim was made. The premises were to be read as being the block and its appurtenant property and nothing more. The tribunal had arrived at the correct conclusion that the claim notice correctly specified the premises which were the subject matter of the claim. The duty imposed by s.80(2) should not normally cause difficulties for a claimant. The claim notice had to specify the premises, and for that purpose premises was a reference to the self-contained building, or part of a building. It was not necessary for the claim notice to specify either that there was appurtenant property or, if there was, what that appurtenant property was. If that were a requirement, it would be impossible to comply with. That was principally because appurtenant property included appurtenances, that was rights pertaining to the property, some of which would be contained expressly in the leases but others of which would take effect only by implication and which would therefore by definition be difficult, and often impossible, to list comprehensively. The claim notice complied with s.80(2) (see paras 29-32, 34-47 of judgment).

MILTONLAND LTD v PLATINUM HOUSE (HARROW) RTM CO LTD, [2015] UKUT 236 (LC), [2016] L. & T.R. 9, Judge Stuart Bridge, UT (Lands).

1386 Right to manage–RTM companies–Notices of invitation to participate–Omission of notes from prescribed form–Validity of notices

[Commonhold and Leasehold Reform Act 2002 (c.15) s.78(1), s.78(2)(d), s.78(3), s.79(2), s.80, s.84]

A landlord appealed against a decision of the First-tier Tribunal that the respondent right to manage (RTM) company was entitled to acquire the statutory right to manage a residential building notwithstanding defects in its compliance with the procedural requirements of the Commonhold and Leasehold Reform Act 2002. The RTM company gave notices of invitation to participate, pursuant to s.78(1) of the Act, to each of the qualifying tenants of the flats in the building. However, those notices omitted the notes that ought to have been included as part of the prescribed form. The RTM company then served a claim notice which was modified to invite service of a counter-notice at the address of its solicitors instead of at its registered office. The landlord challenged the validity of the notices of invitation and the claim notice, and alleged that two of the members of the RTM company were not qualifying tenants. The tribunal found that none of the parties had been prejudiced by the defects and held that the provisions of the Act which related to the content of notices were directory rather than mandatory because there was no reference to any consequences of non-compliance.

Held: Appeal allowed. (1) The correct approach to defects in compliance with statutory schemes for the acquisition of property rights was to ascertain Parliament's intention in respect of the consequences of non-compliance in the light of the statutory scheme as a whole. That was a question of construction which did not depend on the circumstances of an individual case. In some schemes, certain defects would be inconsequential. In others the service of a notice or the provision of information might be critically important to the integrity of the scheme, with the consequence of non-compliance being that the statutory procedure had not validly been invoked, *Newbold v Coal Authority* [2013] EWCA Civ 584, [2014] 1 W.L.R. 1288, [2013] C.L.Y. 2431 and *Natt v Osman* [2014] EWCA Civ 1520, [2015] 1 W.L.R. 1536, [2015] C.L.Y. 1576 followed. The acquisition of the right to manage under the Act fell into the second category of procedures considered in *Osman*, namely those which conferred a property or similar right on a private person, and for which compliance with the strict requirements of the statutory scheme was essential, and substantial compliance was not good enough. Although no interest in land was created or transferred by the acquisition of the right to manage, the same policy of providing certainty in relation to the existence, acquisition and transfer of property interests was fully engaged (see paras 32-33 of judgment). (2) The purpose of a notice of invitation to participate under s.78 was to afford all qualifying tenants the opportunity to become members of the RTM company. A failure to comply with s.78(3) was not to be regarded as one relating to the "particulars" required by s.78(2)(d), but as a failure to comply with the requirements as to the form of the notice. Since Parliament intended that the notices should be in the prescribed form, including all of the notes, the significance of individual pieces of information contained in the notes did not arise for consideration. Therefore, in having regard to the practical consequences of the omission of the notes, and in basing its conclusion on the absence of prejudice, the tribunal had erred in principle. The inclusion of the notes in the prescribed form was essential to the validity of a notice of invitation to participate, and therefore the RTM company was prohibited by s.79(2) from giving a claim notice seeking to acquire the right to manage. Accordingly, the appeal succeeded on that ground (paras 39, 42, 45-47, 55). (3) Neither s.80 nor s.84 of the Act provided that a claim notice had to inform the recipient that any counter-notice was to be served at the registered office of the RTM company. Although it was stated in para.5 of the prescribed form of claim notice that a counter-notice had to be given to the company "at the address in paragraph 1", and para.1 required the company to state the address of its registered office, the sole purpose of identifying an address for service of the counter-notice was to facilitate the receipt by the RTM company of that counter-notice. There was nothing in the statutory scheme to prohibit an RTM company from specifying an alternative address for service (paras 48-50). (4) Section 73 of the Act did not make it a condition of a company's status as an RTM company that its membership should be restricted exclusively to qualifying tenants of flats (para.53).

TRIPLEROSE LTD v MILL HOUSE RTM CO LTD, [2016] UKUT 80 (LC), [2016] L. & T.R. 23, Martin Rodger QC, UT (Lands).

1387 Secure tenancies–Notification–Requirements for creation of tenancies

[Housing Act 1996 (c.52) s.184, s.188, s.193; Housing Act 1985 (c.68) Sch.1 para.4]

The appellant tenant appealed against a decision that she held a property rented from the respondent local authority under a non-secure tenancy. The tenant, her husband and children had vacated their previous property following violent acts by a neighbour. Whilst not accepting that it owed them the full housing duty under the Housing Act 1996 s.193, the local authority was satisfied that they qualified for temporary accommodation pursuant to the interim duty under s.188. The family were initially housed in bed and breakfast accommodation before being offered the property in issue as alternative temporary accommodation. In July 2011, they signed a tenancy agreement, provided by the local authority, for the grant of an introductory tenancy. The form included the provision that "the tenancy will become a secure tenancy at the end of the trial period", and the tenant and her husband signed a certificate of acceptance. The local authority later informed the tenant that the introductory tenancy form had been used in error, and that they should have been granted a non-secure tenancy pending completion of its inquiry into their homelessness status under s.184. The local authority issued possession proceedings, contending that the tenancy had been granted in pursuance of its homelessness function and that it was not and could not have been secure because the tenant had not been notified pursuant to the Housing Act 1985 Sch.1 para.4 that the tenancy was to be regarded as secure. The tenant averred that the tenancy took effect as an introductory tenancy because the notification required by Sch.1 para.4 was provided by the signed certificate contained in the tenancy form. The judge held that the tenancy was granted pursuant to the local authority's homelessness functions and that the certificate did not amount to a notice under Sch.1 para.4 because it did not notify the tenant that the tenancy was "to be regarded" as a secure tenancy. He construed para.4 as requiring a landlord to specify that the tenancy was secure at the date of its grant, not that it would or might become one in the future. He therefore declared that the tenant held the property under a non-secure tenancy. The issue was the legal effect of the parties' agreement in July 2011, and the signed certificate.

Held: Appeal dismissed. The judge's construction of Sch.1 para.4 as requiring a notice to state that the tenancy would be secure at the date of grant and not merely at some unspecified date in the future seemed to be right. However, the main reason why the certificate was unable to function as a proper para.4 notification was that, read as a whole and in context in which it was signed, it could not amount to a notification by the local authority that the tenancy was to be a secure tenancy. It was not any form of notification, whether for the purposes of para.4 or otherwise. Its purpose was to provide a statement by the tenants that they had understood the general statutory provisions governing the grant of an introductory tenancy, and it was impossible to read it as anything more. The judge had been right to declare that the tenancy was a non-secure tenancy (see paras 31, 33 of judgment).

WANDSWORTH LBC v TOMPKINS, [2015] EWCA Civ 846, [2016] P.T.S.R. 102, Patten LJ, CA (Civ Div).

1388 Service charges–Claims–Determination of charges payable–Claim struck out as abuse of process

[Landlord and Tenant Act 1985 (c.70) s.18, s.27A, s.29, s.38]

A married couple appealed against a decision of the First-tier Tribunal to strike out their claim as an abuse of process. The appellants occupied a lodge in a holiday park under a long lease. In 2010, the members of the lodge owners association relating to the park applied to the Southern Rent Assessment Committee for recognition as a tenants' association. The effect of the Landlord and Tenant Act 1985 s.29, s.18 and s.38 was that in order to show that they were "qualifying tenants" the occupants of the lodges had to show that each of them contributed to the same costs by the payment of a "service charge", being an amount payable by a "tenant of the dwelling" in addition to rent. "Dwelling" was defined in s.38 as "a building or part of a building occupied or intended to be occupied as a separate dwelling". The committee declined jurisdiction, finding that the lodges were neither the subject of tenancies nor dwellings for the purposes of the Act. In 2012, the appellants, who had bought their lodge in 2011, applied under s.27A of the Act for a determination of the service charges payable. The First-tier Tribunal struck out the claim on the basis that the appellants were raising issues which had been determined against the lodge owners in the proceedings before the committee. The appellants argued that the tribunal had been wrong to strike out their claim. They were not parties to the earlier proceedings. Further, the tribunal had failed to address their primary case, not put before the committee, that the lodge was a tenant's fixture. Moreover, the tribunal should have drawn a distinction between the collective application made by the association and their own application: the former was a lesser and purely collective right to have the tenants' association recognised, whereas the latter was an application by the parties to a long lease to seek the protection of the Act in relation to the levying of a fair service charge.

Held: Appeal dismissed. (1) The First-tier Tribunal had been correct to strike out the claim. It had taken the appellants' position as successors in title who played no part in the previous litigation into account and weighed that factor in the balance, *Aldi Stores Ltd v WSP Group Plc* [2007] EWCA Civ 1260, [2008] 1 W.L.R. 748, [2007] C.L.Y. 346 considered. Further, the tribunal concluded that the "tenant's fixture" argument made no difference to the basic finding that the lodges were not dwellings within s.27A; it therefore found that the argument was no basis for asserting that the appellants were in any different position from the original applicants. Moreover, no real distinction could be drawn between the position of a party, like the appellants, who was seeking to establish that his lodge was a dwelling for the purposes of s.27A and one who, like the applicants before the committee, was seeking to establish exactly the same thing under exactly the same statutory definition for the purposes of s.29 (see paras 67, 69, 73-74 of judgment).(2) (Obiter) As to whether the appellants' lodge was a building and thus a dwelling, the appropriate test was whether the structure had become something that could only be enjoyed where it was and whether it could be removed elsewhere without a process of demolition, *Elitestone Ltd v Morris* [1997] 1 W.L.R. 687, [1997] C.L.Y. 3304 considered. The appellants' lodge was not a building. It could not only be enjoyed where it was. It could be taken apart and put back together elsewhere without any process of demolition or even any process that could fairly be described as re-erection. It was not attached to the plot in any way that made it a fixture. It had not become part of the realty. It was a *mobile* home (paras 77, 87).

CADDICK v WHITSAND BAY HOLIDAY PARK LTD, [2015] UKUT 63 (LC), [2015] L. & T.R. 16, Judge Mole QC, UT (Lands).

1389 Service charges–Procedural irregularity–Landlord's compliance with procedural requirements of lease

[Landlord and Tenant Act 1985 (c.70) s.27A]

The management company of an apartment block appealed against a decision of the First-tier Tribunal that the tenants' obligation to pay service charges had been vitiated by procedural failures. The apartment block comprised residential flats and a Chinese restaurant. The leases of all the properties provided for the tenants to reimburse a proportion of the costs and expenses incurred by the management companies, including the buildings insurance premium. By clauses 5 and 6 of the seventh schedule, the management company covenanted to obtain audited accounts of all expenses incurred by it in carrying out its obligations under the lease and to serve on the tenants a certificate of those expenses. One of the tenants refused to pay the service charge, complaining that invoices submitted by the management company contained no information as to how the charges or individual costs had been calculated and that charges were being made for work that was not carried out. The management company brought county court proceedings for recovery of the unpaid service charges. The proceedings were transferred to the tribunal, which assessed the service charges at nil. Of its own motion, the tribunal recommended that the landlord ought to take the higher risk posed by the restaurant into account when apportioning the buildings insurance premium between the various properties. The issues were whether the tribunal (i) had wrongly found that compliance with clauses 5 and 6 was a condition precedent to payment of the service charge; (ii) lacked jurisdiction to determine that the demand was invalid, since the question of whether the service charges were recoverable at all was not in issue in the county court proceedings; and (iii) lacked jurisdiction to recommend that the landlord take account of the risk attributable to the restaurant when fixing the apportionment of insurance.

Held: Appeal allowed. (1) The tribunal's interpretation of the effect of clauses 5 and 6 was not in accordance with clause 1 of schedule 5, which clearly provided for payment based on a determination of the amount estimated to be due by the management company. There was nothing in clause 1 which required the provision of audited accounts and there was no reason to imply such a term, *Redrow Homes (Midlands) Ltd v Hothi* [2011] UKUT 268 (LC), [2012] L. & T.R. 8, [2012] C.L.Y. 2045 and *Pendra Loweth Management Ltd v North* [2015] UKUT 91 (LC), [2015] L. & T.R. 30 applied. It followed that the tribunal had been wrong to assess the service charges at nil. It was open to the tenant to apply to the county court for damages or specific performance, or to apply to the Leasehold Valuation Tribunal for determination of the service charges payable (see paras 36-43 of judgment). (2) Bearing in mind that the proceedings were in the county court and that the tenant was a litigant in person, his pleading that the management company was in breach of the lease by failing to provide audited accounts was wide enough to enable him to submit that, as a matter of law, no service charge was payable, *Cain v Islington LBC* [2015] UKUT 117 (LC) applied (paras 46,

50). (3) The tribunal had made the comments regarding the Chinese restaurant of its own motion without evidence as to the insurance ratings. Moreover, its recommendation was not a determination of a service charge within the jurisdiction under the Landlord and Tenant Act 1985 s.27A and therefore could not stand (para.51). (4) The case was remitted to a fresh tribunal to determine the amount payable under the service charges. In the meantime, the management company was directed to submit fully audited accounts within 28 days and the tenant to provide details of which parts of the service charges were challenged (para.54).

ELYSIAN FIELDS MANAGEMENT CO LTD v NIXON; IMPERIAL BUILDINGS MANAGEMENT CO LTD v NIXON *sub nom.* APARTMENTS 52, 53 AND 97, ELYSIAN FIELDS, COLQUITT STREET, LIVERPOOL L1 4DL, RE; APARTMENTS 6, 10, 20 AND 25, IMPERIAL BUILDINGS, HIGH STREET, ROTHERHAM S60 1FF, RE, [2015] UKUT 427 (LC), [2016] L. & T.R. 4, Judge Behrens, UT (Lands).

1390 Service charges–Reasonableness–Existence of money judgment covering service charge–Tribunal's jurisdiction to determine reasonableness

[Landlord and Tenant Act 1985 (c.70) s.18, s.19, s.27A, s.27A(1), s.27A(4)(c)]

A tenant appealed against a First-tier Tribunal's decision that it could not determine the reasonableness of a service charge under the Landlord and Tenant Act 1985 s.19 because a money judgment in the amount of the charge had been entered by the county court. The lease in question contained a service charge provision enabling the respondent landlord to recover the cost of providing a television aerial. By the time of the instant appeal, it was common ground that the charge was a "variable" charge within the meaning of s.19 and the amount recoverable was therefore limited to that which was reasonable. When the tenant failed to pay the amount claimed, the landlord brought possession proceedings in the county court. The district judge entered judgment for the full amount of the charge, despite the tenant's argument that it was unreasonable. While the reasonableness of the service charge would usually be determined by the tribunal on an application under s.27A, the district judge failed to appreciate that the county court had parallel jurisdiction and would usually refer the question to the tribunal. The tenant appealed against the entry of the money judgment and made a s.27A application to the tribunal. A circuit judge dismissed her appeal, holding that the charge was a fixed, rather than a variable, charge and was not susceptible to a determination of reasonableness. Thereafter, the tribunal concluded that it had no jurisdiction to entertain the tenant's s.27A application because the question of the service charge had been determined by the county court. The issue was whether the tribunal had jurisdiction to determine the reasonableness of a service charge when a money judgment for the full amount of the charge had already been entered by the county court. The tenant submitted that it could, on the basis that the county court had not determined the reasonableness of the charge. The landlord argued that the county court decision constituted a s.27A determination and that the tribunal therefore had no jurisdiction.

Held: Appeal dismissed. The money order judgment remained extant. It resolved the questions of liability, the amount payable, and the question of jurisdiction. No sensible distinction could be made between liability to pay and the amount payable. As matters stood, the county court had determined that the charge was not a variable service charge within the meaning of s.18. Therefore, by virtue of s.27A(1) and s.27A(4)(c), the tribunal had no jurisdiction (see paras 16- 17 of judgment).

COWLING v WORCESTER COMMUNITY HOUSING LTD, [2015] UKUT 496 (LC), [2016] L. & T.R. 2, Judge Nigel Gerald, UT (Lands).

1391 Service charges–Reasonableness–Tenant's challenge to service charges paid over previous 12 years–Limitation periods

[Landlord and Tenant Act 1985 (c.70) s.27A, s.27A(4), s.27A(5); Limitation Act 1980 (c.58) s.19, s.8]

A tenant appealed against a preliminary decision that he was not permitted to challenge, under the Landlord and Tenant Act 1985 s.27A, the reasonableness of service charges imposed by the respondent, his landlord, for periods more than six years previous. The tenant had acquired the lease of his flat in 2002. He had paid all service charges. From shortly after his purchase, he had sought general information from the landlord about their make-up and apportionment. However, he raised no challenge until 2014. The tribunal held that the tenant was to be treated as having agreed or admitted each element of the service charge and its apportionment, and that his challenge was debarred by s.27A(4) of the Act. It held, in the alternative, that the tenant's claim was statute-barred because both a six-year limitation period, and the doctrine of laches, applied. The tenant submitted that (1) by virtue of s.27A(5), agreement could not be inferred from his conduct; (2) the tribunal had been wrong about the limitation period and the doctrine of laches.

Held: Appeal dismissed. (1) A tribunal could infer from a series of payments made without protest that the tenant had agreed that the amount claimed was the amount properly payable. People did not generally pay money unless they accepted that it was due, certainly not regularly over a period of time. Even if the tenant had withheld payment, there might still be other facts and circumstances indicating agreement. The effect of s.27A(5) was to preclude any such finding "by reason only of [the tenant] having made any payment". The references to the making of "any payment" and the word "only" indicated that agreement could never be inferred from a single payment on its own; in such circumstances there would have to be other circumstances implying agreement. That was because it was common for tenants to pay an expressly disputed service charge to avoid the risk of forfeiture of the lease. However, the longer the period over which payments had been made, the more readily a tribunal would find that the tenant agreed that which had been demanded. It was the absence of protest which provided the additional evidence from which agreement could be implied, *Shersby v Grenehurst Park Residents Co Ltd* [2009] UKUT 241 (LC) considered. In the instant case, it was not clear precisely what the tenant was challenging in each of the years. However, all the matters seemed to be those which could be challenged without any form of disclosure, so the tenant's explanation that he did not have all the material he needed did not stand scrutiny. His earlier requests for information did not amount to challenges, especially as he had continued to pay the charges without protest. Just the existence of the series of payments justified the tribunal's finding that he had agreed them, but the passage of time before making the challenge served to reinforce that finding. It did not matter that the precise date on which the tenant had agreed the charges could not be pinpointed. The tenant was barred by s.27A(4) from proceeding (see paras 14-26, 30 of judgment). (2) The tribunal's finding about limitation and the doctrine of laches was misconceived. The tribunal had been required to address the reasonableness of the amounts claimed, not whether the sums could be recovered. The limitation period was therefore 12 years pursuant to the Limitation Act 1980 s.8, not six years under s.19. The doctrine of laches only applied to equitable claims where there was no limitation period, such as restitution, *Warwickshire Hamlets Ltd v Gedden* [2010] UKUT 75 (LC) followed (paras 33-34)

CAIN v ISLINGTON LBC, [2015] UKUT 542 (LC), [2016] L. & T.R. 13, Judge Nigel Gerald, UT (Lands).

1392 **Service charges–Repairs–Charge for major works–Landlord's obligation to consider financial impact**

[Housing Act 1985 (c.68); Landlord and Tenant Act 1954 (c.56) s.27; Landlord and Tenant Act 1985 (c.70) s.19]

The appellant tenant appealed by way of review against a decision of the First-tier Tribunal (Property Chamber) that, subject to minor adjustments, she should pay the service charges demanded by the respondent landlord. The landlord had carried out a scheme of major works to the tenant's property at a local authority estate where 850 residents were secure tenants and 140 were long leaseholders under the Housing Act 1985. The landlord demanded that each long leaseholder pay more than £55,000 in service charges towards the work. The tenant applied under the Landlord and Tenant Act 1954 s.27 for a determination of the charges. They were held to be substantially payable.

Held: Application granted in part. Under the lease, the landlord had an obligation to repair and a discretion to improve and was entitled to seek contribution to either from the tenants, but the lease was not clear as to whether the landlord had a separately-expressed power to carry out such improvements. However, under a proper interpretation of the lease there was a power to do so. The question was whether the cost of them was reasonably-incurred (see paras 39-40 of judgment). The Landlord and Tenant Act 1985 s.19 made no express distinction between repairs and improvements, but the approach had to be different: with repairs a landlord fulfilled an obligation under the lease, whereas improvements could be merely a matter of choice. Provided a landlord acted reasonably the choice was his and tenants could not complain because a cheaper method was adopted, but if he went beyond what was needed for repair and asked leaseholders to contribute he should take account of the extent of their interests, their views, and the financial impact made, *Sheffield City Council v Oliver* applied. The local authority landlord had responsibility for its leaseholders as well as to its secure tenants. The right to recover the cost of improvements was not enough to justify embarking on a scheme of very expensive works (paras.41-43). The financial impact on residents was relevant. Improvement went beyond repair. Where, as in the instant case, the scheme was expensive and the resulting structure was wholly different from that originally demised, a landlord should, before proceeding, consider the availability of alternatives and should give greater weight to the views and means of the lessees who would be required to pay (para.46). It was appropriate to decide whether works were repairs, improvements or a mixture. In the instant case, replacing the roof was reasonable and within case-law guidelines, *Post Office v Aquarius Properties Ltd* [1987] 1 All E.R. 1055, [1987] C.L.Y. 2141 and *Quick v Taff Ely BC* [1986] Q.B. 809, [1985] C.L.Y. 1610 followed (paras 47-48). The cost of works to the windows and replacement cladding was significant and the landlord should have made more effort to explore cheaper solutions, and to have considered the financial impact on lessees. The tribunal should not have been satisfied that the landlord's decision to incur the costs was reasonable (paras 49, 54-57). The case was remitted to the tribunal for determination of amount of service charge reduction.

WAALER v HOUNSLOW LBC, [2015] UKUT 17 (LC), [2015] L. & T.R. 24, Siobhan McGrath, UT (Lands).

1393 Service charges–Residential property–Residential service charge costs–Whether relevant agreements qualifying long-term agreements within s.20 Landlord and Tenant Act 1985

[Landlord and Tenant Act 1985 (c.70) s.20, s.20ZA, s.27A(3); Service Charges (Consultation Requirements) (England) Regulations 2003 (SI 2003/1987) Sch.2, Sch.2 para.4, Sch.3, reg.4, reg.7; Public Contracts Regulations 2006 (SI 2006/5) reg.16]

A local authority applied under the Landlord and Tenant Act 1985 s.27A(3) for a determination of the liability to pay residential service charge costs to be incurred in respect of a number of leasehold properties. The properties in question comprised residential apartments held on long leases which provided for payment of a service charge. The local authority, as freeholder of the properties, put forward a schedule of proposed repair works and gave notice to the leaseholders of its intention to enter into Qualifying Long Term Agreements (QLTAs) under the Service Charges (Consultation Requirements) (England) Regulations 2003 Sch.2. The QLTAs would be entered into with building contractors to support the delivery of repairs and maintenance and would be for a period of four years. The value of the contracts was likely to reach £130 million over that period. The landlord followed the restricted procedure under the Public Contracts Regulations 2006 reg.16 and a contract notice was published. The local authority asked the tribunal to consider, among other things, whether it had complied with its obligation to consult under the 1985 Act and the 2003 Regulations. The lessees relied on the Upper Tribunal decision in *London Area Procurement Network v All Right to Buy Lessees* (LAPN) in arguing that the proposed framework agreements were not QLTAs within the meaning of s.20 of the 1985 Act and that the local authority's consultation was inadequate.

Held: Application refused. (1) When considering an application under s.27A(3), the tribunal had jurisdiction to consider whether the correct consultation had been carried out in accordance with the 2003 Regulations (see para.66 of judgment). (2) Having regard to s.20 and s.20ZA of the 1985 Act and to reg.4 of the 2003 Regulations, a QLTA was an agreement entered into by a landlord for a term of more than 12 months where the relevant costs incurred under the agreement for any tenant exceeded £100 in any accounting period. Those requirements were met here. It was not necessary for a landlord to establish that costs in excess of that amount would definitely be incurred or to demonstrate which accounting period they might fall into (paras 70-72). (3) The costs would be incurred "under" the framework agreements because there was a sufficient factual nexus between the subject-matter of the agreement and the works themselves. Such a nexus existed where works were carried out by one of the contractors identified under the terms of the agreement. The framework agreements identified the works to be carried out with sufficient particularity to satisfy that test. Moreover, reg.7 of the 2003 Regulations provided that the requirements of Sch.3 to the 2003 Regulations applied to qualifying works which were the "subject" of a QLTA to which s.20 applied. The word "subject" indicated that a broad construction was appropriate. Thus, the proposed works in the instant case were the "subject" of the framework agreements, which were QLTAs for the purposes of s.20. The instant case was very different from the LAPN case, where the agreements were in draft and agency relationships between the Network and the local authorities threw the issue of nexus into doubt, *LAPN* not followed (paras 73-76 of judgment). (4) It was not necessary to seek dispensation from the public notice requirements of Sch.2 to the 2003 Regulations where a landlord was unable to provide the information set out in reg.4 of those Regulations on the application of s.20 to QLTAs, *Southwark LBC v Leaseholders of Southwark LBC* [2011] UKUT 438 (LC) applied. The fact that the information required by Sch.2 para.4 was not available to be provided to the leaseholders did not mean that dispensation was required; all that was necessary was for the authority to provide the information when it was able to do so. Because of *Southwark*, there was no longer any issue of discretion: either the QLTA was one to which the 2003 Regulations applied or it was not. As those Regulations did apply, consultation would be limited to that required by Sch.3 (paras 46, 67, 77, 79). (5) The consultation requirements were not changed by *Daejan Investments Ltd v Benson* [2013] UKSC 14, [2013] 1 W.L.R. 854, [2013] C.L.Y. 1879: it remained the case that s.20 consultation had to be complied with or dispensed with if a landlord wished to recoup relevant costs, *Daejan* considered (para.80). (6) Since a determination under s.27A(3) was made before works were carried out, it could not be determinative of the standard of the work when completed. However, precision as to the extent and duration of the works and the terms of the lease which supported the obligation to carry them out was nevertheless required, and the local authority had failed to satisfy the tribunal on those matters. As it was impossible to say whether the estimated costs were reasonable, no determination of payability could be made (para.82).

KENSINGTON AND CHELSEA RLBC v LESSEES OF 1-124 POND HOUSE, POND PLACE, LONDON SW23, [2015] UKUT 395 (LC), [2016] L. & T.R. 10, Siobhan McGrath, UT (Lands).

1394 Service charges–VAT–VAT on landlord's payment to managing agent–Recoverability

[Landlord and Tenant Act 1985 (c.70) s.19]

The appellant tenant appealed against a decision that certain VAT charges incurred by the respondent landlord were recoverable as service charges. Under the lease, the landlord was obliged to "employ such number of porters and staff as the Lessors shall from time to time think reasonable in and about the performance of the relevant covenants by the Lessors". The relevant clause continued as follows: "the Lessors may pay to Porters and staff in addition to wages such allowances in respect of uniform rent food and maintenance as the Lessors shall from time to time determine And generally the Lessors may employ and pay such contractors agents or servants (including the Agent) and may incur such costs as they shall think necessary or desirable in and about the performance of the covenants and provisions of this Schedule". The landlord sought to discharge its obligations under that clause by employing a managing agent, which in turn employed caretakers/staff in relation to the development of which the tenant's flat formed part. The invoices submitted by the managing agent to the landlord included VAT on the salaries of the staff in question, and such VAT was included as part of the service charges sought to be recovered from the tenants. The issue was whether the relevant items of VAT included in the service charges fell within the extra-statutory concession set out in VAT Notice 48 para.3.18, which exempted "all mandatory service charges or similar charges paid by the occupants of residential property towards the upkeep of the dwellings or block of flats in which they reside and towards the provision of a warden, caretakers and people performing a similar function for those occupants".

Held: Appeal dismissed. The concession did not apply, as the agent's charges were not "mandatory service charges". The concession did not apply to any charges paid by the landlord (or other person levying the service charge) to third parties for the supply of services even though the cost of those services was passed on to a residential occupier through a service charge. Where a landlord employed staff directly and passed the cost on to the tenants through a service charge, no VAT would be payable on the salaries of such staff. On the other hand, where the same staff were employed by a managing agent who invoiced the landlord for their services, VAT would be payable on the salaries and that could be passed on to the tenants through the service charge. Given that the standard rate of VAT was 20 per cent, that could give rise to significantly increased service charges. That might give rise to an argument as to the reasonableness of properties being managed in that way; it might be said that the VAT thus passed on via the service charge was not reasonably incurred for the purposes of the Landlord and Tenant Act 1985 s.19. However, the tenant had not sought to raise such an argument, so it would be wrong to express any view about it. In the circumstances, the landlord was entitled to claim the disputed items of VAT as service charges (see paras 35, 44-46 of judgment).

INGRAM v CHURCH COMMISSIONERS FOR ENGLAND, [2015] UKUT 495 (LC), [2016] L. & T.R. 6, Judge Alice Robinson, UT (Lands).

1395 Tenancies–Introductory tenancies–Operation and duration of introductory tenancy regime

[Housing Act 1996 (c.52) s.124(1), s.124(5)]

The appellant appealed against a declaration that the respondent local housing authority had elected to operate an introductory tenancy regime. The appellant had been granted a purported introductory tenancy for 12 months from August 2011. In March 2012, following rent arrears, the local authority had issued a claim for possession. A preliminary issue arose as to whether the appellant's tenancy was an introductory tenancy. The judge took account of (i) a September 1997 report from the local authority's director of housing, which recommended the adoption of introductory tenancies, closely monitored by the housing management sub-committee, and a full report on their effect after the first year of operation; (ii) the minutes of the local authority's housing committee's September 1997 meeting, in which the committee had resolved to authorise the director to implement introductory tenancies on a trial basis for one year, to be monitored by the sub-committee, and required a further report to be submitted in six months. The judge found that an introductory tenancy regime had been implemented under the Housing Act 1996 s.124(1), and that the appellant was therefore an introductory tenant. The appellant contended that the housing committee had in September 1997 elected to operate an introductory tenancy regime for a trial period of one year only, after which the regime had ceased to operate in the absence of a further election to extend it. He submitted that his tenancy was therefore a secure tenancy.

Held: Appeal dismissed. The implementation of the introductory tenancy regime for a finite one-year period could be inferred if the words of the committee meeting's minutes were read in isolation. However, those words had to be read in the context of the director's report and the s.124 framework, which enabled the committee to revoke the introductory tenancy regime at any time under s.124(5). The director had not advised the operation of the introductory tenancy regime for only one year, or for a trial period: the report had recommended the implementation of the regime on a trial basis subject to monitoring by the sub-committee for one year. The director was not seeking, and was not granted, authorisation to implement the introductory tenancy regime for one year only: he had asked for and received authorisation to implement an introductory tenancy regime which would be monitored for one year, so that any concerns would be taken back to the committee and the regime revoked if that was appropriate.

GORMAN v NEWARK AND SHERWOOD HOMES *sub nom.* GORMAN v NEWARK AND SHERWOOD DC; NEWARK AND SHERWOOD DC v GORMAN, [2015] EWCA Civ 764, [2015] H.L.R. 42, Lord Dyson MR, CA (Civ Div).

LEGAL ADVICE AND FUNDING

1396 Civil legal aid–Domestic violence–Legal aid for victims of domestic violence–Eligibility

[Civil Legal Aid (Procedure) Regulations 2012 (SI 2012/3098) reg.33; Legal Aid, Sentencing and Punishment of Offenders Act 2012 (c.10) s.12; Children Act 1989 (c.41) s.91(14)]

The appellant charity appealed against a decision (*R. (on the application of Rights of Women) v Lord Chancellor* [2015] EWHC 35 (Admin), [2015] 2 F.L.R. 823, [2015] C.L.Y. 1625) refusing its application for judicial review of the Civil Legal Aid (Procedure) Regulations 2012 reg.33. Regulation 33 specified the supporting evidence which had to be provided by a legal aid applicant who claimed to be the victim of domestic violence. With certain exceptions, it provided that legal aid would not be available unless documentary proof of domestic violence was provided within a period of 24 months before the legal aid application was made. The charity submitted that (1) in imposing reg.33, the Lord Chancellor had exceeded the powers conferred on him to make regulations by the Legal Aid, Sentencing and Punishment of Offenders Act 2012 s.12; (2) alternatively, reg.33 breached the principles in *Padfield v Minister of Agriculture, Fisheries and Food* [1968] A.C. 997, [1968] C.L.Y. 1667 because it frustrated the purpose of the Act.

Held: Appeal allowed. (1) Section 12 of the Act had to be construed according to its terms. It made "provision about conditions which must be satisfied by an applicant before a determination is made". A condition that a GP or other report should be provided had to be within that power. A condition that such a report had to be dated within the previous 24 months also seemed to come within that statutory wording (see paras 35-36 of judgment). (2) It was a matter for the court to ascertain the purpose of the statute from its words. The purpose was partly to withdraw civil legal services from certain categories of case in order to save money, but also to make such services available to the great majority of persons in the most deserving categories. That would be catered for partly by the requirements of financial need and merit, as set out in s.11, but could also be catered for by requirements which the Lord Chancellor was entitled to impose under the s.12 regulation-making power, *R. (on the application of Public Law Project) v Secretary of State for Justice* [2014] EWHC 2365 (Admin), [2015] 1 W.L.R. 251, [2014] C.L.Y. 2021 applied. The House of Commons had rejected a proposed amendment to the effect that no time limit would apply to the forms of evidence that would be accepted in relation to domestic violence. However, that could not absolve the court from considering whether the Regulations, in their final form, did in fact frustrate or thwart their statutory purpose, *Padfield* followed. There were many situations in which victims of domestic violence found themselves involved in legal proceedings more than 24 months after incidents of domestic violence had occurred, but more than 24 months after it was practical to obtain the kind of verification required by reg.33. Examples of such cases were where: (a) the perpetrator had been in prison and brought proceedings for divorce or child contact when released; (b) a non-molestation order, or other injunction, had kept the parties apart for two years; (c) a period of separation had occurred for reasons such as a police caution or other police involvement where criminal proceedings did not result in a conviction; (d) child contact was refused, but the perpetrator of violence served a fresh application on the victim of domestic abuse after the expiry of the two-year period or the court directed, under the Children Act 1989 s.91(14), that no such proceedings should be begun until expiry of the two-year period; (e) a victim of domestic abuse brought proceedings for divorce or financial relief after 24 months had expired, when any practical ability to obtain verification had passed, because her immediate priority had been to make arrangements for her personal safety and that of her children; (f) the domestic abuse was psychological or emotional rather than physical, meaning that the verifications required by reg.33 were much harder to satisfy and there was considerable difficulty for the victim in obtaining the necessary verification after any lapse of time; (g) the victim had suffered financial abuse and therefore would not be able to obtain any of the verifications required by reg.33 at all. Those examples provided a formidable catalogue of areas of domestic violence not reached by a statute which had a purpose of reaching such cases. The 24-month requirement had no rational connection with the statutory purpose. There was no obvious correlation between the passage of such a comparatively short period of time as 24 months and the harm to the victim of domestic violence disappearing or even significantly diminishing. Once it was accepted that part of the statutory purpose was to ensure that legal aid was available to the great majority of domestic violence victims, it was necessary to ask why so many of them were excluded by the 24-month rule. The rule operated in a completely arbitrary manner and there was no safety valve which enabled the victims of domestic violence to explain why they were unable to obtain verification of that violence less than 24 months before proceedings began. For those reasons, reg.33 frustrated the purposes of the Act and was invalid insofar as it imposed a requirement that the verification of the domestic violence had to be dated within a period of 24 months before the application and insofar as it made no provision for victims of financial abuse (paras 37, 41, 43-51).

R. (ON THE APPLICATION OF RIGHTS OF WOMEN) v LORD CHANCELLOR, [2016] EWCA Civ 91, [2016] 1 W.L.R. 2543, Longmore LJ, CA (Civ Div).

1397 Civil legal aid–Eligibility–Lawfulness of residence test

[Legal Aid, Sentencing and Punishment of Offenders Act 2012 (c.10) Sch.1 Pt 1, s.41, s.41(2)(b), s.9, s.9(2), s.9(2)(b)]

The Lord Chancellor appealed against a decision (*R. (on the application of Public Law Project) v Secretary of State for Justice* [2014] EWHC 2365 (Admin), [2015] 1 W.L.R. 251, [2014] C.L.Y. 2021) that his proposed introduction of a residence test that would qualify the provision of civil legal aid would be ultra vires the enabling statute and unjustifiably discriminatory. The Legal Aid, Sentencing and Punishment of Offenders Act 2012 Sch.1 Pt 1 set out the categories of case, other than exceptional cases, in which civil legal aid could be provided. Section 9 of the Act, supplemented by s.41, empowered the Lord Chancellor to amend Sch.1 by statutory instrument. The Lord Chancellor published his intention to introduce the residence test by way of such statutory instrument. To satisfy the residence test, with some exceptions, an applicant would have to be lawfully resident in the UK at the time of application, and would have to have been lawfully resident for a 12-month period at some point before that. The Lord Chancellor submitted that s.9 read with s.41 empowered him to introduce the residence test. The respondent Public Law Project submitted that (1) the Divisional Court had been right to find that the original, needs-based content of Sch.1 Pt 1 defined the scope of the power given by s.9(2), namely that the Lord Chancellor could only "recalibrate" Sch.1 by reference to a criterion or criteria based on need; he could not delete potential recipients for other reasons; (2) in the context of access to justice the court should be vigorous in its judgment of the justification for discrimination such as the residence test.

Held: Appeal allowed. (1) The Lord Chancellor's department's published documentation underlined the focus on need that informed the material provisions of the Act. However, there were also references to the saving of expense. The explanatory notes to the Act identified the purpose of its material part as the fulfillment of the government's aim to review legal aid and make it more efficient. It was obvious that in circumstances of financial stringency choices as to the disposition of public funds would focus on need for the services in question. Thus it was inevitable that Sch.1 Pt 1 listed categories where the need for civil legal aid was pressing. However, that did not mean that the only criterion by which the Lord Chancellor could limit or restrict civil legal aid was the perceived need of its potential recipients. It would be very difficult for the subordinate legislator to draw rational or humane distinctions on grounds of need between the various legal services listed in Pt 1. The terms of the Act did not indicate that its purpose was to be read as narrowly as the Public Law Project would have it. In particular, the inevitable fact that the contents of Sch.1 Pt 1 were needs-based did not suggest, far less require, that the expression in s.41(2)(b) "a particular class of individual" was limited by reference to the needs of the class's members. It was clearly wide enough to encompass characteristics of a class that were material to the heightened efficiency of civil legal aid: an objective that plainly included the saving of public funds. The residence test was well within the scope of such a strategy and within the scope of changes permitted to the Lord Chancellor by s.9(2)(b), read in particular with s.41(2)(b) (see paras 21-23 of judgment). (2) Whether state funding of legal expenses in civil matters should be limited to recipients resident in the UK was essentially a political question on which reasonable people would entertain contrary opinions. Therefore one would expect the law, in setting the criterion by which the discrimination involved might be justified, to allow a very considerable margin of discretion to the government. The test of "manifestly without reasonable foundation", deriving from *Stec v United Kingdom (65731/01)* (2006) 43 E.H.R.R. 47, [2006] C.L.Y. 2089 and established in domestic law, did not cover the whole field of government decisions challenged on grounds of discrimination: the standard of review varied with the context, *Stec* applied, *Humphreys v Revenue and Customs Commissioners* [2012] UKSC 18, [2012] 1 W.L.R. 1545, [2012] C.L.Y. 3093 followed. Certain grounds for discrimination, for example race and sex, would be especially hard to justify, and the law would apply a more intrusive judgment to the justification, *R. (on the application of Carson) v Secretary of State for Work and Pensions* [2005] UKHL 37, [2006] 1 A.C. 173, [2005] C.L.Y. 3835 followed. However, the classes of case where the law would control discrimination with particular vigour were not exclusively defined by reference to the grounds of discrimination: some were defined by reference to the context, most notably the doing of justice and the presumption of individual liberty. The "manifestly without reasonable foundation" test for justification constituted the law's default position in any discrimination case where the subject-matter was one of broad or strategic economic and/or social policy. However, it would be disapplied and a more vigorous approach adopted where either the grounds of discrimination or the context called for the law's special protection. The ground of discrimination in the instant case, namely place of residence, was not a characteristic such as sex or race that was specially protected by the law. The argument based on the context of access to justice faced the difficulty that there was a profound difference between the state's duty on the one hand to ensure fair and impartial procedures and to avoid undue legal obstacles to access to the courts, and on the other a putative duty to fund legal representation. The residence test was not manifestly without reasonable foundation, *Stec* applied (paras 32-39, 44-45).

R. (ON THE APPLICATION OF PUBLIC LAW PROJECT) v SECRETARY OF STATE FOR JUSTICE *sub nom.* R. (ON THE APPLICATION OF PUBLIC LAW PROJECT) v LORD CHANCELLOR; PUBLIC LAW PROJECT v LORD CHANCELLOR, [2015] EWCA Civ 1193, [2016] 2 W.L.R. 995, Laws LJ, CA (Civ Div).

1398 Civil legal aid–Eligibility–Lawfulness of residence test–Ultra vires

[Legal Aid, Sentencing and Punishment of Offenders Act 2012 (c.10) Sch.1 Pt 1, Sch.1 Pt 2, s.11, s.41, s.9]

The appellant Public Law Project (PLP) appealed against the Court of Appeal's decision that the Lord Chancellor's proposed introduction of a residence test for eligibility for civil legal aid was lawful. The Legal Aid, Sentencing and Punishment of Offenders Act 2012 Sch.1 Pt 1 contained sections concerned with the provision of legal aid. Section 9 set out the services for which civil legal aid could be provided, and empowered the secretary of state to amend the services described by statutory instrument. In 2013, he determined to introduce a residence test for eligibility for civil legal aid, to the effect that, with some exceptions, an applicant would have to be lawfully resident in the UK at the time of application and to have been lawfully resident for a 12-month period at some point before that. PLP applied for a declaration that the draft order would be unlawful, in that it would be (i) ultra vires the 2012 Act, and (ii) unjustifiably discriminatory. The Divisional Court held that the draft order was unlawful on both grounds, and it was withdrawn. The Court of Appeal allowed the Lord Chancellor's appeal, holding that the draft order was intra vires and that, while it was discriminatory in its effect, the discrimination could be justified. PLP argued that the exclusion of a specific group of people from the right to receive civil legal services in relation to an issue, on the ground of personal circumstances or characteristics which had nothing to do with the nature of the issue or services involved or the individual's need, or ability to pay, for the services, was not within the scope of the power accorded to the Lord Chancellor by s.9(2)(b), and nothing in s.41 of the Act undermined that contention.

Held: Appeal allowed. PLP's argument was accepted. As a matter of ordinary language, the relevant parts of the draft order did not seek to "vary or omit services" as specified in s.9(2)(b); rather they sought to reduce the class of individuals who were entitled to receive those services by reference to a personal characteristic or circumstance unrelated to the services. The wider statutory context supported the conclusion indicated by the natural meaning of the words of s.9(2)(b) on their own. Each of the services identified in Sch.1 Pt.1 or Pt. 2 was linked to a specific type of legal issue or claim, and had nothing to do with the personal circumstances or characteristics, and in particular the geographical residence, of the potential recipient of the services. That conclusion was supported by the contrast in the wording of the two subsections of s.9. Section 9(1) clearly distinguished between the question whether the particular services qualified and whether the particular individual qualified (see paras 29-31, 33 of judgment). Whereas s.9 was concerned with the issues in respect of which civil legal services were to be available, s.11 appeared to be concerned with identifying the characteristics or circumstances of individuals who were to qualify for civil legal aid. The criteria listed in s.11 were connected to the need of the individual for the services, the cost of the services, the extent and likelihood of the benefit from those services, and the conduct of the individual "in connection with" those services. That suggested that the draft order was attempting to do something which the legislature never had in mind when enacting Sch.1 Pt.1, let alone s.9. While it was true that s.41(2)(b) permitted any order made under s.9(2)(b) to "make provision by reference to....services provided for a particular class of individual", that did not mean that the power to make orders under s.9(2)(b) was thereby extended to exclude a whole class of individuals from the scope of Sch.1 Pt.1 by reference to their residence. Section 41 was intended to grant ancillary powers to those powers which were primarily granted by provisions such as s.9: it was not intended to permit an alteration in the nature of those powers (paras 34, 36). The exclusion of individuals from the scope of most areas of civil legal aid, on the ground that they did not satisfy the residence requirements of the proposed order, involved a wholly different sort of criterion from those embodied in the 2012 Act or the consultation paper on which it was based. Accordingly, the appeal was allowed on the ultra vires issue. The court did not deal with the discrimination issue (paras 37, 39).

R. (ON THE APPLICATION OF PUBLIC LAW PROJECT) v SECRETARY OF STATE FOR JUSTICE *sub nom.* R. (ON THE APPLICATION OF PUBLIC LAW PROJECT) v LORD CHANCELLOR; PUBLIC LAW PROJECT v LORD CHANCELLOR, [2016] UKSC 39, [2016] 3 W.L.R. 387, Lord Neuberger PSC, SC.

1399 Civil legal aid–Exceptional funding–Complexity of exceptional cases funding scheme

[Legal Aid, Sentencing and Punishment of Offenders Act 2012 (c.10) s.10(3); European Convention on Human Rights 1950 art.14, art.8; Equality Act 2010 (c.15) s.149]

The court considered the Official Solicitor's concerns that the exceptional case funding scheme under the Legal Aid, Sentencing and Punishment of Offenders Act 2012 s.10(3) failed to properly deal with claims made by those who lacked capacity. The claimant (S) had sought judicial review of the first defendant's refusal of legal aid to enable him to apply for recognition of his immigration status in the UK. S lacked capacity to engage in litigation. His legal aid application had been refused on the ground that ECHR art.8 was not engaged in immigration cases. His claim was joined to five other claims contending that there had been a systematic failure to comply with the requirements of the 2012 Act. The grounds were that: (i) the operation of the exceptional case funding scheme frustrated the Act's purpose by putting unnecessary obstacles in the path of applicants, which bore particularly severely on disabled persons; (ii) the refusal of funding breached art.8 and art.14 rights as applicants were unable to make an effective application for their position to be recognised; and (iii) there had been a failure to comply with the Equality Act 2010 s.149. The court held that guidance issued by the second defendant indicating how an application for exceptional funding under s.10(3) should be considered was unlawful as it wrongly indicated that art.8 considerations did not apply in immigration cases. It also wrongly indicated that discretion to grant exceptional funding was severely circumscribed and that a refusal would only amount to a breach of Convention rights in rare and extreme cases. That decision was upheld by the Court of Appeal in *R. (on the application of Gudanaviciene) v Director of Legal Aid Casework* [2014] EWCA Civ 1622, [2015] 1 W.L.R. 2247, [2015] C.L.Y. 1626. S had been granted legal aid, but the importance of the issues justified their further consideration.

Held: Judgment accordingly. (1) The basic submission was that the scheme was insufficiently accessible. The prescribed forms were far too complex and the information required excessive. For those without legal assistance, they were almost impossible to understand and complete satisfactorily. A particularly adverse effect of the 2012 Act reforms had been the effect on family cases and the increase in litigants who had to appear in person, *MG v JF (Child Maintenance: Costs Allowance)* [2015] EWHC 564 (Fam), [2016] 1 F.L.R. 424, [2016] 874 considered. A contested family case involving children in which there was no interference with art.8 rights was unlikely. Only rarely, subject to means and merits if properly applied, should legal aid be denied in such cases. The 2012 Act should not be construed to limit grants of legal aid to the highest priority cases. Legal aid had to be granted if, without it, an individual would suffer a breach of his Convention or EU law rights, and might be granted if there was a risk of such breach. The test in *R. (on the application of Gudanaviciene)* had to be followed. The scheme was not providing the safety net s.10 was supposed to provide and the difficulties applied with greater force where children or adults lacking capacity were concerned. Those who were unable to pay for legal assistance were suffering in a way that Parliament could not have intended (see paras 30-80 of judgment). (2) There were two difficulties in the way the merits test was applied. First, the requirement that in all cases there had to be a greater than even chance of success was unreasonable. Second, the manner in which the agency assessed the prospects of success was erroneous. The point of representation was that it would produce the chance of success which would not exist without representation. If a case turned on issues of fact, the ability to challenge apparently unfavourable material and to cross-examine adverse witnesses effectively could turn the case in a party's favour. It was not for the agency to carry out the court's exercise, in effect prejudging the issue to be determined by the court (paras 81-97). (3) The obligation under s.149 was a continuing duty to have due regard to the material need. Provided that the court was satisfied there had been a rigorous consideration of that duty, that there had been a proper appreciation of the potential impact of the policy on equality objectives and the desirability of protecting them, it was for the decision-maker to decide how much weight should be given to various factors informing the policy, *R. (on the application of Greenwich Community Law Centre) v Greenwich LBC* [2012] EWCA Civ 496, [2012] Eq. L.R. 572, [2012] C.L.Y. 2209 and *R. (on the application of Bracking) v Secretary of State for Work and Pensions* [2013] EWCA Civ 1345, [2014] Eq. L.R. 60, [2014] C.L.Y. 2804 applied. The Lord Chancellor had produced an equality impact assessment in May 2012, and the necessary due regard had been had (paras 98-104). (4) There had to be changes to the scheme. The application forms were far too complex for applicants in person. The test in *R. (on the application of Gudanaviciene)* could be set out in the form and applicants or solicitors/providers could be required to give full details of the need for legal assistance. Consideration had to also be given to the provision of Legal Help to enable solicitors/providers to decide whether legal assistance should be granted because a case qualified within s.10. The system was also defective in failing to provide a right of appeal to a judicial body where an individual lacking capacity would otherwise be unable to access a court or tribunal (paras 98-197).

R. (ON THE APPLICATION OF S) v DIRECTOR OF LEGAL AID CASEWORK; DIRECTOR OF LEGAL CASEWORK v IS *sub nom.* IS v DIRECTOR OF LEGAL AID CASEWORK, [2015] EWHC 1965 (Admin), [2015] 1 W.L.R. 5283, Collins J, QBD (Admin).

1400 Civil legal aid–Inquests–Refusal of legal aid for interested person at inquest

[Coroners and Justice Act 2009 (c.25) s.47(2)(f), s.5; Legal Aid, Sentencing and Punishment of Offenders Act 2012 (c.10) s.10(2), s.15; European Convention on Human Rights 1950 art.6, art.6(3)(c); Coroners (Inquests) Rules 2013 (SI 2013/1616) r.22]

The claimant applied for judicial review of the defendant director's refusal of her legal aid application for representation at an inquest. The claimant was 17 years old and had mental health problems and had been assessed by a psychologist as intellectually on the borderline of disability. The inquest was into the death of a firefighter at premises where the claimant and a friend had smoked a cigarette shortly before the fire had started. The claimant was charged but acquitted of arson. For the inquest she was designated as an "interested person" pursuant to the Coroners and Justice Act 2009 s.47(2)(f) as a person who might by any act or omission have caused or contributed to the deceased's death; that entitled her to rights including the examination of witnesses either in person or by a legal representative and to receive relevant documents. Proceedings before a coroner's court did not fall within the definition of "criminal proceedings" under the Legal Aid, Sentencing and Punishment of Offenders Act 2012 s.15. Civil legal aid was only available in limited circumstances, unless the director made an "exceptional case determination" under s.10(2) of the 2012 Act. The claimant submitted that failure to provide her with legal assistance for the inquest would breach her right under ECHR art.6(3)(c) to be defended by a lawyer in the determination of a criminal charge.

Held: Application refused. (1) It was in the interests of justice for the claimant to be legally represented at the inquest. In view of her young age, mental health problems and limited intellectual capacity, without legal representation she would be unable to exercise her rights as an interested person at the inquest meaningfully or effectively. However, the failure to make representation available to her would not be a breach of her Convention rights because she was not a person "charged with a criminal offence" to whom art.6 applied and because an inquest was not a criminal proceeding or part of a criminal proceeding for the purposes of art.6 (see para.24 of judgment). (2) The claimant was no longer being treated as a suspect by the police and was not the subject of any extant criminal investigation. There was a risk that facts brought to light at the inquest could prompt the CPS to consider the possibility of bringing a fresh prosecution against her. That risk was no different from the situation where an inquiry was made into an incident and there was a possibility that a criminal offence might have been committed; that risk was insufficient to engage art.6, *Beghal v DPP* [2015] UKSC 49, [2016] A.C. 88, [2015] C.L.Y. 580 followed and *Bubbins v United Kingdom (50196/99)* (2005) 41 E.H.R.R. 24, [2006] C.L.Y. 2166 applied. Pursuant to s.5 of the 2009 Act the sole purpose of an inquest was to ascertain who the deceased was, how, when, where and in what circumstances he died and any particulars required for registration of the death; it was not aimed at obtaining evidence for use in a criminal prosecution. In any event, findings of a coroner or coroner's jury were not admissible as evidence against any person in subsequent proceedings, *Bird v Keep* [1918] 2 K.B. 692 and *Rogers v Hoyle* [2014] EWCA Civ 257, [2015] Q.B. 265, [2014] C.L.Y. 288 applied (paras 25-26). (3) It was questionable whether it would be open to a coroner's jury to return a verdict of unlawful killing based on evidence about the claimant's conduct. It was strongly arguable that such a verdict would be inconsistent with her acquittal in the earlier criminal proceedings and with the presumption of innocence implicit in art.6(2), which might remain applicable in proceedings following the conclusion of criminal proceedings, Allen v United Kingdom Application No 25424/09, 12 July 2013 applied. Furthermore, because of the principle of double jeopardy, it was generally unfair and/or oppressive to prosecute someone for an offence which arose out of the same or substantially the same facts as an offence for which he had previously been acquitted, and the court had power to stay such proceedings. The Coroners (Inquests) Rules 2013 r.22 conferred a privilege against self-incrimination on a witness at an inquest. Although incriminating admissions made by a witness could expose him to a risk of subsequent prosecution the existence of such a risk was not by itself enough to bring proceedings within the scope of art.6 (paras 27, 29, 32). (4) The claimant was not a person "charged with a criminal offence" for the purposes of art.6(1) and art.6(3) and the inquest was not a proceeding which fell within the scope of art.6 , save potentially as regards the presumption of innocence arising from the claimant's acquittal. As desirable as it was that the claimant should be legally represented at the inquest, it could not be said that she had a Convention right to be provided with free legal assistance. It followed that the director did not have the power to make an exceptional case determination under s.10 of the 2012 Act (para.38).

R. (ON THE APPLICATION OF RJ) v DIRECTOR OF LEGAL AID CASEWORK, [2016] EWHC 645 (Admin), [2016] Inquest L.R. 91, Leggatt J, QBD (Admin).

1401 Conditional fee agreements–Assignment–Assignment of CFA to another firm of solicitors

The appellant (J) appealed against a decision to disallow costs incurred following the purported assignment of a conditional fee agreement (CFA) from one firm of solicitors to another. The respondent cross-appealed against a decision to allow the costs incurred before the assignment. J had been injured in an accident in 2011. She signed a CFA with a firm of solicitors in 2012. The firm went into administration. A second firm agreed to acquire the personal injury portfolio under a deed of assignment, including J's case. J agreed to move to the new firm and signed a separate deed of assignment in January 2014. Her claim was resolved when she accepted a Part 36 offer in October 2014. The respondent denied that J was entitled to any costs, as there was no longer a valid retainer: the CFA was not capable of assignment because it was a contract for personal service, and assignments of the burdens of such contracts were not generally permitted. The respondent considered that an exception to that general rule could be inferred from *Jenkins v Young Brothers Transport Ltd* [2006] EWHC 151 (QB), [2006] 1 W.L.R. 3189, [2006] C.L.Y. 2734 where the contract involved "personal trust and confidence", but that the instant case did not fall within that exception. The district judge held that there had been no personal trust and confidence in the instant case such as there had been in *Jenkins* and that *Jenkins* had left open the question of whether a CFA generally could be assigned. He held that the burden of the instant CFA could not be assigned and so the post-assignment costs would be disallowed. However, he held that the benefit, which was effectively the entitlement to an existing chose in action in the form of future payment of fees, could be assigned, meaning that the pre-transfer fees were recoverable.

Held: Appeal allowed, cross-appeal dismissed. (1) If there was an applicable ratio in *Jenkins*, the instant court was bound by it. A solicitor's retainer involved a contract for personal services and was therefore a personal contract. The judge in *Jenkins* had not sought to qualify the exception to the general rule against the assignment of the burden of a contract to specific situations where "personal trust and confidence" could be established, but had sought to set a context in which it applied to the facts of the case. She had made plain that the benefit of being paid was conditional on and inextricably linked to the burden of performance under the CFA so as to enable an assignment to take place. She had done no more than apply principles from earlier authorities to the facts before her, *Jenkins* considered, *Davies v Jones* [2009] EWCA Civ 1164, [2010] 2 All E.R. (Comm) 755, [2010] C.L.Y. 2744 followed. The district judge had been wrong to regard *Jenkins* as not providing a binding ratio and to proceed on the basis that it was necessary to establish the same context of trust and confidence which had prevailed in *Jenkins*, *Jenkins* followed (see paras 70-75 of judgment). The intentions behind the arrangement in the instant case were impossible to ignore. Rules restricting burden assignment had been devised to protect the non-participating counterparty. Where not only the assignor and assignee agreed to the shifting of the burden, but so too did the recipient of the benefit, and a separate deed of assignment was entered into in relation to her own CFA, it would be unduly restrictive to deny the parties the effect of what they intended. J had had a choice when the old solicitors went into receivership. It should be assumed that she was advised of her best interests when she made her deed of assignment. The court could proceed in confidence that no affected party had been unwitting or unwilling (paras 76-77). (2) The debt under the CFA could be ascertained at any given point in time, even though there could not be certainty that ultimately the debtor would have to pay it. It was properly described as a contingent debt arising out of a presently existing legal relationship in which everything was certain save for ultimate payment. Although a contingent right which might never be realised to receive an unascertainable amount of money at an unknown date had too much uncertainty to amount to a present chose in action, a CFA entitlement did not fall into the same category. There would be an attributable value to any existing CFA which was capable of being assigned from one solicitor to another. The proposition that an assignment of the benefit of a CFA could only be effective in equity at the time the contingency arose would have a chilling effect on the efficacy of business arrangements which legal service providers might wish to enter into; solicitors with CFAs who wished to cease practice could not assign the agreements unless they continued to exist as a legal entity. They would have no value for assignment if the new solicitor could not recover the benefit of the work undertaken (paras 116-119).

JONES v SPIRE HEALTHCARE LTD, [2016] 3 Costs L.O. 487, Judge Graham Wood QC, CC (Liverpool).

1402 Conditional fee agreements–CLS funding–Costs limitation–Enforceability of CFA before discharge of CLS funding certificate

[Access to Justice Act 1999 (c.22) s.10(1), s.22(2)]

The appellant NHS foundation trust appealed against a decision of a costs judge that a conditional fee agreement (CFA) entered into between the respondent and her solicitors (S) was enforceable. The respondent had brought a clinical negligence action against the trust which settled in November 2013. A CLS funding certificate had been issued to her in 2008. In February/March 2013, S undertook a case review which concluded that the cost of the work which had been done was approaching the £43,000 costs limitation in the respondent's certificate and that public funding would therefore be insufficient to bring the case to a conclusion. S advised the respondent to enter into a CFA, which she did on 25 March 2013. By a notice of funding in Form N251 dated 26 March, S advised the trust of the CFA and the associated after-the-event insurance policy. However, S never applied for or obtained a discharge of the funding certificate. The trust argued that the CFA was unenforceable because it amounted to a private retainer running concurrently with public funding, in breach of the Access to Justice Act 1999 s.10(1) and s.22(2). It submitted that there were only two exceptions to that principle, the first being where the work authorised by the certificate had been completed and the second being where the client dispensed with his solicitors and acted in person.

Held: Appeal dismissed. The evidence showed that by February/March 2013 the funding was approaching exhaustion and that the Legal Services Commission had made it clear that there would be no more. S reviewed the position and concluded that the quantum stage (liability had been admitted) could not be completed on a funded basis and that the only way forward was via a CFA. They so advised the respondent. S's conclusion and advice were entirely reasonable and proper. As to the effect of s.10(1) and s.22(2), it would be appropriate to consider the position if the evidence were that the funding limited by the certificate had been completely exhausted by the date of the CFA. In such a situation, the respondent would, as a matter of fact and law, no longer be "an individual for whom services are funded by the Commission" for the purposes of s.10(1) and S would no longer be "a person who provides services funded by the Commission" for the purposes of s.22(2). The position would thus be analogous to the cases where the work authorised by the certificate had been completed: the certificate would be treated as "spent" and the litigant would no longer be assisted/funded. It could not be said that "costs limitation" cases should be distinguished on the basis that the authorised work remained incomplete. What mattered was that the funding was exhausted. Accordingly, in such a case s.10(1) and s.22(2) provided, subject to one qualification, no obstacle to the client and solicitor entering into a private retainer for the work which would have been carried out under the certificate if the funding had not been exhausted. The qualification was that notice of the new funding arrangement had to be given to the other parties to the litigation; the client would continue to be treated as funded until that moment. The position set out above was no different where, as here, the authorised funds were *approaching* exhaustion and the solicitor reasonably concluded that the necessary work could not be carried out without alternative funding. While the correct and wise procedural course would have been to obtain a discharge of the certificate, the position was in substance the same as where the authorised funds had been completely exhausted. The funds were approaching exhaustion, the Legal Services Commission had refused further funding and the case could only proceed if alternative funding was obtained. In those circumstances, there was no question of any abuse of the system. Given those conclusions, there was no concurrency of public funding and private retainer save for the one-day interval between the CFA being entered into and the date of service of Form N251. As notice of a change in funding arrangements could not be issued and served any earlier than the date on which the arrangement was complete, the interval here was de minimis. If that was wrong, the trust had argued that a CFA entered into during any period of concurrency would be entirely unenforceable. That was not so: the effect of s.10(1) and/or s.22(2) was that the solicitor would be precluded from recovering costs under a private retainer only during the period of concurrency (see paras 34, 36-41, 43-44 of judgment).

HYDE v MILTON KEYNES HOSPITAL NHS FOUNDATION TRUST *sub nom.* MILTON KEYNES NHS FOUNDATION TRUST v HYDE, [2016] EWHC 72 (QB), [2016] 4 All E.R. 874, Soole J, QBD.

1403 Conditional fee agreements–Defamation claims–Conditional fee agreement regime in defamation and privacy cases–Compatibility with art.10 ECHR

[European Convention on Human Rights 1950 art.10, art.10(2)]

The court had to determine whether conditional fee agreement (CFA) legislation, which allowed the recovery of additional liabilities in defamation and privacy cases, was incompatible with ECHR art.10. The claimants had sought damages for invasion of privacy after their phones were hacked by the defendant newspaper publisher. Eight of the claimants had gone to trial, where they were successful; 12 other cases were settled. The claimants were awarded costs and sought to recover a success fee uplift provided for under their CFAs, and after the event (ATE) insurance premiums they had paid. Prior to the costs assessments, the instant court was asked to determine whether (i) the CFA scheme, insofar as it allowed the recovery of such additional liabilities in defamation and privacy cases, was incompatible with the defendant's right to freedom of expression under art.10; (ii) in relation to the eight cases decided at trial, the defendant should be debarred from raising the incompatibility point in relation to the uplift on the ground that, at the trial, it had actually relied on the availability of an uplift under the CFAs in order to oppose the claimants' claim for a 10% damages uplift by virtue of *Simmons v Castle* [2012] EWCA Civ 1288, [2013] 1 W.L.R. 1239, [2013] C.L.Y. 782.

Held: Judgment accordingly. (1) In *Campbell v Mirror Group Newspapers Ltd (Costs)* [2005] UKHL 61, [2005] 1 W.L.R. 3394, [2006] C.L.Y. 2739, the House of Lords decided that the overall CFA scheme, which allowed recovery of an uplift, was compatible with art.10 because it was permitted under art.10(2). Although the European Court of Human Rights in *MGN Ltd v United Kingdom (39401/04)* [2011] 1 Costs L.O. 84, [2011] C.L.Y. 1680 reached a contrary view, the laws of precedent required the court to follow the English decision, *Miller v Associated Newspapers Ltd* [2016] EWHC 397 (QB), [2016] 2 Costs L.R. 195, [2016] 579 applied, *Campbell* followed, *MGN* not applied. The position of the ATE premiums was technically different as those were not an issue in *Campbell*. Accordingly, neither the House of Lords nor the ECtHR had ruled on the recovery of those premiums. However, it was very hard to see how they fell to be treated differently, *Miller* applied. Accordingly, on the basis of binding English authority, the English legislative regime which permitted the recovery of additional liabilities was not incompatible with art.10 (see paras 15-19, 37 of judgment). (2) The defendant was debarred from challenging the uplift in relation to the eight cases decided at trial. At that trial, the existence of CFAs and the right of recovery in relation to them was actually being relied on by the defendant. Allowing the defendant to now succeed on its argument that the CFA provisions which allowed for such an uplift were incompatible with art.10 would be allowing it to approbate and reprobate in a manner which was contrary to principle, *Express Newspapers Plc v News (UK) Ltd* [1990] 1 W.L.R. 1320, [1991] C.L.Y. 2978 applied. It was an inconsistency which should not be allowed. Alternatively, it was an abuse of process. Therefore, even if the English legislative regime was incompatible with art.10, the defendant would not be entitled to rely on any incompatibility to resist recovery of an uplift in relation to the eight cases decided at trial, *Simmons* referred to (paras 26-37).

EIGHT REPRESENTATIVE CLAIMANTS v MGN LTD, [2016] EWHC 855 (Ch), [2016] 3 Costs L.O. 413, Mann J, Ch D.

1404 **Conditional fee agreements–Legal aid–Switch from legal aid to conditional fee agreements–Recovery of success fees and after-the-event premiums**

In three conjoined appeals, the appellants, who had been successful in clinical negligence claims, appealed against decisions of costs judges that it had not been reasonable for them to change the funding arrangements of their claims from legal aid to conditional fee agreements (CFAs), with the result that the success fees and after-the-event insurance premiums claimed were not recoverable. The solicitors handling the claims had advised the appellants' litigation friends to switch from legal aid to CFAs shortly before 1 April 2013, being the date from which it would no longer be possible for claimants proceeding under a CFA to recover success fees and after-the-event premiums from the defendant if successful in the litigation. The litigation friends were not advised that taking that step would deprive the appellants of the 10% uplift on general damages provided for in *Simmons v Castle* [2012] EWCA Civ 1039, [2013] 1 W.L.R. 1239, [2012] C.L.Y. 852. Before the costs judges, the effective defendant, the National Health Service Litigation Authority, challenged the decisions to switch to CFAs by asserting that the litigation friend's decision in each case was based on materially unreasonable advice. That argument was based on the proposition that a reasonable person in the position of the litigation friend would have been likely, when making his decision as to whether to change funding, to attach significance to information that the appellant would lose the 10% uplift if there was a change of funding. Reliance was placed, by way of analogy, on *Montgomery v Lanarkshire Health Board* [2015] UKSC 11, [2015] A.C. 1430, [2015] C.L.Y. 1769, in which the Supreme Court reviewed the law on informed consent in the context of a medical practitioner's duty to inform a patient as to the risk involved in proposed treatment. The costs judges accepted that submission and disallowed the success fees and after-the-event premiums claimed.

Held: Appeals allowed in part. (1) The reference to *Montgomery* was a distraction. The issue was simply whether the additional liabilities were reasonably or unreasonably incurred. That question was to be determined by the application of the test in *Wraith v Sheffield Forgemasters Ltd* [1998] 1 W.L.R. 132, [1997] C.L.Y. 540. That test was wholly objective but was to be applied in the context of the individual circumstances of the particular claimant. The question was whether the CFA represented a reasonable choice for the claimant at the time, having regard to all the circumstances applying to him, *Wraith* applied and *LXM v Mid Essex Hospital Services NHS Trust* considered. That test, properly applied, would enable a costs judge to decide whether, in a particular case, the failure to mention the 10% uplift would be likely to have made any difference to the decision to switch to a CFA without any direct evidence from the claimant or the litigation friend. In the vast majority of cases, the costs judge would be likely to conclude that the failure to mention the uplift would have made no difference to the relevant decision. The additional liabilities disallowed by the costs judges would be restored in principle, *Montgomery* considered and *Simmons* cited (see paras 95-96, 107-108 of judgment). (2) The court set out a procedural framework for the way in which the issue of advice (or the lack of it) as to the 10% uplift should be dealt with in similar cases in the future (para.110). (3) In two of the three cases, the costs judge said that if the after-the-event premium had been allowed as recoverable in principle, he would have made a reduction in its amount. In one case, the reduction proposed was from £50,681 to £31,800; in the other, it was from £18,881.78 to £15,000. They considered that the cover of £500,000 in each case was too high. The experience gained by costs judges over the years had to be respected and their decisions on the premiums recoverable should stand (paras 111, 118-121).

SURREY (A CHILD) v BARNET AND CHASE FARM HOSPITALS NHS TRUST *sub nom.* AH v LEWISHAM HEALTHCARE NHS TRUST; YESIL (A CHILD) v DONCASTER AND BASSETLAW HOSPITALS NHS FOUNDATION TRUST, [2016] EWHC 1598 (QB), [2016] 4 Costs L.O. 571, Foskett J, QBD.

1405 **Conditional fee agreements–Settlements–Whether personal injury claimant had won case by settling it with Tomlin order requiring second defendant to pay damages even though only first defendant in contemplation when agreement reached**

The second defendant plumbing company appealed against a decision (*Engeham v London and Quadrant Housing Trust Ltd*) that the outcome of the claimant's personal injury action was a win for her within the terms of the conditional fee agreement she had made with her solicitors. The claimant was injured when her bathroom ceiling fell on her. She entered a CFA with the solicitors whom she had instructed to pursue a claim against the first defendant, her landlord. The CFA was stated to cover her claim against the first defendant, but did not mention the second defendant, which at that point had not been identified as a potential party. It further stated that if the claimant won, she would be liable for the firm's basic charges, disbursements and success fee. The claim was pursued against both defendants and was settled against both under a Tomlin order on payment of £10,000 by the second defendant plus costs to be assessed if not agreed. The claimant sought to recover her costs from the second defendant. A costs officer found that the CFA did not cover the claim against the second defendant and therefore the claimant's solicitors' charges and success fee in respect of that claim were disallowed for breach of the indemnity principle. The Senior Courts Costs Office upheld that decision. The county court overturned it on appeal, holding that the claimant had derived benefit from the claim irrespective of who had to pay, and therefore that she was liable for her solicitors' costs under the CFA, and entitled to recover them from the second defendant. The second defendant submitted that "your claim" in the CFA meant the claim in contemplation of the parties at the time the agreement was concluded, which was only the claim against the first defendant.

Held: Appeal dismissed. It was not realistic to say that the claimant had not won and had not secured an agreement for payment of damages. The parties could not have contemplated that only the first defendant could pay. The Tomlin order was an agreement to pay damages for the purposes of the CFA. It was not relevant that it was the second rather than the first defendant paying. The county court had been correct to allow the claimant to recover her solicitors' costs from the second defendant.

ENGEHAM v LONDON AND QUADRANT HOUSING TRUST LTD, [2015] EWCA Civ 1530, [2016] 3 Costs L.O. 357, Lord Dyson MR, CA (Civ Div).

1406 **Costs–Civil legal aid–Meaning of "costs attributable to the funded part of the proceedings" in reg.5 Community Legal Service (Cost Protection) Regulations 2000**

[Access to Justice Act 1999 (c.22); Community Legal Service (Cost Protection) Regulations 2000 (SI 2000/824) reg.5, reg.5(4)]

The appellant Lord Chancellor appealed against a decision that the Legal Services Commission was liable to pay the respondent's legal costs for the entirety of a claim. The respondent had been the defendant in an action brought against him by a carer (M), who had been employed after the respondent suffered a stroke. Part of her claim in the action was for a share in his flat and investments. The respondent counterclaimed for money and other valuables misappropriated by M. M's legal representation was funded, subject to a short hiatus, by the Commission under the Access to Justice Act 1999. M's claim was dismissed and she was ordered to pay the respondent damages. The respondent was awarded costs on an indemnity basis. He then made a claim against the Commission under the Community Legal Service (Cost Protection) Regulations 2000 reg.5 for the totality of the costs awarded against M. The issue in the instant hearing arose from the fact that there was a period during the course of the proceedings in which M was represented by solicitors who were not named in the funding certificate issued by the Commission. There was therefore a period of shortly over three months during the most fee intensive period that M was not being funded. The Senior Costs Office ruled that M did not have cost protection during that hiatus. The respondent successfully appealed and the judge found that his claim for costs was not limited to the periods in which M was in receipt of funding. The appellant submitted that the test of whether the costs of a non-funded party were "attributable to the part of the proceedings which are funded proceedings" under reg.5(4) of the Regulations was whether they had been incurred during the period that the proceedings were funded, and that in the instant case it had already been held that the proceedings had not been funded during the hiatus period; and that that was the natural reading of the words as a matter of language and having regard to the scheme of the Regulations. The respondent contended that as a matter of ordinary English the word "attributable" connoted a relationship of causation and that it was not apt to a relationship based simply on things happening during the same period, and that if the draftsman had meant what the appellant contended it would have been very easy for him to say so.

Held: Appeal allowed. The appellant's case was to be preferred. The phrase "costs attributable to the funded part of the proceedings" did more naturally mean costs incurred during that part. It did not necessarily follow from the fact that a part of the proceedings was defined in temporal terms that the criterion for attribution was also temporal but the phrase seemed to point in that direction. It was true that the draftsman could have simply referred to "costs incurred during the funded part of the proceedings". But he could also easily have said "costs incurred as a result of the funded services" or "as a result of steps funded by the Commission". The fact that he used ambiguous language was the problem. It was reasonably clear that he had proceeded on the basis that the criteria governing the qualification of the funded party for cost protection and those governing the liability of the Commission for the costs of the unfunded party should match. The draftsman might nevertheless have taken the more sophisticated view that the two criteria should differ, in order to reflect the potential mismatch which was at the heart of the respondent's case between the period when the funded party was protected and the period when the non-funded party might incur costs. However, that would necessarily raise the problem of the Commission being potentially liable for the same costs as the funded party. The whole structure of reg.5 rested on the basis that cost protection was in place as regards the selfsame costs of the unfunded party for which the Commission was to be (potentially) liable. The criteria governing cost protection and the potential liability of the Legal Aid Board mirrored one another, *Burridge v Stafford* [2000] 1 W.L.R. 927, [1999] C.L.Y. 3760 considered. In the instant case the construction of reg.5(4) produced a result where the respondent was unable to recover costs which he had had to incur as a result of the Commission's funding of M in the earlier stages of her case. That was regrettable. But statutes did sometimes adopt criteria which failed to produce a wholly just result in a particular case. The instant case was unusual: it had to be rare for funding to cease at so critical a stage, in circumstances where the non-funded party had no option but to continue to incur very substantial costs. Typically where public funding ceased part-way through a piece of litigation it would be because it had become clear that the merits were insufficient to justify its continuation; in such a case it would generally not be possible for the previously funded party to continue the proceedings and the non-funded party would not have to incur significant further costs and could look to the Commission for any costs already incurred. There might also be cases where the financial circumstances of a funded party improved, so that funding was no longer justified; in which case the non-funded party was in principle at no worse risk of not recovering his later-incurred costs than was inherent in the system generally. There was nothing unsurprising in Parliament proceeding on the broad basis that the interests of a non-funded party were sufficiently protected by his having recourse to the Commission for his costs incurred during the period of funding; and that as regards costs incurred thereafter he had to face the same risk as other litigants. That did not make the untypical case any more palatable to the victim, but it did put the claimed arbitrary effect of the temporal approach into perspective (see paras 50-56 of judgment).

RAYNER v LORD CHANCELLOR, [2015] EWCA Civ 1124, [2015] 6 Costs L.R. 957, McCombe LJ, CA (Civ Div).

1407 Criminal legal aid–Graduated fees–Remuneration under litigator's graduated fee scheme–Requirement to follow R. v Furniss (Michael) [2015] 1 Costs L.R. 151

[Criminal Legal Aid (Remuneration) Regulations 2013 (SI 2013/435) Sch.2 Pt 1 para.2(7)(b); European Convention on Human Rights 1950 art.6]

A firm of solicitors appealed against a determining officer's decision in respect of the remuneration allowed under the Litigator's Graduated Fee Scheme (LGFS). The solicitors had been instructed by a defendant in a criminal trial. The prosecution originally served 6,015 pages of evidence, but subsequently served further electronic evidence consisting of 11,715 pages, making a total of 17,730 pages. The evidence was central to the prosecution case and the judge was satisfied that if the material had been relied upon by the prosecution before the coming of the "digital age" it would have been printed out on paper. The solicitors therefore made a claim in respect of 10,000 pages of prosecution evidence, the maximum which could be claimed under the Criminal Legal Aid (Remuneration) Regulations 2013 Sch.2 Pt 1 para.2(7)(b). That represented the original printed evidence, together with 3,985 pages of the subsequent electronic evidence. However, the decision in *R. v Furniss (Michael)* [2015] 1 Costs L.R. 151, [2015] C.L.Y. 1641 was subsequently handed down, suggesting that the maximum limit of 10,000 pages did not have to be applied where the actual page count vastly exceeded that amount. The solicitors sought a redetermination on the basis of a page count of 17,730, to include all of the electronic material. The agency declined, and the solicitors lodged the instant appeal. The issue was whether the court was bound to follow the decision in *Furniss* so that it was not obliged to apply the maximum limit of 10,000 pages in calculating the solicitors' graduated fee.

Held: Appeal dismissed. Although the decision in *Furniss* had been made by a High Court judge, he had made the decision in his capacity as a Crown Court judge. That decision was not therefore binding, but it was extremely persuasive. The LGFS needed to provide for additional remuneration where the page count was unusually high. It did so by using the concept of special preparation. The effect of the decision in *Furniss* was to require the agency to pay the graduated fee on the first 10,000 pages and to entertain a claim for special preparation for work done in relation to the additional pages. However, the judge had gone further than previous decisions in seeking to remove the test set out in *R. v Napper (Costs)* [2014] 5 Costs L.R. 947, [2015] C.L.Y. 1645 regarding the importance of the documents being considered, *Napper* considered. It had clearly been the judge's view that the method of assessment of special preparation was so arbitrary that defence lawyers had to conclude that they would not be remunerated for work done in respect of page counts above 10,000. He was implicitly concluding that the 10,000 page provision was not a fundamental feature and so was capable of being read down. The current arrangements were not ideal. It was clear that the direction of travel was towards paperless trials and that the concept of pages of prosecution evidence was unlikely to survive long. The LGFS had begun as a limited scheme dealing with short hearings involving a limited amount of paperwork. However, it now dealt with a much wider range of criminal cases including those involving considerably more than 10,000 pages of documents. The use of special preparation was not a particularly attractive solution because it required litigators to record their time and involved an assessment process, which imposed a burden and was contrary to the general tenor of the LGFS. However, the current arrangements had been in place since at least 2007 and the concept of special preparation provided for the prospect of remuneration for all of the work done, even if the litigator did not always accept the determining officer's view of the amount of time reasonably to be paid. Litigators were provided with an appeal route to a costs judge and potentially a High Court judge and it was difficult to argue that such a process was in principle arbitrary. It was uncertain when compared with the graduated fee, but that was true of any summary or detailed assessment of costs and did not make it irrational. The supplementing of the graduated fee by the special preparation arrangements was compatible with the defendant's rights under ECHR art.6 to receive representation that was adequately remunerated. There was no need to read down the cut-off provision in whole or in part, Furniss doubted (see paras 51, 56, 59-68 of judgment).

R. v JAGELO (COSTS), [2016] 1 Costs L.O. 133, Costs Judge Rowley, Sen Cts Costs Office.

1408 **Exceptional funding–Lawfulness of exceptional case funding scheme for administration of legal aid under Legal Aid, Sentencing and Punishment of Offenders Act 2012 s.10**

[Legal Aid, Sentencing and Punishment of Offenders Act 2012 (c.10) s.10, s.4(3)(b); Civil Legal Aid (Merits Criteria) Regulations 2013 (SI 2013/104); European Convention on Human Rights 1950 art.6, art.8]

The Director of Legal Aid Casework and the Lord Chancellor appealed against a declaration (*R. (on the application of S) v Director of Legal Aid Casework* [2015] EWHC 1965 (Admin), [2015] 1 W.L.R. 5283, [2016] 1399) that the exceptional case funding scheme for the administration of legal aid pursuant to the Legal Aid, Sentencing and Punishment of Offenders Act 2012 s.10 was unlawful. The judge below had based his decision on two essential findings; first, that the application form was far too complex, certainly for a lay person and even for solicitors; and second that solicitors with the necessary legal aid contracts were unwilling to help complete the forms because no payment was available for work done on unsuccessful applications. He also found that the Civil Legal Aid (Merits Criteria) Regulations 2013 were unlawful because of the rigidity of the merits test and the manner in which it was applied. He found that parts of the Lord Chancellor's guidance issued under s.4(3)(b) of the Act were unlawful. The appellants submitted that (1) the judge had failed to explain how his criticisms of the scheme condemned it as unlawful within the meaning of the test of inherent unfairness; the scheme was lawful and the judge's criticisms did not establish the contrary; (2) the Regulations did not impose a uniform set of merits criteria, as the outcome of an application to which they applied depended on the type of legal services required and the category of case for which funding was sought; (3) criticisms of the Lord Chancellor's guidance, particularly para.8 regarding prioritisation of resources and para.39 regarding the approach to be adopted to ECHR art.6 and art.8, was unjustified.

Held: Appeal allowed. (1) (Briggs LJ dissenting on the issue of whether the scheme was fair and lawful). The scheme was not inherently or systematically unfair. The judge below had not made clear how it failed to meet the test of inherent unfairness. He had made individual exhortations to improvement, but had not produced a reasoned conclusion, *R. (on the application of Refugee Legal Centre) v Secretary of State for the Home Department* [2004] EWCA Civ 1481, [2005] 1 W.L.R. 2219, [2005] C.L.Y. 2155 and *R. (on the application of Tabbakh) v Staffordshire and West Midlands Probation Trust* [2014] EWCA Civ 827, [2014] 1 W.L.R. 4620, [2015] C.L.Y. 1822 applied. However, that failure could not carry the appeal on its own. The central issue was whether there was so great a deficiency of access to civil legal aid for those entitled to assistance that the scheme was to be condemned as unfair. The dividing line between multiple instances of individual unfairness and an inherent failure in the system was mainly a matter of degree, but the latter could not be established by proof of the former. The evidence did not justify an across-the-board conclusion that the scheme was so unfair as to lay outside the range of lawful choices open to the appellants as to the administration of s.10. There had clearly been real difficulties with the scheme, and their extent was troubling. An important part of the context rested on the fact that the scheme had been operated on a learning curve. There was room for improvement, particularly concerning lay applicants and those with disabilities. However, while the success rate remained low and the number of applications was modest, there had been an improvement since *R. (on the application of Gudanaviciene) v Director of Legal Aid Casework* [2014] EWCA Civ 1622, [2015] 1 W.L.R. 2247, [2015] C.L.Y. 1626, *Gudanaviciene* considered (see paras 11, 14-18, 23-24, 31, 52-57 of judgment). (2) The Regulations were lawful. They offered a balanced, proportionate approach to the grant of legal aid, which could not be condemned as arbitrary. The merits criteria were carefully specified and exceptions were carefully spelt out. There was an internal review procedure, and judicial review was also available and effectively deployed, *Del Sol v France (46800/99)* (2002) 35 E.H.R.R. 38, [2003] C.L.Y. 2118, *Ivison v United Kingdom (39030/97)* (2002) 35 E.H.R.R. CD20 and *Eckardt v Germany (23947/03) (Admissibility)* (2007) 45 E.H.R.R. SE7 applied (paras 62-66). (3) Paragraph 8 of the guidance, which referred to limited resources being refocused on the highest priority cases, did not restrict grants of legal aid to such cases. In any event, it was a legitimate purpose of the Act that the availability of civil legal services be confined to cases judged to be of the greatest need, *R. (on the application of Rights of Women) v Lord

Chancellor [2015] EWHC 35 (Admin), [2015] 2 F.L.R. 823, [2015] C.L.Y. 1625 applied. Paragraph 39 of the guidance was not tainted by any legal error and was not limiting (paras 9, 68-71). (4) (Per Briggs LJ) The defects in the scheme were systematic and inherent because of the combination of an inaccessible application process and the absence of an economic business model sufficient to encourage lawyers to help litigants in person. The fact that many solicitors worked pro bono to assist people in obtaining the funding did not rescue the scheme from inherent unlawfulness (paras 75, 78, 83-84).

R. (ON THE APPLICATION OF S) v DIRECTOR OF LEGAL AID CASEWORK; DIRECTOR OF LEGAL CASEWORK v IS *sub nom.* IS v DIRECTOR OF LEGAL AID CASEWORK, [2016] EWCA Civ 464, [2016] 1 W.L.R. 4733, Laws LJ, CA (Civ Div).

1409 Legal aid–False imprisonment–Claim for false imprisonment against police–Meaning of "abuse of position or powers by a public authority" in Sch.1 Pt 3 para.21(4) Legal Aid, Sentencing and Punishment of Offenders Act 2012

[Legal Aid, Sentencing and Punishment of Offenders Act 2012 (c.10) Sch.1 Pt 3 para.21]

The appellant director appealed against a decision (*R. (on the application of Sisangia) v Director of Legal Aid Casework* [2014] EWHC 3706 (Admin), [2015] 1 W.L.R. 1891, [2015] C.L.Y. 1627) concerning the interpretation of the Legal Aid, Sentencing and Punishment of Offenders Act 2012 Sch.1 Pt.3 para.21(4). The director had refused the respondent's application for legal aid funding for a false imprisonment claim she wanted to bring against the Chief Commissioner of Police for the Metropolis. In judicial review proceedings challenging that refusal, the judge held that the director had misinterpreted para.21(4). The judge stated that para.21(4) was a comprehensive definition of what was entailed in a claim for abuse of position or power by a public authority for the purposes of assessing the availability of civil legal aid funding; it was not a statement of the minimum criteria for such a claim. He also found that, for the purposes of that definition, it was only the arrest itself that had to be deliberate or dishonest, otherwise every request for civil legal aid for false imprisonment would amount to a claim for misfeasance in public office.

Held: Appeal allowed. (1) The judge was wrong in his interpretation of para.21(4). The effect of his characterisation of that paragraph as an exclusive or comprehensive definition was that any deliberate act by a public authority that caused reasonably foreseeable harm to another counted as an abuse of power. He had ignored what it was that was being defined, *Dextra Accessories Ltd v MacDonald (Inspector of Taxes)* [2005] UKHL 47, [2005] 4 All E.R. 107, [2005] C.L.Y. 4026, *Walker v Birmingham City Council* [2007] UKHL 22, [2007] 2 A.C. 262, [2007] C.L.Y. 2768 and *Chartbrook Ltd v Persimmon Homes Ltd* [2009] UKHL 38, [2009] 1 A.C. 1101, [2009] C.L.Y. 722 considered. The fact that a definition of "abuse of position or power" of universal application could not be extracted from the authorities did not mean that the term defined could be ignored. It was equally possible, indeed probable, that Parliament's intention was that it should be left to the courts to develop what the phrase meant. The natural meaning of the term defined might be its meaning in ordinary discourse, or its meaning as a legal concept. The fact that it could not be given a hard-edged definition did not mean that the concept itself was meaningless, *R. v Hillingdon LBC Ex p. Puhlhofer* [1986] A.C. 484, [1986] C.L.Y. 1619, *R. v Secretary of State for Education and Employment Ex p. Begbie* [2000] 1 W.L.R. 1115, [1999] C.L.Y. 1704 and *R. (on the application of Lumba) v Secretary of State for the Home Department* [2011] UKSC 12, [2012] 1 A.C. 245, [2011] C.L.Y. 1727 considered. The judge's interpretation gave no weight at all to the meaning of the phrase "abuse of position or power". Abuse of position or power was a recognised juridicial concept which, like many other public law concepts, was both flexible and context-specific. It should, therefore, be given meaning in para.21(4). That conclusion was supported by the language in which para.21(4) was phrased. There were different kinds of definition, and an exclusionary definition was not the same as a comprehensive definition (see paras 10-23 of judgment). (2) To make an arrest knowing that there was no power to do so would amount to a claim for misfeasance in public office. However, it was not so clear that making an arrest in the honest belief that there was the power to do so, where that belief was not founded on reasonable grounds, would amount to the offence. The causes of action that could potentially amount to abuse of position or power included both intentional and unintentional torts. However, there was no support for a distributive interpretation of the words in para.21(4). Since an intentional tort was by definition unlawful, the selection of unlawfulness as the core content of the phrase "abuse of power" added nothing. Even in the case of the intentional torts, unless the act complained of was deliberate, there was no tort at all; the requirement in para.21(4) that the act in question be deliberate added nothing in the case of an intentional tort. Having accepted that para.21(4) was not an exhaustive or comprehensive definition, it was forensic sleight of hand to say that if an act amounting to an intentional tort was deliberate, it amounted, without more, to abuse of power. Although the various judicial descriptions of "abuse of power" all had a common theme of unlawfulness, that merely meant that unlawfulness was a necessary condition; it did not mean that unlawfulness was a sufficient condition to amount to "abuse of power". Confining the adjective "deliberate" to intentional torts and requiring "dishonest" to cover everything else produced very odd results. "Abuse of power" was a flexible and fact-specific concept which might be incapable of definition. However, something more than an intentional tort was necessary before the impugned act became an "abuse of power", even if it could not be said what that "something more" was (paras 25-28, 30).

R. (ON THE APPLICATION OF SISANGIA) v DIRECTOR OF LEGAL AID CASEWORK *sub nom.* DIRECTOR OF LEGAL AID CASEWORK v R. (ON THE APPLICATION OF SISANGIA), [2016] EWCA Civ 24, [2016] 1 W.L.R. 1373, Elias LJ, CA (Civ Div).

1410 Legal aid–Statutory charge–Waiver of statutory charge at beginning or during case

[Access to Justice Act 1999 (c.22) s.10(7); European Convention on Human Rights 1950 art.5, art.5(4), art.5(5); Human Rights Act 1998 (c.42); Civil Legal Aid (Costs) Regulations 2013 (SI 2013/611) reg.9]

The claimant prisoner applied for judicial review of the defendant Legal Aid Agency's refusal to waive a statutory charge imposed pursuant to the Access to Justice Act 1999 s.10(7). The claimant had been awarded £10,000 in damages by the Court of Appeal as a result of being unlawfully detained contrary to the ECHR art.5(4). The Supreme Court allowed the parole board's appeal against that decision, dismissed the claimant's cross-appeal against the award and his human rights claim, and reduced the award to £6,500. A dispute as to costs in the Supreme Court followed. The claimant asserted that a costs order should be made in his favour as failure to do so or making no order for costs would effectively wipe out his award of damages. The Supreme made a costs order in the parole board's favour. The claimant had received legal aid for his Supreme Court appeal and wrote to the agency seeking waiver of the statutory charge so that his award of damages would remain intact. It declined to waive the charge under the Community Legal Services (Financial) Regulations 2000 reg.47. The claimant submitted that (1) the agency's decision had been based on a flawed interpretation of reg.47 by assuming that waiver should come at the beginning of a case instead of the end; (2) as a result, the agency's decision was contrary to the Human Rights Act 1998 and would leave him without redress for the violation of his art.5 rights.

Held: Claim dismissed. (1) Statutory charges had been a feature of the legal aid scheme since it had begun. The Statutory Charge Manual described the features of the statutory charge. Regulation 44 listed the exemptions from a statutory charge, and reg.46 permitted suppliers to waive a statutory charge where enforcement would cause hardship to a client. Regulation 47, which was badly drafted, was the only other example which permitted waiver. Regulation 47(3) enabled the Legal Services Commission to waive a statutory charge when a case was over, and if a client won there would be no statutory charge. The question was whether in terms of the temporal assessment, events listed in reg.47(2) occurred at the end of the case or at the beginning or during. A clear decision as to whether waiving the statutory charge was in the wider public interest and other cases were to be funded in a different way had to be made at either the start of or during a case. That was the only possible interpretation of reg.47(2), which was made clear by the Civil Legal Aid (Costs) Regulations 2013 reg.9. (2) To conclude that the construction of reg.47 favoured by the instant court violated the claimant's human rights was contrary to the necessary inference that could be drawn from the Supreme Court's order. Further if that particular construction did violate the claimant's human rights and his damages were to be subject to a statutory charge, reg.44 of the 2000 Regulations would list it as an exemption, but it did not. Secondly, the Strasbourg jurisprudence had never criticised the UK costs regime. Thirdly, the principle of the costs regime was that an award of costs would never be for the full amount incurred. Fourthly part 36 offers had not been criticised by Strasbourg, neither had issue-based costs orders. Damages awarded under art.5(5) were very serious, and damages, although modest, should reflect the fact that it was only in art.5(5) that compensation was mentioned. However, an award of damages under the Convention was not in a class apart from other types of damages awarded. Damages under the Convention should not be immunised in a way that other awards of damages would not be; they attracted no special status and were to be treated the same as other awards of damage.

R. (ON THE APPLICATION OF FAULKNER) v DIRECTOR OF LEGAL AID CASEWORK, [2016] EWHC 717 (Admin), [2016] 4 W.L.R. 178, Mostyn J, QBD (Admin).

1411 Legal Ombudsman–Claims management–Complaints

THE LEGAL SERVICES ACT 2007 (CLAIMS MANAGEMENT COMPLAINTS) (FEES) (AMENDMENT) REGULATIONS 2016, SI 2016/92; made under the Legal Services Act 2007 s.174A(3)(5), s.204(3). In force: 29 January 2016.

These Regulations amend the Legal Services Act 2007 (Claims Management Complaints) (Fees) Regulations 2014. The Compensation Act 2006 provides for the designation of a Regulator for regulated claims management services. Where no one is designated as the Regulator and the Secretary of State carries out the function by virtue of s.5(9) of the 2006 Act, the Lord Chancellor may charge periodic fees on those providing regulated claim management services to recover the expenditure incurred by the Lord Chancellor in respect of the Office for Legal Complaints. These Regulations amend the levels of fees set by the 2014 Regulations, for the purposes of the year beginning with 1 April 2016 and subsequent years. This is to ensure that the fees meet the expenditure incurred by the Lord Chancellor.

1412 Legal services–Civil legal aid–Transitional provisions

THE CIVIL LEGAL AID (PROCEDURE) (AMENDMENT) (NO.2) REGULATIONS 2016, SI 2016/561; made under the Legal Aid, Sentencing and Punishment of Offenders Act 2012 s.12(2) , s.41(1)(b)(3)(c). In force: 30 May 2016.

These Regulations amend the Civil Legal Aid (Procedure) Regulations 2012, which make provision about the making and withdrawal of determinations that an individual qualifies for civil legal services under ss.9 and 10 of the Legal Aid, Sentencing and Punishment of Offenders Act 2012. Reg.2(3) of this instrument inserts a new reg.61A (determinations) into Pt 7 (family mediation), providing that a determination that a person qualifies for particular civil legal services relating to family mediation may be backdated where certain criteria apply. Reg.3 of this instrument provides that the amendments made by reg.2(3) do not apply to determinations that an individual qualifies for civil legal services which were provided to that individual on or before 30 May 2016.

LEGAL METHODOLOGY

1413 Precedent–Judicial Committee of the Privy Council–Precedent value of decisions of Judicial Committee of the Privy Council

The court determined issues regarding the precedent value to be given by the courts of England and Wales to decisions of the Judicial Committee of the Privy Council and the approach the Privy Council should take towards decisions of the domestic courts. The judge in the instant case had had to consider a House of Lords decision whose reasoning would lead her to strike out the claim, but also a more recent Privy Council decision whose reasoning would lead her to a different conclusion. She held (*Willers v Gubay* [2015] EWHC 1315 (Ch)) that she was bound by the House of Lords decision and therefore could not follow the Privy Council case. She accepted that she could take a different course if it was a "foregone conclusion" that the Supreme Court would follow the Privy Council decision, but that that was not a foregone conclusion. She therefore struck out the claim.

Held: Judgment accordingly. The Privy Council was not a court of any part of the UK. However, it almost always applied the common law, and either all or four of the five Privy Counsellors sitting on the appeal would almost always be Supreme Court justices. Accordingly, Privy Council decisions could not be binding on any judge of England and Wales and could not override any decision of a court of England and Wales which would otherwise represent a precedent which was binding on that judge. However, subject to that point, any Privy Council decision, at least on a common law issue, should normally be regarded by any judge of England and Wales as being of great weight and persuasive value. The Privy Council should regard itself as bound by any House of Lords or Supreme Court decision, at least when applying the law of England and Wales (see paras 10-12 of judgment). The difficult question was whether the rule that a court should not follow a Privy Council decision if it was inconsistent with a binding decision was an absolute rule, or whether it was subject to the qualification that it could be disapplied where a first instance judge or the Court of Appeal considered that it was a foregone conclusion that the view taken by the Privy Council would be accepted by the higher court. It was more satisfactory that the rule should be absolute, *Doughty v Turner Manufacturing Co* [1964] 1 Q.B. 518, [1964] C.L.Y. 2499 and *R. v James (Leslie)* [2006] EWCA Crim 14, [2006] Q.B. 588, [2006] C.L.Y. 838 considered. The doctrine of precedence should be clear in its terms and simple in its application. There could be much argument as to whether it was a foregone conclusion that the Supreme Court would follow a particular Privy Council decision. There should be no more delay or cost in having a strict and clear rule rather than a more flexible rule (paras 17-18). That rule was subject to one important qualification. There would be appeals where the Privy Council decided that an earlier House of Lords, Supreme Court or Court of Appeal decision was wrong. It would be unfortunate in practical terms if the Privy Council could never effectively decide that the courts of England and Wales should follow its decision rather than the earlier decision. The Privy Council's Practice Direction 3.1.3 and Practice Direction 4.2.2 required an appellant to say whether an appeal would invite the Privy Council to depart from a House of Lords or Supreme Court decision. That should be expanded to apply to Court of Appeal decisions. In cases where the Practice Directions applied, the registrar of the Privy Council should draw the attention of its President to the fact that there might be such an invitation. The President could take that into account when deciding on the constitution of the panel to hear the appeal and, provided that the point was one of English law, the panel members could not only decide that the earlier decision was wrong but could also expressly direct that domestic courts should treat its decision as representing the law of England and Wales, *Tai Hing Cotton Mill Ltd v Liu Chong Hing Bank Ltd (No.1)* [1986] A.C. 80, [1985] C.L.Y. 150 considered (paras 19-21). The traditional view in Scotland was that, subject to possible exceptions, House of Lords judgments in English appeals were at most highly persuasive; it was impossible to see how Privy Council decisions on English law could have greater authority than that. It was likely that precisely the same principles would apply in Northern Ireland as in England and Wales given that the common law applied in the same way (para.22).

WILLERS v JOYCE *sub nom.* WIILLERS v GUBAY, [2016] UKSC 44, [2016] 3 W.L.R. 534, Lord Neuberger PSC, SC.

LEGAL PROFESSION

1414 **Barristers–Costs–Barrister's costs in defending disciplinary proceedings–Barrister acting for herself**

[Civil Procedure Rules 1998 r.48.6, r.48.6(4)(a); Senior Courts Act 1981 (c.54) s.31(5), s.31(5A)]

A barrister appealed against a decision (*R. (on the application of Bar Standards Board) v Disciplinary Tribunal of the Council of the Inns of Court* [2014] EWHC 1570 (Admin), [2015] 1 W.L.R. 2778, [2015] C.L.Y. 1651) that the respondent Bar Standards Board should pay her costs of successfully defending disciplinary proceedings which it had brought against her at a rate of £60 per hour. The barrister was not in practice but had represented herself in the disciplinary proceedings. The Disciplinary Tribunal of the Council of the Inns of Court dismissed the charges against her and appointed an assessor to determine the costs which the board should pay to her. The assessor considered that although the CPR did not apply, they were persuasive as to how he should exercise his discretion. He considered that he was bound by the decision in *Miller v Bar Standards Board* that a barrister acting in person was entitled to be remunerated for such legal work as if she were acting in a professional legal capacity for another and was entitled to costs representing the expenditure of his own time and skill under CPR r.48.6(4)(a). He therefore awarded the barrister her costs at £120 per hour. The Divisional Court quashed that decision, concluding that Miller had been wrongly decided but that, in any event, the CPR did not apply and were not even persuasive authority in cases before the tribunal. It held that the tribunal should have awarded such costs as it thought fit. On that basis, it assessed her costs, deeming £60 per hour to be reasonable. The barrister submitted that (1) the decision in *Miller* was correct and the assessor had not been wrong to follow it; (2) even if any part of the assessor's reasoning was wrong, his decision as to the hourly rate should not have been set aside because it was one that had been open to him, in accordance with *Jafri v Lincoln College* [2014] EWCA Civ 449, [2015] Q.B. 781, [2014] C.L.Y. 1061; (3) the court had no jurisdiction to assess the hourly rate itself and had been bound to remit the matter to the tribunal under the Senior Courts Act 1981 s.31(5) and s.31(5A).

Held: Appeal allowed in part. (1) CPR r.48.6 did not apply to bar disciplinary proceedings. The assessor had therefore been wrong to find that he was bound by the decision in Miller and had erred in failing to exercise the independent discretion conferred upon him by the Bar's Disciplinary Tribunal Regulations 2009 reg.31. Because the CPR did not apply, the best guidance for the tribunal in assessing costs remained the common law. The court had therefore been entirely correct to conclude that the barrister was entitled to claim the costs represented by the expenditure of her professional skill on that basis, *London Scottish Benefit Society v Chorley* (1884) 13 Q.B.D. 872 applied, *Miller* disapproved (see paras 19, 21 of judgment). (2) The judgment in *Jafri* did not support the argument that the court would conclude that if the assessor had exercised his own discretion he would necessarily have reached the same conclusion as to the proper rate of charge for the barrister's work, *Jafri* considered (paras 22-23). (3) A problem arose in the instant case because the court had reached its own determination of the rate of £60 per hour by the express agreement of the parties at the hearing, with the barrister at that point being represented by leading counsel. However, the effect of s.31 of the Act was that it had not been open to the court to fix a new hourly rate itself, even by agreement. It had not had the material to conclude that there would have been only one decision that the tribunal would have reached. Section 31 required that the matter had to be remitted to the tribunal. The appeal would be allowed to the limited extent of ordering that the assessment of costs should be remitted to the tribunal to make its own determination as to the appropriate hourly rate. It should do so in accordance with its own rules, namely by awarding such costs as it thought fit in accordance with reg.31 (paras 25, 27-29, 36).

R. (ON THE APPLICATION OF BAR STANDARDS BOARD) v DISCIPLINARY TRIBUNAL OF THE COUNCIL OF THE INNS OF COURT, [2016] EWCA Civ 478, [2016] 1 W.L.R. 4506, McCombe LJ, CA (Civ Div).

1415 Solicitors–Breach of undertaking–Compromise of costs claim–Damages for loss of chance

[Conditional Fee Agreements Regulations 2000 (SI 2000/692); Courts and Legal Services Act 1990 (c.41) s.58]

The court had to determine a preliminary issue in the course of a firm of solicitors' claim against one of its former partners for an alleged breach of undertaking. The partner had left the firm in 2009 to set up his own practice. The firm transferred certain clients to him and he undertook to preserve a lien over the client files so that the firm could recover fees under their original retainers. He was also obliged to inform the firm of any significant developments in those cases. The instant claim concerned a personal injury client who had instructed the firm in 2003 under a conditional fee agreement and whose file was transferred to the partner. In January 2011, the client's claim against his employer was compromised. The employer was to pay the client's costs, subject to a detailed assessment if they could not be agreed. The partner served a bill for some £84,000, which included both his and the firm's costs. The employer's solicitors made two offers, which the partner rejected. The solicitors also challenged the validity of the firm's conditional fee agreement, questioning whether it complied with the Conditional Fee Agreements Regulations 2000. The partner informed the firm of the rejected offers but did not mention the challenge to the agreement's validity. In November 2011 at a hearing to assess costs, the agreement was ruled unenforceable for non-compliance with reg.4 and all the firm's profit costs were disallowed. The firm believed that if the partner had complied with the undertaking and informed them of the validity challenge, they could have reached a compromise of the costs claim without any need for a validity determination. The issue was whether the firm could seek to recover damages for the loss of a chance to receive a sum for its costs. The partner argued that there had been no such loss as the non-compliant conditional fee agreement was unlawful for being contrary to public policy, or at least unenforceable, and any compromise of the costs claim would have been invalid.

Held: Preliminary issue determined in favour of claimant. The Courts and Legal Services Act 1990 s.58 stated that conditional fee arrangements which did not comply with the Regulations were unenforceable. However, in terms of whether the firm's agreement was also illegal for being contrary to public policy, it was observed in *Awwad v Geraghty & Co* [2001] Q.B. 570, [2000] C.L.Y. 4002 that modern perception was changing as to what kinds of lawyers' fee arrangements were acceptable, *Awwad* considered. Such perception might well have changed in the years since that judgment. Given that illegality would depend on public policy, in the absence of any clear evidence on the issue at the material time, it could not be determined whether in general conditional fee agreements in 2003 were contrary to public policy and only those that complied with the Regulations were lawful. As to whether a compromise of the costs claim would have been valid and enforceable, that was assessed at the date it would or could have been entered into had the partner complied with the undertaking. At that point there had been an issue between the client and employer as to the validity of the conditional fee agreement. On the basis that the partner, as a solicitor and officer of the court, had negotiated with the employer's solicitors in good faith and had a genuine belief that it was reasonably arguable that the agreement was valid, a compromise of the costs claim would have been enforceable, *Binder v Alachouzos* [1972] 2 Q.B. 151, [1972] C.L.Y. 2194 applied. Further, the firm's cause of action was founded in contract and accrued when the breach of the undertaking took place. That was before the ruling on the agreement. Therefore, an enforceable compromise could have been reached irrespective of whether at a later stage the conditional fee agreement was found to be unenforceable or illegal. If the partner had performed his obligation under the undertaking there might have been no determination of the enforceability of the agreement. Accordingly, whether the failure to comply with reg.4 rendered the agreement unenforceable or also illegal did not affect the claim for breach of contract. The firm was permitted to seek to recover damages for their loss of chance (see paras 26, 29-30, 32-33, 35 of judgment).

FPH LAW v BROWN (T/A INTEGRUM LAW), [2016] EWHC 1681 (QB), [2016] 5 Costs L.O. 733, Slade J, QBD.

1416 Solicitors–Conditional fee agreements–Power of Legal Ombudsman to direct repayment of contingency fee

[Legal Services Act 2007 (c.29) s.113, s.12, s.137]

A solicitor applied for judicial review of a decision by the Legal Ombudsman that he should refund a sum of money to a former client whom it was held had been overcharged under a contingency fee agreement. The client sought advice from the solicitor in connection with the administration of an intestate estate of which she was one of three beneficiaries. A contingency fee arrangement was discussed. The solicitor gave notice of the client's beneficial interest in a property comprising the chief asset of the estate to the firm acting in the sale and obtained from that firm an undertaking to hold the proceeds pending determination of her claim. The client attended the solicitor's offices on the day before completion of the sale and signed a contingency fee agreement. According to the solicitor, she had been fully advised on its terms prior to signing. The agreement provided for the client to pay to the solicitor 20% of any compensation and damages that she received in the event that she was successful. The solicitor received the client's share of the sale proceeds and deducted £37,806.88, being the contingency fee plus VAT and disbursements. The client complained that she had been given insufficient advice about the terms and consequences of the contingency fee agreement. The matter came before the Ombudsman, who concluded that the client had been poorly advised and that the manner of funding the case had not been in her best interests given that no litigation had arisen and that the solicitor had not undertaken any significant amount of work on her behalf. Accordingly, he was ordered to refund the sum of £34,000 which was held to have been overcharged. The solicitor submitted that (1) the Ombudsman lacked jurisdiction to direct the repayment; (2) alternatively, the Ombudsman's decision was not founded upon the quality of the advice provided to the client, as he claimed, but rather on the fairness of the contingency fee agreement; (3) the decision to direct repayment was irrational or unreasonable.

Held: Application refused. (1) By the Legal Services Act 2007 s.113, the Ombudsman was entitled to resolve disputes between a solicitor and his client which related to an act or omission of the solicitor in carrying on an activity. The word "activity" had to encompass, at the very least, reserved legal activity and legal activity as defined in s.12. In the absence of any authority to the contrary, the complaints made to the Ombudsman in the instant case constituted complaints relating to acts or omissions in carrying on legal activity on the solicitor's part and the statutory words entitled the Ombudsman to determine that complaint, *Layard Horsfall Ltd v Legal Ombudsman* [2013] EWHC 4137 (QB), [2014] 2 Costs L.O. 277, [2014] C.L.Y. 2054 applied. Moreover, the complaints related to services within r.2.8 of the Scheme Rules published by the Office for Legal Complaints on 1 February 2013, which did not seek to proscribe in any way the meaning to be given to legal activity. The statutory words were clear and unambiguous, and sufficiently widely drawn to confer upon the Ombudsman the power to entertain complaints about the circumstances in which a client came to enter into a contract for services with his or her solicitor and the advice received in relation to that contract as to its terms and consequences (see paras 31-32, 36-37 of judgment). (2) Although the Ombudsman had expressed the view that the contingency fee agreement was unfair or inappropriate, that view was based upon an assessment of the factual circumstances surrounding the making of the agreement and the conclusions he had reached about the adequacy of the advice given to the client. Having determined that the complaint of poor legal advice was justified, he was entitled to reach a view about the fairness and reasonableness of the effect of the contingency fee agreement in determining the complaint under s.137 of the 2007 Act (paras 39-40). (3) The Ombudsman had a wide-ranging discretion to determine complaints and a court would usually be circumspect before labelling a decision of his unreasonable or irrational. On the basis of the solicitor's attendance notes, the advice tendered to the client as to the terms and effects of the contingency fee agreement was at the very least inadequate. Moreover, it was signed at a time when the undertaking had been given and the solicitor knew that the client had an indefeasible right to a share in the sale proceeds. Accordingly, the prospect of litigation was very small by that point. It was open to the Ombudsman to conclude that the client had not been informed of that undertaking and that pressure had been brought to bear on her to enter into the contingency fee agreement. It was also clearly open to him to conclude that the amount of work conducted by the solicitor on the client's behalf was not substantial (paras 42, 44, 46).

EJIOFOR (T/A MITCHELL & CO SOLICITORS) v LEGAL OMBUDSMAN, [2016] EWHC 1933 (Admin), [2016] 4 Costs L.R. 759, Wynn Williams J, QBD (Admin).

1417 Solicitors–Fees–Fairness and reasonableness of fee agreement

[Solicitors Act 1974 (c.47) s.57, s.57(5)]

The claimant solicitors (B) claimed for professional fees under an agreement entered into with the defendant hotel proprietor (T) in respect of non-contentious business. T had previously instructed a specialist adviser to seek compensation on his behalf from a bank under the Financial Conduct Authority redress scheme in relation to an allegedly mis-sold product. His complaint was unsuccessful. T then engaged B to pursue his case. B assessed the prospects of success at less than 50%, given that the redress scheme had no formal appeal process, and that any claim in contract or tort was statute barred. The parties entered into a contingency fee agreement which entitled B to 50% of any compensation recovered. When B informed the bank that they were instructed on behalf of T in relation to the claim, the bank replied that it was already in the process of reconsidering T's case. A month later, the bank offered T compensation of over £380,000. B considered that the offer was insufficient, and pursued the matter further. The bank eventually offered more than £821,000. B claimed fees of over £400,000. It was T's case that B should only be entitled to 50% of the increase on the bank's first offer, since the first offer was the result of the work done by his previous adviser, and was nothing to do with B. The issues were (1) whether B were entitled to 50% of the sum recovered as compensation, irrespective of whether the bank's first offer resulted from their efforts; (2) whether T was induced to enter into the agreement by an actionable misrepresentation as to the strength of his claim against the bank, in relation to advice that the limitation period for any claim had expired, and that the bank's initial decision as to compensation was, for practical purposes, final; (3) whether the terms of the agreement were unfair or unreasonable, such that the court should exercise its power under the Solicitors Act 1974 s.57(5) to set the agreement aside or reduce the fees payable.

Held: Judgment for claimant. (1) The relevant provisions of the agreement made it very clear that the contingency on which B's fee became payable was the objective fact of an offer of compensation during the currency of the agreement, however that offer came about. The agreement, properly construed, did not require that any offer of compensation by the bank need be obtained through B's efforts. There was no basis for implying a term into the agreement to that effect in order to give the agreement business efficacy or to reflect what was said to be the true intention of the parties, *Investors Compensation Scheme Ltd v West Bromwich Building Society (No.1)* [1998] 1 W.L.R. 896, [1997] C.L.Y. 2537 considered (see paras 77-84 of judgment). (2) T was advised that it would be difficult to take the case to court, but not necessarily impossible. The representations made to T were statements of B's opinion as to the legal difficulties presented by the likely expiry of the limitation period. It was an opinion honestly and reasonably held, and was probably correct. In relation to the finality of the bank's initial decision on compensation, there was nothing false or inaccurate in the statement B made to T. It was quite correct that there was no formal appeal procedure under the redress scheme. In any event, it was merely an expression of B's opinion honestly and reasonably held. Had there been any misrepresentations of fact, T would have faced insurmountable difficulties in establishing that he relied upon the statements in entering into the agreement, and insurmountable difficulties in establishing what loss he suffered in consequence (paras 124-130). (3) The issues of fairness and reasonableness had to be considered separately. Fairness related principally to the manner in which the agreement came to be made, whereas reasonableness related principally to the terms of the agreement, *Stuart Ex p. Cathcart, Re* [1893] 2 Q.B. 201 applied. T was a very experienced businessman who knew exactly what he was agreeing to. He was given an accurate assessment of the prospects of success. He was unwilling to pay anything for B's services unless and until compensation was received from the bank. It was an important factor that T was the one who had suggested the figure of 50%. He had deliberately sought to give B an appetite for the case, as he acknowledged in his oral evidence. T had suggested that there was a conflict of interest for B in advising him to enter into a fee agreement which was so strongly to their own advantage. However, it could be said of any contingency fee agreement, where the solicitors' remuneration was proportionate to the amount of recovery, that there was a conflict between the solicitors' wanting to obtain as their fee the largest possible percentage of the compensation recovered and the client's interest in achieving the reverse. There was on the face of it an obvious disquiet in permitting solicitors to recover fees of some £400,000 for work which might otherwise have been billed, on the basis of hourly rates, at only £50,000. However, on a proper analysis, that ignored the commercial realities which faced the parties when the agreement was made. In truth the agreement represented a speculative joint venture in which B were taking all the risk and T was exposed to no risk. It was clear that the agreement was not unfair or unreasonable (paras 157-171).

BOLT BURDON SOLICITORS v TARIQ, [2016] EWHC 811 (QB), [2016] 2 Costs L.R. 359, Spencer J, QBD.

1418 Solicitors–Remuneration–Claim by solicitors for professional fees–Whether contractual interest constituted "additional amount" under r.36.17(4)(d) CPR

[Civil Procedure Rules 1998 Pt 36, r.36.17; Senior Courts Act 1981 (c.54) s.35A]

In the absence of complete agreement between the parties, the court was required to deal with three outstanding issues regarding interest and costs following the order it had made in a claim by the claimant firm of solicitors for professional fees. The defendants had claimed compensation from a bank but had been unsuccessful and had instructed the firm to pursue their claim. The parties had agreed that the firm should receive a contingency fee of 50% of any compensation recovered. The bank told the firm that it had been in the process of re-considering the defendants' claim and offered a sum as compensation. The firm negotiated a higher sum and claimed fees on the contractual interest that had been awarded, as well as on the principal sum. The defendants objected. The firm made two offers under CPR Pt 36. The judgment against the defendants was at least as advantageous as the proposals in the Part 36 offers. The main issue was whether any "additional amount" was payable within the meaning of r.36.17(4)(d) in relation to the firm's award for contractual interest. The claimant submitted that it was plainly entitled, as part of the "additional amount", to 10% of the contractual interest to which it was entitled and which had been awarded, and because it was contractual interest it was part of the "sum awarded to the claimant by the court".

Held: Judgment for claimant. (1) The "additional amount" was, in effect, a further head of damages intended to be a reward of real value where a claimant made a successful Part 36 offer (see para.10 of judgment). The wording of r.36.17(4)(d) was clear. The additional amount was to be calculated by applying the prescribed percentage "to an amount which is ... the sum awarded to the claimant by the court". Whatever the court might do in its discretion, for example pursuant to the Senior Courts Act 1981 s.35A, in the instant case it had awarded interest at 8% as part of the sum to which the claimant was entitled contractually, and which the notes in the *White Book*, 2016 edn (London: Sweet & Maxwell, 2016) at 7.0.10 stated was part of the sum awarded "as a specific sum". The words "excluding interest" were absent, although they appeared in sub-paragraph(a) in relation to special sanctions. As a matter of statutory interpretation, the use of "excluding interest" in one part of a rule and not in another was a strong indication that a difference was intended (paras 18-19). Entitlement to an additional amount was qualified under r.36.17(4) by the words "unless ... [the court] considers it unjust to do so". Under r.36.17.(5) the court had to take into account any other relief to which a claimant was entitled where those provisions were engaged. It had to consider all the circumstances of the case. The contractual entitlement of 8% interest had become part of the overall award, and there had been no claim for enhanced interest under sub-para.4(a). The "additional amount" had clearly been designed as a penal sanction to mark a defendant's failure to accept a Part 36 offer when they should have done and to reward a claimant for a commendable attempt to settle the case. The composition of the overall sum was immaterial. Therefore, in addition to the sums payable under para.2 of the interim order, the defendants had to pay the claimant the sum claimed as part of the "additional amount" to which it was entitled under r.36.17(a)(d) (paras 20-23).

BOLT BURDON SOLICITORS v TARIQ, [2016] EWHC 1507 (QB), [2016] 4 W.L.R. 112, Spencer J, QBD.

1419 Solicitors–Retainers–Provisions of retainer–Whether firm entitled to render final "statute bills" when work still in progress

[Solicitors Act 1974 (c.47) s.70, s.70(4)]

The defendant solicitors firm appealed against a preliminary determination granted in favour of the claimant client. The client had instructed the firm in relation to three matters. The retainer provided at cl. 6.1 that the firm would send a bill for its "charges and expenses at the end of each month" while the work was in progress, and that it would send the client "a final bill after completion of the work". The firm rendered various invoices to the client while the work was in progress, and then in October 2013 sent a letter saying that no further sums were due. The letter also stated if the client did not apply under the Solicitors Act 1974 s.70 for an assessment of the invoices, it would issue proceedings for the recovery of outstanding sums due from the client. The client subsequently applied for an assessment under s.70. The firm's case was that the client's application in respect of some of the invoices was time-barred by virtue of s.70(4). The master held that the provisions of the retainer were ambiguous and had to be interpreted in the client's favour. He therefore concluded that the relevant invoices had not, at the time of payment, constituted "statute bills", and accordingly the time bar under s.70(4) had not bitten. He held that the retainer did not entitle the firm to render statute bills while work was in progress. The firm argued that the master should have concluded that it was contractually entitled to render statute bills while work was in progress. Alternatively, it contended that if the master was right to hold that the "time bar" invoices were not statute bills at the time of payment, then none of the invoices had constituted statute bills with the result that the instant proceedings had been brought prematurely.

Held: Appeal allowed. (1) There was no express statement in the retainer that each interim bill would be a final bill for the period that it covered. To an objective reader without special knowledge of the Act, the only indication in the retainer that any bill was to be final was at cl.6.1, which said that the firm would send the client "a final bill after completion of the work". There was a substantial ambiguity in the retainer. It did not tell the client that the bills "at the end of each month" would be final as to work and expenses during the period covered by the bill (see paras 23-24, 27 of judgment). (2) The crucial issue was whether the October 2013 letter could have caused any change in status of any of the bills. There was no sound basis for construing the letter as having enabled the client to seek assessment immediately upon its receipt. The letter had to be construed in the context of the retainer, which provided at cl.6.1 for a final bill after the work had been completed, but also for interim bills which were not statute bills. Nothing in the letter said that if the interim bills were not statute bills, then the letter was intended to change their status. Rather, it said that there was no proposal to invoice for further amounts, and that in the absence of an application for assessment, proceedings for the amounts already invoiced would be brought. In those circumstances, the mere fact that the letter had informed the client of such matters did not change the nature of the earlier bills. It followed that since there had been no statute bills, the client's application for assessment had been premature (paras 36, 38-39).

VLAMAKI v SOOKIAS & SOOKIAS (A FIRM), [2015] EWHC 3334 (QB), [2015] 6 Costs L.O. 827, Walker J, QBD.

1420 Solicitors' powers and duties–Duty to the court–Alleged failure to pursue immigration proceedings–Undermining of immigration system

The tribunal was required to determine whether a firm of solicitors had engaged in a course of conduct designed to undermine the immigration system which amounted to a persistent abuse of process of the court. The firm had acted on behalf of immigrants and asylum seekers. The five cases before the tribunal showed a pattern whereby without-notice injunctions to restrain imminent removal had been sought but, when granted, were not pursued by the service of proceedings. The pattern suggested a strategy of permitting a case to fade away with the consequence that the failed asylum seeker or immigrant remained in the UK. The firm had also failed to respond to requests from court officials. In each of the five cases, the applications for permission to apply for judicial review were dismissed as without merit and an abuse of process. The firm, its managing director and the relevant caseworkers were required to attend the tribunal to address the concerns. At the hearing, one of the partners failed to attend as he was ill and his representative was unable to offer his assistance as he had not reviewed the files in time.

Held: Judgment accordingly. Solicitors acting on behalf of asylum seekers had to be acutely aware of the need for a thorough understanding of the law, fully appreciating that pursuing litigation without arguable grounds was potentially unprofessional, *R. (on the application of Akram) v Secretary of State for the Home Department* [2015] EWHC 1359 (Admin), [2015] A.C.D. 113 applied. It seemed that the firm had been prepared to advance tenuous or hopeless grounds, simply to provide a platform for the interim relief application which followed. The paramount duty of all legal representatives in judicial review proceedings was to the court and that duty took precedence over the duty owed to clients. Legal representatives applying on a without-notice basis had to comply with the duty of candour but the firm had not placed the full facts before the judges who were hearing the applications for interim relief. All judges hearing such applications should take steps to verify whether there had been delay and to ensure that representatives had put as full a set of facts as they could before the tribunal. Once interim relief had been granted, a legal representative had to serve and pursue the proceedings. It was a serious breach of the professional conduct rules to obtain the relief and then fail to pursue the substantive claim for judicial review. The facts suggested a deliberate disregard for the professional duties that all legal representatives owed to the court. No one from the firm who was able to assist the tribunal had attended the hearing. No formal findings were made against the firm or its solicitors but there were serious concerns that the conduct of its legal representatives had fallen below the minimum standard required in relation to their duty to the court and the tribunal. It was appropriate to refer the firm to the Solicitors Regulation Authority for a fuller investigation (see paras 2-4, 41, 43-44, 46-51 of judgment).

SANDBROOK SOLICITORS, RE, [2015] EWHC 2473 (Admin), [2016] P.N.L.R. 2, Green J, UT (IAC).

1421 Solicitors' powers and duties–Legal advice–Divorcee instructing solicitors after agreeing financial settlement with husband. Solicitors instructed to draw up consent order reflecting agreed terms–Extent of solicitor's duty to advise on agreed terms

The appellant (M) appealed against the dismissal of her claim for negligence against the respondent solicitor (L). M and her husband had divorced and had negotiated a financial settlement. M consulted solicitors and was warned that the husband's offer did not seem satisfactory. She was advised of alternatives, including negotiation, mediation and litigation with full disclosure. However, M decided to adhere to the agreed settlement. She changed solicitors and instructed L to put the agreement into a form that the court could approve. She subsequently regretted signing the consent order and claimed damages for professional negligence on the basis that L had failed to advise or warn her against entering into the agreement. The district judge dismissed the claim on the basis that the retainer was limited and L had been under no duty to provide such further advice. The issue was the extent of the duty to advise in circumstances where the parties had reached agreement and solicitors were being asked to put that agreement into proper form for court approval.

Held: Appeal dismissed. (1) The extent of a solicitor's duty to their client was determined by the retainer. The starting point in every case was to ascertain what the client had engaged the solicitor to do or to advise on. A solicitor's contractual duty was to carry out the task the client had instructed and the solicitor had agreed to undertake, *Midland Bank Trust Co Ltd v Hett Stubbs & Kemp* [1979] Ch. 384, [1978] C.L.Y. 2822 applied. It was implicit in the retainer that the solicitor would proffer advice which was reasonably incidental to the work being carried out, *Credit Lyonnais SA v Russell Jones & Walker* [2002] EWHC 1310 (Ch), [2003] Lloyd's Rep. P.N. 7, [2002] C.L.Y. 3306 applied. In determining what advice was reasonably incidental, it was necessary to have regard to all the circumstances of the case, including the client's character and experience, *Carradine Properties Ltd v DJ Freeman & Co* [1999] Lloyd's Rep. P.N. 483, [1990] C.L.Y. 3283 and *National Home Loans Corp Plc v Giffen Couch & Archer* [1998] 1 W.L.R. 207, [1997] C.L.Y. 3829 applied. In that respect, it was not possible to give definitive guidance. However, an experienced businessman would not wish to pay for being told that which he already knew; an impoverished client would not wish to pay for advice he could not afford; and an inexperienced client would expect to be warned of risks which were apparent to the solicitor but not to the client. The solicitor and client could, by agreement, limit the duties which would otherwise form part of the retainer. As a matter of good practice, the solicitor should confirm such agreement in writing. Otherwise, the court might not accept that any such restriction had been agreed, *Hurlingham Estates Ltd v Wilde & Partners* [1997] 1 Lloyd's Rep. 525, [1997] C.L.Y. 3842 considered (see paras 32-39 of judgment). (2) It would have been good practice for L to expressly confirm in correspondence the limited nature of her retainer. However, the district judge accepted that M's instructions had been limited, having heard the parties' oral evidence, and the court would not go behind that finding of fact. The provision of further advice or warning was not reasonably incidental to the work L was carrying out under the retainer. M was an intelligent woman who had qualified and practised as a chartered accountant. She had, as L knew, taken legal advice about the proposed consent order before instructing L, and had rejected L's warning about the difficulties of enforcement if the husband emigrated. M had made it plain that, despite the risks, she wished to conclude the consent order "as swiftly as possible". L was operating under a defined and limited retainer. Her task was to re-draft the consent order, so as to set out the matters agreed between husband and wife in a form likely to be approved by the court. She did not have a duty to warn M about other matters, or to investigate the question of duress (paras 40-48). (3) (Per King LJ) Legal aid had still been available to parties in financial remedy proceedings when the instant case began. However, it was no longer available, no matter the level of hardship caused or the complexity of the proceedings. Where an unrepresented divorcing couple reached an agreement, they faced the challenge of producing an order reflecting the settlement, the terms of which had to be drafted in proper form to be put before a district judge as a consent order. Such an order was a complex legal document which had to deal with all aspects of the parties' financial lives, present and future. There would be very serious consequences for both the courts and litigants in person generally if solicitors felt unable to accept instructions to act on a limited retainer basis for fear that what they anticipated to be a modest and relatively inexpensive drafting exercise, albeit complex to a lay person, might lead to a far broader duty of care being imposed on them. However, where a solicitor acted on a limited retainer, client care letters, attendance notes and formal written retainers had to be drafted with considerable care to reflect the client's specific instructions. Notwithstanding L's failure to set out with precision the limits of the retainer, she was acting under a limited retainer and had carried out the work M had instructed her to undertake (paras 65-77).

MINKIN v LANDSBERG, [2015] EWCA Civ 1152, [2016] 1 W.L.R. 1489, Jackson LJ, CA (Civ Div).

1422 Solicitors' remuneration–Dishonesty–False invoices

A solicitors' firm brought a claim against the defendant client for unpaid fees allegedly incurred in matters relating to a property he owned. The defendant had engaged the firm to act for him in a county court action and a land registry matter. It also acted for him to discharge a freezing order, and in proceedings against his tenant. The latter was allegedly authorised by an estate agent on the defendant's behalf. Payments were made to the firm from the defendant's accounts. The firm obtained a court order for an interim payment on account, in reliance on an email from the defendant's son allegedly admitting the debt. The firm claimed (1) £131,514.56 for work done on the county court action, chiefly preparation of trial bundles; (2) that the son's email contained a binding admission of debt, and the order to that effect was res judicata on the instant trial; (3) £15,171 for work done on the freezing order; (4) £21,522.50 for work done on the land registry matter; (5) £3,500 for work done on the tenant matter. The defendant counterclaimed for £65,356.89, for the payments received by the firm on his behalf.

Held: Judgment for defendant. (1) The documents contradicted the claim that the firm had prepared the trial bundles. Correspondence showed that the other party in those proceedings had done so. The purported bundles prepared by the firm were unpaginated, unindexed and inappropriate for any hearing. The responsible solicitor had seemed to admit that some costs should not have been billed to the defendant, that the costs charged were excessive and at an inappropriate rate, and that VAT should not have been charged. He gave conflicting accounts of how the bundles were delivered, unsupported by evidence. The firm had not prepared or delivered anything resembling complete trial bundles. It was impossible to say what work it had properly carried out. There were grounds to suspect that an invoice was made up or back-dated. The invoice and bill of costs were false regarding a majority of the fees charged, and the firm must have known that or at least been reckless (see paras 19-21, 25-25B, 30, 34-39 of judgment). (2) The email was not a legally binding admission of debt. It was a statement as to the arithmetical result of the firm's figures. Res judicata did not apply: it was difficult to see how an order for an interim payment on account could be binding on the judge hearing all the issues on the evidence at trial. Even if it was, there would be good reason to depart from that course, given the subsequent issues raised as to improper overcharging, and the instant court's examination of the bills' false elements (paras 42-44). (3) The firm had provided no evidence of the alleged agreement to pay the costs regarding the freezing order. If there was one, the firm ought to have had details and a record. It had shown itself capable of claiming against a client with no proper basis. It might have discharged the freezing order and acted for the defendant or as regards the property for all sorts of reasons regardless of his agreement (paras 47-48). (4) The firm had produced no time sheets or work logs to show that the work was done as claimed. It was very likely that no substantial partner or solicitor time was spent. The vast majority of the work was carried out by caseworkers with lower rates. The bill was false. The firm could not have submitted it without knowing or at least being reckless as to its falsity. It was impossible to determine how much time was properly spent on the matter. The firm's actions connoted an absence of any concern for the truth and a wholly unscrupulous approach. It had wanted to charge a total of £43,732.50 for the matter and made up many of the entries and figures to justify that charge (paras 60-63, 66-71). (5) There was no evidence to show that the defendant had authorised the agent to incur costs on his behalf. In the context of the proceedings, the firm did not deserve the benefit of any doubt as to the extent of the agent's authority. The son denied any authorisation by himself or the defendant (paras 78-79). (6) The payments seemed to have been remittances from the agent out of rent collections from the defendant's tenants. The firm had not disclosed original ledgers, source documents supporting its account spreadsheets, or client and office bank statements. Given the inconsistencies, the firm may well have received monies on the defendant's behalf for which they had not given credit. Its claims in debt were dismissed. It would not receive any further assessment of its recoverable fees and disbursements given its dishonest pursuit of the claims. As for the counterclaim, the consideration for the defendant's payments on account had wholly failed, as they were paid by mistake when he thought the firm was charging honestly for him, and the firm was entitled to be paid only when the work was finished. He was entitled to repayment. The firm's shortcomings were not the result of negligence or eccentricity: its bills were false in the most basic ways, which could only result from a dishonest plan to charge for sums it knew, or was reckless to the fact that, it was not entitled to. Its claims were wholly without merit (paras 82, 87-93, 108-113).

ALPHA ROCKS SOLICITORS v ALADE, [2016] 4 Costs L.R. 657, Murray Rosen QC, Ch D.

LEGISLATION

1423 Byelaws–Revocation–Alternative procedure

THE BYELAWS (ALTERNATIVE PROCEDURE) (ENGLAND) REGULATIONS 2016, SI 2016/165; made under the Local Government Act 1972 s.236A(1)(2)(3)(4). In force: 3 March 2016.

These Regulations prescribe classes of byelaws to which the Local Government Act 1972 s.236 does not apply and make provision about the procedure (the alternative procedure) for the making, coming into force and revocation of such byelaws. In particular the alternative procedure removes the requirement that byelaws must be confirmed by the Secretary of State.

LICENSING

1424 Premises licences–Appeal notices–Licence holder's solicitor mistakenly naming licence holder's parent company on notice–Power to amend notice

[Magistrates' Courts Act 1980 (c.43) s.123]

The licence holder (E) of a bar appealed against a decision (*Essence Bars (London) Ltd (t/a Essence) v Wimbledon Magistrates' Court* [2014] EWHC 4334 (Admin), (2015) 179 J.P. 79, [2015] C.L.Y. 209) that a district judge had rightly concluded that he did not have jurisdiction under the Magistrates' Courts Act 1980 s.123 to amend an appeal notice against the revocation of its premises licence where E's parent company (F) had been mistakenly named as the appellant. The notice of appeal had named F as the complainant, but the description of the licence holder had given the name of the bar, which was E's trading name. The appeal was adjourned while separate proceedings were initiated, also in F's name, to apply for judicial review of the interested party local authority's decision. The application was refused, with no one noticing the erroneous name of the licence holder. The appeal process before the magistrates' court resumed, and by the time it was realised that F was not the licence holder, the time limit for E to appeal against the revocation had expired. The district judge concluded that the court had no jurisdiction to hear an appeal brought by F because authorities on s.123 had established that where it was not a question of misdescription, but separate companies with separate corporate functions, the court could not correct the name. The High Court upheld that decision, stating that by naming F there had been a mistake as to identity of the appellant rather than simply its name. E argued that the district judge and the High Court had erred in concluding that they were bound by the authorities on s.123 to conclude that it was a case of mistake of identity rather than misdescription.

Held: Appeal allowed. The case law relied on by the district judge involved prosecutors proceeding against the wrong member of a corporate group when another member of the group could have been charged appropriately. They gave a narrow construction to s.123 and refused to regard the naming of a different corporate persona as a misdescription of the same person. The instant case was distinguishable from those cases on s.123 because of the reference in the appeal notice to the description of the appellant, as well as the use of a corporate name, *Marco (Croydon) Ltd (t/a A&J Bull Containers) v Metropolitan Police* [1984] R.T.R. 24, [1984] C.L.Y. 1612, *R. v Greater Manchester Justices Ex p. Aldi GmbH & Co KG* (1995) 159 J.P. 717, [1996] C.L.Y. 782 and *Sainsbury's Supermarkets Ltd v HM Courts Service (South West Region, Devon & Cornwall Area)* [2006] EWHC 1749 (Admin), (2006) 170 J.P. 690 not followed. In cases concerning corporate entities the distinction between misdecription and misidentity was particularly elusive but there was no indication that there was an automatic rule that a mistake concerning a corporate entity was a mistake of identity or that where a name and a description was used it was the former that identified the parties in question. There was no reason for not adopting the approach in civil proceedings in the context of the powers to substitute a party under CPR r.19.5 and to amend statements of case under CPR r.17.4 after the limitation period, which took a generous interpretation to the meaning of "mistake as to name", *Adelson v Associated Newspapers Ltd* [2007] EWCA Civ 701, [2008] 1 W.L.R. 585, [2007] C.L.Y. 534 applied. The boundaries of the distinction between such a mistake and a "mistake as to identity" should be determined accordingly. The position should not differ where the matter fell for decision after the end of the period for appealing provided that there was no mistake as to identity, and the other party was not in any reasonable doubt about that. The public nature of the document and the fact that the third parties and the public were affected were strong reasons for saying that it was necessary that there be no reasonable doubt by the respondent and all relevant parties as to the identity of the party whose name had been mistakenly stated on the document. The district judge had erred in his conclusion that the mere fact that there were two corporate entities involved meant that there was a mistake of identity which could not be rectified pursuant to s.123, and the High Court had failed to recognise that error. It did not follow that where a name and a description were both used in a document that it was the former that identified the party in question unless the maker of the mistake realised that the named person was not the person who satisfied the description. The district judge's decision was set aside and the matter remitted to the magistrates' court for redetermination (see paras 34, 39, 56, 64 of judgment).

ESSENCE BARS (LONDON) LTD (T/A ESSENCE) v WIMBLEDON MAGISTRATES' COURT, [2016] EWCA Civ 63, [2016] 1 W.L.R. 3265, Beatson LJ, CA (Civ Div).

1425 **Premises licences–Club premises certificates–Queen's birthday licensing hours**

THE LICENSING ACT 2003 (HER MAJESTY THE QUEEN'S BIRTHDAY LICENSING HOURS) ORDER 2016, SI 2016/591; made under the Licensing Act 2003 s.172(1), s.197(2). In force: 18 May 2016.

This Order is made under the Licensing Act 2003 s.172 and marks the occasion of Her Majesty The Queen's official 90th birthday. It provides for premises licences and club premises certificates to have effect during the period from 10 June to 1h June 2016 (to the extent that this is not already the case) as if specified times were included in the opening hours under the licence or certificate. The specified times are the periods of 2 hours beginning at 11 on each of 10 June and 11 June 2016. The Order only applies to licences and certificates which authorise licensable activities to be carried on up to or after 11pm on each of those days; it does not apply to the sale by retail of alcohol for consumption off the premises, and the supply of alcohol by or on behalf of a club to, or to the order of, a member of the club for consumption off the premises. It permits premises to be used for the provision of late night refreshment at the specified times only if at those times the premises may also be used for the sale or supply of alcohol for consumption on the premises.

1426 **Premises licences–Revocation–Prevention of crime and disorder–Whether prosecution necessary**

[Licensing Act 2003 (c.17)]

The licensing authority appealed by way of case stated against a district judge's decision to reinstate the respondent restaurant's licence. The respondent owned and managed a restaurant that was the subject of a joint police and immigration visit. They found a chef working at the premises who it was accepted by the respondent was an illegal worker with no right to be in or work in the UK. The respondent paid him cash in hand, at less than the minimum wage, he did not keep PAYE records, he purported to deduct tax from the chef's salary and did not account to HMRC for the tax deducted. The police applied for the respondent's licence to be revoked and the licensing sub-committee revoked it. The district judge allowed the respondent's appeal against the revocation. He held that the crime prevention objective had not been engaged because no crime had been committed. One of the questions posed for the High Court was whether the district judge had been correct to conclude that the crime prevention objective had not been engaged. Among other arguments the appellant submitted that the district judge had wrongly held that the crime prevention objective had not been engaged. It argued that the Licensing Act 2003 did not require a crime to have been committed, let alone a prosecution or conviction, before a review application was brought. The appellant argued that the duty of the licensing authority was prospective; it concerned the prevention of crime and disorder, not merely the reaction to it. In any event, the appellant submitted that crimes had been committed, namely failing to pay the minimum wage, tax evasion and employing an illegal worker.

Held: Appeal allowed. The district judge had applied the law erroneously. A prosecution or criminal conviction was not required for the licensing authority's crime prevention objective to be engaged. Each case turned on its own facts, but in the instant case crimes had been committed in any event. The licence should have been revoked.

EAST LINDSEY DC v HANIF (T/A ZARAF RESTAURANT AND TAKEAWAY), [2016] EWHC 1265 (Admin), [2016] C.T.L.C. 81, Jay J, QBD (Admin).

LOCAL GOVERNMENT

1427 Anti-social behaviour orders–Local authorities' powers and duties–Prohibition from engaging in any behaviour likely to cause harassment, alarm or distress to local authority employees–Whether necessary and proportionate

[Crime and Disorder Act 1998 (c.37) s.1(1); European Convention on Human Rights 1950 art.10]

The appellant appealed by way of case stated against the imposition of an anti-social behaviour order (ASBO) and a costs order. The respondent local authority had applied for an ASBO under the Crime and Disorder Act 1998 s.1(1). The judge found that the appellant had verbally attacked various people associated with the local authority, made allegations of serious impropriety against them and had threatened one person with violence. He made an ASBO prohibiting the appellant from engaging in any behaviour likely to cause harassment, alarm or distress to any of the local authority's employees. He also made a costs order of £16,984 against the appellant. The questions for the court were whether the judge had been right to find that (i) the appellant had acted in an anti-social manner which had caused persons harassment, alarm or distress; (ii) an ASBO was necessary, and if so, whether the terms of the ASBO were proportionate and lawful. The judge had also been directed to state a case with regard to the costs decision, but due to time constraints that had not been done. The appellant submitted that (1) the judge had used the wrong standard of proof in deciding the matter, namely the civil rather than criminal standard of proof, and that he had not been entitled to find on the facts that the appellant's behavior amounted to anti-social behaviour; (2) the ASBO was not necessary and proportionate, its terms were so wide so as to offend legal certainty, five years was too long, and the judge had not considered the least restrictive means of achieving the legitimate aim; (3) the costs order was unlawful.

Held: Judgment accordingly. (1) There was no basis for concluding that the judge had failed to apply the criminal standard of proof. There had been threatening and distressing conduct, and he was entitled to conclude that it had been persistent and serious to justify making an ASBO. There had been personal threats, intimidation, allegations of personal abuse, abuse concerning employees' physical disabilities, and the appellant had also accused local authority employees of animal abuse and paedophilia. Having regard to the context, it amounted to anti-social behavior. The judge had been entitled to consider the cumulative effect. The fact that the appellant might have genuinely believed his accusations was irrelevant, as was whether an allegation was true. (2) Although the appellant had been described as a "passionate political activist" the judge had been entitled to make the ASBO for the protection of the public. The judge had observed the appellant and had assessed his grievance and denial. The effect of the ASBO did not infringe the appellant's right to share opinions on political matters, or to attend local authority meetings. A fair balance had to be struck between the interests of the community and individual fundamental rights under ECHR art.10. It was important that local authority employees could carry out their functions without being subjected to threatening behaviour. The appellant had a deep-seated and bitter grievance towards local authority employees, and the judge had been entitled to find that the only way of protecting them from harassment was to encompass all local authority members and employees. The ASBO was necessary and proportionate. As for the duration, five years was not unnecessary, unreasonable or disproportionate. Alternatives, such as barring the appellant from meetings, would only have had a limited effect. (3) As no question in the case stated on costs had been put before the instant court, it had no jurisdiction to deal with the matter. However, as the case stated was supposed to have dealt with that matter, the appeal was adjourned and the district judge directed to amend the case stated to include a question on costs.

R. (ON THE APPLICATION OF CARNEY) v NORTH LINCOLNSHIRE COUNCIL *sub nom.* CARNEY v NORTH LINCOLNSHIRE COUNCIL, [2016] EWHC 676 (Admin), (2016) 180 J.P. 416, Lloyd Jones LJ, QBD (Admin).

1428 Boundaries–Parishes–Flintshire

THE FLINTSHIRE (COMMUNITIES) ORDER 2016, SI 2016/1151; made under the Local Government Act 1972 s.58(2), s.266(2). In force: In accordance with art.1.

His Order, made in accordance with Local Government Act 1972 s.58(2), gives effect, with modification, to proposals of the Local Democracy and Boundary Commission for Wales. The effect of this Order is that there are changes to a number of community areas and some consequential changes in community electoral arrangements. Changes are made to the boundaries of Broughton and Bretton, Halkyn, Higher Kinnerton, Hope, Leeswood, Mold and Pen-y-Ffordd. Consequential electoral changes are made to the electoral divisions within the communities of Broughton and Bretton and Halkyn.

1429 Chargeable dwellings–Households–Whether property containing more than one self-contained unit–Evidence of actual use

[Council Tax (Chargeable Dwellings) Order 1992 (SI 1992/549) art.2, art.3]

The Listing Officer appealed against a decision of the Valuation Tribunal for England ordering an alteration to the valuation list to show one entry for a property instead of two. The property in question was a Grade II listed building which had been built as one dwelling but had been converted into two dwellings on three floors. It was entered on the 1993 valuation list as two separate hereditaments. At that time, one property comprised a kitchen, bathroom, sitting room and dining room on the lower ground floor, plus two ground-floor bedrooms, with outside access solely from the lower ground floor. The other property comprised the remainder of the ground floor, consisting of a kitchen, dining room, bathroom and shower room, and the whole of the first floor. In 2014, the respondents purchased both properties and undertook works to convert them back to a single dwelling. On completion of the works, the ground floor comprised a kitchen, sitting area, dining room, two bedrooms and a shower room, with a hall leading to the main entrance. The first floor comprised a drawing room, study, bedroom and bathroom. A utility room had been installed on the lower ground floor in place of the previous kitchen and bathroom. The listing officer maintained two entries in the valuation list, classing the lower ground floor as a self-contained unit. The tribunal overturned that decision, holding that (i) the lower ground floor was not a self-contained unit because the utility room provided laundry facilities for the whole house and was not for the separate and exclusive use of the lower ground floor; and (ii) the character of the building was that of a Grade II listed building that could not be adapted for use as conventional living accommodation.

Held: Appeal dismissed. (1) The application of the legislative test in the Council Tax (Chargeable Dwellings) Order 1992 art.2 and art.3 as to whether a single property contained more than one "self-contained unit" was a matter of fact and judgment for the specialist tribunal. The focus had to be on the physical characteristics of the building as presently constructed and adapted for use, not on the way in which the occupants were actually using it. Although the test was sometimes referred to as the "bricks and mortar" test, the "physical characteristics of the building" was a more apt description as it included physical facilities installed for essential living functions such as cooking, washing and laundry, *Corkish (Listing Officer) v Wright* [2014] EWHC 237 (Admin), [2014] R.V.R. 233, [2014] C.L.Y. 2086 applied, *Hayes v Humberside Valuation Tribunal* [1998] R.A. 37, [1998] C.L.Y. 4299 followed. In the instant case, the relevant physical characteristics of the building included, in addition to the external structure: the two external doors; the internal layout, including the separate floors; the staircases between each floor and a second staircase linking the kitchen and utility room; bathrooms on each floor; the installation of the lower ground floor utility room and laundry facilities; the installation of a ground floor kitchen; and the absence of a kitchen and cooking facilities on the lower ground floor. Although the manner in which the building was being used by particular occupiers was not the legislative test, evidence of actual use might properly be considered, *Clement (Listing Officer) v Bryant* [2003] EWHC 422 (Admin), [2003] R.A. 133 applied. Thus, it was not impermissible for the tribunal to have regard to the evidence that the house was in use as a single household whose sole kitchen facilities were on the ground floor and sole laundry facilities on the lower ground floor (see paras 22, 28-31, 34-35, 38, 40-41 of judgment). (2) The tribunal had not erred in law in taking into account evidence that there were major restrictions on changes to the construction and layout of the building because of its status as a Grade II listed building. That was a potentially relevant part of the evidential background which the panel was entitled to consider when examining the physical characteristics of the building and asking itself whether it had been "constructed or adapted for use as separate living accommodation" for the purposes of art.2 of the Order. Because of the way in which the building had been adapted, the lower ground floor held the communal laundry facilities for the whole house and was not a separate self-contained unit. Accordingly, the tribunal had not misdirected itself in law (paras 42-44, 46).

COLL (LISTING OFFICER) v MOONEY, [2016] EWHC 485 (Admin), [2016] R.A. 125, Lang J, QBD (Admin).

1430 Codes of conduct–Local authorities

THE LOCAL AUTHORITIES (MODEL CODE OF CONDUCT) (WALES) (AMENDMENT) ORDER 2016, SI 2016/84; made under the Local Government Act 2000 s 50(2)(3)(4)(4E), s.81(2)(3), s.105. In force: 1 April 2016.

This Order amends the Local Authorities (Model Code of Conduct) (Wales) Order 2008 Sch.1 in which is set out a model code as regards the conduct which is expected of members and co-opted members of relevant authorities in Wales under the Local Government Act 2000 s.50(2). Section 50(3) of that Act enables the Welsh Ministers to revise a model code which has been issued.

1431 Combined authorities–Elected mayors–West Midlands

THE WEST MIDLANDS COMBINED AUTHORITY (ELECTION OF MAYOR) ORDER 2016, SI 2016/933; made under the Local Democracy, Economic Development and Construction Act 2009 s.107A, Sch.5B para.3. In force: In accordance with art.1.

The Local Democracy, Economic Development and Construction Act 2009 Pt 6 provides for the establishment of combined authorities for the areas of two or more local authorities in England. Article 3 of this Order creates the position of mayor for the area of the West Midlands Combined Authority. Article 3 further specifies the term of office for the mayor for the area of the West Midlands Combined Authority, and the dates on which elections for the return of a mayor shall take place and the intervals between elections.

1432 Council tax–Disregards–Backdating of carer's disregard

[Limitation Act 1980 (c.58) s.9]

The appellant appealed against a decision of the respondent billing authority concerning the backdating of the carer's disregard to which he was entitled. The appellant had applied for carer's disregard in December 2012, as soon as he became aware of his eligibility. The authority accepted that, for the purpose of assessing his council tax liability, the appellant had in fact become eligible for the disregard in 1996. However, it backdated the disregard only to December 2006.

Held: Appeal allowed. It was for the authority to take reasonable steps to ascertain whether the calculation of the chargeable amount of council tax was subject to a discount. The authority had been aware of the appellant's situation in 1996. The authority's failure to act on such knowledge was significant in two respects. First, it meant that the authority could not claim to have taken reasonable steps to ascertain whether the disregard applied. Second, it absolved the appellant of any responsibility for failing to alert the authority to his situation as a carer. The Limitation Act 1980 s.9, which concerned the time limit governing actions for sums recoverable by statute, applied. Its effect was that the claim had to be commenced within six years of the accrual of the cause of action. That date, for the purpose of these proceedings, was December 2012, when the appellant first became aware of his eligibility for the disregard. Provided the appellant made his claim by December 2018, which of course he had, he was entitled not only to proceed but also to claim the return of the entire amount of overpaid council tax back to 1996 when he first became eligible. The authority should recalculate his council tax bill on the basis that he should have been awarded carer's disregard from 1996 (see paras 4-5, 7-9, 11-12 of judgment).

HS v LEICESTER CITY COUNCIL, [2015] R.A. 565, Graham Zellick QC, VT.

1433 Council tax–Exemptions–Eligibility for student exemption

[Local Government Finance Act 1992 (c.14) Sch.1 para.4, Sch.1 para.5; Council Tax (Discount Disregards) Order 1992 (SI 1992/548) art.4(b), art.5; Council Tax (Exempt Dwellings) Order 1992 (SI 1992/558)]

The appellant (R) appealed against a local authority's decision that she did not qualify for the student exemption from council tax. R was studying full-time in the University of Cambridge's veterinary medicine department for a postgraduate qualification of the European College of Veterinary Pathologists. She was not registered with the university's board of graduate studies and was not a member of a college of the university, because she was not taking a course leading to an award, degree or qualification of the university. The local authority considered that she was not a "student" within the Local Government Finance Act 1992 Sch.1 para.4 and the Council Tax (Discount Disregards) Order 1992 and therefore not exempt under the Council Tax (Exempt Dwellings) Order 1992, on the basis that she was a student not of the university but of the European college, which was not a prescribed educational establishment within art.4(b) of the Discount Disregards Order.

Held: Appeal allowed. The legislation required a person to be studying full-time for the required duration on a course at a prescribed institution, namely an institution established solely or mainly for the purpose of providing higher education. It did not require that the course undertaken had to lead to an award, degree or qualification of the prescribed institution, nor that any other qualification of the awarding body had to be recognised by the relevant authority. The purpose of the provisions specifying degrees and higher education went to the status of the institution, not to the particular course being followed by the student. R was pursuing a full-time course that met the statutory criteria as to duration. She was undertaking that course at the university. The university was established for the purpose of providing higher education. It was clearly a prescribed educational establishment. It was irrelevant that the course and the qualification to which it led were not the university's. It was therefore irrelevant that R was not registered with the board and was not a member of a college of the university. Correspondence received from the university's veterinary department satisfied the requirement for a certificate under Sch.1 para.5 of the Act and art.5 of the Discount Disregards Order. It was wholly irrelevant that the European college was not a prescribed institution and that the qualification was not a degree or qualification recognised by any entity of the British government. R qualified for the exemption (see paras 14-17 of judgment).

RUPP v CAMBRIDGE CITY COUNCIL, [2015] R.V.R. 310, S Rehman, VT.

1434 Council tax–Liability orders–Lawfulness of local authority £125 standard costs charge

[Council Tax (Administration and Enforcement) Regulations 1992 (SI 1992/613) reg.34(7); Audit Commission Act 1998 (c.18) s.17(4), s.8]

The appellant appealed against the respondent auditors' decision not to seek a declaration that an item of account was unlawful, or to issue a report in the public interest, in respect of costs sought by the first interested party. The first interested party was a local authority which had a practice of claiming costs of £125 in each case where it sought a liability order in respect of unpaid council tax. The appellant was an anti-poverty campaigner. The local authority was entitled under the Council Tax (Administration and Enforcement) Regulations 1992 reg.34(7) to seek costs reasonably incurred in seeking a liability order, but the appellant was concerned that the figure of £125 was disproportionate. He wrote to the auditors objecting to the local authority's accounts for the year ending 2014 and inviting them to make an application for a declaration under the Audit Commission Act 1998 s.17(4) or to issue a report in the public interest under s.8 in respect of the £125 charge. The auditors declined to do so, contending that the local authority's calculations were supported by evidence. They stated that the calculations involved the aggregation of staff costs, direct costs, indirect costs and overheads divided by the number of summonses sought in a year. Although a more comprehensive calculation might have provided a better understanding of the figure charged, the auditors were satisfied that the costs were not unreasonable and did not represent an attempt to raise income.

Held: Appeal dismissed. As to the costs sought by the local authority, what mattered was whether they were "reasonably incurred" within the meaning of reg.34. If they were, the local authority was entitled to them as of right. The costs had been reasonably incurred. Importantly, the apportionment carried out by the local authority was focused on the costs of cases in which summonses were issued and on the costs up to the issue of the summons. It expressly did not include the following: costs associated with those who did not pay without any issues; those who paid with some action but before summonses were issued; matters unrelated to the summons processes, such as annual billing; and the costs of staff time spent after the issue of the summons. It was permissible to use the average amount of costs incurred per order obtained as a basis for the costs claimed. In any such exercise, there could not be precise equivalence with the actual costs incurred, but the result could be said to represent costs "reasonably incurred", *R. (on the application of Nicolson) v Tottenham Magistrates* [2015] EWHC 1252 (Admin), [2015] P.T.S.R. 1045, [2015] C.L.Y. 1678 considered. Further, on the local authority's figures, the amount claimed was actually slightly less than the actual costs incurred for each summonsed case. Insofar as the appellant was seeking to revisit the auditors' decision not to issue a report in the public interest, there was no right of appeal. There was a right of appeal under s.17(4) of the 1998 Act in respect of a decision not to seek a declaration, but that required establishing that the auditors' exercise of their discretion was wrong in principle, outside the range of decisions reasonably open to them or made without consideration of the relevant factors. It was clear that the relevant factors were considered. The decision reached involved the exercise of discretionary judgment by an expert in the course of a statutory function. The court would be slow to interfere with the exercise of a discretion in such circumstances. The exercise by the auditors of their discretion was amply justified by the reasons they had given. In particular, once they were satisfied that the local authority was not seeking to deliberately apportion inappropriate costs and to increase its income, that its costs calculations were "not unreasonable" and that the costs claimed were "broadly reasonable", it was difficult to see the public interest in seeking a declaration under s.17(4) (see paras 48, 51, 55, 59-62 of judgment).

NICOLSON v GRANT THORNTON UK LLP, [2016] EWHC 710 (Admin), [2016] 2 Costs L.R. 211, Hamblen LJ, DC.

1435 Council tax–Liability orders–Summons specifying amount of costs that would be claimed if order made–Validity of summons

[Council Tax (Administration and Enforcement) Regulations 1992 (SI 1992/613) reg.23, reg.34(1), reg.34(2), reg.35, reg.53(5); Magistrates' Courts Rules 1981 r.98]

The appellant appealed by way of case stated against an order that he meet a council tax liability and pay the costs of the respondent local authority. Pursuant to the Council Tax (Administration and Enforcement) Regulations 1992 reg.34(2), the local authority had applied for a liability order against the appellant in respect of unpaid council tax. The complaint indicated that the appellant was liable for unpaid council tax. An accompanying schedule, in the form of a computer generated print-out, quantified the unpaid council tax at £975 and indicated that the local authority would be claiming £75 in costs. As required by reg.53(5), the print-out was accompanied by a certificate stating that it was an accurate extract of information held within the computer operated by the local authority, and that the computer operated a LINUX system and had been functioning properly at all material times. The summons issued by the magistrates informed the appellant that he was to show cause why he should not pay unpaid council tax of £975 plus costs of £75. The questions stated were whether the magistrates had been right to (1) find that the application for the liability order was valid, even though the summons included a request for costs; (2) find the appellant liable on the basis of the evidence and the certificate produced by the local authority; (3) conclude that the costs reasonably incurred by the local authority amounted to £75.

Held: Appeal dismissed. (1) The application for the liability order was valid even though the summons included a request for costs. Regulation 23, which fixed a defaulting taxpayer with liability, did not mention costs, and it was clear that the amount referred to in that regulation, and in reg.34(1), was the amount of council tax due, not costs. Therefore, the local authority's complaint had referred only to the failure to pay council tax. The attached schedule made it clear that the sum payable was the £975 unpaid council tax. The summons complied with the requirements of the Magistrates' Courts Rules 1981 r.98. There was nothing in those Rules or in the Regulations to prevent additional information, or a reference to costs, from appearing on the face of the summons. It was not an abuse of process for the summons to include a reference to a claim for costs, and the inclusion of such a reference would not render the summons invalid. The purpose of the reference to costs was simply to inform the appellant of the amount of costs claimed, so he could pay them before the hearing if he chose. Given that that was an option open to him, and given that reg.35(8) enabled him to accept a liability order but contest the amount of costs, information about the amount of the costs claimed was the sort of information that ought to be made available to him. The fact that a costs order would not be made until after the basis for the liability order had been established was not a reason for not telling the taxpayer in advance what sum the local authority would be claiming in costs. Nor did the reference to costs usurp the magistrates' power to determine the quantum of costs reasonably incurred by the local authority. The level of costs had been the subject of evidence and submissions, and the magistrates had not acceded to the claim for £75 without investigation (see paras 23-35 of judgment). (2) The certificate contained sufficient information to comply with the requirements of reg.53(5) in that it adequately identified the computer that had produced the print-out. Computers could be identified in different ways and the Regulations prescribed no particular method. The print-out was admissible; the magistrates had heard oral evidence of the appellant's default; and the appellant was not suggesting that he had any substantive defence. In those circumstances, the magistrates had been entitled to find him liable (paras 46- 54). (3) The Regulations enabled the local authority to recover costs which it had actually and reasonably incurred, and which were genuinely attributable to its use of the enforcement process. Provided that the right types of costs and expenses were taken into account, local authorities could legitimately calculate their costs by determining what they had spent on enforcement proceedings in the previous year and dividing that figure by the number of summonses issued, to arrive at an average cost per head that could be levied in standard cases, *R. (on the application of Nicolson) v Tottenham Magistrates* [2015] EWHC 1252 (Admin), [2015] P.T.S.R. 1045, [2015] C.L.Y. 1678 applied (paras 57-66). That was what the local authority had done in the instant case. It provided a schedule showing that it had incurred costs of £266,102 the previous year, and in that calculation it had legitimately included a proportion of its information technology costs, chip and pin costs and pension deficit costs. There was nothing objectionable about the inclusion of any of those costs. When standardised costs were applied it was inevitable that some types of cost might be incurred in the case of one defaulter, but not in the case of another. Provided that the local authority had taken into account the right types of costs and expenses when calculating the standard cost, that was acceptable (paras 67, 73-74, 76, 79-81, 85-88).

WILLIAMS v EAST NORTHAMPTONSHIRE DC, [2016] EWHC 470 (Admin), [2016] R.A. 191, Alexander Nissen QC, QBD (Admin).

1436 Council tax–Liability orders–Whether costs claimed by local authority representing costs reasonably incurred in obtaining order

[Council Tax (Administration and Enforcement) Regulations 1992 (SI 1992/613) reg.34]

The claimant applied for judicial review of a liability order imposed by the defendant magistrates' court under the Council Tax (Administration and Enforcement) Regulations 1992 reg.34. The order had been made against the claimant on the application of the interested party local authority to enforce payment of unpaid council tax charges in the sum of £137 and £95 in costs. The issue was whether the costs of obtaining the liability order had been reasonably incurred.

Held: Application granted. The order for costs was unlawful and was quashed. The magistrates' court did not have sufficient relevant information before it to reach a proper judicial determination of whether the costs claimed represented costs reasonably incurred by the local authority in obtaining the liability order. The court had erred in failing to make further inquiries into how the £95 was calculated and the claimant had been denied a fair opportunity to challenge the lawfulness of the order before it was made, by reason of the failure to answer his requests for the provision of information as to how the sum of £95 had been arrived at, *R. (on the application of Nicolson) v Tottenham Magistrates* [2015] EWHC 1252 (Admin), [2015] P.T.S.R. 1045, [2015] C.L.Y. 1678 applied. The order made was the aggregate of the costs and the debt, the costs part of the order fell away and so should the balance which went to make up the aggregate. The liability order was also quashed (see paras 7-9, 12 of judgment).

EWING v HIGHBURY CORNER MAGISTRATES' COURT, [2015] EWHC 3788 (Admin), [2016] R.V.R. 174, McGowan J, QBD (Admin).

1437 Council tax–Liability to tax–Uninhabitable property let on 99-year lease–Liability of tenant to pay council tax

[Local Government Finance Act 1992 (c.14) s.6; European Convention on Human Rights 1950 Protocol 1 art.1, art.8]

A tenant appealed against a listing officer's refusal to remove her flat from the council tax valuation list. The tenant had a 99-year lease of a flat. The flat suffered from damp and had twice been flooded. The tenant moved out and had not lived in the flat for several years. She asked for the flat to be removed from the council tax list because it was uninhabitable. The valuation office rejected her request. It did not inspect the inside of the property, but concluded that since the rest of the building was structurally sound, and occupied, there were no structural problems with the flat. However, the tenant's surveyor had concluded that the property was uninhabitable due to damp and faulty electrical wiring, and was beyond economic repair. The tenant appealed to the valuation tribunal. She did not call her surveyor to give evidence as the listing officer had told her that the condition of the flat was not in issue. The tribunal told her that she could ask for an adjournment, but she decided to proceed with the hearing. It decided that despite signs of major damp, the flat was not derelict and it remained a hereditament for council tax purposes. The tenant's application for a review of that decision was refused. The tenant submitted that (1) the hearing was unfair; (2) the tribunal reached the wrong conclusion; (3) even if the tribunal was right, the outcome was wrong and a breach of her human rights.

Held: Appeal dismissed. (1) The tenant accepted that she had been offered an adjournment of the hearing and had refused that offer. The tribunal could not be criticised for continuing with the hearing in that situation, nor could it be criticised for not apprehending that she might have had reservations about continuing, if she did not articulate them. If she thought she would have been helped by the presence of her surveyor, she could have asked for the hearing to be postponed to another date when he could be instructed to attend to give evidence. However, she had suffered no disadvantage from the surveyor's absence, since there was no possibility that the evidence which he was able to give would have enabled the tribunal to reach a different conclusion on the legal issue which it had to decide (see paras 50-51 of judgment). (2) The tribunal had cited *Wilson v Coll (Listing Officer)* [2011] EWHC 2824 (Admin), [2012] P.T.S.R. 1313, [2012] C.L.Y. 2148, in which it was decided that a point might be reached when a property was so derelict as to be incapable of repair. There was a distinction between repair and the complete reconstruction or replacement of a building. If a dwelling could be repaired it was still a hereditament, even if those repairs would be uneconomic. The tribunal had applied the right legal test, *Wilson* applied. On the evidence, it concluded that the flat could be made suitable for occupation if a reasonable amount of repair was done (paras 30, 53). (3) The Local Government

Finance Act 1992 s.6 determined who was liable to pay council tax in respect of any chargeable dwelling. It imposed liability in descending order on, first, a person who was resident in the dwelling and had a freehold interest in any part of it, and then through a chain of people with an interest in, or connection with, the property. If none was resident, the owner was liable. "Owner" was defined as someone who had a "material interest" in the dwelling. Material interest was defined as a freehold or leasehold interest which was granted for a term of six months or more. The effect of those provisions was that if no-one was living in a dwelling, and it was subject to a lease for a term of more than six months, the lessee was liable for council tax in respect of that dwelling. The tenant felt strongly that the legislative scheme was wrong and irrational. However, the decision about who should be liable for council tax on an unoccupied dwelling which was subject to a lease had been made by Parliament. A court had no power to disapply the provisions of primary legislation. Further, the scheme in s.6 was an intelligible and rational scheme. The hierarchy in s.6 showed that Parliament had decided that liability should depend on residence in, and the right to reside in, a dwelling. The interference, if any, with the rights protected by ECHR art.8 and Protocol 1 art.1 was plainly justified (paras 28, 54-58).

BRANWELL v VALUATION OFFICE AGENCY, [2015] EWHC 824 (Admin), [2016] R.V.R. 39, Elisabeth Laing J, QBD (Admin).

1438 **Council tax–Liability to tax–Whether assured shorthold tenancy agreement was single tenancy for minimum term, thereafter terminable by notice, or fixed-term tenancy ending after six months**

[Local Government Finance Act 1992 (c.14) s.6, s.6(6); Law of Property Act 1925 (c.20)]

A local authority appealed against a decision of the Valuation Tribunal concerning liability for council tax. The decision related to five separate properties and five separate appeals. The respondent landlord had used a standard form tenancy agreement when granting assured shorthold residential tenancies in respect of the properties. Under the terms of the agreement, the respective tenants were responsible for council tax "during the tenancy". The agreement stated that the premises were let for a term of six or 12 months "and thereafter continuing on a monthly basis" unless terminated by either party on one month's notice. When the tenants vacated the property, the local authority ceased to regard them as being liable for council tax. However, the landlord asserted that the tenants remained responsible, as the tenancy continued until it was terminated under the terms of the agreement. He claimed that the contracts created a single tenancy whose term was six or 12 months, thereafter continuing as a monthly tenancy. The local authority argued that a single tenancy could not be both a fixed-term tenancy and a periodic tenancy as that would offend the principle of uncertainty. Liability to pay council tax was to be determined having regard to the Local Government Finance Act 1992 s.6. A person liable to pay council tax included a person who was a resident of the dwelling and was a statutory or secure tenant. The tribunal decided in the landlord's favour. On appeal, the landlord submitted that the tenancies were periodic tenancies with a minimum six-month period, thereafter terminable by one month's notice, not a fixed-term ending after six months. The local authority argued that the agreement created two tenancies, a fixed-term of six or 12 months followed by a monthly tenancy, and that at the material time the tenant was holding the premises under the latter, which was not a "material interest" for council tax purposes under s.6(6).

Held: Appeal dismissed. On their face, the words used in the agreement purported to create a single tenancy whose term comprised a fixed period of six or 12 months followed by a period which operated precisely as if it were a new monthly tenancy, but which was described in the document as a continuation of the term originally granted. The issue was whether the tenancy as granted by the plain words of the agreement was invalid because it offended the uncertainty rule. The words used had to be construed in a way which gave effect to the intention of the parties, as deduced from the document itself against the relevant background. That did not include the parties' actual intentions. The document stated its intention as "This agreement is intended to create an assured shorthold tenancy under the provisions of the Housing Act 1988", which was plainly to create one tenancy only. The agreement had to be interpreted in the same way as any other written contract, *Mexfield Housing Co-operative Ltd v Berrisford* [2011] UKSC 52, [2012] 1 A.C. 955, [2012] C.L.Y. 2035 followed. If the words, on their plain meaning, offended the rule against uncertainty, it might be possible to save something of the agreement by interpreting it in another way, as suggested by the local authority, but that would mean that it was not a "material interest" for council tax purposes. The uncertainty rule preserved by *Mexfield* was that a tenancy was invalid for uncertainty if it prevented a party from determining it except if an event occurred which might never happen, *Mexfield* considered. The tenancy as granted by the plain words of the agreement did not offend against that rule. The tenancy agreement created a term which was neither simply a fixed term nor a periodic tenancy, nor one followed by the other. It was a term which had the characteristics of a fixed term followed by a periodic tenancy. Fixed terms and periodic tenancies were both capable of being created under the Law of Property Act 1925 and were not void for uncertainty at common law. There was no reason why a term should become uncertain because it comprised two successive periods of time, each of which was sufficiently certain for the purposes of the relevant rule. There was no prospect of the term being perpetual because its termination depended on an event which might never happen. It was not legally impossible to have a single tenancy comprised of both a fixed and periodic term. The only reason for wishing to define a term in that way appeared to be to secure a benefit for the landlord in relation to his council tax liability. It was a modern contrivance, but the uncertainty rule, which was developed long before anyone considered granting a tenancy in the instant terms, should not be extended to invalidate it (see paras 25-30 of judgment).

LEEDS CITY COUNCIL v BROADLEY, [2016] EWHC 1839 (Admin), [2016] 4 W.L.R. 137, Edis J, QBD (Admin).

1439 Council tax–Non-payment–Suspended committal order with repayment period of over six years–Lawfulness

[Council Tax (Administration and Enforcement) Regulations 1992 (SI 1992/613) reg.47(3)]

The appellant appealed against a decision of a magistrates' court committing him to prison for 90 days, suspended on payment of £100 per month, for failing to pay council tax. The period for which the council tax was due was 1 January 2005 to 31 December 2010. Liability for the payment of the council tax originally fell on the tenants of the property in question, the property being let in multiple occupation. On that fact being discovered in November 2010, the respondent local authority transferred the liability for the sums owing to the owners of the property, namely the appellant and another man. A liability order was made against the appellant under the Council Tax (Administration and Enforcement) Regulations 1992 in the sum of £7397.43. In evidence given to the magistrates during the inquiry into his means, the appellant stated that he had been adjudged bankrupt on 5 January 2006. He accepted that he owned the property in question but asserted that he held it as trustee only and not as a beneficiary. The magistrates' court commented that it had not been addressed on the legal implications of the appellant's bankruptcy. It found that the liability order should be enforced and made the suspended committal order, being satisfied that the appellant had adequate means to pay but had culpably neglected to do so for each of the relevant periods.

Held: Appeal allowed. The suspended committal order was unlawful as the repayment period exceeded six years, which was simply too long. The case would be remitted to the magistrates for rehearing. They should establish when the appellant was discharged from bankruptcy and consider what liability for council tax arose after that date as a result of the appellant's position as trustee of the property. The appellant would remain liable for the council tax in respect of the earlier period. However, in respect of that earlier liability he may not have failed to pay "due to his wilful refusal or culpable neglect" so as to satisfy reg.47(3) of the Regulations. The magistrates would no doubt enquire as to whether his non-payment of the later liabilities for council tax resulted from such a refusal or neglect. If so satisfied, they could then impose a fresh order committing him to prison, suspended on payment of a monthly sum commensurate with their view of his means and always provided that the period for payment was not excessive (see paras 20-23 of judgment).

SOOR v REDBRIDGE LBC, [2016] EWHC 77 (Admin), [2016] B.P.I.R. 766, Irwin J, QBD (Admin).

1440 Council tax–Property bands–Appeal against banding decision settled by agreement to amend banding–Whether agreement precluding later alteration

[Council Tax (Alteration of Lists and Appeals) (England) Regulations 2009 (SI 2009/2270) reg.13, reg.13(7), reg.3(1)(b), reg.4(1)]

A council taxpayer appealed against the refusal of a listing officer to alter the banding of a dwelling in the valuation list. The dwelling was placed in band F in 1993, but the taxpayer disputed that and lodged an appeal. The listing officer accepted the correctness of the challenge. A formal agreement was reached and signed and the valuation list was altered to change the band. The taxpayer was under the impression that the agreement was binding and withdrew his appeal without seeking a consent order from the tribunal. Twenty years later, the listing officer decided that the reduction had been based on mistake and restored the dwelling to band F. The issue was whether the agreement precluded any later alteration by the listing officer.

Held: Appeal dismissed. (1) The Council Tax (Alteration of Lists and Appeals) (England) Regulations 2009 reg.3(1)(b) allowed a listing officer to alter a council tax band if satisfied that a different valuation band should have been determined. It was to be noted that that was not restricted, for example, by the existence of any earlier agreement. It was also to be noted that reg.4(1), which allowed proposals to be made for alteration of the list, made no provision in relation to earlier agreements. Under reg.13(7), an appeal was treated as automatically withdrawn if a listing officer reached an agreement on an alteration of the list. That meant that the only way a consent order could be obtained would be for there to be no agreement under reg.13 and a joint application made to the tribunal by the parties. It therefore had to be acknowledged that reg.13 agreements could not enjoy the imprimatur of the tribunal and would not have whatever durability was conferred by an order of the tribunal. Further, if an alteration to the list pursuant to an agreement precluded a later alteration on the basis that the earlier alteration was based on an error, the listing officer would equally be prevented from reducing the band to the taxpayer's advantage where the error was that the agreed band was higher than it should have been. The draftsman would be unlikely to have intended that result. Read as a whole, the statutory provisions did not prevent the listing officer from correcting a mistake in the valuation list where that entry followed an agreement within the terms of the Regulations. It was understandable that that would cause a sense of grievance to council taxpayers, who would have to instigate the challenge process again when they thought the matter had been settled. However, the circumstances in which an alteration could be made were limited; any misuse or abuse of power by the listing officer was correctable in the Administrative Court; and the taxpayer could appeal to the instant tribunal against the actual valuation (see paras 17, 19, 22, 24, 26-27 of judgment). (2) In future, listing officers should make reference in any written agreement to their power to disregard the agreement in the future should they believe that the entry was erroneous. The burden on the listing officer to show that a mistake had been made should be scrutinised by the tribunal with considerable intensity before endorsing any alteration (para.28).

WARD v COLL (LISTING OFFICER), [2016] R.V.R. 37, Graham Zellick QC, VT.

1441 Council tax–Property bands–Re-banding of property–Refund of overpaid council tax

[Limitation Act 1980 (c.58) s.9, s.9(1); Council Tax (Administration and Enforcement) Regulations 1992 (SI 1992/613) reg.24(2)(a)]

The three appellants appealed against decisions of the respondent billing authority concerning the refunds to which they were entitled following a rebanding of their properties to a lower council tax band. The appellants became liable for council tax in respect of their properties in 1993, 1994 and 1996. In 2014, their properties were rebanded to a lower council tax band. Under council tax law, the rebanding was entered in the list as from 1993, when council tax was introduced, or from the date when the dwelling was first entered in the list, if that occurred later. Following the rebanding, the authority issued revised bills allowing the appellants a refund only for the past six years.

Held: Appeals allowed. Nothing in the Council Tax (Administration and Enforcement) Regulations 1992 or the other council tax legislation imposed any limitation on the refund or the period covered by the refund. The authority had relied on the Limitation Act 1980 s.9(1), which set a six-year time limit for the bringing of an action, starting on "the date on which the cause of action accrued". However, the Act did not set a limit on the number of years in the past in respect of which sums could be recovered. That was the authority's fundamental error. It had simply assumed that s.9, as interpreted and applied in *Arca v Carlisle City Council* [2013] R.A. 248, [2013] C.L.Y. 2002, set a six-year maximum period for refunding overpayments. It did no such thing, *Arca* considered. The only question therefore was whether the appellants had brought these proceedings within six years of the date on which the cause of action accrued. The authority had argued that the cause of action accrued in 1993, 1994 and 1996, when the band was originally fixed. It relied on the fact that none of the appellants had brought proceedings then to challenge their band. That argument had no merit. These appeals were not about the bands; they were about overpaid council tax following a reduction of the banding by the listing officer in the exercise of his statutory duty. The cause of action accrued when the authority issued a new council tax bill to reflect the revised band and declined to give the full refund requested in accordance with reg.24(2)(a) of the 1992 Regulations. The requirement to make a refund of council tax going back some 20 years might seem odd, but it was not the only odd feature of council tax law. It was the result of the failure to have periodic revaluations. The authority should refund the overpaid council tax back to the date when each appellant became liable to council tax on the relevant dwelling (see paras 11, 16-20, 24-25 of judgment).

HOLDSWORTH v BRADFORD MDC, [2015] R.A. 559, Graham Zellick QC, VT.

1442 Council tax–Valuation–Restrictive covenant capable of affecting valuation of self-contained cottage annexed to main property

[Council Tax (Situation and Valuation of Dwellings) Regulations 1992 (SI 1992/550) reg.6, reg.6(2)(c); Law of Property Act 1925 (c.20) s.205(1)(vii)]

The appellant listing officer appealed against the valuation tribunal's determination that a self-contained cottage annexed to a main property was to be treated as band A for council tax purposes. The respondent property owner had acquired a house consisting of a larger main property, and an annexe which lay within the curtilage of the main property. The annex was physically capable of being separate from the main building although it shared electricity and water facilities. The main building and annex were subject to a restrictive covenant, by which the owner could not use the property except for a single private residence in one occupation only. The listing officer treated the main building and the annex as separate dwellings for council tax purposes, putting them in council tax bands F and C respectively. The owner successfully appealed. The tribunal found that the annex should be treated as Band A because the covenant meant that it could not be used or sold separately, and it shared facilities with the main house. The issue was whether it had been wrong in law to find that the restrictive covenant was capable of affecting the annex's value for the purpose of council tax. The listing officer submitted that, following *Dawkins (Valuation Officer) v Ash Bros & Heaton Ltd* [1969] 2 A.C. 366, [1969] C.L.Y. 3019, there was a general principle in non-domestic rating law that human realities were excluded in the valuation exercise in so far as they were "accidental" to the letting of a hereditament, but acknowledged in so far as they were "essential" to the heriditament itself. Accordingly, an owner intending to pull down a property was accidental and did not affect its value, whereas a demolition by a superior power, such as a local authority would, it being an essential characteristic of the hereditament regardless of the owner. The listing officer argued that that principle applied in the instant case, and that the covenant was accidental to the property being valued, it being a private arrangement capable of being removed rather than something inescapably imposed on the property from outside by a superior power. She further argued that that was reinforced by the Council Tax (Situation and Valuation of Dwellings) Regulations 1992 reg.6(2)(c), which provided that for the purpose of council tax valuation, there was an assumption that a dwelling had been sold free from any rent charge or other incumbrance; she contended that "incumbrance" included such a restrictive covenant.

Held: Appeal dismissed. (1) The basic valuation technique under reg.6(1) involved ascertaining a dwelling's market value on 1 April 1991. In undertaking that valuation, what the court in *Dawkins* had had in mind was the effect on valuation of the exercise of a power which the person subject to it could do nothing unilaterally to remove, *Dawkins* followed. For example, the removal of a planning obligation required consent from the local authority. Similarly, removing a covenant imposed by an adjoining land owner required that land owner to be persuaded to agree to remove the restriction. The reality was that the covenant would be enforced, and that affected the value of the property. Unless the 1992 Regulations required otherwise, there was no reason to substitute fiction for reality, *Dawkins* considered. (2) The definition of incumbrance under the Law of Property Act 1925 s.205(1)(vii) referred to a mortgage, lien or other capital or annual sum. The drafters of the 1992 Regulations, had they wanted to exclude such a restrictive covenant in the valuation exercise, could have added words such as "...or any other restriction on the use of the dwelling" as something for which "no regard was to be paid". The fact that they had deliberately chosen a word that had been defined under the 1925 Act suggested that they had not intended for it to include a wider scope. The 1992 Regulations did not require the substitution of fiction for reality. The main building and annex could only be sold with the covenant in favour of the original land owner, and any valuation would have to take the fact that the covenant could be enforced into account. The tribunal had been correct to take into account the restrictive covenant in the valuation exercise and place the annex in the lowest value band for council tax purposes. (3) The instant council tax valuation exercise, which dealt with the capital value of a freehold land rather than the annual letting value, was not the same as the exercise in the non-domestic valuation scheme. The statutory approaches to valuation were not identical. The outcome of the instant appeal had no consequences for the non-domestic rating scheme.

COLL (LISTING OFFICER) v WALTERS, [2016] EWHC 831 (Admin), [2016] R.A. 293, Mitting J, QBD (Admin).

1443 Council tax support–Discrimination–Council tax reduction scheme–Whether breach of art.14 ECHR in conjunction with Protocol 1 art.1

[European Convention on Human Rights 1950 Protocol 1 art.1, art.14; Equality Act 2010 (c.15) s.149]

The claimant sought judicial review of the council tax reduction scheme which had been adopted by the defendant local authority. Faced with financial restraints, the local authority decided to replace the previous 100 per cent reduction for those eligible for council tax support because of their lack of resources with an 85 per cent reduction. The claimant was a 55-year-old man whose health problems made it impossible for him to work. He and his wife, who was his registered carer, received disability living allowance together with employment and support allowance. There were three stages to the defendant's scheme. First, there was an assessment of what earnings and capital should be taken into account when determining the "applicable amount" in respect of any claimant; not all of a disabled person's income was taken into account. Second, premiums and allowances were adopted depending on marital status and other factors. A comparison was then made between actual available income and the applicable amount that the scheme deemed was reasonable for someone in the taxpayer's position to pay. If actual income was below the applicable amount, the maximum council tax support was available under the primary scheme; where actual income exceeded the applicable amount, the taxpayer might be eligible for support on a reduced basis. Third, in any case of exceptional hardship, the taxpayer could apply for discretionary additional support. The claimant was initially subject to the 85 per cent reduction. However, after applying for a further reduction under the discretionary scheme, he was awarded council tax support of 100 per cent. The main issues were (i) whether the scheme amounted to discrimination on grounds of disability or age, in breach of ECHR art.14 taken in conjunction with Protocol 1 art.1; (ii) whether the local authority had had due regard to the public sector equality duty in the Equality Act 2010 s.149.

Held: Application granted in part. (1) The scheme did not breach art.14. First, it applied to all people of working age whose income fell beneath the applicable amount; it was thus overtly neutral with respect to age or disability. Second, while it had greater impact on disabled people under retirement age than on others of a similar age (because more members of that class were likely to be unable to access employment that would result in earnings exceeding the applicable amount), there had not been indirect discrimination on such grounds by the application of a single blanket rule to those whose situations were significantly different. The fact that the scheme had an impact on the disabled was expressly taken into account in the various disregards to income made and the premiums awarded in ascertaining the applicable amount. The different situations of the able-bodied and the disabled with respect to access to the labour market had thus already been acknowledged in the scheme. Once it was recognised that different rules had been established for the disabled in calculating the applicable amount, it did not constitute either a difference in treatment or an unlawful failure to treat people differently to expect that a modest percentage of council tax support would be absorbed in the subsistence budgets of the poor generally, even if the benefits forming that budget were provided because of eligibility through the disability gateway. Further, in the light of the above factors and with the existence of a discretionary scheme to address exceptional hardship, any indirect difference in treatment on the grounds of age or disability was justified, *Burnip v Birmingham City Council* [2012] EWCA Civ 629, [2013] P.T.S.R. 117, [2012] C.L.Y. 3111 distinguished (see paras 34-35, 37-40 of judgment). (2) The equality impact assessment which the local authority had carried out before adopting the scheme was not defective. However, there was insufficient evidence to support the conclusion that due regard was had to the assessment by those who took the decision: the full council consisted of 54 people, but the assessment had not been circulated to all of them. There would be sufficient vindication of the public interest and the claimant's rights for that conclusion to be stated in a declaratory judgment. No other formal relief was needed (paras 9, 32).

R. (ON THE APPLICATION OF LOGAN) v HAVERING LBC, [2015] EWHC 3193 (Admin), [2016] P.T.S.R. 603, Blake J, QBD (Admin).

1444 Council tax support–Prescribed requirements and default scheme

THE COUNCIL TAX REDUCTION SCHEMES (PRESCRIBED REQUIREMENTS AND DEFAULT SCHEME) (WALES) (AMENDMENT) REGULATIONS 2016, SI 2016/50; made under the Local Government Finance Act 1992 s.13A(4)(5), Sch.1B para.2, Sch.1B para.3, Sch.1B para.4, Sch.1B para.5, Sch.1B para.6, Sch.1B para.7. In force: 20 January 2016.

These Regulations amend the Council Tax Reduction Schemes and Prescribed Requirements (Wales) Regulations 2013 and the Council Tax Reduction Schemes (Default Scheme) (Wales) Regulations 2013.

1445 Home Office–Secretaries of State–Transfer of functions

THE TRANSFER OF FUNCTIONS (FIRE AND RESCUE SERVICES) ORDER 2016, SI 2016/162; made under the Ministers of the Crown Act 1975 s.2. In force: 1 April 2016.

This Order provides for the transfer of property, rights and liabilities from the Secretary of State for Communities and Local Government to the Secretary of State for the Home Department (Home Secretary) in consequence of the transfer of functions in relation to fire and rescue services from the Department for Communities and Local Government to the Home Secretary.

1446 Investigations–Standards committees–Functions of monitoring officers and standards committees

THE LOCAL GOVERNMENT (STANDARDS COMMITTEES, INVESTIGATIONS, DISPENSATIONS AND REFERRAL) (WALES) (AMENDMENT) REGULATIONS 2016, SI 2016/85; made under the Local Government Act 2000 s.53(11)(12), s.56(5), s.73(1), s.81(5), s.105(1)(2), s.106. In force: 1 April 2016.

These Regulations amend the Standards Committees (Wales) Regulations 2001, the Local Government Investigations (Functions of Monitoring Officers and Standards

Committees) (Wales) Regulations 2001 and the Standards Committees (Grant of Dispensations) (Wales) Regulations 2001 to implement changes in operation of the system governing member conduct with the aim of improving local democracy.

1447 Local authorities–Combined authorities–West Midlands

THE WEST MIDLANDS COMBINED AUTHORITY ORDER 2016, SI 2016/653; made under the Transport Act 1985 s.85; Local Transport Act 2008 s.84, s.91, s.93; Local Democracy, Economic Development and Construction Act 2009 s.103, s.105, s.114, s.117. In force: 16 June 2016.

This Order establishes the West Midlands Combined Authority.

1448 Local authorities' powers and duties–Children's services–Voluntary sector provision of breaks for disabled children–Decision to cut funding–Lawfulness

[Equality Act 2010 (c.15) s.149; Breaks for Carers of Disabled Children Regulations 2011 (SI 2011/707) reg.3, reg.4; Children and Families Act 2014 (c.6) s.27(2); Children Act 2004 (c.31) s.11]

The claimants applied for judicial review of two decisions made by the defendant local authority concerning cuts to funding for short breaks for disabled children. The local authority had been providing funding to voluntary sector organisations which provided short breaks for disabled children since 2008. Following financial pressures, in 2016 it decided to cut that funding. That decision (Decision 1) was made on 1 March 2016 as part of the local authority's process of setting its own budget. The claimants were given permission to challenge Decision 1. A second decision (Decision 2) made on 31 May 2016 re-affirmed Decision 1. The court had to determine whether the local authority had erred in failing to ask itself the right questions, and/or failed to take into account mandatory relevant considerations (the legality issue), and whether the local authority had given "due regard" to the statutory equality needs described in the Equality Act 2010 s.149. In light of the answers to those questions, the court had to determine what, if any, relief should be granted.

Held: Application granted. (1) *Decision 1* - The court was conscious of the intense pressures, both financial and timing, to which the decision was a response. However, those pressures were not relevant to the legality issue. The only question on that issue was whether the local authority members responsible for making the decision were given the help they needed on the legal issues which they had to consider before making funding cuts. Councillors were entitled to help from full-time expert officers to understand the policy and legal issues which would equip them to make lawful decisions. The materials provided to the members in the instant case would have helped them understand the likely practical impact of the cuts on parents/carers and children. However, the question was whether, despite provision of the necessary factual information, the local authority had failed to have "due regard" to the statutory equality needs listed in s.149. While members were given the text of s.149, they were directed to a formula which did not accurately encapsulate, for the purposes of the decision about short breaks, the effect of s.149. They were also directed to look at factual material in a way that did not help them focus on the right question. Furthermore, there was no reference to the express language, or to the substance, of the Breaks for Carers of Disabled Children Regulations 2011 reg.3 and reg.4, or of the Children and Families Act 2014 s.27(2), or of any relevant guidance. Nor was there any reference to the duty imposed by the Children Act 2004 s.11, or the best value guidance, to which the local authority was required to have regard. Members' attention was not drawn to mandatory relevant considerations. Decision 1 was therefore unlawful (see paras 42-48 of judgment). *Decision 2* - Although the members were equipped to take into account the factors which were relevant to a lawful decision, the way in which the challenge to Decision 1 was presented to them on 31 May gave a clear impression that they were expected to rubber stamp that decision and that they could not decide to rescind in accordance with the local authority's constitution. That state of affairs gave rise to a very clear appearance of predetermination. As a result, Decision 2 did not show that, had the local authority, properly directed, reconsidered Decision 1, the outcome for the claimants would have been the same, or not substantially different. Decision 2 was unlawful and was not effective to replace Decision 1 (paras 49, 64, 76).

(2) The court's provisional view was that, subject to any further written submissions which the parties wished to make, the reduction in funding for short breaks which was decided on 1 March should be quashed. Decision 2 should also be quashed (paras 72, 76).

R. (ON THE APPLICATION OF T) v WEST BERKSHIRE COUNCIL *sub nom.* R. (ON THE APPLICATION OF DAT) v WEST BERKSHIRE COUNCIL, [2016] EWHC 1876 (Admin), (2016) 19 C.C.L. Rep. 362, Elisabeth Laing J, QBD (Admin).

1449 Local authorities' powers and duties–Dangerous premises–Compensation–Meaning of "in default" in s.106(1) Building Act 1984

[Building Act 1984 (c.55) s.106, s.77, s.78; Occupiers' Liability Act 1957 (c.31); Health and Safety at Work etc. Act 1974 (c.37)]

A local authority appealed against a decision that it was liable to pay compensation to the respondent (M) under the Building Act 1984 s.106. M had acquired the rights of a leaseholder (Stylus) which leased a bingo hall and an amusement arcade on Hastings Pier. The freeholder was responsible for the repair and renewal of the pier's structure. In 2004 Stylus obtained an engineering survey of the pier which revealed serious structural problems requiring urgent attention. It sent the report to the freeholder and to the local authority, but no remedial work was carried out. In June 2006 the local authority exercised its emergency powers to close the pier to the public because it was unsafe. It was concerned about large numbers of people due to attend events in the pier ballroom. Stylus attempted to compel the freeholder to carry out the works, and when that failed it carried out the works itself. It then brought a claim against the local authority for compensation under s.106 of the Act. The local authority defended the action on the basis that Stylus could not claim if it was itself in "default". It asserted that Stylus was in default because it had breached its duties under the Occupiers' Liability Act 1957 and the Health and Safety at Work etc. Act 1974. The Technology and Construction Court and the Court of Appeal disagreed, holding that "default" was limited to default under the 1984 Act. The local authority submitted that the courts were wrong to treat the word "default" as confined to default under the 1984 Act.

Held: Appeal dismissed. (1) Section 106 gave a right to compensation to a person who had sustained damage by reason of the exercise of any of the authority's powers under the Act "in relation to a matter as to which he has not himself been in default". It was important to identify (a) the "matter" in relation to which the authority had exercised its powers and (b) whether it was a matter "as to which" the claimant had been in default. The relevant power was the power to take emergency action under s.78. Even a claimant in "default", in the relevant sense, was not precluded from seeking compensation, if the court determined that the authority was not justified in using its emergency power, rather than first seeking an order from the magistrates under s.77 to force the claimant to execute works. The right to compensation provided an important check on the unbridled use of the emergency power under s.78 (see paras 25-26 of judgment). (2) The matter which led the authority to take emergency action, rather than applying first to the magistrates' court, was not the general state of the pier. The authority had been aware of that since the receipt of the report from Stylus, but had not thought it necessary to close the pier, nor to take any legal action at that stage. The matter which triggered the action in June 2006 was the state of the pier combined with fear of possible collapse from crowd-loading during the forthcoming events. Stylus was not legally responsible for the state of the pier, nor was it responsible for the events which triggered the authority's action. It was not "in default" as to the matter which led to the authority's use of s.78. It was therefore entitled to compensation (paras 27-28). (3) When concluding that "default" in s.106 referred only to default under the 1984 Act the courts below had relied on the legislative history; the other references to "default" in the 1984 Act; the wide scope of the factual inquiry implicit in an alternative approach; and the various authorities under the predecessor statutes. None of those factors could support the conclusion that "default" was limited to default under the 1984 Act, rather than extending to other forms of legal default, *Clayton v Sale Urban DC* [1926] 1 K.B. 415 and *Neath Rural DC v Williams* [1951] 1 K.B. 115, [1947-51] C.L.Y. 6972 applied. The courts were right to find that the authority had no defence to the claim for compensation, not because there was no default under the 1984 Act, but because it was not default by Stylus which led to the emergency action under s.78. However, when assessing compensation attributable to the authority's action, the arbitrator could take into account the statutory and common law responsibilities of Stylus to its customers and employees. It was open to the authority to argue that the loss of profit should be substantially reduced due to the structural condition of the pier and the implications it would have had for the continuation of its business quite apart from the effects of the emergency notice (paras 30-37).

MANOLETE PARTNERS PLC v HASTINGS BC *sub nom.* HASTINGS BC v MANOLETE PARTNERS PLC, [2016] UKSC 50, [2016] 1 W.L.R. 3059, Lady Hale DPSC, SC.

1450 Local authorities' powers and duties–Performance indicators–Revocation

THE LOCAL GOVERNMENT (PERFORMANCE INDICATORS) (WALES) (REVOCATION) ORDER 2016, SI 2016/1057; made under the Local Government (Wales) Measure 2009 s.8(1). In force: 24 November 2016.

This Order revokes the Local Government (Performance Indicators) (Wales) Order 2012 which specifies, for Wales, performance indicators by reference to which the performance of county councils and county borough councils, in exercising functions, are measured.

1451 Local authorities' powers and duties–Pet animals–Unlawful sale of pet animals–Cancellation of event at which sale suspected

[Pet Animals Act 1951 (c.35) s.2]

The claimants sought permission to apply for judicial review of what they claimed was the defendant local authority's decision to cancel a meeting which was due to take place at a racecourse. The claimants were the chairman of the Portsmouth Reptile and Amphibian Society and the chairman of the Federation of British Herpetologists. A "Private Breeders' Meeting" had been due to take place at the racecourse, but it was cancelled after the local authority wrote to the racecourse's Operations Manager. The Society had organised and booked the meeting. It was said that the Federation had standing because the issue was the lawfulness of the sale of reptiles and amphibians at such meetings and because it represented the interests of persons involved in the breeding and keeping of such animals. The letter from the local authority referred to the Pet Animals Act 1951, which rendered the sale of animals unlawful if carried out in the "course of a business", and continued as follows: "Councils are responsible for enforcing the law in this area and action will be taken with regard to the forthcoming event so that the Council does not permit any unlawful activity taking place. At an absolute minimum we must insist that ... absolutely no sales of animals can take place at the event. However the event may proceed as an animal exhibition with the sale of dry goods and reptilian/amphibian paraphernalia".

Held: Application refused. The first issue was whether the local authority, if alerted to the risk of unlawful activity, should investigate the matter and pass on its concerns to an organisation such as the racecourse. The answer had to be yes. The local authority was a public body; it had a duty to do what it properly could to prevent the commission of offences by legitimate means. Warning an organisation such as the racecourse that its premises might be hosting an event at which unlawful activity might take place was an entirely proper course to have taken. The second issue was whether the local authority had been right to fear unlawful activity. The answer again was yes. The Animal Protection Agency, the intervener, had written to the local authority expressing its concerns about the impermissible sale of animals at similar events, saying that the same stallholders tended to appear at them. The third issue was whether the local authority had "procured" the cancellation of the event. Its letter might have been more clearly worded, but it did not bear the interpretation put on it by the claimants. In effect, the local authority had taken a decision to advise and the recipients of that advice were in agreement with it. If the decision of the racecourse owner/manager to cancel the event was wrong, the claimants were entitled to bring a private law action against the owner/manager. There was no arguable basis on which the instant claim, even if properly brought, could succeed. Further, it would not be appropriate for the court to accede to a request from the Animal Protection Agency to construe s.2 of the 1951 Act. Notwithstanding the understandable desire of the Agency and others interested in the subject for clarity, it was not for the court to legislate or to determine in advance of a course of conduct what would or would not amount to the commission of a criminal offence. There were exceptional circumstances in which such a course might be appropriate, but it was not appropriate here, *R. (on the application of Haynes) v Stafford BC* [2006] EWHC 1366 (Admin), [2007] 1 W.L.R. 1365, [2006] C.L.Y. 191 applied (see paras 23-29 of judgment).

KENT v ARUN DC, [2015] EWHC 2295 (Admin), [2015] L.L.R. 753, McGowan J, QBD (Admin).

1452 Local authorities' powers and duties–Roads–Power of local authority to rename streets

[Public Health Act 1925 (c.71) s.18, s.8]

A local authority appealed by way of case stated against the rejection of its decision concerning the renaming of streets on a residential estate. The renaming decision was made as part of a redevelopment scheme. Residents of the estate objected to the decision and appealed to the magistrates' court, which issued a summons. The appeal was heard by a district judge who, in the absence of any reported authority on the applicable legislation, namely the Public Health Act 1925 s.8 and s.18, adopted the approach taken in licensing cases. The judge did not consider that the new names had any particular advantage over the old names in terms of public safety and upheld the residents' objections. In doing so he stated that, in order to determine whether the local authority's decision was wrong, it had to be considered whether that decision was made with a view to promoting reasonable and identifiable objectives and whether the local authority had considered alternatives.

Held: Appeal allowed. (1) Since there was no reported authority on the proper construction of s.8 and s.18, the starting point had to be the words of the statute. Section 18 empowered the local authority to alter the name of any street with no precondition other than the giving of notice. Thus, a subjective judgement was required. The right of appeal given by s.8 to those "aggrieved" by an intended order of the local authority did not change the local authority's status as the primary decision-maker. The court's entitlement to make such order as it considered reasonable described the remedies available to it in disposing of the appeal: it did not make the magistrates' court the body charged with the decision whether or not to alter the street name. Since the statute did not restrict the right of appeal, there was no reason to read into s.8 a provision that the appeal should only be allowed where the local authority's decision was outside the ambit of reasonable responses. While it might be of assistance to consider analogous statutory provisions in order properly to apply a statutory scheme previously unconsidered in the case law, it was necessary to exercise caution when doing so. Before determining what order was required, the court first had to determine whether or not the local authority's decision was wrong. Only if it was satisfied that that was the case could it substitute its opinion for that of the local authority, *Stepney BC v Joffe* [1949] 1 K.B. 599, [1947-51] C.L.Y. 5948 and *R. (on the application of Hope & Glory Public House Ltd) v City of Westminster Magistrates' Court* [2011] EWCA Civ 31, [2011] 3 All E.R. 579, [2011] C.L.Y. 2136 applied. In the instant case, the judge was right not to test the local authority's decision by asking whether it was *Wednesbury* unreasonable and it followed that he had adopted the correct approach to the issue before him (see paras 31-37, 39, 42-44 of judgment). (2) However, the judge had fallen into error in the way he applied that approach to the facts, since he had paid little attention to the local authority's opinion and appeared to have regarded the burden of proof as falling on the local authority. Moreover, he had failed to identify where he considered the local authority had gone wrong. He had proceeded on the basis that he was not satisfied that the local authority's decision was right, whereas it was only if that decision was shown to be wrong that he was permitted to substitute his own opinion. While commenting on what he regarded as the limited advantages of the renaming scheme, he had not explained why that vitiated the decision. Therefore, the conclusion he had reached was not one that was properly open to him, *G v G (Minors: Custody Appeal)* [1985] 1 W.L.R. 647, [1985] C.L.Y. 2594 followed (paras 45-47, 49-51).

BASILDON BC v JAMES, [2015] EWHC 3365 (Admin), [2016] P.T.S.R. 377, Garnham J, QBD (Admin).

1453 Local authorities' powers and duties–Special educational needs–21-year-old subject to education, health and care plan–Transport to college–Whether obligation to fund

[Education Act 1996 (c.56) s.15ZA, s.312, s.35, s.508F]

The appellant local authority appealed against the First-tier Tribunal's decision that it was required to provide transportation costs to and from the educational institution of a 21-year-old (H) with special educational needs who was the subject of an Education, Health and Care (EHC) plan. H's EHC plan named only one educational institution. It was not close to her home. The local authority had argued that because H was between age 19 and 25, under the Education Act 1996 s.508F, it did not have an absolute duty to pay for H's travel to and from school and that it only had to do so if it considered it to be necessary. The respondent parents believed that the local authority should be responsible for transport costs, relying on para.9.215 of the Special Educational Needs Code of Practice 2014. The FTT found that H required transportation in order to access her college programme and that that amounted to a form of provision for H's special educational needs. It also found that H's needs were exceptional and that transport was accordingly a special educational need. The issues were whether (1) transport to from the place of education specified in an EHC plan for an adult learner with special educational needs was either a special educational need or a special educational provision; (2) a local authority had a duty under s.508F to pay transportation costs which would enable a young person over the age of 19 with an EHC plan to access the education specified in the plan.

Held: Appeal allowed. (1) It was clear from the wording of s.312 of the 1996 Act, which defined special educational needs and special educational provision, that a special educational need had to arise from a learning difficulty and that the learning difficulty had to call for special educational provision. It could not sensibly be argued that a need for home-to-school transport arose from a learning difficulty in and of itself. Nor could home-to-school transport be classed as a form of special educational provision, *R. v Havering LBC Ex p. K* [1998] 1 F.C.R. 641, [1997] C.L.Y. 2144 applied, *Dudley BC v S* [2012] EWCA Civ 346, [2012] P.T.S.R. 1393, [2012] C.L.Y. 993 followed. That did not mean that transportation issues were irrelevant. In cases where the choice of school was in issue, the cost of transportation was a matter which might be taken into account in deciding whether the parental or local authority choice of school was to prevail. In the instant case the issue was not the choice of school. Section 15ZA reinforced that analysis. The duty was described in terms of "education" and "training". Other matters, such as the location and times at which the education or training was provided, went to the suitability of the education to meet the individual's needs and not to the meaning of education or training themselves. There was nothing in the wording of the above sections which suggested that Parliament intended to change the understanding of those core terms. The FTT had erred in law by finding that transportation to and from school was either a special educational need or a special educational provision to meet such a need (see paras 22-27 of judgment). (2) The local authority argued that the 1996 Act did not impose a duty on a local authority to pay for transport for a person in H's situation even though it maintained an EHC plan for her. A local authority had a duty to secure transportation to school for certain eligible children under s.35 of the 1996 Act. There was no correlative provision for those in the post-19-year-old group. Under s.508F the local authority had a duty to make arrangement for H, as somebody over 19 years old, if it considered that to be necessary having regard to all of the relevant circumstances. That was not a pure discretion. In deciding that question it had to exercise its judgment judiciously and in good faith. If it came to the conclusion that it was necessary, it had to make the necessary arrangements and the transportation had to be free of charge. Paragraph 9.215 of the Code of Practice could be wrongly interpreted as a free-standing rule allowing transport needs to be included in an EHC plan despite s.508F, but if a tribunal found guidance in the Code which contradicted legislative provisions, its duty was to apply the law as laid down by Parliament. It was plain that a tribunal was not permitted to deal with transportation in the manner in which the FTT purported to do. The FTT had been in error of law in deciding that it could bypass s.508F by relying on the Code and in taking jurisdiction over transport where none existed (paras 36-37, 40-41).

STAFFORDSHIRE CC v JM, [2016] UKUT 246 (AAC), [2016] E.L.R. 307, Judge SM Lane, UT (AAC).

1454 Local elections–Elected mayors–Durham

THE TEES VALLEY COMBINED AUTHORITY (ELECTION OF MAYOR) ORDER 2016, SI 2016/783; made under the Local Democracy, Economic Development and Construction Act 2009 s.107A, Sch.5B para.3. In force: 20 July 2016.

This instrument makes essential provision in preparation for the introduction of a directly elected mayor for the area of the Tees Valley Combined Authority. The Order provides that the area of the Combined Authority is to have a directly elected mayor, and for the date of the first and subsequent elections to the role of mayor and the term of office.

1455 Local elections–Elected mayors–Merseyside

THE HALTON, KNOWSLEY, LIVERPOOL, ST HELENS, SEFTON AND WIRRAL COMBINED AUTHORITY (ELECTION OF MAYOR) ORDER 2016, SI 2016/782; made under the Local Democracy, Economic Development and Construction Act 2009 s.107A, Sch.5B para.3. In force: 20 July 2016.

This instrument makes essential provision in preparation for the introduction of directly elected mayors for the area of the Halton, Knowsley, Liverpool, St Helens, Sefton and Wirral Combined Authority. The Order provides that the area of the Combined Authority is to have a directly elected mayor, and for the date of the first and subsequent elections to the role of mayor and the term of office.

1456 Local elections–Elected mayors–South Yorkshire

THE BARNSLEY, DONCASTER, ROTHERHAM AND SHEFFIELD COMBINED AUTHORITY (ELECTION OF MAYOR) ORDER 2016, SI 2016/800; made under the Local Democracy, Economic Development and Construction Act 2009 s.107A, Sch.5B para.3. In force: 22 July 2016.

This Order creates the position of mayor for the area of the Barnsley, Doncaster, Rotherham and Sheffield Combined Authority and specifies the term of office for the mayor for that area, and the dates on which elections for the return of a mayor shall take place and the intervals between elections.

1457 Local government finance–Capital finance and accounting–Local authorities' powers and duties

THE LOCAL AUTHORITIES (CAPITAL FINANCE AND ACCOUNTING) (WALES) (AMENDMENT) REGULATIONS 2016, SI 2016/102; made under the Local Government Act 2003 s.21(1), s.24, s.123(1). In force: 31 March 2016.

These Regulations amend the Local Authorities (Capital Finance and Accounting) (Wales) Regulations 2003 and apply in relation to local authorities in Wales for financial years beginning on and after 1 April 2015.

1458 Non-domestic rates–Agricultural buildings–Meaning of occupied "together with agricultural land", in Sch.5 para.3(a) Local Government Finance Act 1988

[Local Government Finance Act 1988 (c.41) Sch.5 para.3(a)]

A ratepayer appealed against a decision of the Valuation Tribunal for England, upholding a valuation officer's refusal to delete a building from the rating list. The building was originally a retail warehouse, but the ratepayer, a farmer, had used it for the storage of agricultural machinery and silage between June 2010 and January 2012. The building was subsequently converted for use as a supermarket. The use of the building for agricultural purposes was always intended to be temporary and was partly motivated by the aim of obtaining a rates exemption on the basis that the building would be an "agricultural building" for the purposes of the Local Government Finance Act 1988 Sch.5 para.3(a). The issues were whether (1) the building was occupied "together with agricultural land" as required under Sch.5 para.3(a); (2) the building was used "solely in connection with agricultural operations" on the land together with which it was occupied, as required under Sch.5 para.3(a).

Held: Appeal allowed. (1) In *Farmer (Valuation Officer) v Buxted Poultry Ltd* [1993] A.C. 369, [1993] C.L.Y. 3389, Lord Slynn had indicated that in order for a building to be occupied "together with agricultural land", it was necessary to show that the buildings and agricultural land were occupied together so as to form an agricultural unit "in a real sense". However, that did not support the proposition that a use motivated by a desire to obtain exemption from liability to pay non-domestic rates should be disregarded. The words had to be read in the context of the issue in that case, namely whether premises which were separated by considerable distances could nevertheless be described as being "occupied together" by reason of their functional connection as part of a single business enterprise. The words were not intended to introduce considerations of motive, but to emphasise that the issue was fact-sensitive and all relevant factors had to be taken into account, *Farmer* considered. An arrangement should not be treated differently because it existed for the purpose of tax avoidance. The ratepayer's motive in using the building for the storage of silage and agricultural implements was irrelevant to the issue of whether it was occupied together with the adjoining agricultural land, *Kenya Aid Programme v Sheffield City Council* [2013] EWHC 54 (Admin), [2014] Q.B. 62, [2013] C.L.Y. 2035 and *Makro Properties Ltd v Nuneaton and Bedworth BC* [2012] EWHC 2250 (Admin), [2012] R.A. 285, [2012] C.L.Y. 2687 applied. Irrespective of any advantage in reducing liability for non-domestic rates, it was both convenient and beneficial to store silage in the building. The use was temporary and might fairly be described as opportunistic. The ratepayer's primary motivation was fiscal rather than agricultural, and he could have carried on his business as he had previously done, but the use itself was substantial, exclusive, beneficial and prolonged and there was no reason to disregard it. The building was occupied together with the remainder of the holding for the purposes of Sch.5 para.3(a) (see paras 39-43 of judgment). (2) During the period for which exemption was sought the building was used solely in connection with the agricultural operations on the land. The fact that it was not necessary for silage or machinery to be stored in the building was irrelevant. The correct focus was on the use itself, not on the motive for the use or whether the enterprise could have been arranged differently, *W&JB Eastwood Ltd v Herrod (Valuation Officer) (No.2)* [1971] A.C. 160, [1970] C.L.Y. 2404 considered (paras 46-47).

WOOTTON (T/A EF WOOTTON & SON) v GILL (VALUATION OFFICER), [2015] UKUT 548 (LC), [2016] R.A. 49, Martin Rodger QC, UT (Lands).

1459 Non-domestic rates–Amendments–Power of valuation officers to alter rating list of own volition during currency of list

[Local Government Finance Act 1988 (c.41) s.41, s.55(2), s.55(6); Non-Domestic Rating (Alteration of Lists and Appeals) (England) Regulations 2009 (SI 2009/2268) reg.14(5), reg.17]

A ratepayer (B) appealed against a decision (*BMC Properties and Management Ltd v Jackson (Valuation Officer)* [2014] UKUT 93 (LC), [2014] R.A. 309, [2014] C.L.Y. 2127) concerning the date from which an amendment to the rating list took effect. In 2007 B had bought a property divided into self-contained units. The property had been used for holiday lets since 1989, but the exact date of the change in use could not be ascertained. The property had been omitted from the 1990 non-domestic rating list in error. In March 2011, the valuation officer issued a notice of addition to the 2005 rating list. The alteration was stated to take effect from 1 April 2005, the day on which the 2005 list came into force. B submitted that (1) the valuation officer had no power under the Local Government Finance Act 1988 or the Non-Domestic Rating (Alteration of Lists and Appeals) (England) Regulations 2009 to make an alteration during the currency of a rating list; (2) the alteration of the list should not be retrospective because the date that commercial use of the property began could not be readily ascertained and therefore, under the terms of reg.14(5), the alteration should take effect from 22 March 2011.

Held: Appeal dismissed. (1) The 1988 Act did not explicitly empower the valuation officer to make alterations to the list of his own volition. In the 2009 Regulations, the closest to an express authorisation was reg.17, although the drafting seemed to assume that the power of alteration already existed, rather than explicitly conferring it. The scheme of the legislation was to impose a statutory duty on the valuation officer under s.41 to compile and maintain the list, and to take such steps as were reasonably practicable to ensure that it was accurately compiled. It was obvious that the word "maintain" in the context of s.41 had to be read as imposing an obligation on the valuation officer to maintain the list in an accurate state, and not merely to preserve it as an historic snapshot of the position on the date the list came into effect. Both the Local Government Act 1948 and the General Rate Act 1967 had allowed the list to be altered by proposals made by the valuation officer or an interested party. B had produced no obvious or compelling reason why the change in the structure of the legislation should have been intended to deprive the valuation officer of a power to amend the list of his own volition. That was particularly so where the owners and occupiers of rateable property had no obligation to notify the valuation officer of the creation or existence of a rateable hereditament. Insofar as was necessary, a power to alter the list could be implied into the s.41 duty itself, but the court's view was that s.55(2) was an enabling power designed to facilitate the execution of the s.41 duty, and that had been accomplished by reg.17 (see paras 11, 14, 18, 20-21 of judgment). (2) It was clear from s.55(6) that alterations of an existing rating list could be retrospective in effect. Regulation 14(2) was obviously drafted in order to encompass both initial inaccuracies in the list, for example, due to the omission of a rateable hereditament, and subsequent changes of circumstances which rendered the list inaccurate. It defined the effective date of alterations made in order to correct an inaccuracy on the list as "the day on which the circumstances giving rise to the alteration first occurred". The word "circumstances" did not just mean the underlying change of circumstances which lead to the inaccuracy. It also included a subsisting inaccuracy. The inaccuracy in the 2005 list on the day of its compilation was reasonably ascertainable when the alteration was made in 2011. Although it was not possible to identify precisely when the commercial use of the property began, it had started long before 1 April 2005. Regulation 14(5) therefore had no possible application to cases of the instant kind involving changes in circumstances which predated the compilation of the relevant list (paras 27, 40-44).

BMC PROPERTIES AND MANAGEMENT LTD v JACKSON (VALUATION OFFICER), [2015] EWCA Civ 1306, [2016] R.A. 1, Patten LJ, CA (Civ Div).

1460 Non-domestic rates–Appeals–Valuation officer withdrawing appeal–Costs

The appellant valuation officer requested permission to withdraw his appeal against a decision of the Valuation Tribunal for England concerning two ratings valuations of non-domestic premises. The appellant's statement of case had proposed different valuations of the respondent ratepayer's premises, and the appellant maintained his valuations in his reply to the respondent's statement of case. The appeal hearing was fixed, to be held under the simplified procedure, but less than a month before the hearing date the appellant requested permission to withdraw from further proceedings. The appellant accepted that the tribunal's valuations had been correct on the basis of evidence provided to him by the respondent's expert. The respondent did not consent to the withdrawal unless the appellant paid her costs of preparation for the appeal. The appellant submitted that: (1) the respondent had unnecessarily caused costs to be incurred by engaging an expert and preparing a detailed statement of her case, in an appeal which was proceeding under the simplified procedure; (2) there was an element of double counting in the respondent's expert's fees, as he been instructed to act on behalf of other ratepayers in the area, from whom he was also claiming fees; (3) he had not acted unreasonably and had not lengthened the proceedings, as he had sought to withdraw his appeal at the earliest opportunity.

Held: Application granted, costs determined. (1) The respondent was entitled to respond to the appeal in such detail as she saw fit and it was entirely reasonable for her to respond to the appeal. Her statement of case was detailed but it was cogent, relevant and competently presented, and provided the appellant with a substantial amount of useful information. It was extraordinary to suggest that that was not necessary and had lengthened the proceedings. Neither was it disproportionate to use an expert witness. It was only after the expert witness was appointed that the respondent was provided with the information that enabled him to reassess his case. For the appellant to suggest otherwise was absurd and contrary to his own evidence (see paras 32-33 of judgment). (2) There was no suggestion of double counting in the payment of the expert's fees. The fact that he was retained by other ratepayers did not affect the work that he had done for the respondent and he had not charged twice for the same work (para.34). (3) On balance, the appellant had withdrawn his appeal at the earliest that he could reasonably have done so. It had been reasonable to check thoroughly the evidence provided by the respondent's expert. Once the appellant had satisfied himself and the other senior personnel within the Valuation Office Agency that the tribunal's approach had been correct and that the rating list was accurate, he withdrew the appeal without delay and saved the parties the cost of the hearing. The early settlement of disputes was to be encouraged. It would be unhelpful if a party which had reassessed the strength of its case was to be discouraged from withdrawing an appeal in a simplified procedure case by concern that it would automatically become liable for the costs of the respondent. To withdraw an appeal which was believed to have little prospect of success was a reasonable course of action and it should not automatically be penalised. Some additional factor was likely to be necessary in a simplified procedure case, such as a frivolous or a purely tactical appeal, to make it appropriate to order the appellant to pay the respondent's costs. The appellant's conduct was not unreasonable and the circumstances of the case were not so exceptional as to justify an award of costs to the respondent in respect of the substantive issues in dispute, *Tarafdar (t/a Shah Indian Cuisine) v Revenue and Customs Commissioners* [2014] UKUT 362 (TCC), [2014] B.V.C. 533, [2014] C.L.Y. 3037 applied. However, when considering the conduct of a party the tribunal should have regard to whether a party had acted reasonably in pursuing or contesting an issue. The appellant's submissions about the respondent's conduct, including criticism of the presentation of her case and the appointment of an expert were wholly unjustified and unreasonable. Therefore, the appellant should have to pay 50% of the respondent's costs on the indemnity basis of preparing her written representations on the issue of costs (paras 38-42).

MCDONOUGH v O'KEEFFE, [2015] UKUT 74 (LC), [2015] R.V.R. 385, AJ Trott FRICS, UT (Lands).

1461 Non-domestic rates–Cash dispensers–Whether cash dispenser sites separate hereditaments from the properties in which located

The appellants, the operators of retail properties and of automated teller machines (ATMs), appealed against the respondent valuation officers' decisions to enter the sites of ATMs in the rating lists as separate hereditaments from the properties in which they were located. The ATMs were placed in the properties under agreements or licences. They were either within the properties and only accessible when the properties were open, or in holes in the wall and accessible 24 hours a day. The appellants argued that the ATM sites were not hereditaments: they were not physically self-contained, as they could only be found within the host properties, and the ATMs were non-rateable pieces of machinery whose presence could not be relied on to identify the appeal hereditament. They further argued that no leases had been granted to the ATM operators and that both parties to the agreements were obliged to undertake certain arrangements.

Held: Appeals dismissed. The issue was not the rateability of the machinery but of the land on which it was placed. Each site was a self-contained piece of land. Every part was physically accessible from all other parts without having to go onto other property. There was a clear defined physical area. Its definition might not be marked, but it was a physical area which the host premises could not use. The emphasis in the test set out in *Woolway (Valuation Officer) v Mazars LLP* [2015] UKSC 53, [2015] A.C. 1862, [2015] C.L.Y. 1702 was that the hereditament under dispute was self-contained, and that test had been met, *Woolway* followed. The appellants' argument focused on the host store and its relationship with the ATM site instead of identifying the hereditament in dispute and then determining who was in occupation, *Westminster City Council v Southern Railway Co Ltd* [1936] A.C. 511 followed. Although the appeals did not concern buildings, what was being rated was the site of the ATM, a piece of land clearly defined, *Bradford (Valuation Officer) v Vtesse Networks Ltd* [2006] EWCA Civ 1339, [2006] R.A. 427 considered. It had to be determined whether the use of the ATM sites by the operators carved out a separate occupation. It was possible to carve a hereditament out of the site of an ATM, but that was not the end of the matter. *Westminster* required those considering occupation to answer the question of paramount occupation with regard to the position and rights of the occupation of the premises and the purpose of the occupation of the premises. The relevant premises were the ATM sites, rather than the stores. In each appeal the licence or agreement signed by the operator and the host provided for the operator to install and operate an ATM at the site. There was a degree of reciprocity between operator and host in the agreements, but that did not affect paramount control. Frequently leases would place obligations on both parties. They did not mean that the tenant was not in occupation. The ingredients necessary to find rateable occupation were met by the ATM operators: the area was clearly defined, was self-contained, they had exclusive use for their purpose, the possession was of value and ATM sites rarely moved, so the period of possession was not too transient, *Westminster* and *John Laing & Son v Kingswood Assessment Committee* [1949] 1 K.B. 344, [1947-51] C.L.Y. 8292 followed. The merger of two hereditaments was only permissible where they were under the same occupation; the issue did not arise otherwise, *Woolway* followed. The functionality or purpose test suggested by the appellants was therefore not relevant. The appeals could not succeed (see paras 62-83 of judgment). Appeals such as the instant would be decided by identifying the hereditament in dispute; undertaking the geographical/self-contained test; determining who was in occupation, using the *Westminster* and *John Laing* tests; and, if both hereditaments were in the same occupation, following the test in *Woolway* as to whether they should be treated as a single hereditament (para.90). The tribunals in *Lanarkshire Valuation Joint Board Assessor v Clydesdale Bank Plc* 2005 S.L.T. 167, [2005] C.L.Y. 5618 and cases following that had misdirected themselves by focusing on the agreement and not whether the ATM site was separately occupied, *Lanarkshire*, *Assessor for Central Scotland Valuation Joint Board v Bank of Ireland* [2010] CSIH 91, 2011 S.C. 265, [2011] C.L.Y. 4551 and *Selecta UK Ltd v Lothian Valuation Joint Board Assessor* [2010] R.A. 37, [2010] C.L.Y. 4496 doubted (paras 84-89).

SAINSBURY'S SUPERMARKETS LTD v ALEXANDER (VALUATION OFFICER), [2016] R.A. 141, A Clark, VT.

1462 Non-domestic rates–Charitable purposes–Test of whether premises "wholly or mainly used for charitable purposes"

[Local Government Finance Act 1988 (c.41) s.43(5), s.43(6), s.43(6)(a), s.45A, s.45A(2)]

The appellant local authority appealed by way of case stated against a deputy district judge's refusal to make liability orders for non-domestic rates in relation to retail warehouse premises leased by it to the respondent charity. The charity occasionally held public appeals at the premises. On appeal days, the charity used approximately 42% of the available space. Between appeal days, the charity was not in occupation and there was no other use of the premises. The local authority applied for liability orders for non-domestic rates in relation to them. Under the Local Government Finance Act 1988 s.45A(2), there was no liability for rates for an unoccupied hereditament where the ratepayer was a charity and when next in use the hereditament would be wholly or mainly used for charitable purposes. For the appeal days, the effect of s.43(5) of the Act was that the charity would be relieved from paying at least 80% of the rates payable if the condition in s.43(6)(a) was fulfilled, namely that the ratepayer was a charity and the hereditament was wholly or mainly used for charitable purposes. In dismissing the application, the judge held that, on appeal days, the premises were used wholly or mainly for charitable purposes and nothing happened in the remainder. Accordingly, under s.43(6), the charity was liable for only 20% of the rates for those days and, under s.45A, it did not have to pay any rates for the periods between the appeal days. The local authority contended that the judge had not been entitled to find that, on appeal days, the premises were wholly or mainly used for charitable purposes. It submitted that the judge had erroneously interpreted the meaning of "wholly or mainly used"; "mainly" had to mean "more than half". It submitted that the judge had improperly had regard to the fact that the premises were not being used for any other purpose. Accordingly, it claimed that full rates were payable.

Held: Appeal allowed. (1) When considering whether a hereditament was "wholly or mainly used for charitable purposes" under s.43(6) of the Act, the test was not whether the activity conducted on the premises was wholly or mainly charitable, but whether the premises were being used wholly or mainly for charitable activity, *Kenya Aid Programme v Sheffield City Council* [2013] EWHC 54 (Admin), [2014] Q.B. 62, [2013] C.L.Y. 2035 and *Public Safety Charitable Trust v Milton Keynes Council* [2013] EWHC 1237 (Admin), [2013] 2 E.G.L.R. 133, [2013] C.L.Y. 236 applied, *English Speaking Union Scottish Branches Educational Fund v Edinburgh City Council* [2009] CSOH 139, 2009 S.L.T. 1051, [2010] C.L.Y. 4486 considered. If the premises were being used wholly or mainly for charitable purposes, it did not matter that they could have been run more efficiently or that only part of the premises need have been used. The rules on charitable exemption could be manipulated to advantage the owners of business premises and charities leasing them; when determining whether the exemption applied, it was immaterial that the purpose of the arrangement was to reduce or avoid the payment of business rates, *Kenya Aid* applied (see paras 13, 16, 17 of judgment). (2) There was no presumption that once the floor space used was less than half it was perverse to find that the premises were wholly or mainly used for charitable purposes, *Public Safety* applied. The "wholly or mainly" question should not depend on how the premises were arranged for presentational purposes, provided that there was a clearly demarcated area in which the services were being provided, even if the premises were not all actually in use, *English Speaking Union* considered. A broad brush approach was required (paras 25-26). (3) The judge had erred in placing as much weight as he had on the fact that there was no other activity occurring on the premises. If there had been, that would have been material to the "wholly or mainly" question. However, if, having regard to the nature and extent of the use, the conclusion was that the premises could not properly be said to be wholly or mainly used by the charity, that conclusion could not change simply because the rest of the premises were empty. The judge had erroneously assumed that that could be the case. It was not possible to say that the decision would have been the same if that factor had been ignored. Accordingly, the decision was quashed and the matter was remitted to the judge (paras 27-28).

SOUTH KESTEVEN DC v DIGITAL PIPELINE LTD, [2016] EWHC 101 (Admin), [2016] 1 W.L.R. 2971, Elias LJ, QBD (Admin).

1463 Non-domestic rates–Completion notices–Appeals procedure–Notices of appeal–Running of time

[Non-Domestic Rating (Alteration of Lists and Appeals) (England) Regulations 2009 (SI 2009/2268) reg.19, reg.19(1), reg.19(3); Local Government Finance Act 1988 (c.41) Sch.4A para.8]

The applicant, a development owner, applied for an extension of time in which to appeal against 19 completion notices issued by the respondent local authority. The local authority's taxation team had issued the notices in October 2012 with an incorrect completion date of 1 November. The correct date should have been 22 November. The notices were addressed to a firm of surveyors which advised the applicant on landlord and tenant matters but not on rates matters. Neither the landlord and tenant advisers nor the rating advisers were authorised to accept service, a fact of which the respondent was aware. The development was not complete on 1 November 2012, practical completion being around eight months later. In the meantime, the valuation officer had made 19 entries in the rating list and issued rate demands for the period from 1 November 2012. Those demands caused the applicant and its advisers to initiate inquiries. They found no trace of the 19 completion notices. In September 2013, they challenged both the valuations and the effective dates. On 25 September 2013, the respondent sent them duplicate copies of the notices. The applicant and its advisors then searched for the original notices but could not find them. Nothing was done in relation to an appeal until 9 December 2013. The issues were: (1) whether the appeals were out of time, which involved determining the date on which the 28-day appeal period in the Non-Domestic Rating (Alteration of Lists and Appeals) (England) Regulations 2009 reg.19(1) began to run; (2) whether the appeals were valid despite the absence of an appeal notice; (3) if the appeals were out of time, whether the applicant's delay was excusable.

Held: Application granted. (1) The respondent normally sent completion notices by recorded delivery, but had not done so in the instant case. The valuation officer had not received the notices either, which was a statutory requirement. On the balance of probabilities the 19 notices were never issued or, if they were, had gone astray before reaching their destination. The applicant's argument that the 28-day appeal period had therefore never started to run had an inescapable logic. There was also something in the respondent's argument that the appeal period began on 25 September 2013 when the applicant received the copy notices, since otherwise there was no time limit at all, which hardly seemed satisfactory. Assuming that the completion notices were valid, and noting the use of the word "received" as opposed to the word "served" in reg.19(1), the provision was to be read as applying to the situation where the original notices were not received but where copies had subsequently been supplied. Therefore, the 28-day period began to run on 25 September and it was for the applicant to satisfy the tribunal that its failure to act within the period was excusable (see paras 8, 10-11, 18-23 of judgment). (2) Regulation 19(1) required an appeal notice to be lodged and the applicant had not done so. The tribunal was not convinced by the applicant's argument that reg.19(3) was to be construed as impliedly permitting an extension of time to be granted *before* a notice of appeal had been provided, but did not need to decide the point. The respondent's argument that the absence of an appeal notice meant that there was no appeal could not succeed. The requirements of reg.19 had not been met, but several factors had influenced what took place. Not all failures to comply with statutory procedural requirements resulted in invalidity or ineffectiveness, and reg.19 should probably not be enforced with undue rigour (paras 28-29). (3) The applicant's conduct was the primary focus in determining its entitlement to proceed with the appeals, but it would be wrong to exclude other relevant factors including the respondent's actions and, in the instant case, earlier input by the tribunal. Mistakes had been made, all of which started because of the failings surrounding the issue of the completion notices and the failure to serve them in accordance with the Local Government Finance Act 1988 Sch.4A para.8. It was regrettable that there had been no attempt to appeal until 9 December when the appellant could have appealed immediately upon, or within 28 days of, receiving the copy notices. However, it had been reasonable to search for the lost notices, and to assume that the time for appealing had not started to run. That period of delay was therefore excusable. Some significance was to be attached to later delay caused by a reasonable, though mistaken, belief that the time limit either no longer applied or had long since expired, and that as proposals had been made, there was no urgency. However it was in the overall interests of justice to grant the extension of time for appealing (paras 25-26, 33, 35-38).

SAINSBURY'S SUPERMARKETS LTD v EDEN DC, [2016] R.A. 40, Graham Zellick QC, VT.

1464 Non-domestic rates–Completion notices–Name of intended recipient not appearing on completion notice–Validity of notice

[Local Government Finance Act 1988 (c.41) Sch.4A, Sch.4A para.2, Sch.4A para.8, Sch.4A para.8(c)]

The appellant billing authority appealed against a decision of the Valuation Tribunal that a completion notice issued under the Local Government Finance Act 1988 Sch.4A was defective and not validly served. The first respondent ratepayer owned the freehold of the building concerned. In anticipation of the completion of its redevelopment, discussions took place between the appellant and rating agents acting on behalf of the first respondents concerning the service of a completion notice. No agreement was reached on a completion date and the agents declined to confirm the identity of the building's owner. The appellant issued a completion notice addressed to "the owner" at the address of the building. It was delivered on 5 March 2012 by hand to a receptionist at the building who was employed by the facilities management company. Neither that company nor its receptionist had authority to accept service of legal documents on behalf of the first respondent. The receptionist scanned the completion notice and transmitted it electronically to the first respondent which acknowledged that it had received the notice no later than 12 March 2012. The issues for consideration were whether (i) a completion notice was invalid if it failed to state the name of the intended recipient (where it was not suggested that that name could not be ascertained after reasonable enquiry), and (ii) the completion notice delivered to the building addressed to "the owner" was validly served.

Held: Appeal allowed. (1) The completion notice was a valid completion notice, despite the fact that it did not identify the intended recipient by name. The building to which the notice related was specified in the completion notice, which also stated the day which the appellant proposed should be the completion day. The statutory requirements for a valid completion notice were described in Sch.4A para.2(1). No form of completion notice was prescribed and no other information was required to be given. The expectation that a completion notice would be addressed to the intended recipient was not a requirement. In any event, the completion notice was addressed to the owner of the building, although not by name. The identification of the intended recipient of a formal document by reference to a status or capacity was not an uncommon technique, and the adoption of that technique was not inconsistent with the purpose of a completion notice. The modes of service described in Sch.4A para.8 were not mandatory but were permissive, and any other method which brought the completion notice into the hands of the owner would be sufficient. The making of reasonable enquiries was a necessary precondition to reliance on para.8(c) to prove service of a completion notice addressed only to "the owner", but para.8 did not introduce a further requirement as to the form of the notice itself and did not prohibit service of a notice addressed only to "the owner" (see paras 32-33, 35-36 of judgment). (2) The steps taken by the appellant, coupled with the actions of an employee of the owner's agent, brought the completion notice to the attention of the owner of the building. Schedule 4A para.8(c) did no more than permit service by a particular method in specified circumstances. The instant notice was in valid form and it did not become invalid because of the mode of service adopted. Whether that mode of service was effective or ineffective did not depend on the content of the document itself, but on whether it was delivered in such a way as to come into the hands of the intended recipient. Although neither the facilities management company nor the receptionist had authority from the respondent to receive the notice, the receipt of the document was only one step in its passage into the respondent's hands. A document which arrived in the hands of the intended recipient by an unorthodox route was still served, *Townsend Carriers Ltd v Pfizer Ltd* (1977) 33 P. & C.R. 361, [1978] C.L.Y. 1790 considered. The instant notice was not handed to a complete stranger or to a third party with no relevant connection to the intended recipient, and the court did not accept that its onward transmission to the intended destination by one or more stages prevented the eventual receipt from being effective. Furthermore, in circumstances where there was no dispute that the electronic copy was received there was no justification for distinguishing between notices in different forms. The relevant sequence of events did not come to an end when the completion notice was handed to the receptionist: service took place when the electronic copy arrived in the hands of the respondent not later than 12 March (paras 39, 41, 44, 47-50).

UKI (KINGSWAY) LTD v WESTMINSTER CITY COUNCIL *sub nom.* WESTMINSTER CITY COUNCIL v UKI (KINGSWAY) LTD, [2015] UKUT 301 (LC), [2015] R.A. 433, Martin Rodger QC, UT (Lands).

1465 Non-domestic rates–Equestrian facilities–Whether racehorse training constituting intrinsically non-domestic activity for purposes of s.66(1)(b) Local Government Finance Act 1988

[Local Government Finance Act 1988 (c.41) s.66(1), s.66(1)(b)]

Two taxpayers appealed against valuation officers' decisions to enter their equestrian facilities into the non-domestic rating list. The first taxpayer owned a cottage with equestrian facilities and seven to ten racehorses. The second taxpayer owned a house on a farm, an adjacent barn containing stables, other equestrian facilities, and between seven and nine racehorses. The barn had been built before the house. A planning restriction limited the house's use to a person looking after the stables. Both taxpayers complied with the British Horseracing Authority's requirements, entered horses into races and earned winnings. The valuation officers determined that neither of the facilities could be covered by the council tax payment for the nearby dwelling, as it was not an "other appurtenance" to the domestic property within the Local Government Finance Act 1988 s.66(1)(b) since it was not within the curtilage of the dwelling and not used for domestic purposes. The issues were (1) the meaning of "curtilage"; (2) whether s.66(1)(b) required that the appurtenance was used wholly or mainly for domestic purposes; (3) whether the facilities were within the curtilage; (4) whether the training of racehorses at the properties was non-domestic.

Held: Appeals allowed in part. (1) A curtilage was fixed as a matter of law and was not fluid depending on use, although use or function could shed light on whether a building was within the curtilage, along with all other relevant factors. The concept of curtilage did not vary depending on the legal context. That did not mean that the curtilage could never change over time, whether by design or in consequence of other developments, *Seabrook v Alexander (Valuation Officer)* [2014] R.A. 382, [2014] C.L.Y. 2133 applied (see para.17 of judgment). (2) It would not be absurd if s.66(1)(b) did not require domestic use, but it would be surprising. Section 66 defined domestic property for council tax purposes; every type of property identified in s.66(1) was expressed in terms of its residential or domestic use. It was difficult to see why appurtenances should alone be treated as domestic even if manifestly non-domestic in use. It would be odd if predominantly commercial activity within the curtilage of a dwelling escaped entry into the rating list, whereas significant commercial activity in the dwelling would commonly be rated, and if a predominantly commercial activity was to be rated, so too was one that was non-domestic even if not commercial. Although *Levinson (Valuation Officer) v Robeson* [2008] R.A. 379, [2009] C.L.Y. 2678 had held that an element of commercial use did not prevent a garden and outbuildings from escaping rateability, that case was not about an "other appurtenance", and the non-domestic use there was occasional. The judge appeared to have stated that non-domestic use within the curtilage could never take that part of the hereditament outside s.66(1). That was wrong, although it had not been part of the ratio, Levinson considered. Reading words like "wholly used for domestic purposes" into s.66(1)(b) was unnecessary. It was inconceivable that the draftsman had intended to exclude commercial activity otherwise within s.66(1)(b) from non-domestic rates. "Appurtenant" implied a link relating to use, in the instant case relating to a residence and of a domestic character (paras 23-37). (3) The cottage's facilities were within the curtilage. The tribunal rejected the proposition that a horse walker and training circuit were not found in a domestic context and that their presence had to remove it from the ambit of s.66(1)(b). Those were matters of fact and degree (paras 52-55). The barn at the farm was neither within the curtilage nor appurtenant to the house. The house had been built long after the barn, whose scale was so out of proportion to the house that it could not be regarded as within the curtilage. The planning restriction showed that the house had never been intended to be an ordinary domestic residence to which the facilities could be appurtenant. That conclusion was not displaced by the barn's proximity to the house or the lack of a physical boundary between them. The appeal regarding the farm failed (paras 57-59). (4) The valuation officers had argued that the costs of training racehorses pointed to it being non-domestic, but many such costs arose for residents with a single horse used for pleasure riding. They also argued that horse racing was a sport around which an industry had developed. Whether it was a sport or an industry was irrelevant. The tribunal had to have regard to the substance of the matter. Keeping horses was an ordinary adjunct of domestic life. The use to which a particular horse was put did not of itself raise issues as to rateability. If the valuation officers were right, the property of a horse owner who subsequently obtained a permit from the authority and began to train and race it would be a composite hereditament. That could not be correct. It was not possible to start from the proposition that training racehorses was per se non-domestic; all relevant factors had to be brought into consideration. It was the scale or circumstances of the operation that removed it from the domestic sphere, not the intrinsic nature of the activity (paras 62-70). The seven to ten horses at the cottage, although borderline, fell within the range of domestic equestrian activity. The authority's regulatory framework, the intense effort required by the taxpayer, the fact that racing took place elsewhere, and the amount of the taxpayer's winnings did not affect the outcome (paras 71-74).

CORNWALL v ALEXANDER (VALUATION OFFICER); PANVERT v REEVES (VALUATION OFFICER), [2015] R.A. 504, Graham Zellick QC, VT.

1466 Non-domestic rates–Highways–Land forming part of highway operated as car park–Whether local authority occupying land as car park

[Highways Act 1980 (c.66) s.263; Road Traffic Regulation Act 1984 (c.27) s.55]

The appellant local authority appealed against the respondent valuation officer's refusal to delete from the rating list a hereditament comprising a car park. The appeal land formed part of a public highway within the meaning of the Highways Act 1980. It was a highway maintainable at public expense which, by s.263, vested in the appellant as highway authority. The appellant operated the land as a pay and display car park. The appellant argued that the public highway was not in any person's occupation: it was land over which the public had free and unrestricted access and therefore it did not meet in full the four tests of rateable occupation set out in *John Laing & Son v Kingswood Assessment Committee* [1949] 1 K.B. 344, [1947-51] C.L.Y. 8292. The appellant further argued that the fact that the land was vested in it as the highway authority did not make it the occupier of the land. The respondent submitted that a single area of land might have several layers of different uses, each of which might be liable to a rate. He argued that the occupation of the land as a car park on a chargeable basis was a separate and distinct use from the highway use of the land. He further submitted that the appellant's use of the land as a car park constituted rateable occupation because it went beyond the provision of a highway: it added a value to the highway.

Held: Appeal allowed. (1) The reality, both in fact and in law, was that the appellant was not occupying the land as a car park. Rather, it was regulating the flow of traffic and parking on the highway in accordance with its statutory powers and duties as highway authority. Subject to that regulation, the appellant had no power to exclude the public from the land. As it was a highway, the public were free to pass and repass over it and use it for lawful parking. It had to be maintained by the appellant for that purpose. That distinguished the land from an off-street car park on land which was not a highway, *John Laing* and *Pimlico, Peckham and Greenwich Street Tramway Co v Greenwich Union Assessment Committee* (1873-74) L.R. 9 Q.B. 9 considered (see paras 24-26 of judgment). (2) If that conclusion was wrong, and the appellant was in actual occupation and exclusive possession of the land for the purpose of usage as a car park, then such possession was not of value or benefit to the appellant for the purposes of being liable to rating. The tribunal accepted the respondent's submission that there need not be profitable occupation for there to be beneficial occupation for the purposes of rating of land. However, the constraint imposed on a highway authority by the charging regime under the Road Traffic Regulation Act 1984 s.55, whereby any surplus over expenditure on designated parking places had to be applied for certain specific purposes, led to the conclusion that such occupation as might be found could not be beneficial for the purposes of rating, *R. (on the application of Attfield) v Barnet LBC* [2013] EWHC 2089 (Admin), [2014] 1 All E.R. 304, [2013] C.L.Y. 2525 considered. No tenant would give rent for the appeal land as a car park because no tenant would be able to operate the highway as a car park (paras 27-30). (3) The entry of the appeal land in the rating list should be deleted (para.32).

DORSET CC v REEVES (VALUATION OFFICER), [2015] R.V.R. 340, MF Young, VT.

1467 Non-domestic rates–Liability orders–Setting aside–Scope of test in *R. (on the application of Brighton and Hove City Council) v Brighton and Hove Justices* [2004] EWHC 1800 (Admin), [2004] R.A. 277

In an appeal by way of case stated, the appellant property owner appealed against a number of liability orders obtained by the respondent rating authority in respect of its failure to pay non-domestic rates for several of its properties. In December 2011 the appellant had relocated its registered office and arranged for mail to be forwarded to the new address. In April or May 2012, it received correspondence relating to proceedings in the magistrates' court for the liability orders. It attended a hearing in May 2012 and the proceedings were adjourned. The liability orders were made in October 2012 after no further contact between the parties. On 10 October 2012, the rating authority gave notice of its intention to begin winding-up proceedings on the basis of non-payment of the liability orders. As a result of the mail redirection, the appellant did not receive the letter until 6 November. It replied, requesting that the winding-up proceedings be postponed and undertaking to deal with the matter urgently. Between then and 19 December 2012, it disclosed documentation in support of its contention that it had not been liable for rates during the time periods relevant to the liability orders. There was no further contact between the parties until 4 February 2014 when the rating authority notified the appellant of further orders and repeated its intention to begin winding-up proceedings. The appellant applied to set aside the liability orders. A district judge refused, finding that the appellant had not acted with urgency or diligence, as it had not acted promptly upon receiving notice of the rating authority's application, and had not tried to contact or correspond with it between May and September 2012 or between December 2012 and February 2014. She also found that the appellant had failed to supply the rating authority with its new address. She stated a case as to whether she had been entitled to conclude that the test in *R. (on the application of Brighton and Hove City Council) v Brighton and Hove Justices* [2004] EWHC 1800 (Admin), [2004] R.A. 277, [2005] C.L.Y. 3357 was not met.

Held: Appeal allowed in part. The test in *Brighton and Hove* had to be carefully applied in relation to each liability order. The district judge had dealt with all the orders on the basis that, irrespective of when each one had been made, there had been a failure by the appellant to act with urgency and diligence. The issue was whether, had she considered each liability order separately, it would have made any difference to the outcome. The instant court was satisfied that it would not have made a difference in relation to the orders dated October 2012. However, the appellant could not be taken to have failed to act promptly in relation to orders dated July 2013 because it did not know about them until 4 February 2014. The fact that the later orders related to the same properties as in earlier orders, and the fact that the appellant had failed to respond promptly to those earlier orders, did not mean that it could be implied that the appellant had failed to respond promptly to the later orders. That stretched the rule in *Brighton and Hove* too far. The observations about promptness made at para.33 of that case were not designed to capture prospectively future orders when the ratepayer and the rating authority were in dispute about earlier orders in respect of the same property. The later orders related to different periods of liability, in respect of which different factual considerations might arise, and they required separate consideration. The district judge had misdirected herself as to the appropriate application of the test in relation to the later orders. The answer to the stated case was, therefore, that she had been entitled to find that the *Brighton and Hove* test was not met, but only in relation to the earlier liability orders, not in relation to the later ones (see paras 36-43 of judgment).

SLEEKMADE PROPERTY CO LTD v SHEFFIELD CITY COUNCIL, [2015] EWHC 4193 (Admin), [2016] R.V.R. 316, Dove J, QBD (Admin).

1468 Non-domestic rates–Primary schools–Determination of rateable value

The appellant valuation officer appealed against determinations by the Valuation Tribunal for England of the rateable values of the three respondent small independent primary schools in north London. The tribunal had determined the schools' respective rateable values using the contractor's basis. The valuation officer presented 12 comparables and information about five rating assessments of properties in several London boroughs. The collection included two day nurseries, a business providing music lessons and nine independent primary schools, three of which had been the subject of management buy-outs. The valuation officer contended that there was a rental market in small independent primary schools and sufficient evidence in the marketplace for the schools' rateable values to be determined by comparable rents. The schools submitted that the comparables provided were insufficient and the contractor's method should be used.

Held: Appeal dismissed. The rateable value of the three schools would be determined on the contractor's method using the figures which had been set by the tribunal. Although there were no precise rules about how close the comparables had to be, they had to be close enough in locality, type of occupation, size and other aspects to indicate the rental value of the properties to be valued. None of the comparables were useful: the day nurseries were not sufficiently similar, and a rental market in day nurseries did not provide useful information about any rental market in independent schools; the rents on four of the properties, including the nurseries, were not negotiated or there were close connections between the parties agreeing the rent; there was too little information provided for four properties; the localities of one independent school and the music school were not useful comparables; the music school was not a private independent primary school. The flaws in each item in the valuation officer's collection made them either useless or of very limited value. There was no evidence in the rents, individually and taken together, that there was a market in private independent primary schools rather than a collection of rents determined on rent review or otherwise than through negotiation. The quality of each item was such that little or no useful information could be drawn from it as to the rent that any of the respondent schools would fetch on the open market. There were far fewer items of evidence than would be expected, and it resembled evidence that would have been discarded from a much larger collection prior to its use rather than a useful collection in itself. Individually or as a whole, the rental evidence presented by the valuation officer was not sufficient to determine the rateable value of each of the three respondent schools' premises (see paras 7, 22, 25, 37-76 of judgment).

TURNBULL (VALUATION OFFICER) v GOODWYN SCHOOL, [2016] UKUT 68 (LC), [2016] R.A. 85, Elizabeth Cooke, UT (Lands).

1469 Non-domestic rates–Rateable value–Determining rateable value of property in disrepair

In an unopposed appeal, the appellant valuation officer appealed against a decision of the Valuation Tribunal of England that a shop and premises had a rateable value of £0 with effect from 1 April 2010. The appeal property, a two-storey retail unit which was demolished in 2014 as part of a larger redevelopment site, had been occupied and trading until May 2008 when it became vacant. Brown asbestos was exposed as a result of subsequent vandalisation. The original compiled list assessment for the property was £57, 500 with effect from 1 April 2010; on the respondent's proposal, the rateable value of the property was reduced to £0 with effect from 1 July 2013, when demolition works began, on the ground that the property had been sold for redevelopment, was vacant, had been stripped out by vandals, contained disturbed asbestos, and no longer had a value. However, negotiations with the appellant in relation to the period from 1 April 2010 to 30 June 2013 proved fruitless. The valuation tribunal determined that the property had been incapable of beneficial occupation due to the presence of exposed asbestos, because the work required to make the property capable of beneficial occupation would go beyond the works of repair assumed in the statutory rating hypothesis. The rateable value was accordingly reduced to £0 from 1 April 2010. The appellant submitted that the tribunal's reasoning had been overturned by *SJ&J Monk (A Firm) v Newbigin (Valuation Officer)* [2015] EWCA Civ 78, [2015] 1 W.L.R. 4817, [2015] C.L.Y. 2086, where the question of beneficial occupation was irrelevant. Instead, the court should determine whether the property was in a state of disrepair; the works could be characterised as repair; the repairs were economic. He considered that the property's rateable value at 1 April 2010 should be £57,500, and that as the cost of remedial work of £112,000 amounted to less than two years' rental value, the property could be assumed to have been in repair.

Held: Appeal dismissed. It was necessary to consider three questions: were the premises in such repair as would make it reasonably fit for the occupation of a reasonably-minded tenant, having regard to the age, character and locality of the property; if not, were the works required to put the premises into such a condition works of "repair"; and could those repairs be carried out economically, *Newbigin* followed. In the instant case, it was common ground that the property was not reasonably fit under the first question. Works, too, were required to put the property into a state of being reasonably fit for occupation: those works involved "restoration by renewal or replacement of subsidiary parts of a whole" not reconstruction of the entirety or substantially the entirety of the property, and would not produce a building of a wholly different character, *Lurcott v Wakeley & Wheeler* [1911] 1 K.B. 905 and *McDougall v Easington DC* (1989) 21 H.L.R. 310, [1989] C.L.Y. 2121 considered. However, a landlord would regard the repairs as uneconomic: it was highly unlikely that the hypothetical landlord would be willing to spend £112,000 or thereabouts on repairs in circumstances where other properties within the development area had been allowed to become derelict and had been hoarded, and would have been faced with the risk the redevelopment would come forward sooner rather than later. The correct assessment was therefore a rateable value of £0 (see paras 32, 35, 39, 41, 45-46 of judgment).

CEREP III TW SARL v KENDRICK (VALUATION OFFICER) *sub nom.* BARBER (VALUATION OFFICER) v CEREP III TW SARL, [2015] UKUT 521 (LC), [2016] R.A. 20, Judge Alice Robinson, UT (Lands).

1470 Non-domestic rates–Rateable value–Ground floor shop unit in popular tourist town

[Landlord and Tenant Act 1954 (c.56); Local Government Finance Act 1988 (c.41) s.56]

A ratepayer appealed against a decision of the Valuation Tribunal for England confirming that the rateable value of a retail unit (K) was £11,250. K was located in a parade of five shops facing a harbour in a popular tourist town. It was accessed via seven steps to a front balcony area. Its front window was set back behind the balcony. It was subject to a six-year lease at an annual rent of £13,000, and the previous leaseholder had paid a premium of £10,000 at the start of the lease. The lease was contracted out of the security of tenure provisions of the Landlord and Tenant Act 1954. The previous leaseholder had agreed a rateable value of £11,250 with the Valuation Office Agency, including an end allowance of 5% for the steps. The ratepayer took an assignment of K's lease and paid a premium of £5,000 to the previous leaseholder. K and another retail unit (M) were in the same building. M was similarly configured to K and was subject to a seven-year lease at an annual rent of £10,500. Its lease had no premiums attached and enjoyed protection under the 1954 Act. Its rateable value of £11,000 had been agreed by its occupier. The other three units in the parade were at a lower level than K and M, and were accessed by either steps or a sunken forecourt. The ratepayer sought a reduction in the rateable value of the property. The valuation officer considered the rents and rating assessments of all five units in the parade, and found M to be physically the closest comparable to K. He confirmed K's rateable value of £11,250. The ratepayer submitted that (1) K had a hard frontage and should not be valued as a ground-floor shop because a consideration of the average rent of first- and ground-floor properties along the same harbour resulted in a lower rateable value, and a cafe at a lower height had been valued under the first-floor rating scheme; (2) the terms upon which K was let were not compatible with the definition of "rateable value" in the Local Government Finance Act 1988 s.56 because the property was let for a fixed term without security of tenure, meaning that there was no reasonable prospect of continuance; (3) M's rental and assessment evidence should carry little weight because its lease was unreliable as a comparable and its valuation was under appeal.

Held: Appeal dismissed. (1) The Valuation Tribunal had not erred in confirming K's rateable value as £11,250.The hard frontage aspect was a common reason for an end allowance or lower zone rent being adopted for hereditaments without plate glass shop fronts. In the instant case, although there was a flank wall next to the steps up to the property, the property had a plate glass shop front on the balcony area. K was clearly a ground floor shop, albeit one accessed by steps. It was not comparable to the first-floor units along the harbour, all of which were cafes or similar and most of which were at a much higher floor level. It was also not comparable to the cafe which had been valued under the first-floor rating scheme because that was in a completely different, secondary location. Rating lists were a collection of valuations, arrived at on a consistent basis, and a hybrid method was not appropriate in valuing K (see paras 36-41 of judgment). (2) The rent on the property might not be on the statutory hypothetical terms. A letting was very rarely on those terms, but the rent remained a key piece of evidence. The fact that the lease was contracted out of the 1954 Act and that premiums had been paid twice suggested that, if anything, the basic rent was lower than the equivalent rent on the statutory hypothetical basis (para. 36). (3) Most weight had to be placed on the rent and assessment evidence in respect of K and M, and less weight on the three adjoining units. Significant weight had to be placed on K's passing rent. Although the ratepayer had not been a party to the agreement on K's rating assessment, a ratepayer with an informed appreciation of the premises and their location had agreed to it. Similarly, although the ratepayer in respect of M had appealed against M's assessment, she had agreed to it at the time. The rental evidence of K and M was to be preferred to the assessment evidence, and the basis for the valuation officer's valuation was correct. The final rateable value of £11,250 had to be considered in the context that it had been agreed by one previous occupier in respect of a unit where the rent passing was possibly too low, and it had to be assumed that K's physical configuration was reflected in those agreements (paras 36, 42-48).

WILLIAMS v MURDOCH (VALUATION OFFICER), [2015] UKUT 477 (LC), [2016] R.V.R. 105, PD McCrea FRICS, UT (Lands).

1471 Non-domestic rates–Rateable value–Licensed premises–Premises used as bar rather than private members' club

A ratepayer appealed against a decision of the Valuation Tribunal for England that the rateable value of his licensed premises was £11,250 from 1 April 2010. In 2010, the ratepayer had rented the premises under a five-year lease, paying an annual rent of £4,800. Some years previously, there had been court proceedings concerning the rating assessment of the premises. As a result, the premises' description in the 2005 rating list had been amended from "wine bar and premises" to "club and premises". The property had a premises licence which permitted the sale of alcohol for consumption on and off the premises. In 2014, the tribunal determined that the premises were a bar and should be valued on that basis in accordance with Valuation Office Agency guidance. Although the ratepayer ran the premises as a members' club, the tribunal deemed the club to be a town centre proprietary club rather than a non-profit-making club run for the members' benefit. It determined that the property should be assessed by way of turnover. It used an estimate of fair maintainable trade of £150,000 and attached little weight to the low rent because it had been agreed during an economic downturn. The ratepayer submitted that the premises were a private members' club rather than a bar or a proprietary club and that the club's rateable value should therefore have been determined by reference to rents of comparable properties in the region, not by its profits.

Held: Appeal dismissed. It was for the ratepayer to demonstrate, on balance and on the evidence, that the tribunal's decision was wrong. He had provided no evidence as to how his club operated, or what happened to the profits that were shown in the accounts. An inspection of the premises and the comparable evidence left no doubt that the premises were physically similar to the valuation officer's comparables rather than the ratepayer's, which were largely in different settings, often suburban or quasi-residential and in a variety of different types of buildings. The premises were fitted out in such a way that they could easily function as a bar. They were in a location with many bars nearby and would be of interest to licensed premises operators if vacant and to let. It was not appropriate to place weight on the low rent or on the alteration of the description to "club and premises" in the 2005 rating list. That had been an attempt to come to a pragmatic solution in respect of a long-running dispute with the previous ratepayer. Valuation officers should be discouraged from such a practice. The scope of the premises licence was wider than that of a club premises certificate, which would only provide for consumption on the premises. The user clause in the lease was also for a licensed bar rather than a club and the latest planning consent for the premises was for a bar and restaurant. All of those elements pointed to the premises being used as a bar, or akin to a bar, rather than a club. The premises were a bar and should be valued accordingly. A valuation based on an assumed fair maintainable trade of £150,000 was correct. The property would remain in the non-domestic rating list with a rateable value of £11,250 from 1 April 2010 (see paras 40-50 of judgment).

HARRIS v GRACE (VALUATION OFFICER), [2015] UKUT 365 (LC), [2015] R.V.R. 380, PD McCrea FRICS, UT (Lands).

1472 Non-domestic rates–Rateable value–Office and premises units on business park–Rental and settlement evidence

[Local Government Finance Act 1988 (c.41) Sch.6 para.2]

A valuation officer appealed against determinations by the Valuation Tribunal for England of the rateable value of two office and premises units on a business park. In adopting a valuation for main office space of £137 per sq m for the two properties, the tribunal had concluded that there was an issue of oversupply in the rental market on the business park that would be likely to reduce a hypothetical tenant's bid for the purposes of determining rental value. It had also attributed weight to the argument that such an oversupply allowance had been agreed between the Valuation Office Agency in respect of hereditaments in the City of London. The parties agreed that the passing rents were of little assistance for the purposes of the valuation exercise. The issues were whether: (i) lease renewals should be accorded more evidential weight than rent reviews when examining the evidence; (ii) the tribunal had erred in its interpretation of the decision in *Lotus & Delta Ltd v Culverwell (Valuation Officer)* (1976) 239 E.G. 287, [1976] C.L.Y. 2260.9, by placing too much weight on the ratepayer's arguments relating to the alleged oversupply, and in ignoring the comparable rental and ratings settlement evidence.

Held: Appeal allowed. (1) If there was a pecking order between lease renewals and rent reviews then, in principle, lease renewals should come first. A lease renewal was a new letting from which the tenant could walk away, rather than an assumed letting, and the rent agreed on the renewal therefore supplied evidence more closely aligned with the statutory hypothesis of a letting in the open market under the Local Government Finance Act 1988 Sch.6 para.2 (see para.48 of judgment). (2) It was a longstanding principle of rating valuation that reliable rental evidence should be accorded more weight than rating assessments unless there was an established tone of the list. The tribunal had been wrong to ignore the rental and settlement evidence and to attribute a reduction for oversupply, as the hypothetical tenant would have been aware of the situation on the business park on the valuation date. The decline in rental values after the valuation date was not due to oversupply on the park but to the effects of the economic recession. The circumstances under which the agreements were reached with the Valuation Office Agency in London were different and did not apply by means of precedent. The lease renewal and rent review evidence adequately demonstrated the correct figure to be applied as £180 per sq m for the main office space. The evidence from ratings settlements was also sufficient to establish a settled tone of the list at that sum, *Lotus* applied. The first unit's valuation was increased from £19,750 to £25,750, and the second unit's valuation increased from £39,500 to £51,500 (paras 47, 53-55).

BAINBRIDGE (VALUATION OFFICER) v BOLDFIELD LTD; BAINBRIDGE (VALUATION OFFICER) v GREENFIELD SOFTWARE LTD, [2015] UKUT 295 (LC), [2015] R.A. 459, PR Francis FRICS, UT (Lands).

1473 Non-domestic rates–Restaurants–Determination of rateable value

Two ratepayers appealed against the Valuation Tribunal for England's determination of the rateable value of their leasehold property, a licensed restaurant, at £54,000. The ratepayers had previously held a lease of a public house on the site of the restaurant. However, they had entered into an agreement with a developer under which they surrendered their lease so that the public house could be demolished and a new development constructed in its place. The development was a single building comprising a number of commercial and residential units. The appeal property was a restaurant unit which the ratepayers leased in the new development. Under their agreement with the developers, the ratepayers took the lease without the property being openly marketed. The headline rent on the property was £45,000, which was reduced under a concessionary arrangement to £26,954.73 to reflect the surrender of the previous lease. Situated in a popular and affluent holiday area, the property had planning consent as a bar and restaurant, and the user clause under the lease was for a "high class public house". In determining rateable value, the tribunal took the headline rent of £45,000 and applied an increase of 20% to reflect rental value when the property was fitted out, resulting in a rateable value of £54,000. The ratepayers submitted that minimal weight should be attached to the actual rent passing on the property and instead, an adjoining unit which traded as a restaurant should be used as a comparable. The valuation officer submitted that the actual rent passing on the appeal property was the best guide to rateable value because, while the adjoining unit was the only realistic comparable, the appeal property was a restaurant and bar whereas the adjoining property was a restaurant, serving higher quality food at higher prices. He also argued that rents had fallen since the valuation date, which was two years before the letting of the adjoining property.

Held: Appeal allowed in part. The actual rent passing on the appeal property under the concessionary arrangement was of little assistance. It had been arrived at by applying the annual retail prices index increase to the rent passing on the former public house, and accordingly related to the original rent agreed for the public house, rather than having anything to do with the appeal property. It was also tainted by being linked to the surrender of the previous lease. The best evidence was supplied by the open market letting of the adjoining property, which was of identical age, location and aspect. Although the two properties had different planning consents and their leases contained differing user clauses, that was not determinative of mode and category of occupation. Apart from differences in price, the two properties traded in a very similar manner and any differences were of style rather than of substance. The appeal property was trading as a restaurant, not a bar. There was no evidence that rents had deteriorated since the statutory valuation date, and that was unlikely to be the case in a relatively upmarket location. The property should be valued at the same main space rate as the adjoining property. It would be entered into the list at a rateable value of £41,000 with the description "restaurant and premises" (see paras 50- 55, 62-65 of judgment).

TURNER v MURDOCH (VALUATION OFFICER), [2015] UKUT 493 (LC), [2016] R.V.R. 44, PD McCrea FRICS, UT (Lands).

1474 **Takeaways–Sanitary conveniences–Extent of obligation to provide sanitary conveniences–Advice and guidance by primary authority**

[Regulatory Enforcement and Sanctions Act 2008 (c.13) Sch.4 para.1(3); Local Government (Miscellaneous Provisions) Act 1976 (c.57) s.20]

A local authority applied for judicial review of the defendant secretary of state's decision concerning advice which had been given under the primary authority scheme, as set out in the Regulatory Enforcement and Sanctions Act 2008. The local authority had wanted to bring enforcement action against the second interested party (G) under the Local Government (Miscellaneous Provisions) Act 1976 s.20, requiring it to provide toilet and washing facilities at two of its food outlets. However, the first interested party, which had been nominated under the scheme as the "primary authority" for G's business, determined that the proposed action was inconsistent with advice it had previously given. That advice stated that there would be no requirement to provide customer toilets where the main use of the shop was for takeaway sales and no more than 10 seats were provided for occasional customer use; where that was the case, the premises could not be classed as a "relevant place" for the purposes of s.20 of the 1976 Act. The local authority referred the matter to the secretary of state's Better Regulation Delivery Office (BRDO), which concluded that the primary authority's advice was "correct" for the purposes of Sch.4 para.1(3) of the 2008 Act. The decision was the first one made by the BRDO under the scheme. The issues were (1) whether the BRDO was entitled to find that the advice was "correct"; (2) if the primary authority had erred in its advice, whether that error was material.

Held: Application granted. (1) The BRDO had not been entitled to conclude that the primary authority's advice was correct. The advice had proceeded on a clear misconstruction of s.20(9) of the 1976 Act. The primary authority had wrongly stated that G's outlet was not a "relevant place" if it had fewer than 10 seats and if most of the customers took their food away. That was not the law, and a construction which looked to the predominant type of trade, whether sit-down or takeaway, was obviously wrong. If it was normal for customers to sit down and eat on the premises, then the outlet was a "relevant place". The statutory definition could not have more than one correct construction; to do so would be subversive of the rule of law. It was critical that the primary authority got the law right so that the regulated person was not subjected to a different law from that which applied to its competitors. Accordingly, the BRDO had erred in law in upholding as "correct" the primary authority's advice. It had misdirected itself in law by proceeding on the basis that the advice could be "correct" even if it was founded on a misinterpretation, albeit an informed and professional interpretation, of the law (see paras 52, 54-56, 60-61 of judgment). (2) The error was material. The advice that G did not need to have toilet facilities if there were fewer than 10 seats and the trade was mainly takeaway was fundamentally wrong. Claims that the error was irrelevant and that relief should be refused because the two erroneous features of the advice should be treated as discretionary matters which other authorities had to adopt in order to test whether to serve an enforcement notice, had to be rejected. Accordingly, BRDO's decision would be quashed and the primary authority's advice was declared to be flawed by error of law (paras 64-65, 84). (3) (Per curiam) The scheme should operate in the following way. It was for the primary authority to give advice and guidance to the enforcing authority. In doing so, it had to get the law right. The law had to be the same for everyone in the relevant market to avoid unlawful distortion of competition. In advising and giving guidance on the exercise of discretionary powers, the primary authority might suggest what weight should be given to particular factors, such as the number of seats and proportions of take-away and sit-down customers. However, it was fundamental that those discretionary matters were clearly separated from statements of what the law was. The advice and guidance had to be taken seriously by the enforcing authority and in practice it should be followed unless there was a good reason not to do so. If the enforcing authority decided to take enforcement action on the basis of a policy which ignored the primary authority's advice on the discretionary elements of the regime, it was likely, although not inevitable, that it would be stopped from doing so. However, it did not follow that the decision whether to serve an enforcement notice was that of the primary authority and not the enforcing authority; that was not what s.20 said. The enforcing authority, as the decision-maker, would need to satisfy itself that the advice was satisfactory, correct in law and rational in its treatment of discretionary considerations (paras 71-75).

R. (ON THE APPLICATION OF KINGSTON UPON HULL CITY COUNCIL) v SECRETARY OF STATE FOR BUSINESS, INNOVATION AND SKILLS, [2016] EWHC 1064 (Admin), [2016] P.T.S.R. 967, Kerr J, QBD (Admin).

1475 Valuation Tribunal for England–Jurisdiction–Appeals against completion notices–Extent of jurisdiction to entertain

[Local Government Finance Act 1988 (c.41) Sch.4A para.4]

The appellant appealed against a completion notice served on it by the respondent billing authority. The building in question was a four-storey office building which had been built in the 1980s. Major refurbishment work began in 2010. All floors apart from the second were let in 2013. The billing authority served a completion notice in respect of the second floor in May 2014. It specified a completion date of 12 August 2014. The appellant argued that the completion notice was invalid because such a notice could only be served in respect of a new building; this was an existing building which had been refurbished for the purpose of re-letting.

Held: Appeal dismissed. In *R. (on the application of Reeves (Valuation Officer)) v Valuation Tribunal for England* [2015] EWHC 973 (Admin), [2015] R.A. 241, [2015] C.L.Y. 2088, the High Court had ruled that under the Local Government Finance Act 1988 Sch.4A para.4(1) the only ground on which an owner could appeal to the tribunal was that the building had not been completed or could not reasonably be expected to be completed by the date stated in the notice. According to the court, the only matter for the tribunal to determine on such an appeal was the completion date. In the instant case, although the appeal property was not a new building and the appellant was correct to say that the billing authority should not have served a completion notice, the only matter which the tribunal had jurisdiction to address was the completion date. However, that was not in dispute. The only logical conclusion was that the appeal fell to be dismissed, *Reeves* followed (see paras 19-20 of judgment).

ROYAL LONDON MUTUAL INSURANCE SOCIETY v CRAWLEY BC, [2016] R.V.R. 209, E Ebenezer, VT.

1476 Valuation Tribunal for England–Jurisdiction–Billing authority's failure to exercise discretion to reduce council tax–Extent of tribunal's appellate jurisdiction

[Local Government Finance Act 1992 (c.14) s.13A(1)(a), s.13A(1)(c), s.16]

The tribunal had to consider whether the appellant's appeal against her council tax bill should be struck out as having no reasonable prospect of success. The appellant disputed a council tax bill issued on 11 April 2014 in the sum of £1,630.74. That sum included her council tax liability for the year beginning 1 April 2014 as well as a brought-forward balance of £880.87 for the year beginning 1 April 2013. That bill was issued as a result of a downward adjustment to the appellant's council tax reduction from 3 June 2013, recalculated and applied retrospectively as a result of a change in her financial circumstances from that date. The appellant's case was that she had notified that change of circumstances promptly and that the failure to recalculate her council tax reduction until April 2014 was not her fault but was instead the result of an official error on the part of the respondent billing authority; accordingly, she should not have to pay the increased council tax for which she became liable. The Local Government Finance Act 1992 s.13A(1)(a) provided for council tax to be reduced to the extent, if any, required by the relevant authority's council tax reduction scheme. Section 13A(1)(c) provided billing authorities with a discretion to reduce council tax to such extent, or such further extent, as they thought fit.

Held: Appeal struck out. The appellant had conceded that she could not contend that a reduction was "required by the authority's council tax reduction scheme" for the purposes of s.13A(1)(a), as the billing authority's council tax reduction scheme did not give it a discretion to reduce council tax on the basis of an official error. Her case was that the tribunal had jurisdiction to consider determining whether there should be a further reduction in council tax under s.13A(1)(c) in the circumstances of the case. The tribunal did have jurisdiction to entertain an appeal concerning the award of discretionary relief under s.13A(1)(c). Further, an unnoticeable official error could form the basis of discretionary relief. However, the problem for the appellant was s.16 of the Act, which proscribed an appeal unless a grievance had been made which included the matters and grounds on which the person was aggrieved. In the instant case, the appellant had not made a grievance in relation to any failure by the billing authority to exercise the discretionary power under s.13A(1)(c). Her appeal would therefore be struck out (see paras 18, 20, 24, 26, 33, 37, 45 of judgment).

DG v LIVERPOOL CITY COUNCIL, [2016] R.A. 259, F Dickie, VT.

MEDIA AND ENTERTAINMENT

1477 Wireless telegraphy licences–Exemptions

THE WIRELESS TELEGRAPHY (WHITE SPACE DEVICES) (EXEMPTION) (AMENDMENT) REGULATIONS 2016, SI 2016/615; made under the Wireless Telegraphy Act 2006 s.8(3). In force: 9 June 2016.

These Regulations amend the Wireless Telegraphy (White Space Devices) (Exemption) Regulations 2015 Sch.1. The list of organisations in Sch.1 is amended to include additional organisations. These are organisations which may operate databases from which white space devices may obtain master operational parameters and slave operational parameters.

1478 Wireless telegraphy licences–Radio spectrum–Fees

THE WIRELESS TELEGRAPHY (LICENCE CHARGES) (AMENDMENT) REGULATIONS 2016, SI 2016/643; made under the Wireless Telegraphy Act 2006 s.12, s.13(2), s.122(7). In force: 27 June 2016.

These Regulations amend the Wireless Telegraphy (Licence Charges) Regulations 2011 to enable the annual charges payable for licences for use of frequencies in the 28 GHz spectrum band to be payable in 10 equal instalments where the amount payable by a licence holder for any one or more licences held exceeds £100,000. The Regulations also: increase the charges which may be payable for licences in the Aeronautical Sector and for the Local TV DTT Multiplex licence in the Broadcasting Sector; and add new fees for licences for Manually Configurable White Space Devices and for Spectrum Offshore licences.

MENTAL HEALTH

1479 Compulsory admissions–Secure accommodation–Duty to provide accommodation–Patient from Wales detained in hospital in Brighton

[National Health Service (Wales) Act 2006 (c.42) s.3(1); Mental Health Act 1983 (c.20) s.2, s.3]

A patient applied for judicial review of the defendant public authorities' alleged failure to discharge their duty under the National Health Service (Wales) Act 2006 s.3(1) to provide hospital accommodation in Wales. The patient had a complex mental health condition including autistic spectrum disorder and learning disability. Her behaviour was sometimes challenging and she had been compulsorily detained in hospital under the Mental Health Act 1983 s.2 and s.3 on four occasions. On one occasion she was detained in a hospital in Brighton, over 200 miles from her home in Wales, because there had been no appropriate available low secure facility in Wales. The patient alleged that the public authorities had failed to discharge their duty under s.3(1) to provide hospital accommodation "throughout Wales, to such extent as they consider necessary to meet all reasonable requirements". In particular, she argued that no decision had been taken by any of the authorities as to the "reasonable requirements" of women in Wales with both autistic spectrum disorder and learning disability for secure in-patient assessment and treatment, and that no decision had been made as to the level of provision necessary to meet the reasonable requirements found to exist. She further alleged that the authorities had failed to collate the information required to make the decisions.

Held: Application refused. Secure accommodation required under the 1983 Act was "accommodation" within s.3(1) of the 2006 Act. If a public body was obliged to provide accommodation to meet a statutory requirement, it had to ascertain the requirement it was obliged to meet, before deciding how it should be met. The s.3(1) obligation was limited to providing the services identified to the extent that the authority considered them necessary to meet all reasonable requirements. That placed considerable discretion in the authority's hands, *R. v North and East Devon HA Ex p. Coughlan* [2001] Q.B. 213, [1999] C.L.Y. 2643 and *R. (on the application of Forge Care Homes Ltd) v Cardiff and Vale University Health Board* [2015] EWHC 601 (Admin), [2015] P.T.S.R. 945, [2015] C.L.Y. 2376 applied. The authority also had a substantial degree of flexibility as to how it went about its task, *CREEDNZ Inc v Governor General* [1981] 1 N.Z.L.R. 172 considered, *Findlay, Re* [1985] A.C. 318, [1984] C.L.Y. 2756 and *R. (on the application of Khatun) v Newham LBC* [2004] EWCA Civ 55, [2005] Q.B. 37, [2004] C.L.Y. 1907 applied. The margin granted to the authority was particularly wide where the discretion being exercised involved balancing complex socio-economic factors against a policy backdrop (see paras 99-107 of judgment). Before making an assessment of reasonable requirements or necessary services, an authority had to consider whether the information it had was sufficient to make a properly informed decision, but that in itself required an exercise of judgement with which the court would only interfere on public law grounds. The patient had criticised the authorities for not collating data in respect of the group of women requiring secure accommodation because of autistic spectrum disorder and learning disability and, thereafter, for not making decisions concerning the requirements of the individuals in that group. However, it was for the authorities to consider the criteria for the clinical areas in respect of which planning could best be made. It was artificial to create a cohort by reference to a diagnosis of both autistic spectrum disorder and learning disability. A cohort was a group of people with a common characteristic, but individuals with complex diagnoses had varying degrees of mental and physical health disabilities and different treatment needs. Even if they could be properly categorised, the decision about their reasonable requirements and how they might be met could not be made in isolation from the competing needs of other patients. The decision-making could be done in a scheme taking all such requirements into account. NHS Wales had such a scheme (paras 109-111). There was no confusion as to the allocation of responsibilities under s.3(1). The fact that s.3(1) required the Welsh ministers to provide services throughout Wales did not impose an obligation on each Local Health Board and the Welsh Health Specialised Services Committee in respect of the whole of Wales. Each body was only responsible for the functions delegated to it for its own area (paras 113-114). The authorities had had an abundance of data available to them for planning purposes; there was no evidence that they had failed to take it into account (paras 124-126). Section 3(1) did not require the relevant authority to make a formal, discrete decision about the reasonable requirements of the cohort defined by the patient (para.128). Local Health Boards had no statutory duty to collaborate with other Boards other than in respect of certain services. Medium secure provision was such a service and no complaint about the co-ordination of that had been made. Low secure provision was not such a service (para.130). Since the Board and the Committee had not breached s.3(1), there could be no failure on the ministers' part to take steps to prevent such a breach (para.134).

R. (ON THE APPLICATION OF DYER) v WELSH MINISTERS, [2015] EWHC 3712 (Admin), (2016) 19 C.C.L. Rep. 84, Hickinbottom J, QBD (Admin).

1480 Deprivation of liberty–Community treatment orders–Checklist for determining whether community treatment order amounting to unlawful deprivation of liberty.

[European Convention on Human Rights 1950 art.5; Mental Health Act 1983 (c.20) s.17A(5), s.64D, s.72(1)(c); Mental Capacity Act 2005 (c.9)]

A patient who was the subject of a community treatment order appealed against a decision not to order its discharge. The patient had been detained in hospital and later made the subject of a community treatment order and discharged to a care home. The treatment order included conditions that the patient would abide by the care home's regime, which included unescorted leave in the community, provisions for such leave to be stopped if risk factors increased and an absconding protocol. The patient wanted more unaccompanied leave but that was opposed. He sought discharge of the treatment order on the basis that it was an unlawful deprivation of liberty in breach of ECHR art.5. The Mental Health Review Tribunal refused his application, holding that he had not been deprived of his liberty as he was not under continuous supervision and control. It held that the treatment order provided a framework for treatment which had to take precedence over any human rights issues.

Held: Appeal allowed. (1) The tribunal had erred in concluding that the patient had not been deprived of his liberty. *Cheshire West and Chester Council v P* [2014] UKSC 19, [2014] A.C. 896, [2014] C.L.Y. 2189 had identified a test for whether there was a deprivation of liberty with two parts, namely that the person concerned was under continuous supervision and was not free to leave. *Cheshire West* envisaged that a person who was not free to leave might not be under such continuous supervision as to found a deprivation of liberty, but it did not, as the tribunal had, consider the degree of supervision and control in isolation and then not go on to consider whether the patient was free to leave, *Cheshire West* followed. The tribunal had overlooked that the fact that a person might have unescorted leave in the community did not mean that he was not deprived of liberty if the leave was regulated and controlled, and he was not free to leave in the sense of removing himself permanently in order to live where he chose. The tribunal had also overlooked the guidance in *Cheshire West* that the purpose of the relevant conditions was not relevant to the assessment of whether the objective element of a deprivation of liberty was satisfied (see paras 66-74 of judgment). Whether the patient was free to leave on the ground that the conditions were unenforceable had to be considered on the alternative bases that the deprivation of liberty either was or was not lawful. If lawful, it was clear that the patient was not free to leave even though the reality of enforcement was the exercise of the power of recall. If the deprivation was unlawful, the pragmatic risks and consequences of the exercise of the power of recall meant that for the purposes of ECHR art.5 it could not be said that the person was free to leave, although a different view could be taken, *R. (on the application of H) v Mental Health Review Tribunal* [2007] EWHC 884 (Admin), (2007) 10 C.C.L. Rep. 306, [2007] C.L.Y. 2898 considered (paras 78-82). (2) The tribunal had erred in concluding that a tribunal should ignore possible breaches of ECHR rights or permit breaches of ECHR rights to continue. The only basis on which those conclusions could be justified was that tribunals did not have power when applying tests under the Mental Health Act 1983 or exercising a discretion under the Act to take into account a breach of an ECHR right. The language and purposes of the Act did not support that basis, *SH v Cornwall Partnership NHS Trust* [2012] UKUT 290 (AAC), [2012] M.H.L.R. 383, [2013] C.L.Y. 2052, *GA v Betsi Cadwaladr University LHB* [2013] UKUT 280 (AAC), [2014] M.H.L.R. 27 and *NL v Hampshire CC* [2014] UKUT 475 (AAC), [2015] M.H.L.R. 338 not followed. Where the criteria for making a treatment order in s.17A(5) and discharging or upholding an order under s.72(1)(c) referred to appropriate and available medical treatment, they referred to lawful treatment that was lawfully available. When exercising its discretion under s.72(1), and when considering whether to adjourn a hearing, the tribunal had to take into account whether there was a breach of ECHR rights and if so use its powers to bring it to an end (paras 91-113, 136). (3) Tribunals should address the following questions: whether the implementation of the conditions would on an objective assessment result in a deprivation of liberty; if so, whether the patient had capacity to consent to the relevant conditions and the resulting deprivation; if so, whether the patient's consent avoided a breach of art.5; if the patient lacked capacity, whether any objectively assessed deprivation could be authorised by the Court of Protection or under the Mental Capacity Act 2005; if the patient lacked capacity, whether s.64D of the 1983 Act could be relied upon to avoid a breach of art.5; and how the conclusions on those questions should be taken into account in determining whether there should be an adjournment and if not whether the tribunal should discharge or uphold the treatment order (paras 147-154).

PJ (A PATIENT) v A LOCAL HEALTH BOARD, [2015] UKUT 480 (AAC), [2015] C.O.P.L.R. 756, Charles J, UT (AAC).

1481 Deprivation of liberty–Judicial decision-making–Court of Protection authorisation of deprivation of liberty–Guidance on stages of decision-making

[European Convention on Human Rights 1950 art.5]

The appellants appealed against the refusal of the first appellant local authority's application for authorisation of the deprivation of liberty of the first respondent (G). G had complex difficulties including ataxic cerebral palsy, and his behaviour posed a risk to himself and others. He had lived in his ground-floor flat for 10 years and had a support team of 12 workers. The flat was too small for the use of a wheelchair and G mobilised by crawling. Night staff could not sleep there. However, G was able to access the community daily and enjoyed watching the world from his window. He was deprived of his liberty by, amongst other things, being unable to open the front door himself, which was always locked; being unable to go outside on his own because of safety restrictions; and always having one-to-one staffing because of the risk he posed to himself. The local authority had been looking for alternative accommodation for G since 2013 and it was accepted that it would be in G's best interests to move to a less restrictive property which met certain criteria, when one was identified. The judge did not accept that she could authorise deprivation of liberty on the basis that nothing else was available. She stated that the local authority would have to take steps to ensure there was no breach. The second respondent submitted that the judge should have distinguished between whether the deprivation of liberty was in G's best interests and whether the conditions in which it was effected were lawful. The second respondent and the local authority submitted that the judge erred in directing herself to the effect that the fundamental principles as to the limits on the Court of Protection's role, confirmed by *N (An Adult) (Court of Protection: Jurisdiction), Re* [2015] EWCA Civ 411, [2016] Fam. 87, [2015] C.L.Y. 1741, did not apply to cases involving ECHR art.5. The Official Solicitor argued that the current and proposed deprivations of liberty were in breach of art.5. The local authority and second respondent further submitted that the court was attempting to make a decision on G's behalf which, if he had capacity, he would not have been able to make.

Held: Appeals allowed. (1) The decision-making needed to be broken down into two separate questions. First, whether it was in G's best interests to live at the property. It was to be noted that, although he was deprived of his liberty, there was nothing else available offering less restriction and no one had disagreed that it was in G's best interests to live at the property at that time. The deprivation of liberty arising on the implementation of the care package was a necessary consequence of the least restrictive available option which best promoted G's needs. Second, it was necessary to consider whether the accommodation provided was so unsuitable as to be unlawfully provided, breaching G's Convention rights. In that regard, the judge was required to consider the particular type of accommodation in which G was deprived of his liberty and the purpose of the detention. Neither G's property nor the manner in which his care package was delivered was so unsuitable as to be unlawful. Context was everything. The court had to consider the relationship between the ground of permitted deprivation of liberty and the place and conditions of the detention, *R. (on the application of Idira) v Secretary of State for the Home Department* [2015] EWCA Civ 1187, [2016] 1 W.L.R. 1694, [2016] 1104 applied and *Ashingdane v United Kingdom (A/93)* (1985) 7 E.H.R.R. 528, *Aerts v Belgium* (2000) 29 E.H.R.R. 50, [1999] C.L.Y. 3094 and *Mayeka v Belgium (13178/03)* [2007] 1 F.L.R. 1726, [2007] C.L.Y. 2202 considered. Had the judge considered both questions rather than proceeding straight to considering whether the elements of the care package involving a deprivation of liberty were lawful, she would have found it to be in G's best interests to live at the property (see paras 23-27 of judgment). (2) The judge's reasoning in seeking to make a distinction between welfare decisions, as in *Re N*, and decisions involving deprivation of liberty, as in the instant case, was unconvincing. She did not identify any proper basis for asserting that the guidance in *Re N* as to the limits of the Court of Protection's role was irrelevant where art.5 was engaged, *Re N* applied (paras 28-37). (3) G's accommodation and care plan did not breach art.5 and were not inherently unlawful. Article 5 was concerned with the reason for the detention, not its circumstances; there was no suggestion that the deprivation of liberty was arbitrary; the conditions needed to be appropriate, not the most appropriate for the detained person; a balanced determination of G's home would have brought out the many positives and the "devastation" G would experience on moving; the judge did not expressly find any breach of art.5; she had granted interim applications of deprivation of liberty on the same evidence for three-and-a-half years; and the "place and conditions of detention" would have to be "seriously inappropriate", *Idira* applied. (4) The Court of Protection's role was to take, on behalf of those who lacked capacity, the decisions that they would take themselves. G would not have been able to achieve what the judge directed the local authority to do, in the absence of a public law remedy, *Re N* applied (para.44). (5) The judge's intention in refusing the authorisation was to make the local authority provide alternative accommodation for G, which would have put wholly unjustified pressure on it as a public authority, *Re N* considered (paras 46-47).

NORTH YORKSHIRE CC v MAG, [2016] EWCOP 5, [2016] C.O.P.L.R. 346, Cobb J, CP.

1482 **Deprivation of liberty–Standard authorisations–Detained person requiring 24-hour care after sustaining severe injuries in road-traffic accident**

[Mental Capacity Act 2005 (c.9); European Convention on Human Rights 1950 art.5]

A local authority applied for a welfare order authorising the deprivation of liberty of the first respondent (K). K had been severely injured in a road traffic accident. As a result of those injuries, he lacked capacity to make decisions on the regime of care, treatment and support that he should receive. He was awarded substantial damages, which were paid to his property and affairs deputy, the third respondent. He lived at a property that had been bought and adapted for him. His regime of care and support there was provided by private-sector providers. His care regime created, on an objective assessment, a deprivation of liberty. The issue was whether that situation was a deprivation of liberty that had to be authorised by the making of a welfare order. The test that the court would apply in making such an order was whether K's care regime was the least restrictive available option to best promote his best interests. The same test applied to the decision-makers involved in his care. It was common ground that at present K's care regime satisfied that test. If a welfare order was made, it would include provisions concerning when and how it was to be reviewed. It was likely that K's regime of care and support would always create an objective deprivation of liberty and that he would never have capacity to make decisions about it. However, from time to time issues were likely to arise on what changes should be made to that regime to ensure that it remained the least restrictive available option.

Held: Application granted. A welfare order was needed. The critical issue was whether, absent the making of such an order in cases within the class represented by K's case, the amendments to the Mental Capacity Act 2005 directed to filling the

"Bournewood gap" (the lack of procedural regulation identified in *HL v United Kingdom (45508/99)* (2005) 40 E.H.R.R. 32, [2005] C.L.Y. 2109) had achieved that purpose in those cases. The answer was no. A welfare order needed to be made in such cases to provide a procedure that protected the relevant person from arbitrary detention, avoiding a violation of the state's positive obligations under ECHR art.5. That conclusion was based on the premise that the state knew or ought to know of the situation on the ground. That knowledge existed in K's case and would exist in all cases in the class it represented. That was because the court that awarded the damages, the Court of Protection when appointing a property and affairs deputy and the deputy or the trustees or attorney or other person to whom the damages were paid should take steps to ensure (a) that the relevant local authority with duties to safeguard adults knew of the regime of care, and (b) that if, as here, the least restrictive available care regime to best promote the person's best interests created a situation on the ground that satisfied the objective and subjective components of a deprivation of liberty (and so a deprivation of liberty within art.5), a welfare order based on that regime of care was made by the Court of Protection, *Storck v Germany (61603/00)* (2006) 43 E.H.R.R. 6 and *A, Re* [2010] EWHC 978 (Fam), [2010] 2 F.L.R. 1363, [2010] C.L.Y. 3144 applied, *HL* cited (see paras 9-10 of judgment).

STAFFORDSHIRE CC v K *sub nom.* STAFFORDSHIRE CC v SRK, [2016] EWCOP 27, [2016] 3 W.L.R. 867, Charles J, CP.

1483 Deprivation of liberty applications–Representatives–Lack of practically available resource to enable the court to appoint professional representatives

[Court of Protection Rules 2007 (SI 2007/1744) r.3A]

The Court of Protection considered the procedure to be adopted in cases where local authorities had applied for welfare orders to authorise the deprivation of liberty of persons lacking capacity and where there was no family member or friend who could be appointed as a representative under the Court of Protection Rules 2007 r.3A. *Cheshire West and Chester Council v P* [2014] UKSC 19, [2014] A.C. 896, [2014] C.L.Y. 2189 had provided that deprivation of liberty of persons in care lacking capacity could only be made lawful by a welfare order made by the court and stipulated that such persons should have the benefit of regular independent reviews to ensure that their placement, or any restrictions on their liberty, remained in their best interests. Subsequently, *X (Deprivation of Liberty), Re* [2015] EWCA Civ 599, [2016] 1 W.L.R. 227, [2015] C.L.Y. 1720 described a streamlined process for dealing with deprivation of liberty cases. In *P, Re* [2015] EWCOP 59, [2015] C.O.P.L.R. 690, [2016] 1518, the secretary of state had indicated that to enable the court to meet the minimum procedural safeguards in cases where there was no family member or friend who could act as a r.3A representative, it could appoint professional representatives. The court had accepted that that approach would in theory enable the minimum procedural requirements to be met.

Held: Directions given. The instant cases were an opportunity for the secretary of state to show that there were available resources from which professional representatives could be appointed. However, the secretary of state had failed to constructively address the availability in practice of such representatives and so address that aspect of the problems created by the decision in *Cheshire West*. Instead, he had sought to avoid them by asserting that local authorities should provide the extra resources. That approach was unfortunate. The local authorities would not provide the resources, meaning that neither central nor local government was offering to create a practically available resource to enable the court to meet the minimum procedural requirements by appointing professional r.3A representatives (see paras 16-22 of judgment). The Re X streamlined procedure did not meet the minimum procedural requirements in the instant cases, but a procedure in which the person lacking capacity was not joined as a party and there was no hearing would do so if a r.3A representative was appointed, *Re X* distinguished and *Cheshire West* considered. It was not appropriate for the court to direct applicant local authorities to take steps or identify a person or persons who the court could appoint in cases such as the instant. The local authorities had no statutory duty to do that; there was currently no available pool of people who were able to accept such an appointment by the court; and without help from central government, there was no reasonable prospect that any such pool of people would be created by local authorities. The primary responsibility to provide a resource that enabled the court to make such appointments or otherwise meet the minimum procedural requirements fell on the secretary of state, alone or with local authorities, Re P considered (paras 23-24). The court would make an order: (a) joining the Ministry of Justice and the Department of Health as parties; (b) inviting the parties to take steps to either identify a suitable person who was able to accept immediate appointment as the person's r.3A representative, or identify an alternative procedure that was actually available to the court to meet the minimum procedural requirements; (c) staying the applications pending the identification of a practically available procedure that enabled the court to meet the minimum procedural requirements; and (d) giving all the parties liberty to apply, specifically to lift the stay and generally. That order could and should be made by the court in other such cases. If and when the relevant authorities made applications in significant numbers, the likelihood was that that approach would create a backlog comprising a very large number of stayed cases. That was unfortunate but would identify the extent of the problem (paras 25-27).

JM (INCAPACITATED PERSONS) (DEPRIVATION OF LIBERTY: APPOINTMENT OF REPRESENTATIVES), RE, [2016] EWCOP 15, [2016] 4 W.L.R. 64, Charles J, CP.

1484 Deprivation of liberty applications–Representatives–Suggestion of explanatory note for representatives explaining role and proceedings

[Court of Protection Rules 2007 (SI 2007/1744) r.3A; Mental Capacity Act 2005 (c.9) s.4(6)]

The Court of Protection suggested an explanatory note which could, where a package of care and support for a person lacking capacity would result in the person being deprived of their liberty, be sent to the person's family members and friends who had been appointed as their representatives under the Court of Protection Rules 2007 r.3A.

Held: Judgment accordingly. The explanatory note provided a general explanation of the role of representative; described the court documentation the representative would receive; described the steps the representative should take; set out the requirements of the Mental Capacity Act 2005 s.4(6) as to what someone determining what was in a person's best interests had to consider; gave guidance on making a statement; suggested that the representative could want to seek legal advice; and suggested that the relevant local authority could answer any queries.

VE, RE *sub nom.* JM (INCAPACITATED PERSONS) (DEPRIVATION OF LIBERTY: APPOINTMENT OF REPRESENTATIVES), RE, [2016] EWCOP 16, [2016] 4 W.L.R. 64, Charles J, CP.

1485 Deputies–Conflict of interest–Managing conflicts–Application of safeguards in s.19 Mental Capacity Act 2005

[Mental Capacity Act 2005 (c.9) s.16(8), s.19]

An individual (G) asked the court to remove the local authority as the deputy for his mother's property and affairs and to appoint him in its place. The mother, who was 95 and lacked capacity, was a widow with six living children. She had Alzheimer's disease and was living in a residential care home, and the local authority had been appointed as her deputy in 2013. She had a cottage worth around £350,000 and had inherited her eldest daughter's house which, given its state of repair, was worth around £150,000. G had evidence that, if repaired and refurbished, the house could be sold for between £200,000 and £220,000. He was a builder and offered to do the necessary works for £35,000. The local authority declined. G incurred expenses in dealing with his late sister's estate and funeral, but had difficulty in being reimbursed by the local authority. He applied to be appointed deputy in its place, claiming that the local authority's decisions, particularly its disinclination to refurbish the inherited property, did not maximise his mother's estate and were not in her best interests. He asserted that relations between him and the local authority had broken down and it was not in his mother's best interests for her deputy to have such a poor relationship with her family. The local authority submitted that it was in the mother's best interests for it to remain her sole deputy. It argued that it would be a conflict of interest for G to be appointed, since he stood to gain from the refurbishment works and from expenses claims in connection with discharging his duty as a deputy.

Held: Application granted. (1) G would be appointed as his mother's property and affairs deputy in place of the local authority. The court could remove a deputy in the specific circumstances set out in the Mental Capacity Act 2005 s.16(8), and it could also do so pursuant to s.16(7) where it was convinced that it was in the protected person's best interests to do so. It would be sensible to repair and renovate the inherited house so that it could be sold to best advantage. Although the mother would not benefit personally from a greater profit from the sale, her estate would. The best interests test was not confined to the self-interest of the incapacitated person. Altruistic wishes which had, or might have, been formed could be relevant, *G (TJ), Re* applied (see paras 18, 22-27 of judgment). (2) Conflicts of interest were ubiquitous in any mental capacity jurisdiction and while they had to be safeguarded against, it was impossible to eradicate them entirely. The local authority had a conflict of interest in respect of care-funding issues and also because it was deputy for one of the children, who was living rent-free in the mother's cottage. While conflicts of interest frequently arose in family situations, they did not automatically disqualify the family member from being appointed as a deputy, Holt v The Protective Commissioner (1993) 31 NSWLR 227 considered. Although it was not expressly stated in the Act, one of the court's principal functions was to manage conflicts of interest to ensure that decisions were made in the best interests of the incapacitated person. The avoidance of conflicts of interest was built into the principles on which the Act was based and into the Code of Practice issued under the Act. One way to avoid a conflict was to appoint more than one deputy, but that could not be done in the instant case because the local authority had refused to work with G. The court would therefore have to manage the conflict between G's interests and those of his mother by applying the safeguards in s.19 of the Act in the following way: (a) G would be entitled to be reimbursed out of his mother's funds for reasonable expenses in discharging his functions as deputy, but he would be allowed to charge mileage for only four visits a year; (b) he would not receive any remuneration for acting as deputy; (c) he could charge his daily rate of £150, including mileage, in respect of his functions as a builder when refurbishing the inherited house; (d) any anticipated expenditure in excess of the £35,000 budget for refurbishment had to be approved in advance by the court; (e) he would have authority to sell the inherited house, but not his mother's cottage without the court's permission; (f) he would have to give £250,000 security; and (h) he had to account annually to the Public Guardian (paras 31, 39-41).

JW, RE *sub nom.* GGW v EAST SUSSEX CC, [2015] EWCOP 82, [2016] C.O.P.L.R. 36, Senior Judge Denzil Lush, CP.

1486 Detained residents–Habitual residence–Patients detained in hospital in Scotland, transferred to England

[Mental Capacity Act 2005 (c.9) s.15, s.16, s.21A]

The court was required to determine as a preliminary issue whether two patients (D and E) had acquired habitual residence in England. D and E were unrelated. They were born in Scotland in the 1980s. Both had severe learning difficulties, autistic spectrum disorders and a history of aggressive behaviour. D had been detained from the age of 14, and E from the age of 21, for treatment. They were transferred to a hospital in England in 2008 and 2010 respectively, where they had remained until the date of the instant hearing. Neither patient attended any day care services outside the hospital nor had any friends in England outside the hospital. D's family members visited him regularly and wished him to return to Scotland. E had had no contact with his family for over ten years. Their conditions improved while at the English hospital and their detention was revoked and replaced with a standard authorisation. Their advocates applied to set aside the standard authorisation. An alternative placement had been identified for D in Scotland. There was uncertainty about E's future placement. The English local authority and the Scottish authorities submitted that the duration of D and E's stay in England was such that they had each acquired habitual residence.

Held: Preliminary issue determined. (1) The court had jurisdiction under the Mental Capacity Act 2005 s.21A to determine a challenge to a standard authorisation made under Sch.A1 irrespective of whether or not the subject of the proceedings was habitually resident in England and Wales. However, in order for a court to make decisions concerning the care and residence of the individual under its s.15 and s.16

powers, it had to be established that the adult was habitually resident in the English jurisdiction. The approach to be applied when assessing habitual residence in proceedings under the 2005 Act was that set out in *An English Local Authority v SW* [2014] EWCOP 43, [2015] C.O.P.L.R. 29, [2015] C.L.Y. 1751. The court had to analyse properly the nature of the residence of the adult concerned in order to establish whether it had become habitual. That involved a careful consideration of the factors identified in the case law, in order to determine whether the necessary degree of integration had been achieved, *SW*, *A v A (Children) (Habitual Residence)* [2013] UKSC 60, [2014] A.C. 1, [2013] C.L.Y. 1250, *LC (Children) (International Abduction: Child's Objections to Return), Re* [2014] UKSC 1, [2014] A.C. 1038, [2014] C.L.Y. 1378, *Proceedings Brought by A (C-523/07)* EU:C:2009:225, [2010] Fam. 42, [2009] C.L.Y. 1552 and *Mercredi v Chaffe (C-497/10 PPU)* EU:C:2010:829, [2012] Fam. 22, [2011] C.L.Y. 1429 applied (see paras 15-16, 21, 31 of judgment). (2) The duration of D and E's stay in England was substantial; seven-and-a-half years and six years respectively. That was a very significant factor, but was not by itself determinative. A number of factors supported a conclusion that they had acquired habitual residence in England: (a) D and E had remained resident at the hospital throughout their time in England, they had not left the jurisdiction at any point; (b) it was understood in each case that their stay in England would be indefinite, until such time as they were ready to return to Scotland and a suitable place was available; (c) they had each achieved a degree of stability through a steady routine as part of their treatment. The factors pointing the other way were that both D and E were Scottish; it was always intended that they would return to Scotland; their families remained in Scotland; they had not established friendships or other relationships in England beyond the confines of the hospital; and they had no significant access to the local community. D and E's lives in England were not characterised by the degree of social or family integration enjoyed by most people. However, their individual circumstances meant that they were not able to integrate in a family or social environment anywhere in a conventional way. Wherever they resided, their life would be focused on their residential unit. Within those restricted circumstances, and having regard to all the factors above, D and E had achieved a degree of integration at the English hospital. They had acquired habitual residence in England. The court therefore had jurisdiction to determine issues concerning their future welfare (paras 32-37).

DB (A PATIENT), RE; EC (A PATIENT), RE *sub nom.* DB v WORCESTERSHIRE CC; EC v WORCESTERSHIRE CC, [2016] EWCOP 30, [2016] C.O.P.L.R. 450, Baker J, CP.

1487 Detention in hospital–Reasons–Test for adequacy of reasons

[Mental Health Act 1983 (c.20) s.17, s.3]

A patient appealed against the findings of a mental health tribunal that his disorder was such that he required to be detained for treatment under the Mental Health Act 1983 s.3. The patient suffered from mild learning disability and hyperkinetic disorder, associated with seriously irresponsible conduct. His history was cyclical. He had been detained under s.3, then gradually improved until he was released under a community treatment order. His behaviour then deteriorated so that he had to be detained again. He was currently living and receiving one-to-one rehabilitation and care in a residential placement in the community, pursuant to leave to live away from the hospital under s.17. He was required to attend hospital for psychology sessions every fortnight and for the ward round every month. The patient sought a discharge or a community treatment order. The issue was whether a patient who was living and receiving treatment outside hospital, remained "liable to be detained in a hospital for treatment" pursuant to s.3. The patient submitted that although the tribunal had cited the correct cases, its reasons showed that it had misunderstood their purpose because it had cited them on the irrelevant issue of whether the patient's accommodation was a hospital. The patient argued that the tribunal had further erred in finding there was a significant element of treatment in hospital and in the way it described the patient's case, submissions and evidence since almost all of the treatment he received was delivered in the community.

Held: Appeal dismissed. In applying an approach set out in the relevant case law, a tribunal had to avoid reasoning by analogy from the facts rather than applying the principles. Further, a tribunal had to make findings of fact to justify its conclusions, *R.*

(on the application of Epsom & St Helier NHS Trust) v Mental Health Review Tribunal [2001] EWHC Admin 101, [2001] M.H.L.R. 8, *R. (on the application of DR) v Mersey Care NHS Trust* [2002] M.H.L.R. 386, [2002] C.L.Y. 3238 and *R. (on the application of CS) v Mental Health Review Tribunal* [2004] EWHC 2958 (Admin), [2004] M.H.L.R. 355 considered. In the instant case, the tribunal had been wrong to refer to the case law as resolving the issue of whether the patient's accommodation was a hospital. However, the rest of the judgment showed that the tribunal had applied the correct test. It had accurately identified the patient's review meetings as forming a supportive process for the transition from hospital-based to community-based treatment. It had correctly recognised the element of treatment as a significant part of the whole, and it had accurately recorded the importance of the review meetings to the clinical team's decision-making on future treatment. Although the tribunal could have made more detailed findings and provided fuller reasons, that did not mean that its reasons were inadequate. The test that the Upper Tribunal applied was adequacy, not perfection (see paras 35-39, 41 of judgment).

SL v LUDLOW STREET HEALTHCARE, [2015] UKUT 398 (AAC), [2015] M.H.L.R. 390, Judge Jacobs, UT (AAC).

1488 Enduring powers of attorney–Expenses–Remuneration for attorneys' care and travel expenses

[Mental Capacity Act 2005 (c.9) Sch.4 Pt 5 para.16(2)(b)]

The applicant sister and brother applied for the retrospective approval of monthly payments made to themselves and their sister from their parents' funds under two enduring powers of attorney (EPAs). The applicants had been appointed joint attorneys under their parents' EPAs, which had been registered with the Office of the Public Guardian (OPG). The parents were both diagnosed with dementia. The father later died, but the mother continued to live independently. Due to the expense of travelling to see the mother and caring for her, the applicants took £150 per month for each of themselves and their sister out of the parents', and then the mother's, funds. After a disagreement with the sister, she reported them to the OPG, which requested that they apply for retrospective approval of the £450 monthly payment. The claim for payment was based on travelling expenses, remuneration for acting as attorneys, and a "gratuitous" care allowance; they had based their travel expense calculations on a mileage rate of 45p.

Held: Application granted in part. (1) The court would not approve a particular mileage rate; the OPG could give guidance on that if it chose. The applicants had based their rate on those issued by HMRC for "business miles". In the context of journeys made by those acting under EPAs, the person paying was almost invariably a close relative who lacked mental capacity rather than a corporation or business employer. The business mileage rates quoted by HMRC should be substantially discounted to reflect being domestic rates rather than business rates (see paras 28-31 of judgment). (2) The parents had not expressly provided for their attorneys to be remunerated. Although the Mental Capacity Act 2005 Sch.4 Pt 5 para.16(2)(b) provided that the court could direct such remuneration, no specific remuneration would be allowed to the applicants for the actual management of their parents' property and financial affairs. There was nothing to suggest that they had understood that they would be rewarded on a quantum meruit basis, and nothing exceptional about the work undertaken that warranted remuneration (paras 34-35, 38-39). (3) The principles discussed in *ATL v Public Guardian* [2015] EWCOP 77 regarding remuneration for care and case management services provided to incapacitated relatives could apply to individuals who devoted a substantial amount of their time towards caring for an elderly relative. The payments had been in the parents' best interests and were in the mother's best interests because: the services provided were reasonably required; the payments were currently affordable and sustainable; they were a considerable saving on the commercial costs of those services; in the absence of express remuneration in the EPAs, they struck a reasonable balance between ensuring that the applicants were not financially disadvantaged but were not making a profit from their position. The applicants were to be remunerated for the tasks they had performed as care support workers, *ATL* applied. There was a commercial value for many of those tasks, although the court was reluctant to place a specific value on the services absent a professional valuation. The applicants' care support and travelling expenses merited the payment of £150 each per month from the parents' funds. The court retrospectively approved those allowances, and approved their continued payment until further order. It was left to the applicants' discretion to reimburse the sister for reasonable expenditures incurred in providing care support to the mother (paras 40-44, 47).

WP (DECEASED), RE, [2015] EWCOP 84, [2016] C.O.P.L.R. 176, Judge Lush, CP.

1489 Enduring powers of attorney–Revocation–Donor revoking power of attorney–Whether having capacity to revoke

[Mental Capacity Act 2005 (c.9) Sch.4 Pt 5 para.16(3), s.3(1)]

A brother and sister applied for permission to appeal the revocation of an enduring power of attorney (EPA) held by them in respect of their father. The father signed the EPA in 2007, when aged 79, shortly after his wife's death. He subsequently remarried. The applicants became concerned over aspects of his spending and in 2013 acted to restrict his income. Their relationship with their father progressively deteriorated and in March 2014 the father revoked the EPA by deed and applied to confirm the revocation pursuant to the Mental Capacity Act 2005 Sch.4 Pt 5 para.16(3). The application was accompanied by an assessment of capacity completed in March 2014 by a consultant old-age psychiatrist (V) who concluded that the father had the necessary capacity to revoke the EPA. The applicants opposed the application and later served narrative evidence setting out their concerns about their father's capacity to manage his financial affairs. The district judge made a number of orders. Initially, he suspended the EPA and directed the applicants to serve any medical evidence as to the father's capacity upon which they sought to rely. When no medical evidence was filed, he ordered that the EPA be cancelled. The applicants submitted that they would not have been able to obtain any capacity evidence on their father without order of the court. They also argued that as V's evidence did not appear to accord with their own assessment, his conclusions ought to be interrogated by the court.

Held: Permission refused. Permission to appeal was refused as the appeal had no real prospect of success. The district judge's decision was neither wrong nor unjust. In focusing on examples of irregularities or perceived procedural unfairness, the applicants had lost sight of the bigger picture and the duty to respect their father's right to revoke his EPA at any time when he had the capacity to do so. The court must revoke the EPA under the Act if it was satisfied that the donor had done whatever was necessary in law to effect an express revocation and was mentally capable when he did so. There was no doubt that the father had fulfilled the first condition. Further, his evidence of his capacity to revoke the EPA was exemplary and incontrovertible. V was an experienced consultant in old-age psychiatry. There was nothing to suggest that he was given inadequate or incorrect information, or that he did not receive proper instructions or apply the appropriate test. His assessment was both time-specific and decision-specific. He had correctly applied the checklist in s.3(1). With regard to "the information relevant to the decision" that the father needed to be able to understand, retain, and use or weigh, V's evidence was that he understood who the attorneys were, what authority they had, why it was necessary to revoke the EPA and the foreseeable consequences. In contrast, the applicants had filed no medical evidence to support their assertion that their father lacked capacity to revoke the EPA and instead had relied upon their own observations of his uncharacteristic behavior. There was insufficient evidence to entertain a reasonable belief that the father lacked capacity, *F (Mental Capacity: Interim Jurisdiction), Re* [2010] 2 F.L.R. 28, [2010] C.L.Y. 1587 considered. The district judge was satisfied that the father had done whatever was necessary in law to effect an express revocation and was mentally capable when he did so, and as the legislation compelled him to do so in such circumstances, he confirmed the revocation. He had felt the need repeatedly to remind the applicants of the overriding objective of the Court of Protection proceedings and he was right to do so. The applicants and their legal advisers were demanding an in-depth inquiry into how V could have reached the conclusion that their father had capacity to revoke the EPA and were attempting to spin out proceedings in circumstances in which there was, essentially, no contest, *A (Court of Protection: Delay and Costs), Re* [2014] EWCOP 48, [2015] C.O.P.L.R. 1, [2015] C.L.Y. 1718 considered (see paras 38-59 of judgment).

KJP, RE *sub nom.* TB v KJP, [2016] EWCOP 6, [2016] W.T.L.R. 687, Senior Judge Denzil Lush, CP.

1490 Enduring powers of attorney–Revocation–Removal of unsuitable attorney–Appointment of deputy

[Mental Health Act 1983 (c.20) s.117; Mental Capacity Act 2005 (c.9) Sch.4 Pt 5 para.16(2)(b)]

The Public Guardian applied for the revocation of an enduring power of attorney held by the respondent, and the appointment of a deputy to administer the affairs of the respondent's mother. The elderly mother had dementia. The son was appointed as her sole attorney in 2004. The enduring power of attorney was registered in 2009. In 2014, the Public Guardian became concerned that the son (a) had not paid his mother's nursing home fees to the value of £29,000; (b) had not provided a personal allowance to pay for her toiletries, hairdressing and chiropody; and (c) had claimed £117,289.45 in expenses for the time spent pursuing a legal dispute on her behalf, and had charged a daily rate of £400 for visits to check on her wellbeing. The legal dispute was with the local health board as to whether the nursing home fees should have been publicly funded under the Mental Health Act 1983 s.117; the Public Guardian believed that whilst that dispute was ongoing, it would be in the mother's best interests for the son to continue to pay her care fees. The son was concerned that the health board would not refund any monies owed if the dispute was settled in his favour.

Held: Application granted. (1) One would be hard pressed to find a more callous and calculating attorney, who had so flagrantly abused his position of trust. He had resented having to pay for his mother's toiletries because they had been free in her previous nursing home. Furthermore, there was no evidence that the health board would avoid refunding any monies; it had acted in good faith and reimbursed overpaid fees in the past. In relation to the son's claim for reimbursement of out-of-pocket expenses, his mother had not expressly provided for him to be remunerated, and if he intended to charge a daily rate of £400 for acting as her attorney, he should have applied to the court under the Mental Capacity Act 2005 Sch.4 Pt 5 para.16(2)(b)(iii). By not doing so, he behaved in a way that contravened his authority and was not in the donor's best interests. Charging one's elderly mother a daily rate of £400 for visiting and acting as her attorney was repugnant (see paras 34-41 of judgment). (2) The panel deputy would, for the first time in 11 years, place the mother at the centre of the decision-making process, rather than view the preservation and enhancement of the son's inheritance as the paramount consideration (para.42).

PUBLIC GUARDIAN v MF *sub nom.* SF, RE, [2015] EWCOP 68, [2016] W.T.L.R. 355, Judge Lush, CP.

1491 Enduring powers of attorney–Revocation–Removal of unsuitable attorney–Appointment of deputy

A local authority applied for the court to revoke an enduring power of attorney and to appoint a deputy to manage the property and affairs of the donor (R). In 2005 R executed the enduring power of attorney appointing her youngest son (J) to be her sole attorney. Concerns were raised about R's mental health and in February 2015 she was admitted to hospital and formally diagnosed with Alzheimer's dementia. She was then transferred to a care home. In May 2015, having received an anonymous phone call alleging that R's sons were selling her personal effects and were planning to rent her property out, the local authority applied to the court to appoint a particular solicitor as R's deputy. J then applied to register the enduring power of attorney with the Office of the Public Guardian. A social worker made a witness statement that J and his brother (G) had neglected R's needs by allowing her home to fall into disrepair, failing to follow recommendations as to her care needs and, after moving in with her for a short period, leaving her alone in her home. R's daughter (L) made a witness statement expressing her concerns regarding the power of attorney and the behaviour of J and G, including putting R's home up for rent and selling her belongings once she entered the care home. G gave evidence as to the hostility among the family and debts incurred by L in R's name.

Held: Application granted. (1) J had failed to ensure R's basic care needs were provided for, regularly left her without support, care, assistance and basic provisions for a four-month period and removed himself from her home despite being fully aware of her deteriorating mental health and care needs. J demonstrated inertia and a lack of urgency, demonstrated by his failure to ensure R's property was fully insured and the reactive, rather than proactive, registration of the enduring power of attorney. J also gave the impression that he had delegated his decision-making responsibilities to G. Furthermore, the hostility within the family was likely to have an adverse impact on the proper administration of R's estate. Having regard to all the circumstances, J was unsuitable to be R's attorney. The power of attorney would be revoked and the Public Guardian would be directed to cancel its registration. The solicitor was appointed as R's deputy for property and affairs (see paras 31-34, 37-44 of judgment). (2) J's disposal of R's goods and furniture and attempt to let her property after her entry to the care home did not make J unsuitable to be R's attorney. Those functions were entirely within the scope of his authority, and letting the property rather than selling it and investing the proceeds was a sound commercial decision (paras 35-36).

RG, RE *sub nom.* NORTHAMPTONSHIRE CC v RG, [2015] EWCOP 66, [2015] C.O.P.L.R. 794, Senior Judge Denzil Lush, CP.

1492 First-tier Tribunal–Reasons–Guidance on giving of reasons in mental health cases

On an appeal by a mental patient against a decision of the Mental Health Review Tribunal for Wales that he should not be discharged from hospital, the Upper Tribunal provided guidance on the giving of reasons for decisions in mental health cases.

Held: Appeal allowed. (1) The following was intended to assist tribunals when composing reasons in mental health cases. It was not an exhaustive or novel treatise on the art of reason-writing but merely an aide-memoire of those matters which might help in the production of adequate and intelligible reasons. First, it would be helpful if tribunals were to set out their reasons by reference to the relevant criteria for detention. They should consider setting out their reasons under the headings provided by the legal questions they had to determine. That would make it easier to show that the tribunal had dealt with each of the legal criteria it had to address. The First-tier Tribunal (Mental Health) in England had made template decisions using appropriate headings available to tribunal judges to assist them in reason-writing. Second, the tribunal's reasons should address how the tribunal had dealt with any disputes as to either the law or the evidence. If that was not done, the unsuccessful party might believe that the tribunal had ignored important issues. In particular, failing to address explicitly any applications made by one or other of the parties might render a set of reasons inadequate. Such an omission certainly made it more difficult for a party to know why he had been unsuccessful; it would also raise doubt as to whether the tribunal had dealt fairly with his case. However, it was not necessary for a set of reasons to resolve evidential matters which were irrelevant to the legal issues to be determined; a prudent tribunal though might wish to explain briefly why it had not resolved a factual dispute. Third, the reasons themselves had to be clear and unambiguous; it was not for a party to deduce the reasons for a decision. Fourth, rehearsing what each witness told the tribunal was, without more, liable to render a set of reasons erroneous in law. The tribunal should explain what facts it had found as a result of the evidence and what conclusions it had reached on those facts. Fifth, it was not necessary for the tribunal's reasons to mention all the evidence in a case. It was entitled to be selective in its references to the evidence, though it should, as indicated above, identify and resolve evidence and applications which were in dispute (see paras 11-16 of judgment). (2) In the instant case, the tribunal's reasons were defective in a number of respects. Its decision would be set aside and the matter remitted for rehearing by a differently constituted tribunal (paras 18-25).

HK v LLANARTH COURT HOSPITAL, [2014] UKUT 410 (AAC), [2015] M.H.L.R. 88, Judge Knowles, UT (AAC).

1493 Guardianship–Discharge–Application on basis that less restrictive arrangements could be imposed under Mental Capacity Act 2005–Guidance

[Mental Health Act 1983 (c.20) s.18(3), s.2, s.3, s.72; Mental Capacity Act 2005 (c.9)]

A person with a mental disorder (D) appealed against the First-tier Tribunal's rejection of his application under the Mental Health Act 1983 s.72 for discharge of the guardianship to which he was subject. D had been diagnosed with amnesic syndrome, due to extensive alcohol use, which meant that he could not manage the basic skills of daily life because he could not retain information or evaluate risk and benefit. In 2011 he was admitted to hospital under s.2 of the 1983 Act and thereafter detained under s.3. Since 2012 he had been the subject of guardianship. In late 2012 he was transferred to his current placement, a residential care home. In June 2013 he applied for discharge of the guardianship, contending that his care regime included 24-hour supervision and support, that he was not free to leave and that he was not permitted to go out unless accompanied by a member of staff. The First-tier Tribunal rejected that application, concluding that the guardianship was necessary in the interests of D's welfare or for the protection of others. D accepted that he lacked capacity to decide where he should live and the terms of his care plan. He submitted that guardianship was not necessary because alternative and less restrictive arrangements could be imposed under the Mental Capacity Act 2005 and authorised pursuant to a Deprivation of Liberty Safeguards standard authorisation; and the guardianship could not authorise, and so render lawful, the existing restrictions on his liberty.

Held: Appeal dismissed. (1) Albeit that the 2005 Act did not confer on a guardian an express power equivalent to an injunction to prevent a patient leaving his place of residence or to dictate the terms of a care plan, the combination of the express powers conferred on him and s.18(3) of the 1983 Act had the following practical effects: (a) in choosing the place that the patient was to live, the guardian would have regard to, and might require a commitment from the provider of the placement in respect of, the terms of the care plan and its restrictions; (b) if the care plan was changed, the guardian could require the patient to live elsewhere; (c) the patient was required to live at a certain place under a care regime; (d) by requiring the patient to live at a given place a guardian was at least indirectly requiring him to live there under those conditions and restrictions, albeit that he could not impose them on the provider of the care or treatment; it was the care plan not the guardianship that was the basis of a deprivation of liberty, *NL v Hampshire CC* [2014] UKUT 475 (AAC), [2015] M.H.L.R. 338 applied; (e) the power to return the patient to his place of residence had the effect of a requirement or an injunction preventing him from leaving. That power was a more readily available, effective and sensible means of enforcing the result that the patient lived at a certain place than an injunction against a person who lacked capacity to decide where to live, the enforcement of which was problematic (see paras 30-31 of judgment). (2) Engaging the jurisdiction of the FTT to discharge a guardianship under s.72 of the 1983 Act did not require a move from a "deprivation of liberty" to a "restriction of liberty or less". The guardian's powers were to the exclusion of any other person; that meant that the Court of Protection could not override those powers, C v Blackburn and Darwen Borough Council (2011) EWHC 3321 (COP) applied. Therefore the Court of Protection could only a consider a care plan at a placement where the guardian required the person to live and so any authorisation of a deprivation of liberty given by the court could only relate to that placement. That limitation on the Court of Protection's jurisdiction could give rise to issues relating to where disputes were to be decided concerning the placement of a person without capacity to decide where and how he should live or to consent to their consequences (paras 44-47). (3) The FTT had no jurisdiction to authorise or otherwise render lawful a deprivation of a person's liberty during and after discharge of his guardianship. In exercising its statutory discretion it had to take account of practically available, and hence lawful, options. It should not discharge a guardianship if the consequence of doing so would be to bring about an unlawful deprivation of liberty. The tribunal further discussed the parties' and the FTT's approach on applications such as D's, and provided a checklist of questions for FTTs faced with such applications (paras 55-73). (4) It was not clear what lawful alternative arrangements for D there were. Therefore the best that D could have hoped for in the FTT, and on the instant appeal, was an adjournment. However, the FTT had been entitled on the evidence before it to conclude that there was a need for the continued existence of the guardian's power, and that the continuation of the guardianship was the least restrictive available option. It erred only in discussing whether the guardianship should be discharged if a lawful alternative might be or become available; that was not sufficient to found a discharge (paras 74-90). (5) The appropriate course was for D's discharge from guardianship to be dealt with on a new application to the FTT supported by appropriate evidence and arguments (paras 91-94).

KD v A BOROUGH COUNCIL, [2015] UKUT 251 (AAC), [2015] C.O.P.L.R. 486, Charles J, UT (AAC).

1494 Hospital discharges–Conditional discharge–Conditions giving rise to deprivation of liberty–Power of tribunal to direct

[Mental Health Act 1983 (c.20) s.37, s.41, s.73; Mental Capacity Act 2005 (c.9); European Convention on Human Rights 1950 art.5]

The secretary of state appealed against residential conditions imposed by a First-tier Tribunal when it directed that a restricted patient should be conditionally discharged from detention in hospital. After the patient had been convicted of indecently assaulting a girl, he was detained in hospital under the Mental Health Act 1983 s.37 and subjected to special restrictions under s.41. Ten years later, the tribunal found that the patient no longer required detention in hospital for medical treatment, as opposed to mere containment. It concluded that he should be conditionally discharged but, in order to ensure that he did not have any opportunity to offend sexually, he would have to reside at a particular placement and would not be allowed to leave the premises unless accompanied and supervised at all times by a member of staff. The tribunal accepted that those conditions would amount to a deprivation of his liberty. The patient lacked the capacity to consent to his care plan and the deprivation of liberty its implementation would cause. Accordingly, the local authority brought proceedings in the Court of Protection for a personal welfare order under the Mental Capacity Act 2005 to move him to the proposed placement. The secretary of state argued that, following *Secretary of State for Justice v RB* [2011] EWCA Civ 1608, [2012] 1 W.L.R. 2043, [2012] C.L.Y. 2280, a tribunal could not direct a conditional discharge of a restricted patient on conditions that would result in a deprivation of liberty of the patient outside hospital.

Held: Appeal dismissed. (1) Although a tribunal directing a conditional discharge could not impose conditions which when implemented would result in a deprivation of liberty that was unlawful because it would be in breach of ECHR art.5, it could impose conditions that when implemented would give rise to a deprivation of liberty that was lawful because it had been authorised by the Court of Protection under the 2005 Act or its Deprivation of Liberty Safeguards (DOLS) and so complied with art.5, *RB* explained (see paras 19, 80 of judgment). (2) A tribunal would be permitted under s.73 of the 1983 Act to write into the conditions an ability to apply to it for a variation or discharge of protective conditions on the basis of a material change in circumstances if a variation or discharge was refused by the secretary of state or the tribunal agreed to consider the application, and if the tribunal was invited to consider such an application by the Court of Protection or a DOLS decision-maker. Generally it would be sensible for the tribunal to do that to provide a further alternative route of challenge to a continuing deprivation of liberty (para.120). (3) The Court of Protection could only authorise a deprivation of liberty under the 2005 Act if the restricted patient lacked capacity to consent to the relevant conditions and was not ineligible to be deprived of liberty by the Act. Provided that the terms and conditions that gave rise to the deprivation of liberty did not conflict with conditions that the tribunal had decided were necessary and had identified, the restricted patient would not be ineligible and such authorisations could be given under the Act, applying the tests it set out (para.141).

SECRETARY OF STATE FOR JUSTICE v KC, [2015] UKUT 376 (AAC), [2015] C.O.P.L.R. 804, Charles J, UT (AAC).

1495 Hospital discharges–Delegated powers–NHS trust delegating powers to independent panel–Capacity to seek judicial review of panel's discharge decsion

[Mental Health Act 1983 (c.20) s.23, s.23(6), s.3, s.72]

The claimant trust applied for judicial review of an independent panel's decision to discharge the interested party (X) from detention under the Mental Health Act 1983. X was in his sixties and had lived with bipolar affective disorder and personality disorder for most of his adult life. He had been detained under s.3 following an assault on his father. The trust was concerned about the panel's decision to discharge X in light of the views of the clinical team and also a decision of the First-tier Tribunal which had previously decided not to discharge him. The issues were (i) whether the trust had the capacity to seek judicial review of a decision which it could have made itself; (ii) whether the trust had an alternative remedy, namely to re-section X under s.3, so that judicial review should not be granted; (iii) if a claim for judicial review was appropriate, whether the panel had failed to treat the tribunal's decision as a relevant consideration and whether its decision to discharge was irrational.

Held: Application refused. (1) The trust had a patent interest in bringing the claim. However, its capacity to do so was not straightforward. It sought judicial review of a decision which it had the power to take but which was taken by a body to which it had delegated that power. If it had taken the decision itself, judicial review would have been impossible because of the principle about a body not being able to bring a claim for judicial review of its own rules and decisions. However, the legal position changed given the nature of the delegation in the instant case, to a body which Parliament intended to be an independent decision-making entity. Section 23(6) ensured the independence of a panel from an NHS foundation trust by the requirement that members could not be executive directors of its board or employees. Consequently, the panel was sufficiently separate from and independent of the trust to enable the trust to bring a judicial review challenge to its decision. The situation was analogous to a regulatory body bringing a judicial review challenge to one of its own disciplinary committees, *R. v Statutory Committee of the Pharmaceutical Society of Great Britain Ex p. Pharmaceutical Society of Great Britain* [1981] 1 W.L.R. 886, [1981] C.L.Y. 508 considered. Furthermore, the trust ought to be able to bring a judicial review challenge to protect the public in circumstances where it considered a panel had made an unlawful decision (see paras 25-27 of judgment). (2) A responsible clinician might take the view that to re-section a patient after a panel had ordered discharge would be to undermine the panel system. Even if the same result might be achievable through other means, judicial review was an appropriate remedy in the instant case, *R. (on the application of von Brandenburg) v East London and the City Mental Health NHS Trust* [2003] UKHL 58, [2004] 2 A.C. 280, [2004] C.L.Y. 2683 considered (para.30). (3) The tribunal's decision was not a relevant consideration such that the panel had to take it into account. There was nothing on the face of the Act, or the Code of Practice, which elevated a tribunal's decision to the status of a relevant consideration for the purposes of a panel's decision-making. Nor was there anything which made a tribunal's decision something so obviously material that not to take it into account meant that the decision of a trust or its panel was flawed. A tribunal decision not to discharge a patient under s.72 in no way prevented a trust or its panel from exercising its own, separate powers of discharge under s.23 (paras 39-41). All members of the panel had exhibited experience and care in considering X's case. They were aware of the medical professionals' reports and had heard evidence from the clinical team. The decision to discharge was clearly open to the panel on the evidence before it. In particular, it considered the risk X posed to his parents, but balanced that against other factors. Moreover, the decision to discharge was not beyond the range of reasonable decisions open to the panel. X's bipolar state had stabilised; over 30 years it had warranted hospital admission on only two occasions; he had a clear motivation in light of his hospital experience to continue taking his medication in the community; and although his personality disorder was not yet treated he had lived with it for the majority of his adult life without great incident. The panel decided, on an obviously rational basis, that the treatment offered to X in hospital, under compulsory powers, was not treatment addressing his overall needs. That a differently consulted panel might have reached a different decision was beside the point. It was a paradigm case where a panel had disagreed with the clinical team and discharged a patient where it considered that the state's compulsory power of detention could no longer be justified (paras 33-34).

SOUTH STAFFORDSHIRE AND SHROPSHIRE HEALTHCARE NHS FOUNDATION TRUST v ST GEORGE'S HOSPITAL MANAGERS, [2016] EWHC 1196 (Admin), (2016) 19 C.C.L. Rep. 253, Cranston J, QBD (Admin).

1496 Hospital discharges–Persons lacking capacity–Patient with anorexia nervosa–Discharge to community care

[Mental Health Act 1983 (c.20) s.3; Mental Capacity Act 2005 (c.9) s.4, s.4(4); European Convention on Human Rights 1950 art.2, art.5, art.8]

The applicant hospital board applied for an order discharging the respondent (W) into the community with a support package for her and her family. W, aged 28 and currently detained under the Mental Health Act 1983 s.3, had been diagnosed with obsessive compulsive disorder at seven years old, and with anorexia nervosa by the age of 10. From 11 years old to date she had spent six periods as a hospital in-patient variously lasting from nine months to two-and-a-half years and totalling over nine years. At 19 she spent more than a year at university, but at 22 she was readmitted in an emergency with a weight of 25kg and a BMI of 10.8. Recently she had the possibility of a job, but her psychiatrist had had to inform the employer that she was unfit for work. W thought he should not have intervened. All treatment options had been tried, including force feeding. The three current options were: rendering W unconscious for up to six months and feeding her by tube, which was by common consent ethically unacceptable; discharging her to her parents' home or to a flat of her own; keeping her in a specialist unit for some weeks to see if she could gain weight before discharge into the community. There was expert psychiatric evidence that remaining on the specialist unit would be unlikely to prolong her life more than any other alternative and that discharge would at least give her the chance to exercise any control she was capable of over her condition. The Official Solicitor supported the hospital's application. The hospital submitted that W lacked capacity to make decisions about her care and treatment, though she did have it regarding her physical health, and should be discharged into the community with support.

Held: Application granted. The court accepted the board's submission and the specialist medical advice that W, by reason of her severe anorexia, lacked the relevant capacity. It had to identify her best interests with reference to the Mental Capacity Act 2005 s.4 and the terms of the ECHR art.2, art.5 and art.8. The court was only entitled to interfere where a person lacked relevant capacity, Re E (Medical treatment: anorexia) (Rev 1) 2012 EWHC 1639 applied. Under s.4(4) the person had to participate as fully as possible in any decision affecting her, and the court had spoken with her at length. It had followed the proper approach, which was to consider the individual at the particular time, their welfare in the widest sense, the treatment options and prospects of success. It had to put itself in the place of the patient and ask what their attitude was or was likely to be, and to consult carers and those interested in the patient's welfare on those matters, *Aintree University Hospitals NHS Foundation Trust v James* [2013] UKSC 67, [2014] A.C. 591, [2014] C.L.Y. 1526 followed (see paras 7-9, 28-33, 35-47 of judgment). The judicial instinct was directed to giving the highest priority to the preservation of life, *A NHS Foundation Trust v X* [2014] EWCOP 35, [2015] 2 F.C.R. 418, [2015] C.L.Y. 1738 considered. However, the conclusion was that there was no realistic alternative to what the hospital proposed. It was the least worst option for W. Hard as it was to accept, the institutional environment was not therapeutic for her. Services were not being withdrawn and community services would be provided. If W's thinking were to change a reassessment would be made (paras 48-53).

W (MEDICAL TREATMENT: ANOREXIA), RE *sub nom.* BETSI CADWALADR UNIVERSITY LOCAL HEALTH BOARD v W, [2016] EWCOP 13, (2016) 151 B.M.L.R. 220, Peter Jackson J, CP.

1497 Lasting powers of attorney–Interpretation–Provision for appointment, reappointment and replacement of attorneys

[Mental Capacity Act 2005 (c.9) Sch.1 Pt 3 para.19(2), s.10, s.10(8), s.13(5), s.13(6), s.13(7), s.9(4); Lasting Powers of Attorney, Enduring Powers of Attorney and Public Guardian Regulations 2007 (SI 2007/1253)]

The appellants appealed against a Court of Protection decision (*Public Guardian v M* [2014] EWCOP 40, [2015] C.O.P.L.R. 107, [2015] C.L.Y. 1723) on the interpretation and effect of two lasting powers of attorney (LPAs). Both appellants had executed LPAs in similar terms drawn up by the same solicitors for their property and affairs and for health and welfare. The LPAs appointed two attorneys to act jointly for significant decisions and severally for less important decisions, described as a "hybrid" appointment. The intention of the drafter of the LPAs was that if only one of the original attorneys was able and willing to act, that attorney would be reappointed to act alone. A second paragraph then provided for the appointment of a replacement attorney in the event that both of the original attorneys were unable or unwilling to act. The respondent Public Guardian applied to the Court of Protection for guidance as to whether it was possible to reappoint an original attorney to act alone, where a joint appointment had failed, before any substitute attorney acted. The judge ruled that the wording purporting to reappoint a surviving joint attorney was ineffective and should be severed. He relied on the fact that the Mental Capacity Act 2005 made no provision for survivorship or reappointment, nor did the forms prescribed under the Lasting Powers of Attorney, Enduring Powers of Attorney and Public Guardian Regulations 2007.

Held: Appeal allowed. There was nothing in the 2005 Act which precluded the effect which the drafter was trying to achieve, namely to appoint A and B to act as attorneys under s.10, and if one of them was unable or unwilling to act to appoint the remaining attorney as sole attorney, and only if both of the original attorneys were unable or unwilling to act to appoint a replacement attorney, C. There was nothing surprising about that intention, since C was the donor's third choice as attorney. Under s.9(4) the authority conferred by a lasting power of attorney was "subject to any conditions or restrictions specified in the instrument". If a donee was unable or unwilling to act, within s.13(6), that had the effect of terminating the appointment under s.13(5), and revoking the power except, by virtue of s.13(7), where the donee was replaced under the terms of the instrument, or two or more persons had been appointed to act jointly and severally in respect of any matter and there was at least one remaining donee. The fact that, if A and B were appointed under a hybrid appointment, and if one of them was unable or unwilling to act, the remaining attorney would not be able to act in respect of the joint matters did not mean that the remaining attorney could not be appointed or reappointed under s.10(8) to act as sole attorney, so long as the terms of the instrument clearly had that effect. What was said in the respondent's guidance about the failure of joint appointments did not affect that conclusion. The judge had erred in relying on the former Court of Protection rules relating to appointing deputies to act jointly with survivorship. Further, the prescribed forms did not prevent the form of appointment sought to be made. Continuation sheet A2 in particular allowed the donor to indicate how he wanted his replacement attorneys to act. There was no reason to construe the legislation in an unduly restrictive way. The key issue was that of clarity. Any words in the LPAs which were not clear could be excised as ineffective under Sch.1 para.19(2). The judge's solution of having a second contingent LPA was unnecessary and cumbersome. The LPAs, with the unclear wording severed, could properly be construed as providing for a hybrid appointment of two attorneys, followed by the reappointment of the remaining attorney as sole attorney, where one was unable or unwilling to act, followed by the appointment of a third replacement attorney, if both the original attorneys were unable or unwilling to act.

MILES v PUBLIC GUARDIAN *sub nom.* BEATTIE v PUBLIC GUARDIAN, [2015] EWHC 2960 (Ch), [2015] C.O.P.L.R. 676, Nugee J, Ch D.

1498 Lasting powers of attorney–Revocation–Deputies taking advantage of position–Appointment of panel deputy

[Mental Capacity Act 2005 (c.9) s.12, s.22(4)(b); European Convention on Human Rights 1950 art.8]

The Public Guardian applied for an order under the Mental Capacity Act 2005 s.22(4)(b) revoking a lasting power of attorney in respect of the property and financial affairs of a 77-year-old woman (O). O was a widow with three adult children, two sons and a daughter. She had lived alone in her own maisonette until 2010, when her daughter moved in with her. In 2011 she was diagnosed with vascular dementia, and in July 2013 she suffered a stroke. In late 2013 she executed and registered a lasting power of attorney in respect of her property and financial affairs, appointing her daughter and younger son jointly and severally to be her attorneys. In the summer of 2014, O's maisonette was sold for £730,000. She and her daughter moved into a property in Croydon, purchased for £430,000 from the proceeds of sale. A declaration of trust was executed, stating that O had a 20 per cent share in the Croydon property, whereas the daughter and younger son had a 40 per cent share each. Some £200,000 of O's money was then used to discharge the mortgage on, and to pay for repairs to, a property owned by the daughter. In six months, O went from owning a property worth £730,000 to having only a 20 per cent share in the Croydon house and £7,000 in her bank account. O's elder son expressed concerns and the Public Guardian opened an investigation. The attorneys failed to produce a full account of their dealings and the Public Guardian concluded that they had used their powers irresponsibly. When a Court of Protection visitor concluded that O lacked capacity to revoke the lasting power of attorney, the Public Guardian made the instant application. The attorneys indicated that they were willing to stand down so that a panel deputy could be appointed. However, they argued that that the elder brother should not be appointed as a deputy either alone or together with a professional deputy.

Held: Application granted. (1) There was no medical evidence indicating how O's cognitive function had been affected by the stroke, and the Public Guardian appeared to accept that, despite the stroke, she had had the capacity to make the lasting power of attorney. However, questions about O's capacity, whether she had been unduly influenced, and whether any of the transactions should be set aside were matters for another day and another court. O had an immediate need for someone who could manage her property and financial affairs honestly and competently, in her best interests, and free from any conflict of interest or undue influence. The question for the instant court was whether the attorneys had behaved in a way that contravened their authority or was not in O's best interests. They had. Revocation of their appointment could be justified simply on the basis of their failure to keep accounts of the transactions carried out on O's behalf and their failure to produce any record of her income and expenditure. However, they had compounded their culpability by taking colossal advantage of their position and obtaining personal benefits far in excess of those permitted under s.12 of the Act. The daughter had also failed to keep O's money and property interests separate from her own. Since O lacked the capacity to revoke the lasting power of attorney, the court would revoke it for her. To the extent that that interfered with O's rights under ECHR art.8, the interference was in accordance with the law and necessary for the prevention of crime. A panel deputy would be appointed and would be authorised to take such steps as were expedient to restore O's estate, so far as possible, to the position it would have been in but for the attorneys' actions. The elder brother would not be appointed as a deputy. He lacked the detachment and impartiality necessary to manage O's affairs and to ensure that her interests were properly considered. There was a sense that he was motivated by a desire to salvage his own inheritance and a craving for revenge against his siblings. To appoint him to act with a panel deputy would impede the decision-making process and increase the costs incurred by O's estate (see paras 16-19, 33-39 of judgment). (2) In view of the attorneys' conduct, a departure from the general rule as to costs in property and affairs proceedings was justified. There would therefore be no order as to costs (para.40).

OL, RE *sub nom.* PUBLIC GUARDIAN v DA, [2015] EWCOP 41, [2015] W.T.L.R. 1647, Senior Judge Denzil Lush, CP.

1499 Lasting powers of attorney–Revocation–Donee making inappropriate decisions and showing no intention of learning about statutory responsibilities

[Mental Capacity Act 2005 (c.9) s.22, s.22(4)(b), s.23(3)(a), s.58(1)(c); Convention on the Rights of Persons under Disabilities (UN) 2006]

The Public Guardian applied under the Mental Capacity Act 2005 s.22(4)(b) for an order revoking a lasting power of attorney for property and affairs. The executor of the LPA had appointed her daughter and her favourite grandson jointly and severally to be her attorneys for property and affairs. The Office of the Public Guardian removed the grandson as lacking capacity. The executor's estate was a half-share in a seaside bungalow. She had also executed an LPA for health and welfare, appointing her son, his wife and their two daughters (the executor's granddaughters) jointly and severally. The guardian had become concerned at the conduct of the attorney daughter, and later of the rest of the family attorneys. There had been reports of family conflict, even extending to physical violence, and a lack of co-operation in producing information about their decisions under the LPAs. The manager of the executor's previous care home stated that the daughter had wasted money by buying unnecessary and unsuitable food for her mother. The guardian was granted an order under s.23(3)(a) directing that the attorney daughter account for her dealings with the executor's financial affairs over the previous two-and-a-half years; in default of the account, that there be an order under s.22(4)(b) to revoke and cancel the LPA; if the LPA was cancelled, that there be an order to invite a panel deputy to become the executor's deputy. The file was referred to a judge. The guardian's investigator concluded that the daughter, mostly out of ignorance, was not using her mother's assets in her best interests and that the LPA should be revoked and the daughter made a deputy to manage the assets with guidance from the Office of the Public Guardian. The daughter objected to the guardian's application on the basis of what she declared were her mother's wishes. The son also objected, stating that he thought he should be deputy for finance and property.

Held: Application granted. Section 22 allowed the court to revoke an LPA for property and affairs and cancel its registration where it was satisfied that donees' behaviour contravened their authority or was not in the executor's best interests. The human rights of persons with disabilities, including lack of mental capacity, was protected in an international law context by the Convention on the Rights of Persons under Disabilities 2006 (UN) adopted in 2006 and ratified by the UK in 2009. Although not directly part of UK law, it was recognised by European law as part of the international law context within which the guarantees of the ECHR were to be interpreted, *Cheshire West and Chester Council v P* [2014] UKSC 19, [2014] A.C. 896, [2014] C.L.Y. 2189 followed (see paras 33-37 of judgment). The daughter had demonstrated no intention or desire to learn about the Act, about best interests decision-making, or about her fiduciary duties as an attorney, and had exhibited inflexibility in thought and behaviour. She wasted over £250 per month of her mother's money on unnecessary food for her. She insisted that the bungalow, devised to the grandson, was to provide him with a home, but he did not want to live there and it was unoccupied, generating no income and requiring money for its upkeep. It was neither sensible nor in the executor's best interests to leave the daughter in unfettered control of the executor's property and financial affairs. The Public Guardian had no statutory duty to supervise attorneys acting under an LPA, but did have an obligation to supervise deputies appointed by the court under s.58(1)(c).The executor lacked capacity to revoke her LPA, and although the daughter might not have contravened her authority, her behaviour was not in her mother's best interests. The LPA was revoked and the daughter appointed to act as deputy for property and affairs. That respected the executor's rights, will and preferences regarding her choice of decision-maker, while allowing appropriate, effective and proportionate safeguards (paras 40-42, 44-46).

PUBLIC GUARDIAN v ALH *sub nom.* AMH, RE, [2015] EWCOP 70, [2016] W.T.L.R. 571, Judge Lush, CP.

1500 Lasting powers of attorney–Revocation–Hostility between joint attorneys for property and financial affairs–Removal of attorney

[Mental Capacity Act 2005 (c.9) s.1(3), s.4(4)]

The Public Guardian applied for the partial revocation of a lasting power of attorney for property and financial affairs and for the revocation of a lasting power of attorney for health and welfare. The lasting powers of attorney had been made by an elderly man (M) in 2014. As to the lasting power of attorney for property and financial affairs, he appointed his wife, son and daughter as his attorneys. His wife died in 2015. As to the lasting power of attorney for health and welfare, he appointed his daughter as his sole attorney. By the instant application, the Public Guardian effectively sought the daughter's removal under both powers of attorney. It was said that the daughter's continued involvement in the management of M's financial affairs was unworkable due to the poor relationship between her and her brother. Reliance was placed on a report of the Court of Protection General Visitor, who stated that the daughter had been "in a high level of agitation" throughout her meeting with the Visitor and that she saw herself as the victim of a conspiracy. The Visitor also expressed grave doubts about the daughter's ability to make health and welfare decisions in M's best interests. Although M continued to live in his own home, he required support for day-to-day activities. The Visitor had stated that he did not have the mental capacity to revoke or suspend the lasting powers of attorney.

Held: Application granted in part. (1) The daughter should continue to act as M's attorney for health and welfare. She had made proposals in relation to M which showed an awareness of, and a genuine eagerness to apply, the supported decision-making provisions in the Mental Capacity Act 2005 s.1(3) and s.4(4). She had suggested, for example, that M should "have all decisions fully discussed with him, giving him time and support to come to his own decisions". That was commendable conduct and it was unusual to find an attorney attaching such prominence to it in practice. Another important factor was that M specifically chose his daughter to be his sole attorney for health and welfare, whereas in the lasting power of attorney for property and financial affairs he appointed his wife, son and daughter to act jointly and severally as attorneys. The distinction was clearly relevant and it should be treated with respect (see paras 44-46 of judgment). (2) The daughter's continued involvement as one of M's attorneys for property and financial affairs would not be in his best interests, because the hostility between her and her brother had impeded the proper administration of his estate. That hostility was such that they deliberately avoided having any contact with one another; they simply could not work together. That had had the following consequences: M's bank accounts had been frozen; the daughter and son had not obtained a grant of representation to their late mother's estate, of which M was the primary beneficiary; further, any communications between the daughter and son had to be channelled through the daughter's solicitors, causing a delay in the decision-making process. By concentrating on the daughter's negative influence on the management of M's property and finances, the court should not overlook the son's positive impact. He had acted reliably and sensibly in difficult circumstances and seemed to be able to interact satisfactorily with everyone who had an interest in M's welfare, other than his sister. In the circumstances, he should act as M's sole attorney in relation to M's property and financial affairs (paras 53-55, 58).

RM, RE *sub nom.* PUBLIC GUARDIAN v PM, [2016] EWCOP 25, [2016] C.O.P.L.R. 488, Judge Lush, CP.

1501 Lasting powers of attorney–Revocation–Property, affairs and personal welfare deputy not acting in donor's best interests

[Mental Capacity Act 2005 (c.9) s.22]

The Public Guardian applied for the revocation of lasting powers of attorney (LPAs) for property and affairs, and personal welfare in respect of a 93-year-old woman (S) with dementia. S was a widow and mother of three sons and lived with her granddaughter (F). In 2008 S executed LPAs for property and affairs, and for personal welfare in which she appointed her youngest son (R) as her sole attorney. A month later she was diagnosed with dementia and by the time of the instant application was severely impaired and non-communicative. S had moved abroad in 2010 to live with F and R had transferred £15,000 to F from S's funds to support S. F and S returned to the UK two years later. S's eldest son (K) then made several complaints to the Office of the Public Guardian (OPG) about R's conduct. An OPG investigations officer stated that R visited S only once a year, had delegated his functions to F, and had failed to provide a care allowance. K and F were concerned that proper procedures had not been observed in obtaining the LPAs and K requested that F assume control of S's affairs. The Public Guardian invited the court to find that S lacked capacity to revoke the LPAs and make decisions about her property and affairs, sought revocation of the LPAs and asked the court to consider appointing F as deputy. R agreed to be removed as attorney, but wanted to know where the money paid to F when S was living abroad had gone.

Held: Application granted. (1) The court was satisfied that S lacked capacity and that R had behaved in a manner which contravened his authority or was not in her best interests, as set out in the Mental Capacity Act 2005 s.22. R had failed to (a) monitor the money transferred for S's move abroad, and her accounts generally; (b) receive or scrutinise her bank statements; (c) register the LPA for property and affairs until very recently; (d) demonstrate financial prudence in ensuring that all relevant benefits were obtained on S's behalf; (e) provide the agreed allowance for F to care for S. The court had discretion as to whom it appointed as deputy for property and affairs and preferred to appoint a relative or friend if satisfied that that was in S's best interests, *RP, Re* [2016] EWCOP 1 considered. It was not in S's best interests to appoint a professional deputy, who would expect remuneration, as her assets were of minimal value. F was appointed as she had looked after S since 2008 and had sacrificed a lot with little reward. There was no need to investigate how the £15,000 had been disposed of and it had obviously been spent on S's care and living expenses over two years. There were no reasonable grounds to believe that F had financially abused S (see paras 25-32 of judgment). (2) The LPA for personal welfare was revoked as R had been neglectful and had delegated his decision making functions to F. However, there was no need to appoint F as a personal welfare deputy. F could make routine decisions concerning S's day-to-day care. Medical decisions should be made by health care professionals, in consultation with S's sons and F. In the event of disagreement, an application could be made to the Court of Protection, *G v E* [2010] EWHC 2512 (Fam), [2011] 1 F.L.R. 1652, [2011] C.L.Y. 2236 considered (paras 40-43).

PUBLIC GUARDIAN v RL *sub nom.* SH, RE, [2016] EWCOP 2, [2016] W.T.L.R. 719, Judge Lush, CP.

1502 Mental capacity–Consent to treatment

[Mental Capacity Act 2005 (c.9) s.15(1)]

The trust applied for declarations under the Mental Capacity Act 2005 s.15(1) in relation to the respondent patient (B). B was 36 years old and had been diagnosed with paranoid schizophrenia. Doctors were concerned that she had ovarian cancer and advised that she needed surgery. B was told that the surgery would involve a total abdominal hysterectomy, which would mean the loss of her fertility. Despite her desire to have children, B initially consented to the operation. However, following a psychotic episode in theatre, it was cancelled. Since that time, B's psychosis led her to doubt that she had a tumour and, despite compelling evidence to the contrary, she had an entrenched view that she would not experience any harmful consequences by not having the operation. The trust sought declarations that (i) B now lacked the capacity to consent to or to refuse medical treatment for ovarian cancer, specifically a total abdominal hysterectomy and removal of the ovaries and fallopian tubes, with a possible bowel resection and colostomy, general anaesthetic, sedation and ancillary treatment; and (ii) it was lawful being in B's best interests to undergo the proposed surgery.

Held: Declarations granted. (1) It was more likely than not that B had ovarian cancer. Without treatment the disease would progress to the point where she would cease to be a candidate for surgery. Her prognosis for survival without surgery was six months; with surgery, she had the chance of being cured and at least achieving a survival period of between three and five years. B's diagnosis of paranoid schizophrenia fulfilled the diagnostic element of the test for capacity. Florid psychosis which was consequent upon her paranoid schizophrenia rendered her unable to understand certain information relevant to the decision to consent to or refuse surgery. The paranoia consequent upon that psychosis fundamentally undermined her ability to understand the reality and seriousness of her condition, the threat to her life and the urgent need for surgery. Accordingly, she lacked the capacity to consent to or refuse the proposed medical treatment. Even with further treatment for her paranoid schizophrenia, she was unlikely to regain capacity within the narrow timescale in which the surgery had to be performed (see paras 49-56 of judgment). (2) It was in B's best interests for her to undergo the proposed surgery. Such a course of action accorded with that to which she had previously consented when she had capacity. It was a course of action that offered the chance of a significantly prolonged life-span and, perhaps, a cure and was consistent with preserving the sanctity of B's life by administering life-sustaining treatment where responsible medical opinion was of the view that such treatment was in her best interests. Whilst she would lose the ability to have children, her likely prognosis without treatment precluded that in any event, in that without surgery the likelihood was that death would occur in a timescale much shorter than that required to carry a baby to term. Within that context, the chance of continued life outweighed the permanent loss of fertility (paras 57-66).

CAMBRIDGE UNIVERSITY HOSPITALS NHS FOUNDATION TRUST v BF, [2016] EWCOP 26, [2016] C.O.P.L.R. 411, MacDonald J, CP.

1503 Mental capacity–Intellectual disability and autism–Capacity to consent to sex or marriage

[Mental Capacity Act 2005 (c.9) s.3(1)]

The court was required to determine whether the second respondent, a 25-year-old man (R), lacked capacity to consent to marriage and sexual relations, and whether his marriage should be declared non-recognised under English law. R had intellectual disability and autism, causing him to have behavioural and emotional difficulties. He had had previously spent four years in a residential unit after his behaviour had become unmanageable at home. The expert considered R to be operating practically at the level of a 5-8 year old, which indicated moderate learning disability. The applicant local authority had sought a forced marriage protection order, to forestall an anticipated marriage. However, the marriage had already taken place in Pakistan. The issues were whether (i) R lacked the capacity to consent to sexual relations; (ii) R lacked capacity to consent to marry; (iii) if so whether he could gain capacity in those areas; (iv) the court should exercise its discretion to declare the marriage non-recognised under English law.

Held: Judgment accordingly. (1) As to whether R lacked the capacity to consent to sexual relations, the court had to apply the test under the Mental Capacity Act 2005 s.3(1), *M (An Adult) (Capacity: Consent to Sexual Relations), Re* [2014] EWCA Civ 37, [2015] Fam. 61, [2014] C.L.Y. 2175 followed. It was agreed that: R understood the "mechanics" of the sexual act; had some understanding of the use of condoms; had articulated the possibility of "infection"; had made some link between pregnancy and sexual intercourse. However, the expert had considered that the combination of autism and intellectual disability prevented R from making the crucial link between actions and consequences, thus establishing a unifying analysis for his overall behaviour. He had concluded that R did not know the risk of intercourse, except possibly the words "baby" and "infection". The court accepted the expert's evidence, which fitted closely with key aspects of his family's evidence, that R did not have capacity to consent to sexual intercourse and would not have had capacity at the time of the marriage in Pakistan (see paras 20, 23-25 of judgment). (2) To have the capacity to consent to marry, it was not enough that an individual appreciated that he was taking part in a marriage ceremony or understood its words. He had to understand both the nature of the marriage contract, and the duties and responsibilities which normally attached to marriage, *Sheffield City Council v E* [2004] EWHC 2808 (Fam), [2005] Fam. 326 applied. It was clear that R had no significant grasp of the role of husband and wife or the duties of either. Mutuality, reciprocity and the capacity for compromise were indivisible components of marriage. Mutuality and reciprocity were subtle, complex and not easily reducible to easy definition, and R's difficulties rendered him unable to grasp those kinds of responsibilities. The court had already found that he lacked capacity to consent to sexual relations, itself a fundamental requisite of marriage; he also lacked the capacity to marry (paras 27, 30). (3) As to whether R could gain capacity in both areas, the medical evidence was that R's core functioning difficulties, intellectual disability and autism would prevent him from weighing and evaluating abstract concepts. He was unable to grasp the concept of fidelity. There was no real prospect of R gaining the capacity to consent to marriage or sexual relations (paras 31-33, 35). (4) The issue was one of recognition of the Pakistani marriage. The courts had consistently emphasised the importance of autonomy; development of psychological and moral integrity and relationships with other human beings as key aspects of individual human rights, *Pretty v United Kingdom (2346/02)* [2002] 2 F.L.R. 45, [2002] C.L.Y. 2528 and *Niemietz v Germany (A/251-B)* (1993) 16 E.H.R.R. 97, [1993] C.L.Y. 2157 considered. Ultimately, however, capacity was an intrinsic, indivisible facet of both psychological and moral integrity. The absence of R's capacity to consent either to sexual relations or to marriage ultimately compromised the couple's ability to forge the mutual and reciprocal commitment which was an essential component of a marriage. Further, R was subject to the legal obligations of a marriage which he was unlikely to be able to understand or fulfill. In most cases an overseas marriage, entered into by an individual who lacked capacity to consent to sexual relations or marriage, was likely to require the court to make a declaration of non-recognition. Although the interests of justice, fairness and respect for different aspects of individual autonomy might, in certain circumstances, prevail, those circumstances were likely to arise very rarely indeed: they had not done so in the instant case (paras 36, 48-52).

LUTON BC v B *sub nom.* RS (CAPACITY TO CONSENT TO SEXUAL INTERCOURSE AND MARRIAGE), RE; LUTON BC v SB, [2015] EWHC 3534 (Fam), [2016] 1 F.C.R. 461, Hayden J, Fam Div.

1504 Mental capacity–Life-sustaining treatment–Capacity to refuse life-sustaining treatment

[Mental Capacity Act 2005 (c.9) s.15, s.2(1), s.3(1)]

An NHS foundation trust applied for a declaration under the Mental Capacity Act 2005 s.15 that a patient lacked capacity to made decisions about her medical treatment. The patient, aged 50, had lived an unconventional life during which she had placed great emphasis on her looks, social life and material possessions, and on living what she described as a "sparkly" lifestyle. She was treated for breast cancer at the age of 49, and the same year experienced the loss of her home and the acrimonious breakdown of a long-term relationship. She attempted suicide by taking paracetamol tablets with alcohol and suffered kidney failure as a result. However, the medical prognosis was highly positive with the likelihood of full recovery if the patient underwent dialysis treatment. Without that treatment, the patient would not survive more than 10 days. There was an issue as to whether the patient believed that she was likely to recover. Two psychiatric reports concluded that she lacked capacity by reason of being unable to use and weigh the information required as part of the decision-making process about whether to undergo dialysis, that inability being due to her belief system or a personality disorder. A further expert concluded that, although the patient suffered from a narcissistic personality disorder, she had capacity. The Official Solicitor reported that the patient had said that she would refuse treatment even if she knew she was going to get better. According to the patient's daughters, she had said that she did not want to become "old", "ugly" and "poor" and therefore did not want to continue living.

Held: Application refused. (1) A capacitous individual was entitled to decide whether or not to accept medical treatment. The right to refuse treatment extended to declining treatment that would, if administered, save the life of the patient, *T (Adult: Refusal of Treatment), Re* [1993] Fam. 95, [1992] C.L.Y. 2918 followed. The court was only entitled to intervene in such a decision if it was satisfied, on the balance of probabilities, that the patient lacked the mental capacity to decide whether or not to accept or refuse such treatment. However, a person was not to be treated as unable to make a decision merely because he or she made a decision that was unwise, *Heart of England NHS Foundation Trust v JB* [2014] EWHC 342 (COP), (2014) 137 B.M.L.R. 232, [2015] C.L.Y. 1730 applied. Moreover, the outcome of the decision made was not relevant to the question of whether the person making it had capacity for the purposes of the 2005 Act, *R. v C* [2009] UKHL 42, [2009] 1 W.L.R. 1786, [2009] C.L.Y. 806 and *York City Council v C* [2013] EWCA Civ 478, [2014] Fam. 10, [2014] C.L.Y. 2172 followed. The fact that a decision not to have life-saving treatment might be regarded as unwise was not in itself evidence of a lack of capacity to take that decision, notwithstanding the importance placed by society in general on the sanctity of life. For a person to be found to lack capacity there had to be a causal connection between being unable to make a decision by reason of one or more functional elements set out in s.3(1) of the Act and the "impairment of, or a disturbance in the functioning of, the mind or brain" required by s.2(1). Taken as a whole, the evidence showed that the patient had acknowledged that her prognosis was positive if she maintained treatment. She was able to use that information and weigh it in the decision-making process. Statements she had made apparently rejecting her positive prognosis had to be placed in the context of the information she was receiving during her recovery period, when she might not have been receiving uniformly positive and reassuring information concerning her prognosis and the likelihood of her being able to live a life without dialysis. It was important not to confuse her decision to give no weight to her prognosis, having weighed it, with an inability on her part to use and weigh that information. She had given a range of reasons for reaching her decision, including her fear that she would continue to be dependent on dialysis. That fear could not be regarded as irrational (see paras 1, 3, 28-30, 34, 70-73, 81-92 of judgment). (2) While it was accepted that the functioning of the patient's mind was impaired, there was no conclusive evidence as to precise nature of that impairment. The evidence was similarly equivocal as to the question of causation, in particular whether the patient's conduct resulted from the operation of a personality disorder or simply the thought processes of a stubborn individual with unpalatable and highly egocentric views. The case was a finely balanced one in which a number of reasonable interpretations of the available information were possible, *PH v A Local Authority* [2011] EWHC 1704 (Fam) applied. Accordingly, it had not been established that she lacked capacity to decide whether or not to accept dialysis treatment (paras 93-98).

KINGS COLLEGE HOSPITAL NHS FOUNDATION TRUST v C, [2015] EWCOP 80, [2016] C.O.P.L.R. 50, MacDonald J, CP.

1505 **Mental patients–Appropriate treatment test–Guidance for tribunals**

[Mental Health Act 1983 (c.20) s.145(4), s.3(4), s.72(1)(b), s.72(1)(b)(iia)]

A detained patient appealed against a decision of the Mental Health Review Tribunal for Wales that appropriate treatment for his mental disorder was available to him in hospital and he should not be discharged. The patient had dissocial personality disorder and was detained in hospital under the Mental Health Act 1983. Various treatments were tried and his condition was managed by nurses but did not improve. He believed that the tribunal should discharge him under s.72(1)(b)(iia) on the basis that no appropriate treatment was available. The patient's responsible clinician reported to the tribunal that the hospital had no further treatment to offer and recommended the patient's transfer to a rehabilitation hospital, which the patient had visited and was willing to try. The clinician reported that discharge was not possible as a community package would not meet the patient's needs. Two social workers also reported that the patient could not be managed in the community. The tribunal concluded that appropriate treatment was available at the rehabilitation hospital and refused to discharge the patient. The patient argued that the tribunal had erred in that (1) the appropriate treatment had to be available at the hospital in which he was detained; (2) the detaining hospital was not providing appropriate treatment; (3) the reasons for its decision were inadequate.

Held: Appeal allowed. (1) The tribunal had erred in concluding that appropriate treatment was available at the rehabilitation hospital. A tribunal only had jurisdiction to determine the appropriate treatment test under s.72(1)(b)(iia) with regard to the treatment that a patient was receiving at the detaining hospital (see para.47 of judgment). (2) The detaining hospital had provided appropriate treatment. First, medication had been prescribed for relief, and the alleviation of a symptom or manifestation of the patient's disorder fell within medical treatment under s.145(4), *MD v Nottinghamshire Health Care NHS Trust* [2010] UKUT 59 (AAC), [2010] M.H.L.R. 93 applied. Second, his disorder was managed by nursing staff, and he might fall within the *Mental Health Act 1983: Code of Practice for Wales (2008) para.4.14*, which envisaged "... patients with persistent medical disorders for whom management of the undesirable effects of their disorder is all that can realistically be hoped for." Third, rehabilitative planning such as planning a future move to the rehabilitation hospital fell within medical treatment. Fourth, para.4.15 of the Welsh Code recognised that appropriate treatment might consist only of nursing and specialist daily care in a safe environment with a structured regime; it did not have to involve medication or psychological therapy. Also, appropriate treatment could not be judged in isolation: s.3(4) of the Act required tribunals to consider the nature and degree of a patient's mental disorder and all other circumstances. In the instant case, the evidence pointed towards serious consequences for the patient's own mental health and for others if he was discharged. Patients with personality disorders represented a particular challenge for tribunals, especially if receiving the type of care described in para.4.15, but making little progress. However, if the purpose of the treatment was to prevent a worsening of the symptoms or manifestations of a patient's disorder, it was likely to constitute appropriate treatment even if its outcome had little or no beneficial effect on the patient. Precise fact-finding that focused on both the terms of the s.72(1)(b)(iia) test and the particular treatment that a hospital said was available for a patient was essential in helping to ensure that patients were lawfully detained, *DL v Partnerships in Care Ltd* [2013] UKUT 500 (AAC), [2014] M.H.L.R. 241 applied. Tribunals troubled by the issue could also benefit from the approach of *R. (on the application of Epsom & St Helier*

NHS Trust) v Mental Health Review Tribunal [2001] EWHC Admin 101, [2001] M.H.L.R. 8, *Epsom & St Helier* considered (paras 50-56, 58). (3) The tribunal's reasons left much to be desired. It had ignored the guidance on writing reasons in *HK v Llanarth Court Hospital* [2014] UKUT 410 (AAC), [2015] M.H.L.R. 88, [2016] 1492: its reasons were not set out by reference to the relevant criteria for detention, they addressed none of the patient's submissions and it was wholly unclear what evidence had been accepted or rejected and why, HK applied (paras 60-62). (4) No nurse's report had been made available in the instant case. Nursing staff had a great deal more contact with detained patients than doctors or social workers and their written or oral evidence could be crucial for a tribunal's understanding of the patient's circumstances. Also, the reports produced had contained limitations. In 2013, the Senior President of Tribunals in England had issued a *Practice Direction on Statements and Reports in Mental Health Cases*. It contained valuable instruction on the contents of reports from responsible clinicians, nursing staff and those preparing social circumstances reports, often social workers. It would be desirable for the Welsh tribunal to adopt its contents (paras 40-44).

WH v LLANARTH COURT HOSPITAL (PARTNERSHIPS IN CARE), [2015] UKUT 695 (AAC), [2016] M.H.L.R. 245, Judge Knowles QC, UT (AAC).

1506 Mental patients–Hospital discharges–Whether fax constituting proper delivery of discharge notice under reg.3 Mental Health (Hospital, Guardianship and Treatment) (England) Regulations 2008

[Mental Health Act 1983 (c.20) s.25; Mental Health (Hospital, Guardianship and Treatment) (England) Regulations 2008 (SI 2008/1184) reg.3, reg.3(3)(b)(i)]

The claimant patient (K), by his litigation friend (M), his mother, made a habeas corpus application to end his detention under the Mental Health Act 1983. K had a severe form of Asperger's syndrome and had been detained for six years under the 1983 Act. M's view was that K would be better treated at home or elsewhere other than at the defendant hospital (H). As the nearest relative, M served a discharge notice on H under s.25 of the Act. The effect of that notice was that once a 72-hour period had expired the patient had to be released. Within that time urgent steps could be taken by a hospital to prevent release if it was felt that the patient was likely to be a danger to himself or other persons. No further discharge order could then be obtained by a relative for a further six months. Under the Mental Health (Hospital, Guardianship and Treatment) (England) Regulations 2008 reg.3(3)(b)(i), where a patient was liable to be detained in hospital a s.25 notice had to be delivered at that hospital to an officer of the managers authorised by the managers to receive it. M faxed a discharge notice to H. It was put into the in-tray of the hospital administrator (C), who only worked three days a week and given that the 72-hour period included weekends, she was only present to receive notices for three-sevenths of the week. C lodged a barring report preventing K's release which was served within 72 hours of her return to work but not within 72 hours of the receipt of the notice at the fax machine. K submitted that the 72 hours was a mandatory period and as it concerned the continued detention of an individual affecting his human rights and that the absence of a system for dealing with documents while a part-time administrator was not working should not stand in the way of his rights.

Held: Application refused. The question was whether C had received the discharge notice within reg.3(3)(b)(i). The delivery to the fax machine was not a delivery to an officer of the managers authorised by the managers to receive it, *GK (Patient: Habeas Corpus), Re* [1999] M.H.L.R. 128 applied. The risk of non-receipt of the order remained upon K until C had read it when she returned to work; thereafter both C and the hospital had acted with substantial expedition. (2) (Obiter) In future, there should be in all hospitals a proper system in place for receipt of such documents, which could come at any time of the day or night and had to be capable of being dealt with within 72 hours (see para.38 of judgment).

K v KINGSWOOD CENTRE HOSPITAL MANAGERS, [2014] EWHC 2271 (Admin), [2015] M.H.L.R. 68, Burton J, QBD (Admin).

1507 **Mental patients–Recall to hospital–Whether written reasons for recall necessary**

[Mental Health Act 1983 (c.20) s.42(3), s.75(1)(a); European Convention on Human Rights 1950 art.5, art.5(2)]

The appellant appealed against a decision that the secretary of state had lawfully recalled him to hospital under the Mental Health Act 1983 s.42(3). The appellant suffered from a mental disorder and had been made subject to hospital and restriction orders after being convicted of criminal offences. He was detained in hospital, but was conditionally discharged and moved to a care home for ex-offenders. Following his discharge, his social supervisor contacted the National Offender Management Service, raising concerns about his condition. On behalf of the secretary of state, a caseworker issued a warrant for his recall. The warrant gave no reason for the recall, but the social supervisor informed the appellant that the reason was because his mental health had deteriorated. He was taken to hospital and no further explanation was provided until 15 days later, when his responsible clinician read the social supervisor's statement to him and discussed it with him. The appellant was not given any written reasons for his recall. Department of Health guidance on the recall of patients to hospital required that at the time of a patient's return to hospital, he had to be informed in simple terms that he was being recalled, and that within 72 hours of re-admission his responsible clinician had to explain the reasons for the recall and ensure as far as possible that he understood them. The patient also had to be provided with a written explanation of the reasons for his recall within 72 hours. The issues were whether (1) sufficient explanation was given at the time of the recall; (2) the recall was made unlawful by the failure to provide a full written explanation within 72 hours; (3) the breaches of the appellant's rights should be the subject of a formal declaration and damages awarded to him.

Held: Appeal dismissed. (1) Where a public authority issued a policy statement concerning the exercise of one of its functions, a member of the public to whom it applied had a common law right to require the authority to apply the policy. In the instant case, the explanation provided at the time of the recall complied with the policy and contained an accurate summary of the ground for recall. In that respect, there had been no breach of the appellant's common law right. The appellant also had rights under ECHR art.5. In relation to the explanation provided at the time of his recall, the demands of art.5(2) did not extend beyond the demands of the common law. The recall to hospital of a mental patient had special features. It was often effected in an emergency, which might mean that the hospital would be unacquainted with the reasons for the recall until later, *X v United Kingdom (A/46)* (1982) 4 E.H.R.R. 188 considered, *Fox v United Kingdom (A/182)* (1991) 13 E.H.R.R. 157, [1990] C.L.Y. 2526 applied. The explanation provided at the time of recall had been legally sufficient (see paras 17-18, 24-32 of judgment). (2) The secretary of state conceded that he had breached the appellant's common law right to receive an adequate written explanation for the recall within three days in accordance with the published policy. In that respect, he also conceded that he had breached the appellant's right under ECHR art.5(2) to be informed promptly of the reasons for his recall. However, those breaches did not render the appellant's detention unlawful between the third and fifteenth days following his recall. There was no direct link between the lawfulness of the detention and the secretary of state's wrongful failure to provide an adequate explanation for 12 days, *R. (on the application of Lumba) v Secretary of State for the Home Department* [2011] UKSC 12, [2012] 1 A.C. 245, [2011] C.L.Y. 1727 and *R. (on the application of Kambadzi) v Secretary of State for the Home Department* [2011] UKSC 23, [2011] 1 W.L.R. 1299, [2011] C.L.Y. 1733 followed. The failure did not delay the secretary of state's reference of the case to the First-tier Tribunal under s.75(1)(a) of the Act and that provided a statutory mechanism for ensuring that an adequate justification was provided for the detention (paras 21, 39-41). (3) The appellant had suffered no pecuniary loss as a result of the breaches. He reported that in the months following his recall he suffered great distress, but he attributed that to the recall itself and did not identify the failure to provide reasons for 12 days as an additional cause. He was not entitled to damages for the breach of his common law right to receive an adequate explanation within the time identified by the policy. The breach did not amount to a tort and there was nothing to suggest that damages would have been available in any ordinary action against the secretary of state. Damages were not payable for breach of art.5(2) because the appellant had failed to establish that the effects upon him were sufficiently grave, *R. (on the application of Greenfield) v Secretary of State for the Home Department* [2005] UKHL 14, [2005] 1 W.L.R. 673, [2005] C.L.Y. 2066, *R. (on the application of Sturnham) v Parole Board for England and Wales* [2013] UKSC 23, [2013] 2 A.C. 254, [2013] C.L.Y. 2113 and *R. (on the application of Sturnham) v Parole Board for England and Wales* [2013] UKSC 47, [2013] 2 A.C. 254, [2013] C.L.Y. 2112 followed. Further, a formal declaration would not add anything to the recording in the instant judgment of the secretary of state's concessions (paras 42-43, 46).

R. (ON THE APPLICATION OF LEE-HIRONS) v SECRETARY OF STATE FOR JUSTICE *sub nom.* LEE-HIRONS v SECRETARY OF STATE FOR JUSTICE, [2016] UKSC 46, [2016] 3 W.L.R. 590, Lady Hale DPSC, SC.

1508 Mental patients–Social circumstances reports–Adequacy of reports and requirements of authors

[Mental Health Act 1983 (c.20) s.117, s.66; Tribunal Procedure (First-tier Tribunal) (Health, Education and Social Care Chamber) Rules 2008 (SI 2008/2699) r.7(2)(b); European Convention on Human Rights 1950 art.5(4), art.6(1)]

A patient appealed against the First-tier Tribunal's refusal to adjourn his application under the Mental Health Act 1983 s.66 to enable him to seek a social circumstances report. The patient suffered from chronic paranoid schizophrenia. He wanted a social worker or community psychiatric nurse to prepare an independent social circumstances report for the hearing of his s.66 application. Earlier social circumstances reports had been prepared by nursing staff. The patient sought an adjournment on the basis that it was not fair and just to proceed with the hearing in view of the fact that the existing social circumstances report had not been written by a professional from the community mental health team. The tribunal refused an adjournment, taking the view that the respondent trust's policy of having the patient's named nurse prepare social circumstances reports was not inconsistent with the Act. At the hearing, the tribunal had before it two nursing reports and two social circumstances reports written by the same staff nurse. The tribunal refused to discharge the patient's liability to be detained. The patient did not challenge that substantive decision, but asked for the refusal to adjourn to be set aside. The issues were whether (1) a blanket policy for ward nurses to prepare social circumstances reports would lead to the preparation of inadequate reports because the ward nurse would not have access to all relevant information; (2) there was an absolute requirement for the report's author to attend the hearing; (3) the report had to contain an after-care package pursuant to s.117 of the Act, having regard to the Code of Practice, the Tribunal Procedure (First-tier Tribunal) (Health, Education and Social Care Chamber) Rules 2008 and the relevant Practice Direction .

Held: Appeal dismissed. (1) There was nothing in the law that required the social circumstances report to have been written by a social worker or community psychiatric nurse, or that required the nursing report and social circumstances reports to have different authors. The important issue was not the professional title of the report writer, but the relevance and quality of the information provided and thus the writer's position of knowledge in respect of that information. The adequacy of any individual report had to be determined on the facts of the case in which it arose (see paras 38, 45, 56 of judgment). (2) There was no legal requirement for the report's author to attend the hearing. In the instant case, a different nurse had attended and the tribunal had been satisfied that she had a good knowledge of the patient's case (para.49). (3) It was not clear that the Act, the Code of Practice, the 2008 Regulations or Practice Direction (First-tier Tribunal: Health Education and Social Care Chamber: Statements and Reports in Mental Health Cases) (Unreported, 6 April 2012) required the social circumstances report to include details about s.117 after-care in every case. It was at least arguable that the Practice Direction only required that the report contain details of the care pathway and after-care as far as such information was known, *AM v West London MH NHS Trust* [2012] UKUT 382 (AAC), [2012] M.H.L.R. 399, [2013] C.L.Y. 2048 applied. Paragraph 27.9 of the Code of Practice emphasised the need to consider putting preparations in place only where there was a strong possibility that the patient would be discharged if appropriate after-care could be arranged. In any event, under r.7(2)(b) of the 2008 Rules, if a responsible authority failed to comply with a requirement in a practice direction, and if the First-tier Tribunal considered that it needed that information in order to deal with the application before it fairly and justly, then it could require the responsible authority to remedy the failure (paras 14, 50, 52, 55). (4) If a policy or procedure of a responsible authority led to a consistent failure in its ability to provide relevant and complete social circumstances reports such that the tribunal was unable to discharge its statutory functions fairly and justly, then that might have consequences in terms of patients' rights under ECHR art.5(4) and art.6(1). Beyond that, however, any challenge to the lawfulness of such a policy or procedure would have to be brought by way of judicial review, since the appellate jurisdiction of the Upper Tribunal was limited to deciding whether the First-tier Tribunal had materially erred in law in an individual case. In the instant case, there had been no such error in refusing the adjournment (paras 59-60).

AF v NOTTINGHAM NHS TRUST, [2015] UKUT 216 (AAC), [2015] M.H.L.R. 347, Judge Wright, UT (AAC).

1509 **Mental patients' rights–Hospital discharges–Whether conditional discharge violating patient's rights under art.8 ECHR**

[European Convention on Human Rights 1950 art.8]

The appellant patient appealed against a decision of the First-tier Tribunal that his conditional discharge should continue. The patient had been diagnosed with paranoid schizophrenia and was made the subject of hospital and restriction orders following convictions for violent offences in 2010. He was conditionally discharged in 2011. The tribunal decided in 2015 that the conditional discharge should continue and confirmed the conditions that were in place at the time of the hearing, which included that he should abstain from illegal drugs, refrain from the consumption of excess alcohol and submit to random drug testing. The patient submitted that the tribunal had breached his rights under the ECHR art.8 and that there was no justification for the conditions. He argued that he was young when he had offended, he had been on conditional discharge for over three years without recall and had been off medication for a year. He further contended that the condition on consuming alcohol was vague.

Held: Appeal dismissed. The tribunal was under a duty not to act in violation of a patient's Convention rights but that did not mean that it was expected to deal with the issue separately in every case. The conditions were the same as those already in force so the tribunal was entitled to expect that the patient's representative would draw its attention to any part of those conditions that might involve a violation of art.8. Article 8 was not expressly put to the tribunal. Accepting that art.8 was engaged by virtue of the conditions imposed, the issue was whether the interference was authorised under art.8(2). It was understood when conditions were imposed that they would be applied reasonably. The tribunal was more likely to be concerned to ensure that the conditions were reasonable in principle. It had been reasonable for the tribunal to have re-imposed the conditions including some control over alcohol consumption. What mattered was how the conditions were operated and art.8 operated to protect the patient at that stage. An absolute discharge was premature when there was uncertainty as to whether the patient's partner knew he was on conditional discharge and he had only been free from medication for a year (see paras 10- 12, 16, 19-21 of judgment).

RP v DUDLEY AND WALSALL MENTAL HEALTH PARTNERSHIP NHS TRUST, [2016] UKUT 204 (AAC), [2016] M.H.L.R. 270, Judge Jacobs, UT (AAC).

1510 **Mental patients' rights–Restricted patients–Applications for tribunal to make extra-statutory recommendations–Existence of duty on tribunal to hear such applications**

[Mental Health Act 1983 (c.20) s.37, s.41, s.72(1)(b)(iia), s.74(1)(a)]

The appellant patients (X and Y) appealed against decisions of the Upper Tribunal dismissing their appeals against the First-tier Tribunal's refusals to make extra-statutory recommendations in respect of their care and treatment. X and Y were detained under the Mental Health Act 1983 s.37 and subject to restriction orders under s.41, which required their indefinite detention. Following X's discharge and subsequent recall to hospital, the respondent secretary of state referred the case to the FTT pursuant to his duty in s.74(1)(a). At the hearing of that reference, X applied to the tribunal for an extra-statutory recommendation that he be granted leave outside the hospital. Y applied to the FTT for a transfer to less restrictive conditions. In each case the tribunal refused to make a recommendation without hearing evidence. The Upper Tribunal refused X and Y's appeals, holding that while the FTT could make extra-statutory recommendations in relation to restricted patients, it had no legal power to do so and could not be compelled to do so. X and Y submitted (1) in reliance on a parliamentary answer given by a Home Office minister on October 28, 1987, that applicants to the FTT enjoyed a legitimate expectation that it would entertain submissions that a recommendation should be made; (2) as their applications for extra-statutory recommendations were about transfer and leave, which could form an essential part of the FTT's consideration of the availability of appropriate medical treatment under s.72(1)(b)(iia), it had to make findings on those issues.

Held: Appeals dismissed. (1) The ministerial answer was not capable of generating a legitimate expectation. There was no practice of conferring an expectation that such recommendations would be made. Decisions arising out of applications for extra-statutory recommendations might be challengeable. But none of that suggested that there was a procedural right to have requests for recommendations heard. The FTT was a creature of statute so it had no statutory duty to entertain the sort of applications the appellants had made. It was striking that in both cases the sole purpose of the appellant's case was to ask for extra-statutory recommendations. (2) The FTT had to fulfil its duty under s.72(1)(b)(iia), and it had done so in the instant cases. However, the appellants' case before the instant court was put on a new factual basis. If the FTT had been faced with the contention that leave or transfer were necessary or available parts of the patient's treatment, it would have had to consider it. However, that was not the basis on which the appellants had put their cases before the FTT.

EC v BIRMINGHAM AND SOLIHULL MENTAL HEALTH NHS TRUST; K v (1) ST ANDREWS HEALTHCARE (2) SECRETARY OF STATE FOR JUSTICE, [2013] EWCA Civ 701, [2014] M.H.L.R. 23, Laws LJ, CA (Civ Div).

1511 Mentally disordered offenders–Hospital discharges–Correct approach to conditions for discharge

[Mental Health Act 1983 (c.20) s.72(1)]

A mentally disordered offender who had been detained in hospital since committing two robberies in 2002 and 2003 appealed against a refusal of the First-tier Tribunal to authorise his discharge from detention. The offender had a personality disorder. The tribunal had noted his progress, and that it had enabled him to move to a low security unit. It also noted that there had been allegations by three males at three different hospital placements between 2001 and 2007 that the offender had raped and sexually abused them. Criminal investigations had not taken place owing to the vulnerability of the victims. The offender initially denied that the incidents had occurred, eventually conceding that they might have. He had declined to undergo psychosexual assessment and was placed on depot medication. In his evidence to the tribunal he said that he would be prepared to undergo certain treatment, but only if the tribunal conditionally discharged him. The tribunal found as a fact that there was insufficient evidence to establish that the first rape definitely occurred, but that the later two rapes did occur. It found that those rapes fully justified the conclusion that sexual treatment work needed to be undertaken before the offender was conditionally discharged, because without such treatment it was impossible to assess what level of risk he posed. The offender submitted that in deciding whether the rapes had occurred, the tribunal failed to address the evidence with sufficient care and proceeded on the mistaken belief that the second and third alleged rapes had been the subject of criminal proceedings with forensic evidence to support them. He maintained that the tribunal had believed that the existence of two independent allegations, both of which had been taken seriously by the police, increased the probability of each of them having occurred.

Held: Appeal allowed. (1) The tribunal's finding that the two rapes had occurred was central to its decision that the offender needed to undergo sexual treatment work before being discharged. There was a risk that the error of fact had been critical to the outcome of the appeal. It was, therefore, a fundamental error in the light of which the decision could not stand (see paras 15-18 of judgment). (2) The tribunal's bare statement that the two rapes had occurred was not an adequate explanation for the finding. Having found the offender to lack credibility, the tribunal seemed to have simply accepted that the rape allegations were true because they were viewed as credible at the time. It did not follow from the offender's lack of credibility that they were true, *English v Emery Reimbold & Strick Ltd* [2002] EWCA Civ 605, [2002] 1 W.L.R. 2409, [2002] C.L.Y. 301 followed and *R. (on the application of N) v Mental Health Review Tribunal (Northern Region)* [2005] EWHC 587 (Admin), [2005] M.H.L.R. 56, [2005] C.L.Y. 2825 applied. The tribunal had failed to scrutinise the evidence. In particular it had acknowledged neither the difficulties arising from the lack of contemporaneous records nor indications in some of the reports that an account from one of the victims was unreliable. The tribunal's decision had therefore been made in error of law (paras 22-26). (3) The conditions under the Mental Health Act 1983 s.72(1) of which a tribunal had to be satisfied involved mixed questions of fact and judgment. Judgment involved evaluating what was likely to occur, and the evaluation had to be founded on fact, *H (Minors) (Sexual Abuse: Standard of Proof), Re* [1996] A.C. 563, [1996] C.L.Y. 632 applied. That did not mean, however, that the tribunal could only be satisfied as to the risk of sexual violence if it was satisfied that the rapes occurred. It could take account of a whole range of facts, including aspects of his sexual or other history, his behaviour towards others, things he said, and his attitudes (paras 27-33).

AM v PARTNERSHIPS IN CARE LTD, [2015] UKUT 659 (AAC), [2016] M.H.L.R. 214, Judge Markus QC, UT (AAC).

1512 Persons lacking capacity–Best interests–68-year-old objecting to amputation of foot–Amputation necessary to sustain life

The applicant NHS trust sought a declaration that it would be lawful for the doctors treating the respondent, a 73-year-old man with a severely infected leg, to amputate his foot against his wishes in order to save his life. The respondent had a longstanding mental illness, dating from his 20s when both of his parents died, that deprived him of the capacity to make the decision for himself. He suffered from bipolar affective disorder with psychotic symptoms. As a result, he experienced auditory hallucinations that told him whether or not to take his medication. He had said, for example: "If the Lord says it's no, it's no". He had religious beliefs, though he did not follow an established religion. He had been treated with anti-psychotic medication over the years, generally with enough success to allow him to live in the community, though his medical notes described over 10 compulsory admissions for treatment since 1994. He had been fit to work only briefly. Before his admission to hospital, he had lived alone in somewhat squalid conditions. About 12 to 18 months ago, he had developed a chronic foot ulcer which had not healed despite various interventions. He had resisted antibiotics for his foot; he had also resisted medication for diabetes, from which he also suffered. He strongly opposed the proposed operation, without which he would die shortly.

Held: Application refused. (1) Where a patient lacked capacity, it was of great importance to give proper weight to his wishes and feelings and to his beliefs and values. An enforced amputation would not be in the respondent's best interests. He had had a hard life. Through no fault of his own, he had suffered in his mental health for half a century. He was a sociable man who had experienced repeated losses so that he had become isolated. He had no next of kin. No one had ever visited him in hospital and no one ever would. Yet he was a proud man who saw no reason to prefer the views of others to his own. His religious beliefs were deeply meaningful to him and did not deserve to be described as delusions: they were his faith and were an intrinsic part of who he was. It would not be appropriate to define him by reference to his mental illness or his religious beliefs; rather, his core quality was his fierce independence. It was that which was now, as he saw it, under attack. He was on any view in the later stages of his life. His fortitude in the face of death would be the envy of many people in better mental health. He had gained the respect of those who were nursing him. It would not be in his best interests to take away his little remaining independence and dignity in order to replace it with a future for which he understandably had no appetite and which could only be achieved after a traumatic and uncertain struggle which he and no one else would have to endure. There was a difference between fighting on someone's behalf and just fighting them; enforcing treatment in this case would surely be the latter. The application, though rightly brought, would be dismissed (see paras 10, 42-46 of judgment). (2) (Obiter) The court had arranged a face-to-face meeting with the respondent. The advantages of such a course could be considerable and had proved so here. First, the court had obtained a deeper understanding of the respondent's personality and view of the world, supplementing and illuminating the relevant reports. Second, the respondent seemed glad to have the opportunity to get his point of view across. To whatever small degree, the meeting may have helped him to understand something of the process and to make sense of whatever decision was then made. Third, the nurses were pleased that the respondent had had the fullest opportunity to get his point across. A case like this was difficult for the nursing staff in particular, and it was to be hoped that the fact that the respondent had been as fully involved as possible would make it easier for them to care for him at what would undoubtedly be a difficult time (para.18).

WYE VALLEY NHS TRUST v B *sub nom.* X NHS TRUST v B, [2015] EWCOP 60, [2015] C.O.P.L.R. 843, Peter Jackson J, CP.

1513 Persons lacking capacity–Best interests–Decision about residence of 88-year-old woman–Context of bitter family dispute

[Mental Capacity Act 2005 (c.9) s.4]

The court was asked to make a number of decisions in the best interests of a woman (G). G was 88 and in poor health. She lacked capacity to make decisions about where she should live and who she should see. She had four children who were engaged in long-running and acrimonious litigation concerning the family home and business affairs, and her welfare had become a matter of dispute between them. In July 2015 the court determined that it would be in her best interests for her to go into a nursing home following a spell in hospital. By the time of the instant hearing she had been in the home for almost three months. Her children disagreed about whether she should stay there or return to the family home; they were in dispute about which of them should have contact with her; and one asserted that the others had dissipated her finances. The court was therefore required to make decisions about where she should live, who she should see, and whether her finances should be investigated. There was also a preliminary issue. The instant hearing had been conducted in private, though members of the press had attended, having learned of it through an alert issued by a public relations company instructed by a family friend. The court had to decide whether the press should be allowed to report the hearing, and whether should there be a public judgment naming the parties.

Held: Judgment accordingly. (1) The general rule was that Court of Protection hearings were held in private, though the court could, with good reason, allow all or part of the hearing to be held in public, or allow specified information to be published. Decisions about whether the hearing was to be in public or in private should normally be made at the outset, and the court was to be cautious about retrospectively converting a private hearing to a public one. There was no good reason for doing so in the instant case, or for allowing the press to report extracts from the evidence. There was, however, good reason to publish a judgment naming the parties. Very few families descended to the level of acrimony exhibited in the instant case, and it was in the public interest to reveal the consequences and show how the court process operated, and at what cost, in a recognisable case. Such knowledge might deter other families from behaving in a similar way. Moreover, so much information was already in the public domain that anonymising the judgment would be futile. The Chancery Division had already delivered a public judgment concerning another aspect of the dispute, and it was undesirable that there should be any unnecessary difference of approach between courts dealing with different but related aspects of a dispute. The parties had repeatedly chosen to air their differences in court, and while G's right to privacy and dignity was an important consideration, publication of the judgment would not be a significant further intrusion into her privacy (see paras 12-17 of judgment). (2) In making decisions in G's best interests, the court had to apply the Mental Capacity Act 2005 s.4 and take account of all relevant circumstances. It had to consider whether she was likely to regain capacity in relation to the matters in question; encourage her to participate as fully as possible; and consider her past and present wishes and feelings together with the beliefs, values and other factors likely to have influenced her if she had capacity. It also had to take account of the views of anyone caring for her or interested in her welfare as to what would be in her best interests. G was unlikely to regain capacity and had participated as fully as possible: ideally, she would prefer to be at home and to have easy relations with all her children. No weight would be attached to the children's views about her welfare. They had forfeited their right to have their views taken into consideration: they had no insight into her longing for peace, none of those arguing about contact saw how important the others were to her, and their actions were dictated by the wish to get the better of the others (paras 88-94). It would not be in G's interests to return to the family home. She needed the care package on offer at the nursing home and it was impossible to approve an arrangement that returned her to a home which her children had turned into a war zone. Collectively, the family had the means to pay for the nursing home care and should do so. The contact plan supported by the nursing home and the Official Solicitor for separate daily visiting by both sides of the family would be adopted. Outings acceptable to the nursing home could take place, but visits to the family home were to be approached with caution. While G was living in the nursing home there was no need for a welfare deputy; the home'"s management would protect her day-to-day interests. No property or affairs deputy would be appointed, and the Official Solicitor would not be required to carry out further inquiries into G's finances. Such investigations would be complicated, expensive and unlikely to benefit her (paras 95-101). (3) Subject to submissions, there would be no order for costs between the parties, but they would be ordered to pay the Official Solicitor's costs equally and in full (paras 102-104).

AIDINIANTZ, RE *sub nom.* AIDINIANTZ v AIDINIANTZ; AIDINIANTZ v RILEY, [2015] EWCOP 65, [2015] C.O.P.L.R. 643, Peter Jackson J, CP.

1514 Persons lacking capacity–Best interests–Pregnant woman suffering brain injury and post-traumatic amnesia–Whether abortion in best interests

[Mental Capacity Act 2005 (c.9) s.1, s.4, s.4(6), s.4(7)]

A hospital trust applied for permission to terminate the pregnancy of a patient whom it believed lacked capacity to make the decision. The patient had been in a relationship with a partner who allegedly abused her. She became pregnant and told her friends and sister that she wanted an abortion. Her sister agreed to accompany her to a clinic, as she had done when the patient had had an abortion some years earlier. However, before the appointment, the patient was allegedly violently assaulted by her partner and suffered a serious brain injury. Her medical staff reported that she had post-traumatic amnesia and could no longer retain information. She could not remember what stage of pregnancy she was at. At times she indicated that she wanted to keep the baby, but each time she then said that she wanted an abortion. She had problems rehabilitating and occasionally fell over, with one such fall leading to a further head injury. Her obstetrician believed that continuing the pregnancy would involve a greater risk of injury to her physical health than if the pregnancy was terminated. The issues were whether (1) the patient lacked capacity to decide whether to have an abortion; (2) an abortion would be in her best interests.

Held: Application granted. (1) The patient lacked capacity to make the decision. In so concluding, the instant judge had considered the Mental Capacity Act 2005 s.1 to s.4 concerning a person's ability to make a decision for themselves, the Act's Code of Practice para.3.14 as to the likelihood of the person's capacity being restored, the central principles summarised in *CC v KK* [2012] EWHC 2136 (COP), and the causal relationship between the person's mental impairment and their inability to make the decision, *CC v KK* and *York City Council v C* [2013] EWCA Civ 478, [2014] Fam. 10, [2014] C.L.Y. 2172 applied. Owing to her post-traumatic amnesia, the patient could not understand or retain relevant information as to the stage of her pregnancy, the options for termination, her previous views about the pregnancy and her personal circumstances. There was a reasonable prospect that she would regain capacity, but almost certainly not within the limited timescale for an effective termination. She was therefore unable to decide whether to have an abortion (see paras 7-12 of judgment). (2) Regarding the patient's best interests, it was necessary under case law and s.4(6) and s.4(7) to consider her past and present wishes and feelings and the views of anyone engaged in caring for her or interested in her welfare, *Aintree University Hospitals NHS Foundation Trust v James* [2013] UKSC 67, [2014] A.C. 591, [2014] C.L.Y. 1526 applied. Also, considerable weight had to be attached to clearly expressed wishes and feelings of a mother as to whether she wanted a termination, *X (A Child)*

(Capacity to Consent to Termination), Re [2014] EWHC 1871 (Fam), (2014) 139 B.M.L.R. 143, [2015] C.L.Y. 1033 applied. The patient had expressed an intention on a number of occasions prior to her brain injury to terminate her pregnancy and had taken steps towards making an appointment to do so. Her mother and sister believed that if she was able to make a capacitated decision she would still want an abortion. An important factor was that she had previously had a termination. Her clearly expressed views prior to her injury were made while knowing the physical, emotional and psychological consequences of the procedure. Her present wishes were very difficult to ascertain as they had fluctuated since her injury. No significant weight could be attached to them given her patent lack of capacity. Overall, the crucial factors were the clear and unambiguous views that she had expressed prior to her injury. A termination also accorded with her best interests in other ways. Continuing her pregnancy would involve a greater risk of injury to her physical health as it was likely she would become more prone to falls, whereas a termination was likely to promote her physical recovery and rehabilitation. Her best interests lay in authorising the termination. That accorded with her clear wishes prior to her injury and her overall health and welfare (paras 13-22).

CS (TERMINATION OF PREGNANCY), RE *sub nom.* AN NHS TRUST v CS, [2016] EWCOP 10, [2016] C.O.P.L.R. 187, Baker J, CP.

1515 Persons lacking capacity–Deprivation of liberty–Proper construction of Sch.1A Pt 1 para.2 Mental Capacity Act 2005

[Mental Health Act 1983 (c.20) s.3; Mental Capacity Act 2005 (c.9) Sch.1A, Sch.1A Pt 1 para.2, Sch.1A Pt 1 para.3, s.16A]

An NHS trust sought orders and declarations depriving a teenage boy of his liberty for the purposes of administering medical treatment. The boy, who had autism, was detained in a psychiatric hospital under the Mental Health Act 1983 s.3. Before 2011 he had exhibited a relatively high level of functioning. However, his condition had deteriorated sharply since then. He had begun to display psychotic symptoms and a high level of aggressive behaviour, resulting in his detention, and he currently functioned at the level of someone with a moderate learning disability. He was uncommunicative and was cared for in long-term segregation. Despite extensive investigations, the cause of his catastrophic decline remained a mystery. A number of neuro-degenerative diseases had been ruled out. There were other diseases that might be responsible, but they could only be identified with a CT or MRI scan, which the boy would have to undergo under general anaesthetic. The trust therefore sought the authority of the court to carry out the scans and to use such physical restraint as was necessary in doing so. It also sought authorisation to fill a number of the boy's teeth while he was under anaesthetic. It was possible that pain from caries was contributing to his condition, and he was at risk of developing a serious oral infection. The proposed treatment was supported by a consultant psychiatrist, a consultant anaesthetist, a registered mental health nurse and the boy's parents.

Held: Application granted. It might be thought that, given the circumstances, the court could simply make an order declaring that the proposed procedures were in the boy's best interests and authorising the necessary deprivation of liberty. However, the law was not that simple. Instead, the court had to navigate through a thicket of opaque legislative drafting that seemed designed to confuse. Pursuant to the Mental Capacity Act 2005 s.16A, the Court of Protection could not make a welfare order depriving a person of his liberty if, pursuant to Sch.1A of that Act, he was ineligible to be deprived of his liberty. Determining whether a person was ineligible to be deprived of his liberty under Sch.1A involved a two-stage test. First, the court had to decide whether he fell into one of the cases set out in the second column of the table at Sch.1A Pt 1 para.2. If he did, it had then to decide whether one of the entries in the third column of the table provided that he was ineligible. In the instant case, the boy fell within "case B" of the second column by virtue of his being subject to a hospital treatment regime but not detained in a hospital under that regime. Although he was detained under the 1983 Act, he would no longer be so detained once he was transferred to the general hospital for treatment. That was because the 1983 Act did not authorise treatment without the consent of the detained person save for treatment to address a mental disorder. The treatment proposed in the instant case was treatment to address an underlying disease that might be causing a mental disorder. Therefore, once he was in the general hospital, the boy would be subject to a hospital treatment regime, but would not be subject to detention under that regime. Moving on to the second stage of the test, the relevant entry in the third column provided that the boy would be ineligible to be deprived of his liberty if the authorised course of action was not "in accordance with a requirement which the relevant regime impose[d]". In effect, that meant that if the 1983 Act imposed a specific requirement, the Court of Protection could not make a welfare order that was at variance with it. The scheme was plainly intended to prevent any possibility of mutually incompatible courses of treatment being authorised. The treatment proposed in the instant case did not clash with any requirements imposed by the 1983 Act. The boy was therefore not ineligible to be deprived of his liberty. In *A Local Health Board v AB* [2015] EWCOP 31, [2015] C.O.P.L.R. 412, [2015] C.L.Y. 1742, the court had reached the opposite conclusion in a similar case. Paragraph 54 of the judgment read "Under Sch.1A Pt 1 para.3(2) unless the proposed treatment is in accordance with the requirement which the relevant regime imposes, [the subject of the proceedings] is ineligible to be deprived of her liberty...".However, that was precisely the opposite of what Sch.1A Pt 1 para.3(2) actually said, and any future scrutiny of *AB* had to proceed on the basis that para.54 accidentally omitted a negative and mistakenly expressed the opposite of the true construction of Sch.1A Pt 1 para.3(2), *AB* not followed. In conclusion, the boy in the instant case was eligible to be deprived of his liberty for the purposes of the proposed treatment. The Mental Capacity Act: Deprivation of Liberty Safeguards Code of Practice issued by the secretary of state confirmed that interpretation (see paras 8-14 of judgment).

AN NHS TRUST v A, [2015] EWCOP 71, [2016] Fam. 223, Mostyn J, CP.

1516 Persons lacking capacity–Deprivation of liberty–Provison of care, observation and monitoring in own home

[European Convention on Human Rights 1950 art.5; Mental Health Act 1983 (c.20) s.136]

The Court of Protection was asked to determine whether care arrangements in place for a 28-year-old man (B) who lacked capacity constituted a deprivation of his liberty. B suffered from autistic spectrum disorder and mild learning disability and had exhibited extremely challenging and dangerous behaviour. He lived in his own home and staff were with him at all times. He was subject to constant observation and monitoring but was provided with minimal personal care when he was in his home. There were no locks on the doors although there were sensors which would alert staff if B tried to leave; in fact, he had never tried to do so. He required staff support at all times when in the community as he lacked road and traffic awareness. However, with support, he used local transport and was involved in doing his own shopping. There was a particular risk associated with B accessing public toilets, since there had been past incidents of him engaging in inappropriate sexual activity in public places including toilets. As a result, he was supported by staff to use public toilets should he wish to do so. The local authority and B's mother were agreed that the current arrangements were in B's interests and should continue. The court was further asked to decide what contact B should have with his mother.

Held: Judgment accordingly. The intensive support and care that a person required to meet their needs plainly did engage ECHR art.5 which referred to the right to "liberty and security of person": it engaged and gave effect to that right to security, *W City Council v L* [2015] EWCOP 20, [2015] C.O.P.L.R. 337, [2015] C.L.Y. 1745 applied. However, the continuing legal controversy showed how difficult it was to pin down a definition of what was a deprivation of liberty as opposed to a restriction on movement or nothing beyond humane and empathetic care; the difference was merely one of degree or intensity, *Stanev v Bulgaria (36760/06)* (2012) 55 E.H.R.R. 22 considered. B was not being detained by the state. He was not under continuous supervision and he was afforded appreciable privacy. He was free to leave: were he to do so his carers would seek to persuade him to return, but such persuasion would not cross the line into coercion. The deprivation of liberty line would only be crossed if and when the police exercised powers under the Mental Health Act 1983 s.136. Were that to happen then a range of reviews and safeguards would become operative, but up to that point B was a free man. Accordingly, on the specific facts, the acid test was not met: B was not being deprived of his liberty by virtue of the care package which was approved as being in his best interests. So far as contact was concerned, the present monthly supervised contact would be increased to happen much more frequently and after the passage of a reasonable period under the new routine a review was to take place to see if contact could resume on an unsupervised basis (see paras 28-29, 33, 35-37 of judgment).

BS, RE *sub nom.* BOURNEMOUTH BC v PS, [2015] EWCOP 39, (2015) 18 C.C.L. Rep. 486, Mostyn J, CP.

1517 Persons lacking capacity–Deprivation of liberty–Supported living–Constant monitoring, no freedom to leave

[European Convention on Human Rights 1950 art.5; Mental Capacity Act 2005 (c.9) s.4]

The court had to determine issues arising from the placement of a 23-year-old man (P) in supported living accommodation. P had learning disabilities, epilepsy and autism. He frequently self-harmed and required a high level of daily support. During his final year at a residential college, his family and the local authority agreed that the best option for P when he left college would be a supported living placement. The local authority gave P's family a list of care providers that enabled people with complex needs to live in the community. The family chose a provider that proposed a placement with 1:1 support during the day and 1:2 support at night. The local authority agreed to fund that placement, and also a placement for P at a day centre five days a week. P moved into the supported living accommodation, where he was monitored by care staff and could only leave the building if closely supervised. It was common ground that his care arrangements were in his best interests, they were the least restrictive option in terms of his rights and freedom of action, and that he lacked capacity to make decisions about his care arrangements. The issues were (1) whether P was objectively being deprived of his liberty, and, if so, (2) whether that deprivation was imputable to the local authority and thereby the state, bringing it within ECHR art.5. The local authority argued that P's family had chosen his placement and was responsible for any deprivation of liberty.

Held: Judgment accordingly. (1) The objective element of deprivation of liberty consisted of "confinement in a particular restricted place for a not negligible length of time", *Storck v Germany (61603/00)* (2006) 43 E.H.R.R. 6 applied. Applying the approach of *Cheshire West and Chester Council v P* [2014] UKSC 19, [2014] A.C. 896, [2014] C.L.Y. 2189, P's care arrangements satisfied the test for deprivation of liberty. He was obliged to live in a particular place; he was subject to constant monitoring and control; all aspects of his care arrangements were controlled and supervised by his care staff; he was only allowed to leave the building with close supervision; he was not free to leave without permission and would be restrained by the staff if he attempted to do so. The fact that his living arrangements were as comfortable as possible made no difference, and it was irrelevant that he was content and accepted the arrangements without protest, *Cheshire West* applied. His case was different from that of a person who lived in their own home under no control or supervision for large parts of the day, or a person who had appreciable privacy and was free to leave, *W City Council v L* [2015] EWCOP 20, [2015] C.O.P.L.R. 337, [2015] C.L.Y. 1745 and *BS, Re* [2015] EWCOP 39, (2015) 18 C.C.L. Rep. 486, [2016] 1516 considered (see paras 33, 36, 53-56 of judgment). (2) The local authority had at all times been directly responsible for P's care arrangements, and thus the deprivation of liberty was caused by them. It had been actively involved in every stage of the care planning process and had provided the specialist knowledge and commissioning ability to enable P's family to choose his care providers. Whatever choice the family had made would have been subject to the local authority's further approval. The local authority had funded both placements, the providers of the supported living package and the day care facilities were accountable to the local authority, and the services provided were subject to review by the local authority. For the purposes of the Mental Capacity Act 2005 s.4, the local authority was ultimately "the person making the determination" as to what was in P's best interests. It had considered the family's views but those views had not automatically determined the outcome. They were merely a factor that the local authority had to take into account as part of the overall decision-making process (paras 57-60).

HARINGEY LBC v R *sub nom.* R, RE, [2016] EWCOP 33, [2016] C.O.P.L.R. 476, Judge Lush, CP.

1518 **Persons lacking capacity–Deprivation of liberty–Welfare orders–Whether necessary to join incapacitated person as party**

[Mental Capacity Act 2005 (c.9) s.16(2)(a), s.49; Court of Protection Rules 2007 (SI 2007/1744) r.3A; European Convention on Human Rights 1950 art.5; Legal Services Act 2007 (c.29) Sch.2 para.4]

In conjoined cases concerning applications under the Mental Capacity Act 2005 s.16(2)(a) for welfare orders, the court was required to determine various issues arising from the decision in *Cheshire West and Chester Council v P* [2014] UKSC 19, [2014] A.C. 896, [2014] C.L.Y. 2189. *Cheshire West* stipulated that incapacitated people in care should have the benefit of regular independent reviews to ensure that their placement, or any restrictions on their liberty, remained in their best interests. Subsequently, in *X (Deprivation of Liberty), Re* [2015] EWCA Civ 599, [2016] 1 W.L.R. 227, [2015] C.L.Y. 1720, the President of the Court of Protection devised a streamlined process for dealing with deprivation of liberty cases. The instant court had to decide (i) whether the streamlined process should be abandoned or modified; (ii) whether, in order to satisfy fairness requirements, the subject of the proceedings should always be a party, even when proceedings were non-contentious; (iii) the criteria to be applied when selecting a litigation friend so as to ensure the necessary degree of independence; (iv) whether a litigation friend could conduct the proceedings without appointing a solicitor; (v) whether there must always be an oral hearing.

Held: Judgment accordingly. (1) The streamlined process in *Re X* focused on the key issues and was designed to ensure that care packages satisfied relevant requirements. It would be better if the forms in the streamlined process asked for the key provisions of the care package to be summarised so that the questions raised in the forms were answered by reference to that summary. The court outlined what information the summary should contain and listed further issues to be addressed before it could be demonstrated that the care package was the least restrictive available option and one that could be approved without a hearing, *Cheshire West* and *Re X* considered (see paras 223-229 of judgment). (2) The subject of the proceedings did not automatically have to be a party to applications for welfare orders based on care packages whose implementation gave rise to a deprivation of liberty. When there was a family member or friend who could act in a balanced way to promote the best interests of an incapacitated person, they should do the independent checks and reviews without making the subject of the proceedings a party. Most applications were non-contentious; independent checking would only confirm what those supporting the incapacitated person already knew to be in his best interests. Fairness in the Court of Protection did not require treating the subject of the proceedings in the same way as a protected party in adversarial civil proceedings. While aspects of the court's jurisdiction were adversarial, application of the best interests test was largely investigatory. In most cases, however, it would be appropriate to formally appoint a parent, or other family member or friend, as a representative under the newly added Court of Protection Rules 2007 r.3A. That would best satisfy the procedural safeguards required by ECHR art.5. The parent was best placed to provide information about the care package and participate in the proceedings. The parent could also monitor implementation of the plan and initiate any reviews. The best way for the court to obtain further information was to exercise its investigatory jurisdiction under s.49 of the 2005 Act rather than suffering the problems and delay associated with appointing a litigation friend. Such a decision struck the correct procedural balance (paras 33-36, 40-41, 43-47, 111-116, 177, 239, 261-269). (3) Family members or friends were not disqualified by the requirement for independence from acting as a litigation friend, even though they might have been looking after the incapacitated person over his lifetime and have formed firm views about his best interests. The fact that there was no family member or friend who could act as a litigation friend or r.3A representative did not mean that the only solution was to join the incapacitated person into the proceedings and appoint the Official Solicitor as a litigation friend. An independent person who was not involved with the incapacitated person in a professional or remunerated capacity could be involved in decisions about, and reviews of, the care package. The best interests assessor might have that independence. The absence of such a formalised role was a weakness in the streamlined procedure (paras 241- 267). (4) There was no requirement for a litigation friend to act through a solicitor. The phrase "conduct of litigation" in the Legal Services Act 2007 Sch.2 para.4 included a right of audience. The litigation friend was not limited to a strategic or determinative role (paras 135, 139-142, 146, 149-154, 162-164, 167, 170, 230-234). (5) An oral hearing was not a mandatory procedural requirement, *Reilly's Application for Judicial Review, Re* [2013] UKSC 61, [2014] A.C. 1115, [2013] C.L.Y. 2115 and *R. (on the application of Dudson) v Secretary of State for the Home Department* [2005] UKHL 52, [2006] 1 A.C. 245, [2005] C.L.Y. 3775 applied. There were significant problems relating to the funding of legal representation in applications that were presented as non-controversial because they would not satisfy the legal aid criteria (paras 99-108).

P, RE *sub nom.* LM, RE; NR, RE; DPW, RE; MT, RE; EJG, RE; VS, RE; MJW, RE; ML, RE; HR, RE; NRA, RE, [2015] EWCOP 59, [2015] C.O.P.L.R. 690, Charles J, CP.

1519 Persons lacking capacity–Deputies–Appointment of joint deputies

[Mental Capacity Act 2005 (c.9) s.4(7)]

The applicant relatives applied for the appointment of joint deputies for property and financial affairs in respect of a woman lacking capacity (W). W had Alzheimer's disease and lived in a nursing home. Her husband also had Alzheimer's disease. He applied for an order appointing himself and the second and third applicants, who were W's first cousins once removed, jointly to be his wife's deputies. They were very close to the family, and one of them had worked in accounts. They had both already been appointed as the executors of the wills of W and her husband, and as the husband's attorneys under a lasting power of attorney. W and her husband had two sons. The eldest son objected to the application and proposed that he be appointed as joint deputy with the third applicant. He did not consider the second applicant to be a suitable choice. Their younger son submitted a witness statement recommending that his father's request be honoured, but he did not object to his father not being appointed due to his deteriorating health. W's assets consisted of a half-share of the family home, substantial investments, and a half-share of a joint loan which she and her husband had made to their eldest son for him to set up a business. That business had subsequently gone into liquidation.

Held: Application granted in part. (1) The husband would not be appointed as W's deputy because he had his own health issues and would probably prefer to be relieved of the worry. Under the Mental Capacity Act 2005 s.4(7), he would be consulted by the deputies about any decisions as to what was in W's best interests. Further, the eldest son would not be appointed as deputy because he was his parents' principal debtor; it was possible that they would need to realise the funds he owed them in order to provide for their care in later life. The actual conflict between his interest and theirs was too great to enable him to secure their interests and position in a satisfactory manner. Moreover, the views of anyone interested in W's welfare had to be taken into account under s.4(7)(b), and the rest of W's family regarded him as totally unsuitable to be her deputy, because he lacked competence and integrity and because he had a poor track record of managing his company's financial affairs (see paras 27-29 of judgment). (2) The cousins would be appointed as joint deputies because (a) they were suitable relatives who were able and willing to act; (b) they lived locally and could visit W regularly and attend to her needs; (c) W had appointed them to be the executors of her will, which suggested that she trusted them to deal with her financial affairs after her death, and that she thought they would be business-like and capable of coping with the paperwork; (d) the husband clearly trusted them too, as he had appointed them to be his attorneys and had proposed them as deputies for his wife; (e) the younger son considered that their appointment would be in his mother's best interests, and had provided a particularly impressive witness statement, which gave an articulate and balanced account of the family's history and current circumstances. In contrast, the eldest son's witness statements had been rambling, hysterical and vindictive (para.30).

PAW, RE *sub nom.* ARW v IW, [2015] EWCOP 57, [2015] W.T.L.R. 1785, Senior Judge Denzil Lush, CP.

1520 Persons lacking capacity–Deputies–Appointment of successive deputies

[Mental Capacity Act 2005 (c.9)]

The applicant parents sought the reconsideration of an order refusing them permission to apply for an order appointing successive deputies for their 26-year-old daughter (H). H was autistic and had cognitive functioning and adaptive skills in the extremely low range. In addition, she had almost unintelligible speech and very limited communication skills. In August 2014, her parents, who were in their early 50s, applied to be appointed jointly and severally as her deputies for property and affairs and personal welfare. They also applied for the appointment of three successive deputies (X, Y and Z) in the event that they could no longer act themselves. X, Y and Z lived not far from H and knew her extremely well. X and Y were her twin maternal aunts and were aged 41. Z was 44 and had known H for several years; she was now paid to work with H one day a week and occasionally took her to her own home.

Held: Application granted. A balance sheet of the advantages and disadvantages would help the court to decide whether the appointment of successive deputies would be in H's best interests. The following were some of the disadvantages. The application was based on the false premise that, on the death of her parents, the court would appoint someone from outside H's circle of support as her deputy. The persons who constituted H's support network could change at any time. There was currently no infrastructure in the Mental Capacity Act 2005, the Court of Protection Rules or any practice direction governing the procedure to be followed on a successive appointment. The successor deputies might encounter difficulties in getting banks, building societies and other financial institutions to accept the order appointing them. There would be a problem over the amount of security the successor deputies were required to obtain and maintain, especially if H's parents died leaving their combined estates to her absolutely, rather than under a trust. Further, a successive appointment was incompatible with the requirement in international human rights law that any measures affecting a person's legal capacity should apply for the shortest time possible and be subject to regular review. The advantages included the following. There would be a continuity of care and decision-making. There would be continued contact with persons whom H knew. The proposed successive deputies were people who could communicate with H and understand her. The successive deputies would feel a stronger sense of responsibility and commitment towards H. An appointment would reduce the amount of paperwork and bureaucracy which were required. It would give the parents peace of mind, which would filter through to H. No harm would be done to H by appointing successive deputies. It would be appropriate to allow the application. The factor of magnetic importance was that the appointment of successive deputies would give H's parents peace of mind. For the last 26 years, their lives, their needs and their rights had been completely subordinated to H's. When they said that the appointment of successive deputies would be in her best interests, they were to be believed. Moreover, their views in that respect had not changed when they were informed of the problems that were associated with an appointment of this kind. In para.8.43 of its report on Mental Incapacity, the Law Commission had noted that many elderly carers of young disabled persons experienced great anxiety about what would become of the younger person when they, the carers, had gone. If an order appointing successive deputies would relieve H's parents of that anguish, these proceedings would have been worthwhile (see paras 47-52 of judgment).

H, RE, [2015] EWCOP 52, [2015] C.O.P.L.R. 660, Senior Judge Denzil Lush, CP.

1521 Persons lacking capacity–Judicial decision-making–Whether updated capacity assessment and fact-finding hearing necessary

[European Convention on Human Rights 1950 art.8]

A mother appealed against declaratory orders made by the Court of Protection in relation to welfare arrangements for her 30-year-old daughter. The daughter had a moderate learning disability, autistic spectrum disorder and suffered from depression. She lived in a rented property with 24-hour live-in care. In 2011 she alleged that she was being abused physically and emotionally by her mother; allegations were also made that both mother and daughter had abused care workers. The local authority removed the daughter from the property and a deprivation of liberty safeguards authorisation was granted. At a hearing in 2012, the court found that she lacked capacity to litigate and make decisions about residence, care, contact and her finances. At a further hearing in 2013 it declared that (i) the daughter lacked capacity to litigate and to make decisions about residence, care, contact and her finances; (ii) the daughter lacked capacity to enter into or terminate a tenancy arrangement; (iii) it was in the daughter's best interests to reside at a supported living placement and to receive a care package in accordance with her needs; (iv) it was in the daughter's best interests to have contact with her mother and other family members in accordance with her wishes and feelings. The mother argued that the judge had: (1) erred in not conducting an updated assessment of her daughter's capacity before the 2013 hearing; (2) failed to make findings of fact in relation to the events in 2011 that had triggered the proceedings; (3) made a decision as to where her daughter should live which, by the time the order was made, was a fait accompli; (4) acted in breach of ECHR art.8 in directing that contact with her daughter should be heavily supervised.

Held: Appeal dismissed. (1) There was no evidence to suggest that the daughter's capacity was fluctuating, dynamic or likely to alter in the future, and there was no new material before the judge. Court of Protection judges had to concentrate on the issues that really needed to be resolved; they did not need to address every conceivable legal or factual issue, *N (An Adult) (Court of Protection: Jurisdiction), Re* [2015] EWCA Civ 411, [2016] Fam. 87, [2015] C.L.Y. 1741 applied. Although there were cases where expert opinion or observable events pointed to the need to keep the question of capacity under appropriate review, the instant case was not one (see paras 12-18 of judgment). (2) The mother had relied upon *Oxfordshire CC v DP* [2005] EWHC 1593 (Fam), [2005] 2 F.L.R. 1031, [2006] C.L.Y. 1660, *W (Children) (Care Proceedings: Litigation Capacity), Re* [2008] EWHC 1188 (Fam), [2010] 1 F.L.R. 1176 and *LBX v TT* [2014] EWCOP 24, [2014] C.O.P.L.R. 561 to support her argument that there were a number of factors in the case which justified the need for a fact-finding hearing. Those decisions, however, had to be read in the context of the overarching principles articulated in *S (Adult's Lack of Capacity: Carer and Residence), Re* [2003] EWHC 1909 (Fam), [2003] 2 F.L.R. 1235, [2004] C.L.Y. 3648 about whether findings of fact should be made in relation to disputed historical issues in proceedings relating to adults. Those principals fully justified the approach adopted by the judge in the instant case, *BS* applied, *Oxfordshire CC*, *W (Children)* and *LBX* considered. The judge was careful to spell out the legal consequences of having no fact-finding hearing. Furthermore, the decision not to have such a hearing had to be viewed in context. Although the proceedings had been issued against the background of safeguarding concerns arising from various allegations, matters had progressed and the court was faced with a different landscape. The judge correctly recognised that he was looking at the present position and looking to the future. The degree of inquiry undertaken during the 2012 hearing was entirely sufficient to inform the decisions in respect of future planning for the daughter. A lengthy and costly fact-finding hearing would have been entirely disproportionate and there was nothing to suggest that recommendations made by an independent social worker had been adversely influenced by the allegations. Accordingly, the judge had been fully entitled to proceed as he did (paras 23, 29-37). (3) There was no basis for any criticism of the course the judge took. He gave cogent reasons for his decision that the daughter should be moved to the supported living placement. His decision was based on professional and other evidence which he was entitled to accept (para.46). (4) The judge was appropriately sensitive in balancing the daughter's needs and wishes against the mother's understandable and legitimate aspirations. He was anxious to move forward quickly in progressing contact, with a view to both increasing its frequency and reducing the level of supervision. His approach was entirely legitimate and properly respectful of both the mother and daughter's art.8 rights (para.52). (5) (Per curiam) Local authorities had to obtain appropriate judicial authority before moving an incapacitous adult from their home into other accommodation. They also needed to take appropriate steps to minimise the distress and anger caused to someone in the mother's position when initial relief was obtained on the basis of allegations which were not thereafter pursued (paras 56-57).

AG, RE, [2015] EWCOP 78, [2016] C.O.P.L.R. 13, Sir James Munby PFD, CP.

1522 Persons lacking capacity–Medical treatment–Whether hysterectomy in best interests of woman suffering from paranoid schizophrenia

[Mental Health Act 1983 (c.20) s.3; Mental Capacity Act 2005 (c.9) Sch.A1 Pt 1 para.3, s.4]

A hospital trust applied for permission to perform a hysterectomy on a 43-year-old patient suffering from paranoid schizophrenia. The patient had been diagnosed as schizophrenic 18 years previously. She had a long history of violence and aggression and was eventually detained in a mental hospital under the Mental Health Act 1983 s.3. Doctors discovered that she had two ovarian growths and the patient had various delusional beliefs as to their cause. The growths grew bigger and the doctors believed that even if they were not cancerous, they would gradually interfere with the patient's kidney function and without surgery she would die in six or seven years. They considered that the longer the surgery was delayed, the more extensive it would be, increasing the risk of complications. The patient had initially refused surgery but subsequently changed her mind. On the first day of the instant hearing, the judge visited her in hospital, where she made it clear that she wanted the hysterectomy and knew what it would entail.

Held: Application granted. (1) The patient manifestly lacked capacity to make a decision about her treatment under the Mental Capacity Act 2005 and a decision had to be made in her best interests as detailed in s.4. In reaching that decision, it was vital that the wishes and feelings of an incapacitated person were strictly confined to the best interests analysis and did not act subtly to undermine a capacity assessment, *Wye Valley NHS Trust v B* [2015] EWCOP 60, [2015] C.O.P.L.R. 843, [2016] 1512 considered. Where, as in the instant case, there was no doubt about incapacity, the wishes and feelings of the patient could not alter that fact even if they happened to align exactly with a rational decision. However, although by no means decisive, what the patient wanted was very important. Meeting her had been an enlightening experience which was recommended to any judge hearing a similar case. Based on her wishes and feelings and the totality of the medical evidence, the proposed hysterectomy was in her best interests and would therefore be authorised (see paras 12-13, 28, 31, 48 of judgment). (2) It was also necessary to consider whether an ancillary authorisation of deprivation of liberty was required. In that respect, the instant judge rejected criticism he had received from the Court of Appeal in *Rochdale MBC v KW* [2015] EWCA Civ 1054, [2016] 1 W.L.R. 198, [2016] 4 regarding his approach to the question of what amounted to a deprivation of liberty. He repeated his concern that the test set out by the Supreme Court in *Cheshire West and Chester Council v P* [2014] UKSC 19, [2014] A.C. 896, [2014] C.L.Y. 2189 was confusing, *KW* and *Cheshire Council* cited. That confusion was mirrored by the confusion arising from the highly ambiguous wording of Sch.1A para.3(2) of the 2005 Act, which stated that a patient was ineligible to be deprived of liberty by the Act if the authorised course of action was not in accordance with a requirement imposed by the relevant regime. That was open to two directly contradictory interpretations in the instant case. The first was to say that the hysterectomy was not in accordance with a requirement of the regime whereby the patient was detained in a mental hospital. Consequently, she would be ineligible to be deprived of liberty under the Act and the necessary orders would have to be made under the inherent jurisdiction of the High Court. Such a result would be directly contrary to the statute's intention and Code of Practice. The alternative, correct interpretation was to say that the patient would be ineligible to be deprived of her liberty if the regime whereby she was compulsorily detained imposed a specific requirement for dealing with the problem of her ovarian growths but a different procedure was proposed. The regime imposed no such requirement so she was not ineligible, thus the case remained within the statutory powers of the Court of Protection, *An NHS Trust v A* [2015] EWCOP 71, [2016] 3 W.L.R. 119, [2016] 1515 applied. The decision to allow the surgery was intrinsically coercive even though the patient was enthusiastically compliant. It would have been made even if she had been resistant: if she did change her mind, the operation would still have to proceed, and for that purpose restraints could be used. It was therefore necessary to authorise her deprivation of liberty. However, although her situation clearly fell within the Supreme Court's test in *Cheshire Council*, there were still potential scenarios where no such clarity existed (paras 38-48).

A HOSPITAL NHS TRUST v CD, [2015] EWCOP 74, [2016] C.O.P.L.R. 1, Mostyn J, CP.

1523 **Persons lacking capacity–Mental patients' rights–Detention under Mental Health Act 1983–Interaction between Mental Health Act 1983–Mental Capacity Act 2005, Deprivation of Liberty Safeguards**

[Mental Health Act 1983 (c.20) s.131, s.135, s.2, s.5; Mental Capacity Act 2005 (c.9) Sch.A1, s.6; European Convention on Human Rights 1950 art.5(1)(e)]

The appellant (M) appealed against the First-tier Tribunal's refusal to discharge her from hospital following her detention under the Mental Health Act 1983. M, a 78-year-old woman who suffered from depression, had been living in her own home for many years with one of her daughters, when she was removed from her home by a community mental health team on the execution of a warrant under the MHA s.135(1) to carry out a s.2 assessment. The FTT refused M's daughter's application for her discharge from hospital on the basis that M's daughter had had a history of non-cooperation with giving M's medication and with the community support team. A further application for M's discharge was also refused by the FTT; that decision was the subject of the instant appeal, in which it was common ground that M had a mental disorder; she needed a cognitive assessment and treatment in the form of taking tablets, and that she was compliant incapacitated in the sense that she lacked capacity to consent to treatment. At the core of the instant appeal was the nature of the interaction between the MHA and the Mental Capacity Act 2005 and its related Deprivation of Liberty Safeguards (DOLS). The issues were (i) the nature of the relationship between those two regimes; (ii) the steps the FTT had to take in deciding whether a person ought to be detained; (iii) whether the FTT had erred in refusing to discharge M. M submitted that her detention in hospital on the basis of her lack of capacity under the MHA s.2 was unnecessary as she was willing to remain voluntarily under s.5; accordingly, her involuntary detention was neither necessary nor warranted.

Held: Appeal allowed. (1) In order to be compatible with the European Convention on Human Rights 1950 art.5(1)(e), the MHA had to be applied on the basis that for detention to be warranted, it had to be necessary in the sense that the relevant statutory test could not be achieved by less restrictive measures, *Varbanov v Bulgaria (C31365/96)* [2000] M.H.L.R. 263 applied. Accordingly, given that the MCA and its DOLS provided an alternative basis to authorise the deprivation of the liberty of an incapacitated person for a range of purposes including his or her assessment or treatment for mental or physical disorders in hospital, it was for the decision-maker to consider whether an alternative under DOLS existed and whether it ought to be used when applying the necessity test under the MHA in the circumstances of the particular case. In the instant case, the relevant decision-maker was the FTT, which lacked jurisdiction to make decisions under the MCA or its DOLS (see paras 15, 28, 33-34, 36 of judgment). (2) The first question for the FTT was to decide whether a person had the capacity to consent to the arrangements under the MHA s.131: if that capacity was present, the MHA applied; if it was lacking, then the MCA was engaged, and the decision-maker had to consider whether the person was a compliant or non-compliant incapacitated person. The FTT next had to consider whether the relevant person lacked capacity under the MCA: that involved a consideration of whether the relevant person would comply with all the elements of his assessment or treatment under the MHA s.131, and the application of the MCA s.5 and s.6 and DOLS if the objective element of a deprivation of liberty was, or was likely to be, satisfied: here, likely was used in the sense of whether there was a real risk or possibility that the relevant person would be a detained resident under the MCA Sch.A1, *H (Minors) (Sexual Abuse: Standard of Proof), Re* [1996] A.C. 563, [1996] C.L.Y. 632 followed. The DOLS regime therefore applied if it appeared that, judged objectively, there was a risk that could not sensibly be ignored that the circumstances amounted to a deprivation of liberty, *A Local Authority v PB* [2011] EWHC 2675 (Fam) applied. The third question was how the choice between the MHA, and the MCA and DOLS, was to be exercised: in situations such as the instant case where M was a compliant incapacitated person, it was generally but not always more appropriate to rely on DOLS; there could, however, be circumstances in which a person could be treated under the MHA when that person could be treated under the MCA and DOLS. However, the FTT needed to consider the availability of the MCA regime and compare its impact with the impact of detention under the MHA (paras 43-44, 49, 57, 59-60, 68, 72). (3) In the instant case, the FTT had erred in law by either not addressing the compliance issue or explaining with sufficient clarity what they decided on it and why. The case was remitted for a rehearing by a differently constituted tribunal (para.88). (4) The court noted that general propositions in respect of issues that arose concerning the interrelationship between the MHA and the MCA were dangerous, and that it was wrong to say that the MCA should approach the application of the MHA on the basis of an assumption that an alternative solution was not available under the MCA, and that any description of the MHA as having primacy ought to be case specific: in defined circumstances Parliament had created statutory alternatives that were factors for the relevant decision-maker to take into account, *J v Foundation Trust* [2009] EWHC 2972 (Fam), [2010] Fam. 70, [2010] C.L.Y. 2254 overruled in part (paras 76, 78).

AM v SOUTH LONDON & MAUDSLEY NHS FOUNDATION TRUST, [2013] UKUT 365 (AAC), [2014] M.H.L.R. 181, Charles J, UT (AAC).

1524 Persons lacking capacity–Residential accommodation–Whether confinement of 16-year-old in secure residential care facility amounted to deprivation of liberty

[Children Act 1989 (c.41) s.20; European Convention on Human Rights 1950 art.5, art.5(1)]

The court was required to determine whether a 16-year-old boy (D) who was living in a secure residential care unit had been deprived of his liberty. D had conditions including Asperger's Syndrome and a learning disability which made his care in the family home difficult. He was admitted to a secure hospital aged 12. He was assessed as not being competent to consent to his residence and care arrangements or to any deprivation of liberty. The court had held in *D (A Child) (Deprivation of Liberty: Parental Responsibility), Re* [2015] EWHC 922 (Fam), [2016] 1 F.L.R. 142, [2015] C.L.Y. 1747 that D's confinement satisfied the first limb of the three-part test in *Storck v Germany (61603/00)* (2006) 43 E.H.R.R. 6, the test being that (1) the person was confined at a particular place; (2) the person did not, or was unable to, consent; (3) the deprivation of liberty was imputable to the state. The court held that D's parents could consent to his confinement at the hospital and that he had not been deprived of liberty. At age 15 he was moved to a residential unit chosen by the local authority. His placement was funded by the local authority and his care plan was determined by its social work team. His parents had agreed to him being accommodated under the Children Act 1989 s.20. It was accepted that D's residence at the unit constituted an objective confinement satisfying the first limb of *Storck*. The local authority submitted that D's parents had requested and consented to his confinement and that the second and third limbs of the *Storck* test had not been satisfied. D's litigation friend contended that a parent could not consent to the confinement of their child in circumstances which amounted to a deprivation of liberty, or that there was a distinction between children aged 15 and younger and those aged 16 and 17. Further, D's confinement was imputable to the state via the acts of the local authority.

Held: Judgment accordingly. In appropriate circumstances, a parent could give a valid consent to the confinement of their child aged 15 years and younger in what would otherwise amount to a deprivation of liberty. A local authority in whose favour a care order had been made could never give a valid consent to a confinement which would amount to a deprivation of liberty, *AB (A Child) (Deprivation of Liberty: Consent), Re* [2015] EWHC 3125 (Fam), [2016] 1 W.L.R. 1160 considered. Parliament had distinguished the legal status of those younger than 16 from those aged 16 and 17. While parents still had parental responsibility for 16-and 17-year-olds, various international conventions recognised the need for a greater degree of respect for the autonomy of those young people. The parent of a 16-or 17-year-old could not consent to their confinement which, absent a valid consent, would amount to a deprivation of liberty. The age and maturity of a young person were important factors when considering the extent of parental responsibility, *Cheshire West and Chester Council v P* [2011] EWHC 1330 (Fam) considered. A further important factor was the extent to which a young person had the capacity to make their own decisions. In *D (A Child),* D's conditions and his limited ability to make decisions on his own behalf had been material factors in determining which decisions fell within the scope of parental responsibility.

His parents' decision to consent to his confinement in hospital had been a proper exercise of parental responsibility when he was 15. To have held otherwise would have been an unwarranted and unnecessary state interference in his and his parents' family life. The position was different at the age of 16. Young people of 16 or 17 were entitled to the full protection of the ECHR art.5(1) irrespective of their capacity to consent to treatment or living arrangements. No European or domestic authority endorsed the principle of substituted consent in relation to a confinement which, absent a valid consent, would amount to a deprivation of liberty. To accept that D's parents could provide consent would be to wrongly discriminate against him on the grounds of his disability. The fact that his parents could at any stage object to his continued accommodation and remove him from the unit did not provide an answer to the test of imputability to the state. That would ignore the fact that the local authority had identified the unit, assessed D's needs, approved his care regime, and paid for his placement. D's confinement was necessary and in his best interests, but that did not prevent it from amounting to a deprivation of liberty. Accordingly, the local authority had to apply to the court to determine whether he was deprived of his liberty and, if he was, to obtain authorisation for its continuance. The protection of D's art.5(1) rights could not be overridden by consideration of the resource implications for state bodies including the instant local authority. The court declined to give general guidance on the issue of the deprivation of liberty of young people (see paras 100-105, 108-110, 113-124, 131, 135, 146-147 of judgment).

BIRMINGHAM CITY COUNCIL v D (A CHILD), [2016] EWCOP 8, [2016] P.T.S.R. 1129, Keehan J, CP.

1525 Standard authorisations–Local authorities' powers and duties–Duties of local authorities when issuing standard authorisations

[Mental Capacity Act 2005 (c.9) s.1(6)]

A man with autism (P), who lived in a local authority care home, applied for a declaration that it was in his best interests to move to a placement which offered specialist autism services, and that a 10-month standard authorisation issued by the first respondent trust in relation to his current placement was too long. P lived in a local authority care home, having been urgently transferred there in September 2014 when his previous placement broke down. The local authority asked the second respondent commissioning group to assess whether P was eligible for ongoing NHS care. It was decided in November 2014 that he was. An urgent authorisation was issued on 24 November. By that time, P had been in the home for almost 12 weeks without any deprivation of liberty safeguards. The urgent authorisation expired after seven days. Almost three weeks later, on 23 December, a 10-month standard authorisation was issued. In all, P had been unlawfully deprived of his liberty for 14-and-a-half weeks. The main issue was whether the local authority had been right to issue a standard authorisation of 10 months' duration when, at the time of the application, a best interests assessment indicated that the home was not suitable for P, and that although it had been in his best interests for a short period, he would be better placed at an alternative care home which offered specialist autism services.

Held: Declaration granted. In granting a 10-month authorisation, the local authority had failed to take proper account of various factors. It should have noted that the current placement was only suitable on a time-limited basis. It should also have given weight to views expressed by P's mother and the non-appointed advocate about lack of suitability. If it had done so, it would have authorised P's deprivation of liberty for only a short period of time and requested further details about more suitable care alternatives. It had not been open to the local authority to grant such a long authorisation when there was uncontradicted information from multiple sources regarding the long-term unsuitability of the placement. It had placed too much weight on the desirability of sparing P further assessments when there was no evidence that the assessments caused P any distress. Care home managers, best interests assessors and local authorities had to ensure that deprivation of liberty accorded with the least restrictive principles of the Mental Capacity Act 2005 s.1(6). It could not be said that a period totalling one year and six weeks amounted to "a short period of time" or that the 10-month standard authorisation was a short period. It had been incumbent on the best interests assessor to investigate alternative proposals to see whether they offered a less restrictive and more suitable environment. Those alternatives also had to be proactively and independently considered by the local authority as part of its process for issuing standard determinations. Its determination had to be independent of the best interests assessor's recommendations. A tick-box approach to the analysis of the four necessary conditions enunciated in *Hillingdon LBC v Neary* [2011] EWHC 1377 (COP), [2011] 4 All E.R. 584, [2012] C.L.Y. 1669 had not been appropriate given that the best interests assessment stated that the deprivation of liberty would only be in P's interests for a short period, *Hillingdon* considered. Both the best interests assessor and the local authority ought to have asked themselves what harm P might suffer if his continued detention was authorised; what placement would be more appropriate; and how long would it take to investigate a more suitable placement. The local authority had to ask those questions as a detached supervisor of the best interests assessment. In the instant case, there was evidence of some independence of thought by the local authority, but it had not asked itself those questions and its reasons for authorising deprivation of liberty for 10 months were unrelated to the principle of choosing the least restrictive principle. The local authority could not delegate its duty to investigate the availability of a less restrictive alternative to the relevant person's representative or the non-appointed advocate (see paras 17-19, 22, 26-29, 32-33 of judgment).

P v SURREY CC, [2015] EWCOP 54, [2015] C.O.P.L.R. 747, District Judge Cushing, CP.

NEGLIGENCE

1526 **Causation–Cancer–Lung cancer caused by asbestos–Apportionment of liability between employers**

The appellant appealed against a decision (*Heneghan v Manchester Dry Docks Ltd* [2014] EWHC 4190 (QB)) concerning the assessment of damages in respect of his father's death from lung cancer. During his working life, the father had been exposed to asbestos fibres and dust. He had been employed successively by each of the six respondents. He had also been exposed to asbestos by earlier employers who had not been sued. The experts agreed that, on the balance of probabilities, he would not have developed lung cancer if he had not been exposed to asbestos. It was agreed that his exposure to asbestos over the course of his working life could be quantified and that the respondents were responsible for 35.2% of the whole exposure. It was also agreed that biological evidence could not establish which, if any, of the exposures had triggered the cell changes in his body which led to him contracting the disease. The judge awarded damages against each respondent in proportion to the increase in risk for which it was responsible, applying the principle established in *Fairchild v Glenhaven Funeral Services Ltd (t/a GH Dovener & Son)* [2002] UKHL 22, [2003] 1 A.C. 32, [2002] C.L.Y. 2225 to apply to cases of mesothelioma. On that basis, the appellant was awarded damages of £61,600, rather than full damages of £175,000. The appellant submitted that, rather than applying the "Fairchild exception", the judge should have held that each respondent had materially contributed to the cancer and was liable for damages in full.

Held: Appeal dismissed. The broader view of causation in *McGhee v National Coal Board* [1973] 1 W.L.R. 1, [1972] C.L.Y. 2356 had been adopted as a matter of policy in order to find a just solution to the problem which arose where the conventional rules of causation would result in a claimant failing to prove his case and recovering no damages for a defendant's breach of duty, even though the defendant had materially increased the risk that the claimant would suffer injury. To apply the test set out in *Bonnington Castings Ltd v Wardlaw* [1956] A.C. 613, [1956] C.L.Y. 3489 in the instant case would be to ignore the fact that there was a fundamental difference between making a material contribution to an injury and materially increasing the risk of an injury. The decision in *Fairchild* had not been based on the fiction that a defendant who had created a material risk of mesothelioma was deemed to have caused or materially contributed to the contraction of the disease. *Bonnington Castings* applied in cases where the court was satisfied on scientific evidence that the exposure for which the defendant was responsible had, in fact, contributed to the injury. That was readily demonstrated in the case of divisible injuries, the severity of which was proportionate to the amount of exposure to the causative agent. The response of the law to the problem posed in a case where the scientific evidence did not permit a finding that the exposure attributable to a particular defendant contributed to the injury was to apply the *Fairchild* exception. The factors identified in *Fairchild* for the application of the exception existed in the instant case: (a) all the respondents conceded their breach of duty; (b) all the respondents had increased the risk that the father would contract lung cancer; (c) all had exposed the father to the same agency that was implicated in causation, namely asbestos fibres; (d) medical science was unable to determine to which respondent there should be attributed the exposure which actually caused the cell changes which initiated the genetic changes culminating in the cancer. Therefore the judge had been right to apply the *Fairchild* exception. It would be wrong to draw an inference of causation from the epidemiological evidence. The evidence permitted the contribution to the risk of cancer attributable to an individual respondent to be quantified, but it went no further than that. It was not possible to infer that all or any of the respondents had made a material contribution to the father contracting lung cancer. However, all of them had materially contributed to the risk that he would contract lung cancer, *Amaca Pty Ltd v Ellis* [2010] HCA 5, *Jones v Secretary of State for Energy and Climate Change* [2012] EWHC 2936 (QB) and *McGhee* applied, *Bonnington Castings* distinguished, *International Energy Group Ltd v Zurich Insurance Plc UK* [2015] UKSC 33, [2016] A.C. 509, [2015] C.L.Y. 1458 followed (see paras 32, 34-35, 41-50 of judgment).

HENEGHAN v MANCHESTER DRY DOCKS LTD, [2016] EWCA Civ 86, [2016] 1 W.L.R. 2036, Lord Dyson MR, CA (Civ Div).

1527 Causation–Material contribution–Asbestosis–Former employer responsible for 2.3% of total exposure

The appellant former employer appealed against a decision that it was liable to pay damages to the respondent in relation to a personal injury claim. The respondent was 87 years old. He had worked as an electrician and had been negligently exposed to asbestos by a number of employers. He developed asbestosis and also suffered from unrelated conditions which affected his lung function. He alleged that his condition was attributable in part to negligent exposure to asbestos dust whilst in the appellant's employment. The appellant accepted that it was responsible for 2.3% of the respondent's total exposure to asbestos dust. An expert opined that a 2.3% contribution to the respondent's asbestosis was material, "although very small". The judge found that the respondent had suffered damage and injury that was actionable against the appellant and he was awarded damages worth 2.3% of what would have been the full liability value of his claim. The appellant conceded that the 2.3% exposure and contribution to the asbestosis, although very small, was material. However, it argued that since that contribution had made no difference to the respondent's symptoms and condition, the judge should have held that it did not make him worse off and therefore made no material contribution to the damage suffered.

Held: Appeal dismissed. (1) In the context of asbestosis, the words "disease", "impairment", "injury" and "disability" were used interchangeably. That was not helpful. It was unprofitable to consider whether a particular medical condition should be characterised as a "disease" or an "injury". Instead, the focus should be on whether the medical condition had made the claimant worse off. Most diseases or injuries would make a person worse off, but that was not always the case. The use of the word "disability" was perhaps more apposite in that a person suffering from a disability was likely to be worse off as a result of it. But disability might not be an apt word to describe a condition of which a person was unaware but which had caused/continued to cause him some harm. The use of labels to describe a medical condition might be convenient, however it should not distract attention from the only relevant question, namely whether the claimant was materially worse off as a result of the alleged tort, *Grieves v FT Everard & Sons Ltd* [2007] UKHL 39, [2008] 1 A.C. 281, [2007] C.L.Y. 2919 and *Holtby v Brigham & Cowan (Hull) Ltd* [2000] 3 All E.R. 421, [2000] C.L.Y. 5114 considered. The question of whether a claimant had suffered material damage in an asbestosis case where he had been exposed to more than one source of asbestos dust raised no difficulties of principle. It depended on the facts of the particular case (see paras 18-22,

26 of judgment). (2) There was a fundamental contradiction in the appellant's case. On the one hand it argued that the asbestos dust attributable to it made no material contribution to the respondent's asbestosis; the 2.3% had made, and would make, no difference to the respondent's symptoms, disability or prognosis. On the other hand, it accepted that the 2.3% was a material contribution to the entire dose of asbestos dust; that each source of asbestos exposure would have contributed to the development of the respondent's asbestosis (including the risk of his developing it) in approximate proportion to the dose of exposure received in each; and therefore the 2.3% made a material contribution to the respondent's asbestosis. It was not in dispute that asbestosis was a condition which, if more than negligible in severity or extent, caused an individual to be worse off or to suffer damage. It was to be distinguished from benign conditions such as pleural plaques. The appellant emphasised that the 2.3% caused the respondent to suffer no symptoms and the extent of the disease was not measureable. However, the severity of the disease had been increased to a small, albeit not measureable, extent. It was conceded that the increase was material. That concession was critical. In those circumstances, the judge was right to hold that the respondent was slightly worse off as a result of the 2.3% exposure for which the appellant was responsible. That conclusion naturally followed from the appellant's acceptance of the fact that it was responsible for the 2.3% and that that was material (paras 39-40).

CARDER v SECRETARY OF STATE FOR HEALTH *sub nom.* CARDER v UNIVERSITY OF EXETER, [2016] EWCA Civ 790, [2016] Med. L.R. 562, Lord Dyson MR, CA (Civ Div).

1528 Clinical negligence–Breach of duty of care–Failure to deliver part of placenta

The claimant sought damages in respect of the defendant trust's alleged breach of duty of care. The claimant's case was that, after giving birth to her second child, the registrar who had attended her had negligently failed to see on an ultrasound scan that she had failed to deliver a substantial part of the placenta. She alleged that, as a result, she had suffered pain and subsequently had to have the piece of placenta removed under a general anaesthetic, following which she suffered a haemorrhage. She asserted that, as a result, she suffered two periods of adjustment disorder: the first for about a year after the birth of her second child, and the second for about eight months while she was pregnant with her third child. The trust accepted that a small piece of placenta might have been retained but said that it was not substantial. It said that what had been removed was a small piece together with blood which had clotted and accreted around it. The issue therefore was whether the piece of placenta which had been retained was small or substantial. The parties agreed that "small" should be treated as around 2cm and "substantial" about 7cm. The claimant relied on *Wiszniewski v Central Manchester HA* [1998] P.I.Q.R. P324, [1998] C.L.Y. 3961 to argue that the court should draw an adverse inference against the trust because of its omission to call a doctor who had explained the procedure to her on the day of the operation and who had attended the operation.

Held: Judgment for defendant. Considering the evidence as a whole, the piece of placenta which had been retained in the claimant's uterus after the birth was not substantial (see paras 62-63 of judgment). It was not appropriate to draw an adverse inference against the trust because of its omission to call the doctor. In *Wiszniewski*, the absent witness had been the doctor whose negligence was said to have caused the harm. Accordingly, his role had been absolutely central to what the court had to decide. In the instant case, the doctor's position had been far more tangential. She was not the doctor who was alleged to have been negligent, and while she might have been present at the operation to remove the retained piece of placenta, she had not been the surgeon. In any event, the court in *Wiszniewski* had been concerned with whether the trial judge was entitled to draw an adverse inference, whereas the claimant appeared to be suggesting that the instant court was obliged to draw such an inference; *Wiszniewski* did not go so far, *Wiszniewski* considered. The fact-finding process was more nuanced than that (para.63). Since the claimant's success had been dependent on a finding that a substantial amount of the placenta had been retained, it followed that her claim had to be dismissed (para.64).

MANZI v KING'S COLLEGE HOSPITAL NHS FOUNDATION TRUST, [2016] EWHC 1101 (QB), [2016] Med. L.R. 294, Nicol J, QBD.

1529 Clinical negligence–Burden of proof–Hip operation–Negligence of consultant surgeon

An NHS trust appealed against a decision that a consultant surgeon had been negligent in his conduct of the respondent patient's total hip replacement and that she had suffered injury as a result. After the patient's surgery, she had experienced numbness and lack of movement in her leg and foot. A post-operative X-ray showed the presence of a large "blob" of the cement which had been used to secure the acetabular prosthesis in position. During the blob's removal in a second operation, it was found to have been in contact with the left sciatic nerve, causing permanent damage. The patient alleged that the surgeon had been negligent in allowing the blob of cement to be retained, and that she had suffered damage as a result. The issue for the judge at trial was breach of duty. The surgeon was the only witness of fact, and two medical experts also gave evidence. The judge reminded himself that the burden of proof rested on the patient and said that the primary facts did not, without more, give rise to any inference of negligence. He found that a substantial cement extrusion had probably occurred in the area of the transverse acetabular ligament, probably at a time when the surgeon could not see it happening because of the presence of the tool he was using. That such extrusion occurred was not indicative of sub-standard technique, but the surgeon knew or should have known that such extrusion could occur, and should have adopted a rigorous surgical technique which demanded vigilance and careful examination for extrusions at all times. He held that the surgeon's performance or technique fell below acceptable standards because he had not exercised the necessary minimum degree of vigilance. He therefore concluded that the patient had made out her claim because the surgeon had been negligent in failing to see and remove the cement during the hip replacement. The trust contended that (1) despite the judge's direction to himself he had wrongly reversed the burden of proof, requiring proof that the surgery had been conducted with reasonable skill and care; (2) the judge's findings and holding were not supported by the evidence; (3) the trial was unfair due to a serious procedural irregularity, in that the surgeon had not had the opportunity to deal with the allegation that he had negligently cut away the cement extrusion at a time when he did not have a complete view.

Held: Appeal dismissed. (1) The judge's direction on the burden of proof was clearly correct. He had rightly stated that he could draw no inference of negligence from the fact that an extrusion had been retained, and correctly identified and answered the question whether, on the facts, the patient had proved that the surgeon's performance of the operation had fallen below the acceptable standard (see para.34 of judgment). (2) Perversity was always a difficult furrow for an appellant to plough, and it could not possibly be said that, on the basis of the evidence before him, the judge's decision was wrong. His findings of primary fact were, by the end of the hearing, virtually common ground. A substantial extrusion had occurred in the area of the transverse acetabular ligament, probably at a time when the surgeon could not see it because of the tool he was using. That finding was not sensibly open to challenge. The judge's holdings as to the extent of the duty or the standard of care to be expected were almost entirely based on common ground. The experts had agreed that the risk of extrusion was well known and that it was important to remove any extrusion so far as possible. The judge had found that the surgeon had known or ought to have known of the risk that an extrusion might occur and that its extent could not be predicted, and that he should have adopted a technique which demanded vigilance and careful examination at all times: those findings were uncontroversial. The judge could not be faulted for concluding that the surgeon had failed to meet the expected standard. He had been entitled to reach the conclusion he had (paras 36, 42, 44, 46-48). (3) The surgeon's function was as a witness of fact, describing what he had seen and done. He was not an expert whose function was to give an opinion on breach of duty. It could not be a serious procedural irregularity not to put to a witness of fact that a particular action amounted to substandard practice. The case had been conducted thoroughly and fairly and there was no procedural irregularity at all, let alone one which could undermine the fairness of the process (paras 49, 51).

ROYAL WOLVERHAMPTON HOSPITALS NHS TRUST v EVANS *sub nom.* EVANS v ROYAL WOLVERHAMPTON HOSPITALS NHS TRUST, [2015] EWCA Civ 1059, (2016) 147 B.M.L.R. 136, Lord Dyson MR, CA (Civ Div).

1530 Clinical negligence–Causation–Delay–Multiple factor cases–Material contribution test

The claimant GP claimed damages for brain injury arising from alleged clinical negligence by the defendant trust. The alleged negligence concerned two periods of delay in the administration of urgent medical treatment. The claimant had fallen backwards down internal stairs leading to his flat upon returning home from a night out. He was found by a neighbour two hours later, slumped in vomit and unable to say anything intelligible. Upon arrival at hospital just before 07:00 he was resuscitated and the triage doctor arranged for a CT scan. For various reasons, including a cancellation of the triage doctor's booking, the scan was performed more than six hours later at 13:15. That was the first period of delay relied upon by the claimant. The scan showed that the claimant had an acute subdural haematoma requiring urgent neurosurgery. A transfer to a different hospital was immediately arranged. Those arrangements were completed at 14:00. An ambulance was requested at 15:17. While waiting for the ambulance, the claimant had a seizure and lost consciousness. It took doctors between 30 minutes and one hour to stabilise him. The ambulance was sent away around 16:30 and a second one requested just after 17:30. It arrived at 18:40. The delay in transferring him to the second hospital gave rise to the claimant's second allegation of negligence. Having undergone a craniotomy at the second hospital, the claimant suffered a further seizure and also developed an infection. He had further surgery to relieve inter-cranial pressure. He was left with permanent cognitive and neuropsychological impairment, which prevented him from practising as a GP. The claimant's case was that without the trust's two periods of negligent delay, he would have avoided some or all of the inter-cranial pressure which materially contributed to the brain damage sustained in his fall. The trust's case was that only the second period of delay was potentially culpable. It claimed that the first period of delay had not been negligent because the claimant's condition had improved so significantly after arriving at hospital that it had been reasonable to cancel the first scan booking. There was also an issue about whether the correct approach to causation was the "material contribution" test, applying *Bonnington Castings Ltd v Wardlaw* [1956] A.C. 613, [1956] C.L.Y. 3489, *Bailey v Ministry of Defence* [2008] EWCA Civ 883, [2009] 1 W.L.R. 1052, [2008] C.L.Y. 2764 and *Williams v Bermuda Hospitals Board* [2016] UKPC 4, [2016] A.C. 888 or the "but for" test in *Wilsher v Essex AHA* [1988] A.C. 1074, [1988] C.L.Y. 2415.

Held: Judgment for claimant. (1) The evidence supported the claimant's primary case on negligence. Both periods of delay had been negligent: the CT scan should have been performed no later than 10:00, and the second ambulance should have been called soon after 16:30, which was when the claimant had been stable enough to leave the first hospital. The fact that the second ambulance took over an hour to arrive was attributable to the ambulance service, not to the trust (see paras 47-48, 52-59 of judgment). (2) The evidence indicated that, on a balance of probabilities, the claimant had been suffering damaging intra-cranial pressure before his craniotomy, probably from 12.15 onwards, but at the very least from the time of his first seizure. Had he had the scan before 10:00, he would have been operated upon before he had his seizure, and would have avoided a period of raised intra-cranial pressure for around six hours or slightly less. There was no need to consider what would have happened if the second period of delay had been the only negligent act, but it was worth noting that if it had not happened, the claimant would have avoided a period of raised intra-cranial pressure for one hour (paras 68, 71-72, 80). (3) The "material contribution" test was the appropriate approach to causation, even though the instant case concerned a material contribution to damage, rather than a material contribution to risk. The "material contribution" approach applied just as much to multiple factor cases, where causes were sequential or cumulative, as it did to "single agency" cases, *Bonnington and Bailey* applied, *Heneghan v Manchester Dry Docks Ltd* [2016] EWCA Civ 86, [2016] 1 W.L.R. 2036, [2016] 1526, *McGhee v National Coal Board* [1973] 1 W.L.R. 1, [1972] C.L.Y. 2356, *Wilsher* and *Williams* considered. The "material contribution" test having been satisfied, causation was made out, and the claimant was entitled to recover in respect of the entirety of his loss; an apportionment exercise of the sort carried out in *Holtby v Brigham & Cowan (Hull) Ltd* [2000] 3 All E.R. 421, [2000] C.L.Y. 5114 was inappropriate because the evidence could not possibly attribute particular damage to a specific cause, *Holtby* not applied. The claimant was therefore entitled to recover, without deduction, damages for his loss and injury arising from the trust's negligence. The appropriate award was £454, 858.65 including interest (paras 88-89, 95-101, 105, 121). (4) The separate components of the award were: (a) pain and suffering (para.107); (b) care and assistance (para.108); (c) loss of earnings (paras 109-119); (d) travel expenses and future treatment costs (para.120).

JOHN v CENTRAL MANCHESTER AND MANCHESTER CHILDREN'S UNIVERSITY HOSPITALS NHS FOUNDATION TRUST, [2016] EWHC 407 (QB), [2016] 4 W.L.R. 54, Picken J, QBD (Liverpool).

1531 Clinical negligence–Diagnosis–Undiagnosed stroke–Lack of causation

The court had to consider as a preliminary issue whether an NHS trust was liable to a patient for pain, suffering and loss of amenity after she suffered a stroke, and to the patient's husband for psychiatric harm caused by the alleged failure properly to diagnose and treat the patient. According to the patient, she had first awoken at 05.50 on 14 March 2010 and had then returned to bed and slept until 07.00. At that time, she got up feeling unwell. She felt her right arm growing weaker and experienced difficulties with her speech. The patient was admitted to hospital with a suspected stroke. At 08.20, a history was taken by a triage nurse. She was then returned to A&E, where she was seen by a senior house officer (SHO). He discussed the patient's case with another doctor, as he was unsure of the cause of her condition. At 09.40 the patient's condition deteriorated. The SHO accepted that his failure to re-examine her at that time was a significant failure on his part. The patient was discharged from hospital at 11.36, which the trust accepted was negligent. Due to the patient's deteriorating condition, her husband drove her to another hospital. The patient was diagnosed as having suffered a rare type of stroke. She died in August 2014. It was common ground that, in the case of strokes, thrombolysis could be used to break up the blood clot if administered within three hours of the onset of symptoms. According to the trust, however, the patient was suffering from stroke symptoms at the time of awakening and was therefore excluded from thrombolysis treatment on the basis that the three-hour window might have passed. There was no record of the 05.50 incident in the patient's hospital notes. However, the patient claimed that the 05.50 incident showed that she was symptom-free at that time so that the onset of symptoms could not have occurred until later, making her a candidate for thrombolysis. The trust accepted that aspirin should have been prescribed at some point between 10.40 and 11.00, but the patient claimed that that should have been done before 09.40. The claim brought by the patient's husband was based on symptoms of post-traumatic stress disorder that he exhibited after witnessing the events after 09.40.

Held: Preliminary issue determined in favour of defendant. (1) On the balance of probabilities, the 05.50 incident had not occurred. The patient had awoken with some right-sided heaviness and had experienced ataxia immediately after getting out of bed. Accordingly, the neurological deficit probably existed before she awoke and there was no basis on which she should have been thrombolysed (see paras 31, 36, 38-39 of judgment). (2) There had clearly been procedural failings, in particular as to whose responsibility it was to make a diagnosis and to whom a patient should be referred in a difficult case such as the instant one where there were fluctuating symptoms and a stroke could not be excluded. On the balance of probabilities, the nurse's training should have been such that she did not refer the patient back to an SHO on the findings of her examination. The patient should have been seen urgently after 08.20 by a more senior doctor. However, since a stroke diagnosis would probably not have been made at that stage, the trust was not negligent in failing to prescribe aspirin before the 09.40 deterioration, but shortly thereafter. On the expert evidence it was not possible to conclude that, had the patient been prescribed aspirin at any time, she would have had a better outcome. Therefore, it had not been demonstrated that the trust's breach of duty in failing to treat her promptly with aspirin had caused or materially contributed to her eventual outcome (paras 59, 70-72, 91, 121, 123). (3) The patient's husband had a close tie of love and affection with the patient, was close to the incident in time and space and had directly perceived the incident, *Liverpool Women's Hospital NHS Foundation Trust v Ronayne* [2015] EWCA Civ 588, [2015] P.I.Q.R. P20, [2015] C.L.Y. 1799 followed. What he had witnessed from 09.40 was very distressing, consisting of the failure properly to diagnose and treat and the negligent discharge of his wife who was, by then, very seriously ill. However, there was no sudden appreciation of a "horrifying event" by objective standards and by reference to persons of ordinary susceptibility; nor were those events wholly exceptional, *Walters v North Glamorgan NHS Trust* [2002] EWCA Civ 1792, [2003] P.I.Q.R. P16, [2003] C.L.Y. 3132 followed. It followed that the husband's claim as a secondary victim did not succeed (paras 138, 149, 151).

OWERS v MEDWAY NHS FOUNDATION TRUST, [2015] EWHC 2363 (QB), [2015] Med. L.R. 561, Stewart J, QBD.

1532 Clinical negligence–Duty of care–Eye surgery–Appropriate procedure

The claimant brought a claim in clinical negligence against the defendant NHS foundation trust following unsuccessful eye surgery which he had undergone in 2010. The claimant suffered from an inherited condition called EDS Type III/hypermobility syndrome. References in his medical notes also indicated that he had a "posterior vitreous detachment" in his left eye. The purpose of the surgery was to correct a retinal detachment which had occurred in that eye. The procedure used, known as the cryo buckle procedure, was unsuccessful: the claimant's left retina was not re-attached, and the sight in his left eye was not restored. The claimant asserted that in the particular circumstances of his case the surgeons in question should have undertaken a different procedure, namely what was known as a primary vitrectomy. The claimant's expert witness was of the view that in the case of a patient like the claimant who had an abnormal sclera or white of the eye (owing to EDS or pathological myopia), the existence of a posterior vitreous detachment rendered a primary vitrectomy mandatory because the risks attendant on the cryo buckle procedure were unacceptable. The issues were (1) whether the claimant had a posterior vitreous detachment when his left eye was examined before the surgery (if he did not, there would be no negligence on the part of the surgeons); (2) if the answer to (1) was yes, whether it was generally understood in the ophthalmic community in 2010 that EDS Type III carried with it a risk of a friable or thin sclera; (3) whether that risk was such that it was *Bolam* negligent not to perform a primary vitrectomy.

Held: Judgment for defendant. (1) On the strong balance of probability, the claimant did not have a posterior vitreous detachment when his left eye was examined before the surgery. That conclusion was sufficient for the trust's case to prevail on the issue of breach of duty (see paras 112-113 of judgment). (2) The claimant's friable or thin sclera was likely to have been caused by a combination of his EDS and pathological myopia. It was received wisdom in the ophthalmic community in 2010 that a pathologically myopic patient with EDS Type III would be at enhanced risk of complications from a thin or friable sclera (paras 117, 119). (3) A responsible body of ophthalmic opinion could reasonably have concluded in 2010 that the cryo buckle procedure was appropriate to the claimant's particular circumstances. It followed that his case would have failed even if the first issue had been decided in his favour (paras 140, 142).

STUCKEN v EAST KENT HOSPITALS UNIVERSITY NHS FOUNDATION TRUST, [2016] EWHC 1057 (QB), [2016] Med. L.R. 380, Jay J, QBD.

1533 Clinical negligence–Interim payments–Positive causation defence–Supporting evidence

[Civil Procedure Rules 1998 r.25.6(3)(b), r.25.6(4), r.25.6(5), r.25.7(1)(c)]

The appellant doctor appealed against the refusal of her application for permission to appeal against an order requiring her to make an interim payment in a clinical negligence claim commenced by the respondent patient. The doctor admitted that she had been negligent in failing to identify and report on a malignant tumour on the patient's liver. Causation was in dispute and depended on expert evidence. The hearing of the patient's application for an interim payment took place six weeks before the date for exchange of the expert evidence. The patient had served her expert evidence early so the master had it before him at the interim payment hearing; the doctor was still to serve hers. The master found that he had to decide the application on the evidence before him. He held that the patient had proved her case, and the doctor had not discharged the evidential burden upon her of proving that the patient would not succeed in obtaining substantial damages. He held that in order to successfully resist an interim payment, it was not enough for a defendant to simply plead a defence and provide a statement of truth and a witness statement that expert evidence was to follow; there had to be a letter or report from an expert in the case. The doctor's application for permission to appeal against the interim payment failed on the ground that it had no prospect of success, but there was an issue of wider application in respect of which the judge decided to give reasons. The issue was how a judge should respond to an application for an interim payment in a clinical negligence case where a positive causation defence had been pleaded, but where the defendant was not required to serve supporting expert evidence until some weeks after the hearing. The doctor argued that the master's approach had been wrong because if that practice were to be routinely followed, claimants would acquire a weapon to force early exchange of expert evidence when the court had otherwise set a considered timetable for exchange.

Held: Appeal dismissed. By virtue of CPR r.25.6(3)(b) an application for an interim payment had to be supported by evidence. However, r.25.6(4) and r.25.6(5) made clear that there was no obligation on either party to file supporting evidence; there was simply an option to do so. The court would always be alert to the possibility of an interim payment application being made for an improper purpose and would deal with it accordingly, but there was nothing improper about the application in the instant case. The patient had served supporting evidence and the doctor, as was her right, had chosen only to serve limited evidence in response. The master had been right to find that he should decide the application on the evidence before him. It was also clear that, on that evidence and in the absence of anything to the contrary from the doctor, the master had been entitled to find the patient's expert evidence compelling and sufficient to satisfy r.25.7(1)(c). In reaching that decision, he had been doing no more than recognising the apparent strength of the patient's evidence and recognising the need for some contrary reasoning if he was to be persuaded otherwise. He had been entitled to proceed on that basis, *Smith v Bailey* [2014] EWHC 2569 (QB), [2015] R.T.R. 6, [2014] C.L.Y. 2305 applied (see paras 44, 46-49 of judgment).

SELLAR-ELLIOTT v HOWLING, [2016] EWHC 443 (QB), [2016] P.I.Q.R. P13, Sweeney J, QBD.

1534 Clinical negligence–Several tortfeasors–Settlement with one tortfeasor–Liability of hospital as second tortfeasor

A hospital trust applied to strike out a clinical negligence claim brought against it by a roofer who was treated by the hospital after suffering an accident at work. The roofer had been working as a sub-contractor for a roofing company in 2011 when he fell through a skylight and sustained a series of spinal fractures. At the end of his hospital treatment he had suffered a complete spinal cord injury and was a paraplegic. He initiated proceedings against the roofing company for the whole of his loss. The company began negotiations on the basis that he was liable in contributory negligence as he was the senior supervisor on site and was involved in the job's risk assessment. In the meantime, the roofer sent a letter of claim for damages to the hospital trust, claiming that he had suffered negligent treatment that had caused the outcome of his accident to be much worse than it should have been. In September 2014, he reached a compromise agreement in his claim against the roofing company. A substantial discount for contributory negligence was made in agreeing the settlement sum. In November 2014, he informed the hospital trust of the compromise agreement and sent it details of the same. He then issued proceedings against it. The hospital trust argued that the claim should be struck out for abuse of process as the roofer had been compensated in full for his loss by the agreement with the roofing company and there should be no double recovery.

Held: Application refused. There was a pre-clinical negligence element of the damage caused to the roofer for which only the roofing company was liable. That element included the loss which occurred after the clinical negligence but which would have occurred anyway. After the clinical negligence, there was an additional loss which would not have occurred but for the clinical negligence. Both the hospital trust and the roofing company were liable for that additional loss as, by causing the injury, the roofing company had exposed the roofer to the hazard of imperfect medical treatment. However, the roofing company was liable only for the proportion of the additional loss that remained due after the reduction for the roofer's contributory negligence, whereas the hospital trust was liable for all of it. The roofing company and the hospital trust had each made a contribution to the additional loss by a different tortious act in breach of different duties to the roofer. They were therefore concurrent tortfeasors, and the release of one concurrent tortfeasor did not have in law the effect of releasing another, *Heaton v Axa Equity & Law Life Assurance Society Plc* [2002] UKHL 15, [2002] 2 A.C. 329, [2002] C.L.Y. 482 applied. The proper approach to a compromise case was to focus primarily on the construction of the agreement in its appropriate factual context, *Heaton* applied. The test was whether the agreement represented the full measure of the claimant's estimated loss, *Appleby v Northern Devon Healthcare NHS Trust* [2012] EWHC 4356 (QB) applied. In the roofer's case, he had not been fully compensated. Because of the contributory negligence discount, the roofing company was not liable for the whole of the additional loss. It had neither paid nor purported to pay the whole loss caused by the hospital (on the assumption that the roofer's claim against the latter would succeed). It was therefore impossible to construe the compromise agreement in its true factual context as providing full compensation for the loss being claimed against the hospital trust. A settlement with one concurrent tortfeasor did not release the others unless it was clear that it was intended to have that effect, or unless the payment clearly satisfied the whole claim. There was no risk of double recovery as the roofer had agreed that appropriate credit would have to be given for the sum he had received from the roofing company if his claim succeeded (see paras 4, 14, 17-21 of judgment).

WRIGHT v BARTS HEALTH NHS TRUST, [2016] EWHC 1834 (QB), [2016] Med. L.R. 545, Edis J, QBD.

1535 Clinical negligence–Surgeons–Clinical judgment to operate despite patient's psychiatric problems

A patient brought a negligence claim against a hospital trust on the basis that one of its orthopaedic surgeons had wrongly decided to carry out spinal surgery on her. The patient had been sexually abused as a young teenager and had serious psychological problems for which she was seeing a psychiatrist. She had also sustained a back injury during the abuse and suffered constant pain. She was referred to the hospital's orthopaedic department and for three years the surgeon tried to manage her condition with pain relief, physiotherapy and eventually steroid injections. He was reluctant to offer spinal surgery because of her young age. The patient's condition did not improve and in addition she developed leg pain. The surgeon became concerned that she was developing chronic pain syndrome as there was no physical explanation for some of her symptoms. He thought that he should continue to delay surgery until her mental health improved, as her psychiatric problems could adversely affect the outcome. The patient's psychiatrist then wrote to the surgeon advising him not to delay as the patient's back pain was a constant reminder of the abuse she had suffered and was in itself making her mental health problems worse. The surgeon operated on her four months later. Her psychiatric illness subsequently worsened to the point where she lost the feeling in her legs and became a wheelchair user. The patient contended that the problems associated with her psychological symptoms had been overriding and the surgeon had breached his duty of care by offering her surgery without discussing it further with her psychiatrist or getting a second opinion.

Held: Claim dismissed. There had been no breach of duty of care in the patient's case. Several factors supported the action that the surgeon had taken: the patient had had persistent and unresolved pain, the injections had failed to provide her with any long-standing relief and the findings of her MRI scans had supported surgical intervention. Regarding the patient's psychiatric condition, the surgeon had been entitled to approach the psychiatrist's correspondence as a simple, direct and explicit encouragement for the operation to occur. Applying the *Bolam* test, a reasonable body of competent medical opinion would have taken her statement as a "green light" for surgery to be undertaken. The letter had not directly dealt with the patient's psychiatric symptoms as a counter-indication to surgery, but the surgeon had been entitled to assume that the psychiatrist would have communicated any observation that surgery would have a material impact on the patient's mental wellbeing alongside the message that he ought not to wait for her mental health to improve before operating. The letter was in reality positive in respect of undertaking surgery. In addition, the letter had offered the opportunity for further discussion but that did not suggest that it was required. The surgeon had been entitled to proceed without further discussion. As to seeking a second opinion, a reasonable body of competent medical opinion would not have considered it necessary. The decision of whether to operate had been a clinical judgement that the surgeon had been best placed to make given his detailed and extensive knowledge of the patient's case, which stretched over a number of years. He had had regard to all the relevant clinical factors affecting the decision. The treatment that he had given the patient reflected a standard accepted as proper by a responsible body of medical opinion, and it had been reasonable and defensible bearing in mind the risks and benefits that were at stake in assessing its suitability, *Bolitho (Deceased) v City and Hackney HA* [1998] A.C. 232, [1997] C.L.Y. 3789 applied (see paras 64-70 of judgment).

XYZ v WARRINGTON AND HALTON NHS FOUNDATION TRUST, [2016] EWHC 331 (QB), [2016] Med. L.R. 147, Dove J, QBD (Manchester).

1536 Defective premises–Occupiers' liability–Duty to repair–Obligation to repair if object out of repair

[Occupiers' Liability Act 1957 (c.31) s.2; Defective Premises Act 1972 (c.35) s.4]

A widow appealed against the striking out of her negligence claim against the freeholder of a building in which her husband had fallen down a staircase and suffered brain damage before dying two years later. The building was made up of three storeys. In 1987, the freeholder had kept the ground floor for retail premises while granting a lease over the first and second floors to a developer who created residential flats and replaced the staircase between the ground and first floor. The new stairs were steep with no handrail. The husband fell down them in 2007 while visiting a flat on the first floor. The widow claimed that the freeholder had failed to discharge its common law duty of care as occupier to the husband as a visitor under the Occupiers' Liability Act 1957 s.2, and had failed to take reasonable care under the Defective Premises Act 1972 s.4 to see that those likely to be affected by the condition of the staircase were reasonably safe in using it. At a hearing before a High Court master, it was questioned whether the freeholder had demised the staircase to the developer owing to some potentially contradictory wording in the lease. The master applied the principle of corrective interpretation and concluded that the parties had obviously intended a means of access to the first floor to be demised. He therefore found that the freeholder had no control or duty of care over the replacement staircase under the 1957 Act. He also concluded that the staircase was not defective under the 1972 Act. He gave summary judgment against the widow. The widow argued that (1) the construction of the lease was too important to determine on a summary basis and should have been decided at a trial based on evidence of how it was negotiated; (2) the lack of a handrail was a relevant defect that the freeholder as landlord had a duty to repair under s.4 of the 1972 Act.

Held: Appeal dismissed. (1) The master had been correct in his approach to the construction of the lease. It was thoroughly implausible that commercial entities such as the freeholder and the developer would have entered into a lease for the demise of the upper floors of the building without providing for access for the intended residential occupants. The entrance hall and staircase did no more than lead to the upper floors, so there would have been no point in the freeholder retaining them. The purported contradictory wording had plainly been a clumsy error in the drafting of the lease and it was appropriate for the master to invoke the device of corrective interpretation to give effect to the obvious intention of the parties that the staircase was part of the demise. Further, he was right to decide the matter on a summary basis. Evidence of pre-contractual negotiations was generally excluded as an aid to construction unless rectification was sought, and the widow had no standing to seek rectification of a lease to which she was a stranger, *Chartbrook Ltd v Persimmon Homes Ltd* [2009] UKHL 38, [2009] 1 A.C. 1101, [2009] C.L.Y. 722 applied (see paras 32-33, 36 of judgment). (2)

Case law had established that the duty of repair under s.4 of the 1972 Act was not to be equated with a duty to make safe. It was limited to a duty to put right something that was in a worse condition than it was at some previous time. Moreover, s.4 should not be given a wide construction because that could impose a substantial burden on a landlord to put right matters that were under the tenant's control, *Quick v Taff Ely BC* [1986] Q.B. 809, [1985] C.L.Y. 1610, *Ratcliffe v Sandwell MBC* [2002] EWCA Civ 6, [2002] 1 W.L.R. 1488, [2002] C.L.Y. 3059 and *Alker v Collingwood Housing Association* [2007] EWCA Civ 343, [2007] 1 W.L.R. 2230, [2007] C.L.Y. 2738 applied. The obligation to repair therefore did not arise unless the object concerned was out of repair, and in the widow's case there was no evidence that the staircase was other than well constructed. The steep stairs and lack of handrail probably made it unsafe but, given the authorities, potential dangerousness was not the test for a relevant defect under the 1972 Act (paras 55-60, 63).

DODD v RAEBARN ESTATES LTD, [2016] EWHC 262 (QB), [2016] H.L.R. 12, Judge Richard Parkes QC, QBD.

1537 Duty of care–Bankers' references–Counterfeit cheques–Bank's liability to casino for references to agent

A bank appealed against a decision (*Playboy Club London Ltd v Banca Nazionale Del Lavoro SpA* [2014] EWHC 2613 (QB), [2015] L.L.R. 171, [2015] C.L.Y. 1761) that it was liable in negligence for providing a bankers' reference for a customer (B) to an agent for the respondent club. The club operated a casino and used an agent to preserve customer confidentiality. The bank had confirmed to the agent that B was financially sound and trustworthy for up to £1.6 million per week. On the strength of the reference the club exchanged B's cheques for gambling chips. B never held any money in the account, the cheques were returned as counterfeit, and the club lost around £800,000. The judge held that the bank owed a duty of care to the club of which it was in breach, and but for that breach the club would not have accepted the cheques. He found that the club was contributorily negligent to the extent of 15% since the cheques were photocopies and looked odd on their face. The bank submitted that (1) its duty of care extended only to the agent; (2) the scope of that duty did not include the customer's use of counterfeit cheques; (3) any claim should be reduced because of the contributory negligence of the club's employees.

Held: Appeal allowed. (1) On the facts, the bank had assumed no responsibility to the club, *Caparo Industries Plc v Dickman* [1990] 2 A.C. 605, [1990] C.L.Y. 3266 and *Customs and Excise Commissioners v Barclays Bank Plc* [2006] UKHL 28, [2007] 1 A.C. 181, [2006] C.L.Y. 2880 followed, *Hedley Byrne & Co Ltd v Heller & Partners Ltd* [1964] A.C. 465, [1963] C.L.Y. 2416 distinguished on the ground that the bank was only aware that the reference was for the agent and totally unaware, either of the club's existence, or that the purpose of the reference was for gambling. Further, any special relationship was between the bank and the agent alone. Given the club's standard practice of concealing its existence and asking for references in the name of its agent, it was not fair, just, or reasonable to impose liability on the bank (see paras 15, 19-25 of judgment). (2) The fact that the cheques were counterfeit and the bank would not accept them was only an interim problem, the real problem was that B was impecunious when the bank had represented that he was a man of wealth. It was quite different from cases where the problem was wholly extraneous to the defendants' negligence, *NV Koninklijke Rotterdamsche Lloyd v Western Steamship Co Ltd (The Empire Jamaica)* [1955] P. 259, [1955] C.L.Y. 2594 and *South Australia Asset Management Corp v York Montague Ltd* [1997] A.C. 191, [1996] C.L.Y. 4519 distinguished, where the startling blunder in seamanship and the fall in the property market, respectively, were extraneous factors (paras 26-28). (3) As no duty of care arose, the court declined to express an opinion on the issue of contributory negligence (para.29).

PLAYBOY CLUB LONDON LTD v BANCA NAZIONALE DEL LAVORO SPA, [2016] EWCA Civ 457, [2016] 1 W.L.R. 3169, Laws LJ, CA (Civ Div).

1538 Duty of care–Hospitals–Existence of duty to provide patients with accurate waiting times in accident and emergency

The court was required to determine liability in a claim for negligence brought by a patient against the defendant NHS trust. The claimant had been attacked and struck on the head. He attended the hospital's accident and emergency department. He alleged that the reception staff had told him that he would be seen in four or five hours. The staff no longer recalled the incident, but alleged that they would have told him he would be seen by a triage nurse within 30 minutes. He left the hospital without being treated. After he returned home his condition deteriorated, and he suffered a left hemiplegia. The NICE clinical guidelines stated that a patient with a head injury should be assessed by a clinician within 15 minutes of arrival. The court was required to determine: (i) how long the claimant had waited at the hospital and what information had been given to him by the defendant's reception staff; (ii) whether the defendant was in breach of its duty of care in not examining the claimant in triage during the time he was waiting; (iii) whether the defendant was in breach of its duty in failing to give accurate information about waiting times.

Held: Claim dismissed. (1) On the evidence the claimant had left the hospital after being there for a maximum of 19 minutes. Whatever the usual practice of the on-duty receptionists might have been, the claimant was not told that he would be seen within 30 minutes. The only information given to the claimant was that he would have to wait for up to four or five hours. He was not told about being seen earlier by a triage nurse. Had he been told that he would be seen within 30 minutes, he would have waited to be seen, his collapse would have occurred at the hospital and he would have made a full recovery (see paras 4, 26, 35-36 of judgment). (2) On the evidence, the claimant's condition at the hospital was not such as to have alerted non-clinical reception staff to the presence of a serious condition requiring priority attention from a triage nurse. The clinical guidelines stated that a patient should be seen within 15 minutes; the alleged breach of duty was a failure to meet that tight target by four minutes. The consensus amongst the experts was that the longest allowable target was 30 minutes; that was appropriate. The fact that the claimant was not seen in the 19 minutes he was present did not amount to a breach of a clinical duty of care, and in any event did not cause any loss. The damage arose because the deterioration occurred away from the hospital, but the claimant had chosen to leave when he did (paras 50, 60-62). (3) The court had to determine whether the staff had had a duty of care to inform the claimant that he would be seen within 30 minutes. Applying the three-part test from *Caparo Industries Plc v Dickman* [1990] 2 A.C. 605, [1990] C.L.Y. 3266 to identify a duty of care, (a) it was reasonably foreseeable that some patients left A&E departments without being treated, which could lead to harm, and that a person might leave if he believed it would be four or five hours before he would be seen; (b) the issue of proximity was linked to the defendant's duty to guard the claimant from a certain kind of harm, but A&E receptionists were not under a duty to guard patients against harm caused by their failure to wait to be seen, even if such harm could have been prevented by the provision of full and accurate information about waiting times; (c) it would not be fair, just and reasonable to impose liability on the defendant for the harm arising in the instant case from the reception staff's failure to inform the claimant of the likely waiting time. The primary function of a civilian receptionist was to complete registration forms, and the provision of information about waiting times was a courtesy. To impose a legal liability on the defendant in the circumstances would be a step too far. The imposition of a liability would carry a risk that reception staff would be instructed not to do anything other than complete the registration form, which would be a regrettable state of affairs. The conclusion that there was no legal liability could be based on a failure of either the proximity stage or the "fair just and reasonable" stage of the *Caparo* test. Equally, it could be justified because the connection between the inadequate information and the harm suffered was broken because the claimant himself had decided to leave. The defendant was not liable to compensate him, *Rahman v Arearose Ltd* [2001] Q.B. 351 applied, *Caparo* followed (paras 86-88, 90-93).

DARNLEY v CROYDON HEALTH SERVICES NHS TRUST, [2015] EWHC 2301 (QB), [2016] P.I.Q.R. P4, Judge Robinson, QBD.

1539 Duty of care–Jurisdiction–English parent company's liability for personal injury in Zambia

[Regulation 1215/2012 on jurisdiction and the recognition and enforcement of judgments in civil and commercial matters 2012 art.4]

The defendants applied for a declaration that the court did not have jurisdiction to try the Zambian claimants' actions. The first defendant English company applied to stay the proceedings, and the second defendant Zambian company applied for an order setting aside service of the claim form on it out of the jurisdiction. The claimants were numerous Zambian citizens who alleged that they had suffered personal injury, damage to property, loss of income and loss of amenity and enjoyment of land arising out of pollution and environmental damage caused by discharges into the local waterways from a copper mine operated by the Zambian company, which was owned by the first defendant parent company. The issues were whether (1) the claim against the parent company should be stayed on forum non conveniens grounds, because the proceedings were a device to ensure the claims were brought in the UK and were an abuse of EU law, or on case management grounds; (2) service on the Zambian company should be set aside.

Held: Applications refused. (1) The case of *Owusu v Jackson (t/a Villa Holidays Bal Inn Villas) (C-281/02)* EU:C:2005:120, [2005] Q.B. 801, [2005] C.L.Y. 604, which had been followed by domestic authorities, was binding authority for the proposition that forum non conveniens arguments were irrelevant to the claim against the parent company, as Regulation 1215/2012 art.4 provided that persons domiciled in a Member State should be sued in the courts of that Member State, *Owusu* followed. Although the facts in *Owusu* were very different, and it might be capable of criticism, that did not make it less binding. To show an abuse of EU law was a high hurdle: the parent company needed to prove that the sole object of the claim against it was to oust the jurisdiction of another court, or that the basis for joining it to the claim was fraudulent. The claim raised a real issue and could not be labelled as a device. There were also legitimate concerns that the parent company was the architect of the environmental pollution, and about the Zambian company's ability to pay any judgment. In an appropriate case, and notwithstanding the effect of *Owusu,* the court had to be able to exercise its case management powers and procedure, *Pacific International Sports Clubs Ltd v Soccer Marketing International Ltd* [2009] EWHC 1839 (Ch) considered. However, there was no basis for doing so in the instant case (see paras 65-67, 71, 74, 77, 82, 84 of judgment). (2) The claim against the Zambian company had a real prospect of success. For the claimant's to establish that the parent company owed them a common law duty of care, they were required to establish foreseeability, proximity and reasonableness, *Caparo Industries Plc v Dickman* [1990] 2 A.C. 605, [1990] C.L.Y. 3266 followed. Depending on the facts, it was arguable that a claim in negligence against a parent company arising out of the operations of its subsidiary might give rise to liability, *Chandler v Cape Plc* [2012] EWCA Civ 525, [2012] 1 W.L.R. 3111, [2012] C.L.Y. 2400 applied. Such a claim was more likely to succeed if advanced by former employees. However, claims by residents were still arguable, *Lubbe v Cape Plc* [2000] 1 W.L.R. 1545, [2000] C.L.Y. 775 considered. The claim against the parent company was arguable in English and Zambian law, and it was reasonable for the English court to try that issue, *Erste Group Bank AG (London) v JSC (VMZ Red October)* [2015] EWCA Civ 379, [2015] 1 C.L.C. 706 considered. The claims against both defendants were closely bound together and their resolution would require only one investigation. The Zambian company was a necessary and proper party to the claim against the parent company. Although the focus of the claim against the Zambian company was Zambia, England was the appropriate place to try the claims against the Zambian company because of the existence of the claim against the parent company. Further, there was clear and cogent evidence that the claimants would not obtain access to justice in Zambia. Had it been necessary, the court would have exercised its discretion to allow service out of the jurisdiction on the Zambian company (paras 99, 115, 121, 124, 141, 147, 169).

LUNGOWE v VEDANTA RESOURCES PLC, [2016] EWHC 975 (TCC), [2016] B.C.C. 774, Coulson J, QBD (TCC).

1540 Duty of care–Mental disorder–Liability in negligence of person with mental disorder

The appellant appealed against a decision that he was not entitled to damages in negligence in respect of injuries which he sustained when he attempted to prevent his uncle, the first respondent, from setting fire to himself. The uncle had poured petrol over himself and the appellant had unsuccessfully attempted to prevent him from igniting it. The uncle died and the appellant suffered extremely serious burns to his face and body. The uncle was subsequently diagnosed as having suffered from florid paranoid schizophrenia. The incident took place in the uncle's home and there was an issue about whether it was covered by a household insurance policy under which the second respondent insurer had agreed to indemnify the uncle in respect of accidental bodily injury to any person. Two psychiatric experts were instructed. They filed an agreed joint statement, concluding that the uncle's delusional state would have been so overwhelming as to render him incapable of formulating any rational alternative action and that he had not been in control of his actions. The judge at first instance held that the extreme nature of the manifestation of his mental illness meant that the uncle had not been acting voluntarily and therefore owed no duty of care to the appellant. The issue was whether a person was liable in negligence where he was suffering from a mental disorder.

Held: Appeal allowed. There was no principle which required the law to excuse a defendant from liability in negligence where he failed to meet the normal standard of care partly because of a medical problem. The courts had consistently and correctly rejected the notion that the standard of care should be adjusted to take account of the defendant's personal characteristics. The single exception in respect of the liability of children should not be extended. Only defendants whose medical incapacity had the effect of entirely eliminating any fault or responsibility for the injury could be excused. There was no reason for the law of negligence to differentiate between mental and physical illness. The actions of a defendant who was merely impaired by medical problems, whether physical or mental, could not escape liability if he caused injury by failing to exercise reasonable care. To say that a medical condition entirely eliminated any fault or responsibility for the injury simply meant that the defendant himself had done nothing to cause the injury, such as a person whose arm was holding a knife and who was overcome by another forcing him to stab a victim. It was only if the defendant could properly be said to have done nothing himself to cause the injury that he escaped liability. That approach avoided the need for medical witnesses to become engaged with difficult and undefined terms such as "volition", "will", "free choice", "consciousness", and "personal autonomy". Those formulations emanated from the rules applicable to insanity and automatism as defences in criminal law and were not helpful in the circumstances. In the instant case, there had been a troubling proliferation of terms in play, in the judgment and in the experts' evidence. The words "involuntary" and "irrational" had almost been used as synonyms. For example, the judge concluded that so long as incapacity altogether removed rational motivation there was no liability. It was not helpful to refer to cases which considered the position when, for example, the defendant lost control of his actions, lost the power of choice, ceased to act voluntarily, or lost consciousness. The judge at first instance had held that the appellant's ability to think and act rationally had been eliminated. However, no one would suggest that someone should be excused from liability for negligence if they acted irrationally. The uncle had been under a duty of care and the real issue was whether, unwell as he was, he had breached that duty by failing to measure up to the objective standard of care. The experts had said that the uncle lacked control over his actions, but they meant that he did not have rational control. They were not saying that he had no physical control. His mind, although deluded, directed his actions, *Morriss v Marsden* [1952] 1 All E.R. 925, [1952] C.L.Y. 3562 and *Corr v IBC Vehicles Ltd* [2008] UKHL 13, [2008] 1 A.C. 884, [2008] C.L.Y. 2771 applied. His disease did not excuse him from needing to take the care of a reasonable man unless he was not acting or was completely free of any fault, which was not the case. The judge's conclusion had not been open to him. The uncle had breached his duty of care and was liable to the appellant in negligence. The liability was covered by the insurance policy. The policy excluded cover for any acts which were wilful or malicious. However, the injuries were truly accidental and could not have been wilful or malicious because the uncle had clearly lost control of the ability to make choices and could not be said to have intended to injure the appellant (see paras 103-118, 127-139, 144, 146-147 of judgment).

DUNNAGE v RANDALL, [2015] EWCA Civ 673, [2016] Q.B. 639, Arden LJ, CA (Civ Div).

1541 Duty of care–Sporting events–Parking at horse show–Obstruction

[Occupiers' Liability Act 1957 (c.31)]

The claimant brought a claim under the Occupiers' Liability Act 1957 and in negligence against the first defendant (D1) and a claim in negligence alone against the second defendant (D2). D1 was the owner of Hickstead Showground in West Sussex. D2 provided services to D1 which included the managing of parking at horse shows. The claimant suffered serious spinal injuries at one such show. His case was as follows: he had parked his horsebox on the directions of an employee of D2; he left his horse in the horsebox and because it was a very hot day he left the ramp down; when he returned several hours later, he found that someone had put the ramp back up; he began to put the ramp back down by using the hydraulic system on the horsebox, but it fell onto his head, causing him severe injuries; he did not realise that in releasing the ramp to take it down in that way, it would fall; it fell because whoever raised it had done so by manually lifting it into the closed position instead of using the hydraulic controls; the accident occurred because the horseboxes were parked too close to one another and another horsebox driver had had to manually lift the ramp to get out.

Held: Judgment for defendants. A duty of care at common law would be established if it was reasonably foreseeable that personal injury would be suffered as a result of the raising or lowering of horsebox ramps belonging to another. The evidence clearly demonstrated that it was reasonably foreseeable that people might have to raise or lower other people's horsebox ramps. It was also reasonably foreseeable that doing so might cause personal injury. However, in order to establish a breach of the duty of care, the claimant had to show that his horsebox created an obstruction, that that was the reason why whoever lifted it did so and that the obstruction was the result of a breach of duty on the part of D1 and/or D2. The claim failed, as it could not be said that D1 or D2 had done anything which resulted in an obstruction. The evidence revealed that the ramp had been raised to enable whoever raised it to gain quicker egress (by reversing rather than driving forwards) from the showground, not because the claimant's horsebox and ramp were causing an obstruction. Even if there had been an obstruction, it would not have followed that liability would have been established. The mere presence of an obstruction would not amount to a breach of duty provided that there was a reasonable system in place which was designed to prevent obstructions. D2 had a system of parking whereby obstruction was generally avoided; if there was an obstruction, there were measures which were appropriate to deal with it, so as to avoid the need for people to raise ramps on horseboxes belonging to others. The evidence showed that, in relation to the field where the claimant had parked, there was adequate space to allow horseboxes to move forwards when leaving. The system also involved drivers being required to display their telephone numbers on their passes and in the windscreen of their horseboxes, so that they could be contacted. The claimant had done that. The system operated by D2 was entirely reasonable. Given the conclusion that there was no breach of duty by D2, the independent contractor employed by D1 to manage parking at the horse show, it had to follow that D1 could be under no liability to the claimant in respect of what D2 did in relation to parking management (see paras 70-72, 77, 86-87, 89-91, 96 of judgment).

LEAR v HICKSTEAD LTD, [2016] EWHC 528 (QB), [2016] 4 W.L.R. 73, Picken J, QBD.

1542 Duty of care–Taxis–Passenger jumping from moving taxi in attempt to make off without paying–Application of ex turpi causa

The appellants appealed against a decision that the respondent taxi driver was not liable in negligence to them. The appellants, who were both 17, had formed a plan with four other youths to take a taxi from Salford to Manchester city centre and make off without paying the fare. They got into the respondent's taxi. When they reached the city centre, three of the youths got out of the taxi and ran off without paying. The respondent then drove on, knowing that one of the doors of the taxi was open and that the appellants were not wearing seatbelts. The appellants exited from the taxi as it was moving, fell and sustained serious injuries. The judge dismissed their claim in negligence, holding that they had brought about their injuries themselves.

Held: Appeal dismissed. The respondent had been in breach of his duty of care to his passengers. His choice was either to let the remaining three of his passengers out of his vehicle or to drive them to the nearest police station. Although it was entirely understandable that he did not want to lose his comparatively modest fare, that was not an excuse for driving off with an open door when the appellants were not wearing their seat belts. In the circumstances, the judge below had been wrong to say that it was not reasonably foreseeable that the appellants would position themselves with a view to jumping out of the taxi. That was regrettably all too foreseeable once the first three youths had put their part of the criminal enterprise into effect. As to causation and the ex turpi causa maxim, Lord Hoffmann had suggested in *Gray v Thames Trains Ltd* [2009] UKHL 33, [2009] 1 A.C. 1339, [2009] C.L.Y. 2836 that it might be preferable to treat the issue as simply one of causation: could one say that, although the damage would not have happened but for the tortious conduct of the defendant, it was caused by the criminal act of the claimant?; or was the position that, although the damage would not have happened without the criminal act of the claimant, it was caused by the tortious act of the defendant? The former proposition applied here. Even it if could be said that the appellants' injuries would not have happened but for the tortious conduct of the respondent, they were in reality caused by the appellants' own criminal acts of making off without payment. Accordingly, there should be no recovery, *Gray* considered (see paras 18, 22, 25 of judgment).

BEAUMONT v FERRER, [2016] EWCA Civ 768, [2016] R.T.R. 25, Moore-Bick LJ, CA (Civ Div).

1543 Negligent misstatement–Causation–Employment reference for surgeon–Proof that withdrawal of offer due to negligent misstatement

The appellant, a locum surgeon whose offer of a hospital placement had been withdrawn in reliance upon a reference from a colleague, appealed against a decision that he was not entitled to damages for negligent misstatement. The appellant had been offered the placement on the basis of references from the hospital where he was working at the time. A surgeon at the new hospital learnt that the appellant was due to start work in his department and telephoned the respondent, a surgeon with whom he knew the appellant had worked three or four years previously. After that conversation, he had concerns about the appellant's clinical competence, which he referred to a manager. The manager cancelled the locum offer after speaking to the appellant's former colleague himself. The appellant began proceedings. The judge found that there had been two misstatements by the respondent: the first being that there was likely to be a second litigation case relating to the appellant's surgical work when there was only evidence of one; and the second being a suggestion that there had been "about half a dozen" incidences of complications when, in fact, there had only been three. She held, however, that the appellant had failed to establish that the impression given by the respondent that the complications rate was higher than expected was a misstatement. Furthermore, she found that the respondent's comments about the high complication rate to have been at the heart of the manager's decision to withdraw the offer. She therefore concluded that the appellant's claim failed on causation because he had not proved on a balance of probabilities that the withdrawal resulted from either of the negligent misstatements. The appellant submitted that the judge had been wrong to treat the respondent's reference to there being half a dozen patient complications and his impression that the complication rate was high as separate misstatements. He maintained that it was precisely the misstatement of the number of complications which had led to the respondent's opinion about the high complication rate, so that the judge should have found the withdrawal to have been caused by the misstatement.

Held: Appeal dismissed. The judge had been clear in her finding and had been entitled to reach it. She found that the manager's principal concern, which lay at the heart of his decision to withdraw the offer, was that the rate of complications for a relatively short period of time as a locum was higher than would be expected. There had clearly been imprecision in communicating the number of cases concerned, but there was no scope for regarding the two statements as indivisible. The point which registered with the manager was not the number of cases, but the fact that the rate was higher than expected. One would not ordinarily expect a consultant surgeon to act without due care and skill, so it was fanciful to believe that the manager had only been concerned because there were six cases, and that he would not have been concerned if he had known that there were three. It was unreal to think that three cases in four months might be considered expected of a competent and careful surgeon. The appellant had not discharged the burden upon him of proving that the respondent had been incorrect to say that the rate of complications was higher than expected (see paras 23-25 of judgment).

ABDEL-KHALEK v ALI, [2016] EWCA Civ 80, [2016] I.R.L.R. 358, Tomlinson LJ, CA (Civ Div).

1544 Professional negligence–Economic loss–Solicitors' duty to take care in carrying out instructions–Contractual remoteness test

A solicitors' firm appealed against the measure of damages awarded (*Wellesley Partners LLP v Withers LLP* [2014] EWHC 556 (Ch), [2014] P.N.L.R. 22, [2014] C.L.Y. 2214) against them for professional negligence in drafting a partnership agreement. The partnership concerned appealed against the measure of damages and against a finding that the solicitors had not been negligent regarding a related matter. The partnership was a headhunting firm. It instructed the solicitors to draft a new agreement to admit new partners including an investor. The partnership agreed that the investor should have an option to withdraw half its capital after 42 months. As executed, the agreement gave the investor such an option exercisable any time within the first 41 months. The investor exercised that option and the drafting error was revealed. The solicitors initially advised that the investor had made the alteration; they later learned that the error was theirs, but did not immediately advise the partnership of that. The partnership sought damages for profits it would have made by opening a US office, arguing that it would have relied on the investment to achieve that, and that it had been unable to obtain mandates from a bank, Nomura, operating in the US. The judge held the solicitors negligent in the drafting but not in their advice, and awarded damages for the US loss of profits claim. He also awarded damages for one month of the partnership's founder's time spent negotiating with and litigating against the investor. The solicitors argued that the judge had wrongly adopted the tortious test for remoteness regarding the US losses and should have adopted the contractual test. The partnership argued that the judge had wrongly categorised its loss of profits claim as a loss of chance claim; wrongly assessed its prospects of obtaining the Nomura mandates at only 60 per cent; and wrongly held that the solicitors had not been negligent in not informing it of the true source of the drafting error when they discovered it.

Held: Appeals allowed in part. (1) The "reasonable contemplation" remoteness test applicable in contract was more restrictive than the "reasonable foreseeability" test in tort, *Transfield Shipping Inc v Mercator Shipping Inc (The Achilleas)* [2008] UKHL 48, [2009] 1 A.C. 61, [2008] C.L.Y. 3443 followed. The first depended on the circumstances surrounding the making of a contract and the second on the purpose of the rule imposing the tortious duty. Where contractual and tortious duties to take care in carrying out instructions existed side by side, the test for recoverability of damage for economic loss should be the same, namely the contractual one. The basis of the contractual remoteness test was that the parties had opportunity to draw special circumstances to each other's attention at the time of contract formation; they were assumed to be contracting on the basis that liability would be confined to damage of the kind within their reasonable contemplation. It made no sense for the concurrent duty in tort to upset that consensus, *Rubenstein v HSBC Bank Plc* [2012] EWCA Civ 1184, [2013] 1 All E.R. (Comm) 915, [2013] C.L.Y. 2085 applied (see paras 74-80 of judgment). However, that did not result in the solicitors' appeal being allowed. The damages awarded were recoverable under the contractual remoteness test. The damage had been of a kind within the reasonable contemplation of the parties: the solicitors had known the partnership wished to expand into the US and that was a way in which the investment was to be used to make profits. Neither party had known at the time of contract formation any more about how profits would be made; a solicitor drafting the agreement would not have considered the Nomura opportunity to be different from the other contemplated opportunities (paras 81-89). (2) Whilst the partnership had to show that, but for the negligence, it would have opened a US office, the actual loss claimed was dependent on the hypothetical actions of Nomura, a third party, and the chances of Nomura awarding the mandates to the partnership would have to be reflected in the damages, *Allied Maples Group Ltd v Simmons & Simmons* [1995] 1 W.L.R. 1602, [1996] C.L.Y. 4489 applied. Case law the partnership relied on in the instant case did not disagree with that conclusion, *Owners of the Front Ace v Owners of the Vicky 1* [2008] EWCA Civ 101, [2008] 2 All E.R. (Comm) 42, [2008] C.L.Y. 3446, *Parabola Investments Ltd v Browallia Cal Ltd (formerly Union Cal Ltd)* [2010] EWCA Civ 486, [2011] Q.B. 477, [2011] C.L.Y. 857, *Vasiliou v Hajigeorgiou* [2010] EWCA Civ 1475 and *AerCap Partners 1 Ltd v Avia Asset Management AB* [2010] EWHC 2431 (Comm), [2010] 2 C.L.C. 578, [2011] C.L.Y. 556 considered (paras 100-110). (3) The instant court was reluctant to interfere with evaluative judgments of the kind the judge had made in reaching the 60 per cent figure. The assessment was within the broad range of assessment which could reasonably be made on the evidence (paras 125-126). (4) The solicitors had had reason to believe that the information as to the source of the error could be relevant to the course the partnership was contemplating. It was clearly important that the partnership should not negotiate with the investor on an incorrect basis. The solicitors should have corrected their explanation of the drafting error when they found it was erroneous. They had been negligent in not doing so (paras 134-136). The damages awarded in respect of the founder's time was accordingly increased to four months (paras 141-142).

WELLESLEY PARTNERS LLP v WITHERS LLP, [2015] EWCA Civ 1146, [2016] Ch. 529, Longmore LJ, CA (Civ Div).

1545 Professional negligence–Solicitors–Advice on termination of employment of chief executive officer–Failure to identify conditions of service

The claimant companies (C) claimed damages for professional negligence against a firm of solicitors regarding advice given on the termination of employment of a chief executive officer of C. The CEO's employment had been terminated by an agreement about which the firm had given advice, but two years later he brought proceedings regarding his entitlement under a long-term incentive plan agreed when he became a CEO. It had been referred to in a side letter to the termination agreement. The action was compromised for £1,350,000 by a settlement agreement. C claimed that sum in damages from the firm. C submitted that (1) the firm had been asked to give and had given advice about the meaning of the incentive plan clause; (2) the firm should have identified that there were general conditions of employment incorporated into the employment contract that contained a payment in lieu of notice clause, which if discovered would have resulted in more favourable terms for C under the settlement agreement.

Held: Judgment for claimants in part. (1) It was for the court to determine the terms of the retainer, *Minkin v Landsberg* [2015] EWCA Civ 1152, [2016] 1 W.L.R. 1489, [2016] 1421 followed. The relevant standard of skill and care was that of the specialist employment lawyer willing to do work relating to the matters arising when a corporate client was contemplating ending the employment of a chief executive, *Wright v Lewis Silkin LLP* [2015] EWHC 1897 (QB), [2015] P.N.L.R. 32, [2015] C.L.Y. 1793 applied. Further, there was the question of whether, on the balance of probabilities, C would have acted differently with correct advice, and if so, and if negotiations were with a third party, the court had to assess whether C had "a real and substantial chance of a better outcome" and not a speculative one in negotiations and if so to assess it in percentage terms and quantify any loss, *Allied Maples Group Ltd v Simmons & Simmons* [1995] 1 W.L.R. 1602, [1996] C.L.Y. 4489 followed. The court's findings were that the firm was not asked to and did not advise C on interpretation of the incentive plan and did not act in breach of duty by failing to ask for the file (see paras 13-15, 51, 59 of judgment). (2) When advising on the employment settlement agreement the firm was in breach of duty by failing to identify the conditions of service and by not asking for them; if they had, the notice clause would have been identified. Correct advice on its effect on the vesting of the final 25% of the incentive plan would have meant that C's chairman would not have offered it to the former CEO. There was approximately a 35% chance that C would have been able to avoid agreeing to the vesting of the remaining 25% in the settlement agreement and side letter. The valuation of that 25% was 25% of the sum agreed to be paid to the former CEO to settle the action he had brought. That figure, together with the one representing the 35% chance, was the amount of damages awarded (para.110).

COMMODITIES RESEARCH UNIT INTERNATIONAL (HOLDINGS) LTD v KING AND WOOD MALLESONS LLP (FORMERLY SJ BERWIN LLP), [2016] EWHC 727 (QB), [2016] P.N.L.R. 29, Dingemans J, QBD.

1546 Professional negligence–Solicitors–Mortgages–Duty of care to Land Registry

The claimant, the Chief Land Registrar, sought judgment against the defendant law firm in default of the filing of an acknowledgment of service. The defendant had acted for a couple (T) in relation to the discharge of a mortgage in favour of a bank. T supplied the defendant with a discharge form (Form DS1) purportedly signed on behalf of the bank. In fact it was not so signed. T told the defendant that the bank was represented by another firm of solicitors, but that was not true either. The defendant did not contact the bank or the solicitors allegedly instructed by it to verify the Form DS1 or the instruction of solicitors. Instead, it submitted the Form DS1 to the Land Registry with a view to deleting the charge. The Land Registry requested evidence that the person signing the Form DS1 had authority to do so on the bank's behalf. T supplied the defendant with a purported power of attorney apparently appointing four individuals, including one whose name and signature were on the Form DS1, as the bank's attorneys. It was fabricated. The defendant sent a certified copy of the purported power to the Land Registry. The claimant acted on the application and removed the mortgage from the title of the property. The bank was indemnified by the claimant for its loss. By statute, the claimant became entitled to exercise any cause of action which the bank could have exercised had the indemnity not been paid. The claimant relied on two causes of action. First, he asserted that in acting for T in making the application to the Land Registry, the defendant owed a duty of care to the bank to take reasonable care and skill to verify that Form DS1 had been properly completed on the bank's behalf, that the other firm of solicitors had been instructed on its behalf, that the power of attorney was genuine, that the bank wished to discharge the charge and that the property was no longer charged as security for the payment of sums due under the mortgage. Second, he claimed that in making the application for T in the way and using the documents it did, the defendant expressly or impliedly represented to him that it had taken sufficient steps or knew of sufficient facts to satisfy itself that the Form DS1 had been properly executed on the bank's behalf, that the other firm had been instructed on its behalf, that the power of attorney was valid, that the bank wished to discharge the charge and that the property was no longer charged. He also asserted that the defendant owed him a duty to take reasonable care that the representations were true.

Held: Application granted. (1) As to the first cause of action, the defendant did not owe the duty of care alleged. The defendant was never asked to act on the bank's behalf and never thought it was doing so. Its clients were T, not the bank. T were instructing the defendant on their own behalf, not the bank's. The defendant was under a duty by contract to present the document with which it was supplied to the correct person. It was under no duty to a third party to take care to verify the genuineness of the information contained in it. Moreover, the actual act which caused the loss was the act of the claimant in removing the charge, not the defendant's act in supplying the information to the claimant. An analogy could be drawn: suppose a solicitor, on the basis of statements made by the client, initiated a claim, on the assumed facts constituting a good cause of action, against B on behalf of A; by carrying out a simple internet search the solicitor could discover that the claim was bogus. The solicitor would not owe a duty of care to B not to sue him without carrying out a simple check that might expose the worthlessness of the claim; if the solicitor did not know that the claim was bogus in fact, he had no duty to test it before launching it. The problem was that the system of registered land at the time of these events was not secure enough against this kind of fraud. The real question was how the law should allocate the risks of such fraudulent activity where, and in the circumstances in which, it was successfully practised. It was not fair, just or reasonable to make the solicitor in this case responsible to the bank for the risk of fraud within an inherently risky system, *Sebry v Companies House* [2015] EWHC 115 (QB), [2016] 1 W.L.R. 2499, [2015] C.L.Y. 1777 distinguished (see paras 27, 36-37, 42, 45-46 of judgment). (2) The court had been narrowly persuaded that, on the peculiar facts of the case, which might not be replicated in other cases where the solicitors challenged the allegations of express or implied representations that had to be accepted here, it was right to treat the defendant as having assumed a duty to take care in the representations which it made to the claimant, *White v Jones* [1995] 2 A.C. 207, [1995] C.L.Y. 3701 applied. Accordingly, default judgment would given in the claimant's favour on the second cause of action, with damages to be assessed (para.59).

CHIEF LAND REGISTRAR v CAFFREY & CO, [2016] EWHC 161 (Ch), [2016] P.N.L.R. 23, Master Matthews, Ch D.

1547 Professional negligence–Solicitors–Negligent advice causing tax investigation–Settlement not in reasonable range of responses

The claimant company alleged that the defendant firm of solicitors had breached its retainer and given negligent advice to the company's predecessor in title. The predecessor had acquired another company and its subsidiaries. A key part of the tax planning for the transaction was the pushdown of debt to subsidiaries in other jurisdictions in which they could obtain the tax relief available on interest payments in those jurisdictions. The subsidiaries were to bear the debt and claim tax relief on the interest payments. The defendant approved an inter-company loan agreement which was entered into as part of the implementation of the pushdown. As part of the debt pushdown scheme, the predecessor created a subsidiary in Mexico. The pushdown resulted in a very large increase in the subsidiary's liabilities, while its net worth decreased by a substantial amount. A big fall in the value of the Mexican dollar and a weaker performance by the subsidiary meant that its debt was not sustainable as a result of the poor income level that it was capable of generating. Consequently, the Mexican tax authorities commenced enquiries into the tax treatment of the subsidiary's interest payments. The authorities concluded that under the Income Tax Law (Mexico) art.92(1) those payments were in reality dividends and therefore not eligible for the tax relief available to interest payments. The subsidiary issued proceedings in Mexico to challenge the tax authority's determinations, by way of nullity petitions. However, it subsequently decided to settle its tax liabilities and it withdrew its petitions. The claimant claimed the total amount of the tax payments it made, arguing that the defendant was liable because it had advised that the inter-company loan agreement did not engage art.92(1) so as to prevent the interest payments being deductible in accordance with the pushdown strategy.

Held: Judgment for defendants. (1) The defendant had been negligent or had breached its retainer because the claimant should have been advised that part of the wording of the agreement would be challenged by reference to art.92(1). There was no reason why the wording, which provided that the amount drawn and outstanding under the loan would be due from the subsidiary on the initial lender's demand, could not have been removed as not being a crucial part of the agreement. It was absent from the agreement for the Brazilian and Swiss subsidiaries. That it was not in any way fundamental to the structure was made clear by the fact that it was later removed without any difficulty by a subsequent clarification agreement. Furthermore, the defendant's negligence or breach of retainer was an effective and concurrent cause of the Mexican tax authority's investigation which led to the settlement (see paras 54, 58 of judgment). (2) Whether a settlement was in all the circumstances within the range of settlements which reasonable people in the position of the settling party might have made depended on the uncertainties and expenses of litigation, the benefits of settling the case rather than disputing it, whether the settlement was the result of legal advice, and the strength of the claim, Siemens Building *Siemens Building Technologies FE Ltd v Supershield Ltd* [2009] EWHC 927 (TCC), [2009] 2 All E.R. (Comm) 900, [2009] C.L.Y. 671 applied. The claimant had not compared what would be achieved by the compromise with what would result if the proceedings were simply taken forward and lost, or compared it with the very substantial pot which would be recovered for three tax years and with certainty avoided for two tax years. The only independent legal advice on which the claimant relied was that of another law firm which informed it that it would lose if it did not settle; but that advice did not analyse the advantages and disadvantages, and in particular did not point up, particularly while emphasising the unenforceability of the undertaking, the very substantial amount of money that stood to be gained if the claimant were to take the nullity petitions, all ready for decision as they were, to that decision. In the event that art.92(1) was not applicable and the claimant had proceeded with the nullity petitions, it would have succeeded, at any rate in relation to art.92(1), for which alone complaint was made against the defendant in the instant proceedings. The claimant acted unreasonably in abandoning the proceedings which it had a very good chance of winning, and in the event would have won, and in giving up the very good prospect of a recovery which would have avoided the tax losses. Thus the steps taken by the claimant had not been within the reasonable range of responses, and its tax recovery claim therefore failed (paras 17, 68, 79, 87).

SYMRISE AG v BAKER & MCKENZIE (A FIRM), [2015] EWHC 912 (Comm), [2016] 1 All E.R. (Comm) 603, Burton J, QBD (Comm).

1548 Professional negligence–Solicitors–Solicitors' failure to protect settlement sum

The claimant brought an action in professional negligence against the defendant solicitors for recovery of her share of a settlement sum in group litigation. The solicitors had acted for a group of claimants from the Ivory Coast in relation to the discharge of chemical waste from a tanker. The litigation was settled in September 2009 and the settlement sum was paid into an Ivorian bank account nominated by the solicitors. In October 2009, the solicitors were contacted by an individual (G) who claimed to represent a victims' organisation. G obtained a freezing order from the Ivory Coast courts over the funds in the bank account. The funds were ordered to be transferred to the organisation. The solicitors applied unsuccessfully for a stay of the transfer order pending an appeal. They entered into agreements with the organisation, as a result of which the majority of the claimants were paid their share of the settlement sum. The claimant, as representative of those who remained unpaid, brought the instant claim. The claimant's case was that: (i) the payment of the settlement sum into an Ivory Coast bank account left it vulnerable to dishonest claims, including claims by a corrupt judiciary; and (ii) the solicitors had failed to retrieve the funds from the account before the freezing order was made. The claimant relied on the evidence of a witness (W), an Ivory Coast citizen who had assisted the solicitors by liaising with local representatives. Shortly before the settlement, W had sent a newspaper article to members of the solicitors' firm containing allegations of dishonesty against G. The solicitors denied negligence, claiming that there was no causal connection between the loss and the matters complained of, and that the loss was too remote to be recoverable.

Held: Judgment for claimant. (1) The solicitors were under a duty to exercise reasonable skill and care in making safe arrangements for receiving the settlement sum, in safeguarding it pending distribution and in distributing it to the proper recipients. However, they had paid insufficient attention to the newspaper article and had failed to consider whether it had any implications for their plans for distributing the settlement funds. The firm had expertise in organising group litigation for unsophisticated clients in various African countries. However, the plan for managing the settlement monies had apparently been left to two paralegals with no relevant experience, without any proper rigorous analysis of the risks having been undertaken by a senior practitioner and without a proper assessment of the information about corruption in the Ivory Coast. Nor were the paralegals sufficiently closely supervised to compensate for their inexperience. In view of the available information as to the poor economic position of the Ivory Coast, its political instability and corruption among public officials, the solicitors were in breach of their professional duty in deciding to hold the entire settlement sum in an Ivorian account pending distribution. They should have recognised the risk that a large sum such as the settlement fund would be subject to a dishonest claim and that they might not be able to protect the fund without a robust legal system and a judicial system of reliable integrity. In any event, the fund should have been transferred after the events of October 2009 when G asserted his claim to represent the victims (see paras 76-77, 79, 82-83, 97-98, 101-103, 110-112 of judgment). (2) Although the solicitors were in breach of their duties in both contract and tort, the claimant was entitled only to damages that were recoverable in contract, *Wellesley Partners LLP v Withers LLP* [2015] EWCA Civ 1146, [2016] Ch. 529, [2016]

1544 followed. It had to be assessed whether the loss was of a kind or type of loss that satisfied the contractual test, regardless of whether the parties should have reasonably foreseen the particular loss that occurred, *Overseas Tankship (UK) Ltd v Morts Dock & Engineering Co (The Wagon Mound)* [1961] A.C. 388, [1961] C.L.Y. 2343 followed. In the instant case, the type of loss that was suffered was that, as a result of the solicitors' failure properly to protect the settlement sum, the claimant did not receive her share. That was a loss of exactly the kind that would be contemplated as the likely result of their breach of duty. It followed that causation had been established (paras 121-122, 124, 126). (3) The court was not in a position to assess damages as there were too many uncertainties, including the reason why some claimants, but not others, remained unpaid; the possibility that the claimant would not have received her entitlement in any event; and the fees and charges that might have been inapplicable if the solicitors had used an overseas account (paras 131-133).

AGOUMAN v LEIGH DAY (A FIRM), [2016] EWHC 1324 (QB), [2016] P.N.L.R. 32, Andrew Smith J, QBD.

1549 Professional negligence–Solicitors' powers and duties–Mortgages–Duty of solicitor to report to lender

The appellant solicitors appealed against a finding that they were liable to make a contribution to the respondent surveyors for the settlement of a claim by a mortgage lender against the surveyors for the negligent valuation of a property. The borrower purchased the property in September 2005 for £390,000. The surveyors were instructed to produce a valuation in November 2005. The borrower told the surveyors that he had purchased the property six months earlier for £600,000 and the surveyors valued it at £725,000. In December 2005 the borrower applied to the lender for a remortgage, stating that he had purchased the property for £450,000 in October 2005. The application was approved having been considered by three of the lender's underwriters. The solicitors were instructed by the borrower and the lender. The lender's instructions were given on the basis of the Council of Mortgage Lenders Handbook. The solicitors obtained details of the actual purchase price but did not report it to the lender. The borrower defaulted on the mortgage, the lender suffered a loss and a claim against the surveyors was settled. The judge found in favour of the surveyors that the solicitors were under a duty to advise the lender of facts which might have a material bearing on the valuation and that, if they had informed the lender of the discrepancy, the lender would have referred back to the surveyors who would have revised their valuation and suffered no loss. The solicitors disputed the judge's findings on the duty owed and the issue of causation.

Held: Appeal allowed. (1) The starting point for deciding whether the solicitors were under such a duty had to be the express terms of the solicitors' retainer and the instructions given by the lender. The pre-existing law as to the duties of a solicitor were also relevant. The solicitors' duty of care in carrying out their task of investigating title extended to the disclosure of facts which they, as reasonably competent solicitors, ought to have realised would have a material bearing on the valuation or the lending decision, *Mortgage Express Ltd v Bowerman & Partners* [1996] 2 All E.R. 836, [1996] C.L.Y. 4497 followed. The *Bowerman* duty was one of disclosure. The information as to the discrepancy between the purchase price and the valuation clearly affected the adequacy of the lender's security. The question of whether the solicitors were under the *Bowerman* duty depended on whether that duty was excluded by the terms of the solicitors' retainer. The answer was clearly "no". Clause 1.3 of the Handbook was inconsistent wlth Its provisions being a comprehensive and exclusive statement of the solicitors' responsibilities. The suggestion in Tomlinson and Grant, *Lender Claims,* that clause 5.1.2 was not engaged unless the solicitor considered that the information showed fraud, was inconsistent with the express wording of the clause. The provisions of the Handbook were not inconsistent with the *Bowerman* duty as was suggested in Flenley and Leech, *Solicitors' Negligence and Liability (3rd ed).* If a solicitor, instructed on the terms of the Handbook, came into possession of non-confidential information that a reasonably competent solicitor would realise adversely affected the title to the mortgage property or the value of the security, he was under a duty to report it to the lender. The judge correctly found that the solicitors were in breach of that duty (see paras 18, 32-33, 36, 38-43, 52-53 of judgment). (2) On the issue of causation, the facts were unusual in that the lender was already in possession of information which strongly suggested that the valuation of the property was excessive. The judge had reversed the burden of proof in finding that the solicitors should have adduced evidence of the underwriters' failures. It was for the surveyors to establish that the solicitors' breach of duty was a cause of the lender's loss. The judge's finding that there was no evidence of a standard practice for an underwriter to conduct a thorough cross-check contrasted with his earlier finding that an underwriter had scrutinised the information provided by the borrower and nonetheless approved it. The judge did not have the evidence before him to decide whether a reported price of £390,000 would have concerned the underwriters, if a reported price of £450,000 had not. The surveyors had not proved that the lender would have reacted to the information which the solicitors should have provided, which was not materially different from the information they already had. The appeal on the issue of causation was allowed (paras 44, 47-48).

E.SURV LTD v GOLDSMITH WILLIAMS SOLICITORS; GOLDSMITH WILLIAMS SOLICITORS v E.SURV LTD, [2015] EWCA Civ 1147, [2016] 4 W.L.R. 44, Patten LJ, CA (Civ Div).

1550 Professional negligence–Surveyors–Valuations–Whether losses causally related to negligent valuation–Application of "But for" test

A lender appealed against a decision (*Tiuta International Ltd (In Liquidation) v De Villiers Chartered Surveyors Ltd* [2015] EWHC 773 (Ch), [2015] P.N.L.R. 23, [2015] C.L.Y. 344) to grant summary judgment regarding the potential liability of the respondent surveyor for professional negligence. The lender had considered lending money to a property developer in return for security over a development. On the basis of the surveyor's valuation, it advanced money and took a charge over the property. The developer later requested further funds. The surveyor carried out a second valuation. On the basis of that, the lender, instead of varying the original loan agreement, refinanced the facility. It advanced funds to repay the amount outstanding on the first loan, and further funds as the developer drew them down. The loan was not repaid; the lender realised a shortfall on enforcing its security. The lender claimed that the second valuation had been made negligently. It did not impugn the first valuation. The surveyor applied for summary judgment on its assertion that, assuming that the second valuation had been negligent, it could not have caused a greater loss to the lender than the amount by which the indebtedness had increased after the second valuation. The judge held, following *Preferred Mortgages Ltd v Bradford & Bingley Estate Agencies Ltd* [2002] EWCA Civ 336, [2002] P.N.L.R. 35, [2003] C.L.Y. 3025, that the "but for" test of causation applied, meaning that any negligence in relation to the second valuation had not caused losses attributable to the original loan. The lender argued that the second transaction had discharged the original loan and created a new loan created by fresh security, rendering the surveyor liable for all losses flowing from the negligent second valuation. The surveyor argued, citing *Swynson Ltd v Lowick Rose LLP (In Liquidation) (formerly Hurst Morrison Thomson LLP)* [2015] EWCA Civ 629, [2016] 1 W.L.R. 1045, [2015] C.L.Y. 1781, that despite the structure of the transaction, the second loan was in substance merely an increase in the amount of the original loan.

Held: Appeal allowed. (McCombe LJ dissenting) (1) *Swynson* was not authority for the court to disregard the structure of a refinancing transaction in favour of what it regarded as the substance of the case, *Swynson* considered. The lender had been willing to enter into a new facility agreement under which part of the new loan would be used to repay the original. The relevant comparison was between the amount of money lent, which the lender would still have had, and the value of the rights acquired, normally the borrower's covenant and the property's true value, *Nykredit Mortgage Bank Plc v Edward Erdman Group Ltd (Interest on Damages)* [1997] 1 W.L.R. 1627, [1998] C.L.Y. 1432 applied. In the instant case, the developer's covenant had had no value; all the lender had acquired was the property's value. When a lender considered making a fresh loan, part of which was to repay an existing loan, the purpose to which the new loan would be put was irrelevant to the valuer. The valuer was liable for any adverse consequences attributable to any negligent deficiency in the valuation which flowed from the lender's entering into the transaction. The judge's application of the "but for" test failed to take into account the fact that the transaction had been structured so that the second loan paid off the first. The fact that the lender had been the same for each loan did not affect the analysis. The fact that the second loan repaid the first released the surveyor from any potential liability regarding the first valuation. The second loan stood apart from the first; the comparison for ascertaining the loss was between the amount of the second loan and the value of the security. The lender had entered into the second transaction in reliance on the surveyor's valuation. If the valuation had not been negligent, the lender would have suffered no loss on that transaction. It would have been left with the first loan and the security for it, together with any claim it might have had against the valuer. However, that was irrelevant to the surveyor in its capacity as valuer for the second loan. The loss the lender had sustained as a result of entering into the second transaction was the advance of the second loan, less the developer's covenant and the true value of the security. If the property value had been negligently overstated, the surveyor would be liable to the extent that the loss had been caused by its over-valuation. The "but for" test applied, but when correctly applied it led to the conclusion that the surveyor was liable to the lender for the whole of the loss flowing from the second valuation (see paras 15-18, 21 of judgment). (2) *Preferred Mortgages* seemed to reflect the nature of the transactions concerned in that case, *Preferred Mortgages* considered. It was very much doubted whether the court could or should disregard the way commercial parties had chosen to structure a routine business transaction (para.20). (3) The issues raised by the appeal were generally better determined at trial on the basis of findings of fact rather than on a hypothetical basis. If it had been desirable to determine the issue before trial, it would have been better to direct the trial of a preliminary issue, enabling the parties to call evidence and the court to make findings of fact. If the court eventually decided that the surveyor had not negligently over-valued the property, the summary judgment application and the appeal could have wasted time and money (para.22).

TIUTA INTERNATIONAL LTD (IN LIQUIDATION) v DE VILLIERS CHARTERED SURVEYORS LTD, [2016] EWCA Civ 661, [2016] P.N.L.R. 34, Moore-Bick LJ, CA (Civ Div).

1551 Professional negligence–Valuation–Overvaluation–Assessment of loss

The defendant companies (ERL and CBRE) applied for summary judgment on claims in negligence brought against them by the claimant investors. The investors had invested in a trust (T1) which held the freehold of a property and a partnership (P2) with an interest in the acquisition and development of five sites to become regional fire control centres. ERL owned the company which had acquired the freehold or long leasehold interests in the sites. In 2006 a bank had loaned T1 and P2 substantial sums in order to buy and develop the property and centres. The bank engaged CBRE to provide expert valuations for loan security purposes. The valuations were summarised in an information memorandum issued by ERL as totalling over £170 million. The claimants invested almost £27 million. There was a collapse in commercial property values in 2008 and the development of the centres was cancelled in 2010. P2 defaulted on its debt to the bank and entered administration with debts of £123.3 million. The aggregate value of the sites and the property was significantly less than the value ascribed to them in the memorandum and the claimants lost all they had invested in T1. The investors brought a claim against the defendants alleging that the valuations had been materially over-stated. The defendants argued that the investors' losses fell outside the scope of their duty to the investors following the principle in *South Australia Asset Management Corp v York Montague Ltd* [1997] A.C. 191, [1996] C.L.Y. 4519 and were attributable to factors other than the overvaluation such as the financial crisis. The investors had a separate claim against ERL regarding loan notes.

Held: Applications refused. (1) *South Australia* was authority for the proposition that, where a person negligently provided inaccurate information, he would generally only be liable for loss attributable to the inaccuracy and not for all the loss that may have been suffered as a result of entering into a transaction in reliance on that information, *South Australia* followed. A claimant seeking damages for breach of a duty of care had to prove both that he had suffered loss and that the loss fell within the scope of the duty. He had to prove that the loss was a consequence of the incorrect information. The principle was all about the precise scope of the duty. A negligent valuer would typically be liable for loss limited to the extent of the overvaluation, *Nykredit Mortgage Bank Plc v Edward Erdman Group Ltd (Interest on Damages)* [1997] 1 W.L.R. 1627, [1998] C.L.Y. 1432 followed. An assessment was required of the difference between the valuation and the real value at the date of the transaction. The court was required to conduct a two-stage process: to ascertain the basic loss and then to assess the maximum amount of the loss capable of falling within the duty of care. The investors had real prospects of establishing that the loss they had suffered on their investment was attributable, at least in part, to the alleged inadequacies in the memorandum. The case should go to trial (see paras 26, 52, 54, 56-59, 62-63, 70-71, 80 of judgment). (2) The investors' further claim against ERL, regarding ERL's alleged duty to take reasonable care to ensure that loan notes were non-qualifying corporate bonds, was also not suitable for determination on a summary basis. The question of whether ERL owed the pleaded duty of care to the investors could not be determined without a trial (paras 97, 110, 121).

ASTLE v CBRE LTD; AMROLIA v EVANS RANDALL INVESTMENT MANAGEMENT LTD; ABBOTT v EVANS RANDALL INVESTMENT MANAGEMENT LTD, [2015] EWHC 3189 (Ch), [2016] P.N.L.R. 16, William Trower QC, Ch D.

1552 Road traffic accidents–Fraudulent claims–Exclusion of one claimant while other gave evidence

The claimants appealed against the dismissal of their claims for damages following their allegations that the first defendant had negligently driven his car into their motorcycles and damaged them. The second defendant was the insurer of the car and alleged that the accident had been staged to make a dishonest insurance claim. The judge found that the claims were fraudulent and dismissed them. During the trial, the judge excluded the first claimant from court whilst the second was giving evidence on the basis that fraud was alleged and the credibility of both claimants was in issue. The claimants submitted that (1) the judge had wrongly failed to have regard to *Hussain v Hussain* [2012] EWCA Civ 1367, [2013] R.T.R. 11, [2013] C.L.Y. 1728 in relation to the drawing of inferences; (2) the judge had erred in her findings that the claims were fraudulent; (3) as parties to the proceedings, they both had a right, at common law and under ECHR art.6, to be present for the whole trial.

Held: Appeal allowed. (1) The judgment in *Hussain* exemplified how a fraud allegation of the instant type should be approached. However, it did not establish the parameters of appropriate inferences that could be drawn in such cases. What inferences were appropriate depended entirely on the facts of a particular case, *Hussain* considered (see paras 21-22 of judgment). (2) The insurer's pleaded case was that a "single controlling mind" was orchestrating the claims and that the claimants knew the first defendant and had conspired with him. However, the judge made no findings about that or about whether the accident had occurred at all. She referred to a statement, obtained by an investigator, from a woman who described herself as an "ex-friend" of the first defendant. The judge noted that whilst the statement was multiple hearsay, the ex-friend had indicated that the first defendant had never owned a car or a bike. Although that was not explicitly a finding that the first defendant had never owned a car, it might amount to a finding to that effect and there was no doubt that the assertion was influential in the judge's evaluation of the fraud case. That witness's evidence raised a number of difficulties and it had, at the least, been incumbent on the judge to deal with those difficulties in order to explain why she felt able to rely upon it. The judge had also relied on the fact that a moped belonging to one of the claimants had been in a later accident involving another member of the same community and that the same claimant had been involved in three other road traffic accidents. Without further explanation, those facts alone did not contribute to a picture of fraud. The judge had not made sufficient findings or provided sufficient reasoning to substantiate her findings. The fraud finding would therefore be set aside. However, the judge had heard the evidence and it was not appropriate to interfere with her rejection of the claims as not having been proved (see paras 28-32, 34, 36-37 of judgment). (3) The decision in *Al-Rawi v Security Service* [2011] UKSC 34, [2012] 1 A.C. 531, [2011] C.L.Y. 261 was not authority for the proposition that in order for a party to have a fair trial, there was an absolute requirement for him to have the opportunity to be present throughout the hearing. That judgment had acknowledged that there were classes of case where a departure from the norm might be justified. However, the starting point was that a party was entitled to be present throughout the hearing of a civil trial, *Al Rawi* and *Attorney General of Zambia v Meer Care & Desai (A Firm)* [2006] EWCA Civ 390, [2006] 1 C.L.C. 436, [2006] C.L.Y. 516 applied. In the instant case, the judge should not have excluded the first claimant from part of the hearing. Her reasoning was sparse and gave little clue to her thinking about how the exclusion would assist matters. It was difficult to contemplate there being sufficient reason for taking that course in a case such as the instant one. However, the exclusion was not automatically fatal to the entire trial. The fairness of the hearing depended on the proceedings as a whole, *Zambia* applied. The instant case did not involve a claimant being excluded from court whilst an opposing party or an opposing party's witness gave evidence; both claimants were telling essentially the same story, the elements of which they knew from their witness statements. Although the first claimant had lost the opportunity to give immediate instructions which might have shaped his barrister's response to points which arose during the course of cross-examination, it was unlikely during a simple accident claim that material points would have arisen without the barrister realising that he needed to take instructions. The barrister had not applied to be allowed to take instructions and had not pointed to any part of the transcript where things might have been different if the first claimant had been in court. The judge had clearly not intended that the first claimant should be in ignorance of what the second claimant had said because she referred to the possibility of him applying for a transcript of the evidence. The trial as a whole had not been rendered unfair by the judge's decision to exclude the first claimant from court whilst the second claimant gave evidence (paras 59-65).

DA COSTA v SARGACO, [2016] EWCA Civ 764, [2016] C.P. Rep. 40, Black LJ, CA (Civ Div).

1553 Vicarious liability–Prisoners–Liability of Ministry of Justice for prisoner undertaking kitchen work

The Ministry of Justice appealed against a decision (*Cox v Ministry of Justice* [2014] EWCA Civ 132, [2015] Q.B. 107, [2014] C.L.Y. 2343) that it was vicariously liable for injury caused to the respondent (C) by the negligent act of a prisoner undertaking paid kitchen work. C had been a catering manager at a prison. Prisons were required by statute to ensure that prisoners did useful work. The prisoner responsible for the injury had earned a nominal wage. The Court of Appeal, applying the criteria listed in *Various Claimants v Institute of the Brothers of the Christian Schools* [2012] UKSC 56, [2013] 2 A.C. 1, [2013] C.L.Y. 2099 (*Christian Brothers*) for imposing vicarious liability where a relationship was other than one of employment, held the Prison Service, and therefore the ministry, vicariously liable. The ministry argued that the relationship between the Prison Service and prisoners was fundamentally different from an employer/employee relationship in that the Prison Service's primary purpose was not a business or profit, but prisoners' rehabilitation, and prisoners had no interest in furthering the Prison Service's objectives; it was always necessary to ask whether it would be fair, just and reasonable to impose vicarious liability; and there was a risk of further claims arising should vicarious liability be imposed.

Held: Appeal dismissed. (1) The *Christian Brothers* approach extended the scope of vicarious liability beyond an employer's responsibility for the acts of its employees, but did not impose liability where a tortfeasor's activities were entirely attributable to an independent business. The defendant did not have to carry on commercial activities, nor did it need to derive a profit from the tortfeasor's activities. It was sufficient that there was a defendant carrying on activities in furtherance of its own interests. Defendants could not avoid liability by technical arguments about the employment status of the tortfeasor, *Christian Brothers* explained, *Viasystems (Tyneside) Ltd v Thermal Transfer (Northern) Ltd* [2005] EWCA Civ 1151, [2006] Q.B. 510, [2005] C.L.Y. 2890 and *E v English Province of Our Lady of Charity* [2012] EWCA Civ 938, [2013] Q.B. 722, [2012] C.L.Y. 3349 applied (see paras 29-31 of judgment). (2) The Christian Brothers requirements were met and the ministry was vicariously liable, *Christian Brothers* applied. The Prison Service carried on activities in furtherance of its aims. The fact that the aims were not commercially motivated, but served the public interest, was no bar to imposing vicarious liability. Prisoners working in the kitchens were integrated into the operation of the prison, so that the activities assigned to them by the Prison Service formed an integral part of the activities it carried on, in particular the activity of providing meals for prisoners. The prisoners were placed in a position where there was a risk that they could commit a variety of negligent acts within the field of activities assigned to them. Further, they worked under the direction of prison staff. C had been injured as a result of negligence by the prisoner in carrying on the activities assigned to him (para.32). The fact that setting prisoners to work was one means by which the Prison Service sought to rehabilitate prisoners did not alter that conclusion. Rehabilitation was not the only objective: the Prison Service also intended that prisoners should contribute to the cost of their upkeep by providing services. The prisoners' activities formed part of the operation of the prison and were of benefit to the Prison Service itself. It was not essential to the imposition of vicarious liability that the defendant should seek to make a profit. Nor did it depend on alignment of the objectives of the defendant and the tortfeasor. The fact that prisoners were required to serve part of their sentence in prison and to undertake work there for nominal wages, bound them into a closer relationship with the Prison Service than would be the case for an employee. The fact that payments were below commercial level reflected the context in which prisoners worked, but did not mean that vicarious liability should not be imposed. Payment of a wage was not essential, *Christian Brothers* applied. The fact that prison operators were under a statutory duty to provide prisoners with useful work was not incompatible with vicarious liability. The *Christian Brothers* criteria were designed to ensure that vicarious liability was imposed where it was fair, just and reasonable to do so; where the criteria were satisfied, it would not generally be necessary to reassess the fairness of the result. However, where a case concerned circumstances which had not previously been the subject of authoritative judicial decision, it could be valuable to consider fairness. The instant appeal was such a case; however, for the Prison Service to be liable to compensate for negligence by the prison catering team appeared just and reasonable whether the tortfeasor was a civilian or a prisoner. The court rejected arguments based on the risk of further claims being brought (paras 34-45).

COX v MINISTRY OF JUSTICE, [2016] UKSC 10, [2016] A.C. 660, Lord Neuberger PSC, SC.

NUISANCE

1554 Noise–Helicopters–Training operations–Unreasonable and excessive

[Civil Aviation Act 1982 (c.16) s.76(1), s.77(2); Air Navigation Order 2009 (SI 2009/3015)]

The claimant complained of nuisance by noise emanating from the defendant aerodrome. The claimant lived in a substantial detached dwelling with grounds adjacent to the aerodrome. She accepted that a certain level of noise would emanate from the aerodrome, but contended that the noise of helicopters carrying out training operations at a spot close to the aerodrome boundary was excessive and unreasonable. The training involved landing and taking off on a sloping piece of land. The defendant's case was that the area where the training was carried out was uniquely useful for that operation and was the only place where it could be carried out. The claimant argued that the noise was a nuisance and seriously affected her enjoyment of her property in respect of the garden and the major parts of the house. The most important living room and bedrooms faced towards the aerodrome and the noise from the helicopters was very different from other activities, being extremely loud and continuing for what the claimant argued were unacceptable periods. There was a dispute between the parties as to the frequency of the training. The defendant contended that the activity took place on average 1.5 times a week for 15 minutes or so per session. The claimant accepted that that would not be an actionable nuisance, but contended that the activity was far more frequent, and carried on for an unreasonable length of time and was unpredictable, interfering with her enjoyment of the property.

Held: Judgment for claimant. The court had to balance the claimant's right to the undisturbed enjoyment of her property against the defendant's right to use its property for its own lawful enjoyment, *Coventry (t/a RDC Promotions) v Lawrence* [2014] UKSC

13, [2014] A.C. 822, [2014] C.L.Y. 2223 followed. The claimant's evidence about the nature and frequency of the noise was compelling and the defendant's was unconvincing. There had been a regular pattern of complaints about noise nuisance from 1970 onwards. It was impossible to use the gardens with the helicopters performing their operations on the other side of the boundary hedge. Based on the evidence, the court rejected the defendant's case that the helicopter noise was neither unreasonable nor excessive. The right to make a noise nuisance could not in the circumstances be established by prescription as complaints had been made for decades, and the defendant could not therefore establish a right in the nature of an easement to carry on the interference, *Coventry* followed. It was impossible for the defendant to disavow the activities carried on in the aerodrome as it had plainly licensed the complained-of activity and it was therefore liable for all activities carried out by the helicopters on the slope. The defendant did not have statutory defences under the Civil Aviation Act 1982 s.76(1) or s.77(2) as the training exercises on the slope did not amount to flights passing over the area and the activities were not within the permissive activities prescribed by the Air Navigation Order 2009. The training operations did not involve the normal incidents of "taking off and landing", for the purposes of the regulations. The activities carried on by the defendant were an unreasonable nuisance and interfered with the claimant's reasonable use of the property. Two fixed day operations of 15 minutes each would be reasonable and not actionable. The court therefore granted an injunction to limit the activity (see paras 21, 55, 64-65, 70, 81-90, 92-102, 104, 106, 109, 117 of judgment).

PEIRES v BICKERTON'S AERODROMES LTD, [2016] EWHC 560 (Ch), [2016] Env. L.R. 27, Peter Smith J, Ch D.

1555 Private nuisance–Owners–Property owner's liability for failing to abate nuisance

The second defendant property owner (W) appealed against a decision that she was liable in nuisance to the claimants, her next door neighbours. W did not reside at the property but had granted her daughter (E) a bare licence to live there. E had created a nuisance by shouting and by letting her dog bark excessively. In 2009, W became aware that the claimants were alleging that E was creating a nuisance. In September 2010, the claimants wrote a letter before action. W responded rejecting the claim, stating that a landlord was not liable for nuisance committed by a tenant, and that she was not personally involved in the alleged incidents. After the instant proceedings were issued, W served a notice to quit on E, and three months later she obtained a possession order. However, she chose not to enforce it. The judge held that E was liable for the shouting nuisance and the barking nuisance. He also held that W was jointly liable for the barking nuisance from July 2011 onwards, by analogy with the decisions in *Page Motors v Epsom and Ewell BC* 80 L.G.R. 337, [1982] C.L.Y. 2267 and *Winch v Mid Bedfordshire DC*. He found that W had knowledge of the barking nuisance but had done nothing to abate it notwithstanding that she was in complete control of the property. He ordered W to pay all of the claimants' costs jointly and severally with E. W argued that (1) her position as a licensor was akin to that of a landlord, who would not be liable for such nuisance committed by a tenant. The judge made no express finding that she had unduly delayed in abating the barking nuisance, but had simply found her liable from July 2011; (2) she should only have been found liable for part of the costs, since she was not held responsible for most of the incidents of nuisance that were alleged.

Held: Appeal dismissed. (1) There were two possible tests for liability for nuisance: one for landlords of property, and one for those in occupation of property. To be liable for nuisance, a landlord had to either participate directly in the commission of the nuisance, or be taken to have authorised the nuisance by letting the property. The fact a landlord did nothing to stop a tenant from causing the nuisance could not amount to participating in it, *Coventry v Lawrence* [2014] UKSC 46, [2015] A.C. 106, [2014] C.L.Y. 2221 applied. The landlord had limited liability because the tort focused the blame on the person who caused the nuisance. The landlord had neither control over nor possession of the property from which the nuisance emanated. An occupier, however, was in a different position. He would normally be responsible for a nuisance even if he did not directly cause it, because he was in control and possession of the property. An owner might be regarded as an occupier of property for those purposes even if he had allowed others to live or undertake activities on his land. An occupier was liable if he continued or adopted the nuisance by failing to abate it without undue delay after he became aware of it or with reasonable care should have become aware of it, *Sedleigh-Denfield v O'Callagan (Trustees for St Joseph's Society for Foreign Missions)* [1940] A.C. 880 applied. A licensor in W's position was correctly regarded as an occupier of the property for the purposes of the test in *Sedleigh-Denfield.* W was in control of the property, notwithstanding that she did not live there. She allowed E to live there. She knew of the nuisance in 2009. She could have abated the nuisance by enforcing the possession order against E, but chose not to. Instead, she defended the instant proceedings, arguing that she had no legal liability for E's nuisance. W was both in possession and control of the property throughout E's residence there, and the judge was right to hold her liable for the nuisance as he did, *Page* and *Winch* considered (see paras 21-28 of judgment). (2) The costs order the judge made was entirely justified. W was always a necessary party to the claim, as she was the only person who could ultimately abate the nuisance by removing E from the property, which she eventually did after the conclusion of the proceedings. The fact that she was not liable for every act of nuisance alleged did not affect the underlying rationale for the proceedings, which were brought to force her to do something about the persistent conduct of her licensee, of which she was aware for a number of years (para.31).

COCKING v EACOTT, [2016] EWCA Civ 140, [2016] 3 W.L.R. 125, Arden LJ, CA (Civ Div).

1556 Public nuisance–Travellers–Obstruction of highway–Interim injunction

[Criminal Justice and Public Order Act 1994 (c.33) s.77; Highways Act 1980 (c.66) s.130]

The local authority applied for an injunction against a family of travellers. The family had set up an encampment on a road within the borough. The local authority carried out a welfare and environmental assessment and applied for a direction to leave under the Criminal Justice and Public Order Act 1994 s.77. A removal order was executed and the family moved 120 metres along the road, re-establishing their encampment on a common. The local authority issued a claim for possession and applied for an injunction. At the beginning of the hearing the parties agreed on the terms of a possession order. The application for a final prohibitory injunction remained to be determined. The local authority contended that the encampment created a public nuisance in that it produced human waste, noise, unsafe electrical generators and restricted the use of public land. The family argued that a final order should not be made without hearing oral evidence as there were disputed issues of fact, namely that the family was not responsible for all of the alleged nuisance.The local authority submitted that the family had shown that it was prepared to occupy or obstruct parts of the highway, that its behaviour constituted a public nuisance, and that its willingness to move from one site to another within the borough which justified a borough-wide injunction. The family relied on welfare issue, the shortage of authorised traveller sites, and government guidance which encouraged local authorities to tolerate travellers. It was willing to undertake not to set up camp on three specific public areas, but would not undertake not to park on the public highway. It argued that the proposed injunction was unjustifiably wide.

Held: Application granted. The court would have to proceed on the basis of written evidence but, as there were issues of fact material to final relief, oral evidence would have to be heard and tested by cross-examination. An injunction ought to go no further than what was properly justified. It was important that its terms were clear and that those subject to it knew precisely what they were prevented from doing. The court was not attracted by the local authority's suggestion that the family should be barred from parking on all council land in the borough as that was too ambiguous in the absence of further elaboration. The Highways Act 1980 s.130 clearly authorised the local authority to enforce public rights over highways, at least at an interim stage. It had made out its case that there was a real risk that, unless restrained by an injunction, the family would again park caravans in a manner which obstructed the highway. Bearing the family's arguments in mind, it was right and proportionate to give priority to the matters raised by the local authority, namely public health, the enjoyment of public spaces, and the right of the public to use roads unobstructed. Interim injunctive relief, in narrower terms than originally sought, was granted until the trial of the action.

EALING LBC v CONNORS, [2016] EWHC 1387 (QB), [2016] J.P.L. 1100, Nicol J, QBD.

PARTNERSHIPS

1557 Limited liability partnerships–Accounts and audit–Exemptions

THE LIMITED LIABILITY PARTNERSHIPS, PARTNERSHIPS AND GROUPS (ACCOUNTS AND AUDIT) REGULATIONS 2016, SI 2016/575; made under the Limited Liability Partnerships Act 2000 s.15, s.17; European Communities Act 1972 s.2(2); Companies Act 2006 s.396(3). In force: In accordance with reg.2.

The Regulations amend legislation relating to the accounting and audit regulatory framework for limited liability partnerships (LLPs). They also introduce an exemption from certain financial reporting requirements for very small (micro) LLPs, and for very small (micro) partnerships (including limited partnerships) which are "qualifying partnerships" under the Partnerships (Accounts) Regulations 2008.

1558 Limited liability partnerships–Partnership formation–Existence of partnership between founding members of LLP and contractor

[Partnership Act 1890 (c.39) s.1(1)]

The appellant appealed against a decision of the Chief Master granting summary judgment to the first to fourth respondents in proceedings concerning an alleged partnership between the appellant, the respondents and a company. The first four respondents were concerned with the establishment of a private equity business to create funds for investing in African businesses using capital raised from outside investors. The company was to provide seed capital for the project. A limited liability partnership was formed. The appellant entered into a consultancy agreement with the LLP to engage in fundraising and co-ordinating meetings with potential investors. According to the appellant, the project was structured in such a way that the investment professionals would have a significant personal stake in the profits. He claimed that a partnership had arisen from an agreement between the parties to work together with a view to profit. In making that assertion, he relied on the use of the words "partner" and "partnership" at meetings where the project was discussed. The Chief Master held that the appellant had no realistic prospect of establishing the partnership claim. The appellant submitted that the Chief Master had impermissibly conducted a mini-trial on the documents.

Held: Appeal dismissed. (1) A partnership arising under the Partnership Act 1890 required, by virtue of s.1(1), an agreement that the putative partners should carry on business themselves: an agreement that they should merely have an economic interest in a business to be carried on by some other entity was plainly insufficient. In the instant case, the individuals concerned were to own the LLP which was to carry on the business of establishing the fund: the founding partners would work for that business, not for themselves. As a body corporate, the LLP had a separate legal identity from that of its members. The mere fact that parties contemplated that a business would ultimately be run through a corporate body was not necessarily inconsistent with the parties embarking on that business themselves in the period before the corporate body was established. However, work done by those parties to establish the corporate body could not simply be treated as the equivalent of the carrying on a business. Although a partnership might be inferred during a period in which business had already commenced before the legal relationships between the parties were determined, it was far less likely that a partnership could be inferred in a case such as the instant one where the principal trading vehicle had already been incorporated. The use of the words "partner" and "partnership" had little value in determining whether an 1890 Act partnership had come into being, especially where there was an LLP, as members of an LLP were very commonly referred to as partners. There was therefore no support for the notion that the appellant had been invited to participate in an arrangement in which he would personally be carrying on a business with the first four defendants or the company. The Chief Master had examined all the facts relied on and had been entitled to conclude that all the indicators were against a partnership coming into being. Moreover, he had correctly observed that the appellant's failure to explain how the company became a partner with the five individuals concerned was fatal to his case (see paras 6, 16, 18, 30, 40, 50, 58, 80-82, 96, 100, 103-105 of judgment). (2) The Chief Master had correctly observed that the prohibition against conducting a mini-trial was primarily directed at attempts to evaluate disputed evidence or rival versions of events. That did not mean that it was impermissible to examine how a claimant put his case and the material relied on in support of it to see whether such a case had any real prospect of success, *Easyair Ltd (t/a Openair) v Opal Telecom Ltd* [2009] EWHC 339 (Ch) applied. The Chief Master had examined the evidence relied on by the appellant to see whether his claim was fit for trial, not in order to form a view as to where the truth of the disputed facts might lie (paras 111-113).

DUTIA v GELDOF, [2016] EWHC 547 (Ch), [2016] 2 B.C.L.C. 252, Nugee J, Ch D.

PENOLOGY AND CRIMINOLOGY

1559 Controlled drugs–Drug testing–Young offender institutions

THE PRISON AND YOUNG OFFENDER INSTITUTION (AMENDMENT) RULES 2016, SI 2016/583; made under the Prison Act 1952 s.47(1)(3A). In force: 7 June 2016.

These Rules amend the Prison Rules 1999 and the Young Offender Institution Rules 2000 to specify substances or products which are "specified drugs" for the purposes of the Prison Act 1952 s.16A (testing prisoners for drugs).

1560 Drugs–Prisons–Young offender institutions

THE PRISON AND YOUNG OFFENDER INSTITUTION (AMENDMENT) (NO.2) RULES 2016, SI 2016/945; made under the Prison Act 1952 s.47(1)(3A). In force: 17 October 2016.

These Rules amend the Prison Rules 1999 and the Young Offender Institution Rules 2000. The amend the definition of "specified drug" in reg.2(1) of the 1999 Rules and reg.2(1) of the 2000 Rules.

1561 Ministers' powers and duties–Terrorism prevention and investigation measures–Temporal application

THE TERRORISM PREVENTION AND INVESTIGATION MEASURES ACT 2011 (CONTINUATION) ORDER 2016, SI 2016/1166; made under the Terrorism Prevention and Investigation Measures Act 2011 s.21(2)(c). In force: 13 December 2016.

This Order provides that the Secretary of State's Terrorism Prevention and Investigation Measures (TPIM) powers will continue in force for a further five years. The Terrorism Prevention and Investigation Measures Act 2011 provides the Secretary of State with the power to impose terrorism prevention and investigation measures on an individual where the conditions in s.3 of the Act are met. Such measures are imposed by means of a "TPIM notice". In addition to the power to impose a TPIM notice, the Secretary of State has powers to extend and vary a TPIM notice that is in force and power to revive a TPIM notice that has expired.

1562 Parole Board–References by Secretary of State–Procedure to be adopted

THE PAROLE BOARD RULES 2016, SI 2016/1041; made under the Criminal Justice Act 2003 s.239(5), s.330(3)(4). In force: 22 November 2016.

These Rules set out the procedure to be adopted by the Parole Board when dealing with cases referred to it by the Secretary of State. They: revoke the Parole Board Rules 2011 and the Parole Board (Amendment) Rules 2014, and make provisions for the application and interpretation of the Rules: cover procedures which are required in Parole Board proceedings, including the appointment of panels, information and reports to be prepared by the Secretary of State and the giving of directions; set out the timetable and rules for proceedings without a hearing; and set out the timetable and rules for proceedings with an oral hearing.

1563 Prisoners–Disciplinary offences–Alcohol in cell–Defences–Duress was mitigation not defence

[European Convention on Human Rights 1950 art.6; Young Offender Institution Rules 2000 (SI 2000/3371)]

The claimant young offender applied for judicial review of the respondent independent adjudicator's refusal to allow him to raise a defence of duress in disciplinary proceedings. The claimant had been detained at a younger offenders' institution and had told an officer that he had been threatened into keeping alcohol in his cell. The governor referred the case to the independent adjudicator (IA) for disciplinary action. The claimant wanted to advance the defence of duress, stating that he had been threatened with a knife. The IA accepted the claimant's version of events, but held that the duress would only have been available in a criminal trial and was not, as a matter of law, available in prison disciplinary proceedings as such a defence would create difficulty in maintaining prison discipline and because only limited penalties were applicable. He treated the claimant as effectively pleading guilty, the duress as mitigation, and awarded 10 additional days' detention suspended for four months. The claimant submitted that (1) the charge should be characterised as a criminal charge for the purposes of the ECHR art.6 and attract common law criminal defences including duress, or (2) the IA's adjudications were the determination of criminal charges and the Young Offender Institution Rules 2000 should be construed so that substantive common law criminal defences applied.

Held: Claim dismissed. (1) Article 6 provided that in the determination of criminal charges a person was entitled to various rights which enabled a fair trial, but that did not afford any right to a duress defence. It created no rights in respect of the content of substantive law, *R. v G* [2002] EWCA Crim 1992, [2003] 3 All E.R. 206, [2002] C.L.Y. 763 and *Matthews v Ministry of Defence* [2003] UKHL 4, [2003] 1 A.C. 1163, [2003] C.L.Y. 2970 followed (see para.20 of judgment). (2) Three criteria were to be weighed together in deciding whether adjudications on disciplinary offences were the determination of criminal charges; (i) the domestic classification of the offence as criminal, disciplinary or both, (ii) the nature of the offence, (iii) the severity of the penalty, *Engel v Netherlands (A/22) (Compensation)* (1979-80) 1 E.H.R.R. 706 considered. The court accepted that art.6 applied to the instant case, but procedure did not determine the content of the substantive law. The first *Engel* criterion showed that there could be different classifications of an offence for domestic and art.6 purposes. Whether duress was available under the Rules was a question of statutory construction and the art.6 procedural classification was irrelevant. Some offences under the Rules coincided with criminal offences under the general law, but others did not, and proceedings arising from them could not be regarded as a criminal matter, *R. v Board of Visitors of Hull Prison Ex p. St Germain (No.1)* [1979] Q.B. 425, [1979] C.L.Y. 2195 followed. The purpose of the Rules was prison order and discipline. The offences were not criminal under the general criminal law. Even where coincident with criminal offences, they were treated as part of a special non-criminal disciplinary code. There were no special categories by type of offence. The offences were not tried before a criminal court, and did not lead to conviction or permit a defence of autrefois acquit. The fact that the IA determined more serious offences, but still only as disciplinary offences, did not transform the proceedings into criminal proceedings for domestic purposes, and the nature of his adjudication did not alter the applicable substantive law. The procedure and evidential provisions, while art.6 compliant, were deliberately quicker and more informal than a domestic criminal trial, for good reason. The defence of duress was expressly available under the Rules for a select few offences, but was not a generally available defence. Disciplinary offences were intended to be resolved quickly in the interests of order, and with some informality. Prisoners were often transferred and hearings were concluded beforehand for logistic and other reasons. A prisoner might be nearing release and an assertion of duress might require further investigation, involving the investigation of offences allegedly committed by other prisoners. The role of duress as mitigation left much more to the experience and judgment of the governor or IA (paras 21-25, 28, 33, 37).

R. (ON THE APPLICATION OF WILSON) v INDEPENDENT ADJUDICATOR, [2016] EWHC 176 (Admin), [2016] 4 W.L.R. 27, Burnett LJ, DC.

1564 Prisoners–Warrants–Lawfulness of remission warrant to send patient at high security psychiatric hospital back to prison

[Mental Health Act 1983 (c.20) s.50(1); European Convention on Human Rights 1950 art.3]

The claimant life prisoner (P) applied for judicial review of the defendant secretary of state's decision to issue a remission warrant to send him back to prison from a high security psychiatric hospital. P had been imprisoned following his convictions for rape, burglary, and manslaughter on the ground of diminished responsibility. He was subsequently assessed as having a psychopathic disorder within the meaning of the Mental Health Act 1983, and the secretary of state directed that he be transferred by warrant to a high security psychiatric hospital. Several years later, his care team proposed his transfer to a lower security hospital placement. However, the responsible clinician, being satisfied that P no longer required treatment in hospital for a mental disorder and that effective treatment for his mental disorder could not be given in the hospital to which he had been removed, concluded that both the statutory conditions for remission in s.50(1) were made out. Although the First-tier Tribunal concluded that P ought not to be transferred to prison, the secretary of state decided to rely on the views of the responsible clinician. P submitted that the secretary of state had acted unlawfully in departing from the tribunal's findings.

Held: Application refused. Although, under the rule of law, effect should be loyally given to decisions of legally constituted tribunals in accordance with what they decided, in the instant case the tribunal had not been entrusted with the determination of what should happen to P, *R. (on the application of von Brandenburg) v East London and the City Mental Health NHS Trust* [2003] UKHL 58, [2004] 2 A.C. 280, [2004] C.L.Y. 2683 distinguished. Section 50(1) specifically identified that whilst a tribunal could notify that it considered the preconditions were satisfied, it was not the sole relevant body which could give such a notification. It had no power to veto transfer if notified by somebody else, and the ultimate decision as to whether the individual should be transferred lay in the hands of the secretary of state. Furthermore, the secretary of state had had good reason to depart from the tribunal's finding because the responsible clinician had reached the view that the treatment suggested to the tribunal by other clinicians was inappropriate, and his view had been supported in a peer review by three personality disorder teams. Thus, there was no basis on which the secretary of state's decision or reasons could be impugned as being unlawful. The secretary of state had objective justification for the conclusion that P no longer required treatment in hospital for mental disorder and that there was no effective treatment for his disorder which could be given in the hospital. Moreover, the secretary of state reached a justified conclusion that if P were remitted to prison it was not more likely than not that he would suffer treatment so damaging as to amount to inhuman or degrading treatment within the meaning of the European Convention on Human Rights 1950 art.3 (see paras 30-32, 36, 38, 41, 51, 59 of judgment).

R. (ON THE APPLICATION OF PENDLEBURY) v SECRETARY OF STATE FOR JUSTICE, [2013] EWHC 3613 (Admin), [2014] M.H.L.R. 234, Recorder Fordham QC, QBD (Admin).

1565 Prisoners' rights–Hospital orders–Delay in implementing conditional discharge–Whether breach of state's obligation to provide speedy resolution

[Mental Health Act 1983 (c.20) s.47, s.49, s.74(1)(b)]

The claimant (L) applied for judicial review of the second defendant Parole Board's failure to conduct an expedient review of her detention under the Mental Health Act 1983 s.47 following a tribunal's recommendation that she be conditionally discharged. L had received an indeterminate sentence following her conviction for arson. She had a history of mental health problems and was assessed as suffering from a personality disorder. In July 2010, the first defendant secretary of state directed her transfer to a secure hospital under s.47 and directed that her discharge be restricted under s.49. In May 2011, L applied to the tribunal for review of her detention. In December, the tribunal notified the secretary of state that L would, if subject to a restriction order rather than a restriction direction, have been entitled to be conditionally discharged from detention in hospital, and that such discharge should be deferred until the necessary arrangements had been made. In the event that L was not discharged, the tribunal recommended her continued detention in hospital under s.74(1)(b). The secretary of state did not discharge L following the notification; therefore, it fell to the Board to consider her release. In January 2012, the Board's public protection casework section received L's case and, in March, a dossier was prepared and sent to the Board for consideration. In July, L was transferred to a residential hospital (X) which had been identified as her desired destination to which she would be conditionally discharged. In March 2013, following a review of her progress at X and on the basis of psychiatric reports, the Board concluded that there was a significant risk of reoffending if she was released into the community because of her mental health problems and history of disturbed behaviour: it declined to direct her release or transfer to open conditions. L submitted that in a situation where there were to be two hearings before two bodies, namely the tribunal and the Board, the state had a legal obligation to ensure expedition throughout the whole process.

Held: Application refused. The facts of the case were complex, the position was fluid and the eventual outcome uncertain. The tribunal's order was for a conditional discharge once any future arrangements and dispositions had been made. The tribunal had focused only on L and her mental disorder, not on the wider risks she posed to the community. The Board was not simply remaking the tribunal's decision. The Board had taken into account the judge's sentencing remarks and made clear that there was a risk associated both with L's mental disorder and with wider considerations about her background and previous offending, going beyond her mental disorder. The two aspects of the case were interconnected, but it would be wrong to characterise L's case as being one where all the risks were associated with her disorder. It followed that, whether the case fell to be decided by one tribunal or two, a great deal more work was required to be done as at December 2011, before discharge from the secure mental hospital could have been achieved. There had been multiple causes of short delays. However, the essential timetable of the cases was determined by the need to observe L once she had been transferred to X. The period following transfer was set by the advice of appropriately qualified clinicians and it was advice which was bound to be followed. In reality, in relation to all of the time before the move to the residential hospital and thereafter, the time necessary for assessment of L's progress, could not be ascribed to delay by either defendant. Even if everything had moved with alacrity, the outcome would have been the same. Although it took a considerable time to be resolved, there was no breach of the obligation on the part of the state to provide a speedy resolution.

R. (ON THE APPLICATION OF LV) v SECRETARY OF STATE FOR JUSTICE, [2014] EWHC 1495 (Admin), [2015] M.H.L.R. 29, Irwin J, QBD (Admin).

1566 Prisons–Telecommunications restriction orders

THE TELECOMMUNICATIONS RESTRICTION ORDERS (CUSTODIAL INSTITUTIONS) (ENGLAND AND WALES) REGULATIONS 2016, SI 2016/830; made under the Serious Crime Act 2015 s.80. In force: 3 August 2016.

These Regulations are made under the Serious Crime Act 2015 s.80 and provide a mechanism whereby the county court may make an order, namely a "telecommunications restriction order", requiring the disconnection of communication devices within prisons and other custodial institutions without authorisation.

1567 Release on licence–Breach of statutory duty–Elderly prisoner still in custody 18 months after Parole Board direction for his release–Whether breach by secretary of state or probation service

[Offender Management Act 2007 (c.21) s.2(1); Care Act 2014 (c.23) s.6]

The claimant prisoner applied for judicial review of his continued detention despite the Parole Board's direction for his release on licence. The claimant had pleaded guilty in

1974 to murdering a 14-year-girl and having sexual intercourse with her body. He was sentenced to life imprisonment with a minimum term of 18 years which he completed in 1992, but he was not released. He was 77 years old and had spent 40 years in prison. He had had a heart attack and a stroke, was deaf in both ears, incontinent and unable to walk for any distance. In 2014 the Parole Board directed his release to a hostel for male offenders once funding was put in place to meet his care needs in the community. It recommended that on his release his licence should include conditions requiring him to reside permanently at the hostel and not to leave except in the company of a staff member. The claimant was not released to the hostel as the necessary funding was not put in place. Eighteen months after the Parole Board had given its direction for his release, the claimant still remained in custody. The claimant submitted that (1) the secretary of state and the probation service were in breach of statutory duty, namely the Offender Management Act 2007 s.2(1) and the Care Act 2014 s.6 and/or duties to comply with published policies; (2) his continued detention was a result of age and/or disability discrimination.

Held: Application refused. (1) The claimant could not establish a breach of duty on the part of the secretary of state under s.2 of the 2007 Act. Section 2 did not create a duty to provide any particular assistance to any individual. It was framed in general terms. It referred to the secretary of state's "function", which connoted a general responsibility rather than any specific duty. It was clear from its wording that the section was dealing with the overall sufficiency of the provision made for probation services and not whether or what specific provision should be made for the benefit of any particular individual, *R. (on the application of Irving) v London Probation Board* [2005] EWHC 605 (Admin), [2006] 1 Prison L.R. 209 applied. Under the 2007 Act it was for the secretary of state to decide what provision ought to be made for any of the probation purposes and to decide what provision was sufficient. That question necessarily involved judgments about how the various probation purposes could most effectively be furthered using the resources available. It was not within the expertise or part of the constitutional function of the courts to make judgments of that nature. They were for the executive to make. Providing accommodation and services for the resettlement in the community of offenders whose release on licence had been approved by the Parole Board was part of the probation purposes. However, no arguable basis had been put forward for disputing that the secretary of state was entitled to regard the provision currently made as sufficient. Neither s.6(1) of the 2014 Act nor the policy statement relied upon by the claimant could require the National Offender Management Service (NOMS) to fund any services which fell outside the secretary of state's functions under s.2 of the 2007 Act; it was not part of that function to meet social care needs resulting from an offender's disabilities. However, there was an area of potential overlap between rehabilitation and social care. Even where an offender had a need for assistance which fell within that grey area, it could not realistically be contended that either s.6(1) or policy imposed an obligation on the secretary of state through NOMS to fund the provision of services where a local authority would not. Section 6(1) must have been intended to prevent a situation in which, where support was needed which both a local authority and a "relevant partner" might be expected to provide, neither did so because each took the position that the provision of such support was the responsibility of the other so that the individual concerned "fell within the cracks". The defendants were not in breach of duty in the instant case (see paras 24-27, 33-35 of judgment). (2) There was no valid basis for the allegation that the claimant had suffered from discrimination. Even though a prisoner had not been released 18 months after the Parole Board had given a direction which was intended to result in his release on licence, the delay had not been caused by any breach of duty on the part of the secretary of state or the probation service (paras 46, 73).

R. (ON THE APPLICATION OF TAYLOR) v SECRETARY OF STATE FOR JUSTICE, [2015] EWHC 3245 (Admin), [2016] P.T.S.R. 446, Leggatt J, QBD (Admin).

1568 Release on licence–Imprisonment for public protection–Test for re-release of determinate sentence prisoners recalled after reoffending–Parole Board guidance

[Legal Aid, Sentencing and Punishment of Offenders Act 2012 (c.10); Criminal Justice Act 2003 (c.44) Pt 12 s.255B(3), Pt 12 s.255B(5), Pt 12 s.255C(3), Pt 12 s.255C(5)]

The appellant, a determinate sentence prisoner who had been recalled to custody after re-offending, appealed against a decision ([*R. (on the application of King) v Parole Board for England and Wales* [2014] EWHC 564 (Admin), [2014] A.C.D. 103) that the respondent Parole Board had applied the correct test when considering whether to re-release him. The appeal concerned the lawfulness of the guidance given by the board to its panels in December 2013, one year after the coming into force of the Legal Aid, Sentencing and Punishment of Offenders Act 2012, which made major changes to the law on recall and release of such prisoners. The relevant part of the guidance stated that before directing release, the board should be satisfied that detention was no longer necessary "in order to protect the public from serious harm (to life and limb)". A second sentence stated: "it is not a requirement to balance the risk against the benefits to the public or the prisoner of release". The issues were (1) whether the first part of the guidance wrongly directed panels to apply the "public protection test" contained in the Criminal Justice Act 2003 Pt 12 s.255B(3) and s.255C(3) when making their directions under s.255B(5) and s.255C(5); (2) whether the advice in the second sentence was wrong so that it was appropriate to conduct a balancing exercise in appropriate cases.

Held: Appeal dismissed. (1) Neither s.255B(5) nor 255C(5) expressly replicated the tests contained in s.255B(3) and s.255C(3). However, it was implicit from the language used in s.255B and s.255C that Parliament intended the test applied by the board to be the same as that applied by the secretary of state when exercising the power to release without a board direction. If Parliament had intended the board to operate a different test, it would have explicitly identified one. Furthermore, there was no rational justification for requiring two different tests. Parliamentary intention must have been that a prisoner was either suitable for release or not suitable, regardless of whether the board or the secretary of state was performing the determination. The test in s.255C(3) was, therefore, the test to be applied by the board when exercising its power under s.255B(5) to order the release of a prisoner (see paras 10, 20-27 of judgment). (2) The question whether the December 2013 guidance was correct in saying that it was not necessary to balance a risk of offending against the benefits of early release involved construing the public protection test to determine whether it featured such a balancing exercise. That test was flexible in that the public could be protected in various ways from dangers posed by prisoners. Early release might afford more protection than release at the end of a sentence because early release would be subject to supervision. Parliament would not have intended to prevent the board from considering such public interest factors. However, as a matter of ordinary language, the words "necessary for the protection of the public" did not entail any kind of balancing exercise. The goal and the means of achieving it were clear: to protect the public by the continued confinement of the prisoner. When enacting s.255B and 255C, and re-enacting them in the 2012 Act, Parliament would have been aware of the direction issued by secretary of state to the board in May 2004, which was in language materially different from the public protection test, and which directed the board to consider "primarily the risk to the public of a further offence being committed at a time when the prisoner would otherwise be in prison and whether any such risk is acceptable". The omission of the reference to a balancing act must have been deliberate. A further supporting factor was that the public protection test which existed before Parliament introduced a statutory test did not permit the board to balance a risk of harm to the public against other matters, *R. (on the application of Sturnham) v Parole Board for England and Wales* [2013] UKSC 47, [2013] 2 A.C. 254, [2013] C.L.Y. 2112 applied, *R. v Parole Board for England and Wales Ex p. Watson* [1996] 1 W.L.R. 906, [1996] C.L.Y. 4576, *R. v Parole Board for England and Wales Ex p. Bradley* [1991] 1 W.L.R. 134, [1991] C.L.Y. 2993 and *R. v Parole Board for England and Wales Ex p. Wilson* [1992] Q.B. 740, [1992] C.L.Y. 3643 considered. The 2013 guidance correctly stated that s.255B(3) and s.255C(3) did not require or permit the risk of offending to be balanced against the benefits of release (paras 10, 28-29, 31-41).

R. (ON THE APPLICATION OF KING) v PAROLE BOARD FOR ENGLAND AND WALES, [2016] EWCA Civ 51, [2016] 1 W.L.R. 1947, Lord Dyson MR, CA (Civ Div).

1569 Spent convictions–Rehabilitation of offenders–Exemptions

THE REHABILITATION OF OFFENDERS ACT 1974 (EXCEPTIONS) ORDER 1975 (AMENDMENT) (ENGLAND AND WALES) ORDER 2016, SI 2016/824; made under the Rehabilitation of Offenders Act 1974 s.4(4), Sch.2 para.4. In force: 4 August 2016.

This order amends the Rehabilitation of Offenders Act 1974 (Exceptions) Order 1975. It makes amendments in relation to current regulated activities under the Safeguarding Regulated Activity Act 2006, certain members of staff and commissioners of the Independent Police Complaints Commission and candidates seeking appointment to judicial office.

PENSIONS

1570 Contracting out–Contributions Equivalent Premium

THE PENSIONS ACT 2014 (CONTRIBUTIONS EQUIVALENT PREMIUM) (CONSEQUENTIAL PROVISION) AND (SAVINGS) (AMENDMENT) ORDER 2016, SI 2016/252; made under the Pensions Act 2014 s.53(1)(2), s.54(5)(6), s.56(8). In force: 6 April 2016.

This Order clarifies the legislation at the point when contracting-out is abolished on 6 April 2016, in order to prevent a Contributions Equivalent Premium payment being made when contracting-out ends and the member remains in the scheme.

1571 Deferred pensions–Entitlement to deferred pension from staff pension fund–Documentary evidence

[Pension Schemes Act 1993 (c.48) s.145]

The appellant (M) appealed against the Pensions Ombudsman's refusal to uphold his complaint against the respondent that he was entitled to a deferred pension from a staff pension fund (MMC). M's case was that he was a member of a previous staff pension scheme (DCF) to which the MMC scheme was a successor, and that he was entitled to a deferred pension under the rules of the DCF scheme. DCF was a well-known firm of actuaries. He was employed by it as an actuary and was an experienced and knowledgeable pensions professional. He left in September 1978. At that time he did not think that he was entitled to a deferred pension and therefore did not keep any records of his employment or of his membership of the DCF scheme, other than a scheme booklet. The business of DCF was later acquired by MMC, and the assets and liabilities of the DCF scheme were transferred to a scheme run by one of its subsidiaries. The respondent was the trustee administering that scheme. While the MMC scheme had records of a number of former employees of DCF from the 1970s, who were entitled to deferred pensions, and for whom a transfer payment had been made from the DCF scheme, there was no mention of M. The Ombudsman's decision letter concluded that there was "... no evidence whatsoever that [M] was a participating member of the DCF scheme" and, on the balance of probabilities, there was no evidence to support his claim.

Held: Appeal dismissed. In circumstances where there was no documentary evidence of M's entitlement under the fund, it was for him to establish that entitlement. A pension scheme could not be expected to provide proof of the negative proposition that an individual of whom it had no record was not a member. The operation of the burden was not quite as it would have been in court proceedings, since the Ombudsman had an investigatory function that the court did not have, pursuant to the Pension Schemes Act 1993 s.145. M would be entitled to rely on any information discovered by the Ombudsman in the course of his investigation which showed that he was a member of the DCF scheme (see para.13 of judgment). It was not literally true that there was no evidence that M was a member of the DCF scheme, because he had given his own evidence to that effect. However, it was a conclusion of fact which it was open to the Ombudsman to take on the material before him. It was for him to assess the relative weight of M's statement as against the documentary record. The Ombudsman was entitled to conclude at the end of his investigations that the mere possession of a copy of the DCF scheme booklet was not itself evidence that M was a member of that scheme (paras 22-24). It was difficult to be certain about matters that happened some 40 years ago in the absence of contemporary records. In 1978, M did not consider that he was entitled to a deferred pension and it was impossible to know whether he was wrong at that time, although that would be surprising considering his profession and expertise, or whether he was right for a reason he had forgotten. Whatever the explanation, he had not shown any error of law in the Ombudsman's determination (para.28).

MCSHEE v MMC UK PENSION FUND TRUSTEES LTD, [2016] EWHC 1574 (Ch), [2016] Pens. L.R. 239, Judge David Cooke, Ch D.

1572 Employer-financed retirement benefit schemes–Unfunded unapproved schemes–Shareholder approval–Whether pension schemes fell within s.320 Companies Act 1985

[Companies Act 1985 (c.6) s.320, s.320(1)(a), s.346(3)(b), s.739(2)]

The claimant pension scheme employer (Granada) sought to recover from the defendant trustee gilts worth more than £40 million which it had given as security for its obligations under a supplementary pension scheme. The trustee counterclaimed for a declaration of its right to an indemnity regarding its legal costs. From June 1989, an "earnings cap" was introduced, which limited the total amount of pensionable earnings which could be taken into account in calculating the benefits payable to members of an approved pension scheme. Companies whose senior executives earned salaries in excess of the cap entered into top-up schemes to ensure that those executives could continue to earn pension entitlement based on their full salaries. In 2000 Granada entered into an unfunded unapproved retirement benefit scheme, which involved it promising to top up the relevant member's benefits at retirement, but without making ongoing contributions into a trust fund. Granada's non-executive directors resolved that Granada should give security, which could be enforced if it failed to pay the promised top-up pensions. Granada's case was that the arrangements were a substantial property arrangement within the Companies Act 1985 s.320, so that the top-up scheme was voidable because shareholder approval had not been obtained. The issues were (i) whether, for the purposes of s.320(1)(a), the claimant's directors had acquired a non-cash asset of the requisite value; (ii) whether the trustee acquired the charge over the gilts in the capacity of trustee of a pension scheme.

Held: Judgment for defendant. (1) The purpose of s.320 was to ensure that where a transaction involved a non-cash asset of significant value, the company should have the protection of the arrangements being scrutinised at a general meeting rather than being left to the directors' judgement. The reference in the provision to "arrangements" was deliberately wide; directors did not need to be party to the transaction, but the section was triggered if it caused them to acquire, at the time or in the future, non-cash assets above the requisite value. That value was £100,000 in the instant case. The extended definition of "non-cash asset" in s.739(2) meant that the director's interest did not have to be a proprietorial interest, but might include some other right which was capable of being valued. It could not include, however, personal rights against a trustee, such as the right to compel him to administer the trust properly. Section 320(1)(a) applied to a director or "a person connected with such a director". The exception in s.346(3)(b) of the Act meant that Parliament had not intended to include trustees in the definition of "connected persons". Therefore, s.320(1)(a) did not apply where a non-cash asset was held in trust for a director by somebody other than the company, except possibly where the trust was a bare trust. The instant arrangement did not involve a bare trust. It was to be inferred that pension scheme arrangements were altogether outside the scope of s.320: Granada's directors had no beneficial interest in the gilts themselves, or in the charge over the gilts; they had only an interest in the cash proceeds of the gilts and, until retirement, a personal right to compel the trustee to administer the trust correctly, *Forde & McHugh Ltd v Revenue and Customs Commissioners* [2014] UKSC 14, [2014] 1 W.L.R. 810, [2014] C.L.Y. 2950 applied. By virtue of s.739(2), that right was not a right "over" the gilts for the purposes of s.320. The fact that it was also a right which was incapable of being measured by any reliable methodology reinforced that view (see paras 38, 40, 44-60, 70-74 of judgment). (2) It was common ground that the trustee would fall within the definition of "connected person" but for the exemption in s.346. The Act contained no definition of the phrase "pension scheme" in s.346(3)(b) which would assist in construing the exception to the "connected persons" provisions. There was no justification for applying a special or restricted interpretation to the words, as it was Parliament's intention that such schemes, however structured, should fall outside s.320, *Thirty-Eight Building Ltd, Re* [1999] B.C.C. 260, [1999] C.L.Y. 3362 applied. It was clear that the security element of the top-up arrangement accorded with the employer's obligations under the special terms of the pension scheme. In taking the security, the trustee had not been acting as an agent, but had merely been performing its trustee duties (paras 75, 81, 83-85, 88-90). (3) Under the terms of the trust deed, the trustee was entitled to cover its costs on an indemnity basis (paras 91-98).

GRANADA GROUP LTD v LAW DEBENTURE PENSION TRUST CORP PLC, [2015] EWHC 1499 (Ch), [2015] Bus. L.R. 1119, Andrews J, Ch D.

1573 Occupational pensions–Pension protection–Employer's insolvency–Reference to European Court–Whether art.8 Directive 80/987 had direct effect

[Directive 80/987 on the protection of employees in the event of the insolvency of their employer 1980 art.8; Pensions Act 2004 (c.35) Sch.7, Sch.7 para.26, s.143, s.144; Pensions Act 1995 (c.26) s.73]

An employee appealed against a decision that Directive 80/987 art.8 did not oblige Member States to ensure that members of occupational pension schemes received at least half of their scheme benefits in the event of their employer's insolvency. Pursuant to the Pensions Act 2004 s.144, the board of the Pension Protection Fund had approved a valuation of the assets and protected liabilities of an occupational pension scheme provided by the employer. The board had obtained the valuation in order to determine whether it was obliged to assume responsibility for the scheme following the employer's insolvency in 2006. The employee had been a member of the scheme until his redundancy in 1998 at the age of 51. Under Sch.7 of the Act he was entitled to compensation in respect of the benefits he would have received under the scheme. However, because he had not reached pensionable age at the date of the insolvency, his compensation was subject to a cap imposed by Sch.7 para.26. That cap limited his compensation to about 26% of the pension to which he was contractually entitled. He brought proceedings against the board, arguing that art.8, as interpreted by *Robins v Secretary of State for Work and Pensions (C-278/05)* EU:C:2007:56, [2007] E.C.R. I-1053, [2007] C.L.Y. 3021 and *Hogan v Minister for Social and Family Affairs (C-398/11)* EU:C:2013:272, [2013] 3 C.M.L.R. 27, obliged Member States to ensure that measures were in place to guarantee that employees of insolvent companies would receive compensation representing at least half the benefits to which they were entitled under their occupational pension scheme. At a trial of preliminary issues, the judge held that art.8 did not mandate a minimum level compensation. He held that *Hogan* simply applied the decision in *Robins*, which, he found, did not stipulate a universal minimum entitlement in terms of pension protection. The board submitted that the judge was right. It argued that art.8 protected employees as a class, did not create obligations to individual claimants, and did not confer a minimum level of compensation in each individual case. It argued that the cap was lawful in principle, even if it meant some members receiving less than half of their contractual entitlement.

Held: Questions referred to ECJ. (1) While it was right to say that the court in *Hogan* was simply applying the decision in *Robins* to the facts before it, that left open the question of what *Robins* actually decided. The importance of *Hogan* lay in its apparent confirmation, at para.51 of the judgment, that *Robins* established a minimum level of protection that was of universal and individual application. In that paragraph the court said that, following *Robins*, the correct transposition of art.8 required an employee to receive at least half of the benefits to which he was contractually entitled. However, the judge below had declined to read para.51 literally, finding it inconceivable that the court would have held that it was unlawful per se to impose a cap on protected benefits. The instant court was split on the question, the majority disagreeing with the judge and considering that para.51 meant what it said, *Hogan* and *Robins* considered. If the majority was correct, the Sch.7 capping provisions did not properly transpose the provisions of art.8 into domestic law. Given that the point was not free from doubt, it would be referred to the European Court of Justice (see paras 38-39 of judgment). (2) If art.8 mandated a minimum level of compensation, the question was whether it was enforceable. Because the employee could not pursue *Francovich* damages, he had had to take the more indirect route of challenging the s.143 valuation. At best, he could obtain a declaration that art.8 established a minimum level of protection and was directly enforceable. However, there appeared to be an actuarial surplus of the scheme's assets over the protected liabilities, which meant that it would continue to be administered by the trustees. Because art.8 had no direct effect against the trustees, they would be bound by the relevant provisions of the Act and by the Pensions Act 1995 s.73, unless those provisions could be read down on *Marleasing* principles. The question was whether it was possible to interpret the provisions so as to give effect to the Directive without destroying their structure and fabric. In carrying out the interpretive exercise, the court was not entitled to override or set aside what appeared to be fundamental or important features of the domestic legislation. To disapply the Sch.7 cap would be to remove a fundamental feature of the 2004 Act. It was therefore not possible to enforce art.8 by adopting a *Marleasing*-compliant construction of the 2004 Act (paras 40-43, 47-50). (3) It was not clear whether art.8 was sufficiently clear and precise to have direct effect. The parties disagreed about whether direct effect was to be judged solely by reference to the terms of art.8 without recourse to how it had been interpreted by the ECJ, and whether art.8 specified the guarantor of the protected liabilities. The question of whether art.8 had direct effect would therefore form part of the reference to the ECJ (paras 50-59).

HAMPSHIRE v BOARD OF THE PENSION PROTECTION FUND, [2016] EWCA Civ 786, [2016] Pens. L.R. 281, Patten LJ, CA (Civ Div).

1574 Occupational pensions–Pension Protection Fund–Compensation

THE PENSION PROTECTION FUND AND OCCUPATIONAL PENSION SCHEMES (LEVY CEILING AND COMPENSATION CAP) ORDER 2016, SI 2016/82; made under the Pensions Act 2004 s.178(1)(6), s.315(2)(5), Sch.7 para.26(7), Sch.7 para.27(2)(3). In force: In accordance with art.1(2).

This Order specifies the levy ceiling and the amount of the compensation cap for use in relation to the Pension Protection Fund in the financial year beginning on 1 April 2016.

1575 Occupational pensions–Pension Protection Fund–Lump sum payments

THE PENSION PROTECTION FUND AND OCCUPATIONAL AND PERSONAL PENSION SCHEMES (MISCELLANEOUS AMENDMENTS) REGULATIONS 2016, SI 2016/294; made under the Pension Schemes Act 1993 s.113(1)(3), s.181(1), s.182(2)(3); Pensions Act 1995 s.74(2)(3)(e), s.91(5)(c)(iii), s.124(1), s.174(2)(3); Pensions Act 2004 s.122(5), s.129(1)(b)(1A)(b)(3), s.130(5)(b), s.135(4), s.138(9B), s.170(2), s.315(2)(4)(5), s.318(1), Sch.7 para.24(1)(2), Sch.7 para.25(1), Sch.7 para.33; Pension Schemes Act 2015 s.83. In force: 6 April 2016.

These Regulations make amendments in relation to the payment of pension lump sums by occupational pension schemes (Part 2), the Pension Protection Fund (Part 3), and the provision of information by occupational and personal pension schemes (Part 4). Some of these amendments are consequential on changes introduced by the Taxation of Pensions Act 2014 and the Pension Schemes Act 2015.

1576 Occupational pensions–Pension scheme trustees–Trustees' powers and duties

THE OCCUPATIONAL PENSION SCHEMES (CHARGES AND GOVERNANCE) (AMENDMENT) REGULATIONS 2016, SI 2016/304; made under the Pensions Act 2014 s.54(5)(6), Sch.18 para.1(1)(3)(5), Sch.18 para.3(1)(2). In force: 6 April 2016.

These Regulations amend the Occupational Pension Schemes (Charges and Governance) Regulations 2015. They: insert new definitions into reg.2(1) of the 2015 Regulations, including definitions of "adviser" and "service provider"; correct a typographical error; and set out that charges may not be imposed on members of certain occupational pension schemes where they are used to pay an adviser or to reimburse the service provider for a payment that they have made to an adviser.

1577 **Occupational pensions–Public sector employees–Pensionable earnings**

THE PUBLIC SERVICE PENSIONS REVALUATION (EARNINGS) ORDER 2016, SI 2016/95; made under the Public Service Pensions Act 2013 s.9(2)(3). In force: 1 April 2016.

The Public Service Pensions Act 2013 s.9 applies to public service pension schemes established under that Act which require a revaluation of pensionable earnings, or a portion of such earnings accrued as a pension, by reference to a change in prices, earnings or both. This Order specifies an increase in earnings of 2 per cent in relation to the period of 1 April 2015 to 31 March 2016 inclusive. This figure is based on a measure of the year on year change in average weekly earnings to September 2015.

1578 **Occupational pensions–Rectification–Rectification granted without hearing–Confidential information**

[Civil Procedure Rules 1998 Pt 24, r.5.4]

The claimant trust applied for rectification of a definitive deed for a new occupational defined benefit pension scheme. The new scheme was to take a bulk transfer of past service benefits from an old scheme that was part of The Pensions Trust for Charities and Voluntary Organisations (the pensions trust). The first defendant trustee of the new scheme produced an initial draft of the definitive deed, but certain amendments were agreed and a second version was produced. The deed had to be approved by the pensions trust. The deed was executed by the claimant and the trustee, but it was later discovered that it did not include the required amendments and rectification was sought. The second defendant representative scheme member wished to advance her stance by reference to an opinion of counsel, but did not wish to waive privilege. All parties agreed to rectification.

Held: Application granted. (1) The claimant had to demonstrate that it and the trustee had a common, continuing, objectively established intention in respect of the matter which by mistake had been omitted from the deed, and that had the deed been executed in its intended form the pensions trust could not have objected to it, *IBM Pension Plan, Re* [2012] EWHC 2766 (Ch), [2012] Pens. L.R. 469, [2013] C.L.Y. 2168 applied. The jurisdiction under CPR Pt 24 was available in rectification cases, and the court could dispose of an application without a hearing if that would save time and expense and a hearing was not necessary. Rectification of a pension scheme would ordinarily require a hearing because it was often not an efficient use of court time for a judge to consider complex material unassisted by oral representations, and because it was important that ordinary scheme members should not be left with any sense that there had been some deal done in a dark corner. The court could in exceptional circumstances consider evidence tendered on a confidential basis and not available to other parties. The agreement of the other parties to the evidence remaining confidential did not prevent the court from deciding that after judgment it ought to be available for inspection by scheme members (see paras 8, 12-13, 16-17 of judgment). (2) There was no real prospect of arguing that the claimant and trustee had not intended to enter into a deed in the terms of the second version. Summary judgment was granted without a hearing. Counsel's opinion would not be open to unrestricted inspection after judgment. The evidence without the opinion was full and had been scrutinised and tested: justice would have been done in public if it was ordered that it should be open to inspection by any scheme member or beneficiary. When the opinion had been written the possibility of disclosure outside a restricted circle had not been considered. The judgment adequately set out the relevant facts on which the opinion drew. The opinion should be placed in a sealed envelope, not to be opened without leave under CPR r.5.4 (paras 45-46, 51). (3) For the future, any party seeking to rectify a mistake in the expression of a pension scheme by obtaining a summary judgment order without a hearing had to understand that it was likely that the court would insist that after judgment all evidence be open to inspection. If that was not acceptable, the summary judgment application had to be listed for a public hearing, with permission to vacate if no scheme member gave notice of intention to attend, *University of Wales, Trinity St David v Davies* applied (para.50).

GIRLS' DAY SCHOOL TRUST v GDST PENSION TRUSTEES LTD, [2016] EWHC 1254 (Ch), [2016] Pens. L.R. 181, Norris J, Ch D.

1579 Occupational pensions–Rules–Rate of annual increases to pensions in payment–Construction of amended rule

The court was required to determine the correct construction of a rule of a pension scheme in proceedings brought by pension trustees. Under rule 16(e) of the previous terms of the scheme, pensions in payment were increased each year by 3 per cent on a compound basis. On 20 June 1991 a deed of amendment purported to delete rule 16(e) and replace it with a new rule that pensions in payment would be increased by "the lesser of 5 per cent ... or such increase in the Government's Index of Retail Prices since the immediately preceding anniversary date". A proviso in the scheme rules prevented changes which would prejudicially affect pensions in payment or members' accrued rights. The scheme had 2,200 deferred members and 1,588 pensioner members, a large number of whom had accrued benefits in respect of service prior to June 1991. The potential increase in the scheme's liabilities was between £5 million and £17 million, depending on the effect of the 1991 deed. The employer submitted that the pre-20 June 1991 element of a pension should be calculated separately from the post-1991 element, so that the different percentages under each rule could be applied.

Held: Judgment for claimants. (1) The amended rule 16(e) breached the proviso in respect of benefits accrued prior to 20 June 1991 in that it purported to remove the right to increases under the old rules in a way which was prejudicial. Amended rule 16(e), subject to the proviso, should be construed so as to give reasonable and practical effect to the scheme. Technicality should be avoided, and it should be borne in mind that if the consequences of a construction were impractical, it was likely that the interpretation was not the right one. Further, the amendment should be considered against the circumstances and factual situation prevailing in 1991, together with the relevant background. In determining the meaning that the rule would convey to a reasonable person with all of the background knowledge, it was necessary to consider the provision in the context of the 1991 deed as a whole. The matter should be approached without any particular predisposition as to the correct philosophical approach, *Stevens v Bell* [2002] EWCA Civ 672, [2002] O.P.L.R. 207, [2002] C.L.Y. 3390 followed (see paras 12, 25 of judgment). (2) The amended rule 16(e) subject to the proviso amounted to a single right to annual increases in pensions in payment but derived from more than one provision or source. No question of windfall arose. The proviso preserved what was necessary of the old rule 16(e) to avoid the member being prejudiced. The 1991 deed had to be construed as having effect subject to the limitation contained in the proviso. It was easier to view the position as a composite or blend of amended rule 16(e) and the old rule 16(e) to the extent necessary to prevent prejudice to the member, rather than an "underpin", *Betafence Ltd v Veys* [2006] EWHC 999 (Ch), [2006] Pens. L.R. 137, [2006] C.L.Y. 2987 applied. Overall, the amended rule 16(e) should be construed to mean that part of a pension which accrued as a result of service pre 20 June 1991 must be increased annually by the greater of 5 per cent/RPI and 3 per cent. That was the most natural meaning of the amended rule 16(e) subject to the proviso which prevented the member from being prejudiced should the 5 per cent/ RPI increase prove less beneficial than the entitlement under the old rule 16(e). Both versions of the rule required the pension in payment on the anniversary date to be increased. Such a construction also avoided technicality and would have been straightforward to operate in 1991. It also provided for annual increases in pensions at no less than 3 per cent per annum compound at each anniversary of the pension having come into payment, which was consistent with the effect of the proviso, given the meaning it would convey to a reasonable person. The fact that such a construction resulted in a pension which was more valuable than that to which the member was originally entitled was hardly surprising (paras 44-47, 54). (3) The court rejected the employer's submission that increases at 3 per cent should be kept separate from the 5 per cent/RPI increases. The amended rule was a composite, and an attempt to separate out the original sources led to an attempt to give more weight to one than the other, and to calculate increases from the date of retirement rather than on an annual basis. The fact that on that basis the actual increase rate could fall below 3 per cent was a clear indicator that that construction was incorrect. It was clearly contrary to the proviso. It would have made the administration of the scheme particularly complicated in 1991. By comparison, the construction set out above was simple to implement and would have been so in 1991 (paras 50-52).

DUTTON v FDR LTD, [2015] EWHC 2946 (Ch), [2015] Pens. L.R. 569, Asplin J, Ch. D.

1580 Occupational pensions–Statutory interpretation–Qualification for transfer credits–Meaning of "earner" in s.181 Pensions Schemes Act 1993

[Pension Schemes Act 1993 (c.48) s.181; Social Security Contributions and Benefits Act 1992 (c.4) s.112, s.3, s.4]

The appellant (H) appealed against the Pension Ombudsman's dismissal of her complaint against the respondent pensions administrator. H was a member of a personal pension scheme and an occupational pension scheme. The respondent administered the personal scheme. Under that scheme, H had acquired a right to the cash equivalent of the accrued benefits. She asked the respondent to use the cash equivalent to acquire transfer credits for her occupational scheme. The respondent refused. The Ombudsman upheld that refusal on the basis that H was not an "earner" within the statutory definition of "transfer credits", because she was not earning an income from the employer under the occupational scheme. She earned income from other sources. The relevant statutory provisions were in the Pension Schemes Act 1993, which incorporated a definition of "earner" from the Social Security Contributions and Benefits Act 1992. H submitted that the Ombudsman had wrongly construed the definition of "earner" and "transfer credits", because she did not need to be earning remuneration from the occupational scheme employer.

Held: Appeal allowed. (1) The interpretation adopted by the Ombudsman involved reading words into the definition of transfer credits in s.181 of the 1993 Act. It was sometimes possible for a court to supply missing words in a statutory provision, but before doing so the court had to be "abundantly sure" of three matters: (a) the intended purpose of the statute in question; (b) that by inadvertence the draftsman and Parliament had failed to give effect to that purpose in the relevant provision; (c) the substance of the provision Parliament would have made, had the error been noticed, *Inco Europe Ltd v First Choice Distribution* [2000] 1 W.L.R. 586, [2000] C.L.Y. 220 followed. The court was not satisfied that the *Inco* criteria were met. It was therefore not able to read words into the definition of "transfer credits". Accordingly, the Ombudsman's interpretation of that definition could not be accepted (see paras 28-29, 31 of judgment). (2) In the absence of any other identified meaning for the word "earner", the court gave it its general meaning in accordance with s.3, s.4 and s.112 of the 1992 Act. It was agreed that H was an earner by reason of her earnings from another source or sources. It followed that she was entitled to require the respondent to transfer the cash equivalent of her accrued rights under her personal scheme so that she would be awarded transfer credits in relation to her occupational scheme (paras 31, 32).

HUGHES v ROYAL LONDON MUTUAL INSURANCE SOCIETY LTD, [2016] EWHC 319 (Ch), [2016] Pens. L.R. 69, Morgan J, Ch D.

1581 Occupational pensions–Transfer of assets–Certification process under reg.12(3) Occupational Pension Schemes (Preservation of Benefit) Regulations 1991–Security of benefits

[Occupational Pension Schemes (Preservation of Benefit) Regulations 1991 (SI 1991/167) Sch.3, reg.12, reg.12(3); Pension Schemes Act 1993 (c.48) s.73]

Pension scheme trustees brought a Part 8 claim arising out of the proposed transfer of the scheme's assets and liabilities to a new occupational pension scheme. The original scheme was a defined benefit occupational pension scheme in severe deficit. It was suggested that, unless the proposed transfer took place, the employer would be placed in administration and the scheme would go into the Pension Protection Fund resulting in a reduction in members' compensation levels. It was undisputed that the new scheme offered greater security than the original one. In relation to the transfer, the scheme actuary had to certify, in accordance with the Occupational Pension Schemes (Preservation of Benefit) Regulations 1991 reg.12 and Sch.3, that transfer credits to be acquired by the members under the new scheme were at least equal in value to the rights to be transferred from the original scheme. The trustees submitted that (1) when determining whether the transfer credits in the new scheme were "broadly no less favourable" than the rights under the original scheme, pursuant to Sch.3 para.1, the actuary should take into consideration the security of the benefits in each of the schemes and, therefore, the likelihood of the benefits being paid; (2) even if reg.12(3) did not require security to be taken into account where the transferring scheme was ongoing, that issue became relevant where that scheme was being wound up.

Held: Judgment accordingly. (1) Construed in the light of the 1991 Regulations as a whole and of the Pension Schemes Act 1993 s.73, from which that provision emanated, reg.12(3) did not include the security of benefits as a factor to be taken into account by the actuary in the certification process. The actuary was required to compare transfer credits to be acquired and rights to be transferred in terms of the packages of rights and to form the opinion that the transfer credits were "broadly no less favourable" than the rights. No express reference was made to the security of the rights or transfer credits. Had it been intended that such a factor be taken into account, the Regulations would have made that clear. Moreover, the security of the benefits was not implicit in Sch.3 para.1, nor was the exercise of opinion sufficiently wide as to permit the actuary to take that factor into account in any event. The word "opinion" in Sch.3 para.1 was merely used to signify the need to apply professional judgement in the certification task. If the actuary were required to take security into consideration, that task would require information to be obtained which might be highly commercially sensitive and which would not necessarily be readily available to the actuary (see paras 79-82, 85, 101 of judgment). (2) There was no scope for a different construction of reg.12(3) where the transferring scheme was in winding up. Such a construction would create anomalies according to timing, in the sense that different results would occur where the certification was carried out in a scheme where winding up had been triggered and in a scheme which was extremely poorly funded but not in winding up. Nor did s.73 and s.74 of the 1993 Act effect a reduction in the right to benefits for the purposes of reg.12. Those provisions established a priority order for the payment of benefits in the event of a winding up where it was envisaged that there might not be sufficient assets to meet the liabilities in full: however, the fact that benefits in payment were reduced was not an indicator that the right to the benefits had itself been reduced as a result of the practical consequences of an insufficiency of assets (paras 118-122, 127). (3) The trustees had taken a broad range of professional advice and had concluded that, subject to the determination of the court on the legal issues, it would have been in the best interests of the members of the original scheme to enter into the proposed transaction. They had undertaken a careful and proper review of all the relevant issues and had not taken account of any irrelevant considerations. Therefore, had a different view been taken in relation to the legal issues, their decision to enter into the proposed transaction would have been approved (paras 130, 137-138).

POLLOCK v REED, [2015] EWHC 3685 (Ch), [2016] Pens. L.R. 129, Asplin J, Ch D.

1582 Pension schemes–Automatic enrolment–Seafarers working on cruise ships–Ordinarily working in Great Britain

[Pensions Act 2008 (c.30) s.1, s.35]

An employer applied for judicial review of a decision of the Pensions Regulator that the certain seafarers who worked on its cruise ships fell within the territorial scope of the Pensions Act 2008 and therefore qualified for automatic enrolment into a pension scheme. The employer was a company incorporated in Bermuda and had no place of business in the United Kingdom, but was a wholly owned subsidiary of an English company. The crew lived on board the cruise ships to which they were assigned during any particular tour of duty and spent a significant majority of their time outside UK territorial waters. Some of the crew resided in the UK and some outside. Under the Act, an employer was required to automatically enrol an eligible jobholder into a pension scheme. A jobholder was defined by Pensions Act 2008 s.1 as a worker who, among other things, was working or was ordinarily working in Great Britain under a contract. The Regulator issued a compliance notice under s.35 to the employer requiring it to enrol workers who lived in the UK if they joined and left their ships from ports within the UK or, if not, the days they spent travelling to and from ports outside the UK were treated as days of work for the purposes of entitlement to pay and leave. After the employer requested a review of the notice, the Regulator affirmed it and the employer sought judicial review of that affirmation.

Held: Application granted in part. An employee's base was the place where he should be regarded as ordinarily working, within the meaning of s.1(1)(a) , even though he might spend time working overseas. The question of where a peripatetic worker was based was not necessarily settled by the terms of the worker's contract but would generally depend on how the contract was in fact being operated at the relevant time, *Todd v British Midland Airways Ltd* [1978] I.C.R. 959, [1978] C.L.Y. 1138, *Lawson v Serco Ltd* [2006] UKHL 3, [2006] 1 All E.R. 823, [2006] C.L.Y. 1390 applied, *Wilson v Maynard Shipbuilding Consultants AB* [1978] Q.B. 665, [1978] C.L.Y. 981 distinguished. As applied to a peripatetic worker, the concept of a base was that of a place from which the worker set off at the start and to which the worker returned at the end of a period when the worker was travelling in the course of his work. A ship was not such a place; rather it was a means of transport from one place to another. Therefore, the ship on which a seafarer worked was not that worker's base. However, not every peripatetic worker had to have a base which was to be regarded as the place where he ordinarily worked. A key question in determining whether a peripatetic worker was based in Great Britain and hence could be regarded as ordinarily working in Great Britain was where his tours of duty began and ended. In the instant case, each tour of duty for a seafarer employed under a permanent contract of employment started when the seafarer joined the ship to which he was assigned to work and ended when he left the ship. Accordingly, the Regulator had been correct in the view that a seafarer who lived in the UK but spent several weeks away working in foreign waters and joined and left that vessel from a port within the UK should be assessed as ordinarily working in the UK, even though most of his tour of duty might be spent outside the UK. However, the Regulator had been incorrect to conclude that a seafarer who began and ended his tour of duty at ports outside the UK was also ordinarily working in the UK if travelling to and from those foreign ports was treated as days of work (see paras 24, 50, 60, 68-72 of judgment).

R. (ON THE APPLICATION OF FLEET MARITIME SERVICES (BERMUDA) LTD) v PENSIONS REGULATOR, [2015] EWHC 3744 (Admin), [2016] 2 Lloyd's Rep. 35, Leggatt J, QBD (Admin).

1583 Pension schemes–Deeds–Validity of amendments to pension scheme deed and rules–Retrospective effect

The trustees of a pension scheme sought the determination of issues regarding the validity and effects of deeds by which amendments had purportedly been made to the scheme's deed and rules. The first defendant (V) had taken actions as the scheme's principal employer until 1997, and had been appointed again by a 2003 deed of novation. It agreed to a 1995 deed which set out the scheme's rules. There was an issue as to whether another company (M), which became V's holding company in 1994, had become the principal employer that year by the retrospective effect of a 1999 deed or a 2002 deed of novation, or whether it became principal employer in 1999. M agreed to a further deed in 2001 intended to rectify an error in the rules introduced under the 1999 deed. Legal actions were pending regarding the scheme.

Held: Judgment accordingly. (1) *The 1999 deed, and whether it appointed M principal employer retrospectively Whether r.10.10 of the 1995 rules, requiring the consent of the existing principal employer to the appointment of a new principal employer, required V's formal written consent:* The language used in r.10.10 could not be interpreted as meaning that written consent was required. Nor was it necessary to imply any requirement of formality. Although it might have been sensible to have some documented record, the scheme could operate without one (see paras 58-62 of judgment). *Whether the r.10.10 power could be exercised retrospectively:* Retrospectivity depended on the power's scope, which depended on what the parties to the 1995 deed had envisaged as to the circumstances of its exercise. That depended on the effect of retrospective exercise of the power. Before the exercise of the power, the principal employer would have been performing the acts required of it under the scheme; appointing a new principal employer with retrospective effect could invalidate acts which were valid when done. It was impermissible to exercise a power so as adversely to affect accrued rights, falsify something effective when done, or validate something that when done was a breach of trust, *PNPF Trust Co Ltd v Taylor* [2010] EWHC 1573 (Ch), [2010] Pens. L.R. 261, [2010] C.L.Y. 2338 and *Dalriada Trustees Ltd v Faulds* [2011] EWHC 3391 (Ch), [2012] 2 All E.R. 734, [2012] C.L.Y. 2385 applied. It could not reasonably be considered to have been within the contemplation of the parties to the 1995 deed that the power would be capable of exercise retrospectively (paras 63-77). *Had the r.10.10 power been validly exercised?* The relevant parties had understood in 1999 that M was not already the principal employer, but was, under the 1999 deed, to become the principal employer with retrospective effect to 1994. The rules amendments made by the 1999 deed were only valid if it also made M principal employer. The question was whether the deed itself constituted the necessary agreement of the relevant parties to M becoming principal employer, although that could not be with retrospective effect. V had not been a party to the deed. However, as V was M's wholly-owned subsidiary, M could take decisions on V's behalf, *Duomatic Ltd, Re* [1969] 2 Ch. 365, [1969] C.L.Y. 412 applied. V had therefore ceded its role as principal employer to M. The deed had effect as an exercise of the r.10.10 power (paras 89-96). If that was wrong, there was to be imputed to the trustees and M the intention to exercise the power to appoint M so that the rule changes would have effect, *Davis v Richards and Wallington Industries Ltd* [1990] 1 W.L.R. 1511, [1991] C.L.Y. 1727 applied (paras 97-102). (2) *The 2001 deed* The trustees had unsuccessfully attempted to amend r.61.4(a) of the 1999 rules in 2000. There was a question as to whether, by reciting the 2000 attempt, the 2001 deed had amended r.61.4(a) even though it did not expressly do so. That raised a question as to the circumstances in which the law would impute the exercise of a power that could have been exercised but had not been exercised in terms. There had to be sufficient evidence on M's part to exercise its power to amend r.61.4(a). That evidence could be derived from the recital of a previously ineffective exercise of the power, *Shinorvic Trust, Re* [2013] W.T.L.R. 337 considered (paras 111-119). (3) *The 2002 deed of novation Did the 2002 deed make M principal employer with effect from 1994 using the power in r.32 of the 1999 rules to substitute the principal employer?* The purported exercise of the r.32 power was of no effect. M had already been principal employer in 2002. Rule 32 did not empower the principal employer to agree with a previous principal employer to be treated as principal employer from an earlier date than that on which it had been appointed. The 2002 deed therefore did not invalidate the 1995 deed. In any event, a new principal employer could not have been appointed retrospectively under r.32 so as to invalidate prior actions validly made by V (paras 122-125). (4) *The 2003 deed of novation Did r.32 permit V to be re-appointed principal employer with retrospective effect under the 2003 deed?* The parties could not have intended that a principal employer which had acted as such could be displaced retrospectively so as to create a fiction that that person had not been the principal employer. The 2003 deed had not made V the principal employer before the date of its execution (paras 137-141).

SHANNAN v VIAVI SOLUTIONS UK LTD, [2016] EWHC 1530 (Ch), [2016] Pens. L.R. 193, Timothy Fancourt QC, Ch D.

1584 Pension schemes–Loans–Loan received by member of self-investment personal pension scheme–Unauthorised member payment

[Finance Act 2004 (c.12) s.160(2), s.161, s.164, s.175, s.208, s.209, s.279(2)]

A pension scheme member appealed against an unauthorised payment charge and surcharge imposed by the Revenue concerning his receipt of a loan that he was repaying from the proceeds of his pension fund. In 2009 the appellant, then 41 years old, had wanted to access part of his pension fund without incurring income tax. To that end, he became a member of a registered self-invested personal pension scheme (H) to which he transferred his existing pension funds of approximately £35,000. He then instructed H to invest the funds by purchasing shares in a wholesale lending company (K). Based on that investment, a further company (G) agreed to loan him around £18,000 to be repaid from the net proceeds of his pension. The Revenue decided that the loan was an unauthorised payment under the Finance Act 2004 and was subject to an income tax charge and surcharge under s.208 and s.209 respectively. The issues were (1) whether the loan could be classed as a "payment"; (2) if so, whether it had been made by a registered pension scheme to one of its members as defined by s.160(2) having regard to the interpretation provisions in s.279(2) and s.161.

Held: Appeal dismissed. (1) The loan was a payment, and given that it did not fall within the list of authorised payments in s.164, it was an unauthorised payment, *Dalriada Trustees Ltd v Faulds* [2011] EWHC 3391 (Ch), [2012] 2 All E.R. 734, [2012] C.L.Y. 2385 applied. Further, if a loan was not a payment, there would have been no need to include "authorised employer loans" in the class of "authorised employer payments" in s.175 (see para.58 of judgment).(2) At first sight, as the loan had been made by G rather than H, it appeared that it could not properly be regarded as a payment by the pension scheme of which the appellant was a member. However, the interpretation provision in s.279(2) made it clear that references to payments by a pension scheme were to be interpreted as payments "made from sums or assets held for the purpose of the pension scheme". That set the scene for the provision in s.161(3), which stated that a payment should be interpreted as such when it was made "in connection with an investment ... acquired using sums or assets held for the purposes of a registered pension scheme". In the appellant's case, it was clear that the shares in K acquired by H were such an investment. It was also apparent that the investment was inextricably linked to the loan made by G. The entire arrangement had been orchestrated from beginning to end to ensure that the appellant received his expected loan as a result of transferring his pension funds to H and instructing it to invest them in K. There was nothing objectionable about a loan being advanced to a pension scheme member on the basis that they were expected to repay that loan out of, for example, an anticipated tax-free cash lump sum arising under the pension arrangements. However, the appellant's case had contained extra features not included in normal arrangements, namely the requirement to transfer his pension fund into a new scheme and authorise its investment in specified investments as a condition of accessing the loan. The loan had been an unauthorised payment within s.160(2) and was therefore subject to the income tax charge and surcharge (paras 37-41, 59, 61).

DANVERS v REVENUE AND CUSTOMS COMMISSIONERS, [2016] UKFTT 3 (TC), [2016] Pens. L.R. 49, Judge Kevin Poole, FTT (Tax).

1585 Pension schemes–Pension benefits–Normal pensionable age–Alteration to be effected by deed

[Treaty establishing the European Economic Community 1957 (pre-Union Treaty) (as amended) 1957 art.119; Treaty on the Functioning of the European Union 2008 art.157; Pensions Act 1995 (c.26) s.62]

A company claimed against the first respondent, a representative member of its pension scheme, and the second respondent scheme trustees for a declaration that the normal pensionable age had been amended to 65 in 1991 by an announcement subsequently confirmed by a 1996 amending deed. The company's final salary benefits pension scheme was set up under a 1984 deed which stipulated a normal pensionable age (NPA) of 60 for female and 65 for male members. Clause 19 contained a power of amendment which could be applied retrospectively. As a result of the decision in *Barber v Guardian Royal Exchange Assurance Group (C-262/88)* EU:C:1990:209, [1991] 1 Q.B. 344, [1990] C.L.Y. 1915, EU law required that such schemes had to have the same NPA for all members, and that during the period until a scheme was formally amended (the "Barber window") the benefit for the disadvantaged sex had to be levelled up. The NPA for men during that period would therefore be 60. The company informed members in November 1991 that the NPA for women was shortly to be raised to 65 to match that of men. The company effected those changes in December 1991. Subsequently those amendments were formalised in a deed dated 2 May 1996, which wholly superseded the 1984 trust deed and rules. At the time, the principle of equal pay was laid down in EC Treaty art.119 (now TFEU art.157) which required benefits in respect of service from 17 May 1990 until 30 November 1991 to be equal. The issue was whether the 1991 announcement and letters had been effective to introduce a common NPA of 65 so as to satisfy the requirements of EU equality law in respect of service after 1 December 1991 and, if not, whether the NPA for men, the disadvantaged class, had been levelled up by law to 60 to match that of the advantaged class of women for the period between December 1991 and the date of the 1996 deed. A very considerable sum depended on the answer. The company submitted that (1) the effect of cl.19 of the 1984 deed was to make the 1991 announcements and letters effective to alter the members' benefits and that amendment was retrospectively confirmed by the 1996 deed; (2) if not, then the Pensions Act 1995 s.62 from its entry into force on 1 January 1996 had brought about the required equal treatment by law so that art.119 had no relevance to the validity of the 1996 deed.

Held: Judgment for defendants. (1) Clause 19 was clear and unambiguous in that any alteration or addition to the trust's powers and provisions of the scheme had to be effected by deed. The 1991 notices had not changed the normal pensionable age of women. They were only effective in conjunction with the amending power of the 1996 deed, even if under domestic law the relevant amendment could take effect from 1991. The announcements could not therefore constitute "measures" sufficient to comply with the EU legal requirement concerning equal treatment without the endorsement of the 1996 deed, *Barber* applied (see paras 115, 120-125, 129 of judgment). (2) *Smith v Avdel Systems Ltd (C-408/92)* EU:C:1994:349, [1994] E.C.R. I-4435, [1995] C.L.Y. 1998 had decided that it was wrong in principle to reduce benefits to equalise treatment during "the Barber window". It was not possible to distinguish *Avdel* on the basis of a difference in the wording of the respective powers of amendment, *Avdel* applied. There was also a general principle against retrospective levelling down in the line of EU cases, *Harland & Wolff Pension Trustees Ltd v Aon Consulting Financial Services Ltd* [2006] EWHC 1778 (Ch), [2007] I.C.R. 429, [2006] C.L.Y. 2960 applied and *Coloroll Pension Trustees Ltd v Russell (C-200/91)* EU:C:1994:348, [1994] E.C.R. I-4389, [1995] C.L.Y. 2001 considered. The company's purpose could not be achieved by levelling up the benefits for men and then using cl.19 to reduce the equalised benefit without infringement of art.119. It was impossible to divorce the two steps and to say that the first step constituted the "measures" required by EU law but that the second step could be ignored. Even if s.62 operated as if the scheme had already been amended, it did not fully implement art.119 so as to eliminate any further reliance by a member on its direct effect. The 1996 deed was ineffective to retrospectively introduce a common NPA of 65 for men and women from 1 December 1991 to 2 May 1996 and both men and women were entitled to benefits in respect of that period based on an NPA of age 60 (paras 140-146, 150-153).

SAFEWAY LTD v NEWTON, [2016] EWHC 377 (Ch), [2016] Pens. L.R. 79, Warren J, Ch D.

1586 Pension schemes–Rectification–Mistake–Deed of amendment did not reflect intention of parties

The claimant company applied for summary judgment on its claim for rectification of a deed of amendment to a pension scheme. The company and the pension trustees had resolved to amend the rules of the scheme in 1998 to reduce the rate at which annual increases were made to benefits in payment and in deferment. By mistake the administrators of the scheme drafted the deed of amendment so that it changed the benefits in payment only. The first defendant beneficiary of the pension scheme did not oppose the relief sought.

Held: Judgment for claimant. The first defendant was an appropriate person to represent the members of the scheme and he was right to accept that, on the evidence before the court, there was no arguable defence to the claim nor other good reason for the trial to take place. Every possible defence had been investigated and rejected. The evidence leading up to and post-dating the deed compellingly established that a mistake had been made in drafting the deed. The intention of the company and the trustees to amend the pension scheme in relation to benefits in payment and in deferment had been defeated, *IBM Pension Plan, Re* [2012] EWHC 2766 (Ch), [2012] Pens. L.R. 469, [2013] C.L.Y. 2168 applied. The court granted the declaration sought (see paras 23-26, 28-29 of judgment).

HOGG ROBINSON PLC v HARVEY, [2016] EWHC 129 (Ch), [2016] Pens. L.R. 61, Timothy Fancourt QC, Ch D.

1587 Pension schemes–Rectification–Rectification of pension deed

[Pensions Act 1995 (c.26)]

The claimant employer and trustee applied unopposed for summary judgment in a claim for rectification of a pension deed through the adoption of a replacement definitive deed. The claimants' pension scheme, which had been established on January 1 1959, had provided for pension benefits on a defined contribution basis and on a defined benefit basis. Following the coming into force of the Pensions Act 1995, the claimants instructed their pension administrators in 1996 to prepare a new deed to implement the minimum changes necessary, which came into effect in 2001. The 2001 deed was intended to amend two rules in the schedule to the deed: the relevant rules governed the normal retirement pension and were amended to reflect a definitive increase on April 6 1997 at the lesser of 5% pa compound interest or the relevant percentage increase in the retail price index, which was an increase from 3%. The deed failed, by mutual mistake, to distinguish between pensionable service falling before and after April 6 1997. In support of the contention that there had been a mutual mistake, the claimants relied on various contemporaneous documents as reflecting the common intention of the parties, including: a letter from the administrators to the trustees in October 1996 confirming what had been decided in a meeting between the trustees and the company, namely that a distinction between pre and post-April 1997 pensionable service had been intended; letters sent to members telling them of the differences in benefit prior to and post-April 1997, and extracts from actuarial valuation reports. The issues were whether (1) rectification should be granted; (2) it was right that the scheme should bear the costs of the instant application, in light of the claimants' separate claim against the adminstrators for tortious damages.

Held: Rectification granted. (1) The party seeking rectification had to show that: the parties had a common continuing intention, whether or not amounting to an agreement, in respect of a particular matter in the instrument to be rectified; there was an outward expression of accord; the intention continued at the time of the execution of the instrument sought to be rectified, and that, by mistake, the instrument did not reflect that common intention, *Chartbrook Ltd v Persimmon Homes Ltd* [2007] EWHC 409 (Ch), [2007] 1 All E.R. (Comm) 1083, [2007] C.L.Y. 806 followed and *CIT Group (UK) Ltd v Gazzard* [2014] EWHC 2557 (Ch) considered. The contemporaneous documents all pointed in the one direction that there was to be a split in the maximum increases: the various witnesses' evidence supported that contention too. The criteria for rectification of the deed with the replacement definitive deed had been made out: the changes had been only those required by the 1995 Act, and no one had given the deed a contrary construction. Further support for that conclusion had been the way in which the scheme had been administered. The defendant had no prospect of successfully defending the claim and there was no reason why the claim ought to proceed to trial. (2) The court questioned whether it was appropriate that the scheme should bear the costs of the instant application, which were to be decided on an indemnity basis if not agreed. The usual order in a case such as the instant was that the costs be borne by the fund: the administrators could, however, argue that they did not owe a duty of care to the company and were therefore not liable for the company's costs. In that light, it seemed right that the fund should bear the costs in order to forestall that possibility in the separate proceedings. The court's concern that the scheme would be thereby depleted was assuaged by the fact that there would be a small surplus in the current year so that any increases would be limited to a maximum of 3% or 5% under the deed as rectified.

ST MODWEN PROPERTIES PLC v HERBERT, [2016] EWHC 428 (Ch), [2016] Pens. L.R. 113, Rose J, Ch D.

1588 Pension schemes–State retirement pension–Contracting out

THE PENSIONS ACT 2014 (ABOLITION OF CONTRACTING-OUT FOR SALARY RELATED PENSION SCHEMES) (CONSEQUENTIAL AMENDMENTS AND SAVINGS) ORDER 2016, SI 2016/200; made under the Pensions Act 2014 s.53, s.54(5)(6). In force: In accordance with art.1.

The Pensions Act 2014 creates a new state pension for people reaching pensionable age after implementation on 6 April 2016. The new pension will be paid at a single weekly rate, replacing the current state pension which has two components: a basic state pension and an additional state pension. s.24 and Sch.13 of the Act therefore make amendments to existing primary legislation to abolish contracting-out of the additional state pension for salary-related pension schemes. This Order makes consequential amendments to subordinate legislation.

1589 Pension sharing–Transitional provisions–Transitional rate state pension

THE PENSIONS ACT 2014 (PENSION SHARING ON DIVORCE ETC.) (TRANSITIONAL PROVISION) ORDER 2016, SI 2016/39; made under the Pensions Act 2014 s.56(8). In force: 6 April 2016.

This is the first transitional provision Order made in respect of the Pensions Act 2014 Pt 1. It makes transitional provision in relation to the coming into force on 6 April 2016 of ss.13 to 15 of, and Schs.8 to 11 to, that Act. These provisions allow for the continuation of state pension sharing on divorce or nullity of a marriage or dissolution or annulment of a civil partnership for people who reach state pension age on or after 6 April 2016 and are entitled to the new state pension at the transitional rate.

1590 Pensions Act 2014 (c.30) Commencement No.8 Order

THE PENSIONS ACT 2014 (COMMENCEMENT NO.8) ORDER 2016, SI 2016/203; made under the Pensions Act 2014 s.56(1)(4)(7). Commencement details: bringing into operation various provisions of the 2014 Act on 23 February 2016.

This is the eighth Commencement Order made under the Pensions Act 2014. This Order brings into force provisions relating to the new state pension for people reaching pensionable age on or after 6 April 2016.

1591 Pensions management–Local government pension schemes

THE LOCAL GOVERNMENT PENSION SCHEME (MANAGEMENT AND INVESTMENT OF FUNDS) REGULATIONS 2016, SI 2016/946; made under the Public Service Pensions Act 2013 s.1(1), s.3(1)(4), Sch.3. In force: 1 November 2016.

These Regulations make provision in relation to the management and investment of pension funds held by administering authorities required to maintain such funds by the Local Government Pension Scheme Regulations 2013.

1592 Registered pension schemes–Provision of information–Consequential amendments

THE REGISTERED PENSION SCHEMES (PROVISION OF INFORMATION) (AMENDMENT) REGULATIONS 2016, SI 2016/308; made under the Finance Act 2004 s.251. In force: 6 April 2016.

These Regulations amend the Registered Pension Schemes (Provision of Information) Regulations 2006 to change information requirements for scheme administrators of a registered pension scheme in consequence of the introduction of a tapered reduction in the amount of the annual allowance for individuals with income of over £150,000 from 6 April 2016.

1593 Social security administration–State pension–Transitional rate state pension

THE STATE PENSION REVALUATION FOR TRANSITIONAL PENSIONS ORDER 2016, SI 2016/1141; made under the Social Security Administration Act 1992 s.148AC(3), s.189(1)(4). In force: In accordance with art.1.

This Order is made following a review under Social Security Administration Act 1992 (c.5) (revaluation for transitional pensions under Pensions Act 2014) s.148AC(1). This Order specifies the increase in the general level of prices during the review period as 1.0 per cent for the purposes of Social Security Administration Act 1992 ss.48AC(3) and (4) and brings into force on 19 December 2016 for the purpose of making an advance award of state pension under Social Security (Claims and Payments) Regulations 1987 reg.15.

1594 State pension–Isle of Man

THE SOCIAL SECURITY (RECIPROCAL AGREEMENT) (ISLE OF MAN) ORDER 2016, SI 2016/157; made under the Social Security Administration Act 1992 s.179(1)(a)(2)(3)(5), s.189(4)(5)(6). In force: 6 April 2016.

Part 1 of the Pensions Act 2014 creates a new benefit called state pension to which people in the UK reaching pensionable age on or after 6 April 2016 may be entitled.

This Order provides that the Social Security Administration Act 1992, the Social Security Contributions and Benefits Act 1992, Pt 1 of the Pensions Act 2014 and regulations made under those Acts or that Part, are to be modified to give effect to the provisions of the Agreement made with the Government of the Isle of Man set out in the Schedule to this Order.

1595 State pension–Social security–Reciprocal agreements

THE SOCIAL SECURITY (RECIPROCAL AGREEMENTS) ORDER 2016, SI 2016/158; made under the Social Security Administration Act 1992 s.179(1)(b)(2)(5) , s.189(4)(5). In force: 6 April 2016.

Part 1 of the Pensions Act 2014 creates a new benefit called state pension to which people reaching pensionable age on or after 6 April 2016 may be entitled. This Order provides that Pt 1 of the Pensions Act 2014, regulations made under it and other social security legislation, are to be modified to give effect to: the alterations in Sch.1, which are proposed to the agreements in the Schedules to the Orders in Council listed in Sch.2; and the alterations in Sch.3, which are proposed to the agreements in the Schedules to the Orders in Council referred to in Sch.3.

1596 Trustees' powers and duties–Interpretation–Order under s.48 Administration of Justice Act 1985–Trustees permitted to administer trust on basis of court's construction of trust deed

[Administration of Justice Act 1985 (c.61) s.48, s.48(1)(b)]

The trustee of an occupational pension plan sought an order under the Administration of Justice Act 1985 s.48 authorising it to administer the plan in a particular way. The plan had been established in 1996 by an interim trust deed. A final trust deed and rules were drawn up in 1998 and a deed of alteration was entered into in 2005. In 2011 a consolidated trust deed was executed. Rule 23 of the original rules, which dealt with annual pension increases, became r.22 of the consolidated rules. However, some of the words from the original r.23 were omitted from the new r.22. The trustee claimed that that resulted in confusion about how, in any particular case, the annual pension increase should be calculated. Having obtained an opinion from leading pensions counsel in accordance with s.48(1)(b) of the Act, it contended that r.22 should be construed as if it included the words included in the original r.23. The Pensions Act 1995 s.67 prevented it from unilaterally amending r.22 because, if r.22 did not mean what the trustee thought it meant, the amendment might have a significant financial effect on individual members of the plan. Therefore, the trustee sought an order authorising him to administer the plan on the basis that r.22 contained the omitted words.

Held: Application granted. (1) The same principles of construction applied to pension scheme documents as to any other documents, *ICM Computer Group Ltd v Stribley* [2013] EWHC 2995 (Ch), [2013] Pens. L.R. 409, [2014] C.L.Y. 2278 applied. The question was what meaning would be conveyed to a reasonable reader in possession of all the background knowledge reasonably available to the parties when the instrument was executed. The courts would correct mistakes as a matter of construction as long as the mistake was clear on the face of the instrument and it was clear what correction was required to cure it, *Chartbrook Ltd v Persimmon Homes Ltd* [2009] UKHL 38, [2009] 1 A.C. 1101, [2009] C.L.Y. 722 followed. In deciding whether there was a clear mistake, the court was not confined to reading the document without regard to its background or context, and earlier contractual documents, though not drafts produced in negotiation, could be used as part of the background, *Cherry Tree Investments Ltd v Landmain Ltd* [2012] EWCA Civ 736, [2013] Ch. 305, [2013] C.L.Y. 2454 applied. That said, the principles outlined in *Chartbrook* were not a broad invitation for the courts to rewrite commercial contracts, *ING Bank NV v Ros Roca SA* [2011] EWCA Civ 353, [2012] 1 W.L.R. 472, [2012] C.L.Y. 627 followed. The court would not, as a matter of construction, read into a document whole clauses omitted in error if the document made sense without them, *Cherry Tree* applied (see paras 19-23 of judgment). (2) While the trustee's subjective intention and the fact that he had been administering the plan as if r.22 contained the omitted words was not admissible on the question of construction, the terms of the original rules and the 2005 deed of alteration were admissible background, *KPMG v Network Rail Infrastructure Ltd* [2007] EWCA Civ 363, [2007] Bus. L.R. 1336, [2007] C.L.Y. 2748 followed. It was self-evident that there had been a mistake in the drafting of r.22. Both on its face and read in light of the background and context, it did not make sense and represented a radical change to the plan. Such a radical change would not have been intended as part of a consolidation exercise. If it had been, it would have been preceded by detailed advice, financial modelling and consultation with members. The nature of the mistake and the construction necessary to cure it were obvious, and the fact that the correction involved reading a whole sub-paragraph into r.22 did not offend against the *Cherry Tree* principle. The inclusion of that sub-paragraph was necessary to make the consolidated rules work (paras 28-34). (3) It was appropriate to authorise the trustee to administer the plan on the basis that r.22 included the omitted words. However, in making an order under s.48 the court was not making any declaration or granting any relief that bound the plan's members or potential beneficiaries. They were not parties to the s.48 proceedings and no representation order had been made. The order would protect the trustee against any complaint that, by administering the plan in accordance with the court's construction of r.22, it was wrongly administering it. However, members were free to contend that a different construction of r.22 should apply (paras 35-36). (4) It would be wrong in principle to make the s.48 order conditional upon the giving of notice to members or the granting of liberty to apply to set it aside. The order did not bind members and its implementation would maintain the increases in the benefits that the trustee had been paying. However, the trustee would be required to notify the members of the order and the reasons for it. While there should be some scope for dispensing with or modifying the notification requirement in an appropriate case, if a s.48 order directly related to the level of benefits payable to the members then they were to be told of it unless there were compelling reasons to the contrary. In the instant case, the trustee proposed that notice be given in its next planned communication to the members. That was a sensible and proportionate method of notification, provided that an appropriate form of wording was used; any electronic communication contained a link to the order and the judgment, any hard-copy communication offered to provide hard copies of the judgment and order; and both types of communication offered hard copies of all the non-confidential evidence before the court (paras 41-43).

BCA PENSION TRUSTEES LTD, RE, [2015] EWHC 3492 (Ch), [2016] 4 W.L.R. 5, Snowden J, Ch D.

PERSONAL INJURY

1597 Causes of action–Asbestos–Joint tortfeasors–Actionable injury resulting from totality of exposure

In a claim for general damages for asbestos-induced diffuse pleural thickening, where the claimant had died and his claim was pursued by his executor, the court was required to determine issues of contribution and apportionment, and to assess damages. The deceased had been exposed to asbestos during the 1950s and early 1960s during periods of employment with each of the three defendants. He had issued proceedings against all three, but only the second defendant had been served because the other two had no insurance. The deceased's death was unrelated to his asbestos-induced disease. Medical evidence was undisputed and showed an overall disability of between 70% and 80%. The pleural thickening was agreed to account for 5% of that disability. It had not prevented him from doing things which he would otherwise have been able to achieve, nor had it necessitated a significantly increased level of care. Its impact upon the deceased's life expectancy was agreed at between one and three months. It was also agreed that the second defendant had contributed 8.16% of the deceased's total asbestos exposure. The issues were whether the deceased (1) had proved that he had suffered an actionable injury resulting from the totality of his exposure to asbestos; (2) needed to prove that the second defendant had made a material contribution giving rise to a discernible or measurable injury.

Held: Judgment for claimant. (1) The overall 5% disability was clearly actionable notwithstanding the deceased's other medical conditions. A contribution of 8.16% to that actionable injury was small but nevertheless material (see para.31 of judgment). (2) A suggestion that claimants had to go on to prove that the particular contribution gave rise to a discernible or measurable injury, as maintained by the second defendant, was unwarranted and unsupported by authority. Such a requirement would ignore the totality of the exposure during a claimant's working life and the quantifiable disability caused by that exposure. It would not accord with either the reality of the industrial disease or with common sense, and it would lead to uncertainty, unfairness, and arbitrary results. In the instant case, the medical evidence and percentage calculations of the individual contributions demonstrated that none of the separate contributions of the three defendants would have been perceptible by the deceased. Accepting the second defendant's submissions would mean that the deceased had no cause of action despite suffering an actionable injury. The court in *Holtby v Brigham & Cowan (Hull) Ltd* [2000] 3 All E.R. 421, [2000] C.L.Y. 5114 had never intended such an outcome and the decision could not be said to lend support to the second defendant's submissions, *Holtby* explained and *Carder v Secretary of State for Health* [2015] EWHC 2399 (QB) applied (paras 21-22, 32-34). (3) The correct approach to assessing damages was to assess the damages otherwise awardable for the 5% disability and then to apportion an amount to the second defendant relative to its contribution to the overall asbestos exposure. The appropriate award was 8.16% of £12,600, namely £1,208 (paras 35-36).

MAYNE v ATLAS STONE CO LTD, [2016] EWHC 1030 (QB), [2016] I.C.R. 957, Cox J, QBD.

1598 Clinical negligence–Babies–Birth management–Death of baby due to aspiration of meconium

A mother and father brought claims against an NHS trust for damages for bereavement and psychiatric injuries following the death of their baby. The mother arrived at hospital in labour at 08.00. A cardiotocograph (CTG) was started at 08.27. A slightly accelerated foetal heart rate, albeit still within the normal range, was recorded. There were decelerations in the fetal heart rate from 08.56, which were attributed to maternal vomiting. The heart rate recovered partially but did not return to its earlier level. The membranes were ruptured at 10.00 and it was noted that the baby had passed meconium. However, according to the NICE Guidance, that was not necessarily an indication for a caesarean section. The CTG trace was reviewed again at 10.20 and was noted to have improved. At 10.40 the CTG was abnormal. It was reviewed at 10.45. An attempt was made at obtaining a foetal blood sample, in accordance with the NICE Guidance, but that was unsuccessful. At 11.15, a decision was taken to perform a caesarean section. The baby was delivered at 11.53 with no signs of respiratory effort and was pronounced dead. The parents' expert stated that the CTG trace at 08.48 showed a "wavy" unstable baseline foetal heart rate indicating ongoing hypoxia, and was highly critical of the decision to undertake a foetal blood sample. The parents claimed that, in view of the CTG readings and the clinical picture, any reasonable doctor would have carried out a caesarean section in response to the 08.56 deceleration. The trust denied liability.

Held: Judgment for defendant. (1) The evidence of the parents' expert as to whether all reasonable practitioners should have carried out a caesarean section in response to the 08.56 deceleration did not indicate that he had appreciated the differences between best practice, reasonable practice and practices which no reasonable practitioner would carry out. His reference to the "wavy" nature of the CTG trace appeared to have been formulated with the benefit of hindsight and was not indicative of any real appreciation of how a reasonable doctor might interpret that trace. Moreover, there was nothing in the NICE Guidance to suggest that the "wavy" nature of the CTG was likely to be a problem. Accordingly, the care provided to the mother during or in response to the 08.56 deceleration could not be criticised. Nor was there any indication of hypoxia which should have been apparent to the reasonable practitioner. The fact that the NICE Guidance suggested that a foetal blood sample should be taken was strong evidence of the reasonableness of undertaking that procedure. The parents' expert had been influenced by hindsight and had placed interpretations on the CTG which would not have been shared by a reasonable practitioner at the time. Accordingly, there had been no breach of duty on the trust's part (see paras 28, 63-65, 67, 69-70, 72 of judgment). (2) Having regard to the findings of the post mortem examination, aspiration of meconium was likely to have occurred at some time after 11.00. Therefore, if there had been a culpable failure at 10.20 to make the decision to carry out a caesarean section, which would have been performed by 10.50, causation would have been established (para.77). (3) Had negligence been established, the mother would have been a primary victim because the aspiration of the meconium, and therefore the negligence, would have occurred at a time when the mother and child were still one person. Had liability been established, the mother would have been entitled to general damages for the adjustment disorder that she suffered after her baby's death. The father would have been a secondary victim if it were found that there had been a sudden, shocking event arising from witnessing the death of or extreme danger to his child, *Liverpool Women's Hospital NHS Foundation Trust v Ronayne* [2015] EWCA Civ 588, [2015] P.I.Q.R. P20, [2015] C.L.Y. 1799 followed. However, there was no such shocking event in the sense of an assault on the senses or sudden appreciation. The father's claim for psychiatric injury would therefore have been rejected (paras 83-86).

WELLS v UNIVERSITY HOSPITAL SOUTHAMPTON NHS FOUNDATION TRUST, [2015] EWHC 2376 (QB), [2015] Med. L.R. 477, Dingemans J, QBD (Winchester).

1599 Clinical negligence–Causation–Brain damage at birth–Delay in delivery

A child, acting by his mother and litigation friend, claimed damages for injury and loss caused by the defendant's alleged negligent mismanagement of his birth, which resulted in him suffering brain damage and spastic cerebral palsy. The child's case was that there had been negligent delay at the end of his mother's labour in that the midwives failed to realise, owing to inadequate monitoring, that his heartbeat had dropped to a dangerous level. He alleged that once they had discovered the problem, they should have called for medical assistance minutes earlier than they did, and that the doctor who then arrived should have decided to perform an emergency caesarean section at least two minutes before she did. His case was that but for the negligent delay, his delivery would have been between six and nine minutes earlier, which would have been sufficient to reduce the period of damaging hypoxia to a materially less damaging injury.

Held: Judgment for defendant. (1) On the evidence there had been a maximum of three minutes of negligent delay in the child's delivery. The child failed to prove that, absent that delay, his brain damage would not have been sustained, or that the damage would have had a materially less severe impact on his ability and capacity. Even on his case that there had been a delay of six to nine minutes, the expert evidence was that his motor functions would not have been materially different. Although there was understood to be a relationship between the duration of an acute profound hypoxic episode and the severity of the resulting brain injury, the relationship was not simple to define. Before his birth, the child was apparently a healthy and robust foetus. In fact, he suffered hypoxia for at least 39 minutes, but probably longer. Making an allowance for the generally accepted 10 minutes of non-harmful hypoxia, he had suffered at least 29 minutes of injurious hypoxia. He displayed a less profound injury than might have been expected after that period of exposure. Common sense suggested that a reduction in exposure by six to nine minutes would have made a difference to the child's cognitive abilities, but it was difficult to be certain that the difference would have been material. On the balance of probabilities, a saving of nine minutes would have made a material difference but a saving of six minutes would have made a proportionally minor difference. A saving of three minutes would have had no impact (see paras 150, 196-197 of judgment).

DS v NORTHERN LINCOLNSHIRE AND GOOLE NHS FOUNDATION TRUST, [2016] EWHC 1246 (QB), [2016] Med. L.R. 339, Cheema-Grubb J, QBD.

1600 Clinical negligence–Causation–Diabetic eye disease–Surgeon entitled to treat intraocular pressure medically rather than by operating

The claimant brought a claim for damages for personal injuries suffered as a result of the alleged clinical negligence of staff at an eye hospital operated by the defendant NHS trust. The claimant, who was born in 1978, was diagnosed at the age of 10 with diabetes. In 2000, bilateral background diabetic retinopathy was noted. The claimant's condition deteriorated over the next few years and he was treated by a consultant ophthalmic surgeon (S1). In 2008, the claimant's vision was getting worse and S1 diagnosed aggressive neovascular disease. He performed a left vitrectomy and indirect laser treatment on the claimant's right eye. Ten days later, the claimant experienced pain in his left eye and attended the hospital. A different consultant ophthalmic surgeon (S2) at the hospital advised treating the intraocular pressure (IOP) in the claimant's left eye with drugs. When the claimant saw S1 a few days later, he was told that he would have operated within 24 hours of medical treatment if the pressure had not alleviated. S1 perfomed a left vitrectomy the following day but the claimant's sight in his left eye did not improve. The claimant was referred to a specialist for his right eye in 2009 but the decision was made not to operate on it. The claimant had hemorrhages in his right eye in 2011 and an operation was performed on his right eye in 2013 which was only of limited success. The claimant had lost 90 per cent of his vision with a 25 per cent chance of loss of all functional vision over the next 10 years. The claimant submitted that (1) the defendant and its employees were negligent in failing to operate within 24 hours of the medical treatment; (2) if his left eye had been treated effectively, there would have been earlier treatment and surgery on his right eye so that he would have suffered less loss of vision. The defendant contended that the medical treatment was reasonable in the circumstances and that the claimant would have lost useful vision in any event due to his diabetic eye disease.

Held: Judgment for defendant. (1) S2 had a reasonable belief that the claimant was suffering from suprachoroidal hemorrhage which would increase the complications of surgery. S1's evidence did not rule out the possibility that, though he would have performed surgery earlier, a different view could have been taken by a responsible clinician. S2 was not negligent in pursuing the medical treatment. It was a logical and justifiable clinical judgment. The contention that surgery was mandatory was rejected. Whilst the claimant's elevated IOP involved risks, surgery also carried risks and it was reasonable to regard the risks of surgery as outweighing the risks of medical treatment, albeit a responsible body of opthalmological opinion might have taken a different view. S2 accepted that he had not offered the claimant the alternative option of surgery but the claimant had given evidence that he would have followed medical advice which would have been to proceed with medical treatment. The claimant had not established that the breach of duty to advise a patient had caused any loss or damage. It had not been established that the cause of loss of vision in the claimant's left eye was the period when he suffered elevated IOP as opposed to damage arising from his proliferative diabetic retinopathy but it had made a contribution to it. It was not accepted that the claimant's sight would have been better in his left eye if surgery had been performed in 24 hours (see paras 127, 140, 151, 158, 160, 163-164, 169, 178-179 of judgment). (2) The fact that there was no vision in the claimant's left eye played a part in the medical decisions with regard to his right eye but there was no causal link between the alleged negligence and the loss of vision in the right eye. The loss of vision was solely the consequence of the proliferative retinopathy. Earlier decisions not to operate on the right eye were made on the basis of the state of the right eye at the time (paras 181, 196).

BARRETT v SANDWELL AND WEST BIRMINGHAM HOSPITALS NHS TRUST, [2015] EWHC 2627 (QB), (2016) 147 B.M.L.R. 151, Blair J, QBD (Birmingham).

1601 Clinical negligence–Causation–Judge's findings as to cause of injury to patient's femoral nerve–Judge had not drawn unlawful inferences

An NHS trust appealed against a decision that one of its surgeons had negligently caused injury to the respondent patient's left femoral nerve during an abdominal operation. The patient had developed a vesicovaginal fistula and a surgeon employed by the trust had operated to repair it. He did so by cutting open the abdomen and using a device to hold the abdomen wall open. In order to repair the fistula, he needed to move the sigmoid colon out of the way. That involved dissecting the colon from the pelvic wall and dissecting the colon from the vaginal side of the fistula. After the operation, it emerged that the patient had sustained injury to the left femoral nerve. Various experts agreed that the most likely cause of the injury was some form of surgical trauma. Some experts originally considered that the injury could have been caused by the device used to hold the abdomen wall open. They also indicated that it could have been caused by dissection of the sigmoid colon, but described that as less likely. However, they later discounted the possibility of the injury being caused by the device on the basis of the surgeon's description of the manner in which he had used the device. A pain management expert initially expressed the view that the regional anaesthetic block administered during the operation had caused the damage but subsequently decided that was unlikely after learning about the technique used by the consultant who had anaesthetised the patient. At trial, the trust applied for permission to call an expert anaesthetist. The judge refused permission and the trial went ahead. The judge found that the injury to the femoral nerve had been negligently caused during the process of dissection. The trust submitted that the judge: (1) had erred in refusing the application to adduce additional expert evidence; (2) ought to have found that the dissection was one of two possible explanations, the other being the anaesthetic block.

Held: Appeal dismissed. (1) The views of the expert witnesses had developed as more factual evidence became available and as discussions between them proceeded. The fact that some of the experts had changed their opinions did not entitle the trust to bring in a new expert witness. Further, the application for permission to call an additional expert was made at the latest possible stage. Granting the application would have meant adjourning the trial with consequential delay and massive extra costs. That could not be justified, *Denton v TH White Ltd* [2014] EWCA Civ 906, [2014] 1 W.L.R. 3926, [2014] C.L.Y. 454 applied (see paras 48-54 of judgment). (2) Where a trial judge heard direct evidence and made findings of fact, appellate courts would seldom interfere. Where, however, the judge made findings based on inference, an appellate court might, in an appropriate case, examine the judge's process of inference. The judge had not misinterpreted or read too much into the expert evidence. There were inconsistencies between the evidence of the surgeon who operated on the patient and that of one of the experts in relation to the likelihood of causing direct damage to the femoral nerve during dissection. However, both parties had the opportunity to put the surgeon's evidence to the expert during cross-examination. The judge had preferred the expert's evidence and the appellate court could not go behind that. The judge had gone beyond the evidence in referring to "possible difficulties with visualisation" in the use of the device. However, that was not a significant factor in his overall decision. The judge had not misinterpreted a letter which the surgeon had sent to the patient's GP and had merely referred to that letter as providing some support for the conclusions which he had reached on the basis of other evidence. The judge had been entitled to entirely dismiss the anaesthetic explanation. He had received a range of different views on that matter and had assessed them and reached a conclusion for which there was abundant support. He had not been obliged to keep the anaesthetic explanation in play as a possible, though unlikely, cause of the injury. He had not based his crucial finding of blunt trauma injury during the dissection stage simply on the fact that all other possible explanations had been eliminated. He had based that finding on the totality of the evidence which he heard. He had treated the absence of any other plausible explanation as supporting his conclusion, not as providing the sole basis for it. The fact that the trust had not proffered any plausible explanation for the patient's injury consistent with the exercise of due care did not convert the case into one of res ipsa loquitur. Nor did it reverse the burden of proof. Nevertheless, it was a material factor which the judge had been entitled to take into account. The judge had in mind the limitations of res ipsa loquitur and the principles set out in *Rhesa Shipping Co SA v Edmunds (The Popi M)* [1985] 1 W.L.R. 948, [1985] C.L.Y. 3207. He had made his finding on the balance of probabilities, without relying upon res ipsa loquitur, *Ratcliffe v Plymouth and Torbay HA* [1998] P.I.Q.R. P170, [1998] C.L.Y. 3972 and *Thomas v Curley* [2013] EWCA Civ 117, [2013] Med. L.R. 141, [2013] C.L.Y. 2191 applied, *Rhesa Shipping* followed (paras 63-64, 72-73, 75-87).

O'CONNOR v PENNINE ACUTE HOSPITALS NHS TRUST, [2015] EWCA Civ 1244, [2016] Med. L.R. 11, Jackson LJ, CA (Civ Div).

1602 Clinical negligence–Cerebral palsy–Court ordered interim payment to 13-year-old boy

The claimant (L) applied for an interim payment in his claim against the defendant NHS trust for damages for clinical negligence. L was aged 13. He had suffered hypoglycaemia following his birth, which the trust failed to treat appropriately. He suffered serious neurological damage resulting in cerebral palsy, learning difficulties, epilepsy, visual problems and behavioural problems. The trust admitted liability. An interim payment of £250,000 was made in 2014. A trial to assess damages was listed for February 2017 and L served a schedule of loss calculated up to that date. L's behavioural problems increased; it was unclear whether they meant that he would need one or two carers. The cost difference between one and two carers was £2.5 million. The 2017 hearing was vacated and the claim stayed so that the position could become clearer. L sought a further interim payment of £1.75 million. The trust considered that the interim payment should not exceed £1 million.

Held: Application granted in part. The court could have a high degree of confidence that accommodation costs would be awarded as a capital sum. Thus, in stage 1 of the process for ordering interim payments described in *Eeles v Cobham Hire Services Ltd* [2009] EWCA Civ 204, [2010] 1 W.L.R. 409, [2009] C.L.Y. 414, it was appropriate to consider, on a conservative basis, the likely awards for general damages, special damages, interest and accommodation costs. A trial was likely to be able to take place in June 2020; the instant application would be approached by first determining the likely capital award on a conservative basis as at that date. The court would assess a conservative figure for each head of loss, rather than apply an overall percentage reduction to the figures (see paras 16-18 of judgment). *General damages:* L's injuries fell within the category of moderately severe brain injury. The appropriate award was £200,000; with interest up to June 2020 it was £228,000 (para.20). *Past losses up to February 2017:* Family care: £162,000 reflected the hours of extra care provided by L's parents above those a child would normally need, and reflected the fact that a lower rate than a commercial rate was appropriate, because the care had been provided by L's parents. Miscellaneous losses: £60,000 for the purchase of a Land Rover and the cost of a holiday. Equipment costs: £4,253. Costs of deputyship and Court of Protection: £8,398. Accommodation costs: £10,000. Interest: The total of past losses was £244,000. L had claimed 22% interest, but that was reduced to 15% to give credit for the 2014 interim payment, the interim payment to be made as a result of the instant application, and the length of time over which losses had occurred. Interest of 15% produced £36,600. Total past losses: £281,000 (paras 21-27). *Future losses between February 2017 and June 2020:* Such losses had to be assessed as they would form part of the past losses as at the predicted trial date. Care and case management: It was likely that the trial judge would allow for paid carers including sleep-in care for four or five nights per week, with perhaps a small daily amount of extra care by the parents. The care costs would be £295,000. Costs of deputyship and Court of Protection: £46,500. Aids and equipment: £35,000. Transport: £5,000. Therapies: £31,375, covering psychological input for L's behavioural problems and speech therapy. Extra cost of holidays: £18,000. Education appeal: L had claimed £25,000 in respect of the legal costs of a possible appeal regarding his educational placement. That was highly speculative and would not be awarded. Assistive technology: £10,000. Total losses between February 2017 and June 2020: £440,875 (paras 28-39). *Accommodation costs for life:* It was reasonable for L to purchase a property now for his long term needs. Taking a multiplier of 31.2 and having regard to the parties' arguments that L had a life expectancy of 78 and that, but for his injuries, he would have rented a property until age 30, when he would have bought a property, a total of £707,000 was assessed, *Roberts v Johnstone* [1989] Q.B. 878, [1989] C.L.Y. 1202 followed (paras 40-46). The *Eeles* stage 1 total was £1.66 million, less than the amount sought by way of interim payment. The question arose of whether, under Eeles stage 2, elements of future loss could be included in assessing the likely final capital amount so as to bring the total above the amount sought. The court did not have a high degree of confidence that the trial judge would award future loss by way of a capital sum, and there was no real need for an interim payment in the amount sought, *Eeles* followed. There would be an interim payment of £1.1 million; when that was added to the £250,000 already paid, the interim payments represented 81% of the total likely capital award. That interim payment would not fetter the discretion of the trial judge (paras 48-49).

LAT (A CHILD) v EAST SOMERSET NHS TRUST, [2016] EWHC 1610 (QB), [2016] Med. L.R. 438, Judge Reddihough, QBD.

1603 Clinical negligence–Findings of fact–Judge entitled to prefer evidence of patient over medical notes of a ward round

The defendant NHS trust appealed against a finding of fact made by the trial judge in the claimant's action for clinical negligence. The claimant, who had had rectal cancer which had resulted in his having a stoma and colostomy bag, attended the trust's hospital suffering from abdominal pain and a history of non-functioning stoma. He was diagnosed as suffering from a parastomal hernia with sub-acute obstruction. A consultant general surgeon, assisted by a surgical registrar (Z), conducted a laparoscopic repair of the parastomal hernia with mesh repair. The claimant alleged clinical negligence by both doctors, but the instant appeal was concerned only with the claim in respect of Z. The claimant's discharge was scheduled for two days after the operation. On that day, Z saw the claimant on a morning ward round. A note of that attendance, made by a more junior doctor (D), recorded that the claimant was "well", and that the stoma was "normal colour". The claimant was discharged later that morning. Over the next two days his pain increased until he could bear it no longer, and he returned to hospital. He had surgery to remove the stoma, which was by then necrotic and perforated, and to create a new one. He had had abnormal stoma function since. The claimant's case was that at the ward round he had been in some pain and was feeling sick, and that his stoma was much darker than its normal colour. His secondary case was that he had told Z that he was concerned about the colour of his stoma but that Z advised him that it was just bruising and not to worry. The claimant contended that he should not have been discharged but should have been kept in hospital and had further surgery, which would have led to recovery and normal stoma function. The judge accepted that case, finding that the written record of Z's attendance on the claimant at the ward round was inaccurate, while the evidence of the claimant and his wife was persuasive, and that the claimant's discharge amounted to a breach of duty. The trust submitted that that finding was one to which no rational judge could have come, as was demonstrated by the absence in the judgment of any reason for the rejection of the contemporaneous clinical record or for the preference of the demonstrably unreliable evidence of the claimant.

Held: Appeal dismissed. When assessing the evidence of witnesses about what they said, or what was said to them, or what they saw or heard, it was essential to test their veracity or reliability by reference to the objective facts proved independently of their testimony, in particular by reference to contemporary documentary evidence, *Onassis v Vergottis* [1968] 2 Lloyd's Rep. 403, [1969] C.L.Y. 3352 followed, *Grace Shipping Inc v CF Sharp (Malaya) Pte* [1987] 1 Lloyd's Rep. 207, [1987] C.L.Y. 427 applied (see para.10 of judgment). It was plain that the judge had recognised that the claimant's evidence had to be assessed in the light of the apparently contemporaneous clinical note. Indeed that note was doubly important: not only did the claimant's evidence fall to be evaluated in the light of it, it also represented the full extent of the evidence that Z could give as to what was said and observed on his ward round, as he had no other recollection of it. Simply because a document was apparently contemporary did not absolve the court of deciding whether it was reliable and what weight to give it. Some records, such as medical records, were by their nature likely to be reliable. The difficulty for the judge was that he had no evidence of the circumstances in which the medical note had been made, and no evidence from D. Furthermore, it was unclear whether D had been present when Z spoke to and examined the claimant and unclear when precisely he had prepared the note, *W v Johnson* [2015] EWHC 276 (QB) approved (paras 11-13). The judge's fact-finding process had been properly conducted. He had made proper use of the advantage afforded to him of seeing the claimant and his wife give their evidence. It might be that in the light of the wife's unchallenged evidence and in the absence of any evidence from D, the judge could hardly have reached any other conclusion. Nevertheless, his conclusion that the clinical note recording the ward round was unreliable, in fact incorrect in certain respects, was entirely open to him on the basis of the evidence and well within the ambit of reasonable decision-making. He had had in mind and weighed in the balance as part of a single compendious fact-finding exercise the inherent possibility of what he had been asked to decide. He had taken into account the totality of the evidence and in light of it he had been entitled to conclude that the clinical record was in the respects identified inaccurate (para.27).

SYNCLAIR v EAST LANCASHIRE HOSPITALS NHS TRUST, [2015] EWCA Civ 1283, [2016] Med. L.R. 1, Tomlinson LJ, CA (Civ Div).

1604 Criminal injuries compensation–Persons lacking capacity–Award held on trust–Application to Court of Protection

[Mental Capacity Act 2005 (c.9) s.16, s.20(3)(a), s.20(3)(c)]

The appellant (P), a victim of crime who lacked capacity, appealed against a decision that an order of the Court of Protection was required before the Criminal Injuries Compensation Authority (CICA) could pay an award to the trustees of a trust set up to receive the award. In 1993, when he was a baby, P had suffered non-accidental head injuries. His mother was in the pool of potential perpetrators, but the local authority was content for him to remain in her care. He would never be capable of independent living and continued to live with his mother. In 2002, a deputy appointed by the Court of Protection applied on P's behalf for compensation under CICA's compensation scheme established in 1990. CICA determined that any award should be paid into a trust. Following stays on the proceedings, an award was ordered in 2012. CICA did not pay, on the basis that an order from the Court of Protection was required to establish the necessary trust. It drafted a trust deed including a provision that the mother could not benefit from the award. A judge upheld CICA's decision to withhold payment. CICA argued that an order under the Mental Capacity Act 2005 s.16 was required to set up the trust because the applicant for the award, P, was the settlor and the award was his property; alternatively, s.20(3)(a) and/or s.20(3)(c) precluded a deputy from creating a trust of P's property, so that had to be done by court order.

Held: Appeal allowed. (1) In its practice concerning capacitous applicants, CICA did not require the applicant to make a declaration of trust. Where CICA required a declaration of trust, it was executed only by trustees. When a trust was required by CICA, that was a condition of the award. When it decided to include that condition, CICA would not pay the sum awarded to the applicant until it had been agreed by the applicant or agreed on his behalf. Those points showed that when CICA required the award to be paid to trustees, the applicant never became entitled to the award, so it was never the applicant's property to settle or deal with in another way. Instead, the trusts were created by the acceptance of the award because that finalisation of the claim provided that the award had to be paid to trustees. Accordingly, CICA's practice concerning capacitous applicants ran contrary to the judge's conclusion that the applicant was always the settlor. The question therefore arose of why a different process for creating the relevant trust was needed if the applicant lacked capacity. The Court of Protection, a deputy or an attorney would accept an award on behalf of the applicant on the basis that it was to be paid to trustees. The question was whether a deputy was precluded from doing so by s.20(3)(a) and/or s.20(3)(c). A deputy could accept an award on the applicant's behalf. Section 20(3)(c) was not directed against powers that anyone had, such as a power to accept compensation; rather, it was directed to powers conferred by something, such as a mortgage or trust. The power to accept an award from CICA was not given to the applicant by the relevant scheme but something he could do as an individual. When the applicant did not have capacity to make that decision, someone else could do it for him just as they could make a range of decisions on the applicant's behalf. Section 20(3)(a) did not prevent the deputy from accepting an award because the award did not involve the applicant's property being settled. There was no need for an application to the Court of Protection to finalise an award that CICA had decided should be held on trust. A deputy could be authorised to negotiate and finalise the terms of an award (see paras 60-83 of judgment). (2) (Obiter) It was arguable that the term preventing the mother benefiting from the award did not reflect a proper interpretation of the scheme because it had not taken account of all relevant factors having regard to the underlying purposes of the scheme and that it was unduly harsh and could present difficulties because P lived with and was cared for by his mother. There did not appear to have been a finding that the mother had inflicted the injuries; the possibility that she was a perpetrator could not be relied on to find a risk that P was likely to suffer harm in her care. There was therefore a mismatch between what had been found to be P's best interests and terms governing the award that hindered the application of the compensation to best promote his welfare. Those points merited the deputy seeking to agree different terms with CICA (paras 93-95).

V v ASSISTANT DIRECTOR ADULT SOCIAL CARE NEWCASTLE CITY COUNCIL *sub nom.* PJV v ASSISTANT DIRECTOR ADULT SOCIAL CARE NEWCASTLE CITY COUNCIL; ASSISTANT DIRECTOR ADULT SOCIAL CARE NEWCASTLE CITY COUNCIL v PJV, [2015] EWCOP 87, [2016] Fam. 229, Charles J, CP.

1605 Duty of care–Local authorities' powers and duties–Claim by children in negligence against local authority

[Children Act 1989 (c.41); Human Rights Act 1998 (c.42); European Convention on Human Rights 1950]

Two children appealed by their litigation friend against the striking out of their claims for damages in negligence against the local authority. Both children were minors and one was severely disabled and a protected party. They had both suffered prolonged abuse, and anti-social and criminal behaviour perpetrated by members of a family who lived on the same council estate. That family had been reported to the local authority for causing trouble before the children and their mother moved in. Their claim was struck out on the basis that there was no common law duty of care imposed by the Children Act 1989. It was submitted for the children that the master had wrongly struck out their claims on the ground that no duty of care arose, in reliance on the case of *X (Minors) v Bedfordshire CC* [1995] 2 A.C. 633, [1995] C.L.Y. 3452 and the Tenth Edition of "Charlesworth & Percy on Negligence".

Held: Appeal allowed. The principal issue was whether the decision in *JD v East Berkshire Community Health NHS Trust* [2003] EWCA Civ 1151, [2004] Q.B. 558, [2003] C.L.Y. 3004 had been impliedly overruled by *Mitchell v Glasgow City Council* [2009] UKHL 11, [2009] 1 A.C. 874, [2009] C.L.Y. 2848 or *Michael v Chief Constable of South Wales* [2015] UKSC 2, [2015] A.C. 1732, [2015] C.L.Y. 2062. Since the decision in *X v Bedfordshire*, which had been reached on policy grounds, *JD v East Berkshire* had reviewed the impact of the Human Rights Act 1998 on the common law principles of negligence and had determined that when considering a child's claim in negligence the court had to take into account their rights under the ECHR. Further, following developments in domestic jurisprudence, the effect of the *X v Bedfordshire* case was restricted to the core proposition that decisions by a local authority whether or not to take a child into care were not reviewable by way of a claim in negligence, *JD v East Berkshire* followed. The references to *JD v East Berkshire* in para.7 of *Mitchell* and in *Michael* were all to the appeals of the parents and did not affect the dicta of the Court of Appeal in the cases concerning the children, except for para.191 in *Michael* where in the dissenting judgment of Baroness Hale she had accepted that *JD v East Berkshire* provided an exception to the general rule that public authorities which failed to perform their duties did not owe a duty of care in negligence towards individuals who suffered harm thereby. As neither *Mitchell* nor *Michael* had implicitly overruled *JD v East Berkshire,* it remained binding authority, *Mitchell* and *Michael* considered. The children's claims had been wrongly struck out and were reinstated (see paras 40-44 of judgment).

CN v POOLE BC, [2016] EWHC 569 (QB), [2016] H.L.R. 26, Slade J, QBD.

1606 Fatal accident claims–Future loss–Correct date as at which to assess multiplier–Date of trial not date of death

[Fatal Accidents Act 1976 (c.30)]

A widower appealed against a decision (*Knauer v Ministry of Justice* [2014] EWHC 2553 (QB)) as to the damages he had been awarded for future loss following the death of his wife. The widower's wife had died from mesothelioma aged 46, having contracted it from being exposed to asbestos during her employment by the respondent ministry. The ministry admitted liability in the widower's claim brought under the Fatal Accidents Act 1976. The damages assessed included an annual figure, or multiplicand, for the value of the income and services lost as a result of the wife's death. The judge held that the multiplier, namely the number of years by which the multiplicand was to be multiplied, was to be calculated from the date of death rather than the date of trial, following the House of Lords' decisions in *Cookson v Knowles* [1979] A.C. 556, [1978] C.L.Y. 713 and *Graham v Dodds* [1983] 1 W.L.R. 808, [1983] C.L.Y. 979. The issues were (1) whether the *Cookson* and *Graham* approach properly reflected the principle of full compensation; (2) if not, whether the instant court should depart from that approach, applying the *Practice Statement (HL: Judicial Precedent)* [1966] 1 W.L.R. 1234, [1966] C.L.Y. 9921.

Held: Appeal allowed. (1) The normal approach was to calculate losses up to the date of trial and award a lump sum in respect of those. Future losses were calculated on the multiplier/multiplicand approach. The multiplier reflected the normal life expectancy of the victim, based on actuarial tables which included a discount to take account of the risk of an earlier death. There was also a discount to reflect the value to the claimant of receiving a lump sum now to cater for future losses which would have been suffered over a number of years in the future. Calculating damages for loss of dependency upon the deceased from the date of death, rather than from the date of trial, meant the claimant suffered a discount for early receipt of the money when in fact the money would not be received until after trial. That resulted in under-compensation in most cases. The current approach in fatal accidents cases involved taking a multiplier as at the date of death and then deducting from it the time which elapsed between death and trial. That mixed up a calculation based on properly considered actuarial principles with an arbitrary arithmetical deduction. The Law Commission had recommended that, as in personal injury cases, actuarially calculated multipliers should be used for calculating future losses in fatal accident cases from the date of trial. *Cookson* and *Graham* had been decided in a different era, when the calculation of damages for personal injury and death had been nothing like as sophisticated as it had become. The approach at the time, relying on the intuition of the barristers and judges in the cases, was wholly unscientific. The Ogden tables had not existed when the cases had been decided. *Wells v Wells* [1999] 1 A.C. 345, [1998] C.L.Y. 1446 had laid to rest any doubts about using the tables in the courts, *Wells* considered. The tables included fatal accident calculations based on the Law Commission's recommended approach, although they could not yet be used (see paras 6-18 of judgment). (2) The instant court should be very circumspect before invoking the *Practice Statement*. However, it had no hesitation in concluding that it should do so in the instant case. At least in the current legal climate, the application of *Cookson* and *Graham* was illogical and resulted in unfair outcomes. That had encouraged courts to distinguish them on unfair grounds, meaning that certainty and consistency were being undermined, *A v Hoare* [2008] UKHL 6, [2008] 1 A.C. 844, [2008] C.L.Y. 385 applied. Above all, the change in the legal landscape, namely *Wells* and the adoption of the Ogden tables, when taken with the other factors, gave rise to an overwhelming case for changing the law. The Act provided for over-compensation in some cases. That resulted from legislative choices, not judicial decisions. The Law Commission had recommended that they be modified by legislation. However, the instant claimant should not be deprived of the compensation to which on ordinary principles he would be entitled because some other claimants, as a result of understandable legislative choices, received more than they would on those ordinary principles. The solutions regarding those choices had to lie with Parliament. However, the law on the issue in the instant case had been made by judges; unless there was good reason to the contrary, it should be corrected by judges. The matter would not be left to Parliament to change the law. The court refused to follow *Cookson* and *Graham*: the correct date at which to assess the multiplier when fixing damages for future loss in claims under the Act should be the date of trial, not the date of death, *Cookson* and *Graham* not followed, *Practice Statement* applied (paras 23-27).

KNAUER v MINISTRY OF JUSTICE, [2016] UKSC 9, [2016] A.C. 908, Lord Neuberger PSC, SC.

1607 Fatal accident claims–General damages–Court declined to make award for loss of intangible services

[Law Reform (Miscellaneous Provisions) Act 1934 (c.41); Fatal Accidents Act 1976 (c.30)]

The court assessed damages in a claim under the Law Reform (Miscellaneous Provisions) Act 1934 and Fatal Accidents Act 1976 brought by a widow after her husband's death following a prolonged illness with mesothelioma. The deceased had been exposed to asbestos while working for the defendant between 1963 and 1964. After that period, he was self-employed. Primary liability was admitted and the claimant obtained judgment for damages to be assessed. The defendant alleged that any damages should be reduced on account of the deceased's contributory negligence during his period of self-employment. The defendant disputed certain heads of damage.

Held: Damages assessed. *Contributory negligence.* The defendant had established that the deceased was self-employed at the material time, but was unable to establish that he had breached the duty he owed himself to take reasonable care to avoid the risk associated with asbestos exposure. The allegation that the deceased was contributory negligent was rejected (see paras 31-34 of judgment). *General damages.* The Judicial College Guidelines gave a bracket of between £53,200 to £95,700 for mesothelioma cases. The instant case lay within the upper half of the most severe category for asbestos-related disease. The deceased had suffered severe pain and gross impairment of function and quality of life. His pain and suffering lasted for longer than was typical in these cases. He underwent repeated pleural drainage, repeated investigations, six cycles of chemotherapy, radiotherapy and surgical removal of parts of the pleura. His disease did not involve the peritoneum, which caused the most severe pain. The deceased had also continued working until April 2013, had tolerated the chemotherapy reasonably well, had been able to take a holiday in October 2013, and had given evidence in November 2013. His last witness statement was provided eight days before his death. The case fell in the upper half of the appropriate category, but it was not at the very top. The appropriate amount general damages was £85,000 (paras 42-47). *Funeral expenses.* It was not reasonable to claim for the cost of a memorial bench or for clothing to be worn at the funeral, *Gammell v Wilson* [1982] A.C. 27, [1981] C.L.Y. 581 followed (paras 49-50). *Probate costs.* There was no reference to probate costs in the 1934 Act and no basis on which such a claim could be read into the Act. There was no other basis for allowing probate costs (para.51). *Past loss of earnings.* The widow claimed £15,915 in respect of sick pay paid to the deceased during his lifetime by his former employers. The defendant should pay the sums claimed and the claimant would hold those sums on trust for the former employers, *Dennis v London Passenger Transport Board* [1948] 1 All E.R. 779, [1947-51] C.L.Y. 2500 applied (paras 52-54). *Bereavement award.* From April 2013, the appropriate award under the 1974 Act increased from £11,800 to £12,980 (paras 55-56). *Loss of services.* The deceased provided valuable services to his family, including gardening and general home maintenance. Considering the likely cost of having those services provided commercially, an amount of £1,500 per annum with a multiplier of five was granted (paras 62-64). *Loss of intangible benefits.* This was a claim for the inconvenience of paying for the services under the loss of services claim and using the damages to purchase them. The defendant alleged that it was not a valid head of claim. The making of such an award was increasingly commonplace. However, there was no proper jurisprudential foundation for it. Damages for personal injury were intended to put the claimant in the position they would have been had the tort not occurred. There could be no precise equivalence in money terms of every loss that flowed from an injury or a death. In the case of claims for services, the award was the best estimate of the value, rather than the cost, of services lost. The court had already made an award in respect of loss of services. That was done by estimating the cost of providing commercially what would otherwise have been provided by the deceased. The award recognised the advantages and disadvantages of having services provided commercially rather than by the deceased. There was no room for an additional award for the loss of intangible benefits over and above the claim for lost services. The claimant was seeking further compensation for the inconvenience of paying someone to do what her husband would have done voluntarily. That was a claim of the sort which bereavement damages were intended to cover, as described in William Latimer-Sayer, *Personal Injury Schedules: Calculating Damages*, 3rd edn (London: Bloomsbury Professional). Where the consequence of bereavement could be valued in financial terms it could be separate head of claim. Where they could not be financially valued, they fell to be regarded as part of bereavement damages. In those circumstances, the claim for intangible services was not a proper claim in law. Even if it were recognised in law, there was no unusual circumstance to justify an additional award, *Beesley v New Century Group Ltd* [2008] EWHC 3033 (QB) considered (paras 66-80).

MOSSON v SPOUSAL (LONDON) LTD, [2016] EWHC 53 (QB), [2016] 4 W.L.R. 28, Garnham J, QBD.

1608 **Loss of earnings–Adjustment of awards–Injury resulting in minor disability–Determination of damages for loss of future earning capacity–Appropriateness of Smith v Manchester approach**

[Equality Act 2010 (c.15)]

The Ministry of Defence appealed against a decision awarding damages (*Billett v Ministry of Defence* [2014] EWHC 3060 (QB)) after it had admitted liability in respect of a non-freezing cold injury sustained by the respondent (B). B was aged 30. He had been employed by the ministry as a lance corporal and suffered the injury in February 2009 when undertaking physical exercises in cold weather. He claimed that his condition had been caused by the army's failure to provide suitable footwear. Following treatment, he was found to be medically fit for deployment, but he left the army in October 2011. He immediately found new employment as a lorry driver. He maintained that he continued to suffer various symptoms in cold weather. The judge accepted his evidence that he had difficulty in doing various household tasks and always stayed inside in cold weather, limiting his ability to do various things such as play and engage with his children, undertake gardening and DIY, swim and play rugby. He conceded that he continued to go fishing and clay pigeon shooting all year round, but only in good weather. B's principal claim related to loss of future earning capacity. His earnings as a lorry driver were the same as his earnings before his injury. However, two experts agreed that although he had an excellent driving qualification and a good CV, if he lost his present job he would be at a disadvantage in finding new employment because of his injury. The judge found that B's injury was minor and that he was "disabled", as that term was defined in the explanatory notes to the Ogden tables, but only just. He determined B's future earning capacity by using the Ogden Tables A and B, suitably adjusted. He awarded damages for loss of future earning capacity of £99,062.04 and general damages for pain, suffering and loss of amenity of £12,500. The ministry submitted that (1) an award of £12,500 for general damages was outside the permissible range for B's minor injury; (2) B was not "disabled" within the definition in the Ogden Tables, but even if he was, damages would have been more appropriately assessed using the *Smith v Manchester* method.

Held: (1) The award for general damages might have been too high if the court had been proceeding on the basis of a minor non-freezing cold injury. However, the judge had accepted B's evidence about the continuing effects of his injury and the interference with his normal life. The instant court could not go behind the judge's findings of fact concerning his continuing symptoms. The judge had properly carried out the exercise of identifying where B's injuries fitted within the conventional framework for determining general damages. He had not moved outside the permissible bracket (see paras 44-48 of judgment). (2) The explanatory notes to the Ogden Tables stated that a person was disabled if his condition substantially limited his ability to carry out normal day to day activities within the meaning of the Equality Act 2010. However, the secretary of state's guidance notes on s.6(5) of the Act were of limited assistance because they tended towards the extreme. It was appropriate to adopt the approach set out in *Aderemi v London and South Eastern Railway Ltd* [2013] I.C.R. 591, [2013] C.L.Y. 962. B had no difficulty working as a lorry driver and could go fishing and clay pigeon shooting all year round, provided the weather was good. However, the focus had to be on what he could not do as a result of his injury. The judge had accepted that he could not undertake DIY and gardening in cold weather; that he could not play rugby or swim regularly; and that he could not play with his children outside when it was cold. In view of that, the judge had been entitled to reach the conclusion that B's injury had a substantial adverse effect on his ability to carry out normal activities and that his condition qualified as a disability, even if only just, *Aderemi* applied (paras 85-92). There would be many instances where the use of Tables A to D would be a valuable aid to determining a claimant's loss of earning capacity. However, the instant case was not one of them. Some of the bands in the tables were, of necessity, extremely wide and "disability" covered a very broad spectrum. B was at the outer fringe of that spectrum and his disability affected his ability to pursue his chosen career much less than it affected his activities outside work. Because of that, there was no rational basis for determining how the reduction factor should be adjusted. If the Ogden Tables A to B were applied without any adjustment, the result would be a hopelessly unrealistic award of about £200,000. B was pursuing his chosen career as a lorry driver with virtually no hindrance from his disability and the judge had commented that he was likely to be sought after by employers. In his case, determining an appropriate adjustment to the reduction factor was a matter of broad judgement which was no more scientific than the broad brush judgement which the court made when carrying out a *Smith v Manchester* assessment. The instant case was a classic example of a case where a conventional *Smith v Manchester* award was appropriate. An appropriate award for future loss of earnings would be two years' earnings, which amounted to £45,000 (paras 93-96, 98-100, 104).

BILLETT v MINISTRY OF DEFENCE, [2015] EWCA Civ 773, [2016] P.I.Q.R. Q1, Jackson LJ, CA (Civ Div).

1609 Measure of damages–Care costs–Pre-existing needs–Defendant liable for additional needs

The defendant NHS trusts appealed against a decision (*Reaney v University Hospital of North Staffordshire NHS Trust* [2014] EWHC 3016 (QB), [2015] P.I.Q.R. P4, [2015] C.L.Y. 1891) that they were liable for all of the claimant's care needs. The claimant at the age of 61 had contracted transverse myelitis which left her paralysed below the mid-thoracic level. As a T7 paraplegic her needs would have been met initially by the provision of a few hours care each week rising to 31.5 hours of care after the age of 75. With such care she could have led a largely independent life. However, during her hospitalisation, she had developed a number of deep pressure sores with consequent osteomyelitis, hip dislocation, serious contractures of the lower limbs and increased lower limb spasticity. Her seating posture had been permanently damaged by the hip dislocation so that she was unable to use a standard wheelchair safely. She was also left with a large area of vulnerable skin where the pressure sores had healed. As a result she needed 24 hour care from two carers. The defendants admitted negligence in relation to the pressure sores. The judge held that the defendants were liable for all of the claimant's care needs resulting from the pressure sores and their consequences. The defendants contended that they were liable for the claimant's care needs less the needs that she would have had but for the negligence.

Held: Appeal allowed. The judge should have held the defendants liable to meet the cost of the claimant's needs but only to the extent that her needs were increased as a result of the negligence, *Performance Cars v Abraham* [1962] 1 Q.B. 33, [1961] C.L.Y. 2345, *Baker v Willoughby* [1970] A.C. 467, [1970] C.L.Y. 1862 and *Halsey v Milton Keynes General NHS Trust* [2004] EWCA Civ 576, [2004] 1 W.L.R. 3002, [2004] C.L.Y. 291 followed. If the defendants' negligence caused her to have care and other needs which were substantially of the same kind as her pre-existing needs, then the damage caused by the negligence was only the additional needs. If the needs caused by the negligence were qualitatively different from her pre-existing needs, then those needs were caused in their entirety by the negligence. The judge's findings did not support a conclusion that the significant care package required as a result of the negligence was qualitatively different from what would have been required but for the negligence. His decision that all of her care and physiotherapy needs were caused by the defendants' negligence could not stand (see paras 15-26 of judgment). The judge had erred to the extent that he had relied on the decision in *Sklair v Haycock* [2009] EWHC 3328 (QB) in reaching his decision on causation: the judge in *Sklair* had confused the question of the need for care, which was a question of causation, with the question of who would have to pay for it; however, the decision in Sklair could be explained and supported on the basis that the care required as a result of the accident in that case was qualitatively different from that which would have been required but for the accident, *Sklair* explained (paras 30-33). There was no doubt about the claimant's condition before the negligence or about the injuries she suffered as a result of the negligence. It was therefore not necessary to modify the "but for" test and consider whether the negligence had made a "material contribution" to the claimant's condition, *Bailey v Ministry of Defence* [2008] EWCA Civ 883, [2009] 1 W.L.R. 1052, [2008] C.L.Y. 2764 considered (paras 34-36).

REANEY v UNIVERSITY HOSPITAL OF NORTH STAFFORDSHIRE NHS TRUST, [2015] EWCA Civ 1119, [2016] P.I.Q.R. Q3, Lord Dyson MR, CA (Civ Div).

1610 Measure of damages–Sexual abuse–Teachers–Grooming and sexual abuse of 16-year old female student

The claimant (C) claimed damages against the defendant company for personal injuries allegedly caused while she was a pupil at its special school by her sexual abuse by the Part 20 defendant (W), a member of the school staff. C developed severe epilepsy at the age of 18 months. She was excluded from mainstream education as a result of her behaviour and attended the special school. She had communication and memory problems. C's family was dysfunctional and she was placed on the child protection register because of emotional and physical abuse at home. A staff member found indecent images of C and inappropriate texts from W on her mobile phone. W pleaded guilty to possession of the images in a magistrates' court and was sentenced to a community order. C alleged that W had groomed her when she was aged about 16 by listening sympathetically to her problems, spending time with her, talking to her on the telephone, encouraging her to send indecent images of herself to him, exchanging text messages of a sexual content and, eventually, sexually assaulting her by indecent touching, digital penetration, oral sex and rape. W strongly denied the allegations, except those relating to the indecent images and the texts. After the images were disclosed C took an overdose. She suffered from acute distress, panic attacks and anxiety and she threatened self-harm. She was diagnosed with adjustment disorder and personality disorder. The company accepted vicarious liability and sought 100 per cent contribution from W for any damages payable. C claimed damages for the assaults but, if the court found against her on the assaults and the abuse was limited to the texts and indecent images, then she claimed damages for the intentional infliction of harm under the principles in *Wilkinson v Downton* [1897] 2 Q.B. 57 as reformulated in *O v A* [2015] UKSC 32, [2016] A.C. 219, [2015] C.L.Y. 2537. W argued that it had been the disclosure of the abuse, rather than the abuse itself, which had caused C's mental health problems.

Held: Judgment for claimant. (1) On the basis of the texts, the indecent images and the evidence, in particular that of W, it was clear that he had been actively encouraging C to send indecent photographs to him, he had a sexual motive and he was grooming her for sexual activity (see paras 33-36 of judgment). (2) W was a wholly untrustworthy witness but there were also aspects of C's evidence which were not wholly reliable. As the burden of proof was on C and there was a substantial conflict of evidence, her claims had to be treated with considerable caution, *Armagas Ltd v Mundogas SA (The Ocean Frost)* [1985] 3 W.L.R. 640, [1985] C.L.Y. 27 followed. The court determined that sexual touching, fondling, and digital penetration of C had taken place over a matter of months. However, the allegation of rape was very serious and the evidence was insufficient to establish that penetrative sexual intercourse or oral sex had taken place (paras 74-77). (3) Family conflict had been another source of C's mental health problems but it was clear that the abuse had caused her diagnosed psychiatric condition of an adjustment order which continued after 2010, and manifested as increased anxiety, increased self-harm, social difficulties with peers and a decrease in self-confidence and self-esteem. It did not matter that it was the disclosure of the abuse, rather than the abuse itself, which had initiated C's serious mental health problems. It was in the very nature of successful grooming that a victim might become infatuated, and accept the abuse in exchange for the continuation of the relationship. This was especially so where W became a father figure, substituting himself for the father with whom C could not get on. The expert evidence was that the abuse had caused 30 per cent of C's symptoms and that they would diminish over the next few years with the help of therapy and more stable relationships, *C v D* [2006] EWHC 166 (QB) and *JL v Bowen* considered. The court was satisfied that each of the three elements of the tort of intentional infliction of harm were made out, *Wilkinson v Downton* and *O v A* followed. Total damages of £51,370 were assessed as below: pain, suffering and loss of amenity £35,000 (had it only been an *O v A* case it would have been £25,000); handicap on the labour market £10,000; psychological treatment £6,370 (paras 80-84, 89, 92, 105).

C v WH, [2015] EWHC 2687 (QB), [2016] E.L.R. 1, Sir Robert Nelson, QBD.

1611 Mesothelioma–Employers' liability–Exposure to asbestos–Widow not discharged burden of proof

[Mines and Quarries Act 1954 (c.70) s.74; Civil Evidence Act 1995 (c.38) s.4]

The claimant (W), on behalf of the estate of her deceased husband (H), brought a claim for damages for personal injury against the defendant secretary of state. H had been employed as a colliery worker in the 1970s and 1980s and died from mesothelioma in 2008. Before his death he stated that he had been exposed to asbestos while inspecting conveyor belts at a colliery between 1979 and 1984. H alleged that friction brakes containing asbestos were used to control the belts during that period and that their pads created dust to which he was exposed. The instant court heard evidence that those brakes were phased out and replaced with an anti-rollback system which did not contain asbestos. It also heard that the brakes were protected by guards and did not fail regularly, and, while H inspected them, he was not a mechanic and did not carry out repairs. The issue was whether H had been exposed to asbestos dust while working at the colliery and, if so, whether he had been exposed to a level which was likely to be injurious. The secretary of state submitted that H's statement was riddled with errors and was undermined by previous inconsistent statements.

Held: Claim dismissed. (1) The secretary of state had owed H a common law duty of care to not expose him to material which was likely to cause reasonably foreseeable injury, subject to the standard of knowledge prevailing at the relevant time, and a stricter statutory duty of care was also owed under the Mines and Quarries Act 1954 s.74. (2) A note from H's solicitor to a coroner which stated that the anti-rollback system had been in use during H's employment was double hearsay which was unsworn and untested by cross-examination. H had had no opportunity to confirm or correct its contents and under the Civil Evidence Act 1995 s.4 it was to be given little or no weight. There were several errors of fact in H's statement which W contended could be excused by his age and poor health, but while that could be taken into account, there were other matters which undermined his reliability. (3) There was no reason to doubt that friction brakes were in use in 1979, but the evidence was that they ceased to be used in 1982 or 1983. There was no evidence of regular brake failure and, while H would have occasionally observed repairs, he would not have been close to any dust. While the actual level of exposure to asbestos dust was never measured or monitored, there was no evidence that any, let alone significant, amounts of brake-pad dust had been allowed by the mechanics who had carried out repairs to accumulate on the floor. H had been very occasionally or intermittently exposed to dust on the very few occasions of brake failure when the guards which prevented the dust from escaping were removed, but that exposure had diminished over three years as the friction brakes were phased out of use. H had been exposed to asbestos, but the level of exposure was considerably lower than he had claimed and the burden of proof on W had not been discharged.

ATKINSON v SECRETARY OF STATE FOR THE DEPARTMENT OF ENERGY AND CLIMATE CHANGE, [2014] EWHC 3773 (QB), [2014] Inquest L.R. 209, Judge Gore QC, QBD.

1612 Personal injury claims–Conditional fee agreements–Insurer making settlement offers direct to claimants–Insurer required to pay solicitor's fees

[Cancellation of Contracts made in a Consumer's Home or Place of Work etc. Regulations 2008 (SI 2008/1816)]

A firm of solicitors (G) appealed against the dismissal (*Gavin Edmondson Solicitors Ltd v Haven Insurance Co Ltd* [2014] EWHC 3062 (QB), [2015] R.T.R. 14, [2015] C.L.Y. 1909) of its claim against the respondent insurer. G had entered into conditional fee agreements (CFAs) to represent six clients in personal injury claims against the insurer. The insurer had settled the claims directly with the clients on an inclusive basis, meaning that G had been deprived of their costs. G had therefore brought the instant claim in order to recover their fees, disbursements and success fees from the insurer.

They sought equitable intervention by the court, claiming that the insurer had wrongfully prevented them from establishing a lien on the settlement sums for their costs. The CFAs incorporated a Law Society document which provided that a client who won the claim would pay G's charges, disbursements and a success fee, which it could claim from its opponent. However, each client also received a client care letter which indicated that if the client won, G would be able to recover their fees, disbursements and success fee from the opponent and had the right to take recovery action in the client's name. Each CFA was subject to the Cancellation of Contracts made in a Consumer's Home or Place of Work etc. Regulations 2008, meaning that each client had the right to cancel his retainer within a seven-day period. In the case of two of the clients, the insurer made the offer to compromise within that seven-day period. The issues were whether: (i) the principle of equitable intervention set out in *Khans Solicitors v Chifuntwe* [2013] EWCA Civ 481, [2014] 1 W.L.R. 1185, [2013] C.L.Y. 332 could operate only where a defendant had express notice of a lien; (ii) a lien could arise in circumstances where the clients were under no personal liability to pay G's fees; (iii) the insurer's liability was affected by the fact that an offer might have been made at a time when a retainer could still be cancelled.

Held: Appeal allowed. (1) There was no reason in principle why implied, rather than express, notice of a lien should not be sufficient for the operation of the principle of equitable intervention. In any event, express notice had been given in the instant case. It was apparent from transcripts of telephone calls that the insurer had intended to avoid paying G's costs by entering into a settlement directly with the clients. The insurer's knowledge of and participation in the scheme established by the Pre-Action Protocol for Low Value Personal Injury Claims in Road Traffic Accidents meant that it was well aware of G's interest in receiving its fixed costs and other sums due under the scheme, *Khans* applied (see paras 25-26, 28-29 of judgment). (2) There was a tension between the provisions in the CFAs. The provision in the client care letter had to prevail because it was expressed to be for the avoidance of doubt. That meant that G had no recourse against their clients for the fees and were limited to what they could recover from the losing side. In those circumstances, they would not have a lien over assets received in their clients' account because the clients had no underlying liability to them. However, under the normal course of events, G would have an entitlement to recover the fixed costs and other sums payable under the Protocol scheme. That was either an entitlement of the solicitors themselves or, alternatively, an entitlement to bring proceedings in the name of the clients to recover those sums. In either case, G had an interest which equity could protect and which was deserving of protection. The insurer was aware of that interest because of its knowledge of and participation in the Protocol scheme. That might involve an extension of the principle in *Khans*, but there was no reason why that principle should not apply in the circumstances of the case. The Protocol scheme was not mandatory and it was therefore open to the insurer to enter into compromise agreements with the claimants outside the Protocol. However, that was not what had happened. In each case, the client had authorised G to commence the Protocol process on his behalf and the insurer had voluntarily entered into the Protocol process. Neither the clients nor the insurer had formally exited the process before entering into the compromise agreements. The insurer had acted with the intention of defeating G's entitlement under the scheme, *Khans* applied (paras 18, 30-32). (3) The fact that an offer might have been made at a time when a retainer could still be cancelled could not relieve the insurer of liability. It would have been open to the insurer to make the offer conditional upon cancellation of G' retainer within the permitted period, but it did not do so. In each case, the insurer assumed the risk that its offer might be accepted after the expiry of the cancellation period. In any event, in none of the underlying cases was the retainer cancelled or otherwise terminated (paras 21, 34-37). (4) The insurer entered into each compromise agreement with notice of G's entitlement and the principle of equitable intervention required it to pay to G the sums payable on settlement under the Protocol scheme (para.38).

GAVIN EDMONDSON SOLICITORS LTD v HAVEN INSURANCE CO LTD, [2015] EWCA Civ 1230, [2016] 1 W.L.R. 1385, Laws LJ, CA (Civ Div).

1613 Quantum–Brain damage at birth

Held: Damages approved. N, a boy, newborn at the date of the incident and seven years old at the date of the child settlement approval hearing, developed kernicterus (brain damage from excessive levels of bilirubin) as a result of jaundice in the newborn period which went undetected and untreated. N was left with severe dyskinetic cerebral palsy with intellectual impairment and hearing loss. N was and would continue to be fully dependent on others for all activities of daily living. He had very limited mobility and would always require the use of wheelchairs. His upper and lower limbs were severely impaired, the bulbar musculature was severely affected and he was fed by a gastrostomy tube. His level of disability was GMFCS V. Intellectually, at age 7, N functioned in the 12 to18 month range. His agreed life expectancy was to age 31, a further 24 years. There was no prospect of improvement. Out of Court Settlement (approved): Total Damages: £8,050,335. General Damages: £300,000. Future losses: Care and case management: £4,692,070 (paid as PPO's); Accommodation: £1,200,000; Holidays: £110,000; Therapies: £216,115; Medical care: £42,000; Loss of Earnings: £120,000; Assistive technology: £100,000; Deputyship costs: £180,000 (paid as PPO's); Aids & Equipment: £500,000. Future care and case management were to be paid as periodical payments, index linked to ASHE 6115 at the 80th centile, as follows: £217,000 per annum to age 11; £235,000 per annum from age 11 to age 19; £300,000 per annum from age 19. Future Deputyship costs were to be paid as periodical payments, linked to RPI, at £11,500 per annum. The lifetime multiplier used was 18.11, being the Table 28 multiplier for a fixed period of 24 years. Breakdown of special damages: Past gratuitous care: £152,000; Past paid care: £150,000; Past accommodation costs: £47,000; Past travel and expenditure: £19,500; Past Deputyship costs: £10,000.

N (A CHILD) v LEWISHAM AND GREENWICH NHS TRUST, Green J, QBD.

1618 Quantum–Digestive organs

Held: Damages assessed. B, the claimant, brought an action on behalf of his brother, the deceased (X). X had presented at A&E in February 2008 with symptoms of a gastric ulcer. It was alleged that X should have been admitted overnight and arrangements made for an outpatient gastroscopy. Instead, X was discharged home with the correct medication and instructions to attend his GP to arrange a gastroscopy. Liability was successfully defended at trial but the recorder assessed quantum for completeness. X suffered a deep chronic ulcer and eventual resection of his transverse colon and gastrectomy. Damages for pain, suffering and loss of amenity were assessed for the eight weeks leading up to the surgery. X suffered a loss of weight, admission to HDU, blood transfusions, biopsies and four weeks of severe pain, suffering and loss of amenity following surgery. General Damages: £15,000.

AB v ST HELENS AND KNOWSLEY TEACHING HOSPITALS NHS TRUST, Recorder Heaton, CC (Liverpool).

1624 Quantum–Poisoning food

Held: Damages assessed. C, male, aged 13 at the date of the injury and 16 at the date of the hearing, was on a two week holiday in Morocco when he became unwell on the fourth day of the holiday. He experienced stomach cramps, diarrhoea, vomiting, headaches, nausea and sweats. For the first few days, C experienced diarrhoea at least eight times a day and it troubled him at night as well. By the time that C returned to the UK, his residual symptoms consisted of loss of appetite and tiredness. In all C suffered from acute gastroenteritis with symptoms lasting about two-and-a-half weeks. General Damages: £1,700.

D (A CHILD) v BROADWAY TRAVEL, Deputy District Judge Orme, CC (Bristol).

1625 Quantum–Sacrum, pelvis and hip

Held: Damages assessed. P, male, aged 40 years old at the date of the accident and 41 at the date of the hearing, sustained soft tissue injuries to his pelvis, lower back and right leg when he was involved in a low speed collision. P experienced severe shock for one day, as well as mild travel anxiety and travel discomfort for six months. P's pelvic injury caused moderate pain at the time of the accident, which was described as mild to moderate at the time of the medical examination at five months after the accident. Six sessions of physiotherapy were recommended and four were undertaken. P's lower back pain and right leg pain were mild from the onset and resolved within eight weeks. P visited his GP and received painkillers, which he still took occasionally at five months after the accident. P took one week off work. His ability to do household chores was initially severely restricted for three weeks. His pelvic pain was expected to resolve completely within eight months of the accident. *Simmons v Castle* [2012] EWCA Civ 242 10 per cent uplift: applied. General Damages: £3,250.

PIRATHABAN v LUCAF, District Judge Smith, CC (Dartford).

1626 Road traffic accidents–Apportionment–Causative potency and blameworthiness–Apportionment of liability for collision between motorist and pedestrian

A motorist appealed against the extent to which a judge had reduced the damages awarded to the respondent pedestrian for injuries sustained in a road traffic accident. The judge's findings were that the pedestrian got out of a car which was parked a few metres beyond a pedestrian crossing on a busy suburban road with shops either side. She moved to the rear of the parked car, then looked at the road and saw the motorist's car approaching at normal speed. She misjudged its position and thought there was enough time to cross the road. The motorist had a clear view of her as he approached, but did not see her. The front offside of his car struck her when she was almost four metres into the carriageway. She suffered very significant injuries including a traumatic brain injury. The judge found that the motorist's failure to pay proper attention had caused the accident, but that the pedestrian's share of responsibility was 25 per cent. The motorist submitted that the judge had substantially understated the extent of the pedestrian's responsibility because the fact that she had made a considered but flawed decision to cross the road was more negligent than simply crossing the road without looking. He also asserted that the finding was out of line with the approach taken in other decided cases that a pedestrian who stepped into the path of an oncoming car attracted a greater share of the responsibility.

Held: Appeal dismissed. There were two aspects to apportioning liability between the parties to a road traffic accident: their respective causative potency and their blameworthiness. Motorists had a high burden of causative potency because a car usually did more damage to a person than a person did to a car. The destructive potential of a car, even one driven at a moderate speed, was also relevant to blameworthiness, and made it rare for a pedestrian to be found more responsible than a driver. Driving a car without keeping a proper lookout where pedestrians were reasonably expected to be present indicated a considerable degree of blameworthiness, *Jackson v Murray* [2015] UKSC 5, [2015] 2 All E.R. 805, [2015] C.L.Y. 1797 followed and *Eagle v Chambers (No.1)* [2003] EWCA Civ 1107, [2004] R.T.R. 9, [2003] C.L.Y. 2964 considered. The principle suggested by the motorist that pedestrians took a greater share of the responsibility if they stepped in front of an oncoming car could not be stated quite so baldly. In the instant case, the court could not accept that the pedestrian had taken a deliberate risk. Crossing a busy road usually involved an element of deliberate risk-taking, but "deliberate risk-taking" in the instant context meant conduct such as the pedestrian setting off to cross the road when an accident was likely unless the motorist took avoiding action, *Belka v Prosperini* [2011] EWCA Civ 623 followed. There had been no finding that the pedestrian had set out on an obviously unsafe errand. She was clearly blameworthy because she misjudged her own safety, but she had not put the motorist in danger or in an emergency situation; he ought reasonably to have seen her and taken his foot off the accelerator. Not only did he fail to do that, but he failed to see her at all for a period significantly longer than the benchmark. Both the causal potency and the blameworthiness of his conduct were very substantially greater than that of the pedestrian. The judge's assessment of how the pedestrian's damages should be reduced having regard to her share in the responsibility for the damage was reasonable and should not be interfered with. It was not demonstrably out of line with the approach taken in previously decided cases, *Clifford v Drymond* [1976] R.T.R. 134, [1976] C.L.Y. 2434, *Lunt v Khelifa* [2002] EWCA Civ 801 and *McCluskey v Wallace* 1998 S.C. 711, [1998] C.L.Y. 6103 considered (see paras 12-13, 15-18 of judgment).

SABIR v OSEI-KWABENA *sub nom.* OSEI-KWABENA v SABIR, [2015] EWCA Civ 1213, [2016] R.T.R. 9, Arden LJ, CA (Civ Div).

1627 Tripping and slipping–Highway authorities' powers and duties–No duty under s.41(1) Highways Act 1980 to ensure highways clear of moss

[Highways Act 1980 (c.66) s.36(2), s.41(1)]

A local authority appealed against a decision that it had a duty under the Highways Act 1980 s.41(1) to ensure that its highways were clear of moss and algae. The respondent had slipped on a patch of moss on the footpath outside his home. He brought a personal injury claim against the local authority on the basis that it had breached its duty under s.41(1) to keep the fabric of the highway in repair. It was not disputed that the footpath constituted a "highway" and was maintainable at public expense under s.36(2). The judge held that the local authority had breached its duty under s.41(1) to remove moss which constituted a danger to highway users. The judge reasoned, referring to *Thomas v Warwickshire CC* [2011] EWHC 772 (QB), that moss put down roots and adhered to the surface, thus becoming part of the roadway. The judge also found that there had been no contributory negligence on the respondent's part. The local authority submitted that (1) its s.41(1) duty did not extend to removing moss and algae from the footpath; (2) there was no evidence that the moss was rooted in the footpath surface; (3) the judge had erred in failing to make a finding of contributory negligence.

Held: Appeal allowed. (1) The s.41(1) duty was to "repair" and "keep in repair" the highway, *Goodes v East Sussex CC* [2000] 1 W.L.R. 1356, [2000] C.L.Y. 4237 followed. It included a duty to keep the drains and substructure of the highways clear and in good repair, *Burnside v Emerson* [1968] 1 W.L.R. 1490, [1968] C.L.Y. 1762 and *Mott MacDonald Ltd v Department of Transport* [2006] EWCA Civ 1089, [2006] 1 W.L.R. 3356, [2006] C.L.Y. 3531 followed. It did not include a duty to remove surface-lying material, accretions, obstructions or spillages, regardless of whether they were dangerous, *Valentine v Transport for London* [2010] EWCA Civ 1358, [2011] B.L.R. 89, [2011] C.L.Y. 2729 followed. Whether a particular problem, defect, contaminant or accretion would render a road, pavement or pathway "out of repair" such as to engage s.41(1) depended on the precise nature of the particular problem, defect, contaminant or accretion, *Hereford and Worcester CC v Newman* [1975] 1 W.L.R. 901, [1975] C.L.Y. 1546 applied. Relevant considerations included whether it was permanent or transient; amounted to, or comprised, material disturbance or damage to the road, pavement or pathway or the surface thereof; and could be said to have become part of the fabric of the road, pavement or pathway, *Thomas* applied (see paras 14-24 of judgment). None of those principles or criteria applied to the instant case. *Thomas* and *Newman* were plainly distinguishable on their facts, *Thomas* and *Newman* considered. The judge had erred in finding that because moss "puts down roots" it therefore "becomes part of" the surface or roadway, that there was any relevant comparison between moss and concrete bonded to the highway, in assuming that there was anything permanent about moss, and in regarding the fact that the local authority had taken steps to remove moss as relevant to the question of statutory construction. The scope of a highway authority's absolute duty under s.41 did not extend to the removal of moss. The judge failed to consider whether the imposition of a duty to prevent or remove moss from every highway and byway of the UK was something which Parliament could sensibly have had in mind. It rationally could not. The absolute nature of the s.41(1) duty plainly militated against any such conclusion, *Haydon v Kent CC* [1978] Q.B. 343, [1978] C.L.Y. 1547 applied. The judge's decision, if allowed to stand, would lead to the absurd situation whereby a highway authority would be obliged to consider removing or preventing the propagation of every patch of moss or algae on every road, pavement and pathway in the country in order to avoid being in breach of its duty to "repair". That would not be practical, sensible, or affordable (paras 27-33). (2) The judge had stated that whereas lichen was "epithetic" and took its moisture from the air, moss had roots which had to go into the "substrata". A judge was entitled, within reasonable limits, to use his personal knowledge of matters within the common knowledge, *Reynolds v Llanelly Associated Tin Plate Co* [1948] 1 All E.R. 140, [1947-51] C.L.Y. 11100 applied. However, it was doubtful whether the fact that lichen could be categorised as epithetic was within common knowledge. The fact that moss had some sort of shallow root structure was probably within most people's common knowledge, and was something to which the judge could have regard from his own knowledge. However, the fact that it had roots which might have gripped the path surface did not mean that the moss had become "part of the fabric" of the footpath or pavement, still less a permanent part of it, *Thomas* considered (paras 35-38). (3) The respondent had admitted in cross-examination that he had been aware of the moss before the accident and had considered it to be dangerous. He said that there had been no room to avoid it. However, the photographic evidence showed that there were clear strips on both sides of the path where people habitually walked and the moss had been worn away. Although an appeal court was reluctant to interfere with a judge's findings regarding contributory negligence, the decision was plainly wrong. The judge should have held that the respondent's personal responsibility for the accident was significant and made an apportionment of 50% for contributory negligence (paras 41-42).

ROLLINSON v DUDLEY MBC, [2015] EWHC 3330 (QB), [2016] R.T.R. 19, Haddon-Cave J, QBD.

1628 Uninsured drivers–Applicable law–Persons injured in other EU state–France

[Motor Vehicles (Compulsory Insurance) (Information Centre and Compensation Body) Regulations 2003 (SI 2003/37) reg.13, reg.13(1), reg.13(2); Regulation 864/2007 on the law applicable to non-contractual obligations (Rome II) 2007 art.4, art.4(1), art.4(3)]

In actions commenced following a road traffic accident in France, the court was required to determine preliminary issues in relation to the applicable law relating to issues of liability, questions of liability under French law, and whether the Motor Insurers' Bureau was liable under the Motor Vehicles (Compulsory Insurance) (Information Centre and Compensation Body) Regulations 2003. An uninsured Peugeot car driver had hit two British nationals (M and P) as they were standing behind a Ford Fiesta car and trailer, while the trailer was being attended to by a recovery truck on the side of a motorway. P had been driving the Fiesta, and M was his passenger. After hitting M and P, the Peugeot collided with the trailer, shunting it into the Fiesta which in turn was shunted into the recovery truck. P was thrown forward by the impact with the Peugot and landed clear of the vehicles. He suffered serious injuries. M was thrown off the front of the Peugeot, and the trailer fell on his leg. He died at the scene. The Fiesta was registered in the UK and insured by RSA; the recovery truck was registered in France and insured by Generali. Two actions were commenced. The first was brought by M's widow (W) against the MIB, relying upon the 2003 Regulations. The MIB denied liability on the basis that under French law, liability lay with P and RSA, as driver and insurer of the Fiesta, and Generali, as insurer of the recovery truck. Its case was that its equivalent in France, the FdG, was not liable to compensate W, and therefore it had no liability. P and Generali were added as defendants. The second action was brought by P against the MIB. Again, the MIB denied liability and claimed that Generali was liable to P. The issues were (i) whether French or English law applied to the issue of liability; (ii) if French law applied, whether the Fiesta and recovery truck were "involved" within the meaning of the applicable French statute, the Loi Badinter, and (iii) whether the MIB was liable under the 2003 Regulations.

Held: Preliminary issue determined. (1) The applicable law was to be determined by reference to Regulation 864/2007 art.4. The general rule under art.4(1) was that the applicable law was the law of the country in which the damage occurred. It was common ground that for all the claims, the damage occurred in France. Article 4(2) provided an exception to that general rule, that where the parties had their habitual residence in the same country at the time when the damage occurred, the law of that country would apply. Article 4(3) provided that where it was clear from all the circumstances that the tort was more closely connected with a country other than that indicated in (1) or (2), the law of that country applied. Thus, under art.4(3), a governing law mandated by art.4(1), but excluded by art.4(2), might be required by art.4(3). In the instant case it was clear that the tort was manifestly more closely connected with France rather than England and thus French law applied to the issue of liability for the claims before the court (see paras 9-23 of judgment). (2) The Loi Badinter imposed a liability to compensate persons injured in a road traffic accident on the insurer of any vehicle which was "involved". A vehicle was involved in an accident if it intervened in "any capacity whatsoever". That went beyond a causal link, but there were still limits; mere presence of a vehicle at the time of the accident was not enough. In respect of M, the Fiesta was involved as M had ended up trapped underneath the trailer at a time when he was alive. The recovery truck was also involved as the trailer fell on M when it was prevented from travelling forward by the truck's presence. Thus, both RSA, as insurer of the Fiesta, and Generali, as insurer of the recovery truck, were liable to W under French law. In respect of P, although there was no contact between him and the Fiesta or trailer, both were involved in his accident. However, the recovery truck was not involved as there was no collision or contact between it and P and, although it was present at the time of the collision, there was nothing out of the ordinary in what the recovery truck had done so far as P was concerned. Neither RSA nor Generali was liable to P (paras 24-54). (3) In those circumstances, the FdG was liable to P and thus the MIB was liable to compensate him under the 2003 Regulations. The question remained as to whether the MIB was liable to W under reg.13. W contended that as it was common ground that the preconditions in reg.13(1) had been satisfied, the MIB was liable to compensate her under reg.13(2). The court did not accept that. The FdG was not liable to make payments to W under French law as liability lay with both RSA and Generali under the Loi Badinter. In those circumstances, under the terms of re.13(2), the MIB was not liable to compensate W, *Jacobs v Motor Insurers' Bureau* [2010] EWCA Civ 1208, [2011] 1 W.L.R. 2609, [2011] C.L.Y. 1922 and *Bloy v Motor Insurers' Bureau* [2013] EWCA Civ 1543, [2014] Lloyd's Rep. I.R. 75, [2014] C.L.Y. 2559 considered (paras 55-71).

MARSHALL v MOTOR INSURERS' BUREAU; PICKARD v MOTOR INSURERS' BUREAU, [2015] EWHC 3421 (QB), [2016] Lloyd's Rep. I.R. 400, Dingemans J, QBD.

1633 Whiplash injury–Expert reports–Governmental reforms to process of handling whiplash claims–MedCo system not irrational or anti-competitive

[Competition Act 1998 (c.41) Sch.3]

The claimant applied for judicial review of the defendant secretary of state's reforms to the process for handling soft tissue whiplash claims. The claimant was a medical reporting organisation (MRO) which arranged for medical reports to be prepared for litigation. The reforms under challenge included a requirement for personal injury solicitors to identify and instruct independent, accredited medical experts for the provision of initial medical reports via an online portal administered by a company known as MedCo. The MedCo system distinguished between Tier 1 MROs, namely high volume national MROs such as the claimant, and Tier 2 MROs, namely regional MROs. It stated that anyone using the portal would be offered a selection of MROs to choose from in the ratio of one Tier 1 MRO to six Tier 2 MROs. The claimant's case was that the new system had had an adverse effect on its business. It argued that the system was irrational because although its purpose was to maintain consumer choice without preventing Tier 1 MROs from developing their businesses, its effect was that consumers were left unable to choose experts as freely as they could previously, and Tier 1 MROs were prevented from developing their businesses beyond a certain level. It further submitted that the policy was unlawful because it was anti-competitive contrary to national and European competition law. In particular, it contended that the offer ratio of one Tier 1 MRO to six Tier 2 MROs, and the criteria for Tier 1 and Tier 2 MROs, meant that there was no way of controlling the system's anti-competitive effects.

Held: Application refused. (1) The rationality challenge to aspects of the MedCo system did not get off the ground. There had been extensive consultation with those likely to be affected by the reforms, including Tier 1 MROs like the claimant, and there had been many round-table meetings with representatives across the sector. The government had received support for its proposals from the major representative bodies whose members were involved with the production and use of medical reports commissioned for whiplash injuries. Those representatives had not only responded to the government's consultations and participated in round-table meetings, but had also taken the initiative to suggest how the medico-legal reporting system might be changed to meet the government's policy objectives. As with any exercise in public policy-making, the outcome might not be ideal. The problem might not have been precisely identified and, even if it had been, the solution chosen might not be the most effective or efficient to address it. However, given the process of policy formulation, it could not be said to be irrational. The fact that the reforms had adversely affected the claimant's business did not alter that conclusion. The policy did not prevent the claimant and other Tier 1 MROs from developing their businesses (see paras 44, 47-48, 50 of judgment). (2) It could not be reasonably argued that MedCo was abusing a dominant position in the relevant market by administering a system in accordance with the requirements imposed by the government. MedCo was not active in the market where MROs and medical experts competed to provide expert reports for whiplash claims. MedCo was not an MRO, it did not provide medical reports, it had no commercial interests in that market, and it derived no direct or indirect economic or other advantage from distorting competition. Rather, it was a regulator acting in the public interest and implementing a policy of the secretary of state, who equally was not active in the relevant market and had no financial or other interest in the market, *SELEX Sistemi Integrati SpA v Commission of the European Communities (T-155/04)* EU:T:2006:387, [2006] E.C.R. II-4797, [2007] C.L.Y. 652 considered. The MedCo portal was the avenue mandated in the CPR for obtaining medical reports for whiplash claims. It had acted in accordance with the governmental policy and was effectively complying with the type of legal requirement recognised under the Competition Act 1998 Sch.3. Even if MedCo had acted in a way which restricted competition, or there was a risk that it would do so, there was objective justification for its actions. In those circumstances, the claimant's challenge had to be refused (paras 61-62, 65, 68, 72, 76).

SPEED MEDICAL EXAMINATION SERVICES LTD v SECRETARY OF STATE FOR JUSTICE, [2015] EWHC 3585 (Admin), [2016] E.C.C. 13, Cranston J, QBD (Admin).

1637 Quantum–Sacrum, pelvis and hip

Held: Damages assessed. S, male, aged 54 at the date of the accident and 57 at the date of the hearing, was injured whilst using a piece of equipment at the gym. The equipment was attached to the wall and required S to pull down on a bar and then return the bar to the up position. As S proceeded to pull down, the bar and the equipment fell from the wall and landed on top of S's left hip, forcing his knee down towards the floor. S sustained a severe and high impact fracture and dislocation of his left hip. S had one month off work and two further months on light duties. He also required care and assistance for two months. S underwent two surgical procedures, the first to reduce the dislocation and the second to fix the fracture with metal plates and screws. S required the use of crutches for three months and underwent physiotherapy. The medical expert confirmed that S had made a significant recovery at 18 months post-accident but continued to suffer from some pain and discomfort in his left hip, which occasionally disturbed his sleep, along with pain in the right shoulder blade area. The expert also concluded that S had a five to ten per cent risk of developing osteoarthritis within the next 15 to 20 years and that if he did develop that condition he would require a total hip replacement. *Simmons v Castle* [2012] EWCA Civ 1288, [2013] 1 W.L.R. 1239, [2013] C.L.Y. 782 ten per cent uplift: applied. General Damages: £19,000.

SMITH v ACTIVE NATION UK LTD, Deputy District Judge Walder, CC (Oxford).

1638 Road traffic accidents–Contributory negligence–Collision between two vehicles in Poland–Appropriate approach to determining contributory negligence and quantum

[Regulation 864/2007 on the law applicable to non-contractual obligations (Rome II) 2007 art.15]

The court determined contributory negligence and quantum in proceedings concerning a collision between two vehicles in Poland. Judgment on primary liability had been entered against the second defendant. The 37-year-old claimant had been a rear seat passenger in the other car. He had not been wearing a seatbelt. He was catapulted from the car upon impact. He suffered a moderately severe brain injury resulting in a personality change. He also suffered impaired intellectual and cognitive efficiency, memory and central executive functioning. The consequences were permanent. His physical injuries included fractures to his pelvis and spine, leading to urological problems; a partial tear of the thoracic aorta, leading to a 10-15 per cent reduction in pulmonary function; fractures to the right hand, and difficulties with balance which caused foot pain and problems walking. Contributory negligence and quantum were agreed to fall for determination under Polish law. The defendants bore the burden of proving that Polish law differed from English law. Regarding contributory negligence the defendants relied on the Polish Civil Code art.361.1, under which a person obliged to pay damages was only liable for the "ordinary effects" of an action which the damage resulted from. The defendants submitted that the "ordinary effect" of wearing a seat belt was to prevent or reduce injury, and the burden was therefore on the claimant to establish the extraordinary converse. They also submitted that the Polish percentage reduction for contributory negligence was more severe than in English law, and argued for 30 per cent. Regarding pain and suffering, the claimant maintained that Polish law was vague and uncertain so that the defendants could not discharge the burden of proving that it was different from English law, and English law should therefore prevail.

Held: Damages assessed. (1) *Contributory negligence* - The burden of proof was determined by art.6 of the Polish Civil Code. The defendants had to establish on the balance of probabilities that the claimant's admitted fault caused him to suffer injuries which would have been avoided or lessened if he had been wearing a seat belt. Article 361 had not featured prior to the hearing and the defendants did not explain how it could be squared with the unqualified language of art.6. The court was not persuaded that art.361 reflected the true position in Polish law or that the Polish law on the wearing of seat belts was any more fundamental than in English law. There was a finding in related criminal proceedings that the claimant had been in the middle rear seat, which had only a lap restraint. The defendants considered it more likely that he was sat in a side seat with both lap and diagonal restraint and that it would have been negligent to sit in a seat with limited restraint. Both experts agreed that if he had been belted into a side seat, he would have been restrained by the lap belt, but at risk of sliding sideways out of the diagonal belt, so that there was a high risk of his head colliding forcefully with the door frame and a considerable risk of him suffering serious head and/or neck injury and a low risk of chest or lower spinal injury. On the evidence, the claimant was most likely to have been sat in the middle seat. It was not negligent to have done so. He would have been ejected through the side window, suffering his injuries when he struck the road. If he had been wearing the lap restraint, he would have struck his head in the way suggested by the experts. That would have caused head, brain and aortic injuries at least as severe as those which occurred. However, the orthopaedic and urological injuries would have been avoided. The overall deduction for contributory negligence should be five per cent (see paras 9-16, 19, 24-27, 33-35, 38-39, 240-241 of judgment). (2) *Pain and suffering* - Under Polish law there were no fixed scales or guidelines applicable to the claimant's injuries. Judges were to assess a "relevant amount". In practice, they calculated damages according to a table in an Ordinance produced under social insurance legislation for non-fault injuries. The defendants maintained that despite criticism by the Supreme Court of Poland, that practice continued. The word "law" in Regulation 864/2007 art.15 had been construed to include practice and convention. Therefore, the defendants had established a relevant Polish law which differed from English law. It would be wrong for the instant court to find that damages were calculated solely on the basis of the Ordinance, because that practice was unlawful in light of the Polish court's criticisms. However it was clear that regard to the Ordinance remained part of the lawful practice of Polish courts. Therefore the instant court had to take into account that the highest award known to have been made for pain and suffering was the equivalent of some £133,000 (paras 41, 44-48). (3) *Damages assessed* - The court assessed (a) pain and suffering at a "relevant amount" of £50,000 (paras 96-105); (b) past loss of earnings including deduction of benefits (paras 107-153); (c) future loss of earnings (paras 154-167); (d) care (paras 168-196); (e) case management (paras 197-200); (f) therapies, medication and monitoring (paras 201-210); (f) orthotics (paras 211-212); (g) rehabilitation (paras 213-219; (h) aids and equipment (paras 220-224); (i) Domestic help (paras 225-230; (j) car expenses and other items (paras 231-239).

SYRED v POWSZECNNY ZAKLAD UBEZPIECZEN (PZU) SA, [2016] EWHC 254 (QB), [2016] 1 W.L.R. 3211, Soole J, QBD.

1639 Uninsured drivers–Applicable law–Person injured in other EU state–Greece

[Motor Vehicles (Compulsory Insurance) (Information Centre and Compensation Body) Regulations 2003 (SI 2003/37) reg.13, reg.13(2)(b); Directive 2000/26 on insurance against civil liability in respect of the use of motor vehicles 2000 art.7]

The Motor Insurers' Bureau (MIB) appealed against a decision of the High Court that the compensation due to the respondent, an English national who had been seriously injured in an accident involving an uninsured driver while she was on holiday in Greece, was to be assessed in accordance with English law. The respondent had brought a claim against the MIB under the Motor Vehicles (Compulsory Insurance) (Information Centre and Compensation Body) Regulations 2003 reg.13 and liability was admitted. The compensation payable under Greek law would be lower than that which was payable under English law. In holding that compensation was to be assessed in accordance with English law, the High Court followed the decision of the Court of Appeal in *Jacobs v Motor Insurers' Bureau* [2010] EWCA Civ 1208, [2011] 1 W.L.R. 2609, [2011] C.L.Y. 1922. In *Jacobs*, the court found that reg.13(2)(b) distinguished between liability and heads of damage on the one hand and the measure of compensation on the other, such that compensation was to be assessed by reference to the law of the victim's state of residence. The decision in *Jacobs* was endorsed by the Court of Appeal in *Bloy v Motor Insurers' Bureau* [2013] EWCA Civ 1543, [2014] Lloyd's Rep. I.R. 75, [2014] C.L.Y. 2559.

Held: Appeal allowed. In construing the 2003 Regulations, the starting point was that they should, so far as possible, be interpreted in a sense which was not in any way inconsistent with the Directives which they were intended to implement. There was no suggestion in the Regulations or the Explanatory Note or elsewhere of any intention on the part of the domestic legislator to do anything other than faithfully implement and give effect to those Directives. On that basis, two questions were central to the appeal. The first was whether the Directives prescribed any particular approach to the scope or measure of recovery applicable in a claim against a compensation body under Directive 2000/26 art.7. The second was whether, if they did, the language of reg.13(2)(b) of the Regulations reflected that approach or mandated some different approach. The scheme of the Directives was clear. They did not leave it to individual Member States to provide for compensation in accordance with any law that such states might choose. On the contrary, they proceeded on the basis that a victim's entitlement to compensation would be measured on a consistent basis, by reference to the law of the state of the accident, whichever of the routes to recovery provided by the Directives he or she invoked. Moreover, the language of reg.13(2)(b) of the Regulations reflected that approach and did not mandate a different approach, *Jacobs* and *Bloy* overruled. Accordingly, the scope of the MIB's liability to the respondent was to be determined in accordance with the law of Greece (see paras 26, 28-29, 39, 41, 43 of judgment).

MORENO v MOTOR INSURERS' BUREAU, [2016] UKSC 52, [2016] 1 W.L.R. 3194, Lord Mance JSC, SC.

1645 Quantum–Back and neck: whiplash injury: no previous condition

Held: Damages assessed. G, female, aged 37 at the date of the road traffic accident and 38 at the date of the hearing, sustained injuries to her neck, back and shoulders in May 2015. G was driving her vehicle when the defendant collided with it to the rear causing G to be jolted within the confines of her seatbelt. After the accident, G experienced pain. She was not absent from her work as a receptionist but did experience some difficulties with movements whilst working. Her sleep and capacity to attend to her personal care were affected. She also experienced restrictions in her social life, her ability to undertake DIY tasks, shopping, carrying and lifting although her abilities in all such activities did improve. The accident also affected her enjoyment of a holiday. G's symptoms were moderately severe. By the date of the medical examination, approximately three months after the accident, they had improved to a mild to moderate and intermittent nature. G was advised by her GP to take analgesia and to undertake mobilisation techniques. She regularly took analgesia for eight weeks and thereafter she took it when required. C also underwent a course of physiotherapy. The medical expert anticipated that all G's injuries would resolve by approximately 10 months after the accident. As liability was admitted, the matter was assessed pursuant

to Practice Direction 8B para.11: Pre-Action Protocol for Low Value Personal Injury Claims: Stage 3 procedure. General Damages: £3,000.
GORMAN v SABRE INSURANCE CO LTD, District Judge Davies, CC (Derby).

1647 Quantum–Cerebral palsy

Held: Damages approved. C, female, newborn at the date of the incident and 24 at the date of the approval hearing, suffered brain damage during her birth in 1991. C suffered a period of up to a maximum of 25 minutes of profound hypoxic-ischaemia immediately prior to her delivery leading to her suffering from quadriplegic choreoathetoid cerebral palsy. C was fully dependent on others for all activities of daily living. She had very limited mobility and would always require the use of wheelchairs. C suffered from significant involuntary movements, primarily of the upper limbs, and suffered pain as a result and due to limb stiffness and spasticity. She had severe dysarthric speech. Despite her severe physical disabilities, C was a keen horse rider competing in various competitions at national level. She was also studying textile design at university at the time of settlement. C had impaired cognitive function. She was assessed as lacking capacity to manage her financial affairs and a deputy was appointed. Liability was admitted. Out of Court Settlement (approved): £3,250,000 plus periodical payments. Periodical payments comprised care and case management for life of £130,345, index linked to ASHE 6115 80th centile; loss of earnings to age 68 of £22,000, index linked to ASHE all female earnings, and therapies and court of protection costs for life of £32,000, index linked to RPI. *Simmons v Castle* [2012] EWCA Civ 24210 per cent uplift applied. General Damages: £250,000.
AZB v SECRETARY OF STATE FOR HEALTH, Judge Turner, QBD.

1652 Quantum–Cerebral palsy–Delay in diagnosis or treatment

Held: Damages approved. C, male, newborn at the date of the incident and ten at the date of the approval hearing, sustained injuries following his delivery in 2006. A day before C was born, his mother had tested positive for Group B Streptococcus infection, but she was not provided with antibiotic therapy during labour and there was no prescription of antibiotic therapy to C following his delivery. C suffered from GBS infection-related meningitis causing subsequent neurological injury and cerebral palsy. His severe cerebral palsy affected all four limbs, worse on his left side. He suffered from epilepsy (which was largely controlled on medication), significant cognitive impairment and behavioural difficulties. C could walk 20 metres unaided, but otherwise required the use of a walking frame or wheelchair. He had limited use of his upper limbs with reduced range of movement and poor coordination and fine motor skills. He suffered from hypermetropia and a left convergent squint. Due to his learning difficulties he did not have a functioning level of numeracy or literacy and had high levels of inattention and distractibility. He could be aggressive and violent. He was generally continent. He slept very poorly, required 24-hour care and was incapable of employment. C underwent orthopaedic surgery at eight years of age by way of a medial shift calcaneal osteotomy and reefing of the tibialis posterior tendon followed by plaster casting. C's position would not improve and would only worsen. He would lose the ability to walk independently by 15 years; by 20 years he would require the use of a wheelchair indoors when unwell or tired; by 45 years he would be almost entirely dependent on a wheelchair and by 60 years would require intermittent hoisting for transfers. He had a life expectation to 81.5 years. Out of Court Settlement (approved): £3.25 million lump sum plus periodical payments for care and case management of: £86,000 to age 12; £120,000 from age 12 to age 19; £208,000 from age 19 and for the remainder of his life. General Damages for pain, suffering and loss of amenity: £220,000. Interest on general damages: £10,000; future loss of earnings: £334,000; future accommodation costs: £718,000; future therapy costs: £227,000; future aids and equipment costs: £305,000; future assistive technology costs: £66,000; future travel and transport costs: £242,000; future holiday costs: £230,000; future Court of Protection and deputyship costs: £406,000; future education costs: £31,000; future surgery costs: £20,000; future DIY/gardening costs: £26,000. *Simmons v Castle* [2012] EWCA Civ 1288, [2013] 1 W.L.R. 1239, [2013] C.L.Y. 782 10 per cent uplift: applied. Breakdown of special damages: past care and case management costs: £195,000;

past travel costs: £62,000; past accommodation costs: £82,000; past therapy costs: £32,000; past aids and equipment: £15,000; past Deputyship costs: £9,000; past miscellaneous costs: £8,000; interest: £12,000.

R v EAST KENT HOSPITALS UNIVERSITY NHS FOUNDATION TRUST, Judge Laing, QBD.

Personal Injuries or Death–*Quantum*

Details have been received of the following cases in which damages for personal injuries or death were awarded. The classification and sequence of the classified awards follows that adopted in *Kemp and Kemp: The Quantum of Damages*, Vols 3 and 4. In most cases, the age of the plaintiff is reported at the date of injury and at the time of the court hearing. If the age is only stated once, unless there is a statement to the contrary, the age is at the date of the hearing. The cases are classified according to injury type adopted in *Kemp and Kemp* and arranged in descending order of quantum. Unless specified the damages are stated on the basis of full liability, i.e. ignoring any deduction made for contributory negligence. Likewise, any deduction made on account of an applicant in criminal injury compensation cases is ignored unless otherwise specified. The sum is the total amount of the damages awarded unless otherwise stated.

For a cumulative guide to quantum of damages cases reported in *Current Law*during 2016, see the Quantum of Damages table. We must stress that we are entirely dependent on the contributor for the accuracy of his or her report. We welcome contributions and are most grateful for all the reports received. We would appreciate reports of any alterations to awards noted here, either on, or in anticipation of, appeal.

1614 **Quantum–Brain damage: very severe**

Held: Damages approved. L, male, aged 27 at the date of the accident and 33 at the date of the approval hearing, suffered a traumatic brain injury when he was knocked down by a bus as he was crossing the road. L's injuries were catastrophic. He was left with a very severe cognitive defect such that he was only able to communicate with simple words, gestures and grunts. He was rendered tetraplegic and required 24-hour care. There would be no improvement in his condition. Liability was agreed 57.5/42.5 in L's favour and the award reflected the deduction for contributory negligence. The claim was settled, and approved with a lump sum of £2,000,000 with periodical payments of £135,413 per annum. On a capitalised basis, before deduction for contributory negligence, the sum would have been at least £9,100,000. A key issue was the impact of the liability split on the provision of care. L could not elect to be self-funding but the parties agreed to treat the damages as "topping up" the gap between L's care need and the funding the state provided. Breakdown of General Damages: £250,000 before deduction for contributory negligence (£143,750 after deduction). Future losses: PPO's of £135,413 for future care (£235,500 before reduction for contributory negligence). Lump sum of £2,000,000 (£3,478,260 before reduction) for all other heads of loss both past and future.

L (A PROTECTED PARTY) v ARRIVA LONDON NORTH LTD, Judge Coe QC, QBD.

1615 **Quantum–Brain damage: very severe**

Held: Damages approved. M, male, aged 19 at the date of the accident and 30 at the date of the approval hearing suffered an extremely severe head injury following a high speed motorway crash in which he was travelling as a rear-seat passenger. M required a partial right frontal lobotomy, and was left with the front half of his skull missing. There were attempts to replace bone flap with titanium plate but those failed because of recurrent infection. As a consequence, M was left with very obvious cosmetic disability. M's rehabilitation was prolonged and stormy. He experienced seizures and there was a real risk of falls from balance problems, which increased his vulnerability arising from the craniectomy. He had to wear a helmet when away from home. There were severe emotional, behavioural and cognitive consequences from the brain injury, particularly with paranoia and the control of anger and temper. Initial family support led to a belief he was being exploited, as a result of which he was prosecuted and imprisoned for assaulting family members. On release M was accommodated under a Guardianship Order with 24-hour support. Arrangements were gradually made to move him to his own accommodation in the community with daily support and case management. M's life expectancy was anticipated to be to age 80-85. The life time multiplier was assessed at 29.63. There were guarded prospects of increased independence but M would remain vulnerable to breakdowns and crises for which additional support would be required. He was unable to complete a university course or to pursue paid employment, and required continuing daily support with case management. Out of Court Settlement (approved): £3 million total damages. General Damages: £165,000. Past losses: interim payments of £493,000 were made for care, therapies and case management. Total past losses including earnings were assessed at £583,000. Future losses: earnings: £556,000; care, case management, mentoring/counselling: £38,000 per annum; Court of Protection costs: £10,000 per annum; travel: £30,000; DIY, decoration and gardening: £59,000; holidays: £15,000; neuropsychology and neuropsychiatry: £50,000. Breakdown of special damages: loss of earnings: £120,000; family care: £75,000; paid care: £250,000; case management: £50,000; Deputyship: £21,000; Travel: £28,000.

YM v AK , Judge Denyer, QBD.

1616 Quantum–Cerebral palsy

Held: Damages approved. K, male, aged 9 years old at the date of the approval hearing, suffered brain damage leading to quadriplegic cerebral palsy at the time of his birth. K had had an abnormal fetal heart rate and his head was delivered with a loop of umbilical cord looped around his neck. He suffered acute profound asphyxia. K's cerebral palsy was predominantly dystonic, with overt upper limb involuntary athethoid movements, truncal hypotonia and overt dystonia affecting all four limbs. He was immobile except for directional wiggling on his back. He had a small amount of head control and was able to stand when supported in a standing frame. He did not have any fine motor function and his attempts to use his hands were impeded by his involuntary upper limb movements. He was wholly fed by a gastrostomy, using bolus feeds, and his speech was incomprehensible. He had multiple learning difficulties and his communication skills were limited to making various noises and pointing using his eyes. K's condition was permanent. His life expectancy was reduced to 39 years old. He would require constant care and feeding by gastrostomy for the rest of his life. He would need expert professional care, adapted accommodation and a range of equipment. He would never be able to sit independently, stand or walk. When an adult, he was unlikely to have any independent mobility, be able to live independently or to manage his own household. He would not have any mental capacity as an adult and would not be able to obtain paid employment. It was expected that K's ultimate level of intellectual functioning would be within the low end of the moderate range of intellectual disability (IQ 35-50). However, it was expected that with increased assistive communication, he would be better able to communicate and his cognitive abilities would significantly progress. Out of Court Settlement (approved): £2,675,000 lump sum and annual payments of £150,000 per annum until K was 19 years old and £201,800 per annum thereafter for the remainder of his life. Future costs: psychological therapy costs: £25,806; physiotherapy costs: £57,071; speech and language therapy costs: £84,169; aid and equipment costs: £171,322; communication aid and assistive technology costs: £135,292; transport costs: £108,229; loss of earnings: £168,706; accommodation costs: £429,584; education costs: £12,500; deputyship costs: £171,306. General Damages: £285,000. *Simmons v Castle* [2012] EWCA Civ 1288, [2013] 1 W.L.R. 1239, [2013] C.L.Y. 782 10 per cent uplift : applied.

K (A CHILD) v UNIVERSITY HOSPITALS OF LEICESTER NHS TRUST, Nicola Davies J, QBD.

1617 Quantum–Cerebral palsy

Held: Damages approved. S, female, aged 7 at the date of the approval hearing, sustained severe hypoxic ischemia, resulting in four limb asymmetric dystonic cerebral palsy at the time of her birth. S was born by emergency caesarean with an Apgar score of 0 at 1 minute and 6 at five minutes. There was no heartbeat and S was resuscitated and intubated. Regular resuscitation was achieved after 30 minutes. S was transferred to the special care baby unit where she remained for five days. She then spent a further two days on the ward, before being discharged. Initially S had mild hypoxic signs with some hypertonia, but there were no seizures or significant organ problems. S had good cognitive abilities although she would remain vulnerable due to concerns over her working memory. S's left side was most affected and she had difficulty with fine motor skills that limited her ability with activities of daily living. She had poor balance and relied on a walking frame and wheelchair to assist her in mobility for longer distances or uneven surfaces. S had some dysarthria of speech but had good comprehension and vocabulary. She spoke slowly and found it difficult to compete with her peers in terms of volume. S could feed independently. Her sleep pattern was very poor and she often woke during the night and required assistance. The settlement was approved by the court. Past losses: Care and Case Management: £86,000; Equipment: £6,500; Therapies: £3,404; Holidays: £7,500; Travel: £25,000; Accommodation: £16,000; Trustee costs: £5,000. Future Care and Case management: to secondary school: £42,000 per annum; to higher education: £52,000 per annum; to age 60: £100,000 per annum; for life: £118,729 per annum. Future losses: Loss of Earnings: £120,000; Aids and Equipment: £154,577; Occupational Therapy: £47,897; Physiotherapy: £95,000; Assistive Technology: £50,000; Speech and Language Therapy: £14,390; Accommodation: £838,737; Travel: £203,000; Educational Psychology: £7,000; Holiday Costs: £118,650; Trustee costs: £85,000; Pension: £30,000. General Damages: £264,000.

S (A CHILD) v N NHS FOUNDATION TRUST, District Judge Hassall, QBD.

1619 Quantum–Excretory organs: bowels

Held: Damages assessed. M, male, aged 55 years at the date of the accident and 56 at the date of the hearing, was involved in a rear-end shunt road traffic accident. M suffered a neck strain, headaches and a flare up of his pre-existing Crohn's disease. His headaches lasted for eight days and he suffered with symptoms of his neck strain for a period of six weeks. His flare up of Crohn's disease lasted for a period of six months. M had suffered from Crohn's disease for 30 years prior to his accident. His symptoms prior to the accident were described in the medical report as mild. After the collision, for a period of six months, M suffered constipation, diarrhoea and fatigue. However, the medical evidence stated that M had suffered no significant effect on his work, social, or domestic life as a result. The medical evidence was that the flare up of his Crohn's symptoms was 65% attributable to the collision and 35% attributable to his pre-existing condition. The judge considered that the relevant category of the JC Guidelines for a flare up of pre-existing Crohn's Disease symptoms was Chapter 6(G)(b). As recovery took place within six months, rather than "within a few days or weeks" as stated in 6(G)(b)(iv), the judge found that bracket 6(G)(b)(iii) was the most appropriate. The judge awarded £3,500 for the Crohn's symptoms, which was then discounted by 35% to £2,275, in accordance with the medical evidence. General Damages: £3,275. Total Damages: £3,290.

MALLOY v COLLINS, District Judge Gill, CC (Medway).

1620 Quantum–Facial scarring

Held: Damages approved. B, a schoolboy, aged six at the date of the accident and eight at the date of the child settlement approval hearing, sustained a laceration to his left cheek. B was playing on a field which formed part of his school. A metal container had been placed on the field by the defendant, who was carrying out remedial work. As B was running by the container he caught his left cheek on a piece of protruding metal. B sustained a 22mm by 2.2mm laceration to his left cheek. He was absent from school for one week and was unable to use his quad bike for six weeks. B was left with a scar on his left cheek. Although the scar improved over the 17 months following the accident, it was permanent and was visible at conversational distance. The district judge reminded himself that the scar would continue to grow as B's head grew. General Damages: £10,000.

BST (A CHILD) v ANWYL, District Judge Humphreys, CC (Welshpool & Newtown).

1621 **Quantum–General psychiatric disorders**

Held: Damages assessed. C, female, aged 35 at the date of the incident and 39 at the date of the award, suffered psychological injury in the form of a psychotic breakdown in January 2009 arising out of bullying and harassment by other employees. C had been employed by the defendant ambulance service (D) as a business administration manager in its fleet and logistics department. In 2007, the department was functioning poorly and she found ambulances lacking MOTs and proper servicing on the road in an illegal condition. She received no support from her line managers who were rude and obstructive, and had over the years told her that she was a "dummkopf", had bad breath, was a "woman in a man's world", and commented on her breast size. In March 2008 she was signed off sick for a short period with reactive depression but received little support. She was subsequently appointed to a new post as business administration manager (BAM). However a new director (L) was appointed to D's fleet and logistics department. He awarded a contract to his girlfriend (M) for a post which overlapped with C's role so that staff due to be supervised by C were instead supervised by M. C was told to perform a project role, and never worked on her substantive role. A senior manager told her that she was "a monster" who "nobody wants to work with", and that he was "pissed off" with her. She was very upset by that and told another manager that she was considering suicide. After C reported her problems to another director, she was seconded to a different department and enjoyed her work there. However, D later terminated all external contracts and secondments. C returned to her substantive post, but M's contract was not terminated. She sought clarification of her role from human resources, but they were unable to advise her of her true position. In January 2009, her new line manager told her that the BAM role was obsolete and she was asked to do project work. C saw her GP who prescribed anti-depressants and wanted to sign her off work with a depressive illness. C experienced delusions and hallucinations and was referred to a mental health crisis team who attended her for two weeks. She never returned to work. She was set to make a graduated return to work in April 2011 but D put her on special leave and made her redundant in December 2011. The judge held that D had breached its duty and rejected D's case that a relationship breakdown was the cause of her illness. He held that D's breach of duty materially contributed to her psychotic illness. C suffered from continuing depression and a permanent increased vulnerability to future depressive episodes. General Damages: £27,500; Future loss of earnings: £178,539; Loss of future car benefit: £92,419; Loss of chance of enhanced earnings: £17,508; Loss of pension: £110,253; Loss of chance of enhanced pension: £37,473. Breakdown of Special Damages: Past loss of earnings: £121,128; Interest on past loss of earnings: £1,672; Past loss of car benefit: £17,921; Loss of congenial employment: £5,000; Interest on loss of congenial employment: £1,904.

PHILLIPS v GREAT WESTERN AMBULANCE SERVICE NHS TRUST, Judge Blunt QC, QBD (Bristol).

1622 **Quantum–General psychiatric disorders–Neck: whiplash injury: no previous condition**

[Civil Procedure Rules 1998 r.36.14(3)(a), r.36.14(3)(d)]

Held: Damages assessed. K, male, aged 39 at the date of the road traffic accident and 44 at the date of trial, was driving along a carriageway when the defendant drove out of a side road and collided with his nearside front corner bumper. K sustained pain in his right shoulder, tension-type headaches and pain in the nape of his neck. He also suffered from an adjustment disorder with anxiety and depression. A consultant orthopaedic spinal surgeon and consultant orthopaedic shoulder surgeon agreed that K "suffered from significant psychological problems following the accident which would have compounded his perception of his level of disability and had an impact on his recovery". Prior to the accident, K was a highly-motivated, driven man who coped with a very demanding job, together with his family responsibilities, which included maintaining the garden and carrying out decorating in the home. He was involved in the running of the house as his wife had rheumatoid arthritis. He was also actively involved in martial arts training. Following the accident K could only provide limited assistance within and around the house. He was also unable to continue with his martial arts training. K's pain and symptoms were ongoing at the time of the award and the court heard evidence from orthopaedic specialists and psychologists. In relation to future loss of earning capacity, the court found that K, being in his early forties with previous employment experience in the high-pressured area of sales, with a record of absences due to ill-health, would find it extremely difficult to find any employer prepared to offer him employment. Further, he had ongoing problems which were likely to be long term. Future loss of earning capacity was calculated applying a multiplicand of £43,200 with a multiplier of 15.44 years. His residual earning capacity was calculated as £7,800 p.a. on the basis of 20 hours per week at the level of the national minimum wage. A multiplier of 17.55 years was applied with a secondary discount of 0.33 resulting in a multiplier of 5.79. In respect of costs, K beat his own offer and pursuant to CPR r.36.14(3)(a) he received enhanced interest on his damages, which was agreed at 7.5 per cent per annum. Pursuant to CPR r.36.14(3)(d), in addition to the indemnity costs and interest to which K was entitled, he received a prescribed percentage uplift of 15 per cent (10 per cent on the first £500,000 and 5 per cent thereafter) on his past and future damages. Future loss of earning capacity: £621,846; Future care and domestic assistance costs: £33,800; Future assistance with decorating and DIY costs: £12,000. Breakdown of Special Damages: Policy excess: £250; Past gardening costs: £885; Past medical treatment and investigations costs: £11,446; Past gratuitous care costs: £12,480; Past cleaning costs: £100; Past employer's outlay: £14,256; Past prescription costs: £466; Past painkiller costs: £50; Past carpet cleaning costs: £300; Past additional parking costs: £677; Past physiotherapy treatment costs: £1,170; Past pain management clinic swimming programme costs; £50; Past TENS machine cost: £34; Past cost of attendance on PALS scheme at leisure centre: £86; Past decorator costs: £1,400; Interest on past losses: £982. General Damages for pain, suffering and loss of amenity: £40,000. Total Damages: £791,109.

KASHIF v SIMPSON, Recorder Knapton, CC (Bradford).

1623 Quantum–Head

Held: Damages assessed. C, a schoolboy, aged nine at the date of the road traffic accident and 11 at the date of the hearing, was injured when the vehicle in which he was travelling was hit from the rear by the vehicle driven by the defendant. The car in which C was travelling was shunted into the car in front. C's forehead collided with the interior of the vehicle and he suffered pain and bruising. On examination it was noted that C's bruising, which was described as a red mark, had resolved over seven days. C did not miss any school as a result of his injury but he was unable to participate in football training for a period of one week. He did not suffer from any psychological symptoms following his accident. General Damages: £450.

D (A CHILD) v HARJI, Deputy District Judge Jeffries, CC (Cardiff).

1629 Quantum–Back and neck: whiplash injury: no previous condition

Held: Damages assessed. S, male, aged 43 at the date of the road traffic accident and 44 at the date of the hearing, suffered soft tissue injuries to his neck and lower back. His symptoms were severe for two weeks before improving. By the date of the medical examination at two months after the accident his symptoms and pain were moderate and constant. His symptoms were aggravated by movements of his head from side to side or up and down as well as sitting or standing for long periods. The pain was worse when the weather was cold, particularly in the morning. S struggled with strenuous tasks at work, including lifting items. His domestic lifestyle was affected, including domestic chores, shopping, lifting items, sleep, childcare and his social life, particularly in the first few weeks. Upon examination at two months, there was a 76 to 99 per cent restriction of movement in the neck and back as well as some tenderness over the trapezius muscles as well as at the interspinous ligaments and over the vertebral muscles in the back. The medical expert expected a full recovery of the neck and lower back whiplash injuries by 12 months after the accident. S gave evidence that he had made a full recovery by nine months after the accident and the judge assessed the injury on that basis. Six sessions of physiotherapy were recommended and undertaken. General Damages: £3,100. Total Damages: £3,512.

SHARIF v DARASZ-SMULSKA, Deputy District Judge Oldroyd, CC (Blackpool).

1630 **Quantum–Back and neck: whiplash injury: no previous condition**

Held: Damages assessed. G, male, a truck driver, aged 62 at the date of the road traffic accident and 63 at the date of the hearing, was injured when his car, which was stationary at a set of traffic lights, was hit to the rear by another vehicle. G was jolted backwards and forwards by the impact. He left the vehicle unaided. He did not seek medical attention but took painkillers regularly for six weeks afterwards and thereafter as required. He experienced shock for four days and pain to his neck and lower back which was severe at onset and moderate by the time he was medically examined five months after the accident. On that examination, his movement was 90 to 99% of normal and appeared to cause pain and muscle spasms in the neck and lower back. G also experienced travel anxiety, especially when other vehicles appeared to be close to him. That was initially moderate and had resolved by 12 weeks after the accident. G's sleeping, personal care, social life and walking were initially severely restricted, and were moderately restricted at the time of the medical examination. As a truck driver, G found long journeys difficult. It was recommended that G undertake eight sessions of physiotherapy. G had six sessions before being discharged. The prognosis was that his neck and lower back injuries would resolve by 12 months after the accident. General Damages: £3,600. Physiotherapy: £415. Total Damages: £4,025.

GWILLIAM v KALLY, District Judge Trent, CC (Leeds).

1631 **Quantum–Back and neck: whiplash injury: no previous condition–Knee**

Held: Damages assessed. L, male, aged 27 at the date of the road traffic accident and 28 at the date of the hearing, sustained injuries when the vehicle which he was driving was involved in a rear-end shunt. L suffered soft tissue injuries to his neck, shoulder, back and knee. L's vehicle was written off. He was transferred by ambulance to A&E and thereafter attended his GP on two occasions. He took one week off work and worked reduced hours as a civil servant for one month. At three months after the accident, on examination, the medical expert observed that there was discomfort and a restriction of neck movements by about 20 to 30 per cent and discomfort and restriction of upper limb, back and left knee movements by 30 to 40 per cent. L's physical symptoms were described as improved but moderate. He also suffered from headaches and travel anxiety and those had not improved. His household activities such as cleaning, cooking, carrying bags, ironing, lifting items and shopping, as well as his sleep and social life, were moderately restricted. He had not returned to his pre-accident activities of fitness training, football, gym and kickboxing. The medical expert was of the view that all L's symptoms should fully resolve by 13-15 months post-accident and eight sessions of physiotherapy were recommended. L underwent 10 sessions of physiotherapy. When he was discharged from that treatment at 11 months after the accident, he was still experiencing some pain. At the hearing, at about 13 months after the accident, L described mild ongoing symptoms, experienced every other day, and that he had not been able to return to his pre-accident sporting activities. General Damages: £4,300. Total Damages: £5,151.

LALY v ADMIRAL INSURANCE CO LTD, Deputy District Judge Pickup, CC (Preston).

1632 **Quantum–Back and neck: whiplash injury: no previous condition–Shoulder**

Held: Damages assessed. S, female, aged 36 at the date of the accident and 38 at the date of the hearing, suffered soft tissue injuries to her neck, thoracic spine and right shoulder when she was injured as a passenger on a bus that was involved in a road traffic accident. S was stiff in the mornings and used analgesia. She found that carrying her shopping or heavy items at work, such as confidential waste bags, caused her pain. Washing her hair was painful and she could not sit for long periods without experiencing back pain. S suffered right shoulder pain when getting dressed, particularly when putting her bra on. She experienced headaches for 10 days. On examination at two months after the accident there was limitation of movement of all injured areas. The prognosis was that a full recovery was expected by 14 months after the accident. Physiotherapy was recommended but not undertaken. The prognosis was borne out. General Damages: £4,000. Total Damages: £4,115.

STARR v AVIVA INSURANCE UK LTD, Deputy District Judge Thexton, CC (Stockport).

1634 Quantum–Facial scarring

Held: Damages assessed. F, male, aged 65 at the date of the accident and 66 at the date of the hearing, sustained a laceration to his right eyebrow in a road traffic accident due to an impact with the open windscreen. C was in his stationary vehicle when it was hit from the rear by another vehicle. C attended A&E for treatment. The injury required cleaning, wound dressing and steristrips. C took over the counter painkillers for two days. Upon examination at 10 weeks after the accident, a 0.5cm in diameter, faint pink, round, scar was noted on F's eyebrow. No further treatment was required. It was noted that the scar had "faded well". The expert concluded that any residual scarring was best judged at twelve months after the accident. There was no impact on C's lifestyle or hobbies and no restrictions on personal care or home life. C also suffered moderate travel anxiety for one month. The judge explained his assessment by referring to the Judicial College Guidelines (13th edition), Chapter 9(B)(b), Facial Disfigurement, and commented that "leaving aside political correctness, an older man is likely to be less troubled than a young female" in regards to such scarring, which he found, in any event, was on "the low end of the scale, in terms of severity". He noted that as the scar was on the eyebrow, it was likely to be covered by C's eyebrow hairs. It did not appear that C had any concerns about how the scar looked. The judge also considered two authorities, noting that while he always approached such authorities with caution, they were of some assistance in the instant case as they did involve trivial scarring on the area of the eyebrow, *Maqsood v Peace* [2008] C.L.Y. 2889 and *Grant v Hampshire CC* [1992] C.L.Y. 1766 considered. The judge found that the circumstances justified an award falling just below the bracket set out in Chapter 9(B)(b)(v), trivial scarring (£1,430 to £2,940 with 10 per cent uplift). He found that the anxiety did not add much to that assessment. *Simmons v Castle* [2012] EWCA Civ 242 10 per cent uplift: applied. General Damages: £1,300.

FURMAN v HOLT, Deputy District Judge Stockdale , CC (Leeds).

1635 Quantum–Neck: whiplash injury: no previous condition

Held: Damages assessed. H, female, aged 32 years old at the date of the accident and 33 at the date of the hearing, sustained a whiplash injury to her neck when her vehicle was involved in a rear-end shunt. H also suffered with pain in her shoulders. H was restricted in her domestic activities, notably lifting and carrying. Those restrictions were ongoing at the time of the medical examination that took place three months after the accident. H made a full recovery within eight months. She also suffered from shock for two days and experienced travel anxiety for eight months. *Simmons v Castle* [2012] EWCA Civ 242 10 per cent uplift: applied. General Damages: £2,600.

HAYES v DAVIES, Deputy District Judge Evans, CC (Blackwood).

1636 Quantum–Neck: whiplash injury: no previous condition

Held: Damages assessed. K, female, aged 26 years at the date of the accident and 27 at the date of the hearing, sustained soft tissue injuries to her neck in a road traffic accident. K was a front seat passenger in a vehicle that was stationary at a roundabout when it was involved in a rear-end shunt. K experienced difficulties washing and dressing, difficulties in carrying out housework and discomfort whilst watching television. K was a housewife and those restrictions impacted on her day-to-day functioning significantly, although she gave evidence that she had not hired a cleaner or any other domestic assistance following the accident. On examination at two months after the accident, the medical expert found that K's symptoms were severe and noted that her movements were painful. K visited her GP once following the accident. Twelve sessions of physiotherapy were recommended by the medical expert and those were undertaken by February 2015. The physiotherapy discharge report, dated some three months after the accident, gave K's continuing pain at three out of ten, reduced from initial pain of seven out of ten. However, it noted that K had reported that her pain could reach five to six out of ten when her injury was aggravated. In evidence she explained that that was through performing tasks such as hoovering and heavier housework. The medical expert considered that K would recover from her injuries by 13 months after the accident; however, at the time of the hearing K reported ongoing minor and occasional symptoms of which the judge took account. K also reported feeling anxious about her pain, particularly because as a result of her injuries she had suffered from sleep disturbance for approximately 12 months. *Simmons v Castle* [2012] EWCA Civ 1039, [2013] 1 W.L.R. 1239, [2012] C.L.Y. 852 10 per cent uplift applied. General Damages: £4,250.

KHATUN v EUI LTD, District Judge Taylor, CC (Cambridge).

1640 Quantum–Arm: less severe injuries

Held: Damages assessed. B, female, aged 48 at the date of the road traffic accident and 49 at the date of the hearing, sustained soft tissue injuries to her neck, left shoulder and upper arm in November 2015. B was driving her vehicle when the defendant collided with it to the rear, causing her to be jolted within the confines of her seatbelt. Her neck and shoulder symptoms were described as being moderate in intensity but resolved within a week of the accident. Her pain in her arm was moderate for two weeks and thereafter mild in intensity. B did not seek medical attention but took paracetomol for four weeks. She was able to undertake all work, domestic and recreational activities without restriction but her sleep was affected. On examination at two months after the accident only mild arm symptoms persisted with tenderness only on palpation. A recovery was anticipated within three months from the date of the accident. General Damages: £1,750.

BATCHELOR v BUTLER, District Judge Humphreys, CC (Basildon).

1641 Quantum–Back and neck: whiplash injury: no previous condition

Held: Damages assessed. C, a schoolboy, aged 10 at the date of the road traffic accident, suffered injuries to his neck and upper back in a road traffic accident. D suffered from symptoms for a two week period. The defendant's offer fell below £1,000 and arguments were raised to have proceedings transferred to the small claims track. At a Stage 3 hearing, the court awarded C a sum of £800 for general damages for pain, suffering and loss of amenity. The defendant submitted that C should be limited to small claims costs on that basis. The judge agreed and awarded £80 small claims costs plus disbursements. General Damages: £800.

D (A CHILD) v SKINNER, District Judge Smith, CC (Dartford).

1642 Quantum–Back and neck: whiplash injury: no previous condition

Held: Damages assessed. B, female, a sales assistant, aged 41 years old at the date of the road traffic accident and 42 at the date of the hearing, suffered soft tissue injuries to her neck and lumbar spine, as well as travel anxiety, in a rear-end shunt road traffic accident in July 2015. B suffered with referred pain in her left shoulder and associated headaches. She described her symptoms as being of an initially moderate severity and the symptoms persisted at that level for five weeks, before improving, such that by the time of the medico-legal examination at 10 weeks post-accident they were described as mild to moderate and intermittent in nature. B had attended once upon her own GP and, at the time of examination, she continued to undertake self-help exercises and to take analgesia. She reported that her ability to carry her shopping was restricted, as was her ability to exercise, and her sleep was affected. She also reported that her work aggravated her symptoms somewhat. She recovered within six months. The district judge stated that he would not make a separate award in respect of the travel-related anxieties, but that those were accounted for in determining where to place the claim within the applicable physical injury brackets in the JC Guidelines. General Damages: £3,600. Physiotherapy-related costs: £125. *Simmons v Castle* [2012] EWCA Civ 1288, [2013] 1 W.L.R. 1239, [2013] C.L.Y. 782 10 per cent uplift: applied.

BARLOW v TESCO UNDERWRITING, Deputy District Judge Downton, CC (Walsall).

1643 Quantum–Back and neck: whiplash injury: no previous condition

Held: Damages assessed. W, male, an industrial cleaner, aged 22 at the date of the accident and 23 at the date of the hearing, sustained injuries when the vehicle he was driving was involved in a rear-end shunt. W suffered whiplash injuries to his neck and back. He was on restricted duties at work for four weeks and his domestic activities, ability to lift heavy items, sleep, swimming and other sporting activities were initially severely restricted. On examination at five weeks after the accident, all symptoms and loss of amenity had reduced and were described as moderate. He had 50 per cent restriction of movement in all directions of the neck, back and shoulders as well as experiencing pain and tenderness upon palpation. The medical expert was of the opinion that his neck, back and shoulder injuries would resolve within 11 to 13 months, 12 to 14 months and 2 to 4 months of the accident respectively. Six to ten sessions of physiotherapy were recommended. W also suffered from travel anxiety and that was expected to resolve by five months after the accident. General Damages: £3,700.

WAINE v WHITELOCKS, District Judge Clarke, CC (Burnley).

1644 Quantum–Back and neck: whiplash injury: no previous condition

Held: Damages assessed. S, male, aged 35 at the date of the road traffic accident and 38 at the date of the hearing, suffered injuries to his neck and lower back. The accident occurred in July 2013. S was travelling on his scooter when the vehicle in front of him stopped in the centre of the road and the passenger door was opened. S's scooter subsequently collided with the door causing the scooter to swerve. S managed to keep his scooter upright but was injured. S sustained a soft tissue injury to his neck and an acute moderate sprain to his lower back with associated bilateral sciatica. He also suffered psychological trauma and required CBT. S took three weeks off work following the accident. He had restrictions in relation to domestic, household and personal tasks for which he needed assistance for one month. He also suffered from disturbed sleep. S's neck injury resolved 16 months after the accident and his back symptoms resolved 19 months after the accident. The case was dealt with at a Stage 3 Oral Hearing. When considering general damages, the District Judge took into consideration S's sciatica as a significant aggravating factor and considered that the appropriate Judicial College Guideline bracket was Chapter 7(B)(c)(ii), minor back injuries and Chapter 13(C). General Damages: £6,000. Total Damages: £10,842.

STEVENSON v KHAN, District Judge Hugman, CC (Wandsworth).

1646 Quantum–Back and neck: whiplash injury: no previous condition–Shoulder

Held: Damages assessed. R, male, aged 27 at the date of the road traffic accident and 30 at the date of the hearing, was driving his car when he was hit from the passenger side by a van driven by the defendant. He was jolted forwards and to the right before recoiling into his seat. He was able to exit the vehicle without assistance and he attended A&E. R suffered soft tissue injuries resulting in pain and stiffness to his neck, both shoulders, thoracic and lumbar spine and his right thumb. He was prescribed paracetomol, cocodamol and ibuprofen and he underwent a course of osteopathy. He was absent from his job in sales and administration for one week. He was restricted in lifting and carrying, personal care and he suffered from disturbed sleep. The initial prognosis was that he would recover from his injuries within five months, but the spinal and shoulder injuries in fact took 10 months before full recovery was achieved. R described his pain as severe for one month and moderate for a further eight months. In addition to his soft tissue injuries, R felt shocked and shaken for three days, suffered headaches for one month and he experienced travel anxiety for four months. He described the latter as moderate for one month and mild to moderate thereafter. The district judge was of the opinion that each of the injuries to the neck, back and shoulder would have been worth around £3,000 on their own according to the JC Guidelines. There was bound to be some overlap as simply adding them up and reaching a figure of £12,000 would be too high. The judge felt that £6,000 was an appropriate figure. The judge considered the thumb injury and the travel anxiety separately and noted that the JC Guidelines suggested awards of £1,750 and £750 respectively. *Simmons v Castle* [2012] EWCA Civ 242 10 per cent uplift: applied. General Damages: £8,500.

RUSSELL v AGER, Deputy District Judge Campbell, CC (Horsham).

1648 Quantum–Back and neck: whiplash injury: no previous condition

Held: Damages assessed. B, male, aged 36 at the date of the road traffic accident and 37 at the date of the assessment hearing, sustained soft tissue injuries to his neck, shoulders and lower back in March 2015. B was driving his vehicle when the defendant's vehicle collided with it to the rear, causing him to be jolted within the confines of his seatbelt. Following the accident, B developed symptoms in his neck, shoulders and low back which he initially described as severe in intensity. He did not seek medical attention and did not require any treatment; he medicated with over the counter painkillers. B had no time off work and while he remained able to attend the gym as normal, that was moderately restricted as a result of his injuries. B's neck and shoulder symptoms resolved within four months and his back symptoms resolved within six months of the date of the accident. Liability was admitted and the matter was assessed pursuant to Practice Direction 8B para.11: Pre-Action Protocol for Low Value Personal Injury Claims in Road Traffic Accidents. General Damages: £2,500.

BENNETT v AGEAS INSURANCE LTD, District Judge Watson, CC (Wolverhampton).

1649 Quantum–Back and neck: whiplash injury: no previous condition

Held: Damages assessed. H, female, a teacher, aged 36 at the date of the road traffic accident and 37 at the date of the hearing, sustained injuries when the defendant (D) collided with the rear of her stationary vehicle. H suffered soft tissue injuries to her neck, upper back and left shoulder. H reported that her neck symptoms had initially been severe, but had improved to a moderate level by the time of the medico-legal examination, approximately two months after the accident. She also reported that her back and shoulder symptoms had never been greater than a moderate severity and had improved to a mild nature by the time of the examination. C was absent from work for a day and attended her GP once, who prescribed analgesia and anti-inflammatories. C also attended eight physiotherapy sessions. C had missed a party on account of her injuries, her ability to attend to her personal care had been restricted for three weeks and her capacity to undertake heavy lifting, cooking, shopping, DIY and child care had all been restricted. The prognosis was for recovery from the neck symptoms within ten months, and other symptoms within eight months from the date of the accident. C had claimed £510 in respect of physiotherapy related costs. D contended that it had made an offer to supply treatment at a lesser cost than that which had been incurred by C and that therefore only the lesser cost should be allowed. C, relying upon *Copley v Lawn* [2009] EWCA Civ 580, [2010] 1 All E.R. (Comm) 890, [2009] C.L.Y. 970, responded that, D's offer letter had not established what the cost to D would otherwise have been and therefore that C had not failed to mitigate, as there was no way that C could have gauged which had been the better deal. The judge ruled that *Copley* applied but that there was duplication between two assessments claimed and that C could not claim the costs of a treatment discharge report that had not been filed and served, *Copley* applied. Physiotherapy costs: £425. General Damages: £3,000.

HEALD v FULLER, District Judge O'Regan, CC (Birmingham).

1650 Quantum–Back and neck: whiplash injury: no previous condition

Held: Damages assessed. G, male, aged 45 at the date of the road traffic accident and 46 at the date of the hearing, suffered injuries to his neck and lower back. G was stationary at a set of traffic lights on a roundabout when a vehicle driven by the defendant entered the roundabout and collided with G. He was wearing a seatbelt at the time but was aware of being jolted within his vehicle. G suffered from severe pain in his neck and lower back for six weeks after the accident. That reduced to moderate pain for seven and a half months. He required care and assistance in relation to domestic and household duties, and was significantly restricted in relation to his regular hobbies. G underwent seven sessions of physiotherapy and suffered from sleep disturbance. The judge took into account the level of pain that G had been in when he was examined two months after the accident, along with the level of care and assistance that he required, medication and the prognosis period given. Due to the substantial recovery period of approximately two months, he considered that the correct JC Guideline was Chapter 7: Neck and Back injuries: (c) minor (ii). General

Damages: £3,000. *Simmons v Castle* [2012] EWCA Civ 1288, [2013] 1 W.L.R. 1239, [2013] C.L.Y. 782 10 per cent uplift : applied. Physiotherapy costs: £541; Hire costs: £900; Miscellaneous costs: £60. Total Damages: £4,501.

GRAHAM v JACKSON, Judge Wood, CC (Newcastle).

1651 Quantum–Back and spine: acceleration or exacerbation of pre-existing symptomatic condition–Head

Held: Damages assessed. H, female, aged 39 at the date of the road traffic accident and 40 at the date of the hearing, suffered injuries to her head and lower back. H was involved in a rear-end shunt while she was stationary at a roundabout. H was jolted backwards and forwards in her vehicle. She was wearing a seatbelt at the time. H suffered severe stress induced headaches following the accident. She also suffered pain and stiffness in her lower back due to an exacerbation injury, and fear of travel. H was severely restricted in relation to household and domestic tasks and exercising. She took two days off work following the accident and underwent a course of physiotherapy treatment. Her headaches resolved within three weeks of the accident date. Her exacerbation injury to her lower back returned to its pre-accident status 12 months after the accident. H's fear of travel resolved seven months after the accident with no further treatment. General Damages: £3,700.

HILL v PERRY, District Judge Humphries, CC (Basildon).

1653 Quantum–Claims for death of husband–General psychiatric disorders

Held: Damages approved. KH was the personal representative of the deceased (X), her husband, who died aged 42. X was admitted to hospital after the sudden onset of chest pain. He was kept in hospital over the weekend and continued to suffer pain. He was diagnosed with gastro-oesophageal reflux disorder and discharged. The day after he was discharged, D was at home with his eight year old son (AH). D collapsed as a result of a ruptured thoracic aortic aneurysm. He was writhing around on the floor and shouting in pain. AH dialed for an ambulance. KH and the couples eldest son (JH) arrived home and witnessed X's significant and disturbing pain and distress. X was transferred by ambulance but died in the ambulance and could not be resuscitated. It was KH's case that if X's aortic aneurysm had been identified on the date he was admitted to hospital he would have undergone aneurysm repair and, given his young age and the fact that he did not suffer from any other significant co-morbities, he would have had very good prospects of survival. Liability was admitted. The primary issue for determination was what X's life expectancy would have been if his aortic aneurysm had been identified and treated. X's aneurysm had been in the descending aorta and the medical experts agreed that, but for the negligence, X would have had a further life expectancy of 10 years. KH and her two sons suffered psychiatric injuries as a result of witnessing X's collapse. They were expected to make a good recovery from their psychiatric injuries with time and treatment. X was the breadwinner of the family and KH and X had three children. The settlement was agreed and approved. General Damages: X: £3,000; KH: £10,800; JH and AH: £14,200. Future loss of earnings: £128,000. Loss of pension: £30,000. Future loss of services: £30,000. Future counselling costs: £6,100. Intangible benefits: KH: £5,400; JH: £5,400; AH: £6,200. Bereavement award: £11,800. Total Damages: £400,000.

KH v UNIVERSITY HOSPITALS BRISTOL NHS FOUNDATION TRUST, Judge Denyer, QBD (Bristol).

1654 Quantum–General psychiatric disorders

Held: Damages assessed. B, a boy, aged one year and five months at the date of the accident and three years and seven months at the date of the hearing, was a passenger in a vehicle that was involved in a road traffic accident. As a result of the accident, B was diagnosed with insomnia. The defendant sought to strike out the claim on the basis that the statement of case disclosed no reasonable grounds for bringing a claim. The defendant alleged that B did not have a compensable injury and that the medical evidence did not support the diagnosis of any recognisable psychiatric or psychological condition. The defendant sought to rely upon *Nicholls v Rushton* Times, June 19, 1992, [1992] C.L.Y. 3252, where the Court of Appeal had concluded that a claimant needed to have suffered from a recognisable psychological disorder in order to be entitled to an award for damages. The defendant denied that B had suffered any physical injury for which compensation was payable pursuant to *Nicholls*. The judge found that although he was bound by the findings in *Nicholls*, he was able to distinguish B's case. He accepted that insomnia was far more significant than mere fear and anxiety and that it was a recognisable disorder under F51.1 as a Non-Organic Insomnia of the World Health Organisation International Classification of Mental and Behavioural Disorders, 10th Edition. The defendant's application to strike out B's claim was dismissed, *Nicholls* distinguished and *Hicks v Chief Constable of South Yorkshire* [1992] 2 All E.R. 65, [1992] C.L.Y. 1554 considered. Following the accident, B suffered severe shock for 24 hours and the onset of severe insomnia. He was frustrated and showed aggression towards his older brother for about a month following the accident. His insomnia had improved and was considered moderately severe at the date of the medical examination, 11 months after the accident. It was anticipated that B's insomnia would resolve over the next six months, that is within 17 months of the accident date. General Damages: £1,375.

B (A CHILD) v THOMAS, District Judge Fraser , CC (Pontypridd).

1655 Quantum–Neck: whiplash injury: no previous condition

Held: Damages assessed. C, female, aged 37 at the date of the road traffic accident and 38 at the date of the hearing, sustained soft tissue injuries to her neck and right shoulder with associated headaches in December 2015. C was the driver of a vehicle, when the defendant collided with it to the rear, causing her to be jolted within the confines of her seatbelt. She was attended to by paramedics at the scene and was subsequently seen in the Accident and Emergency Department as well as by her GP on one occasion. As well as her soft tissue injuries, C sustained a burn to her right hand and bruising around her eyes and suffered from driver anxiety. She medicated with analgesics, anti-inflammatory medication and muscle relaxants. Her symptoms were initially described as moderate in intensity. She was absent from work for two weeks and childcare, cooking, shopping, sleep and sexual intercourse were all restricted during that period. The bruising and burn resolved without complication within two to three weeks. Her shoulder symptoms resolved within a month. By the time of medical examination at two months after the accident, her neck symptoms had improved but there remained tenderness and restriction of movement. A full recovery from her travel anxiety was anticipated within five months of the accident and from her neck injury within eight months. General Damages: £3,600.

OADES v ELEPHANT INSURANCE SERVICES, District Judge Heppell, CC (Rotherham).

1656 Quantum–Neck: whiplash injury: no previous condition

Held: Damages assessed. C, male, aged 27 at the date of the road traffic accident and 28 at the date of the assessment hearing, sustained moderate soft tissue injuries to his neck, shoulder, back and ankle in August 2015. C was the driver of a vehicle, when the defendant collided with it to the rear, causing him to be jolted within the confines of his seatbelt. His neck, shoulder and ankle symptoms were initially described as moderate in intensity and his lower back symptoms were described as mild. He attended his GP on one occasion and medicated with Co-Codamol for three weeks. His lower back symptoms resolved after two weeks. The neck, shoulder and ankle symptoms were acute for two weeks and thereafter reduced in intensity and were considered mild but constant. C had no time off work but was restricted in his duties for three weeks. At the time of the medical examination, eight weeks after the accident, C's residual symptoms had improved albeit tenderness and restricted range of movement was noted. C had still not resumed his hobby of playing football. A full recovery from the residual symptoms was anticipated within four months of the accident. General Damages: £2,800.

CHRYSTAL v AGEAS INSURANCE LTD, District Judge Nicolle, CC (Nottingham).

1657 Quantum–Neck: whiplash injury: no previous condition

Held: Damages assessed. N, female, aged 33 years old at the date of the road traffic accident and 35 years at the date of the hearing, suffered a soft tissue whiplash type injury to her neck in April 2015. N was driving her vehicle and approaching a roundabout when a vehicle driven by the defendant abruptly changed lanes and collided with the offside of her vehicle. N suffered symptoms and associated headaches for nine months before those resolved. The district judge considered the JC Guidelines and found that her injuries fell within Chapter 7(A)(c)(ii) on the basis of the length of her recovery. The judge considered that the lower end of the tariff applied on the basis that N required no medical treatment and there was no significant impact on her work, social life or domestic functioning. General Damages: £1,950.

NARRAMORE v ADMIRAL INSURANCE CO LTD, Deputy District Judge Priddis, CC (Torquay & Ntn Abbott).

1658 Quantum–Neck: whiplash injury: no previous condition–Knee

Held: Damages assessed. H, male, aged 43 years old at the date of the road traffic accident and 44 at the date of the hearing, suffered soft tissue injuries to his neck and knees, with contusion injuries to his chest and thighs, as well as travel-related anxieties. H was a front seat passenger in a car, when the defendant collided with it to the front, causing him to be jolted within the confines of his seatbelt. H reported that all of his symptoms were of moderate severity. He had attended once at the local A&E Department and also once upon his own GP and received a course of physiotherapy. The chest and lower limb injuries resolved entirely within a month, but the neck symptoms and anxieties continued at a mild to moderate, albeit intermittent, level by the time of the medico-legal examination, approximately two months after the accident. At that time, he was still undertaking physiotherapy. He reported to the medical expert that he continued to take analgesia as required and that his ability to carry his shopping remained restricted. He recovered within six months. *Simmons v Castle* [2012] EWCA Civ 1288, [2013] 1 W.L.R. 1239, [2013] C.L.Y. 782 10 per cent uplift: applied. General Damages: £2,650.

HODGSON v FOSTER, Deputy District Judge Nix, CC (Kingston upon Hull).

1659 Quantum–Neck: whiplash injury: no previous condition–Shoulder

Held: Damages assessed. K, female, aged 33 at the date of the road traffic accident and 36 at the date of the hearing, suffered injuries when the vehicle she was driving was involved in a rear-end shunt. K was approaching a junction when she came to a stop in a line of traffic. The defendant failed to stop and collided with the rear of K's vehicle, shunting K into the rear of the vehicle in front of her. K sustained a muscular strain to her neck and a soft tissue injury to her right shoulder. K experienced restrictions at work with lifting heavy objects and in relation to domestic and household tasks. She underwent a course of physiotherapy and was prescribed analgesics from her GP. The muscular strain to her neck resolved within 24 months of the accident and the injury to her right shoulder was given a 24-month prognosis. The district judge took into account the significance of the shoulder injury and felt that the 24-month prognosis was appropriate but stated that the neck injury could be subsumed with the shoulder injury and so an enhanced award would not be appropriate. General Damages: £6,000.

KELLY v KAUR, Deputy District Judge Smart, CC (Newcastle).

1660 Quantum–Neck: whiplash injury: no previous condition–Shoulder

Held: Damages assessed. T, female, a kitchen worker, aged 73 at the date of the road traffic accident and 74 at the date of the hearing, suffered injuries when the defendant collided with the rear of her stationary vehicle. The accident occurred in December 2014. T's vehicle was turned on its right side and she had to be assisted from her vehicle by the emergency services. She was wearing a seatbelt. T sustained soft tissue whiplash-type injuries to her neck and right shoulder, as well as bruising to her chest. T suffered moderate pain for the first month following the accident and then she suffered intermittent, mild to moderate pain for 11 months. She was prescribed painkillers and analgesics for the first month and underwent a course of physiotherapy. T was reduced to light duties. Her ability to carry out housework and lift objects was moderately restricted and her sleep was disturbed. T made a full recovery from the injuries to her neck, right shoulder and chest within 12 months from the date of the accident. General Damages: £3,970.

THORNHILL v HUDD, District Judge Ralton, CC (Swindon).

1661 Quantum–Nose

Held: Damages assessed. C, female, aged 27 at the date of the operation and 33 at the date of the hearing, underwent a septorhinoplasty performed by a private cosmetic surgeon in April 2010. C alleged that the operation was carried out negligently and/or her consent had not been obtained. As a consequence, C suffered painful after-effects, including bleeding. She was left with a distorted and functionally impaired ("Polly Beak") nose, as well as constriction of her internal nasal valves and alar collapse on the lower third of the nose. She had a broad columella and narrowed airways due to alar reduction and lack of support in the mid-third of the nose. There was obvious scarring to the columella and in the alar grooves. She was unable to breathe properly, either at day or at night. She also had to sleep with her mouth open, resulting in a dry throat and lips, and causing her to wake frequently. Her voice had acquired a nasal tone. Her breathing difficulties had had an adverse impact on her relationship with her boyfriend and had also caused her difficulties in her work as a hairdresser. C had also suffered an adverse psychological reaction, with symptoms of post-traumatic stress, anxiety and depression. She underwent a revision operation in August 2013. That operation restored her cosmetic appearance to one with which she was relatively happy, but she was left with a compromised nasal airway. She was advised that any further revision surgery would be "unpredictable" in its overall result. She was also left with residual psychological effects, which she was advised could be alleviated with cognitive behavioural therapy. C's evidence at trial was that whilst she was relatively happy with the cosmetic appearance, she still had difficulty breathing through her nose. That caused a number of problems: she snored at night and did not attend the gym as she had done prior to her first operation. She said that if funds were made available she would seek advice about a further operation as well as undertaking psychological treatment. Further, she was still distressed by her experiences. The defendant did not engage with the litigation and judgment in default was entered. The judge commented that he had found the Judicial College Guidelines of little assistance. General Damages: £17,500. Past treatment: £6,980. Past loss of earnings: £19,539. Future cognitive behavioural therapy: £1,300. Future treatment: £3,500.

C v MORACI, Judge Collender QC, CC (City of London).

1662 Quantum–Shoulder

Held: Damages assessed. S, female, aged 45 years old at the date of the road traffic accident and 46 at the date of the hearing, suffered injury to her right shoulder in April 2015. S was a front seat passenger in a stationary car when the defendant's vehicle collided with it at the front, causing her to be jolted within the confines of her seatbelt. Liability was admitted and the matter was assessed pursuant to Practice Direction 8B para.11: Pre-Action Protocol for Low Value Personal Injury Claims. S described her initial symptoms as being severe, but reported that they had improved to a moderate to severe nature at the time of the medical examination, at two months after the accident. S worked in chiropody services and suffered pain whilst at work. Additionally she suffered discomfort when driving and her sleep was affected. She was also unable to attend the gym. The medical expert anticipated a complete recovery within four months of the examination, approximately six months after the accident date. General Damages: £2,500.

SWEENEY v BATES, District Judge Potts, CC (Nottingham).

PERSONAL PROPERTY

1663 **Chattels–Co-ownership–Collection of porcelain–Division between joint owners pursuant to s.188(1) Law of Property Act 1925**

[Civil Procedure Rules 1998 Pt 8; Law of Property Act 1925 (c.20) s.188, s.188(1)]

The court was required to determine the appropriate division of a valuable collection of Chinese porcelain as between the claimants and defendants (D1 and D2). The parties were siblings. They jointly owned the collection. All but one of the pots had been purchased by their father (F). The majority of them were gifted to the parties by a deed of gift executed in 1987 by F and their mother (M), as joint owners and donors, and that gift was added to by smaller gifts annually over five subsequent years. The siblings had agreed that, at least during F's lifetime, the collection would be preserved as a collection and would be available for scholarly study and exhibition. In 1995 and 1996, two pots from the collection were sold at auction: D2 maintained that he was not paid his quarter share of the net proceeds. F died at the end of 2013 and disagreement between the siblings about what should happen to the collection surfaced almost immediately. The claimants issued a CPR Pt 8 claim seeking an order for division on the basis that the siblings took turns in selecting a pot until there were none left in the collection, with the result that each sibling's joint interest in the collection would be converted to an absolute interest in those pots selected by that sibling. The legal foundation for the order sought was the Law of Property Act 1925 s.188(1). The defendants submitted, as a preliminary issue, that the claimants had no standing to bring proceedings under s.188 and their claim had to fail because they were not "interested in a moiety or upwards". They argued that D2 had an interest or entitlement in the collection exceeding one quarter which, when aggregated with D1's share, resulted in the claimants having an interest falling short of a moiety and thus they did not meet the qualifying criteria as applicants for an order under s.188.

Held: Judgment for claimants. (1) The gift in 1987, and supplementary gifts, were of individual items, not of a collection. On the evidence, D2 knew of the proposed sale of pots in 1995 and 1996 and did not oppose it; he knew of but chose not to present cheques representing his share of the proceeds; the claimants were interested in a moiety of the collection and therefore had standing to apply for an order under s.188 (see para.42 of judgment). (2) Parliament had enacted s.188 as a provision to assist the court in doing justice as between co-owners unable to agree between themselves what was to become of their jointly owned property. The court was empowered by s.188 to take a flexible and case by case approach aiming to deliver justice according to the particular circumstances of the case. It was a fact that, by the deed and subsequent annual gifts, F and M made a positive decision not to cause the collection to be preserved as a collection for scholarship and appreciation, or at least not to prioritise that aim, but instead made a positive decision to pass on the items comprising the collection to their children in a tax efficient manner, or at least prioritised that aim (paras 73-74). The evidence showed that the motives of each sibling were genuine and rational. There was nothing in the conduct of any of the siblings that should influence the court's decision in a way adverse to either the claimants or the defendants. Since the parties were in deadlock as to what to do with and about the collection, and relations between the claimants and defendants were sour if not acrimonious, there were compelling reasons for making an order. The appropriate order was that sought by the claimants. The collection was readily divisible between the parties. There was no evidence that a 1-2-3-4 selection process would produce an unjust result whether by reference to value or otherwise (paras 78-79, 90, 98).

BUTLER v BUTLER, [2016] EWHC 1793 (Ch), [2016] 4 W.L.R. 133, Judge Simon Barker QC, Ch D.

1664 Personal chattels–Bankrupt's estate–Extent of bankrupt's propriety rights–Chattels purportedly gifted shortly before bankruptcy

A trustee in bankruptcy applied for a declaration as to the extent of the first respondent bankrupt's proprietary rights in items in his home and in other properties registered in his sole name. The administration of the bankruptcy had not run smoothly. The bankruptcy order had been made on the bankrupt's own petition. He asserted that he had no material assets. HMRC sought to prove for over £2.67 million. The trustee indicated that the bankrupt had been obstructive, dishonest, contentious and uncooperative and that it was appropriate to treat his evidence with scepticism. A key issue in the case was whether relatives had acquired ownership of the disputed items by gift. The second and third respondents were close family members who claimed ownership of some of the items. Other family members had also been called to give evidence of ownership.

Held: Declaration granted. (1) The court found many aspects of the case to be unsatisfactory: not all of the people asserting ownership of the disputed items had been joined into the proceedings, which could compromise the finality of the judgment; there were 102 disputed items and insufficient time to deal with the matter justly; no effort had been made to value the disputed items; the trustee was relying on *South Staffordshire Water Co v Sharman* [1896] 2 Q.B. 44 and *Cohen (Deceased), Re* [1953] Ch. 88, [1953] C.L.Y. 1651 as authority for the proposition that chattels on premises belonged to the registered owner of the premises when it was questionable whether those cases were relevant to the bankrupt's situation, as it was hard to accept that everything in a family home was owned by the father, *South Staffordshire* and *Re Cohen* considered (see paras 4-5, 8, 12, 14, 16-17, 19-20, 24-25 of judgment). (2) To obtain ownership of a chattel by gift, there had to be an intention by the donor to make the gift and also delivery of it to the donee. The authors of *Law of Personal Property,* edn 1 (London: Sweet & Maxwell) suggested at para.8-25 that judicial scepticism of ownership by gift might be especially marked where there had been no unequivocal act of delivery and where the donor had subsequently become bankrupt and the gift was being challenged by the trustee in bankruptcy. On the whole, the evidence given by the respondents and those on their behalf was unconvincing and unimpressive, and it positively attracted the judicial scepticism referred to in the Law of Personal Property (see paras 41, 43, 86 of judgment). (3) The court made findings as to ownership of the disputed items (see appendices to judgment).

WOOD v LOWE, [2015] EWHC 2634 (Ch), [2015] B.P.I.R. 1537, Judge Saffman, Ch D (Leeds).

PLANNING

1665 Agricultural dwellings–Agricultural workers–Dependants–Whether "dependants" in planning condition required financial dependency

The appellant husband and wife appealed against a decision (*Shortt v Secretary of State for Communities and Local Government* [2014] EWHC 2480 (Admin), [2015] J.P.L. 75, [2015] C.L.Y. 1940) that the word "dependants" in an agricultural dwelling condition pertaining to their home did not mean only persons who were financially dependent on an agricultural worker. The wife ran the small farm on which she, her husband and their children had lived for 21 years. She spent only some of her time running the farm and it had always made a loss; the family lived on the husband's earnings. The planning condition to which their dwelling was subject limited its occupation to agricultural workers "... and the dependants (which shall be taken to include a widow or widower) of such persons." It was not in dispute that the wife was an agricultural worker. The appellants sought to argue that because the husband and children were not dependants of the wife, given that they were not even in part financially dependent on her, they had always been in breach of the condition and therefore were immune from enforcement action. A planning inspector, and then a judge, rejected that argument, taking a broad view of the meaning of "dependants" in the planning condition. The judge reasoned that the House of Lords' decision in *Fawcett Properties Ltd v Buckingham CC* [1961] A.C. 636, [1960] C.L.Y. 3110 was equivocal as to whether "dependant" in the statutory context from which the condition in that case derived necessarily required an element of financial dependency. The appellants submitted that the planning condition must have been imposed because the local authority was satisfied of the need for a dwelling for occupation by a person employed in agriculture to generate an income, and that the dependency of that person's "dependants" had to stem at least in part from that agricultural income. They submitted that any other approach would defeat the purpose of the condition and would be open to abuse.

Held: Appeal dismissed. The decision in *Fawcett Properties* was of little assistance. What Lord Keith said about "dependants" in the planning condition in that case was not intended to be a definitive interpretation, the condition was differently worded from that in the instant case, and the decision was not binding, *Fawcett Properties* distinguished. It provided little support for the contention that "dependants" in a condition of the instant kind meant persons who were financially dependent on the agricultural worker. As a matter of ordinary language, "dependants" was capable of referring to relationships involving a non-financial dependency. Within a family home, spouses could sensibly be described as dependent on each other, and children as dependent on both parents, irrespective of the respective contribution of each spouse/parent to the family finances: emotional support and care could be just as important. On the face of it, the condition contained no requirement as to financial dependency on the agricultural worker, which it easily could have done had it been intended, but was equally apt to cover a non-financial dependency such as existed in a family relationship. That a family relationship was in contemplation was shown by the express inclusion of a widow or widower (see paras 23-25 of judgment). The underlying policy also pointed towards interpreting "dependants" as encompassing a spouse and children living as a family with the agricultural worker, irrespective of the degree of financial contribution made by the agricultural worker. There was no obvious reason why the condition should be read as applying only where the agricultural worker provided financial support to the family members living with him or her. Indeed, it would be very surprising if the intention was to permit an agricultural worker to have family members living with him or her only as long as the agricultural business was profitable or to require family finances to be organised in such a way as to channel profits from the agricultural business into meeting the family's ordinary living expenses rather than, for example, allowing them to be reinvested in the agricultural business while relying on the spouse's income to meet the living expenses (para.26). It was true that Planning Policy Guidance 7 made clear that before permission was given for a new rural dwelling on the basis of need for accommodation for an agricultural worker, a local planning authority should scrutinise the application thoroughly, with the possibility of abuse in mind, and should be satisfied as to the economic viability of the agricultural enterprise in question. However, that did not support the appellants' reasoning. The condition in issue did not tie occupation to a particular agricultural enterprise, let alone impose a requirement as to its continuing profitability (para.27).

SHORTT v SECRETARY OF STATE FOR COMMUNITIES AND LOCAL GOVERNMENT, [2015] EWCA Civ 1192, [2016] 1 P. & C.R. 15, Richards LJ, CA (Civ Div).

1666 Appeals–Fresh evidence–Valuation evidence in compulsory purchase proceedings

The applicant sought permission to appeal against a number of decisions made in compensation proceedings. The proceedings started in 2007 following a compulsory purchase order made in relation to a redundant mill owned by the applicant. Preliminary issues were determined by the tribunal in 2010 and a final decision was made in 2012. The applicant was awarded compensation of £2.045 million, reduced to £2.013 million on appeal, and he was ordered to pay most of the local authority's costs. He subsequently tried to get the outcome of the proceedings overturned, and wanted to admit a number of documents, obtained as a result of a freedom of information request in 2013, as fresh evidence. According to the applicant, the documents demonstrated that in 2004 the local authority's expert (M) had provided a "preliminary valuation estimate" of the mill in the sum of £2.8 million; those documents demonstrated that M had lied when he later valued the property in 2005 at £2 million and, for the purposes of the proceedings, at the much lower sum of £650,000. The applicant claimed that the local authority knew of all three valuations and therefore had conducted the valuation proceedings in reliance upon what it knew was false evidence. The applicant also sought to admit fresh evidence based upon entries in the local authority's solicitors' bill of costs to support his case for an appeal against the refusal of his wasted costs application against those solicitors. The court had to determine whether the fresh evidence should be admitted for the purposes of appeals against the valuation decision; the preliminary issues decision; and the refusal of his wasted costs application.

Held: Applications refused. (1) *Valuation decision* - The main question was whether the applicant had any real prospect of persuading the court to admit the fresh evidence applying the tests in *Ladd v Marshall*. Applying the first test, the fresh evidence could have been obtained by the applicant, exercising reasonable diligence, before the valuation decision in 2012. He knew that M had provided an estimate in 2004; reasonable diligence would have enabled him to obtain that estimate by way of a request for disclosure. Furthermore, the applicant knew of the £2.8 million preliminary valuation well before the hearing of the appeal against the valuation decision, yet did nothing to pursue any case based upon it. The second and third *Ladd v Marshall* conditions asked whether, if admitted, the fresh evidence would have an important influence on the outcome, and whether the evidence was inherently credible. The difficulty with answering either of those questions in the affirmative was that the 2004 document was only a "preliminary valuation estimate" reflecting M's initial thoughts, after an exercise undertaken without full information or detailed investigation. M's later £2 million valuation was supported by detailed calculations and analysis. The real difficulty for the applicant was that the fresh evidence did not demonstrate that M was lying when he gave the £2 million value in 2005. There was no real prospect that the applicant would be able to demonstrate that it was a case of fraud, still less a fraudulent conspiracy in which M, the local authority and its solicitors were all complicit. Although the tribunal had been critical of M's lack of candour in presenting an expert report valuing the mill at £650,000 without at the same time disclosing his £2 million valuation, that had been remedied by the time of the hearing, when his full workings were made available (see paras 21-28 of judgment). (2) *Preliminary issues decision* - The material relevant to the preliminary issues could have been obtained before the hearing by an application for disclosure. In relation to the second preliminary issue, it could not be said that reasonable diligence would have revealed the information in question in time for the preliminary issues hearing. But the second and third *Ladd v Marshall* tests remained unsatisfied (paras 29-35). (3) *Wasted costs application* - It had been the applicant's case that the bill of costs revealed dishonest or improper practices perpetrated by the firm in the conduct of the litigation, including colluding in the dishonest preparation of M's expert evidence. However, there was no real prospect that the court would find anything to fault the tribunal's exercise of its discretion whether to make a wasted costs order (paras 26-28).

THOMAS NEWALL LTD v LANCASTER CITY COUNCIL, [2016] EWCA Civ 31, [2016] R.V.R. 254, Briggs LJ, CA (Civ Div).

1667 Certificates of lawful use or development–Outline planning permission–Proposed houses not within layout approved by earlier outline permission

The claimant challenged a planning inspector's decision dismissing his appeal from the refusal of the second defendant planning authority to grant a certificate of lawful use or development for two houses at a site near Windermere. In March 1957 outline planning permission had been granted for the "layout of nine houses south of Keldwith", a house near Windermere. Condition 1 required "Satisfactory detail plans, sections and elevations of the proposed buildings, showing their siting, design and external appearance and any existing or proposed means of access". Condition 2 related to vehicular access. In September 1957 a second permission was granted, the essential change being as to the vehicular access in condition 2. The layout was shown on an attached plan. A number of houses had been built following that layout, but there was a dispute as to whether that had been pursuant to the outline permissions or pursuant to further freestanding applications in respect of the relevant houses. The claimant then applied for a certificate of lawful use or development for two further houses on a site south of Keldwith but which was not within the layout of the 1957 permissions. The Lake District National Park Authority refused a certificate and the inspector upheld that decision. He concluded that the 1957 permissions were no longer extant, but that even if they were the appeal site was not within the layout. The claimant argued that the 1957 permissions permitted construction south of Keldwith and did not limit the layout or siting to an area excluding the appeal site, and that the inspector had been wrong to find that the 1957 permissions had not been implemented before they expired.

Held: Claim dismissed. The inspector was entitled to hold that the 1957 planning permissions were not just for nine houses south of Keldwith but also for their "layout", *R. v Ashford BC Ex p. Shepway DC* [1999] P.L.C.R. 12, [1999] C.L.Y. 4249 and *Koumis v Secretary of State for Communities and Local Government* [2014] EWCA Civ 1723, [2015] J.P.L. 682, [2015] C.L.Y. 1969 considered. The permissions incorporated by reference the plan attached. If the permissions had been for the number of houses only, there would have been no need to use the word "layout". That conclusion was not inconsistent with the fact that "siting" was mentioned as a reserved matter in condition 1, *I'm Your Man Ltd v Secretary of State for the Environment* (1999) 77 P. & C.R. 251, [1998] C.L.Y. 4215 considered. The conclusion that the layout in the plan was part of the permission was consistent with the fact that there was no description of the site in the permission. The inspector was accordingly entitled to conclude that the 1957 permissions did not include the appeal site which was not within the approved layout. That conclusion made it unnecessary to decide whether the 1957 permissions had been implemented before they expired.

R. (ON THE APPLICATION OF KEMBALL) v SECRETARY OF STATE FOR COMMUNITIES AND LOCAL GOVERNMENT, [2015] EWHC 3338 (Admin), [2016] J.P.L. 359, Holgate J, QBD (Admin).

1668 Certificates of lawful use or development–Planning permission–Listed building consent–Ability to apply within time limit for implementation

[Planning (Listed Buildings and Conservation Areas) Act 1990 (c.9) s.26H; Town and Country Planning Act 1990 (c.8) Pt VII s.192; Town and Country Planning (Development Management Procedure) (England) Order 2015 (SI 2015/595) art.40]

The claimant sought permission to apply for judicial review of two lawful development certificates issued by the defendant local authority to the second interested parties (IP2) in April 2015 in respect of their leasehold property. The first interested parties (IP1) owned the freehold of IP2's property and the neighbouring property, whose leasehold belonged to the claimant. After carrying out some work on their property IP2 had sought certificates of lawful use. The first certificate, issued to IP2 under the Planning (Listed Buildings and Conservation Areas) Act 1990 s.26H, provided that the works authorised by listed building consents granted in August 2008 and November 2010 might lawfully be carried out under those consents; the second certificate, issued under the Town and Country Planning Act 1990 Pt VII s.192, provided that the development authorised by planning permission granted in August 2000 might lawfully be carried out under that permission. The claimant contended that (1) the certificates were ultra vires, because they purported to certify the lawfulness of works already carried out, whereas s.192 and s.26H might only be used to certify the lawfulness of proposed works; (2) the local authority had erred in granting the certificates because the works relied upon were referable to the requirements of the lease between IP1 and IP2 rather than by the planning permission and listed building consent; (3) the local authority had failed to obtain information from IP1 before issuing the certificates; (4) the certificates had been issued without any prior consultation with or notification to IP1 and the claimant, in breach of their legitimate expectations; (5) the s.26H certificate had been granted in breach of the principle in *FG Whitley & Sons Co Ltd v Secretary of State for Wales* (1992) 64 P. & C.R. 296, [1993] C.L.Y. 3941, namely that development started before pre-commencement conditions were fully discharged was unauthorised, because of non-compliance with pre-conditions contained in the 2008 listed building consent which had been incorporated into the 2010 consent; (6) the local authority had failed to enter the s.192 certificate on its planning register in breach of the Town and

Country Planning (Development Management Procedure) (England) Order 2015 art.40. The local authority accepted that it had not complied with that obligation until June 2015.

Held: Application granted in part. (1) On their proper construction, s.192 and s.26H enabled a landowner to apply for a certificate of lawful development so long as the time limit for the works' implementation had not yet expired (see para.47 of judgment). (2) A developer's purpose in carrying out works, such as to comply with obligations under a lease, was irrelevant in applications for certificates, *Staffordshire CC v Riley* [2001] EWCA Civ 257, [2002] P.L.C.R. 5, [2002] C.L.Y. 3725 applied. In any event, even if the works had been necessary to comply with the lease, it did not follow that they could not also qualify as works for the implementation of a planning permission or a listed building consent (paras 55-56). (3) Obtaining information from IP1 would only have led to the disclosure of material which the local authority could not lawfully take into account (para.61). (4) Whilst the local authority followed the standard practice of notifying neighbouring properties of applications for planning permission or listed building consent, it had no established practice of notifying or consulting with neighbours on any other application made under planning legislation, including applications for certification that proposed works would be lawful. There was no legitimate expectation that it would do so (paras 73-74). (5) Conditions could not be implied into a planning permission or a listed building consent, and the 2010 consent was clearly freestanding and had not incorporated the 2008 consent's conditions. The claimant's contention that the s.26H certificate had been granted in breach of the *Whitley* principle simply because of non-compliance with pre-conditions contained in the 2008 listed building consent was unarguable, *Whitley* considered. The claimant was refused permission to apply for judicial review in relation to its first five grounds (paras 107-110, 120). (6) Given the absence of any obligation to publicise, or notify third parties of, the making of an application for a s.192 certificate, it was important that the statutory duty to enter the certificate on the register was complied with. If that was not done then very real difficulties might be created for a member of the public or a body wishing to ascertain whether a certificate had been granted, and if so in what terms, so that they might consider whether to make an application for judicial review. The claimant was granted permission on its sixth ground and its application was successful in that respect, although it could not found an application to quash the s.192 certificate. Accordingly, it was appropriate to grant declaratory relief only (paras 121, 123).

FRANCE v KENSINGTON AND CHELSEA RBC, [2015] EWHC 3437 (Admin), [2016] J.P.L. 387, Holgate J, QBD (Admin).

1669 Change of use–Conservation areas–Offices changed to residential-led development–Impact of local plan

[Planning (Listed Buildings and Conservation Areas) Act 1990 (c.9) s.72]

The claimant applied for judicial review of a local authority's decision to grant planning permission to a developer for a residential-led mixed-use development in a conservation area. The developer had been given permission to change the use of an existing tower block of shops and offices to residential accommodation and also to make alterations and additions to the building, as well as erect other buildings. The claimant argued that (1) the planning officer's report to the local authority's planning committee had not applied properly the tall building policy contained in the emerging local plan to the development, which included the erection of an additional tall building alongside the existing tower block; (2) although the local authority had correctly acknowledged that the materiality of any fall-back position for the developer depended on its viability and feasibility, the report had not considered whether there was any realistic prospect of the developer actually implementing the permitted development right it had already acquired if its application were refused; (3) the local authority had failed to recognise a clear breach of the local plan policy, which provided that a change of use from offices would only be acceptable if the site had been actively marketed as offices for at least two years; (4) the local authority's refusal to adjourn its determination of the application so as to allow objectors the time to address late marketing evidence from the interested party had been unfair, contrary to the principles of natural justice and the requirements for fair consultation; (5) the local authority's approach to compliance with the Planning (Listed Buildings and Conservation Areas) Act 1990 s.72 had been legally deficient.

Held: Application refused. (1) The officer's report had not failed to take into account the tall building policy or erred in its approach to the policy. The report expressly referred to the policy and it had been apparent to the committee that the new building was eight storeys high. The committee had to look at the development as a whole and decide whether it was acceptable, which it did. When the report was read as a whole, there was no failure by the officers or the committee to take the policy into account and no unlawful interpretation of the policy (see paras 37, 40-41 of judgment). (2) Where an applicant for planning permission already had permission to develop the land in some other way, the existence of that fall-back position could be a material consideration, *Samuel Smith Old Brewery (Tadcaster) v Secretary of State for Communities and Local Government* [2009] EWCA Civ 333, [2009] J.P.L. 1326, [2010] C.L.Y. 2600 applied. In the instant case, in circumstances where it had not been suggested that there was no possibility of the prior approval being implemented, the committee had been entitled on the evidence before it to treat the prior approval as a material consideration. The officers and the committee had been entitled to conclude that the prior approval was a material fall-back option and attach some weight to it (paras 17, 53). (3) A finding of compliance or conflict with the development plan and the basis for it needed to be made so that the decision-maker could proceed to undertake the planning balance in an informed way, *Tiviot Way Investments Ltd v Secretary of State for Communities and Local Government* [2015] EWHC 2489 (Admin), [2016] J.P.L. 171, [2016] 1685 applied. The legal requirement was to determine the application against the development plan as a whole. The committee had been advised that the marketing had taken place for only seven months and so it knew that the two-year requirement had not been met. Nevertheless, the planning officer's report had advised that the proposal was in accordance with the development plan as a whole, despite that breach of policy (paras 15, 59, 62, 64). (4) In determining planning applications, local authorities were required to act fairly. In the instant case, the local authority's statement of community involvement stated that the authority would, where appropriate, consult on specific details. However, the committee had been perfectly entitled on the evidence before it to take the view that the marketing evidence did not raise any new points that necessitated consultation and refuse the application to adjourn the meeting. There had been no procedural unfairness (paras 18-19, 77-78). (5) The local authority had not failed in its duties under s.72.The requirement under that provision was to have special regard to the desirability of preserving or enhancing the character or appearance of the conservation area; it was not that a development had to perform a preserving or enhancing function, *South Lakeland DC v Secretary of State for the Environment* [1992] 2 A.C. 141, [1992] C.L.Y. 4186 applied (paras 84-85, 89).

R. (ON THE APPLICATION OF KVERNDAL) v HOUNSLOW LBC *sub nom.* KVERNDAL v HOUNSLOW LBC, [2015] EWHC 3084 (Admin), [2016] P.T.S.R. 330, Supperstone J, QBD (Admin).

1670 Change of use–Enforcement notices–Unauthorised change of use from offices to residential accommodation–Previous permission to change use to holiday homes

[Town and Country Planning Act 1990 (c.8) s.179, s.180(1); Town and Country Planning (Use Classes) Order 1987 (SI 1987/764)]

The appellants appealed against their conviction for an offence of failing to comply with a planning enforcement notice contrary to the Town and Country Planning Act 1990 s.179. The appellants owned a property with a number of outbuildings which they had converted to units capable of residential use. The enforcement notice was issued in respect of an unauthorised change of use of the outbuildings from farm offices and facilities to residential accommodation. An appeal against that enforcement notice was dismissed on the ground that residential use was contrary to the development plan. The appellants obtained planning permission for a change of use from office and staff facilities to holiday homes. That permission was subject to a condition that the appellants submit a scheme to ensure that the converted buildings were used only as short-term holiday accommodation and to demonstrate that they would not be permanently occupied as residential dwellings. When the appellants failed to comply with that condition, they were prosecuted for failure to comply with the enforcement notice. According to the appellants, the grant of planning permission had the effect of allowing permanent residential use of the units because the purported restriction to holiday home use was ineffective. The appellants argued that the condition did not require the local authority to approve any submitted scheme or require the appellants to comply with the terms of any approved scheme. Further, dwellinghouses for short-term holiday lets and for permanent residential use both came within the same class of the Town and Country Planning (Use Classes) Order 1987, so that planning permission for a change of use from one to the other was not required.

Held: Appeal dismissed. (1) The permitted use of the units was for farm offices and facilities: permission had never been given for residential use. The appellants had applied for planning permission for holiday homes, not residential accommodation. The meanings of the grant of permission for change of use from offices to holiday homes, and of the planning condition, were clear and unambiguous. No permission had been granted for permanent occupation as residential dwellings, and it had been made clear on the face of the document that such occupation would be contrary to the development plan which the local authority was under a statutory duty to comply with. It was not necessary to define "holiday homes" or "holiday accommodation". The meaning of those terms was clear, as was the difference between "short-term holiday accommodation" and "permanent occupation as a residential dwelling". The onus was on the appellants to ensure that future lettings complied with the terms of the planning permission, and the scheme had to be prepared and submitted before any lettings could take place. It was their failure to comply with the condition that made it ineffective; the fact that the scheme was not subject to local authority approval did not deprive it of its force. The condition met the general criteria for the validity of planning conditions summarised in Planning Circular 11/95 (see paras 25, 27-31 of judgment). (2) Although both permanent residences and short-term holiday homes fell within Class C3 of the 1987 Order, a material change of use might occur where both former and new use fell within C3, depending on the facts, *Moore v Secretary of State for Communities and Local Government* [2012] EWCA Civ 1202, [2012] 3 E.G.L.R. 91, [2013] C.L.Y. 2314 followed. It was for the planning decision-maker to make that planning judgment, subject to the supervisory jurisdiction of the courts. No such decision had been made either way in the instant case. A planning authority was entitled to attach conditions to a planning permission which had the effect of restricting the use of a dwellinghouse to use as a holiday home, *R. v Tunbridge Wells BC Ex p. Blue Boys Development* (1990) 59 P. & C.R. 315, [1990] C.L.Y. 4440.1 applied. The appellants had not disputed that the unit in question was never let as a holiday home; therefore, they had never established a lawful existing use on which to base a change to residential use under the 1987 Order. Since the planning permission for change of use from offices to holiday homes did not cover residential use, the enforcement notice could not cease to have effect, for the purposes of s.180(1) of the 1990 Act, in respect of residential use. The trial judge was therefore entitled to hold that the enforcement notice remained in force requiring the appellants to cease using the unit as residential accommodation. There was sufficient evidence of breach of that notice on which a jury could convict (paras 34-36, 39, 42-44, 46).

R. v AKHTAR (SYED MOSHIN); R. v AKHTAR (ILYAS FATIMA), [2015] EWCA Crim 1430, [2016] J.P.L. 164, Davis LJ, CA (Crim Div).

1671 Compulsory purchase–Compensation–Certificates of appropriate alternative development–Likelihood of residential development

[Land Compensation Act 1961 (c.33) s.14(5)(a), s.17]

The appellants, landowners whose properties had been subject to an employment site compulsory purchase order (CPO), appealed against certificates of appropriate alternative development (CAADs) issued by the respondent local planning authority. Under the Land Compensation Act 1961 s.17, the first appellant had requested a positive certificate for his entire site (site B) for residential or industrial use, or a mix of the two. The local authority issued a CAAD certifying that, if the CPO had not been made, planning permission would have been granted for the development of business and industrial units on part of the site but considered that residential development would be contrary to the local development plan, which allocated further development to settlements in accordance with a sustainable strategic settlement framework (SSSF). It contended that adequate land had been allocated to meet the housing element and the development of the entire site would lead to an over-provision of housing. The second appellant applied for a positive CAAD for his entire site (site M) for residential use. Finding that the proposed development would be contrary to the SSSF, the authority issued a CAAD certifying that planning permission would have been granted for residential development only in respect of a 50m wide strip of the land fronting the road. The appellants relied on the fact that the plan showed the sites as falling within a local regeneration site (PDB31) stated to offer potential for employment use and which the appellants contended expanded the urban area. However, the local authority submitted that the cancellation assumption under s.14(5)(a) of the Act required that parts of the plan supporting the scheme of development underlying the acquisition were to be ignored if they would contradict the assumption. The appellants submitted that residential development of the sites would not prejudice the SSSF as that policy incorporated a large margin of flexibility in relation to possible population growth and the number of housing units that could be erected on the sites would not be disproportionate, given the size of the total housing allocation. The issues were (1) whether the allocation of PDB31 had to be ignored when considering what planning permission would have been granted for the sites; (2) whether, as contended by the local authority, the fact that both sites were shown on the plan as outside the settlement boundary and in the countryside was of material significance; (3) the merits of the local authority's objection that the proposals would lead to an over-provision of housing; it considered that there was more than a five year land supply.

Held: Appeal allowed. (1) The allocation of PDB31 should not be ignored. If the local authority was correct, any employment allocation for the whole of the scheme area would be removed from the plan. In that case, one would be considering a CAAD for development where there was effectively no relevant development plan; a planning void. That was not the correct position, as indicated by the fact that the stated reason for the local authority's refusal of a positive CAAD in each case was a conflict with the SSSF. On a proper reading of the SSSF, the elements of the development plan allocation upon which the appellants relied were integral and not to be regarded as non-applicable merely because the scheme was cancelled (see paras 88-89, 91 of judgment). (2) The local authority had not considered the settlement boundary to be of material significance when considering proposals for development in the area. Firstly, PDB31 had been allocated on the plan for employment use even though it was outside the boundary. Secondly, the authority had not relied on that boundary when issuing the CAADs. Thirdly, it had issued a positive certificate for an extension of the existing business park into a section of site B which was itself outside the boundary. Fourthly, there were other significant areas beyond that boundary which were allocated for residential development (para.94). (3) The SSSF sought a balance between directing new development to growth areas and to smaller settlements. Any residential development on the appeal sites would have been at a density of 33 units per hectare. In considering applications for residential development, it was important to bear in mind that the sites were in an area selected for growth. Whilst there was a considerable degree of flexibility in the plan, the fact that the local authority considered that there was a five year land supply and the end of the plan period was approaching would have made it cautious about permitting extensive residential development projects on any site not already allocated for the purpose. Residential planning permission would have been granted for a total of 1.74ha on site M, comprising the part for which the original CAAD included a positive certificate and a further 1.15ha. In relation to site B, permission would have been granted for residential development of 1.15ha. At a density of 33 units per hectare, that would have produced a total of 95 units on the sites; development of that scale would not have prejudiced the SSSF. In relation to site B, the traffic associated with the extension of the positive certificate for industrial development to the entire site would cause unacceptable damage to the amenity of nearby houses and accordingly planning permission would not have been granted for such development. The CAADs would be cancelled and two new CAADs would be issued (paras 96, 98, 100-103, 105).

BONNELL (DECEASED) v CARMARTHENSHIRE CC, [2014] UKUT 413 (LC), [2016] R.V.R. 194, NJ Rose FRICS, UT (Lands).

1672 Compulsory purchase–Compensation–Landowner's entitlement to basic loss payment

[Housing Act 1985 (c.68) s.17; Land Compensation Act 1973 (c.26) s.29, s.33A, s.33E]

An acquiring local authority referred to the tribunal the question of the compensation payable to the claimant freehold landowner on a compulsory purchase of a residential property. The local authority acquired a residential property via a compulsory purchase order under the Housing Act 1985 s.17. The landowner was served with a notice to treat, followed by a notice of entry, and the acquiring local authority took possession of the property. The condition of the property suggested that it had been unoccupied for some time. The landowner did not respond to the notice to treat, did not submit a claim or provide any evidence, and did not attend the hearing. The local authority submitted that (1) a home loss payment under the Land Compensation Act 1973 s.29 was not payable because there was no evidence that the landowner was in occupation of the property in the year before the local authority displaced her; (2) while it appeared that the landowner was entitled to a basic loss payment under s.33A of the 1973 Act, no written claim had been made for that in accordance with s.33E, and the award of compensation should not include such a payment.

Held: Compensation assessed. (1) The landowner was not entitled to a home loss payment. There was no evidence that the landowner was in occupation of the property throughout the period of one year ending with her date of displacement. Nor was she in occupation at that date and she therefore did not qualify for consideration of a discretionary payment under s.29(2) (see para.44 of judgment). (2) A basic loss payment required the landowner to apply in writing to the acquiring authority. Since no such application had been made, there would be no award of compensation for a basic loss payment. However, the landowner could still make an application under s.33E for a basic loss payment after the tribunal's determination of the market value of the property, provided such an application complied with the limitation period referred to in s.33E(4) (paras 45-46). (3) Adopting as a preferred method a direct comparison with the sale of a comparable property, the open market value of the property at the valuation date was determined at £650,000 (para.42).

PARMAR v BARNET LBC, [2015] UKUT 510 (LC), [2016] R.V.R. 9, AJ Trott FRICS, UT (Lands).

1673 Compulsory purchase–Compensation–Rights to lay and use pipeline under land–Nil compensation

[Land Compensation Act 1961 (c.33) s.5(6); Compulsory Purchase Act 1965 (c.56) s.7]

An owner of land claimed compensation from the acquiring authority for its compulsory acquisition of rights to lay, use, maintain, repair and replace a high-pressure natural gas pipeline under the owner's land. The site consisted of undeveloped and disused brownfield land. The owner sought compensation of more than £4.5 million on the basis that it had suffered (i) loss due to disturbance and damage during the occupation and use by the acquiring authority; (ii) loss due to being prevented from extracting or working the surface and below-ground mineral deposits, and diminution in the land's value due to sterilisation of the land from development; (iii) diminution in value of a restrictive covenant over part of the land.

Held: Compensation assessed. (1) The claim for disturbance and damage had been made on the basis of standard payments which the acquiring authority made to landowners and damages. However, the standard payments were made purely by agreement with landowners and there had been no such agreement in the instant case. The acquiring authority had made an offer to the landowner on the standard basis, but it had been rejected and no claim had been subsequently made seeking a higher sum. The other part of the claim was a damages claim, over which the tribunal had no jurisdiction, and not on the basis of disturbance that fell within the Land Compensation Act 1961 s.5(6), over which the tribunal did have jurisdiction. Even if it were treated as a disturbance claim under s.5(6), there was not a scintilla of evidence that the landowner had suffered any loss as a result of the occupation of part of the land before, during or after the construction of the pipeline. The land throughout that period was disused. Compensation would be determined at nil (see paras 44-49 of judgment). (2) The landowner's right to compensation for the injurious affection of its mineral rights and the land's value would be under the Compulsory Purchase Act 1965 s.7 and so any injury had to have been caused by the exercise of the powers conferred by the Act. In assessing the injury for the purposes of injurious affection, it was necessary to have regard not only to the rights as exercised initially but also to how those rights might realistically, in practice, be exercised in the future in terms of ongoing maintenance, repair and possible replacement. The crux of the matter regarding the issues under those heads was what a prospective purchaser would have known, or could realistically have found out, at the valuation date about what was going to be installed under the land and what restrictions on the potential for development that might mean. Such a purchaser would have been able to find out that it was to be a heavy wall pipe, as that information had been in the public domain for a long time before the valuation date. The prospective purchaser would know that he could not construct houses on the strip but that roads and services could go over it, and it could be used for gardens, public open spaces or other uses related to the potential residential development. He would also have been told by the acquiring authority that he would be able to take deposits off the easement strip surface and possibly also be permitted to open-cast mine. The purchaser would not have had any undue concerns that the pipe's installation or what might happen to it in the future would cause any injury by the sterilisation of potential development prospects. Thus, the exercise of the powers conferred by the compulsory purchase order would not have been anticipated to cause, and had not in fact caused, damage to the landowner compensatable under s.7 of the 1965 Act. It was to be concluded that the landowner had suffered no loss as a result of the compulsory purchase order, and compensation for injurious effect would be assessed at nil (paras 50-51, 79-80, 87-88). (3) The restrictive covenant prevented certain types of development of part of the land which was being sold to a rugby club, so if the club ever wanted to develop the land for, say, residential purposes, it would have to pay compensation for a modification or discharge of the restriction. Although the landowner maintained that the value of that covenant had been diminished, given the finding that there had been no sterilisation, and thus no loss of potential development value, the landowner's claim had also to fail. Compensation for diminution of the covenant's value would also be determined at nil (paras 29, 90-92).

ELITESTONE LTD v NATIONAL GRID GAS PLC, [2015] UKUT 452 (LC), [2015] R.V.R. 392, PR Francis FRICS, UT (Lands).

1674 Compulsory purchase–Development consent orders–Land use

THE HORNSEA TWO OFFSHORE WIND FARM ORDER 2016, SI 2016/844; made under the Planning Act 2008 s.114, s.120. In force: 7 September 2016.

This Order grants development consent for, and authorises the construction, operation and maintenance of up to 2 offshore wind farms with a combined capacity of up to 1,800 megawatts in the North Sea approximately 89 km off the coast of Yorkshire together with associated development. It imposes requirements in connection with the development and authorises the compulsory purchase of land (including rights in land) and the right to use land and to override easements and other rights. It also grants deemed marine licences under the Marine and Coastal Access Act 2009 Pt 4 in connection with the wind farms. The marine licences impose conditions in connection with the deposits and works for which they grant consent.

1675 Compulsory purchase–Land use–Electricity lines

THE NORTH WALES WIND FARMS CONNECTION ORDER 2016, SI 2016/818; made under the Planning Act 2008 s.114, s.120. In force: 19 August 2016.

This Order authorises SP Manweb PLC (referred to in this Order as the undertaker) to install and keep installed, use and maintain, a 132 kV electric line above ground, approximately 17.4 km in length in North Wales. The Order permits the undertaker to acquire, compulsorily or by agreement, rights in land and to use land for this purpose.

1676 Compulsory purchase orders–Public inquiries–Parties' costs of aborted inquiry into order made before 25 June 2013

[Local Government Act 1972 (c.70) s.250(5); Acquisition of Land Act 1981 (c.67) s.5, s.5(4); Growth and Infrastructure Act 2013 (c.27); Growth and Infrastructure Act 2013 (Commencement No. 2 and Transitional and Saving Provisions) Order 2013 (SI 2013/1488)]

The claimant applied for judicial review of the defendant secretary of state's decision refusing its application for an award of costs against the interested party highway authority. The authority had acquired rights to land owned by the claimant under a compulsory purchase order made in October 2012. The claimant had objected to the CPO and it was sent to the secretary of state for confirmation. The secretary of state announced that an inquiry would be held in July 2013. In April 2013, the authority withdrew the order and the inquiry was cancelled. The claimant applied to the secretary of state for an order that the authority pay its abortive costs. The application was refused on the basis that the statutory power to award costs to "the parties at an inquiry" under the Local Government Act 1972 s.250(5), as applied by the Acquisition of Land Act 1981 s.5, only arose when an inquiry was actually held. It acknowledged that the Growth and Infrastructure Act 2013 had introduced a new s.5(4) to the 1981 Act providing for costs to be awarded where an arranged public inquiry did not take place but stated that, under the Growth and Infrastructure Act 2013 (Commencement No. 2 and Transitional and Saving Provisions) Order 2013, that provision did not apply to a compulsory purchase order made before 25 June 2013, and the contested CRO was thereby excluded. An issue arose as to the correct interpretation of s.250(5) of the 1972 Act. The claimant contended that s.250(5) was capable of meaning that the power to award costs in favour of a party to a CPO inquiry existed whether or not an inquiry was convened. It submitted that the provision was engaged when an inquiry was caused to be held, and that an inquiry was not confined to the oral exchange before an inspector but included the process of written exchange of statements of case and evidence. It argued that the reference in s.250(5) to "the parties at the inquiry" did not necessarily connote physical presence at a convened public inquiry and was, in context and as a matter of plain English, capable of meaning the parties to an inquiry which had been caused to be held. It asserted further that it was impossible to conceive of any reason why Parliament would have wished to exclude the possibility of an award of costs in circumstances such as those in the instant case.

Held: Application refused. It was clear from the words used in s.250(5) and the statutory context that "the inquiry" was a public local inquiry which was an event to which the public had access. An inquiry was not the whole process prior to that event; that process was pre-inquiry procedure to secure the efficient running of the inquiry when it transpired. The words used in both the 1972 and 1981 Acts envisaged some physical attendance or representation by parties at a convened public local inquiry. Until the inquiry was opened, there was no inquiry. Accordingly, the secretary of state's discretionary power to make orders as to costs of the "parties at the inquiry" did not arise when the inquiry was "caused to be held". Whilst it was difficult to think of any reason why Parliament would have wished to exclude the possibility of a costs award where the need for an inquiry fell away, there had to be some event that triggered entitlement to a costs order. Historically, that had been the inquiry. The consequence of the statutory scheme in force at the relevant time meant that the secretary of state's decision was correct. It was, however, reassuring that the statutory amendment to s.5 of the 1981 Act meant that parties would no longer be placed in the unfortunate position which the claimant had found itself in (see paras 35-36, 39-40, 42, 47, 51 of judgment).

R. (ON THE APPLICATION OF BEDFORD LAND INVESTMENTS LTD) v SECRETARY OF STATE FOR TRANSPORT, [2015] EWHC 3159 (Admin), [2016] P.T.S.R. 31, Patterson J, QBD (Admin).

1677 Compulsory purchase orders–Quashing orders–Court's power to quash compulsory purchase order under s.24(2) Acquisition of Land Act 1981–Quashing of whole order

[Town and Country Planning (General Development Procedure) Order 1995 (SI 1995/419) art.10(3); Acquisition of Land Act 1981 (c.67) s.24(2)]

The Port of London Authority appealed against a decision (*Grafton Group (UK) Plc v Secretary of State for Transport* [2015] EWHC 1083 (Admin)) upholding the respondent landowner's challenge to a compulsory purchase order (CPO) made by it. Together with the secretary of state it also appealed against the quashing (*Grafton Group (UK) Plc v Secretary of State for Transport* [2015] EWHC 1889 (Admin)) of the order. The land in question was a derelict wharf on the River Thames. It was subject to a safeguarding direction under the Town and Country Planning (General Development Procedure) Order 1995 art.10(3), but the landowner had hoped to develop it for residential use at some stage. The authority had made the CPO to bring the land back into active use as a wharf, handling river-borne aggregates. Planning permission for the development required for that activity was refused on the basis of its harmful impact on the character and appearance of the area. Following an inquiry, the inspector recommended that the refusal of planning permission should be upheld. Nevertheless, he recommended confirmation of the CPO on the basis that, with some design changes, a more acceptable scheme was likely to be put forward. The secretary of state accepted his recommendations, finding that there was a reasonable prospect of some form of aggregates-handling permission being granted. The judge upheld the landowner's challenge to the confirmation of the CPO. He held that the secretary of state had confirmed the CPO on a different basis from that promoted during the inquiry; that he had done so without sufficient evidence; and that the decision was unfair to the landowner. Pursuant to the Acquisition of Land Act 1981 s.24(2), he quashed the CPO in its entirety, finding that it was not open to him to quash only its confirmation. The appellants submitted that the judge had erred in finding that (1) the court's power under s.24(2) was limited to quashing the whole of the CPO, and there was no scope to quash only its confirmation; (2) there was insufficient evidence to support the confirmation of the CPO; (3) the decision to confirm was unfair to the landowner.

Held: Appeals allowed in part. (1) The judge was correct in his interpretation of s.24(2). Under that subsection it was the whole of the CPO that had to be quashed, not just its confirmation. The secretary of state's argument was that "to quash" meant "to deprive of legal effect", and since a CPO assumed legal effect only once confirmed, the quashing related only to the confirmation. However, the long-accepted rule was that a quashing order rendered the instrument in question as if it had never been. If only the confirmation were quashed, the CPO as made would remain in place, with legal effect. The term "CPO" meant the instrument so called from first to last, and had Parliament intended quashing to relate only to its confirmation, it would have said so (see paras 18-20 of judgment). The only remedy available on a challenge to a CPO was that given by s.24, and the court had no inherent power to grant any different form of relief. Section 24 might be a blunt instrument, but it did not purport to oust judicial review and put in its place a remedy that was so ineffective as to amount to no remedy at all, *R. (on the application of Cart) v Upper Tribunal* [2009] EWHC 3052 (Admin), [2010] 2 W.L.R. 1012, [2010] C.L.Y. 70 considered (paras 22-24). (2) The judge had erred in finding that there was insufficient evidence to support the confirmation of the CPO. The confirmation of a CPO was not necessarily tied to any particular scheme for which planning permission was simultaneously sought, and the CPO in the instant case could, in principle, be confirmed despite the dismissal of the planning appeal. The judge's finding rested on the premise that the inspector would have to have seen the detail of an alternative design in order to find that there was a reasonable prospect of planning permission being granted for some level of aggregate-handling development. However, given his appreciation of the details of the proposed development, his criticisms of its scale and design, and his legitimate emphasis on the benefits of the wharf's reactivation, the inspector was entitled to conclude that there was sufficient probability of an alternative scheme being put forward. That was quintessentially an exercise of planning judgment (paras 29-30, 34-37). (3) The judge had correctly concluded that the decision was unfair to the landowner. At the inquiry it had not been part of the Port of London Authority's case that an alternative design might be adopted.

Nevertheless, the inspector had concluded that the refusal of planning permission on account of poor design should not necessarily lead to non-confirmation of the CPO. He did not ask the planning witnesses whether a redesign could be accomplished with only a minor reduction in throughput, and he did not suggest that that was the basis upon which he might recommend confirmation of the CPO. Indeed, the proposition that a better design would be likely to come forward was never put to the parties. The landowner had thus had no opportunity to address the basis upon which the secretary of state confirmed the CPO (paras 38-42). (4) The CPO had been unfairly and unlawfully confirmed, and written submissions on relief would be invited (paras 43-44).

GRAFTON GROUP (UK) PLC v SECRETARY OF STATE FOR TRANSPORT, [2016] EWCA Civ 561, [2016] C.P. Rep. 37, Laws LJ, CA (Civ Div).

1678 Compulsory purchase orders–Reasons–Need for reasons to be comprehensible to citizens without professional assistance

[Town and Country Planning Act 1990 (c.8) s.106]

A representative of market traders appealed against a decision (*Horada v Secretary of State for Communities & Local Government* [2015] EWHC 2512 (Admin)) upholding the secretary of state's confirmation of a compulsory purchase order (CPO) contrary to the recommendation of his planning inspector. The CPO was made to regenerate the established Shepherd's Bush market and secure its long-term future through mixed-use development. The market currently provided an affordable trading environment for a diverse ethnic mix of independent traders. The local planning authority granted outline planning permission for its redevelopment, subject to conditions. The developer entered into a Town and Country Planning Act 1990 s.106 agreement. Following a public inquiry, the inspector concluded that it was unclear whether the new trading conditions would be sufficiently affordable or suited to the needs of the current traders. She was also concerned that the design information regarding the stalls, would only be confirmed when the condition was discharged and there was no indication that the railway arch areas, which were a key original feature, were to be upgraded. The inspector recommended that the CPO should not be confirmed as the guarantees and safeguards were inadequate. The secretary of state confirmed the CPO, stating that sufficient safeguards were in place to protect traders through planning conditions and the s.106 agreement. The Planning Court judge found no error of law. The issues were whether the secretary of state had correctly identified the principal important controversial issues and had provided adequate reasons for disagreeing with the inspector. The developer and the secretary of state argued that his decision letter was addressed to parties well aware of the issues and of the arguments advanced so that no elucidation was required.

Held: Appeal allowed. Though there was no formal standard which the secretary of state had to apply when disagreeing with the conclusions of an inspector and he had no duty to provide a detailed response paragraph by paragraph, there was authority suggesting that fuller reasons were required where the decision maker was disagreeing with an inspector's considered and reasoned recommendation, *Save Britain's Heritage v Number 1 Poultry Ltd* [1991] 1 W.L.R. 153, [1991] C.L.Y. 3494, *South Buckinghamshire DC v Porter (No.2)* [2004] UKHL 33, [2004] 1 W.L.R. 1953, [2004] C.L.Y. 3087, *R. (on the application of Ling (Bridlington) Ltd) v East Riding of Yorkshire Council* [2006] EWHC 1604 (Admin), [2007] J.P.L. 396, [2007] C.L.Y. 3273, *R. (on the application of Telford Trustee No.1 Ltd) v Telford and Wrekin Council* [2011] EWCA Civ 896, [2012] P.T.S.R. 935, [2012] C.L.Y. 2601 and *R. (on the application of Siraj) v Kirklees MC* [2010] EWCA Civ 1286, [2011] J.P.L. 571, [2011] C.L.Y. 2564 applied. Further, a higher standard was expected from a decision letter of the secretary of state than from the local authority's summary of reasons, *R. v Secretary of State for Transport Ex p. Cumbria CC* [1983] R.T.R. 129, [1983] C.L.Y. 3299 applied (see paras 36-37, 40 of judgment). It was true that the decision letter was addressed to a factually well-informed readership but the reader would have had to have been not only well-informed but also psychic to have extracted the secretary of state's reasoning from the two laconic sentences. The secretary of state was required to explain why he rejected the inspector's view. However, it was unclear whether he was saying that the safeguards were adequate to ensure existing traders returned in sufficient numbers to preserve the unique character of the market so that the inspector's concerns were unfounded; or whether he was saying that existing traders did not matter because new traders of a similar nature would be protected. It was similarly unclear whether he thought there was certainty about the design information so that the inspector's concerns were unfounded; or that the level of uncertainty that the inspector thought was unacceptable was in fact an acceptable level. With regard to the arches, it was striking that he did not mention them at all. It was unclear whether he thought they were unimportant, or whether he accepted the inspector's view that they were important but thought that their upgrading was assured (paras 51-53). (Per Lord Thomas of Cwmgiedd, CJ) It was important that the reasons for decisions were explained in plain English in terms the affected citizen could understand. Using terms that were familiar to other experts was not permissible when explaining the reasons for a decision to others, however well informed. Experts had to guard against using terms which could only be understood through the intermediary of a lawyer or other professional. In the instant case, it was particularly important that a proper and easy to understand explanation for rejecting the Inspector's recommendation was given. The livelihoods of the market traders were put at risk by the proposed development. The inspector had given her reasons on a matter of vital concern to the traders in a way that could readily be understood by them and the secretary of state had to do the same (paras 57-59).

HORADA v SECRETARY OF STATE FOR COMMUNITIES & LOCAL GOVERNMENT, [2016] EWCA Civ 169, [2016] P.T.S.R. 1271, Lord Thomas LCJ, CA (Civ Div).

1679 Construction projects–Development consent–Marine licences

THE WALNEY EXTENSION OFFSHORE WIND FARM (AMENDMENT) ORDER 2016, SI 2016/810; made under the Planning Act 2008 Sch.6 para.2(1)(9). In force: 28 July 2016.

This Order amends the Walney Extension Offshore Wind farm Order 2014, a development consent order under the Planning Act 2008, following an application under paragraph 2 of Schedule 6 to that Act for a non-material change to article 5 (Benefit of the Order) to make provision for the Secretary of State to grant consent to the transfer of the benefit, in part, of the deemed marine licences included in the Order, and notice requirements associated with such transfer. The change to the Order takes effect from the date specified in the Order.

1680 Deemed applications–Judicial review–Avenue for challenging refusal of deemed application for planning permission–S.289 Town and Country Planning Act 1990

[Town and Country Planning Act 1990 (c.8) s.174(2)(a), s.177(5), s.288, s.289; Planning and Compulsory Purchase Act 2004 (c.5) s.38(6)]

The applicant (D) applied for permission to appeal against a decision of the respondent secretary of state, by his planning inspector, upholding an enforcement notice issued by the local authority. The enforcement notice related to a piece of land in open countryside. The local authority asserted that D had changed the use of the land without permission and was using it for the open storage of building materials and equipment. The land was adjacent to a site on which a dwelling was under construction, and D claimed that he had express permission to store building materials and equipment on part of the land subject to the enforcement notice. He also claimed that, pursuant to the Town and Country Planning Act 1990 s.174(2)(a), planning permission should be granted for that use for the whole of the land. Pursuant to s.177(5) he was deemed to have made such an application. The inspector rejected his arguments, but concluded that he had permitted development rights in respect of part of the land. He declined to grant permission for the change of use because of a possible flood risk and because the storage of building materials and equipment conflicted with development plan policy SET 03 in the 2006 local plan. Pursuant to the Planning and Compulsory Purchase Act 2004 s.38(6), permission was not to be granted for development that conflicted with the development plan unless material considerations indicated otherwise. D argued that (1) the inspector had not given due regard to the express permission for the storage of materials and equipment on part of the land; (2) policy SET 03 was inconsistent with the National Planning Policy Framework, and that inconsistency was a material consideration militating against the refusal of planning permission; (3) the inspector had acted unfairly by, without warning, choosing not to grant planning permission rather than to grant it subject to a condition requiring a satisfactory flood risk assessment.

Held: Application refused. (1) The alleged breach of planning control was the use of the whole of the land for storage, and it was irrelevant that part of the land had express permission for storage (see para.19 of judgment). (2) The inspector had to make his decision in accordance with the development plan, and policy SET 03 permitted development in the countryside only if there was an overriding need for it or if it was development of an appropriate type. The use of the land for the storage of building materials and equipment was in conflict with that policy and therefore had to be refused. The inspector had been right to reject D's argument that the SET 03 policy of safeguarding undeveloped rural land was inconsistent with the Framework's approach of supporting economic growth in rural areas. Determining the extent to which there was any inconsistency between the two policies involved two elements: interpreting the policies themselves, which was a matter for the court; and evaluating the policies and their objectives in the context of a particular development, which was a matter for the planning decision-maker. As to the latter, there was nothing in the inspector's evaluation that amounted to an error of law. As to the former, there was no inconsistency in terms of interpretation between SET 03 and the Framework. The basic thrust of both policies was to encourage development in the location most appropriate for it. The open storage of building material and equipment was not encouraged in the countryside either specifically or because of any other particular feature of rural support set out in the Framework. It did not fit into any of the developments set out in para.28 of the Framework as developments that should be supported by policy. The difference between "safeguarding the countryside" in SET 03 and "recognising its intrinsic character and beauty" in the Framework was very unclear. The concept of intrinsic character and beauty recognised that all of the countryside would have some such qualities, and the concept had to involve some element of protection or safeguarding (paras 23-34). (3) The land lay in an area identified by the Environment Agency as a flood zone, and both the local plan and the Framework required a site-specific flood-risk assessment covering the risk to development on site and the effect of the development on flood risks elsewhere. A sufficiently specific assessment had not been carried out in the instant case, despite the inspector having given D the opportunity to undertake one. The inspector had refused planning permission on the basis that he could not be sure that any risk would be abated by the imposition of conditions. He had been entitled to approach the flood-risk issue on the basis that the Environment Agency was not satisfied with the assessment. In the absence of an assessment satisfying the Environment Agency, the obvious conclusion was that there could be no certainty that the use of the land for open storage would satisfy the policies in the local plan and the Framework (paras 36-41). (4) The only avenue for challenging the refusal of a deemed application for planning permission was s.289 of the 1990 Act. Section 288 was of no application (paras 9-14).

DE SOUZA v SECRETARY OF STATE FOR COMMUNITIES AND LOCAL GOVERNMENT, [2015] EWHC 2245 (Admin), [2016] J.P.L. 85, Ouseley J, QBD (Admin).

1681 Development–Cycle tracks–Whether cycle superhighway was development within s.55(1) Town and Country Planning Act 1990

[Town and Country Planning Act 1990 (c.8) s.55(1), s.55(2)(b); Highways Act 1980 (c.66) s.65]

The claimant, a representative body for licensed taxi drivers in London, applied for judicial review of a decision of the defendant highway authority (TfL) to construct a "cycle superhighway" without planning permission. The cycle superhighway was a segregated cycle lane that was to run continuously for 9.5km on local authority roads and the TfL road network. Its construction involved, amongst other things, reducing the number of vehicular traffic lanes along its route; redesigning junctions; changing parking and loading arrangements; and improving lighting and pedestrian facilities. It was a key element of the Mayor of London's 2012 transport strategy. Public consultation began in September 2014, and the claimant made representations. In January 2015, TfL published its response to the consultation together with an environmental evaluation report. Concluding that the construction of the superhighway would not have any significant adverse impact on the environment, it approved the proposal. Work began in April 2015. TfL took the view that planning permission was not required because the works were not "development" within the meaning of the Town and Country Planning Act 1990 s.55(1). Its case was that, as road improvement works that would not have significant adverse environmental impact, the works were exempted by s.55(2)(b). The claimant argued that the works would have a significant adverse impact. It initially sought a declaration to the effect that TfL was in breach of planning control by carrying out the works without planning permission. During the hearing it amended its application so as to seek instead a declaration that TfL had acted unlawfully by failing to either request a screening opinion or submit an environmental statement to the relevant local planning authorities. The issues were (1) whether the works were "development" within the meaning of s.55(1); (2) if they were, whether declaratory relief should be granted.

Held: Application refused. (1) The works were not "development" within the meaning of s.55(1) and therefore planning permission was not required. That was not to say that planning permission might not be required for certain minor works within the scheme, or for other cycle superhighways. Each scheme would need to be judged on its own facts. The works in issue fell within s.55(2)(b) in that they were being carried out within the boundaries of a road by a highway authority. It was common ground that they were improvement works: a cycle track constituted an improvement to a highway by virtue of the Highways Act 1980 s.65. The phrase "any works" was used twice in s.55(2)(b) and was intended to mean the same thing each time, and a judgement had to be made about whether the works as a whole might have a significant adverse effect on the environment. The only evidence of the environmental effect of the works was that contained in TfL's environmental evaluation report. That report, which was supported by detailed modelling work, concluded that there would be significant impacts, both beneficial and adverse, in localised areas. However, read fairly and as a whole, it supported TfL's assertion that the works would, overall, have no significant effect on the environment. Assessing whether a proposal would have an adverse environmental effect was an exercise of planning judgement and was not a matter for the court, *R. v Rochdale MBC Ex p. Milne (No.2)* [2001] Env. L.R. 22, [2001] C.L.Y. 4680 applied. The issue for the court was whether TfL's conclusion on that matter was erroneous or irrational, and it was not (see paras 55-64 of judgment). (2) If the foregoing was wrong and planning permission was required, the court would nevertheless exercise its discretion to refuse to grant declaratory relief. The declaration as originally sought might well offend against the scheme established by the 1990 Act. Since most of the works could be lawfully carried out without recourse to a local planning authority, it was unlikely that a court would grant a declaration in those terms. Moreover, as environmental effect was a matter of planning judgement, it would be inappropriate for the court to usurp the role of the local planning authority. The court had no power to declare that the work carried out had been in breach of planning control; that power resided with the local planning authority. Furthermore, the claimant had not issued proceedings until some six months after the superhighway was approved, and it had not raised the issue of lawfulness during the consultation. By the time of the instant hearing, construction had been ongoing for seven months and £18.4 million of public money had been spent on the project. Challenges to planning decisions had to be brought within six weeks, and although the decision to proceed with the superhighway was not a planning decision, the rationale for the time limit, namely the need for certainty, was equally applicable, *R. (on the application of Champion) v North Norfolk DC* [2015] UKSC 52, [2015] 1 W.L.R. 3710, [2015] C.L.Y. 2027 applied (paras 79-87). The amended application raised the issue of a screening opinion and an environmental statement, neither of which had formed part of the case before the instant court. Argument had not been heard on them, and it would be inappropriate to grant a declaration in such terms (paras 88-89).

R. (ON THE APPLICATION OF LICENSED TAXI DRIVERS ASSOCIATION) v TRANSPORT FOR LONDON, [2016] EWHC 233 (Admin), [2016] R.T.R. 29, Patterson J, QBD (Admin).

1682 **Development consent orders–Nationally significant infrastructure projects–New material concerning strategic merits–Requirements of s.104(7) Planning Act 2008 on secretary of state**

[Planning Act 2008 (c.29) s.104, s.104(7), s.118; Directive 85/337 on the assessment of the effects of certain public and private projects on the environment 1985; Directive 2001/42 on the assessment of the effects of certain plans and programmes on the environment 2001]

The claimants renewed their applications for permission to appeal against the refusal to grant permission to apply for judicial review of the grant of a development consent order (DCO) for an infrastructure project to deal with effluent in London. The project was the subject of strategic examination through the formation of a national policy statement under the Planning Act 2008. The structure of the Act was such that statements were subject to obligations of publicity and consultation, and there was a power to mount legal challenges in relation to them. An application for a DCO had been made to the secretary of state. It was examined by an examining authority, which decided not to entertain representations for strategic alternatives to the project that had not been advanced at the time of development of the statement. Under s.104 of the Act, the secretary of state had to decide the DCO application in accordance with any relevant national policy statement unless, under s.104(7), he was satisfied that the adverse impact of the proposed development would outweigh its benefits. The first claimant's assertion that s.104(7) obligated the secretary of state and the examining authority to consider at that time whether there were any strategic alternatives to the project had been rejected as unarguable in the context of the Act, because such task would have already been undertaken during development of the national policy statement. The second claimant's application for judicial review was refused because he had failed to fulfil the requirements of s.118, which required any judicial review proceedings to be brought during the period of six weeks beginning with the day on which the DCO was published. The first claimant submitted that s.104(7) and Directive 85/337 (EIA Directive) required the secretary of state to consider new material concerning the strategic merits of the project or reopen and examine the strategic merits. The second claimant argued that the secretary of state had provided him with the incorrect date for filing.

Held: Applications refused. (1) In a genuine case where new circumstances arose, it was open to a person to approach the secretary of state to invite him to revisit the national policy statement. That was the proper way in which such matters should be taken into account, because revisiting the strategic need for a project would mean that the procedural protections which applied in relation to the formation of a statement would apply again to ensure proper consideration was given to the alleged change of circumstances and the impact they might have on the statement. The legal provisions were clear and there was no arguable case in favour of the claimant's interpretation of the Act, nor was there any other compelling reason why permission to appeal should be granted on that ground (see paras 14-20 of judgment). Directive 2001/42 (SEA Directive) allowed for a full assessment in terms of environmental acceptability of options at the strategic level. The EIA Directive allowed for consideration of environmental impacts in relation to the application for particular planning consents taking as read the strategic options which had ex hypothesi already been subject to examination under the SEA Directive. There was no requirement that the EIA Directive should be given the expansive interpretation for which the claimant contended, and to do so would be contrary to the overall structure of European law in this area (para.22). (2) While it was regrettable that the secretary of state had incorrectly advised the second claimant of the relevant filing date, it was not a matter capable of being brought into account so as to create jurisdiction for the court which, by reason of s.118, did not have. Nothing that the secretary of state said or did was, in terms of law, capable of altering the operation of the statutory provision (para.29).

R. (ON THE APPLICATION OF THAMES BLUE GREEN ECONOMY LTD) v SECRETARY OF STATE FOR COMMUNITIES AND LOCAL GOVERNMENT; R. (ON THE APPLICATION OF BLUE GREEN LONDON PLAN) v SECRETARY OF STATE FOR THE ENVIRONMENT, FOOD AND RURAL AFFAIRS, [2015] EWCA Civ 876, [2016] J.P.L. 157, Sales LJ, CA (Civ Div).

1683 Development plan documents–Duty to co-operate–No duty on local authority after independent examination stage under s.20 Planning and Compulsory Purchase Act 2004 s.20

[Planning and Compulsory Purchase Act 2004 (c.5) s.19, s.20, s.20(7C), s.23, s.33A]

A landowner appealed against a decision (*Samuel Smith Old Brewery (Tadcaster) v Selby DC* [2014] EWHC 3441 (Admin), [2015] P.T.S.R. 719, [2015] C.L.Y. 2045) refusing its application for judicial review of the adoption of a development plan document. The local authority had presented a draft core strategy for independent examination under the Planning and Compulsory Purchase Act 2004 s.20. When it became apparent early on that the core strategy was not sound, the planning inspector suspended the examination for six months to enable the local authority to propose changes. During the suspension, s.33A of the 2004 Act came into force, imposing on local authorities a duty to co-operate in relation to strategic planning matters. When the examination resumed, the inspector ruled that the duty did not apply after the core strategy had been submitted for examination. He found the core strategy to be sound if subjected to modifications, including those the local authority proposed as a result of its work during the suspension. The local authority consequently adopted the core strategy. A judge upheld the inspector's ruling on the basis that the s.33A duty only applied to the stage of preparing documents under s.19, not the examination stage under s.20.

Held: Appeal dismissed. The judge had correctly held that the duty to co-operate was not engaged. That conclusion flowed from the natural construction of s.19, s.20 and s.23, governing the preparation, examination and adoption of local development documents. The preparation of a document, as provided for in s.19, and independent examination, as provided for in s.20, were separate from each other. Preparation came to an end before examination began. In the examination stage, the decision of what should happen to the plan was the planning inspector's. Section 33A itself reinforced the separation between preparation and examination. The activities to which the duty to co-operate in s.33A related included "the preparation of development plan documents"; that plainly corresponded to s.19. By contrast, the activity in s.20 did not match any of the activities in s.33A. The duty to co-operate was a duty of the local authority in preparing the plan, which it must have performed at that stage to the satisfaction of the inspector who later carried out the examination; it was not a duty for the local authority to perform, or perform again, after the examination stage had begun. The provisions of s.20 put that understanding of the statutory scheme beyond doubt. They showed that in the examination, the inspector was concerned with whether the development plan document itself satisfied the statutory requirements, rather than whether the local authority had complied with the relevant procedural requirements. The preparation of the plan was regarded as having been completed before the plan was submitted for examination. Although a local authority might undertake further work, which might qualify as preparation, once the examination stage was underway, that did not displace the inspector's role in conducting the examination. The notion that the duty to co-operate might be engaged during the suspension of an examination, but not if the examination continued, would lead to an arbitrary distinction in the statutory arrangements. The interpretation of the relevant sections in line with their natural sense did not create a significant gap in a local authority's responsibility to engage with neighbouring authorities when considering potential modifications to propose to an inspector under s.20(7C). There was no policy need which could justify a strained reading of the provisions. A degree of co-operation with neighbouring authorities was required as an aspect of satisfying an inspector as to the soundness of a development plan document, quite apart from s.33A. The practical effect of not applying the s.33A duty to work done in the examination stage was to leave the inspector to review a local authority's co-operative engagement with other authorities in relation to any further work and make a fact-specific assessment as to its impact on the overall soundness of the plan. That served the public interest of promulgating satisfactory planning policy documents in good time. The s.33A duty had not been engaged, and there had been no failure on the local authority's part to comply with that duty (see paras 26-48 of judgment).

SAMUEL SMITH OLD BREWERY (TADCASTER) v SELBY DC, [2015] EWCA Civ 1107, [2016] P.T.S.R. 146, Moore-Bick LJ, CA (Civ Div).

1684 **Development plans–Environmental impact assessments–Hydro-electric generation–Local authority's compliance with s.38(6) Planning and Compulsory Purchase Act 2004–Impact on heritage assets**

[Planning and Compulsory Purchase Act 2004 (c.5) s.38(6); Planning (Listed Buildings and Conservation Areas) Act 1990 (c.9) s.66; Town and Country Planning (Environmental Impact Assessment) Regulations 2011 (SI 2011/1824) Sch.2]

The claimants applied for judicial review of the defendant local authority's decision to grant planning permission for a hydro-electric generating facility at a weir. The claimants, who owned or had an interest in nearby land, opposed the development. The local authority approved the application, subject to conditions including a noise mitigation scheme setting out noise levels within which the facility could operate. The issues were whether (1) the local authority had complied with its duty under the Planning and Compulsory Purchase Act 2004 s.38(6) to make its determination in accordance with the local plan; (2) the local authority had properly considered the development's impact on heritage assets as required by the Planning (Listed Buildings and Conservation Areas) Act 1990 s.66; (3) the application should have been screened under the Town and Country Planning (Environmental Impact Assessment) Regulations 2011 to decide whether the proposal concerned Environmental Impact Assessment (EIA) development; (4) the local authority had failed to have regard to material considerations by basing its decision solely on matters relating to noise; (5) the noise condition was too imprecise to be enforceable.

Held: Application refused. (1) The absence of any express reference to s.38(6) in the local authority's planning officers' reports was immaterial because it was obvious that they had concluded that the proposal conformed with the development plan. The reports were addressed to a knowledgeable readership with substantial local, background knowledge of the area and knowledge of the statutory test for determining planning applications, *R. v Mendip DC Ex p. Fabre* (2000) 80 P. & C.R. 500, [2000] C.L.Y. 4508 and *R. v Selby DC Ex p. Oxton Farms* [1997] E.G. 60 (C.S.), [1997] C.L.Y. 4114 applied. It was clear from the reports that the officers had appreciated and understood the important planning issues and relevant policies in the case, *South Somerset DC v Secretary of State for the Environment* (1993) 66 P. & C.R. 83, [1993] C.L.Y. 3927 applied. The proposed development was considered to add an element of visual interest and had an overall design in character with the weir's operational structure which did not conflict with the local plan (see paras 34, 38-40, 43 of judgment). (2) The local authority had considered the relationship between the proposed development and adjoining heritage assets and concluded that it would not have an adverse impact. That was a planning judgment for the local authority, and the reasons for its decision were comprehensible and sufficient (paras 57-59). (3) The question whether the proposed development fell within Sch.2 of the Regulations, thereby requiring a screening opinion, depended on how much electricity the scheme would generate. The local authority's principal planning officer had been satisfied that the output was not sufficient to engage Sch.2: he had been entitled to reach that conclusion on the basis of the material before him and for the reasons he had given. The local authority had applied its mind to the relevant provisions of the Regulations and reached a reasonable conclusion (paras 68-72). (4) The local authority's planning committee had, as it was required to do, considered all the representations on various issues received in relation to the proposal, *R. (on the application of Kides) v South Cambridgeshire DC* [2002] EWCA Civ 1370, [2003] 1 P. & C.R. 19, [2002] C.L.Y. 3662 applied. It had, therefore, had regard to all the material considerations (paras 73, 78). (5) A judicial review application was not a forum for resolving issues between the parties on technical matters such as the assessment of noise: those were matters of judgment for the local planning authority, *R. (on the application of Nicholson) v Allerdale BC* [2015] EWHC 2510 (Admin) applied. In any event, the noise condition was sufficiently clear and precise (paras 89, 92-93).

R. (ON THE APPLICATION OF LENSBURY LTD) v RICHMOND UPON THAMES LBC, [2016] EWHC 980 (Admin), [2016] Env. L.R. 29, Supperstone J, QBD (Admin).

1685 Development plans–Green wedge–Refusal of permission for residential development–Secretary of state's failure to apply s.38(6) Planning and Compulsory Purchase Act 2004 when finding that development accorded with development plan

[Planning and Compulsory Purchase Act 2004 (c.5) s.38(6)]

A property development company applied to quash the first defendant secretary of state's decision dismissing its appeal against the second defendant local authority's refusal of planning permission for residential development. The planning application had been refused by the local authority despite a recommendation for approval by planning officers. As the proposed development involved residential development of more than 150 units on a site of more than 5 hectares, a planning enquiry was held by the secretary of state. A planning inspector concluded that the development accorded with the development plan and recommended that the company's appeal should be allowed. The secretary of state agreed with the inspector that the development plan did not support the conclusion that the land was within a designated green wedge. He disagreed with the inspector's view that, if the land had been within a green wedge, the development would leave sufficient green wedge to adequately maintain the separation of two conurbations, thereby finding a conflict with core strategy policy CS10(3). He also concluded that the development would have a materially harmful effect on the character of the area, also in conflict with CS10(3). The secretary of state conceded that his decision should be quashed. However, the local authority did not. The company submitted that the secretary of state had wrongly applied the Planning and Compulsory Purchase Act 2004 s.38(6), and had unlawfully concluded that the development conflicted with CS10(3) and the strategic objective of providing a maintaining green wedge between conurbations. The local authority argued that to treat CS10(3) as the most relevant policy was an acceptable approach. It argued that it was evident that the s.38(6) duty had been discharged, that conflict with s.38(6) occurred due to conflict with CS10(3), and that the development proposals complied with the other relevant policies and there had been no need to refer to them.

Held: Application granted. (1) A finding of compliance or conflict with the development plan, and the basis for that finding, needed to be made so that the decision-maker could undertake the planning balance in an informed way. Such a step enabled the decision-maker and the recipient of the decision to understand that the s.38(6) duty had been properly discharged. The difficulty with the local authority's approach was that it did not show the decision-maker engaging with whether the proposal complied with the development plan as a whole. A decision had to be made on the right basis and in relation to the development plan overall. That did not mean employing a mechanistic approach of judging the proposals against each and every policy that might be prayed in aid of a development or against it, but an evaluation of main policy areas within the development plan that were relevant to the proposal to be determined, and an assessment of how the proposal fared against them. The process to be followed was for the individual decision-maker. However, it needed to be clear at the culmination of the decision-taking process what the eventual judgment was against the development plan as a whole. Only by carrying out that exercise could evaluation of the planning balance be properly undertaken. It was important to recall the actual wording of s.38(6) and the exercise to be undertaken. To determine whether a proposal was in accordance with the plan, the decision-maker needed to have regard to all of the relevant policies. The secretary of state appeared to have reached his decision in respect of one policy only, material though it was. The finding that a conflict with CS10(3) sufficient to give rise to substantial weight against the proposal, without any prior evaluation of development plan policies being engaged with, was an inadequate and incomplete attempt to discharge the s.38(6) statutory duty, *R. (on the application of Hampton Bishop PC) v Herefordshire Council* [2014] EWCA Civ 878, [2015] 1 W.L.R. 2367, [2015] C.L.Y. 2031 distinguished, *R. v Rochdale MBC Ex p. Milne (No.2) (Application for Permission to Appeal)* considered (see paras 27-36 of judgment). (2) The secretary of state's finding that there was no development plan support for a conclusion that the land was a designated green wedge was the starting point for consideration of where policy CS10(3) applied. Once it was accepted that the key diagram set out the geographical extent of the green wedge in indicative terms, as an aid to interpretation of policy CS10, and that the appeal site was clearly outside the indicative extent on any interpretation, there was no basis for the application of CS10 to the appeal site. The secretary of state's clear and unambiguous finding meant that there was no basis for applying CS10. It might be a perfectly valid exercise in terms of the effect of the development on the general appearance of the area, but not in development plan policy terms given the very clear finding regarding the application of CS10. It had therefore not been possible for the secretary of state to conclude that the scheme conflicted with CS10(3). He had clearly misunderstood and/or misapplied the policy. The decision would be quashed (paras 45-54).

TIVIOT WAY INVESTMENTS LTD v SECRETARY OF STATE FOR COMMUNITIES AND LOCAL GOVERNMENT, [2015] EWHC 2489 (Admin), [2016] J.P.L. 171, Patterson J, QBD (Admin).

1686 Electricity generation–Development consent

THE PALM PAPER MILL GENERATING STATION ORDER 2016, SI 2016/166; made under the Planning Act 2008 s.114, s.120. In force: 12 February 2016.

This Order grants Palm Paper Ltd development consent for a gas-fired generating station on the site of the paper mill at Saddlebow Industrial Estate, King's Lynn, Norfolk.

1687 Enforcement notices–Address for service–Planning department entitled to rely on proprietorship register for address

[Town and Country Planning Act 1990 (c.8) s.171B(2), s.179(2), s.285(2)]

A local authority appealed by way of case stated against two magistrates' court decisions acquitting the respondent (M) of breaching an enforcement notice. In 2007, M purchased a property. The planning department received information from the finance department indicating that the property had been subdivided into two self-contained flats without planning permission. On 24 September 2010, it served an enforcement notice on M at the property address, the occupants of the flats, and the mortgagee, requiring the current use to be ceased and the reconversion of the property into one home. On 5 July 2012, the local authority sent a non-compliance letter to M at another address. Earlier letters had been sent to M at the property. In September 2012, the local authority brought proceedings against M alleging that he had breached the enforcement notice on 10 November 2011 contrary to the Town and Country Planning Act 1990 s.179(2). The lay justices accepted a submission of no case to answer. On appeal the High Court stated that the justices erred in their decision. The local authority brought further proceedings in the magistrates' court alleging that between 12 July 2012 and 6 January 2015, M was in breach of s.179(2). The court acquitted M on the basis that he satisfied s.285(2), namely that he did not know and could not reasonably have expected to know that the notice had been issued. M also successfully invoked the four-year time bar in s.171B(2) on the basis that the conversion of the property occurred before he purchased it. A tenant who lived in the property for three months in 2005 gave evidence that he lived in the top floor flat and that someone else was living downstairs, but he could not say who. The issues were whether (i) the notice had not been served on M at "his usual or last place of abode" when it was delivered to the property on 24 September 2010; (ii) the correct test had been applied in deciding that it was too late to issue the notice in September 2010 and if there was sufficient evidence on which a reasonable tribunal could have found that it was too late to issue it on that date; (iii) with regard to the second offence only, had the court been entitled to find that M did not know, and could not have reasonably been expected to know, that the notice had been issued.

Held: Appeal allowed. (1) The issue of a person's usual place of abode or last known address was a question of fact and law. The statutory framework clearly pointed to the knowledge of the planning department being relevant as regards service of an enforcement notice, not the authority as a whole. That knowledge came from the proprietorship register. The planning department did not need to trawl through the records of other departments to locate another address. Further, if another address was located it would not always be evidence which was the current address for service. M had been properly served in September 2010. He did not satisfy s.285(2) and could not challenge the validity of the notice. Moreover, he could not invoke the defence under s.179(7)(a) that he was unaware of the notice (see paras 20-21, 23 of judgment). (2) The justices had focused on the date of conversion and failed to address the extent to which the property was used as flats during the immunity period. M did not adduce evidence to satisfy the relevant test. The tenant who lived in the property in 2005 was unable to give any evidence as to the use of any part of the property either before or after his three-month tenancy. The justices accepted that there had been periods during M's ownership when the flats were vacant. M had no definite evidence of the use of the flats after he acquired the property. There was simply no evidence on which a reasonable tribunal could have found that it was too late for the local authority to issue the enforcement notice on 24 September 2010. Applying the correct test, no reasonable tribunal could have concluded that a two-flat use had been ongoing at the property continuously for a four-year period prior to that date (para.32). (3) For the purposes of the defence under s.179(7), the relevant date for knowledge was the date of the alleged offence, *Sanger v Newham LBC* [2014] EWHC 1922 (Admin), [2015] 1 W.L.R. 332, [2014] C.L.Y. 2379 followed. The same had to be true in respect of the date for the state of knowledge under s.285(2)(c)(i). Where a defendant was unable to use s.179(7) because the notice was on the required register, as in the instant case, s.285(2) could be invoked. However, it would be strange if a defendant could use a different route to a successful defence merely by virtue of not having been aware of the enforcement notice at an early stage, when he did in fact know of it when the alleged offence took place. The second offence was alleged to have commenced on 12 July 2012. M had accepted that he received the non-compliance letter delivered to his home address on 5 July. By that date he knew that the enforcement notice had been issued. In relation to the second offence, he could not satisfy s.285(2)(c) and could not challenge the validity of the notice under s.285(1) (paras 35-36). (4) The matter was remitted to the magistrates' court and was to be heard by a district judge (para.39).

NEWHAM LBC v MIAH, [2016] EWHC 1043 (Admin), [2016] P.T.S.R. 1082, Cranston J, QBD (Admin).

1688 Enforcement notices–Appeals–Inspector's power under s.174(2)(f) Town and Country Planning Act 1990 to determine planning merits

[Town and Country Planning Act 1990 (c.8) s.174(2)(a), s.174(2)(f), s.177(5); Localism Act 2011 (c.20)]

A restaurateur appealed against a decision (*Miaris v Secretary of State for Communities and Local Government* [2015] EWHC 1564 (Admin)) upholding an enforcement notice issued by the second respondent local authority. The enforcement notice had alleged a breach of planning control by way of an unauthorised change of use from that of a restaurant to include its use as a drinking establishment and nightclub. The notice required the restaurant to stop (a) its use as a drinking establishment; (b) its use as a nightclub; (c) DJs from performing at the premises. His appeal against the notice was brought solely under the Town and Country Planning Act 1990 s.174(2)(f), that the enforcement notice exceeded what was necessary to remedy any breach of planning control, or to remedy any injury to amenity. He did not appeal under s.174(2)(a) that planning permission ought to be granted. The inspector declined to consider his representations on the planning merits, holding that they were not appropriate in a ground (f) appeal where there was no appeal under ground (a) and where there had been no deemed application for planning permission. The issue was whether, when planning permission was not sought under s.174(2)(a), the secretary of state could entertain an appeal against a notice on the basis that its requirements exceeded what was necessary to remedy any injury to amenity caused by the breach, as opposed to remedying the breach itself. The restaurateur submitted that the deputy judge had been wrong to conclude (1) that the inspector had properly understood the extent of his powers; (2) that the conditions in the enforcement notice were merely seeking to remedy the injury to amenity caused by the breach.

Held: Appeal dismissed. What the restaurateur was seeking to achieve by his appeal was not approval of the use of the premises as a restaurant, drinking establishment and nightclub, which was the subject of the enforcement notice, but planning approval for its future mixed use as a restaurant and drinking establishment, or at least future use as a restaurant with a substantial ancillary use as a drinking establishment. Both the inspector and the judge had been correct to decide that an appeal under ground (f) alone could not achieve that, in the absence of an appeal on ground (a) and a deemed application for planning permission, *Wyatt Bros (Oxford) Ltd v Secretary of State for the Environment, Transport and the Regions* [2001] EWCA Civ 1560, [2002] P.L.C.R. 18, [2002] C.L.Y. 3678 and *Ioannou v Secretary of State for Communities and Local Government* [2014] EWCA Civ 1432, [2015] 1 P. & C.R. 10, [2015] C.L.Y. 1965 followed. There was a substantial difference in scope between appeals on ground (a) and appeals on the second limb of ground (f), which had not been reduced by the changes to the statutory scheme caused by amendments to s.177(5) introduced by the Localism Act 2011, which meant that there was no longer a deemed application for planning permission unless an appeal had been made on ground (a). Nor was there any provision in the statutory scheme for a discretion to grant planning permission where the only ground of appeal was ground (f) (see paras 21-22, 27, 31, 34-36 of judgment). (2) "Injury to amenity" was an imprecise concept, not being defined in the 1990 Act or in case law. However, the notice had clearly stipulated planning harm going beyond injury to amenity and including the effects of increased pedestrian movements and noise on the health and well-being of nearby residents (paras 42-44).

MIARIS v SECRETARY OF STATE FOR COMMUNITIES AND LOCAL GOVERNMENT, [2016] EWCA Civ 75, [2016] J.P.L. 784, Longmore LJ, CA (Civ Div).

1689 Enforcement notices–Building extensions–Agreement between local authority and applicant that extension was residential annex–Inspector's failure to give parties opportunity to address his finding

[Town and Country Planning (General Permitted Development) Order 1995 (SI 1995/418); Town and Country Planning Act 1990 (c.8) Pt VII s.191, Pt VII s.192]

The appellant appealed against a decision of the first respondent secretary of state, by his planning inspector, refusing his appeal against an enforcement notice concerning an extension to a garage. The appellant had lived on a farm which had outbuildings, including a garage block, and was in the green belt. The garage block was initially extended to house the appellant's classic cars. It was later converted into a residential annex, which extended further into the green belt. The local authority issued an enforcement notice in respect of the annex, stating that its erection was an unauthorised extension that did not fall within permitted development rights and that it breached the tolerance for curtilage under the Town and Country Planning (General Permitted Development) Order 1995 Sch. 2 class E; it required its removal within three months. The local authority and the appellant had previously agreed that the extension was within the curtilage of the main house, and the appellant had a certificate of lawful use and development (CLUD) stating that the annex was to be used ancillary to the main house. The appellant appealed against the enforcement notice and the inspector directed written representations. The appellant's fallback position was that he had a lawful use of the existing garage block for ancillary garaging and storage, and that he should be entitled under Class E to construct additional buildings to replace the lost garage and storage space if the enforcement notice was upheld. He advised the inspector to consider the aim of the green belt against the fall-back position. The inspector dismissed the appeal, concluding that the annex was actually a new independent and separate dwelling and was being used as such, and that there were no special circumstances outweighing the harm to the green belt. The appellant submitted that planning permission should have been granted for the new extension and that three months to comply with the enforcement notice and convert the garage fell short of what should have reasonably been allowed.

Held: Appeal allowed. The parties had agreed that the new extension was within the curtilage and was for residential use. The inspector had rejected the concept of an ancillary dwelling as a contradiction in terms; however, there was no indication as to what evidence he had referred in drawing that conclusion. The fall back position turned on whether the use could be accommodated in part of the original garage block in accordance with the CLUD and whether the appellant was entitled under Class E to construct an additional building to replace the lost garage and storage space. In holding that the CLUD only certified lawfulness at the date of the application, the inspector had confused the CLUD for existing use of development under the Town and Country Planning Act 1990 Pt VII s.191. The CLUD for the proposed development under s.192 was conclusive unless there was a material change before the development began.

Similarly, in relation to the fall-back position, the inspector had rejected the reliance on the fact that the local authority had unusually accepted the lawfulness of other developments because they could be repeated elsewhere. The inspector's conclusion, that the conversion to a dwelling was in line with the CLUD and would do less damage to the green belt than retaining the unauthorised extension, still left open the question of the appellant's ability to construct replacement storage pursuant to Class E. The inspector had considered the fall-back position weak in part because the appellant was repeating the sequence of development and there was doubtful justification concerning the extent of the curtilage of the original dwelling and to the use of the buildings. The inspector noted that a failure to apply the special circumstances test would encourage development as the appellant would be able to continue to construct buildings by reference to the requirements and qualifications of Class E. However, that did not adequately address the appellant's point. The inspector was aware that the local authority agreed with the appellant's stance on Class E and therefore should have given the parties an opportunity to deal with that issue. As it had been the inspector, and not the parties, that had raised the issue of the extension being a new and independent dwelling, fairness required that the appellant was given an opportunity to argue against that proposition, *R. (on the application of Ashley) v Secretary of State for Communities and Local Government* [2012] EWCA Civ 559, [2012] J.P.L. 1235, [2012] C.L.Y. 2570 followed. Further representations might have affected the inspector's decision and accordingly the matter was remitted.

PITT v SECRETARY OF STATE FOR COMMUNITIES AND LOCAL GOVERNMENT *sub nom.* R. (ON THE APPLICATION OF PITT) v SECRETARY OF STATE FOR COMMUNITIES AND LOCAL GOVERNMENT, [2015] EWHC 1931 (Admin), [2016] J.P.L. 20, Robin Purchas QC, QBD (Admin).

1690 Enforcement notices–Intensification of use–Notice limiting use to certified existing lawful use

[Town and Country Planning Act 1990 (c.8) s.177(1)(c); Town and Country Planning (Enforcement) (Determination by Inspectors) (Inquiries Procedure) (England) Rules 2002 (SI 2002/2685) r.16]

The appellant appealed against a decision of a planning inspector to uphold an enforcement notice issued by the second respondent local authority. The site in question was in the metropolitan green belt. It had the benefit of a certificate of lawfulness of existing use which enabled two small areas to be used for the storage of up to four vehicles and two storage containers. In the enforcement notice it was alleged that there had been intensification of use by the presence of more than four vehicles and more than two storage containers "along with the use of the land as a whole for the storage of vehicles and containers, the hire of containers for self-storage and the storage of builders/building materials, waste and equipment and other non-horticultural/forestry materials". The appellant argued, among other things, that (1) the inspector had erred by taking into account the off-site impact of the existing use, the parties having agreed in the statement of common ground that that was not an issue; (2) the inspector had also erred by failing to consider, pursuant to the Town and Country Planning Act 1990 s.177(1)(c), whether to issue a further certificate of lawfulness of existing use, modifying the existing one; further, by endorsing the enforcement requirements of the notice, the inspector had breached the doctrine in *Mansi v Elstree Rural DC* 62 L.G.R. 172, [1964] C.L.Y. 3580 that an enforcement notice could not lawfully remove existing lawful uses.

Held: Appeal allowed in part. (1) The fact that the inspector took into account the off-site impact of the existing use when the parties had agreed in the statement of common ground that that was not an issue was a breach of natural justice. The inspector was not bound to accept the parties' stance, but if the matter appeared important to him, he needed to draw their attention to that fact so that they could address him on it. In the context of a planning appeal, there was the additional problem that an inspector who strayed into an area covered by the statement of common ground, without any indication to the parties that he proposed to do so, would be deviating from the requirements of the procedure rules. The Town and Country Planning (Enforcement) (Determination by Inspectors) (Inquiries Procedure) (England) Rules 2002 r.16 made the statement of common ground compulsory, with the clear intention that the inspector would not generally have to inquire into matters on which the parties were agreed. Moreover, the inspector had treated the off-site impact of the existing use as relevant to the materiality of the change of use. Accordingly, insofar as the decision stated that there was an intensification amounting to a material change of use, it could not stand (see paras 14-15, 19-20 of judgment). (2) The inspector had not been required to issue a further certificate of lawfulness of existing use pursuant to s.177(1)(c). First, the word "may" was used in the sub-section, giving the inspector a discretion. Second, a certificate could only be issued under s.177(1)(c) if (for present purposes) "any existing use of the land was lawful". The inspector had decided that the existing use of the land was not lawful. There was no provision in s.177 requiring or even allowing an inspector to issue a certificate setting out a use which would be lawful. The appellant had relied on *Mansi* in arguing that because of the certificate an intensification of lawful use that did not amount to a material change of use would have been a lawful use of the site, so that confirmation of the enforcement notice limiting the use of the land to that certified as lawful in the certificate was in fact a restriction on the lawful uses of the land. That submission was unsound. Extended in the way suggested, the *Mansi* doctrine would prevent an enforcement notice from ever being based on the terms of the certificate itself. The authority issuing the enforcement notice, and any decision-maker on appeal, would need to investigate precisely what level of intensification was permitted and in what circumstances. Save where an actual existing use was held to be lawful, that investigation was impossible. If an appellant claimed that he was entitled to use the land more intensively than the certificate permitted, he could make an application for planning permission or raise a specific objection to the terms of the enforcement notice, asserting that it was too wide. If the use of the land continued at a modestly intensified level, he might be able to resist enforcement on the basis that the intensified use was lawful. Here, the local authority had been entitled to issue an enforcement notice based on the certificate, *Mansi* considered (paras 27-28, 31-32).

TURNER v SECRETARY OF STATE FOR COMMUNITIES AND LOCAL GOVERNMENT, [2015] EWHC 1895 (Admin), [2015] J.P.L. 1347, CMG Ockelton, QBD (Admin).

1691 Enforcement notices–Traveller sites–Lawfulness of planning authority's decision to clear unauthorised site in green belt

[Town and Country Planning Act 1990 (c.8) s.178]

The appellant Romany Gypsies appealed against a decision (*Eastwood v Windsor and Maidenhead RLBC* [2014] EWCA Civ 963) dismissing their claim for judicial review of the respondent local planning authority's decision to use its enforcement powers under the Town and Country Planning Act 1990 s.178 to clear land which they occupied. Since 2009, the appellants had been occupying caravans on a green belt site without planning permission. In December 2009, the planning authority had issued an enforcement notice requiring cessation of use of the land for residential purposes. The secretary of state had dismissed an appeal against the enforcement notice, refused to grant planning permission for use of the land as a residential site, and had allowed a period of 18 months for compliance with the enforcement notice. That period had expired and the appellants had not cleared the land. Within the local authority, there was insufficient provision for traveller sites which could accommodate the caravans and the occupants indicated that if they were evicted, they would be driven to camp at the roadside. In April 2013, the planning authority decided to use its powers under s.178 to clear the land of the caravans. The appellants submitted that (1) the planning authority's decision to use its s.178 powers was irrational or perverse because it was a fundamental premise of the secretary of state's decision to uphold the enforcement notice that an 18-month compliance period had been allowed, so that another site would be available before the enforcement notice took effect; (2) the planning authority should have waited until it had investigated more fully whether an alternative site might be found, particularly when it had just received a new list of potential sites; (3) the judge had erred in treating the exercise of s.178 powers as a matter of planning judgement in which the planning authority had a significant degree of discretion.

Held: Appeal dismissed. (1) The 18-month compliance period was not predicated on any assumption that a proper alternative site would necessarily have been found by the time the enforcement notice took effect. The inspector had indicated in terms that the unmet need and the absence of alternative sites should be left to the balance to be struck, meaning that they should be treated as a factor to be weighed against other factors when striking a balance to find a reasonable period for compliance. The inspector had expressly contemplated that if the appeal were dismissed there would be a risk that the occupants might be expelled from the land with no alternative site to go to, and he had not suggested that such a problem would be met by a compliance period of 18 months. On a fair reading of the inspector's report and the secretary of state's decision letter, all that the 18-month compliance period was intended to achieve was the allowance of a reasonable opportunity to make alternative arrangements. It plainly did not mean that the inspector thought that the appellants could only be removed once an appropriate alternative site had been found (see paras 17-18, 38 of judgment). (2) It was clear why the planning authority had decided not to wait any longer before acting. It had already waited a considerable period of time to implement the enforcement notice and during that time, serious harm to the public interest had continued by reason of the caravan encampment on green belt land. The compliance period had expired and there was a continuing breach of planning control in contravention of the criminal law. It was speculative whether any new site on the list would even be suitable for a traveller site or would result in a new location with proper planning permission which the appellants could move to in the near future. It had therefore been proportionate for the planning authority to proceed to implement the enforcement notice. It could not be said that it was irrational or perverse for it to do so (paras 39-41). (3) The exercise of enforcement powers under s.178 was not a matter in which the court should make up its own mind, giving little or no weight to the decision of the planning authority. The planning authority was a public authority deciding how it should act in the exercise of enforcement powers which had been directly conferred upon it by Parliament under s.178. In deciding how to exercise those powers, it had discretion. In the instant case, its decision had been a rational and lawful one (para.43).

R. (ON THE APPLICATION OF EASTWOOD) v WINDSOR AND MAIDENHEAD RLBC, [2016] EWCA Civ 437, [2016] H.L.R. 22, Arden LJ, CA (Civ Div).

1692 Enforcement notices–Use classes–Definition of "builder's merchants with ancillary sales"

The appellants appealed by way of case stated against their conviction for using a site as a builder's merchants with ancillary sales, contrary to an enforcement notice issued by the respondent local authority. The site was permitted for B8 use (storage and distribution). The local authority, concerned that the site was being used as a builder's merchants, issued the notice. One year later, a local authority inspector visited the site and noted that it was still being used in contravention of the notice. A warning was issued. When he visited again three months later, the site had been stripped of all materials. However, the local authority concluded that it was still being used as a builder's merchants as sales were still being transacted there. The appellants were prosecuted for breaching the notice. The Crown Court refused their appeal against conviction on the basis of the following: (i) after the site was stripped, the inspector visited twice more and found a substantial amount of building materials, a working cash register, a computer connected to a printer, and a working credit/debit card machine; (ii) there was evidence of a working website advertising that the company carried out trade and retail sales; (iii) items on the premises were marked with barcodes; (iv) test sales were carried out whereby an individual purchased building materials. The High Court ordered the Crown Court to state a case. The issues were whether (1) the Crown Court had failed to define the meaning of "builder's merchants"; (2) the Crown Court was right to decide that the meaning of "use as a builder's merchant with ancillary sales" was a question of fact rather than a mixed question of fact and expert judgment; (3) the Crown Court was right to admit the inspector's evidence and to take the view that it was not expert evidence; (4) there had been sufficient evidence to reasonably conclude that trade sales and ancillary sales had taken place during the relevant period; (5) the advertisement of the premises for trade sales was evidence that the site had been used for trade sales during the relevant period.

Held: Appeal dismissed. (1) The parties had always been broadly agreed that the definition of "a builder's merchant" was "the supplier of building materials". That was expressly accepted in the appellants' expert's report. Although he had sought to qualify that meaning by reference to wholesale rather than retail sales, the general definition was agreed. Further, the parties had agreed that sales were the critical element of the operation of a builder's merchants. The definition agreed did not require any further definition. It was in accordance with *R. (on the application of CW Young Ltd) v Secretary of State for the Environment, Transport and the Regions* [2001] EWHC Admin 141, [2001] J.P.L. 1321 (Note), *CW Young Ltd* considered (see paras 11-13 of judgment). (2) It was a matter of fact as to whether a particular site was being used in a particular way during the relevant period. Expert evidence could have no place in reaching such a decision. The appellants' expert evidence went to various arguments of law to the effect that sales might be ancillary to the use of the site for storage and distribution, or that sales might be de minimis, or that sales might not be wholesale. None of those were matters of expert evidence at all. At best, they were opinions on various aspects of planning law. Their inclusion in the appellants' expert's report meant that he was attempting to set himself up in place of the Crown Court. That evidence was inadmissible (paras 16-17). (3) The Crown Court would not have admitted the inspector's evidence as expert evidence because the issue was rightly regarded as not requiring expert evidence. His evidence had been allowed as to matters of fact, and there could be no question that it had been properly adduced. There was no expert evidence in his statement. The proof of that could be seen in the case stated itself. There was no finding there, no reason for the Crown Court's decision as to whether the site was being used as a builder's merchants, that was based in any way on any expression of the inspector's opinion. His opinion was simply not relevant (paras 19-20). (4) The evidence overall, as summarised in the case stated, was sufficient to justify dismissal of the appeal. Given the history of the site and its prior use as an unauthorised builder's merchants, the terms of the enforcement notice and the failure to comply with it, the evidence concerning the test purchase and the sophisticated sales paraphernalia, and the wide terms of the advertisement, the Crown Court was plainly entitled to conclude that the sales were ancillary to the unauthorised use of the premises as a builder's merchants (paras 27, 30-33). (5) The advertisement was part and parcel of the background, and made plain the appellants' continuing intention to sell construction supplies from the site. That intention was plainly expressed in terms of wholesale and retail sales. The website had advertised the site as being a builder's merchants. The Crown Court was obviously obliged to take that into account (para.34).

MATSONS LTD v LEICESTER CITY COUNCIL, [2016] EWHC 642 (Admin), (2016) 180 J.P. 302, Coulson J, QBD (Admin).

1693 Green belt–Change of use–Interpretation of para.89 National Planning Policy Framework

[Town and Country Planning Act 1990 (c.8) s.75]

A local authority applied to quash a decision of the respondent secretary of state, by his planning inspector, granting planning permission for the redevelopment of land already being used for a livery business. The proposed development involved retaining part of the livery business but building a new barn and associated workers' dwellings, and also constructing a number of houses. The local authority had refused planning permission on the basis that the proposed development constituted inappropriate development within the green belt. However, the planning inspector disagreed and found that the development was appropriate. The National Planning Policy Framework (NPPF) para.89 set out exceptions to the general policy that new buildings were inappropriate development in the green belt. Indent six provided an exception for "limited infilling or the partial or complete redevelopment of previously developed sites (brownfield land), whether redundant or in continuing use (excluding temporary buildings), which would not have a greater impact on the openness of the Green Belt and the purpose of including land within it than the existing development". The local authority submitted that under the sixth indent of para.89, applications that were not only for operational development for new buildings, but also involved material changes of use for those buildings could not be appropriate development in the green belt. It therefore argued that it had been an error for the inspector to treat the proposal as appropriate development because the construction of new houses involved a material change of use to residential or mixed residential and equestrian use. Alternatively, the local authority submitted that if para.89 did not preclude all material changes of use, the only changes of use permitted were those specifically mentioned in para.89.

Held: Application refused. It was unnecessary to gloss the para.89 exceptions. They should be read naturally and in the context that under the Town and Country Planning Act 1990 s.75, permission for new buildings would always carry with it permission for the use of those buildings, whether that was the use specified in the permission or the use for the purpose for which the building was designed. To include changes of use with respect to those new buildings did not involve contradicting the decision in *Timmins v Gedling BC* [2015] EWCA Civ 10, [2016] 1 All E.R. 895, [2015] C.L.Y. 1974 because that case was concerned with whether there was an unstated general category of appropriate development comprising a material change of use of land. The reasoning in *Timmins* was based on the fact that what was appropriate development was set out in the NPPF and the NPPF made no provision for a material change of use as a freestanding category of appropriate development. There was nothing inherent in the concept of a material change of use which led the court in *Timmins* to consider that it was not suitable in principle to be appropriate development, *Timmins* considered. Reading para.89 according to its language and purpose, the new buildings set out in the six indents were all concerned with new buildings which were defined in an individual manner according to the category in which they fell. It was clear that the Government must have had in mind their use given the frequent reference to the use of the new buildings. In only one case, namely indent four, did the policy seek to restrict the new buildings to their current use. Providing that new buildings fell within the use and other restrictions of the applicable indent of para.89, the mere fact that permission for a new building might also involve a material change of use did not mean that it ceased to be appropriate development. To read para.89 as though it introduced a general material change of use of land category would be to read into the paragraph an additional restriction which was not present. Further, an alternative approach whereby the only changes of use permitted under para.89 were those where the uses were specifically mentioned was not consistent with the meaning or purpose of para.89. The partial recognition of changes of use would make less sense than precluding changes altogether since the local authority's argument sought to restrict those categories of appropriate development where the policy did not seek to restrict the use of the new building itself but imposed some other means of preventing an adverse impact on the green belt. The categories of appropriate development were confined to what was expressly set out in the NPPF and those categories were intended to be restrictive. The inspector had not erred in concluding that the development was appropriate in the green belt, *Timmins* and *Fordent Holdings Ltd v Secretary of State for Communities and Local Government* [2013] EWHC 2844 (Admin), [2014] 2 P. & C.R. 12, [2014] C.L.Y. 2394 applied (see paras 12, 21-23, 33-34, 36-37, 41, 47-48, 53-54 of judgment).

BROMLEY LBC v SECRETARY OF STATE FOR COMMUNITIES AND LOCAL GOVERNMENT, [2016] EWHC 595 (Admin), [2016] P.T.S.R. 1186, David Elvin QC, QBD (Admin).

1694 Green belt–Gypsies–Refusal of planning permission on unauthorised travellers site–No very special circumstances

The appellant appealed against a decision (*Connors v Secretary of State for Communities and Local Government* [2014] EWHC 2358 (Admin), [2015] J.P.L. 196, [2015] C.L.Y. 1972) upholding the first respondent secretary of state's refusal of planning permission and issuing of an enforcement notice. The appellant was a Romani Gypsy who occupied an unauthorised site on the green belt with her family. She had sought planning permission for the change of use of the site for the retention and siting of a residential mobile home. The second respondent local authority had refused her application and imposed an enforcement notice. She appealed against those decisions and a planning inspector recommended that the enforcement notice should be quashed and a three-year temporary planning permission granted. The inspector accepted that the development amounted to inappropriate development in the green belt. However, he determined that very special circumstances existed to outweigh the harm to the green belt because it was likely that if the appeals failed, the appellant would move to another unauthorised site in the green belt, to the detriment of her daughter's health and her children's education. The secretary of state agreed that the appellant was likely to move to another unauthorised site if her appeals were dismissed, but did not agree that very special circumstances existed. He upheld the refusal of planning permission and the enforcement notice. The appellant unsuccessfully challenged those decisions in the High Court. The appellant submitted that the judge had been wrong not to address her contention that the secretary of state had failed to take account of the inspector's conclusion that if the appeals were dismissed, she and her family were likely to move to another unauthorised green belt site, which was bound to cause as much harm to the environment as continued occupation of the existing site. She relied on the decision in *Moore v Secretary of State for Communities and Local Government* [2013] EWCA Civ 1194, [2014] J.P.L. 362, [2014] C.L.Y. 2383 in support of that argument.

Held: Appeal dismissed. The judgment in *Moore* did not throw significant light on the issue in the instant case. The judge in that case had made it clear that the issue in that appeal was fact-specific rather than of wider importance. In *Moore*, the inspector had failed to make any relevant finding about the likelihood that the appellant and her children would have to resort to roadside camping if temporary permission was refused. In the instant case, however, the secretary of state had accepted the inspector's findings as to the likelihood of the family moving to another unauthorised site if the appeals were dismissed, *Moore* not applied. It had not been necessary for the secretary of state to specifically refer to the likelihood that the unauthorised site would be in the green belt. His decision letter was not bound to replicate every word of the inspector's report. In practice, it would have been plain to those reading the decision letter, with knowledge of the underlying facts, that the unauthorised site would necessarily have been in the green belt. The judge had dealt with the point sufficiently and had not erred in his conclusion that the decision not to grant planning permission pursued a legitimate and highly important aim and was proportionate to that aim (see paras 20-24 of judgment).

LEE v SECRETARY OF STATE FOR COMMUNITIES AND LOCAL GOVERNMENT, [2016] EWCA Civ 558, [2016] J.P.L. 1230, Jackson LJ, CA (Civ Div).

1695 Green belt–National Planning Policy Framework–Development's impact on openness–Visual impact as consideration

A landowner appealed against a decision (*Turner v Secretary of State for Communities and Local Government* [2015] EWHC 2728 (Admin)) upholding a determination of a planning inspector appointed by the first respondent secretary of state that planning permission should not be granted for a residential development in the green belt. The landowner owned a site in the green belt on which was situated a static caravan and a yard from which he ran a business storing, repairing and selling commercial vehicles. Certificates of lawful use existed for the caravan and for the storage of 11 lorries on the yard. The landowner sought permission to replace the caravan and storage yard with a three-bedroom bungalow, and to use land adjacent to the site to continue his business. The local authority refused permission on the ground that the proposal constituted inappropriate development in the green belt. The landowner appealed, arguing that his proposal was not inappropriate development because it would have no greater impact on the openness of the green belt than the existing development and so fell within the exception in NPPF para.89, bullet point 6. The planning inspector upheld the local authority's refusal of permission. He found that although the volume of the bungalow might be the same as that of the caravan and lorries, the impact of the two developments could not be judged simply by measured volume. He found that the bungalow would have a greater visual impact on the openness of the green belt than did the existing development. The landowner submitted that when considering bullet point 6 the inspector had failed to carry out a proper volumetric comparison of the existing and proposed developments and had wrongly conflated the concepts of openness and visual impact.

Held: Appeal dismissed. The inspector had addressed his mind to the comparative exercise required by bullet point 6 and had made an evaluative, comparative assessment of the existing and proposed developments. The central issue was whether in making that comparison he had taken an improper approach to the question of openness. He had not. Assessing openness was not limited to measuring the volume of the existing and proposed structures on the site. Many factors were relevant, including how built-up the green belt was currently and how built-up it would be if the proposed development went ahead. On the natural meaning of the language of para.89, visual impact was implicitly part of the concept of openness, and that interpretation was reinforced by the general guidance in NPPF paras 79-81. The visual dimension of the green belt was an important part of the point of designating land as green belt land. In stating in *Timmins v Gedling BC* [2014] EWHC 654 (Admin) that there was a clear conceptual distinction between openness and visual impact and that it was wrong in principle to arrive at a conclusion on openness by reference to visual impact, Green J had erred. That part of his judgment was not to be followed. He had not focused sufficiently on the language of NPPF s.9 and had placed excessive weight on the previous policy guidance on development in the green belt (PPG 2) in interpreting the NPPF. Moreover, he had purported to rely on *R. (on the application of Heath & Hampstead Society) v Camden LBC* [2007] EWHC 977 (Admin), [2007] 2 P. & C.R. 19, [2007] C.L.Y. 3286. However, his conclusion was not supported by that case, which concerned the application of the test in PPG 2 para.3.6 to a building which represented a spatial, but not a visual, intrusion. PPG 2 para.3.6 did not refer to the concept of openness in the green belt and did not correspond to the text of bullet point 6. It was therefore not appropriate to treat that case as giving authoritative guidance on the interpretation of bullet point 6, *Heath & Hampstead* considered, *Timmins* doubted. The NPPF was a self-contained, national planning policy that replaced the proliferation of policy guidance documents preceding it and set out national planning policy afresh. Nevertheless, it was not intended to weaken or change the central policy in PPG 2 that inappropriate development in the green belt was not to be allowed. In the instant case, the planning inspector had not erred. He had made a legitimate comparison of the existing and proposed developments and had carried out an evaluative assessment. That evaluation was a matter of planning judgement and was not irrational. The planning inspector had been entitled to conclude that there was a difference between a permanent physical structure in the form of a bungalow and a shifting body of lorries, and he had been entitled to take account of the difference in the level of visual intrusion presented by both developments on the openness of the green belt (see paras 12-27 of judgment).

TURNER v SECRETARY OF STATE FOR COMMUNITIES AND LOCAL GOVERNMENT, [2016] EWCA Civ 466, [2016] J.P.L. 1092, Arden LJ, CA (Civ Div).

1696 Green belt–Very special circumstances–Mixed use development–Need for new housing–Limited options for meeting need

[Civil Procedure Rules 1998 r.52.11]

The appellant appealed against a decision (*R. (on the application of Smech Properties Ltd) v Runnymede BC* [2015] EWHC 823 (Admin)) upholding the first respondent local authority's grant of planning permission for a mixed use development on a green belt site. The second respondents owned the site and wanted to develop it. The appellant owned land close to the site. A draft local plan core strategy (LPCS) set out policies for provision of a five-year supply of new housing. It identified that the local authority was constrained by the fact that green belt land amounted to 79% of the land in its area. Although the evidence base indicated that there was a need for an average of 595 new homes per year in the five-year-period, the LPCS proposed that only 220 new dwellings should be provided each year. The LPCS was withdrawn because it did not comply with the local authority's statutory obligations. A planning officer's report stated that the local authority would only be able to demonstrate a five-year housing supply with the inclusion of the residential provision of 200 houses on the application site. However, that report appeared to be based on the proposal for 220 homes per year in the draft LPCS. In any event, a technical paper made it clear that there was an adequate housing supply to meet that low figure without any need for additional housing on the site. The officer's report was therefore misleading, but planning permission was granted on the basis that very special circumstances existed to justify development in the green belt, under the National Planning Policy Framework para.87. The judge at first instance acknowledged the misleading advice, but declined to quash the planning permission, concluding that the planning committee would still have granted the permission if it had not been misled. The appellant submitted that no oral evidence had been given at trial and the court was therefore as well placed as the judge to assess the evidence for itself. It argued that the court should find that the judge's decision was wrong because it was not inevitable that the planning committee would have made the same decision without the misleading advice.

Held: Appeal dismissed. The general rule in CPR r.52.11 had not been displaced. The appeal was limited to a review of the decision of the lower court rather than a re-hearing. It was therefore necessary to ask whether the judge had legitimate and proper grounds for reaching the decision she did, rather than approach the matter afresh. Where an appeal was to proceed by way of a review of the judgment below rather than a re-hearing, it would often be appropriate for the court to give weight to the assessment of the facts made by the judge below, even where that assessment had been made on the basis of written evidence which was also available to the appeal court. The weight to be given to the judge's own assessment would vary depending on the circumstances. The weight to be accorded to the considered view of a judge at first instance might also be enhanced where the judge had a particular expertise in the area or where the judge had had a fuller opportunity to understand the case in the round. Both factors applied in the instant case. The judge at first instance had expertise in planning matters. The hearing before her lasted two days, in contrast with the half day spent before the instant court. It also involved consideration of other grounds of challenge and deeper consideration of the case as a whole (see paras 27-30 of judgment). It had not been shown that the judge's decision was "wrong". She had directed herself by reference to the relevant test as laid down in *Simplex GE (Holdings) Ltd v Secretary of State for the Environment* (1989) 57 P. & C.R. 306, [1989] C.L.Y. 3578. The LPCS had not been approved or adopted and the local authority had therefore remained obliged to seek to meet its full objectively assessed housing needs, namely 595 new homes a year. In such a situation, the judge had correctly directed herself by reference to *Hunston Properties Ltd v Secretary of State for Communities and Local Government* [2013] EWCA Civ 1610, [2014] 1 E.G.L.R. 79, [2014] C.L.Y. 2432. She had addressed the question of whether there were "very special circumstances" such as to justify permission for development in the green belt by reference to the full, objectively assessed needs of the area, *Hunston* applied. She had plainly understood the nature of the case presented by the appellant and her implicit assessment that the creation of 200 new homes was a significant contribution to meeting the pressing housing need in the area was one which she was fully entitled to make. There was great pressure of need for new housing and very limited options for meeting that need. The site was suitable for development. It was extensively covered in dilapidated buildings, meaning that the impact of the development upon the openness of the green belt would be limited. Moreover, the site was especially well suited for the proposed development because of the existing main railway line which served it. The judge had been entitled and correct to conclude that it was inevitable that if the planning committee had been properly advised in relation to housing need, it would have made the same decision, *Simplex* applied (paras 31-36, 39-40).

R. (ON THE APPLICATION OF SMECH PROPERTIES LTD) v RUNNYMEDE BC *sub nom.* SMECH PROPERTIES LTD v RUNNYMEDE BC, [2016] EWCA Civ 42, [2016] J.P.L. 677, Tomlinson LJ, CA (Civ Div).

1697 Highway improvement–Trunk roads–Tyne and Wear

THE A19/A1058 COAST ROAD (JUNCTION IMPROVEMENT) DEVELOPMENT CONSENT ORDER 2016, SI 2016/73; made under the Planning Act 2008 s.114, s.115, s.117, s.120, s.122, Sch.5 para.1, Sch.5 para.2, Sch.5 para.3, Sch.5 para.10, Sch.5 para.11, Sch.5 para.12, Sch.5 para.13, Sch.5 para.14, Sch.5 para.15, Sch.5 para.17, Sch.5 para.19, Sch.5 para.21, Sch.5 para.22, Sch.5 para.26, Sch.5 para.33, Sch.5 para.36, Sch.5 para.37. In force: 18 February 2016.

This Order authorises Highways England to improve the A19 junction with the A1058 in North Tyneside and carry out all associated works in order to reduce congestion and improve road safety.

1698 Home loss payments–Uprating

THE HOME LOSS PAYMENTS (PRESCRIBED AMOUNTS) (ENGLAND) REGULATIONS 2016, SI 2016/789; made under the Land Compensation Act 1973 s.30(5). In force: 1 October 2016.

These Regulations increase the amount of home loss payments payable in England under the Land Compensation Act 1973 s.30.

1699 Injunctions–Public nuisance–Use of buildings in breach of planning control

The claimant local authority applied for an injunction to prevent alleged nuisances caused by the defendant tenants. The defendants were tenants of five units on an industrial estate. Planning controls restricted the sites' usage to light industrial and storage. The defendants had used one site for religious worship and four others for social and educational purposes, including hiring them out as venues for parties. A local resident complained that loud music regularly emanated from the sites into the early hours of the morning. Local authority officers gave evidence that they had attended the scene and witnessed loud music, parties and obstructive parking. They confirmed an intrusive level of noise at the resident's house. The local authority issued abatement notices onto the defendants, and one was convicted for three breaches of a notice. It served enforcement and stop notices but the activities continued. The defendants' applications for retrospective planning permission were refused, as were their subsequent appeals. The defendants accepted that they had breached planning controls for approximately five years. Their case was that they had sound-proofed the relevant buildings. Upon service of the injunction application, some of the defendants had made a fresh application for planning permission. The defendants submitted that (1) they had not used the group of units as a place of worship for the previous two years and the balance of convenience lay against an injunction because of the public interest in the religious, educational and social uses to which the sites had been put, and because an injunction would cause them to breach contracts hiring out the units for social events; (2) the instant proceedings should be adjourned pending determination of their fresh planning permission applications.

Held: Applications granted. (1) The defendants must have known that their use was a breach of planning control, whether it caused a statutory nuisance or not. There was a difference between the withdrawal of an existing entitlement, and the commencement of proceedings seeking to reverse that withdrawal, and the instant situation. It was difficult to accept that the defendants had believed that planning permission had somehow been de facto granted so that they could behave as if their applications had succeeded. It was abundantly clear that there was a serious triable issue that a nuisance had been caused at the units. The defendants had also admitted breaching planning control over several years. They clearly wanted to continue in breach unless restrained by a court order. The local authority's measures had not succeeded. Making every allowance for the defendants, they had at least simply hoped that the various proceedings would go away. There was no evidence to show that damages would be an adequate remedy. Although there was a significant measure of social utility in the sites' activities, the balance of convenience lay in ensuring that the planning control system was properly maintained and not flouted in the pursuit of a different objective. Notwithstanding the public interest in the activities, they had been largely commercial ventures. A person in breach of planning control, who entered into commercial contracts which would lead to further breaches, could not rely on the fact that enforcement of planning regulations would cause them to breach their commercial contracts. (2) The fresh planning permission applications had come far too late and there was no good reason why they could not have been made months or years previously. It was not a coincidence that the applications had been made once the application for an injunction had been served. Allowing an adjournment pending the planning applications would be lengthy, which was inappropriate. (3) It was just and convenient to grant the injunction, but that would be stayed for one week in fairness to the defendants so that they could make the necessary arrangements.

GREENWICH RLBC v OGBUKA HOUSING LTD, [2015] EWHC 2707 (QB), [2015] L.L.R. 706, Holroyde J, QBD.

1700 Judicial review–Local authorities' powers and duties–Local authority's duty to court and role in proceedings where it lacked funds to defend planning decision

A supermarket owner challenged a local authority's grant of planning permission to a developer for an out-of-town-centre retail store. The supermarket was in a town centre in the local authority's area. Planning permission for a store on the site of the proposed development had been refused by the secretary of state after he had noted the significant harm that the development would cause an already vulnerable town centre. The local authority twice gave planning permission for a store on the site. Each permission was later quashed on judicial review. Officers for the local authority's planning committee prepared a report regarding a further planning application. The committee gave permission. The supermarket argued that the local authority had failed to consider the true harm to the town centre and had adopted an inconsistent approach to the s.106 contributions offered by the developer.

Held: Application granted. (1) There was a fundamental defect in the analysis in the officers' report. The full impact on the town centre and in particular on the existing supermarket was not clearly set out. It had not gone far enough in making clear that the proposed store would remove half the supermarket's turnover. Those were matters that had been emphasised in a previous judgment, but the officers' report had still not informed the planning committee of the extent of the harm likely to result from the development. The balancing judgement performed by the committee was vitiated by that error, *North Wiltshire DC v Secretary of State for the Environment* (1993) 65 P. & C.R. 137, [1993] C.L.Y. 3930 and *R. v Selby DC Ex p. Oxton Farms* [1997] E.G. 60 (C.S.), [1997] C.L.Y. 4114 followed (see paras 99-101 of judgment). The officers' report had stated that the s.106 benefits were necessary to make the development acceptable in planning terms. However, nowhere in the report was it explained why the benefits were necessary. Further, it was stated elsewhere in the report that the benefits could be ignored and the development would still be acceptable. Accordingly, the balancing judgement was again flawed (paras 116-117). (2) (Obiter) The local authority had taken no active part in the instant proceedings and had left the developer to defend its decision. That would not be unusual if the local authority had conceded the claim, but it had not conceded the claim. It had stated that, since it could not afford to take an active part in the proceedings, it supported the developer in its resistance to the challenge. That stance could lead to tension with fundamental aspects of the way judicial review proceedings were conducted. Such proceedings were not to be conducted in the same way as ordinary civil litigation because the relationship between a public authority defendant and the court was not the same as that between an ordinary litigant and the court. In particular, a public authority had a duty of candour and co-operation so as to assist the court in understanding its decision-making process and dealing with the issues fairly, *R. v Lancashire CC Ex p. Huddleston* [1986] 2 All E.R. 941, [1986] C.L.Y. 1141 considered. It should conduct the litigation with its cards face upwards: it acted in the public interest, not merely to protect a private commercial interest. There were circumstances in which an interested party would also be subject to the duty of candour, but that would not necessarily meet all the practical issues which could arise. If a public authority could not, for financial reasons, defend its decision in judicial review proceedings, and in particular where it could not file a skeleton argument or make oral submissions at a substantive hearing, it should at least consider the following: whether it had complied with its duty of candour and co-operation, by disclosing all relevant documents; whether that duty required it to file a witness statement to assist the court in understanding its decision-making process and dealing with the claim fairly; whether it should file an acknowledgement of service, with summary grounds of resistance, even if only in outline form; and whether a representative, not necessarily a lawyer, should be present in court at any hearing (paras 148-151).

R. (ON THE APPLICATION OF MIDCOUNTIES CO-OPERATIVE LTD) v FOREST OF DEAN DC, [2015] EWHC 1251 (Admin), [2015] B.L.G.R. 829, Singh J, QBD (Admin).

1701 **Local planning authorities–Reasons–Inadequately reasoned screening opinion not rectified by supplying information in witness statement in proceedings**

[Town and Country Planning (Environmental Impact Assessment) (England and Wales) Regulations 1999 (SI 1999/293) reg.2]

A local resident appealed against the dismissal (*Jedwell v Denbighshire CC* [2014] EWHC 1633 (Admin), [2015] Env. L.R. D2) of his application for judicial review of the first respondent local authority's grant of planning permission for the erection of two wind turbines at a farm in Wales. Although the application site was not within any specially protected area, it was within an area that had been evaluated as having a high visual and sensory aspect of regional importance. It was also close to a national park, areas of outstanding natural beauty and special scientific interest, and existing and proposed wind farms. The local authority's planning officer had issued a negative screening opinion, stating that no environmental impact assessment was required, and she had recommended that planning permission be refused. In February 2013, the planning committee granted planning permission. The resident challenged that decision, arguing that an EIA should have been obtained, the screening opinion was inadequately reasoned, and the grant of planning permission was unlawful. In May 2013 he wrote to the local authority asking for contemporaneous reasons for the screening opinion. The local authority sent him the covering letter that had accompanied the opinion and indicated that it had nothing further to add. The resident issued his claim form in August 2013. The judge rejected his challenge, finding that although the screening opinion was inadequately reasoned, the local authority was saved by a witness statement made by the planning officer in October 2013, supplying reasons. He reached that conclusion on the papers, declining to allow the resident to cross-examine the planning officer with a view to showing that her evidence was merely an ex post facto justification of her decision. The issues were:(i) whether the screening opinion was adequately reasoned;(ii) whether the May letter was a valid request for reasons;(iii) whether the local authority's response discharged its duty to give reasons;(iv) if not, whether the planning officer's witness statement saved the local authority;(v) whether the judge should have required the planning officer to attend for cross-examination;(vi) whether the judge had erred by failing to consider the meaning of "significant effect" in the Town and Country Planning (Environmental Impact Assessment) (England and Wales) Regulations 1999 reg.2 in the context of the opinion of the *Sweetman v An Bord Pleanala (C-258/11)* EU:C:2013:220, [2014] P.T.S.R. 1092.

Held: Appeal allowed. (1) The Regulations, which remained in force in Wales, obliged the local authority to give reasons only where the screening opinion concluded that an EIA was required. They did not require reasons to be given for a negative screening opinion. However, EU law did, either in the decision itself or in a subsequent communication following a request from an interested party, *R. (on the application of Mellor) v Secretary of State for Communities and Local Government (C-75/08)* EU:C:2009:279, [2010] P.T.S.R. 880, [2010] C.L.Y. 1246 applied. The reasons had to demonstrate that the author had understood and considered the issues, and that proper consideration had been given to the possible environmental effects of the development. They also had to be sufficient to enable the interested party to understand why the decision had been made and to decide whether to challenge it, *R. (on the application of Bateman) v South Cambridgeshire DC* [2011] EWCA Civ 157, [2011] N.P.C. 22 followed. The instant screening opinion stated its conclusion but contained no reasoning at all. It did not indicate why the planning officer thought that no EIA was needed, and it did not demonstrate that she had applied her mind to the relevant questions (see paras 21-34 of judgment). (2) The May letter was a valid request for contemporaneous reasoning. It was plainly the kind of request contemplated in *Mellor* (para.35). (3) The local authority had not provided any proper reasons in response to the May letter and, when the claim form was issued, it was in breach of its duty to give adequate reasons (para.36). (4) The planning officer's witness statement could not cure that deficiency. One of the purposes of requiring the local authority to give reasons for a negative screening opinion was to enable the interested party to decide whether to challenge it in legal proceedings. Reasons had to be given within a reasonable time of the request. However, if a reasonable time had elapsed but proceedings had not been commenced, the local authority might still cure any deficiency by supplying further reasons before the commencement of proceedings.

However, in the instant case, the contents of the planning officer's witness statement had not been disclosed before the resident issued his claim form and could not rescue the local authority from its breach of duty, *R. (on the application of Burridge) v Breckland DC* [2013] EWCA Civ 228, [2013] J.P.L. 1308, [2014] C.L.Y. 2425 considered (paras 37-47). (5) The judge should have required the planning officer to attend for cross-examination. While cross-examination was rare in judicial review cases, it could be permitted in an appropriate case, *O'Reilly v Mackman* [1983] 2 A.C. 237, [1982] C.L.Y. 2603 and *Trim v North Dorset DC* [2010] EWCA Civ 1446, [2011] 1 W.L.R. 1901, [2011] C.L.Y. 2507 followed. The instant case, where the question of fact was whether the planning officer's evidence was an ex post facto justification of her decision, was such a case. The judge's order could not stand and the matter would be remitted to the Administrative Court (paras 50-59). (6) The judge had not erred by failing to consider the opinion of the Advocate General in *Sweetman. Sweetman* concerned the Habitats Directive, and the reasoning could not be read across into the EIA Directive, *Sweetman* considered and *R. (on the application of An Taisce (National Trust For Ireland)) v Secretary of State for Energy and Climate Change* [2014] EWCA Civ 1111, [2015] P.T.S.R. 189, [2014] C.L.Y. 1188 followed (para.61).

R. (ON THE APPLICATION OF JEDWELL) v DENBIGHSHIRE CC *sub nom.* JEDWELL v DENBIGHSHIRE CC, [2015] EWCA Civ 1232, [2016] P.T.S.R. 715, Moore-Bick LJ, CA (Civ Div).

1702 Local planning authorities–Strategic planning–Qualifying expenditure

THE STRATEGIC PLANNING (COMPOSITION OF PANELS AND QUALIFYING EXPENDITURE) (WALES) REGULATIONS 2016, SI 2016/18; made under the Planning and Compulsory Purchase Act 2004 s.122, Sch.2A para.5, Sch.2A para.16. In force: 16 March 2016.

These Regulations make provision about the gender composition of a strategic planning panel and about the qualifying expenditure of a panel which is to be met by its constituent local planning authorities.

1703 Local plans–Residential development–Sustainability appraisals–Revision of green belt boundary

[Environmental Assessment of Plans and Programmes Regulations 2004 (SI 2004/1633) reg.12(2); Planning and Compulsory Purchase Act 2004 (c.5) s.20(5)]

The applicant asked the court to quash a local plan. The options for housing development which the local authority had considered when preparing the local plan had included a town-focused development on two sites, which would require building on the green belt, and a new settlement option to create a village outside the green belt. The applicant was the promoter of the latter development. However, the local authority adopted a local plan containing the former option after its sustainability appraisal indicated that the new village option was less sustainable than the two developments taking land out of the green belt. The applicant submitted that (1) the inspector appointed to examine the local plan failed to determine whether the local authority's sustainability appraisal complied with the relevant legal and procedural requirements; (2) important aspects of the sustainability appraisal could not be understood and so there had been a breach of the requirement in the Environmental Assessment of Plans and Programmes Regulations 2004 reg.12(2) for the local authority to identify, describe and evaluate the likely significant effects on the environment of its proposals and the alternatives; (3) the inspector, when considering whether it was appropriate to alter the green belt boundaries by releasing the two sites for housing, had not asked himself whether the alteration was necessary.

Held: Application refused. (1) A planning inspector's report had to be read sensibly and in a down-to-earth way, *South Somerset DC v Secretary of State for the Environment* (1993) 66 P. & C.R. 83, [1993] C.L.Y. 3927, *Clarke Homes Ltd v Secretary of State for the Environment* (1993) 66 P. & C.R. 263, [1993] C.L.Y. 3925 and *South Buckinghamshire DC v Porter (No.2)* [2004] UKHL 33, [2004] 1 W.L.R. 1953, [2004] C.L.Y. 3087 applied. Although, in the instant case, the inspector had stated that it was not his role to comment on the legality of the sustainability appraisal but rather to establish whether it was a reliable piece of evidence, that had been in response to the applicant's submission that the evidence had brought into question the credibility and reliability of the sustainability appraisal as a robust evidence base. Furthermore, the inspector had, in fact, been faced with legal issues at the hearings and had reached conclusions on the issues relevant to the lawfulness of the sustainability appraisal. In considering the competing submissions on whether the sustainability appraisal was a reliable piece of evidence, the inspector was addressing the competing legal submissions and meeting his duty under the Planning and Compulsory Purchase Act 2004 s.20(5). And at the end of his report, he concluded that there was legal compliance, specifically of the sustainability appraisal (see paras 19, 37-38 of judgment). (2) The inspector had conceded that the sustainability appraisal was not a simple document, that it was hard to understand and that the local authority had, at times, had to resort to additional explanatory notes to explain the intricacies. However, it was significant that he had added that the local authority had needed to do so only when the document was subjected to forensic examination, that its main points were clearly drawn out in the non-technical summary and that it was a reliable piece of evidence (para.48). (3) For redefinition of a green belt, exceptional circumstances were required which necessitated a revision of the boundary. The question of whether circumstances were exceptional required an exercise of planning judgment, *Gallagher Homes Ltd v Solihull MBC* [2014] EWHC 1283 (Admin), [2014] J.P.L. 1117 applied. The inspector had stated the test of exceptional circumstances and the statutory need to promote sustainable patterns of development. He had identified that the question of whether circumstances were exceptional for those purposes required an exercise of planning judgment. He had not then failed to apply the test of exceptional circumstances or invoked instead a simple planning balance. Indeed, he had summarised in his report the exceptional circumstances as he had found them (paras 51, 54).

IM PROPERTIES DEVELOPMENT LTD v LICHFIELD DC, [2015] EWHC 2077 (Admin), [2015] P.T.S.R. 1536, Cranston J, QBD (Admin).

1704 Motorways–Sites of Special Scientific Interest–Motorway's likely significant effect on environment–Consideration of alternatives

[Directive 2001/42 on the assessment of the effects of certain plans and programmes on the environment 2001 art.5; Environmental Assessment of Plans and Programmes (Wales) Regulations 2004 (SI 2004/1656); Wildlife and Countryside Act 1981 (c.69) s.28G; Planning (Listed Buildings and Conservation Areas) Act 1990 (c.9) s.66]

An environmental organisation applied for judicial review of the defendant Welsh Ministers' decision to adopt a plan which provided for the construction of a new section of motorway across several sites of special scientific interest (SSSIs) in Wales. The new motorway section was to be built to the south of Newport on the M4. The plan was formulated with regard to the Welsh Transport Planning and Appraisal Guidance (WelTAG), the aim of which was to ensure that transport proposals contributed to the wider policy objectives for Wales. According to the environmental organisation, the decision-making process leading to the adoption of the plan was unlawful for failure to comply with Directive 2001/42, which required assessment of the significant environmental effects of both the preferred option and all potential viable alternatives (SEA assessment). The Directive was implemented in Wales by the Environmental Assessment of Plans and Programmes (Wales) Regulations 2004. The environmental organisation argued that (1) the decision to construct a highway across the protected sites had been taken before the SEA assessment process began, which frustrated the Directive's objective of integrating environmental considerations into the preparation and adoption of plans, and that the Ministers had applied the wrong test for "reasonable alternatives" within art.5(1) of the Directive; (2) contrary to the Wildlife and Countryside Act 1981 s.28G, no reasonable steps had been taken to further conservation and enhancement of the flora and fauna of the SSSIs over which the proposed route ran.

Held: Application refused. (1) Neither the Directive nor the Regulations defined "reasonable alternatives" to the implementation of a plan or programme likely to have significant effects on the environment. However, art.5(1) of the Directive required the environmental report to identify, describe and evaluate all, and not merely a selection, of the alternatives capable of meeting the plan objectives, *R. (on the application of*

Buckinghamshire CC) v Secretary of State for Transport [2013] EWHC 481 (Admin), [2013] P.T.S.R. D25 applied. Moreover, the Directive required reasons to be given for the selection of an option, *Heard v Broadland DC* [2012] EWHC 344 (Admin), [2012] Env. L.R. 23, [2012] C.L.Y. 2535 applied. An option other than the preferred option that was capable of meeting the objectives of the plan, as determined by the relevant decision-maker, was the truest and most helpful formulation. However, an option which the decision-maker considered "viable", having regard to the full planning context, was also a helpful and appropriate way to characterise "reasonable alternatives", *Ashdown Forest Economic Development LLP v Secretary of State for Communities and Local Government* [2014] EWHC 406 (Admin), [2015] Env. L.R. D1 applied. It was primarily for the Minister to identify objectives, give each appropriate weight, and determine whether they were met by a particular option. If a particular plan was incapable of meeting the identified objectives such that in practice it would never be pursued, there was no point in subjecting it to an environmental assessment. In the instant case, other than the plan and the alternatives assessed in the SEA report, none of the options considered came close to meeting the objective of solving the problems of the M4 around Newport. It was clear from both the SEA report and the WelTAG appraisals that the options discarded before the SEA assessment had been rejected because they would not significantly improve the position. Thus, the Welsh Ministers had used the correct legal test and had chosen the option which they considered best met the transport planning objectives under the WelTAG. They had included, as reasonable alternatives, other options which they considered to be capable of meeting those objectives. The decisions they had made with regard to the selection of objectives, the weight given to each, and the selection of the preferred option and reasonable alternatives were all in accordance with the relevant legal tests, rational and otherwise lawful (see paras 78, 85-86, 93, 99, 105-109, 113-115 of judgment). (2) The obligation imposed by s.28G of the 1981 Act did not take the form of a general duty whereby the decision-maker had to have particular regard to the desirability of protecting and preserving SSSIs. The duty imposed by the Planning (Listed Buildings and Conservation Areas) Act 1990 s.66 to have special regard to the desirability of protecting and preserving listed buildings did not apply by analogy to SSSIs. The s.28G duty did not seek to protect SSSIs by weighting the desirability of their protection as against other factors by requiring relevant authorities to take reasonable steps. In the instant case, the SEA assessment had properly considered the potential harm to the SSSIs and the available mitigation measures, and its conclusion that the plan would give rise to minor negative harm overall was unassailable as a matter of law (paras 130, 132, 137).

R. (ON THE APPLICATION OF FRIENDS OF THE EARTH ENGLAND, WALES AND NORTHERN IRELAND LTD) v WELSH MINISTERS, [2015] EWHC 776 (Admin), [2016] Env. L.R. 1, Hickinbottom J, QBD (Admin).

1705 National Planning Policy Framework–Heritage property–Paragraph 14 National Planning Policy Framework–Balancing exercise between harm to heritage asset and benefits of any proposed development

The claimant local authority sought to quash a decision of the first defendant secretary of state, by his inspector, granting the second defendant developer outline planning permission for a residential development. The proposed development was close to a farm house complex, including Grade II listed buildings, which was a designated heritage asset. The local authority had refused permission and the developer appealed. The inspector found that the development would cause less than substantial harm to the farm's setting. He held that para.14 of the National Planning Policy Framework applied to the case because the local authority's local development plan was out of date due to its inability to show a five-year housing supply. He stated that para.14 made it clear that where there was an outdated plan, planning permission should be granted unless any adverse impacts of doing so would significantly and demonstrably outweigh the benefits, when assessed against the NPPF's policies taken as a whole. He concluded that the limited number of adverse impacts arising from the proposed development would not significantly and demonstrably outweigh its considerable economic, social and environmental benefits when assessed against the NPPF's policies. He therefore granted permission. The local authority contended that the inspector had failed to consider the interaction between para.14 of the NPPF and para.134 and had consequently applied the wrong test when balancing the development's harm and benefits. The secretary of state accepted that contention and also requested that the decision be quashed.

Held: Judgment for claimant. Paragraph 14 of the NPPF provided that "At the heart of the National Planning Policy Framework is a presumption in favour of sustainable development ... For decision-taking this means ... where the development plan ... or relevant policies are out-of-date, granting permission unless: adverse impacts of doing so would significantly and demonstrably outweigh the benefits, when assessed against the policies in this Framework taken as a whole; or specific policies in this Framework indicate development should be restricted." Footnote 9 gave examples of those policies, one of which was identified as relating to designated heritage assets. Paragraph 134 provided that "Where a development proposal will lead to less than substantial harm to the significance of a designated heritage asset, this harm should be weighed against the public benefits of the proposal, including securing its optimum viable use" (see paras 7, 18 of judgment). Paragraph 134 was a policy indicating that development should be restricted. Throughout the NPPF, there was a presumption in favour of sustainable development, and therefore in favour of granting permission. That was the default setting. However, certain specific policies within the NPPF indicated situations where that presumption did not apply and where, instead, development should be restricted. Paragraph 134 was one such policy. It provided for a balancing exercise to be undertaken, between the "less than substantial harm" to the designated heritage asset on the one hand, and the public benefits of the proposal on the other. The presumption in favour of development was not referred to and did not apply. Paragraph 134 was thus a particular policy restricting development, and the second limb of para.14 applied. Accordingly, on a proper interpretation of the NPPF, the exercise at para.134 and the second limb of para.14 had to be undertaken when there was less than substantial harm to the significance of a designated heritage asset (paras 25-26, 32). When a development would harm a listed building or its setting, the decision-maker had to give that harm considerable importance and weight; that harm alone gave rise to a strong presumption against the grant of planning permission, *R. (on the application of Forge Field Society) v Sevenoaks DC* [2014] EWHC 1895 (Admin), [2015] J.P.L. 22, [2015] C.L.Y. 2018 applied. Since the inspector had not undertaken the ordinary balancing exercise required by para.134, it followed that the considerable weight to be given to the preservation of listed buildings, let alone the presumption against granting permission in such situations, had been at best diluted, and at worst lost altogether, and there was a real risk that the important guidance in *Forge Field* was not fully followed. The inspector had thereby erred in law (paras 38-40, 47). It was unclear whether that error had made any difference to the outcome of the developer's appeal: it might have made no difference, but it might have made a very significant difference. In those circumstances, it was proper to quash the decision, *Europa Oil and Gas Ltd v Secretary of State for Communities and Local Government* [2014] EWCA Civ 825, [2014] P.T.S.R. 1471, [2015] C.L.Y. 1996 considered (para.52).

FOREST OF DEAN DC v SECRETARY OF STATE FOR COMMUNITIES AND LOCAL GOVERNMENT, [2016] EWHC 421 (Admin), [2016] P.T.S.R. 1031, Coulson J, QBD (Admin).

1706 **National Planning Policy Framework–Housing–Meaning of "relevant policies for the supply of housing" in NPPF–Wide interpretation**

In conjoined appeals against decisions relating to planning permission for residential development (*Hopkins Homes Ltd v Secretary of State for Communities and Local Government* [2015] EWHC 132 (Admin) and *Cheshire East BC v Secretary of State for Communities and Local Government* [2015] EWHC 410 (Admin)), the court was required to determine the meaning and effect of the National Planning Policy Framework (NPPF) para.49. Paragraph 49 stated that housing applications should be considered in the context of the presumption in favour of sustainable development and that "relevant policies for the supply of housing should not be considered up-to-date if the local planning authority could not demonstrate a five-year supply of deliverable housing sites". The issues were (i) the meaning of "relevant policies for the supply of housing"; (ii) how the policy in para.49 was to be applied.

Held: First appeal dismissed, second appeal allowed. (1) The court's interpretation of para.49 had to be faithful to the words of the NPPF, read in their full context and not in isolation from it. The broad context was the Government's aim of providing the supply of housing to meet the needs of present and future generations, reflected generally in the policies for sustainable development, plan-making and decision taking. The more specific context was set by the housing development policies in the paragraphs immediately preceding and following para.49. Underlying them all was the basic imperative of delivery (see paras 20-30 of judgment). "Relevant policies for the supply of housing", construed objectively in their proper context, meant relevant policies "affecting" the supply of housing. A "relevant" policy was simply one relevant to the application for planning permission before the decision-maker. That should not be interpreted narrowly and was not confined to policies in the development plan that provided positively for the delivery of new housing in terms of numbers and distribution or the allocation of sites. It had a wider interpretation: the concept extended to plan policies whose effect was to influence the supply of housing land by restricting the locations where new housing might be developed, including policies for the Green Belt and the general protection of the countryside. Restrictive policies might have the effect of constraining the supply of housing land. If a local planning authority was unable to demonstrate the requisite five-year supply of housing land, both the policies of its local plan that identified sites for housing development and policies restrictive of such development were liable to be regarded as not up-to-date under para.49. Otherwise, Government policy for the delivery of housing might be undermined by decisions in which development plan policies that impeded a five-year supply of housing were treated as up-to-date. In the court's view, those first instance judgments which had rejected the "wider" interpretation of the policy had not been correctly decided on that point, *William Davis Ltd v Secretary of State for Communities and Local Government* [2013] EWHC 3058 (Admin), and *Wenman v Secretary of State for Communities and Local Government* [2015] EWHC 925 (Admin) disapproved (paras 31-41). (2) When determining an application for planning permission for housing development, the NPPF presented the decision-maker with a simple sequence of steps. The first step, under the policy in para.49, was to consider whether "relevant policies of the supply of housing" in the development plan were out-of-date because the local planning authority could not demonstrate a five-year supply of deliverable housing sites. Provided he acted on the correct understanding of the policy in para.49, it was for the decision-maker to judge whether the plan policy was a relevant policy for the supply of housing. If he found that the relevant policies were out-of-date, then he applied the presumption in favour of sustainable development in accordance with para.14. The policies in paras14 and 49 did not make "out-of-date" policies for the supply of housing irrelevant in the determination of a planning application. Nor did they prescribe how much weight should be given to such policies in the decision. One might infer from para.49 that the Government's view was that less weight should be given to such policies, however the weight to be given was not dictated by Government policy in the NPPF. It would be for the decision-maker to judge, in the particular circumstances of the case, how much weight should be given to those policies. The policies in paras14 and 49 were not intended to punish a local planning authority when it failed to demonstrate the requisite five-year supply of housing land. They were, however, clearly meant to be an incentive (paras 42-48). (3) In the first appeal, the planning inspector had adopted a "narrow" interpretation of para.49 and the judge had been right to find that he had therefore neither interpreted it correctly, nor applied it lawfully (paras 49-55). In the second appeal, the planning inspector had proceeded on a correct understanding of the policy in para.49 and of the relevant development plan policies. He had exercised his own judgment when resolving which of those policies were within the scope of para.49 and how much weight he should give to them when applying the policy presumption in favour of sustainable development. He had made no error of law and his decision should not have been quashed (paras 66-71).

SECRETARY OF STATE FOR COMMUNITIES AND LOCAL GOVERNMENT v HOPKINS HOMES LTD; RICHBOROUGH ESTATES PARTNERSHIP LLP v CHESHIRE EAST BOROUGH COUNCIL *sub nom.* SUFFOLK COASTAL DC v HOPKINS HOMES LTD, [2016] EWCA Civ 168, [2016] P.T.S.R. 1315, Jackson LJ, CA (Civ Div).

1707 National Planning Policy Framework–Written ministerial statements–Lawfulness of ministerial introduction of exemptions from need to include affordable housing on small sites

[Equality Act 2010 (c.15) s.149, s.149(1); Town and Country Planning Act 1990 (c.8); Planning and Compulsory Purchase Act 2004 (c.5)]

The claimant local authorities applied for judicial review of the defendant secretary of state's decision to alter national policy in respect of planning obligations for affordable housing. The National Planning Policy Framework required local planning policies to make provision for affordable housing. Following government concerns about the decline in the small-scale house building industry, the secretary of state carried out a consultation exercise and subsequently amended national planning practice guidance, by way of a ministerial statement, so that, inter alia, developments of 10 units or 1,000 square metres or less would be excluded from affordable housing levies and tariff-based contributions, with a threshold of five units or less applying in designated rural areas. The claimants were concerned that the new policy would reduce the provision of affordable housing by relieving smaller sites from any obligation to provide affordable housing, thereby resulting in a windfall for landowners and/or developers, and would effectively negate or "trump" local plans and policies. They contended that (1) the new national policy was inconsistent with the statutory scheme and its purposes; (2) the consultation process had been unfair; (3) the secretary of state had failed to take into account material considerations; (4) in deciding to adopt the new national policy, the secretary of state had failed to comply with the public sector equality duty (PSED) in the Equality Act 2010 s.149.

Held: Application granted. (1) It was for Parliament and ministers to determine the objectives of planning policy and to set out those objectives in legislation, ministerial directions and in planning policy guidelines, *R. (on the application of Holding & Barnes Plc) v Secretary of State for the Environment, Transport and the Regions* [2001] UKHL 23, [2003] 2 A.C. 295, [2001] C.L.Y. 4761 followed. A prerogative power could not, however, be exercised incompatibly with, or so as to frustrate, the relevant statutory scheme, *Laker Airways Ltd v Department of Trade* [1977] Q.B. 643, [1977] C.L.Y. 150 applied. A key issue in the instant case was whether the new policy was unlawful on grounds of inconsistency with the statutory scheme, which was a matter for judicial review in the courts. The secretary of state's common law powers to promulgate planning policies could not be used incompatibly with the statutory code, *R. (on the application of Cala Homes (South) Ltd) v Secretary of State for Communities and Local Government* [2011] EWCA Civ 639, [2011] 2 E.G.L.R. 75, [2011] C.L.Y. 2574 applied. The substance of the new policy was materially different from the national policies currently in force, in that it was not devised to be taken into account alongside local plans, but displaced them. The exemptions from affordable housing contributions were incompatible with the statutory framework of the Town and Country Planning Act 1990 and the Planning and Compulsory Purchase Act 2004, which presumed that planning applications would be determined in accordance with adopted local plan policies formulated on the basis of local circumstances, and were therefore unlawful, *Laker Airways* and *Cala Homes* applied. Moreover, the new policy was not calculated to promote the policy of the legislation and was also unlawful on that basis, *Padfield v Minister of Agriculture, Fisheries and Food* [1968] A.C. 997, [1968] C.L.Y. 1667 and *R. v Braintree DC Ex p. Halls* (2000) 32 H.L.R. 770, [2000] C.L.Y. 3943 applied (see paras 109, 117-119, 124- 126, 136-139,143 of judgment). (2) The driver for the change in national policy was the view that affordable housing requirements imposed a disproportionate burden on small sites, but the consultation paper had not explained what that disproportionate burden was thought to be, nor the basis for that view, including any supporting evidence. Consequently, local planning authorities had not had an opportunity to give a meaningful, intelligent response on that key justification for the proposed policy. The rationale for the policy was not properly defined. The secretary of state had also failed to take the product of consultation conscientiously into account. It had thereby failed to meet the criteria for a proper consultation, *R. (on the application of Moseley) v Haringey LBC* [2014] UKSC 56, [2014] 1 W.L.R. 3947, [2014] C.L.Y. 2087 considered (paras 144, 152-153, 157, 160-161). (3) Considerations that were obviously material to the decision to adopt the new policy included (a) the main benefits and disadvantages of the proposed exemptions from affordable housing requirements; (b) the relevant statutory provisions relating to the formulation of local plan policy; (c) the determination of planning applications and the implications of those provisions for the use of the policy-making power. The secretary of state's failure to have regard to them rendered the new policy unlawful (paras 165-168, 173). (4) The secretary of state had failed to comply with the PSED because adequate steps to obtain relevant information in order to comply with the PSED had not been taken, and/or the duty was not fulfilled in substance and with rigour, and/or the extent and risk of certain adverse impacts upon persons with protected characteristics and falling within s.149(1) had not been assessed, and the exercise had not been carried out with a sufficiently open mind (paras 197-198). (5) The appropriate relief was to make a declaration as to the new policy's unlawfulness (para.216).

R. (ON THE APPLICATION OF WEST BERKSHIRE DC) v SECRETARY OF STATE FOR COMMUNITIES AND LOCAL GOVERNMENT *sub nom.* WEST BERKSHIRE DC v DEPARTMENT FOR COMMUNITIES AND LOCAL GOVERNMENT; SECRETARY OF STATE FOR COMMUNITIES AND LOCAL GOVERNMENT v WEST BERKSHIRE DC, [2015] EWHC 2222 (Admin), [2016] P.T.S.R. 215, Holgate J, QBD (Admin).

1708 National Planning Policy Framework–Written ministerial statements–Lawfulness of ministerial introduction of exemptions from need to include affordable housing on small sites

[Equality Act 2010 (c.15) s.149; Planning and Compulsory Purchase Act 2004 (c.5) s.38(6); Town and Country Planning Act 1990 (c.8) s.70(2)]

The secretary of state appealed against a decision (*R. (on the application of West Berkshire DC) v Secretary of State for Communities and Local Government* [2015] EWHC 2222 (Admin), [2016] P.T.S.R. 215, [2016] 1707) that a planning policy communicated by way of written ministerial statement, to alter national policy in respect of planning obligations for affordable housing, was unlawful. The respondent local authorities were concerned that the new policy would reduce the provision of affordable housing by relieving smaller sites from any obligation to provide affordable housing, thereby resulting in a windfall for landowners and/or developers, and would effectively negate or "trump" local plans and policies. The judge upheld the respondents' challenge on four grounds: (i) the ministerial statement was inconsistent with the statutory planning regime; (ii) the secretary of state had failed to take into account necessary material considerations; (iii) the secretary of state's consultation upon the proposals was legally inadequate; (iv) the secretary of state had failed to properly assess the impact of the proposal on persons with protected characteristics, pursuant to the Equality Act 2010 s.149. The secretary of state sought to overturn the judge's conclusions on all four grounds.

Held: Appeal allowed. (1) The question was whether the written ministerial statement on its face sought to countermand or frustrate the effective operation of the Planning and Compulsory Purchase Act 2004 s.38(6) and the Town and Country Planning Act 1990 s.70(2); or if it merely expressed the secretary of state's substantive planning policy in unqualified though trenchant terms. It was the language of the policy that counted. Once it was accepted that the articulation of planning policy in unqualified or absolute terms was not in principle repugnant to the proper operation of s.38(6) of the 2004 Act, that use of language was unobjectionable. The ministerial statement was in mandatory terms. The policy outlined in the ministerial statement was not to be faulted on the grounds that it did not use language which indicated that it was not to be applied in a blanket fashion, or that its place in the statutory scheme of things was as a material consideration for the purposes of s.38(6) of the 2004 Act and s.70(2) of the 1990 Act, and no more. It did not countermand or frustrate the effective operation of those provisions. The judge conflated what the policy said with how it could lawfully be deployed (see paras 24-25, 30 of judgment). (2) The statutory planning context prevented the secretary of state from introducing into planning policy matters which were not proper planning considerations at all. Subject to that, his policy choices were for him. The planning legislation established a framework for the making of planning decisions: it did not lay down merits criteria for planning policy or establish what the policy-maker should or should not regard as relevant to the exercise of policy-making. The secretary of state was not obliged to go further than he did into the specifics, and in consequence was not to be faulted for a failure to have regard to relevant considerations in formulating the policy set out in the written ministerial statement (paras 36-37). (3) A consideration of whether a non-statutory consultation process contravened the requirements of procedural fairness would always be fact and context sensitive. The test was whether the process had been so unfair as to be unlawful. The Court of Appeal found that the consultation was fair, and that appropriate consideration was given to the consultation responses (paras 60-64). (4) The considerations in s.149(1)(a)-(c) of the 2010 Act had not been addressed prior to the making of the written ministerial statement. However, a formal Equality Statement, produced on 5 February 2015, demonstrated a consideration of the potential for adverse impacts on protected groups. The process required by s.149 did not require a precise mathematical exercise to be carried out in relation to particular affected groups. Whilst it could be said that the Equality Statement took a relatively broad brush approach, compliance with the terms of s.149 was achieved by what was done in the instant case. As the Equality Statement satisfied the statutory requirements, the fact that it was not prepared as part of the policy decision, and post-dated it, did not warrant the quashing of the decision, *R. (on the application of C) v Secretary of State for Justice* [2008] EWCA Civ 882, [2009] Q.B. 657, [2008] C.L.Y. 2692 considered (paras 66-68, 73, 77, 83 , 85-88).

R. (ON THE APPLICATION OF WEST BERKSHIRE DC) v SECRETARY OF STATE FOR COMMUNITIES AND LOCAL GOVERNMENT *sub nom.* WEST BERKSHIRE DC v DEPARTMENT FOR COMMUNITIES AND LOCAL GOVERNMENT; SECRETARY OF STATE FOR COMMUNITIES AND LOCAL GOVERNMENT v WEST BERKSHIRE DC, [2016] EWCA Civ 441, [2016] 1 W.L.R. 3923, Lord Dyson MR, CA (Civ Div).

1709 Nationally significant infrastructure projects–Criteria for development

THE DEVELOPMENTS OF NATIONAL SIGNIFICANCE (SPECIFIED CRITERIA AND PRESCRIBED SECONDARY CONSENTS) (WALES) REGULATIONS 2016, SI 2016/53; made under the Town and Country Planning Act 1990 s.62D, s.62H. In force: 1 March 2016.

These Regulations specify the criteria for development which is of national significance for the purposes of the Town and Country Planning Act 1990 s.62D.

1710 Neighbourhood development plans–Referendums

THE NEIGHBOURHOOD PLANNING (REFERENDUMS) (AMENDMENT) REGULATIONS 2016, SI 2016/934; made under the Town and Country Planning Act 1990 s.333(2A), Sch.4B para.16(1)(2)(c); Planning and Compulsory Purchase Act 2004 s.38A(3). In force: 1 October 2016.

These Regulations amend the Neighbourhood Planning (Referendums) Regulations 2012. The 2012 Regulations make provision for the conduct of referendums held in accordance with the Town and Country Planning Act 1990 Sch.4B paras 14 and 15 in relation to the question of whether a neighbourhood development plan, neighbourhood development order or a community right to build order should be made in relation to a neighbourhood area in England.

1711 Permitted development–Building extensions–Exclusion of house extensions of more than one storey

[Town and Country Planning (General Permitted Development) (England) Order 2015 (SI 2015/596) Sch.2 Pt 1 para.A1(h)]

A local authority applied to quash decisions of the respondent secretary of state, by his planning inspectors, allowing two appeals against the refusal of certificates of lawful use or development in respect of basement extensions to residential properties. Both applications for certificates of lawful use or development related to the excavation and formation of single storey basements, one beneath a two-storey house and the other beneath a three-storey house. In both appeals no part extended beneath the perimeter of the existing house. In the first application the development would have been up to the rear wall and boundary of the house. In the second it would have been 5.4m from the rear boundary of the curtilage of the house. The local authority refused both applications on the grounds that the enlarged part of the house would have more than a single storey and be within 7m of the curtilage opposite the rear wall of the house contrary to the Town and Country Planning (General Permitted Development) (England) Order 2015 Sch.2 Pt 1 para.A1(h). In the first appeal the inspector held that the proposed basement would not have more than one storey so para.A1(h) did not apply. In the second appeal the inspector held that although the enlarged part of the house would have more than one storey it would not be within 7m of the boundary of the curtilage of a house opposite the rear wall of the house as there was no house in that position. The issues concerned the correct interpretation of para.A1(h), particularly whether (1) the phrase "the enlarged part of the dwelling house would have more than a single storey" included the original dwelling house or referred to that part of the house for which permission was granted; (2) the phrase "the enlarged part of the dwelling house would be within 7 metres of any boundary of the cartilage of the dwelling house opposite the rear wall of the dwelling house" referred to the dwelling house being developed or another dwelling house opposite that one.

Held: Application refused. (1) Paragraph A1(h) distinguished between "the enlarged part of the dwelling house" and the "original dwelling house". The "enlarged part" referred to the development permitted under the Order and the "original dwelling house" was defined in accordance with art.1. It was artificial to submit that "enlarged part" incorporated the original and that submission offended the natural language used. Paragraph A1(h) dealt with enlargement or alterations to the original house; each step of development had to be judged against that baseline so that incremental development would be caught each time it was proposed. "Part" could not be characterised as meaning the whole of the house as enlarged. The original house and the enlarged part of the house might combine to make a house as enlarged, but they were two separate components. That interpretation had the advantage of being both straightforward and consistent with the language used. There was no distinction between storeys above or below ground and in both appeals the enlarged part of the house once built would not have more than one storey. The "enlarged part of the dwelling house" was referring solely to that which was the subject of permission granted under the development order. What was proposed did not contravene para.A1(h) (see paras 32-46 of judgment). (2) If the draftsman had intended to refer to another dwelling house than the one which was the subject of the application, he could have said so, but he had not. There was nothing in the plain and ordinary use of the words to suggest any reference to two separate dwelling houses. From a consideration of the other permissible material, the permitted development regime sought to control impacts without reference to neighbouring properties as that had the advantage of avoiding measurements to those properties and the reference to the distance from the extension to the curtilage boundary was a reference to the measurement from the application house rather than any neighbouring property. Technical guidance to the contrary was wrong (paras 53-60). (3) Relief would be refused as the grant of the certificate was inevitable and the errors in the inspector's decision were immaterial as all other relevant conditions of Class A were satisfied (paras 63-66).

KENSINGTON AND CHELSEA RLBC v SECRETARY OF STATE FOR COMMUNITIES AND LOCAL GOVERNMENT, [2015] EWHC 2458 (Admin), [2016] J.P.L. 148, Patterson J, QBD (Admin).

1712 Permitted development–Electronic communications networks–Permitted development rights relating to electronic communications infrastructure

THE TOWN AND COUNTRY PLANNING (GENERAL PERMITTED DEVELOPMENT) (ENGLAND) (AMENDMENT) (NO.2) ORDER 2016, SI 2016/1040; made under the Town and Country Planning Act 1990 s.59, s.60, s.61, s.333(7). In force: 24 November 2016.

The Town and Country Planning (General Permitted Development) (England) (Amendment) (No. 2) Order 2016 amends the Town and Country Planning (General Permitted Development) (England) Order 2015 to introduce and extend permitted development rights in relation to electronic communications infrastructure.

1713 Planning (Wales) Act 2015 (anaw 4)–Commencement No.3 and Transitional Provisions Order

THE PLANNING (WALES) ACT 2015 (COMMENCEMENT NO.3 AND TRANSITIONAL PROVISIONS) ORDER 2016, SI 2016/52; made under the Planning (Wales) Act 2015 s.58(4). Commencement details: bringing into operation various provisions of the 2015 Act on 1 March 2016 and 16 March 2016.

This Order is the third commencement order made by the Welsh Ministers under the Planning (Wales) Act 2015. It brings the following sections of the 2015 Act into force on 1 March 2016: section 17 (requirement to carry out pre-application consultation); section 18 (requirement to provide pre-application services); section 19 (developments of national significance: applications for planning permission); section 20 (developments of national significance: secondary consents); section 21 (developments of national significance: local impact reports); section 22 (timetable for determining applications); and section 49 (costs on applications, appeals and references).

1714 Planning appeals–Error of law–Errors in inspector's grant of permission–Court's discretion under s.288(5)(b) Town and Country Planning Act 1990–Whether decision same in any event

[Town and Country Planning Act 1990 (c.8) s.288(5)(b), s.78]

The secretary of state appealed against the quashing (*South Gloucestershire Council v Secretary of State for Communities and Local Government* [2014] EWHC 4555 (Admin)) of a planning inspector's decision to grant planning permission to the second respondent for the stationing of a mobile home on green belt land. The inspector found that the second respondent's personal circumstances were exceptional and a material consideration. The local authority applied under the Town and Country Planning Act 1990 s.78 to quash the decision. The judge held that the inspector, when concluding that the local authority could not demonstrate a five-year supply of housing land as required by the core strategy, had seriously erred. First, by failing to take into account the core strategy inspector's conclusions that the accrued shortfall in housing land supply should be annualised over the remainder of the core strategy period, rather than "front-loaded" into the first five years. Second, that, if the inspector had considered those conclusions, he had failed to adequately explain why he had departed from them. Third, that he had misunderstood and misapplied the Government's Planning Practice Guidance. The local authority initially opposed the secretary of state's appeal. However, an agreed statement explained that the local authority had challenged the inspector's decision because it considered the issue regarding its five-year supply of housing land to have "significant implications for its development control decisions relating to residential development across its administrative area". The secretary of state did not dispute the "serious errors of law" in the inspector's decision discerned by the judge, but challenged the judge's exercise of his discretion.

Held: Appeal allowed. (1) There was no suggestion that the judge had misunderstood the relevant legal principles. He rightly observed that it was not for the court "normally to pre-empt" what the outcome of a s.78 appeal would be if errors of law had not been made. If the court was to exercise its discretion not to grant relief where unlawfulness had been found, it had to be satisfied that the decision-maker would necessarily have reached the same decision but for the legal error. That was a stringent test. It was not enough for the court to be persuaded that the decision almost certainly would have been the same but for the error. That was consistent with perhaps the most elementary principle of planning law, that the exercise of planning judgment was a matter for the decision-maker and not for the court, *Tesco Stores Ltd v Secretary of State for the Environment* [1995] 1 W.L.R. 759, [1995] C.L.Y. 4784 followed (see paras 24-25 of judgment). (2) Although the inspector stated that the absence of an up-to-date five-year housing land supply weighed in the second respondent's favour, he had not mentioned that factor as a specific consideration in determining the crucial issue of "whether the harm to the green belt by reason of inappropriateness, and any other harm, [was] clearly outweighed by other considerations so as to amount to the very special circumstances necessary to justify the development". There was therefore no real possibility that the presence of a five-year supply of housing land could have affected the outcome of the appeal. Whether the requisite five-year supply existed or not, the addition of a single dwelling could not have made any material difference. Given the extraordinary strength of the considerations weighing in favour of the grant of permission, it was inconceivable that the inspector's decision might have been different if he had dealt with the housing land supply issue correctly. The errors in his handling of that issue went to an important theme of national planning policy, namely the requirement for a local planning authority being able to show at all times a five-year supply of housing land. That requirement had its own distinct significance in the specific policies set out in the National Planning Policy Framework. Those policies were amplified in the Planning Practice Guidance, which the inspector had failed to properly understand and apply. The adequacy of the supply of housing land was clearly a matter of considerable importance to the local authority. It led the judge to conclude that if the inspector's decision was allowed to stand, it could be relied on as a precedent to cast doubt on the efficacy of its core strategy, and was clearly a powerful factor in the exercise of his discretion. The judge's concern was understandable. However, his very careful discussion of, and cogent and indisputably correct conclusions on, the grounds of challenge to the inspector's analysis of the housing land supply issue, and his identification of the inspector's "serious errors of law" were such as to prevent any future reliance on that analysis in support of planning permission applications. That conclusion was reinforced by the fact that the inspector's errors in his approach were no longer a matter of dispute between the parties, and the secretary of state had not sought to defend the inspector's analysis. In any event, the "precedent" factor should not have been a consideration in the judge's exercise of his discretion. In the extremely unusual circumstances, the judge had erred in the exercise of his discretion in such a way as to justify the setting aside of the decision. Rather than remit the case, the instant court exercised its own discretion to uphold the inspector's decision. The instant case was one of those exceptional cases in which the court, in exercising its discretion under s.288(5)(b) should have refrained from quashing an inspector's decision flawed by legal error (paras 26-31).

SOUTH GLOUCESTERSHIRE COUNCIL v SECRETARY OF STATE FOR COMMUNITIES AND LOCAL GOVERNMENT *sub nom.* SECRETARY OF STATE FOR COMMUNITIES AND LOCAL GOVERNMENT v SOUTH GLOUCESTERSHIRE COUNCIL, [2016] EWCA Civ 74, [2016] J.P.L. 798, Lindblom LJ, CA (Civ Div).

1715 Planning appeals–Locus standi–Meaning of "person aggrieved" in s.288(1)(b) Town and Country Planning Act 1990

[Town and Country Planning Act 1990 (c.8) s.288, s.288(1)(b)]

The claimants applied under the Town and Country Planning Act 1990 s.288 to quash a decision of the defendant secretary of state, by his planning inspector, allowing a property developer's appeal against a local authority's refusal to grant planning permission for a residential development. The two claimants lived in properties adjoining the proposed development site. The developer's appeal under s.78 of the Act had proceeded by way of the inquiry procedure. Neither claimant had written to the inspector or made any representations at the inquiry to object to the appeal proposals. Under s.288(1)(b), "any person" who was "aggrieved" by a decision on appeal could make an application under s.288. The issue was whether the claimants were "aggrieved persons".

Held: Application refused. It was common ground that the leading authority on the meaning of the term "person aggrieved" under s.288(1)(b) was *Walton v Scottish Ministers* [2012] UKSC 44, [2013] P.T.S.R. 51, [2013] C.L.Y. 3703. Lord Reed JSC, delivering the first judgment, stated at paras 86-87 that "persons will ordinarily be regarded as aggrieved if they made objections or representations as part of the procedure which preceded the decision challenged". He stated that there were circumstances in which a person who had not participated could nonetheless be "aggrieved", but ordinarily it would be relevant to consider whether an applicant's objection was stated at the appropriate stage of the statutory procedure. It had not been contended that any such circumstances existed. It was not disputed that the procedure preceding the inspector's decision was the appeal procedure under s.78. The claimants had not actively participated in that process (see paras 10, 13-14, 16). The claimants had sought to rely on further passages by Lord Reed in *Walton*, as well as passages in the judgments of Lord Carnwath and Lord Hope. However, none of those passages could assist. The words "person aggrieved" in s.288(1)(b) had to be interpreted in accordance with Lord Reed's judgment at paras 86-87, with which all their Lordships had been in agreement, *Walton* followed. Neither claimant had made objections or representations during the appeal procedure and they therefore had no standing to bring the instant application (para.28).

CRAWFORD-BRUNT v SECRETARY OF STATE FOR COMMUNITIES AND LOCAL GOVERNMENT, [2015] EWHC 3580 (Admin), [2016] J.P.L. 573, Supperstone J, QBD (Admin).

1716 Planning applications–Change of use–Fees

THE TOWN AND COUNTRY PLANNING (FEES FOR APPLICATIONS, DEEMED APPLICATIONS AND SITE VISITS) (WALES) (AMENDMENT) REGULATIONS 2016, SI 2016/62; made under the Town and Country Planning Act 1990 s.303, s.333(2A). In force: 16 March 2016.

These Regulations amend the Town and Country Planning (Fees for Applications, Deemed Applications and Site Visits) (Wales) Regulations 2015. Regulation 2 makes provision for fees payable in respect of requests for pre-application services made to local planning authorities and Regulation 3 makes minor amendments in relation to applications for approval of reserved matters.

1717 Planning applications–Local planning authorities–Service provision

THE TOWN AND COUNTRY PLANNING (PRE-APPLICATION SERVICES) (WALES) REGULATIONS 2016, SI 2016/61; made under the Town and Country Planning Act 1990 s.61Z1, s.61Z2, s.333(2A). In force: 16 March 2016.

These Regulations make provision under the Town and Country Planning Act 1990 ss.61Z1 and 61Z2 for the provision of services by local planning authorities before a qualifying application is made.

1718 Planning applications–Nationally significant infrastructure projects

THE DEVELOPMENTS OF NATIONAL SIGNIFICANCE (APPLICATION OF ENACTMENTS) (WALES) ORDER 2016, SI 2016/54; made under the Town and Country Planning Act 1990 s.75A. In force: 1 March 2016.

This Order applies various enactments to applications made to the Welsh Ministers for planning permission for development which is of national significance.

1719 Planning applications–Nationally significant infrastructure projects–Payment of fees

THE DEVELOPMENTS OF NATIONAL SIGNIFICANCE (FEES) (WALES) REGULATIONS 2016, SI 2016/57; made under the Town and Country Planning Act 1990 s.303, s.333(2A). In force: 1 March 2016.

These Regulations provide for the payment of fees in respect of: (1) pre-application services provided by the Welsh Ministers and local planning authorities under the Developments of National Significance (Wales) Regulations 2016; and (2) notifications of proposed applications under the Town and Country Planning Act 1990 s.62D.

1720 Planning applications–Planning authorities' powers and duties

THE TOWN AND COUNTRY PLANNING (SECTION 62A APPLICATIONS) (AMENDMENT) REGULATIONS 2016, SI 2016/944; made under the Town and Country Planning Act 1990 s.62A, s.76C; Small Business, Enterprise and Employment Act 2015 s.28(2)(a). In force: 21 October 2016.

These Regulations amend the Town and Country Planning (Section 62A Applications) (Procedure and Consequential Amendments) Order 2013 and the Town and Country Planning (Section 62A Applications) (Written Representations and Miscellaneous Provisions) Regulations 2013 with the effect of making new provision in respect of the circumstances in which an authority may be designated under the Town and Country Planning Act 1990 s.62A, and where, as a consequence, an applicant making certain types of application for planning permission may make those directly to the Secretary of State, rather than to the local planning authority. The Regulations also specify the respective obligations of the Secretary of State and the local planning authority in relation to publicising the making of such an application.

1721 Planning conditions–Interpretation–Condition prohibiting "industrial or commercial activities" at bus depot outside of specified hours–Whether running of bus engines out of hours constituted breach–Application of ejusdem generis principle to interpretation of planning conditions

A bus company appealed against a decision (*R. (on the application of XPL Ltd) v Harlow Council* [2014] EWHC 3860 (Admin)) upholding a breach of condition notice issued by the respondent local authority. The local authority had granted planning permission for the bus company to use a site as a bus depot. The permission included a condition prohibiting the "repairs or maintenance of vehicles or other industrial or commercial activities (other than the parking of coaches and other vehicles)" outside specified hours. The local authority later issued a breach of condition notice requiring the bus company to cease the running of engines of coaches and buses outside the specified hours. The engines had been run early in the mornings because they needed to run for several minutes before a bus moved off to enable air brakes and suspension to operate. The bus company argued that (1) the condition had prohibited repairs and maintenance, and similar activities, outside the specified hours, but not any other activities, in accordance with the principle of ejusdem generis; further, the parking of buses, permitted by the condition, included "un-parking", or driving buses away; (2) the breach of condition notice was unlawful as it purported to prevent an activity, namely the running of engines, which was not prohibited by the condition.

Held: Appeal dismissed. (1) The condition was obviously intended to preclude a wide range of activities outside the specified hours and the obvious purpose was to ensure that the amenity of neighbouring residents was not harmed. The restrictions were not confined to the "repairs or maintenance of vehicles" but extended to other activities potentially harmful to residential amenity. The prohibition of "other industrial or commercial activities" would have been unnecessary if the restrictions had been limited to the activities involved in repairing and maintaining vehicles. The condition had been intended to protect neighbouring residents from noise generated by the permitted use of the site as a bus depot. The most obvious source of noise associated with that use was the buses themselves. "Other" in "other industrial or commercial activities" meant that the activities were themselves "industrial or commercial activities". The sole specific exception was the parking of vehicles. Whether parking was regarded as an industrial or a commercial activity did not matter; it was one or the other, because it was explicitly an exception to the generality of those activities. Further, it was not an activity similar to "repairs or maintenance"; it was an "industrial or commercial" activity of a quite different kind. The ejusdem generis principle had no place in the interpretation of planning conditions. In any event, there was no need to resort to it in the instant case. The court had to construe the words used in order to give the condition a sensible meaning as a restriction on a use approved by the planning permission. "Repairs or maintenance" did not represent a "genus" limiting the sense of "other industrial or commercial activities". One should not read into the phrase some qualifying word to make it, for example, "other similar industrial or commercial activities". Accordingly, the phrase could include activities quite unlike "repairs or maintenance". "Parking" in the condition did not include the removal of a vehicle from the place where it had been parked. That was to distort the natural meaning of the word. The parking exception related to the parking of buses when they returned to the depot in the evening, not to their engines being started before they departed at the start of the day. The correct interpretation of the condition was that it restricted to the specified hours any industrial or commercial activity at the site, including the repair and maintenance of buses, but with the exception of the parking of vehicles (see paras 24-33 of judgment). (2) The breach of condition notice was lawful. The notice was not concerned with the parking of vehicles. The condition expressly permitted that activity, and the notice did not require that activity to cease. The focus was on the concept of the running of bus engines outside the permitted hours, which was the only activity attacked by the notice. The court had to consider whether running the engines outside the permitted hours, in preparation for the vehicles to be driven from the site for some commercial purpose, was inextricably part of that commercial purpose and hence within the scope of "other industrial or commercial activities" in the condition. Running the engines was a necessary activity in preparing to use the vehicles for commercial purposes and so was itself a commercial activity or at least indispensably part of a commercial activity. It was therefore restricted by the condition, and the notice had been properly made (paras 36-40).

R. (ON THE APPLICATION OF XPL LTD) v HARLOW COUNCIL, [2016] EWCA Civ 378, [2016] J.P.L. 878, Jackson LJ, CA (Civ Div).

1722 Planning conditions–Removal–Removal of condition limiting periods of use of multi-use games area–Condition having no useful purpose as noise from games area neither unreasonable nor substantial

The appellant resident appealed against a decision (*R. (on the application of May) v Rother DC* [2014] EWHC 456 (Admin), [2014] L.L.R. 535) dismissing judicial review proceedings challenging the respondent local authority's removal of a planning condition limiting the hours during which a multi-use games area could be used. The appellant's house and garden adjoined the games area, which consisted of a hard-surfaced, fenced games court next to which there was a youth shelter, basketball hoops and goal posts. Although the hours during which the games area could be used had been restricted, the local authority, following a trial period during which the use of the games area was unrestricted, removed the condition, having determined that a curfew did not solve the noise problem, there was not unreasonable noise or substantial noise emanating from the games area and that while activity was audible, it was not excessive to warrant restricted usage. The appellant submitted that the local authority had failed to consider the National Planning Policy Framework para.123, which required it to "mitigate and reduce to a minimum other adverse impacts on health and quality of life arising from noise from new developments", and that there was a real and substantial difference between that requirement and the Rother District Local Plan policy GD 1 (ii), which the local authority did take into account. That policy required that development should be "in keeping with" and "not unreasonably harm the amenities of adjoining properties".

Held: Appeal dismissed. (1) The appellant's argument treated the NPPF and the local policy as if they were statutory texts; although there were textual differences between the two, they were no more than semantic differences and NPPF para.123, once read in the light of a noise policy statement to which it cross-referred, was not materially different to the local policy, *Tesco Stores Ltd v Dundee City Council* [2012] UKSC 13, [2012] P.T.S.R. 983, [2012] C.L.Y. 2595 followed. The NPPF para.123 was to be interpreted as minimising noise as far as reasonably practicable; the policy statement made it clear that noise considerations did not trump everything else (see paras 15-16, 18-19 of judgment). (2) Whether the imposition of a condition was a reasonable step was one of planning judgment for the planning authority. Such a decision might take into account the position of a would-be developer as well as those affected by the development; neither NPPF [123] nor the local policy prohibited a decision-maker from balancing those conflicting considerations (para.18). (3) In the instant case, the essence of the planning committee's reasoning was that the condition did not solve the problem; the noise itself was neither unreasonable nor substantial and the condition no longer served a useful purpose. Once the committee had reached that conclusion it was difficult to see how it could have justified retaining the condition. Although the answer to the question as to whether the condition did serve a useful purpose might have been highly controversial, it was one of fact or planning judgment which did not reveal an error of law (para.24).

R. (ON THE APPLICATION OF MAY) v ROTHER DC *sub nom.* MAY v ROTHER DC, [2015] EWCA Civ 610, [2015] L.L.R. 853, Lord Dyson MR, CA (Civ Div).

1723 Planning control–Enforcement–Nature of planning enforcement order procedure

[Town and Country Planning Act 1990 (c.8) s.171B, s.171BA, s.171BC; Localism Act 2011 (c.20) s.124]

In conjoined appeals the appellant developers appealed against decisions (*Jackson v Secretary of State for Communities and Local Government* [2015] EWHC 20 (Admin), [2015] 2 P. & C.R. 8, [2015] C.L.Y. 1968 and *R. (on the application of Bonsall) v*

Secretary of State for Communities and Local Government [2014] EWHC 2022 (Admin)) that the time limits in the Town and Country Planning Act 1990 s.171B for enforcing their breaches of planning control did not apply because they had deceived the planning authority about the nature of their developments. In *Welwyn Hatfield Council v Secretary of State for Communities and Local Government* [2011] UKSC 15, [2011] 2 A.C. 304, [2011] C.L.Y. 2510 the Supreme Court held that the s.171B time limits did not apply in cases of positive deception designed to avoid enforcement action. Shortly thereafter, by the Localism Act 2011 s.124, Parliament inserted s.171BA to s.171BC into the 1990 Act, creating a procedure whereby, in cases of deliberate concealment, planning authorities could apply for a planning enforcement order (PEO) permitting enforcement action outside the time limit. The instant cases had been determined after the enactment of s.171BA to s.171BC. The planning authority had not used the PEO procedure in either case, opting instead to take enforcement action after the expiry of the time limit. Both appellants were found to have deliberately deceived the planning authority about the nature of their developments. In each case the planning inspector relied on *Welwyn* and found that the time limit for enforcement did not apply. The issue was whether *Welwyn* survived the enactment of s.171BA to s.171BC, or whether, in cases of deliberate concealment, local planning authorities seeking to enforce outside the time limit had to follow the PEO procedure. The appellants' case was that where a PEO was available, planning authorities could not rely on the *Welwyn* principle. They submitted that: (1) where a PEO was available there was no justification for disapplying s.171B on grounds of public policy, and that the words of s.171B should given their obvious and unqualified meaning; (2) where Parliament had legislated exhaustively for a particular area and set out a procedure to be followed, the legislation should not be construed in a way that allowed that procedure to be sidestepped.

Held: Appeals dismissed. (1) In *Welwyn*, the Supreme Court had interpreted s.171B and, using public policy as a principle of interpretation, had held that the time limits for enforcement did not apply in cases of positive deception. It had not relied on public policy to depart from the true meaning of s.171B, but had read the apparently unqualified language of the section as being subject to an implied limitation. On the appellants' case, the meaning of s.171B must have changed upon the introduction of the PEO procedure. However, there was nothing in either s.171BA to s.171BC or the 2011 Act to suggest a legislative intention to change the meaning of s.171B. Had Parliament wanted to remove the effect of *Welwyn*, it could have amended the Localism Bill, but it had not done so. Moreover, nothing said by the Supreme Court in *Welwyn* suggested that the members of the court considered themselves to be applying a short-term fix that would fall away once the PEO procedure was introduced. They were concerned simply with the interpretation of the existing s.171B, and the instant court was to be very slow to conclude that the meaning they gave it was altered sub silentio by the introduction of the PEO procedure (see paras 42-44 of judgment). (2) By introducing the PEO procedure, Parliament had not legislated exhaustively in respect of enforcement in cases of deception. While there was some overlap between the PEO procedure and the *Welwyn* principle, it was far from complete; the PEO procedure was narrower than the *Welwyn* principle in some respects, and wider in others. On the appellants' argument, Parliament must have intended that the PEO procedure should prevail within the area of overlap, but that the *Welwyn* principle could apply outside the area of overlap. That was a strained interpretation of the legislation. The appellants were not assisted by cases such as *De Keyser's Royal Hotel Ltd, Re* [1920] A.C. 508, *B v Forsey* 1988 S.C. (H.L.) 28, [1988] C.L.Y. 4521, *Marcic v Thames Water Utilities Ltd* [2003] UKHL 66, [2004] 2 A.C. 42, [2004] C.L.Y. 2763, and *R. (on the application of Best) v Chief Land Registrar* [2015] EWCA Civ 17, [2016] Q.B. 23, [2015] C.L.Y. 2091. In those cases, the decision that the statutory scheme was intended to displace other powers or causes of action was based on the need to avoid absurdity, inconsistency or arbitrary effects that would otherwise arise. There was no absurdity, inconsistency or arbitrariness in s.171B continuing to have the meaning it was held to have in *Welwyn; De Keyser's, Forsey, Marcic and Best* considered. Nor did it help to point to the checks and balances inherent in the PEO procedure to ensure compliance with the ECHR. The *Welwyn* principle could equally be applied in a Convention-compliant manner. Finally, the survival of the *Welwyn* principle in relation to cases of deliberate concealment would not drive a coach and horses through the PEO regime. The PEO procedure was an alternative and additional means of permitting enforcement outside the time limit in cases of deliberate concealment. There was nothing in either of the appellants' cases to cause any concern about the continued ability of planning authorities to rely on the *Welwyn* principle in such contexts (paras 45-52).

JACKSON v SECRETARY OF STATE FOR COMMUNITIES AND LOCAL GOVERNMENT *sub nom.* BONSALL v SECRETARY OF STATE FOR COMMUNITIES AND LOCAL GOVERNMENT, [2015] EWCA Civ 1246, [2016] Q.B. 811, Richards LJ, CA (Civ Div).

1724 Planning inspectors–Procedural impropriety–Decision made on basis of issues not raised at inquiry

[Town and Country Planning Act 1990 (c.8) s.70(2); Planning and Compulsory Purchase Act 2004 (c.5) s.38(6)]

The claimant developer sought to quash decisions of the first defendant secretary of state's inspector to uphold the second defendant local authority's refusals to grant planning permission for residential development on two sites. The developer's appeals against the refusals were conjoined. The inspector had found that there was a shortfall in the five-year supply of housing land for the local authority's district as a whole, so that the presumption in favour of development under the National Planning Policy Framework para.14 applied. However, he held that (i) there was an adequate supply of housing land in the areas of the proposed developments; (ii) the rate of housing growth within the areas of the proposed sites was significantly biased towards the beginning of the local plan period, and such "front-loading" of the supply of housing land might leave the local authority unable to respond appropriately to future, unforeseen needs, contrary to the "monitor and manage principle" underlying the local plan system; (iii) the proposals would divert development pressure away from the city of Bath so as to dilute or undermine the local authority's strategy of directing the main initiatives for growth to Bath. The inspector dismissed the appeals, having concluded that those adverse factors outweighed the para.14 presumption. The developer contended that (1) the inspector had taken account of an irrelevant consideration, namely that the supply of housing land in the developments' areas was adequate, since the concept of a five-year supply of housing land related to the local authority area as a whole; (2) the inspector's conclusion that the appeal proposals would undermine the spatial strategy for directing the main growth initiatives to Bath by diverting development pressure away from it was not based on any evidence or submissions at the inquiry: the inspector had thereby acted unfairly by relying on that consideration in dismissing the appeals; (3) "frontloading" had not been raised by the inspector as an issue for the inquiry to consider.

Held: Judgment for claimant. (1) Although the NPPF required a local authority to demonstrate a five-year supply of housing land for the whole of its area, it did not follow that if such a supply could not be demonstrated, then it was legally irrelevant for a decision-maker to consider the distribution of housing land supply in parts or sub-areas of the district. Any consideration relating to the use and development of land, or which served a planning purpose in that it related to the character of the use of land, was legally capable of being a relevant planning consideration, *Westminster City Council v Great Portland Estates Plc* [1985] A.C. 661, [1984] C.L.Y. 3413 and *Stringer v Minister for Housing and Local Government* [1970] 1 W.L.R. 1281, [1970] C.L.Y. 2778 applied (see paras 36-37 of judgment). (2) Under the Town and Country Planning Act 1990 s.70(2) and the Planning and Compulsory Purchase Act 2004 s.38(6), if the statutory development plan raised a relevant consideration then ordinarily the decision-maker was obliged to take it into account, whether or not the matter had been referred to by a party to an appeal or in representations, *R. (on the application of St James Homes Ltd) v Secretary of State for the Environment, Transport and the Regions* [2001] EWHC Admin 30, [2001] P.L.C.R. 27, [2001] C.L.Y. 4684 considered. However, there was no reason why the statutory obligation to take into account the development plan should necessarily absolve the decision-maker from complying with the normal principles of procedural fairness. Nothing in the inspector's decision letter indicated that the "Bath point" had been raised at the inquiry, and he had not produced a witness statement to indicate that the subject was raised in some way at the inquiry or in the written representations which he had received. Whilst *R. (on the application of Bleaklow Industries Ltd) v Secretary of State for Communities and Local Government* [2009] EWCA Civ 206, [2009] 2 P. & C.R. 21, [2010] C.L.Y. 2574 propounded the principle that even if a particular point was not raised at an inquiry there might be no procedural unfairness if the "point" fell within the ambit of a "topic" which was raised, the application of that approach was plainly fact-sensitive; in general terms, fairness required that the parties should be aware of the points to be addressed and have a reasonable opportunity to deal with them, *Bleaklow* considered, *Hopkins Developments Ltd v Secretary of State for Communities and Local Government* [2014] EWCA Civ 470, [2014] P.T.S.R. 1145, [2014] C.L.Y. 2411 applied. In the instant case, there had been no discussion of whether allowing the appeals would divert development away from Bath or impede the strategy of directing a certain level of growth to Bath. Since that topic had not been raised at the inquiry, the developer had been unfairly denied the opportunity to present any relevant evidence and argument in that respect and to have it assessed and taken into account by the inspector (paras 51-54, 57, 60-61, 63). (3) The local authority had raised no concern in respect of "frontloading" as a reason for opposing the developments. There had been material prejudice to the developer and procedural unfairness because the inspector had relied on the frontloading point as a further reason for dismissing the appeals, without the point being raised as an issue to be addressed. The inspector's decisions were quashed (paras 68, 70, 73, 79).

EDWARD WARE HOMES LTD v SECRETARY OF STATE FOR COMMUNITIES AND LOCAL GOVERNMENT, [2016] EWHC 103 (Admin), [2016] J.P.L. 767, Holgate J, QBD (Admin).

1725 Planning permission–Bias–Permission for development including affordable housing–Councillor voted in favour was director of housing association likely to be awarded contract

[Localism Act 2011 (c.20) s.31]

The claimant applied for judicial review of the defendant local authority's decision to grant the interested party developers planning permission for a residential development, including some affordable housing. The developers had identified a local housing association as a prospective partner to provide the affordable housing segment of the proposed development. One of the councillors (M) involved in the subsequent planning committee meeting was a director of the association. He declared that he was a member of its board but, because it was only a prospective partner rather than the applicant for permission, he decided to vote on the planning application, which was passed by one vote. Had he withdrawn from the debate and not voted, the application would have been refused. The association subsequently became the developers' preferred bidder for the affordable housing. The claimant contended, inter alia, that the decision to grant permission was unlawful because of M's participation. He submitted that (1) M was automatically disqualified because of his directorship; (2) M was subject to statutory disqualification under the Localism Act 2011 s.31 because of a disclosable pecuniary interest; (3) the decision was tainted by apparent bias.

Held: Application granted. (1) The rule on automatic disqualification for pecuniary or proprietary interest was stated in *Dimes v Grand Junction Canal Proprietors* 10 E.R. 301, and was first applied to planning decisions in *King, The v Hendon Rural DC Ex p. Chorley* [1933] 2 K.B. 696, *Dimes* and *Chorley* considered. However, unlike in *Chorley*, M had no direct or pecuniary interest in the planning application so as to be automatically disqualified from participating in the decision, *Chorley* considered. The planning committee's decision did not lead to M obtaining any benefit: there were too many contingencies between the committee's decision and any benefit to him as a director of the association for the rule to have any purchase (see paras 41-42 of judgment). (2) M had no disclosable pecuniary interest in the matter to be considered, as the association was not the applicant for planning permission and, when the decision was made, had no contract with the developers. Accordingly, he was not disqualified under s.31 (para.45). (3) The legal test for apparent bias was whether the fair-minded and informed observer, having regard to all material facts, would conclude that there was a real possibility of bias, *Porter v Magill* [2001] UKHL 67, [2002] 2 A.C. 357, [2002] C.L.Y. 3185 applied. The principle of apparent bias applied to local government decision-making, *R. (on the application of Lewis) v Redcar and Cleveland BC* [2008] EWCA Civ 746, [2009] 1 W.L.R. 83, [2008] C.L.Y. 2935 applied. M's participation in the planning meeting gave rise to an appearance of potential bias. It was plainly in the association's interests, and those of M as director, for the planning application to be approved. The association had committed time, resources and expertise in working with the developers on the affordable housing. It was highly unlikely that it would have done so unless it believed that it would be awarded a contract once permission was granted. Apparent bias could arise even in a case where a councillor had not voted, *Darker Enterprises v Dacorum BC* [1992] C.O.D. 465, [1993] C.L.Y. 2598 considered. M's private interests were engaged by the vote and it had been wrong for him to have participated in the meeting. The decision to grant planning permission was, accordingly, quashed (paras 46, 50, 52-53, 72).

KELTON v WILTSHIRE COUNCIL, [2015] EWHC 2853 (Admin), [2016] J.P.L. 273, Cranston J, QBD (Admin).

1726 Planning permission–Community infrastructure levy–Local authority treating separate applications as one–Permitted works constituting development liable to authority's levy

[Community Infrastructure Levy Regulations 2010 (SI 2010/948) reg.6(1)(c); Town and Country Planning Act 1990 (c.8) s.55; Town and Country Planning (Development Management Procedure) (England) Order 2015 (SI 2015/595) art.44]

The owner of a unit in a shopping centre applied for judicial review of a local authority's decision that it had to pay a community infrastructure levy after making alterations to the unit. Following two simultaneous, but separate, planning applications by the owner, the local authority granted it planning permission to install a mezzanine floor and planning permission to make external alterations to the unit. The mezzanine created an extra 1,709 square metres of retail floor space, but the external alterations created no additional floor space. The local authority sent the owner a liability notice and then a demand notice requiring payment of the levy. The owner contended that it had deliberately made two separate applications so that neither permission would be liable to the levy: the mezzanine planning permission would be exempt because it fell within the exemption in the Community Infrastructure Levy Regulations 2010 reg.6(1)(c) and the external planning permission because it created no floor space. The local authority maintained that the two permissions should be treated as one because the works were linked, and the relevant legislation was to be construed purposively so as to preclude avoidance of the levy.

Held: Application granted. (1) Regulation 6(1) set out those works that were not to be treated as development in respect of which a local authority could charge the levy. Regulation 6(1)(c) exempted work on an existing building for which planning permission was required only because of the Town and Country Planning Act 1990 s.55(2A). Section 55(2A) empowered the secretary of state to specify the circumstances in which works such as those which affected only the interior of the building would involve development requiring planning permission. By the Town and Country Planning (Development Management Procedure) (England) Order 2015 art.44, the secretary of state specified that internal operations which increased the floor space of a building by more than 200 square metres, if that building was used for the retail sale of goods, was development which required planning permission. Therefore, without art.44, a mezzanine floor inserted into a building for use for the retail sale of goods of more than 200 square metres would not require planning permission at all. It followed that if the mezzanine floor planning permission was considered by itself, it would not constitute development under reg.6(1)(c) and so would not be chargeable development. On the plain and ordinary meaning of the words used within reg.6(1)(c), it was clear that the levy was not chargeable on the mezzanine planning permission (see paras 44-48 of judgment). (2) There was nothing on the face of the mezzanine planning permission to link it with the planning permission for external alterations. Further, each permission would be entered separately upon the planning register that the local planning authority was required to maintain. Nothing on that public record would indicate that the two separate permissions should be seen as one. There was, therefore, no basis in the statutory provisions or in planning law which supported the local authority's argument that the two permissions should be treated as one (paras 53-54). (3) There had been no manipulation of the system for any ulterior or illegal motive. Rather, the owner had taken advantage of the legislative scheme which permitted it to submit two separate planning applications for each act of operational development that it wished to pursue. If it was not the intention of the legislature to permit that to occur then it was for the legislature to change it. Furthermore, despite pressing a purposive intention of the statutory provisions in general, the local authority had not identified which particular provision entitled it to act as it did in charging the levy (paras 73-74). (4) Accordingly, the local authority had not acted lawfully in demanding the levy under its liability and demand notices by interpreting the two separate planning permissions as one (paras 76-77).

R. (ON THE APPLICATION OF ORBITAL SHOPPING PARK SWINDON LTD) v SWINDON BC, [2016] EWHC 448 (Admin), [2016] P.T.S.R. 736, Patterson J, QBD (Admin).

1727 Planning permission–Conditions–Interpretation by implication

[Electricity Act 1989 (c.29) Sch.9 para.3, s.36, s.5, s.6]

The appellant company, which owned a golf club and linked resort, appealed against a ruling (*Trump International Golf Club Scotland Ltd v Scottish Ministers* [2015] CSIH 46, 2015 S.L.T. 369, [2015] 8 C.L. 315) upholding a decision of the respondent Scottish Ministers to grant consent under the Electricity Act 1989 s.36 for the construction and operation of a wind farm in the vicinity of the resort. The appellant argued that (1) Sch.9 para.3 of the Act gave rise to a necessary implication that only holders of licences to generate electricity or exempt persons (the party which had been granted consent was neither) could be granted a s.36 consent; (2) condition 14 attaching to the consent, which required the submission and approval of a design statement, was void for uncertainty.

Held: Appeal dismissed. (1) (Per Lord Hodge) It was not the case that only licence-holders or exempt persons could be granted a s.36 consent. The appellant's interpretation was not supported by the structure of the Act, its language or its policy background. As to the policy background, it was relevant, among other things, that it had been the established practice in both of the British jurisdictions for commercial organisations to apply for and obtain s.36 consents before they sought a licence to generate electricity under s.6 of the Act or an exemption under s.5. No evidence had been presented that such a practice had resulted in unsuitable persons applying for and obtaining s.36 consents or in any failure to protect the environment (see paras 13, 19, 21 of judgment).(2) (Per Lord Hodge) Even if condition 14 were invalid, important elements of the benefits which it promoted were contained within the supplementary environmental information statement which had been prepared. The Scottish Ministers could insist on compliance with that document in the construction of the development. The scope of the development was defined by Annex 1 of the consent, and the supplementary environmental information statement set out the principles governing the size and location of the turbines. Condition 14 therefore could not be seen as a fundamental condition which determined the scope and nature of the development and which, if invalid, would in turn invalidate the consent. Further, when one read condition 14 in the context of other conditions (13 and 24), it was clear that the conditions envisaged that the Scottish Ministers could use both the construction method statement (the subject of condition 13) and the design statement to regulate the detailed design of the wind farm in the interests of environmental protection and require those constructing the generating station to comply with those statements (paras 26, 30).(3) (Per Lord Carnwath) It was appropriate to comment on the planning cases which had been relied on in support of the appellant's strict interpretation of condition 14. Those cases were said to support the submission that it was not possible by implication to add to the condition a requirement that the development be completed in accordance with the approved design statement. Planning permissions and conditions were not in a special category when it came to using implication as a technique of interpretation. It was not right to regard the process of interpreting a planning permission as differing materially from that appropriate to other legal documents. Any such document had of course to be construed in its particular legal and factual context. One aspect of that context was that a planning permission was a public document which might be relied on by parties unrelated to those originally involved. It had also to be borne in mind that planning conditions could be used to support criminal proceedings. Those were good reasons for a relatively cautious approach, for example in the well-established rules limiting the categories of documents which might be used in interpreting a planning permission. But such considerations arose from the legal framework within which planning permissions were granted. They did not require the adoption of a completely different approach to their interpretation, *Sevenoaks DC v First Secretary of State* [2004] EWHC 771 (Admin), [2005] 1 P. & C.R. 13, [2005] C.L.Y. 3303 disapproved (paras 45, 60, 66).

TRUMP INTERNATIONAL GOLF CLUB SCOTLAND LTD v SCOTTISH MINISTERS, [2015] UKSC 74, [2016] 1 W.L.R. 85, Lord Neuberger JSC, SC.

1728 Planning permission–Daylight and sunlight–Development adjacent to listed public house used for film and photography–Loss of light

The owner of a public house and licensed music venue appealed against a decision upholding a planning inspector's grant of planning permission for a mixed commercial and residential development on adjacent land. Planning permission was granted by the inspector for the demolition of a single storey building and the erection in its place of a three storey building with commercial uses on the ground floor and six flats above. The pub owner had opposed permission on the grounds that noise complaints from new residents would prejudice her late night licence and the loss of daylight would destroy her subsidiary business hiring out the upstairs as a location for filming and photography. The inspector held that noise insulation in the new building would be sufficient given a planning condition that required the local authority to be satisfied that suitable sound insulation had been installed before the new building could be occupied. In the case of the light, even the developer's expert had accepted that the proposed development would almost totally extinguish the morning sunlight falling on the pub's eastern elevation, which lit the main shooting location of the staircase. The owner submitted that (1) in assessing the risk to her business of complaints of noise from the new residents the inspector had failed to consider the fact that residents would open their windows; (2) the inspector had not dealt with the loss of natural light to the eastern flank of the pub.

Held: Appeal allowed. (1) The impact of a prospective planning permission on the viability of a neighbouring business could amount to a material planning consideration. However, the owner had failed to provide an evidence-based case to support the alleged effects of the proposed development (see paras 16, 22-26 of judgment). (2) Although an inspector's decisions were to be read with a certain latitude, in the instant case he had failed to deal with the owner's point about the loss of daylight and sunlight despite being bound to do so, *Bloor Homes East Midlands Ltd v Secretary of State for Communities and Local Government* [2014] EWHC 754 (Admin) considered. The appeal was allowed on the light issue only and the grant of planning permission quashed (paras 27-32).

FORSTER v SECRETARY OF STATE FOR COMMUNITIES AND LOCAL GOVERNMENT, [2016] EWCA Civ 609, [2016] J.P.L. 1220, Laws LJ, CA (Civ Div).

1729 Planning permission–Development management procedure

THE DEVELOPMENTS OF NATIONAL SIGNIFICANCE (PROCEDURE) (WALES) ORDER 2016, SI 2016/55; made under the Town and Country Planning Act 1990 s.59, s.61, s.62, s.65, s.69, s.71, s.61Z, s.62E, s.62I, s.62J, s.62K, s.62L, s.62R, s.71ZA, s.71ZB, s.333; Planning and Compulsory Purchase Act 2004 s.54. In force: In accordance with art.1.

This Order makes provision for the manner in which applications for planning permission in respect of such development are to be dealt with by the Welsh Ministers.

1730 Planning permission–Development plans–Material considerations–No quashing of decision despite error

[Planning and Compulsory Purchase Act 2004 (c.5) s.38(6)]

A local resident appealed against a local authority's decision to grant a developer planning permission for the erection of a building for office, light industrial or warehouse use at a former nursery site. The developer had previously been granted planning permission for the building, but the High Court allowed the resident's first appeal and quashed the planning permission because a condition limiting occupation to the developer had been invalid. The High Court dismissed the resident's other grounds of appeal. In particular, it found that although the development was not in accordance with the local plan, other material considerations, including the National Planning Policy Framework, indicated that planning permission should be granted. On the instant appeal against the new grant of planning permission, the resident argued that the local authority (1) erred in concluding that, contrary to the court's previous decision, the development was in accordance with the development plan; (2) ought to have referred the application to the secretary of state under the Town and Country Planning (Consultation) England Direction 2009 art.9.

Held: Appeal dismissed. (1) Under the Planning and Compulsory Purchase Act 2004 s.38(6), the determination of a planning application had to be made in accordance with the development plan unless material considerations indicated otherwise. The principal policy that was relevant in the local plan provided that proposals for small-scale expansion of existing businesses outside defined development areas would be permitted provided they met certain criteria. Since the proposed development was not small-scale, it was difficult to see how that policy allowed the local authority to conclude that the development was in accordance with the development plan. While conflict with one policy did not mean that the proposal could not accord with the development plan as a whole, it was not clear what policy the proposal complied with which weighed against its non-compliance with the small-scale policy so as to enable it to be said that the proposal accorded with the development plan read as a whole. It would appear that the local authority had concluded that the proposal accorded with the development plan on the basis that the crucial policy on small-scale development should be given less weight because it was not wholly consistent with the National Planning Policy Framework para.28. That was not a lawful approach: the framework was but another material consideration and while it might mean that conflict with the development plan was to be given less weight, it could not bear upon whether the conflict existed in the first place. Nevertheless, although the decision to grant planning permission was flawed, it would not be quashed on that basis. Even though it had been wrong to give the policy reduced weight on account of its not having been wholly consistent with the framework when considering whether the proposal accorded with the local plan, as it was irrelevant to that issue, the local authority would have been fully entitled to give it exactly that same reduced weight as it did when considering whether material considerations indicated a determination otherwise than in accordance with the development plan. The decision would have been exactly the same, the same reasoning would have been deployed and no additional factors would have been brought into play. That was clearly the balance that it intended to and did strike. The analytical framework would have been different, but its legal correctness could not logically have affected its output. That view was reinforced by the fact that when the local authority had originally concluded that the proposal was not in accordance with the local plan but granted permission, it came to that decision without error of law. That also meant that the local authority's error of not taking the High Court's first judgment into account in relation to whether the proposal accorded with the development plan also should not lead to the quashing of the decision (see paras 4, 10, 43-44, 48-49 of judgment). (2) Under art.9 of the Direction, the local planning authority had to consult the secretary of state if it was not minded to refuse planning permission for a type of development to which the Direction applied. Under art.5(1)(c)(ii), the Direction applied to retail, office and leisure developments outside town centres where the floor space of an extension or new development of 2,500sq m or more, when aggregated with existing floor space, would exceed 5,000sq m. Taking existing floorspace to mean only so much of the floorspace as was in retail, leisure or office use rather than all existing floorspace, the proposal did not fall within art.5(1)(c)(ii) (paras 60-64).

SIENKIEWICZ v SOUTH SOMERSET DC *sub nom.* R. (ON THE APPLICATION OF SIENKIEWICZ) v SOUTH SOMERSET DC, [2015] EWHC 3704 (Admin), [2016] P.T.S.R. 815, Ouseley J, QBD (Admin).

1731 **Planning permission–Environmental impact assessments–Planning authority granting planning permission after obtaining screening opinion to effect that environmental impact assessment not needed–Secretary of state subsequently issuing positive screening direction–Whether grant of planning permission rendered unlawful**

[Town and Country Planning (Environmental Impact Assessment) Regulations 2011 (SI 2011/1824) Sch.2, reg.3(4), reg.4(3)]

The claimant applied for judicial review of the defendant local authority's decision to grant planning permission for a development to support the reopening of a quarry. The dormant, gabbro quarry was within an Area of Outstanding Natural Beauty on the Lizard peninsular. The quarry's owner, the first interested party, had applied for permission to erect buildings and facilities to provide infrastructure for the operation of the quarry. The claimant was a local resident and proprietor of a nearby local organic farm and business. She registered objections to the planning application, indicating that, since the proposed development was within an AONB, it amounted to a development within the Town and Country Planning (Environmental Impact Assessment) Regulations 2011 Sch.2 and therefore had to be screened in order to see whether it required an environmental impact assessment. The local authority adopted a screening opinion which found that the application concerned a Sch.2 development, but concluded that there were not likely to be significant environmental effects such as to warrant the preparation of an environmental impact assessment. The claimant urgently requested a screening direction from the secretary of state in relation to the proposed development. The local authority noted that the claimant had submitted an environmental impact assessment request to the secretary of state, but resolved to approve the development and grant permission. A month later, the secretary of state published his screening direction under reg.4(3) stating that the proposal would be likely to have significant effects on the environment and that the risk of significant harm justified an environmental impact assessment. The claimant contended that (1) in the light of the secretary of state's binding screening direction that the proposal was environmental impact assessment development, the grant of consent was unlawful under reg.3(4) because it was not accompanied by environmental information; (2) it was irrational for the local authority to have proceeded to grant planning permission without awaiting the outcome of the secretary of state's screening direction process.

Held: Application granted. (1) The grant of permission for environmental impact assessment development was rendered unlawful by the secretary of state's subsequent positive screening direction (see para.37 of judgment). The reg.3(4) prohibition on granting permission for environmental impact assessment development without environmental information was a matter for the court's determination on the basis of the material available when it considered that question. In the instant case, the material before the court included an unchallenged decision of the secretary of state to issue a direction that the development was environmental impact assessment development. The Regulations did not suggest that the question whether a development was environmental impact assessment development, and the secretary of state's jurisdiction under reg.4(3) to direct that the development was environmental impact assessment development, came to an end on the grant of planning permission (para.38). The secretary of state's decision as to whether a development was environmental impact assessment development was conclusive and, under reg.3(4), planning permission could not be granted until the environmental information contained in an environmental impact assessment had been taken into account by the planning authority. If the planning authority chose to grant consent prior to the resolution of a direction requested of the secretary of state, it ran the risk that if that direction was positive it would have granted a planning consent which was infected with illegality (para.39). (2) It followed from that analysis that no reasonable planning authority, knowing when it formed a resolution to grant planning permission that there was an outstanding request of the secretary of state to make a determination on a screening direction, would proceed to grant planning permission without knowing the outcome of that screening direction process (para.39). The grant of planning permission was quashed (para.42).

R. (ON THE APPLICATION OF ROSKILLY) v CORNWALL COUNCIL, [2015] EWHC 3711 (Admin), [2016] Env. L.R. 21, Dove J, QBD (Admin).

1732 **Planning permission–Environmental impact assessments–Whether residential development and link road separate projects for purposes of assessment**

[Directive 2011/92 on the effects of public and private projects on the environment 2011; Town and Country Planning (Environmental Impact Assessment) Regulations 2011 (SI 2011/1824)]

The appellant property developer appealed against the dismissal (*R. (on the application of Larkfleet Ltd) v South Kesteven DC* [2014] EWHC 3760 (Admin), [2015] Env. L.R. 16, [2015] 5 C.L. 187) of its application for judicial review of a grant of planning permission by the respondent local authority to a highways authority, the interested party. The appellant had property development interests in the north of Grantham. The planning permission related to the construction of a section of road (the link road) to complete a by-pass to the south of the town. The building of the by-pass was one of the local authority's long-standing planning policy objectives, and the core strategy in the local plan identified a site to the south of the town that was suitable for residential development. The strategy stated that if the site, which was owned by a rival of the appellant, were to be developed, access would be dependent on the construction of the link road. A "masterplan" adopted by the local authority showed the link road skirting the site and providing access to it via a roundabout and "stub" road which could later be extended into the site. The by-pass, including the link road section, was to be publicly funded, though the strategy contemplated that a significant part of the cost would be recouped from the developer of the residential site. The highway authority proposed to construct the link road as shown on the masterplan, and its application for planning permission was accompanied by an environmental statement prepared pursuant to Directive 2011/92 and the Town and Country Planning (Environmental Impact Assessment) Regulations 2011. In terms of environmental impact, the statement treated the construction of the link road as a separate "project" from the residential site development. It did, however, recognise that the two might have cumulative environmental effects, and it addressed them. Before granting permission, the planning committee was given a joint presentation by the highway authority and the developer of the residential site showing how the link road related to the proposals for the site. The appellant submitted that planning permission should not have been granted because (1) the link road and residential development were so interconnected that they constituted a single project and the environmental statement did not provide the information required for such an integrated project; (2) even if the link road was a separate project, the environmental statement failed to adequately address its cumulative effects in combination with the proposed residential development.

Held: Appeal dismissed. (1) The Directive's objective was the protection of the environment. What was in substance a single project could not be divided into a series of smaller projects which each fell below the threshold criteria for environmental impact assessment scrutiny, *Ecologistas en Accion-CODA v Ayuntamiento de Madrid (C-142/07)* EU:C:2008:445, [2009] P.T.S.R. 458 followed. However, the Directive was clear that the fact that two sets of proposed works might have a cumulative effect on the environment did not make them a single project for environmental impact assessment purposes. It contemplated that they might constitute two potential projects but with cumulative effects which needed to be assessed. The Directive and the CJEU recognised that it was legitimate for different development proposals to be brought forward at different times, even though they might have a degree of interaction, if they were different projects. Where two or more distinct, but linked, sets of works were contemplated, the Directive's environmental protection objective was sufficiently secured by considering as far as possible their cumulative effects when permission for the first project was sought, combined with scrutiny for each subsequent project. Urban development projects within the meaning of Annex II s.10 para.b of the Directive often included the construction of roads, and whether the construction of a road was a distinct project required an evaluative judgment. The link road proposal was a project for environmental impact assessment purposes and was distinct from the proposed residential development. The most important feature was the strong independent planning need for the link road to complete the by-pass, whether or not the residential site was developed. The residential site could not be developed without the link road, but the converse was not true. It was simple planning good sense to have the link road skirt the residential site and to include the roundabout and stub to avoid extra costs in the future. The fact that funding for the link road depended to a significan degree on contributions from the developer of the residential site did not mean that the two developments were part of a single project. The public funding reflected the strong public need for the road, which could not wholly be attributed to the private developments linked to it. The highway authority was not a private developer and had no commercial interest in the residential site, which also indicated that the two projects were distinct (see paras 35-39, 44, 46, 48-49, 51-52 of judgment). (2) The environmental statement supplied as much information as it reasonably could about the cumulative effects, taking account of the uncertainty which existed about the precise details of the residential development. Uncertainty in relation to a later proposed project affected what cumulative effects could be said to be likely at the time when the application for the earlier development was being considered (para.55).

R. (ON THE APPLICATION OF LARKFLEET LTD) v SOUTH KESTEVEN DC, [2015] EWCA Civ 887, [2016] Env. L.R. 4, Moore-Bick LJ, CA (Civ Div).

1733 Planning permission–Extensions of time

THE TOWN AND COUNTRY PLANNING (OPERATION STACK) SPECIAL DEVELOPMENT (AMENDMENT) ORDER 2016, SI 2016/564; made under the Town and Country Planning Act 1990 s.59, s.60. In force: 31 May 2016.

This Order extends the planning permission granted by the Town and Country Planning (Operation Stack) Special Development Order 2015 for a further eighteen months. The planning permission granted by the 2015 Order will now cease at the end of 31 December 2017.

1734 Planning permission–Extrinsic evidence–Decision regarding ambiguity in planning permission–Consideration of extrinsic evidence not limited to application for permission

[Town and Country Planning Act 1990 (c.8) s.195]

A university applied to quash a decision of the first defendant secretary of state, by his planning inspector, dismissing its appeal against the second defendant local authority's refusal to grant a certificate of lawful use under the Town and Country Planning Act 1990 s.195. The certificate was sought in relation to the mixed used of a halls of residence for student accommodation and for conferences. The halls had been built pursuant to planning permissions granted in 2004 and 2005. The application for each permission and the resulting permissions referred to "student accommodation". A local authority officer's report for the 2004 permission, a s.106 agreement, correspondence between the highway authority and local authority, and objection letters from local residents all referred to the intended conference use. The local authority refused to grant a certificate because neither permission expressly permitted conference use. Before the planning inspector, the university's project manager gave uncontradicted evidence that conference use had always been intended. The inspector considered that the permissions were ambiguous as to use and looked to extrinsic evidence, namely the applications for clarity. However, neither referred to an existing or proposed conference use. He did not consider that the project manager's evidence was helpful to an objective interpretation. The university argued that the inspector should have concluded that on the basis of the extrinsic evidence that conference use had been intended to be included in the 2004 permission and, if that was right, then the 2005 permission also permitted such use.

Held: Application granted. Previous authorities suggested that where there was ambiguity in a planning permission, it was permissible to look at the extrinsic evidence, including but not limited to the application form and the documentary evidence, *R. v Ashford BC Ex p. Shepway DC* [1999] P.L.C.R. 12, [1999] C.L.Y. 4249 applied, *Trump International Golf Club Scotland Ltd v Scottish Ministers* [2015] UKSC 74, [2016] 1 W.L.R. 85, [2016] 1727 and *Wood v Secretary of State for Communities and Local Government* [2015] EWHC 2368 (Admin) considered. All relevant extrinsic evidence could be referred to depending on the circumstances of the case. While the permission application could be the first port of call in any examination of extrinsic evidence, it did not follow that the decision maker had to ignore all other extrinsic material. In some cases the permission would resolve the ambiguity, in other cases it would not. When it did not, other extrinsic material could be referred to, and such evidence could include the way in which the permission was actually implemented. Plainly the uncontradicted evidence of the project manager, the officer's report, the minutes of the committee meeting, the correspondence and the s.106 agreement were relevant extrinsic material for the purposes of resolving the ambiguity in the planning permission. The inspector had recognised that the 2005 permission was intended to be an amended version of the 2004 permission, and that it was to be interpreted as permitting the same use at the 2004 permission. If there was a need to resolve ambiguity then the inspector should have referred to all the extrinsic evidence on which the university had relied. With regard to the s.106 agreement, the 2005 permission expressly referred to the fact that the grant of permission was conditional on the terms of the agreement. The s.106 agreement shed light on the 2004 permission, there being no suggestion that the 2004 and 2005 permissions were to be for different uses. The s.106 agreement therefore assisted with the interpretation of both permissions. The inspector had erred in concluding that both permissions permitted student accommodation use only. The 2004 permission was ambiguous and he had erred in limiting his consideration of extrinsic material to the application for permission. Had he considered the other relevant material he would inevitably have concluded that mixed use had been permitted. The 2005 permission amended the 2004 permission and as such was to be interpreted as permitting the same uses (see paras 42, 72-78 of judgment).

UNIVERSITY OF LEICESTER v SECRETARY OF STATE FOR COMMUNITIES AND LOCAL GOVERNMENT, [2016] EWHC 476 (Admin), [2016] J.P.L. 709, Supperstone J, QBD (Admin).

1735 Planning permission–Green belt–Inappropriate development–Meaning and effect of National Planning Policy Framework for construction of agricultural buildings

[Planning and Compulsory Purchase Act 2004 (c.5) s.38(6); Directive 92/43 on the conservation of natural habitats and of wild fauna and flora 1992 art.6; Conservation of Habitats and Species Regulations 2010 (SI 2010/490) reg.61]

The appellant park authority appealed against a decision (*R. (on the application of Lee Valley Regional Park Authority) v Epping Forest DC* [2015] EWHC 1471 (Admin), [2016] Env. L.R. 8) dismissing its challenge to the respondent local authority's decision to grant the interested party planning permission for a substantial glass house development on land within the green belt close to a Special Protection Area (SPA). The interested party had submitted two previous applications for similar proposals, both of which had been refused by the local authority. Its third proposal proposed a glass house extending partly into a shallow artificial lake used by wintering wildfowl, and included ecological mitigation to include the reshaping of the lake and the creation of a new pond. The appellant was consulted and objected to the application on the basis of the development's impact on the landscape of the regional park and the green belt. Natural England was also consulted: it indicated that, subject to the imposition of conditions to secure the ecological mitigation, it did not object to the proposal. The application was considered by the local authority's district development control committee in the light of a report by a planning officer. The committee accepted her recommendation that planning permission should be granted. The local authority granted planning permission subject to conditions related to the proposed ecological mitigation measures. The appellant's claim for judicial review was based on the harm it said the development would cause to the green belt, alleged conflict with policy in the National Policy Framework (NPPF) and in the development plan, and the effects the development might have on the SPA. The judge rejected the claim on all grounds. The issues on appeal were whether the judge was wrong: (i) to conclude that the local authority had not misinterpreted and misapplied relevant national and local policy, including policies relevant to the openness of the green belt; (ii) to reject the argument that the local authority had failed to perform the decision-maker's duty under the Planning and Compulsory Purchase Act 2004 s.38(6) to determine the application in accordance with the development plan unless material considerations indicated otherwise, and that it had also misunderstood and misapplied the NPPF policy for the "presumption in favour of sustainable development"; (iii) to conclude that the local authority had properly discharged its duty under Directive 92/43 art.6 on the conservation of natural habitats and of wild fauna and flora and the Conservation of Habitats and Species Regulations 2010 reg.61, to consider whether it was necessary to undertake an "appropriate assessment" of the implications of the development for the SPA.

Held: Appeal dismissed. (1) The true position in respect of national policy for the green belt was that development that was not, in principle, "inappropriate" in the green belt was development "appropriate to the green belt". On a sensible contextual reading of the relevant policies in paras 79 to 92 of the NPPF, development appropriate in - and to - the green belt was regarded as not inimical to the fundamental aim of green belt policy "to prevent urban sprawl by keeping land permanently open", or to "the essential characteristics of green belts", namely "their openness and their permanence", or to the five purposes served by the green belt. That was the real significance of a development being appropriate in the green belt, and the reason why it did not have to be justified by "very special circumstances". The planning officer's report showed that she understood both NPPF and local plan policy for development in the green belt correctly and applied the relevant policies lawfully. In accepting her advice and recommendation, the committee adopted her interpretation and application of the relevant policies. Accordingly, the judge was correct: the local authority did not in any respect misinterpret relevant national and local policy, or apply it unlawfully (see paras 24, 30, 43 of judgment). (2) The planning officer's conclusion in her report, together with the analysis in the preceding sections, showed how she had formed the crucial planning judgment: that despite the proposal's conflict with the local plan and the harm the development would cause, its benefits as "sustainable economic development" were sufficient to justify the grant of planning permission. She gave to each consideration, on either side of the balance, the weight she thought it should have. Weight was a matter for her and, in the light of her advice, the committee. Her use of the phrase "the presumption in favour of sustainable economic development" was, at worst, infelicitous: it did not expose a wrong or misleading approach. The proposal was not given the full benefit of the policy "presumption in favour of sustainable development" in the NPPF, but the officer's advice throughout her report was loyal to the statutory presumption in favour of the development plan in s.38(6) (paras 53-54). (3) The judge was right to conclude that the local authority had lawfully discharged its duties under the Habitats Directive and the Regulations, and had properly concluded that there was no need for an "appropriate assessment". He was correct to acknowledge the role of Natural England as an appropriate consultee, to conclude that the local authority had been entitled to adopt and rely on its conclusions, and to find that it had reached its conclusions on the possibility of there being any significant effect on the SPA in accordance with the correct legal tests (paras 65, 67).

R. (ON THE APPLICATION OF LEE VALLEY REGIONAL PARK AUTHORITY) v EPPING FOREST DC, [2016] EWCA Civ 404, [2016] Env. L.R. 30, Treacy LJ, CA (Civ Div).

1736 Planning permission–Green belt–Proposal to convert stables to office block–Inappropriate development in conflict with policy and local plan

[Planning and Compulsory Purchase Act 2004 (c.5) s.38(6)]

A developer applied to quash a decision of the respondent secretary of state, by his inspector, upholding the second respondent local authority's refusal to grant him planning permission to convert a stable block to offices. The land was in the green belt and an "area of great landscape value". The developer's case was that the conversion would generate three jobs and would benefit the local economy. The inspector identified the main issues as being whether the proposed change of use represented inappropriate development in the green belt and, if so, whether the harm caused by the development would be outweighed by other considerations; and the effect of the development on the character and appearance of the countryside and the living conditions of the occupants of neighbouring properties. He considered the green belt policies in the National Planning Policy Framework as they related to the re-use of existing buildings and concluded that the development was inappropriate because it represented an encroachment of urban-type development into the countryside. He indicated that the limited employment opportunities generated by the development would not clearly outweigh the substantial harm that it would cause. He also found that the development conflicted with policies in the local plan which required development to have no adverse effect on the landscape character and setting of an area of great landscape value and on general or residential amenity. The developer submitted that the inspector had (1) failed to have regard to his duty under the Planning and Compulsory Purchase Act 2004 s.38(6) to determine the application in accordance with the development plan unless material considerations indicated otherwise; (2) failed properly to interpret and apply para.89 of the Framework with respect to the re-use of buildings in the green belt; (3) either failed to have regard to a previous appeal decision relating to the site, or failed to give adequate reasons for departing from it.

Held: Application refused. (1) On a fair reading of the decision letter as a whole, the inspector had found that the development did not accord with the development plan. He properly identified that the development plan comprised the local plan review, and that its relevant policies appeared to be consistent with the main thrust of national policy in the Framework and should be afforded substantial weight. There was no tension between the green belt policies in the Framework and those in the local plan review, and it was clear that if the development was contrary to the policies in the Framework, it would also be contrary to the more restrictive policies in the local plan review. The inspector referred to the relevant local plan policies and found that the development conflicted with them. Most fundamentally, he found that the development was inappropriate development in the green belt because it was an encroachment of urban-type development into the countryside; was not outweighed by the limited number of jobs it created; and was not justified by very special circumstances. Although the NPPF green belt policies post-dated the local plan review, the inspector considered that the local plan policies were consistent with the main thrust of the NPPF policies. Inspectors were not required to include in their decisions express conclusions on whether a proposal accorded with the development plan, or to adopt any particular mantra, *R. (on the application of Hampton Bishop PC) v Herefordshire Council* [2014] EWCA Civ 878, [2015] 1 W.L.R. 2367, [2015] C.L.Y. 2031 followed, *Dartford BC v Secretary of State for Communities and Local Government* [2014] EWHC 2636 (Admin), [2015] 1 P. & C.R. 2, [2015] C.L.Y. 2046 applied, and *Tiviot Way Investments Ltd v Secretary of State for Communities and Local Government* [2015] EWHC 2489 (Admin), [2016] J.P.L. 171, [2016] 1685 considered. The inspector in the instant case had been aware of his s.38(6) obligation and had discharged it by finding implicitly that the proposal was not in accordance with the development plan and that the material considerations did not indicate that planning permission should be granted (see paras 18-25 of judgment). (2) Paragraph 89 of the Framework was irrelevant to the proposal before the inspector. It was not engaged where the development did not involve the construction of a new building. In any event, the inspector explicitly found that the development would be inappropriate because it represented an encroachment of urban-type development into the countryside. Therefore, the exception to inappropriateness set out in para.89 did not apply (para.31). (3) The inspector did not refer to the earlier appeal decision in his decision letter. However, that proposal was significantly different from the one before him. It was in a different, although close, location and comprised the construction of a new dwelling on the site of a barn. An assessment of the impact of a new building in one location was different from an assessment of the effect of a change of use of an existing building in another. The earlier decision was not sufficiently material as to oblige the inspector to deal with it in his decision letter (para.40).

GILL v SECRETARY OF STATE FOR COMMUNITIES AND LOCAL GOVERNMENT, [2015] EWHC 2660 (Admin), [2016] J.P.L. 262, Rhodri Price Lewis QC, QBD (Admin).

1737 Planning permission–Listed buildings–Approach to reasons required by decision-maker in cases involving listed buildings

[Planning (Listed Buildings and Conservation Areas) Act 1990 (c.9) s.66(1)]

The appellant landowner appealed against a decision (*Jones v Mordue* [2015] EWHC 539 (Admin)) quashing the grant of planning permission for the erection of a single wind turbine. The turbine would affect views of listed buildings, including a church. The second respondent secretary of state's inspector had found that the turbine would harm the church's setting, but that the harm would be less than substantial, and that it would have a negligible harmful effect on other buildings. He considered that, whilst the harm to the heritage assets' settings was less than substantial, the proposed development was nevertheless in conflict with local planning policy and the National Planning Policy Framework para.134. He concluded, however, that the harm that would be caused by the development was outweighed by the environmental benefits of the renewable energy scheme, and granted permission. The first respondent, the chairperson of a local group objecting to the turbine, challenged that decision. The judge accepted her contention that the inspector had failed to demonstrate in his reasons that he had referred to and applied the Planning (Listed Buildings and Conservation Areas) Act 1990 s.66(1), which required him to give considerable weight to the desirability of preserving the setting of the church and other listed buildings. The judge considered that he was bound to reach that conclusion by *East Northamptonshire DC v Secretary of State for Communities and Local Government* [2014] EWCA Civ 137, [2015] 1 W.L.R. 45, [2014] C.L.Y. 2388, which he treated as authority for the proposition that the normal burden of proof was reversed in respect of the s.66(1) requirement, so that there was an onus on a decision-maker positively to demonstrate by the reasons given that considerable weight had been given to the desirability of preserving the setting of relevant listed buildings, notwithstanding that that was contrary to the general position on reasons explained in *Save Britain's Heritage v Number 1 Poultry Ltd* [1991] 1 W.L.R. 153, [1991] C.L.Y. 3494 and *South Buckinghamshire DC v Porter (No.2)* [2004] UKHL 33, [2004] 1 W.L.R. 1953, [2004] C.L.Y. 3087. He therefore quashed the grant of planning permission. The appellant contended that the judge had misunderstood the judgment in *East Northants*, and that the inspector had given sufficient reasons for his decision.

Held: Appeal allowed. The decision in *Save Britain's Heritage* was authority regarding the standard of reasons to be expected where a planning decision was taken granting permission for development which had a detrimental impact upon listed buildings: the question which the court had to ask itself whenever a planning decision was challenged on the ground of a failure to give reasons was whether the applicant's interests had been substantially prejudiced by the deficiency of the reasons given, *Save Britain's Heritage* applied. That guidance was followed by the summary of the relevant principles in *South Bucks* that the reasons for a decision had to be intelligible and adequate so as to enable the reader to understand why the matter was decided as it was and what conclusions were reached on the principal important controversial issues, disclosing how any issue of law or fact was resolved; reasons could be briefly stated, the degree of particularity required depending entirely on the nature of the issues falling for decision, *South Bucks* applied (see paras 19-20 of judgment). The judge had read too much into the *East Northants* judgment. Read in context, it was not intended to state an approach to the reasons required to be given by a decision-maker dealing with a case involving application of s.66(1) which was at variance from, and more demanding than, that stated in *Save Britain's Heritage* and *South Bucks*, *East Northants* explained. The relevant standard to be applied in assessing the adequacy of the reasons given in the instant case was indeed the usual approach explained in *Save Britain's Heritage* and *South Bucks* (para.26). Reasons for planning decisions had to be read as a whole in their proper context, and there would inevitably be differences of context, expression and nuance between cases which might be highly relevant. Reading other decision letters (and the judgments in relation to them) could take up considerable time and effort without adding value for the determination of the particular case before the court. The relevant principles in relation to the giving of reasons were well-established and very well known, and it should be sufficient for a judge to be reminded of them and taken to the reasons in the case before him to assess them in light of those principles, without any need for exegetical comparison with reasons given in relation to other planning decisions (para.27). If one applied the correct approach in the present case, as set out in *Save Britain's Heritage* and *South Bucks*, it could not be said that the inspector's reasoning gave rise to any substantial doubt as to whether he had erred in law. On the contrary, his express references to local policy and para.134 of the NPPF were strong indications that he had in fact had the relevant legal duty according to s.66(1) in mind and had complied with it. Paragraph 134 appeared in part of the NPPF which lay down an approach which corresponded with the duty in s.66(1). Generally, a decision-maker who worked through those paragraphs in accordance with their terms would have complied with the s.66(1) duty. The inspector's decision was upheld (paras 28-29).

JONES v MORDUE *sub nom.* MORDUE v SECRETARY OF STATE FOR COMMUNITIES AND LOCAL GOVERNMENT, [2015] EWCA Civ 1243, [2016] 1 W.L.R. 2682, Richards LJ, CA (Civ Div).

1738 Planning permission–Lobbying–Local MP opposed to wind farm–Effect on secretary of state's grant of permission

The claimant sought an order quashing a decision of the first defendant secretary of state upholding the refusal of the second defendant local authority to grant planning permission for a wind farm. Permission had initially been refused in 2011. The application was not finally determined until December 2014, when, after calling in the matter for determination by himself, the secretary of state refused permission. In April 2014, the planning inspector had recommended that permission be granted. He concluded that the renewable electricity generation which would result from the proposal weighed heavily in favour of it. He stated that the matter was finely balanced but that the adverse impacts which he had identified would not significantly and demonstrably outweigh the benefits of the scheme. The secretary of state agreed with the inspector's conclusion that the benefits and disadvantages of the proposal were finely balanced. However, he disagreed with the inspector's overall conclusion, finding that the benefits were not sufficient to outweigh the likely adverse impacts, "in particular the identified harm to the [heritage assets] as well as the character and visual amenity of the area". The local MP (L) had campaigned against onshore wind farms generally. She expressed opposition to the claimant's proposal throughout. Among other things, she wrote a number of letters to both the secretary of state and the chief executive of the Planning Inspectorate. The claimant argued that L's intervention rendered the secretary of state's decision unlawful. Among other things, the secretary of state had failed to inform it of correspondence passing between L, on the one hand, and Eric Pickles, the secretary of state, and Kris Hopkins, the Housing Minister, on the other; further, Mr Hopkins had allowed L to speak with him about the matter in the House of Commons tea room and lobby.

Held: Application refused. Ministers were lobbied by MPs about constituency issues. That took place through correspondence and other avenues. Because ministers were Parliamentarians, MPs used the opportunity to lobby them in person through informal encounters on the Parliamentary estate. That was part of our Parliamentary democracy, and generally there could be no lawful objection to it. Planning was an area where ministers were sometimes the primary decision-maker. There was nothing unlawful in their being lobbied by an MP on a constituency planning matter so long as they acted fairly and consistently with the standards of propriety set by the Planning Inquiries Rules, the Ministerial Code and the planning propriety guidance. In the instant case, the claimant had failed to establish that the ministerial decision against planning permission for its proposed wind farm was unlawful, either through unfairness, bias or a material breach of planning propriety standards. L's letters did not raise any new matters. Moreover, they were not treated by the secretary of state as the basis for his disagreement with the planning inspector. As to the meetings between L and Mr Hopkins in the House of Commons, they were of no consequence; among other things, there was evidence that both parties were aware of the propriety boundaries of what Mr Hopkins could say or do in response to L's lobbying (see paras 39, 42, 48-49 of judgment).

BROADVIEW ENERGY DEVELOPMENTS LTD v SECRETARY OF STATE FOR COMMUNITIES AND LOCAL GOVERNMENT, [2015] EWHC 1743 (Admin), [2015] J.P.L. 1355, Cranston J, QBD (Admin).

1739 Planning permission–Lobbying–Planning decision by secretary of state–Lobbying by parties to planning process or by local MPs

An energy company appealed against a decision that the fact that the local MP had lobbied against its proposed wind farm did not render the refusal of planning permission by the first respondent secretary of state unlawful. Permission had initially been refused in 2011. The application was not finally determined until December 2014, when, after calling in the matter for determination by himself, the secretary of state refused permission. In April 2014, following a public inquiry, the planning inspector had recommended that permission be granted. He concluded that while the matter was finely balanced, the adverse impacts would not significantly outweigh the benefits of the scheme. The secretary of state agreed that the matter was finely balanced but he disagreed with the inspector's overall conclusion. The local MP (L) had campaigned against onshore wind farms generally. She expressed opposition to the company's proposal throughout. Among other things, she wrote to the secretary of state and Kris Hopkins, the Housing Minister to whom the secretary of state had delegated the decision, both before and after the planning inspector's decision. The company had argued that L's intervention rendered the ministerial decision unlawful as the secretary of state had failed to inform it of the correspondence and, further, the correspondence showed that Mr Hopkins had allowed L to speak to him about the matter in the House of Commons tea room and lobby. The judge found that there was nothing unlawful in Ministers being lobbied by an MP on a constituency planning matter so long as they acted fairly and consistently with the standards of propriety set by the Planning Inquiries Rules, the Ministerial Code and the planning propriety guidance. He concluded that the decision was not unlawful, either through unfairness, bias or a material breach of planning propriety standards.

Held: Appeal dismissed. There had been no breach of the Rules. The secretary of state had not differed from the planning inspector on any question of fact material to the inspector's conclusion nor did he take into account any new evidence or fact. L's correspondence had not raised any new matters. The obligation to notify any such difference or new evidence to interested parties and permit fresh representations did not therefore arise. To the extent that the guidance reflected that requirement of the Rules, it was not contravened. However, the guidance also stated that privately made representations should not be entertained unless other parties had been given the chance to consider and comment on them. That was an obvious application of the fundamental principle that a decision-maker must listen to and take into account both sides of an argument. The principle had to be applied sensibly: if representations were merely repetitive of matters already raised at the inquiry there should be no obligation to inform other parties of the contents. The guidance drew no difference between written and oral representations. However, any judge was acutely aware of the difference oral advocacy could make, particularly if it occurred in the absence of the other side. In those circumstances, it was incumbent on a Minister taking a planning decision to make clear to any person who tried to make oral representations to him that he could not listen to them. If the inquiry had concluded, he could add that anything that such persons wanted to say could be put in writing and sent to the Planning Casework Division. L's letter following the tea room conversation asserted that she had made several points to Mr Hopkins and finished by saying that she appreciated he could not comment on individual applications. However, there was no evidence that Mr Hopkins had said that he could not listen to what she was saying. He ought to have done so. The court did not endorse the judge's finding that the lobbying of Ministers by MPs was part and parcel of the representative role of a constituency MP with its implication that such lobbying was permissible even when the Minister was making a quasi-judicial decision in relation to a planning application. However, it was impossible to conclude that the conversation played any part in Mr Hopkins' decision-making process. He did not have to make his decision until nearly a year after the conversation took place. The breach of natural justice in failing to cut off the conversation was at the most a technical breach which could not have made any difference to his ultimate decision. Further, a well-informed observer would not consider that there was a real possibility of bias on the part of Mr Hopkins. Nevertheless, the accusation of bias showed how important the principle was that Ministers who made planning decisions should not allow themselves to be lobbied by parties to the planning process or by local MPs (see paras 25-37 of judgment).

BROADVIEW ENERGY DEVELOPMENTS LTD v SECRETARY OF STATE FOR COMMUNITIES AND LOCAL GOVERNMENT, [2016] EWCA Civ 562, [2016] J.P.L. 1207, Longmore LJ, CA (Civ Div).

1740 Planning permission–Local plans–Inspector giving local policies reduced weight because of age

[Town and Country Planning Act 1990 (c.8) s.70(2); Planning and Compulsory Purchase Act 2004 (c.5) s.38(6)]

The local authority applied to quash a decision of the first defendant secretary of state, by his planning inspector, allowing the second defendant developer's appeal against the refusal of its application for planning permission for 121 dwellings. The proposed site was 7.72 hectares, comprising three fields outside a village. The National Planning Policy Framework para.12 stated that the starting point for decision making was the development plan, and that if a proposed development conflicted with an up-to-date local plan it should be refused unless material considerations indicated otherwise. Under para.14, there was a presumption in favour of sustainable development and, where a development plan was out of date, permission was to be granted unless the adverse impacts of the proposal significantly and demonstrably outweighed the benefits when assessed against the policies in the NPPF as a whole. The local authority refused permission because the proposal was contrary to saved local policies restricting large scale development outside the village, and development in open countryside. The saved policies were seen as dating from 1997 and they were saved in 2007. In his decision allowing the developer's appeal, the inspector held that as the local authority could demonstrate a five-year housing land supply then, under para.49, the presumption in favour of sustainable development did not apply. In reaching his decision, he gave the saved policies "reduced weight" on account of their age and their lack of consistency with para.49. The local authority argued that the planning inspector had failed to determine the application in accordance with the development plan and had misapplied the NPPF.

Held: Application granted. Under the Town and Country Planning Act 1990 s.70(2) and the Planning and Compulsory Purchase Act 2004 s.38(6), a decision maker had to have regard to the provisions of the development unless material considerations indicated otherwise. The NPPF was a material consideration. It was policy, not statute, and did not displace the presumption in favour of the development plan. The inspector's decision demonstrated a series of errors in his approach to the saved policies. He had failed to apply para.215 of the Framework, under which he was required to analyse in what way and to what extent the policies were inconsistent with the NPPF. He then failed to assess the extent to which the policies were consistent with the policies in the NPPF. The local policies were not inconsistent with the NPPF just because they had been adopted years earlier, against the background of a structure plan that had been superseded. The inspector had failed to take account of the differences between para.49 and para.215 and thus fell into error. There were two key differences between para.49 and para.215. The sole focus of para.49 was the supply of deliverable housing sites pursuant to the policy in para.47. In contrast, para.215 had a broader ambit which required assessment of the extent to which the saved policies were consistent with all NPPF policies. The other difference was that para.49 was mechanistic. If the minimum figure was not reached then the policy was automatically out of date. However, para.215 provided that "due weight" should be given to relevant plans according to their degree of consistency with the NPPF. Not only did that require a careful assessment but it also meant that the inspector had to specify the weight which was to be accorded to each policy. Weight was typically addressed as limited, moderate or substantial. The term "reduced" was not sufficiently clear. The inspector had erred in the law in the way he discharged his duty under s.70(2) of the 1990 Act and s.38(6) of the 2004 Act, and in his application of the NPPF (see paras 38-41, 47-52, 56 of judgment).

DAVENTRY DC v SECRETARY OF STATE FOR COMMUNITIES AND LOCAL GOVERNMENT *sub nom.* GLADMAN DEVELOPMENTS LTD v DAVENTRY DISTRICT COUNCIL, [2015] EWHC 3459 (Admin), [2016] J.P.L. 578, Lang J, QBD (Admin).

1741 Planning permission–Material considerations–Applicant's offer to make annual community donation wrongly treated as material consideration

The claimant applied for judicial review of a grant of planning permission by the defendant planning authority to the interested party. The interested party was an energy company which had applied for change of use of agricultural land so as to install a wind turbine. In its application, it expressed an intention to make an annual community donation based on 4% turnover, which would be spent on projects, activities and initiatives for the benefit of the community as determined by a panel of people selected from the community. It provided detail of a similar, already operational, scheme nearby, where the donations had funded socio-economic benefits such as church maintenance, creation of a village handyman service, provision of waterproof clothing to a playgroup, maintenance of village defibrillators and a meals club for older citizens. It was accepted that, in granting planning permission, the offer of the local community donation had been treated as a material consideration in favour of the proposal. It was a condition of the grant of planning permission that the development would be undertaken via a Community Benefit Society to ensure that the benefit was legally guaranteed and properly delivered. The issue was whether it had been lawful for the planning authority to treat the offer of a local community donation as a material consideration when granting planning permission. The claimant submitted that it was not lawful, because the donation was merely financial, did not serve a planning purpose, was not related to land use, and had no real connection with the proposed development.

Held: Application granted. A consideration had to pass the legal test in *Newbury DC v Secretary of State for the Environment* [1981] A.C. 578, [1980] C.L.Y. 2667 before a decision-maker could legitimately take it into account: it had to be for a planning purpose, and be fairly and reasonably related to the proposed development. The starting point was, therefore, to identify the nature of the donation. It involved the provision of a significant sum of money, derived from the operation of the development, which could be used for anything which benefitted the local community. It was an off-site, purely financial, contribution, which did not in any way regulate how the development might operate, and which was not designed to address some impact on social or physical infrastructure, or an adverse land use consequent upon the grant of planning permission. The fact that a Community Benefit Society would be used to deliver the benefit did not alter how the nature of the donation was to be understood. The society would have extremely wide-ranging purposes; it would be able to pay money to any individual, organisation or business for any project, activity or initiative considered to be of community benefit. The interested party's reference to how a comparable community donation had been spent demonstrated that none of the expenditure had been for a planning purpose or fairly and reasonably related to the proposed development. The fact that the National Planning Policy Framework referred to supporting "local strategies to improve health, social and cultural wellbeing for all" and to delivering "sufficient community and cultural facilities and services to meet local needs" could not make a consideration material if, as a matter of law, it was not material. The Framework's objectives had to be met in the context of the lawful regulation of land use; just because a contribution was for community benefit and touched upon issues of health and social and cultural wellbeing did not mean that it would inevitably be a material consideration in development control or forward planning. It was incumbent upon the decision-maker to scrutinise all elements of the proposed development and its package of benefits to establish that each of the benefits passed the legal test of properly amounting to a material consideration, *Newbury*, *R. v Plymouth City Council Ex p. Plymouth and South Devon Cooperative Society* (1994) 67 P. & C.R. 78, [1994] C.L.Y. 4462, *Tesco Stores Ltd v Secretary of State for the Environment* [1995] 1 W.L.R. 759, [1995] C.L.Y. 4784 and *R. (on the application of Sainsbury's Supermarkets Ltd) v Wolverhampton City Council* [2010] UKSC 20, [2011] 1 A.C. 437, [2010] C.L.Y. 2553 applied, *R. (on the application of Welcome Break Group Ltd) v Stroud DC* [2012] EWHC 140 (Admin) considered. In the instant case, the community donation did not pass the *Newbury* test because, being irrelevant to the issues engaged by the exercise of land use planning, it was not an on-site feature of the development designed to make it more attractive. Furthermore, its application was too open-ended (see paras 26, 31-34, 38, 41-42, 47-56 of judgment).

R. (ON THE APPLICATION OF WRIGHT) v FOREST OF DEAN DC, [2016] EWHC 1349 (Admin), [2016] J.P.L. 1235, Dove J, QBD (Admin).

1742 Planning permission–Material considerations–Permission for crematorium on potential habit for protected species–Officer's failure to tell committee about alternative site

[Conservation of Habitats and Species Regulations 2010 (SI 2010/490) reg.41; Directive 92/43 on the conservation of natural habitats and of wild fauna and flora 1992 art.12(1)]

The claimant applied for judicial review of a decision by the local planning authority to grant planning permission for a crematorium. A joint committee of local authorities applied for planning permission for a crematorium on a site north of Aylesbury (the Bierton site). The claimant applied for planning permission for another crematorium in the same area (the Watermead site). It was agreed that the area could not support more than one crematorium. The claimant objected to the Bierton application on the ground that it was not the best site available to meet the identified need, whereas, according to the officer report, the Bierton site had been identified as the most suitable site available. Shortly before the grant of permission, the regional archaeological service advised the local authority that the Bierton site was of potential archaeological significance, requiring archaeological investigations prior to the grant of planning permission. The local authority proposed a planning condition that development would only take place in accordance with a pre-approved written scheme of archaeological investigation. That condition was accepted by the archaeological service and planning permission was granted for the Bierton site. The claimant contended that (1) the officers had wrongly failed to take the planning application back to committee following the contact from the archaeological service; (2) the failure to advise the committee that the Watermead site was available as an alternative to the Bierton site was a material error in the officer report; (3) the officer report had failed to have regard to the fact that the Bierton site was a potential habitat for a European protected species, namely great crested newts.

Held: Application granted. (1) The response from the archaeological service could not reasonably have been anticipated because it had not been a formal consultee to the planning application. Had the archaeological service continued to ask for an investigation prior to determination of the application, that might have amounted to a material consideration. However, since it had conceded that its position could be dealt with by the proposed condition, its response could not tip the balance in relation to the decision whether to grant planning permission. It followed that the final position was such that the response of the archaeological service did not amount to a new material consideration requiring planning permission to be taken back to committee, *R. (on the application of Kides) v South Cambridgeshire DC* [2002] EWCA Civ 1370, [2003] 1 P. & C.R. 19, [2002] C.L.Y. 3662 followed (see paras 42-45 of judgment). (2) To hold that a decision-maker had erred in failing to have regard to alternative sites it was necessary to find some legal principle that compelled, and did not merely empower, him to do so, *Derbyshire Dales DC v Secretary of State for Communities and Local Government* [2009] EWHC 1729 (Admin), [2010] 1 P. & C.R. 19, [2010] C.L.Y. 2595 applied. There was no statutory or policy requirement to that effect in the instant case. Nor was there any conflict with development plan policies, since the local plan had no specific policies dealing with crematoria. Both sites were able to fulfil the identified need for a crematorium in North Aylesbury; it was not the role of the planning system to inhibit competition. There was therefore no material error in the officer report in its advice to members on the consideration of the Bierton application about the relevance of the Watermead site (paras 71-77). (3) Under the Conservation of Habitats and Species Regulations 2010 reg.41(1)(d), it was an offence to destroy or damage the nesting place of a European protected species. However, it was possible to carry out works pursuant to a licence granted by Natural England if there was no satisfactory alternative. Planning permission for a development should normally be granted if it was found acceptable on its planning merits unless it would be likely to offend against Directive 92/43 art.12(1) and would be unlikely to be licensed under the derogation powers, *R. (on the application of Morge) v Hampshire CC* [2011] UKSC 2, [2011] 1 W.L.R. 268, [2011] C.L.Y. 1233 followed, *Cheshire East Council v Secretary of State for Communities and Local Government* [2014] EWHC 3536 (Admin), [2015] Env. L.R. 10, [2015] C.L.Y. 2026 and *R. (on the application of Prideaux) v Buckinghamshire CC* [2013] EWHC 1054 (Admin), [2013] Env. L.R. 32, [2013] C.L.Y. 1158 applied. In the instant case, the officer report on the Bierton application had stated that there were no satisfactory alternatives to the site proposed. However, the existence of the Watermead site, which did not require a derogation, was material to that test and should have been brought to the attention of the committee, which might have decided to defer its decision and seek further information. To close off consideration of the Watermead site significantly misled the members and that error had not been corrected orally. It could not be said that the committee's decision would have been the same if the error had been corrected; therefore, it was not appropriate for the court to exercise its discretion against quashing the permission (paras 78-79, 87, 91-94, 98-99).

R. (ON THE APPLICATION OF WESTERLEIGH GROUP LTD) v AYLESBURY VALE DC, [2015] EWHC 885 (Admin), [2016] Env. L.R. 11, Patterson J, QBD (Admin).

1743 Planning permission–Noise–Grant of permission for conversion of public house into retail and residential units–Noise impact from adjoining nightclub–Whether planning authority taking proper account of material representations about noise and heritage assets

[Town and Country Planning Act 1990 (c.8) s.62(1), s.62(2), s.62(3); Planning (Listed Buildings and Conservation Areas) Act 1990 (c.9) s.66, s.72(1)]

The claimant nightclub operator applied for judicial review of the defendant local authority's grant of planning permission to the interested party authorising the conversion of a public house to retail and residential use. The claimant operated a nightclub and live music space in a Grade II listed building of national importance and special interest which shared a party wall with the relevant site. It was concerned that new residents would complain about noise from its space, which might affect its business. It submitted written representations about heritage issues, and a noise survey from its own consultant. Following the planning officer's report, the local authority's environmental health officer wrote to the senior planning officer, recommending that the report be amended to take into account previous noise complaints about a nightclub across the street, and noting that the local authority's noise survey did not take traffic noise into account. The development control committee resolved to grant planning permission, subject to certain conditions. Subsequently, environmental health officers informed the senior planning officer that the noise conditions were not satisfactory and should be rejected, and suggested new conditions. The local authority later granted planning permission. The claimant submitted that (1) the officer's report had failed to assess the heritage impact of the proposed development; (2) the assessment of noise impact was flawed by the local authority's failure to take into account material representations made by its own environmental health officer; (3) the proposed amended conditions should have been reported back to the committee; (4) the local authority's approach to the conditions was irrational and unlawful; (5) the local authority had breached a procedural requirement under the Town and Country Planning Act 1990 s.62(3) by failing to include heritage and noise assessments contrary to its own requirements for planning applications.

Held: Application granted. (1) The local authority had complied with the Planning (Listed Buildings and Conservation Areas) Act 1990 s.72(1) in that it had paid special attention to the desirability of preserving or enhancing the character or appearance of the area. However, s.66 required a local authority to have special regard to the desirability of preserving the building or its setting and give considerable importance and weight to that factor, *East Northamptonshire DC v Secretary of State for Communities and Local Government* [2014] EWCA Civ 137, [2015] 1 W.L.R. 45, [2014] C.L.Y. 2388 and *R. (on the application of Forge Field Society) v Sevenoaks DC* [2014] EWHC 1895 (Admin), [2015] J.P.L. 22, [2015] C.L.Y. 2018 applied. That material consideration was not brought to the committee's attention in the officer's report, nor had the report assessed the significance of the heritage assets as required. Those were material considerations which had not been considered, and the decision was therefore flawed (see paras 14-15 of judgment). (2) The officer's report had not recorded the environmental health officer's statement that the noise report had to be amended to take into account noise from the other nightclub. That should have been put before the committee. The committee was also not told that an assessment of traffic noise should be made and could be dealt with by condition. The tenor of the officer's report on that subject was not accurate. The overall effect of the report in relation to noise significantly misled the committee about material matters which were left uncorrected before the planning decision was taken (para.26). (3) The conditions suggested after the committee's resolution were entirely different in character from what had been approved. There was nothing in the resolution or any other document permitting officers to reword the conditions. If the officers had wished to remove or amend the conditions they were under a duty to return to the committee to have that done,*R. (on the application of Kides) v South Cambridgeshire DC* [2002] EWCA Civ 1370, [2003] 1 P. & C.R. 19, [2002] C.L.Y. 3662 considered. The officers had no power to redraft the conditions and, in any event, the conditions as approved were regarded by the environmental health officers as wholly inadequate, and the application should have been referred back to the committee (paras 35, 37-40). (4) An applicant alleging that an inspector had reached a Wednesbury unreasonable conclusion on matters of planning judgment faced a particularly daunting task, *R. (on the application of Newsmith Stainless Ltd) v Secretary of State for the Environment, Transport and the Regions* [2001] EWHC Admin 74 considered. The noise consultant's report said that the conditions could not possibly fulfil the aims they sought to achieve. The local authority had provided no evidence to refute his points. A brief witness statement explaining why it had taken issue with the report's conclusions might have been sufficient, but the court was left with a detailed report alleging irrationality and nothing of real substance to begin to counteract it (paras 42-43). (5) Under s.62(3), a local planning authority might require an application for planning permission to include such evidence in support of anything or relating to the application as it thought necessary. However, s.62(1) and s.62(2) affected the natural construction of s.62(3). They used the word "provision" as a term of art, and the local authority's requirement for an applicant to include heritage and noise assessments was not a "provision" made under s.62(3) as it was not a document made under a development order which, under s.62(1), might make "provision" as to applications for planning permission. The final ground failed (paras 44-46).

OBAR CAMDEN LTD v CAMDEN LBC, [2015] EWHC 2475 (Admin), [2015] L.L.R. 782, Stewart J, QBD (Admin).

1744 Planning permission–Noise–Mixed commercial and residential development–Suitability of conditions to protect future residents from noise from music venue

The claimant sought to quash planning permission granted to the third defendant developer by the first defendant secretary of state's inspector. The developer had applied for permission to demolish a single-storey building, formerly used as a nightclub, and erecting a three-storey building with commercial uses on the ground floor and flats above. The claimant, who owned the neighbouring tavern, objected to the proposed development on the basis that residents of the new dwellings might complain about the noise from the tavern's use as a public house and for live music, film-making and other activities. The second defendant local authority refused planning permission on the basis that the development's future residents would be detrimentally affected by reason of general disturbance and significant noise from the tavern. The developer appealed, submitting an expert acoustic assessment review and report which concluded that planning approval should not be rejected on the basis of noise. It stated that external patron noise was not considered problematic to existing local residents, and that internal noise levels could be effectively controlled with the provision of high specification glazing and specific construction methods. The claimant was refused further time to procure her own expert's report to counter that assessment. The inspector identified the main issue in the appeal as being whether the proposed scheme's future residents would be subjected to unreasonable levels of noise. He concluded that, with suitable conditions, they could be protected from noise generated locally. He therefore granted planning permission, subject to the condition that construction works should not begin until a scheme for protecting future residents from noise had been approved by the local authority. The resulting condition required the local authority to carry out testing so as to be satisfied that suitable sound insulation had been achieved before the new building could be occupied. The claimant contended that (1) the inspector had wrongfully regarded himself as bound to accept the acoustic report's conclusions, and should have formed his own judgment on the likely effects of noise generated by and associated with the tavern's use on the development's future residents; (2) she had been unfairly denied the opportunity to present her own acoustic report, and the appeal had wrongly proceeded on the basis that the conclusions in the developer's report were uncontentious; (3) the planning condition imposed was not an effective and enforceable means of ensuring that adequate sound insulation would be put in place in the new building; (4) even if the condition was effective, the inspector had failed to have regard to the potential harm to the operation of the tavern as an established business, since there was no guarantee that future residents would not complain about noise coming from the tavern, which might lead to an abatement notice being served, the revocation of the tavern's late night music licence, or an injunction being granted to prevent a private nuisance.

Held: Judgment for defendants. (1) There was nothing in the inspector's decision suggesting that he had regarded himself as bound by the acoustics report. He was entitled to have regard to the expert assessment and conclusions in that report, and he plainly did so. At no stage had he said, or implied, that he regarded the report as relieving him of the task of applying his own judgment to the noise-related issues that he had to deal with. The inspector had exercised his own judgment on the noise-related issues, having had regard to all of the relevant evidence before him, and the reasons for his conclusion were intelligible and adequate (see paras 38, 40, 49 of judgment). (2) There was no unfairness in the planning inspectorate adhering to its normal and well-advertised procedure in written representations appeals when it had refused the claimant's request for further time to procure an expert's report to counter the developer's expert's assessment and conclusions. When an assertion of procedural unfairness in a planning appeal was made, the court had to consider whether the party complaining of procedural unfairness had been aware of the case that he had to meet and had had a reasonable opportunity to bring before the decision-maker evidence in response to that case and to make any submissions relevant to it, *Hopkins Developments Ltd v Secretary of State for Communities and Local Government* [2014] EWCA Civ 470, [2014] P.T.S.R. 1145, [2014] C.L.Y. 2411 followed. It was impossible to conclude that the claimant was unaware of the case she had to meet, either in so far as it related to noise or generally, or that she was denied a reasonable opportunity to bring forward evidence of her own and make such submissions as she wished to make on the matters of concern to her (paras 54, 56). (3) The planning condition was not legally flawed or in any way inadequate to achieve the purpose the inspector had had in mind for it. Its effect was that the development could not be lawfully occupied until the protective scheme had been approved, implemented, and tested to the local authority's satisfaction (paras 69, 72-73). (4) The inspector had grasped the true nature of the claimant's objection to the proposed development, namely its possible effect on her business. That was, in effect, the central question in the appeal and the inspector had tackled it fully, having made all of the necessary planning judgments on the specific issues arising from the claimant's objection (paras 77-79).

FORSTER v SECRETARY OF STATE FOR COMMUNITIES AND LOCAL GOVERNMENT, [2015] EWHC 2367 (Admin), [2015] L.L.R. 677, Lindblom J, QBD (Admin).

1745 Planning permission–Planning conditions–Sidestepping of conditions–Wind turbines

A local resident applied for judicial review of two decisions by the local authority to grant planning permission to the interested party for the installation of a wind turbine. Permission was first granted in September 2014, and then again in January 2015. Both decisions permitted the installation of a single turbine of specified dimensions. Because the intended access route during the construction phase involved narrow country lanes with high-sided embankments, trees and hedgerows, a number of habitat, ecological, bird and tree surveys had been conducted and an "abnormal access route" report had been obtained. That report identified a number of points where the highway would have to be modified, subject to ecological mitigation and compensation measures. There was initially some doubt about whether the modifications required at point 14 related to land that was owned by the local authority or by a neighbouring landowner. To the extent that the neighbouring landowner's land was involved, he refused to consent to any modifications, and the route was revised so as to avoid point 14. The latest evidence was, however, that all the required modification areas were within the control of either the developer or the highway authority. A screening opinion concluded that an environmental impact assessment was unnecessary because no significant environmental impacts were anticipated and all possible impacts could be assessed within the planning application process. Before granting permission, the planning committee had a site visit, considered the planning officer's report and heard oral representations. Twenty nine conditions were attached to the first permission. Condition 21 specified particular dimensions for the turbine, "unless given the written approval of the local planning authority". Condition 24 required that "prior to the commencement of the development" there should be a trial run of the abnormal loads and that, thereafter, proposals for any highway improvements were to be submitted to the local planning authority for approval. The resident argued that (1) the "unless" clause in condition 21 allowed safeguards about the turbine's dimensions to be sidestepped; (2) condition 24 was unlawful in that it was a positively-worded condition requiring works to be carried out on land that was not within the local authority's control; (3) there was an error in the screening opinion that was only rectified as a result of his having brought the instant proceedings, and that the opinion should therefore be declared unlawful; (4) the local authority misinterpreted and misapplied policy UT6 of its urban development plan, which provided that permission would be granted for wind turbines provided that they did not cause demonstrable harm to the amenity of any residents; (5) permission should have been refused because the neighbouring landowner had refused to consent to the modifications; (6) the local authority had breached its statutory duty to conserve biodiversity by failing to conduct adequate ecological assessments of the alternative route.

Held: Application granted in part. (1) Condition 21 was central to the permission, and all parties acknowledged that the turbine's dimensions were significant in terms of its environmental impact. The "unless" clause allowed the local authority to approve variations that could result in a turbine whose scale and impact were greater than those for which permission had been granted. The permission had been the subject of public debate and democratic decision-making, and it would be wrong if the safeguards in condition 21 could be side-stepped. The "unless clause" therefore had to be severed from condition 21, *R. (on the application of Midcounties Co-operative Ltd) v Wyre Forest DC* [2009] EWHC 964 (Admin) applied (see paras 33-35 of judgment). (2) The argument about condition 24 was based in part on the faulty premise that the modifications would involve third-party land. The latest evidence was that they would not. Moreover, on a benevolent construction, the words "prior to the commencement of the development" could mean that all the requirements in condition 24 had to be performed before the commencement of the development, *Hulme v Secretary of State for Communities and Local Government* [2011] EWCA Civ 638, [2011] N.P.C. 55 applied (paras 38-39). (3) The resident's screening opinion argument revealed him to be under a misconception about the nature of judicial review. If, as a result of the proceedings, the decision-maker corrected an error in the opinion, that was the end of it and the matter was relevant only to costs. In any event, the first screening opinion was not unlawful and had applied the correct test in concluding that an environmental impact assessment was unnecessary. The assessment of likely significant effects did not involve a detailed assessment of the factors relevant to the grant of planning permission, and nor did it require all considerations to be mentioned, *R. (on the application of Bateman) v South Cambridgeshire DC* [2011] EWCA Civ 157, [2011] N.P.C. 22 followed and *R. (on the application of Plant) v Pembrokeshire CC* [2014] EWHC 1040 (Admin), [2015] Env. L.R. D4 applied (paras 40-44). (4) Policy UT6 was straightforward, requiring demonstrable harm to residential amenity. The committee had been told that, and it had made its decision after a site visit. The policy had not been misunderstood and the committee had not been misled (paras 45-47). (5) The best available evidence was that any work during the construction phase would not affect the neighbouring land (paras 49-51). (6) The committee knew of the alternative route, had had professional advice about its ecological implications, and had been told that a further ecological assessment was unnecessary. Therefore, it had no duty of inquiry (paras 52-53).

R. (ON THE APPLICATION OF HUBERT) v CARMARTHENSHIRE CC *sub nom.* HUBERT v CARMARTHENSHIRE CC, [2015] EWHC 2327 (Admin), [2016] P.T.S.R. 162, Cranston J, QBD (Admin).

1746 Planning permission–Power to decline to determine–Site subject to enforcement notice–Permission relating to development constituting the planning breach–Power under s.70C Town and Country Planning Act 1990

[Town and Country Planning Act 1990 (c.8) s.70C; Localism Act 2011 (Commencement No. 4 and Transitional, Transitory and Saving Provisions) Order 2012 (SI 2012/628) art.13(1), art.13(1)(a), art.13(1)(b); European Convention on Human Rights 1950 art.8, art.8(1)]

The claimant Irish traveller applied for judicial review of the defendant local authority's refusal to determine her application for planning permission for a change of use of a site to a gypsy and traveller pitch. The claimant and her family had stationed caravans on the site without obtaining planning permission. In 2005, the local authority served an enforcement notice requiring residential use of the site to cease. The claimant's husband appealed against the notice, but subsequently withdrew the appeal. The enforcement notice came into force but was not complied with. In 2006, the husband applied for planning permission for a change of use. That was refused in 2007 and the husband appealed. An inspector dismissed the appeal in 2008. In 2012, the claimant applied for planning permission for a change of use. That was refused, and in 2014 an inspector upheld that decision. A third application for planning permission was made in 2015. The local authority declined to determine it under the Town and Country Planning Act 1990 s.70C on the basis that the site was subject to a pre-existing enforcement notice and the permission related to development constituting the breach of planning control. The legislation conferring the s.70C power came into effect on 6 April 2012 and applied to planning applications made on or after that date, subject to certain saving provisions, including those under the Localism Act 2011 (Commencement No. 4 and Transitional, Transitory and Saving Provisions) Order 2012 art.13(1). The claimant contended that (1) her case fell within the art.13(1) saving provisions since there had been an appeal against the enforcement notice before 6 April 2012, pursuant to art.13(1)(a), and, under art.13(1)(b), an application for planning permission for the land subject to the notice had been made after the notice was issued; (2) the impact of s.70C amounted to an unjustified interference with her rights under the ECHR art.8.

Held: Application refused. (1) The saving provisions in art.13(1) only applied if both the enforcement notice had been served before 6 April 2012 and the relevant requirement in art.13(1)(a) or art.13(1)(b) was also satisfied before that date. Accordingly, an enforcement notice had to have been issued before 6 April 2012 and an application for planning permission had to have been made after the issue of the notice but before 6 April 2012. The reason for introducing the s.70C power was to ensure that an applicant could not insist on having two separate considerations of a site's underlying planning merits. The wording and purpose of s.70C applied to the instant case. The local authority had issued an enforcement notice determining that the stationing of caravans on the site for residential use constituted a breach of planning control. The claimant was able to insist on only one consideration of the underlying planning merits, and that was to be done by appealing against the enforcement notice. The local authority was not obliged to determine a subsequent application for planning permission. Whilst an enforcement notice had been served before 6 April 2012, the application for planning permission had not been made until 2015: the claimant's case did not, therefore, fall within art.13(1)(b). In relation to art.13(1)(a), an enforcement notice needed to have been served before 6 April 2012 and an appeal, lodged before that date, had to have been in existence on that date for that saving provision to apply. Since the husband's appeal against the enforcement notice had been withdrawn, there had been no appeal in existence within art.13(1)(a). The claimant's case did not fall within the saving provisions of art.13(1) (see paras 27, 41, 44, 55-60, 70-71 of judgment). (2) The claimant had not advanced any reasons why s.70C involved any infringement within the meaning of art.8(1) of the Convention (para.64).

R. (ON THE APPLICATION OF O'BRIEN) v SOUTH CAMBRIDGESHIRE DC, [2016] EWHC 36 (Admin), [2016] J.P.L. 656, Lewis J, QBD (Admin).

1747 **Planning permission–Residential development–Adverse effect of nitrogen emissions on protected heathland–Lack of evidence that developer would mitigate effect**

[Conservation of Habitats and Species Regulations 2010 (SI 2010/490) reg.61, reg.61(5)]

The claimant local authority applied to quash the first defendant secretary of state's decision, by his planning inspector, to grant the second defendant developer planning permission for housing and associated development in an area of natural beauty (AONB). The local authority had refused planning permission in 2013, concluding that the development would have an adverse effect on the integrity of special areas of conservation within Ashdown Forest, the edge of which was 2.4km from the proposed site. It was common ground that parts of the forest were covered by the Conservation of Habitats and Species Regulations 2010 due to the presence of extensive areas of lowland heath. The developer had agreed to pay Strategic Access Management and Monitoring Strategy (SAMMS) contributions and a heathland management contribution. On appeal, the inspector found that nitrogen emissions from vehicle exhausts would have an adverse effect on the forest, but that the developer's contributions to habitat management would outweigh any harm from nitrogen deposits. He further found that, applying National Planning Policy Framework para.116, there were exceptional circumstances in the public interest why planning permission should be granted and that alternative sites proposed by the local authority were not realisable alternatives. The issues were whether the inspector had erred in (1) concluding under the Conservation of Habitats and Species Regulations 2010 reg.61 that the proposals would have no significant effect on the special areas of conservation; (2) his consideration of NPPF para.116 when concluding that there were no alternative sites to meet the need for the proposed development.

Held: Application granted. (1) Under reg.61(5), a local authority could only agree to a development after having ascertained to a high standard of investigation that it would not adversely affect the integrity of the protected site, *R. (on the application of Champion) v North Norfolk DC* [2015] UKSC 52, [2015] 1 W.L.R. 3710, [2015] C.L.Y. 2027 followed. The inspector had made a mistake in finding that heathland management would mitigate nitrogen deposits as part of the agreed SAMMS projects funded by the developer's contributions. There was clear evidence that the SAMMS projects would be directed at mitigating the potential harm to the forest and the protected bird species as a result of increased recreational use of the forest by residents of the proposed development, but there was no suggestion that it would be directed at reducing nitrogen deposits. The local authority had informed the inspector that no formal agreement had been reached on that issue. Further, the inspector's conclusion on the nitrogen issue had been reached without giving any proper consideration to the local authority's evidence which raised a number of concerns about heathland management as a means of mitigation. His finding that the proposed development was not likely to have significant effects on the special areas of conservation was unlawful by reason of his flawed decision-making process. He could only properly exclude the risk of significant effects in reliance upon mitigating proposals if he was sure, on the basis of objective information, that there would be no significant harmful effects, *Smyth v Secretary of State for Communities and Local Government* [2015] EWCA Civ 174, [2015] P.T.S.R. 1417, [2016] 1759 followed. The inspector had failed to meet the requirements of lawful decision making, *Secretary of State for Education and Science v Tameside MBC* [1977] A.C. 1014, [1976] C.L.Y. 829 followed (see paras 31, 34, 47-48, 56, 59, 62-63, 77 of judgment). The evidence was too uncertain to say that an inspector properly directing himself on the evidence would have reached the same decision in any event, bearing in mind the importance of the special areas of conservation and the legal requirements of the Regulations. The local authority was undertaking a further, ongoing investigation of the impacts of nitrogen deposition in the forest. It would be wrong to conclude that the inspector's conclusions were correct when a much more comprehensive review was underway (paras 79, 85-56). (2) On the issue of need, the inspector was not required to specify the objectively-assessed housing need, or the affordable housing need, in precise figures. For the purposes of NPPF 116, it was sufficient for him to assess and record the need in broad terms, which he had done. However, the inspector had not adequately investigated or assessed whether the development could be located at an alternative site, and so had not properly applied NPPF 116. Given the high level of protection afforded to AONBs under national planning policy, that was a significant failure. It was possible that a suitable alternative site might be identified, which could alter the overall judgment made on whether the presumption against development ought properly to be rebutted in respects of the development. The inspector's decision was quashed (paras 112, 121, 123).

WEALDEN DC v SECRETARY OF STATE FOR COMMUNITIES AND LOCAL GOVERNMENT, [2016] EWHC 247 (Admin), [2016] Env. L.R. 19, Lang J, QBD (Admin).

1748 **Planning permission–Residential development–Proposals for development plan affecting appeal site**

[Town and Country Planning Act 1990 (c.8) s.78]

A local planning authority applied to quash a decision of the secretary of state, by his planning inspector, allowing an appeal under the Town and Country Planning Act 1990 s.78 against the refusal of outline planning permission for a residential development. The appeal site was on the edge of a large village. Permission for the proposed development was refused on the grounds that the site was not allocated for development on the statutory development plan and that the proposed development would extend into the adjacent countryside, contrary to the existing local plan. The local authority had decided to abandon the Site Allocations Development Plan Document (DPD) and had begun the process of preparing a local plan for the period to 2031. An appeal was brought before the planning inspector, who held that there was a policy vacuum on the issue of site allocations in the larger villages and that the development plan was silent on the question of the allocation of dwellings in such villages. She also stated that she did not need to consider whether the relevant policies for the supply of housing should be considered up to date. The local authority argued that the inspector had (1) failed properly to apply the National Planning Policy Framework para.14, which provided for a presumption in favour of sustainable development where the development plan was absent or silent or relevant policies were out of date; (2) failed to take into account a material consideration, namely the harm that would be caused by making a decision in advance of the new plan coming forward.

Held: Application refused. (1) In addition to the matters of first principle set out by Lindblom J. in *Bloor Homes East Midlands Ltd v Secretary of State for Communities and Local Government* [2014] EWHC 754 (Admin), a planning inspector conducting an appeal had to determine a proposal in accordance with the development plan unless material considerations indicated otherwise. The inspector also had to apply national policy unless he or she gave reasons for not doing so. If it was shown that the decision-maker had had regard to an immaterial consideration or failed to have regard to a material one, the decision would be quashed unless the court was satisfied that the decision would necessarily have been the same, *Simplex GE (Holdings) Ltd v Secretary of State for the Environment* (1989) 57 P. & C.R. 306, [1989] C.L.Y. 3578 followed. As a statement of government policy, the NPPF was a material consideration and was therefore relevant to the determination of an appeal, *Secretary of State for Communities and Local Government v Hopkins Homes Ltd* [2016] EWCA Civ 168, [2016] P.T.S.R. 1315, [2016] 1706 followed. The policies in para.14 and para.49 of the NPPF did not make out-of-date policies for the supply of housing irrelevant in the determination of a planning application or appeal, nor did they prescribe how much weight should be given to such policies in the decision, *Hopkins* followed. A qualitative planning judgment had to be made at the time the decision was made. In the case of the development plan in issue, the mechanism by which its housing requirement figures were intended to be translated into actual allocations was the DPD, which the local authority had abandoned. There was no distinction to be drawn between an argument that the policies in the development plan were silent because there was no DPD and the argument that the plan was out of date because there was no DPD. It was held in *Bloor* that "silent" within para.14 meant an absence of relevant policy. Accordingly, the inspector had determined that there was no body of policy sufficient to enable the development to be judged acceptable, that being a planning judgment that was open to her to make, *Bloor* applied. In any event, it was plain that the relevant policies in the development plan were out of date, given the abandonment of the mechanism by which the sites were to be allocated (see paras 85-101 of judgment). (2) The planning code of the Act permitted development to occur following a grant of permission on sites which were not allocated in the development plan. There was nothing in the Act which gave any particular status to emerging plans in development control. The NPPF emphasised the importance of planning being "genuinely plan led" but also encouraged the grant of permission to sustainable housing development. It followed that there were often cases where a planning application had to be considered in a location where there were proposals to bring forward a plan. Whether the approval of the application would cause harm to the process of development plan preparation was then a matter of planning judgment for the decision-maker. In the instant case, allocated development sites were not coming forward in a timely manner because the local authority had abandoned the mechanism for doing so. The inspector had concluded that any harm to the plan-led system was overridden by the silence of the development plan on the issue of allocations in the larger villages. In so concluding, she had done no more than state the effect of para.14 of the NPPF (paras 108-110).

SOUTH OXFORDSHIRE DC v SECRETARY OF STATE FOR COMMUNITIES AND LOCAL GOVERNMENT, [2016] EWHC 1173 (Admin), [2016] J.P.L. 1106, Gilbart J, QBD (Admin).

1749 Planning permission–Solar power–Statements of community involvement–Existence of legitimate expectation of neighbour notification

[Civil Procedure Rules 1998 Pt 54; Senior Courts Act 1981 (c.54) s.31(6); Town and Country Planning (Development Management Procedure) (England) Order 2010 (SI 2010/2184) art.13]

The local authority and two linked renewable energy companies appealed against a decision (*Gerber v Wiltshire Council* [2015] EWHC 524 (Admin), [2015] Env. L.R. 33, [2015] C.L.Y. 2044) quashing planning permission for a solar farm built on agricultural land. Planning permission was granted under delegated powers for the 22 hectare site in June 2013. The owner of a nearby Grade II* listed building did not see the planning notices and only became aware of the installation when work started. He immediately contacted the local authority on 19 March 2014 but did not apply for judicial review until October 2014. The solar farm was completed in June 2014. It was common ground that the companies would have to spend £1.5 million in dismantling the panels and restoring the land, and would lose expenditure of £10.5 million. The appellants submitted that that the judge had erred (1) in holding that the local authority had created a legitimate expectation of neighbour notification by reason of its Statement of Community Involvement (SCI); (2) in his assessment of the significance of the delay by the owner in commencing his claim under both CPR Pt 54 and the Senior Courts Act 1981 s.31(6); (3) in the exercise of his discretion to quash the planning permission.

Held: Appeal allowed. (1) The SCI did not contain an unambiguous promise that any neighbour would be consulted about the application for planning permission. The judge had been wrong to run together para.5.6 of the SCI with its Appendix 1. Paragraph 5.6 was limited to properties adjoining the development site rather than neighbouring properties such as that of the householder. There had been no breach of his legitimate expectation (see paras 40-44 of judgment).(2) The judge's error regarding legitimate expectation had affected the exercise of his discretion to extend time to bring the claim. The householder had no reasonable explanation for his lengthy delay in bringing judicial review proceedings. In the light of a developer's detrimental reliance on permission, it was incumbent on an objector to bring proceedings without delay. Proper notice of the application for planning permission had been given pursuant to the Town and Country Planning (Development Management Procedure) (England) Order 2010 art.13 and it was inappropriate to extend time for bringing a legal challenge simply because an objector did not notice what was happening, or because of reliance on incorrect legal advice, *Finn-Kelcey v Milton Keynes BC* [2008] EWCA Civ 1067, [2009] Env. L.R. 17, [2009] C.L.Y. 3033 applied (paras 45-49, 52-56).(3) Even if time were to be extended, the judge's exercise of his discretion under s.31(6) of the 1981 Act was also flawed. Given the long delay for which there was no good excuse; the major financial detriment which would be suffered by the companies; the lesser harm to the householder's amenity; the balance of factors affecting good administration, including the importance of renewable energy in the national interest, and the need for certainty and finality, his order quashing the planning permission had to be set aside.

GERBER v WILTSHIRE COUNCIL *sub nom.* R. (ON THE APPLICATION OF GERBER) v WILTSHIRE COUNCIL, [2016] EWCA Civ 84, [2016] 1 W.L.R. 2593, Lord Dyson MR, CA (Civ Div).

1750 Planning permission–Special Protection Areas–Environmental impact assessments–Series of development projects close to special protection areas–Timing of environmental impact assessment

[Directive 92/43 on the conservation of natural habitats and of wild fauna and flora 1992 art.6(3)]

An environmental group appealed against the refusal (*Forest of Dean Friends of the Earth v Forest of Dean DC* [2014] EWHC 1353 (Admin)) of its challenge to a grant of outline planning permission by the respondent local authority for the development of two sites within the Forest of Dean. The planning permission was for housing and mixed business development. It was envisaged that the two sites would be connected by a spine road, for which planning permission had been granted as part of a separate development (the Northern Quarter). Each site had access to the existing highway network without any need for the spine road. The area was home to a large proportion of the total population of lesser horseshoe bats in England and Wales. The appellant thought that the spine road would disrupt the bats' flight paths. The main issue was whether the local authority had properly complied with its duty under Directive 92/43 art.6(3) to assess the impact of the proposed development on the Special Protection Areas. A judge found that the local authority had discharged its duties. The appellant argued that the local authority had not discharged its duties because, as the development of the two sites, when combined with development of the spine road, was likely to have a significant effect on the Special Protection Area, it should have performed an appropriate assessment, and had failed to do so.

Held: Appeal dismissed. An assessment under art.6(3) would be required if a particular development proposal might be detrimental to a protected site. In such situations, a strict precautionary approach was required, including assessment of any "in-combination" effects. However, where a series of development projects was contemplated, the strict precautionary approach would be complied with if the first project would not, by itself, have a detrimental impact on a protected site, and if there would be future opportunity to consider measures arising from a later project, so as to identify any "in-combination" effects of the two together, *Smyth v Secretary of State for Communities and Local Government* [2015] EWCA Civ 174, [2015] P.T.S.R. 1417, [2016] 1759 applied and *Commission of the European Communities v United Kingdom (C-6/04)* [2005] E.C.R. I-9017 considered. The latter case did not require a full environmental assessment of all projects to be undertaken when planning permission for the first project was sought; a staged approach was lawful. In the instant case, the development of the two sites was independent of the construction of the spine road. By themselves, the sites would have no significant effect on the Special Protection Area, nor were they likely to have an adverse effect when viewed in combination with any other plan or project. A separate legal challenge to development of the Northern Quarter had been dismissed. The grant of the instant planning permission created no presumption, and added no force to any contention, that planning permission should be granted for the spine road (see paras 10-19, 23 of judgment).

R. (ON THE APPLICATION OF FOREST OF DEAN (FRIENDS OF THE EARTH)) v FOREST OF DEAN DC, [2015] EWCA Civ 683, [2015] P.T.S.R. 1460, Longmore LJ, CA (Civ Div).

1751 Planning permission–Sustainable development–Presumption in para.14 National Planning Policy Framework in favour of sustainable development

The claimant local authority sought to quash a decision of the first defendant secretary of state, by his inspector, to grant the second defendant developer outline planning permission for up to 60 dwellings. The local authority had refused planning permission on the ground that it constituted unsustainable development on land allocated as open countryside. The developer appealed. The local authority conceded that its local plan was effectively out-of-date since it lacked a five-year supply of housing land. Under the National Planning Policy Framework para.14, where a development plan was out-of-date there was a presumption in favour of granting planning permission for sustainable development unless its adverse impacts would significantly and demonstrably outweigh its benefits when assessed against the NPPF's policies taken as a whole. The inspector considered that the main issue was whether the proposal amounted to sustainable development within para.14. He found that the adverse impacts of the proposed development would not significantly and demonstrably outweigh its benefits, namely its contribution to meeting unmet need for market and affordable housing arising from the lack of an adequate housing supply and the very limited harm that it would cause. He concluded that the proposal had therefore to be regarded as sustainable development to which the para.14 presumption applied, and granted outline permission. The local authority contended that para.14 had been designed to create an enhanced presumption in favour of development which had already been assessed to be sustainable, and to allow para.14 to define that question was illogical and amounted to an error of law.

Held: Judgment for defendants. The NPPF gave guidance to decision-makers, and the guidance given in para.14 was that a proposal should be approved as sustainable development unless its adverse impacts clearly and significantly outweighed its benefits. Another way of putting the matter was that the scales, or the balance, was weighted, loaded or tilted in favour of the proposal. That was what the presumption in favour of sustainable development meant: it was a rebuttable presumption, yielding only in the face of significant and demonstrable adverse impacts. In practice, there would be questions of fact and degree. If, for example, the planning advantages were assessed to be non-existent, the presumption was likely to be easily displaced. The stronger the planning benefits were assessed to be, the more tenaciously the presumption would operate and the harder it would be to displace. There was no question of assessing whether the proposal amounted to sustainable development before applying the presumption within para.14. That was not what para.14 said, and would be unworkable. Rather, para.14 taught decision-makers how to decide whether the proposal, if approved, would constitute sustainable development (see paras 20-23 of judgment). The instant court disagreed with the decision in *William Davis Ltd v Secretary of State for Communities and Local Government* [2013] EWHC 3058 (Admin) to the effect that determining the issue of sustainable development was a matter anterior to, or at least independent from, para.14 of the NPPF, *William Davis* doubted, *Dartford BC v Secretary of State for Communities and Local Government* [2014] EWHC 2636 (Admin), [2015] 1 P. & C.R. 2, [2015] C.L.Y. 2046 considered (paras 33-37). Having found that the adverse impacts of the proposed development would not, in his view, significantly and demonstrably outweigh the benefits, the inspector had been entitled to find that it amounted to sustainable development to which the para.14 presumption applied. Even if the assessment of the proposal's sustainability should have been carried out independently from para.14, and the tilted balance contained within it, the preponderance of planning considerations would have favoured the development (paras 40-41).

CHESHIRE EAST BC v SECRETARY OF STATE FOR COMMUNITIES AND LOCAL GOVERNMENT, [2016] EWHC 571 (Admin), [2016] P.T.S.R. 1052, Jay J, QBD (Admin).

1752 Planning permission–Waste treatment sites–Facility for recycling incinerator bottom ash

The claimant applied for judicial review of the defendant local authority's decision to grant the interested party planning permission for a facility for recycling incinerator bottom ash (IBA). The interested party intended to process IBA produced from an incinerator at a nearby energy recovery facility. The recycling process would produce incinerator bottom ash aggregates for use in road construction. An environmental statement accompanying the planning application provided that the IBA to be stored and processed at its site would be non-hazardous, and Natural Resources Wales (NRW) had granted a permit to carry out the recycling operation at the site on that basis. A detailed "dust assessment" provided that the impact of dust arising from the stored IBA would be negligible. The planning officer's report stated that the proposal complied with the general principles of waste strategy set out in the national documents by recycling 100% of the IBA produced by the local incinerator, which was classified as a non-hazardous waste material that would otherwise be sent to landfill, to produce a usable secondary aggregate product that could reduce the need for quarried stock material for aggregate and cement production. The local authority accepted the report's recommendation and granted permission. The claimant contended, inter alia, that whilst most IBA was likely to be classified as non-hazardous, if it was found to possess a hazardous property it would be categorised as hazardous waste, and the statement in the officer's report that IBA was classified as non-hazardous was therefore misleading and amounted to a fatal flaw in the decision-making process. It submitted that the local authority had also failed to take into account risks to human health even where IBA was classified as non-hazardous, and the officer's report had not dealt with health questions. It argued that there was also inadequate, and therefore unlawful, consultation with Public Health Wales (PHW) and an unlawful failure to consider consulting, and then to consult, the local health board.

Held: Application refused. (1) Rather than referring to the properties of IBA in general, the planning officer was referring to the particular IBA that was going to be brought to the interested party's site, stored at that site, and subjected to the recycling process at that site. Accordingly, the officer's report was not misleading: it reflected, as the planning committee would have known that it reflected, the specific proposal for that particular site. Moreover, the fact that the IBA brought to, stored and used on that site was non-hazardous, was reflected in the NRW permit which made plain that hazardous waste, including hazardous IBA, should not be accepted. Planning officers' reports were addressed to a knowledgeable readership and the adequacy of their reasoning had to be considered against that background; the courts should not impose too demanding a standard on officers' reports, otherwise their whole purpose would be defeated, *R. v Mendip DC Ex p. Fabre* (2000) 80 P. & C.R. 500, [2000] C.L.Y. 4508 and *R. (on the application of Hayes) v Wychavon DC* [2014] EWHC 1987 (Admin), [2015] J.P.L. 62, [2015] C.L.Y. 2012 applied, *R. (on the application of Morge) v Hampshire CC* [2011] UKSC 2, [2011] 1 W.L.R. 268, [2011] C.L.Y. 1233 followed. It would be excessively legalistic, and would ignore the knowledgeable readers to whom the report was addressed, to say that the planning officer should instead have said that IBA was generally classified as non-hazardous, but might sometimes be classified as hazardous. The local authority's planning committee had known that, although IBA could theoretically be classified as hazardous, that was not a matter with which they needed to concern themselves, given that the interested party was only entitled, by the express terms of the permit, to bring non-hazardous IBA onto the site. The local authority was entitled to rely on NRW's regulation of the site (see paras 32-34, 42-47 of judgment). (2) Taking into account all of the information available to the planning committee, there was no solid evidential foundation to suggest that the proposed use of the site posed a risk to human health, and/or that it had not taken account of any relevant material relating to human health. There was no arguable deficiency in the decision-making process. The dust assessment recorded that dust would not spread from the site, and it followed that there would be no or minimal risk to health (paras 55-56). (3) In respect of the sufficiency of consultation, it was for the decision-maker, subject to *Wednesbury* review, to decide on the manner and intensity of inquiry to be undertaken into any relevant factor, *Hayes* applied. The claimant's complaint about the consultation process trespassed into areas which were uniquely a matter for the decision-maker. In any event, PHW had not responded to the consultation and the local health board was not a body with whom the local authority was obliged to consult. There was nothing wrong with the consultation in the instant case (paras 29, 60-61, 65-66).

R. (ON THE APPLICATION OF SURRINGER) v VALE OF GLAMORGAN COUNCIL, [2016] EWHC 494 (Admin), [2016] Env. L.R. 25, Coulson J, QBD (Admin).

1753 Planning policy–Core strategy–Special Protection Areas–Requirement for new residential developments close to area to contribute to "suitable alternative natural greenspaces"

[Environmental Assessment of Plans and Programmes Regulations 2004 (SI 2004/1633) reg.12]

The appellant appealed against a decision (*Ashdown Forest Economic Development LLP v Secretary of State for Communities and Local Government* [2014] EWHC 406 (Admin), [2015] Env. L.R. D1) dismissing its challenge to part of a core strategy adopted by the first respondent local authority. The policy challenged in the core strategy concerned the protection of Ashdown Forest, which was a special protection area and a special area of conservation. Concerned at the effect that increased visitor numbers would have on the ecological integrity of the forest, the local authority included in the policy provision for a 7km zone around the forest where new residential development would be required to contribute to "Suitable Alternative Natural Greenspaces". The appellant was a corporate vehicle controlled by four landed estates whose property interests were affected by the core strategy. It brought a claim seeking to quash the core strategy in whole or in part. The judge dismissed the claim, holding that the "Habitats Regulations Assessment" carried out by the local authority showed that it had taken a proper approach to the issue of the 7km zone. The appellant argued that the local authority had failed to comply with its duty under the Environmental Assessment of Plans and Programmes Regulations 2004 reg.12 to assess reasonable alternatives to the 7km zone.

Held: Appeal allowed. The identification of reasonable alternatives was a matter of evaluative assessment for the local planning authority, subject to review by the court on normal public law principles, including *Wednesbury* unreasonableness. In order to make a lawful assessment, however, the authority did at least have to apply its mind to the question. A fundamental difficulty faced by the local authority in this case was that there was no evidence that it did give any consideration to the question of reasonable alternatives to the 7km zone. The local authority's case that the question of reasonable alternatives was considered depended on inferences to be drawn from the Habitats Regulations Assessment. However, it was not the function of that assessment to consider alternatives. What mattered for the purposes of that assessment was that the core strategy should not lead to any adverse effects on the integrity of the Ashdown Forest Special Protection Area. The avoidance and/or mitigation measures recommended in it were put forward in accordance with the precautionary principle with the aim of eliminating the risk of adverse effects. They were considered to meet that aim. It did not follow that there were no alternative means of ensuring the necessary protection of the special protection area. Further, the judge below had been wrong to conclude that reasonable alternatives to the 7km zone had been considered in the assessment. No one had suggested alternatives. However, it remained the local authority's duty to consider the issue. Had it done so, it might have concluded, in the absence of any suggestions to the contrary, that there were no reasonable alternatives and have given reasons in support of that conclusion. The fact that nobody suggested alternatives could not, however, validate the local authority's failure to consider the question at all. A quashing order would be granted, limited to the part of the policy which related to the 7km zone (see paras 42, 44-47, 50, 60 of judgment).

ASHDOWN FOREST ECONOMIC DEVELOPMENT LLP v SECRETARY OF STATE FOR COMMUNITIES AND LOCAL GOVERNMENT *sub nom.* ASHDOWN FOREST ECONOMIC DEVELOPMENT LLP v WEALDEN DC, [2015] EWCA Civ 681, [2016] P.T.S.R. 78, Richards LJ, CA (Civ Div).

1754 Planning policy–Flood risk–Proper approach under National Planning Policy Framework and Planning Practice Guidance

[Planning and Compulsory Purchase Act 2004 (c.5) s.38(6)]

In conjoined applications for judicial review, the claimant local residents' group challenged the defendant local authority's decisions to grant the interested party developer conditional planning permission for a residential development, and later to discharge certain conditions. The claimant had objected to the proposed development on the grounds of flooding, on the basis that the application site was regularly inundated with water which often spread onto the land of existing adjacent properties. The developer submitted a flood and draining assessment (FDA) in support of its application, including the suggested provision for a storage facility for flood water. The local authority's planning officer concluded that the proposed flood mitigation measures were reasonable and met the appropriate regulatory requirements. The local authority subsequently granted planning permission, subject to conditions requiring the developer to provide details of and implement flood mitigation measures before commencing the development. The developer later applied to the local authority to discharge a number of the conditions on the ground that it had satisfied their requirements. The local authority was advised that the "flood storage provided equates to 50% more than what the site currently provides to the catchment". The conditions were discharged. The claimant contended that (1) the local authority had misinterpreted or misapplied the relevant policies of the National Planning Policy Framework and the Planning Practice Guidance in relation to issues of flooding; it submitted that, on their proper construction, those policies required opportunities to be taken to reduce existing flood risk, and the developer had not done that; (2) the developer had failed to comply with condition 5 which, interpreted properly, required flood mitigation measures to be carried out exactly in accordance with the details specified in the FDA; (3) the statement as to the increase in the developer's provision of flood storage was misleading and incorrect, since it left out of account the additional requirement for storage for storm water arising from the impermeable parts of the site. The local authority and the developer asserted that the reference to provision of flood storage was not a suggestion that there was a 50% increase in the net storage capacity of the site: the statement was limited to the creation of additional surface storage features.

Held: Applications refused. (1) The Planning and Compulsory Purchase Act 2004 s.38(6) required a local authority to determine planning applications in accordance with the development plan unless material considerations indicated otherwise. The interpretation of planning policy, as opposed to its application, was a matter for the court, *Tesco Stores Ltd v Dundee City Council* [2012] UKSC 13, [2012] P.T.S.R. 983, [2012] C.L.Y. 2595 applied. The question in the instant case was whether the NPPF and the PPG required, in the development control context, a proposal to seek out and provide opportunities to reduce flood risk. It did not. For the purposes of planning applications the test was to ensure that flood risk was not increased elsewhere, although if a development proposal offered the benefit of reducing flood risk that would plainly be a positive factor in the planning balance weighing in favour of the grant of planning permission. There had been no misinterpretation or misapplication of the planning policy in the instant case (see paras 31-32, 38-41 of judgment). (2) The approach to the construction and interpretation of planning conditions was no different from that which should be undertaken in relation to any legal document, *Trump International Golf Club Scotland Ltd v Scottish Ministers* [2015] UKSC 74, [2016] 1 W.L.R. 85, [2016] 1727 applied. It was necessary to interpret the words of condition 5 on the basis of what a reasonable reader would understand them to mean, reading the condition as a whole and in context. Properly construed, the words of condition 5 contemplated the alteration of specific values within the FDA, albeit in the context of the framework of the drainage principles set out within it. There had been no misdirection or error in the approval of the details under condition 5. The details reflected the kind of additional work that would be necessary within the overall framework of the principles set out in the FDA (paras 34, 45-46, 49). (3) Even if taken on its face, the representation to the local authority as to the increase in storage provision had been honoured, since there was in fact a 50% increase in storage provision for the development site's watercourse (para.54).

R. (ON THE APPLICATION OF MENSTON ACTION GROUP) v BRADFORD MDC *sub nom.* MENSTON ACTION GROUP v BRADFORD MDC, [2016] EWHC 127 (QB), [2016] P.T.S.R. 466, Dove J, QBD.

1755 Power stations–Electricity generation–Ferrybridge Multifuel 2 Power Station

THE FERRYBRIDGE MULTIFUEL 2 POWER STATION (CORRECTION) ORDER 2016, SI 2016/737; made under the Planning Act 2008 Sch.4 para.1(4)(8). In force: 13 July 2016.

This Order corrects errors identified in the Ferrybridge Multifuel 2 Power Station Order 2015, which granted development consent under the Planning Act 2008, following a written request from Multifuel Energy Limited under para.1(5)(a) of Sch.4 to that Act.

1756 Rail network–Listed buildings–New elevated urban railway–Harm to listed buildings outweighed by public benefits

[Planning (Listed Buildings and Conservation Areas) Act 1990 (c.9) s.16(2), s.66(1), s.72(1)]

The appellant appealed against a decision (*Whitby v Secretary of State for Transport* [2015] EWHC 2804 (Admin)) dismissing his claim challenging the proposed route of an elevated chord railway. The railway was to run between Manchester and Salford. It was accepted that it would bring considerable transport benefits but that it would also cause substantial harm to several listed buildings. The appellant objected and presented the case for an alternative alignment, called "Option 15". Option 15's route would largely avoid harm to listed buildings, but it ran through a large site which had been identified as a key opportunity for comprehensive redevelopment in Salford. An inquiry was held into the railway company's proposals. The inspector considered the National Planning Policy Framework (NPPF) paras 132 and 133 and found that although the harm to heritage assets would be very great, the primary assets would remain intact; further, that Option 15 was not a reasonable means of achieving the public benefit because of the harm it would cause to the regeneration of Salford. He ultimately found that the harm to the buildings would be outweighed by the public benefits of the railway, and recommended that planning permission and listed building consent for the demolition and alteration of listed buildings affected by the works should be granted. Those recommendations were accepted by the secretaries of state. The issue was whether the decisions were unlawful because they had not been taken consistently with the decision-makers' statutory duties relating to listed buildings and conservation areas and/or because the secretaries of state had misunderstood or misapplied the relevant national policy and guidance. The claimant submitted that the secretaries of state had failed to take their decisions in accordance with the duties in the Planning (Listed Buildings and Conservation Areas) Act 1990 s.16(2), s.66(1) and s.72(1) on listed building consent, the NPPF paras 132 and 133 on heritage assets, and the Planning Policy Statement 5 (PPS5) para.91.

Held: Appeal dismissed. The need for the project, the urgency of that need and the significance of the public benefits associated with it were uncontroversial. The secretaries of state had not failed to discharge the requirements for decision-makers in s.16(2), s.66(1) and s.72(1) of the 1990 Act. The transport secretary, in agreeing with the inspector that the listed building consents should be granted, could be taken to have adopted his conclusions on the statutory duties. The inspector had expressly acknowledged the requirement that considerable importance and weight had to be given to the desirability of preserving a listed building or its setting. It could not be argued that either the inspector or the secretaries of state had failed to grasp what the statutory duties required. Further, they had in mind the requirements of the NPPF paras 132 and 133. The inspector had acknowledged that substantial harm to heritage assets of the highest significance should be "wholly exceptional". An inspector's report and a secretary of state's decision letter had to be read fairly and as a whole, and not with undue rigour, *South Buckinghamshire DC v Porter (No.2)* [2004] UKHL 33, [2004] 1 W.L.R. 1953, [2004] C.L.Y. 3087 followed. On a fair and unselective reading of the report, the inspector had not misinterpreted or misapplied policy and guidance. His reference to the need for a "reasonable" alternative also corresponded to the guidance in PPS5 para.91. He had faithfully applied that guidance, which amplified the policy in the NPPF para.133, and had not been simply undertaking a conventional comparison between alternative sites without heed to the relevant statutory imperatives, relevant national policy and guidance. The inspector had not imposed on the appellant the onus of demonstrating the superiority of Option 15. The decisive factor was the harm that a railway on the Option 15 route would cause to the proposed Salford development and the serious consequences for regeneration of that area. That was a classic exercise of decision-making judgment, wholly in line with the policies in the NPPF paras 132 and 133 and PPS5 para.91. It was essential to consider the potential harm to regeneration associated with Option 15 in deciding whether it was in the public interest for the proposed works to be approved. The inspector's conclusions, accepted by the secretaries of state, found that the harm to regeneration associated with Option 15 was decisively greater than the harm to heritage assets in the principal scheme. That represented an entirely reasonable exercise of planning judgment. The appellant's arguments fell a long way short of establishing any error of law (see paras 41-44, 47, 49-50, 52-54 of judgment).

WHITBY v SECRETARY OF STATE FOR TRANSPORT; R. (ON THE APPLICATION OF WHITBY) v SECRETARY OF STATE FOR TRANSPORT, [2016] EWCA Civ 444, [2016] J.P.L. 980, Simon LJ, CA (Civ Div).

1757 Residential development–Housing supply–Inspector's approach to housing supply and policy

The claimant local authority challenged the decision of the first defendant secretary of state's inspector allowing the second defendant developer's appeal against the refusal of planning permission for a residential development. The developer had sought permission to build up to 129 dwellings with vehicular access, associated public open space, landscaping and drainage work. The local authority had refused permission. During the appeal process, the developer submitted revised plans for 90 dwellings. The inspector considered that the local core strategy no longer provided an appropriate basis for calculating the deliverable five-year housing supply required by the National Planning Policy Framework, and identified the housing need figure as 833 dwellings per year. He found that the revised proposal would constitute sustainable development and that its limited adverse environmental impacts were outweighed by its benefits. He concluded that, in the light of that and the presumption in favour of sustainable development, permission should be granted. The local authority contended that the inspector had wrongly (1) treated the core strategy's housing policies as out-of-date; (2) identified the housing need figure and treated it as an absolute consideration rather than one that was a relative matter of weight; (3) applied no weight to the housing land supply policies and little weight to the emerging development plan document, and thereby failed to apply the correct planning tests, including how the overall planning balance applied; (4) failed to give adequate reasons for his decision.

Held: Judgment for defendants. (1) The planning policy guidance advised that evidence drawn from revoked regional strategies might not be up-to-date and that significant weight should be given to local plan housing figures unless significant new evidence came to light. As the inspector had explained, significant new evidence in terms of population and household projections along with jobs growth forecasts had become available. The inspector had been entitled to find that the annual housing requirement figure in the core strategy was out-of-date and no longer provided an appropriate basis for calculating the five-year housing supply (see paras 41, 43 of judgment). (2) The developer had produced evidence which the inspector had considered to be material to his decision on the housing need figure. The inspector had been required to have regard to that evidence in the absence of up-to-date figures in the core strategy, and had done so. He was required to identify an annual housing requirement in the district: if he had failed to do so, he would not have been able to identify whether the local authority could demonstrate a five-year supply of housing land. Having rejected the core strategy figure, the inspector had explained how he came to the figure of 833 dwellings per annum as an appropriate point in calculating a five-year housing requirement. The weight he gave to the figure was a matter of planning judgment for him (paras 49, 52-53). (3) The inspector had clearly dealt with all the matters that the NPPF required him to, and considered that the proposal did not conflict with key policies in the development plan. He had been entitled to give the emerging development plan, covering the period from 1991 to 2006, little weight in terms of a planning decision about development needs in 2015. He had made no error of law (paras 57-59). (4) The inspector's reasons on the principal important controversial issues were clear and adequate, *South Buckinghamshire DC v Porter (No.2)* [2004] UKHL 33, [2004] 1 W.L.R. 1953, [2004] C.L.Y. 3087 considered (para.61).

WEST BERKSHIRE DC v SECRETARY OF STATE FOR COMMUNITES AND LOCAL GOVERNMENT, [2016] EWHC 267 (Admin), [2016] A.C.D. 50, Supperstone J, QBD.

1758 Residential development–Self-build and custom housebuiding–Time for compliance and fees

THE SELF-BUILD AND CUSTOM HOUSEBUILDING (TIME FOR COMPLIANCE AND FEES) REGULATIONS 2016, SI 2016/1027; made under the Self-build and Custom Housebuilding Act 2015 s.2A(3). In force: 31 October 2016.

The Self-build and Custom Housebuilding Act 2015 requires a relevant authority to keep a register of individuals and associations of individuals who are seeking to acquire serviced plots of land in the authority's area. Section 2A of the Act imposes a duty on relevant authorities to grant sufficient development permissions in respect of serviced plots of land to meet the demand as evidenced by the number of entries on the register in a base period. Paragraph 6 of the Schedule to the Act allows regulations to enable relevant authorities to charge fees in connection with their functions in connection with maintaining the register and complying with the duty in s.2A.

1759 Residential development–Special Protection Areas–Development on agricultural land close to special protection area for birds

[Directive 92/43 on the conservation of natural habitats and of wild fauna and flora 1992 art.6(3); Community Infrastructure Levy Regulations 2010 (SI 2010/948)]

The appellant (S) appealed against a decision (*Smyth v Secretary of State for Communities and Local Government* [2013] EWHC 3844 (Admin)) refusing to quash a grant of planning permission for residential development. The proposed development site was located close to a special protection area for birds, which incorporated a special area of conservation and was also designated as a site of special scientific interest. S was chair of an association of local residents which objected to the development. The area was protected under EU law, in particular for the purposes of Directive 92/43. The principal ground of appeal focused on whether the grant of permission complied with the requirements set out in art.6(3) of the Directive. The local authority had carried out the two stages of assessment provided for by art.6(3), a "screening assessment" and an "appropriate assessment". It considered that the development would be likely, in combination with other projects carried out by other local planning authorities in the vicinity, to have a significant effect on the area and therefore carried out an appropriate assessment. It concluded that, having regard to certain mitigation measures, the development proposal would have no significant adverse impact. Natural England endorsed that assessment. The local authority refused permission for reasons unrelated to application of the Directive. An ecology expert stated that it was legitimate to bring mitigation measures into account for the screening assessment required by the first limb of art.6(3). The planning inspector followed that analysis and concluded that there was no risk of significant harm to the area, which meant that no further appropriate assessment was required. S's challenge to the decision was rejected. S submitted that the inspector had failed properly to comply with the strict precautionary approach required under art.6(3) as he could not be certain to the required standard that there would be no possibility of adverse effects on the area. S further submitted that the mitigation measures relied on by the inspector were too vague and uncertain.

Held: Appeal dismissed. (1) There was force in S's submissions, but they could not be accepted in relation to the specific circumstances the inspector had been required to address. Two preliminary points needed to be made. First, it appeared from the local authority's assessments that it was only because of the potential in-combination effects of the proposed development, together with other very substantial residential developments contemplated under local development frameworks of the local planning authorities in the vicinity of the special protection area, that the proposed development was likely to have a significant effect on the area. Those were legitimate and sustainable assessments, and the inspector had been entitled to proceed on the basis of them. The proposed development was small and involved only a very limited increase of population in an area which was already reasonably well populated. The relevant assessments available to the inspector agreed on the absence of significant impact from the development alone, and the inspector had accepted those assessments, as he was entitled to do. The critical question for the inspector, therefore, was whether there was sufficient assurance from the mitigation adopted by the local planning authorities, and the approach to mitigation and the taking of preventive safeguarding measures which it contemplated, to allow him to be sure that there would be no significant in-combination adverse effects on the area if planning permission was granted. The inspector had to be sure to the required standard under the first limb of art.6(3). That led to a second preliminary point. In the instant case, the inspector was conducting an inquiry for the purpose of art.6(3) which, to a significant degree, was informed by work done for the local authority when it was the relevant competent authority considering whether to grant permission. The inspector had further information, including the evidence from the ecology expert, and was particularly well-placed therefore to consider the position at the screening assessment stage under the first limb of art.6(3). If the very full information available to him properly enabled him to make the screening assessment, he was not obliged to require an "appropriate assessment" to be carried out under the second limb of art.6(3), *R. (on the application of Hart DC) v Secretary of State for Communities and Local Government* [2008] EWHC 1204 (Admin), [2008] 2 P. & C.R. 16, [2008] C.L.Y. 2967 applied. The inspector was entitled to make the assessment that the proposed development, even in combination with other development projects, would not be likely to give rise to any significant effects on either the special protection area or the special area of conservation. He was entitled to find that the uncertainties regarding possible future in-combination effects relevant to the site were adequately catered for by the mitigation arrangements and the associated safeguards. Those arrangements meant that there was sufficient assurance that future preventive safeguarding measures would have to be in place, to the satisfaction of relevant competent authorities and Natural England, before any future in-combination effects could actually arise. That evaluative judgment did not involve any compromise of the strict precautionary approach under art.6(3), *Landelijke Vereniging tot Behoud van de Waddenzee v Staatssecretaris van Landbouw, Natuurbeheer en Visserij (C-127/02)* EU:C:2004:482, [2004] E.C.R. I-7405, [2005] C.L.Y. 1439 applied, (see paras 87-102 of judgment). (2) Further grounds based on the Directive, on alleged misapplication of the National Planning Policy Framework, on criticism of the inspector's reasons and on his alleged failure to properly apply the Community Infrastructure Levy Regulations 2010 were also dismissed (paras 103-121).

SMYTH v SECRETARY OF STATE FOR COMMUNITIES AND LOCAL GOVERNMENT, [2015] EWCA Civ 174, [2015] P.T.S.R. 1417, Richards LJ, CA (Civ Div).

1760 Residential development–Sustainable development–Presumption in favour of sustainable development–Consideration of development plan

[Planning and Compulsory Purchase Act 2004 (c.5) s.38(6)]

The claimant local authority applied to quash a decision of the defendant secretary of state's planning inspector to grant planning permission for the development of 32 residential dwellings. The area in question had a Local Plan GD1, which stated that most new development up to 2011 would be accommodated and would be within defined development boundaries and/or on allocated sites. The interested party developer's application for planning permission was in direct conflict with the GD1, as it was for a site outside the settlement boundary. The local authority did not determine the application so the developer appealed to the planning inspector. The inspector granting planning permission concluded that, contrary to what the developer argued, GD1 was in date and retained its full weight as part of the statutory development plan; it was possible for a material consideration to outweigh the development plan; the policies and objectives of the National Planning Policy Framework (NPPF) were important material considerations; the proposed development constituted sustainable development having regard to the NPPF, and the benefits of development outweighed the identified limited harm and the conflict with GD1 and so the presumption in favour of sustainable development applied. The secretary of state conceded that the decision should be quashed. Paragraph 14 of the NPPF stated that the presumption in favour of sustainable development was the golden thread running through the plan-making and decision-taking. The local authority submitted that (1) the inspector had not addressed whether GD1 was out-of-date and so might not have given it its full weight or priority under the Planning and Compulsory Purchase Act 2004 s.38(6); (2) there was legitimate doubt that the inspector had applied the s.38(6) test; (3) the inspector had created two incorrect presumptions in relation to sustainable development and boosting housing supply.

Held: Application refused. (1) The inspector had expressly found that there was a development plan and he had rejected the developer's criticism that it was out of date. The suggestion that there was ambiguity over the inspector's approach to the plan was contrived. The inspector had noted that the plan was not entirely consistent with the NPPF, but that was correct and in no way detracted from the full weight he gave to GD1. The balancing exercise conducted did not suggest a reduction in weight (see paras 31-34 of judgment). (2) It might have been better if the inspector had explained that what he called the "full weight" to be given to GD1 meant that the statutory priority in s.38(6) was being applied, but that was a counsel of perfection and not a criticism of substance. The inspector was writing to an informed audience who would have known that "full weight" was a reference to s.38(6) (para.36). (3) In respect of the presumption in favour of sustainable development, the inspector had to balance the statutory priority of GD1 against the other material considerations in accordance with s.38(6) and paras 11-13 of the NPPF, which he did. The local authority argued that the inspector had failed to apply the approach to decision-taking in NPPF para.14. However, both parties had agreed that the decision-taking envisaged in para.14 did not apply. Therefore that argument fell away. It had been wrong to say that a presumption favouring sustainable development did not exist outside of para.14. Other paragraphs in the NPPF referred to that presumption, and it was the golden thread running through the NPPF. The inspector had had proper regard to it as an important material consideration, *Crane v Secretary of State for Communities and Local Government* [2015] EWHC 425 (Admin) considered. Paragraph 14 did not offer a true definition of "presumption". It explained the effect of presumption. Had the local authority been right about the inspector creating an incorrect presumption relating to sustainable development, the presumption favouring sustainable development would only apply if the development plan was silent or absent, or if the relevant policies went out-of-date. Had that been the intention of the NPPF to limit the "golden thread" in such a way, it would have said so explicitly. Where there was a conflict between a proposal and a development plan, the NPPF policies, including the presumption of sustainable development, were important material considerations to be weighed against the statutory priority of the development plan. The inspector had had proper regard to para.47 of the NPPF, which dealt with the need to boost significantly the supply of housing, as a material consideration. Paragraph 47 of the NPPF applied to both decision-taking and plan-making, *Daventry DC v Secretary of State for Communities and Local Government* [2015] EWHC 3459 (Admin), [2016] J.P.L. 578, [2016] 1740 considered. The inspector had regarded para.47 as no more than a material consideration (paras 38-49). (4) Had the court been wrong about the inspector's approach it still would have exercised its discretion in favour of not quashing his decision. The inspector had not said in terms that the balancing act he undertook was pursuant to s.38(6) or that the presumption was a material consideration, but even if he had worded his letter more clearly he would have reached the same decision (paras 50-53).

WYCHAVON DC v SECRETARY OF STATE FOR COMMUNITIES AND LOCAL GOVERNMENT, [2016] EWHC 592 (Admin), [2016] P.T.S.R. 675, Coulson J, QBD (Admin).

1761 Right to buy–Rural areas–Shropshire

THE HOUSING (RIGHT TO BUY) (DESIGNATED RURAL AREAS AND DESIGNATED REGIONS) (ENGLAND) ORDER 2016, SI 2016/587; made under the Housing Act 1985 s.157(1)(c)(3). In force: 20 June 2016.

This Order designates the parishes listed in the Schedule to the Order as rural areas under the Housing Act 1985 s.157(1)(c), and provides for each of the regions of Chichester, Malvern Hills, Shropshire and Wychavon to be a designated region under s.157(3) of the Act in relation to dwelling-houses in the designated rural areas falling within the district.

1762 **Screening opinions–Duty to provide reasons–Guidance on giving reasons for negative screening opinion**

[Town and Country Planning (Environmental Impact Assessment) (England and Wales) Regulations 1999 (SI 1999/293)]

The court was required to determine, as remitted issues, whether a planning officer's later statement had provided her contemporaneous reasons or an ex post facto justification for issuing a negative screening opinion, and the appropriate relief following the defendant local authority's established breach of duty to give reasons within a reasonable time. The interested party developers had applied for planning permission for the erection of two wind turbines at a site close to several specially protected areas, an existing wind farm and a proposed wind energy development. In March 2012, the planning officer, on behalf of the local authority, issued a screening opinion stating that no environmental impact assessment would be required: her reasons were that the proposed development would not give rise to significant effects. She went on maternity leave in December 2012. The local authority granted permission in February 2013. The claimant, a local resident opposed to the development, sent the local authority pre-action protocol letters complaining of the negative screening opinion's lack of reasoning, in particular as to the proposed development's cumulative impact with the existing nearby windfarm and the other one proposed. The local authority declined to give further reasons for the decision, having stated that it was inconceivable that the planning officer had failed to have regard to cumulative effects and that there was no requirement under the Town and Country Planning (Environmental Impact Assessment) (England and Wales) Regulations 1999 to give reasons for a negative screening opinion. That view was mistaken, as an obligation to give reasons for a negative screening opinion was confirmed as a matter of European law by the ECJ in *R. (on the application of Mellor) v Secretary of State for Communities and Local Government (C-75/08)* EU:C:2009:279, [2010] P.T.S.R. 880, [2010] C.L.Y. 1246. The claimant issued judicial review proceedings, seeking to quash the planning permission on the basis that the screening opinion was inadequately reasoned. By a witness statement made in October 2013, the planning officer explained that she had paid regard to the impact of the proposed development in the light of the existing and other proposed windfarms, but considered that it was unlikely to have significant environmental effects, so that a negative screening opinion was appropriate. The judge accepted that the screening opinion was inadequately reasoned, but found that its deficiency in reasoning was "cured" by the planning officer's statement. In doing so, he had refused permission to cross-examine the planning officer on the basis that her statement adequately set out her contemporaneous reasons for giving a negative screening opinion. The claimant appealed. The Court of Appeal found that the screening decision was inadequately reasoned, that the claimant's first pre-action protocol letter amounted to a valid request for reasons and that the local authority's response did not satisfy its legal duty to give reasons, although it was unclear whether the planning officer's statement remedied that position. It held that the judge should have permitted her to be cross-examined in order to establish whether the reasons given in her witness statement were contemporaneous or an ex post facto justification of the decision. It remitted that issue, and the question of remedy, to the instant court. The planning officer gave oral evidence and was cross-examined.

Held: Judgment accordingly. (1) The planning officer was a credible and truthful witness. Having heard her oral evidence under cross-examination, there was no real possibility that her statement had set out a rationalisation of her decision as opposed to her contemporaneous reasoning. The local authority had undoubtedly been in breach of its duty to give reasons for a negative screening opinion within a reasonable time of a request, *Mellor* applied. However, since adequate reasons had now been given, the instant case was not one in which it would be appropriate to give substantive relief. As a result of that breach, the claimant had not been deprived of any right or opportunity granted to him as a member of the public by European law, and he had suffered no prejudice in the planning process. The judicial review claim was therefore allowed, but the substantive relief was restricted to a declaration that the local authority was in breach of its *Mellor* duty to give reasons for its negative screening decision within a reasonable time of the claimant's request (see paras 83-86, 95 of judgment). (2) Whilst every case was necessarily fact-specific, the following propositions in relation to the giving of reasons in a negative screening case under the Regulations could be derived from principle and the authorities: (a) a local planning authority was required to give reasons for a negative screening opinion within a reasonable time of a request; in other words, it bore the *Mellor* duty. Those had to be the reasons in its mind at the time of the decision, and not an ex post facto justification. If it failed to give reasons within a reasonable time of request, it would be in breach of duty. Given the possibility of a request coming in perhaps months or even years after the EIA screening decision was taken, authorities would no doubt wish generally to maintain a note of the decision-maker's reasons for any negative screening decision, so that those reasons could be sent out if and when any request was made; (b) once proceedings were issued, whilst it would be too late for an authority to avoid a breach by providing reasons, if the authority thereafter provided reasons, and the court was persuaded that they were indeed the reasons in the local authority's mind at the time of the decision, the court was likely to be slow to quash the planning permission. That was because it was unlikely that interested parties would have been denied any right or opportunity to participate in the planning process given by European law, or that anyone would have been materially prejudiced by the delay in providing reasons. In those circumstances, the court might, however, penalise the authority in costs; (c) if no contemporaneous reasons were forthcoming (including, a situation where the court rejected the submission that reasons put forward were contemporaneous), then in accordance with usual public law principles, the planning permission should be quashed unless the authority could show that the decision would inevitably have been the same if the breach had not occurred; or, if remitted, the decision would now be the same. The burden was on the authority, and whether it had discharged it would be dependent upon the evidence, particularly the evidence it had adduced in those issues. The court would be wary of the possibility that, in producing such evidence, the authority might be under some pressure, conscious or unconscious, to maintain the planning permission decision (para.94).

R. (ON THE APPLICATION OF JEDWELL) v DENBIGHSHIRE CC, [2016] EWHC 458 (Admin), [2016] 2 C.M.L.R. 49, Hickinbottom J, QBD (Admin).

1763 Screening opinions–Residential development–Outline planning permission

[Town and Country Planning (Environmental Impact Assessment) Regulations 2011 (SI 2011/1824) Sch.2, Sch.3, reg.4(9); Town and Country Planning (Environmental Impact Assessment) (Amendment) Regulations 2015 (SI 2015/660) reg.3]

A local householder appealed against a decision (*Mackman v Secretary of State for Communities and Local Government* [2013] EWHC 3396 (QB)) refusing to quash the first respondent's inspector's decision to uphold the grant of conditional planning permission for a development of 73 dwellings on land near Great Dunmow in Essex by the second respondent local authority. The local authority's planning officer had adopted a screening opinion under the Town and Country Planning (Environmental Impact Assessment) Regulations 2011 to the effect that the development did not require an environmental impact assessment. The local authority refused the planning application and the third respondent developer appealed. The inspector allowed the developer's appeal and granted permission. On appeal, the judge below determined that the planning officer had fully considered the cumulative impact of other local development in making her screening opinion, despite not having expressly mentioned that factor and, therefore, there had been a lawful screening opinion before the grant of planning permission. The householder submitted that the inspector's decision had been tainted by the preceding screening opinion, which had been unlawful because (1) although an express reference to cumulative impact was not required, there had to be something in the opinion's wording to show such impacts had been considered; the likely knowledge of other local decisions and the expertise of the officer alone could not be sufficient; (2) even if the cumulative impact had been considered, the officer had failed to give clear reasons why the development, and other development nearby, would not significantly affect the environment.

Held: Appeal dismissed. (1) The officer had produced a detailed report referring to other local developments for the Planning Inspectorate shortly after completing her screening opinion. The judge had been correct to consider it most improbable that she would have been unaware of the other local planning decisions. When drafting her opinion, she had carefully followed the guidance in Circular 02/99 and Sch.3 of the 2011 Regulations. It was inherently unlikely that she had ignored para.46 of the Circular which referred directly to the cumulative effects. On a fair reading of the opinion it was clear that the officer had considered all the factors in Sch.3 despite referring explicitly only to the visual impact. That had been mentioned as the only factor that she had considered might significantly affect the environment but she had determined that it did not (see paras 10-15 of judgment). (2) The judge had been correct to hold that although the officer's reasons were brief, they were adequate. The level of detail required in a screening opinion depended upon the complexity of the issues to be considered and the test was whether the reasons were adequate for the particular application, *R. (on the application of Bateman) v South Cambridgeshire DC* [2011] EWCA Civ 157, [2011] N.P.C. 22 distinguished, as unlike *Bateman* there was nothing in the instant case requiring further explanation (paras 18-21). (3) The judge also had been correct to determine that she would exercise her discretion to refuse to quash the inspector's decision, even if the screening opinion had been legally flawed. Since the inspector's decision, sch.2 of the 2011 Regulations had been amended by the Town and Country Planning (Environmental Impact Assessment) (Amendment) Regulations 2015 reg.3, which had raised the threshold for residential development to more than 150 dwellings or an overall area in excess of five hectares. It was common ground that if the inspector's decision was quashed and the appeal remitted for redetermination, the secretary of state was bound to conclude that the proposed development was not Sch.2 development. The householder's argument that the secretary of state would exercise his discretion under reg.4(9) of the 2011 Regulations was ingenious but wholly unrealistic. Circular 02/99 para.77 made it clear that such power would only be exercised exceptionally and there was nothing exceptional about the instant case (paras 23-28).

MACKMAN v SECRETARY OF STATE FOR COMMUNITIES AND LOCAL GOVERNMENT, [2015] EWCA Civ 716, [2016] Env. L.R. 6, Sullivan LJ, CA (Civ Div).

1764 Section 106 agreements–Contributions–Development completed under second planning permission granted without s.106 obligation

[Town and Country Planning Act 1990 (c.8) s.106]

A highway authority appealed against a decision (*R. (on the application of Robert Hitchins Ltd) v Worcestershire CC* [2014] EWHC 3809 (Admin), [2015] P.T.S.R. D5) that the respondent developer (R) was not required to contribute towards transport infrastructure costs pursuant to an agreement under the Town and Country Planning Act 1990 s.106 where the development had been implemented under a second permission granted without the s.106 obligation. R had been granted planning permission to develop a site by the local planning authority, the interested party. The permission contained a s.106 obligation that R pay the highway authority a contribution towards the transport infrastructure and services in three instalments. R subsequently sold its interest in the site to another company (B), having agreed that it would perform the s.106 payment obligations for as long as they were enforceable, and that it would submit a second application for the site in identical terms except for the s.106 obligation. B began developing the site, and R paid the first instalment under the s.106 agreement. The second planning application became subject to an inquiry, and the planning inspector concluded that the development's impact was not severe enough to require a s.106 contribution. A second planning permission was therefore granted without that obligation, subject to reserved matters approval. B made a unilateral undertaking to the local authorities to implement the second permission. It provided that, following the reserved matters approval, B would "dispense with the implementation" of the first permission. Approval was given and the undertaking came into effect in September 2014. The judge rejected the highway authority's arguments that B had not been able as a matter of law to choose to complete the development under the second permission rather than the first, and had not in fact chosen to do so. The highway authority argued that (1) in covenanting in the unilateral undertaking to dispense with the "implementation" of the first permission, B had covenanted to dispense with the beginning of the development, but since the development had already begun, that provision was of no effect; (2) the judge's finding that B had chosen to complete the development from September 2014 under the second permission was inconsistent with his earlier finding that the fact that operations had continued after September 2014 could not of itself answer the question of which permission the operations had been performed under; (3) operations could not be carried out fully in accordance with the second permission because part of the development had already been built under the first permission, meaning that any operations under the second permission were unlawful, as discussed in *Sage v Secretary of State for the Environment, Transport and the Regions* [2003] UKHL 22, [2003] 1 W.L.R. 983, [2003] C.L.Y. 3386.

Held: Appeal dismissed. (1) Since the unilateral undertaking was not a bilateral commercial contract but a unilateral deed with the status of a public document, appropriate adjustment had to be made to the principles of contractual interpretation in *Arnold v Britton* [2015] UKSC 36, [2015] A.C. 1619, [2015] C.L.Y. 1606. However, since it was enforceable as a contract and had been entered into in connection with a commercial development, the principles remained applicable in their essential features, *Arnold* applied. "Implementation" in relation to planning permission was not the subject of statutory definition and did not have a single specific meaning. There were strong reasons for rejecting the highway authority's construction that "implement" was to be interpreted as "begin". B could not have intended to dispense with the beginning of the first permission when it knew that development under that permission had already begun. Further, it was obvious from the background that B had intended to cease development under the first permission and continue under the second. In the sale agreement between R and B, references to "implementing" the planning permission were ambiguous, but B had clearly agreed that from the time of reserved matters approval under the second permission, it would carry out development under the second, not the first, permission. The provision should be given a meaning that avoided ineffectiveness (see paras 29-33 of judgment). (2) There was no inconsistency between the judge's earlier finding and his ultimate finding that the operations had been carried out from September under the second permission. The undertaking was clear-cut evidence in support of that conclusion. Accordingly, it did not matter that it was impossible to tell from evidence on the ground which permission operations were being carried out under. One would not expect any difference in the operations themselves, since the permissions were identical (paras 35-36). (3) The highway authority had taken the relevant passage in *Sage* out of context. The point in *Sage* had been that if a building operation did not accord with the permission for it, the whole of that operation was unlawful; it was not saying that if a building was built in a way conforming with the permission but was not completed, the whole building was unlawful, nor was it addressing the situation where a building was completed pursuant to two identical permissions, *Sage* considered. A development could be commenced but not completed and still remain lawful (paras 48-50).

R. (ON THE APPLICATION OF ROBERT HITCHINS LTD) v WORCESTERSHIRE CC, [2015] EWCA Civ 1060, [2016] J.P.L. 373, Richards LJ, CA (Civ Div).

1765 Self-build and Custom Housebuilding Act 2015 (c.17)–Commencement Regulations

THE SELF-BUILD AND CUSTOM HOUSEBUILDING ACT 2015 (COMMENCEMENT) REGULATIONS 2016, SI 2016/113; made under the Self-build and Custom Housebuilding Act 2015 s.6(3). Commencement details: bringing into operation various provisions of the 2015 Act on 1 April 2016.

These regulations bring into force the provisions of the Self-build and Custom Housebuilding Act 2015 that are not yet in force on 1 April 2016. The Act places duties on certain public authorities to keep a register of individuals and associations of individuals who are seeking to acquire serviced plots of land in the authority's area in order to bring forward self-build and custom housebuilding projects, and to have regard to that register in carrying out their planning and other functions.

1766 Sports and leisure facilities–Noise–Noise impact of college's sports fields used outside school hours

[Town and Country Planning Act 1990 (c.8) s.96A]

A local resident applied for judicial review of a decision by the defendant local authority to grant planning permission for a synthetic pitch and associated facilities, including floodlights, on the existing sports fields of a community college. The claimant lived approximately 120m from the site. A member of his family suffered from a condition resulting in sleep difficulties, which benefited from darkness and a quiet environment. The proposal was for use of the new pitch during school hours and during the daytime at weekends for team sports. The pitch would be fenced with timber-boarded acoustic screening and the floodlights would not be used after 21.30. The playing fields were already used for team sports. The claimant instructed various noise consultants, who disagreed on a number of points, including methodology. One consultant regarded the new activity "outside daylight hours" as introducing a new noise to the environment which would be more noticeable than the effect of new road traffic. The consultants' reports were considered by the local authority. An environmental health officer expressed concern regarding the use of whistles outside school hours and spectator noise. The planning officer's report dealt with noise and health issues and recommended approval subject to conditions. Planning permission was granted subject to conditions, including conditions relating to the use of the floodlights, the erection of noise barriers, and one preventing the use of the pitch for competitive matches between 19.00 and 08:00. The claimant challenged the local authority's treatment of the issue of the noise generated by use of the new pitch. He also challenged the legality of a condition related to a community use agreement. The claimant contended that the planning officer's report failed to deal adequately or fairly with the evidence about potential noise generation.

Held: Application granted in part. (1) There were two issues regarding the planning officer's report: whether the committee had been provided with sufficient material on which to address the noise impact of the proposal, and whether it had been misled about the environmental health officer's concerns. It was helpful to bear in mind the test set out in *R. v Selby DC Ex p. Oxton Farms* [1997] E.G. 60 (C.S.), [1997] C.L.Y. 4114, namely whether the overall effect of the report had significantly misled the committee about material matters which thereafter were left uncorrected. The purpose of scientific assessments and predictions regarding noise was to provide the decision-maker with information which might assist them in reaching a judgment. Some issues could not be understood without scientific input; for example, a layman could not be expected to know the degree of attenuation a particular shape or height of barrier provided or the shape of the noise contours for a new major piece of infrastructure such as a road, railway or runway. Such issues could involve complex discussions, in which conclusions uninformed by expert assessment would carry much less weight. There were also cases where the nature of the noises were very familiar, and the question of their impact much more subjective. The instant proposal involved exactly the same use that had existed on the site for many years. The difference was that it would be usable for longer in the evenings. The current user involved matches, training and whistles, and the committee did not need experts' reports to be able to form a judgment on those issues. It was also hard to imagine that committee members needed an expert's report to point out that a whistle made a more distinctive and audible sound than the generality of noises, or to know that players and supporters could shout during a match. Once competitive matches outside normal hours were substantially reduced by the effect of the specific condition, the incidence of spectator noise in the evening was reduced to an occasional event. While it would have been possible, therefore, for the committee to have been told of differences in methodology in the planning officer's report, it would have added nothing to the issues debated. The committee had accepted that noise impacts existed unless steps were taken to limit use. The committee was also aware from the officer's report that the environmental health officer had sought a condition related to the use of whistles. It knew that the proposal would extend the hours of use and that whistles would be used, and had all the information it needed to make a decision, *Oxton Farms* applied, *R. (on the application of Trashorfield Ltd) v Bristol City Council* [2014] EWHC 757 (Admin) considered (see paras 63-76 of judgment). (2) The claimant considered the community use agreement condition to be unintelligible. The court had suggested to the local authority that part of the condition was patently deficient and had invited correction. No correction had been made. Following the instant judgment, which included the conclusion that the condition as drafted was unenforceable, both parties accepted that the proper course was to adjourn the final formal giving of judgment until an application had been made under the Town and Country Planning Act 1990 s.96A to amend the condition, and for the court to make a declaration that the claimant's application had been successful to that extent. However, no order would be made quashing the planning permission *R. (on the application of Nicholson) v Allerdale BC* [2015] EWHC 2510 (Admin) applied, *Hunt v North Somerset Council* [2015] UKSC 51, [2015] 1 W.L.R. 3575, [2015] C.L.Y. 251 followed (paras 78-81).

R. (ON THE APPLICATION OF HILL) v CORNWALL COUNCIL, [2016] EWHC 1264 (Admin), [2016] J.P.L. 1145, Gilbart J, QBD (Admin).

1767 Waste disposal–Enforcement notices–Rubble brought into former quarry to create access road–Difference between tipping waste and using it as part of process

A landowner appealed against a planning inspector's decision to uphold an enforcement notice issued by a local authority requiring him to remove rubble which he had imported on to his land to create an access road. The land, which had formerly been a quarry, was authorised for use as woodland. To remove felled trees, the landowner needed to construct an access road into the site. He therefore imported the rubble to use it as hardcore. The local authority issued the enforcement notice on the ground that, without planning permission, the use of the land had been changed from woodland to mixed use, involving the importation and disposal of waste. The notice required the landowner to cease importing waste to the land, remove the waste that had already been imported and restore the land to its previous condition. The landowner appealed, arguing that the rubble was no longer waste as it had been fully recovered by being incorporated into a road. The inspector found that at the time of the enforcement notice, the rubble remained waste as it had not been incorporated into the access road; and it remained waste after it had been incorporated because there was no evidence that it had been decontaminated. The landowner, whilst accepting that the rubble was waste, submitted that the inspector's conclusion that he had disposed of it was irrational.

Held: Appeal allowed. There was a substantial difference between tipping waste into a former quarry as landfill and depositing it temporarily on the land before using it in a process which, when complete, would no longer be waste, subject to the issue of whether the waste included contaminated materials. If the local authority considered that it was expedient to take enforcement action against importing and depositing waste pending its re-use, it could and should have said so in its notice and identified that as the specific activity which breached planning control. The evidence before the inspector had indicated that the local authority's case on breach of planning control had been disposal by tipping of the waste as a final activity and not depositing it temporarily with a view to recovering it. However, the landowner had not been intending to dispose of rubble by tipping it and would not have sought planning permission for that purpose. Having regard to the terms of the enforcement notice read in the context of the planning history and the reasons for enforcement action given by the local authority at the inquiry, the landowner's activity was not that which the local authority alleged had taken place. Accordingly, there had been misdirection by the inspector as to the form of disposal referred to in the enforcement notice. Since her decision was flawed, the matter would be remitted to the secretary of state for further consideration of the appeal against the enforcement notice (see paras 27-29, 40 of judgment).

COLLINS v SECRETARY OF STATE FOR COMMUNITIES AND LOCAL GOVERNMENT, [2016] EWHC 5 (Admin), [2016] Env. L.R. 28, Blake J, QBD (Admin).

POLICE

1768 Disclosure–Enhanced criminal record certificates–Failure to conduct reasonable statutory compliant independent review of reliability of material

[European Convention on Human Rights 1950 art.8; Police Act 1997 (c.50) s.117A, s.119B(9)]

The claimant applied for judicial review of the defendant independent monitor's review of the interested party police service's review of the information that it considered was relevant and ought to be included in an enhanced criminal record certificate. The claimant had applied for a certificate in order to apply to recommence work as a licensed hackney carriage taxi driver. The police service supplied information that the claimant had come to their notice on five occasions over 15 years earlier in respect of alleged indecent assaults on female passengers of a London taxi. One allegation had resulted in a charge, but that had been discontinued. The claimant made detailed objections to disclosure of the information based on serious deficiencies in the identification evidence. A review of the disclosure decision by the police and then by the independent monitor upheld the decision. The independent monitor said that there had been five definitive allegations in relation to which the claimant had been identified, that there was no reason to doubt the credibility of the allegations and that disclosure was necessary and proportionate under ECHR art.8. The claimant argued that the independent monitor had failed to deal properly with his allegations, make the requisite enquiries to resolve disputed issues of fact and give sufficient reasons.

Held: Application granted. In order for allegations to feature in the assessment of proportionality the decision-maker had to reach a conclusion about their reliability so as to afford them the correct weight when balancing the conflicting interests of the need to protect vulnerable groups from the risk of harm and an applicant's right under art.8, *R. (on the application of L) v Commissioner of Police of the Metropolis* [2009] UKSC 3, [2010] 1 A.C. 410, [2010] C.L.Y. 2633 followed. When conducting a review of a police decision the independent monitor exercised an independent monitoring review under the Police Act 1997 s.117A and had to apply the same statutory guidance that governed the police, which stated that allegations should not be included without taking reasonable steps to ascertain whether they were more likely than not to be true, *RK v Chief Constable of South Yorkshire* [2013] EWHC 1555 (Admin), [2013] A.C.D. 121 considered. The independent monitor had the ability to assess the merits of the police's conclusions and the statutory authority under s.119B(9) to demand from the police information that he might reasonably require in connection with exercising his review function. In the instant case the independent monitor was not required to investigate ab initio the claimant's grievances about the credibility and reliability of the allegations, but his decision revealed that he had not undertaken what was required of him in reviewing the police disclosure decision given the extent of the claimant's detailed objections. He had not undertaken the independent review required of him in accordance with his statutory obligations and applying the statutory guidance. His analysis of the disputed material was even more forcefully pitched against the claimant than that of the police reviewing officer and could not withstand the *Wednesbury* test of reasonableness. Given the dangers that could arise in relation to mistaken identification of assailants, the independent monitor was obliged to scrutinise with a high degree of forensic care the material said to incriminate the claimant. He had to then assess its weight with care. Only once he had reached a conclusion as to its weight could he undertake the balancing exercise necessary to justify an interference with the claimant's art.8 rights. The claimant had not had the benefit of a reasonable, statutorily compliant, independent review by the independent monitor of the reliability of the material that was the foundation of the information said to be relevant and disclosable (see paras 19, 24, 27, 30, 48-52 of judgment).

R. (ON THE APPLICATION OF MS) v INDEPENDENT MONITOR OF THE HOME OFFICE, [2016] EWHC 655 (Admin), [2016] 4 W.L.R. 88, Judge Blair QC, QBD (Admin).

1769 Disclosure–Enhanced criminal record certificates–Scheme concerning disclosure of convictions and cautions–Compatibility with art.8 ECHR

[Police Act 1997 (c.50) Pt V; Police Act 1997 (Criminal Record Certificates: Relevant Matters) (Amendment) (England and Wales) Order 2013 (SI 2013/1200); European Convention on Human Rights 1950 art.8; Rehabilitation of Offenders Act 1974 (Exceptions) Order 1975 (SI 1975/1023); Rehabilitation of Offenders Act 1974 (Exceptions) Order 1975 (Amendment) (England and Wales) Order 2013 (SI 2013/1198)]

The claimants sought declarations that (i) the scheme under the Police Act 1997 Pt V, as amended by the Police Act 1997 (Criminal Record Certificates: Relevant Matters) (Amendment) (England and Wales) Order 2013, was incompatible with ECHR art.8, and (ii) the Rehabilitation of Offenders Act 1974 (Exceptions) Order 1975, as amended by the Rehabilitation of Offenders Act 1974 (Exceptions) Order 1975 (Amendment) (England and Wales) Order 2013, was incompatible with art.8. Part V of the 1997 Act created a new machinery for the disclosure of criminal records held by the police where the information was required to assess the suitability of persons for employment or engagement in particular types of positions of trust or sensitivity, including positions involving contact with children. Under the Act, the Disclosure and Debarring Service was required to issue a criminal record certificate or an enhanced criminal record certificate to any person who applied for such a certificate. The Act required the disclosure of all convictions and cautions, whether current or spent and whatever the nature of the offence or offences to which they related. In *R. (on the application of T) v Chief Constable of Greater Manchester* [2014] UKSC 35, [2015] A.C. 49, [2014] C.L.Y. 1637, the Supreme Court held that the disclosure provisions of the Act were incompatible with art.8. The Act was modified by the amending Order as follows: where there were two or more convictions, they would always be disclosable on certificates; further, where a conviction was of a specified kind or resulted in a custodial sentence or was "current", it would always be disclosable. The 1975 Order provided for certain exceptions to the statutory exemption from disclosing "spent" convictions and cautions, for example in relation to those intending to work with children or vulnerable adults. The amending Order sought to modify the blanket applicability of those exceptions. The first claimant was a former teacher who had two convictions, one for a minor shoplifting offence and the other for failing to surrender, both of which had been committed at a time, 16 years ago, when she had mental-health problems. The second claimant was a 51-year-old finance director who had been convicted, at the ages of 17 and 18, of theft and driving without insurance. Both were caught by the legislation.

Held: Judgment accordingly. (1) In *T*, the Supreme Court moved the domestic understanding of the requirement for an interference with art.8 rights to be "in accordance with the law" a significant distance from what had previously been understood: the question now was whether the 1997 Act afforded the individual adequate protection against arbitrariness; further, for an interference with art.8 rights to be "in accordance with the law", there had to be adequate safeguards which had the effect of enabling the proportionality of the interference to be adequately examined. It could be seen from this and other cases that the present rules could give rise to some very startling consequences. Such results were properly to be described as "arbitrary". No doubt in many cases rules requiring the indefinite disclosure of certain serious offences would be seen as far from arbitrary, in that such offences would clearly be relevant to anyone considering a person's suitability for engagement in a sensitive post requiring an enhanced criminal record certificate. However, when the rules were capable of producing such questionable results, there ought to be some machinery for testing the proportionality of the interference if the scheme was to be "in accordance with the law". If the present scheme was not in accordance with the law, the state's "margin of appreciation" fell away. The deference that a judge would always feel towards a scheme expressly sanctioned by Parliament could not be engaged. Equally, questions of administrative convenience could have no operative place in assessing the lawfulness of the interference with Convention rights. In any event, the court was far from convinced that a review scheme would be unworkable. The issue of whether the interference with art.8 rights was "necessary" did not strictly arise. However, there was no reason for thinking that the convictions in issue bore, for the claimants' entire lifetimes, a rational relationship with the objects sought to be achieved by the disclosure provisions of the Act, simply because in the case of each claimant there was more than one conviction, *T* applied (see paras 84-89 of judgment). (2) As to the 1975 Order as amended, the court should go no further than did the Supreme Court in *T*, when it held that the interference in issue was not necessary in a democratic society to attain the aim pursued (paras 54, 90-91).

R. (ON THE APPLICATION OF P) v SECRETARY OF STATE FOR JUSTICE; R. (ON THE APPLICATION OF A) v SECRETARY OF STATE FOR JUSTICE, [2016] EWHC 89 (Admin), [2016] 1 W.L.R. 2009, McCombe LJ, QBD (Admin).

1770 **Disclosure–Reprimands and warnings–Statutory regime requiring disclosure of historic reprimands to potential employers–Compatibility with art.8 ECHR**

[Rehabilitation of Offenders Act 1974 (c.53); Police Act 1997 (c.50); Human Rights Act 1998 (c.42); European Convention on Human Rights 1950 art.8]

The claimant applied for judicial review of the disclosure scheme for convictions and cautions. The claimant had been issued with two reprimands for offences of sexual activity with a child when he was 13 years old. The incidents involved other boys who were two to three years younger than him and appeared to have been consensual and non-exploitative, and involved sexual experimentation. The claimant was the only one over the age of criminal responsibility. The claimant's mother was given an inaccurate and incomplete leaflet which led her to conclude that the record of his reprimands would not be retained after five years if there was no subsequent offending during that time. When the claimant was 18 years old he applied for employment that required enhanced disclosure. By that time reprimands given to juveniles were treated as cautions. By way of exemption from the principle of non-disclosure in the Rehabilitation of Offenders Act 1974, convictions and cautions were required to be disclosed in certain circumstances. By the terms of the Police Act 1997 disclosure was required if an employer asked the data subject to obtain enhanced disclosure. A change in policy meant that such reprimands would remain on the police national computer indefinitely or until the individual was 100 years old. The claimant asked the Chief Constable to exercise her discretion to expunge the record of the reprimands having regard to the circumstances of the offending and the Crown Prosecution Service's guidance on rape and sexual offences. The Chief Constable decided that the reprimands were lawfully administered, and there was insufficient reason within the terms of the policy to erase the records. The claimant submitted that the Chief Constable's refusal to erase the data was flawed as the reprimands should never have been issued. If that submission failed he sought a declaration of incompatibility against the defendant secretaries of states under the Human Rights Act 1998 for unjustified interference with his ECHR art.8 rights. He submitted that a disclosure scheme without sufficient safeguards to assess relevance and proportionality was not in accordance with the law.

Held: Declaration granted in favour of claimant. (1) The challenge to the legality of the decision to issue the reprimands failed. The prosecutor had not failed to have regard to the CPS guidance or otherwise reached a decision that was irrational or unlawful. The guidance had to be read as a whole and no single paragraph was dispositive. The fact that no force had been used and the younger boys had agreed to participate and may have had some previous sexual encounters before voluntarily engaging in the activity with the claimant were relevant but not conclusive factors against a reprimand being issued. The prosecutor was also entitled to note that the younger boys were under 13, incapable of giving consent and that such young children needed particular protection from sexual experiences that they were unlikely to have fully understood. The activity was not confined to a single incident or a single child and had carried on for over a year, and some expression of official concern was needed (see paras 30, 32 of judgment). (2) If there were insufficient safeguards to ensure that the data retained was relevant to and necessary for the purpose for which it was disclosed to the third party, then, despite the existence of the filtering process under the more recent national measures, the overall regime for disclosure could not be said to have the characteristics that the ECHR required in order for the interference with private life caused by the transmission to be in accordance with the law, *R. (on the application of P) v Secretary of State for Justice* [2016] EWHC 89 (Admin), [2016] 1 W.L.R. 2009, [2016] 1769 and *MM v United Kingdom (24029/07)* Times, January 16, 2013 applied. The claimant's offences were serious enough to require disclosure and the claimant was seeking an individualised assessment scheme that had been rejected as impractical in the discussions leading to the amendments. The claimant had a highly arguable case that despite the statutory scheme, as amended, disclosure of the data to a third party was not relevant and proportionate. The claimant had a compelling case that a review mechanism was needed and was practicable. He fell within a class of people within the criteria set out in *MM* where the European Court of Human Rights had concluded that the nature of the offence, the disposal in the case, the time that had elapsed since the offence took place or the relevance of the data to the employment sought, might reasonably result in a decision by a public authority applying human rights principles that disclosure was not relevant or necessary, *MM* applied. There were insufficient safeguards and the interference with the claimant's art.8 rights was not in accordance with the law. The absence of any procedure enabling a decision-maker to examine all the relevant considerations resulted in the statutory regime being incompatible with the claimant's rights. The claimant was entitled to declaratory relief (paras 43, 45, 47-48, 50- 51).

R. (ON THE APPLICATION OF G) v CHIEF CONSTABLE OF SURREY; R. (ON THE APPLICATION OF G) v SECRETARY OF STATE FOR THE HOME DEPARTMENT, [2016] EWHC 295 (Admin), [2016] 4 W.L.R. 94, Blake J, QBD (Admin).

1771 Elections–Police and crime commissioners

THE POLICE AND CRIME COMMISSIONER ELECTIONS (RETURNING OFFICERS' ACCOUNTS) (AMENDMENT) REGULATIONS 2016, SI 2016/488; made under the Police Reform and Social Responsibility Act 2011 s.55(10). In force: 4 May 2016.

This instrument amends the Police and Crime Commissioner Elections (Returning Officers' Accounts) Regulations 2012, which set out the manner and form in which returning officers at police and crime commissioner elections must submit an account of their charges. In particular, it reduces the deadline for submission of accounts and amends the definition of "accounting officer" to whom an account must be addressed (such that it must now be submitted to the Cabinet Office rather than the Home Office).

1772 Enhanced criminal record certificates–Presumption of innocence–Inclusion of details of acquittal on rape charge had not undermined correctness of acquittal

[European Convention on Human Rights 1950 art.6(2), art.8]

The appellant appealed against a decision (*R. (on the application of R) v Chief Constable of Greater Manchester* [2013] EWHC 2721 (Admin)) refusing his application for judicial review challenging the lawfulness of the contents of an enhanced criminal record certificate issue by the first respondent chief constable. The appellant had applied for the certificate when applying for work as a private hire taxi driver. The certificate stated that the appellant had been tried and acquitted of raping a 17-year-old woman who had been a passenger in his taxi. On appeal, a reviewing officer concluded that the disputed information was relevant and ought to be included because the CPS had believed there to be a realistic prospect of a conviction, which indicated that the allegation was more likely to be true than false. The appellant sought judicial review on the grounds that it breached his right to the presumption of innocence in ECHR art.6(2) and that it would adversely affect his family life in breach of art.8. The judge held that it did not breach art.6(2) to imply that notwithstanding an acquittal a person might have committed the act complained of in the criminal charge. He found that despite proceeding on the false basis that the allegation was likely to be true, the reviewing officer's comments overall had been fair.

Held: Appeal dismissed. (1) Once it was accepted that art.6(2) was engaged on the facts of a particular case, there was nothing materially inconsistent in the approaches of the Supreme Court and the European Court of Human Rights, *Allen v United Kingdom (25424/09)* (2016) 63 E.H.R.R. 10, [2014] C.L.Y. 1630 applied, *R. (on the application of Adams) v Secretary of State for Justice* [2011] UKSC 18, [2012] 1 A.C. 48, [2011] C.L.Y. 794 followed. Lord Hope's short summary of the principles in *Adams*, that it was not open to the state to undermine the effect of an acquittal, represented in broad terms how English law was to decide problems of the present type. It was important to have in mind the general principles set out in *Allen*, that the presumption of innocence remained after acquittal, and that whenever the question of the applicability of art.6(2) arose in subsequent proceedings, the applicant had to demonstrate the existence of a link between the concluded criminal proceedings and the subsequent proceedings. Public officials must not treat acquitted persons as if they were guilty of the criminal charges of which they had been acquitted. However, there was to be no single approach to ascertaining whether there had been a violation in proceedings post acquittal. Much depended on the context of the decision to be taken. In the instant case, there had been no violation of art.6(2). There was no aspersion cast on the correctness of the acquittal, nor was it suggested that the appellant was guilty. It went too far to suggest that the fact of an acquittal could never feature in an enhanced criminal record certificate. There was some unfortunate language in the reviewing officer's reasoning, but art.6(2) had only been applied by the ECtHR to public statements of state organs and not documents such as the reviewing officer's reasons which were not in the general public domain. The ECtHR had not previously found a violation of art.6(2) in a situation such as the instant case, and the instant court should not go beyond the limits of the previous cases decided in the ECtHR, *R. (on the application of Ullah) v Special Adjudicator* [2004] UKHL 26, [2004] 2 A.C. 323, [2004] C.L.Y. 2009 applied (see paras 54-58 of judgment). (2) A failure to consult the appellant before issuing the certificate had not breached the procedural requirements of art.8, *R. (on the application of L) v Commissioner of Police of the Metropolis* [2009] UKSC 3, [2010] 1 A.C. 410, [2010] C.L.Y. 2633 applied. In relation to the alleged substantive breaches of art.8, the role of the first-instance judge was to conduct a high intensity review of the original decision, and decide whether the decision reached a proportionate result. The appellate court would only consider proportionality itself if the judge had made a significant error of principle. In the instant case the judge had made no such error (paras 66, 74-75).

R. (ON THE APPLICATION OF R) v CHIEF CONSTABLE OF GREATER MANCHESTER, [2016] EWCA Civ 490, [2016] 1 W.L.R. 4125, Lord Dyson MR, CA (Civ Div).

1773 Football banning orders–Right to respect for private and family life–Justification–Necessary for prevention of crime and disorder

[Football Spectators Act 1989 (c.37) s.14(4), s.14B(4), s.14G; European Convention on Human Rights 1950 art.8, art.8(2)]

The appellant police appealed by way of case stated against a magistrates' court's decision to impose a football banning order on the respondent with a limitation. The appellant had applied for a football banning order against the respondent. The order was granted for a three-year period however, in relation to matches in the UK the magistrates inserted a limitation that the order would only be in relation to matches between three football teams whether at home or away. The effect was that the respondent was free to attend regulated football matches which did not involve the three named clubs. The appellants contended that there was no power to impose a prohibition limited in that way. The question was whether the magistrates had power to make a football banning order under the Football Spectators Act 1989 s.14B(4) limited to matches between the three teams. The respondent submitted that any interference with his ECHR art.8 private life had to be the least which would meet the legitimate aim of controlling violence at football matches. He argued that if the justices had found that he only presented a risk at certain matches, it had to be disproportionate and therefore unlawful to impose a ban which prevented him from attending any other matches. He contended that if the 1989 Act said otherwise, it had to be read down so as to comply with art.8.

Held: Appeal allowed. (1) Banning orders could engage art.8, but that had to be understood as relating to the power to impose additional requirements in addition to the mandated terms of a banning order defined by s.14(4). It did not mean that an order simply in those mandatory terms was capable of engaging art.8, at least where the subject of the order was simply a spectator at football matches. The protection afforded by art.8 was confined to the private sphere of a person's existence and did not extend to engagement in sporting activities which, by their very nature, were conducted in public with social aspects involving the wider community, *R. (on the application of Countryside Alliance) v Attorney General* [2007] UKHL 52, [2008] 1 A.C. 719, [2007] C.L.Y. 204 followed. Article 8 was not engaged where a person was prevented from attending as a spectator, an event to which the public were invited in return for payment, and subject to contractual terms. It was simply not arguable that the freedom to attend professional football matches as a paying spectator enjoyed the protection of art.8 from interference by the state. There was no human right protected by the ECHR to attend football matches as a spectator. That did diminish the importance of football and other entertainment in society, but to involve human rights in that sphere would, undermine the importance to be attached to those rights in areas where they were genuinely engaged. In any event, the rights, if they were engaged, were not unqualified. If a football banning order interfered with an individual's right to respect for private life under art.8, that interference was justified under art.8(2) on the grounds that it was necessary for the prevention of crime and disorder, *Gough v Chief Constable of Derbyshire* [2002] EWCA Civ 351, [2002] Q.B. 1213, [2002] C.L.Y. 1579 followed. The 1989 Act created a narrow tailored jurisdiction. If two threshold conditions were found to have been established an order had to be made. The person affected must have caused or contributed to violence and the evidence had to show that making the banning order would help prevent violence or disorder at football matches. If those two conditions were met, the court had no discretion as to how to proceed. It had to make the order and no other order. Having made the order, the court should then go on to decide whether to impose any additional requirements under s.14G. The court's power and discretion was narrowly limited until the s.14G stage (see paras 15-17, 19-22 of judgment). (2) No comparison could be made with the legislation for anti-social behaviour orders. There was no principle to be carried over from a provision which gave a court a wide power to make a variety of orders to a provision which gave the court no power to choose what order to make if the threshold conditions were met (para.27). (3) The answer to the question posed in the case stated was "No".

COMMISSIONER OF POLICE OF THE METROPOLIS v THORPE, [2015] EWHC 3339 (Admin), [2016] 4 W.L.R. 7, Edis J, QBD (Admin).

1774 Human trafficking–Enforcement officers–Codes of practice

THE MODERN SLAVERY ACT 2015 (CODE OF PRACTICE) REGULATIONS 2016, SI 2016/823; made under the Modern Slavery Act 2015 Sch.2 para.5(6). In force: 8 August 2016.

This instrument brings into force a Code of Practice to be followed by constables and enforcement officers when arresting a person under the maritime enforcement powers set out in the Modern Slavery Act 2015 in relation to the England and Wales slavery and human trafficking offences.

1775 Independent Police Complaints Commission–Investigations–Commission entitled to re-open investigation

[Police Reform Act 2002 (c.30) Sch.3, s.10]

The appellant police commissioner appealed against a decision (*R. (on the application of Demetrio) v Independent Police Complaints Commission* [2015] EWHC 593 (Admin), [2015] P.T.S.R. 1268, [2015] C.L.Y. 2056) that the respondent IPCC was entitled to re-open an investigation against a police officer which it had recommended the commissioner close. The IPCC had conducted an investigation into events that had occurred in a police van following the arrest of a suspect (D). The IPCC's report concluded that there was no case to answer in regard to an allegation that a police officer had put his hands around D's neck and tried to strangle him. It did, however, find a case to answer in respect of other allegations arising out of the incident. Consequently, the commissioner thought that there should be no disciplinary action relating to the strangling allegation, and the IPCC agreed. Subsequently, the IPCC considered re-opening the investigation of the strangling allegation. The commissioner contended that the functus officio principle was applicable as the IPCC had already made a determination in respect of the strangling allegation. The IPCC issued a decision notice to re-open the investigation. The commissioner applied for judicial review seeking to quash the IPCC's decision notice, and restraining the IPCC from carrying out further investigation into the strangling allegation. The Divisional Court, in dismissing the application for judicial review, held that the IPCC was entitled to re-open the investigation. The commissioner submitted that the IPCC had no power to re-open its decision not to recommend or direct disciplinary action because it was functus officio: the Police Reform Act 2002 Sch.3 contained express provisions for review in certain cases, so it could not have intended the IPCC to have such a power when none was expressly provided for. The IPCC submitted that it only finally discharged its functions when all criminal and disciplinary proceedings arising from a complaint had been finally concluded.

Held: Appeal dismissed. The appeal was academic, as the investigation had been re-opened. However, it was appropriate for the court to hear the appeal; two public authorities had had a fundamental disagreement about an important point of public law, and it was in the public interest for it to be resolved. The IPCC's functions and responsibilities were defined in the Police Reform Act 2002 s.10. Schedule 3 gave the IPCC ultimate control over the progress of an investigation and any disciplinary and criminal proceedings that followed. However, complaints were not resolved until any proceedings agreed or directed by the IPCC had been concluded. Schedule 3 set out a regime for the holistic handling of police complaint matters from end to end. There were intermediate stages in the handling of such matters, but the process was not to be regarded as a number of self-contained steps that had to undertaken without regard to the overall statutory objective to deal with matters efficiently, effectively and with public confidence. The IPCC's handling of D's complaint had been ongoing when it recommended that proceedings should not be brought against the officer in respect of the strangling allegation. The complaint had not been resolved or concluded, and the IPCC's functions in respect of it were far from over. Functio officio meant that a judicial, ministerial or administrative actor had performed a function in circumstances where there was no power to revoke or modify it. For there to be a power to revoke, the function must have been performed. D's complaints were still in progress, and so it could not be said that the IPCC had "performed" its function. The fact that there was no express provision for review in sch.3 was not sufficient to outweigh the clear definition of the IPCC's functions and to allow for an interpretation of the steps in Sch.3 that would make every one irrevocably concluded without the possibility of review if such a course was later shown to be desirable and in the public interest. It was undesirable for the IPCC to be stuck with a questionable decision until, at least, the entire handling of a complaint had been concluded. Any decision by the IPCC to re-open would need a compelling reason and, in the instant case, there had been one (see paras 34-35, 37, 42-43, 45 of judgment).

R. (ON THE APPLICATION OF DEMETRIO) v INDEPENDENT POLICE COMPLAINTS COMMISSION; R. (ON THE APPLICATION OF COMMISSIONER OF POLICE OF THE METROPOLIS) v INDEPENDENT POLICE COMPLAINTS COMMISSION, [2015] EWCA Civ 1248, [2016] P.T.S.R. 891, Gloster LJ, CA (Civ Div).

1776 Investigatory powers–Authorisations–Right of journalist to protect identity of source–Breach of complainant's Convention rights

[European Convention on Human Rights 1950 art.10; Regulation of Investigatory Powers Act 2000 (c.23) s.22; Police and Criminal Evidence Act 1984 (c.60); Human Rights Act 1998 (c.42) s.6]

A newspaper group and three of its journalists brought a complaint against the Commissioner under the ECHR art.10. Communications data had been sought and obtained by the police during an investigation into an incident which took place in September 2012 when the Government Chief Whip was prevented from leaving Downing Street on his bicycle through the main gate. Shortly after the altercation the gate officer wrote an email to his superiors, setting out a detailed account of the incident. Later that day a source telephoned the news desk of one of the complainant newspapers to report the incident. Two days later an article about the incident appeared on the front page of that paper. The claim was made in respect of four authorisations issued under the Regulation of Investigatory Powers Act 2000 s.22, the purpose of which was to enable the police to obtain communications data which might have revealed the sources of information obtained by the journalists. They were prepared by a detective constable and assessed by an officer designated and trained to facilitate the lawful acquisition of communications data. At the relevant time, the 2007 Code of Practice related to the exercise of the power conferred by s.22. A revised Code in 2015 required that an application by a police force for communications data designed to identify a journalists's source should be made under the Police and Criminal Evidence Act 1984 which required judicial authorisation. The issue was whether the obtaining of the communications data was prescribed by law and necessary in a democratic society so as to comply with the requirements of art.10.

Held: Judgment accordingly. (1) Whether the art.10 rights had been infringed was an objective question, which did not depend on the procedural propriety of the decision-making process or the adequacy of reasoning of the designated person granting the authorisation. There had been reasonable grounds to suspect a conspiracy by a number of police officers to discredit a government minister, and the applications had been made for the purpose of investigating that serious criminal offence. The authorisations thus pursued a legitimate aim, *R. (on the application of Malik) v Manchester Crown Court* [2008] EWHC 1362 (Admin), [2008] 4 All E.R. 403, [2008] C.L.Y. 408 applied. In the circumstances, it was honestly and reasonably believed by those making the application, and the designated person when he approved it, that it was reasonable to take steps to identify the source of the leak. If prior enquiries had been made of the newspaper group, the journalists would have declined to disclose their sources. However, before the third authorisation was made the police had already discovered the source and thus it was not supported by a compelling case that disclosure of the data was necessary to make the investigation effective. There might have been a proper investigative purpose, but it did not justify the serious step of obtaining access to communications data which might identify a journalist's sources. Accordingly, the first, second and fourth authorisations were both necessary and proportionate; the third authorisation was neither necessary nor proportionate to the legitimate aim which it pursued and there was thus an infringement of Convention rights in that respect (see paras 65-71, 73-77, 79-83 of judgment). (2) Although there were other alternative measures which could have been adopted to obtain the data, the 2000 Act was, at the relevant time and under the provisions of the 2007 Code, reasonably considered to be the appropriate means for the police to obtain communications data. The issue of proportionality was directed to the effect of the infringement in question, not to the procedure by which an order or authorisation was obtained. It was the intrusion which had to be justified under the principle of proportionality, *Ernst v Belgium (33400/96)* (2004) 39 E.H.R.R. 35, [2005] C.L.Y. 2048 considered (paras 89-91). (3) Section 22 did comply with the principle of legal certainty, *Gillan v United Kingdom (4158/05)* (2010) 50 E.H.R.R. 45, [2010] C.L.Y. 1746 applied. The discretion granted to a designated person under s.22 was not unfettered: it was subject to review by an independent commissioner and, in the event of a complaint, by a tribunal. The power conferred by s.22 was thus subject to protection against arbitrary use for the general run of criminal cases. However, cases directly engaging freedom of the press required different treatment. The 2015 Code recognised the need for judicial authorisation in respect of communications data disclosing journalists' sources. Importantly it required that an authorisation which might reveal a journalist's source was dealt with under the 1984 Act, ensuring that a proper balancing exercise would be conducted independently of the police force making the application. Accordingly, the legal regime under s.22 did not contain effective safeguards to protect art.10 rights in a case in which the authorisations had the purpose of obtaining disclosure of the identity of a journalist's source (paras 97, 103-104, 109-111). (4) Applying the Human Rights Act 1998 s.6, the commissioner did not act unlawfully in making the first, second and fourth authorisations under s.22. However, s.6(2) did not preclude a finding in favour of unlawfulness in respect of the third authorisation which did not comply with the requirements of s.22 (paras 120, 126).

NEWS GROUP NEWSPAPERS LTD v COMMISSIONER OF POLICE OF THE METROPOLIS, [2016] 2 All E.R. 483, Burton J, IPT.

1777 PACE codes of practice–Police interviews–Suspects

THE POLICE AND CRIMINAL EVIDENCE ACT 1984 (CODES OF PRACTICE) (REVISION OF CODE E) ORDER 2016, SI 2016/35; made under the Police and Criminal Evidence Act 1984 s.67(5). In force: 2 February 2016.

This Order brings into force a revised code of practice under the Police and Criminal Evidence Act 1984 s.60(1)(a) which will supersede the existing code of practice issued under that subsection.

1778 Police and crime commissioners–Returning officers–Specified services and expenses

THE POLICE AND CRIME COMMISSIONER ELECTIONS (LOCAL RETURNING OFFICERS' AND POLICE AREA RETURNING OFFICERS' CHARGES) ORDER 2016, SI 2016/514; made under the Police Reform and Social Responsibility Act 2011 s.55(1)(2), s.154(5). In force: In accordance with art.1.

This Order specifies: the overall maximum amount and the maximum amounts for specified services and specified expenses that may be recovered by a local returning officer in respect of a voting area at a police and crime commissioner (PCC) election; the overall maximum amount and the maximum amounts for specified services and specified expenses that may be recovered by a police area returning officer in respect of a police area at a PCC election; and the maximum amounts that may be recovered (instead of the amounts referred to previously) where an election is uncontested.

1779 Police authorities–Riot–Section 2(1) Riot (Damages) Act 1886–Compensation only for physical damage to property

[Riot (Damages) Act 1886 (c.38) s.2(1)]

The appellant police authority appealed against a decision (*Mitsui Sumitomo Insurance Co (Europe) Ltd v Mayor's Office for Policing and Crime* [2014] EWCA Civ 682, [2015] Q.B. 180, [2014] C.L.Y. 2448) concerning its liability to pay compensation for losses caused by riot damage. The appeal arose from three conjoined claims brought against the police authority pursuant to the Riot (Damages) Act 1886 s.2(1). During a period of rioting in August 2011, a gang of youths had broken into a distribution warehouse, looted it and burnt it down. The owner of the warehouse, its occupier and three companies which had stored goods there all sustained losses as a result of the looting and the fire. Their losses included the physical loss of the warehouse and its contents together with consequential loss including business interruption losses, loss of profits and loss of rent. The respondents, who comprised the three companies and the insurers of the owner and occupier, sought to recover those losses from the police authority under s.2(1). At first instance, the judge held that s.2(1) provided compensation only for physical damage to property and not for consequential losses such as loss of profits or rent. The Court of Appeal reversed that finding. The police authority argued that it had been wrong to do so.

Held: Appeal allowed. The words of the 1886 Act should be construed in the light of the prior legislation. The Riot Act 1714 used open-textured wording, requiring the payment of "damages" to persons injured or damaged by the demolition of their houses. The courts' liberal interpretation of that Act extended the liability of the "hundred" (hundreds being predecessors of police authorities) to cover physical damage to household goods and furniture but no further. That limited extension was incorporated into the Seditious Meetings Act 1817. Over time, statutory innovations extended the scope of the compensation to cover agricultural buildings, mills, commercial and industrial buildings, the contents of those buildings, and mines and collieries. There was nothing in the wording of the 1886 Act that supported an intention to extend the scope of the compensation to cover consequential loss. The wording suggested a contrary intention. There was no provision for compensation for personal injury or for injury to property other than buildings and their contents; that indicated that it was not correct to interpret the words "sustained loss by such ... destruction" in s.2(1) as creating an unqualified causal test to which the normal rules of causation in tort could readily be applied. There was also an unusual provision for compensation to be reduced according to very broad assessments of the conduct of the person seeking compensation. The Act's provisions supported the conclusion that it, like its predecessors, created a self-contained statutory scheme which did not mirror the common law of tort (see paras 16, 34 of judgment).

MITSUI SUMITOMO INSURANCE CO (EUROPE) LTD v MAYOR'S OFFICE FOR POLICING AND CRIME *sub nom.* MAYOR'S OFFICE FOR POLICING AND CRIME v MITSUI SUMITOMO INSURANCE CO (EUROPE) LTD; ROYAL AND SUN ALLIANCE INSURANCE PLC v MAYOR'S OFFICE FOR POLICING AND CRIME; LACE

INTERNATIONAL LTD v MAYOR'S OFFICE FOR POLICING AND CRIME, [2016] UKSC 18, [2016] 2 W.L.R. 1148, Lord Neuberger PSC, SC.

1780 Police officers–Pensions–Policeman suffering from recurrent depressive disorder–Entitlement to pension under Police Pensions Regulations 1987–Permanent disability

[Police Pensions Regulations 1987 (SI 1987/257) Pt A reg.12, Pt B reg.3]

The claimant police officer (S) applied for judicial review of the interested party board's decision that he was not entitled to a pension under the Police Pensions Regulations 1987. S had been a serving police officer for 15 years until his resignation. He was a member of the police pension fund throughout his time in office. S's career was characterised by periods of good performance, but he also had long periods off work as a result of psychiatric illness. After his resignation S applied for an ill health award under Pt B reg.3 on the ground that he was permanently disabled from being able to perform all of the duties of a police officer. As required by the Regulations, the Chief Constable referred the decision to a selected medical practitioner who recorded a diagnosis of recurrent depressive disorder but noted that S was functioning at a reasonable level in terms of everyday activity. The board decided that S was not permanently disabled within the meaning of Pt A reg.12. S's appeal was based on an expert's report that described him as having a "paranoid attitude" and liable to develop a psychiatric disorder under stress, and stated that if S returned to work he would become unable to work and to perform his ordinary duties. S's appeal was dismissed by a second board.

Held: Application granted. (1) In the light of Pt A reg.12, in order to determine whether an officer was entitled to an ill health award it was necessary to ask three questions. The police officer would be entitled to an award if, and only if, the answer to each question was affirmative (see paras 32-33 of judgment). The first was whether the officer was suffering from an infirmity of the mind or body. The definition of infirmity in Pt A reg.12(5) was wide and included "mental disorder, injury and condition". There was no restriction on the mental disorders covered in the definition. The board ought to have held that S's recurrent disorder was an infirmity within the meaning of Pt A reg.12(5). It was unnecessary and wrong to go on to consider whether S's paranoid attitude was also an infirmity. It was a cause of the infirmity, not the infirmity itself. It had crossed the line and was a recognised medical condition, *R. (on the application of Northumbria Police Authority) v Broome* [2005] EWHC 2644 (Admin), [2006] I.C.R. 555, [2006] C.L.Y. 3403 considered (paras 34, 47). (2) The second question was whether that infirmity caused S to be unable to perform his duties as a police officer. The board's decisions did not deal with causation in any great detail. In the second decision the causation question was combined with the permanence question. It did not seek to answer the question whether the recurrent depressive disorder caused S to be unable to carry out his normal duties. S was unable to carry out his duties during the extensive periods off work when the recurrent depressive disorder was not in remission. Substantial inability to perform any of a police officer's duties as a result of the infirmity should enable an officer to be classified as disabled. However, that required the board to form a view as to whether the inability was substantial. That required an assessment of the effect of the disability when not in remission and the likelihood of recurrence. The board had not attempted such an assessment in either of its reports (paras 58, 60-61, 63-65). (3) The third question was whether S's inability to perform his normal duties was permanent. The second board's view was that a "paranoid attitude" was not a permanent disablement; diagnosis of recurrent depression by itself was not sufficient to render an officer permanently disabled; the additional element of a permanent attitude did not make S's case a permanent disablement; and it did not consider such an attitude to be immutable. The question whether a paranoid attitude was an infirmity was not relevant to the issues before the board. The paranoid attitude was one of the causes of the severity of the recurrent depressive disorder that S suffered. It was accepted that a recurrent depressive order might not, in itself, be a permanent disablement, but might be. The questions for the board had been whether S's recurrent depressive disorder was sufficiently serious to amount to a permanent disablement. That involved a consideration of the effect on S of previous incidents of recurrent depressive disorder, the likelihood of recurrence if S returned to work, the likely effect on him of future incidents including the extent to which he would recover from any further incidents. That was plainly a matter for the board but there was no indication that it had considered those matters. Although the board's reports were not written by lawyers and should not be construed as legal documents, they had to be written so that those reading them could understand the basis for its decision. S had been entitled to know the reasons why the board decided that the paranoid attitude was immutable. The report was silent on that issue and contained no assessment of the likelihood that S's paranoid attitude would change prior to his normal retirement age. If the likelihood was very small then it would not prevent S's disability from being permanent. The statement that the paranoid attitude was not immutable was insufficient to determine the permanence of S's disability. The decision was quashed and a rehearing before a differently constituted tribunal was directed (paras 66-70)

SHARP v CHIEF CONSTABLE OF WEST YORKSHIRE, [2016] EWHC 469 (Admin), (2016) 149 B.M.L.R. 163, Judge Behrens, QBD (Admin).

1781 **Police powers and duties–Authorised persons–Certificate issued under s.20 Road Traffic Offenders Act 1988 signed by prosecuting clerk–Certificate valid**

[Road Traffic Offenders Act 1988 (c.53) s.20]

The appellant appealed by way of case stated against a magistrates' court decision convicting him of speeding. The appellant had notice of the trial date but had not attended the trial. The chief constable served the trial documents he relied on on the appellant prior to the trial. Included was a certificate pursuant to the Road Traffic Offenders Act 1988 s.20 signed by the Prosecutions Clerk (W); it included details of the recording device and the speed the camera had recorded. Section 20(1) stated that evidence of a fact relevant to proceedings for an offence could be given by the production of (a) a record produced by a prescribed device, and (b) a certificate as to the circumstances in which the record was produced signed by a constable or by a person authorised, by or on behalf of, the chief officer of police for the police area in which the offence had been allegedly committed. Section 20(7) stated that a document purporting to be a record of the kind mentioned in s.20(1) or to be a certificate or other document signed as mentioned, was deemed to be such a record, or to be so signed, unless the contrary was proved. The justices accepted the certificate as evidence and were satisfied that the appellant had exceeded the speed limit. The appellant's case was that the magistrates had erred in law in relying on the s.20 certificate when there was no evidence that W had been authorised to sign it. The question was whether the court had been entitled to treat the certificate as in accordance with s.20. The appellant argued that reading s.20(1) with s.20(7) there was a requirement for the certificate to state on its face that it had been signed by either the chief constable or a person authorised by, and on behalf of, the chief constable and that when the certificate was not signed by the chief constable it should be stated on its face that the person signing had been authorised by the chief constable to do so.

Held: Appeal dismissed. Once it was clear that s.20(1) did not require a person who was authorised to say in the certificate that he was authorised, that implication could not be read in as a result of s.20(7). Looking at the matter as a whole there were indications on the face of the certificate that it emanated from the constabulary and by a prosecutions clerk of that constabulary who was cognisant with s.20 and he was satisfied of its requirements. The appellant's contention could not be accepted as a proper construction of the provision. Section 20(7) did not impliedly insert a further requirement. It had been open to the parties, including the justices to enquire further but that had not been done.

CRADER v CHIEF CONSTABLE OF HAMPSHIRE *sub nom.* CRADER v DPP, [2015] EWHC 3553 (Admin), (2016) 180 J.P. 199, Blake J, QBD (Admin).

1782 **Police powers and duties–Disclosure–Teacher's past sexual misconduct with students–Failure to verify information against police database records–Disclosure unlawful**

[European Convention on Human Rights 1950 art.8; Police Act 1997 (c.50); Data Protection Act 1998 (c.29)]

A teacher applied for judicial review of the disclosure by the defendant chief constable of information about his dismissal from a college teaching post. He also challenged a decision that the police had not acted unlawfully in disclosing the information. The teacher had been dismissed in September 2010 for gross misconduct, having made inappropriate sexual comments to female students. The college relied on the General Teaching Council code of conduct, which required appropriate professional boundaries between teachers and children. However, the teaching council found the incident to fall short of unacceptable professional conduct. A year later, the teacher obtained another position at a girls' school. He disclosed his previous dismissal, but explained that it had not been ratified by the teaching council. At the time of the dismissal, the defendant's child abuse unit had been helping the college with the dismissal of another staff member. The unit was not involved with the teacher's case, but the college nevertheless notified it of his dismissal. The unit asked for details for its database. The college emailed the teacher's name and stated the reason for dismissal as "inappropriate behaviour and comments towards female students". In time, the unit learnt of the teacher's new post. An officer told the defendant's public protection department that there was a safeguarding issue, as the teacher had two previous dismissals, one of which was for "touching pupils and getting them to touch him". That was untrue in two respects: the teacher had been dismissed only once, and in respect of an incident which did not involve touching. The information was communicated to the Local Authority Designated Officer, who notified the teacher's employer. The school terminated the teacher's employment. The teacher made a data access request to discover the source of the information. The police officer relied on an entry in his police notebook dated October 2010, which referred to the teacher having had an erection in front of school children. He said he had received that information from the college when following up on the nature of the teacher's misconduct. The teacher complained to the defendant's professional standards department that the officers had not followed the Disclosure and Barring Service formal reporting procedures. The defendant decided that the police officer had not breached his legal safeguarding duties. The decision was upheld on appeal. The court was required to determine whether the disclosure was in breach of the teacher's rights under ECHR art.8 and whether the police complaints procedure had been properly conducted.

Held: Application granted. (1) The police had common law powers to obtain and store information for policing purposes. The Data Protection Act 1998 prevented interference with art.8 rights and the Police Act 1997 provided relevant safeguards for disclosure of information about enhanced criminal record certificates, *R. (on the application of L) v Commissioner of Police of the Metropolis* [2009] UKSC 3, [2010] 1 A.C. 410, [2010] C.L.Y. 2633 and *R. (on the application of A) v Chief Constable of Kent* [2013] EWCA Civ 1706, (2014) 135 B.M.L.R. 22, [2014] C.L.Y. 2444 and [*R. (on the application of Catt) v Association of Chief Police Officers of England, Wales and Northern Ireland* [2015] UKSC 9, [2015] A.C. 1065, [2015] C.L.Y. 1298 considered. Unlike disclosure prompted by a specific request, however, the instant case concerned a proactive measure carried out by the officer. He would clearly have known that it would have repercussions for the teacher's employment. Neither the fact that the disclosure was to the Local Authority Designated Officer nor the statutory safeguarding provisions absolved the defendant from having to consider whether disclosure was necessary and proportionate. Before deciding to disclose, each officer should have considered the criteria in the 1997 Act, even though they were not in a situation involving an enhanced criminal record certificate (see paras 53, 55-57, 66-68, 70-73, 75, 84-85 of judgment). (2) The disclosure had been made on an entirely false basis and was unlawful because it failed to have sufficient regard to the teacher's art.8 rights. Not only was the disclosed information untrue, but it was also not the information which the college had provided. It was the officer's mistaken belief that the teacher had previously committed sexual offences upon young females which had led to him contacting the public protection department. Although safeguarding issues were then believed to be in play, both the officer and the public protection department dealt with child protection issues and knew that the teacher would have had to obtain an enhanced criminal record certificate. A proportionate step would have been to ascertain from the Disclosure and Barring Service what information had already been disclosed on the teacher's certificate. If there was nothing, it would have been clear that further enquiries needed to be made, which would have triggered the officer to look at the emails from the college on the police database, which would have led him to realise his mistake (paras 78-83, 87-89). (3) The police accorded importance to the making of contemporaneous records, yet there was no indication that those dealing with the teacher's complaint about the officer's conduct had considered the lack of contemporaneous recording. They had also failed to appreciate that the complaint concerned disclosure of false information, which suggested a serious lack of thoroughness in the investigation. The failure to conduct an appropriate and sufficient investigation was sufficiently procedurally unfair so as to render the resulting decision unlawful (paras 92-95).

R. (ON THE APPLICATION OF B) v CHIEF CONSTABLE OF HAMPSHIRE *sub nom.* R. (ON THE APPLICATION OF AB) v CHIEF CONSTABLE OF HAMPSHIRE, [2015] EWHC 1238 (Admin), [2015] 1 W.L.R. 5250, Jeremy Baker J, QBD (Admin).

1783 **Police powers and duties–Investigations–Deaths following use of force by police officers–2014 College of Policing guidance**

[European Convention on Human Rights 1950 art.2]

The claimants (Z and D) applied for judicial review challenging the lawfulness of guidance relating to the post-incident management of investigations into deaths following the use of force by police officers. Z's son had suffered a cardiac arrest and died soon after being forcibly restrained and detained by police officers. D's son was shot dead by police officers who had stopped the car in which he had been travelling. The challenge was to the 2014 College of Policing guidance, although it was not in force at the time of the deaths of the claimants' sons. The 2014 guidance provided that "principal" officers and key police witnesses should not be separated as a matter of course but that separation should be considered where it was both necessary and practicable and where there were no implications for the safety of the public or officers. Z and D's claim was that in failing to require the immediate separation of the officers who either used force or witnessed its use, the guidance was unlawful, because of the risk of deliberate collusion or innocent contamination of evidence if officers had an opportunity to confer with one another before they made statements for the purposes of the investigation. The Independent Police Complaints Commission (IPCC) had not issued actual guidance, but rather a consultation draft regarding how police should achieve best evidence in death or serious injury matters. Z and D submitted that the policy created an unacceptable risk that an investigation into a death would fail to meet the procedural requirements of ECHR art.2 and was therefore unlawful, in particular because (1) the guidance would not provide for an adequate investigation, because it did not require the separation of officers immediately after the incident and until they had given their detailed accounts to the IPCC; (2) the guidance would not provide for an independent investigation, because it failed to provide that first accounts would not be taken until IPCC investigators had arrived.

Held: Applications refused. (1) In a case of death following the use of force by police officers, a failure to separate the officers who used or witnessed the use of force might impair the adequacy of the investigation because of the risk of deliberate collusion or innocent contamination. However, whether it did so to any material extent would depend on the circumstances, including other safeguards in place. The risk of collusion was only one factor relevant to the question of whether an investigation was adequate under art.2. A failure to keep officers separate would not necessarily render an investigation inadequate, *Ramsahai v Netherlands (52391/99)* (2006) 43 E.H.R.R. 39 considered, *R. (on the application of Saunders) v Independent Police Complaints Commission* [2008] EWHC 2372 (Admin), [2009] 1 All E.R. 379, [2008] C.L.Y. 3000 applied. The approach taken in the IPCC's draft guidance had much to commend it in terms of art.2; it would minimise the risk of collusion. That did not mean, however, that the 2014 guidance, in particular by taking a different approach towards separation of officers, created an unacceptable risk of breach of art.2. Nor did it mean that the IPCC should adopt its draft guidance; that was entirely its own decision. The 2014 guidance was an imperfect document. For example, its provisions regarding the circumstances in which officers should be separated lacked clarity and precision. However, if it was properly applied it went a long way towards reducing the risk of collusion. There were two areas of concern: one was the absence of a requirement of separation of officers at the scene and while the officers were conveyed back to the station. However, there were strong reasons to doubt the practicality of separation in the generality of cases. The other concern was the unsupervised interval between initial and detailed accounts being given. There could be no effective requirement of separation at that point; the problem could and should be addressed instead by ensuring that initial accounts contained a reasonable amount of detail. The 2014 guidance left open a greater risk of collusion than would be left by the IPCC draft guidance, thereby creating a greater risk that an investigation carried out in accordance with the guidance would fail to meet the art.2 procedural requirements. But in the light of the safeguards that the guidance did provide, and bearing in mind that the adequacy of an investigation for the purposes of art.2 would have to be assessed by reference to all the investigation's features, the risk of breach of art.2 was relatively low, and was not unacceptable such as would make the guidance unlawful (see paras 55-57, 59, 61-62 of judgment). (2) The guidance did not breach the art.2 requirement of independence in failing to provide that first accounts were not taken until the IPCC investigators were present to supervise them. It could take several hours for them to arrive and there was no reason why an officer should not make his initial account before then. The guidance ensured that it would be made in controlled conditions under the supervision of a senior officer. The procedure could not realistically be said to prejudice the independence of an investigation (para.63).

R. (ON THE APPLICATION OF DELEZUCH) v CHIEF CONSTABLE OF LEICESTERSHIRE, [2014] EWCA Civ 1635, [2014] Inquest L.R. 267, Moore-Bick LJ, CA (Civ Div).

1784 Police powers and duties–Special police services–Provision of policing two roads adjoining football stadium

[Police Act 1996 (c.16) Pt I s.25]

A football club claimed that the defendant police service had not been entitled to charge for the provision of policing in two roads adjoining the club's stadium. Around 20,000 supporters typically attended matches at the stadium. The club had a good record of supporter behaviour. It had a traffic control order (TCO) in place over the two roads, where turnstiles and exit gates were located. The roads were closed during matches to allow stewards to control the crowds. By agreement between the club and the police, matches were graded according to the risk of disorder. Some matches had no police presence. At others, the police attended inside the stadium and in the TCO area. The parties agreed that the services within the stadium amounted to special police services (SPS) under the Police Act 1996 Pt I s.25, for which the police could charge the club, but disagreed as to the services provided in the TCO area.

Held: Judgment for defendant. (1) The court found that: the club had primary responsibility for ensuring safety and public order in the stadium; those in the TCO area during matches were predominantly supporters and not the general public; the club had exclusive but not absolute control over the TCO area, and primary responsibility for safety, public order and traffic control within it; stewards' activities in the TCO area were the corollary of those within the stadium before and after matches; the club also used the TCO area for commercial activity by permission of the local authority; police services in the TCO area were by request, overwhelmingly preventative, and a natural extension of police services inside the stadium; the need for reactive policing in the TCO area was rare (see para.87 of judgment). (2) Several principles could be distilled from the case law. Section 25 divided police services into operational duties, which were free, and SPS. There were no hard and fast rules differentiating them. Core operational services embraced both preventative policing, which could be operational or SPS, and reactive policing, which might never be SPS. Preventative policing on private premises or land controlled by the recipient was prima facie SPS; the legal relationship of the recipient to the land was important but not dispositive. Preventative policing on public land or highways was prima facie part of the operational duty. If the police decided not to allocate preventative resources somewhere, a private person could request those services as SPS. The identity and nature of the recipient was relevant but not conclusive; it might be significant if the beneficiary was a private person acting for a private gain. Police services were not SPS simply because they would not have been provided "but for" the existence of the relevant event, *Glasbrook Bros Ltd v Glamorgan CC* [1925] A.C. 270, *Harris v Sheffield United Football Club Ltd* [1988] Q.B. 77, [1987] C.L.Y. 2869, *Reading Festival Ltd v West Yorkshire Police*

Authority [2006] EWCA Civ 524, [2006] 1 W.L.R. 2005, [2006] C.L.Y. 3408 and *Leeds United Football Club Ltd v Chief Constable of West Yorkshire* [2013] EWCA Civ 115, [2014] Q.B. 168, [2013] C.L.Y. 2388 followed (paras 115-126). (3) The TCO area was not private land which the club could preclude the police from entering. A service provided away from private land could be SPS. Control of the TCO area was relevant, *Leeds United* followed. Control could include a licence or permission over the land. If a private party controlled land to some relevant degree, used it for a commercial purpose, and requested the police to provide low-level preventative services to instil a sense of order, that had the hue of SPS, especially where the area was contiguous to land over which the recipient exercised a fuller proprietary interest, and where there was a strong nexus between policing activities in the controlled land and on the private land. The club had a high degree of control over the TCO area, which was contiguous with the stadium, and the purpose of policing services in the TCO area had a strong nexus to those inside the stadium. That was a significant consideration in favour of preventative services in the area being SPS (paras 136-139). (4) The risk of serious disorder at the stadium was low and the norm was preventative policing. The hot-risk spots were away from the stadium. The police's purpose was generally to establish a presence and tone for spectators. Within the TCO area the police supported the stewards who had principal responsibility for safety, order and traffic (paras 143-145). (5) The test of who benefitted from the services was not determinative. The preventative service in the TCO was secondary and supportive to the stewards, provided pursuant to a request. It was the corollary of services provided within the stadium, and thus directed at the club and its paying spectators. When the police did not attend, the club managed disorder issues adequately, reinforcing the contention that regulating order in the TCO area was a stewarding function with the police providing a service directed to the club for its benefit (paras 148-149). (6) A request was a necessary but not sufficient condition under s.25. The club had made requests, as required by its safety certificate. Even if a request was made to comply with regulatory duties, that did not change its character. The club benefitted materially from making the request, as it met its regulatory requirements (para.150). (7) Taking all factors into account, the services in the TCO area were SPS (para.153).

IPSWICH TOWN FOOTBALL CLUB CO LTD v CHIEF CONSTABLE OF SUFFOLK, [2016] EWHC 1682 (QB), [2016] 4 W.L.R. 118, Green J, QBD.

1785 Police powers and duties–Stop and search–Power to stop and search under s.60 Criminal Justice and Public Order Act 1994–Compatibility with art.5 and art.8 ECHR

[Criminal Justice and Public Order Act 1994 (c.33) s.60; European Convention on Human Rights 1950 art.5, art.8; Human Rights Act 1998 (c.42) s.6(1); Equality Act 2010 (c.15)]

The appellant (R) appealed against a decision (*R. (on the application of Roberts) v Commissioner of Police of the Metropolis* [2014] EWCA Civ 69, [2014] 1 W.L.R. 3299, [2014] C.L.Y. 2461) that the stop and search powers conferred by the Criminal Justice and Public Order Act 1994 s.60 were compatible with ECHR art.5 and art.8. R was a woman of African-Caribbean heritage. She had been travelling on a bus in the London borough of Haringey without a ticket. She gave the ticket inspector a false name and address and told him that she was not carrying any proof of identity. The ticket inspector called the police. A police officer noted that R kept a tight hold of her bag and appeared nervous. The officer considered that she might be carrying an offensive weapon. Due to recent gang-related violence in the area, a s.60 authorisation was in force, empowering uniformed police officers to stop and search any pedestrian for offensive weapons or dangerous instruments. Pursuant to that authorisation, the police officer decided to search R's bag. When R tried to resist, she was handcuffed and her bag was searched. R claimed that s.60 was incompatible with art.5 and art.8 of the Convention.

Held: Appeal dismissed. (1) A police officer's powers under s.60 depended upon a general authorisation given by an officer of the rank of inspector or above, for a period of up to 24 hours, within a particular locality, where the senior officer reasonably believed that one or more of the three grounds set out in s.60(1) existed. Section 60(5) made it clear that the individual police officer operating under such an authorisation did not have to have any grounds for suspecting that the person or vehicle stopped and searched was carrying offensive weapons. However, his purpose had to be to search for such things (see para.6 of judgment). (2) It was common ground that the power to stop and search, without grounds for suspicion, was an interference with the right to respect for private life protected by art.8. The power pursued the legitimate aim of preventing disorder or crime. The issue was whether it was "in accordance with the law" as required by art.8(2) (para.3). (3) Any random "suspicionless" power of stop and search carried with it the risk that it would be used in an arbitrary or discriminatory manner. However, it was the randomness of the search which had the deterrent effect, and increased the chance that weapons would be detected. The power had to be lawfully used and the Human Rights Act 1998 s.6(1) made it unlawful for a police officer to act in a manner which was incompatible with the Convention rights of any individual. That had to be read in conjunction with the Equality Act 2010 which made it unlawful for a police officer to discriminate on racial grounds in the exercise of his powers. It was said that, without the need to have reasonable grounds for suspecting the person stopped to be carrying a weapon, it was hard to judge the proportionality of the stop. However, the 1994 Act, PACE and the police standard operating procedures guarded against the risk that the officer would not have good reasons for the decision. The result of breaching them would, in many cases, be to render the stop and search unlawful, and expose the officers concerned to disciplinary action (paras 41-43). (4) The requirements attached to the s.60 authorisation, the operation and the actual encounter on the street, in particular the requirement to give reasons both for the authorisation and for the stop, made it possible to judge whether the action "was necessary in a democratic society ... for the prevention of disorder or crime". No system of safeguards could guarantee that no one would ever act unlawfully, but if they did so, the individual would have a remedy. The law under s.60 was not incompatible with Convention rights, *Colon v Netherlands (49458/06* (2012) 55 E.H.R.R. SE5 and *Beghal v DPP* [2015] UKSC 49, [2016] A.C. 88, [2015] C.L.Y. 580 applied.

R. (ON THE APPLICATION OF ROBERTS) v COMMISSIONER OF POLICE OF THE METROPOLIS, [2015] UKSC 79, [2016] 1 W.L.R. 210, Lady Hale DPSC, SC.

1786 Police powers and duties–Suspects–Death–Firearms officer shooting suspect–Lawfulness

[Criminal Justice and Immigration Act 2008 (c.4) s.76(4)]

The claimant police officer (E7) applied for permission to seek judicial review of a report of a public inquiry conducted by the defendant chairman into the death of a suspect (AR). The interested parties supported E7's application. E7 was a specialist firearms officer who had participated in an operation to stop and detain men believed to be carrying automatic weapons. The suspects' car was forced to a halt by three police vehicles. E7 was travelling in a police vehicle which stopped on the offside of the suspects' vehicle. He stated that AR had ducked down in the car as if he was reaching for something. Fearing that AR had picked up an automatic weapon, E7 fired a number of shots. Six shots struck AR, the last four of which were fatal. Three firearms were subsequently found in the vehicle. The public inquiry concluded that E7 had fired 0.06 of a second after his car had stopped, AR had not made the movements described, and E7 could not rationally have believed that AR had picked up a gun and was about to use it. Accordingly, it had not been proportionate or lawfully justified to open fire on him. The inquiry went on to find that even if E7 had believed that AR had picked up a weapon, there had been no basis for firing the fatal fifth to eighth shots and shooting so as to kill. E7 submitted that the chairman's findings were irrational. The first interested party submitted that the shot-by-shot analysis adopted by the chairman ignored what E7 could reasonably have been expected to know and appreciate at the time, and was unfair.

Held: Permission refused. (1) Unchallenged expert evidence and unchallenged timings derived from the video footage set an essential context to the evidence given orally by E7. His first opportunity to see AR was limited to what could be seen through the rear window of the suspects' car. The police car initially impacted the suspects' rear offside door in such a position that E7 could not have seen through the rear offside door window. The suspects' car was then shunted forward by a rear impact from another police car. During that shunt, E7 still could not see through the rear offside door window. However, E7 had given two accounts in which he said he was looking through the rear offside window when he saw AR duck down and move back up again; he assessed that as a threat and then fired. The chairman was justified in concluding that was not consistent with the unchallenged evidence that firing began within 0.06 seconds of E7's car coming to a halt. That finding was not irrational or perverse (see paras 35, 43-46 of judgment). (2) There was considerable force in the interested parties' concern that a minute dissection of fractions of a second with the benefit of hindsight would discourage an appropriate response to threats, in real time, thereby resulting in potentially increased danger to those involved in such difficult operations. The Criminal Justice and Immigration Act 2008 s.76(4) required a court to determine the genuinely held belief of the individual in question when considering whether the degree of force used was reasonable, and, if the belief in question was mistaken, whether it was reasonable. The reasonableness or otherwise of a belief was only relevant to the question of whether it was genuinely held. That inevitably required consideration of a dynamic situation and militated against an analysis by fractions of a second. However, that issue had not arisen in the inquiry because E7's evidence was rejected and the report's primary decision was one which was entirely open to the chairman. It was arguably inappropriate to embark on an alternative analysis by relying on E7's assertion that he aimed each shot without also recognising the timeframe and the consequences which flowed from it. However, there was no value in granting permission for that to be further argued as it did not advance the investigation into AR's death and would not change the fundamental conclusion of the inquiry (paras 54-56, 59).

E7 v HOLLAND, [2014] EWHC 452 (Admin), [2014] Inquest L.R. 124, Sir Brian Leveson PQBD, DC.

1787 Search warrants–Seized property–Judicial review proceedings–Application under s.59 Criminal Justice and Police Act 2001for retention of seized property

[Criminal Justice and Police Act 2001 (c.16) s.59]

The court had to consider a claim for judicial review in proceedings concerning the legality of search warrants and the retention of seized property. The claimants asserted legal professional privilege over material that had been seized under search warrants. They asked for an undertaking from the police not to examine that material pending resolution of the privilege issue. Although there appeared to have been an understanding to the contrary, the examination nevertheless continued. Following a complaint by the claimants, the police conceded that the warrants were open to challenge but indicated their intention to issue an application under the Criminal Justice and Police Act 2001 s.59 for the retention of the seized property. The claimants applied for judicial review, seeking the quashing of the warrants, the return of the property seized and a declaration that the seizures were unlawful. On 29 July 2015, an order was made for limited use of the seized material pending a final decision in the judicial review claim. The police applied for an order under s.59. A circuit judge refused a cross-application by the claimants, who argued that the Crown Court could not determine the s.59 application until the Divisional Court had determined the nature and extent of the police's unlawful conduct in respect of the warrants. At the hearing of the s.59 application, it was held that the initial unlawfulness of the warrants did not displace the public interest in allowing the police to retain the seized material. Relying on *C v Nottingham and Newark Magistrates' Court* [2013] EWHC 3790 (Admin), [2014] A.C.D. 55, the claimants argued that the quashing of the warrants was a prerequisite to the exercise of the Crown Court's powers under s.59.

Held: Judgment accordingly. (1) The Crown Court had a remedial jurisdiction to entertain applications by the police to retain material seized pursuant to a warrant which was either acknowledged to be invalid or had been quashed by the court, *R. (on the application of Panesar) v Central Criminal Court* [2014] EWHC 2821 (Admin), [2015] 4 All E.R. 754, [2014] C.L.Y. 2467 applied. Where a warrant was acknowledged to be invalid or was quashed, the High Court might permit or refuse an application to be made to the Crown Court under s.59 of the 2001 Act. In deciding whether to permit such an application to be made, the court would weigh the public interest in preventing the misuse of powers conferred on state agencies against the need to prevent the overall interests of justice from being defeated by what might be technical issues in relation to warrants. The task of the Crown Court on hearing a s.59 application was to weigh the public interest in the retention of property for the purposes of a criminal investigation against the countervailing public interest in the due legal process of granting and executing search warrants. Bad faith and an unscrupulous approach to the drawing up and execution of warrants would weigh heavily against the exercise of the court's discretion in favouring retention, *R. (on the application of El-Kurd) v Winchester Crown Court* [2011] EWHC 1853 (Admin), [2011] Lloyd's Rep. F.C. 469, [2011] C.L.Y. 818 and *R. (on the application of Chatwani) v National Crime Agency* [2015] EWHC 1283 (Admin), [2015] A.C.D. 110 applied. Although only the High Court had the power to declare warrants unlawful and to quash them, a claimant could not insist on a case remaining in the Administrative Court until every issue was either conceded in its favour or resolved by a decision, *C v Nottingham* considered. Nor did the determination of the validity of a warrant necessarily preclude the making of an order leading to a s.59 application. Since the undecided issues in relation to the first claim were not such as to prevent the hearing of a s.59 application, the Divisional Court had been entitled to make the order of 29 July. The circuit judge had carried out a full and careful analysis and had heard evidence in a way which could not have happened in the Administrative Court, where hearings in relation to the legality of warrants were conducted entirely by reference to witness statements. He had rejected the allegations of bad faith made against the police and attributed the matters of complaint to inefficiency. There were no legitimate grounds for challenging that decision. The warrants were quashed and the parties invited to make submissions as to the outstanding issues (see paras 63-72, 84 of judgment).

R. (ON THE APPLICATION OF HS) v SOUTH CHESHIRE MAGISTRATES COURT; R. (ON THE APPLICATION OF HS) v CROWN COURT AT MANCHESTER; R. (ON THE APPLICATION OF AM) v SOUTH CHESHIRE MAGISTRATES COURT; R. (ON THE APPLICATION OF MU) v NORTH CHESHIRE MAGISTRATES COURT, [2015] EWHC 3415 (Admin), [2016] 4 W.L.R. 74, Simon LJ, DC.

1788 Welsh Language Standards–North and South Wales FRA

THE WELSH LANGUAGE STANDARDS (NO.5) REGULATIONS 2016, SI 2016/406; made under the Welsh Language (Wales) Measure 2011 s.26, s.27, s.39, s.150(5). In force: 22 March 2016.

These Regulations specify standards in relation to the conduct of the bodies listed in Schedule 6 to the Regulations (which are referred to in the Regulations as "bodies"). The bodies are: the chief constables of the police forces that operate in Wales (the British Transport Police, the Civil Nuclear Constabulary, Dyfed-Powys Police, Gwent Police, North Wales Police and South Wales Police); the British Transport Police Authority; the Civil Nuclear Police Authority; the Police and Crime Commissioners for Dyfed-Powys, Gwent, North Wales and South Wales; the Independent Police Complaints Commission; the Fire and Rescue Authorities ("FRA") that operate in Wales (Mid and West Wales FRA, North Wales FRA and South Wales FRA).

PROFESSIONS

1789 EU law–Free movement of persons–Health care

THE EUROPEAN QUALIFICATIONS (HEALTH AND SOCIAL CARE PROFESSIONS) REGULATIONS 2016, SI 2016/1030; made under the European Communities Act 1972 s.2(2). In force: 18 November 2016.

These Regulations, which are made under powers contained in the European Communities Act 1972, implement, in part, amendments to Directive 2005/36, which concerns the recognition of professional qualifications. The essential aim of the Directive is to facilitate the free movement of persons between Member States of the European Union, by setting out principles and procedures which Member States are to apply in determining the rights of migrants to pursue professions which require professional qualifications.

PUBLIC PROCUREMENT

1790 Public procurement procedures–Suspension–Automatic suspension of tendering process under reg.47G Public Contracts Regulations 2006–Suspension set aside

[Public Contracts Regulations 2006 (SI 2006/5) reg.47G, reg.47H]

The defendant local authority applied to set aside the automatic suspension of its tendering process, in which the claimant company had participated. The local authority had run a procurement competition to provide and maintain a CCTV and number plate recognition system to improve road safety and reduce pollution. The company and several competitors tendered. The local authority declared its intention to award the contract to a competitor; the company came second. It alleged that the local authority had applied non-published criteria in its assessment, and issued proceedings. Under the Public Contracts Regulations 2006 reg.47G, the contract-making procedure was automatically suspended. The local authority applied under reg.47H for an interim order ending the suspension; the test under reg.47H(2) was whether, if the suspension were not applicable, it would be appropriate to make an interim order preventing the local authority from entering into the contract. The company submitted that an interim order maintaining the suspension was appropriate, since damages would be an inadequate remedy because it would be unduly difficult to assess (1) loss of chance; (2) loss of reputation by reason of not being awarded the contract. The local authority submitted that (3) damages would be an inadequate remedy for it because the delay in entering into a contract would have negative health and safety repercussions for the local population; (4) the public interest tipped the balance of convenience towards lifting the suspension.

Held: Application granted. (1) Even if the allegation about non-published criteria opened the way for a hypothetical re-run of the tender process, that did not raise a real prospect that the calculation of damages would be technically difficult. There was no reason to suppose others would leapfrog over the company and it was speculative to suggest that additional competitors would have tendered if the criteria had been disclosed. The tender specification set out the contract's scope and did not support the suggestion that assessing damages would be unacceptably difficult. The amount of maintenance was not subject to the local authority's discretion, as in a typical framework contract. The court was used to assessing damages attributable to losing contracts in such circumstances. The mere fact that damages would be assessed for loss of chance did not render them an inadequate remedy (see paras 32, 46-49 of judgment). (2) Loss of reputation did not normally sound in damages because it was speculative and legally too remote. It was unlikely to be of consequence unless the court was reasonably confident that not imposing interim relief would lead to significant financial losses irrecoverable as damages. A party arguing for a continuing suspension would have to show a real prospect of loss retrospectively attributable to the contract's loss but not recoverable in damages, *Alstom Transport v Eurostar International Ltd* [2010] EWHC 2747 (Ch), [2011] Eu. L.R. 229, [2011] C.L.Y. 2638, *DWF LLP v Secretary of State for Business, Innovation and Skills* [2014] EWCA Civ 900 and *NATS (Services) Ltd v Gatwick Airport Ltd* [2014] EWHC 3133 (TCC), [2015] P.T.S.R. 566, [2015] C.L.Y. 2078 considered. Traffic management contracts were likely to be relatively common. All or most of the tenderers must have previously failed to obtain contracts. If the competitor failed to deliver, it and not the company would suffer loss of reputation. The loss of the contract would not cause the company financial loss through reputational harm that would be significant and irrecoverable as damages (paras 37-39, 55, 57-58). (3) Implementing an improved system was in the public interest, and the delay would not sound in damages if the company were unsuccessful. However, the local authority's reliance on that argument was exaggerated. The incremental effect of the new system would be lost but the old system already captured many infringements. The benefits' importance was overstated and did not justify a conclusion that damages would be an inadequate remedy for the local authority (paras 61, 64-66). (4) There was frequently a public interest in contracting authorities being able to go ahead with their plans promptly, which fell to be considered if and when the court gave separate consideration to the balance of convenience, *Alstom* applied. However the local authority had overstated the effect of the delay as a factor in the balance of convenience. The availability of a prompt remedy of review did not bring the balance down in favour of continuing the suspension. Where damages were an adequate remedy, the period to trial should generally not be an influential factor, and the court should be cautious about looking at the nature of the remedy as a reason to maintain an interim suspension. The Regulations established a procedure that did not suggest that suspension should be the norm, *Bristol Missing Link Ltd v Bristol City Council* [2015] EWHC 876 (TCC), [2015] P.T.S.R. 1470, [2015] C.L.Y. 2077 and *Edenred (UK Group) Ltd v HM Treasury* [2014] EWHC 3555 (QB) considered. If the suspension were maintained and the company succeeded, in addition to damages the local authority's decision would be set aside; the most the company could obtain was another chance. That had some weight in the balance of convenience, but not enough to justify maintaining the suspension. The company was not being deprived of existing market presence but of the chance of increasing it, which was a transient and minor disadvantage. The matters identified did not tilt the balance one way or the other; damages were an adequate remedy for both parties and the suspension was lifted (paras 16, 21-22, 25-27, 67-70).

OPENVIEW SECURITY SOLUTIONS LTD v MERTON LBC, [2015] EWHC 2694 (TCC), [2015] B.L.R. 735, Stuart-Smith J, QBD (TCC).

1791 Suspension–Application by local authority to lift automatic suspension under reg.96(1) Public Contracts Regulations 2015–Application refused

[Public Contracts Regulations 2015 (SI 2015/102) reg.24(1), reg.96, reg.96(1)]

The defendant local authority applied to lift an automatic suspension under the Public Contracts Regulations 2015 reg.96(1) that had been in place since the service of the substantive proceedings. The local authority had conducted a tender for the procurement of substance misuse treatment and harm reduction services. A not-for-profit organisation had provided the clinical aspect of substance misuse services since 2013 under an existing contract. The claimant (C), who had tendered with two other consortium members via a special vehicle, was unsuccessful in the procurement process, while the previous contract holder, an NHS trust (N), was the successful tenderer. C initiated proceedings claiming that the procurement process was unlawful; in breach of EU regulations, and that there was an implied tender contract. C specifically alleged that the local authority had breached reg.24(1) by failing, inter alia: to take measures to identify and remedy a conflict of interest of a member of the procurement panel, who had been the contract manager for the existing contract; to follow the published award criteria and marking inconsistently against the relevant specifications; to understand C's bid. C sought declarations that the local authority had acted unlawfully and that C be awarded the new contract and/or damages. With the issue of those proceedings on November 17 2015, an automatic suspension came into being under reg.95. The current model of addressing alcohol and substance misuse had three providers. If the suspension were to be lifted in the instant proceedings, N would be operational in March 2016; if the application were unsuccessful, N would not be operational until the summer of 2016. The local authority submitted that there was an urgent need to lift the suspension in light of the fact that there was no serious issue to be tried: there had been a lengthy tender document, specifications and a questionnaire and that there was no conflict of interest with the panel member as he had no personal interest which would compromise his impartiality, there was no evidence to show that his impartiality had been undermined, and that the member had in fact been named as a referee in C's tender application. C contended that on any view there was a serious issue to be tried; that on the balance of convenience it should continue until an expedited trial scheduled for March 2016; that the provision of a safe and reliable service was its raison d'etre; that if the local authority had legitimate concerns about the current service it was odd that it had not communicated them before the instant litigation had been initiated; that there had been errors and unfairness in the scoring process, and that in the circumstances no cross-undertaking was required.

Held: Application refused. (1) In considering whether to lift the suspension under reg.96, the *American Cyanamid* principles in considering whether to grant interim relief were applicable, that was, it had to be determined whether there was a serious issue to be tried, and whether damages would be an inadequate remedy, *American Cyanamid Co v Ethicon Ltd (No.1)* [1975] A.C. 396, [1975] C.L.Y. 2640 followed. The exercise was not weighted in favour of maintaining the suspension and the court would lift the suspension unless it was otherwise appropriate to grant interim relief. The test had two stages: firstly, to identify whether there was a serious issue to be tried, and secondly, whether on the balance of convenience it ought to be granted; the adequacy of damages was considered at the second stage, *NATS (Services) Ltd v Gatwick Airport Ltd* [2014] EWHC 3133 (TCC), [2015] P.T.S.R. 566, [2015] C.L.Y. 2078, *Bristol Missing Link Ltd v Bristol City Council* [2015] EWHC 876 (TCC), [2015] P.T.S.R. 1470, [2015] C.L.Y. 2077 and *National Commercial Bank Jamaica Ltd v Olint Corp Ltd* [2009] UKPC 16, [2009] 1 W.L.R. 1405 considered. There was a serious issue to be tried in relation to the potential conflict of interest: reg.24 was relatively new and there was no relevant authority to date. It was not only arguable that the local authority had failed to identify a conflict of interest in allowing the particular member to be on the panel; that could be perceived as having compromised the panel's partiality. C's claim of errors and unfairness in the scoring process was also not hopeless, frivolous or vexatious; it was necessary to consider each method statement question and what score would have been given in the circumstances. The issue of causation was difficult to assess; C was not in a position to address the issue of causation satisfactorily, *Bristol Missing Link* considered. For those reasons, and as full disclosure had not yet taken place, there was a serious issue to be tried. However, although there was a serious issue to be tried, it was neither so strong nor so weak that it was a material factor: rather, it was neutral in effect. (2) C's claim to damages was readily calculable; it could be calculable on the basis of the loss of a chance.. However, that was not the gravamen of C's position: if the suspension were to be lifted then the workforce would be lost and it would take years to develop skills that were not available in the wider market. The court had sympathy with C's position: although there was no evidence that the local authority would suffer any loss, and C was a not-for-profit organisation, giving a cross-undertaking was standard if not commonplace. (3) There was no dispute that public interest was an important factor in the balance of convenience, *Alstom Transport v Eurostar International Ltd* [2010] EWHC 2747 (Ch), [2011] Eu. L.R. 229, [2011] C.L.Y. 2638 and *Solent NHS Trust v Hampshire CC* [2015] EWHC 457 (TCC) applied. There was a public interest in the local authority complying with EU legislation, *Covanta Energy Ltd v Merseyside Waste Disposal Authority* [2013] EWHC 2922 (TCC), 151 Con. L.R. 146, [2014] C.L.Y. 2477 considered. The current service did not create such a risk to the users of the service that the public interest outweighed the prejudice to C if the suspension were lifted: there was no suggestion that the service was in a desperate situation; on the local authority's case, there had been problems with the service for two years and there had been no need for immediate action. From a public interest viewpoint, protection and support for service users was currently in place, and the service was "less than ideal" at worst. A further delay of two to three months in the lead up to trial could not sensibly be said to be critical and the risk of staff leaving was not great. Considering all of the factors together, on the balance of convenience, the automatic suspension should not be lifted, but it should rather continue until trial on the terms of the limited undertaking C had offered.

COUNTED4 COMMUNITY INTEREST CO v SUNDERLAND CITY COUNCIL, [2015] EWHC 3898 (TCC), 164 Con. L.R. 230, Carr J, QBD (TCC).

1792 Tenderers–Standstill periods–Unsuccessful tenderers–Issuing proceedings under reg.47C Public Contracts Regulations 2006 not pre-condition to availability of damages

[Public Contracts Regulations 2006 (SI 2006/5) reg.47C, reg.47J; Directive 89/665 on the application of review procedures to the award of public supply and public works contracts 1989; Directive 2004/18 on the coordination of procedures for the award of public works contracts, public supply contracts and public service contracts 2004]

A tenderer appealed against a decision (*Energy Solutions EU Ltd v Nuclear Decommissioning Authority* [2015] EWHC 73 (TCC), [2015] P.T.S.R. 1106, [2015]

C.L.Y. 2074) determining preliminary issues in its claim for damages arising from its unsuccessful tender to decommission nuclear installations for the respondent public authority. After learning that its bid had been unsuccessful, it would have been open to the tenderer to issue proceedings under the standstill provisions of the Public Contracts Regulations 2006 reg.47C. However, it did not do so and the standstill period expired. The tenderer then issued a claim for damages for loss of profits, alleging that the authority had breached its obligations under the Regulations. The court below was asked to decide whether the tenderer should be deprived of its damages because it had failed to issue proceedings within the standstill period and had thereby deprived itself of the opportunity to ensure that the authority had to refrain from entering into the contract pending determination of the dispute. The judge determined that it was inappropriate to determine that question without evidence. The judge was also asked to determine whether the award of damages under reg.47J was discretionary. He held that ordinary English law principles applied and that once a breach of the Regulations was established, the award of damages was not discretionary. The authority submitted that: (1) under EU law, a claimant which failed to avail itself of all available legal remedies might be deprived of its damages; (2) the claim was one for Francovich damages and was therefore subject to the requirement for the breach to be sufficiently serious, which made the award of damages discretionary.

Held: Appeal allowed in part. (1) Questions of mitigation of damages were matters for national law. Neither party had been able to point to any English law authority whereby a claimant had been deprived of damages on the basis that it failed to seek an interlocutory injunction. In *Brasserie du Pecheur SA v Germany (C-46/93)* EU:C:1996:79, [1996] Q.B. 404, [1996] C.L.Y. 2803, the ECJ said that in order to determine the loss or damage for which reparation might be granted, the national court might inquire whether the injured person showed reasonable diligence in order to avoid the loss or damage or limit its extent. However, it was not laying down any principle that was mandatorily applicable. There was nothing in Directive 89/665 or the Regulations to suggest that a person whose rights under those instruments had been infringed should be deprived of damages because of the failure to invoke any other available remedy, *Brasserie du Pecheur* applied. If the legislators had wished to make the standstill regime a pre-condition to the availability of damages, it could easily have said so. The tenderer's failure to issue and alert the authority to a claim form before the authority entered into the contract did not break the chain of causation between any breaches of the authority's obligations that might be established and any loss caused to the tenderer in consequence of them. The appeal would be allowed on that issue (see paras 71, 73-78 of judgment). (2) The tenderer's claim pleaded only breaches of the Regulations and no direct breaches of duties owed under Directive 2004/18 or Directive 89/665. The court was therefore concerned with a series of alleged breaches of statutory duty arising under the domestic law provisions of the Regulations, *Matra Communications SA v Home Office* [1999] 1 W.L.R. 1646, [1999] C.L.Y. 482 applied. Those Regulations were, however, enacted in order to implement the EU law provisions of those Directives. The *Francovich* conditions were a minimum standard for damages for breach of an EU law right and were always subject to the principle of equivalence. The liability and assessment of those damages would be a matter for national law, but national law might inquire whether the claimant showed reasonable diligence to avoid the loss and might inquire whether the claimant had availed himself of all legal remedies available to him. The domestic legal system did not have to impose such requirements, even in a claim for pure *Francovich* damages, *Brasserie du Pecheur* explained, *Commission of the European Communities v Portugal (C275/03)* EU:C:2004:632, *Manfredi v Lloyd Adriatico Assicurazioni SpA (C-295/04)* EU:C:2006:461, [2007] Bus. L.R. 188, [2007] C.L.Y. 622, *Stadt Graz v Strabag AG (C-314/09)* EU:C:2010:567, [2011] 1 C.M.L.R. 26, *Danske Slagterier v Germany (C-445/06)* EU:C:2009:178, [2009] E.C.R. I-2119, [2009] C.L.Y. 1407, *Combinatie Spijker Infrabouw-De Jonge Konstruktie v Provincie Drenthe (C-568/08)* EU:C:2010:751 and *Kone AG v OBB-Infrastruktur AG (C-557/12)* EU:C:2014:1317, [2014] 5 C.M.L.R. 5 applied. If national law laid down criteria which provided a less restrictive remedy in damages than would be provided by the application of the *Francovich* conditions, national law would prevail for the benefit of those harmed by the relevant infringements. It did not make any difference whether the infringement alleged was one of directly enforceable EU law or one of the domestic laws enacted to give effect to the EU law obligations. The primary claim under the Regulations was a private law claim for breach of statutory duty. That claim was not discretionary. There was no requirement in English law for a breach of statutory duty to be shown to be "sufficiently serious" before damages had to be awarded. Once a breach was established, the victim was entitled to be put in the position he would have been in had there been no breach. The third *Francovich* condition, requiring a "direct causal link" between the breach and the loss sustained was not suggested to be any different in principle from the causation requirement in English law. The English court had no discretion about whether to make an award of damages to the tenderer if it was shown to have suffered loss as a consequence of breaches of duty established against the authority under the Regulations. The appeal would be dismissed on that issue (paras 45-46, 55-60, 62-68, 78).

ENERGY SOLUTIONS EU LTD v NUCLEAR DECOMMISSIONING AUTHORITY *sub nom.* ENERGYSOLUTIONS EU LTD v NUCLEAR DECOMMISSIONING AUTHORITY, [2015] EWCA Civ 1262, [2016] P.T.S.R. 689, Lord Dyson MR, CA (Civ Div).

RATES

1793 Non-domestic rates–Uprating

THE NON-DOMESTIC RATING (MISCELLANEOUS PROVISIONS) (NO.2) REGULATIONS 1989 (AMENDMENT) (ENGLAND) REGULATIONS 2016, SI 2016/777; made under the Local Government Finance Act 1988 s.143(1)(2), Sch.6 para.2(8). In force: 1 September 2016.

These Regulations amend Non-Domestic Rating (Miscellaneous Provisions) (No. 2) Regulations 1989 reg.2 in relation to England in respect of hereditaments shown in a rating list compiled for a billing authority in England on or after 1 April 2017.

REAL PROPERTY

1794 Beneficial interests–Constructive trusts–Parties' contributions–Fresh evidence

The appellant appealed against a decision of the First-tier Tribunal rejecting his challenge to a restriction registered by the respondent in respect of a property. The respondent had worked for the appellant and they were close friends. A property was purchased that required refurbishment before being rented out. The property was registered in the appellant's sole name and the respondent carried out work at the property. The respondent claimed that the property had been jointly bought as an investment which he had relied on to his detriment by contributing to the mortgage payments through deductions from his wage slips and by working on the property. At the hearing before the FTT, the respondent was unrepresented. The FTT held that there was a constructive trust arising from express agreement on which the respondent relied to his detriment and that the two parties owned the flat in equal shares. The FTT gave two further decisions: refusing to review its initial decision and refusing permission to appeal. The appellant submitted that (1) fresh evidence should be admitted, namely wage slips allegedly showing that the deductions from the respondent's pay had begun before the flat was bought, bank statements showing the appellant"s discharge of the mortgage, and a completion statement to demonstrate that only a very small deposit was paid; (2) the two further decisions of the FTT were contradictory as the initial decision had found that the respondent had not been able to fund a substantial deposit, while the later decisions said that it was unlikely that any significant deposit had been paid; (3) the judge's decision had been wrong in law; (4) the FTT had been biased.

Held: Appeal allowed. (1) For fresh evidence to be admitted on appeal, it had to be shown that it could not have been obtained with reasonable diligence for use at the trial, it had to be likely to have an important influence on the result of the case and it had to be credible, *Ladd v Marshall* [1954] 1 W.L.R. 1489, [1954] C.L.Y. 2507 followed. The bank statement and completion statement could easily have been obtained and should have been put before the FTT. It was a case about a resulting or constructive trust. The funding of the purchase was fundamental to the argument that had been bound to take place and was basic material that the appellant should have presented to the FTT. With regard to the wage slips, they could have been produced without much diligence at all. However, the respondent's case that the deductions from his wages were contributions to the mortgage should have been made clear in his statement of case, well before the FTT hearing. He was unrepresented at the time and it was right that the evidence was heard, but the appellant should have been able to adduce evidence to answer that point because the respondent's evidence on it was crucial to the FTT decision. It went to the respondent's credibility and to detrimental reliance. It was not right that that finding was made on the basis of unexpected evidence which the appellant had not had an opportunity to answer. That fresh evidence should be admitted as a matter of common sense and justice, *Mulholland v Mitchell (No.1)* [1971] A.C. 666, [1971] C.L.Y. 3232 followed (see paras 12-13, 16, 20, 24 of judgment). (2) The reasoning of the first instance decision and the two further decisions presented a confusing picture. At the very least the reasoning surrounding the deposit required to be articulated, and as things stood the overall impression was contradictory. It was a crucial point, being the basis of the FTT's findings about the appellant's reasoning and intentions at the time of purchase. The contradiction made it impossible to see the basis of the decision, and the appeal should be allowed on that point (para.30). (3) The judge's finding of a common intention constructive trust was based upon a careful consideration of the evidence. The findings made by the FTT as to detrimental reliance were sufficient to found a common intention constructive trust, although the elements of detrimental reliance would have to be looked at again in the light of the fresh evidence to be adduced at the re-hearing (paras 34-36). (4) The judge's remarks did not indicate bias or pre-judgment. He had had to take care to ensure a level playing field and to give proper assistance to the respondent who was unrepresented. That could include intervention in the form of questions that the judge felt might have been put in cross-examination had the respondent been represented (para.39). (5) The matter was remitted to the FTT for re-hearing (para.43).

DAVIS v WIGGETT, [2016] UKUT 358 (TCC), [2016] W.T.L.R. 1563, Judge Elizabeth Cooke, UT (Tax).

1795 Beneficial ownership–Oral contracts–Common understanding between cohabitants

[Law of Property (Miscellaneous Provisions) Act 1989 (c.34) s.2(1)]

The appellant cohabitee appealed against a declaration as to the extent of the beneficial interests which she and the respondent, her partner, held in their family home. The respondent had bought the property in his sole name in 1987 and the parties moved in together and had children there. The appellant made no contribution to the purchase price. When the relationship broke down eight years later, the respondent asked the appellant to move out, but she refused. He issued possession proceedings, which she defended on the basis that they owned the beneficial interest in the property in equal shares, as was the common intention at the time of purchase. A letter sent by the respondent's solicitors to the appellant's solicitors on 14 August 2007 recorded an agreement that the respondent held the property on trust for himself for life, with a remainder of 80% to his heirs and 20% to the appellant. It also recorded that the appellant was entitled to occupy the property for as long as her mother and aunt, who also lived there, were alive. In 2014, when they had both died, the respondent issued the instant proceedings. In reliance on the 14 August agreement, he sought declaratory relief and an order for sale. The appellant denied that she and the respondent had reached a final agreement in August 2007. She accepted that settlement negotiations had occurred, but said that they were not binding because both parties appreciated that a final agreement would need to be in writing. She claimed to have discussed her position regarding the property with the respondent every year for the first few years of living there, and asserted that he had always reassured her that "what is mine is also yours". She sought a declaration that the respondent owned the property on trust for them both in equal shares. The respondent replied that he had abided by the terms of their 2007 agreement, and that if it lacked the necessary formalities, it took effect by way of constructive trust or gave rise to a proprietary estoppel. The judge rejected the appellant's evidence in favour of that of the respondent. He found that the 14 August letter clearly contemplated the drawing up of a formal settlement agreement and associated trust deed, but that executing those was merely a matter of mechanics whereby the parties' clearly stated objectives would be realised. He considered that there was enough clarity for a proprietary estoppel to arise. He made a declaration in the terms sought by the respondent. The appellant submitted that the judge had failed to appreciate that the respondent's case was based entirely on oral discussions which took place before 14 August 2007, and that when the letter was written, the negotiations had been incomplete and uncertain and could not amount to a binding agreement satisfying the Law of Property (Miscellaneous Provisions) Act 1989 s.2(1).

Held: Appeal dismissed. The judge had been entirely justified in rejecting the appellant's account. The nature of her case was not simply that settlement discussions had been underway and in need of further progress; her case was that the 14 August letter had been generated by the solicitors without any input from her, and that she had not met with the respondent until after she had received it. Those submissions were not acceptable. While the letter contemplated the drawing up of a written agreement, and a later letter to the court stated that the parties were "relatively close" to reaching agreement, neither letter precluded the possibility that the parties had agreed the terms of a compromise which they intended to be binding upon them. The 14 August letter was sufficiently clear to be capable of forming the basis of a binding agreement in a case which did not concern a commercial transaction, but involved two persons trying to resolve costly litigation following their estrangement. The appellant had not identified any matters upon which the parties still had to agree. On the evidence, when the parties met just before the 14 August letter was written, they had had a common understanding as to the extent of their respective interests in the property. Both parties had acted consistently with that understanding and he respondent had acted to his detriment in reliance upon it. All that had remained to be done was to put in place what the judge described as the mechanics necessary to achieve the parties' stated objectives. The appellant's interest was therefore limited to that which the judge had defined in his declaration. It would be unconscionable for her to assert to the contrary, and she was estopped from doing so, *Cobbe v Yeoman's Row Management Ltd* [2008] UKHL 55, [2008] 1 W.L.R. 1752, [2008] C.L.Y. 3081 and *Herbert v Doyle* [2010] EWCA Civ 1095, [2011] 1 E.G.L.R. 119, [2011] C.L.Y. 2710 considered (see paras 40-44 of judgment)

ELY v ROBSON, [2016] EWCA Civ 774, [2016] W.T.L.R. 1383, Sir Brian Leveson PQBD, CA (Civ Div).

1796 Coastal access–Footpaths–Kent

THE ACCESS TO THE COUNTRYSIDE (COASTAL MARGIN) (CAMBER TO RAMSGATE) ORDER 2016, SI 2016/669; made under the Countryside and Rights of Way Act 2000 s.3A(10). In force: In accordance with art.1.

This Order appoints the day on which the access preparation period ends in relation to land which is coastal margin as a result of the approval by the Secretary of State of Natural England's proposals contained in two reports relating to coastal access along the long-distance route in East Sussex and Kent which (taking the two reports together) runs from Camber to Ramsgate.

1797 Coastal access–Footpaths–North Yorkshire

THE ACCESS TO THE COUNTRYSIDE (COASTAL MARGIN) (FILEY BRIGG TO NEWPORT BRIDGE) ORDER 2016, SI 2016/670; made under the Countryside and Rights of Way Act 2000 s.3A(10). In force: 21 June 2016.

This Order appoints the day on which the access preparation period ends in relation to land which is coastal margin as a result of the approval by the Secretary of State of Natural England's proposals contained in a report relating to coastal access along the long-distance route in North Yorkshire and Teesside from Filey Brigg to Newport Bridge.

1798 Compulsory purchase–Compensation–Business owner with security of tenure–Compulsory purchase of premises and extinguishment of business

[Landlord and Tenant Act 1954 (c.56) s.39(2); Compulsory Purchase Act 1965 (c.56) s.20, s.25]

The tribunal had to determine the compensation payable to the claimant following the compulsory purchase of its premises and the extinguishment of its business. The reference property formed part of a cold store facility which was owned and operated by a company (F). In 2002, a sale and leaseback transaction took place with F's lease expiring on 31 December 2008. The lease was contracted out of the security of tenure provisions of the Landlord and Tenant Act 1954, so that F could break the lease at any time upon six months' notice. In 2003, F sublet part of the cold store to the claimant. The sublease was intended to be for a term up to 30 September 2008 and to be contracted out of the 1954 Act, but the documents were never signed and the claimant took up occupation under a periodic tenancy. The defendant compulsorily acquired the claimant's leasehold interest in the reference property in 2005. In March 2006, F went into administration but remained in occupation of the cold stores. The acquiring authority agreed with the administrators that F would continue to operate up to July 2007. The claimant tried unsuccessfully to find suitable alternative premises. Although it had operated at a loss initially, it had become profitable by the time of the compulsory purchase and in the final 10 months of trading its turnover had increased by 22%. The claimant's business was extinguished on 22 June 2007. It applied for compensation under the Compulsory Purchase Act 1965 s.20 on the basis that it would have negotiated a renewal of its lease irrespective of F's situation. The claimant's director and sole shareholder valued the business at £847,857 and it also put forward expert evidence. The acquiring authority's expert had regard to the fact that two sets of accounts had been filed at Companies House, the first of which was inconsistent with the profit and loss figures presented as part of the claim. His valuation of £59,000 to £98,400 was based on assumptions about which he was highly sceptical.

Held: Judgment accordingly. (1) Although, as a matter of law, it had to be assumed that the freeholder would have terminated the claimant's business tenancy at the earliest opportunity by the service of a "hostile" notice under s.25 of the 1965 Act on the valuation date, that assumption did not extend to ignoring the claimant's right to protection under the 1954 Act. It was likely that the claimant would have had a short period of grace after the expiry of the six-month notice period, even if only until a court hearing had taken place. That period might have been four to six months. It was unlikely that the claimant would have been successful in applying for a new lease. Therefore, its position was precarious at the valuation date. In the absence of any evidence as to what might have been the value of the leasehold interest, the claimant was entitled to compensation to the extent that the compensation under s.20 of the 1965 Act was increased by that which would have been payable under s.39(2) of the 1954 Act. To that amount was added a basic loss payment of 7.5% (see paras 55-58 of judgment). (2) In a claim for compensation following compulsory acquisition, it was for the claimant to show that it had suffered a loss and that the amount claimed was reasonable. The weight to be accorded to the evidence in support of the claim depended on matters which included the credibility of the party submitting it, their expertise and the existence and credibility of any other evidence. In the instant case, the evidence of the acquiring authority's expert was to be preferred. He was the only witness to have reflected that a potential purchaser of the claimant's business would have had concerns about the reliability of the revised accounts information. He was right to be sceptical about the assumptions on which his valuation was based, and which could not be safely relied upon. Accordingly, the valuation of the business was nil and no award of compensation was made for extinguishment (paras 97-98, 105-106).

BLUEFOOT FOODS LTD v GREATER LONDON AUTHORITY, [2015] UKUT 208 (LC), [2016] R.V.R. 182, PD McCrea FRICS, UT (Lands).

1799 Compulsory purchase–Compensation–Compensable loss–Sufficiency of evidence

[Land Compensation Act 1973 (c.26) s.29(2), s.33C, s.37, s.38(1)(a)]

The tribunal was required to determine whether the eighth claimant (H) had provided sufficient evidence to sustain his reference for compensation following the compulsory acquisition of land by the defendant acquiring authority. The acquiring authority had compulsorily acquired land and buildings at a site in London. When the general vesting declaration was served in 2006, the buildings were being used for a combination of commercial and residential purposes by the first claimant (R) and various of his associates. The acquiring authority took possession in October 2006, demolishing all the buildings on the site. Sixteen claimants made a reference for compensation, authorising R to act on their behalf. They included H and a business run by him (Apex). Their evidence was limited, and they did not instruct a valuer. The only evidence filed by H was a pro forma statement which asserted that he had occupied premises on the site at various times between 1972 and 2006 for residential and business purposes. The acquiring authority filed expert evidence which suggested that only R and two of his associates had any valuable interest in the site. The reference was heard in September 2014, when a settlement was reached. The settlement provided for a payment of compensation to R in full and final settlement of all the claims except H's, H not having been present when the compromise was reached. The determination of H's reference was adjourned. On 2 October 2014 the tribunal gave H permission to file a witness statement setting out "full details of his claim". The order provided that if he failed to file such a statement within 28 days, his reference would stand dismissed. He filed a statement to the effect that he had taken occupation of a bedroom in one of the buildings on the site (no.316) under an "irrevocable licence" granted by R. He claimed that he had remained in occupation for 18 years, paying no rent, utility bills or council tax. He claimed that as well as occupying the room in no.316, he enjoyed communal living facilities at no.318 and was permitted to park on vacant land at the site. He sought a home-loss payment pursuant to the Land Compensation Act 1973 s.29(2); an occupier's loss payment pursuant to s.33C; a disturbance payment pursuant to s.37; and compensation for loss of profits arising from the closure of Apex.

Held: Application struck out. (1) The task of the instant tribunal was to determine whether H's evidence was sufficient to support a claim for compensation. There was nothing in his statement which justified his assertion that he had an "irrevocable licence" to occupy the premises. The reality appeared to be that he was an employee or business associate of R, and that while he had occupied part of the premises with R's consent, he had no security of any kind. He asserted no legal interest, did not suggest that he had made any financial contribution to the acquisition of any of the properties, and gave no account of a specific grant of rights by R. His statement did not even support a claim that he was a rent-free tenant of a room in no.316 with rights to use the remaining space within the property for living and working. He did not assert that he was entitled to the exclusive use of any part of the premises. He described himself as a licensee, and nothing in his statement provided any ground for thinking that that was not a proper description (see paras 23, 28-29 of judgment). (2) H had failed to provide sufficient evidence to sustain any claim for compensation. To be entitled to a home-loss payment, he needed an interest recognised by s.29(2) of the Act, and as a gratuitous licensee he did not have such an interest. To be entitled to an occupier's loss payment, he needed a freehold or leasehold interest, but he not asserted either. He could show that he met the three requirements set out in s.37 for entitlement to a disturbance payment. However, s.38(1)(a) limited the amount of any such payment to the reasonable expenses incurred in removing from the land, and there was no evidence that H had incurred any such expenses. Nor was he entitled to any disturbance payment in respect of losses sustained by Apex. Apex had participated in the reference as a claimant in its own right and had authorised R to represent its interests. In any event, H had failed to provide full details of his claim as required by the order of 2 October and therefore the reference stood dismissed as of 30 October 2014 (paras 30-34).

RAPOSE v WANDSWORTH LBC, [2015] UKUT 172 (LC), [2015] R.V.R. 388, Martin Rodger QC, UT (Lands).

1800 Compulsory purchase–Compensation–Distribution company forced to relocate–Quantum of loss

The court was required to determine the compensation payable to the claimant company for losses alleged to have occurred following the enforced relocation from its operating premises to replacement premises occasioned by The London Development Agency (Lower Lea Valley, Olympic & Legacy) Compulsory Purchase Order 2005. The acquiring authority had compulsorily acquired the land from which the claimant operated its business as a distributor of packaging materials. The claimant relocated to a new site but brought compensation claims for the freehold value of the site and for costs incurred in connection with the relocation, which were settled by negotiation at £9.7 million. The remaining issue for determination was the compensation for loss of profits, which was divided into four categories: (1) losses allegedly caused by loss of customers who were said to have ceased trading with the claimant due solely to the compulsory acquisition and its subsequent move (the lost customer claim valued at £2,703,277); (2) increased costs incurred at the replacement premises which were alleged not to provide value for money (the increased costs claim valued at £1,912,603); (3) loss of profits allegedly due to the amount of management time which the directors had to expend in connection with the compulsory acquisition, distracting them from their principal duties (the management time claim valued at £231,570); and (4) temporary losses due to storage costs and the temporary loss of four customers (the temporary loss claim valued at £105,429).

Held: Compensation assessed. (1) There was no compensation payable under the lost customer claim. There was nothing to show that any of the short-term loss of turnover suffered by the claimant in the relevant years was caused by the purchase order and it was far more likely to have been caused by the recession or other factors, especially as evidence had been produced which confirmed similar businesses suffered dips in their turnover in those same years. A payment of further compensation would offend the principle of equivalence which in that case required that the dispossessed owner should be paid neither less nor more than his loss, *Horn v Sunderland Corp* [1941] 2 K.B. 26 applied. The claimant's case on lost customers was unproven and no causal connection had been established (see paras 100-114 of judgment). (2) The increased costs claim was based on a one-off service charge, increased business rates liability and notional rent. The claimant could only receive compensation for increased operating costs where it had no alternative and received no benefit as a result. The replacement site offered significant benefits to the claimant over the old site and its turnover and profit had increased since the move, which was most likely due to the fact that the new premises were modern, purpose built and conveniently located. In terms of the increased costs claimed for notional rent and business rates the claimant had achieved value for money and no compensation was payable. An element of the one-off service charge should be compensated to the value of £60,429) (paras 115-128). (3) There was no lack of evidence as to loss due to management time and the claimant had provided a detailed breakdown of the time spent on matters related to the purchase order, together with evidence of the directors' remuneration. Whilst it would not be appropriate to compensate the directors for every single hour they had spent on matters relating to the purchase order, it would not be fair to refuse any compensation for their diversions just because, subsequent to the move, they had become supremely successful. Had they not been distracted it was likely that the reduced profitability would have been less or to some extent negated. Fair compensation for the losses caused by the distractions to management time was valued at £115,000 (paras 116-136). (4) Storage costs in the sum of £13,120 should be reimbursed. There was no compensation payable for the temporary loss of customers because there was no evidence to support that part of the claim. In addition the claimant was entitled to £172,047 compensation for professional fees (paras 137-149).

KENDON PACKAGING LTD v GREATER LONDON AUTHORITY, [2015] UKUT 354 (LC), [2015] R.V.R. 355, PR Francis FRICS, UT (Lands).

1801 Compulsory purchase–Compensation–Factual issues concerning credibility, extent of compulsory purchase scheme, shadow period losses, injurious affection, disturbance

[Land Compensation Act 1973 (c.26) s.37, s.38; Land Compensation Act 1961 (c.33) s.9]

The tribunal was required to determine factual matters in a claim for compensation following the compulsory purchase of a property by the respondent acquiring authority. The claimants were members of the same family. One of them had purchased the property (No.15) for £40,000 in 1996. It had been registered in the name of another family member in 2001. He claimed to have paid £250,000 for it. It consisted of a fish and chip shop on the ground floor and a flat on the first floor. The freeholder claimed to have granted three leases in 2001 of various parts of the property to three family members who claimed to have carried on businesses from those parts of the property. The leases were granted shortly after the local authority first indicated that it was likely to purchase the property compulsorily. As well as claiming compensation for the acquisition of the leases under the compulsory purchase order (CPO) in 2002, the business owners claimed compensation for disturbance for the relocation of the businesses to a nearby property (No.4) also owned by the freeholder, who claimed to have granted leases of that property to other family members. The acquiring authority attacked the claimants' credibility and contended that the 2001 transfer of No.15 and the leases were not genuine transactions. It denied the existence of the businesses other than the fish and chip shop. It also said that the leases of No.4 were of no effect and challenged claims for construction work at No.4 and for injurious affection and loss of business profits. The parties agreed that the tribunal should rule on factual matters before hearing the expert evidence.

Held: Judgment accordingly. (1) In the absence of corroboration, the tribunal did not accept that £250,000 had been paid for the freehold of No.15 in 2001 (see para.81 of judgment). The 2001 leases of No.15 were shams, *AG Securities v Vaughan* [1990] 1 A.C. 417, [1989] C.L.Y. 2145 followed and *National Westminster Bank Plc v Jones* [2001] 1 B.C.L.C. 98, [2000] C.L.Y. 3471 considered. They were a family arrangement not intended to be implemented in practice according to their provisions and obligations. The rents reserved were uncommercial and there was no corroboration of rental payment and receipt. The purported leases were badly drafted and not intended to create any interest assignable to a third party. The leases were a device intended to increase the compensation claim (para.103). In the circumstances the leases did not take effect in equity and confer on the claimants any compensatable equitable interest, *Cobbe v Yeoman's Row Management Ltd* [2008] UKHL 55, [2008] 1 W.L.R. 1752, [2008] C.L.Y. 3081 considered (paras 104-105). However, the claimants were in lawful occupation as licensees of the freeholder and were therefore entitled to disturbance payments under the Land Compensation Act 1973 s.37 and s.38 (para.112). The purported leases of No.4 were family arrangements and were not genuine contractual agreements intended to create a binding landlord and tenant relationship. They were shams and of no effect (para.133). The relevant claimants' occupation of No.4 was not under those leases but as informal licensees (para.134). (2) The claimants failed to prove the existence of other businesses trading from No.15, namely a convenience store and a clothing and jewellery business. There was only one business carried on from No.15 and then from No.4, namely the fish and chip business, which primarily sold hot food takeaways but also a range of ancillary, non-food items (paras 155-156). (3) The acquiring authority had accurately identified discrepancies in the claimants' accounts. Those were not exhaustive. The accounts were not a reliable starting point upon which to base expert accountancy evidence. The claimants' accountant was in the best position to explain the discrepancies but he was not called as a witness by the claimants (para.174). (4) The claimants' tax returns were not a reliable source of information because they contained unexplained discrepancies and there was no evidence that the tax was actually paid. The discrepancies might have been satisfactorily explained had the claimants called their accountant to give evidence about how he prepared both the accounts and the tax returns (para.195). (5) After the CPO had been implemented there was still a busy night life in the vicinity of No.4. There was new residential development but that did not necessarily make it more difficult to achieve extended opening hours for the fish and chip shop (paras 211-212).

An indication that the relevant land was likely to be acquired, for the purposes of the Land Compensation Act 1961 s.9, was first given when the authority approached the claimants in April 2001 to see whether they would be prepared to sell the property (paras 250). Where it was claimed that the scheme had depreciated rather than increased the value of the land to the owner, the *Pointe Gourde* principle added nothing to the application of the statutory disregard under s.9, *Pointe Gourde Quarrying & Transport Co v Sub-Intendent of Crown Lands* [1947] A.C. 565, [1947-51] C.L.Y. 1435 and *Spirerose Ltd v Transport for London* [2009] UKHL 44, [2009] 1 W.L.R. 1797, [2009] C.L.Y. 3135 considered (para.252). (6) The claimants' accounts for the year 2000 were not sufficiently representative or reliable to form an appropriate base year for assessing business losses (para.263). (7) Any losses which arose before the land was acquired ("shadow period losses") were compensatable if they arose "in consequence of the compulsory acquisition of the land or threat of it" but not if they were caused by the construction of the scheme or imminent threat of construction underlying the acquisition of the land, *Ramac Holdings Ltd v Kent CC* [2014] UKUT 109 (LC), [2014] R.V.R. 207, [2014] C.L.Y. 2357 considered (para.285). (8) The common ownership of No.15 and No.4 was not sufficient in itself to establish a claim for injurious affection. The test was whether possession and control of the freehold interests gave an enhanced value to them both. That issue could not be decided without hearing the expert evidence (para.304). (9) It was reasonable for the claimants to move the fish and chip shop from No.15 to No.4 and they were entitled to claim for loss of profits sustained as a result of that relocation, but they were not entitled to claim in respect of a further move occasioned by failure to obtain longer opening hours. There was no causal connection between the acquisition and the second move, *Director of Buildings and Lands v Shun Fung Ironworks Ltd* [1995] 2 A.C. 111, [1995] C.L.Y. 664 applied (paras 330-336). (10) The claim originally presented for personal time spent on the relocation was utterly unconvincing and obviously exaggerated. A fair and reasonable allowance for management time in relation to the first move was 100 hours. The hourly rate should be the cost to the claimants of employing staff to cover for them. The rate should be the adult national minimum wage of £4.50 in force at the valuation date (paras 385, 395-396).

MOHAMMED v NEWCASTLE CITY COUNCIL, [2015] UKUT 439 (LC), [2016] R.V.R. 212, AJ Trott FRICS, UT (Lands).

1802 Compulsory purchase–Compensation–Temporary possession–Timing of claim

[Crossrail Act 2008 (c.18) Sch.5 para.1(4)]

The compensating authority applied to strike out the claimant's reference for compensation for the authority's temporary possession of a London building's basement. The claimant's interest in the building comprised a number of leases. The authority took temporary possession of the basement in January 2010 in connection with the Crossrail project, with an anticipated return to the claimant in 2018. The claimant had sought compensation on the basis that, but for the authority's temporary possession of the building, it would have begun to redevelop the site in January 2011 and would have completed its project by the end of 2013. It claimed that it would then have had a valuable asset in respect of which it would have received rental income, which it could have refinanced to enable it to make further investments in the property market. By deferring the site's redevelopment for approximately eight years, the claimant contended that it had been denied the benefit of that redeveloped asset; its loss was therefore the deferment of the opportunity for redevelopment until the beginning of 2019. The claimant also asserted that by the time it commenced the reference it had already incurred separate losses in excess of £4 million in wasted planning and design costs for its previous development scheme which would be redundant by 2019, and in holding costs and the relevant costs of preparing the claim. The authority submitted that the proceedings should be struck out because they were premature and had no reasonable prospect of success since, as yet, the claimant had no cause of action. It argued that there could be no claim for loss sustained as a result of a period of temporary possession until that period had ended: until then, it was impossible to know whether a loss would be sustained because of the need to give credit for any change in the building's value while redevelopment was prevented by the taking of temporary possession. As no loss could be pleaded, no cause of action could exist. The authority contended that it was not a matter of quantification of loss, but more fundamentally whether there would be a loss at all. Additionally, any attempt to calculate the claimant's loss up to 2018 in advance of that date would be speculative because it was impossible to predict intervening events which might have a profound impact on the claimant's position.

Held: Application refused. Under the Crossrail Act 2008 Sch.5 para.1(4), the authority was liable to pay compensation to the owners and occupiers of land of which possession was taken "for any loss which they may suffer" by reason of that exercise. The statutory language was prospective and did not support a general contention that when proceedings were brought all events which gave rise to liability to pay compensation had already to have occurred, *Yorkshire Electricity Board v British Telecommunications Plc* [1986] 1 W.L.R. 1029, [1986] C.L.Y. 2000 considered. The tribunal was not prevented from assessing loss prospectively. In any event, a significant element of the claim was in respect of costs which had already been incurred, and for losses which were continuing at a known rate. There was no element of speculation in the quantification of those sums. More significantly for the claim as a whole, the claimant's case on the facts was that it would have redeveloped the building, would have retained it and, by refinancing and reinvesting in further development opportunities, would have benefited from any general growth in the property market until 2018. There was no reason why the tribunal should not assess that factual case on the basis of evidence presented at a hearing in 2015, before the return of possession of 2018. If after hearing its evidence the tribunal was persuaded by the claimant's case on the facts, it was unlikely that it would be appropriate to require the claimant to give credit for any increase in the building's value as a redevelopment opportunity; any such increase would not have been created by the authority and would have been available to the claimant if temporary possession had not been taken. The claimant's case was properly arguable and had a reasonable prospect of success, and no case had been made out for striking out the reference (see paras 17, 21, 23-25, 28 of judgment).

BPP (FARRINGDON ROAD) LTD v CROSSRAIL LTD, [2015] UKUT 195 (LC), [2016] R.V.R. 113, Martin Rodger QC, UT (Lands).

1803 Compulsory purchase–Compensation–Unexercised purchase option agreement between landowner and acquiring local authority determining price–Effect on tribunal's jurisdiction

[Land Compensation Act 1961 (c.33) s.1]

A local authority applied for a determination that the tribunal had no jurisdiction to determine compensation for a compulsory purchase of land. The landowner applied for a direction that the authority should make an advance payment of 90% of the authority's assessment of the sum payable in compensation. The authority had entered into an option agreement to purchase land at a price, to be determined by an expert as the market value of the land plus all other sums the landowner would be entitled to if the land was acquired compulsorily. The authority sought to exercise the option and the expert determined a price. However, the sale was not completed as the landowner was dissatisfied with the expert's determination and sought to withdraw. The authority then acquired the land through the use of its compulsory powers. The authority submitted that (1) the tribunal had no jurisdiction to determine the compensation payable for the land, as the expert's binding determination of the contractual purchase price meant that there was no question of "disputed compensation" capable of being referred to the tribunal under the Land Compensation Act 1961 s.1; (2) there was an implied term of the option agreement that any price determination by the expert would remain binding between the parties in the event of compulsory purchase.

Held: Applications refused. (1) The landowner was clearly entitled to refer the determination of the compensation to the tribunal under the Act. The expert's determination was irrelevant to the question whether the tribunal had jurisdiction to entertain the reference. The land was acquired by the exercise of compulsory powers and there had been no agreement between the parties on the compensation payable in respect of that acquisition. The expert's determination had been made for a different purpose. Even if the price determined by the expert included a sum reflecting statutory compensation, there had been no agreement by the landowner to treat that determination as conclusive of the value of its entitlement, BP Oil UK Ltd v Kent County Council [2003] EWCA Civ 798 considered (see paras 31-32 of judgment). (2) There was no implied term. It was neither necessary nor obvious that the expert's determination of the contractual purchase price would have been intended by reasonable people in the position of the parties to be determinative also of the claimant's statutory entitlement in the event of the land being acquired by the exercise of compulsory powers. It could not be said that the contract would lack commercial or practical coherence without such an implied term, *Marks & Spencer Plc v BNP Paribas Securities Services Trust Co (Jersey) Ltd* [2015] UKSC 72, [2016] A.C. 742, [2016] 1377 applied (para.33). (3) The tribunal had no jurisdiction to make an order requiring an advance payment to be made. All the tribunal could do was to consider whether the behaviour of an authority in relation to the making or withholding of an advance payment should be taken into account when determining liability for the costs of the reference, or the appropriate basis of assessment (para.43).

PHOENIX DEVELOPMENTS (JPJ) LTD v LANCASHIRE CC, [2016] UKUT 38 (LC), [2016] R.V.R. 296, Martin Rodger QC, UT (Lands).

1804 Compulsory purchase–Compensation–Valuation on basis of existing use as scrap yard–Lack of hope or ransom value

The tribunal was required to determine the amount of compensation payable to the claimant following the compulsory acquisition of land by the respondent local authority. The land had been owned and operated by the claimant as a scrap yard at the valuation date. The local authority acquired it under a compulsory purchase order (CPO) for the purpose of creating a public park. When it took possession of the land it transferred it to a developer for a nominal consideration. The CPO had been connected to the developer's proposal for a corporate business centre for which outline planning permission had been granted. The developer had been obliged, for a certain period of time, to seek to acquire the claimant's land and to improve its appearance so that it was compatible with a public park. The claimant contended that while the developer was required to cease the land's use as a scrap yard, it could carry out a residential development, compatible with the park, which would have been welcomed by a planning authority and that that would significantly affect the land's value. The developer had been recognised as a special purchaser in respect of neighbouring land in an earlier related case, *Potter v Hillingdon LBC* [2010] UKUT 212 (LC), [2010] R.V.R. 271, [2010] C.L.Y. 2550, and the claimant argued that her land had been an essential consideration in securing planning consent for the office development scheme and it would therefore have been prepared to pay whatever was necessary to secure her land. The claimant submitted that compensation should be assessed on the basis of the land's ransom value or hope value or existing use value plus a disturbance amount for clearing the land.

Held: Compensation assessed. (1) The court rejected the ransom basis of valuation. While the land at one time had had a value to the developer as a special purchaser by virtue of its obligation to seek to acquire it, that had ended long before the valuation date. The developer had ceased to be a special purchaser because the planning permission had not prohibited the continuing use of its office development in the absence of acquiring the claimant's land (see paras 59-60 of judgment). (2) In relation to hope value, in view of the land's location within the green belt, and having regard to unfavourable market conditions, any prospective developer would have discounted the chances of securing an acceptable planning permission for residential or industrial development when bidding for the land at the valuation date to such an extent that he would inevitably have been outbid by a hypothetical purchaser interested in acquiring the land for its existing use as a scrap yard (para.61). (3) Despite a lack of reliable comparable evidence in relation to the value of the land in its existing use as a scrap yard, the court reached a figure which represented what the land would have been worth per acre at the valuation date. The higher value for the land as a scrap yard within the green belt further reduced the likelihood that any potential hope value for alternative, and perhaps more valuable, uses might have been more than the existing use value. In respect of the disturbance claim, the court awarded an amount less than that claimed as the claimant had continued to buy and sell scrap after the CPO while her possession of the land was precarious. Any loss of stock suffered in the course of clearing the land was the product of her wholesale failure to mitigate as she had wanted to profit from the continuing use of the scrap yard for as long as possible (paras 62, 67-68).

HALL v HILLINGDON LBC, [2015] UKUT 606 (LC), [2016] R.V.R. 155, Judge Hodge QC, UT (Lands).

1805 Compulsory purchase–Costs–Power of Upper Tribunal to award costs on reference for compensation for temporary possession

[Crossrail Act 2008 (c.18) Sch.5 para.1(5); Land Compensation Act 1961 (c.33) s.39(1), s.4; Tribunal Procedure (Upper Tribunal) (Lands Chamber) Rules 2010 (SI 2010/2600) r.10(6)(a), r.10(6)(b)]

The Upper Tribunal was required to determine whether it had power to award costs in a reference by the claimant for compensation for the taking of temporary possession of land under the Crossrail Act 2008. The compensating authority had taken temporary possession of the basement of a building for use as a work site for over eight years during the building of a new railway. The issues were whether the tribunal had power to order costs (i) under the Land Compensation Act 1961 s.4 if the award did not exceed a settlement offer made by the acquiring authority, or if the claimant failed to indicate the amount sought to enable an offer to be made; (ii) because the proceedings were for injurious affection of land within the Tribunal Procedure (Upper Tribunal) (Lands Chamber) Rules 2010 r.10(6)(b); because the proceedings were for compensation for compulsory purchase within r.10(6)(a) of the Rules.

Held: Judgment accordingly. (1) Although the expression "acquiring authority" in s.4 was not particularly apt to refer to a statutory undertaker exercising rights of temporary possession, the definitions in s.39(1) were stated to apply "except where the context otherwise requires", and the context of s.4 clearly required that the "acquiring authority" be understood to mean the nominated undertaker who was obliged to pay compensation. Further, sch.5 para.1(5) to the 2008 Act expressly provided for determination of such disputes "in accordance with Part 1" of the 1961 Act. Accordingly, the costs regime in s.4 of the 1961 Act was available to the parties to the instant reference. It functioned independently of the tribunal's Rules and the restrictions imposed by r.10(2)(a) of the Rules did not apply to it. It did not, however, give the tribunal an unrestricted jurisdiction in relation to costs (see paras 24-27 of judgment). (2) The phrase "injurious affection" in r.10(6)(b) should be given a wider meaning that did not depend on the use of that expression in the statute giving rise to the claim for compensation. Injurious affection connoted damage to land that would have been wrongful but for the existence of statutory powers, and damage to land caused by activity conducted elsewhere. It was not apt to describe activity which, but for statutory authority, would amount to trespass. The essence of injurious affection was that a claimant had to show that but for the statute he would have had an action in damages for public or private nuisance, *Wildtree Hotels Ltd v Harrow LBC* [2001] 2 A.C. 1, [2000] C.L.Y. 4293 applied. It followed that a claim for compensation for loss suffered as a result of the exercise of a power to enter and take possession of land was not properly described as a claim in proceedings for injurious affection of land. The loss sustained by the claimant was not consequent on damage to land, but was the result of the claimant being kept out of its land for the duration of the works (paras 53-54). (3) As a matter of ordinary language, the compensating authority had exercised a power compulsorily to acquire a right over the claimant's land for which it was liable to pay compensation; it had purchased that right for the duration of its requirement for land as a work site. Possession conferred control of the land and the duration of it did not justify a conceptual distinction between temporary and permanent acquisition. There was no policy reason for distinguishing between possession for a temporary rather than permanent period for costs purposes. The reference in r.10(6)(a) to proceedings for compensation for compulsory purchase was wide enough to include proceedings for temporary possession (paras 63-66).

BPP (FARRINGDON ROAD) LTD v CROSSRAIL LTD, [2015] UKUT 356 (LC), [2016] R.V.R. 117, Martin Rodger QC, UT (Lands).

1806 Compulsory purchase–Policies–Policy on re-acquisition of compulsorily acquired land–Interpretation

[Crossrail Act 2008 (c.18)]

The claimant railway company applied for judicial review of the decision of the defendant not to offer to sell land to him or to a consortium that included him. The claimant had had a leasehold interest in a flat within a block which had been compulsorily acquired by the defendant under the Crossrail Act 2008. A land disposal policy had been put before Parliament which dealt with the circumstances where the previous landowners could seek to re-acquire land after it had been compulsorily acquired but was no longer required for the full extent for which it was acquired. The policy constituted an extension of the policy in the Crichel Down Rules. The defendant wrote to all the qualifying interests (as defined) in respect of the site, including the claimant, requesting expressions of interest in purchasing the site. It explained that, in accordance with para.5.2 of the policy, where only one expression of interest was received from the holder of a qualifying interest that person would be given the opportunity, within set timescales, to acquire the site but that if there was more than one competing bid the invitation to acquire the land would be withdrawn and the site would be sold on the open market in accordance with para.5.3. Expressions of interest were received from the claimant and two interested parties. The defendant wrote to the claimant to say that as there was more than one expression of interest the site would be sold on the open market. The claimant replied to say that he was part of a consortium with one of the interested parties so that the defendant was required to assess its financial and development capability. The defendant replied that even if the parties had demonstrated the necessary financial and development expertise as there was more than one expression of interest the site would be offered on the open market. The claimant submitted that the defendant had misinterpreted the policy and failed to apply it in order to enable him to re-acquire the land. He argued that the defendant's approach to and interpretation and application of the policy had been unlawful. He submitted that before separate expressions of interest could be regarded as competition the defendant had to ascertain whether they were in fact competition or wished to work together as a consortium.

Held: Application refused. The position was quite clear. The starting point was the way in which the procedures were intended to work, which was that where there was more than one expression of interest the property would be sold on the open market. Although para.5.2 could have used different language it was clear that the policy meant on its wording that two or more expressions of interest were competing bids. The open market phase came after the competing bids. The claimant's interpretation of the policy would require more words to be read in than was appropriate. It would require a specific obligation on the defendant to identify who the expressions of interest were and invite them to consider forming a consortium. A consortium with which the defendant could deal might be formed within the short time scale in the policy. However, the procedure envisaged a two-month period where expressions of interest should be agreed. What the claimant was requesting was for a further period when negotiations could take place. The position on analysis was clear; several expressions of interest amounted to a competitive bid. To have a further stage went beyond the policy and introduced aspects that it did not cover. The defendant had taken the approach that it said it would and on which basis Parliament had accepted the policy.

R. (ON THE APPLICATION OF PRITCHETT) v CROSSRAIL LTD, [2015] EWHC 3474 (Admin), [2016] R.V.R. 109, Ouseley J, QBD (Admin).

1807 Compulsory purchase orders–Compensation–Claim by one of two personal representatives–Extent to which binding both

The Upper Tribunal was required to determine preliminary issues in a claim for compensation in respect of a property which had been acquired under a compulsory purchase order. A local authority had made a compulsory purchase order in relation to a dwelling house and outbuildings which were unoccupied. The owner had died intestate and letters of administration were granted to the claimant and his sister. The claimant sought compensation in respect of the property, and the local authority made an advance payment of compensation to the claimant and his sister. Correspondence between the claimant and the local authority indicated that the claimant was prepared to accept the local authority's proposals for a settlement in respect of the compensation claim at a figure of £118,000. The claimant subsequently made a notice of reference to the tribunal seeking a claim for compensation in the sum of over £145,000. The local authority contended that the claimant and his sister had accepted its proposal settling the compensation payable and that the claim should have been brought by both the claimant and his sister as personal representatives.

Held: Preliminary issues determined. (1) The evidence demonstrated that a compromise was reached on the payment of compensation. The negotiations by exchange of correspondence between the parties had crystallised into a contractually binding agreement whereby the claim for payment of compensation was agreed between the claimant and the local authority (see para.9 of judgment). (2) The general rule was that personal representatives had to act unanimously when exercising their discretion or making decisions relating to a deceased's estate, thus one personal representative could not exercise judgment and discretion on behalf of another unless permitted to do so under the terms of a will, letters of administration or by statute. A second general rule was that executors' authority over pure personalty was several as well as joint. That rule probably applied to joint administrators so that the acts of one were binding on the other subject to certain exceptions, thus the claimant could seek to make a claim for compensation which was binding on his sister (paras 10-11).

DEVINE v TRAFFORD BC, [2015] UKUT 340 (LC), [2016] R.V.R. 147, Judge Edward Cousins, UT (Lands).

1808 Contracts for sale of land–Conditions precedent–Condition obliging buyer to obtain "acceptable planning permission"–Extent of obligation

[Town and Country Planning Act 1990 (c.8) s.73]

The court was required to determine whether the claimant supermarket had been entitled to terminate a contract with the defendant football club for the purchase of its stadium. The supermarket had entered into a conditional agreement to purchase the club's stadium in order to redevelop it as a store. A condition precedent was that the supermarket had to obtain an "acceptable planning permission", which did not restrict the delivery and dispatch of goods. The agreement provided that the supermarket would use "all reasonable endeavours" to obtain planning permission, and that it was obliged to appeal against a planning refusal if the appeal had at least a 60 per cent chance of being successful before an agreed cut off date. The appeal was to be conducted "with due diligence" and in a "good and efficient manner". The agreement also specified that if the conditions precedent were not satisfied by the long stop date of 14 December 2014, either party could terminate it. Planning permission was granted, but it restricted delivery times and was therefore treated as a deemed planning refusal for the purposes of the agreement. The parties agreed that the supermarket would apply under the Town and Country Planning Act 1990 s.73 to vary the permission. That agreement overrode the term of the contract which obliged the supermarket to appeal against a planning refusal. By the time of that application, it considered that the proposed store was not financially lucrative and wanted to terminate the agreement. The local authority refused the s.73 application and the supermarket did not appeal, believing that it had become entitled to terminate the agreement. The dispute centred on whether the supermarket had been entitled to end the agreement after a single s.73 application. The issues were whether (i) there had been an appeal against the planning refusal as required by the terms of the agreement; (ii) the obligation under the agreement to use all reasonable endeavours to procure the grant of acceptable planning permission continued beyond the cut-off date; (iii) the effect of the long-stop date was to extinguish the contractual obligations of good faith, mutual assistance and reasonable endeavours.

Held: Judgment for claimant. (1) The supermarket's s.73 application had been an "appeal" for the purposes of the agreement. The parties had acted on that shared assumption; it would be unjust and unconscionable for the supermarket to go back on that. It had, however, only agreed to one s.73 application being made and had been under no obligation to lodge an appeal against the result (see paras 42-44, 79, 117 of judgment). (2) There was nothing in the language of the agreement to suggest that the definition of the cut-off date had any contractual significance beyond its connection to the date on which the parties acquired the right to serve a termination notice. Where a buyer obtained a contractual monopoly as to the conduct of a planning application, the obligation to use all reasonable endeavours was the quid pro quo for the seller's surrender of its own right to make the planning applications. If, instead of serving a termination notice, the parties elected to continue pursuing the agreement's objectives after the cut-off date, the reasonable endeavours obligation would continue unless and until until the termination notice had taken effect, *Simons Records Ltd v WEA Records Ltd* [1980] F.S.R. 35, [1980] C.L.Y. 381 and *CPC Group Ltd v Qatari Diar Real Estate Investment Co* [2010] EWHC 1535 (Ch), [2010] C.I.L.L. 2908 followed, *Yewbelle Ltd v London Green Developments Ltd* [2007] EWCA Civ 475, [2008] 1 P. & C.R. 17, [2008] C.L.Y. 659 applied (see paras 70-74 of judgment). (3) The supermarket should have engaged with local councilors and objectors and kept the club informed of the likely refusal of its s.73 application, but there was no link between such engagement or information and the success of the planning application. On the evidence, the application would have failed in any event because it had been brought at a politically inexpedient time. An acceptable store planning permission could not have been obtained before the termination date because the club unequivocally assented to the timing and terms of the s.73 application and because planning counsel had not approved an appeal (paras 119-121, 156).

SAINSBURY'S SUPERMARKETS LTD v BRISTOL ROVERS (1883) LTD *sub nom.* BRISTOL ROVERS (1883) LTD v SAINSBURY'S SUPERMARKETS LTD, [2015] EWHC 2002 (Ch), [2016] 1 P. & C.R. 6, Proudman J, Ch D.

1809 Conveyancing–Breach of trust–Fraudulent vendor–Loss to purchaser–Liability of purchaser's conveyancer and vendor's solicitor

[Trustee Act 1925 (c.19) s.61]

The claimant sought damages for breach of trust against the first defendant solicitors and the econd defendant conveyancer. The claim arose out of the purported sale to the claimant of a property by a fraudster who claimed to be, but was not, the registered proprietor of the property. By the time the fraud was discovered, the whole of the £470,000 purchase price had been paid to the conveyancer who had been retained by the claimant to act on his purchase of the property, who had paid it to the solicitors who acted for the fraudster, who had paid it on the fraudster's instructions to an account in Dubai. None of the money was recovered. No genuine completion of the transaction took place. It was common ground that the monies paid away by the conveyancer and the solicitors were payments made in breach of trust. Evidence was heard that the fraudster had supplied the solicitors with utility bills showing him living at a different address, and a forged passport. The fraudster had told the solicitors that the property had been left to him by his father and that he needed a quick sale. The Land Registry showed a different address for the registered proprietor but no further enquiries were made by the solicitors. In answer to enquiries, the solicitors had informed the conveyancer that they had no documents relating to the property from the fraudster. An earlier sale of the property had been stopped by the fraudster when the purchaser had asked for proof of where he worked in Abu Dhabi. Both defendants sought relief under the Trustee Act 1925 s.61. The solicitors submitted that a more favourable reasonableness test should be applied to a vendor's solicitor seeking to rely on s.61. The claimant argued that the conveyancer was also liable in contract and tort for failing to advise him of the unsatisfactory response to his enquiries and failing to provide him with the information he needed to make an informed decision on the sale.

Held: Judgment for claimant. (1) The solicitors knew that: the property was unoccupied; unencumbered; of high value; fast completion was requested; an alternative address for service was shown at the Land Registry; instructions had not been obtained from the fraudster as to the alternative address; no documentation had been supplied which showed a link between the fraudster and the property; the fraudster had not told the solicitors that he worked abroad; there was inconsistency between the information supplied by the fraudster in relation to building works at the property and information which came to light from a local authority search; and the first sale was withdrawn following a request for information as to the fraudster's employment. The Law Society's Conveyancing Handbook warned practitioners of a rising incidence of fraudsters and the importance of taking a risk-based approach to due diligence particularly in light of the circumstances of the sale. The submission that a lesser standard of reasonableness should be applied to a vendor's solicitor than a purchaser's solicitor was mistaken. The issue was not whether the vendor's solicitor owed a duty of care in tort. The vendor's solicitor was as much a trustee of the purchase money while it was in his possession pending completion as was the purchaser's solicitor. There was an absolute obligation not to release the money before completion. Once it was found that a vendor's solicitor was a trustee of purchase money and had parted with it in breach of trust, there was no obvious justification for interpreting s.61 more leniently than for a purchaser's solicitor. The same standard of reasonableness applied to both, though what each had to do in order to fulfil that standard might be different, *Santander UK v RA Legal Solicitors* [2014] EWCA Civ 183, [2014] Lloyd's Rep. F.C. 282, [2014] C.L.Y. 2058 followed. The solicitors and conveyancer had failed to discharge the burden to establish that they had acted reasonably, and were not entitled to the benefit of s.61. A reasonable solicitor carrying out due diligence and adopting a risk-based approach ought to have clearly considered whether the fraudster was the owner of the property in order to assess whether the transaction was lawful. The solicitors had failed to carry out their money laundering obligations and that failure increased the loss by fraud (see paras 19, 32-33, 39-41, 43, 53, 55, 58-59 of judgment). (2) The conveyancer had also been in breach of contract and/or duty to the claimant in failing to inform him that the enquiries had not verified a link between the fraudster and the property. The claim for damages for breach of contract and negligence succeeded (paras 49, 52). (3) The solicitors and conveyancer had to bear equal liability for the loss. The conveyancer was acting for the claimant and under a professional obligation to ensure that the claimant proceeded at all times on an informed basis and it was the responsibility of the solicitors to carry out risk-based due diligence which they had made no serious attempt to do (paras 63-64, 66, 68).

PURRUNSING v A'COURT & CO, [2016] EWHC 789 (Ch), [2016] 4 W.L.R. 81, Judge Pelling QC, Ch D.

1810 Disclaimer of lease–Bona vacantia–Effect of disclaimer following vesting of property in Crown as bona vacantia

[Companies Act 2006 (c.46) s.1012, s.1013, s.1029(1)(b), s.1034; Insolvency Act 1986 (c.45) Sch.B1, Sch.B1 para.84(1)]

A bank applied for the restoration of a company to the register under the Companies Act 2006 s.1029(1)(b) to enable the freehold of a property owned by the company to be sold. The bank had provided a loan facility to the company, secured by a legal charge over the property. The company defaulted. The bank appointed receivers, who pursued rent from leasehold tenants which had been paid to a connected company. Administrators appointed under the Insolvency Act 1986 Sch.B1 following a recommendation from the receivers, settled a claim for the unpaid rent. They gave notice for the company to move from administration to dissolution under Sch.B1 para.84(1), stating in their final report that there were no further assets to be realised. However, the same report also referred to the company's continued ownership of the property. The para.84(1) notice was registered and the company was recorded as being dissolved. Any assets remaining in the company's ownership vested in the Crown as bona vacantia under s.1012 of the 2006 Act. The tenants served notice on the Crown of a claim for a new lease. Under s.1013, the Crown disclaimed its interest in the property. The company had ceased to exist by virtue of its dissolution and, because of the disclaimer, its freehold interest in the property was deemed not to have vested in the Crown but to have been terminated. The bank contended that the effect of the dissolution of the company and the Crown's disclaimer was that the land reverted to the Crown.

Held: Application granted. (1) The bank's contention was correct. The disclaimer did not extinguish the Crown's ultimate right to the land, only the Crown's title to it under s.1012, *Scmlla Properties Ltd v Gesso Properties (BVI) Ltd* [1995] B.C.C. 793 applied. Notwithstanding the dissolution of the company and the termination of the freehold, the registered freehold title had not been closed. It was just to order restoration if the effect was that the property might be more readily realised for the benefit of the bank as a secured creditor. Section 1012(1), which deemed such property to be bona vacantia, had effect under s.1012(2) "subject to the possible restoration of the company to the register". The general effect of restoration was that the company was retrospectively deemed to have continued in existence as if it had not been dissolved, on which hypothesis the property never would have become bona vacantia. Subject to the possible effect of s.1034 if the Crown had, in the meantime, made a disposition of the property, the company was deemed always to have been the owner, as if it had never been dissolved. There was no reason to regard a Crown disclaimer of a freehold as operating differently from that of a leasehold. It operated by way of extinguishment of the freehold estate such that "the Crown becomes the owner of the land in question freed from the previous freehold interest", rather than by way of transfer of the freehold to the Crown, *Scmlla* applied. The operation of the disclaimer as it related to interest disclaimed was the same whether the interest was a freehold or a leasehold estate, even if the nature of the superior interest freed from that estate was different. That difference had no bearing on the instant matter; it did not mean that the rights removed from the company were transferred to, or accrete to, the Crown, simply that they no longer existed to bind the Crown. With regard to policy considerations, it would be highly undesirable to interpret the statute as having a different effect dependent on the nature of the interest disclaimed. There was also less reason to seek to protect the Crown from uncertainty caused by Crown disclaimer, given that (a) the disclaimer was the Crown's own act; and (b) if the Crown had in mind any dealing with the land that might be at risk on an unexpected restoration, it had the more straightforward option of disposing of the bona vacantia interest rather than disclaiming it. The Crown disclaimer was not therefore a "disposition" and the effect of restoration was that the freehold estate was retrospectively recreated and re-vested in the company in all respects as if it had never been dissolved, and as if the freehold had never been disclaimed, *Allied Dunbar Assurance Plc v Fowle* [1994] B.C.C. 422, [1995] C.L.Y. 572 applied. It followed that it was just to make the restoration order (see paras 12-23 of judgment). (2) (Obiter) It was surprising that the application had to be made. There were several alternative possibilities for future consideration, the most obvious being that, if assets remained to be realised and were expected to produce value for creditors, the company should not be put into dissolution, even if it was technically proper to do so (para.25).

FIVESTAR PROPERTIES LTD, RE *sub nom.* WEST BROMWICH COMMERCIAL LTD, RE, [2015] EWHC 2782 (Ch), [2016] 1 W.L.R. 1104, Judge David Cooke, Ch D.

1811 Easements–Rights of way–Necessary for land to be used as contemplated by parties

[Law of Property Act 1925 (c.20) s.62]

The claimant receivers of a company's property sought a declaration that the property had the benefit of a right of way over a pathway on adjacent land owned by the defendant, the company's former director. The company had purchased land and a factory in a business park. The defendant intended to let the property and later sell it for a profit. For tax reasons some land around the factory was conveyed to the defendant personally. The factory had three fire doors which exited on to a pathway which ran along the edge of the building and led on to a concrete clearing on the company's land, and on to a highway. When leases were granted to two companies (T and M) the issue of whether there was proper access from the fire doors across the pathway arose, given that the pathway belonged to the defendant rather than the company. A right of egress over the path in case of emergency was granted to T and M. Receivers were later appointed over the company's land and they sought to establish that such a right of way had already existed under the Law of Property Act 1925 s.62, or the rule in *Wheeldon v Burrows*, or by the intention of the parties to the transfer of the land to the company and the defendant.

Held: Declaration granted. (1) The case concerned not a reservation of a right on a conveyance, but the creation of a right. All of the land had been conveyed simultaneously, the major part to the company and the smaller part to the defendant. Section 62 could create a right of way by express grant if the necessary conditions were fulfilled. The question was whether the right of way was demised, occupied or enjoyed by the company at the time of the conveyance of the land to it. The claimant struggled to establish a regular pattern of use for a reasonable period before the transfer. The units ultimately rented to T and M had been vacant for more than two years at the time of the demise. There was no evidence that there was any user, and no evidence sufficient to be able to say that there should be an implied user. Section 62 did not create new easements, it converted quasi-easements into easements if there was evidence of use in any period prior to the date of demise. The previous owners had stopped using the factory three years before the demise and M and T had not occupied any part of the land before the demise. The court did not accept that the nature of a fire escape and the right of egress around a fire escape route was such that it was enjoyed by reason of being there. Section 62 did not apply (see paras 24, 26, 33-35 of judgment). (2) For the rule in *Wheeldon v Burrows* to apply the claimant had to establish not only that the easement was apparent by reason of its physical features but that there was evidence of user. There was no such evidence and the rule did not assist the claimant. User for the purposes of the rule was not satisfied simply by reason of the existence of the right of way. The mere existence of something that appeared to be a right of access combined with fire exits did not itself satisfy the rule (para.40). (3) The court had to determine whether the easement was necessary for the land to be used in the way contemplated by the parties. The common intention was that the land be fully occupied to maximise profit. When it became necessary to divide up the occupation of the property, then it should have been used to its full extent without the addition of further escape routes interfering with the property's floor area, or for parties to have to travel over property within the demise of another party. The common intention was that the fire doors and pathway were to be used by the occupiers. There was no evidence that there had been an intention to remove the fire doors or pathway upon the demise of the land to the defendant. All evidence pointed to the plain common intention being for the land to continue to enjoy the benefit of the exits and pathway. While the use of the fire exits was reasonable, desirable, or even to be expected, that was not sufficient as it was not necessary for the use and enjoyment of the land. The determination of what was necessary was not simply what was necessary for any use and enjoyment of the property, but that which was necessary for the use and enjoyment in the way contemplated by the parties. It was their common intention that the property be used in a way that included the use of the fire exits and the pathway. An easement was implied because it was necessary to give effect to that common intention. There was no need to declare that the claimant was entitled to a right of way from the three doorways to the building at all times for the purpose of egress in the event of an emergency. What should be declared was a right of way in similar terms to that which had been granted expressly when the issue arose when at the demise to M and T (paras 50-55).

LINVALE INVESTMENTS LTD v WALKER *sub nom.* LINVALE INVESTMENT LTD v WALKER, [2016] 2 P. & C.R. 12, Judge Walden-Smith, Ch D.

1812 Easements–Sports and leisure facilities–Extent to which sporting and recreation rights taking effect as easements

Timeshare unit owners sought a declaration regarding their rights to enjoyment of easements in respect of sporting and leisure facilities on adjoining land. The first claimant company owned the freehold of the land containing the timeshare units (the timeshare land) and held the land on trust for the timeshare owners. The second to fifth claimants represented the interests of the individual timeshare owners. The first defendant company owned an adjacent estate which had sporting and leisure facilities. The timeshare land was transferred to the first claimant company's predecessor in 1981. The rights granted by the transfer included the right for the "Transferee its successors in title its lessees and the occupiers from time to time of the property" to use the sporting and leisure facilities on the "adjoining estate". The defendants disputed the contention that the timeshare owners were entitled to use the facilities free of charge. The timeshare owners could not enforce their rights as leasehold covenants, there being no privity of estate between them and the defendants, and had to establish that the rights took effect as easements. The issues were (1) whether the rights took effect as easements; (2) whether the rights amounted to no more than mere rights of recreation; (3) the various claimants' entitlement to declaratory or other relief.

Held: Judgment for claimants in part. (1) If the right to use the facilities took effect as an easement, the facilities were available free of charge. The timeshare land was the dominant tenement and the estate was the servient tenement. They had been owned by different persons since the 1981 transfer. The adjacent facilities were connected with, and part of, the normal enjoyment of the timeshare land, and had to therefore be regarded as accommodating that land. There was nothing vague or of excessive width in the present rights, which clearly extended to all recreational and sporting facilities on the estate. To construe the rights as limited to the actual facilities, or those planned, in 1981 was unrealistic and might inhibit the servient owner from adding facilities which would be for everyone's benefit. If the rights did not extend to new or replacement facilities, any alteration to the facilities might amount to a substantial interference with the timeshare owners' existing rights. That could not have been intended. There was no practical difficulty in framing and applying rules and regulations applicable to all users of the facilities. The defendants, who were in possession and control of the estate, were entitled to regulate the use of the facilities in the interests of good management. The timeshare owners accepted that they had to comply with the regulations governing their use of the facilities. The rights took effect as easements, *Ellenborough Park, Re* [1956] Ch. 131 applied (see paras 25-36, 38-52 of judgment). (2) An easement permitting the dominant owner to walk over all parts of the servient tenement purely for pleasure could exist in law, *Ellenborough Park* applied. It was a relatively small step to extend that to the enjoyment of sporting and other recreational facilities. The objection that a mere right of recreation could not take effect as an easement was therefore apt to mislead, unless the limits of the proposition were understood. The key might lie in the use of "mere", which could connote a right which did not benefit dominant land at all because there was none, *Mounsey v Ismay* 159 E.R. 621 considered. It could also connote a right which was wholly extraneous to, and independent of, the use of the dominant land as such. Outside those examples, rights of recreation could take effect as easements, provided that they accommodated dominant land, were not too wide and vague, did not amount to rights of joint occupation and did not deprive the servient owner of proprietorship or legal possession. There was no English, or Scottish, authority determining whether an easement could exist to use, for example, a golf course, swimming pool or tennis court. However, there was no legal impediment to the grant of such an easement, provided that the intention to grant an easement, as opposed to a merely personal right, was evident on the proper construction of the grant construed in the light of the material surrounding circumstances, *Ellenborough Park* applied. The rights formed part of a group of rights, the first two of which, rights of way and of passage, were clearly easements. Also, the rights were expressed to benefit successors and occupiers form time to time, and to construe the rights as purely personal would produce the unexpected consequence that the rights fell away on the transfer of the timeshare land. The timeshare owners were entitled to appropriate declaratory relief confirming that they had the easement rights claimed, and that they could not be required to pay for the use of those rights (paras 54-65). (3) The court also dealt with issues concerning the various claimants' entitlement to declaratory or other relief and a number of monetary claims (paras 66-89). (4) The timeshare owners were entitled to damages for nuisance in the amount of payments made for use of the facilities. All other financial claims were dismissed.

REGENCY VILLAS TITLE LTD v DIAMOND RESORTS (EUROPE) LTD, [2015] EWHC 3564 (Ch), [2016] 4 W.L.R. 61, Judge Purle QC, Ch D (Birmingham).

1813 Electricity lines–Agricultural land–Compensation–Date of valuation

The appellant electricity company appealed against the Upper Tribunal's determination of the date on which compensation under the terms of a deed of grant should be valued. The respondent was the owner of agricultural land and the successor in title to the grantor who had granted the right to construct and maintain overhead electricity lines over the land to the appellant's successor. A clause in the deed provided that if the grantor obtained planning permission for industrial or residential development of the land, the grantee would within six months of being notified pay compensation for any diminution in its value attributable to the lines. Outline planning permission was granted in 2001, it was varied in 2004 and reserved matters were approved in 2007. In 2008 the respondent notified the appellant that planning permission had been granted and a dispute arose in respect of compensation. The tribunal which decided as a preliminary issue that the correct valuation date for the assessment of compensation under the deed was the date of approval of reserved matters in 2007. The issues were whether (i) the correct valuation date was that on which planning permission had been granted or the date on which the appellant had been notified; (ii) planning permission was to be taken as having been granted in 2007 for the purposes of the clause.

Held: Appeal dismissed. (1) The language of the clause pointed to the grant of planning permission as being the event which triggered the respondent's entitlement to compensation. The obligation to pay compensation did not arise until notice of the planning permission had been given, but that was a matter of practicality. The structure of the obligation was that if the grantor obtained planning permission, the grantee would, within six months of being notified, pay compensation. The event on which the obligation was conditional was the obtaining of planning permission. That triggering event seemed most naturally to be the date by reference to which the diminution in value should have been ascertained. The tribunal had been correct. (2) The planning permission was the outline planning permission obtained in 2001 supplemented by the approval of reserved matters in 2007. The asset to be valued was the land with the full benefit of the planning permission, including the reserved matters which were a necessary ingredient affecting the value. The tribunal had been correct that the date of planning permission for the purposes of the clause was therefore in 2007.

G PARK SKELMERSDALE LTD v ELECTRICITY NORTH WEST LTD *sub nom.* ELECTRICITY NORTH WEST LTD v G PARK SKELMERSDALE LTD, [2015] EWCA Civ 1157, [2016] R.V.R. 152, Laws LJ, CA (Civ Div).

1814 Enfranchisement–Houses–Scope of definition of "house" in s.2(1) Leasehold Reform Act 1967

[Leasehold Reform Act 1967 (c.88) s.2(1)]

The appellant tenant appealed against a decision that premises did not constitute a house in the definition in the Leasehold Reform Act 1967 s.2(1) so that it was not entitled to enfranchise. The premises consisted of a purpose-built ground-floor shop and a two-bedroom flat above, both of approximately the same size. It formed part of a parade of similar shops built in the 1920s. When built, the shop was not self-contained and could be accessed via an internal staircase leading to the first floor or from the flat's kitchen and scullery, which were at the rear of the ground floor. In about 1970 the ground floor kitchen and scullery were incorporated into the shop, and the internal stairs were replaced by external stairs. The judge decided that the question to decide was not whether it was possible but whether it was reasonable to call the premises a house. He decided that it was not: that it did not look like a house, and was not built as a house but as part of a parade of shops, and that the residential and commercial elements had been separate for 40 years. Section 2(1) provided that "'house' includes any building designed or adapted for living in and reasonably so called, notwithstanding that the building is not structurally detached, or was or is not solely designed or adapted for living in...". The basis of the appeal was that the judge had failed properly to apply the s.2(1) definition, as interpreted and explained in the decisions in *Tandon v Trustees of Spurgeons Homes* [1982] A.C. 755, [1982] C.L.Y. 1767 and *Day v Hosebay Ltd* [2012] UKSC 41, [2012] 1 W.L.R. 2884, [2013] C.L.Y. 2439. It was common ground that commercial use of part of the premises was not a bar in itself to it being a house within s.2(1). The respondent landlords submitted that the decision in *Henley v Cohen* [2013] EWCA Civ 480, [2013] H.L.R. 28, [2013] C.L.Y. 1875 meant that two types of building were excluded from s.2(1): buildings looking like a house but used for non-residential purposes, and buildings with some residential use but which did not look like a house. On that basis, they submitted, a distinction could be made between the premises under consideration in *Tandon* and mixed units like the instant premises where there was no internal linking or sharing of accommodation.

Held: Appeal allowed. (1) The definition of "house" in s.2 of the Act, although representing in many ways the common understanding of that word, operated and was clearly intended to operate as a purpose-made and therefore extended definition of that term designed to implement policy. It was therefore not Parliament's intention to exclude the right of enfranchisement in the case of buildings that were designed or adapted in part for non-residential use or which were wholly residential but internally divided into flats. There was no right to enfranchise properties such as the one in the instant case unless the whole building including the ground floor shop element could reasonably be called a house. The width of the extended definition in s.2(1) created by the proviso beginning with the words "notwithstanding" meant that the more difficult cases fell to be determined by the words "reasonably so called". As a matter of construction, that phrase qualified and had to be satisfied in relation to any property in respect of which a claim to enfranchise was made even if its potential inclusion as a house depended on the application of the terms of the proviso. The interpretation and application of the "reasonably so called" condition would therefore often be the critical limiting factor in determining whether the Act applied (see paras 14-16 of judgment). (2) The distinction contended for by the respondents was precluded as a matter of authority. The replacement of the internal staircase with external stairs to the flat did not take the building outside the scope of what could reasonably be called a house. Until the alterations in 1970 the premises, although not identical to those considered in *Tandon*, were in substance the same in terms of layout and use. That did not change merely because the shop space was increased and the means of access to the flat was changed. If a purpose-built shop with ancillary accommodation was within the definition of a house for the policy reasons identified in *Tandon*, that position could not be materially changed by the staircase works, *Tandon* followed (para.38). *Henley v Cohen* was an exceptional case because until shortly before the notice of enfranchisement there was no residential use of the building and the upper floor was linked and used in conjunction with the next door premises, *Henley v Cohen* doubted (para.39). The endorsement and explanation of the decision in *Tandon* by the Supreme Court in *Hosebay* as one turning on use meant that claims to enfranchise buildings comprising shops with accommodation above should not be dismissed for non-compliance with the "reasonably so called" condition in s.2(1) either because the building was, as a matter of ordinary speech, best described as a shop or because the accommodation was not linked internally to the remainder of the building, *Hosebay* followed. *Tandon* established that shops with accommodation above were, as a matter of law, reasonably to be described as houses for the purpose of s.2(1) provided that a material part of the building was designed or adapted for and used for residential purposes. County court judges would be adept at dismissing cases where the conversion of part of premises to residential use was not genuine or substantial or where the premises were not of the type that as a matter of policy Parliament intended to fall within the 1967 Act. A block of offices with a caretaker's flat would be such a case. However, those cases apart, there should be no warrant for distinguishing between similar types of building solely on the basis of their external appearance or their internal layout, as the judge had incorrectly done in the instant case (paras 40-41).

JEWELCRAFT LTD v PRESSLAND, [2015] EWCA Civ 1111, [2015] H.L.R. 48, Patten LJ, CA (Civ Div).

1815 Estate agents–Prohibition orders–Local authority's function as lead enforcement authority under Estate Agents Act 1979–Propriety of procedure denying opportunity of making oral representations about fitness to act as estate agent

[Estate Agents Act 1979 (c.38) Sch.2 Pt I para.2, Sch.2 Pt I para.2(3)(b), Sch.2 Pt I para.3, Sch.2 Pt I para.4, s.3(1), s.3(2)]

The claimants (L) applied for judicial review of a decision made further to the Estate Agents Act 1979 as amended to deny them the opportunity to make direct, face to face oral representations regarding their fitness to work as estate agents. The powers and duties under the Act had belonged originally to the Director General of Fair Trading, including the power to make an order prohibiting an unfit person from doing any estate agency work or certain such work, and the Office of Fair Trading (OFT) had devised a procedure for its exercise. It involved an initial investigatory stage by an investigator, followed by a decision-making stage by an adjudicator who decided on behalf of the OFT whether to make the order. It was the adjudicator who was the actual decision-maker. The procedure was clear that any oral representations by the person affected would be made directly to, and face to face with, the adjudicator at a hearing where a lawyer and others could attend and speak, and evidence could be given. Those powers and duties passed via public competition to the respondent local authority, which became the "lead enforcement authority" referred to in the Act. It was free to devise its own procedure within the terms of the Act and it replicated the OFT's concept of investigator and adjudicator. It clearly delegated the decision-making to the adjudicator. In the claimants' case it proposed that their oral representations be made directly to, and face to face with, the investigator, and that an audio recording and verbatim transcript of them should be passed to the adjudicator, who would not see the claimants. The claimants wanted to make the representations directly to the adjudicator. The issue was whether they could be heard by the investigator, or whether they had to be heard directly and face to face by the adjudicator.

Held: Application granted. The division of roles was merely the procedural machinery devised by the director general and later by the local authority. The Act did not provide expressly for a division, which meant that the local authority's "adjudicator" was the effective decision-maker. The function was administrative, but s.3(1) and s.3(2) made it clear that the decision-maker was required to act in a judicial manner, namely to determine the presence of one of the trigger facts, and then to determine the fitness of the applicant, which required making a discretionary decision, i.e. a judgment. An applicant had the right under Sch.2 para.2(3)(a) to submit written representations as to why a prohibition order should not be made. Under Sch.2 para.2(3)(b) he had the right to give notice to the local authority that he "wishes to make such representations orally". The word "hearing" was not mentioned and the identity of the hearer was not specified (see paras 28-30, 32 of judgment). However, Sch.2 para.3 and Sch.2 para.4 headed, "Hearing and representations" clearly contemplated something with the hallmarks of a hearing, even if inquisitorial rather than adversarial, and evidence could be called (paras 31, 33-34). Parliament must have intended the Sch.2 paragraphs to confer some advantage on the applicant and the proceedings, and those advantages could only be those ensuing from the dialogue between the decision-maker and the applicant. That was especially so considering the gravity of the decision to be made. It could not have been intended that the oral representations should take place before anyone other than the decision-maker. Otherwise, logically, the schedule would be satisfied without the decision-maker actually receiving the recorded representation. Even if the local authority merely sent the adjudicator the recording, it would subvert the legislative intention and open the door to possible absurdities, e.g. fulfilling the requirement to give the applicant not less than 21 days' notice of the date, time and place when it would be heard, when a busy adjudicator might be listening to it at any convenient opportunity. The overall position was the same under the amended Act as under the original (paras 35-38, 40, 42). Parliament must have intended the local authority to follow its own procedure, which it had declared to be for the laudable aim of protecting and reinforcing the adjudicator's independence, *R. v Local Government Board Ex p. Arlidge* [1915] A.C. 120 followed. That independence was not compromised by hearing the oral representations and evidence directly and face to face rather than by listening to a recording, and there was no evidence that when the OFT was operating the process there was any such difficulty. In fact, the separation of roles might restrict the adjudicator's independence, as he had no control over the course of the hearing of oral representations. The local authority's procedure did not comply with the act and was unlawful, and its adjudicator had to personally and face to face conduct the hearing of oral representations for the purpose of Sch2 (paras 44, 46).

LITTLEWOOD v POWYS CC, [2015] EWHC 2125 (Admin), [2016] P.T.S.R. 45, Holman J, QBD (Admin).

1816 Leases–Premiums–Valuation of premium payable for extended lease–Status of "non-guidance" cases

[Tribunal Procedure (Upper Tribunal) (Lands Chamber) Rules 2010 (SI 2010/2600)]

In a matter concerning the valuation of the premium payable for an extended lease and the appropriate deferment rate, the court was required to address to what extent the First-tier Tribunal might rely upon decisions of the Upper Tribunal. The leasehold valuation tribunal had determined the premium for an extended lease of a flat in the West Midlands. When setting the deferment rate, the tribunal had taken as a starting point the 5 per cent rate for flats that the Lands Tribunal had concluded was appropriate and of general applicability in *Earl Cadogan v Sportelli* [2007] 1 E.G.L.R. 153. However, it adopted a higher rate of 5.75 per cent in light of the decision in *Zuckerman v Calthorpe Estates Trustees* [2009] UKUT 235 (LC), [2011] L. & T.R. 12, [2010] C.L.Y. 2062. In *Zuckerman*, the Upper Tribunal had considered that an upward adjustment of the rate for the West Midlands was appropriate. On appeal to the Upper Tribunal in the instant case, the tribunal found that while the deferment rates identified in *Sportelli* provided a starting point for tribunals outside prime central London, such tribunals did not have to find "compelling" evidence to justify departing from them and those tribunals were entitled to take account of the conclusions in *Zuckerman*. The issue was what status was to be accorded to Upper Tribunal decisions which were not "guidance" cases and whether those "non-guidance" cases were no more than factual decisions which ought not to be followed without more by the First-tier Tribunal.

Held: Appeal dismissed. The Tribunal Procedure (Upper Tribunal) (Lands Chamber) Rules 2010 made it clear that a previous decision of the Upper Tribunal was admissible evidence of what it decided. The question was what weight a subsequent tribunal should give it. The Immigration and Asylum Chamber issued "country guidance" cases. While those were not binding precedent, they should be applied except where they did not apply to the particular facts of an individual case. Country guidance cases had the flexibility to accommodate individual cases, changes, fresh evidence and other circumstances. Decisions of the Lands Chamber did not have the same sort of formal designations. Nor did those of its predecessor, the Lands Tribunal. Indeed, *Sportelli* was the first case in which the Lands Tribunal had said in terms that its decision was intended to give general guidance. Moreover, the guidance that it gave was expressed as guidance to leasehold valuation tribunals (now the First-tier Tribunal) and not as guidance to the Lands Tribunal itself. The Lands Tribunal was not a superior court of record, unlike the Upper Tribunal. In the Court of Appeal decision in *Sportelli*, the court said that it would be for the Upper Tribunal to lay down guidelines as to the precedent effect of its decisions for different purposes. That had not as yet been done, but the mere fact that the Upper Tribunal had not yet taken the formal step of proclaiming that its decision was to be treated as a "guidance case" did not rob it of value for a subsequent tribunal. With regard to the weight that should be given to it, the extent to which the previous decision was a decision on general points of interest rather than specific facts and the cogency of the reasoning would be of relevance, but that would be a matter for the subsequent tribunal. In the instant case, therefore, it was for the leasehold valuation tribunal and the Upper Tribunal to decide what weight to give to *Zuckerman*. That was a question of fact for the tribunal in question and was not a point of law on which an appeal lay to the instant court (see paras 20-26 of judgment). Further, the leasehold valuation tribunal's selection of the appropriate deferment rate was not simply based on the decision in *Zuckerman*. It also relied upon the specialised general knowledge of a valuer. It could not be said that there was no evidence upon which the tribunal came to its conclusion. Nor could it be said that its judgment was perverse. Whether the decision was right or wrong on the facts, it did not reveal any error of law. Since the only permitted ground of appeal to the instant court was an error of law, if followed that the appeal should be dismissed, *Zuckerman* and *Sportelli* considered (para. 27).

SINCLAIR GARDENS INVESTMENTS (KENSINGTON) LTD, RE *sub nom.* SINCLAIR GARDENS INVESTMENTS (KENSINGTON) LTD v RAY, [2015] EWCA Civ 1247, [2016] 1 P. & C.R. 14, Moore-Bick LJ, CA (Civ Div).

1817 Legal charges–Power of sale–Meaning of "owner's powers in relation to a registered estate or charge" in s.23, s.24 Land Registration Act 2002

[Land Registration Act 2002 (c.9) s.23, s.23(2)(a), s.24, s.51; Law of Property Act 1925 (c.20) s.101, s.106, s.136(1)]

The seventh defendant, a buyer who had contracted to purchase land, and the claimant, the registered owner of the land, each applied for the summary disposal of aspects of the litigation. The claimant had acquired the land from a family partnership. The partnership took a charge pending payment of the purchase price by instalments. A few years later the partnership called in its security. At the same time it assigned the charge to another company (the assignee). The assignee entered into the contract of sale with the seventh defendant. The claimant's case was that the sale agreement was invalid because the assignee was not the registered proprietor of the charge and therefore not entitled to exercise a statutory power of sale. It also relied on deficiencies in service of the notice of assignment, and alleged breach of duty against the partnership. It asked the court to enter summary judgment in its favour. The seventh defendant applied for the case against it to be struck out. Alternatively it applied for summary judgment on the ground that the claimant's allegations were not adequate to impugn the sale agreement and that, as equitable mortgagee, the assignee had been entitled to enter into the agreement. The main issue was whether the assignee, as beneficial owner of the partnership's registered charge, was entitled to exercise the same rights over the property as the partnership.

Held: Claimant's application refused; seventh defendant's application granted. (1) An assignee of a registered charge had to be registered as the proprietor of the charge before the assignment was effective at law. However, under the Land Registration Act 2002 s.24, an assignee could exercise "owner's powers" after execution of the assignment, and before it was registered. That being so, the assignee must have had power, in accordance with s.23(2)(a), "to make a disposition of any kind permitted by the general law in relation to an interest of that description, other than a legal sub-mortgage". The issue was whether "owner's powers" were restricted to powers over the charge, or whether they extended to powers over the charged property. The answer, for a variety of reasons outlined by the court at para.47 of its judgment, was that "owner's powers" in s.23(2) of the Act were quite extensive and encompassed powers exercisable in relation to the charged land. The power of sale could be an aspect of a chargee's "owner's powers". The starting point for determining precisely what "owner's powers" comprised was s.51 of the Act, the wording of which confirmed that the registered proprietor's powers included the power of sale conferred by the Law of Property Act 1925 s.101 on a mortgagee in the case of a mortgage by deed. However, under the doctrine that a person could not grant a greater interest than they themselves possessed, the extent of the "owner's powers" of "a person entitled to be registered as the proprietor" of a charge depended on whether the person had acquired ownership of the charge at law; an equitable assignee did not automatically acquire legal title because an equitable owner of land could not grant a legal interest, *North East Property Buyers Litigation, Re* [2012] EWCA Civ 17, [2012] 1 W.L.R. 1521, [2012] C.L.Y. 2734 applied and *Bank of Scotland Plc v King* [2007] EWHC 2747 (Ch), [2008] 1 E.G.L.R. 65, [2008] C.L.Y. 3082 considered. It followed that s.24 of the 2002 Act could not mean that the powers of a person entitled to be registered as a proprietor were automatically the same as those of a registered proprietor: the former had to demonstrate not only that he could have exercised the power had he been the registered proprietor, but also that the power was exercisable by an equitable owner under "the general law". The distinction between legal and beneficial ownership therefore continued to matter. Somebody lacking legal ownership could only exercise the powers conferred on a registered owner if the statute or other instrument conferring it expressly permitted it. That meant, in the instant case, that the assignee, as equitable owner of the charge, would only have a power of sale if that power was granted by s.106 of the Law of Property Act 1925 and/or by the powers of attorney conferred by the charge (see paras 37-38, 41-59 of judgment). (2) Under s.106, a power of sale was exercisable by a person entitled to receive and give discharge for the mortgage money. Under s.136(1) of the same Act, the assignment of a debt would not take effect at law unless the debtor was given notice of it. In modern times, however, equitable assignees were considered to have the "substantive legal right to sue for the assigned debt", *National Westminster Bank Plc v Kapoor* [2011] EWCA Civ 1083, [2012] 1 All E.R. 1201, [2012] C.L.Y. 1864 applied. The assignee had therefore been entitled to "receive and give discharge for the mortgage money" by the date of the sale agreement with the buyer, regardless of whether the notice of assignment satisfied the requirements of s.136 or had been properly served. The assignee had therefore had power under s.101 to sell because it was entitled to receive and give good discharge for the mortgage money under s.106 (paras 60-67 of judgment). (3) The power of attorney granted by the charge could not validate the sale agreement but, given the conclusion on s.106, that did not affect the outcome of the case (para.75).

SKELWITH (LEISURE) LTD v ARMSTRONG, [2015] EWHC 2830 (Ch), [2016] Ch. 345, Newey J, Ch D.

1818 Mortgages–Completion–Requirements for completion of remortgage

A bank appealed against a decision that its claim against the respondent borrower for repayment of sums due following a remortgage transaction should be dismissed on the ground that the transaction had not been completed. The borrower had applied for a loan to be secured on properties then registered in the name of his sister and charged to another lender a security for existing loans made to her. The sister wished to transfer the properties to the borrower as a gift subject to the charges; the purpose of the loan was to redeem the existing charges. The bank offered the loan on terms that it would obtain a first legal charge over the properties. Its solicitors required the borrower's solicitors (X) to give undertakings governing the payment to them of the mortgage advance in anticipation of completion. They included an undertaking to use the advance to redeem the existing charges. The sister transferred the properties to the borrower and the advance was released to X, but X misappropriated the advance instead of using it to redeem the charges. The charges remained in place and the bank had no security. The judge dismissed the bank's claim on the basis that the borrower had never become contractually liable, the mortgage transaction not having been completed. The bank argued that once the monies had left its solicitors' client account, they belonged to the payee; the payee's failure to comply with its undertakings regarding future use of the monies did not necessarily mean that the transaction had not been completed.

Held: Appeal dismissed. The production of a suitable undertaking by the existing chargee to release its security on payment of the redemption monies would be sufficient to enable the lender's solicitors safely to release the redemption monies, but it was difficult to see how the remortgage could be said to have been completed if, instead of paying the money to the chargee, the solicitor misappropriated it. The court had to consider the terms on which the parties had contracted and on which the solicitors had been instructed. In an ordinary purchase involving the redemption of a prior charge on the vendor's title, completion would often take place when the vendor's solicitors provided the purchaser's solicitors with the executed transfer and a suitable undertaking to use the purchase price after completion to discharge the existing mortgages. Absent some specific provision in the contract of sale, it would be difficult to contend that completion had not taken place until the existing mortgage had been discharged. A remortgage was different because the property providing the security for the new mortgage would usually already belong to the borrower. Although that was not true in the instant case, the factual difference was immaterial: the borrower was not a purchaser of the properties; they had been gifted to him subject to the existing charges so that on completion of the remortgage the only additional formality was the release of the transfers. The critical issue was whether completion of the remortgage transaction required X not merely to have in their possession the redemption statement and undertaking from the chargee, but also to have used the bank's mortgage advance in the payment of the redemption monies. Under the terms on which the monies had been sent to X, X had held the advance on trust for the bank as the agents of the bank's solicitors until the mortgage transaction was completed. X's undertakings stated that they would comply with the bank's solicitors instructions. Part of those instructions was that the advance should be used to redeem the existing charges and that thereafter the DS1 forms executed by the chargee should be sent to the bank's solicitors. Since the release to the bank's solicitors of completed forms could only take place once the payment required under the redemption statement had been made, it was impossible to construe the instructions as giving X authority to release any of the advance other than to redeem the charges. That was consistent with the bank's instructions to its solicitors and with the contract between bank and borrower. Completion of a remortgage transaction ordinarily included the redemption of the prior charges, *AIB Group (UK) Plc v Mark Redler & Co Solicitors* [2013] EWCA Civ 45, [2013] P.N.L.R. 19, [2013] C.L.Y. 227 considered. The essence of the transaction was the creation of a new first legal charge. The discharge of the existing borrowings was a critical part of that process and a necessary component of completion (see paras 19-26 of judgment).

ALDERMORE BANK PLC v RANA, [2015] EWCA Civ 1210, [2016] 1 W.L.R. 2209, Sir Terence Etherton C, CA (Civ Div).

1819 Possession–Proprietary estoppel–Trust property–Beneficiary spending money on property and claiming right of occupation

[Trusts of Land and Appointment of Trustees Act 1996 (c.47) s.12, s.6]

The claimant trustees sought an order for possession of a pub against the defendant beneficiary. The defendant's mother's will provided for her freehold interest in the pub to be held on trust. It stated her wish that the pub be run by her husband and the defendant for as long as the trustees saw fit and then to be left in equal shares to her three children. She died in 1997 and her husband and the defendant ran the pub until her husband was unfit to do so. The defendant undertook substantial renovations to the pub using money provided by his company, the second defendant. The defendant submitted that he had a right to stay in occupation of the pub on the basis of a proprietary estoppel equity. He argued that he had spent money on the pub and had acted to his detriment with the knowledge and encouragement of the trustees on the understanding that he would be entitled to occupy the pub for as long as he wished. He stated that one of the trustees had agreed that any money the defendant put into the business would be repaid out of the proceeds when the pub was sold or refinanced and that the beneficiaries, who were his siblings, had agreed to that. The trustees contended that it was impossible for them, even acting jointly, to have created a proprietary estoppel binding on the trust estate and beneficiaries.

Held: Judgment for claimants. (1) An issue arose as to whether the promise on which the defendant relied was that of both trustees or only one of them. The defendant's allegation was made against only one of them. There were sufficient allegations against the one trustee to found a proprietary estoppel if proved on the evidence but not against the other trustee. On the evidence, the beneficiaries and the one trustee knew of the renovation works beforehand and no one had any objection. They knew that the defendant was funding the works. The trustees as trustees of the building would have had to have been formally involved if the defendant's loan had been to the property rather than to the business and they had not been. The defendant had made a loan to the business not to the will trust. Everyone had agreed that the defendant would be repaid but there was not an agreement with the one trustee that the will trustees would be liable to repay the costs of the works out of the proceeds of sale or refinancing of the building and that the defendant could occupy the pub for as long as he wished. The one trustee had no authority to bind the second trustee of the will trust at the times of his alleged promises, *Fielden v Christie-Miller* [2015] EWHC 87 (Ch), [2015] W.T.L.R. 1165, [2015] C.L.Y. 2570 applied. The question of whether the defendant acted in reliance on such a promise did not arise (see paras 14-15, 19, 38-41, 83, 86-87, 94, 104, 117, 127-129 of judgment). (2) Neither trustee powers under the Trusts of Land and Appointment of Trustees Act 1996 s.6 nor beneficiary rights under s.12 authorised proprietary estoppel claims binding on beneficiaries who had not at least acquiesced in them. The words of s.6(1) were wide and the proper protection of beneficiaries required that the words be confined to formally and substantively complete transactions. A bargain for an interest in land which failed as a contract because of a lack of formality was not within s.6 and did not bind the beneficiaries as an exercise of the trustees' powers. A contractual licence could be created which was potentially binding on the trust estate and therefore on the beneficiaries (paras 44-55).

PREEDY v DUNNE, [2015] EWHC 2713 (Ch), [2015] W.T.L.R. 1795, Master Matthews, Ch D.

1820 Possession orders–Overriding interests–Sale of flat at undervalue set aside as unconscionable bargain–Seller's equitable interest overreached by grant of mortgage

[Land Registration Act 2002 (c.9) Sch.3 para.2, s.116, s.26; Law of Property Act 1925 (c.20) s.2, s.34, s.35]

The appellant appealed against a possession order made in favour of the respondent mortgage company. The appellant had owned a flat worth £120,000 but could not make mortgage repayments. Two buyers offered to buy it for £30,000 and let her continue living there indefinitely. She agreed. The buyers applied to the respondent for a mortgage, naming the flat's value at £120,000. The respondent asked about any overriding interests; the appellant did not mention her continuing occupancy. She sold it with a full title guarantee under a contract providing for vacant possession on completion. The mortgage went unpaid and the respondent appointed receivers, who began possession proceedings against the appellant. The judge set aside the sale on the ground that it was an unconscionable bargain, but decided that that entitlement was not binding on the respondent, and made the possession order. The issues were (1) whether the appellant was entitled to pursue her alternative claim to a leasehold interest in the flat; (2) the legal character of the right to set aside the sale as an unconscionable bargain, how that fitted into the scheme of land registration, and whether the appellant was precluded from asserting her claim against the respondent.

Held: Appeal dismissed. (1) The appellant was no longer entitled to pursue the alternative claim, which was founded on the continuing effectiveness of the bargain with the buyers. That had been set aside. The appellant's notice only disputed the charge to the respondent. She had elected to pursue that route and could not rely on the alternative claim, *Tang Man Sit (Deceased) v Capacious Investments Ltd* [1996] A.C. 514, [1996] C.L.Y. 3789 followed (see paras 14-15 of judgment). (2) A right to set aside a transaction for misrepresentation or undue influence was "an equity" or a "mere equity". The right to set aside an unconscionable bargain was no different. The equity did not arise only on completion of the sale; it was a right to set aside the bargain, which existed at the exchange of contracts. Under the Land Registration Act 2002 s.116, a mere equity was an interest capable of binding successors in title. Sch.3 para.2 of the 2002 Act set out certain overriding interests but did not create rights, it merely preserved existing ones. If the rights of a person in actual occupation did not give priority over the registered estate holder, Sch.3 para.2 did not change those rights. There were exceptions to the general proposition that an interest belonging to a person in actual occupation was overriding. An equitable right to rectification of a lease was capable of enduring through successive ownerships, and hence of sufficient proprietary character to qualify as an overriding interest, *Nurdin & Peacock Plc v DB Ramsden & Co Ltd (Rectification Claim)* [1999] 1 E.G.L.R. 119, [1998] C.L.Y. 3658 applied. A right to have an unconscionable bargain set aside was no different. In principle, the appellant's right to have the sale set aside was capable of being an overriding interest, and was proprietary in character. Since the buyers were joint registered proprietors, they held the legal estate as trustees of land under the Law of Property Act 1925 s.34 and s.35. Once completion took place they were entitled to charge the estate, free from any limitation affecting the validity of the disposition, subject to the exceptions in s.26 of the 2002 Act. An overriding interest would not affect the validity of the grant of the mortgage, which would take effect subject to it. The purpose of s.26 was to prevent the disponee's title being called into question. The respondent contended that the appellant could not call its title into question, because if the right asserted as an overriding interest was a right to impugn the title acquired by the disponee, it was defeated by s.26. That was strongly supported by the Report of the Law Commission and HM Land Registry at the time of the 2002 Act's creation. Additionally, under s.2 of the 1925 Act, where there was a sale or mortgage made by two trustees, and the capital monies were paid to both, what would amount to an overriding interest was shifted from the land to the sale or mortgage proceeds. The question was whether the appellant's interest was capable of being overreached. Section 116 of the 2002 Act assimilated mere equities and other more traditional equitable interests. Therefore, if the appellant had an interest that was potentially an overriding interest, it was overreached by the grant of the mortgage by two trustees (paras 16-18, 21-32, 36-39). (3) If it had been necessary to decide, the appellant had not disclosed the right she asserted before the grant of the mortgage. The contract had provided for vacant possession and she gave a full title guarantee. It would have been reasonable for her to disclose that she was not in fact giving vacant possession. If the occupier did not reveal their rights, they could not thereafter assert them. Even if the respondent had had notice of the undervalue, the philosophy behind the 2002 Act was that notice was irrelevant, *Williams & Glyn's Bank Ltd v Boland* [1981] A.C. 487, [1980] C.L.Y. 1847 followed. The allegation of the respondent's notice was the sole reason advanced for disabling it from relying on her failure to disclose the true arrangement. As that reason was not a good one, the appellant did not have an overriding interest that bound the respondent (paras 40-44).

MORTGAGE EXPRESS v LAMBERT, [2016] EWCA Civ 555, [2016] 3 W.L.R. 1582, Lewison LJ, CA (Civ Div).

1821 Prescription–Car parks–Acquisition of right to use car park–Landowner's signs stating that car park private

The appellants appealed against a finding that they had not acquired by prescription the right to park on a car park belonging to the respondents. The car park had been owned by a club until 2010. Since 1998 the appellants had operated a fish and chip shop adjacent to the car park entrance. Suppliers and customers of the shop would use the car park. The respondents purchased the land in 2010 and let the building in 2012 to a tenant who obstructed access to the car park. Until 2007 there had been a sign attached to the wall of the car park which stated "Private car park. For the use of club patrons only". There had been a similar sign in the club's window. The First-tier Tribunal found that the appellants had established their claim to parking rights as a result of use over a number of years. The Upper Tribunal allowed the respondents' appeal. The issue was whether the signs were sufficient to prevent the appellants acquiring a right to use the land as a car park or whether the landowners had acquiesced in such use so as to entitle the appellants to such a right, notwithstanding the presence of signs.

Held: Appeal dismissed. The appeal was concerned with what constituted "protest" on the part of the landowner. In the instant case, the signs were by themselves sufficient to make contentious the parking of cars by the appellants, their suppliers and their customers, *Betterment Properties (Weymouth) Ltd v Dorset CC* [2012] EWCA Civ 250, [2012] 2 P. & C.R. 3, [2012] C.L.Y. 2763 followed. The authorities did not support the proposition that a servient owner had to back his objection either by physical obstruction or by legal action. The presence of signs clearly indicated the landowner's continuing objection to unauthorised parking. The signs were a proportionate protest. Anyone reading the signs would understand their meaning and effect; that persons other than club patrons were not allowed to park there. Where a landowner made his position entirely clear through the erection of clearly visible signs, the unauthorised use of the land could not be said to be "as of right". Those who chose to ignore such signs should not thereby be entitled to obtain legal rights over the land (see paras 13, 19, 23, 31, 36-37, 40, 41 of judgment).

WINTERBURN v BENNETT, [2016] EWCA Civ 482, [2017] R.T.R. 5, Sharp LJ, CA (Civ Div).

1822 Rentcharges–Registrability–Whether rentcharge lease mortgages by demise

[Land Registration Act 2002 (c.9) s.4; Law of Property Act 1925 (c.20) s.121, s.121(4), s.85; Rentcharges Act 1977 (c.30)]

Two directors of the third appellant company appealed against a decision cancelling their applications to the Land Registry to register rentcharge leases. The leases of the respondent house owners' properties had been granted to the directors as trustees by the company, following the non-payment of rentcharges by the owners. Pursuant to the Land Registration Act 2002 s.4, certain property rights, including a lease granted for a term of more than seven years, could not take full effect unless registered at HM Land Registry. A rentcharge was a property right, which could be bought and sold. The company was in the business of buying and managing rentcharges and owned about 15,000. These small fixed annual sums had been severely eroded by inflation but the Law of Property Act 1925 s.121 provided a number of remedies for non-payment of the rentcharge for over 40 days, including taking possession of the property and using the income from it to clear the arrears, or the grant to trustees of a lease of the property to compel payment of the rentcharge and the costs of recovery, which usually far exceeded the rentcharge itself. Those remedies were available whether or not the owner had been asked to pay the rentcharge. The Rentcharges Act 1977 had prevented any new rentcharges from being created, had provided a mechanism for statutory redemption, and would extinguish them all in 2037. However, the 1977 Act made no provision for a rentcharge lease to end if the arrears were cleared. The rentcharge lease amounted to a stranglehold on an owner's freehold which thus became worthless. The directors had caused the company to grant them 99-year leases and sought to register them. The Land Registry normally registered such leases notwithstanding any owner's objections, but had referred the particular leases to the tribunal. The tribunal determined that the leases were actually mortgages by demise and therefore not registrable pursuant to the 2002 Act. The directors submitted that the judge had erred in finding the rentcharge leases to be mortgages by demise, because the Law of Property Act 1925 s.85 required such mortgages to be "subject to a provision for cesser on redemption".

Held: Appeal allowed. (1) A rentcharge lease continued in existence even when the arrears had been repaid unless it was surrendered voluntarily. There was no question of it coming to an end, or of it being held on trust as the judge had supposed. Section

121(4) of the 1925 Act provided that once a rentcharge lease was in place, the rentcharge holder could continue to make use of it to recover future payments. Moreover, the rentcharge lease would continue notwithstanding any statutory redemption of the rentcharge itself, and even beyond the extinguishment of rentcharges in 2037. A rentcharge lease was a remedy, not a security right. The rentcharge itself was the security for the liability and the creation of a rentcharge lease was the realisation of that security. The rentcharge lease was not a mortgage by demise for that general reason, as well as for the technical reason that it was not subject to a provision for cesser on redemption (see paras 24-25 of judgment). (2) The passage of time and the effects of inflation meant that the grant of a rentcharge lease was a wholly disproportionate remedy. Although s.121(4) of the 1925 Act had been an efficient and useful provision when it was drafted, inflation had made it toxic. The draconian remedy was out of all proportion to the wrong and it was unfortunate that the Rentcharges Act 1977 had not reformed the remedies available to a rentcharge holder (paras 32-33).

ROBERTS v LAWTON, [2016] UKUT 395 (TCC), Judge Elizabeth Cooke, UT (Tax).

1823 Resulting trusts–Beneficial interests–Spouses–Property in husband's name–Wife failing to establish contributions to purchase price

[Charging Orders Act 1979 (c.53) s.3(5)]

The second defendant wife (W) applied under the Charging Orders Act 1979 s.3(5) for a variation of a final charging order over a property (P) held by her first defendant husband (H) in order to correctly record her alleged beneficial interest in that property. The claimants (C), following their successful petition to declare the election of H as mayor of a London borough void, had been awarded their costs. As an interim payment of £25,000 remained unpaid, they secured a final charging order over H's interest in P. W applied to be joined in order to determine the extent of her beneficial interest in P, if any. Although C obtained interim charging orders in relation to other properties owned by H and W individually, C were unable to pursue their rights under the interim orders due to H's bankruptcy, which was granted on his own petition. H did not appear at the instant trial, nor was he represented. In support of her assertion of a beneficial interest, W exhibited an unregistered declaration of trust evidencing that she held a 74% interest in P. She was only, on her case, able to provide H's bank records in a heavily redacted form. W also failed to call H to give evidence; she felt that his evidence would be discounted on the basis of adverse findings made against him by the Electoral Commissioner. The issues were (1) the intended effect of the declaration of trust; (2) whether a resulting trust analysis should be applied; (3) whether the declaration of trust was a sham.

Held: Judgment accordingly. (1) The intended effect of the declaration of trust was to declare the legal position which had already arisen by virtue of W's contribution of 74% of the purchase price. It was therefore not to be seen as a document which created a new legal position at the date of execution: it purported to evidence a trust which came into being as a consequence of the legal effect of having made the contribution (see para.32 of judgment). (2) As H and W did not purchase P as their home, the extent of W's interest turned on the extent of her contribution to the purchase price under resulting trust principles, *Laskar v Laskar* [2008] EWCA Civ 347, [2008] 1 W.L.R. 2695, [2008] C.L.Y. 3104 followed. W's cavalier attitude to disclosure was symptomatic of her approach to evidence generally: she was willing to alter her case when challenged, and no real effort had been made to explain her case about the receipt of rental payments that was coherent. She also failed to make any proper effort to ensure that the court had a full unredacted set of H's bank statements. Given her failure to call H as a witness, and her failure to obtain unredacted bank statements, it was appropriate, where a party sought to establish a beneficial interest in a property by virtue of contributions made years ago, to draw an adverse inference where there had been a failure to obtain evidence which could have been obtained without any real difficulty without an adequate explanation, *Petrodel Resources Ltd v Prest* [2013] UKSC 34, [2013] 2 A.C. 415, [2013] C.L.Y. 1300 followed. Given that property had been acquired to let, the burden rested on W to show on the balance of probabilities that she made a contribution to the purchase of P: she failed to discharge that burden and therefore failed to establish that there had been a resulting trust. The declaration of trust had been based on the premise that she made a contribution of 74% to the purchase price; however, that did not reflect the reality. The declaration of trust also did not amount to a gift of a beneficial interest to W and its purported effect to declare that she had a 74% interest based on a contribution of that proportion was a fiction. Moreover, it was impossible to know how the figure of a 74% interest had been reached (paras 38, 41, 67-68, 70-71, 75-76). (3) (Obiter) There was ample basis for concluding that the declaration of trust was a sham, which was borne out by the absence of any registration and the way in which H and W dealt with the property between themselves: they had acted at all times as if P was beneficially 100% owned by H and they had represented to the outside world that the property was his (para.82). (4) A declaration was granted that H held a 100% beneficial interest in P (para.83).

ERLAM v RAHMAN, [2016] EWHC 111 (CH), [2016] B.P.I.R. 856, Chief Master Marsh, Ch D.

1824 Rights of common–Prescription–Failure register rights within requisite period–Whether rights extinguished

[Commons Registration Act 1965 (c.64) s.1(2)(b); Commons Act 2006 (c.26) Sch.3 para.2(2)(a)]

The appellant farmers appealed against the dismissal (*R. (on the application of Littlejohns) v Devon CC* [2015] EWHC 730 (Admin), [2015] Q.B. 869, [2015] C.L.Y. 2106) of their claim for judicial review of the respondent local authority's refusal to register their rights of common over registered common land owned by the Duchy of Cornwall. The farmers and their predecessors in title had grazed livestock on common land adjacent to their farms for decades. The common land was registered under the Commons Registration Act 1965. In 1968, L's father filed with the local authority a formal notice of intention to register rights of common under the Act, but the local authority's records indicated that no formal application had ever been made and no rights were registered. L discovered this in 1984 but continued to graze livestock on the land until 2001. In 2010, L applied to the local authority to amend the register to record their rights of common, pursuant to the Commons Act 2006 Sch.3 para.2(2)(a). The basis of their application was that, after January 2, 1970 and before October 1, 2008, the relevant dates in para.2(2)(a), they had grazed livestock for more than 20 years on the specified common land and had thus acquired a prescriptive right of grazing. The local authority refused the application on the ground that a right of common could not be created by prescription after January 2, 1970 over land that had been registered as common land. The judge held that the purpose of sch.3 was to provide a brief window for updating and correcting the commons register by adding any registrations which could have been, but had not been, made under the 1965 Act; and that thereafter any unregistered rights would be extinguished. The issues were (i) whether it was possible after 2 January 1970 to acquire a right of common over land registered under the Commons Registration Act 1965 on or before 31 July 1970 by virtue of an express grant, or by user, and (ii) if so, whether such a right would be immediately extinguished by s.1(2)(b) of the Act. The farmers submitted that the term "*such land*" in s.1(2)(b) applied only to the situation on the ground in 1970 and had no future application. The local authority argued that the section had continuing application.

Held: Appeal dismissed. (Sir Terence Etherton C dissenting). The purpose of the 1965 Act was to establish a definitive register of common land and of existing rights of common over it. After the operative date, any common land which had not been registered would cease to be common land and any rights of common which had not been registered would be extinguished. The term "*such land*" in s.1(2)(b) did not mean, as the farmers argued, either land actually registered under the 1965 Act or land capable of being registered under the Act. The words referred only to land registered under the Act. That meant that unregistered rights of common were not exercisable over land already registered under the 1965 Act as common land. If such rights could not be exercised, then a person who claimed to have acquired a prescriptive right of grazing over registered common land was precluded from establishing such a right by s.1(2)(6). The general principle was that an easement or profit could not be acquired by doing something prohibited by a public general statute, *Neaverson v Peterborough Rural DC* [1902] 1 Ch. 557, *Bakewell Management Ltd v Brandwood* [2004] UKHL 14, [2004] 2 A.C. 519, [2004] C.L.Y. 3224 and *R. (on the application of Newhaven Port and*

Properties Ltd) v East Sussex CC [2015] UKSC 7, [2015] A.C. 1547, [2015] C.L.Y. 2128 followed. Section 1(2)(b) of the 1965 Act prevented a landowner from lawfully granting a right of common over such land, so such a right could not be acquired by prescription, *Oxfordshire CC v Oxford City Council* [2006] UKHL 25, [2006] 2 A.C. 674, [2006] C.L.Y. 3456 applied (see paras 101-103, 126-129,133-139 of judgment).

R. (ON THE APPLICATION OF LITTLEJOHNS) v DEVON CC, [2016] EWCA Civ 446, [2016] 3 W.L.R. 743, Sir Terence Etherton C, CA (Civ Div).

1825 Rights of way–Proprietary estoppel–Right of way over garden–Common assumption

A local authority appealed against a decision that the respondent company was entitled to a right of way on the basis of proprietary estoppel. The company leased an upper floor of a property owned by the local authority. It agreed to also lease the basement, which was to be converted into a residential apartment. The basement could be accessed by an internal door from the main entrance, through a fire exit which led into a walled garden, and by a separate route through the car park. The company obtained planning permission for the conversion and prepared a plan, plan A, for the proposed works, including the planned access routes. It also needed to obtain a licence for alterations from the local authority as freeholder of the property. The plan was agreed with the local authority and the lease agreement signed. The lease was granted without the licence and the only right of way granted was through the car park. The company reconsidered its conversion plans and prepared a new plan, plan B, which made the garden the main access route. The parties discussed the changes and the local authority's representatives indicated that the arrangement was likely to be acceptable. Further correspondence between the parties discussed plan B. The alterations licence was granted, which contained obligations to carry out the works in accordance with plan B. The internal access route was used by the company with occasional use made of the garden access, without objection, for three years. The company surrendered its lease of the upper floor and blocked the internal access. It sold the basement flat. The purchaser was concerned that no formal right of way via the garden was granted by the lease. The company's attempts to agree a deed of variation with the local authority were unsuccessful. It successfully sought a declaration regarding the existence of the garden right of way. The local authority contended that the judge had erred in (1) finding that the company believed that it had, or would have, a right of way over the garden; (2) concluding that it had allowed or encouraged the company to believe that it would be granted such a right; (3) his conclusions on detrimental reliance; (4) finding that it had acted unconscionably.

Held: Appeal dismissed. (1) There was no justification for interfering with the judge's finding of fact that the company had believed that it had or would have a right of way via the garden access. The local authority's argument that the judge's formulation of his finding regarding the company's belief, namely that it "had or would have" a right of access, was not sufficient for a finding of proprietary estoppel by acquiescence, was rejected. The judge was not expressing any uncertainty regarding the company's belief in an existing right, and the submission did not hold good outside pure acquiescence cases, the instant case not being such a case, *Ramsden v Dyson* (1866) L.R. 1 H.L. 129 considered (see paras 61-63 of judgment). (2) The focus was on whether the company's belief that it had a right of way over the garden was through encouragement by the local authority or through an independent hope without any encouragement. It was not right to analyse the local authority's inactivity and failure to act separately from its acts of encouragement. A proprietary estoppel did not have to fit neatly into the pure acquiescence-based pigeon hole or the assurance one, *Taylor Fashions Ltd v Liverpool Victoria Trustees Co Ltd* [1982] Q.B. 133, [1979] C.L.Y. 1619 and *Thorner v Major* [2009] UKHL 18, [2009] 1 W.L.R. 776, [2009] C.L.Y. 3723 applied. The local authority's reliance on *Brinnand v Ewens* (1987) 19 H.L.R. 415, [1987] C.L.Y. 1448 for its argument that it could not encourage a belief that it was unaware of was misplaced, *Brinnand* and *Willmott v Barber* (1880) 15 Ch. D. 96 considered. It was possible by words and conduct to encourage another to believe or assume that they had a right or interest over property when what was encouraged was only consistent with them having some such a right. Overt acts by the local authority, including its indication at the meeting and in subsequent correspondence that access across the garden was likely to acceptable, coupled with its silence on the issue of what was to happen when the internal door was closed, amounted to encouragement to the company to hold the belief that it had (paras 71-75). (3) There was no error in the judge's conclusions on detrimental reliance. What was critical was not so much the local authority's knowledge of the company's reliance, but the fact that it must have appreciated that plan B was critically dependent on a garden right of way being granted. That was what had been discussed at the meeting and was what it had approved and encouraged thereafter. The entire project had proceeded on that common assumption that there would be such a right of way (paras 80-85). (4) To deny the existence of a right of way via the garden rendered the existing configuration of the flat highly inconvenient, given that the only means of access would be through a small bedroom. It was unconscionable for the local authority to approve and encourage the construction according to plan B, which both parties recognised was only consistent with a right of way through the garden, and then to refuse to recognise it (paras 89-94).

HOYL GROUP LTD v CROMER TOWN COUNCIL, [2015] EWCA Civ 782, [2015] H.L.R. 43, Longmore LJ, CA (Civ Div).

1826 Rights of way–Public rights of way–Meaning of "private" in Inclosure Consolidation Act 1801 s.10

The appellant (X) appealed against a refusal (*R. (on the application of Andrews) v Secretary of State for the Environment, Food and Rural Affairs* [2014] EWHC 1435 (Admin), [2014] 4 All E.R. 718, [2015] C.L.Y. 2101) to set aside the respondent secretary of state's decision that the local authority had been right to refuse his application for the modification of its definitive map to include a public bridleway. A local inclosure act had been passed for the relevant area in 1816. That local act incorporated the terms of the Inclosure Consolidation Act 1801 and appointed an inclosure commissioner. In 1841 the commissioner made an inclosure award including a public bridleway across land. The bridleway was not recorded on the definitive map. The local authority, relying on the construction of s.10 of the Act in *R. v Secretary of State for the Environment Ex p. Andrews* (1996) 71 P. & C.R. 1, [1996] C.L.Y. 5018, refused to modify the map on the ground that the commissioner had not had power to set out a public bridleway. The court at first instance agreed that the word "private" in s.10 governed not merely roads, but also bridleways and footpaths and that it conferred a power only to create private bridleways. The issue was the correct interpretation of s.10, looking at the Act as a whole and in the light of the evidence of its pre-enactment history.

Held: Appeal allowed. The Act was not drafted with the degree of accuracy and consistency of language that was found in modern statutes. Even in relation to those modern statutes, the courts adopted a purposive, in preference to a literal, interpretation so as to give effect to Parliament's intention. A purposive interpretation was all the more appropriate in a statute which was couched in less consistent and more imprecise language (see paras 30-34 of judgment). The purpose of the 1801 Act was to consolidate in one statute the clauses usually contained in earlier private enclosure acts so that subsequent local enclosure acts could incorporate its provisions by reference. Most of the pre-1801 acts authorised commissioners to appoint public, as well as private, bridleways. It seemed unlikely that Parliament would not have intended to give commissioners the power under the 1801 Act to set out public bridleways (paras 36-41). Even if no account was taken of pre-enactment practice, unless the statutory language compelled the court to interpret s.10 as applying only to private bridleways, a purposive interpretation led to the contrary conclusion for three reasons. First, in an era before the car and when carriages and carts were expensive, public rights of way on foot and on horseback were as important for the public in getting around the local area as were the public carriageway for vehicular traffic. It would have made no sense for Parliament to include a standard set of powers in relation to private, but not public, bridleways. Second, under the scheme of the 1801 Act and with particular reference to s.35, the whole commissioner process was intended to lead to the creation of an award, incorporating a map, which was definitive. The natural inference was that Parliament intended the commissioner to have full power to deal with all relevant rights with respect to the land for the future, including the power to set out and appoint all public bridleways whether pre-existing, with altered course, or new. Third, the object of inclosure was to create new private estates over areas of land which previously had been held in common. The physical landscape was to be changed in radical ways and there was likely to be a strong need to redraw the network of footpath and bridleway public rights of way. It would make no sense if that did not include the power for commissioners to create new public bridleways and footpaths pursuant to s.10 (paras 43-50). The court accepted the contention that if s.10 was looked at in isolation the natural grammatical construction of the word "private" before the list that followed it was that it applied to all items in that list, rather than simply to the first item, namely "roads". However, in the context of a statute that was drafted at the beginning of the 19th century, with linguistic imperfections, that argument had limited force. It was not impossible to read the word "private" as governing only the first item and to read the remaining items, including bridleways, as being unqualified, that is, either public or private. *Andrews* was therefore wrongly decided, *Andrews* overruled. Section 10 did authorise a commissioner to set out and appoint public bridleways and footpaths in an award and the local authority should not have rejected X's application (paras 51-62).

R. (ON THE APPLICATION OF ANDREWS) v SECRETARY OF STATE FOR THE ENVIRONMENT, FOOD AND RURAL AFFAIRS, [2015] EWCA Civ 669, [2016] 3 All E.R. 1022, Lord Dyson MR, CA (Civ Div).

1827 Settlements–Setting aside–Transfer of wife's share in family home for no consideration–Mistake as to tax consequences

[Finance Act 2006 (c.25)]

The claimant (H) applied for an order to set aside a settlement and a transfer of title to a property to the second defendant (W) who was his wife. H and W had been the joint freehold owners of a substantial house, where they had lived. On 24 March 2006, H and W executed a transfer of the title to the house to H alone, for no consideration. On 27 March H executed a deed of settlement whereby he settled the house on the terms of that deed and appointed himself and W as trustees of the settlement. H also executed a transfer of the title to the house to himself and W as the trustees of the settlement. An unintended consequence of those steps was that H became liable to pay a substantial sum of inheritance tax and to pay a further charge on every 10th anniversary of the date of the transfer. Those changes in the law were effected by the Finance Act 2006 following a budget announcement. The relevant amendments had retrospective effect from 22 March 2006. H and W were unaware of the announcement and that the steps they had taken would result in an immediate charge to tax or a 10-year anniversary charge. H maintained that the settlement and the transfer should be set aside on the basis that he had been mistaken as to the tax consequences of creating the settlement. The issue was whether the case was governed by the common law rules for declaring a contract to be void by reason of mistake, or the equitable rules for setting aside a gift for mistake. H argued that the settlement and transfer were voluntary distributions to which the equitable rules applied.

Held: Judgment for claimant. (1) The difference between cases where the equitable rules applied turned on whether consideration had been given for the benefit conferred by the transaction. If the effect of rescission (or a declaration that a transaction was void) would deprive a party of a benefit for which he had given consideration, then the common law rules applied and there was no separate equitable jurisdiction to order rescission. Conversely, if the effect of rescission would deprive a party of a benefit for which he had given consideration, then there was a separate equitable jurisdiction to order rescission, *Pitt v Holt* [2013] UKSC 26, [2013] 2 A.C. 108, [2013] C.L.Y. 3173 followed. Considering the transactions as a whole the position was that before 24 March 2006 H and W, as the legal and beneficial owners of the property, wished to settle the property on themselves and their children and remoter issue. By taking two steps on 24 and 27 March they implemented their intentions. The position of the two of them acting together was no different from the position of a sole legal and beneficial owner settling his property on himself and members of his family. H and the other beneficiaries had not given consideration for the settlement. It was a unilateral transaction and all the beneficiaries were volunteers. The equitable rules applied to the claim to set aside the transactions (see paras 31, 36-37, 40 of judgment). (2) Applying those rules the position was as follows: (a) H and W had made a mistake when they entered into the transfer on 24 March and the settlement and transfer of 27 March; they were ignorant of the budget announcement; that ignorance could not be regarded as "mere ignorance" which would not give rise to a relevant mistake because the ignorance led to a false belief or assumption that the creation of the settlement did not involve a chargeable transfer so that inheritance tax would be payable as a result: (b) they would not have entered into the transactions if they had not made those mistakes; (c) their mistake did not involve them running a risk about a possible liability to pay inheritance tax by reason of the creation of the settlement; they believed that there was to be no question of a charge to tax by reason of the creation of a settlement; (d) the fact that the mistake was a mistake about tax was irrelevant. H and W were entitled to an order setting aside the transfer and the settlement (paras 41, 48).

VAN DER MERWE v GOLDMAN, [2016] EWHC 790 (Ch), [2016] 4 W.L.R. 71, Morgan J, Ch D.

1828 **Tenants in common–Beneficial interests–Common intention to vary beneficial interests in property–Imputation of intention as to respective shares**

[Trusts of Land and Appointment of Trustees Act 1996 (c.47) s.14]

The appellant appealed against a decision regarding the beneficial shares held in a property jointly owned with the respondent as tenants in common. The parties had been in a relationship since 1983 and had two children. In 1996 they bought a property as joint tenants. The appellant was self-employed. He paid the mortgage and some of the bills. The respondent worked full-time, except when the children were very young when she worked part-time. During their relationship, the appellant bought three investment properties registered in his name. In early 2005, he had debt problems and they remortgaged the jointly held property. Repayment of the existing mortgage and the appellant's debts effectively used all the remortgage funds. The parties separated in 2005. The respondent sought a declaration under the Trusts of Land and Appointment of Trustees Act 1996 s.14. The judge found that, on the purchase of the property, the parties' intention was that they were joint tenants in law and in equity, and that both were contributing equally. However, he found that the appellant had received almost 25 per cent of the net equity in the property following the remortgage, and imputed an intention at that stage that the property was to be held in shares of 75 per cent and 25 per cent, in the respondent's favour. He then considered that a further adjustment was required for the period from 2008, when the respondent had sole responsibility for the mortgage. She also had financial responsibility for the children, though the appellant made some contribution to child support. The judge held that the parties' shares were 85 per cent and 15 per cent, in favour of the respondent. The appellant submitted that it had not been open to the judge to impute a common intention that the shares be unequal, having found that there was no agreement by the parties to change their beneficial interests.

Held: Appeal dismissed. (1) The judge's use of "impute" was intentional and appropriate. He was seeking to determine the shares in which the parties were to own the property following a change in the basis on which their beneficial interests were held. The imputation of intention was entirely permissible in that context where it was not possible to infer the parties' intention. Imputation was not permissible at the stage of determining whether there had been a common change of intention, only at the second stage of determining the respective shares where inference was not possible, *Jones v Kernott* [2011] UKSC 53, [2012] 1 A.C. 776, [2012] C.L.Y. 2705 followed. It was strongly arguable that the judge had concluded that there had been a common intention to vary the shares, despite that stage of reasoning being absent from his judgment. In those circumstances, it was open to the instant court to consider whether a common intention to vary should be inferred. The weight of the evidence supported an inference that the parties had intended to alter their shares in the property. The remortgage in 2005 was entered into for the appellant's sole benefit, to pay off debts incurred in his personal capacity. Virtually all of the money remaining after repayment of the original mortgage went to him. A month later, the relationship ended and the appellant left the property. In those circumstances, where nearly 25 per cent of the equity in the property had been paid to the appellant for his own purposes, and the relationship ended almost immediately afterwards, there was to be inferred a common intention at that point to vary their respective interests in the property. Both parties had contributed to the mortgage repayments between June 2005 and January 2008. After

January 2008, the respondent alone made the repayments. That also supported an inference that there was a common intention to vary their interests in the property. The appellant could only legitimately have taken that stance and acted in that way if there had been such a change. A common intention should therefore be inferred to the parties at separation to vary their beneficial interests in the property (see paras 20-35 of judgment). (2) Having inferred a common intention to vary the respective interests, the judge entirely appropriately imputed an intention to the parties regarding their respective shares. The appellant's receipt of almost 25 per cent of the equity very shortly before the parties separated warranted an adjustment to the beneficial shares in the property. The judge had also correctly concluded that subsequent events required a further adjustment in the intention to be imputed to the parties. He properly took account of their respective positions, and in particular the mortgage repayments and repairs. The appellant had failed to contribute towards the mortgage repayments for the six years up to trial (paras 36-37). (3) It should be open to a court to take account of financial contributions, or the lack of them, to child maintenance as part of the financial history of the parties, save in circumstances where it was clear to do so would result in double liability, *Stack v Dowden* [2007] UKHL 17, [2007] 2 A.C. 432, [2007] C.L.Y. 3367 and *Jones* followed. There was no danger of double liability in the instant case (paras 38-41).

BARNES v PHILLIPS, [2015] EWCA Civ 1056, [2016] H.L.R. 3, Longmore LJ, CA (Civ Div).

1829 Transactions defrauding creditors–Beneficial ownership–Transfer of beneficial interest in properties to spouse not publicly registered–Inference of intention to place assets beyond reach of creditors

[Insolvency Act 1986 (c.45) s.423]

A lender applied for a deed of trust made by the first respondent husband in favour of the second respondent wife to be set aside under the Insolvency Act 1986 s.423. On 16 November 2006, the husband had been registered as proprietor of a property, although he claimed to have bought the property in 1995 in his sole name. In May 2007 the lender granted the husband a loan, secured by a charge on the property. The charge was registered. In December 2006 the husband had been registered as proprietor of a second property and in October 2007 the lender granted to loan to the husband secured by a registered charge on that property. The husband defaulted on the loans and the lender brought possession proceedings regarding both properties. The husband produced a deed dated December 2006 under which the beneficial interest in the properties was transferred to the wife. In the instant proceedings, the husband and wife produced a further deed dated 1996 in identical terms to the 2006 deed, except that it only referred to the second property. After closing speeches, the lender reviewed its documents and discovered a transfer dated 10 November 2006 whereby the husband and wife as joint proprietors had transferred the first property to the husband alone. The lender argued that (1) the 2006 transfer should be admitted as evidence; (2) the husband's purpose in entering into the deeds had been to place assets beyond the reach of creditors.

Held: Application granted. (1) The 2006 transfer would be admitted. At the time the transfer was sought to be introduced, the court had not made its assessment of the evidence and the trial had not concluded. It would be an affront to common sense and to any sense of justice to exclude the transfer, *Mulholland v Mitchell (No.1)* [1971] A.C. 666, [1971] C.L.Y. 3232 applied. Further, neither husband nor wife could properly object to its being adduced. Their evidence had been that the 2006 deed was simply an updating of the 1996 deed to include extra property. That was liable to mislead, because the 2006 deed was in truth a restatement of the 1996 deed, which had effectively been set aside by the 2006 transfer. It was a litigant's duty, having led the court to believe a fact to be true, to correct it when he or she discovered it to be false, *Vernon v Bosley (No.2)* [1999] Q.B. 18, [1997] C.L.Y. 456 applied. The transfer could fairly be admitted because the husband and wife had been given the chance to put in further witness statements, which they had taken, and had declined to be cross-examined further. Having admitted the transfer, the court found it to be an authentic and effective document. It was therefore unnecessary to consider the 1996 deed, since whatever its effect, it had been undone by the transfer (see paras 26-29 of judgment).

(2) The lender had established on the balance of probabilities that a real and substantial purpose of the husband in entering into the 2006 deed was to place assets beyond the reach of those who might have a claim against him. It could be inferred from the chain of events that the husband had understood the importance of the borrower being the beneficial owner at the time of borrowing: that was why the first property had been transferred to him in November 2006 to enable him to borrow to help fund the acquisition of the second property, and why that property had been acquired in his sole name with the aid of further borrowing. Despite appreciating that, he had not publicly registered the true ownership, instead keeping the deed in a safe and controlling to whom its effect was disclosed. That was a very significant factor in determining the substantial purposes of the transaction, *Inland Revenue Commissioners v Hashmi* [2002] EWCA Civ 981, [2002] B.C.C. 943, [2003] C.L.Y. 4484 followed. The court was entitled to ask why the husband had chosen to undertake the transaction without using a conveyancing solicitor and had not communicated with the Land Registry, and, in the absence of a compelling answer, to infer that one reason was to keep knowledge of the transaction private. The 2006 deed prejudiced the interests of those who might have a claim against the husband. An inference was raised that that obvious result was its purpose to a substantial degree. That was not outweighed by any evidence adduced by the husband. Accordingly, there would be an order restoring the position to what it would have been had the transaction not been entered into: the 2006 deed would be set aside, thus revesting both properties in the husband beneficially (paras 30-40).

SWIFT ADVANCES PLC v AHMED, [2015] EWHC 3265 (Ch), [2016] B.P.I.R. 197, Norris J, Ch D.

1830 Transfer of land–Legitimate expectation–Claim for specific performance of contractual obligation to transfer land to local authority

[Law of Property (Miscellaneous Provisions) Act 1989 (c.34) s.2]

A community association appealed against a decision (*Dudley Muslim Association v Dudley MBC* [2014] EWHC 296 (Ch)) striking out its defence to the respondent local authority's claim for specific performance of a contractual obligation. The association had acquired the freehold of a site to build a mosque and community centre. Development covenants provided that the property would transfer back to the local authority if the development was not completed by a particular date. The association applied promptly for planning permission, but delays ensued. The local authority referred in writing to delays due to factors beyond the association's control and stated that the completion deadline was unrealistic and that a new target date should be set once planning permission was resolved. Planning permission was refused. The local authority rejected the association's request to extend the deadline, which subsequently expired. The local authority issued proceedings claiming specific performance of the obligation to transfer the land. The association argued that it had a legitimate expectation that it would be allowed to develop the site within a reasonable timeframe given the delays caused by what it asserted to be the local authority's failings. The issues were whether (i) the association had such a legitimate expectation; (ii) the local authority had abused its power by making an irrational and unreasonable decision and/or acting unfairly.

Held: Appeal dismissed. (1) The case was not about the local authority's unilateral exercise of a statutory power, but about the implementation of a commercial bargain. The association's defence gave rise to the question of whether a public law defence based on legitimate expectation was, in principle, an available defence to a claim to enforce a contract. The case was a purely contractual dispute. There might be cases in which a true public law defence vitiated a contractual claim and, in the exercise of its supervisory jurisdiction, the court might quash a decision made in bad faith. However, the authority would be free to take the decision again, in good faith, and the contract would be enforceable. The association's case was that the legal effect of the contract had changed, or been suspended. There was no public law defence available to it based on legitimate expectation or a general appeal based on abuse of power. If it could not assert a variation of the contract or a promissory estoppel, which it had not attempted to do, the contract was enforceable according to its terms. Even if either of those defences were to be asserted, there was a further obstacle in the association's way, under the Law of Property (Miscellaneous Provisions) Act 1989 s.2. The obligation to transfer the site to the local authority was a contract for the disposition of an interest in land. It was an executory, and initially conditional, promise to transfer the freehold to the local authority in exchange for a stipulated sum of money. The obligation to transfer was therefore within the ambit of s.2. Even if the association had been able to plead, and prove, a defence of promissory estoppel, it would not have overcome the problem arising under s.2(1), *MP Kemp Ltd v Bullen Developments Ltd* [2014] EWHC 2009 (Ch) applied. The claim based on legitimate expectation also failed on the facts. The association relied on what it stated to be a specific promise by the local authority. However, the letter relied on was one of a series of communications between the parties. One could not cherry pick the parts which favoured one side; the communications had to be looked at as a whole, *R. v Secretary of State for Education and Employment Ex p. Begbie* [2000] 1 W.L.R. 1115, [1999] C.L.Y. 1704 applied (see paras 30-41 of judgment). (2) The abuse of power argument was another way of seeking to inject public law defences into what was essentially a private law claim, which the court had already concluded was impermissible. A citizen could rely on an allegation of abuse of power to impugn a public authority's decision, even if there had been no clear representation creating a legitimate expectation, *R. v Inland Revenue Commissioners Ex p. Unilever Plc* [1996] S.T.C. 681 applied. However, the local authority had done nothing unlawful and abuse of power was not a freestanding ground on which a court could act in the absence of unlawful action. It was necessary, therefore, to identify the power being abused. The instant case concerned contractual rights and obligations, and it could not usually be an abuse of power to exercise contractual rights freely conferred. The context in respect of "fairness" was a commercial contract entered into by parties with the benefit of legal advice. Promissory estoppel was not relied on by the association. The defence of abuse of power, if available, also failed on the facts (paras 42-50).

DUDLEY MUSLIM ASSOCIATION v DUDLEY MBC, [2015] EWCA Civ 1123, [2016] 1 P. & C.R. 10, Lewison LJ, CA (Civ Div).

1831 Transfer of land–Rescission–Rescission for unilateral mistake–Third party rights

The claimants, who were father and son, made a claim to rescind two transfers of land on the grounds of mistake. The claimants had farmed together in partnership. They were concerned about possible claims to the partnership land from other members of the family. They claimed that their solicitors advised them to create a discretionary trust of the land, and advised them that there would be no capital gains tax chargeable on the transfer of the land into that trust. The trust was created and the land was transferred to the trustees in June 2011. It transpired that capital gains tax was chargeable on the transfers. The claimants sought to set aside on the ground of mistake the transfer of part of the land, namely land at Seamer Grange Farm. At a hearing in September 2015 the judge granted the relief sought. He was satisfied that there had been a distinct mistake made by the claimants, as opposed to mere ignorance; that the mistake was basic to the transaction; that the claimants had not deliberately run the risk of being wrong; and that it would be unconscionable or unjust to leave the mistake uncorrected. He was also satisfied that there were no effective bars to rescission; in particular, it was not a bar to rescission that relief was being sought only in relation to part of the property transferred. The judge gave the claimants permission to re-amend the claim form to allow them to make similar claims to set aside two further transfers of land (Harker Hill and Fox Covert) into the trust. Harker Hill and Fox Covert had been transferred in June 2011 along with Seamer Grange Farm; however, they had later been sold by the trustees. The proceeds of sale had been used to acquire new land. The father died shortly after the September 2015 hearing, and his executor was substituted for him in the proceedings. The claimants accepted that the purchasers of Harker Hill and Fox Covert were good faith purchasers and that there was no prospect of the court's making an order rescinding the purchases by those third parties. They submitted that the new land substantially represented Harker Hill and Fox Covert, and that the court should make an order "restoring" the new land to the claimants' beneficial ownership.

Held: Declaration granted in favour of claimants. (1) Rescission was usually seen as an all or nothing remedy, *TSB Bank Plc v Camfield* [1995] 1 W.L.R. 430, [1995] C.L.Y.

2447 considered. However, the remedy awarded was fact-sensitive, and permitted what was practically just, *O'Sullivan v Management Agency and Music Ltd* [1985] Q.B. 428, [1984] C.L.Y. 388 and *Cheese v Thomas* [1994] 1 W.L.R. 129, [1995] C.L.Y. 842 considered. The judge at the earlier hearing had held that there was no reason why, in a non-contractual case, relief could not be sought in relation to part of the property transferred subject to a vitiating factor, and not all of it, *Kennedy v Kennedy* [2014] EWHC 4129 (Ch), [2015] B.T.C. 2, [2015] C.L.Y. 2566 considered (see paras 20-22 of judgment). (2) Another way to look at rescission was to see it as a foundation for a claim to other property than that which was originally transferred. In The Law of Tracing, OUP 1997, 365-67, Prof Lionel Smith referred to that idea as a "proprietary base by avoidance". That could be seen in the fact that the right to rescind was an equity which attached to the property in whosoever's hands it might be, unless and until it came to the hands of a good faith purchaser for value without notice. So it was binding on a donee of that property. But it was also facilitated by virtue of a process of tracing through the products of the original property. In *Shalson v Russo* [2003] EWHC 1637 (Ch), [2005] Ch. 281, [2003] C.L.Y. 3611 it was held that, upon rescission of a contract for misrepresentation, the beneficial title which passed to the representor under the contract revested in the representee, and the representee could trace through the products of the original property. It did not matter that the line of authorities discussed in *Shalson* was concerned with rescission for misrepresentation, whereas the instant case was concerned with mistake. The consequence of the rescission was the same whether it took place because of fraudulent or negligent misrepresentation, or because of causative and basic unilateral mistake. The property transferred under such a mistake revested beneficially in the transferor, subject to third party rights. In a case where third party rights could not be disturbed, there was no reason not to apply the tracing process to exchange products of the transferred property in order to find other assets to which to make a claim instead, *Shalson* and *Pearce v Beverley* [2013] EWHC 2627 (Ch), [2014] W.T.L.R. 85, [2014] C.L.Y. 2844 applied, *National Crime Agency v Robb* [2014] EWHC 4384 (Ch), [2015] Ch. 520, [2015] C.L.Y. 217 considered. It was not only in cases of fraudulent misrepresentation that the idea of a "proprietary base by avoidance" and the tracing process could be prayed in aid. The principle was wide enough to cover other vitiating factors too, including mistake. It was open to the claimants to make a claim to the new land: the court would make an appropriate declaration giving effect to the rescission of the transfers of Harker Hill and Fox Covert (paras 24-32, 43).

BAINBRIDGE v BAINBRIDGE, [2016] EWHC 898 (Ch), [2016] W.T.L.R. 943, Master Matthews, Ch D.

1832 Unmarried couples–Constructive trusts–Determining common intention

The court was required to determine whether the respondent (H) had acquired a beneficial interest in property owned by the appellant (C). C and H had lived together for 20 years. C took over H's frozen food business after he was made bankrupt. Ten years after the beginning of their relationship, C purchased a property (Sunnyside). The property was purchased with an interest-only mortgage in C's sole name, and the deposit came from her business earnings. She later purchased another property (Beaumont). H set up his own company. The relationship between the parties began to break down. C asserted that she had agreed to transfer her business to H's company in exchange for a weekly payment of £750. She moved out of Sunnyside, and H continued to live, and run the frozen food business, there. H paid C £750 per week for several years. He asserted a beneficial interest in Sunnyside. The judge concluded that there was no agreement that H should have a beneficial interest in Sunnyside, but she concluded that by reason of H's contribution to the business, he had acquired a beneficial interest of 25 per cent. She also found that H held the issued shares of the company on trust for himself and C with a 65:35 split in his favour.

Held: Appeal allowed, cross-appeal dismissed. (1) In relation to unmarried cohabitees, where an asset was owned in law by one person, but another claimed to share a beneficial interest in it, a two-stage analysis was necessary to determine whether a common intention constructive trust had arisen. First, the person claiming the beneficial interest had to show that there was an agreement that he should have a beneficial interest, even if there was no agreement as to the precise extent of that interest. Second, if such an agreement could be shown to have been made, but there was no agreement on the extent of the interest, the court could impute an intention that the person was to have a fair beneficial share in the asset, *Oxley v Hiscock* [2004] EWCA Civ 546, [2005] Fam. 211, [2004] C.L.Y. 3196, *Stack v Dowden* [2005] EWCA Civ 857, [2006] 1 F.L.R. 254, [2005] C.L.Y. 3391 and *Jones v Kernott* [2011] UKSC 53, [2012] 1 A.C. 776, [2012] C.L.Y. 2705 considered. The court was not entitled to impute an intention to the parties at the first stage in the analysis; an actual agreement had to be found to have been made (see paras 16-17 of judgment). (2) The judge had erroneously elided the two stages. She had imputed an intention to the parties for the first stage of the analysis rather than identifying an actual agreement that H should have any beneficial interest in Sunnyside. No actual agreement to that effect had ever been made between the parties. C was the sole legal and beneficial owner of Sunnyside and Beaumont. H had no valid claim to a beneficial interest in either of those properties (paras 18-23). (3) H was the sole legal and beneficial owner of the shares in the company, and C had no beneficial interest in them. She had sold the business to H's company in 2007 in return for a payment by H of £750 per week. The company was the sole owner of the business, and C had no beneficial interest in the business or the company. The payment of £750 per week was agreed to last while H was in occupation of Sunnyside or until the interest-only mortgage expired in 2019, whichever was sooner. There was a strong probability that Sunnyside would have to be sold by C in 2019 in order to repay the mortgage, as contemplated by the parties (paras 24, 26, 28).

CAPEHORN v HARRIS, [2015] EWCA Civ 955, [2016] 2 F.L.R. 1026, Sir Brian Leveson PQBD, CA (Civ Div).

1833 Village greens–Appropriation–Registration of village green–Application of implied doctrine of appropriation

[Commons Act 2006 (c.26) s.15(2); Local Government Act 1972 (c.70) s.122]

The claimant applied for judicial review of an inspector's refusal of an application to register an area of land as a town or village green. In 1984, a local authority had owned a parcel of land, the most southerly third of which, it was proposed, should be allocated for employment use and a link road proposal (the land). That land encompassed railway sidings. In 1989, the local authority formally appropriated the land from a recreation use to be held for development purposes and then disposed of for industrial use. The allocation of the land was carried forward in two local plans adopted in 1983 and 2005. In 2012, the local authority consulted the public in relation to the retention and continuation of the land for employment development and the construction of the link road. In the meantime, the claimant had applied to register the land, together with adjoining land, as a town or village green under the Commons Act 2006 s.15(2). Under that provision, a significant number of the inhabitants of any locality, or of any neighbourhood within a locality, had to have indulged "as of right" in lawful sports and pastimes on the land for a period of at least 20 years and continue to have done so at the time of the application. In the instant case, an inspector tentatively concluded that the land had been appropriated in 1989, and, together with the railway sidings land, was re-appropriated to open space use by 2006-2007 by inference, and that the use by local inhabitants of the land for lawful sports and pastimes was therefore by right for a substantial part of the 20-year period. As those conclusions were tentative, the inspector went on to conclude that if the land had been held for planning purposes, or industrial development purposes, it was reasonable to conclude that the temporary licensing of the activities that took place there would have alerted a reasonable person to the fact that the land, when access could be gained, was being used by permission. Although the inspector was satisfied of all the statutory ingredients, he was not satisfied therefore that the use of the land had been "as of right" rather than "by right". The application was accordingly refused. The issues were whether the inspector had (i) erred in law and misdirected himself in concluding that reliance could be placed on an inferred re-appropriation in relation to the land; (ii) failed to have regard to two material considerations, namely the public ownership of the land, and the nature and quality of the events which had been held on it.

Held: Application granted. (1) The authority the inspector relied on as creating a doctrine of inferred appropriation by conduct was not capable of being interpreted as broadly as he did: appropriation could not be inferred by conduct alone, *Oxy Electric*

Ltd v Zainuddin [1990] E.G. 128 (C.S.) explained. The Local Government Act 1972 s.122 required some conscious deliberative process to ensure that the statutory powers under which the land was held was clear and appropriation from one use to another could not be simply inferred from how a local authority managed or treated the land, *R. (on the application of Malpass) v Durham CC* [2012] EWHC 1934 (Admin) and *Western Power Distribution Investments Ltd v Cardiff City Council* [2013] EWHC 1407 (Admin) applied, *R. (on the application of Barkas) v North Yorkshire CC* [2014] UKSC 31, [2015] A.C. 195, [2014] C.L.Y. 2526 explained. The inspector's decision consequently contained a clear legal misdirection and was fatal to his case. In any event, a factual finding on the material which had been before the inspector that appropriation could be inferred was not justified. That conclusion inferred that it could be implied from the local authority's conduct that the land was no longer required, that being the test under s.122 of the 1972 Act. Such a conclusion was wholly at odds with the local authority's conduct as a local planning authority (see paras 25-27, 29, 35, 43-44, 46 of judgment). (2) The inspector had failed to take account of two material considerations in relation to the implied licence, namely the fact that the land in the instant case had been in public ownership, and the character and nature of the events that had taken place on the land. That was sufficient to justify a conclusion that his decision was based on an error of law *R. (on the application of Mann v Somerset CC* applied (paras 51-53).

R. (ON THE APPLICATION OF GOODMAN) v SECRETARY OF STATE FOR ENVIRONMENT, FOOD AND RURAL AFFAIRS, [2015] EWHC 2576 (Admin), [2016] 2 All E.R. 701, Dove J, QBD (Admin).

1834 Village greens–Registration–Successful applications for registration–Duty of registration authority to inform objectors of reasons for decision

[Commons Act 2006 (c.26) s.15; European Convention on Human Rights 1950 art.6]

The claimant company sought judicial review of a decision of the defendant local authority to register a parcel of woodland (the land) as a town or village green under the Commons Act 2006 s.15. At all relevant times, the land had formed part of land held by one of various NHS bodies. The land was held for defined statutory health-related purposes, although it had not to date actually been used for such purposes. The land was currently owned by the claimant. The local authority granted an application to register the land as a town or village green, having concluded that the criteria in s.15 of the 2006 Act were met. Those criteria were that "a significant number of the inhabitants of any locality, or neighbourhood within a locality, indulged as of right in lawful sports and pastimes on the land for a period of at least 20 years". The claimant had objected to the application, arguing, among other things, that there was an incompatibility between the statutory purposes for which the land was held and registration under s.15. The local authority did not appear to have addressed that submission when reaching its decision. The main issues were (1) whether the local authority was under a duty to give reasons for its decision; (2) if it was, the standard of reasoning required; (3) whether the local authority had given adequate reasons; (4) whether the local authority's finding that there was a "neighbourhood" for the purposes of s.15 was one which it could reasonably make; (5) given the absence of any consideration or reasoning relating to the question of statutory incompatibility, whether the local authority had shown that there was no basis for concluding that there was statutory incompatibility.

Held: Application granted. (1) The giving of reasons was required to achieve compliance with ECHR art.6, which was engaged as registration involved a determination of civil rights and obligations. Common law also required the giving of reasons. A landowner was at risk of losing his freedom to do as he wished with his land. He needed to know whether the decision to register was made on lawful grounds and whether he had grounds for challenging it (see paras 100, 104 of judgment). (2) The starting point was that the reasons given had to be intelligible and deal adequately with the substance of the arguments advanced. The local authority would need to set out whether the applicant for registration had shown that the s.15 criteria had been met and why the criteria had been met or not. In a case where an objection had been made on a ground known to law, the local authority should state whether that objection was well founded and why it was or was not well founded. The losing party should be left knowing why he had lost and the legal justification for rejecting his submissions (paras

108-109, 111). (3) The local authority had erred by failing to consider the issue of statutory incompatibility and giving no reasons for rejecting the claimant's case as an objector (para.143). (4) The local authority had considered whether the identified "neighbourhood" had the necessary quality of cohesion and its finding that there was a neighbourhood was a decision which it could reasonably make (paras 115, 119). (5) The claimant's objection to registration on the basis of statutory incompatibility was well founded. It was not necessary that the land in question was used for a purpose incompatible with use as a village green. What mattered was whether, as a matter of statutory construction, the relevant statutory purpose was incompatible with registration. Here it was. The erection of buildings or facilities to provide treatment, or the erection of buildings for the administration of those facilities, or the creation of car parking, would plainly conflict with recreational use, *R. (on the application of Newhaven Port and Properties Ltd) v East Sussex CC* [2015] UKSC 7, [2015] A.C. 1547, [2015] C.L.Y. 2128 applied (paras 127, 133, 143).

R. (ON THE APPLICATION OF NHS PROPERTY SERVICES LTD) v SURREY CC, [2016] EWHC 1715 (Admin), [2016] 4 W.L.R. 130, Gilbert J, QBD (Admin).

RESTITUTION

1835 Unjust enrichment–Local authorities' powers and duties–Local authority failing to provide mental health after-care services–Patient paying privately for services

[Mental Health Act 1983 (c.20) s.117, s.2, s.25A, s.3; Civil Procedure Rules 1998 Pt 7, r.54.3]

The defendants, a local authority and an NHS commissioning group, applied to strike out the claimant's claim for restitution. The claimant had been detained in hospital on several occasions under the Mental Health Act 1983 s.2, and later under s.3. The responsible medical officer completed a supervision application under s.25A, allowing for the claimant to be supervised after leaving hospital in order to receive after-care services under s.117. The application was meant to include details of the after-care services. The relevant NHS commissioning group had a duty to provide those after-care services. The medical officer's application provided for the claimant's attendance at an outpatient clinic, and cooperation with a care plan, but did not include the details of the after-care services. No s.117 after-care plan had come to light. After his discharge, the claimant's deputy moved him to a care home, and then to his own home with full-time carers; the costs were paid by the claimant privately. He claimed for restitution, seeking to recover the £644,645.87 spent by the deputy on his behalf, on the basis that the defendants had failed to provide the services that they had considered should be supplied. The issues were (1) whether it was in principle possible for the claimant to bring a restitutionary claim; (2) if so, whether the claim should have been brought by way of judicial review, rather than as a CPR Pt 7 claim. On the second issue, the claimant submitted that he was not challenging the defendants' assessment of his needs or decisions as to what after-care should be provided.

Held: Application refused. (1) The case of *Clunis v Camden and Islington HA* [1998] Q.B. 978, [1998] C.L.Y. 3937 established that s.117 did not create a private law cause of action for failure to carry out a statutory duty. However, *Clunis* had not considered the availability of a claim in unjust enrichment, *Clunis* distinguished. The Act did not evince an intention to exclude any common law claim for unjust enrichment that would otherwise exist. There was no comprehensive and conclusive scheme for the correction and consequences of mistaken benefit awards, *R. (on the application of Child Poverty Action Group) v Secretary of State for Work and Pensions* [2010] UKSC 54, [2011] 2 A.C. 15, [2011] C.L.Y. 3157 considered. However, the fact that the Act did not exclude a claim for unjust enrichment did not imply that the claimant had such a claim. A successful unjust enrichment claim depended on establishing an "unjust factor", *Deutsche Morgan Grenfell Group Plc v Inland Revenue Commissioners* [2006] UKHL 49, [2007] 1 A.C. 558, [2007] C.L.Y. 3973 and *Test Claimants in the FII Group Litigation v Revenue and Customs Commissioners* [2012] UKSC 19, [2012] 2 A.C. 337, [2012] C.L.Y. 3251 followed. The claimant's claim was based on the proposition that payments made on his behalf had relieved the defendants of their s.117 liabilities. Failure to perform a public law duty had not, to the court's knowledge, of itself been held to be an unjust factor in an unjust enrichment claim, or a sufficient basis for any other restitutionary claim. The claimant also alleged that his deputy had made the payments under mistake, an accepted unjust factor. The payments were not to the defendants, so there was no scope for a conventional claim to recover money paid under mistake, but that was not necessarily fatal. It was seriously arguable that the defendants had been enriched at the claimant's expense (see paras 32-37 of judgment). (2) There were exceptions to the rule that challenges to public authorities' decisions should normally be by way of judicial review, *O'Reilly v Mackman* [1983] 2 A.C. 237, [1982] C.L.Y. 2603 followed. It was relevant whether the claimant had suffered an infringement of a private law right, *Wandsworth LBC v Winder (No.1)* [1985] A.C. 461, [1985] C.L.Y. 9 and *Boddington v British Transport Police* [1999] 2 A.C. 143, [1998] C.L.Y. 89 followed. It was also relevant whether the private law right only arose if the claimant could show that a public law decision was unlawfully made, *R. v Secretary of State for the Home Department Ex p. Shingara (No.2)* [1999] Imm. A.R. 257, [1999] C.L.Y. 3196 and *Jones v Powys Local Health Board* [2008] EWHC 2562 (Admin), (2009) 12 C.C.L. Rep. 68, [2009] C.L.Y. 341 considered. However, *Jones* was not the same as the instant case; in that case the claimant could not get reimbursement without establishing that the relevant authority had erred in assessing him as entitled to continuing care, and the complaints about the authority had been "central, explicit and suitable for determination by judicial review". In the instant case the claimant was permitted to pursue his restitutionary claim. He was asserting a private law claim, albeit one that raised a question as to whether the defendants had failed to perform their statutory duty to assess and determine his needs. While CPR r.54.3 allowed restitution to be claimed within judicial review applications, such applications could not be for restitution alone, and the claimant's concern was to obtain financial redress rather than any other relief. It was not clear that a private law claim for restitution should be subject to the strict judicial review time limits (paras 41-50).

RICHARDS v WORCESTERSHIRE CC, [2016] EWHC 1954 (Ch), [2016] Med. L.R. 534, Newey J, Ch D (Bristol).

ROAD TRAFFIC

1836 Disabled persons' badges–Mobility impaired persons–Identification

THE DISABLED PERSONS (BADGES FOR MOTOR VEHICLES) (WALES) (AMENDMENT) REGULATIONS 2016, SI 2016/453; made under the Chronically Sick and Disabled Persons Act 1970 s.21. In force: 1 October 2016.

These Regulations amend the Disabled Persons (Badges for Motor Vehicles) (Wales) Regulations 2000 to provide a description of disabled persons that captures people with a temporary but substantial disability that is expected to affect their mobility for at least twelve months.

1837 Driving Instructors (Registration) Act 2016 (c.16)

An Act to make provision about the registration of driving instructors.

1838 Highway construction–Bridgwater & Taunton Canal Bridge–Somerset

THE COUNTY COUNCIL OF SOMERSET (BRIDGWATER & TAUNTON CANAL BRIDGE) SCHEME 2015 CONFIRMATION INSTRUMENT 2016, SI 2016/1018; made under the Highways Act 1980 s.106(3). In force: In accordance with art.1.

This instrument confirms a scheme to construct over the navigable waters of the Bridwater & Taunton Canal the bridge specified in the Schedule to this Scheme as part of the highway which they are proposing to construct and improve between Marsh Lane/Showground Road junction and Parrett Way in the District of Sedgemoor in the County of Somerset.

1839 Highway construction–River Parrett Bridge–Somerset

THE COUNTY COUNCIL OF SOMERSET (RIVER PARRETT BRIDGE) SCHEME 2015 CONFIRMATION INSTRUMENT 2016, SI 2016/1019; made under the Highways Act 1980 s.106(3). In force: In accordance with art.1.

This instrument confirms a scheme to construct over the navigable waters of the River Parrett the bridge specified in the Schedule to this Scheme as part of the highway they are proposing to construct and improve between Marsh Lane/Showground Road junction and Parrett Way in the District of Sedgemoor in the County of Somerset.

1840 Highway maintenance–Danger–Defect on edge of road–Whether danger to cyclists

[Highways Act 1980 (c.66) s.41; Occupiers' Liability Act 1957 (c.31)]

A cyclist appealed against the dismissal of his claim for damages from the local highway authority for breach of its duty to maintain the highway under the Highways Act 1980 s.41 after he fell off his bicycle and suffered injuries. In May 2009, the cyclist had been cycling along a high mountain road, under 4m wide, with gradients of between 14% and 20%. There was gravel and vegetation along it, and changes of camber and gradient. Whilst cycling downhill, he rounded a bend and came upon some debris. He changed direction to avoid it and came upon a defect on the edge of the left side of the road. He was catapulted from his bike and suffered cuts and wounds. The local authority inspected the road twice a year. It had last been inspected in February 2009 when the defect was there. The local authority was guided by its code of practice, Well-Maintained Highways, which divided road defects into different categories. Category 1 defects required prompt action because they were an immediate or imminent hazard but their categorisation as such depended on a range of factors and, pursuant to para.9.5.3 of the code, was to be informed by local knowledge. The judge held that the defect was not a danger. The issue was whether the highway was dangerous, with the cyclist arguing that the defect fell into category 1 of the local authority's code of practice.

Held: Appeal dismissed. (1) The judge asked the right question, which was posed in *Mills v Barnsley MBC* [1992] P.I.Q.R. P291, [1993] C.L.Y. 2967 , namely whether the highway was dangerous "in the sense that in the ordinary course of human affairs danger [might] reasonably be anticipated from its continued use by the public", *Mills* followed. However, that did not of itself mean that he gave the right answer. It was necessary to look at what considerations he did or did not take into account in giving his answer. The judge made findings as to the nature of the road and the extent of its use by cyclists, which were relevant in analysing the dangerousness of any supposed defect in it. He also took into account that the defect was at the very edge of the road and was visible from about 21m from around the bend. Whilst the cyclist was entitled to be on any part of the road, the site of the defect was a material consideration. In the circumstances, it was open to the judge to find that the possibility of a cyclist riding into the defect was remote, particularly as, when coming round the corner, he would not be expected to be going too fast and to be watching carefully what was ahead due to the general state of the road. He encountered the defect because of the peculiar circumstance that he swerved to avoid some stones and manure. The judge was entitled to find that danger was not reasonably to be anticipated from the continued use, by members of the public who were likely to use it, of a road with such a defect. Although the question was an objective one, the judge was also entitled to have his view reinforced by the fact that a man who lived along the road had been aware of the defect since December 2008 without reporting it and the cyclist did not report the matter either. Further, the judge took into account the character of the road and that such defects could be found for miles on hill roads, and that such an unremarkable feature in such a location could not properly be regarded as a danger to those likely to use it. He also took into account, as he was required to do by *Mills*, the burden that a finding of dangerousness would impose on the local authority, *Mills* followed (paras 28-34 of judgment). (2) The local authority's policy of when it would intervene was not determinative of whether the test of dangerousness was satisfied. In relation to the duty of care under the Occupiers' Liability Act 1957, the court noted that the test was whether the judge, being a reasonable person, thought the local authority had taken all reasonable steps to keep a person reasonably safe, *Esdale v Dover DC* [2010] EWCA Civ 409 applied. Further, the local authority's policy as set out by its officer, was that 60mm represented a guideline for an actionable category 1 but that the officer also took into account all the circumstances. As the judge found, the officer did not treat the case as falling into category 1 because he did not think that it did so (paras 35-37).

GRIFFITHS v GWYNEDD CC, [2015] EWCA Civ 1440, [2016] R.T.R. 15, Christopher Clarke LJ, CA (Civ Div).

1841 Highway maintenance–Trees–Roadside tree felling–Whether "development" for purposes of s.55 Town and Country Planning Act 1990

[Highways Act 1980 (c.66); Town and Country Planning Act 1990 (c.8) s.211, s.55, s.55(2)(b); Town and Country Planning (Tree Preservation)(England) Regulations 2012 (SI 2012/605); Directive 85/337 on the assessment of the effects of certain public and private projects on the environment 1985 Annex II]

The claimant, a resident within the defendant local authority, applied at a "rolled-up" hearing for permission to challenge roadside tree felling by the local authority as part of its duty to maintain its highways. He also applied for an injunction preventing further felling until there had been proper consultation. The local authority had outsourced its statutory highway maintenance obligations and powers to the interested party (Amey). Between August 2012 and February 2016, Amey had removed more than 3,600 trees and replaced them with smaller ones. Another 1,000 had been identified as needing replacement. Trees were assessed against six criteria. All of the trees at issue had been categorised as "damaging", either to kerbs, or because they were rooting into the highway. The claimant complained that there had been wholesale felling of trees which were attractive and environmentally valuable when not all had been unhealthy or dangerous; that the replacement trees were too small, and that other methods falling short of felling could have been used. By June 2015, the local authority had received very many such objections, which it considered at various council meetings. In November 2015, it set up an "independent tree panel" comprising impartial experts who would liaise with residents and the local authority, and advise on the issues. The issues were: (1) the extent of the highway authority's powers and duties; (2) whether planning permission, Conservation Area consent, and an environmental impact assessment were needed; (3) whether the local authority was under a duty to consult before felling.

Held: Permission refused. (1) It was surprising and most unfortunate that the claimant's case had failed to address the local authority's powers and duties as a highway authority. The nature and effect of those duties were important because they set the context for considering the works done, the effect of the Town and Country Planning Act 1990 and matters concerning environmental assessment. The Highways Act 1980 was a comprehensive code dealing with the role of highway authorities. If a tree on a highway, pavement or verge was a source of danger or obstruction, or needed moving in order to facilitate highway repairs, there was a statutory obligation on the highway authority to remove it. There was no statutory defence available to the authority that such trees had landscape, aesthetic or ecological value. The claimant's case also overlooked the fact that a dangerous or obstructive tree adjoining a highway would be a public nuisance (see paras 16-18, 20, 24, 152-153, 160 of judgment). (2) Only acts of development required planning permission. By virtue of s.55(2)(b) of the 1990 Act, repair works to a highway did not involve "development" and therefore no planning permission was needed. It was plain from the second clause of that provision that the question of whether significant adverse effects would be caused by the works arose only where the works were not exclusively for the maintenance of the road. The claimant's argument that substantial work was not "maintenance" but "improvement" so that planning permission and environmental assessments were needed, was unsustainable. Both the 1980 and 1990 Acts drew a clear distinction between maintenance (including repair), which it was the authority's *duty* to perform, and improvement, which it had a *power* to carry out. The duty to maintain was directed at the fabric of the highway and the interests of passage and re-passage, not at retaining the trees growing within it. Provided tree felling was carried out under a duty to maintain, no consent under s.211 of the 1990 Act was needed. The requirement in the Town and Country Planning (Tree Preservation)(England) Regulations 2012 for environmental assessment applied only to projects of deforestation on sites of at least one hectare in size, and the instant project could not be called deforestation. At most, the fact that a tree could contribute to the appearance and character of a Conservation Area could be a material consideration, but there was no evidence that Amey or the local authority had failed to take it into account. Furthermore, Directive 85/337 Annex II para.13, which referred to an environmental assessment being needed where there was a "change ... which may have significant adverse effects on the environment" was not directed at highway maintenance or repair, but only applied where a feature of the road was replaced by something different. Removing a tree from a highway did not amount to such a change (paras 18, 20, 155-159, 161-163, 166, 168-171, 174-175, 178, 181-182, 187). (3) As the works did not amount to "development" within s.55 of the 1990 Act, and as no environmental impact assessment was required, there was no duty of consultation at any point: not before the local authority subcontracted its duties to Amey, nor when the tree assessment criteria were drafted, nor before the felling was started. The setting up of the independent tree panel had not given rise to a legitimate expectation of consultation. It had been a means of assessing residents' views, not a consultation exercise. The local authority might have been more adroit in predicting resistance, but it was not a case where there had been a failure to consult where fairness demanded it (paras 193-194, 197, 205-209).

R. (ON THE APPLICATION OF DILLNER) v SHEFFIELD CITY COUNCIL, [2016] EWHC 945 (Admin), [2016] Env. L.R. 31, Gilbart J, QBD (Admin).

1842 Street works–Workers–Qualifications of operatives and supervisors

THE STREET WORKS (QUALIFICATIONS OF OPERATIVES AND SUPERVISORS) (ENGLAND) REGULATIONS 2016, SI 2016/1147; made under the New Roads and Street Works Act 1991 s.67, s.104(1). In force: 6 April 2016.

These Regulations prescribe the qualifications needed for the types of work being executed by trained operatives and supervisors. They also allow for the operation of rules for the recognition of equivalent qualifications in relation to trained operatives and supervisors found in the European Union (Recognition of Professional Qualifications) Regulations 2015.

1843 Traffic management–Parking–Civil enforcement officers

THE CIVIL ENFORCEMENT OF PARKING CONTRAVENTIONS DESIGNATION ORDER 2016, SI 2016/586; made under the Traffic Management Act 2004 Sch.8 para.8(1), Sch.10 para.3(1). In force: 13 June 2016.

This Order designates part of the area of each of The Council of the City of Wakefield, The Borough Council of Gateshead and The Dorset County Council as a civil enforcement area for parking contraventions and as a special enforcement area for the purposes of the Traffic Management Act 2004 Pt 6.

SALE OF GOODS

1844 Agreements to sell–Future goods–Seller's acquisition of goods depending on contingency–Validity of agreement to sell

[Sale of Goods Act 1979 (c.54) s.29(3), s.5, s.8(1)]

A customer appealed against a decision that he had not entered into a contract with the respondent car dealer. H had learnt that Porsche was to manufacture a limited edition of its 911 GT3 RS4 model. He emailed the dealer, stating that he would like to place an order for the new model. A few days later, a sales executive advised the customer that he needed to visit the dealership premises that day to pay an "expression of interest deposit" of £10,000 to increase his chances of obtaining a vehicle. He did so and also signed a document headed "Vehicle Order Form" which stated that he agreed to purchase the vehicle subject to the terms and conditions in the form. The document stated: "This document contains the terms of a contract and includes the Terms and Conditions attached". It also indicated that the seller was not obliged to fulfil orders in the sequence in which they were placed. However, a few days after the customer signed the order form, the sales executive emailed him, confirming that he had placed an order and confirming that he would get the first vehicle which the dealer was allocated by Porsche. The dealer subsequently received a vehicle, but supplied it to another customer. The judge found that there was no contract, only an agreement to agree because price, specification and delivery date had not been agreed. He also found that the customer could not prove any loss because there was no indication of the price he would have been willing to pay. The customer submitted that (1) the judge had been wrong to find that there was no binding agreement; (2) there was a collateral contract that if Porsche supplied a vehicle to the dealer, it would be allocated to him; (3) it was possible to quantify his loss with reference to the price of the nearest equivalent vehicle.

Held: Appeal allowed. (1) The customer had entered into a binding agreement with the dealer. The judge's conclusion that the customer had done no more than express his wish to purchase a vehicle was contrary to what had happened. To characterise the order form as an expression of interest with no contractual force belied what was contained in it. The terms and conditions in the document had all the hallmarks of what would be expected in an agreement to sell a vehicle. The specification details for the vehicle were to follow, but the terms and conditions expressly contemplated that eventuality and set out a procedure for it. Under the Sale of Goods Act 1979 s.5, there could be an agreement to sell future goods, which included goods to be acquired by the seller after the making of the contract. There could also be a contract for the sale of goods even though the seller's acquisition of those goods depended on a contingency which might or might not happen. Similarly, s.8(1) stated explicitly that the price of goods might be left to be fixed in a manner agreed by the contract. The terms and conditions of the order form covered the issue of price, providing that once a vehicle was available for delivery, a purchaser had to pay the balance of the purchase price, being the difference between the importer's recommended retail price and any deposits paid. Further, the provisions of s.29(3) meant that the failure to specify a delivery date was irrelevant to the existence of a contract. The agreement was for the sale of a Porsche 911 GT3 RS4, subject to the contingency of Porsche allocating one to the dealer (see paras 28-30 of judgment). (2) The parties had entered into a collateral contract at the time when the customer signed the order form. The customer had ordered the vehicle from the dealer and paid the deposit because of the assurance that he would be first in the queue if Porsche allocated one to the dealer. The statement was intended to have contractual effect, the consideration for it being entry into the main, written agreement. That collateral contract varied the clause in the terms and conditions conferring a discretion on the dealer not to fulfil orders in the sequence in which they were received, *Wake v Renault (UK) Ltd* (1996) 15 Tr. L.R. 514, [1996] C.L.Y. 1250 applied. The dealer had breached that collateral contract when it sold the vehicle it was allocated to someone else (paras 31-33, 35). (3) It was not possible to assess the measure of damages according to s.51(3) because there was no available market in the goods and the experts had been unable to find the relevant model for sale. It was therefore necessary to apply the first limb of the test in *Hadley v Baxendale*, namely that the measure of damages was the loss directly and naturally resulting from the seller's breach of contract. That did not require any resale, but could turn on other evidence. The value of the customer's lost chance was the difference between the contract price and the cost of the nearest equivalent vehicle. It could be assumed that he would have paid £135,000 for the vehicle. The evidence about the cost of the nearest equivalent vehicle was deficient because the market had been illiquid after the model's launch. However, a resale price of £170,000 would be adopted. The customer would therefore be awarded damages of £35,000 (paras 36-40).

HUGHES v PENDRAGON SABRE LTD (T/A PORSCHE CENTRE BOLTON), [2016] EWCA Civ 18, [2016] 1 Lloyd's Rep. 311, Richards LJ, CA (Civ Div).

1845 Contracts of sale–Retention of title–Contract for supply of bunker fuel containing retention of title clause–Whether contract for sale of goods

[Sale of Goods Act 1979 (c.54) s.12(1), s.2(1), s.49]

The appellant buyer, a vessel owner, appealed against a decision (*PST Energy 7 Shipping LLC v OW Bunker Malta Ltd* [2015] EWHC 2022 (Comm), [2015] 2 Lloyd's

Rep. 563) that a contract with the first respondent for the supply of bunker fuel was not a contract of sale within the meaning of the Sale of Goods Act 1979 s.2(1). The disputed contract was the first in a chain of supply contracts. It provided for payment 60 days after delivery. A retention of title clause stated that ownership of the fuel did not pass to the buyer until full payment had been made. However, the contract expressly provided that the buyer could use the fuel straight away. The first respondent had obtained the fuel through three sub-sellers. The contracts incorporated retention of title clauses and differing periods of credit. The dispute arose when the first respondent suffered financial difficulties and its bank became the assignee of the debt. It fell to be determined which of the sub-sellers in the chain had title to the fuel. All the fuel had been consumed by the end of the 60-day credit period in the initial contract, and the buyer had not yet paid. Arbitrators determined that the retention of title clause and the right to use the fuel during the credit period meant that the contract was not one for the sale of goods. They held that the bank could not recover the debt under the Sale of Goods Act 1979 s.49, but could recover it as a simple debt. The buyer appealed on grounds relating to the first respondent's ability to pass title at the time of payment. The court affirmed the arbitrators' decision. It held that the first respondent had never undertaken to pass title to the buyer upon payment because both parties had envisaged that some, if not all, of the fuel would have been consumed by then, and it was impossible to pass title of something which did not exist. The court found that the true nature of the parties' bargain was that the first respondent would arrange for delivery of the fuel, and the buyer was entitled to use it straight away. The buyer submitted that the language of the contract indicated that it was an agreement to sell the full quantity of the fuel on terms that property in it would pass retrospectively upon payment, even if some or all of the fuel had been consumed by the time payment fell due.

Held: Appeal dismissed. The language of the first respondent's standard terms suggested that the parties were thinking in terms of a sale and purchase of the fuel. However, the judge had been correct that in order to decide whether the buyer was relieved of liability to pay the debt, it was necessary to identify carefully what the parties had undertaken to do. If one party had agreed to transfer property to another in return for a money payment, the Act would apply, together with the implied condition in s.12(1) that the seller could sell the goods. If the transfer of property was not of the essence of the contract, it was necessary to identify the essential benefit for which the buyer had agreed to pay. The critical contractual terms were those concerning the credit period, the retention of title clause, and the right to use the fuel from the moment of delivery. The parties had contemplated that the fuel would be consumed within the credit period and would cease to exist. Authority existed to support a submission that the courts had consistently regarded contracts for the sale of goods, which contained a retention of title clause, as falling within the Act's scope even where the buyer could use or dispose of the goods before payment. However, none concerned the question whether property could pass retrospectively at a time when the goods, or part of them, had ceased to exist, *Borden (UK) Ltd v Scottish Timber Products Ltd* [1981] Ch. 25, [1979] C.L.Y. 2390 and *Armour v Thyssen Edelstahlwerke AG* [1991] 2 A.C. 339, [1991] C.L.Y. 3193 considered. It was not possible to transfer property in goods once they had ceased to exist. Even if the goods had been only partly consumed, it was still not possible to transfer title in the whole of the goods covered by the contract. Whatever label were attached to the contract, its essential nature was clear: the buyer took delivery of the goods as bailee with a licence to consume them, and the seller agreed to sell any quantity remaining at the date of payment in return for money consideration. The commercial background and the contract terms made it clear that the buyer had contracted for delivery of the fuel, not for the transfer of its title. The retention of title clause provided the seller with an ever diminishing degree of security for the payment due. The transfer of property in the fuel was not the essential subject matter of the contract. The failure to do so did not relieve the vessel owners of the obligation to pay for them (see paras 17, 20, 24, 31-34 of judgment).

PST ENERGY 7 SHIPPING LLC v OW BUNKER MALTA LTD, [2015] EWCA Civ 1058, [2016] 2 W.L.R. 1072, Moore-Bick LJ, CA (Civ Div).

1846 Contracts of sale–Retention of title–Contract for supply of bunker fuel containing retention of title clause–Whether contract for sale of goods

[Sale of Goods Act 1979 (c.54) s.2(1), s.2(3), s.2(6), s.49]

Vessel owners appealed against a decision (*PST Energy 7 Shipping LLC v OW Bunker Malta Ltd* [2015] EWCA Civ 1058, [2016] 2 W.L.R. 1072, [2016] 1845) that a contract for the supply of fuel bunkers was not a contract for the sale of goods within the meaning of the Sale of Goods Act 1979 s.2(1). The contract provided for the supply of bunkers with payment to be made within 60 days of the presentation of an invoice. It was subject to the seller's general terms, which provided that until full payment was made, title remained with the seller, and that the buyer was in possession of the bunkers solely as the seller's bailee, and would not be entitled to use the bunkers other than for the propulsion of the vessel. The owners received and consumed the bunkers but did not make payment. The seller did not make payment to its own suppliers. The seller became insolvent and the owners were concerned that they could be exposed to paying both the seller and the suppliers, who could have claimed rights under a reservation of title. The owners commenced arbitration proceedings for a declaration that they had no liability to pay the seller for the bunkers, on the basis that the contract was a contract for sale within s.2(1) of the Act, meaning that the Act applied to the contract and they could defeat an action for the contract price, as the case was not within s.49, which set out circumstances in which a seller could bring an action for the price of goods. The arbitrators rejected that argument. The owners argued that the contract (1) was a contract of sale within s.2(1); (2) included an implied term that the seller had performed its obligations to its supplier by making payment timeously.

Held: Appeal dismissed. (1) The basic form of the contract was one of sale. However, "sale" could be used in an expanded sense, since the general terms were stated to apply to all agreements and services and subsequent contracts "of whatever nature". Further, the terms showed that the contract had special features in providing for retention of title pending payment. They provided that the buyer would not be entitled to use the bunkers, with the qualification "other than for the propulsion of the Vessel". The qualification reflected reality: bunker suppliers knew that bunkers were for use. If they granted relatively long credit periods combined with a reservation of title pending payment, it was unsurprising that they combined that with a qualification authorising use in propulsion, since standard terms prohibiting any use would be uncommercial. In those circumstances, the contract could not be a straightforward agreement to transfer the property in the bunkers to the owners for a price. It was in substance an agreement, first, to permit consumption prior to payment and without any property ever passing in the bunkers consumed, and, second, but only if and so far as bunkers remained unconsumed, to transfer the property in the bunkers so remaining to the owners in return for the owners paying the price. That price was not the price of the bunkers in respect of which property was passing; it was the price payable for all the bunkers, whether consumed before or remaining at the time of payment (see paras 26-28 of judgment). The contract could not be regarded as an agreement, in accordance with s.2(3) and s.2(6), to transfer property conditional on the bunkers remaining unburned when payment was made. That interpretation categorised the whole agreement by reference to only one possibility relating to only one part of the bunkers, namely the possibility of some bunkers surviving unused. Section 2(3) and s.2(6) could be applied where there was a condition regarding the passing of property to which all the goods covered by an agreement were subject, but that was not the instant case. There was no condition governing the transfer of property in the bunkers used before payment; that was never agreed to be transferred. Further, the agreement was a single contract to pay a single price for all the bunkers sold, not later than 60 days after delivery, whatever had happened to the bunkers in the meantime. It could not be treated as divisible (para.29). The contract was not one of sale within s.2, meaning that the owners could have no possible defence under s.49 to the claim for the price (para.37). (2) There was no need for the implied duty argued for by the owners. Given the nature of the bargain, the seller's only implied undertaking regarding the bunkers it permitted to be used in propulsion prior to payment was that the seller had the legal entitlement to give such permission. The seller had not needed to have title to the bunkers to give such permission; it had merely needed the right to authorise use (paras 38-39). (3) (Obiter) Section 49 was not a complete code of situations in which the price could be recoverable, *FG Wilson (Engineering) Ltd v John Holt & Co (Liverpool) Ltd* [2013] EWCA Civ 1232, [2014] 1 W.L.R. 2365, [2014] C.L.Y. 2586 doubted, *Harry & Garry Ltd v Jariwalla*considered. The section would have been no bar to a claim by the seller for payment of the agreed price (paras 58, 60).

PST ENERGY 7 SHIPPING LLC v OW BUNKER MALTA LTD, [2016] UKSC 23, [2016] A.C. 1034, Lord Neuberger PSC, SC.

1847 FOB contracts–Grain and Feed Trade Association–Buyer nominating substitute vessel–Requirement for compliance with terms of contract of sale

The seller under an FOB contract of sale concerning a cargo of maize appealed against a decision of the GAFTA Board of Appeal that the buyer had validly nominated a substitute vessel to take delivery of the cargo. The contract provided for delivery in the period from 15 to 31 March 2013. The buyer was to provide the seller with not less than 10 days' "pre-advice" of, among other things, the collecting vessel's name, dimensions and estimated time of arrival. The contract also stated that the terms of GAFTA 49 would apply. The "Period of Delivery" clause in GAFTA 49 stated as follows: "Buyers shall serve not less than ... consecutive day's [sic] notice of the name and probable readiness date of the vessel and the estimated tonnage required. The Sellers shall have the goods ready to be delivered to the Buyers at any time within the contract period of delivery. Buyers have the right to substitute the nominated vessel, but in any event the original delivery period and any extension shall not be affected thereby. Provided the vessel is presented at the loading port in readiness to load within the delivery period, Sellers shall if necessary complete loading after the delivery period, and carrying charges shall not apply". On 20 March 2013, the buyer sent a message nominating a vessel, Puffin, to load the cargo, giving an estimated time of arrival at the loading port of 26/27 March. On 26 March, the buyer sent another message nominating another vessel, Sea Way, in place of Puffin, giving an estimated time of arrival of 28 March. The seller asserted that the nomination of Sea Way was invalid and terminated the contract. The issues were (i) where a buyer of goods FOB nominated a substitute vessel pursuant to its right under the GAFTA "Period of Delivery" clause in GAFTA 49, whether it was required to comply with the terms of the contract of sale as to nomination and pre-advice in respect of the substitute vessel; (ii) whether, on a true construction of the contract of sale, the buyer's nomination of Sea Way was valid.

Held: Appeal allowed. (1) Where a buyer of goods FOB nominated a substitute vessel pursuant to its right under GAFTA 49, it had to comply with the terms of the contract of sale as to nomination and pre-advice in respect of the substitute vessel. The buyer had argued that GAFTA 49 was a complete code defining and limiting the right to substitution and that there was therefore no requirement for pre-notice in respect of the substitute vessel. That was not so. The natural interpretation of the requirement in the first sentence in GAFTA 49 about the nomination of the vessel was that it referred to the vessel that was to load the cargo: that was the only vessel whose name and "probable readiness date" could possibly matter. It was true that the seller was to have the goods "ready to be delivered to the Buyers at any time within the contract period of delivery", but that did not mean that it would not be interested in receiving information about when the vessel that was to carry the cargo would probably be ready. Similar considerations applied to the pre-advice provisions in the contract: for example, the seller might want the dimensions and draft of the vessel so as to arrange a safe berth. That interpretation left a sensible commercial purpose for the substitution provisions. It made express the implied right to substitute but went on to qualify it by giving the seller a remedy if the buyer changed the nomination after the seller had relied on it, *Cargill UK Ltd v Continental UK Ltd* [1989] 2 Lloyd's Rep. 290, [1990] C.L.Y. 4030 applied (see paras 19, 21, 23-24 of judgment).(2) On a true construction of the contract, the buyer's nomination of Sea Way was invalid (para.24).

RAMBURS INC v AGRIFERT SA, [2015] EWHC 3548 (Comm), [2016] Bus. L.R. 135, Andrew Smith J, QBD (Comm).

1848 Repurchase agreements–Warehouse receipts–Tender of endorsed warehouse receipts–Whether effective re-delivery

[Sale of Goods Act 1979 (c.54) s.29(4)]

The claimant metal traders (M) brought proceedings relating to sales and repurchases of metal under master agreements entered into with the defendant banking companies (C). The master agreements provided for C to purchase metal from M, and for C to sell and M to repurchase equivalent metal at a specified future date at a higher price. The intended commercial effect of the transactions was that C was to provide finance to M on the security of M's inventory of metal. The common expectation and practice was that the same metal would be delivered and re-delivered without leaving the warehouse in which it was stored. Nevertheless the agreements provided that on a sale of metal to C, notwithstanding any arrangements relating to the forward sale of equivalent metal, full title to and ownership of the metal would pass to C. Following purchases of metal from M, C held warehouse receipts evidencing ownership and the right to possession of aluminium and copper stored in warehouses in the Chinese ports of Qingdao, Penglai and Shanghai. Evidence then began to emerge of a significant fraud in relation to metal supposed to be stored at Qingdao and Penglai. It appeared that substantial quantities of metal were missing or the subject of multiple pledging. As a result C served "bring forward" notices under the master agreements, bringing forward the sale date of all the forward transactions to one banking day after receipt of the notices. C subsequently suspended the notices in relation to metal stored in Shanghai and M voluntarily repurchased that metal early. M then served notice under the agreements, declaring a termination event, which had the effect of requiring C to deliver equivalent metal before M was obliged to pay the price. C purported to deliver the metal to M by tendering the warehouse receipts, endorsed in blank. C had not issued release instructions to the warehouse operators, who had not attorned to M, by acknowledging that they held the metal on M's behalf. M sought declarations that the notices served by C were invalid and/or superseded by its own notice and that, in any event, C had not performed its delivery obligations by tendering endorsed warehouse receipts. C counterclaimed for the price specified in the forward sales, and further claimed that it was entitled to terminate the master agreements. In one transaction relating to copper cathodes stored in Qingdao, M had paid the repurchase price and C had purported to effect delivery by endorsing and delivering the warehouse receipts to M. M had been unable to obtain the metal or an attornment from the warehouse operator.

Held: Judgment accordingly. (1) The forward sale confirmations, pursuant to the master agreements, provided for delivery by means of in-warehouse transfer "without the need for any confirmation from the owner/operator of the storage facility". However, that wording, which purported to exclude the need for a release confirmation or other attornment from the warehouse operator, was inconsistent with the preceding wording, the intended meaning and effect of the master agreements and the overall commercial scheme of the transactions and their operation. The parties could not have intended that that unheralded wording in the confirmations would fundamentally change the nature of C's delivery obligation as set out in the master agreement. As the words were repugnant and could not be harmonised, they had to be rejected. Accordingly, the court rejected C's argument that the tender of endorsed warehouse receipts to M constituted "deemed" delivery for the purposes of the forward sales and master agreements. In the absence of an attornment from the warehouse operators, as required by the Sale of Goods Act 1979 s.29(4), C had not made valid delivery of the metal within the meaning of the master agreements (see paras 76-77 of judgment). (2) C was not entitled to invoke cl.7.2(B) of the master agreements which would permit it to satisfy its obligations in respect of the transactions, where it was unable to deliver the metal, by assigning such rights as it had in the metal to M. It had not yet attempted to deliver in the required manner by giving release instructions to the warehouse operators, and if such instructions did not result in delivery that was likely to be because of the occurrence in relation to C of a termination event, which would prevent C relying on cl.7.2(B) (paras 81-84). (3) In respect of the copper cathode transaction, C had not made valid delivery, but since M had not treated that as a repudiatory breach it was limited to a claim for damages for non-delivery. In respect of the remaining forward sales, although C had not made effective delivery, it was not in breach of any obligation to do so (paras 86-90). (4) At the time of the bring forward notices C held the reasonable opinion required by cl.9.1(C) of the master agreements that the storage facilities were no longer able to store the metal safely and satisfactorily. The notices were therefore valid and effective (paras 93-123, 127). (5) M's obligation to pay the prices in respect of the forward sales brought forward by the notices was not suspended by the declaration of a termination event. Under cl.10.3(B) the declaration of a termination event permitted a party to refuse to make further payments or deliveries as they fell due but did not have the effect of suspending accrued debts, *Lomas v JFB Firth Rixson Inc* [2012] EWCA Civ 419, [2012] 2 All E.R. (Comm) 1076, [2012] C.L.Y. 259 applied. (6) M was in breach of contract in failing to pay the price, but had a good defence of circuity of action to C's claim for the price, since C could not make good delivery, giving rise to an immediate claim for the price paid (paras 134-139). (7) C had a right to terminate the master agreements in accordance with their terms, and at common law because of M's repudiation. It had not lost the contractual or common law right to terminate. It was entitled to exercise the right to terminate, even though it could not deliver (paras 140-157).

MERCURIA ENERGY TRADING PTE LTD v CITIBANK NA, [2015] EWHC 1481 (Comm), [2015] 1 C.L.C. 999, Phillips J, QBD (Comm).

SENTENCING

1849 Arson–Intimidation–Campaign of intimidation against former partner–Undue leniency

The Attorney General referred to the court as unduly lenient a total sentence of three years and eight months' imprisonment imposed on the offender following guilty pleas to arson being reckless as to whether life was endangered, arson, and breach of a suspended sentence order. After the offender and his former partner (L) had separated, the offender began a campaign of criminality directed at L and her new partner. He assaulted L and was sentenced to a community order and made the subject of a restraining order. He breached that order by threatening to kill L and her new partner. He also made numerous threatening phone calls. He was charged with breaching the restraining order and was remanded on bail. He then went to L's home one night and set fire to her car. He was subsequently sentenced to 12 weeks' imprisonment, suspended for two years, for breaching the restraining order. Around a month after the arson, the offender entered L's home, which was empty at the time, and set a fire which caused extensive damage. The offender had 10 previous convictions for 22 offences. The pre-sentence report indicated that he had minimised or denied responsibility for the offences. The report addressed the issue of dangerousness, concluding that the offender posed a significant risk to L and any of her future partners. The judge imposed consecutive sentences of three years' imprisonment for the offence of arson being reckless as to whether life was endangered, six months' imprisonment for the offence of arson, and two months' imprisonment for breaching the suspended sentence order. The Attorney General drew attention to the following aggravating features: the offences of arson and arson being reckless as to the endangerment of life were the culmination of a deliberate campaign of intimidation, and were premeditated attacks borne out of revenge; the offence of arson being reckless as to the endangerment of life involved the offender unlawfully entering L's house and was committed while he was on bail, in breach of a restraining order, and subject to a suspended sentence order.

Held: Reference allowed. (1) The pre-sentence report, quite properly, had addressed the issue of dangerousness. For some reason, counsel for the prosecution did not raise the point with the judge, and the judge himself made no reference to it. The Attorney General had indicated that he did not seek to pursue any finding of dangerousness or the imposition of an extended sentence. However, the matter should have been expressly discussed in the court below (see para.33 of judgment). (2) The arson offences were bad cases of their kind: they were revenge attacks committed at night, either during the currency of a community order and a restraining order, or while the offender was on bail and the subject of a suspended sentence order. On the count of arson being reckless as to whether life was endangered, given all the circumstances, it could be expected that a starting point of approaching eight years would have been taken had there been a trial. The consecutive six-month sentence imposed for the arson offence was, in itself, a lenient sentence: a sentence in the order of 15 months could have been expected had there been a trial. In the circumstances, and having regard to considerations of totality, the sentence of three years for the offence of arson being reckless as to whether life was endangered would be quashed and replaced with a sentence of six years. The consecutive sentence of six months imposed for the arson offence would be retained. The sentence with regard to the breach of the suspended sentence order would stand, but would run concurrently to the other sentences. The overall sentence was therefore increased to six and a half years' imprisonment, *Attorney General's Reference (No.68 of 2008)* [2008] EWCA Crim 3188, [2009] 2 Cr. App. R. (S.) 48, [2009] C.L.Y. 3337 considered (paras 31-37).

ATTORNEY GENERAL'S REFERENCE (NO.39 OF 2016) *sub nom.* R. v HITCHENS (ALAN), [2016] EWCA Crim 794, [2016] 2 Cr. App. R. (S.) 34, Davis LJ, CA (Crim Div).

1850 **Arson–Recklessness–Fire started outside house causing risk of harm to property and residents–Undue leniency**

The Attorney General referred to the court as unduly lenient a sentence of two years' imprisonment following a guilty plea to arson being reckless as to whether life was endangered. The offender (H) lived with his partner in a mid-terrace house. His father had recently died and their three young children had been adopted due to their parents' heroin addiction. Following an argument one night with his partner, H set fire to a wheelie bin outside their house and fuelled it with wood and rubbish. A neighbour told him to stop, but he continued. The flames grew and reached the top of the ground floor window. H left the scene. Neighbours, whose children were asleep in their beds, called the fire brigade. Had they not attended it was likely that the fire would have spread. H made no comment in interview other than to deny causing the fire. The pre-sentence and psychiatric reports suggested he had caused the fire due to the stress of losing his father and children. The judge noted that H had not set out to burn down his home and stated that the offence had been low on the scale of seriousness. The Attorney General submitted that the sentence was unduly lenient and pointed to Attorney General's Reference No.68 of 2008 R v Myrie (2009) Cr App R (S) 48, which set out guidelines for the offence. He noted as aggravating features the fact that the fire had been started against the wall of a mid-terrace house, posing a significant risk that it would spread and endanger others; the offence was at night; H had been under the influence of drink and drugs and had left the scene without doing anything to raise the alarm. In mitigation, he said the fire had been started outside with no accelerant, it had not spread and H had pleaded guilty.

Held: Reference allowed. It was necessary to distinguish between cases where a fire set outside posed a high risk to propery and residents, such as in the instant case, and cases where the risk to others was far removed. Taking into account all the circumstances of the offence, the starting point after a trial should have been four-and-a-half years. Taking into account the credit for a guilty plea, the appropriate sentence should have been three years.

ATTORNEY GENERAL'S REFERENCE (NO.56 OF 2015) *sub nom.* R. v HILTON (RYAN), [2015] EWCA Crim 1442, [2016] 1 Cr. App. R. (S.) 9, Macur LJ, CA (Crim Div).

1851 **Burglary–Persistent offenders–Third offence–Whether unjust to pass statutory minimum sentence**

[Powers of Criminal Courts (Sentencing) Act 2000 (c.6) s.111]

The appellant appealed against a sentence of three years' imprisonment imposed after his guilty plea to a domestic burglary. While living in supported accommodation, the appellant had entered another resident's bedsit and stolen a games console. He was caught on CCTV. He pleaded guilty at the preliminary hearing. At the time of the offence he was aged 44 and had 42 previous convictions for 93 offences. Of those offences, 55 were for theft and similar offences, and two involved domestic burglaries. The judge concluded that the appellant was subject to the minimum sentencing provisions because of his previous convictions for domestic burglary, but concluded that he would have sentenced the appellant to three years' imprisonment in any event because of his previous record. The appellant submitted that it was unjust to pass the statutory minimum sentence, and the judge had failed to take into account his early plea of guilty.

Held: Appeal allowed. By virtue of his previous convictions the appellant was liable to receive a minimum sentence of three years' imprisonment pursuant to the Powers of Criminal Courts (Sentencing) Act 2000 s.111, unless the court was satisfied that it was unjust to impose such a sentence. While the appellant had a poor criminal record, it would be unjust to impose the minimum sentence required by statute. The previous domestic burglaries were 11 and 9 years prior to the index offence, and the nature of the offence itself was not the most severe of its kind. The appropriate sentence was 27 months' imprisonment. Given that the appellant had pleaded guilty at the first available opportunity, full credit was given for his guilty plea. The sentence was therefore 18 months' imprisonment.

R. v FLETCHER (LEE), [2015] EWCA Crim 1709, [2016] 1 Cr. App. R. (S.) 28, Davis LJ, CA (Crim Div).

1852 Burglary–Residential property–Offender ransacking house over several days, breaking through roof to escape police, throwing roof tiles at cars below

The appellant appealed against a sentence imposed after his late guilty plea to a residential burglary. The appellant had discovered that his girlfriend's neighbours were away on holiday. He smashed through the rear door of their home and, over the course of several days, stole approximately £56,000 of property including specialist electronic equipment, computers containing family photographs and jewellery. When police were called to the property he was drunk and hiding in the attic. He broke through onto the roof, ripped off roof tiles and threw them at cars below, damaging three civilian cars and two police cars. When the home owners returned they found that their house was a shell, stripped of all valuables, covered in broken glass, with a hole in the roof. It was uninhabitable for several weeks. Their young son had to delay starting school and was traumatised by what had happened. The appellant received a 10 per cent discount for pleading guilty on the day of trial. The judge concluded that the offence fell into category 1 of the sentencing guidelines and sentenced him to five-years-and-four-months' imprisonment. He also activated a 12-month suspended sentence imposed for assault and ordered it to run consecutively. The appellant was aged 26 at the time of the offence with numerous previous convictions for robbery, criminal damage, burglary of commercial premises and public order offences. The appellant submitted that: (1) the judge was wrong to find that the burglary fell at the top end of category 1; (2) the suspended sentence should not have been activated in full; (3) the total sentence was manifestly excessive.

Held: Appeal dismissed. (1) There was no doubt that the burglary was within category 1 of the relevant sentencing guidelines. It was an offence of the greatest harm by reason of the significant degree of loss and ransacking, and of higher culpability because of the deliberate targeting. His previous convictions were a statutory aggravating factor. Other aggravating factors were that the victims had to leave their home for a time and he was under the influence of drink when committing the offence. There were no mitigating factors. No separate penalty had been imposed for affray and criminal damage. The judge was entitled to reflect the appellant's culpability in relation to those offences in the sentence for the burglary offence, as they represented further aggravating features of the burglary. A sentence of six years after a trial was just and proportionate, and appropriate credit had been given for the late guilty plea (see paras 11-12 of judgment). (2) The activation of the suspended sentence was entirely just given the seriousness of the appellant's further offences, as was ordering the sentence to be served consecutively. The appellant had committed the offences when only one-quarter of the way through the modest operational period of 12 months (para.13). (3) The total sentence reflected considerations of totality. There was no error of principle, nor was the sentence manifestly excessive (para.14)

R. v BARNETT (JONATHAN), [2015] EWCA Crim 1760, [2016] 1 Cr. App. R. (S.) 29, Beatson LJ, CA (Crim Div).

1853 **Child sex offences–Extended sentences–Stepfather abusing children under 12 over number of years**

The appellant (W) appealed against a total sentence of 17 years and two months' imprisonment with an eight-year extension period imposed for child sex offences following a guilty plea. W had abused his step-daughter from when she was aged six to eleven years old. The abuse involved vaginal and oral rape in her home and in his car, filming her whilst he made her perform oral sex on him, performing oral sex on her, taking indecent photographs of her and making her watch pornographic films. W had ejaculated on occasions and had pressured his step-daughter not to report what had happened. He also abused her 12-year-old cousin, who suffered from autism, by raping her orally. The abuse only stopped when W's wife, his step-daughter's mother, saw him taking a picture of her daughter naked from the waist down. W pleaded guilty to the offences. The pre-sentence report noted that W acknowledged that the offences might have caused some distress, but minimised them. He was assessed as presenting a high risk to children. When sentencing the judge placed the rapes in category 2A of the sentencing guidelines, and noted that the offences involved planning and isolating the step-daughter, a gross abuse of trust, the vulnerability of the victims because of their age and because one suffered from autism and had caused one victim severe psychological harm. The judge took a 26-year starting point for the rapes, and applying full credit for W's guilty plea, reduced the determinate element of the sentence to 17 years and 2 months. Finding that W was dangerous, the judge also imposed an eight-year extended sentence for the protection of the public. W submitted that the judge had taken too high a starting point.

Held: Appeal dismissed. The judge's approach to sentencing could not be faulted. His sentencing remarks had been clear and succinct, as had his summary of the aggravating features. W had carried out a sustained and systemic campaign of abuse against his step-daughter and her cousin, which had only ended when his wife discovered it. The judge had been entitled to make a finding of dangerousness and a lengthy sentence was justified. Although the net determinative sentence passed by the judge was severe, it was not excessive (see paras 23-24, 26-29 of judgment).

R. v W (A), [2015] EWCA Crim 1877, [2016] 1 Cr. App. R. (S.) 39, Davis LJ, CA (Crim Div).

1854 **Child sex offences–Indecent assault–Historic offences committed against young boys when offender aged 11 and 14–Young offenders–Undue leniency**

The Attorney General referred to the court as unduly lenient a two-year suspended sentence which had been imposed on the offender (X) following his conviction for two offences of indecent assault. The offences had been committed decades ago. As to the first offence, X, who was 11 at the time, had forced a three-year-old boy to perform oral sex on him. As to the second offence, X , who was then 14, had played with the penis of a five-year-old boy before placing it in his (X's) mouth. The victim of the first offence said that the offence had had a significant and lasting effect on him. The sentencing judge decided to suspend the sentence because of the passage of time, X's age at the time of the offences and his good character.

Held: Reference dismissed. The focus had to be on the seriousness of the offences, the harm caused and X's culpability. The evidence suggested an 11-year-old boy and then a 14-year-old boy taking advantage of opportunities that presented themselves when playing with younger boys, rather than any act of grooming or deliberate isolation. The two-year length of the sentence was not unduly lenient. If, as the judgment in *R. v H* [2011] EWCA Crim 2753, [2012] 1 W.L.R. 1416, [2012] C.L.Y. 3016 made clear, the passage of time since the offence, the age of the offender at the time he committed the offence and the fact that the offender had not subsequently been convicted of any offence were all factors to be considered when assessing sentence generally, there was no good reason why they might not be relevant to the question of suspension. It would be for the sentencing judge to make a judgment on all the facts before him. The mitigation available to X was considerable. There was no principle of sentencing that all offences of this kind had to be met by immediate terms of imprisonment, whatever the circumstances. As the Definitive Guideline on Sexual Offences made clear, as serious as these offences were, there might be exceptional cases where a non-custodial sentence was appropriate. It was clear that the judge was acutely conscious of the seriousness of the offences, the impact of the offences on the victims and the relevant guidelines. He did not take the decision to suspend the sentence lightly. He took a measured and balanced approach with which the instant court did not intend to interfere, *R. v H* applied (see paras 31, 33-35, 37-38 of judgment).

ATTORNEY GENERAL'S REFERENCE (NO.32 OF 2016) *sub nom.* R. v B, [2016] EWCA Crim 572, [2016] 2 Cr. App. R. (S.) 20, Hallett LJ, CA (Crim Div).

1855 Child sex offences–Rape–78-year-old man pleading guilty to historic sexual offences against daughter

The appellant (G), who had pleaded guilty to two offences of indecent assault, three offences of rape and one offence of aiding and abetting rape, appealed against his sentence of 18 years' imprisonment. The victim of the offences was G's daughter. The offending began when she was five or six and continued into her teenage years. It escalated in seriousness from indecent assaults to the extent where G had full sexual intercourse with his daughter and allowed another man to have sex with her. The sentencing judge adopted a starting point of 24 years. He made a one-third deduction for G's guilty plea, arriving at a sentence of 16 years' imprisonment. However, shortly thereafter he increased the sentence to 18 years under the slip rule, having concluded that G had had several opportunities over the years to admit his offending but had failed to take them. The judge commented that if G had admitted the indecent assaults years previously, his daughter's life might well have been different. On that basis, he reduced the discount to which G was entitled from eight to six years, resulting in the 18-year sentence. Leave to appeal was granted on the basis of the decision in *R. v Nodjoumi (Benham)* (1985) 7 Cr. App. R. (S.) 183, [1986] C.L.Y. 864, in which Lawton L.J. observed that the power to adjust a sentence under the slip rule should not be exercised solely because the original sentence was regarded as inadequate. G argued that there was no basis for reducing the discount: he had never previously been charged with sexual offending and had pleaded guilty at the first available opportunity.

Held: Appeal allowed. (1) The procedure adopted by the criminal courts 30 years ago no longer reflected the power of the Attorney General to refer sentences as unduly lenient and the court's resulting power to increase such sentences. That meant that the power to exercise discretion under the slip rule was no longer encumbered by the approach outlined in *Nodjoumi*, *Nodjoumi* not followed (see para.16 of judgment). (2) To the argument that had G admitted indecent assault years previously his daughter's life might have been different, the simple answer was that he was not now being sentenced simply for the indecent assaults but for a catalogue of the most appalling sexual criminality over a very substantial period of time. It was that substantial criminality that led to the starting point of 24 years. Nobody had suggested that that starting point was wrong. The judge was not entitled to increase the sentence by reducing the discount for the guilty plea simply because G had previously refused to take the opportunity of admitting his offending. That fact was reflected in the 24-year starting point, which also took account of G's age (he was now 78) and the other circumstances of the case. The sentence was correctly assessed by the judge on the first occasion and the 16-year sentence would be restored (paras 18-20).

R. v G, [2016] EWCA Crim 541, [2016] 4 W.L.R. 124, Sir Brian Leveson PQBD, CA (Crim Div).

1856 Child sex offences–Rape of child under 13–Whether exceptional circumstances justifying non-custodial sentence for 19-year-old offender–Undue leniency

The Attorney General referred to the court as unduly lenient a community order with a two-year rehabilitation and activity requirement following a guilty plea to rape of a child under 13. The offender, aged 19, had been in a relationship with the 12-year-old victim. He asked her to have sex with him. She refused, but when he asked her again she agreed. They had sex on one occasion. The offender knew that the victim was 12 and asked her not to tell anyone about their relationship. Although they used a condom, it split and the victim became pregnant. She had a termination. The judge emphasised the fact the offender had not used force or coercion and that the victim had willingly engaged in the sexual act. The victim had written a letter to the court, blaming herself for the offender's predicament and stating that she did not want him to go to prison and that she missed him. The Attorney General submitted that the offence warranted an immediate custodial sentence and that there had been no exceptional circumstances that justified a non-custodial sentence. He identified as an aggravating feature the fact that the offender had told the victim not to tell anyone about the relationship. In mitigation the Attorney General said that the offender had no previous convictions, he had shown remorse, he had learning difficulties and was immature and he had pleaded guilty.

Held: Reference allowed. The judge had been wrong to assess the case as being exceptional and to have imposed a non-custodial sentence. The law was there to protect young children, both from others and from themselves. To emphasise the lack of force used, missed the point. A 12-year-old child could not legally consent to sexual intercourse. The offender had taken advantage of the victim's willingness to engage in sexual activity, he knew she was only 12, he knew what he was doing was wrong and he asked her not to tell anyone about it. The offender had powerful mitigation and it was relevant that no force was used. The starting point should have been six years, with full credit for the guilty plea. Further consideration had to be given to the fact that the offender faced a prison sentence and to the positive engagement he had had with probation. The sentence should have been three-and-a-half years' imprisonment.

ATTORNEY GENERAL'S REFERENCE (NO.142 OF 2015) *sub nom.* R. v BROWN (JACK JOSEPH), [2016] EWCA Crim 80, [2016] 1 Cr. App. R. (S.) 68, Davis LJ, CA (Crim Div).

1857 Child sex offences–Sexual assault of child under 13–Judge wrongly restricting sentence for repeated historic offences to maximum for single offence–Undue leniency

The Attorney General referred to the court as unduly lenient a sentence of nine years' imprisonment imposed following convictions for three offences of sexual assault. The offender (L) had carried out a series of historic sexual assaults against the same child victim over three-and-a-half years between 2000-2003. At the time the victim had been aged between five and nine and L had been aged between 29-33. L had been in a relationship with the girl's mother at the time and they had been living with him. L abused the victim several times a week, forcing her to give him oral sex to the point of ejaculation and making her swallow the ejaculant. He threatened her that if she told anyone, she would go to prison and would never see her mother again. The offences had a considerable and lasting psychological effect on the victim. She was diagnosed with depression, self-harmed, had low esteem and anxiety attacks. L had no previous convictions, but continued to show no remorse and remained in denial about the offences. He had a good employment record, had committed no further offences and had been a carer to his elderly and disabled parents. At the time the offences were committed, the maximum sentence for each was 10 years' imprisonment. In his sentencing remarks the judge indicated that he was constrained by a maximum sentence of 10 years. The Attorney General submitted that the sentence failed properly to reflect the overall offending and its gravity, combined with aggravating features. The Attorney General identified among the aggravating features the age and vulnerability of the victim, the significant psychological harm caused, the abuse of trust, the number of offences committed over a lengthy period of time and the fact that the victim had been degraded by being forced to swallow semen.

Held: Reference allowed. In sentencing historic offences, the court was limited to the maximum sentence available at the time an offence was committed, but it should have reflected modern sentencing attitudes and guidelines when sentencing historic offences, *R. v H* [2011] EWCA Crim 2753, [2012] 1 W.L.R. 1416, [2012] C.L.Y. 3016 followed. The modern equivalent offence was rape of a child under 13. The offence fell in category 2A and had a starting point of 13 years. But caution should have been exercised in using this guideline, which had a maximum sentence of life imprisonment. Regard should have been had to the guidelines for sentencing offences of causing a child under 13 to engage in a sexual act, which carried a maximum sentence of 14 years' imprisonment, with a starting point of eight years and a range of five to 20 years. The judge had been wrong to constrain himself to a maximum of 10 years. That maximum had been for a single offence and in the instant case the rapes had been repeated and frequent. The sentence passed failed to reflect the overall gravity of the offending. The least sentence that should have been passed was one of 14 years' imprisonment. The original sentence was quashed and replaced with a total of 14 years'.

ATTORNEY GENERAL'S REFERENCE (NO.75 OF 2015) *sub nom.* R. v L, [2015] EWCA Crim 2116, [2016] 1 Cr. App. R. (S.) 61, Treacy LJ, CA (Crim Div).

1858 Child sex offences–Young offenders–16-year-old offender in relationship with 12-year-old victim

A young offender (H) appealed against an 18-month detention and training order imposed following his guilty pleas to four offences of rape of a child under 13. H, 16 at the time of the offences, had been in a relationship with the 12-year-old victim since meeting at school. H was 15 when they first met. Initially, he thought the victim was 14 and told his parents that was her age, but at all material times he was aware of her true age. The sexual activity involved oral and vaginal intercourse on a number of occasions. H pleaded guilty to four specimen counts at the first opportunity in the youth court and his case was committed for sentence. He pleaded guilty on the accepted basis that the offences had commenced shortly after he became 16; that, if the victim had had the capacity to consent, the activity was consensual; and that there had been no use of force. The judge emphasised the victim's age, the gap in age between the parties, the number of occasions of offending, H's misleading of his parents and the purpose of the legislation to protect children under 13 from themselves. H was of previous good character. He had expressed remorse and stated that he had felt he was in a genuine relationship. A social worker assessed him as being emotionally immature and as a low risk of reoffending.

Held: Appeal allowed. The relevant category of the sentencing guidelines for an adult was category 3B, with a starting point of eight years' custody and a range of six to 11 years. The guideline included specific reference to the context of a young offender. It stated that the guideline might not be appropriate where the sentencer was satisfied that, on the available evidence and in the absence of exploitation, a young and/or particularly immature offender genuinely believed on reasonable grounds that the victim was aged 16 or over and that they were engaging in lawful sexual activity. That last observation did not apply in the instant case, but it was necessary for any court sentencing a young offender to pay close attention to the circumstances of the offender as well as to the facts of the case. That approach was reinforced by the Sentencing Guideline Council's guidance in relation to young offenders and the emphasis on the avoidance, wherever possible, of custodial sentences. There were many mitigating factors in the instant case. What took place was not forced. H's behaviour and family circumstances had otherwise given no cause for concern. He had educational ambitions and had shown a readiness while in custody to engage with rehabilitative and preventative work. He had been frank and apparently remorseful, and had pleaded guilty at the earliest opportunity. The reference to his emotional immaturity and low risk of reoffending were balanced by the disparity in age between the parties and the evidence that H knew that what he was doing was wrong. What took place was not mere experimentation but a settled and relatively frequent course of conduct which took place over several months. There was no coercion or obvious exploitation. However, the victim's participation had to be seen in the context of someone of her chronological age who might need to be protected from her own immature urges and inclinations. The sentencing guidelines were primarily concerned with single offences, not multiple offending. The imposition of a custodial sentence was not wrong, even when regard was had to the guideline for young offenders. The judge made very considerable reductions in the term imposed to reflect the facts of the case and H's guilty pleas. However, he had not made sufficient allowance for the available mitigation and the need to keep custody to a minimum. The 18-month term would be reduced to a 12-month detention and training order, to run concurrently on each count.

R. v H, [2015] EWCA Crim 1579, [2016] 1 Cr. App. R. (S.) 13, Treacy LJ, CA (Crim Div).

1859 Community orders–Non-compliance–Appropriateness of custodial sentence for single breach of community order imposed for robbery

The appellant, who had breached a community order, appealed against his sentence of 18 months' imprisonment. Following his conviction for robbery, the appellant had been sentenced to an 18-month community order with an 18-month supervision requirement, a 275-hour unpaid work requirement and a 10-month curfew requirement. The recorder who imposed the sentence warned the appellant that if he breached the community order he would receive a custodial sentence. The recorder imposed a sentence of 18 months for an admitted breach of the community order which took the form of two unjustified failures to report. The curfew had been complied with for over 40 weeks without incident. Otherwise, compliance had been patchy. The appellant had completed 113 hours of unpaid work. The breach report prepared by the Probation Service had expressed a wish for the community order to continue.

Held: Appeal allowed. The definitive guideline applicable to breaches of community orders provided that the primary objective when sentencing for a breach of requirements under such an order was to ensure that those requirements were completed. It also stated that custody should be the last resort, reserved for those cases of deliberate and repeated breach where all reasonable efforts to ensure that the offender complied had failed. The sentence passed by the recorder departed from that approach. By the time the appellant was resentenced, a very considerable amount of resources had been invested in working with him, and he had not reoffended. While the breach report did not make good reading, it was significant that the Probation Service still felt able to work with the appellant and that there had been progress. Putting an offender subject to a community order before the court in relation to a breach was an important tool available to the Probation Service to ensure that orders worked effectively. There might be a reluctance to place an offender before the court in circumstances such as this if the report from the Probation Service was not given very considerable weight in deciding the manner of disposal. The Probation Service had to deal with difficult offenders whose response was often not entirely positive. At a breach hearing, the following matters were important: whether there had been any reoffending, whether the risk presented by the offender had been reduced and whether the Probation Service felt that its work with the offender might usefully continue. The appellant's failure to heed the recorder's firm warning of inevitable custody in the event of any breach did not justify a departure from the definitive guideline in the circumstances of the case. The sentence imposed by the recorder would be quashed. In its place there would be a sentence of seven days' custody, which would result in the appellant's immediate release (see paras 11-15 of judgment).

R. v ASLAM (AQIB), [2016] EWCA Crim 845, [2016] 2 Cr. App. R. (S.) 29, Simon LJ, CA (Crim Div).

1860 Conspiracy–Sentencing guidelines–Relevance of guideline for substantive offence–Undue leniency

The Solicitor General referred to the court as unduly lenient sentences imposed on three offenders (C, M and F) following their guilty pleas in respect of a conspiracy to burgle dwelling houses. C was aged 25, M was 42 and F was 44. They were alleged to have conspired to burgle 19 houses over eight months. The burglaries were committed at night when the houses were unoccupied. The total value of property stolen was over £200,000. In one case, firearms and live ammunition were stolen. Those items, and most of the stolen property, had not been recovered. In six burglaries, the offenders took car keys from the house and stole the occupants' cars. The offenders were arrested shortly after committing the last burglary. The prosecution accepted a basis of plea stating that C had committed at least 13 burglaries, M 13 burglaries and a theft from a motor vehicle, and F five burglaries. Regarding C and M, the judge took a starting point of seven-and-a-half years' imprisonment; giving full credit for their guilty pleas, he imposed a sentence of five years. The starting point for F, given his lesser involvement, was five years and the sentence imposed was three years and four months. The Solicitor General argued that the judge had placed too much reliance on the sentencing guideline for burglary offences, whereas that guideline had little, if any, import in a conspiracy case. He argued that a number of aggravating features were present, not all of which had been referred to by the judge: the length and organisation of the conspiracy; the fact that the houses had been damaged to gain entry; the fact that some houses had been ransacked or vandalised; the significant loss; the theft of firearms; the traumatisation of some victims; and the fact that all the offenders had previous convictions. He acknowledged the mitigating factors of the houses having been unoccupied and the offenders having expressed remorse.

Held: Reference allowed. It was not correct to say that in the case of a conspiracy a judge should disregard completely the sentencing guidelines applicable to the substantive offence. Such guidelines, while not binding upon the judge sentencing for a conspiracy, could well provide a valuable and important touchstone (see para.24 of judgment). The Solicitor General had correctly identified the aggravating and mitigating features. The judge had failed to give sufficient weight to the adverse impact of the aggravating features of the substantive burglary offences. However, the conspiracy was not merely reflected in the execution of the actual substantive offences but had been persistent and only brought to an end by police intervention. Whatever approach was adopted, the starting point should have been in double figures because of the nature and number of the burglaries, the items stolen and the offenders' respective culpability. F had entered the conspiracy later and his participation in its execution had been lesser, but the degree of distinction drawn by the judge appeared to have no objective basis. The correct starting point for C and M was 10 years and for F it was eight years. Giving credit for the pleas, C and M's sentence would be six years and eight months; F's would be five years and four months (paras 25-30).

R. v COPELAND (RICHARD TORN); R. v FROOM (IAN); R. v MILBURN (GLENN ALAN), [2015] EWCA Crim 2250, [2016] 1 Cr. App. R. (S.) 56, Macur LJ, CA (Crim Div).

1861 Conspiracy to defraud–Financial traders–Manipulation of LIBOR

The court set the sentences to be served by four men (D1, D2, D3 and D4) who had been convicted of conspiracy to defraud. The defendants were LIBOR submitters or US dollar traders who had got together to manipulate the market for their own benefit and, as a result, to the benefit of the bank for which they worked. They took that action to improve the position on their own books, knowing that that would cause loss to the counterparties.

Held: Judgment accordingly. The offending fell within the "high culpability" category in the sentencing guidelines: the defendants had abused their positions of trust; the offending had been carried out over a significant period of time; and there was a large number of victims. As to the loss caused, it had been impossible to calculate the actual loss. However, the risk of loss could be judged to run into millions of pounds. The case therefore fell within category 2 of Harm A in the guidelines. The offending was aggravated by the effect that it had had: the defendants had damaged the confidence in and the integrity of a market rate that was relied on globally. The defendants had played different roles, D2 being the most culpable, and could rely on various matters by way of mitigation. For example, D4 had been involved for a shorter period than the others. D1, unlike the others, had pleaded guilty. All four were of previous positive good character. The appropriate sentences were as follows: D1, four years' imprisonment; D2, six-and-a-half years' imprisonment; D3, four years' imprisonment; D4, two years and nine months' imprisonment (see paras 13, 17-18, 21, 23, 26, 29, 33, 36, 41 of judgment).

R. v JOHNSON (PETER), [2016] Lloyd's Rep. F.C. 529, Judge Leonard QC, Crown Ct (Southwark).

1862 Conspiracy to defraud–Seriousness of offence–Vulnerability of victims relevant to assessment of culpability and harm

The appellants appealed against their sentences for conspiracy to commit fraud. The conspiracy had involved defrauding vulnerable householders by falsely representing that they needed remedial building works and grossly overcharging for the work. The frauds involved eight separate complainants, one of whom had changed his will to give the second appellant half of his estate in payment for the bogus works. The value of the potential losses was estimated at £285,000. The actual loss was just over £100,000.

The appellants had previous convictions for similar offences. The judge considered that the appellants' culpability was in category A, the intended loss was near the top of category 2 and the victim impact was one of high impact sufficient to move the offence up a category in the sentencing guidelines to category 1. He arrived at a starting point of seven years. The first and third appellants were sentenced to seven years' and the second appellant received five years and three months' imprisonment. The appellants submitted that the starting point was manifestly excessive and the judge had erred in sentencing within category 1. They argued that there was an element of double-counting in regarding the victims' vulnerability as a factor relating to harm and as a factor in placing the case in the high culpability category.

Held: Appeals dismissed. The double-counting argument was misconceived. The assessment of seriousness involved an evaluation of culpability and harm. When the targeting of vulnerable victims resulted in harm to them, there was no flaw in an approach that treated the victims' vulnerability as a relevant factor for both purposes. The guideline expressly envisaged that approach. It was a methodical and appropriate application of the guidelines and the sentences were not manifestly excessive.

R. v WHARF (DAX); R. v WILLIAMS (TONY); R. v DOE (BILLYSAM), [2015] EWCA Crim 2320, [2016] 1 Cr. App. R. (S.) 51, Sharp LJ, CA (Crim Div).

1863 Credit for time served–Curfew requirements–Necessity of following guidance in R v Hoggard (Barrie) [2013] EWCA Crim 1024, [2014] C.L.Y. 2611 and R v Thorsby (Adrian Kenneth) [2015] EWCA Crim 1, [2015] C.L.Y. 2200

[Criminal Justice Act 2003 (c.44) s.240A; Criminal Appeal Act 1968 (c.19) s.11(3)]

The appellant and the first and second applicants asked the court to determine the number of days counting towards their sentences in consequence of time spent on remand subject to a qualifying curfew, pursuant to the Criminal Justice Act 2003 s.240A. When the first applicant's sentence was imposed, the form of words specified in *R. v Hoggard (Barrie)* [2013] EWCA Crim 1024, [2014] 1 Cr. App. R. (S.) 42, [2014] C.L.Y. 2611 concerning credit for time spent on curfew was not used. The matter was re-listed before the Crown Court in the mistaken belief that the Court of Appeal had refused to deal with it. The judge purported to direct that 54 days, being half of the 108 days that the first applicant had spent on a qualifying curfew, should count towards his sentence. In the appellant's case, an administrative error meant that he was given insufficient credit for time spent on tagged curfew. The correct form of words was used, enabling the sentence to be amended administratively pursuant to *R. v Thorsby (Adrian Kenneth)* [2015] EWCA Crim 1, [2015] 1 W.L.R. 2901, [2015] C.L.Y. 2200. However, the number of days was not agreed. In the second applicant's case, the fact that he had been subject to a qualifying curfew condition for a period of 96 days was not drawn to the recorder's attention at the time of sentencing.

Held: Appeal allowed, applications granted. (1) Since the coming into effect of s.240A, sentencing courts had to specify the number of days that would count towards sentence in consequence of time spent on remand subject to a qualifying curfew. The instant court had been convened in order to re-affirm and re-emphasise the principles in *Hoggard* and *Thorsby* concerning the procedure to be adopted in the Court of Appeal, since the guidance given in those cases was not being followed (see paras 1-2 of judgment). (2) The procedure in the magistrates' court was to add up the days spent on qualifying curfew and then deduct the days on which the defendant was also being monitored with a tag or on temporary release from custody, along with any days when he had broken the curfew or tagging condition. The resulting number was divided by two and, if necessary, rounded up to the nearest whole number. The court in *Hoggard* had provided a form of words for sentencers to use. If the judge did not use those words, defence representatives should try to have the case re-listed within 56 days under the slip rule. If the error materialised after 56 days, an application had to be made to the Court of Appeal. However, if the *Hoggard* formula was used, the Crown Court retained jurisdiction, even after 56 days, *Hoggard* followed (paras 4-8). (3) According to *Thorsby*, the Court of Appeal procedure was for the applicant's representatives to try and agree the number of days' credit with the prosecution after making enquiries with the lower court and the monitoring company. Applicants had to explain in a witness statement explaining when and how they became aware of an error in the court's calculations or order. If the calculations were agreed, the single judge would be able to give leave and send the matter to the full court for a declaration without any need for representation. If the calculations were not agreed, the matter might be referred to the full court for resolution without the granting of leave or the making of a representation order. Practitioners had a duty to comply with the court's requirements, especially where the liberty of the subject was at stake. If they continued to ignore them, they risked being reported to their professional body and penalised in costs. In future, if the *Thorsby* requirements were not complied with, the Criminal Appeal Office would no longer process applications on behalf of represented applicants, *Thorsby* followed (paras 10-11, 13-14). (4) In relation to the first applicant, the Crown Court had had no jurisdiction to make a direction under s.240A outside the 56 days allowed for the slip rule. The unlawful order had resulted in an additional 12 days' credit and his early release from prison. However, the Criminal Appeal Act 1968 s.11(3) prevented the court from passing a sentence that would result in a harsher sentence overall. Accordingly, it would be disproportionate to pursue the matter any further. A lawful direction under s.240A for 54 days was substituted. In the appellant's case, he should have been given the opportunity to address the court, since the number of days in issue materially affected his sentence. The second applicant was entitled to 48 days' credit (paras 25-29, 38, 40, 44-45).

R. v MARSHALL (RAYMOND MARTIN) *sub nom.* R. v RAMOS (CHRISTOPHER); R. v HUSSAIN (SARAJ MAHMOOD), [2015] EWCA Crim 1999, [2016] 1 Cr. App. R. (S.) 45, Hallett LJ, CA (Crim Div).

1864 Criminal behaviour orders–Anti-social behaviour orders–Transitional provisions in the Anti-social Behaviour, Crime and Policing Act 2014 for replacement of anti-social behaviour orders with criminal behaviour orders

[Anti-social Behaviour, Crime and Policing Act 2014 (c.12) s.33(1)(a), s.33(2)(a)]

The appellant young offender appealed against a criminal behaviour order which had been substituted for an anti-social behaviour order. The offender had pleaded guilty to drugs offences in September 2014. On 21 October he received a custodial sentence, suspended for 24 months, and an anti-social behaviour order set at five years and containing three conditions. The day before, on 20 October, the Anti-social Behaviour, Crime and Policing Act 2014 had abolished anti-social behaviour orders and replaced them with criminal behaviour orders. In November 2014, the offender's case was re-listed under the slip rule and the judge made the substitution complained of. The issue was whether the judge had had power to impose the anti-social behaviour order in the first place given that such orders had effectively been abolished the day before. The offender also criticised the length of the order and its conditions. In January 2015, he breached one of the conditions, which activated his custodial sentence.

Held: Appeal allowed in part. Notwithstanding the effective repeal of anti-social behaviour orders on 20 October 2014, the combined effect of s.33(1)(a) and s.33(2)(a) of the Act was that the court retained power to impose such orders after that date if the relevant "criminal proceedings" began before that date. The Act neither defined "criminal proceedings" nor indicated when the transitional provisions should treat such proceedings as commencing. However, the proceedings in the instant case clearly began before the relevant date because the offender had already been convicted by then on his own guilty plea. The judge had, therefore, had power to impose the anti-social behaviour order (see para.8 of judgment). Furthermore, the judge would not have been able to impose a criminal behaviour order when sentencing the offender on 21 October, even though the operative parts of the Act were then in force. That was because s.22(1) made "conviction" a necessary precondition, and a "conviction" would be one after the coming into force of the Act on 20 October. The offender's conviction, through his guilty plea, had occurred a month before that date. The judge had not been entitled to convert the anti-social behaviour order into a criminal behaviour order in November 2014 (paras 9-10, 19). The offender's main submission about the unsuitability of an anti-social behaviour order for an 18-year-old who had matured and who was taking steps towards rehabilitation fell away in light of the fact that his recent conduct had activated the custodial sentence. However, on the facts, the five-year duration was too long and was reduced to three. Two of the conditions were also unnecessary, *R. v Briggs (Sharon)* [2009] EWCA Crim 1477 considered. The criminal behaviour order was varied to a three-year anti-social behaviour order with only a single condition (paras 12-13, 19)

R. v SIMSEK (ONUR), [2015] EWCA Crim 1268, (2016) 180 J.P. 192, Sir Brian Leveson PQBD, CA (Crim Div).

1865 Criminal behaviour orders–Duration–Self-employed gardener fraudulently overcharging elderly customer

[Anti-social Behaviour, Crime and Policing Act 2014 (c.12) s.22, s.22(9), s.27]

The appellant (J), who had been convicted of fraud, appealed against the criminal behaviour order which had been imposed on him. J, a self-employed gardener, was found to have significantly overcharged a man in his eighties for work done at his home. The Crown's case was that the victim had been defrauded of the sum of £7,850. The criminal behaviour order prohibited J from touting for business for a period of 10 years. In imposing the order, the sentencing judge stated that, for the purposes of the Anti-social Behaviour, Crime and Policing Act 2014 s.22, he was satisfied that J had engaged in behaviour that had caused or was likely to cause harassment, alarm or distress. He also considered, in the words of the statute, that the making of the order would help in preventing J from engaging in such behaviour in the future. J argued that the order was wrong in principle in being made after one-off offending against a single victim and against a background of his having worked as a self-employed gardener for over 20 years without similar offending; further, the order was disproportionate as it prevented him from working to provide for himself and his family in his normal occupation.

Held: Appeal allowed in part. There was nothing wrong in principle in making an order of the type imposed on J. Section 22 did not require proof of a sustained course of conduct. Section 22(9) provided that prohibitions and requirements in a criminal behaviour order should, so far as practicable, be such as to avoid any interference with the times at which the offender normally worked; that might imply that such orders should not prevent an offender from working "so far as practicable". However, where the conduct established derived from the very performance of work or took place in the course of it, there was no reason not to make an order in an appropriate case. There was nothing in the order made that would prevent J from seeking work upon his release in employment by others, provided he did not engage in conduct covered by the order, namely touting. Indeed, it would "help" to prevent the conduct for which he was prosecuted if he were to be under the control of a supervising employer. If difficulties proved to be insuperable, he could apply to vary the order under s.27 of the Act. However, the duration of the order was excessive: the order should last for three years rather than 10 (see paras 17-20 of judgment).

R. v JANES (JOHN), [2016] EWCA Crim 676, [2016] 2 Cr. App. R. (S.) 27, McCombe LJ, CA (Crim Div).

1866 Custodial sentences–Historic offences–Appropriateness of custodial sentence imposed on 68-year-old man for child sex offences committed when 15–Young offenders

[Children and Young Persons Act 1933 (c.12) s.41]

The appellant (B) appealed against a total sentence of 15 months' imprisonment imposed following his guilty pleas to incest and indecent assault. B was 68 years old. When aged 14 he had sexually abused his 13-year-old sister over a six-month period. He would lift her bed sheets, reach under the covers, touch her between her legs, including the outside of her vagina, and insert his fingers into her vagina. Aged 15 he had committed incest by having sexual intercourse with his sister, who was then 14. The victim first reported the matter in 2013, over 50 years after the offending. In sentencing, the judge referred to the guidelines for sentencing adult offenders.

Held: Appeal allowed. The judge had been misled in that he had not been referred to the relevant guidelines in relation to sentencing young offenders. None of the aggravating factors referred to in the guidelines were present in B's case. However, the assaults were part of a series of such offences, which was an aggravating factor. The small disparity in age between B and the victim was a mitigating factor. Whenever sentencing a youth pursuant to the Children and Young Persons Act 1933 s.41 and the

Sentencing Guidelines Council's Definitive Guideline on the Overarching Principles of Sentencing Youths, regard had to be had to the offender's welfare. B was not being sentenced as a 15-year-old youth, and it was necessarily artificial for a court to put itself into the position of sentencing an offender who was a young teenager at the time of the offence but was over 50 years older at the time of sentence. However, the court had to do its best. It was common ground that in the absence of aggravating factors of the kind referred to in the guidelines, a 15-year-old boy who offended in such a way might be made the subject of a non-custodial sentence. The issue was whether the judge was justified in imposing a far harsher sentence on B than would have been imposed if he had been a 15-year-old boy at the time of sentencing. B's behaviour had not added to the victim's reasons for not revealing what had happened, over and above the natural reluctance of a victim of a sexual assault to come forward. Further, as an adult, he had led an honest and industrious life for 50 years. He had been of considerable assistance to all his family, including the victim and her immediate family. He was remorseful, and had acknowledged what he had done and been punished. Bearing in mind all the circumstances, it would be wrong in principle to impose an immediate custodial sentence. It was appropriate to quash the existing sentence and impose a community penalty instead (see paras 18-21 of judgment).

R. v GB, [2015] EWCA Crim 1501, [2016] 1 Cr. App. R. (S.) 17, Hallett LJ, CA (Crim Div).

1867 Custodial sentences–Mental disorder–Offender damaging property being reckless as to whether life endangered–Evidence that actions attributable to mental disorder–Appropriateness of sentence of life imprisonment with hospital and limitation directions

[Mental Health Act 1983 (c.20) s.37, s.41, s.45A]

The appellant (Q) appealed against a sentence of life imprisonment with a minimum term of six years, coupled with hospital and limitation directions under the Mental Health Act 1983 s.45A, following his guilty pleas to eight counts of damaging property being reckless as to whether life was endangered. Q had three times travelled to a bridge over a busy motorway and thrown rocks and other heavy objects. Arrested after the third incident, he admitted the offences but stated that he had only wanted to "disrupt" people. Aged 63 at the time of the instant appeal, he had a long history of the same kind of offending. There was medical evidence that he suffered from an autistic spectrum disorder. A consultant forensic psychiatrist did not recommend a hospital order. However, a doctor at the hospital to which Q had been admitted advised that his behaviour was underpinned by his condition and recommended an order under s.37 and s.41. The judge found that despite his condition, Q's culpability was high. Q argued that (1) a custodial sentence was wrong, as an order under s.37 and s.41 would have been sufficient, the judge had been wrong to assess his culpability as high where the medical evidence indicated that his criminal actions were entirely attributable to his mental disorder, and the judge had failed to acknowledge that imprisonment was not appropriate to his medical condition; (2) if a custodial sentence was appropriate, the minimum term was excessive.

Held: Appeal dismissed. (1) The judge's evaluation of Q's culpability was one properly open to him. He had not been bound by the doctor's opinion, and there had been other opinions expressing doubt as to the appropriateness of a hospital order. The judge had been entitled to conclude that Q's culpability remained high. There had been a clear element of planning in his conduct, and when apprehended he had sought to minimise or conceal his wrongdoing. He had known what he was doing and that what he was doing was highly dangerous and wrong. Although such awareness was possibly not entirely to be equated with responsibility, those matters could not simply be disassociated from the assessment of culpability. The judge had been entitled to place reliance on the doctor's observations with regard to a s.37 and s.41 disposal in the context of the possibility of a safe discharge into the community. Although that had not been considered at all a likely prospect, it had not been ruled out; where culpability was high, it was a matter properly taken into account in deciding whether to impose a custodial sentence, albeit with a s.45A direction and limitation attached. In the circumstances, the judge had been justified in imposing a life sentence coupled with a s.45A direction and limitation. The potential impact of a custodial sentence on Q had been a matter requiring the judge's consideration, and the judge had considered it, as was clear from his sentencing remarks. That Q could be treated better in hospital than in prison could not be determinative in the instant case (see paras 38-40 of judgment). (2) Given all the circumstances and the previous convictions, the six-year specified minimum term was not excessive (para.41).

R. v QUIRK (PETER), [2014] EWCA Crim 1052, [2015] M.H.L.R. 22, Davis LJ, CA (Crim Div).

1868 Deferred sentences–False statements–Sentence deferred on basis of false mitigation–Reduction of credit for guilty plea

The appellant appealed against a sentence of four years' imprisonment imposed following his plea of guilty to putting a person in fear of violence by harassment. The appellant had been abusive and threatening towards staff at a hotel. He had a lengthy criminal record, and had previously been imprisoned for offences of harassment and battery which took place at the same hotel. Sentence was deferred for six months in the light of a pre-sentence report which indicated that the appellant had a long history of alcohol misuse but had not been able to engage with support, and that he had been in the Royal Marines but had been discharged on health grounds due to shrapnel in his legs and post-traumatic stress disorder (PTSD). During the period of deferment the appellant committed offences of theft and being drunk and disorderly. The deferred sentence report indicated that, in fact, the appellant had not been involved in active service in the Royal Marines, and did not have a diagnosis of PTSD. The recorder took the early guilty plea into account but held that the argument that the appellant was suffering from PTSD because of his experience on active service had been shown to be an attempt to deceive the court, and that operated to substantially diminish the credit otherwise due to him for his early plea. The appellant submitted that the sentence was manifestly excessive. He argued that it was appropriate for the court to take into consideration the fact that it had been misled when considering the appropriate level of credit for plea, but it was not appropriate for the court to pass a sentence for the initial offence which in any way reflected punishment for misleading the court.

Held: Appeal allowed. The reduction principle derived from the need for the effective administration of justice via the shortenings and savings resulting from an early plea. Although there was an early plea in the instant case, the proceedings were thereafter prolonged by the way in which the court was knowingly misled by the appellant into ordering a deferment when otherwise it would not have done so. It was plainly in the interests of the administration of justice that the mitigation which was put forward on behalf of an offender was true. Equally, it was not in the interests of the administration of justice that an offender who should have been sent to custody immediately was released and during the period of release went on to commit further offences. However, it was not appropriate for the sentence imposed for the initial offence to reflect any punishment, as such, for the misleading of the court. The recorder had been entitled to reduce the credit for plea to nothing in the light of the way in which the court had been misled. Nevertheless, the sentence of four years' imprisonment was too long. The correct sentence, taking into account the aggravating and mitigating features, was one of two-and-a-half years. The appeal would be allowed to that extent.

R. v WENDT (PAUL), [2015] EWCA Crim 2241, [2016] 1 Cr. App. R. (S.) 53, Sweeney J, CA (Crim Div).

1869 Deprivation orders–Dangerous driving–Reasonableness of order depriving offender of car

[Powers of Criminal Courts (Sentencing) Act 2000 (c.6) s.143, s.143(5)]

The appellant (H) appealed against a deprivation order, imposed following his guilty plea to dangerous driving. H had been driving between 70 and 90mph through red lights in a 30mph speed zone. He crashed into a tree while being chased by police cars. He was sentenced to 12 months' imprisonment suspended for two years, with a requirement to carry out 240 hours of community service. He was also disqualified from driving for two years, and ordered to pay £500 towards the prosecution costs and a £100 victim surcharge. In addition, the recorder made an order under Powers of

Criminal Courts (Sentencing) Act 2000 s.143 depriving H of his rights in the car that he had been driving when he committed the offence. The Crown had mentioned the deprivation order at its opening of the facts; nothing more was said at that stage. In sentencing, the recorder did not refer to the order until being prompted by the Crown. The issue was whether the order could not stand because there had not been the proper investigation, as required under s.143(5), of the vehicle's value or the impact on H of depriving him of it. The appellant submitted that the sentencing remarks had not indicated that the recorder had considered the likely financial and other effects on H; in particular that the car was worth £10,000 and that H had intended to sell it in order to pay off an informal loan from his father. The Crown submitted that the recorder had had ample information in the pre-sentence report, even though he had not referred specifically to it the s.143(5) provisions.

Held: Appeal allowed. The Crown had to lay some evidence before the judge before an order was made, *R. v Pemberton (Thomas)* (1982) 4 Cr. App. R. (S.) 328, [1983] C.L.Y. 808 applied. Although the recorder did have some of the relevant material before him, that could not be equated with proper consideration of the matters that he had been required by statute to consider. If it had always been the recorder's intention to incorporate a deprivation order as part of the overall sentence, he would have referred to it as part of his sentencing remarks; instead, it was an afterthought when prompted by the Crown. On the facts of the case and considering that H was a man of hitherto unblemished character, the suspended sentence of imprisonment, an unpaid work requirement, fine and disqualification was sufficient punishment. The deprivation order, equating to a further financial penalty of £10,000, was manifestly excessive. Further, on the assumption that H did owe his father money and intended to pay him back from the car's sale proceeds, the order would put him substantially into debt. However, that would not of itself have led the court to quash the order; the totality point was critical, *R. v Highbury Corner Magistrates Court Ex p. Di Matteo* [1991] 1 W.L.R. 1374, [1991] C.L.Y. 1125 applied. Had the recorder been aware of all those matters, and had his attention drawn to the authorities and the obligation to consider the likely financial and other effects on H, the order would not have been made (see paras 8-9, 15-19 of judgment).

R. v HAMLETT (MATTHEW WILLIAM), [2015] EWCA Crim 1412, [2016] R.T.R. 4, Davis LJ, CA (Crim Div).

1870 Directors disqualification–Misconduct–Judge failing to identify misconduct rendering director unfit

[Company Directors Disqualification Act 1986 (c.46) s.2, s.6; Consumer Protection from Unfair Trading Regulations 2008 (SI 2008/1277) reg.9]

The appellant company director (C) appealed against an order disqualifying him from being a director for five years pursuant to the Company Directors Disqualification Act 1986 s.2. C's company had acquired two motor vehicles in a car auction. The vehicles were later advertised for sale on eBay with mileage that was substantially less than the actual mileage. C pleaded guilty to three regulatory offences of engaging in a commercial practice which was a misleading action, contrary to the Consumer Protection from Unfair Trading Regulations 2008 reg.9. In his basis of plea he indicated that a company employee had altered the mileage on the vehicle pedometers without his knowledge, however he accepted liability as managing director for the misrepresentations even though he had no personal knowledge of them. The judge imposed fines of £1,250 for each offence with a period of 10 weeks' imprisonment in default and a victim surcharge order. Without warning, the judge then made the disqualification order.

Held: Appeal allowed. The judge had not identified the conduct which was said to have made C unfit to be a company director for the purposes of s.6 of the Act. That problem was exacerbated because three offences of fraud which were also on the indictment, and which prima facie might have been evidence of such misconduct, were not pursued and were abandoned in favour of the regulatory offences. The regulatory offences were ones of strict liability incurred as a director; they did not suggest any personal misconduct by C (see para.11 of judgment). It was always possible that there had been misconduct by C's failure to supervise the commercial activities of the company for which he had responsibility. However, without any further investigation, there was nothing in the basis of plea that would have founded a factual basis of misconduct. The judge was not bound by the basis of plea, but if he was going to depart from it he should have indicated his intention and given C an opportunity to give evidence and address the particular issues. That was not done (para.12). Furthermore, C's previous conviction for fraudulent use of a vehicle licence registration document was disregarded by the judge and thus could not form the basis of the relevant misconduct (para.13). If the judge had reminded himself of the authority of *Sevenoaks Stationers (Retail) Ltd, Re* [1991] Ch. 164, [1991] C.L.Y. 401, to which he had referred, he would not have, and could not have, proceeded in the manner which he did, *Sevenoaks* considered. If he was going to pursue a director's disqualification, he needed to ensure that C had proper notice of what allegations of misconduct within the meaning of the statute he faced and had an opportunity to make informed submissions about them, *Lo-Line Electric Motors Ltd, Re* [1988] Ch. 477, [1988] C.L.Y. 316 and *Secretary of State for Trade and Industry v McTighe (No.2)* [1997] B.C.C. 224, [1997] C.L.Y. 806 applied. The disqualification was something of an afterthought, not anticipated when mitigation was addressed, and not something that had been sought by the prosecuting authority. Accordingly, the disqualification order was quashed (paras 14-15).

R. v CHANDLER (LLOYD), [2015] EWCA Crim 1825, [2016] B.C.C. 212, Lloyd Jones LJ, CA (Crim Div).

1871 **Disqualification from driving–Custodial sentences–Disqualification and custodial sentence imposed simultaneously–Guidance on approach to sentencing under s.35A and s.35B Road Traffic Offenders Act 1988**

[Road Traffic Offenders Act 1988 (c.53) s.34, s.35, s.35A, s.35B; Coroners and Justice Act 2009 (c.25) Sch.16, s.137; Criminal Justice and Courts Act 2015 (c.2) s.30]

The Court of Appeal was required to consider the effect of the Road Traffic Offenders Act 1988 s.35A and s.35B on offenders who were disqualified from driving and had a custodial sentence imposed at the same time. The provisions were originally inserted by the Coroners and Justice Act 2009 s.137 and sch.16, but were not brought into force at that time. They were amended by the Criminal Justice and Courts Act 2015 s.30 and, as amended, came into force on 13 April 2015. In broad terms, they did not apply to offences committed before that date. They related to situations where a person was to be disqualified under s.34 (disqualification for specific offences) or s.35 (totting up disqualification) of the 1988 Act.

Held: Judgment accordingly. (1) The purpose of the legislation was to avoid offenders who were disqualified from driving and had a custodial sentence imposed at the same time, serving all or part of their disqualification while in custody. The clear intention of Parliament was that periods of disqualification should be served by an offender while he or she was at liberty in the community. Sections 35A and 35B employed different mechanisms for achieving that purpose(see paras 2-3 of judgment). (2) Section 35A applied where a person was convicted of an offence for which the court (a) imposed a custodial sentence and (b) ordered the person to be disqualified under s.34 or s.35. In those circumstances, the order of disqualification comprised a "discretionary" disqualification period and the appropriate "extension" period (para.16). (3) Section 35B came into play, in addition to s.35A, where other offences were involved. Where s.35B applied, in determining the length of disqualification, the court had to have regard, if and to the extent that it was appropriate to do so, to the diminished effect of disqualification as a distinct punishment on a person who was also detained pursuant to a custodial sentence. The court thus had greater discretion in fixing the term than what was achieved by the extension period mechanism under s.35A (paras 25-26, 30). (4) The Court of Appeal set out a checklist of steps as to the approach in respect of s.35A and s.35B: did the court intend to impose a "discretionary" disqualification under s.34 or s.35 for any offence; did the court intend to impose a custodial term for that same offence; did the court intend to impose a custodial term for another offence (which was longer or consecutive) or was the defendant already serving a custodial sentence; did the court intend to impose a custodial term for another offence or was the defendant already serving a custodial sentence (para.31). (5) The Court of Appeal discussed issues relating to the imposition of periods of disqualification: credit for curfew or remand; minimum periods of disqualification; early release arrangements;

guilty plea; start of disqualification; extended re-test; impact on other provisions; impact on sentencing guidelines (paras 32-46). (6) It was important that there was a degree of clarity in judges' sentencing remarks so that others could identify the correct extension period pursuant to s.35A and any uplift pursuant to s.35B. Such information would be important for police, the courts and the DVLA in terms of record-keeping. Accordingly, the judge in sentencing under s.35A should state the total period of disqualification but break that period down into the discretionary and extension periods. He should also give brief reasons for the length of the discretionary disqualification. When sentencing under s.35B, the court should state the total period of disqualification imposed but explain how the legislative steer of the section had been taken into account by indicating the period added by way of upward adjustment for the purposes of s.35B. Brief reasons should be given for the imposition of both those elements (paras 47-48).

R. v NEEDHAM (PAUL MAURICE); R. v ALI (SHAFIQ); R. v WILLIAMS (MICHAEL); R. v SMYTHE (LEE); R. v DEAKIN (LLOYD); R. v AITKEN (TONY); R. v KHAN (SADDIQ), [2016] EWCA Crim 455, [2016] 1 W.L.R. 4449, Treacy LJ, CA (Crim Div).

1872 Drug offences–Conveying prohibited articles–Conveying drugs into prison–Failure to award full credit for early indication of guilty plea

The appellant (O) appealed against a sentence of two-and-a-half-years' imprisonment, which included a two-year sentence imposed for two offences of conveying articles into or out of a prison and the activation of a suspended sentence. O visited his incarcerated cousin. He was behaving suspiciously and fidgeting with his trousers. He declined the prison officers' request to search him. The police attended and on the way to the police station he admitted that he had subutex down his trousers. When searched, subutex and a cannabis substitute were found in a package wrapped around a mobile phone, charger and SIM card. O admitted that the drugs were his but denied intending to pass them onto a prisoner. He had numerous previous convictions, including drug offences for which he had received 12 months' imprisonment suspended for two years. The pre-sentence report noted that O thought that his offending outweighed the risk, he had a lack of regard for the courts and others, it was his fourth breach of a community order, he had engaged positively with his current community order, and sought to address issues connected with drug misuse. The judge did not give O full credit for his guilty plea as he had declined formally to plead guilty in the magistrates' court but had pleaded guilty in the Crown Court.

Held: Appeal allowed. (1) Mobile phones were of significant value in prison. Those who smuggled or sought to smuggle such items into prison had to expect lengthy deterrent sentences. There was a difference between the hard-pressed family member persuaded to bring illegal drugs into prison and the sophisticated and experienced criminal who behaved in that way, which was the category into which O fell. The gravity of the offending was in relation to the prison setting and consequently the drugs guideline was not appropriate. The judge had been entitled to approach sentencing on the basis that he had (see paras 11-12 of judgment). (2) Given that the offences were indictable only, O was not able to enter a plea in the magistrates' court, but had indicated that he would plead guilty in the Crown Court. As a result, O should have been given the full discount for his guilty plea. Accordingly O's sentence was reduced to 20 months' imprisonment and the consecutive six-month sentence, although lenient, stood (para.13).

R. v ORMISTON (DAMIAN), [2016] EWCA Crim 363, [2016] 2 Cr. App. R. (S.) 4, Sir Brian Leveson PQBD, CA (Crim Div).

1873 Drug offences–Conveying prohibited articles–Single mother coerced into taking class A drugs into prison

[Prison Act 1952 (c.52) s.40B]

The appellant appealed against her sentence of three years' imprisonment for an offence of conveying a List A article into a prison contrary to the Prison Act 1952 s.40B. The appellant had handed over 6.88g of cocaine to an inmate in prison during a visit. She was a single mother of two children, one of whom had ADHD, who had been introduced to the inmate over the telephone. She considered them to be a couple and he had put pressure on her to bring the drugs. She had previously been in an abusive relationship and was a vulnerable person. The judge observed that the Sentencing Council guidelines for drug offences applied to her case and that the supply of drugs in prison was an aggravating feature. He used a starting point of four-and-a-half years based on a category 3 significant role classification for a class A drug. Her early guilty plea and mitigation brought her sentence down to three years. The judge held that a deterrent sentence was required.

Held: Appeal allowed. It was legitimate to have regard to the definitive guidelines on drugs offences when dealing with Prison Act cases involving drugs, *Attorney General's Reference (No.75 of 2002)* [2002] EWCA Crim 2383, [2003] 1 Cr. App. R. (S.) 109, [2003] C.L.Y. 3696 doubted. The appellant was a vulnerable person who had been prevailed upon by emotional pressure to give in to a request to smuggle class A drugs into prison. The guideline made provision for those who became engaged in the supply of drugs by coercion and not for gain. Theirs was a lesser role. However it could still be aggravated by the fact that the supply was into a prison so that the top of that range should apply. Category 4 applied for class A drugs weighing about 5g. For an offender playing a lesser role, the starting point after trial was 18 months' imprisonment. The top end of the category range was three years and the bottom end was a high-level community order. The judge took too high a starting point. Taking into account the impact of the sentence on the appellant's children, a starting point of 27 months was appropriate, *R. v Petherick (Rosie Lee)* [2012] EWCA Crim 2214, [2013] 1 W.L.R. 1102, [2013] C.L.Y. 2749 followed. Given her guilty plea, her sentence was reduced to 18 months' imprisonment (see paras 14, 16-19 of judgment).

R. v HAMILTON (KELLY MARIE), [2016] EWCA Crim 78, [2016] 2 Cr. App. R. (S.) 2, Treacy LJ, CA (Crim Div).

1874 Drug offences–Drug trafficking–Appropriate sentencing guideline category for offender acting as "sole trader"

An offender appealed against a sentence of 15 months' imprisonment imposed following his guilty plea to possessing a Class C drug, namely steroids, with intent to supply, and against a consecutive sentence of 15 months imposed following his guilty plea to importing steroids. The offender, aged 35 at the time of appeal, had bought steroids over the internet from China. He acted as a "sole trader". He knew those to whom he supplied the drugs. The quantity of the steroids was such that it fell into category 3 of the relevant sentencing guideline. They had a street value of some £58,000 and the offender might have made around £20,000 from his dealing, although evidence of that was not clearly put before the sentencing judge. The plea and case management hearing had not taken place until five months after the case was committed for trial, and it had then taken some time for counsel and the offender to consider the papers. He had pleaded guilty two months after the hearing. The judge allowed a 10% discount for the guilty plea. The offender argued that the judge had erred in his approach to determining his culpability, that he had not given a sufficient discount, and that consecutive sentences were inappropriate because he had engaged in one course of conduct.

Held: Appeal allowed. The categories used in the sentencing guidelines, for example leading role, significant role and lesser role, were not easily applicable to a sole trader. The offender's role, in the circumstances, lay somewhere between a significant role and a leading role: he had obvious knowledge of the importation in which he was involved, he had been going to make a significant financial gain and he had known precisely to whom he was supplying. However, it was importation and dealing by someone acting on his own account as a sole trader. Given the delay, the 10% discount had been on the low side. There had essentially been one course of conduct, namely importing the drugs with a view to selling them. However, the offence was serious. A significant sentence was required to emphasise that the conduct, which was easy to perform, of buying steroids over the internet and selling them was conduct which the courts would treat severely. Taking into account the steroids' value, because of the paucity of the evidence before the judge, and taking into account the offender's role and the fact that the discount had been low, the sentences would be quashed. A sentence of 20 months would be imposed on each count, but the sentences would be concurrent.

R. v PEARCE (STEPHEN DAVID), [2015] EWCA Crim 1291, [2015] 2 Cr. App. R. (S.) 70, Lord Thomas LCJ, CA (Crim Div).

1875 Drug offences–Drug trafficking–Large-scale conspiracy to import cocaine

The first appellant (S), who had pleaded guilty to conspiring to import cocaine and conspiring to import ammunition, appealed against his sentence of 30 years' imprisonment. The second appellant (X), who had pleaded guilty to conspiring to import cocaine, appealed against his sentence of 21 years' imprisonment. The third and fourth appellants (B and O), who had pleaded guilty to conspiring to supply cocaine, appealed against their sentences of 13 years' imprisonment. The appellants had taken part in an enterprise to import cocaine from Mexico via transatlantic flights. On arrival in the UK, the drugs, disguised as innocuous packages, would be unloaded in a warehouse facility and then collected by couriers using false documents for cutting, distribution and consumption. The success of the scheme depended on the participation of corrupt British Airways employees. There were two importations. The first involved cocaine and 100 rounds of live ammunition. The second involved cocaine alone. The two consignments of cocaine had a combined weight of almost 40kg and a wholesale value of over £2 million. S and X were involved in both importations; B and O took part only in the second. The sentencing judge stated that S had played a leading role in the conspiracy, being closely linked to the original source of the drugs. He was sentenced to 25 years for the cocaine offence and to a consecutive term of five years for the ammunition offence. The judge described X as S's trusted aide or lieutenant and as a leader in his own right. As to B and O, the judge stated that they played significant roles in the second importation, having had operational and management functions and having arranged couriers and the collection of money for S and X.

Held: Appeals allowed. The judge did not indicate what credit he was giving for any of the pleas of guilty. Given the circumstances in which, and the stage at which, the pleas were given, S was entitled to a discount of one sixth, while the others were entitled to a discount of 20%. This had been a very serious conspiracy involving nearly 40kg of high-purity cocaine, a relatively sophisticated international smuggling operation extending over several months and the corruption of airport staff. Nevertheless, each sentence should be reduced to a limited extent. As to S, although he played a leading role in the conspiracy, he was not its mastermind. Further, the quantity of 40kg, though eight times the indicative quantity for Category 1 in the sentencing guidelines, was not as great as some of the importations which had come before the courts. Those two factors in combination meant that the starting point of 30 years which the judge must have adopted was wrong. The appropriate starting point on the drugs charge was 27 years. Applying a discount of one sixth, the sentence on that count should be 22.5 years. The appropriate consecutive sentence for the ammunition offence was three-and-a-half years, making 26 years in total. The starting point in X's case should have been 24 years. A reduction of 20% would give a figure of just over 19 years. A sentence of 19 years' imprisonment would be substituted for the 21-year sentence imposed by the judge. The starting point in the cases of B and O should have been 14 years. A reduction of 20% would give a figure of just over 11 years. Sentences of 11 years' imprisonment would be substituted for the 13-year sentences imposed by the judge, *R. v Welsh (Christopher Mark)* [2014] EWCA Crim 1027, *Attorney General's Reference (Nos 99, 100, 101 and 102 of 2004)* [2005] EWCA Crim 294, [2005] 2 Cr. App. R. (S.) 82, [2005] C.L.Y. 3750 and *Attorney General's Reference (Nos 15, 16 and 17 of 2012)* [2012] EWCA Crim 1414, [2013] 1 Cr. App. R. (S.) 52, [2013] C.L.Y. 2621 considered (see paras 18-21, 33-36 of judgment).

R. v SANGHERA (HARVINDER); R. v ATKAR (SAVDEEP SINGH); R. v BROWN (DAVID); R. v O'MEARA (STEPHEN), [2016] EWCA Crim 94, [2016] 2 Cr. App. R. (S.) 15, Bean LJ, CA (Crim Div).

1876 Drug offences–Possession with intent to supply–Mentally disordered offender possessing class B drugs with intent to supply

The appellant (C), who had pleaded guilty to possessing Class B drugs with intent to supply, appealed against his sentence of 14 months' imprisonment. C had been stopped by the police while driving south from Liverpool. He admitted having drugs in his car. Police found cannabis valued at £57,540. C's basis of plea, not challenged by the prosecution, was that he had been asked to collect a consignment of cigarettes from Liverpool; he was not to be paid; he had no idea that the consignment was drugs until he arrived in Liverpool; he only agreed to carry the consignment because he was put under pressure and was concerned about the consequences for himself and his family if he refused; he accepted that the pressure fell short of duress. He told the author of the pre-sentence report that he was trying to help a friend's family who had been threatened over a debt; he had offered to repay the debt himself; he denied any financial motive and said that he had acted out of a misguided sense of morality. C, who was 48, had appeared in court on 25 previous occasions for 55 offences. In 2004, he had been sentenced to 10 years' imprisonment, varied on appeal to seven-and-a-half years, for conspiracy to supply heroin. It was said in the pre-sentence report that he had a significant mental health condition and a history of committing offences under the influences of others. He told the author of the report that he had been drug-free for at least five years. The sentencing judge stated that he was prepared to accept that C did not know precisely what he was entering into until he collected the drugs, but that at that point he must have realised that he was involved in serious criminality. He concluded that under the Sentencing Council Guideline the offence fell somewhere between a significant and lesser role and somewhere between a Category 2 and 3 offence. The appropriate starting point was 18 months' imprisonment. That starting point was increased to two years as he had previously been involved in serious drug dealing. The judge reduced the sentence to one of 14 months to take account of C's plea and the mitigation available to him.

Held: Appeal allowed. As to the quantity of drugs involved, the case fell just into Category 2. As to C's role, one of the characteristics identified by the guideline to demonstrate a "significant" role was some awareness and understanding of the scale of the operation. That was no doubt behind the judge's comment that once C collected the drugs he must have known that serious criminality was involved. At that point he knew the situation because, as the judge said, he was no stranger to the supply of drugs. His previous drugs offence was a serious aggravating factor. However, regard should be had to the substantial personal mitigation available to C: he had serious mental health problems and a low IQ. The judge worked back from his two-year starting point to take those matters into account. However, C's sentence for the previous drugs offence had been reduced substantially, primarily, it seemed, because of his mental health difficulties. The judge should have accorded greater weight to that factor. The appropriate sentence was one of 10 months' imprisonment, and such a sentence would be substituted for the sentence imposed (see paras 9-10 of judgment).

R. v CLAYTON (MARTIN), [2014] EWCA Crim 557, [2015] M.H.L.R. 325, Elias LJ, CA (Crim Div).

1877 Drug offences–Supply of drugs–Guidance on approach to issue of prevalence of drug dealing in local area

The appellant (B) appealed against a total sentence of four years and 10 months' detention following his guilty pleas to three counts of supplying Class A drugs and one count of being concerned in the supply of a Class A drug. B was 20 years old. On three separate dates over a two-week period in 2015, he supplied crack cocaine and heroin to an undercover police officer who was taking part in an operation targeting drug dealing. At the sentencing hearing, a statement from the operation's senior investigating officer was read to the court. In it, the officer considered the nature and effect of organized drug dealing networks within the local area and referred to the harm caused by drug dealing and the associated violence, intimidation and targeting of vulnerable people. In passing sentence, the judge commented on the serious drug problem in the local area and took a starting point of six-and-a-half years. In addition to the sentence imposed, a six-month suspended sentence imposed in 2014 for other drug offences was also activated in full and ordered to run consecutively. B argued that the starting point was unduly harsh and that the judge had wrongly increased it because of the prevalence of drug offences in the area.

Held: Appeal allowed. (1) Sentencing levels set in guidelines such as the Drugs Guideline took account of collective social harm. In the case of drugs supply, that covered the detrimental impact of drug dealing upon communities. Offenders should normally be sentenced by a straightforward application of the guidelines without increasing the sentence for the fact that their activity contributed to a harmful social effect. In ordinary circumstances, judges should not increase a sentence by reason of prevalence or in response to their own personal view that there was "too much of this sort of thing going on in this area" (see para.10 of judgment). If, however, the Crown intended to invite the court to consider the issue of prevalence, it had to expressly say so at the hearing, identifying the materials upon which it relied as evidence and referring the judge to the relevant guideline. If a judge of his or her own motion was contemplating prevalence as a factor, he or she should clearly identify that as a matter to be addressed in submission to the court. A judge would only be entitled to treat prevalence as an aggravating factor if he was satisfied that (a) the level of harm caused in a particular locality was significantly higher than that caused elsewhere; (b) that the circumstances could properly be described as exceptional; and (c) that it was just and proportionate to increase a sentence for such a factor. Only if the evidence placed before the court demonstrated a level of harm which clearly exceeded the well understood consequences of drug dealing by a significant margin should the courts be prepared to reflect that in sentencing. Any sentence imposed should identify if prevalence had been a factor and provide reasoning so that the parties could understand how it had influenced the sentencing decision. However, courts should be hesitant before increasing a sentence by reason of prevalence. Judges were well aware of the types of harm caused by drug dealing and would not be assisted by obvious statements (paras 11, 19). (2) In relation to the instant case, the starting point given in the sentencing guidelines of four-and-a-half years could properly be increased to reflect the two types of drug involved and the commission of offences on three separate dates. However, B was a relatively young offender who was not previously heavily convicted and an increase in sentence to six-and-a-half years before credit for guilty plea was not justified. The judge must have included some part of that increase to reflect prevalence, even though the officer's statement did not reveal a picture significantly different from that obtaining in other parts of the country, and there were doubts as to whether the circumstances were exceptional. It was not satisfactory to take account of prevalence both on the basis of the evidence available and in the circumstances of B's hearing. A sentence of a little over five years was appropriate. With credit for a guilty plea that resulted in a sentence of three years and six months to which six months should be added to run consecutively in activation of the suspended sentence. That gave a total of four years (paras 20-22).

R. v BONDZIE (MARCO) *sub nom.* R. v BONDIZE (MARCO), [2016] EWCA Crim 552, [2016] 1 W.L.R. 3004, Treacy LJ, CA (Crim Div).

1878 Drug offences–Supply of drugs–Non-commercial supply of class A drugs amongst addicts

The appellant (G) appealed against concurrent sentences of 16 months' imprisonment imposed after he pleaded guilty to two counts of supply of drugs. G's basis of plea stated that he was a heroin addict, he had purchased some heroin with another addict for personal use, at the time of his arrest he was handing over his friend's share, and that there was no financial gain. G had handed over four wraps, two of heroin and two of cocaine. Each wrap contained single street level doses. There was no accurate figure for the weight of drugs involved but in all likelihood four wraps would not exceed 1g in weight. The sentencing judge noted that G had committed a large number of very serious offences and many drug offences throughout his life. In recent years there was constant low-level shoplifting. G had tried to inform the judge that the last very serious offence was one of robbery committed in 1998 and that until October 2015 his record contained only one drugs offence. The judge did not let him speak. The pre-sentence report recommended a suspended term of imprisonment with a nine-month medium-intensity drug rehabilitation activity requirement, a 10-day rehabilitation activity requirement and a curfew. The judge took a starting point of three years' imprisonment, assigning G a lesser role for the purposes of the relevant guideline. She noted that the range was two to four years, meaning that the offence was in category 3. The sentence was reduced to two years before discount for G's guilty pleas. The judge stated that G did not qualify for any of the requirements proposed and imposed an immediate custodial term. She took note of the fact that following his arrest for the instant offences, he had committed more offences. G submitted that the judge ought to have imposed a suspended sentence with appropriate requirements as recommended in the pre-sentence report and that she failed to characterise his criminal history accurately.

Held: Appeal allowed. The judge had rightly assigned a lesser role to G given that the supply was not for financial gain. The basis on which the case was placed in category 3 was unclear. That classification depended on quantity unless the offence was one of street dealing, defined as "selling directly to users". G had not sold to anyone. The quantity involved was less than 5g which took the case to category 4 which had a starting point of 18 months' custody and a range of a high-level community order to three years' custody. G's antecedent history and the fact that he offended on bail meant that a decision to impose a prison sentence rather than the high-level community order was appropriate. The fact that the appropriate range did not require a prison sentence in all cases taken together with the guidance on the types of sentence available was relevant in deciding whether a sentence could properly be suspended. While G's history meant that a community order was inappropriate, it did not require a sentence in excess of the 18-month starting point in the correct range in the guideline. He was entitled to a one-third discount for plea. The judge had failed to have regard to the fact that one month earlier the magistrates' court had imposed a community order with a drug rehabilitation requirement which had been complied with "so far". The original sentence was quashed and replaced with concurrent 12-month sentences, suspended for two years, together with the recommendations made in the pre-sentence report except the curfew (see paras 10-13 of judgment).

R. v GHALGHAL (ABRAZAK), [2016] EWCA Crim 140, [2016] 1 Cr. App. R. (S.) 66, Thirlwall J, CA (Crim Div).

1879 Drug offences–Supply of drugs–Supply of cannabis to undercover police officer

The appellant appealed against a sentence of 32 months' imprisonment following his guilty plea to an offence of supplying cannabis. An undercover police officer had approached the appellant and told him that he wanted to buy drugs. The appellant referred him to a co-offender standing nearby and the officer bought a small amount. At the officer's request the appellant gave him a mobile phone number to use to buy cannabis in the future; the number was used to arrange to buy cannabis. About three weeks later the police stopped two co-offenders and found the appellant in a nearby car with three mobile phones, including the one with the number the officer had been given. The appellant also had £670 on him. He was arrested and bailed in respect of those offences. Six weeks later the officer returned to buy cannabis; he spoke to a co-offender and was told to wait. The appellant arrived and supplied £20 of cannabis to the co-offender who sold it on to the officer. The appellant fell to be sentenced for the latter offence only, but the judge referred to the background and context of the offending. He had committed that offence while subject to a suspended sentence of 26 weeks' imprisonment for possessing an offensive weapon in a public place. His records also included public order offences and two previous offences of supplying cannabis. When sentencing, the judge said that he did not need to decide whether the appellant was an "organiser", or had a "leading role" or was "merely at the top of street dealing" because he considered that the significant fact was that it was the third time the appellant had been dealing in cannabis. He concluded that because of that and the appellant's general background, after a trial, the offending would have attracted a sentence of four years' imprisonment. The court ordered that the suspended sentence be activated for only 18 weeks, to be served concurrently with the 32-month sentence. The sentence reflected a starting point before credit for a plea of 48 months. The appellant submitted that the starting point was too high for the single offence to which he pleaded guilty. He argued that the judge either disregarded or paid insufficient attention to the applicable definitive guideline and did not stipulate whether he considered the appellant to have played a "leading" or "significant" role in the offending.

Held: Appeal dismissed. The recommendations of the definitive guidelines were that in respect of Category 3 dealing of a Class B drug, the starting point for those with a leading role was four years' custody, with a range of suggested sentences of between two years six months and five years' custody. For a significant role, the starting point was one years' custody and a range of 26 weeks to three years' custody. The judge's observations could be interpreted as meaning that the appellant's offending did not fall sufficiently clearly into that of" leading" or "significant" role to specify which side of the line it fell. He could not be criticised for that view. The judge had been entitled to approach the sentencing exercise as he did without specifying the appellant's role by reference to the guideline. The starting point of four years was longer than an offence of supplying that amount of cannabis would generally warrant. However, the sentence was justified because (a) the appellant had organised others with regard to conducting the supply and had provided a mobile phone for the undercover officer to make regular purchases; (b) the appellant was on bail at the time of the offending; (c) the appellant's record, in particular his previous offences of supplying cannabis; and (d) the order on the suspended sentence justified the overall disposal of the appellant's case. The sentence was not excessive (see paras 10-13 of judgment).

R. v ARSLAN (SAYGAN), [2016] EWCA Crim 321, [2016] 2 Cr. App. R. (S.) 8, Lindblom LJ, CA (Crim Div).

1880 Drug offences–Totality of sentence–Guilty plea to cultivating cannabis when already serving custodial sentence for possession of Class A drugs with intent to supply

[Powers of Criminal Courts (Sentencing) Act 2000 (c.6) s.110]

The appellant (C) appealed against a sentence of 18 months' imprisonment imposed after his guilty plea to cultivation of a class B drug, namely cannabis. At the time of sentencing, C was already serving a prison sentence of five years and eight months' imprisonment for possession of Class A drugs with intent to supply. That sentence was a prescribed custodial term under the Powers of Criminal Courts (Sentencing) Act 2000 s.110, it being his third qualifying conviction for such an offence. The sentencing judge took a starting point of two years' imprisonment and applied a discount of 25 per cent for C's guilty plea to arrive at a sentence of 18 months' imprisonment, which she ordered to run consecutively to the sentence for the possession offence, resulting in a total sentence of seven years and two months' imprisonment.

Held: Appeal allowed. It appeared as though the judge had considered totality before making any reduction for the guilty plea. Had the judge approached sentencing in the correct order and considered the reduction for guilty plea before totality, it would have been clear to her that the resulting, total sentence of seven years and two months' imprisonment was manifestly excessive. Insufficient weight had been given to totality. It would have been wrong to make the sentence for the cultivation offence concurrent because it would have watered down the impact of s.110. However, the term of 18 months was manifestly excessive and it was appropriate to reduce it to nine months' imprisonment, to run consecutively to the sentence for the possession offence.

R. v CHAPLIN (CHERALDO), [2015] EWCA Crim 1491, [2016] 1 Cr. App. R. (S.) 10, Macur LJ, CA (Crim Div).

1881 Extended sentences–Dangerousness–Reliance on insufficient material and speculative reasoning for assessment of sexual offender

[Criminal Justice Act 2003 (c.44)]

The appellant (O) appealed against an extended sentence, comprising an 11-year custodial term and a five-year licence period, imposed for rape by way of vaginal penetration, rape by way of oral penetration, assault by penetration and false imprisonment. The complainant (S) had met O and others on a night out. She drank a significant amount and ended up at O's house where she fell asleep. When she awoke he subjected her, over three hours, to the ordeal represented by the four convictions. He had locked her in the house. At one point he threatened her with a cleaver and suggested that she phone her daughter as it might be the last time they spoke. She was able to put the cleaver in her handbag. O called a taxi for her and she left. S reported the matter to the police. O claimed that S had consented. The sentencing judge considered that the case fell within category 1B of the guideline for vaginal rape, with a starting point of 12 years' custody and a range of 10 to 15 years. No separate sentence was passed on the other offences. The judge recognised that each was "grave and serious" and treated them as aggravating the vaginal rape. O argued that (1) the sentence was too severe; (2) there was no proper basis for concluding that he was dangerous within the meaning of the Criminal Justice Act 2003 Pt 12 Ch.5.

Held: Appeal allowed. (1) The judge had been entitled to put the vaginal rape in category 1 in terms of harm given that separate sentences were not passed for the other offences. The oral rape and digital penetration were additional degradation/humiliation of a particularly grave kind. The threat with the cleaver and reference to S's call to her daughter being her last were highly relevant to the categorisation. In evidence, S had stated that O referred to killing himself and her, and after raping her he said "don't wind me up or I'll get the knife". The kidnapping was also relevant; S had been locked in the house for several hours. The custodial term of 11 years was justified (see paras 7-8 of judgment). (2) The judge had had a pre-sentence report before him but he did not refer to it to support his conclusion of dangerousness, or at all. The report had noted O's lack of victim empathy. A clinical psychologist's report led the judge to conclude that O had a deeply worrying personality. In reaching his decision, the judge referred to delusional behaviour and concluded that O presented a significant risk to women through the commission of further specified offences and that an extended sentence was required. He did not explain what constituted delusional behaviour. The prosecution suggested that the judge might have been referring to O thinking that he might have been able to form a relationship with S and S's evidence about him killing himself, but it was difficult to regard that as delusional. Before the instant court was a prison report and a forensic psychiatrist's report which referred to O's engagement with prison services and noted that he did not display any symptoms suggestive of any personality disorder and no active features of psychopathy such as lack of empathy. The psychiatrist's report concluded that O's risk of violent offending was low, that his risk to women, including any sexual offending, was low to medium, and that he was not dangerous for the purposes of the extended sentence provisions. There was no proper basis for the finding of dangerousness and, accordingly, no proper basis for the extended sentence. The material was too thin and the reasoning too speculative to justify that conclusion. The extended sentence was quashed and replaced with a determinate 11-year sentence (paras 10-18).

R. v OGUNTOKUN (JOHN), [2016] EWCA Crim 331, [2016] 2 Cr. App. R. (S.) 5, Lindblom LJ, CA (Crim Div).

1882 Extended sentences–Dangerousness–Risk of commission of further offences causing serious harm

The appellant (S) appealed against his extended sentence of nine years and three months' imprisonment. S and two others had punched and kicked a taxi driver. The taxi driver gave them money but the perpetrators continued to assault him until he handed over the safe. The victim suffered bruises, swelling and a minor head injury. In a victim impact statement, the driver said that since the attack he had been nervous about picking up passengers and wanted to leave his job. S pleaded guilty at the case management hearing and received a 25 per cent discount. He had previous convictions for violence and robbery. He accepted that he had been drinking alcohol and taking cocaine at the time of the offence, and was assessed as posing a high risk of causing serious harm when intoxicated. The judge took a starting point of seven years, which was at the top of the range of category 2 in the sentencing guidelines. He imposed a custodial sentence of five years and three months' imprisonment, with a three year extended sentence after finding that S was dangerous. S submitted that the custodial term was too high and that there was no justification for the dangerousness finding.

Held: Appeal allowed. The offence had involved a number of aggravating features: S had been intoxicated, it had taken place at night, a lone taxi driver had been targeted and subjected to racist abuse, the driver had been traumatised, and S had relevant previous convictions. The judge was right to have taken a starting point of seven years. As for dangerousness, the judge had to be satisfied that there was a serious risk of S causing serious harm by committing further specified offences. The risk identified had to be significant, *R. v Lang (Stephen Howard)* [2005] EWCA Crim 2864, [2006] 1 W.L.R. 2509, [2006] C.L.Y. 3836 applied. A serious risk that he would commit further offences did not necessarily mean that there was a serious risk of serious harm being caused. S had never tried to cause serious harm: in the instant case he had used his fists but could have inflicted far more serious harm on the victim. There was undoubtedly a serious risk of him committing further serious offences, but there was insufficient evidence that those offences would cause serious harm. The extended sentence was quashed so that the total sentence was five years and three months' imprisonment.

R. v SEDDON (DARREN EDWARD), [2015] EWCA Crim 2141, [2016] 1 Cr. App. R. (S.) 50, Elias LJ, CA (Crim Div).

1883 Fines–Enforcement notices–Guilty plea to non-compliance with planning enforcement notice–Offender profiting by renting property to tenants during four-year period of non-compliance–Whether fine punishing offender for benefit already taken account of in confiscation order

[Town and Country Planning Act 1990 (c.8) s.179(2)]

The appellant appealed against a fine of £190,000 imposed on him following his guilty plea to an offence contrary to the Town and Country Planning Act 1990 s.179(2) and (8) of non-compliance with a planning enforcement notice. In 2007 the appellant had constructed an outbuilding comprising six residential units at the rear of his property without planning permission. He was refused retrospective planning permission. He failed to comply with an enforcement notice issued by the council in 2009 requiring him to demolish the outbuilding. In 2010 planning permission was granted for use of the outbuilding as ancillary to the main building but not for separate residential units. The appellant did not cease residential use and the council issued an enforcement notice requiring the removal of kitchens and bathrooms from the outbuilding by February 2012. Two informations were laid by the council in 2013: the first for non-compliance with the 2009 enforcement notice; the second for non-compliance with the 2010 notice. The first information was withdrawn on the basis that partial planning permission had been granted after service of the 2009 enforcement notice. In 2014, the appellant removed the kitchens and bathrooms from the units a week before the Crown Court hearing. The judge made a confiscation order of £76,562 which represented the benefit the appellant had obtained from renting out the units between the dates identified in the information. He imposed a fine of £190,000 on the basis that the appellant had made a profit for four years, until the 2010 enforcement notice took effect, while flouting planning controls.

Held: Appeal allowed in part. On a proper interpretation of s.179, the criminal offence only arose after the end of the period given for compliance with the enforcement notice. That date was February 2012. The prosecution of any one offence was limited to the period ending with the date set out in the information, which was October 2013. If there was a failure to comply after that period, a further offence had to be charged. Accordingly the appellant was only liable to be sentenced for the period from February 2012 until October 2013. Since the council had withdrawn the first information, it would be an abuse to sentence him in respect of that earlier period on the second information. There had been no finding of guilt in respect of that earlier period and he had not pleaded guilty to that offence. It would be wrong in principle to impose a fine in respect of the financial benefit from the offence if it had already been the subject of a confiscation order, *R. v Rance (Piers)* [2012] EWCA Crim 2023, [2013] 1 Cr. App. R. (S.) 123, [2013] C.L.Y. 2630 applied. It was not lawful to fine the appellant £175,000 by reference to the financial benefit received from renting the units prior to February 2012. The benefit which the appellant had gained from his offence between February 2012 and October 2013 was fully recognised in the confiscation order. Taking into account the appellant's course of conduct, his disregard of planning controls for personal gain and his failure to comply with enforcement notices, a fine of £30,000 was appropriate, with a 20 per cent discount for his guilty plea making a fine of £24,000 (see paras 33-43 of judgment).

R. v KOHALI (DAVID), [2015] EWCA Crim 1757, [2016] 1 Cr. App. R. (S.) 30, Davis LJ, CA (Crim Div).

1884 Firearms offences–Possession of firearms–Appropriateness of immediate imprisonment for possession of prohibited firearm with sentimental attachment

The appellant (B) appealed against a total sentence of two years' imprisonment following his guilty pleas to possessing a prohibited firearm and possessing ammunition without a firearm certificate. B had been found in possession of a British Enfield revolver and 50 rounds of ammunition, both dating from the Second World War. In interview, he admitted knowing that it was illegal to have the gun and ammunition, but said that he felt a sentimental attachment to them because they had belonged to his father. He had no previous convictions. B submitted that the judge had given insufficient consideration to whether a suspended sentence was appropriate.

Held: Appeal allowed. Given that B knew it was illegal to be in possession of the gun and ammunition, a sentence of two years' imprisonment was not of itself inappropriate. As to whether the judge should have suspended the sentence, the issue was whether B's immediate imprisonment had been necessary. It had not been in the circumstances, and so it was appropriate to quash the sentence of two years' immediate imprisonment and to replace it with a sentence of two years' imprisonment suspended for two years (see paras 13-14 of judgment).

R. v BENSON (JONATHAN NICHOLAS), [2016] EWCA Crim 339, [2016] 2 Cr. App. R. (S.) 9, Lindblom LJ, CA (Crim Div).

1885 Firearms offences–Possession of firearms–Departure from statutory minimum sentence where no exceptional circumstances–Undue leniency

The Attorney General referred to the court as unduly lenient a sentence of three-and-a-half years' imprisonment, following a conviction for possession of a firearm. Police had attended the home of the offender (G) in relation to a separate matter. G volunteered the presence of a gun in the flat and retrieved it. She told the police that a drug dealer had asked her to store the weapon and that she had done so because she was afraid of him. G gave the drug dealer's name to the police. The gun was in poor condition, but was capable of being fired in an unorthodox manner, although it had not been used. G, aged 33 and a drug addict, had numerous previous convictions, including possession of drugs, but none for gun-related offences. The offence carried a minimum sentence of five years' imprisonment save in exceptional circumstances. The judge said that he had applied a holistic approach to sentencing and found there were exceptional circumstances because the gun was in poor condition, G had been its custodian rather than its owner, she had volunteered its presence and location, she had been vulnerable due to her drug addiction and had named the drug dealer who had asked her to store the gun. The Attorney General submitted that the sentence failed to reflect the seriousness of the offence or G's culpability as the gun had been held for a known criminal, and that the judge had wrongly found there had been exceptional circumstances which allowed him to depart from the statutory minimum.

Held: Reference allowed. The judge had tried his best to tailor the sentence to G, but parliament had decided that, absent exceptional circumstances, a minimum sentence of five years should be imposed for the instant offence. The Court of Appeal had given a clear steer that exceptional circumstances will only be found in rare cases and that sentencing judges should not be guided by sympathy for the offender;*Attorney General's Reference (No.43 of 2009)* [2009] EWCA Crim 1925, [2010] 1 Cr. App. R. (S.) 100, [2010] C.L.Y. 2882 and *Attorney General's Reference (No.37 of 2013)* [2013] EWCA Crim 1466, [2014] 1 Cr. App. R. (S.) 62, [2014] C.L.Y. 2639, followed. Taking the most positive view of G's circumstances and the instant offence, it did not come close to amounting to exceptional circumstances. The minimum sentence should have been five years' imprisonment.

ATTORNEY GENERAL'S REFERENCE (NO.115 OF 2015) *sub nom.* R. v GREENFIELD (CHERYL), [2016] EWCA Crim 765, [2016] 2 Cr. App. R. (S.) 23, Hallett LJ, CA (Crim Div).

1886 Firearms offences–Prohibited firearms–Large-scale conspiracy to transfer prohibited weapons and ammunition–Undue leniency

The Attorney General referred to the court as unduly lenient sentences imposed on 17 men who had pleaded guilty or been convicted of conspiracy to transfer prohibited weapons and ammunition. Between March 2014 and January 2015, there had been a sophisticated criminal enterprise in Birmingham involving the supply of firearms and lethal ammunition to criminals in the West Midlands and elsewhere in the UK. The police recovered eight firearms and 492 live rounds of ammunition. They identified six men as being involved in the enterprise. They were referred to by the sentencing judge as the leader, the armourer and four key facilitators. The judge set the sentence he would have passed on the leader at 19.5 years (before the discount for his guilty plea). The starting points for the others were between 17.5 and 11 years. The remaining offenders were individuals who had purchased guns and weapons or who had assisted the purchaser. The judge set the sentence he would have passed on the purchasers at between 11 and 7.5 years, before a discount for a guilty plea. As to those who assisted the purchaser, the starting points were between 12 and 5 years.

Held: Judgment accordingly. It would not be appropriate to revisit the judge's decision not to impose a life sentence. However, criminals who were prepared to deal in lethal weapons invariably represented a serious public danger and therefore a sentence of life imprisonment should always be considered. If a life sentence was not passed, the courts should impose long determinate sentences commensurate with the role played in any activity in relation to the supply of guns. Sentences had to reflect the hierarchy of the supply enterprise, the role played in individual transactions and any previous gun-related convictions. For the leader of the enterprise, a very long determinate sentence was required. It appeared to have been assumed, based on the decision in *Attorney General's Reference (No.43 of 2009)* [2009] EWCA Crim 1925, [2010] 1 Cr. App. R. (S.) 100, [2010] C.L.Y. 2882, that the maximum determinate sentence for involvement in a large-scale enterprise concerning the supply of guns was 22 years. No such maximum was indicated by the court in that case, and 22 years should not be regarded as the maximum. A materially longer sentence would be appropriate if there was any previous conviction for offences involving guns. Nor could it make any difference that the criminal enterprise here was engaged in converting or acquiring guns rather than importing them; the same level of sentence was appropriate, as the essence of the criminality was the organisation of a criminal enterprise to supply guns and lethal ammunition to customers. The court should assess all the circumstances, including the number and type of weapons involved, whether lethal ammunition had been provided, the period of time over which the enterprise operated, the level of sophistication employed, the geographic range of the enterprise and any specific factors connecting the criminal enterprise to a locality where gun crime was particularly serious. The appropriate sentence for the leader here was 25 years, before a discount for his plea. Those engaged in the criminal enterprise under him should have received sentences reflecting his sentence (before any discount for a plea), depending on the role they played. As to the purchasers, they must have required the gun and lethal ammunition to kill, maim, terrorise or intimidate. Two were engaged in the supply of Class A drugs. The appropriate sentences should have been in the region of 15 years (before any discount). Significantly longer sentences were required where the purchaser had previous gun-related convictions. The role played by those who assisted in the purchases varied, but as Parliament had stipulated a minimum sentence of five years for those in possession of a gun, it was inappropriate to pass sentences with a starting point of less than eight years for those who assisted in putting guns into circulation. Their criminality lay in assisting in putting guns and lethal ammunition into the hands of a purchaser. Sentences materially longer were required in cases where the assistance was significant. Here, the sentences should have ranged from 12 to 8 years (before any discount), depending on the role played and any previous association with guns. The adjusted sentences were severe but reflected Parliament's intention to punish gun crime in a manner that would deter criminals from engaging in dealing in guns and lethal ammunition, *Attorney General's Reference (No.43 of 2009)* considered (see paras 6-8, 21 of judgment).

ATTORNEY GENERAL'S REFERENCE (NOS 128 TO 141 OF 2015 AND 8 TO 10 OF 2016) *sub nom.* R. v STEPHENSON (NOSAKHERE); R. v NAZRAN (SUNDISH SINGH); R. v MCDERMOTT (LOUIS JUNIOR); R. v WIGGAN (THEODORE JUNIOR); R. v GUL (ROWAN); R. v DUCRAM (FITZROY); R. v MATTU (JOGA SINGH); R. v MIAH (MOHAMMED SELU); R. v GHALIB (AMAR); R. v ABDIN (JOYNAL); R. v HUSSAIN (IFRAN); R. v HUSSAIN (USMAN); R. v FEDAR (MOHAMMED); R. v MOHAMMED (JANED); R. v OFFICER (CLINTON); R. v SMITH (JAMAL SHAKA); R. v MENTORE (DARREN), [2016] EWCA Crim 54, [2016] 4 W.L.R. 83, Lord Thomas LCJ, CA (Crim Div).

1887 Fraud–Credit cards–Systematic, persistent use of stolen credit cards

The appellant (X), who had pleaded guilty to a number of offences involving dishonesty, appealed against his sentence of five years and six months' imprisonment. As to the first offence, X had used a stolen credit card to pay for goods and hotel charges. The total loss incurred by the use of that card was £10,800. As to the remaining offences, X had on five separate occasions used stolen credit cards in attempting to purchase expensive watches or jewellery. On two occasions he was successful. Watches valued at over £72,000 were taken on the first occasion, while diamonds with a value of £32,000 were taken on the second. The shop assistant who sold the watches to X was deeply upset by the offence. He had difficulty going back to work for a time and continued to be extremely hesitant about doing his job because he feared that somebody else might attempt to defraud him in a similar way. The diamonds were taken from the shop of a sole trader. He made a victim impact statement setting out how deeply he had been affected, both personally and financially, by X's actions. X, who was now 40, had a bad record, which included offences of dishonesty. Counsel in the court below agreed that this was a Category 2 offence within the definitive guideline on fraud, bribery and money laundering offences, as the combined value of the items taken or attempted to be taken by fraud fell between £100,000 and £500,000. They also agreed that culpability should be set at the highest point within that level. A combination of those two features gave a category range of three to six years' custody with a starting point of five years' custody.

Held: Appeal dismissed. While the sentence was towards the higher end of the range, it was not manifestly excessive. These were systematic, persistent offences, targeting shops which on occasions were run by individuals vulnerable to this sort of fraud. The offences were relatively sophisticated, to the extent that on two occasions X almost certainly was working with somebody else who would make a call to the shop's landline and offer comfort and assurance by way of an authorisation code for the credit card. The offences were carried out with a degree of bravado and confidence. Moreover, the five later offences were committed while X was on bail for the first offence. Further, there were very serious detrimental effects on the victims, both financial and otherwise (see paras 22-23 of judgment).

R. v AHMED (AKBAR), [2016] EWCA Crim 104, [2016] 2 Cr. App. R. (S.) 7, Macur LJ, CA (Crim Div).

1888 Grievous bodily harm–Mentally disordered offenders–Uncertain psychiatric status at sentencing–Subsequent diagnosis of mental disorder and recommendation for hospital and restriction orders

[Mental Health Act 1983 (c.20) s.41, s.45A]

The appellant (M) appealed against a sentence of imprisonment for public protection imposed following his pleas of guilty to causing grievous bodily harm with intent and two counts of having an offensive weapon. M had subjected a neighbour to an unprovoked attack using a kitchen knife, which resulted in numerous stab wounds, including a wound to the neck requiring urgent surgical intervention. When police attempted to arrest M he produced another kitchen knife, initially refused to drop it, and struggled with officers as they attempted to restrain him. Eventually a taser had to be used. In the period prior to the offence, M had displayed uncharacteristically agitated and aggressive behaviour giving cause for concern. Given his mental state, M was sectioned under the Mental Health Act 1983. When the matter came before the sentencing judge there was conflicting medical opinion as to whether M was suffering from a mental disorder, with no recommendation made for a hospital order or suggestion of any hospital treatment being available at that time. The judge, observing that if there was an underlying mental disorder the risk of reoffending had to be considered as high, but noting the uncertainty surrounding M's psychiatric status, concluded that M was dangerous and imposed the sentence of imprisonment for public protection, with a minimum term of four years. Following subsequent psychiatric assessment, M's treating psychiatrist (S) reported that M suffered from paranoid schizophrenia characterised by auditory hallucinations and delusions of persecution, and recommended that the court should consider a s.41 restriction order. S gave evidence that M suffered from a mental disorder that should respond to treatment and that a disposal under s.45A was inappropriate.

Held: Appeal allowed. In light of the medical opinion and the fact that an order under s.45A might amount to the imposition of a more severe penalty than had been imposed at the Crown Court, the most appropriate course was to quash the sentence of imprisonment for public protection and impose a hospital order coupled with a restriction order without limit of time. M was clearly very dangerous. Risks could not be taken with the public simply because a patient appeared to respond to treatment in a structured environment. The court was satisfied that S was very conscious of that and would ensure that any recommendations regarding M's future discharge would be given the most careful consideration, with the risk to the public uppermost in the minds of all concerned. No criticism was made of the sentencing judge as he had not had the benefit of the medical opinion before the instant court.

R. v MARINOS (IOAANNIS), [2013] EWCA Crim 652, [2014] M.H.L.R. 20, Hallett LJ, CA (Crim Div).

1889 Grievous bodily harm–Undue leniency–Unlawful variation of sentence under s.155 Powers of Criminal Courts (Sentencing) Act 2000–Appropriateness of considering new information available since original imposition of sentence

[Criminal Justice Act 1988 (c.33) s.36; Powers of Criminal Courts (Sentencing) Act 2000 (c.6) s.155; Criminal Procedure Rules 2014 (SI 2014/1610) r.42.4]

The appellant (N) appealed against an extended sentence of 11 years which had been imposed following his guilty pleas to offences of attempting to cause grievous bodily harm with intent and possession of an offensive weapon. N had assaulted a woman at night as she walked home. He had been disguised in a full burka and had struck her to the head and eye with a rock and tried to strangle her. Months later he was arrested in the same area wearing a similar disguise and carrying a hammer. He was originally sentenced to four years and four months' imprisonment. The Attorney General made a reference under the Criminal Justice Act 1988 s.36, and the Crown applied to vary the sentence under the Powers of Criminal Courts (Sentencing) Act 2000 s.155. The Crown's s.155 application was ultimately reconsidered by the same judge outside the 56-day time limit and in the light of new information that the victim had known N and that she had been deliberately targeted. N was re-sentenced to the extended sentence of 11 years' imprisonment, comprising a seven-year custodial term and a licence period of four years.

Held: Judgment accordingly. (1) There had been no power to extend the 56-day time limit, either under s.155 or the Criminal Procedure Rules 2014 r.42.4, so that all that had flowed afterwards had been undertaken without jurisdiction. It followed that the sentence in fact imposed on N remained that initially passed, namely four years and four months' imprisonment (see para.8 of judgment). (2) The starting point taken by the judge must have been too low. It could not have been less than between seven-and-a-half and eight years prior to mitigation for the guilty plea and the other elements of the case. The sentence in relation to the assault offence could not have been less than four-and-a-half years, which itself would have permitted the imposition of an extended sentence. In those circumstances, the sentence was unduly lenient (para.32). (3) Once the court had decided that a sentence had been unduly lenient based on the facts as known to the sentencing judge at the time, it was the appellate court's responsibility to pass the appropriate sentence. In doing so, it was at the very least open to it to take into account whatever new information was available. The court had to proceed on the up-to-date information that had become apparent after the initial sentence had been imposed, including that N and the victim had known one another. The additional material made it abundantly clear that, in misleading the court as he had, N was not demonstrating the true remorse the judge had initially accepted that he did. The only proper assessment was that he was a dangerous offender presenting a significant risk of committing further specified offences. The judge had assessed the appropriate sentence as being one of seven years' imprisonment. Having regard to all that had happened since the original sentencing, it was not appropriate to increase the sentence beyond that which had subsequently been wrongly imposed by the judge. The appropriate course was to quash the sentence of four years and four months' imprisonment and to replace it with sentences of seven years' imprisonment with an extension of four years in relation to the assault offence, and two years concurrent in relation to the possession offence (paras 14, 40, 42-43).

ATTORNEY GENERAL'S REFERENCE (NO.79 OF 2015) *sub nom.* R. v NGUYEN (HONG), [2016] EWCA Crim 448, [2016] 4 W.L.R. 99, Sir Brian Leveson PQBD, CA (Crim Div).

1890 Hospital orders–Restriction orders–Psychiatric advice that restriction order unnecessary

[Mental Health Act 1983 (c.20) s.37, s.41]

The appellant (D) appealed against a hospital order with restrictions imposed pursuant to the Mental Health Act 1983 s.37 and s.41. D had been committing offences since she was 17. She had committed an offence of wounding in 2011 when she had struck a passer-by in the face with a brick. By the time that sentencing for that offence took place a year-and-a-half later, she had committed and been dealt with for various other offences. The sentencing judge decided that D did not appear to have symptoms of psychosis and passed a three-year community order. Within weeks of that order, D committed various offences, including possession of an offensive weapon, namely a seven-inch kitchen knife. The medical opinion of the two psychiatrists instructed was that the appropriate sentence was a s.37 hospital order, on the basis that D had been suffering from a severe and enduring psychotic illness for several years. The judge decided that, additionally, there should be a s.41 restriction order. He concluded that, notwithstanding that one of the psychiatrists thought that a s.41 order was unnecessary because D was responding to treatment and there had been no incidents or difficulties within the previous three months, it was necessary for the public's protection to make such an order. D submitted that, in making the s.41 order, the judge had relied on the incorrect understanding that only one psychiatrist had thought that such an order was unnecessary, when in fact both of the psychiatrists had taken such a view. Since the judge's decision, a third psychiatrist had prepared a report opining that a s.41 order was unnecessary in D's case.

Held: Appeal allowed. At the time of the instant hearing, it had been about a year since D had started to make progress under her medication and treatment. All three psychiatrists had concluded that a s.41 restriction order was unnecessary. In the light of all the material and notwithstanding the judge's concerns, the addition of a s.41 order had been unnecessary. It was appropriate to remove it, leaving the s.37 hospital order in place alone (see para.15 of judgment).

R. v DANIELS (JADE LOUISE), [2014] EWCA Crim 2009, [2015] M.H.L.R. 91, Wyn Williams J, CA (Crim Div).

1891 Immigration offences–Possession of articles for use in fraud–Conspiracy to facilitate breach of immigration law–Undue leniency

The Solicitor General referred to the court as unduly lenient respective custodial sentences of five years and two-and-a-half years imposed on two offenders (B and H) convicted of conspiracy to facilitate the commission of a breach of immigration law by non-EU citizens; B was also convicted of possession of articles for use in fraud. For approximately a year, B had recruited non-EU students seeking post-study work visas to attend lectures at the college where he worked or a university with which the college had links; the students paid him course fees and received false certificates for use in their visa applications. Some were deported as a result, including some who genuinely believed they had completed a university or college course. B possessed false university acceptance letters, certificates and visa letters. H, an external examiner at the university, had handed out the fraudulent certificates. In sentencing, the recorder assessed the value of the fraud at around £300,000. She found that B had acted in a leading role, and H's role in providing the required legitimacy was no less important. The Solicitor General argued that the recorder had imposed sentences that were lenient even under the guidelines for offences of fraud, despite the limited relevance of those guidelines and the additional aggravating feature of the dire consequences for several innocent victims.

Held: Reference allowed. The recorder had turned first to the guidelines and then to the authorities; however, the guidelines were of secondary assistance in such cases.

The offences were designed to circumvent the immigration rules, which was a matter of grave public concern, *Attorney General's Reference (No.28 of 2014)* [2014] EWCA Crim 1723 considered. That was the gravamen of the case, not the profit margin or the fraudulent behaviour. The cynical and callous disregard for UK immigration law and the determination to circumvent it over a period of months were central to sentencing; also relevant was the acute human misery visited on the victims who were dedicated to educational advancement. The authorities provided a helpful guide for the appropriate range, *R. v Kao (Junjie)* [2010] EWCA Crim 2617, [2011] 2 Cr. App. R. (S.) 4, [2011] C.L.Y. 2907 and *R. v Olivieira (Milusca Theresita)* [2012] EWCA Crim 2279, [2013] 2 Cr. App. R. (S.) 4, [2013] C.L.Y. 2674 considered. Both sentences were unduly lenient. B's sentence was increased to eight years, and H's was increased to five years (see paras 24, 29-30 of judgment).

ATTORNEY GENERAL'S REFERENCE (NOS 49 AND 50 OF 2015) *sub nom.* R. v HOWARD (JOHN); R. v BAKHT (KENAN), [2015] EWCA Crim 1402, [2016] 1 Cr. App. R. (S.) 4, Rafferty LJ, CA (Crim Div).

1892 Imprisonment for public protection–Appeals against sentence–Whether sentences imposed in accordance with Criminal Justice Act 2003

[Criminal Justice Act 2003 (c.44)]

Thirteen offenders applied for extensions of time in which to apply for leave to appeal against sentences of imprisonment or detention for public protection which had been imposed between 2005 and 2008 under the Criminal Justice Act 2003. All the applicants had been either detained in custody long after the expiry of the relevant minimum term or recalled to prison for breach of their licences. Some were very young when their sentences were imposed. The applicants argued that the imposition of the sentences was not justified by the statutory criteria in the 2003 Act as explained by the court's case law.

Held: Applications refused. In all 13 cases, the sentencing judge had correctly applied the law and passed a sentence in accordance with the 2003 Act as interpreted in the decisions of this court. If similar applications were brought in the future and the judge had done that, the instant court would refuse an extension of time without more, unless clear new points were raised. The instant court was a court of review: its function was to review sentences imposed by courts at first instance, not to conduct a sentencing exercise of its own from the beginning. The review of sentences in the light of events occurring long after the original sentence was a matter for the Parole Board or, if a change was required for the regime for release, for the Executive and Parliament. As the principles on which the instant court exercised its jurisdiction were clear and as the judges had passed sentences faithfully and properly following the clear terms of the 2003 Act, it was not permissible to set aside the sentences imposed. The court was mindful of the substantial criticism that years after the expiry of minimum terms, some of a very short period, many of those sentenced to imprisonment or detention for public protection remained in custody or had been recalled to custody for breach of their licence conditions. There was some evidence that the effect of long periods of imprisonment or the recall to prison of those sentenced to imprisonment or detention for public protection under their licence requirements might be either impeding their rehabilitation or increasing the risk they posed. However, it was Parliament which had legislated to establish a regime of sentences of imprisonment or detention for public protection in terms which the courts had faithfully and properly applied. In our democracy and in accordance with the rule of law, it had to be for Parliament to correct that problem (see paras 19, 21, 41-45, 47 of judgment).

R. v ROBERTS (MARK); R. v DOWE; R. v WAKELING; R. v BYRNE; R. v DIVENEY; R. v FAY; R. v WARWICK; R. v GARBUTT; R. v POWNEY; R. v GITTENS; R. v WOODWARD; R. v QUAGLIA; R. v PRECADO, [2016] EWCA Crim 71, [2016] 1 W.L.R. 3249, Lord Thomas LCJ, CA (Crim Div).

1893 Imprisonment for public protection–Grievous bodily harm–Offender suffering from undiagnosed serious mental illness at time of offending–Appropriateness of hybrid sentence under s.45A Mental Health Act 1983

[Mental Health Act 1983 (c.20) s.37, s.41, s.45A]

The appellant (F) appealed against a sentence imposed for offences of kidnapping and causing grievous bodily harm with intent comprising imprisonment for public protection with a minimum term of eight years, together with hospital and limitation directions made pursuant to the Mental Health Act 1983 s.45A and s.41. F had also been sentenced for related offences of inflicting grievous bodily harm, assault occasioning actual bodily harm, burglary, dangerous driving and aggravated vehicle taking. F had forcibly taken control of a car belonging to his girlfriend (L), and driven it at speed into a forest, where he had punched and kicked L and another passenger (E), inflicting life threatening injuries to L, including severe brain damage, and serious injuries to E. F drove off, leaving E and L in the forest, and crashed the car. He then walked to a residential property, entered the occupants' bedroom and demanded car keys. He was arrested shortly afterwards. A breath analysis revealed alcohol in his system. Subsequent psychiatric reports indicated that at the time of the offending F had been suffering from undiagnosed paranoid schizophrenia and experiencing auditory hallucinations commanding him to harm L. F was convicted of causing grievous bodily harm with intent and burglary, having pleaded guilty to the other offences. He had some old previous convictions for violence. A further psychiatric report stated that F's volatility and inability to control his anger placed him at risk of committing further acts of violence, which risk was likely to increase if he became severely psychotic and did not receive proper care and treatment. It also indicated that if F absconded he would represent a high risk, particularly towards the victims of his offending. By the time of sentence, medical opinion was that F's illness had become treatment resistant. He had been prescribed the only available anti-psychotic drug for treatment resistant schizophrenia, and required close medical supervision for its continued use. The medical expert witnesses were unanimous in recommending a hospital order under s.37 of the 1983 Act, together with a s.41 restriction order for the protection of the public. Two medical experts expressed the view that if F was transferred to prison in the future, there would be a high risk of relapse. F argued that (1) in light of his psychiatric condition and in view of the medical evidence and opinion, imprisonment for public protection was wrong in principle and manifestly excessive; (2) the minimum term was also manifestly excessive.

Held: Appeal dismissed. (1) Imprisonment had not been wrong in principle, and in the circumstances it would be wrong to interfere with the judge's finding that imprisonment for public protection was justified, *R. v Drew (Anthony James)* [2003] UKHL 25, [2003] 1 W.L.R. 1213, [2003] C.L.Y. 3773, *R. v Staines (Paula)* [2006] EWCA Crim 15, [2006] 2 Cr. App. R. (S.) 61, [2006] C.L.Y. 3777 and *R. v Cooper (Benjamin Alan)* [2010] EWCA Crim 2335, [2010] M.H.L.R. 240, [2011] C.L.Y. 2928 applied. It was quintessentially a matter for his judgment in light of the evidence and counsel's submissions. When passing sentence, the judge had clearly taken into account that at the relevant time F was suffering from a serious undiagnosed mental illness. However, whilst that was an important factor in deciding sentence, it was not the only factor. Criminal culpability had clearly not been wholly absent. Through the jury's guilty verdicts, it was implicitly accepted that F's will had not entirely been overborne by the voices in his mind, and the consequences of the violence that he had unleashed were very serious. Whilst the judge had not precisely quantified the degree of culpability attributed to F, upon reading the sentencing remarks as a whole in the context of the circumstances, he had clearly found that F's culpability was significant enough to justify a hybrid sentence under s.45A. Moreover, the instant case was a paradigm example of the kind of case that Parliament had had in mind as being suitable for a hybrid order. F's argument that the sentence would engender a vicious cycle of F being moved backwards and forwards between hospital and prison, and that therefore the s.45A disposal was inappropriate, was rejected. There was no material distinction between the circumstances of the instant case and those in *Cooper*, in which the court had stated that it had no basis for concluding that ways could not and would not be devised for the appellant to demonstrate that he did not pose a risk to the public, *Cooper* considered. The degree of harm and the significant risk to the public of serious harm being caused by F's future commission of specified offences were such that a custodial sentence was required in the public interest (see paras 48, 50-52, 62-65 of judgment). (2) The judge had concluded that the appropriate degree of punishment called for a minimum term of eight years, meaning that was the minimum term he was entitled to impose. It would have been wrong to reduce the minimum term to allow for the possibility of F's recovery in a shorter time. That did not mean that F's mental illness was not a mitigating factor in the overall sentencing exercise; plainly it was, and there was no reason to think that the judge had left it out of account (para.67).

R. v FOX (WAYNE ANTHONY), [2011] EWCA Crim 3299, [2015] M.H.L.R. 12, Davis LJ, CA (Crim Div).

1894 Indecent photographs of children–Sentencing guidelines–Late guilty plea to distribution of indecent photograph of a child

The appellant (B), who had pleaded guilty on the day of his trial to distributing an indecent photograph of a child, appealed against his sentence of 16 months' imprisonment. Using a false name, B had made contact over the internet with a 17-year-old youth (J). Because of his autism, J functioned as a 12-year-old. During the internet conversations, B showed J what B made out was a live sex scene; it was in fact a video which showed an adult male engaging in sexual activity with a female child. B invited J to show the female child his penis, but J refused. The offence came to light a few days later when J's father came across the internet conversations.

Held: Appeal dismissed. (1) It was agreed that the sexual activity in the video involved non-penetrative sex. It followed that the case fell within category B of the relevant sentencing guideline. That yielded a starting point of one year's custody with a range going from 26 weeks to two years. The sentencing judge must have taken as his starting point a term of about 18 months. That was justified. This was not just the distribution of an image. It was distribution for a particular purpose. B's aim had been to engage J in sexual activity. B was entitled to no more than a 10% credit for his late plea. The end result was a severe sentence but not one that was manifestly excessive (see paras 6, 9, 11 of judgment). (2) B had also been made subject to a sexual harm prevention order. The question for the judge was whether such an order was necessary for the purpose of protecting the public, or any particular members of the public, from sexual harm. The requirement of necessity should not be diluted, but this was not just a case of simple distribution: it was distribution to a young person, a stranger, for a particular purpose, namely to entice him to expose his penis. There was ample evidence to satisfy the requirement of necessity (paras 13, 15).

R. v BINGHAM (DEAN), [2015] EWCA Crim 1342, [2016] 1 Cr. App. R. (S.) 3, Macur LJ, CA (Crim Div).

1895 Indecent photographs of children–Sentencing guidelines–Making and possessing vast quantities of indecent and prohibited images of children

The appellant (N), who had pleaded guilty to making indecent photographs of children, possessing such photographs and possessing prohibited images of children, appealed against his sentence of five years' imprisonment. Police officers had executed a search warrant at N's home as a result of information they had received that a computer at that address had accessed indecent images of children. There were 4.2 million images in all, downloaded over two years. Over 1.1 million were capable of being graded according to established criteria. Of those, 10,000 images were actually graded. Five thousand were in Category A (the most serious category involving penetrative sexual activity), 643 were in Category B and 2009 were in Category C. In addition, there were 60 prohibited images. There were also 463 Category B and 1,000 Category C moving images and 27 prohibited moving images. N was 64. He had one previous conviction for showing or distributing an indecent photograph or pseudo-photograph of a child. When imposing the five-year sentence, the sentencing judge gave N credit for the candour and remorse he had shown, his early guilty plea and the assistance he had given to the police.

Held: Appeal allowed. The definitive guideline for the instant offences characterised offending according to the nature of the images. The judge was fully entitled to treat the offences as involving a very large number of images in Category A, as there was a vast amount of images of penetrative sexual activity. The judge was also right to treat the offending as involving possession rather than distribution or production. On that basis, as he recognised, the guidelines indicated a starting point of 12 months and a range of 26 weeks to three years. The judge's starting point must have been more than seven-

and-a-half years, as he had acknowledged other features of the mitigation, such as N's candour and contrition, before he gave full credit for the guilty plea. The reason why the judge took the starting point he did was the quantity of still and moving images, particularly of those in the most serious category. While the judge was fully entitled to treat the sheer quantity of the images as taking the offending outside the range in the definitive guideline, the offending did not justify a starting point in the order of seven-and-a-half to eight years. That sort of starting point should usually be reserved for those who were involved in the production of such images. The appropriate starting point was four years. Giving N maximum credit for his plea, a term of two years and eight months' imprisonment would be substituted for the five-year sentence (see paras 11-14 of judgment).

R. v NESTOROS (COSTOS), [2015] EWCA Crim 1424, [2016] 1 Cr. App. R. (S.) 5, Simon J, CA (Crim Div).

1896 Life imprisonment–Mental disorder–Treatability of condition–Effect on sentence of fresh psychiatric evidence

[Mental Health Act 1983 (c.20) s.37, s.41, s.47, s.49; Criminal Appeal Act 1968 (c.19) s.23]

The appellant (E) appealed against a sentence of life imprisonment imposed following her guilty plea to an offence of arson being reckless as to whether life was endangered. E had suffered psychiatric illness in her youth. At 13 she began a long period of overdoses, self-harm, depression and admission to hospital. She spent nine months in a psychiatric unit. In 1998, when she was in a rehabilitation centre for people with mental health issues, she set fire to two baskets in the laundry room. The fire did not spread beyond the laundry room and there was no injury. E admitted the offence in interview. She had four previous convictions for nine offences between 1995 and 1998, principally damage to property, and on no occasion had she lost her liberty. Psychiatric reports concluded that she had an untreatable psychopathic disorder. In sentencing her, the judge took account of her age, 21 at the date of sentence, convictions, that she was an untreatable psychopath and reminded himself of the psychiatric reports. He determined that there was a high risk of further serious offences. After sentencing, E was transferred under the provisions of the Mental Health Act 1983 s.47 and s.49 from prison to hospital. Her responsible clinician (S) concluded that there was evidence for a diagnosis of emotionally unstable personality disorder, but that in 1998, at sentence, there would have been available a body of respectable medical opinion that E was treatable. E submitted that the discretionary life sentence was wrong in principle. She contended that the medical evidence at sentence, that her condition was not treatable, was wrong, and that S's evidence should be received as fresh evidence. She argued for the substitution of a disposition under s.37 and s.41.

Held: Appeal allowed. S's evidence passed the tests for the admissibility of fresh expert evidence, pursuant to the Criminal Appeal Act 1968 s.23. Medical science and research had moved on, and what at sentence might have been seen as not amenable to treatment could now be seen as amenable. S opined that only four years after the imposition of sentence it was plain that treatment was available and was already achieving some success. He made the point that E's response to treatment had been what he would have expected, a gradual and purposeful move toward significant engagement with therapists and with the regime offered. Her progress after treatment had led to a significant reduction of the risk she posed (see paras13-17 of judgment). Had the judge been informed that E was treatable, it was overwhelmingly likely that he would have imposed orders under s.37 and s.41, *R. v De Silva (Charles)* (1994) 15 Cr. App. R. (S.) 296, *R. v Roden (Jason)* [2006] EWCA Crim 1121 and *R. v Beatty (David William)* [2006] EWCA Crim 2359, (2006) 92 B.M.L.R. 22, [2007] C.L.Y. 3626 considered. The term of life imprisonment was quashed and orders under s.37 and s.41 were substituted (paras 20-23).

R. v EVANS (JAIMIE ANGELA), [2013] EWCA Crim 1193, [2014] M.H.L.R. 285, Rafferty LJ, CA (Crim Div).

1897 **Manslaughter–Diminished responsibility–Appropriateness of life sentence for mentally disordered offender's killing of parents**

[Mental Health Act 1983 (c.20) s.41, s.45A]

An offender (D) applied for permission to appeal against a minimum term of 19 years and 73 days imposed in respect of a sentence of life imprisonment following his guilty pleas to two counts of manslaughter on the grounds of diminished responsibility. A hospital and limitation direction was also made under the Mental Health Act 1983 s.45A for D to be transferred to a secure hospital and to be subject to special restrictions under s.41. D had killed his parents in a knife attack after smoking cannabis and taking amphetamines. He was charged with murder. The psychiatric evidence was that the criteria for a defence of diminished responsibility were met; that D was dangerous; and that he suffered from a mental disorder which made hospital detention appropriate. He had been hospitalised under the Act four years earlier after having had an acute transient psychotic episode and had been regularly monitored since then. The judge concluded that D's culpability was significant, notwithstanding his diminished responsibility. He stated that D had known that his mental illness caused a serious danger to others, particularly his parents; that he knew his condition was adversely affected by his drug use; and that he had been aware that his mental health was deteriorating but had continued to take drugs and concealed that fact from the community psychiatric nurse. The judge further stated that had it been a double murder without mental illness the starting point would have been increased because of the aggravating features, which included a clear intention to kill both victims, the significant degree of premeditation and the fact that it was a particularly savage and sustained attack. D submitted that the judge had erred in (1) taking as a starting point the appropriate sentence relating to two victims, as it had been one attack and he had treated his victims as one entity; (2) making insufficient allowance for his diminished responsibility; (3) increasing the minimum term to reflect the risk he posed to the public; (4) giving insufficient credit for his guilty pleas.

Held: Application refused. (1) The serious aggravating factor of more than one killing with an intention to kill had an impact on sentence. Where there were two deaths, culpability was likely to be significantly higher. In the instant case, the level of residual responsibility was significant, *Attorney General's Reference (No.34 of 2014)* [2014] EWCA Crim 1394, [2014] 2 Cr. App. R. (S.) 84, [2015] C.L.Y. 2239 applied, *R. v Dighton (Daniel)* [2011] EWCA Crim 1372, [2012] 1 Cr. App. R. (S.) 30, [2012] C.L.Y. 2943 considered (see para.22 of judgment). (2) The medical evidence did not establish that D's drug misuse was the consequence, as opposed to the cause, of his mental illness. The majority medical opinion was that D's mental problems were drug induced and that he was aware of the effect on his mental health of taking drugs and the danger he posed, yet continued to take them. It was therefore open to the judge to find that the level of responsibility required a discount of one fifth as opposed to one third (para.23). (3) The suggestion that the minimum term had been increased to reflect the fact that D was dangerous was based on a misunderstanding of the judge's sentencing remarks. He had set out his assessment of the risk D posed to explain the imposition of a life sentence and the making of the s.45 order with restrictions. He did not wrongly inflate the length of the minimum term to protect the public (para.24). (4) It had been open to the judge to reduce the amount of credit given to D because of the overwhelming case against him. No complaint could legitimately be made of the minimum term imposed. The offences were extremely serious and the judge had conducted an impeccable sentencing exercise (paras 25-28).

R. v DANTES (KAMIL), [2016] EWCA Crim 733, [2016] 2 Cr. App. R. (S.) 25, Hallett LJ, CA (Crim Div).

1898 **Manslaughter–Diminished responsibility–Appropriateness of sentence of life imprisonment**

[Mental Health Act 1983 (c.20) s.41, s.45A(3); Criminal Justice Act 2003 (c.44) Pt 12 s.225(1)(b), Pt 12 s.225(2)]

The appellant (G) appealed against a sentence of life imprisonment imposed on him following his guilty plea to manslaughter on the basis of diminished responsibility. The trial judge had sight of reports from three psychiatrists. In sentencing, he noted that, although G's mental illness was a significant contributory factor in causing him to act as he did, there were elements of rationality in his behaviour at the time of the killing such that the abnormality of mental functioning did not literally overwhelm him. The judge stated that he had taken account of the requirement for public confidence in his sentencing decision, and the appreciation of the different release regimes which applied to indeterminate sentences. He considered that the appropriate sentence was one of life imprisonment with a minimum term of seven-and-a-half years and made directions under the Mental Health Act 1983 s.45A(3). In his sentencing remarks, the judge had not expressly determined that G was a dangerous offender under the Criminal Justice Act 2003 Pt 12 s.225(1)(b), neither had he made any express reference to s.225(2) nor stated that the minimum term took into account G's guilty plea. The single ground of appeal initially relied on was that the judge was wrong to have imposed an indeterminate sentence of imprisonment, rather than a hospital order with restrictions under s.37 and s.41 of the Act. However, on appeal G accepted that a finding of dangerousness was an inevitable conclusion and he did not challenge the minimum term. G submitted that since the psychiatrists were of the opinion that the appropriate sentence was a hospital order with restrictions, there was insufficient justification for the imposition of a sentence of life imprisonment, and the lack of express reference by the judge to s.225(2) underlined that the correct sentence was a hospital order with restrictions.

Held: Appeal allowed. (1) At one time the general approach to the sentencing of those suffering from mental disorder, where it was recommended by the psychiatrist, was the making of a hospital order with, if necessary, a restriction order under s.41. However, more recently there had been a general movement away from that approach as a result of a greater understanding of the need to take into account wider factors including both the culpability of the offender and the need to adequately protect the public from future harm, *R. v Vowles (Lucinda)* [2015] EWCA Crim 45, [2015] 1 W.L.R. 5131, [2015] C.L.Y. 2234 followed and *R. v Birch (Beulah)* (1990) 90 Cr. App. R. 78, [1991] C.L.Y. 1136 applied. *Vowles* provided general guidance as to the approach which should be taken to the sentencing of individuals suffering from mental disorders (see paras 16-20 of judgment). (2) Prior to the instant offence, G had no previous convictions, nor was there any other evidence of a violent or aggressive personality. However, it was not a case in which G's culpability had been entirely extinguished by his mental disorder, such as would have been the case with a finding of insanity. Rather it was one in which aspects of his mental responsibility had been impaired, albeit substantially. G retained some significant elements of rationality and, as the circumstances of the offence reflected, he retained a significant degree of culpability for the killing. There was nothing wrong in principle with the sentence imposed. G had conceded that he fulfilled the criteria for being considered dangerous. Although the judge did not express the sentence as being passed under s.225(2), it was implicit that it was and the length of the minimum term properly reflected G's culpability and his guilty plea. However, when imposing a minimum term the judge failed to order that the period which G had spent on remand should be deducted from the term. Therefore, to that extent only, the minimum term would be expressed to be seven years and six months less 218 days on remand (paras 21-24).

R. v GRACIANO (FAUSTO), [2015] EWCA Crim 980, [2016] M.H.L.R. 104, Macur LJ, CA (Crim Div).

1899 Manslaughter–Discretionary life imprisonment–Compatibility of minimum term with art.7 ECHR

[European Convention on Human Rights 1950 art.7; Criminal Justice Act 2003 (c.44) Sch.21; Criminal Justice Act 1991 (c.53)]

The appellant (B) appealed against his minimum term of 12 years after being sentenced to life imprisonment following his guilty plea to manslaughter on the grounds of diminished responsibility. At the time of the killing in 2000, B had suffered from psychosis. The victim had gone to B's flat where he had repeatedly struck her with a hammer and stabbed her. He then dismembered and buried her body. In 2014, B confessed to the police. In determining that life imprisonment was appropriate, the recorder had to apply the law as it was in 2000. He then considered whether the minimum term should be calculated with reference to the principles in place in 2000, or the current regime. The judge applied the reasoning in *R. v H* [2011] EWCA Crim 2753, [2012] 1 W.L.R. 1416, [2012] C.L.Y. 3016, where the court, in considering the correct approach towards sentencing historic sex abuse cases, concluded that the sentence should be imposed on the basis of current legislative provisions and practice, while respecting the maximum sentences that applied at the time of commission of the offence. The issue was whether ECHR art.7 had been breached because the recorder should have fixed the minimum term in accordance with the courts' practice in 2000. B submitted that (1) the recorder should have followed *R. v Sullivan (Melvin Terrence)* [2004] EWCA Crim 1762, [2005] 1 Cr. App. R. 3, [2004] C.L.Y. 3401, which had determined that where the court imposed a mandatory life sentence for a murder committed before the commencement of the Criminal Justice Act 2003, it could not impose a minimum term that would be longer than the minimum term imposed at the time that the offence was committed; in 2000 it was likely that he would only have received a minimum term of six years; (2) had he pleaded guilty to murder rather than manslaughter in 2014, he would have received a shorter minimum term, and so the sentence was manifestly excessive.

Held: Appeal dismissed. (1) *R. v Sullivan (Melvin Terrence)* [2004] EWCA Crim 1762, [2005] 1 Cr. App. R. 3, [2004] C.L.Y. 3401 was a case of murder and not manslaughter, *Sullivan* distinguished. The 2003 Act had introduced an entirely new structure for the calculation and imposition of minimum terms which only applied to mandatory life sentences in murder cases. After the abolition of the death penalty for murder, the penalty of life imprisonment changed from being initially a compulsory sentence involving no active judicial consideration, to the statutory regime imposed in the Criminal Justice Act 1991. Even then, there was a clear statutory distinction between the regime for release of mandatory life prisoners and that for discretionary life prisoners. In the 2003 Act Parliament imposed a statutory structure on the judiciary when setting the minimum terms of mandatory life sentences, and judicial discretion had to be exercised lawfully, having regard to the guidance set out in Sch.21, *Sullivan* applied. The judge was bound by statute to follow the guidance. The minimum term in murder cases, authorised by statute, was recognised to potentially impose a penalty greater than would have been imposed prior to the commencement of the 2003 Act, and transitional provisions were brought in by Parliament so as not to breach art.7. However, the calculation of the minimum term in manslaughter cases was entirely an exercise in judicial discretion, and had not been imposed by Parliament, *Sullivan* considered. The word "applicable" in art.7 referred to penalties which the law had authorised the court to impose at the time the offence was committed, and art.7(1) was only infringed if a sentence was imposed which constituted a heavier penalty than that which could have been imposed on the defendant under the law in force at the time he committed the offence, *R. (on the application of Uttley) v Secretary of State for the Home Department* [2004] UKHL 38, [2004] 1 W.L.R. 2278, [2004] C.L.Y. 3428 followed. The sentence for manslaughter that was "applicable" both in 2000 and in 2014 was life imprisonment. The recorder had been correct to follow *R. v H* [2011] EWCA Crim 2753, [2012] 1 W.L.R. 1416, [2012] C.L.Y. 3016, *H* applied. Further, it could be argued that B had chosen to put it out of the authorities' ability to bring him to justice in 2000 by his own actions (see paras 37-41, 43, 46-47, 51, 53 of judgment). (2) The basis of the Crown's acceptance of the diminished responsibility plea was that the psychosis meant that B suffered more than trivial, but less than total diminution of responsibility. If B had pleaded guilty to murder, the highest he could have put his mitigation was that the psychosis was trivial. The guilty plea was more than offset by 14 years of silence, concealment and lies. Thus, the minimum tariff for murder would have exceeded the sentence imposed by the recorder and would have been around 16 years (paras 58-59). family procedure rules

R. v BELL (MARTIN CHRISTOPHER), [2015] EWCA Crim 1426, [2016] 1 W.L.R. 1, Macur LJ, CA (Crim Div).

1900 Manslaughter–Mentally disordered offenders–Effect of new psychiatric evidence on disposal of case

[Mental Health Act 1983 (c.20) s.37, s.41, s.45A, s.47, s.49; Offences Against the Person Act 1861 (c.100) s.20]

An offender (X) appealed against a sentence of life imprisonment imposed following his conviction for manslaughter on the grounds of diminished responsibility. X also applied to adduce further psychiatric evidence. In 2005, he had stabbed a friend three times during an unprovoked attack. The psychiatric evidence at trial was that X was suffering from a severe depressive episode with psychotic symptoms, but that his condition was not of such a nature or degree for him to be detained under the Mental Health Act 1983. The judge found X to be dangerous and imposed the life sentence with a minimum term of three-and-a-half years. In 2011, while in prison, X attacked another prisoner and, following almost a year in hospital under s.47 and s.49 of the 1983 Act, pleaded guilty to wounding contrary to the Offences Against the Person Act 1861 s.20. A hospital order under s.37 and a restriction order under s.41 of the 1983 Act were imposed. The fresh evidence consisted of psychiatric assessments dating from 2012 to 2015. One of the psychiatrists who gave evidence at trial had revisited his 2006 opinion and diagnosis, concluding that X suffered from schizo-affective disorder. X had already served the minimum term of his life sentence.

Held: Application granted, appeal allowed. (1) The judge had correctly concluded on the medical evidence available that an order under the 1983 Act was not open to him. However, the new psychiatric evidence revealed the course of a deteriorating mental condition. X's conduct at the time of the killing was the first manifestation of what had become an enduring and relapsing condition. He had not developed a new or different disorder in prison; the original diagnosis had been proved wrong by the course of his illness over many years. It was necessary in the interests of justice to admit the fresh evidence (see paras 8, 19-23 of judgment). (2) The instant court had the advantage of detailed and cogent evidence of the course of X's illness and the effect of treatment over many years. There was no doubt that X had a mental disorder which required continuing hospital treatment, that he responded to treatment and that it had been successful in controlling his illness. The conditions in s.37(2)(a) were therefore met; the issue was whether an order under s.37, having regard to s.37(2)(b), was the most suitable method of disposal, *R. v Vowles (Lucinda)* [2015] EWCA Crim 45, [2015] 1 W.L.R. 5131, [2015] C.L.Y. 2234 applied. While X's condition was untreated, he had offended or engaged in highly anti-social behaviour in prison. Since receiving appropriate treatment he had not offended, been disruptive or anti-social. Confinement and supervision in hospital, rather than prison, was the context for the change and improvement, and provided effective control of his disorder. That did not mean that he bore no responsibility for the killing, his responsibility was diminished, not eliminated, but meant that his mental health would be the fundamental issue when his release was considered by the Parole Board or the First-tier Tribunal. X's illness was life-long. The seriousness of the 2005 and 2011 offences demonstrated that when his illness was untreated he was very dangerous. Comparing the supervision regimes for release on life licence and conditional discharge under a restriction order, public safety could be better secured on X's eventual release under a restriction order. An order under s.45A directing hospital admission could not be imposed alongside the life sentence, as s.45A had only been in force since 2008 and was not therefore available to the original sentencing court, but would not be the right disposal anyway. Although the medical experts did not expect X's health to deteriorate in the short or medium term, deterioration at some stage was inevitable and it was imperative that he was subject to appropriate expert supervision on release. That was not possible under s.45A. It was therefore appropriate to impose a hospital order and a restriction order (paras 24-36).

R. v AHMED (SABER MOHAMMED), [2016] EWCA Crim 670, [2016] M.H.L.R. 282, Gross LJ, CA (Crim Div).

1901 Mitigation–Personality disorders–Setting of minimum term on mandatory life sentence for murder–Whether lack of remorse, intention to kill and dangerousness aggravating factors–Relevance of anti-social personality disorder as mitigating factor

[Criminal Justice Act 2003 (c.44) Sch.21]

The appellant (M) appealed against the setting of a 24-year minimum term on his mandatory life sentence following his conviction for murder. M, who was 39, had a long history of serious offending, and previous psychiatric and psychological reports indicated that he had a serious anti-social personality disorder as a result of a traumatic childhood and upbringing, manifested in persistent abnormally aggressive and irresponsible behaviour. M had met the victim (W) amongst a group of street drinkers. They left the group and walked together to a loading bay at the back of a supermarket. M then kicked and stamped on W's upper body and head, causing fatal traumatic brain injury. M twice interrupted the attack, once to buy alcohol and cigarettes, before resuming the assault. Finally, M dropped a refrigerator repeatedly on W's head. He then went home, shaved off his distinctive haircut and burned his clothes. When arrested, M initially denied any involvement and claimed amnesia, but he later admitted attacking W because he had mistreated his dog. At his murder trial, M's defence of diminished responsibility was rejected. The judge had a number of new psychiatric and psychological reports from experts instructed by M and the prosecution. M's expert stated that at the time of the offence, M was suffering from an anti-social personality disorder which provided an explanation for his killing of W, that the disorder impaired his ability to form rational judgments and exercise self control, and that it was a significant contributing factor in causing the fatal attack. The prosecution's expert maintained that the disorder was descriptive of M's offending not explanatory. In determining the minimum term for M's mandatory life sentence, the judge took a starting point of 15 years, and then considered the various aggravating and mitigating factors. He rejected M's motive for the murder and found that it was a senseless attack. He concluded that M was dangerous and that whilst the personality disorder had caused him to act compulsively and aggressively, it did not lower his culpability. The judge therefore imposed a 24-year term. M contended that the minimum term was excessive. He submitted that the judge had overstated his culpability and had made insufficient allowance for his personality disorder as a mitigating feature within the Criminal Justice Act 2003 Sch.21. The prosecution argued that the aggravating factors justifying the 24-year term included the sustained and brutal nature of the attack, M's lack of remorse, his dangerousness and his intention to kill W.

Held: Appeal allowed. (1) The aggravating and mitigating factors in Sch.21 of the Act were not an exhaustive list of what the court had to take into account when deciding a minimum term. The brutal nature of the attack on W was an aggravating factor, but others raised by the prosecution were not. The lack of remorse was a result of M's personality disorder and amounted to an absence of mitigation, rather than an aggravating factor. Similarly, whilst the lack of intention to kill could be a mitigating factor, an intention to kill was not an aggravating factor. The finding of dangerousness was not an aggravating factor because it was subsumed by the mandatory imposition of a life sentence, and M would not be released after serving the minimum term if he remained a risk. (2) Given the broad approach to be taken to mitigating factors under Sch.21, personality disorders, in addition to mental disorders, could be relevant as mitigating factors, *R. v McDowell (Thomas)* [2006] EWCA Crim 1836, [2007] 1 Cr. App. R. (S.) 56, [2007] C.L.Y. 3702 and *R. v Levey (Alan Kenneth)* [2012] EWCA Crim 657, [2012] M.H.L.R. 268, [2013] C.L.Y. 2702 applied. On the psychiatric and psychological evidence, M's anti-social personality disorder was potentially relevant as a mitigating factor. The judge had rejected M's reason for attacking W, which left the offence entirely unmotivated. The judge had been wrong to leave the disorder entirely out of account and should have had regard to it as a relevant mitigating factor with some bearing on M's actual offending, even if it had not substantially diminished his responsibility. The 24-year term was, accordingly, too long. It was quashed and replaced with a minimum term of 21 years.

R. v MCFLY (CAMERON LEE), [2013] EWCA Crim 729, [2014] M.H.L.R. 159, Davis LJ, CA (Crim Div).

1902 Murder–Attempts–Appropriateness of life sentence minimum terms imposed on young offenders following joint enterprise knife attack–Undue leniency

[Criminal Justice Act 2003 (c.44) Pt 12 s.225]

The Attorney General referred to the court as unduly lenient sentences which had been imposed on three offenders (D1, D2 and D3). D1, D2 and two other offenders (D4 and D5) sought leave to appeal against their sentences. In the early hours of the morning, a man (V) had gone into a supermarket in order to buy drinks. Inside the shop, he was attacked by D1, D2, D4 and D5. D3, who had driven the others to the area, did not enter the shop. As V went to the till, D1 punched him three times to the head. He was then set upon in a joint attack. D5 drew a knife and plunged it into V's back. D2 punched V. D4 also drew a knife and stabbed V in the lower back area. V staggered towards the entrance to the supermarket and fell to the ground. D4, D5 and D2 continued to attack him, with D2 kicking him. D5 then repeatedly stabbed him in the stomach area, while D4 repeatedly stabbed into the areas of the stomach and chest. D2 left the shop. Eventually D1 managed to drag D4 away from the victim. V sustained life-changing injuries and survived the attack only because of the skill and speed of the emergency services. D1, D2, D4 and D5 were all convicted of attempted murder following a trial. D3 was convicted of wounding with intent. The following sentences were imposed: D1, life imprisonment with a minimum term of 10 years; D2, youth custody for life with a minimum term of seven-and-a-half years; D3, 10 years' imprisonment; D4, youth custody for life with a minimum term of 15 years; D5, youth custody for life with a minimum term of 13 years and six months. All but D3 were now aged 19 or 20. D3 was 27. D1, D2, D4 and D5 all had several previous convictions.

Held: Judgment accordingly. It would not be appropriate to interfere with any of the sentences, even though D2's sentence was lenient. In a multi-handed case such as this, considerable weight would be given to the view taken by the judge, who had the benefit of trying the case. With a complex sentencing exercise involving a number of defendants, the judge would have formed a picture of their relative roles and responsibility. That picture, at least unless displaced, would be better than anything available to an appellate court. The sentencing judge had adopted a discernible, logical and coherent sentencing approach. On the jury's verdict, while all five offenders were party to a joint enterprise involving the use of knives, the intent to kill must have been formed by D1, D2, D4 and D5 after leaving the car, hence the verdict on D3. As between D1, D2, D4 and D5, D4 and D5 stabbed the victim. The judge was entitled to find that D4 was the leader and hence to distinguish between him and D5. As to D1 and D2, D1 began the attack and D2 joined in. There should be no minimising the gravity of their offending but it did not involve actual stabbing. The actual use of the knives was sufficient to justify differentiating between D4 and D5, on the one hand, and D1 and D2, on the other. As between D1 and D2, D1 was more heavily convicted and he began the attack. In addition, D2 left before he did. A life sentence was one of last resort, and a pause for reflection was required when passing a life sentence on a young offender. However, the life sentences passed on D1, D2, D4 and D5 were fully justified. CCTV footage of the attack showed that the judge was entitled to conclude that the "seriousness" condition in the Criminal Justice Act 2003 s.225 was satisfied. There was no telling when the offenders would cease to pose a danger to the public, not least because no truthful explanation for the attack on V had ever been proffered. However, the minimum terms set in the cases of D1, D2, D4 and D5 would be reduced to take into account the time they had spent on remand (see paras 48, 51-54, 57 of judgment).

R. v SHAIF (SAAD ABDEEQ); R. v MOHAMED (MOHAMED ISHMAIL); R. v IBRAHIM (ZACKIRYA); R. v MOHAMED (HANAD); R. v MOHAMED (ABDI WAHAM) *sub nom.* ATTORNEY GENERAL'S REFERENCE (NOS 22, 23 AND 24 OF 2016), [2015] EWCA Crim 575, [2016] 2 Cr. App. R. (S.) 22, Gross LJ, CA (Crim Div).

1903 Murder–Attempts–Imposition of hospital order with limitation direction–Undue leniency

The Attorney General referred to the court as unduly lenient a sentence of 14 years' imprisonment with a hospital order and limitation direction imposed on an offender (W) who had pleaded guilty to attempted murder. The victim (V) was a friend of tenants living in the same flats as (W) needed somewhere to live. W's landlord suggested, without consulting W, that he move into the spare room in his flat. V was openly gay and often wore women's clothes and make-up. A few weeks before V moved in W had been heard making homophobic remarks. W helped V to move in and a witness said they had been getting on well together. On the first night after V moved in, W struck him on the head with a claw hammer while he was asleep, causing serious and lasting injuries. W telephoned the emergency services reporting that there was a dead man, whom he did not know, in his flat. He said that he had killed him and that his own mental health had deteriorated. The judge formed the view that W's mental health was a contributing factor, but not the sole factor, to the offence. Applying the sentencing guidelines the judge said that the offence was aggravated by an element of hostility to V due to his sexual orientation and V's vulnerability as he had been asleep at the time of the attack. He put the offence in the second level of seriousness and chose the highest of the three ranges in that level. He took a starting point of 20 years and reduced that to 14 because of W's mental health, young age and lack of relevant previous convictions. The Attorney General argued that the sentence was unduly lenient because the offence feel in the highest level with a range of 17-25 years, it did not adequately reflect the aggravating features, and that there could be residual dangerousness when W was released from hospital which required an extended or life sentence to protect the public.

Held: Appeal allowed. The appropriate range was 17-25 years and the starting point was 20 years after a trial. The judge was not at fault for reducing the sentence by six years from the starting point given the unusual facts of the case that related to W's mental health. It was not certain that the offence was motivated by antipathy to V's sexual orientation; it could equally have been the case that W did not want to share his flat with anyone. As the judge considered that W's dangerousness was not confined to his mental illness, he should have passed an extended sentence to protect the public in the event that the criteria for the hospital order and restrictions were no longer satisfied, but the offender remained a risk to the public. An extended period of five years was added to the 14-year sentence. The hospital direction with restrictions remained unchanged.

ATTORNEY GENERAL'S REFERENCE (NO.91 OF 2014) *sub nom.* R. v WILLIAMS (JOSEPH), [2014] EWCA Crim 2891, [2015] M.H.L.R. 518, Fulford LJ, CA (Crim Div).

1904 Murder–Minimum term–Murder, kidnap, false imprisonment and conspiracy to supply class A drugs–Undue leniency

The Attorney General referred to the court as unduly lenient a life sentence with a minimum term of 16 years, following the offender's (D) convictions for murder, kidnap, false imprisonment and conspiracy to supply class A drugs. D had pleaded guilty on the first day of the trial to conspiracy to supply class A drugs. The deceased had been a drug addict. He and another man (S) were recruited by D and another (P) to sell drugs on their behalf. Instead of selling the drugs, S and the deceased took them themselves. When they discovered this, P and D detained S in a flat until he could settle the debt. When it became apparent that S could not do so, P produced a sawn off shotgun and a knife and threatened to kill him and the deceased. P then decided to kill the deceased in order to teach S a lesson. So they kidnapped the deceased and took him and S to a secluded area. Both men were forced to kneel down. The deceased resisted and was P shot him point blank range in the upper thigh. D followed this by punching the deceased in the face. The deceased fell down a steep bank into a river, where his body was discovered the following day. S was released. P was convicted and sentenced to life imprisonment with a minimum term of 32 years. D was 22 years old and had convictions for drugs and firearms offences. In sentencing him the judge gave weight to the following mitigating factors: D's age, the fact that his role was less than P's and his previous convictions were less serious than P's. The Attorney General submitted that the minimum term given by the judge did not give sufficient weight to the seriousness of the murder and gave undue weight to the offender's role as a secondary party and to his age. The Attorney General identified the following among the aggravating factors: the offence was a punishment killing committed using a sawn off shotgun, it was done for financial gain and the gun was not recovered.

Held: Reference allowed. The judge gave too much weight to the mitigating factors and the sentence failed adequately to reflect the aggravating features or the seriousness of the offence. The minimum term was increased to 20 years.

ATTORNEY GENERAL'S REFERENCE (NO.73 OF 2015) *sub nom.* R. v DORE (XAVIER), [2015] EWCA Crim 1803, [2016] 1 Cr. App. R. (S.) 31, Sir Brian Leveson, CA (Crim Div).

1905 Permission to appeal–Loss of time directions–Appropriateness of counsel request for loss of time indication prior to permission application

The applicant (O) applied for permission to appeal against a total sentence of eight years' imprisonment imposed following his guilty pleas to offences of aggravated burglary, assault occasioning actual bodily harm, and having an offensive weapon, and following his conviction after trial for wounding with intent. In sentencing, the judge took a starting point of 12 years' imprisonment which he reduced by one-third on account of O's guilty pleas at the plea and case management hearing. Permission to appeal against sentence was refused on paper; in doing so, the judge indicated that the court should consider making a loss of time order if the application was renewed unsuccessfully. At the instant hearing, when O's counsel stood up to begin his submissions, he invited the court to indicate whether it would be minded to make a loss of time order if his application was ultimately unsuccessful, the implication being that if the court indicated that it was so minded, he would apply to withdraw the permission application in order to avoid the risk of a loss of time order being made. The court refused to give any such assurance.

Held: Application refused. (1) The judge had been right to take a 12-year starting point. The reduction of four years to take account of the plea and other mitigation was very fair in the circumstances. Permission to appeal was refused (see paras 16-17 of judgment). (2) O was only 20 when he pleaded guilty, and therefore he should have been sentenced to detention in a young offender institution. The sentence was corrected in that regard (para.18). (3) (Per curiam) It was for counsel and solicitors advising an applicant to consider the possibility of a loss of time order being made when deciding whether to renew an application for permission to appeal. It was wholly inappropriate to ask the court to indicate whether it would be minded to make a loss of time order in order to decide whether to apply to withdraw the application rather than pursue it. By that time, the vice to which loss of time orders were intended to be directed, namely the pursuit of hopeless applications with the effect that they had on the court's business and other litigants, had already occurred. Once a permission application was before the court, the court would, if necessary, consider making a loss of time order, regardless of whether permission was sought to withdraw the application (para.22).

R. v O'LEARY (PATRICK WILLIAM), [2015] EWCA Crim 1706, [2016] 1 Cr. App. R. (S.) 18, Beatson LJ, CA (Crim Div).

1906 Perverting the course of justice–Deterrence–Deliberate misleading of police over lengthy period of investigation into motoring offence

The appellant (R) appealed against a sentence of 15 months' imprisonment following his guilty plea to an offence of doing acts tending and intended to pervert the course of justice. A car bearing R's number plate had been detected contravening a red light by a camera. The following day R had reported his number plate as stolen. He subsequently sent photographs of his car to the police on request which were found to have been altered with a view to deceiving the police into believing that his car was not the one which had been captured by the red light camera. R later told the police that he had purchased a new number plate. R denied the offence in interview but ultimately pleaded guilty at an adjourned plea and case management hearing. He had a significant number of previous convictions, including for theft and driving offences. In sentencing, the judge took a starting point of 19 months' imprisonment to which he applied a 20% reduction for the guilty plea. R submitted that the judge had taken too high a starting point and had failed to give sufficient credit for the mitigating factors or his guilty plea.

Held: Appeal dismissed. Cases of perverting the course of justice almost inevitably called for custodial sentences. Such offending struck at the heart of the administration of justice and accordingly deterrence was called for. Sometimes the necessary deterrence could be found in the making of an immediate custodial sentence and not one necessarily requiring a term of imprisonment of any great length; all would depend on the circumstances of the particular case. It was also well-established that, amongst other matters to be taken into account, it was ordinarily appropriate to consider the seriousness of the underlying offence, the length of time during which the deception had been continued, the nature of the deception practised, and the success or otherwise of the deception. The deception in the instant case had been swiftly initiated by R, he doubtless appreciated from the camera flash that his car had been detected going through a red light. Thereafter he had deliberately and over a lengthy period of time pursued that deception. He had not only repeated to the police and others that his number plate had been stolen, but had also cunningly and with a degree of preparation submitted a doctored photograph designed to support his case and mislead the police. He had further sought to bolster his story by the purported purchase of a fresh number plate. All such matters, as well as R's previous convictions, plainly distinguished the case from those such as *R. v Burney (Kevin Charles)* [2007] EWCA Crim 1658, [2008] 1 Cr. App. R. (S.) 57, [2008] C.L.Y. 3349, *Burnley* distinguished. While it was true that R had not sought to implicate some other named person, he had clearly sought to say that someone other than himself had been driving the car at the relevant time. In all those circumstances, while the 19-month starting point was very severe, it was not manifestly excessive. The judge had had appropriate regard to the mitigation available. As to the reduction for guilty plea, it was in his discretion to decide how much credit to give, and there was no basis for criticising the 20% figure chosen (see paras 13, 17-22 of judgment).

R. v RATCLIFFE (DEAN ROBERT), [2016] EWCA Crim 27, [2016] 1 Cr. App. R. (S.) 65, Davis LJ, CA (Crim Div).

1907 Perverting the course of justice–Mitigation–Inaccurate references provided to sentencing judge–Undue leniency

The Attorney General referred to the court as unduly lenient a sentence of four months' imprisonment following a conviction for doing acts likely to pervert the course of justice. In 2007 the offender (J) had been convicted of soliciting to murder and public order offences relating to his participation in demonstrations outside the Danish Embassy in London. In 2012 J had pleaded guilty to three offences under the Terrorism Act 2000 s.58 after the police had found documents on his laptop. Those documents had been on his computer when the police seized it in relation to the 2007 offences. J had not looked at the documents since 2007, one had been in Arabic, a language he did not speak, and the documents were available on the internet. J's wife acquired references for the judge who sentenced J for the 2012 terrorism offences. While not totally false, the references were misleading and inaccurate. However, they had not gone to the heart of the judge's sentencing decision and the terrorism offences were not the most serious. The aggravating features were the underlying terrorism offences, the persistent and calculated conduct and the impact that the references had had on his sentence. However, J had amended his ways since 2007, there had been a delay in the case coming to trial and he had a young family and a wife who suffered difficulties. The Attorney General submitted that the gravamen of the offence of perverting the course of justice went to the heart of administration of justice and demanded a deterrent sentence, particularly given the serious nature of the underlying offences.

Held: Reference dismissed. There were no guideline cases or sentencing guidelines for the offence and the circumstances of such cases varied widely. Providing false references was a serious offence and offenders should expect immediate custodial sentences with a deterrent aspect. In the instant offence the culpability was not at the highest level because the references had not been entirely false and bogus and had not gone to the heart of the judge's sentencing decision. The judge had been entitled to make a substantial reduction for the delay and the other mitigation. Taking into account all matters, eight months' imprisonment would have been appropriate after trial. A four-month sentence was lenient, but unduly so. Aside from the references, other material showed that J had changed his ways since 2007. He had a young family, had shown exemplary conduct in prison and was due to be released in three days. No useful purpose would have been served by extending his prison sentence for a few weeks. But it must be understood that immediate custody is expected for those who provide the court with false references.

ATTORNEY GENERAL'S REFERENCE (NO.123 OF 2015) *sub nom.* R. v JAVED (UMRAN), [2016] EWCA Crim 28, [2016] 1 Cr. App. R. (S.) 64, Davis LJ, CA (Crim Div).

1908 **Possession of firearms–Suspended sentences–Short period of possession in attempt to hide evidence from police–Undue leniency**

[Firearms Act 1968 (c.27) s.51A]

The Attorney General referred to the court as unduly lenient a sentence of two years' imprisonment suspended for two years, imposed on the offender (G) following her plea of guilty to possessing a prohibited firearm. G had committed the offence following the arrest of her friend's son for drugs offences. Immediately after the arrest she had gone to the friend's house where she was handed a plastic bag and an item wrapped in a sock. When police officers arrived moments later, they found that the bag contained a quantity of cannabis and the sock contained a small revolver. G was charged with possession of a prohibited firearm and possession of cannabis with intent to supply. She pleaded guilty to the former and was acquitted of the latter. At trial, the judge found that she had not known that there was a gun at the house, and that she had gone there either to warn her friend of the imminent arrival of the police or to help dispose of drug-related items. She sentenced G for the firearms offence on the basis that she had not known that the sock contained a prohibited weapon. G was 54 and had previous convictions for two drugs offences dating from 1992. She was the sole carer for her adult son, who had physical and psychological injuries. She had cancer and had had a colostomy, leaving her with significant functional problems. She also suffered from clinical depression and panic attacks. The judge found that there were exceptional circumstances justifying a departure from the minimum sentence of five years' imprisonment mandated by the Firearms Act 1968 s.51A. She sentenced G to two years' imprisonment suspended for two years, with a 16-hour "structured supervision for women" requirement. The Attorney General identified the following aggravating features: the firearm was real, was in working order and had been intended to facilitate drug dealing, and G had been involved in attempting to hide evidence from the police. In mitigation were G's guilty plea; her lack of recent convictions; her health problems and caring responsibilities; her positive response to the structured supervision order; the fact that she had not known she was handling a firearm; the lack of any evidence that the firearm had been used; and the delay between plea and sentence. The Attorney General submitted that the judge (1) had erred in finding that the circumstances were exceptional; (2) was guilty of an element of double-counting by reducing the sentence to two years and also suspending it.

Held: Reference dismissed. (1) Sentencing G was not straightforward. Parliament intended s.51A to have a deterrent effect, and to that the mandatory minimum term applied even to those in possession of a firearm for just a short time. The courts had to interpret "exceptional circumstances" strictly. Generosity would create the risk of those with unfortunate personal circumstances being recruited by others to move firearms around the country, *R. v Edwards (Michelle Marie)* [2006] EWCA Crim 2833, [2007] 1 Cr. App. R. (S.) 111, [2008] C.L.Y. 3292 considered. G had been on the periphery of the incident and she had acted in a misguided attempt to help her friend. She had been in possession of the gun for a few minutes at most, without knowing what it was, she had powerful personal mitigation and she had pleaded guilty. On the other hand, by going to the house she had taken a chance that she might be involved in clearing it of incriminating items. A holistic approach had to be taken to determining whether the circumstances were exceptional, *R. v Rehman (Zakir)* [2005] EWCA Crim 2056, [2006] 1 Cr. App. R. (S.) 77, [2005] C.L.Y. 3693 applied. Moreover, the appellate court would not interfere with the judge's decision unless it was clearly wrong. In G's case, the judge had not been plainly wrong to find exceptional circumstances; that conclusion was open to her on the basis of the cumulative effect of G's plea, her compelling personal mitigation, and the circumstances of the offence (see paras 25-28 of judgment). (2) The judge might have been guilty of an element of double-counting in reducing the sentence to two years and also suspending it. Those who involved themselves in the possession of firearms had to expect to go to prison. A sentence of two years' immediate imprisonment might have been merciful, but would not have been unduly lenient. However, the two-year suspended sentence was unduly lenient and might have been overturned were it not for the fact that G had spent time on a qualifying curfew entitling her to 223 days credit towards any sentence. That credit, plus the fact that G deserved some credit for her positive response to the supervision requirement, meant that although the sentence was unduly lenient in principle, it would be wrong to interfere with it (paras 29-30).

ATTORNEY GENERAL'S REFERENCE (NO.91 OF 2015) *sub nom.* R. v GOLDEN (CATHERINE MARY), [2015] EWCA Crim 1990, [2016] 1 Cr. App. R. (S.) 43, Hallett LJ, CA (Crim Div).

1909 Possession with intent to supply–Basis of plea–Lack of clarity about whether supply for financial gain

The appellant (B) appealed against a total sentence of three years and nine months' imprisonment imposed after he pleaded guilty to possession of cocaine with intent to supply (count 1) and production of cannabis (count 2). Police had found 21 cannabis plants at B's house. They were in the early stage of growth and had a yield of £12,600. B was searched and a bag of cocaine and five wraps were found. The cocaine weighed 13.61g and had a street value of £890. Scales and plastic bags were also recovered from the house. In his basis of plea, B claimed that he was a regular user of cocaine and that the amount found had been mainly for his own use, he had placed it in bags to ration it out, and he thought that he would probably supply his friends with some on a weekend away. The basis of plea did not refer to count 2. B had 25 previous convictions for 57 offences, one of which was for possession of amphetamine. A pre-sentence report noted that B, aged 50 at the time, had been using drugs since he was 25. He confirmed the account in the basis of plea and claimed that the cannabis was for his own use. The recorder placed count 1 into category three of the relevant sentencing guideline, with B in a significant role. The starting point was four-and-a-half years' custody, with a range of three-and-a-half years to seven years. Credit was given for B's guilty plea, but it was limited to 15 per cent. A sentence of three years and nine months was imposed for count 1, and six months concurrent for count 2. B argued that the judge had failed to give sufficient weight to the basis of plea in respect of count 1, that the quantity of cocaine put the offence just outside category four of the guideline and that he should have been categorised as being in a lesser role.

Held: Appeal allowed. The basis of plea stated that B "would have supplied some of the drugs to a few of my friends on the trip". It did not state whether that supply would have been for financial gain or otherwise. The recorder had failed to question the meaning of the word "supply" in the context of the basis of plea. The starting point for a lesser role in category three was three years' custody with a range of two to four-and-a-half years. The offence was on the borderline of the lesser and significant roles, bearing in mind all the circumstances, in particular the basis of plea and the quantity of drugs recovered. The recorder had taken too high a starting point. It was possible for an offence to straddle more than one category and the characteristics present could fall under different role categories. It had been incumbent on the recorder to make an overall assessment of B's culpability. In circumstances where the meaning of "supply" had not been considered, the correct notional sentence after trial was three-and-a-half years' imprisonment, reduced by 15 per cent to three years for B's guilty plea (see paras 9-13 of judgment).

R. v BAKEWELL (JEFFREY), [2015] EWCA Crim 1807, [2016] 1 Cr. App. R. (S.) 34, Treacy LJ, CA (Crim Div).

1910 Reduction of sentence–Assisting investigations–Assistance given to prosecution in unrelated case

[Serious Organised Crime and Police Act 2005 (c.15) s.73, s.75]

The appellant (E) appealed against a sentence imposed after his guilty plea to dishonesty offences, through a reference from the Criminal Cases Review Commission. E had pleaded guilty to six offences of fraud, and one of making off without payment. He was aged 34 and had convictions for 39 previous offences of dishonesty. He was sentenced to 33 months' imprisonment. However, the sentencing judge was not informed of the assistance he had given to the Crown in a case of attempted rape. E gave evidence for the prosecution twice, once before his sentencing and once afterwards. His evidence of a cell confession by the man accused of attempted rape helped to secure a conviction. However, he had also helped the accused put together a false defence statement. E appealed against his sentence, but again failed to mention the assistance he had given to the prosecution and his appeal was dismissed. He submitted that his sentence should be reduced because of the assistance he gave to the prosecution.

Held: Appeal allowed. (1) The Court of Appeal would always look carefully at any attempts to rely on mitigation arising post sentence. Assistance given to the police or the Crown post sentence would normally be too late. However, there was a public interest in giving credit to those who had given evidence for the Crown in serious cases. Where assistance had been given by an offender but, by some oversight, the judge was ignorant of it, the mitigation which should have been before the Crown Court would be taken into consideration on appeal, *R. v H* [2009] EWCA Crim 2485, [2010] 2 Cr. App. R. (S.) 18, [2011] C.L.Y. 2841 applied (see paras 17, 27 of judgment). (2) The material relied on by E was not all post-sentence since he had already given evidence at the first trial by the time of his sentence. Further, the evidence given at the retrial represented a continuation of that process. To some extent, the situation had arisen from E's own failure to give clear instructions to his solicitors. However, what occurred before the sentencing judge could properly be viewed as the sort of oversight or misadventure referred to in *R v H*. The interests of justice would be served by receiving the evidence relating to the assistance given on both occasions (paras 18, 20). (3) Where assistance was given outside the framework of the Serious Organised Crime and Police Act 2005 s.73 to s.75, the level of credit to be given depended on the facts of the individual case, *R. v P* [2007] EWCA Crim 2290, [2008] 2 All E.R. 684, [2008] C.L.Y. 3356 applied. Important considerations included the quality and value of the assistance given, and whether it brought to justice persons who might not otherwise have been brought to justice. E had given assistance in a serious case, and had contributed to a conviction. The extent of his contribution was limited given that another prisoner also gave evidence of the cell confession, and the victim had given powerful evidence; that should not deprive E of credit, although it affected the overall weight to be attached to it. E's actions in helping the offender create a false defence statement also significantly reduced available credit. However, the court could not say that his evidence had made no difference. If his assistance had been known to the judge at the time of sentence it would have had some, albeit a limited, effect. E's sentence was therefore reduced by three months (paras 21-23, 26-28).

R. v EMSDEN (KEVIN RUSSELL), [2015] EWCA Crim 2092, [2016] 1 Cr. App. R. (S.) 62, Treacy LJ, CA (Crim Div).

1911 Reduction of sentence–Assisting police–Effect of assistance provided after time of sentence

[Serious Organised Crime and Police Act 2005 (c.15) s.73, s.75]

The court was asked to consider reducing the minimum term of the applicant's life sentence for murder. The applicant had been convicted of murder and other serious offences. A number of years later, after the Serious Organised Crime and Police Act 2005 s.73 to s.75 came into force, the police asked him to assist them in matters which had arisen a significant period of time after his conviction. He did so, and his help was significant. Before the coming into force of the 2005 Act, the courts had taken assistance offered to law enforcement authorities into account when sentencing, in accordance with well-established principles as set out in *R. v A* [1999] 1 Cr. App. R. (S.) 52, [1998] C.L.Y. 1267. The scheme under the 2005 Act permitted a sentence to be reduced for assistance given after sentencing. That scheme did not apply to the applicant because he was convicted of an offence for which the sentence was fixed by law, and he did not plead guilty. Thus, the position at common law had to be considered. The applicant submitted that, in the current circumstances and in the light of the decision by Parliament in the 2005 Act to allow a sentence to be reduced on account of assistance provided after sentence, the common law principle should recognise the utilitarian and pragmatic rationale behind the common law. He submitted that it was clear that the principle of reducing sentences for assistance provided did not operate on the basis of remorse: on the contrary it operated on pragmatic considerations that a reduction should be offered whenever it might encourage a person to provide the necessary assistance to the authorities, whether before or after sentence.

Held: Judgment accordingly. In *R. v A,* Lord Bingham made it clear that if a defendant denied guilt but was convicted and sentenced following a contested trial without supplying valuable information before sentence, or expressing willingness to do so, the Court of Appeal would not ordinarily reduce his sentence to take account of information supplied to the authorities after sentence. In *R. v H* [2009] EWCA Crim 2485, [2010] 2 Cr. App. R. (S.) 18, [2011] C.L.Y. 2841, the judge observed that where an offender wished to limit his co-operation, it was normally unrealistic for him to anticipate any reduction in sentence on appeal to the court if he had pleaded not guilty and had not set in motion the process for providing assistance to the authorities by the time of sentencing. Good reasons would be needed before the common law principle, so clearly established, could be changed. The arguments based on utilitarianism and pragmatism had always been present. There was no good reason to depart from established principles, *R. v A* followed, *R. v H* and *R. v A* [2006] EWCA Crim 1803, [2007] 1 Cr. App. R. (S.) 60, [2007] C.L.Y. 3667 considered. There were also two countervailing considerations. First, the instant court would not be acting as a court of review, but rewarding someone for good behaviour during his sentence. Second, experience had shown that some individuals might be motivated to manufacture assistance after conviction in the hope of a reduction in a long sentence. Nothing should be done which might encourage that (see paras 8-20 of judgment).

R. v ZTR, [2015] EWCA Crim 1427, [2016] 1 Cr. App. R. (S.) 15, Lord Thomas LCJ, CA (Crim Div).

1912 Religiously aggravated offences–Harassment–Suspended sentences with rehabilitation activity requirements–Undue leniency

[Crime and Disorder Act 1998 (c.37) s.31(1)]

The Attorney General referred to the court as unduly lenient sentences of six months' imprisonment, suspended for 12 months with a rehabilitation activity requirement, imposed on the offenders (F and R) after they pleaded guilty to religiously aggravated intentional harassment, alarm or distress contrary to the Crime and Disorder Act 1998 s.31(1), and a concurrent two-month suspended sentence imposed on R for assault. The offenders, who were with R's, and a friend's, children, had been in a park drinking alcohol. They saw a married Muslim couple and their two children start to pray nearby. One of the offenders shouted "Not in Plymouth" and they both walked to within 2m of the family and urinated with their backs to them. When the offenders walked away they swore at, and made coarse remarks towards, the family, referring to their religion. A witness confronted them. R became aggressive towards him and pushed him in the chest. She was drunk and slurring her words. Both offenders had previous convictions but neither had been imprisoned. R had long-term alcohol addiction and psychiatric problems. F's pre-sentence report noted that alcohol misuse was linked to the offending behaviour and recommended a 12-month community order with a rehabilitation activity requirement. It referred to her remorse and embarrassment. R's report noted that she had denied any religious or racially offensive behaviour. Following imposition of the sentences, the offenders had engaged positively with probation services and had confronted their alcohol-related problems. The Attorney General argued that given the nature of the offending, which involved serious elements of religious and racial hostility and a lack of respect to the victims, only an immediate custodial sentence would suffice.

Held: Reference dismissed. The offenders' conduct was offensive and disgusting. They were drunk in a public place, accompanied by children of their own and a friend. They deliberately and offensively exposed themselves, making coarse and offensive remarks, and urinated in the presence of the victims. Their conduct and remarks were based on the race and religion of the family whilst they were engaged in the course of prayer. Their conduct was designed to cause maximum offence. The custodial threshold was passed and a deterrent sentence was necessary. However, whether or not to suspend a sentence of imprisonment was a matter of discretion. The offenders' drunken state did not provide mitigation for their actions. Such behaviour when drunk could be revealing of their true underlying attitudes, notwithstanding their protestations that they had no racist feelings. F was lightly convicted. R had a significantly worse record, and clearly had anger management and behavioural problems when drunk. Neither had been imprisoned before or received a custodial sentence. Each had children at home. In deciding to suspend the sentences, the recorder had given weight to the offenders' personal circumstances, their expressions of remorse and shame, and recommendations made in the pre-sentence reports. He had also had regard to the need to assist them both in rehabilitation and in confronting their alcohol and other related problems. He had been entitled to give weight to those matters. While other judges might have imposed an immediate custodial sentence, it did not follow that the recorder was obliged to do so. He had a discretion and exercised it in a way which was open to him. The fact that a judge exercised mercy was not in any way necessarily to be equated with the outcome being unduly lenient (see paras 33-40 of judgment).

ATTORNEY GENERAL'S REFERENCE (NOS 143 AND 144 OF 2015) *sub nom.* R. v FARRELL (CLAIRE); R. v RICHARDSON (NATALIE), [2016] EWCA Crim 21, [2016] 1 Cr. App. R. (S.) 69, Davis LJ, CA (Crim Div).

1913 Restriction orders–Risk–Offender suffering from depressive psychosis when committing offences–Imposition of hospital and restriction orders–Whether appropriate to quash restriction order given offender's good response to treatment

[Mental Health Act 1983 (c.20) s.37, s.41, s.41(1), s.48, s.49]

The appellant (T) appealed against the imposition of a restriction order under the Mental Health Act 1983 s.41 following his guilty plea to three offences of attempting to cause actual bodily harm. T had, on the same day, carried out three random, unprovoked attacks on members of the public. In each case, he had wrapped a cable or belt around the victim's neck. Upon his arrest, there was concern as to his mental health and he was remanded in custody then sent to a secure psychiatric hospital under s.48 and s.49 of the Act. T subsequently pleaded guilty to three counts of attempting to cause actual bodily harm. He was tried but acquitted of attempting to commit grievous bodily harm with intent. In sentencing T, the judge had evidence from T's doctor that he was suffering from depressive psychosis at the time of the offences, but had responded well to medication and his condition was under control. The doctor indicated that a hospital order would be sufficient to reduce the risk of further offending. A detailed antecedent history recording T's extensive record of many instances of domestic violence against his partners since 2002, including a caution and a conviction for common assault, was also provided. The judge considered that T's offences were very serious and potentially dangerous and it was only by good fortune that none of the victims had been significantly harmed. He imposed a hospital order under s.37 and a s.41 restriction order on the basis that, given that the risk of further offending was so great were T to fail to take his medication and relapse, that was also necessary to protect the public. T contended that the progress in his treatment meant that the s.41 order was unnecessary. An up-to-date medical report from T's doctor stated that T had been transferred to a low security mental hospital, that there were no concerns as to his mental state or behaviour, that his anti-depressive and anti-psychotic medication had been tailed off or ended completely, and that he was an appropriate candidate for escorted community leave. The report indicated that T intended to continue to engage with the health team and did not want to leave hospital until he was ready to do so. In the doctor's opinion, a restriction order was no longer necessary.

Held: Appeal allowed. It was for the sentencing judge, applying s.41(1) of the Act, to decide whether a restriction order was necessary for public protection, and he was not bound to follow the recommendations of medical professionals, *R. v Royse (Irene Olive)* (1981) 3 Cr. App. R. (S.) 58, [1981] C.L.Y. 525.107 applied. It was understandable, in light of the antecedent history, for the judge not to have accepted the recommendation of T's doctor. He had been perfectly entitled, in sentencing T, to have made a restriction order in addition to the hospital order. However, the court was now satisfied that, in the circumstances, the restriction order could be removed and that T's care needs could adequately be met by the hospital order alone. The s.41 order was, accordingly, quashed, although the s.37 order remained in force.

R. v TALARICO (RICARDO), [2013] EWCA Crim 2798, [2014] M.H.L.R. 202, Rafferty LJ, CA (Crim Div).

1914 Road traffic offences–Causing death by dangerous driving–Effect of multiple aggravating features on sentencing guidelines starting point and sentence–Undue leniency

The Solicitor General referred to the court as unduly lenient a sentence of four-and-a-half years' imprisonment following guilty pleas to causing death by dangerous driving and causing serious injury by dangerous driving. The offender had been approaching a blind bridge. Road signs warned drivers to slow, but the offender had driven in the middle of the road and, travelling at 57 mph, had collided head-on with another car. The offender had made no attempt to brake. He left the scene following the accident, was later found under the influence of alcohol and drugs, and claimed that he had not been the driver but only a passenger. The victims, a married couple, were taken to hospital where the husband eventually died of his injuries. The wife sustained internal injuries and was left with limited mobility. The offender had 57 previous convictions for 169 offences of dishonesty, some of which related to driving. It was not until the plea and case management hearing that he pleaded guilty. The judge found that the offender had driven after taking diazepam, cocaine and a low level of alcohol. He concluded that the case fell within category 2 of the sentencing guidelines and reduced the offender's sentence by 30% as credit for his guilty pleas. The Solicitor General submitted that the sentence failed to take proper account of the nature of the offences and the aggravating features of the case which he identified as the fact that despite warnings the offender had been driving at 57 mph, the offender had had three different drugs in his system, his conduct at the scene, the consequences of the offending, his lack of driving licence or insurance, his large number of previous convictions for driving offences and his initial lie. He submitted that they elevated the offence from category 2 of the sentencing guidelines to category 1 and the appropriate starting point to one above eight years.

Held: Reference allowed. The nature of the driving in isolation positioned the offence within category 2 of the sentencing guidelines. However, the multiplicity of aggravating features dictated that the offence should be moved into category 1. They also required the starting point to be elevated above eight years; the appropriate starting point was ten years. The discount of 30% for the offender's guilty plea was over-generous; the appropriate discount was 25%. Accordingly, the sentence was quashed and a sentence of seven-and-a-half years' imprisonment was imposed.

ATTORNEY GENERAL'S REFERENCE (NO.150 OF 2015) *sub nom.* R. v FREEMAN (SHAUN RICHARD), [2016] EWCA Crim 459, [2016] 2 Cr. App. R. (S.) 16, Rafferty LJ, CA (Crim Div).

1915 Road traffic offences–Causing death by dangerous driving–Racing at high speed against another vehicle after alcohol consumption

The appellant (M) appealed against a total sentence of eight years' imprisonment imposed after he pleaded guilty to causing death by dangerous driving and causing serious injury by dangerous driving. M and a co-accused had been racing each other along a 40mph dual carriageway at between 80 to 90mph. They were undertaking and overtaking other vehicles. As the co-accused slowed down, M continued at high speed. He lost control of the vehicle and crashed into a bus shelter. A woman waiting at the bus stop was killed instantly. Another sustained grave injuries, including multiple fractures to her pelvis, and upper and lower limbs, punctured lungs, and a serious traumatic brain injury. She would be seriously disabled for the rest of her life. M told a paramedic that he had been travelling at 40mph. CCTV cameras revealed he had reached 101mph. M provided a breath specimen that was positive for alcohol. He refused to provide a specimen of blood at the hospital. At interview, M claimed that the co-accused had overtaken him at speed and that he had lost control of the car after steering to avoid a collision. In another interview, he denied seeing the co-accused's car. Victim impact statements from the victims' parents described the devastation caused by the incident. The judge put the case in level 1 of the relevant sentencing guideline. The aggravating features were that the victims were vulnerable road users; M was speeding in an area demanding extra care given the presence of junctions, a pedestrian crossing, a bus lane and a bus stop; M had consumed alcohol; and there were two victims. The appropriate sentence after trial would have been 12 years' imprisonment. Giving full credit for a guilty plea, a sentence of eight years' imprisonment was imposed for causing death by dangerous driving and a concurrent three-year sentence for causing serious injury by dangerous driving. M submitted that although the aggravating features elevated the sentence, the judge had taken too high a starting point and the offences fell within level 2 of the guideline.

Held: Appeal dismissed. The five factors in the guidelines relevant to determining seriousness were clearly identified in the instant case. First, there was excessively risky driving. There was a plain awareness of risk caused by the prolonged, persistent and deliberate course of very bad driving. Second, there had been consumption of alcohol. M had deliberately failed to provide a specimen after providing an earlier positive breath test. Third, M's vehicle was being driven at hugely excessive speed and he was racing against another person. Fourth, his behaviour was seriously culpable. Fifth, the victims were vulnerable. Each and every determinant of seriousness was present. The judge had plainly had regard to the specific guideline to causing death by dangerous driving. It indicated that a level 1 offence would be towards the top of the sentencing range where it involved a prolonged, persistent and deliberate course of bad driving and consumption of substantial amounts of alcohol or drugs leading to gross impairment, particularly if accompanied by aggravating factors such as multiple deaths or injuries. M's driving was highly criminal in its culpability, causing death and serious injury. As such, he should expect to be punished very severely (see paras 13-22 of judgment).

R. v MANNAN (SUKVINDER SINGH), [2016] EWCA Crim 1082, [2016] 2 Cr. App. R. (S.) 37, Jones LJ, CA (Crim Div).

1916 Robbery–Extended sentences–Violent robbery of vulnerable woman in own home

The appellant (N) appealed against an extended determinate sentence of 14 years imposed following his guilty plea to robbery. The victim was a 63-year-old widow with mental health issues. She had let N live in her house and had lent him money. One night, while under the influence of drink and drugs, N attacked the victim while she was asleep. He placed a towel over her head and pinned her down. N pretended that others were present during the attack and were telling him to get money from her. She handed over some cash and her bank card. N asked for her PIN and subsequently withdrew £130 from her account. N, who was 50 years old, had 12 previous convictions, including convictions in 2003 and 2004 for robbery. Based upon the nature and circumstances of the attack; a previous risk assessment following the 2004 robbery which stated that N posed a significant risk of serious harm to the public, but particularly to vulnerable females; and an indication in the pre-sentence report, the judge concluded that N was dangerous. She imposed an extended sentence comprising 10 years' imprisonment and an extension period of four years on licence. N submitted that the judge: (1) had erred in making her finding of dangerousness; (2) took too high a starting point so that the sentence of 10 years' imprisonment was manifestly excessive.

Held: Appeal allowed in part. (1) The judge's rationale in finding dangerousness could not be faulted. Given the troubling nature of the attack, the judge was right to look carefully at N's history and risk profile. When ordering the pre-sentence report, she asked specifically that the question of dangerousness be considered. The overall finding of the author of the report and her professional opinion were clear, namely that N posed a high risk of serious harm to the public. The fact that the previous risk assessment had been downgraded from a high risk to a medium risk after N's completion of his licence period for the 2004 robbery was irrelevant. The circumstances of the instant offence were also a potent factor which the judge was entitled to take fully into account. The very unpredictability of N and his willingness to resort to violence after long periods of quiescence made him potentially dangerous (see paras 19-23 of judgment). (2) The aggravating features were (a) the breach of trust by N; (b) that it was a despicable attack on a vulnerable, elderly, single lady with mental health issues carried out at night while she was asleep in bed; (c) that it was an extremely frightening attack which had a lasting effect on the victim. The case was clearly not in the category of *R. v O'Driscoll (James)* (1986) 8 Cr. App. R. (S.) 121, [1987] C.L.Y. 1042 at the top of the sentencing range. Nor was it at the bottom of the range as in *R. v Alexander*

(Alex Stuart) [2014] EWCA Crim 1768 where a street robbery took place just inside a person's flat, *O'Driscoll*, *Alexander* and *R. v Roe (Michael)* [2010] EWCA Crim 357, [2011] 4 All E.R. 773, [2011] C.L.Y. 3021 considered. Taking all the matters into account, the correct starting point for the determinate element of the sentence would have been 10 years. When full credit was given for an early plea, that equated to a determinate net sentence of 6 years and 8 months. The finding of dangerousness and the extension of four years on licence were upheld. Accordingly, the sentence substituted was an extended determinate sentence of 10 years and 8 months, made up of a custodial term of 6 years and 8 months and an extension period of four years on licence (paras 27-34).

R. v NEVILLE (NEIL JOSEPH), [2015] EWCA Crim 1874, [2016] 1 Cr. App. R. (S.) 38, Lloyd Jones LJ, CA (Crim Div).

1917 Robbery–Grievous bodily harm–Serious assault of elderly couple during robbery at home

[Criminal Justice Act 2003 (c.44) s.226A]

The appellant (N), who had pleaded guilty to robbery, possessing an imitation firearm, causing grievous bodily harm with intent and causing grievous bodily harm, appealed against the extended sentence of 15 years which had been imposed on him. The extended sentence comprised a custodial term of 10 years and eight months and an extended licence period of four years and four months. The victims of the offences were an elderly couple (H and W) who were aged 90 and 86 respectively. They knew N, as he had done some maintenance work for them. N arrived unannounced at their home. After chatting to H for some time, N grabbed him by the throat, gripping his neck with such force that he passed out. Shortly afterwards, W entered the room. She was extremely concerned and knelt down beside H to see whether he was all right. As she did so, N grabbed her by the throat and placed his hand over her mouth. She struggled but lost consciousness. After H had regained consciousness, N demanded money from him, producing what looked like a handgun. It was in fact an imitation firearm. He threatened H that if he did not comply with his demand for money he would shoot W. H gave N £6,000. N then noticed a small safe and told H to open it. H was able to press a panic alarm, causing N to flee. At that stage, H discovered that W was lying in a pool of blood. H had injuries consistent with strangulation, bruising to the tongue, injuries to the neck, chest and back of the head, and extensive tenderness over the neck. W had suffered a small bleed at the front of her brain. She also had a cut to her eye, bruising and a fractured rib. The sentencing judge concluded that N was dangerous. The judge had regard to the fact that he had told untruths to a psychologist who had been asked to prepare a report. The judge stated that N had given the psychologist the false impression that the offences were impulsive when in fact they were "cold-eyed, calculated and thoroughly premeditated". The judge also noted the psychologist's view that N had a capacity for minimisation and distortion, was uncritical of his own behaviour and lacked insight. The judge concluded that N had "fundamental shortcomings in [his] thought processes and thinking skills and profound deficits in [his] internal control mechanisms which [were] way outside of societal norms and [were] wholly inconsistent with conventional standards". N argued that the judge had been wrong to find that he was dangerous and therefore to impose an extended sentence.

Held: Appeal dismissed. It was quite plain from the careful and detailed analysis to which the judge subjected the reports before the court and the facts of the offences that he took great care in the sentencing exercise. It was also plain that he reflected carefully on the requirements of the Criminal Justice Act 2003 s.226A. His analysis of the evidence could not be faulted and his conclusions were reasoned and justifiable. It followed that his conclusion as to the danger posed by N was one that was open to him. A determinate sentence would not have sufficed. The purpose of the sentence was public protection. The judge could not know at what stage N would no longer be dangerous and he was entitled to conclude that a determinate sentence would not be adequate. Accordingly, he was right to impose an extended sentence. The extension period of four years and four months was near the maximum but not too long. The judge plainly considered that N needed the long-term supervision that would not have been available with a determinate sentence. The extension period was an additional safeguard for the public for a man who had behaved in a most extraordinary way.

Counsel had made no complaint about the length of the custodial period. He had mitigated, quite properly, by reference to N's youth (he was now 23), the fact that he had been desperate for money, the fact that he had no criminal record and his guilty plea. All of that was reflected in the custodial period imposed by the judge (see paras 19-21 of judgment).

R. v NEWLAND (HARLEY), [2016] EWCA Crim 351, [2016] 1 Cr. App. R. (S.) 74, Elias LJ, CA (Crim Div).

1918 Robbery–Sentencing guidelines–Cash-in-transit robbery–Undue leniency

The Solicitor General referred to the court as unduly lenient sentences imposed on three offenders (C, M and H) for a cash-in-transit robbery. H applied for permission to appeal against his sentence. C and M had attacked a security guard as he was taking a cash box to his van. Both wore masks and M had stabbed at the driver with a knife. Although none of the blows made contact, C and M were able to make off with the box, which contained £12,000. H was the getaway driver. All three had planned the robbery, undertaking reconnaissance and stealing a car for the purpose. C and M entered early guilty pleas while H was convicted after a trial. C was 20 at the time of the offence and had convictions for relatively minor matters. A pre-sentence report indicated that he had been taken advantage of by M and H and had become involved to gain kudos amongst his peers. M was 30 at the time of the offence and had a substantial criminal history which included two convictions for robbery. H was 34 at the time of the offence and had a long criminal record which included six convictions for robbery and attempted robbery. Weapons had been used in four of those offences, and a pre-sentence report assessed him as presenting a medium risk of serious harm to the public. He committed the instant offence whilst on licence. The judge described the robbery as a professionally planned, commercial one falling within Part 2 of the relevant sentencing guideline, which had a starting point of eight years' custody and a range of seven to 12 years. He sentenced C to two years and eight months' imprisonment, M to five years and four months' imprisonment, and H to an extended sentence comprising 10 years' custody and a three-year extension period. The Solicitor General submitted that the sentences were unduly lenient in that they failed to reflect the seriousness of the offence and the offenders' culpability. H argued that the judge had erred in finding that he was dangerous.

Held: Reference allowed, application refused. (1) The judge was right to find that the offence fell within Part 2 of the guideline. It was a carefully planned robbery involving a weapon, and the security guard had been targeted and attacked at the most vulnerable point of his operation. The fact that M and H had previously been involved in significant commercial robberies tended to demonstrate that the instant offence was not an unsophisticated attempt by relative amateurs. The reconnaissance, the preparation of disguises and the obtaining of a stolen vehicle all added to the picture of something more sophisticated, *R. v Adeojo (Simon)* [2008] EWCA Crim 1552, [2009] 1 Cr. App. R. (S.) 66, [2009] C.L.Y. 3533 considered. That said, it was not the most serious type of commercial robbery, which typically involved firearms and very high money values. For that type of offence, Part 2 referred to *R. v Turner (Bryan James)* (1975) 61 Cr. App. R. 67, [1975] C.L.Y. 559, which indicated a term of about 15 years' custody. However, it had to be noted that that case was out of date as a sentencing authority, and sentencing levels for top-bracket robberies would now be significantly higher, *Turner* and *R. v Thomas (Thomas)* [2011] EWCA Crim 1497, [2012] 1 Cr. App. R. (S.) 43, [2011] C.L.Y. 3027 considered. The fact that 15 years was no longer the ceiling had to be taken into consideration in assessing where less serious Part 2 robberies fell in the sentencing spectrum (see paras 20-31 of judgment). (2) The judge was right to categorise H as dangerous. He was entitled to regard him as a serial robber who was prone to involvement in the carrying of a weapon such as a knife, and to conclude that there was a significant risk of serious harm resulting from a further such offence. However, bearing in mind that there was no credit to be given for a guilty plea, a custodial term of 13 rather than 10 years was appropriate (paras 33-35, 38). M's record was somewhat less serious, and a sentence of eleven years' imprisonment would have been appropriate after a trial. Taking into account his guilty plea, that would give a sentence of seven years and four months' imprisonment (para.39). C had the mitigation of age and lack of previous criminal experience. The picture in his case was one of naivety, foolishness and some element of manipulation. A sentence of five-and-a-half years' imprisonment would have been appropriate after a trial. Credit for his guilty plea would reduce that to three years and eight months' imprisonment (paras 40-42).

ATTORNEY GENERAL'S REFERENCE (NOS 53, 54 AND 55 OF 2015) *sub nom.* R. v CHOWDHURY (NAVIS AHMED); R. v HUSSAIN (SHAH); R. v MOHAMMED (ASAD), [2015] EWCA Crim 1580, [2016] 1 Cr. App. R. (S.) 14, Treacy LJ, CA (Crim Div).

1919 Robbery–Sentencing guidelines–Robbery committed in home–Approach to sentence–New sentencing guideline replacing 2006 guideline

The appellant (C), who had been convicted of robbery, appealed against his sentence of 10 years' imprisonment. Three men (N, M and C), together with others, had travelled to the home of a woman with the intention of robbing her boyfriend. When the door was opened, they pushed in and accosted the woman. Some of them went upstairs and found her boyfriend, who fought back and put them to flight but not before they had taken £200 and some computer equipment. N, M and C all had significant previous convictions. N was initially sentenced to nine years' imprisonment and M and C to 10 years' imprisonment. The Court of Appeal subsequently allowed the appeals of N and M, reducing N's sentence to seven years and M's to eight.

Held: Appeal allowed. (1) There was no real difference between the cases of M and C and it would not be just for the court to take a different course in the case of C than was taken in the case of M. Accordingly, C's sentence would be reduced to one of eight years' imprisonment (see para.9 of judgment). (2) The robbery guideline published by the Sentencing Guidelines Council in 2006 had now been replaced but it contained a well-known gap: it gave no guidance about the significance of an offence of robbery being committed in a home, except where serious violence was used. In the instant case, the judge had regard to the aggravated burglary guidance in the definitive guideline on burglary. That approach had been expressly approved by the Court of Appeal in recent decisions, *Attorney General's Reference (No.18 of 2015)* [2015] EWCA Crim 950 and *R. v Smith (Claire Louise)* [2015] EWCA Crim 1047, [2015] 2 Cr. App. R. (S.) 35, [2015] C.L.Y. 2277 followed. However, the new robbery guideline should reduce the need for such an approach (paras 11-13, 17).

R. v CHE (VIN), [2016] EWCA Crim 827, [2016] 2 Cr. App. R. (S.) 35, Treacy LJ, CA (Crim Div).

1920 Robbery–Seriousness of offence–Threat to use weapon but none produced–Categorisation of offence in terms of sentencing guidelines

An offender appealed against a sentence of four years' imprisonment imposed following his guilty plea to robbery. The offender had pretended to buy some goods in a petrol station shop at night and then threatened the cashier when she refused to give him a refund or to open the till. She said that he put his hand into his pocket in a manner which she thought meant that he had a weapon. No weapon was produced. The cashier opened the till and the offender took the contents, approximately £120. The cashier stated that she felt vulnerable, scared and violated. The offender was identified by CCTV evidence. He made admissions when arrested and pleaded guilty at a preliminary hearing. He was 30 and had previous convictions for theft, burglary, affray and possession of a firearm with intent. The recorder assessed the offence as a level 2 robbery within the sentencing guidelines. Level 2 included "Use of weapon to threaten and/or use of significant force", expanded to mean "A weapon is produced and used to threaten and/or force is used which results in injury to the victim". The starting point, for an offender of good character, was four years' imprisonment with a range of two to seven years. The recorder stated that the threat of unknown force could not be minimal, and interpreted "weapon" as including "a harmless toy and is therefore capable of including a disguised weapon, real or imagined". He adopted a starting point of six years before applying the full one-third credit for the guilty plea. The issue was the categorisation of a robbery offence within the guideline where the threat to use a weapon was made, but no weapon was produced. The offender contended that the offence properly fell within level 1, which included "threat and/or use of minimal force", with a starting point of 12 months' imprisonment and a range up to three years.

Held: Appeal allowed. On an initial view, pretending to have a weapon was not "producing and using a weapon to threaten". However, the description of the activity for each level was not to be treated as if the words were contained in a statute to be interpreted strictly and in isolation from the rest of the guideline. An offender might fall to be sentenced for a level 2 robbery even if the prosecution could not prove production and use of a weapon. It depended on the judge's assessment of the seriousness of the offence. That was determined by a number of factors: degree of force and/or nature and duration of the threats; degree of injury to the victim; degree of fear experienced by the victim; and the value of the property taken. The Sentencing Guidelines Council had stated expressly that whether a weapon used was real or imitation was not "a major factor" because the amount of fear created in the victim was likely to be the same. The victim in the instant case had experienced a very high degree of fear; she believed that the offender had a weapon. She was also in a very vulnerable position. Such vulnerability explained why the Council had added in the introduction to "Levels of Seriousness" the statement: "The levels apply to all three categories of robbery but it will be very rare for robberies of small businesses or less sophisticated commercial robberies to have the features of the lowest level of seriousness". The instant case did not come into that very rare category. Also, under the heading "Aggravating and mitigating features", the guideline indicated that if the aggravating features were exceptionally serious, the case could move to the next level of seriousness. The offender had chosen an opportune moment, when the victim was alone at night and was particularly vulnerable. The impact on her was very considerable. He had relevant previous convictions and the offence was more serious than a level 1 offence. However, any element of double-counting of aggravating factors which put the offence into level 2 had to be carefully avoided. It was not the most sophisticated robbery of its kind and, balancing all the relevant factors, four-and-a-half years' imprisonment was appropriate before credit was given for a guilty plea. Allowing full credit for the offender's admissions in interview and his guilty plea at the first reasonable opportunity, three years' imprisonment was appropriate.

R. v ROBINSON (WAYNE), [2015] EWCA Crim 1839, [2016] 1 Cr. App. R. (S.) 35, Hallett LJ, CA (Crim Div).

1921 Robbery–Totality of sentence–Robbery and attempted robbery of four boys in park while carrying a knife–Young offenders

[Powers of Criminal Courts (Sentencing) Act 2000 (c.6) s.91]

The appellant (M) appealed against a total sentence of four years' detention in a young offender institution imposed after he pleaded guilty to three counts of robbery, one of attempted robbery and one of assault, and not guilty to having a bladed article. M, aged 17 at the time, and three friends had robbed four boys, aged 14 to 15, in a park. M showed one of the victims that he had a knife in the waistband of his trousers. On arrest, M gave a no comment interview and was released on bail. Two months later M and two others attacked a man who had been in a dispute with one of M's associates. The attackers ran off. M denied the allegation in interview but pleaded guilty on the day of trial. A pre-sentence report noted that M had a conviction for possession of cannabis which was subsequent to the instant offences. He lived with his mother and had been nine months into an apprenticeship at a care home. The offences occurred when he was on sick leave after suffering injuries in a street assault. The author of the report noted a need for M to prove himself to his peers. A number of supportive references were submitted. The recorder observed that M and his friends had gone out with the intention of robbing people. While M had not produced a knife, he had shown it, and violence was used by his peers. The victims' experience had to have been terrifying. Further, M had offended whilst on bail. In mitigation, M had pleaded guilty to the robberies and assault, and they were his first offences. He was a young man that people had spoken positively of. He was a carer and would miss the birth of his baby as result of his inevitable custodial sentence. The judge imposed concurrent three-year sentences for the robberies, one year consecutive for having a bladed article, and eight weeks concurrent for the assault. M argued that (1) the knife was taken into account as an aggravating factor for the robbery offences and a consecutive sentence indicated an element of double-counting; (2) the total sentence failed to have sufficient regard to totality bearing in mind his youth and his guilty pleas to the robberies.

Held: Appeal allowed. (1) Before considering the merits, there was a technical point to be addressed regarding M's age at the time of the offences. He had pleaded guilty when he was aged 17 and fell to be sentenced as a 17-year-old. Detention in a young offender institution was not available. If the offences merited custody, which they did, detention under the Powers of Criminal Courts (Sentencing) Act 2000 s.91 was available for the grave crimes of robbery but not for the other offences. The appropriate course on the authorities was that a term of detention commensurate with the seriousness of all the offences ought to be imposed for the robbery offences. The offence of possession of a bladed article did not simply reflect that M was armed with a knife at the time of the robberies, it also reflected that he was armed with a knife at all. It was undoubtedly the case that the presence of a knife was a factor in the categorisation of the robberies and the assessment of the starting point for the sentence (see paras 7, 9 of judgment). (2) The appeal turned on M's second submission. There were a number of aggravating factors: several offenders were involved; there was a degree of planning or coordination; M was carrying a weapon; M was on bail at the time; and he had contested that he was carrying a knife. In mitigation, M was aged 17 and had no criminal history. It was his first experience of custody and it was hoped to have a salutary effect. In all the circumstances, the total sentence was excessive. Concurrent terms of three years' detention under s.91 would be imposed for the robbery offences. Those terms reflected the overall criminality involved in all of the offences and there would be no separate penalty for the assault or having a bladed article (paras 10-11).

R. v MATTIS (JORDAN), [2016] EWCA Crim 151, [2016] 1 Cr. App. R. (S.) 67, Davis LJ, CA (Crim Div).

1922 Robbery–Totality of sentence–Robbery of vulnerable victim by offender with physical and mental difficulties whilst under suspended sentence

An offender (X) applied for permission to appeal against a total sentence of three years and two months' imprisonment imposed following his guilty plea to robbery and the activation of a suspended sentence. X was sentenced to two years and nine months for the robbery. A suspended nine-month sentence imposed for attempted robbery was activated, with a reduced consecutive term of five months. X had stolen a rucksack from a woman waiting for a bus to travel to work early in the morning. The victim was knocked to the ground and hit and kicked repeatedly. She suffered bruising and headaches and required hospital treatment. The rucksack was retrieved, damaged but with no items missing. The victim was afraid to travel alone following the incident and had to be accompanied by her boyfriend when travelling to work. X pleaded guilty on the accepted basis that he had been the victim of a robbery involving three males who had pressurised him to commit a robbery to obtain the return of his property. He was 24 years old and suffered from congenital curvature of the spine. A psychological report concluded that although he had a low IQ, placing him at the borderline of intellectual functioning, he did not have a learning disability. The judge indicated that he would normally have adopted a four-year starting point, but reduced that to three years given the basis of plea. He gave X reduced credit for his late guilty plea. X submitted that he had been given insufficient credit for his plea as the Crown had been given notice that such a plea would be tendered. He further submitted that the judge had paid insufficient heed to the psychological report.

Held: Permission refused. The judge accepted that X had been under some pressure from bullies who had taken his personal belongings, which must have been embarrassing, difficult and humiliating for him. The judge placed the offence lower in the scale of seriousness because of that pressure, but it did not excuse X's actions. He had targeted a lone vulnerable woman in the early hours of the morning. Not only did he snatch her bag, he attacked her, hitting and kicking her repeatedly. The judge took into account the contents of the psychological report, pointing out that X had several physical and intellectual challenges while indicating that they were not of the utmost seriousness and did not explain or excuse his conduct. No greater heed should have been taken of the report. Some judges might have given a greater discount for the guilty plea. However, the judge's starting point of four years was very substantially reduced and the sentence had to be viewed as a whole, bearing in mind that the consecutive term from the activated suspended sentence was reduced to five months. The total sentence of three years and two months was entirely merited (see paras 9-15 of judgment).

R. v ADEOGUN (OLAMIDE JOHN), [2015] EWCA Crim 1873, [2016] 1 Cr. App. R. (S.) 40, Simon LJ, CA (Crim Div).

1923 **Sentencing–Custodial sentences–Guidance on application of Pt 12 s.236A Criminal Justice Act 2003 when sentencing for specified offences**

[Sexual Offences Act 1956 (c.69) s.14(1); Sexual Offences Act 2003 (c.42) s.6; Criminal Justice Act 2003 (c.44) Pt 12 s.236A]

The applicants (F and S) applied for permission to appeal against sentences of imprisonment imposed for child sex offences. In 2016, F, aged 59, received a total sentence of six years' imprisonment after pleading guilty to two counts of indecent assault against two girls contrary to the Sexual Offences Act 1956 s.14(1). One count was equivalent to an offence under the Sexual Offences Act 2003 s.6 (SOA). The judge did not apply the Criminal Justice Act 2003 Pt 12 s.236A (CJA) which related to sentencing for specified offences. In 2016, S, aged 59, received a total 14-year custodial sentence with a further one-year licence period under s.236A following his conviction for 19 counts against two girls. Two counts were equivalent to an offence under SOA 2003 s.6 and four counts were historic indecent assaults.

Held: Applications refused. (1) Where a person aged 18 or over was convicted of an offence listed in Sch.18A CJA 2003 on or after 13 April 2015 and the court did not impose a life sentence or an extended sentence, s.236A(2) required the court to impose a sentence equal to the aggregate of the appropriate custodial term and a further one-year licence period. Passing an ordinary determinate sentence was not an option. Schedule 18A included s.6 SOA 2003 offences and abolished offences. Historic offences under the 1956 Act that were the equivalent of a s.6 SOA 2003 offence were therefore caught by s.236A. Section 236A prisoners were not automatically released halfway through their sentence. Under s.244A, if the Parole Board did not direct release during the period of the appropriate custodial term, the prisoner had to be released at the end of that term. If an offender was released during the course of their sentence, the effect of s.236A was that they would be on licence for the remainder of the sentence plus one further year. Where consecutive s.236A sentences were imposed, consecutive further licence periods had to follow. Judges therefore had to give careful consideration to the structuring of their sentences as decisions as to whether to make sentences concurrent or consecutive would impact on the length of the further licence period. While that issue did not arise in the instant case, it was appropriate to give guidance on it (see paras 1-7, 24 of judgment). Practitioners and judges had failed to apply s.236A in a significant number of cases. Practitioners appearing before the courts, particularly prosecutors, had a duty to ensure that they assisted the judges. The following checklist of points should be considered: (a) whether the offence was listed in Sch.18A; (b) if the offence was a repealed historic sexual offence, whether it involved rape or penetration of a child under 13; (c) whether the offender was 18 or over when the offence was committed; (d) s.236A could not apply if a life sentence or extended sentence was imposed for the offence or associated offence; (e) a sentence was to be expressed as a single term comprising the custodial element and a further one-year licence period; (f) each offence qualifying under s.236A had to be sentenced in the terms set out in (e); (g) if the s.236A sentences were to run concurrently, the overall custodial term for those offences plus the one-year licence period had to be stated at the end of sentencing; (h) if the s.236A sentences were to run consecutively, the total custodial term for those offences as well as the total licence period had to be stated at the end of sentencing (paras 26-27). (2) There was no merit in F's grounds of appeal. The judge should have passed sentence under s.236A in respect of the SOA 2003 s.6 equivalent offence. The custodial sentence of three years and four months on that count was appropriate but a further one-year licence period should have been added to it. It was not possible to make that sentence more severe by ordering the further licence period, nor was the instant court disposed to reduce the overall custodial term. Accordingly, the sentence remained unchanged. F's case was an illustration of the consequences of a failure to apply s.236A: F had been dealt with more lightly than

Parliament intended (para.40). (3) In S's case, the judge was alert to s.236A but failed to deal with it correctly. Having structured the sentencing with a mix of concurrent and consecutive sentences to reflect the fact that the offences were committed against separate victims, the judge wrongly stated that S would be released after serving half of his sentence in custody. Such error did not invalidate the sentence. The judge failed accurately to state the effect of the further licence period and did not identify the offences to which the further licence period attached. For a valid sentence to be passed, the judge should have attached the further licence period to the relevant counts, being the s.6 equivalent offences and the historic sexual offences. Having imposed ordinary determinate sentences and decided to impose consecutive but internally concurrent sentences, the judge should have identified those offences falling within s.236A and passed s.236A-style sentences in relation to those counts. However, the irregularities in expressing and recording the sentence did not give S any ground of appeal. It was fully understood at the time of the hearing that a 15-year sentence had been imposed, comprising a 14-year custodial term plus a further one-year licence period (paras 54-58).

R. v LF; R. v DS, [2016] EWCA Crim 561, [2016] 1 W.L.R. 4432, Treacy LJ, CA (Crim Div).

1924 Sentencing guidelines–Young offenders–Consideration of appropriate sentence for young offender in comparison with adult in similar situation

[Powers of Criminal Courts (Sentencing) Act 2000 (c.6) s.101; Magistrates' Courts Act 1980 (c.43) s.133]

The appellant youth (B) appealed by way of case stated against his total sentence for seven offences as compared with what an adult would have received in that situation. B's sentence for seven offences had comprised: a four-month detention and training order for aggravated vehicle-taking; no separate penalty for driving without insurance; another and consecutive four-month detention and training order for aggravated vehicle-taking; a concurrent four-month detention and training order for handling stolen goods on the same occasion; no separate penalties for a public order offence and two offences of criminal damage. B pleaded guilty at the first opportunity. He had been 16 at the time of one criminal damage offence, and 17 in the case of all the other offences. He had served three weeks on remand. On appeal, the Crown Court quashed the four-month detention and training orders and replaced them with three-month ones, but when the appellant pointed out that under the Powers of Criminal Courts (Sentencing) Act 2000 s.101 the minimum duration of such an order was four months, it dismissed the appeal. The issue for the instant court was the implications for youths of restrictions on the powers of magistrates' courts to sentence adult offenders. B submitted that under the Sentencing Guidelines Council's Overarching Principles for Sentencing Youths a young person should generally be dealt with less severely than an adult, albeit that the distinction diminished as an offender approached 18, and that his case resembled *P v Leeds Youth Court* [2006] EWHC 2527 (Admin) where the Divisional Court held that a four-month detention and training order imposed on a 17-year-old had been unlawful. B argued that his sentence should be tested by considering the effect of the Magistrates' Courts Act 1980 s.133, namely that in the case of an adult the magistrates would have been entitled to impose a sentence exceeding six months only where there were two or more offences triable either way, whereas in his case there was only one. B contended that, applying the Sentencing Guideline on Reduction in Sentence for a Guilty Plea para.5.7, and considering time on remand, he had received a total sentence of double that for an adult in his circumstances.

Held: Case remitted to magistrates' court. For the reasons B gave, it would not have been right to sentence him, had he been an adult, to a custodial sentence of more than four months as an absolute maximum, so his total sentence of eight months was unlawful, *P v Leeds Youth Court* applied. It was quashed and the case remitted to the magistrates' court for reconsideration (see para.21 of judgment). (Per Simon, LJ) For the same reasons, it was clear that the Crown Court had fallen into error in relation to its jurisdiction and had proceeded to re-sentence on that basis, which amounted to an error of law. Additionally, the sentence imposed fell so far outside the normal discretionary limits as to enable the instant court to say that its imposition must involve an error of law, those being the two approaches set out by the High Court in *R. v St*

Albans Crown Court Ex p. Cinnamond [1981] Q.B. 480, [1981] C.L.Y. 396, *Cinnamond* applied.

B v LEEDS CROWN COURT *sub nom.* B v CROWN PROSECUTION SERVICE, [2016] EWHC 1230 (Admin), (2016) 180 J.P. 282, Simon LJ, QBD (Admin).

1925 Sentencing powers–Maximum sentences–Counsel's duty to properly prepare cases for sentence and to inform judge where necessary of sentencing powers

[Criminal Justice Act 1988 (c.33) s.160(1), s.160(2A)]

The appellant (H) appealed against concurrent extended sentences of seven-and-a-half years imposed following his pleas of guilty to three counts of possession of indecent photographs of children. Each sentence was made up of a two-and-a-half year custodial period with an extended licence period of five years. H's pleas of guilty placed him in breach of a 24-week suspended sentence imposed in December 2013 for 11 offences of making indecent photographs of children and two offences of possessing an indecent photograph of a child. The suspended sentence was activated in full, but ordered to run concurrently. H had previously been convicted of offences of making and possessing indecent photographs of children in 2012, and was given a three-year community order. He was made the subject of a sexual offences prevention order in 2012. H submitted that an extended sentence was wrong in principle, and the overall length of the sentence, in particular the custodial term, was manifestly excessive.

Held: Appeal allowed. (1) Pursuant to the Criminal Justice Act 1988 s.160(2A), the maximum sentence for an offence under s.160(1) was five years' imprisonment. H's sentences of seven-and-a-half years exceeded the maximum and were unlawful. It was unfortunate that no-one had pointed that out to the judge at the time. Counsel were reminded of their duty properly to prepare cases for sentence and to remind a judge where necessary of the scope of his powers; that included reminding the judge of the maximum sentence (see para.3 of judgment). (2) H's offences were serious, as the judge had found. Furthermore, H had treated his previous sentences and the sexual offences prevention order with contempt. However, the judge had not been entitled to find that H was dangerous, *R. v Guest (Darren)* [2011] EWCA Crim 1762 and *R. v Terrell (Alexander James)* [2007] EWCA Crim 3079, [2008] 2 All E.R. 1065, [2008] C.L.Y. 3314 applied. In *Guest,* the court was satisfied that an offender involved in the sophisticated distribution of images could not be categorised as dangerous. In *Terrell*, the court stated that the link between the offending act of downloading indecent images and the possible harm which might be done to children was too remote to satisfy the requirement that the offender's reoffending had to cause serious harm (paras 11-13). (3) The appropriate sentence had to be a custodial one. The judge was bound to reflect the totality of the offending in a sentence at the top of the range. A custodial term of two-and-a-half years in respect of all the offending was entirely correct. The extended sentences were quashed and replaced with concurrent sentences of two-and-a-half years' imprisonment on each count (paras 14-15).

R. v HAYES (CHRISTOPHER), [2016] EWCA Crim 663, [2016] 2 Cr. App. R. (S.) 24, Elias LJ, CA (Crim Div).

1926 Sexual harm prevention orders–Indecent photographs of children–Offences not involving direct contact with children–Proportionality and necessity of order

[Sexual Offences Act 2003 (c.42) s.103A, s.103A(3)(b)(i)]

The appellant appealed against a sexual harm prevention order imposed following his guilty plea to making and possessing indecent photographs of children. The appellant had been a music teacher at an independent school. He also had pastoral duties as an assistant house master. Police found images and videos on his home computer in categories A, B and C. The judge concluded that he might be rehabilitated. He therefore imposed a three-year community order, with requirements for supervision and rehabilitation. A five-year sexual harm prevention order was made prohibiting him from unsupervised contact with children under the age of 16 and from using devices capable of accessing the internet, unless the device retained the history of its use and was made available upon request for police inspection. The appellant submitted that the order was not necessary or proportionate because he had not behaved inappropriately towards children, and any risk of him doing so was purely speculative. He also argued that monitoring his use of email was excessive. The Crown sought to rely on a risk assessment carried out after sentencing, and argued that the appellant had been viewing indecent material for the bulk of his teaching career, and there was an obvious risk that he might seek contact with a child.

Held: Appeal dismissed. (1) The court could not say that there could be no case in which it would be appropriate to consider material adverse to the interests of an appellant which did not exist at the time sentence was passed. However, the court would not take such material into account in the instant case (see para.16 of judgment). (2) The appellant was a qualifying offender for an order under the Sexual Offences Act 2003 s.103A, but the court had to be satisfied that the requirements under s.103A(3)(b)(i) were also met. The issue was the perception of risk as it appeared to the judge at the time sentence was passed. It was plainly foreseeable that unsupervised contact with children could lead to offending given the appellant's acknowledged sexual attraction to young children. The pre-sentence report had made it clear that the appellant needed to develop skills to avoid re-offending (paras 11, 16-18). (3) The sexual offences prevention order contained the standard provisions approved in *R. v Smith (Steven)* [2011] EWCA Crim 1772, [2012] 1 W.L.R. 1316, [2012] C.L.Y. 3019. There were no authorities in which the standard *Smith* prohibitions had been successfully challenged in order to protect private emails from inspection. If emails were excluded from the prohibition, it would enable offenders to set up email accounts at will in order to access children on chat lines, or receive images which would remain undetected. The prohibitions contained in the order were necessary and proportionate in order to protect children from sexual harm from the appellant, *Smith* applied. However, if the appellant made good progress on the sexual offender treatment programme he could apply at the end of the community order for a variation or discharge of the provisions of the sexual harm prevention order (paras 20-21).

R. v MCDONALD (JOHN), [2015] EWCA Crim 2119, [2016] 1 Cr. App. R. (S.) 48, Jackson LJ, CA (Crim Div).

1927 Sexual offences–Sexual assault–Effect of co-defendant's acquittal on offender acting "together with others to commit the offence" for sentencing guidelines categorisation–Undue leniency

The Attorney General referred to the court as unduly lenient a total sentence of two years' imprisonment imposed on an offender (S) for offences of kidnapping, committing an offence with intent to commit a sexual offence, and sexual assault. S and another (X) had led an intoxicated girl from a nightclub to a flat where S had forcibly run the victim's hand across his groin. The victim remembered trying to pull away but that S was too strong. X was jointly charged on all three counts but was acquitted. The judge decided that the sexual assault fell within category 1 of the relevant guidelines. As to culpability, he had regard to the fact that S had acted with another. He concluded that while there were grounds for placing the sexual assault in category 1A, it was properly to be placed on the borderline of categories 1A and 1B. S submitted that the offending did not fall within category 1A because he had not "acted with others to commit the offence" within the wording of the guidelines, as evidenced by the fact that his co-accused had been acquitted of all charges.

Held: Reference allowed. (1) The wording in the guidelines was that the "offender acts together with others to commit the offence". The words "to commit the offence" sensibly and practicably related to the offender. Where others had been present and acting with the offender, more often than not they too would be intending to commit the offence. However, in cases where that could not be shown or inferred, that did not prevent the offending from being within culpability categorisation A. The wording had to be read both objectively and sensibly. From the victim's point of view, if another or others were present at the relevant time and acting with the offender, a degree of menace, force or assistance was conveyed. A co-accused's lack of intent might have some bearing on the ultimate overall assessment of the position for sentencing purposes, but that did not of itself remove it from categorisation under culpability A (see para.26 of judgment). (2) The judge's approach was puzzling. In his view the case fell somewhere on the cusp of categories 1A and 1B. The top of the range for category 1B was four years' custody, and the bottom of the range of category 1A was three years' custody, yet the judge had arrived at a total sentence of two years' custody. Even allowing for mitigation, that was a surprising result. However, it was important to be neither over-refined nor mechanistic in applying the guidelines to the circumstances of the particular offending. The sexual assault had not just occurred in the flat without any preceding conduct, but had been preceded by the abduction of the victim, who was almost totally insensible through drink. That was a very serious matter, and accordingly it would be wrong to sentence S solely by reference to a strict and self-contained application of the guidelines for sexual assault offences. The aggravating features of the case were such that the matter fell well within the range indicated in category 1A. The sentence imposed was unduly lenient, and it was appropriate to replace it with one of five years' imprisonment (paras 27-31).

ATTORNEY GENERAL'S REFERENCE (NO.113 OF 2015) *sub nom.* R. v SENUSSI (ALI), [2016] EWCA Crim 38, [2016] 1 Cr. App. R. (S.) 70, Davis LJ, CA (Crim Div).

1928 Sexual offences–Sexual assault–Element of breach of trust aggravated by victim's vulnerability and repeated nature of behaviour

The appellant (X), who had pleaded guilty to three offences of sexual assault, appealed against his sentence of two years and three months' imprisonment. X, who was homosexual and 36 at the time of the offences, ran a gay bar with his partner. The victim (G), who was heterosexual and 18, had been offered some bar work by X. After G had finished work one night, he and X began drinking together. G became very drunk and fell asleep. X then carried out three sexual assaults on him. He performed oral sex on him (the first assault). Some 20 minutes later, he pulled down G's trousers, put his hand between his buttocks and touched his anus (the second assault). He then knelt down and licked G's anus (the third assault). In a victim personal statement, G stated that the offences had caused anger issues, heavy drinking, depression and suicidal thoughts. The sentencing judge placed the offences in category A of the sentencing guidelines, given the breach of trust involved. He adopted a starting point of two years and six months' imprisonment and applied a reduction of 10 per cent to reflect X's late guilty plea.

Held: Appeal dismissed. In the social setting in which the offences were committed, and given the situations and ages of the parties, this was not a case of a formal breach of trust by reason of an abuse of X's position due to his status and/or standing. However, there was not total equality between the parties, and G's age and circumstances were something that should be reflected in the sentence as far as X's culpability was concerned. The offences fell within category 2B of the guidelines, which provided for a starting point of one year and a range of a high-level community order to two years' custody. The offences were right at the top of that range. Although not a formal breach of trust, the offences were significantly aggravated by G's situation and vulnerability and by the repeated nature of the behaviour. Although the offences were committed within a short period of time, they involved separate occasions on which X assaulted G in different ways. They were serious offences in themselves and had had a significant impact on G. The judge could properly have imposed consecutive sentences. A total sentence of two years and three months reflected the overall criminality and was just and proportionate (see paras 24-26 of judgment).

R. v ASHTON (ROBERT VINCENT), [2015] EWCA Crim 1799, [2016] 1 Cr. App. R. (S.) 32, Beatson LJ, CA (Crim Div).

1929 Supply of drugs–Conspiracy–Leading roles in conspiracy to supply class A drugs

[Criminal Justice Act 2003 (c.44) s.153(2), s.166(3)(b)]

The appellants (L and R) appealed against sentences imposed after their guilty pleas to conspiracy to supply a class A drug. The conspiracy concerned almost 3 kg of cocaine between 65 and 73% purity and worth in the region of £120,000. R had been in possession of the cocaine and L was alleged to be the potential wholesale buyer. Cutting agents were found in L's home. L had a previous conviction for possession of MDMA with intent and had been on licence at the time he committed the instant offence. He was sentenced to nine-years-and-eight-months' imprisonment, with a consecutive sentence of six months for possession of cannabis with intent to supply. R had been convicted in Spain of supplying one ton of cocaine. He had been sentenced to nine years' imprisonment for that offence but had absconded. The judge took that into account by increasing his sentence. She imposed a sentence of 15 years' imprisonment. L submitted that his sentence was excessive and he was lower in the hierarchy than the judge had assumed. R submitted that the judge was not entitled to increase his sentence to take account of the Spanish sentence, and that offence was not an "associated offence" under the Criminal Justice Act 2003 s.153(2).

Held: Appeals allowed. (1) In both L and R's cases there were three or four of the characteristics to determine culpability of a leading role as set out in the Sentencing Council definitive guidelines on drug offences, namely directing or organising, buying and selling on a commercial scale, substantial links to and influence on others in the chain, and close links to the original source. The cocaine was of a high purity and would inevitably be cut substantially before it reached the street. There was also the expectation of a substantial gain (see para.8 of judgment). (2) L had committed the offence when on licence for a similar offence which was a significant aggravating factor. When considering the level within the guidelines it would be appropriate to move upwards within the bracket. The judge had started with a figure of 14 years. She sought to reduce it by a full discount for his guilty plea. That must have meant one third, which should lead to a term of nine years and four months rather than nine years and eight months. Whilst the difference could not be said to be manifestly excessive, it was the sentencing judge's apparent intention. Therefore, L's sentence was reduced to nine years and four months, with six months consecutive, making the total term nine-years-and-ten-months' imprisonment (paras 13, 20). (3) In respect of R, the judge's intention was to ensure that he did not receive a benefit from absconding from his nine-year Spanish sentence. He would thereby have avoided a substantial part of that sentence unless the judge took that fact into account, but she could not impose a sentence consecutive to the Spanish sentence as he was not yet serving it and the position of extradition to Spain remained unclear. She therefore imposed an additional term, in effect, of five years and eight months. It was accepted by R's counsel at the sentencing hearing that the Criminal Justice Act 2003 s.166(3)(b) entitled the judge to look at the aggregate term in that manner. The judge was not powerless in reflecting the Spanish conviction in the sentence for the instant offence. Having reached a notional figure for sentence based on harm and culpability, the judge was entitled to take into account the statutory aggravating feature of a like previous conviction. The fact that R had sought to avoid service of the previous sentence was a further aggravating feature. The judge had taken an appropriate starting point of 14 years. Given that she was entitled to approach the Spanish offence as an aggravating factor, that would have increased the notional sentence to sixteen years. From that should be deducted the discount of a third for the plea. The sentence should therefore be 10 years and eight months (paras 16, 18-19).

R. v LUCIANO (GIOVANNO); R. v ROTHERY (ROBERT), [2016] EWCA Crim 195, [2016] 1 Cr. App. R. (S.) 73, Elias LJ, CA (Crim Div).

1930 Suspended sentences–Activation–Breach of unpaid work and supervision requirements–Investigation of post-breach history

The appellant (R) appealed against the activation of a suspended sentence. R had received a sentence of six months' imprisonment, suspended for 12 months, with supervision and 120 hours' unpaid work requirements. He failed to attend unpaid work or supervision on at least five occasions, had been late for several appointments and rearranged others. The probation service had not investigated R's reasons for non-compliance. The breach report, completed after R had completed 22 hours of work, noted that R's engagement was sporadic and his motivation fluctuated. While he was positive, polite and had not reoffended, he did not appreciate the seriousness of the order. At the time of the court hearing, R had completed 36.15 hours of work. The recorder was required to activate the suspended sentence in its original form or with a reduction in term, or he could amend the terms of the order overall. He made his decision on the basis of the position at the time of the breach report and concluded that R had half-heartedly committed to the requirements and had wasted the chances he had been given. The length of the prison term was reduced from six months to 22 weeks, to reflect the extent of R's compliance with the order. During the hearing, the probation service had requested an adjournment so it could investigate R's explanations for not attending the post-breach appointments. The recorder proceeded to sentence R on the basis of events leading up to the breach report and disregarded subsequent events. R argued that the recorder had not properly taken into account all the relevant circumstances.

Held: Appeal allowed. The recorder should have adjourned so that further investigations into the post-breach history could be made and he could make his decision on the full facts and give credit for the hours of unpaid work that had been completed. The activation period was reduced to 50 days, which had already been served.

R. v REYNOLDS (DANIEL), [2015] EWCA Crim 1796, [2016] 1 Cr. App. R. (S.) 33, Rafferty LJ, CA (Crim Div).

1931 Suspended sentences–Activation–Further offence indicating failure to gain benefit from programmes forming part of suspended sentence

The appellant (W) appealed against a total sentence of 14 months' imprisonment. W was sentenced to six months' imprisonment following his conviction for common assault. In addition, a term of eight months' imprisonment, which was the full term of a suspended sentence previously imposed, was ordered to be activated in full and to run consecutively. As to the common assault, W had punched his partner during an argument. He denied the offence at the time and continued to deny it. He had been before the courts many times for offences involving violent and aggressive behaviour. In 2014, for an offence of affray, which dated back some considerable time, W was sentenced to eight months' imprisonment, which was suspended for 18 months. He was ordered to attend a thinking skills programme, to undertake alcohol treatment for three months and to continue under supervision for the total term of 18 months. The pre-sentence reports that were before the sentencing judge made it clear that the thinking skills programme, although completed, had not worked and that any alcohol treatment, if it had ever worked, had not continued to work beyond the end of the three months. W argued that while it might have been appropriate to activate the suspended sentence in part, the judge had been wrong to activate it in full, because no credit was given for the fact that he had already complied with the conditions imposed as part of that sentence.

Held: Appeal dismissed. It was right to observe that the offence for which the suspended sentence was imposed had occurred some years before the commission of the index offence. That said, W had gone back to (if he had ever left) alcohol, had carried out a significant assault on his partner and had continued to deny the offence, despite the presence of independent witnesses and the obvious injury which his partner had sustained. All of those features, together with others taken into account by the judge in passing sentence, demonstrated a total failure on W's part to gain any benefit from the terms of the various conditions which were imposed as part of his suspended sentence. Those conditions were designed to be therapeutic rather than punitive. While W appeared to have complied in the sense of attending and completing courses, he certainly had not succeeded in putting what he had learnt into practice. The fact that he had got through most of the 18-month period of suspension was not such as to create a sliding scale at the end of which the judge should have reduced the term imposed (see paras 9, 11 of judgment).

R. v WOLSTENHOLME (MARK ANTHONY), [2016] EWCA Crim 638, [2016] 2 Cr. App. R. (S.) 19, Sharp LJ, CA (Crim Div).

1932 Terrorist offences–Preparation of terrorist acts–Significant degree of planning and premeditation prior to travelling to Syria to commit terrorist acts

[Terrorism Act 2006 (c.11) s.5(1)]

The appellants appealed against extended sentences imposed following their guilty pleas to an offence of engaging in conduct in preparation for acts of terrorism contrary to the Terrorism Act 2006 s.5(1). In May 2013 they had travelled from the UK to Turkey and on to Syria where they were involved with Islamist forces, returning to the UK in January 2014 when they were arrested. The significant planning prior to their departure was identified by the prosecution as supporting its case that this was a well-planned operation put into action for sinister reasons. Social networking activity provided more evidence that the real purpose of the journey to Syria was to commit acts of terrorism. On their return to the UK, memory cards were found in their luggage containing images taken in Syria close to combat areas, and traces of high explosive were found on their clothes and belongings. The thrust of the bases of plea was that the appellants had not in fact been involved in armed combat in Syria, although there was an acceptance that they had been involved in armed activity close to combat zones, falling short of actual combat. The prosecution case was that they had been involved in armed activity in combat areas. The appellants entered guilty pleas on the second day of trial, but prior to the jury being sworn in. The judge held that they were fundamentalists who had become deeply committed to violent extremism, and it made no difference to the gravity of the offence that the intention was to be achieved abroad rather than in the UK. He made a finding of dangerousness and concluded that they were equally responsible. He imposed extended sentences of 17 years 8 months comprising a custodial term of 12 years 8 months and an extended licence period of five years. The judge granted 20 per cent credit for their guilty pleas, meaning that the custodial term after trial would have been 16 years. The appellants submitted that the judge had erred in finding them dangerous and imposing extended sentences. They argued that their admitted involvement with the Free Syria Army represented a less blameworthy form of the offence and should be regarded as some form of noble cause terrorism. They further contended that there should have been a Newton hearing since the prosecution did not accept their bases of plea and put the case forward on a different basis.

Held: Appeal allowed. (1) There was no basis for criticising the judge's conclusion that the appellants were equally involved. There were no sentencing guidelines for such an offence since the facts of individual cases were likely to be very different from one another. A s.5 offence was committed when a person engaged in acts of terrorism in the UK for the purpose of giving effect to an intention to commit acts of terrorism which could take place in the UK or abroad. By their guilty pleas, the appellants had acknowledged that their conduct met that definition. The starting point for sentence was the sentence that would have been imposed if the objective had been achieved, in other words if the intended acts of terrorism had actually been carried out. However, the ultimate sentence would largely be determined by the factual nexus between the offender's conduct in the UK in preparation for acts of terrorism and the potential acts of terrorism, *R. v Dart (Richard)* [2014] EWCA Crim 2158, *R. v Khan (Usman)* [2013] EWCA Crim 468 and *Attorney General's Reference (No.7 of 2008)* [2008] EWCA Crim 1054 considered. The offences were characterised by a significant degree of planning and persistence. The fact that the target of their intentions was not in the UK did not mean that the criteria for a consideration of dangerousness did not apply. The combination of extensive planning and premeditation coupled with repeated expressions of alignment with radical Muslim fundamentalism, followed by the appellants acting on such views, confirmed that the judge was correct in his finding of dangerousness and in passing an extended sentence (see paras 24-25, 28-30 of judgment). (2) So-called noble cause terrorism could not be regarded as a mitigating factor. Preparatory activity with a view to fighting UK forces was not present as an aggravating feature, but it had to be borne in mind that the absence of aggravation did not constitute positive mitigation, *R. v F* [2007] EWCA Crim 243, [2007] Q.B. 960, [2007] C.L.Y. 925 considered. In any event, s.5 applied whether or not the intended activity was to take place within the UK. Further, while the prosecution accepted that the appellants had no specific intention of attacking civilians, the position was not that clear-cut and it would be unrealistic to conclude that there would be no harm to civilians (paras 41-46). (3) Given the way the prosecution had put the case, there was no basis for the judge to reject the bases of plea as manifestly false. Accordingly, he erred in forming the conclusion he did without hearing evidence. There was a substantial nexus between the preparatory activity and what transpired once the appellants went abroad. Nonetheless, the finding of involvement in combat activity improperly made by the judge made some difference to the sentence imposed (paras 48, 50-53). (4) The appellants showed a deep commitment to the jihadist cause maintained over a substantial period and resorted to subterfuge in order to achieve their aim. Both were nearly 21 when they left the UK. Neither had any previous convictions, but the offences were grave and the mitigation of good character carried correspondingly less weight in the circumstances, *R. v Khawaji (Imran)*considered. The starting point of 16 years was too high and was reduced to 13 years. A 20 per cent credit for guilty pleas resulted in a custodial term of 10 years 3 months. The five-year extension period was appropriate (paras 37-38, 47, 55-57).

R. v SARWAR (YUSUF) *sub nom.* R. v AHMED (MOHAMMED), [2015] EWCA Crim 1886, [2016] 1 Cr. App. R. (S.) 54, Treacy LJ, CA (Crim Div).

1933 Terrorist offences–Sentencing guidelines–Guidance on imposition of sentences under s.5 Terrorism Act 2006

[Terrorism Act 2006 (c.11) s.5; Criminal Justice Act 2003 (c.44) Pt 12 s.236A, s.244A; Counter-Terrorism Act 2008 (c.28) s.47, s.56]

While considering one Attorney General's reference and five appeals against sentence for terrorism related offences, the Court of Appeal provided guidance on sentencing for offences committed under the Terrorism Act 2006 s.5.

Held: Judgment accordingly. (1) As the range of conduct covered by s.5 was broad, it was appropriate to divide it into levels of criminality. Those levels were differentiated by (a) the culpability of the offender by reference to his proximity to carrying out the intended act(s), and (b) the harm caused measured in terms of the impact on immediate victims and the wider public. The judge should identify where on the scale the offending fell, taking into account the following levels (in each instance, the range identified related to the sentence after trial, and the cases were cited as illustration of conduct which came within the relevant level): *Level 1* - the highest level was where the offender had taken steps which amounted to attempted multiple murder, or to a conspiracy to commit multiple murder. A sentence of life imprisonment with a minimum term of 30 to 40 years or more was appropriate, *R. v Ibrahim (Muktar)* [2008] EWCA Crim 880, [2009] 1 W.L.R. 578, [2008] C.L.Y. 700, *R. v Ali (Abdulla Ahmed)* [2011] EWCA Crim 1260, [2011] 3 All E.R. 1071, [2011] C.L.Y. 812 and *R. v Barot (Dhiren)* [2007] EWCA Crim 1119, [2008] 1 Cr. App. R. (S.) 31, [2007] C.L.Y. 3691 considered. *Level 2* - those who might not get quite so near in preparation or where the harm which might have been caused was not quite as serious. In such cases a life sentence would generally be called for with a minimum term in the range of 21 to 30 years or a very long determinate sentence and an extension period of five years, *R. v Khyam (Omar)* [2008] EWCA Crim 1612, [2009] 1 Cr. App. R. (S.) 77, [2009] C.L.Y. 807, *R. v Asiedu (Manfo Kwaku)* [2008] EWCA Crim 1725, [2009] 1 Cr. App. R. (S.) 72, [2009] C.L.Y. 3347, *R. v Karim (Rajib)* [2011] EWCA Crim 2577, [2012] 1 Cr. App. R. (S.) 85, [2012] C.L.Y. 3021 and *R. v Jalil (Abdul Aziz)* [2008] EWCA Crim 2910, [2009] 2 Cr. App. R. (S.) 40 considered. *Level 3* - cases where the offender travelled abroad and participated in actual combat. The offender would invariably be dangerous. The appropriate sentence would be a life sentence with a minimum term of 15 to 20 years or a long determinate sentence of 20 to 30 years or more with an extension period of five years, *R. v Khan (Parviz)* [2009] EWCA Crim 1085, [2010] 1 Cr. App. R. (S.) 35, [2010] C.L.Y. 2990 and *R. v Khan (Usman)* [2013] EWCA Crim 468 considered. *Level 4* - offenders who joined or supported a terrorist organisation, usually engaged in a conflict overseas, and either participated on the periphery of the combat or trained to that end or with a view to carrying out acts in the UK. Such an offender was likely to be dangerous and a determinate sentence in the range of 10 to 20 years or more with an extension period of five years was likely to be appropriate, *R. v Sarwar (Yusuf)* [2015] EWCA Crim 1886, [2016] 1 Cr. App. R. (S.) 54, [2016] 1932 and *R. v Dart (Richard)* [2014] EWCA Crim 2158 considered. *Level 5* - offenders who set out to join an overseas terrorist organization but did not complete their journey or offenders who made extensive preparations, but did not get very far. Where the offender was not dangerous, the range of a determinate sentence was likely to be five to 10 years, *R. v Tabbakh (Hassan)* [2009] EWCA Crim 464, (2009) 173 J.P. 201, [2009] C.L.Y. 935 and *Attorney General's Reference (No.7 of 2008)* [2008] EWCA Crim 1054 considered. The Criminal Justice Act 2003 Pt 12 s.236A / s.244A also applied. *Level 6* - the typical offender would be one who never set out to join a terrorist organisation, or who set out, but the circumstances were such that it was unlikely that he would go very far, or returned without going far, or who had a minor role in relation to intended acts at the lowest end of seriousness in the UK. Sentences in the range of 21 months to five years were likely to be appropriate. Section 236A / s.244A of the 2003 Act also applied.

Whatever the sentence imposed, the notification requirements under the Counter-Terrorism Act 2008 s.47-s.56 applied (see paras 23-35 of judgment). (2) The court also considered more general issues including (a) the wide definition of terrorism; (b) the use of s.5 where specific offences could have been charged; (c) the purpose or aim of the terrorism; and (d) the factors relevant to sentencing in cases under s.5 (paras 3-22). (3) The Attorney General's reference was allowed and the sentence was increased to eight years' imprisonment. The appeal by Ziamani was allowed to the extent that his extended sentence of 27 years' imprisonment was reduced to 24 years' imprisonment made up of a custodial term of 19 years and an extended licence period of five years. The application for leave to appeal by Khan was allowed to the extent that the minimum term of the sentence of life imprisonment was reduced from 25 to 23 years. The appeal of Eshati was dismissed and the applications of Rashid and Ozcelik were refused (para.182).

R. v KAHAR (MOHAMMED ABDUL); R. v ZIAMANI (BRUSTHOM); R. v ESHATI (ABDURRAOUF); R. v RASHID (YAHYA); R. v OZCELIK (SILHAN); R. v KHAN (SANA), [2016] EWCA Crim 568, [2016] 1 W.L.R. 3156, Lord Thomas LCJ, CA (Crim Div).

1934 Theft–Assault–Theft from jewellers involving assault of intervening customer–Young offenders

The appellant (M), who had pleaded guilty to theft and assault by beating, appealed against his sentence of two years' detention. M, who was now 20, and an accomplice had forced their way into a small jewellery shop. They ran towards the window display and took a watch selling for £6,500. The owner of the shop and the customer with him tried to detain the men. The accomplice escaped with the watch but M was detained. There was a short struggle during which the customer was wrestled to the ground and received cuts to his hands. M had appeared before the courts on eight previous occasions for 11 offences between 2009 and 2013. He had convictions for possessing a Class B drug with intent to supply, possession of cannabis and amphetamine, violent disorder, burglary and possessing a prohibited weapon, an automatic weapon and ammunition. The sentencing judge took 30 months as the starting point for the theft and six months (the maximum for the offence) for the assault. He gave full credit for M's plea.

Held: Appeal dismissed. Having regard to the sentencing guidelines concerning thefts from shops, which stated that the offence would be aggravated by the use or threat of force, the sentence for the theft could not be considered manifestly excessive. As to the assault, this was undoubtedly a category 1 case of greater harm and higher culpability. When imposing the maximum sentence of six months consecutive to the sentence for theft, which took into account the use or threat of violence, the judge did not double count; a consecutive sentence was merited. M and his accomplice had forced their way into the premises. The shop-owner would have felt threatened and fearful in continuing his business. That was in addition to, and separate from, the actual assault on the customer, which in itself had the additional aggravating feature of his being injured while trying to prevent a crime. M's convictions were an additional aggravating feature in respect of the assault offence. The sentences were not manifestly excessive either individually or cumulatively (see paras 6-8 of judgment).

R. v MIAH (HELAL), [2015] EWCA Crim 1231, [2016] 1 Cr. App. R. (S.) 1, Rafferty LJ, CA (Crim Div).

1935 Theft Act offences–Going equipped to steal–Going equipped for burglary and theft

The appellant (H) appealed against a sentence of 20 months' imprisonment following his guilty plea to going equipped for burglary and theft. Whilst being searched on suspicion of drug offences H had been found in possession of a pair of bolt croppers, rubber gloves, a face mask and a camouflage hat. H had 12 previous convictions, including for robbery. The sentencing judge indicated that following trial the appropriate sentence would have been two years' imprisonment, and applying the one-sixth discount for the guilty plea, he arrived at a sentence of 20 months.

Held: Appeal dismissed. It was not helpful to refer to the definitive sentencing guidelines for offences of going equipped, because they had only come into force after H was sentenced, *R. v Boakye (Christiana)* [2012] EWCA Crim 838, [2013] 1 Cr. App. R. (S.) 2, [2013] C.L.Y. 2620 applied (see para.9 of judgment). The judge had been right to conclude that H was in possession of the items found with the intention of going equipped for burglary. He had indicated that what was planned was an offence of burglary at least, which meant that in his view the collection of items was consistent only with burglary or a more serious offence, namely robbery. He had been entitled to draw that inference. Whilst individually the items recovered might lend themselves to some lesser offence, when considered cumulatively it was difficult to conceive of their use other than in a burglary or robbery (para.10). The instant case was considerably more serious than *R. v Shariff (Idrees)* [2012] EWCA Crim 768: H had been in possession of a face mask and hat and had plainly been contemplating an offence involving at least the possibility of contact with a third party. He also had relevant previous convictions and was on licence at the time of his arrest, *Shariff* considered. The judge had been entitled to conclude that it was a serious example of going equipped. Accordingly, while the sentence was severe, it was not outside the range available to the judge (paras 13-14).

R. v HODGKINS (BEAU ANTHONY), [2016] EWCA Crim 360, [2016] 2 Cr. App. R. (S.) 13, Gross LJ, CA (Crim Div).

1936 Trespass with intent–Sexual offences–Appropriate starting point–Use of knife balanced against early guilty plea and previous good character

The appellant (M) appealed against a total sentence of six years' imprisonment imposed after he pleaded guilty to trespass with intent to commit a sexual offence (count 1) and having an article with a blade or point (count 2). M, aged 33 at the time, had followed the complainant into her house and threatened her with a knife. She thought that he was going to rape her or take money from her. M fled from the property. When police officers attended his house he said "I just tried to rape someone" and told them where the knife was. A victim impact statement noted that the complainant's life had fallen apart since the attack. She had lived at the house for 33 years but had been unable to sleep there for two weeks after the incident and was planning to move. She had not returned to work for some weeks. A pre-sentence reported noted that M had been under the influence of drink and drugs, and could not explain why he had a knife with him. He had apologised for his behaviour. The report considered that M lacked understanding of the physical, psychological and emotional harm that he had caused, which was a significant risk factor. He was assessed as posing a high risk of reoffending and a medium to high risk of harm to females, especially if he continued to use alcohol and drugs. A three-year community sentence was recommended. The sentencing judge noted that the offence was in category 1 of the relevant guideline with a starting point of six years' imprisonment. He took into account that the attack occurred in the victim's home, the use of a weapon and the intention of committing an offence which, had it been committed, would have carried a maximum sentence of life imprisonment. In mitigation, M had no previous convictions, had expressed genuine remorse and was of previous good character. The judge considered that he was bound to take account of the extreme effect of the offences on the complainant. A sentence of six years' imprisonment was imposed for count 1, and a concurrent three-year sentence for count 2. A restraining order and notification requirements were also imposed. M argued that the judge had taken a starting point of nine years for count 1, which was too high.

Held: Appeal allowed. The sentencing guidelines suggested a starting point of six years with a range of four to nine. The offence was very serious with a number of aggravating features: M had violated the complainant's home; a knife was carried and used against the complainant's face and neck; the complainant was caused grave psychological harm. In mitigation, M was of previous good character, he admitted the offence immediately and entered his plea at the earliest opportunity thus relieving the complainant from giving evidence. The use of a knife justified increasing the starting point. However, the nine-year starting point was too high and M should have been given greater credit for his previous good character and immediate admission of the offence. The appropriate starting point was seven-and-a-half years. Making a full reduction for the guilty plea, the appropriate sentence was five years' imprisonment. The six year sentence on count 1 was quashed and replaced (see paras 17-18 of judgment).

R. v MIAH (MUKITH), [2015] EWCA Crim 1628, [2016] 1 Cr. App. R. (S.) 27, Lloyd Jones LJ, CA (Crim Div).

1937 Wounding–Aggravating features–Unlawful wounding including racial threat but not charged as racially aggravated offence

[Crime and Disorder Act 1998 (c.37) s.29(1)(a)]

An appellant appealed against a total sentence of eight years' imprisonment imposed following his guilty pleas to offences of assault with intent to rob and unlawful wounding. The three offences took place during the course of one evening, when the appellant repeatedly armed himself with knives which he used to intimidate two victims who were in sole charge of convenience stores. Both victims suffered physical injuries and psychological harm as a result of the attacks which were captured on CCTV. In the second attack, while brandishing a knife, the appellant told his victim that he wanted to kill a Muslim. He had previous convictions for assault occasioning actual bodily harm, common assault, racially threatening behaviour, harassment and possessing an offensive weapon. In sentencing, the judge referred to a number of aggravating features, including the significant psychological harm caused to the victim of the unlawful wounding due to the racial nature of the threat to him. He assessed the assault as a level 2 offence with a starting point of four years' imprisonment; he determined the pre-plea starting point to be six years and eight months, and deducted 25 per cent to reflect a reduced discount for plea because of the overwhelming nature of the CCTV evidence. In relation to the unlawful wounding, the judge assessed the offences as falling within category 1 with a starting point of three years; he determined the pre-plea starting point to be four years' imprisonment and, for the same reasons, made a similar discount for plea. The appellant argued that, in the absence of a conviction of an offence of racially aggravated unlawful wounding contrary to the Crime and Disorder Act 1998 s.29(1)(a), the judge was not entitled to treat racial motivation as a factor which increased the seriousness of the unlawful wounding.

Held: Appeal dismissed. There was clear evidence on which the judge had been entitled to conclude to the criminal standard that the offence was racially motivated, and in the circumstances he was entitled to treat the matter as a factor which increased the seriousness of the offence. However, that was not an endorsement of the view that the prosecution were thereby relieved of their duty to consider the indictment with care. In the majority of cases where the evidence supported an aggravated form of assault, it should be placed upon the indictment, *R. v Khan (Imran Mohammed)* [2009] EWCA Crim 389, [2010] 1 Cr. App. R. (S.) 1, [2010] C.L.Y. 2936 considered. It was an extremely serious series of offences; at least one of the offences was racially aggravated and the victims had suffered lasting psychological harm. The circumstances merited the overall sentence passed (see paras 16-19 of judgment).

R. v O'LEARY (MICHAEL PATRICK), [2015] EWCA Crim 1306, [2016] 1 Cr. App. R. (S.) 11, McCombe LJ, CA (Crim Div).

1938 Wounding with intent–Biting–Offender biting victim's eyebrow and flesh

An offender appealed against a total sentence of eight years and two months' imprisonment imposed following his convictions for wounding with intent and witness intimidation and his guilty plea to handling stolen goods. The offender, aged 39 at the time of appeal, had attended a rugby club fundraising day. He had argued with the victim, the owner of a bouncy castle, after the victim had spoken to the offender's son about his behaviour. The victim had later been attacked outside the club and went inside to confront a man he believed to be responsible. The offender intervened in that confrontation, knocked the victim to the ground and bit his eyebrow, biting away part of his flesh. The victim required plastic surgery and had a permanent scar; he also suffered severe psychological consequences. While on bail, the offender intimidated the victim. He also had stolen goods in his house. Following the offender's convictions, and his guilty plea on the handling stolen goods count, the judge considered the appropriate category for the wounding offence within the relevant sentencing guideline.

He placed the case in category 2 on the basis that there was greater harm, in that the injury was "serious in the context of the offence" within the terms of the guideline, but lower culpability. He noted aggravating factors: the offender's previous convictions for violence; the ongoing effect on the victim; the presence of a large number of people, including children, during the attack; the fact that the attack had breached a community order to which the offender was subject; and the fact that he had been intoxicated. He also held that there had been an element of premeditation. He imposed sentences of seven years' imprisonment for the wounding, 12 months consecutive for the intimidation and two months consecutive for the handling offence. The offender argued that the wounding offence had been wrongly placed in category 2, and even if that category was correct, there was no reason to impose a sentence 12 months longer than the six-year starting point.

Held: Appeal dismissed. The judge had been wrong to hold that the offence was one of greater harm because, within the scale of grievous bodily harm, the case fell somewhat short of injury "serious in the context of the offence". However, the judge had also erred in his conclusion that the case was one of lesser culpability. Use by the offender of his teeth should be regarded as the use of a "weapon equivalent" within the guideline, *R. v Wagner (Carl David)* [2013] EWCA Crim 529 and *Attorney General's Reference (No.6 of 2015)* [2015] EWCA Crim 625, [2015] 2 Cr. App. R. (S.) 24, [2015] C.L.Y. 2302 applied. Accordingly, albeit by a different route than that taken by the judge, the court arrived at the same conclusion, namely that the case should be in category 2. The aggravating features identified by the judge clearly resulted in a significant increase in the starting point. There was little, if anything, in the offender's favour. There had been no provocation or presumed provocation; nor could the case be regarded as entirely lacking in premeditation. The sentence for the wounding was not manifestly excessive. No challenge had been made to the other sentences and there was no reason to reduce them (see paras 21-23 of judgment).

R. v THOMPSON (DALE), [2015] EWCA Crim 1575, [2016] 1 Cr. App. R. (S.) 26, Holroyde J, CA (Crim Div).

1939 Wounding with intent–Imprisonment for public protection–Appropriateness of indeterminate sentence for sudden knife attack on 64-year-old causing serious injury

[Criminal Justice Act 2003 (c.44)]

The appellant (J) appealed against a sentence of imprisonment for public protection with a minimum term of seven years imposed following his conviction for wounding with intent. J had followed a 64-year-old man and suddenly attacked him, repeatedly stabbing him. The man suffered eight stab wounds so deep that his bowels were protruding and seriously damaged. J had been four times over the drink drive limit. A medical expert (X), who had not seen J's psychiatric records, believed that J had a schizoaffective disorder and that his acts had been the consequence of psychosis rather than a criminal motive. The judge directed an independent report and the medical expert (Y), who had seen J's records, disagreed with X and stated that J had a borderline personality disorder. He said that J posed a significant risk of harm to others in the future, based on J's long-running intrusive thoughts about stabbing and hurting other people, and that there was a high risk of future severe violence. X assessed J again and disagreed with Y's diagnosis on the basis that J appeared to be responding to anti-psychotic medication, suggesting that J stop taking the medication to allow for a clearer diagnosis. A third expert, who saw J after a year of his not taking the medication, concluded that J had an emotional unstable personality disorder, and that there was no link between the disordered mental state and the commission of the offence. The sentencing judge found there to be a significant risk of serious harm being caused in the future and that J was likely to represent a significant risk upon release. He assessed the offence as being within category 1, with a range of 12 to 16 years' imprisonment. He found greater harm indicated by the injuries being extremely serious and resulting from a sustained attack, and higher culpability indicated by the use of a weapon, pre-meditation, and the targeting of a vulnerable victim. The existence of a previous offence of robbery with a knife, seven years before, was an aggravating factor. The judge gave a notional determinate term of 14 years, hence the seven-year minimum term. J submitted that (1) the medical evidence showed that his risk was not significant within the meaning of the Criminal Justice Act 2003; (2) an extended sentence could and should have been imposed as his mental health was improving; (3) the notional determinate term was too long as the judge had failed to consider the specific guideline mitigating factor of his mental state, with the medical evidence showing that his acts were primarily a consequence of his psychosis rather than a criminal motive.

Held: Appeal dismissed. (1) The judge's task had been to reach a conclusion on all of the evidence including J's background and all the available medical evidence. The judge had been entitled to reach his conclusion about dangerousness and the material showed that he had been correct (see para.11 of judgment). (2) J's difficulties went back over 20 years. There were two serious offences which were separated by a seven-year gap. There were difficulties in monitoring somebody, even under supportive terms, as part of a licence under an extended sentence. Notwithstanding J's progress, the judge was entitled to conclude that the risk of serious harm upon release, whenever that would be, could not be excluded. That uncertainty militated against imposing an extended sentence (para.13). (3) The specific guideline mitigating factor was not one where a mental disorder had caused or contributed to the offence. It was expressed in terms of a mental disorder or learning disability not linked to the commission of the offence. If the mental disorder had to be taken into account, consideration would have to be given to the balancing, significantly aggravating factor of the offence being committed under the influence of an enormous quantity of alcohol. The judge had been entitled to reject X's view about the psychosis and its relationship to the commission of the offence, which stood alone, in favour of the contrary expert opinions. The notional determinate term was entirely appropriate and the consequent minimum term was not manifestly excessive (paras 17-19).

R. v ATKINSON (JAMES), [2014] EWCA Crim 2010, [2015] M.H.L.R. 492, Sharp LJ, CA (Crim Div).

1940 Wounding with intent–Imprisonment for public protection–Offender later diagnosed as having personality disorder at time of offence–Commission of later offences for which hospital order received–Appropriateness of imprisonment for public protection for wounding with intent

[Mental Health Act 1983 (c.20) s.37, s.41, s.45A]

The appellant (X) appealed against a sentence of imprisonment for public protection with a minimum term of seven-and-a-half-years' imprisonment for wounding with intent. X had met the complainant (C) at a bar. He realised that C was vulnerable and arranged to meet at a later date. X met C at his home and took the co-accused (Y) with him. X asked to borrow money from C and all three went to the cash point to see if he had any. C did not so they all returned to his flat where X and Y attacked C and asked for his wallet and phone. X slit C's throat three times, attempted to suffocate him by stuffing a sock in his mouth and holding a pillow over his head, which he took a picture of, and then slit his throat again. Y hit C over the head twice and cut his arm. X and Y effectively left C for dead. The sentencing judge noted that the appropriate determinate sentence would have been 15 years' imprisonment, but that as X was "dangerous", imprisonment for public protection with a minimum term of seven-and-a-half-years was the appropriate sentence. Whilst in prison for the index offence, X tied up his cellmate and threatened to cut his throat with a razor blade. X gagged him and held him hostage for a number of hours in anticipation of his demands being met, but eventually gave in. X pleaded guilty to false imprisonment and making threats to kill. Two doctors prepared reports on X. They both agreed that he had a personality disorder but disagreed on the sentencing options, one favouring a hospital order under the Mental Health Act 1983 s.37 with a s.41 restriction and the other favouring a hospital and limitation direction under s.45A. X was transferred to a high security hospital and his treating doctor also recommended a s.45A hospital and limitation direction, as there was a strong possibility that X would disengage from treatment. The judge imposed an order under s.37 with a s.41 restriction order stating that it operated independently of the earlier order of imprisonment for public protection and that a s.45 order was not appropriate as X's offending was connected to his mental illness. X submitted that, in light of his diagnosis and later offences, the term of imprisonment for public protection for the index offence was wrong in principle and that the most appropriate sentence was a s.37 hospital order with a s.41 restriction.

Held: Appeal dismissed. The later offences were intrinsically linked to X's personality disorder. X's responsibility was diminished to a certain extent by his disorder but there still remained a strong element of criminality; the index offence was committed with another person who did not suffer from a personality disorder or mental health condition. There was a strong risk of return to criminality, even if X's personality disorder could be adequately treated and alleviated. The fact that X would be recalled under a hospital order, if one was imposed for the index offence, if he reoffended was not sufficient protection for the public given the risk that X posed. Further, the treatment that X was currently receiving would not be interfered with by the existing order for imprisonment for public protection or hospital order under sections 37 and 41. Accordingly, even in the light of the later offences and subsequent sentence, it could not be said that the sentence for the index offence was wrong in principle (see paras 25, 28, 31-32 of judgment).

R. v ANDERSON (DARREN GABRIEL), [2013] EWCA Crim 2212, [2014] M.H.L.R. 324, Lloyd Jones LJ, CA (Crim Div).

1941 Wounding with intent–Knives–Victim stabbed three times and kicked whilst on ground–Undue leniency

The Attorney General referred to the court as unduly lenient a sentence of 18 months' imprisonment following an offender's guilty plea to wounding with intent. The offender, who was aged 23, and the victim had both separately attended a party. They knew each other but not well. When the party ended the victim left with his friends and the offender with his. The offender approached the victim with a knife which had a 17cm-long blade and began stabbing him. A fight ensured and the offender stabbed the victim twice to his lower back and once to his shoulder. The victim fell to the ground where the offender kicked him. He lost consciousness. The victim's two sisters tried to help but the offender scratched one with the knife and punched her to the forehead, and kicked the other in the back. He said that if the victim did not die then, he would kill him later. The victim suffered three stab wounds, damage to a kidney and loss of blood. At a hearing to extend custody time limits, the offender asked the judge for an indication as to sentence. At the following *Goodyear* hearing, the prosecution submitted that the offence fell within category 2 of the relevant sentencing guideline for such an assault, which had a starting point of six years' imprisonment and a range of five of nine years. The judge indicated that the maximum sentence following a guilty plea would be 18 months' imprisonment. The offender pleaded guilty. In sentencing him, the judge took into account the offender's age, plea and lack of previous convictions. The offender argued that the level of injustice involved in interfering with the sentence, bearing in mind that he was due to be released imminently, would be beyond that which could be rectified by applying any discount for double jeopardy. The Attorney General submitted that the case was one of higher culpability, that there were several aggravating features, including the use of a knife three times, and that the case fell towards the top end of the range of category 2 of the guideline.

Held: Reference allowed. (1) The offender came close to saying that the more a sentence was unduly lenient, the less the court should interfere. That could not be accepted as a proposition. Where a sentence was unduly lenient, the court would normally intervene. Obviously, justice would not have been done. The positions of the victim and of society had to be taken into account, just as much as that of the individual offender (see para.28 of judgment). (2) The court was in no doubt that the sentence was unduly lenient. Whilst the offender was relatively young and had no relevant previous convictions, the case remained well within the range indicated in the sentencing guideline. It was a bad case of its kind. There were a number of aggravating factors; in particular, that a knife was used and used three times, that the victim was kicked on the ground, and the circumstances in which that occurred. Balancing the aggravating and mitigating factors, and having regard to the facts, a starting point of seven years, or perhaps more, would have been appropriate. A notional and generous credit of 25% for the offender's guilty plea would be accorded. The lowest sentence that the court could impose in the circumstances was five years' imprisonment (paras 29-31).

ATTORNEY GENERAL'S REFERENCE (NO.126 OF 2015) *sub nom.* R. v BILY (JONAS), [2016] EWCA Crim 37, [2016] 1 Cr. App. R. (S.) 71, Davis LJ, CA (Crim Div).

1942 Wounding with intent–Offender suffering from autism–Whether indeterminate sentence should be replaced by hospital and restriction orders

[Mental Health Act 1983 (c.20) s.37, s.41, s.45A, s.47]

The applicant (R) applied for an extension of time within which to seek leave to appeal against sentences of detention for public protection. The sentences had been imposed in November 2007 and May 2008. As to the first sentence, R had pleaded guilty to three offences of wounding with intent, one offence of having a bladed article and one offence of having an offensive weapon. The later sentence had been imposed following R's plea of guilty to two offences of making a threat to kill. Both sentences were subject to limitation directions made under the Mental Health Act 1983 s.45A. Under those directions, R was sent to Broadmoor Hospital. He now resided at a specialist medium-secure unit handling patients who suffered from autistic spectrum disorder. R had been under 21 at the time of the offences.

Held: Application granted. As s.45A applied only when a sentence of imprisonment was being imposed, the court did not have the power to make the limitation directions. The issue was whether, had the judge known of the absence of the power, the sentence would or should have been one of detention for an indeterminate period or orders under s.37 and s.41 of the 1983 Act. Had there remained a significant risk that R might be released while he was a danger to the public, it would have been appropriate to leave the indeterminate sentence undisturbed and rely on the secretary of state to exercise his power under s.47 of the Act to transfer R to hospital. However, having regard to the written evidence of two properly certified medical practitioners, it had been established that R should be detained at the unit where he was staying under s.37. Further, by reason of the clear danger that he presented to the public, he should be made the subject of a restriction order under s.41 (see paras 3, 33, 38 of judgment).

R. v RUBY (IAN), [2013] EWCA Crim 1653, [2014] M.H.L.R. 205, Pitchford LJ, CA (Crim Div).

1943 Wounding with intent–Sentencing guidelines–Level of harm necessary to place offence within Category 1 of sentencing guideline

[Offences Against the Person Act 1861 (c.100) s.18]

The appellant (S) appealed against sentences imposed for wounding with intent and burglary. S's wife had started a relationship with another man. S broke into his home and struck him with a baseball bat. The victim collapsed onto a bed. S then struck him again with such force that the bat broke into pieces. The victim suffered lacerations to his head, which required stitches, and a fractured arm. S pleaded guilty to burglary and was convicted of the wounding offence after trial. The judge considered that the wounding offence fell within Category 1 of the relevant sentencing guideline as it involved greater harm and higher culpability. He sentenced S to 12 years' imprisonment for the wounding, and six years' imprisonment for burglary, to be served concurrently. S argued that the wounding offence fell within Category 2 of the guideline because the victim had not suffered greater harm.

Held: Appeal allowed. (1) Three factors were referred to in the guideline under Category 1: the nature of the injury; the vulnerability of the victim and whether the attack was sustained or repeated. (a) With regard to the victim's injury, the question was whether the injury was serious "in the context of the offence". The purpose behind those words was to distinguish between the level of violence inherent in a standard offence under the Offences Against the Person Act 1861 s.18, and that which went beyond what could be viewed as standard. The starting point for a Category 1 offence was 12 years' custody, and for a Category 2 offence it was six years. Given the marked disparity in the starting points, the sort of harm and violence which would justify placing a case within Category 1 had to be significantly above the level of harm which was normal for the purpose of s.18. In the instant case, there was one blow which amounted to a s.18 offence, inflicted when the victim was on the bed, prone and defenseless. The blow was delivered with sufficient force to break the bat. It necessitated three stitches to the back of the victim's head but, following the blow, the victim had been able to rise from the bed and pursue S out of the house. It was a serious attack, but it could not be said to be serious in the context of the offence standing alone. However, that single blow had followed on from a previous blow which caused a fracture to the victim's arm and lacerations to his head. It was relevant as context to take all the blows into account. Viewed in that light, the violence was more serious and involved materially more harm, taking it much closer to Category 1 (see paras 14-16 of judgment); (b) In relation to the victim's vulnerability, the obvious categories of vulnerability were extraneous to the offence, such as age, medical condition or infirmity. However, the category of vulnerability was not limited only to extraneous considerations. An attack on a person who at the point of attack was already dazed, prone and not able to defend himself by reason of events directly connected to the offence might also make that victim vulnerable. His personal circumstances at that particular point in time included the condition he had been placed in by the prior attack (para.17); (c) An assault might be "sustained" because it continued over the course of a significant period of time, even though it did not involve a substantial number of blows. An assault could be "repeated" because it involved multiple blows over a short period of time. The instant case involved two blows. It was doubtful whether the difference between one blow and two could justify moving the starting point from six years to 12. The concept of sustained or repeated imported some degree of persistent repetition. To comply with the test of proportionality, the facts warranting the higher sentence should reflect the difference in the guidelines. Two blows, one of which did not amount to a s.18 offence, would not normally amount to a sustained or repeated assault (para.18). (2) Overall, S's offence was not a clear Category 1 case. It was either at the top end of Category 2, or on the borderline between the categories. A starting point of nine years was appropriate, with a range of seven to 11 years. S had broken into the victim's home in the middle of the night and attacked him in the presence of his partner. The fact that the victim was prone on the bed at the time of the final blow was a further aggravating consideration. S's mitigation included his lack of previous convictions, that the injuries were not serious and that the incident was out of character. A sentence of nine years' imprisonment was therefore appropriate (paras 20-21, 24).

R. v SMITH (GRANT CHRISTOPHER), [2015] EWCA Crim 1482, [2016] 1 Cr. App. R. (S.) 8, Macur LJ, CA (Crim Div).

SHIPPING

1944 Bills of lading–Delivery orders–Use of electronic release system

[Carriage of Goods by Sea Act 1992 (c.50) s.1(4)]

The claimant claimed against the first defendant shipping company (M) for damages for breach of contract. The claimant had contacted with M to have three containers shipped to Antwerp under a negotiable bill of lading. The claimant's agents (S) were to take delivery. The bill contained an express term that an endorsed original bill had to be surrendered to the carrier in exchange for the goods. However, the cargo was handled under an electronic release system (ERS) at Antwerp, under which carriers provided electronic pin codes. Holders of bills then presented the codes at the terminal to take delivery of goods. The claimant had previously made successful shipments to Antwerp for which M would email a release note and pin code to S. In respect of the instant shipment, M sent S a code for each of three containers, but S's hauliers were informed that two had already been collected. S produced a copy of the bill and M, arguing that it was obliged to exchange it for either the goods or a delivery order, provided a delivery order. The claimant argued that it had not been aware that the ERS was being used and that M should have delivered the cargo only on presentation of an endorsed bill. M submitted that S's knowledge of the use of ERS was to be imputed to the claimant, that providing S with the pin codes had constituted a delivery order and that it had handled the cargo in accordance with the express term of the bill. Alternatively, an implied term permitted ERS use, or S had agreed on the claimant's behalf to vary the term. M further submitted that it had given no undertaking with regard to delivery, or if it had, it was only that the goods would be delivered to whoever presented the right codes, and that the claimant was estopped from complaining by reason of previous dealings.

Held: Judgment for claimant. (1) The claimants had not known that M had been using the ERS. S was not the claimant's agent for the purpose of entering into contracts, and S's knowledge was not relevant to determining the contractual intention evinced by the claimant when it made the contract. "Delivery order" had to be interpreted in its context in the bill. The parties had to be taken to be referring to what was commonly called a "ship's delivery order", defined in the Carriage of Goods by Sea Act 1992 s.1(4). An essential feature of such a delivery order was that it contained an undertaking by the carrier to deliver the goods to the other party, *Waren Import Gesellschaft Krohn & Co v Internationale Graanhandel Thegra NV* [1975] 1 Lloyd's Rep. 146, [1975] C.L.Y. 3145 considered. The purpose of agreeing that a delivery order might be delivered rather than the goods in exchange for a bill was usually to expedite the performance of contracts and allow bulk cargoes to be split into parcels without issuing substitute bills. It was improbable that the holder of the bill would agree to a term where it might surrender its rights against the carrier without receiving the goods or a substitute undertaking (see paras 19 and 23 of judgment). (2) Negotiable bills were addressed to, and had to be understood by, various persons other that the original parties. Original parties were taken to have intended that bills should be given the meaning conveyed by their wording in the light of knowledge available to the range of persons to whom they were addressed, *Homburg Houtimport BV v Agrosin Private Ltd (The Starsin)* [2003] UKHL 12, [2004] 1 A.C. 715, [2003] C.L.Y. 3896 followed. The parties would not have expected a range of addressees to know of their previous dealings and were not to be taken to have intended that previous dealings should inform the interpretation of the bill (para.22). (3) M had to show that when it provided pin codes for previous shipments it had been taken to have fulfilled its responsibilities and had no further liability. The previous dealings provided no support for that proposition. Even if the claimant had been content for the ERS to be used, it did not follow that it would have agreed that delivery was made on receipt of pin codes rather than goods. The port authority's operator's covenant contemplated that delivery occurred only when the code was used to take goods from the port, and that receipt of a code conferred a right of delivery, not actual delivery. M had not, in exchange for the bill, given a delivery order of the kind required by the bill and had not expressly complied with its obligations (paras 24-25). (4) The parties had agreed that M might surrender goods against a delivery order. However, an agreement to such a limited relaxation made it difficult to suppose that they intended to go further, *Johnson v Unisys Ltd* [2001] UKHL 13, [2003] 1 A.C. 518, [2001] C.L.Y. 2253 followed. There was no reason to imply a term that by providing a pin code M had fulfilled its obligations (paras 27, 29). (5) S did not have authority to vary the contract by accepting the terms of the release note stating that M was not required to effect delivery in the usual sense. S might have been impliedly authorised to use the ERS, but it did not follow that S was entitled to agree that M could complete delivery otherwise than in accordance with the bill (para.31). (6) The complaint was not that M had breached the contract by delivering the cargo on presentation of pin codes; it was that the cargo had not been delivered. The claimant had not let it be understood that it would be content for the goods to be delivered to anyone who presented the correct pin code and estoppel did not arise (para.33).

GLENCORE INTERNATIONAL AG v MSC MEDITERRANEAN SHIPPING CO SA, [2015] EWHC 1989 (Comm), [2015] 2 Lloyd's Rep. 508, Andrew Smith J, QBD (Comm).

1945 Bills of lading–Hague-Visby Rules–Whether cargo owners claim confined to damages limited by reference to the Hague-Visby Rules

The appellant cargo-owners appealed against a finding (*Yemgas FZCO v Superior Pescadores SA Panama* [2014] EWHC 971 (Comm), [2014] 1 Lloyd's Rep. 660, [2014] C.L.Y. 2706) that they were confined to recover damages limited by reference to the Hague-Visby Rules in their claim against the respondent shipowners. Cargo had been loaded on the vessel in Belgium in 2008. The shipowners had issued six bills of lading in the Conline form. A paramount clause on the reverse of the bills of lading stated that the Hague Rules as enacted in the country of shipment applied to the contract. Significant damage was caused to the cargo on the voyage and the cargo-owners suffered losses. In 2012, an insurance company gave a letter of undertaking to the cargo-owners to pay such sum as was agreed or adjudged in respect of the claim and further agreed on the shipowners' behalf that the claim would be subject to English law. That law included the Carriage of Goods by Sea Act 1971 which rendered the Hague-Visby Rules applicable. The cargo-owners' particulars of claim relied on the clause paramount as a contractual incorporation of the Hague Rules and pleaded that they were entitled to the higher sums provided for by those rules. The judge held that the paramount clause incorporated the Hague Rules, not the Hague-Visby Rules, but that it did not operate as an agreement for a higher limit pursuant to the Hague-Visby Rules and that the cargo-owners were confined to recover damages limited by reference to r.5(a) of the Hague-Visby Rules.

Held: Appeal dismissed. The correct approach was to ask what the phrase "paramount clause" meant to shipping men, *Nea Agrex SA v Baltic Shipping Co Ltd (The Agios Lazarus)* [1976] Q.B. 933, [1976] C.L.Y. 2534 followed. The actual paramount clause identified the Hague Rules but provided that it was those Rules as enacted in the country of shipment. The country of shipment was Belgium which adhered to the Hague-Visby Rules in 1978. *Wilford Coghlin & Kimball, Time Charters* had been correct to say that since 1977 a typical paramount clause, which did not differentiate in terms between the two sets of rules, would be taken by shipping men to incorporate the Hague-Visby Rules in a Baltime charter governed by English law and, by extension, to other charters and to bills of lading subject to such a clause, such as the Conline bills in the instant case. The judge had relied on *Parsons Corp v CV Scheepvaartonderneming Happy Ranger* [2002] EWCA Civ 694, [2002] 2 All E.R. (Comm) 24, [2002] C.L.Y. 4090 as authority for holding that in the bills of lading the Hague Rules rather than the Hague-Visby Rules had been incorporated, *Parsons* considered, *Parsons Corp v CV Scheepvaartonderneming Happy Ranger* [2002] 1 All E.R. (Comm) 176 explained. Retrospective agreement that English law governed the claim had the effect of rendering the Hague-Visby Rules applicable by reason of Sch.1 art.X of the 1971 Act. Any case in which a bill of lading was issued in 2008 incorporating the Hague Rules as enacted in the country of shipment and in which the country of shipment had enacted the Hague-Visby Rules should be regarded as a case which was subject to the Hague-Visby Rules rather than the Hague Rules. The judge's conclusion that the Hague-Visby limit applied was upheld although the Court of Appeal's reasons differed from the judge's (see paras 17, 21-22, 30, 32, 37, 42, 47, 49 of judgment).

YEMGAS FZCO v SUPERIOR PESCADORES SA PANAMA, [2016] EWCA Civ 101, [2016] 2 All E.R. (Comm) 104, Longmore LJ, CA (Civ Div).

1946 Charterparties–Arbitration awards–Permission to appeal

[Arbitration Act 1996 (c.23) s.69, s.69(2)(b), s.69(3)(a)]

The defendant charterers sought to appeal against an arbitrator's decision that they were liable to the claimant shipowners for the detention of a vessel. The shipowners had let the vessel to the charterers. Clause 28 of the charterparty provided that "no voyage shall be undertaken, nor any goods or cargoes loaded, that would expose the vessel to capture or seizure by rulers or governments". Other clauses limited the parties' liabilities for certain events, and there was a clause providing for dispute resolution under the Arbitration Act 1996, with an "appeal to the High Court on any question of law arising out of an award". The charterers subchartered the vessel for a crude oil shipment from Venezuela to the United States. They gave employment orders to the vessel's master with instructions to contact the subcharterers' agents. The charterers received a false document purporting to be an authorisation from the state oil company for cargo loading. Venezuelan port officers arrested an individual for forging it and detained the vessel as part of the criminal investigation. The shipowners and charterers went to arbitration over compensation for the detained vessel. The arbitrator held that the charterers had breached clause 28, amongst others, and were liable to the shipowners. The issues were (1) whether there was an error of law in the arbitrator's decision; (2) whether the charterers required permission to appeal.

Held: Judgment accordingly. (1) The court did not wish to endorse the correctness of the charterers' proposition that the question of whether the voyage exposed the vessel to capture or seizure was to be answered prospectively at the time that the voyage order was given by the charterers. Clause 28 made no reference to voyage orders, but merely to the undertaking of a voyage. If the increased risk materialised during a voyage, the clause came into effect irrespective of whether it arose subsequently to the original voyage orders. As for the arbitrator's reasoning, it was expressed concisely, but the findings of fact were dispositive of the issue and no question of law arose. The findings meant that the charterers' order was not merely to proceed to a load port to await orders, but to proceed to the Venezuelan terminal for the purposes of loading the subcharterer's unlawful cargo. As a direct consequence, the vessel's master was ordered to communicate with the agents, and the vessel received the false authorisation which led to the detention. There was therefore the necessary causative link between the order and the detention. The arbitrator's conclusion, that there was no reason to suppose that on the date of the order the intended cargo was any more authorised than it was later, had not involved an error of law. It reflected what was inherent in the findings of fact: the increased risk of the vessel's arrest existed on the date of the charterers' order because at that stage the agents intended to use the vessel to export an unlawful cargo. That put the charterers in breach of clause 28. The charterers' case attempted to dress up an appeal against findings of fact as one which turned on questions of law. That was sufficient to dispose of the appeal because the charterers could not succeed under the other clauses if the detention was caused by the breach of clause 28 (see paras 31-36 of judgment). (2) The remaining issue was whether the order should be to refuse the charterers permission to appeal, or to dismiss their appeal. The arbitration clause was clearly drafted with the terms of s.69 in mind. Its scope was limited to a question of law whose determination might serve a useful purpose for the parties. The statutory context of s.69(3)(a) suggested that the criterion should be that the question would, as opposed to might, substantially affect the parties' rights. It was for a party asserting that it did not need the court's permission under s.69(2)(b) of the Act, on the grounds that it had an agreement falling within s.69(1)(a), to establish that fact by adducing evidence with the application. The charterers had not fulfilled those criteria. Accordingly, permission to appeal was required, and was refused because the statutory requirement in s.69(3)(a) was not fulfilled (paras 42-44).

ST SHIPPING AND TRANSPORT PTE LTD v SPACE SHIPPING LTD, [2016] EWHC 880 (Comm), [2016] Bus. L.R. 703, Popplewell J, QBD (Comm).

1947 Charterparties–Contract terms–Whether ship owners entitled to court order that protection and indemnity club increase sum insured to cover shortfall in security–"Liberty to apply" clause in letter of undertaking

The claimant ship owners applied for summary judgment on an issue in its claim against the defendant protection and indemnity (P&I) club, of whom the charterers were members. The chemical tanker, "FSL NEW YORK" was damaged during loading in Indonesia causing an escape of cargo. The vessel was on charter and both owners and charterers claimed against each other, with the owners threatening to arrest other vessels owned by companies in the charterer's group of companies. The initial impasse was resolved by the mutual provision of security by way of three letters of undertaking (LOU), one of which was provided to the owners by the charterer's P&I club in the sum of $3,500,000. The LOU allowed for adjustment if the security proved to be inadequate, in the following terms: "*It is agreed that both Charterers and Owners shall have liberty to apply if and to the extent the Security Sum is reasonably deemed to be excessive or insufficient to adequately secure Owners' reasonable Claims.*" The LOU was subject to English law and jurisdiction. A London arbitration was commenced pursuant to the terms of the charterparty but the arbitral tribunal had no power to order security. It was common ground that the owners were under-secured and the issue was whether they were entitled to look to the P&I club directly to make good the shortfall. The owners submitted that the clause gave both owners and charterers liberty to apply to each other and to the court to adjust the security if necessary. The charterers argued that an application to increase or reduce the secured amount had to be an application to the court and to be directed to the other party not directly to the P&I club.

Held: Judgment for defendant. It was correct that the clause was symmetrical, giving charterers the right to reduce the security, and owners the concomitant right to increase it but the charterers were not a party to the LOU and had no rights under it. The standard terms of a P&I club LOU would ordinarily prevent a beneficiary from arresting the assets of the party with which it was in dispute. However, the parties could agree otherwise. Construing the liberty to apply the clause consistently with business common sense they had done so, *Rainy Sky SA v Kookmin Bank* [2011] UKSC 50, [2011] 1 W.L.R. 2900, [2012] C.L.Y. 637 followed. A reference to standard English admiralty procedure was irrelevant as that applied only between the parties and the club was not a party. Similarly the club was not in breach of contract as it had not refused to pay and had never undertaken to increase the security. Further, it was inherently unlikely that a P&I club, or any other financial institution, would issue an instrument giving a court the right to increase its liability on the application of the beneficiary, thus leaving it exposed on an unsecured basis (see paras 14-18, 19-23, 25-34 of judgment).

FSL-9 PTE LTD v NORWEGIAN HULL CLUB, [2016] EWHC 1091 (Comm), [2016] 2 All E.R. (Comm) 576, Blair J, QBD (Comm).

1948 Charterparties–Incorporation by reference–Bill of lading–Express terms

[Arbitration Act 1996 (c.23) s.44; Senior Courts Act 1981 (c.54) s.37]

The claimant vessel owners applied to continue an anti-suit injunction preventing the defendant charterers from bringing proceedings in China. The parties had agreed a time charterparty, dated 11 April 2013, that included a London arbitration clause. They had also agreed a vessel charterparty with a different date. The bill of lading stated that freight was to be payable "as per the charterparty" and that all the terms and conditions of the charterparty "dated as overleaf" were incorporated. The overleaf contained the date, "11 April 2013". An accident occurred during the voyage, damaging the cargo which had to be salvaged. The claimant took delivery of the cargo and sold it to a third party, alleging that it incurred a loss of $1.2 million. It issued arbitration proceedings against the defendant, claiming breach of charterparty and/or an indemnity. The claimant later received notification that the defendant had issued proceedings in China, seeking damages in respect of the shipment loss and its portion of the salvage fees. The claimant obtained a without notice anti-suit injunction to prevent the Chinese proceedings. The defendant's insurers in China had refused its claim on the basis that there had been moisture in the cargo. The defendant submitted that (1) there was a sufficient degree of uncertainty such that the court might be persuaded that, on its true construction, the bill of lading was intended to refer to the voyage charterparty; (2) the court's power to order an injunction was, under the Arbitration Act 1996 s.44, available only for the purposes of, and in relation to, arbitral proceedings, which were not yet afoot; that had to be satisfied even if the injunction was being granted under the Senior Courts Act 1981 s.37; (3) there were strong reasons for refusing to grant an injunction as the defendant was likely to lose its insurance claim in China if it was unable to bring the substantive proceedings there; damages were a sufficient remedy where the only loss was the exposure to the cost of the Chinese proceedings; the defendant was the innocent party, as it had suffered the loss following the problems with the cargo.

Held: Application granted. (1) Where a bill of lading made a blank reference to a charterparty, it was to be inferred that a voyage charterparty was intended to have been incorporated, *Bangladesh Chemical Industries Corp v Henry Stephens Shipping Co and Tex-Bilan Shipping Co (The SLS Everest)* [1981] 2 Lloyd's Rep. 389, [1982] C.L.Y. 2888 considered. However, there was no bar to finding that a time charterparty had been incorporated by reference in a bill of lading, *Sotrade Denizcilik Sanayi Ve Ticaret AS v Amadou LO (The Duden)* [2008] EWHC 2762 (Comm), [2009] 1 Lloyd's Rep. 145, [2009] C.L.Y. 3558 applied. The reference to a charterparty dated 11 April 2013 was entirely clear and unambiguous. There was no reason to doubt that the time charterparty had been incorporated as per the express terms of the bill of lading. The court would not accept the suggestion that it should approach the matter as doubted unless there was a concrete suggestion of an agreement to the contrary or some other extraneous reason. The claimant was entitled to rely on the express terms. The arbitration clause had been incorporated. (2) Where an injunction was sought to restrain foreign proceedings in breach of an arbitration agreement the source of the power to grant such an injunction was s.37 of the 1981 Act, not s.44 of the 1996 Act. Such an injunction was not in relation to arbitral proceedings, but for the purposes of the promise in the arbitration agreement not to bring foreign proceedings *AES Ust-*

Kamenogorsk Hydropower Plant LLP v Ust-Kamenogorsk Hydropower Plant JSC [2013] UKSC 35, [2013] 1 W.L.R. 1889, [2013] C.L.Y. 97 followed. (3) The defendant need not lose its insurance claim if the injunction was granted. The claimant had said that it would undertake to waive any time bar in respect of any fresh claims in the arbitration. Insurance contracts were typically regarded as matters which were not relevant to the relationship between claimant and defendant. Even if pursuing a London arbitration did deprive the defendant of certain rights against the claimant, that was not a reason for denying a claimant that forum. The position was stronger where the right or interest which a defendant might lose was against a third party and was not something for which the claimant was responsible or interested in. It was not clear that the defendant had a valid insurance claim in any event. Damages were insufficient as the claimants would lose their contractual right to be sued in the agreed forum. An anti-suit injunction was usually sought to prevent an "injured" or "innocent" party from the "guilty" litigant. Whoever was in the right or wrong was a matter for the arbitrator's determination. The fact that the defendant claimed to be an aggrieved party was not unusual, nor a strong reason for refusing the injunction.

SOUTHPORT SUCCESS SA v TSINGSHAN HOLDING GROUP CO LTD, [2015] EWHC 1974 (Comm), [2016] 2 All E.R. (Comm) 403, Phillips J, QBD (Comm).

1949 Charterparties–Shipbrokers–Repudiation of charterparty–Shipbroker's authority to enter into guarantee on behalf of principal–Enforceability of guarantee

[Statute of Frauds 1677 (c.3)]

The claimant shipowner claimed damages under an alleged contract of guarantee against the defendant company following termination of a long-term charter of a vessel. London-based shipping brokers had contacted the shipowner about the company's interest in hiring a deadweight bulk carrier on a ten-year charter. After lengthy negotiations a charterparty was agreed, with the charterer expressed to be a nominee guaranteed by the company. Both the nominee and the company were based in Goa. The charterparty was subject to English law, and any dispute was to be referred to London arbitration. The charterparty was performed for over three years before the charterer terminated it alleging that the vessel was unsuitable for alternate loading of iron ore. The shipowner began arbitration proceedings against the charterer, and began the instant proceedings seeking the same sum from the company as guarantor. Expert evidence was produced about the gross daily hire rate as at the date of repudiation. A signed copy of a contract of guarantee could not be found. The issues were (i) whether the company had agreed to guarantee the charterer's performance of the charterparty; (ii) whether the guarantee satisfied the Statute of Frauds 1677 that it be in writing and signed by the guarantor; (iii) whether the company was in breach of the guarantee; (iv) quantum; (v) whether it should be declared that the English court had jurisdiction.

Held: Judgment for claimant. (1) The brokers were a well-established broking firm that had held itself out as acting for the company and clearly had actual authority to enter into the guarantee on the company's behalf. That was supported by the correspondence, individually and collectively. There was a consistent thread running through the negotiations that the brokers had actual authority. Such facts gave rise to a binding guarantee, *Golden Ocean Group Ltd v Salgaocar Mining Industries Pvt Ltd* [2012] EWCA Civ 265, [2012] 1 W.L.R. 3674, [2012] C.L.Y. 3047 applied. The company had promised to be responsible for the due performance of the charterer's obligations and if the charterer failed to comply with its obligation, or pay damages, the shipowner was entitled to claim damages from the company, *Vossloh AG v Alpha Trains (UK) Ltd* [2010] EWHC 2443 (Ch), [2011] 2 All E.R. (Comm) 307, [2011] C.L.Y. 548 considered. (2) The requirement that a guarantee had to be in writing could be satisfied even if it was not contained in a single document but in a series of documents taken as a whole, *Golden Ocean* applied. In the instant case, the correspondence between the brokers and the company taken as a whole demonstrated an agreement in writing. Regarding a signature, other evidence could be relied on when a written guarantee could not be found. On the balance of probabilities, the guarantee had to have been signed by the brokers acting with actual authority. (3) The charterer had wrongfully repudiated the charterparty and the defences it had raised were without merit. The shipowner was entitled to claim damages against the company from the date of wrongful repudiation. (4) The company was only liable to the extent that the charterer was liable under the charterparty. The expert's figure for the gross daily hire rate was a reasonable assessment of the market for an equivalent charter of the vessel. Damages were to be assessed from the date of repudiation until the end of the hire period. Credit was to be given for off-hire periods of 10 days per year, *Zodiac Maritime Agencies Ltd v Fortescue Metals Group Ltd (The Kildare)* [2010] EWHC 903 (Comm), [2011] 2 Lloyd's Rep. 360, [2011] C.L.Y. 3117 applied. Credit was also to be given for catastrophic contingencies of 1.5 per cent, and for the charterer's set-off claims for overpaid hire and bunkers on redelivery. It was appropriate to make a lump sum award, but it was to be further reduced by 1.5 per cent to reflect accelerated receipt, *The Kildare* and *Koch Marine Inc v d'Amica Societa di Navigazione arl (The Elena d'Amico)* [1980] 1 Lloyd's Rep. 75, [1980] C.L.Y. 640 applied. (5) A declaration was made that the English court had jurisdiction. England was the appropriate forum to determine the claim: the terms of the guarantee conferred jurisdiction on the English courts, the guarantee was subject to English law, and the agents had operated in England.

MITSUI OSK LINES LTD v SALGAOCAR MINING INDUSTRIES PRIVATE LTD, [2015] EWHC 565 (Comm), [2015] 2 Lloyd's Rep. 518, Eder J, QBD (Comm).

1950 Charterparties–Time charters–"One time charter trip"–Process for determining scope of charter

The owners of a vessel appealed against a decision made in arbitration proceedings concerning a charter trip. Under the charterparty, the owners agreed to let, and the charterer agreed to hire, the vessel for a "one time charter trip" via good and safe ports to other good and safe ports. The vessel loaded and discharged cargoes at permitted ports. After the last load had been discharged, the charterer ordered the vessel to proceed to the port of Sohar to load a new cargo. It was the owner's case that the charterer was not contractually entitled to give that order under the charter. The tribunal held that the charterer was so entitled. On appeal, the issue was whether, on the true construction of the charterparty, the charterer was entitled to order the empty vessel to another port to perform a further trip/voyage or whether it was only entitled to order the vessel to proceed to the agreed charter redelivery place having completed the agreed one time charter trip.

Held: Appeal dismissed. (1) The charter was a time charter. Time charters could be divided into two main categories: term time charters, where the charter period was agreed in advance, and trip time charters, where the charter period was defined by a trip within a geographical range. In both cases, the defining characteristic of the charter was that the vessel was under the directions and orders of the charterer as regards her employment for the charter period, *Martrade Shipping & Transport GmbH v United Enterprises Corp* [2014] EWHC 1884 (Comm), [2015] 1 W.L.R. 1, [2014] C.L.Y. 2711 applied. There was no single definition as to what constituted a "trip" or "one trip", and the fact that the charter in the instant case was for a "one" time charter trip was of little assistance. The scope of any "trip time charter" depended upon the particular terms agreed between the parties. The charterer's entitlement to give directions and orders could be restricted by whatever was agreed between the parties with regard, for example, to period, trading limits, geographical route and even number and designation of loading and discharging ports or ranges. Any such restriction would have to be specifically agreed and would require clear words (see paras 8, 12-13 of judgment). (2) In light of those observations, the question in the instant case did not involve any general point of public importance but turned on a rather narrow question of construction of the specific charter and, in particular, whether it contained sufficiently clear words to exclude Sohar as a loading port. The charterer was not, as a matter of language, restricted to loading the vessel at a single port. The charter specified a delivery port/range and a redelivery port/range. By and within that range, it specified a route. The charterer was, in principle, entitled to call at such ports as it wished provided that the calls were within the trading limits and the route was not inconsistent with the contractual route; proceeding to Sohar was not inconsistent with the contractual route. The word "via" which simply meant "by way of"; and the word "to" which simply denoted the contractual route, did not restrict the charterer's general entitlement to give orders and directions with regard to loading and discharging (paras 14-16, 18).

SBT STAR BULK AND TANKERS (GERMANY) GMBH CO KG v COSMOTRADE SA, [2016] EWHC 583 (Comm), [2016] 2 Lloyd's Rep. 170, Sir Bernard Eder, QBD (Comm).

1951 Charterparties–Time charters–Vessel underperforming under time charter–Application of warranty–Defences to underperformance

A ship owner appealed against a decision by arbitrators to dismiss its claim for hire after its charterers made deductions from the hire cost to set-off damages for breach of the charterparty. The ship owner hired its vessel to a head charterer, which fixed the vessel to a sub-charterer. Under clause 29 of the charterparty, the owner warranted that the vessel would be capable of maintaining certain average speeds on all sea passages under fair weather conditions. During the sub-charterer's trading, the vessel spent four weeks in tropical waters while it waited to receive its next cargo. Consequently, the hull and propeller suffered marine fouling by barnacles, reducing the vessel's speed and breaching clause 29. The arbitrators concluded from three authorities that the marine growth was fair wear and tear incurred in the ordinary course of trading. They found that the owner had assumed the risk of a drop in performance as a result of marine fouling, and the general rule that a ship owner had an implied right of indemnity against a time charterer concerning the consequences of complying with the charterer's orders as to the ship's use did not apply. They awarded the sub-charterer judgment against the head charterer, who in turn was awarded judgment against the owner. At the instant hearing, the owner referred to the leading textbook, Terence Coghlin et al, *Time Charters*, 7th edn (UK, Informa law, 2014), which stated that it was a defence for owners to prove that an underperformance of their vessel resulted from compliance with the charterers' orders. The textbook cited *Bulfracht (Cyprus) Ltd v Boneset Shipping Co Ltd (The Pamphilos)* [2002] EWHC 2292 (Comm), [2002] 2 Lloyd's Rep. 681, [2003] C.L.Y. 3894 as support, in which the ship's failure to achieve the promised performance had resulted from marine fouling, which had resulted from the owners' compliance with the charterers' order to wait for 21 days at a tropical port. The owner submitted that the textbook and *The Pamphilos* showed that it should not be liable for the reduced performance, and clause 29 should only apply where the hull and propeller remained clean.

Held: Appeal dismissed. The speed warranty in clause 29 was expressed in wide and unqualified terms. However, the parties had included an express restriction on the extent of the vessel's performance in terms of limiting it to passages under fair weather conditions. They could have also excluded the speed warranty in respect of voyages after the vessel had been waiting in warm water ports. Such clauses were commonly included in time charters. The owner was therefore seeking to construe the warranty as containing a restriction that the parties had chosen not to include. There was no basis for that construction as the language was clear and unambiguous. Further, where no right to an implied indemnity arose because the risks were assumed by the owner, such as usual and expected marine fouling during legitimate deployment of the vessel, it was difficult to see why the warranty should be read as not applying where performance was affected as a consequence of such an assumed risk. The owner had given the continuing warranty at the same time as assuming that risk, without excluding it from the warranty, so the warranty had to be taken to apply with full force. Although the opposite view was expressed in The Pamphilos, that was in the context of refusing leave to appeal under the Arbitration Act 1996 s.69 and was only reported because the application for leave was dealt with at the end of a judgment on an appeal under s.68. Further, the terms of the speed warranty in that case were not set out in the report and it did not appear that the authorities on the application of the implied indemnity were cited, *Triad Shipping Co v Stellar Chartering & Brokerage Inc (The Island Archon)* [1995] 1 All E.R. 595, [1994] C.L.Y. 4059, *Action Navigation Inc v Bottiglieri di Navigatione SpA (The Kitsa)* [2005] EWHC 177 (Comm), [2005] 1 Lloyd's Rep. 432, [2005] C.L.Y. 3814 and *Santa Martha Baay Scheepvaart and Handelsmaatschappij NV v Scanbulk A/S (The Rijn)* [1981] 2 Lloyd's Rep. 267, [1981] C.L.Y. 2495 applied, *The Pamphilos* considered. For all those reasons, the proposition stated in Terence Coghlin et al, *Time Charters* (2014) was too widely stated. Where a vessel had underperformed, it was not a defence to a claim on a continuing performance warranty for the owner to prove that the underperformance resulted from compliance with the time charterers' orders unless the underperformance was caused by a risk which the owner had not contractually assumed and for which they were entitled to be indemnified by the charterers (see paras 26-31 of judgment).

IMPERATOR I MARITIME CO v BUNGE SA; BUNGE SA v C TRANSPORT PANAMAX LTD, [2016] EWHC 1506 (Comm), [2016] Bus. L.R. 876, Phillips J, QBD (Comm).

1952 **Collisions at sea–Apportionment–Claim against owner of vessel in respect of collision at sea–Liability apportioned between all four vessels involved in collision, whether or not owners parties to action**

[Merchant Shipping Act 1995 (c.21) s.187]

The claimant shipowner brought an action against the defendant, the owner of a container vessel, in respect of damage to its ship in a collision at sea. The claimant's ship had been heading away from port while the defendant's vessel and three warships owned by the Government of India had been heading towards port. After narrowly avoiding a collision with the defendant's vessel, the claimant's ship collided with one of the warships while in a dredged channel used by vessels to access the port. The claimant alleged that the collision had been caused by the negligence of the crews of the defendant's vessel and the three warships. The defendant argued that those on board the claimant's ship and the warships were at fault.

Held: Judgment accordingly. (1) Under the Merchant Shipping Act 1995 s.187, if there was fault by two or more vessels, the court had to apportion liability in proportion to the degree to which each vessel was at fault. That was so even if, as in the instant case, the owner of some of those vessels was not a party to the action. The claimant sought to hold the defendant liable for the damage to its ship, but unless the court took account of the degree to which the Government of India's warships were at fault, the proportion in which the defendant's vessel was held liable would exceed the degree to which it was at fault. Although the court could not give judgment against the Government of India to make good the damage in proportion to the degree to which its warships were at fault because it was not a party, it still had to take into account the degree to which those warships were at fault, *Bovenkerk, The* [1973] 1 Lloyd's Rep. 63, [1973] C.L.Y. 3122 considered. Apportionment depended on an assessment of the causative potency and culpability of the vessels, *Owners of the Crystal Jewel v Owners of the British Aviator* [1965] 1 Lloyd's Rep. 271, [1965] C.L.Y. 3628 and *Owners and/or Bareboat Charterers and/or Sub Bareboat Charterers of the Samco Europe v Owners of the MSC Prestige* [2011] EWHC 1580 (Admlty), [2011] 2 Lloyd's Rep. 579, [2012] C.L.Y. 3051 applied (see paras 4, 144-151 of judgment). (2) The collision had been caused by the claimant's ship, the defendant's vessel and two of the warships. The claimant's ship had been guilty of three faults that were causative of the collision: breaching the International Regulations for Preventing Collisions at Sea 1972 r.9 by not keeping as near to the outer limit of the dredged channel on her starboard side as was safe and practicable; breaching r.6 by proceeding in her wrong water towards three vessels in their correct water without reducing her speed to no more than steerage way so she could navigate with caution; and breaching r.5 by failing to keep adequate look-out. The first warship had been guilty of two causative faults: a poor lookout and an attempt to cross ahead of the claimant's vessel. The second warship had been guilty of altering her heading significantly to port and of increasing her speed. The defendant's vessel had been guilty of three faults: poor lookout, requesting a green-to-green passing with the claimant's vessel, and going to port immediately thereafter. The faults of the second warship and the defendant's vessel had probably contributed to the collision in that their movements distracted the claimant's ship (paras 137-143). (3) In terms of causative potency, the primary fault was the failure of the claimant's ship to comply with r.9, and her failure to slow down added to its causative potency. By contrast, the first warship had complied with r.9. Her fault lay in her reaction to the dangerous situation created by the claimant's ship. The faults of the defendant's vessel and the second warship had contributed to the collision, but their causative potency was very much less than that of the claimant's ship and significantly less than that of the first warship. The claimant's ship had deliberately chosen not to navigate in accordance with r.9, and that was seriously culpable. Her fault was at least three times greater than that of the first warship, which in turn was significantly greater than that of the defendant's vessel and the second warship. Liability would be apportioned as 60% to the claimant's vessel, 20% to the first warship and 10% each to the second warship and the defendant's vessel (paras152-156, 160).

OWNERS AND/OR DEMISE CHARTERERS OF THE NORDLAKE v OWNERS OF THE SEAEAGLE (NOW NAMED ELBELLA), [2015] EWHC 3605 (Admlty), [2016] 2 All E.R. (Comm) 449, Teare J, QBD (Admlty).

1953 Collisions at sea–Claim forms–Proceedings issued and served out of time

[Merchant Shipping Act 1995 (c.21) s.190(5), s.190(6); Civil Procedure Rules 1998 Pt 36, r.3.10, r.61.4, r.7.6]

The claimants applied for an order confirming that their claim had been compromised. Alternatively, they sought an extension of time for serving a claim form pursuant to the Merchant Shipping Act 1995 s.190(5) or s.190(6), or an order under CPR r.3.10 remedying their failure to serve their claim form in time. The defendants cross-applied for a declaration that the claim form had not been validly served and that the court had no jurisdiction to hear the claim. In April 2012, vessels belonging to the claimants and defendants had collided in fog. The claimants sought damages from the defendants. Each provided security and agreed not to arrest the other's vessel. They entered into two agreements extending time for the issue and service of proceedings. The second extended the deadline to 28 April 2015. In March 2015 the defendants offered to settle. The offer was expressed to be in accordance with CPR r.61.4 "and/or" Pt 36 and indicated that it would remain open for 21 days following receipt, after which it would remain open on the same terms but with costs penalties. It was sent under cover of an email which made it clear that the 28 April deadline would not be extended unless the offer was accepted beforehand. Negotiations took place but the claimants neither accepted the offer nor served a claim form before the deadline. On 15 May they purported to accept the offer and on 24 June they served a claim form. The principal issue was whether the claimants were entitled to accept the offer when they did because the 28 April deadline had ceased to have effect, had been overridden by the offer, or had been waived.

Held: Applications refused. (1) Although the offer was expressed to be a r.61.4 offer "and/or" a Pt 36 offer, it could not be both. Rule 61.4 offers and Pt 36 offers were different both in their nature and in their consequences. The defendant's offer was not a Pt 36 offer and, if r.61.4(10) concerned only post-commencement offers, it was not a r.61.4 offer either. Its meaning had to be ascertained by applying ordinary principles of construction without attempting to shoehorn it into any particular category. The relevant background and context had to be taken into account, and if the offer was intended to be effective in accordance with r.36 or r.61.4 then it should, if reasonably possible, be given such effect, *C v D* [2011] EWCA Civ 646, [2012] 1 W.L.R. 1962, [2011] C.L.Y. 359 and *Investors Compensation Scheme Ltd v West Bromwich Building Society (No.1)* [1998] 1 W.L.R. 896, [1997] C.L.Y. 2537 followed. Ultimately, the question was how a reasonable person would understand the offer, taking account of the background and context. In the instant case, a reasonable person would have taken account of the extension agreement, the covering email, and the fact that the offer was expressed to be in accordance with r.61.4 and/or Pt 36. The extension agreement was a sensible commercial agreement which included a clear deadline for the service of any claim form, and the covering email made it clear that the deadline would not be extended unless the offer had been accepted beforehand. A reasonable person would therefore not consider that the offer could be accepted at any time. The offer was consistent with both the requirements of r.61.4 and the continuing validity of the extension agreement. If r.61.4 could apply to a pre-action offer, it had to be open to the parties to require proceedings to be issued and served within the limitation period. Even if the continuing validity of the deadline was not consistent with r.61.4, it was so clear that the defendants intended it to continue in force that the offer could not be construed as overriding it (see paras 40-55 of judgment). (2) The defendants had not waived their right to rely on the deadline by continuing to correspond with the claimants after it became clear that service could not take place in time. They had clearly stated their intention to rely on the deadline, and there was no evidence of reliance on any waiver (paras 57-60). (3) The claimants were not entitled to an extension of time under s.190(5) or s.190(6). Those sections were concerned with extensions of time for the bringing of proceedings, whereas the claimants needed an extension to validate their invalid service. Such extensions were governed by CPR r.7.6. So far as it was relevant to consider the requirements of s.190(5) and s.190(6), they had not been met. Section 190(6) did not apply where the parties had concluded a jurisdiction agreement and had agreed not to arrest each others' vessels, *Owners of the Stolt Kestrel v Owners of the Niyazi S* [2015] EWCA Civ 1035, [2016] 1 All E.R. (Comm) 843, [2016] 253 applied. Nor was there any good reason to extend time as required by s.190(5). Since the requirements of r.7.6 were no more onerous than those of s.190(5) and the claimants had not taken all reasonable steps to serve the claim form in time, any application under r.7.6 would fail (paras 61-75). (4) The claimants' failure to serve proceedings by 28 April was not an error of procedure that could be remedied under CPR r.3.10. That rule could not be used to circumvent the requirements of r.7.6(3) or s.190(5), *Vinos v Marks & Spencer Plc* [2001] 3 All E.R. 784 followed (paras 77-79). (5) The claimants' application for an order confirming that liability for the collision had been settled would be dismissed, as would their applications for an extension of time or a r.3.10 remedy. The claim form had not been validly served and the court had no jurisdiction to hear the claim (para.80).

FORMER OWNERS OF THE MELISSA K (NOW NAMED JASMINE I) v FORMER OWNERS OF THE TOMSK (SUBSEQUENTLY NAMED PURE ENERGY AND NOW NAMED THAYER), [2015] EWHC 3445 (Admlty), [2016] 1 Lloyd's Rep. 503, Males J, QBD (Admlty).

1954 EU law–Marine equipment–Implementation

THE MERCHANT SHIPPING (MARINE EQUIPMENT) REGULATIONS 2016, SI 2016/1025; made under the European Communities Act 1972 s.2(2); Merchant Shipping Act 1995 s.85(1)(3)(5)(6)(7), s.86(1), s.302; Merchant Shipping (Prevention of Oil Pollution) Order 1983 (SI 1983 1106) art.3. In force: 5 December 2017.

These Regulations implement Directive 2014/90 on marine equipment. Part 1 (Regulations 1-4) contains introductory provisions and a power to designate notified and nominated bodies. Regulation 2 contains interpretation provisions. Regulation 3 applies the Regulations to all United Kingdom ships wherever they may be. Regulation 4 gives the Secretary of State a power to designate notified and nominated bodies to carry out conformity assessment procedures.

1955 Freight–Contracts of carriage–Breach of contract by charterer–Shipowner deprived of right to payment of freight–Substantial loss

A shipowner appealed against the decision of an arbitration tribunal to award it nil damages in respect of a breach of contract by the respondent charterer. The parties had made a contract of affreightment in 2008 under which the charterer would make shipments of bulk commodities in 2009, 2010 and 2011. The charterer breached the contract. Its breaches in 2009 and 2010 were dealt with in an earlier arbitration. The owner had become insolvent by 2011 and substantial claims had been brought against it, leading to risks to its monetary assets. It therefore used two companies, owned by the shipowner's directors, to receive inward freight earned under the contract. The instant proceedings concerned the charterer's breaches in 2011 when it failed to nominate cargoes for six shipments. The owner sought damages in respect of its expected profit for the shipments not made, some US $3 million. The tribunal found that the owner had suffered no loss because the freight would not have passed through its hands in any event, but been paid straight to the two companies.

Held: Appeal allowed. The owner had had a contractual right to a payment of freight from the charterer and, because of the charterer's breach, it had been deprived of that right. The right had had a value: the right to receive freight under the contract in respect of the voyages for which the charterer had failed to nominate cargoes had a substantial value of $3 million. The tribunal had held that the owner had not suffered a $3 million loss because, in circumstances where it would have directed the charterer to pay the freight to the two companies, it would never have received any sum on account of freight. However, the owner had been entitled to dispose of the fruits of its rights to receive freight under the contract. A shipowner with a right to receive freight was entitled, once it had received the freight, to pay it to another. It was also entitled to direct the charterer to pay it to another. If the charterer failed to ship cargo with the result that the owner was deprived of the right to receive freight, the owner was deprived of the right to dispose of the freight and of the benefits attaching to the right to receive the freight. To conclude that the owner had suffered no loss would amount to saying that the right to receive freight was valueless. The value of the freight was not any less because the owner had decided for its own reasons, even if they involved turpitude, that the freight would be paid to another company with the result that the freight would never have been transferred to it. To award the owner $3 million damages would not put the owner in a better position than it would have been in had the charterer performed its obligations. The tribunal had erred by failing to hold that by being deprived of its right to receive freight, the owner had suffered a loss (see paras 17-19, 25-27 of judgment).

GLORY WEALTH SHIPPING PTE LTD v FLAME SA, [2016] EWHC 293 (Comm), [2016] 2 All E.R. (Comm) 151, Teare J, QBD (Comm).

1956 General average adjustment–Ransoms–Piracy–Expenses

The appellant cargo owners appealed against the court's interpretation of the York-Antwerp Rules 1974 Rule F. Pirates had taken possession of a ship and demanded a ransom of $6 million. After negotiations lasting 51 days, the first respondent shipowner paid an agreed ransom of $1.85 million, and the vessel continued her voyage. The cargo was carried under a bill of lading which stated that "General Average, if any, shall be settled in accordance with the York-Antwerp Rules 1974". All parties accepted that the ransom payment was allowable in general average under Rule A of those Rules. The dispute centred upon whether vessel operating expenses incurred during the negotiation period were also allowable, under Rule F. An adjuster determined that they were. He reasoned that instead of meeting the initial ransom demand, the shipowner had taken the alternative course of negotiating, which had saved $4.15 million, which would otherwise have been recoverable in general average under Rule A. He therefore held that substituted expenses up to that sum were allowable under Rule F, which included crew wages and maintenance, and bunker consumption, and that professional media response services were recoverable under Rule A. The cargo owners disagreed and brought proceedings for repayment of their contribution towards the expenses. A judge upheld the adjuster's decision and reasoning. The issues were whether:(1) the judge had been right to find that negotiation had been an alternative course of action to paying the initial ransom demand; (2) the judge had been right to find that if the initial ransom demand had been paid without negotiation, the sum would still have been "reasonably incurred" for the purposes of Rule A; (3) the consumption of bunkers was properly an "expense" for the purposes of Rule F; (4) the media response costs were properly recoverable under Rule A, given that they had been incurred for various purposes, not all of which were for the vessel's "common safety".

Held: Appeal allowed in part. (1) Substituted expenses within Rule F had to be "in place of" another expense. That implied making a choice between two or more alternative courses of action. There was no evidence that the shipowners had ever considered that they faced a choice. Their goal from the outset had been to obtain release of the vessel upon payment of a ransom, but in a reduced amount. The failure to recognise any choice reflected the reality that whether the ransom was paid on demand, or after negotiation, the two were simply different ways of going about the same course of action. Negotiation had not been an alternative, but had been the only course of action; wherever the negotiations led, vessel and crew costs would be incurred regardless. The only difference was the extent of the costs. If the court regarded payment on demand as an alternative course of action to negotiation, anomalies would arise. It might seem to accord with equity and natural justice for the ransom saving to be generally shared within general average, but its recoverability depended on proper interpretation and application of the Rules. Rule F presupposed some real choice being made, and none had been made. The appeal would be allowed on that issue (see paras 38-40, 43-55 of judgment). (2) Rule F required a finding that if the alternative course of action had been followed, it would have involved expenditure which would have been "allowable as general average". The instant issue therefore fell to be considered on the basis that payment of the initial ransom demand had been an alternative course of action. The question was in what sense did the hypothetical alternative course of action have to be "reasonable" in order to fulfil the requirements of Rule A, given that the course of action actually taken, namely negotiation, must have appeared the most reasonable and economical choice? The judge below had rightly rejected the shipowner's argument that the court should adopt the approach in *Marida Ltd v Oswal Steel (The Bijela)* [1994] 1 W.L.R. 615, [1994] C.L.Y. 4077, which was a case concerning Rule XIV (temporary repairs) and Rule X (expenses at port of refuge). The wording, context and applicability of those rules were materially different. The judge had also been right to hold that the reasonableness requirement was to be interpreted with a degree of latitude so as to give Rule F practical effect, and to find that payment of the initial ransom sum, without negotiation, would have been reasonable. If, as stated in *Masefield AG v Amlin Corporate Member Ltd* [2010] EWHC 280 (Comm), [2010] 2 All E.R. 593, [2010] C.L.Y. 1925, "the safest, most timely and effective means to secure the release" of a ship and crew was to pay a ransom, it followed that the safest, most timely and effective means of doing so was to pay as soon as possible so as to avert danger to the vessel, cargo and crew, *Marida* considered and *Masefield* approved (paras 31, 56-57, 64-65, 70-76, 81-84). (3) Bunker consumption had been correctly characterised as an expense (paras 85-89). (4) As long as one of the purposes of incurring the expenditure was the "common safety" of the vessel, that was sufficient to bring it within Rule A. The judge had been right to find that expenditure did not need to be solely or exclusively in the interests of common safety to be recoverable under that Rule (paras 92-95).

MITSUI & CO LTD v BETEILIGUNGSGESELLSCHAFT LPG TANKERFLOTTE MBH & CO KG, [2016] EWCA Civ 708, [2016] 2 Lloyd's Rep. 375, Kitchin LJ, CA (Civ Div).

1957 Harbour authorities–Designation

THE HARBOUR DIRECTIONS (DESIGNATION OF HARBOUR AUTHORITIES) ORDER 2016, SI 2016/820; made under the Harbours Act 1964 s.40A(4)(b). In force: 1 October 2016.

This order designates the harbour authorities in respect of three harbours in England and one harbour (non-fishery) in Wales, which are described in the Schedule to the Order, for the purpose of giving harbour directions.

1958 Harbour authorities–Designation

THE HARBOUR DIRECTIONS (DESIGNATION OF HARBOUR AUTHORITIES) (AMENDMENT) ORDER 2016, SI 2016/821; made under the Harbours Act 1964 s.40A(4)(b). In force: 1 October 2016.

This Order amends the description of Mostyn Docks Harbour in the Schedule to the Harbour Directions (Designation of Harbour Authorities) Order 2015 which designated the harbour authority for Mostyn Docks with the power to give harbour directions.

1959 Harbours–Development consent–Durham

THE YORK POTASH HARBOUR FACILITIES ORDER 2016, SI 2016/772; made under the Planning Act 2008 s.114, s.115, s.117, s.120, s.122, s.135(2), s.149A(4), 36 and 37. In force: 10 August 2016.

This Order authorises the construction and operation of a quay, associated onshore facilities and other development to be situated on the River Tees.

1960 Harbours–Reconstitution of Dover Harbour Board

THE DOVER HARBOUR (CONSTITUTION) REVISION ORDER 2016, SI 2016/250; made under the Harbours Act 1964 S.14(1)(3). In force: 25 March 2016.

This Order reconstitutes the Dover Harbour Board on the new constitution date. It provides for the Board to consist of a body of nine members with experience in relevant matters. Three members will be appointed by the Secretary of State one of whom will be appointed as the chair. Four members will be appointed by the Board, two of whom will be appointed as having particular knowledge or experience of, or ability in, the position of the port within the local community and local economy.

1961 Houseboats–Inland waterways–Meaning of "vessel" in art.2 Environment Agency (Inland Waterways) Order 2010

[Environment Agency (Inland Waterways) Order 2010 (SI 2010/699) art.2]

The Environment Agency appealed against a Crown Court decision that the respondents' houseboats moored on the River Great Ouse in Huntingdon were not "vessels" within the Environment Agency (Inland Waterways) Order 2010 art.2. The respondents' houseboats were structures that had been constructed at the marina where they were moored. The living quarters of the structures were built on a raft made of blocks of polystyrene and concrete bolted together. The corners of the raft had round brackets through which poles were driven into the bed of the marina to hold the structure in place and allow it to move up and down with changes in water level. The structures were connected to mains electricity, sewage and water. Council tax was paid in respect of them. The structures did not have a keel or ballast and there was no space for them to be fitted. They had no means of propulsion. The structures could be moved but it would be difficult to do so, as two boats would be needed to guide and support and to provide the necessary stability. The respondents had been convicted by the magistrates of keeping or using a vessel on a waterway when it was not registered with the appellant Agency. The Crown Court allowed an appeal, holding that although the definition of a vessel in art.2 of the 2010 Order was wide since it included "every description of vessel with or without means of propulsion of any kind and ... anything constructed or used to carry persons, goods, plant and machinery, or to be propelled or moved, on, in or by water", the houseboats were not capable of being properly described as vessels. The respondents submitted that the essence of a vessel was its ability to navigate over water whilst carrying people or loads. The appellant submitted that the houseboats, though used for the purpose of residential accommodation, remained boats or vessels since they floated and were capable of being moved from one mooring to another.

Held: Appeal dismissed. The issue was whether the structures in question were vessels within art.2 of the 2010 Order. The court gained only limited assistance from definitions of a "vessel" to be found in other statutory codes and corresponding case law, although the authorities were helpful to the extent that they provided a general understanding of what a vessel might be (see paras 24, 41, 87 of judgment). The ability to navigate or to be navigated was inherent in the ordinary meaning of the word vessel, *Steedman v Scofield* [1992] 2 Lloyd's Rep. 163, [1992] C.L.Y. 3954 considered (paras 47, 89). The Crown Court was right to find that the houseboats were not vessels within the definition in art.2. The salient facts were the construction of the living quarters on top of a raft made of polystyrene and concrete blocks without a keel or ballast or means of propulsion. The structures once assembled lacked navigability and could not easily be moved. The houseboats were actually floating houses. They were constructed, and were used, as homes on water, not to carry people or things or to be propelled or moved across the water. On a realistic view of the facts they were not vessels for the purposes of the 2010 Order (paras 33, 66-74, 99). The court rejected the Agency's argument that there was a public interest in a simple system of registration which would include the houseboats as vessels; the draftsman of the Order had used the concept of a vessel, albeit widely defined, rather than "floating objects" or "floating structures" (paras 72, 100).

ENVIRONMENT AGENCY v GIBBS, [2016] EWHC 843 (Admin), [2016] 2 Lloyd's Rep. 69, Lindblom LJ, DC.

1962 Marine insurance–Oil pollution–Liability insurance

THE MERCHANT SHIPPING ACT 1995 (AMENDMENT) ORDER 2016, SI 2016/1061; made under the European Communities Act 1972 s.2(2); Merchant Shipping Act 1995 s.185(2C), s.306A. In force: 30 November 2016.

This Order amends the Merchant Shipping Act 1995 s.164(1A) which makes provision for the issue by the Secretary of State of a certificate where there is in force insurance or other security satisfying the International Convention on Civil Liability for Bunker Oil Pollution Damage 2001 art.7. It also: substitutes a new para.1 into art.6 in Sch.7 Pt.1 to the Act; and sets out the provisions of the Convention on Limitation of Liability for

Maritime Claims 1976 as amended by the Protocol of 1996 to amend the Convention on Limitation of Liability for Maritime Claims 1976.

1963 Maritime liens–Conversion–Cargo discharged into storage by shipper for failure of cargo owner to present bill of lading–Claim in conversion against shipper based on creation of lien in favour of warehouse operator

The holder of a bill of lading brought a claim for the conversion of a cargo of iron ore carried from Iran to China by the defendant shipper. The shipper counterclaimed for storage charges incurred on the cargo. The bill of lading had been issued "to order" with no named consignee under a charterparty arrangement. By a letter of indemnity, the shipper was requested to discharge the cargo to the bill of lading holder's agent, who was to release it against presentation of the bill of lading. A dispute arose between the bill of lading holder and the buyer of the cargo, as a result of which no bill of lading was presented at the discharge port. The shipper directed the cargo to be discharged into storage in China. The storage charges eventually exceeded the value of the cargo, which was never collected. The warehouse operator refused to release the cargo without payment. The bill of lading holder accepted that the shipper had been entitled to discharge the cargo into storage, but claimed that it had converted the cargo because (i) a lien for storage charges was created in favour of the warehouse operator without its authority; and (ii) statements had been made by the warehouse operator and the agent which amounted to denying it access to the cargo, regardless of whether it presented the bill of lading. The shipper denied conversion and maintained that the bill of lading holder was responsible for the storage charges.

Held: Claim dismissed, counterclaim upheld. (1) In principle, goods might be converted by a person who created a lien without the authority of the owner, *Syeds v Hay* 100 E.R. 1008 applied. A goods owner who authorised a bailee to deliver goods into storage had to be taken to authorise the creation of a lien where that was a reasonable and foreseeable incident of the storage contract which the bailee was authorised to conclude, *Morris v CW Martin & Sons Ltd* [1966] 1 Q.B. 716, [1965] C.L.Y. 178 followed, *Pioneer Container, The* [1994] 2 A.C. 324, [1994] C.L.Y. 255 applied. It was long established that if a bill of lading holder did not claim delivery within a reasonable time, the master was entitled to warehouse the cargo and the shipowner to charge the cargo owner with expenses incurred in so doing, *ENE 1 Kos Ltd v Petroleo Brasileiro SA Petrobras (The Kos)* [2012] UKSC 17, [2012] 2 A.C. 164, [2012] C.L.Y. 3075 followed. As the shipper had been entitled to warehouse the cargo, it was not unreasonable of it to agree to a term in the storage contract which conferred a lien on the warehouse operator for its charges. That was an obvious commercial reality. Moreover, the charterparty incorporated into the bill of lading expressly permitted the discharge and storage of the cargo, so that the creation of a lien was a reasonable and foreseeable incident of the storage contract which the shipper was authorised to conclude. It followed that the claim by the bill of lading holder for conversion by reason of the creation of a lien was unfounded (see paras 45-46, 48-49, 51-52 of judgment). (2) A denial of access to goods might be capable of constituting the tort of conversion, depending on whether the conduct of the defendant amounted to a deliberate encroachment of the rights of the owner so as to exclude him from use and possession of the goods, *Kuwait Airways Corp v Iraqi Airways Co (No.6)* [2002] UKHL 19, [2002] 2 A.C. 883, [2002] C.L.Y. 4540 followed. However, the matters relied upon by the bill of lading holder as constituting denial of access fell far short of that. Even if the statements in issue were intended to assert that it would not get its cargo if it presented the bill of lading, they had never been put to the test because the bill of lading holder had never presented the bill. Moreover, those statements were a long way from being so final and unequivocal that it would have been futile for the bill of lading holder to have pressed for delivery thereafter. Therefore, it was simply not the case that it had been deprived of the use and possession of its cargo; the cargo had always been available on presentation of the bill of lading and payment of the accrued charges (paras 56-64). (3) There was no failure on the shipper's part to mitigate its loss by selling the cargo because the bill of lading would have been needed for any such sale and for the cargo to be cleared through customs. The bill of lading holder was therefore liable to reimburse the shipper for the storage charges owed to the warehouse operator (paras 75-76).

SANG STONE HAMOON JONOUB CO LTD v BAOYUE SHIPPING CO LTD, [2015] EWHC 2288 (Comm), [2016] 1 Lloyd's Rep. 320, Males J, QBD (Comm).

1964 Protected areas–Wrecks

THE PROTECTION OF WRECKS (DESIGNATION) (ENGLAND) (NO.2) ORDER 2016, SI 2016/841; made under the Protection of Wrecks Act 1973 s.1(1)(2). In force: 16 August 2016.

This Order designates an area within 50 metres of the wreck site of the vessel "HMT Arfon", just under four kilometres south of St. Alban's Head, Dorset, as a restricted area for the purposes of the Protection of Wrecks Act 1973. The Secretary of State is satisfied that that site ought to be protected from unauthorised interference on account of the historical and archaeological importance of the vessel. Under s.1(3) of the Act, it is a criminal offence for a person to engage in certain activities in a restricted area otherwise than under the authority of a licence issued by the Secretary of State.

1965 Sale of ships–Commission–Broker's claim to commission–Whether express or implied agreement to sell at material time or effective cause of sale

The appellant yacht broker appealed against a decision (*Moran Yacht & Ship Inc v Pisarev* [2014] EWHC 1098 (Comm), [2014] 2 Lloyd's Rep. 88, [2014] C.L.Y. 2728) dismissing its claim to commission on the sale of a luxury yacht. The yacht had been owned by the first respondent through the second respondent company, and the appellant had been appointed its exclusive chartering broker in 2009. In May 2010, a wealthy Russian (X) came aboard the vessel at the invitation of one of the appellant's employees, but expressed no interest in purchasing it. In September 2010, the first respondent instructed the appellant to market the yacht for sale. It did so, but no sale had been made by the time the chartering agreement was terminated in October 2011. In January 2012, the first respondent met X and offered the yacht for sale. X bought it for €19.8 million. The judge rejected the appellant's claim to commission on the sale, having found that there was no express or implied agreement for it to sell the yacht at the material time and, in any event, it was not the effective cause of the sale. The appellant contended that there was an implied term in the charter agreement that if someone had been shown round the vessel as a potential charterer and purchased it within two years, it was entitled to commission.

Held: Appeal dismissed. The appellant's contention failed for a number of reasons. The situations in which the respondents had to pay commission to the appellant under the 2009 chartering agreement could not be expanded in that way. In any event, the appellant was unable to challenge the judge's finding that it was not the cause of the sale. Moreover, the appellant had enjoyed excessive latitude in asserting its entitlement to commission: that point had never been pleaded and should not be allowed to be taken on appeal.

MORAN YACHT & SHIP INC v PISAREV, [2016] EWCA Civ 317, [2016] 1 Lloyd's Rep. 625, Sir Terence Etherton C, CA (Civ Div).

1966 Salvage remuneration–Notice of abandonment–Whether cost of recovery or repair of vessel before notice of abandonment served could be included in total loss calculation

[Marine Insurance Act 1906 (c.41) s.60, s.60(2)(ii), s.62(3)]

Ship owners brought a claim against their insurers for recovery under a hull and machinery insurance policy. The owners' vessel was insured under a hull and machinery insurance policy which incorporated the Institute Time Clauses - Hulls (1/10/83). They also had the benefit of an increased value policy with the first defendant. That policy incorporated the Institute Time Clauses - Hulls Disbursement and Increased Value (Total Loss Only) Clauses (1/10/83). The insured vessel sustained damage after a fire in the engine room in August 2012. It was initially unclear whether the vessel could be repaired or whether it was a constructive total loss. The owners received conflicting repair quotations. The owners gave notice of abandonment to the insurers on 1 February 2013 and claimed that they were entitled to be indemnified on a constructive total loss basis. The insurers maintained that they were only entitled to be indemnified on a partial loss basis. Salvage operations were necessary to recover the vessel and the salvors were engaged under the terms of a special compensation protection and indemnity clause (SCOPIC). Paragraph 15 of that clause stated that any liability "to pay SCOPIC remuneration shall be that of the Shipowner alone and no claim...shall be made...under the vessel's Hull and Machinery Policy by owners of the vessel". The court was required to determine whether (1) the notice of abandonment was given too late; (2) the cost of recovery or repair before notice of abandonment should be included in the total loss calculation; (3) the owners' liability to pay remuneration to salvage operators under the special clause should be included in the total loss calculation; (4) a contingency figure for repairs after notice of abandonment should be 5 or 10% .

Held: Judgment for claimants. (1) The owners had met the requirements of the Marine Insurance Act 1906 s.62(3) and had not given notice of abandonment too late. The nature of the event was such that achieving reliable information of the loss would be a complex task and would take time. What mattered was the receipt of reliable information of the loss. Measured against the standard of reasonable diligence set by the 1906 Act, the owners had taken no more than a reasonable time. The notice of abandonment was effective and the vessel was a constructive total loss (see paras 8-11, 20, 24-26, 98 of judgment). (2) There was no basis, on the wording of the relevant clauses or in principle, for limiting the cost of recovery and repair to recovery and repair after notice of abandonment. Under the 1906 Act there were circumstances where the assured elected to abandon but there was no notice of abandonment. It was stated in *Robertson v Petros M Nomikos Ltd* [1939] A.C. 371 that "notice of abandonment was not an essential ingredient of a constructive total loss." To argue that it was would confuse constructive total loss with the right to claim for a constructive total loss, Robertson followed. The relevant Institute Time Clauses contemplated that the cost of recovery and repair of the vessel was to be compared with the insured value. The 1906 Act did not require any different conclusion because (a) the wording of s.60(2)(ii) referred to the cost of repairing the damage to the ship, not some part of that cost, or that cost for a period commencing other than when the ship was damaged; (b) the word "future" in that sub-section simply provided that account was to be taken of the expense of salvage operations and of any general average contributions to which the ship would be liable where they were in the future. It did not exclude the expense of such operations and contributions where they were not in the future. If the decision in *Hall v Hayman* [1912] 2 K.B. 5 held that s.60(2)(ii) excluded costs before a notice of abandonment from "the cost of repairing the damage", then that was wrong, Hall and *Helmville Ltd v Yorkshire Insurance Co Ltd (The Medina Princess)* [1965] 1 Lloyd's Rep. 361, [1965] C.L.Y. 3651 not followed (paras 31-32, 38-46). (3) SCOPIC remuneration was payable to salvors in respect of necessary salvage operations arising from the insured event. It was an indivisible part of an item the balance of which the insurers accepted was a "cost of repair". Approaching the matter in accordance with ordinary principles of construction, its inclusion in the assessment of whether there was a constructive total loss did not fall with the terms of para.15 of the special clause (paras 51-53). (4) Allowing a general contingency of the order of 10% was not too generous to the owners. Whether one talked of contingency or margin, suitable allowance for uncertainty was properly to be made, *Suez Fortune Investments Ltd v Talbot Underwriting Ltd* [2015] EWHC 42 (Comm), [2015] 1 Lloyd's Rep. 651, [2015] C.L.Y. 1467 applied (paras 89-90).

CONNECT SHIPPING INC v SVERIGES ANFGARTYGS ASSURANS FORENING (THE SWEDISH CLUB), [2016] EWHC 1580 (Comm), [2016] Bus. L.R. 1184, Knowles J, QBD (Comm).

1967 Shipbuilding–Breach of contract–Refurbishment contract for cruise ship–Failure of port main engine lubricating oil coolers during ship's inaugural cruise–Claim for damages for cancellation of cruise and delay

A shipowner claimed damages against the defendant shipbuilder for the breach of a refurbishment contract relating to its cruise ship. There were two claims. The first related to a catastrophic failure of the port main engine lubricating oil coolers during the ship's inaugural cruise a few weeks after completion of the refit. Investigation revealed that the tubes of both coolers were heavily corroded and needed replacing. As the engine could not run without a functioning cooler, the cruise had to be abandoned and passengers sent home. The next scheduled cruise had to be delayed. The shipowner claimed that an "overhaul" of the coolers had specifically fallen within the remit of the contract, and that "retubing" was the only effective method of overhaul. It claimed that on a true construction of the contract, the defendant had been obliged to advise of the need for retubing and to perform that process. The second claim was for €770,000 in liquidated damages in respect of the defendant's two-week delay in redelivering the vessel. That sum represented the amount of the cap on liquidated damages agreed at the time of the vessel's re-delivery. The defendant denied the claimant's construction of the contract, denying that it had been obliged to notice whether retubing was required. Its case was that it had only been contracted to clean the coolers. The essence of the dispute related to the correct interpretation of the "specification" and appendix 11. The former contained the technical specifications of the contract, and the latter incorporated the parties' later agreement as to price. The claimants regarded appendix 11 as having primacy and noted that it made many references to an "overhaul" of the coolers. The defendant considered that appendix 11 concerned only price not the scope of work. The court was required to ascertain the objective meaning of the contract against the relevant background.

Held: Judgment for claimants. *Construction* - the specification and appendix 11 had to be read together, in the round and not hierarchically. What the parties had objectively intended was for the defendant to (a) do an in situ overhaul, short of retubing the coolers; and (b) do whatever was necessary to enable the shipowner to make an informed decision as to whether retubing was necessary. The defendant needed to open the coolers to clean and test them. That imported an obligation to inspect them, at least for the purpose of ascertaining the necessary level of cleaning. The defendant was not entitled, having examined the coolers, to simply redeliver them without mentioning that they were defective because they obviously needed retubing. The defendant had not been under a duty to positively advise for or against retubing. Neither the specification nor appendix 11 contained specific advisory wording. Given that failure of the coolers would normally be gradual, retubing was a judgement call. On the facts, the coolers had been significantly corroded, but had not raised the "red flag" for incipient failure. The corrosion had still been visible after cleaning. The defendant had been duty-bound to report anything material to the question of retubing. Its obligation was to advise by reporting, not by recommending. It had failed in that duty. It had also failed to perform a competent clean of the coolers (see paras 51-56, 59, 107, 109-110, 112-113, 118-119, 326 of judgment). *Causation* - the primary cause of the cooler failure was long-standing corrosion, probably caused by inadequate water treatment by previous owners. That corrosion had not been adequately cleaned away by the defendant, but its breaches did not cause the failure. It could have done no more than advise the shipowner as to the existence of corrosion. It did not do so because it concluded that the coolers would last another two years. The shipowner's evidence was that if it had been advised of the corrosion, it would have authorised retubing. However, it was implausible that a report up the chain of command would have been made and/or that retubing would have been ordered (paras 136-137, 141, 143, 145-147, 326). *Damages for cancellation of the first cruise* - given the conclusion on causation, these did not arise, but the court set out its conclusions in the event that they became relevant at a later stage (paras 147-226, 326). *The delay claim* - the shipowner was entitled to €770,000 in liquidated damages. The court considered the correct approach to construing the apparent scheme of the contract, with its separate clauses for liquidated damages and permissible delay. It preferred the defendant's construction because it was consistent with the approach adopted in many construction contracts, particularly on the issue of concurrent causes, *De Beers UK Ltd (formerly Diamond Trading Co Ltd) v Atos Origin IT Services UK Ltd* [2010] EWHC 3276 (TCC), [2011] B.L.R. 274, [2011] C.L.Y. 540 considered. The defendant was responsible for a number of delays and could not rely on delays for which the shipowner was responsible as stopping time running under the liquidated damages clause, *Adyard Abu Dhabi v SD Marine Services* [2011] EWHC 848 (Comm), [2011] B.L.R. 384, [2011] C.L.Y. 532 applied (paras 238-242, 245, 248-251, 326).

SAGA CRUISES BDF LTD v FINCANTIERI SPA, [2016] EWHC 1875 (Comm), 167 Con. L.R. 29, Sara Cockerill QC, QBD (Comm).

1968 Shipbuilding–Fitness for purpose–Seller providing 12-month guarantee–Buyer complaining about defect three years after taking delivery–Effect of guarantee on time limits for making complaint

[Sale of Goods Act 1979 (c.54) s.14(3), s.55]

The buyer of a ship appealed against an arbitrator's decision that its complaint about the ship was time-barred under its contract with the seller, and a broad fitness for purpose term could not be implied. The contract had been for the design, build and supply of a bulk carrier, to include cranes rated for continuous operation with the capacity to handle 30-tonne cargoes. The seller guaranteed that the vessel "will be seaworthy and contractual in all respects, and will be free from all defects which are due to defective design, construction, calculation, material or workmanship (collectively "Guarantee Defects") ..." upon delivery and for 12 months from delivery. More than three years after delivery, the buyer complained that the crane bearings were subject to excessive wear and it had had to limit their use. The seller replied that it was not obliged to address the complaint as its contractual liability was limited to the 12-month period from delivery. At the arbitration hearing, the buyer submitted that the guarantee clause could be split such that it could cover two types of claim: the first part related to the vessel being "seaworthy and contractual in all respects"; the second part listed defects collectively known as "Guarantee Defects". The buyer argued that the cranes' inadequate performance fell under the first part of the clause and was governed by the normal six-year limitation period; only claims under the second part were related to the guarantee period and the limitation of liability clause. The buyer also submitted that as the seller knew that the vessel's intended use included dealing with heavy cargoes via the continuous use of the cranes, the contract contained an implied term as to fitness for that purpose under the Sale of Goods Act 1979 s.14(3). The arbitrator rejected both of the buyer's constructions.

Held: Appeal dismissed. (1) Regarding the construction of the guarantee clause, the instant judge agreed with the arbitrator's conclusion. The buyer's submission depended on there being a real dichotomy between two different types of claims. It would be a difficult and unnecessary task to characterise failures of performance or a defective selection of parts as not amounting to any one of the other specified defects. Creating a category of claims that was to be excluded from the guarantee period, the careful procedure for remedying defects and the limitation of liability clause was wholly artificial. There was no commercial or other justification for there being two different schemes. Accordingly, the 12-month time-bar provision applied to any and all claims whatsoever, including the buyer's claim (see paras 23-24 of judgment). (2) Regarding implied terms under s.14(3), the problem in the buyer's case was that its submission had referred broadly to an implied term that the vessel would be fit to handle "heavy cargoes"; it had not clarified or limited the submission to the 30 tonnes expressly specified in the contract. The arbitrators had thereby been entitled to find that such an implied term was inconsistent with the express terms of the contract and was consequently excluded under s.55. If an implied term had been formulated that on its face was consistent with, and put into effect, the terms of the vessel's specification, the result would almost certainly have been different. The matter would have been referred back to the arbitrator to consider the implied term in a clarified or limited form had the buyer's claim not been time-barred (paras 33, 36-40).

NEON SHIPPING INC v FOREIGN ECONOMIC 7 TECHNICAL CORP CO OF CHINA, [2016] EWHC 399 (Comm), [2016] 2 Lloyd's Rep. 158, Burton J, QBD (Comm).

1969 Time charters–Jurisdiction clauses–Whether charterer dealing as principal or acting as agent for trader–Whether trader bound by English jurisdiction clause

The owner of a vessel applied for an anti-suit injunction to restrain a trading company from bringing proceedings in Nigeria on the ground that the agreement between them contained an English jurisdiction clause. The trader cross-applied for a declaration that the English court lacked jurisdiction. The trader chartered the vessel under a time charter which contained an English jurisdiction clause. The charterer was a Bermudan company. On 5 January 2015, the vessel loaded its cargo in Nigeria but became grounded when leaving port. According to the trader, the delay in resuming the voyage resulted in the cargo being sold at a substantial loss. The charter was terminated prematurely when the charterer tendered notice of redelivery of the vessel, asserting a contractual right of termination. The owner treated the redelivery as a repudiation of the charter. The trader issued proceedings in Nigeria based on a contract of carriage with the owner said to be evidenced by the bill of lading issued in Nigeria on 5 January 2015. Those proceedings were served out of the jurisdiction on the owner on 2 July 2015. By those proceedings, the trader claimed that the owner was liable for the consequences of the grounding. On 14 July 2015, the owner commenced proceedings against the charterer in the instant court, claiming damages for the repudiation of the charter. The owner brought the instant application on 21 December 2015. The owner submitted that (1) the charterer had entered into the charter as the trader's agent, so that the trader, as undisclosed principal, was bound by the English jurisdiction clause; (2) alternatively, the bill of lading issued on 5 January 2015 should be rectified to incorporate the terms and conditions of the charter, including the jurisdiction clause; (3) in the further alternative, a free-standing jurisdiction agreement had been reached between the owner and the trader during negotiations for the charter.

Held: Application refused, cross-application granted. (1) In establishing whether the trader was an undisclosed principal, the question was whether the supposed agent had communicated to the supposed principal an intention to contract on its behalf, *Garnac Grain Co Inc v HMF Faure & Fairclough Ltd* [1968] A.C. 1130, [1967] C.L.Y. 587 followed. When a contract was made by or on behalf of a named legal person and there was nothing in the terms of the contract or surrounding circumstances to indicate to the other contracting party that the named person was making the contract as an agent, then it had to be presumed that the named person was contracting as a principal. In the instant case, the evidence did not support the owner's case that the charterer was acting as the trader's agent and there was therefore nothing to displace the presumption that the charterer was dealing as a principal. It followed that the trader was not bound by the English jurisdiction clause (see paras 16-18, 28-29, 36 of judgment). (2) There was nothing in the bill of lading to incorporate into it the terms of the time charter, nor was there any evidence of an agreement to refer disputes under the bill of lading to the jurisdiction of the English courts. General words of incorporation of charter terms in a bill of lading were insufficient to incorporate a jurisdiction clause which referred only to disputes under the charter and which could not, without verbal manipulation, be applied to disputes under the bill of lading. Even if the parties would have agreed to English jurisdiction had they noticed that the bill of lading evidenced a contract between the trader and the owner which was separate from the charter, the doctrine of rectification enabled a document to be corrected so as to reflect an actual, objectively expressed prior consensus of the parties: it did not enable a document to be altered so as to accord with a hypothetical consensus which the parties would have reached in circumstances which did not actually arise (paras 39, 46, 51-53). (3) Even if it could be demonstrated that negotiations for the charter had resulted in a consensus as to jurisdiction, a non-contractual consensus would not give the owner any legal right not to be sued in Nigeria, let alone a right capable of being enforced by an anti-suit injunction. To establish such a right, there would have to be a binding contract of which the trader's suit against the owner constituted a breach. It followed that the instant court had no jurisdiction to try the trader's cargo claim and the owner had no contractual right not to be sued on that claim in Nigeria (paras 55-56, 59). (4) Even if the instant court had jurisdiction to try the owner's claim, its application for an injunction would have been refused because there had been fatal delay in making the application. Once the proceedings were served on 2 July 2015, prompt action was called for and there was no justification for waiting until 21 December (paras 60, 63).

MAGELLAN SPIRIT APS v VITOL SA, [2016] EWHC 454 (Comm), [2016] 2 Lloyd's Rep. 1, Leggatt J, QBD (Comm).

1970 Time charters–Off-hire clauses–Vessel under arrest and unable to discharge–Whether arrest occasioned by personal act or omission or default of charterers or agents

A charterer (C) appealed against a decision (*NYK Bulkship (Atlantic) NV v Cargill International SA (The Global Santosh)* [2014] EWCA Civ 403, [2014] 2 Lloyd's Rep. 103, [2014] C.L.Y. 2739) on the construction of an off-hire clause in a time charter with the respondent shipowner (N). N had chartered a vessel to C, who sub-chartered it under a voyage charter for a cargo which had been sold by a company (T) to another company (X). X was responsible for unloading the cargo and was liable to pay demurrage to T if unloading was delayed. When the vessel arrived at port on 15 October 2008, she was held on anchor for almost two months because of congestion caused partly by problems with X's unloader. She was called in to berth on 18 December, but was sent back because T had obtained an arrest order on the cargo to secure a claim for demurrage against X. The order mistakenly directed the arrest of the vessel. Discharge eventually took place in January 2009. C withheld hire for the period of arrest in reliance on cl.49 of the charter, which provided that the vessel would be off-hire during any period of detention or arrest, unless such arrest was "occasioned by any personal act or omission or default of the Charterers or their agents". Arbitrators rejected N's argument that the vessel's detention had been occasioned by the personal act or omission of T, as agent for C, and held that the vessel was off-hire during the relevant period. N successfully appealed. The Court of Appeal held that the delay fell within C's sphere of responsibility, because the dispute which caused the delay did not involve N and arose out of C's "trading arrangements concerning the vessel".

Held: Appeal allowed. (1) References in a time charter to acts of the charterer's "agents" in the course of performance was not necessarily limited to persons doing those acts on his behalf in the strict legal sense of the term, or to those standing in any direct legal relationship with him. As between the owner and the time charterer, the latter's rights were made available to those further down the contractual chain, and some at least of the time charterer's obligations were satisfied by the acts of sub-contractors, *Mediolanum Shipping Co v Japan Line Ltd (The Mediolanum)* [1984] 1 Lloyd's Rep. 136, [1984] C.L.Y. 3174, *Trade Star Line Corp v Mitsui & Co Ltd (The Arctic Trader)* [1996] 2 Lloyd's Rep. 449, [1996] C.L.Y. 5313 and *Merit Shipping Co Inc v TK Boesen A/S (The Goodpal)* [2000] 1 Lloyd's Rep. 638, [2000] C.L.Y. 4694 considered. Under the time charter in the instant case, C enjoyed the facility of directing where and when to discharge. The parties ultimately entitled to the benefit of that facility were T and X. They were for that purpose "agents" of C. However, that did not mean C was responsible for anything T or X might do which resulted in the detention of the ship. There had to be some nexus between the occasion for the arrest and the function which T or X was performing as "agent" of C (see paras 14-21 of judgment). (2) The effect of the parties' arrangements was that such cargo handling operations as occurred, although carried out by X, were carried out on C's behalf. It was the vicarious exercise of a right of C under the time charter, which C indirectly made available to X. However, the defective performance of cargo handling operations was one thing: an absence of cargo handling operations was another. X's failure to discharge the cargo between the giving of notice of readiness on 15 October and the commencement of discharge three months later could not meaningfully be regarded as the vicarious exercise by X of some right of C under the time charter. Any responsibility of C under the time charter for X's acts or omissions in the conduct of cargo handling operations at the port of discharge extended only to acts or omissions in the actual performance of those operations while they were in progress. The arrest had been occasioned by a dispute between T and X about demurrage. Incurring or enforcing a liability for demurrage under a sub-contract could not possibly be regarded as the vicarious exercise of any facility made available to C under the time charter. The proviso to cl.49 did not apply. The vessel was off-hire during the period of arrest (paras 27-30). (3) The distinction drawn by the Court of Appeal between C's and N's spheres of responsibility was not helpful in the present context, *Hyundai Merchant Marine Co Ltd v Furness Withy (Australia) Pty (The Doric Pride)* [2006] EWCA Civ 599, [2006] 2 All E.R. (Comm) 188, [2006] C.L.Y. 3917 considered. Although the proviso to cl.49 was, broadly speaking, concerned with matters for which C might be regarded as responsible, that did not reveal what those matters were. Where the range of matters for which the time charterer was responsible depended on what functions he had delegated to a sub-contractor, it was necessary to identify the extent of the delegation. The Court of Appeal seemed to have regarded the delegation as extending to everything that arose out of C's "trading arrangements concerning the vessel". That amounted to saying that anything T or X might choose to do which resulted in the arrest of the vessel became C's responsibility if the occasion for doing it would not have arisen but for their having come in at the end of a chain of contracts which C initiated. Such a test was impossible to justify, since it depended simply upon the status of the sub-charterer or receiver, and would not necessarily require any nexus between the acts leading to the arrest and the performance of functions under the time charter (para.31).

NYK BULKSHIP (ATLANTIC) NV v CARGILL INTERNATIONAL SA, [2016] UKSC 20, [2016] 1 W.L.R. 1853, Lord Neuberger PSC, SC.

1971 Voyage charters–Cancellation–Contract terms

The appellant charterers appealed against a decision of arbitrators that the cancelling provisions of cl.17 of the BEEPEEVOY3 form did not apply where charterers had nominated a revised loading port under cl.24. The respondent owners chartered their vessel on the BEEPEEVOY3 form. The charter was novated to the appellants. It provided that, subject to the provisions of cl.24, the vessel would proceed to "1/2 safe port(s) Black Sea excl Bulgaria, Romania, Turkey". The charterers nominated Tuapse as the first loading port. Three days later they gave a revised order nominating Batumi as the loading port. The vessel's estimated time of arrival at Batumi was after the cancelling date in cl.17 of the charter ("Laydays/Cancelling"). On the basis that owners' ETA for Batumi would be after the cancelling date, the charterers purported to cancel the charter. The owners treated the purported cancellation as a repudiatory breach of the charter and claimed damages. The arbitrators found that the owners' claim succeeded. They concluded that following the revised order under cl.24, the cancellation provisions of cl.17 ceased to apply and, in particular, did not apply to the re-nominated loading port of Batumi. They further held that, if the right to cancel survived, the charterers could not cancel if, as in the instant case, the re-nominated loadport was one which the vessel, at the time of the re-nomination, could not have reached by the cancelling date. The charterers appealed on two questions of law: (i) whether the right to cancel under cl.17 survived a re-nomination of the first loadport pursuant to cl.24; (ii) if it did, whether they were nevertheless not entitled to cancel where the re-nomination was made at a time when the ETA for the re-nominated port was after the cancelling date.

Held: Appeal dismissed. (1) The charterers had a strong argument based on the commercial value to them of the cancelling clause, but it was not of such force as to knock out the owners' rival contentions as to the commercial undesirability of losing the certainty associated with an irrevocable nomination while remaining exposed to cancellation rights (see paras 94-102 of judgment). The wording of cl.24 varied the cl.17 regime for laytime and demurrage where charterers gave revised orders, but not the cancellation regime. The draftsman or the parties, had that been the intention, could have introduced a provision applying the cancellation provision or a variation of it, in such a case (paras 103-108). There was an inconsistency between charterers' acceptance that an initial loadport nomination could not be given so late that it would cause the vessel to miss the cancelling date and their contention that a re-nomination under cl.24 was not so fettered. That undermined their contention that cl.24 was intended to equate a re-nominated first loadport with an originally nominated first loadport, thus conferring on charterers in relation to the re-nominated first loadport all the entitlements which the charterparty conferred on them in relation to the originally nominated first loadport (paras 109-118). Had there been an intention that cancellation rights should survive, express words would have been used to that effect (para.126). The tribunal was entitled to hold that the simplest solution, consistent with established principle, was that the liberty given to vary the first loadport under cl.24 was too wide to carry with it any continued ability to rely on the cancelling date. The survival of the cancelling regime would give rise to complexities that would have to have been expressly addressed. The arbitrators were right that the right to cancel under cl.17 did not survive a re-nomination of the first loadport under cl.24 (paras 136-139, 161). (2) When the charterers nominated Tuapse as the first loadport, it became the contractual loadport. It was not to be regarded as a provisional nomination, merely because of the existence of the right to give revised orders in cl.24. It would be uncommercial and unsatisfactory if, following the original nomination of Tuapse, the vessel was obliged not only to proceed there but also to proceed as if any other port within the charterparty range might be substituted by a revised order. Unless and until a re-nomination was made owners were entitled to proceed on the basis that Tuapse was the first loadport. Where the vessel had proceeded in accordance with the contract, the duty of co-operation logically required that charterers could not cancel if the re-nominated first loadport was a port for which, at the time of the re-nomination, the ETA was after the cancelling date, *Mackay v Dick* (1881) 6 App. Cas. 251 considered. If the vessel had arrived late at the re-nominated port, the cause would have been the late re-nomination at a time when owners were not in breach of contract. Thus the arbitrators were also right on the second issue (paras 141-154, 161).

ST SHIPPING AND TRANSPORT INC v KRITI FILOXENIA SHIPPING CO SA, [2015] EWHC 997 (Comm), [2015] 2 Lloyd's Rep. 609, Walker J, QBD (Comm).

1972 Voyage charters–Repudiation–Charterer's repudiation of voyage charter–Loss of charter freight–Loss of benefit of two transatlantic voyages

The appellant charterer appealed against the quantum of an arbitral tribunal's award of damages made in favour of the respondent shipowner. The appellant had chartered a ship to carry a cargo of crude/refined vegoil within a range of load ports in South America to one safe berth at 1-4 safe ports in the Gibraltar-Rotterdam range. After that, it was planned that the ship would carry a cargo of urea ammonium nitrate from the Baltic to the US, and then a chemical cargo from the US to Europe. However, the ship's previous employment had taken her to the Democratic Republic of Congo where she became grounded at Boma. That led to delay, and following exchanges between the parties, the shipowner accepted the charterer's latest message as a repudiatory breach which brought the charter to an end. The ship then sailed towards South America, and after a lengthy delay, was fixed with a substitute voyage from Argentina to Rotterdam, and discharged its cargo of sunflower oil and soya methyl ester in Rotterdam on 12 April 2011. If the voyage charter had been performed, it would have been completed on 17 March 2011. The arbitrators accepted the owners' contention that damages should consist of the difference between the profit which the ship would have earned if not only the contract voyage but also the next two voyages had been performed and the profit actually earned on the substitute charter to Europe. The issue was whether the arbitrators had been wrong to award compensation for the loss of the ship's follow-on fixtures. The charterer submitted that (1) the prima facie compensatory principle in *Smith v Thomas M'Guire* 157 E.R. 589 did not extend to consequential losses; (2) the arbitrators had failed to keep distinct the owner's loss and the mitigatory steps which reduced that loss; (3) the basis of the arbitrators' comparative reasoning was too speculative given that if the calculation did not end when the contract voyage did, there was no other logical end point for the calculation of damage; (4) the award was contrary to the allocation of responsibility under a voyage charter because the charterers had not assumed, in an implied term, responsibility for losses after the period when the contract voyage would have been completed.

Held: Appeal dismissed. (1) The charterer's breach caused two distinct heads of loss: the owners lost the charter freight and had to make do with the lesser freight under the substitute charter, but they also suffered a delay in repositioning the ship in Europe and thereby lost the benefit of two transatlantic voyages which, on the arbitrators' findings, the vessel would have been able to perform in about the same time as the substitute fixture. As there was no reason in law why damages for the consequences of the ship's delay should not be awarded in addition to the loss of profit from performing the contract voyage, the application of the compensatory principle required that such damages be awarded. The arbitrators had effectively found that the damages which they awarded represented appropriate compensation for both heads of loss which the owners sustained, *Smith v M'Guire* and *Dalwood Marine Co v Nordana Line SA* [2009] EWHC 3394 (Comm), [2010] 2 All E.R. (Comm) 802, [2010] C.L.Y. 3003 considered (see paras 24-27, 41-45, 65, 67 of judgment). (2) Although it was typical that a substitute fixture might extend beyond the date when a contract voyage would have terminated, the *Smith v McGuire* measure of damages did not represent losses other than the loss of the profit that would have been earned from performing the contract voyage; it did not represent compensation for losses such as those which the owners sustained in the instant case, *Smith v McGuire* considered (para.69). (3) The arbitrators had not failed to keep separate the owner's loss and steps taken in mitigation: once it was recognised that the arbitrators were awarding damages for two kinds of loss, it was apparent the losses consisted of the net freight which would have been earned under both the contract voyage and the two follow-on transatlantic voyages, against which credit needed to be given for the net freight earned in mitigation under the substitute charter (para.70). (4) Although in some cases there might not be a logical end point for the calculation of damage where the uncertainty and unpredictability of maritime trade would make a valid comparison difficult, that was not the instant case. The arbitrators had made firm findings as to what the ship would have done if the contract was performed, given the trading options open and the prevailing market conditions, and found that the ship would have been notionally back in Europe at about the same time as she did in fact complete discharge under the substitute fixture. There was, therefore, no need for calculations extending into the distant future, let alone to the end of the vessel's working life. The only calculations necessary concerned events about which the arbitrators were able to make findings with some degree of certainty (para.71). (5) The implied term for which the charterer contended either would not assist them or was far too wide, and, in any event, the charterer had not obtained the findings of fact which they needed for their argument to succeed. Accordingly, there was no basis on which to conclude that the charterer did not assume responsibility for loss of the kind suffered in the instant case, nor could it be said that, in the absence of relevant findings, such loss was necessarily irrecoverable as a matter of law (paras 73, 76).

LOUIS DREYFUS COMMODITIES SUISSE SA v MT MARITIME MANAGEMENT BV, [2015] EWHC 2505 (Comm), [2016] 1 Lloyd's Rep. 197, Males J, QBD (Comm).

SOCIAL SECURITY

1973 Administration of benefits–Computation of earnings

THE SOCIAL SECURITY BENEFIT (COMPUTATION OF EARNINGS) (AMENDMENT) (NORTHERN IRELAND) REGULATIONS 2016, SI 2016/268; made under the Social Security Contributions and Benefits (Northern Ireland) Act 1992 s.3(2)(3), s.133(1), s.171(3)(b)(ii). In force: 6 April 2016.

These Regulations amend the Social Security Benefit (Computation of Earnings) Regulations (Northern Ireland) 1996. The 1996 Regulations make provision for the calculation or estimation of income so as to enable the Department to determine the amount of benefit a claimant should be awarded.

1974 Armed forces independence payments–Descriptors for incapacity–Interpretation

THE ARMED FORCES AND RESERVE FORCES (COMPENSATION SCHEME) (AMENDMENT) ORDER 2016, SI 2016/557; made under the Armed Forces (Pensions and Compensation) Act 2004 s.1(2). In force: 31 May 2016.

This Order amends the Armed Forces and Reserve Forces (Compensation Scheme) Order 2011, which provides for benefits to be payable to or in respect of a person by reason of injury, illness or death which is caused (wholly or partly) by service in the regular or reserve armed forces. Article 2 inserts a meaning for the term "operative treatment". Article 3 amends Sch.3 Table 2 by replacing the existing descriptors for non-freezing cold injuries with three new descriptors and adds a new bilateral complex injury descriptor that was awarded as a temporary award in June 2015. Article 4 amends Sch.3 Table 8 by inserting a meaning for the term "with complications".

1975 Carer's allowance–Disability discrimination–Lawfulness of failure to exempt carers of severely disabled adult family members from benefit cap–Whether indirect discrimination against disabled people

[Housing Benefit Regulations 2006 (SI 2006/213) Pt 8A; European Convention on Human Rights 1950 Protocol 1 art.1, art.14, art.8]

Beneficiaries of carer's allowance applied for judicial review of the Housing Benefit Regulations 2006 Pt 8A, which had reduced their income by operation of the benefit cap. Carer's allowance was available to those caring for a severely disabled person for at least 35 hours per week. Part 8A, introduced by a statutory instrument made by the secretary of state and approved by Parliament under the affirmative resolution procedure, applied the benefit cap, including recipients of carer's allowance but exempting those who received disability allowance or who were caring for a partner or young person in receipt of disability living allowance. The first and third claimants cared for adult family members so were not exempt. The second claimant was cared for by the first claimant. The claimants gave evidence of hardship caused by the cap. The second claimant did not wish to be cared for by someone outside her family and was concerned that if the first claimant was no longer able to care for her, she would have to move to a home; in that case, the state would have to pay more than would be saved by imposing the cap. The claimants argued that (1) not to exempt those caring for disabled adult family members was disproportionate; (2) there was unlawful discrimination contrary to ECHR art.14 in the impact on carers and those for whom they cared.

Held: Application granted. (1) The claimants had argued that the appropriate test was proportionality rather than irrationality, on the basis that the common law no longer required the uniform application of the *Wednesbury* irrationality test. However, *Wednesbury* irrationality, rather than proportionality, continued to apply outside the ECHR and EU law, *R. v Secretary of State for the Home Department Ex p. Brind* [1991] 1 A.C. 696, [1991] C.L.Y. 71 and *Council of Civil Service Unions v Minister for the Civil Service* [1985] A.C. 374, [1985] C.L.Y. 12 followed. However, the claimants did not need to argue that proportionality applied as a common law principle to all cases: ECHR rights were engaged in the instant case. Depriving the first and third claimants of their allowances engaged ECHR Protocol 1 art.1 since the right to receive the benefit was a possession within the meaning of Protocol 1 art.1. Further, the second claimant's art.8 rights were engaged: a disabled person's desire for care to be administered by a particular family member was clearly connected with their human dignity and would almost always be likely to fall within art.8, *Pretty v United Kingdom (2346/02)* [2002] 2 F.L.R. 45, [2002] C.L.Y. 2528 applied. There were therefore fundamental rights involved regarding all three claimants. That affected the intensity of the review the court should apply, but however intense the review, the common law test remained one of irrationality. The fact that both Houses of Parliament had approved the statutory instrument meant that whether the traditional approach or one of proportionality was used would not affect the result. The court had power to pass judgment on such a provision, but public finance was a particularly inapt subject for judicial scrutiny, *Bank Mellat v HM Treasury* [2013] UKSC 38, [2014] A.C. 700, [2014] C.L.Y. 48 and *R. v Secretary of State for the Environment Ex p. Nottinghamshire CC* [1986] A.C. 240, [1986] C.L.Y. 27 followed. The court had to be equally circumspect in applying proportionality or irrationality. The secretary of state's decision as approved by Parliament had been based on political objectives but had had regard to material matters. That a policy could produce hardship in individual cases was not a reason to find it unlawful. Nor did the incidence of greater hardship than expected render it unlawful. The Regulations would not be declared unlawful. However, consideration should be given to an amendment which exempted at least individual family carers such as the claimants since they were very few and the cost to public funds if the cap was to be maintained was likely to significantly outweigh the cost of granting the exemption (see paras 42-57 of judgment). (2) The question regarding discrimination was whether there was discrimination against the disabled. As a result of the cap, a significant number of those cared for in a family context were unable to have that care continue. That would inevitably have an adverse effect on the disabled. The relevant difference in status was between the disabled being cared for by family members and the disabled who were not in that position. There was indirect discrimination. The question was therefore whether it was objectively justifiable. The policy had legitimate aims of reducing expenditure and incentivising work, *R. (on the application of JS) v Secretary of State for Work and Pensions* [2015] UKSC 16, [2015] 1 W.L.R. 1449, [2015] C.L.Y. 2338 followed. Regarding whether the policy was proportionate to those aims, it was noteworthy that the effect on the disabled of the loss of family carers had not been raised in the impact assessments or put before Parliament. Regarding state benefits, the normally strict level of scrutiny of justification gave way to a test which respected the Government's policy choices unless they were manifestly without reasonable foundation, *SG* and *Humphreys v Revenue and Customs Commissioners* [2012] UKSC 18, [2012] 1 W.L.R. 1545, [2012] C.L.Y. 3093 applied. Social and economic policy was pre-eminently the function of the democratically elected institutions, but that consideration would not fully apply unless the particular discriminatory effect had been considered. It had not been in the instant case. The failure to exempt at least individual family carers from the cap was unlawful because it amounted to indirect discrimination which was not objectively justifiable (paras 63-74).

R. (ON THE APPLICATION OF HURLEY) v SECRETARY OF STATE FOR WORK AND PENSIONS *sub nom.* HURLEY v SECRETARY OF STATE FOR WORK AND PENSIONS, [2015] EWHC 3382 (Admin), [2016] P.T.S.R. 636, Collins J, QBD (Admin).

1976 Council tax benefit–Exemptions

THE BENEFIT CAP (HOUSING BENEFIT AND UNIVERSAL CREDIT) (AMENDMENT) REGULATIONS 2016, SI 2016/909; made under the Welfare Reform Act 2012 s.96(1)(4)(a)(c)(g)(5)(5B)(10), s.97(1); Welfare Reform and Work Act 2016 s.34. In force: 7 November 2016.

These Regulations amend the Housing Benefit Regulations 2006, the Universal Credit Regulations 2013, the Housing Benefit and Council Tax Benefit (Decisions and Appeals) Regulations 2001, and the Universal Credit (Transitional Provisions) Regulations 2014. These Regulations make amendments in connection with the Welfare Reform and Work Act 2016 and introduce new exemptions to the benefit cap.

1977 Disability Living Allowance–Personal Independence Payment–Conditions

THE SOCIAL SECURITY (DISABILITY LIVING ALLOWANCE AND PERSONAL INDEPENDENCE PAYMENT) (AMENDMENT) REGULATIONS 2016, SI 2016/556; made under the Social Security Administration Act 1992 s.73(1)(b), s.189(1)(4)(5); Welfare Reform Act 2012 s.86, s.93, s.94(1)(2)(3)(a)(4), Sch.10 para.1(1), Sch.10 para.3(1)(a)(c). In force: 29 June 2016.

These Regulations, which come into force on the 29 June 2016, amend the Social Security (Disability Living Allowance) Regulations 1991 ("the DLA Regulations"), the Social Security (Personal Independence Payment) Regulations 2013 ("the PIP Regulations") and the Personal Independence Payment (Transitional Provisions) Regulations 2013 ("the PIP Transitional Regulations"). Reg.8 and 12A of the DLA Regulations make it a requirement, for receipt of disability living allowance care component and mobility component respectively, that the person in respect of whom it is paid is not maintained free of charge while undergoing medical or other treatment as an in-patient in an NHS or Defence Council hospital or other similar institution. There is an equivalent provision in reg.29 of the PIP Regulations.

1978 Disability living allowance–Residence–Whether person entitled to receive disability living allowance under UK domestic law after move to other Member State–British national ceased all occupational activity before move–Remained insured against old age under UK social security system

[Regulation 1408/71 on the application of social security schemes to employed persons and their families moving within the Community 1971 art.1, art.10, art.13, art.19, art.22]

The secretary of state appealed against a decision (*Tolley (Deceased) v Secretary of State for Work and Pensions* [2013] EWCA Civ 1471)) that the respondent British national (T) was entitled to continue to receive disability living allowance (DLA) even though she had moved to Spain. T had been awarded the care component of DLA on an indefinite basis in 1993. She had previously made national insurance contributions. She moved to Spain in 2002. She was not employed or self-employed there. The secretary of state decided that she was no longer entitled to DLA. The Upper Tribunal held that T was entitled to the benefit by virtue of Regulation 1408/71 art.22. It held that she was an "employed person" for the purposes of the Regulation, she had become entitled to sickness benefits under UK legislation, and she had transferred her residence to another Member State. *Dodl v Tiroler Gebietskrankenkasse (C543/03)* EU:C:2005:364, [2005] E.C.R. I-5049, [2006] C.L.Y. 3977 had held that a person was an "employed person" for the purposes of art.1(a)(ii) of the Regulation where he was covered, even if only in respect of a single risk, on a compulsory or optional basis, by a general or special social security scheme mentioned in art.1(a), irrespective of the existence of an employment relationship. The Court of Appeal upheld the UT's decision, holding that it was bound by *Revenue and Customs Commissioners v Ruas* [2010] EWCA Civ 291, [2010] P.T.S.R. 1757, [2010] C.L.Y. 3063, which applied *Martinez Sala v Freistaat Bayern (C-85/96)* EU:C:1998:217, [1998] E.C.R. I-2691, to hold that T was an "employed person". The secretary of state argued that T could not be an "employed person" just because she was insured against the risk of old age under UK legislation and thus fell within the interpretation of art.1(a)(ii) in *Dodl* and *Sala*. He argued that that reasoning made a nonsense of the careful distinctions drawn in Title III Ch.1 of the Regulation between people who were employed or self-employed, and "unemployed persons", whose rights to export sickness and maternity benefits were severely limited. The secretary of state submitted that the specific provisions in Title III were lex specialis overriding the general provisions in the Regulation. The secretary of state's alternative argument was that T fell within art.13(2)(f), because the legislation of the UK had ceased to be applicable to her, without the legislation of another Member State becoming applicable. He submitted that, in the light of *Kuusijarvi v Riksforsakringsverket (C275/96)* EU:C:1998:279, [1998] E.C.R. I-3419, the UK was entitled to make her right to remain subject to its legislation dependent upon her continued residence in the UK; hence she was subject to the legislation of Spain.

Held: Questions referred to ECJ. (1) In *Commission of the European Communities v European Parliament (C-299/05)* EU:C:2007:608, [2007] E.C.R. I-8695, the care component of DLA was categorised as a "cash sickness benefit" for the purpose of EU law. Although the point had not been argued, the principled solution to a case such as the instant case would be to treat the care component of DLA as an invalidity benefit, and thus freely exportable under art.10, leaving the detailed provisions of Title III Ch.1 to deal with sickness benefits in the narrow sense, *Commission v European Parliament* considered. The broad characteristic of the benefits in art.10 was that they were long-term or one-off payments in respect of permanent conditions, such as disability, old age or death, rather than short-term benefits in respect of potentially temporary conditions, such as sickness, maternity or unemployment (see para.24 of judgment). (2) None of the cases relied upon by T was concerned with whether, in the light of the specific provisions of Title III relating to unemployed persons, the broad definition in *Dodl* could apply to the provisions relating to "employed persons". It might be thought surprising if people who were economically inactive were treated more favourably than people who were actively seeking work in a Regulation which was designed to facilitate the free movement of workers, *Dodl*, *Sala*, *Ruas* and *Kuusijarvi* considered (para.25). (3) Three questions were referred to the ECJ: (i) Whether the care component of DLA was properly classified as an invalidity rather than a cash sickness benefit; (ii) Whether a person who ceased to be entitled to DLA under UK domestic law because she had moved to another Member State, and who had ceased all occupational activity before the move, but remained insured against old age under the UK social security system, ceased to be subject to the legislation of the UK for the purpose of art.13(2)(f). Also, whether such a person in any event remained subject to the legislation of the UK in the light of Point 19(c) of Annex VI of the Regulation. If such a person had ceased to be subject to the legislation of the UK, whether the UK was obliged or merely permitted by virtue of Point 20 of Annex VI to apply the provisions of Title III Ch.1 of the Regulation to her; (iii) Whether the broad definition of an employed person in *Dodl* applied for the purposes of art.19 to art.22 of the Regulation, where the person had ceased all occupational activity before moving to another Member State, notwithstanding the distinction drawn in Title III Ch.1 between employed and self-employed persons, and unemployed persons; if it did apply, whether such a person was entitled to export the benefit by virtue of either art.19 or art.22. Also, whether art.22(1)(b) operated to prevent a claimant's entitlement to the care component of DLA being defeated by a residence requirement imposed by national legislation on a transfer of residence to another Member State (para.27).

SECRETARY OF STATE FOR WORK AND PENSIONS v TOLLEY (DECEASED), [2015] UKSC 55, [2016] 1 All E.R. 40, Lady Hale DPSC, SC.

1979 Electronic communications–Telephone calls–Making claim for industrial injuries benefit

THE SOCIAL SECURITY (CLAIMS AND PAYMENTS) AMENDMENT REGULATIONS 2016, SI 2016/544; made under the Social Security Administration Act 1992 s.5(1)(a)(i), s.189(1)(4)(5)(5A)(6), s.191. In force: 15 June 2016.

These Regulations amend a number of provisions in the Social Security (Claims and Payments) Regulations 1987. The amendments allow the use of the telephone or an electronic communication when making a claim for industrial injuries benefit.

1980 Employment and support allowance–Freedom of movement for workers–EU citizens with no right to reside in UK–Entitlement to employment and support allowance–Whether employment and support allowance paid predominantly for purpose of facilitating access to labour market

The appellant, a Dutch citizen living in the UK, appealed against a decision of the Upper Tribunal that she was not entitled to receive employment and support allowance (ESA). The appellant had been in the UK since 2010. She had initially received jobseeker's allowance, but that was discontinued when she became unable to sign on for work because of ill health. Thereafter, the secretary of state refused her claim for ESA on the basis that she had no right to reside in the UK. The appellant argued that ESA was a benefit intended to facilitate access to the labour market and that, under EU law, the secretary of state was not entitled to deny such benefits to EU citizens who were in the UK as job seekers and met the financial conditions for eligibility. The Upper Tribunal held that although the secretary of state could not deny the appellant access to benefits intended to facilitate her access to the labour market, ESA was not such a benefit. It held that ESA was "social assistance" and that, as such, it could properly be withheld under EU law. The issues were (1) the test for distinguishing between social assistance and labour-market related benefits; (2) the application of that test to the facts, (3) whether it was possible to divide ESA into social assistance and labour-market related components and apply the test to the latter.

Held: Appeal dismissed. (1) The test for determining whether a benefit was labour-market related was whether it was paid predominantly for the purpose of facilitating access to the labour market, *Jobcenter Berlin Neukolln v Alimanovic (C-67/14)* EU:C:2015:597, [2016] Q.B. 308 followed. If the predominant function of the benefit was to cover the minimum subsistence costs necessary to lead a life in keeping with human dignity, then the benefit could not be said to be intended to facilitate access to the labour market. The ECJ took a narrow approach to defining labour-market related benefits and excluded mere subsistence benefits from the definition. That reduced the amount of benefits that an EU citizen could claim in every Member State and potentially created two tiers of EU citizens in a single Member State: those entitled to social assistance and those not so entitled. However, that was a logical consequence of the fact that social benefits were only available to claimants claiming by virtue of their EU citizenship where they were workers or job seekers exercising their right to freedom of movement. EU law was not a passport to the same social benefits in every Member State in every situation. There was a place for separate national benefit systems in which claimants from other Member States could not always participate (see paras 5, 22-30 of judgment). (2) Applying that test, ESA was social assistance and was not a labour-market related benefit. ESA was primarily provided for those who could not work by reason of some disability or past episode. Some claimants might be able to work in future, and one of the aims of the benefit was to provide facilities that would enable them to do so. However, facilitating an entry into work was not the predominant function of the benefit. Roughly 87% of those receiving it had a limited capability for work and were not required to do any work-related activity, and it made no sense to treat the benefit paid to them as being intended to facilitate their access to the labour market. The rationale of the EU law requirement that nationals of other Member States should participate equally in benefits paid to facilitate access to the labour market was to support the internal market by putting job seekers from other Member States on an equal footing with those resident in the Member State in question. It was not to put those with a limited capability for work into the same position as regards training and preparation for work as those in different Member States. The fact that one of the aims of ESA was to help some people back into work where possible did not make it a labour-market related benefit (paras 42-45). (3) ESA was not the sort of benefit that could be separated into component elements. Some claimants had limited capability to undertake both work and work-related activity, whereas others could undertake work-related activity but not work. However, one of the aims of the benefit was to make the two groups "porous" so that claimants could move from one to the other at different points in time depending on their capability. There was thus no need to decide whether, if the benefit paid to those who could undertake work-related activity were a separate benefit, it would be a labour-market related benefit (paras 52-55).

ALHASHEM v SECRETARY OF STATE FOR WORK AND PENSIONS, [2016] EWCA Civ 395, [2016] 3 W.L.R. 853, Arden LJ, CA (Civ Div).

1981 Employment and support allowance–Jobseeker's allowance–Reduction of benefit

THE SOCIAL SECURITY (JOBSEEKER'S ALLOWANCE, EMPLOYMENT AND SUPPORT ALLOWANCE AND UNIVERSAL CREDIT) (AMENDMENT) REGULATIONS 2016, SI 2016/678; made under the Jobseekers Act 1995 s.6J(5)(b)(6), s.6K(4)(b)(5)(b), s.19(4)(b)(5), s.19A(4)(b)(5)(b), s.19B(1)(4)(b)(6), s.35(1), s.36(4)(a); Welfare Reform Act 2007 s.11J(3)(b)(4)(b)(7), s.12(3)(4)(c), s.13(3)(4)(c), s.24(1), s.25(5)(a); Welfare Reform Act 2012 s.19(2)(d), s.26(6)(b)(7)(8)(c), s.27(4)(b)(5)(b)(9)(c), s.28(1)(2)(f), s.37(6), s.40, s.42(1)(3)(a). In force: 25 July 2016.

These Regulations amend the Jobseeker's Allowance Regulations 1996, Employment and Support Allowance Regulations 2008, Universal Credit Regulations 2013, Jobseeker's Allowance Regulations 2013 and Employment and Support Allowance Regulations 2013. Regs 3, 4, 5(5) to (9), 6 and 7 amend the sanctions provisions in those Regulations. In each case, a table setting out the reduction periods that apply depending on the circumstances in which the failure has occurred is substituted for the existing provisions so as to ensure that in all cases where a failure has occurred within 14 days of a previous one the reduction period for the subsequent failure is for the same duration as the previous reduction period. The length of the actual reduction periods is not altered. The amendments in those regulations will apply to a failure that occurs on or after 25 July 2016 and which is sanctionable under s.6J, 6K, 19, 19A or 19B of the Jobseekers Act 1995, s.11J, 12 or 13 of the Welfare Reform Act 2007 or s.26 or 27 of the Welfare Reform Act 2012.

1982 Housing benefit–Discrimination–Under-occupancy–Lawfulness of scheme under Housing Benefit (Amendment) Regulations 2012

[Housing Benefit Regulations 2006 (SI 2006/213) reg.B13; Housing Benefit (Amendment) Regulations 2012 (SI 2012/3040); European Convention on Human Rights 1950 art.14; Equality Act 2010 (c.15) s.149]

The appellants (R, T and X) appealed against decisions (*Rutherford v Secretary of State for Work and Pensions* [2014] EWHC 1631 (Admin) and *R. (on the application of A) v Secretary of State for Work and Pensions* [2015] EWHC 159 (Admin)) concerning the lawfulness of the Housing Benefit Regulations 2006 reg.B13. T was a child with a severe disability who lived with R, his grandparents. He required 24-hour care. R were in poor health and received respite care twice a week from carers who stayed with them overnight. They lived in a three-bedroom housing association property which had been adapted for T's needs. X was a victim of domestic violence who lived with her son in a three-bedroom local authority house. The house had been adapted to make it secure under the sanctuary scheme. Until the Housing Benefit (Amendment) Regulations 2012 came into force, introducing reg.B13 of the 2006 Regulations, R, T and X had all received housing benefit which covered their full rent. However, their benefit was reduced because the number of bedrooms in their properties exceeded the number they were entitled to under the criteria in reg.B13 and they were therefore deemed to be under-occupying their houses. They all received discretionary housing payments which made up the shortfall in their housing benefit. However, they contended that they ought to come within the defined classes of persons set out in reg.B13 and that the failure to make provision for them breached their rights under ECHR art.14. In particular, X argued that the failure to make provision for female victims of domestic violence amounted to sex discrimination because it had a disproportionate effect on a group which was overwhelmingly female. She also maintained that the secretary of state had breached his public sector equality duty under the Equality Act 2010 s.149. In both cases, the judge concluded that, looking at the overall scheme, the policy of dealing with those affected by discretionary housing benefit payments was not manifestly without reasonable foundation. In X's case he also found that the secretary of state had not breached his public sector equality duty because it was unnecessary to look at every eventuality for the discharge of that duty. The issues were whether (1) the failure to make provision in reg.B13 for female victims of domestic violence living in accommodation adapted under the sanctuary scheme was unlawful sex discrimination which breached art.14; (2) the secretary of state had complied with his public sector equality duty in respect of those living in accommodation under the sanctuary scheme; (3) provision under reg.B13 ought to have been made for overnight carers of a child in the same way that it had been made for overnight carers of an adult.

Held: Appeals allowed. (1) Those who were within the sanctuary scheme and in need of an adapted "safe" room were few in number and capable of easy recognition. There would be little prospect of abuse and little need for monitoring if they were included within the defined categories in reg.B13. Regulation B13 discriminated against women within the sanctuary scheme. The question was whether that discrimination was justified. The Master of the Rolls in *R. (on the application of MA) v Secretary of State for Work and Pensions* [2014] EWCA Civ 13, [2014] P.T.S.R. 584, [2014] C.L.Y. 2757 had found that there was an objective and reasonable justification for the scheme. However, he had only been able to approach the matter in that way because he had distinguished *Burnip v Birmingham City Council* [2012] EWCA Civ 629, [2013] P.T.S.R. 117, [2012] C.L.Y. 3111 on the facts of the case. He had not said that *Burnip* had been wrongly decided. *MA* had made a clear distinction between a broad class for which discretionary housing payments were appropriate and a narrow class for which they were not. X's case was within the narrow class covered by the decision in *Burnip*. In those circumstances, the secretary of state had failed to show that his reasons amounted to an objective and reasonable justification for the admitted discrimination in reg.B13, *Burnip* and *MA* followed (see paras 8, 47-49, 53-56 of judgment). (2) Those within the sanctuary scheme who would be adversely affected by reg.B13 were few in number. The secretary of state had addressed the issue of gender-based discrimination. In the circumstances, it was not a breach of the public sector equality duty to fail to identify that tiny and specific group in the equality impact assessment. When the group had been identified, the problem had been addressed by the provision of discretionary housing payments (paras 59-60). (3) The best interests of children in T's position should have been a primary consideration for the secretary of state in devising the Regulations. That was underlined by the way in which the Master of the Rolls in MA had acknowledged that the secretary of state had been entitled to provide for a greater degree of protection for children than for adults who were in the materially similar situation of having a disability-related need for an additional bedroom. There was a difference in treatment in reg.B13 concerning accommodation needed for carers of disabled adults and accommodation needed for carers of disabled children. The secretary of state had not addressed how that difference could be justified by reference to the best interests of the child. Discretionary housing payments were intended to provide the same sum of money, but that did not justify the different treatment of children and adults in respect of the same essential need within the same Regulation. Neither the Regulation nor the policy behind it addressed the best interests of the child as a primary consideration. R and T's appeal therefore succeeded for those reasons as well as those which applied to X (paras 72-74).

RUTHERFORD v SECRETARY OF STATE FOR WORK AND PENSIONS; R. (ON THE APPLICATION OF A) v SECRETARY OF STATE FOR WORK AND PENSIONS *sub nom.* R. (ON THE APPLICATION OF RUTHERFORD) v SECRETARY OF STATE FOR WORK AND PENSIONS, [2016] EWCA Civ 29, [2016] H.L.R. 8, Lord Thomas LCJ, CA (Civ Div).

1983 Income support–EU nationals–Temporary or permanent inability to work–Whether Polish national entitled to income support–Whether Austrian national entitled to housing assistance

[Accession (Immigration and Worker Registration) Regulations 2004 (SI 2004/1219); Immigration (European Economic Area) Regulations 2006 (SI 2006/1003); Treaty on the Functioning of the European Union 2008 art.21; Directive 2004/38 on the right of citizens of the Union and their family members to move and reside freely within the territory of the Member States amending Regulation (EEC) No 1612/68 and repealing Directives 64/221/EEC, 68/360/EEC, 72/194/EEC, 73/148/EEC, 75/34/EEC, 75/35/EEC, 90/364/EEC, 90/365/ 2004 art.24, art.7(1)]

The appellants (M and S) appealed against decisions (*Mirga v Secretary of State for Work and Pensions* [2012] EWCA Civ 1952 and *Samin v Westminster City Council* [2012] EWCA Civ 1468, [2013] 2 C.M.L.R. 6, [2013] C.L.Y. 1526) upholding determinations that they were not entitled to income support and housing assistance respectively. M was a Polish national who had spent much of her life in England. Although she had worked at various times, she was refused income support after becoming pregnant. The secretary of state's position was as follows: at the time she applied for income support, M was ineligible for income support because she was a "person from abroad"; that was on the basis that she could not claim to be a "worker" as she was a Polish national who had not completed 12 months' registered employment under the Accession (Immigration and Worker Registration) Regulations 2004 and thus could not be a "qualifying person" for the purpose of the Immigration (European Economic Area) Regulations 2006; there was no question of her having been a "jobseeker", a "self-employed person" or a "student" under the 2006 Regulations, nor could she claim to be a "self-sufficient person". S was an Austrian citizen who had come to the UK in 2005. He was in poor health and had not worked since 2006. He applied for housing under the homelessness provisions of the Housing Act 1996, but his application was refused. The local authority's position was as follows: S was not a "worker" within the 2006 Regulations, as he was now permanently incapable of work; in any event, he could not claim to be a "worker", as he had not worked for 12 months in the UK; accordingly, he was not a "qualified person" under the Regulations, from which it followed that he was "ineligible" for housing assistance; further, he could not claim to be "a self-sufficient person" within the Regulations, as he had no assets and no health insurance. The issues were (1) whether the domestic Regulations which had led to the impugned decisions infringed the right under Treaty on the Functioning of the European Union art.21(1) to "reside freely" within the EU and/or the right under art.18 not to be discriminated against on nationality grounds; (2) whether there should have been an investigation as to whether it was proportionate to refuse M and S income support and housing assistance.

Held: Appeals dismissed. (1) The appellants' TFEU rights had not been infringed. The right accorded by art.21(1) (relied on by M), although fundamental and broad, was qualified by the words "subject to the limitations and conditions laid down in the Treaties and in the measures adopted to give them effect". The "measures" included Directive 2004/38, which was concerned with "the right of citizens of the Union and their family members to move and reside freely within the territory of the member states". They also presumably included the Treaty on Accession 2003, under which 10 countries, including Poland, acceded to the EU. It was a significant aim of the Directive that EU nationals from one Member State should not be able to exercise their rights of residence in another Member State so as to become "an unreasonable burden on the social assistance system". Article 7(1) limited the right of residence after three months to those who were workers, self-employed, students or persons with sufficient resources and health insurance "not to become a burden on the social assistance system of the host member state". Under art.24, EU nationals' right of equal treatment in host Member States was "subject to ... secondary law" and they could be refused social assistance "where appropriate". Having regard to the 2003 Treaty and the Directive, because M had not done 12 months' work in this country, she could not claim to be a "worker", and, because she was not a "jobseeker", "self-employed", a "student" or "self-sufficient", she could validly be denied a right of residence in the UK and therefore could be excluded from social assistance. In those circumstances, it had to follow that art.21(1) could not assist her. The position was similar in relation to art.18, on which S had relied. The art.18 right did not constitute a broad or general right not to be discriminated against. First, its ambit was limited to "the scope of the Treaties", which meant that it only came into play where there was discrimination in connection with a right in the TFEU or another EU Treaty. Second, the art.18 right was "without prejudice to any special provisions contained [in the Treaties]". Further, the point raised by the appellants had to be rejected as *acte eclare* following the Grand Chamber judgments in *Dano v Jobcenter Leipzig (C-333/13)* EU:C:2014:2358, [2015] 1 W.L.R. 2519 and *Jobcenter Berlin Neukolln v Alimanovic (C-67/14)* EU:C:2015:597, [2016] Q.B. 308, *Dano* and *Alimanovic* applied (see paras 43-45, 47-48 of judgment). (2) Where a national of another Member State was not a worker, self-employed or a student, and had no, or very limited, means of support and no medical insurance, it would severely undermine the whole thrust and purpose of the 2004 Directive if proportionality could be invoked to entitle that person to have the right of residence and social assistance in another Member State, save perhaps in extreme circumstances. It would also place a substantial burden on a host Member State if it had to carry out a proportionality exercise in every case where the right of residence (or indeed the right against discrimination) was invoked (para.69).

MIRGA v SECRETARY OF STATE FOR WORK AND PENSIONS; SAMIN v WESTMINSTER CITY COUNCIL, [2016] UKSC 1, [2016] 1 W.L.R. 481, Lord Neuberger JSC, SC.

1984 Jobseeker's allowance–Service personnel–Higher level sanctions

THE JOBSEEKER'S ALLOWANCE (MEMBERS OF THE FORCES) (NORTHERN IRELAND) (AMENDMENT) REGULATIONS 2016, SI 2016/622; made under the Jobseekers (Northern Ireland) Order 1995 (SI 1995 2705) art.24 , art.36(2). In force: In accordance with reg.1.

These regulations insert references to higher level sanctions into the Jobseeker's Allowance (Members of the Forces) (Northern Ireland) Regulations 1997 in relation to the provisions of the Welfare Reform (Northern Ireland) Order 2015.

1985 Jobseeker's allowance–Work capability assessments

THE JOBSEEKER'S ALLOWANCE (EXTENDED PERIOD OF SICKNESS) AMENDMENT REGULATIONS 2016, SI 2016/502; made under the Jobseekers Act 1995 Sch.1 para.2(1); Welfare Reform Act 2012 s.37(3)(6). In force: 23 May 2016.

These Regulations amend the Jobseeker's Allowance Regulations 1996 (the 1996 Regulations) and the Jobseeker's Allowance Regulations 2013 (the 2013 Regulations) concerning the circumstances in which a claimant is treated as capable of work (or as not having limited capability for work) on account of a period of disease or disablement.

1986 National insurance contributions–Apprentices–Statutory definition

THE SOCIAL SECURITY (CONTRIBUTIONS) (AMENDMENT) REGULATIONS 2016, SI 2016/117; made under the Social Security Contributions and Benefits Act 1992 s.9B(9), s.175(3); Social Security Contributions and Benefits (Northern Ireland) Act 1992 s.9B(9), s.171(3). In force: 6 April 2016.

These Regulations prescribe "an apprentice" for the purposes of the Social Security Contributions and Benefits Act 1992 s.9B and the corresponding Northern Ireland legislation.

1987 National insurance contributions–Earnings–Consequential amendments

THE SOCIAL SECURITY (CONTRIBUTIONS) (AMENDMENT NO. 4) REGULATIONS 2016, SI 2016/1067; made under the Social Security Contributions and Benefits Act 1992 s.3(2)(3), s.10(9)(a), s.120(1), Sch.1 para.6(1)(2); Social Security Contributions and Benefits (Northern Ireland) Act 1992 s.3(2)(3), s.10(9)(a), Sch.1 para.6(1)(2). In force: 28 November 2016.

These Regulations make a number of consequential amendments to the Social Security (Contributions) Regulations 2001. The Contributions Regulations set out how to calculate an individual's earnings for the purpose of earnings-related National Insurance contributions. Schedule 3 of the Contributions Regulations provides for certain payments to be disregarded for these purposes. In particular, paras 4A to 4D of

Pt VIII of Sch.3 to the Contributions Regulations provide that certain payments of travel, subsistence and accommodation costs and expenses in connection with an employment, some or all of the duties of which are performed overseas, are to be disregarded for this purpose.

1988 National insurance contributions–Rectification

THE SOCIAL SECURITY (CONTRIBUTIONS) (AMENDMENT NO.3) REGULATIONS 2016, SI 2016/647; made under the Social Security Contributions and Benefits Act 1992 s.3(2)(3); Social Security Contributions and Benefits (Northern Ireland) Act 1992 s.3(2)(3), s.171(10). In force: 6 July 2016.

These Regulations amend the Social Security (Contributions) Regulations 2001 by substituting a new sub-paragraph (a). This is a technical amendment which corrects an error in the Social Security (Contributions) (Amendment) (No. 2) Regulations 2016.

1989 Social security–Administration of benefits–Computation of earnings

THE SOCIAL SECURITY BENEFIT (COMPUTATION OF EARNINGS) (AMENDMENT) REGULATIONS 2016, SI 2016/267; made under the Social Security Contributions and Benefits Act 1992 s.3(2)(3), s.122(1), s.175(3). In force: 6 April 2016.

These Regulations amend the Social Security Benefit (Computation of Earnings) Regulations 1996. The 1996 Regulations make provision for the calculation or estimation of income so as to enable the Secretary of State to determine the amount of benefit a claimant should be awarded.

1990 Social security–Reciprocity–Northern Ireland reciprocal arrangements

THE SOCIAL SECURITY (NORTHERN IRELAND RECIPROCAL ARRANGEMENTS) (AMENDMENT) REGULATIONS 2016, SI 2016/1050; made under the Northern Ireland Act 1998 s.87(4)(6)(9); Social Security Administration Act 1992 s.189(1)(4)(5). In force: In accordance with reg.1.

These Regulations give effect in Great Britain to reciprocal arrangements between Great Britain and Northern Ireland relating to social security. These arrangements, which are contained in the exchange of letters set out in the Schedule, amend earlier reciprocal arrangements relating to social security.

1991 Social security administration–National insurance contributions–Consequential amendments

THE SOCIAL SECURITY (CREDITS, AND CREDITING AND TREATMENT OF CONTRIBUTIONS) (CONSEQUENTIAL AND MISCELLANEOUS AMENDMENTS) REGULATIONS 2016, SI 2016/1145; made under the Social Security Contributions and Benefits Act 1992 s.22(5), s.122, s.175(1)(3)(4), Sch.1 para.8(1)(d)(1A); Jobseekers Act 1995 s.35, Sch.1 para.18; Social Security Act 1998 s.9(1), s.10(3), s.79(1)(4)(6)(7), s.84; Welfare Reform Act 2007 s.24, Sch.2 para.11. In force: 1 January 2017.

These regulations amend the Social Security (Credits) Regulations 1975, the Social Security and Child Support (Decisions and Appeals) Regulations 1999, the Social Security (Crediting and Treatment of Contributions, and National Insurance Numbers) Regulations 2001 and the Universal Credit, Personal Independence Payment, Jobseeker's Allowance and Employment and Support Allowance (Decisions and Appeals) Regulations 2013. The amendments are consequential on the changes made by the National Insurance Contributions Act 2015 (c.5) to reform the payment and collection of Class 2 contributions, and the introduction of accelerated payment of contributions by that Act. These Regulations also make various tidying-up miscellaneous amendments.

1992 Social security administration–State pension–Consequential amendments

THE PENSIONS ACT 2014 (CONSEQUENTIAL AMENDMENTS) ORDER 2016, SI 2016/931; made under the Pensions Act 2014 s.53. In force: In accordance with art.1.

This Order makes amendments to the Social Security Administration Act 1992 and the Social Security Act 1998 which are consequential on the introduction of the State

Pension for persons reaching pensionable age on or after 6 April 2016 by the Pensions Act 2014.

1993 **Social security benefits–Universal credit–Tax credits**

THE UNIVERSAL CREDIT (TRANSITIONAL PROVISIONS) (AMENDMENT) REGULATIONS 2016, SI 2016/232; made under the Welfare Reform Act 2012 s.42(2)(3), Sch.6 para.1(1), Sch.6 para.6. In force: 1 April 2016.

Regulation 12(4) of the Universal Credit (Transitional Provisions) Regulations 2014 modifies the operation of the Tax Credits Act 2002 s.29(4) to provide alternative means of recovery in cases where a person entitled to a tax credit claims universal credit. This currently provides for recovery by deductions from universal credit. These Regulations substitute a new version of reg.12(4) which provides for recovery by deductions from benefit (including universal credit) under the Social Security Administration Act 1992 s.71ZC, deductions from earnings under s.71ZD of that Act or through court action etc. as set out in s.71ZE of that Act.

1994 **Tax credits–Child benefit**

THE TAX CREDITS AND CHILD BENEFIT (MISCELLANEOUS AMENDMENTS) REGULATIONS 2016, SI 2016/360; made under the Tax Credits Act 2002 s.7(8)(9) , s.8(2), s.12(4), s.65(1)(7) , s.67, s.29(4), s.65(2)(7) , s.67; Social Security Contributions and Benefits Act 1992 s.142(2) , s.175, Sch.9 para.1; Social Security Contributions and Benefits (Northern Ireland) Act 1992 s.138(2) , s.171, Sch.9 para.1(1). In force: 6 April 2016.

These Regulations amend various Regulations concerning tax credits and child benefit.

1995 **Universal credit–Care leavers–Looked-after children**

THE UNIVERSAL CREDIT (CARE LEAVERS AND LOOKED AFTER CHILDREN) AMENDMENT REGULATIONS 2016, SI 2016/543; made under the Welfare Reform Act 2012 s.4(3), s.11(4), s.40, s.42(3). In force: 26 May 2016.

These Regulations make a number of amendments to the Universal Credit Regulations 2013 in relation to looked after and formerly looked after children and young persons.

1996 **Universal credit–Self-employment–Surpluses and Self-employed Losses**

THE UNIVERSAL CREDIT (SURPLUSES AND SELF-EMPLOYED LOSSES) (CHANGE OF COMING INTO FORCE) REGULATIONS 2016, SI 2016/215; made under the Welfare Reform Act 2012 s.42(2)(3), Sch.1 para.4I1)(3)(a)(4). In force: 23 March 2016.

The Universal Credit (Surpluses and Self-employed Losses) (Digital Service) Amendment Regulations 2015 amended the Universal Credit Regulations 2013 by making further provision for the calculation of earned income for the purposes of calculating an award of universal credit. These Regulations postpone the coming into force of those Regulations from 6 April 2016 until 3 April 2017.

1997 **Welfare Reform Act 2012 (c.5)–Commencement No.13, 14, 16, 19, 22, 23 and 24 and Transitional and Transitory Provisions (Modification) Order**

THE WELFARE REFORM ACT 2012 (COMMENCEMENT NO.13, 14, 16, 19, 22, 23 AND 24 AND TRANSITIONAL AND TRANSITORY PROVISIONS (MODIFICATION)) ORDER 2016, SI 2016/596; made under the Welfare Reform Act 2012 s.150(3)(4)(a)(b)(i)(c). In force: 23 May 2016.

This Order modifies a series of prior Orders bringing into force provisions of the Welfare Reform Act 2012 relating to universal credit and the abolition of income-related employment and support allowance and income-based jobseeker's allowance.

1998 **Welfare Reform and Work Act 2016 (c.7)–Commencement No.2 Regulations**

THE WELFARE REFORM AND WORK ACT 2016 (COMMENCEMENT NO.2) REGULATIONS 2016, SI 2016/610; made under the Welfare Reform and Work Act

2016 s.36(6). Commencement details: bringing into operation various provisions of the 2016 Act on 9 June 2016.

These Regulations appoint 9 June 2016 as the day for the coming into force of the Welfare Reform and Work Act 2016 s.10 (benefit cap: Social Security Advisory Committee).

1999 Welfare Reform and Work Act 2016 (c.7)–Commencement No.3 Regulations

THE WELFARE REFORM AND WORK ACT 2016 (COMMENCEMENT NO.3) REGULATIONS 2016, SI 2016/910; made under the Welfare Reform and Work Act 2016 s.36(3)(b)(8). Commencement details: bringing into operation various provisions of the Welfare Reform and Work Act 2016 on 7 November 2016.

Regulation 2(1) of these Regulations appoints the 7 November 2016 as the day for the coming into force of the Welfare Reform and Work Act 2016 ss.8 (benefit cap) and 9(1)-(5) (review of benefit cap) to the extent they are not already in force on that day.

SOCIAL WELFARE

2000 Adult social care–Local authorities' powers and duties–Allegations of financial impropriety against accredited provider of direct payment support services–Suspension

[Care Act 2014 (c.23) s.1, s.42, s.42(1)(c)]

The claimants, who were the recipients of social care, applied for permission to seek judicial review of a decision of the defendant local authority to suspend the interested party (D) from being an accredited provider of direct payment support services. Under the direct payment scheme, the money intended for social care was paid to accredited providers such as D. Those providers would then be responsible for the administration of the money on behalf of recipients of social care. The local authority suspended D from its list of accredited providers after being informed by the Trading Standards Department that it was pursuing a criminal investigation into alleged fraudulent dealings by D in relation to service-users' accounts. The claimants argued, among other things, that (1) the local authority had acted in breach of the Care Act 2014 s.1, which imposed a general duty in relation to the well-being of service-users; (2) the local authority had acted in breach of s.42 of the Act, which imposed a duty to begin enquiries where there was reasonable cause to suspect that an adult with needs for care and support was experiencing or at risk of abuse, including financial abuse; (3) the local authority's policy only to have accredited providers was unlawful and contrary to statutory guidance.

Held: Application refused. (1) It was unarguable that s.1 had been breached. Given the risk of abuse to service-users arising from possible financial impropriety, the local authority had acted reasonably in suspending D from its list of accredited providers. There was no basis for deferring suspensory action to await the outcome of any criminal charges; had the local authority done that, public money might have been put at risk and the local authority might have been guilty of maladministration (see paras 22-23, 25 of judgment). (2) There was no basis for arguing that there had been any breach of the s.42 duty. There was clear evidence that the service-users were at risk of financial abuse. What had been uncovered was a widespread issue and there was an ongoing criminal investigation. As a result, it was appropriate for the local authority to commence safeguarding enquiries and act in response to those enquiries. Its decision to suspend D was part of that safeguarding duty. The claimants had argued that, for the purposes of s.42(1)(c), they were not unable to protect themselves against abuse or neglect or the risk of it. That submission was unarguable. The local authority was dealing with vulnerable service-users and the evidence was, in relation to at least two of the three claimants, that Trading Standards had information which provided a basis for concluding that there may well have been financial impropriety in relation to their accounts. The fact that those claimants may have been unaware of that taking place, or had not taken any action in relation to it, was clear evidence that they were unable to protect themselves from either actual abuse or the risk of the abuse which may have taken place (paras 28-30). (3) As to the local authority's policy of only having accredited providers, the claimants had argued that their choice was circumscribed by the fact that they had to use another provider from the list. They relied on the statutory guidance, which indicated that limited lists of providers did not fit within the Government's vision for social care after the passing of the 2014 Act. The local authority's case was that it had a list of accredited providers in April 2011; that number had reduced to seven, including D, by August 2015; it was in fact in the throes of reviewing the list when the issues arising from D came to its attention; as a result, it took the view that it was better to maintain the list, given the entirely exceptional circumstances that it was dealing with, as providing some indication of other providers with appropriate experience and probity; as a result, it took the action that it did. It was quite right that, in the face of the statutory guidance, to restrict a choice to accredited providers was not consistent with the new approach to social care provision. However, guidance could be departed from if there was a good reason for doing so. Here, there was a good reason. The local authority was dealing with an exceptional circumstance and it was entirely appropriate for it to take the action that it did in seeking to move on the service-users to other providers from the list. What the local authority was doing was seeking to protect the well-being of the service-users in a very difficult position (paras 31-33).

R. (ON THE APPLICATION OF COLLINS) v NOTTINGHAMSHIRE CC, [2016] EWHC 996 (Admin), (2016) 19 C.C.L. Rep. 494, Patterson J, QBD (Admin).

2001 Adult social care–Local authorities' powers and duties–Reduction of care provision

[Local Authority Social Services Act 1970 (c.42) s.7]

A user of community care services applied for judicial review of a local authority's decision to reduce his social care support. The service user was a 23-year-old man with learning difficulties, communication difficulties, Down's syndrome and general developmental delay. The local authority had been paying £74 for him to receive six hours of support a week. It increased payment temporarily to £296 so that he could be provided with 24 hours of support a week pending an assessment of the level of support he needed. However, that provision ended before the assessment was carried out and there ceased to be any care package at all. The service user sought judicial review of the local authority's apparent decision to reduce his care provision to less than 24 hours per week. The service user submitted that the local authority had failed to review his needs and provide a revised support plan, contrary to the Department of Health's guidance issued under the Local Authority Social Services Act 1970 s.7; had failed to give reasons for the reduction in care, contrary to the statutory guidance; and had failed to take all reasonable steps to reach agreement as to his care, contrary to the Community Care Assessment Directions 2004.

Held: Application granted. On the evidence, the payments had come to a complete halt and there was no care package at all. The assessment had not been carried out when it should have been and no further assessment had since taken place. There had never been any explanation as to why if it had been appropriate to allow 24 hours' community care per week, it had then ceased to be appropriate. There was no evidence at all of any assessment at any stage of whether the day-care solution was appropriate. Thus the service-user's first ground was made out: there was no evidence whatsoever of any assessment or any appropriate support plan to deal with his care needs after the temporary support funding ended. The second ground was also made out: the situation cried out for an explanation by the local authority as to its approach when the assessment did not take place. Given the local authority's lack of transparency and confusion, there was substance to the third ground, but it did not seem to be the real point of concern, which was that the authority never came forward with any assessment of what would be an appropriate care package after the temporary support ended. Therefore, the local authority's decision to reduce the care provision to less than 24 hours per week would be quashed and the local authority would be required to reassess the service user's community care needs (see paras 39, 55-61, 65 of judgment).

H v BEXLEY LBC *sub nom.* OH v BEXLEY LLP, [2015] EWHC 1843 (Admin), (2015) 18 C.C.L. Rep. 375, Roger Ter Haar QC, QBD (Admin).

2002 Adult social care–Need–Whether "care and support" under Care Act 2014 encompassed simple need for accommodation

[Care Act 2014 (c.23) s.8; Care and Support (Eligibility Criteria) Regulations 2015 (SI 2015/313); Localism Act 2011 (c.20) s.1; European Convention on Human Rights 1950 art.3; Nationality, Immigration and Asylum Act 2002 (c.41) Sch.3]

The 49-year-old claimant applied for judicial review of the defendant local authority's refusal to provide her with accommodation. The claimant was a Swiss national who was wheelchair dependent and had severe mental health problems. She had been homeless in Switzerland before arriving in the UK. She was assessed by psychiatrists who agreed that she did not have the mental capacity to decide whether to return to Switzerland or consent to mental health treatment. The local authority provided her with temporary accommodation but the claimant said it was unsuitable for wheelchair access. The local authority conducted a needs assessment to see whether she was entitled to care and support under the Care Act 2014 according to the Care and Support (Eligibility Criteria) Regulations 2015. The claimant painted a more positive picture of her physical abilities than was actually the case, hoping that she would be given alternative accommodation if she was not considered too much trouble. The local authority decided that her sole need was accommodation, which did not fall within the 2014 Act and which it concluded it had no power to provide. The claimant was later awarded a weekly personal independence payment but was not entitled to any other benefits. The claimant submitted that "care and support" was broad enough to include a need for simple accommodation, as could be seen by references to accommodation in s.8 of the 2014 Act and in the Regulations. She further submitted that the local authority had the power to help her under the Localism Act 2011 s.1 and its refusal amounted to inhuman or degrading treatment in breach of ECHR art.3. The local authority argued that there was no breach as she could use her weekly benefit to find accommodation.

Held: Application granted. (1) A need for accommodation did not amount to a "need for care and support" under the 2014 Act. Under the Act's predecessor, local authorities could provide residential accommodation for those in need of "care and attention". Case law had decided that that phrase had to mean something more than "accommodation", *R. (on the application of M) v Slough BC* [2008] UKHL 52, [2008] 1 W.L.R. 1808, [2008] C.L.Y. 2090 and *R. (on the application of Wahid) v Tower Hamlets LBC* [2002] EWCA Civ 287, [2003] H.L.R. 2, [2003] C.L.Y. 2046 considered. The principles derived from those cases applied to the 2014 Act, *R. (on the application of SG) v Haringey LBC* [2015] EWHC 2579 (Admin), (2015) 18 C.C.L. Rep. 444, [2016] 2012 applied. The ordinary meaning of "care and support" did not include a need for accommodation on its own. Section 8 mentioned the provision of accommodation in a care home, but that section listed examples of how care and support might be provided; it was not a list of examples of what constituted a need for care and support. The Regulations required local authorities to assess whether an adult was able to make use of their home safely and maintain a habitable home environment, but they did not support a need for accommodation as a "need"; they envisaged accommodation that existed. Other legislation existed to provide accommodation for those in need of it. Accordingly, given that the claimant's requirement was for accommodation alone, there was no obligation on the local authority under the 2014 Act (see paras 22-29, 49-50 of judgment). (2) Under the Nationality, Immigration and Asylum Act 2002 Sch.3, the claimant was not eligible for support or assistance under s.1 of the 2011 Act. However, Sch.3 provided that the local authority had a duty to act to the extent that it was necessary to avoid breaching the claimant's rights under the ECHR. Lack of accommodation alone did not necessarily result in a breach of art.3, but the claimant was vulnerable and social stressors around accommodation and finances exacerbated her mental condition, including suicidal ideation. Her potential social isolation, physical disabilities, pain, mental health condition and the physical difficulties she encountered were such that if she became homeless it would breach art.3. Hers was a case of serious suffering that reached the high threshold in *R. (on the application of Limbuela) v Secretary of State for the Home Department* [2005] UKHL 66, [2006] 1 A.C. 396,

[2006] C.L.Y. 2217, *Limbuela* applied. Further, there was no accommodation available that was suitable for her physical disabilities within the means provided by her weekly benefit. If she put her entire weekly benefit payment into accommodation, she would be unable to fund other necessities, *Limbuela* applied. Accordingly, the local authority's decision not to exercise its power under s.1 of the 2011 Act had been unlawful (paras 52, 75, 78).

R. (ON THE APPLICATION OF GS) v CAMDEN LBC, [2016] EWHC 1762 (Admin), [2016] H.L.R. 43, Peter Marquand, QBD (Admin).

2003 Care–Carers–Power to promote well-being

THE SOCIAL SERVICES AND WELL-BEING (WALES) ACT 2014 (CONSEQUENTIAL AMENDMENTS) REGULATIONS 2016, SI 2016/413; made under the Social Services and Well-being (Wales) Act 2014 s.198. In force: In accordance with reg.2.

These Regulations make provision about improving the well-being outcomes for people in Wales who need care and support and carers who need support. They amend primary legislation that currently underpins the provision of care and support for people and support for carers in Wales.

2004 Care–Complaints–Consequential amendments

THE SOCIAL SERVICES AND WELL-BEING (WALES) ACT 2014 (CONSEQUENTIAL AMENDMENTS) (SECONDARY LEGISLATION) (AMENDMENT) REGULATIONS 2016, SI 2016/351; made under the Social Services and Well-being (Wales) Act 2014 s.198. In force: 5 April 2016.

These Regulations correct an error in the Social Services and Well-being (Wales) Act 2014 (Consequential Amendments) (Secondary Legislation) 2016. They amend the 2016 Regulations to omit reference to two sets of regulations from Sch.2 to the 2016 Regulations (regulations disapplied in relation to Wales).

2005 Care plans–Needs assessments–Parent carer–Local authority's general duty to provide services for children in need

[Children Act 1989 (c.41) s.17(1)]

A 15-year-old boy who had autism applied for judicial review of the local authority's assessment of his needs and those of his mother, who was his primary carer. The boy lived with his mother in a two bedroom maisonette on an upper floor of a block of flats. In 2005, the local authority assessed him as needing 12.5 hours of support a week, which it provided in the form of direct payments. The boy was educated at home by his mother, but between September 2010 and July 2014 he attended an independent school for one-and-a-half days a week. In February 2015, the local authority undertook a fresh assessment of his needs and recommended that he should attend a local special school and should be referred to a challenging behaviour team and other support schemes. His mother was advised to bid for alternative accommodation under a scheme for allocating properties. The assessment report did not recommend an increase in the number of hours of support needed. The boy submitted that the assessment underestimated the extent of his need for support and supervision, his inability to look after himself and his challenging behaviour.

Held: Application refused. (1) Local authorities were under a duty to take reasonable steps to identify children in need within their areas, to produce a care plan specifying how those needs were to be met, and to provide the services identified in that plan, *R. (on the application of KM) v Cambridgeshire CC* [2012] UKSC 23, [2012] 3 All E.R. 1218, [2012] C.L.Y. 3164 followed. The plan had to be realistic and had to address the needs of parent carers as an integral feature: providing services which met the needs of parents was often the most effective means of promoting the welfare of children in need. The maximum timeframe for the assessment to be produced was to be no longer than 45 working days from the date it was commissioned (see paras 8-9 of judgment). (2) In the instant case it was reasonably open to the social worker who prepared the 2015 assessment to reach the conclusions she did about the number of hours of support the boy needed each week. In relation to the mother's needs, it was reasonable to conclude that the need for overnight care was best met by the boy's staying overnight occasionally at a specialist short break service, coupled with a referral to the challenging behaviour team to address his interrupted sleeping. It was also reasonable to conclude that the amount of supervision he needed during the day could be met without increasing the number of hours of support he was already receiving. If the boy went to school full time, his mother would have more time to herself and would not need to engage a carer as often. Moreover, since he only occasionally needed to use a wheelchair, it was reasonable to conclude that the limited resource of a ground floor flat should be reserved for more needy cases. Even if the current flat had been assessed as inadequate, any duty on the local authority's part to meet that need could only have arisen under the Children Act 1989 s.17(1), which imposed a general duty to provide services for children in need. That general duty was not owed to every individual child, and the local authority was not obliged to meet every child's assessed needs regardless of resources, *R. (on the application of G) v Barnet LBC* [2003] UKHL 57, [2004] 2 A.C. 208, [2004] C.L.Y. 3643 followed (paras 29, 31-33, 37-38). (3) The recommendations which concluded the assessment could not be characterised as a care plan, as they were drafted in very general terms with no concrete proposals about how the desired outcomes could be achieved. However, it was reasonable for the local authority to await the outcome of the challenge to the lawfulness of the assessment before producing a care plan, which might otherwise need to be quashed and a new assessment prepared (paras 39, 41).

R. (ON THE APPLICATION OF MM) v HOUNSLOW LBC, [2015] EWHC 3731 (admin), (2016) 19 C.C.L. Rep. 141, Sir Brian Keith, QBD (Admin).

2006 Childminding–Registration

THE CHILD MINDING AND DAY CARE EXCEPTIONS (WALES) (AMENDMENT) ORDER 2016, SI 2016/96; made under the Children and Families (Wales) Measure 2010 s.19(4)(5). In force: 1 April 2016.

This Order amends the Child Minding and Day Care Exceptions (Wales) Order 2010 to extend the circumstances in which a person whose activity would otherwise fall within the definition of "child minding" or "day care for children" is excepted from it and who is not therefore required to register.

2007 Children–Local authorities' powers and duties–Refusal of accommodation for teenage girl as child in need of accommodation–Issues of radicalisation

[Children Act 1989 (c.41) s.17(10), s.20, s.23A, s.23C, s.23E; Children (Leaving Care) Act 2000 (c.35); Children (Leaving Care) (England) Regulations 2001 (SI 2001/2874)]

The applicant teenager applied for judicial review of the defendant local authority's refusal to provide her with accommodation as a child in need. C had been referred to the defendant local authority after presenting herself as homeless. She indicated that her family lived within the defendant's area but that she did not wish to return to them. She gave a generalised account of incidents of domestic violence and explained that she had been abroad for two months and had just returned to the UK. It became apparent that C had previously been detained at an airport after leaving her family home without her family's consent and had travelled through Turkey to the Syrian border. The defendant's records indicated that C's case was regarded as high profile because of concerns around radicalisation. An assessment was conducted, and it was concluded that C was not homeless as she was able to return to her parents, and that as she was not homeless she could not be in need pursuant to the Children Act 1989 s.17(10). Following the assessment C was again detained by police at the airport whilst seeking to travel to Bulgaria with a significant amount of money. C was granted interim relief ordering the local authority to provide her with accommodation and support under s.20 of the 1989 Act. C had since turned 18 years old. She claimed that she was a child in need of accommodation and support under s.20, and that the local authority should treat her as if she were a former relevant child, therefore triggering the responsibilities arising pursuant to the Children (Leaving Care) Act 2000.

Held: Application granted. (1) The concept of need under s.17 covered a wide spectrum of issues relating to the welfare of a child. The 1989 Act imposed a duty both to promote and to safeguard the welfare of children. It was also important under the Act to ascertain the wishes and feelings of a child regarding the provision of a range and level of services appropriate to the child's needs. The older the child and the greater her understanding, the more the weight that had to be given to her wishes and feelings, particularly where the child was requesting support. The local authority had not truly analysed C's case within the framework of the Act. The risks to C by virtue of her views and belief structure and the concerns that she was within a spectrum of radicalisation, undoubtedly placed her securely within the contemplated reach of s.17. To that could be added preparation for marriage to a much older man, which her parents were apparently unable to prevent; two occasions in which she travelled extensively and alone in dangerous parts of the world; C's allegations of being locked in her home against her will for considerable periods of time; direct requests to the local authority from C's parents that she be found somewhere safe to live; very significant periods when C's whereabouts were not known at all and allegations made by C to the effect that she had been subjected to disproportionate degrees of force from her father. The court's view was reinforced by the guidance from the Family Division entitled *Radicalisation Cases in the Family Courts*. Those types of cases were recognised as a new facet of safeguarding and child protection. It was hard to envisage any circumstances where issues such as those that arose in the instant case would not fall within the ambit of s.17. Many children who were at risk or in need lived with parents or carers who themselves presented a risk, or as in the instant case were unable to protect them. That such parents continued to offer a home to their children was often understandable but frequently irrelevant. The local authority's decision-making had been fundamentally flawed (see paras 35-37, 42 of judgment). (2) A child that had been accommodated for more than 13 weeks after the age of 14, including at least some time after the age of 16, was an eligible child while aged 16 or 17 under the 1989 Act and the Children (Leaving Care) (England) Regulations 2001. If he was no longer accommodated some time after the age of 16 he was a relevant child (s.23A of the 1989 Act). The provisions provided a gateway to a raft of provisions for care and support including care and accommodation which a local authority was obliged to provide to an eligible or relevant child throughout childhood. Once eligible or the relevant child reached the age of 18, they acquired the status of former relevant children, which had considerable legal significance, as it established an entitlement to a wide range of support under the "leaving care" provisions in s.23C to s.23E of the 1989 Act until the age of 21, or 24 if they remained in education. Had C not turned 18 she would have fallen within those provisions and would have achieved the status of "former relevant child" in any event. There were no foreseeable circumstances where it would have been fair to exclude her from consideration of the entire range of services that would have been open to her. That was not to say that her entitlement to services was necessarily regarded as automatic, it was inextricably linked to the identification of her welfare requirements. In that respect she was to be regarded as if she were a former relevant child, *R. (on the application of GE (Eritrea)) v Secretary of State for the Home Department* [2014] EWCA Civ 1490, [2015] 1 W.L.R. 4123, [2015] C.L.Y. 2388 followed (paras 45, 56-57).

R. (ON THE APPLICATION OF A) v ENFIELD LBC *sub nom.* A v ENFIELD LBC, [2016] EWHC 567 (Admin), [2016] H.L.R. 33, Hayden J, QBD (Admin).

2008 Children's services–Children's welfare–Unitary authority's failure to rehouse two severely autistic children–Local authorities' duty to co-operate in relation to provision of services for children in need

[Children Act 1989 (c.41) s.27]

Two severely autistic children applied for judicial review of the defendant unitary authority's failure to rehouse them. The children were aged 9 and 10, and lived with their respective mothers in local authority accommodation. They required close supervision and lacked a sense of danger, but their bedrooms were on the first floor, which posed a risk because they were likely to try to jump out of the window. They sought transfers to properties with ground-floor bedrooms and gardens. However, the local authority decided that their need for transfer was not urgent and that the risks could be managed with safety precautions. The children submitted that (1) the requirement under the Children Act 1989 s.27, for authorities to co-operate in relation to the provision of services for children in need, could apply to different departments within a unitary authority; (2) in the instant case, the local authority's system did not equate to that required by s.27 because there was no social services input into the question of whether a child in need went onto the housing risk register.

Held: Application refused. (1) The natural meaning of the words in s.27 indicated that it was aimed at co-operation between different authorities when the authority which dealt with social services, and so the welfare of children, in one did not have responsibility for dealing with other matters, such as housing. It might be assumed that Parliament considered that unitary authorities would ensure that there was the necessary co-operation between their various departments so that there would be no need for a statutory requirement to achieve it, *R. v Tower Hamlets LBC Ex p. Byas* (1993) 25 H.L.R. 105, [1993] C.L.Y. 2065 considered and *R. (on the application of C) v Hackney LBC* [2014] EWHC 3670 (Admin), [2015] P.T.S.R. 1011, [2015] C.L.Y. 46 applied. Nevertheless, it was unnecessary for the children to argue that s.27 applied to different departments within a unitary authority: the government's guidance, *Working Together to Safeguard Children,* should be read to require that the same degree of co-operation between departments in a unitary authority was given as would be required by s.27 between different authorities. Therefore, whilst s.27 did not apply directly, its requirements were to be applied indirectly (see paras 8, 14-15 of judgment). (2) It was clear that the authority's system involved all relevant professionals, and it was apparent from the evidence that it was open to anyone in children's services to raise any concerns about risk in existing housing. The system in operation did comply with the indirect application of s.27. The system was lawful and its implementation in the instant case had not been unlawful: the continuing absence of housing transfer was not irrational (paras 40, 42, 44).

R. (ON THE APPLICATION OF M) v ISLINGTON LBC *sub nom.* M v ISLINGTON LBC, [2016] EWHC 332 (Admin), [2016] H.L.R. 19, Collins J, QBD (Admin).

2009 Direct payments–Care homes–Staffordshire

THE CARE AND SUPPORT (DIRECT PAYMENTS) (AMENDMENT) REGULATIONS 2016, SI 2016/167; made under the Care Act 2014 s.33(1)(2), s.75(7), s.125(7)(8). In force: 1 April 2016.

These Regulations amend Sch.2 of the Care and Support (Direct Payments) Regulations 2014 and make transitional provision in relation to that amendment so that Staffordshire County Council is not permitted to make direct payments for the purpose of securing long term accommodation in a care home for adults who are not already receiving direct payments for such a purpose before 1 April.

2010 Investigations–Complaints–Public Services Ombudsman for Wales

THE REGULATION AND INSPECTION OF SOCIAL CARE (WALES) ACT 2016 (COMMENCEMENT NO.1) ORDER 2016, SI 2016/467; made under the Regulation and Inspection of Social Care (Wales) Act 2016 s.188(1). Commencement details: bringing into operation various provisions of the 2016 Act on 6 April 2016.

This is the first Commencement Order made by the Welsh Ministers under the Regulation and Inspection of Social Care (Wales) Act 2016. It provides powers for the Public Services Ombudsman for Wales (PSOW) to investigate complaints relating to listed authorities. It also requires listed authorities to give publicity for complaints procedures.

2011 Local authorities' powers and duties–Residential accommodation–Mother in UK without leave to remain–Local authority's duty to provide accommodation in order to safeguard son's right to enjoy family life with her

[Children Act 1989 (c.41) s.17; Nationality, Immigration and Asylum Act 2002 (c.41) Sch.3 para.1, Sch.3 para.3; European Convention on Human Rights 1950 art.8]

A mother, who was homeless and in the UK without leave to remain, applied for a mandatory order that the defendant local authority provide accommodation for her and her eight-year-old son. The mother had been 14 years old when her son was born. They lived periodically with the father, a British citizen, until the relationship broke down in 2013. A residence order was made in favour of the father, but there were ongoing proceedings in the Family Court to determine contact and the son's long term residence owing to concerns about the father's criminality and quality of parenting.

Assessments indicated that the son was likely to suffer harm without social services intervention, and that the mother's parenting capacity was good. As well as a mandatory order for the provision of accommodation, she sought a declaration that the local authority had acted unlawfully in failing to assess her son under the Children Act 1989 s.17. It was common ground that the mother's lack of leave to remain meant that she was ineligible for housing or other support by virtue of the Nationality, Immigration and Asylum Act 2002 Sch.3 para.1, and that she could not therefore invoke s.17. The mother argued that Sch.3 para.3 of the 2002 Act, when read with s.17 of the 1989 Act, compelled the local authority to provide her with accommodation so as to safeguard her son's welfare, which was the court's paramount consideration. She maintained that the local authority had a duty to take positive action under ECHR art.8 to ensure that there was no interference with her son's right to enjoy a family life with his mother.

Held: Judgment accordingly. The mother's reliance on her son's art.8 rights was a difficult, but logical and legally arguable route to bringing herself within the grace of the local authority. However, it would not be right or possible to make the order sought because it would be both conditional and uncertain. It was the mother's immigration problem which was at the heart of her claim. The court was faced with a circular conundrum: first, the local authority had no power to offer the mother accommodation unless accommodation were necessary to prevent interference with the son's right to family life. Second, the exercise of any such power could not be contemplated in the absence of an order from the Family Court granting the mother at least shared residence. Third, without accommodation, the Family Court would not grant the mother shared residence. There was a plain need for certainty as to the Family Court's intentions for the son. That court was best placed to determine whether a s.17 assessment was required. The mother's claim would be transferred to the Family Division for a case management hearing (see paras 5, 9, 25-26 of judgment).

R. (ON THE APPLICATION OF F) v BARKING AND DAGENHAM LBC, [2015] EWHC 2838 (Admin), (2015) 18 C.C.L. Rep. 754, Bobbie Cheema QC, QBD (Admin).

2012 Local authorities' powers and duties–Residential accommodation–Refusal of accommodation to asylum seeker in need of accommodation-related care and assistance–Local authority's lack of consideration of the need to provide accommodation

[Immigration and Asylum Act 1999 (c.33) s.95; National Assistance Act 1948 (c.29) s.21; Care Act 2014 (c.23) s.67(2), s.9; Care Act 2014 (Transitional Provision) Order 2015 (SI 2015/995) art.2(5); Care and Support (Independent Advocacy Support) (No. 2) Regulations 2014 (SI 2014/2889)]

The claimant applied for judicial review of two decisions of the defendant local authority refusing her accommodation. The claimant, an Afghan national, had applied for asylum in the UK. She was a victim of torture and abuse who suffered from severe mental health problems, spoke no English and was illiterate. She struggled with basic tasks and required support with daily life. She had been provided with asylum support, including accommodation, under the Immigration and Asylum Act 1999 s.95. She applied to the local authority for accommodation shortly before being granted asylum. The local authority initially refused her accommodation under the National Assistance Act 1948 s.21. After the Care Act 2014 came into force, the local authority completed an assessment under s.9, though without an independent advocate present, and in its second decision it refused her care and support, including accommodation, under the 2014 Act. The claimant submitted that (1) at the date of the first decision, the local authority had been required to provide her with accommodation pursuant to s.21 of the 1948 Act as she had a need for accommodation-related care and assistance; (2) the second decision was flawed because she had been entitled to but had not had an independent advocate when she was assessed under the 2014 Act; (3) the local authority had a duty to provide her with accommodation under the 2014 Act, and had not asked itself the correct questions in the second decision.

Held: Application granted. (1) Once a review referred to under the Care Act 2014 (Transitional Provision) Order 2015 art.2(5) had taken place, that prevented any continued application of the 1948 Act. A "review" included a local authority's decision that a person did not require care and support (see paras 36-37 of judgment). (2) Section 67(2) of the 2014 Act was clear regarding the need for an independent advocate. The detailed criteria set out in the Care and Support (Independent Advocacy Support) (No. 2) Regulations 2014 testified to the importance of that protection for essentially vulnerable persons. There might be cases where an advocate's presence was unlikely to affect the outcome, but the instant case was a paradigm case where an advocate was required, as in the absence of one the claimant had been in no position to influence matters. The assessment was flawed as a result and had to be redone (paras 38-40). (3) The authorities stood for several propositions which continued to apply under the 2014 Act: (a) services provided by the local authority had to be accommodation-related for accommodation to be potentially a duty; (b) in most cases the matter was best left to the local authority's good judgment and common sense; (c) "accommodation-related care and attention" was of a sort that was normally provided in the home or that would be effectively useless if a claimant had no home, *R. (on the application of M) v Slough BC* [2008] UKHL 52, [2008] 1 W.L.R. 1808, [2008] C.L.Y. 2090 and *R. (on the application of SL) v Westminster City Council* [2013] UKSC 27, [2013] 1 W.L.R. 1445, [2013] C.L.Y. 2951 followed. The only suggestion that the local authority had considered whether it was under a duty to provide accommodation was in the pre-action letter. There was no evidence that it had asked itself whether, even if services could have been provided in a non-home environment, they would have been rendered effectively useless if the claimant were homeless. The care plan had to be redone. It was not appropriate for those carrying it out to take into account the accommodation being provided elsewhere. Two aspects of the services provided to the claimant were accommodation-related: she was visited at home and her home environment checked, and she was assisted with domestic and practical tasks in the home. While it was within the local authority's discretion to decide that notwithstanding those services it was not appropriate to meet her needs through the provision of accommodation, the local authority's decision-making was defective as it was not clear that it had actually given consideration to the need to provide accommodation. The second decision was quashed (paras 20-21, 47-55).

R. (ON THE APPLICATION OF SG) v HARINGEY LBC, [2015] EWHC 2579 (Admin), (2015) 18 C.C.L. Rep. 444, John Bowers QC, QBD (Admin).

2013 Local authorities' powers and duties–Social services–Codes of practice

THE SOCIAL SERVICES CODES (APPOINTED DAY) (WALES) ORDER 2016, SI 2016/142; made under the Social Services and Well-being (Wales) Act 2014 s.146(4)(b). In force: 6 April 2016.

This Order appoints 6 April 2016 as the day on which codes issued by the Welsh Ministers under s.145(1) of the Social Services and Well-being (Wales) Act 2014 come into force. The codes impose requirements and include guidelines setting out aims, objectives and other matters in relation to the exercise of social services functions under the 2014 Act; s.145(3) of the 2014 Act requires local authorities to act in accordance with any relevant requirements contained in a code issued under s.145(1) and to have regard to any relevant guidelines contained in it.

2014 Regulation and Inspection of Social Care (Wales) Act 2016 (anaw 2)

An Act to reform the regulatory regime for care and support services; provide for a regulatory framework that requires an approach to the regulation of care and support services focused on outcomes for service users; reform the inspection regime for local authority social services functions; provide for the reconstitution and renaming of the Care Council for Wales as Social Care Wales and the broadening of its remit; and reform the regulation of the social care workforce.

2015 Residential accommodation–Families–Local authority providing accommodation and financial support to family seeking assistance under s.17 Children Act 1989–Whether flawed policy or practice followed

[Children Act 1989 (c.41) s.17; European Convention on Human Rights 1950 art.8; Immigration and Asylum Act 1999 (c.33) s.4, s.95]

A family appealed against the dismissal of their claim for judicial review of the respondent local authority's decisions concerning the lawfulness of the type of accommodation and level of support provided to them. The family, a mother and her three children, were Nigerian nationals who had been refused leave to remain in the UK. They had no right of recourse to public funds. The local authority undertook a number of assessments of need under the Children Act 1989 s.17 and two financial support assessments. It provided accommodation and financial support in cash and in kind, through payment of utility bills and payments for school transport and clothing. The issue was whether the local authority had inappropriately fettered its discretion by following a flawed policy or practice in its provision of financial support to those seeking assistance under s.17, thereby breaching the appellants' ECHR art.8 rights. The family submitted that the support provided had been wrongly based on the local authority's position that a rate equivalent to child benefit and payments to asylum seekers under the Immigration and Asylum Act 1999 s.4 and s.95 was lawful.

Held: Appeal dismissed. (1) The s.17 scheme did not create a specific or mandatory duty owed to an individual child; it was a target duty which created a discretion to make a decision to meet a child's assessed need. The focus had to be on whether the information gathered by a local authority was adequate for the purpose of performing its statutory duty. A local authority was acting under its powers as a children's services authority, not as a local social services authority performing functions relating to homelessness and its prevention, and not as a local housing authority, *Blackburn-Smith v Lambeth LBC* [2007] EWHC 767 (Admin), (2007) 10 C.C.L. Rep. 352, [2007] C.L.Y. 3941 applied. The limited nature of the local authority's power was important. Accordingly, the local authority had provided accommodation and financial support under s.17 and not as a consequence of any other statutory scheme. The secretary of state had issued guidance to local authorities regarding assessments of need for s.17 purposes, to be followed save in exceptional circumstances. There was a generic assessment framework with identifiable factors. In the instant case, the local authority did not have a written policy in relation to the assessment of children of families with no recourse to public funds. To have such a policy would be difficult given that each child's needs were to be individually assessed by reference to the framework. There was, however, a need for a rational and consistent approach to decision-making, *R. (on the application of PO) v Newham LBC* [2014] EWHC 2561 (Admin), (2014) 17 C.C.L. Rep. 325, [2015] C.L.Y. 2385 considered. That permitted of appropriately phrased internal guidance or cross-checking consistent with the guidance, but not of a policy or practice of fixing financial support by reference to that available under other statutory schemes. The starting point for a decision had to be an analysis of all appropriate evidential factors, and any cross-checking must not constrain the obligation to have regard to the impact on the child's welfare and the proportionality of that impact. In the instant case, the financial support provided exceeded child benefit rates and s.4 support rates for most of the period in question. There had been repeated assessments and consequential changes to the level of support provided. Given the quality of the bespoke assessments on which the local authority's decisions were based, there was insufficient material on which to conclude that the financial support payments were made by reference to an irrational or inflexible rate. There was a substantial difference between an appropriate and lawful cross-check and an inflexible fixing of rates, whether by the use of an extraneous and inappropriate rate as a starting point or an inflexible policy or practice. Payments made at a rate greater than the allegedly fixed rate suggested that a de facto policy or practice of inflexible fixing did not exist, that a discretion was being exercised and, in any event, that the evidence of the rate of payment was inconsistent with a policy or a practice. There was therefore no basis to challenge the local authority's decisions based on a flawed policy or practice of inflexibly fixing its support payments. It would have been equally inappropriate for the local authority to have benchmarked its payments under s.17 to any other statutory scheme, including that applicable under the 1999 Act. There had been no breach of art.8 founding an entitlement to damages (see paras 12-30 of judgment). (2) If wrong about the local authority's decisions, there was a question as to whether art.8 imposed a positive obligation on the state in the factual circumstances complained of. If a local authority failed to provide services in accordance with an assessment of need, it was arguable that an immediate and direct link was capable of being established between the measures requested and the appellant's private life. However, the local authority's decisions were well within the margin of appreciation that the state enjoyed even if that had been the case, *R. (on the application of McDonald) v Kensington and Chelsea*

RLBC [2011] UKSC 33, [2011] 4 All E.R. 881, [2011] C.L.Y. 3207 followed, *Anufrijeva v Southwark LBC* [2003] EWCA Civ 1406, [2004] Q.B. 1124, [2004] C.L.Y. 1986 considered (paras 31-32).

R. (ON THE APPLICATION OF C) v SOUTHWARK LBC, [2016] EWCA Civ 707, [2016] H.L.R. 36, Moore-Bick LJ, CA (Civ Div).

2016 **Residential accommodation–Local authorities' powers and duties–Whether child whose grandmother voluntarily undertook care of him whilst mother was in prison waschild in need requiring accommodation**

[Children Act 1989 (c.41) s.20, s.23(2); Fostering Services Regulations 2002 (SI 2002/57)]

The claimant grandmother applied for judicial review challenging the defendant local authority's failure to provide her with support to care for grandson (R), as a looked-after child. R had lived in the local authority's area from his birth in 2011. He was made the subject of a child protection plan and visited the claimant one weekend per month. On 17 October 2012 when R was 18-months-old his mother (M) was arrested. The claimant had thought that her care of R would be short-term until M was bailed or released from custody. However, on 26 October 2012 M pleaded guilty to a number of offences and was sentenced to 27 months' imprisonment. By that time the claimant was aware that the local authority would not offer her support as it viewed R's living arrangement with the claimant as voluntary. The claimant continued to care for R even after M was released from prison. The local authority submitted that R never appeared to it to require accommodation as M chose to make her own private family arrangements for his care in respect of which it took no part, therefore no duty arose under the Children Act 1989 s.20 to accommodate R.

Held: Application refused. The local authority had always maintained that it had never reasonably appeared to it that R had acquired accommodation as a result of M's inability to provide accommodation because of her detention in prison. The question was whether that was a lawful position for the local authority to have taken. Whether there was an exercise of statutory duty or a private fostering arrangement was a question of fact, requiring analysis as to what the local authority in fact did, *R. (on the application of D) v Southwark LBC* [2007] EWCA Civ 182, [2007] 1 F.L.R. 2181, [2007] C.L.Y. 1777 followed. On 17 October 2012, the local authority did nothing to encourage or facilitate the arrangement whereby R was taken in by the claimant. The events had to be looked at in a common sense way. M's arrest prompted an immediate crisis so far as R's care was concerned; and the claimant, commendably and understandably, stepped in and agreed to take R as an emergency. At that stage, although M had been arrested, it did not reasonably appear to the local authority that R required accommodation because he was staying with his grandmother and it was hoped, at least by her, that after a short period, M would be released and R would be able to live with her. At that stage it would have been open to the claimant not to have agreed to a voluntary arrangement. Had she done so, it was likely that the local authority's s.20 obligations would have arisen immediately, but she agreed to R staying with her on a short-term basis. The local authority had no part in that arrangement. The position changed when M pleaded guilty to a number of serious charges. She was remanded in custody and faced a substantial prison sentence. At that stage it was no longer possible for R merely to stay with the claimant as he needed a permanent home. With M's approval, the claimant offered R a home in the full knowledge that the local authority did not consider itself under any obligation to support her doing so. It would have been open to her then to say that, whilst she had been prepared for R stay with her short-term, she was not prepared to offer to look after him longer term and to offer her house to him as his home during that time. Without encouragement or facilitation by the local authority, and with M's approval, she continued to look after R in that role. A local authority did not exercise its statutory powers and duties by facilitating a private arrangement for a child's accommodation by merely not objecting to it. The local authority did not facilitate the arrangements: it did not suggest that the claimant might get support if she continued to look after R. To the contrary the claimant knew that the local authority would not support her on the basis that it was a purely voluntary arrangement. The local authority did not act as if there was a placement under s.23(2) and never suggested it; nor did it attempt to fulfil its obligations under the Fostering

Services Regulations 2002, which applied to such placements. The local authority was reasonable to conclude throughout that it did not appear to it that R required accommodation. The arrangements the claimant made for R's care were purely voluntary and did not come about by any exercise of any statutory power or fulfilment of any duty by the local authority (see paras 33-40 of judgment).

R. (ON THE APPLICATION OF T) v HERTFORDSHIRE CC *sub nom.* R. (ON THE APPLICATION OF PC) v HERTFORDSHIRE CC, [2015] EWHC 1936 (Admin), (2015) 18 C.C.L. Rep. 632, Hickinbottom J, QBD (Admin).

2017 Social services–Codes of practice–Role of Director of Social Services

THE SOCIAL SERVICES CODE (ROLE OF THE DIRECTOR OF SOCIAL SERVICES) (APPOINTED DAY) (WALES) ORDER 2016, SI 2016/414; made under the Social Services and Well-being (Wales) Act 2014 s.146(4)(b). In force: In accordance with art.2.

This Order appoints 6 April 2016 as the day on which the code of practice on the role of the director of social services comes into force. This code was issued by the Welsh Ministers under the Social Services and Well-being (Wales) Act 2014 s.145(1) on 16 March 2016.

2018 Social workers–Age assessments–Victim of human trafficking–Social workers' failure to allow opportunities to explain inconsistencies

The claimant (N) challenged a decision of the defendant local authority that he was an adult born in July 1990. N asserted that his actual birth date was 13 May 1997, so that he had only just turned 18. N's account of his life, largely accepted by the local authority, was as follows. He was born and lived in Vietnam until the age of 13. Owing to domestic violence, his mother suddenly left the family home in 2008; he understood that she had gone to England. His father died in February 2010. He then went to live with one of his father's friends. However, it became clear that he could not stay in Vietnam because his father owed money to a criminal gang. His father's friend therefore arranged for an agent to take him out of Vietnam so that he could ultimately come to the UK to look for his mother. He came here via Russia, Hungary, the Czech Republic and France. In Hungary, he was detained in prison for several months. After arriving in the UK, he was placed in foster care. Shortly thereafter, he was taken by two Vietnamese people to work in a cannabis factory. He was detained there for just over two years before managing to escape. He was interviewed by an immigration officer and then placed into foster care, where he remained for over a year until the local authority assessed his age as being that of an adult. The Home Office had written a "Positive Reasonable Grounds" letter stating that there were reasonable grounds to believe that N had been trafficked. The local authority's position was as follows: N's evidence concerning his age was not credible; there were a number of inconsistencies in the accounts given by him over the course of a range of different interviews; it was hard to believe that a boy of 13 could have gone through the experiences which, on his account, he had gone through in travelling from Vietnam via Russia, Hungary, the Czech Republic and France; further, the age assessment carried out by the two relevant social workers was "*Merton* compliant" and the conclusion reached in it that N was 23 at the time was fully justified.

Held: Judgment for claimant. Where an age assessment was disputed, the role of the court was to inquire and, on the available evidence, to make a decision on a balance of probabilities. It was appropriate to have regard to a Home Office document entitled "Victims of human trafficking - competent authority guidance". Specifically, the court should consider (a) whether N's evidence as to the material facts was "coherent and consistent with any past written or verbal statements" and (b) how well it fitted together or whether it contradicted itself. N's evidence was coherent and truthful. It also fitted together and was not self-contradictory. The inconsistencies in his accounts were fewer than suggested and, where they existed, were either capable of being explained or not so significant as to make a conclusion that he lacked credibility either inevitable or even appropriate. N's evidence was also supported by the testimony of his most recent foster carer. Her evidence was compelling. She had vast experience as a foster parent as well as substantial experience as both a mother and a grandmother. She had also had direct experience of N over the course of more than a year. It was not appropriate to attach substantial weight to the conclusion which the social workers had reached in the age assessment process. It was not in doubt that they had tried hard to treat N fairly and that they had acted at all times in what they considered to be his best interests. However, the age assessment was rendered unlawful by their failure to give N a proper opportunity to deal with certain adverse points. At their final meeting with him, they had begun by telling him that they had decided that he was over 18, preventing him from addressing certain important matters. Those matters included perceived inconsistencies in his accounts of his relationship with his father and the relationship between his mother and his father, and in what had been said about his computer skills. He should also have been given the opportunity to deal with matters more generally. In particular, the social workers were clearly sceptical that a boy of 13 could have made the journey which N described, including the periods of detention in Hungary, without displaying signs of trauma. That was another important matter which should have been raised with N in such a way as to enable him to comment and at a time when a final decision had not yet been reached. The fact that he was not given that opportunity was a significant omission, *R. (on the application of Z) v Croydon LBC* [2011] EWCA Civ 59, [2011] P.T.S.R. 748, [2011] C.L.Y. 1803 applied. In the circumstances, it was appropriate to hold that N's date of birth was the one he had given, namely 13 May 1997 (see paras 46, 131-135, 155, 157-162, 164-165, 167-169 of judgment).

MVN v GREENWICH LBC, [2015] EWHC 1942 (Admin), (2015) 18 C.C.L. Rep. 645, Picken J, QBD (Admin).

SPORT

2019 Sport–Statutory interpretation–Definition of "sport" requiring element of physical activity–Statutory construction and construction of Royal Charters

[Physical Training and Recreation Act 1937 (c.46) s.3]

The English Bridge Union applied for judicial review of a decision by the English Sports Council to adopt a definition of "sport" which excluded games such as bridge. The council was established by Royal Charter, as a result of the Physical Training and Recreation Act 1937 and previous Charters, to encourage the development of "sport and physical recreation". It was responsible for distributing sports funding received from the secretary of state and from the national lottery. In its recognition policy, the council adopted the definition from the European Sports Charter, which defined "sport" as a form of physical activity. It therefore excluded "mind sports" which did not have a physical element. The Bridge Union submitted that the council had (1) misconstrued the phrase "physical training and recreation" in s.3 of the 1937 Act; (2) misconstrued its Royal Charter in adopting a definition that incorporated a requirement of physical activity.

Held: Application refused. (1) The starting point for ascertaining the meaning of statutory provisions was to consider the ordinary meaning of the words in question. However, it was also permissible, if not essential, to have regard to documents such as any Explanatory Memorandum published alongside the legislative provisions. Regard should also be had to the historical context of the situation leading to its enactment, *R. (on the application of Quintavalle) v Secretary of State for Health* [2003] UKHL 13, [2003] 2 A.C. 687, [2004] C.L.Y. 3274 followed. It was permissible to have regard to parts of an Act which had been repealed in seeking to understand the will and purpose of Parliament in relation to the parts which remained in force. It was perfectly clear from the 1937 Memorandum that the phrase "physical training and recreation" was focused on physical activity and was intended to encompass physical recreation rather than any other kind of recreation. It was noteworthy that s.1(1) of the Act, subsequently repealed, established National Advisory Councils with a duty to advise in relation to "the maintenance and improvement of the physical wellbeing of people by means of exercise and recreation". Those matters, taken together, presented a compelling case that the phrase "physical training and recreation" meant physical training and physical recreation. It was true that the meaning of statutory words could change and develop over time, but there was no warrant in the instant case to reinterpret the statutory phrase as a result of the passage of time. The inclusion of activities promoting mental activity and mental agility would require amendment to the legislation (see paras 35, 37, 39, 41-44 of judgment). (2) The approach to establishing the legal meaning of a Royal Charter was to seek to understand what the document would convey to a reasonable reader with knowledge of the factual background of how it came into being, alongside its purpose and the purpose of the body which it incorporated. Such a meaning was not contingent on dictionary definitions of its individual words. The circumstances surrounding the need for the Royal Charter formed part of a reasonable person's understanding of the objects and powers as defined within the Royal Charter. While the correct interpretation of the 1937 Act was not itself determinative of the correct interpretation of the Royal Charter, it was an important starting point for consideration of the phrase "sport and physical recreation" in the Charter. It was consistent with the correct interpretation of s.3(1)(a) of the Act to understand the phrase in the Royal Charter as being similarly limited to physical activity. It was also consistent with the scope of the work and objects of the council's predecessors. There was a continuous unbroken history from 1937 to the present day of the council and its predecessors' work being confined to engaging with physical activities. There was no reason to suppose that the phrase "sport and physical recreation", when it re-emerged in the 1996 Charter, was to be understood differently from when it appeared in the 1971 charter. Accordingly, the council's decision to adopt the European Sport Charter definition of "sport", which required an element of physical activity, was entirely consistent with the proper understanding of its Royal Charter. The correct interpretation of the phrase in the 1996 Charter incorporated an essential element of physical activity. The fact that other international organisations had recognised bridge as a sport was of limited relevance in determining the legal questions which arose in the instant case (paras 32, 46-48, 51).

R. (ON THE APPLICATION OF ENGLISH BRIDGE UNION LTD) v ENGLISH SPORTS COUNCIL, [2015] EWHC 2875 (Admin), [2016] 1 W.L.R. 957, Dove J, QBD (Admin).

2020 Stadiums–Football spectators–Providing seated accommodation

THE FOOTBALL SPECTATORS (SEATING) ORDER 2016, SI 2016/629; made under the Football Spectators Act 1989 s.11. In force: 1 July 2016.

This Order directs the Sports Grounds Safety Authority to include an "all-seater" condition in any licence granted to admit spectators to the London Stadium at the Queen Elizabeth Olympic Park, the home ground of West Ham United Football Club. This condition requires that only seated accommodation be provided for spectators at designated football matches, and spectators only be admitted to watch a designated football match from seated accommodation.

SUCCESSION

2021 Administration of estates–Forfeiture rule–Application to interests under family trusts

[Forfeiture Act 1982 (c.34) s.1(1), s.2]

The claimant, who had been convicted of the manslaughter of his mother, applied for an order modifying the common law "forfeiture rule", which prevented him from inheriting his mother's estate. The claimant was 62 years old. The deceased, believing that he had been born with a hereditary brain illness, had kept him isolated from other people and subject to a strict domestic routine. He had lived with her all his life. She died from injuries sustained in a severe assault at their home. The claimant pleaded not guilty to murder on the basis of an absence of intention to kill. He pleaded guilty to manslaughter and was sentenced to detention in hospital for the urgent treatment of a serious mental disorder. A restriction order was also made. There was evidence that the claimant had suffered mental health problems for a few years and that he had been violent towards his mother on several occasions. Medical examinations of the claimant after his mother's death revealed that his mental disorder was a combination of moderate depression, a learning disorder and autistic spectrum disorder, which had made him unable to cope easily with the role reversal when his mother started needing care. She had made a will leaving her entire estate to the claimant. Since the claimant had caused the deceased's death by his own criminal act, it was accepted that the forfeiture rule, as defined in the Forfeiture Act 1982 s.1(1), applied. However, the house, which had at one time been in the joint names of the deceased and the claimant, was in family protection trusts. The deceased's trust transferred her interest in the house to solicitor trustees and named herself, her nephew and the claimant as beneficiaries. The claimant's trust was a mirror image except with different beneficiaries. The claimant sought: (i) a declaration that the forfeiture rule did not apply to interests held under the trusts; (ii) a modification of the forfeiture rule under s.2 of the Act in relation to his acquisition of property passing under the deceased's will.

Held: Claim dismissed. (1) The interests that the claimant stood to acquire under the deceased's trust did not result from her death. Insofar as he was a discretionary beneficiary of her trust, the claimant had acquired that status upon execution of the trust and his interest was neither created nor enlarged by her death. Anything which he received would be as a result of the trustees' decision and not by virtue of the death itself. The forfeiture rule therefore did not apply to any interest existing under either of the trusts, and the trustees were not prevented from exercising their discretion in the claimant's favour (see paras 17-18 of judgment). (2) The power to modify the forfeiture rule was discretionary. The court had to be satisfied that the "justice of the case" required the particular modification. The Act contained no guidance about which matters should be taken into account other than the conduct of the offender and the deceased, *Dunbar v Plant* [1998] Ch. 412, [1997] C.L.Y. 4729 considered. The assault which killed the deceased was very serious and was further aggravated by the fact that it was the culmination of a series of attacks. The claimant's culpability was lessened by his relatively low IQ and the difficulties he faced in having to assume a carer role when the deceased became too old to look after him. He clearly did not have the life skills to do so. There was no medical evidence as to the extent of his mental disorder or autism, but even if he was on the borderline of such disorders, they may have contributed to his actions and so lessened his culpability. His culpability remained high however: he had had mental capacity at all times, had been fit to plead in the criminal proceedings, and had not pleaded diminished responsibility. He knew that his assaults were wrong, but continued them and bullied the deceased into silence and denial. She had protected him throughout his life and part of her motivation in concealing the assaults might have been a misguided loyalty to him. The claimant would benefit from additional money and, even after what had happened, the deceased would want him to benefit from her estate and be taken care of. But those things were of relatively low weight. The claimant would continue to benefit from his own trust and might do so under his mother's if the trustees were sympathetic. Sympathy was not the guiding factor for the court: justice did not require modification of the forfeiture rule (paras 20-22, 54-60).

HENDERSON v WILCOX, [2015] EWHC 3469 (Ch), [2016] 4 W.L.R. 14, Judge David Cooke, Ch D (Birmingham).

2022 Administration of estates–Insolvent estates–Non-provable debts–Proper interpretation of art.4(1) Administration of Insolvent Estates of Deceased Persons Order 1986

[Administration of Insolvent Estates of Deceased Persons Order 1986 (SI 1986/1999) art.4(1); Insolvency Rules 1986 r.12.3; Child Support Act 1991 (c.48) s.43A]

The mother of a deceased person (D) sought directions, as administrator of his estate, about whether his estate should make provision for payment of three contested liabilities. The first liability was a claim by the mother that D owed her £325,000 after she had transferred her house into their joint names, with a trust deed declaring that D held no beneficial interest in the property. They had obtained a loan of £325,000, using the property as security. The mother claimed that she had loaned the money to D in order to help him raise finance for an investment, but that D had agreed to be responsible for paying the mortgage instalments. She maintained that he had failed to do so, meaning that she had to sell the house to discharge the mortgage. The second liability arose from a consent order following D's divorce. He had undertaken to continue paying the premiums under a life insurance policy so that its proceeds could be held on trust for his ex-wife (the first defendant), and his son. The policy would have produced a payment of £100,000 upon his death. However, D had stopped paying the premiums and the policy had lapsed. The third liability concerned child maintenance arrears of £103,441.73 which D had failed to pay to the Child Support Agency. If those liabilities were payable, D's estate would become insolvent. The issues were whether the estate should make provision for payment of (1) the £325,000 which the mother claimed to have loaned to D; (2) the £100,000 which would have been payable under the life insurance policy; (3) the child maintenance arrears.

Held: Judgment accordingly. (1) The documentation was far more consistent with the mother making a loan to her son than with her personally making an investment. The debt claimed by the mother was payable (see paras 73, 75, 78-79 of judgment). (2) The liabilities arising from the policy premiums and the CSA arrears were not provable under the Insolvency Rules 1986 r.12.3. If D had been made bankrupt while he was alive, he therefore would not have been discharged in relation to them. Because there had been no insolvency process when he died, however, it was necessary to consider the Administration of Insolvent Estates of Deceased Persons Order 1986 art.4(1), which incorporated the statutory regime for "debts and liabilities provable" but made no reference to discharge from liability in relation to non-provable debts. It seemed that the legislation might not have considered the deceased insolvent individual who died without a bankruptcy order having been made, with liabilities which would be non-provable in the case of a living bankruptcy (paras 123-126, 136). D was in breach of "an order made in family proceedings" for the purpose of r.12.3(2)(a) because he had failed to pay the policy premiums. However, he was also in breach of an implied obligation to notify his ex-wife if he was about to miss any payment, so that she could make it promptly. That obligation was implied as a result of an agreement, recorded as a preamble to the order, that if D was unable to pay any premium and his ex-wife paid it instead, the payment would be treated as a loan which D had to repay to her. It arose under a freestanding agreement between the parties and there was no breach of an order made in family proceedings. The debt was therefore provable. In any event, the policy considerations which rendered court-ordered maintenance a non-provable debt in the case of a living bankrupt could not apply logically to the insolvent estate of a deceased person. Moreover, drawing on the underlying principles of the United Nations Convention on the Rights of the Child as an aid to interpretation of art.4(1), there was an obligation to ensure that children were properly provided for by a parent. It would be bizarre if a statutory provision which was designed to ensure that a father always paid was being turned on its head so that he did not have to pay at all once he had died. The reference to provable debts and liabilities in art.4(1) was to the system of submitting proofs and not to a distinction between provable and non-provable debts. There was a potential gap in the drafting of art.4(1) and it was not clear how much of the bankruptcy code dealing with a living bankrupt applied to the estate of an insolvent deceased person where there had been no formal bankruptcy process. The estate had to meet D's liability for £100,000, whether or not it was a provable debt. In any event, it was appropriate to interpret art.4(1) in order to preserve D's obligation to his child, *Child Maintenance and Enforcement Commission v Beesley* [2010] EWCA Civ 1344, [2011] 1 W.L.R. 1704, [2011] C.L.Y. 1868 applied (paras 93, 130-134, 141, 147-152). (3) Child support maintenance was assessed and enforced through a self-contained statutory regime. It was not enforceable through the civil courts and arrears were not legally characterised as a "debt" during the life of a paying parent. However, the Child Support Act 1991 s.43A enabled the recovery of arrears as a debt payable from a deceased's estate. That was a different concept from an obligation arising under a child support maintenance assessment under r.12.3(2)(a) of the Rules. The arrears were a provable debt which could be recovered from the estate. It made no difference that the estate was insolvent (paras 156-167).

BERRY v CHILD SUPPORT AGENCY *sub nom.* BERRY v GARCIA; TOVEY (DECEASED), RE, [2016] EWHC 1418 (Ch), [2016] B.P.I.R. 1256, Judge McCahill QC, Ch D (Bristol).

2023 **Administration of estates–Insolvent estates–Proprietary claims–Prospects of success**

[Insolvency Act 1986 (c.45) s.284]

The ninth to eleventh defendant trustees applied to strike out proprietary claims made by the claimant (G) in relation to the estate of her deceased long-term partner (B). G and B had been in a relationship since 1991 and had lived in the UK since 2001. They had two children. They owned a large property in the UK, the family home. B was a successful businessman. His business partner (X) died unexpectedly in 2008, resulting in cash-flow problems for B. He commenced proceedings against X's family and was also conducting litigation on a number of other fronts. G was aware of the litigation and helped to finance it, including agreeing to remortgage the family home. B and G's relationship deteriorated and they discussed a financial separation. G understood she would receive one-third of B's wealth. A document, the litigation deed reflecting discussions regarding the sale of the family home, was drafted by B's lawyers and signed by both parties. Following a significant litigation defeat, B entered into settlement negotiations with X's family. He entered into a further agreement with G, the litigation agreement. He then reached a settlement agreement with X's family and made a new will, under which G and their children were the major beneficiaries. He died nine days later. The trustees were appointed over his estate. X's family made payments under the settlement agreement to B's estate, which had significantly more liabilities than assets. The trustees resolved proprietary claims made in respect of separate litigation. G submitted that, by virtue of the litigation deed and the litigation agreement, the trustees held one-third of B's rights under the settlement agreement with X's family on trust for her. The trustees argued that the words used in the deed and the agreement did not create any trust; that the subject matter of the supposed trust was too uncertain; and that any trust would be void pursuant to the Insolvency Act 1986 s.284.

Held: Application granted. (1) The wording of the litigation deed did not evidence an intention on B's part to create a trust of any property recovered through the litigation, let alone of B's rights under the settlement agreement. The wording did not evidence an intention to make an immediate disposition of the beneficial interest in specified property. On the contrary, they amounted to a promise to pay one-third of "the value of" property recovered, which was inconsistent with a declaration of trust. It was intended that B should receive any property recovered through the litigation beneficially, not as trustee for G. G's case amounted to an attempt to re-write the deed. With regard to the uncertainty of the subject-matter, the deed was a formal document drafted by B's lawyers which appeared to have been carefully worded, and G was unable to point to anything in either the wording of the deed or in the admissible background which suggested that the inclusion of "the value of" was a mistake. The argument amounted to a plea that the court should ignore part of the document because it was inconsistent with G's case. The litigation deed did not refer to the settlement agreement, which was not at that date in prospect. Nor did it refer to B's rights under any settlement of any of the litigation. It did refer to (one third of the value of) property recovered through the litigation agreement. Accordingly, any trust was of the property when received. In respect of the monies received from X's family after B's death, any such trust was void by virtue of s.284 (see paras 60-65 of judgment). (2) The wording of the litigation agreement also did not evidence an intention on B's part to create a trust of any monies received under the agreement. The words used did not evidence an intention to make an immediate disposition of the beneficial interest in specified property. They amounted to a conditional agreement on B's part to transfer any monies received under the settlement agreement which were free from encumbrances or restrictions. It was therefore predicated on receipt of the monies by B beneficially, which was inconsistent with B declaring himself a trustee of such monies. The litigation agreement was a promise to make a future gift of monies, if and when those monies were received. G's case again amounted to an attempt to re-write the agreement. The subject matter of the supposed trust was uncertain because of the words "free from encumbrances and restrictions". G appeared to admit in her amended particulars of claim that, although she had understood at the time of the litigation agreement that sums would be paid out of the sums payable under the settlement agreement, further debts payable were encumbrances or restrictions on the sums received under that agreement. It would not have been possible to quantify those sums at the date of the litigation agreement. The litigation agreement had not created a trust of B's rights under the settlement agreement (paras 66-71). (3) G was refused permission to re-amend her particulars of claim to introduce claims of equitable assignment, rectification, proprietary estoppel, constructive trust and other estoppels (paras 74-112).

GORBUNOVA v BEREZOVSKY'S ESTATE *sub nom.* ELENIN (DECEASED), RE, [2016] EWHC 1829 (Ch), [2016] W.T.L.R. 1591, Arnold J, Ch D.

2024 Administration of estates–Trustees' powers and duties–Different classes of beneficiary–Extent of duty to account

[Trustee Act 2000 (c.29) s.31(1); CPR PD 46 (Fast Track Trial Costs) 2000 para.1.1]

The claimant charities sought an order that the second defendant solicitor provide them with estate accounts. The first and second defendants were the executors of a will. The will created two life interests for adult beneficiaries. Upon both their deaths, the estate would fall into the possession of trusts for the benefit of the claimants. The estate was administered in 1996 and one of the adult beneficiaries was still alive. The defendants provided some estate accounts in 2007, but despite several requests by the claimants during 2014 and 2015 for more information, none was provided. The instant proceedings were brought on 2 February 2016. By that time, the first defendant had died, unbeknown to the claimants. They successfully applied for an order removing his name from the proceedings, so that the obligation to provide trust information fell on the second defendant. The claimants sought disclosure of "proper particulars and accounts of (i) the property comprising the trust estate; and (ii) the income, expenditure and distributions of the trust, in each case for the period since 1 October 2007". They also sought costs. The second defendant did not take part in the proceedings.

Held: Judgment accordingly. Trustees had to be ready to account to their beneficiaries for what they had done with the trust assets. Every beneficiary, whether in possession or in reversion, was entitled to an accounting, and to see the documents which justified that accounting, *Armitage v Nurse* [1998] Ch. 241, [1997] C.L.Y. 4940 applied. However, the issue in the instant case was what kind of accounting different classes of beneficiary were entitled to. Not all documents had to be disclosed to all beneficiaries; disclosure depended on what was needed in the circumstances for the beneficiaries to appreciate, verify and, if needed, vindicate their own rights against the trustees in respect of the administration of the trust. That would vary according to the facts of the case. In the instant case, the claimants' entitlement was only to capital on the death of both life tenants. There was no basis for the claimants having an accounting as to the income accrued or paid to the income beneficiaries, one of whom was still alive and presumably receiving it. The same applied to expenses being charged to income. If the defendants did not pay the income to the remaining life tenant, only she, and not the claimants, could complain about it; the claimants did not need that information in order to protect their interests, *Nestle v National Westminster Bank Plc* [2000] W.T.L.R. 795, [2001] C.L.Y. 5531 considered. There was no objection in principle to the claimants obtaining an accounting as to the capital in which they were interested as remaindermen. So far as expenses and distributions were concerned, the accounting to the claimants as to capital would obviously show what capital expenses and capital distributions had been made. Accordingly, the claimants were entitled to the accounts of capital and list of investments since 1 October 2007. They were also entitled to a breakdown of trustees' fees and expenditure, but only so far as the trustees sought to deduct such fees and expenditure from trust capital. They were also entitled to information confirming the identity of the present trustees and to be informed when their interests fell into possession. Once the second life interest beneficiary died, the claimants would also be entitled to the income accruing thereafter, and would be entitled to an accounting of everything, capital and income, for the future (see paras 11-15, 22, 24, 30-31 of judgment). (2) The claimants' application for costs in relation to their application to remove the first defendant from the proceedings was made out. Had the second defendant responded to correspondence and informed the claimants that the first defendant had died, the claimants would not have included him in the proceedings and it would have been unnecessary to apply for an order removing him. The costs of that application, assessed summarily, were £1,000 (paras 32, 42). The claimants were also entitled to costs of the claim itself. There had been a long and egregious refusal by the defendants to engage at all with the claimants. That refusal was quite unwarranted. The fact that the claimants originally asked for disclosure in relation to income did not make any real difference, *Skinner, Re* [1904] 1 Ch. 289 considered. Furthermore, it was clear that the second defendant in failing to account to the claimants over so many years acted for a benefit other than that of the estate, and in failing to take part in the instant proceedings, acted unreasonably. Any costs incurred by the second defendant were not "properly incurred" within the Trustee Act 2000 s.31(1) and CPR PD 46 para.1.1 and therefore he was not entitled to be reimbursed out of the trust fund in respect of them. The costs of the claim itself, assessed summarily, were £7,980 (paras 33, 36, 40, 43).

ROYAL NATIONAL LIFEBOAT INSTITUTION (RNLI) v HEADLEY, [2016] EWHC 1948 (Ch), [2016] W.T.L.R. 1433, Master Matthews, Ch D.

2025 Beneficiaries–Locus standi–Extent of beneficiary's right to bring claim on behalf of estste

[Civil Procedure Rules 1998 r.19.8, r.19.8(1); Administration of Estates Act 1925 (c.23) s.28]

The claimant applied to be appointed as personal representative of the deceased's estate. The first defendant applied for the claim to be struck out. The claimant claimed to be the son of the deceased, who had died in England in 2012. The first defendant, was the deceased's former wife, and denied the claimant's paternity. The claim concerned the alleged use by the first defendant of a power of attorney dated 2010 and made by the deceased. In 2014, the claimant obtained letters of administration in Nigeria to the deceased's estate, but was restrained from using the letters by a Nigeria injunction pending litigation over the disputed will. His application in the UK for an interim injunction to restrain the first defendant from using the power of attorney and for summary judgment was refused. The first defendant gave an undertaking not to use the power until trial or further order. The judge noted that the claimant had failed to establish that he had any title to sue, and that the proper parties were not before the court, there being no representative of the deceased's estate. The issues were whether (1) the claimant should be appointed as personal representative of the deceased's estate under CPR r.19.8(1); (2) the claim should be struck out. With regard to strike out, the first defendant submitted that the claimant had no right to bring a claim in his own name to complain of wrongs done to the deceased's estate. The claimant submitted that he could maintain his claim against the first defendant as she had constituted herself an executor de son tort.

Held: Judgment accordingly. (1) The starting point was that, subject to the application of procedural rules such as CPR r.19.8, an action brought on behalf of a deceased's estate by a person as administrator, who at the date of commencing the claim did not have a grant, was a nullity, *Ingall v Moran* [1944] K.B. 160 applied. The words "person who had an interest in a claim had died" in r.19.8(1) applied only to the case where the claim in question had already commenced, and then the claimant or a person with an interest in it had died, *Millburn-Snell v Evans* [2011] EWCA Civ 577, [2012] 1 W.L.R. 41, [2011] C.L.Y. 394 followed. Accordingly, r.19.8(1) did not assist the claimant, as the deceased had died in 2012 and the claim was only commenced in 2015: it was therefore not open to the court to appoint the claimant as personal representative of the estate for the purpose of the claim under r.19.8(1). The claimant's argument that there were "special circumstances", namely that he, as a beneficiary, should be able to bring a claim on behalf of the estate against an alleged wrongdoer where there was no personal representative able to take action against others, was misconceived. To allow, in every case where a representative had not been appointed, that any beneficiary of the estate might bring their own legal action to "protect" it would be a recipe for confusion, duplication of effort, lack of supervision and waste of resources (see paras 20, 24, 33 of judgment). (2) To allow a putative estate beneficiary to bring a claim personally violated the principle that no such beneficiary had a proprietary interest in estate assets until the administration was complete; every estate asset had to be available to the personal representative for administration purposes. The claimant argued that a "burglar" of estate assets became an executor de son tort. However, unlike an executor de son tort, who did something to intervene in the administration so as to assume the obligations of a trustee or executor, a burglar never intended to intervene in the administration; they just wanted to take the assets and run away. The Administration of Estates Act 1925 s.28 extended the liability of an executor de son tort to persons who were not otherwise such executors but who received assets of the deceased from the duly appointed administrator as part of a fraud on creditors or without paying full value for them. A person might become an executor de son tort if he intermeddled with the assets in such a way as to denote an assumption of the authority or an intention to exercise the functions of an executor, Halsbury, Laws of England, 5th ed. 1264 of vol 103. A burglar, however, did not so assume or intend. In any event, the deceased had to already have died by the time of the acts complained of, because one could not inherit from a living person. The allegations made against the first defendant were either alleged to have been committed during the deceased's lifetime or were not alleged to have been committed at a specific time. Accordingly they could not found a claim of executor de son tort, because they had not allegedly occurred after the deceased's death. The claimant, not being a personal representative, had no right, even in his claimed but disputed capacity as beneficiary of the deceased's estate, to sue the first defendant. The claim was struck out as not disclosing any reasonable grounds for bringing the claim (paras 41-42, 62, 78, 81-82, 84).

HAASTRUP v OKORIE, [2016] EWHC 12 (Ch), [2016] W.T.L.R. 803, Master Matthews, Ch D.

2026 Distribution of estates–Creditors' rights–Directions for distribution where risk of contingent debt

The claimant executor applied for directions permitting him to distribute the deceased's assets to the defendant sole beneficiary. The beneficiary was the deceased's son. The principal assets of the estate had been shares of a partnership between the beneficiary and the deceased, and shares in other companies of which the beneficiary was also a shareholder. The deceased had entered into film partnership investment schemes that were purportedly tax efficient. The investments were funded by substantial loans, and the schemes were intended to be self-financing in that shares in the partnership's income would match the liabilities. The Revenue challenged the schemes, giving rise to potential liabilities for the estate for historic tax and tax upon future income. The executor had been granted probate nearly four years before the instant hearing. However, he had been unable to distribute the estate's assets without the court's directions where the estate had potential liabilities to creditors, lest he incur personal liability. The loans were due to be fully repaid in six years' time. The beneficiary stated that his business interests were inextricably linked to the estate and that he needed the assets to properly manage his business. The executor's view was that there was adequate provision to cover the capital under the loans and that, with indemnities in place, the estate would only be exposed if the partnership was wound up and ceased to generate income. The issues were whether (i) a charge the beneficiary suggested in the sum of £2 million over one of his properties, which was actually worth in excess of £5.6 million, would be appropriate; (ii) a retention of cash in the sum of £400,000, sought by the executor, should be ordered to give further security to potential creditors.

Held: Directions given. (1) It was clear that the beneficiary's link to the estate was so close that the current situation caused practical difficulties in operating a successful business. That could continue for many years, would be costly and was not in the best interests of the business being run most efficiently. The executor had a duty to distribute assets to creditors before beneficiaries and could be personally liable if he failed to do so, though it was possible for him to look to the overpaid beneficiary for an indemnity. It was possible to retain a sum to meet the risk of a contingent debt, or seek security from a prospective beneficiary. The court had to seek to achieve a fair balance between the risk of creditors' debts being unmet and the beneficiary being kept out of an interest to which he was entitled, *Yorke (Deceased), Re* [1997] 4 All E.R. 907, [1997] C.L.Y. 4724 applied. It was unlikely that the loans would become due and the more likely exposure was tax liability. The beneficiary's suggested charge seemed to be appropriate to cover the potential liability. Upon taking that security, the executor and the beneficiary would no longer have personal liability arising from the schemes. (2) Whilst the beneficiary was asset rich, he was not cash rich and retention of a large sum of cash would have a real impact on his ability to run his business. That would undermine the purpose of the directions at the instant stage for distributing assets. The tax liabilities were a relatively small sum for which it would be proper to order a cash retention, but that would be limited to cover the estimated costs of the liabilities that the estate was likely to have, namely £90,000.

INGREY v KING, [2015] EWHC 2137 (Ch), [2016] W.T.L.R. 131, Judge Walden-Smith, Ch D.

2027 Distribution of estates–Personal injury claims–Payments in accordance with court-approved scheme for payment of sexual abuse claims

[Limitation Act 1980 (c.58) s.33]

The court was asked to approve a distribution from the estate of the late Jimmy Savile in the implementation of a scheme which had been approved by the court in 2014. The scheme had been set up to deal with claims by a significant number of individuals that they had been sexually abused by Savile. The claims were made against the claimant bank, being Savile's executor, and against certain third parties on whose premises the alleged abuse had taken place. The scheme provided for the making and processing of claims and the assessment of compensation where claims were admitted. It also provided for compensation to be calculated by reference to particular tariffs, the amount of compensation depending on the seriousness of the assault. The scheme also made provision for the costs of claimants. It provided for the payment of £10,000 per claimant for certain claimants where those costs were incurred before the approval of the scheme. Future costs were provided for by a tariff. In each case, a claimant was entitled to recover the costs subject to the approval by a Chancery judge of the agreement of the bank to such costs. The scheme also stipulated that any agreement to the payment of a claim would only be made if approved by a Chancery judge and that no distribution of the estate would be made without the approval of a Chancery judge.

Held: Application granted. Given the evidence the court had heard about the scrutiny given to the claims and the manner in which settlements were reached, it would be appropriate to approve the agreements by the bank to make payment. Although the court had a discretion to refuse to approve a settlement which fell within the tariff, it was not appropriate to go behind the tariff amounts given that acceptance of liability for a particular type of assault listed in the tariff was justified. Similarly, it was not appropriate to go behind the costs tariff contained in the scheme. Accordingly, the amounts of the settlement agreements and the amounts of costs would be approved. Approving the distribution of the estate in the manner sought by the bank would mean that the claims of potential claimants whose claims were not satisfied by the distribution would be irrecoverable. The claims affected were out-of-time claims already intimated, claims which had been rejected and out-of-time claims not yet intimated. A line had to be drawn somewhere. The bank could not be expected to retain assets indefinitely against the possibility of proceedings being commenced in relation to any of the three types of claim. As to the first two types, they were all now time-barred subject to the power under the Limitation Act 1980 s.33 to extend the time for bringing proceedings. Those potential claimants had known of, and had intimated their claims, months, and in some cases, years ago. They had had every opportunity to bring claims but had not done so; and they had failed to do so notwithstanding that they knew, or must be taken to have known, the time for bringing claims under the scheme. Importantly, by raising claims under the scheme, the individual concerned had shown that he had knowledge of a claim which could, in the alternative, have been made in court proceedings. Once the claim under the scheme was rejected (whether on its merits or because it was out of time), it was incumbent on the claimant to get on with his claim, seeking as part of his proceedings an extension of time under s.33. If a claimant delayed in taking proceedings, as all the relevant claimants had done, he could not expect the court to delay the distribution of the estate. The position of potential claimants who had not yet intimated a claim was even weaker. The scheme had been widely advertised and, quite apart from such advertisement, the media exposure was so great that it was difficult to imagine that a person with a claim did not know that he could make it through the scheme. In any case, the bank had made formal advertisement for claims. The statutory protection for an executor who distributed after such advertisement in the absence of knowledge of a claim pointed strongly to the conclusion that the court should approve the distribution notwithstanding potential claims of the third type. Authorisation would therefore be given for payment by the bank of the agreed settlement amounts and associated costs out of the estate (see paras 31-34, 54 of judgment).

NATIONAL WESTMINSTER BANK PLC v LUCAS, [2016] EWHC 1934 (Ch), [2016] W.T.L.R. 1413, Warren J, Ch D.

2028 **Persons lacking capacity–Statutory wills–Permission to execute statutory will–Application under r.38 Court of Protection Rules 2007 to dispense with service–Guidance on proper approach**

[Court of Protection Rules 2007 (SI 2007/1744) r.159, r.3, r.38; European Convention on Human Rights 1950 art.6, art.8]

The Official Solicitor appealed against an order made in favour of the respondent and dispensing with service of an application for permission to execute a statutory will. The respondent, who was the mother of a 30-year-old man (D) was applying for permission to execute a statutory will. D had been awarded £3.1 million in damages after birth complications had left him with athetoid cerebral palsy. He was intestate and lacked the capacity to make a will. He had a normal life expectancy, and on his death his estate would be divided equally between his mother and father. Under the proposed statutory will, D's mother and his siblings would be beneficiaries but his father would not. At the mother's request, the court made an order under the Court of Protection Rules 2007 r.38 dispensing with the requirement for service of the application on D's father. The judge took into account the mother's assertions that she did not know where D's father was; that he had not had contact with D for some 22 years; that she would have to spend around £5,000 tracking him down; and that the prospect of contacting him caused her anxiety. He concluded that because D's father was unlikely to succeed in opposing the will, the cost of tracing him was not proportionate. The Official Solicitor invited the court to approve guidance to the effect that (1) an application to dispense with service was not to be determined only by reference to the best interests of the incapacitated person; (2) the court had to have regard to the overriding objective in r.3 of the Rules; (3) ECHR art.6 and art.8 might be engaged; (4) dispensing with service might mean the court deciding the substantive application without all the relevant material; (5) the apparent merits of the substantive application should not be used to justify dispensing with service; (6) fears about the consequences to the applicant or the incapacitated person could be ameliorated by the redaction of relevant details; (7) the consequences of a successful application for the person not served should be considered; (8) before deciding to dispense with service because of practical difficulties, the court should consider service by alternative means; (9) cases in which it would be appropriate to dispense with service on an individual who was directly and adversely affected were likely to be exceptional; (10) different factors might apply where the application was to dispense with service on the incapacitated person, or where there was genuine urgency and a need to balance the prejudice of proceeding in the absence of an affected party against the prejudice to the incapacitated person or another party of not proceeding at all.

Held: Appeal allowed. (1) The guidance suggested by the Official Solicitor would be approved. The question of dispensing with service had been considered by the courts a number of times and the decisions consistently favoured notifying those adversely affected save in exceptional circumstances, *HMF (Mental Patient: Will), Re* [1976] Ch. 33, [1975] C.L.Y. 3577, *B (CP: Notice of Proceedings), Re* [1987] 1 W.L.R. 552, [1987] C.L.Y. 2422 and *AB, Re* [2014] C.O.P.L.R. 381 applied (see paras 27-34, 45 of judgment). (2) The instant case not exceptional and there were no compelling reasons why the court should depart from its usual practice of joining those who were materially and adversely affected by the substantive application. The judge had given undue prominence to the cost of searching for D's father, and his concern about that was unjustified given the magnitude of the principle at stake and the extent to which D's father stood to be disinherited. Natural justice deterred judges from making decisions impacting adversely on the rights of individuals without giving them the opportunity to be heard. If a court agreed to dispense with service because it would be cheaper, more convenient or less discomfiting for the applicant, it would be failing in its duty to manage conflicts of interest and provide for appropriate and effective safeguards to prevent abuse in accordance with international human rights law. The perceived merits of the substantive application and the apparent weakness of any objection D's father might have did not detract from his right to be served (paras 45-60). (3) It would be unfair to order D's mother to pay her own costs. There was no reason to invoke r.159 and depart from the general rule that the costs would be paid by the incapacitated person or charged to his estate. Although it might be sad that D's mother had acted unreasonably in applying to dispense with service, she had succeeded twice in the court below (there having been an interim hearing before the decision under appeal). She had had no option but to respond to the appeal, and she had not been warned that she might have to pay her own costs. However, the fact that the Official Solicitor had urged the court to order D's mother to pay her own costs indicated that he might in future seek costs orders against applicants who, in unexceptional circumstances and for no compelling reason, applied to dispense with service on someone who was materially and adversely affected by an application for the execution of a statutory will (paras 61-68).

D, RE *sub nom.* I v D, [2016] EWCOP 35, [2016] C.O.P.L.R. 432, Judge Lush, CP.

2029 Probate–Contentious probate claims–Locus standi–Creditor of beneficiary

[Civil Procedure Rules 1998 r.57.7; Inheritance (Provision for Family and Dependants) Act 1975 (c.63); Senior Courts Act 1981 (c.54) s.121]

A husband appealed against a decision (*Randall v Randall* [2014] EWHC 3134 (Ch), [2015] W.T.L.R. 99, [2015] C.L.Y. 2412) that he lacked standing to bring a probate claim in respect of the will of his ex-wife's mother. In the parties' divorce settlement, they agreed that if the wife were to inherit more than £100,000 from her mother, she would keep the £100,000 and the balance would be split equally between the parties. The mother left £100,000 to the wife in her will and the balance of her estate to the wife's children. The husband brought a probate claim to challenge the validity of the will. If the will was invalid, the husband would be entitled to around £75,000. A master decided as a preliminary issue that the husband had no standing to bring a claim because he had no sufficient interest in the will as required by CPR r.57.7. The master concluded that the creditor of a beneficiary of an estate had no interest in the estate, holding that the decision in *White (Deceased), Re*to that effect was inconsistent with the proposition in *Menzies v Pulbrook and Ker* 163 E.R. 605 that the creditor of an estate had no right to oppose a will.

Held: Appeal allowed. The master had been wrong to assimilate the position of a creditor of a beneficiary of an estate with that of a creditor of an estate. That meant that he had been wrong to conclude that *White* was wrongly decided on the grounds of inconsistency with *Menzies*, *White* approved, *Dixon v Allinson* 164 E.R. 1397 considered. There was no doubt that a creditor of an estate did not have sufficient interest in an estate to bring a probate claim, *Menzies* approved. However, the interests of the two types of creditor were fundamentally different. The interest of the creditor of a beneficiary was to ensure that the beneficiary received what was due to him or her under the will or an intestacy. The interest of a creditor of an estate was to ensure that there was due administration of the estate. The creditor of the estate was not interested in which beneficiary received what. The court in *Seagrave (Deceased), Re* [2007] EWHC 788 (Ch), [2007] 1 W.L.R. 2002, [2007] C.L.Y. 3953 had correctly adopted a broad construction of "interest" and held that there was no decided case which was inconsistent with such a broad construction, *O'Brien* approved. *O'Brien* was not authority only for the proposition that a person with a claim under the Inheritance (Provision for Family and Dependants) Act 1975 had a sufficient interest to bring a probate claim, *O'Brien* explained. Absent binding authority or cogent arguments requiring a more narrow interpretation, justice required that "interest" should extend to include a person such as the husband. If there had been any doubt about whether the husband would have had an interest before the introduction of the CPR, that was resolved by the CPR's requirement to give effect to the overriding objective: justice required the husband to be able to bring the claim (see paras 15, 22-24, 28 of judgment). If the husband had not had an interest in the deceased's estate, there would be in practice no route by which his claim that the will was invalid could be brought before the court. The master had said that the Senior Courts Act 1981 s.121 provided a mechanism for the court to intervene on the basis that a grant of probate had been wrongly made or contained an error. However, if the husband was not party to a probate claim because he did not have an interest, it was difficult to see how he would be able to bring his claim to the court's attention so as to engage s.121 (paras 25-26). The question of whether a person had a sufficient interest was a matter of procedural, rather than substantive, law. Whether a person had a good claim was a matter of substantive law; whether the person had the right to bring a claim before a court was a question of procedure (para.27).

RANDALL v RANDALL, [2016] EWCA Civ 494, [2016] 3 W.L.R. 1217, Lord Dyson MR, CA (Civ Div).

2030 Reasonable financial provision–Jurisdiction–Establishing place of deceased's domicile at death–Domicile of choice overriding domicile of origin

[Inheritance (Provision for Family and Dependants) Act 1975 (c.63)]

The claimant wife made a claim under the Inheritance (Provision for Family and Dependants) Act 1975 following the death of her husband. The deceased, who had an English domicile of origin, had moved to Gambia in 1994. He had married the claimant, originally a Gambian citizen, in Gambia in 2000. In 2001, their daughter was born in England where they lived for much of that year. By 2003, the marriage was in difficulty and from 2004 at the latest the deceased remained for the majority of his time with his daughter in Gambia, whilst retaining access to a flat in England where the claimant lived. The deceased allegedly divorced the claimant in 2004, but the claimant claimed not to have been told about the divorce. The evidence was that the deceased had intended to permanently reside in Gambia and that he wished to be buried there. The evidence of one of his three daughters was that he had asked her not to allow him to be repatriated for an English funeral. The defendants, the deceased's two daughters by his first marriage and his friend, argued that the claimant had no claim under the Act as the deceased had died domiciled in Gambia. The issue was whether the deceased had intended to live in Gambia permanently, or at least indefinitely. The claimant argued that: the deceased had not acquired Gambian citizenship; he had regularly visited England; he had paid for her UK citizenship; his English business interests, including investment properties, meant that he had not severed all ties; two executors of his will were English; and it was unlikely that someone would wish to abandon domicile in one of the richest countries in the world in favour of domicile in one of the poorest countries.

Held: Claim dismissed. Citizenship was not decisive of domicile, *Henwood v Barlow Clowes International Ltd (In Liquidation)* [2008] EWCA Civ 577, [2008] B.P.I.R. 778, [2008] 8 C.L. 58 followed. The court had to look at all of the facts of the deceased's life and determine whether or not a clear case had been made out that his domicile had changed, *Cyganik v Agulian* [2006] EWCA Civ 129, [2006] 1 F.C.R. 406, [2006] C.L.Y. 4082 followed. The picture that emerged from 2004 onwards was of the deceased making his life in Gambia, backed up by numerous statements to friends and family emphasising his wish to live there indefinitely or permanently. His visits to England were referable to his daughter's need to see her mother and were no more than temporary visits; the flat to which the deceased had access in England could not be regarded as any sort of home. The fact that he had paid for the claimant's UK citizenship said little or nothing about his domicile; it was equally, if not more, consistent with the deceased cementing the distance between them. The fact that someone's ties were not wholly severed did not prevent the formation of an intention to live permanently or indefinitely elsewhere. In any case, the deceased had ceased to be involved in the running of the business. The investment properties did not require the deceased's presence in England and their existence was of little materiality in considering domicile. Although the claimant was never told about it during the deceased's lifetime, there had been what purported to be a divorce and it was ludicrous to regard them as husband and wife in any meaningful sense from 2003 onwards. Whilst the fact that two of the executors were English was a factor to be considered, it was not a strong indication of domicile. The unlikelihood of someone wishing to abandon domicile in one of the richest countries in the world for domicile in one of the poorest countries was a factor to be considered, but there was an overwhelming body of evidence to suggest that that was exactly what the deceased had done. The court had to be wary about relying on statements as to a person's intentions about where he would live in the future. However, the deceased's conduct was consistent with a settled intention to remain and live indefinitely in Gambia. The deceased had died domiciled in Gambia; the links that he had had up until his death with England were insufficient to override the very strong evidence that Gambia was his permanent home (see paras 5, 10-11, 21-22, 30, 32-33, 37,39, 47-48, 55-56, 60-63, 65 of judgment).

KEBBEH v FARMER, [2015] EWHC 3827 (Ch), [2016] W.T.L.R. 1011, Judge Purle QC, Ch D (Birmingham).

2031 Reasonable financial provision–Maintenance–Whether "maintenance" under s.1(2)(b) Inheritance (Provision for Family and Dependants) Act 1975 could include transfer at full consideration

[Inheritance (Provision for Family and Dependants) Act 1975 (c.63) s.1(1)(ba), s.1(1)(e), s.1(2)(b), s.1(3)]

A beneficiary appealed against a decision to grant relief under the Inheritance (Provision for Family and Dependants) Act 1975. The appellant was the daughter of the deceased. Under the deceased's will, the appellant inherited the entire estate. The deceased and her partner (W) had cohabited in the deceased's home for 20 years before her death. W was aged 91 and had expected to die before the deceased. He accepted that there was never any understanding that he would have an interest in the deceased's estate. He had the means to buy a house if necessary but he wished to remain in the home where he had lived with the deceased, because he was in poor health and was assisted by his neighbours. The appellant commenced proceedings for possession and W brought a claim under the 1975 Act. The recorder concluded that he should be given the option to purchase the house from the estate for £385,000. That figure was based on a valuation of the property obtained by the appellant. A joint expert had concluded that the property was worth £340,000. The appellant submitted that the recorder had erred by (1) treating W's claim as made under s.1(1)(e) of the Act; (2) failing to apply the law correctly, because W had no need for financial provision; (3) making an order which he had no power to make.

Held: Appeal dismissed. (1) Those who could apply under the Act included, under s.1(1)(e), persons who were being maintained by the deceased immediately before the deceased's death and, by virtue of s.1(1)(ba), a person who had, for two years up to the death of the deceased, been living in the same household as the husband or wife of the deceased. The evidence did not justify a finding that W had been "maintained" by the deceased within the meaning of s.1(3). However, the recorder had not treated W as having applied under s.1(1)(e). He was making the point that the fact that the will did not contain anything to allow W to remain in his home meant that it had failed to make reasonable financial provision for his "maintenance" within the meaning of s.1(2)(b) (see paras 6, 17-19 of judgment). (2) In the majority of cases "financial provision" for an applicant's "maintenance" would involve an overall transfer of value from the estate to the applicant, *Dennis (Deceased), Re* [1981] 2 All E.R. 140, [1981] C.L.Y. 2887 considered. Arrangements for full value would not support a claim to have been "maintained" by the deceased for the purposes of s.1(1)(e). However, "maintenance" was not defined in the Act and the courts had shied away from providing a precise explanation of the word, In *Coventry (Deceased), Re* [1980] Ch. 461, [1979] C.L.Y. 2807 and *Ilott v Mitson* [2015] EWCA Civ 797, [2016] 1 All E.R. 932, [2015] C.L.Y. 2413 considered. On balance, "maintenance" could exceptionally encompass an arrangement for full consideration. The word "maintenance" suggested the provision of assistance to enable a person to meet the requirements of his daily life. Someone of ample financial means would not normally need any such help. In principle, however, "maintenance" was not necessarily confined to support with a person's cost of daily living. It was capable of referring to other forms of assistance with the requirements of daily life. If, therefore, a person was in want of a particular thing to sustain a reasonable quality of life, the provision of it could represent "maintenance" regardless of his financial means. There was no absolute bar on the provision of something for full consideration representing "financial provision" for a person's "maintenance". The recorder had concluded that the fact that the deceased's will did not allow W to keep the roof over his head meant that it failed to make reasonable provision for him. That was not an error of principle (paras 22-26, 29-30). (3) If it was correct that the will failed to make reasonable provision for W, it must have been open to the recorder to give effect to his view by exercising his powers under s.2 to compel the appellant to transfer the house to W (para.34).

LEWIS v WARNER; WARNER v LEWIS, [2016] EWHC 1787 (Ch), [2016] 3 W.L.R. 1545, Newey J, Ch D.

2032 Statutory wills–Best interests–Elderly man lacking testamentary capacity

[Mental Capacity Act 2005 (c.9) s.18(1)(i), s.4; Inheritance and Trustees' Powers Act 2014 (c.16) s.1; Inheritance (Provision for Family and Dependants) Act 1975 (c.63)]

The applicants applied under the Mental Capacity Act 2005 s.18(1)(i) for authority to execute a statutory will on behalf of an 81-year-old intestate man (J) who suffered from dementia and lacked testamentary capacity. The applicants were his wife of more than 40 years (W) and a solicitor. J had one child, his 56-year-old daughter (D) from a previous marriage, who lived in Canada. She had suffered from addiction and mental health problems and serious financial difficulties. Since she was 13 she had seen J only once, when she was 23, and again in the past year; otherwise there had been only infrequent telephone contact. J's estate was worth about £2.3 million. If he died intestate, the effect of the Inheritance and Trustees' Powers Act 2014 s.1 was that, following the statutory legacy of £250,000 plus personal chattels to W, she and D would each receive half of the remainder of the estate. The Official Solicitor, for J, submitted that it was in his best interests that a statutory will be made to enable independent professional executors to be appointed and to avoid the intestacy provisions, which gave too much weight to D's limited involvement in J's life and failed adequately to provide for W given their long marriage.

Held: Judgment accordingly. (1) For many people it was in their best interests to be remembered with affection by their family as having done the right thing by their will. The court was entitled to take that into account alongside the other factors in s.4 of the 2005 Act. However, where a person with capacity had recently made a will excluding a potential beneficiary and/or had expressed views that he disliked them and did not want them to share in his estate, and that person then became incapacitated, a third-party decision-maker could not "correct" his wishes by substituting his own or society's view as to what he rightfully should have done. To do so would run counter to testamentary freedom and the wishes, feelings, beliefs and values provisions of the 2005 Act, and lead to inconsistent and arbitrary outcomes. The onset of mental incapacity was not an opportunity for moral correction. That left room for the kind of case where the court authorised a statutory will that made good the patient's omissions but did not seek to correct his considered acts and decisions. In the absence of clear evidence to the contrary, it could be assumed that if a patient had given proper thought to his pending incapacity and intestacy, he would have wanted to put his house in order and make a will, *P (Statutory Will), Re* [2009] EWHC 163 (Ch), [2010] Ch. 33, [2009] C.L.Y. 3727, *M (Statutory Will), Re* [2009] EWHC 2525 (Fam), [2011] 1 W.L.R. 344, [2010] C.L.Y. 3212, *G, Re* [2010] EWHC 3005 (Fam), [2011] Med. L.R. 89, [2011] C.L.Y. 2234, *Meek, Re* [2014] EWCOP 1, [2014] C.O.P.L.R. 535, [2014] C.L.Y. 2829, *Aintree University Hospitals NHS Foundation Trust v James* [2013] UKSC 67, [2014] A.C. 591, [2014] C.L.Y. 1526 considered (see paras 59, 60, 62-67 of judgment). (2) J had done what many people would regard as the wrong thing in respect of his estate by not providing for D or making a will providing for W's future despite having had 40 years to do so. He had intended that W and D would both benefit from his estate in due course but preferred to retain control of his money and relationships for as long as possible. D had always loved him and they had a close and loving relationship until they were separated. The absence of her visits was explained by her sensitivity, fragile mental health and financial circumstances, and by his unapproachability, rather than by a lack of interest on her part. J loved her, and had stated that he intended to include both her and W in a will. The fact that he had not made a will did not demonstrate that he wished to limit W's inheritance to what she would receive under intestacy or by way of the Inheritance (Provision for Family and Dependants) Act 1975. It was likely that he intended to arrange for her to receive the greater part of his estate whilst making reasonable provision for D in due course. If he knew that legitimate arrangements for his estate could no longer be postponed it was improbable that he would not include D among the beneficiaries. The receipt of a significant sum would have a life-changing effect on her and, given the size of the estate, no significant effect on his or W's well-being. W's share of the estate should be around 75 per cent and D's around 25 per cent. An overall provision of about £625,000 for D in the form of a lifetime gift, to enable the purchase of a home, followed by a legacy, was appropriate. It was in J's best interests for a statutory will to be made on his behalf and for neutral and independent professional executors to be appointed (paras 69, 94-97, 108, 119-120, 125-132).

JONES, RE, [2014] EWCOP 59, [2016] W.T.L.R. 661, District Judge Eldergill , CP.

2033 Wills–Executors–Exexutors unable to work together–Removal and replacement

[Administration of Justice Act 1985 (c.61) s.50]

The claimant applied for the removal of the defendant, her brother, as an executor of their late mother's estate and for him to account for rent in respect of the property which was the main asset of the estate. The claimant and her brother were appointed executors of their late mother's estate under her will. The estate was to be divided equally between them. The defendant lived in the same street where his mother had lived in Colchester. The claimant lived in Cornwall and rarely saw her brother. The estate consisted of the mother's house, which was in poor condition, and other money and investments. The claimant agreed that the defendant could administer the estate on the basis that he kept her informed. The defendant refused to involve solicitors in the administration of the estate on the basis that that was in accordance with his mother's wishes. He allowed the grandson of his partner to live in the house and proposed to sell it to him. He did not respond to letters or a telephone call from the claimant's solicitors. The claimant lodged a caveat which prevented him obtaining a grant of probate and selling the house. The claimant issued proceedings to remove the defendant as an executor and for him to account for rent in respect of the property. The defendant failed to comply with procedural directions and the deputy master gave judgment in default in respect of the claim for the defendant to account for the market rent of the property plus interest.

Held: Judgment for claimant. It was clear that the parties were effectively strangers and could not get on with one another. There was a clash of personalities and lack of confidence. That had led to a standstill for three years. It was clearly appropriate to remove them both under the Administration of Justice Act 1985 s.50, *Steel (Deceased), Re* [2010] EWHC 154 (Ch), [2010] W.T.L.R. 531, [2010] C.L.Y. 3205 applied. If the parties agreed, the court was prepared to appoint the claimant's son and the defendant's partner as joint administrators. Failing agreement there would have to be an appointment of a local, independent probate solicitor. In respect of the rental income claim, it had been reasonable for the defendant to allow his partner's grandson to occupy the property rent-free for a period while carrying out improvements. Thereafter he was liable for the market rent for 33 months with interest. The defendant was liable to pay the costs of the claim on the standard basis.

WILBY v RIGBY, [2015] EWHC 2394 (Ch), [2015] W.T.L.R. 1845, Judge Hodge QC, Ch D.

2034 Wills–Interpretation–Whether testatrix intending to include real property in residuary estate

[Administration of Justice Act 1982 (c.53) s.21]

The claimant executors asked the court to construe a will or rectify it. The testatrix's last will and that of her husband were in mirror terms with all to the spouse in the event of the spouse surviving and various gifts to other individuals and named charities in the event of the spouse pre-deceasing. The testatrix's husband pre-deceased her and his estate passed to her. By her will the testatrix gave all her personal property to her trusts on trust to pay her debts, funeral and testamentary expenses and then for her husband absolutely provided that if he should not survive the trustees should hold the residuary estate for ten named individuals or charities. Before making a distribution the executors asked the court to confirm their interpretation of the will or rectify it. Their case was that it was not clear that the residuary estate included real property; that the 10 gifts were of a one-tenth share even though the will referred sometimes to one-tenth and sometimes to one part; that correct numbers were given for some charities but incorrect names; and that two of the charities were wrongly named.

Held: Judgment accordingly. (1) The court was satisfied that the testatrix intended to include real property in her will and that it should be construed accordingly under the Administration of Justice Act 1982 s.21, *Marley v Rawlings* [2014] UKSC 2, [2015] A.C. 129, [2014] C.L.Y. 2835 followed. It would be surprising if the intention had not been to include the matrimonial home as it was probably the most valuable asset. Although the residuary estate was not defined, it should be regarded as comprising the whole of the estate after paying the debts, funeral and testamentary expenses and inheritance tax. (2) The use of two different terms, one-tenth and one part, suggested different meanings. However, there were ten gifts and if one part was construed as one-tenth that would dispose of the entire residuary estate. Each gift was contained in one of ten separate sub-clauses. The correct interpretation was that one part equalled one-tenth. (3) A gift to "Newbury Hospital" at a given address would be construed as a gift to the West Berkshire Community Hospital which was at that address and was colloquially referred to as Newbury Hospital. Similarly in the case of other charities where a correct number was given but the name was given incorrectly the court would construe the gifts by reference to the number. The charities were clearly misnamed. (4) The final gift was to "West Berkshire Ambulance Hospital" which was a nonsense. For the purposes of rectification the court had to be satisfied not just that the will did not reflect the testatrix's intentions, but also what those intentions were. There was little available evidence but notes in the instructions for the drawing up of the wills did refer to a gift to "air rescue ... West Berks area". There was no other relevant gift in the will. The court was satisfied that the testatrix intended to make a gift to the air ambulance service covering West Berkshire. That was the Thames Valley and Chiltern Air Ambulance. The will was rectified accordingly. (5) The firm of solicitors which drafted the will was joined to the proceedings for the purpose of costs only and a costs hearing was directed.

HARTE (DECEASED), RE, [2015] EWHC 2351 (Ch), [2015] W.T.L.R. 1735, Judge Hodge QC, Ch D.

2035 Wills–Knowledge and approval–Testator vulnerable and suggestible but having capacity–Will made without knowledge and approval

[Wills Act 1837 (c.26) s.9]

The claimants challenged a will executed by their brother (D) and sought proof in solemn form of his earlier will. D had been in an accident and later spent time in a mental health hospital. The first defendant was his live-in carer and was paid by the local authority. D received damages of over £1 million from his accident claim. A solicitor was appointed to manage his financial affairs. The second defendant was D's partner with whom he had lived for several years, before living with the first defendant again. The solicitor discussed D's testamentary wishes and expressed caution about a proposed gift to the first defendant. A doctor assessed D as having testamentary capacity in February 2012 and D executed a will, leaving money to the claimants, their children, D's partner and several charities, but not to the first defendant. The first defendant made several complaints about the solicitor and maintained that D wanted to change the will. At D's alleged request, the first defendant prepared a new will in December 2012 that left 95% of the estate to the first defendant and 5% to D's partner. It was witnessed by two neighbours. D died in early 2013. The claimants challenged the December will and sought proof in solemn form of the February will. The claimants submitted that (1) the December will was not duly executed; (2) D had lacked testamentary capacity; (3) the will was made without D's knowledge and approval; (4) the February will was valid.

Held: Judgment for claimants. (1) The Wills Act 1837 s.9 required that the testator sign the will in presence of at least two witnesses. The claimants alleged that two witnesses were not present when D signed the will. One witness had stated that she had witnessed D's signature on 29 December, although the will was dated 26 December. She later said that she had been present with the other witness on 26 December. The presumption in favour of an apparently duly executed will was very strong, *Wright v Rogers (No.1)* (1865-69) L.R. 1 P. & D. 678 applied. The claimants were inviting the court to find that although the witnesses positively affirmed that they had been present together, their testimony should be disbelieved due to previous inconsistent statements. It was right to submit that their explanations did not make sense. However, all the positive evidence supported the position that both had been present on 26 December, and in those circumstances, whatever doubts there were about their credibility, it could not be said that there was "the strongest" evidence against due execution. The court was bound to find that the will was duly executed (see paras 94-103 of judgment). (2) Not every case required a contemporaneous formal capacity assessment. D had been formally assessed in February 2012; the doctor's opinion was that he was likely to continue to have capacity. The solicitor, who had experience of D's condition, believed that D had retained testamentary capacity. D's mental capacity was not entirely normal: he was vulnerable and prone to suggestibility, particularly in relation to money. An issue as to whether a testator required an explanation to properly understand the nature and effect of what he was doing was better considered under knowledge and approval, rather than capacity. If he was capable of understanding the relevant matters, even if only when they were suitably explained, he was to be treated as having testamentary capacity. D had had capacity at the time of executing the December will (paras 105-114). (3) D had understood that he was executing a will; the question was whether he sufficiently understood its contents and effects. Particular caution was required where the will was prepared by a person who stood to benefit under it. It was obvious that the first defendant could not satisfy the burden. D, a vulnerable and suggestible person, had made a will in which the great bulk of his estate was given to a person on whom he had been dependent for his care, and the will was drafted by that same person. The concerns were magnified where previous gifts to family members and charities were removed altogether and the gift to D's partner reduced by half. The evidence that D fully understood the will came only from the first defendant and was self-serving. He had not read over the will's terms to D. Given D's vulnerability and difficulties in recalling beneficiaries without being reminded, the court would not have been satisfied unless it had been drawn to his attention that the will removed the family and charity gifts and reduced the partner's gift. There was only the first defendant's unsupported word that that had been discussed. There was a substantial risk that he sought to pursue his own interests. He had used his relationship with D to isolate D from others, with the motive of preventing the influence of those who questioned his actions, especially the solicitor. He had failed to discharge the burden of showing that D knew and approved of the will's terms, and it was not valid (paras 115-117, 121-126, 135). (4) There was no challenge to the formalities of execution of the February will. The solicitor took careful steps to take instructions for it and to confirm that it represented D's wishes and that D knew and approved of its contents. D made his own decision and was not coerced into doing so (para.139).

POOLE v EVERALL, [2016] EWHC 2126 (Ch), [2016] W.T.L.R. 1621, Judge David Cooke, Ch D (Blackburn).

2036 Wills–Reasonable financial provision–Unmarried couples–Jointly-owned property

[Inheritance (Provision for Family and Dependants) Act 1975 (c.63) s.2]

The claimant sought an order under the Inheritance (Provision for Family and Dependants) Act 1975 s.2 for reasonable financial provision to be made for her from the estate of a man (M) with whom she had lived for many years. M had died unexpectedly in 2012 at the age of 69. The case of the claimant, who was now 69, was that for 18 years she and M had been living in the same household as man and wife, giving her standing to bring a claim under the Act. The defendant was M's wife. Although the two were married in 1967, M had lived with the claimant since 1994. M made a will in 1986 under which he left his entire estate to his wife. In 1994, he moved out of the matrimonial home and went to live with the claimant. They lived together until his death. Some three years before his death, he and the claimant bought a property together. The claimant continued to live there. The property was currently worth in the region of £320,000. The wife continued to live in the former matrimonial home, which was said to be worth around £420,000. The claimant had intended to retire in 2012 but owing to M's death had had to continue working. Her salary was modest. She said that M had assured her that she would be looked after in the event of his death and that he had intended to change his will but never got around to doing so. M's net estate comprised his one-half interest in the property bought jointly with the claimant, £20,000 and a small share of another property.

Held: Judgment for claimant. The claimant and M had lived in the same household as man and wife for 18 years. Theirs was an intimate, committed and loving relationship, and they had intended to spend the rest of their lives together. M had failed to make reasonable financial provision for the claimant in his will. The claimant currently struggled to make ends meet and would be unable to do so once she retired. Of particular importance as far as her position was concerned was the length and quality of the relationship she had with M, the contribution she had made towards his welfare and the heightened obligation and responsibility he had towards her, as evidenced by the assurances he had given her before his untimely death and the disproportionately high level of financial contribution he made towards their joint expenditure. The appropriate order was to vest in the claimant absolutely M's beneficial interest in the property which the two had bought together (see paras 98, 130, 141, 151 of judgment).

WILLIAMS v MARTIN, [2016] W.T.L.R. 1075, Judge Gerald, CC (Central London).

2037 Wills–Rectification–Clerical error

The claimants (C1 and his wife, C2) sought a declaration as to the proper construction of a will or, alternatively, rectification of it. The defendant was the deceased's sister-in-law. They owned a house as tenants in common. The deceased's last will was dated 2011. Clause 3 provided that that the defendant was to have a right of occupancy of the house, rent-free, as long as she paid for its maintenance. At the deceased's request, the trustees were to sell the house and apply the proceeds to another investment. Upon the defendant's death, the house fund was to be held upon trusts in respect of the deceased's "Residuary Estate", which was undefined. Clause 5 dealt with the deceased's "Residuary Fund", providing for an absolute gift to the defendant or, if she predeceased the deceased, the residue was to pass to the claimants and to C1's two brothers in equal shares absolutely. An earlier will, dated 2006, was in substantially the same form, but provided that upon the defendant's death, the house fund passed to C1 and his brothers in equal shares absolutely, rather than passing into residue. The 2006 will was amended in manuscript, striking through the provision passing the house fund to C1 and his brothers. The solicitor who drafted the will gave evidence that the effect of the 2011 will was that the deceased's share in the house fell into residue, and that on that basis the property would pass on to the defendant absolutely on her death, so that cl.3 served no purpose. He considered that the manuscript amendment to the 2006 will and the deletion of the beneficiaries' names had been in error. The claimants' case was that a literal reading of cl.5 of the 2011 will rendered cl.3 otiose, and that the deceased had intended that, after the defendant's lifetime, the house fund would pass to themselves and to C1's brothers. The claimants submitted that (1) the presence of an apparently defined term, namely "Residuary Estate", which was not defined, was a paradigm example of an ambiguity, particularly where there was a similar term which was defined, namely "Residuary Fund", so that the court should construe the terms as meaning the same thing; (2) the court should rectify the will so that it carried out the deceased's intentions.

Held: Judgment for claimants. (1) Reading "Residuary Estate" to mean the same as "Residuary Fund" was not the natural reading of the will. The court was not engaged in the exercise of seeking to avoid an absurd result. There was nothing odd about the 2011 will as it stood. There was a doubt as to whether the court should construe the will in the manner alleged, and the claim for construction therefore failed. (2) The deceased's solicitor had admitted an error in preparing the will and the current effect of the 2011 will could have been achieved in a simpler phrase. The 2006 will provided for the house fund to pass to C1 and his brothers following D's death. There was nothing in the notes of the meeting with the solicitor to indicate that instructions were given to change that. The discussion had been about whether the property should be divided four ways, with C2 getting a share. At first the deceased had not intended such a change, but later instructed that C2 was to be added. The failure to correctly record those instructions in the draft will was a clerical error; the will was to be rectified, *Marley v Rawlings* [2014] UKSC 2, [2015] A.C. 129, [2014] C.L.Y. 2835 followed.

GLEDHILL v ARNOLD, [2015] EWHC 2939 (Ch), [2016] W.T.L.R. 653, Proudman J, Ch D.

2038 Wills–Testamentary capacity–Elderly lady with signs of some mental impairment

The appellants appealed against a decision that a will made by the deceased (B) in July 2005 was valid. The appellants were grandchildren of B. Their father (AB) had recently died. Under the 2005 will, B's estate was left to AB and his brother (CB), the respondent, in equal shares. B had made an earlier will in 2003, under which AB was to receive a larger share of her estate. AB had challenged the validity of the 2005 will on the basis that B lacked testamentary capacity at the date of its execution and did not know and approve of its contents. The evidence indicated that by 2003, when B was 83, her mental condition was giving rise to sufficient concern on AB's part for him to approach social services. Assessments known as "Mini Mental State Examinations" were carried out in October 2003 and May 2005, and an occupational therapy assessment was carried out in May 2005. A geriatrician concluded on the basis of those assessments that B was "poorly orientated as to where she was in time and place, had poor recall ... and ... had problems with analysis and simple task planning". The judge concluded that B had the requisite testamentary capacity in 2005 and that she knew and approved the contents of the later will. He made the following findings: the assessments, while valuable, had been prepared with a view to the provision of care packages and assessments of risk in daily life; the objective evidence in late 2004, when B gave written instructions to her solicitor in the terms of the 2005 will, showed that she could still determine "crucial parts of her life" and that she was still essentially independent of mind on issues that were important to her; she understood, in late 2004, what she was asking the solicitor to do; there was poor management by the solicitor of the meeting with B in July 2005 when she signed the will; for example, he had not complied in certain respects with the "golden rule" which applied in the case of a testator whose capacity might be doubtful (the solicitor should have prior knowledge of the testator, consider whether the will should be witnessed by an approved medical practitioner, examine any earlier will, discuss proposed departures from any earlier will, ask non-leading questions and ensure that the reading through of the will was not an idle ceremony); however, as an experienced solicitor, he would probably have been alerted to any serious question about B's capacity; further, B knew that the document she was signing was the will that she had requested in late 2004.

Held: Appeal dismissed. The judge had been entitled to pronounce in favour of the 2005 will. He adequately identified the criteria for the determination of testamentary capacity. He was also well aware of the "golden rule". However, that "rule" was a prudent guide for solicitors, not a rule of law. The evidence clearly raised doubts as to B's testamentary capacity both in late 2004 and in July 2005. However, the judge decided the case primarily on the basis that capacity had been established in late 2004, when the instructions were given and the draft will was approved, finding that B had at the least capacity to recognise that what she was signing in July 2005 was a will in the form instructed by her in 2004. Thus, validity of the 2005 will was established under the rule in *Parker v Felgate* (1883) 8 P.D. 171, *Parker* considered. He also found, in very brief terms, that B had capacity in July 2005. The evidence entitled him to make those findings. The undisputed events of late 2004 amounted to sufficient evidence to meet the burden of proof on CB that B genuinely intended in that period to revoke the 2003 will and make a will dividing her entire estate between her two sons. Such a disposition would clearly have been a rational one and a simple one to comprehend and state. B attended the offices of her former solicitors in person to collect documents to achieve such an end. Her actions and the unchallenged letters that she wrote and/or to which she put her signature at that time were sufficient material entitling the judge to reach the conclusion he did as to her capacity in that period. There was some concern over the judge's failure to articulate the countervailing considerations arising from the various assessments and the geriatrician's interpretation of them. However, the judge clearly had those matters well in mind. As to the issue of B's approval and knowledge, CB's involvement in the 2005 will (he accompanied B to certain appointments and benefited from the change to the 2003 will) together with the fact that B displayed some traits of mental impairment were circumstances giving rise to some suspicion calling for affirmative proof of knowledge and approval of the 2005 will. However, the judge had approached the matter correctly. The evidence, which he accepted, was that B was seen alone by the solicitor, who, although not searching in his enquiries, read the simple will over to her. He was an experienced solicitor in this type of business and clearly reached the view that B understood and approved the will's contents (see paras 46-50, 54-55, 57 of judgment).

BURNS (DECEASED), RE *sub nom.* BURNS v BURNS, [2016] EWCA Civ 37, [2016] W.T.L.R. 755, Longmore LJ, CA (Civ Div).

2039 Wills–Testamentary capacity–Evidence of solicitor dealing with will

The claimant sought an order pronouncing for the validity of the will of the deceased (J). J made the will in February 2012, some six months before he died. The claimant, with whom J had been in a relationship, was the sole beneficiary. J left nothing to his wife, their children or the first defendant, his daughter from a relationship which predated his marriage. The solicitor (M) who prepared the will had known J for many years and was his brother-in-law. At the time of J's death, divorce proceedings were taking place. In a certificate dated 19 July 2012, a medical expert assessed J as lacking capacity to conduct those proceedings. The issues were (1) whether J had testamentary capacity when he executed the will; (2) if he had such capacity, whether he executed the will with the requisite knowledge and approval of its contents.

Held: Judgment for claimant. (1) J had the necessary testamentary capacity to make the will. In *Key (Deceased), Re* [2010] EWHC 408 (Ch), [2010] 1 W.L.R. 2020, [2010] C.L.Y. 3214, Briggs J. had said that persons with failing or impaired mental faculties might, for perfectly understandable reasons, seek to conceal what they regarded as their embarrassing shortcomings from persons with whom they dealt, so that a friend or professional person such as a solicitor might fail to detect defects in mental capacity which would be or become apparent to a trained and experienced medical examiner. That risk arose in the instant case. However, the fact that M knew J so well meant that he would have been in a better position than most to judge whether there were signs of deterioration in J's mental acuity. M was not simply a friend, a family member or a solicitor interviewing an aged client for the first time. He was a long-standing friend and family member who also happened to be a solicitor. It was clear from his evidence that he was alive to the need to be sure that J understood what he was doing in making the testamentary disposition that he made and its consequences. Moreover, at least three other solicitors had interacted with J during the subsequent months and none had noted any signs of mental deterioration or raised any concerns about his mental capacity or powers of understanding or decision-making. It was clear that J knew what he was doing and the consequences of what he was doing, *Re Key* considered (see paras 61, 63, 69 of judgment). (2) Given that the will had been duly executed and that J had the necessary testamentary capacity, the presumption arose that he knew and approved of the will's contents. Nothing had arisen from M's cross-examination which displaced that presumption. Further, there were no other suspicious circumstances raising a doubt as to whether the will represented J's testamentary intention. There was plenty of evidence via his various conversations with solicitors that the will did represent his firm intention, however disappointing that might prove to members of his family. Accordingly, he had the requisite knowledge and approval of the will's contents (paras 73, 75-77).

ELLIOTT v SIMMONDS *sub nom.* JORDAN (DECEASED), RE, [2016] EWHC 732 (Ch), [2016] W.T.L.R. 1355, Edward Murray, Ch D.

TAX

2040 Accounting standards–Securitisation companies

THE SECURITISATION COMPANIES (APPLICATION OF THE FINANCE ACT 2005 S.83(1) : ACCOUNTING STANDARDS) (AMENDMENT) REGULATIONS 2016, SI 2016/1182; made under the Finance Act 2005 s.83(7A)(7B). In force: 28 December 2016.

The Finance Act 2005 s.83(1) required securitisation companies to use UK generally accepted accounting practice as it stood at 31 December 2004 as the basis for tax computations for periods of account beginning on or after 1 January 2005 and ending before 1 January 2008. These Regulations amend the principal Regulations to further extend the application of s.83(1) to periods of account ending before 1 January 2037, subject to a company electing that the extension should not apply.

2041 Advance corporation tax–Foreign income dividends–Restitution–Lawfulness of tax under EU law

[Civil Procedure Rules 1998 r.24.4(1A), r.24.4(2)]

Claimants in a group litigation applied for summary judgment on their claims for restitution of advance corporation tax (ACT) paid on foreign income dividends (FIDs). The claimants had paid ACT under the FID regime between 1994 and 1999. In *Test Claimants in the FII Group Litigation v Revenue and Customs Commissioners* [2014] EWHC 4302 (Ch), [2015] S.T.C. 1471, [2015] C.L.Y. 2422 (*FII (High Court) II*), the judge held that it was clear beyond argument that the FID regime breached EU law. He reached that decision in the light of *Test Claimants in the FII Group Litigation v Inland Revenue Commissioners (C-446/04)* EU:C:2006:774, [2012] 2 A.C. 436, [2007] C.L.Y. 3971 (*FII (ECJ) I*) and *Test Claimants in the FII Group Litigation v Revenue and Customs Commissioners* [2010] EWCA Civ 103, [2010] S.T.C. 1251, [2010] C.L.Y. 3268 (*FII (CA) I*). He found that the test claimants were entitled to recover the time value of the ACT which they had paid under the FID regime. The claimants in the instant case wished to replicate that success. The appeal from *FII (High Court) II* was due to be heard in June 2016. HMRC intended to seek permission to appeal on the issue of FIDs at the forthcoming appeal hearing. The issues in the instant case were (1) whether the unlawfulness under EU law of the FID regime had been established so clearly that there was no real prospect of HMRC successfully defending the claims. HMRC argued that there was a real prospect that the Court of Appeal would grant them permission to appeal and would take a different view of the law from that taken in *FII (High Court) II*; (2) whether HMRC could object to the instant applications on the ground that the claimants had never applied to lift the stay previously imposed on their claims by the group litigation order; (3) whether, if the stay persisted, the instant applications were barred by CPR r.24.4(1A) on the basis that HMRC's time for filing a defence to the claims had not expired. The claimants argued that HMRC's time for filing a defence began to run again when directions were given at a case management conference in January 2015, and although HMRC could rely on the permissive extension of time in r.24.4(2) pending the summary judgment hearing, it could not rely on the bar in r.24.4(1A) once the standard 14 or 28-day period had elapsed.

Held: Applications granted in part. (1) In *FII (ECJ) I*, the ECJ had given a definitive ruling that the FID regime as a whole was unlawful. The only issue left outstanding was the possible application of the standstill provision to third country FIDs, and that question had been definitively answered in the claimants' favour in *FII (CA) I*. Accordingly, all of the claimants in the FII group litigation which paid FIDs, and which received refunds of ACT following a matching of the FIDs with either EU or third country dividends, were entitled to restitution of the time value of the unlawful ACT which they paid. The whole of the ACT on the matched FIDs had to be regarded as unlawful, because it was paid pursuant to a regime which the ECJ had held to be unlawful. There was no reason to depart from the conclusions in *FII (High Court) II* in relation to the FID claims of the test claimants. HMRC's arguments to the contrary would not have a real prospect of success (see paras 39-44, 47, 54, 59-63 of judgment). (2) HMRC must be taken to have waived its right to object to the summary judgment applications on the ground that the stay had not been lifted: it must have been aware of its right to object on that ground, but it refrained from asserting that right either at the case management hearing or when the applications were listed for trial. At the lowest, the facts established a waiver by acquiescence, and arguably a promissory estoppel upon which the claimants acted by taking steps to list the applications for hearing, *Kammins Ballrooms Co Ltd v Zenith Investments (Torquay) Ltd (No.1)* [1971] A.C. 850, [1970] C.L.Y. 1525 applied (para.75). (3) Time had started to run again for service of HMRC's defences when directions were given in January 2015, and each claimant was able to rely on an application notice for summary judgment which was either re-issued, or issued in amended form, at least 28 days after that date. Although the interaction between r.24.4(1A) and r.24.4(2) was not altogether clear, it would be wrong to construe the provisions as preventing an application for summary judgment against the Crown in any case where the general period for filing a defence had expired but the Crown wished to take advantage of the permissive extension of time provided by r.24.4(2). Such a construction would turn a purely permissive provision into a positive requirement that no application could be made against the Crown for summary judgment until after a defence had actually been filed (paras 77-79). (4) The claims for summary judgment succeeded save in relation to those for compound interest in respect of the periods after repayment or utilisation of the unlawfully paid ACT, and in relation to a claim which was subject to pending proceedings before the First-tier Tribunal (paras 82-84).

EVONIK DEGUSSA UK HOLDINGS LTD v REVENUE AND CUSTOMS COMMISSIONERS *sub nom.* FII GROUP LITIGATION, RE, [2016] EWHC 86 (Ch), [2016] B.T.C. 4, Henderson J, Ch D.

2042 Banking–Surcharges–Regulations

THE BANKING SURCHARGE (INFORMATION) REGULATIONS 2016, SI 2016/566; made under the Taxes Management Act 1970. In force: 1 June 2016.

The instrument sets out the additional information banking companies must provide when providing written notification of payments of banking surcharge.

2043 Capital gains tax–Discovery assessments–Failure of tax avoidance scheme–Requirements of s.29(5) Taxes Management Act 1970

[Taxes Management Act 1970 (c.9) s.29(1), s.29(5)]

A taxpayer appealed against a decision (*Sanderson v Revenue and Customs Commissioners* [2013] UKUT 623 (TCC), [2014] S.T.C. 915, [2014] C.L.Y. 2891) upholding a discovery assessment made by HMRC under the Taxes Management Act 1970 s.29(1). The taxpayer's late self-assessment tax return had disclosed a chargeable gain which was off-set by losses resulting from his involvement in a scheme designed to reduce his capital gains tax liabilities. HMRC's Special Compliance Office investigated the scheme. The taxpayer accepted that the scheme was ineffective and that, to that extent, his return was insufficient for the purposes of s.29(1). He argued that his participation in the scheme, and its ineffectiveness, had been known to HMRC before he submitted his return. The First-tier Tribunal concluded that HMRC had been entitled to raise the discovery assessment. The issue was whether the second condition imposed by s.29(5) for the exercise of the power to issue a discovery assessment, namely that the officer could not have been reasonably expected, on the information available, to be aware of the insufficiency, had been satisfied.

Held: Appeal dismissed. (1) Part of the taxpayer's argument was based on eliding the requirement in s.29(1) for an officer to "discover" an insufficiency with the s.29(5) condition. However, s.29(1) and (5) did not import the same test, and HMRC's power to raise an assessment was therefore directly dependent on the level of awareness the notional officer would have based on the s.29(6) information. The exercise of the s.29(1) power was made by a real officer who had to come to a conclusion about a possible insufficiency based on all the available information at the time when the discovery assessment was made. Section 29(5) placed a restriction on the exercise of that power by reference to a hypothetical officer who had to carry out an evaluation of the adequacy of the return at a fixed and different point in time, on the basis of a fixed and limited class of information. The purpose of that condition was to test the adequacy of the taxpayer's disclosure, not to prescribe the circumstances which would justify the real officer in exercising the s.29(1) power. Although there would inevitably be points of contact between the real and hypothetical exercises, the tests were not the same, *Langham (Inspector of Taxes) v Veltema* [2004] EWCA Civ 193, [2004] S.T.C. 544, [2004] C.L.Y. 3789 and *Revenue and Customs Commissioners v Lansdowne Partners LP* [2011] EWCA Civ 1578, [2012] S.T.C. 544, [2012] C.L.Y. 3295 applied (see paras 17-25 of judgment). (2) The scope of the available s.29(6) information was not agreed and the taxpayer's argument before the Upper Tribunal had been in three parts, each of which assumed a different level of information and knowledge on the part of the hypothetical officer, namely where the officer had only the tax return; where he also had knowledge of HMRC's publicly stated views about the scheme; and where he also had attributed to him the results of HMRC's investigations into the scheme (para.26). The UT was entitled to conclude that the information contained in the return was not enough to have made the officer aware of an insufficiency. It was not a simple case as presented in the return, and the non-disclosure of the self-cancelling nature of the scheme's transaction was not compensated for by other factors disclosed. The fact that the information in the return might have been sufficient to cause the officer to ask further questions was not enough. That part of the taxpayer's case had been raised for the first time in the UT, and it was therefore for the UT to assess whether the s.29(5) condition was fulfilled. Its decision had been open to it on the facts and disclosed no error of principle in relation to the application of s.29(5) (paras 27-35). There had been no published determination about the effectiveness of the scheme until the decision in *Corbally-Stourton v Revenue and Customs Commissioners* [2008] S.T.C. (S.C.D.) 907, [2008] C.L.Y. 3649. There was no proper basis for attributing to the officer what might have been the thinking at the time in HMRC's Special Compliance Office. The exercise postulated by s.29(5) was a consideration by the officer of the information disclosed by the taxpayer by reference to the relevant legal principles, not by reference to what some particular department or officer at HMRC might at the time have thought about the efficacy of the scheme then under investigation, *Corbally-Stourton* considered (paras 36-37). The taxpayer's argument was based on s.29(6)(d)(i). However, the case was not concerned with information supplied by the promoters of the scheme, which was readily available through a link in the taxpayer's own disclosure and could therefore be treated as part of the taxpayer's disclosure. The information the taxpayer was seeking to have attributed to the officer was information obtained by a department within HMRC as a result of its investigations into the scheme. There was nothing in the return to indicate that the scheme had been under investigation, or that relevant information about a possible insufficiency was in HMRC's possession. It would have been highly speculative, rather than a matter of inference from the return, for the officer to have concluded that another branch of HMRC might have relevant information on the effectiveness of the scheme. There was no basis on which the existence of such information could reasonably be expected to be inferred from the limited disclosure in the return, *Revenue and Customs Commissioners v Charlton* [2012] UKFTT 770 (TCC), [2013] S.T.C. 866, [2013] C.L.Y. 3006 applied (paras 38-42).

SANDERSON v REVENUE AND CUSTOMS COMMISSIONERS, [2016] EWCA Civ 19, [2016] 4 W.L.R. 67, Patten LJ, CA (Civ Div).

2044 Capital gains tax–Discovery assessments–Tax avoidance scheme–Meaning of "discovery" in s.29(1) Taxes Management Act 1970–Tax officer's level of knowledge at relevant cut-off date

[Taxes Management Act 1970 (c.9) s.29, s.29(1), s.29(5)]

A taxpayer appealed against a decision of the First-tier Tribunal upholding an assessment made by HMRC under the Taxes Management Act 1970 s.29 based on the discovery of an insufficiency of tax. The taxpayer entered into a tax avoidance scheme for the 2004 tax year involving the use of capital redemption contracts (CRCs). In October 2006, he was identified as a possible participant in arrangements whose sole or main purpose was the avoidance of tax. At that stage, the HMRC officer concerned did not consider that there was a sufficient basis on which to raise an assessment but an investigation was commenced. In June 2009, the Court of Appeal found in favour of HMRC in *Drummond v Revenue and Customs Commissioners* [2009] EWCA Civ 608, [2009] S.T.C. 2206, [2010] C.L.Y. 3248 and permission to appeal was refused. Following that judgment, according to which CRC schemes were held to be ineffective, HMRC claimed to be satisfied that there was an insufficiency in the taxpayer's case. The taxpayer appealed to the tribunal, which held that the insufficiency had been discovered between June and November 2009 for the purposes of s.29(1). The tribunal also held that the assessment was not "stale", notwithstanding that it had not been submitted until shortly before the deadline of 31 January 2010. The taxpayer (1) argued that the tribunal had erred in proceeding on the basis that a discovery could comprise a "series of discoveries", and that "staleness" was determined by the statutory time limits; (2) challenged the tribunal's finding as to when the discovery was made; (3) challenged the tribunal's conclusion that the test in s.29(5) was satisfied.

Held: Appeal dismissed. (1)(a) For the purposes of s.29(1), the process of discovering that more tax was owing than had been assessed might not involve the HMRC officer reflecting on the matter or conducting further research after forming initial suspicions. The tribunal was not saying any more than that when it referred to a "series of discoveries" having been made by HMRC as a consequence of the series of judgments in *Drummond*. The reference to a "series of discoveries" was plainly a reference to the earlier stages of the legal process in *Drummond* and the thinking within HMRC which had developed in association with that, *Drummond* considered (see paras 41, 44-45 of judgment). (1)(b) Once the discovery was made, HMRC had to act with reasonable diligence if it was to make an assessment; otherwise the discovery became "stale" and the right to make an assessment was lost. The requirement for the discovery to be acted on while it remained fresh arose on the natural meaning of s.29(1) itself, *Charlton v Revenue and Customs Commissioners* [2011] UKFTT 467 (TC), [2011] S.F.T.D. 1160, [2012] C.L.Y. 3223 and *Corbally-Stourton v Revenue and Customs Commissioners* [2008] S.T.C. (S.C.D.) 907, [2008] C.L.Y. 3649 applied. However, the decision in each case was fact-sensitive. In the instant case, the tribunal had not directed itself properly to that issue and had elided the concept of staleness with that of time bar (paras 47, 52-55). (2) It was clear from the tribunal's decision that it understood the level of knowledge required for the purpose of a discovery within the terms of s.29(1). It had also understood that the test was a subjective one and had heard evidence from the HMRC officer concerned. There was no reason to question the tribunal's conclusion that, although that officer had had suspicions at an earlier stage, those suspicions did not lead him to form a view that there was an insufficiency until the Court of Appeal decision in *Drummond* (para.62). (3) Section 29(5) provided that HMRC, on discovering an insufficiency, was only entitled to make a further assessment where, at the time of completing the enquiry or at the time when the deadline for such enquiries had expired, the officer concerned could not reasonably have been aware of the insufficiency. The tribunal had applied the test of the hypothetical officer having a general knowledge of tax law and practice. Such an officer, at the cut-off date of 31 January 2006, would not have had any real understanding of CRCs and would not have been able to identify, from the tax return in issue, that an ineffective tax avoidance scheme was being used and had given rise to an insufficiency (paras 82-83). (4) (Obiter) Were it not for the wealth of authority in that area, the court would have adopted a construction of s.29(5) which did not depend on the identification of a hypothetical officer but which instead focused on the knowledge and expertise reasonably expected of the officer whose awareness was in question. On that approach, s.29(1) and (5) would be read together so that the test for awareness under s.29(5) was the same as the test for discovery under s.29(1). In the instant case, that would mean that s.29(5) would be satisfied unless it could be shown that the officer's lack of awareness was unreasonable, which was a conclusion that could not have been reached on the tribunal's findings (paras 79, 81).

PATTULLO v REVENUE AND CUSTOMS COMMISSIONERS, [2016] UKUT 270 (TCC), [2016] S.T.C. 2043, Lord Glennie, UT (Tax).

2045 Capital gains tax–Qualifying corporate bonds–Exemptions–Meaning of "sterling" in s.117(1)(b) Taxation of Chargeable Gains Act 1992

[Taxation of Chargeable Gains Act 1992 (c.12) s.117, s.117(1)(b), s.117(2)(b), s.21(1)(b)]

HMRC appealed against a decision of the First-tier Tribunal that corporate bonds purchased by the respondent taxpayer were qualifying corporate bonds within the meaning of the Taxation of Chargeable Gains Act 1992 s.117 and were therefore exempt from capital gains tax. The bonds were all issued, denominated and redeemable in sterling. Each contained one of two "future-proofing" clauses providing for conversion or redenomination in the event of the UK adopting the euro as its currency. The issue was whether the inclusion of the clauses prevented the bonds from being exempt from capital gains tax as "qualifying corporate bonds". HMRC argued that the bonds were not qualifying corporate bonds because the clauses were provisions for conversion into, or redemption in, "a currency other than sterling" within the meaning of s.117(1)(b). The taxpayer argued that "sterling" in s.117(1)(b) should be interpreted purposively as "the lawful currency of the UK", so that if the UK adopted the euro as its currency, the euro would not be "a currency other than sterling". The tribunal held that "sterling" meant British pounds sterling and not "the lawful currency of the UK from time to time". However, it held that the clauses did not prevent the bonds being qualifying corporate bonds either because the statutory disregard in s.117(2)(b) applied or because, upon any monetary union, sterling would cease to exist. The issues were (1) the construction of "sterling" in s.117(1)(b); (2) the scope of the disregard in s.117(2)(b); (3) the construction of the phrase "currency other than sterling" in s.117(1)(b); (4) the application of s.117 to the bonds.

Held: Appeal allowed. (1) The modern approach to statutory construction was to have regard to the purpose of the provision and to interpret its language, so far as possible, to give effect to that purpose, *Barclays Mercantile Business Finance Ltd v Mawson (Inspector of Taxes)* [2004] UKHL 51, [2005] 1 A.C. 684, [2005] C.L.Y. 3988 followed. Regard had to be had to the context and the legislative scheme as a whole, and the literal meaning of the statutory language could not be ignored (see paras 12-16, 33-35 of judgment). It was clear from s.21(1)(b) that "sterling" as used in s.117(1)(b) was the unit of measurement for the purpose of capital gains tax, *Goodbrand (Inspector of Taxes) v Loffland Bros North Sea Inc* [1998] S.T.C. 930, [1998] C.L.Y. 4619 considered. For capital gains tax purposes, currency other than sterling was not "money" but "money's worth" whose value had to be computed in sterling. The definition of qualifying corporate bonds did not cover normal commercial loan securities that were expressed in sterling but where the amount was determined by reference to the value of another currency or was convertible or redeemable in another currency. That was because such securities could generate gains or losses attributable to the fluctuation of currencies relative to sterling. Parliament intended that the UK's lawful currency should be the unit of measurement for capital gains tax purposes, and it gave effect to that intention by referring in s.117(1)(b) to the lawful currency, namely the pound sterling, and not by referring to any other currency that might in future become that lawful currency. No amount of purposive construction could result in "sterling" being construed as "the lawful currency of the UK from time to time" (paras 38-50). (2) The purpose of s.117(2)(b) was to apply a limited exception to s.117(1)(b). It meant that in assessing whether a bond contained a provision for conversion into, or redemption in, a currency other than sterling, a provision could be disregarded if the rate of exchange to be applied was that which ruled at the date of redemption. The exemption from capital gains tax was limited to sterling bonds, the redemption of which would not give rise to currency gains and losses, and redemption in a foreign currency at the rate of exchange prevailing at redemption was tantamount to redemption in sterling. The purpose of the legislation was to exclude from the exemption securities containing provisions for conversion or redemption into foreign currency, except in so far as those provisions were, in substance, no more than redemption in the currency at the exchange rate on redemption. The purpose of s.117 as a whole was to draw a clear dividing line between chargeable and exempt debt securities, and Parliament could not have intended the s.117(2)(b) disregard to apply to conversions going beyond redemption (paras 53-58). (3) A currency other than sterling was any currency that was not the pound sterling, irrespective of whether the pound sterling was in existence at the relevant time. The distinction between the two was not a distinction between money and money's worth (paras 58-60). (4) The future-proofing clauses were provisions for conversion into a currency other than sterling. It was immaterial that they were contingent, *Harding v Revenue and Customs Commissioners* [2008] EWHC 99 (Ch), [2008] S.T.C. 1965, [2008] C.L.Y. 3656 applied. It could not be said that when they became operative the effect of their application would not be a conversion of the bonds, *Klincke v Revenue and Customs Commissioners* [2010] UKUT 230 (TCC), [2010] S.T.C. 2032, [2010] C.L.Y. 3245 considered. Nor could it be said that any possible conversion would be a conversion at a time when the euro was the same currency as the pound sterling. It followed that the bonds were not qualifying corporate bonds (paras 62-71).

TRIGG v REVENUE AND CUSTOMS COMMISSIONERS *sub nom.* REVENUE AND CUSTOMS COMMISSIONERS v TRIGG, [2016] UKUT 165 (TCC), [2016] S.T.C. 1310, Asplin J, UT (Tax).

2046 **Capital gains tax–Reliefs–Lloyd's underwriters**

THE LLOYD'S UNDERWRITERS (ROLL-OVER RELIEF ON DISPOSAL OF ASSETS OF ANCILLARY TRUST FUND) (TAX) REGULATIONS 2016, SI 2016/597; made under the Finance Act 1993 s.182(1)(b). In force: 16 June 2016.

Changes to the rules of Lloyd's have had the effect of reducing the capital gains tax relief available to individual members of Lloyd's who convert to underwriting through successor companies and individual partners in Lloyd's partnerships that similarly convert. These Regulations ensure individual members and individual partners in Lloyd's partnerships remain entitled to broadly the same capital gains tax relief which would have been available if the Lloyd's rule changes had not been made.

2047 **Capital gains tax–Taper relief–Application of Enterprise Investment Scheme relief to disposal of mixed-use property**

[Taxation of Chargeable Gains Act 1992 (c.12) Sch.5B, Sch.A1 para.3]

A taxpayer appealed against a decision of the Upper Tribunal (*Stolkin v Revenue and Customs Commissioners* [2014] UKUT 165 (TCC), [2014] S.T.C. 2672, [2014] C.L.Y. 2857) that he was not entitled to divide the gain accruing on the disposal of mixed-use properties into business and non-business gains before applying enterprise investment scheme (EIS) relief. The taxpayer's 2005/2006 tax return had included chargeable gains in respect of two mixed-use properties. He divided the gain arising on the disposal of the properties between business and non-business use in accordance with the statutory provisions dealing with taper relief. He sought to apply EIS relief against the full amounts of the non-business gains, thereby deferring those chargeable gains to a subsequent tax year, and applying taper relief to the business gains, so far as not relieved by the EIS relief. Conversely, HMRC applied the EIS relief to the gains on the mixed-use assets, without any prior sub-division into business and business use. The balance was then separated into business and non-business elements and taper relief applied. Accordingly, not all of the balance of the gain benefited from the rate of taper relief for business use. The First-tier Tribunal found that the taxpayer's approach was correct. However, the Upper Tribunal held that HMRC's method was correct.

Held: Appeal dismissed. The taxpayer had erred in using the deeming provision in the Taxation of Chargeable Gains Act 1992 Sch.A1 para.3, which dealt with separate periods of business and non-business use, in the application of EIS relief so as to produce separate net gains in respect of notional business and non-business assets. That approach was not based on a correct interpretation of how the EIS and taper relief provisions were intended to operate. EIS relief applied in priority to taper relief. The first task in the case of a mixed-use asset was to calculate the overall gain on the sale of the real asset and apply EIS relief to calculate the gain accruing in the year of assessment. It was to that net gain that taper relief applied. The net gain had then to be divided according to the proportions of business and non-business use. At that stage the taper relief was to be calculated on the basis of the fiction that there had been separate disposals of separate assets giving rise to separate gains, applying the provisions of s.2A. That did not mean that there were deemed to be separate disposals of separate assets at the earlier EIS stage. Schedule 5B provided no basis for a notional sub-division of assets into business and non-business uses at the stage of the application of EIS relief. There was no provision for selectively applying EIS relief to gains on separate notional business and non-business assets (see paras 28-35 of judgment).

STOLKIN v REVENUE AND CUSTOMS COMMISSIONERS *sub nom.* REVENUE AND CUSTOMS COMMISSIONERS v STOLKIN, [2016] EWCA Civ 447, [2016] S.T.C. 1731, Floyd LJ, CA (Civ Div).

2048 **Capital gains tax–Transactions–Conversion of securities–Whether disposal for cash by taxpayers of two loan notes brought into charge accrued capital gain**

[Taxation of Chargeable Gains Act 1992 (c.12) s.116, s.116(1)(b), s.116(10), s.117, s.126(1)(a), s.132]

HMRC appealed against a decision (*Hancock v Revenue and Customs Commissioners* [2014] UKFTT 695 (TC), [2014] S.F.T.D. 1163, [2014] C.L.Y. 2851) that a disposal for cash by the respondent taxpayers of two loan notes did not bring into charge an accrued capital gain. The taxpayers had held the share capital of a company which they sold in August 2000. The initial consideration was given as loan notes (the 08/00 notes). The conditions, providing for repayment in US dollars, prevented the notes from being qualifying corporate bonds (QCBs) for the purposes of the Taxation of Chargeable Gains Act 1992 s.117. Further notes (the 03/01 notes) were issued in 2001. In 2002 those were varied to remove the rights to redemption in US dollars. The revised 03/01 notes were QCBs. In May 2003 both the 08/00 notes and the revised 03/01 notes were exchanged for two secured discounted loan notes, which were QCBs. The taxpayers redeemed those successor notes for cash in June. HMRC considered that that redemption generated a chargeable gain in respect of the capital gain accruing on the total value of the successor notes. HMRC argued that (1) there had been two relevant conversions. The first, the conversion of the 08/00 notes into successor notes, engaged s.116 because no QCBs were included in the holding of "original shares" for the purposes of that conversion, and, following the disposal of the QCBs in June 2003, s.116(10) triggered the charge in respect of the frozen gain. The second conversion, that of the revised 03/01 notes into successor notes, would not have engaged s.116, but since s.116 had applied on the earlier removal of the dollar redemption provision, s.116(1) triggered the charge on the frozen gain. The First-tier Tribunal had held that there had been a single composite conversion, the "original shares" for which had included QCBs, meaning that s.116(1)(b) had not been met; (2) alternatively, the conversion into successor loan notes should be disregarded under the principle in *WT Ramsay Ltd v Inland Revenue Commissioners* [1982] A.C. 300, [1981] C.L.Y. 1385 so that the 08/00 notes were treated as having been redeemed for cash. The tribunal had rejected that argument.

Held: Appeal allowed. (1) Section 116 directed that the transaction to which sections 127-130 would apply in the absence of s.116 should be identified. The relevant route into s.116 in the instant case was s.132. The first task was therefore to identify what the transaction was. "Transaction" in s.116 could not encompass more than one conversion of securities where the route to sections 127-131 was through s.132. Such a construction of "transaction" would be inconsistent with s.116(2), which provided that "transaction" included any conversion of securities within the meaning of s.132. The "transaction" in s.116(1) was the conversion of securities as defined in s.132, not some broader transaction that could include more than one conversion. Each "conversion" within s.132 was a different "transaction" within s.116(1) (see paras 37-40 of judgment). The next question was whether there had been one or more conversion of securities. Section 132 defined "the conversion of securities" non-exhaustively as including a conversion of a security which was a non-QCB into a security which was a QCB, and vice versa. It was significant that the examples given only encompassed unmixed conversions. Each original single asset or single security should be treated as the subject of a conversion whenever s.132 provided for that. That accorded with the structure of the provisions for the rollover of gains in cases such as reorganisations. The provisions addressed the situation where there would be a chargeable disposal of some asset for capital gains purposes; their purpose was to nullify that disposal but then to attach the latent gain or loss in respect of the original shares or securities to the new assets that then represented the original shares or securities (paras 41-43). The tribunal had considered that the reference in s.126(1)(a) to the original shares being "shares concerned in the reorganisation" suggested that different shares should be aggregated together if they were concerned in the reorganisation. However, the reference simply stated that the original shares had to have been held before the reorganisation and had to have been affected by it. In the case of conversions addressed by s.132, there was no such difficulty as was posed by the potential contrast between the "transaction" in s.116 and the "reorganisation" in s.126: in s.132, there was no such wider overall term and the various transactions that could occasion "conversions" did not envisage aggregation (paras 45-47). The 08/00 loan notes' conversion into successor notes was one conversion in which s.116(1) applied so that on the redemption of the successor notes, the frozen gain was realised under s.116(10). The redemption of the successor notes following the conversion of the revised 03/01 notes had triggered the gain calculated at the earlier point of the removal of the dollar redemption provision (para.50). (2) The tribunal had been right to reject

HMRC's secondary argument. The loan notes' conversion into successor notes, and the existence of those notes, could not be ignored, *Ramsay* considered (paras 65-66).

HANCOCK v REVENUE AND CUSTOMS COMMISSIONERS, [2016] UKUT 81 (TCC), [2016] S.T.C. 1433, Rose J, UT (Tax).

2049 Closure notices–HMRC guidance–Taxpayer's reliance on HMRC advice–Whether HMRC's decision to resile from guidance an abuse of power

[Taxation of Chargeable Gains Act 1992 (c.12) s.144ZA, s.17; Finance Act 2003 (c.14) s.158; Taxes Management Act 1970 (c.9) s.29]

A taxpayer applied for judicial review of four closure notices from HMRC rejecting his claims for capital losses between 1999 and 2002. As part of his remuneration the taxpayer had received options in an unapproved employee share option scheme at a nominal price. Such schemes were widespread in the banking sector at the time, but were investigated by HMRC as designed by employers to avoid tax and national insurance contributions. Those investigations led to settlements with all the respective employers and the issues were never litigated. The taxpayer had exercised his options on the same day as he had received them and had completed his tax returns on the basis of no gain or loss in accordance with the "market value rule" (as it was then understood), pursuant to the Taxation of Chargeable Gains Act 1992 s.17. Following the decision in *Mansworth (Inspector of Taxes) v Jelley* [2002] EWCA Civ 1829, [2003] S.T.C. 53, [2003] C.L.Y. 4161 that the grant of an option and its exercise were deemed to be a single transaction, HMRC published its 2003 guidance stating that the effect of that case would be to deem the acquisition cost for capital gains tax purposes to include the amount charged to income tax. The taxpayer applied to amend his return to claim a capital tax loss which he sought to offset against subsequent capital gains. His claims, and those of many others employed by banks, were kept open pending investigation into the schemes with the relevant employers, for the next 11 years. In the meantime, the Finance Act 2003 s.158 enacted a new s.144ZA to the 1992 Act to close the loophole for new claims. In 2009 HMRC published revised guidance, RCB 30/09, which reversed that of 2003. The taxpayer was one of that subset of taxpayers whose claims had remained open and were therefore not out of the reach of HMRC by virtue of the statutory protection under the Taxes Management Act 1970 s.29. The taxpayer contended that (1) he had a legitimate expectation that his claims would be dealt with consistently with the published 2003 guidance and HMRC's decision to resile from that guidance was so unfair as to amount to an abuse of power; (2) HMRC's refusal to recognise his claims when other taxpayers who had used employment related share options had been taxed in accordance with the 2003 guidance was unfair and inconsistent; (3) keeping the enquiry open for eleven years and then issuing closure notices was an unlawful use of the statutory power to enquire into a taxpayer's affairs. HMRC argued that its primary and overarching duty was to collect tax due.

Held: Application granted. (1) The authorities established the principle that HMRC should be held to its published statements because their publication was in the public interest, provided certainty for taxpayers, was part of the co-operative relationship with the public, and was part of the tax collection function, *R. v Inland Revenue Commissioners Ex p. MFK Underwriting Agents Ltd* [1990] 1 W.L.R. 1545, [1990] C.L.Y. 2651 applied and *R. (on the application of Davies) v Revenue and Customs Commissioners* [2011] UKSC 47, [2011] 1 W.L.R. 2625, [2011] C.L.Y. 3419 followed. HMRC could resile from its earlier guidance but, if it did, the circumstances had to be considered under the doctrine of legitimate expectation. The taxpayer had relied on the 2003 guidance and had a legitimate expectation that his claim for capital losses on the disposal of his shares would be taxed in accordance with it (see para.42 of judgment). (2) HMRC had to consider the fairness of withdrawing its 2003 guidance and to conduct a balancing exercise between the legitimate interests of taxpayers' and the public interest in collecting tax. There was evidence that the majority of *Mansworth* claims had been accepted by HMRC and only those in the financial sector had been made subject to enquiries that kept them open. The fact that some taxpayers had been treated differently made it not just a matter of private complaint but an issue of public interest. Further, HMRC should not be able to profit from its mistake, *Cameron v Revenue and Customs Commissioners* [2012] EWHC 1174 (Admin), [2012] S.T.C. 1691, [2012] C.L.Y. 3277, *R. (on the application of Rashid) v Secretary of State for the Home*

Department [2004] EWHC 2465 (Admin), Times, November 17, 2004 and *Mansworth* applied (paras 59-61, 71-73). (3) Although there had been no improper motive on the part of HMRC, the taxpayer was entitled to expect his tax affairs to be resolved more swiftly (para.74). (4) The duty to collect tax was a broad duty with a wide managerial discretion. HMRC could be required to forgo tax in an appropriate case where continuing to apply the wrong tax treatment would ensure consistency, and the alternative would be conspicuously unfair and an abuse of power, *Davies* followed. The closure notices were quashed (para.43).

R. (ON THE APPLICATION OF HELY-HUTCHINSON) v REVENUE AND CUSTOMS COMMISSIONERS, [2015] EWHC 3261 (Admin), [2016] S.T.C. 962, Whipple J, QBD (Admin).

2050 Construction industry scheme–Sub-contractors–Cancellation of registration for gross payment–Relevant factors in exercise of discretion under s.66 Finance Act 2004

[Finance Act 2004 (c.12) Sch.11 Pt 3 para.12, s.66; European Convention on Human Rights 1950 Protocol 1 art.1]

HMRC appealed against a First-tier Tribunal's decision (*JP Whitter (Waterwell Engineers) Ltd v Revenue and Customs Commissioners* [2012] UKFTT 639 (TC)) that it had failed to take into account a relevant factor when it cancelled a company's registration for gross payment under the construction industry scheme. The company received most of its business from contractors who were only prepared to work with sub-contractors registered for gross payment. For three years running, the company made several late payments of PAYE amounting to non-compliance with the conditions of its gross payment registration under the Finance Act 2004 Sch.11 Pt 3 para.12, thereby putting its registration at risk. HMRC allowed the company's appeals for the first two years, but in the third year of non-compliance it cancelled the company's registration and refused its appeal. At the tribunal hearing, the company stated that the cancellation would have a significant detrimental effect on its business and the hardship caused would be disproportionate to its failures. The tribunal decided that was a relevant factor which HMRC should have taken into account when exercising its discretion to cancel a gross payment registration under s.66 of the Act. It allowed the company's appeal but decided that it did not have jurisdiction to substitute its own view. The company submitted that HMRC's exercise of its s.66 discretion should comply with ECHR Protocol 1 art.1 and had to be proportionate. HMRC argued that its discretion focused on past compliance and the expectation of future compliance, and had nothing to do with the consequences of non-compliance.

Held: Appeal allowed. (1) Protocol 1 art.1 had no part to play in the exercise of HMRC's power under s.66. Case law demonstrated that the previous version of the construction industry scheme had involved no breach of the Protocol, and that reasoning applied equally to the current scheme, *Shaw (Inspector of Taxes) v Vicky Construction Ltd* [2002] EWHC 2659 (Ch), [2002] S.T.C. 1544, [2003] C.L.Y. 4251 and *Barnes (Inspector of Taxes) v Hilton Main Construction Ltd* [2005] EWHC 1355 (Ch), [2005] S.T.C. 1532, [2005] C.L.Y. 4036 applied. Nor was there any reason to take Convention rights into account when ascertaining the scope of the power or the identification of matters to be taken into account. Those were matters purely for domestic law, *Bank Mellat v HM Treasury* [2013] UKSC 39, [2014] A.C. 700, [2013] C.L.Y. 194 considered (see paras 30-31, 37, 40 of judgment). (2) The financial consequences of the cancellation of a taxpayer's registration for gross payment were not a relevant factor to be taken into account by HMRC when deciding how to exercise its s.66 discretion. The purpose of the power to cancel had to be emphasised. The construction industry scheme was a collection scheme, not a scheme for the imposition of tax. The strict conditions required to obtain registration for gross payment reflected the balance that Parliament considered appropriate to ensure the effective collection of tax: a sub-contractor was entitled to receive gross payment but only if they could show a good track record of compliance. Similarly, registration should only continue if the sub-contractor continued to show an adequate track record. The power to cancel the registration was there principally to ensure compliance with the substance of the scheme. There might be circumstances where HMRC might decide that there was no need to cancel a registration notwithstanding non-compliance, such as where it was satisfied that the failure would not be repeated. In contrast, the financial consequences of a decision to cancel registration were irrelevant to any issue of future compliance. Further, all sub-contractors who were registered for gross payment were taken to know of the risk of cancellation if they did not meet the compliance test. A taxpayer whose business would be destroyed by cancellation could not repeatedly fail in its compliance obligations and then rely on that inevitable destruction as a ground for challenging the decision to cancel (paras 63-67). (3) The tribunal had correctly concluded that it had a supervisory function, which was what might be expected in a case where HMRC was exercising a discretion, and that it could not substitute its own decision for that of HMRC. Further, a decision by HMRC to cancel a taxpayer's registration for gross payment that had not been properly made should ordinarily be quashed and not remitted, *Piers Consulting Ltd v Revenue and Customs Commissioners* [2011] UKFTT 613 (TC) and *Cardiff Lift Co v Revenue and Customs Commissioners* [2011] UKFTT 628 (TC), [2012] S.F.T.D. 85, [2012] C.L.Y. 3319 applied (paras 76-83).

JP WHITTER (WATERWELL ENGINEERS) LTD v REVENUE AND CUSTOMS COMMISSIONERS *sub nom.* REVENUE AND CUSTOMS COMMISSIONERS v JP WHITTER (WATERWELL ENGINEERS) LTD, [2015] UKUT 392 (TCC), [2016] S.T.C. 204, Warren J, UT (Tax).

2051 Corporation tax–Accelerated payment notices–Contributions to employer-finance retirement benefit schemes–Whether implementation of accelerated payment notice regime abuse of power

[Corporation Tax Act 2009 (c.4) s.1292(5); Finance Act 2011 (c.11); Finance Act 2014 (c.26) s.219, s.220; European Convention on Human Rights 1950 Protocol 1 art.1]

The claimant taxpayers applied for judicial review of the defendant HMRC's decision to issue accelerated payment notices (APNs) requiring them to make payments equal to their disputed corporation tax liabilities. The taxpayers had set up employer-financed retirement benefit schemes (EFRBS). They claimed relief from corporation tax for payments that they had made to the EFRBS on the basis that the payments were "qualifying benefits" under the Corporation Tax Act 2009 s.1292(5). The Finance Act 2011 amended the definition of "qualifying benefit" to exclude employer contributions unless they gave rise to an employment income tax charge. HMRC's position was that employer contributions to EFRBS might be earnings and that schemes entered into before 6 April 2011 did not enable companies to claim relief from corporation tax for employer contributions paid as qualifying benefits. HMRC issued APNs to the taxpayers under the Finance Act 2014 s.219 on the basis that a tax enquiry was open and the EFRBS were "disclosure of tax avoidance schemes" arrangements which had resulted in a tax advantage. The taxpayers argued that (1) HMRC's decisions to issue APNs were ultra vires the 2014 Act because HMRC had not determined whether the taxpayers had a tax liability and because the taxpayers had been unaware of HMRC's legal position; (2) the notice requirements of s.220 of the 2014 Act had not been met; (3) the court should depart from *R. (on the application of Rowe) v Revenue and Customs Commissioners* [2015] EWHC 2293 (Admin), [2015] B.T.C. 27, [2015] C.L.Y. 2512 and *Walapu v Revenue and Customs Commissioners* [2016] EWHC 658 (Admin), [2016] 4 All E.R. 955, [2016] 2115 in which claims for judicial review of HMRC's decisions to issue APNs had been dismissed; (4) issuing the APNs had violated ECHR Protocol 1 art.1, breached the principles of natural justice and was otherwise unreasonable and unfair.

Held: Application refused. (1) There was no convincing explanation for why HMRC's position on the statutory construction of "qualifying benefits" had not been litigated and decided upon before the 2014 Act had introduced APNs. HMRC should avoid further delays in resolving the correct interpretation of "qualifying benefits", because such clarification would resolve similar cases involving EFRBS without the need for detailed examination of complicated schemes, or would at least limit or focus investigations in such cases. Nevertheless, in the instant case, the taxpayers' assertions that HMRC had not formed a view on the efficacy of their claim for relief and that they had been unaware of its legal position had no foundation. They had entered into the EFRBS on advice regarding their effectiveness in achieving corporation tax deductions. They had not been unaware of HMRC's published views and that their claims for relief were questionable, or of the possibility of a situation in which relief from corporation tax would be available yet no PAYE and national insurance contributions would be paid on the contributions because they were time-barred. The assessments issued by HMRC were protective and did not show that it had changed its interpretation of the underlying legislation. HMRC's expressed view was that the interpretation relied on by the taxpayers to claim relief was incorrect; accordingly their claims were disputed (see paras 52, 55-56, 59-77, 88 of judgment). (2) On both a linguistic and purposive approach, the notice requirement for the issue of a valid APN could not be satisfied unless, to the best of a designated officer's information and belief, he was not satisfied that the claimed tax advantage was lawfully available and should be allowed so that he had determined that the claimed tax advantage was disputed. The officer could act on HMRC's published view and intention to argue its point, and on the basis that the taxpayers' claims for relief were disputed. The notice requirement was accordingly met (paras 35, 79-82). (3) The taxpayers' argument that *Rowe* and *Walapu* should be departed from was based on the same mirage relied on to establish that HMRC had not reached a decision on the efficacy of their individual schemes, and therefore failed. In any event, the decisions in *Rowe* and *Walapu* were not plainly wrong and would not be departed from on issues relating to legality, necessity and proportionality, *Rowe* and *Walapu* considered (paras 84-86). (4) The taxpayers had known the case against them and the reasons for the assessments for some time. The assessments were protective rather than unfair or abusive. The implementation of the APN regime in their cases was not an abuse of power. It reversed the cash flow advantage of further delay, which was what Parliament had intended, and it included protective assessments (paras 87-88).

R. (ON THE APPLICATION OF VITAL NUT CO LTD) v REVENUE AND CUSTOMS COMMISSIONERS, [2016] EWHC 1797 (Admin), [2016] 4 W.L.R. 144, Charles J, QBD (Admin).

2052 Corporation tax–Cessation of business–Transfer of potential relief to successor company–Meaning of "trade" in s.343(3) Income and Corporation Taxes Act 1988

[Income and Corporation Taxes Act 1988 (c.1) s.337, s.343, s.343(1), s.343(3), s.393(1)]

HMRC appealed against the First-tier Tribunal's decision that the respondent taxpayer (L) was entitled to relief under the Income and Corporation Taxes Act 1988 s.393(1). L, a retailer, had acquired the entire issued share capital of another company (C) which carried on a similar trade. C's business was hived up to L, and C became dormant. C had accumulated trading losses of about £3 million. L maintained that it was entitled, pursuant to s.343 and s.393, to obtain relief for those losses by setting them off against the income of the enlarged business. HMRC decided that L could only set the losses against any income generated by what was formerly C's business, and given that that part of the business remained unprofitable, no relief was available. The issue before the tribunal was whether the terms of s.343(3) required L to undertake "streaming" of the income of the combined trade, so as to identify separately the income derived from C's former business and the income derived from L's continued trade. L advanced two hypotheses, the "trade" hypothesis (that the loss was to be treated as having been sustained by the successor, rather than the predecessor, in carrying on the trade), and the "quantum" hypothesis (that the amount of the loss was the amount for which the predecessor would have been entitled to relief had it continued to carry on the trade), to support its argument that there was no proper basis on which s.343(3) could be interpreted in the manner for which HMRC argued. The tribunal accepted L's argument that there was no legislative basis for undertaking a streaming exercise, that to do so would pose practical difficulties, and that L's approach was more closely aligned to commercial reality. HMRC submitted that the tribunal had committed an error which undermined its reasoning: after outlining L's "trade hypothesis", it had observed that "the successor should be treated as having incurred the losses in question". That error led it to the further incorrect proposition that "any subsequent entitlement to losses under s.393 could only be an entitlement of" the combined trade. It was plain that the "trade" mentioned in s.343(3) must be the predecessor's trade; the provision could not be read as if the trade was the combined trade of the successor. There was no need for any mention of streaming in s.343(3), because it was implicit in the words used that the relief was available only by reference to the income of the predecessor's continued trade.

Held: Appeal allowed. (1) Section 343(3) represented an exception to the finality of s.337, without which the potential relief in respect of accumulated losses would be forfeited on cessation of the trade by the predecessor. Its purpose was not to put the successor in a better position than the predecessor would have been in had it carried on the trade, but to transfer the potential for relief, without change, to the successor in a case falling within s.343(1). It was clear that "the trade" to which s.343(3) referred was the same trade as that to which s.343(1) referred, namely the predecessor's trade. The predecessor could not have carried on the enlarged trade, but only its own, smaller, trade, and it was only by reference to the profits, if any, of that trade that it would have been entitled to relief for accumulated losses. The draftsman had not included any provision for streaming because it was unnecessary to do so (see paras 28-29 of judgment). (2) The taxpayer's argument that s.343 gave rise to two hypotheses had set the tribunal on the wrong track. There was nothing hypothetical about the amount, or quantum, for which relief was available. It was, as s.343(3) made clear, the "amount for which the predecessor would have been entitled to relief". There was no need for a trade hypothesis when the meaning of the subsection was clear, but it was probably that argument which led the tribunal to the observation that "[t]he basic premise of the relieving provision in s 343(1) (combined with s 337) is that if one company ceases to carry on a trade and another begins to carry it on, the trade of the original company has disappeared"; and, from it, and the absence of an express streaming provision in s.343(3), to the conclusion that relief was available by reference to the income of the enlarged trade (para.30). (3) The tribunal had erred in its consideration of the commercial reality of the situation. It was not permissible to disregard the words of a statute because of a perception of practical difficulty. Moreover, the difficulty could be avoided or minimised by careful record-keeping. The policy reasons behind the restriction of the successor to relief only in those circumstances in which relief would have been available to the predecessor were obvious: if it were otherwise there would be ample opportunity for abuse (para.31).

LEEKES LTD v REVENUE AND CUSTOMS COMMISSIONERS *sub nom.* REVENUE AND CUSTOMS COMMISSIONERS v LEEKES LTD, [2016] UKUT 320 (TCC), [2016] S.T.C. 1970, Roth J, UT (Tax).

2053 Corporation tax–Closure notices–Scope of appeal to First-tier Tribunal defined by conclusions in closure notice–Whether HMRC restricted on appeal to process of reasoning by which it reached those conclusions

[Finance Act 1996 (c.8) Sch.9 para.13, Sch.9 para.19A, Sch.9 para.19A(3)]

The appellant company (F) appealed against a decision (*Fidex Ltd v Revenue and Customs Commissioners* [2014] UKUT 454 (TCC), [2015] S.T.C. 702, [2015] C.L.Y. 2435) that it was not entitled to claim a trading loss under a tax avoidance scheme. F had adopted a tax avoidance scheme designed to create a tax loss which could be surrendered to other companies in its group. The group acquired F's shares before F issued preference shares to its tax adviser. Those shares had rights which matched various bonds held by F and they conferred upon the tax adviser an entitlement to 95% of the amounts which F had received from the corresponding bond. F then changed its accounting principles for the year ending 31 December 2005, indicating that it would now use International Financial Reporting Standards (IFRS). As a consequence, when it prepared its 2005 accounts, neither the preference shares nor 95% of the bonds were shown on its balance sheet since the terms of the preference shares and the economic qualities of the bonds cancelled each other out and IFRS accounting policy required them to be "derecognised". Under the Finance Act 1996 Sch.9 para.19A, on a change of accounting policy, where the carrying value of a loan relationship in a company's accounts changed between the end of one accounting period and the beginning of the next, the difference had to be treated as deductible or taxable in the later year. F therefore claimed a debit of €84 million, giving rise to a corresponding trade loss although it had not suffered any economic loss. HMRC issued a closure notice reducing the amount available for F to surrender as group relief by €84 million on the basis that there was no difference or debit under para.19A(3). F appealed to the First-tier Tribunal and HMRC raised a new argument that F should be denied the benefit of any debits arising under para.19A because it had an unallowable purpose in being party to a loan relationship within the meaning of Sch.9 para.13. F argued that the tribunal had no jurisdiction to hear any argument based on para.13 because that had not been mentioned in the closure notice. The tribunal found (*Fidex Ltd v Revenue and Customs Commissioners* [2011] UKFTT 713 (TC)) that it had jurisdiction to hear the issue, but nevertheless decided that F should be allowed to bring the debit into account. The Upper Tribunal agreed that the terms of the closure notice did not preclude HMRC from arguing that Sch.9 para.13 applied. It went on to overturn the tribunal's decision and find that Sch.9 para.13 did operate to deny F the benefit of that loss. The issues were whether (1) the terms of the closure notice precluded HMRC from raising the para.13 issue; (2) the UT had erred in finding that the debit was wholly attributable to an unallowable purpose.

Held: Appeal dismissed. (1) In relation to closure notices, it was necessary to apply the following principles, which had been set out in *Tower MCashback LLP 1 v Revenue and Customs Commissioners* [2011] UKSC 19, [2011] 2 A.C. 457, [2011] C.L.Y. 3277: (a) the scope and subject matter of an appeal were defined by the conclusions stated in the closure notice and by the amendments required to give effect to those conclusions; (b) what mattered were the conclusions set out in the closure notice, not the process of reasoning by which HMRC had reached those conclusions; (c) the closure notice had to be read in context in order to properly understand its meaning; (d) subject to the requirements of fairness and proper case management, HMRC could advance new arguments before the tribunal to support the conclusions set out in the closure notice, *Tower McCashback* followed (see para.45 of judgment). HMRC had been free to deploy new arguments in support of its conclusions, subject to the tribunal's exercise of its case management powers to ensure that F was not ambushed. There had been no suggestion of any ambush and no suggestion that F had not been fully able to present its case. The tribunal had considered the closure notice in context and had identified the conclusions which it contained. It had properly directed itself by reference to the principles set out in *Tower McCashback* and had proceeded to consider the closure notice in the context of the enquiry which it completed. It had noted that the enquiry was not some kind of roving investigation into F's tax returns, but a focused consideration of whether, having regard to the loan relationships code in Sch.9, the implementation of the scheme served to increase the loss shown in F's self-assessment tax return. It was not unfair to F to hold that the issue should be examined as widely as might be necessary to determine whether it was entitled to what it had claimed. The tribunal did have jurisdiction to hear HMRC's argument based on para.13 (paras 61-64, 68). (2) The debit arose from and was entirely attributable to the tax avoidance scheme. Without that scheme there would have been no debit at all. The UT had come to the correct conclusion that on a just and reasonable apportionment, the debit was wholly attributable to an unallowable purpose for which the bonds were held (paras 74-75).

FIDEX LTD v REVENUE AND CUSTOMS COMMISSIONERS, [2016] EWCA Civ 385, [2016] S.T.C. 1920, Arden LJ, CA (Civ Div).

2054 Corporation tax–Dividends–Corporation tax levied in breach of EU law–Mistake-based restitutionary cause of action

[Civil Procedure Rules 1998 Pt 35]

The second claimant taxpayer applied for summary judgment on its claim to recover corporation tax levied in breach of EU law, together with compound interest, or for an interim payment. The claim related to certain dividends paid to the taxpayer by its wholly-owned Dutch subsidiary in the accounting periods ending 30 September 1993, 1996 and 1997. The taxpayer sought to recover corporation tax under Sch.D Case V which it said had been levied on the dividends in breach of EU law, together with compound interest from the dates when the tax was paid until judgment. The claim relied on the cause of action established in *Woolwich Equitable Building Society v Inland Revenue Commissioners* [1993] A.C. 70, [1992] C.L.Y. 2508 and the mistake-based restitutionary cause of action, as developed and applied in the context of the Franked Investment Income group litigation so as to provide the test claimants in that group litigation with an effective remedy for recovering tax which the European Court of Justice had held to be unlawfully levied. HMRC submitted that the fact that permission to appeal to the Court of Appeal on issues of law relevant to the taxpayer's claim had been granted in *Test Claimants in the FII Group Litigation v Revenue and Customs*

Commissioners [2014] EWHC 4302 (Ch), [2015] S.T.C. 1471, [2015] C.L.Y. 2422 meant that it could not be said that HMRC had no real prospect of successfully defending the claim, on those and similar issues. HMRC further submitted that, although the taxpayer was entitled to an interim payment in respect of part of its claim, parts of the dividends sourced from revaluation adjustments, exempt profits on the liquidation of a subsidiary, and the return of share premium were not subject to Dutch corporation tax so that the taxpayer would not be entitled to a tax credit in respect of them.

Held: Application granted in part. (1) It was inappropriate to grant summary judgment for the reasons given by HMRC. The claim turned to a significant extent on questions of law which were either already under appeal in the *FII* proceedings, or were sufficiently similar that their ultimate resolution was likely to be heavily influenced by the outcome of that appeal. The test for granting permission to appeal was the same as that for summary judgment and the court accordingly could not be satisfied that HMRC had no realistic prospect of successfully defending the claim. There was a further reason why the court could not grant summary judgment: the claim depended heavily on evidence of Dutch tax law, and the relevant Dutch law had not been pleaded, and no expert evidence had been adduced in accordance with CPR Pt 35 (see paras 35-36 of judgment). (2) HMRC's argument about the revaluation adjustments was most unlikely to succeed at trial. It seemed clear that the relevant adjustments formed part of the taxpayer's accounting profits and as such fell within the basic charge to Dutch corporation tax. The adjustments were then excluded from the taxable amount, with the result that the tax base was correspondingly narrowed and the effective rate of tax was reduced. The exclusion of the adjustments fell squarely within the reasoning of the ECJ which led it to conclude that a tax credit would have been needed in order to achieve equivalence between the exemption system for domestic dividends and the imputation system for foreign dividends which the UK then operated, *Test Claimants in the FII Group Litigation v Inland Revenue Commissioners (C-35/11)* EU:C:2012:707, [2013] Ch. 431 considered. It followed that the taxpayer would succeed at trial on its claim to be entitled to a tax credit on the dividends in so far as they were sourced from profits arising from the revaluations. For similar reasons, an interim payment should also be made in respect of part of the 1997 dividends derived from profits on the liquidation of a subsidiary which were in principle within the charge to Dutch corporation tax, although they were excluded from the taxable amount by virtue of a participation exemption. However, HMRC's arguments were likely to succeed in relation to part of the 1997 dividends paid out of share premium reserve, which could not in principle be regarded as liable to Dutch corporation tax. It followed that the claim for an interim payment succeeded, save in relation to those parts of the 1997 dividends which were sourced from share premium account (see paras 47-62).

SIX CONTINENTS LTD v INLAND REVENUE COMMISSIONERS, [2015] EWHC 2884 (Ch), [2015] B.T.C. 29, Henderson J, Ch D.

2055 Corporation tax–Double tax relief–Companies' acquisition of partnership interests in addition to normal trading activities–Acquisition and funding costs revenue expenditure incurred wholly and exclusively for purpose of companies' sole trades

[Income and Corporation Taxes Act 1988 (c.1) s.114, s.393A, s.797, s.798]

Two financial dealing companies in the Investec group appealed against a decision of HMRC refusing to allow them to offset their costs of acquiring interests in highly tax positive leasing partnerships. The appellants acquired interests in leasing partnerships as part of a tax mitigation scheme in which the leases were terminated to realise profits. The appellants sought to claim double tax relief in the UK for tax they had paid in Hong Kong as a result of one of the transactions. The appellants claimed that, as financial dealers, they should be able to deduct the costs of purchasing the partnership interests from the rental income or the sale proceeds of the rentals received whilst they were partners. They claimed that they were conducting only one trade consisting of their sole financial trades which encompassed their participation in the partnerships; alternatively, they claimed that, if they were conducting one sole trade and a second trade in partnership, they should be permitted to deduct the same costs and offset them against the partnership income so as to end up paying tax solely on the overall net profit. HMRC issued a closure notice on the basis that the profits of the sole trades and the participation in the partnership trades should be computed separately. The issues were whether (1) the appellants were conducting one trade or two separate trades; (2) the expenditure of purchasing and funding partnership interests was capital expenditure, and if not whether that expenditure was incurred wholly and exclusively for trading purposes; (3) the commissioners were precluded by the closure notices from raising the issue of whether the dealing expense of buying and funding the partnerships could diminish the taxable profits in the partnerships on the receipt or sale of rentals, such that the appellants were taxable only on their net profits; (4) the commissioners could challenge the basis on which the appellants had claimed credit for Hong Kong tax.

Held: Judgment accordingly. (1) Although the appellants had acquired interests in partnerships which were conducting leasing trades, the costs they had incurred in acquiring those partnership interests had nothing to do with the generation of profits in the leasing business. The appellants had no interest in participating as active partners in the leasing business: the sole aim of the transactions was to effect the pre-planned step of terminating the leases so as to receive the distributions. Thus, for tax purposes, the appellants' roles in the partnership trades were distinct from their other sole trades and it followed that they had two separate trades (see paras 44, 46-47, 53, 71 of judgment). (2) The costs of acquiring and funding the partnership interests was revenue expenditure, made in order to further the short-term venture of co-operating with the former lessors to terminate the leases and profit from the proceeds. That conclusion was reinforced by the appellants' position as financial trading companies which periodically dealt in receivables. All the disputed expenditure was incurred wholly and exclusively for the purpose of each of the sole trades of the appellants (paras 95, 99-100). (3) The intended effect of the closure notice was to advance HMRC's primary contention that the costs should be disallowed and that the partnership profits attributable to each partner under the Income and Corporation Taxes Act 1988 s.114 should constitute the total relevant taxable profits. The statutory machinery provided no way of drafting a closure notice with one conclusion and related adjustments which then enabled HMRC to advance different arguments relating to the same subject matter. However, having regard to the context of the discussions between the parties and references to other potential issues made in both the closure notice and its covering letter, HMRC were not precluded from raising other contentions in relation to the treatment of the partnership transactions. In calculating the profits of the appellants' sole trades, it was appropriate to deduct from the gross income the amount already taxed under s.114. Relief for those expenses or losses in the sole trades could be obtained by offsetting against other sole trade profits or by carrying the losses forward or, by virtue of s.393A, offsetting them against the s.114 partnership profits, *Inland Revenue Commissioners v FS Securities Ltd* [1965] A.C. 631, [1964] C.L.Y. 1810 followed (paras 112, 124-126, 148-149). (4) Section 797 and s.798 of the Act effectively provided that the limit on credit for foreign tax in relation to income was the corporation tax attributable to the income, and that the amount of corporation tax attributable to trade income was calculated by taking into account deductions or expenses which would be allowable in the computation of the taxpayer's liability. On the basis of the "two trades" analysis, there was no limitation on double tax credit relief in relation to the Hong Kong tax, save for a reduction in the event of the appellants being able to claim offsetting of the sole trade losses against the partnership profits under s.393A (paras 157-158).

INVESTEC ASSET FINANCE PLC v REVENUE AND CUSTOMS COMMISSIONERS; INVESTEC BANK PLC v REVENUE AND CUSTOMS COMMISSIONERS, [2016] UKFTT 356 (TC), [2016] S.F.T.D. 677, Judge Howard M Nowlan, FTT (Tax).

2056 Corporation tax–Double tax relief–Payment of dividends between related group companies–Whether dividends were source of profits throughout chain

[Income and Corporation Taxes Act 1988 (c.1) Sch.D, s.799(1), s.801(1), s.802(2); Finance Act 2000 (c.17); Finance Act 2001 (c.9)]

A UK company (P) appealed against a decision (*Peninsular & Oriental Steam Navigation Co v Revenue and Customs Commissioners* [2015] UKUT 312 (TCC),

[2015] S.T.C. 2393, [2015] C.L.Y. 2438) upholding HMRC's reduction of its claim for double tax relief. P was the parent company of a group of companies. It had claimed double tax relief on a dividend received from a foreign subsidiary, but originating from a UK subsidiary. The dividend was taxable under the Income and Corporation Taxes Act 1988 Sch.D. P was entitled to credit for foreign tax suffered by the paying company and its subsidiaries. P sought to maximise the amount of credit in response to changes in the law under the Finance Act 2000 and the Finance Act 2001. The 2000 Act limited the amount of foreign tax credit to the maximum amount of UK corporation tax via a "mixer cap" by amending the double tax code in the 1988 Act. The 2001 Act sought to mitigate the effects on multi-national companies by allowing credit for tax that would have been paid by the UK subsidiary of a foreign subsidiary if the UK subsidiary had not been relieved from paying UK tax at the full rate. The purpose of the 2001 Act was said to be to put the UK subsidiary of a foreign subsidiary of a UK parent into the same position as the UK subsidiary of a UK parent which paid a dividend to that parent. That dividend payment was not subject to UK corporation tax, which was considered unfair. HMRC argued that underlying tax had to have been paid for double tax relief to be given, the "tax borne" argument, and that the dividend paid by the UK subsidiary had to flow through to the parent company, namely be the source of profits for successive dividends up the chain, the "disappearing dividend" argument.

Held: Appeal allowed in part. (1) There were two preliminary points. First, the proper approach to interpreting the statutory code was to read it as a whole piece of prose, not to pull out phrases, potentially without their context, or to overcomplicate the matter with, necessarily, selective examples of the operation of the provisions. Second, one had to be cautious before accepting any assertion of purpose of an Act of Parliament, not set out in any provision of the Act itself, made by a party propounding a particular statutory interpretation. Such assertions could be self-fulfilling or examples of "confirmation bias". Exceptions could be made for assertions of purpose deducible by implication from the legislative scheme or clearly stated in some material which was admissible as an aid to interpretation (see paras 57-60 of judgment). (2) The legislation contained a trilogy of statutory hypotheses. The first was in s.801(1) of the 1988 Act. It treated third country and UK taxes payable by an overseas subsidiary as taxes payable under the law of the country in which that company was resident. UK tax therefore became notionally foreign tax. The second hypothesis was in s.802(2). It stated that "underlying tax payable by the third company [the UK subsidiary]" was to be treated for the purpose of s.801(1) as tax paid by the overseas company. The third hypothesis was in the tailpiece to s.801(2), "to the extent that it would be taken into account under this Part if the dividend had been paid by a company resident outside the [UK] to a company resident in the [UK] and arrangements had provided for underlying tax to be taken into account." The underlying tax attributed to the UK company by the second hypothesis underwent a further transformation because the dividend was treated as paid by an overseas company and as qualifying to be taken into account for double tax relief purposes. P's scheme failed not because of that statutory trilogy, but because of the way in which it was implemented. It failed because of the disappearing dividend argument. High level dividends had to flow through to the UK parent company to some extent. In the instant case, the UK subsidiary had paid a lawful dividend to the overseas subsidiary, but the dividend had ceased to form part of the profits of the foreign subsidiary because it had used most of it to write down its investment in the UK subsidiary (paras 66-67, 71-75). (3) It was very attractive to read the words "tax borne" in tax legislation as meaning "tax paid". Tax "borne" was generally tax suffered. However, when the hypotheses in s.801 were given effect, the underlying tax payable was correctly described as deemed underlying tax payable for the purpose of s.801(1), and, therefore, for the purposes of s.799(1). The underlying tax payable produced by the hypotheses was treated as underlying tax paid and there was no need to discount the actual underlying tax by any amount if it was not in fact payable because it was relieved by group relief or capital allowances or whatever it might have been. The hypotheses prescribed the only facts which could be taken into account in the hypothetical world. As the Upper Tribunal had remarked, the idea that double tax relief would be available under s.801(2) if only £1 was paid, but not if tax was fully relieved by capital allowances, was capricious. It was unreal to conclude that Parliament would have provided for foreign tax credit in a group situation in all cases except the common one where a subsidiary had, for reasons of sensible group financial management, taken advantage of available relief (para.68).

PENINSULAR & ORIENTAL STEAM NAVIGATION CO v REVENUE AND CUSTOMS COMMISSIONERS, [2016] EWCA Civ 468, [2016] S.T.C. 2001, Arden LJ, CA (Civ Div).

2057 Corporation tax–Foreign income dividends–Portfolio holdings–Dividends paid on shares in foreign companies held as investments–Tax credit to which taxpayer entitled by way of reduction of unlawful charge to corporation tax on foreign dividends

[Income and Corporation Taxes Act 1988 (c.1) Sch.D, s.790]

The appellant HMRC appealed against a judge's findings in the respondent's claim (*Prudential Assurance Co Ltd v Revenue and Customs Commissioners* [2013] EWHC 3249 (Ch), [2014] S.T.C. 1236, [2014] C.L.Y. 2874) to recover tax unlawfully levied. The case related to portfolio holdings, dividends paid on shares in foreign companies held as investments, where the investor held less than 10% of the voting power in the company in question. *Test Claimants in the FII Group Litigation v Inland Revenue Commissioners (C-446/04)* EU:C:2006:774, [2012] 2 A.C. 436, [2007] C.L.Y. 3971 established that the UK's tax treatment of dividends received by UK companies was in breach of the EC Treaty art.56, and hence unlawful, to the extent that it discriminated between dividends paid by UK companies and dividends paid by foreign companies. The judge held that EU law required a tax credit for the higher of tax actually paid and the foreign nominal rate of tax of the dividend-paying company capped at the UK corporation tax rate. He concluded that the UK legislation would have been compliant with EU law if it had provided for a dual credit in respect of portfolio dividends and that a conforming interpretation could be given to the Income and Corporation Taxes Act 1988 s.790 by construing it as providing for the grant of a tax credit for foreign dividends to the extent necessary to comply with EU law. HMRC submitted that EU law required a credit for the actual tax rate paid capped at the UK corporation tax rate and that the judge had been wrong to reject pro-rating methodology.

Held: Appeal allowed in part. (1) The judgment was a masterpiece of exposition and reasoning. The judge had correctly analysed the decision in *Test Claimants in the FII Group Litigation v Inland Revenue Commissioners (C-35/11)* EU:C:2012:707, [2013] Ch. 431, *FII Group Litigation* followed. The issue in relation to the correct rate concerned the amount of the tax credit to which a taxpayer was entitled by way of reduction of the unlawful charge to corporation tax on foreign dividends under Sch.D Case V. The contention that credit should be at the actual rate could not stand with the decision in *C-35/11*. The exemption from tax in respect of dividends from UK companies was treated as an exemption at the nominal rate of tax in the UK, in effect amounting to a tax credit at the nominal rate; and it was treated as being at that rate because the profits of the paying company were taxed at the nominal tax rate also. Such an approach had the benefit of simplicity of operation and avoided the mischief identified in *C-35/11*. Whether the credit should be at the nominal or the actual rate of tax did not depend on whether the dividends were portfolio dividends. The same principles applied to portfolio and subsidiary dividends. The judge had been right to take the higher of the actual or nominal rate since the foundation of the jurisprudence was that there should be credit for at least the tax actually paid (see paras 11, 51, 65-71, 76, 78 of judgment). (2) The judge's ruling, that foreign-sourced dividends had to be treated as having been fed into the domestic advance corporation tax (ACT) system at the water's edge carrying the tax credit to the extent required by EU law, stood. The unlawful ACT was identified by operating the domestic ACT system on the assumption that the foreign-sourced dividends would have carried the tax credit required by EU law, and would have been franked investment income to that extent (para.89). (3) HMRC's pro-rating methodology was correct in principle. The presumption in favour of applying the pro-rating approach correctly identified by the judge had greater normative force than he had given it in his judgment. HMRC's appeal against that part of the judgment was allowed. The judge's initial reaction to the issue of the resulting repayment of ACT where a company had received excess franked investment income (FII) had been correct. The ACT against which the FII was carried back might comprise an element of lawful and unlawful ACT. The fair course was to treat the FII payment as attributable pro rata to the unlawful ACT element and the lawful ACT element. There was no good reason to prioritise the notional repayment of lawful ACT as compared with unlawful ACT. A fair approach was that excess FII in Q4 should be treated as repayment of the lawful and unlawful ACT in Q2 on a pro rata basis as argued by HMRC. The judge's rulings on those issues were set aside (paras 118, 122, 127, 131-133, 143).

PRUDENTIAL ASSURANCE CO LTD v REVENUE AND CUSTOMS COMMISSIONERS, [2016] EWCA Civ 376, [2016] S.T.C. 1798, Lewison LJ, CA (Civ Div).

2058 Corporation tax–Foreign tax–Profits arising from exploitation of patents

THE CORPORATION TAX ACT 2010 (PROFITS ARISING FROM THE EXPLOITATION OF PATENTS) FOREIGN TAXES DESIGNATION REGULATIONS 2016, SI 2016/1181; made under the Corporation Tax Act 2010 s.375BP(8)(d). In force: 31 December 2016.

In accordance with the Corporation Tax Act 2010 s.357BP (meaning of "new qualifying IP right" and "old qualifying IP right"), a right or exclusive licence is a "new qualifying IP right" for the purposes of Pt 8A of the Act (profits arising from the exploitation of patents) if the right is assigned or the licence is granted on or after 2 January 2016 and the conditions set-out in s.357BP subs.(8) are met. One of the conditions in s.357BP(8) is that the person who assigned the right or granted the licence was not liable at the time of the assignment or grant to a designated foreign tax. These Regulations designate the foreign taxes listed in reg.2 for the purposes of s.357BP.

2059 Corporation tax–Group relief–Surrendering and claiming companies were not under the same control

[Corporation Tax Act 2010 (c.4) s.1124(2), s.152, s.154, s.155B; Restrictive Trade Practices Act 1956 (c.68) s.6]

Two companies appealed against HMRC's refusal to allow their claims for group relief. The appellant companies and another (P) were subsidiaries of a parent company for the purposes of the Corporation Tax Act 2010 s.152. In June 2011, P went into receivership, and a bank appointed receivers over the whole of its property. The bank's rights flowed from its appointment as security trustee under a deed of debenture. In 2014 the appellant companies submitted corporation tax returns claiming group relief in respect of sums surrendered to them by P. HMRC rejected their claims on the basis that, on a proper interpretation of s.154 of the Act, the surrenders were invalid.

Held: Appeals dismissed. (1) The purpose of s.154 was simply to make group relief unavailable where the surrendering and claiming companies were not under the same control. Section 154 was not an anti-avoidance provision and there was no need to read it narrowly so as to deny group relief only where there had been some manipulation or disposition of an abnormal, undesirable or exploitative character, or where the arrangements were artificial and had been contrived simply to secure group relief. Section 154(3) effect 2 was intended to apply to transactions whereby the control of two companies came to be in separate hands, irrespective of the underlying motive, *Pollen Estate Trustee Co Ltd v Revenue and Customs Commissioners* [2013] EWCA Civ 753, [2013] 1 W.L.R. 3785, [2013] C.L.Y. 3128 applied (see paras 13, 44-47 of judgment). (2) The circumstances of the instant appeals constituted "arrangements" for the purposes of s.154. The term "arrangements" was expressed compendiously in s.154 and it was significant that it was in the plural. Arrangements could be of any kind, and there was no justification for reading into the term the concept of "a combination for a singular purpose". The discussion of the meaning of "arrangements" in *British Basic Slag Ltd's Agreements (No.1), Re* [1963] 1 W.L.R. 727, [1963] C.L.Y. 3475 was unhelpful because it was predicated on the definition of "agreement" in the Restrictive Trade Practices Act 1956 s.6, which connoted an element of mutuality, *British Basic Slag* considered. Section 154 was designed to be of straightforward and practical application, requiring no inquiry into concepts such as consensus or a meeting of minds. The term "arrangements" was therefore to be read widely. Section 155B, read both literally and as an aid to interpreting s.154(3), clearly pointed to the deed of debenture as constituting "arrangements" within the meaning of s.154(3), at least once the receivers had been appointed. A wide interpretation of "arrangements" was also consistent with the approach in *Scottish and Universal Newspapers Ltd v Fisher (Inspector of Taxes)* [1996] S.T.C. (S.C.D.) 311, [1996] C.L.Y. 1308 and *Barclays Bank Plc v Revenue and Customs Commissioners* [2006] S.T.C. (S.C.D.) 100, [2006] C.L.Y. 4210, *Scottish and Universal* and *Barclays* applied (paras 48-56). (3) The correct approach to s.154(3) was simply to ask whether P and the appellant companies were under the same control. It was common ground that the receivers did not control the appellant companies, so it was helpful to ask whether they controlled P. If they did, then P and the appellant companies were not under the same control. The appointment of a receiver deprived a company of its powers to enter into contracts in relation to its business or to dispose of property under the receiver's control, *Moss Steamship Co Ltd v Whinney* [1912] A.C. 254 followed. The whole of P's property had been put into the hands of the receivers, who had extensive powers. They had the power to carry on P's business, do whatever they considered appropriate in relation to the secured assets, and to do everything necessary for the realisation of P's property. In practical terms, all of P's affairs had been put into the receivers' hands. There were no relevant powers outside the scope of the receivership, and although P's directors remained in office, they were unable to exercise any management powers. The receivers controlled P within the meaning of s.1124(2). Once they had been appointed, P's affairs were no longer being conducted in accordance with the wishes of the appellant companies' shareholders. That was sufficient to de-group P. Thus, at the relevant time, P was not a member of the same group as the appellant companies and could not validly surrender group relief to them (paras 57-63, 67-72).

FARNBOROUGH AIRPORT PROPERTIES CO LTD v REVENUE AND CUSTOMS COMMISSIONERS, [2016] UKFTT 431 (TC), [2016] S.F.T.D. 826, Judge Christopher McNall, FTT (Tax).

2060 Corporation tax–Interest rate swaps–Sale or transfer of derivatives between related companies–Disregard provisions in Sch.26 Pt 6 para.28 Finance Act 2002

[Finance Act 2002 (c.23) Sch.26 Pt 6 para.28, Sch.26 Pt 6 para.28(1), Sch.26 Pt 6 para.28(2); Finance Act 1998 (c.36) Sch.18 Pt IV para.32]

HMRC appealed and a company (B) cross-appealed against decisions of the Upper Tribunal (*Revenue and Customs Commissioners v Bristol & West Plc* [2014] UKUT 73 (TCC), [2014] S.T.C. 1048, [2014] C.L.Y. 2970) made in litigation concerning the appropriate corporation tax treatment of a premium paid to the company upon its novation of interest-rate swaps. In August 2003, B novated a portfolio of interest-rate swaps to another company in the same group and received a premium of £91 million. Seeking to secure the benefit of the "disregard" in the Finance Act 2002 Sch.26 Pt 6 para.28, it left the premium out of account for the purposes of corporation tax when submitting its tax return for the relevant period. HMRC took the view that the disregard did not apply to the novation and opened an enquiry. At the same time, it sought to end another enquiry it was conducting into returns issued by other companies in the same group. In October 2007 it purported to issue a closure notice under the Finance Act 1998 Sch.18 Pt IV para.32 in respect of that other enquiry. However, by some mistake, it instead triggered the issue of a closure notice stating that no amendment would be made to B's tax return. It immediately emailed B informing it that it would be receiving a closure notice in error. In November it wrote to B explaining that it would be amending its return, and in December it amended B's return to bring the premium into account. B appealed. The Upper Tribunal held that HMRC had issued a valid closure notice and therefore could not challenge the application of the para.28 disregard to the premium. It went on to hold that the disregard did not apply to the premium and that, but for the closure notice, B would have been liable to pay corporation tax on it. HMRC appealed against the former decision and B cross-appealed against the latter. The issues were whether (1) HMRC had issued a valid closure notice; (2) the disregard applied to the premium.

Held: Appeal allowed, cross-appeal dismissed. (1) HMRC had not issued a valid closure notice and its appeal on that point would be allowed. There was no prescribed form for a closure notice under Sch.18 Pt IV para.32 of the 1998 Act, but it had to be in writing and had to state that HMRC had completed its enquiry and set out its conclusions. Once it had issued a closure notice, HMRC could not unilaterally withdraw it and it could not amend the tax return in question other than to give effect to its stated conclusions. Neither the erroneously issued notice nor the November letter, nor a combination of the two amounted to the issue of a valid closure notice in relation to the enquiry into B's tax return. A reasonable person in B's position and having B's knowledge of any relevant context would not have understood them to constitute a valid closure notice, *Mannai Investment Co Ltd v Eagle Star Life Assurance Co Ltd* [1997] A.C. 749, [1997] C.L.Y. 3256 applied. The November letter neither purported to be a closure notice nor contained HMRC's conclusions, and the notice had to be read alongside the email warning B that it was about to receive a closure notice in error. An inconsistent document could invalidate an apparently valid notice if it formed part of the contextual background, *Barclays Bank Plc v Bee* [2001] EWCA Civ 1126, [2002] 1 W.L.R. 332, [2001] C.L.Y. 4156 applied and *Saxon Weald Homes Ltd v Chadwick* [2011] EWCA Civ 1202, [2012] H.L.R. 8, [2012] C.L.Y. 2022 considered. The email plainly formed part of the relevant factual context for the purposes of interpreting the notice. It invited B not to treat the notice as a statement that HMRC had completed its enquiry and was sufficient to invalidate it. It did not put the notice into some sort of agreed suspension, and in the absence of any such agreement, HMRC had no power to deliver a closure notice on a suspended basis. The legislative scheme required HMRC to decide to close its enquiry, decide what amendments were to be made to the return, and then communicate both those decisions to the taxpayer; there was no scope for HMRC to send a closure notice before deciding that its enquiry was complete (see paras 24-26, 29-40 of judgment). (2) The company's cross-appeal in relation to the applicability of the disregard in Sch.26 Pt 6 para.28 of the 2002 Act had to be dismissed. The Upper Tribunal was correct in its conclusion that the disregard did not apply to the premium. It was common ground that the novation satisfied the conditions in para.28(1) and para.28(2). However, para.28(3) referred to the credits and debits to be taken into account "in the case of the two companies", and it was clear that para.28 could only operate where both the transferor company and the transferee company were subject to Sch.26. The requirement that para.28(3) should apply in the case of the transferor and the transferee, and the requirement both companies "shall be deemed ... to be the same company" left no room for any other interpretation. The purpose of para.28 was not to ensure that no charge arose as a result of an intra-group transaction, but was to achieve tax neutrality in relation to intra-group transfers. In the instant case, para.28(3) could not be applied to the accounts of both B and the company to which it novated the swaps because Sch.26 took effect only in relation to accounting periods beginning on or after 1 October 2002. While the novation fell within B's accounting period commencing 1 April 2003, it fell within the transferee's accounting period starting 1 September 2002 (paras 41-42, 48-50, 57-59).

REVENUE AND CUSTOMS COMMISSIONERS v BRISTOL & WEST PLC, [2016] EWCA Civ 397, [2016] S.T.C. 1491, Black LJ, CA (Civ Div).

2061 Corporation tax–Restitution–Challenge to Corporation Tax Act 2010 Pt 8C–Amendment of Particulars of Claim–First-tier Tribunal as appropriate forum

[Corporation Tax Act 2010 (c.4) Pt 8C, s.357YO, s.357YQ; European Convention on Human Rights 1950]

The claimant taxpayers applied to amend their particulars of claim in order to challenge the lawfulness of the restitution interest tax provisions in the Corporation Tax Act 2010 Pt 8C. The taxpayers had brought a claim against HMRC for the repayment of corporation tax allegedly levied in breach of EU law. HMRC was ordered to make an interim payment in respect of most of the claim. The payment was made four days before Pt 8C came into force; the withholding tax obligation in s.357YO therefore did not apply and the payment was received gross. However, it was the taxpayers' case that the forthcoming trial would yield a judgment in their favour, including a large amount of compound interest to which the Pt 8C provisions would apply. They sought the amendment to argue that the provisions were unlawful by reason of their incompatibility with EU law and the ECHR. Alternatively, they sought to argue that any restitution and/or compensation awarded had to be increased so as to take account of the tax which would be charged under the provisions, and further that they were entitled to compensation from the state for the breaches of EU law. HMRC submitted that the taxpayers' application was premature because the trial had not been concluded and, as such, there was no "restitution interest" under Pt 8C. They also argued that the First-tier Tribunal had exclusive jurisdiction to deal with the proposed challenges to Pt 8C in accordance with the principles in *Autologic Holdings Plc v Inland Revenue Commissioners* [2005] UKHL 54, [2006] 1 A.C. 118, [2005] C.L.Y. 4056. Relying on observations made in Autologic, the taxpayers submitted that even if HMRC's jurisdictional objections were accepted, the appropriate course would still be to grant permission for the amendments to be made, but for the court to stay the issues until further order.

Held: Application refused. (1) HMRC's linked objections of prematurity and jurisdiction were compelling and pointed strongly towards the conclusion that the taxpayers should not be permitted to challenge the validity of the provisions in the High Court, at a stage before any judgment had been given in their favour. If and when they obtained judgment for a sum which included actual or potential restitution interest, the question of validity would arise. However, save perhaps in exceptional circumstances, the only appropriate forum for resolution of that issue was the tribunal in the context of an appeal brought by the taxpayers against either a withholding of tax under s.357YO or an assessment under s.357YQ. That was the machinery provided by Parliament and there was no good reason for departing from it, *Autologic* followed (see para.36 of judgment). (2) The position might have been different if the taxpayers were able to persuade the court that it was necessary to consider and rule upon the validity of the provisions before deciding on the quantum of restitution. However, there was no plausible argument why that might be the case. The suggestion that it might be appropriate to gross up the recovery by the amount of tax under Pt 8C which was prospectively payable on the interest element of the restitution was misconceived and ran the risk of over-compensating the taxpayers. If the provisions were valid, or to the extent that they might be held to be valid, that had to be because the challenges to them under EU law and/or human rights law had failed. In those circumstances, they would be binding on the taxpayers in the same way as other primary UK tax legislation, and there would be no more reason to increase the restitution or compensation in order to take future Pt 8C tax charges into account, than there would be to take account of the basic charge to corporation tax which admittedly already applied to the interest element of the restitution. If, on the other hand, the provisions were wholly or partly invalid, the taxpayers would be able to recover any overpaid tax under the statutory appeal machinery, and there would again be no proper basis for grossing up the restitution awarded to them (para.39). (3) The tribunal would not have jurisdiction to entertain a claim for compensation from the state. However, it could not be seen how such a claim could sensibly be brought before the invalidity of Pt 8C had been established, and before the taxpayers had suffered any loss as a result of the imposition of the unlawful tax (para.40). (4) The observations in *Autologic* were made in a context where the relevant claims related to past events, and had already been made albeit in the wrong forum. In those circumstances, it was considered prudent to keep the High Court proceedings alive in order to cater for unforeseen contingencies. However, the instant case was very different: no claims had yet crystallized; the statutory machinery would be available to resolve any future appeals; and if some good reason for claiming relief in the High Court emerged, fresh proceedings could be commenced for that purpose, *Autologic* distinguished. It would be wrong to permit the proposed amendments in order to cater for hypothetical problems which might never arise. The proper function of pleadings was to formulate concrete issues which arose on existing facts, not to provide a springboard for the resolution of hypothetical and unforeseen future issues (para.44).

SIX CONTINENTS LTD v INLAND REVENUE COMMISSIONERS *sub nom.* SIX CONTINENTS LTD v REVENUE AND CUSTOMS COMMISSIONERS, [2016] EWHC 169 (Ch), [2016] B.T.C. 7, Henderson J, Ch D.

2062 Corporation tax–Restitution–Corporation Tax Act 2010 Pt 8C–First-tier Tribunal as appropriate forum

[Corporation Tax Act 2010 (c.4) Pt 8C; European Convention on Human Rights 1950 Protocol 1 art.1, art.14]

On an application by the claimants for permission to seek judicial review of the restitution interest tax provisions set out in the Corporation Tax Act 2010 Pt 8C, the court had to consider the effect of parallel proceedings in the First-tier Tribunal. Both claimants were parties to what was known as the Franked Investment Income Group Litigation, which had been ongoing for many years. Each had received an interim payment of restitution interest reflecting the taxpayers' success to date in the litigation. The provisions being challenged imposed corporation tax at 45% on restitution interest. Their effect was to impose a tax on compound interest payments paid by HMRC; that tax became due at the point that (and only if) the court finally determined compound interest to be payable by HMRC or any final settlement to that effect was reached. The claimants were potentially liable to pay tax under the provisions if the group litigation was finally resolved in the taxpayers' favour. They relied on the following grounds in their challenge to the provisions: the provisions breached the UK's obligation under EU law to provide them with an adequate and effective remedy in respect of taxes unlawfully levied; the provisions also contravened the established EU law and human rights principles of legal certainty, non-retroactivity and the protection of legitimate expectations; by seeking to reverse the effect of final judicial rulings as to the appropriate and necessary remedy, the provisions constituted an unjustified interference by the state in judicial proceedings contrary to general principles of EU and human rights law; further, the provisions breached specific provisions of EU and human rights law, such as ECHR art.14 and Protocol 1 art.1. Another company had brought an appeal to the First-tier Tribunal in relation to the restitution interest tax provisions.

Held: Application stayed. The First-tier Tribunal was the appropriate forum for a challenge to the restitution interest tax provisions. The proceedings there were further advanced. The issues of law in both sets of proceedings were the same. There were real advantages in the challenge being considered by the tribunal. First, the appeal was against a withholding actually made, so that the tribunal could consider whether the appellant's fundamental rights under EU and human rights law had been infringed. Any evidence required, or arguments advanced, would be tailored to the specific facts; by contrast, the claimants' case was hypothetical because there was no withholding or assessment yet in existence. Second, the tribunal was a specialist tax tribunal, with knowledge of the background issues giving rise to the appeal and the wider arguments about compound interest. That familiarity would assist in the efficient disposal of the appeal. There were disadvantages in the instant court considering the challenge to the restitution interest tax provisions before or in preference to the tribunal. The legal challenge to the provisions was just one aspect of the claim. The court would also have to address the Treasury and HMRC's arguments based on the prematurity of the claim, the availability of an alternative remedy in due course in the tribunal and the consequent lack of jurisdiction for the court to hear the claim. Those were difficult issues, which would take time and careful analysis to resolve. They did not arise in the tribunal. If the Treasury and HMRC were correct in their arguments on those threshold issues, the court might never rule on the more fundamental issues of law raised by the claimants. Moreover, if the instant claim was to go ahead, there was no guarantee that the appeal in the tribunal would be put on hold. In the circumstances, it would be appropriate to stay the instant claim pending the outcome of the appeal in the tribunal or until further order (see paras 24-28, 30, 34 of judgment).

R. (ON THE APPLICATION OF IMPERIAL CHEMICAL INDUSTRIES LTD) v HM TREASURY *sub nom.* R. (ON THE APPLICATION OF IMPERIAL CHEMICAL INDUSTRIES LTD) v REVENUE AND CUSTOMS COMMISSIONERS, [2016] EWHC 279 (Admin), [2016] B.T.C. 9, Whipple J, QBD (Admin).

2063 Corporation tax–Small and medium-sized enterprises–Enhanced research and development relief–Institutional investors

[Corporation Tax Act 2009 (c.4) s.1044; Recommendation 2003/361 on the definition of micro, small and medium-sized enterprises 2003]

The appellant company appealed against a decision of HMRC that it was not entitled to research and development tax deductions at the rate of 75% under the Corporation Tax Act 2009 s.1044. The appellant designed and distributed loudspeakers. In 2007, there had been a management buy-out: the appellant bought the entire issued share capital of a company called Monitor Audio Holdings Ltd from its existing shareholders.

The buy-out was funded through a number of different routes. Among other things, the appellant obtained £8.7 million in secured credit facilities from a bank, RBS, and £2.6 million in equity from a company within the RBS group (T). In 2009, a debt-for-equity swap was agreed between the appellant and RBS. RBS converted £10.7 million of its outstanding debt into shares in the appellant. The appellant also retained a five-year loan of £5.5 million with RBS. RBS transferred its shareholding in the appellant to one of its (RBS's) subsidiaries (W). T also transferred its shareholding to W. The result was that W held 43.75% of the shares in the appellant and 26.22% of the voting rights. W was given the right to appoint a non-executive director of the appellant as "Investor Director". The Investor Director's consent was required for any variations to share capital, and all lending, borrowing, acquisitions and disposals over a certain threshold, among other things. The relief under s.1044 was available to small or medium-sized enterprises, as defined in Recommendation 2003/361. Pursuant to the rules in the Recommendation, the appellant would cease to be treated as a small or medium-sized enterprise eligible for the relief if an upstream "partner enterprise" such as W held more than 25% of its capital or voting rights, unless W could be treated either as an "institutional investor" or as a "venture capital company".

Held: Appeal allowed. (1) An institutional investor was an institution whose function was to invest on behalf of others in a wide range of ways. It would not be involved in the day-to-day management of its target investments. A comparison could be made between private and institutional investors, with the former more likely to take a direct interventionist role in the management of the companies in which they invested. The essential test here was whether RBS and/or W were, by their structural or strategic involvement in the appellant, putting it in a stronger market position than other small or medium-sized enterprises. The answer was no. The extent of the involvement of W and/or RBS in the day-to-day management of the appellant was very little. Although the Investor Director had a right to block a wide range of decisions taken by the appellant, that right represented not a positive involvement in deciding how the company was run but a negative veto against decisions not considered to be favourable to W, the lead investor. Moreover, the evidence showed that the Investor Director was not in practice involved in making day-to-day decisions about how the appellant was run and that in some cases he failed to exercise the rights which he did have. RBS was clearly an institutional investor. As a 100% subsidiary of RBS with policies set by its parent, W shared RBS's character and there was nothing to suggest that a different conclusion should be reached if W were viewed in isolation. Both RBS and W could properly be described as institutional investors in the appellant, with the result that it was entitled to the relief under s.1044 (see paras 63, 65, 67 of judgment). (2) A venture capital company was a company whose strategy was to invest in high-risk, high-return ventures. It, too, would not be involved in the day-to-day management of its target investments. Only limited evidence had been provided about W's activities, strategies and risk appetite for the relevant periods. The concept of a venture capital company entailed more than establishing what was done for one particular investment and went to the character of all the investments held by it. The tribunal had very limited information about W. The appellant had not therefore shown that W could be treated as a venture capital company for the relevant periods (paras 63, 72-73).

MONITOR AUDIO LTD v REVENUE AND CUSTOMS COMMISSIONERS, [2015] UKFTT 357 (TC), [2016] S.F.T.D. 1, Judge Rachel Short, FTT (Tax).

2064 Corporation tax–Tax avoidance–Connected companies–Claims for loan relationship debts–Unallowable purpose provisions in Sch.9 para.13 Finance Act 1996

[Finance Act 1996 (c.8) Sch.9 para.13, s.103(1), s.91B]

The first and second appellants appealed against HMRC's decision to disallow their claims for loan relationship debits under the Finance Act 1996 s.91B. The second appellant was a subsidiary of the first appellant. They were members of a large company group which had been looking to reduce its number of active subsidiaries in early 2008. The first appellant was informed of a potential tax advantage to be gained through making the second appellant dormant. The process involved the first appellant obtaining shares in the second appellant and entering into a total return swap with another of the group's members regarding those shares. The swap triggered loan relationship provisions under s.91B, where the shares were treated as if they were rights under a creditor relationship. Solicitors then confirmed that if a further group member novated its loan liabilities to the second appellant to strip out the latter's reserves, the first appellant could use its creditor relationship with the second appellant to bring into account the resultant reduction in the value of its shareholding. The novations were duly effected and the first appellant made its claim for the debit. The second appellant's claim was for debits concerning the interest payable on the novated loans. HMRC disallowed the debits on the basis that they were attributable to tax avoidance, which was an unallowable purpose under Sch.9 para.13. The first appellant argued that its creditor relationship was a "deemed" loan relationship by virtue of s.91B, and the subjective test of purpose under Sch.9 para.13 could apply only to actual relationships. It further argued that in any event its purpose in holding the shares had been unequivocally commercial, regardless of any potential tax advantage. The second appellant submitted that the novations giving rise to its claim had resulted from the commercial purpose of extracting its reserves and making it dormant.

Held: Appeals dismissed. (1) Regarding the first appellant, Sch.9 para.13 did apply to a deemed loan relationship. A creditor relationship was, by definition under s.103(1), a loan relationship. The investing company came to be treated as being party to a loan relationship only by satisfying the conditions in s.91B(1), which it had to continue to satisfy to remain so treated. Logically, therefore, the investing company's purposes in bringing about and maintaining the satisfaction of those conditions were the relevant purposes to be tested against Sch.9 para.13. In applying para.13 in that way to the first appellant's case, the event that had triggered s.91B and had brought the deemed loan relationship into existence was its entry into the total return swap while continuing to hold shares in the second appellant. It was clear that one of the main purposes of that event had been a tax avoidance purpose, which had continued to be the case until the swap was terminated. Therefore, the first appellant had had an unallowable purpose throughout the period for the creditor relationship it was deemed to have had by reason of s.91B(2). If that conclusion was wrong and it was instead necessary to examine the first appellant's purpose in holding the shares, it might have had a perfectly sound business and commercial purpose for doing so, but that did not alter the fact that its hoped-for use of those shares to obtain the debit constituted another main purpose under para.13(4), being tax avoidance. The debit was therefore wholly excluded (see paras 56-61, 65-69, 72 of judgment). (2) As to the second appellant, the question was whether its debtor loan relationships that had arisen from the novations had had an unallowable purpose under Sch.9 para.13. Crucially, under para.13(5), "tax avoidance purposes" referred to any purpose that consisted in securing a tax advantage, whether for the company or any other person. The second appellant had become party to the loan relationships only after the solicitors had advised that the novations would result in a tax benefit for the first appellant. One of its main purposes had been to secure that tax advantage, and given the method that it had chosen to achieve the extraction of its reserves, it was very hard to attribute the resulting debits to anything other than that unallowable purpose. Therefore, they were disallowed in full (paras 74-77, 81-82).

TRAVEL DOCUMENT SERVICE v REVENUE AND CUSTOMS COMMISSIONERS, [2015] UKFTT 582 (TC), [2016] S.F.T.D. 186, Judge Kevin Poole, FTT (Tax).

2065 Corporation tax–Tax returns–Company's voluntary return and self-assessment of corporation tax liability–Notice issued under Sch.18 Pt II para.3 Finance Act 1998

[Finance Act 1998 (c.36) Sch.18 Pt II para.3, Sch.18 Pt V para.46, Sch.18 Pt VI para.51, Sch.18 para.88, Sch.18 para.97; Income and Corporation Taxes Act 1988 (c.1) s.393(1)]

A company appealed against the corporation tax charged, and the penalties determined, for its 2005 and 2007 accounting periods. The company was German-incorporated but had been UK-resident between March 2003 and March 2012. During that time it had been liable to pay corporation tax in the UK. However, it did not appreciate that until March 2010, when it sent HMRC an "error or mistake" claim under the Finance Act 1998 Sch.18 Pt VI para.51. In September 2010, HMRC issued notices under Sch.18 para.3 requiring the company to file company tax returns for its 2004-2009 accounting periods. The company complied and also filed a voluntary return for 2003. It claimed that it had incurred trading losses in 2003 and 2004 periods, which it could carry forward under the Income and Corporation Taxes Act 1988 s.393(1) and offset against any 2005 and 2007 profits. Since it had made no profits in 2005 and 2007, it claimed that no tax was payable. HMRC concluded that given the four-year time limit in Sch.18 para.46 of the 1998 Act, the 2003-2005 returns were out of time, which meant that the company could not establish its 2003 and 2004 losses so as to carry them forward. The central issue was whether the 2003 and 2004 losses could be carried forward. The company argued that by virtue of s.393(1) of the 1988 Act they were automatically available for set off without the need for any return or self-assessment. HMRC argued that, pursuant to Sch.18 para.7 of the 1998 Act, trading losses could only be established by self-assessment through a valid company tax return submitted within the time limit. The issues for the tribunal were whether (i) the company's March 2010 notification was an in-time assessment of its liability for 2003 and 2004; (ii) a company could make a voluntary return and self-assessment of its tax liability; (iii) the Sch.18 para.46 time limit applied to a company tax return submitted pursuant to a Sch.18 para.3 notice; (iv) the company's entitlement to set off its 2005 and 2007 trading depended on them being included in valid returns for 2003 and 2004.

Held: Appeals allowed. (1) The March 2010 notification was not an in-time assessment of its liability. It did not purport to be a tax return, but merely indicated that returns were being prepared and that losses had been incurred in 2003 and 2004. A company tax return had to comply with specific requirements, and the self-assessment included in the return had to be the outcome of the computation specified in Sch.18 para.8, based on the information contained in the return. There was nothing in Sch.18 to suggest that a self-assessment could be in some other form and submitted outside the return (see paras 86-90, 137 of judgment). (2) Sch.18 did not allow for a company to make a voluntary return and self-assessment of its tax liability. A company's obligation to deliver a return and self-assess tax depended on it receiving notice from HMRC to that effect, *R. (on the application of Higgs) v Revenue and Customs Commissioners* [2015] UKUT 92 (TCC), [2015] S.T.C. 1600, [2015] C.L.Y. 2487 considered. The company could not, therefore, establish its 2003 trading losses by reference to its 2003 return, because that return had not been required by a Sch.18 para.3 notice (paras 99-104, 127, 137). (3) The Sch.18 para.46 time limit did not apply to the submission of a company tax return submitted pursuant to a Sch.18 para.3 notice. The provisions of Sch.18 para.97 did not extend to para.46, and while para.46 applied to an "assessment", it did not apply to a "self-assessment". The company could therefore establish its 2004 trading losses by reference to its 2004 return (paras 106-111, 114-116, 125-127, 137). (4) The company's entitlement to set off trading losses in 2005 and 2007 did not depend on those losses being included in valid in-time returns for 2003 and 2004. Section 393 of the 1988 Act entitled the company to relief for trading losses incurred in an earlier period. The information required on the tax return included brought-forward trading losses irrespective of whether they had been included in a previous tax return. Schedule 18 para.88 provided for "an amount stated in a company tax return for an accounting period which is required to be included in the return" and which affected the tax payable for another accounting period. The amount in question was conclusively determined in relation to that other period. If the return did not require trading losses to be included, para.88 would not apply and the amount would not be taken to be conclusively established for a later period. HMRC could not use the form of the return as a way of depriving a company of relief to which it was entitled under the Corporation Tax Acts. Because HMRC had not required the company to produce a return for 2003, para.88 could not apply to that period. HMRC could not deny that the 2003 return was valid and at the same time rely on para.88 to say that the company had no established losses for that period. The 2003 return either counted as a return, in which case the trading losses were included in it, or it did not, in which case there had been no amount stated in a company tax return for the 2003 period and there was nothing that could be conclusively determined as envisaged by para.88. Given that the 2005 and 2007 returns allowed the company to claim trading losses for earlier periods, it could set off its 2003 losses in computing its profits for 2005 and 2007 (paras 130-137).

BLOOMSBURY VERLAG GMBH v REVENUE AND CUSTOMS COMMISSIONERS, [2015] UKFTT 660 (TC), [2016] S.F.T.D. 205, Judge Malcolm Gammie QC, FTT (Tax).

2066 Corporation tax–Trading income–Interpretation of s.103(1) Income and Corporation Taxes Act 1988–Whether charge to tax applied to recipient of post-cessation receipt regardless of recipient being original trader

[Income and Corporation Taxes Act 1988 (c.1) Sch.D, s.103, s.103(1), s.103(2), s.106(1), s.106(2)]

A retail group (S) appealed against a decision (*Shop Direct Group v Revenue and Customs Commissioners* [2014] EWCA Civ 255, [2014] S.T.C. 1383, [2014] C.L.Y. 2886) upholding an assessment to corporation tax made by the respondent HMRC. S was part of a VAT group which had made substantial overpayments of VAT. The relevant supplies had been made between 1978 and 1996 by a number of companies within the group, including S. In 2007, HMRC made a VAT repayment to S as the nominated member of the group. By that time, the group had undergone a reorganisation and the companies making the relevant supplies had transferred their business and permanently discontinued their trades. HMRC assessed S to corporation tax on the repayment on the basis that it was a post-cessation receipt within the meaning of the Income and Corporation Taxes Act 1988 s.103. S submitted that if it was liable to corporation tax on the repayment at all, then it was liable only for such sums as related to the supplies it had made itself because (1) s.103 imposed a tax charge only on the trader from whose trading the sum had arisen; (2) if the receipt of a sum equivalent to the repayment arose from an intra-group transfer without any assignment of rights to the recipient, s.103 did not impose a charge; (3) if the receipt of that sum were the result of a transfer of the right to the receipt, s.106 precluded any charge to tax on the recipient.

Held: Appeal dismissed. (1) Section 103 did not impliedly restrict the charge to tax on post-cessation receipts to the former trader whose trade was the source of the income. First, there was nothing in the wording of either s.103(1) or s.103(2) to necessitate such an implication. The charge to tax was clear: where a trade had been permanently discontinued, corporation tax was charged on sums arising from trades made before the discontinuance. All that s.103(1) required was that the sums should be received after discontinuance. While it specified the source of the sums falling within the charge, it imposed no limit on the recipient and thus the person liable to the charge. Secondly, s.103 sought to tax sums arising from "the fruit of the trade". It brought the fruit of discontinued trade into the charge to tax not only in the hands of the former trader, his personal representatives and heirs, but also in the hands of those to whom the rights to the post-cessation receipts had been assigned or those who were otherwise entitled to receive and keep such receipts. The purpose of s.103 was to ensure that sums arising from a discontinued trade were brought into a charge to tax, and there was no sound policy reason for confining the charge to the former trader and his personal representatives. Thirdly, s.105 and s.108 drew a distinction between the person chargeable to tax and the person who had previously carried on the trade. That gave rise to the inference that the former was not confined to the latter (see paras 19-23, 27 of judgment). (2) The court rejected S's submission that the sum equivalent to the repayment was the result not of a trade but of an intra-group arrangement, which was either a transfer for no consideration of that sum or a transfer for no consideration of the rights to the repayment. Section 103 focused on the original source of the receipt, which was not altered by arrangements within the VAT group about which company was to receive the repayment. The question was simply whether the sum received arose from the trade before its discontinuance (paras 24, 27). (3) Section 106(1) also supported a wide interpretation of the scope of the s.103 charge. It related to transfers for value, quantified the s.103 charge at the amount of the consideration or the market value of the rights to future receipts at the point of transfer, and imposed the charge on the former trader. Section 106(2) dealt with the situation where a trade was treated as having been discontinued by reason of its having being transferred to new traders together with the right to receive post-cessation receipts. Section 106(2) disapplied s.103 and substituted Sch.D Case 1 only if the transferee was carrying on the business when it received the fruits of the deemed-discontinued trade (paras 25-27). (4) Applying those principles to the facts of the instant case led to the conclusion that repayment was subject to a charge to corporation tax in S's hands. It was clear that the VAT group's affairs had been organised so that S would receive the repayment as its beneficial owner. S had received sums arising from the carrying on of the trade of those companies making relevant supplies before the discontinuance, and those sums were not otherwise chargeable to tax (paras 27-31).

SHOP DIRECT GROUP v REVENUE AND CUSTOMS COMMISSIONERS, [2016] UKSC 7, [2016] 1 W.L.R. 733, Lord Neuberger PSC, SC.

2067 Costs orders–Case management directions–First-tier Tribunal's power to order sharing of costs of preparing single appeal bundle

[Tribunal Procedure (First-tier Tribunal) (Tax Chamber) Rules 2009 (SI 2009/273) r.10(1), r.10(1)(a), r.10(1)(b), r.10(1)(c), r.10(1)(c)(ii), r.10(3), r.23, r.5(3)]

A taxpayer appealed against a decision that the First-tier Tribunal lacked jurisdiction to order that the costs of preparing a trial bundle should be shared between the taxpayer and HMRC where the taxpayer had requested that the proceedings be excluded from potential liability for costs or expenses under the Tribunal Procedure (First-tier Tribunal) (Tax Chamber) Rules 2009 r.10(1)(c). The taxpayer appealed against a closure notice. The appeal was allocated as a complex case under the Tribunal Procedure (First-tier Tribunal) (Tax Chamber) Rules 2009 r.23. The taxpayer made a request under r.10(3) of the Rules to invoke the no costs-shifting regime under r.10(1)(c). The tribunal gave directions for the procedure leading up to the hearing, As the parties were unable to agree a bundle of documents, the tribunal gave an oral direction for the taxpayer to prepare the bundle with the costs to be shared (the order). The taxpayer prepared an extensive bundle running to over 700 lever-arch files, three copies of which were served on HMRC and on the tribunal respectively. The taxpayer's appeal on the closure notice was dismissed and it invoiced HMRC in the sum of £108,395 for half the cost of preparing the bundles. HMRC sought to set aside the order as to the sharing of costs on the ground that the tribunal had had no jurisdiction to give it in the light of r.10 of the Rules. The matter came before the Court of Appeal, which held that the tribunal would have had a broad jurisdiction as to costs if no request under r.10(1)(c)(ii) had been made. However, since such a request had been made, the effect of r.10(1)(c) was that the tribunal could only make an order for costs if either r.10(1)(a) or r.10(1)(b) applied, concerning wasted costs and unreasonable behaviour respectively. Accordingly, the Court of Appeal upheld the decision that the tribunal lacked jurisdiction. The taxpayer submitted that (1) the order was not a true order for the payment of costs, but only for the sharing of costs; (2) it was inherent in the case management powers set out in r.5(3) of the Rules that orders made by the tribunal under that provision could include terms as to costs.

Held: Appeal dismissed. (1) Even though the payment of half the taxpayer's expenses in preparing the bundles could fairly be described as the "sharing" of costs, it also undoubtedly involved the payment of costs by HMRC in the sense of reimbursing the taxpayer for half the expenses it had incurred. The step of recovering half the expense from HMRC was plainly an order for the recovery of costs, albeit a partially proleptic one (see para.15 of judgment). (2)(a) The taxpayer's interpretation of r.5(3) robbed r.10(1) of much of its force, given that the purpose of the latter provision was to preclude the tribunal from making cost-shifting orders in all ordinary cases, and that even in complex cases the taxpayer could opt to avoid cost-shifting. If, as the taxpayer suggested, the tribunal was able to attach a costs order every time it made a direction under one of the subparagraphs of r.5(3) or under the more general powers contained in r.5(2), even in the absence of unreasonable behaviour, that would greatly reduce the effectiveness of the no costs-shifting regime in r.10(1) (para.18). (2)(b) The taxpayer's argument was inconsistent with r.10(3) to r.10(7), which contained rules for the assessment and recovery of any costs awarded by the tribunal pursuant to r.10(1). Since there were no provisions governing the assessment and recovery of costs under r.5, the taxpayer's argument would mean that there was a lacuna in the Rules (para.19). (2)(c) Rejecting the taxpayer's case did not mean that the tribunal could not give permission to amend or grant an adjournment on terms that one party pay the other's costs wasted or incurred as a result of such amendment or adjournment (para.20). (2)(d) Rule 16(2)(b), which enabled the tribunal to provide for the costs of a witness to be paid by the other party, did not support the taxpayer's argument that r.10(1) was not an absolute code. Rather, r.16(2)(b) demonstrated that the Rules made it clear where they intended to enable the tribunal to render a party liable for costs (para.21). (3) It was irrelevant that the tribunal could have ordered both parties to prepare the bundles jointly so that the taxpayer would have been able to recover the sum of £108,395 on the basis of a contribution between jointly liable parties. Since the taxpayer was liable for the preparation of the bundles, it was not possible to characterise the order as having any effect other than requiring HMRC to pay some of the taxpayer's costs, which order was precluded by r.10(1) (para.24).

ECLIPSE FILM PARTNERS NO.35 LLP v REVENUE AND CUSTOMS COMMISSIONERS *sub nom.* REVENUE AND CUSTOMS COMMISSIONERS v ECLIPSE FILM PARTNERS NO.35 LLP, [2016] UKSC 24, [2016] 1 W.L.R. 1939, Lord Neuberger PSC, SC.

2068 Discovery assessments–Validity–Burden of proof

[Taxes Management Act 1970 (c.9) s.29, s.29(8), s.34(2), s.36; Finance Act 1998 (c.36) Sch.18 Pt V para.41, Sch.18 Pt V para.42, Sch.18 Pt V para.42(3), Sch.18 Pt V para.43, Sch.18 Pt V para.46, Sch.18 Pt V para.46(3)]

The appellant taxpayers appealed against a decision confirming the respondent HMRC's demands for income and corporation tax based on discovery assessments. The first appellant had been assessed under the Taxes Management Act 1970 s.29 for income tax in relation to alleged failures to return profits of his business as a sole trader. The second appellant company had been assessed under the Finance Act 1998 Sch.18 Pt V para.41, para.42 and para.43 for corporation tax on alleged under-declarations of profits. The First-tier Tribunal decided that, with one exception, there were undeclared profits and upheld the assessments. The appellants did not challenge the tribunal's substantive finding that they had under-declared their profits for the relevant periods, but contended that it had made errors of law in failing to consider the underlying validity of the assessments by considering whether (i) the relevant conditions for the issue of a discovery assessment under s.29 and paras 41-43, namely that the appellants' conduct had been deliberately fraudulent or careless, had been met: the "competence" issue; (ii) the assessments were in time, by reference to s.36 of the 1970 Act and Sch.18 Pt V para.46 to the 1988 Act: the "time limit" issue. HMRC submitted that they had understood, from the way the appellants had raised their case before the tribunal, that only the substantive issue required determination, and there was no obligation on them to raise the competence and time limit issues. They argued that those issues were new points of law not argued before the tribunal, and that the appellants should not be permitted to raise them.

Held: Appeal allowed. (1) The tribunal had not dealt with the competence and time limit issues. The scope of an appeal did not have to be conclusively determined by reference to the case put by an appellant, *Hargreaves v Revenue and Customs Commissioners* [2014] UKUT 395 (TCC), [2015] S.T.C. 905, [2014] C.L.Y. 2890 explained. The scope of an appeal, and the issues that fell to be determined by the tribunal, had to be established by reference to all the circumstances, including the legislative framework and the burden of proof in relation to relevant issues, and the way in which the parties' respective cases had been put. In relation to the legislative framework, both for discovery assessments and time limits, objections to the making of an assessment might only be made on an appeal against the assessment. That was expressly provided in s.29(8) of the 1970 Act and Sch.18 Pt V para.42(3) to the 1988 Act, in relation to discovery assessments, and s.34(2) and Sch.18 Pt V para.46(3) for time limits. Those provisions did not require an appellant to make an express objection or challenge to the assessment's validity for competence and time limits to be in issue. In relation to the competence and time limit issues relevant to the instant appeal, the burden of proof rested with HMRC, *Hankinson v Revenue and Customs Commissioners* [2011] EWCA Civ 1566, [2012] 1 W.L.R. 2322, [2012] C.L.Y. 3268 distinguished. There was no obligation on the appellants' part to raise those issues. In the circumstances, neither the competence or time limit issues could be regarded as new issues of law, *Jones v MBNA International Bank Ltd* considered. They were issues in respect of which HMRC had the burden of proof, and which, for them to succeed, had to form part of their own case; they were not issues that the appellants had to raise, and so could not be regarded as points not taken by the appellants before the tribunal, for which the UT's permission was required. For HMRC to succeed before the tribunal, either the competence and time limit issues had to be determined in their favour, or those issues had to have been conceded by the appellants. There was no such express concession and none could be inferred. In the absence of a positive case put by HMRC in relation to the competence and time limit issues, the tribunal had erred in law in not finding that HMRC had failed to discharge the burden of proof in those respects such that the assessments could not be regarded as having been validly made. The tribunal's decision was set aside (see paras 17, 36-38, 43, 47-49, 53, 57 of judgment). (2) In the absence of HMRC having put a positive case to the tribunal on the competence and time limit issues, the only course open to the tribunal had been to allow the appeal. In those circumstances, to remit the appeal would allow HMRC to have a second bite of the cherry, which was not in the interest of justice and fairness. The assessments were reduced to zero (paras 58-60).

BURGESS v REVENUE AND CUSTOMS COMMISSIONERS *sub nom.* BRIMHEATH DEVELOPMENTS LTD v REVENUE AND CUSTOMS COMMISSIONERS, [2015] UKUT 578 (TCC), [2016] S.T.C. 579, Judge Roger Berner, UT (Tax).

2069 Employee benefit trusts–Disclosure–Participation in special disclosure facility–Legitimate expectation–Unfairness of change of policy by HMRC

The claimants, operators of employee benefit trust (EBT) schemes which had been challenged as tax avoidance schemes, sought judicial review of HMRC's decisions to limit the benefits available to them under the Liechtenstein Disclosure Facility (LDF), under which UK taxpayers with assets in Liechtenstein could be assessed to UK tax with a limited penalty and period of assessment and with a composite tax rate. The LDF's purpose was to bring liabilities were "disguised" by Liechtenstein law into UK tax; it was originally aimed at tax frauds. Taxpayers could obtain the benefits available under the LDF in return for disclosing relevant liabilities. Taxpayers were invited to apply for registration; HMRC registered them if eligible. HMRC began enquiries into EBT schemes. In 2011, the claimants began correspondence with HMRC regarding whether the LDF could be used to settle disputed liabilities arising from EBTs. In discussions, HMRC indicated that that was possible. In July 2013, HMRC said that they were reviewing the benefits available under the LDF. The claimants applied for registration in late 2013. HMRC put the applications on hold pending the review; the claimants were not registered. In 2014, HMRC told the claimants that the LDF's full benefits were not available where, as in the claimants' case, there had been an ongoing enquiry into a taxpayer's EBT arrangements when the application was made. Limited benefits remained available. Notwithstanding the change in practice, HMRC continued to grant full benefits to "category 2 taxpayers", who had registered under the LDF but whose affairs were not yet settled. The claimants argued that (1) HMRC had treated them with conspicuous unfairness in "leading them up the garden path" by inducing them to believe that they could benefit from the full benefits but then withdrawing many benefits; (2) HMRC had acted comparatively unfairly in that category 2 taxpayers, in a materially identical situation, had been given the full benefit of the LDF.

Held: Application refused. (1) The claimants had conceded that they had no legitimate expectation to any substantive benefit under the LDF: the LDF was an invitation to taxpayers to apply for registration and offered no promise that the application would be accepted. It was only if HMRC granted the taxpayer a registration certificate that the taxpayer might have a legitimate expectation of entitlement to the benefits described within the LDF. Having accepted that they had no legitimate expectation, the claimants would struggle to show conspicuous unfairness in the refusal to bestow the LDF benefits because they had had no expectation that they would get those benefits in the first place (see paras 71-73 of judgment). There was some truth in the assertion that the claimants had been led up the garden path. HMRC had encouraged them to use the LDF and to believe that using it could settle their EBT liabilities. However, the claimants got nowhere near showing that HMRC had treated them with conspicuous unfairness. No guarantee had been given to any claimant that the LDF would be available to them. HMRC had been at liberty to withdraw the benefits at any time because the claimants had had no legitimate expectation of any substantive benefit. Without a guarantee or promise, the refusal to confer the tax treatment sought was not so outrageously unfair that it should not be allowed to stand, *R. v Inland Revenue Commissioners Ex p. Unilever Plc* [1996] S.T.C. 681 applied (paras 76-80). (2) To determine whether HMRC had acted with comparative unfairness, it was first necessary to establish whether HMRC had known or ought to have known of the alleged disparate treatment at the time the decision was made. If not, the challenge failed. If that knowledge was established, it was necessary to establish whether HMRC had considered there to be a material difference between the two groups of taxpayers justifying the different tax treatment. If no material difference had been identified, it was difficult to see how HMRC's decision could stand. If HMRC had identified a material difference, the court should examine the asserted difference to determine whether it was rational and defensible, or material, such as to justify the different tax treatment, *British Sky Broadcasting Group Plc v Customs and Excise Commissioners* [2001] EWHC Admin 127, [2001] S.T.C. 437, [2001] C.L.Y. 5605 applied, *R. (on the application of Weston) v Inland Revenue Commissioners* [2004] EWHC 1069 (Admin), 76 T.C. 207, [2004] C.L.Y. 3695 considered (paras 67-69). The category 2 taxpayers had been in a different position because they had been registered, not because of the timing of their applications. That meant that they had had a legitimate expectation of receiving the full benefits of the LDF in its unaltered state. The existence of the legitimate expectation was a valid discriminator. HMRC had concluded that there was a material difference, namely that the category 2 taxpayers had been registered, and that distinction had been rational, *British Sky Broadcasting* applied. There had been no inconsistent treatment (paras 84-86). (3) (Obiter) In *R. (on the application of Hely-Hutchinson) v Revenue and Customs Commissioners* [2015] EWHC 3261 (Admin), [2016] S.T.C. 962, [2016] 2049 a taxpayer's comparative unfairness challenge had been granted. One problem there had been the lack of evidence filed by HMRC to explain their change of policy. Where comparative unfairness was alleged, the court was likely to be heavily dependent on HMRC's evidence. In the instant case, HMRC had given a full account of their internal discussions leading to the change of policy; that approach was the better working model, *Hely-Hutchinson* considered (para.70).

R. (ON THE APPLICATION OF CITY SHOES WHOLESALE LTD) v REVENUE AND CUSTOMS COMMISSIONERS, [2016] EWHC 107 (Admin), [2016] S.T.C. 2392, Whipple J, QBD (Admin).

2070 Energy conservation–Plant and machinery allowances

THE CAPITAL ALLOWANCES (ENERGY-SAVING PLANT AND MACHINERY) (AMENDMENT) ORDER 2016, SI 2016/927; made under the Capital Allowances Act 2001 s45A(3)(4). In force: 6 October 2016.

This Order amends the Capital Allowances (Energy-saving Plant and Machinery) Order 2001 (the Principal Order). The Principal Order implemented legislation to introduce a scheme for 100% first-year capital allowances to encourage businesses to invest in energy-saving plant or machinery.

2071 Environmental impact–Plant and machinery allowances

THE CAPITAL ALLOWANCES (ENVIRONMENTALLY BENEFICIAL PLANT AND MACHINERY) (AMENDMENT) ORDER 2016, SI 2016/926; made under the Capital Allowances Act 2001 s.45H(3)(5). In force: 6 October 2016.

This Order amends the Capital Allowances (Environmentally Beneficial Plant and Machinery) Order 2003 (Principal Order). The Principal Order implemented legislation to introduce a scheme for 100% first-year allowances to encourage businesses to invest in environmentally beneficial plant and machinery.

2072 Excise duty–Tobacco products–Regulations

THE FINANCE ACT 2016, SECTION 179 (APPOINTED DAYS) REGULATIONS 2016, SI 2016/1171; made under the Finance Act 2016 s.179(5)(6) (England and Wales (UKEW)). In force: In accordance with reg.2.

These Regulations appoint the days on which the amendments made by the Finance Act 2016 s.179 come into force. The amendments introduce a scheme prohibiting any person from carrying out any activity involving raw tobacco, unless the person holds an approval given by HMRC.

2073 **Finance Act 2016 (c.24)**

An Act to grant certain duties, to alter other duties, and to amend the law relating to the National Debt and the Public Revenue, and to make further provision in connection with finance.

2074 **HMRC–HMRC powers–HMRC's obligation under s.8Taxes Management Act 1970 to give notice requiring submission of tax return–Whether voluntary or unsolicited submission by taxpayer amounting to waiver of HMRC's obligation**

[Taxes Management Act 1970 (c.9) s.115, s.28A, s.28C, s.34, s.7, s.8, s.9, s.9A; Interpretation Act 1978 (c.30) s.7]

The appellant taxpayer appealed against the respondent HMRC's decision to close its enquiry into his self-assessment and make amendments so as to increase the tax due. HMRC had conducted a reconciliation of the taxpayer's PAYE records over a number of years, which showed significant underpayment. HMRC sent a self-assessment return to the taxpayer for the year ending 2009. The taxpayer did not complete it because he did not receive it as he no longer lived at the address to which it had been sent; he had tenants there. A P60 issued prior to the self-assessment showed a different address but HMRC's records had not been updated with that address. The taxpayer received other correspondence from HMRC at his old address which was passed on to him. HMRC sent to his old address an unsigned return from 2009. The taxpayer had not received it as his tenants had sent it back to HMRC blank and unsigned. Using the correct address, HMRC sent the taxpayer a duplicate return but by that time the Taxes Management Act 1970 s.34 time limit had expired and so HMRC relied on the fact that the first return was a valid notice under s.8. HMRC purported to issue a notice of determination in relation to the underpayment of tax to protect its position for the year in question pursuant to s.28C. The taxpayer then submitted a return in order to supersede that determination. HMRC purported to open an enquiry into the return and, following completion, issued a closure notice. The taxpayer contended that it was not open to HMRC to open an enquiry because no valid request to file a self-assessment return pursuant to s.8 had ever been made, and consequently the closure notice was also invalid.

Held: Appeal allowed. HMRC's initial request to the taxpayer to make and deliver a self-assessment was not served in compliance with s.115, as when it was made the address at which it was served was no longer the taxpayer's last-known address, since HMRC had received a more up to date address through the taxpayer's P60 months earlier. Nor was there any suggestion that HMRC had tried to deliver to his place of business or employment. Accordingly, the presumption of service in the Interpretation Act 1978 s.7 could not apply. The wording of s.7, s.8, s.9, s.9A and s.28A was clear and provided no basis for HMRC's submission that by making an unsolicited tax return a taxpayer had waived the requirement for a notice under s.8. Notice of the 2008/2009 self-assessment return had not been given pursuant to s.8 and therefore there was no valid determination under s.28C. The determination could not therefore be superseded because it was invalid and because the self-assessment was not delivered following a validly made request pursuant to s.8. The taxpayer's return was to be correctly categorised as a notice of liability pursuant to s.7 rather than a return. Had the s.34 time-limit not expired, HMRC could have issued a request for a return pursuant to s.8 in response. The consequence of HMRC's failings was that there was no opportunity to open an enquiry; the only route available would have been to make a discovery assessment had the statutory conditions been satisfied. Accordingly both the notice of enquiry and the closure notice were invalid, and the tax assessment had to be discharged (see paras 32, 38-39, 41-44 of judgment).

REVELL v REVENUE AND CUSTOMS COMMISSIONERS, [2016] UKFTT 97 (TC), [2016] S.F.T.D. 618, Judge Timothy Herrington, FTT (Tax).

2075 **HMRC officers–Confidentiality–Commissioners' off-the-record interview with journalists–Proper construction of s.18(2)(a)(i) Commissioners for Revenue and Customs Act 2005**

[Commissioners for Revenue and Customs Act 2005 (c.11) s.18(2)(a)(i)]

The appellants, a firm of chartered accountants and its chief executive officer, appealed against the refusal of their application for judicial review of disclosures by HMRC of confidential information. The appellants specialised in the media and entertainment industry. They promoted film investment schemes which utilised film tax relief. In June 2012, after an off-the-record interview with a senior HMRC officer, a newspaper published two articles about film schemes and tax avoidance. The appellants were named and the articles contained direct quotes about them and their tax activities. There was no dispute that the information had been disclosed during the off-the-record interview. The first instance judge refused the appellants' judicial review application, stating that he could not intervene unless satisfied that the officer could not rationally believe that speaking to the journalists would assist HMRC in the exercise of its tax collection functions. The judge held that the rationality standard was flexible and that the disclosures, being limited and made "off the record", had been legitimate and proportionate. The Court of Appeal rejected the appellants' arguments that the disclosures had not been made "for the purposes of a function of the Revenue and Customs" within the Commissioners for Revenue and Customs Act 2005 s.18(2)(a)(i), and that the judge had adopted the wrong standard of review. It held that s.18(2)(a) should be widely construed, and upheld the decision below that it was not for the court to review the facts as if it were the primary decision-maker. The issues were (1) the proper construction of s.18(2)(a)(i); (2) the proper approach of the court in judging the officer's conduct; (3) the significance of the officer's understanding that the interview was "off the record".

Held: Appeal allowed. (1) The appellants' claim was effectively a straightforward claim for breach of the common law duty of confidentiality. It was long-established that HMRC owed such a duty to taxpayers. It was entitled to hold their confidential financial information for the purpose of its primary function of revenue collection and management. Total confidentiality was a vital element in the working of the system, *R. v Inland Revenue Commissioners Ex p. National Federation of Self Employed and Small Businesses Ltd* [1982] A.C. 617, [1981] C.L.Y. 1433 applied and *Marcel v Commissioner of Police of the Metropolis* [1992] Ch. 225, [1992] C.L.Y. 3581 approved. The *Marcel* principle could be overridden by explicit statutory provisions, and s.18(2)(b) *did* permit disclosure of taxpayer information for various specific purposes other than HMRC's primary function. A wide interpretation of s.18(2)(a)(i) would mean, however, that those specific exceptions were otiose. More fundamentally, the vague wording would significantly erode the protection otherwise given to taxpayers by the duty of confidentiality, and that would run counter to the principle of legality, *R. v Secretary of State for the Home Department Ex p. Simms* [2000] 2 A.C. 115, [1999] C.L.Y. 4105 applied. In passing the Act, Parliament could not be supposed to have envisaged that it was authorising HMRC officials to discuss its views of individual taxpayers in off-the-record discussions whenever they thought it would be expedient for some collateral purpose connected with its functions, such as developing its relations with the press. Section 18(2)(a)(i) should be narrowly interpreted as reflecting the ordinary principle of taxpayer confidentiality. It only permitted disclosure to the extent necessary for HMRC to fulfil its primary function (see paras 14, 17-19, 22-25 of judgment). (2) It was for the court to decide whether there had been a breach of the duty of confidentiality, applying established legal principles to its own judgement of the facts. That principle applied equally to public law. Public bodies susceptible to judicial review were not immune from the ordinary application of the common law. Common law was multi-faceted and remained the bedrock of the English legal system. It was therefore for the court to approach the disclosures made by HMRC as if it was the primary decision-maker (paras 26-29). (3) Like many idioms "off the record" could bear different shades of meaning. The first instance judge found that the HMRC officer had understood the phrase to mean that the interview was a "background briefing" intended to influence journalists' views but without being published. There had been no appeal against that finding. However, nothing turned on what the officer intended: an impermissible disclosure of confidential information was no less impermissible just because it was passed on in confidence. The fact that the officer did not anticipate his comments being reported was no justification for making them. The officer's disclosure was not justified and the court would hear further submissions about the appropriate form of order (paras 30-31, 35).

R. (ON THE APPLICATION OF INGENIOUS MEDIA HOLDINGS PLC) v REVENUE AND CUSTOMS COMMISSIONERS, [2016] UKSC 54, [2016] 1 W.L.R. 4164, Lady Hale DPSC, SC.

2076 Income–Holiday accommodation–Income from furnished holiday lettings–Whether property income or trading income for tax purposes

[Income Tax (Trading and Other Income) Act 2005 (c.5) s.10, s.10(1), s.268, s.5; Income Tax Act 2007 (c.3)]

The First-tier Tribunal was required to determine whether income received by the appellant taxpayer was property income or trading income. In 2009, the appellant was gifted an estate. The estate included a manor house, gardens, a farmyard area which included working farm buildings, and holiday accommodation units. Lettings of the units were generally for two weeks or less. Each unit comprised one or more bedrooms, a sitting room and kitchen. Cooked breakfasts and a daily cleaning service were offered for an additional charge. Additional facilities available to guests included the recreational grounds; guided farm tours for children; a "concierge" service; a pool and pool house, and a games area. Guests were given a "licence to use the property for the purposes of a holiday" and the proprietors were "entitled to enter the property at any time if we deem it necessary". The appellant's 2009-10 tax return treated the income from the units as income from a trade. However, HMRC concluded that the income was property income from furnished holiday lettings. The taxpayer appealed. The tribunal had to determine: (i) whether the income was property income or trading income; (ii) to what extent the taxpayer's activities could be distinguished from HMRC's settled practice of taxing hotels and bed and breakfasts as trades; (iii) whether the income fell within the Income Tax (Trading and Other Income) Act 2005 s.10; (iv) if the taxpayer's activities constituted a furnished holiday lettings business within the Income Tax Act 2007, what effect, if any, that had on issues (i) to (iii).

Held: Appeal dismissed. (1) HMRC's default position was that income from the exploitation of property was to be taxed as property income. In certain situations, the taxpayer might be able to establish that the activities giving rise to the income constituted a trade, *Fry (Inspector of Taxes) v Salisbury House Estate Ltd* [1930] A.C. 432 and *Griffiths (Inspector of Taxes) v Jackson* [1983] S.T.C. 184, [1983] C.L.Y. 1978 considered. However, consideration of the relevant case law showed that the normal "badges of trade" had not been found to be of particular assistance. The tribunal had to determine "what is let, paid for and used", *Colman v Governors of the Rotunda Hospital, Dublin* 7 T.C. 517 applied. In reaching that determination, the nature and level of any services offered by the taxpayer would be important if the "cardinal principle" was to be displaced. Whether or not the taxpayer remained in occupation of the premises would also be relevant. However, there was no authority for the proposition that those two issues were determinative, *Westminster City Council v Southern Railway Co Ltd* [1936] A.C. 511, *Croft (Inspector of Taxes) v Sywell Aerodrome Ltd* [1942] 1 K.B. 317, *Gittos v Barclay* [1982] S.T.C. 390, [1982] C.L.Y. 1625, *MacLean v Revenue and Customs Commissioners* [2007] S.T.C. (S.C.D.) 350, [2008] C.L.Y. 3657, *Griffiths* and *Fry* considered. It was unclear whether "occupancy" meant legal or paramount occupancy, as argued by the appellant, or whether it was a question of fact and should be given its normal meaning. In any event, the appellant did not "occupy" each of the units, however occupancy was properly defined. Furthermore, while the additional services provided by the appellant were extensive, they were not such as to "change the whole picture", *Croft* considered. They were in large part consistent with the services normally provided by a landlord of furnished holiday accommodation. The recreational facilities offered were in substance features intended to increase the attractiveness of the units for letting, rather than additional services. The breakfasts and daily cleaning which were offered for an additional fee were insufficient to change the profit derivation from the exploitation of property to a package of services comprising a trade (see paras 34-85 of judgment). (2) The dividing lines between various types of rental accommodation had become increasingly fluid. In determining "what is being paid for", the spectrum was broad. However, the tax treatment of other businesses could not operate to convert the appellant's activity into a trade if there was no trade on the facts. To have described the units as a hotel or bed and breakfast to potential guests would have been confusing and misleading (paras 86-88). (3) Section

10(1) provided that the commercial occupation of land in the UK was treated for income tax purposes as the carrying on of a trade. Consideration of the statutory predecessors to s.10 showed that it was intended to apply where the commercial occupation of land fell short of amounting to a trade on basic principles. It was not intended to cut across s.5 and s.268 of the 2005 Act (paras 90-94). (4) The 2007 Act contained a special regime for UK furnished holiday lettings (FHL) businesses. Where the relevant conditions were satisfied the taxpayer was treated as trading for certain tax purposes, although he was not carrying on a trade on basic principles. The fact that the conditions might be satisfied did not preclude the taxpayer from establishing that his activity was in fact a trade. However, a taxpayer who could prove a trade need not in general avail himself of the quasi-trading benefits provided by the FHL rules. There was no evidence in the instant case that HMRC had failed to consider whether the appellant's activities amounted to an actual trade for tax purposes, either because it had pigeon-holed those activities as an FHL business or for other reasons (paras 95-97).

NOTT v REVENUE AND CUSTOMS COMMISSIONERS, [2016] UKFTT 106 (TC), [2016] S.F.T.D. 628, Judge Thomas Scott, FTT (Tax).

2077 Income tax–Barristers–Barrister subject to transitional regime of moving from cash to "true and fair" basis of recognising profits for tax purposes–Avoidance of double taxation on same profits–Peaceful enjoyment of possessions

[Finance Act 1998 (c.36) s.42; Taxes Management Act 1970 (c.9) s.29; European Convention on Human Rights 1950 Protocol 1 art.1; Human Rights Act 1998 (c.42) s.3]

A barrister appealed against discovery assessments made by HMRC in respect of the 2005/06 and 2007/08 tax years and against penalties related to those assessments. The appellant was in the "transitional regime" applicable to barristers moving from the cash to the "true and fair" basis of recognizing profits for tax purposes under the Finance Act 1998 s.42 for the three tax years 2005/06, 2006/07 and 2007/08. It was found that he had underpaid tax for the years 2005/06 and 2007/08 but had overpaid for the year 2006/07. He was informed by HMRC that any claim for overpayment relief for the 2006/07 year was out of time. HMRC then raised discovery assessments under the Taxes Management Act 1970 s.29 for the 2005/06 and 2007/08 tax years on the basis that the appellant had been "careless". It was the appellant's case that those assessments should take account of the overpayment of tax for the 2006/07 tax year, which should be offset against the tax due in the discovery assessments so that there would not be a double charge to tax in respect of the same profits. He based his claim on his rights under ECHR Protocol 1 art.1, as applied by the Human Rights Act 1998 s.3.

Held: Appeal allowed in part. (1) Although the tribunal had no supervisory jurisdiction over the conduct of HMRC, it had jurisdiction (and was indeed obliged) to consider whether the assessments had been properly issued pursuant to s.29. In determining that question, it was obliged to read the power conferred on HMRC by s.29 as being to issue an assessment which made good the loss of tax but only where assessing that amount did not breach the relevant taxpayer's rights under Protocol 1 art.1 to the extent that giving effect to those rights did not go against the "grain of the legislation" (see para.34 of judgment). (2) The appellant had satisfied the tribunal that the provisions of s.29, prior to any Protocol 1 art.1 override, were not consistent with his rights under Protocol 1 art.1. In applying UK tax legislation there was a presumption of avoiding double taxation on the same profits, [*R. v Inland Revenue Commissioners Ex p. Woolwich Equitable Building Society* [1990] 1 W.L.R. 1400, [1991] C.L.Y. 2084 applied. Furthermore, subjecting the same profits to tax twice could not reasonably be said to be pursuing a legitimate aim in the public interest or striking a fair balance between the demands of the general interest of the community and the protection of the individual's rights, *Lobler v Revenue and Customs Commissioners* [2015] UKUT 152 (TCC), [2015] S.T.C. 1893, [2015] C.L.Y. 2486 and *NKM v Hungary (66529/11)* [2013] S.T.C. 1104 applied. It was not proportionate for the consequence of the appellant's carelessness to result in what was effectively a 100% penalty in respect of the tax payable on the doubly-assessed profits. Furthermore, it was hard to see how assessments which included profits in respect of which tax had already been paid reflected a reasonable relationship between the means employed and the aims pursued or involved a fair balance between the general interest - that each taxpayer should pay his or her fair share of tax - and the appellant's Protocol 1 art.1 right not to be deprived of his possessions, *AXA General Insurance Ltd, Petitioners* [2011] UKSC 46, [2012] 1 A.C. 868, [2011] C.L.Y. 473 applied, *Barrett v Revenue and Customs Commissioners* [2015] UKFTT 329 (TC), [2015] S.T.I. 2968 considered (paras 56, 58). Were the assessments not to be reduced to avoid double taxation, the appellant would potentially be in a worse position than if he had not filed tax returns at all (para.63). (3) As regards the appropriate remedy, the aggregate profits included in the assessments for the underpayment tax years should be reduced so that the aggregate amount of tax payable in respect of the two underpayment tax years, taking into account, in respect of each underpayment tax year, the tax rates, personal allowance and band limits applicable to profits assessable in respect of the relevant tax year, was reduced by the overpaid tax. In that way, the appellant effectively obtained a credit for the tax which he had already paid but neither gained nor lost from the fact that he paid his tax on the profits in question in respect of the wrong tax year. The best way to achieve that was to allow the appeal in relation to the assessment in respect of the tax year 2005/06 but uphold the assessment in respect of the tax year 2007/08 (paras 71, 74). (4) The penalty in respect of the tax year 2005/06 would be reduced to 5% of the tax which remained subject to assessment in respect of that tax year following the necessary adjustments to the assessment for that tax year. The penalty in respect of the tax year 2007/08 would not be changed given that the assessment in respect of that tax year was upheld (para.78).

FESSAL v REVENUE AND CUSTOMS COMMISSIONERS, [2016] UKFTT 285 (TC), [2016] S.F.T.D. 585, Judge Tony Beare, FTT (Tax).

2078 Income tax–Business expenses–Deductibility of payment made by solicitor to settle German litigation

[Income Tax (Trading and Other Income) Act 2005 (c.5)]

HMRC appealed against a decision of the First-tier Tribunal (*Vaines v Revenue and Customs Commissioners* [2013] UKFTT 576 (TC)) that a payment made by the respondent solicitor to settle litigation was deductible for income tax purposes. HMRC had disallowed a deduction of £215,455 claimed in the respondent's 2007-08 self-assessment tax return at a time when he was a member of a limited liability partnership (S). Until December 2005, the respondent had worked as a solicitor in the London office of a law firm (H) which had offices in Germany and elsewhere. H ceased to trade, owing substantial sums to, among others, a German bank (B). The respondent believed that the risk of challenging B through the German courts was unacceptably high because if B succeeded he would be made bankrupt and lose his position as a partner in S. Following negotiations with B, the respondent agreed to pay it £215,455 to release him from all claims. He sought a deduction of the payment against his share of the profits of S. In finding that the payment was deductible for income tax purposes, the tribunal concluded as follows: the effect of the provisions of the Income Tax (Trading and Other Income) Act 2005 which concerned limited liability partnerships and partnerships in general was that it was the partners who were treated as carrying out the trade, not the firm itself, so that each partner was carrying on a trade, albeit collectively with others, with the result that his profits were taxed on him individually; the respondent's purpose in making the payment was to preserve and protect his career or trade, which meant that it had been made wholly and exclusively for the purposes of his trade; further, the payment was of a revenue, rather than a capital, nature.

Held: Appeal allowed. (1) The tribunal had erred in finding that the respondent's profits were taxed on him individually. It was the profits of the trade carried on collectively by the partnership that had always been recognised as the subject-matter of computation and charge. That had not changed with the enactment of the 2005 Act. It was in the context of the partnership trade conducted collectively that the respondent had to justify the deduction of his payment (see para.31 of judgment). (2) The tribunal had also been wrong to conclude that the payment had been made wholly and exclusively for the purposes of the respondent's trade. The "trade" in this context was the trade of S conducted collectively by its members as partners. The payment was a liability that had arisen from the respondent's previous engagement with H and in that respect had nothing whatsoever to do with the business of S. The respondent's decision to make the payment was a personal decision that he needed to make unless he was to risk bankruptcy and his continuing membership of S. Further, the respondent had to be able to establish that preserving and protecting his career was not just a purpose but his only purpose in making the payment. Professional considerations could not have been his sole consideration. The payment inevitably resolved what was a personal matter. The payment inevitably disposed of a potential liability that did not arise from his "trade" with S and necessarily brought with it the wider and personal benefits of avoiding extensive litigation and the risk of possible bankruptcy. It was therefore not possible to conclude that the respondent made the payment wholly and exclusively for the purposes of his trade with S (paras 37-39, 44, 58, 60). (3) Given the conclusions reached above, it was unnecessary to deal with the issue of whether the respondent's payment to B was a capital or a revenue expense. A variety of authorities established that payments designed to protect or preserve a person's trade or profession might be deductible as revenue expenditure and were not necessarily to be disallowed as capital expenditure. Had the respondent succeeded on the first two issues, a decision in his favour might have been reached on this issue (para.61).

VAINES v REVENUE AND CUSTOMS COMMISSIONERS *sub nom.* REVENUE AND CUSTOMS COMMISSIONERS v VAINES, [2016] UKUT 2 (TCC), [2016] S.T.C. 1201, Judge Malcolm Gammie QC, UT (Tax).

2079 Income tax–Discovery assessments–Appeal by personal representatives of deceased taxpayer–Discovery assessments made under extended time limits in s.36(1A) Taxes Management Act 1970–Right to fair trial

[Taxes Management Act 1970 (c.9) s.36(1A), s.36(1A)(a), s.95; European Convention on Human Rights 1950 art.6; Finance Act 2008 (c.9); Limitation Act 1980 (c.58) s.32]

The appellant personal representative of a deceased taxpayer appealed against a decision that discovery assessments made against the taxpayer by the respondent HMRC under the extended time limits in the Taxes Management Act 1970 s.36(1A) should not be set aside. Before his death the taxpayer had admitted an under-declaration of income with a view to taking advantage of an HMRC disclosure opportunity for medical professionals known as the tax health plan. HMRC were not satisfied that his disclosure came within the terms of the tax health plan and issued assessments for the tax years 1992-2006. The taxpayer appealed but later died. After being informed of the taxpayer's death HMRC cancelled the penalties, and the appellant requested that the protective assessments should be discharged. The tribunal found that requiring the appellant to contest the disputed assessments would not breach her human rights under ECHR art.6 because the making of the disputed assessments under the extended time limits conferred by s.36 of the 1970 Act did not constitute a taxpayer being charged with a criminal offence. The appellant submitted that the tribunal's decision involved errors of law in that *Director of the Assets Recovery Agency v Customs and Excise Commissioners* [2005] EWCA Civ 334 and *O'Rorke v Revenue and Customs Commissioners* [2013] UKUT 499 (TCC), [2014] S.T.C. 279, [2014] C.L.Y. 2772 had been misapplied because the application of s.36(1A)(a) did not simply enable HMRC to recover tax that the taxpayer should have paid and that the nature of HMRC's powers to assess under s.36(1A)(a) over a period of up to 20 years was penal; the changes to the law brought about by the Finance Act 2008 resulting in s.36(1A) were an instance of the use of state power to punish individuals for wrongdoing; the indicia of a sanction of a penal nature and serious personal consequences of involvement in alleged deliberate conduct were present.

Held: Appeal dismissed. (1) There was no analogy between s.36(1A)(a) and the penalty provisions of the Taxes Management Act 1970 s.95. Although HMRC had stated that the penalties were discharged because the taxpayer would not have a fair trial because of his death, the correct legal basis for cancelling penalties after a taxpayer's death was that criminal liability did not survive the person who had committed the criminal act and inheritance of the guilt was not compatible with the presumption of innocence required by art.6(2). The court had to determine whether s.36(1A)(a) was penal in nature by reference to the features of that provision alone. The key issue was whether it could be regarded as imposing a punishment to deter offending (see paras 57-58 of judgment). (2) Section 36(1A)(a) operated in a similar manner to the Limitation Act 1980 s.32. It was a gateway through which the path to a discovery assessment could be opened and it extended the time limit for the making of an assessment that was otherwise time-barred. The provision under consideration in *O'Rorke* simply enabled HMRC, upon proof of fraud, to recover from the taxpayer that which he should have paid. Likewise, s.36(1A)(a) was simply a provision which enabled HMRC to recover from the taxpayer the correct amount of tax, provided that it could demonstrate a loss of tax caused deliberately. In relation to *Charrington*, s.36 could not be characterised as the use of state power to punish an individual for wrongdoing. It was a mechanism to enable tax that might be due to be assessed and did not involve any formal penalty. The allegation of deliberate behaviour could not be equated to a criminal charge. Section 36(1A)(a) clearly operated as an incentive for a taxpayer to submit his returns in a timely fashion and the extended time limit might act as a deterrence against non-compliance with that obligation, but that kind of deterrence could not be construed as a punishment of the type necessary to make a provision penal in nature. It was not the purpose of s.36(1A)(a) to recover more tax than was properly due. The appellant was in no different position to any other taxpayer in having the burden to displace an assessment. She would have the opportunity to adduce evidence and HMRC would have to demonstrate that there had been a loss of tax caused as a result of deliberate behaviour. It was not unreasonable that the burden should then shift to the appellant to displace the presumption that the assessments were accurate. The impact of the burden on HMRC to prove both a loss of tax and deliberate behaviour on the part of the late taxpayer should not be underestimated. Section 36(1A)(a) was not penal in nature and did not engage art.6(1), O'Rorke and Charrington considered (paras 58-71).

WOOD (DECEASED) v REVENUE AND CUSTOMS COMMISSIONERS, [2016] UKUT 346 (TCC), [2016] B.T.C. 515, Morgan J, UT (Tax).

2080 Income tax–Discovery assessments–Correctness of refusal to determine competence of discovery assessment as preliminary issue

[Taxes Management Act 1970 (c.9) s.29, s.29(2), s.29(4), s.29(5), s.29(8); Civil Procedure Rules 1998 Pt 11]

A taxpayer appealed against a decision (*Hargreaves v Revenue and Customs Commissioners* [2014] UKUT 395 (TCC), [2015] S.T.C. 905, [2014] C.L.Y. 2890) refusing to order a preliminary hearing to determine the competence of a discovery assessment issued by the respondent HMRC. The taxpayer had claimed to be non-resident in the UK for tax purposes for the purposes of his self-assessment tax return. HMRC issued the discovery assessment under the Taxes Management Act 1970 s.29 on the basis that the taxpayer was not entitled to be treated as neither resident nor ordinarily resident in the UK. The taxpayer asserted that HMRC had issued the discovery assessment when it lacked the power to do so as it had not satisfied the conditions set out in s.29(4) or s.29(5) of the Act (the competence issue). The Upper Tribunal upheld the First-tier Tribunal's refusal to order a preliminary hearing to decide the competence issue. It held that the evidence on the substantive issue of whether the taxpayer had been resident in the UK during the relevant period was plainly relevant to the competence issue. It determined that it would need to hear evidence on the two issues together and that it was possible to have a single hearing. The taxpayer submitted that (1) it was to be inferred that meeting the conditions of s.29(4) and s.29(5) had to be dealt with as a threshold matter because on an appeal, the tribunal's power under s.50(6) was merely to reduce an assessment, not to quash it, meaning that s.29(8) must, by necessary implication, confer the power to quash a discovery assessment if the relevant conditions were not met; (2) the purpose of the legislation was to give the taxpayer the right not to have to present his case under s.29(2) until HMRC had proved that the competence conditions were met, but if the competence issue were determined during the substantive appeal he would lose that right; (3) the power to make a discovery assessment was penal in its effect because if a taxpayer made a small mistake, the door was open to HMRC to reopen the computation of all tax for the relevant period; (4) the position regarding the preliminary issue of competence was analogous to that arising in an objection to jurisdiction under CPR Pt 11 and was also analogous to criminal proceedings.

Held: Appeal dismissed. (1) Section 29(8) was dealing with the procedure the taxpayer had to adopt, not the powers of the tribunal. Further, the tribunal's power to reduce an assessment under s.50(6) clearly included a power to reduce it to nil. There was no reason why Parliament should provide for the remedy that might be given in judicial review proceedings. The Court of Appeal had decided that the conditions in s.29(4) and s.29(5) were not a precondition to the validity of a discovery assessment, *Hankinson v Revenue and Customs Commissioners* [2011] EWCA Civ 1566, [2012] 1 W.L.R. 2322, [2012] C.L.Y. 3268 applied. In any event, the procedure in s.29 was not a two-stage process because s.29(8) required any objection to the competence of a discovery assessment to be dealt with on an appeal (see para.38 of judgment). (2) The decision in *Dixon & Gaunt Ltd v Inland Revenue Commissioners* [1947] 1 All E.R. 723, [1947-51] C.L.Y. 8008 did not support the proposition that in appeals against discovery assessments, HMRC always had to call its evidence first, *Dixon & Gaunt Ltd* considered. There were no legislative provisions which established a rule as to which party was to begin in every case. The taxpayer would only be directed to open the appeal where the tribunal considered that to be a just way of proceeding and it was difficult to see how it would reach that conclusion in the instant case (paras 40-43). (3) The door was not open to HMRC to reopen the computation of all tax for the relevant period once it had shown that the competence conditions were met. Rather, once HMRC had shown that the competence conditions were met, the burden rested on the taxpayer to establish that the assessment was wrong, *Hurley v Taylor (Inspector of Taxes)* [1999] S.T.C. 1, [1998] C.L.Y. 4668 applied (para.47). (4) In dealing with the statutory code, the court should not be dictated to by any analogies. Further, a criminal analogy did not assist the court in determining whether the taxpayer had a right to a separate hearing because the issue was one of statutory interpretation. Section 29 was not penal. Even if there were a single issue in a criminal trial in relation to which the burden of proof fell on the defendant, the defendant would not necessarily be required to call evidence first. Nor would a defendant in criminal proceedings be prevented from making a submission of no case to answer on any issue for which the prosecution had the burden. Section 29 did not impose criminal liability. On the appeal under s.29, the taxpayer would have the privilege against self-incrimination but the wider right to silence did not arise as he was not subject to any criminal charge (paras 49, 53, 56-57). (5) Under s.29, the taxpayer could not establish the right to require a separate trial to determine whether the competence issue was satisfied. He received the protection to which he was entitled on the hearing of the appeal through the tribunal's exercise of its powers of case management (paras 5, 60-61, 63).

HARGREAVES v REVENUE AND CUSTOMS COMMISSIONERS, [2016] EWCA Civ 174, [2016] 1 W.L.R. 2981, Arden LJ, CA (Civ Div).

2081 Income tax–Double taxation treaties–Deep sea diver resident for tax purposes in South Africa but employed to undertake diving activities in UK–Whether income chargeable to UK income tax–Business profit

[United Kingdom-South Africa Double Taxation Convention 2002; Income Tax (Trading and Other Income) Act 2005 (c.5) s.15; Double Taxation Relief (Taxes on Income) (South Africa) Order 2002 (SI 2002/3138) Sch.1; Taxation (International and Other Provisions) Act 2010 (c.8) s.6; Vienna Convention on the Law of Treaties 1969 art.31, art.32; Income Tax (Earnings and Pensions) Act 2003 (c.1) s.6(5)]

The tribunal was required to determine, as a preliminary issue, the correct interpretation of the United Kingdom-South Africa Double Taxation Convention 2002. The appellant was a South African resident employed as a deep sea diver in the UK. HMRC had assessed him for tax under art.14 of the Convention, which concerned income from employment, and had therefore determined that his diving income was chargeable to UK income tax. The appellant's case was that his income constituted business profits within art.7 of the Convention and was therefore exempt from UK income tax because he had no permanent establishment in the UK within the meaning of art.5. He relied upon the Income Tax (Trading and Other Income) Act 2005 s.15, which deemed employed seabed divers to be carrying on a UK trade, even though they might have employee status. Whether the appellant was an employee or self-employed during the relevant tax years was for determination in the substantive appeal. The issue for the instant tribunal was whether, if s.15 of the Act applied to the appellant's diving activities so that he was deemed to be self-employed, he was liable to tax under art.7 or art.14 of the Convention.

Held: Preliminary issue determined in favour of appellant. Under the Taxation (International and Other Provisions) Act 2010 s.6, double taxation agreements had effect "despite anything in any enactment ... in relation to income tax and corporation tax so far as the arrangements provide ... for taxing income of non-UK resident persons that rises from sources in the UK". Double taxation agreements had to be interpreted in accordance with the Vienna Convention on the Law of Treaties 1969 art.31 and art.32, *Anson v Revenue and Customs Commissioners* [2015] UKSC 44, [2015] 4 All E.R. 288, [2015] C.L.Y. 2462 applied (see paras 18-19, 26-28 of judgment). Deeming provisions, such as s.15 of the Act, were common in UK tax law, but the exact purpose of s.15 was difficult to discern. Its real purpose was to be found in the more relaxed rules, when compared with those for employment income, for deductibility of expenses in the calculation of trading income. The question was how far the effect of the deemed treatment in s.15 extended. That issue depended on the interpretation of art.7 and art.14 of the 2002 Convention. Their interpretation had to be in accordance with art.3(2) of the 2002 Convention, which mandated that any term not defined within the Convention "shall" have the meaning attributed to it by domestic tax laws. In art.7 of the 2002 Convention, the words "enterprise" and "business" were not defined; in art.14, the words "salaries, wages and other similar remuneration derived .... in respect of an employment" were not defined. Those words therefore had to be determined in accordance with synonymous terms in UK tax law, *Squirrell v Revenue and Customs Commissioners* [2005] S.T.C. (S.C.D.) 717, [2006] C.L.Y. 4254 applied (paras 93-101, 105-108). The phrase "profits of an enterprise" in art.7 included the charge to income tax on the "profits of a trade, profession or vocation" in s.5 of the 2005 Act, and also included the profits arising from the deemed trade pursuant to s.15 of that Act. The clear purpose of s.15 was to re-characterise "for income tax purposes" what would otherwise be the exercise of employment duties as the carrying on of a trade. The result of the s.15 treatment was that the appellant's income constituted profits within art.7 of the 2002 Convention. Moreover, the Income Tax (Earnings and Pensions) Act 2003 s.6(5) excluded income falling within s.15 from the charge to income tax, which meant that, under the UK tax law which corresponded to art.14 of the 2002 Convention, the appellant's income was not employment income and could not fall within art.14. The phrase "for income tax purposes" in s.15 would include s.6 of the 2010 Act, which provided that double taxation arrangements had effect "in relation to income tax ... so far as the arrangements provide". That was another factor in support of s.15 having effect in relation to the 2002 Convention (paras 111-114, 118). Provisions such as art.3(2) of the 2002 Convention that allowed a contracting state to rely on a deemed domestic meaning did not amount to allowing it to unilaterally change its law to expand its Convention taxing rights. If a contracting state changed its domestic law *after* the conclusion of a double tax treaty to change the effect of the treaty's distributive rules for a certain type of income, that could contravene the requirements of good faith imposed by art.31(1) of the Vienna Convention and by international law generally. A breach of the obligation of good faith could override the words "at any time" in art.3(2) of the 2002 Convention. In the instant case, the predecessor of s.15 was enacted long before the 2002 convention was concluded, so there was no reason to exclude the meaning which it gave to the appellant's income (paras 115-117).

FOWLER v REVENUE AND CUSTOMS COMMISSIONERS, [2016] UKFTT 234 (TC), [2016] S.F.T.D. 535, Judge Guy Brannan, FTT (Tax).

2082 Income tax–Earnings and pensions–Car fuel benefits

THE VAN BENEFIT AND CAR AND VAN FUEL BENEFIT ORDER 2016, SI 2016/1174; made under the Income Tax (Earnings and Pensions) Act 2003 s.170(1A)(2)(5)(6). In force: 31 December 2016.

This Order amends of the Income Tax (Earnings and Pensions) Act 2003 ss.150(1), 155(1B) and 161(b). Where an employee receives fuel for a car or van as a result of their employment and they are chargeable to tax in respect of that vehicle under the Act ss.120 or 154, the cash equivalent of the benefit of that fuel is treated as earnings under the Act ss.149 and 160.

2083 Income tax–Emoluments–Payment to employee for client business brought with him to new employer–Whether emolument payment from employment liable to income tax

[Income Tax (Earnings and Pensions) Act 2003 (c.1) s.9; Taxation of Chargeable Gains Act 1992 (c.12)]

HMRC appealed against a decision that a payment made to an employee for client business he brought with him when he joined his new employer did not constitute earnings from his employment liable to income tax. The first respondent employer was part of a group of companies operating in the financial services sector. The second respondent employee had built up a customer portfolio for another employer (B). He and his team were offered employment by the first respondent. The offer letter stated that they would also receive payment for bringing client business to the group from their previous employment. Eight months later they entered into a contract with another company in the group (C2), under which they would receive a "goodwill payment" for bringing client business to the group. The sum was payable after two years' employment with the group. The issue was whether that payment was an emolument from employment liable to income tax under the Income Tax (Earnings and Pensions) Act 2003 s.9, or whether it was capital consideration for disposal of an asset under the Taxation of Chargeable Gains Act 1992. HMRC considered that it was the former, but the First-tier tribunal concluded that it was the latter as the contracts were separate and had been negotiated independently. For accounting purposes, the group had treated the sum as payment for an asset.

Held: Appeal allowed. (1) There had been errors in the tribunal judge's reasoning: (a) he had attached too much weight to the fact that the contract of employment and the contract for payment for client business were separate. It was clear that the two contracts had derived from the single objective of transferring B's clients to C2 and from a single arrangement articulated in the covering letter accompanying the job offer. The two elements went together: the employee and his team would not have been employed unless they were to bring their clients with them; (b) he had lost sight of the ultimate question in issue, being whether the payment for the client business was "from" the employee's employment; (c) he had wrongly attached importance to the perceptions of the parties, seeing the arrangements made as reflecting their subjective intentions rather than assessing the effect of those arrangements objectively. Therefore, his decision was set aside (see paras 43, 53, 67-69, 82 of judgment). (2) Following *Shilton v Wilmshurst (Inspector of Taxes)* [1991] 1 A.C. 684, [1991] C.L.Y. 2092, the starting point was whether the payment was for being or becoming an employee. Where the payment was made by a third party, the question was whether it was motivated by a desire to see that the employee entered into or continued in the employment of another, *Shilton* followed. The employee was clearly employed by the first respondent in the hope and expectation that at least some of his clients would follow him from B to C2. C2 clearly had an interest in the performance of the employment contract (para.163). (3) The payment was a reward for providing a service in introducing those clients and procuring, or assisting in procuring, their transfer. That did not equate to goodwill. The employee had not owned nor had any legal interest in the business carried on by B or the goodwill of that business. His client connections had not been a right to sell customer portfolios or a right of ownership or management of the assets; rather, they had been personal relationships, *Asprey & Garrard Ltd v WRA (Guns) Ltd (t/a William R Asprey Esquire)* [2001] EWCA Civ 1499, [2002] E.T.M.R. 47, [2002] C.L.Y. 2785 applied, *Kirby (Inspector of Taxes) v Thorn EMI Plc* [1988] 1 W.L.R. 445, [1987] C.L.Y. 277 and Ho*Hose v Warwick* 27 T.C. 459 considered (paras 111, 116, 164-167). (4) The payment by C2 to the employee was linked to and arose from his employment by the first respondent, *Kuehne & Nagel Drinks Logistics Ltd v Revenue and Customs Commissioners* [2012] EWCA Civ 34, [2012] S.T.C. 840, [2012] C.L.Y. 3299 followed. It was therefore liable to income tax (para.168).

REVENUE AND CUSTOMS COMMISSIONERS v SMITH & WILLIAMSON CORPORATE SERVICES LTD, [2015] UKUT 666 (TCC), [2016] S.T.C. 1393, Warren J, UT (Tax).

2084 Income tax–Employee benefits–Employer providing employees with lease cars–Extent to which arrangement giving rise to liability to income tax

[Income Tax (Earnings and Pensions) Act 2003 (c.1) s.114, s.120, s.62]

HMRC appealed against a decision (*Apollo Fuels Ltd v Revenue and Customs Commissioners* [2014] UKUT 95 (TCC), [2014] B.T.C. 510, [2014] C.L.Y. 2911) that car-leasing arrangements entered into by the respondents were not liable to income tax. The first respondent employer had entered into car leases with the second respondent employees who used the cars for business and private purposes. The employees were paid for business mileage at the same rate as employees who used their own cars for business purposes. The sums due to them as mileage allowances were set off against the rentals owed to the employer under the car leases. HMRC accepted that the rental paid by the employees was an arm's length commercial rental, similar to what the employees would pay if they leased a car from a third party. The issue was whether the arrangements fell within the Income Tax (Earnings and Pensions) Act 2003 s.114. For s.114 to apply, the car had to have been "made available (without any transfer of the property in it) to [the] employee". Section 120 provided that the cash equivalent of "the benefit of the car" was to be treated as earnings. The Upper Tribunal concluded that the leases did not involve a transfer of property in the car, but the application of s.114 was excluded by virtue of s.114(3) and s.62. It found that s.114 was also inapplicable because fair bargains were excluded from the regime for taxing benefits under s.120. The court was required to determine whether: (1) the leases had involved a transfer of property in the car;(2) there was no "benefit of the car" within the meaning of s.120 because the employees paid the full market rental for the cars;(3) the application of income tax was excluded by s.114(3) and s.62.

Held: Appeal dismissed. (1) *Transfer of property* - Section 114(1)(a) did not refer to the creation or transfer of a proprietary interest in the car but to "any transfer of the property in it". The property in a chattel, such as a car, was the legal title to it. It meant the absolute ownership interest. While the absolute ownership interest could be subject to other interests, such as a charge or mortgage, "the property" in a chattel was not constituted by an equitable or limited propriety interest. Contractual rights under the lease agreement might have created a proprietary interest in favour of the hirer, but they did not involve the transfer of the property in the chattels to the hirer. They merely qualified the owner's general property in the chattels. Accordingly, the UT's decision that there was no transfer of the property in the leased car, and that s.114(1)(a) was satisfied, was correct, but not for the reasons it gave (see paras 30, 33 of judgment). (2) *Benefit of the car* - Parliament had used the phrase "the benefit of the car" in s.114(2) and s.120(1) without defining it. The choice of the word "benefit", without any definition altering its ordinary meaning, was intended to show that before a charge to income tax could arise, there had to be a benefit to the employee in the ordinary sense of that word. It was established in *Mairs (Inspector of Taxes) v Haughey* [1992] S.T.C. 495 and *Wilson (Inspector of Taxes) v Clayton* [2004] EWCA Civ 1657, [2005] S.T.C. 157, [2005] C.L.Y. 4071 that the law did not tax an employee in respect of a fair bargain. While those decisions concerned a different provision, the statements were applicable to the word "benefit" in other parts of the tax code. The UT was right to decide that a charge to income tax would arise under Chapter 6 and s.114 only if the terms on which a car was leased to an employee conferred a benefit on the employee in the ordinary sense of that word. The employees in the instant case received no such benefit, *Mairs* and *Wilson* applied (paras 43, 45, 50-51, 71-73). (3) *Section 114(3)* - Since no charge to income tax arose under Chapter 6 in respect of the cars, it was not strictly necessary to consider the s.114(3) issue. However, the court expressed the following view: the section was intended to prevent double taxation, and s.62 concerned something that was capable of being converted into money, or of direct monetary value. If the car was leased to an employee at less than the market rate, the employee could derive a benefit by sub-hiring the car at a full market rate. The cars had been leased to the employees at full market value and therefore no charge to income tax would arise in consequence of section 62. However, the UT had accepted that a nil amount arising under section 62 was nonetheless "an amount constituting earnings" in respect of the benefit of the car. That was incorrect. Nil was not a number or an amount, but the absence of a number or an amount (paras 76-80, 82).

APOLLO FUELS LTD v REVENUE AND CUSTOMS COMMISSIONERS *sub nom.* REVENUE AND CUSTOMS COMMISSIONERS v APOLLO FUELS LTD, [2016] EWCA Civ 157, [2016] 4 W.L.R. 96, Sharp LJ, CA (Civ Div).

2085 Income tax–Enterprise investment scheme–Preferential rights of ordinary shareholders

[Income Tax Act 2007 (c.3) Pt 5, s.173(2)(aa), s.205]

A company appealed against HMRC's refusal to authorise it to issue compliance certificates confirming that its ordinary shares could benefit from enterprise investment scheme tax relief. The company needed to raise revenue from its shareholders and decided to reorganise its capital. It issued 1,657,000 ordinary shares which raised the necessary funds. The company's share capital was divided into ordinary shares and deferred shares. The new articles of association gave the ordinary shares a preferential right to a return of assets of the company on a liquidation or otherwise. The company submitted a Form EIS1 to HMRC declaring that, at no time since the ordinary shares had been issued, had they carried any preferential rights to its assets on a winding up. Form EIS1 was a "compliance statement" under the Income Tax Act 2007 s.205, which certified that the requirements for enterprise investment scheme relief on the issue of the ordinary shares were satisfied. Part 5 of the Act set out the details of the scheme, which provided for relief when individuals subscribed for shares in qualifying companies. Section 173(2)(aa), located in Part 5, provided that the shares could not carry "any present or future preferential right to a company's assets on its winding up". HMRC responded that the shares carried a preferential right under the new articles. The company submitted that (1) the preferential right fell within the de minimis principle; (2) applying *WT Ramsay Ltd v Inland Revenue Commissioners* [1982] A.C. 300, [1981] C.L.Y. 1385, s.173(2)(aa) had to be construed purposively and the ordinary shares were the kind of shares that Parliament intended to benefit from such relief as they carried the majority of the risk in its business; (3) HMRC's published guidance stated that such ordinary shares were not necessarily to be regarded as carrying a preferential right.

Held: Appeal dismissed. (1) The de minimis principle could, in appropriate situations, apply as an aid to the construction of a taxing statute. However, the principle had to yield to any contrary intention. The ultimate question, whether phrased in terms of the *Ramsay* approach to statutory construction or the application of the de minimis principle, was whether Parliament intended the ordinary shares to satisfy the condition set out in s.173(2)(aa), even though they carried some, albeit small, preferential rights to a return of capital on a winding up. Part 5 set out a number of detailed conditions that the investor, the company being invested in and the shares issued had to satisfy. Many of those conditions contained qualifications and exceptions. The fact that Part 5 was a "closely articulated" set of statutory provisions led to the conclusion that if Parliament had intended small or insignificant preferential rights to be ignored when applying s.173(2)(aa), it would have made express provision to that effect, *Collector of Stamp Revenue v Arrowtown Assets Ltd* 6 I.T.L. Rep. 454 considered. That conclusion did not mean that the de minimis principle was incapable of application in any circumstances in which Parliament had not made specific provision. That would deprive the maxim of effect. However, the fact that Parliament had not made specific provision in a "closely articulated" statutory regime was evidence of the necessary contrary intention that would prevent the de minimis principle from applying in the instant case. Some inferences could be drawn from the statutory procedure that had to be followed to enable an investor to claim relief. Before a company could issue a certificate of compliance, it had to first certify to HMRC that all of the conditions of enterprise investment scheme relief, including the s.173(2)(aa) condition, were satisfied. Parliament therefore required a company to make a formal declaration to HMRC that the shares being issued did not carry any preferential rights to assets on a winding up. While lawyers might be aware of the existence of the de minimis principle, directors of companies which could benefit from such relief would probably not be. If Parliament had truly intended that a company could properly make a compliance statement even if the shares being issued carried some, albeit small, preferential rights, that was a further reason why it would have said so expressly (see paras 53-59 of judgment). (2) With regard to the argument that a purposive construction of s.173(2)(aa) should lead to the conclusion that relief was available, Parliament intended relief to be available in connection with shares that carried "genuine economic risk" only where those shares did not also carry any preferential right to assets on a winding up, *Ramsay* considered (para.60). (3) The extracts from HMRC's published manuals did not affect the matter. The extracts set out HMRC's view of the law rather than binding principles of law. They also seemed to be aimed at a completely different situation, namely where the rights of a deferred share to a return of assets on a winding up were so contingent as not to be meaningful. While the preferential right in the instant appeal was small, it was definitely not contingent and would apply on any winding up of the company (para.61).

FLIX INNOVATIONS LTD v REVENUE AND CUSTOMS COMMISSIONERS, [2015] UKFTT 558 (TC), [2016] S.F.T.D. 173, Judge Jonathan Richards, FTT (Tax).

2086 Income tax–Enterprise investment scheme–Preferential rights of ordinary shareholders

[Income Tax Act 2007 (c.3) s.173(2)(aa)]

A company appealed against a First-tier Tribunal decision that HMRC were correct in refusing to authorise it to issue compliance certificates confirming that its ordinary shares could benefit from enterprise investment scheme relief. The company had decided to reorganise its share capital to enable investment in the business. Following the reorganisation, the company's share capital consisted of ordinary shares and deferred shares. The company's shareholders adopted new articles of association which gave the ordinary shares a preferential right to a return of assets of the company on a liquidation or otherwise. It required holders of ordinary shares to receive payment of the nominal value of £0.0001 per share before the holders of deferred shares. The company submitted a Form EIS1 to HMRC, declaring that the ordinary shares had never carried any preferential rights to its assets on a winding-up. HMRC decided, however, that the shares did carry such a preferential right and did not therefore qualify for relief. The company appealed. It claimed that the meaning of "preferential right" in the Income Tax Act 2007 s.173(2)(aa) should be construed purposively and/or in accordance with the de minimis principle, and that the shares should not be excluded from EIS relief because of an insignificant preferential right. The tribunal concluded that if Parliament had intended small or insignificant preferential rights to be ignored it would have done so expressly.

Held: Appeal dismissed. (1) Section 173(2)(aa) referred to "any ... preferential right". Giving those words their ordinary meaning, that was a clear indication that any description of preferential right disqualified the shares in question from benefiting from EIS relief. The word "any" was an indication of a contrary Parliamentary intention, namely an intention to exclude the application of the de minimis rule, *Boxmoor Construction Ltd v Revenue and Customs Commissioners* [2016] UKUT 91 (TCC), [2016] B.V.C. 508, [2016] 2196 applied. Although the general policy of the EIS legislation was to limit relief to ordinary shares which carried the risk and reward of ownership, Parliament implemented that policy by limiting relief, inter alia, to those ordinary shares which did not carry any present or future preferential rights to assets on a winding-up. Parliament did not say that the right to relief was restricted only as regards shares where the preference rights were significant or material; it specifically said that the relief was denied if any preferential right to a return of capital existed. Purposive construction could not be used to give effect to a perceived wider policy in cases where the words used would not bear the meaning, *Trigg v Revenue and Customs Commissioners* [2016] UKUT 165 (TCC), [2016] S.T.C. 1310, [2016] 2045 applied. Part 5 of the 2007 Act was, as the tribunal found, "closely articulated" legislation. The fact that the relevant legislation was highly detailed, prescriptive or "closely articulated" did not exclude the general principle that the statutory words had to receive a purposive construction, *Trigg* applied. Nonetheless, it was true that highly prescriptive or formulaic legislation would often give less scope for a purposive interpretation resulting in a meaning which was different from the literal meaning, *Berry v Revenue and Customs Commissioners* [2011] UKUT 81 (TCC), [2011] S.T.C. 1057, [2011] C.L.Y. 3366 applied. In the instant case, the tribunal correctly concluded that, given the "highly articulated" provisions of Part 5, it was unlikely that Parliament would have intended to permit a small or insignificant preferential right to be ignored in applying s.173(2)(aa) without doing so expressly. In the context of the highly detailed provisions of Part 5, and the use of the word "any" in s.173(2)(aa), it was impossible to ignore the preferential rights carried by the ordinary shares. To do so would be to rectify the language of the statute rather than to construe it purposively. The requirement that a company had to certify to HMRC that all the conditions of EIS relief, including the condition in s.173(2)(aa), were satisfied was much easier for a company officer to understand than a test which required an application of the de minimis test, or a test which required "a normal commercial interpretation" of the words "carry ... any ... preferential right" (see paras 36-50 of judgment). (2) The tribunal had also concluded, noting that it was not necessary for its decision, that if there was scope for small preferential rights to be ignored, the preferential right in the instant case would be de minimis and sufficiently small to be ignored. However, when the preference on the ordinary shares was compared with the nominal share capital on the deferred shares, it could not be described as de minimis (paras 51-54).

FLIX INNOVATIONS LTD v REVENUE AND CUSTOMS COMMISSIONERS, [2016] UKUT 301 (TCC), [2016] S.T.C. 2206, Mann J, UT (Tax).

2087 Income tax–Exemptions–Employer-Financed Retirement Benefits

THE EMPLOYER-FINANCED RETIREMENT BENEFITS (EXCLUDED BENEFITS FOR TAX PURPOSES) (AMENDMENT) REGULATIONS 2016, SI 2016/1036; made under the Income Tax (Earnings and Pensions) Act 2003 s.393B(3)(d)(4A). In force: 1 December 2016.

These Regulations amend the Employer-Financed Retirement Benefits (Excluded Benefits for Tax Purposes) Regulations 2007 which exempt specified benefits under an employer-financed retirement benefits scheme from the charge to tax under the Income Tax (Earnings and Pensions) Act 2003 s.394. They exempt the provision of trivial benefits to or in respect of a former employee that would have been exempted under ss.323A and 323B of the 2003 Act had they been provided to or in respect of a current employee. They provide that the amendments made by this instrument have effect for the tax year 2016-17 and subsequent tax years. Power to make legislation with retrospective effect is contained in s.393B(4A) of the 2003 Act which allows Regulations made under s.393B(3)(d) to include provision having effect in relation to times before they are made. In addition they insert a new Part 3 para.22 of the Schedule to the 2007 Regulations to include an exemption for the provision of trivial benefits to or in respect of a former employee that would have been exempted had they been provided to or in respect of a current employee.

2088 Income tax–Income-related benefits

THE SOCIAL SECURITY (SCOTTISH RATE OF INCOME TAX ETC.) (AMENDMENT) REGULATIONS 2016, SI 2016/233; made under the Social Security Contributions and Benefits Act 1992 s.123(1)(a)(d), s.136(3(4)(5)(a), s.137(1), s.175(3); Jobseekers Act 1995 s.12(1)(2)(3)(4)(a), s.35(1), s.36(2); Welfare Reform Act 2007 s.17(1)(2)(3)(a), s.24(1), s.25(3). In force: 6 April 2016.

These Regulations amend various sets of existing legislation relating to income-related social security benefits to reflect the introduction, by the Scottish Government, of a Scottish rate of income tax for Scottish taxpayers, from 6 April 2016, being the start of the 2016/17 tax year.

2089 Income tax–Indexation–Consumer Prices Index

THE INCOME TAX (INDEXATION) ORDER 2016, SI 2016/1175; made under the Income Tax Act 2007 s.57(6). In force: 5 December 2016.

This Order fulfils the indexation requirement in the Income Tax Act 2007 s.57 that certain allowances and limits are increased by reference to the Consumer Prices Index. These increases have effect for the 2017-18 tax year.

2090 Income tax–Information notices–Lack of meaningful response–Punitive penalty under Sch.36 Pt 7 para.50 Finance Act 2008

[Finance Act 2008 (c.9) Sch.36 Pt 7 para.50; Tribunal Procedure (Upper Tribunal) Rules 2008 (SI 2008/2698) r.42, r.43]

A taxpayer applied to set aside a decision (*Revenue and Customs Commissioners v Tager* [2015] UKUT 40 (TCC), [2015] S.T.C. 1687, [2015] C.L.Y. 2483) imposing tax-related penalties for a failure to comply with three HMRC information notices. The penalties, totalling £1,246,020, were issued under the Finance Act 2008 Sch.36 Pt 7 para.50. Two notices related to income tax and capital gains tax self-assessment returns. The third related to the late delivery of an inheritance tax account following the death of the taxpayer's father, the taxpayer being his father's personal representative. HMRC applied for tax-related penalties to be imposed. The tribunal allowed the taxpayer further time to comply, with undertakings given by him. When the matter came back before the tribunal, there had been some compliance with the notices. The taxpayer accepted that he had no reasonable excuse for failing to fully comply. He had previously argued that the amounts of tax estimated by HMRC were excessive and that his failure to comply with the notices was attributable to difficulties in securing the necessary information. The taxpayer made the instant application, having fully complied with the information notices. The taxpayer submitted that procedural errors in the decision relating to the tribunal's approach to determination of the level of penalty warranted it being set aside under the Tribunal Procedure (Upper Tribunal) Rules 2008 r.43. HMRC agreed that the assessment of the tax at risk was incorrect, but argued that the necessary amendments should be made under r.42, the slip rule, and that the jurisdiction to set aside and re-make the decision was not engaged.

Held: Judgment accordingly. (1) Rule 43 was not engaged. Although it might be in the interests of justice to correct a decision which did not accurately reflect the evidence, and that, correspondingly, r.43(1)(a) was met, the conditions in r.43(2) were not satisfied. The taxpayer's argument was that the tribunal's misunderstanding or misinterpretation of the evidence amounted to "some other procedural irregularity" under r.43(2)(d) and that that phrase should be given a wide interpretation. Although the phrase invited a wide interpretation, and made it clear that r.43(2)(a) to (c) did not represent an exhaustive list of conditions, it was apparent from the manner in which the conditions were set out that r.43(2)(d) had to be read in its context, and interpreted consistently with what preceded it. The error on which the taxpayer relied, the tribunal's failure to understand the evidence or to make a finding supported by the evidence, was a judicial rather than a procedural error. Rule 43(2)(d) was clearly intended to apply only in the case of failings which led to a flawed hearing, and could not be extended to encompass judicial errors. Rule 42 was also not applicable. It was designed for the correction of minor errors, such as spelling mistakes, the transposition of digits, errors in dates, or other slips which, although warranting correction, were accidental mistakes made while committing the decision to writing. In practice, such corrections were commonly suggested by the parties during the seven-day period between the sending of the draft decision to them and its public release. They were usually uncontroversial. Rule 42 did not lend itself to the correction of errors which included some element of dispute. It was not permissible to deploy r.42 where the finding might be erroneous but the record of it was not. That was even more so when the parties did not agree on what the correction should be (see paras 15-23 of judgment). (2) The errors could still be addressed without the need for an appeal. HMRC's original application had not been finally determined because of the outstanding matter of the taxpayer's failure to comply with his undertakings. The tribunal was still seised of the matter and the overriding objective required the assessment of the tax at risk to be revisited. That had to be the appropriate course when the question was the correct application of a penal provision. If agreement on the amount of inheritance tax payable could be reached, the pragmatic course would be for the parties to agree on the amount of tax "which has not been, or is not likely to be, paid by" the estate. That was not necessarily the same as the total amount payable. An argument that the tribunal's approach to the assessment of the penalty was flawed had to be advanced by way of appeal, as it was an attempt to re-argue the case on a materially different basis from that previously advanced. The taxpayer's conduct was not to be equated with carelessness. A persistent failure to deal with information notices could not be so characterised, even if, as argued, it was not a deliberate and considered refusal to co-operate. The appropriate course was for the parties to agree the correct amount of inheritance tax at risk, to enable the tribunal to determine the penalty due for the failure to comply with the relevant notice, or to return for further argument if agreement was not possible (paras 24-29). (3) There was no breach of the undertaking relating to the income tax notices. There had been late and incomplete compliance with the inheritance tax notice and the taxpayer had breached his undertaking in respect of that notice. However, it was unnecessary to impose a further financial penalty. The taxpayer had agreed to adopt a certain course of action, not publicly disclosed, which would be burdensome and represented sufficient recognition of the gravity of his behaviour (paras 31-32).

TAGER v REVENUE AND CUSTOMS COMMISSIONERS, [2015] UKUT 663 (TCC), [2015] B.T.C. 538, Judge Colin Bishopp, UT (Tax).

2091 Income tax–Interest–Determination of where interest payments arose–Weight given to debtors' residence and to substantive or actual source of funds for payment

[Income Tax Act 2007 (c.3) s.874]

A company (C) and an individual (P) each appealed against separate decisions of the First-tier Tribunal (*Ardmore Construction Ltd v Revenue and Customs Commissioners* [2014] UKFTT 453 (TC), [2014] S.F.T.D. 1077 and *Perrin v Revenue and Customs Commissioners* [2014] UKFTT 223 (TC), [2014] S.F.T.D. 919) that interest paid on loans arose in the UK and they were liable for tax that should have been deducted. P was resident and domiciled in the UK. He was the managing director of a UK company which made contributions to a retirement benefits scheme via two trusts. One of the trusts made loans to P, payment of which was made from the trust's Isle of Man bank account to P's Isle of Man bank account. The law of the underlying loan agreement was that of the Isle of Man and it was the jurisdiction in which judgment could have been obtained. P made two interest payments from funds in his Isle of Man account, but the tribunal concluded that other interest payments would have been funded from other non-Isle of Man accounts. The tribunal determined that P's obligations to pay would have been enforced or would have substantially originated from the UK. It found that the factors of P's residence in the UK and the source of funds for payment or enforcement in the UK outweighed that of the Isle of Man's jurisdiction and actual payments there, and therefore the interest payments arose in the UK for the purposes of the Income Tax Act 2007 s.874. In the case of C, a UK company, two Gibraltar trusts lent funds to it pursuant to facility agreements. C also entered into loan agreements with British Virgin Islands companies owned by the trusts. Interest payments were made from C's bank account in the UK, funded by income from C's UK trading activities. In determining the source of the interest, the tribunal referred to C's residence in the UK and found that the UK, as well as being the source or origin of the funds for payment, was the place of enforcement of the debt. Relying on *National Bank of Greece SA v Westminster Bank Executor & Trustee Co (Channel Islands)* [1971] A.C. 945, [1971] C.L.Y. 5739, the appellants submitted that the source of the interest should properly be found by ascertaining the "nationality" or "residence" of the relevant loan instrument, or the place where the credit was provided, and the tribunal had erred in applying a multi-factorial test. Alternatively, if the multi-factorial test was the proper one, the tribunal erred by affording too much weight to C and P's residence.

Held: Appeals dismissed. (1) The nationality of a document could not be identified save from its relevant circumstances, which was a multi-factorial question. In *National Bank of Greece*, the court was stating that it was the source of the obligation that had to be ascertained by a multi-factorial enquiry, not the nationality of the loan instrument, *National Bank of Greece* explained. In view of the binding nature of that authority, it was not open to the instant tribunal to find that, as a matter of law, the source of the interest was to be found by reference to the single factor of the place where the credit was provided. No single test could be applied in all cases. In the case of a simple debt, the debt was the source of the interest and there was no authority for a test which focused on where the creditor's activities took place, *Inland Revenue Commissioner v Orion Caribbean Ltd (In Voluntary Liquidation)* [1997] S.T.C. 923, [1997] C.L.Y. 1084 applied. The legal situs of the debt was not a relevant factor for income tax purposes. Residence of the debtor was a factor regardless of whether it was the jurisdiction in which the parties could bring proceedings (see paras 28-36, 42-53 of judgment). (2) The tribunal was fully entitled on the evidence in both cases to find that the substantive source of the interest payments was in the UK. It was correct to adopt a multi-factorial approach. The proper law of the agreement, the jurisdiction in which judgment could be obtained, and the place where payment was made were factors of limited, if any, weight having regard to their lack of significance in *National Bank of Greece*. The tribunal was correct to have given weight to the residence of P and C and to the source of funds for payment and enforcement. The place where the credit was provided was not a relevant factor. The place where the money was lent should not be regarded as the commercial source. The place where payments were received was not relevant and the place from which payments were made was of little or no significance, compared to the substantive or ultimate source of payment in respect of the obligations associated with the debt. The absence of security over UK assets was a neutral factor (paras 65-68, 90-92).

ARDMORE CONSTRUCTION LTD v REVENUE AND CUSTOMS COMMISSIONERS, [2015] UKUT 633 (TCC), [2016] S.T.C. 1044, Morgan J, UT (Tax).

2092 Income tax–Partnerships–Carry-back reliefs–Losses in film partnerships–Enquiries by HMRC into partnership returns

[Taxes Management Act 1970 (c.9) Sch.1A para.5, Sch.1B para.2, s.42(2), s.54, s.8, s.8(1B), s.9, s.9A; Partnership Act 1890 (c.39) s.6; Income and Corporation Taxes Act 1988 (c.1) s.380]

Two taxpayers appealed against a decision (*R. (on the application of de Silva) v Revenue and Customs Commissioners* [2014] UKUT 170 (TCC), [2014] S.T.C. 2088, [2014] C.L.Y. 2860) upholding HMRC's refusal to accept their claims for carry-back loss relief and upholding its decision to make amendments to their tax returns in earlier years. HMRC cross-appealed the finding that partnership settlement agreements made under the Taxes Management Act 1970 s.54 precluded the taxpayers from contending for the full loss reliefs. The taxpayers were partners in a number of limited film partnerships which participated in marketed tax avoidance schemes. Their aim was to carry back losses in film partnerships to be offset against income received from other sources in earlier years. Following extensive investigations, HMRC disallowed the losses and the claims for relief. The taxpayers' appeals against those decisions were eventually compromised in s.54 partnership settlement agreements between the general partner and HMRC in which some carry-back losses at a reduced level were allowed and the individual partnership returns were statutorily amended. HMRC argued that the taxpayers as partners were bound by the s.54 agreement because such partnerships were transparent entities for tax law purposes. The taxpayers relied on *Revenue and Customs Commissioners v Cotter* [2013] UKSC 69, [2013] 1 W.L.R. 3514, [2014] C.L.Y. 2931 to submit that a claim under Sch.1B to the 1970 Act could only be made by way of a "stand-alone claim" under Sch.1A, or could only be investigated by means of an enquiry under paragraph 5(1) of Schedule IA to the Act. Thus their carry-back claims for relief were stand-alone claims made in the earlier years which could only be the subject of enquiry under Sch.1A para.5(1), not claims made in a personal tax return under s.8 of the 1970 Act and, because no such enquiry had been initiated by HMRC within the relevant time period, any further enquiry was time-barred.

Held: Appeal dismissed, cross-appeal allowed. (1) HMRC were correct that the s.54 partnership settlement agreements with the general partner, including the agreement to claim only limited sums by way of relief in respect of partnership losses, were contractually binding on the taxpayers as limited partners because, pursuant to the Partnership Act 1890 s.6, such partnerships were transparent entities for tax law purposes (see paras 41-44 of judgment). (2) Sch.1B para.2(2) of the 1970 Act acted only to disapply s.42(2), which held that if a claim could be made in a return, then it had to be. Removal of that restriction meant that a Sch.1B claim could be made either in a return, or in a stand-alone claim. Further, s.8(1B) and s.9 of the 1970 Act and the Income and Corporation Taxes Act 1988 s.380 stipulated that no matter how a claim for relief had initially been made, the claim for relief was required to be included in the return of the individual taxpayer for the year in which the losses were actually made by the partnership, here the later year's return. The judge had been correct to find that the inclusion of estimated losses in the earlier year returns were "inchoate" as they were unsubstantiated until the relevant partnership statements for the later years had been filed, *Cotter* considered. Even if, contrary to that view, the earlier year tax returns were stand-alone claims, it was not the case that HMRC were obliged to make an enquiry under Sch.1A para.5(1) and if it failed to do so within the time limits it was precluded from making an enquiry under s.9A of the 1970 Act. It was true that if HMRC chose to challenge an earlier stand-alone claim under Sch.1A para.5(1) then it could not subsequently open a s.9A enquiry after the self -assessment return had been filed, but that was not the case here, *Cotter* distinguished on its facts as it was considering a stand-alone claim for carry-back relief where no claim had been made in either earlier or later years' tax returns (paras 48-53).

R. (ON THE APPLICATION OF DE SILVA) v REVENUE AND CUSTOMS COMMISSIONERS, [2016] EWCA Civ 40, [2016] S.T.C. 1333, Arden LJ, CA (Civ Div).

2093 Income tax–PAYE–Collection and recovery of income tax

THE INCOME TAX (PAY AS YOU EARN) (AMENDMENT NO.3) REGULATIONS 2016, SI 2016/1137; made under the Income Tax (Earnings and Pensions) Act 2003 s.684(1)(2). In force: 19 December 2016.

These Regulations amend the Income Tax (Pay As You Earn) Regulations 2003 which make provision for the assessment, charge, collection and recovery of income tax in respect of pay as you earn income.

2094 Income tax–Penalties–Daily penalty for late filing of tax return–Conditions in Sch.55 para.4(1) Finance Act 2009

[Finance Act 2009 (c.10) Sch.55 para.18(1)(c), Sch.55 para.4(1); Taxes Management Act 1970 (c.9) s.114(1)]

A taxpayer appealed against a penalty imposed for the late filing of his tax return. The tax return had been due on 31 October 2011. HMRC's policy was to levy a daily penalty on all taxpayers who were at least three months late in filing their return under the Finance Act 2009 Sch.55 para.4(1). HMRC sent the taxpayer a reminder, stating that he had already incurred a £100 penalty and would incur daily £10 penalties from 31 January 2012 for a maximum of 90 days. A second reminder was sent to the taxpayer, stating that the daily penalties would begin on 1 February for a maximum of 90 days. The taxpayer did not file his return until more than six months after it was due. HMRC imposed a £300 penalty for filing more than six months late, and £900 in daily penalties. The notice did not indicate the dates for which the daily penalty was imposed. Schedule.55 para.4(1) stated a taxpayer would be liable to daily penalties only if (a) the taxpayer's failure continued for more than three months; (b) HMRC "decide that such a penalty should be payable" and (c) HMRC gave "notice to [the taxpayer] specifying the date from which the penalty is payable". Paragraph 18(1)(c) stated that the notice should state "the period in respect of which the penalty is assessed". The taxpayer submitted that (1) the decision had to relate to the particular taxpayer, and the conditions in para.4 had to be complied with in chronological order, therefore the policy decision taken by HMRC years earlier could not meet the requirements of para.4(1)(b); (2) the reminder letters did not meet the requirement in para.4(1)(c) to give notice as they merely stated that daily penalties "might" be applied; (3) the letters and the penalty notice failed to state the period in respect of which the penalty was assessed, in breach of para.18(1)(c).

Held: Appeal dismissed. (1) It was inherently unlikely that Parliament intended that HMRC should be required to make a decision by exercising a discretion on an individual taxpayer-by-taxpayer basis. Parliament had addressed the issue of the individual circumstances at Sch.55 para.23, by setting out that liability would not arise if the taxpayer had a reasonable excuse for his failure. The order in which the three conditions were set out in para.4 did not show that Parliament intended that they should be chronological. There were no words such as "then" or "after" to indicate a specific sequence; and there was nothing in the structure of para 4(1)(b) to support it either. The draftsman had gone no further than to make the three requirements cumulative. Accordingly, a generic policy decision of the kind taken by HMRC a few years earlier was a decision which satisfied the requirement of para 4(1)(b) (see paras 15-17 of judgment). (2) The notices had not merely informed the taxpayer that he "might" be liable to a penalty. They both stated in terms that he would be liable to a £10 daily penalty for every day after 31 January 2012 that the return was not filed. Further, it was wrong to say that the notice could not be given until the taxpayer became liable for the penalty. There was nothing in the language of sub-para (c) which restricted the timing of a notice in that way (para.21). (3) In some contexts the phrase "period in respect of which the penalty is assessed" was the relevant tax year, but in the context of a daily penalty, the most natural interpretation of the phrase was the period over which the penalty had been incurred. The taxpayer needed that information to enable him to decide whether to challenge the assessment of the penalty. The notice sent to the taxpayer had stated that he was liable for the maximum penalty of £900 calculated at the rate of £10 per day for a maximum of 90 days. That was not sufficient to satisfy the requirements of para.18(1)(c). The notice should have specified the three month period, at least by stating when it started. However, the failure to state the period was saved by the Taxes Management Act 1970 s.114(1). Although the period was not stated, it could be worked out without difficulty from the notice and the reminders. The taxpayer could have been in no doubt as to the period over which he had incurred a liability for daily penalties. The omission was therefore one of form and not substance. The effect of s.114(1) was that the omission did not affect the validity of the notice (paras 25-29).

REVENUE AND CUSTOMS COMMISSIONERS v DONALDSON *sub nom.* DONALDSON v REVENUE AND CUSTOMS COMMISSIONERS, [2016] EWCA Civ 761, [2016] 1 W.L.R. 4521, Lord Dyson MR, CA (Civ Div).

2095 Income tax–Repayments–Time limits for claims for repayment of overpaid tax–Reasonable excuse for claiming out of time

[Taxes Management Act 1970 (c.9) Sch.1AB, Sch.1AB(3), s.118(2)]

A taxpayer appealed against a decision of the First-tier Tribunal (*Raftopoulou v Revenue and Customs Commissioners* [2014] UKFTT 818 (TC)) striking out her appeal against HMRC's refusal to repay overpaid income tax. The taxpayer had made her claim for repayment under the Taxes Management Act 1970 Sch.1AB. The claim was made outside the four-year time limit in Sch.1AB(3) and HMRC responded by letter, refusing to make any repayment on the basis that the claim was late. The tribunal struck out the taxpayer's appeal, holding that it did not have jurisdiction to hear it in the absence of any statutory provision to extend or appeal against the time limit. The taxpayer argued that the tribunal had failed to consider the deeming provision in s.118(2) of the Act, which would give it jurisdiction if it was satisfied that she had a reasonable excuse for not making the claim in time. The issues were whether (i) on an appeal against a strike-out decision, the appellant merely had to show an arguable case; (ii) there was any statutory right of appeal to the tribunal; (iii) the deeming provision in s.118(2) applied to claims for repayment under Sch.1AB.

Held: Appeal allowed. (1) There was no basis for the taxpayer's contention that she merely had to show an arguable case, *Fairford Group Ltd Plc (In Liquidation) v Revenue and Customs Commissioners* [2014] UKUT 329 (TCC), [2015] S.T.C. 156, [2014] C.L.Y. 3063 considered. The issue was whether the tribunal had erred in law, and the Upper Tribunal had to determine the material questions of law in answering that question (see paras 24-25 of judgment). (2) Any appeal to the tribunal had to have a statutory basis, and in the instant case Sch.1A provided for an appeal against a closure notice. That required a claim within the meaning of Sch.1A, an enquiry by HMRC, and a closure notice. An out-of-time claim was not a claim within the meaning of Sch.1A and did not trigger the appeal provision in that section, *Portland Gas Storage Ltd v Revenue and Customs Commissioners* [2014] UKUT 270 (TCC), [2014] S.T.C. 2589, [2014] C.L.Y. 2978 applied. The taxpayer had therefore not made a claim within the meaning of Sch.1A unless s.118(2) applied so as to deem it as having been made in time (paras 27-29, 34-36). (3) Whether the deeming provision in s.118(2) applied depended on the proper construction of the words "required to be done". The question was whether that phrase connoted something that the taxpayer was compelled to do, or whether it also connoted something that he could choose to do, but having so chosen had to do within a particular time. There was nothing in s.118(2) to limit the words to mandatory acts. Giving them their ordinary meaning, they properly applied to voluntary acts which had to be done within a certain time. Failure to do what was required had to have a consequence, but that did not have to be a financial penalty. Sch.1AB(3) was saying that if a claim was to be made, it was "required to be done" within the stated time limit. Thus, s.118(2) could apply to it, *Ames v Revenue and*

Customs Commissioners [2015] UKFTT 337 (TC), [2015] S.T.I. 3041 doubted. If the taxpayer had a reasonable excuse for not filing his claim within the time limit and had made the claim without unreasonable delay after the excuse ceased, then s.118(2) deemed the claim to have been filed in time. A deemed in-time claim was a claim within the meaning of Sch.1A and could found an appeal (paras 39, 55-72). (4) By its letter responding to the taxpayer's claim, HMRC had both opened an enquiry and issued a closure notice. The decision in *Portland Gas* established that the opening and closing of enquiries did not require any particular formality; the word "enquire" bore its natural and ordinary meaning and included "scrutinising"; and that the information sent by HMRC to the taxpayer had to make it clear that an enquiry had been opened. Similarly, HMRC had to make it clear that an inquiry was being closed. The instant tribunal could not agree with obiter remarks in *Portland Gas* to the effect that if all the relevant information was contained in the claim, any conclusion which HMRC drew from it was not the result of an "enquiry", *Portland Gas* considered. Whether HMRC had made an enquiry would always be a question of fact, but situations in which HMRC had reached a conclusion and amended a claim without scrutiny or enquiry were likely to be exceptional. Moreover, *Portland Gas* did not address the situation in the instant case, where one letter purported to both open and close the enquiry. The legislation did not prescribe any minimum length for an enquiry and did not prevent one document from both opening and closing an enquiry. The requirement in Sch.1A that HMRC should give notice of its intention to begin an enquiry did not mean that the notice had to be prospective, it could equally be retrospective. A single letter could constitute both notice of enquiry and closure notice as long as the taxpayer could clearly understand it as having that effect. In the instant case, HMRC's letter could clearly be understood as opening and closing an enquiry. The tribunal had therefore erred in law by failing to consider whether the taxpayer had a reasonable excuse for the late submission of her claim and the matter would be remitted for reconsideration (paras 89-91, 93-103, 107, 111).

RAFTOPOULOU v REVENUE AND CUSTOMS COMMISSIONERS, [2015] UKUT 579 (TCC), [2016] S.T.C. 656, Judge Roger Berner, UT (Tax).

2096 Income tax–Share dealing–Pharmacist conducting second business as day trader–Losses from share activities set against profits of pharmacy business–Whether share activities commercial trade under s.66 Income Tax Act 2007

[Income Tax Act 2007 (c.3) s.66]

The appellant taxpayer appealed against penalties imposed by HMRC for incorrect returns. The taxpayer was a pharmacist who had been using the profits of his successful pharmacy business to buy and sell shares as a day trader. He had a business plan and a strategy for his share activities and spent most of his time day trading from an office above his pharmacy. He had treated his share activities as a separate trade and had claimed for losses from his share activities to be treated as trading losses and set against his general income. HMRC disallowed losses generated by his share activities and imposed penalties. The taxpayer submitted that his share activities comprised the carrying on of a trade and that the trade was commercial under the Income Tax Act 2007 s.66. He argued that his share activities satisfied the badges of trade based on the high frequency of his transactions in short periods and the amount of time and effort expended in gaining knowledge and experience of trading. HMRC contended that the taxpayer's share activities were no more than speculative investment over a prolonged period.

Held: Appeal allowed. The taxpayer's activities bore the classic hallmarks of trading. The badges of trade supported a finding of trading. It was clear that the courts were wary of awarding trading status to an individual speculating in shares or gambling transactions, *Salt v Chamberlain* [1979] S.T.C. 750, [1980] C.L.Y. 1503 and *Lewis Emanuel & Son Ltd v White* 42 T.C. 369 considered. However, the taxpayer's activities did not add up to gambling transactions. His business plan was a decisive fact, along with the finding that he had pursued it in a sufficiently organised manner, which dislodged the prima facie presumption that individuals engaging in share speculation were not trading. The taxpayer had a deliberate and organised scheme of profit-making and was carrying on a trade in undertaking his share activities during the tax years in question. Both limbs of s.66(2) were satisfied: the taxpayer's trade was not uncommercial but was seriously interested in profit, *Wannell v Rothwell (Inspector of Taxes)* [1996] S.T.C. 450, [1996] C.L.Y. 3398 followed. The taxpayer's trade was commercial for the purposes of s.66 for each of the tax years in question (see paras 48-51, 54, 58, 61-64 of judgment).

ALI v REVENUE AND CUSTOMS COMMISSIONERS, [2016] UKFTT 8 (TC), [2016] S.F.T.D. 335, Judge Zachary Citron, FTT (Tax).

2097 Income tax–Tax avoidance–Dividends–Construction of deeming provision in s.730 Income and Corporation Taxes Act 1988

[Income and Corporation Taxes Act 1988 (c.1) s.730]

A limited liability partnership appealed against a closure notice issued by the respondent HMRC reducing its trading losses to nil. The partnership had been created to make a profit other than by means of investment, principally through the acquisition of short-dated securities. The partnership had bought the right to receive a share dividend from a company (H) in respect of shares owned by another company (D). D obtained a loan to make a capital contribution to H, which treated it as a share premium available for distribution. H declared a dividend and paid it to the partnership. The partnership claimed that under the Income and Corporation Taxes Act 1988 s.730 the dividend was deemed to be D's income as it remained the owner of the shares. The partnership had excluded the dividend from its accounts, which showed a trading loss. The issues were whether (1) the partnership had been carrying on a trade in the relevant accounting period; (2) if so, the dividend transactions had been trading transactions; (3) a distribution within s.730 was to be treated as the income of the owner of the shares, and was not deemed to be the income of any other person.

Held: Appeal dismissed. (1) The tribunal had to assess the effect of what the partnership had in fact done. If its acts had been equivocal as to the question of whether it had carried on a trade as opposed to an investment activity, its subjective purpose might be a material factor, *Iswera v Inland Revenue Commissioners* [1965] 1 W.L.R. 663, [1965] C.L.Y. 1930 applied. Trading required an intention to trade, *Simmons (Liquidator of Lionel Simmons Properties) v Inland Revenue Commissioners* [1980] 1 W.L.R. 1196, [1980] C.L.Y. 1481 applied. The perception of persons participating in the relevant market would be that the partnership's activities in the market were such as could be recognised as a trade. Applying the test in *Inland Revenue Commissioners v Livingston* 1927 S.C. 251, the partnership's activities in the market had been of the same kind, and carried on in the same way, as those that were characteristic of ordinary trading in short-dated securities, *Livingston* applied. However, it could not be concluded simply by an application of the *Livingston* test that its acts unequivocally demonstrated that it had been trading. On all the evidence, the acts had been equivocal, so it was necessary to look at the subjective intention, which had been to make a profit other than by means of investment. The partnership had been carrying on a trade of dealing in short-dated securities in the relevant accounting period (see paras 87-92 of judgment). (2) The purchase of rights to dividends and payment of those dividends were a single composite transaction that could not be regarded as a trading transaction, *WT Ramsay Ltd v Inland Revenue Commissioners* [1982] A.C. 300, [1981] C.L.Y. 1385 and *Lupton (Inspector of Taxes) v FA & AB Ltd* [1972] A.C. 634, [1971] C.L.Y. 1919 applied. They had been artificial arrangements to enable the partnership to claim a tax loss pursuant to its interpretation of s.730 (paras 101-103). (3) In construing a deeming provision the words had to be taken to have their ordinary and natural meaning consistent with the policy of the Act and the purposes of the provisions so far as they could be ascertained, *Marshall (Inspector of Taxes) v Kerr* [1993] S.T.C. 360, [1993] C.L.Y. 335 applied. The policy and express purpose of s.730 was the prevention of tax avoidance by transferring the right to distributions from shares without transferring the shares themselves. The partnership was endeavouring to use s.730, intended to prevent tax avoidance, as an engine of tax avoidance. Section 730 did not have the effect of relieving the partnership from tax on the dividends. That was supported by the amendment of s.730 to remove a provision by which there was a prohibition on treating a distribution as the income of any person other than the owner of the shares. Further, there had been no real sale of the right to receive the dividends by D to the partnership within the meaning of s.730. The authoritative comments in *UBS AG v Revenue and Customs Commissioners* [2016] UKSC 13, [2016] 1 W.L.R.

1005, [2016] 2098 concerning the interpretation of exemption provisions were of general application to the construction of tax legislation where avoidance of tax was sought by using a provision apparently providing for a tax exemption by its application to transactions having no connection to the real world of business, such as the transactions in the instant case, *USB* applied (paras 120-128).

CLAVIS LIBERTY FUND 1 LP v REVENUE AND CUSTOMS COMMISSIONERS, [2016] UKFTT 253 (TC), [2016] S.F.T.D. 558, Judge John Walters QC, FTT (Tax).

2098 Income tax–Tax avoidance–Employees awarded shares in special purpose offshore company–Restricted securities–Validity of scheme

[Income Tax (Earnings and Pensions) Act 2003 (c.1) Pt 7, Pt 7 s.425(2), s.423(1)]

HMRC appealed against a decision (*UBS AG v Revenue and Customs Commissioners* [2014] EWCA Civ 452, [2014] S.T.C. 2278, [2014] C.L.Y. 2969) that tax avoidance schemes set up by the respondent banks (UBS and DB) in order to award tax-free bonuses to employees were effective. The schemes sought to avoid their employees' income tax liability by taking advantage of the Income Tax (Earnings and Pensions) Act 2003 Pt 7 Ch.2. The banks had used the amount of the employees' bonuses to pay for redeemable shares in an offshore company set up solely for the purpose of the scheme. The shares were awarded to the employees in place of the bonuses. Conditions were attached to the shares which were intended to make them "restricted securities" within s.423(1) and so to enable them to benefit from the exemption from income tax under s.425(2). The restrictions involved a contingency which was unlikely to occur but which might conceivably do so. UBS provided that the shares in its scheme would immediately be sold if the FTSE 100 share index exceeded a certain level within a three-week period. DB provided that the shares would be forfeited if the employee's employment was terminated within a certain period. Once the exemptions accrued, the restrictions were removed and the shares were redeemable by the employees for cash. The issue was whether the Act should be interpreted purposively and the *Ramsay* principle should be applied so as to disregard the conditions for the purpose of deciding whether the shares were restricted securities.

Held: Appeals allowed. (1) Part 7 of the Act was concerned with issues arising when employees were remunerated in shares and other securities. Its purposes were (a) to promote employee share ownership, particularly by encouraging share incentive schemes; (b) since such schemes required benefits to be contingent on future performance, creating a problem if tax was charged on the acquisition of the shares, to wait and see in such cases until the contingency had fallen away; and (c) to counteract consequent opportunities for tax avoidance, *Grays Timber Products Ltd v Revenue and Customs Commissioners* [2010] UKSC 4, [2010] 1 W.L.R. 497, [2010] C.L.Y. 4580 followed. The background to Ch.2 supported that view: it had been enacted to address aspects of previous provisions which had left them vulnerable to avoidance or created anomalies. It was in that context that it was necessary to consider the scope of the exemption conferred by s.425(2), and more specifically whether, in s.423(1), "any contract, agreement, arrangement or condition which makes provision to which any of subsections (2) to (4) applies" referred to "provision" with a genuine business or commercial purpose. The fact that Ch.2 had been introduced partly to forestall tax avoidance schemes self-evidently made it difficult to attribute to Parliament an intention that it should apply to schemes which were carefully crafted to fall within its scope purely for the purpose of tax avoidance. Further, it was difficult to accept that Parliament could have intended to encourage by exemption from taxation the award of shares to employees where the award of the shares had no purpose other than the obtaining of the exemption, a matter which was reflected in the fact that the shares were in a company which was brought into existence merely for the purposes of the scheme. The background to the legislation indicated that the s.425(2) exemption was designed to address the problem of valuing a benefit which was, for real-world business or commercial reasons, subject to a restrictive condition involving a contingency. Nothing suggested that Parliament had intended that s.423(2) should apply to transactions having no real-world business connection. Accordingly, adopting a purposive construction, the reference in s.423(1) to "any contract, agreement, arrangement or condition which makes provision to which any of subsections (2) to (4) applies", was to be construed as being limited to provision having a business or commercial purpose, and not to commercially irrelevant conditions whose only purpose was the obtaining of the exemption (see paras 74-78, 85 of judgment). (2) The condition in UBS's case was arbitrary and had no business or commercial rationale beyond tax avoidance. Such a condition was not relevant to the application of s.423. The condition was to be disregarded, meaning that the shares were not restricted securities within s.423. The restrictive condition in DB's case was equally artificial. The forfeiture provision had operated for only a short period, during which the possibility that it might be triggered lay largely within the control of the employee who would be adversely affected. It had no business or commercial purpose, *Barclays Mercantile Business Finance Ltd v Mawson (Inspector of Taxes)* [2004] UKHL 51, [2005] 1 A.C. 684, [2005] C.L.Y. 3988 and *Scottish Provident Institution v Inland Revenue Commissioners* [2004] UKHL 52, [2004] 1 W.L.R. 3172, [2005] C.L.Y. 4158 applied. The conditions were to be disregarded for the purpose of deciding whether the shares were restricted securities, *Furniss (Inspector of Taxes) v Dawson* [1984] A.C. 474, [1984] C.L.Y. 270 applied (paras 86-89). The employees therefore fell to be taxed in respect of their receipt of the shares in accordance with ordinary taxation principles. The shares could not be valued for income tax purposes without regard to the conditions. The conditions had reduced the shares' value on the date of acquisition by a small amount. Value had to be assessed as at the date of acquisition, taking the conditions into account (paras 90-95).

UBS AG v REVENUE AND CUSTOMS COMMISSIONERS; DB GROUP SERVICES (UK) LTD v REVENUE AND CUSTOMS COMMISSIONERS *sub nom.* DEUTSCHE BANK GROUP SERVICES (UK) LTD v REVENUE AND CUSTOMS COMMISSIONERS, [2016] UKSC 13, [2016] 1 W.L.R. 1005, Lord Neuberger PSC, SC.

2099 Income tax–Tax avoidance–Payments to employees and/or former employees routed through other companies and limited liability partnership as profit shares and dividends–Source of payments–Whether taxable as employment income or dividends

The appellant taxpayers appealed against a decision of the First-tier Tribunal dismissing conjoined appeals against assessments in respect of income tax and national insurance contributions. The third appellant was the sole director of the first appellant company, Darvel. The appellants were involved in a number of arrangements to avoid tax. In the first a company, Services, was incorporated and shares were issued to participating employees of Darvel. Those employees agreed to their pay from Darvel being reduced to the level of the national minimum wage. The balance of their previous pay was paid by way of dividends from Services. The second arrangement involved another company, Retail, initially owned by the third appellant, and a limited liability partnership. Employees of Darvel who wished to participate became members of the LLP and shareholders in Retail, which was also a member of the LLP. Darvel paid the LLP a share of its profits. The LLP's profits were distributed among its members, including Retail. Retail paid its shareholders dividends, and, on an annual basis, redeemed shares in it, owned by participants, and allotted further shares for the following year. A third arrangement involved Services providing a car for the third appellant, and Darvel, then the LLP, providing cars for the second and fourth appellants. The tribunal held that the sums received as dividends from Services and by way of profit share or dividend from the LLP were all received as emoluments of employment referable to the recipients' employment with Darvel; the cars provided to the individual appellants were also referable to their employment with Darvel. Accordingly Darvel was liable to pay income tax and national insurance contributions, and the individual appellants were liable to income tax in respect of the cars. The appellants argued that the tribunal had erred because (1) having concluded that payments to the participants by Services were income from employment, it should have gone on to consider whether they were also dividends, since the provisions which charged dividends to income tax took precedence over and precluded the application of the provisions charging employment income to income tax, in cases of overlap; (2) it had failed properly to take into account the fact that the LLP was a properly constituted entity that provided services to Darvel and that the participants who had become members of the LLP and Retail had given up their employment with Darvel; (3) it had failed to give adequate reasons for holding that the cars were benefits-in-kind provided by Darvel.

Held: Appeal allowed in part. (1) The tribunal applied the correct test and came to the correct conclusion that the true source of the payments received by the appellants was their employment by Darvel. The question was one of substance, not form, *Hochstrasser (Inspector of Taxes) v Mayes* [1960] A.C. 376, [1959] C.L.Y. 1543 followed. Such payments could be provided by a third party, *Shilton v Wilmshurst (Inspector of Taxes)* [1991] 1 A.C. 684, [1991] C.L.Y. 2092 followed. The source of employment income was not the employer but the employment relationship. The real source from which the income was derived was employment by Darvel and once that source had been identified, the income was to be taxed as employment income and not as dividends, *Fry (Inspector of Taxes) v Salisbury House Estate Ltd* [1930] A.C. 432 and *PA Holdings Ltd v Revenue and Customs Commissioners* [2011] EWCA Civ 1414, [2012] S.T.C. 582, [2012] C.L.Y. 3300 followed. There was no error of law in the tribunal's finding that the total sums received by the appellants from Services, whether by way of wages or dividends, represented income from their employment with Darvel (see paras 33-44 of judgment). (2) The tribunal had been entitled to find that the participants in Retail and the LLP nevertheless remained in an employment relationship with Darvel. Viewing the matter objectively, the participants continued to provide services to Darvel. The tribunal was entitled to infer a contract of employment between the parties, *Hall (Inspector of Taxes) v Lorimer* [1994] 1 W.L.R. 209, [1994] C.L.Y. 2546 and *Autoclenz Ltd v Belcher* [2011] UKSC 41, [2011] 4 All E.R. 745, [2011] C.L.Y. 1074 followed. Darvel, Retail and the LLP were all controlled by the third appellant. The object of the arrangement was to facilitate the payment of wages/salaries to Darvel's employees with a tax saving. The total sums received from the LLP, whether by way of profit share or dividend from Retail, represented a reward for services to Darvel, and had been calculated by reference to their entitlement under their contracts of employment with Darvel. There was no proper distinction between the operation as a whole and a separate part that the LLP was carrying out. The tribunal was entitled to hold that it was no more than a cog in the machine and that the appellants were being paid for services rendered to Darvel under a contract of service (paras 65-71). (3) The tribunal had failed to deal with the argument that the third appellant was Services' company secretary and that the car was remuneration for that, and to deal with evidence that the cars provided to the other appellants were provided by the LLP. That part of the appeal was allowed and remitted to the tribunal for reconsideration (paras 76-77).

JAMES H DONALD (DARVEL) LTD v REVENUE AND CUSTOMS COMMISSIONERS, [2015] UKUT 514 (TCC), [2016] S.T.C. 616, Lord Jones, UT (Tax).

2100 Income tax–Tax avoidance–Tax avoidance scheme involving Isle of Man partnership and trust–Interpretation of s. 858(4) Income Tax (Trading and Other Income) Act 2005

[Income Tax (Trading and Other Income) Act 2005 (c.5) s.858(4)]

The appellant (H) appealed against a decision of HMRC concerning the correct interpretation of the Income Tax (Trading and Other Income) Act 2005 s.858(4). H had entered into a tax avoidance scheme which involved setting up an Isle of Man trust in which he had a right to income. The trust became a partner in an Isle of Man partnership which entered into a contract with H under which H provided his services and received an annual fee. H also received a share of the partnership profits as a beneficiary under the trust. The scheme purported to exploit the terms of the UK-Isle of Man Double Taxation Arrangement so that H would pay no income tax or national insurance on sums paid to him as beneficiary of the trust. It was intended that H's income from the trust would be treated as being of the same nature as the underlying trust income, namely a share in the partnership profits. Because he would not be a member of the partnership, it was intended that s.858 would not operate to prevent reliance on the double taxation arrangement. The issue was whether s.858(4) prevented H from benefiting under the scheme. HMRC submitted that the reference to "income of the firm" in s.858(4) was intended to include profits of the firm.

Held: Appeal dismissed. It might have been clearer if Parliament had referred to profits rather than income in s.858(4). However, it had used the term "income" to refer not to a share in the income or gross receipts of a partnership, but to a share in the profits of a partnership. It would be extraordinary if Parliament had intended s.858(4) to refer to a person having a share in the gross income of a partnership. Section 858 was clearly an anti-avoidance provision initially aimed at schemes involving a share of profits. It was necessary to give s.858(4) a purposive construction, *Berry v Revenue and Customs Commissioners* [2011] UKUT 81 (TCC), [2011] S.T.C. 1057, [2011] C.L.Y. 3366 applied. The Act contained a number of examples from which it was clear that, in some contexts, the term "income" could be construed as meaning profits. In the context of income tax, it was not unnatural to refer to an entitlement to income from a partnership when meaning an entitlement to a share of the profits of the partnership. That was particularly the case in the context of a beneficiary's entitlement to trust income which comprised the trust's share of the profits of a partnership in which it was a partner. H's scheme was caught by s.858 (see paras 81-90 of judgment).

HUITSON v REVENUE AND CUSTOMS COMMISSIONERS, [2015] UKFTT 448 (TC), [2016] S.F.T.D. 37, Judge Jonathan Cannan, FTT (Tax).

2101 Income tax–Termination of employment–Settlement–Payment for injury to employee's feelings–Whether taxable income

[Income Tax (Earnings and Pensions) Act 2003 (c.1) s.401, s.403, s.406(b)]

An employee appealed against a decision of the First-tier Tribunal (*Moorthy v Revenue and Customs Commissioners* [2014] UKFTT 834 (TC), [2015] I.R.L.R. 4, [2015] C.L.Y. 2496) upholding the respondent HMRC's decision that compensation paid to him by his former employer was taxable income. After the employee was made redundant he brought proceedings for unfair dismissal and age discrimination. Pursuant to a compromise agreement, his employer paid him £200,000 in full and final settlement. It treated the first £30,000 as exempt from tax by virtue of the Income Tax (Earnings and Pensions) Act 2003 s.403 but deducted income tax at the basic rate from the remainder. The employee completed his self-assessment tax return for the relevant year on the basis that the whole of the settlement sum was tax free. HMRC disagreed and issued a closure notice. On appeal, the tribunal found that the whole of the settlement sum had been paid in connection with the termination of his employment, fell within the scope of s.401, and was chargeable to income tax pursuant to s.403. The central issues were whether the settlement sum was (1) a payment in connection with the termination of employment within the meaning of s.401; (2) taken out of the charge to tax by s.406(b) on the basis that, insofar as it compensated the employee for injury to his feelings, it was a payment made on account of injury to an employee.

Held: Appeal dismissed. (1) The whole of the settlement sum fell within the scope of s.401. The language of that section was clear and its scope was wide. It applied to payments and other benefits received directly or indirectly in consideration, in consequence of, or otherwise in connection with the termination of a person's employment. It applied to payments made even where the termination was fair and lawful; it was not restricted to payments made under a contractual entitlement; and it applied to non-pecuniary awards, such as damages for injury to feelings. The fact that the sum paid might exceed the statutory maximum that could be awarded for unfair dismissal did not mean that the excess was unconnected with the termination of the employment. The tribunal in *Oti-Obihara v Revenue and Customs Commissioners* [2010] UKFTT 568 (TC), [2011] I.R.L.R. 386, [2011] C.L.Y. 3386 was wrong in concluding that compensation paid on the termination of employment for discrimination was taxable only to the extent that compensated for financial loss suffered by reason of the termination, and that compensation for the infringement of the right not to be discriminated was not taxable. Its decision was based on its view that *Walker v Adams (Inspector of Taxes)* [2003] S.T.C. (S.C.D.) 269, [2004] C.L.Y. 3764 was authority for that proposition, but that was a misunderstanding of *Walker*. *Oti-Obihara* was wrongly decided and was not to be followed, *Oti-Obihara* overruled and *Walker* considered (see paras 5, 38, 52-56 of judgment). (2) The settlement sum was not taken out of the charge to tax by s.406(b). It was not a payment on account of injury to an employee within the meaning of that subsection. The meaning of "injury" was context-specific and as used in s.406 it did not include injury to feelings. Insofar as *Vince-Cain v Orthet Ltd* [2005] I.C.R. 374, [2004] C.L.Y. 1186 and *Timothy James Consulting Ltd v Wilton*

[2015] I.C.R. 764, [2015] C.L.Y. 860 held that "injury" in s.406 included injury to feelings, they were wrongly decided and the obiter reasoning in *Horner v Hasted (Inspector of Taxes)* [1995] S.T.C. 766, [1996] C.L.Y. 3379 was to be preferred, *Horner* considered. In *Orthet*, the tribunal's analysis of s.406 was flawed. The lack of any discussion in *Vento v Chief Constable of West Yorkshire* [2002] EWCA Civ 1871, [2003] I.C.R. 318, [2003] C.L.Y. 1306 about the tax treatment of awards for injury to feelings did not mean that such awards fell within s.406, and the fact that the Court of Appeal regarded damages for injury to feelings as being analogous to awards for pain, suffering and loss of amenity in personal injury claims did not support the view that "injury" in s.406 included injury to feelings, *Vento* considered. While "injury" in s.406 included personal injury, that did not mean that it included injury to feelings, *Orthet* not followed. Section 406 was not a general exemption from tax for payments made on account of injury to an employee. Because it was only relevant where a payment was made in connection with the termination of employment, the instant tribunal disagreed with Singh J.'s observation in *Timothy James* that the phrase "injury to... an employee" in s.406(b) was not qualified by the words "in connection with the termination of employment". That subsection could not be read as exempting all payments made by an employer in respect of an injury to an employee. The word "injury" fell to be interpreted together with "death" and "disability" in s.406, because it had to be something leading to the termination of employment or to a change in duties or the level of earnings, *Timothy James* not followed. Finally, the side-note to s.406 supported the interpretation of "injury" as meaning a medical condition resulting in the termination of employment or a change in duties or earnings. That did not include injury to feelings (paras 5, 57-63).

MOORTHY v REVENUE AND CUSTOMS COMMISSIONERS, [2016] UKUT 13 (TCC), [2016] S.T.C. 1178, Rose J, UT (Tax).

2102 Inheritance tax–Charitable gifts–Exempt tranfers

[Inheritance Tax Act 1984 (c.51) s.23, s.23(6); Income Tax Act 1918 (c.40) s.37; Income Tax Act 2007 (c.3) s.989]

The executors of an estate appealed against a High Court decision upholding a determination by HMRC that a disposition in a will was not exempt from inheritance tax. The deceased was domiciled in Jersey. She left her residuary estate on trust, under a trust established under and subject to Jersey law, to be distributed to a charity. HMRC considered that the gift did not qualify for the charitable gifts exemption in the Inheritance Tax Act 1984 s.23. The executors appealed. It was not disputed that the trust had only charitable purposes as a matter of English law. However, the phrase "trust established for charitable purposes only" in the Income Tax Act 1918 s.37 had been held in *Camille and Henry Dreyfus Foundation Inc v Inland Revenue Commissioners* [1956] A.C. 39, [1955] C.L.Y. 304 to contain an implicit limitation such that it only included trusts governed by UK law and subject to the jurisdiction of the UK courts. The executors accepted that s.23 required the "charity" to be established under UK law. However, they contended that there was no such requirement in the phrase "held on trust for charitable purposes only" in s.23(6). The judge considered it incongruous to require a court to ascertain whether the purposes of a body governed by foreign law were charitable as a matter of UK law. She decided that Parliament had intended that the interpretation in *Dreyfus* of "trust established for charitable purposes only" should have the same meaning in s.23, and that the executors had not provided good reason why the second limb of s.23 should be so much broader than the first. The executors argued that the estate was plainly "held on trust for charitable purposes only" because it could only be applied for purposes which were charitable as a matter of UK law. They further argued that the judge had erred in importing into the second limb of s.23 the limitation that the trust had to be governed by UK law and subject to the jurisdiction of the UK courts.

Held: Appeal dismissed. The first limb of s.23 exempted a transfer if the property became the property of any body of persons or trust established for charitable purposes only; the second limb exempted the transfer if the property was held on trust for charitable purposes only. The second limb had to be seen in the context of the whole provision, which required the trust to be governed by UK law, *Barras v Aberdeen Steam Trawling & Fishing Co Ltd* [1933] A.C. 402 applied. The executors' interpretation would result in the second limb having a much broader scope. The first limb applied to bodies or trusts established for charitable purposes only, provided they were governed by UK law. By contrast, the second limb would, on the executors' interpretation, apply to both UK and foreign trusts provided they held the property for charitable purposes. That interpretation also discriminated between foreign law charities which were incorporated and were excluded unless they held the property on trust, and those formed under trust, which were not. There was no good reason why Parliament might have chosen to draw such distinctions. Moreover, those distinctions were far more significant than the ones which arose on HMRC's interpretation. The practical difficulties inherent in considering whether a foreign law trust held property on trust for charitable purposes only, or was established for charitable purposes only, provided a further reason to question whether Parliament intended s.23 to have the meaning for which the executors contended, *Camille and Henry Dreyfus Foundation Inc v Inland Revenue Commissioners* [1954] Ch. 672, [1954] C.L.Y. 391 applied. It was no answer to that point to say that, on the facts of the instant case, concerning as it did a Jersey trust, that did not present any particular difficulty. Such a broad and open-ended interpretation might in other cases necessitate an abstruse and controversial enquiry, *Dreyfus [1954]* applied. The judge was entitled to attach the weight she did to the structure of s.23. Section 23(1) was the primary exempting provision and concerned transfers of property to charities. "Charities" were defined in the Income Tax Act 2007 s.989 in terms which called for a UK link. The broader notion of the meaning of "property which was given to charities" was introduced by the definition in s.23(6). Insofar as the terms of s.23(6) were ambiguous, the phrase so defined did shed light on the meaning of those terms. It suggested a UK link of the kind the judge below had identified. With regard to the use of the term "trust" and the expression "held on trust" elsewhere in the1984 Act, HMRC had never disputed that, when used elsewhere, those words could denote a foreign trust. However, the phrase with which the instant court was concerned was "held on trust for charitable purposes only" and that had the meaning for which HMRC contended, *Dreyfus [1956]* applied (see paras 13, 37-43 of judgment).

ROUTIER v REVENUE AND CUSTOMS COMMISSIONERS, [2016] EWCA Civ 938, [2016] S.T.C. 2218, Moore-Bick LJ, CA (Civ Div).

2103 Inheritance tax–Disclosure–Transfer of property before death at alleged undervalue–Third-party disclosure of deceased woman's medical records–Whether public interest in proper collection of taxes outweighed right to privacy

[Inheritance Tax Act 1984 (c.51) s.2, s.221, s.221(2), s.3; Taxes Management Act 1970 (c.9) s.28B; Human Rights Act 1998 (c.42)]

The applicant HMRC applied for third-party disclosure of a deceased woman's medical records. The deceased had died in February 2007 and in April 2014 HMRC issued a notice of determination on the respondent executors under the Inheritance Tax Act 1984 s.221. The executors appealed against that notice and a review was carried out. In the course of preparing for the hearing of the substantive appeal HMRC applied for copies of all the deceased's medical records that related to either emphysema or heart failure from February 2002 for a period of five years. The primary cause of death recorded was emphysema and the secondary cause of death was heart failure. The executors submitted that the tribunal had no jurisdiction to order disclosure if it was not relevant to an issue in the proceedings and that none of the circumstances justified the invasion of privacy of the deceased and her family in having her medical records made available to HMRC and the tribunal. HMRC contended that the transfer of her freehold farm, made 17 days before her death, was ineffective or was a transfer at an undervalue and therefore a transfer of value on which an IHT liability arose and that the medical records were relevant to that issue, and that the right to privacy was outweighed by the public interest.

Held: Application granted. (1) The medical records were only relevant to the second issue of whether the transfer had been at an undervalue because it was HMRC's case that the deceased's life expectancy to her knowledge at the date of transfer was such that the annuity she received in return was worth very little. It had no relevance to the effectiveness of the transfer. The first question was whether *Tower MCashback LLP 1 v Revenue and Customs Commissioners* [2011] UKSC 19, [2011] 2 A.C. 457, [2011]

C.L.Y. 3277 had any relevance to a s.221 determination. *Tower MCashback* concerned a closure notice issued after a Taxes Management Act 1970 s.28B enquiry which merely required the closure notice to state that the enquiries were complete and the officer's conclusions. A notice of determination could only be issued where HMRC considered that a transfer of value had been made and then it had to state that HMRC had determined the matters specified in the notice. Section 221(2) set out what matters could be specified but it was a permissive section. However, despite the different wording of the sections, s.221 was effectively the same as s.28B insofar as the latter was about the conclusions of an officer and the former about a determination of an officer. What had been said in *Tower MCashback* and *Fidex Ltd v Revenue and Customs Commissioners* [2014] UKUT 454 (TCC), [2015] S.T.C. 702, [2015] C.L.Y. 2435 about how a closure notice should be interpreted was relevant to a s.221 determination. HMRC had a duty to make closure notices as informative as possible, but that was not an absolute duty. The tribunal had to fairly balance the competing interests of the taxpayer and general public and should look at the context of the notice of determination. The instant determination had to be interpreted as determining that the executors ought to pay IHT on the value of the farm; and although it did not state any reasoning relying on s.2 and s.3 of the 1984 Act, HMRC were entitled to rely on such reasoning as the executors were well aware that was an issue between the parties. The tribunal would determine whether the executors were liable for IHT on the value of the farm and in doing so would consider both whether the deceased had made an effective transfer of it and whether it had been at an undervalue. The medical records were therefore relevant, *Tower MCashback* and *Fidex* considered (see paras 5-37 of judgment). (2) While a tribunal could not act in breach of a person's rights under the Human Rights Act 1998, the right to privacy was caveated and was balanced against other public interests. People had the right in general to expect their medical records to remain confidential even after their death. The deceased's family also had a right to a private life in that regard. But those rights had to be balanced against the public interest in the collection of the right amount of tax. Having decided that the question of whether there had been a transfer of value by the deceased days before her death when she sold the farm in return for the benefit of an annuity was an issue, it followed that her medical condition and in particular what she knew about her medical condition might be critical to determine whether the sale was at an undervalue. There was a public interest in the full facts being known in order that the tribunal was more likely to reach the right conclusion on whether there was tax liability on the executors in respect of the transfer of the farm (paras 38-55).

EDWARDS-MOSS v REVENUE AND CUSTOMS COMMISSIONERS, [2016] UKFTT 147 (TC), [2016] S.F.T.D. 500, Judge Barbara Mosedale, FTT (Tax).

2104 Inheritance tax–Trusts–Whether value of testator's estate before death reduced by transfer of house to discretionary trust–Beneficial entitlement at date of death

[Inheritance Tax Act 1984 (c.51) s.49, s.53]

The appellant, who was the personal representative of his deceased mother, appealed against a notice of determination issued by the respondent HMRC. The appellant's mother had died in February 2006, leaving a will which left the appellant all of her property. In February 2007 the appellant submitted an "IHT 200" account of his mother's estate. One of the assets shown was a house, the mother's former matrimonial home. The appellant sold the house in March 2007 but failed to pay the inheritance tax due in respect of it. In September 2012 HMRC issued a notice of determination. The following month the appellant unsuccessfully appealed, HMRC finding that he was not challenging the amount of tax said to be due. In June 2014 the appellant submitted an amended IHT 200 which asserted that the house was not part of his mother's estate, and in August 2015 he asked HMRC to treat the new IHT 200 as an out-of-time notice of appeal. His case was that the house had been owned by his late father, whose will had given the mother an interest in possession in relation to the house and the residue; that in 1998 his mother had signed a deed transferring the house to a discretionary trust of which he was the sole beneficiary; and that the house was therefore not part of the estate for the purposes of inheritance tax. HMRC argued that either the mother's interest in possession had continued until she died, in which case a charge arose on its full value upon her death, or she had transferred it to the trust whereupon it became property subject to a reservation of benefit and a charge arose on its full value at the date of her death.

Held: Appeal dismissed. (1) The appellant would be given permission to appeal out of time. The purpose of the time limit for appealing was to bring efficiency to the conduct of appeal proceedings and to discourage stale appeals. There had been a lengthy delay on the appellant's part, but refusing to allow him to appeal out of time would put an end to his case. The case was not straightforward, but both parties had arrived at court prepared to argue it. The balance weighed in favour of allowing the appellant to present his appeal, *Data Select Ltd v Revenue and Customs Commissioners* [2012] UKUT 187 (TCC), [2012] S.T.C. 2195, [2012] C.L.Y. 3428 applied (see paras 6-7 of judgment). (2) Although the appellant believed that he was entitled to the trust assets, he was not. The deed signed by his mother made it clear that he could be removed as a beneficiary or joined by other beneficiaries. Therefore, he was not the owner of the trust assets. The central question was what asset, if any, was the subject of the trust declared in the deed. The appellant's mother had only had an interest in possession in the house and the residue, and she had nothing capable of being transferred to anybody else. Her interest was a right to occupy which would cease if she stopped living permanently in the house, and such an interest could not be the subject of a trust of the type declared in the deed. Had the house been sold in 1998, or had the mother ceased to live there permanently, then it or its proceeds would have become subject to her further life interest in the residue, which was an interest in possession for the purposes of the Inheritance Tax Act 1984 s.49. The termination of her first interest would have been exempt from inheritance tax as a result of s.53 of the Act, but only if she became entitled to a further interest in possession in the house or in property representing it. However, she had continued to live in the house, her interest in possession continued and she remained beneficially entitled to the house up until her death. She could not have given away her right to occupy the house, and she had nothing else to give away while she continued to occupy it. As a result of s.49 she was therefore treated as being beneficially entitled to the house when she died, and it therefore formed part of her estate for inheritance tax purposes (paras 27-30, 36-47).

SUSSMAN v REVENUE AND CUSTOMS COMMISSIONERS, [2016] UKFTT 523 (TC), [2016] W.T.L.R. 1447, Judge Judith Powell, FTT (Tax).

2105 Land transactions–Stamp duty land tax

THE FINANCE ACT 2003, SECTION 66 (PRESCRIBED STATUTORY PROVISIONS) ORDER 2016, SI 2016/558; made under the Finance Act 2003 s.66(2). In force: 26 May 2016.

This Order exempts from the charge to stamp duty land tax, land transactions which are effected under the Housing and Regeneration Act 2008 ss.51 or 53A (schemes to transfer property to the Homes and Communities Agency or the Welsh Ministers) if either the purchaser or the vendor is a public body within the meaning of the Finance Act 2003 s.66.

2106 Landfill tax–Repayments–Repayments of landfill tax in respect of "fluff" layers of landfill–Legitimate expectation

Two taxpayers applied for judicial review of HMRC's reversal of its decision to make repayments of landfill tax in respect of certain elements of landfill. The taxpayers operated landfill sites. Disposal of material as waste in landfill attracted landfill tax liability. Rubbish was placed in lined cells. Landfill operators sorted rubbish so that layers not containing sharp or heavy objects, known as base fluff and side fluff, covered the base and sides of the cells, protecting the lining. In *Waste Recycling Group Ltd v Revenue and Customs Commissioners* [2008] EWCA Civ 849, [2009] S.T.C. 200, [2008] C.L.Y. 3818 (*WRG*), material used, not discarded, at landfill sites was held not to be taxable. HMRC issued Brief 58/08, which gave examples of non-taxable use, and invited claims for repayment of tax. Landfill operators including the taxpayers claimed repayment of tax paid on base and side fluff. HMRC wrote to the taxpayers acknowledging that tax was repayable on base and side fluff. It made substantial repayments to the second taxpayer. HMRC received claims for "top fluff", which it did not consider legitimate. Considering that the industry was pushing the boundaries of what was taxable, it decided to resist paying base and side fluff claims. The taxpayers challenged that decision on the basis that they had a legitimate expectation to repayments. Tribunal appeals against the decision that fluff was taxable were pending; the instant application proceeded on the assumption that fluff was taxable.

Held: Applications refused. The instant case differed from cases where guidance had been issued first and taxpayers had arranged their affairs accordingly. The taxpayers had initially paid tax on the basis that base and side fluff was taxable; they relied on subsequent representations by HMRC that fluff was not taxable after all in order to found repayment claims. Unfairness seemed less strong in that case. That did not mean that the principle of legitimate expectation was inapplicable. It depended on the facts (see paras 104-109 of judgment). Brief 58/08 had not made a clear representation that fluff was not taxable. It had not been published in order to give guidance on the taxability of fluff. The hypothetical landfill operator would have read the brief as providing an argument that fluff was material used on a landfill site, hence qualifying for repayment, but would not have read it as unambiguously indicating that HMRC accepted that that was the case (paras 117-121). HMRC's letters to the taxpayers had constituted acceptance that base and side fluff was not taxable and that repayments would be made. In the case of the second taxpayer, the repayments made confirmed that the tax paid was in principle repayable (paras 122-129). It had not been shown, on the evidence, that either taxpayer had "failed to place its cards face up on the table" so as to preclude a repayment claim. They had each established a legitimate expectation of being repaid (paras 130-151). Whether conduct was "conspicuously unfair", so that effect should not be given to it, depended on whether it was a good deal more unfair than just a little bit unfair, *R. v Inland Revenue Commissioners Ex p. Unilever Plc* [1996] S.T.C. 681 and *R. v Inland Revenue Commissioners Ex p. MFK Underwriting Agents Ltd* [1990] 1 W.L.R. 1545, [1990] C.L.Y. 2651 considered. The fact that HMRC considered that its original guidance conflicted with what it later considered to be the true application of statute was not by itself sufficient to justify frustrating a legitimate expectation, but it could be a factor to be taken into account, *R. (on the application of GSTS Pathology LLP) v Revenue and Customs Commissioners* [2013] EWHC 1801 (Admin), [2013] S.T.C. 2017, [2014] C.L.Y. 3084 considered. When considering fairness, the court was to take into account the matters HMRC had taken into account at the time of its decision, rather than whether giving effect to its decision would be unfair in the light of matters it now relied on. The amount of tax at stake could not itself be justification for resiling from a promise. However, in citing the sector-wide challenge to the tax, HMRC relied not on the amount of tax, but on the boundary-pushing behaviour of the industry. The base and side fluff claims had been attempts to extend the *WRG* principle. HMRC had sought to signal to the industry that it would resist challenges to landfill tax. That was a legitimate aim. Since *WRG*, the tax had been challenged by accountants and lawyers; many challenges had been such as to undermine the policy objectives of the tax, *WRG* referred to (paras 156, 162, 166, 172-184). The court had to consider whether the decision was conspicuously unfair not by reference to the industry as a whole but by reference to the individual taxpayers, since the expectations had been generated by the individual letters, not by the brief. The decision had not been conspicuously unfair to the second taxpayer: it had received substantial repayments; failure to repay was unlikely to leave it open to claims from its customers; and its detrimental reliance on the expectation had been limited. Nor had there been conspicuous unfairness to the first taxpayer. Although there had been some detrimental reliance, it had not been extensive. It was appropriate to take into account any comparative unfairness: there was unfairness in the first taxpayer not having received any repayments while all its major competitors had received at least some. However, while other companies might have been fortunate to receive payment before HMRC's decision, that did not make it conspicuously unfair for the first taxpayer not to have done (paras 188-201, 213-216).

R. (ON THE APPLICATION OF VEOLIA ES LANDFILL LTD) v REVENUE AND CUSTOMS COMMISSIONERS; R. (ON THE APPLICATION OF VIRIDOR WASTE MANAGEMENT LTD) v REVENUE AND CUSTOMS COMMISSIONERS, [2016] EWHC 1880 (Admin), [2016] B.T.C. 29, Nugee J, QBD (Admin).

2107 Liability to tax–Agreements–Whether HMRC barred from pursuing company for PAYE and NIC on basis of agreement and undertaking given by HMRC

The appellant company appealed against the First-tier Tribunal's decision that the respondent HMRC was entitled to pursue certain PAYE and national insurance contributions (NIC) liabilities against it. The company had ceased trading in 2005. The dispute before the FTT had related to the company's liability to pay PAYE and NIC in respect of a £900,000 bonus payment to its director and his brother, and payment of salaries of £178,230. In August 2006, the company, acting through its sole director, resolved retrospectively to make a £900,000 bonus payment to the director and his brother. That sum was reflected in the company's cessation accounts. The company had declared and paid no PAYE and NIC in respect of any director or employee and the payments were not mentioned in the personal tax returns of the director or his brother. In January 2007, HMRC opened enquiries into the company's accounts for the 2004/2005 tax year. The company contended that in July 2007 it entered into a binding agreement with HMRC whereby no PAYE or NIC would be demanded from the company in respect of the bonus payment. The agreement had stated that the bonus payment would be disallowed for corporation tax purposes and in return HMRC would not demand PAYE, NIC or income tax on it. In August 2007, the company was struck off the register of companies. HMRC successfully applied for its restoration, and gave an undertaking that it would make no further demands on the company in relation to "outstanding enquiries" and issued closure notices in respect of the "outstanding enquiries" into the company's liabilities. HMRC subsequently issued PAYE notices of determination and NIC decisions on the £900,000 bonus payment. The FTT found that the undertaking did not cover PAYE or NIC determinations. The issues were whether HMRC had been barred from pursuing the company for PAYE and NIC liabilities on the basis of the terms of (1) the agreement of July 2007; (2) the undertaking given by HMRC.

Held: Appeal allowed. (1) There had been a binding agreement between HMRC and the company in 2007. The FTT had wrongly concluded that that HMRC was unlikely to be willing to agree to a final settlement of the tax position in relation to the £900,000 bonus payment while it was still awaiting information from the director. On the contrary, a final settlement might be regarded as more rather than less likely if there was uncertainty about the underlying facts. However, the agreement reached was conditional. HMRC had agreed to an arrangement whereby if the £900,000 bonus payment in the company's accounts was treated as a paper transaction which was not to have effect on reducing the company's profits then PAYE and NIC would not be levied. That condition had been broken by the company. The director was claiming a tax loss of £2.4m, calculated on the basis of obtaining relief in respect of the £900,000. The FTT had been right to find that HMRC was not precluded by the July 2007 agreement from charging PAYE and NIC in respect of the £900,000 bonus (see paras 27-28 of judgment). (2) The undertaking should have been construed in the same way as any legal document, adhering as far as possible to the plain meaning of the words used in the way in which they would have been understood by the parties. At the time that the undertaking had been given, it could not have been intended in an unduly technical sense. It was obvious that the reference to "outstanding enquiries" was intended to be a reference to the enquiries into the company's corporation tax liabilities initiated in 2007. HMRC had been entitled to conclude those outstanding enquiries by issuing closure notices and assessments in respect of those outstanding enquiries. It was an undertaking on HMRC's part to make no further demands of the company in relation to those enquiries and to raise no further enquiries into the company's trade to that date. Apart from any assessment made on the closure of that enquiry, HMRC could not raise any other assessments in relation to the company's trade. The FTT's finding that assessments did not cover PAYE or NIC determinations smacked of over-literalism. The undertaking was not intended to draw such fine semantic distinctions; its clear intention was that the outstanding enquiry could be brought to a conclusion. HMRC were precluded by their undertaking from seeking to claim the sums which were the subject of the instant appeal (paras 37-39).

SPRING SALMON & SEAFOOD LTD v REVENUE AND CUSTOMS COMMISSIONERS, [2016] UKUT 313 (TCC), [2016] B.T.C. 511, Lord Glennie, UT (Tax).

2108 Remote gaming duty–Freedom to provide services–UK tax regime–Compatibility with art.56 TFEU

[Finance Act 2014 (c.26); Treaty on the Functioning of the European Union 2008 art.56]

A trade association based in Gibraltar (G) applied for judicial review of a UK tax regime relating to remote gambling introduced by the Finance Act 2014. Under the new regime, a duty was charged on participation in remote gaming whether the providers of those services were established in the UK or anywhere else in the word, whereas under the previous regime providers established in Gibraltar had paid no tax in the UK on the provision of such services. The effect of the new regime was that Gibraltar providers would pay tax in both the UK and Gibraltar on the same business activity with UK persons. G had brought an earlier claim for judicial review which was directed to a new regulatory framework that required companies to obtain a licence in order to provide remote gaming services to UK consumers. It was accepted that that regulatory framework engaged TFEU art.56. The earlier judicial review was dismissed on the grounds that the new regulatory framework was justified under EU law as having a legitimate aim and was not disproportionate or discriminatory. However, that judicial review did not address the issue of whether a company established outside the EU could rely on EU law to avoid the impact of UK legislation. By the instant application, G claimed that the new tax regime was incompatible with art.56.

Held: Questions referred to ECJ. (1) The constitutional issue of the application of art.56 to Gibraltar entities was a matter for the Courts of Justice of the European Union (CJEU). In relation to whether art.56 was engaged, the fundamental starting point was to consider the nature and effect of the taxes imposed under the new regime. That regime applied equally to operators established in the UK and those established elsewhere in the world, creating a "level playing field" between all suppliers in that market. Member States were entitled, by their tax legislation, to charge tax on remote gaming services and thus to tax an economic activity relating to the supply of goods or services which took place in two states, by reference to the place where the supplier or the consumer was established. It was open to the UK to charge tax on that supply on a point-of-consumption (POC) basis. Therefore, the new tax regime was a POC tax regime on the supply of such services by reference to where they were consumed, and was not a tax on the profits of the suppliers. The question of the fundamental starting point to the art.56 issues also involved issues of EU law that were not *acte clair* and necessitated a reference to the CJEU (see paras 17-23, 34, 39, 64, 73 of judgment). (2) The Revenue had consistently stated that one of the aims of the new tax regime was to ensure that the UK could exercise proper fiscal supervision over the remote gaming market, which included minimising the risk of gambling service providers avoiding tax which would otherwise fall due on their economic activity with UK consumers by relocating offshore. The purpose of the new regime was to rectify what was perceived as the non-taxation of an economic activity within the jurisdiction and to ensure that that activity was taxed on an equal basis among all service providers. It remained for the CJEU to determine whether the imposition of duties such as those introduced by the new regime was within the UK's fiscal competence over which it was entitled to exercise its sovereignty, and whether the disadvantages to foreign providers resulting from the new regime could be characterised as consequences of Member States' parallel exercise of such competence (paras 91, 93-94). (3) It was only in exceptional cases that the court would, in its discretion, entertain a claim for judicial review if there was an alternative remedy. However, the judge granting permission had not reserved the issue of whether there existed an appropriate alternative remedy to the main hearing of the application. In any event, G was not an individual taxpayer and could therefore only bring proceedings by way of judicial review. Moreover, there was no principle of administrative law that the court should refuse to hear a claim by a party who had standing simply because a different party would have an alternative remedy. The situation in the instant case was different from that in *Autologic Holdings Plc v Inland Revenue Commissioners* [2005] UKHL 54, [2006] 1 A.C. 118, [2005] C.L.Y. 4056 because G was not a taxpayer and the companies in that case had already been assessed for tax and did not appeal to the tribunal, *Autologic* distinguished (paras 97, 101). (4) Relief might be obtained by a party who did not have directly effective EU law rights, *R. v Secretary of State for Employment Ex p. Equal Opportunities Commission* [1995] 1 A.C. 1, [1994] C.L.Y. 1981 followed, *R. (on the application of Age UK) v Secretary of State for Business, Innovation and Skills* [2009] EWHC 2336 (Admin), [2010] 1 C.M.L.R. 21, [2010] C.L.Y. 2150 applied (para.104).

R. (ON THE APPLICATION OF GIBRALTAR BETTING & GAMING ASSOCIATION LTD) v REVENUE AND CUSTOMS COMMISSIONERS, [2015] EWHC 1863 (Admin), [2016] S.T.C. 151, Charles J, QBD (Admin).

2109 **Stamp duty land tax–Chargeable transfers–Anti-avoidance provisions–Subsales**

[Finance Act 2003 (c.14) Pt 4, s.42(1), s.43(1), s.45(3), s.46, s.71A, s.75A(1)(c)]

The appellant company appealed against a decision (*Project Blue Ltd v Revenue and Customs Commissioners* [2014] UKUT 564 (TCC), [2015] S.T.C. 745, [2015] C.L.Y. 2509) that it was liable pursuant to the Finance Act 2003 to pay stamp duty land tax (SDLT) in connection with its acquisition of the former Chelsea Army Barracks from the Ministry of Defence. The company purchased the site for £959m but the tax consequences of the transaction were complicated by the fact that it decided to obtain finance for the acquisition and development of the site in a way which was compliant with Sharia law. It did so by contracting to sell the site to a Qatari bank, for approximately £1.25bn. The contract with the bank was completed contemporaneously with the completion of the company's contract with the MoD. On the same day, the bank granted the company a lease of the site and the parties entered into various put and call options which would entitle the company in due course to re-acquire the freehold of the site from the bank. Other steps included the bank's lease-back of the land to the company. The Upper Tribunal held that SDLT was payable by the company in the sum of £38.36m based on a consideration of £959m. The company argued that it had no liability for any SDLT on the transaction and that the party liable for the tax was the bank, but that the commissioners were now out of time for making any determination or assessment in order to recover it. The commissioners contended that the company was the taxable party but that the chargeable consideration in respect of which SDLT was payable should be the £1.25bn paid by the bank to the company rather than the £959m paid by the company to the secretary of state.

Held: Appeal allowed, cross-appeal dismissed. (1) SDLT was chargeable under s.42(1) on "land transactions", which meant "any acquisition of a chargeable interest" pursuant to s.43(1). The charge applied, if at all, to the acquisition of a chargeable interest on the transfer of the freehold or leasehold interest to the mortgagor and not to the financing arrangements which followed. The Ijara form of Sharia financing transaction utilised in the instant case provided for the property in question to be acquired by the financial institution as its property and then leased to the person seeking the finance in exchange for agreed rental payments which gave the financial institution a return on its money. The evidence indicated that the Ijara transaction itself was comprised in the lease and the option agreement (see paras 5-8 of judgment). The entry into the contract between the MoD and the company was not a land transaction, nor was the entry into the contract between the company and the bank or the lease agreement between the bank and the company. The put and call options were land transactions under s.46 but no charge to SDLT arose because they were granted for no consideration. The existence of the sale on to the bank meant that under s.45(3) the substantial performance or completion of the sale to the company was disregarded leaving the completion or substantial performance of the deemed secondary contract to the bank as the only possible acquisition of a chargeable interest. There would have been a land transaction in respect of the completion of the sale to the bank but none in respect of the company's own acquisition of an interest on completion of the contract with the MoD, *DV3 RS Ltd Partnership v Revenue and Customs Commissioners* [2013] EWCA Civ 907, [2014] 1 W.L.R. 1136, [2013] C.L.Y. 3130 applied (paras 13, 16-17). (2) Section 71A accommodated Sharia-compliant financing arrangements according to the Ijara model which depended upon the financial institution being the owner of the property in question. It provided a blanket exemption from a charge to SDLT in cases where the property already belonged to the customer seeking the finance and was then sold to the bank for the purpose of the Ijara (paras 20-21). The architecture of the relevant transaction in a case covered by s.45(3) was part of what was identified in *DV3* as the central provisions of Part 4 of the Act and s.71A fell to be construed by reference to and in conformity with them. The alternative was that the exemption from charge which it conferred fell to be determined in the non-SDLT world by reference to transactions which had no existence in relation to the creation of the charge to which the exemption related (para.30). The obvious construction of s.71A was that cases falling within s.45(3) were intended to be treated as direct acquisitions by the financial institution from the third party vendor in terms of their tax consequences. The bank was therefore liable for SDLT on completion of the secondary contract under s.45(3) and was not entitled to claim s.71A relief. It was payable on the completion of the transaction which gave rise to the charge. The availability of the relief could not depend on how the claim for relief was subsequently determined or dealt with by the commissioners. The s.75A(1)(c) condition was not therefore satisfied (para.35).

PROJECT BLUE LTD (FORMERLY PROJECT BLUE (GUERNSEY LTD)) v REVENUE AND CUSTOMS COMMISSIONERS, [2016] EWCA Civ 485, [2016] S.T.C. 2168, Patten LJ, CA (Civ Div).

2110 Tax–Domicile of origin–Justification for preliminary hearing determining taxpayer's domicile of origin

[Tribunal Procedure (First-tier Tribunal) (Tax Chamber) Rules 2009 (SI 2009/273) r.2]

The appellant taxpayer appealed against a case management decision of the First-tier Tribunal refusing his application for his domicile of origin to be determined as a preliminary issue in advance of the main hearing of his appeal against determinations made by the respondent HMRC. The taxpayer was born in the Republic of Ireland but had lived in the UK and spent increasing amounts of time in Switzerland. HMRC had issued notices of determination to the effect that he was domiciled in the UK during 2000-2008. The taxpayer appealed to the tribunal and applied for the issue of his domicile during the tax years in question to be decided at a preliminary hearing. The tribunal refused on the basis, inter alia, that a hearing would be required to determine the substantive issue between the parties in any event and there was little prospect of finding the time for a preliminary hearing before the appeal. The taxpayer submitted that the tribunal had been plainly wrong to have refused to grant a preliminary hearing on the issue of domicile as it was a discrete issue which could dispose of the case either by settlement or by him walking away and would make a real difference to the approach to the rest of the case.

Held: Appeal dismissed. (1) The Upper Tribunal should be slow to interfere with a tribunal's case management decisions. The power to order a preliminary hearing should be used sparingly, particularly as regards an issue of mixed fact and law. The overriding test had to be what was fair and just in the circumstances of the case having regard to the factors listed in the Tribunal Procedure (First-tier Tribunal) (Tax Chamber) Rules 2009 r.2, *Tilling v Whiteman* [1980] A.C. 1, [1979] C.L.Y. 1624, *McLoughlin v Grovers* [2001] EWCA Civ 1743, [2002] Q.B. 1312, [2002] C.L.Y. 3307 and *SCA Packaging Ltd v Boyle* [2009] UKHL 37, [2009] 4 All E.R. 1181, [2009] C.L.Y. 4260 followed, *Steele v Steele* [2001] C.P. Rep. 106, [2001] C.L.Y. 440 considered. Key principles to consider included that the power should only be exercised where there was a succinct knockout point which would dispose of the case or an aspect of it and that the point should be a succinct one which was capable of being decided without significant delay. It was not clear that the tribunal had applied all the correct principles, taken all relevant considerations into account and made no error in the balancing exercise. It appeared that the tribunal had principally relied on two factors, namely that a further hearing would be necessary and that the tribunal could not accommodate a preliminary hearing before the substantive appeal, but they were not the only factors. The concerns were sufficiently material to conclude that the decision involved making an error on a point of law. The UT would remake the decision (see paras 9-10, 25, 28, 33, 41, 43 of judgment). (2) In remaking the decision, the balancing exercise came out in favour of refusing to direct a separate or preliminary hearing on the issue of the taxpayer's domicile of origin. There was no clear justification for it in the instant case. A conclusion on the taxpayer's domicile of origin would not dispose of the whole case or a separate aspect of it. It was not a succinct point in the circumstances of the case and it would increase the time and resources needed to resolve the dispute. The prospect of a delay was a material factor. The difference it might make to the taxpayer's pre-trial preparation was not a material consideration given that the factual enquiry remained the same and the taxpayer had a choice as to the evidence he wished to present. There was no indication that HMRC would settle if the issue was resolved and there was no certainty as to whether the taxpayer would walk away. To accord particular weight to that factor risked tribunal resources being employed for purposes other than those for which it had jurisdiction, namely to resolve the actual dispute before the tribunal (para.68).

WROTTESLEY v REVENUE AND CUSTOMS COMMISSIONERS, [2015] UKUT 637 (TCC), [2016] S.T.C. 1123, Judge Timothy Herrington, UT (Tax).

2111 Tax–Upper Tribunal–Upper Tribunal's power to order payment for costs in respect of pro bono representation

[Legal Services Act 2007 (c.29) s.194, s.194(10); Tribunals, Courts and Enforcement Act 2007 (c.15) s.25, s.29; Tribunal Procedure (Upper Tribunal) Rules 2008 (SI 2008/2698)]

A taxpayer applied for pro bono costs to be awarded under the Legal Services Act 2007 s.194 against HMRC following her successful appeal in *Raftopoulou v Revenue and Customs Commissioners* [2015] UKUT 579 (TCC), [2016] S.T.C. 656, [2016] 2095. The taxpayer had been represented pro bono. It was her case that the Upper Tribunal had the power to make an order for a payment in respect of pro bono representation and, as the appeal had been successful, such an order should be made for a payment in favour of the Access to Justice Foundation, a prescribed charity for the purposes of s.194. She submitted that the power was available by virtue of the effect that should be given to the Tribunals, Courts and Enforcement Act 2007 s.25, namely that s.25 avoided the need for Parliament to have to legislate expressly to transfer the High Court's powers to the tribunal in matters which would only arise from time-to-time. She placed s.194 into that category and argued that that section did not need to be updated to include the Upper Tribunal because of the effect of s.25.

Held: Application refused. (1) The tribunal did not have inherent jurisdiction to award pro bono costs. Nor could any power to award costs, whether in the Tribunals, Courts and Enforcement Act 2007 s.29 or in the Tribunal Procedure (Upper Tribunal) Rules 2008, be construed so as to provide a power to make an order for payment such as that in s.194, where no costs had been incurred by the pro bono party. Furthermore, the jurisdictional limitation in s.194 excluded reliance on s.194 directly. The expression "civil court" was restrictively and exclusively defined by s.194(10) and it was not possible to construe that sub-section to include the Upper Tribunal (see paras 5-6 of judgment). (2) Section 25 could not have the effect argued for by the taxpayer. The power of the High Court to make an order for payment in respect of pro bono representation had its basis in statute, and was thus conditioned by statute. The power afforded to the High Court by s.194 was therefore confined by the limitations inherent in s.194 itself, in particular the jurisdictional limitation which Parliament saw fit to impose. Section 25 could not be construed so as to permit an extension beyond those express jurisdictional boundaries, *IB v Information Commissioner* [2011] UKUT 370 (AAC) applied. The possible rationale for the enactment of s.25 canvassed by the court in *R. (on the application of Cart) v Upper Tribunal* [2010] EWCA Civ 859, [2011] Q.B. 120 did not answer the question as to the scope and delineation of the powers to which s.25 could apply. The scope of the relevant power in the instant case was expressly delineated by s.194 so as not to be capable of being exercised in any jurisdiction other than those within the meaning of "civil court" under s.194(10). As that expression was defined by reference to particular jurisdictions, and did not include the Upper Tribunal, that limited the exercise of any power under s.194. That jurisdictional limitation could not be overridden by s.25, *Cart* considered. There was no inconsistency between that finding and the position in respect of the power to order security for costs, where it had been accepted in *Blada Ltd (In Liquidation) v Revenue and Customs Commissioners* that s.25 enabled the tribunal to make such an order, notwithstanding the absence of an express power to do so. In contrast to the position of an order for payments in respect of pro bono representation, there was no jurisdictional limitation imposed by statute on orders for security for costs, *Blada* considered. Accordingly, the tribunal did not have the power to make an order for payment in respect of pro bono representation (paras 14-18). (3) (Per curiam) It was hoped that urgent consideration would be given to the Costs Review Group's recommendation that the provisions of s.194 be extended to tribunals. The taxpayer's submissions represented a powerful argument why the tribunal should be empowered to make such an order. Appeals to the tribunal were on questions of law and it would be contrary to the interests of justice if there was anything which discouraged the availability of pro bono representation for self-represented parties who often appeared in such cases. There was no reason why, where the tribunal had full costs-shifting powers which could result in a party represented pro bono being ordered to pay the costs of the other, represented, party, the playing field should not be levelled so as to permit an analogous order to be made against the represented party. There was a public interest in such orders being made where permitted and where appropriate, *E, Re* and *S (Children) (Appeal from Care and Placement Orders), Re* [2015] UKSC 20, [2015] 1 W.L.R. 1631, [2015] C.L.Y. 1001 considered (paras 20-21).

RAFTOPOULOU v REVENUE AND CUSTOMS COMMISSIONERS, [2015] UKUT 630 (TCC), [2015] B.T.C. 535, Judge Roger Berner, UT (Tax).

2112 Tax and Chancery Chamber–Protective costs orders–Whether taxpayer liable for costs of HMRC in application for protective costs order

The Upper Tribunal was required to determine the costs of an unsuccessful application for a protective costs direction made by the appellant. The appellant had unsuccessfully appealed to the First-tier Tribunal against a penalty for the late filing of a tax return. She obtained permission to appeal to the UT. She applied for a direction that no costs award should be made whatever the outcome of the appeal. It was suggested that the matter be dealt with on written submissions alone, but the UT held that that was not appropriate. It refused the application; its reasons could be taken as establishing the principle that a protective costs direction would be made only in limited circumstances and usually, although not invariably, when HMRC were the appellants. The appellant argued that she should not have to pay HMRC's costs because she had not asked for a hearing and because the hearing of the substantive appeal would have taken no longer than the application.

Held: No order for costs made. The appellant was mistaken in suggesting that the hearing of the appeal would have taken no longer than the application. However, there had been no prior authority directly in point and HMRC had therefore established the principle for which they had argued. It would not be appropriate to direct the appellant to contribute towards the costs of their doing so.

PINE v REVENUE AND CUSTOMS COMMISSIONERS, [2016] UKUT 257 (TCC), [2016] B.T.C. 508, Judge Colin Bishopp, UT (Tax).

2113 Tax assessments–Bankrupts–Appeal notices–Whether undischarged bankrupt had locus standi to bring appeal–Prior authority from trustee in bankruptcy

[Taxes Management Act 1970 (c.9) s.49F(2), s.54]

An undischarged bankrupt applied for permission to notify appeals to the tribunal against various HMRC assessments and penalties after the statutory time limit for doing so had expired. The issue was whether the bankrupt had standing to bring the proceedings, and argue the appeals if permission were granted, in view of the fact that he had not obtained prior authority from his trustee in bankruptcy.

Held: Application struck out. (1) The bankrupt had no standing to bring the appeals against HMRC assessments because that right had vested in his trustee in bankruptcy, *Soul v Inland Revenue Commissioners* 43 T.C. 662, [1967] C.L.Y. 1906, *McNulty v Revenue and Customs Commissioners* [2012] UKUT 174 (TCC), [2012] S.T.C. 2110, [2012] C.L.Y. 3331 and *Ahajot (Count Artsrunik) v Waller (Inspector of Taxes)* [2005] B.P.I.R. 82, [2005] C.L.Y. 4061 applied. Under *McNulty,* the bankrupt also had no standing to appeal against the HMRC penalties for the same reason. Furthermore, the case of *R. (on the application of Singh) v Revenue and Customs Commissioners* [2010] UKUT 174 (TCC), [2010] S.T.C. 2020, [2010] C.L.Y. 74 strongly suggested that as an undischarged bankrupt had no standing to bring judicial review proceedings, an application to notify appeals late should be treated in an identical way, *Singh* considered (see paras 8, 11, 13, 15, 27-28 of judgment). (2) The application to notify the appeals late would be struck out for want of jurisdiction so that the appeals would automatically fall. Had the bankrupt had standing to bring the appeals, the tribunal would have granted him permission to do so, but would have upheld HMRC's assessments and penalties. However, contrary to HMRC's assertions, the grant of permission would have undone the agreement under the Taxes Management Act 1970 s.54 to settle the appeal, which was deemed by s.49F(2) to have been reached (paras 29-31).

ALI v REVENUE AND CUSTOMS COMMISSIONERS, [2015] UKFTT 464 (TC), [2015] B.P.I.R. 1348, Judge Richard Thomas, FTT (Tax).

2114 Tax assessments–Gaming duty–Payments on account

THE GAMING DUTY (AMENDMENT) REGULATIONS 2016, SI 2016/943; made under the Finance Act 1997 s.12(4). In force: 31 October 2016.

The Gaming Duty Regulations 1997 reg.5 specifies the amount of the payment on account of gaming duty. Payments on account are required to be made for the first three months of a six month accounting period that a registered provider (as defined in reg.2) is required to make for the first three months of any six month accounting period. These Regulations substitute a new table to reflect the changes made by the Finance Act 2016 s.152 increasing the bands of gross gaming yield to which the rates of gaming duty apply in the Finance Act 1997 s.11(2) in line with inflation and will have effect in relation to payments on account of gaming duty payable on or after 31 October 2016.

2115 Tax avoidance–Accelerated payment notices–Disputed sums in hands of state during enquiry and assessment process–Public interest outweighing limited private interest in retention of money pending formal assessment

[Finance Act 2004 (c.12) Sch.42, s.308(5); Finance Act 2014 (c.26) Pt 1; European Convention on Human Rights 1950 Protocol 1 art.1, art.6; Taxes Management Act 1970 (c.9) s.28A(4); Tax Avoidance Schemes (Prescribed Descriptions of Arrangements) Regulations 2006 (SI 2006/1543) reg.1(2)(a)]

A taxpayer applied for judicial review of HMRC's power to issue an accelerated payment notice requiring him to make a payment on account of his unassessed tax liability. The taxpayer entered into a tax avoidance scheme (the syndicates scheme) which had been notified to HMRC under to the Disclosure of Tax Avoidance Schemes regime introduced by the Finance Act 2004 Sch.42. The promoter of that scheme had notified an earlier scheme to HMRC (the partnerships scheme) which, according to the taxpayer, was substantially similar to the syndicates scheme in economic and financial terms. The partnerships scheme was not notifiable under the legislation in force at the relevant time. The syndicates scheme made a net business loss attributable to the taxpayer for the purposes of his 2008 tax return, which he submitted in 2008. He received a substantial repayment of tax. HMRC raised an inquiry, and in 2015 the taxpayer received the notice requiring repayment of the tax pending a final assessment. The taxpayer submitted that the Finance Act 2014 Pt 1 Ch.3 failed to confer a right of representation, frustrated his legitimate expectations, operated in an unlawfully retroactive manner, and violated ECHR art.6 and Protocol 1 art.1. He also submitted that HMRC lacked power to issue the notice on the basis that the syndicate scheme was not notifiable.

Held: Application refused. (1) Chapter 3 of the 2014 Act had the legitimate objective of altering the economics of tax avoidance by ensuring that the disputed tax remained with HMRC, rather than with the taxpayer, pending formal assessment. The imposition of an accelerated payment notice prior to a full assessment greatly reduced the liquidity benefit of participation in tax avoidance schemes and thus acted as a disincentive (see paras 6, 49 of judgment). (2) The 2014 Act created a statutory right of consultation which afforded the addressee a right to representation prior to the notice becoming effective. In any event, the remedy of judicial review existed if the representation process was inadequate (paras 8, 67-68, 74). (3) There had never been any promise or representation that a payment notice would only be issued following assessment. The Treasury had consulted all affected persons on the proposal to empower the issuance of payment notices during inquiries and there had been no suggestion that the consultation was unfair or inadequate. Moreover, there had been no detrimental reliance, since if HMRC was correct in regarding the scheme as unlawful then the taxpayer would have to pay the sum anyway. The issue was therefore one of liquidity only. Even if any legitimate expectation had arisen, it was fair and not an abuse of power for it to be thwarted. Unlawful tax avoidance was a substantial problem which the provisions of the 2014 Act were designed to address. Therefore, the policy reasons far outweighed the relatively limited private interest in retention of the money pending formal assessment (paras 91-95). (4) The application of the new payment rules under the 2014 Act was only retroactive in the very limited sense that the rules changed the consequences of acts or omissions from those which would have been expected. In the context of tax avoidance, that was a change justified by a legitimate policy and was fair and reasonable in all the circumstances, *R. (on the application of Rowe) v Revenue and Customs Commissioners* [2015] EWHC 2293 (Admin), [2015] B.T.C. 27, [2015] C.L.Y. 2512 applied (para 97-98). (5) A tax dispute pre-assessment was not a "civil" dispute, since tax matters formed part of the hard core of public authority prerogatives and disputes involving them were between citizen and state. Therefore, ECHR art.6 was not engaged. Even if the instant dispute was "civil", the taxpayer had not been denied access to a court because the remedy of judicial review was available. Moreover, he had the right under the Taxes Management Act 1970 s.28A(4) to compel HMRC to issue a closure notice, triggering the normal rights of appeal, *Rowe* applied (paras 8, 101-110). (6) A tax dispute did not give rise to an asset protectable under ECHR Protocol 1 art.1, *R. (on the application of Huitson) v Revenue and Customs Commissioners* [2011] EWCA Civ 893, [2012] Q.B. 489, [2011] C.L.Y. 3384 followed. Even if the dispute did entail property of the taxpayer, there was no deprivation, but only a requirement that the taxpayer pay money to HMRC which would be returned if he won his case. If he lost, it was rightly retained by the state. In any event, the proportionality of the measure in issue met the four-part test in *Bank Mellat v HM Treasury* [2013] UKSC 39, [2014] A.C. 700, [2013] C.L.Y. 194, *Bank Mellat* followed (paras 118, 120-121). (7) The promoter was not exempt under s.308(5) of the 2004 Act from notifying the syndicate scheme on the basis of substantial similarity. The syndicate scheme did not fall within the transitional arrangements provided for by the Tax Avoidance Schemes (Prescribed Descriptions of Arrangements) Regulations 2006 reg.1(2)(a), which only covered schemes already in existence as at the date on which the Regulations came into force and did not extend to future schemes of a similar nature which remained within the parameters of the old schemes. Even if s.308(5) did apply, Parliament had consciously ensured that the two schemes were fundamentally different in legal terms, notwithstanding their economic and financial similarities (paras 123, 132, 146-151, 167-170).

WALAPU v REVENUE AND CUSTOMS COMMISSIONERS, [2016] EWHC 658 (Admin), [2016] 4 All E.R. 955, Green J, QBD (Admin).

2116 Tax avoidance–Accelerated payment notices–Interim relief–Public interest in collection of tax weighed in balance of convenience against granting of interim relief

[European Convention on Human Rights 1950 Protocol 1 art.1; Taxes Management Act 1970 (c.9) s.55]

Taxpayers applied for permission to appeal, and interim relief if permission were granted, following a decision that they should have to pay sums required under advance payment notices. The taxpayers had challenged the notices on grounds including retrospectivity, the applicability of ECHR Protocol 1 art.1 and legitimate expectation. The issues were whether (1) permission to appeal should be granted given that the taxpayers in *R. (on the application of Rowe) v Revenue and Customs Commissioners* [2015] EWHC 2293 (Admin), [2015] B.T.C. 27, [2015] C.L.Y. 2512, which raised similar issues, had applied to the Court of Appeal for permission to appeal; (2) HMRC should be precluded, pending determination of the claims, from enforcing the amounts specified in the notices if permission were granted.

Held: Judgment accordingly. (1) There was no clear demarcation between *Rowe* and the instant case, *Rowe* referred to. However, in relation to legitimate expectation, there was potentially a separate issue of law in the instant case on the interpretation of the Taxes Management Act 1970 s.55. Further, the taxpayers had raised real points in relation to the correctness of *Rowe*. The Court of Appeal considering the permission application in *Rowe* was going to be considering the points raised by the taxpayers in the instant case in criticism of the judgment in *Rowe*. The instant court would be very concerned about the instant claim proceeding without the judge having seen what had happened in *Rowe*. Sufficient had been made out for permission to be granted. However, the claim would be stayed until the application in *Rowe* was determined (see paras 2-4 of judgment). (2) The central issue as to interim relief was where the balance of convenience lay. Parliament had imposed a specific regime: it had taken the view that tax avoidance arrangements had enabled taxpayers, for a substantial length of time, to defer tax, and that that was contrary to the public interest in the collection of tax. The advance payment notice provisions were there to discourage artificial tax arrangements and to remove the advantages to taxpayers of the delay that would occur before the tax could be levied. The court therefore had to consider the merits of the proposed claim more critically than it would in a different context. The ultimate prospects of success in the claim were relatively low. It would not be conducive to the public interest to grant any interim relief. The taxpayers had had the advantage of income that, on one strong view, should have been subject to tax in the instant jurisdiction many years earlier. If they had spent the money on current consumption or the acquisition of assets that had fallen in value, one had sympathy, but that was not a determinative factor on the balance of public interest. Even had the court been prepared to grant interim relief, it would have done so only on terms that the penalty regime should continue to be operative. If the claim were successful, no penalty would be collectable, but if it were not it would not be right to have deferred the triggering of the penalty provisions pending the claim's determination (paras 7-8, 18-20).

R. (ON THE APPLICATION OF ASTON) v REVENUE AND CUSTOMS COMMISSIONERS, [2015] EWHC 3118 (Admin), [2016] B.T.C. 1, Kenneth Parker J, QBD (Admin).

2117 Tax avoidance–Accelerated payment notices–Whether partnerships notifiable under applicable disclosure of tax avoidance schemes provisions–Transitional provisions in reg.1 Tax Avoidance Schemes (Prescribed Descriptions of Arrangements) Regulations 2006

[Finance Act 2014 (c.26) s.219(1), s.219(3), s.219(5); Tax Avoidance Schemes (Prescribed Descriptions of Arrangements) Regulations 2006 (SI 2006/1543) reg.1; Finance Act 2004 (c.12) s.308(1), s.308(3), s.308(5), s.313(1)(b)]

The claimants sought to challenge the legality of accelerated payment notices and partner payment notices issued by the respondent Revenue pursuant to the Finance Act 2014. The claimants were individuals who had participated in tax avoidance schemes, namely Liberty Partnerships 5-8 and 6-8 or Liberty Syndicates schemes. The Revenue issued the notices on the basis that the claimants had avoided the payment of tax by their use of those schemes. The court had to determine whether any of the Liberty Fund Partnerships were notifiable under the applicable disclosure of tax avoidance schemes (DOTAS) provisions, having regard to the transitional provisions in the Tax Avoidance Schemes (Prescribed Descriptions of Arrangements) Regulations 2006 reg.1. The claimants submitted that none of the partnerships were notifiable. They argued that Condition C in s.219(1) of the 2014 Act was not satisfied because for all the partnerships the relevant first date for notifying any notifiable arrangements under the Finance Act 2004 s.308(3) fell before 1 August 2006. The Revenue submitted that, for the purposes of s.308(3), the promoter of each partnership had a duty to notify when he became aware of any transaction forming part of the particular arrangements for each specific partnership. For each of partnerships 5-8 that date inevitably fell after 1 August 2006, because no relevant transactions in respect of any of those partnerships had been implemented before August 2006.

Held: Claim dismissed. (1) For fiscal purposes, the focus had to be on each specific partnership. Section 219(3) of the 2014 Act referred to a particular tax advantage resulting from particular arrangements, being DOTAS arrangements. The chosen DOTAS arrangements could only be the particular arrangements for each partnership, with the particular tax advantage being the alleged trading loss for each individual partnership. Under s.313(1)(b) of the 2004 Act a person who was party to any notifiable arrangements had to provide the Board with prescribed information relating to "The time when he obtains or expects to obtain by virtue of the arrangements an advantage in relation to any relevant tax." In the circumstances of the instant case, that provision could sensibly apply only if the "arrangements" in question comprised the particular partnership that the taxpayer had entered, or firmly intended to enter. It was clearly essential that the Revenue should know when a taxpayer had entered, or intended to enter, into particular arrangements and the specific characteristics of those arrangements, in the instant case the individual partnership. Before the 2006 Regulations were introduced, any arrangements implementing proposals that pre-dated 18 March 2004 were not notifiable. That constituted favourable treatment of some taxpayers, because other arrangements, being substantially the same and having the same alleged tax advantages, were notifiable simply because they implemented "proposals" made on or after 18 March 2004. The position had since changed, in that "arrangements" were notifiable where they were implemented on or after 1 August 2006, even if the proposal was made before that date but on or after 18 March 2004. That result was less favourable to certain taxpayers, but it was not difficult to see why it might be considered more effective in terms of legislative policy, a greater number of individual tax avoidance arrangements being made notifiable; and as promoting greater equality of treatment of taxpayers seeking to exploit tax avoidance opportunities (see paras 35, 37-38, 41 of judgment). (2) In respect of the relevant Liberty Fund Partnerships 5-8, there was a duty to notify prescribed information about the first partnership under s.308(3), because (a) such a partnership constituted "notifiable arrangements" under s.308(3); and (b) the promoter first became aware of a transaction forming part of such arrangements after 1 August 2006 when those arrangements began to be implemented; and (c) those arrangements did not implement a proposal in respect of which notice had been given under s.308(1) of the 2004 Act. As regards Liberty Fund Partnerships 6-8, each constituted notifiable arrangements under s.308(5) of the 2004 Act, being substantially the same as the arrangements constituted by Liberty Fund Partnership 5, and there was no separate duty to notify provided that the arrangements of Liberty Fund Partnership 5 had been duly notified. In any event, each of the Liberty Fund Partnerships 5-8 fell within s.219(5) of the 2014 Act as "DOTAS arrangements". Condition C was, therefore, satisfied in each case (paras 42-44).

R. (ON THE APPLICATION OF GRAHAM) v REVENUE AND CUSTOMS COMMISSIONERS, [2016] EWHC 1197 (Admin), [2016] B.T.C. 23, Sir Kenneth Parker, QBD (Admin).

2118 Tax avoidance–Information notices–Validity of third party information notices

[Finance Act 2008 (c.9) Sch.36, Sch.36 Pt 1 para.2, Sch.36 Pt 1 para.3, Sch.36 Pt 1 para.3(3)(e); European Convention on Human Rights 1950 art.6, art.8]

The appellant UK registered companies (D) appealed against a decision (*R. (on the application of Derrin Brothers Properties Ltd) v Revenue and Customs Commissioners* [2014] EWHC 1152 (Admin), [2014] S.T.C. 2238, [2014] C.L.Y. 2973) upholding the approval of third party information notices issued by the respondent Revenue in connection with a tax avoidance investigation into an Australian taxpayer. The notices issued under the Finance Act 2008 Sch.36 Pt 1 para.2 were sent at the request of the Australian Tax authorities to 24 companies associated with a taxpayer suspected of avoiding some A$230m. The notices were approved by the First-tier Tribunal (FTT) and sent to third party accountants and banks asking for business records and confidential documents belonging to D. D received copies of the notices and summary details explaining the nature of the investigation, and that information held by the third parties was believed to be directly relevant to the investigation. D submitted that the notices were ultra vires and invalid as they were in breach of the requirements of Sch.36 and had been applied unfairly in breach of their ECHR art.6 and art.8 rights. In particular, the condition in para.3(3)(e) was not satisfied because all 24 appellants should have been treated as taxpayers and the summary of reasons provided had been inadequate and served with insufficient time for D to make representations to the FTT.

Held: Appeal dismissed. (1) D did not claim that Sch.36 itself was incompatible with the Convention but that Sch.36 had been applied unfairly. However, Parliament had clearly distinguished between a taxpayer, a third party, and a non-taxpayer. On a purposive interpretation of Sch.36 there was no requirement for third parties or non-taxpayers to be given any further information. Such a requirement would be inconsistent with Sch.36 itself and with the intention of Parliament, which was to balance the Revenue's power to investigate possible tax avoidance with controls on the executive. D had been informed of the nature of the allegations by the third parties and some of them were parties to Australian proceedings challenging the notices. They had adequate knowledge in time to make representations but had not done so (see paras 80-81, 83-89 of judgment). It was for HMRC to decide who was a taxpayer for the purposes of the third party notices. The mere fact that the documents and information relating to non-taxpayer entities were also relevant to their own tax affairs did not make them taxpayers within Sch.36 para.2 and para.3 (paras 98-99). Identification of specific documents was not an express requirement of para.3(3)(e) neither was it implicit because of the need for the Revenue to be able to obtain documents without prejudicing an investigation, *R. v Macdonald (Inspector of Taxes) Ex p. Hutchinson & Co Ltd* [1998] S.T.C. 680, [1998] C.L.Y. 4692 considered (paras 68, 105). (2) Parliament had provided a statutory judicial monitoring scheme which balanced private interests against the interests of the wider community and that process, combined with judicial review, was sufficient to satisfy D's art.6 rights combined with art.8. The judicial review process was adequate to review compliance with the statutory pre-conditions for judicial approval of third party notices under schedule 36, both in relation to law and fact, *Tsfayo v United Kingdom (60860/00)* (2009) 48 E.H.R.R. 18, [2008] C.L.Y. 1955 and Ravon v France (18497/03) 21.5.2008 considered (paras 67-68, 80, 116-121).

R. (ON THE APPLICATION OF DERRIN BROTHERS PROPERTIES LTD) v REVENUE AND CUSTOMS COMMISSIONERS *sub nom.* R. (ON THE APPLICATION OF DERRIN BROTHER PROPERTIES LTD) v JUDGE OF THE FIRST-TIER TRIBUNAL (TAX CHAMBER), [2016] EWCA Civ 15, [2016] 1 W.L.R. 2423, Sir Terence Etherton C, CA (Civ Div).

2119 Tax avoidance–Limited liability partnerships–Whether partnership payment notices applied to limited liability partnerships as well as general partnerships

[Finance Act 2004 (c.12) s.308; Finance Act 2014 (c.26) Sch.32 para.3; Limited Liability Partnerships Act 2000 (c.12) s.1; Taxes Management Act 1970 (c.9) s.12AA, s.12AA(6), s.12AC, s.12AC(1)]

The claimants applied for judicial review of HMRC's decision to issue them with partnership payment notices. Each claimant was a member of either a general or limited liability partnership. The partnerships had been set up by an investment company that promoted a tax avoidance scheme. The company acted as the partnerships' consultant and two of its affiliates were the nominated partners responsible for filing the tax returns. The company informed HMRC of the scheme under the disclosure of tax avoidance schemes in the Finance Act 2004 s.308. HMRC requested further information and corresponded with the company for over 18 months. Partnership returns were submitted and HMRC sent notices of enquiry to the company and the partners named on the returns. The affiliates had not been identified as members of the partnerships on the returns; consequently, no notices of enquiry were sent to them. HMRC concluded that understated partner tax was payable and issued partnership payment notices under the Finance Act 2014 Sch.32 para.3. The claimants submitted that the payment notices were invalid because (1) in terms of the limited liability partnerships, the ordinary law of partnership did not apply to them under the Limited Liability Partnerships Act 2000 s.1 unless specific provision was made, and Sch.32 made no such provision; (2) in terms of both types of partnership, HMRC had not issued a notice of enquiry to the partners who had made and delivered the tax returns, being the affiliates, in accordance with the Taxes Management Act 1970 s.12AC(1), so had not satisfied the conditions of Sch.32.

Held: Application refused. (1) The words in tax legislation had to be interpreted in light of the context and scheme of the Act as a whole, avoiding a formalistic approach, *Barclays Mercantile Business Finance Ltd v Mawson (Inspector of Taxes)* [2004] UKHL 51, [2005] 1 A.C. 684, [2005] C.L.Y. 3988 followed. Whatever the legal character of limited liability partnerships under the 2000 Act, that could not be determinative when considering the meaning that the words of Sch.32 conveyed. The purpose of Sch.32 was to make tax avoidance less advantageous. There was no reason to think that Parliament would have intended for it to apply to general partnerships but not limited liability partnerships when the latter could also be used for tax avoidance schemes. Further, Sch.32 was meshed with s.12AA-s.12AC of the 1970 Act. There was no distinction between a general partnership and limited liability partnership in those provisions and case law had decided that they applied to both, *Tower MCashback LLP 1 v Revenue and Customs Commissioners* [2011] UKSC 19, [2011] 2 A.C. 457, [2011] C.L.Y. 3277 followed. Given those factors, Sch.32 applied to both general and limited liability partnerships and their members (see paras 59-62 of judgment). (2) Contrary to the mandatory requirement of s.12AA(6) of the 1970 Act, the partnership tax returns made no mention of the affiliates as either partners or as filing partners attesting to their accuracy and completeness. Those that failed to comply with a legal obligation to identify their existence to a public authority, and to attest to the truth of what they were stating, could not then complain when the public authority did not send them a notice of enquiry into the information proffered. The parliamentary intention behind s.12AC(1) was to ensure that the taxpayer knew in writing of the enquiry and had the opportunity to put their case. As long as they knew of HMRC's decision to conduct an enquiry, that was sufficient, and in the instant case, the partnerships and their members knew of the enquiries and the notices, *Flaxmode Ltd v Revenue and Customs Commissioners* [2008] S.T.C. (S.C.D.) 666, [2008] C.L.Y. 3824 applied. In addition, as a matter of formal legal analysis, the affiliates had delegated the administration of the partnerships' tax affairs to the investment company. Given its ensuing correspondence with HMRC, there could be no doubt that the company was aware of the notices of enquiry into the partnership tax returns. Notice to the company was notice to its principals, the partnerships, in particular to those who had made and delivered the returns. They had not received the formal notices of enquiry, but their knowledge of the enquiry was sufficient for the purposes of the legislation, *El-Ajou v Dollar Land Holdings Plc (No.1)* [1994] 2 All E.R. 685, [1994] C.L.Y. 416 followed (paras 69-75).

R. (ON THE APPLICATION OF SWORD SERVICES LTD) v REVENUE AND CUSTOMS COMMISSIONERS *sub nom.* SWORD SERVICES LTD v REVENUE AND CUSTOMS COMMISSIONERS, [2016] EWHC 1473 (Admin), [2016] 4 W.L.R. 113, Cranston J, QBD (Admin).

2120 Tax avoidance–Manufactured overseas dividends–Application of Sch.23A para.4 Income and Corporation Taxes Act 1988 and regs 2B(3) and 2B(4) Income Tax (Manufactured Overseas Dividends) Regulations 1993

[Income and Corporation Taxes Act 1988 (c.1) Sch.23A para.4, s.338(2)(a), s.349(1); Income Tax (Manufactured Overseas Dividends) Regulations 1993 (SI 1993/2004) reg.2B, reg.2B(3), reg.2B(4)]

A taxpayer appealed against an amendment to his self-assessment tax return by HMRC, disallowing a deduction from his total income. The taxpayer's entitlement to make the deduction depended on two payments totalling some £303,000 which he made to a company as manufactured overseas dividends, as defined in the Income and Corporation Taxes Act 1988 Sch.23A para.4. The taxpayer claimed that the payments were annual payments within s.349(1) and as such, were deductible from his total income for that year. HMRC's case, based on the Ramsay principles, was that the payments were not deductible because they had been made as part of a tax avoidance scheme with the result that neither Sch.23A para.4(1) nor the Income Tax (Manufactured Overseas Dividends) Regulations 1993 reg.2B applied. The Regulations disapplied Sch.23A para.4 where the transfer of the overseas security and the payment of the manufactured overseas dividends was made in the context of a loan relationship. HMRC's argument failed before the First-tier Tribunal, but succeeded before the Upper Tribunal. The taxpayer had never sought to present the scheme transactions as anything other than a series of circular payments that had no commercial purpose and were designed to produce deductible payments which qualified as manufactured overseas dividends. The taxpayer challenged the UT's construction of Sch.23A para.4 and reg.2B(3). The issue was whether the provisions should be treated as conferring tax relief even where the securities lending was part of a scheme which had no commercial benefit and was designed purely for the purpose of obtaining that relief.

Held: Appeal dismissed. Regulation 2B(3) and reg.2B(4) were critical provisions where manufactured overseas dividends had been made in the context of a loan agreement. Individuals who were not trading so as to be required to include the dividends in their calculation of profits were allowed to treat the dividends as annual payments under s.349(1) for the purposes of self-assessment, and were not obliged to deduct and account for tax on the payments. That involved a variation of the position under s.349(1), which required the annual payments to which it applied to be paid after deduction of tax. The dividend recipient, if not a trader, was taxed under reg.2B(4) on the gross amount of the payment. An obvious purpose of being able to treat the dividends as deductible annual payments under reg.2B(3) was to prevent the taxpayer from being taxed on the dividends or interest received during the period of the loan. It was an established principle that annual payments were not generally deductible from the payer's income unless they had been paid with a deduction of tax, *Inland Revenue Commissioners v Frere* [1965] A.C. 402, [1964] C.L.Y. 1845 considered. However, the rule had to yield to the particular legislation under which the annual payments arose. In the instant case, the concluding words of reg.2B(3) removed the obligation to deduct tax, but that cannot have been intended to remove the borrower's right to deduct the annual payment from total income. Otherwise the deeming of the dividends as annual payments served no purpose (see paras 11, 13, 15, 22, 24 of judgment). The UT had been wrong to treat reg.2B(3) as subject to the principle in *Frere*. Regulation 2B(3) was intended to give the borrower tax relief on overseas dividends. Whether that tax treatment was intended to apply to taxpayers in the appellant's situation depended on how tax legislation was applied to scheme transactions and with what effect. That was essentially a matter of statutory construction. Various useful cases described how the Ramsay principle or the approach to construction had developed over time, *Collector of Stamp Revenue v Arrowtown Assets Ltd* 6 I.T.L. Rep. 454, *Furniss (Inspector of Taxes) v Dawson* [1984] A.C. 474, [1984] C.L.Y. 270, *Barclays Mercantile Business Finance Ltd v Mawson (Inspector of Taxes)* [2004] UKHL 51, [2005] 1 A.C. 684, [2005] C.L.Y. 3988 considered and *UBS AG v Revenue and Customs Commissioners* [2016] UKSC 13, [2016] 1 W.L.R. 1005, [2016] 2098 applied. Contrary to the appellant's assertions, the payments in the instant case were not analogous with the interpretation of the word "payment" in s.338(2)(a), *MacNiven (Inspector of Taxes) v Westmoreland Investments Ltd* [2001] UKHL 6, [2003] 1 A.C. 311, [2001] C.L.Y. 5199 considered (paras 26, 29-34, 36, 38-40, 42). The appellant was also wrong in his analysis of Sch.23A and the Regulations creating a complete tax code designed to avoid double taxation of manufactured overseas dividends so that neither provision had to be given a purposive or restricted meaning in order to exclude tax avoidance. Regulation 2B was intended to benefit the parties to real-world, commercial transactions involving the lending of marketable securities, not parties engaging in transactions which lacked those characteristics, and whose only purpose was to obtain tax relief (para.44).

CHAPPELL v REVENUE AND CUSTOMS COMMISSIONERS, [2016] EWCA Civ 809, [2016] S.T.C. 1980, Sir Terence Etherton C, CA (Civ Div).

2121 Tax avoidance–Tax avoidance schemes–Assessment

THE TAX AVOIDANCE SCHEMES (PRESCRIBED DESCRIPTIONS OF ARRANGEMENTS) (AMENDMENT) REGULATIONS 2016, SI 2016/99; made under the Finance Act 2004 s.306(1)(a)(b), s.317(2). In force: 23 February 2016.

These Regulations amend the Tax Avoidance Schemes (Prescribed Descriptions of Arrangements) Regulations 2006. They extend the scope of the confidentiality and premium fee hallmarks to include inheritance tax; make changes to aspects of the standardised tax products and losses hallmarks; and introduce a new hallmark relating to financial products.

2122 Tax avoidance–Trustees' powers and duties–Decision by interim managers of charity to discontinue gift aid appeal–Correct approach to applications by Charity Commission under s.78(5)(b) Charities Act 2011 for directions sanctioning decisions made by interim managers

[Charities Act 2011 (c.25) s.76(3)(g), s.78(5), s.78(5)(b); Income Tax Act 2007 (c.3) s.416]

The claimant commission sought a direction under the Charities Act 2011 s.78(5) sanctioning a decision by interim managers of a charity known as "the Cup Trust". The trust was involved in a tax avoidance scheme which enabled UK taxpayers, who were clients of a firm providing tax advice, to claim higher rate tax relief on what were portrayed as charitable donations to the trust. The trust had also made claims totaling £46 million for gift aid on the "donations" from the taxpayers, but the claims had been rejected by HMRC on the basis that they failed to satisfy the requirements of the Income Tax Act 2007 s.416. The first defendant company, which was the sole corporate trustee of the trust, wanted the trust to appeal. However, the interim managers, who had been appointed under s.76(3)(g) of the 2011 Act, decided to discontinue the trust's gift aid appeal and sought the court's sanction of their proposed decision. In making that decision, the interim managers had sought advice from counsel who considered that the prospects of success for the trust's appeal were negligible. The first defendant argued that the appeal should not be discontinued. Its director offered to personally fund the pursuit of the claims on the condition that the first defendant could choose counsel to represent the trust. The commission submitted that the court should give a direction sanctioning the decision to discontinue the gift aid appeal provided it was satisfied that it was a decision that a reasonable body of trustees, properly instructed, could reasonably have arrived at. It argued that it could be so satisfied having regard to the detailed analysis of the options that the interim managers had gone through prior to reaching the decision, the advice given by counsel, and the insufficiency of the funding proposals by the first defendant.

Held: Application granted. Where issues arose in the conduct of the affairs of a charity by interim managers, there should be no need or justification for involving the court. However, there were some situations where the court did need to become involved. Applications to the court made by trustees had been classified in *Public Trustee v Cooper* [2001] W.T.L.R. 901, [2001] C.L.Y. 5527, and the instant application had a good deal in common with the second category discussed in that case, namely the interim managers had decided what they wanted to do, but the sanction of the court was sought because the decision was recognised as being a "momentous" one for the trust. There was a real question over whether the court should "bless" what were essentially business decisions, but there were plainly exceptional circumstances in the instant case that justified the commission having referred the matter to the court. The facts were highly unusual in the context of a charity and the potential amounts at stake were large. Moreover, controversy surrounded the trust and there had been a challenge to the appointment of the interim managers. In light of those factors, the commission was justified in seeking an independent review of the decision that its appointees wished to take, Cooper applied (see paras 57-74 of judgment). (2) In deciding whether the decision to discontinue the appeal was one that a reasonable body of trustees could properly have reached, the first and central issue was the advice given by counsel as to the merits of the appeal. That advice was competent and persuasive. It also correctly stated that in fulfilling the role of charity trustees, the interim managers did not have the freedom to "take a punt" on speculative litigation. Second, protection against an adverse costs order was not absolute. Third, it was entirely reasonable, and in accordance with the reasons for, and terms of, the appointment of the interim managers, that they should take the view that the first defendant or those connected with it should not be involved in directing how the appeal should be pursued. Even having regard to the very large amount of the gift aid claims, the interim managers were not obliged to accept funding and pursue an appeal against HMRC on the terms offered by the first defendant. The decision not to accept such funding and to discontinue the gift aid claims was within the range of decisions to which rational charity trustees could properly come (paras 75-89).

CHARITY COMMISSION FOR ENGLAND AND WALES v MOUNTSTAR (PTC) LTD *sub nom.* CUP TRUST, RE, [2016] EWHC 876 (Ch), [2016] Ch. 612, Snowden J, Ch D.

2123 Tax enquiries–Discovery assessments–Agreement as to no understatement of tax–Closure notice

[Finance Act 1998 (c.36) Sch.18 Pt V para.41; Taxes Management Act 1970 (c.9) s.54(1)]

The appellant company appealed against the First-tier tribunal's decision to refuse to direct the respondent HMRC to issue a closure notice in respect of its enquiry into the company's 2011/2012 tax return. HMRC had opened an enquiry into the company's tax return for the year 2010/2011. It issued a closure notice in respect of that enquiry, concluding that the company had understated its profits. The officer considered, relying on the presumption of continuance, that it was likely that the company had understated its tax liability for 2011/2012 in the same way and issued a discovery assessment under the Finance Act 1998 Sch.18 Pt V para.41. The company asked for a review of both decisions, which were conducted by a different HMRC officer (M). M reduced the tax decision for 2010/2011 and cancelled it in respect of 2011/2012. The company appealed to the tribunal in respect of M's decision regarding 2010/2011 but not against his decision in respect of 2011/2012. That matter was therefore regarded as settled by agreement under the Taxes Management Act 1970 s.54(1). HMRC subsequently opened an enquiry into the company's 2011/2012 tax return. The company applied to the tribunal for a direction that HMRC close the enquiry. The tribunal refused, holding that the particular matter that had been agreed under s.54(1) between the company and HMRC was that a presumption of continuity did not justify the additional assessment; however, that did not mean that HMRC had agreed that the company's profits were correctly reported and so it was reasonable that it should seek to determine whether there had been any understatement of profits. The issue was what had been agreed under s.54(1) of the 1970 Act.

Held: Appeal allowed. The question was not why M had arrived at his conclusion, but rather what that conclusion was, *Scorer (Inspector of Taxes) v Olin Energy Systems Ltd* [1984] 1 W.L.R. 675, [1984] C.L.Y. 450 followed. The starting point was the making of the discovery assessment pursuant to Sch.18 para.41 of the 1998 Act. The company's appeal was against the assessment and not against the reasons behind the assessment. M's conclusion had been that the 2011/2012 tax decision was cancelled. An objective observer would have concluded from that decision, read in the context of the statutory process, that: HMRC's decision that there had been a deliberate understating by the company for the year 2011/2012 should be cancelled; that conclusion should be treated as if the parties had agreed to cancel the tax assessed; that agreement should be treated as if the tribunal had determined that the discovery assessment had been cancelled; the determination was final and conclusive. HMRC was bound by M's cancellation of the discovery assessment not to assert again that the company had understated its business takings in respect of the 2011/2012 year. That was the particular matter at issue that had been agreed between the parties. The tribunal should have directed that HMRC close the enquiry into the company's 2011/2012 tax return because the parties were to be treated as having agreed that there had been no understatement of profits for that year (see paras 42, 44, 47-49, 51 of judgment)

EASINGHALL LTD v REVENUE AND CUSTOMS COMMISSIONERS, [2016] UKUT 105 (TCC), [2016] S.T.C. 1476, Rose J, UT (Tax).

2124 Tax enquiries–Privilege against self-incrimination–Suspected tax fraud on part of company director–Enquiries into corporation and self-assessment tax returns

[Finance Act 2008 (c.9) Sch.36; European Convention on Human Rights 1950 art.6; Tribunal Procedure (First-tier Tribunal) (Tax Chamber) Rules 2009 (SI 2009/273) r.5(3)(k); Tribunals, Courts and Enforcement Act 2007 (c.15); Civil Evidence Act 1968 (c.64) s.14]

In proceedings where HMRC had opened an enquiry and issued notices under the Finance Act 2008 Sch.36 against a taxpayer suspected of fraud, the court had to consider preliminary issues concerning: (i) the First-tier Tribunal's jurisdiction to close the enquiry; (ii) HMRC's use of its civil powers to obtain information for the purposes of a possible criminal prosecution; (iii) the taxpayer's right against self-incrimination. HMRC advised the taxpayer that it was enquiring into his affairs under Code of Practice 9 (COP9), meaning that he was suspected of tax fraud. The COP9 documentation provided the taxpayer with an opportunity to admit that he had been involved in fraud and to agree to make full disclosure, in which event a criminal investigation would be avoided. The taxpayer refused that offer and denied fraud. HMRC opened enquiries into the taxpayer's self-assessment tax returns and the corporation tax returns of companies of which he was a director. Schedule 36 notices to provide documents were issued against the taxpayer and his companies. Penalties were also issued under Sch.36 for failure to comply with the notices. The taxpayer applied to the tribunal for the closure of the COP9 enquiry and appealed against the notices and penalties. The taxpayer argued that (1) by analogy with its power to direct the closure of corporation tax and self-assessment enquiries, the tribunal could also direct the closure of a COP9 enquiry; (2) the sending of the COP9 documentation and his refusal of the full disclosure option meant that he had been "charged" with a criminal offence for the purposes of ECHR art.6.

Held: Preliminary issues determined. (1) The taxpayer's argument that the tribunal's powers could be inferred ran directly counter to the fact that those powers had their source in specific statutory provisions, *Oxfam v Revenue and Customs Commissioners* [2009] EWHC 3078 (Ch), [2010] S.T.C. 686, [2010] C.L.Y. 3488 considered. The tribunal had no general supervisory power over HMRC's power to carry out an enquiry and no jurisdiction to close the COP9 enquiry. The only way to challenge that enquiry was by judicial review at the Administrative Court. The tribunal had no power to move the case to that court because it was clear from the Tribunal Procedure (First-tier Tribunal) (Tax Chamber) Rules 2009 r.5(3)(k) that it could only direct that cases be transferred between tribunals and not to courts. Moreover, that rule was expressly subject to the Tribunals, Courts and Enforcement Act 2007, which included specific provisions relating to transfers between the Upper Tribunal and the High Court but did not permit transfers from the First-tier Tribunal to the Administrative Court (see paras 43, 62, 65, 69, 77-80 of judgment). (2) The term "criminal offence" extended to the imposition of civil penalties for the fraudulent evasion of tax. A person who refused to engage in the full disclosure procedure was meant to understand from the COP9 documentation that there was now a likelihood of prosecution or civil penalties. It followed that the taxpayer had been "charged" with a criminal offence within the meaning of art.6 (paras 113, 116). (3) Requiring a person to provide documents by a Sch.36 notice did not breach the right not to self-incriminate, *Saunders v United Kingdom (19187/91)* [1997] B.C.C. 872, [1997] C.L.Y. 2816 considered. Accordingly, although the taxpayer had been "charged" with a criminal offence so as to engage art.6, he could not rely on that article to refuse to provide the information required by a Sch.36 notice, *Funke v France (A/256-A)* [1993] 1 C.M.L.R. 897, [1994] C.L.Y. 2431 considered, *Jalloh v Germany (54810/00)* (2007) 44 E.H.R.R. 32, [2007] C.L.Y. 2200 applied. The privilege against self-incrimination under the Civil Evidence Act 1968 s.14 did not apply to Sch.36 notices issued by HMRC or to proceedings before the tribunal. Nor did the common law privilege against self-incrimination apply to Sch.36 notices, as it would frustrate the statutory purpose of that provision if a person could refuse to comply with them on the basis that his compliance carried a real and appreciable danger of prosecution, *R. v Boyes* 121 E.R. 730 applied, *Bishopsgate Investment Management Ltd (In Provisional Liquidation) v Maxwell* [1993] Ch. 1, [1992] C.L.Y. 2557 and *R. v Hertfordshire CC Ex p. Green Environmental Industries Ltd* [2000] 2 A.C. 412, [2000] C.L.Y. 2300 followed. Therefore, the tribunal could not strike out the Sch.36 notices issued against either the taxpayer or his companies. The same reasoning applied to the penalties, which also engaged art.6 but could not be appealed on the basis of any right to rely on the taxpayer's privilege against self-incrimination. Similarly, the taxpayer could not rely on that privilege to refuse to respond to the questions asked by HMRC as part of their enquiries, although at the substantive hearing it would be for HMRC to show that there were reasonable grounds to continue those enquiries (paras 130-131, 133, 138, 163, 188-189, 200, 208, 214-215, 220-226, 229, 253, 272, 278, 282).

GOLD NUTS LTD v REVENUE AND CUSTOMS COMMISSIONERS, [2016] UKFTT 82 (TC), [2016] Lloyd's Rep. F.C. 249, Judge Anne Redston, FTT (Tax).

2125 Tax returns–Termination payments–Refusal of foreign service deduction on termination payment received from taxpayer's former employer

[Income Tax (Earnings and Pensions) Act 2003 (c.1) s.404(3)(a), s.414; Finance Act 2007 (c.11) Sch.24]

A taxpayer appealed against an assessment to tax and penalties imposed by the respondent commissioners following the refusal of a foreign service deduction on a termination payment received from his former employer. From 2004, the taxpayer was employed by a United States investment bank (E1). In March 2008, E1 was acquired by another bank. The taxpayer was initially offered employment with the acquiring bank, but in May 2008 he was told he would be joining a different bank (E2) on identical terms to the offer from the acquiring bank. The merger between E1 and the acquiring bank was completed in July 2008 and the taxpayer took up employment with E2 on 1 September. He was transferred with the whole of his previous business unit, including all the employees who had not been made redundant. However, his employment contract did not refer to E1 and was not conditional on the acquisition by E2 of any part of E1's business. The transfer did not take place under the TUPE Regulations. In 2010, the taxpayer left E2 and received a termination payment, which he reported in his tax return for 2011. He claimed foreign service relief against that payment, pursuant to the Income Tax (Earnings and Pensions) Act 2003 s.414, in respect of the period when he was employed by E1. HMRC held that foreign service relief was not available. An assessment was raised for additional tax and penalties were charged for an inaccurate return under the Finance Act 2007 Sch.24 for failure to take reasonable care. The taxpayer argued that E2 was the "successor" to E1 for the purposes of s.404(3)(a) of the 2003 Act and could therefore be classed as his employer.

Held: Appeal allowed in part. (1) In order for the taxpayer to be entitled to foreign service relief, he had to show that his employment with E2 was connected with his employment at E1 for the purposes of s.404 of the 2003 Act, and that part of the termination payment was referable to his service with E1. As there was no statutory definition of "successors", the ordinary meaning of the word had to be applied and construed in the context of the legislation. Part 6 Ch 3 of the 2003 Act was intended to operate either in circumstances where an employee was employed by different members of the same group of companies, where there was an overarching common ownership, or where there was continuity in the existence of a business entity on a change of ownership. The key element was the continuation of the whole business or a discrete part of it, whether or not in combination with another business. It was not sufficient that all the employees were transferred. There was insufficient evidence that the taxpayer's business unit had been transferred from E1 as an identifiable economic entity to E2; thus, E2 could not be regarded as the "successor" to E1 for the purposes of the foreign service provisions (see paras 48, 62, 64, 67, 69 of judgment). (2) The tribunal in *Hanson v Revenue and Customs Commissioners* [2012] UKFTT 314 (TC), [2012] W.T.L.R. 1769, [2013] C.L.Y. 3133 had set out the correct test for establishing whether a taxpayer who used an agent to complete his tax return had taken reasonable care to avoid an inaccuracy. The essential elements were that the taxpayer had consulted an adviser he reasonably believed to be competent, had provided the adviser with the relevant information and documents, had checked the adviser's work to the extent that he was able to do so, and had implemented the advice, *Hanson* applied. The taxpayer could not necessarily be expected to identify an error by the adviser in relation to complex legal points. Where a piece of legislation was open to different interpretations and its application was uncertain, the adviser was entitled to take a view and advise the taxpayer on that basis. Provided that the view taken was a reasonable one, the taxpayer was entitled to rely on that advice. Where there was scope for a different view on certain legislative provisions, the taxpayer was not obliged to consult another adviser or HMRC, as the situation was inherently uncertain and might need to be resolved by the tribunals or courts. In the instant case, the taxpayer had adopted advice which had been properly sought and given and had therefore taken reasonable care to avoid an inaccuracy. The penalty imposed under the 2007 Act was therefore not due (paras 102, 115-116, 119-126).

GEDIR v REVENUE AND CUSTOMS COMMISSIONERS, [2016] UKFTT 188 (TC), [2016] W.T.L.R. 775, Judge Marilyn McKeever, FTT (Tax).

2126 Taxable income–Termination payments–Payment representing settlement of threatened claim for race discrimination

[Income Tax (Earnings and Pensions) Act 2003 (c.1) s.62]

The appellant taxpayer appealed against a decision of HMRC to amend his self-assessment tax return for 2008-9. The amendment concerned a payment of £600,000 which the appellant had received under a compromise agreement entered into with his employer upon the cessation of his employment. The appellant, who was non-European, had worked as a trader for a European bank. His case was that the bank had made the payment in settlement of a threatened claim for race discrimination, which took the form of unfair treatment in his receipt of low or no bonuses over several years and the failure to increase his salary. HMRC asserted that the payment represented "earnings" within the meaning of the Income Tax (Earnings and Pensions) Act 2003 s.62, as it had been designed to make good shortfalls in bonuses and salary.

Held: Appeal allowed in part. (1) It was relevant to look at the provisions which founded the claim for damages. If an employee received a payment in a race discrimination claim, he would receive it not in return for his services but because it had been decided that his employer had acted unlawfully by discriminating against him. Where damages were calculated by reference to underpaid earnings, while the discrimination may have manifested itself through the way in which the employee was remunerated, the damages arose not because he was under-remunerated but because the underpayment was discriminatory. An award in those circumstances could not be described as a reward for services. The award was paid for some reason other than the employment and was not earnings. In a case such as this, proof of discrimination was not required. Instead, the appellant had to produce sufficient evidence from which it could be inferred that the reason why the payment was made was to compensate for an actual or potential action for discrimination. The appellant had done that, even though the bank had not admitted race discrimination. By the time the payment was made, it was clear that the appellant's complaint and the proceedings he was threatening against the bank were for race discrimination. A race discrimination questionnaire had been served on the bank, and its service had been instrumental in the bank's decision to put in place the compromise agreement and to offer to pay the sum of £600,000. That sum did not therefore represent "earnings" under s.62 of the 2003 Act (see paras 79, 81, 94, 120, 123-124, 152, 154 of judgment). (2) The appellant had also appealed against a penalty assessment in the sum of £739.72 in relation to the tax year 2008-9. The penalty concerned redundancy payments of £48,898 and £1,650 which HMRC said had been omitted from the appellant's tax return despite his having received advice that those sums were taxable. HMRC had been justified in imposing that penalty: while the appellant had no intention of falsely representing his income, his error had been "careless" (paras 155, 182, 190).

A v REVENUE AND CUSTOMS COMMISSIONERS, [2015] UKFTT 189 (TC), [2015] I.R.L.R. 962, Judge Swami Raghavan, FTT (Tax).

2127 Tonnage tax–Payments–Training requirements

THE TONNAGE TAX (TRAINING REQUIREMENT) (AMENDMENT) REGULATIONS 2016, SI 2016/819; made under the Finance Act 2000 Sch.22 para.29, Sch.22 para.31, Sch.22 para.36. In force: 1 October 2016.

These Regulations further amend the Tonnage Tax (Training Requirement) Regulations 2000 by increasing the amount of the payments which fall to be made in lieu of training and which are payable to the Maritime Training Trust.

2128 Trust income–Discovery assessments–Taxpayer's claim for double tax relief–Failure to disclose trust's tax return contained information relevant to insufficiency in taxpayer's return

[Taxes Management Act 1970 (c.9) s.29(1), s.29(5), s.29(6)(d)(i), s.34, s.36]

The appellant appealed against a discovery assessment raised against him by HMRC. The appellant was a UK taxpayer. He was the life tenant of a trust he had established in Guernsey during the tax year 2006-07. In his 2006-07 tax return, he declared his income of £755,573 as life tenant and claimed 100% tax relief on it under the UK-Guernsey double tax treaty. The trust later completed a return for the same period disclosing that it had traded in partnership in the UK, which precluded the appellant from double tax relief. In 2009 HMRC began investigating tax avoidance schemes involving the treaty, and in March 2011 it found that the appellant's 2006-07 tax assessment had been insufficient. It raised the discovery assessment under the Taxes Management Act 1970 s.29(1) on the basis that it met the condition in s.29(5) for raising such assessments as its officer could not have been reasonably expected to be aware of the insufficiency. Such expectation was based on the information made available to an officer before the enquiry window into a tax return closed. In the appellant's case, the trust's tax return was filed before the enquiry window into his own return closed. The appellant argued that the discovery assessment was unlawful in that (1) the trust's tax return fell within information made available under s.29(6)(d)(i) as HMRC could reasonably have been expected to infer its existence and relevance to the insufficiency in his return; (2) HMRC should have been aware from his own return that he was not entitled to double tax relief; (3) the assessment was not made promptly after discovery.

Held: Appeal dismissed. (1) Section 29(6)(d)(i) distinguished a document's contents from the document itself. A tax return was not "information": it was its contents that amounted to information. A hypothetical HMRC officer could have inferred from the appellant's return that he had received a substantial income as the life tenant of a trust known to HMRC, that that trust might have made a timely tax return for the same period and that that tax return might contain information that might explain the appellant's claim to relief under the double tax treaty. However, inferences of possible existence and relevance were not sufficient to fix HMRC with knowledge of the information contained in the trust's return: the officer had to have been in the position that they ought reasonably to have inferred that the information did exist and was relevant. There was nothing in the appellant's tax return that indicated that there would be relevant material in the trust's tax return. It would have been mere speculation on the officer's part that the information existed and was relevant. Moreover, if Parliament had intended for the contents of a relevant trust return to be deemed as known to the officer considering the taxpayer's return, it could have said so, *Trustees of the Bessie Taube Discretionary Settlement Trust v Revenue and Customs Commissioners* [2010] UKFTT 473 (TC), [2011] S.F.T.D. 153, [2011] C.L.Y. 3356 applied. Instead, the taxpayer had to draw HMRC's attention to it, and the appellant had not done so (see paras 29-30, 34-35, 48, 51-53 of judgment). (2) The appellant's disclosure was inadequate. When the enquiry window closed, the law was clear that as a life tenant of a trust trading in partnership in the UK, he was not entitled to relief under the double tax treaty. However, his tax return had not mentioned that the trust traded in partnership. The hypothetical HMRC officer might have suspected an insufficiency in his return but would not have been aware of actual insufficiency, *Langham (Inspector of Taxes) v Veltema* [2004] EWCA Civ 193, [2004] S.T.C. 544, [2004] C.L.Y. 3789 and *Sanderson v Revenue and Customs Commissioners* [2016] EWCA Civ 19, [2016] 4 W.L.R. 67, [2016] 2043 applied. The appellant had shown a large income as wiped out by a relief but he had not disclosed the crucial element that the trust traded in partnership, and it was not for HMRC to infer such crucial elements of the appellant's scheme (paras 105-108). (3) In *Revenue and Customs Commissioners v Charlton* [2012] UKFTT 770 (TCC), [2013] S.T.C. 866, [2013] C.L.Y. 3006, it was suggested obiter that a discovery assessment should not be made too long after the discovery, *Charlton* considered. That reasoning was flawed. There was nothing on the face of s.29(1) that imported any prohibition against a time lag between the discovery and the assessment. Parliament quite clearly intended the time limits in s.34 and s.36 to apply to s.29 assessments, *Gakhal v Revenue and Customs Commissioners* [2016] UKFTT 356 (TC) applied. To import a "staleness" time limit into s.29 would in many cases make those limits otiose. It was discovered in March 2011 that the appellant had received income from a trust trading in partnership, and the assessment was raised that same month. However, even if the discovery had been made earlier when investigations began in 2009, it would still have entitled HMRC to raise the assessment later on within the s.34 time limit that applied in the appellant's case (paras 140-147).

MIESEGAES v REVENUE AND CUSTOMS COMMISSIONERS, [2016] UKFTT 375 (TC), [2016] S.F.T.D. 719, Judge Barbara Mosedale, FTT (Tax).

TELECOMMUNICATIONS

2129 Electronic communications networks–Electronic communications code–Conditions and restrictions

THE ELECTRONIC COMMUNICATIONS CODE (CONDITIONS AND RESTRICTIONS) (AMENDMENT) REGULATIONS 2016, SI 2016/1049; made under the Communications Act 2003 s.109(1)(3), s.402(3). In force: 24 November 2016.

This instrument amends the Electronic Communications Code (Conditions and Restrictions) Regulations 2003. The requirements relating to the notice to be given by electronic communications code operators to planning authorities, certain landowners and other interested parties before installing electronic communications apparatus are amended.

2130 EU law–Radio spectrum

THE 1452-1492 MHZ AND 3400-3800 MHZ FREQUENCY BANDS (MANAGEMENT) REGULATIONS 2016, SI 2016/495; made under the European Communities Act 1972 s.2(2). In force: 6 May 2016.

These Regulations: implement Decision 2015/750 and Decision 2008/411; and revoke and replace the 3400-3800 MHz Frequency Band (Management) Regulations 2008, which implemented Decision 2008/411 prior to its amendment.

2131 Radio spectrum–Wireless telegraphy licences–Fees

THE WIRELESS TELEGRAPHY (LICENCE CHARGES FOR THE 900 MHZ FREQUENCY BAND AND THE 1800 MHZ FREQUENCY BAND) (AMENDMENT AND FURTHER PROVISIONS) (AMENDMENT) REGULATIONS 2016, SI 2016/794; made under the Wireless Telegraphy Act 2006 s.12, s.13(2), s.122(7). In force: 12 August 2016.

These Regulations amend the Wireless Telegraphy (Licence Charges for the 900 MHz frequency band and the 1800 MHz frequency band) (Amendment and Further Provisions) Regulations 2015, which revised the level of fees payable to the Office of Communications in respect of the licences of the Public Wireless Networks licence class granted under the Wireless Telegraphy Act 2006 s.8 for the use of the frequencies in the bands 880.0-960.0 MHz and 1710.0-1880.0 MHz.

2132 Wireless communications–Exemptions

THE WIRELESS TELEGRAPHY (EXEMPTION) (AMENDMENT) REGULATIONS 2016, SI 2016/486; made under the Wireless Telegraphy Act 2006 s.8(3) , s.122(7). In force: 28 April 2016.

These Regulations amend the Wireless Telegraphy (Exemption) Regulations, inserting the definition of "body" and introducing additional circumstances in which the exemption in reg.4(1) of the principal Regulations shall apply.

TORTS

2133 Breach of contract–Gambling–Dishonoured cheque signed by gambler in exchange for gambling chips–Lawfulness of casino's provision of credit

[Gambling Act 2005 (c.19) s.33]

The claimant casino sought to recover money in respect of a dishonoured cheque which had been signed by the defendant in exchange for gambling chips. The defendant counterclaimed alleging that the casino had breached its duty of care to not harm or exploit him. The defendant was a regular gambler at London casinos and in 2009 had signed a voluntary self-exclusion agreement (VSE) in respect of the claimant casino. He contended that he had done so in an attempt to control his serious gambling addiction. The claimant argued that he had signed the VSE as a reaction to a dealer behaving disrespectfully toward him. The defendant sought to be readmitted on a number of occasions stating that he did not have a gambling problem and that he had simply been upset with the dealer. The casino took advice from the Gambling Commission and readmitted the defendant in 2010. After a further dispute with a dealer, the casino withdrew the defendant's membership in 2011, but he returned the next year following discussions during which he confirmed that his previous self-exclusion had not been as a result of problem gambling. The defendant had also self-excluded himself from, and sought readmission to, other London casinos following disagreements with dealers, and took legal action to recover losses from another establishment citing problem gambling. On an evening in 2014 the defendant had requested £2 million in chips from the claimant, signed a cheque and gambled them all away on the claimant's roulette tables. He was refused a further £5 million and demanded to sign another VSE. The issues were whether (i) provision of chips had been illegal; (ii) readmission following the 2009 VSE was a breach of contract; (iii) the casino had acted negligently and in breach of its statutory duty. The defendant submitted that the chips had been provided in breach of the Social Responsibility Code of the Gambling Commission's Licence Conditions and Codes of Practice 2012 s.2.5, and therefore in breach of the casino's gaming licence, rendering the provision of gambling facilities illegal under the Gambling Act 2005 s.33.

Held: Judgment for claimant. (1) The defendant's illegality argument turned on the proper construction of the Gambling Commission's codes of practice. They did not address periods of self-exclusion and were silent on revocation. There was no need to fill that lacuna with an implication that a VSE was irrevocable. Revocation was a bilateral process; there had to be a request and a reasoned decision about whether to accede to it. Provided that any agreed revocation was on reasonable grounds, reflecting the non-absolute nature of the licensee's requirements to "have and put into effect procedures for self-exclusions" and "take all reasonable steps" to refuse service or prevent a self-excluded person from participating, there was no reason why a self-exclusion could not be lifted by an agreed revocation. That did not undermine the efficacy of the VSE system. It respected individual autonomy and was consistent with the limited wording of the Social Responsibility Code that required the taking of reasonable steps. Whether in a particular case it was reasonable for a casino to agree to lift a revocation depended on the facts and circumstances of that case. The claimant had acted reasonably in revoking the VSE as: the defendant's conduct did not suggest a gambling problem; there were grounds to believe that the VSE had been made for another reason; the defendant repeatedly sought its revocation; the defendant confirmed orally and in writing that he had no gambling disorder; the claimant had sought advice from the Gambling Commission. There had been no breach of the licence's conditions or the codes of practice (see paras 124-128, 132-133 of judgment). (2) The claimant had not acted unlawfully in readmitting the defendant to the casino in 2010 and the VSE had not given rise to a contract. Such an alleged agreement was without consideration as nothing had moved from the defendant to the claimant, *Calvert v William Hill Credit Ltd* [2008] EWHC 454 (Ch), [2008] L.L.R. 583 considered. Even if it had been a contract, it had been lawfully rescinded when the parties to it agreed that it should be revoked (paras 136-137). (3) The court doubted that a private law cause of action for breach of statutory duty arose, *X (Minors) v Bedfordshire CC* [1995] 2 A.C. 633, [1995] C.L.Y. 3452 followed. The statute provided remedies for its breach and afforded appropriate means of securing the protection which was intended to be conferred. It established a regulatory body to enforce compliance and criminal offences. That was not conclusive, but it was strongly indicative. However, it was unnecessary to reach a view on the issue given the conclusion that the claimant had not acted unlawfully in breach of its licence conditions in readmitting the defendant in 2010. No broad common law duty of care was owed by the claimant to the defendant, *Calvert* considered. A narrower duty of care might arise where a customer's behaviour was extreme and a gambling establishment had expressly undertaken to prevent further gambling, but the defendant's evidence that he had a gambling disorder was rejected. The VSE had not given rise to a voluntary assumption of responsibility by the claimant to prevent the defendant from gambling after its lawfully agreed revocation (paras 139-144).

RITZ HOTEL CASINO LTD v AL GEABURY, [2015] EWHC 2294 (QB), [2015] L.L.R. 860, Simler J, QBD.

2134 Breach of contract–Unlawful means conspiracy–Sub-contractor fabricating documents to refute unjustified allegations against it–Absence of fraud

The claimant contractor brought various claims against the defendants. The claimant had been awarded a contract for the cleaning and maintenance of reservoirs. As it had insufficient directly employed labour to carry out the works, it entered into a sub-contract with the first defendant company (C). The claimant appointed the third defendant (BC), one of its employees, as the contract manager. BC was the brother of the second defendant (AC), who ran C. BC's responsibilities included authorising the payment of labour invoices. Those invoices also had to be authorised by another employee of the claimant. BC and that employee (K) were in a relationship, a fact of which the claimant claimed to have been unaware. The claimant's case was that AC, BC and K had acted in concert in a conspiracy and fraud which involved BC and K ensuring that C was paid for work invoiced without timesheets, which were required under the sub-contract; through those invoices, the claimant had been deliberately and fraudulently overcharged in respect of standard work done and overtime; further, BC and AC had fabricated timesheets and a letter from BC to C authorising overtime. The claim was formulated as follows: C, AC and BC were liable for unlawful means conspiracy; BC and AC were liable in deceit and for procuring or inducing a breach of the contract between the claimant and C; further, C was in breach of contract in failing to provide timesheets with the invoices, a condition precedent to payment.

Held: Judgment for claimant in part. The evidence indicated that C's timesheets and BC's letter authorising overtime by C's staff had been fabricated after the dispute between the parties arose. However, deliberate fraud, conspiracy and deceit had not been established. The most likely explanation for the backdated documents was that there had been a misguided and wrongful attempt to meet allegations of fraud which AC and BC considered to be wholly unjustified. They were acting in response to what had been shown to be an unfounded allegation. They knew that they had no documents and therefore attempted to reconstruct them to bolster what they believed to be the proper position. It was likely that most, if not all, of the work for which invoices were submitted was carried out. However, there had been a breach of contract by BC in not requiring timesheets to be provided, a breach of contract by C in not providing them and a procuring or inducing of a breach of contract in that respect by both BC and AC (see paras 43, 53, 66, 68-69, 71 of judgment).

J BROWNE CONSTRUCTION CO LTD v CHAPMAN CONSTRUCTION SERVICES LTD, [2016] EWHC 152 (QB), 165 Con. L.R. 175, Judge Taylor, QBD.

2135 Breach of fiduciary duty–Confidential information–Software company developing technology for storage of confidential personal data–Former directors and employees using and selling similar product–Interim injunctions

The claimant software development company applied for an interim injunction preventing the defendant former directors and employees from using its confidential information and intellectual property and from carrying on a trade similar to its own. The claimant had developed technology for the storage of important or confidential personal data. Its claim was that the defendants, who had all worked on the development of the storage system, had left to set up a new company developing and selling a similar product, and to poach its customers. It claimed damages under various heads, including breach of fiduciary duty and breach of contractual covenants. It sent letters before action in January 2015, which was when it became clear that it had lost staff and established contracts. It did not apply to court however, for two months, and then only on the basis of anticipated proceedings and without having issued a claim form. The defendants denied that they were using the claimant's confidential information or intellectual property. They asserted that the covenants relied on were too broad to be enforceable, that most computer programming companies would, on some level, compete with the claimant, and that the balance of convenience weighed against injunctive relief.

Held: Application granted in part. (1) It seemed clear that the basic business idea developed by the claimant was the same as that developed by the new company, even if there were differences in their respective technologies. Competition, in itself, was not precluded; whether the conduct of departing directors and employees was permissible or not was fact-sensitive, *Hunter Kane Ltd v Watkins* [2003] EWHC 186 (Ch) and *Foster Bryant Surveying Ltd v Bryant* [2007] EWCA Civ 200, [2007] Bus. L.R. 1565, [2007] C.L.Y. 562 applied. The claimant's non-competition and non-solicit covenants were broad; they reinforced obligations which might otherwise be implied, but they did not define what information was properly to be characterised as confidential (see paras 12, 53-55, 57, 59-60 of judgment). The court had to seek to protect rights and expectations which were arguably enforceable, the breach of which could not be properly compensated by damages. In doing so, the *American Cyanamid* test of whether there was a serious question to be tried was only to be departed from in extreme circumstances, *Cayne v Global Natural Resources Plc* [1984] 1 All E.R. 225, [1984] C.L.Y. 2656 considered. Despite the claimant having included a term in its customer contracts that intellectual property rights vested in the customer, the evidence disclosed an at least arguable case raising a serious issue to be tried that the work done in relation to its storage system, and the system itself, was the claimant's intellectual property, which was confidential. Therefore any use of it by the defendants would be a serious breach of the claimant's legal rights and a serious breach of an ex-director's fiduciary duty. The claimant had a good arguable case against all the defendants that their implied duties of good faith and fidelity as employees included a duty not to make preparations during their employment to compete with the claimant after their employment ended, and not to solicit other employees to leave, *QBE Management Services (UK) Ltd v Dymoke* [2012] EWHC 80 (QB), [2012] I.R.L.R. 458, [2012] C.L.Y. 1141 applied (paras 66-72, 78-79, 98-100, 103, 108, 110-112). (2) Factors against granting an injunction were that the claimant might not benefit from it, as it had lost its entire workforce and was in a perilous financial position, and the new company appeared interested in only one of the claimant's customers so leakage of information elsewhere was unlikely. An injunction could therefore backfire on the claimant because if the new company was allowed to continue trading, it was more likely to be able to pay damages than if it was forced out of business. Those factors were outweighed by seven factors in favour of granting injunctive relief. It was not, however, appropriate to prevent the new company from developing its storage system and fulfilling its contract with the claimant's former customer so long as it did so without the use of any property or confidential information belonging to the claimant. It was appropriate to grant injunctive relief with that proviso, and to order an expedited trial of the proceedings (paras 118-120, 125). (3) In light of the court's assessment of the balance of convenience, it was not strictly necessary to consider what should be taken as the status quo for the purpose of the *American Cyanamid* test. Normally the relevant status quo was that immediately prior to when the breaches started. However, the claimant had delayed seeking relief. Delay was not, of itself, a bar, but the longer the "last change" had gone unchallenged, the more likely that it would be established as the new status quo. The claimant had taken a risk in waiting two months after issuing its first challenge to the defendants, and that was another reason for the provisos in the injunctive relief granted (paras 152-157).

ALLFILED UK LTD v ELTIS, [2015] EWHC 1300 (Ch), [2016] F.S.R. 11, Hildyard J, Ch D.

2136 Economic loss–Loss of earnings–Claim by employee for pure economic loss–No actionable injury–Requirement of physical injury in claim for substantive damages including financial losses suffered as a result of such injury

Five chemical process operators appealed against a decision (*Greenway v Johnson Matthey Plc* [2014] EWHC 3957 (QB), [2015] P.I.Q.R. P10, [2015] C.L.Y. 1779) that their claims against the respondent employer arising out of their exposure to platinum salts in the workplace were claims for pure economic loss not personal injury. Chlorinated or halogenated platinum salts were produced during the refining process undertaken at the employer's chemical factory. Owing to the risk of sensitisation through exposure to the salts, the employer required employees to undergo regular skin prick testing. The appellants were found to have become sensitised and were removed from work involving contact with platinum. They claimed substantial damages for loss of earnings. Platinum sensitisation was symptomless and did not adversely affect day-to-day life. However, it created a susceptibility to developing a platinum allergy if exposure continued. The employer accepted that it had failed in its statutory duties regarding workplace cleaning. The appellants claimed in tort and contract. The judge held that they had not suffered any physical injury as necessary to give them a cause of action in tort. He found that the losses they claimed to have suffered were outside the scope of the relevant contractual duty owed to them and that they could only recover nominal damages for breach of contract.

Held: Appeal dismissed. *The claim in tort* - the judge had been right to find that the appellants had not suffered an actionable injury, *Cartledge v E Jopling & Sons Ltd* [1962] 1 Q.B. 189, [1961] C.L.Y. 5055 explained, *Cartledge v E Jopling & Sons Ltd* [1963] A.C. 758, [1963] C.L.Y. 2023 and *Grieves v FT Everard & Sons Ltd* [2007] UKHL 39, [2008] 1 A.C. 281, [2007] C.L.Y. 2919 applied. *Cartledge* involved employees contracting pneumoconiosis, which was asymptomatic under ordinary circumstances, but was capable of being diagnosed by an X-ray, which revealed scarring to the lung tissue. That scarring was part of a disease which could have a significant impact on the individual's ordinary life. *Grieves* concerned workers contracting asbestos-induced pleural plaques, which were not harmful and did not constitute a physical change which would increase susceptibility to other diseases or reduce life expectancy. The judge below had been right to find that the reasoning in *Grieves* applied to the appellants. They believed that they had suffered actionable physical injury because of a physiological change in their bodies revealed by the skin prick test, but platinum sensitisation was not harmful in itself in any relevant sense. Unlike the situation in *Cartledge*, it was not a "hidden impairment" potentially giving rise to detrimental physical effects in the course of ordinary life. The appellants suggested that the judge in the lower hearing of *Cartledge* had treated the reduction in future earning capacity as a salient feature of the injury. He had not; he had merely reiterated the conventional and accepted position that damages for personal injury could include loss of earnings resulting from the injury. The appellants' removal from their jobs was financially detrimental, but the presence of such economic loss did not convert a physiological change falling short of an actionable injury into one which was sufficient to found an action in tort (see paras 11, 16-18, 21-33, 53-55 of judgment). *The claim in contract* - the judge had been right to find that the appellants could not claim their financial losses as damages for breach of their contracts of employment, *South Australia Asset Management Corp v York Montague Ltd* [1997] A.C. 191, [1996] C.L.Y. 4519 applied. The employer had breached its duty to take all necessary and reasonable steps to ensure its employees' safety at work, but that duty, whether in contract or tort, was focused on protecting employees from physical injury, not from economic harm. A standard term or duty of care requiring an employer to protect an employee from economic loss could not be implied into contracts of employment. Furthermore, the instant employer had entered into a collective agreement providing for an ex gratia compensation payment where employees had to leave as a result of platinum allergy. It could not reasonably or fairly be said that the employer should be taken to have assumed any wider responsibility for its employees' financial welfare, *Reid v Rush & Tompkins Group* [1990] 1 W.L.R. 212, [1990] C.L.Y. 1903 and *Crossley v Faithful & Gould Holdings Ltd* [2004] EWCA Civ 293, [2004] 4 All E.R. 447, [2004] C.L.Y. 1203 applied. The employer also bore no liability for the appellants not being able to work in other environments involving exposure to platinum salts (paras 34-42, 44, 53-55). *Damages for pure economic loss* - the court should be slow to extend the categories of case in which a duty to protect against pure economic loss would be found to arise. Where the nexus between parties was founded in contract, that contract was the primary source and reference point for their respective rights and obligations. Although a duty of care in tort might run parallel, it was difficult to see how it could impose more extensive obligations, *Crossley* and *Scally v Southern Health and Social Services Board* [1992] 1 A.C. 294, [1992] C.L.Y. 1917 applied, *Spring v Guardian Assurance Plc* [1995] 2 A.C. 296, [1994] C.L.Y. 1918 considered (paras 47-51).

GREENWAY v JOHNSON MATTHEY PLC, [2016] EWCA Civ 408, [2016] 1 W.L.R. 4487, Lord Dyson MR, CA (Civ Div).

2137 Foreseeability–Causation–Damage due to water abstraction

[Water Resources Act 1991 (c.57) s.48A]

The claimants, who owned an area of land in rural Norfolk, sought damages and injunctive relief against the defendants, who owned an adjoining area of land. The defendants had excavated four lakes on their land. The claimants' case was that that had caused a significant decrease in the water levels in the lakes on their own land, affecting the viability of the commercial fishery which they operated. The claimants made a claim under the Water Resources Act 1991 s.48A for loss and damage suffered by them as a result of the defendants' abstraction of water resulting from the construction of the lakes. They also claimed that the excavation of the lakes created a nuisance and/or that the defendants had acted negligently in excavating the lakes, as a result of which they had suffered loss and damage. In relation to the claim under s.48A, two issues arose, namely (1) whether foreseeability of the loss or damage in question was required and (2) the correct test for causation.

Held: Judgment for defendants. (1) The proper interpretation of s.48A was that foreseeability of the loss or damage in question was not required. The words in s.48A(1) were clear. There was no limitation or qualification in relation to the loss or damage or its type. There was no reason to override the clear words of the section and read into it a necessity for foreseeability of loss or damage on the part of the abstractor. The abstraction of water might well cause loss or damage and so s.48A put the risk on the abstractor: if his abstraction caused any loss or damage, he had to take the consequences and would be strictly liable for all loss and damage caused whether he could have foreseen it or not (see para.23 of judgment). (2) The approach (argued for by the claimants) in disease and clinical negligence cases of only having to establish a material contribution to the injury could not properly be extended to a case such as this, where the factual situation was very different. The defendants had been correct in submitting that the normal "but for" causation test should be applied. The essence of the claimants' case was that a reduction of the water levels in the lakes on their own land had caused their alleged loss and damage. Thus they had to prove on the balance of probabilities that, but for the defendants' excavation of the lakes on the defendants' land, their loss and damage would not have occurred (para.33). (3) Having regard to the evidence, primarily that of the experts, the claimants had failed to prove on the balance of probabilities that, but for the excavation of the lakes, the water levels in their own lakes would not have reduced to an extent where loss and damage occurred. The expert evidence supported the view that various factors, primarily climatic variation, had caused the lowering of water levels in the claimants' lakes. The claim under s.48A therefore failed (paras 131-132). (4) The claims in negligence and nuisance failed for the same reason. They failed for an additional reason: it had been held in *Langbrook Properties v Surrey CC* [1970] 1 W.L.R. 161, [1970] C.L.Y. 2444 and *Stephens v Anglian Water Authority* [1987] 1 W.L.R. 1381, [1988] C.L.Y. 2446 that a landowner had a right to abstract subterranean water flowing in undefined channels beneath his land regardless of the consequences to his neighbours, *Langbrook* and *Stephens* followed (para.132).

CHETWYND v TUNMORE, [2016] EWHC 156 (QB), [2016] 3 W.L.R. 1159, Judge Reddihough, QBD.

2138 Fraudulent misrepresentation–Personal injury–Setting aside settlement of claim–Insurers influenced by misrepresentations

The appellant insurer appealed against a decision upholding a settlement which had been reached in a personal injury claim brought by the respondent. The respondent had injured his back as a result of an accident at work. He claimed that he suffered from continuing serious back pain which restricted his mobility and that his ability to work was seriously impaired. The insurer conducted the defence on the employer's behalf. Relying on video evidence which showed the respondent undertaking heavy work at home, it argued that he had exaggerated the consequences of his injury. The parties reached an agreement under which the insurer agreed to pay £134,973 in full and final settlement of the claim. About two years later, the respondent's neighbours approached the employer to say that from their observation of his conduct and activities they believed that he had entirely recovered from his injury at least a year before the settlement was reached. The insurer claimed damages for deceit, asserting that the statements which the respondent had made about the extent of his injury in his particulars of claim and witness statements constituted fraudulent misrepresentations. The judge at first instance set the settlement agreement aside. The respondent was awarded damages of £14,720 and he was ordered to repay the settlement sum, less that amount. The Court of Appeal reversed that decision. It held that for a fraudulent misrepresentation to be the basis of a claim to rescind a contract, the claimant had to have been induced into making the contract by a perception that it was true; for that reason, where a defendant entered into an agreement to settle a claim, having positively asserted that statements in the claimant's particulars of claim and witness statements were dishonestly advanced (being the insurer's stance in the instant case on the basis of the video evidence), it implicitly agreed not thereafter to seek to have the settlement set aside on the basis that statements made in support of the claim were false. The main issue was whether, in order to show the requisite influence by or reliance on the misrepresentation in a claim to set aside a compromise on the basis of fraudulent misrepresentation, the defrauded representee had to prove that it settled because it believed that the misrepresentation was true.

Held: Appeal allowed. The answer to that question was no. It was not necessary, as a matter of law, to prove that the representee believed that the representation was true. There was no clear authority to the contrary. However, that was not to say that the representee's state of mind might not be relevant to the issue of inducement. Indeed, it could be very relevant. If the representee did not believe that the representation was true, he might have serious difficulty in establishing that he had been induced to enter into the contract or that he had suffered loss as a result. However, inducement was a question of fact. The judge at first instance had been entitled to adopt the proposition in *Clerk and Lindsell on Torts* that "the claimant must have been influenced by the misrepresentation". The judge found that the representations made by the respondent did influence the insurer in its decision on how much to pay him in settlement. He found that although the insurer might not have believed the representations to be true, it did believe that they would be put before the court as true and that there was a real risk that the court would accept them in whole or part and consequently make a larger award than it (the insurer) would otherwise have considered appropriate. The judge had been correct to make those findings. The fact that the representee (here, the insurer) did not wholly credit the fraudster (the respondent) and carried out its own investigations did not preclude it from having been induced by the representations in question. Qualified belief or disbelief did not rule out inducement, particularly where those investigations were never going to find out the evidence that subsequently came to light. That depended only on the respondent's neighbours coming forward. Only then did the insurer find out the true position. As the respondent knew, the insurer was settling on a false basis. The court had also been asked to rule on a second issue, namely whether suspicion by the defendant of exaggeration for financial gain by the claimant would preclude unravelling a settlement when fraud was subsequently established. The answer followed from the conclusions above: it was difficult to envisage any circumstances in which mere suspicion that a claim was fraudulent would preclude unravelling a settlement when fraud was subsequently established (see paras 15, 18, 25, 30, 40, 48 of judgment).

HAYWARD v ZURICH INSURANCE CO PLC, [2016] UKSC 48, [2016] 3 W.L.R. 637, Lord Neuberger PSC, SC.

2139 Harassment–Neighbour disputes–Diminution in value of property–Damages for distress and loss of amenity–Double recovery

The appellants appealed against a decision (*Raymond v Young*) awarding damages in favour of the respondents for diminution in the value of their property. The appellants owned a cottage, and the respondents owned an adjacent farmhouse. The farmhouse had originally been owned by the father of the first appellant (Y), but it had been sold on the father's retirement. It was eventually purchased by the respondents as a holiday home. The recorder found that the appellants had been responsible for continuous acts of harassment, trespass and nuisance against the respondents over a period of many years. Those acts included obstructing the respondents' driveway, vandalising their property, burning noxious materials causing smoke, dumping rubbish and physical intimidation. He found that the acts were motivated by Y's resentment at acquisition of the farm as a weekend home. The recorder granted a permanent injunction to prevent further nuisance. He made a composite award of £20,000 for distress and loss of amenity. He found that the appellants' actions had caused a diminution in the value of the farm of 20 per cent, amounting to £155,000 and he made a further award in that sum. The appellants submitted that the recorder was wrong to have made an award for diminution in value, because the injunction was sufficient to prevent any future acts of nuisance.

Held: Appeal allowed in part. (1) The assessment of loss might be complicated by the fact that the nuisance was transitory or time-limited, *Dennis v Ministry of Defence* [2003] EWHC 793 (QB), [2003] Env. L.R. 34, [2003] C.L.Y. 3038 considered. It was contemplated in *Hunter v Canary Wharf Ltd* [1997] A.C. 655, [1997] C.L.Y. 3865 that in such cases the measure of damages should reflect the diminution in the value of the right to live in the property during the relevant period, *Hunter* followed. However, the recorder had found that the appellants' conduct could not be described as transitory, by which he meant that it was likely to continue to be a facet of Y's character and behaviour, so far as not restrained by the injunction. Therefore, the grant of a permanent injunction was not likely to be treated by a potential purchaser as a guarantee that they would not be subjected to the same treatment. The benefit of the injunction was personal to the respondents and, on a sale, the protection it afforded would end. Any repetition of the same sort of conduct towards the incoming purchaser would necessitate fresh proceedings for an injunction. The recorder was therefore entitled to make an award of £155,000 for diminution in value calculated on the basis that the threat of a nuisance to future purchaser would continue (paras 29, 34, 38 of judgment). (2) The recorder was wrong to have awarded damages of £20,000 for loss of amenity along with the full measure of capital loss of £155,000. That amounted to double recovery, as the sums were alternative methods of calculating the diminution in value of the respondents' property. If damages were awarded for loss of capital value, then damages for loss of amenity were excluded. Further, even if the £20,000 was treated as damages for distress rather than loss of value, there was still double counting, because damages for distress were not recoverable separately in nuisance from an award for loss of value. Damages for diminution in value were intended to compensate the landowners for the distress and loss of amenity which they experienced as a result of the nuisance, but only in terms of the consequent loss in the use value of the property. It was not appropriate to make separate awards of damages for distress in cases of nuisance, *Hunter* followed. The distress suffered by the respondents was reflected in the damages awarded for loss of value. The damages were therefore reduced by £20,000 to eliminate double recovery (paras 27-28, 38-40).

RAYMOND v YOUNG, [2015] EWCA Civ 456, [2015] H.L.R. 41, Patten LJ, CA (Civ Div).

2140 Malicious prosecution–Civil proceedings–Applicability to malicious and groundless prosecution of civil claim causing damage

The appellant (W) appealed against a decision to strike out his claim for malicious prosecution against the respondent (G). W was a former director of a company which was assumed, for the purposes of the hearing, to be controlled by G. W alleged that G had caused the company to pursue a claim against him for breach of contractual and fiduciary duties and that G had known that the claim was brought without reasonable cause. The company withdrew its claim shortly before trial. W claimed damages for loss of reputation, health and earnings, and for his legal expenses over the amount awarded to him in costs. The judge in the malicious prosecution claim held that she was bound to follow the House of Lords' decision in *Gregory v Portsmouth City Council* [2000] 1 A.C. 419, [2000] C.L.Y. 5117 and therefore to conclude that English law recognised no cause of action of malicious prosecution in respect of civil proceedings. She reached that decision having determined that she should not follow the later Privy Council decision of *Crawford Adjusters (Cayman) Ltd v Sagicor General Insurance (Cayman) Ltd* [2013] UKPC 17, [2014] A.C. 366 where such a cause of action had been found. The precedent value of Privy Council decisions would be addressed in a separate Supreme Court judgment.

Held: Appeal allowed. (Lords Mance, Neuberger, Sumption and Reed dissenting) The case law on malicious prosecution showed how the courts had fashioned the tort to do justice in various situations in which a person had suffered injury in consequence of the malicious use of legal process without reasonable basis, *Savile v Roberts* 91 E.R. 1147, *Quartz Hill Consolidated Gold Mining Co v Eyre* (1883) 11 Q.B.D. 674 and *Berry v British Transport Commission* [1962] 1 Q.B. 306, [1961] C.L.Y. 5397 considered. The instant court had to decide whether the tort should apply to the malicious and groundless prosecution of a civil claim causing damage. That required consideration of the justice and practical consequences whichever way the question was decided (see para.42 of judgment). It seemed unjust for a person to suffer injury as a result of malicious prosecution and yet not be entitled to compensation. The question was whether there were countervailing factors such that the tort's applicability to civil proceedings should be limited to an assortment of instances where it had previously been applied. *Obsolescence:* The suggestion that malicious prosecution of criminal proceedings was obsolescent as a tort, and should not be considered in civil proceedings, was rejected: such prosecutions were far from a thing of the past.

Deterrence: There was no way of testing whether those with valid claims might be deterred from pursuing them for fear of a subsequent malicious prosecution claim, and it was intrinsically unlikely. *Finality:* The public interest in avoiding satellite litigation was insufficient reason for disallowing malicious prosecution claims regarding criminal proceedings. *Duplication of remedies: Gregory* had suggested that manifest injustice arising from groundless civil proceedings was or could be covered by other torts; *Crawford* and the instant case showed that that was not so, *Gregory* and *Crawford* considered. *Inconsistency with witness immunity from civil liability:* If that were a valid objection it would apply to all forms of malicious prosecution. *Inconsistency with absence of duty of care towards an opposing party:* There was a great difference between imposing a duty of care and imposing a liability for maliciously instituting proceedings. *Tort should be confined to persons exercising state power:* Malicious prosecution was not a public law tort as that argument suggested. *Reciprocity:* There was no need for a reciprocal right to sue for malicious defence of a civil claim; there was a distinction between the initiation of the legal process and later steps which might involve bad faith (paras 43-51). The suggested countervailing factors did not outweigh the argument that simple justice dictated that the claim should be sustainable (para.57). The claim to recover excess costs was not an abuse of process. It was understandable that the costs on the company's claim should have been assessed on the standard basis, but the notion that the costs order had necessarily made good the injury caused by the claim was almost certainly a fiction. Although W's claim would take up further court time, that was not a good reason for him to accept a loss (para.58). (Per Lord Mance) The pre-*Crawford* authorities fell into only a limited number of categories: prosecution of criminal proceedings, institution of coercive measures instituted ex parte, and petitions for insolvency. It had never been accepted that there was a general right to claim damages for the malicious prosecution of a civil action. That position should be maintained as a matter of policy, having regard to the illogic of creating the tort, the potential consequences, what role malice should have, and the damage recoverable (paras 128-146).

WILLERS v JOYCE, [2016] UKSC 43, [2016] 3 W.L.R. 477, Lord Neuberger PSC, SC.

2141 Misuse of private information–Newspapers–Phone hacking–Damages payable for infringements of privacy rights

[Human Rights Act 1998 (c.42); European Convention on Human Rights 1950 art.8; Legal Aid, Sentencing and Punishment of Offenders Act 2012 (c.10) s.44(5)]

The court was required to assess the damages payable to claimants for infringements of privacy rights arising primarily from phone hacking by the defendant newspaper proprietor, and to give guidance on damages payable in other phone hacking cases. The claimants were persons in the public eye, such as actors and sportsmen or people associated with them. The defendant had conceded liability for infringements of privacy rights by obtaining confidential or private information from phone hacking and private investigators which, apart from one claimant, had led to the publication of articles in its newspapers; the articles were themselves an invasion of privacy rights and would not have been published but for the earlier invasions which provided material for them. The claims were also based on the substantial hacking which did not result in articles. The claimants gave evidence as to their horror, distaste and distress at discovering that the defendant's journalists had been frequently listening to aspects of their personal, medical and professional lives by hacking into their voicemails, and they described the effect on their lives caused by the distrust that the defendant's newspapers' activities had engendered in them and those around them.

Held: Damages assessed. (1) The privacy right to which the UK was obliged to give effect under the Human Rights Act 1998 was reflected in, though not itself created by, ECHR art.8. A regime in which damages were confined to damages for distress would, to a degree, render privacy rights illusory and fail to provide an effective remedy. To award damages to reflect infringements of privacy rights in themselves would not amount to the wrongful reintroduction of vindicatory damages; such damages would be truly compensatory, *R. (on the application of Lumba) v Secretary of State for the Home Department* [2011] UKSC 12, [2012] 1 A.C. 245, [2011] C.L.Y. 1727 considered, *Halford v United Kingdom (20605/92)* [1997] I.R.L.R. 471, [1997] C.L.Y. 2795 applied.

Compensation could therefore be given not only for distress and injury to feelings, but also for infringements of privacy rights in themselves, so far as the defendant's acts had impacted on the values protected by those rights (see paras 110, 113, 132-133, 144 of judgment). (2) The court had to compensate a claimant properly and fairly for the wrong sustained. In some cases a global award would be appropriate; in others a more divided-up approach would meet that aim. In the instant case, it was not appropriate to grant a global sum to compensate those claimants about whom articles had been published as the wrongs they had sustained had too great a degree of separation. As a starting point, each article should be treated separately in terms of an award of damages. The activities of private investigators merited separate awards, and it would also be right to reflect general levels of distress, including distrust of and damage to relationships arising out of the whole pattern of conduct, in a separate award (paras 154-159). (3) The 10 per cent uplift to non-pecuniary damages required by *Simmons v Castle* [2012] EWCA Civ 1288, [2013] 1 W.L.R. 1239, [2013] C.L.Y. 782 was a substitute for the loss of the opportunity to claim CFA success fees, which had been removed by the Legal Aid, Sentencing and Punishment of Offenders Act 2012 s.44(5), *Simmons* considered. The claimants had the benefit of CFAs but the litigation was of a class in which success fees were still potentially recoverable notwithstanding the Act's reforms. In assessing damages, no provision should be made for the *Simmons* 10 per cent uplift (paras 163-166). (4) Damages in privacy cases should compensate not merely for distress but also, if appropriate, for the loss of privacy or autonomy arising out of the infringement by hacking or other mechanism. That might include a sum to compensate for meaningful damage to dignity or standing, so far as that was not already within the distress element. In the instant case, the loss of privacy or autonomy element would be significant. Existing case law showed an increasing tendency to appreciate and give effect to the seriousness of invasions of privacy, but no previous cases involved the award of sums approaching those claimed by the claimants. The scale of the invasions of privacy in the instant case was very much greater than in any of the reported cases: the invasions had been carried out on a daily basis and had resulted in a number of articles over a period, but some had not resulted in any form of publication and none of the reported cases involved that. Those were very important distinguishing factors which made the direct application of any of the figures in previous cases inappropriate (paras 167-169, 184). (5) A parallel could not be drawn with the bands of damages for harassment claims set out in *Vento v Chief Constable of West Yorkshire* [2002] EWCA Civ 1871, [2003] I.C.R. 318, [2003] C.L.Y. 1306. The nature of the wrong in harassment cases, compared with the wrongs in the instant case, made direct application of the *Vento* bands inappropriate, *Vento* considered (paras 190-193). (6) The defendant's practice of phone hacking had been widespread, institutionalised, long-standing and covert, and the defendant had initially adopted a posture of denial. That conduct was capable of being an aggravating factor (paras 208-215). (7) Apologies tendered by the defendant were not relevant to the totality of hurt suffered by the claimants. The apologies were a sensible tactical move for the purposes of the litigation rather than being born purely of a genuinely litigation-independent contrition and desire to make amends. They had done nothing to mollify the claimants or reduce their level of hurt (para.216). (8) In assessing the individual claims, the following principles were applicable: (a) the disclosure of certain types of private information was more significant than others; (b) information about mental and physical health and significant private financial matters attracted a higher degree of privacy, and therefore compensation; (c) information about social meetings attracted a lower degree of privacy and compensation; (d) information about matters internal to a relationship would be treated as private, and disclosures which disrupted a relationship or were likely to adversely affect a couple's attempts to repair it were likely to be treated as a serious infringement deserving substantial compensation; (e) the appropriate compensation would depend on the nature of the information, its significance as private information, and the effect on the victim of its disclosure; (f) the effect of repeated intrusions by publication could be cumulative; (g) in relation to distress, the "egg-shell skull" principle applied, so that a thinner-skinned individual might be caused more upset, and therefore receive more compensation, than a thicker-skinned individual who was the subject of the same intrusion; (h) for each year of serious levels of phone hacking the starting point was an award of £10,000 (paras 229-230). (9) Alan Yentob, the claimant about whom no articles had been published, was entitled to a global award of £85,000. The remaining awards were aggregate sums. Lauren Alcorn, who had been in a relationship with a footballer, was awarded £72,500; Robert Ashworth, a television producer who had been married to an actress, received £201,250; Lucy Taggart, an actress known as Lucy Benjamin, was awarded £157,250; the actress Shobna Gulati was awarded £117,500; the entertainer and actor Shane Roche, known as Shane Richie, was entitled to £155,000; Paul Gascoigne, a well-known football personality, was awarded £188,250; Sadie Frost, an actress and businesswoman, received £260,250. Those awards were greater than any other publicly available award because the invasions of privacy involved were so serious and prolonged. None of the articles in respect of which compensation was awarded would have been published had it not been for the underlying prolonged phone hacking, which was known to be wrongful. People whose private voicemail messages were hacked so often and for so long, and had very significant parts of their private lives exposed and then reported on, were entitled to significant compensation (paras 252, 292, 364, 435, 480, 537, 599, 701-702). (10) The claimants experienced significant disquiet from not knowing what private information had been listened to or discovered by unlawful means. In principle, if justice and the facts required it, the court had jurisdiction to order some sort of inquiry as to what information the defendant had acquired about the claimants. Further awards might be made if there was to be no investigative relief, but the parties should not assume that they would be great, if they were awarded at all (paras 704, 707, 711).

GULATI v MGN LTD; TAGGART v MGN LTD; YENTOB v MGN LTD; ALCORN v MGN LTD; ROCHE v MGN LTD; GASCOIGNE v MGN LTD; ASHWORTH v MGN LTD; FROST v MGN LTD *sub nom.* REPRESENTATIVE CLAIMANTS v MGN LTD, [2015] EWHC 1482 (Ch), [2016] F.S.R. 12, Mann J, Ch D.

2142 Misuse of private information–Privacy–Paparazzi photographs of well-known musician and children on family day out–Photographs published in newspaper–Reasonable expectation of privacy

[European Convention on Human Rights 1950 art.10, art.8]

A newspaper publisher appealed against a decision (*Weller v Associated Newspapers Ltd* [2014] EWHC 1163 (QB), [2014] E.M.L.R. 24, [2014] C.L.Y. 842) that it had misused private information by publishing paparazzi photographs of the respondents, the three children of a well-known British musician. It also appealed against the grant of an injunction restraining it from further publication of the photographs (*Weller v Associated Newspapers Ltd* [2014] EWHC 2127 (QB)). The photographs showed the musician on a day out in Los Angeles with his 16-year-old daughter and twin 10-month-old sons. The pictures showed the family out in public, shopping and visiting a cafe. The children's faces were clearly shown and captions identified them by surname. The photographs had been taken without consent. Indeed, the musician had asked the photographer to stop and had been told that the children's faces would be pixelated. The musician, who regarded himself as a private person when not performing, had mentioned his family in interviews but had not given in-depth interviews about his private life. His daughter had done some modelling, including a photo-shoot for a magazine, but the judge found that she was genuinely embarrassed by the paparazzi photographs. He held that they had been published in circumstances where the children had a reasonable expectation of privacy; that although publication would have been lawful in California, that did not prevent a reasonable expectation of privacy in relation to their publication in England; and that the children's rights under ECHR art.8 outweighed the publisher's right to freedom of expression under art.10. The issue was whether he had erred in reaching those conclusions.

Held: Appeals dismissed. (1) The starting point for determining whether there had been a misuse of private information was the two-stage test in *Campbell v Mirror Group Newspapers Ltd* [2004] UKHL 22, [2004] 2 A.C. 457, [2004] C.L.Y. 2673. First, the court had to ask whether the person had a reasonable expectation of privacy. If it concluded that he did, it had to balance his art.8 right against the publisher's art.10 right to freedom of expression. Those were questions of fact, *Campbell* followed. The appellate court would not interfere with the first-stage decision unless satisfied that the lower court's findings were unsupported by the evidence or its decision was one that it could not reasonably have made. The second-stage balancing exercise was analogous to the exercise of a discretion and the appellate court would not interfere unless the court below had erred in principle or reached a conclusion which was plainly wrong or outside the ambit of reasonable conclusions (see paras 15, 56-57 of judgment). The judge had been right to conclude that the children had a reasonable expectation privacy in respect of the photographs. There were some matters about which a person could have a have a reasonable expectation of privacy notwithstanding that they occurred in public. The photographs depicted a family activity belonging to that part of life which was protected by the broader right of personal autonomy recognised by Strasbourg jurisprudence. The children's father had not consented to the taking or publishing of the photographs, which, critically, identified the children by name. Two of the children were less than a year old. They had not laid themselves open to the possibility of being photographed in the context of an activity that was likely to be reported, and nor had their parents courted publicity for them. The fact that a child had a celebrity parent did not necessarily mean that they should have less of a reasonable expectation of privacy. Indeed, it might make them particularly vulnerable. In considering the impact of publication, the judge had properly considered the best interests of the children, who were to be protected from the risk of embarrassment, bullying, and more serious threats to their safety, *Murray v Express Newspapers Plc* [2008] EWCA Civ 446, [2009] Ch. 481, [2008] C.L.Y. 1984 and *JR38's Application for Judicial Review, Re* [2015] UKSC 42, [2016] A.C. 1131, [2015] C.L.Y. 1301 followed (paras 20, 29-38, 59-66). (2) The weight to be given to the lawfulness of the taking and publication of the photographs under Californian law was a matter for the judge, and he had been entitled to give it little weight. He had heard little argument about the impact of the children's connection with California and, on any view, the fact that publication would have been lawful in California was not determinative (paras 67-71). (3) In balancing the children's art.8 rights against the publisher's art.10 rights, the court had considered the five criteria in *Von Hannover v Germany (40660/08 and 60641/08)* [2012] E.M.L.R. 16 and had been entitled to find that the balance came down in favour of the children's art.8 rights. The publication of the photographs did not contribute to a current debate of general interest; the children had little or no public profile and were only of interest to the publisher because of their father; the photographs related exclusively to their private lives and had the sole purpose of satisfying public curiosity; the mere fact that their father had mentioned them in interviews could not justify publication; images of the younger children's faces had not previously been published; and the father had genuine security concerns, *Von Hannover* applied (paras 72-80). (4) The judge had granted the injunction because, although there was no evidence that the publisher would publish the photographs again, there were "grounds for concern" that there might be future publication. While there was force in the publisher's argument that the identified grounds for concern were insufficient to justify the grant of an injunction, the decision was an exercise of discretion and it could not be said that the judge had reached a decision that was not reasonably open to him (paras 84-88).

WELLER v ASSOCIATED NEWSPAPERS LTD, [2015] EWCA Civ 1176, [2016] 1 W.L.R. 1541, Lord Dyson MR, CA (Civ Div).

2143 Misuse of private information–Public figures–Reassignment of Navy commanding officer following proven allegations of bullying–Details leaked to press by fellow employee–Whether commanding officer having reasonable expectation of privacy

[European Convention on Human Rights 1950 art.8]

The claimant naval officer brought a claim for misuse of private information and/or breach of confidence against the defendant. In 2004 the claimant had been the Commanding Officer of a ship. Complaints of bullying had been made against him which were upheld following an investigation and he was reassigned. Documents in relation to the investigation were marked "Restricted - Staff". Articles were published in the media at the time about the allegations. In 2013 the third party newspaper group publisher disclosed that a source within the MoD had been paid for the stories. She pleaded guilty to conspiracy to commit misconduct in public office. The claimant alleged that he had a reasonable expectation of privacy or confidentiality in respect of the allegations and their outcome and that the publication of the information was an actionable interference with that reasonable expectation and/or his rights under the

ECHR art.8 for which the MoD was vicariously liable. The MoD denied liability and argued that the claim concerned the claimant's performance of a very public role representing the UK and any change in who performed the role would be publicly known or shared by those on board.

Held: Judgment for defendant. (1) The claimant did not have a reasonable expectation of privacy in the information on which he relied. The case concerned the claimant's role in a very public position; there could have been no reasonable expectation of privacy in his removal from his command as it was a public fact; it was a highly unusual case and the reasons for his removal were likely to have become publicly known; it was relevant, but not conclusive, that the internal investigation had been private; the claimant had accepted that he had bullied officers; it would have been acceptable for the officers to have told their parents of the situation; the security markings on the documents did not estop the MoD from arguing that the claimant did not have a reasonable expectation of privacy, *Campbell v Mirror Group Newspapers Ltd* [2004] UKHL 22, [2004] 2 A.C. 457, [2004] C.L.Y. 2673 followed, *Yeo v Times Newspapers Ltd* [2015] EWHC 3375 (QB), [2017] E.M.L.R. 1 considered (see paras 35, 44-49, 64 of judgment). (2) The claimant could not maintain a distinct claim for breach of confidence because he could not show that the source at the MoD owed him any duty to keep any material confidential. She owed a duty to the Crown and to the MoD but not to the claimant, *Fraser v Evans* [1969] 1 Q.B. 349, [1968] C.L.Y. 3133 followed (paras 68-70). (3) The claim under art.8 did not assist the claimant given the finding in relation to the claim for misuse of private information (para.73).

AXON v MINISTRY OF DEFENCE, [2016] EWHC 787 (QB), [2016] E.M.L.R. 20, Nicol J, QBD.

2144 Occupiers' liability–Breach of duty of care–Sheer drop at site not obvious danger–Failure to provide warning signs for protection of visitors

[Occupiers' Liability Act 1957 (c.31) s.2]

English Heritage appealed against a decision that an injury suffered by the respondent (T) when visiting one of its sites was caused by a breach of its common duty of care under the Occupiers' Liability Act 1957 s.2. T, aged 60, had been visiting a castle when he fell and suffered a serious head injury. A designated walk on the site ran around the tower fortifications. There was an elevated cannon firing platform. Directly below the platform, at the base of a steep slope, was a grass pathway. There was also an informal path down the slope from the platform to the pathway. On the other side of the pathway, beyond a bastion wall, was a dry moat. T had set off down the informal path, lost his footing and fallen across the grass pathway and over the wall into the moat. A central issue was whether anyone contemplating going down the steep slope to the pathway could have seen that there was a sheer drop into the moat, such that there was an obvious danger. T claimed that the accident was caused by English Heritage's negligence and/or its breach of s.2. The recorder visited the site before finding that English Heritage had breached s.2 in failing to warn visitors, by means of a sign, of the danger which gave rise to the accident. He also found that T was 50% to blame. English Heritage challenged the recorder's findings regarding the breach of s.2, causation and the apportionment of blame. It submitted that, if the decision was upheld, it and similar public organisations would be under pressure to adopt an unduly defensive approach to the guardianship of historic sites, leading to an unwelcome proliferation of unsightly warning signs that was contrary to the public interest.

Held: Appeal dismissed. (1) English Heritage's arguments advanced for reversing the decision regarding the breach of s.2 were rejected. The sheer drop was not an obvious danger and English Heritage should have taken reasonable steps to protect visitors against it (see paras 16-21 of judgment). (2) The recorder was entitled to find that, on the balance of probabilities, causation was established. The risk that T took was that he would lose his balance and fall over on a steep grassy slope. That would have been most unlikely to cause him to suffer a serious head injury. The risk of falling 12 feet down a sheer drop was of a different magnitude, involving a real and obvious risk of serious injury. A sign warning of the sheer drop would have been likely to influence the behaviour of most sensible individuals (paras 22-24). (3) When determining the issue of contributory negligence, the recorder had to balance the degree of fault and causation of injury. A 50/50 apportionment was reasonable, *Clare v Perry (t/a Widemouth Manor*

Hotel) [2005] EWCA Civ 39, (2005) 149 S.J.L.B. 114 and *Jackson v Murray* [2015] UKSC 5, [2015] 2 All E.R. 805, [2015] C.L.Y. 1797 considered. It was relevant that English Heritage's fault was of longstanding, whereas T's was momentary (paras 26-27). (4) The decision was a straightforward application of the principle that adult visitors did not require warnings of obvious risks except where they did not have a genuine and informed choice, *Tomlinson v Congleton BC* [2003] UKHL 47, [2004] 1 A.C. 46, [2003] C.L.Y. 4360 followed. There was no basis for interfering with the recorder's finding that the sheer drop from the pathway into the moat was not an obvious danger. The question of whether a danger was obvious might not always be easy to resolve, and might present an occupier of land with a difficulty. However, there were many areas of life in which difficult borderline judgments had to be made. That was well understood by the courts and was taken into account in deciding whether negligence or a breach of s.2 had been established. In that context, it was highly relevant that the common duty of care was to take such care "as in all the circumstances [was] reasonable" to see that the visitor was "reasonably" safe in using the premises for the purpose for which he was invited or permitted by the occupier to be there. The court was, therefore, required to consider all the circumstances. Those would include how obvious the danger was and, in an appropriate case, aesthetic matters. If an occupier was in doubt as to whether a danger was obvious, it might be advised to take reasonable measures to reduce or eliminate the danger. The steps needed to be no more than reasonable steps, which was why the decision in the instant case should not be interpreted as requiring occupiers like English Heritage to place unsightly warning signs in prominent positions all over sensitive historic sites. The recorder found the existence of a breach of the common duty of care on a very specific basis, namely the failure to provide a sign warning of a sheer drop which was not obvious (paras 28-31).

ENGLISH HERITAGE v TAYLOR, [2016] EWCA Civ 448, [2016] P.I.Q.R. P14, Lord Dyson MR, CA (Civ Div).

2145 Unlawful means conspiracy–Contempt of court–Whether contempt of court constituted "unlawful means" for purposes of tort of conspiracy to injure by unlawful means–Jurisdiction

[Lugano Convention on Jurisdiction and the Enforcement of Judgments in Civil and Commercial Matters 2007 art.5(3), art.6(1)]

The second defendant (D2) applied to set aside a claim form issued by the claimant bank. The bank's claim arose in the context of long-running litigation between it and its former chairman (D1). Much of that litigation had concerned the bank's attempts to enforce a worldwide freezing order against D1. The bank established that D1 had breached the order, but when it sought his committal for contempt, he fled to France. The bank obtained judgments in default against him and began proceedings against D2, his son-in-law, on the basis of the tort of conspiracy to injure by unlawful means. It claimed that D1 and D2 had conspired to prevent it from making any substantial recovery, alleging that they had breached the freezing order by creating and using false and misleading documents. It thus relied on contempt of court as the unlawful means for the purposes of the tort. Because D2 was domiciled in Switzerland, the Lugano Convention 2007 dictated that he be sued there unless the bank could establish that the instant court had jurisdiction pursuant to art.6(1) or art.5(3). The issues were whether (1) contempt of court could constitute unlawful means; (2) the court had jurisdiction to hear the bank's claim.

Held: Application refused. (1) The bank relied on *Surzur Overseas Ltd v Koros* [1999] 2 Lloyd's Rep. 611, [1999] C.L.Y. 528. However, that case simply suggested, but did not decide, that breaches of a freezing order could amount to unlawful means, *Surzur* considered (see paras 8-10 of judgment). It was necessary to consider whether there was a positive common law rule preventing the court from awarding damages to one party following another's breach of a court order. The law of contempt was concerned with maintaining the authority of the court in the public interest. Since it was not focussed on compensating litigants who had suffered loss, principle suggested that it did not confer a power to award damages. While some authorities suggested that there was jurisdiction to award damages for contempt, none expressly decided the point and none grappled with the principle that the contempt jurisdiction was concerned with the public interest rather than private redress. Even *Chapman v Honig* [1963] 2 Q.B. 502,

[1963] C.L.Y. 2729, which was often referred to as having decided the issue, simply identified the opposing arguments without resolving them, *Chapman* considered. The observations of the House of Lords in *Customs and Excise Commissioners v Barclays Bank Plc* [2006] UKHL 28, [2007] 1 A.C. 181, [2006] C.L.Y. 2880 were a very clear indication that damages could not be awarded for contempt, and the instant court had to apply them. The argument from principle was compelling: the court had no power to order damages for contempt, *Hudson, Re* [1966] Ch. 209, [1966] C.L.Y. 9978 considered and *Barclays Bank* applied (paras 16-21, 72-77). However, that simply meant that damages could not be awarded where contempt was the only basis for the claim. Where the claim was based on a conspiracy to injure by unlawful means, namely a contempt, the contempt was not the only basis of the claim. *Barclays Bank* did not preclude the court from regarding a contempt as unlawful means: while a third party with knowledge of a freezing order was not liable in negligence for damages caused by his failure to obey its terms, that did not mean that a third party who conspired to breach the terms of a freezing order was not liable in the tort of conspiracy to injure by unlawful means. Moreover, the reasoning in *Customs and Excise Commissioners v Total Network SL* [2008] UKHL 19, [2008] 1 A.C. 1174, [2008] C.L.Y. 3907 provided strong support for the conclusion that a contempt could amount to unlawful means, *Total Network* applied. Although the court in *Digicel (St Lucia) Ltd v Cable & Wireless Plc* [2010] EWHC 774 (Ch) had refused to extend unlawful means to non-criminal breaches of Regulations, contempts of court were sufficiently reprehensible to justify treating them as unlawful means, *Digicel* considered. The bank had a good arguable case that D2 had committed the tort of conspiracy to injure by unlawful means (paras 22-26). (2)(a) The bank's art.6(1) argument on jurisdiction was that when the proceedings were issued against D2, D1 was domiciled in England, which meant that D2 could be sued in England. However, at that time, D1 had abandoned England as his country of residence and hence domicile. Although he had been domiciled in England until his flight to France, he was in custody in France fighting extradition to Russia when the proceedings against D2 were issued. It was unlikely that he would return to England were he not extradited to Russia: he had fled England once, had no connections there, and was liable to arrest and detention there (paras 28-30, 33-36). (2)(b) The court did, however, have jurisdiction under art.5(3), England being the place "where the harmful event occurred". That phrase encompassed the place where the damage occurred and the place of the event giving rise to the damage, *Handelswekerij GJ Bier BV and Stichtung Reinwater (The Reinwater Foundation) v Mines de Potasse d'Alsace SA (4320/74)* [1979] E.C.C. 206 applied. The damage did not occur in England, because the assets were held abroad and bank's loss was the receivers' inability to realise those assets, *AMT Futures Ltd v Marzillier, Dr Meier & Dr Guntner Rechtsanwaltsgesellschaft mbH* [2015] EWCA Civ 143, [2015] Q.B. 699, [2015] C.L.Y. 438 applied (paras 38-44). However, the bank had much the better argument that England was the place of the event giving rise to the damage in respect of part of the claim. That event was the implementation, rather than the hatching,of the conspiracy, *Domicrest Ltd v Swiss Bank Corp* [1999] Q.B. 548, [1998] C.L.Y. 770 considered. Up until February 2012, the conspiracy had been implemented by instructions given by D1 in London (paras 45-54).

JSC BTA BANK v ABLYAZOV, [2016] EWHC 230 (Comm), [2016] 3 W.L.R. 659, Teare J, QBD (Comm).

2146 Vicarious liability–Employers' liability–Unprovoked assault on customer by sales assistant–Whether employer vicariously liable

A supermarket customer appealed against a decision (*Mohamud v Wm Morrison Supermarkets Plc* [2014] EWCA Civ 116, [2014] 2 All E.R. 990, [2014] C.L.Y. 3000) that the respondent supermarket was not vicariously liable for an assault perpetrated by one of its employees. The customer had attended a petrol station kiosk run by the supermarket and had approached one of the staff members (K) with an enquiry. K, whose job was to serve customers and see that the petrol pumps and kiosk were kept in good running order, responded with foul-mouthed abuse and ordered the customer to leave. He then followed him onto the forecourt where he told him to keep away and subjected him to a violent and unprovoked assault. The customer brought proceedings against the supermarket, claiming that it was vicariously liable for the assault. The trial judge held that it was not liable because there was no sufficiently close connection between the assault and what K was employed to do. The Court of Appeal upheld his decision, finding that while K's employment involved interaction with customers, that was insufficient to fix the supermarket with vicarious liability for his violence: his duties did not involve him being placed in situations where there was a clear possibility of confrontation. The customer submitted that there should be a new test of vicarious liability in which the courts applied a "representative capacity" rather than a "close connection" test. He argued that the question should be whether a reasonable observer would consider the employee to be acting in the capacity of a representative of the employer at the time of committing the tort.

Held: Appeal allowed. (1) After reviewing the development of the doctrine of vicarious liability, the court indicated that the "close connection" test adumbrated in *Lister v Hesley Hall Ltd* [2001] UKHL 22, [2002] 1 A.C. 215, [2001] C.L.Y. 5359 and *Dubai Aluminium Co Ltd v Salaam* [2002] UKHL 48, [2003] 2 A.C. 366, [2003] C.L.Y. 3046 had been followed in a line of cases, including several at the highest level. There was a risk in attempting to lay down criteria for determining what precisely amounted to a sufficiently close connection to make it just for an employer to be held vicariously liable. A simplification of the essence was more desirable, and in its simplest terms, two matters had to be considered: (a) what functions had been entrusted by the employer to the employee (which had to be addressed broadly); and (b) whether there was sufficient connection between the employee's wrongful conduct and the position in which he was employed to make it right for the employer to be fixed with vicarious liability. The cases in which the necessary connection had been found to exist were those in which the employee had used or misused his position in a way which injured the third party, *Lloyd v Grace Smith & Co* [1912] A.C. 716, *Pettersson v Royal Oak Hotel* [1948] N.Z.L.R. 136, [1947-51] C.L.Y. 3607 and *Warren v Henlys Ltd* [1948] 2 All E.R. 935, [1947-51] C.L.Y. 3604 considered. There was nothing wrong with the close connection test as such and the law would not be improved by a change of vocabulary, *Lister* and *Dubai Aluminium* followed (see paras 42- 46 of judgment). The test should only be abrogated or refined if a demonstrably better test could be devised. However, the proposed "representative capacity" test was hopelessly vague. Moreover, while the instant court had suggested in *Various Claimants v Institute of the Brothers of the Christian Schools* [2012] UKSC 56, [2013] 2 A.C. 1, [2013] C.L.Y. 2099 that the law of vicarious liability was on the move, such change was a response to changes in the legal relationships between enterprises and members of their workforces, *Christian Brothers* referred to. There had been no changes in societal conditions requiring a change in the law governing the circumstances in which an employer should be held vicariously liable for the torts of an employee (paras 53-55). (2) It was K's job to attend to customers and respond to their inquiries. His conduct in answering the claimant's request in a foul-mouthed way and ordering him to leave was inexcusable but was within the field of activities assigned to him. What happened thereafter was an unbroken sequence of events. It was not right to regard K as having metaphorically taken off his uniform when he followed the customer onto the forecourt. Moreover, once on the forecourt, K had repeated his order to leave. That was not something personal between him and the customer; he was ordering him to keep away from his employer's premises, and he reinforced that order by violence. In doing so he was purporting to act in the furtherance of his employer's business. While it was a gross abuse of his position, it was in connection with the business in which he was employed. Since the supermarket had entrusted him with the position of serving customers it was just that it should be held responsible for his abuse of that position. Finally, it was irrelevant that it looked as if K was motivated by personal racism rather than a desire to benefit his employer's business (paras 47-49, 57). (3) Although the claims and issues in the instant case were separate from those in *Cox v Ministry of Justice* [2016] UKSC 10, [2016] A.C. 660, [2016] 1553, that and the instant judgment were intended to be complementary in their legal analysis. The instant court agreed with the reasoning and conclusion of Lord Reed in that case (para.1).

MOHAMUD v WM MORRISON SUPERMARKETS PLC, [2016] UKSC 11, [2016] A.C. 677, Lord Neuberger PSC, SC.

TRANSPORT

2147 Carriage by sea–Personal injury–Whether Athens Convention 1974 extended to claims against carrier for contribution to liability of others–Nature of time-bar in art.16 Athens Convention 1974

[Athens Convention relating to the Carriage of Passengers and their Luggage by Sea 1974; Civil Liability (Contribution) Act 1978 (c.47) s.1(3)]

The appellant employer appealed against a decision that its claim for contribution against the respondent to a personal injury claim brought by one of its employees was barred under the Athens Convention 1974. The employee had been injured during a work team-building outing on a rigid inflatable boat owned and operated by the respondent. The employee sued the employer for damages for personal injury and the employer issued a Part 20 claim against the respondent seeking a contribution to any liability. The respondent filed a defence that the contribution claim was barred because it had not been issued within the two-year time limit in art.16 of the Convention. A district judge granted the respondent summary judgment on the ground that the employee's right to pursue the employer had been extinguished by the time limit expiring, and that therefore under the Civil Liability (Contribution) Act 1978 s.1(3) there was nothing on which the contribution claim could rely. On appeal, the judge did not distinguish between the personal injury claim and the contribution claim and held that the contribution claim had been extinguished. The issues were (i) whether the Convention was directly applicable to the contribution claim; (ii) the nature of the time bar under art.16.

Held: Appeal allowed. (1) The Convention dealt with claims by passengers against carriers and with nothing else. It did not purport to be a complete code governing all liability of sea carriers in respect of carriage of passengers and their luggage, *Abnett v British Airways Plc* [1997] A.C. 430, [1997] C.L.Y. 220 applied. Rights of recourse between carriers and other parties were not mentioned in the Convention. An action in which a claim for contribution from the carrier was sought in respect of the employer's liability for personal injury to its employee was not "an action for damages for... personal injury to a passenger... brought against a carrier". The claim to contribution was autonomous and derived from the English domestic statutory entitlement to contribution. It was unsurprising that the claim in itself was unaffected by the provisions of the Convention. On the other hand, the carrier's liability to contribute was critically dependent on its own liability to the passenger, which in turn was governed by the provisions of the Convention, including those as to limitation (see paras 15-16, 21 of judgment). (2) The language of art.16 did not extinguish the right on which the claim was based: it was remedy-barring as opposed to right-extinguishing. However, it was appropriate to approach the effect of art.16 having regard to the fact that it was the language of an international convention rather than a domestic statute. There was no corpus of international understanding pursuant to which the language of art.16 should be regarded as extinguishing the right of action. The ultimate question was what the words meant, which was prompted by an exclusively domestic enquiry of whether the statutory right to contribution was excluded by reason of s.1(3) of the 1978 Act. Whilst the words used in art.16 had an international or Convention provenance, they did not have an autonomous and internationally understood meaning that was different in effect from that which they naturally bore in the English language and as understood in English law (paras 22, 28, 44-45).

SOUTH WEST SHA v BAY ISLAND VOYAGES *sub nom.* FEEST v SOUTH WEST SHA, [2015] EWCA Civ 708, [2016] Q.B. 503, Laws LJ, CA (Civ Div).

2148 Compulsory purchase–Diversion of highways–Trafford Park extension

THE TRANSPORT FOR GREATER MANCHESTER (LIGHT RAPID TRANSIT SYSTEM) (TRAFFORD PARK EXTENSION) ORDER 2016, SI 2016/1035; made under the Transport and Works Act 1992 s.1, s.5, Sch.1 para.1, Sch.1 para.5, Sch.1 para.7,

Sch.1 para.11, Sch.1 para.13, Sch.1 para.15, Sch.1 para.17. In force: 24 November 2016.

This Order authorises Transport for Greater Manchester to construct and operate a transit system in the borough of Trafford, being an extension to the existing Manchester Metrolink system by way of a new route joining existing tramway routes from the existing Pomona Metrolink stop through Trafford Park and terminating at the Trafford Centre retail and leisure complex. For that purpose, the Order also authorises the compulsory purchase and temporary use of land, the diversion of existing rights of way, street works and ancillary works.

2149 Inland waterways–Tolls–Tolls payable pursuant to Norfolk and Suffolk Broads Act 1988 in respect of vessels moored, used or navigated on adjacent waters as well as in navigation area–Whether toll payable in respect of houseboat moored in private marina

[Norfolk and Suffolk Broads Act 1988 (c.4); Harbours Act 1964 (c.40) s.26, s.27]

The appellant authority appealed by way of case stated against a Crown Court decision setting aside the respondent's conviction for failing to pay a toll demanded by the authority. The authority was established by the Norfolk and Suffolk Broads Act 1988 and under byelaw 19 of the Vessel Registration Byelaws 1997 the appropriate toll had to be paid in order to moor, use or navigate a vessel on waters within the navigation area. The Broads Authority Act 2009 amended s.13 of 1988 Act to provide that the authority could determine and recover tolls in respect of vessels moored, used or navigated on adjacent waters as well as in the navigation area. Section 25(1) of the 1988 Act was amended to provide that "toll" meant a charge levied by the authority under the Harbours Act 1964 s.26 including any levied in respect of a vessel moored, used or navigated on any adjacent waters. The respondent kept an unpowered houseboat on adjacent waters, namely a private marina. The authority required him to pay a toll of £552 to moor his vessel there. He was convicted in the magistrates' court of infringing the byelaws by failing to pay the toll. The Crown Court set aside his conviction accepting an argument, based on *Forth Conservancy Board v Inland Revenue Commissioners* [1931] A.C. 540, that the demand for a toll was invalid because the respondent personally derived no benefit from the authority's activities.

Held: Appeal allowed. The Crown Court had erred in concluding that it was unlawful to impose a toll on the respondent because he did not, and could not, use his vessel in the navigation area, *Forth Conservancy Board* considered. There was nothing in that case that could affect the express wording of the 1988 Act as amended by the 2009 Act. It was unfortunate that the legislative amendments were opaque and that the byelaws had not been updated. However, it was clear that the 1988 Act as amended expressly authorised the authority to impose tolls in respect of vessels moored in adjacent waters. The respondent's interpretation of the provisions was untenable since it would require the authority to show that a person had personally benefited before it could lawfully impose a toll. The respondent also argued that the byelaw was uncertain because it referred merely to the appropriate toll. However, on the authorities, establishing the necessary uncertainty was a very high hurdle to surmount. It had to be shown that the provision had no ascertainable meaning and was incapable of application, *Kruse v Johnson* [1898] 2 Q.B. 91, *Fawcett Properties Ltd v Buckingham CC* [1961] A.C. 636, [1960] C.L.Y. 3110 and *Percy v Hall* [1997] Q.B. 924, [1996] C.L.Y. 5688 followed. The tolls were set annually and posted on the authority's website. The byelaw was not invalid by reason of uncertainty. The case was remitted to the Crown Court for reconsideration. That would include the issue whether, as seemed likely, s.27 of the 1964 Act applied, which required harbour charges, apart from certain excepted charges, to be reasonable.

BROADS AUTHORITY v FRY, [2015] EWHC 4139 (Admin), [2016] 2 Lloyd's Rep. 61, Beatson LJ, DC.

2150 Public transport–Acquisition of land

THE MIDLAND METRO (BIRMINGHAM CITY CENTRE EXTENSION, ETC.) (LAND ACQUISITION AND VARIATION) ORDER 2016, SI 2016/545; made under the Transport and Works Act 1992 s.1, s.5, Sch.1 para.1, Sch.1 para.2, Sch.1 para.3,

Sch.1 para.4, Sch.1 para.5, Sch.1 para.7, Sch.1 para.8, Sch.1 para.9, Sch.1 para.10, Sch.1 para.11, Sch.1 para.12, Sch.1 para.13, Sch.1 para.15, Sch.1 para.16, Sch.1 para.17. In force: 14 June 2016.

This Order confers further powers of compulsory acquisition on the West Midlands Passenger Transport Executive (the Executive) for the purpose of the works authorised by the Midland Metro (Birmingham City Centre Extension, etc.) Order 2005 (the 2005 Order). Powers for compulsory acquisition under the 2005 Order expired on 22 July 2010.

TRUSTS

2151 Breach of fiduciary duty–Law firms–Investment monies paid by investors into client account of firm of solicitors–Immediate loans to single purpose company operating property investment scheme–Whether monies held on trust for investors

The appellant firm of solicitors (B) appealed against a decision (*Challinor v Juliet Bellis & Co* [2013] EWHC 347 (Ch)) that it had breached its fiduciary duty as a trustee. The respondent investors (C) had invested in a property investment scheme operated by a single purpose company (X). The offering documents consisted largely of two emails from X. C paid monies into B's client account. B used most of the money to reduce X's short-term bank borrowing. The scheme was unsuccessful and X was placed in administration. C sought recovery of their money from B. They claimed breach of an escrow agreement and, alternatively, that B had received the monies on trust for C and had advanced them in breach of that trust. C also claimed in restitution. The judge rejected the claim in respect of the escrow agreement, but held that there had been an implied resulting trust analogous to a *Quistclose* trust, and a resulting trust arising from the fact that B had received the monies without authority from X. The judge indicated that he would also probably have upheld C's restitutionary claim. The issues were whether (i) C had advanced the money on trust pending the satisfaction of ill-defined conditions, or had made immediate loans to X by paying the money to B as X's agents; (ii) B had X's authority to receive and disburse C's money and, if not, whether the money was therefore held by B on a resulting trust for C; (iii) C had a restitutionary claim against B in respect of unjust enrichment.

Held: Appeal allowed. (1) The issue regarding C's objective intention had to be addressed by reference to the offering documents. As those documents constituted the whole of the invitation material to which C had responded, they lay at the heart of the analysis of what, if any, restrictions C had sought to place on the use that could be made of their money. The offering documents invited interested investors to make immediate payments to B's client account by way of loan to X, in return for promised loan notes in which X acknowledged its immediate obligations as borrower. The clear implication was that B was being identified as X's agent for the receipt of loan monies, and X as B's client for that purpose. The identification of B's client account was an ordinary incident of an arrangement to pay a commercial counter-party through a solicitor agent. The risk taken by investors responding to X's emails was that the scheme might be seriously undersubscribed, and then dissolved without them obtaining control through an equity share. The fact that X might prove to be insolvent was a risk investors would take even if they obtained proportionate equity shares. Absent insolvency, in the event of failure of the scheme the investors would be repaid in full by X, albeit probably after considerable delay. The risk C took of the scheme not being fully subscribed did not permit the offering documents to be interpreted as proffering something completely different from what they described. On the judge's findings of fact, C made their payments to B as immediate loans to X. Subject to the agency issue, B received those payments into its client account as trustee for X, and had not breached any obligation owed to C when it disbursed them for X's benefit (see paras 67-92 of judgment). (2) As to whether there was a resulting trust due to lack of authority, C had to be taken as having intended that the money should belong beneficially to X from the moment it reached B's client account, as it would if C had paid X direct. B were X's solicitors by the time the payments were made and C's payments had been disbursed for X's benefit before any repayment request was made by C. It could not be right that the law compelled a conclusion that C's monies were held on immediate resulting trust for them, such that B's application of them at X's direction constituted a breach of that trust. The resulting trust argument adopted by the judge, based on the payments having been made to B's client account, was wrong, *Westdeutsche Landesbank Girozentrale v Islington LBC* [1996] A.C. 669, [1996] C.L.Y. 4149 followed, *Vandervell v Inland Revenue Commissioners* [1967] 2 A.C. 291, [1967] C.L.Y. 1975 considered (paras 95-110). (3) There were two insuperable obstacles to the restitutionary claim. First, from receipt B held C's monies on client account trust for X. B was therefore not enriched by the receipts. Second, B would have had a change of position defence if a restitutionary claim had otherwise been available. The judge had provisionally rejected such a defence on the ground that, by disbursing the monies without sufficient certainty as to the basis on which the payments had been made, B had not acted in a commercially acceptable way. However, B had owed no duties or responsibilities to C, because they had advanced the monies by way of immediate loan to X. There was force in the judge's criticism of B, namely that C's monies had been disbursed without checking the precise terms on which they had been solicited. However, as more diligent enquiry would only have confirmed the understanding that the monies constituted loans, any lack of diligence could not be treated as commercially unacceptable conduct, *Niru Battery Manufacturing Co v Milestone Trading Ltd (No.1)* [2002] EWHC 1425 (Comm), [2002] 2 All E.R. (Comm) 705 applied (paras 111-120).

CHALLINOR v JULIET BELLIS & CO *sub nom.* BELLIS (A FIRM) v CHALLINOR, [2015] EWCA Civ 59, [2016] W.T.L.R. 43, Moore-Bick LJ, CA (Civ Div).

2152 Constructive trusts–Beneficial interests–Cohabitee's claim for share of properties held by former partner in his sole name

The appellant (P) appealed against an order dismissing her claim for a share in three properties acquired by the respondent (B) and held in his name, and a kennels business conducted from the kennels attached to one of the properties. P and B met in around 1977 to 1978 and were in a relationship from that time until 2010. P did not move in to live with B until 2002. The properties were purchased during that time. It was common ground that, because all the properties were held in B's name, P bore the legal burden of proving that she was entitled to a share; there was no express agreement. P's case at trial was that she had made significant financial contributions by using her wages from which payments of household bills, including mortgage repayments, were made. The judge was not persuaded that P had made any contribution from her earnings; her earnings were too small for her to have done so. In respect of the second property, when P had raised the question of her having a share in it B had told her that it was too expensive for her name to be on the property (the excuse); it was P's case that that statement was impliedly made on the basis that B accepted that, but for the expense, she would be an owner of the house. The judge made important findings as to credibility, and concluded that she preferred B's account of events to that of P. P appealed on the basis that the judge was wrong (i) to discount her evidence and to prefer that of B; (ii) in assessing the excuse by reference to subjective factors; (iii) to focus on financial contributions; (iv) not to find that the business was a partnership; (v) to rely on incomplete disclosure of documents by B.

Held: Appeal dismissed. (1) The failure at trial largely turned upon the judge's view of the facts. Her finding on B's credibility envisaged that she would have to exercise caution when considering his evidence; that meant that she would on some matters accept and on others reject it. That did not amount to inconsistency. There was no suggestion that her acceptance or rejection of his evidence was against the weight of the evidence so that it was not open to her. She was not for that reason wrong to accept B's evidence at times in her judgment (see paras 3, 32 of judgment). (2) The judge's interpretation of events surrounding the excuse was an evaluation by her of all the relevant facts and circumstances. The court could only properly interfere if the judge was wrong. The parties were not living together when the excuse was given, and did not do so until many years later. Although that was not conclusive, taken with the absence of significant contribution it constituted material which supported the judge's finding. Moreover, there was no material to gainsay the judge's finding. Accordingly, the judge's interpretation of the excuse could not be set aside as a misinterpretation of events. Given that P and B were not living together and the absence of significant contribution by P, it was clear that the judge applied the objective test in her interpretation of the excuse, *Grant v Edwards* [1986] Ch. 638, [1986] C.L.Y. 3034 considered (paras 41-42). (3) The judge expressly went beyond mere financial contributions (para.50). (4) There was no partnership agreement and the judge found that there was no documentary evidence to support it. Thus, the question whether there was a partnership turned on the parties' intention. The judge made clear findings of fact and gave reasons for her decision. There was no basis on which the instant court could interfere (paras 51, 54). (5) It was clear from the sequence of events described by B that the judge was entitled to proceed in the way she did (para.57).

CURRAN v COLLINS, [2015] EWCA Civ 404, [2016] 1 F.L.R. 505, Arden LJ, CA (Civ Div).

2153 Corporate trustees–Trust funds–Wrongful transfer of funds by trustee company into bank account–Investigation into company dealings–Scope of s.236(2) Insolvency Act 1986

[Insolvency Act 1986 (c.45) s.236, s.236(2), s.236(2)(c), s.236(3); Civil Procedure Rules 1998 Pt 6, r.6.15; CPR PD 6B (Service out of the Jurisdiction) 2000 para.3.1(a)]

The applicant official receiver, acting as the provisional liquidator of the trustee company of an occupational pension scheme (the trust), applied for permission to serve applications outside of the jurisdiction, and by means of an alternative service. The company had transferred a significant sum of trust money into an account held at the first defendant bank. The account holder's identity was unclear, but was connected to another trust ("the recipient trust"). The receiver's case was that there was no legitimate basis for the transfer and that the money had to be returned. He sought an order under the Insolvency Act 1986 s.236(2) that the bank produce documents explaining the receipt into, and dealings on, the account. The receiver also sought similar orders under s.236(2) against the second and third defendants, who were connected to the recipient trust, seeking their summons for examination as persons capable of giving information as to the company's dealings, affairs or property. There was a suggestion that the second and third defendants were resident in Hong Kong. The receiver stated that legal advisors in Hong Kong had told him that service was normally required to be in person, but that email was not prohibited. The issues were whether (i) the bank fell within the scope of s.236(2)(c) as a person capable of giving information concerning the business, dealings, affairs or property of the company; (ii) there was a good reason to serve on the second and third defendants by an alternative method of service, namely email; (iii) there was a realistic basis for arguing that s.236 had extraterritorial effect insofar as the requirement to provide documents, so that there should be permission to serve out of the jurisdiction; (iv) service by email was permitted out of the jurisdiction.

Held: Application granted. (1) There had been doubt as to whether the trust money concerned "property of the company" as it constituted funds held by a trustee. However, the statutory language was wide enough to cover the beneficial interest held on trust by the company for another. As between the beneficiaries and the company, the company had legal title and was therefore entitled to maintain a claim against third parties into whose hands trust money came. The court was satisfied bank possessed the documents sought within the meaning of s.236(3). (2) There was a good reason to authorise service by email under CPR r.6.15; the second and third defendants had not supplied addresses and had each made themselves available to the receiver by email only; any email communications would therefore be received. There was insufficient information to enable formal service on them personally. (3) Under CPR PD 6B para.3.1(a) the court could grant permission to serve out of the jurisdiction if the claim was made under an enactment which allowed proceedings to be brought and those proceedings were not covered by any of the other grounds referred to in that paragraph. The argument as to whether s.236 had extraterritorial effect was moot and the matter had been left open, *Casterbridge Properties Ltd (No.2), Re* [2002] B.C.C. 453 considered. The issue required more careful argument. It could not be said that the argument was hopeless; it had a reasonable prospect of success. It was therefore appropriate to give permission to serve out of the jurisdiction. (4) In *Civil Procedure*, 2015 edn (London: Sweet & Maxwell, 2014), para.6.15.7 it was observed that, where none of the general methods of service outside of the jurisdiction had been adopted, the question was not whether the method of service adopted was good service by a method permitted by CPR Pt 6 (for example under the law of the state in which the document was to be served) but whether in an individual case there was good reason to declare that the method used, being ipso facto not a permitted method, was to be treated as good service, *Abela v Baadarani* [2013] UKSC 44, [2013] 1 W.L.R. 2043, [2013] C.L.Y. 425 followed. On the basis that service by email was permissible in Hong Kong, the order would be made. The receiver undertook to file a witness statement the following day setting out the legal advice he had received from Hong Kong.

OMNI TRUSTEES LTD, RE *sub nom.* OFFICIAL RECEIVER v HBOS PLC, [2015] EWHC 2122 (Ch), [2015] B.C.C. 644, Judge Pelling QC, Ch D.

2154 Declarations of trust–Criminal injuries compensation–Trustees powers and duties–Amended trust terms referred to Court of Protection for approval

[European Convention on Human Rights 1950 art.8]

The court gave further consideration to points that arose from directions given to a deputy at a previous appeal hearing (*V v Assistant Director Adult Social Care Newcastle City Council* [2015] EWCOP 87, [2016] Fam. 229, [2016] 1604) concerning a compensation award by the Criminal Injuries Compensation Authority. The judge had made a declaration which was subject to further amendments that could be negotiated in the terms of the trust. On appeal the court stated that the points had, or potentially had, widespread impact and hoped that the CICA would be true to its position that it would cooperate with the Court of Protection in ensuring that they would be addressed. The court stated that the judgment below had to be qualified to make it clear that CICA decisions were not "entirely" in its discretion, as it had to decide on a correct interpretation of the relevant scheme, and its exercise of discretion under it was subject to challenge applying public law principles; that meant that an applicant and so the COP, or a deputy or attorney, did not have to accept the CICA's decision and could challenge quantum and the terms the CICA sought to require. The court said that, although there was a risk that a challenge could result in an award not being made or being delayed, the CICA, as a body governed by public law principles, was bound to act fairly and that was likely to preclude a commercial negotiating stance. The court also raised the issue of the imposition of a term in a trust which was directed to the risk that a perpetrator would benefit from the award. That seemed to merit the deputy seeking to agree different terms with the CICA and raised points of general importance for child victims, as those points were relevant to the promotion of their best interests, their well-being and their rights under the ECHR art.8. There were also issues regarding the terms of appointment of a deputy, a review of the merits of declaratory relief following the appeal court's disagreement with the terms of the declaration, and the issue of a Peters undertaking. The question was what part, if any, the Court of Protection should play in the finalisation of the award of compensation under the relevant scheme decided upon by the CICA, and which the local authority had agreed was to be held on trust.

Held: Further amendments approved. (1) The matters raised had, or potentially had, widespread impact (see para.2 of judgment). The parties had addressed them. The wording, as in part 1 of the schedule to the order, was agreed for the appointment of a deputy and should form a useful precedent or starting point for other cases. The deputy was authorised to accept the CICA award on the basis that it was to be held on, and subject to, the trusts set out in part 2 of the schedule thereto. As the appointment of the deputy was discharged, it was agreed that there was no need for a *Peters* undertaking (paras 3-5). (2) The terms of the trust were agreed and were anonymised save for the identity of the original trustee. The terms did not include the appellant's mother within the definition of excluded persons; did not exclude, and so included her within persons in favour of whom an appointment by deed or will could be made; did not exclude her from the trusts in default and from being a trustee. That solution addressed the problems relating to indirect benefit raised in the earlier appeal judgment and meant that an appointment could be made in her favour. It was clear that the appellant would never have capacity to make any such appointment and so it would have to be made on his behalf by the COP; in that case the court should take account of the source of the trust moneys, namely a CICA award, and so the underlying purposes of the 1990 scheme, and should give the CICA an opportunity to make submissions on what was proposed. That approach to the way the appellant's mother could benefit directly and indirectly under the trusts, together with her exclusion from the default trusts and from being a trustee, addressed the public interest points raised by the CICA and provided a result in the best interests of the appellant by avoiding problems relating to indirect benefit and enabling the COP to make an appointment on his behalf in favour of his mother, having regard to all the relevant circumstances. The power to appoint new trustee invested in the appellant would have to be exercised by the COP (paras 6-12). (3) The parties had reached a sensible and pragmatic result (para.13 and schedule).

V v ASSISTANT DIRECTOR ADULT SOCIAL CARE NEWCASTLE CITY COUNCIL *sub nom.* PJV v ASSISTANT DIRECTOR ADULT SOCIAL CARE NEWCASTLE CITY COUNCIL, [2016] EWCOP 7, [2016] Fam. 229, Charles J, CP.

2155 Declarations of trust–Title to land–Acquisition of property by partnership which subsequently dissolved–Whether letters between partners about status of property amounting to declarations of trust–Significance of using word "trust"

The appellant appealed against an order that his beneficial interest in a property was limited to 50%. The appellant and respondent had formed a partnership for acquiring properties and had purchased the relevant property as part of their portfolio. The parties fell out and the partnership was dissolved. The appellant subsequently claimed to hold 100% of the beneficial interest in the property and relied in that regard on three letters the respondent had written to him which referred to the respondent holding the property "on trust" for him. The judge rejected the appellant's proposition that the letters had constituted declarations of trust entitling him to 100% of the beneficial interest in the property, and instead ruled that the appellant held 50% of the beneficial interest.

Held: Appeal dismissed. It was appropriate to bear in mind when considering the evidence that it was inherently improbable that the respondent would have given the appellant the entire beneficial interest in the property by way of trust. None of letters amounted to declarations of trust. Although it was true that the word "trust" did not have to be used in order for a trust to be formed, it did not follow that if the parties had used the word "trust" the relevant document had to be a trust. The court would look at the true effect of the documents. The language of the letters was inconsistent with them being trusts. The judge had therefore been correct to hold that none of the letters constituted declarations of trust entitling the appellant to 100% of the beneficial interest in the property.

SINGHA v HEER *sub nom.* HEER v SINGHA, [2016] EWCA Civ 424, [2016] W.T.L.R. 1189, Arden LJ, CA (Civ Div).

2156 Protectors–Trustees' powers and duties–Challenge to validity of appointment–Late application for re-amendment of defence

[Trustee Act 1925 (c.19) s.41(1)]

The second defendant, the purported protector of two settlements, applied for permission to re-amend his defence and bring a counterclaim in an action brought by the claimant beneficiaries challenging the validity of his appointment as protector. The settlements were established upon discretionary trusts in favour of a class of beneficiaries which included the settlors' children and remoter issue. The claimants were the settlors' children. By deeds of appointment made in 2003, the trustees established a protectorship regime. Under that regime, the protector was able to give or withhold consent to any exercise by the trustees of their powers of appointment, remove any trustee from office, and appoint new trustees and protectors. In 2004, the settlors appointed the third defendant as the first protector of each settlement. In 2013, the second defendant (the protector) was appointed to act jointly with the third defendant. Relations between the settlors and their children broke down. The claimants brought proceedings challenging the validity of the protectoral regime and seeking a declaration that the 2003 appointments were void. Alternatively, they sought a declaration that the protector's appointment was invalid or, in the further alternative, an order for his removal. The protector defended the claim and the trial was fixed for early

April 2016. The protector made the instant application in July 2015, raising significant new issues as to the alleged maladministration of the trusts and seeking removal of the current trustees. The application was heard on 15 December 2015.

Held: Application refused. (1) Late applications to amend attracted a much stricter approach by the court, particularly if the result of granting permission to amend would be to lose or jeopardise the trial date, *Quah v Goldman Sachs International* [2015] EWHC 759 (Comm) applied. The question had to be judged at the time when the application was heard, not when the application was issued. However, the proposed amendments in the instant case had to be characterised as very late. There was no realistic way in which the trial date could have been held, even if permission to amend had been granted at the conclusion of the hearing on 15 December 2015. Given the issues raised by the proposed re-amendments, much fuller particularisation would be needed before they could satisfy the stringent criteria laid down in *Swain Mason v Mills & Reeve* [2011] EWCA Civ 14, [2011] 1 W.L.R. 2735, [2011] C.L.Y. 389, *Swain Mason* considered. As it was, the trustees were being asked to face what amounted to an entirely new cross-application for their removal which had previously formed no part of either the claim or the protector's original defence. Moreover, the protector had not explained why he had raised those issues at such a late stage. Furthermore, even if the allegations against the trustees were to be formulated with the necessary particularity, there would then have to be an adequate opportunity for the trustees, the third defendant and the claimants to respond. It followed that permission for the re-amendments had to be refused (see paras 42-43, 46-48, 51, 66 of judgment). (2) Since the protector was alone in seeking the removal of the trustees, without the concurrence of the third defendant, he had no standing to seek that relief. Moreover, it was implicit in the Trustee Act 1925 s.41(1) that nobody other than a trustee or beneficiary had standing to seek the appointment of new trustees under that Act. Since the claimants and their adult children had made it clear that they had confidence in the trustees, it was fanciful to suppose that the court would be willing to remove them on the application of the protectors even if they were acting jointly. In any event, there was no evidence which might suggest that the trustees were guilty of misconduct such as to jeopardise the interests of possible future beneficiaries. Thus, the protector lacked standing to bring the relevant claims and his proposed counterclaim offered no reasonable prospect of success (paras 57-59, 65). (3) A full review of the trusteeship and protectorate was needed and the immediate priority was for the protector's status to be resolved by the court. Until his standing to act had been confirmed, there would be no justification for having a trial of the issues raised by his re-amended defence (para.67).

DAVIDSON v SEELIG, [2016] EWHC 549 (Ch), [2016] W.T.L.R. 627, Henderson J, Ch D.

2157 Trust funds–Variation–Life insurance policy in trust for deceased's adult children–Whether court satisfied that variation beneficial

[Inheritance (Provision for Family and Dependants) Act 1975 (c.63); Variation of Trusts Act 1958 (c.53)]

The claimant asked the court to approve a variation of two trusts declared by the deceased. The claimant was the second wife of the deceased and a trustee of the second trust. Both trusts were for the benefit of the deceased's three children from his first marriage. When the deceased and his first wife had divorced, he had undertaken to execute a declaration of trust in respect of a policy of insurance on his life in favour of the children, on terms to be agreed with his first wife. In 2005 he made a unilateral declaration of trust to the effect that he held the insurance policy on trust for the children for as long as any one of them remained in full-time education, and that once they had all ceased full-time education the proceeds of the policy would revert to him. In 2006 he executed a further declaration of trust by which he appointed the claimant and another as trustees, assigned the policy to them and declared that they should hold it on trust for the benefit of the children. In 2013, when the deceased died and the proceeds of the policy became payable, the youngest child was still in full-time education. A dispute arose as to who was entitled to the income and capital of the policy proceeds and whether the youngest child had a claim under the Inheritance (Provision for Family and Dependants) Act 1975. After mediation, the parties agreed that the 2005 declaration should be treated as effective, but that it should be altered to provide for the immediate payment of one-third of the fund to each of the older children, with the remaining third being held on trust for the youngest until she reached 23 or graduated from university, whichever was the sooner. The claimant therefore applied under the Variation of Trusts Act 1958 to vary whatever applicable trust affected the policy proceeds.

Held: Application granted. The court had to be satisfied that the proposed arrangement was more beneficial to the youngest child than were the 2005 and 2006 declarations. The 2005 declaration was an effective declaration of trust entitling the children to the benefit of the policy in equal shares for so long as any of them remained in full-time education. It entitled each child to a share of the income arising from any investment of the policy proceeds, but not to any capital. Once the youngest child ceased full-time education their interest would end and the proceeds of the policy would form part of the deceased's estate. The 2006 declaration was an effective assignment of the legal title to the trustees. Because the deceased had already settled the benefit of the policy, he could not declare fresh trusts except in relation to his estate's reversionary entitlement to the policy proceeds upon the youngest child ceasing full-time education. The 2006 declaration was therefore effective to that extent. The proposed variation contained a fresh assignment of the policy and a declaration that the trustees would hold it and any monies arising under it on trust for the children in equal shares until each reached 23, whereupon their shares would be held absolutely and paid over in the event of the policy monies becoming payable. During the hearing, the court indicated that it could not approve the variation as drafted. First, there was no need to provide for an assignment of the policy: the policy no longer existed, all that existed was a fund representing its proceeds. Second, the arrangement did not vest the youngest child's share in her upon her reaching 23; rather it gave her an absolute right to call for it when she reached 18. Third, if the aim was to make her entitlement to capital contingent upon her reaching 23, insufficient consideration had been given to the tax consequences of achieving that outcome. Following that indication, the parties therefore agreed that the youngest child's interest should vest at 18. That was undoubtedly for her benefit in that it secured for her an absolute interest in a fund in which she currently had only a terminable interest in the income. That was a clear financial advantage, and there was no evidence to suggest that she would deal imprudently with her share (see paras 8 -16 of judgment).

COLLINS v COLLINS, [2016] EWHC 1423 (Ch), [2016] W.T.L.R. 1145, Norris J, Ch D.

2158 Trustees–Appointments–Re-appointment of trustees by court

[Trustee Act 1925 (c.19) s.41(1); Civil Procedure Rules 1998 r.64.2(a)]

The claimants sought an order that they be re-appointed as trustees of a cricket foundation. The president (C) of a cricket club had made a will whereby one fifth of the residue of his estate, together with a cricket ground and a pecuniary legacy, was intended for the benefit of the club. C died in 2001. As the will was complex and confusing, the executor brought proceedings for the determination of issues of validity and construction. The cricket foundation was established as a trust by a court order in 2004. The trust deed, also made in that year, provided that the power to appoint a new trustee or trustees would be vested in the trustee or trustees for the time being. It also provided that trustees would be appointed for a period of five years. The first to fourth claimants, the second defendant and another individual, who retired in 2007, were the original trustees. The assets due to them under C's will were duly transferred to them. The fifth and sixth claimants were later appointed as additional trustees, in 2005 and 2006 respectively. The instant application had been brought because the five-year terms of the six claimants had expired and they had not been re-appointed. Apart from the usual questions of internal administration that needed to be carried on, there was an urgency in establishing who the trustees were, because the process had been started of acquiring two properties as investments. All the claimants wished to be re-appointed, or to continue, as trustees. The second defendant did not. The first defendant, a member of the club, had been put forward to represent the members generally. Both defendants supported the application.

Held: Application granted. Under the Trustee Act 1925 s.41(1), the court had the power to appoint a new trustee or trustees when "it [was] found inexpedient difficult or impracticable so to do without the assistance of the court". The court also had the power under its inherent jurisdiction to appoint new trustees in any administration action; the advantage was that it would not have to consider the restriction imposed by the words "inexpedient difficult or impracticable". In cases where the court's inherent jurisdiction over trusts and trustees was to be invoked, it was formerly common to add to the claim form a claim "for administration, if and so far as may be necessary" in order to quell any doubts that the court did in fact have such jurisdiction. That was strictly unnecessary, as RSC Ord.85 r.2 provided that an action could be brought for the determination of any question or for any relief which could be determined or granted in an administration action, and a claim did not need to be made in the action for the administration or execution under the direction of the court. CPR r.64.2(a) now proceeded on the same basis. The inherent jurisdiction of the court to appoint trustees was therefore exercisable even where there was no formal claim for administration on foot. In any event, it was clear that the reference in the claim form to the appointment of trustees under "the inherent jurisdiction of the court" performed the same function as a claim to administration "if and so far as may be necessary". The evidence was to the effect that the finances and other affairs of the foundation were in good order, and there was nothing to suggest that any maladministration had taken place or that any of the trustees were in any way unfit or unsuitable to be re-appointed. The best course was to appoint the claimants for a further five-year term in substitution for themselves and the second defendant. That would be done under the court's inherent jurisdiction, making it unnecessary to consider whether it was "inexpedient difficult or impracticable" to make the appointment without the assistance of the court. Had it been necessary, the court would have held that it was indeed both inexpedient and impracticable, in the circumstances, to make the appointment out of court, and so the court could have made the order under s.41 also (see paras 12-16 of judgment).

BARCLAY v SMITH, [2016] EWHC 210 (Ch), [2016] W.T.L.R. 583, Master Matthews, Ch D.

2159 Trustees–Estoppel by convention–Appellant raising new case of estoppel by convention for first time on appeal

A beneficiary under a will (J) and two companies run by him appealed against an order for possession made in favour of the respondents, the trustees of the will. Until her death in 1977, the testator, J's mother, had run a pub in partnership with her husband (B). She left the pub to her executors to hold on trust for J and his siblings, allowing B to run it during his lifetime. B ran the pub by himself until 2001 when he sold half of it to J. Thereafter, he and J ran it together until his death in 2013. In the early 2000s, J spent over £300,000 renovating the pub after the beneficiaries tried and failed to obtain a loan for that purpose. After B's death, J claimed a proprietary estoppel, alleging that he had paid the money on the understanding that he would be entitled to occupy the pub for as long as he wished. His wider case was that the beneficiaries had agreed that he should not to have to pay personally for works that maintained and benefitted the pub. The trustees brought possession proceedings, arguing that J had loaned the business the cost of the renovations, that the renovations had been undertaken for the benefit of the business, and that because J was running the business with B, he had had the benefit of them. The judge found in favour of the trustees, rejecting J's case of proprietary estoppel. On appeal, J asserted that the judge should have found that he had made the loan to the trustees as partners in the business, and not to the business itself. He argued that the judge should have concluded that there was an estoppel by convention between him and the trustees on the basis of a common assumption that the trustees were partners in the business with a 50% share, and that they were jointly and severally liable to repay any loans made by J to the business. The issues were whether (1) a new case of estoppel by convention was open to J; (2) an estoppel by convention was made out.

Held: Appeal dismissed. (1) Although J had not advanced a case of estoppel by convention at trial, he had pleaded the important elements of an estoppel by convention, albeit not fully, and the basic allegation of a mutual understanding had been before the judge. The judge had considered J's wider case that the beneficiaries had agreed that he should be repaid the cost of the renovations, and while that was not the same as the allegation of a loan to the trustees, it was not far from it. J had expressly been given permission to advance his new case on appeal, and since he was not asking the instant court to decide additional facts there was no reason why it could not fairly decide the issues raised (see paras 20, 43-46 of judgment). (2) Given the contemporaneous documents and the judge's findings, it was impossible to conclude that J and the trustees made the common assumption that J had made the loan to the trustees as partners in the business. The judge was entitled to find as a fact that J had made the loan to the business and not to the trustees. There was nothing to suggest that the trustees considered themselves to be partners in the business, and while the judge did not say expressly that they had not proceeded on the basis that they were partners, that was clearly implied: he made the point that it was inconceivable that the trustees, then a solicitor and an accountant, would have taken a substantial loan without a formal agreement and discussion with the beneficiaries. J's wider case, that the beneficiaries had agreed that he should not have to bear the cost of the renovations himself, had much to recommend it in terms of common sense. However, the correspondence made it clear that nothing had been agreed and there was no shared understanding of how the monies expended by J were to be treated. Although estoppels were intended to meet the justice of the case, they had to be based on legal principle, not a vague idea that someone who had expended monies for a worthy purpose would somehow be able to recoup them. J's problem was that he had paid for the renovations without securing any clear repayment commitment from anyone. His estoppel claims foundered on the need for promises, or at least expectations created or acquiesced in by the persons he sought to make liable. No such promises had been made and no expectations legitimately created. There was no common understanding that the trustees were partners in the business or that they were jointly and severally liable to repay any loans made by J to the business. Moreover, there was no evidence that J had relied on any such understanding in paying for the renovations (paras 53, 55-61).

PREEDY v DUNNE, [2016] EWCA Civ 805, [2016] C.P. Rep. 44, Longmore LJ, CA (Civ Div).

2160 Trustees' powers and duties–Breach of trust–High-risk investment for trust funds invested on behalf of minor beneficiaries–Trustees' duty to act prudently–Advice from independent financial advisers

[Trustee Act 1925 (c.19) s.61; Trustee Act 2000 (c.29) s.1]

Beneficiaries under a will trust brought a claim against the trustees for breach of trust arising from their reliance on the advice of independent financial advisers. The testator died in 1999. The executors and trustees (T1 and T2) were two partners in a firm of solicitors. The value of the estate was over £3 million. In February 2000, a third partner in the firm (T3) contacted a firm of investment advisers which the firm had used previously and asked for recommendations with a realistic risk profile. He told them that they were looking for a "growth portfolio" rather than one which would yield a lot of income. According to the course of dealings between T3 and the investment advisers, the expression "growth portfolio" meant one comprising around 80% equities and 20% non-equities. The trust fund performed poorly between 2000 and 2002. The beneficiaries sought compensation in the sum of £1,467,076, claiming that the trustees had failed to take appropriate care to invest in a properly diversified investment portfolio and had wrongly relied on the advice and recommendations of the investment advisers. The trustees denied breach of trust; alternatively, they claimed to have acted honestly and reasonably so that the court ought to relieve them of personal liability for any such breach pursuant to the Trustee Act 1925 s.61. According to the beneficiaries, T1 and T2 had impermissibly delegated their functions to T3.

Held: Judgment for defendants. (1) Whether the claim was based on equitable duty or, after the coming into effect of the Trustee Act 2000 s.1 in February 2001, on the statutory duty of care set out in that provision, the award of equitable compensation in a case such as the instant one resembled the award of damages at common law. Although those remedies were based on separate legal obligations, they had the same broad aim. Where trustees were alleged to have been at fault in making particular investments, it was necessary to establish on the balance of probabilities what loss had resulted from each breach of duty (see paras 52-53, 158 of judgment). (2) Trustees had a duty to act prudently, *Nestle v National Westminster Bank Plc* [1993] 1 W.L.R. 1260, [1993] C.L.Y. 1849 followed. The decision to opt for a portfolio comprising 80% equities reflected a high level of risk and was one which no trustee, complying with the duty to act prudently, could reasonably have made (paras 38, 155-156, 162-164). (3) There did not appear to be any direct authority as to the extent to which trustees were entitled to rely upon advice from independent financial advisers, *Locke v Camberwell HA* [1991] 2 Med. L.R. 249, [1992] C.L.Y. 4086 considered. In the instant case, there was no basis for saying that the trustees had acted unreasonably in relying on the advice of responsibly chosen investment advisers. Although they were at fault in believing that it was in keeping with a realistic risk strategy to invest in what they termed a "growth portfolio", the initial investment in equities was below 30% of the value of the trust assets and was spread over 10 different companies. In fact, the percentage of the total value of the assets which was held in equities never reached the headline figure of 80%. Accordingly, the beneficiaries had established some breaches of duty in the early stages of the relevant period but had failed to prove that they suffered loss as a result of those breaches,*Wight v Olswang (No.2)* [2000] Lloyd's Rep. P.N. 662, [2000] C.L.Y. 5270 applied (paras 58, 168-169, 180, 183-184). (4) Even if the trustees were liable for breach of trust, there would be scope for the application of s.61 of the 1925 Act since they had acted to the best of their abilities and in reliance on what they reasonably believed to be competent professional advice. The degree of harm which any breaches of trust had occasioned to beneficiaries was to be taken into account when deciding whether trustees ought to be excused under s.61. In the instant case, even if the beneficiaries had suffered loss, it was appreciably less than the amount claimed (paras 185-186). (5) Although, under the 2000 Act, it was permissible for trustees to delegate their asset management functions, in the instant case there had been no lawful delegation to T3 because the requirements of s.15 of the 2000 Act were not satisfied. However, the trustees had involved their fellow partner in good faith and any impermissible delegation had not resulted in losses which would not otherwise have occurred, *AIB Group (UK) Plc v Mark Redler & Co Solicitors* [2014] UKSC 58, [2015] A.C. 1503, [2015] C.L.Y. 167 followed (paras 75, 188-190).

DANIEL v TEE, [2016] EWHC 1538 (Ch), [2016] 4 W.L.R. 115, Richard Spearman QC, Ch D.

2161 Trustees' powers and duties–Variation–Fiduciary power to benefit core beneficiaries

[Variation of Trusts Act 1958 (c.53)]

The court was required to determine an application to vary the trusts made under a will and a settlement. The core beneficiaries of the trusts were members of the same family, including their spouses and children. However, a wide remoter class of potential beneficiaries existed, including unborn and unascertained persons and charitable entities. They were not represented before the court and were not parties to the proceedings. The main purpose of the proposed variation was to extend the perpetuity period to 2141.

Held: Application granted. (1) Due to the nature of the trusts it was highly unlikely that any non-party other than members of the specified class would ever benefit under the trusts. The entire arrangement funds were intended to be applied for the benefit of the parties and the specified class. Ordinarily, that would not eliminate the need for a variation affecting potential beneficiaries to be agreed by adults and approved by the court on behalf of unborn and unascertained persons. However, the trustees had proposed a method of eliminating the need for such involvement. The trustees were to execute deeds releasing their powers, but only to the extent that it deprived the members of the wider class, who were not members of the narrower class, of any right which they might otherwise have had to challenge the arrangement. In practical terms, the result of the release was that it removed such persons as potential beneficiaries for the instant before the arrangement took effect, so that their consent and the court's approval were not required, and reinstated them immediately after the arrangement took effect according to the terms of the varied trusts. There was no doubt that a power of appointment could be released, *Christie Miller's Marriage Settlement Trusts, Re* [1961] 1 W.L.R. 462, [1961] C.L.Y. 8169 applied. If the persons entitled in default of the exercise of the power agreed a variation of the trusts, it would not be necessary to release the power altogether. It could be released to the extent necessary to allow the variation to take effect (see paras 21-23, 26, 28 of judgment). (2) In the instant case, the powers concerned were fiduciary powers. The trustees could only exercise their powers of appointment, release and revocation for proper purposes. However, the trustees' powers included power to benefit the core beneficiaries. The trustees clearly considered that the variation was in the interests of the core beneficiaries; they did not wish to cut out the wider class from potential benefit. It was also arguable that the arrangement benefited the wider class as it preserved valuable assets for the future in the remote circumstance of their ever benefiting. It did not matter whether the arrangement was seen as a partial or total release, subject to reinstatement of modified powers of appointment. On either view, on the facts of the instant case it was perfectly proper for the trustees to effect the partial releases, and no fraud on a power was involved. The method of dispensing with the need for representation of the wider class was effective, and was a sensible approach to the application. The court approved the arrangement under the Variation of Trusts Act 1958 (paras 30-34).

A v B, [2016] EWHC 340 (Ch), [2016] W.T.L.R. 745, Warren J, Ch D.

2162 Trusts–Variation orders–Proper exercise of English court's jurisdiction to vary trusts of foreign settlement

[Variation of Trusts Act 1958 (c.53) s.1; Hague Convention on the Law Applicable to Trusts and their Recognition 1986 art.7, art.8(h)]

A beneficiary applied to the court to approve, on behalf of minor beneficiaries and all unborn and unascertained persons who might become beneficially interested, the variation of the trusts of four family settlements and the compromise of an issue as to the validity of the two most recent of those settlements. The first two settlements were made in 1932 and 1950 by the first respondent's late father, while the third and fourth were made by the first respondent in 1996. The 1950 settlement was governed by the law of Kenya. The other three settlements were governed by English law. The applicant and the first and second respondents, who were husband and wife, were beneficiaries of all four settlements. The first respondent's minor sons were also beneficiaries of the 1932 settlement and his nephew was a beneficiary of the 1950 and 1996 settlements. None of the respondents contested the proceedings.

Held: Application granted. (1) The terms of the compromise were for the benefit of the minor beneficiaries and all unborn and unascertained persons who might become interested under the trusts of the settlements created in 1932 and 1996, save for any future wife and future born child of the first respondent. Therefore, the terms of compromise would be approved on behalf of the minor respondents and the represented parties. The terms should be binding on them, while the applicant and, in their capacity as trustees, the first and sixth respondents should carry those terms of compromise into effect. The proposed arrangement was also for the benefit of the minor respondents and all unborn and unascertained persons who might become beneficially interested in the property subject to the trusts of any of the four family settlements. The arrangement did not give rise to a resettlement of the trust property subject to any of those settlements. Therefore, the proposed variation and arrangement would be approved under the Variation of Trusts Act 1958 s.1 on behalf of the minor respondents and the relevant unborn and unascertained persons (see paras 10-12 of judgment). (2) The applicable law regarding the 1950 settlement was the law of Kenya which, under the Hague Convention on the Law Applicable to Trusts and their Recognition 1986 art.8(h), was to govern the variation of a trust. Nevertheless, a court still retained the power under the 1958 Act to vary a trust governed by foreign law, subject to two limitations: (a) the court should be cautious in assuming jurisdiction where there were substantial foreign elements in the case, *Paget's Settlement, Re* [1965] 1 W.L.R. 1046, [1965] C.L.Y. 3579 considered and (b) the court should apply the substantive law of the country governing the trust identified by reference to art.6 or art.7 of the Convention. It should not exercise the jurisdiction under the 1958 Act to make a variation if the applicable law did not permit variation. The Kenyan Trustee Act 1929 referred to "the court" having power to effect a variation. "The court" meant the High Court of Kenya. If the English court decided on that ground that it could not exercise the foreign power, it would be applying only a truncated form of foreign law, and not the whole of it, as the Convention prescribed. Since, in the instant case, since a Kenyan court would have power to vary the trusts of the 1950 settlement under its legislation, the English court similarly had jurisdiction under the 1958 Act. It was therefore appropriate to exercise that jurisdiction in the instant case. The variation of the trusts created by the 1950 settlement was intimately associated with the variation application in relation to the other three settlements, which were all governed by English law. It would be wholly unreasonable and disproportionate to require a separate application to be made to the Kenyan courts (paras 22, 29-31, 40-41, 44-45).

C v C, [2015] EWHC 2699 (Ch), [2016] W.T.L.R. 223, Judge Hodge QC, Ch D.

2163 Will trusts–Trustees–Appointment of replacement trustees–Conflict of interest

The defendants, who were relatives of a man (W) who had died in 2008, sought an order appointing replacement trustees under certain will trusts created by W's will. W had run a successful company. His will provided that 50 per cent of his shares in the company should go to employees, as long as they were working for the company at the date of his death; the remaining shares were left to family members. The executors named under the will were W's sister, his solicitor (J), the first claimant, and his accountant (M), the second claimant. W's sister had renounced probate. The executors were to act as trustees of the will trusts. The will trusts involved in the instant application were those relating to the shares in the company which benefited W's daughters and grandchildren. Tension had arisen between the family and employee beneficiaries. M had acted as a de facto director of the company and still acted for it; he was seen by some family members as being in a different camp from that of the family, who sought his and J's replacement.

Held: Application granted. The family were entitled to voice concerns in relation to the position of M and J as will trustees. Looking at the matter objectively, a well-informed observer would see M's position as impossible or, at least, seriously compromised in the event of a conflict of interest arising between the interests of those in day-to-day control of the company and the family beneficiaries. M and J's role as trustees would require regular contact with the directors and employees of the company. Family members would obviously wish the will trustees to maximise the return from the investment in the company. Against that, the company would or might need to deploy its finite resources for other business purposes and the proper reward of its workforce. There thus remained a potential for conflict between the interests of the directors and employees of the company and the interests of the family beneficiaries which M, as someone perceived to have acted as a de facto director, was not ideally suited to deal with as trustee of the will trusts. Given further that J had now joined forces with M in the sense of taking out a joint grant of probate with him, the two of them would be seen objectively, not just by the family, as being more inclined to the company's camp than the family's. M and J were not against being replaced; they had proposed to appoint two other individuals, one an accountant and the other a solicitor, to act in their place. The defendants had sought an order that the first and second defendants, who were W's daughters, and the probate solicitor now acting for them should be appointed. The will trusts should be administered by those who were indisputably within the family camp. Trusts were better administered in an atmosphere of harmony, not disharmony. The better chance of harmony would be achieved by appointing the family members, with the probate solicitor of their choice, as trustees rather than anyone else. That was also likely to be significantly cheaper than the appointment of two professionals of different, albeit complementary, disciplines. It was therefore appropriate to accede to the instant application. The appointment of the new trustees would take place immediately upon completion of the administration (see paras 26, 33, 35-36, 56, 59, 61 of judgment).

WEETMAN (DECEASED), RE *sub nom.* JAMES v WILLIAMS, [2015] EWHC 1166 (Ch), [2015] W.T.L.R. 1745, Judge Purle QC, Ch D (Birmingham).

2164 Wills–Interpretation–Exoneration clause relieving trustees of personal liability for breaches of duty

The appellants (B and G) appealed against the dismissal of their claim for equitable compensation against the respondent (P). P and his brother had owned a business and property portfolio. Following the brother's death, P and the appellants were appointed as executors. Negotiations for a demerger took place with the aim of dividing the organisation so that, broadly, P acquired the business assets and G acquired the property assets. Prior to the demerger it was discovered that some of the businesses had possible claims for VAT repayments arising from judgments pending in the ECJ. Following the demerger, the appellants considered that P had misled them as to the value of the VAT repayment claims that he would acquire as part of the business assets. The appellants contended that P had acted in breach of fiduciary duty by acting in breach of the self-dealing rule and failing to disclose all relevant information concerning the VAT repayment to them. The court held that P was covered by an exoneration clause which stated that "in the professed execution of the trusts ... no trustee shall be liable for any loss to the trust premises arising by reason of any improper investment made in good faith ... or by reason of any other matter or thing except wilful and individual fraud or wrongdoing on the part of the trustee ...". The appellants argued that (1) the exoneration clause did not apply to the self-dealing rule because only the transactions clause modified the impact of that rule; (2) the exoneration clause did not apply because P had not acted "in the professed execution of the trusts and powers" of the will; (3) in giving effect to the demerger, P had engaged in "wilful and individual fraud or wrongdoing" and could not rely on the exoneration clause, and "wilful" translated to "intentional".

Held: Appeal dismissed. (1) (Per The Chancellor of the High Court) The exoneration clause in the instant case was in common use and, up to the final proviso, was to be found in the Encyclopedia of Forms and Precedents. It was untenable to argue that it had no application because the transactions clause was a self-contained code on self-dealing. The transactions clause and the exoneration clause addressed different matters. The former conferred powers of self-dealing if the conditions therein were satisfied. If the conditions were not satisfied, the transaction was voidable by any beneficiary as of right. The latter, as appeared from its express wording, addressed the issue of personal liability of the defaulting trustee for loss to the trust consequent on breach of the trustee's duty (see paras 46-47 of judgment). (2) The appellants' argument that P had never consciously thought that he was acting pursuant to the transactions clause in the discussions and decisions concerning the treatment of the VAT repayments in the context of the demerger was incorrect in fact and law. That argument would turn the analysis in *Walker v Stones* [2001] Q.B. 902, [2000] C.L.Y. 5268 on its head by depriving an honest and conscientious non-professional trustee, who acted without a particular provision of the trust deed in mind, of the benefit of the exoneration clause even though the breach of trust was entirely unconscious or accidental, *Walker* considered. The only capacity P thought he was acting in was as executor of the will. The discussion with B and the decision about entitlement to the VAT repayments took place in the context of the demerger for the purposes of administering the estate. Further, P formally and expressly executed the relevant documents relating to the demerger in his capacity as executor (paras 48-51).. (3) The meaning of the words "wilful wrongdoing" required an awareness of wrongdoing, *Armitage v Nurse* [1998] Ch. 241, [1997] C.L.Y. 4940 considered. The fact that "wilful" governed "fraud" as well as "wrongdoing" supported the conclusion that "wilful" imported a requirement of conscious wrongdoing. The expression "wilful fraud" in the exoneration clause made it clear that such conduct would only fall outside the scope of the clause if it had been carried out with awareness that it was wrongful. The exoneration clause divided into five parts: (a) an improper investment made in good faith; (b) the negligence or fraud of any agent employed by the trustee; (c) any mistake or omission made in good faith by the trustee; (d) any other matter or thing except wilful and individual fraud; (e) provided that nothing exonerates a remunerated professional trustee from liability for negligence or other wrongdoing. The appellants' interpretation produced an inconsistency between (a) and (c) on one hand, and (d) on the other. If that was correct, the trustee was not exonerated in relation to any other breach of duty if the act was intentional, even if the trustee acted in complete honesty and good faith and even in reliance on legal advice. There was no logic to such a distinction. Further, since (d) comprised the largest category of breaches, it would deprive a non-professional trustee of the most practical benefit of the exoneration clause. P had not deliberately held back information from B knowing that he ought to disclose it, and he was not deliberately or consciously acting in a way he knew to be wrong (paras 54-67), *Walker* considered.

BARNSLEY v NOBLE, [2016] EWCA Civ 799, [2016] W.T.L.R. 1501, Sir Terence Etherton C, CA (Civ Div).

UTILITIES

2165 Water charges–Local authorities' powers and duties–Water and sewerage supplied by water utilities company to unmetered properties occupied by local authority tenants–Overcharging by local authority

[Water Industry Act 1991 (c.56)]

The claimant tenant claimed that the defendant local authority had overcharged her for water and sewerage services. Since 2000, when an agreement was signed between the local authority and a water utilities supplier (X), the local authority had collected charges for water and sewerage services supplied by X to many of its tenants including the claimant. The agreement applied to unmetered properties and referred to X as the " provider" and the local authority as the "customer". Recitals to the agreement explained that X provided water and sewerage services to the premises managed by the customer in its capacity as local housing authority and that X and the local authority agreed that the latter would pay for the services in respect of some of the premises in accordance with the agreement. The local authority reviewed its arrangements with X and entered into a deed of clarification and amendment in 2013 when doubts were cast upon it in unrelated proceedings. It was common ground that if the 2013 deed was effective, the local authority was not a water "re-seller" and was not subject to the Water Resale Order 2006, made pursuant to the Water Industry Act 1991. The claimant contended that the 2013 agreement was invalid because the local authority failed to follow certain procedures and to consult its tenants. However, as X was not a party to the instant case, any decision on the validity of the deed was adjourned to enable X to be joined. The issue was whether the Water Resale Order 2006 applied to the arrangements and, if so, whether the local authority had charged tenants more than was permissible under the Order. The claimant submitted that the 2000 Agreement involved X supplying the local authority with water and sewerage services and the local authority's tenants buying such services from the local authority. Consequently, the local authority was a "re-seller" within the meaning of the Order and, as such, was not entitled to recover from its tenants more than the maximum charges set by the Order. The local authority submitted that on its true construction, the 2000 agreement operated to make the local authority X's agent.

Held: Judgment for claimant. The key question was whether the 2000 agreement gave rise to an agency relationship under which the local authority was to collect water and sewerage charges from its tenants as X's agent or whether it involved the local authority buying water and sewerage services from X and re-selling them to its tenants, *Lambeth LBC v Thomas* (1998) 30 H.L.R. 89, [1997] C.L.Y. 2750 and *Rochdale BC v Dixon* [2011] EWCA Civ 1173, [2012] P.T.S.R. 1336, [2012] C.L.Y. 2053 considered. Unless and until the 2013 deed took effect the relationship between X and the local authority was not one of principal and agent but involved the local authority buying water and sewerage from X and re-selling it to its tenants. As a result, the 2006 Order applied and served to limit what tenants could be charged. The amounts that the local authority had charged at least between 2000 and 2013 had exceeded the maximum charge under the 2006 Order (see paras 52-58 of judgment).

JONES v SOUTHWARK LBC, [2016] EWHC 457 (Ch), [2016] P.T.S.R. 1011, Newey J, Ch D.

2166 Water mains–Agricultural land–Compensation payable to landowners

[Water Industry Act 1991 (c.56) Sch.12]

The Upper Tribunal was required to determine the amount of compensation payable to the claimant landowners under the Water Industry Act 1991 Sch.12. The defendant company had installed a water main under the claimants' land. The pipe was laid by digging six holes of varying sizes, with the pipe being installed by way of a "mole". The claimants were asked to remove their stock from the land for the duration of the work, which took place over 10 days, and when the soil was reinstated, the topsoil and subsoil were not kept separate. The claimants sought a total of £14,621.28 compensation.

Held: Compensation assessed. The amount of compensation awarded under the different heads was as follows: *Loss of production* - The claimants were awarded £382.30 in respect of the area of land that was affected by the company's machinery and which the claimants could not use for grazing for a period of two years following the work. *Subsequent loss / weed control* - The claimants were awarded £270.93 to cover the additional costs of loss of use of the land and the cost of further work required to eradicate weeds from the areas affected over a subsequent three-year period. *Consequential loss* - The claimants were awarded £37.05 to cover the cost over two winters for which sheep agistment was required. *Reinstatement* - The claimants were awarded £3,983.88 for the cost of removing the incorrectly laid topsoil/subsoil mix, refilling with fresh topsoil and reseeding. That sum also included the cost of peripheral items including stone picking and rolling. *Fees* - The company agreed to pay fees based on Ryde's Scale plus 30%. The aggregate of the awards to the claimants so far totaled £4,674.16. That lay between the parameters of £4,500 and £4,999 in Ryde's Scale, for which the appropriate fee was £740. Adding 30% meant that £962 would be awarded to the claimants. *Inconvenience / Goodwill* - The appropriate amount of compensation for disturbance was £250. The total amount of compensation payable by the company to the claimants was therefore £5,886.16 (see paras 11-31 of judgment).

SURTEES v UNITED UTILITIES WATER PLC, [2015] UKUT 384 (LC), [2016] R.V.R. 149, PD McCrea FRICS, UT (Lands).

2167 Water quality–Water supply–Fees payable

THE WATER QUALITY AND SUPPLY (FEES) ORDER 2016, SI 2016/303; made under the Water Industry Act 1991 s.86ZA(1)(4). In force: 1 April 2016.

This Order provides for fees to be payable, and sets out how the amounts of such fees are to be determined, for the exercise of certain functions under the Water Industry Act 1991 by an inspector appointed under that Act.

2168 Water supply–Water quality and supply fees

THE WATER QUALITY AND SUPPLY (FEES) (UNDERTAKERS WHOLLY OR MAINLY IN WALES) ORDER 2016, SI 2016/843; made under the Water Industry Act 1991 s.86ZA(2)(4). In force: 8 September 2016.

This Order provides for fees to be payable, and sets out how the amounts of such fees are to be determined, for the exercise of a function by an inspector appointed by the Welsh Ministers under the Water Industry Act 1991 s.86.

VAT

2169 Carousel fraud–Statements of case–Whether allegations by HMRC in its statement of case amounted to allegation of dishonesty

[Tribunal Procedure (First-tier Tribunal) (Tax Chamber) Rules 2009 (SI 2009/273) r.27]

The Upper Tribunal had to consider conjoined appeals in which taxpayers (E and C), who were the subject of missing trader intra-community fraud proceedings, claimed that HMRC had failed to plead its statements of case with sufficient particularity. E also sought disclosure of documents by HMRC. E was a large online retailer of electrical goods and C was a global financial institution involved in EU emissions allowances trading. In proceedings before the First-tier Tribunal, HMRC alleged that the taxpayers had been involved in transactions which formed part of an overall scheme to defraud the Revenue; that the schemes involved an orchestrated and contrived series of transactions; and that there were features of those transactions which demonstrated that the taxpayers "knew or should have known" that that was the case. The taxpayers argued that HMRC's statements of case failed to satisfy the requirements of civil fraud pleadings because they were insufficiently particularised and contained no proper plea of fraud, notwithstanding that dishonesty was being alleged. According to HMRC, the pleadings did not have to be particularised in the manner contended for by the taxpayers because they did not amount to an allegation of dishonest behaviour. The tribunal found in favour of HMRC in E's case, but in C's case it held that HMRC had failed to clarify whether it was alleging a dishonest state of mind. It directed HMRC to either expressly allege dishonesty or disclaim it. The issue was whether, in a case where HMRC chose to allege actual knowledge of a fraud under the first limb of the test in *Kittel v Belgium (C-439/04)* EU:C:2006:446, [2008] S.T.C. 1537, [2008] C.L.Y. 4052, such an allegation was tantamount to an allegation of dishonesty.

Held: Appeals allowed in part. (1) In *Kittel*, the Court of Justice of the European Union had laid down a test of whether a taxpayer "knew or should have known" that transactions in which it had engaged were connected to fraud. That test was one of knowledge and was not to be regarded as synonymous with dishonesty, *Kittel* applied. The test was to be applied in accordance with the guidance given by the Court of Appeal in *Mobilx Ltd (In Administration) v Revenue and Customs Commissioners* [2010] EWCA Civ 517, [2010] S.T.C. 1436, [2010] C.L.Y. 3502 and *Fonecomp Ltd v Revenue and Customs Commissioners* [2015] EWCA Civ 39, [2015] S.T.C. 2254, [2015] C.L.Y. 2592. However, where HMRC relied on the first limb of *Kittel* and alleged that the taxpayer actually knew that it was taking part in a transaction connected with fraudulent evasion of VAT, that would very often amount to an accusation of conduct that would be regarded as dishonest by an English court, *Megtian Ltd (In Administration) v Revenue and Customs Commissioners* [2010] EWHC 18 (Ch), [2010] S.T.C. 840, [2010] C.L.Y. 3496 applied (see paras 61, 85-86 of judgment). (2) In the context of ordinary civil litigation, there was clear authority that a rolled-up plea of "knew or should have known" did not necessarily make alternative allegations, one of knowledge and, alternatively, one that the relevant facts should have been known, *Armitage v Nurse* [1998] Ch. 241, [1997] C.L.Y. 4940 followed. However, in the instant case, HMRC was seeking to rely on both limbs of *Kittel* by making such alternative allegations. The natural meaning of the allegation was that C knew both that there was an overall scheme involving an orchestrated and contrived series of transactions to defraud the Revenue, and that its transactions were part of that scheme. The tribunal was fully justified in concluding that that amounted to an allegation of dishonest conduct. HMRC's position was unclear: it was willing to allege that C knew that its transactions formed part of a fraudulent scheme, but was unwilling to accept that it was alleging dishonesty. It had used the same rolled-up plea E's case, and therefore a similar allegation of dishonest conduct was being made against E. It followed that E was entitled to proper particulars of what it was alleged to have known and the facts on which the case against it was based. E's case was therefore remitted to the tribunal to decide which of its requests for further information were justified and proportionate, *Mobilx* and *Fonecomp* followed (paras 91-97, 100-105). (3) Although the Tribunal Procedure (First-tier Tribunal) (Tax Chamber) Rules 2009 r.27 demonstrated that disclosure in the tribunal did not simply mirror that in ordinary civil litigation, the limitations of that rule should not preclude a request for wider disclosure where it was proportionate to the importance of the case, the complexity of the issues, the anticipated costs and the resources of the parties. The instant case was highly complex and of great importance to the taxpayer. Therefore, it was appropriate for HMRC to disclose not only the material that it wished to rely on, but also any other material uncovered in the course of its investigations which might undermine its case (paras 108-109).

E BUYER UK LTD v REVENUE AND CUSTOMS COMMISSIONERS; REVENUE AND CUSTOMS COMMISSIONERS v CITIBANK NA, [2016] UKUT 123 (TCC), [2016] S.T.C. 1533, Nugee J, UT (Tax).

2170 Costs–Withdrawal of VAT appeal–Costs following event

The Upper Tribunal was required to determine costs after the withdrawal of an appeal. The issue on the appeal had been whether building works undertaken by the appellant had been zero-rated or standard-rated. The First-tier Tribunal decided the issue against the appellant. The appellant obtained leave to appeal to the UT, seeking a direction that there should be no risk of its being subject to an adverse costs direction. That application was dismissed and the appellant withdrew its appeal. The issue was whether the appellant should pay HMRC's costs.

Held: Costs determined. The general rule was that costs followed the event. The UT could only exercise its discretion to deviate from the rule when a cogent reason had been demonstrated, and there was no such reason in the instant case. There was some force in the argument that the amount claimed was excessive, but it was not enough to warrant the additional cost of detailed assessment. The parties would be left to agree on a figure if they could, returning to the UT for summary assessment if they could not.

GATESHEAD JEWISH NURSERY v REVENUE AND CUSTOMS COMMISSIONERS, [2016] UKUT 237 (TCC), [2016] B.V.C. 519, Judge Colin Bishopp, UT (Tax).

2171 Exempt supplies–Colleges–College associated with university–Whether necessary integration to fall within Sch.9 Pt II Group 6 Value Added Tax Act 1994

[Value Added Tax Act 1994 (c.23) Sch.9 Pt II Group 6]

HMRC appealed against a First-tier Tribunal's decision that supplies of education made by the UK subsidiary of a global creative media group were exempt from VAT. The media group provided higher education and training in media technologies through subsidiary companies in various countries. The group worked closely with a university in England with which it had built a relationship, entering into agreements whereby the university validated the group's courses and the group's students were able to use their qualifications as credit towards one of the university's degrees. The university received 7.5% of the revenues generated by the subsidiary from the courses covered by the agreements. Eventually, the subsidiary was granted status as an "associated college". HMRC issued assessments to VAT concerning the education supplied by the subsidiary. The subsidiary appealed on the basis that it was exempt under the Value Added Tax Act 1994 Sch.9 Pt II Group 6, item 1 as it was an eligible body providing education. It considered that its associated status fell within the meaning of Note 1(b), which described an eligible body as being a UK university and any college of such a university. The tribunal examined the evidence at length, applying the factors cited in *School of Finance and Management (London) Ltd v Customs and Excise Commissioners* [2001] S.T.C. 1690, [2002] C.L.Y. 4740 to decide that the subsidiary, as the UK representative of the media group, was a college of the university. HMRC argued that the tribunal's findings were not supported by the evidence and there was insufficient integration of the subsidiary with the university to fall within the Sch.9 exemption.

Held: Appeal allowed. Where the university was not of a traditional collegiate structure, a flexible approach was required to determine whether the putative college fell within the VAT exemption, *Customs and Excise Commissioners v Leicester University Students Union* [2001] EWCA Civ 1972, [2002] S.T.C. 147, [2002] C.L.Y. 4741 applied. It was necessary to adopt a multi-step evaluation of the relationship between the two bodies. First, the bodies had to have a common understanding of their relationship. Second, that understanding had to be that they were in a relationship of university and college, not some different relationship such as partnership. Third, the relationship had to be sufficiently close that the college was a college "of" the university. Only at that point did the School of Finance and Management factors become relevant, *School of Finance and Management* considered. Fourth, the college had to have similar objectives to those of the university. In the instant case, the tribunal had erred in its approach to the first and second steps, meaning it was appropriate for the instant tribunal to intervene, *Pendragon Plc v Revenue and Customs Commissioners* [2015] UKSC 37, [2015] 1 W.L.R. 2838, [2015] C.L.Y. 2612 and *Fage UK Ltd v Chobani UK Ltd* [2014] EWCA Civ 5, [2014] E.T.M.R. 26, [2014] C.L.Y. 1889 applied. It had not distinguished between the university's relationship with the media group and its relationship with the subsidiary. All of the relevant agreements had been made with the media group, and it was clear that the university did not regard the media group as a college of itself. The media group had a wholly independent existence. Whether the relationship was a partnership or association, there was no element of integration between them. It followed that the subsidiary could not be a college of the university either, given that it carried the same status as the media group. The tribunal had failed to analyse what was meant by the use of the term "associate college". The agreements referred to collaboration between the university and the subsidiary, indicating a relationship similar to partnership between two independent organisations. By contrast, the relationship between a university and a constituent college was not one of partnership. Rather, the university was an umbrella organisation, implying that it and the college had rather different statuses, *University of Leicester* applied. The only realistic conclusion from the evidence was that the university and the subsidiary had a relationship that fell short of constituting the latter a college of the former (see paras 104-111, 115-116, 120-127 of judgment).

SAE EDUCATION LTD v REVENUE AND CUSTOMS COMMISSIONERS *sub nom.* REVENUE AND CUSTOMS COMMISSIONERS v SAE EDUCATION LTD, [2016] UKUT 193 (TCC), [2016] S.T.C. 1837, Judge Colin Bishopp, UT (Tax).

2172 Exempt supplies–Dental services–Whether services provided by dental plan administrator to dentists' patients exempt from VAT

[Directive 2006/112 on the common system of VAT 2006 art.135]

HMRC appealed against a decision of the First-tier Tribunal (*DPAS Ltd v Revenue and Customs Commissioners* [2013] UKFTT 676 (TC), [2014] S.T.I. 385) that the respondent dental plan administrator provided supplies of services to dentists' patients which were exempt from VAT. Until 2012, the agreement to provide dental services under the dental plan was made between the dentists and their patients. The patient would make monthly payments by direct debit which were intended to cover the amount due to the dentist, the cost of insurance and the respondent's costs of managing the plan. The respondent restructured the contractual arrangements of the plans with the intention that it would, from 1 January 2012, make supplies of services to the patients as well as to the dentists. All patients were sent a "DPAC Acceptance Form" authorising the respondent to deduct and retain from the monthly payments a charge for its management and administration services, which included the insurance previously payable. Patients were assured that the level of their monthly payments would not be affected and were told that if they did not sign and return the form, it would be assumed that they agreed to the changes. Roughly 30 per cent of the forms were returned. The First-tier Tribunal made the following findings: since 2012, the respondent made a supply of services to the patients for a consideration; that supply fell within the exemption for transactions concerning payments or transfers in Directive 2006/112 art.135(1)(d); the supply was not excluded from exemption by reason of being "debt collection"; a £10 registration fee which was charged to patients upon entry into the plan was an ancillary part of the exempt supply; the respondent's changes to its contractual arrangements did not amount to an abusive practice.

Held: Appeal allowed in part. (1) The DPAS Acceptance Form provided for an agreement between the respondent and the existing patients who signed and returned the form under which the respondent would provide services to the patients in return for consideration, namely the charges deducted from the monthly payments. The First-tier Tribunal had been right to hold that the respondent made a supply of services to those patients for a consideration. The tribunal had been wrong, however, to make such a finding in relation to the patients who did not sign and return the form: it was not possible to conclude that those patients accepted the new arrangements by silence or conduct (see paras 51, 61 of judgment). (2) In two other cases, references had been made to the Court of Justice of the European Union which might assist the instant tribunal in determining the next two issues, namely the applicability of the exemption under art.135(1)(d) and whether what the respondent did amounted to "debt collection". The final determination of the VAT liability of the supplies made by the respondent to the patients would be reserved until after the CJEU had given its rulings (paras 72, 80). (3) The issue was whether the registration fee was consideration for a separate standard-rated supply of registration services or for an exempt supply of payment services. It was obvious that patients paid the registration fee to join the dental plan primarily in order to obtain dental care and not to obtain payment services from the respondent. The only possible conclusion was that the supply by the respondent in return for the registration fee was separate from the supplies of services made by it in return for the charges that it retained from the monthly payments made by the patients. The supply of registration on the dental plan was therefore chargeable to VAT at the standard rate (paras 84, 86). (4) HMRC had argued that the new arrangements were an abusive practice in that they were contrary to the purpose of Directive 2006/112: the purpose of the Directive generally was that single supplies should not be artificially split into multiple supplies with a view to reducing the overall VAT payable. However, if, as had been found, the respondent made supplies of services to the patients (other than those who did not sign and return the form) both as a matter of contract and in economic and commercial reality, it was impossible to view such transactions as artificial. Nor had the principle of fiscal neutrality been breached. That principle precluded treating similar goods and supplies of services, which were thus in competition with one another, differently for VAT purposes. However, the supplies in question had to be identical or similar from the point of view of the consumer and meet the same needs of the consumer. Here, the supplies of services under the old arrangements were not identical or similar from the point of view of the consumer precisely because the consumers were different. Previously, the only consumers of the services supplied by the respondent were the dentists. From 2012, the respondent supplied services to the dentists and to the patients. Moreover, the point of view of the two consumers was different because they received the services in different capacities, namely as payer and payee (paras 93, 95-96).

DPAS LTD v REVENUE AND CUSTOMS COMMISSIONERS *sub nom.* REVENUE AND CUSTOMS COMMISSIONERS v DPAS LTD, [2015] UKUT 585 (TCC), [2016] S.T.C. 857, Warren J, UT (Tax).

2173 Exempt supplies–Educational institutions–Whether body eligible within Sch.9 Group 6 Note 1(b) Value Added Tax Act 1994–Compliance with Directive 2006/112 art.132

[Value Added Tax Act 1994 (c.23) Sch.9 Group 6; Directive 2006/112 on the common system of VAT 2006 art.132]

The appellant appealed against a decision (*Finance and Business Training Ltd v Revenue and Customs Commissioners* [2013] UKUT 594 (TCC), [2014] S.T.C. 900, [2014] C.L.Y. 3045) that certain educational services it provided were not exempt from VAT under the Value Added Tax Act 1994 Sch.9 Group 6 Item 1. A university had accredited the appellant as a provider of education to a sufficient standard to prepare and examine candidates for its degrees. The First-tier Tribunal had found that although the appellant provided a university education, for its services to fall within the VAT exemption for the supply of university education in Group 6 Note 1(b), it had to show that it was an integrated part of the university. The tribunal considered the factors for ascertaining whether a body claiming exemption as a "college or hall" of a university was sufficiently integrated with the university as set out in *School of Finance and Management (London) Ltd v Customs and Excise Commissioners* [2001] S.T.C. 1690, [2002] C.L.Y. 4740. It found that the appellant did not qualify as the provision of university education was only a minor part of its activities and the relationship between the appellant and the university was not close enough. The Upper Tribunal upheld that decision. The issue was whether, although the appellant was not entitled to the education exemption from VAT in the same way as a university under UK VAT law, it was nevertheless entitled to the exemption under Directive 2006/112 art.132 as a provider of university courses. The appellant contended that domestic legislation was inconsistent with the exemption as interpreted by the CJEU in *Minister Finansow v MDDP sp z oo Akademia Biznesu sp komandytowa (C-319/12)* EU:C:2013:778, [2014] S.T.C. 699. It submitted that, to the extent that it supplied the same service as a university, it should be treated for the purposes of VAT in the same way under the EU principle of fiscal neutrality. It further argued that Group 6 Note 1(b) did not comply with the EU principle of legal certainty because it did not lay down the conditions which an institution had to satisfy to be treated in the same way as a university.

Held: Appeal dismissed. (1) The appellant's submissions proceeded on the basis that Parliament had not set conditions for the education exemption in compliance with EU law. It was now clear from *MDDP* that a Member State could and should set the conditions for bodies which were entitled to the education exemption; how it set those conditions was a matter for national law, *MDDP* applied. Parliament did not have to use any particular form of words to set those conditions, and it was therefore open to it to exercise the UK's option by deciding which bodies were to qualify and then including a list of them in the relevant legislation. That was what Parliament had done in Group 6 Note 1(b). Parliament was obviously constrained by art.132 as to what bodies it could include and had decided to draw the line, in the case of universities, to those colleges, halls and schools which were integrated into universities. For the appellant to show that its exclusion from that group was a breach of the fiscal neutrality principle would require it to show that it belonged to the same class as those institutions which met the integration test in Group 6 Note 1(b). Neither the tribunal nor UT had made any findings that would support that conclusion (see paras 53-56 of judgment). (2) The combination of Group 6 Note 1(b) and the *School of Finance* factors provided the criteria for determining whether a body qualified for the education exemption, *School of Finance* considered. Those factors met the principle of legal certainly since they were neutral, abstract and defined in advance. By applying them, it was possible to know what supplies and which suppliers qualified for exemption. The appellant had failed to show that domestic VAT law did not comply with art.132 or the principles of fiscal neutrality and legal certainty (paras 57, 59).

FINANCE AND BUSINESS TRAINING LTD v REVENUE AND CUSTOMS COMMISSIONERS, [2016] EWCA Civ 7, [2016] 4 W.L.R. 47, Arden LJ, CA (Civ Div).

2174 Exempt supplies–Educational institutions–Whether supplies of restaurant and entertainment services by educational establishment to paying members of public "closely related" to provision of education within art.132(1)(l) Directive 2006/112–Supplies facilitated by students in course of and as essential part of education

[Directive 2006/112 on the common system of VAT 2006 art.132(1)]

The Revenue and Customs Commissioners appealed against a decision of the Upper Tribunal (*Revenue and Customs Commissioners v Brockenhurst College* [2014] UKUT 46 (TCC), [2014] S.T.C. 1332, [2014] C.L.Y. 3042) that supplies of restaurant services and entertainment services provided to paying members of the public by the students at the respondent college were exempt from VAT. The college taught courses in catering and hospitality, and in performing arts. It ran a restaurant in which all functions were undertaken by the catering and hospitality students, in order for them to learn skills in a practical context. Similarly, to enable the performing arts students to gain practical experience, the college staged concerts and performances for the paying public. The issue was whether the college's supplies of restaurant and entertainment services were exempt for VAT purposes pursuant to Directive 2006/112 art.132(1)(i) because they were "closely related" to the provision of education. The First-tier Tribunal held that they were exempt, and the Upper Tribunal dismissed the commissioners' appeal, rejecting their central argument that the exemption required the students to have benefited from the subject matter of the supply rather than from participating in the making of the supply. The parties were in agreement that the instant appeal turned entirely on the resolution of important issues of Community law that could not be described as *acte clair*, and that had not been addressed before in any reported case in a UK court or in the European Court of Justice. Hence they supported a reference to the ECJ for a preliminary ruling.

Held: Question referred to ECJ. In the absence of any direct authority and in light of the commissioners' submissions, the interpretation and application of the exemption in art.132(1)(i) on the instant facts was not *acte clair*. The facts were not unusual so the decision had a potentially wide impact. A reference to the ECJ was appropriate (see para.28 of judgment).

REVENUE AND CUSTOMS COMMISSIONERS v BROCKENHURST COLLEGE, [2015] EWCA Civ 1196, [2016] S.T.C. 2145, Sir Terence Etherton C, CA (Civ Div).

2175 **Exempt supplies–Gaming–"Spot the ball" competitions–Inter-player participation**

[Finance Act 1972 (c.41); Value Added Tax Act 1983 (c.55); Value Added Tax Act 1994 (c.23); Gaming Act 1968 (c.65) s.52(6)]

The appellants (F) appealed against a decision of the Upper Tribunal that "spot the ball" competitions were not games of chance attracting exemption from VAT. F were operators of "spot the ball" competitions. They provided competitors with a picture of a football game but with the ball blanked out. Competitors had to place a cross where he or she thought the ball was and return the coupon to the operator. The competitors' efforts were not compared with the actual location of the ball: a panel of football experts determined the most likely location of the ball. "Spot the ball" was presented to the public as involving skill and judgment and elements of chance. The games were subjected to VAT. F sought to recover VAT paid between 23 April 1979 and 31 December 2006. To fall within the gaming exemption in the Finance Act 1972, the Value Added Tax Act 1983 and the Value Added Tax Act 1994 "spot the ball" had to be a "game of chance" within the Gaming Act 1968: the dispute between the parties was over the word "game" and the words "of chance". The First-tier Tribunal rejected the argument that a "game" required interaction between the players, and held that "spot the ball" was a "game of chance". The Upper Tribunal determined that playing a game involved some sort of engagement with other players, and that accordingly the FTT had erred in law by holding that "spot the ball", where that element was absent, could involve playing a game: it did not need to consider whether "spot the ball" was a game of "chance".

Held: Appeal allowed. (1) There was little dispute that, in general, the question whether a competition was a "game" for the purposes of the 1968 Act was a question of fact, and that "game" was to be given a wide meaning. In respect of the word "game", the three most important authorities were the bingo cases of *DPP v Regional Pool Promotions* [1964] 2 Q.B. 244, [1964] C.L.Y. 1626, *Adcock v Wilson* [1969] 2 A.C. 326, [1968] C.L.Y. 1712 and *Armstrong v DPP* [1965] A.C. 1262, [1965] C.L.Y. 1745. None of them established that there could not be a game unless there was inter-player interaction or that inter-player interaction had normally to exist. It depended on the facts. The cases of *Adcock* and *Armstrong* clearly contemplated that there could be a game without contestants being in communication with each other. Accordingly, the FTT was correct in holding that there was no inter-player interaction rule. It rightly took the view that, apart from the need for a degree of active participation, the authorities only established two matters: what was a game was primarily a question of fact, and there was no need for competitors to be assembled together, *Regional Pool*, *Adcock* and *Armstrong* applied. Its self-direction was correct. There was no requirement that the competitors had to respond to each other's moves. The authorities showed no more than that the relationship between competitors was a relevant factor. The FTT's decision was one drawn from the totality of its findings and there was material in its very detailed analysis of the evidence and findings which entitled it to reach the conclusion it did. In such circumstances, where the correct analysis depended on the facts, there could be no "ordinary" rule, although past cases could help if facts recurred. The FTT made no error of law on the question of what was a "game". Nor did it err in law in its reasoning on s.52(6). There was no distinction in the Act between single-player and multi-player games, and therefore the FTT was entitled to rely on what it saw as a characteristic of a single-player game which also threw light on the meaning of "game" in the context of a multi-player game such as "spot the ball" (see paras 22-23, 29, 38-43, 48, 56 of judgment). (2) In concluding that "spot the ball" was a game "of chance", the FTT was entitled to go beyond the contractual documentation. It applied English domestic legislation, and the dictum of Lord Hailsham in the *News of the World v Friend* [1973] 1 W.L.R. 248, [1973] C.L.Y. 1539, that "in these cases the court will look at the realities of the offer and the competition and will not allow itself to be deceived, whether innocently or otherwise, by delusive appearances or descriptions", which was of general application, *News of the World* applied (paras 10, 65).

REVENUE AND CUSTOMS COMMISSIONERS v IFX INVESTMENT CO LTD *sub nom.* IFX INVESTMENT CO LTD v REVENUE AND CUSTOMS COMMISSIONERS; 'SPOTTING THE BALL' PARTNERSHIP v REVENUE AND CUSTOMS COMMISSIONERS; SPORTECH PLC v REVENUE AND CUSTOMS

COMMISSIONERS, [2016] EWCA Civ 436, [2016] 1 W.L.R. 3952, Arden LJ, CA (Civ Div).

2176 Exempt supplies–Music–VAT status of membership subscriptions paid to charity organising music concerts–Application of philanthropic exemption within Sch.9 Group 9 Item 1(e) Value Added Tax Act 1994–Zero rating

[Value Added Tax Act 1994 (c.23) Sch.9 Group 9]

The appellant society appealed against a refusal of the respondent commissioners to repay output tax in relation to members' subscriptions. The society, a registered charity, claimed a repayment of output tax. Its aim was to promote the study, practice and knowledge of the art of music worldwide by arranging and giving concerts and by other means. Members paid a monthly subscription with various rights and benefits attaching to that membership, namely the right to vote and receive the annual accounts. Other benefits included receiving various publications, priority booking for tickets, membership to another club, and membership to another mailing list. The public were entitled to purchase subscriptions to certain concert series and obtained priority booking rights as a result. The society also took part in various educational and community programmes. The issues were (i) whether the grant of membership was a supply within the scope of VAT; (ii) if there so, whether it was a single supply or multiple supplies; (ii) the extent to which any supplies fell within the philanthropic exemption within the Value Added Tax Act 1994 Sch.9 Group 9 Item 1(e) or fell to be zero rated as supplies of publications.

Held: Appeal allowed. (1) Whenever the nature of a supply was being considered it was necessary to have regard to the economic and commercial reality of the transaction, *Esporta Ltd v Revenue and Customs Commissioners* [2014] EWCA Civ 155, [2014] S.T.C. 1548, [2014] C.L.Y. 3090 applied. Members paid their subscription to receive at least corporate rights and so it followed that there was a supply of corporate rights. The members were not receiving any proprietary interest or right to income in the society and so the supply was within the scope of VAT, *Kretztechnik AG v Finanzamt Linz (C-465/03)* EU:C:2005:320, [2005] 1 W.L.R. 3755, [2005] C.L.Y. 4363 and *KapHag Renditefonds 35 Spreecenter Berlin-Hellersdorf 3 Tranche GbR v Finanzamt Charlottenburg (C-442/01)* EU:C:2003:381, [2005] S.T.C. 1500, [2006] C.L.Y. 4502 considered. If the right to vote and receive copies of accounts fell outside the scope of VAT, the court would have to consider whether the other benefits of membership were incidental to those rights. Whether the additional benefits brought the transaction within the scope of VAT was a question of degree. A service only became taxable where a legal relationship existed between the provider and the recipient to which there was reciprocal performance. Part of the motivation for people becoming members of the society was its charitable nature. However, the court still had to consider the economic and commercial reality of what was supplied in return for the membership, and whether it was characterised by the right to vote or by the additional benefits. Very few members exercised their right to vote, but it was the existence and supply of the right that mattered, not the extent to which it was used. Subscription was paid for the whole bundle of rights and benefits which attached to membership. The additional rights were not de minimis compared to the corporate rights. The additional benefits were not de minimis in terms of their cost to the society or their value to members, neither were they ancillary to the corporate rights. No part of the package of rights, as suggested by the society, could be regarded as predominating over the other. The supply of corporate rights and additional benefits were both within the scope of VAT (see paras 81-89, 91-97, 104 of judgment). (2) There was a single supply of a package of rights and benefits arising from membership. It was an indivisible economic supply and would be artificial to split it. The supply could be described as a supply of membership rights and benefits which included corporate rights. The rights and benefits had changed over the course of the claim, but the court was not satisfied that the nature of the supply had changed over the course of the claim (paras 105-110). (3) There was no statutory definition of "philanthropy", and its meaning as found in the case of *Macduff, Re* [1896] 2 Ch. 451 posed real problems. The court was concerned with the meaning of philanthropy in the context of the Sixth Directive. It had to be given a strict but fair interpretation, *InsuranceWide.com Services Ltd v Revenue and Customs Commissioners* [2010] EWCA Civ 422, [2010] S.T.C. 1572, [2010] C.L.Y.

3480 applied. The setting up of and funding of an orchestra to put on free or subsidised concerts amounted to philanthropy. The society had aims of a philanthropic nature throughout the period of the claim and the supplies made to its members therefore fell within the philanthropic exemption for those periods following the introduction of that exemption (paras 126-130).

HALLE CONCERTS SOCIETY v REVENUE AND CUSTOMS COMMISSIONERS, [2016] UKFTT 294 (TC), [2016] S.F.T.D. 650, Judge Jonathan Cannan, FTT (Tax).

2177 Exempt supplies–Political activities–Whether membership subscriptions to not-for-profit political club exempt from VAT–Application of political activities exemption in art.132(1)(l) Directive 2006/112 and Sch.9 Pt II Group 9 Item1(e) Value Added Tax Act 1994

[Directive 2006/112 on the common system of VAT 2006 art.132(1)(l); Value Added Tax Act 1994 (c.23) Sch.9 Pt II Group 9; Tribunals, Courts and Enforcement Act 2007 (c.15); European Communities Act 1972 (c.68)]

A not-for-profit political club sought repayment of output tax on the basis that its membership fees were exempt from VAT. The club's rules stated that its aims were to carry on the business of a club and, in so doing, to promote the principles of Conservatism and the implementation of Conservative Party policies. Members received the right to attend the premises and use the leisure and sports facilities, and the opportunity to support and participate in political events and campaigning. The club argued that (1) its membership subscriptions, or an element of them, were exempt from VAT under the political activities exemption contained in Directive 2006/112 art.132(1)(l) and the Value Added Tax Act 1994 Sch.9 Pt II Group 9 Item 1(e); (2) alternatively, it could rely on Extra Statutory Concession 3.35 in relation to the 30% of its subscription income which was referable to its political aims.

Held: Appeal dismissed. (1) The club's main aim had to be political in order for services provided in return for the membership subscription to come within the exemption. Although the motive for the establishment of the club was political, in that it was intended as a local focal point for recruiting and organising members of the Conservative Party, the most significant of its activities during the period in question was providing social amenities to its members. A single supply of services in return for a membership subscription was not exempt merely because one of the club's aims had the requisite political character, *Institute of the Motor Industry v Customs and Excise Commissioners (C-149/97)* EU:C:1998:536, [1998] S.T.C. 1219, [1998] C.L.Y. 4901 and *United Grand Lodge of England v Revenue and Customs Commissioners* [2014] UKFTT 164 (TC), [2014] S.T.I. 953 applied. The services supplied had also to be referable to the body's political aims and objectives. Otherwise, any supplies made by a body with political aims would be exempt, even if the supplies were nothing to do with the political aims, *British Association of Leisure Parks, Piers and Attractions Ltd v Revenue and Customs Commissioners* [2013] UKUT 130 (TCC), [2013] S.T.C. 1410, [2013] C.L.Y. 3195 applied. The club's political motives in making the supplies were not relevant. What was relevant was the nature of the supplies actually made and whether they were mainly referable to political aims, *BLP Group Plc v Customs and Excise Commissioners (C-4/94)* EU:C:1995:107, [1996] 1 W.L.R. 174, [1995] C.L.Y. 5059 applied. The membership benefits constituted a single supply comprising multiple elements. A single fee was paid and it was not possible to be entitled to one benefit without being entitled to them all. It was also clear that the leisure and political activities provided by the club were inextricably linked, *Levob Verzekeringen BV v Staatssecretaris van Financien (C-41/04)* EU:C:2005:649, [2006] S.T.C. 766, [2006] C.L.Y. 4501 applied. The emphasis of the club was social rather than political and the political benefits to the members were not the main aim of the club. It was not possible to say that the membership subscriptions were for services mainly referable to the club's political aims. The subscriptions were paid more for the social services provided. The supply made in return for the membership subscriptions was therefore not within art.132(1)(l) or Sch.9 Group 9 Item 1(e) (see paras 26, 33, 35, 38, 41, 43, 46, 67-68, 75-76 of judgment). (2) The tribunal had to apply the law and the concession was not part of the law. The club could only rely on it to the extent it gave rise to legitimate expectations under public law, and then only in a court or tribunal permitted to take public law considerations into account. The effect of the decision in *Trustees of the BT*

Pension Scheme v Revenue and Customs Commissioners [2015] EWCA Civ 713, [2016] S.T.C. 66, [2015] C.L.Y. 2516 was that the instant tribunal did not have jurisdiction to consider matters of public law. That decision was based on an interpretation of the Tribunals, Courts and Enforcement Act 2007, which conferred jurisdiction on the tribunal in both direct and indirect tax matters. There was no reason to distinguish the instant case from *BT Pension Scheme* merely because it concerned indirect rather than direct taxes. The only material difference between VAT cases and others was that the European Communities Act 1972 had to a great extent subordinated domestic VAT law to EU VAT law. That was what the Court of Appeal had in mind in *BT Pension Scheme* when it refused to consider whether *Oxfam v Revenue and Customs Commissioners* [2009] EWHC 3078 (Ch), [2010] S.T.C. 686, [2010] C.L.Y. 3488 had been wrongly decided. It had recognised that the 2007 Act had to be read in a way consistent with the 1972 Act and that might mean that if EU law would, in a particular context, give effect to legitimate expectations of taxpayers in a VAT context, then the Act might have to be read as giving the instant tribunal jurisdiction to give effect to them. In the instant case, however, the concession was inconsistent with the Directive and the club could not rely on any legitimate expectation arising from the concession, *Oxfam* not applied, *BT Pension Scheme* applied (paras 83, 91-93, 95-96). (3) (Obiter) The concession was intended to apply wherever an element of a single composite supply would, if supplied separately, be exempt. In the instant case, if an element of the single supply referable to the club's political aims was supplied separately, it would be exempt. A proportion of the subscription would therefore be entitled to exemption under the concession (para.111).

SHANKLIN CONSERVATIVE AND UNIONIST CLUB v REVENUE AND CUSTOMS COMMISSIONERS, [2016] UKFTT 135 (TC), [2016] S.F.T.D. 513, Judge Barbara Mosedale, FTT (Tax).

2178 Exempt supplies–Sale of property–Sale of property by trustee of self-invested pension plan–Exercise of option to tax

[Value Added Tax Act 1994 (c.23) Sch.10 Pt 1 para.30, Sch.10 para.3, Sch.10 para.3(1)(a), Sch.10 para.3(6), Sch.10 para.3(9)]

The appellants appealed against a decision of the First-tier Tribunal (*Hills v Revenue and Customs Commissioners* [2014] UKFTT 646 (TC), [2014] S.T.I. 2600) that the sale of a property to them by the trustee of a self-invested pension plan was chargeable to VAT. The trustee had bought the property on 30 March 2004. On 31 March, it granted a lease on the property and charged VAT on the rental payments from that date. Six years later, it notified HMRC that it had opted to tax the property with effect from 30 March 2004. HMRC formally accepted the trustee's late notification. In December 2011, the trustee sold the property to the appellants who used it to run their dental practice. HMRC stated that the sale was chargeable to VAT. The appellants appealed. One of the issues before the tribunal was whether the option to tax had been validly exercised given that the trustee had not sought HMRC's permission before exercising it, as required by the Value Added Tax Act 1994 Sch.10 para.3(9). HMRC issued a notice stating that if prior permission had been required, then it had exercised its discretion under Sch.10 Pt 1 para.30 to dispense with the requirement. The tribunal accepted HMRC's case and found that prior permission had not been required. The appellants argued that (1) HMRC's prior permission had been required in accordance with para.3(9); (2) HMRC's purported dispensation sought to change the effects of an invalid election to opt to tax, which infringed the principle of legal certainty, and it also infringed the principle of legitimate expectation.

Held: Appeal dismissed. (1) The day on which an election to opt to tax had effect in para.3(9) was a reference back to the earlier sub-paragraphs of para.3, in particular para.3(1)(a) and (6). The purpose of para.3(9) was that it should apply to exempt supplies made or intended to be made before the election took effect and that exempt supplies after that time would be dealt with under the usual partial exemption rules. In the instant case, the day on which the election to opt to tax was intended to have effect was 30 March 2004. Therefore, para.3(9) only required prior permission of HMRC in respect of exempt supplies before that date. The grant of the lease took place the following day on 31 March. It followed, therefore, that the prior permission issue had to be decided in favour of HMRC (see paras 54-55 of judgment). (2) The dispensation issued by HMRC did not offend against principles of legal certainty as para.30 was already in existence when the appellants bought the property. Furthermore, HMRC gave no assurance to the appellants that the sale of the property to them would be anything other than a taxable transaction. Therefore, the principle of legitimate expectation could not assist them (paras 69-72).

HILLS v REVENUE AND CUSTOMS COMMISSIONERS, [2016] UKUT 189 (TCC), [2016] B.V.C. 513, Judge Greg Sinfield , UT (Tax).

2179 Fraudulent evasion of VAT–Dishonesty–Failure to conduct VAT affairs in a satisfactory manner–Whether taxpayer acted dishonestly to evade VAT–Civil standard of proof

[Value Added Tax Act 1994 (c.23) s.60]

KENDRICKS PLANNING LTD v REVENUE AND CUSTOMS COMMISSIONERS; KENDRICK v REVENUE AND CUSTOMS COMMISSIONERS, [2014] UKFTT 767 (TC), [2014] S.T.I. 2737, Judge Malcolm Gammie QC, FTT (Tax).

2180 Fraudulent evasion of VAT–Missing trader fraud–Standard of proof

A trader appealed against a decision that it could not deduct input tax that it had incurred in 21 transactions because it had known, or should have known, that the transactions were connected with missing trader fraud and with the fraudulent evasion of VAT. The trader had been one of six companies involved in back-to-back buying and selling of mobile phones. The First-tier Tribunal dismissed the trader's appeal. It found that most of the companies involved would not have had the resources to buy the phones without immediately receiving the money from their subsequent buyers. That synchronisation of funding, along with other factors, led the tribunal to conclude that the trader had actual knowledge of the connection with fraud; it was therefore unnecessary to determine whether the trader had constructive knowledge. The trader submitted that (1) the tribunal had concluded on the balance of probabilities that it had known of the fraud whereas, applying *Unipetrol as v European Commission (T-45/07)* EU:T:2011:359, [2011] 5 C.M.L.R. 26, the tribunal needed to have had a firm conviction that it had known; (2) the finding of actual knowledge was perverse, as the evidence was incapable of supporting that finding.

Held: Appeal dismissed. (1) Entitlement to the right to deduct input tax would be denied where it was ascertained that the taxable person knew or should have known that, by his purchase, he was participating in a transaction connected with fraudulent evasion of VAT, *Kittel v Belgium (C-439/04)* EU:C:2006:446, [2008] S.T.C. 1537, [2008] C.L.Y. 4052 applied. The standard of proof to be satisfied by Customs in relation to *Kittel* knowledge was the civil standard of the balance of probabilities, *Mobilx Ltd (In Administration) v Revenue and Customs Commissioners* [2009] EWHC 133 (Ch), [2009] S.T.C. 1107, [2009] C.L.Y. 4062 applied. Therefore, although in the instant case there had been no issue before the tribunal about the standard of proof, if it was assumed that the tribunal had applied the civil standard, it had been correct to do so. The trader's argument that EU law required its own, different standard to be applied in such a case was misconceived. Whilst it was true that the *Kittel* criteria were creatures of EU law, that was very far from saying that when national courts assessed whether those criteria were established as a matter of fact, they had to apply an EU standard of proof. The well-established principle of procedural autonomy meant that, in the absence of a direction from the Court of Justice of the European Union, or other binding EU rule, national procedural and evidential rules were normally applicable when national courts were enforcing EU rights and obligations, *Rewe Zentralfinanz eG v Landwirtschaftskammer fur das Saarland (33/76)* EU:C:1976:188, [1976] E.C.R. 1989, [1977] C.L.Y. 1248, *Courage Ltd v Crehan (C-453/99)* EU:C:2001:465, [2002] Q.B. 507, [2001] C.L.Y. 783 and *Bulicke v Deutsche Buro Service GmbH (C-246/09)* EU:C:2010:418, [2010] E.C.R. I-6999 applied and *Unipetrol* distinguished (see paras 22, 28, 38-40, 43 of judgment). (2) There had been objective evidence before the tribunal on the basis of which it had been clearly entitled to reach the conclusion that the trader knew that the transactions were connected with the fraudulent evasion of VAT. That conclusion was not perverse (para.68).

EXCEL RTI SOLUTIONS LTD v REVENUE AND CUSTOMS COMMISSIONERS, [2015] UKUT 552 (TCC), [2015] B.V.C. 532, Barling J, UT (Tax).

2181 Input tax–Basic Payment Scheme–Whether purchase by farming company of Single Farm Payment Entitlement units referable to company's business–Repayment of VAT paid when purchasing units

HMRC appealed against a decision that the purchase by the respondent farming company of Single Farm Payment Entitlement units was referable to the company's business, with the result that the company was entitled to a repayment of the VAT paid when purchasing the units. Single Farm Payments were agricultural subsidies paid to holders of Single Farm Payment Entitlements. The company had purchased around £7.7 million entitlements, intending to use the income generated by them to settle its overdraft and diversify its business. It was charged VAT on the purchase. The entitlement units yielded payments of £1.7 million in 2011 and £2.4 million in 2012, which the company held in cash in its bank account. It claimed repayment of the VAT, but HMRC refused. The First-tier Tribunal held that the company's intentions were critical. Having found that there was evidence of exploratory work into wind farm development and preparation for the construction of new farm buildings, it concluded that the use of the capital, and the services connected with raising it, could not be linked to any specific output transactions, but were attributable to the company's economic activity as a whole. HMRC submitted that no right of deduction arose because the company's acquisition and retention of the units had been carried out solely for the purpose of obtaining the Single Farm Payments, rather than for the purpose of a taxable transaction, and that such a use was a non-economic activity outside the scope of VAT. It submitted in the alternative that the tribunal had been wrong to find that there was a direct and immediate link between the cost of acquiring the units and the company's taxable economic activity.

Held: Appeal dismissed. (1) The case fell within the principle established in *Abbey National Plc v Customs and Excise Commissioners (C-408/98)* EU:C:2001:110, [2001] 1 W.L.R. 769, [2001] C.L.Y. 5586 and *Kretztechnik AG v Finanzamt Linz (C-465/03)* EU:C:2005:320, [2005] 1 W.L.R. 3755, [2005] C.L.Y. 4363, *Abbey National* and *Kretztechnik* followed, *Securenta Gottinger Immobilienanlagen und Vermogensmanagement AG v Finanzamt Gottingen (C-437/06)* EU:C:2008:166, [2008] S.T.C. 3473, [2009] C.L.Y. 4058 and *University of Southampton v Revenue and Customs Commissioners* [2006] EWHC 528 (Ch), [2006] S.T.C. 1389, [2006] C.L.Y. 4471 distinguished. There had been ample evidence on which the tribunal could find that the financing opportunity afforded by purchasing the units was not an end in itself, but formed part of the company's economic activity. It had been entitled to find that the purchase did not form a distinct business activity but was a wholly integrated feature of the farming enterprise. The key element in *Abbey National* and *Kretztechnik* was that the respective operations were found to have been carried out for the benefit of the taxpayer's economic activity in general. By contrast, the costs in respect of which input tax was incurred in *Securenta* were attributable to economic and non-economic activities carried out simultaneously, and the costs in *University of Southampton* had not been expended for the university's general economic activity but for the benefit of a separate activity which did not form part of its VAT business. It was fundamental to the VAT system that the right to deduct arose immediately upon the incurring of the charge to tax, and that it could be exercised in respect of goods and services *intended to be used* in connection with taxable transactions, *Belgium v Ghent Coal Terminal NV (C37/95)* EU:C:1998:1, [1998] S.T.C. 260, [1998] C.L.Y. 4918 applied (see paras 19-20 of judgment). (2) In establishing whether there was a direct and immediate link between the cost of the units and the company's taxable business supplies, the starting point was to determine whether the cost in respect of which the input tax was charged was incurred for the purposes of its economic activity in general. If it was, then on the analysis following *Abbey National* and *Kretztechnik,* it must be part of the company's overheads and was to be considered a cost component of the company's products. The necessary direct and immediate link was therefore established, *Volkswagen Financial Services (UK) Ltd v Revenue and Customs Commissioners* [2015] EWCA Civ 832, [2016] S.T.C. 417, [2015] C.L.Y. 2584 applied (paras 21-22).

FRANK A SMART AND SON LTD v REVENUE AND CUSTOMS COMMISSIONERS *sub nom.* REVENUE AND CUSTOMS COMMISSIONERS v FRANK A SMART AND SONS LTD, [2016] UKUT 121 (TCC), [2016] S.T.C. 1956, Lord Tyre, UT (Tax).

2182 Input tax–Exempt supplies–HMRC wrongly treating standard-rated supplies as exempt–Entitlement to input tax recovery–Absence of VAT invoices

[Directive 2006/112 on the common system of VAT 2006 art.168, art.180; Value Added Tax Act 1994 (c.23) s.19(2)]

A business customer appealed against a decision that it was not entitled to claim input tax recovery on supplies that had wrongly been treated as exempt from VAT. The customer used the supplier's services to send mail orders and distribute advertisements. Both the supplier and HMRC believed that the postal supplies made were exempt from VAT. No output tax was paid by the supplier. The contract between the customer and the supplier was silent as to VAT, and the relevant invoices indicated that the supplies were exempt from VAT. However, the Court of Justice of the European Union subsequently ruled, in *TNT Post UK Ltd v Revenue and Customs Commissioners (C-357/07)* EU:C:2009:248, [2009] S.T.C. 1438, [2009] C.L.Y. 4109, that the postal exemption was limited and that postal services were not exempt if they were individually negotiated, which the instant services were. The customer therefore claimed for recovery of input tax and HMRC rejected its claim. The customer argued that (1) VAT on the relevant supplies was "due or paid" within the meaning of Directive 2006/112 art.168 because under the Value Added Tax Act 1994 s.19(2), the terms of the contract were irrelevant and what was actually paid under a standard-rated contract must have comprised an element of VAT; (2) HMRC was obliged to exercise its discretion under art.180 of the Directive to admit other evidence of a charge to VAT, and had to overlook the absence of VAT invoices from the supplier.

Held: Appeal dismissed. The words "due or paid" in art.168 referred to VAT due from or paid by the customer, to the supplier, *PPUH Stehcemp sp j Florian Stefanek, Janina Stefanek, Jaroslaw Stefanek v Dyrektor Izby Skarbowej w Lodzi (C-277/14)* EU:C:2015:719, [2015] B.V.C. 48 and *TNT* applied. The customer did not have to show that what it paid to the supplier expressly included an element of VAT. Section 19(2) of the Act was general in its application and related to the supply to the customer as well as the supply by the supplier. None of the authorities dealt with the situation where the supplier had not actually paid VAT to the tax authority. On the present state of the authorities it was unlikely that the contract was determinative of whether or not VAT was included in the price and whether a person who had not borne the economic burden of VAT was entitled to be regarded as receiving supplies subject to VAT "due or paid" within the meaning of art.168(a), *Tulica v Agentia Nationala de Administrare Fiscala - Directia Generala de Solutionare a Contestatiilor (C-249/12)* EU:C:2013:722, [2013] B.V.C. 547, *Simpson & Marwick v Revenue and Customs Commissioners* [2013] CSIH 29, [2013] S.T.C. 2275, [2014] C.L.Y. 3809 and *T-Mobile Austria GmbH v Austria (C-284/04)* EU:C:2007:381, [2008] S.T.C. 184, [2008] C.L.Y. 4055 considered. However, if input tax was to be deducted, the supplier was required to issue a VAT invoice to the customer including the amount of VAT charged. As the customer held no VAT invoices, it had no right to input tax deduction under art.178, *Petroma Transports SA v Belgium (C-271/12)* EU:C:2013:297, [2013] S.T.C. 1466 and *Terra Baubedarf-Handel GmbH v Finanzamt Osterholz-Scharmbeck (C152/02)* EU:C:2004:268, [2005] S.T.C. 525, [2005] C.L.Y. 4365 applied (see paras 25, 43-44, 56-58 of judgment). (2) The question of the economic burden of VAT was relevant when HMRC was considering whether or not to exercise its discretion to allow input tax recovery in circumstances where no VAT invoice was held. It was correct to consider the reason why a VAT invoice was not held. The reason was that the supply was treated as exempt and the appellant did not pay any amount representing VAT. The decision not to accept other evidence in lieu of a VAT invoice could not be impugned (paras 66-69).

ZIPVIT LTD v REVENUE AND CUSTOMS COMMISSIONERS, [2016] UKUT 294 (TCC), [2016] S.T.C. 1782, Proudman J, UT (Tax).

2183 Input tax–Missing trader fraud–Trader seeking VAT repayment in connection with large-scale purchase of razor blades–Knowledge

HMRC appealed against a decision of the Upper Tribunal (*Davis & Dann Ltd v Revenue and Customs Commissioners* [2013] UKUT 374 (TCC), [2014] S.T.C. 39, [2013] C.L.Y. 3213) that the respondent taxpayers were entitled to a repayment of input tax paid on their purchases of razor blades. The sole issue was whether the taxpayers ought to have known that their purchases were connected with the fraudulent evasion of VAT. The taxpayers traded in "fast-moving consumer goods" in the grey market. In 2003, HMRC had warned them about missing trader fraud, particularly in connection with razor blades, telling them what to look out for and making them aware that large back-to-back deals involving export to Europe required particular care. Three years later, a wholesaler made an unsolicited approach to the taxpayers, offering to sell a large quantity of a particular brand of razor blade on very generous credit terms. At the same time, a Spanish buyer offered to buy the same quantity of razor blades from the taxpayers. A credit check revealed that the wholesaler had been trading for less than a year, was not an authorised distributor of the razor blades and had not previously traded in toiletries. The taxpayers bought the razor blades, sold them to the Spanish buyer and sought repayment of over £8 million in input tax. HMRC refused. Before the First-tier Tribunal, it was common ground that the transactions were connected to a VAT fraud perpetrated by an "upstream" buyer. However, no fraud was alleged against the wholesaler or the Spanish buyer. The FTT held that, on the totality of the evidence, the taxpayers ought to have known that the only reasonable explanation for the transactions was that they were connected with VAT fraud. The UT disagreed, holding that in the context of the taxpayers' business in the grey market, the transactions could be seen as ordinary market transactions. The issues were whether the UT (1) should have looked at the totality of the evidence, including that relating to the wholesaler and the Spanish buyer; (2) had properly considered the implications of HMRC's warnings about missing trader fraud; (3) had been right to hold that the transactions had been concluded in the normal course of business; (4) had exceeded its appellate function by dealing with questions of fact.

Held: Appeal allowed. (1) The UT had over-compartmentalised the factors to be taken into consideration. It had viewed the abnormally large repayment position as merely a consequence of the transactions, when in fact it was capable of supporting knowledge to the requisite standard. In that respect, it had erred in law. Moreover, just because no fraud was alleged against the wholesaler and Spanish buyer, that did not mean that the circumstances surrounding them could not be taken into account. Tribunals could rely on any circumstance capable of being probative of knowledge (see paras 60- 65 of judgment). (2) The fact that the taxpayers had prior knowledge of the risks of missing trader fraud was something to be taken into account when assessing what a reasonable person ought to have concluded about the transactions. However, the UT had not considered the implications of HMRC's warnings and had missed the point: all the characteristics of which the taxpayers had been warned were present in the transactions at issue. That was an error of law. It could not be argued that the warnings did not apply because the wholesaler and Spanish buyer were not alleged to have been involved in the fraud. Such warnings applied to acquisition fraud as well as to carousel fraud (paras 66-70). (3) The course of the taxpayers' business was relevant to the question of whether the transactions were ordinary market transactions. Findings capable of rebutting knowledge on the part of the taxpayers had to be findings about what was in the normal course of business among grey market traders, and what was in the normal course of the taxpayers' business. Relying on the taxpayers' prior knowledge, the unusually high repayment position, the warning signs surrounding the wholesaler, the coincidence of the approaches by the wholesaler and the Spanish buyer, and the extraordinary quantity and value of the razor blades, the FTT had found that the transactions were not in the ordinary course of the taxpayers' business. Its findings of primary fact had not been challenged. The UT's conclusion that the taxpayers had conducted the transactions on the same terms as they ordinarily conducted their business was unsupported by any evidence. As a matter of commercial common sense, it was inherently improbable that the wholesaler's extended credit terms were in the ordinary course of business. In those circumstances, the burden of adducing evidence to show that the transactions were normal market transactions moved to the taxpayers, and they had adduced no such evidence (paras 82- 94). (4) The UT was restricted to determining points of law, and its task was to decide whether the facts found by the FTT justified the finding that the taxpayers had had the requisite knowledge of fraud. That involved a categorisation of the facts, which constituted a question of law. The FTT had been entitled to evaluate the facts in the way it did, and the UT had erred in setting that evaluation aside. The findings of the FTT would therefore stand (paras 95-101, 106).

DAVIS & DANN LTD v REVENUE AND CUSTOMS COMMISSIONERS, [2016] EWCA Civ 142, [2016] S.T.C. 1236, Arden LJ, CA (Civ Div).

2184 Input tax–Newspapers–Newspaper publisher's provision of free vouchers redeemable at certain retailers–Whether publisher entitled to deduct input tax on the supply

[Value Added Tax (Supply of Services) Order 1993 (SI 1993/1507) art.3; Value Added Tax Act 1994 (c.23) Sch.10A para.4; Directive 2006/112 on the common system of VAT 2006 art.168(a)]

The commissioners appealed against a First-tier Tribunal decision that a newspaper publisher's provision of free vouchers redeemable at certain retailers was not a supply of services and so no output VAT was due. The commissioners also appealed against the tribunal's subsequent decision that the publisher was entitled to deduct any input VAT that had arisen on its purchase of the vouchers from both the retailers and intermediaries. As part of a promotional scheme designed to enhance the sales circulation of its newspapers, the publisher bought retailer vouchers from popular retailers. The vouchers were issued by the retailers directly to the publisher, and at a discount to their face value. The publisher would give a free voucher to customers who took its titles for a requisite period of time. A second promotional scheme was managed by an intermediary, from which the publisher purchased some of the vouchers at cost; it bought other vouchers directly from the retailers. In its first decision, the tribunal concluded that the provision of vouchers was not a supply of services in the course or furtherance of the publisher's business, for the purposes of the Value Added Tax (Supply of Services) Order 1993 art.3, and it was accordingly not subject to a liability to account for output VAT in that respect. In its second decision, the tribunal concluded that the publisher could recover the input tax it had incurred when it purchased the vouchers. The commissioners submitted that (1) the publisher was not entitled to deduct input tax on its purchases (a) from the retailer or intermediary because the input tax was directly and immediately attributable to the provision of the vouchers by the publisher free of charge, which was therefore outside the scope of VAT or (b) directly from the retailer because, under the Value Added Tax Act 1994 Sch.10A para.4(2), the consideration would be disregarded and so there was no input tax on that supply; (2) under art.3 of the Order, the publisher's provision of the free vouchers to its customers was to be treated as a supply in the course or furtherance of its business, so there would be a charge to output VAT on the publisher on its deemed supply of an amount equal to the input VAT which it would be entitled to deduct.

Held: Appeals allowed in part. (1)(a) A taxable person might have a right to deduct input tax where there was a direct and immediate link between a particular input transaction and a particular output transaction or transactions giving rise to entitlement to deduct, *Investrand BV v Staatssecretaris van Financien (C-435/05)* EU:C:2007:87, [2008] S.T.C. 518, [2008] C.L.Y. 4037 applied. In the instant case, the vouchers were acquired for the purpose of the business promotion scheme to increase newspaper circulation and to facilitate the associated sales of advertising. It was to that element of the publisher's economic activity which the acquisition of the vouchers and any input tax attributable to that acquisition was directly and immediately linked. No such link could be established with the provision of the vouchers by the publisher to its customers for no consideration, and the immediate use of the vouchers acquired by the publisher in providing those vouchers to its customers free of charge could not affect the direct and immediate link with its economic activity. The costs associated with the acquisition of the vouchers were cost components of the sales of the newspapers and of advertising, and thus cost components of transactions within the scope of the publisher's taxable activities. The output supplies by the publisher in that respect were taxable supplies, and input tax was accordingly, in principle, deductible (see paras 45,

73-74 of judgment). (b) Under Directive 2006/112 art.168(a), the right to deduct could arise only with respect to VAT due or paid in respect of supplies to the taxable person of goods or services. The fact, therefore, that the consideration paid by the publisher for the acquisition of the voucher included an amount that, on redemption, would satisfy the VAT element of the price for the goods or services supplied to the customer redeeming the voucher did not render the publisher the consumer of the relevant supply. The consumer of that supply was the customer to whom the publisher had provided the voucher. The supply to the publisher was the supply of the voucher on which, by virtue of Sch.10A para.4(2), no VAT was chargeable at all (para.88). (c) Accordingly, the publisher would be able to recover input tax on its acquisition of vouchers from an intermediary, but not on its acquisition from the retailer (para.92). (2) The tribunal made no error of law in determining that the publisher's provision of the vouchers was for strictly business-related purposes and accordingly was not deemed to be a supply of services in the course or furtherance of its business pursuant to art.3 of the 1993 Order. In consequence, no obligation to account for output tax arose (para.138).

ASSOCIATED NEWSPAPERS LTD v REVENUE AND CUSTOMS COMMISSIONERS *sub nom.* REVENUE AND CUSTOMS COMMISSIONERS v ASSOCIATED NEWSPAPERS LTD, [2015] UKUT 641 (TCC), [2016] S.T.C. 1143, David Richards LJ, UT (Tax).

2185 Input tax–Supply of services–Recovery of input tax in relation to fees paid to accountants by company in financial difficulties–Tripartite contract between accountants, company and institutions to which company indebted

The appellant company appealed against a decision (*Airtours Holiday Transport Ltd (formerly My Travel Group) v Revenue and Customs Commissioners* [2014] EWCA Civ 1033, [2015] S.T.C. 61, [2014] C.L.Y. 3061) that it was not entitled to recover input tax in respect of services supplied by a firm of accountants (P). The appellant had faced a financial crisis that threatened the continuation of its business. It was indebted to banks and other institutions. In order to facilitate a refinancing package, those institutions invited a number of accountancy firms to submit proposals for carrying out advisory work. P was engaged pursuant to a contract contained in a letter of engagement. The contract was a tripartite contract between the appellant, P and the institutions. P invoiced the appellant in respect of its fees for work carried out under the engagement letter, and payment was duly made by the appellant to P. The appellant sought to deduct the VAT thereon as input tax in its VAT return for the relevant periods. However, HMRC maintained that P's services had not been supplied to the appellant but rather to the institutions, with the result that the appellant was not entitled to deduct the VAT on P's fees as input tax. The issues were (1) whether P had a contractual obligation to the appellant to provide the relevant services to the institutions (if it did, the appellant would have the right to recover input tax); (2) if not, whether there was nonetheless a supply of services to the appellant.

Held: Appeal dismissed. (Lords Clarke and Carnwath dissenting) (1) P did not have a contractual obligation to the appellant to provide the relevant services to the institutions. P's commitment to provide the services as described in the contract was a contractual commitment to the "Engaging Institutions", not to the appellant. It was significant, among other things, that the letter of engagement was addressed "To the Engaging Institutions", not to the appellant. It was also stated that it was those institutions which had retained P and that any reports were "for the sole use of [those] institutions" which had countersigned. It was also said that P's report was to be provided to the institutions; the appellant was merely to be provided with a copy, and that copy could be redacted (see paras 23-25 of judgment). (2) There was no supply of services to the appellant. The domestic authorities and those of the European Court of Justice made it clear that where the person who paid the supplier was not entitled under the contractual documentation to receive any services from the supplier, then, unless the documentation did not reflect the economic reality, the payer would have no right to reclaim by way of input tax the VAT in respect of the payment to the supplier. On that analysis, the appellant's case failed. The contract did reflect the economic reality and was not in any way an artificial arrangement. It was true that the appellant benefited from the contract, but the benefit was not so much the services from P but the enhanced possibility of funding from the institutions for its restructuring. And it was to improve the prospects of refinancing that it was prepared to pay for the provision of P's report (paras 50-51). (3) (Per Lord Clarke) The judgment of the majority gave too little attention to the legal relationship between P and the appellant and to the economic realities of that relationship. Treating the institutions as the only entities supplied with P's services was much too narrow a view. The appellant was at least as much a beneficiary of those services as were the institutions. The appellant's right to have P carry out the work in question provided real additional value to it in its struggle for financial survival. The presentation to the institutions, which were considering the withdrawal of credit facilities, of the appellant's own figures, without review or validation by an independent third party such as P, would have been highly unlikely to have satisfied those institutions (paras 61, 66, 77).

AIRTOURS HOLIDAY TRANSPORT LTD (FORMERLY MY TRAVEL GROUP) v REVENUE AND CUSTOMS COMMISSIONERS *sub nom.* AIRTOURS HOLIDAYS TRANSPORT LTD v REVENUE AND CUSTOMS COMMISSIONERS; REVENUE AND CUSTOMS COMMISSIONERS v AIRTOURS HOLIDAY TRANSPORT LTD, [2016] UKSC 21, [2016] 4 W.L.R. 87, Lord Neuberger PSC, SC.

2186 Input tax–Supply of services–Scheme to avoid irrecoverable input tax on supplies of advertising services to loan broking business–Liability for VAT–Supply of services to Jersey company not United Kingdom business

[Directive 77/388 on turnover taxes - Common system of value added tax: uniform basis of assessment 1977]

The commissioners appealed against a decision of the First-tier Tribunal (*Newey (t/a Ocean Finance) v Revenue and Customs Commissioners* [2010] UKFTT 183 (TC), [2010] B.V.C. 2311, [2010] C.L.Y. 3515) that an offshore scheme to recover otherwise irrecoverable input tax was not an abuse of Directive 77/388. The respondent (N) had traded in the UK as a loan broker under the name "Ocean Finance". Because the business was making only exempt supplies it was not registered for VAT, and therefore expended irrecoverable input tax on advertising that it purchased. N therefore created a Jersey company (Alabaster), to which he transferred the business. Alabaster traded under the Ocean Finance name. It used UK-based lenders, and all the loan processing work was carried out in the UK by N as its sub-contractor. It advertised in the UK media, purchasing the supplies of advertising in Jersey. N claimed that it was Alabaster, and not he, who was making and receiving supplies of services. The commissioners considered that the scheme was abusive because it did not accord with economic and commercial reality; its essential aim was to obtain a tax advantage; and it resulted in avoidance of irrecoverable input tax. The tribunal disagreed, holding that although the aim of the scheme was to gain a tax advantage, there was no abuse because it was not contrary to the purposes of the Directive. The commissioners appealed, and the Upper Tribunal referred six questions to the Court of Justice. The CJ gave judgment in June 2013 (*Revenue and Customs Commissioners v Newey (t/a Ocean Finance) (C-653/11)* EU:C:2013:409, [2013] S.T.C. 2432, [2013] C.L.Y. 3231). The commissioners submitted that the CJ had given new guidance on the approach to abuse, namely that the court was to assess the economic and commercial reality of the transactions, with the contractual arrangements being merely one factor to be taken into account. They argued that the tribunal had erred by assigning undue weight to the contractual structure over the economic reality. N argued that the CJ was simply restating existing principles, which the tribunal had applied correctly.

Held: Appeal dismissed. (1) The CJ's judgment applied the established jurisprudence to a new factual situation and provided some further guidance, but did not depart from the principles in *Halifax Plc v Customs and Excise Commissioners (C-255/02)* [2006] Ch. 387, [2006] C.L.Y. 4467, *Halifax* and *Newey* followed. Unlike the tribunal, the CJ had not addressed the abuse issue separately from the characterisation of the supplies and the circumstances in which it would be appropriate to depart from the contractual position. It was not saying that in all cases where the contractual terms did not wholly reflect the economic and commercial reality of the transactions, abuse was established or it was appropriate to depart from the contractual arrangements in identifying the supplier and the recipient (see paras 49-55 of judgment). (2) It would only be permissible to depart from the contractual position in the instant case if the contractual arrangements were wholly artificial, set up with the sole aim of obtaining a tax advantage. In order to depart from the contractual provisions, the arrangements had to be abusive. Even if that analysis was wrong, the tribunal had still been entitled to find that the supplies had been made by and to Alabaster. None of the transactions constituted abusive conduct and there could therefore be no redefinition of the contractual arrangements. Since the structure within which the parties operated was not an abuse, it governed the supplies and established who had made and received them for VAT purposes (paras 213- 216). (3) Two points emerged from the CJ judgment. The first was the description of abuse as including a case in which the contractual terms constituted purely artificial arrangements which did not correspond with the economic and commercial reality of the transactions. The second was that, in principle, there could be abuse even if the abusive transactions had not simply been inserted into an existing structure, but a completely new structure had been adopted. The fact that Alabaster traded on its own account did not necessarily mean that, for VAT purposes, supplies to and by it could not be treated as having been made by and to N. That was so even if the structure was not a sham. In order to establish abuse, there had to be a tax advantage. However, it was not right to compare a structure that a trader had adopted in the past with the one adopted at present and to conclude that, if the latter was more favourable for VAT purposes than the former, then it must be contrary to the purposes of the Directive. In considering the first element of the *Halifax* test, the existing arrangements had to be viewed on their own merits, without comparison with previous arrangements. The question was whether the structure gave rise to abuse in the context of the overall factual matrix; not whether the change in structure resulted in a tax advantage as compared with the pre-existing structure. Whether the scheme comprised wholly artificial arrangements and had been set up with the sole aim of obtaining a tax advantage had to be answered by reference to the same objective criteria as applied in *Halifax*. There was no abuse in the instant case simply because there was a supply in the UK of loan broking services to UK lenders who made loans to UK borrowers following introductions arising as result of advertising in UK media. The Alabaster arrangements did not comprise wholly artificial arrangements which did not reflect economic and commercial reality. Nor could the scheme be said to result in the accrual of a tax advantage contrary to the purposes of the Directive (paras 217-244).

NEWEY (T/A OCEAN FINANCE) v REVENUE AND CUSTOMS COMMISSIONERS *sub nom.* REVENUE AND CUSTOMS COMMISSIONERS v NEWEY (T/A OCEAN FINANCE), [2015] UKUT 300 (TCC), [2015] S.T.C. 2419, Warren J, UT (Tax).

2187 Input tax–Taxable supplies–Services provided gratuitously–Intention to make taxable supplies–Whether consideration given

[Value Added Tax Act 1994 (c.23) s.5(2); Directive 2006/112 on the common system of VAT 2006 art.2(1); Value Added Tax Regulations 1995 (SI 1995/2518) reg.90]

A company appealed against a decision that it had not made taxable supplies to its subsidiaries in the relevant VAT accounting periods and was therefore not entitled to recover input tax. The company had operating subsidiaries which carried out mining operations. In its application to register for VAT, the company's intended business activity was described as the re-charging of running costs to the subsidiaries in the form of a management charge. Contrary to its original intention, the company did not charge management fees to the subsidiaries. However, it sought to recover input tax. HMRC took the view that the company was in reality an investment company. The judge held that the company was actively engaged in managing its subsidiaries and that the services it provided to them were in principle capable of amounting to a taxable supply. However, it found that there was a "rather vague intention" to levy unspecified charges and no common understanding of what was payable. Accordingly, it held that the services were not being made for consideration for the purposes of the Value Added Tax Act 1994 s.5(2) and Directive 2006/112 art.2(1) and the company was not engaged in an economic activity during the relevant period. For that reason, it concluded that there was no entitlement to recover input tax. The company submitted that the judge had not been entitled, on the evidence, to make the findings that he did, and that an intention that payment should be made in respect of supplies was enough to establish consideration. It also relied on the provisions of the Value Added Tax Regulations 1995 reg.90.

Held: Appeal dismissed. (1) For a supply to amount to "consideration" within art.2(1) of the Directive, there had to be a direct link between the services provided by the supplier and the payment made by its customers, so that the remuneration received by the supplier constituted the value given by the customer in return for the services, *Lebara Ltd v Revenue and Customs Commissioners (C-520/10)* EU:C:2012:264, [2012] S.T.C. 1536 followed. The term "economic activity" was very wide and had to be interpreted objectively. The receipt of a payment did not in itself mean that a given activity was economic in nature, *Commission of the European Communities v Finland (C-246/08)* EU:C:2009:671, [2009] E.C.R. I-10605 followed (see paras 41-43, 51-52, 124 of judgment). (2) The judge had been entitled to find that there was no agreement about payment other than what he described as a "vague intention", although he accepted that there was a genuine intention at the relevant time that fees would be payable. Since he had been entitled to make the findings of fact which he did, it was not open to the company to argue that the evidence did not support the findings, *Edwards (Inspector of Taxes) v Bairstow* [1956] A.C. 14, [1955] C.L.Y. 417 considered (paras 113-114, 117). (3) Where a taxpayer relied on an intention to make future taxable supplies on the basis of reg.90 concerning services which were "separately and successively applied", it would need to be shown that the future continuous supplies would be for a consideration which was determined or payable periodically, *Esporta Ltd v Revenue and Customs Commissioners* [2014] EWCA Civ 155, [2014] S.T.C. 1548, [2014] C.L.Y. 3090 followed. In the instant case, however, the supplies were made gratuitously. It could not be argued that supplies were made for consideration simply because there had, at an earlier stage, been an intention to do so. Moreover, an intention merely to make supplies was not a sufficient basis on which to recover input tax. What had to be established was an intention to make taxable supplies, namely supplies for a consideration. However, even if it was correct to say that there was an intention, before any services were provided, that they would be made for payment, and even if it was correct that an intention to make payment for those services continued into the future, that was not enough to demonstrate either an intention to make taxable supplies, or that the services provided were in fact taxable supplies. In either case, the link required by EU law had to be established. Having evaluated the evidence, the judge did not consider that, at the time when the input tax was incurred, there was a direct and immediate link between the supplies and intended supplies on the one hand, and any payment in respect of those supplies on the other. An appellate court should be slow to interfere with the fact-finding tribunal's multi-factorial evaluation. On the facts found by the judge, it could not be said that the intended payment would be full cost recovery; thus, the company was unable to establish either that consideration was given for the services actually provided during the relevant period, or that there was an intention to make taxable supplies in the future (paras 109, 118-120, 123, 126, 128, 130-131, 133-137).

NORSEMAN GOLD PLC v REVENUE AND CUSTOMS COMMISSIONERS, [2016] UKUT 69 (TCC), [2016] S.T.C. 1276, Warren J, UT (Tax).

2188 Missing trader fraud–Admissibility–Whether judge justified in striking out evidence

[Value Added Tax Regulations 1995 (SI 1995/2518) reg.14(1)]

The appellant commissioners appealed against a decision of a judge to strike out certain evidence which they had sought to introduce in appeals brought by the respondent company. The appeals concerned a decision of the commissioners that six invoices were invalid in that they failed to satisfy the requirements of the Value Added Tax Regulations 1995 reg.14(1). The invoices related on their face to certain phones. The commissioners' case was that the phones in question had not actually been manufactured when the goods were ostensibly bought and sold. They alleged that the respondent had not acted in good faith and that it had failed to take every reasonable step to ensure that its supplies did not lead to participation in tax evasion. However, no particulars of such allegations were provided. The commissioners had sought to adduce evidence that various officers of one of the respondent's suppliers had been found guilty of cheating the revenue. They also sought to adduce evidence that implied fraud on the respondent's part.

Held: Appeal dismissed. The judge had been justified in striking out the evidence in question. The fact of conviction counted for nothing in this case. The commissioners were proceeding on the basis that the burden of proof in the appeals was on the respondent. That was not so. In accordance with established principles, if it was alleged that there was wrongdoing or a failure to take reasonable care, the burden was on the party alleging that. The case was in an unsatisfactory state. It involved what were undoubtedly missing trader frauds, but the evidence did not implicate the respondent. The commissioners should set out the basis of their case against the respondent. Thus they should provide full particulars of every fact or matter relied on for the allegation that the respondent did not act in good faith. If they were going to allege fraud, they had to give full particulars of fraud to the like extent; an allegation of bad faith was tantamount to an allegation of fraud on established authority. Further, they had to give full particulars of every fact or matter relied on for the allegation that the respondent did not take every reasonable step to ensure that its supplies did not lead to its participation in tax evasion (see paras 9, 15, 24, 28, 35, 37 of judgment).

REVENUE AND CUSTOMS COMMISSIONERS v INFINITY DISTRIBUTION LTD (IN ADMINISTRATION), [2015] UKUT 219 (TCC), [2015] S.T.C. 2374, Peter Smith J, UT (Tax).

2189 Output tax–Repayments–Amendment of claim for repayment of output tax–Change of basis of groundsof claim constituted new claim

[Value Added Tax Act 1994 (c.23) s.80, s.80(1), s.80(2); Value Added Tax Regulations 1995 (SI 1995/2518) reg.37]

HMRC appealed against a First-tier Tribunal's decision to allow a company to rely on new grounds in its VAT repayment claim. The company had written to HMRC stating that it had incorrectly accounted for output tax and claiming a VAT repayment. The letter detailed the reasons for, and calculation of, the claim, which related to a loyalty card scheme. HMRC rejected the claim and the company appealed. While the appeal was pending, the company made further repayment claims for the same tax periods. Those claims were based on accounting errors that had nothing to do with the loyalty card scheme. Moreover, they were out of time. The company then sought to amend the grounds of its loyalty card claim so as to encompass the grounds on which the new claims were based. Although those grounds gave rise to a higher value claim, the company did not seek to increase the amount originally claimed. In a preliminary ruling, the tribunal held that nothing in the Value Added Tax Act 1994 s.80 prevented the reasons for a claim being amended or changed. It concluded that the company could rely on the new grounds to justify its original claim provided that it confined itself to the original amount. HMRC contended that, given that the reasons and method of calculation were materially different, the company was aiming to advance a completely new claim that would ordinarily have been out of time.

Held: Appeal allowed. In determining whether the amended grounds were permissible, the starting point was to identify the elements of a claim. The focus of s.80(1) was an amount of output tax that had been brought into account but was not due, together with the supplies relevant to that amount. A claim under s.80(2) was not simply for a sum of money in abstract; it related to particular transactions in respect of which output tax had been accounted for. It was not possible for the taxpayer to rely on that claim as including a claim related to entirely different transactions. Therefore, the company's later claims could not be subsumed into its original loyalty card claim (see paras 47-52 of judgment). If that conclusion by reference to s.80 alone was wrong, it was necessary to consider the interaction of s.80 with the Value Added Tax Regulations 1995 reg.37. From that interaction, it was clear that a claim was not identified by its amount alone; the method of calculation was equally important and both elements defined a claim's character. Applying *Reed Employment Ltd v Revenue and Customs Commissioners* [2013] UKUT 109 (TCC), [2013] S.T.C. 1286, [2013] C.L.Y. 3220, a claim could be amended as long as its fundamental character was unchanged. Errors and omissions could be corrected provided that the correction did not enlarge the scope of the claim by adding elements that were not contemplated when it was originally made. In the instant case, the company wished to change the entire basis of its claim. That was not a permissible course and amounted to an attempt to circumvent the time limit imposed on s.80 claims, *Reed Employment* applied. The tribunal's decision would therefore be set aside (paras 53-57, 61-64 of judgment).

VODAFONE GROUP SERVICES LTD v REVENUE AND CUSTOMS COMMISSIONERS *sub nom.* REVENUE AND CUSTOMS COMMISSIONERS v VODAFONE GROUP SERVICES LTD, [2016] UKUT 89 (TCC), [2016] S.T.C. 1064, Warren J, UT (Tax).

2190 Output tax–Repayments–Overall amount claimed relating to several prescribed accounting periods–Quantification of claims

[Value Added Tax Act 1994 (c.23) s.80, s.80(1), s.80(2), s.80(4ZA), s.80(6); Value Added Tax Regulations 1995 (SI 1995/2518) reg.37]

A company appealed against a decision of the First-tier Tribunal (*Bratt Auto Services Ltd v Revenue and Customs Commissioners* [2014] UKFTT 676 (TC), [2014] S.F.T.D. 1120, [2014] C.L.Y. 3076) which had the effect of dismissing in part its VAT repayment claim while a second, associated, company appealed against the tribunal's decision that its repayment claim should be dismissed. HMRC appealed against the partial success of the first company's claim. The companies were in the car rental and leasing business. They had written to HMRC on the penultimate day of the time limit for making a claim to say that they wanted to recover output tax that they had incorrectly accounted for concerning two aspects of the car industry. Their claims were based on *Argos Distributors Ltd v Customs and Excise Commissioners (C-288/94)* EU:C:1996:398, [1997] Q.B. 499, [1996] C.L.Y. 5909 and *Commission of the European Communities v Italy (C-45/95)* EU:C:1997:315, [1997] S.T.C. 1062, [1997] C.L.Y. 4988, which had prompted many such actions for VAT repayments. The letter set out the first company's *Elida Gibbs*-based claim, claiming a repayment of £1,293,750 for the year ended 1989 as a whole and enclosing its accounts for that year. It indicated its intention to claim for other relevant years but offered no amounts or accounts for those. The second company did not quantify its *Elida Gibbs* claim and had no supporting documents. Neither company quantified or supplied supporting documents for their *Italy* claims. The letter indicated that further information could be provided later. HMRC rejected all the claims, deciding that the letter provided insufficient detail to satisfy the Value Added Tax Act 1994 s.80 and the Value Added Tax Regulations 1995 reg.37. The First-tier Tribunal judge concluded that the first company's *Elida Gibbs* claim was valid as the letter had stated the amount claimed and method of calculation and was supported by documentary evidence. He dismissed the other claims for lack of detail. The companies argued that as the *Elida Gibbs* and *Italy* cases were well-known bases for VAT repayment claims, the letter should be deemed sufficient and a purposive approach should be used to give them the chance to gather full details, albeit outside the time limit. HMRC argued that the first company's *Elida Gibbs* claim was invalid because it had claimed a global amount for 1989 instead of an amount for each prescribed accounting period for that year as required by s.80(1).

Held: Companies' appeals dismissed, HMRC's appeal allowed. (1) Taken together, s.80(2), s.80(6) and reg.37 meant that a claim could only be treated as a claim if it satisfied the requirements of form and manner that were prescribed. Compliance with reg.37 was mandatory and there was no room within it for a claim to be made without the specification of an amount or the method of calculation on the basis that they would be provided later, *Nathaniel & Co Solicitors v Revenue and Customs Commissioners* [2010] UKFTT 472 (TC) and *R. (on the application of Building Societies Ombudsman Co Ltd) v Customs and Excise Commissioners* [2000] S.T.C. 892, [2000] C.L.Y. 5318 applied. The companies' submission as to a purposive interpretation of the legislation did not change that conclusion. An effective remedy had been available to them but they had failed to exercise it within the time limit. Therefore, the letter had not constituted an *Elida Gibbs* claim for the second company or an *Italy* claim for either company, *Elida Gibbs* and *Italy* cited (see paras 37-39 of judgment). (2) HMRC was right to point out that s.80(1) was directed at an amount of VAT for a single prescribed accounting period. The provision in s.80(2) for a claim for repayment of "an amount under this section" had to be the same "amount" as was mentioned in s.80(1). It was possible to make claims relating to several prescribed accounting periods, *Reed Employment Ltd v Revenue and Customs Commissioners* [2013] UKUT 109 (TCC),

[2013] S.T.C. 1286, [2013] C.L.Y. 3220 applied. However, the taxpayer had to comply with s.80(6) and reg.37 in respect of each period. Therefore, where an overall claim related to several prescribed accounting periods, the taxpayer had to make a separate claim for each, identifying the period, the amount of repayment sought and its method of calculation. Such separation was required to determine whether the time limit for making a claim had passed under s.80(4ZA). Consequently, the global amount put forward for the first company's *Elida Gibbs* claim had not constituted a claim under s.80 (paras 41-43).

BRATT AUTO SERVICES LTD v REVENUE AND CUSTOMS COMMISSIONERS *sub nom.* REVENUE AND CUSTOMS COMMISSIONERS v BRATT AUTO CONTRACTS LTD, [2016] UKUT 90 (TCC), [2016] S.T.C. 1463, Warren J, UT (Tax).

2191 Overdeclarations–Limitations–National time limit on repayment of VAT–Proportionality of three-year cap–Compliance with EU principles

A local authority appealed against a decision (*Leeds City Council v Revenue and Customs Commissioners* [2013] UKUT 596 (TCC), [2014] S.T.C. 789, [2014] C.L.Y. 3077) upholding HMRC's restriction on the repayment of overpaid VAT to only that accounted for before 4 December 1996. HMRC's decision was based on the Value Added Tax Act 1994 s.80(4), in force from 4 December 1996, which had imposed a three-year limitation period for the making of claims for the repayment of wrongly paid VAT together with the Finance Act 2008 s.121, which had disapplied that limitation period in respect of VAT paid before 4 December 1996, provided that a claim had been made by 1 April 2009. Under Directive 77/388 art.4.5, which had not been transposed into domestic law but was directly effective, the local authority was not taxable for certain activities where it was acting as a public authority. It had sought repayment of output tax it had paid in error. The local authority relied on the EU law principles of effectiveness, equivalence, certainty and legitimate expectation to argue that the domestic limitation period was invalid and submitted that the Upper Tribunal had been wrong to distinguish the ECJ decision in *Banca Antoniana Popolare Veneta SpA v Ministero dell'Economia e delle Finanze (C-427/10)* EU:C:2011:844, [2012] S.T.C. 526. It submitted that there were special factors involved, namely: (i) that the UK had not implemented art.4.5; (ii) art:4.5 was very difficult both to understand and to apply; (ii) HMRC's published position at the time had not only been wrong in law, but had led a reasonably attentive trader astray because it had failed to mention art.4.5, instead focussing on whether the supply had been made for a consideration and whether it had been made in the course of business; (iv) when the claims had been made the limitation period was, for all practical purposes unknown and unknowable.

Held: Appeal dismissed. The real issue was whether the local authority had been given a readily ascertainable prospective opportunity of a reasonable length in which to bring its claims. If so, in the absence of special factors, none of the applicable principles of EU law had been breached. As the live claims all related to VAT in accounting periods after 4 December 1996, those claims had never had a longer limitation period than the three years allowed, therefore, there had not been a retrospective alteration of the limitation period *Fleming (t/a Bodycraft) v Customs and Excise Commissioners* [2008] UKHL 2, [2008] 1 W.L.R. 195, [2008] C.L.Y. 4016 followed (see paras 26-28 of judgment). It was therefore necessary to establish if there had been any special factors involved: (1) The fact that a Member State had not properly transposed a Directive did not preclude the taxing authorities from relying on a limitation period against a person asserting a directly effective EU right, *Fantask A/S v Industriministeriet (Erhvervsministeriet) (C188/95)* EU:C:1997:580, [1997] E.C.R. I-6783, [1998] C.L.Y. 655 applied. (2) The fact that a piece of European legislation was difficult to understand or apply could not justify an extension of the limitation period. (3) There was no rule of EU law which required a limitation period to be deferred until the existence of a right to recover the payment had been judicially established. It was not uncommon for a claim to repayment to have become time-barred in domestic law while proceedings were still in progress to determine whether the member state was in breach of EU law.(4) The argument depended on an erroneous first instance decision in *Scottish Equitable Plc v Revenue and Customs Commissioners* [2006] B.V.C. 2515, [2006] C.L.Y. 4442 which had been flatly contradicted by *Fleming* and had itself been overturned by consent in the Inner House, *Scottish Equitable* overruled (paras 41-45).

With regard to the case of *Banca Antoniana*, there the bank had been specifically disadvantaged by a disparity in limitation periods, whereas in the instant case the local authority's claims had always been subject to a prospective three-year limitation period. Further, when it had made the supplies, the local authority had fully expected to pay the VAT because of the way HMRC had interpreted the law at the time, so there had been no breach of legitimate expectation. Any changes to HMRC's position had been progressively favourable to the local authority, whereas in *Banca Antoniana* the change had increased the bank's economic burdens, *Banca Antoniana* distinguished (paras 35-39). Whether there had been an infringement of the principles of effectiveness and equivalence was a question of fact for determination by the domestic court. Those questions had been determined by a specialist tax tribunal whose reasoning had subsequently been confirmed by the binding decision in *Littlewoods Retail Ltd v Revenue and Customs Commissioners* [2015] EWCA Civ 515, [2016] Ch. 373, [2015] C.L.Y. 2613, *Littllewoods* followed (paras 47, 50-51).

LEEDS CITY COUNCIL v REVENUE AND CUSTOMS COMMISSIONERS, [2015] EWCA Civ 1293, [2016] S.T.C. 2256, Lewison LJ, CA (Civ Div).

2192 Repayments–Time limits–Claim for repayment outside time limit in s.80(4) Value Added Tax Act 1994–Proper interpretation of s.80–Reliance on reg.38 Value Added Tax Regulations 1995

[Value Added Tax Act 1994 (c.23) s.80, s.80(4); Directive 77/388 on turnover taxes - Common system of value added tax: uniform basis of assessment 1977 art.11:(C)(1); Value Added Tax (Accounting and Records) Regulations 1989 (SI 1989/2248) reg.7; Value Added Tax Regulations 1995 (SI 1995/2518) reg.38; Finance Act 1989 (c.26) s.24]

The commissioners appealed against a decision of the First-tier Tribunal upholding the respondent's claim for a repayment of overpaid VAT made outside the statutory period provided for in the Value Added Tax Act 1994 s.80(4). The respondent charged and accounted for VAT on its sales of commercial vehicles. Between 1 January 1978 and 31 December 1989 (the claim period), it paid rebates to purchasers of the vehicles. Directive 77/388 art.11(C)(1), which was in force throughout the claim period, provided that where the price of a supply was reduced after the supply had taken place, the value of the supply had to be reduced accordingly under conditions laid down by the Member State concerned. In 2011, the respondent claimed a repayment of VAT charged on vehicles sold to reflect the rebates given during the claim period. HMRC rejected the claim on the basis that it had been made outside the four-year time limit specified in s.80(4). The tribunal allowed the respondent's appeal, holding that the claim was not subject to the statutory time limit or otherwise time-barred. Article 11C(1) was implemented in the UK on 1 January 1990, when the Value Added Tax (Accounting and Records) Regulations 1989 reg.7 came into effect; it was subsequently replaced by the Value Added Tax Regulations 1995 reg.38. The Finance Act 1989 s.24 also came into force on 1 January 1990 and provided that persons who had overpaid VAT could claim a repayment, subject to a six-year time limit from the date of overpayment. Section 24 became s.80 of the 1994 Act on consolidation. It was common ground that art.11C(1) had direct effect, notwithstanding the absence of implementing legislation. It was also undisputed that reg.38 only allowed adjustments in relation to rebates paid after January 1990. Following the decision in *Fleming (t/a Bodycraft) v Customs and Excise Commissioners* [2008] UKHL 2, [2008] 1 W.L.R. 195, [2008] C.L.Y. 4016, a transitional period was introduced disapplying the time limit to claims for overpaid VAT in accounting periods ending before 4 December 1996, provided that the claim was made before 1 April 2009 (the *Fleming* window). The respondent's position was that, until it made its claim to assert its directly effective rights, there was no relevant "claim" for the purposes of s.80 of the 1994 Act; therefore, time did not start to run until that claim was made. The commissioners argued that the tribunal had erred in holding s.80 of the 1994 Act inapplicable and in seeking to interpret reg.38 so as to give effect to any reduction pursuant to art.11C(1).

Held: Appeal allowed. (1) There was no scope for the application of reg.38 in the case of a price reduction before 1 January 1990; therefore, that provision had no direct application to the reductions made in the claim period. However, there was no difficulty in interpreting s.80 in such a way as to give effect to the directly effective rights of a taxpayer under art.11C(1) in relation to matters occurring before 1 January 1990 and, in particular, reductions in taxable amounts taking place before that date. Moreover, art.11C(1) was sufficiently clear, unconditional and precise to give rise to directly effective rights. Therefore, unless and until domestic legislation provided otherwise, that provision gave rise to a reduction in the taxable amount at the time when the price reduction took place. It followed that the respondent should have made its claims by the end of the *Fleming* window at the very latest, *Fleming* followed (see paras 17, 42-43, 51, 66, 72-73 of judgment). (2) The structure of reg.38 included its own inherent time limit and there was no scope for late implementation of that provision. Reading s.80 and reg.38 together, the respondent was precluded from using reg.38 at any time in the future. Instead, applying the *Marleasing* principle, s.80 had to be interpreted so as to reflect the respondent's directly effective rights. Thus, s.80 applied on the basis that the reduction in the taxable amount and the consequent overpayment of VAT arose on the occasion of each price reduction (paras 76-77, 103). (3) Prior to 1 January 1990, there was no legislation which could have been interpreted in accordance with the *Marleasing* principle to give effect to the respondent's directly effective rights. Nonetheless, if the respondent had sought to enforce those rights before 1 January 1990, the English courts would have had to find a way to give effect to them. It was likely that the right to receive payment would have been treated as a claim in restitution with a limitation period of six years from the accrual of the cause of action (paras 79, 86). (4) The respondent's cause of action against HMRC arose when its right to assert its directly enforceable rights arose: the commencement of the running of time was not postponed to the time when the directly effective rights were first asserted, *Revenue and Customs Commissioners v British Telecommunications Plc* [2014] EWCA Civ 433, [2014] S.T.C. 1926, [2014] C.L.Y. 3038 followed. All of the respondent's claims based on price reductions occurring before 1 January 1984, being six years before the coming into force of s.24 of the 1989 Act, were time-barred by 1 January 1990. Section 24 and reg.7 of the 1989 Regulations did not have the effect of reviving such claims. Accordingly, the overpaid VAT ceased to be due for repayment as the result of the expiry of the limitation period and there was no amount recoverable under s.80 (paras 88, 93-95).

IVECO LTD v REVENUE AND CUSTOMS COMMISSIONERS *sub nom.* REVENUE AND CUSTOMS COMMISSIONERS v IVECO LTD, [2016] UKUT 263 (TCC), [2016] S.T.C. 1754, Warren J, UT (Tax).

2193 Self-supply–Cars–Supply of cars by car manufacturer to itself

[Value Added Tax Act 1983 (c.55) Sch.4 para.7; Value Added Tax Act 1994 (c.23) Sch.6 para.6(2)]

The commissioners appealed against a decision (*General Motors UK Ltd v Revenue and Customs Commissioners* [2013] UKFTT 443 (TC), [2013] S.T.I. 3166) that a car manufacturer had overpaid VAT when it supplied its cars to itself between 1987 and 1996. Directive 77/388 art.11A(1) provided that the taxable amount of a self-supply would be the purchase price of the goods or of similar goods or, in the absence of a purchase price, the cost price, determined as at the time of supply. That provision was transposed incorrectly by the Value Added Tax Act 1983 Sch.4 para.7, which stated that the taxable amount was the cost price. However, an amendment in 1992 rectified the provision, which was afterwards consolidated in the Value Added Tax Act 1994 Sch.6 para.6(2). For the purpose of calculation, the commissioners and the industry had accepted that the cost price was two-thirds of the list price. After the decision in *Commission of the European Communities v Italy (C-45/95)* EU:C:1997:315, [1997] S.T.C. 1062, [1997] C.L.Y. 4988, it was recognised that the subsequent sale of self-supplied cars was in fact exempt from VAT as a result of art.13B(c) of the Directive. The manufacturer in the instant case therefore claimed repayment of the VAT it had overpaid in relation to self-supplies of cars from 1987 until 1996, arguing that the self-supply charge should have been calculated by reference to the cost of the cars used and that that cost was less than the two-thirds proxy. The commissioners rejected the claim and the manufacturer appealed. The tribunal held that, with regard to the part of the claim relating to 1992-1996, following the amendment of Sch.4 para.7, the VAT due on the self-supplies was to be calculated according to the purchase price for which the manufacturer could have purchased the cars from a third party. Although that notional purchase price for UK-manufactured cars was no lower than the proxy price on which the manufacturer had accounted for VAT, an alternative measure of the purchase price was the import price of UK-manufactured cars where they could be purchased from a sister company. As that import price was less than two-thirds of the UK list price, the manufacturer's claim succeeded in respect of such cars. As to the part of the claim relating to 1987-1992, when the cost price was agreed to be an available alternative measure of the deemed consideration for the self-supplies, the tribunal held that the cost of the UK-manufactured cars was less than two-thirds of their list price. The commissioners argued that (1) the price of imported vehicles could not be relied on as an alternative measure of the price of UK-manufactured cars in 1992-1996; (2) the tribunal had erred in its approach to determining cost price for 1987-1992 because it had misconceived its role as having been to provide a solution rather than to determine whether the manufacturer's claim had been proved on the balance of probabilities; (3) the tribunal erred in accepting a model-based approach to the question of the cost of manufacturing cars in the UK during the claim period as it did not conform to the minimum requirements for justification and validation accepted by experts in the field of econometrics and so the methodology had insufficient probative value to found findings to the civil standard of proof.

Held: Appeal dismissed. (1) There was nothing in the relevant post-1992 legislation which prevented the purchase price of identical imported goods from being used as a measure of the consideration for the self-supply of the UK-manufactured vehicles (see para.44 of judgment). (2) Although the tribunal had had to be satisfied that the manufacturer had overpaid VAT between 1987 and 1992, as a step in the reasoning which might lead it to that conclusion, it had had to consider and evaluate the methodology for ascertaining the ratio of the cost of production of the cars to their list price. The tribunal had stated that its duty was to determine, or at least to set out the principles for determining, how much tax, if any, was likely to have been overpaid. There had thus been no misdirection of law. Accordingly, the tribunal's general approach to its task had involved no fault (paras 67, 78-80). (3) The exercise which the tribunal had had to perform was essentially a unitary one. It did not first have to decide whether the econometric evidence met a particular qualitative threshold, but rather had to assess it together with all the other evidence before delivering its answer on a balance of probabilities. Its overriding duty was to ascertain, if it properly could, the true amount of VAT due during the claim period, drawing for that purpose on its own experience and expertise as well as the evidence presented to it. If the performance of that duty involved an element of subjectivity, that meant no more in the present context than that the tribunal had to bring its own skill and judgment to bear on the problem, and it was not bound by the standards of evaluation which would apply if the same question arose in an academic context. The tribunal had discharged its duty carefully and conscientiously, and with a full awareness of the potential weakness of the data which underlay the model (para.142).

REVENUE AND CUSTOMS COMMISSIONERS v GENERAL MOTORS (UK) LTD, [2015] UKUT 605 (TCC), [2016] S.T.C. 985, Henderson J, UT (Tax).

2194 Supply of goods–Zero rating–Supply of kit for caravan

[Value Added Tax Act 1994 (c.23) Sch.8 Pt II Group 9]

SCANDINAVIAN LOG CABINS DIRECT LTD v REVENUE AND CUSTOMS COMMISSIONERS, [2016] UKFTT 563 (TC), [2016] S.T.I. 2326, Judge Jane Bailey, FTT (Tax).

2195 Supply of services–Vehicle leasing–Whether vehicle finance lease agreements constituted supply of goods or services for VAT purposes–Interpretation and application of art.14(2)(b) Directive 2006/112

[Directive 2006/112 on the common system of VAT 2006 art.14(2)]

HMRC appealed against a decision (*Mercedes-Benz Financial Services UK Ltd v Revenue and Customs Commissioners* [2014] UKUT 200 (TCC), [2014] S.T.C. 2558, [2014] C.L.Y. 3086) that a vehicle finance lease agreement with an option to purchase at the end of the contract constituted a supply of services for VAT purposes, as opposed to a supply of goods, under Directive 2006/112 art.14(2)(b). The respondent financial services company entered into "Agility" hire purchase contracts with its customers for the supply of motor vehicles. It was one of three financial products provided by the company, the other two being "hire purchase" and "leasing" contracts. Under a leasing contract there was no option to purchase at the end of the term, and it was not disputed that such contracts constituted a supply of services. Under the hire purchase contracts, the customer had paid the vehicle price and the credit amount by the end of the term and such contracts constituted a supply of goods. The Agility contract differed from the hire purchase contract in that the monthly payments were calculated by reference to the difference between the purchase price and its anticipated residual value at the end of the term plus interest, which meant that a substantial amount of the original purchase price would remain unpaid. The company argued that the Agility contracts were to be treated as a supply of services for VAT purposes; HMRC issued a VAT assessment on the basis that the contracts constituted a supply of goods. The First-tier Tribunal agreed with HMRC. The Upper Tribunal concluded that art.14(2)(b) required an economic analysis of the transaction. It held that the reference to ownership of goods passing "in the normal course of events" meant that art.14(2)(b) was not concerned with every contract under which there was a possibility of ownership passing, but only with those contracts where that could be described as "the normal outcome". It declined to refer the question of the interpretation of art.14(2)(b) to the European Court of Justice. HMRC contended that the UT had erred in adopting the test of economic purpose in *Customs and Excise Commissioners v Mirror Group Plc (C-409/98)* EU:C:2001:524, [2002] Q.B. 546, [2001] C.L.Y. 5602 as the correct principle to be applied in relation to the meaning and effect of art.14(2)(b).

Held: Questions referred to ECJ. The appeal tribunal's conclusion was a possible interpretation of "in the normal course of events", but it posed difficulties in defining how it was to be accommodated within the established principles of construction. Those principles required determination at the date of the contract of whether the supply was one of goods or services and the exclusion of consideration of the customer's subjective intent in opting for that method of financing. As recognised by the appeal tribunal, the test of economic reality, if it was to be workable, needed to be able to identify which types of hire contract with an option to purchase constituted a supply of goods simply on an objective assessment of the contract at the date when it was made, and without reference to any available evidence as to the percentage of Agility customers who chose to exercise the option to purchase. The focus, therefore, had to be on the provisions of the contract itself when determining whether ownership would pass "in the normal course of events". That raised the difficulty, identified by HMRC, that the Agility contract did not specify whether the option was likely to be exercised. The appeal tribunal had wrongly declined to refer the question to the ECJ. The issue was not so clear as to not require argument. Although art.14(2)(b) was directed to what the relevant contract of hire provided, there was much less certainty regarding whether the qualifying phrase "in the normal course of events" required a tax authority to do no more than to identify the existence of an option which was not exercisable later on payment of the final instalment, or to go further and determine the economic purpose of the contract in accordance with the test outlined in *Mirror Group*, *Mirror Group* considered. Guidance was required from the ECJ as to whether that was the appropriate test to adopt and, if not, further guidance regarding the correct interpretation and application of art.14(2)(b). The questions to be included in the reference would be agreed following further liaison with the parties (see paras 11-15, 26-28 of judgment).

MERCEDES-BENZ FINANCIAL SERVICES UK LTD v REVENUE AND CUSTOMS COMMISSIONERS *sub nom.* REVENUE AND CUSTOMS COMMISSIONERS v MERCEDES-BENZ FINANCIAL SERVICES UK LTD, [2015] EWCA Civ 1211, [2016] 2 All E.R. 163, Sir Terence Etherton C, CA (Civ Div).

2196 Supply of services–Zero rating–Substantial demolition of property–Supplies made by building contractor in course of construction of residential property incorporating remaining part of façade of original building–Whether supplies zero rated

[Value Added Tax Act 1994 (c.23) Sch.8 Group 5, Sch.8 Pt II Group 5]

A building contractor appealed against a decision of the First-tier Tribunal (*Boxmoor Construction Ltd v Revenue and Customs Commissioners* [2014] UKFTT 833 (TC), [2014] S.T.I. 2770) that supplies it had made whilst carrying out works on a residential property were not zero-rated within the Value Added Tax Act 1994 Sch.8 Group 5 Item 2. Planning consent had been obtained for alterations and extensions at the property. The works involved the demolition of the whole of the original house, except for a projecting bay on the front facade. The contractor then built a new property on the site which incorporated the projecting bay. The contractor considered that it had made supplies in the course of the construction of a building designed as a dwelling in accordance with Item 2, and treated those supplies as zero-rated. HMRC, however, concluded that the supplies were chargeable to VAT at the standard rate because the original house had not been completely demolished to ground level. The contractor appealed on the ground that the original house had ceased to be an existing building because it met the condition in Note 18(b) to Group 5 of Sch.8, namely that the retention of the projecting bay was a condition or requirement of planning consent or similar permission. The tribunal dismissed the appeal. The Upper Tribunal had to determine (1) whether the tribunal was entitled to conclude that the retention of part of the front facade was not a condition or requirement of statutory planning consent or similar permission; (2) if so, whether the retained part of the original house should be regarded as de minimis and therefore disregarded for the purposes of Note 18(a); (3) even if the original house had not ceased to be an existing building, whether the construction works were the conversion, reconstruction, alteration, enlargement or extension of the previous house and therefore excluded from zero-rating by Note 16 to Group 5 of Sch.8.

Held: Appeal dismissed. (1) There was nothing in the planning consent itself, or the plans, which required the retention of the projecting bay. Furthermore, an architect's letter stating that the demolition of the bay would have nullified the planning consent did not show that retention of the bay was a condition or requirement of the planning consent; it was merely a warning about possible nullification. Nor did that letter reveal any similar permission to vary the planning consent to include a condition or requirement that the projecting bay had to be retained; it merely revealed that the planning authorities were concerned that the existing planning consent should not be nullified rather than providing any similar permission for a revised planning consent, *Wilson v Revenue and Customs Commissioners* [2014] UKFTT 320 (TC) considered. Accordingly, the tribunal was entitled to conclude, on the available evidence, that the planning consent did not require the retention of the projecting bay, and there was no evidence to conclude that such a condition was imposed by subsequent discussions with the planning authorities that amounted to a similar permission (see paras 39-41 of judgment). (2) There was nothing in the language of Note 18(a) to indicate that the de minimis principle was excluded. In the context of Note 18 as a whole, the retention of a facade could not be regarded as de minimis, since otherwise there would be no need for the specific exemption in Note 18(b). However, Note 18(b) did not show that something much smaller than a facade, such as a single brick, could not be considered to be de minimis. What was de minimis in a particular case depended on the circumstances of that case and the nature of the statutory provision. The projecting bay in the instant case could not be considered to be de minimis; it was capable of being a facade for the purposes of Note 18(b) and was clearly of real substance. Even in the absence of Note 18(b), the retained facade meant that the building could not be regarded as having been completely demolished even if its retention were a condition of planning consent or similar permission. Furthermore, the fact that what was left was enough to prevent the building being completely demolished from the point of view of the planning authority provided additional support for the view that it could not be regarded as de minimis (paras 48-50). (3) The tribunal noted that the planning consent was for alterations and extensions. It held that the retention of the projecting bay was to ensure that the planning authorities would accept that the works did not contravene the planning consent. It was implicit in the decision that the tribunal formed the view that the works were the alteration and extension of the original house within Note 16, and therefore not the construction of a building (para.55).

BOXMOOR CONSTRUCTION LTD v REVENUE AND CUSTOMS COMMISSIONERS, [2016] UKUT 91 (TCC), [2016] B.V.C. 508, Judge Greg Sinfield , UT (Tax).

2197 Taxable persons–Local authorities' powers and duties–Recovery of VAT on public charges for off-street parking–Taxable persons

[Value Added Tax Act 1994 (c.23) s.80; Directive 77/388 on turnover taxes - Common system of value added tax: uniform basis of assessment 1977 art.4(5)(2); Road Traffic Regulation Act 1984 (c.27) s.122; Local Government Finance Act 1988 (c.41) s.91]

The appellant local authorities appealed against a decision (*Isle of Wight Council v Revenue and Customs Commissioners* [2014] UKUT 446 (TCC), [2015] S.T.C. 460, [2015] C.L.Y. 2603) that they were not taxable persons for the purposes of recovering VAT on public charges for off-street car parking (OSCP). The respondent HMRC had refused the local authorities' claims to recover VAT under the Value Added Tax Act 1994 s.80 in respect of OSCP supplies. The issue for the First-tier Tribunal on appeal was whether local authorities were entitled to be treated as non-taxable persons, which depended upon whether treating them as non-taxable persons would lead to significant distortions of competition within the meaning of Directive 77/388 art.4(5)(2), which was in force during the relevant period. The tribunal found that the non-taxation of local authorities would distort competition in the OSCP market in the areas of pricing and outsourcing, so that fewer commercial car parks would remain open and more local authority car parks would open in pursuance of the local authorities' duty to ensure adequate parking provision under the Road Traffic Regulation Act 1984 s.122. The local authorities appealed to the Upper Tribunal, contending that the tribunal had misunderstood the legal framework governing the setting of local authority OSCP charges. They argued that there was no causal connection between increased revenue through non-taxation and lower OSCP charges and that the tribunal had wrongly inferred that they could set OSCP charges at a level which would raise income for other traffic management purposes. The UT found that if local authority OSCP was not taxed, local authorities would not need to consider raising their charges in the event of a VAT increase, whereas commercial providers would be compelled to do so, which supported the tribunal's finding, as a fact, that the absence of taxation would reduce upward pressures on local authority charging. As to the provision of outsourcing, the UT held that there would be a significant difference of approach if commercial provision was taxed but local authority provision was not. It concluded that the tribunal's finding that local authorities did not disregard the incidence of taxation when deciding whether and how to outsource a car park or its management was a finding of fact not based on any misunderstanding of the relevant law. It therefore dismissed the appeal. The local authorities contended that the tribunal and UT had failed to take into account two overriding considerations: first, that the OSCP charges were paid into, and expenditure for OSCP was taken from, a local authority's general fund established under the Local Government Finance Act 1988 s.91 and, secondly, that the pricing of OSCP was informed by numerous policy considerations related to the policy objectives in s.122. They submitted that had those matters been properly considered, the tribunal and UT would have been bound to conclude that HMRC could not discharge the burden on it of showing that in the hypothetical, notional market for OSCP, in which there was no VAT payable on local authority provision of OSCP, the absence of VAT would have a causal connection with a significant distortion of competition.

Held: Appeal dismissed. The critical issue was whether the tribunal had made an error of law in the light of its legitimate factual findings, *Procter & Gamble UK v Revenue and Customs Commissioners* [2009] EWCA Civ 407, [2009] S.T.C. 1990, [2009] C.L.Y. 4129 considered. The tribunal's conclusion that, in a hypothetical world in which VAT had never been imposed on OSCP charges, those charges would have been lower, was based on two principal matters: (a) in fixing the level of charges, local authorities were bound to have regard to the need to meet costs; (b) if VAT had never been payable on OSCP charges, local authorities would have been able to, and would have wished to, keep charges lower in order to boost the local economy by attracting shoppers with cars while maintaining the same spending priorities and the same allocation of the general fund as between the different activities financed out of the general fund. Local authorities had to be permitted to set OSCP charges with a view at least to covering the cost of operating loss-making or free car parks. It was impossible to say that the tribunal's conclusions were plainly wrong or outside the bounds within which reasonable disagreement was possible: they should not be disturbed on appeal, *Assicurazioni Generali SpA v Arab Insurance Group (BSC)* [2002] EWCA Civ 1642, [2003] 1 W.L.R. 577, [2003] C.L.Y. 2480 considered (see paras 63, 65, 69-74 of judgment). The submission that the tribunal had failed properly to take into account that a local authority's general fund was an undifferentiated fund, out of which many activities were financed, and that it would be a matter of discretion for the local authority as to how the funds no longer required to pay VAT on OSCP charged would be expended, missed the point. That submission was based on the scenario of an existing fund budgeted to meet VAT which was no longer required to meet that liability; that was a "change" scenario as opposed to the correct approach in the instant case, namely a hypothetical one in which there never was a VAT liability (para.75).

ISLE OF WIGHT COUNCIL v REVENUE AND CUSTOMS COMMISSIONERS *sub nom.* REVENUE AND CUSTOMS COMMISSIONERS v ISLE OF WIGHT COUNCIL, [2015] EWCA Civ 1303, [2016] P.T.S.R. 620, Sir Terence Etherton C, CA (Civ Div).

2198 VAT–BBC–Whether BBC entitled to VAT exemption for educational services under art.13(A)(1)(i) Directive 77/388

[Directive 77/388 on turnover taxes - Common system of value added tax: uniform basis of assessment 1977 art.13(A)(1), art.4(5)]

HMRC appealed against a decision of the Upper Tribunal (*Open University v Revenue and Customs Commissioners* [2015] UKUT 263 (TCC), [2015] S.T.C. 2324, [2015] C.L.Y. 2608) dismissing its appeal against a decision that the BBC was entitled under Directive 77/388 art.13(A)(1)(i) to VAT exemption for educational services provided to the respondent university (O). The BBC had sought repayment of VAT on supplies of services to O, namely the production and broadcasting of television and radio programmes, as exempt supplies of children's and young people's education, school or university education, vocational training or retraining under art.13A(1)(i). The First-tier Tribunal held that the BBC was not directly entitled to the exemption in art.13A(1)(i) because it was not a body governed by public law, and that it did not have the educational aims required by art.13A(1)(i), but that nevertheless it could benefit from the exemption for other reasons. The UT agreed that the BBC was not a public body, but found that the BBC had "similar objects" to that of a public body with the requisite educational aims within the meaning of art.13A(1)(i) and could therefore benefit from the exemption. The issues were whether (1) the BBC was a body governed by public law within the meaning of art.13A(1)(i): O argued that the UT had been wrong in its heavy reliance on the meaning of "other bodies governed by public law" in art.4(5), and the BBC Charter and the ECJ decision in *Saudacor - Sociedade Gestora de Recursos e Equipamentos da Saude dos Acores SA v Fazenda Publica (C-174/14)* EU:C:2015:733, [2016] S.T.C. 681 led to the conclusion that the BBC was a body governed by public law; (2) the BBC was an organisation with "similar objects" to the requisite educational aims; (3) the BBC was an organisation that had been "defined" by the UK as having similar objects to the requisite educations aims.

Held: Appeal dismissed. (1) Everything pointed in favour of an identical meaning of the expression "other bodies governed by public law" in art.4(5) and art.13A(1)(i), *University of Cambridge v Revenue and Customs Commissioners* [2009] EWHC 434 (Ch), [2009] S.T.C. 1288, [2009] C.L.Y. 4121 approved. The case law on art.4(5) culminating in *Saudacor* showed that the distinction was between bodies that were part of the public administration and pursued a relevant economic activity in fulfilment of that role, and bodies that independently carried on an economic activity otherwise than as part of the public administration. The UT's conclusion that the BBC was not a body governed by public law was a multi-factorial evaluation in respect of which the UT did not make any error of law and which was not plainly wrong. *Saudacor* was not authority for the proposition that a private law body was a body governed by public law if it had been created by the state in order to perform a public service and had operational and management autonomy but the state was in a position to exercise decisive control, nor for the proposition that the state had decisive control if it owned all the shares in a private body and provided its finances. The ECJ in *Saudacor* had merely described those as ingredients of an evaluative exercise on the facts of the case, *Saudacor* considered. The BBC was not comparable to Saudacor. The BBC had operational and editorial independence from the state. Notwithstanding provisions concerning the Crown and secretary of state's powers, the promotion of the public benefit, the BBC's funding, and the fact that it was governed by royal charter and had to report and account to Parliament, during the relevant period the BBC had not been carrying on its activities as part of the public administration and was not a body governed by public law (see paras 61-62, 81-82, 85 of judgment). (2) The UT had been right to hold that the BBC had "similar objects" for art.13A(1)(i) purposes. A two-way teacher/student exchange was not an essential element in education or vocational training within art.13A(i). The essence of art.13A(1)(i) education and training was the imparting of knowledge, information and instruction with a view to educating and training the recipient. There was some evidence of an interactive element to the BBC's educational activities, but it was sufficient that the supply of such services was part of the BBC's objects as a matter of legal vires and operational reality. The BBC provided the whole framework of facilities, teaching materials, technical resources, educational policy and organisational infrastructure to deliver its distance learning direct to children and young people and those seeking vocational training or retraining, *Stichting Regionaal Opleidingen Centrum Noord-Kennemerland/West-Friesland (Horizon College) v Staatssecretaris van Financien (C-434/05)* EU:C:2007:343, [2008] S.T.C. 2145, [2008] C.L.Y. 4003 applied(paras 107-110). (3) It was unnecessary to decide whether the UK had defined the BBC as having similar objects. During the relevant period the BBC had the same objects as public bodies specified in the first part of art.13A(1)(i). Either the UK had defined the BBC as having similar objects within art.13A(1)(i) or, if not, the BBC and O were entitled to rely directly on art.13A(1)(i) because the UK had failed to implement the Directive. The object of the VAT exemption had been intended to increase access to the educational services in art.13A(1)(i) by avoiding the increased costs that would result if they were subject to VAT. To exclude the BBC from the exemption would be both contrary to the Directive's objective and the principle of fiscal neutrality, *JP Morgan Fleming Claverhouse Investment Trust Plc v Revenue and Customs Commissioners (C-363/05)* EU:C:2007:391, [2008] S.T.C. 1180, [2008] C.L.Y. 4002 applied (para.123).

REVENUE AND CUSTOMS COMMISSIONERS v OPEN UNIVERSITY, [2016] EWCA Civ 114, [2016] S.T.C. 2273, Sir Terence Etherton C, CA (Civ Div).

2199 VAT–Costs–Determination of costs after withdrawal of application for judicial review

The Upper Tribunal was required to determine costs after the withdrawal of an application for judicial review of a First-tier Tribunal decision. The tribunal had dismissed the applicants' appeals against information notices served on them by HMRC. The applicants did not comply with the notices and began judicial review proceedings of the tribunal's decision. HMRC participated in the judicial review proceedings as an interested party. HMRC subsequently issued an assessment against one of the applicants despite not having received the requested information. The applicants then decided to supply the requested information since it would be necessary to do so in an appeal against the assessment. They made such an appeal to the tribunal. Since the applicants had disclosed the information, the judicial review proceedings served no purpose and they withdrew them. The applicants argued that the fact that HMRC had made an assessment against one of them showed that the information requested had not been necessary and they had therefore been justified in bringing the proceedings. They argued that, in any event, the UT should not make a decision on the costs application before the appeal in the tribunal had been determined, since the tribunal would decide whether the assessment had been justified, which was relevant to the reasonableness of the parties' conduct regarding the information notices.

Held: Costs determined. The fact that there was an outstanding appeal before the tribunal was irrelevant. The question in that appeal was not whether HMRC had been justified in asking for the information but whether they had been justified in making the assessment. That appeal was not the forum for deciding whether the request for information had been oppressive, or whether the applicants had been justified for some other reason in resisting it. That was the issue in the instant judicial review proceedings. There was no basis on which to defer a costs decision and no reason to refuse HMRC their costs.

R. (ON THE APPLICATION OF WHITEFIELDS GOLF CLUB LTD) v FIRST-TIER TRIBUNAL *sub nom.* R. (ON THE APPLICATION OF WHITEFIELDS GOLF CLUB LTD) v REVENUE AND CUSTOMS COMMISSIONERS, [2016] UKUT 235 (TCC), [2016] B.V.C. 518, Judge Colin Bishopp, UT (Tax).

2200 VAT–Exemptions–Unincorporated association–Payment of VAT on members' subscriptions

[Directive 2006/112 on the common system of VAT 2006 art.132, art.132(1)(l)]

The appellant unincorporated association (U) appealed against a decision (*United Grand Lodge of England v Revenue and Customs Commissioners* [2014] UKFTT 164 (TC), [2014] S.T.I. 953) that supplies made to its members in return for their subscriptions were not exempt from VAT under Directive 2006/112 art.132. U drew together those practising Freemasonry in a manner recognised by its rules. The tribunal found that it had aims of a philosophical, philanthropic and civic nature for the purposes of art.132(1)(l). However, it concluded that it had "other aims", such as social aims, aims of self-improvement, ritual and mutual benevolence, and that those aims were not merely incidental or ancillary, so that U fell outside the words of the exemption in art.132(1)(l). In reaching its decision, the tribunal commented that although Freemasonry had changed since 2000 and had become more outward looking and involved in charity work for the benefit of non-Freemasons or dependents, the charitable spending by Masonic charities was to some extent analogous to that of a mutual insurance company and was thus not wholly philanthropic. It also found that only a small part of U's aims were of a civic nature. U submitted that the tribunal had not first determined what its main aim or aims were; "main" meant principal, primary or predominant and it was possible to have more than one main aim; the second step was to assess the nature of the main aim or aims in order to determine whether they qualified under the exemption. U submitted that, instead, the tribunal had asked itself whether the "other aims" were "minor, insignificant or incidental or ancillary" to the qualifying aims. U argued that, had the correct approach been adopted, the tribunal would have found that U's main aim was to promote the practice of Freemasonry and that that aim fell within the heads of "philosophical, philanthropic or civic nature". U also submitted that the tribunal's determination of whether the aims fell within the relevant exemption was not justified on the evidence or was otherwise perverse. Further, it submitted that the aims described as "other aims" were minor and insignificant and could not prevent the main aim of furtherance of Freemasonry from falling within art.132(1)(l).

Held: Appeal dismissed. (1) The tribunal had not erred in law in the way it approached the statutory question. It had accurately summarised the decisions in *Expert Witness Institute v Customs and Excise Commissioners* [2001] EWCA Civ 1882, [2002] 1 W.L.R. 1674, [2002] C.L.Y. 4757 and *British Association for Shooting and Conservation Ltd v Revenue and Customs Commissioners* [2009] EWHC 399 (Ch), [2009] S.T.C. 1421, [2009] C.L.Y. 4047, *Expert Witness* and *British Association for Shooting* applied. It noted that it was permissible to approach an organisation's activities on the basis that it had a main aim which categorised its fiscal treatment, and that identifying the main object of an organisation was one element in deciding whether it fell within an exemption. The tribunal had not been required, as a mandatory first step, to identify U's main aim or aims. Where there were numerous aims which had the potential to qualify under more than one category in art.132(1)(l), and in relation to which it was conceded that there could be an aggregation of aims in order to render them the main aim or aims, and in which it was necessary to evaluate the nature and relative predominance of the aims over a lengthy period, the tribunal was entitled to adopt the approach which it took. The tribunal had not erred in law in seeking to test U's aims in order to determine the proportion which fell within the categories of exemption and then to decide whether those which fell outside were of sufficient magnitude to prevent the qualifying aims from being main aims (see paras 60-63 of judgment). (2) The tribunal had not erred in the sense described in *Edwards (Inspector of Taxes) v Bairstow* [1956] A.C. 14, [1955] C.L.Y. 417. It came to conclusions upon the evidence before it. It was fully entitled to come to those conclusions and they were not perverse, *Edwards* applied. The conclusion that after 2000 Freemasonry became more outward looking was entirely consistent with the evidence. Furthermore, there was no error in its inference that not all of U's promotion of charitable giving had a philanthropic aim. Given that around 75% of charitable spending was directed to Masons or their dependants and that the interests of family were seen as paramount, it could not be said that that conclusion was perverse or otherwise subject to challenge on *Edwards* grounds. The tribunal had also been entitled on the evidence to find that only a small part of U's aims were of a civic nature. It was clear from *Expert Witness* that aims of a civic nature had to concern the relationship between the citizen and the State, rather than citizens with each other, *Expert Witness* applied. The charitable activities of Freemasons were largely unrelated to any relationship of citizens with the State. In relation to the treatment of "other aims", the tribunal's decision on social aims was not perverse. Its conclusion that ritual was an integral part of teaching Freemasonry and binding people together was not inconsistent with the conclusion that some part of U's aim was the promotion of Masonic ritual and ceremony. Any challenge on the basis of *Edwards* unreasonableness, whether to the conclusion that ritual was an aim of U or that when added with other non-qualifying aims they were not insignificant, had to fail (paras 66-67, 69-72).

UNITED GRAND LODGE OF ENGLAND v REVENUE AND CUSTOMS COMMISSIONERS, [2015] UKUT 589 (TCC), [2016] S.T.C. 888, Asplin J, UT (Tax).

2201 VAT–Late payments–No reasonable excuse–Imposition of default surcharge

[Value Added Tax (Payments on Account) Order 1993 (SI 1993/2001) art.4, art.5, art.6]

The appellant taxpayer appealed against a decision [*Marsdens Caterers of Sheffield Ltd v Revenue and Customs Commissioners* [2014] UKFTT 645 (TC)] dismissing its challenge to a default surcharge imposed by the respondent HMRC in respect of late payment of VAT. The taxpayer operated takeaway food outlets. The 09/11 quarter was the first quarter in respect of which HMRC had notified the taxpayer that it was henceforward to pay VAT under the payment on account (POA) regime. HMRC contended that all three payments required under the POA regime for the 09/11 quarter were made late. When calculating the surcharge to be paid, HMRC took into account its contention that the taxpayer had already made two late payments in respect of previous quarters so a surcharge penalty of 5% applied. On appeal, the tribunal rejected the taxpayer's submission that it had had a reasonable excuse for being late with its payments in respect of the period ending 09/11 because its group financial controller had left abruptly in July 2011. The taxpayer submitted that (1) HMRC was wrong to assert that it fell within the POA regime for the quarter 09/11 because its liability had not exceeded the relevant threshold in 03/11 and thus two of its payments had not been late; (2) HMRC's refusal to grant it a seven-day extension that it had granted to other traders was contrary to the EU law principle of equal treatment; (3) the tribunal had been wrong to conclude that it did not have a reasonable excuse for the late payment.

Held: Appeal dismissed. (1) The taxpayer fell within the Value Added Tax (Payments on Account) Order 1993 art.6 after 31 March 2011 because in the reference year which ended on 31 March 2011 it had a VAT liability higher than the £2 million threshold applicable at that date. The taxpayer became subject to an obligation under art.4 to make POA for the prescribed accounting periods (PAPs) ending 30 June 2011, 30 September 2011, 31 December 2011 and 31 March 2012. That obligation was not affected by the fact that by the time it came to make the POAs in those PAPs, the threshold had increased to £2.3 million and its VAT liability in the reference year ending 31 March 2011 did not exceed the new threshold. The reference year was very clear looking at art.5: it was the year comprising the PAPs the ends of which fell within the period of one year ending on the last day of the taxpayer's PAP ending before the previous December (see paras 30-38, 44 of judgment). (2) POA traders were not comparable to ordinary traders or to large traders who had opted to be outside the POA regime. HMRC applied a number of different payment regimes to different categories of trader and each regime had a bundle of obligations which had to be considered together. The regimes had to be looked at as a whole. The taxpayer was not in a comparable position so the question of objective justification did not arise (paras 64,

67). (3) It was more difficult for a large company like the taxpayer to show that the departure of a single employee provided a reasonable excuse for late payment than it was for a smaller company, *Armkor Ltd v Revenue and Customs Commissioners* [2014] UKFTT 140 (TC) considered. The issue did not raise a point of law on which to interfere with the tribunal's conclusion (para.76).

MARSDENS CATERERS OF SHEFFIELD LTD v REVENUE AND CUSTOMS COMMISSIONERS, [2016] UKUT 88 (TCC), [2016] B.V.C. 507, Rose J, UT (Tax).

2202 VAT–Repayments–Bonuses paid by car manufacturers

The appellant car dealer appealed against a decision of the First-tier Tribunal (*Why Pay More For Cars Ltd v Revenue and Customs Commissioners* [2013] UKFTT 497 (TC), [2013] S.T.I. 3428) upholding HMRC's refusal of its claim for a repayment of VAT that it claimed had been overpaid in various VAT periods between 1973 and 1997. Car manufacturers had supplied demonstrator vehicles and courtesy cars to the appellant. If the appellant met certain conditions in relation to the cars, the manufacturers would pay it a bonus in respect of each car. The appellant would account for VAT output tax on the bonus payments on the basis that they were consideration for a taxable supply of services by it to the manufacturers. Following the decision of the European Court of Justice in *Elida Gibbs Ltd v Customs and Excise Commissioners (C-317/94)* EU:C:1996:400, [1997] Q.B. 499, [1996] C.L.Y. 5908, HMRC accepted that the bonus payments should always have been treated as a discount on the original price of the cars; it invited claims from car dealers who believed that they had overpaid VAT. On the basis of direct evidence in relation to manufacturers' accounting practices over the relevant years, HMRC compiled a table (the *Elida* table) which was intended to facilitate such claims. The *Elida* table was not exhaustive: there were periods in respect of which no entry appeared on the table (silent periods) because, although bonuses may have been paid in those periods, HMRC did not have specific evidence that dealers had accounted for VAT on the receipt of such bonuses. The appellant's claim was for VAT overpaid on bonuses received from various car manufacturers in silent periods between June 1973 and March 1997. It was unable to produce any direct evidence as to its VAT treatment of bonuses during those periods. HMRC refused the repayment claim and its decision was upheld by the First-tier Tribunal. The tribunal rejected the appellant's assertion that because the *Elida* table recognised that dealers accounted for VAT on bonuses received from a specific manufacturer in a particular period or periods, it could be inferred that they had accounted for VAT on bonuses received from the same manufacturer in the silent periods. It found that during the relevant period there were inconsistent approaches among manufacturers and that individual manufacturers changed their practices.

Held: Appeal dismissed. The First-tier Tribunal had decided that it was not satisfied that the fact that the *Elida* table showed that VAT had been accounted for on bonuses paid by a manufacturer in one period meant that, on the balance of probabilities, VAT had also been accounted for during the silent periods. That conclusion was based on the tribunal's evaluation of the evidence, and the appellant had not shown that that evaluation was one which the tribunal was not entitled to make, *Edwards (Inspector of Taxes) v Bairstow* [1956] A.C. 14, [1955] C.L.Y. 417 applied. The tribunal had been entitled to decline to infer that the appellant had accounted for VAT on bonuses paid during the silent periods, *Elida* cited (see para.35 of judgment).

WHY PAY MORE FOR CARS LTD v REVENUE AND CUSTOMS COMMISSIONERS, [2015] UKUT 468 (TCC), [2016] S.T.C. 254, Newey J, UT (Tax).

2203 VAT–Tax avoidance–Whether lease and leaseback arrangement entered into under tax mitigation scheme designed to mitigate VAT liability resulted in tax advantage amounting to abuse of rights

A university appealed against a decision that a lease and leaseback arrangement which it had entered into as a VAT-saving scheme resulted in a tax advantage that was inconsistent with anti-avoidance legislation and amounted to an abuse of rights. The university had wanted to refurbish one of its properties. It recognised that it would have to pay input VAT on the cost of the works and would only be able to recover a small amount back given that it was a supplier of mainly exempt supplies. It entered into a tax mitigation scheme, whereby a discretionary trust was created. The trust was a shell and was controlled by the university. The university opted to waive exemption from VAT in relation to the property, which the trust also did after the university granted it a taxable lease. The trust then granted a taxable underlease to the university, and the university paid for the refurbishment, which was completed in 1998. The lease and underlease were both terminated in 2004. The commissioners assessed the university for under-declared VAT representing the input tax on the refurbishment costs, stating that it did not regard it as having been incurred for the purposes of the university's taxable supply of the lease of the property to the trust. The tribunal found that the purpose of the university's transactions had been to facilitate VAT planning, that the transactions amounted to a deferral scheme with a built-in feature that allowed an absolute saving of VAT at a later date, and that there had been no abuse of rights. The Upper Tribunal reversed that decision. It identified the tax advantage, not as a means of deferring VAT, but as an entitlement to claim 100% of the input tax as a deduction rather than the much smaller percentage which the university would have been able to deduct under normal circumstances. The issue was whether the scheme amounted to an abuse of rights.

Held: Appeal dismissed. The principle of abuse of rights rested on two tests, both of which had to be satisfied. First, the transactions, although formally valid under the VAT code, had to result in the accrual of a tax advantage the grant of which would be contrary to the purpose of its provisions. Second, the essential aim of the transactions had to be to establish a tax advantage (see para.12 of judgment). The second test was undoubtedly met. Whether the first test was met involved identifying (a) the tax advantage which the scheme gave to the university and (b) the relevant part of the VAT code. It was then necessary to compare the purpose and objectives of the part of the tax code allegedly being abused with the purpose and results achieved by the activity at issue. If the tax advantage resulted from a choice that the VAT code intended to give to the taxable person, there would be no abuse (paras 13-14). The university's contention that, under *Revenue and Customs Commissioners v Weald Leasing Ltd (C-103/09)* EU:C:2010:804, [2011] S.T.C. 596, [2011] C.L.Y. 3535, tax advantages that were intrinsic features of normal leasing arrangements were not abusive even if obtained solely for fiscal purposes did not advance its case. In *Weald* the taxable person had to choose between leasing or buying an asset which it did not own, whereas in the instant case there was no question of the university choosing between buying or leasing because it already owned the asset. The university's assertion that choosing leasing arrangements which procured a fiscal advantage could not be criticised as long as the correct VAT treatment of the leasing arrangement was followed was too wide an interpretation of *Weald* and did not reflect the fact that the court in that case was discussing commercial choices. Contrary to the university's submissions, *Weald* required an examination of the object and effects of the impugned transactions, as well as their purpose, *Weald* considered (paras 23-29). The UT had correctly identified the tax advantage as the ability to deduct the whole of the input tax rather than a VAT deferral. The lower tribunal had been wrong to characterise it as a deferral in view of its finding that the university had always intended to make an absolute saving by entering into the scheme. Furthermore, if there was a "built-in feature" allowing an absolute saving to be made, that feature had to have been part of the scheme from the outset (paras 38-41). The UT had also been right to find that the tax advantage was incompatible with the purposes of the VAT code, *Halifax Plc v Customs and Excise Commissioners (C-255/02)* [2006] Ch. 387, [2006] C.L.Y. 4467 applied. The object of the scheme had been to secure a VAT advantage by introducing steps which had no other purpose or commercial effect. Having found that both tests for abuse of rights were met, it had redefined the transactions by disregarding the artificial steps, such as the creation of the trust and the leasehold structure. That had been the right approach. The tribunal's job was to remove the abusive elements of the scheme, not to replace them with a different non-abusive scheme which could have been adopted but had not been (paras 43-48).

UNIVERSITY OF HUDDERSFIELD HIGHER EDUCATION CORP v REVENUE AND CUSTOMS COMMISSIONERS *sub nom.* REVENUE AND CUSTOMS COMMISSIONERS v UNIVERSITY OF HUDDERSFIELD HIGHER EDUCATION CORP, [2016] EWCA Civ 440, [2016] 4 All E.R. 652, Lewison LJ, CA (Civ Div).

2204 **VAT–Tax Chamber–Upper Tribunal's reversal of First-tier Tribunal decision to debar HMRC from proceedings–Whether stricter approach to compliance with rules and directions made under CPR applied to cases in tax tribunals**

[Civil Procedure Rules 1998 r.3.9]

A taxpayer appealed against the Upper Tribunal's reversal of a First-tier Tribunal decision to debar HMRC from the proceedings before it. The taxpayer had appealed against a VAT decision made by HMRC. HMRC delayed service of its statement of case and failed to plead the facts on which it relied. The taxpayer made a request for further information, which HMRC did not comply with. The tribunal ordered HMRC to file its reply, failing which it would be debarred. HMRC failed to comply. The tribunal, having regard to the stricter approach to compliance with rules and directions applicable under the CPR following *Mitchell v News Group Newspapers Ltd* [2013] EWCA Civ 1537, [2014] 1 W.L.R. 795, [2014] C.L.Y. 445 and *Denton v TH White Ltd* [2014] EWCA Civ 906, [2014] 1 W.L.R. 3926, [2014] C.L.Y. 454, debarred HMRC. HMRC appealed to the UT. The UT allowed the appeal, applying its reasoning in *Leeds City Council v Revenue and Customs Commissioners* [2014] UKUT 350 (TCC), [2015] S.T.C. 168, [2014] C.L.Y. 2983 that it was not open to a tribunal to apply by analogy changes in the CPR as if they had been made to the tribunal rules. The taxpayer argued that the tribunal had been bound by the UT's decision in *Revenue and Customs Commissioners v McCarthy and Stone (Developments) Ltd* [2014] UKUT 196 (TCC), [2014] S.T.C. 973, [2014] C.L.Y. 9 to apply the stricter approach.

Held: Appeal allowed. The tribunal had not directly applied the CPR or the authorities on r.3.9. It had made clear that its consideration was limited to whether the guidance in the authorities was relevant by analogy to the application of the overriding objective in the tax tribunal rules. In circumstances where the tribunal rules were silent, the question was whether the tribunal had erred in according the efficient conduct of litigation at a proportionate cost and compliance with rules, practice directions and orders significant weight as part of its consideration of the overriding objective. The answer was that it had not erred and the UT should not have intervened (see paras 32-33 of judgment). *McCarthy & Stone* and *Leeds* were conflicting UT authorities on whether the stricter approach to compliance with rules and directions made under the CPR as set out in *Mitchell* and *Denton* applied to cases in the tax tribunals. The stricter approach was the right approach, *Mitchell* and *Denton* applied, *McCarthy & Stone* approved and *Leeds* disapproved. The UT, as a superior court of record, was not precluded from giving guidance on practice and procedure simply because the tribunal procedure committee had not done so in the form of a rule. Nothing in the wording of the relevant rules justified a different or particular approach in the tax tribunals to compliance or the efficient conduct of litigation at a proportionate cost. Nothing in the wording of the tax tribunal rules' overriding objective was inconsistent with the general legal policy described in *Mitchell* and *Denton*. There was no justification for a more relaxed approach to compliance with rules and practice directions in the tribunals. A more relaxed approach would risk non-compliance having to be tolerated on some rational basis. The correct starting point was compliance unless there was good reason to the contrary, which should, where possible, be put in advance to the tribunal (paras 16, 35-38). HMRC's approach to compliance had been disturbing. At times it had come close to arguing that, since it was a state agency, the constraints of austerity should excuse its unacceptable behaviour. A state party should not work on the basis that it had some preferred status in the tribunals. If HMRC had a difficulty with compliance, it should, where possible, apply to the tribunal to be relieved of compliance on the basis of some alternative proposal which should be canvassed with the taxpayer before the application; the reasons for non-compliance and the merits of the alternative should be explained (paras 39-43).

BPP HOLDINGS LTD v REVENUE AND CUSTOMS COMMISSIONERS, [2016] EWCA Civ 121, [2016] 1 W.L.R. 1915, Moore-Bick LJ, CA (Civ Div).

2205 **VAT–Tax refunds–Development corporations**

THE VALUE ADDED TAX (REFUND OF TAX TO THE OLD OAK AND PARK ROYAL DEVELOPMENT CORPORATION) ORDER 2016, SI 2016/307; made under the Value Added Tax Act 1994 s.33(3)(k). In force: 1 April 2016.

This Order, which comes into force on 1 April 2016, provides that the Old Oak and Park Royal Development Corporation (the Corporation) is specified for the purposes of the Value Added Tax Act 1994 s.33. The effect of this Order is that it entitles the Corporation to claim refunds of value added tax charged on supplies to, and acquisitions or importations by it, provided that those supplies, acquisitions or importations are not for the purpose of a business carried on by it.

2206 **VAT–Telecommunications–Calculation of VAT payable on charges for calls, messages and data services incurred by mobile phone users whilst visiting non-EU countries**

[Value Added Tax Act 1994 (c.23) Sch.4A Pt 1 para.8; Directive 2006/112 on the common system of VAT 2006]

The claimant telecommunications companies (T) applied for judicial review of a decision by HMRC that they should change how they calculated VAT payable on charges for calls, messages and data services incurred by mobile phone users whilst visiting non-EU countries. Under the Value Added Tax Act 1994 Sch.4A Pt 1 para.8, telecommunications services provided in the UK but "effectively used and enjoyed" in a non-EU country were not chargeable to UK VAT. Between 2008 and 2014, T calculated the value of non-EU network access using a calculation called "revenue methodology". That involved looking at the sums paid by customers for "additional services" (services not included in their regular monthly plan), and determining what proportion related to services received in non-EU countries. HMRC considered that method distortive because additional services in non-EU countries were more expensive than additional services in the UK and the EU, and so would account for a much higher proportion of the total cost than their volume justified. HMRC favoured the "usage methodology" calculation, which was based on actual phone usage and involved comparing the number of minutes used on overseas networks to the total number of minutes used in the month. It resulted in a much smaller proportion of the monthly line rental charge escaping VAT. T submitted that: (1) the usage methodology was unlawful because it was contrary to Directive 2008/8 art.59a (amending Directive 2006/112) and Sch.4A para.8(3) of the Act, which were concerned with economic use and enjoyment, not volume of usage; (2) the decision breached T's legitimate expectation based on a clear assurance from HMRC in a 2008 letter that it could use the revenue methodology until there was a material change in the law or its business, which there had not been; (3) HMRC had had a common law duty to consult T before depriving it of the benefit of being able to use the revenue methodology.

Held: Application refused. (1) The purpose of art.59a and Sch.4 para.8(3) was to determine the place of supply of the service. Neither provision stated that economic use was the only relevant factor. Nor did they explicitly or impliedly prohibit HMRC's usage methodology. In any assessment of use it was essential to consider economic reality in the light of the observable terms and features of the taxpayer's business. However, physical use might also be relevant to the determination, *London Clubs Management Ltd v Revenue and Customs Commissioners* [2011] EWCA Civ 1323, [2012] S.T.C. 388, [2012] C.L.Y. 3395 applied. The reference to "enjoyment" did not mean that some concept of the value of the services to the customer had to be imported into the consideration of where the services were supplied. The starting point was to identify the supply. In the instant case it was the ability to access a telecommunications network in the UK and elsewhere. The next step was to decide the meaning of "effective use and enjoyment" of the ability to access the network. "Effective" implied actual enjoyment of the ability rather than the mere opportunity to do so. Some actual use of the network whilst in the non-EU country was therefore required if a person was to be regarded as having "effectively used and enjoyed" the service. The final step was to determine how the monthly network access charge was to be apportioned between EU and non-EU locations. As "effective use and enjoyment" was measured by actual access to the network, the most accurate method was to base apportionment on the amount of time, in each monthly charging period, a customer spent with a mobile phone, with roaming switched on. The fact that customers paid more to access the network when outside the EU did not mean that they valued the ability to do so more highly than when in the EU. There was also no evidence that the actual costs to T of providing access to networks outside the EU correlated with the costs of providing the actual calls made by customers from outside the EU. T had not established that HMRC's methodology was unlawful (see paras 44-59 of judgment). (2) No legitimate expectation had been generated by HMRC's letter or by its acceptance of the revenue methodology over a number of years. The correspondence did not suggest that T had been seeking an assurance about the future, nor had it given any reason why it needed such an assurance. Even if HMRC had given an assurance in 2008, it would have been justified in resiling from it. There was no unfairness or abuse of power resulting from the change to the way in which VAT adjustments were calculated, *R. v Inland Revenue Commissioners Ex p. MFK Underwriting Agents Ltd* [1990] 1 W.L.R. 1545, [1990] C.L.Y. 2651, *R. (on the application of GSTS Pathology LLP) v Revenue and Customs Commissioners* [2013] EWHC 1801 (Admin), [2013] S.T.C. 2017, [2014] C.L.Y. 3084, *Cameron v Revenue and Customs Commissioners* [2012] EWHC 1174 (Admin), [2012] S.T.C. 1691, [2012] C.L.Y. 3277 and *Paponette v Attorney General of Trinidad and Tobago* [2010] UKPC 32, [2012] 1 A.C. 1 considered (paras 65-75, 80-82, 84, 87, 92, 99). (3) HMRC had a duty to consult T, *R. (on the application of Niazi) v Secretary of State for the Home Department* [2008] EWCA Civ 755, Times, July 21, 2008, [2008] C.L.Y. 70 and *R. (on the application of Moseley) v Haringey LBC* [2014] UKSC 56, [2014] 1 W.L.R. 3947, [2014] C.L.Y. 2087 applied. However, it had properly discharged that duty because it gave it an adequate opportunity to make representations and explain why it could not implement the usage methodology (paras 101-105, 112, 115).

R. (ON THE APPLICATION OF TELEFONICA EUROPE PLC) v REVENUE AND CUSTOMS COMMISSIONERS, [2016] UKUT 173 (TCC), [2016] S.T.C. 1614, Rose J, UT (Tax).

2207 VAT–Unjust enrichment–Non-profit making golf clubs–Output tax on green fees

[Directive 2006/112 on the common system of VAT 2006 art.132, art.133, art.134]

The appellant non-profit members' golf clubs sought repayment from HMRC of output tax on green fees. HMRC had contended before the First-Tier Tribunal that they were entitled to exclude the supply of green fee rounds of golf to non-members by such clubs as the appellants from the exemption under Directive 2006/112 art.133 or art.134(b). The Upper Tribunal referred the question to the European Court of Justice which held in *Revenue and Customs Commissioners v Bridport and West Dorset Golf Club Ltd (C-495/12)* EU:C:2013:861, [2014] S.T.C. 663 that the UK was not entitled to rely on art.134(b) or art.133(d) to exclude the supply of green fee golf by non-profit making clubs from the exemption. Following that decision HMRC paid the claim in full, but other similar non-profit making clubs also then sought repayment of output tax on green fees. As HMRC wished to consider whether to raise a defence of unjust enrichment, the instant appellants were chosen to represent all the claims. Each side instructed experts to calculate the economic loss borne by the appellants.

Held: Judgment accordingly. The experts agreed that the clubs had suffered an economic loss through the incorrect imposition of VAT on green fees and that the economic loss comprised the VAT absorbed by the clubs which had not been passed on to the green fee visitors and the net profit on rounds of green fee golf that would have been played had some potential visitors not been deterred by the increased price due to the imposition of the VAT. However, they disagreed as to the extent of that loss and how it should be calculated. One of the key issues in the instant case was the make-up of the cost of an additional round of green fee golf and its relation to the green fee charged, from which the club's net profit on each green fee round of golf was derived. HMRC had not shown that the tribunal should assume that, for the purposes of calculating the economic loss to the clubs of incorrectly imposing VAT, the cost of the clubs' supplying an additional round of green fee golf (and allowing for a return on capital) was equal to the green fee. The tribunal preferred the argument that the green fee market, while competitive, was not a perfectly competitive but an oligopolistic market and, as such, it had to consider the actual costs incurred by the clubs in supplying additional rounds of green fee golf to the number of visitors that would have played had they not been deterred by the imposition of VAT increasing the green fee. On the basis of the evidence before the tribunal, the clubs would be unjustly enriched if the whole of their claims were to be repaid. Having regard to all the circumstances of the case, a restriction of 10% should be applied to each of the claims to take account of the fact that the clubs would have incurred some costs in providing rounds of green fee golf to the additional number of visitors who would have turned up to play had the green fees been lowered by the amount of VAT incorrectly imposed (see paras 170-179 of judgment).

BERKSHIRE GOLF CLUB v REVENUE AND CUSTOMS COMMISSIONERS, [2015] UKFTT 627 (TC), [2016] S.F.T.D. 244, Judge John Brooks, FTT (Tax).

2208 **VAT–Value–Genealogical website requiring purchase of creditsin advance to view and download documents–Whether company supplying genealogical documents**

[Value Added Tax Act 1994 (c.23) Sch.10A para.1, s.6(3), s.6(4)]

A company appealed against a decision of the First-tier Tribunal (*Brightsolid Online Technology Ltd v Revenue and Customs Commissioners* [2014] UKFTT 1040 (TC), [2014] S.T.I. 3557) upholding HMRC's rejection of its claim for repayment of overpaid VAT. The company ran a website providing genealogy information. Customers could search the website for free, but had to pay to view or download documents. They either paid a subscription or bought pay-as-you-go credits, which were valid for a fixed period. Any credits not used within that time would expire. The company applied to HMRC for the repayment of VAT which, it claimed, it had accounted for incorrectly on unredeemed credits between 2008 and 10 May 2012. It claimed that in the case of unredeemed credits, there was no taxable supply and therefore no VAT liability. Its claim did not extend beyond 10 May 2012 because on that date the law changed to make VAT due on single-purpose face-value vouchers at the time of their issue. It was common ground that at the relevant time the company was supplying a service; that under the Value Added Tax Act 1994 s.6(3) the time of supply was when the service was provided; and that under s.6(4), if payment was made before the service was supplied, the supply would be treated as taking place when payment was received. HMRC rejected the company'"s claim and its decision was upheld by the tribunal. The central issue was whether the company was supplying genealogical documents, in which case VAT was chargeable only when credits were used to view or download those documents; or whether, as the tribunal concluded, the company was supplying a package of rights enabling the customers to search for, select and view documents, the package was supplied when the credits were purchased, and VAT was chargeable at the time of purchase. The appeal would succeed only if the company could establish that it was supplying only the documents and either that the credits were face-value vouchers within the meaning of Sch.10A para.1 of the Act and fell to be treated in accordance with s.6(4), or that the purchase of the credits was not a pre-payment for the supply.

Held: Appeal allowed. (1) The company was supplying genealogical documents. When customers bought credits they were not being supplied with a package which gave them the right to search for, as well as to access and download, documents. The search facility was free, and customers did not have to buy credits in order to use it. They could search the website to see what was available before deciding whether to buy credits. The service was supplied when individual documents were viewed or downloaded. There had to be a link between the consideration and the supply of services, and there was no link between the payment for credits and the use of the search facility, *Lebara Ltd v Revenue and Customs Commissioners (C-520/10)* EU:C:2012:264, [2012] S.T.C. 1536 applied (see paras 18-22 of judgment). (2) The credits were face-value vouchers within the meaning of Sch.10A para.1. They were tokens, stamps or vouchers in electronic form and represented a right to receive goods or services. There was no reason why "electronic form" could not cover a website entry showing a customer's remaining unused credits, and the fact that a credit was for a particular service and was non-transferable did not militate against it representing a right to receive goods or services. The credits represented the right to receive services "to the value of an amount", and that amount was stated on them. An email sent by the company to the customer confirming the purchase and listing the number of credits available could, when taken with knowledge of the amount paid for the credits, be sufficient to render the credit a face-value voucher. Similarly, a list of unused credits on the customer's online account could be understood as representing money's worth and qualified as a face-value voucher, and the credit balance shown on the account represented the right to access documents up to that amount. The fact that the account recorded the credit balance in terms of credits rather than monetary value was irrelevant. It was sufficient for the customer to know that he had a certain number of credits, *Leisure Pass Group Ltd v Revenue and Customs Commissioners* [2008] EWHC 2158 (Ch), [2008] S.T.C. 3340, [2009] C.L.Y. 4116 considered. Although the monetary value of the unused credits was not shown on the account, what each credit cost was a matter of record, and the monetary value of the remaining credits could be ascertained by the company from its records. That was sufficient to meet the Sch.10A para.1 requirement that the amount should be recorded on the credit (paras 32-36). (3) Although the question of whether the purchase of the credits was a pre-payment for the services was academic, the tribunal nevertheless set out its opinion. The cost of viewing and downloading documents varied, some required more credits than others. Customers would not know how many credits were required for a particular document until they accessed it. Moreover, since the company reserved the right to alter the price of any particular document or category of documents, it could not be said that the price of the services was clearly identified when the customer bought credits. While the nature of the supply was clear at the time of purchase, the precise specification of the documents that could be viewed or downloaded with the credits could not be fixed until the documents were identified and the credits used. It followed that payment for the credits was not a pre-payment triggering a charge to VAT at that point (paras 43-45).

FINDMYPAST LTD (FORMERLY DC THOMSON FAMILY HISTORY LTD) v REVENUE AND CUSTOMS COMMISSIONERS *sub nom.* FINDMYPAST LTD (FORMERLY BRIGHTSOLID ONLINE TECHNOLOGY LTD) v REVENUE AND CUSTOMS COMMISSIONERS, [2016] UKUT 17 (TCC), [2016] S.T.C. 1107, Lord Glennie, UT (Tax).

2209 VAT–Zero rating–Drugs

THE VALUE ADDED TAX (DRUGS, MEDICINES, AIDS AND CHARITIES, ETC.) ORDER 2016, SI 2016/620; made under the Value Added Tax Act 1994 s.30(4). In force: 28 June 2016.

This Order, which comes into force on 28 June 2016, amends Groups 12 and 15 of the Value Added Tax Act 1994 Sch.8 (zero-rating). The effect of this Order is to maintain the current application of the zero rate of VAT in Group 12 and Group 15 of Schedule 8 to the Value Added Tax Act 1994 following changes to the structure of health services in England and Northern Ireland made by the Health and Social Care Act 2012 and the Health and Social Care (Reform) Act (Northern Ireland) 2009 and a change to the departmental responsibility for health services in the Isle of Man government made by the Transfer of Functions (Health and Social Care) Order 2014.

2210 VAT–Zero rating–Whether supply of distance-learning courses zero rated for VAT purposes–Learning by reading printed material supplied

[Value Added Tax Act 1994 (c.23) s.79]

The court had to consider appeals relating to the VAT rating of a supply of distance-learning courses and ancillary services. The appellant provided courses consisting of a supply of manuals with support from tutors. No qualification or accreditation was available on completion of the course, but some customers went on to seek third-party qualifications. The role of the tutors was to direct customers to relevant parts of the manual, but in practice very little use was made of the facility to contact them. As a further add-on service, customers were able to attend a short practical course to enable them to practise their skills. The appellant claimed that it provided a single supply of manuals which was zero rated for VAT purposes, whereas the commissioners argued that the aim of the appellant's customers was to secure education and obtain a qualification. In 2000, an agreement was reached between the parties to split the supplies so as to classify them as 25% standard rated and 75% zero rated. In 2006, the appellant made a repayment claim resulting from a substantial bad debt. HMRC refused the repayment and held that, following the decision in *College of Estate Management v Customs and Excise Commissioners* [2005] UKHL 62, [2005] 1 W.L.R. 3351, [2006] C.L.Y. 4449, all the appellant's supplies for the relevant period should have been standard rated as supplies of education. HMRC made back assessments but refrained from pursuing them in recognition of the appellant's legitimate expectation that the agreed method would be maintained until its withdrawal in August 2009. HMRC therefore made a payment in respect of the appellant's claim for the 2006 period, but did so late. The appellant demanded the repayment supplement under the Value Added Tax Act 1994 s.79. It also claimed that the commissioners' new analysis of the correct method to charge VAT should not be applied in the run-off period to contracts entered into before August 2009 for which finance was in place and for which the consideration had already been fixed.

Held: Appeal allowed. (1) The end result sought by customers was to learn by reading the printed material supplied and not to pass an examination or obtain a qualification, *College of Estate Management* distinguished. The manuals were sufficient to achieve that end and were therefore the appellant's principal provision, with the add-on items being ancillary. In practice, the majority of customers made no use of those ancillary services. The few staff who were involved in responding to customer contact were essentially there to refer customers back to the manuals, not to provide further or different education. In the event that some customers aimed to obtain third-party qualifications after finishing the courses, those ends were not part of the supply offered by the appellant. It could not be said, therefore, that the end sought by the average customer was an education. It followed that there was a single, zero-rated supply of books with ancillary services (see paras 64, 96-98, 103-105, 110, 120-122 of judgment). (2) If the conclusion on the principal issue were to withstand an appeal, the repayment supplement claimed by the appellant would be due as a matter of law because its supplies would be zero rated and HMRC's payment was late. However, should the decision on the principal issue be overturned on appeal, the appellant would have no VAT credit consisting of an excess of input deductions over output liability, and therefore no entitlement to the repayment supplement (paras 137-139). (3) In relation to contracts entered into before August 2009 under finance arrangements, the appellant would have had no means of changing the agreed consideration payable by customers to take account of the additional VAT that would have become payable if the commissioners' case had succeeded. Although a legitimate expectation did not modify the statutory position, it was a legal right capable of founding a judicial review claim. However, the authorities demonstrated a general trend to the effect that the First-tier Tribunal's function was to arbitrate on the strict legal position in relation to the application of the tax provisions rather than judicial review considerations. Accordingly, express wording in the statutory provisions would be required to confer jurisdiction on the tribunal over such considerations, *Hollinger Print Ltd v Revenue and Customs Commissioners* [2013] UKFTT 739 (TC), [2014] S.T.I. 451 applied (paras 142, 147-149). (4) If the instant tribunal had had jurisdiction to deal with the appellant's claim in relation to the supplies under the pre-August 2009 contracts, HMRC's acceptance of the appellant's legitimate expectation in relation to pre-August 2009 supplies should have extended to the treatment of the pre-August 2009 contracts in their run-off period. Since the appellant would have been unable to recover from the customers the cost of an increase in the VAT rate during the life of those contracts, it followed that they should have been protected from any change in basis (paras 172-175).

METROPOLITAN INTERNATIONAL SCHOOLS v REVENUE AND CUSTOMS COMMISSIONERS, [2015] UKFTT 517 (TC), [2016] S.F.T.D. 134, Judge Howard M Nowlan, FTT (Tax).

2211 VAT groups–VAT registration–Retrospective inclusion of group companies in VAT group

[Value Added Tax Act 1994 (c.23) s.43B(4)]

The appellant house building group of companies appealed against HMRC's refusal to concede the retrospective inclusion of two group companies into the appellant's VAT group. The matter had been remitted to HMRC for reconsideration following a successful appeal (*Copthorn Holdings Ltd v Revenue and Customs Commissioners*

[2013] UKFTT 190 (TC), [2014] S.F.T.D. 1, [2014] C.L.Y. 3054) by the appellant. The group's finance and VAT affairs were in some chaos at the relevant time and several administrative errors had led to a general mistaken assumption that the two companies in question were members of the VAT group. All transactions were recorded consistently with that assumption. Subsequent enquiries by HMRC led to the realisation that the two companies were not in the VAT group. The appellant suffered a serious forfeiture of what should have been a routine deduction for input tax in a sum exceeding £2 million. The issue arose from a sub-sale to one of the two companies in question of a site for development purchased by another group company, and from the monthly on-supply of services to the two companies by a group company which was invoiced by the third party supplier. The group company elected to waive VAT exemption in relation to the sub-sale but no notice of election to tax was given to HMRC. The appellant recovered the whole of the input VAT, the sub-sale being disregarded. The on-supplies appeared to have been ignored and the input deductions claimed by the appellant. Retrospective inclusion was designed to make the VAT treatment conform to the way in which matters had been reported and so eliminate the incoherent VAT treatment that the actual mistakes occasioned. The first appeal had been successful on the ground that HMRC had an open discretion under the Value Added Tax Act 1994 s.43B(4) to retrospectively include companies in a VAT group and it was wrong for that discretion to have been surrendered in the way it had in the published policy. Following that decision, HMRC announced changes to its policy which reduced the period within which applications might be backdated, limited applications to those made in the most exceptional circumstances, and changed the wording defining exceptional circumstances. The appellant argued that the changes to the policy had further added to the bar on making retrospective applications.

Held: Appeal allowed. On the evidence, the VAT filings and the fact that the appellant itself recovered the input VAT in relation to the sub-sale could only be explained on the basis that the two companies were generally assumed to be part of the VAT group. The third party supplies were treated as generating input deductions for the representative member which suggested that the group operated on the assumption that the on-supplies were disregarded for VAT purposes because the two companies were members of the VAT group. Although HMRC had made changes to the policy, the whole tenor remained the same and effectively the policy was unchanged. There should be some reluctance to allow retrospective additions to VAT groups where that necessitated changes to earlier VAT returns, but such changes were unnecessary where the addition was designed to validate a group's assumption that a company was in the group and when the filings had been made on that basis. That could support a retrospective inclusion, particularly where the mistake had been honest and it had affected several aspects of VAT treatment for some time. It was particularly compelling if the inclusion occasioned an entirely sensible and coherent result. In the instant case, the refusal occasioned considerable and complex revisions to earlier filings. There was an obvious distinction between cases where groups had simply changed their mind as to the inclusion of a company in a VAT group, and cases where companies were assumed to be in a VAT group and the application was to make matters conform to the assumptions that had prevailed throughout. Generally, the effect and the intention of VAT groupings was not to alter the overall incidence of tax. In the instant case, the result of not filing the option to tax and the assumption as to inclusion in the VAT group occasioned a substantial loss of input tax where there should not have been any net cost to the group. That might be exceptional. The primary mistake might have been the failure to file, but the retrospective inclusion of the company into the VAT group was the only way to correct the error. The policy required exceptional circumstances for retrospective additions outside a prescribed 30-day period. The decision letters had indicated that "exceptional" required something rare and not common. A very high bar, possibly insurmountable, had been set. The policy significantly fettered the open discretion granted to HMRC in an unacceptable manner. It was futile for the matter to be remitted between HMRC and the First-tier Tribunal continuously, but the policy was still too restrictive of the open discretion conferred on HMRC notwithstanding the very marginal changes. The applications were remitted for reconsideration by HMRC, *Customs and Excise Commissioners v Save and Prosper Group Ltd* [1979] S.T.C. 205, [1979] C.L.Y. 2749 considered. The tribunal outlined the facts to which it considered

HMRC should give attention by reconsidering the application (see paras 6, 16, 18, 27-29, 53, 55-60, 62-64, 66, 75-77 of judgment).

COPTHORN HOLDINGS LTD v REVENUE AND CUSTOMS COMMISSIONERS, [2015] UKFTT 405 (TC), [2016] S.F.T.D. 17, Judge Howard M Nowlan, FTT (Tax).

2212 VAT schemes–Tax refunds–DIY builder's scheme–Consideration of s.35 Value Added Tax Act 1994 and application of Note 2(c) in Sch.8 Group 5

[Value Added Tax Act 1994 (c.23) Sch.8 Pt II Group 5, s.35, s.35(1A)(a), s.35(4)]

HMRC appealed against a decision allowing a property owner to claim a VAT refund under the DIY builder's scheme in the Value Added Tax Act 1994 s.35 in circumstances where it had refused the claim. The property owner had bought land containing a lake and created a fishery. He later obtained planning permission to build a dwelling so as to provide round-the-clock supervision and management of the fishery enterprise and enable expansion of the business. A planning condition stipulated that occupiers had to be employees of the fishery or their widows and dependants. After the house was built, the property owner submitted a claim to HMRC for a VAT refund of some £8,500. HMRC rejected the claim on the ground that it failed to satisfy the construction requirements in s.35(4) of the Act, which referred to Sch.8 Group 5. Note 2(c) of Sch.8 Group 5 stated that the refund was applicable to buildings designed as a dwelling "if the separate use or disposal of the dwelling was not prohibited by ... any covenant, statutory planning consent or similar provision". HMRC maintained that the dwelling could not be used "separately" from the fishery. The property owner appealed to the First-tier Tribunal, which held that "separate use or disposal" of the building was not "prohibited" by the terms of the planning consent, and that Note 2(c) was satisfied. The issue at the instant hearing was the meaning and application of Note 2(c) including (1) the proper construction of "separate use"; (2) the proper construction of "not prohibited"; (3) whether the occupancy description prohibited a use of the dwelling which was separate from the fishery business; (4) whether a description in a planning application or planning permission of a particular land use could amount to a prohibition of a separate use of a dwelling.

Held: Appeal allowed. (1) HMRC was correct that the phrase "separate use" meant "separate from" that of the main building, rather than merely distinct use, or use as a separate household, *Lunn v Revenue and Customs Commissioners* [2009] UKUT 244 (TCC), [2010] S.T.C. 486, [2010] C.L.Y. 3513 applied (see paras 30-34 of judgment). (2) HMRC was also correct that the phrase "not prohibited" had to be construed the same whether it appeared in the context of s.35 or in an issue relating to Group 5 zero rating. In the latter context, a strict construction was imposed by EU law because Group 5 was a derogation from the general application of VAT. Section 35 was not, on its face, a provision implementing EU law so it seemed paradoxical to make it subject to an EU rule of construction. However, EU law was applicable to s.35 by proxy, because the EU rule of construction applied to Group 5 and s.35(4) provided that the notes to Group 5 "shall apply for construing this section as they apply for construing that Group". There was not much scope for a "strict" construction of "not prohibited": a use which was a breach of planning consent terms would be prohibited in that sense (paras 38-40). (3) In the instant case, the separate use of the dwelling was prohibited by the occupancy condition with the result that the building was not "designed as a dwelling" for the purposes of s.35(1A)(a) of the Act and Note 2(c). It did not therefore attract a VAT refund. The occupancy restriction was sufficiently clear and mandatory to amount to a prohibition. It was designed to ensure that the accommodation was retained for the purposes of the fishery business. The condition was not disqualified by the fact that the category of occupiers extended beyond fishery employees; occupants still had to have a connection with the fishery. Nor did it matter that the restriction was not framed expressly as a prohibition, *Swain v Revenue and Customs Commissioners* [2013] UKFTT 316 (TC), [2013] S.T.I. 2185 and *Wendels v Revenue and Customs Commissioners* [2010] UKFTT 476 (TC), [2010] S.T.I. 3136 approved, *Lunn* considered (paras 63-67, 77, 93-96, 98-100) (4) (Obiter) The description of a development in a planning application or planning consent could constitute a prohibition on a certain use without an express mandatory condition or equivalent provision. However, a cautious approach should be taken to construing such a description in that way. That was because the word "prohibited" and its equivalents of "forbidden" or "out of bounds" carried a requirement for legal certainty and it would be rare for a description alone to meet the necessary level, *Shields v Revenue and Customs Commissioners* [2014] UKUT 453 (TCC), [2015] S.T.C. 643, [2015] C.L.Y. 2627 and *Telford and Wrekin Council v Secretary of State for Communities and Local Government* [2013] EWHC 79 (Admin), [2013] 1 E.G.L.R. 87, [2013] C.L.Y. 2333 considered. In the instant case, neither the description in the application nor the inspector's decision would have given rise to a prohibition on separate use or disposal of the dwelling (paras 53-57).

BURTON v REVENUE AND CUSTOMS COMMISSIONERS, [2016] UKUT 20 (TCC), [2016] B.V.C. 502, Barling J, UT (Tax).

2213 Zero rating–Beverages–Supplies of flavoured powders designed for adding to milk–Social policy objections–Principle of fiscal neutrality in art.110 Directive 2006/112

[Value Added Tax Act 1994 (c.23) Sch.8; Directive 2006/112 on the common system of VAT 2006 art.110]

A taxpayer appealed against a decision by the respondent HMRC to refuse its claim for the repayment of output tax which the taxpayer considered it had over-declared on sales of flavoured powders designed for adding to milk. The Value Added Tax Act Sch.8 Pt II Group 1 set out a list of zero-rated goods and supplies which included "food of a kind used for human consumption". It was undisputed that the product in question fell within that description. There followed, in Group 1, a list of items which were excepted from zero rating and a list of items overriding the exception. The products included in the list of overriding items related to the excepted items and were zero rated. Excepted item 4 was "beverages including ... powders ... or other products for the preparation of beverages". According to the taxpayer, its product did not fall within excepted item 4, because the term "beverages" was to be construed as excluding overriding item 6, namely "milk and preparations and extracts thereof", which related to excepted item 4, whereas the product in question was for adding to milk to be consumed as a milk drink. Alternatively, it was argued that adding the product to milk did not create a "beverage" but merely flavoured the milk. According to HMRC, the overriding items did not operate as interpretative provisions. It took the view that the product fell within excepted item 4 because the term "beverages" was not to be read as subject to overriding item 6: it would only be excluded from excepted item 4 if the product itself fell within overriding 6. However, the product was not within overriding item 6 because it did not contain milk. Further, HMRC argued that the addition of the product to milk created a distinct beverage which sufficed for it to be regarded as "for the preparation of beverages". The taxpayer argued that its interpretation of the legislative provisions was clearly supported by social policy objectives and fiscal neutrality considerations in accordance with Directive 2006/112 art.110: respectively, the encouragement of milk-drinking and the requirement for the zero-rating of supplies to be in accordance with EU law.

Held: Appeal dismissed. (1) Having regard to the natural meaning of the provisions in issue, there was no basis for the taxpayer's view that the term "beverages" in excepted item 4 had to be interpreted as subject to overriding item 6 to mean "beverages other than milk and preparations and extracts thereof". The use of the term "overriding" did no more than indicate that, if a supply of an item which fell into the category of excepted items also fell within the related category of overriding item, the standard-rated treatment of supplies of that item was overridden. The overriding items did not function as general interpretative provisions. Although it was clear from overriding item 6 that Parliament intended to zero-rate supplies of milk and milk products, it did not follow that it must have intended also to zero-rate a powder for adding to milk which did not itself contain any milk (see paras 125-129 of judgment). (2) In interpreting the term "powder for the preparation of beverages", the natural meaning had to be applied. It was not appropriate to apply tests or complex analyses in distinguishing between products. In most cases, the type of product envisaged by the provisions in issue would be added to what would commonly be viewed as a drink or "beverage" which could be consumed with no further additions. Applying that test in the instant case, the product was a "powder for the preparation of beverages" within the meaning of excepted item 4 (paras 133, 136, 139-140, 142). (3) When construing VAT exemptions, it was relevant to have regard to the social policy behind them, *Marks & Spencer Plc v Customs and*

Excise Commissioners (C-309/06) EU:C:2008:211, [2008] S.T.C. 1408, [2008] C.L.Y. 4060 followed. Although the drinking of a certain amount of milk might have certain health benefits, that was not necessarily the reason why milk was included in the zero-rating provisions (paras 144, 152-154). (4) Article 110 allowed Member States a discretion to continue providing for zero rating, provided that those arrangements did not infringe the principle of fiscal neutrality. That principle precluded Member States from treating similar goods and supplies of services, which were thus in competition with each other, differently for VAT purposes. The UK's discretion would be deprived of useful effect if the principle of fiscal neutrality meant that supplies of all types of "food of a kind used for human consumption" had to be regarded as similar. The differences between the product in issue and ready-made drinks were likely to have a significant influence on the consumer in making a choice. Therefore, supplies of the product were not sufficiently similar to supplies of ready-make drinks to breach the principle of fiscal neutrality. They were thus standard-rated supplies, *Revenue and Customs Commissioners v Rank Group Plc (C-259/10)* EU:C:2011:719, [2012] S.T.C. 23, [2012] C.L.Y. 3388 followed. Accordingly, the taxpayer was not entitled to repayment of the VAT accounted for (paras 155, 157, 178, 192, 207-209).

NESTLE UK LTD v REVENUE AND CUSTOMS COMMISSIONERS, [2016] UKFTT 158 (TC), [2016] S.F.T.D. 438, Judge Harriet Morgan, FTT (Tax).

2214 Zero rating–Community facilities–Construction of clubhouse by rugby club–Intention to provide social or recreational facilities for local community–Actual use following construction

[Value Added Tax Act 1994 (c.23) Sch.8]

A rugby club appealed against HMRC's decision that supplies made in the course of the construction of a clubhouse did not attract zero-rating. The club, a registered charity, held a lease at a peppercorn rent from the local authority over land which included playing fields used for rugby. The club embarked on a project to build a clubhouse on the grounds. The building was mainly occupied by changing rooms, a main hall area, a kitchen area that doubled as a bar when functions were held, and toilets. The funds required to build the clubhouse came from the Scottish sports agency, from various trusts and community funds, and from fundraising by the club. The club's constitution contained a clause stipulating that the club provided a community benefit, and in fact the clubhouse was used extensively for dance and exercise classes and by a choir, a band and other community associations. It was also used for social and fundraising events unconnected with the club. The club argued that the supplies fell to be zero-rated because the building was intended to be used "as a village hall or similarly in providing social or recreational facilities for a local community" within the meaning of the Value Added Tax Act 1994 Sch.8 Group 5 para.6(b). HMRC submitted that there was no evidence from the funding application forms that the intended use of the building at the time of its construction was for broader community use.

Held: Appeal allowed. (1) The words "intended for use" in para.6(b) referred to the intention at the time of construction of the building. However, where a building had been used in a certain way from the time it was built, that might lead to a strong inference that that was the intended use at the time of construction, absent evidence to the contrary. In the instant case, the general intention that the clubhouse would be available for use by other clubs was supported by the funding applications, despite HMRC's contentions, and appeared consistent with the club's constitution. When any building was constructed with an intended use of "village hall or similar", it would often be impossible to know in advance exactly which groups would use it, and to what extent, over the long term. On the evidence as a whole, the actual usage of the clubhouse following its construction was consistent with what was intended at the time it was built, even if the actual amount of usage by other groups was not foreseeable in all its detail and might have significantly exceeded expectations (see paras 71-72, 74-76 of judgment). (2) As a sporting facility was a "recreational facility", that definition would be satisfied even if the clubhouse were used for nothing other than playing rugby (paras 77-78). (3) In a rural area, the geographic size of a "local community" might be significantly larger than in an urban area. In any event, minor usage of facilities by persons from outside the local community would not of itself prevent the "local community" requirement from being satisfied. Therefore, having regard to the geography of the area and the circumstances as a whole, there was sufficient evidence that the facilities in the instant case were provided to a "local community" (paras 79-80). (4) The facilities were also used, and were at the time of construction intended to be used, as a "village hall or similarly", as evidenced by such matters as the diverse community groups which used the clubhouse, the non-commercial basis on which it was constructed and managed, and the location of the clubhouse on council-owned land for a peppercorn rent. It was not decisive that the clubhouse was managed by one of the groups that used it and could choose to grant or deny others access, as there was no requirement that a "village hall" had to be owned, organised and administered by the local community, *Jubilee Hall Recreation Centre Ltd v Customs and Excise Commissioners* [1999] S.T.C. 381, [1999] C.L.Y. 5031 followed. It was also immaterial that the club gave priority to its own needs, weighed against its characterisation as a "village hall or similar". Given that 90% of the usage of the clubhouse was by groups other than the club itself, it could not be said that use by groups other than the club was secondary. Accordingly, all the requirements of para.6(b) were met (paras 45, 81-83).

CAITHNESS RUGBY FOOTBALL CLUB v REVENUE AND CUSTOMS COMMISSIONERS, [2015] UKFTT 378 (TC), [2015] S.F.T.D. 1078, Judge Christopher Staker, FTT (Tax).

2215 Zero rating–Community facilities–Rugby club's intention to provide social or recreational facilities for local community in new clubhouse–Community not body directing or controlling use–Interpretation of Sch.8 Group 5 Item 2 Note 6(b) Value Added Tax Act 1994

[Value Added Tax Act 1994 (c.23) Sch.8; Directive 67/228 on turnover taxes - Structure and procedures for application of the common system of value added tax 1967 art.17]

HMRC appealed against a decision of the First-tier Tribunal that the construction by the respondent rugby club of a new clubhouse was zero-rated for VAT purposes. The club was a registered charity. HMRC refused to treat the construction works as zero-rated on the basis that use for a relevant charitable purpose "as a village hall or similarly" in the Value Added Tax Act 1994 Sch.8 Group 5 Item 2 Note 6(b) was a requirement that was separate and additional to the requirement of "social or recreational facilities for a local community". Therefore, according to HMRC, the provision of social or recreational facilities to a local community was not in itself sufficient; the building had to be in some sense at the disposal of the community. The tribunal held that there had been very substantial use of the clubhouse for a wide variety of sporting, social and recreational activities in addition to the rugby club's own use, and that the actual use of the building was consistent with what had been intended at the time of its construction, namely use as a "village hall or similarly". Accordingly, it held that the requirement in Note 6(b) was satisfied. HMRC argued that the tribunal had made a material error of law when determining whether the building had been intended solely for use by the club as a village hall or similarly; instead, it was a prerequisite of Note 6(b) that there be local community direction or control of the use of the building.

Held: Appeal dismissed. Note 6(b) had to be interpreted consistently with Directive 67/228 art.17 and with the judgment in *Commission of the European Communities v United Kingdom (416/85)* EU:C:1988:321, [1990] 2 Q.B. 130, [1989] C.L.Y. 1685. According to art.17, provisions for reduced rates or exemptions were only to be made for clearly defined social reasons and for the benefit of the final consumer. There was nothing in art.17 or in *Commission v United Kingdom* to support the proposition that the degree of closeness between the consumer and the supply would necessarily be insufficient to make the consumer the final consumer unless he had direction over or control of the goods or services, or a building in which they had been incorporated, *Commission v United Kingdom* considered. That conclusion was not altered by the judgment in *Jubilee Hall Recreation Centre Ltd v Customs and Excise Commissioners* [1999] S.T.C. 381, [1999] C.L.Y. 5031. On a proper reading of *Jubilee Hall*, it did not state that the direction or control by a local community of the use of the building in which construction services had been incorporated was essential for zero-rating in terms of Note 6(b); rather, it supported the proposition that the existence or non-existence of direction or control over the use of a building was a relevant circumstance, but not necessarily a decisive one, *Jubilee Hall* followed. Something more was required than mere use for the provision of social or recreational facilities for the local community; otherwise, the reference in Note 6(b) to use as a "village hall or similarly" would be devoid of purpose. The use of a building might be intended to be at the disposal of a local community, even though the community was not the body directing or controlling its use. Accordingly, it had been open to the tribunal to make the findings it had, *Yarburgh Children's Trust v Customs and Excise Commissioners* [2002] S.T.C. 207, [2002] C.L.Y. 4811 and *New Deer Community Association v Revenue and Customs Commissioners* [2015] UKUT 604 (TCC), [2016] S.T.C. 507, [2016] 2217 followed (see paras 11, 19-21, 25, 28, 34-36 of judgment).

REVENUE AND CUSTOMS COMMISSIONERS v CAITHNESS RUGBY FOOTBALL CLUB *sub nom.* CAITHNESS RUGBY FOOTBALL CLUB v REVENUE AND CUSTOMS COMMISSIONERS, [2016] UKUT 354 (TCC), [2016] S.T.C. 2028, Lord Doherty, UT (Tax).

2216 Zero rating–Further education colleges–Construction of new building by college with charity status–Whether building's use solely charitable

[Value Added Tax Act 1994 (c.23) Sch.8 Group 5; Directive 2006/116 on the term of protection of copyright and related rights 2006 art.2]

HMRC appealed against a First-tier Tribunal judge's decision that supplies made to a college for the construction of a new campus building were zero-rated for VAT under the Value Added Tax Act 1994 Sch.8 Group 5 Item 2. The college was a charity whose primary source of income was grant funding. As the new building was intended to provide further education, the majority of which was grant funded, the college believed that its use amounted to a relevant charitable purpose under Sch.8 Group 5 and its construction was thereby zero rated. HMRC refused to authorise the zero rating as it considered that the building's use was not solely charitable as required by Group 5 because the college also supplied education to fee-paying students, some of whom paid the full tuition fee while some made part-payments as they were entitled to a remission based on their personal circumstances. The tribunal judge decided that as the part-payments varied depending on personal circumstances, the link between them and the education supplied was not sufficiently direct for the part-payments to amount to consideration within the meaning of Directive 2006/116 art.2(1)(c). He therefore concluded that those supplies did not amount to business use, drawing a comparison with *Commission of the European Communities v Finland (C-246/08)* EU:C:2009:671, [2009] E.C.R. I-10605, where legal aid supplied by a public legal aid office, which varied depending on the recipient's income and level of contribution, was not a business activity. HMRC submitted that the tribunal judge had not addressed the distinction it had made between the students who qualified for remission and the students who paid the full fee, and there was a direct link between payment and supply in the latter group. The college argued that the full fee was subsidised and was less than the cost of the course, so there was no real distinction between the two groups.

Held: Appeal allowed. (1) It was unclear whether the tribunal judge had rejected HMRC's distinction between the two groups of students, and failed to explain why, or overlooked it. His failure to address the point was a material error. There was a clear analogy between the legal aid recipients in *Commission v Finland* and the students who were entitled to a remission, but the question remained whether the full fee paid by the other students was subsidised such that there was no distinction to be drawn between the two groups. The court in *Hotel Scandic Gasaback AB v Riksskatteverket (C-412/03)* EU:C:2005:47, [2005] S.T.C. 1311, [2005] C.L.Y. 4392 had decided that a supply made for consideration less than cost was not a determining factor, although in *Commission v Finland* it thought that there had to be a point where the disparity between the value of the payment and the cost of supply was so great that the direct link between supply and consideration was lost. However, that latter view had followed on from the court's observation that the amount paid by the legal aid recipient was determined by two factors: the cost of the supply and the extent of the recipient's resources. The court's conclusion that the supply was not taxable had been dependent on that combination of factors: without the variation of payment according to means, the link between supply and payment would not have been broken. In the instant case, the students who paid the full fee had to pay it irrespective of their means and the direct link remained in place. The fact that the fee was less than the cost of the supply did not mean that it did not amount to consideration. There was a direct link and there was also reciprocity of obligation. It followed that the college's supplies to those students were made in the course or furtherance of a business and the building was not used solely for a relevant charitable purpose, *Commission v Finland, Hotel Scandic, Tolsma v Inspecteur der Omzetbelasting, Leeuwarden (C-16/93)* EU:C:1994:80, [1994] S.T.C. 509, [1994] C.L.Y. 4962 and *Apple and Pear Development Council v Customs and Excise Commissioners (102/86)* EU:C:1988:120, [1988] 2 All E.R. 922, [1988] C.L.Y. 1572 applied (see paras 45-50, 52-53 of judgment). (2) (Per curiam) It was unlikely that Parliament would have intended a capricious system where a charity providing education for young people could escape a tax burden on the construction of a building intended for its charitable purpose if it kept the extent of its income earned in particular ways below an arbitrary threshold, but was otherwise compelled to suffer not some but all of the burden. The legislation should be reconsidered. It could not be impossible to relieve charities of an unintended tax burden while protecting commercial organisations from unfair competition and preventing abuse (para.56).

WAKEFIELD COLLEGE v REVENUE AND CUSTOMS COMMISSIONERS *sub nom.* REVENUE AND CUSTOMS COMMISSIONERS v WAKEFIELD COLLEGE, [2016] UKUT 19 (TCC), [2016] S.T.C. 1219, Barling J, UT (Tax).

2217 Zero rating–Sports and leisure facilities–Whether building used as village hall or similarly within meaning of Sch.8 Group 5 Item 2 Note(6)(b) Value Added Tax Act 1994

[Value Added Tax Act 1994 (c.23) Sch.8]

The appellant community association appealed against a decision of the First-tier Tribunal (*New Deer Community Association v Revenue and Customs Commissioners* [2014] UKFTT 1028 (TC), [2014] S.T.I. 3548) that the construction of a new building should not, subject to one qualification, be zero rated for VAT purposes. The appellant's objects included maintaining and managing a pleasure park. The pleasure park was a sports pitch on which there had been a small hut providing changing facilities. The appellant decided to replace the hut and pitch with a new pavilion together with an all-weather surface and car park. The new building comprised an entrance area and foyer; four changing rooms, each with an adjoining shower area and WC; two smaller "referee rooms", each with a shower; three WCs; and a meeting room/kitchen. There was also an adjacent equipment-storage area. The entrance and foyer made up 22% of the total floor area; the figure for the meeting room/kitchen was 4.4%. The building was used by persons taking part in sport on the adjacent pitch. There was also evidence that it had been used for play groups, birthday parties and meetings of the British Legion. The issue was whether the building was intended for use solely for a "relevant charitable purpose". Use for such a purpose was defined as use by a charity in one of two ways, including use "as a village hall or similarly in providing social or recreational facilities for a local community" (the Value Added Tax Act 1994 Sch.8 Group 5 Item 2 Note(6)(b)).

Held: Appeal dismissed. As to the interpretation of Note(6)(b), the words "or similarly" related back to the word "use". The enquiry therefore had to focus on whether the use or intended use of the building was similar to use of a building as a village hall, rather than, for example, on whether the building was similar to a village hall. Further, the need for "local" use was made clear by the reference to provision of social or recreational facilities "for a local community". The reference to use similar to that of a village hall had therefore to be to something other than use by or for persons who lived in the vicinity of the building. The focus was on local community use rather than on local community control, *Caithness Rugby Football Club v Revenue and Customs Commissioners* [2015] UKFTT 378 (TC), [2015] S.F.T.D. 1078, [2016] 2214 approved. It was also clear that something more was required than mere use for the provision of social or recreational facilities for the local community; otherwise, the reference to use "as a village hall or similarly" would be emptied of content. Attention had to focus on the nature of the activities conducted or intended to be conducted. The question was whether they were similar to the type of social or recreational activities that one would expect to be conducted in a village hall for the benefit of a local community, *Jubilee Hall Recreation Centre Ltd v Customs and Excise Commissioners* [1999] S.T.C. 381, [1999]

C.L.Y. 5031 considered. It was not, however, a necessary requirement that there should be a "mix" of activities such as one might find carried on in a traditional village hall; note(6)(b) merely required use "similar to" that of a village hall. The carrying on of a mixture of activities might lead to a finding that the use of the relevant building was similar to that of a village hall, but a single use might qualify if it consisted of providing social or recreational facilities for the local community. What was essential, however, was that the activities carried on in the building be similar to use of a building as a village hall. The building here was not itself, subject to a de minimis exception for occasional use of the meeting room/kitchen or the entrance/foyer area, used in providing social or recreational facilities; rather, it was used as an adjunct to the social or recreational facilities provided for the local community by the sports pitch. The tribunal had made no finding that the building itself was used to any material extent by the local community for social or recreational activities. On the contrary, the tribunal emphasised the lack of suitability of the entrance and foyer for any form of use similar to that of a village hall. The tribunal had correctly focused on the potential uses of the building itself rather than on its facilitation of use of the sports pitch. The tribunal held, correctly, that the design of the building was relevant to the extent that it dictated what uses were reasonably practicable. It was entitled to find that a building used primarily to provide changing-room facilities and storage for sporting equipment was not used "as a village hall or similarly". As to the qualification to its finding, the tribunal had been entitled to find that the meeting room/kitchen was "capable [of] use by the whole community for social or recreational facilities, such use being similar to a village hall". It had therefore been entitled to allow zero rating for the 4.4% floor area represented by that room (see paras 8, 17-20 of judgment).

NEW DEER COMMUNITY ASSOCIATION v REVENUE AND CUSTOMS COMMISSIONERS, [2015] UKUT 604 (TCC), [2016] S.T.C. 507, Lord Tyre, UT (Tax).

WATER LAW

2218 **EU law–Bathing water–Management of bathing water quality**

THE BATHING WATER (AMENDMENT) (ENGLAND) REGULATIONS 2016, SI 2016/600; made under the European Communities Act 1972 s.2(2). In force: 20 June 2016.

These Regulations amend the Bathing Water Regulations 2013 which implement, in England and Wales, Directive 2006/7 of the European Parliament and of the Council concerning the management of bathing water quality and repealing Directive 76/160.

2219 **EU law–Implementation–Fitness for human consumption**

THE PRIVATE WATER SUPPLIES (ENGLAND) REGULATIONS 2016, SI 2016/618; made under the Water Industry Act 1991 s.67, s.77(3)(4), s.213(2); European Communities Act 1972 s.2(2). In force: 27 June 2016.

These Regulations, which apply in England, transpose requirements of Directive 98/83 on the quality of water intended for human consumption and Directive 2013/51 laying down requirements for the protection of the health of the general public with regard to radioactive substances in water intended for human consumption. They revoke and replace the Private Water Supplies Regulations 2009.

2220 **EU law–Water supply–Fitness for human consumption**

THE WATER SUPPLY (WATER QUALITY) (AMENDMENT) REGULATIONS 2016, SI 2016/410; made under the European Communities Act 1972 s.2(2); Water Industry Act 1991 s.67, s.69, s.77(3)(4), s.213(2). In force: 14 April 2016.

These Regulations amend the Water Supply (Water Quality) Regulations 2010 so as to implement Directive 2013/51 on the protection of the health of the general public with regard to the radioactive substances in water intended for human consumption in relation to water supplied by water undertakers whose areas are wholly or mainly in Wales.

2221 **Internal drainage boards–Dissolution–March West and White Fen Internal Drainage Board**

THE MARCH WEST AND WHITE FEN INTERNAL DRAINAGE BOARD ORDER 2016, SI 2016/482; made under the Land Drainage Act 1991 s.3(5)(7). In force: In accordance with reg.1.

This Order confirms a Scheme submitted by the Environment Agency making provision for: the abolition of the March and Whittlesey Internal Drainage District and Board; the abolition of the White Fen District Commissioners and the White Fen District; and the constitution of the March West and White Fen Internal Drainage District and Board.

2222 **Internal drainage boards–River Ouse**

THE RIVER OUSE (SUSSEX) INTERNAL DRAINAGE DISTRICT ORDER 2016, SI 2016/791; made under the Land Drainage Act 1991 s.3(5)(7). In force: 31 March 2017.

This Order confirms a Scheme submitted by the Environment Agency making provision for the abolition of the River Ouse (Sussex) Internal Drainage District.

2223 **Reservoirs–Natural Resources Body for Wales**

THE RESERVOIRS ACT 1975 (CAPACITY, REGISTRATION, PRESCRIBED FORMS, ETC.) (WALES) REGULATIONS 2016, SI 2016/80; made under the Reservoirs Act 1975 s.A1(4), s.2(2)(2C)(2D)(2E), s.3(1), s.5, s.11, s.20(1), s.21(1), s.21B. In force: 1 April 2016.

For the purposes of the Reservoirs Act 1975 these Regulations make provision for: calculating capacity; the information about a large raised reservoir that must be registered; notification of changes to, and the keeping and inspection of, the Welsh register; and the making and content of reports by the Natural Resources Body for Wales to the Welsh Ministers.

2224 **Water companies–Water quality–Water supply**

THE WATER SUPPLY (WATER QUALITY) REGULATIONS 2016, SI 2016/614; made under the Water Industry Act 1991 s.67, s.69, s.77(3)(4), s.213(2); European Communities Act 1972 s.2(2). In force: 27 June 2016.

These Regulations provide the legislative framework for drinking water quality in respect of public supplies provided by water companies and licensed water suppliers.

NORTHERN IRELAND

ADMINISTRATION OF JUSTICE

2225 Access to information–Court documents

THE COURT FILES PRIVILEGED ACCESS RULES (NORTHERN IRELAND) 2016, SR 2016/123; made under the Public Records Act 1923 s.9(1). In force: 30 March 2016.

These Rules enable the Department to establish procedures to allow privileged access to information contained in court files.

2226 Coroners–Coroners' powers and duties

The applicant (H) applied to strike out a coroner's appeal against the quashing of a verdict of an inquest. An inquest had taken place into the death of H's son (V), who was shot during a joint police and army surveillance operation. In judicial review proceedings (*Jordan's Applications for Judicial Review, Re* [2014] NIQB 11, [2014] Inquest L.R. 1, [2016] 2237) a judge had quashed the inquest verdict on the basis that the police and the coroner had failed to disclose relevant documents, the police had caused unreasonable delay in the hearing of the inquest, the coroner should not have decided to sit with a jury and should have discharged a particular juror. The police and the coroner appealed. H submitted that it was not appropriate for the coroner to participate as an adversarial party in the judicial review proceedings and he should not be permitted to bring an appeal.

Held: Application refused. (1) Coroners were independent judicial officer holders. Whether sitting alone or with a jury they had to act impartially and their conduct of an inquest must not be affected by bias. Inquest proceedings were inquisitorial rather than adversarial but there was generally no issue of apparent bias in the conduct of either kind of proceedings, *Porter v Magill* [2001] UKHL 67, [2002] 2 A.C. 357, [2002] C.L.Y. 3185 considered. The Divisional Court had a supervisory role in respect of inquest proceedings by way of judicial review. Such proceedings were generally adversarial. In many inquest cases the family of the deceased was the applicant and the coroner was the respondent. The danger was that participation by the coroner in such adversarial proceedings might give rise to a perception on the part of the family that the coroner was predisposed against their interests. The coroner should, where possible, assist the court by deposing as to what took place before him, setting out the reasons for his decisions and, if appropriate, appearing in court to assist in an amicus role. The opposing parties should then conduct the adversarial argument. No perception of bias could arise in those circumstances, *R. v HM Coroner for Lincoln Ex p. Hay* (1999) 163 J.P. 666, [1999] C.L.Y. 36 applied. However, on occasion there might be no opposing party concerned with coronial decisions. In those circumstances, if the supervisory jurisdiction of the Divisional Court was invoked the coroner might be the only realistic opposing party. There were also circumstances where an applicant raised in judicial review proceedings an issue of general importance to coroners concerning the substantive or procedural law governing the conduct of inquests. In such cases a coroner might feel it appropriate to support a particular view and thereby enter into the adversarial argument. The occasions on which the coroner would choose to become involved as an adversarial party would be limited as a result of the considerations outlined above, but the decision as to whether to participate, and the manner of doing so, was for the coroner. The coroner's access to the court should not be limited. Where there was a perception of bias as a result of the participation of the coroner, or it was otherwise in the interests of justice, the court could direct that the proceedings should be conducted by another coroner. That was the appropriate method of securing the independence and impartiality of the coroner hearing the inquest, *Darley's Application, Re* [1997] N.I. 384, [1999] C.L.Y. 5265 considered (see paras 14-21 of judgment). (2) The respondent in the instant proceedings was the coroner who heard the inquest. It was his responsibility to decide whether to appeal the judicial review decision and, if so, on what grounds. It would be inappropriate for that decision to be made by the Coroner's Service since in certain circumstances that might debar all of the coroners from hearing any further proceedings in respect of V's death. The coroner should not be prevented from participating in proceedings as he deemed appropriate (para.22).

JORDAN'S APPLICATIONS FOR JUDICIAL REVIEW, RE, [2014] NICA 36, [2016] N.I. 107, Morgan LCJ, CA (NI).

2227 Coroners and Justice Act 2009 (c.29)–Commencement No.2 (Northern Ireland) Order

THE CORONERS AND JUSTICE ACT 2009 (COMMENCEMENT NO.2) (NORTHERN IRELAND) ORDER 2016, SR 2016/23; made under the Coroners and Justice Act 2009 s.182(5)(6). Commencement details: bringing into operation various provisions of the 2009 Act on 29 February 2016.

This Order brings into force the Coroners and Justice Act 2009 s.49(2), which introduces Sch.11 of the Act. Schedule 11 substitutes new sections 17A to 17C for section 17 of the Coroners Act (Northern Ireland) 1959. Sections 17A to 17C make provision concerning witnesses, evidence and related offences at inquests in Northern Ireland.

2228 Coroners' courts–Coroners' powers and duties–Inquest into fatal shooting

[Coroners Act (Northern Ireland) 1959; European Convention on Human Rights 1950 art.2]

The court had to consider a number of appeals in judicial review proceedings arising from an inquest into the fatal shooting of an individual (P) in Northern Ireland by the police in 1992. P's father (J), who pursued the judicial review proceedings, disputed that the use of lethal force was appropriate. The police involved in the incident had been debriefed by officers (M and V) who had been involved in shootings in 1982. Before the inquest, which took place in 2012, a judicial review hearing resulted in a refusal to disclose reports of an investigation into an alleged cover-up by the police of their role in the 1982 shootings. At the inquest, the coroner summoned a jury pursuant to the Coroners Act (Northern Ireland) 1959 s.18(2) and prepared a series of questions for the jury designed to promote a narrative verdict as to the circumstances of P's death which, according to J, pointed the jury towards the conclusion that the force used was justified. It was held that the coroner had erred in refusing to disclose the reports, contrary to the procedural aspect of ECHR art.2; had not put in place sufficient safeguards to diminish the risk of jury bias; and had wrongly accepted the jury's outcome as a verdict, even though it had not reached a unanimous decision on contentious matters.

Held: Appeals allowed in part. (1) The concept of material being potentially relevant to an inquest imported a broad ambit to the obligation of disclosure in the particular context of the reports, *McKerr v United Kingdom (28883/95)* (2002) 34 E.H.R.R. 20 applied. The credibility of M and V was potentially relevant in determining the scope of the inquest. However, because he had not recognised the relevance or potential relevance of the documents in question, the coroner did not arrive at the stage of determining the scope of the inquest (see paras 21, 34-35, 41-43, 46 of judgment). (2) It was for the coroner to choose the questions to be put to the jury and his formulations of those questions should not be disturbed by the court in the absence of strong grounds, *R. (on the application of Middleton) v HM Coroner for Western Somerset* [2004] UKHL 10, [2004] 2 A.C. 182, [2004] C.L.Y. 37 followed. The trial judge had been correct to reject the challenge to the coroner's questions, which were capable of leading to a full and meaningful verdict and did not lead the jury in any particular direction (paras 59-60). (3) The risk of juror intimidation, partisan juries and perverse verdicts in Northern Ireland had long been recognised and had to be addressed in the context of s.18(2). In order to be assured that the inquest process would be capable of conducting an objective and impartial investigation as required by ECHR art.2, a coroner had to consider the facts of the case and then decide if there was a real possibility that a jury would be biased. In the instant case, the coroner had clearly recognised that there was a real risk of a perverse verdict and had taken certain steps, such as ensuring random selection of jurors and checking their backgrounds. However, he had not asked himself whether those steps had removed the risk to a fanciful or remote level. The need for such an approach was particularly important in cases where there had been a long delay since the death occurred and the safety net of a rehearing in the event of a hung jury would not afford the timely resolution demanded by the investigation (paras 84-88). (4) Coroners had to interpret the meaning of s.31(2) of the 1959 Act in a manner consistent with the principles set out by Lord Bingham in *Middleton*. In considering whether a jury had failed to agree on a verdict, the coroner ought ordinarily to determine whether or not the outcome of its deliberations had culminated in an expression on the disputed factual issues at the heart of the case, *Middleton* followed. If not, the coroner had to address his obligation under s.31(2) to consider whether to discharge the jury and summon another. In the instant case, the coroner had misdirected himself on the proper interpretation of s.31(1). The mere fact that the jury had made some findings did not mean that a verdict had been brought in within the terms of s.31(2) and the instant court could not be certain what the coroner's conclusion would have been if he had directed himself properly (paras 107, 110, 115-117). (5) The verdict was quashed and the matter remitted to a different coroner (para.18). (6) (Obiter) Deficiencies in the existing coronial system adversely affected the conduct of inquests and the coroner's inquisitorial role. The impact of those deficiencies was most pronounced in the conduct of legacy inquests. The UK would continue to breach the requirement of reasonable expedition in relation to its art.2 investigatory obligations in such cases and incur considerable public expense unless there was a new approach, such as taking all the legacy cases out of the inquest system and considering them in a time-bound inquiry with facilities for independent investigation and powers of compulsion in respect of witnesses and documents (paras 120-121, 124).

JORDAN'S APPLICATIONS FOR JUDICIAL REVIEW, RE, [2014] NICA 76, [2016] N.I. 116, Morgan LCJ, CA (NI).

2229 County courts–Court of Judicature of Northern Ireland–Jurisdiction

THE RULES OF THE COURT OF JUDICATURE (NORTHERN IRELAND) (AMENDMENT) 2016, SR 2016/299; made under the Judicature (Northern Ireland) Act 1978 s.55, s.55A. In force: In accordance with Rule 1.

These Rules amend the Rules of the Court of Judicature (Northern Ireland) 1980 to take account of the Justice Act (Northern Ireland) 2015 Pt 1 which creates a single jurisdiction for county courts and magistrates' courts whereby the jurisdiction and powers of those courts are exercisable throughout the whole of Northern Ireland.

2230 County courts–Court rules–Jurisdiction

THE MAGISTRATES' COURTS (MISCELLANEOUS AMENDMENTS) RULES (NORTHERN IRELAND) 2016, SR 2016/303; made under the Magistrates' Courts (Northern Ireland) Order 1981 (SI 1981 1675) art.13. In force: In accordance with Rule 1.

These Rules amend a number of rules to take account of the Justice Act (Northern Ireland) 2015 Pt 1 which creates a single jurisdiction for county courts and magistrates' courts whereby the jurisdiction and powers of those courts are exercisable throughout the whole of Northern Ireland.

2231 County courts–Court rules–Jurisdiction

THE COUNTY COURT (AMENDMENT) RULES (NORTHERN IRELAND) 2016, SR 2016/302; made under the County Courts (Northern Ireland) Order 1980 art.47. In force: In accordance with rule 1.

The purpose of the Statutory Rule is to amend the County Court Rules (Northern Ireland) 1981 in consequence of Part 1 of (and Schedule 1 to) the Justice Act (Northern Ireland) 2015 which creates a single territorial jurisdiction for the county courts and the magistrates' courts in Northern Ireland.

2232 Court rules–Crown Court–Jurisdiction

THE CROWN COURT (AMENDMENT) RULES (NORTHERN IRELAND) 2016, SR 2016/297; made under the Judicature (Northern Ireland) Act 1978 s.52(1), s.53A. In force: In accordance with rule 1.

These Rules amend the Crown Court Rules (Northern Ireland) 1979 to take account of Part 1 of the Justice Act (Northern Ireland) 2015 which creates a single jurisdiction for county courts and magistrate's courts whereby the jurisdiction and powers of those courts are exercisable throughout the whole of Northern Ireland.

2233 Court rules–Jurisdiction–Miscellaneous amendments

THE COUNTY COURT (MISCELLANEOUS AMENDMENTS) RULES (NORTHERN IRELAND) 2016, SR 2016/300; made under the County Courts (Northern Ireland) Order 1980 (SI 1980 397 (NI.3)) art.47. In force: In accordance with Rule 1.

These Rules amend: the Water Supplies and Sewerage (Northern Ireland) County Court Rules 1955; the County Court (Summoning of Witnesses in Criminal Proceedings and Appeals) Rules (Northern Ireland) 1966; and the County Court (Affidavit of Service) Rules (Northern Ireland) 1972 to take account of the Justice Act (Northern Ireland) 2015 Pt 1 which creates a single jurisdiction for county courts and magistrates' courts whereby the jurisdiction and powers of those courts are exercisable throughout the whole of Northern Ireland.

2234 Court rules–Magistrates' courts–Jurisdiction

THE MAGISTRATES' COURTS (AMENDMENT NO.2) RULES (NORTHERN IRELAND) 2016, SR 2016/304; made under the Magistrates' Courts (Northern Ireland) Order 1981 (SI 1981 1675) art.13. In force: In accordance with Rule 1.

These rules amend the Magistrates' Courts Rules (Northern Ireland) 1984 to take account of the Justice Act (Northern Ireland) 2015 Pt 1 which creates a single jurisdiction for county courts and magistrates' courts whereby the jurisdiction and powers of those courts are exercisable throughout the whole of Northern Ireland.

2235 Financial Provisions Act (Northern Ireland) 2014 (c.6)–Commencement No.3 Order

THE FINANCIAL PROVISIONS (2014 ACT) (COMMENCEMENT NO.3) ORDER (NORTHERN IRELAND) 2016, SR 2016/312; made under the Financial Provisions Act (Northern Ireland) 2014 s.13(2). Commencement details: bringing into operation various provisions of the Financial Provisions Act (Northern Ireland) 2014 on 22 August 2016.

This Order brings the Financial Provisions Act (Northern Ireland) 2014 s.8 into operation on 22 August 2016.

2236 Inquests–Delay–Fatal shooting by police officers–Claim for damages made out of time

[European Convention on Human Rights 1950 art.2; Human Rights Act 1998 (c.42) s.7(5), s.7(5)(b)]

The court was required to determine appeals against decisions (*Jordan's Application for Judicial Review, Re* [2014] NIQB 71) concerning an inquest into the fatal shooting of an individual by the police in Northern Ireland in 1992. The inquest did not take place until 2012. By then the victim's family had been pursuing litigation concerning the inquest for over 10 years. In judicial review proceedings the judge determined that the coroner was not responsible for the delay which occurred in the conclusion of the inquest, but that the Police Service of Northern Ireland had delayed progress of the inquest in breach of ECHR art.2. He made an award of £7,500 to the victim's father in respect of that breach. The PSNI appealed the award of damages and the victim's father cross-appealed the decision regarding the coroner. The PSNI submitted that the victim's father had not instituted proceedings for delay within the limitation period set out in the Human Rights Act 1998 s.7(5).

Held: Judgment accordingly. (1) The judge in *Jordan's Application for Judicial Review, Re* [2009] NIQB 76, [2010] Inquest L.R. 12, [2011] C.L.Y. 3598 had been satisfied that the repeated delays up to 2009 in implementing the inquest were entirely due to the continuing efforts of the PSNI to avoid providing the next of kin with the documents they sought. A new coroner was appointed, but the inquest did not proceed in January 2010 as it emerged that the police officer had been involved in three previous shootings and the coroner decided that he should view all the personnel files of other police witnesses. In April 2010 he ruled that a search of the Stevens database was necessary. His decision not to proceed in the absence of that search was based on the real possibility that the database contained material which was potentially relevant to the inquest, and the submission of the PSNI that it was not in a position to confirm that its duty of disclosure had been discharged without such a search. The inquest was listed for October 2011, but there was further late disclosure concerning two police witnesses and a further delay due to a failure of the security services to produce the necessary risk assessments. However, none of those factors showed any lack of expedition on the part of the coroner. The considerable delays were a result of obstacles and difficulties created by the PSNI. The father's cross-appeal was therefore dismissed (see paras 13-17 of judgment). (2) Delay in the hearing of inquest proceedings could constitute a breach of the Convention and thus entitle an aggrieved party to bring proceedings for breach of that Convention right. The appropriate remedy for such a breach would depend on the circumstances of what constituted just satisfaction, but might include an award of damages. Declaratory relief or mandamus might be enough to secure that right. In the instant case, it had been ordered that the inquest proceed before a different coroner. If that inquest did not take place within a reasonable timeframe, that would constitute a fresh breach of the Convention for which a remedy, including damages, might be available. Only when that inquest had been completed would it be possible to examine all of the circumstances surrounding any claim for delay and the court would then be in a position to determine whether adequate redress required an award of damages and, if so, against which public authority and in what amount. Therefore, in legacy cases, the issue of damages against any public authority for breach of the adjectival obligation in art.2 ought to be dealt with within one year of the inquest being completed, *Somerville v Scottish Ministers* [2007] UKHL 44, [2007] 1 W.L.R. 2734, [2008] C.L.Y. 4963 and *A v Essex CC* [2010] UKSC 33, [2011] 1 A.C. 280, [2010] C.L.Y. 989 applied. Each public authority against whom an award was sought should be joined. It might be necessary to rely on s.7(5)(b). The principle that the court should be aware of all the circumstances and the prevention of even further litigation in legacy cases were compelling arguments in favour of it being equitable in the circumstances to extend time if required. Where proceedings had been issued within 12 months of the conclusion of the inquest, time should be extended (paras 25-26).

JORDAN'S APPLICATIONS FOR JUDICIAL REVIEW, RE, [2015] NICA 66, [2015] Inquest L.R. 257, Morgan LCJ, CA (NI).

2237 Inquests–Joint police and army surveillance operation–Fatal shooting–Duty to undertake effective investigation

[European Convention on Human Rights 1950 art.2]

The claimant (H) applied for judicial review of decisions made by a coroner during an inquest into the death of his son (V). In November 1992 police and the army were monitoring the location of a suspected IRA bomb-making factory. V, a suspected IRA member, was shot and killed by a police officer (P1) during the operation. Several officers had been involved in previous incidents in 1982 and 2003 in which suspects were killed. In the 1982 incidents, officers were debriefed before being interviewed by CID and were instructed not to reveal the involvement of special branch, or the fact that it had been a planned operation. The officers thereafter made false statements. Two officers (P2 and P3) had conducted a debrief after V's death. P2 had been involved in all the previous incidents and P3 in the 1982 incidents. The reports into the 1982 incidents (the Sampson reports) were disclosed to the coroner in V's inquest. He decided they were not relevant, and they were not disclosed to H. P2 and P3's witness statements concerning the earlier incidents were disclosed. The coroner refused to allow the police ombudsman's report concerning the 2003 incident to be used to cross-examine P2 and another officer (P4) during V's inquest. A police witness was asked for his opinion on the actions of P1. A juror sent a note to the coroner which stated "is an opinion necessary for the jury. I feel this inquest is very unfair". The coroner gave further directions to the jury but did not discharge the juror. H submitted that the Sampson reports and the ombudsman's report should have been disclosed to him and used in V's inquest. He argued that the coroner should not have conducted the inquest with a jury because of the risk of a perverse verdict, and he should have discharged the juror who sent the note.

Held: Application granted. (1) The test for disclosure was potential relevance, *Chief Constable of Northern Ireland's Application for Judicial Review, Re* [2010] NIQB 66, [2010] Inquest L.R. 97, [2011] C.L.Y. 3599 applied. Potentially relevant documents included those potentially relevant to the credibility of witnesses at the hearing, and any documents potentially relevant as similar fact evidence (see paras 69-74 of judgment). The Sampson reports were relevant to a number of matters in V's inquest including (a) the reason P2 had lied in witness statements in the previous incidents; (b) whether P2 had been told that debriefs should not take place before officers were interviewed by CID; (c) the circumstances in, and dates on, which P3 made additional statements to correct his false statements; (d) the credibility of P2 and P3; (e) the role played by P3 in the fabrication of false accounts; (f) enabling H to make submissions to the coroner as to the scope of the inquest. The reports should have been disclosed to H. No reason had been given as to why H was treated differently from the next of kin in the prior incidents. He had been denied access to the confidential material and to the coroner's court when the material was discussed. He could not follow the arguments as to why particular lines of cross-examination were not permitted. Those effects were inconsistent with the requirement to hold an inquest compliant with the European Convention on Human Rights 1950 art.2, *Jordan v United Kingdom (24746/94)* (2003) 37 E.H.R.R. 2, [2001] C.L.Y. 3575 and *Nachova v Bulgaria (43577/98)* (2006) 42 E.H.R.R. 43, [2006] C.L.Y. 2168 applied. Accordingly, the decision not to permit parts of the report to be deployed was quashed. The inquest verdict was also quashed because the evidence might have been admissible and its potential impact could have been significant (paras 78, 140-145, 151, 154, 165, 168, 177, 182, 186-189). For material to be admitted there was a two-stage inquiry. The first stage was relevance, and the second stage was the "control" stage, *O'Brien v Chief Constable of South Wales* [2005] UKHL 26, [2005] 2 A.C. 534, [2005] C.L.Y. 302 followed. The coroner had held that the reports were not relevant and therefore he did not rule on the control stage. The outcome of the control stage of the test was not inevitable but was a matter which would have to be decided at a future inquest (paras 88, 190). (2) The ombudsman's report concerning the 2003 incident, and the underlying statements of P2 and P4, were potentially relevant in that they demonstrated a lack of planning by P2 and P4 who had performed broadly similar roles in 2003 and in V's shooting. Those documents should have been disclosed to H (paras 209-212, 218-219). (3) In security and terrorist cases in Northern Ireland there was a real possibility of perverse jury verdicts either for or against the security services or those involved in terrorist activities. V's death involved both security and terrorist issues and there was clearly a risk of a perverse verdict. The coroner should not have conducted the inquest with a jury. That was an additional ground upon which the verdict should be quashed (paras 244-248). (4) Based on the juror's note, a fair-minded and informed observer would conclude that there was a real possibility of bias, *Porter v Magill* [2001] UKHL 67, [2002] 2 A.C. 357, [2002] C.L.Y. 3185 followed. The coroner should have discharged the juror (paras 264, 269-270). (5) The state had an obligation under art.2 to carry out an effective and prompt investigation into the circumstances of deaths, *Jordan* and *Nachova* applied. The police service had created obstacles which prevented progress in the inquest (paras 78, 349-359). (6) The verdict of the inquest was quashed.

JORDAN'S APPLICATIONS FOR JUDICIAL REVIEW, RE, [2014] NIQB 11, [2014] Inquest L.R. 1, Stephens J, QBD (NI).

2238 Inquests–Witness anonymity orders–Ability to challenge ruling on witness anonymity

[European Convention on Human Rights 1950 art.2; Coroners Act (Northern Ireland) 1959]

The applicant (M) applied for judicial review of two procedural rulings in connection with the inquest into the death of her husband (H). H had died in prison from a heart attack. Shortly before his death he had been subject to a control and restraint procedure by prison officers. The post-mortem found that he had suffered injuries, including neck compression, consistent with an assault rather than an authorised control and restraint procedure. At the inquest, the coroner granted anonymity to all the prison service witnesses and allowed them to be screened from the public while they gave their evidence. The jury found that it was probable that H had been grabbed by the neck and had sustained the injuries found at post-mortem during the initial restraint. It found that the neck compression and restraint had contributed to his heart attack. It further found that the prison service had not explained the injuries and that excessive force had been used. M welcomed the jury's verdict but challenged (1) the coroner's decision to grant the prison service witnesses anonymity and screening; (2) the coroner's decision, after the inquest, that he was functus officio for the purposes of reviewing the anonymity decision.

Held: Application refused. (1) The context of M's application was vitally important. Significantly, she was not challenging the jury's verdict, which raised the question of whether it was open to her to challenge the rulings made during the inquest. Rulings in relation to anonymity and screening could not generally be challenged during the inquest by the next of kin. They were generally expected to wait until the end of the inquest, when it could be best assessed whether a disputed ruling had undermined the ultimate verdict. However, M was happy with the verdict. Allowing an application such as hers would yield the real prospect of almost endless litigation at public expense in respect of procedural rulings which had had no bearing on the effectiveness of the inquest or its outcome. Such a prospect seemed inconsistent with the decision in *C's Application for Judicial Review, Re* [2012] NICA 47, [2013] N.I. 221, which was intended to prohibit or discourage unnecessary satellite litigation, *C's Application for Judicial Review* followed. Further, the proceedings had been attended by a raft of important safeguards: the officers (while anonymous and screened from the public) had given their evidence in public, they had not been screened from the coroner or the jury, and they had given their evidence in sight of H's family and their lawyers, *Bubbins v United Kingdom (50196/99)* (2005) 41 E.H.R.R. 24, [2006] C.L.Y. 2166 applied. The coroner's rulings were not inconsistent with M's rights under the European Convention on Human Rights 1950 art.2 and had not undermined the integrity of the verdict (see paras 8-9, 14-17 of judgment). (2) The inquest having been completed, the coroner had been functus officio for most purposes and had no power to reopen his rulings on anonymity and screening, *Bradley's Application for Judicial Review, Re* [2007] NIQB 98 applied. He was a creature of statute. His powers and duties derived from the Coroners Act (Northern Ireland) 1959 and there was no provision in that Act that would permit him to embark on any procedure to reconvene the inquest (paras 20-22).

MCDONNELL'S APPLICATION FOR JUDICIAL REVIEW, RE, [2014] NIQB 66, [2014] Inquest L.R. 150, Treacy J, QBD (NI).

2239 Justice Act (Northern Ireland) 2015 (c.9)–Commencement No.7 and Saving Provisions Order–Northern Ireland

THE JUSTICE (2015 ACT) (COMMENCEMENT NO.7 AND SAVING PROVISIONS) ORDER (NORTHERN IRELAND) 2016, SR 2016/387; made under the Justice Act (Northern Ireland) 2015 s.102(8), s.106(2). Commencement details: bringing into operation various provisions of the Justice Act (Northern Ireland) 2015 on 31 October 2016.

This Order brings the provisions of the Justice Act (Northern Ireland) 2015 specified in art.2 into operation on 31 October 2016. Sections 1 to 6 make provision in relation to the establishment of a single jurisdiction for the county courts and magistrates' courts. The provisions in s.53 enable witnesses to give evidence from outside the United Kingdom to a magistrates' court in Northern Ireland in certain proceedings by way of live television link to the courtroom. The provisions in s.92 are enabling powers to allow secondary legislation to be prepared to create a statutory framework for the management of cases.

ADMINISTRATIVE LAW

2240 Inquiries–Legitimate expectation–Historic abuse at care home

The claimant (L) applied for judicial review of the defendant Inquiry's refusal to provide her with a copy of the evidence she gave at an Acknowledgement Forum. L had claimed damages in respect of abuse she allegedly suffered in a care home between 1971 and 1976. She attended the forum and gave her account confidentially and in private. She later asked for a copy of the "statement" she had given, but was refused. The court had to determine whether L had a right to a copy of the Inquiry record of what she said at the forum and whether the Inquiry was subject to the concomitant duty to provide her with a transcript thereof or a disc. L submitted that she had a right to a copy of the record of her evidence to the forum and that absent an express statutory provision preventing the Inquiry from providing a copy, she had a legitimate expectation of its provision.

Held: Application refused. There was no authority to support the proposition that L had the asserted right with the concomitant obligation on the Inquiry to provide her or her solicitors with a copy of the record of her evidence whether by transcript or disc. The recording made by the Inquiry was the property of the Inquiry, *R. v HM Coroner for Hammersmith Ex p. Peach* [1980] Q.B. 211, [1980] C.L.Y. 385 , *Mailey, Re* [1980] 6 N.I.J.B., [1981] C.L.Y. 1876 and *Devine's Application, Re*considered. Nor was there a legitimate expectation of being provided with a copy of the record of her evidence. L was told at the start of the meeting by its chairman that a copy of the recording would not be provided to her or made available beyond the forum unless she wanted to speak to the Statutory Inquiry, in which case it would be made available to the Inquiry's legal team. Such confidentiality was an essential prerequisite for the forum to operate effectively; the Inquiry's confidential procedure was not intended as an evidence gathering forum for claimants and their lawyers. No arguable public law grounds had been established to impugn the chairman's decision. Furthermore, L's application was out of time and there was no reason why the time limit should be extended (see paras 5-11 of judgment).

LP'S APPLICATION FOR JUDICIAL REVIEW, RE, [2014] NIQB 40, [2014] Inquest L.R. 148, Treacy J, QBD (NI).

2241 Legal Complaints and Regulation Act (Northern Ireland) 2016 (c.14)

An Act to make provision for the establishment of the office of the Legal Services Oversight Commissioner for Northern Ireland; to make provision as regards complaints against members of the legal profession in Northern Ireland; and for connected purposes.

2242 Public inquiries–Murder–Legitimate expectation

The applicant wife (F) of Patrick Finucane, a solicitor murdered in 1989 by a protestant paramilitary group, applied for judicial review of a decision of the secretary of state for Northern Ireland to hold an independent review into the murder instead of the promised public enquiry. The core allegation was that the British Army, the Royal Ulster Constabulary and its Special Branch, and the British security services had colluded in the murder of a number of Catholics, including that of Patrick Finucane. Further, that those state agencies had seriously impeded subsequent investigations by the police under Sir John Stevens, by Anthony Langdon, and by Justice Cory. In 2001 in the Anglo-Irish political talks at Weston Park, the British government of the day had agreed that it would abide by the recommendations of Justice Cory. In 2004 Justice Cory recommended that a public inquiry with the power to compel witnesses was required in the cases that he investigated. Although public enquiries had been held in all the other cases, no public inquiry was held into Patrick Finucane's murder. On 11 July 2011 a ministerial meeting took place attended by the Prime Minister, the Deputy Prime Minister, the Defence, Home, and Justice Secretaries, the Secretary of State for Northern Ireland and the Attorney General which decided on a collective basis to hold an independent review under Sir Desmond da Silva instead of a public enquiry. The terms of reference of the review did not include oral hearings. F submitted that she had a substantive legitimate expectation that a public inquiry of the kind recommended by Judge Peter Cory would be established to examine the murder of her husband.

Held: Application granted in part. (1) F had established a promise to hold a public inquiry as a clear and unambiguous representation devoid of relevant qualifications (see paras 161-164 of judgment). (2) However, five public interest factors constituted overriding interests which justified the frustration of F's expectation, namely, (i) the conclusions of reviews and investigations into the case and the extent to which the case had caused public concern; (ii) the experience of the other inquiries established after the Weston Park commitments; (iii) the delay that had occurred since the 2004 announcement and the potential length of any inquiry; (iv) political developments that had taken place in Northern Ireland since 2004; (v) the potential cost of any inquiry and the current pressures on the UK government's finances (para.166). (3) It was clear that the decision lay in the macro-political field. Although F was a crucial person to whom the promise had been made, it had also been made to a wide range of bodies including governments. Because the impugned decisions lay in the macro-political field, the overall intensity of judicial review was limited, *R. v Secretary of State for Education and Employment Ex p. Begbie* [2000] 1 W.L.R. 1115, [1999] C.L.Y. 1704 applied (paras 15, 167-168). (4) Fairness to F required the fulfilment of her legitimate expectation based on an international agreement supported by Judge Cory. It had been made in the context of a breach of the most fundamental obligation of the state to protect the life of its citizen, where there had also been undoubted collusion by servants of the state who had neither been prosecuted nor disciplined. None of the previous investigations had had the power to compel witnesses or suspects to answer any questions. The need for oral evidence was to be set against deficiencies in the written documentation, which was often contradictory or missing, and the fact that a number of key witnesses were now dead. However, overall the frustration of F's expectation and the decision to proceed by way of a review was not so unfair as to be a misuse of the secretary of state's power (paras 170, 173-186). The application for judicial review was dismissed except in so far as it related to a continuing procedural obligation on the state to investigate the murder of Patrick Finucane, in respect of which a declaration was granted (para.218).

FINUCANE'S APPLICATION FOR JUDICIAL REVIEW, RE, [2015] NIQB 57, [2015] Inquest L.R. 111, Stephens J, QBD (NI).

AGRICULTURE

2243 **Animal products–Inspections–Safety**

THE ANIMALS AND ANIMAL PRODUCTS (EXAMINATION FOR RESIDUES AND MAXIMUM RESIDUE LIMITS) REGULATIONS (NORTHERN IRELAND) 2016, SR 2016/54; made under the European Communities Act 1972 s.2(2), Sch.2 para.1A; Food Safety(Northern Ireland) Order 1991 (SI 1991 762) art.15(1)(a)(b)(f), art.15(3), art.16(1)(2), art.25(1)(2)(a)(b)(3), art.26(3) , art.30(9) , art.31(3) , art.32(1)(2)(c)(d)(e)(f)(h), art.44(1)(2), art.47(2), Sch.1 para.3(1)(b), Sch.1 para.7. In force: 31 March 2016.

These Regulations replace provisions formerly contained in the Animals and Animal Products (Examination for Residues and Maximum Residue Limits) Regulations (Northern Ireland) 1998 and Amending Regulations.

2244 **EU law–Food hygiene–Feedingstuffs**

THE ANIMAL FEED (HYGIENE, SAMPLING ETC. AND ENFORCEMENT) REGULATIONS (NORTHERN IRELAND) 2016, SR 2016/5; made under the Agriculture Act 1970 s.66(1), s.74A(4), s.79(9), s.84. In force: 14 February 2016.

These Regulations provide for the continuing execution and enforcement of Regulation 183/2005 of the European Parliament and of the Council laying down requirements for feed hygiene and Regulation 152/2009 laying down the methods of sampling and analysis for the official control of feed.

2245 EU law–Food safety–Genetically modified organisms

THE ANIMAL FEED (COMPOSITION, MARKETING AND USE) REGULATIONS (NORTHERN IRELAND) 2016, SR 2016/4; made under the Agriculture Act 1970 s.66(1), s.68(1), s.74A(1), s.84. In force: 14 February 2016.

These Regulations, which apply in relation to Northern Ireland only, provide for the continuing enforcement or implementation of EU Regulations and Directives on feed safety, genetically modified feed, feed additives, the marketing and use of feed, undesirable substances (contaminants) in feed and feed for particular nutritional purposes.

2246 EU law–Imports–Licences

THE SEED MARKETING REGULATIONS (NORTHERN IRELAND) 2016, SR 2016/244; made under the European Communities Act 1972 s.2(2); Seeds Act (Northern Ireland) 1965 s.1(1)(2A), s.2. In force: 14 July 2016.

These Regulations, which apply in Northern Ireland, implement Directive 66/401, Directive 66/402, Directive 2002/54, Directive 2002/55 and Directive 2002/56. They partially implement Directive 2008/62, Directive 2009/74 and Directive 2009/145. They set out requirements for the marketing, licensing and record keeping with respect to seeds.

ANIMALS

2247 Animal health–Northern Ireland Poultry Health Assurance Scheme–Fees for activities required under Directive 2009/158

THE NORTHERN IRELAND POULTRY HEALTH ASSURANCE SCHEME (FEES) (AMENDMENT) ORDER (NORTHERN IRELAND) 2016, SR 2016/118; made under the European Communities Act 1972 s.2(2); Diseases of Animals (Northern Ireland) Order 1981 (SI 1981 1115) (NI 22) art.8(1)(2)(5). In force: 1 April 2016.

This Order amends the Northern Ireland Poultry Health Assurance Scheme (Fees) Order (Northern Ireland) 2012 to make provision for the Department to charge fees for activities required under Directive 2009/158. The activities and fees are listed in the Schedule.

BANKING AND FINANCE

2248 Credit Unions and Co-operative and Community Benefit Societies Act (Northern Ireland) 2016 (c.16)

An Act to make provision about credit unions and co-operative and community benefit societies; and for connected purposes.

2249 Loans–Spouses–Loan to family partnership–Whether statutory demand imposed on wife could be set aside

The bank appealed against a decision (*O'Neill v Ulster Bank Ltd* [2014] NICh 29) to set aside a statutory demand imposed on the respondent wife. The wife's husband was a self-employed builder. Between 1989 and 2006 his business had been modest and had mainly carried out renovations and one-off new builds using small loans from the bank. In 2005, the wife, along with her sons, was made a partner in the business, although she had no formal dealings with it. After 2006, the nature of the business changed and the bank lent almost £1.5 million so it could buy and develop land. The loans were secured against the family home and other properties. When repayments were not made, the bank issued a statutory demand against the wife as a partner, on the basis that the sums were advanced for the joint benefit of all the partners and not for the sole benefit of her husband. The demand was later set aside on the grounds that it was arguable that a loan to a partnership including a wife was analogous to a loan to a company in which a wife was a shareholder, and that the change of character of the business and the increased loan amounts should have placed the bank on inquiry as to the possibility of undue influence exerted on the wife by her husband. The bank argued that there was nothing to indicate that the loans were other than for the joint benefit of the partners and therefore it had no constructive notice and so was not placed on any inquiry as to possible undue influence.

Held: Appeal dismissed. (1) The observations of Lord Nicholls in *Royal Bank of Scotland Plc v Etridge (No.2)* [2001] UKHL 44, [2002] 2 A.C. 773, [2001] C.L.Y. 4880 did not necessarily exclude transactions such as those in the instant case from the lender's obligation to inquire. It was arguable that a joint loan to purchase lands, which were in reality to be used by the husband for what were effectively his own purposes in a business controlled and operated by him, were not necessarily on the "wrong side of the line" for inquiry. It was also arguable that the partnership arrangement into which the wife was introduced shortly before the lending pattern radically altered was, in substance, no different from the provision of surety for a company's loans by a wife who also had some shareholding in the company, but where the activities of the company were in reality conducted by and for the husband alone. There was an arguable case that the bank had been put upon inquiry as to whether the loans were in fact for the husband's sole purposes, *Etridge* applied (see paras 16-17 of judgment). (2) The identified matters that supported that case included the modest nature and extent of the husband's previous jobbing builder business over many years; the historic low level of bank borrowings over those years consistent with the modest needs of that business; the minimal personal relationship between the wife and the bank, consisting of only one visit over the period of many years and that visit in the company of her husband; and the very significant alteration in the scale and intended purposes of the unprecedentedly large loans negotiated solely by the husband and all advanced during the period of one year. None of those were matters upon which the court had reached any conclusion. It was not the role of the court in statutory demand proceedings to decide that issue; it simply had to ask itself whether an arguable defence, namely a defence with some prospect of success, had been raised, *Irish Bank Resolution Corp Ltd v Dolan*applied. The court also bore in mind the fact that evidential issues had not, by reason of the statutory demand procedure, been examined by a court. The threshold at which a lender was placed upon inquiry varied according to the particular facts on a continuum between the absence of any such obligation, as in the holiday home example of *CIBC Mortgages Plc v Pitt* [1994] 1 A.C. 200, [1994] C.L.Y. 3293, and the obligation that almost certainly arose in a normal surety case, *Pitt* considered. The court did not feel able to say that the authorities obliged it to preclude the wife from making her case at a trial that the bank was, in the particular circumstances upon which she relied, placed upon inquiry, *Etridge* applied (paras 17-19).

O'NEILL v ULSTER BANK LTD, [2015] NICA 64, [2016] B.P.I.R. 126, Morgan LCJ, CA (NI).

CIVIL PROCEDURE

2250 **Mortgages–Correspondence–Delivery up of documents**

The applicant mortgage company applied for the delivery up of documents in the possession and custody of the respondent solicitors in respect of a mortgage over a property (X). X had been transferred from a father (F) to his son (S) absolutely for natural love and affection. S had taken out a mortgage on X with the applicant's predecessor in title (P). P had retained the solicitor to perfect and register the mortgage. S's wife (W) had claimed a beneficial interest in X on the basis that the occupier's consent form which she had signed had been procured through undue influence. P had issued proceedings against S and W to enforce the mortgage. The mortgage had transferred to the applicant who was trying to find out if it could make a case of negligence against the solicitor in respect of the consent form. The applicant sought the original file, and the solicitor provided some documentation. The applicant asked to see much more detailed documentation, and in the absence of a response, applied for delivery up of all papers, documents and title deeds in the possession or custody of the solicitor. The solicitor contended that all documents to which the applicant was entitled had been disclosed, and that it was not entitled to the attendance notes on W because they related to her and contained her confidential information, were the solicitor's property and did not form part of any file which belonged to the applicant. The applicant replied that as the solicitor acted for both S and P it should be entitled to see all documents, and drew attention to the waiver of confidentiality or privilege which S had signed when he applied for the mortgage. The solicitor contended that its correspondence (i) with F was part of the purchase file, not the mortgage file, and belonged to F; (ii) with S formed part of the work carried out for S and belonged to him, not the lender; (iii) with W belonged to W, and that all documentation relating to the execution of the occupier's consent form was privileged.

Held: Judgment accordingly. (1) The solicitor was not obliged to disclose its working papers as they did not belong to the clients, but to the solicitor. The relationship was one of a professional man, not that of principal and client, and the solicitor was not bound to hand those papers over, *Chantrey Martin & Co v Martin* [1953] 2 Q.B. 286, [1953] C.L.Y. 2793 and *Leicestershire CC v Michael Faraday and Partners, Ltd* [1941] 2 K.B. 205 considered (see paras 18, 26 of judgment). (2) When a borrower and a lender retained the same solicitor, there was a several, not a joint, retainer. In such a case there was no implied waiver of confidentiality or privilege by one party in favour of the other, or any implied authorisation by the solicitor to make disclosure to one party of documents passed between it and the other party, *Nationwide Anglia Building Society v Various Solicitors (No.1)* [1999] P.N.L.R. 52, [1998] C.L.Y. 356 and *Mortgage Business Plc and Bank of Scotland Plc (t/a Birmingham Midshires) v Thomas Taggart and Sons* [2014] NICh 14 considered (para.20). (3) S had expressly waived privilege in respect of any documents held by the solicitor and he had agreed to do anything reasonably considered necessary by P under the mortgage. Any correspondence between the solicitor and S was therefore to be disclosed (para.26). (4) Insofar as the solicitor had acted for F, it did so on a separate retainer, namely the transfer of his interest in X to S. There was no evidence that F had ever waived any privilege to any document, and no evidence that he had given up ownership of the documents in his file. Those documents were not to be handed over. Any documents in the file belonging to S which related to correspondence by the solicitor as S's agent to F concerning the transfer of F's interest were to be disclosed because S had waived privilege to all documents that were confidential to him and he had appointed P as his attorney to do anything which P might have considered reasonably necessary in the exercise of rights under the mortgage, and he had agreed to hand over whatever document the applicant considered relevant to P's decision to lend (para.26). (5) When the solicitor advised W about her rights of occupation and obtained her signed consent form, the position was akin to advising a wife about a guarantee given in respect of her husband's borrowing. In such a situation the solicitor's only client was the wife, *Royal Bank of Scotland Plc v Etridge (No.2)* [2001] UKHL 44, [2002] 2 A.C. 773, [2001] C.L.Y. 4880 considered. W had not waived privilege and there was no obligation on her to hand over any documents which belonged to her and were generated by her retainer of the solicitor. However, correspondence to W from the solicitor as S's agents belonged to S and was to be handed over (paras 25-26).

PEPPER (UK) LTD (T/A ENGAGE CREDIT) v FOX, [2016] NICh 1, [2016] P.N.L.R. 27, Horner J, Ch D (NI).

COMPANY LAW

2251 **Directors–Employment status–Remuneration paid in dividends–Whether "employee" under art.3 Employment Rights (Northern Ireland) Order 1996**

[Employment Rights (Northern Ireland) Order 1996 (SI 1996/1919) art.3]

The defendant Department for Employment and Learning appealed against an industrial tribunal's decisions that the claimant had been a company's "employee" for the purposes of the Employment Rights (Northern Ireland) Order 1996 art.3. The claimant had purchased 50% of the company's shares and entered into an employment contract which described him as an "employee director". The contract provided that he was entitled to take his remuneration as dividends instead of salary, and also included other clauses relevant to holiday entitlement, sick leave absence and termination. The claimant opted to receive payment by way of dividends and under the PAYE scheme. The company later ceased trading due to financial difficulties and the claimant lost his job. He applied to the defendant for redundancy payment, notice pay, holiday pay and arrears of pay, but the defendant rejected his application on the basis that he had not been an employee of the company for the purposes of art.3. The tribunal stated that looking at the substance and not the form of the money received by the claimant, it was satisfied that the "dividends" he had been paid were in fact an emolument for services he had rendered to the company, and that they should therefore be treated as a salary. In particular, it relied on its findings that: the claimant had entered into a written contract to provide services to the company in exchange for an annual salary; the contract had provided that the claimant was entitled to take remuneration as dividends instead of a salary; the contract had contained many other clauses consistent with the status of an employee; the claimant had conducted himself according to the contract's terms; there was nothing in the claimant's actions that had been inconsistent with him having an employment contract; the payments had been made as dividends and the claimant had declared the dividends; the dividends had not been related to the company's current profitability; the dividends paid had reflected the claimant's salary entitlement under the employment contract; and the contract had not been a sham. The tribunal subsequently upheld its decision on review.

Held: Appeal dismissed. The question was whether the payments made in the form of dividends were made for services rendered by an employee on foot of an employment contract, Eyres (Surveyor of Taxes) v Finnieston Engineering Company Limited [1916] 7 TC 74 and *PA Holdings Ltd v Revenue and Customs Commissioners* [2011] EWCA Civ 1414, [2012] S.T.C. 582, [2012] C.L.Y. 3300 considered. That was a question of fact for the tribunal. It had applied the correct principles, including the factors set out in *Secretary of State for Business, Enterprise and Regulatory Reform v Neufeld* [2009] EWCA Civ 280, [2009] 3 All E.R. 790, [2009] C.L.Y. 1199, and had set out the reasons for its decisions, *Neufeld* considered. It had not reached a conclusion that was irrational, perverse or erroneous in law. Its decision did not offend the statutory scheme for a minimum wage and had addressed appropriately the factors in *Crawford v Department for Employment and Learning* [2014] NICA 26, [2014] I.R.L.R. 626, [2014] C.L.Y. 3143, *Crawford* considered. There was accordingly no basis for interfering with the tribunal's decisions (see paras 20, 28 of judgment).

DEPARTMENT FOR EMPLOYMENT AND LEARNING v MORGAN, [2016] NICA 2, [2016] I.R.L.R. 350, Gillen LJ, CA (NI).

CONSTRUCTION LAW

2252 **Construction Industry Training Board–Industrial training levies**

THE INDUSTRIAL TRAINING LEVY (CONSTRUCTION INDUSTRY) ORDER (NORTHERN IRELAND) 2016, SR 2016/243; made under the Industrial Training

(Northern Ireland) Order 1984 (SI 1984 1159) (NI.9) art.23(2)(3), art.24(3)(4). In force: 31 August 2016.

This Order gives effect to proposals submitted by the Construction Industry Training Board to the Department for the Economy for the imposition of a further levy upon employers in the construction industry for the purpose of raising money towards the expenses of the Board. The levy is to be imposed in respect of the fifty-second levy period, commencing on 1 September 2016 and ending on 31 August 2017. The levy will be assessed by the Board and will be payable in two instalments. There will be a right of appeal against an assessment to an industrial tribunal. The levy rate of 0.65% in respect of relevant earnings is the same as the rate operating during the preceding levy period which expires on 31 August 2016.As in the previous levy period there will be no remission of levy given to employers in the industry. An employer will be exempt from levy in the fifty-second levy period where the relevant earnings are less than £80,000.

CRIMINAL LAW

2253 Controlled drugs–Exemptions

THE MISUSE OF DRUGS (AMENDMENT) REGULATIONS (NORTHERN IRELAND) 2016, SR 2016/29; made under the Misuse of Drugs Act 1971 s.7, s.10, s.22, s.31. In force: 1 March 2016.

These Regulations amend the Misuse of Drugs Regulations (Northern Ireland) 2002, by including within the definition of "health prescription" contained in reg.2(1) of the 2002 Regulations a nurse independent prescriber, a pharmacist independent prescriber, and a supplementary prescriber as persons who may issue such a prescription.

2254 Licensed premises–Children–Nightclubs

[Licensing (Northern Ireland) Order 1996 (SI 1996/3158) art.58(1), art.58(1)(c)(i), art.58(1)(c)(ii), art.58(13), art.58(2)]

The appellant (M) appealed by way of case stated against his conviction for two offences of allowing a person under the age of 18 to be on licensed premises during the permitted hours contrary to the Licensing (Northern Ireland) Order 1996 art.58(1)(c)(ii). M was a director of a hotel complex. Part of the complex was licensed for the sale and consumption of alcohol and could be hired for events such as wedding receptions. On Saturday nights it functioned as a nightclub for adults, and alcohol was sold and consumed. One Friday night each month it hosted an under-18s disco. Although the discos took place during permitted hours, the bar was closed for the sale of alcohol. No alcohol was on display, none was sold, and none was consumed. The issue was whether, during the discos, under-18s were present in premises that were used exclusively or mainly for the sale and consumption of alcohol within the meaning of art.58(1)(c)(ii). The district judge found that they were, because, overall, the main purpose of the premises was the sale and consumption of alcohol. The central questions stated were whether he had been right to conclude that (i) art.58(1)(c)(ii) prohibited under-18s from attending alcohol-free functions on licensed premises even if the premises were not, at the material time, being used for the sale or consumption of alcohol; (ii) the main use of the instant premises was for the sale and consumption of alcohol.

Held: Appeal dismissed. (1) The objective of art.58(1) and art.58(2) was to safeguard children by restricting their access to licensed premises. The breadth of the prohibition was underscored by the carefully constructed and limited exceptions in art.58(13), none of which applied in the instant case. Moreover, art.58(1)(c) contained two separate prohibitions; it prevented minors being on licensed premises that either contained an open bar or was used exclusively or mainly for the sale of alcohol. The contention that alcohol-free events for under-18s were exempt ignored those two distinct prohibitions. Such an event might not offend against art.58(1)(c)(i) because there was no open bar, but it would fall foul of the additional protection in art.58(1)(c)(ii). It was not possible to say that premises were exclusively or mainly used for the sale and consumption of alcohol for some parts of the day but not for others, *Pilkington v Ross* [1914] 3 K.B. 321 applied. Had the legislature wanted to exempt such events, it could have said so (see paras 18-23 of judgment). (2) Whether licensed premises were used exclusively or mainly for the sale and consumption of alcohol was a matter of fact and degree which depended on the usage of the premises overall, not at a particular time. The district judge had been entitled to find that the premises in question were so used, the core event being the regular Saturday nightclub (paras 24-25).

MORRIS v DPP, [2015] NICA 49, [2015] L.L.R. 772, Morgan LCJ, CA (NI).

CRIMINAL PROCEDURE

2255 Court rules–Crown Court–Jurisdiction

THE CROWN COURT (CRIMINAL PROCEDURE AND INVESTIGATIONS ACT 1996) (TAINTED ACQUITTALS) (AMENDMENT) RULES (NORTHERN IRELAND) 2016, SR 2016/298; made under the Judicature (Northern Ireland) Act 1978 s.52(1), s.53A. In force: In accordance with rule 1.

The purpose of the Statutory Rule is to amend the Crown Court (Criminal Procedure and Investigations Act 1996) (Tainted Acquittals) Rules (Northern Ireland) 1997 in consequence of Part 1 of (and Schedule 1 to) the Justice Act (Northern Ireland) 2015 which creates a single territorial jurisdiction for the county courts and the magistrates' courts in Northern Ireland, similar to that which already exists for the High Court, Crown Court and Coroners' Courts.

2256 Human trafficking–Forced labour–Duty to co-operate with Independent Anti-slavery Commissioner

THE MODERN SLAVERY ACT 2015 (DUTY TO CO-OPERATE WITH COMMISSIONER) (NORTHERN IRISH PUBLIC AUTHORITY) REGULATIONS (NORTHERN IRELAND) 2016, SR 2016/48; made under the Modern Slavery Act 2015 s.43(8), s.58(6)(7). In force: 1 April 2016.

This statutory rule specifies public authorities in Northern Ireland which are subject to a statutory duty to co-operate with the Anti Slavery Commissioner for the purposes of the Commissioner's functions.

2257 Jury service–Eligibility–Excusal

THE JUSTICE (2015 ACT) (COMMENCEMENT NO.6) ORDER (NORTHERN IRELAND) 2016, SR 2016/247; made under the Justice Act (Northern Ireland) 2015 s.106(2). Commencement details: bringing into operation various provisions of the Justice Act (Northern Ireland) 2015 on 1 July 2016.

This Order brings the Justice Act (Northern Ireland) 2015 (c.9 (N.I.)) ss.77 and 81 into operation on 1 July 2016. The provisions make a number of amendments to the Juries (Northern Ireland) Order 1996, in particular by removing the upper age limit for jurors and by updating the lists of those who are disqualified for, ineligible for, or excusable as of right from jury service.

2258 Justice Act (Northern Ireland) 2016 (c.21)

An Act to make provision about enforcement of the payment of fines and other penalties; to provide for the appointment and functions of a Prison Ombudsman for Northern Ireland; to amend the law relating to lay visitors for police stations, the possession of extreme pornographic images and the early removal from prison of prisoners liable to removal from the United Kingdom.

2259 **Proceeds of crime–Benefit from criminal conduct–Confiscation orders**

THE PROCEEDS OF CRIME ACT (APPEALS UNDER PART 4) (AMENDMENT) ORDER (NORTHERN IRELAND) 2016, SR 2016/245; made under the Proceeds of Crime Act 2002 s.237(2), s.238(2), s.459(2)(7A). In force: 25 July 2016.

This Order amends the Proceeds of Crime Act (Appeals under Part 4) Order 2003 by inserting into Part 3 (appeal to Supreme Court) of the 2003 Order an appeal under the Proceeds of Crime Act 2002 s.163B.

DAMAGES

2260 **Measure of damages–Fatal accidents**

THE DAMAGES FOR BEREAVEMENT (VARIATION OF SUM) (NORTHERN IRELAND) ORDER 2016, SR 2016/74; made under the Fatal Accidents (Northern Ireland) Order 1977 (SI 1977 1251 (NI.18)) art.3A(5). In force: 1 April 2016.

This Order, which applies only to causes of action accruing on or after 1 April 2016, amends the Fatal Accidents (Northern Ireland) Order 1977 art.3(A3), increasing the sum which may be awarded for damages for bereavement in Northern Ireland from £11,800 to £14,200.

EDUCATION

2261 **Addressing Bullying in Schools Act (Northern Ireland) 2016 (c.25)**

An Act to address bullying in grant-aided schools.

2262 **Education Authority–Complaints tribunal–Curriculum and related matters**

THE COMPLAINTS TRIBUNAL (CURRICULUM AND RELATED MATTERS) REGULATIONS (NORTHERN IRELAND) 2016, SR 2016/111; made under the Education (Northern Ireland) Order 2006 (SI 2006 1915) art.25(1)(4), art.43(5). In force: 1 August 2016.

These Regulations provide for the constitution and procedure of complaints tribunals. Under the Education (Northern Ireland) Order 2006 art.25, the Education Authority (EA) is required, in accordance with Regulations, to appoint a complaints tribunal to hear and determine any complaint made on or after the coming into operation of that Article which is to the effect that the EA or Board of Governors of a relevant school has acted or is proposing to act unreasonably with respect to the exercise of any power conferred or the performance of any duty imposed on it.

2263 **Full-time students–Suspension–Sexual offences prevention order**

[European Convention on Human Rights 1950 art.6(1)]

A student (S) applied for judicial review of decisions made by the respondent University to temporarily withdraw him from his course for the duration of a sexual offences prevention order imposed following his conviction for making and possessing indecent images of children. S had completed the first two years of a five-year chemical engineering course. During his first year he admitted possession of indecent images of children to police. He was released on bail. Conditions were imposed banning use of a computer or the internet and unsupervised contact with children. He did not inform the university despite much of his course only being accessible via a computer, there being a number of students aged under 18 at the university and many school children visiting the campus. A year later, S was convicted following his guilty plea. The university was alerted through press reports and immediately imposed an emergency suspension, finding S in breach of good faith in not notifying it when first charged. S was later sentenced to a probation order and a SOPO, which contained conditions preventing use of the internet and any contact with children, and was to last for five years. The university's review panel decided to temporarily withdraw S from his course for the term of the SOPO, allowing him to apply for re-admission on its expiry. A review appeals panel subsequently upheld that decision, but informed S that he was entitled to petition the board of visitors. S applied for judicial review of both decisions. S argued that the board of visitors was not the appropriate forum and would infringe his rights under the ECHR, and that those rights had been infringed by the review panel hearings, particularly his rights under art.6(1).

Held: Application refused. The board was the appropriate body to determine whether S should be precluded from completing his studies. In considering the Convention issues, the court had to look at the whole process, including the hearing before the board and the right to the review of such a hearing by the court on certain limited grounds. Any breaches of common law by the review panels could be cured by a fair and independent tribunal and S enjoyed the right to an appeal hearing before an independent and experienced board. Furthermore, any decision of that board was subject to review by the court. As a public authority, the board was obliged to comply with the Convention and there was no reason to doubt that it would act in accordance with the common law in reaching its conclusions. The court could not determine whether S's rights had been infringed and it should not try to do so prior to a full hearing before the board. The availability of legal aid was not critical to whether proceedings before the board were compliant with the Convention. The test was whether a party could have effective access to the board without legal representation so as to ensure a just decision. Legal representation before the board was likely to be less expensive than before a court and the board members' experience with personal litigants would ensure that S received a fair hearing and would have full and effective access to the process. The board had legal and higher education expertise and S enjoyed the right of access to an independent and impartial tribunal whose worth had been proved over hundreds of years. The board's role should not be devalued by the court when Parliament had taken the deliberate decision to retain visitorial jurisdiction in Northern Ireland. Clear and unambiguous findings of fact had not been made in respect of the issues to be addressed in determining whether the risk S posed could be managed and the terms of the SOPO could be complied with should he return to the university. Those findings should be made by an independent and objective tribunal. Although the board's procedure stated that it would not normally make findings of fact, it might consider the instant case was exceptional and that it was well-placed to make those findings where the independence and objectivity of its conclusions were not open to challenge. Leave to apply for judicial review would not have been granted had the court known the basis upon which the visitors to the board had been appointed and their independence from the university. A hearing before the board was a much better alternative to remitting it back to the university, being the procedure suggested by S, *R. (on the application of Maxwell) v Office of the Independent Adjudicator* [2011] EWCA Civ 1236, [2012] P.T.S.R. 884, [2012] C.L.Y. 968 considered. The board had exclusive jurisdiction to hear S's appeal unless it exceeded its jurisdiction, abused its powers, breached the principles of natural justice and/or did not protect a party's Convention rights. If the court was wrong and the board did not have exclusive jurisdiction, then the court declined to grant any relief until S had exhausted his right to petition the board (see paras 2, 9-17, 24-29, 31-34, 36-37, 39 of judgment).

CS'S APPLICATION FOR JUDICIAL REVIEW, RE, [2015] NIQB 36, [2016] E.L.R. 23, Horner J, QBD (NI).

2264 Further education–Appointments–Governing Body of Institution of Further Education

THE FURTHER EDUCATION (GOVERNING BODY OF INSTITUTION OF FURTHER EDUCATION) ORDER (NORTHERN IRELAND) 2016, SR 2016/391; made under the Further Education (Northern Ireland) Order 1997 (SI 1997 1772) Sch.3 para.2(3). In force: Shall come into force in accordance with art.1.

These Regulations amend the Further Education (Northern Ireland) Order 1997 to remove the requirement on the Department for the Economy to appoint two persons nominated by the Education Authority (formerly the Education and Library Boards) to each of the Governing Bodies of the Northern Ireland Further Education Institutions. In addition, they allow for existing Education Authority appointments to continue within the confines of their terms of appointment.

2265 Grants–Grant-maintained schools–Grant-maintained integrated schools

THE EDUCATION (1998 ORDER) (COMMENCEMENT NO.9) ORDER (NORTHERN IRELAND) 2016, SR 2016/211; made under the Education (Northern Ireland) Order 1998 (SI 1998 1759) art.1(3). Commencement details: bringing into operation various provisions of the 1998 Order.

This Order brings into operation the Education (Northern Ireland) Order 1998 art.69, which provides for payment by the Department of Education of capital and special purposes grants to grant-maintained integrated schools.

2266 Shared Education Act (Northern Ireland) 2016 (c.20)

An Act to make provision in relation to shared education.

2267 Special Educational Needs and Disability Act (Northern Ireland) 2016 (c.8)–Commencement No.1 Order–Northern Ireland

THE SPECIAL EDUCATIONAL NEEDS AND DISABILITY (2016 ACT) (COMMENCEMENT NO.1) ORDER (NORTHERN IRELAND) 2016, SR 2016/327; made under the Special Educational Needs and Disability Act (Northern Ireland) 2016 s.18(2). Commencement details: bringing into operation various provisions of the Special Educational Needs and Disability Act (Northern Ireland) 2016 on 30 September 2016.

This Order brings into operation the Special Educational Needs and Disability Act (Northern Ireland) 2016 s.6 which provides that parents have 22 days in which to make representations, or provide written evidence, when the Education Authority notifies them that it has received a referral to make a statutory assessment under the Education (Northern Ireland) Order 1996 art.15. The Authority can, with the parent's consent, proceed to the next stage before the 22 days has expired.

EMPLOYMENT

2268 Employment tribunals–Litigant with Asperger's Syndrome–Failure to take disability into account–Failure to make reasonable adjustments–Whether fair hearing

The appellant employee appealed against a decision dismissing his claim against the respondent employer. The appellant, who suffered from Asperger's Syndrome, had been employed by the respondent as a composite operator until his employment was terminated for gross misconduct based on two incidents. In the first incident he was alleged to have thrown an item of work equipment behind him and in the second he was alleged to have repeatedly shouted an abusive word at an occupational health doctor. He brought claims against the respondent for unlawful racial discrimination, unlawful disability discrimination, victimisation, harassment on grounds of his disability and nationality, detriment and unfair dismissal. He initially had legal representation but was not represented by the time of the tribunal hearing and no-one requested that any adjustments should be made due to his disability. A clinical psychologist's report that had been commissioned by the respondent was not before the tribunal. The appellant submitted that he had not had a fair hearing because the tribunal had failed to take his disability and his medical evidence into account in circumstances where he had not been represented at the tribunal hearing. He argued that a range of tribunal acts were tainted with unlawfulness such as: failure to make reasonable adjustments for his disability; unreasonably failing to adjourn the case on a number of occasions; placing unfair demands on him in relation to the hearing; striking out all claims except his unfair dismissal claim; proceeding to hear his unfair dismissal claim in his absence and in the face of medical evidence supportive of an adjournment; and dismissing his unfair dismissal claim.

Held: Appeal allowed. The instant issues were governed by the obligation of every tribunal and court to act fairly, *Reilly's Application for Judicial Review, Re* [2013] UKSC 61, [2014] A.C. 1115, [2013] C.L.Y. 2115 applied. The instant case should have been recognised immediately as one involving a person under a disability of mental health and a ground rules case management discussion should have occurred to meet the specific challenges of his condition. Had this been done, the sort of measures that surfaced in *Rackham v NHS Professionals Ltd* would have arisen, such as how the evidence was to be taken and whether greater latitude should have been given to the timeframe, *Rackham* considered. No positive thought had been given to the need to obtain a report on the appellant's condition. It was not sufficient to state that no application for adjustment had been made. The tribunal had a duty to make its own decision and there had been clear indications of observed agitation on the appellant's part which should have put the tribunal on notice of the need to investigate his condition. The instant case highlighted the need for there to be better training of the judiciary and legal profession in the needs of the disabled. Everyone had been aware that there was a disability of some kind from an early stage but there had been a complete failure to record the nature of the syndrome. Even if the report had not been available there was no reason why one of the other doctors could not have attended the tribunal. No reference had been made to the Equal Treatment Bench Book and it did not appear to be part of the culture of the hearings. That was a circumstance which had to fundamentally change with a structural correction to ensure that the instant situation did not recur. No attempt had been made to explore the possibilities of alternative representation for the appellant once he lost his solicitor's services. Steps ought to have been taken at least to appraise him of the possibilities of getting pro bono assistance. There was clear medical evidence that the appellant had not been in a position to proceed. The tribunal had observed the distress and agitation being exhibited by him and the determination that his failure to attend was deliberate was patently unjustified. The requirements of procedural fairness had not been met and the matter was remitted to a differently constituted tribunal (see paras 47-63 of judgment).

GALO v BOMBARDIER AEROSPACE UK, [2016] NICA 25, [2016] I.R.L.R. 703, Morgan LCJ, CA (NI).

2269 EU law–Implementation–Posting of workers

THE POSTED WORKERS (ENFORCEMENT OF EMPLOYMENT RIGHTS) REGULATIONS (NORTHERN IRELAND) 2016, SR 2016/242; made under the European Communities Act 1972 s.2(2). In force: 18 June 2016.

These Regulations implement provisions of Directive 2014/67 on the posting of workers in the framework of the provision of services.

ENERGY

2270 Energy efficiency–Home energy efficiency scheme–Grants

THE DOMESTIC ENERGY EFFICIENCY GRANTS (AMENDMENT) REGULATIONS (NORTHERN IRELAND) 2016, SR 2016/333; made under the Social Security (Northern Ireland) Order 1990 (SI 1990 1511) art.17. In force: 7 October 2016.

These Regulations amend the Domestic Energy Efficiency Grants Regulations (Northern Ireland) 2009 by changing the eligibility criteria so that households with an annual income of less than £20,000 may be eligible to receive assistance under the Affordable Warmth grant scheme. They also clarify the conditions under which a Boiler Replacement grant may be payable.

2271 EU law–Offshore installations–Offshore Safety Directive

THE OFFSHORE INSTALLATIONS (OFFSHORE SAFETY DIRECTIVE) (SAFETY CASE ETC.) REGULATIONS (NORTHERN IRELAND) 2016, SR 2016/406; made under the European Communities Act 1972 s.2(2); Health and Safety at Work (Northern Ireland) Order 1978 (SI 1978 1039) art.17(1)(2)(3)(4)(5)(6), art.55(2), Sch.3

para.1(1)(2), Sch.3 para.7, Sch.3 para.8, Sch.3 para.13, Sch.3 para.14, Sch.3 para.15. In force: 19 December 2016.

These Regulations replace, in relation to Northern Ireland external waters, the Offshore Installations (Safety Case) Regulations (Northern Ireland) 2007 to provide for the preparation of safety cases for offshore installations and the notification of specified activities to the competent authority.

2272 Renewable heat incentive–Department of Enterprise Trade and Investment–Suspension notices

THE RENEWABLE HEAT INCENTIVE SCHEMES (AMENDMENT) REGULATIONS (NORTHERN IRELAND) 2016, SR 2016/47; made under the Energy Act 2011 s.113. In force: 17 February 2016.

This Statutory Rule establishes a mechanism for the Department of Enterprise, Trade and Investment to suspend, by notice, renewable heat incentive schemes established by the Domestic Renewable Heat Incentive Scheme Regulations (Northern Ireland) and the Domestic Renewable Heat Incentive Scheme Regulations (Northern Ireland) 2014.

2273 Renewables obligations–Use of biomass to generate electricity

THE RENEWABLES OBLIGATION (AMENDMENT) ORDER (NORTHERN IRELAND) 2016, SR 2016/84; made under the Energy (Northern Ireland) Order 2003 (SI 2003 419) art.52, art.53, art.54, art.55, art.55A, art.55B, art.55C, art.55D, art.55E, art.55EA, art.55EB, art.55F, art.66(3). In force: 1 March 2016.

This Order amends the Renewables Obligation (Northern Ireland) Order 2009. Most of the amendments relate to the use of biomass to generate electricity.

ENVIRONMENT

2274 Environmental Better Regulation (2016 Act)–Commencement No.2 Order–Northern Ireland

THE ENVIRONMENTAL BETTER REGULATION (2016 ACT) (COMMENCEMENT NO.2) ORDER (NORTHERN IRELAND) 2016, SR 2016/332; made under the Environmental Better Regulation Act (Northern Ireland) 2016 s.27(2). In force: Brings into force various provisions of the 2016 Act on 10 October 2016.

This Order brings the Environmental Better Regulation Act (Northern Ireland) 2016 ss.15, 16, 26(2) and Sch.3 into operation to enable fireplaces and fuels which cause only limited amounts of smoke pollution to become officially designated for use in smoke control areas in Northern Ireland without the need for legislation to be compiled. The fuels and fireplaces are designated as being suitable for use in smoke control areas once added to lists kept by the Department of Agriculture, Environment and Rural Affairs, and published in a manner that it considers appropriate. In addition, the following are impliedly revoked by this Order: the Smoke Control Areas (Authorised Fuels) (Amendment) Regulations (Northern Ireland) 2015, the Smoke Control Areas (Exempted Fireplaces) (Amendment) Regulations (Northern Ireland) 2015; and the Smoke Control Areas (Exempted Fireplaces) (Amendment No.2) Regulations (Northern Ireland) 2015.

2275 Environmental Better Regulation Act (Northern Ireland) 2016 (c.13)

An Act to enable provision to be made for protecting and improving the environment; to provide for an integrated environmental permitting system; to provide for a review of powers of entry and associated powers and for the repeal or rewriting of such powers and for safeguards in relation to them; to provide for the repeal or rewriting of offences connected with the exercise of any such powers and for the preparation of a code of practice in connection with such exercise; to amend the Clean Air (Northern Ireland) Order 1981 to provide for a new method for authorising fuels for use in a smoke control area and for exempting fireplaces from the provisions of art.17 of that Order; to amend the Environment (Northern Ireland) Order 2002 to remove the requirement on district councils to make an assessment of air quality under art.13 of that Order; to amend the Water and Sewerage Services (Northern Ireland) Order 2006 to transfer certain functions to the Department of the Environment from the Department for Regional Development; and for connected purposes.

2276 Environmental protection–Regulation–Powers of entry

THE ENVIRONMENTAL BETTER REGULATION (2016 ACT) (COMMENCEMENT NO.1) ORDER (NORTHERN IRELAND) 2016, SR 2016/212; made under the Environmental Better Regulation Act (Northern Ireland) 2016 s.27(2). Commencement details: bringing into operation various provisions of the 2016 Act.

This Order brings into operation the Environmental Better Regulation Act (Northern Ireland) 2016 ss.7 to 14.

2277 EU law–Emissions–Integrated pollution prevention and control

THE POLLUTION PREVENTION AND CONTROL (INDUSTRIAL EMISSIONS) (AMENDMENT) REGULATIONS (NORTHERN IRELAND) 2016, SR 2016/309; made under the Environment (Northern Ireland) Order 2002 (SI 2002 3153) art.4(1), Sch.1. In force: 22 August 2016.

These Regulations amend the Pollution Prevention and Control (Industrial Emissions) Regulations (Northern Ireland) 2013 and implement Directive 2014/99 which amends Directive 2009/126 as regards the test methods to certify petrol vapour recovery systems for use in service stations and the test methods to verify the operation of such systems.

2278 EU law–Groundwater–Fitness for human consumption

THE GROUNDWATER (AMENDMENT) REGULATIONS (NORTHERN IRELAND) 2016, SR 2016/119; made under the European Communities Act 1972 s.2(2). In force: 20 June 2016.

These Regulations amend the Groundwater Regulations (Northern Ireland) 2009 to: take account of amendments made by Directive 2014/80; include the provision for the Department to review authorisations at anytime and where necessary update the authorisation irrespective of the date of when the authorisation was granted; and take account of amendments made to Directive 2006/118 by Directive 2014/80 and to amend the "lead" parameter threshold to bring it in line with the drinking standard set in Directive 98/83.

2279 EU law–Waste management licences

THE WASTE MANAGEMENT LICENSING (AMENDMENT) REGULATIONS (NORTHERN IRELAND) 2016, SR 2016/96; made under the Waste and Contaminated Land (Northern Ireland) Order 1997 (SI 1997 2778) art.4(3). In force: 5 September 2016.

These Regulations amend the Waste Management Licensing Regulations (Northern Ireland) 2003.

2280 Greenhouse gas emissions–Inspections–Enforcing authority for emissions limit

THE EMISSIONS PERFORMANCE STANDARD MONITORING AND ENFORCEMENT REGULATIONS (NORTHERN IRELAND) 2016, SR 2016/28; made under the Energy Act 2013 s.60(2), Sch.5. In force: 15 March 2016.

These Regulations: make provision for the chief inspector to be the enforcing authority for the emissions limit duty; set out the circumstances in which a fossil fuel plant operator must supply a notification to the chief inspector; and make provision for notifications to be given to the chief inspector stating when an exemption for a complete Carbon Capture and Storage system, including to which generating units any exemption should apply.

FAMILY LAW

2281 **Child support–Consequential amendments–Deduction from earnings orders**

THE CHILD SUPPORT (DEDUCTION FROM EARNINGS ORDERS, AMENDMENT AND MODIFICATION AND MISCELLANEOUS AMENDMENTS) REGULATIONS (NORTHERN IRELAND) 2016, SR 2016/390; made under the Child Support(Northern Ireland) Order 1991 (SI 1991 2628) art.29(2)(3), art.32(1)(2)(n)(5), art.47(1), art.48(4); Child Maintenance Act (Northern Ireland) 2008 s.36(1)(2), 6(1)(2). In force: 18 November 2016.

These Regulations amend and modify the Child Support (Collection and Enforcement) Regulations (Northern Ireland) 1992. They amend the Child Support (Meaning of Child and New Calculation Rules) (Consequential and Miscellaneous Amendment) Regulations (Northern Ireland) 2012 and the Child Support (Ending Liability in Existing Cases and Transition to New Calculation Rules) Regulations (Northern Ireland) 2014. Regulation 2 adds a new circumstance in which a deduction from earnings order can be discharged, namely where this appears to the Department to be appropriate as liability has ceased to accrue because the case has been closed under the Ending Liability Scheme. This will apply to all cases, regardless of whether a subsequent application is made to the 2012 child maintenance scheme.

2282 **County courts–Court rules–Family proceedings**

THE FAMILY PROCEEDINGS (AMENDMENT) RULES (NORTHERN IRELAND) 2016, SR 2016/301; made under the Family Law (Northern Ireland) Order 1993 (SI 1993 1576) art.12. In force: In acordance with Rule 1.

These Rules amend the Family Proceedings Rules (Northern Ireland) 1996 to take account of the Justice Act (Northern Ireland) 2015 Sch.1 and Pt 1, which creates a single jurisdiction for county courts and magistrates' courts whereby the jurisdiction and powers of those courts are exercisable throughout the whole of Northern Ireland.

FISHERIES

2283 **Fisheries Act (Northern Ireland) 2016 (c.27)**

An Act to make provision about fisheries.

2284 **Fishing–Carlingford Area**

THE CARLINGFORD AREA (DEFINITION OF THE MOUTH OF THE CLANRYE RIVER) REGULATIONS 2016, SR 2016/346; made under the Foyle Fisheries Act (Northern Ireland) 1952 s.13(1)(j); Foyle Fisheries Act 1952 s.13(1)(j). In force: 1 November 2016.

These Regulations define the mouth of the Clanrye River. It is an offence for any person (other than the owner of a several fishery within the limits thereof) to shoot, draw, or use any net for taking salmon at the mouth of any river or within 805 metres seaward or 805 metres inwards or along the coast from the mouth of any river.

FOOD

2285 **EU law–Infectious disease control–Enforcement**

THE FOOD HYGIENE (AMENDMENT) REGULATIONS (NORTHERN IRELAND) 2016, SR 2016/345; made under the European Communities Act 1972 s.2(2), Sch.2 para.1A. In force: 15 October 2016.

These Regulations make various amendments to the Food Safety and Hygiene Regulations (Northern Ireland) 2016 to provide for the execution and enforcement in Northern Ireland of Regulation 2015/1375 laying down specific rules on official controls for Trichinella in meat.

2286 EU law–Labelling–Caseins and caseinates Regulations

THE CASEINS AND CASEINATES REGULATIONS (NORTHERN IRELAND) 2016, SR 2016/415; made under the Food Safety (Northern Ireland) Order 1991 (SI 1991 762) art.15(1), art.16(1), art.25(1)(2)(e)(3), art.26(3), art.32(1), art.47(2). In force: 22 December 2016.

These Regulations will revoke and replace the Caseins and Caseinates Regulations (Northern Ireland) 1986 and the Caseins and Caseinates (Amendment) Regulations (Northern Ireland) 1990. These Regulations implement Directive 2015/2203 on the approximation of the laws of the Member States relating to caseins and caseinates intended for human consumption.

2287 Food Hygiene Rating (2016 Act) (c.3)–Commencement Order–Northern Ireland 2016

THE FOOD HYGIENE RATING (2016 ACT) (COMMENCEMENT) ORDER (NORTHERN IRELAND) 2016, SR 2016/328; made under the Food Hygiene Rating Act (Northern Ireland) 2016 s.21(3). Commencement details: bringing into operation various provisions of the 2016 Act on 7 October 2016.

This Order provides for the coming into operation of the Food Hygiene Rating Act (Northern Ireland) 2016 on the 7 October 2016.

2288 Food Hygiene Rating Act (Northern Ireland) 2016 (c.3)

An Act to provide for the operation of a food hygiene rating scheme in Northern Ireland.

2289 Food hygiene ratings–Northern Ireland

THE FOOD HYGIENE RATING REGULATIONS (NORTHERN IRELAND) 2016, SR 2016/313; made under the Food Hygiene Rating Act (Northern Ireland) 2016 s.1(6), s.2(7), s.7(1), s.12(2), s.19(1), Sch.1 para.14(b)(c). In force: 7 October 2016.

These Regulations make provision in relation to food hygiene ratings under the Food Hygiene Rating Act (Northern Ireland) 2016 by: exempting specified food business establishments from rating under the Act; prescribing the form of a Food Hygiene Rating Sticker to be issued under s.2(2) and responsibility for the cost of producing the sticker; specifying the location and manner of display of a Food Hygiene Rating Sticker by the operator of a food business establishment required to display by s.7(1); specifying the information that district councils must send to operators of new food business establishments under s.12(2) of the Act explaining the requirements of the Act and regulations made under it, as well as the operators rights under the Act, for example to appeal or request re-rating; and specifying the form and method of payment of a fixed penalty notice issued under s.11(1) of the Act.

2290 Food hygiene ratings–Transitional provisions–Northern Ireland

THE FOOD HYGIENE RATING (TRANSITIONAL PROVISIONS) ORDER (NORTHERN IRELAND) 2016, SR 2016/314; made under the Food Hygiene Rating Act (Northern Ireland) 2016 s.18(1)(3), s.19(1). In force: 7 October 2016.

This Order provides transitional provisions to allow district councils to treat an existing food hygiene rating as a food hygiene rating under the Food Hygiene Rating Act (Northern Ireland) 2016 s.1.

GOVERNMENT ADMINISTRATION

2291 Government departments–Commencement

THE DEPARTMENTS (2016 ACT) (COMMENCEMENT) ORDER (NORTHERN IRELAND) 2016, SR 2016/89; made under the . Commencement details: bringing into operation various provisions of the 2016 Act on 8 May 2016.

This Order provides for the coming into operation of the following provisions of the Departments Act (Northern Ireland) 2016: ss.1 and 2 and the Schedules on 8 May 2016.

2292 Government departments–Transfer of functions orders

THE DEPARTMENTS (TRANSFER OF FUNCTIONS) ORDER (NORTHERN IRELAND) 2016, SR 2016/76; made under the Departments (Northern Ireland) Order 1999 (SI 1999 283) art.8. In force: In accordance with art.1.

This Order transfers certain functions of Northern Ireland departments to other Northern Ireland departments.

2293 Rural Needs Act (Northern Ireland) 2016 (c.19)

An Act to impose a duty on public authorities to consider rural needs; and for connected purposes.

HEALTH

2294 Electronic documents–Health records

THE GENERAL DENTAL SERVICES (AMENDMENT) REGULATIONS (NORTHERN IRELAND) 2016, SR 2016/334; made under the Health and Personal Social Services (Northern Ireland) Order 1972 (SI 1972 1265) art.55A(1)(a), art.61(1)(2), art.106, art.107(6). In force: 10 October 2016.

These Regulations amend the Health and Personal Social Services General Dental Services Regulations (Northern Ireland) 1993 which regulate the terms on which general dental services are provided under the Health and Personal Social Services (Northern Ireland) Order 1972. They make amendments to reflect the new numbering of determinations relating to matters set out in the Statement of Dental Remuneration following the ceasing of commitment payments to dentists; and change the dentists' terms of service to enable a dentist to keep all referred forms of records detailed in the Regulations, including the practice record form, in computerised form.

2295 Health (Miscellaneous Provisions) Act (Northern Ireland) 2016 (c.26)

An Act to regulate the sale of nicotine products and tobacco, to amend the Health and Personal Social Services (Northern Ireland) Order 1972 and the Health (Miscellaneous Provisions) Act (Northern Ireland) 2008 in relation to the provision of health care; and for connected purposes.

2296 Health and Social Care (Control of Data Processing) Act (Northern Ireland) 2016 (c.12)

An Act to make provision about control of data processing in relation to health and social care.

2297 Medical treatment–Compensation–Recovery of health services charges

THE RECOVERY OF HEALTH SERVICES CHARGES (AMOUNTS) (AMENDMENT) REGULATIONS (NORTHERN IRELAND) 2016, SR 2016/105; made under the Recovery of Health Services Charges (Northern Ireland) Order 2006 (SI 2006 1944) art.5(2)(5) and 19(3) , art.19(3). In force: 1 April 2016.

The Recovery of Health Services (Northern Ireland) Order 2006 provides for a scheme for the recovery of charges in cases where an injured person who receives a compensation payment in respect of his injury has received hospital treatment or ambulance services. These Regulations maintain the current charges for incidents occurring before 1 April 2016.

2298 NHS–Medical services–Health professionals

THE HUMAN MEDICINES (AMENDMENT) REGULATIONS 2016, SR 2016/407; made under the European Communities Act 1972 s.2(2)(5). In force: 1 April 2016.

These Regulations amend the Human Medicines Regulations 2012. They update the general interpretation provisions in the 2012 Regulations to insert a new definition of therapeutic radiographer independent prescribers and to add registered dietitians to the list of health professionals who are included in the definition of a supplementary prescriber and amends the 2012 Regulations to ensure that the new provisions relating to therapeutic radiographer independent prescribers, orthoptists and midwives are subject to review by the Secretary of State.

2299 Optical appliances–Optical charges–Vouchers

THE OPTICAL CHARGES AND PAYMENTS (AMENDMENT) REGULATIONS (NORTHERN IRELAND) 2016, SR 2016/335; made under the Health and Personal Social Services (Northern Ireland) Order 1972 art.62, art.98, art.106, art.107(6), Sch.15. In force: 10 October 2016.

These Regulations further amend the Health and Personal Social Services (Optical Charges and Payments) Regulations (Northern Ireland) 1997 which provide for payment to be made, by means of a voucher system, in respect of costs incurred by certain categories of persons in connection with the supply, replacement and repair of optical appliances. The amendments: increase the redemption value of a voucher issued towards the cost of replacement of a single contact lens and to increase the maximum contribution by way of a voucher to the cost of repair of a frame; increase the value of vouchers issued towards the costs of supply and replacement of glasses and contact lenses; increase the additional values for vouchers for prisms, tints, photochromic lenses and special categories of appliances; increase the value of vouchers issued towards the cost of repair and replacement of optical appliances; and provide that the increases apply only in relation to vouchers accepted or used on or after 10 October 2016.

2300 Regional Health and Social Care Board–Disciplinary procedures–Doctors

THE HEALTH AND SOCIAL CARE (DISCIPLINARY PROCEDURES) REGULATIONS (NORTHERN IRELAND) 2016, SR 2016/104; made under the Health and Personal Social Services (Northern Ireland) Order 1972 (SI 1972 1265) (NI 14) art.61, art.62, art.63 , art.106; Health and Medicines(Northern Ireland) Order 1988 (SI 1988 2249) art.10. In force: 1 Apirl 2016.

These Regulations provide for the investigation and determination by the Regional Health and Social Care Board (the Regional Board) of questions whether chemists, dentists, ophthalmic medical practitioners and opticians providing services under Pt VI of the Health and Personal Social Services Order (Northern Ireland) 1972 have failed to comply with their terms of service, and for the consideration and determination of appeals by the Department of Health, Social Services and Public Safety from determinations of the Regional Board.

HOSPITALITY AND LEISURE

2301 Premises licences–Stadiums–Sale of intoxicating liquor

THE MAGISTRATES' COURTS (LICENSING) (AMENDMENT) RULES (NORTHERN IRELAND) 2016, SR 2016/405; made under the Magistrates' Courts (Northern Ireland) Order 1981 (SI 1981 1675) art.13; Licensing (Northern Ireland) Order 1996 (SI 1996

3158) Sch.4 para.4, Sch.5 para.2, Sch.6 para.3, Sch.9 para.3 , Sch.10 para3. In force: 19 December 2016.

These Rules amend the Magistrates' Courts (Licensing) Rules (Northern Ireland) 1997 in consequence of the Licensing Act (Northern Ireland) 2016 which adds an outdoor stadium to the types of premises for which a court may grant a licence for the retail sale of intoxicating liquor. In particular, to prescribe the procedure for an application to attach, vary or remove conditions in respect of a licence for an outdoor stadium.

HOUSING

2302 Houses in Multiple Occupation Act (Northern Ireland) 2016 (c.22)

An Act to make provision for and in connection with the licensing of houses in multiple occupation.

2303 Housing (Amendment) Act (Northern Ireland) 2016 (c.17)

An Act to make provision for the better sharing of information relating to empty homes or to anti-social behaviour; and to provide for the registration of certain loans as statutory charges.

2304 Landlords–Landlord registration scheme–Provision of information

THE LANDLORD REGISTRATION SCHEME (AMENDMENT) REGULATIONS (NORTHERN IRELAND) 2016, SR 2016/257; made under the Private Tenancies (Northern Ireland) Order 2006 (SI 2006 1459) art.65A(1)(2), art.73(1). In force: 1 September 2016.

These Regulations amend the Landlord Registration Scheme Regulations (Northern Ireland) 2014 to require that information held by the registrar and not included in the register of landlords shall, on request from an authorised officer, be disclosed to the Department for Communities for certain purposes.

HUMAN RIGHTS

2305 Abortion–Right to respect for private and family life–Prohibition on termination of pregnancy with fatal foetal abnormality or where pregnancy resulted from sexual crime–Whether breach of art.8 ECHR

[European Convention on Human Rights 1950 art.14, art.3, art.8; Offences Against the Person Act 1861 (c.100) s.58, s.59; Criminal Justice Act (Northern Ireland) 1945 s.25; Coroners Act (Northern Ireland) 1959 s.14(1)]

The applicant Commission applied for a declaration that the law on termination of pregnancy in Northern Ireland was incompatible with the ECHR. The law relating to abortion in Northern Ireland had been set out in *Family Planning Association of Northern Ireland v Minister for Health, Social Services and Public Safety* [2004] NICA 37, [2005] N.I. 188. Procurement of an abortion in Northern Ireland was a criminal offence punishable by a maximum sentence of life imprisonment, unless the pregnancy would cause a risk to the mother's life or cause serious, long-term harm to her physical or mental health. Termination where there was a serious malformation of the foetus (SMF), including fatal foetal abnormality (FFA), or where the pregnancy was a consequence of a sexual crime rendered the person who performed the abortion, and potentially the mother, liable to prosecution. The government had published draft guidelines for public consultation on the limited circumstances for a lawful termination, but the Commission complained about ongoing delay in presenting a consultation document and that when such a document was eventually issued it had not addressed the issues of SMF, FFA, or pregnancy as a result of rape or incest. The Commission sought a declaration that the Offences Against the Person Act 1861 s.58 and s.59 and the Criminal Justice Act (Northern Ireland) 1945 s.25 were incompatible with the ECHR art.3, art.8 and art.14 as they related to access to termination of pregnancy services for women in cases of SMF, FFA, rape or incest. The evidence was that in 2013 abortions had been provided in England and Wales to nearly to 2,000 women from Northern Ireland, a proportion of whom had been pregnant as a result of rape or incest or had been carrying foetuses with SMFs and FFAs. Evidence filed on behalf of the Commission in respect of the experiences those who had been denied abortions was not challenged.

Held: Declaration granted. (1) A foetus was not a legal person in England and Wales, *Paton v British Pregnancy Advisory Service Trustees* [1979] Q.B. 276, [1978] C.L.Y. 1588 and *Evans v Amicus Healthcare Ltd* [2004] EWCA Civ 727, [2005] Fam. 1, [2004] C.L.Y. 1673 considered. There were no grounds for concluding that the common law in Northern Ireland was any different, although pre-natal life did have statutory protection under the Coroners Act (Northern Ireland) 1959 s.14(1) which required an inquest to be held into a foetus in utero which was capable of being born alive and which lost its chance of life as a result of an offence (paras 103, 106, 108-109). (2) Article 3 prevented the infliction of ill-treatment on individuals, but the state was not responsible for a woman having an FFA or being impregnated as a result of rape. While no procedures or services in Northern Ireland allowed women who become pregnant in those circumstances to have terminations, there was no question that the state inflicted any ill-treatment on them. Women received the best medical attention during pregnancy and the state did not prevent them from travelling for abortions, *Pretty v United Kingdom (2346/02)* [2002] 2 F.L.R. 45, [2002] C.L.Y. 2528 considered. Having to leave the jurisdiction caused additional stress and expense, but the court was entitled to take judicial notice of the fact that women received the best health care either within the NHS in England or elsewhere privately. There was no convincing evidence that there were victims or potential victims who were able to satisfy the minimum threshold of severity necessary to allow a court to conclude that there had been a breach of their art.3 rights (paras 111, 117-121). (3) If abortion was immoral in Northern Ireland, it did not protect morals to export the problem. It placed women who had to travel under greater stress and the law made it more difficult for those of limited means to travel. Continuing a pregnancy was a decision belonging to the sphere of private life and autonomy, engaging art.8 rights, *Tysiac v Poland (5410/03)* [2007] 1 F.C.R. 666, [2007] C.L.Y. 2244 considered. While each state had a wide margin of appreciation, it was illegitimate and disproportionate to prohibit the abortion of both a foetus doomed to die because of an FFA, or a viable foetus conceived as a result of rape, but incapable of an independent existence. In the case of FFA, a mother's inability to access abortion constituted a gross interference with her personal autonomy. The foetus was doomed. There was nothing to weigh in the balance and no human life to protect. Sexual crime was a gross intrusion on a woman's autonomy in the vilest of circumstances and a resulting pregnancy was not a voluntary act. Weighed on the scales was the right of life of the foetus, which did not have any art.2 rights. It had limited protection provided by statute when it could exist independently of the womb. The law placed a disproportionate burden on the victim of sexual crime and, by imposing a blanket ban on abortion, reinforced with criminal sanctions, it effectively prevented any consideration of the interests of any woman whose personal autonomy in those circumstances had been so vilely and heinously invaded. A law so framed could never be said to be proportionate. The position in respect of SMF was different. It was not possible to either define SMF or to say that the failure to provide an exception for SMFs under the impugned provisions was not proportionate (paras 142, 144, 148, 160-162, 166). (4) The criminalisation of pregnant women applied with equal force to anyone who became pregnant in Northern Ireland. The Court of Appeal had concluded that the differential treatment of women from Northern Ireland compared to those in England and Scotland did not amount to discrimination under art.14, *R. (on the application of A (A Child)) v Secretary of State for Health* [2014] EWHC 1364 (Admin), [2014] Med. L.R. 246, [2014] C.L.Y. 1482 considered (paras 170-171).

NORTHERN IRELAND HUMAN RIGHTS COMMISSION'S APPLICATION FOR JUDICIAL REVIEW, RE *sub nom.* LAW ON TERMINATION OF PREGNANCY IN NORTHERN IRELAND, RE, [2015] NIQB 96, [2016] 2 F.C.R. 418, Horner J, QBD (NI).

2306 Attorney General–Human rights guidance–Cooperation and operational independence

THE ATTORNEY GENERAL'S HUMAN RIGHTS GUIDANCE (COOPERATION AND OPERATIONAL INDEPENDENCE) ORDER (NORTHERN IRELAND) 2016, SR 2016/386; made under the Justice (Northern Ireland) Act 2004 s.8(3)(c). In force: 19 December 2016.

This Order brings into operation guidance by the Attorney General for Northern Ireland, pursuant to the Justice (Northern Ireland) Act 2004 s.8, which was laid before the Assembly on 5 October 2016. The Attorney General has, in pursuance of s.8(1) of the Justice (Northern Ireland) Act 2004, issued guidance on international human rights standards relevant to cooperation and institutional independence in respect of the Police Service of Northern Ireland, the Public Prosecution Service for Northern Ireland and Forensic Science Northern Ireland.

INSOLVENCY

2307 Debt relief orders–Debt relief restrictions orders–Disqualification provisions

THE DEBT RELIEF ACT (NORTHERN IRELAND) 2010 (CONSEQUENTIAL AMENDMENTS) ORDER (NORTHERN IRELAND) 2016, SR 2016/108; made under the Debt Relief Act (Northern Ireland) 2010 s.5. In force: 7 March 2016.

This order makes consequential amendments to or in connection with disqualification provisions to take account of debt relief order and debt relief restrictions orders.

2308 Individual voluntary arrangements–Creditors' meetings–Breaches of statutory regime–Northern Ireland

[Insolvency Act 1986 (c.45); Insolvency (Northern Ireland) Order 1989 (SI 1989/2405) art.230A(3); Insolvency Rules (Northern Ireland) 1991 (SR 1991/364) Pt 5 (2) r.5.05]

A creditor applied for an order that a creditors' meeting, called to consider an individual voluntary arrangement proposed by the respondent debtors, was materially irregular. The insolvency practitioner acting as the debtors' nominee had acted in accordance with the Insolvency Act 1986, which applied in England, rather than the Insolvency (Northern Ireland) Order 1989 and the Insolvency Rules (Northern Ireland) 1991. Accordingly, he did not endorse the proposal as received on a specified date as required by r.5.05 of the Rules and did not submit a report to the High Court within 14 days of receiving the proposal as required by art.230A(3) of the Order. The creditor argued that the breaches of the statutory regime rendered the meeting invalid.

Held: Application granted. The Order and the Rules provided a highly prescribed mechanism for the proposal of an IVA and the timescales within which the various steps were to be taken. The statutory purpose of the endorsement of the date of receipt of the proposal and the lodging in court was to impose a timescale on any nominee asked to consider such a report. Where the statutory architecture put in place a highly regulated mechanism to deal with any proposal for an IVA any material departure from the machinery was likely to render anything done after the departure invalid, *Vlieland-Boddy v Dexter Ltd* [2003] EWHC 2592 (Ch), [2004] B.P.I.R. 235, [2004] C.L.Y. 2157 applied. There had been a failure to deliver the proposal to the court, as a result of which it was impossible to operate the statutory mechanism. That was a critical departure which rendered it impossible to hold a creditors' meeting in accordance with the statutory procedures. The meeting was invalid and any decision taken at it was of no effect.

BANK OF IRELAND MORTGAGE BANK v SHERIDAN, [2015] NICh 12, [2015] B.P.I.R. 1001, Morgan LCJ, Ch D (NI).

2309 Insolvency–Debt relief orders–Monetary limits

THE INSOLVENCY (MONETARY LIMITS) (AMENDMENT) ORDER (NORTHERN IRELAND) 2016, SR 2016/418; made under the Insolvency (Northern Ireland) Order 1989 (SI 1989 2405) art.362(1)(b). In force: In accordance with art.1.

This Order makes amendments to the Insolvency (Monetary Limits) Order (Northern Ireland) 1991. Article 3 increases the maximum amount of debt and maximum total value of property which a person may have in order to be eligible for a debt relief order. Property excludes a debtor's domestic motor vehicle up to a value of £1,000.

LANDLORD AND TENANT

2310 Statutory tenancies–Protected tenancies–Rent control

THE REGISTERED RENTS (INCREASE) ORDER (NORTHERN IRELAND) 2016, SR 2016/255; made under the Private Tenancies (Northern Ireland) Order 2006 (SI 2006 1459) art.55(5)(6). In force: 1 August 2016.

The purpose of the Order is to allow for increases in rents of statutory and protected tenancies in those properties that meet the housing fitness standard. Rents entered on the register during 2April 2007 and 3 April 2016 will be entitled to be increased by 1.3 percent.

LEGAL ADVICE AND FUNDING

2311 Access to justice–Legal representation–Consequential amendments

THE CIVIL LEGAL SERVICES (GENERAL) (AMENDMENT) REGULATIONS (NORTHERN IRELAND) 2016, SR 2016/337; made under the Access to Justice (Northern Ireland) Order 2003 (SI 2003 435) art.15. In force: 11 October 2016.

These Regulations amend the Civil Legal Services (General) Regulations (Northern Ireland) 2015. They make consequential amendments which are linked to the Civil Legal Services (Scope) Regulations (Northern Ireland) 2016 to provide that civil legal services funding for representation (lower courts) under the Access to Justice (Northern Ireland) Order 2003 is available for proceedings.

2312 Civil Legal Services–Legal representation–Remuneration

THE CIVIL LEGAL SERVICES (REMUNERATION) (AMENDMENT) ORDER (NORTHERN IRELAND) 2016, SR 2016/336; made under the Access to Justice (Northern Ireland) Order 2003 (SI 2003 435) art.12(3), art.47. In force: 11 October 2016.

This Order amends the Civil Legal Services (Remuneration) Order (Northern Ireland) 2015 by inserting new provisions to provide that remuneration is available under civil legal services for representation in those proceedings referred to in arts 3 and 4.

2313 Legal representation–Legal services–Publicly-funded clients

THE CIVIL LEGAL SERVICES (FINANCIAL) (AMENDMENT) REGULATIONS (NORTHERN IRELAND) 2016, SR 2016/338; made under the Access to Justice (Northern Ireland) Order 2003 (SI 2003 435) art.13. In force: 11 October 2016.

These Regulations amend the Civil Legal Services (Financial) Regulations (Northern Ireland) 2015 by inserting new provisions to provide that civil legal services funding for representation under the Access to Justice (Northern Ireland) Order 2003 is available without an assessment of an individual's financial resources for proceedings under: the Police and Criminal Evidence (Northern Ireland) Order 1989 arts 44 or 45; and the Terrorism Act 2000 Sch.8 paras 29 or 36.

2314 Slavery and trafficking prevention orders–Summary jurisdiction

THE CIVIL LEGAL SERVICES (SCOPE) (NO.2) REGULATIONS (NORTHERN IRELAND) 2016, SR 2016/416; made under the Access to Justice (Northern Ireland) Order 2003 (SI 2003 435) art.12(6). In force: 1 December 2016.

These Regulations amend the Access to Justice (Northern Ireland) Order 2003 Sch.2 regarding the proceedings which may be funded as civil legal services. The effect of these amendments is to provide that representation in a court of summary jurisdiction relating to applications for Slavery and Trafficking Prevention Orders and applications for Violent Offences Prevention Orders may be funded as civil legal services.

LICENSING

2315 Licensing Act (Northern Ireland) 2016 (c.24)

An Act to make provision for the granting of licences to authorise the sale of intoxicating liquor at outdoor stadia.

2316 Licensing committees–Procedural irregularity–Amusement arcades

[Betting, Gaming, Lotteries and Amusements (Northern Ireland) Order 1985 (SI 1985/1204)]

The appellant amusement arcade company appealed against the refusal of an application for judicial review of the respondent local authority's decision to grant a provisional amusement permit to another party (the notice party). The notice party had obtained planning permission restricting a proposed amusement arcade to slightly less than half of the ground floor of three-storey premises. The appellant's amusement arcade was a short distance away. It objected to the grant of a permit under the Betting, Gaming, Lotteries and Amusements (Northern Ireland) Order 1985 on the basis that it would have a directly adverse impact upon its business. The local authority's licensing committee arranged a meeting to consider the permit application and the objections. The appellant was invited and told that he might be heard at the committee's discretion. He protested that his solicitors would be unavailable to represent him as he had received only six days notice, which was not common practice. After hearing the other objectors' representations, the appellant indicated that he had nothing to add, but requested an adjournment for legal representation. The committee refused that request, with one member expressing a concern at the prospect of the timing of meetings being determined by solicitors' diaries. The committee granted the permit in respect of the premises, stating that to be "as outlined in the licensing officer's report". The appellant's application for judicial review of that decision was refused. The appellant submitted that (1) the refusal to adjourn was so procedurally unfair as to be unlawful, as although there was no statutory obligation to hear orally from objectors, the committee's own policy and standing orders confirmed that objectors would be given an opportunity to be heard; (2) the permit referred to the entire premises; the 1985 Order specified that the premises in question had to be used "wholly or mainly" for the provision of amusements, whereas the only portion of the building identified to be used was an area occupying less than half of the ground floor.

Held: Appeal dismissed. (1) The decision whether to adjourn a local authority meeting was a matter for the exercise of that local authority's discretion. The court had to be satisfied that the local authority had wrongly exercised that discretion in principle, or had acted upon a significant self-misdirection, *R. v Panel on Take-overs and Mergers Ex p. Guinness Plc* [1990] 1 Q.B. 146, [1989] C.L.Y. 3671 followed. The appellant's solicitors had formally lodged written objections to the permit and, at the meeting, the appellant had stated that he had nothing to add. The solicitors' presence at the meeting would not have impacted upon the form of the decision. The defect articulated in the appellant's second ground of appeal would not have become apparent until the permit had actually been drafted. The court emphasised the importance of affording objectors a fair hearing. The individual committee member's reference to solicitors' diaries did him no credit. The advent of reconstructed local authorities should present an opportunity for those bodies to discuss and rationalise the amount of notice to be afforded in the instant type of case (see paras 16-17 of judgment). (2) It was clear from the licensing officer's report and the committee's minutes that the committee members concerned had been properly informed and were satisfied that the area to which the application related was the portion of the ground floor outlined in the drawings annexed to the planning permission, *R. v Secretary of State Ex p. Anderson* applied. The format of the permit did not raise any doubt as to the legal validity of the committee's decision. The matter was remitted to the committee to consider redrafting the permit.

LEISURE ARCADES LTD'S APPLICATION FOR JUDICIAL REVIEW, RE, [2015] NICA 36, [2015] L.L.R. 761, Morgan LCJ, CA (NI).

2317 Premises licences–Prescribed forms–Stadiums

THE LICENSING (FORM OF LICENCE) (AMENDMENT) REGULATIONS (NORTHERN IRELAND) 2016, SR 2016/295; made under the Licensing (Northern Ireland) Order 1996 (SI 1996 3158) art.33. In force: 1 September 2016.

These Regulations amend the Licensing (Form of Licence) Regulations (Northern Ireland) 1997 by prescribing the form of licence which is issued by a court to authorise the retail sale of intoxicating liquor in an outdoor stadium under the Licensing (Northern Ireland) Order 1996.

2318 Premises licences–Stadiums–Liquor licence

THE LICENSING (DESIGNATION OF OUTDOOR STADIA) (NO.2) REGULATIONS (NORTHERN IRELAND) 2016, SR 2016/296; made under the Licensing (Northern Ireland) Order 1996 (SI 1996 3158) art.2AA(c). In force: 1 September 2016.

These Regulations designate the National Football Stadium for Northern Ireland at Windsor Park, Belfast as an outdoor stadium of importance to the whole of Northern Ireland. This designation allows the Irish Football Association to apply to the courts for a liquor licence at the stadium.

2319 Premises licences–Stadiums–Liquor licence

THE LICENSING (DESIGNATION OF OUTDOOR STADIA) REGULATIONS (NORTHERN IRELAND) 2016, SR 2016/294; made under the Licensing (Northern Ireland) Order 1996 (SI 1996 3158) art.2AA(C). In force: 1 September 2016.

These Regulations designate the main stadium of the Irish Rugby Football Union in Ulster at 85 Ravenhill Park, Belfast as an outdoor stadium of importance to the whole of Northern Ireland. This designation allows the Ulster Branch of the Irish Rugby Football Union to apply to the courts for a liquor licence at the stadium.

LOCAL GOVERNMENT

2320 Rates (Amendment) (2016 Act) (c.6)–Commencement No.1 Order–Northern Ireland

THE RATES (AMENDMENT) (2016 ACT) (COMMENCEMENT NO.1) ORDER (NORTHERN IRELAND) 2016, SR 2016/331; made under the Rates (Amendment) Act (Northern ,Ireland) 2016 s.6(1). Commencement details: bringing into operation various provisions of the 2016 Act on 19 September 2016.

This Order provides for the coming into operation of certain provisions of the Rates (Amendment) Act (Northern Ireland) 2016.

2321 Rates (Amendment) Act (Northern Ireland) 2016 (c.6)

An Act to amend the Rates (Northern Ireland) Order 1977 to enable regulations to be made permitting an increase in the level of reduction in the normal rate to 100% for certain hereditaments used for prescribed recreation; to provide that certain hereditaments are not to be treated for the purposes of the Order as occupied by reason only of them containing certain window displays; and for connected purposes.

2322 Rates (Amendment) Act (Northern Ireland) 2016 (c.6)–Commencement No.2 Order–Northern Ireland

THE RATES (AMENDMENT) (2016 ACT) (COMMENCEMENT NO.2) ORDER (NORTHERN IRELAND) 2016, SR 2016/388; made under the Rates (Amendment) Act (Northern Ireland) 2016 s.6(1). Commencement details: bringing into operation various provisions of the Rates (Amendment) Act (Northern Ireland) 2016 on 26 October 2016.

This Order provides for the coming into operation of the Rates (Amendment) Act (Northern Ireland) 2016 s.1, which was partially commenced for regulation-making purposes by the Rates (Amendment) (2016 Act) (Commencement No.1) Order (Northern Ireland) 2016. This Order now commences that section for all other purposes.

MENTAL HEALTH

2323 Detention in hospital–Discharge–Paranoid schizophrenic

[Mental Health (Northern Ireland) Order 1986 (SI 1986/595) art.2(4), art.4, art.77]

The claimant (H), a paranoid schizophrenic, applied for judicial review of the defendant tribunal's decision that he should not be discharged under the Mental Health (Northern Ireland) Order 1986 art.77 from detention. H had attacked a consultant psychiatrist while driven by his paranoid psychotic ideation and was detained for assessment under art.4. He then attacked another patient who he believed was conspiring with the consultant. H applied to the tribunal to be discharged but it directed that he should remain detained. He commenced anti-psychotic medication and his mental health improved. He re-applied to the tribunal. The evidence before the tribunal from the experts and H's family members was that, despite his claim that he would remain as a voluntary patient, he would abscond from hospital; he would fail to take his prescribed medication; his mental health would deteriorate; and there was a real probability that he would act on his delusions. As a consequence, there was substantial likelihood of serious harm to others. The tribunal found that H continued to hold the core delusional beliefs and there remained very real potential for him to act on those delusions resulting in serious physical harm to others. H submitted that the tribunal had failed to (i) adopt the narrow focused approach required under art.2(4); (2) take into account his stated intention which was to remain in hospital as a voluntary patient if discharged from detention.

Held: Application refused. (1) Under art.2(4)(b), the tribunal was required to focus on H's past behaviour and whether he had behaved violently towards other persons. The evidence was that he had behaved violently towards others when he had not been closely supervised and had failed to take his prescribed medication. The overwhelming evidence before the tribunal was that, despite his stated intention, he was likely to leave hospital, as he had done in the past on at least five occasions, if he were not detained. Once living in the community he would fail to adhere to his treatment regime, suffer increased paranoid ideation as a consequence and then act on those delusions by attacking the consultant psychiatrist or anyone he believed was assisting him. On the basis of that evidence, not only was the tribunal correct to reach such a conclusion, but to have reached a different one would have been wholly unreasonable (see paras 30-31 of judgment). (2) On the question of whether H would remain in hospital as a voluntary patient if discharged, it was necessary to weigh the opinion of H's treating consultant psychiatrist, social worker and family members against the intention of H, who recently had been suffering from increased paranoid ideation, unsupported by any expert opinion. The only possible conclusion for the tribunal, therefore, was that if H were to be discharged from detention he would not remain as a voluntary patient (paras 32, 34).

MH v MENTAL HEALTH REVIEW TRIBUNAL FOR NORTHERN IRELAND, [2014] NIQB 87, [2015] M.H.L.R. 53, Horner J, QBD (NI).

2324 Detention in hospital–Patient suffering paranoid ideation–Likelihood of serious physical harm

[Mental Health (Northern Ireland) Order 1986 (SI 1986/595) art.12, art.2(4)(a)(ii), art.2(4)(b)(ii), art.4]

The claimant (R) applied for judicial review of the defendant trust's decision to detain him in hospital against his will for assessment and treatment pursuant to the Mental Health (Northern Ireland) Order 1986 art.4 and art.12. The trust had detained R for assessment under art.4 on the basis that, within the meaning of art.2(4)(a)(ii), his judgement was so affected that he was, or would soon be, unable to protect himself from serious physical harm and that reasonable provision for his protection was not available in the community. It subsequently detained him for treatment under art.12 on the basis that, within the meaning of art.2(4)(b)(ii), his behaviour had placed other persons in reasonable fear of serious physical harm. R submitted that there was no evidence that he would be unable to protect himself or cause others reasonable fear.

Held: Application granted. (1) A man such as R, who was suffering paranoid ideation with disordered thought processes, and who had no electricity or food in his home and could not explain why that was so, could reasonably be considered to be suffering from judgement so affected that at a minimum he was, or would soon be, unable to protect himself from serious physical harm. R was creating for himself a situation where serious physical harm was inevitable, and he did not seem to have done anything about it. He clearly met the test and his detention under art.4 was lawful (see paras 44-45 of judgment). (2) The responsible medical officer's report contained no acceptable evidence making out the ground that failure to detain R would create a substantial likelihood of serious physical harm to himself or others, his having behaved in a way that other persons were placed in reasonable fear of serious physical harm. Further, the medical officer had failed to specify, in accordance with art.12(1)(d), whether other methods of dealing with R were available and, if so, why they were not appropriate. Thus, no lawful detention under art.12 had been effected (paras 47, 50, 53).

RS'S APPLICATION FOR JUDICIAL REVIEW, RE, [2014] NIQB 88, [2015] M.H.L.R. 61, Treacy J, QBD (NI).

2325 Mental Capacity Act (Northern Ireland) 2016 (c.18)

An Act to make new provision relating to persons who lack capacity; to make provision about the powers of criminal courts in respect of persons with disorder; to disapply Pt 2 of the Mental Health (Northern Ireland) Order 1986 in relation to persons aged 16 or over and make other amendments of that Order; to make provision in connection with the Convention on the International Protection of Adults signed at the Hague on 13 January 2000; and for connected purposes.

2326 Mental patients' rights–Nearest relative orders

[Mental Health (Northern Ireland) Order 1986 (SI 1986/595) art.32, art.36; European Convention on Human Rights 1950 art.8; Human Rights Act 1998 (c.42) s.3]

The claimant patient (H) sought a declaration that the Mental Health (Northern Ireland) Order 1986 art.32 and art.36 were unlawful and should be amended. H was a 34-year-old mental health patient who had been detained for treatment. At the time of his detention he indicated that he did not wish his mother to be appointed as his nearest relative. His sister was appointed instead. She lived in England and did not visit H. H wished his cousin (C) to be appointed as his nearest relative. C lived in Northern Ireland, visited H fortnightly and phoned him several times a week. The art.32 definition of "relative" did not include cousins. Under art.36 the county court could appoint an alternative person to exercise the rights of the nearest relative on application by a relative, an approved social worker or a person with whom the patient resided. The application could only be made on specified grounds, including the inability of the nearest relative to act, and the nearest relative's exercise of the power to discharge the patient without due regard to the patient's welfare. H submitted that the absence of a mechanism allowing him to apply to change his nearest relative represented an infringement of his human rights and was not justified or proportionate; and his reasons for preferring C as his nearest relative were sound. He also argued that identical provisions in England and Wales had been declared incompatible with the European

Convention on Human Rights 1950 art.8 and had been amended to give the patient locus standi to apply to change his nearest relative.

Held: Declaration granted in favour of claimant. (1) It could not be doubted that the role of the nearest relative involved many functions which touched upon a patient's private life, *R. (on the application of M) v Secretary of State for Health* [2003] EWHC 1094 (Admin), [2003] U.K.H.R.R. 746, [2003] C.L.Y. 2959 and *JT v United Kingdom (26494/95)* [2000] 1 F.L.R. 909, [2000] C.L.Y. 4181 considered. The wide-ranging powers given to the nearest relative, which would otherwise infringe the patient's art.8 rights, were saved from illegality because they pursued a legitimate aim. However, the absence of any input from the patient himself in the selection of the nearest relative did not pursue a legitimate aim. The nearest relative was designed to protect the best interests of the patient. The decision of who was best placed to assess and represent those interests had necessarily to take into account the views of the patient where he had the capacity to express such views, or there was the possibility of a complete disconnect between the important safety mechanism and the actual best interests of the patient. The inability of the patient to be heard on the issue of the identity of his nearest relative was therefore an infringement of the patient's art.8 rights which did not pursue a legitimate aim (see paras 46-50 of judgment). (2) The obligation under the Human Rights Act 1998 s.3 to interpret legislation compatibly with the Convention was wide-ranging. However, the obligation had limits, for example where the interpretation contended for was contrary to some fundamental aspect of the legislation or where it would create some far-ranging practical effects which would be outwith the competency of the judiciary, *Ghaidan v Godin-Mendoza* [2004] UKHL 30, [2004] 2 A.C. 557, [2004] C.L.Y. 2538 followed. It would not go against the grain of the statutory provisions to read the words "or the applicant" into the list of people entitled to apply to the county court for a change of the nearest relative. The list of grounds for a change of nearest relative should to be read so as to include "that the nearest relative of the patient is otherwise not a suitable person to act as such" as per the English legislation. Neither of those interpretations undermined the purpose of the scheme, and they did not lead to practical effects which the court was not equipped to consider. Extending the provisions in that way would not alter the procedure to be undertaken by the county court. It remained a matter for the county court to decide on the evidence if the nearest relative should be changed. Accordingly, the court granted a declaration that art.32 and art.36 should be read as outlined above (paras 51-58).

HM'S APPLICATION FOR JUDICIAL REVIEW, RE, [2014] NIQB 43, [2015] M.H.L.R. 326, Treacy J, QBD (NI).

NEGLIGENCE

2327 Professional negligence–Solicitors–Property transactions–Whether breach of duty to mortgage lender–Whether breach caused loss

The claimant lender claimed damages against the defendant solicitors' firm for breaches of its duties in respect of property transactions. The firm had acted for a company in its purchase of several properties from the company's sole director and shareholder, which was part of a tax avoidance scheme. It also acted for the lender. The lender had funded the purchase. The application for finance had been described as a mortgage application and had contained inconsistent information about the nature of the transaction. The lender had instructed the firm to prepare and complete a first legal charge. The company had purchased the properties but had not paid the full amount of consideration, using part of the loan to pay stamp duty and other transaction costs. The balance of the purchase price had been provided in the form of issued share capital in the company rather than cash. The lender had lost money when the property market collapsed and claimed to be unaware that the transaction was a purchase rather than a re-mortgage. It contended that if it had known its true nature, about which the firm had been duty bound to inform it, it would not have provided finance. The lender did not adduce evidence from its underwriters as to whether they knew that the transaction was a purchase. The issues were (1) whether the firm had breached its duties to the lender under its retainer or the Council of Mortgage Lenders' Handbook; (2) if so, whether the lender had proved that the firm's breach of duty had caused the loss it had suffered as a result of entering into the transaction.

Held: Claim dismissed. (1) The test was whether a solicitor of ordinary competence would have considered that the information obtained by him would cause the lender to have second thoughts, *Mortgage Express Ltd v Bowerman & Partners* [1996] 2 All E.R. 836, [1996] C.L.Y. 4497 applied. In the light of the requirements of the CML handbook, there were a number of matters that the lender could reasonably have expected the firm to pass on: (a) the transaction was a sale by an individual to his own company and not a re-mortgage; (b) part of the consideration involved shares in the company; (c) the full consideration was not being paid; and (d) the seller's legal costs were being paid out of the moneys loaned. The firm should have expressly drawn all of those matters to the lender's attention unless it was wholly satisfied that the lender already had the requisite knowledge. That was not the position and the firm had breached its duties to the lender under the retainer (see paras 32, 36-37 of judgment). (2) The lender should, at the very least, have realised that the transaction was not a re-mortgage but a sale to a company. The onus was always on a claimant to prove its case, including causation. That required the underwriter to give evidence and to satisfy the court that the lender would not have proceeded with the transaction if it had known all of the details, *E.Surv Ltd v Goldsmith Williams Solicitors* [2015] EWCA Civ 1147, [2016] 4 W.L.R. 44, [2016] 1549 applied. In the absence of the underwriter's evidence, the court could not know. The lender had failed to discharge the onus of proof (paras 38, 43-44). (3) If the court was wrong that the lender had failed to prove its case, then the lender had also been at fault, that fault was causative of its damage, and it would be just and equitable for the damages to be reduced by 66.7%, *Omega Trust Co Ltd v Wright Son & Pepper (No.2)* [1998] P.N.L.R. 337, [1998] C.L.Y. 4016 considered (paras 46-48). (4) The lender should have mitigated its loss by seeking to enforce the guarantee provided by the seller, which appeared to be a clear claim, rather than seeking to recover all the loss from the solicitors' firm (paras 49-53).

CAPITAL HOME LOANS LTD v HEWIT & GILPIN SOLICITORS LTD, [2016] NIQB 13, [2016] P.N.L.R. 24, Horner J, QBD (NI).

2328 Professional negligence–Valuation–Valuation of development site–Appropriateness of valuation method used–Northern Ireland

The court had to determine as a preliminary issue whether the valuation of a site purchased by the plaintiff fell within a tolerance of 10 per cent either side. In December 2006 the plaintiff, a housing association, entered into a provisional agreement to buy the subject site by way of sub-sale from a developer, who had acquired it on the open market for £6.525 million in October 2006. The defendant valuer had provided an open market valuation of the site for the developer's bank at £10.5 million as a development opportunity. In July and December 2006, two adjacent sites were sold for £3.125 million and £5.12 million per acre respectively. In March 2007, on the plaintiff's instructions, the defendant provided a new valuation of the subject site at £10 million as a development opportunity. Its valuation report made no reference to the developer's acquisition of the site for £6.525 million or to the valuation it had provided to the bank; nor did it identify any other transactions involving the sale of comparable sites in the vicinity. The report referred to the grant of planning approval for 200 apartments as being a viable commercial proposition, but made no reference to documentation from planning consultants and architects concerning the effect of a mix of private and social housing on the number of units that might be built. In reliance on that valuation, the plaintiff purchased the site for £9.75 million (£7.67 million per acre). In August 2007, the Northern Ireland property market collapsed. At the date of the instant hearing, the site was worth approximately one-tenth of the price paid by the plaintiff. The plaintiff brought proceedings. The issue was whether the valuation of the site fell within the broad range of plus or minus 10 per cent, although the defendant contended for a 15 per cent tolerance margin.

Held: Preliminary issue determined. (1) It was clear beyond any doubt that the defendant should have disclosed to the plaintiff that it had valued the site for the bank which was funding the developer in 2006. It was duty bound by the conflict of interest provisions set out in Appendix 1.1 of the RICS Red Book in that regard (see para.33 of judgment). (2) The Red Book also stated that any Special Assumptions which were necessary in order to adequately provide the client with a valuation had to be agreed and confirmed in writing to the client before the report was issued. Although Special Assumptions might include the grant of planning permission for development, there was nothing in the instant case to confirm that planning permission for 200 units would be forthcoming. Accordingly, the market value in the defendant's report could not be said to be based on a Special Assumption that such planning permission would be obtained in the future (paras 37, 43, 45). (3) It was a matter for developers exercising their own reasonable professional judgement to decide what valuation method to use. The comparable method involved looking at similar transactions and making adjustments to allow the index site to be compared. The residual method involved assessing the value of the scheme as completed and deducting the costs of development to arrive at the underlying land value. In the instant case, the defendant had erred in choosing the residual method and then proceeding on the assumption that planning permission would be granted for 200 residential units, notwithstanding that the expert evidence in that regard was hedged with caveats. It had also used values for the finished units which did not reflect location. If the defendant had used the comparable method, even as a check, it would have seen that its assessment was totally out of kilter with the market and in particular the sale of the same site a few months earlier, which should have formed the basis of any valuation subsequently carried out. Moreover, the off-market sales of the adjacent sites suggested that the defendant's valuation was grossly excessive. It was also a material omission on the defendant's part that it had failed to obtain specific planning advice as to whether a mix of private and social housing on the site would have achieved a greater density of units, inter alia by affecting the number of parking spaces that would be required. The defendant should have ascertained the number of private residential units which could be lawfully accommodated on the site (paras 46-49, 51, 56, 63). (4) The valuation was outside the permissible range of plus or minus 10 per cent and was also outside the defendant's suggested range of plus or minus 15 per cent (para.64).

HELM HOUSING LTD v MYLES DANKER ASSOCIATES LTD, [2015] NIQB 73, [2016] P.N.L.R. 4, Horner J, QBD (NI).

PENOLOGY AND CRIMINOLOGY

2329 Trafficked victims–Human trafficking and exploitation–Vocational training

THE HUMAN TRAFFICKING AND EXPLOITATION (CRIMINAL JUSTICE AND SUPPORT FOR VICTIMS) (INDEPENDENT GUARDIAN) REGULATIONS (NORTHERN IRELAND) 2016, SR 2016/410; made under the Human Trafficking and Exploitation (Criminal Justice and Support for Victims) Act (Northern Ireland) 2015 s.21(5), s.27(6); Health and Personal Social Services (Quality, Improvement and Regulation) (Northern Ireland) Order 2003 (SI 2003 431) art.23(1)(2)(d)(f)(5)(a)(c)(7)(a), art.48(2). In force: 19 December 2016.

These Regulations, which are made under the Human Trafficking and Exploitation (Criminal Justice and Support for Victims) Act (Northern Ireland) 2015 s.21(5), make provision for the first time for the training and qualifications required for a person to be eligible for appointment as an independent guardian and the support to be provided for, and the supervision of, an independent guardian.

PENSIONS

2330 Annuities–Additional voluntary contributions–Police Service of Northern Ireland

THE POLICE PENSIONS (ADDITIONAL VOLUNTARY CONTRIBUTIONS) (AMENDMENT) REGULATIONS (NORTHERN IRELAND) 2016, SR 2016/82; made under the Public Service Pensions Act (Northern Ireland) 2014 s.1(1)(2)(g), s.3(1)(2)(3)(5); Superannuation (Northern Ireland) Order 1972 art.14, art.15. In force: 29 February 2016 except for reg.2 and Sch.1 on 6 April 2015.

These Regulations mean that members of the Police Service of Northern Ireland with a protected pension age retiring before age 55, or those retiring members aged 55 or over, are no longer required to purchase an annuity from their additional voluntary contribution pension provider with effect from 6 April 2015.

2331 **Northern Ireland Public Services Ombudsman–Occupational pensions–Public sector employees**

THE PUBLIC SERVICE PENSIONS (NORTHERN IRELAND PUBLIC SERVICES OMBUDSMAN) REGULATIONS (NORTHERN IRELAND) 2016, SR 2016/340; made under the Public Service Pensions Act (Northern Ireland) 2014 s.1(1)(2)(a), s.3(1)(3), s.25(3). In force: 11 October 2016.

These Regulations specify persons employed by the Northern Ireland Public Services Ombudsman as persons to whom the scheme, established under The Public Service (Civil Servants and Others) Pension Regulations (Northern Ireland) 2014, may potentially relate, in accordance with the Public Service Pensions (Northern Ireland) Act 2014 s.25(3). It has retrospective effect from 1 April 2016 by virtue of s.3(3)(b) of the 2014 Act.

2332 **Occupational pensions–Additional voluntary contributions–Annuities**

THE POLICE PENSIONS (CONSEQUENTIAL PROVISIONS) (AMENDMENT) REGULATIONS (NORTHERN IRELAND) 2016, SR 2016/24; made under the Public Service Pensions Act (Northern Ireland) 2014 s.1(1)(2)(g), s.2(1), s.3(1)(2)(3)(a)(4). In force: In accordance with reg.1(2).

These Regulations allow members of the Police Service of Northern Ireland who are retiring with a protected pension age before 55 or aged 55 or over, to no longer be required to purchase an annuity from their AVC pension provider with effect from 6 April 2015, the beginning of the 2015-16 tax years.

2333 **Occupational pensions–Contracting out**

THE OCCUPATIONAL PENSION SCHEMES (SCHEMES THAT WERE CONTRACTED-OUT) REGULATIONS (NORTHERN IRELAND) 2016, SR 2016/107; made under the Pensions (Northern Ireland) Order 1995 (SI 1995 3213) art.90(6), art.166(3); Pension Schemes (Northern Ireland) Act 1993 s.3, s.5, s.7(5), s.8A(4), s.8D, s.12(3)(4), s.13(6), s.16(1)(3), s.17, s.20B(5), s.20C, s.21(2), s.30, s.32(6), s.33(1), s.33A(1)(c), s.46(1B), s.47(2)(4), s.49(3), s.151, s.152(2), s.177(2)(3)(4), s.178(1), Sch1 para.1, Sch.1 para.2, Sch.1 para.3. In force: In accordance with reg.1.

These Regulations revoke and replace most of the Occupational Pension Schemes (Contracting-out) Regulations (Northern Ireland) 1996 in consequence of provision made by the Pensions Act (Northern Ireland) 2015.

2334 **Occupational pensions–Contracting out–Savings provisions**

THE PENSIONS (2015 ACT) (SAVINGS) ORDER (NORTHERN IRELAND) 2016, SR 2016/106; made under the Pensions Act (Northern Ireland) 2015 s.53(5). In force: 6 April 2016 until 6 April 2019.

This Order saves certain provisions of the Pension Schemes (Northern Ireland) Act 1993 Pt 3, repealed by the Pensions Act (Northern Ireland) 2015 Sch.13 which abolishes contracting-out for salary related schemes.

2335 **Occupational pensions–Pensions Regulator Code of practice**

THE PENSIONS (2005 ORDER) (CODE OF PRACTICE) (GOVERNANCE AND ADMINISTRATION OF OCCUPATIONAL TRUST-BASED SCHEMES PROVIDING MONEY PURCHASE BENEFITS) (APPOINTED DAY) ORDER (NORTHERN IRELAND) 2016, SR 2016/330; made under the Pensions (Northern Ireland) Order 2005 (SI 2005 255) art.86(7). Commencement details: bringing into operation various provisions of the 2005 Order on 21 September 2016.

This Order appoints the day for the purposes of the Pensions (Northern Ireland) Order 2005 art.86(7) for the coming into operation of the Pensions Regulator Code of practice no. 13: Governance and administration of occupational trust-based schemes providing money purchase benefits: Second issue as 21 September 2016.

2336 Occupational pensions–Public sector employees–Revaluation

THE PUBLIC SERVICE PENSIONS REVALUATION (EARNINGS) ORDER (NORTHERN IRELAND) 2016, SR 2016/50; made under the Public Service Pensions Act (Northern Ireland) 2014 s.9(2)(3). In force: 1 April 2016.

This Order specifies an increase in earnings of 2% in relation to the period of 1 April 2015 to 31 March 2016 inclusive. This figure is based on a measure of the year on year change in average weekly earnings figure to September 2015.

2337 Occupational pensions–Public sector employees–Superannuation

THE HEALTH AND PERSONAL SOCIAL SERVICES (SUPERANNUATION), HEALTH AND SOCIAL CARE (PENSION SCHEMES) (AMENDMENT) REGULATIONS (NORTHERN IRELAND) 2016, SR 2016/384; made under the Superannuation (Northern Ireland) Order 1972 art.12(1)(2), art.14(1)(2)(3), Sch.3; Public Service Pensions Act (Northern Ireland) 2014 s.1(1)(2)(e), s.3, Sch.1 para.5, Sch.2 para.5, Sch.3. In force: 17 November 2016.

These Regulations amend the Health and Personal Social Services (Superannuation) Regulations (Northern Ireland) 1995, the Health and Social Care (Pension Scheme) Regulations (Northern Ireland) 2008 and the Health and Social Care Pension Scheme Regulations (Northern Ireland) 2015. Part 1 provides for citation, commencement and effect, including that the provisions of this rule are to take effect before the date of commencement. Parts 2, 3 and 4 make similar amendments in respect of the 1995 Regulations, the 2008 Regulations and the 2015 Regulations.

2338 Occupational pensions–Qualifying periods–Teaching assistants

THE LOCAL GOVERNMENT PENSION SCHEME (NURSERY ASSISTANTS) (AMENDMENT) REGULATIONS (NORTHERN IRELAND) 2016, SR 2016/329; made under the Public Service Pensions Act (Northern Ireland) 2014 s.1, s.3, Sch.3. In force: 16 October 2016.

These Regulations amend the Local Government Pension Scheme Regulations (Northern Ireland) 2002, the Local Government Pension Scheme (Administration) Regulations (Northern Ireland) 2009, the Local Government Pension Scheme (Benefits, Membership and Contributions) Regulations (Northern Ireland) 2009 and the Local Government Pension Scheme (Amendment and Transitional Provisions) Regulations (Northern Ireland) 2014. They will protect nursery assistants' pensions by changing the denominator of the fraction used to calculate their pension entitlement from a whole-time equivalent of 32.5 hours per week to 36 hours per week. Nursery assistants employed by the Education and Library Boards who accrued pension rights on the basis of a whole-time equivalent of 32.5 hours per week during the period from 1 January 1995 to 27 March 2015 (inclusive) will have those rights protected. Thereafter their pension rights will be accrued on the basis of the whole-time equivalent of 36 hours per week.

2339 Occupational pensions–Superannuation–Northern Ireland Public Services Ombudsman

THE SUPERANNUATION (NORTHERN IRELAND PUBLIC SERVICES OMBUDSMAN) ORDER (NORTHERN IRELAND) 2016, SR 2016/339; made under the Superannuation (Northern Ireland) Order 1972 art.3(4)(7). In force: 11 October 2016.

This Order adds employment by the Northern Ireland Public Services Ombudsman to the kinds of employment listed in the Superannuation (Northern Ireland) Order 1972 Sch.1, for which the Department of Finance may make pension schemes. It has retrospective effect from 1 April 2016 by virtue of art.3(7) of the 1972 Order.

2340 Pension schemes–Civil Service–Northern Ireland Civil Service pension scheme

THE PUBLIC SERVICE (CIVIL SERVANTS AND OTHERS) PENSIONS (CONSEQUENTIAL PROVISIONS) (AMENDMENT) REGULATIONS (NORTHERN

IRELAND) 2016, SR 2016/34; made under the Public Service Pensions Act (Northern Ireland) 2014 s.1(1)(2)(a), s.2(1), s.3(1)(2)(3)(a)(4). In force: In accordance with reg.1.

The Regulations modify the effect of other statutory provisions in their application to Northern Ireland Civil Service pension scheme. This amendment is necessary to ensure the protection of increases in guaranteed minimum pensions after the abolition of contracting out.

2341 Pension Schemes Act (Northern Ireland) 2016 (c.1)

An Act to make provision about pension schemes, including provision designed to encourage arrangements that offer people different levels of certainty in retirement or that involve different ways of sharing or pooling risk.

2342 Social security–State pension–Transitional rate state pension

THE STATE PENSION REVALUATION FOR TRANSITIONAL PENSIONS ORDER (NORTHERN IRELAND) 2016, SR 2016/419; made under the Social Security Administration (Northern Ireland) Act 1992 s.130AC, s.165(1)(4). In force: In accordance with art.1.

This Order, which corresponds to an Order made by the Secretary of State for Work and Pensions under the Social Security Administration Act 1992 s.148AC, specifies 1% as the percentage to be used as the revaluing percentage for a "protected payment" under the new state pension. This is the first time the power to make the Order has been used.

2343 State pensions–Amendments

THE STATE PENSION (AMENDMENT NO.2) REGULATIONS (NORTHERN IRELAND) 2016, SR 2016/88; made under the Pensions Act (Northern Ireland) 2015 s.3(1). In force: 6 April 2016.

These Regulations set the full rate of the new state pension by amending the State Pension Regulations (Northern Ireland) 2015. The Pensions Act (Northern Ireland) 2015 creates the new state pension for people reaching pensionable age on or after 6 April 2016. It replaces the existing state pension for those people. The full rate is set at £155.65 per week.

2344 State pensions–Supplemental provisions

THE PENSIONS (2015 ACT) (CONSEQUENTIAL, SUPPLEMENTARY AND INCIDENTAL AMENDMENTS) ORDER (NORTHERN IRELAND) 2016, SR 2016/25; made under the Pensions Act (Northern Ireland) 2015 s.50. In force: In accordance with art.1.

The Pensions Act (Northern Ireland) 2015 creates a new state pension for people reaching pensionable age on or after 6 April 2016. This Order makes consequential, supplementary and incidental amendments to provisions of secondary legislation. It inserts references into: the Health and Personal Social Services (Injury Benefits) Regulations (Northern Ireland) 2001; the Employment Equality (Age) Regulations (Northern Ireland) 2006, and the Provision of Health Services to Persons Not Ordinarily Resident Regulations (Northern Ireland) 2015, which currently refer to the old state pension so as to include references to the new state pension.

2345 State pensions–Transitional provisions

THE PENSIONS (2015 ACT) (TRANSITIONAL AND TRANSITORY PROVISIONS) ORDER (NORTHERN IRELAND) 2016, SR 2016/195; made under the Pensions Act (Northern Ireland) 2015 s.53(5). In force: 6 April 2016.

This Order makes transitional and transitory provision in connection with the coming into operation of the Pensions Act (Northern Ireland) 2015 Pt 1. Part 1 creates a new state pension for people reaching pensionable age on or after 6 April 2016.

PLANNING

2346 Development–General development procedure–Consequential amendments

THE PLANNING (GENERAL DEVELOPMENT PROCEDURE) (AMENDMENT) ORDER (NORTHERN IRELAND) 2016, SR 2016/115; made under the Planning Act (Northern Ireland) 2011 s.32, s.56(1). In force: 9 May 2016.

This Order amends the Planning (General Development Procedure) Order (Northern Ireland) 2015 by substituting a new schedule 3 to take account of the restructuring of Government Departments as a consequence of the Departments Act 2016 and the Departments (Transfer of Functions) Order (Northern Ireland) 2016. This reflects the consequent revised roles and responsibilities of planning authorities and statutory consultees in the development management process of the planning system.

2347 Development plans–Local development plans–Transitional provisions

THE PLANNING (LOCAL DEVELOPMENT PLAN) (AMENDMENT) REGULATIONS (NORTHERN IRELAND) 2016, SR 2016/27; made under the Planning Act (Northern Ireland) 2011 s.247(6). In force: 29 February 2016.

These Regulations amend the transitional provisions in the Planning (Local Development Plan) Regulations (Northern Ireland) 2015 to include development plans prepared and adopted by the Department under the Planning (Northern Ireland) Order 1972 within the definition of a departmental development plan under the Planning Act (Northern Ireland) 2011.

2348 Land Acquisition and Compensation (Amendment) Act (Northern Ireland) 2016 (c.28)

An Act to amend the Land Acquisition and Compensation (Northern Ireland) Order 1973 to provide for additional payments for loss following the compulsory acquisition of land.

2349 Planning control–Listed buildings–Consequential amendments

THE PLANNING (LISTED BUILDINGS) (AMENDMENT) REGULATIONS (NORTHERN IRELAND) 2016, SR 2016/117; made under the Planning Act (Northern Ireland) 2011 s.80(5), s.86(4)(c) , s.95(2)(b) , s.247(1). In force: 9 May 2016.

These Regulations amend the Planning (Listed Buildings) Regulations (Northern Ireland) 2015 as a consequence of the Departments (Transfer of Functions) Order (Northern Ireland) 2016. These Regulations take account of the restructuring of Government Departments and reflect the consequent revised roles and responsibilities of planning authorities and statutory consultees in the listed building process of the planning system.

2350 Planning obligations–Hazardous substances–Consequential amendments

THE PLANNING (HAZARDOUS SUBSTANCES) (NO.2) (AMENDMENT) REGULATIONS (NORTHERN IRELAND) 2016, SR 2016/116; made under the Planning Act (Northern Ireland) 2011 s.109(4) , s.247(1). In force: 9 May 2016.

These Regulations amend the Planning (Hazardous Substances) (No.2) Regulations (Northern Ireland) 2015 as a consequence of the commencement of the Departments (Transfer of Functions) Order (Northern Ireland) 2016.

POLICE

2351 Police officers–Complaints–Disciplinary procedures

THE POLICE (CONDUCT) REGULATIONS (NORTHERN IRELAND) 2016, SR 2016/41; made under the Police (Northern Ireland) Act 1998 s.25, s.26, s.59(8). In force: 1 June 2016.

These Regulations apply where an allegation comes to the attention of an appropriate authority which indicates that the conduct of a member may amount to misconduct or gross misconduct. This includes an allegation contained within a complaint by a member of the public or a matter referred to the Police Ombudsman for Northern Ireland, by the Northern Ireland Policing Board, the Department of Justice or the Secretary of State or investigated by the Ombudsman of his own motion.

2352 Police officers–Disciplinary procedures–Performance management

THE POLICE (PERFORMANCE AND ATTENDANCE) REGULATIONS (NORTHERN IRELAND) 2016, SR 2016/42; made under the Police (Northern Ireland) Act 1998 s.25, s.26. In force: 1 June 2016.

These Regulations establish procedures for proceedings in respect of unsatisfactory performance or attendance of members of the rank of chief superintendent or below (excluding probationers).

2353 Police officers–Police Appeals Tribunal–Appeals

THE POLICE APPEALS TRIBUNALS REGULATIONS (NORTHERN IRELAND) 2016, SR 2016/43; made under the Police (Northern Ireland) Act 1998 s.25, s.26. In force: 1 June 2016.

These Regulations set out the circumstances in which a member of the Police Service of Northern Ireland (PSNI) may appeal to a police appeals tribunal. They also set out the procedures governing such an appeal.

2354 Police Service of Northern Ireland–Promotion

THE POLICE SERVICE OF NORTHERN IRELAND (PROMOTION) (AMENDMENT) REGULATIONS 2016, SR 2016/413; made under the Police (Northern Ireland) Act 1998 s.25(2)(b), s.72(2). In force: 31 December 2016.

These Regulations amend the Police Service of Northern Ireland (Promotion) Regulations 2008 to introduce the Constable to Inspector Fast Track Programme. The amendments to the 2008 Regulations have the effect of permitting constables and sergeants participating in the Programme to be promoted more quickly than if they were not participating in the Programme. The Schedule to the 2008 Regulations is also amended to permit constables and sergeants participating in the programme to take their qualifying assessments for promotion earlier than if they were not participating in the Programme.

RATES

2355 Non-domestic rates–Religious groups–Shop used for religious meetings–Whether exempt from rates

[Rates (Northern Ireland) Order 1977 (SI 1977/2157) art.41, art.41(2)(c)]

The appellant brought an appeal challenging the valuation list entry of a property of which he was one of the owners. The property comprised a traditional shop unit. However, during the relevant period it had been used on regular occasions by a religious group for the holding of religious meetings. The appellant argued that as the property was being used as a place of public religious worship it should be exempt from rates under the Rates (Northern Ireland) Order 1977 art.41(2)(b)(i) or art.41(2)(c).

Held: Appeal dismissed. The first issue was not the applicability of the exemption but who had been in rateable occupation of the property during the relevant period. If the religious group had not been in rateable occupation, the exemption could not be invoked. The group had not been in rateable occupation, as it did not have exclusive occupation. There was no agreement, written or otherwise, between the registered owners and the group as to its use and occupation of the property. It had no legal entitlement to be there and paid no rent. The appellant facilitated the group's use and occupation of the property as he was a member of the group. The appellant had also conceded that if the owners had received a bona fide offer to lease the property during the relevant period they would have accepted the offer and gained possession for that purpose. The registered owners had at all times been in paramount control of the property. The presumption therefore was that they were the rateable occupiers. It had not been shown by the appellant that they had parted with occupation to someone else (see paras 14, 19-20 of judgment).

MAYERS v COMMISSIONER OF VALUATION, [2016] R.V.R. 210, Henry Spence, Lands Tr (NI).

2356 Rateable value–Admissibility–Appeal against rating valuation–Admissibility of entries in Net Annual Valuation List

[Rates (Northern Ireland) Order 1977 (SI 1977/2157) Sch.12 Pt 1, art.52, art.54]

The court was required to determine as a preliminary issue whether the Lands Tribunal could, in determining a rating appeal *Debenhams Plc v Commissioner of Valuation for Northern Ireland*, consider later valuations entered in the Net Annual Valuation List. The respondent company (D) occupied a hereditament at a shopping centre. In September 2008, the district valuer issued a certificate revising the NAV list to include that hereditament. D's appeal against that decision was dismissed by the appellant commissioner. D then appealed to the tribunal. Two other hereditaments were entered in the list 13 months after the valuation date of D's hereditament. They were not considered by the valuer or the commissioner. The tribunal determined, as a preliminary issue, that the evidence relating to the two other hereditaments was admissible.

Held: Preliminary issue determined. (Higgins LJ dissenting) There was an inevitable issue of relativity within a class in the NAV list, *Dawkins (Valuation Officer) v Ash Bros & Heaton Ltd* [1969] 2 A.C. 366, [1969] C.L.Y. 3019 applied. The fact that a hereditament's valuation had to be determined by way of comparison with the respective valuations of the other hereditaments in the list demanded a focus, not on the current true value, but, on achieving a proportional and uniformly balanced valuation of the properties. At the time of a general revaluation no NAVs could be entered until all hereditaments had been assessed, and without any NAVs of comparable hereditaments in the list at that point, the concept of comparables could not play any part in the assessment process, *McKeown Vintners v Commissioner of Valuation* [1991] R.V.R. 223, [1991] C.L.Y. 4310 considered. However, different principles applied when a revision of an entry in the list arose for consideration at a later stage, particularly the principle of comparability under the Rates (Northern Ireland) Order 1977 Sch.12 Pt I para.2(1). If actual rental values and turnover figures were used in the revision of an entry in the list, that entry would inevitably be increased to a level significantly different from other entries. There had to be a limiting factor. That was provided by Sch.12 para.2(1), which produced "a tone of the comparables" to ensure fairness and uniformity to meet the issue of relativity referred to in *Dawkins*. Under art.54(2), all entries in the list were deemed correct until the contrary was shown. The combination of art.54(2)and sch.12 Pt I para.2(1) underpinned the tone of the list, *McKeown Vintners* and *Trustees of Glenkeen Orange Hall v Commissioner of Valuation for Northern Ireland*considered. It was significant that the valuer adopted different methods of valuation for D, and for one of the other two later entries, which resulted in an apparently lower valuation for the latter. In September 2008, the valuer had evidence from the valuation of other hereditaments in the list. He had to have regard to the tone of the list emerging from the existing entries. At the time of the appeal to the commissioner, there were new entries in the list. Under art.52, the commissioner had a duty to investigate which required a systematic enquiry into the subject matter of the appeal set in its overall context. Article 52(4)(b) referred to the objective of ensuring proportionality and uniformity in the valuation of hereditaments. That conformed to the principle of "tone of the list". The commissioner's field of enquiry was not limited. The investigation was not restricted such that only evidence up to the valuation date could be considered. The appropriate NAV was assessed without regard to the actual value of the premises at the assessment date. It was a valuation moderated by the "tone of the list", leading to a valuation that was not current at the assessment date. Its value was in comparison to the respective values of the other hereditaments in the list. Valuations after September 2008 must have been assessed in the light of the "tone of the list" and must also have been intended to meet the objective of a uniform and proportionate set of valuations to which "tone of the list" referred. The tribunal had, under art.54(2), the same powers as the commissioner. D was entitled to pursue its evidence and present its case in any way it wished in challenging the NAV attributed to its hereditament. It was for the tribunal to determine the weight to be attached to any such evidence. Questions of weight and admissibility were not to be confused. In the instant case, the commissioner could not establish that the evidence relating to the later NAVs was so clearly irrelevant such as to justify its exclusion (see paras 24, 26, 28-30 of judgment).

COMMISSIONER OF VALUATION FOR NORTHERN IRELAND v DEBENHAMS PLC *sub nom.* DEBENHAMS PLC v COMMISSIONER OF VALUATION FOR NORTHERN IRELAND, [2014] NICA 49, [2016] N.I. 29, Higgins LJ, CA (NI).

2357 Small business rate relief–Extensions of time

THE RATES (SMALL BUSINESS HEREDITAMENT RELIEF) (AMENDMENT) REGULATIONS (NORTHERN IRELAND) 2016, SR 2016/26; made under the Rates (Northern Ireland) Order 1977 (SI 1977 2157) (NI 28) art.31C. In force: 1 April 2016.

These Regulations amend the definition of "qualifying year" in the Rates (Small Business Hereditament Relief) Regulations (Northern Ireland) 2010 to provide for an extension of the small business rate relief scheme until 31 March 2017.

ROAD TRAFFIC

2358 Disabled persons' badges–Badges for Motor vehicles

THE DISABLED PERSONS (BADGES FOR MOTOR VEHICLES) (AMENDMENT) REGULATIONS (NORTHERN IRELAND) 2016, SR 2016/30; made under the Chronically Sick and Disabled Persons (Northern Ireland) Act 1978 s.14. In force: 1 April 2016.

These Regulations further amend the Disabled Persons (Badges for Motor Vehicles) Regulations (Northern Ireland) 1993 by changing the fee for a disabled person's badge to £10 and by including additional specifications for the form of the badge with effect from 1 April 2016.

2359 EU law–Exemptions–Seat belts

THE MOTOR VEHICLES (WEARING OF SEAT BELTS) (AMENDMENT) REGULATIONS (NORTHERN IRELAND) 2016, SR 2016/414; made under the Road Traffic (Northern Ireland) Order 1995 (SI 1995 2994) art.23(1)(2)(e), art.110(2). In force: 1 March 2017.

These Regulations amend the Motor Vehicles (Wearing of Seat Belts) Regulations (Northern Ireland) 1993 reg.6(1) by inserting an exemption from the requirement to wear a seat belt for persons riding in a motor ambulance while that person is providing medical treatment to a patient which due to its nature or the medical condition of the patient cannot be delayed. The amendment to reg.6(1) will add a further exemption in respect of the emergency services within the bounds permitted by the derogation set out in Directive 91/671 art.6 in order that health care professionals riding in motor ambulances can carry out their duties properly.

2360 Motor Vehicles–Construction and use–Increasing speed threshold of category T tractors

THE MOTOR VEHICLES (CONSTRUCTION AND USE) (AMENDMENT) REGULATIONS (NORTHERN IRELAND) 2016, SR 2016/160; made under the Road Traffic (Northern Ireland) Order 1995 (SI 1995 2994) art.55(1)(2)(6), art.110(2). In force: 18 April 2016.

These Regulations amend the Motor Vehicles (Construction and Use) Regulations (Northern Ireland) 1999 to increase the speed threshold at which category T tractors are required to comply with higher standards of vehicle construction and use under the 1999 Regulations from 20 mph to 40 km/h in respect of a number of components and characteristics.

SENTENCING

2361 Forfeiture–Motorcycles–Motorcycle used in criminal activity–Legal title for motorcycle held by finance company

The appellant (M) appealed against a forfeiture order imposed in respect of a motorcycle following his guilty pleas to possessing an explosive substance and possessing ammunition with intent. M's brother had bought the motorcycle on hire purchase terms and had made the payments due under the agreement to a finance company. M had borrowed the motorcycle and used it to commit the offences. M's brother continued to make the payments due under his agreement with the finance company after the motorcycle was seized in connection with M's offending.

Held: Appeal allowed. Three parties had differing interests in the motorcycle. Under the agreement, the legal title to the motorcycle remained vested in the finance company until the moneys due and payable were discharged. M's brother was the hirer with an entitlement to possession and control of the motorcycle while he maintained payments, and he would become the outright owner on completion of the payments due. Under the agreement, once one-third of the payments had been made, the finance company could only recover possession of the motorcycle pursuant to a court order. M's brother had made the motorcycle available to M and had continued to make the payments. However, by virtue of the principle nemo dat quod non habet, he could not make a gift of the vehicle to M so as to pass title to him. M's interest was that of a possessory bailee who could assert no title as against the finance company. Both the brother's and M's interests in the motorcycle were subject to the finance company's prior interest and legal title, even if that legal title was qualified by the need to obtain a court order to recover the motorcycle after one-third of the moneys due had been paid. The instant case fell within the principles enunciated in *R. v Troth (Jack)* (1980) 71 Cr. App. R. 1, [1980] C.L.Y. 574 and *R. v Kearney (Kieran Andrew)* [2011] EWCA Crim 826, [2011] 2 Cr. App. R. (S.) 106, [2011] C.L.Y. 2840, *Troth* and *Kearney* applied. Because of the complications of the finance company's interest, the fact that M had no title to or recoverable interest in the motorcycle, and the uncertainty of the practicability of realising the property, a forfeiture order should not have been made. Indeed, the motorcycle would be unsellable in the absence of a release by the finance company of its interest. The seizure of the motorcycle had de facto deprived M of the use of the motorcycle which he had used for criminal activity, and he would be unable to use the motorcycle during his custodial sentence. The continued or future use of the motorcycle for criminal activity had therefore been effectively frustrated. The finance company's interest was protected by the terms of the hire purchase agreement. The return of the motorcycle to M's brother, who remained subject to the terms of the agreement, did not give rise to any injustice. In those circumstances, it was appropriate to quash the forfeiture order (see paras 17-18 of judgment).

R. v MACKLE (GABRIEL), [2015] NICA 5, [2016] N.I. 171, Girvan LJ, CA (NI).

2362 **Justice Act (Northern Ireland) 2015 (c.9)–Commencement No.8 Order**

THE JUSTICE (2015 ACT) (COMMENCEMENT NO.8) ORDER (NORTHERN IRELAND) 2016, SR 2016/417; made under the Justice Act (Northern Ireland) 2015 s.102(8), s.106(2). Commencement details: bringing into operation various provisions of the 2015 Act on 1 December 2016.

This Order brings into operation provision made in the Justice Act (Northern Ireland) 2015 Pt 8 for the Violent Offences Prevention Order (VOPO), and as listed in art.2 of this Order, to the extent that they are not already in force. The provisions of this Order come into operation on 1 December 2016.

SOCIAL SECURITY

2363 **Benefit cap–Universal credit**

THE UNIVERSAL CREDIT REGULATIONS (NORTHERN IRELAND) 2016, SR 2016/216; made under the Welfare Reform (Northern Ireland) Order 2015 (SI 2015 2006) art.5, art.7(2), art.9(2)(3)(5)(7), art.9(5)(a), art.10, art.11(1)(3), art.12(2)(3), art.13(3), art.14(2)(3), art.15(2)(5), art.16(3)(5), art.17, art.19(5), art.20(2), art.22(3)(4), art.23(3)(5), art.24(2)(d)(3)(4), art.25(1), art.27(2), art.29(1)(7)(8), art.30, art.31(2)(a)(6)(8), art.32(4)(5)(9), art.33, art.36, art.38, art.43(3)(7), art.45(3)(a), art.46, art.48, art.101, Sch.1 para.1, Sch.1 para.2, Sch.1 para.3(2), Sch.1 para.4, Sch.1 para.5, Sch.5 para.2, Sch.5 para.3. In force: In accordance with reg.1.

These Regulations contain provisions in relation to universal credit under the Welfare Reform (Northern Ireland) Order 2015 Pt 2. They also include provision for a benefit cap under art.101 of the Order.

2364 **Child support–Lump sum payments–Mesothelioma**

THE SOCIAL SECURITY, CHILD SUPPORT AND MESOTHELIOMA LUMP SUM PAYMENTS (DECISIONS AND APPEALS) (AMENDMENT) REGULATIONS (NORTHERN IRELAND) 2016, SR 2016/208; made under the Child Support(Northern Ireland) Order 1991 (SI 1991 2628) art.22(2A)(2C)(4), art.22(3A)(3C)(5), art.13(2A)(5), art.28(3); Social Security (Northern Ireland) Order 1998 (SI 1998 1506) art.2(2) , art.10(1) , art.13(3A)(5A), art.74(3)(5)(6); Mesothelioma, etc., Act (Northern Ireland) 2008 s.4(2), s.5(1A)(4), s.9(1)(2). In force: In accordance with reg.1.

These Regulations amend the Child Support (Maintenance Assessment Procedure) Regulations (Northern Ireland) 1992, the Social Security and Child Support (Decisions and Appeals) Regulations (Northern Ireland) 1999, the Mesothelioma Lump Sum Payments (Claims and Reconsiderations) Regulations (Northern Ireland) 2008 and the Child Support Maintenance Calculation Regulations (Northern Ireland) 2012.

2365 **Disability living allowance–Attendance allowance–Carer's allowance**

THE SOCIAL SECURITY (DISABILITY LIVING ALLOWANCE, ATTENDANCE ALLOWANCE AND CARER'S ALLOWANCE) (AMENDMENT) REGULATIONS (NORTHERN IRELAND) 2016, SR 2016/229; made under the Social Security Contributions and Benefits (Northern Ireland) Act 1992 s.64(1), s72(8), s.70(4), s.171(1)(3)(a)(b)(ii)(iii)(4), s.113(1)(a)(2), s.121(1); Social Security Administration (Northern Ireland) Act 1992 s.71(1)(b) , s.165(1). In force: In accordance with reg.1.

These Regulations amend existing rules in Disability Living Allowance (DLA), Attendance Allowance (AA) and Carer's Allowance (CA) relating to: residence and presence conditions for all three benefits; temporary absence rules for DLA and AA; payability of benefit for certain DLA and AA claimants in hospitals and care homes; the upper age limit for claiming DLA with effect from 6 December 2018; and the introduction of a "genuine and sufficient link" provision for claimants subject to certain EU co-ordination Regulations.

2366 **Disability living allowance–Eligibility**

THE SOCIAL SECURITY (DISABILITY LIVING ALLOWANCE AND PERSONAL INDEPENDENCE PAYMENT) (AMENDMENT) REGULATIONS (NORTHERN IRELAND) 2016, SR 2016/235; made under the Social Security Administration (Northern Ireland) Act 1992 s.71(1)(b) , s.165(1)(4)(5); Welfare Reform (Northern Ireland) Order 2015 (SI 2015 2006) art.91, art.98 , art.99(1)(a), Sch.10 para.1(1), Sch.10 para.3(1)(a)(c). In force: 6 July 2016.

These Regulations amend the Social Security (Disability Living Allowance) Regulations (Northern Ireland) 1992, Personal Independence Payment Regulations (Northern Ireland) 2016 and Personal Independence Payment (Transitional Provisions) Regulations (Northern Ireland) 2016 following the Supreme Court's judgment in Mathieson v Secretary of State for Work and Pensions. Regs 8 and 12A of the Disability Living Allowance Regulations provide that for a person to receive payment of disability living allowance, that person is not maintained free of charge while undergoing medical or other treatment as an in-patient in a Health Service or Defence Council hospital or other similar institution. There is an equivalent provision in reg. 29 of the Personal Independence Payment Regulations. The effect of the amendments is that these provisions will no longer apply to any person who was under the age of 18 on the day on which that person's current period as an in-patient in a hospital or similar institution began.

2367 **Disability living allowance–Personal independence payments**

THE PERSONAL INDEPENDENCE PAYMENT (TRANSITIONAL PROVISIONS) REGULATIONS (NORTHERN IRELAND) 2016, SR 2016/227; made under the Welfare Reform (Northern Ireland) Order 2015 (SI 2015 2006) art.98, art.99, Sch.10. In force: 20 June 2016.

These Regulations provide the legislative detail for transitional arrangements to support the phasing out of Disability Living Allowance and the introduction of Personal Independence Payment (PIP). In particular, the Regulations set out the process for assessing Disability Living Allowance (DLA) claimants aged between 16 and 64 on 20 June 2016, or who reach age 16 after that date, for entitlement to PIP.

2368 **Disability premiums–Compensation**

THE WELFARE SUPPLEMENTARY PAYMENT (LOSS OF DISABILITY-RELATED PREMIUMS) REGULATIONS (NORTHERN IRELAND) 2016, SR 2016/254; made under the Welfare Reform (Northern Ireland) Order 2015 (SI 2015 2006) art.137. In force: 20 July 2016.

These Regulations introduce welfare supplementary payments to mitigate impacts as defined in the document "A Fresh Start the Stormont Agreement and Implementation Plan" arising from the implementation of welfare reform.

2369 **Employment and support allowance–Enforcement–Sanctions for failures to take part in work-focused interview**

THE EMPLOYMENT AND SUPPORT ALLOWANCE (SANCTIONS) (AMENDMENT) REGULATIONS (NORTHERN IRELAND) 2016, SR 2016/240; made under the Social Security (Northern Ireland) Order 1998 (SI 1998 1506) art.2(2) , art.11(6), art.74(3)(5); Welfare Reform Act (Northern Ireland) 2007 s.12(2)(3)(4), s.13(2)(4)(6), s.16, s.16A, s.25(2). In force: In accordance with reg.1.

These Regulations amend the Employment and Support Allowance Regulations (Northern Ireland) 2008 in relation to sanctions for failures to take part in a work-focused interview or to undertake work-related activity.

2370 **Employment and support allowance–Housing costs element**

THE SOCIAL SECURITY (HOUSING COSTS AMENDMENTS) REGULATIONS (NORTHERN IRELAND) 2016, SR 2016/44; made under the Social Security Contributions and Benefits (Northern Ireland) Act 1992 s.122(1)(a), s.131(1), s.171(1)(3)(4); Jobseekers (Northern Ireland) Order 1995 (SI 1995 2705) art.6(5), art.36(2); Welfare Reform Act (Northern Ireland) 2007 s.4(2)(a), s.25(2). In force: 1 April 2016.

These Regulations amend the Income Support (General) Regulations (Northern Ireland) 1987, the Jobseeker's Allowance Regulations (Northern Ireland) 1996 and the Employment and Support Allowance Regulations (Northern Ireland) 2008 to increase the waiting period before housing costs (including help with mortgage interest) can be met to 39 weeks from 13 weeks.

2371 Employment and support allowance–Jobseeker's allowance–Overpayment of benefits

THE SOCIAL SECURITY (OVERPAYMENTS AND RECOVERY) REGULATIONS (NORTHERN IRELAND) 2016, SR 2016/224; made under the Social Security Administration (Northern Ireland) Act 1992 s.69(4)(6)(a)(b)(8)(9A)(9C), s.69ZA, s.69ZB(2)(b)(5), s.69ZC(1)(2)(3), s.69ZD, s.69ZF, s.69ZG, s.69ZH, s.72(2), s.73(4)(5)(a)(8)(10), s.74(2)(3B)(3C)(3D), s.109B(4A), s.165(1)(4)(5)(6); Welfare Reform (Northern Ireland) Order 2015 (SI 2015 2006) art.38(1). In force: In accordance with reg.1.

These Regulations set out the processes governing the calculation and recovery of overpayments of Universal Credit, certain Tax Credits and contributory Jobseeker's Allowance and Employment and Support Allowance where the claim for those latter two benefits was made on or after the introduction of Universal Credit.

2372 Employment and support allowance–Personal independence payments–Claims and payments

THE UNIVERSAL CREDIT, PERSONAL INDEPENDENCE PAYMENT, JOBSEEKER'S ALLOWANCE AND EMPLOYMENT AND SUPPORT ALLOWANCE (CLAIMS AND PAYMENTS) REGULATIONS (NORTHERN IRELAND) 2016, SR 2016/220; made under the Child Support(Northern Ireland) Order 1991 (SI 1991 2628) art.40(1)(2); Social Security Administration (Northern Ireland) Act 1992 s.1(1)(1C), s.5(1)(a)(b)(c)(d)(g)(i)(j)(k)(l)(m)(n)(q)(r)(1A)(2B), s.5A(2)(b), s.13A(2)(3), s.105A(1A)(d)(1B)(d)(1D)(c)(1E)(c), s.106(1A)(d)(1B)(d)(1C)(c)(1D)(c), s.165(1)(4)(5)(6), s.167(1); Welfare Reform (Northern Ireland) Order 2015 (SI 2015 2006) art.38, art.97, Sch.1 para.3. In force: In accordance with reg.1.

These Regulations concern claims and payments in relation to a number of benefits administered by the Department for Social Development. This instrument supports the introduction of Universal Credit and Personal Independence Payment. It also supports the administration of contributory-only Jobseeker's Allowance and Employment and Support Allowance.

2373 Employment and support allowance–Regulations

THE EMPLOYMENT AND SUPPORT ALLOWANCE REGULATIONS (NORTHERN IRELAND) 2016, SR 2016/219; made under the Social Security Administration (Northern Ireland) Act 1992 s.5(1A), s.165(4)(6); Social Security (Northern Ireland) Order 1998 (SI 1998 1506) art.21(1)(a); Welfare Reform Act (Northern Ireland) 2007 s.2(1)(a)(c)(4)(a)(c), s.3(1)(c)(2)(b)(d)(3), s.8(1)(3)(4)(a)(b)(5)(6), s.9(1)(3)(4)(a)(b), s.11A(5), s.11B(2)(3), s.11D(2)(d), s.11E(1), s.11H(7)(8), s.11J(3)(4)(8), s.17(1)(2)(3)(a)(b), s.18(1)(2)(4), s.20(2)(7), s.24(1)(2)(b)(3), s.25(1)(2), Sch.1 para.1(3)(4), Sch.1 para.3(2), Sch.1 para.4(1)(a)(c)(3)(4), Sch.2 para.1, Sch.2 para.4A, Sch.2 para.5, Sch.2 para.6, Sch.2 para.9, Sch.2 para.10; Welfare Reform (Northern Ireland) Order 2015 (SI 2015 2006) art.5, Sch.5 para.2(3), Sch.5 para.3. In force: In accordance with reg.1.

These Regulations provide for a social security benefit to be known as an employment and support allowance (ESA), which replaces the existing benefit of the same name. The new benefit is for people who have a health condition or disability which limits their capability to work. People will only be able to claim the new benefit where they have made sufficient National Insurance contributions. People will no longer be able to claim ESA where they have low or no other income but have not made sufficient National Insurance contributions. Many rules for the existing benefit are replicated in these Regulations for the new benefit.

2374 Housing benefit–Assessment–Reduction of benefits

THE HOUSING BENEFIT (AMENDMENT) REGULATIONS (NORTHERN IRELAND) 2016, SR 2016/258; made under the Social Security Contributions and Benefits (Northern Ireland) Act 1992 s.122(1)(d), s.129A(2)(3)(4), s.133(1)(2)(h), s.171(1)(3)(4)(5); Social Security (Northern Ireland) Order 1998 (SI 1998 1506) art.74(3)(6). In force: 2 January 2017.

These Regulations amend the Housing Benefit Regulations (Northern Ireland) 2006, Housing Benefit (Persons who have attained the qualifying age for state pension credit) Regulations (Northern Ireland) 2006 and Housing Benefit (Consequential Provisions) Regulations (Northern Ireland) 2006. They introduce a new method of calculating the eligible rent when determining the appropriate maximum housing benefit of a working age claimant in the social rented sector whose housing benefit is determined under the Housing Benefit Regulations, by making an appropriate deduction from housing benefit where a claimant occupies a dwelling that has more bedrooms than they require.

2375 Housing benefit–Back payments–Family premium

THE HOUSING BENEFIT (ABOLITION OF THE FAMILY PREMIUM AND DATE OF CLAIM) (AMENDMENT) REGULATIONS (NORTHERN IRELAND) 2016, SR 2016/310; made under the Social Security Contributions and Benefits (Northern Ireland) Act 1992 s.122(1)(d), s.131(1), s.132(1)(3)(4), s.171(1)(3)(4); Social Security Administration (Northern Ireland) Act 1992 s.5(1)(b), s.165(1)(5); Child Support, Pensions and Social Security Act (Northern Ireland) 2000 s.60(1)(2)(3)(4). In force: 5 September 2016.

These Regulations amend the Housing Benefit Regulations (Northern Ireland) 2006 and the Housing Benefit (Persons who have attained the qualifying age for state pension credit) Regulations (Northern Ireland) 2006.

2376 Housing benefit–Disability living allowance

THE HOUSING BENEFIT (MISCELLANEOUS AMENDMENTS) REGULATIONS (NORTHERN IRELAND) 2016, SR 2016/230; made under the Social Security Contributions and Benefits (Northern Ireland) Act 1992 s.122(1)(d), s.132(3)(4), s.133(1) , s.171(1)(3); Social Security Administration (Northern Ireland) Act 1992 s.5(1)(a), s.165(1)(4)(6); Social Security (Northern Ireland) Order 1998 (SI 1998 1506) art.74(3); Child Support, Pensions and Social Security Act (Northern Ireland) 2000 Sch.7 para.4(3)(5), Sch.7 para.20(1) , Sch.7 para.23(1). In force: 20 June 2016.

The instrument amends The Housing Benefit (Decisions and Appeals) Regulations (Northern Ireland) 2001 to ensure that housing benefit entitlement continues and claimants are not adversely affected during the transition from Disability Living Allowance to the Personal Independence Payment.

2377 Housing benefit–Income support–Income-based employment and support allowance

THE UNIVERSAL CREDIT (TRANSITIONAL PROVISIONS) REGULATIONS (NORTHERN IRELAND) 2016, SR 2016/226; made under the Welfare Reform (Northern Ireland) Order 2015 (SI 2015 2006) art.38, art.48(1)(2), Sch.6 para.1(1)(2)(b), Sch.6 para.3(1)(a)(b)(c), Sch.6 para.4(1)(a), Sch.6 para.5(1)(2)(c)(d)(3)(a). In force: In accordance with reg.1.

These Regulations make provision for the second phase of the replacement of certain "existing benefits" by universal credit, a new benefit established by the Welfare Reform (Northern Ireland) Order. The existing benefits are income-based jobseeker's allowance, income-related employment and support allowance, income support, housing benefit, working tax credit and child tax credit.

2378 Industrial injuries benefits–Extension of eligibility

THE INDUSTRIAL INJURIES BENEFIT (EMPLOYMENT TRAINING SCHEMES AND COURSES) REGULATIONS (NORTHERN IRELAND) 2016, SR 2016/238; made under the Social Security Contributions and Benefits (Northern Ireland) Act 1992 s.95A, s.121(1) , s.171(1)(3)(5); Welfare Reform (Northern Ireland) Order 2015 (SI 2015 2006) art.72(3). In force: In accordance with reg.1.

These Regulations make provision in relation to the extension of eligibility for industrial injuries benefits to people participating in certain employment training schemes and employment training courses.

2379 Industrial injuries benefits–Transitional provisions

THE INDUSTRIAL INJURIES BENEFIT (INJURIES ARISING BEFORE 5TH JULY 1948) REGULATIONS (NORTHERN IRELAND) 2016, SR 2016/239; made under the Welfare Reform (Northern Ireland) Order 2015 (SI 2015 2006) art.70(3). In force: 31 October 2016.

These Regulations provide for the payment of industrial injuries benefit to persons to whom compensation or benefits were previously payable under the Social Security Contributions and Benefits (Northern Ireland) Act 1992 Sch.8 and s.11, in respect of injuries arising before 5 July 1948.

2380 Jobseeker's allowance–Enforcement

THE JOBSEEKER'S ALLOWANCE (SANCTIONS) (AMENDMENT) REGULATIONS (NORTHERN IRELAND) 2016, SR 2016/241; made under the Jobseekers (Northern Ireland) Order 1995 (SI 1995 2705). In force: In accordance with reg.1.

These Regulations amend the Jobseeker's Allowance Regulations (Northern Ireland) 1996. They implement the powers in the Jobseekers (Northern Ireland) Order 1995 arts 21, 21A and 21B as inserted by the Welfare Reform (Northern Ireland) Order 2015 in relation to sanctions for failures to comply with requirements under the Order and the 1996 Regulations. They also make consequential changes to various other sets of regulations.

2381 Jobseeker's allowance–Ill health–Work capability assessments

THE JOBSEEKER'S ALLOWANCE (EXTENDED PERIOD OF SICKNESS) (AMENDMENT) REGULATIONS (NORTHERN IRELAND) 2016, SR 2016/233; made under the Jobseekers (Northern Ireland) Order 1995 (SI 1995 2705) Sch.1 para.2(1). In force: 23 May 2016.

These Regulations amend the Jobseeker's Allowance Regulations (Northern Ireland) 1996 concerning the circumstances in which a claimant is treated as capable of work (or as not having limited capability for work) on account of a period of disease or disablement.

2382 Jobseeker's allowance–Northern Ireland

THE JOBSEEKER'S ALLOWANCE REGULATIONS (NORTHERN IRELAND) 2016, SR 2016/218; made under the Social Security Contributions and Benefits (Northern Ireland) Act 1992 s.167D, s.171(3)(5); Social Security Administration (Northern Ireland) Act 1992 s.5(1)(j)(k)(1A), s.165(4)(5)(6); Jobseekers (Northern Ireland) Order 1995 (SI 1995 2705) art.2(2)(4), art.4(1)(c)(2A)(3B)(a), art.6(1)(b)(2)(4), art.7(3), art.8A(5), art.8B(2), art.8D(4), art.8E(3)(5), art.8F(1), art.8H(1)(a)(7)(8), art.8I, art.8J(5)(7), art.8K(4)(5)(9), art.14(1)(4)(a)(b), art.36(1)(2), Sch.1; Welfare Reform (Northern Ireland) Order 2015 (SI 2015 2006) Sch.5 para.2(3), Sch.5 para.3. In force: In accordance with reg.1.

These Regulations provide for a social security benefit to be known as a jobseeker's allowance. The benefit is for people who are out of work and are seeking employment. People will only be able to claim the benefit where they have made sufficient National Insurance contributions.

2383 Loss of benefits–Welfare reform

THE SOCIAL SECURITY (LOSS OF BENEFIT) (AMENDMENT) REGULATIONS (NORTHERN IRELAND) 2016, SR 2016/225; made under the Social Security (Northern Ireland) Order 1998 (SI 1998 1506) art.74(3)(4)(5)(6); Social Security Fraud Act (Northern Ireland) 2001 art.10(1), art.8. In force: 26 September 2016.

These Regulations amend the Social Security (Loss of Benefit) Regulations (Northern Ireland) 2002 to support changes introduced by the Welfare Reform (Northern Ireland) Order 2015. The Order introduced more severe penalties to reduce benefit entitlement when claimants commit benefit offences. The Order introduced more severe penalties to reduce benefit entitlement when claimants commit benefit offences. The Regulations prescribe those offences which will be considered "relevant offences" which will incur an immediate 3 year loss of benefit penalty, on first offence, following a benefit fraud conviction for a serious case of organised fraud or identity related fraud.

2384 Northern Ireland Housing Executive–Universal credit–Local housing allowance

THE UNIVERSAL CREDIT HOUSING COSTS (EXECUTIVE DETERMINATIONS) REGULATIONS (NORTHERN IRELAND) 2016, SR 2016/222; made under the Welfare Reform (Northern Ireland) Order 2015 (SI 2015 2006) art.16, art.38(1) , art.48(2)(b). In force: In accordance with reg.1.

These Regulations require the Northern Ireland Housing Executive to determine broad rental market areas and local housing allowance rates to be used in calculating entitlement to the housing costs element of Universal Credit for tenants renting in the private sector.

2385 Personal independence payments–Entitlement conditions and assessment criteria

THE PERSONAL INDEPENDENCE PAYMENT REGULATIONS (NORTHERN IRELAND) 2016, SR 2016/217; made under the Welfare Reform (Northern Ireland) Order 2015 (SI 2015 2006) art.82(3), art.83(3)(4), art.84(3)(4), art.85(1)(4)(5)(a)(c), art.86(1)(3)(b)(4) 99(1)(a), art.88(3), art.90(1)(5)(6), art.91(1)(3), art.92, art.97(1), art.99(1)(a). In force: 20 June 2016.

These Regulations provide the legislative detail on the main rules, entitlement conditions and assessment criteria to support the introduction of personal independence payments.

2386 Personal independence payments–Supplementary provisions and consequential amendments

THE PERSONAL INDEPENDENCE PAYMENT (SUPPLEMENTARY PROVISIONS AND CONSEQUENTIAL AMENDMENTS) REGULATIONS (NORTHERN IRELAND) 2016, SR 2016/228; made under the Welfare Reform (Northern Ireland) Order 2015 (SI 2015 2006) art.97. In force: 20 June 2016.

Personal Independence Payment (PIP) will replace Disability Living Allowance (DLA) for people who are aged 16 to 64 on or after 20 June 2016. Entitlement to a particular rate or component of DLA acts as one of the qualifying criteria for various other schemes and benefits. These are commonly referred to as passporting arrangements. The purpose of these Regulations is to ensure that PIP claimants will be able to benefit from the same passporting arrangements, wherever possible.

2387 Social security–Reciprocity–Reciprocal arrangements between Great Britain and NI

THE SOCIAL SECURITY (GREAT BRITAIN RECIPROCAL ARRANGEMENTS) (AMENDMENT) REGULATIONS (NORTHERN IRELAND) 2016, SR 2016/393; made under the Northern Ireland Act 1998 s.87(5)(6)(10); Social Security Administration (Northern Ireland) Act 1992 s.165(1)(4)(5). In force: In accordance with reg.1.

These Regulations give effect in Northern Ireland to reciprocal arrangements between Great Britain and Northern Ireland relating to social security. The arrangements are made between the Minister of State for Employment on behalf of the Secretary of State for Work and Pensions, with the consent of the Treasury, of the one part and the Minister for Communities in Northern Ireland, with the consent of the Department of Finance, of the other part. These arrangements are contained in the exchange of letters set out in the Schedule to these Regulations.

2388 Social security benefits–Benefit cap

THE WELFARE SUPPLEMENTARY PAYMENT (BENEFIT CAP) REGULATIONS (NORTHERN IRELAND) 2016, SR 2016/389; made under the Welfare Reform (Northern Ireland) Order 2015 (SI 2015 2006) art.137. In force: 7 November 2016.

These Regulations amend the Welfare Supplementary Payments Regulations (Northern Ireland) 2016, which were introduced to mitigate impacts from the implementation of the Welfare Reform (Northern Ireland) Regulations 2015 as defined in the document "A Fresh Start the Stormont Agreement and the Implementation Plan". The Regulations provide for making mitigation payments on the reduction of the benefit cap (as provided for in Art.5 of the Welfare Reform and Work (Northern Ireland) Order 2016).

2389 Universal credit–Contribution-based employment and support allowance–Contribution-based jobseeker's allowance

THE UNIVERSAL CREDIT, PERSONAL INDEPENDENCE PAYMENT, JOBSEEKER'S ALLOWANCE AND EMPLOYMENT AND SUPPORT ALLOWANCE (DECISIONS AND APPEALS) REGULATIONS (NORTHERN IRELAND) 2016, SR 2016/221; made under the Social Security Administration (Northern Ireland) Act 1992 s.5(1A), s.139D(1)(6), s.165(1)(4)(5)(6), s.167(1); Social Security (Northern Ireland) Order 1998 (SI 1998 1506) art.2(2), art.8(6), art.10(1)(4)(6), art.11(3)(6), art.11A, art.12(1), art.13(2)(3)(3A)(3B)(5A)(6), art.16(1), art.17, art.18(1), art.20(2), art.21(1)(2)(3), art.22, art.23, art.24(3)(b)(5)(c), art.26(6)(c), art.28(1), art.31(2), art.74(1)(3)(4)(5)(6), Sch.2 para.9, Sch3 para.1, Sch.3 para.4, Sch.3 para.9, Sch.4. In force: In accordance with reg.1.

This instrument makes provision in relation to the administration of Universal Credit, Personal Independence Payment, contribution-based Jobseeker's Allowance and contributory Employment and Support Allowance. In particular, the Regulations make provision as to the making of decisions and in relation to rights of appeal.

2390 Universal credit–Income-based employment and support allowance–Income-based jobseeker's allowance

THE UNIVERSAL CREDIT (CONSEQUENTIAL, SUPPLEMENTARY, INCIDENTAL AND MISCELLANEOUS PROVISIONS) REGULATIONS (NORTHERN IRELAND) 2016, SR 2016/236; made under the Child Support(Northern Ireland) Order 1991 (SI 1991 2628) Sch.1 para.4(1)(b), Sch.1 para.5(4); Social Security Contributions and Benefits (Northern Ireland) Act 1992 s.70(7) , s.131(1)(5)(6); State Pension Credit Act (Northern Ireland) 2002 s.2(3)(b)(7); Jobseekers (Northern Ireland) Order 1995 (SI 1995 2705) art.6(5); Welfare Reform Act (Northern Ireland) 2007 s.4(2); Welfare Reform (Northern Ireland) Order 2015 (SI 2015 2006) art.38, art.48(1)(2), art.101(4)(c), Sch.1 para.4(3). In force: In accordance with reg.1.

These Regulations make consequential, supplementary, incidental and miscellaneous provision in relation to the provisions of the Welfare Reform (Northern Ireland) Order 2015 Pt 1 that relate to the introduction of universal credit and the abolition of income-related employment and support allowance and income-based jobseeker's allowance.

2391 Universal credit–Payments on account

THE SOCIAL SECURITY (PAYMENTS ON ACCOUNT OF BENEFIT) REGULATIONS (NORTHERN IRELAND) 2016, SR 2016/223; made under the Social Security Administration (Northern Ireland) Act 1992 s.5(1)(s), s.165(1)(4)(5)(6), s.167(1); Social Security (Northern Ireland) Order 1998 (SI 1998 1506) Sch.2 para.9, art.2(2) , art.74(1)(5). In force: In accordance with reg.1.

These Regulations make provision for two new types of payment on account of benefit to replace the loans available through the current system and the criteria which the Department must use when determining whether or not to make them. The new types of payment on account introduced by these Regulations are: Advances of benefit: these will replace Interim Payments and Social Fund Crisis Loan alignment payments for Universal Credit and legacy benefit claimants (covered in Part 2 of the regulations); and Budgeting Advances: which replace Social Fund Budgeting Loans for eligible Universal Credit claimants (covered in Part 3 of the Regulations).

2392 Welfare Reform (Northern Ireland) Order 2015 (SI 2015 2006)–Commencement No.1 Order

THE WELFARE REFORM (NORTHERN IRELAND) ORDER 2015 (COMMENCEMENT NO.1) ORDER 2016, SR 2016/46; made under the Welfare Reform (Northern Ireland) Order 2015 (SI 2015 2006) art.2(2)(4). Commencement details: bringing into operation various provisions of the 2015 Order on 17 February 2016, 4 April 2016, 13 June 2016 and 16 January 2017.

This Order brings into force provisions of the Welfare Reform (Northern Ireland) Order 2015 relating to, in particular: employment and support allowance; benefit cap; recovery of benefits; penalties; information sharing; and discretionary payments.

2393 **Welfare Reform (Northern Ireland) Order 2015 (SI 2015 2006)–Commencement No.2 Order**

THE WELFARE REFORM (NORTHERN IRELAND) ORDER 2015 (COMMENCEMENT NO.2) ORDER 2016, SR 2016/166; made under the Welfare Reform (Northern Ireland) Order 2015 (SI 2015 2006) art.2(2). Commencement details: bringing into operation various provisions of the Welfare Reform (Northern Ireland) Order 2015 on 17 March 2016.

This Order: brings into force provisions of the Welfare Reform (Northern Ireland) Order 2015 relating to requirements to consider revising a decision before appeal; and amends the Welfare Reform (Northern Ireland) Order 2015 (Commencement No. 1) Order 2016 in respect of provision relating to employment and support allowance.

2394 **Welfare Reform (Northern Ireland) Order 2015 (SR 2016 215)–Commencement No.3 Order**

THE WELFARE REFORM (NORTHERN IRELAND) ORDER 2015 (COMMENCEMENT NO.3) ORDER 2016, SR 2016/215; made under the Welfare Reform (Northern Ireland) Order 2015 (SI 2015 2006) art.2(2). Commencement details: bringing into operation various provisions of the 2015 Order on 2 May 2016.

This Order brings into force provisions of the Welfare Reform (Northern Ireland) Order 2015 relating to, in particular: universal credit; jobseeker's allowance; and personal independence payment.

2395 **Welfare Reform (Northern Ireland) Order 2015 (SR 2016 234) Commencement No.4 Order**

THE WELFARE REFORM (NORTHERN IRELAND) ORDER 2015 (COMMENCEMENT NO.4) ORDER 2016, SR 2016/234; made under the Welfare Reform (Northern Ireland) Order 2015 (SI 2015 2006) art.2(2). Commencement details: bringing into operation various provisions of the Welfare Reform (Northern Ireland) Order 2015 on 1 June 2016.

This Order brings into force provisions of the Welfare Reform (Northern Ireland) Order 2015 relating to, in particular: jobseeker's allowance; employment and support allowance; and industrial injuries benefit.

SOCIAL WELFARE

2396 **Health and Personal Social Services (Amendment) Act (Northern Ireland) 2016 (c.23)**

An Act to make provision about the Northern Ireland Social Care Council and other provision about social care workers.

TELECOMMUNICATIONS

2397 **EU law–Energy efficiency–Electronic communications networks**

THE BUILDING (AMENDMENT) REGULATIONS (NORTHERN IRELAND) 2016, SR 2016/412; made under the European Communities Act 1972 s.2(2); Building Regulations (Northern Ireland) Order 1979 (SI 1979 1709) (NI 16) art.3, art.5(1)(2)(3), art.5A(1), art.8. In force: 28 November 2016.

These Regulations amend the Building Regulations (Northern Ireland) 2012 (as amended) (the principal Regulations) and they come into operation on 28 November 2016. The regulations provide definitions from Directive 2014/61 art.2 on measures to reduce the cost of deploying high-speed electronic communications networks. These Regulations also clarify Directive 2010/31 arts 3,4 and 9 on the energy performance of buildings.

TRANSPORT

2398 Drivers–Public service vehicles–New duties for drivers regarding disabled passengers

THE PUBLIC SERVICE VEHICLES (AMENDMENT) REGULATIONS (NORTHERN IRELAND) 2016, SR 2016/344; made under the Road Traffic (Northern Ireland) Order 1981 (SI 1981 154) (NI 1) art.66(1), art.218(1). In force: 31 October 2016.

These Regulations amend the Public Service Vehicles Regulations (Northern Ireland) 1985 to introduce new duties for drivers of regulated public service vehicles in relation to passengers who are disabled.

2399 EU law–Passenger and goods vehicles–Tachographs

THE PASSENGER AND GOODS VEHICLES (TACHOGRAPHS) (AMENDMENT) REGULATIONS (NORTHERN IRELAND) 2016, SR 2016/343; made under the European Communities Act 1972 s.2(2), Sch.2 para.1A; Road Traffic (Northern Ireland) Order 1981 (NI.1) art.83(1). In force: 31 October 2016.

These Regulations facilitate the implementation of Regulation 165/2014 which sets out obligations in relation to construction, installation, use, testing and control of tachographs used in road transport, reflecting the fact that tachographs now use global positioning system technology. It also sets out the conditions and requirements under which the information and data, other than personal data, recorded, processed or stored by tachographs may be used. Northern Ireland's domestic legislation is updated by these Regulations to ensure it makes appropriate provision for the enforcement of the EU Regulation which is directly applicable in Member States.

2400 Infrastructure–Licensing–Railways

THE RAILWAYS INFRASTRUCTURE (ACCESS, MANAGEMENT AND LICENSING OF RAILWAY UNDERTAKINGS) REGULATIONS (NORTHERN IRELAND) 2016, SR 2016/420; made under the European Communities Act 1972 s.2(2). In force: 23 January 2017.

These Regulations, which implement Directive 2012/34 establishing a single European railway area (Recast), grant access rights to operators of international passenger and freight services to the Northern Ireland rail network, impose certain separation requirements between infrastructure managers and railway undertakings, set out the structure for the charging of fees for use of railway infrastructure, set out the framework and timetable for the process of allocating infrastructure capacity, allocate certain regulatory functions to the Office of Rail and Road (ORR), provide a right of appeal to the ORR for applicants aggrieved with various aspects of the allocation of capacity and the fees charged for the use of that capacity, set out the arrangements for enforcement by the regulatory bodies, impose requirements for licensing of railway undertakings, make provision for enforcement and penalty powers, and stipulate the accounting information required by the ORR.

SCOTLAND

ADMINISTRATION OF JUSTICE

2401 Children's hearings–Legal representatives–Exclusion of legal representatives while children's views heard–Whether justified

[Children's Hearings (Scotland) Act 2011 (asp 1) s.76, s.77, s.77(1)(a); European Convention on Human Rights 1950 art.6]

The mother (G) and maternal grandfather (J) of two boys aged nine and seven (collectively X) who had been subject to compulsory supervision, appealed against a decision of the children's hearing (H) excluding their respective legal representatives (L) while X's views were being sought in relation to contact. G and J submitted that the test in the Children's Hearings (Scotland) Act 2011 s.77 had not been met as L's presence would neither have impeded the expression of X's views nor caused them distress, L were not strangers to X and both had been present at previous hearings when X had articulated their views without evident difficulty.

Held: Appeals allowed. H's decision to exclude L from the hearing was not justified where adequate reasons had not been given therefor, H's written reasons neither disclosed that it was presently or currently being prevented from obtaining X's views as per the wording of the statutory power of exclusion under s.77(1)(a), nor the perceived cause of the alleged impediment, and there was no evidential basis upon which H might properly exercise its power of exclusion under s.77 of the 2011 Act: L's exclusion was an error of law which could properly be characterised as constituting a substantive unfairness given that the unauthorised exclusion of a party's legal representative from the hearing infringed a person's right of effective access to justice, the right of equality of arms and the right to a fair hearing in the presence of the party affected, and while none of the aforementioned elements of the right under ECHR art.6 was absolute, the interference therewith in the present case was neither justified nor proportionate. *Opinion*, that *esto* L's exclusion was properly characterised as a procedural irregularity, said irregularity was material in nature because it had a significant effect upon the conduct of the hearing itself by excluding L from part of the proceedings during which significant and contentious evidence was heard, the evidence heard outwith their presence was itself in significant contention and ultimately a highly potent and influential factor upon the outcome of the hearing, and it had caused significant prejudice to G and J. *Observed*, that provided it proceeded upon credible, reliable, specific and contemporaneous information, of sufficient quality, provided to it by others, a hearing could legitimately conclude that the attendance of a relevant person, or representative, was preventing a hearing from obtaining a child's views and on that basis, the hearing might exercise its powers of exclusion under s.76 and/or s.77 of the 2011 Act as appropriate, there was no need for a confrontation to be manufactured in the presence of the hearing between the child and relevant person.

G v CHILDREN'S REPORTER, 2016 S.L.T. (Sh Ct) 293, Sheriff S Reid, Sh Ct (Glasgow).

2402 Court fees–Miscellaneous amendments

THE COURT FEES (MISCELLANEOUS AMENDMENTS) (SCOTLAND) ORDER 2016, SSI 2016/332; made under the Courts Reform (Scotland) Act 2014 s.107(1)(2). In force: 28 November 2016.

This Order replaces the existing Tables of Fees in Sch.3 of previous Court Fees Orders with substituted Tables of Fees from the schedules of this Order. Some fees are to be increased beyond the figures in existing Sch.3 whereas in other cases the fees are to remain as they have been from 1 April 2016. Other textual amendments were made.

2403 Court rules–Upper Tribunal for Scotland–Rules of procedure

THE UPPER TRIBUNAL FOR SCOTLAND (RULES OF PROCEDURE) AMENDMENT REGULATIONS 2016, SSI 2016/333; made under the Tribunals (Scotland) Act 2014 Sch.9 para.4(1)(b)(2). In force: 1 December 2016.

These Regulations amend the Upper Tribunal for Scotland (Rules of Procedure) Regulations 2016 Sch. r.29 to provide that a request by a party for written reasons for an oral decision must be in writing.

2404 Devolved legislation–First-tier Tribunal for Scotland–Time limits

THE SCOTTISH TRIBUNALS (TIME LIMITS) REGULATIONS 2016, SSI 2016/231; made under the Tribunals (Scotland) Act 2014 s.55(1), s.79(1)(a), Sch.9 para.4(2). In force: 1 December 2016.

These Regulations set time limits for applications for permission to appeal to the First-tier Tribunal or the Upper Tribunal against that Tribunal's own decision or to the Upper Tribunal against a decision of the First-tier Tribunal where permission to appeal has already been refused by the First-tier Tribunal.

2405 First-tier Tax Tribunal for Scotland–Homeowner Housing Committees–Transfer of functions

THE FIRST-TIER TRIBUNAL FOR SCOTLAND (TRANSFER OF FUNCTIONS OF THE HOMEOWNER HOUSING COMMITTEES) REGULATIONS 2016, SSI 2016/335; made under the Tribunals (Scotland) Act 2014 s.20(2), s.28(2)(6), s.79(1), s.80(1). In force: 1 December 2016.

These Regulations make provision for the transfer to the First-tier Tribunal for Scotland of the functions of the Homeowner Housing Committees. They also make consequential amendments to the Property Factors (Scotland) Act 2011, largely substituting references to the Homeowner Housing Committees+ with references to the First-tier Tribunal, with similar amendments made to the Code of Conduct of Property Factors. Transitional provisions are made to manage the transfer of on-going casework.

2406 First-tier Tribunal Chambers–First-tier Tribunal for Scotland

THE FIRST-TIER TRIBUNAL FOR SCOTLAND (CHAMBERS) REGULATIONS 2016, SSI 2016/341; made under the Tribunals (Scotland) Act 2014 s.20(2). In force: 1 December 2016.

These Regulations divide the First-tier Tribunal for Scotland into 5 chambers: the Mental Health Chamber; the Housing and Property Chamber; the Health and Education Chamber; the General Regulatory Chamber; and the Tax Chamber.

2407 First-tier Tribunal for Scotland–Housing and Property Chamber–Upper Tribunal for Scotland

THE FIRST-TIER TRIBUNAL FOR SCOTLAND HOUSING AND PROPERTY CHAMBER AND UPPER TRIBUNAL FOR SCOTLAND (COMPOSITION) REGULATIONS 2016, SSI 2016/340; made under the Tribunals (Scotland) Act 2014 s.38(1), s.40(1). In force: 1 December 2016.

These Regulations make provision as to the composition of the First-tier Tribunal for Scotland when dealing with a case in the Housing and Property Chamber. They also make provision as to the composition of the Upper Tribunal for Scotland when hearing appeals or referrals from the First-tier Tribunal for Scotland Housing and Property Chamber.

2408 First-tier Tribunal for Scotland–Property Chamber–Procedure

THE FIRST-TIER TRIBUNAL FOR SCOTLAND HOUSING AND PROPERTY CHAMBER (PROCEDURE) REGULATIONS 2016, SSI 2016/339; made under the Tribunals (Scotland) Act 2014 s.55(1), Sch.9 para.4(2); Housing (Scotland) Act 1988 s.17(1)(3), s.19(3), s.24(1)(3), s.32(2)(4), s.34(1), s.48(2), s.53(3). In force: 1 December 2016.

These Regulations set out rules of procedure in respect of proceedings before the First-tier Tribunal for Scotland Housing and Property Chamber relating to homeowners and the private housing sector. They also provide forms for certain purposes of the Rent (Scotland) Act 1984 and the Housing (Scotland) Act 1988, and for the purpose of proceedings before the First-tier Tribunal.

2409 First-tier Tribunal for Scotland–Transfer of functions–Homeowner Housing Panel

THE FIRST-TIER TRIBUNAL FOR SCOTLAND (TRANSFER OF FUNCTIONS OF THE HOMEOWNER HOUSING PANEL) REGULATIONS 2016, SSI 2016/336; made under the Tribunals (Scotland) Act 2014 s.20(2), s.28(2), s.79(1), s.80(1), Sch.2 para.1(1). In force: 1 December 2016.

These Regulations make provision for the transfer into the First-tier Tribunal for Scotland of the functions and members of the Homeowner Housing Panel. They also make consequential amendments to the Property Factors (Scotland) Act 2011, largely substituting references to the Homeowner Housing Panel with references to the First-tier Tribunal, with similar substituted references made to the Code of Conduct of Property Factors. Transitional provisions are made to manage the transfer of on-going casework.

2410 Lyon Court–Fees–Devolved functions

THE LYON COURT AND OFFICE FEES (VARIATION) (DEVOLVED FUNCTIONS) ORDER 2016, SSI 2016/390; made under the Public Expenditure and Receipts Act 1968 s.5. In force: 1 January 2017.

This Order varies the fees payable in respect of devolved functions in the Lyon King of Arms Act 1867 Sch.B by replacing them with the fees listed in Schs.1 to 3 of this Order for set periods of time. The fee levels for the period from 1 January 2017 to 31 December 2017 are set out in Sch.1 and are given effect by art.2(2).

2411 Private rented housing committees–Transfer of functions

THE FIRST-TIER TRIBUNAL FOR SCOTLAND (TRANSFER OF FUNCTIONS OF THE PRIVATE RENTED HOUSING COMMITTEES) REGULATIONS 2016, SSI 2016/337; made under the Tribunals (Scotland) Act 2014 s.20(2), s.28(2), s.79(1), s.80(1). In force: 1 December 2016.

These Regulations make provision for the transfer to the First-tier Tribunal for Scotland of the functions of the private rented housing committees. These Regulations also make consequential amendments to legislation, largely substituting references to the Private Rented Housing Committees with references to the First-tier Tribunal, Transitional provisions are made to manage the transfer of on-going casework.

2412 Private Rented Housing Panel–Scotland–Transfer of functions

THE FIRST-TIER TRIBUNAL FOR SCOTLAND (TRANSFER OF FUNCTIONS OF THE PRIVATE RENTED HOUSING PANEL) REGULATIONS 2016, SSI 2016/338; made under the Tribunals (Scotland) Act 2014 s.20(2), s.28(2)(6), s.79(1), s.80(1), Sch.2 para.1(1). In force: 1 December 2016.

These Regulations make provision for the transfer to the First-tier Tribunal for Scotland of the functions and members of the Private Rented Housing Panel. These Regulations also make consequential amendments to legislation, largely substituting references to the Private Rented Housing Panel with references to the First-tier Tribunal, with similar amendments made to documents issued in terms of the Housing (Scotland) Act 1988 s.30A, comprising the Tenant Information Pack.

2413 Sheriff Appeal Court–Courts Reform–Consequential amendments

THE COURTS REFORM (SCOTLAND) ACT 2014 (RELEVANT OFFICER AND CONSEQUENTIAL PROVISIONS) ORDER 2016, SSI 2016/387; made under the Courts Reform (Scotland) Act 2014 s.107(4), s.137. In force: 28 November 2016.

This Order makes provision in consequence of the coming into force of certain provisions of the Courts Reform (Scotland) Act 2014. This Order comes into force on 28 November 2016 which is the date that certain provisions of the 2014 Act come into force. One of the key provisions is to add the auditor of the Sheriff Appeal Court to the list of "relevant officers" in s.107(3) of the 2014 Act.

2414 **Sheriff officers–Fees**

ACT OF SEDERUNT (FEES OF SHERIFF OFFICERS) 2016, SSI 2016/100; made under the Courts Reform (Scotland) Act 2014 s.106(1). In force: 1 April 2016.

This Act of Sederunt substitutes a new Table of Fees for the Table of Fees in Schedule 1 to the Act of Sederunt (Fees of Sheriff Officers) (No. 2) 2002. The fee levels in the new Table of Fees represent an increase of 1.3% on the existing fees. This increase takes effect from 1 April 2016.

2415 **Upper Tribunal for Scotland–Rules of procedure**

THE UPPER TRIBUNAL FOR SCOTLAND (RULES OF PROCEDURE) REGULATIONS 2016, SSI 2016/232; made under the Tribunals (Scotland) Act 2014 Sch.9 para.4(1)(b)(2). In force: 1 December 2016.

These Regulations make the Upper Tribunal for Scotland Rules of Procedure 2016 regulating the practice and procedure to be followed in proceedings in the Upper Tribunal for Scotland.

2416 **Vocational training–Continuing professional development–Justices of the peace**

THE JUSTICES OF THE PEACE (TRAINING AND APPRAISAL) (SCOTLAND) ORDER 2016, SSI 2016/329; made under the Criminal Proceedings etc. (Reform) (Scotland) Act 2007 s.69, s.81(2). In force: 28 November 2016.

This Order revokes arts 8 to 17 of the Justices of the Peace (Scotland) Order 2007, and introduces a new framework for the training of justices of the peace ("JPs"). Article 3 provides that every JP must undertake at least 12 hours of mandatory training each year, and must undertake 6 hours of training delivered by the Judicial Institute every 3 years.

ADMINISTRATIVE LAW

2417 **Criminal injuries compensation–Time–Exclusion of claims for injuries occurring before 1979–Lawfulness of rule**

[Human Rights Act 1998 (c.42) s.6(1); European Convention on Human Rights 1950 Protocol 1 art.1, art.14]

M petitioned for judicial review of the refusal by the Criminal Injuries Compensation Authority of her claim for compensation under the Criminal Injuries Compensation Scheme 2008, para.7(b) on the basis that the injury had been sustained before 1 October 1979 and she and the assailant, namely her mother, had been living together at the same time as members of the same family. M sought declarator that the claims officer who had decided her claim had acted unlawfully in terms of the Human Rights Act 1998 s.6(1) by withholding compensation on the basis of para.7(b), reduction of that decision, declarator that the Secretary of State had acted unlawfully by including para.7(b) within the 2008 scheme, reduction of para.7(b), and the expenses of the petition. M argued that para.7(b) and the decisions taken thereunder were unlawful, being in breach of the ECHR Protocol 1 art.1, and s.6 of the 1998 Act, and that para.7(b) discriminated on the basis of her status contrary to art.14: the claim constituted a possession within the meaning of art.1 of Protocol 1; her situation as a member of the household in which she was assaulted was a status within the meaning of art.14; and there was no reasonable and objective justification for the discrimination other than the avoidance of an unquantifiable financial burden on publically funded schemes if all same roof claim were to be admitted for pre-1979 incidents but said burden was unquantified and, from the terms of a report, it appeared the number of claimants would be small.

Held: Petition dismissed. (1) M had an interest with an economic value in the form of her claim for compensation which fell within the ambit of art.1 of Protocol 1, in conjunction with art.14, her situation was a status within the meaning of the latter, there was sufficient to demonstrate a difference in treatment between persons in analogous situations where, had M's mother assaulted a friend of M's at the same time, that child would be entitled to advance a claim, and M was not complaining of a difference in treatment on any of the core grounds referred to in art.14 but in the context of an award of compensation provided by the State as a matter of policy to victims of crime, *Stec v United Kingdom (Admissibility) (65731/01)* (2005) 41 E.H.R.R. SE18, *S v Criminal Injuries Compensation Appeal Panel* [2007] CSIH 49, 2007 S.C. 748, [2007] C.L.Y. 5447, *R. (on the application of M) v Secretary of State for Work and Pensions* [2008] UKHL 63, [2009] 1 A.C. 311, [2008] C.L.Y. 3527, *Mathieson v Secretary of State for Work and Pensions* [2015] UKSC 47, [2015] 1 W.L.R. 3250, [2015] C.L.Y. 2342 and *AL (Serbia) v Secretary of State for the Home Department* [2008] UKHL 42, [2008] 1 W.L.R. 1434, [2008] C.L.Y. 2024, *considered.* (2) The same roof rule imposed a bright line rule which excluded claims for injuries occurring before the relevant date and it was thus discriminatory but, having regard to the fact that it had not been thought possible to estimate the cost of abolition and that the rule assisted in making the scheme sustainable, and the deference the court ought to pay to such a policy decision in an area of general public interest, it could not be said that the same roof rule contained in the 1979 scheme was manifestly without foundation; it was a proportionate response to the criticisms made of the rule and one within the legitimate exercise of the discretion afforded to Parliament.

M, PETITIONER, [2016] CSOH 115, 2016 S.L.T. 911, Lord Burns, OH.

2418 Independent schools–Requests for information–Time for compliance

THE FREEDOM OF INFORMATION (SCOTLAND) ACT 2002 (TIME FOR COMPLIANCE) REGULATIONS 2016, SSI 2016/346; made under the Freedom of Information (Scotland) Act 2002 s.10(4)(5), s.21(7). In force: 1 December 2016.

These Regulations modify the period within which independent special schools and grant aided schools are required to respond to requests for information (and requests for reviews of responses to such requests for information) under the Freedom of Information (Scotland) Act 2002. Independent special schools and grant aided schools must comply with requests under that Act within twenty working days not including any working day which is not also a school day, or within sixty working days, whichever is the earlier.

2419 Inquiries into Fatal Accidents and Sudden Deaths etc. (Scotland) Act 2016 (asp 2)

An Act of the Scottish Parliament to make provision for the holding of public inquiries in respect of certain deaths.

2420 Inquiries into Fatal Accidents and Sudden Deaths etc. (Scotland) Act 2016 (asp 2)–Commencement No.1 and Transitional Provision Regulations

THE INQUIRIES INTO FATAL ACCIDENTS AND SUDDEN DEATHS ETC. (SCOTLAND) ACT 2016 (COMMENCEMENT NO.1 AND TRANSITIONAL PROVISION) REGULATIONS 2016, SSI 2016/196; made under the Inquiries into Fatal Accidents and Sudden Deaths etc. (Scotland) Act 2016 s.42(2)(3). Commencement details: bringing into operation various provisions of the 2016 Act on 1 September 2016.

These Regulations bring into force certain provisions of the Inquiries into Fatal Accidents and Sudden Deaths etc. (Scotland) Act 2016 on 1 September 2016. Reg.2 specifies the appointed day on which ss.8, 12, 16(4), 18, 27(4), 36 (in so far as not already in force) and 39(2) and Sch.2 para.16 come into force. Reg.3 contains transitional provision to require the family liaison charter prepared under s.8 of the 2016 Act to apply to inquiries held under the Fatal Accidents and Sudden Deaths Inquiry (Scotland) Act 1976 applied for on or after the date on which these Regulations come into force. This is because inquiries will continue to be held under the 1976 Act until such time as the remainder of the 2016 Act is brought into force.

2421 Judicial review–Locus standi–Father petitioning for judicial review of local authority's welfare decisions

[European Convention on Human Rights 1950 art.3]

A father (B) of two children (C) reclaimed against a decision of the Lord Ordinary refusing his petition for judicial review of welfare decisions of a local authority (E) in respect of C (*B v Edinburgh City Council* [2015] CSOH 120, 2015 G.W.D. 29-485). The Lord Ordinary found that B had neither standing as C's representative nor in a personal capacity and also sustained E's plea of *mora*.

Held: Reclaiming motion refused. (1) In so far as B relied on *Scozzari v Italy (39221/98)* [2000] 2 F.L.R. 771, [2001] C.L.Y. 3557, the circumstances therein were that there was a conflict between the natural parent and the person appointed by the court as the child's guardian, which was neither the position under Scottish procedure nor in the present case, there was nothing to infer conflict of the type in *Scozzari*, C's interests had been protected by *curators ad litem* and they had now instructed solicitors to represent their interests, further, B was a party to the proceedings in the sheriff court, there had also been a referral to the reporter to the children's hearing, and although B's parental rights were limited, his right to be a party to any proceedings brought by the reporter to the children's panel had expressly been preserved, accordingly, B did not have the requisite standing to represent C's interests, *Scozzari, considered*. (2) There were no averments that B had been a victim of a violation of ECHR art.3, which was for him to establish, any complaint by B of interference with his art.3 rights was to the effect that he was an indirect victim, however, any averments as might be construed as instructing a case that B's art.3 rights had been infringed were not of factors which could amount to a relevant case engaging art.3 or demonstrating its breach, *AXA General Insurance Ltd, Petitioners* [2011] UKSC 46, [2012] 1 A.C. 868, [2011] C.L.Y. 473 and *Cakici v Turkey (23657/94)* (2001) 31 E.H.R.R. 5, [2001] C.L.Y. 3569, *considered*. (3) No issue could be taken with the Lord Ordinary's approach in observing that there had been a 16 month delay in raising the petition, which remained unexplained and that it was relevant to take account of the fact that the petition related to the interests of children, thus delay was undesirable and was apt to create uncertainty and confusion in their lives; it was not conducive to effective and efficient administration to countenance judicial review proceedings that concerned children's interests after such a delay, and B had been in receipt of legal advice since spring 2011 but had taken until April 2014 to commence proceedings, 16 months was an unreasonable delay, there was no difficulty in holding that there had been taciturnity and in inferring acquiescence, and having done so, the court did not require to find separately that there had been prejudice, *Hendrick v Chief Constable of Strathclyde* [2014] CSIH 22, 2014 S.C. 551, [2014] C.L.Y. 3300, *applied*.

B v EDINBURGH CITY COUNCIL, [2015] CSIH 84, 2016 S.L.T. 180, Lord Menzies, Lady Smith, Lord Drummond Young, IH (Ex Div).

2422 Judicial review–Procedure–Guidance as to correct procedure under Act of Sederunt (Rules of the Court of Session 1994) 1994 Sch.2 Ch.58

[Act of Sederunt (Rules of the Court of Session 1994) 1994 Sch.2, Sch.2 para.58.11]

In petitions by three foreign nationals (X) seeking judicial review of decisions of the Secretary of State for the Home Department curtailing X's leave to remain where permission for the petitions had been granted under the new Act of Sederunt (Rules of the Court of Session 1994) 1994 Sch.2 Ch.58, the Lord Ordinary advised on the procedure to be followed thereunder. X had failed to comply with the orders pronounced at the permission stage, in particular, one or more of X had neither lodged any relevant documents nor marked them up to indicate those parts on which they intended to rely, as envisaged by r.58.11(2)(f)), or had failed to lodge the bundle of authorities, or, if lodged, had failed to mark up the cases with the passages on which they intended to rely, as envisaged by r.58.11(2)(g). Furthermore, notwithstanding that it was envisaged in the new Ch.58 rules that the manner of substantive hearing was to be determined at the procedural hearing, none of the counsel appearing on X's behalf was the counsel principally instructed in the matter, which had hampered the discussion in court at the procedural hearing about the nature and scope of the substantive hearing to be fixed.

Held: Guidance issued. *Observed*, (1) that the Ch.58 procedure was designed to filter out cases with no real prospect of success or an insufficient interest on the part of the petitioner at the permission stage, and to identify and define the arguments in those cases granted permission to proceed, with an emphasis on a focused, disciplined analysis of the issues at an early stage resolved by a swift and efficient judicial procedure; (2) that where permission was granted, orders would usually be pronounced under r.58.11(2) requiring parties to lodge notes of argument and/or statements of issues, and to lodge bundles of documents and of authorities with the passages to be relied upon having been marked up; such bundles ought to be joint, assembled according to some ordering principle, be properly paginated with no duplication of cases or documents and ought not to contain documents or cases unlikely to be relied upon, those items were to be reviewed by the Lord Ordinary in advance of the procedural hearing and ought to be lodged accordingly; (3) that petitioners' principal legal representatives ought to appear at the procedural hearing and where that was not possible, the legal representative appearing in lieu thereof required to be appropriately briefed and prepared.

OKM v SECRETARY OF STATE FOR THE HOME DEPARTMENT; O v SECRETARY OF STATE FOR THE HOME DEPARTMENT; P v SECRETARY OF STATE FOR THE HOME DEPARTMENT *sub nom.* M v SECRETARY OF STATE FOR THE HOME DEPARTMENT, [2015] CSOH 177, 2016 S.L.T. 280, Lady Wolffe, OH.

2423 Lobbying (Scotland) Act 2016 (asp 16)

An Act of the Scottish Parliament to make provision about lobbying, including provision for establishing and maintaining a lobbying register and the publication of a code of conduct.

2424 Public authorities–Freedom of information

THE FREEDOM OF INFORMATION (SCOTLAND) ACT 2002 (DESIGNATION OF PERSONS AS SCOTTISH PUBLIC AUTHORITIES) ORDER 2016, SSI 2016/139; made under the Freedom of Information (Scotland) Act 2002 s.5(1). In force: 1 September 2016.

This Order makes provision for the extension of coverage of the Freedom of Information (Scotland) 2002 Act under section 5 of that Act.

AGRICULTURE

2425 Common agricultural policy–Direct payments

THE COMMON AGRICULTURAL POLICY (DIRECT PAYMENTS ETC.) (SCOTLAND) AMENDMENT REGULATIONS 2016, SSI 2016/104; made under the European Communities Act 1972 s.2(2). In force: 24 March 2016.

These Regulations amend the Common Agricultural Policy (Direct Payments etc.) (Scotland) Regulations 2015, which make provision in Scotland for the administration of Regulation 1307/2013 establishing rules for direct payments to farmers under support schemes within the framework of the common agricultural policy.

2426 Crofts–Croft House Grant–Registration

THE CROFT HOUSE GRANT (SCOTLAND) REGULATIONS 2016, SSI 2016/63; made under the Crofters (Scotland) Act 1993 s.42(6). In force: 1 April 2016.

These Regulations revoke and replace the Croft House Grant (Scotland) Regulations 2006.

2427 EU law–Common agricultural policy–Direct payments

THE COMMON AGRICULTURAL POLICY (DIRECT PAYMENTS ETC.) (SCOTLAND) AMENDMENT (NO.2) REGULATIONS 2016, SSI 2016/178; made under the European Communities Act 1972 s.2(2). In force: 18 May 2016.

These Regulations amend the Common Agricultural Policy (Direct Payments etc.) (Scotland) Regulations 2015, which make provision in Scotland for the administration of Regulation 1307/2013, and other associated EU regulations as referred to in reg.2(1) of the principal Regulations.

2428 Producer organisations–Recognition–Withdrawal of producer organisation's recognition under EU's fresh fruit and vegetable scheme–Right to reparation

[Regulation 1234/2007 2007]

An action by a fruit and vegetable marketing company (G) and its grower members (M) against the Scottish Ministers (S) seeking reparation for loss and damage incurred as a consequence of S's breach of EU law came before the court for a preliminary debate on the issues of whether M had title to sue or advance claims for damages and whether the breach founded upon was sufficiently serious to give rise to state liability. G had been recognised in terms of Regulation 1234/2007 as a producer organisation under the EU's fresh fruit and vegetable aid scheme. The Rural Payments Agency (R), acting on S's behalf, alleged breaches by G of Regulation 1580/2007 art.25 and suspended G from the scheme. G implemented changes to comply with R's concerns, and R indicated that suspension would be lifted upon receipt of documentary evidence thereof. R wrote to G stating that developments in European law regarding shared facilities meant that the suspension could not be lifted. R subsequently notified G that its recognition as a producer organisation was withdrawn in terms of Regulation 1580/2007 art.116(1), proceeding upon the basis that a breach of any of the articles referred to in art.116(1) of itself constituted grounds for derecognition, where the Commission must have regarded them as essential to the nature of a producer organisation so that breach had to amount to either serious negligence or a deliberate act. R's decision was upheld at both stage 1 and stage 2 reviews, although the stage 2 review panel considered that it was not qualified to consider legal issues and disregarded G's legal submissions. G appealed to the Scottish Land Court, and S accepted that the legal interpretation of art.116(1) upon which R had proceeded was wrong in law but maintained that G's breaches had been substantial and constituted serious negligence. The Land Court determined that the only breach established was not substantial and that serious negligence had not been established, it allowed G's appeal and set aside R's decision to withdraw recognition (*Angus Growers Ltd v Scottish Ministers* 2012 S.L.C.R. 1, [2013] 2 C.L. 425). S requisitioned a special case in the Court of Session, and the First Division decided that the Land Court had not erred in holding that the breach was not substantial and had not resulted from serious negligence (*Angus Growers Ltd v Scottish Ministers* [2012] CSIH 92, 2013 S.L.T. 611, [2013] C.L.Y. 3502). S did not dispute that withdrawal of recognition from G was unlawful or that it had disabled G from qualifying for scheme assistance, and R made payment of all scheme payments withheld from G after its suspension. G and M sought damages in terms of *Francovich v Italy (C-6/90)* EU:C:1991:428, [1991] E.C.R. I-5357, [1992] C.L.Y. 4815: G's claim was for legal, management and consultancy costs and M's claims were for lost scheme payments and lost profits. S submitted *inter alia* that (1) the scheme rules bestowed right and responsibilities on producer organisations not on their members, and it was not necessary in order to achieve the scheme's objectives to confer such rights on M; (2) the threshold of sufficiently serious breach had not been reached; (3) at the time when the decision to derecognise G was made, there was no authoritative guidance from the courts on certain key issues of interpretation of the Regulations, but the European Court of Justice's judgment in *Fruition Po Ltd v Minister for Sustainable Farming and Food and Animal Health (C-500/11)* EU:C:2013:849 had since demonstrated that their approach was correct.

Held: Case put out by order. (1) M had a relevant claim against S for *Francovich* damages: it would be an unduly narrow approach to interpret the Regulations as conferring rights only on producer organisations, the purpose of the scheme was the benefit to individual growers that arose from strengthening their position in the market, and the result prescribed by the Regulations, i.e. recognition of producer organisations entitled to financial assistance for operational programmes, entailed the grant to member producers of rights identifiable as the right of each grower that their producer organisation be recognised under the scheme and not unlawfully derecognised by the relevant member state; any trading or capital losses were incurred by M, and conferring a right only on G itself would confer a right which was largely devoid of substance, which would not accord with community law principles, *Francovich* and *Dillenkofer v Germany (C-178/94)* EU:C:1996:375, [1997] Q.B. 259, [1996] C.L.Y. 2802, *applied*; *Poole v HM Treasury* [2007] EWCA Civ 1021, [2008] 1 All E.R. (Comm) 1132, [2008] C.L.Y. 2208, *considered.* (2) The breach of community law occasioned by withdrawal of

G's recognition as a producer organisation was sufficiently serious to confer a right to reparation in accordance with *Francovich* and the conditions for imposition of state liability were fulfilled: (i) the provisions of art.116(1) were sufficiently clear and precise, and the interpretation adopted by R was beyond the range of reasonable interpretations as it failed to take account of the graded approach to sanctions in art.116, where only seriously negligent or deliberate failures leading to substantial breaches of the scheme justified derecognition; (ii) R had to have known that derecognition would have had significant financial consequences for M; (iii) there was no reason to assume that had court's view in *Fruition* been known prior to R's decision it would have resulted in G's derecognition, it was more likely that recognition would at worse have been suspended pending the issuing of guidance, and there had been an inexcusable error of law in regarding the factors founded upon as justifying derecognition; (iv) it was relevant in assessing the seriousness of S's breach of community law to take account of the fact that they took the drastic step of derecognising G against a background of inconsistent and incoherent analysis of the ways in which G's operations gave rise to failures to respect the criteria for recognition; (v) the breach of community law could not be said to have been caused or contributed to by a position taken by any community institution and S's actions were not excusable on that basis, *Brasserie du Pecheur SA v Germany (C-46/93)* EU:C:1996:79, [1996] Q.B. 404, [1996] C.L.Y. 2803 and *R. v Secretary of State for Transport Ex p. Factortame Ltd (No.5)* [2000] 1 A.C. 524, [1999] C.L.Y. 2259, *applied*; *Fruition PO Ltd*, *considered*. (3) The case would be put out by order for discussion of further procedure.

ANGUS GROWERS LTD v SCOTTISH MINISTERS, [2016] CSOH 26, 2016 S.L.T. 529, Lord Tyre, OH.

ARBITRATION

2429 Arbitration agreements–Sports governing bodies–Removal of sportsman from membership of governing body–Appointment of arbitrator in terms of governing body's articles of association to determine lawfulness of decision to remove

[Arbitration (Scotland) Act 2010 (asp 1) Sch.1]

A competitive squash player (T) made an application seeking an order in terms of the Arbitration (Scotland) Act 2010 Sch.1 r.7(6) for the court to appoint an arbitrator to determine whether T's removal by the governing body responsible for squash and racketball in Scotland (S) from all categories of its membership had been irrational, unjustified and unlawful. T had been a registered member of S in terms of its articles of association, para.80 of which provided *inter alia* that S's suspension or expulsion of a member would be effective from the date upon which notice thereof was given to that member. In July 2012, T had become subject of a police complaint in relation to alleged criminal activity within premises which was a full corporate member of S. On 3 December 2012, S had suspended T pending a future investigation. T had received no further substantive correspondence until 22 October 2014 when S had notified him that he had been removed from its membership. On 12 November 2014, T had notified S that he had sought the appointment of an arbitrator regarding its decision, founding on para.81 of the articles of association. On 15 December, S had informed T that he was not a member and it had not accepted his notice of arbitration.

Held: Application dismissed. Considering the terms of the applicable agreement to arbitrate in the context of *Heyman v Darwins Ltd* [1942] A.C. 356, *Willis v Wells* [1892] 2 Q.B. 225 and *Judson v Ellesmere Port Ex-Servicemen's Club* [1948] 2 K.B. 52, [1947-51] C.L.Y. 4832, the arbitration agreement in para.81 referred to disputes involving members, the wording did not include any matters arising from, in respect of, with regard to, or under and in terms of, the articles of association, and in view of its wording, following S's intimation of 22 October 2014 removing T from all categories of membership, he was not entitled to seek the appointment of an arbitrator in terms of para.81, *Heyman*, *Willis* and *Judson*, *considered*.

TOLLAND v SCOTTISH SQUASH AND RACKETBALL LTD, 2016 S.L.T. (Sh Ct) 141, Sheriff W Sheehan, Sh Ct (Lothian) (Edinburgh).

AVIATION

2430 Delayed flights–Compensation–Passenger seeking compensation for delay of over six hours–Whether airline took all reasonable measures to avoid delay

[Regulation 261/2004 2004]

An airline passenger (D) raised an action against an airline (E) seeking 400 Euros as compensation under Regulation 261/2004 after her flight was delayed. D had been due to travel on a flight from Glasgow to Malaga operated by E. E's aircraft had been scheduled to depart Gatwick for Bologna in the morning and had been delayed by approximately six hours due to air traffic management's decisions to delay the flight because of adverse weather conditions. As a result the aircraft's return to Gatwick had been delayed, as had the next leg of its journey from Gatwick to Glasgow and D's scheduled evening flight to Malaga on that aircraft had departed and arrived over six hours late, although there had been no adverse weather conditions or air traffic control delays from Glasgow or Malaga airports. E's employee gave evidence that E had had four spare aircraft that day and there had been a possibility of calling upon a linked company's spare aircraft, however all such spare aircraft had already been in use operating other delayed flights, with three of the spare aircraft diverted due to unexpected flight safety shortcomings.

Held: Decree granted. (1) The underlying delay had been caused by extraordinary circumstances in that the aircraft could not leave Gatwick because of an air traffic control decision, and it was clear from recital 15 of the 2004 Regulation that it was not for the court to look behind whether that decision had been correct or not, the fact that the decision had been made leading to a delay or cancellation was self-evidently extraordinary circumstances, although there came a point where extraordinary circumstances ceased to exist or at least the longer between the circumstances causing the original delay coming to an end and the continuation of delays, the weaker the extraordinary circumstances exception had to be, it was not the case that there had been a lengthy gap such that the extraordinary circumstances exception was too remote, and the view in *Jager v Easy Jet*, Cheshire County Court, 16 September 2013, unreported, that knock on delays did not constitute extraordinary circumstances, was too general, *Jager v Easy Jet, disapproved*. (2) The unexpected flight safety shortcomings might have led to delays but they had not been caused by weather conditions in south east England, and without such shortcomings the spare aircraft would have been available to replace the aircraft which had been due to carry D. No information had been provided as to what had constituted the shortcomings and in the absence of clearer specification it did not have the necessary weight to discharge E's onus of proof. (3) Although the original delay between Gatwick and Bologna had been caused by extraordinary circumstances, and by the time of D's flight had been due to depart the extraordinary circumstances had continued, E had not taken all reasonable measures to avoid the delay, thus the limit or exclusion of liability set out in recitals 14 and 15 were not invoked due to deemed extraordinary circumstances not existing. The delay had been known about for many hours, it had been approximately 15 hours from the start of the delays before D's flight had finally taken off, and other measures could have been taken to minimise D's delay, such as using other aircraft.

DUNBAR v EASYJET AIRLINE CO LTD, 2015 S.L.T. (Sh Ct) 249, Sheriff D Livingston, Sh Ct (North Strathclyde) (Paisley).

BANKING AND FINANCE

2431 Bankruptcy (Scotland) Act 2016 (asp 21)

An Act of the Scottish Parliament to consolidate the Bankruptcy (Scotland) Act 1985, the Bankruptcy (Scotland) Act 1993, the Bankruptcy and Diligence etc. (Scotland) Act

2007 Pt 1, the Home Owner and Debtor Protection (Scotland) Act 2010 Pt 2, the Bankruptcy and Debt Advice (Scotland) Act 2014, the Protected Trust Deeds (Scotland) Regulations 2013 and related enactments.

CIVIL EVIDENCE

2432 **Retrials–Fresh evidence–Whether jury's verdict unsafe in face of guilty verdict for giving perjured evidence at trial**

[Court of Session Act 1988 (c.36) s.29; Act of Sederunt (Rules of the Court of Session 1994) 1994 Sch.2 para.39.1; Law Reform (Miscellaneous Provisions) (Scotland) Act 1968 (c.70) s.12]

A newspaper group (G) enrolled a motion for a new trial following a jury finding in favour of a then member of the Scottish Parliament and leader of the Scottish Socialist Party (S), in his action of damages for defamation in respect of certain newspaper articles published in 2004. S had denied all the allegations and the issue was whether the statements in the articles published by G falsely and calumniously stated that S had inter alia committed adultery, participated in orgies, drunk champagne when he claimed to be teetotal, and meant that he was thereby a hypocrite and abuser of his position of power as a party leader to S's loss, injury and damage. G pled justification in that the articles were true, or at least substantially true and lodged a counter issue to that effect. The jury answered in the affirmative to the issue for S, and in the negative to G's counter issue. G's motion was appointed to the summar roll; criminal proceedings against S and his wife ensued, in particular investigations into allegations that they had given perjured evidence during the civil jury trial; and in September 2007, G's motion for a new civil jury trial was sisted. In December 2010, S was found guilty of giving perjured evidence in relation to certain matters during the civil jury trial for which he was sentenced to three years' imprisonment. S immediately lodged an appeal which was refused at first and second sift; he then applied to the Scottish Criminal Cases Review Commission seeking to have his perjury conviction re-investigated and referred to the High Court of Justiciary with a view to having the conviction quashed. A motion to recall the sist was granted and G moved the court to set aside the jury's verdict and remit the case to a Lord Ordinary, submitting that (1) it was essential to the justice of the cause that the verdict be quashed: on any view the verdict was not safe, on the basis of the true evidence S was, at the very least, an adulterer, a liar and a hypocrite; and he had perpetrated a fraud on the court and as a result of the conviction for perjury he fell into the category of a dishonest litigant with all the consequences; (2) the verdict was contrary to the evidence: it had been essential to S's success that he was accepted as honest and that his evidence was accepted as credible and reliable; (3) *res noviter veniens ad notitiam*, namely the fact of the perjury conviction, and new evidence. In relation to further procedure, G argued the better course was to remit to a Lord Ordinary to proceed as accords: it was competent to do so in terms of the Court of Session Act 1988 s.29 and the Act of Sederunt (Rules of the Court of Session 1994) 1994 Sch.2 para.39.1; the evidential effect of the conviction for perjury was sacrosanct and could not be challenged in the present proceedings by virtue of the Law Reform (Miscellaneous Provisions) (Scotland) Act 1968 s.12; and as questions of law were in dispute, any new inquiry should be by a judge and not by jury.

Held: Motion refused. (1) S's existing criminal conviction for perjury could not be ignored or set aside where his case had neither been referred to nor accepted by the High Court of Justiciary; the jury in 2006 were well informed having heard all the evidence and the court should be slow to interfere with any verdict reached thereby; the method by which the jury were to give their verdict was to answer the issue and counter issue with a simple yes or no and their answers were consistent with doubt as to S's general credibility and did not necessarily imply their total acceptance of all of S's evidence. (2) The court was not persuaded that evidence of perjury at a trial opened the door to an argument that the verdict was contrary to the evidence within the meaning of s.29(1)(c) of the 1988 Act: the plain meaning of a reference to a decision "contrary to the evidence" meant contrary to the evidence actually before the jury and evidence of subsequent developments such as a conviction for perjury could provide an argument under *res noviter*. (3) Any party seeking a new trial in terms of s.29 had to satisfy the overarching test by demonstrating that one of grounds (a)-(e) was made out such that it was essential to the justice of the cause that the verdict be set aside and a new trial ordered: for the purposes of s.29, S's conviction was adequate evidence of his perjury, regardless of the applicability of s.12 of the 1968 Act, and it followed that it had to be taken into account, as a separate matter, that S lied about the matters relevant thereto in the civil jury trial; the jury in 2006 were entitled to conclude that S had lied in some respects but not in relation to the allegations which tended to lower his reputation in the estimation of right thinking members of society, and if that was the jury's approach, evidence about S's conviction for perjury and the matters in respect thereof, would only endorse their assessment and the court was thus not persuaded that the conviction would import any new feature into the case, nor that the conviction made it essential to the justice of the cause that the verdict reached in 2006 should be quashed and a new trial ordered; the proposed new evidence regarding S's visits to sex clubs or sexual affairs would similarly fail to import any new feature into the case or put a new complexion thereon.

SHERIDAN v NEWS GROUP NEWSPAPERS LTD, [2016] CSIH 67, 2016 S.L.T. 941, Lady Paton, Lord Drummond Young, Lord McGhie, IH (Ex Div).

2433 Special measures for witnesses–Children–Procedure when considering child witness notice–Child's wishes and risk of prejudice to fairness of proceedings

[Vulnerable Witnesses (Scotland) Act 2004 (asp 3) s.12(1)(b), s.12(3), s.12(4)(a), s.12(4)(b), s.14(2), s.19; Act of Sederunt (Sheriff Court Ordinary Cause Rules) 1993 Sch.1]

In the course of an action by a father (M) against his former partner (B), a party litigant, seeking *inter alia* interdict, a non harassment order, residence and interim residence in relation to their three children, (W), aged 15, (X), aged 11 and (Y), aged 10 (collectively Z), and an order depriving B of her parental rights and responsibilities in respect of Z, B lodged child witness notices in terms of the Vulnerable Witnesses (Scotland) Act 2004 s.12(1)(b) inviting the court to direct that Z give evidence without the benefit of special measures.

Held: B's applications in respect of W granted and in respect of X and Y refused, and hearing assigned. (1) The procedure to be followed when considering a child witness notice where the court was invited to make an order under s.12(1)(b) of the 2004 Act involved two distinct exercises under s.12(4)(a) and (b), in respect of one of which the court required to be satisfied in order to proceed without special measures; in respect of s.12(4)(a), that the child witness had expressed a wish to give evidence without the benefit of any special measure and that it was appropriate for them so to give evidence; and with regard to s.12(4)(b), that the use of any special measure for the purpose of taking the evidence of the child witness would give rise to a significant risk of prejudice to the fairness of the proceedings or otherwise to the interests of justice and that risk significantly outweighed any risk of prejudice to the interests of the child witness if the order was made; and the statute made it clear that was the court satisfied that the requirements of either subsection were met, it retained a discretion not to make an order under s.12(1)(b). (2) Neither X nor Y had expressed a wish to give evidence without special measures thus the s.12(4)(a) test was not satisfied. (3) Taking into account that W wished to give evidence without special measures, the court was obliged to give greater weight to his views where M's views differed thereto, and that the curator *ad litem* to Z was of the view that W ought to be permitted to give evidence without special measures, and having regard to the matters upon which W was likely to be questioned, it was in his best interests, and appropriate, that he be permitted to give evidence without the benefit of any special measure, thus the test in s.12(4)(a) of the 2004 Act was satisfied, and with regard to s.12(1)(b), there were no circumstances justifying the court nonetheless exercising its discretion not to make such an order. (4) Where B was a party litigant, the use of any special measure in s.12(3), namely either the use of a television link from another part of the court building, the use of a screen, or the use of a supporter in conjunction with either of those measures, would not be appropriate, where the vulnerable witness would not be afforded the protection envisaged by the legislation, and the only special measure realistically available would be the taking of X and Y's evidence by a commissioner in terms of s.19 of the 2004 Act, and further, the circumstances amounted to sufficient cause not to dispense with interrogatories in terms of the Act of Sederunt (Sheriff Court Ordinary Cause Rules) 1993 Sch.1 para.45.11(3). (5) Proceeding by way of a commissioner with interrogatories would place limitations upon the manner in which B conducted her defence, however, her interests required to be balanced against X and Y's, and the taking of their evidence in that manner did not give rise to a significant risk of prejudice either to the fairness of the proceedings or otherwise to the interests of justice, it was in X and Y's best interests that there be special measures in place, accordingly, the test in s.14(2)(c) of the 2004 Act was not satisfied. (6) An order would be made under s.12(1)(a) to the effect that X and Y's evidence would be taken by commissioner with interrogatories, further, where X and Y had both expressed a wish for a supporter, that would be authorised and an order to that effect made under s.12(1)(a). (7) A hearing would be assigned for parties to be heard on the approval of the interrogatories and cross interrogatories, the settlement of any dispute as to their contents, and the fixing of a diet or diets for the execution of the commission to examine X and Y.

M v B, 2016 S.L.T. (Sh Ct) 279, Sheriff C Turnbull, Sh Ct (North Strathclyde) (Dumbarton).

CIVIL PROCEDURE

2434 Civil appeals–Jurisdiction–Appellant seeking to appeal on obiter dicta views

[Tribunals, Courts and Enforcement Act 2007 (c.15) s.13(1); Social Security (Disability Living Allowance) Regulations 1991 (SI 1991/2890) reg.12(1A); Social Security Contributions and Benefits Act 1992 (c.4) s.73(1AB); Disability Discrimination Act 1995 (c.50) s.49A; Equality Act 2006 (c.3)]

The Secretary of State for Work and Pensions (S) appealed under the Tribunals, Courts and Enforcement Act 2007 s.13(1) against a decision of the Upper Tribunal (U) regarding S's decision that a disabled person (R), who was virtually blind, was only entitled to the mobility component of disability living allowance at the lower rate. At the relevant date when R's visual acuity had been measured, S had found that she had not had severe visual impairment, as prescribed by the Social Security (Disability Living Allowance) Regulations 1991 reg.12(1A) for the purposes of the Social Security Contributions and Benefits Act 1992 s.73(1AB), and thus had not met the relevant statutory criteria for entitlement to the higher rate of the mobility component of disability living allowance. On appeal, the First-tier Tribunal (F) had revised S's decision and found R entitled to the higher rate on the basis that her visual acuity would meet the requirements of reg.12(1A)(a). S appealed to U, which set aside and remade F's decision to state *inter alia* that R had no entitlement to the higher rate of the mobility component but remained entitled to the lower rate for an indefinite period. U thereafter discussed *inter alia* that the effect of reg.12(1A) was discriminatory for the purposes of ECHR art.14 and was accordingly *ultra vires*, moreover, in making the regulation, S had not had due regard to the equality duty as provided by the Disability Discrimination Act 1995 s.49A, read with the Equality Act 2006, and therefore the regulation was separately *ultra vires*, although U made no formal decision that the regulation was a nullity because it had no jurisdiction to reduce it or set it aside. Due to doubts as to the competency of an appeal by S against a decision in his favour, the court appointed an *amica curiae*.

Held: Appeal dismissed. (1) The only basis upon which U could decide the appeal was whether or not R had the degree of severe visual impairment prescribed by reg.12(1A) such that she was entitled to payment of the mobility component of the disability living allowance at the higher rate, which it had done, and its views as to the legality of the regulation were irrelevant in deciding R's entitlement to benefit; had R qualified under the regulation, as properly construed, she would have been entitled to succeed in her appeal, irrespective of U's views on *vires*. (2) With regard to s.13(1) of the 2007 Act, the matter which S wished to make subject of appeal was not an appeal on any point of law arising from a decision made by U; U had acknowledged that it had no jurisdiction to make a decision as to the *vires* of the regulation and had not done so, its views on the *vires* of the regulation had formed no part of the reasoning which had brought it to its decision but had been *obiter dicta*, accordingly, the making of the decision by U had not involved the making of an error on the point of law which S wished to bring under appeal. U had made its decision not because the regulation was *ultra vires* but because R's condition, as measured in the only relevant manner, had not met the criterion set out in the regulation for payment of the higher rate, and the court had no jurisdiction to entertain the appeal. Observed, that although S had stated that in obedience to the rule of law, were the appeal not permitted to advance, he would feel bound by U's expression of view as to the *vires* of reg.12(1A), that was a matter for him and could not confer on the court a jurisdiction that it did not otherwise have.

SECRETARY OF STATE FOR WORK AND PENSIONS v ROBERTSON, [2015] CSIH 82, 2016 S.L.T. 52, Lady Smith, Lord Brodie, Lady Clark of Calton, IH (Ex Div).

2435 Civil appeals–Time limits–Appeal to Sheriff Appeal Court lodged outwith 28-day time limit–Competence of late appeals

[Act of Sederunt (Sheriff Appeal Court Rules) 2015 (SSI 2015/356) r.2.1, r.6.3, r.6.4; Courts Reform (Scotland) Act 2014 (asp 18)]

H and S (collectively X) lodged motions seeking to lodge notes of appeal outwith the 28 day time limit in the Act of Sederunt (Sheriff Appeal Court Rules) 2015 r.2.1. X had provided an explanation and reasons for their appeals being lodged late. The court required to determine the preliminary question of whether it was competent to appeal late, whatever the reason, standing the terms of rr.6.3 and 6.4, and whether the court might exercise its discretion to relieve a party of the consequences of failing to comply with the 28 day time limit, and where X were unrepresented, the court appointed an *amicus curiae*.

Held: S's motion granted and H's motion refused. (1) The Courts Reform (Scotland) Act 2014 made no provision for the time limit within which an appeal required to be made, that time limit was set by the Sheriff Appeal Court Rules and was within 28 days after the date on which the decision appealed against was given and might be found in r.6.3. (2) Rule 6.4 of the 2015 Rules, which applied where the enactment under which the appeal was made specified a period for lodging an appeal, only applied where an appeal was being brought under a statutory provision and only when the legislation itself specified the time applicable to the appeal and where it provided that an application to appeal out of time could competently be made; r.6.4 did not apply as neither r.6.4(1)(a) nor (b) was engaged, thus X's appeals were subject to the r.6.3 28 day time limit. (3) Rule 2.1, which was concerned with relief for failure to comply with rules, applied to the 28 day time limit, accordingly, the court might consider whether to exercise its discretion under r.2.1 to relieve X of their failure to lodge their appeals timeously because that time limit was a requirement of the rules themselves and was not imposed by the statute under which the appeals had been taken, which reasoning accorded with the previous practice in appeals to the sheriff principal, however, the r.2.1 dispensing power could not normally be used to excuse a failure to comply with a time limit imposed by a statute or other enactment whose time limit for bringing an appeal had to be complied with, *Graham v John Tullis & Son (Plastics) Ltd (No.1)* 1992 S.L.T. 507, [1992] C.L.Y. 6127 and *Graham Builders Merchants Ltd v Mann Engineering Ltd* 2003 S.C. 479, [2004] C.L.Y. 4574, *considered*. (4) S sought to appeal the sheriff's decision of 10 February 2016 granting decree against him, he had known of the 28 day time limit and had presented his note of appeal at Inverness sheriff court and when he had discovered that it required to be lodged at the Sheriff Appeal Court in Edinburgh, he had faxed it but had been unable to lodge it timeously; in those circumstances, it was appropriate to grant the motion to allow his appeal to be lodged late and the delay was excusable. (5) H had failed to attend timeously for proof on 15 February 2016, the action was dismissed and the decree of dismissal was extracted once the appeal days had passed, there was no suggestion that the extract decree had been improperly or incompetently issued thus the general rule that there could be no appeal against an extracted interlocutor applied, accordingly, the court was unable to exercise its discretion in favour of allowing H's appeal late. *Observed*, that any party wishing to appeal required either to seek legal advice or, if he represented himself, to comply with the rules of court.

HAMILTON v GLASGOW COMMUNITY AND SAFETY SERVICES, [2016] SAC (Civ) 3, 2016 S.L.T. (Sh Ct) 367, Sheriff Principal M M Stephen, QC, Sheriff Principal D C W Pyle, Sheriff Principal M Lewis, SAC.

2436 Civil proceedings–Apologies–Exemptions

THE APOLOGIES (SCOTLAND) ACT 2016 (COMMENCEMENT AND TRANSITORY PROVISION) AMENDMENT REGULATIONS 2016, SSI 2016/395; made under the Apologies (Scotland) Act 2016 s.5(2)(3). In force: 16 December 2016.

These Regulations amend the Apologies (Scotland) Act 2016 (Commencement and Transitory Provision) Regulations 2016, with the effect that the Apologies (Scotland) Act 2016 comes into force on 19 June 2017 in so far as not already in force. The Bill for the Act received Royal Assent on 23 February 2016. Ss.5 and 6 came into force on the following day. Ss.2(4) to (6) came into force on 22 September 2016.

2437 Civil proceedings–Breach of interdict–Proceedings following upon breach of interdict–Whether civil proceedings as envisaged by s.3 Sheriff Courts (Scotland) Act 1907

[Sheriff Courts (Scotland) Act 1907 (c.51) s.3, s.3(d); Sheriff Courts (Scotland) Act 1876 (c.70); Courts Reform (Scotland) Act 2014 (asp 18) s.110, s.136, s.47]

In the course of an appeal by a former partner (L) in a firm of chartered surveyors (S) against a decision of the sheriff principal dismissing as incompetent L's appeal against the sheriff's decision finding L in breach of interim interdict and fining him £500, a tension between *Forbes v Forbes* 1993 S.C. 271, [1993] C.L.Y. 5803 and *MacIver v MacIver* 1996 S.L.T. 733, [1996] C.L.Y. 7329 was brought to the court's attention and a full bench was convened. *Forbes* held that proceedings following upon a breach of interdict were not civil proceedings as envisaged by the Sheriff Courts (Scotland) Act 1907 s.3, whereas *Maciver* found that s.3(d) was sufficiently wide to include proceedings which were taken by initial writ for breach of interdict. The sheriff principal had considered that he was bound by *Forbes* and had observed, under reference to *M v S* [2009] CSIH 44, 2011 S.L.T. 918, [2010] C.L.Y. 4517 and *G v B* [2011] CSIH 56, 2011 S.L.T. 1253, [2012] C.L.Y. 3833, that a sheriff's decision in relation to both a finding of contempt and a subsequent sentence were reviewable only by petition to the nobile officium.

Held: Appeal allowed and matter remitted to sheriff principal to proceed as accords. *Maciver* doubted the *ratio* in *Forbes,* the fact that proceedings were described as quasi criminal did not prevent them from being civil proceedings in terms of the 1907 Act, and *Forbes* had been wrongly decided; the 1907 Act had not materially changed the pre-existing position set out in Sheriff Courts (Scotland) Act 1876, both before and after the 1907 Act there was ample authority for the proposition that a finding of contempt or a breach of interdict by a party to the cause was appealable in the normal way, *Forbes, overruled* and *Maciver, approved.* Observed, that the position in relation to contempt by third parties might be different but the matter would shortly be governed, so far as sheriff court civil contempts and sentences were concerned, by the Courts Reform (Scotland) Act 2014 ss.47, 110 and 136.

J&E SHEPHERD v LETLEY, [2015] CSIH 87, 2016 S.L.T. 31, The Lord Justice Clerk (Carloway), Lady Paton, Lord Menzies, Lady Smith, Lord Bracadale, IH (2 Div).

2438 Civil proceedings–Court rules–Courts' powers and duties

ACT OF SEDERUNT (RULES OF THE COURT OF SESSION 1994 AND SHERIFF COURT RULES AMENDMENT) (NO.2) (MISCELLANEOUS) 2016, SSI 2016/229; made under the Courts Reform (Scotland) Act 2014 s.103(1), s.104(1). In force: 28 November 2016.

This Act of Sederunt amends the Ordinary Cause Rules 1993 and the Summary Cause Rules 2002 to set out the procedure for applying for an order under the Courts Reform (Scotland) Act 2014 s.87. It also: makes a minor amendment to r.36.L1 of the Ordinary Cause Rules to correct errors in the paragraph numbers referred to in that rule; amends the Rules of the Court of Session 1994 to set out the procedure which will apply when a person who is the subject of an order under s.100 of the 2014 Act seeks permission to either institute civil proceedings or take a specified step in specified ongoing civil proceedings; and corrects numbering errors in the Act of Sederunt (Sheriff Court Rules Amendment) (Personal Injury Pre-Action Protocol) 2016.

2439 Civil proceedings–Court rules–Sheriff Appeal Court

ACT OF SEDERUNT (SHERIFF APPEAL COURT RULES 2015 AND SHERIFF COURT RULES AMENDMENT) (MISCELLANEOUS) 2016, SSI 2016/194; made under the Courts Reform (Scotland) Act 2014. In force: 7 July 2016.

This Act of Sederunt amends the Act of Sederunt (Sheriff Appeal Court Rules) 2015 and various sheriff court rules, principally to address issues that have arisen since the Sheriff Appeal Court assumed its civil jurisdiction and competence on 1 January 2016.

2440 Civil recovery proceedings–Proceeds of crime–Lord Ordinary recalling two prohibitory property orders–Whether good arguable case that property obtained by unlawful conduct

[Proceeds of Crime Act 2002 (c.29) Pt 5 s.255A]

The Scottish Ministers (S) reclaimed against a decision of the Lord Ordinary recalling two prohibitory property orders in relation to heritable and moveable property belonging to M. In the first petition, S had made reference to M's criminal record, which included convictions for assault, and had averred that that did not however reflect M's involvement in crime and they had police intelligence that he had been involved for many years in organised crime. Evidence was led that in his tax returns for 1997-2000, M had declared no income, for 2000-2003 he had declared an annual income of between £10,000 and £16,000 from various businesses, for 2003-2005 an annual income of £50,000-£60,000 from various businesses, and from 2005-2012, of £4,000-£130,000 from property and either a business (D) or its successor (K), the figures for 2005/06, 2006/07 and 2007/08 being £52,289, £4,035 and £19,620, respectively. In 2008, M had obtained a loan from a bank (B) and in his loan application had stated that he had been self employed in retail sales, earning more than £193,000 in 2004/05, £251,000 in 2005/06 and £272,000 in 2006/07. In a letter dated 13 November, on B's request, chartered certified accountants (G), confirmed that from M's books, records, information and explanations, his income from all sources had been as stated in the loan application. S averred that having regard to the figures declared in his tax returns the loan funds had been obtained by fraud, namely by overstatements of M's legitimate income. In December 2008, M had bought two properties (X and Y, collectively Z), financed by a bank transfer from his account into which the loan funds from B had been paid, and the balance of the purchase prices had been paid from an account held by M, which had in turn been funded by a payment of £303,000 from D's account, which had itself been provided from an unknown account, in turn funded by another of D's accounts into which a deposit of £240,000 had been paid. Rent in respect of Y, from which D operated, amounting to £111,000, had been paid to M in 2009/10, from May 2010, rent of £1,500 per week had been paid to him, averred by S to be profits accruing from recoverable property. In July 2010, a company (G) controlled by M had purchased a property (L), which had been paid from M's accounts or those of D or K, thus there was a good arguable case that Z and L, along with certain amounts in one of M's bank accounts, were recoverable. S also averred that M had bought a club (E) in November 2013, which had been paid for from his bank account, into which money had been paid by *inter alia* a company then controlled in part by M, with the balance coming from rental income from the business operated from X and K, thus there was a good arguable case that E was recoverable property. The Lord Ordinary held inter alia that following the approach in *Scottish Ministers v Stirton* [2008] CSOH 20, 2008 S.L.T. 505, [2008] C.L.Y. 4681, he could not categorise the case as a good arguable one with a good prospect of succeeding, with the strength and quality required to prove fraud, as the documentation did not demonstrate a fraud, and there was an inevitable lacuna in S's case where S had proceeded upon the basis that M required to explain the discrepancies in the figures, which was not the correct approach.

Held: Reclaiming motion allowed. The Lord Ordinary had erred in attempting to place a gloss upon, or redefine using different terms, the Proceeds of Crime Act 2002 Pt 5 s.255A, following the same error in *Stirton*; the test was not whether the case had a good prospect of succeeding, with the strength and quality required to prove fraud but whether it was a good arguable one, and a prohibitory property order was an interim order, preserving the status quo pending inquiries, thus the threshold was not exacting and might be met purely on the basis of averment, and as the Lord Ordinary had applied the wrong test, the matter fell to be re-assessed, *Stirton*, *disapproved*, *Scottish Ministers v Stirton* 2006 S.L.T. 306, [2006] C.L.Y. 5227, *applied* and *Ninemia Maritime Corp v Trave Schiffahrts GmbH & Co KG (The Niedersachsen)* [1983] 1 W.L.R. 1412, [1984] C.L.Y. 2646, *considered.* (2) It was unfortunate that S had made general averments regarding M's involvement in crime when they had not been in a position to support them, however, with regard to the averments of fraud, the facts were not in dispute, M's formal representation to the tax authorities of the extent of his legitimate income in the fiscal years 2005-2008 had referred to the source of his income being D or K but in the loan application, M had stated his income to be well in excess of that declared to the tax authorities, the veracity thereof being supported by G, and one obvious inference to be drawn therefrom was that the figures in the loan application had not represented the extent of M's legitimate income but had been false, thus the application had been fraudulent and the funds made available became recoverable property as did any assets purchased by them, which was a good arguable case, even were the inference not ultimately drawn. (3) M's argument that the higher figures in the loan application were accurate because they represented money which he might have withdrawn from D and K in fact confirmed the nature of the fraud, in so far as it proceeded upon an acceptance that the figures given to B had not represented his actual income during the three year period.

SCOTTISH MINISTERS v MACDONALD, [2016] CSIH 21, 2016 S.L.T. 471, The Lord President (Carloway), Lord Bracadale, Lord Drummond Young, IH (1 Div).

2441 Commission and diligence–Medical reports–Documents prepared by psychiatric hospital in relation to admission of patient–Policy consideration that organisations should not be inhibited from carrying out legitimate investigations

In the course of an action of damages by a state hospital detainee (C) against a local health board (T) for *inter alia* solatium in respect of the loss of his wife (W), C moved the court to grant commission and diligence for (i) all documents prepared by a hospital psychiatrist (X) at or about the time of events in 14 and 15 July 2011 available to, and relied upon by, T's significant clinical event analysis review relative to the treatment provided to C in the period prior to, and including, 15 July, the circumstances surrounding C's road traffic accident on 15 July and the circumstances surrounding W's death on the same day, (ii) the incident report form raised on 15 July relative to C's care and treatment, (iii) the documentation and statements from T's staff with regard to the care and treatment provided to C on 14 July. C had a lengthy history of serious mental disorder and following a worsening of his symptoms, had been examined by X on 14 July who concluded that C should be re-admitted to a psychiatric hospital for in-patient care. No bed had been immediately available for C locally but one was available elsewhere and the dispute centred on whether C had been informed of said availability. The following day, C killed W and had attempted to commit suicide by driving his car into another vehicle. C was acquitted of W's murder by reason of insanity. C claimed that, but for X's negligence in failing to advise him of the availability of a bed, he would not have gone on to kill W and attempt suicide. C submitted that while there was a reference to a fishing diligence in the opposition to the motion, the real issue related to whether the report and the documents on which it was based fell within the *post litem motam* rule such that it was not susceptible to recovery but the court should find an analogy with the circumstances in *Komori v Tayside Health Board* [2010] CSOH 30, 2010 S.L.T. 387, [2010] C.L.Y. 3975.

Held: Motion refused. (1) The situation in the present case was not comparable with that in *Komori*: the purpose of the review was very much wider and its terms of reference did not take the underlying material outwith the *post litem motam* rule, *Komori, considered*. (2) A strong policy consideration underlay the general rule, namely that an organisation should not be inhibited from carrying out legitimate investigations and it would be undesirable to paralyse the taking of remedial measures which might thereby be identified, and those considerations would seem to apply in a hospital setting where a psychiatric patient was not admitted to hospital on seeing a psychiatrist before killing his wife the next day. *Opinion*, that a different conclusion might have been reached had C amended his specification so as to include only the kind of spontaneous reporting by employees to T which fell within the recognised exception.

CUMMING v TAYSIDE HEALTH BOARD, [2016] CSOH 58, 2016 Rep. L.R. 85, Temporary Judge J Beckett, QC, OH.

2442 Contempt of court–Findings–Minute seeking finding of contempt dismissed at hearing on proportionality–Whether proof necessary

[Administration of Justice (Scotland) Act 1972 (c.59) s.1]

A company (M) reclaimed against a decision of the Lord Ordinary dismissing its minute seeking a finding of contempt of court against two individuals (K and G) in the course of its petition seeking certain recoveries in terms of the Administration of Justice (Scotland) Act 1972 s.1 in relation to a franchise agreement (*Martin & Co (UK) Ltd v Stenhouse* [2014] CSOH 33, 2014 G.W.D. 9-168). The commissioner (C) had attended at certain premises in the morning and had been met with non-co-operation by K and G such that he had been unable to commence his duties till later in the day, having obtained and exhibited an interlocutor containing a power of arrest. C had thereafter attended at two other premises but had found no files, documents or computers relating to the franchise such that M had been unable to make any further progress and had decided to take no further proceedings, one of K and G having become bankrupt, however, it had been concerned that there had been a major contempt of court and had instructed the minute, to which K and G had lodged answers denying that they had obstructed C. M sought a proof and at a hearing on proportionality the Lord Ordinary made no finding of contempt but found that even had K and G been in contempt, it would not be proportionate for the minute and answers to continue.

Held: Reclaiming motion allowed. The Lord Ordinary had erred in several respects: (i) evidence necessarily required to be led where there were disputed issues of fact to establish, after proof, what had occurred and whether, and to what extent, C had in fact been obstructed in carrying out his duties, issues of credibility and reliability, and matters involving the weight of any evidence, would require to be resolved and it had not been open to the Lord Ordinary to rule out the possibility that the evidence might establish that C had been significantly impeded; (ii) the appropriate test was whether, were all of M's averments to be proved, it was plain that the behaviour in question was so trivial and unimportant that it did not merit any further court procedure, and assessing matters on the basis of the averments, which described aggressive, threatening, and disrespectful language and behaviour aimed directly at C with a view to keeping files, papers, and computers out of his reach, it could not be said that the minute was bound to fail, or that no reasonable Lord Ordinary, having heard the evidence, would conclude that what had occurred was serious and not trivial; the alleged language and behaviour struck at the heart of the dignity and the power of the court and its officers and were likely to interfere with the course of justice, and the discontinuation of the proceedings ran the risk of encouraging the parties to treat the court's orders as being of little importance, moreover, the bankruptcy of an alleged contemnor was irrelevant where the court was not restricted to monetary penalties; (iii) in concluding that no prejudice had been caused by the delay in the commission and that M had failed to demonstrate that the documents removed had been important to it making progress, the Lord Ordinary had focused solely upon the private interests of the parties, and had given no consideration to the public interest, in particular the upholding of the rule of law by protecting or enforcing the authority of the court, the preservation of the due and impartial administration of justice, the question of whether any conduct had been persisted in to the point at which it had been likely to interfere with the course of justice and the question of whether the discontinuation of the minute and answer proceedings risked encouraging parties to treat the court's orders as being of little importance, furthermore, files which might have fallen within the calls which the court had authorised in terms of its interlocutor had been removed from the premises despite C's attempt to prevent it, and his authority had thus been flouted at the very outset of the commission. Opinion, that where the circumstances in *Sovereign Dimensional Survey Ltd v Cooper* [2009] CSIH 12, 2009 S.C. 382, [2009] C.L.Y. 4546 were particular to that case, no novel protocol in relation to contempt proceedings had been, or had been intended to be, introduced, and the well established procedure whereby allegations of contempt of court, if not admitted, had to be the subject of a proof, remained unaltered, *Sovereign*, *considered*.

MARTIN & CO (UK) LTD v STENHOUSE *sub nom.* MARTIN & CO (UK) LTD, PETITIONER, [2015] CSIH 86, 2016 S.L.T. 45, Lady Paton, Lady Smith, Lady Dorrian, IH (Ex Div).

2443 Court rules–Simple procedure cases–Procedure to be followed

ACT OF SEDERUNT (SIMPLE PROCEDURE) 2016, SSI 2016/200; made under the Scottish Commission for Human Rights Act 2006 s.14)7); Courts Reform (Scotland) Act 2014 104(1). In force: 28 November 2016.

This Act of Sederunt makes provision about the procedure to be followed in simple procedure cases. It comes into force on 28 November 2016, when the first set of cases will become subject to simple procedure. Those will be cases which formerly would have proceeded as a small claim, but which have a value of £5,000 or less.

2444 Courts Reform (Scotland) Act 2014 (asp 18)–Commencement No.7, Transitional and Saving Provisions Order

THE COURTS REFORM (SCOTLAND) ACT 2014 (COMMENCEMENT NO.7, TRANSITIONAL AND SAVING PROVISIONS) ORDER 2016, SSI 2016/291; made under the Courts Reform (Scotland) Act 2014 s.138(2)(3). Commencement details: bringing into operation various provisions of the Courts Reform (Scotland) Act 2014 on 28 November 2016.

This Order brings into force provisions of the Courts Reform (Scotland) Act 2014. The provisions specified in column 1 of the table in the schedule of the Order come into force on 28th November 2016.

2445 Expenses–Abandonment–Abandonment of action seeking appointment of enforcement administrator–No obvious miscarriage of justice

[Proceeds of Crime Act 2002 (c.29) s.128, s.92; Misuse of Drugs Act 1971 (c.38) s.4(3)(b); Proceeds of Crime (Scotland) Act 1995 (c.43); Act of Sederunt (Rules of the Court of Session 1994) 1994 Sch.2 para.29.1, Sch.2 para.29.3; Legal Aid (Scotland) Act 1986 (c.47) s.17; Civil Legal Aid (Scotland) Regulations 2002 (SSI 2002/494) reg.40]

The partner (M) of a convicted person (X) reclaimed against an interlocutor of the Lord Ordinary refusing her motion for expenses against the Lord Advocate in his petition seeking the appointment of an enforcement administrator under the Proceeds of Crime Act 2002 s.128. In September 2009, X had been convicted of being concerned in the supply of controlled drugs, contrary to the Misuse of Drugs Act 1971 s.4(3)(b), and on 20 August 2010, the High Court had made a confiscation order of £20,000 in respect of X in terms of s.92 of the 2002 Act, which had been erroneously stated as having been imposed under the repealed Proceeds of Crime (Scotland) Act 1995 and was consequent upon a joint minute entered into between X and the Lord Advocate which had agreed X's proceeds of crime at approximately £225,000, with his realisable assets being £20,000 equity in a house (H) owned by M. X had failed to pay within the prescribed period and the Lord Advocate had sought the appointment of an enforcement administrator, however, the hearing of 16 May 2014 had been discharged and prior to the next hearing date, X had paid the balance. On the Lord Advocate's motion, the petition was dismissed and X was found liable in the expenses of the Lord Advocate. M submitted that (1) the Lord Ordinary had erred in exercising his discretion under Act of Sederunt (Rules of the Court of Session 1994) 1994 Sch.2 para.29.3 where the usual consequences of abandonment of an action was payment of the expenses, such payment was required by r.29.1(2) as a condition precedent to decree of dismissal and there was no distinguishing factor in the present proceedings by reason of them having been brought by petition; (2) H was not realisable property, having been registered in M's name, and the petition had not stated that it was a tainted gift; (3) the confiscation order was incompetent where it bore to be under the repealed 1995 Act; (4) the Lord Ordinary had failed to give proper weight to the fact that M might lose H by virtue of the legal aid claw back provisions in the Legal Aid

(Scotland) Act 1986 s.17 and the Civil Legal Aid (Scotland) Regulations 2002 reg.40(3)(iv).

Held: Reclaiming motion refused. (1) Rule of Court 29.3(2) provided that the court might grant a motion for abandonment of a petition subject to such conditions as to expenses or otherwise, and the penalty as to expenses to be imposed upon a petitioner who had abandoned his petition was wholly within the discretion of the judge; in that context, there was no requirement to award M her expenses, even had the case involved abandonment of the petition, which it had not, it had ceased to have practical merit because X had paid the money and the petition had been dismissed on that basis and where the petition had been necessitated by X's failure to pay, M's expenses ought to fall on him, however, M had made no such application. (2) It had been reasonable for the Lord Advocate to proceed on the basis that H had been acquired by M with the assistance of funds provided by X, M's title had been registered on 29 November 2005 and where the criminal proceedings had been instituted against X in February 2009, H might have fell to be regarded as a tainted gift; prior to the petition, the court had granted restraint orders against X and M, identifying H as realisable property, which M had not challenged. (3) The confiscation proceedings had proceeded in terms of the Proceeds of Crime Act 2002, there was no suggestion that the erroneous heading had given rise to any confusion or dubiety as to what was required and the error in the date of the statute could not be accepted as carrying the effect contended for, in any event, the order had been satisfied on or before 11 December 2014, and that being so, there was no live issue carrying any practical consequences. (4) The application of the legal aid claw back provisions was not a relevant factor and the manner in which M chose to enter the proceedings and her funding arrangements were immaterial. (5) In the whole circumstances, there was no manifest injustice in the Lord Ordinary's interlocutor such as would justify interference by the court and the order of no expenses due to or by either the Lord Advocate or M was appropriate. *Observed*, that reclaiming motions solely on a question of expenses were severely discouraged and ought not to be entertained except where there had been an obvious miscarriage of justice; expenses were incidental to a cause and the terms of an award were at the discretion of the judge before whom the cause had been heard, *Miller v Chivas Brothers Ltd* [2014] CSIH 65, 2015 S.C. 85, [2015] C.L.Y. 2895 and *Caldwell v Dykes (Expenses)* (1906) 8 F. 839, *considered.*

LORD ADVOCATE v MACKIE *sub nom.* LORD ADVOCATE v MCCOLM, [2015] CSIH 88, 2016 S.L.T. 118, The Lord Justice Clerk (Carloway), Lord Bracadale, Lord Malcolm, IH (2 Div).

2446 Expenses–Junior counsel–Settlement of personal injuries action–Reasonableness of employment of counsel

[Courts Reform (Scotland) Act 2014 (asp 18) s.108]

Following the settlement of an action of damages raised by the parent and guardian (V) of a child (X), aged 11, against theme park premises owners (M), V moved under the Courts Reform (Scotland) Act 2014 s.108 to certify the cause as suitable for the employment of junior counsel. On 12 October 2014, X had slipped on wooden steps at M's premises and the exposed metal tip of a golf club which he had been carrying had pierced his chin. X had required stitches, had required to attend the plastic surgery outpatient clinic for approximately a year, and had suffered permanent facial disfigurement which might require further corrective surgery. V had intimated a claim on 2 February 2015, M had intimated that liability was not accepted, the action was raised in October 2015 and a proof allocated for June 2016. On 29 December 2015, V's agents had instructed junior counsel to consult, adjust and value the claim, which had resulted in a consultation, the drafting by counsel of substantial adjustments, a specification for the recovery of documents and a statement of valuation of the claim. On 21 January 2016, a tender of £10,000 was lodged, and following a further consultation, the action had settled for £12,500.

Held: Motion granted. (1) The reasonableness test was of objective reasonableness considered at the time of the motion, having regard to both V and M's interests, and s.108(3) required the court to have regard to whether the proceedings were such as to merit the employment of counsel and the desirability of ensuring that no party gained an unfair advantage by virtue of the employment of counsel, and in relation to the former, the court had to have particular regard to the difficulty or complexity or likely difficulty or complexity of the proceedings and the importance or value of any claim in the proceedings. (2) Applying the s.108 approach to the present case: the proceedings had not been especially difficult or complex and had not been such as to merit the employment of counsel on their own, consideration of likely complexity was not apposite where the case had been concluded and the actual complexity was known, despite X's age and the unpleasant nature of the injury, the claim had no greater importance to him than to any other pursuer, and there was no suggestion that V had gained an unfair advantage by virtue of having employed counsel; however, where liability had been disputed, V had had to approach the matter on the assumption that the case would have required to go to proof on both liability and quantum, consequently, X would have required to give evidence about both the accident and his injury, and given the permanent and obvious nature of his injury, he might have found that difficult and special skill would have been required in taking his evidence effectively, accordingly, it was reasonable to have any proof conducted by counsel, and the proceedings had been such as to merit the employment of counsel. (3) Although no proof had been fixed by the time the action had settled, it would have been unreasonable to expect X to have coped with the introduction into the case, at a late stage, of counsel whom he had not previously met, thus it was reasonable to sanction the employment of counsel for all the work which he had been instructed to do, at the time he had been instructed to do it.

J'S PARENT AND GUARDIAN v M & D (LEISURE) LTD, 2016 S.L.T. (Sh Ct) 185, Sheriff P J Braid, Sh Ct (Lothian) (Edinburgh).

2447 Expenses–Junior counsel–Settlement of personal injuries action–Sanction for junior counsel for single consultation

[Courts Reform (Scotland) Act 2014 (asp 18) s.108]

Following the settlement of a personal injuries action raised by D against her employers (M) for injury sustained to her elbow during the course of her employment, D lodged a motion *inter alia* seeking sanction for junior counsel, which M opposed. Sanction was sought for the purpose of a single consultation by D with junior counsel in January 2016, which had been decided by D's principal agent (X), who had precognosed D and who was an experienced solicitor with particular knowledge and experience in relation to personal injury cases, where valuation of D's claim had been complex due to the wide variation of possible figures for loss of employability, and given the importance of the value of the claim to D where she suffered from a pre-existing blood disorder and was properly to be regarded as disabled for the purposes of discrimination legislation, she and her husband were reliant on her income to live and there was a threat of redundancy.

Held: Motion granted. (1) Having regard to the Courts Reform (Scotland) Act 2014 s.108, and considering all the available information, in the circumstances of the case, the proceedings were such as to merit the employment of counsel for the purposes of the single consultation, and it had been reasonable for X to have employed counsel for that purpose; the complexity of the issue of loss of employability, and the particular importance and value of the case to D had been such that it was reasonable to sanction the employment of counsel for the limited purpose of the January 2016 consultation. (2) Sanction would be granted for junior counsel's employment for the purposes of the opposed motion.

DOW v M & D CROLLA LTD, 2016 S.L.T. (Sh Ct) 191, Sheriff F L Reith, QC, Sh Ct (Lothian) (Edinburgh).

2448 Expenses–Lands Tribunal for Scotland–Tenant unsuccessful in right to buy litigation–Whether landlord's conduct justified departure from general expenses rule

[Housing (Scotland) Act 1987 (c.26) s.62, s.71; Housing (Scotland) Act 2001 (asp 10) s.49]

A secure tenant (B) and a housing authority landlord (S) each moved for expenses against the other following dismissal by the Lands Tribunal (L) of B's application in terms of the Housing (Scotland) Act 1987 s.71 (*Boyle v South Lanarkshire Council*

2015 S.L.T. (Lands Tr) 189, [2015] 9 C.L. 302). L had found that B had not been entitled to a discount based upon the preserved right to buy as originally provided under s.62 of the 1987 Act, but rather on the less favourable provisions of s.62 as amended by the Housing (Scotland) Act 2001 s.49, after B had been prioritised for relocation by S due to being subjected to antisocial behaviour. B submitted that (1) recourse to L was not normal litigation, and had S complied with its duties to adequately and effectively deal with the antisocial tenants, she would have remained at her previous address and would have had no difficulty in retaining the discount under the preserved right to buy scheme; (2) B was of limited means; (3) any expenses granted to S ought to be restricted to those permitted to a party litigant.

Held: B's motion dismissed and S's motion granted. (1) The general rule was that expenses followed success unless some element of the successful party's conduct which required to be taken into account pointed to a different conclusion, however, no conduct by S had been established to justify a departure from the general rule; the root cause of the general dispute was S's alleged inability to deal with antisocial behaviour, it was not the immediate cause of the litigation, which concerned a dispute about the statutory formula for the discount. (2) There appeared to be no rule that impecuniosity was a reason for withholding expenses. (3) S could not be treated as a party litigant; it had been represented by its in house solicitor and there was no basis for drawing a distinction between in house and independent solicitors, *Ladak v DRC Locums Ltd* [2014] I.R.L.R. 851, [2014] C.L.Y. 1073, *Wiggins Alloys v Jenkins* [1981] I.R.L.R. 372 and *MacBeth Currie & Co v Matthew* 1985 S.L.T. (Sh. Ct.) 44, [1985] C.L.Y. 4136, *considered*.

BOYLE v SOUTH LANARKSHIRE COUNCIL, 2015 S.L.T. (Lands Tr) 205, R A Smith, QC, A Oswald, FRICS, Lands Tr (Scot).

2449 Expenses–Modification–Employee's claim for damages–Employee's conduct depriving defender of opportunity of pre-litigation settlement

G moved for decree in terms of a minute of tender and acceptance in his action of damages against his employers (M), which M opposed. M submitted that G's motion for expenses ought to be refused and those modified to nil; the litigation had been premature and unnecessary and G's conduct had been unreasonable in that he had failed to disclose to M the available medical reports prior to raising a Court of Session action against them, and M's insurers (X) had been put to the expense of framing defences, X had sought to resolve the case by admitting liability early, and were signatories to the protocol, of which G had been aware, G had refused to disclose the medical evidence even after the Court of Session action had been raised on the basis that earnings information was unavailable, without which a proper valuation of the claim was impossible, however, it represented only 4% of the settlement figure, and *Brown v Sabre Insurance Co Ltd* [2014] CSOH 51, 2014 G.W.D. 18-342 was distinguishable as there had been a refusal to follow the protocol. G submitted *inter alia* that without the earnings information, his claim could not be properly valued, there had been disclosure of pre-accident earnings but no voluntary disclosure of his post accident earnings by M, and even had the medical reports been disclosed, it would not have been possible to value the claim in the absence of earnings information.

Held: Motion granted. (1) M had made numerous efforts to obtain information from G, which, taken with the early admission of liability, ought to have made it apparent that M were seeking to value the claim and negotiate a resolution. (2) When the Court of Session action had been raised, liability had been admitted, M had sought in vain to obtain information about valuation of the claim, G's agents (Y) knew, or ought to have known, that M were seeking to resolve the matter without litigation, G had medical reports which had not been disclosed to M, G had given M no ultimatum or time limit in correspondence, and where the justification for raising the Court of Session proceedings had been M's failure to provide up to date earnings information, although M had failed to provide the information, they had not refused to do so, to allow only four weeks to elapse between requesting the earnings information and raising the Court of Session proceedings against a background of co-operation and the absence of any reminder, time limit, ultimatum, or threat of proceedings, could not properly be justified, and Y had made no inquiry themselves as to G's earnings; had it been thought necessary to proceed with the action to recover earnings information, it would have been appropriate to give a specific warning that was the information sought not produced timeously, proceedings would ensue, and it had been unreasonable of G to commence court proceedings at that stage without further warning. (3) The medical evidence could, and ought to, have been disclosed before the Court of Session and present actions had been raised, and the failure to do so was inexcusable. (4) Had the medical evidence been disclosed at the correct time, M would have been able to value the claim, despite other information being incomplete, and had a pre-litigation offer been made, Y would have been bound to take instructions thereon, however, against that had to be balanced the fact that earnings information had still not been produced by M prior to the raising of the present action and that M had in effect issued an invitation to M's agents to proceed with a specification of documents. (5) The failure to disclose the medical reports had been unreasonable and had deprived X of a genuine opportunity to settle the claim pre-litigation, and there had been a reasonable chance that had disclosure been made, the claim would have been capable of settlement, however, although Y's conduct had been such that the court ought to mark its disapproval thereof, given that the chance of pre-litigation settlement could not be quantified with precision and that the failure to disclose the medical reports had not been the sole cause of the litigation and its attendant costs, G's motion would be granted but the award of expenses modified by two thirds.

GIBSON v MENZIES AVIATION (UK) LTD, 2016 S.L.T. (Sh Ct) 179, Sheriff K J McGowan, Sh Ct (Lothian) (Edinburgh).

2450 Expenses–Protective costs orders–Variation–Expenses of reclaiming motion

In the course of a petition by the owner (G) of an estate for judicial review of a decision of the Scottish Ministers (S) not to hold a public inquiry and to grant consent for the construction and operation of a wind farm to an energy company (C), in which G had been granted a protective expenses order by the Inner House, having successfully reclaimed against the Lord Ordinary's refusal thereof, G moved the court to (i) find S and C jointly and severally liable in expenses, (ii) award G an additional fee under Rule of Court 42.14(a), (b), (c), (e), and (g), (iii) have the expenses made payable separately from the sums in the protective expenses order (*Gibson v Scottish Ministers* [2016] CSIH 10, 2016 S.L.T. 319, [2016] 2451).

Held: Motion granted in part. (1) There was no basis for any modification of the general award of expenses in G's favour, the fact that a particular point might not have been fully raised, or raised at all, in the Outer House was of little moment where G was ultimately successful in obtaining his protective expenses order, his motion had been opposed by S and C and he was entitled to an award of expenses against them. (2) G's application had been relatively straightforward and the fact that parties had elected to lodge substantial documentation, and to analyse it in depth, had not implied that those documents, or the analysis, were reasonably required for the resolution of the issue, and the court was not satisfied that grounds for an additional fee had been made out in relation to any of the heads claimed, in any event, the recoverable fees might be a matter for the auditor to determine should the parties proceed to taxation and in so doing, the auditor would have regard to the fact that applications ought to be dealt with expeditiously, upon limited material in a relatively short motion roll hearing. (3) Having regard to the principles of the Aarhus Convention, the expenses of the reclaiming motion and the Outer House ought not to be encompassed in the figures determined, and an order, that the ceiling of £30,000 referred to in the interlocutor ought not to include the expenses of obtaining the order, would be pronounced.

GIBSON v SCOTTISH MINSTERS, [2016] CSIH 31, 2016 S.L.T. 675, The Lord President (Carloway), Lady Paton, Lord Menzies, IH (1 Div).

2451 Expenses–Protective costs orders–Whether proceedings prohibitively expensive–Lord Ordinary failing to properly consider subjective and objective tests

[Act of Sederunt (Rules of the Court of Session 1994) 1994 Sch.2]

The owner (G) of an estate reclaimed against the refusal of his motion for a protective expenses order in the course of his petition for judicial review of a decision by the Scottish Ministers (S) not to hold a public inquiry and to grant consent for the construction and operation of a wind farm (*Gibson v Scottish Ministers* [2015] CSOH 41, 2015 G.W.D. 13-224). The wind farm development was located approximately 4.2 km from the main house and the nearest proposed turbine would be 4.6 km from the Scottish Dark Sky Observatory which was located within the boundary of the estate and said to be one of only eight dark sky parks in the world. The anticipated cost of the litigation was estimated at £173,000 and significant evidence was led relating to G's financial circumstances and the estate.

Held: Reclaiming motion allowed and protective expenses order granted. It was clear that when considering whether proceedings were prohibitively expensive for the applicant in terms of the Act of Sederunt (Rules of the Court of Session 1994) 1994 Sch.2 Ch.58A, the court had to apply both a subjective and an objective test, but the Lord Ordinary, in his consideration of the former, appeared to have addressed whether G was able to meet the expenses when the test was whether it was reasonable that G be required to do so, and he did not appear to have considered the latter which rendered the matter open to review: while G might have been considered a wealthy man, having regard to his individual circumstances, including the fact that the worth of his estate lay in its unfragmented state, thus to sell parts of it to fund the proceedings would be to destroy exactly what G sought to preserve, G's only income was £18,000 which he drew annually from the estate, and that it would have been unreasonable to require him to withdraw £170,000 from his pension fund, the proceedings were prohibitively expensive and a protective expenses order should be made; applying the objective test, G's individual economic interests were unlikely to be significantly affected by either the wind farm development or the proceedings, the importance of what was at stake for the protection of the environment was considerable and having regard to all the factors and the fact that it was not disputed that the total costs might exceed £170,000, the proceedings were prohibitively expensive, *R. (on the application of Edwards) v Environment Agency* [2013] UKSC 78, [2014] 1 W.L.R. 55, [2014] C.L.Y. 333, *European Commission v United Kingdom (C-530/11)* EU:C:2014:67, [2014] Q.B. 988, [2014] C.L.Y. 1222, and *Carroll v Scottish Borders Council* [2014] CSOH 30, 2014 S.L.T. 659, [2014] C.L.Y. 3338, *considered. Opinion*, that concern had to be expressed for the length of time that the application had taken and the expense incurred by the lengthy hearings before both the present court and the Lord Ordinary: applications for a protective expenses order had been few and far between in Scotland but considering the particular circumstances of the case, a more expeditious disposal ought to have been achieved; it was hoped that such applications could be disposed of more quickly in the future with submissions for all parties being concluded within a total of 1.5 hours, they ought to be dealt with by motion with a limited amount of documentary material required in support thereof, it was not an opportunity for a respondent to subject an applicant to intrusive and detailed investigation of financial circumstances, and the court ought to be able to give an immediate *ex tempore* judgment.

GIBSON v SCOTTISH MINISTERS, [2016] CSIH 10, 2016 S.L.T. 319, Lady Paton, Lord Menzies, Lady Clark of Calton, IH (Ex Div).

2452 Expenses–Scottish Legal Aid Board–Payment out of Scottish Legal Aid Fund–Whether just and equitable

[Legal Aid (Scotland) Act 1986 (c.47) s.19(1); Act of Sederunt (Civil Legal Aid Rules) 1987 (SI 1987/492) r.6]

The Secretary of State for the Home Department (S) moved for expenses following her successful reclaiming motion against a decision of the Lord Ordinary setting aside her rejection of an asylum application by a Pakistani national (X) (*AAA (Pakistan) v Secretary of State for the Home Department* [2015] CSIH 31, 2015 S.C. 602, [2015] C.L.Y. 3144). The motion consisted of three parts: the first to find X liable in the expenses of the reclaiming motion as taxed, the second concerned expenses in the Outer House, and in the third S sought an order in terms of the Legal Aid (Scotland) Act 1986 s.19(1) requiring payment out of the Scottish Legal Aid Fund (F) on the basis that it was just and equitable in all the circumstances. The first part was granted but only to the extent of finding X liable in the expenses of the reclaiming motion as an assisted person, and the second part was granted by interlocutor in which X was found liable for Outer House expenses as an assisted person and his liability was modified to nil. S was ordered to lodge a statement on oath of the grounds for claiming payment of expenses out of F and an account of expenses, and to intimate all relevant documents and a copy of the motion to the Scottish Legal Aid Board (B), which had been delayed until that point because of the relevant terms of the Act of Sederunt (Civil Legal Aid Rules) 1987 r.6. B submitted that (1) it should not be regarded as *dominus litus* where it did not run the litigation and in ordinary course was not found liable in expenses; (2) s.19 of the 1986 Act afforded a wide discretion, S had to satisfy its threshold criteria and it was not enough to have won; (3) S's approach was flawed in that it inverted the onus where S was required to show why it was just and equitable to make the award; (4) although in *B v Secretary of State for the Home Department* [2015] CSIH 43, 2015 S.C. 667, [2015] C.L.Y. 2896 the court had departed from any suggestion that an award should not be made in favour of one public body against another, the fact that the payment would be made from public funds was relevant; (5) B had a statutory function for the securing of legal advice and assistance and it could not refuse to fund a party where the relevant statutory criteria were satisfied.

Held: (1) Although expenses would be paid from a government agency to a department of government, that was not a factor which pointed to it being unjust or inequitable to make the award, nor was it one which carried any weight, *B v Secretary of State for the Home Department* and *Bell v Fife CC* 1975 S.L.T. (Notes) 4, [1975] C.L.Y. 3803, *considered.* (2) An application under s.19(1) could be made where the appellate stage was caused by the unassisted party and, if that party could show that it was just and equitable to grant it, the court could do so. (3) The normal rule that expenses followed success weighed in favour of granting the application, and S was entitled to have the court take into account that had X also been unassisted, he would have been found liable in the usual way without the protection of legal aid. S's winning argument was clearly articulated in both the grounds of appeal and her note of argument, which gave B repeated opportunities to assess the likelihood of X being able to resist the reclaiming motion and whether it was appropriate for opposition to be maintained at public expense. (4) The purpose of s.19(1) was to enable the court to do justice by making the funder pay even though that funder did not direct the litigation, and by granting the application there was no question of the court holding B to be *dominus litus.* (5) Nothing set out in the statement on oath or articulated by S in oral submission involved an inversion of onus, the case advanced was that the circumstances demonstrated that it was just and equitable to grant the application and that was sufficient. (6) Although B was fulfilling its statutory duty, that did not mean that it could not be found liable under s.19(1), and S had demonstrated that it was just and equitable to grant the application and make an award against B in relation to the whole expenses of the reclaiming motion. Observed, that an application for expenses under s.19(1) could be streamlined to operate more efficiently: there was no good reason for delaying intimation to B until the second stage where it had an interest from the outset, and no requirement to have a two stage process or the formality of a statement on oath; it might suffice for a note to accompany the motion setting out why the applicant considered it just and equitable that the award be made.

A v SECRETARY OF STATE FOR THE HOME DEPARTMENT *sub nom.* AAA (PAKISTAN) v SECRETARY OF STATE FOR THE HOME DEPARTMENT, [2016] CSIH 1, 2016 S.L.T. 353, Lord Menzies, Lady Smith, Lord McGhie, IH (Ex Div).

2453 Jury directions–Objections–Pursuer intimating desire to take exception to judge's charge–Jury deliberations already in progress

[Act of Sederunt (Rules of the Court of Session 1994) 1994 Sch.2 para.37.7]

In the course of an action for damages by a pedestrian (B) against the insurers of a driver (D) whose vehicle had struck her, an exception was taken by B to the Lord Ordinary's charge to the jury on the appropriate level of damages for solatium. The action had proceeded to jury trial and at the close of the evidence, in accordance with the procedure described in *Hamilton v Ferguson Transport (Spean Bridge) Ltd* [2012] CSIH 52, 2012 S.C. 486, [2012] C.L.Y. 4206, the Lord Ordinary had invited parties to address on the appropriate level of damages for solatium. The Lord Ordinary declined B's invitation to provide the jury with the widest possible range into which her case might fall, taking the view that the procedure recommended in *Hamilton* had intended to provide an opportunity for parties to assist the judge in his guidance to the jury rather than the other way around. At the close of the judge's charge, the jury was invited to retire and consider their verdict on the issue and counter issue which had been lodged and approved, at which stage, neither party had sought to take exception. After the jury had been deliberating for over an hour, B had intimated her desire to take exception to the charge on the basis that the range suggested to the jury was too low and amounted to a misdirection which could be cured by a supplementary direction. The Lord Ordinary had refused either to record and certify a note of exception or to give any further directions to the jury, and issued a note in response to a request by counsel in case it might be of assistance in the development of post-*Hamilton* practice in civil jury trials.

Held: Note issued. (1) B's intimation of her desire to take exception came too late where the Act of Sederunt (Rules of the Court of Session 1994) 1994 Sch.2 para.37.7 explicitly required intimation to be made immediately on the conclusion of the charge, similarly, r.37.7(3) envisaged that any further directions be given before the jury considered its verdict, and there was no scope for latitude in interpretation of the word "immediately" in post-*Hamilton* practice; in any event, interruption of the jury in the course of their discussions might result in their attaching undue weight to the supplementary direction at a late stage in their assessment of the evidence. (2) B's proposed exception did not relate to a direction on a point of law as required by r.37.7: as a generality, non-binding guidance to the jury on quantification of damages was not a direction in law; *Hamilton* required the trial judge to expressly inform the jury that the spectrum suggested was for their assistance only, which was met in the present case; no issue of law had arisen in the circumstances of the case and no relevant basis had been advanced for the recording and certification of a note of exception, *Hamilton*, *considered*.

BRIDGES v ALPHA INSURANCE A/S, [2016] CSOH 114, 2016 S.L.T. 859, Lord Tyre, OH.

2454 Limitation periods–Fatal accident claims–Death following diving accident–Action for damages under Athens Convention 1974

[Athens Convention relating to the Carriage of Passengers and their Luggage by Sea 1974; Prescription and Limitation (Scotland) Act 1973 (c.52) s.18, s.18(2), s.18(3)]

The widow (W) of a diver (X) raised an action of damages against the owners and operators (S) of a vessel in respect of X's death following a diving accident. X had chartered the vessel for a one week diving trip commencing 11 August 2012 and had died on 14 August 2012, and it was agreed that he would have disembarked no later than 18 August 2012. On 17 April 2013, W's agents (M) had written to S and had intimated a claim for damages on behalf of W and her child and on 14 May 2015, the action had been signetted. W averred that she had not been aware that X's death had been caused by an act or omission attributable to S until the publication of an accident investigation report in December 2013. The action came to debate before the Lord Ordinary on S's preliminary plea that the action had become time barred on 18 August 2014 where actions for damages under the Athens Convention 1974 required to be brought within two years in terms of art.16.1. W submitted *inter alia* that (1) art.16.3 provided that the law of the court seized of the case ought to govern the grounds for suspension and interruption of limitation periods; (2) W had not become aware that liability was attributable to S until December 2013, and in terms of s.18(2)(b) that was when the action had accrued; (3) W's claim on behalf of her son had been interrupted through nonage in terms of the Prescription and Limitation (Scotland) Act 1973 s.18(3). S submitted that (1) art.16 was a limitation period not a prescription; (2) the Athens Convention regulated the start dates for the running of the time period and s.18 did not apply thereto.

Held: Action dismissed. (1) The commencement of the time period was governed by art.16.2 and not by s.18(2) of the 1973 Act, to hold otherwise would be to invert the rule of statutory construction; *Martin (Sean) v HM Advocate* [2010] UKSC 10, 2010 S.C. (U.K.S.C.) 40, [2010] C.L.Y. 533, *considered*. (2) Section 18(2) set out commencement dates from which the three year time period ran but did not suspend or interrupt a time period which was already in train, *Higham v Stena Sealink Ltd* [1996] 1 W.L.R. 1107, [1996] C.L.Y. 825, *considered*. (3) Section 18(3) related to the computation of the time period in s.18(2) and could not apply to other standalone provisions in other enactments, in any event, nonage was not a suspension or interruption of a time period already in train, and the action was time barred. *Opinion*, that M's letter dated 17 April 2013 had demonstrated the requisite knowledge for the purposes of s.18(2).

WARNER v SCAPA FLOW CHARTERS, [2016] CSOH 101, 2016 S.L.T. 918, Lord Boyd of Duncansby, OH.

2455 Limitations–Defamation claims–Clear claim made by way of formally stated plea to court of proper jurisdiction–Whether sufficient to interrupt running of prescription

[Prescription and Limitation (Scotland) Act 1973 (c.52) s.18A, s.19A, s.6; European Convention on Human Rights 1950 art.6(1)]

An insured (W) reclaimed against a decision of the Lord Ordinary granting declarator that any obligations on the part of a specialist insurance company (E) arising under W's insurance policy had been extinguished in terms of the Prescription and Limitation (Scotland) Act 1973 s.6 and dismissing W's counterclaim for defamation (*Ecclesiastical Insurance Office Plc v Whitehouse-Grant-Christ* [2015] CSOH 23, 2015 G.W.D. 7-140). In 2000, W submitted an insurance claim arising from a fire at her home, E rejected the claim on the basis that it was entitled to repudiate the policy on the grounds of non-disclosure and it raised an action seeking to avoid the policy. W defended the action and set out her reasons for disputing E's right to avoid the policy. In 2002, she intimated adjustments and included a plea that decree should be granted requiring E to perform its obligations under the policy, and the action was sisted at her instance to allow her to apply for legal aid. W suffered from ill health thereafter, E made no attempt to recall the sist, and in 2012, W lodged a counterclaim which included the defamation claim. In terms of the counterclaim, the Lord Ordinary held that there was no timeous claim under s.18A of the 1973 Act, and his refusal to exercise discretion under s.19A was based on an assessment of the claim's value and the fact that there had been no indication that W had sought any remedy against the newspapers involved in the alleged defamation. E submitted *inter alia* that before a claim could be accepted as a relevant claim within the meaning of s.6 it had to be a claim by way of a conclusion in an initiating writ or in a proper counterclaim. W submitted *inter alia* that (1) the Lord Ordinary had erred in the exercise of his discretion not to permit her to bring the defamation action late and override the time limit in terms of s.19A of the 1973 Act; (2) her rights under ECHR art.6(1) had been breached because of the long delay and E's failure to prosecute its claim.

Held: Case put out by order. (1) W's plea was capable of falling within the language of s.6 of the 1973 Act and was sufficient to interrupt the running of prescription: it was a relevant claim in the sense that it was a claim related to enforcement of the specific obligation in dispute, namely E's obligation to indemnify under the policy, it had been made in appropriate proceedings where it was a plea asking a court of competent jurisdiction for a remedy, there was nothing in the 1973 Act which required the claim to be made in a particular form and the precise form of any claim made in defences was a procedural matter determined by subordinate legislation; all that was needed to serve the legislation's purpose, of a means of extinguishing stale claims while preserving claims insisted on in a formal way, was plain notice, E was aware at all times that W was seeking to be indemnified and no question of prejudice arose, *Highlands and Islands Airports Ltd v Shetland Islands Council* [2015] CSIH 30, 2015 S.C. 588, [2015] C.L.Y. 2927 and *Link Housing Association Ltd v PBL Construction Ltd* [2009] CSIH 54, 2009 S.C. 653, [2010] C.L.Y. 3996, *considered*. (2) The Lord Ordinary was entitled to conclude that there was no adequate explanation for the delay in bringing the proceedings, he was entitled to look at the whole period of delay, to take account of the potential measure of damages and to consider whether W should have been allowed to make a claim out of time against one wrongdoer rather than another, and his decision under s.19A was one he was entitled to make and there was no justification for interfering therewith. (3) There was no basis upon which W's contention that the action be dismissed because of delay could succeed where she had the dominant interest in the outcome of the litigation, the cause had been sisted on her motion and she could have recalled the sist at any time, she had not set forth any basis upon which the delay had prejudiced her ability to deal with the issues in dispute, and no breach of her rights under art.6 could be identified. (4) The Lord Ordinary's interlocutor would be recalled, a proof before answer would be required to deal with the merits, the case would be put out be order for further hearing, and the counterclaim would be sisted until the principal action was decided.

ECCLESIASTICAL INSURANCE OFFICE PLC v WHITEHOUSE-GRANT-CHRIST, 2016 S.L.T. 990, Lady Paton, Lord Drummond Young, Lord McGhie, IH (Ex Div).

2456 Limitations–Knowledge–Solicitors' allegedly defective drafting of notices to quit–Pursuer's awareness of loss

[Prescription and Limitation (Scotland) Act 1973 (c.52) s.11(3), s.6]

The owners (T) of three fields (Z) reclaimed against a decision of the Lord Ordinary granting decree of absolvitor in their action of damages against their solicitors (C) (*Gordon's Trustees v Campbell Riddle Breeze Paterson LLP* [2015] CSOH 31, 2015 G.W.D. 12-216). C had advised T to bring existing agricultural tenancies over Z to an end in 2004 and T had instructed C to serve notices to quit on the tenant (X), to take effect on 10 November 2005, however, X had not complied therewith and in February 2006, T had lodged three applications with the Scottish land court seeking X's removal. On 24 July 2008, the land court had refused T's applications in respect of two of Z on the ground that there were defects in the notices to quit. On 17 May 2012, T had raised their action against C on account of C's alleged breach of contract by drafting ineffective notices to quit. C averred *inter alia* that any obligation incumbent on them to make reparation to T had prescribed in terms of the Prescription and Limitation (Scotland) Act 1973 s.6, placing particular reliance on the fact that the heads of loss included legal fees paid to C prior to May 2007 in respect of the land court proceedings. The Lord Ordinary found that on the strength of *David T Morrison & Co Ltd (t/a Gael Home Interiors) v ICL Plastics Ltd* [2014] UKSC 48, 2014 S.C. (U.K.S.C.) 222, [2014] C.L.Y. 2470, it was not relevant to prove that until the land court decision, T could not have regarded the legal expenses as a loss, to do otherwise was to introduce a subjective consideration which had no place in terms of s.11(3) of the 1973 Act, and the obligation to pay the bills had not been latent damage, thus the prescriptive period had begun when T had known that they had incurred a liability in respect of the fees and outlays, not when they had become aware that they had sustained a compensatable loss in the reparation sense.

Held: Reclaiming motion refused. Section 11(3) of the 1973 Act addressed only latent damage, given T's knowledge of the costs, they could not easily be categorised as latent damage, and it was not possible to uphold T's appeal and remain consistent with Lord Reed's reasoning in *David T Morrison*; the *injuria* was the service of the defective notices and the *damnum* included the liability in legal fees, which had been paid more than five years prior to the commencement of the action; it was not the task of the present court to evaluate the competing views expressed in *David T Morrison* but rather to understand and, if applicable, follow the approach of the majority, and an application of the interpretation of s.11(3) adopted by the majority in that case required that T's reclaiming motion be refused, *Dunlop v McGowans* 1980 S.C. (H.L.) 73, [1980] C.L.Y. 3497, *applied*. Per Lady Paton, that T had been alerted to the fact that something had gone wrong by C's letter of 10 November 2005, therefore, as soon as T had received it, they had had clear intimation that they were suffering, and would continue to suffer, loss, injury or damage. Opinion, that the Supreme Court Justices might reach a different view on the present, or a similar, case, they might opine that the intention in *David T Morrison* was to confine the latent/patent analysis to cases where it would be apparent to anyone who was aware of the circumstances now claimed to be a recoverable head of loss, that they represented an injurious event, or at least something untoward such as would prompt inquiry into the cause and might take the view that the circumstances of the present case were not covered by the reasoning and the decision in *David T Morrison*, *David T Morrison, followed*.

GORDON'S TRUSTEES v CAMPBELL RIDDLE BREEZE PATERSON LLP, [2016] CSIH 16, 2016 S.L.T. 580, Lady Paton, Lord Bracadale, Lord Malcolm, IH (Ex Div).

2457 Multiplepoinding–Proceeds of sale–Solicitors' firm raising action of multiplepoinding in relation to sale proceeds of heritable property owned by company–No joint and unequivocal instruction from company's directors and shareholders

A solicitors' firm (M) raised an action of multiplepoinding seeking *inter alia* judicial authority for the consignation of sale proceeds in the hands of the sheriff clerk. M had acted for a company (W) in the sale of its heritable property which had generated free proceeds of £229,000. W's two directors and equal shareholders (B and D, collectively X) had had a disagreement and M averred that it had no joint and unequivocal instruction from X, as W's agents, regarding disbursement of the sale proceeds. D submitted that the action was incompetent as (1) there were no competing claims to the sale proceeds; the admitted rightful recipient was W itself; (2) M merely held the sale proceeds as W's agent; (3) M was not exposed to double distress.

Held: Case put out by order. (1) Over the years, the prerequisite for double diligence, that the holder of the fund required to be subject to multiple arrestments or poindings, appeared to have been modified such that mulitplepoinding was now competent where there was a double claim, namely, competing claims to one fund on separate and hostile grounds, however, a practice had developed whereby, when considering the competency of a multiplepoinding, a much greater latitude was afforded to a pursuer who was the holder of the fund and asserted no claim thereon, *W. G. L. Winchester v John W. Blakey* (1890) 17 R. 1046, *considered*. (2) M were entitled to raise an action of multiplepoinding: (i) having obtained the money on W's behalf, as its client, M held the fund *in medio* in trust for W and was obliged to account to it therefor but those in whose power it was to permit W to receive the fund and grant a discharge in M's favour were unable or unwilling to do so; there was no necessity for a party who held a fund *qua* trustee and who was prevented from obtaining a discharge extrajudicially to establish double distress arising from competing claims on the fund, and a trustee such as M was not obliged to hold the fund in perpetuity or, at least, indefinitely, pending resolution of the disagreement; (ii) *esto* M did not hold the fund as trustee, the action remained competent because there were, properly understood, competing claims on the fund; in the context of multiplepoinding, competing claims on a fund did not require to be confined to disputed assertions of ownership but could arise from a conflict in the assertion of a right to manage, control or direct the distribution of the fund, such as in the present case, *Commercial Union Assurance Co Ltd v Globe Co Ltd* 1916 1 S.L.T. 343 and *Adam Cochran & Co v Conn* 1989 S.L.T. (Sh. Ct.) 27, [1989] C.L.Y. 4974, *distinguished*. (3) X's pleas to the competency would be repelled, the fund *in medio* would be approved, with M liable only in one single payment thereof, and M would be ordained forthwith to consign the fund *in medio* in the hands of the sheriff clerk with a view to obtaining their judicial discharge, meantime, a case management conference would be appointed to determine further procedure.

MACALLANS v W BURRELL HOMES LTD, 2015 S.L.T. (Sh Ct) 243, Sheriff S Reid, Sh Ct (Glasgow).

2458 Permission to appeal–Scottish Legal Complaints Commission

[Legal Profession and Legal Aid (Scotland) Act 2007 (asp 5) s.21, s.21(3); Act of Sederunt (Rules of the Court of Session 1994) 1994 Sch.2 para.4.2(5)]

Y made an application under the Legal Profession and Legal Aid (Scotland) Act 2007 s.21 for leave to appeal a decision of the Scottish Legal Complaints Commission (S). Y had submitted a complaint to S in July 2014, identifying five issues, with S finding that the first and last were without merit and the second, third and fourth were time barred, S's determination being sent to Y on 21 November 2014. Thereafter, Y's appeal had not been made within 28 days as set out in s.21 of the 2007 Act; Y had been unrepresented and had been granted the necessary order to initiate the appeal process in terms of the Act of Sederunt (Rules of the Court of Session 1994) 1994.r.4.2(5) on 9 January 2015, with the application for leave to appeal and a covering letter sent to Y which stated that he could proceed to lodge his application with the Inner House and was required to lodge a court process along with the appropriate fee, however, the application had not been registered after being lodged with the court by Y until 9 September, when he had been fee exempt. Y submitted that he had experienced financial, personal and legal difficulties, there was a public interest in having the type of complaint and its seriousness determined by the appropriate body, and he had made efforts to proceed with the appeal against a background of personal problems, such that cause had been shown.

Held: Application refused. There had been no cause shown for the purposes of s.21(3) of the 2007 Act; the court letter of 9 January 2015 had made it plain to Y what he required to do, and although sympathy could be had with Y in relation to his personal and financial difficulties, there was an important public interest in court proceedings and other complaints proceedings being progressed timeously, the specific statutory time limit of short duration in relation to the appeal existed for a good reason, and there had been significant and unacceptable delay in the appeal process and the application was out of time.

Y v SCOTTISH LEGAL COMPLAINTS COMMISSION, [2016] CSIH 9, 2016 S.L.T. 249, Lady Clark of Calton, IH.

2459 Personal injury claims–Allocation of jurisdiction–Claim by deceased's relatives against deceased's former employer located in England–Plea to relevancy

[Damages (Scotland) Act 2011 (asp 7) s.4; Private International Law (Miscellaneous Provisions) Act 1995 (c.42) s.14(1), s.9(1); Regulation 864/2007 on the law applicable to non-contractual obligations (Rome II) 2007; Fatal Accidents Act 1976 (c.30)]

An action of damages raised by the widow (W) and 23 relatives (R) of a deceased person (D) against his former employers (S and E) for injuries sustained during the course of his employment came before the Lord Ordinary on the procedure roll for a debate on E's preliminary plea to the relevancy. D had been a mechanical fitter and had served an engineering apprenticeship with S between 1941 and 1947, and between 1954 and 1979, he had been employed by E at its plant in Wilton on Teesside. R averred that X had been exposed to substantial quantities of asbestos dust in both positions, as a result of which he had developed asbestosis and pleural plaques, and sought damages under the Damages (Scotland) Act 2011. E sought dismissal of the action against it and submitted *inter alia* that (1) any alleged wrongdoing by it had occurred prior to the Private International Law (Miscellaneous Provisions) Act 1995 or Regulation 864/2007; (2) the remedy to which W was entitled was regulated by the *lex loci delicti* which was England, and the proper remedy was under the Fatal Accidents Act 1976.

Held: Case put out by order. (1) The issue fell to be determined under the common law where the alleged acts had pre-dated the Private International Law (Miscellaneous Provisions) Act 1995 ss.9(1) and 14(1), and where it had been agreed that the Rome II Regulations did not apply; applying *McElroy v McAllister* 1949 S.C. 110, [1947-51] C.L.Y. 1614, it was clear that the claim against E under the 2011 Act had to fail, R had confused the issue of jurisdiction with the application of the proper law, joint and several liability had not established the applicable law or answered the question as to how the sum sued for was to be assessed, and individual liability for the claim first required to be established, *McElroy, applied*. (2) There was nothing in the 1979 and 2011 Acts which assisted R where those Acts emphasised that the particular remedies therein were available only under the law of that country, *Cox v Ergo Versicherung AG (formerly Victoria)* [2014] UKSC 22, [2014] A.C. 1379, [2014] C.L.Y. 825, *considered*. (3) A claim under s.4 of the 2011 Act vested in the relatives of the deceased, which was in contrast to the position in England under the 1976 Act, where the right to bring an action rested with the executor or administrator of the deceased and the number of people who might bring a claim was much more limited; the action as drafted against E was irrelevant and would be dismissed in so far as it had been brought by R. (4) The case would be put out by order to enable W to consider a minute of amendment to bring a claim under the 1976 Act.

DOCHERTY v SECRETARY OF STATE FOR BUSINESS INNOVATION AND SKILLS, [2015] CSOH 149, 2015 S.L.T. 858, Lord Boyd of Duncansby, OH.

2460 Personal injury claims–Barristers–Claim against former employer for pleural plaques caused by exposure to asbestos–Sanction for employment of counsel

[Courts Reform (Scotland) Act 2014 (asp 18) s.108(3)(a)(i), s.108(3)(a)(ii)]

In the course of a personal injuries action by an employee (C) against his employers (S) for the development of pleural plaques as the result of his exposure to asbestos during the course of his employment with S between June 1988 and December 2014, C lodged a motion for decree in terms of a tender and acceptance and for sanction for the employment of counsel, which was opposed by S in relation to the latter.

Held: Motion granted. (1) In relation to the Courts Reform (Scotland) Act 2014 s.108(3)(a)(i), the proceedings had been such as to merit the employment of counsel having regard to the difficulty or complexity thereof; C's exposure to asbestos had been in the course of three different types of situation during his employment with S, liability was denied and had never been conceded, S's defences had included a number of detailed calls upon C and it had been reasonable for counsel to be instructed for the purposes of the consultation, the drafting of adjustments and a statement of valuation of C's claim, and in relation to the question of advising on the tender when it had been received, and it could not be said that it would have been reasonable for C to have sought to sist the cause on receipt of defences *inter alia* for S to conclude investigations, a further complication had been the requirement to advise about the issue of provisional damages and C being faced with having to give up the right to seek further damages, and further, despite C's failure to produce an HMRC schedule, as sought by S, the action had not been raised prematurely, over two years having elapsed since C's diagnosis in October 2013. (2) With regard to s.108(3)(a)(ii), C had been very anxious and concerned about his condition, related to the fact that he had had a number of work colleagues who had also contracted asbestos related conditions and that his understanding was that two of his former colleagues had died as a result, there was no proper basis for interpreting s.108(3)(a)(ii) to read that because the C's anxiety had provided a basis for seeking compensation for the diagnosis of pleural plaques, that had exhausted the issue of anxiety such that it could not also be taken into account by the court in considering matters under s.108(3)(a)(i), where the issue of a pursuer's anxiety had also been relevant to the question of whether he would be entitled to an award of compensation at all in the principal claim, moreover, C's agents were specialist solicitors and it had been reasonable of them to assess that counsel ought to be instructed once defences disputing liability had been lodged and had included the aforementioned detailed calls. (3) In all the circumstances of the present case, it was reasonable to sanction the employment of junior counsel.

CUMMING v SSE PLC, 2016 Rep. L.R. 75, Sheriff F L Reith, QC, Sh Ct (Lothian) (Edinburgh).

2461 Personal injury claims–Decrees by default–Lord Ordinary imposing sanction of decree by default–Defender's conduct undermining proper functioning of Ch.43 procedure

[Act of Sederunt (Rules of the Court of Session 1994) 1994 Sch.2 Pt 4 para.43.9, Sch.2 para.38.9]

An employer (F) reclaimed against a decision of the Lord Ordinary awarding decree by default in favour of its employee (M) in his action for damages in respect of hand arm vibration syndrome sustained as a result of the use of vibratory tools and machinery during the course of his employment (*Moran v Freyssinet* [2014] CSOH 173). F had failed to prepare a statement of valuation for the pre-trial meeting with M, it had sought to discharge the proof a few days prior to commencement and at the proof it had not lodged any productions or a list of witnesses, its defence had remained skeletal and it had not had a valuation of M's claim. F sought to lodge a nil valuation and had thereafter sought to lodge a valuation which valued past and future solatium at £5,000. F's motion to allow the valuation to be received late was refused and the Lord Ordinary granted decree for the sum sought by M, namely £30,000, as a sanction in terms of the Act of Sederunt (Rules of the Court of Session 1994) 1994 Sch.2 Pt 4 para.43.9(7)(b). F submitted *inter alia* that (1) the Lord Ordinary had strayed outside the reasonable exercise of his discretion and had erred in awarding decree for the sum sued for where he ought to have expressed any censure by an award of expenses; (2) the court was not confined to reviewing the Lord Ordinary's discretion but could exercise its own discretion, and in the circumstances it ought to do so.

Held: Reclaiming motion refused. (1) The Lord Ordinary's interlocutor was a decree by default where r.43.9 expressly referred to the defenders as being in default by failing timeously to lodge their statement of valuation of claim, and the court was satisfied that r.38.9 applied to F's reclaiming motion. (2) In a case involving a decree by default resulting from a failure by one party to lodge a document required by the rules, it was unlikely that the first instance judge would not be aware of the reasons for, and circumstances of, the default, moreover, and where the default was of consequence to the progress of the case, the appellate court ought to be confined to the principles for review of an exercise of discretion set out in *Thomson v Glasgow Corp* 1962 S.C. (H.L.) 36, [1962] C.L.Y. 3636 and on that basis, the court was not persuaded that the high test set out therein had been met; the Lord Ordinary had had regard to the circumstances and history of the case, the point of Ch.43 procedure was early, full and open disclosure by all parties, with the statement of valuation being a cornerstone of the procedure, and while it might have been possible to continue without F's compliance with the rules, the benefits of the Ch.43 procedure had been lost and the Lord Ordinary had been entitled to form the views he had and had not erred in the exercise of his discretion, *Thomson, considered.* (3) F's conduct had undermined the proper functioning of Ch.43, there had been persistent failures, suggestive of a casual approach to the rules, and the court, when applying r.38.9, was not to apply the guiding principle of what would do justice between the parties in the circumstances, or limit itself to searching for a substantial defence, rather it was to have regard to the interests of the public and court users generally, and where necessary to impose a sanction to mark the court's disapproval of failure to comply with the rules. In the present case, it had been appropriate for the court in its discretion to mark F's serious and sustained failure to comply with the Ch.43 procedure by imposing the sanction of decree for an amount not exceeding the amount of M's valuation; it was only through the imposition of sanctions, where necessary, that the Ch.43 procedure would continue to prove efficient and effective in the resolution of personal injuries disputes, *Flaherty v Hyslop* 1933 S.C. 588 and *McKelvie v Scottish Steel Scaffolding Co Ltd* 1938 S.C. 278, *considered.* (4) The court could see no reason to select a figure different from that selected by the Lord Ordinary, M's valuation had been almost twice the sum sued for and bearing in mind the breakdown of the figures contained in M's valuation and all the circumstances of the case, the sanction of decree restricted to approximately 50 per cent thereof was appropriate.

MORAN v FREYSSINET LTD, [2015] CSIH 76, 2015 S.L.T. 829, Lady Paton, Lady Clark of Calton, Lord McGhie, IH (Ex Div).

2462 Personal injury claims–Limitations–Minute of amendment convening 16 additional defenders–Whether time-barred

[Prescription and Limitation (Scotland) Act 1973 (c.52) s.17, s.17(2), s.19A]

An action of damages by a kart club member (H) against the kart club (C) and the governing body of motorsport in Great Britain (R) came before the Lord Ordinary for debate on the procedure roll. H had raised his action shortly prior to the expiry of the triennium in February 1998, with C designed as the club and five named persons (P) at their home addresses being C's office bearers as representing C and as individuals. The action came before the Lord Ordinary on C, P and R's pleas to relevancy and specification and in November 2000, the Lord Ordinary dismissed the action in so far as directed against C and P and allowed H, P and R a proof before answer (*Harrison v West of Scotland Kart Club* 2001 S.C. 367, [2001] C.L.Y. 6813). H reclaimed and R cross appealed. On 19 December 2001, the Inner House allowed H's minute of amendment to be received in which he sought to attach fault to, and convene, 16 named individuals (N) as additional defenders, being C's office bearers and committee members as representing C and as individuals. On 11 February 2004, the Inner House allowed H's minute of amendment. On 30 March 2004, the Inner House refused the reclaiming motion and cross appeal and adhered to the terms of the Lord Ordinary's interlocutor, and noted that when expenses had been disposed of, the case would require to be remitted to the Lord Ordinary, which course was thereafter followed and the cause appointed to the procedure roll on C's motion, with H and R's consent (*Harrison v West of Scotland Kart Club* 2004 S.C. 615, [2005] C.L.Y. 5576).

Held: Action against N dismissed, quoad ultra proof before answer allowed. (1) The action in so far as directed at N was time barred by reason of the Prescription and Limitation (Scotland) Act 1973 s.17(2); the action as originally framed had made no suggestion of individual fault, N had never been previously named in the action, there was nothing in the action disclosing that N had might have any liability in damages towards H because of the accident, in so far as N might be described as defenders to the action, that was only due to being C's members, and it had been conceded that membership of a club did not *per se* result in a duty of care being owed by one member to the others, and the raising of the summons against C and P as representing C and as individuals was insufficient to enable H to bring an action against N after the expiry of the triennium and the action against N would be dismissed. (2) There had been an elapse of nearly seven years between the accident and the attempts at service of the minute of amendment on N without an explanation for the delay, the passage of time since the accident until any proof took place would have an adverse impact on the recollection of witnesses, there had been no attempt to explain how expeditious H had been in seeking advice and intimating a claim of damages or why he had no alternative remedy against his legal advisers, it was difficult to envisage what prejudice would accrue to H by the court exercising its discretion under s.19A in N's favour and against H, and it would not be equitable to allow H to maintain his action against N.

HARRISON v WEST OF SCOTLAND KART CLUB, [2008] CSOH 33, [2008] L.L.R. 317, Lord Menzies, OH.

2463 Personal injury claims–Remittal–Remittal to sheriff court–Unnecessary expense, delay and uncertainty for pursuer

[Courts Reform (Scotland) Act 2014 (asp 18) s.39, s.41, s.93; Law Reform (Miscellaneous Provisions) (Scotland) Act 1985 (c.73) s.14; Act of Sederunt (Rules of the Court of Session 1994) 1994 Sch.2, Sch.2 para.32.1; All-Scotland Sheriff Court (Sheriff Personal Injury Court) Order 2015 (SSI 2015/213)]

The Advocate General for Scotland (G) lodged a motion to remit a personal injuries action to the sheriff personal injuries court in terms of the Courts Reform (Scotland) Act 2014 s.93. The action had been raised and signetted on 14 September 2015 and sought a conclusion for £25,000. G had accepted liability and the only issue remaining was quantum. G accepted that s.93 did not apply to the action as it had been raised prior to the coming into force of the Courts Reform (Scotland) Act 2014 s.39, and the motion proceeded under the Law Reform (Miscellaneous Provisions) (Scotland) Act 1985 s.14 and the old Act of Sederunt (Rules of the Court of Session 1994) 1994 Sch.2 para.32.1. G submitted that the criteria in *McIntosh v British Railways Board (No.1)* 1990 S.C. 338, [1990] C.L.Y. 5624 had been met. The party raising the action (W) submitted *inter alia* that the motion as enrolled was incompetent.

Held: Motion refused. (1) The sheriff personal injuries court was established by the Courts Reform (Scotland) Act 2014 s.41 and the All-Scotland Sheriff Court (Sheriff Personal Injury Court) Order 2015; neither of those provision had been cited and the court did not have full and sufficient submissions to determine the competency of G's motion. (2) Was the motion competent, it would not be appropriate to remit the case to the sheriff court; the Courts Reform (Scotland) Act 2014 had raised the privative jurisdiction of the sheriff court to £100,000, Parliament had not provided that cases that had been raised in the Court of Session prior to the commencement of the 2014 Act but would after the commencement fall within the privative jurisdiction of the sheriff court ought to automatically be transmitted to the new court, and any motion which was brought to remit to the sheriff court required to apply the principles in *McIntosh*, *McIntosh*, *considered*. (3) G's motion was an attempt to effect a general redistribution of work, the effect of remit in this case would create uncertainty for both W and other pursuers in other actions currently before the court, it would give rise to unnecessary expense and delay and the fact that a claim is small and straightforward was not enough to justify remit to the sheriff court; in the present case, the practical advantages were firmly with W and remittance would deprive W of the choice of court which he had validly exercised, it would lead to procedural uncertainty as to how the case would proceed in the sheriff court and might lead to delay and further costs.

WAKEFORD v ADVOCATE GENERAL FOR SCOTLAND, [2016] CSOH 4, 2016 S.L.T. 161, Lord Boyd of Duncansby, OH.

2464 Personal injury claims–Sist–Defender proposing sist of eight weeks to allow pursuer to provide statement with view to settlement–Relevance of Court of Session's approach

[Act of Sederunt (Sheriff Court Ordinary Cause Rules) 1993 Sch.1]

In the course of an action of damages by G against his former employers (F) for the development of pleural plaques during the course of his employment, F moved to sist the action for eight weeks and to suspend the timetable for that period in order that G's statement could be produced and considered with a view to making settlement proposals. Such motions had also been made in 17 other actions of damages regarding pleural plaques and all parties were agreed that all the motions ought to be disposed of in the same manner. Prior to the creation of the sheriff personal injury court and the increase in the privative limit of the Court of Session to £100,000, pleural plaques actions had been raised in the Court of Session and had been regulated by the Lord President's Direction No.2 of 2012, which had provided for new pleural plaques actions to be sisted and to remain so until the parties had complied with certain provisions, including the delivery to the defender of *inter alia* a summary of the pursuer's employment history, an explanation of the pursuer's trade or other employment activity which had exposed him to asbestos and a copy of his up to date medical records, following delivery of which a defender had had eight weeks to intimate whether it proposed to settle the claim and, if so, the direction had provided for a further four weeks for parties to agree the terms thereof. F submitted *inter alia* that the Court of the Session procedure had incentivised early release of evidence from pursuers and had been with a view to maximising pre-litigation settlements and minimising the number of cases that required to proceed to litigation and the duration of cases of those which had, and F merely sought the opportunity in the new sheriff court to settle pleural plaques claims without litigation, equivalent to the procedure in the Court of Session, and without the production of statements, defenders could not take an informed view as to whether or not to litigate a case or to settle it.

Held: Motions refused. (1) The motions required to be decided in accordance with established legal principles and the provisions of the Act of Sederunt (Sheriff Court Ordinary Cause Rules) 1993 Sch.1 Ch.36, and however desirable it might be that so far as possible, the sheriff personal injury court ought to endeavour to follow the same approach as had the Court of Session, actions proceeding in the sheriff court were governed by sheriff court rules and procedure. (2) A general principle of civil procedure was that an action ought to be litigated without interruption to a conclusion in conformity with a set of rules of practice and procedure, qualified by the court's power to sist, which was a matter of discretion for the sheriff who ought not, by following a practice of adopting a fixed rule of policy, to disable himself from exercising his discretion in the light of the particular circumstances of each case. (3) The actions had already had timetables fixed and proofs had been assigned in some, there was neither any steps in G's case which fell to be taken within the proposed eight week period of sist, nor was it submitted by F in any of the other actions that there was a step due to be taken by them within the eight weeks, which they were unable to take, and a sist could have no practical effect in those circumstances and would not give F any more time than they currently had within which to attempt to effect a settlement. (4) To adopt F's approach would be to adopt a blanket policy, which was neither appropriate nor competent in the context of deciding whether or not to sist each action. (5) Many of the perceived difficulties relied upon by F were the pursuers' alleged potential difficulties in complying with the various timetables, however, had a pursuer any such difficulty, the onus was on that pursuer to raise the matter by lodging a motion to have the timetable varied on cause shown, and if he failed to do so and to comply with a timetabled step, it would be open to F to seek an appropriate remedy. Observed, that although the motions had been refused, that was not to say that genuine issues might not have been identified which might require to be dealt with elsewhere, whether by practice note, if competent, changes to the rules, protocols or otherwise. *Opinion reserved*, on whether even the sheriff principal had the power to issue a practice note similar to that made by the Lord President.

GOLIGHER v FLOW PART LTD, 2016 S.L.T. (Sh Ct) 301, Sheriff P J Braid, Sh Ct (Lothian) (Edinburgh).

2465 Pleadings–Relevance–Inconsistent averments–Relevancy

An action for damages raised by a businessman (G) against the surviving partners (P) of a solicitors' firm (K) came before the Lord Ordinary for a debate on preliminary issues. G had acquired property reservations via a property investment company owned by K's former agent (E) and K subsequently concluded missives on G's behalf in respect of three properties. The missives were rescinded following G's failure to pay the purchase price and the developers raised an action for breach of contract against G. P alleged that they had received G's instructions via E. G's defence, namely that he was not contractually bound as K had acted without authority in concluding missives, was rejected by the sheriff, who found *inter alia* that K had had the authority to transact. G settled the case and thereafter sought to recover his losses from P on the basis that he had not instructed P to conclude missives, *esto* he had instructed P, they had acted negligently. P averred that they had fulfilled all duties incumbent upon them. K submitted that (1) G's averments were inconsistent and it would not be in the interests of justice to allow them to go to proof; (2) G's pleadings failed to give fair notice of the causal connection between K's alleged breach of duty and G's claimed loss; (3) G's alternative case was irrelevant and his whole claim ought to be dismissed.

Held: Proof before answer allowed. (1) Inconsistent averments could be tabled, provided they were presented in the alternative, unless it was incompatible with substantial justice to do so, and it was not contrary to the substantive justice of the situation to allow G to attempt to prove both his cases. (2) The issue was not about instructions actually given but whether K ought to have sought confirmation from G directly, whether K ought to have sought specific instructions and what would have happened had specific instructions been sought and given, and there was adequate notice. (3) G's primary case was unequivocal, his alternative case was a contingent one, and the weaker alternative rule did not apply, in any event, G's alternative case was not irrelevant and would not be excluded from probation. (4) The whole averments made in answer to the primary case were capable of supporting the inference that G, through E, had authorised P to transact on his behalf. (5) P's formulaic explanation in respect of their duties did not require to be deleted, there were genuine questions about the facts and P was entitled to put G to proof on that question, however, P's inspecific averment might preclude them from opening specific, positive lines of evidence.

GREIG v DAVIDSON, [2015] CSOH 44, 2015 S.C.L.R. 722, Lord Stewart, OH.

2466 Recording of proceedings–Civil evidence–Challenge to sheriff's approach to evidence led at child welfare hearing–Evidence not recorded so no transcript available

[Act of Sederunt (Sheriff Court Ordinary Cause Rules) 1993]

L appealed against a sheriff's decision to grant a residence order in terms of the Children (Scotland) Act 1995 s.11(2)(c) that a child reside with his father, seeking to challenge the sheriff's approach to the evidence led at a child welfare hearing on the basis that the sheriff had erred in making certain findings in fact, although no transcript of evidence was available.

Held: Appeal refused. The appeal was entirely devoid of merit where no relevant or meaningful argument was presented to challenge the sheriff's conclusions on the evidence and it was a matter of surprise that the appeal should have been marked at all. *Opinion*, per Sheriff Morrison, QC, that in the present case, not recording the evidence was agreed to because legal aid was refused for the cost thereof and the case highlighted the dangers in agreeing to such a procedure. *Observed,* per Sheriff Principal Scott, QC, (1) that a prospective appellant ought to be aware that when the evidence had not been recorded, the sheriff's findings in fact were not open to challenge, they were binding on the court which could not make different, or further, findings in fact; (2) that where the findings in fact could not be challenged, in order for the sheriff's decision to be the subject of a viable appeal, an appellant had to be able to point to a clear error of law on the sheriff's part or to conclusions which were plainly wrong or unwarranted. *Observed,* per Sheriff Morrison, QC, that there was no such process as an evidential child welfare hearing provided for in the Act of Sederunt (Sheriff Court Ordinary Cause Rules) 1993 where one might have either a child welfare hearing or a proof, and were it possible to have an evidential child welfare hearing, it might only be with the consent of the parties: such a hearing, without the recording of evidence, would restrict a party's grounds of appeal to questions of law only; it did not automatically attract the provisions of Ch.29, in particular the authority to cite witnesses and the rules which arose from it, or the recording of evidence; it so restricted the grounds of appeal because, without the recording of evidence, an appellate court could not go behind the facts found by the sheriff; neither r.33.22A(4) nor r.33A.23(4) of the Ordinary Cause Rules 1993 appeared to entitle a sheriff to restrict a party's right of appeal by ordering this procedure without consent. *Opinion reserved,* per Sheriff Principal Scott, QC, and Sheriff Principal Lewis on the general use of evidential child welfare hearings where it was never suggested that such procedure had caused the court to err and while the procedure restricted the scope of an appeal, it did not follow that the case was wrongly decided at first instance, and the expedience of determining discrete issues in family actions through evidence being led in the context of a child welfare hearing.

A v H, [2016] SAC (Civ) 2, 2016 S.L.T. (Sh Ct) 277, Sheriff Principal C A L Scott, QC, Sheriff Principal M Lewis, Sheriff N M P Morrison, QC, SAC.

2467 Reduction–Non-parties–Beneficiary under will seeking reduction of sheriff's decree in action of count, reckoning and payment brought by other beneficiaries–Whether averments amounting to exceptional circumstances

A beneficiary (B) under the will of her late father (F) sought a proof before answer in her action seeking reduction of a decree of the sheriff principal, allowing an appeal against a decision of the sheriff in relation to an action of count, reckoning and payment raised by two of F's sons (P), as beneficiaries under the will, against F's two other sons, as trustees and executors of F's will (*Auchnie v Auchnie* 2014 G.W.D. 27-552). P sought dismissal of B's action. No warrant had been sought or granted to intimate either the proceedings before the sheriff or the appeal to the sheriff principal to B. Thereafter, B had lodged a minute of sist seeking leave to enter the process as a party minuter and to lodge defences, which had been refused by the sheriff, and her appeal against that decision had been refused by the Inner House (*Auchnie v Auchnie* [2014] CSIH 102, 2015 S.C. 320, [2015] C.L.Y. 2889).

Held: Action dismissed. B, by her own admission and with the benefit of legal advice, had known that the proceedings had been raised, what had been involved therein and that their outcome might materially affect her interests, however, she had not sought to be sisted thereto until after the decision of the sheriff principal had been issued. That situation did not amount to exceptional circumstances justifying reduction of the sheriff principal's decree and it could not be said that reduction was required to avoid a miscarriage of justice. B had been the author of her own alleged misfortune and the fact that she had chosen not to be a party to proceedings of which she had been fully aware did not materially distinguish her position from that of a party seeking reduction who had been a party to the proceedings. The remedy of reduction remained one for the discretion of the court, having regard to the equities of the matter, and *inter alia* the conduct of the person seeking the exceptional remedy, and B's averments did not amount to exceptional circumstances which might justify the exercise of the court's discretion in granting reduction.

AUCHNIE v AUCHNIE, [2016] CSOH 70, 2016 S.L.T. 740, Lord Clarke, OH.

2468 Reduction–Pleadings–Property purchaser's action of reduction–Whether sufficiently relevant or specific

[Consumer Protection from Unfair Trading Regulations 2008 (SI 2008/1277) Pt 4A; Directive 2005/29 on unfair business-to-consumer commercial practices in the internal market 2005]

A property purchaser (R) raised an action against a property development company (S) seeking reduction of (i) a court decree, (ii) missives relating to a plot of land (X), (iii) a settlement agreement, together with damages for S's alleged breach of missives. R and S had concluded missives in respect of X on approximately 23 December 2008 and the settlement agreement was signed on 11 May 2011. S raised an action seeking (i) declarator that R and S were bound by the settlement agreement, (ii) payment of X's purchase price, and was granted decree on 10 December 2012. R averred *inter alia* that he had subsequently become aware that part of the common parts might be contaminated land, of which S had been aware, and its omission to provide that information had precluded him from raising the issue in the first action. S lodged a plea of competent and omitted. R submitted *inter alia* that (1) a plea of competent and omitted was not available to S; (2) S's omission to provide him with information, together with its representation to the local authority in respect of its intentions for certain parts of the land, amounted to *res noviter* and disclosed exceptional circumstances supporting reduction; (3) he had been induced to enter into the missives as a result of S's failure to disclose the existence of contaminated land.

Held: Action dismissed. (1) There was no impediment to a plea of competent and omitted being taken by S; R could not challenge a judgment regularly pronounced against him on the grounds that there was a defence which was competent to him but which he had omitted to set up, *The Earl of Perth v Lady Willoughby de Eresby's Trustees* (1875) 2R 538, *applied*. (2) R's averments fell short of *res noviter* and his pleadings did not disclose sufficiently relevant and specific circumstances to justify reduction on the grounds of exceptional circumstances. (3) R's averments in respect of being a consumer and the alleged ownership of common property were of doubtful relevancy, however, he had offered to prove them and they were sufficient for proof before answer on those limited points. (4) R's averments in respect of his knowledge of the contaminated land, the alleged exceptional circumstances and the material information which S required to provide were lacking in relevance and specification, in any event, R's claims based on the Consumer Protection from Unfair Trading Regulations 2008 and Directive 2005/29 were not supported on averment; neither the 2008 Regulations nor the Directive conferred any direct right of action upon R in the current action, the rights of redress conferred on consumers by Pt 4A of the 2008 Regulations related solely to contracts entered into, or payments made, on or after 1 October 2014. (5) R's averments were not sufficiently relevant or specific to support his claims and averments, and S's plea of competent and omitted would be sustained.

RAMSDEN v SANTON HIGHLANDS LTD, [2015] CSOH 65, 2016 S.C.L.R. 89, Lord Kinclaven, OH.

2469 Reduction–Pleadings–Relevancy and specification

[Conveyancing and Feudal Reform (Scotland) Act 1970 (c.35) s.19(6), s.24(1D)]

An action raised by a debtor (M) seeking reduction of a sheriff court decree granting a finance company (P) warrant to enter into possession of and sell subjects (H) came before the Lord Ordinary for debate on the relevancy of M's pleadings. In 2007, M had granted a standard security over H in favour of a bank (B) and in 2009, that security had been assigned to P. M had failed to maintain the monthly repayments and P had unsuccessfully attempted to serve a calling up notice via recorded delivery, which, on 14 May 2012, had been deemed to be served by being sent to the Extractor of the Court of Session in accordance with the Conveyancing and Feudal Reform (Scotland) Act 1970 s.19(6). P had thereafter raised an action in the sheriff court in terms of s.24(1D) of the 1970 Act and at the evidential hearing, M had *inter alia* objected to P's failure to provide the principal documents of indebtedness, which the sheriff had refused on the basis *inter alia* that that defence had not previously been intimated, M had left the courtroom during the hearing and decree had been pronounced. P had thereafter refused to accept a cheque from M which bore to be drawn from an unregulated bank. M sought reduction on the basis that (1) his consent to the assignation by B to P had not been sought or obtained; (2) he had had no knowledge of the calling up notice; (3) his requests to P for exhibition of original documents had been refused; (4) the sheriff had no jurisdiction to hear the case, *esto* he had no jurisdiction in the absence of verified documents and witnesses to their authenticity; (5) M was not in default and P's calculations were incorrect; (6) P was not entitled to refuse to accept his cheque.

Held: Action dismissed. (1) It was unnecessary for either B or P to seek or obtain M's consent to the assignation of his debt, and he neither had any legal entitlement to have the principal assignation exhibited to him nor was he entitled to demand sight of the principal loan agreement as a condition of settling any debt due by him to P as B's assignee. (2) M had had knowledge of the calling up notice when the sheriff court action had been raised and defended by him. (3) The sheriff had jurisdiction to hear the action at P's instance in terms of s.24(1D) of the 1970 Act, which expressly provided for an application by a creditor for warrant to exercise its statutory remedies to be made by summary application in the sheriff court, and M had no right to demand that the case be heard in the Court of Session. (4) P's application had contained no conclusion seeking payment and any contention by M that the sum said to be due by him had been incorrectly calculated was irrelevant to P's entitlement to seek warrant to enforce the calling up notice. (5) The fact that M had attempted to sell H after he had failed to have the sheriff court decree set aside on appeal, rather than seeking reduction, was a factor which weighed against the exercise of the court's discretion in his favour, furthermore his attempt to persuade P to accept payment in cheque form had no bearing on the issue with which the proceedings were concerned, namely whether the interests of justice required the sheriff court decree to be reduced, in any event, P was entitled to refuse to accept payment otherwise than in legal tender, *Child Maintenance and Enforcement Commission v Wilson* [2013] CSIH 95, 2014 S.L.T. 46, [2014] C.L.Y. 3347, *considered*. (6) P's failure to present evidence of the requisite quality at the evidential hearing before the sheriff was an issue of substance and not a technicality, however, that was not sufficient to constitute exceptional circumstances in which reduction of the decree might be necessary in order to achieve substantial justice, having regard to the fact that the calling up notice returned to P stamped with the extractor's receipt was in P's possession at the time of the evidential hearing and had since remained in its possession, and to the land register title sheet which disclosed the registration of (i) M's standard security of B, (ii) the assignation in favour of P, M had failed to raise for inquiry any real issue as to the validity of the documentary foundation of P's action, or any possibility that there were irregularities in the procedure leading up thereto, and M had failed to state a relevant case.

MCLEOD v PRESTIGE FINANCE LTD *sub nom.* MCLEOD v PRESTIGE CREDIT LTD, [2016] CSOH 69, 2016 Hous. L.R. 43, Lord Tyre, OH.

2470 Removal–Pleadings–Order for removal of protesters camped within grounds of Scottish Parliament–Relevancy and specification

[Court of Session Act 1988 (c.36) s.46; Scotland Act 1998 (c.46); European Convention on Human Rights 1950 art.10, art.11; Land Reform (Scotland) Act 2003 (asp 2) s.1]

The Scottish Parliamentary Corporate Body (S) sought decree *de plano* in its petition for an order under the Court of Session Act 1988 s.46 for removal of a pro-independence group (G) camped within the grounds of the Scottish Parliament, on the basis that G's averments were irrelevant *et separatim* lacking in specification. S contended *inter alia* that G's members had been continuously occupying part of the grounds of the property of the Scottish Parliament without right or permission since 29 November 2015, and G had publicly stated that it intended to maintain C until Scottish independence was declared. G averred *inter alia* that any land or property owned by the Parliament through S belonged to, and was owned in common by, the people of Scotland, S, as a public body, was not able to assume private rights which were in conflict with the public interest and its purely administrative role meant that it could only exercise its property rights to a limited degree and only for the public good, the open area around the Parliament comprised an area of common ownership and was S's order granted, it would constitute an act of dispossession and would diminish the rights and freedoms historically enjoyed by the Scottish people. G further averred that any right given to S by statute which purported to give it the power to undermine any rights previously enjoyed by the people of Scotland was not in conformity with the Treaty of Union, in so far as the Scotland Act 1998 had provided for S's creation, with the power to own property, it had not done so in a manner which was for the evident utility of the Scottish people, thus the court could declare that the 1998 Act was invalid, and further, the United Nations Declaration on the Rights of Indigenous Peoples 2007 provided that indigenous peoples had the right to maintain and strengthen their distinctive relationship with their traditionally owned or occupied lands and other resources, and had the right to redress or compensation for lands, territories and resources which had been confiscated, taken, occupied etc. without free, prior and informed consent. One of G's members (X), designed as a member of the government of Scotland, averred *inter alia* that S, being a body corporate, was neither able to own or hold property nor to exercise any other private law rights, the ground on which C was located was public land which S was incapable of acquiring a right to, there was neither a law of trespass known to Scotland, nor was there any encroachment on the land in question, there was a right to roam, the 1988 and 1998 Acts were subservient and their authority ought not to be recognised, and in any event, statute law was not proper law.

Held: Case put out by order. (1) The law of Scotland had long recognised the legal status of non-natural entities and their right to own property and exercise rights of ownership, thus S was entitled to hold or own property, S had produced a copy of its registered title, the contention that the Scottish Parliament had been paid for by the Scottish taxpayer and that any land or property which it owned through S therefore belonged to the people of Scotland, and was owned in common by them, had no legal substance, in any event there was no analysis of the contention that the Scottish taxpayer could be identified as the sole contributor to the cost of the Parliament, and S was the legal owner of the property known as the Scottish Parliament and the surrounding grounds, which was sufficient to reject G's other contentions that the grounds concerned comprised open public parkland, or grounds held in common ownership. (2) The 1998 Act gave S a right to acquire property and further the general law of land ownership in Scotland entitled S to have exclusive use of its property, to resist encroachment thereupon and to otherwise regulate the use thereof, and S's unchallenged averments established that C's presence constituted trespass and encroachment on S's property and an interdict might be sought against a trespasser who did not leave; it would be competent for the court to grant the order sought under s.46 of the 1988 Act. (3) G had made no relevant averments establishing any rights held by it, or by the people of Scotland in general, which had been infringed or altered in some manner to their detriment, no averments offered a valid foundation for a claim of common ownership, or any other right to property legally owned by S and no further legal basis for the presence of any such right as claimed by G had been identified in submissions to the court; the underlying contention upon which G advanced its argument about the impact of the Treaty of Union had no force and would be dismissed. (4) United Nations conventions such as the 2007 Declaration were not binding in international law and created no rights which could be enforced before domestic courts, moreover, G and X had a completely misguided understanding of the meaning of "indigenous" in the context of the Declaration, and it was clear that any attempt on G's part to oppose the order sought by placing reliance on 2007 Declaration was entirely misplaced. (5) No direct reliance was placed on the Land Reform (Scotland) Act 2003 and the right of access given by s.1 thereof was a right to be on land for limited purposes, none of which were present in the circumstances of the occupation by C. (6) ECHR arts 10 and 11 were engaged in the present proceedings; the rights recognised therein were vital but were nevertheless subject to some constraints, including restrictions, provided they were prescribed by law and necessary in a democratic society, the question for the court would be whether the interference with G's rights entailed in granting an order would be lawful, necessary and proportionate, consequently, G was entitled to have the proportionality of the making of the order sought by S assessed by the court; no evidence had been led on the extent to which G did, or did not, constitute an interference with the rights of others to access the grounds of the Scottish Parliament, or on any other matter which might fall to be weighed in a proportionality assessment, C presently appeared to occupy a small area at the very edge of the grounds at the furthest point from the entrance to the Parliament building and it was neither immediately obvious that C's presence inhibited the use of the grounds by others nor that there were any real security or logistical concerns which might weigh the proportionality balance in S's favour, *Mayor of London v Hall* [2010] EWCA Civ 817, [2011] 1 W.L.R. 504, [2010] C.L.Y. 395 and *City of London Corp v Samede* [2012] EWCA Civ 160, [2012] 2 All E.R. 1039, [2012] C.L.Y. 460, *considered.* (7) The question of the proportionality of granting the order sought had been raised and that was sufficient to bar the court from granting S's order until satisfied thereon, therefore, decree *de plano* would be refused and an order would be made requiring the case to call at a procedural hearing in order to identify the scope of further procedure. Observed, that the question of what was "for the evident utility" of the people was a matter of political judgment and not one which was justiciable before the court, *Gibson v Lord Advocate* 1975 S.C. 136, [1975] C.L.Y. 3824, *considered. Opinion reserved*, on whether the court would have jurisdiction to consider the question of whether legislation concerned with private right was incompatible with the Treaty of Union, *MacCormick v Lord Advocate* 1953 S.C. 396, [1953] C.L.Y. 597, *considered.*

SCOTTISH PARLIAMENTARY CORPORATE BODY v SOVEREIGN INDIGENOUS PEOPLES OF SCOTLAND, [2016] CSOH 65, 2016 S.L.T. 761, Lord Turnbull, OH.

2471 Settlement–Agreements–Without prejudice correspondence–Whether extra-judicial settlement reached

A local authority (G) sought declarator that an extrajudicial settlement had been reached in its action for payment against a board member (S) of a school (X). X had closed in 2010 with a deficit of £4.7 million in its pension fund. G had sought a cessation payment from the trustees (T) who held title to the land on which X stood, the board of managers and S, who was the sole remaining member of the board, and following unsuccessful negotiations, in December 2013, it raised an action for payment. The case was subsequently sisted for negotiation and at a meeting on 4 September 2014, G and S had discussed settlement in certain terms, namely that G would consent to recall of the interim interdict, discharge of the inhibition and decree of absolvitor, in return for payment of £1 million, and that G would convey a triangular strip of land to T. On 11 September, S had emailed G setting out the proposed settlement options, which had included an overage requirement not previously discussed, and to which G had replied requesting further information. G had sent a further email on 28 October which had *inter alia* requested that the position be formalised by counsel and confirmed that settlement would be scheduled to take place on 28 November, all things being equal. G contended that an extrajudicial settlement had been agreed by means of the 11 September email, which had been the offer, and the email of 28 October, which had been the acceptance.

Held: Minute dismissed. (1) S's email of 11 September had not constituted an offer but had been a recap of the position, the dispute could not have been concluded on the terms agreed because no agreement had been reached at the meeting on 4 September and G's agent would not have concluded a deal until she had obtained the approval of senior counsel and had ensured that G's interests had been secured; the clear inference was that G's agent had made the bargain subject to contract, and in the absence of agreement in respect of the payer's identity, the bargain could not be enforced. (2) While the court was entitled to look at the terms of without prejudice correspondence to decide whether or not agreement had been reached, the use of "without prejudice" on the relevant emails had tended to indicate that G and S were reserving their respective positions. (3) The language of the email of 28 October was not that of a counter offer, a final position had not been reached, and G and S had not reached a binding extrajudicial settlement.

GLASGOW CITY COUNCIL v SMITH, [2015] CSOH 143, 2015 S.L.T. 800, Lord Woolman, OH.

2472 Sexual offences prevention orders–Breach–Sufficiency of evidence–Corroboration

B appealed against conviction for breaching a sexual offences prevention order by approaching a girl (J), aged 15 (charge 2), and against the imposition of 18 months' detention and a nine month supervised release order. B had also been charged with approaching another girl (C), aged 15 (charge 1) on a serparate occasion. In terms of the order, B was *inter alia* prohibited from having any contact with any person under the age of 16 save for inadvertent or unavoidable contact. C and J had given evidence that B had approached them as he had known them prior to the offences and had spoken to them for approximately five minutes, having walked away from C when she had informed him that she was only 15. B admitted having contact with C and J but claimed that he had been unaware that they were under 16, and that J had in fact approached him. The sheriff directed the jury in relation to corroboration, including standard directions on the doctrine in *Moorov (Samuel) v HM Advocate* 1930 J.C. 68, and they found charge 1 not proven and convicted him of charge 2. B submitted that (1) by acquitting of charge 1, the jury had not accepted the evidence of both C and J, thus there could be no corroboration and they had not been entitled to convict on charge 2; (2) the sentence imposed was excessive where the contact had been of very limited duration, there had been no evidence of alarm, distress or upset and no suggestion of inappropriate behaviour.

Held: Appeal against conviction refused and appeal against sentence allowed. (1) There had been a sufficiency of evidence at the close of the Crown case; in respect of each charge, the contact or engagement had been spoken to by two independent sources, and the jury had not required to rely upon the *Moorov* doctrine but had been entitled to apply the basic rules of corroboration as explained by the sheriff in his charge; the jury had been entitled to conclude that B had not had the necessary *mens rea* for the offence libelled in charge 1 but, on the evidence, to form a different view in relation to charge 2 and convict thereof, and while there had been an inaccurate direction by the sheriff, the charge read as a whole had given the jury sufficient guidance to enable them to proceed as they had and no miscarriage of justice had occurred, *Moorov*, *considered*. (2) Breach of a sexual offences prevention order was a serious matter and the sheriff had been correct to treat the conviction on that basis, nevertheless, the incident involving J had not merited the length of sentence imposed, and the sentence would be quashed and a custodial sentence of 12 months with a supervised release order of six months substituted.

BEUCKMANN (CHRISTOPHER) v HM ADVOCATE, [2015] HCJAC 104, 2016 S.C.L. 118, Lady Paton, Lord Bracadale, Lord Turnbull, HCJ.

2473 Sheriff Court Rules–Pre-action protocols–Personal injury claims

ACT OF SEDERUNT (SHERIFF COURT RULES AMENDMENT) (PERSONAL INJURY PRE-ACTION PROTOCOL) 2016, SSI 2016/215; made under the Courts Reform (Scotland) Act 2014 s.104(1). In force: 28 November 2016.

This Act of Sederunt amends the Ordinary Cause Rules and Summary Cause Rules in respect of personal injury actions. It introduces a requirement on parties to certain actions of damages for personal injury to follow a Personal Injury Pre-Action Protocol with a view to settling the action before proceedings are raised.

2474 Sheriff courts–Simple procedure

THE SHERIFF COURT SIMPLE PROCEDURE (LIMITS ON AWARD OF EXPENSES) ORDER 2016, SSI 2016/388; made under the Courts Reform (Scotland) Act 2014 s.81. In force: 28 November 2016.

This Order prescribes categories of simple procedure cases in which the award of legal expenses is limited. Simple procedure is a new form of sheriff court procedure established by the Courts Reform (Scotland) Act 2014 Ch.1 Pt 3.

2475 Summonses–Amendments–Amendment to first defender's company name–Correction or substitution

[Prescription and Limitation (Scotland) Act 1973 (c.52) s.6; Act of Sederunt (Rules of the Court of Session 1994) 1994 Sch.2]

In an action of damages by a local authority (P) against a water company (S) for flood damage, P enrolled a motion to amend the summons in respect of S's designation. The summons had been signetted on 12 February 2015 and had convened as first defenders "Scottish Water Ltd". S had intimated its defence on 31 August 2015 and P thereafter sought leave to amend. P conceded that the quinquennial period had expired on or about 21 July 2015, and that if the motion was not allowed, its claim would have prescribed in terms of the Prescription and Limitation (Scotland) Act 1973 s.6. S opposed the motion and submitted that the courts discretion ought to be exercised according to the practice set out in *Link Housing Association Ltd v PBL Construction Ltd* [2007] CSIH 4, 2007 S.C. 294, [2008] C.L.Y. 4591.

Held: Motion allowed. (1) The court might deploy its discretionary power to put right errors and omissions where there was a reasonable excuse and where the balance of prejudice favoured excusal, taking a broad view of the interests of justice, however, in terms of the Act of Sederunt (Rules of the Court of Session 1994) 1994 Sch.2 para.24, where a claim had become time limited or time expired, the court would not ordinarily have the power to substitute one party for another, and in the absence of power to waive or extend time limits, the discretion was not available or should not be exercised where the effect of substitution would be to defeat the statutory extinction of a claim by prescription: the essential question was whether P's proposed amendment was a correction or substitution, such characterisation depended on the nature of the error to be corrected and was both subjective and objective, *McCullough v Norwest Socea Ltd* 1981 S.L.T. 201, [1981] C.L.Y. 3328, *considered*. (2) Objectively, S and "Scottish Water Ltd" were separate legal entities, however, the only difference in the names was the suffix "Ltd", clerical error could not be ruled out and both parties had been careless as to the specific name; where the present case was based on a statutory duty which had only ever rested with S and where S was already in the action, in reality if not in name, the rational conclusion was that P's proposed amendment was a correction rather than a substitution and it was open to the court to exercise its discretion, *Link Housing, distinguished*. (3) P had tendered a reasonable excuse and if the amendment was not allowed, its claim would be lost, and where S's hypothetical lost advantage was a windfall benefit, little weight ought to be given to its loss; the prejudice suffered by the nominal first defenders was zero, no other prejudice had been asserted, and it was fair and reasonable, and in the interests of justice, to allow the amendment.

PERTH AND KINROSS COUNCIL v SCOTTISH WATER LTD, [2015] CSOH 138, 2015 S.L.T. 788, Lord Stewart, OH.

2476 Transfer of proceedings–Court of Session–Action against bank seeking payment of sums in settlement of PPI misselling claims–Whether complex or novel point of law

[Courts Reform (Scotland) Act 2014 (asp 18) s.112(2)]

In the course of an appeal by a creditor (D) against a decision of the sheriff to exclude certain of her averments from probation in her action against a bank (B) seeking payment of sums allegedly due in settlement of three claims concerning the misselling of payment protection insurance (PPI), B lodged a motion for remit of the cause to the Court of Session in terms of the Courts Reform (Scotland) Act 2014 s.112(2) (*Donnelly v Royal Bank of Scotland Plc* 2016 S.L.T. (Sh Ct) 307, [2016] 2694). B sought remit on the basis that the appeal dealt with many complex and novel points of law and there was a paucity of direct authority on the points to be addressed, the subject matter of the appeal was of great importance to B and had wider implications for it and other lenders, and the financial implications thereof substantially exceeded the sum sued for.

Held: Motion refused. (1) Whilst s.112(2) of the 2014 Act permitted the court to remit an appeal to the Court of Session there was no necessity to do so even if the appeal raised a complex or novel point of law. (2) The court agreed with the sheriff's assessment that the action raised a number of interesting and novel issues, however, whilst the factual/legal matrix was also far from straightforward, on the strength of the submissions, the points of law involved were not complex or, at least, sufficiently complex to merit the appeal being remitted directly to the Court of Session; the sheriff had described with great clarity each discrete legal question involved and had broken down and analysed the various issues, they were not particularly complex, and it might be said that there really was only one main issue, namely, B's entitlement or otherwise to plead set off in the whole circumstances of the case. (3) The present litigation might be of interest to those having a financial stake of one sort or another, nevertheless, that did not equate to the involvement of national or wide ranging issues of public concern, the present dispute was limited to largely private interests within a particular part of the financial sector, moreover, the parties' submission were silent as to the longer term prospects of the case. (4) The court shared the sheriff's view that the complexity or novelty of the points of law arising together with the allegedly wider importance of the cause had been overstated, and the matter would proceed to an appeal hearing before the court.

DONNELLY v ROYAL BANK OF SCOTLAND PLC, [2016] SAC (Civ) 4, 2016 S.L.T. (Sh Ct) 333, Sheriff Principal C A L Scott, QC, Sheriff I R Abercrombie, QC, Sheriff P Arthurson, SAC.

2477 Transfer of proceedings–Court of Session–Four actions for damages arising out of use of pelvic mesh products–Sheriff court unable to deal with such cases in same manner as Court of Session under newly-issued practice direction

[Act of Sederunt (Rules of the Court of Session 1994) 1994 Sch.2 para.2.2, Sch.2 para.2.2(2), Sch.2 para.32.2B; Courts Reform (Scotland) Act 2014 (asp 18) s.92(4); Consumer Protection Act 1987 (c.43)]

Four damages actions arising from the insertion of vaginal tape and mesh products for the treatment of urinary incontinence or prolapse came before the Lord Ordinary by order in terms of the Act of Sederunt (Rules of the Court of Session 1994) 1994 Sch.2 para.32.2B following the sheriff's request to allow the proceedings to be remitted to the Court of Session under the Courts Reform (Scotland) Act 2014 s.92(4). The manufacturers of the products concerned were defenders common to all four actions and the case against them founded on their alleged breach of the Consumer Protection Act 1987. The local health board were defenders in three of the cases and in the fourth, the defender was a private healthcare company together with a medical practitioner employed by them, the cases against them averring a breach of duty to give warnings about the use of pelvic mesh products founding on *Montgomery v Lanarkshire Health Board* [2015] UKSC 11, [2015] A.C. 1430, [2015] C.L.Y. 1769.

Held: Proceedings remitted. (1) There were presently approximately 350 cases in the Court of Session arising out of the use of pelvic mesh products and only the four present cases had been raised in the sheriff court. (2) The Lord Justice Clerk, exercising the powers of the Lord President, had issued a direction (No.2 of 2015) under r.2.2(2) of the 1994 rules directing that proceedings arising from the use of vaginal tape and female pelvic mesh to treat stress urinary incontinence and pelvic organ prolapse ought to be dealt with in accordance with that direction, and in making such a direction he required to be satisfied that the procedure which would otherwise apply was unsuitable for the disposal of such proceedings: there was no power in the sheriff court equivalent to r.2.2, accordingly, the sheriff court was unable to deal with such cases in the same manner as the Court of Session under the practice direction, the conduct of those cases in the Court of Session was subject to a practice direction which was designed to ensure that the cases were dealt with in a consistent and efficient manner, there was considerable public interest in the wider issues raised by the cases and cause had been shown for remit of the present proceedings to the Court of Session.

B v NHS AYRSHIRE AND ARRAN, [2016] CSOH 120, 2016 S.L.T. 977, Lord Boyd of Duncansby, OH.

2478 Writs of sequestration–Debt Arrangement Scheme–Interpretation of reg.30 Debt Arrangement Scheme (Scotland) Regulations 2011

[Bankruptcy (Scotland) Act 1985 (c.66) s.12; Debt Arrangement Scheme (Scotland) Regulations 2011 (SSI 2011/141) reg.19(2)(b), reg.20, reg.30]

M petitioned for D's sequestration under the Bankruptcy (Scotland) Act 1985. Prior to the presentation of the petition, an entry had been made in the debt arrangement scheme register in respect of a program which had included the debt forming the basis of the petition. D had applied for the program under the Debt Arrangement Scheme (Scotland) Regulations 2011 reg.20 and it had been entered in the register under reg.19(2)(b), but had not yet been approved. D submitted *inter alia* that M's petition was incompetent in terms of reg.30 of the 2011 Regulations because it followed upon an application for a program having been entered in the register. M submitted *inter alia* that D's interpretation of reg.30 conflicted with s.12(2) of the 1985 Act, which did not allow the sheriff discretion to refuse.

Held: Petition granted. (1) The court was not persuaded that the provisions were in conflict; to petition for sequestration was not the same as presenting a sequestration petition to the court and the legal meaning of reg.30 was that M could not move the court to award sequestration during the period following D's application having been entered into the register, that accorded with the legislative intention, namely the prevention of an award of sequestration in the period before a debt payment programme was approved, and properly understood, reg.30 did not prevent a creditor from seeking warrant to cite. (2) In the circumstances, the court was bound by s.12(2) to grant a warrant to cite: D was in Spain and his agent was unable to provide any information in respect of his return date, and given that personal service was likely to prove impossible and that D's agent was bound to report the date of the sequestration hearing to D, it was appropriate not to require personal service; intimation of the petition would also be made to D's solicitor as a precaution. *Opinion*, that even had the court's interpretation of reg.30 represented a strained construction, the circumstances of apparent conflict with s.12(2) of the 1985 Act justified that construction where delegated legislation could not override an Act, except where the enabling Act had provided therefor, *Davis, Re* (1871-72) L.R. 7 Ch. App. 526, *considered*.

MACKIN v MACKIN, 2016 S.L.T. (Sh Ct) 95, Sheriff A F Deutsch, Sh Ct (Glasgow).

COMPANY LAW

2479 Directors disqualification–Payments–Care home company director–Misapplication of funds

[Company Directors Disqualification Act 1986 (c.46) s.6]

The Secretary of State for Business, Innovation and Skills (S) petitioned for a disqualification order in terms of the Company Directors Disqualification Act 1986 s.6 in respect of the director (H) of a care home company (C). In 2008, H had entered into an agreement with a business acquaintance (N), who was one of three partners in a private investment partnership (E), which was an equal shareholder in C with H, that E would purchase care homes and lease them back to be operated by C. In March 2010, C failed to make payment of a quarterly instalment of rent for three care homes, with a late part payment being made in April 2010. In May 2010, E was informed that C was unable to finance staff wages and C requested £50,000 financial assistance in order to do so. C then defaulted on the June rental. Thereafter, C also defaulted in respect of two sets of loan notes, for which it never made any repayment. In September 2010, E carried out investigations which revealed that H had taken substantial unauthorised payments from C, which he maintained N was aware of and had authorised. C went into administration in December 2010 and H was sequestrated in December 2012. S claimed that H's conduct as a director of C made him unfit to be concerned in the management of a company; he caused or permitted the misapplication of C's funds *viz.* unauthorised payments to himself, settling liabilities incurred by him in respect of personal expenses using C's credit cards and settling liabilities incurred by himself and third parties.

Held: Petition granted. (1) C's articles of association provided that the director's remuneration was to be determined by ordinary resolution of C, and, as was accepted by H, there had been no such resolution. Moreover, H had failed to prove the requisite knowledge and assent on E's part and his evidence that N and E were aware of, and agreed to, the payments being made to him, let alone as remuneration, could not be accepted. (2) The information in C's accounts for year end to September 2009 did not provide a sound basis for concluding that the reader thereof would have been fully informed that H had taken the benefit of all the payments that he had that year, and it could not be said that E was aware that by being asked to approve the accounts, it was being asked to approve the remuneration to which H claimed he was entitled. It was clear that H had not provided E with full details of expenditure, of the precises purposes thereof, that it was for his own non-business purposes and was being taken as remuneration, he was selective in what he reported, he concealed the manner in which C's funds were being used, his evidence as to his tax returns was vague, evasive and unsatisfactory, his attitude to the rent due for the care homes was irresponsible, and none of C's members had made an informed and unanimous decision to approve the additional remuneration to be paid to him. (3) On the evidence, from March 2010, H instructed that those entitled to repayment of free personal care payments ought to be treated in the same manner as any other ordinary creditor, he regarded payment of those creditors within eight weeks as satisfactory, and he had used free personal care payments, which ought to have been repaid, as C's working capital, with the sums consistently exceeding £50,000 between April and October 2010. (4) H's misapplication of funds, which was on a significant scale, and his retention of free personal care payments, were both misconduct and made him unfit to be concerned in the management of a company. (5) H's conduct had materially contributed to C becoming insolvent, the misapplication of funds was to the prejudice of C's creditors, materially contributed to C not being able to pay its debts as they fell due, and was continued by H nothwithstanding that he was aware that C was in its predicament. H's conduct was serious and the period of disqualification ought to be near the top of the middle bracket described in *Sevenoaks Stationers (Retail) Ltd, Re* [1991] Ch. 164, [1991] C.L.Y. 401, and the appropriate disqualification period was nine years, *Sevenoaks*, *considered.*

SECRETARY OF STATE FOR BUSINESS, INNOVATION AND SKILLS v HAMILTON, [2015] CSOH 46, 2016 S.C.L.R. 19, Lord Doherty, OH.

2480 Misfeasance–Directors' liabilities–Company's sole director ordained to compensate company following misapplication of sums owing to it–Court's discretion as to mode and amount of repayment

[Insolvency Act 1986 (c.45) s.212, s.212(3); Act of Sederunt (Sheriff Court Company Insolvency Rules) 1986 (SI 1986/2297) r.36]

The sole director (G) of a company in liquidation (B) appealed against a decision of the sheriff finding that G had misapplied certain sums owing to B under a contract and ordaining G to compensate B therefor. B's liquidator (L) had raised proceedings against G in terms of the Insolvency Act 1986 s.212. The sheriff had found that G had paid the sums, or had caused them to be paid, to another company (W), of which G was also the sole director, thus he had been guilty of misfeasance with B's funds and had wrongly preferred W's claims over those of B's other creditors, in particular, Her Majesty's Revenue and Customs (H), accordingly, in terms of s.212(3) of the 1986 Act, it was appropriate that G was compelled to compensate B for the sums diverted away from it. G submitted that (1) proceedings in terms of s.212 were procedural in nature, thus the sheriff had erred in finding that B had become liable to make payment to B; (2) the measure of any payment to B by G ought to be based on any loss to B caused by G's actings and where no overall loss had resulted, the sheriff had erred in ordering payment to B of the amounts which G admitted had been paid to W rather than B as it had placed B in a better financial situation than it would have been had the contractual payments due to the B been paid. L raised an objection to the competency of the appeal on the basis *inter alia* that the latter of the sheriff's two interlocutors had been pronounced on joint motion and therefore of consent.

Held: Appeal refused. (1) With regard to the Act of Sederunt (Sheriff Court Company Insolvency Rules) 1986 r.36, the sheriff's latter interlocutor was the operative order of the court which brought the subject matter of the application to a conclusion and made the judgment final, the appeal had been marked timeously, and L's objection would be repelled. (2) Section 212 of the 1986 Act was procedural in nature but it also provided a summary remedy where there had been a wrongful act by a director or other officer of the company. (3) Standing the sheriff's findings in fact that at the date when B was likely to have become insolvent, a large debt had been outstanding to H, and that the sums due to B in terms of the contract had been diverted or misapplied to W's bank account, which was controlled by G, he had been entitled to come to the conclusion that G had misapplied sums contractually owing to B by paying them or causing them to be paid directly to W and that that had constituted a misfeasance with B's funds; on any view G's actings had constituted both misfeasance and a breach of his duties as B's director and to the general body of creditors, and the sheriff had been entitled to proceed to consider the appropriate remedy in terms of s.212(3). (4) There was no requirement that the court have regard only to actual loss to B, it was required to examine G's conduct and to consider a remedy in terms of s.212(3); once a misfeasance or breach of fiduciary duty was established the court might order or impose one of the remedies set out in s.212(3), it had a discretion as to the mode and amount of repayment or compensation, and there was no requirement to assess that compensation by reference to any established loss to the company. (5) The compensatory payment had been made by reference to the amounts misapplied or diverted from B by G, his assertion that B had suffered no loss was not accepted, those assertions and the claim that W was B's creditor remained to be verified, accordingly, the compensatory payment ordered by the sheriff related directly to the sums diverted from B to W, which was wholly controlled by G, which sums ought to be available to L for the benefit of B's creditors, which the sheriff's order sought to achieve, *Derek Randall Enterprises Ltd, Re* [1990] B.C.C. 749, [1991] C.L.Y. 410, *considered*.

LIQUIDATOR OF GLASGOW AND WEIR BLACKSMITHS LTD v GLASGOW, 2016 S.L.T. (Sh Ct) 171, Sheriff Principal M M Stephen, QC, Sh Ct (Lothian) (Edinburgh).

2481 Share transfers–Share valuation–Unfairly prejudicial conduct–Implementation of bad leaver provisions

[Companies Act 2006 (c.46) s.994, s.996]

A shareholder (G) and another (collectively X) reclaimed against a Lord Ordinary's decision ordaining a company (B) to purchase the shares held therein for the aggregate sum of £2,444,000 (*Gray v Braid Group (Holdings) Ltd* [2015] CSOH 146, 2015 G.W.D. 37-588). G had petitioned the court in terms of the Companies Act 2006 s.994 for an order pursuant to s.996 seeking the purchase of his shares in B on the ground that B's affairs had been conducted in a manner that was unfairly prejudicial to his interests. The Lord Ordinary held that conduct unfairly prejudicial to G's interests had been proved and having heard competing valuation evidence, concluded that B might reasonably be valued at £32,000,000, on which basis, the cumulative value of X's holdings would be £20,614,400. The Lord Ordinary thereafter gave effect to B's submission that, because of G's participation in bribery offences involving B, he was a bad leaver in terms of B's articles of association and was entitled, on disposal of his shares, to be paid only whichever was the lesser of their fair value or their subscription or par value and that to give appropriate relief under s.996, an order should be made for the purchase at par value. It was argued *inter alia* that the order had failed to give relief in respect of the matters complained of where, having decided that B's affairs had been conducted in a manner prejudicial to X's interests, the effect of the order was to grossly enrich those responsible and it did not fall within the proper bounds of discretion conferred on the Lord Ordinary by s.996. Further, G was not a leaving shareholder and did not qualify for consideration as a bad leaver, the mechanisms for determining the sale price for compulsory sale shares contained in art.6.8.2.2 of B's articles of association were thus inapplicable; should the other members of B seek to remove G as a director, in respect of which they had taken no steps, the mechanism which would require to be followed was found in the shareholders' agreement which prevailed over the articles in the event of conflict; in any event, even was G a leaving shareholder, the compulsory transfer provisions in art.6.8 were not automatic but art.6.8.1 made express provision for the board resolving not to implement them which was not a matter investigated in evidence at the proof. *Esto*, the aforementioned arguments were not accepted, art.6.8.2.2 was, in law, an unenforceable penalty clause and could not form a model for the court's disposal of the matter: it was clear from *Makdessi v Cavendish Square Holdings BV* [2015] UKSC 67, [2016] A.C. 1172, [2016] 437 that the law on penalty clauses applied not just to a specific fixed sum in the event of breach of contract but to a range of circumstances including that in which a person was required to give up or surrender property at other than value.

Held: Reclaiming motion refused. (Lord Menzies *dissenting*). Parties were in sharp disagreement as to the correctness of the sum selected by the Lord Ordinary as the price at which B should purchase the shares but no issue was taken with the steps taken to arrive thereat: art.6.8.2.2 did not constitute a penalty, bearing in mind parties' freedom to contract on such terms as they wished, and in order for a provision to amount to a penalty with the result that a contractual term adopted by parties after careful negotiation was held by the court to be unenforceable, the adverse consequence with the secondary obligation imposed had to be entirely disproportionate to the interest in proper performance of the primary obligation and as there were interests to protect, the secondary obligation selected to protect them could neither be said to be exorbitant nor unconscionable; the question had to be tested by reference to the state of affairs at the time of the agreement and the bad leaver provisions were a legitimate and proportionate response to the issues and problems likely to arise if, and when, circumstances justified their implementation; the bad leaver provision was capable of being enforced and the Lord Ordinary, having found that G had been guilty of gross misconduct and been the proper subject of investigation, was correct to have regard to the bad leaver provisions in fixing the purchase price for the share transfer and had not gone too far in finding them applicable, *Cavendish*, *considered*. Per Lord Malcolm, that the proceedings and related actions by G amounted to a failed attempt to extricate himself from the agreed consequences of his gross misconduct which was the implementation of the bad leaver provisions and ss.994 and 996 of the 2006 Act did not provide a reason for the court to interfere with the freely negotiated terms of the parties' agreement in this regard and thereby give a windfall to G. Per Lord Menzies, *dissenting*, that (1) neither party had taken issue with the Lord Ordinary's exercise of his discretion (i) that he should make an order, (ii) that an order under s.996(2)(e) was appropriate and the court had a wide discretion throughout the exercise which it had to carry out in terms of s.996, including the fixing of a price for the purchase of shares in terms of subs.(2)(e), and was entitled to assess the effect of the unfairly prejudicial conduct and to consider issues of proportionality, as well as have regard to G's conduct, but the Lord Ordinary did not have a solid evidential basis for his conclusion that he was faced with circumstances in which the consequence of G's conduct was that the bad leaver provisions of the articles had become applicable and had thereby exercised his discretion wrongly: nothing other than the provisions of art.6.8.2.2 provided a justification for a transfer price of £2,444,000 in respect of X's shareholding of 64.42% of B, a company with a valuation of £32,000,000, and the order could not be said to amount to the giving of relief in respect of the matters complained of; (2) an order for the purchase of the shares in B held by X respectively for the aggregate sum of £18,000,000 would be an appropriate order for giving relief in respect of the matters complained of in terms of s.996(1) of the 2006 Act which amounted to a reworking of the figures before the Lord Ordinary to remove the consequences of G's misconduct from those responsible therefor. *Opinion* per Lord Menzies, that (1) properly characterised, the primary obligation in considering the bad leaver provisions in art.6.8.2.2 was that the employee would not commit an act of gross misconduct or persistently under perform and in the event of a breach thereof, the bad leaver provisions would be triggered, and the secondary obligation was the compulsory transfer of the bad leaver's shares at subscription price, the article could not properly be categorised as providing for a conditional primary obligation, *Cavendish, distinguished*; (2) on whether art.6.8.2.2 was an unfair and unenforceable penalty provision, and considering B's legitimate interests, the provision that where the reason for ceasing to be employed or to act as a director was fraud or misconduct, the sale price should be the lower of 75% of the fair value or the subscription price, was exorbitant or unconscionable, and unjustified by the innocent party's interest in the performance of the contract and had it been necessary to do so, art.6.8.2.2 would have been found not to have been a proper model for an order in the terms of the petition.

GRAY v BRAID GROUP (HOLDINGS) LTD, [2016] CSIH 68, 2016 S.L.T. 1003, Lord Menzies, Lord Brodie, Lord Malcolm, IH (Ex Div).

CONSTRUCTION LAW

2482 Contractual liability–Risk–Employer's action for payment and breach of contract–Whether contractor's liability displaced by joint insurance policy

An action by an energy company (S) against a construction company (H) for *inter alia* payment of the cost of remedial works in respect of an electricity generation scheme came before the Lord Ordinary on a preliminary point relating to insurance. S had employed H to build *inter alia* two tunnels. The contract provided that each party was to indemnify the other against claims, proceedings, compensation and costs due to an event which was at his risk, and further required H to take out a joint insurance policy in respect of contractor's risk events to endure from the starting date until the defects certificate was issued, namely 104 weeks after the completion date. H issued the completion certificate in February 2009 and on 6 August, S issued a defects notice stating that there was inadequate support in part of the tunnel. Subsequent investigations disclosed a significant blockage in the tunnel caused by a collapse. S instructed H to remedy matters within a reasonable time, however, H regarded the collapse as an employer's risk event and considered that it would therefore be entitled to be paid in full for any work carried out in that respect. H submitted *inter alia* that the insurance policy had supplanted contractual liability and S was barred from raising the present proceedings.

Held: Case put out by order. (1) There was neither an implied term preventing an action for damages nor an irrebuttable presumption that the parties had no liability to one another because a joint names policy was in place, the contractual provision for joint insurance had not displaced liability and S was not barred from bringing the present action, *Cooperative Retail Services Ltd v Taylor Young Partnership Ltd* [2002] UKHL 17, [2002] 1 W.L.R. 1419, [2002] C.L.Y. 678, *considered*. (2) A by order hearing would be fixed to consider further procedure. *Observed*, that parties had waived subrogation rights in respect of the directors and employees of the joint insured and where the waiver of such rights in respect of each other was a more significant matter, one would expect such a waiver to be likewise in express terms.

SSE GENERATION LTD v HOCHTIEF SOLUTIONS AG, [2015] CSOH 92, [2015] B.L.R. 774, Lord Woolman, OH.

2483 Performance bonds–Notice–Notice given by local authority under performance guarantee bond–Validity

[Town and Country Planning (Scotland) Act 1997 (c.8) s.75]

A financial institution (F) reclaimed against a decision of the Lord Ordinary that a local authority (C) had validly given notice to F under a performance guarantee bond (*South Lanarkshire Council v Coface SA* [2015] CSOH 8, 2015 G.W.D. 4-79). In June 2009, C and a coal mining company (S) had been granted planning permission to develop an opencast coal mine (M) and had entered into an agreement with regard thereto in terms of the Town and Country Planning (Scotland) Act 1997 s.75, which had required S to restore M at the conclusion of mining operations and to provide a performance guarantee bond in respect thereof. F had agreed to stand as guarantor and executed the bond, which was to endure until 1 August 2014, with liability based upon the amount of restoration work that C estimated would be required subject to a maximum aggregate liability of approximately £4.5 million. On 29 April 2013, the court ordered that S be wound up on the ground of insolvency, and on 1 May 2013, C had written to F stating *inter alia* that the liquidators had ceased all works at M, S was in breach of its planning obligations and C was likely to call up the bond. F had not responded and C had written to F again on 29 May 2013 and had enclosed a notice in terms of the bond stating that S was in breach of the s.75 agreement and stating the cost of the restoration works to be £9,199,892. On 25 July 2014, C had sent two further letters to F purported to be demands for payment, one seeking £4,499,411 and the other £1,271,230.65. Before the Lord Ordinary, F had submitted that (1) where cl.3.1 of the bond referred to a notice in writing and cl.3.2 referred to a written demand for payment, the bond prescribed a two stage procedure and C had to serve a notice specifying the breach and the cost of the works, followed by a demand for payment; (2) the notice enclosed with C's letter of 29 May was deficient in that it failed to provide the cost to C in terms of cl.2.2 of the bond and it did not qualify as a demand because that term was not used, instead C had simply provided the total cost of the restoration works. The Lord Ordinary had rejected F's construction of the bond.

Held: Reclaiming motion refused and matter remitted to Lord Ordinary to proceed as accords. (1) C's notice of 29 May 2013 satisfied the requirements of cl.3.1 of the bond; the covering letter stated that the notice was sent in terms of cl.3 of the bond, the notice itself was on C's writing paper and bore to be signed by C's manager and proper officer, the notice indicated that S was in breach of its restoration obligations under the s.75 agreement, which breach gave rise to a liability under cl.2 of the bond, it was sufficiently clear, and it provided an indication of the cost of the restoration work, in compliance with the second requirement of cl.3.1, thus it complied strictly with the terms of cll.2 and 3 of the bond. (2) There was no commercial purpose in F's contemplated two stage procedure; once the cost of the restoration works had been provided, as required by cl.3.1, the calculation of the amount actually due was straightforward, using the schedule and the index linking provisions in cl.5.4, and could be performed by F as well as C, thus a second document was otiose, further, any such procedure would give rise to uncertainty as to when the bond was realisable, which commercial common sense suggested was unnecessary and undesirable. (3) F's emphasis on the provisions of cl.3.2, which used the expressions "claim" and "written demand for payment", was misplaced; the first part of cl.3.2 had to be construed in accordance with the fundamental purpose of a normal performance bond, that the granter of the bond ought not to be obliged to investigate the underlying facts but ought to be entitled to proceed on the basis of a written demand for payment and any documents or statements of fact that were specified in the relevant clause of the bond, which cl.3.2 achieved; the second part of cl.3.2 was a procedural provision that specified the form that the notice under cl.3.1 ought to take, namely a demand for payment from an authorised official, which would be sufficient evidence of any sum due, and that was in accordance with the fundamental working of a performance bond. (4) Clause 3.1 merely required notice in writing of any breach; in the present case, the breach had occurred at an anticipatory stage, where it had become apparent before the termination of mining operations that S was insolvent and would be unable to carry out the restoration works, therefore, it was impossible to give specification of the breach beyond stating that the restoration obligations could not be carried out, and to require more would fly in the face of commercial common sense. Moreover, the 29 May notice referred to S being in provisional liquidation, and the 1 May letter had referred to the winding up proceedings and the appointment of liquidators, which would obviously mean that nothing would be done by S towards implement of the restoration obligations. (5) The Lord Ordinary had been correct to hold that the notice served by C on 29 May 2013 was in accordance with the requirements of the bond, however, he had further noted that F had not accepted that the signatory to the notice of 29 May 2013 was C's authorised signatory and had therefore allowed a proof before answer to enable further consideration thereof, and the action would be remitted to the Lord Ordinary to proceed as accords.

SOUTH LANARKSHIRE COUNCIL v COFACE SA, [2016] CSIH 15, [2016] B.L.R. 237, Lord Menzies, Lady Smith, Lord Drummond Young, IH (Ex Div).

CONTRACTS

2484 Breach of contract–Loss–Faiilure to pay sums due to employees–Whether award to be made gross or net

Two employees (X and Y, collectively Z) of a children's residential care home operator (J) appealed against a decision of the sheriff assoilzieing J from Z's action seeking payment of sums due to them in terms of their contracts of employment. The sheriff had found that X and Y had each not received half of their wages between 9 October and 31 December 2010, were each entitled to 5% annual cost of living increase, Y was entitled to receive a 10% share of profit, and *in cumulo*, X had established a gross loss of £8,702.74 and Y of £44,622.13, however, they had failed to prove their net loss, thus he had dismissed their claims. Z averred that the sheriff had erred in finding that while they had led evidence of gross loss, they had failed to prove their net loss with reference to the incidence of taxation and in relation to Y, that her profit share entitlement was payable as profits akin to the terms of a joint venture.

Held: Appeal allowed. (1) In claims, it was important to understand whether the sums payable would be taxable or not in the hands of the recipient, and it was regrettable that that had not been properly addressed in the present case; the sums claimed for breach of contract were taxable and any sums awarded to Z as loss of earnings were subject to tax. (2) The sheriff had not fallen into error in not awarding decree for the gross loss of earnings; in making a net award, Z would receive the sum which they would have received from J had it been timeously paid, namely a net sum, moreover, a pursuer would be overcompensated if they were to be entitled to interest in the gross sum when a proportion of that sum had to be accounted for to Her Majesty's Revenue and Customs (HMRC), however, that did not resolve the difficulties in relation to enforcement where a judgment creditor required to know what they were to pay to satisfy the decree where, in addition to paying the net sum to the successful party the unsuccessful party had to account to HMRC for deductions for income tax and national insurance through the PAYE system, which could be best addressed by setting out in a decree in addition to the sum awarded that the unsuccessful party was also bound to account to HMRC for those deductions, thus the successful party would have a basis to take action to recover such sums in the event of the defender not making payment to HMRC, therefore the awards to Z ought to be made in respect of a net sum. (3) The sheriff had only been provided with updated schedules of loss by Z in the course of submission and Z had only had regard to the requirement to consider net loss when faced with the draft written submissions by J, and having resolved the issues of liability, the sheriff would have been entitled to have adopted an approach in line with *Clark v Chief Constable of Lothian and Borders* 1993 S.C. 320, [1993] C.L.Y. 5189 and made a broad axe percentage deduction absent evidence or agreement, however, despite Z's evidence being deficient at proof, there had been a sufficiency to allow the court to establish a net sum from the findings made, alternatively, the sheriff could have encouraged the parties to seek to agree such deductions or invited J to respond to Z's schedules, and in failing to follow either course, the sheriff had fallen into error; it defied logic that he had concluded that he had been unable to make an award to pursuers who he had found to have sustained gross losses. (4) Parties had been able to agree net loss figures of £7,000 for X and £31,500 for Y and it was appropriate to modify the sheriff's interlocutor to grant decree in Z's favour for those amounts; utilising net figures as agreed by the parties was preferable to adopting a broad brush percentage deduction, with regard to the requirement for certainty in the level of award made, best practice would be for the gross loss to be narrated in the decree with the anticipated deductions and consequent net sum also being specified, and the sheriff's interlocutor would be recalled to the extent necessary to find X and Y entitled to £7,000 and £31,500 respectively, those sums to be paid after the required deduction by J for income tax and national insurance through PAYE to be paid to HMRC, *Clark, considered.* (5) The judicial rate of 8% ought to apply to interest; absent averments and information on the rates that might be applicable to parties, there was no reason to modify either the judicial rate of interest or the standard position that interest at the judicial rate ought to be payable to the successful party from the date of citation. (6) The parties would be given an opportunity to make further submissions on expenses.

MORGANS v JULIA STEWART LTD, 2016 S.L.T. (Sh Ct) 351, Sheriff Principal D L Murray, Sh Ct (North Strathclyde) (Paisley).

2485 Breach of contract–Missives–Rescission of agreement to purchase land–Relevancy of pleadings

An action for breach of contract raised by a company (P) against a local authority (G), came before the Lord Ordinary for a debate the relevancy of P's pleadings. Pursuant to negotiations in respect of the purchase of subjects (S) owned by G, in 2006, P had instructed investigations which revealed that S was relatively free from hazardous waste. A 2011 survey report noted the presence of additional earth on S, and G confirmed that spoil from surrounding sites had been deposited thereon between June 2009 and January 2010. G and P signed an option agreement in 2011 and in 2012, G removed the spoil, which included a substantial amount of hazardous waste. The agreement provided *inter alia* that the effective date was 9 December 2011, as soon as reasonably practicable therefrom and no later than the settlement date, G required to instruct contractors to prepare the site waste management plan and the material management plan (collectively X) and to provide X to P as soon as reasonably practicable on receipt thereof (cl.4). The missives within the agreement provided that P required to pay the purchase price on the date of settlement, G required to provide certain documents including collateral warranties upon receipt thereof and in the event of nonpayment for 20 working days, G had the right to rescind the missives and the option agreement, and condition 1.7 provided that G was not entitled to rescind where any delay in payment was due to G's failure to implement its obligations under the missives timeously. P exercised the option in December 2012 with a settlement date of 11 April 2013. On 12 February, P requested copies of X, G refused on the basis that it was not obliged to provide X prior to settlement, and P subsequently failed to pay the initial purchase price on the settlement date, maintaining that it was not obliged to do so in light of G's failure to deliver X. Following delivery of X on 5 June 2013, P failed to pay the purchase price and on 4 July, G rescinded the agreement. P presented its claim on alternative bases: regarding breach of contract, it claimed loss of profits for

G's failure to provide X and certain other documents, averring that but for that failure, it would have obtained the necessary funding for S's purchase; in the alternative, it claimed abortive costs incurred in connection with the purchase for G's negligent misrepresentations regarding the hazardous waste, averring that but for those misrepresentations, it would not have exercised the option.

Held: Action dismissed and case put out by order. (1) Clause 4.1 had imposed a duty of instruction, not one of delivery, to impose an obligation on G to deliver X on or before the settlement date would be to insert words into the provision, and the words therein were straightforward and easily understood, while P's construction involved the rewriting of the contract and fell to be rejected. (2) Condition 1.7 of the missives had not been extended to include a breach of the option agreement, accordingly, the inquiry was a narrow one; parties had prescribed the circumstances in which G would lose its right to rescind, which had not included a breach of cl.4.1, and P was not entitled to withhold the purchase price, *Macari v Celtic Football & Athletic Co Ltd* 1999 S.C. 628, [2000] C.L.Y. 6221, *considered.* (3) Having regard to the wording of the agreement, P's rights depended on it fulfilling its obligation to pay and unless and until that had occurred, G had no obligation to deliver. (4) The present case did not feature the two factors in *Smart v Bargh* 1949 S.C. 57, [1949] C.L.Y. 5003, P ought to know whether it would have exercised the option, its pleadings indicated that the present case was a no transaction case, and it was incompatible with substantial justice to allow P's breach of contract claim to proceed to proof on the basis of one sentence which contradicted its other pleadings; G was entitled to know the case against it and P could only claim for abortive costs, *Smart, London & Caledonian Marine Insurance Co v London & Edinburgh Shipping Co* (1867) 5 M. 982 and *Clarke v Edinburgh & District Tramways Co Ltd* 1914 S.C. 775, *considered.* (5) A by order hearing would be fixed to determine further procedure.

PIP 3 LTD v GLASGOW CITY COUNCIL, [2015] CSOH 119, 2016 S.C.L.R. 361, Lord Woolman, OH.

2486 Contracts of sale–Implied terms–Failure to give notice of cancellation of payment–Business efficacy

An importer and distributer of alcohol (G) raised an action against a company (C) which produced, bottled and packaged whisky to G's order under two brand names, one (X) under G's own brand name and the other (Y) under the brand name of G's customer. G sought repetition of the price paid for X and Y but that C had not shipped, damages representing the loss of profit it would have made had the whisky been supplied, and damages in respect of breach of contract for remedial costs incurred in remedying label defects on bottles of X. C counterclaimed seeking payment of the purchase price due under contracts for the sale of X and Y, failing which damages for breach thereof. G submitted orders to C offering to purchase the whisky specified therein. If C agreed to supply all or part of the order it issued an invoice in respect of that quantity, and a separate contract of sale was concluded on the issuing of each invoice. The acceptance provided that the payment terms were 100 per cent prepayment and that G was obliged to pay shipping costs. G admitted that it was an implied term of each contract that it would make payment within a reasonable time after the contract's conclusion, and sought to amend such admission to reflect its argument that in practice it only paid a few days before shipping dates provided by C. Evidence was led that some of the bottles of X shipped to G had labels peeling off, misaligned or with air bubbles and that a small number of bottles had minor dents or blemishes. By 2 December 2011, there were eight contracts for the supply of Y and two contracts for the supply of X where G had paid for the goods but they had not yet been shipped. On 6 December 2011, G instructed a SWIFT payment for eight containers of Y and emailed C a copy of the receipt. Evidence was led that G subsequently cancelled the SWIFT payment and its orders. On 8 December 2011, C emailed G stating *inter alia* that payment had not been received, that stock of Y had already been produced and materials had been purchased, refuting G's suggestion that labels had partially peeled off and stating that it had placed G's account on hold. In subsequent correspondence G offered to settle accounts by letter of credit rather than by prepayment. G and C were unable to resolve their disputes and C decanted the whisky and invoiced G for costs incurred.

Held: Case put out by order. (1) G's motion to amend its pleadings would be refused where it would have been unfair and prejudicial to C to have allowed G to found upon practice to maintain that the terms of the contracts relating to payment differed from the admitted term; evidence of practice was a relevant factor in determining whether G was in breach of its obligations to make payment within a reasonable time but it was not necessary for it to amend its pleadings to found upon evidence of practice for that purpose. (2) Although it was not necessary in order to give business efficacy to the contracts that a term be implied requiring that G would not cancel SWIFT transfers which it had instructed and exhibited to C, in the whole circumstances business efficacy required an implied term that where intimation of a SWIFT payment was made but the payment was cancelled, G was obliged to inform C immediately of the cancellation. Reasonable business persons would have known that on receipt of evidence of SWIFT payment instructions, C would have been very likely to have incurred expenditure in relation to the contract, and in failing to give C immediate notice of the cancellation, G was in material breach of the implied term, which entitled C to rescind those contracts. (3) A reasonable person would not have regarded the bottles with peeling labels as being of satisfactory quality but would also not have regarded a bottle as being of unsatisfactory quality unless the misalignment of, or air bubbling under, the labels was clearly noticeable, and very minor dents or blemishes would not have had the effect of unsatisfactory quality. The bottles identified as having peeling labels, and a proportion of the bottles identified as having misaligned labels, air bubbles under the labels or damaged bottle tops, were of unsatisfactory quality, and C was in material breach of contract. (4) In the contracts where C withheld performance of its obligations to supply goods, G had duly performed its corresponding obligation to pay for the goods, and there was no legitimate basis for C to have suspended performance of its supply obligations. The alleged failure of performance related to other distinct contracts, and nothing in the terms or surrounding circumstances indicated an intention that C's supply obligations under a particular contract were dependant on payment for goods supplied under other contracts. C was not entitled to withhold performance and was in material breach of those contracts. (5) G was not entitled to withhold performance of its payment obligations under certain of the contracts either on the basis that C had not performed its obligations to supply goods G had paid for under other contracts or that the bottles of X were not of satisfactory quality. Nothing indicated an intention that C's obligations to supply the goods under certain contracts and G's obligations to pay under different contracts were counterpart obligations. The fact that some of the goods under earlier contracts for the sale of X might have been of unsatisfactory quality did not entitle G to withhold performance of later distinct contracts relating to X or Y, and such withholding of payment was a material breach of those contracts. (6) G's cancellation of the SWIFT payment taken together with its subsequent correspondence indicating that it did not intend to honour its contractual obligations was an anticipatory material breach of the contracts relating to that payment and of all other contracts where payment had not been made. (7) The case would be put out by order for parties to address the court as to the terms of an appropriate interlocutor and further procedure.

GLEN CLYDE WHISKY LTD v CAMPBELL MEYER & CO LTD, [2015] CSOH 97, 2016 S.C.L.R. 341, Lord Doherty, OH.

2487 Oral contracts–Leases–Verbal lease in respect of petrol station forecourt shop–Validity

[Requirements of Writing (Scotland) Act 1995 (c.7) s.1(2)(a)(i), s.1(2)(b), s.1(3), s.1(4)]

The son in law (G) of the owner (X) of a petrol station (P) raised an action against P's executor (E) seeking (1) delivery of certain moveable equipment (M), which failing, payment of M's value; (2) damages in respect of profits lost due to an alleged material breach of a verbal lease between G and X. In autumn 2004, P had been in financial difficulties and X and G had agreed *inter alia* to G converting P's forecourt shop (F) into a chip shop (C) and leasing C from X, in relation to which G had obtained £50,000 funding. In early 2005, G and X had verbally agreed a lease in respect of F, the terms being that (i) the parties were G and X, (ii) the property to be leased would be F, (iii) F would be converted into C, (iv) the rent for F would be that G would be responsible for

P's staffing and running costs, save for the purchase of new fuel, (v) the lease's duration would be 15 years from when C opened for business. The verbal lease had never been reduced to writing. G had used the £50,000 funding to convert F into C, which had included purchasing and installing M and C had opened in July 2005. G had operated C in compliance with the conditions of the verbal lease until 20 October 2012 when, due to a deterioration in G and X's relationship, and following a verbal confrontation between them, X had cut the electricity supply to C and had refused to let G into C, as a result of which C had been forced to cease trading, and X had thereafter declined all of G's repeated requests to reconnect the power to C and to allow G back into C, and he had retained possession of M. C's average annual net profit had been £19,000 and the majority of M had a life span of 15 years and had been valued at £16,000.

Held: Procedural hearing fixed. (1) On the basis of the evidence, G owned M, and the weight of the evidence, although limited, pointed to E currently being in possession and control of M, however, E had led no evidence about the three elements or four factors identified in Reid, *The Law of Property in Scotland,* in order for accession to have taken place, and in those circumstances, his defence to the action of delivery could not succeed. (2) The action for delivery was directed against E only in his representative capacity and he ought to have been sued for the purposes of delivery in his individual capacity as possessor rather than as judicial successor in title, and P remained liable for the value of the equipment unless and until it was vindicated from E as subsequent possessor; the alternative remedy of payment of the value of the equipment was not affected by the action only being directed against E in his representative capacity, however, it was not supported by a plea in law; given that the first crave was framed in the alternative and a problem had arisen in relation to both remedies sought therein, a procedural hearing would be fixed for the sheriff to be addressed on, and give further consideration to, the proper disposal of the first crave. (3) On the evidence, G and X had agreed a verbal lease which on the one hand was a contract for the creation of a real right in land, and on the other hand was capable of creating a real right in land, and it could not be described as creating purely personal rights, therefore, on the authorities, the verbal lease fell within the Requirements of Writing (Scotland) Act 1995 s.1(2)(b) such that G could not rely on the personal bar provisions in s.1(3) and s.1(4), thus, the verbal lease had been invalid and P had been entitled to withdraw therefrom, accordingly, G's claim for damages for loss of profits had to fail, *Advice Centre for Mortgages Ltd v McNicoll* 2006 S.L.T. 591, [2006] C.L.Y. 5548 and *Gyle Shopping Centre General Partners Ltd v Marks & Spencer Plc* [2014] CSOH 122, 2015 S.C.L.R. 171, [2014] C.L.Y. 3631, *applied* and *Caterleisure Ltd v Glasgow Prestwick International Airport Ltd* 2006 S.C. 602, [2006] C.L.Y. 5160, *distinguished.* Opinion, that had the verbal lease fallen within s.1(2)(a)(i) of the 1995 Act, the conditions in s.1(4) would have been satisfied and s.1(3) would have applied in relation to the verbal lease, and decree would have been granted in terms of the second crave, awarding damages of £141,117 to G, in terms of a forensic accountant's calculations for C's loss of profit.

GRAY v MACNEIL'S EXECUTOR, 2016 S.L.T. (Sh Ct) 250, Sheriff C Dickson, Sh Ct (Grampian) (Lochmaddy).

2488 Partnership agreements–Contract terms–Whether employee leaving partnership was "competing leaver"–Whether actual or deemed competition between former and current employers

A company (C) in an investment group (G) reclaimed against a decision of the Lord Ordinary granting declarator that G's employee (B) was an ordinary leaver in terms of several limited partnership agreements (X) (*Bishop v 3i Investments PLC* [2014] CSOH 152, 2014 G.W.D. 33-634). G's business model was to establish limited partnerships in which senior employees had become partners and contributed personal funds, which had been invested by the limited partnership. B had invested in several such partnerships which were managed by C and regulated by X, which had provided that any employee classified as a competing leaver was not entitled to receive the carried interest therefrom. X had further provided *inter alia* that a competing leaver was an ordinary leaver who had taken up employment in a competitive capacity with, or provided competitive services to, C's competitor within 24 months of leaving, and that a business would be deemed a competitor where it operated, intended to operate or was likely to operate in any geographical areas and investment product sectors/business lines in which C operated, or intended to operate. B had obtained employment with another investment company (E), and prior to his departure from C, he was informed that he was a competing leaver. Evidence had been led that since 2009, C's investment profile had advertised that it's investments ranged from £25 million to £150 million, and in that year a government report (R) had identified a gap in the financial services market in the band £2 million to £10 million, created by C's move to the higher banding, and that E had been created to meet that problem. The Lord Ordinary had found that there had been no actual or deemed competition between C and E and concluded that B was not a competing leaver. C submitted *inter alia* that (1) it was appropriate to give a wide meaning to competition where the purpose of X was to retain management staff; (2) the Lord Ordinary had given insufficient weight to the deemed competition provision; (3) the differences in banding had not precluded competition between C and E, and all enterprises engaged in private equity business were capable of competing with each other for deals, funds and staff; (4) the contractual provisions ought to be construed by reference to the date on which each contract had been concluded; (5) the expression "investment product sector/business line" ought to be construed as a reference to the totality of C's business; (6) the notion of a disproportionate burden on B was irrelevant where B was only one of several partners within each limited partnership.

Held: Reclaiming motion refused. (1) The definition of a competing leaver indicated that competition with C was crucial; that element of competition was the reason for excluding B from future growth of the limited partnerships and the purpose of the definition was to exclude employees who left C to work for a competitor. (2) The expression "business line" did not add anything of significance to "investment product sector", that expression was flexible and its meaning was highly dependent on context. (3) Issues of competition were to be determined at the time of operation and not when the contract was concluded, anything else would have rendered the clause arbitrary and unpredictable in its effectiveness, and to construe the earlier limited partnership agreements without any reference to the limit adopted in 2009 would fundamentally distort the operation of X. (4) The Lord ordinary's findings, which had not been challenged, justified the proposition that banding was an important differentiating feature in the investment market; the deficiency identified in R indicated that the band in which E operated was a different market from C's band, which was the fundamental reason for the recommendation that gave rise to E's creation and it could not be said that there was competition between C and E. (5) C had raised funds through shareholders and investors while E was funded by five clearing banks, and it was doubtful whether competition in recruiting staff was within the contemplation of the definition of competing leaver. (6) In light of the different banding within which C and E operated, it could not be said that there was any deemed competition between them, particularly where E had been created to meet the problem of funding left by C's departure therefrom. (7) The notion of excessive or disproportionate burdens was of general application to commercial contracts, which ought to be construed in such a way that benefits might be expected to accrue to both parties and one party was not subject to an excessive or disproportionate burden, *Grove Investments Ltd v Cape Building Products Ltd* [2014] CSIH 43, 2014 Hous. L.R. 35, [2014] C.L.Y. 3630, *considered.* (8) Where the definition had relied on actual and deemed competition by reference to C's activities, the deeming provision had not been included to avoid uncertainty, *Greck v Henderson Asia Pacific Equity Partners (FP) LP* 2008 G.W.D. 8-155, *distinguished. Opinion*, that had competition for staff been relevant to the definition of a competing leaver, there might have been a serious question as to whether the restrictions in the competing leaver clause were contrary to public policy.

BISHOP v 3I INVESTMENTS PLC, [2015] CSIH 66, 2016 S.C.L.R. 398, Lady Paton, Lady Dorrian, Lord Drummond Young, IH (Ex Div).

CRIMINAL EVIDENCE

2489 Admissibility–Collateral evidence–Defence of consent to rape–Evidence going to complainer's character

[Criminal Procedure (Scotland) Act 1995 (c.46) s.275, s.275(1)(b), s.275(2)(b)(i)]

K, charged with raping X on 6 June 2011, appealed against the refusal by the preliminary hearing judge of an application under the Criminal Procedure (Scotland) Act 1995 s.275 seeking to elicit or admit certain evidence. K had lodged a special defence of consent, and the evidence sought to be admitted was that X had menstruated between 1 and 6 June 2011, that from approximately 24 June she had falsely claimed to work colleagues that she was pregnant with K's child and to have had a termination performed on 11 July, and that following the alleged rape, X would constantly bring the matter up in conversations with work colleagues, despite their efforts not to speak about it and appeared to enjoy discussing the alleged incident, which was relevant to the proper assessment of X's credibility, demonstrating that she had persistently lied in relation to matters directly connected with, and flowing from, her sexual encounter with K and that that she had persisted therein. The preliminary hearing judge had proceeded on the basis that the behaviour might be relevant to X's credibility and thus to whether K was guilty of the offence charged, thus s.275(1)(b) of the 1995 Act was established, however, before the jury could consider whether the allegation of rape had been part of attention seeking behaviour on X's part they would have to weigh and consider much disputed evidence which would not be directly related to the allegations in the indictment, that given that the complaint of rape had been made very soon after the incident, and when X had been intoxicated, the relevance of the alleged subsequent behaviour to the question of consent was very limited, and X's medical records would require to be examined in detail, and that where under s.275(2)(b)(i) the proper administration of justice included the appropriate protection of X's dignity and privacy, any probative value which the evidence might have did not outweigh any risk to the administration of justice.

Held: Appeal refused. (1) Although the preliminary hearing judge had been content to proceed on the basis that the requirements of s.275(1)(b) had been met, that was not the case where the only significance of the evidence would have been to support an argument that having lied, X's credibility in relation to her assertion that intercourse with K had not been consensual had been suspect and she had lied about the course of events, the evidence was clearly of character and was thus inadmissible because it was collateral to the issues for decision as defined in the libel, *Brady (Joseph) v HM Advocate* 1986 J.C. 68, [1986] C.L.Y. 3815 and *M v HM Advocate (No.2)* [2013] HCJAC 22, 2013 S.L.T. 380, [2013] C.L.Y. 3558, *applied*. (2) Even proceeding on the basis that the evidence was admissible, as the preliminary hearing judge had, he had been correct in deciding that it would be of such little evidential weight value that it could not be said that its probative value outweighed the risk to the administration of justice from its admission; there was a great deal of speculation in the matter, there was significant dispute as to the nature and extent of the evidence, a great deal of time would likely be taken up with examination of medical records and other matters incidental to the trial, all at the expense of X's privacy and dignity, and in any event, there had been ample reason to refuse the application and the court would not interfere with the preliminary hearing judge's decision, being satisfied that the conclusion he had reached had been one within a reasonable exercise of his judgment.

KERSEBOOM (MICHEL) v HM ADVOCATE, [2016] HCJAC 51, 2016 S.C.L. 839, Lady Smith, Lady Dorrian, Lord Bracadale, HCJ.

2490 Admissibility–Expert evidence–Evidence of detective constable with prior operational involvement in case–Independence and impartiality

[Misuse of Drugs Act 1971 (c.38) s.4(3)(b); Customs and Excise Management Act 1979 (c.2) s.170(2); Criminal Procedure (Scotland) Act 1995 (c.46) s.71(2)]

J, charged with 11 charges involving controlled drugs and allegations of contraventions of the Misuse of Drugs Act 1971 s.4(3)(b) and the Customs and Excise Management Act 1979 s.170(2), appealed against the sheriff's decision repelling his minute of objection in terms of the Criminal Procedure (Scotland) Act 1995 s.71(2) to the admissibility of the evidence of a detective constable (D). The sheriff had heard evidence from D as to his qualifications and experience and, having regard to *Kennedy v Cordia (Services) LLP* [2016] UKSC 6, [2016] 1 W.L.R. 597, [2016] 1027, had found that the form and content of D's evidence exposed him to the prospect of considerable challenge under cross examination, and although D's evidence was in certain respects unprofessional and that much of the content was based upon factual assumption or hearsay statements which ought to be differently phrased, that went to the quality of the evidence, which was for the jury to assess, and D's evidence could not be said to be inadmissible by being incapable of meeting the required criteria. J claimed that D's evidence was inadmissible on the basis that he did not have the relevant qualification, competence, expertise and experience necessary to provide an expert opinion in relation to the issues arising in the case, *separatim*, D was not an independent witness who provided an impartial opinion based upon the facts presented to him and accordingly ought not to be regarded as an expert witness in the present case.

Held: Appeal refused. (1) On the basis of the evidence heard by the sheriff, the attack on D's evidence was unfounded; D's evidence was based on sufficient expertise and knowledge to allow him to give opinion evidence in relation to *inter alia* the drugs involved in the charge. (2) The informed observer, seized of all the relevant circumstances, would not infer that D was neither independent or impartial because of his involvement at an early stage of the investigation and because he had only been asked to provide his report by the procurator fiscal the day before it had been required and had been informed that the case would fall if he did not do so; the fact that a police officer had had prior operational involvement in a case did not *per se* render his opinion evidence subsequently inadmissible, and the circumstances of D's report reflected poorly on the Crown but it would not cause the reasonably informed observer to conclude that D was lacking in impartiality or independence by producing the report in that timescale.

JONES (ANDREW RICHARD) v HM ADVOCATE, [2016] HCJAC 65, 2016 S.C.L. 743, Lord Menzies, Lord Bracadale, Lady Cosgrove, HCJ Appeal.

2491 Admissibility–Fresh evidence–Appeal against conviction for using lewd, indecent and libidinous practices towards child–Admissibility and relevance of fresh evidence

G appealed against conviction for using lewd, indecent and libidinous practices towards X, aged between seven and 11, on numerous occasions between 1 December 1999 and 30 August 2003, on the basis that there was fresh evidence which, had it been before the jury, they would have been bound to acquit, or their verdict reached in ignorance thereof had to be regarded as a miscarriage of justice. X had lived in family with G, the partner of her mother (M), who she had believed to be M's husband, for many years. In 2005 and 2009, X had alleged to M that G had sexually abused her. The allegation of rape had first been made in 2014, following which proceedings had commenced. The fresh evidence was that (i) approximately a month after G's trial, M had stated to her estranged husband (E) that she was satisfied with the verdict and that she had had her revenge, (ii) in relation to property transactions that had taken place in 2004, M had alleged in court proceedings in 2014 that her signature had been forged, and in March 2015, when confronted with documentary evidence, she had alleged that G had hacked into her account, and the following day, had also accused X of having done so.

Held: Appeal refused. (1) The evidence in relation to the hacking allegation was not admissible as it was an entirely collateral matter unrelated to the issues in the trial, and in any event, it had no evidential worth. (2) The revenge statement consisted of one statement with no context other than the view expressed by E, the remark was equally consistent with a vehement satisfaction at justice being done from a person with a reasonable basis for harbouring animosity towards G, and E's evidence had not overall been of such a kind and quality that a reasonable jury, properly directed, would have found it to be of material assistance. (3) It could not be said that the jury's verdict, reached in ignorance of the evidence in question, had to be regarded as a miscarriage of justice.

G v HM ADVOCATE, [2016] HCJAC 53, 2016 S.C.L. 640, Lady Dorrian, Lord Menzies, Lord Pentland, HCJ.

2492 Admissibility–Police interviews–Appellant waiving right of access to solicitor–Appellant allegedly suffering from mental disorder

[Sexual Offences (Scotland) Act 2009 (asp 9) s.3; Criminal Procedure (Scotland) Act 1995 (c.46) s.15A(3), s.15A(6)]

B appealed by stated case against conviction for a contravention of the Sexual Offences (Scotland) Act 2009 s.3 and an assault to injury. At the trial, B had raised a compatibility issue minute, namely whether his police interview ought to be inadmissible where he had been suffering from a mental illness at the time. The sheriff had found that B had been duly cautioned and advised of his right of access to a solicitor, which he had declined, and the police had had no reason to suspect that B had been suffering from mental illness where a police surgeon had stated that B was fit to be interviewed. B submitted that (1) the interview should not have been admitted because it had been unfairly obtained and he had been a vulnerable adult when he was detained and had been incapable of granting an informed waiver of his right of access to a solicitor; (2) the sheriff had erred in placing too much emphasis upon the police officers' ignorance, and too little weight on B's mental illness.

Held: Appeal refused. (1) In terms of the Criminal Procedure (Scotland) Act 1995 s.15A(3) and s.(6), a suspect had to be advised that he was entitled to access to a solicitor prior to being interviewed by the police, however, he was able to waive that right and to be valid, such waivers required to be informed, voluntary and unequivocal; B had confirmed several times to P that he had not wished to exercise his right of solicitor access, determining whether a suspect had understood the implications of refusing legal assistance was a question of fact for the court of first instance and where there had been no evidence before the sheriff that B had been unfit to be interviewed, he had been entitled to reach the conclusion of fact which he had. (2) B had validly waived his right of access to a solicitor and the statements made by him had been fairly obtained.

BARCLAY v HARVIE, [2015] HCJAC 110, 2016 S.C.L. 101, The Lord Justice Clerk (Carloway), Lord Bracadale, Lord Malcolm, HCJ.

2493 Admissibility–Previous convictions–Whether unduly prejudicial

[Criminal Procedure (Scotland) Act 1995 (c.46) s.266(4)(b)]

M, convicted *inter alia* of assaulting his neighbour (X), appealed against a decision of the sheriff granting a motion in terms of the Criminal Procedure (Scotland) Act 1995 s.266(4)(b) permitting the procurator fiscal to ask questions of M tending to show that he had been convicted of offences other than that with which he was charged. M had lodged a special defence of self defence. When giving evidence, M had stated that X had had a volatile relationship with his girlfriend (Y), who had been expelled by X from his property for stealing money from him, and later, in response to a question from his agent, had suggested that X had a quarrelsome nature, talked of fighting and drank too much. In granting the s.266(4)(b) application, the sheriff had considered that in the context of a defence of self defence, the remarks in relation to X were not such as to justify M's cross examination as to his criminal record where it would be unduly prejudicial to do so on previous convictions for offences of violence or the possession of weapons even if the purpose was only to go to his credibility, however, having impugned Y's credibility it would not be unduly prejudicial to M for the jury to be aware that M had also committed acts of dishonesty, accordingly, M's cross examination on his convictions had been permitted but only in relation to offences of dishonesty.

Held: Appeal allowed. The sheriff had erred in the exercise of her discretion where it seemed that she had ultimately based her decision solely on the remarks in relation to Y; it had been a passing remark made in the context of an explanation as to the circumstances in which Y had come to be living in the property, no direct attack had been mounted on X's character and the answer had not been completely unrelated to the question asked and the prior convictions were of a significant nature, it was difficult to suggest that they would not have had a significant effect on the jury's assessment, and the potential prejudice to M had been out of all proportion to any potential effect of the remark made by him, *Leggate (Rodger James) v HM Advocate* 1988 J.C. 127, [1988] C.L.Y. 3887, *applied.*

MCLEISH (ANDREW) v HM ADVOCATE, [2016] HCJAC 74, 2016 S.L.T. 960, The Lord Justice Clerk (Lady Dorrian), Lady Paton, Lady Clark of Calton, HCJ.

2494 Admissibility–Stop and search–Diamorphine recovered during stop and search–Whether reasonable suspicion on part of police

[Misuse of Drugs Act 1971 (c.38) s.23]

B, indicted for trial on drugs offences, appealed against a decision of a single judge repelling his objection to the admissibility of evidence of diamorphine recovered during a stop and search of his vehicle by a police officer (P) in terms of the Misuse of Drugs Act 1971 s.23. In the course of a large scale police operation investigating the supply of class A drugs within central Scotland, an investigating officer (O) had informed P that B's car contained controlled drugs. P thereafter stopped B and informed him that he was being detained under s.23 of the 1971 Act. O had arrived immediately thereafter and had also informed B that he was being detained under s.23. B submitted that P had had no reasonable grounds to suspect, rendering the purported detention unlawful, and nothing done thereafter had repaired that irregularity.

Held: Appeal refused. P had been informed by O, a detective officer engaged in an active, ongoing surveillance operation that O was aware that B's car was carrying drugs and that was sufficient in the context of the present case for a reasonable suspicion to have been formed, without the requirement for further interrogation of the source officer; in *McAughey (Charles Gray) v HM Advocate* [2013] HCJAC 163, 2014 S.C.L. 165, [2014] C.L.Y. 3391, the detaining officer had had information conveyed to him second hand that the Scottish Crime and Drug Enforcement Agency thought that a particular car might be carrying drugs whereas in the present case, P had had information conveyed to him directly from O that there were drugs in B's car, and not that O had suspected that there might be. While it was not enough for a superior officer, who had reasonable suspicion, to order a detention by another officer as the detaining officer ought to have his own reasonable suspicion, that suspicion could come from hearsay information emanating from another officer, *McAughey, distinguished* and *McKenzie v Murphy* [2014] HCJAC 132, 2015 S.C.L. 194, [2015] C.L.Y. 2932, *considered.*

BORLAND (ROBERT) v HM ADVOCATE, [2015] HCJAC 95, 2016 S.C.L. 32, The Lord Justice Clerk (Carloway), Lady Paton, Lord Bracadale, HCJ.

2495 Corroboration–Identification–Mutual corroboration–Identification by inference

An employee (N) of a children's home (H), convicted of lewd and libidinous practices (charges 2, 3, and 12), indecent assaults (charges 4, 7, 8, and 10), attempted penetration of a child's anus with his penis (charge 5) and sodomy (charges 9 and 11), appealed against conviction on the basis that the trial judge had misdirected the jury. Evidence in relation to charge 9 had been led from a resident (D) of H that he had returned to H intoxicated, N had taken him to his bedroom, he had woken up on three occasions without any clothes on whereas he usually wore pyjamas, on one of those occasions, N had been in the bed with him, and when he woke up the next day, his anus had been painful, and he had not remembered N doing anything inappropriate. The trial judge had directed the jury *inter alia* that they had been entitled to consider D's evidence from charge 9 when deciding whether or not to apply the *Moorov* doctrine, and that, in relation to charges 2, 3, and 12, the issue was not whether the acts were done deliberately or inadvertently but whether they had been done at all. The trial judge had further directed the jury on speculation and reasonable inference from circumstantial evidence using a fictitious example. N submitted that (1) the trial judge's charge had directed the jury to ignore the defence contention that the complainers had been motivated by money; (2) the trial judge had erred in repelling his submission of no case to answer in respect of charge 9; (3) for the *Moorov* doctrine to be applicable, there had to be at least two independent incidents with direct evidence relating to the *actus reus* in each incident, furthermore, the evidence of each incident had to be independently acceptable; (4) the trial judge had misdirected the jury in relation to speculation and reasonable inference from circumstantial evidence; (5) the trial judge's direction had not made clear that conduct amounting to lewd and libidinous behaviour required to be deliberate; (6) the trial judge had misdirected the jury in relation to the assessment of credibility and reliability in the contect of the possible application of the *Moorov* doctrine.

Held: Appeal refused. (1) The judge's charge required to be read as a whole: the challenged words had occurred when the trial judge had explained to the jury the well established rule that if they did not accept certain evidence, that did not mean that the opposite was true but rather that they ought to set that evidence aside, in any event, there was no other evidence to support N's claim that the complainers had been making up the allegations for money and the judge's charge could not be criticised. (2) There was nothing in the authorities to suggest that there had to be direct eye witness evidence of a particular criminal act before that act might be used as a component in mutual corroboration: it was clear from *Lindsay (Robert) v HM Advocate* 1994 S.L.T. 546, [1994] C.L.Y. 5524 and *Mason (Murray Kenneth) v HM Advocate* [2008] HCJAC 29, 2008 S.L.T. 656, [2008] C.L.Y. 4696 that identification by inference might found mutual corroboration and there was no reason in logic or principle why the position ought to be any different in relation to the commission of a crime; D's evidence in respect of charge 9 was sufficient for the jury to draw the inference that D, while drunk, lying in bed naked and drifting in and out of consciousness, had been sodomised by N, and the judge had not erred in repelling N's s.97 submission, *Lindsay*, *Mason* and *Lees (Sean) v HM Advocate* [2016] HCJAC 16, 2016 S.C.L. 377, [2016] 2558, *considered.* (3) The evidence relating to charge 9 entitled the jury to draw an inference and if the jury found D credible and reliable, and if they drew that inference, they were entitled to use the evidence relating to charge 9 together with such evidence as they found credible and reliable relating to charges 5 and/or 11, such that they could apply the *Moorov* doctrine if they so chose, and find corroboration by that means; the *obiter* views in *Begg (Duncan WIlliam) v HM Advocate* [2015] HCJAC 69, 2015 S.L.T. 602, [2015] C.L.Y. 2943 or the comments by Sir Gerald Gordon on *E v HM Advocate* 2002 J.C. 215, [2002] C.L.Y. 5526 had no direct bearing on the present case where the question raised in the appeal was the sufficiency of the evidence relating to charge 9 in the context of *Moorov*, rather than any attempt to bolster D's credibility or reliability by reference to what other witnesses said; while the judge had referred to other complainers in his charge to the jury, the charge as a whole gave the jury a proper structured approach for them to adopt when considering the *Moorov* doctrine, in particular, the jury were given a clear warning that they could not use D's evidence for the application thereof unless they accepted him as credible and reliable and, reading the charge as a whole, any reference to other complainers did not amount to a misdirection; *esto* his reference thereto were considered a misdirection, the nature and volume of the evidence was such that no miscarriage of justice had occurred. (4) The trial judge's fictitious example was neither inappropriate nor erroneous, it emphasised that the jury ought not to guess or reach conclusions without any evidential basis, that it was their task to consider the evidence, decide what they accepted, and then in a rational manner decide whether an inference might properly be drawn from facts established by the evidence which they had accepted, and the judge had not misdirected the jury, *Begg* and *E (AJ), considered.* (5) There had been no ambiguity in the trial judge's charge which might have resulted in confusion on the part of the jury, the acts which the jury had found proved to have been committed in those charges were all acts which, of their nature, had been done deliberately. (6) The passage complained of was a recapitulation of the condition precedent of finding corroboration by way of the *Moorov* doctrine, namely, that the jury must have already found the particular complainer or complainers credible and that passage, set in context, was not a misdirection.

NEWMAN (BRIAN) v HM ADVOCATE, [2016] HCJAC 46, 2016 S.C.L. 602, Lady Paton, Lord Menzies, Lady Clark of Calton, HCJ.

2496 Corroboration–Moorov doctrine

G appealed against conviction for two charges of using lewd, indecent and libidinous practices and behaviour towards two pre-pubescent girls between 1977 and 1990 (charges 2 and 3). The time lapse between the charges was approximately 11 years and they depended upon the application of the doctrine of mutual corroboration. The complainer in charge 2 testified to G having abused her on two occasions between 1977 and 1978 when she was aged between nine and 10; her parents were friends of G and his wife and on both occasions, G had come into her bedroom following a night out with her parents. The complainer in charge 3 was G's granddaughter and she testified to abuse on various occasions between 1998 and 1990 when she was aged between four and seven, the abuse having occurred when she visited her grandparents' house. The sheriff repelled G's submission of no case to answer, having concluded that there was no specific rule of law as to the interval of time between the charges which rendered the doctrine of mutual corroboration inapplicable, and charged the jury that a lengthy time gap was not decisive in itself and he did not consider there to be a fixed rule of law requiring him to direct the jury to find extraordinary, special or compelling features before they could convict of two similar charges separated by a long interval. The appeal was heard with *L v HM Advocate* [2016] HCJAC 61, 2016 S.C.L. 715, [2016] 2498 and the opinion should be read in conjunction therewith.

Held: Convictions quashed. (1) The law would not permit the application of the *Moorov* doctrine to the circumstances of the case and the appeal had to succeed: the similarities were superficial and the differences substantial; and there was nothing in the evidence which presented any compelling picture suggestive of a course of conduct systematically pursued by G, *Cannell (Paul) v HM Advocate* [2009] HCJAC 6, 2009 S.C.L. 484, [2009] C.L.Y. 4744, *considered.* (2) A direction to the jury that they had to find special features in the evidence that made the similarities compelling despite the long interval was unnecessary where they jury could have been in no doubt that (a) it was not sufficient merely to have two credible witnesses speaking to similar crimes, (b) the individual conduct, and all the circumstances, required to be examined not just for similarities but similarities which bound them together, (c) they had to apply the rule with caution, (d) a general disposition was not sufficient, (e) they required to be satisfied that those were not simply isolated incidents but that each was a link in a course of conduct systematically pursued by G, (f) any interval of time was a relevant factor to take into account when determining whether they could draw that conclusion, and (g) a great deal of time could separate incidents and might speak against there being a single course of criminal conduct.

G v HM ADVOCATE *sub nom.* RG v HM ADVOCATE, [2016] HCJAC 60, 2016 S.C.L. 709, The Lord Justice Clerk (Lady Dorrian), Lord Bracadale, Lady Clark of Calton, HCJ.

2497 Corroboration–Moorov doctrine–11-year time gap between incidents–Whether jury entitled to infer necessary underlying unity of intent

F, charged with *inter alia* raping his partner's sister on an occasion between 27 February 1991 and 6 March 1991 (charge 7), using lewd, indecent and libidinous practices towards his daughter (Y), born 7 May 1998, on an occasion between 7 May 2001 and 6 May 2003 (charge 8), using lewd, indecent and libidinous practices towards Y on an occasion between 7 May 2002 and 6 May 2004 (charge 9) and using lewd, indecent and libidinous practices towards his son, born 14 July 1989, on an occasion between 19 July 2000 and 13 July 2001 (charge 10), appealed against his conviction in respect of charges 7, 8 and 9 on the basis that the trial judge had erred in rejecting his submission of no case to answer. The lapse in time between charges 7 and 8 had been approximately 11 years, that between charges 7 and 10 had been approximately 9 or 10 years, and that between charges 7 and 9 had been approximately 11 years. The trial judge had repelled F's submission of no case to answer on the basis that there were coincidences in the conduct alleged and *Moorov* applied, notwithstanding the time gap. F had been convicted of 11 charges in total involving the physical and sexual abuse of family members between 1976 and 2004, however, he had been acquitted of charge 10. F submitted that (1) the trial judge had erred in rejecting his submission of no case to answer in relation to charge 7 where charges 8, 9 and 10 had not evidenced a course of conduct systematically pursued and the doctrine of mutual corroboration could not apply; (2) *esto* the trial judge had been correct to reject F's submission of no case to answer, the jury had not been entitled to find corroboration in the circumstances of charge 8 where F had been acquitted of charge 10 and the lapse of time between charges 7 and 8 was even greater than that between 7 and 10, particularly where there were neither any compelling or extraordinary features nor was there an explanation for the gap in time, and given that there had been two young children within the family setting during the time lapses and there were no allegations that they had been sexually abused by F, the lapses could not be explained by lack of opportunity.

Held: Convictions quashed. (1) Whilst a submission of no case to answer ought not to be sustained where the trial judge considered that there was sufficient evidence to entitle the jury to conclude that the accused was guilty of the crimes alleged, the connection that the evidence required to demonstrate was, and remained, evidence which met the requirements in *Moorov*, further, the authorities had not indicated that it was only in an extreme case that a no case to answer submission would be upheld, the question was one of sufficiency and where the Crown relied on the principle of mutual corroboration, the question was whether it might apply, whether it might properly be inferred that there was an underlying unity of intent connecting the separate acts, and there was no presumption that it would apply unless the case was an extreme one, which is what the advocate depute seemed to suggest. (2) There were no special or extraordinary features in the charges, further, there were dissimilarities, there was no explanation for the substantial lapse of time and, given the evidence regarding other children, the later events had not been the first opportunities to resume the alleged course of conduct; accordingly, there was no proper basis on which the jury would have been entitled to infer the necessary underlying unity of intent, *Moorov* could not apply and F's submission of no case to answer ought to have been upheld and the conviction on charges 7, 8 and 9 would be quashed.

F v HM ADVOCATE, [2016] HCJAC 52, 2016 S.L.T. 746, Lady Smith, Lady Dorrian, Lord Bracadale, HCJ.

2498 Corroboration–Moorov doctrine–Physical and sexual abuse of three teenage girls–Single course of criminal conduct

L appealed against conviction for three charges involving the physical and sexual abuse of his daughter (D), younger cousin (C), and stepdaughter (S) between October 2006 and April 2014 (charges 3, 6 and 11). Charge 11 was independently corroborated but charges 3 and 6 depended upon the application of the *Moorov* doctrine for mutual corroboration. The appeal was directed against charge 3 which involved D who testified to L coming back to the family home when she was off school recovering from illness aged 14 and sexually abusing her on various occasions over a three month period, in respect of which L contended that the *Moorov* doctrine was inapplicable given the lapse of time between charges 3 and 6, namely six years and six months, and charge 11, almost seven years. Charge 6 involved L abusing C when he was visiting her family home when she was aged 13; charge 11 involved S with whom L started having regular sexual intercourse when she was aged 14 having moved in to her family home following the commencement of a relationship with S's mother. The trial judge repelled a submission of no case to answer, concluding that there was sufficient evidence that L had pursued a common course of criminal conduct against all three complainers and identified the similarities between the circumstances of the offences, namely that the complainers were all teenage girls of similar age at the material times, L was in a position of trust in relation thereto, and the abuse was penetrative and had taken place in a domestic setting. The appeal was heard with *G v HM Advocate* [2016] HCJAC 60, 2016 S.C.L. 709, [2016] 2496, 2016 G.W.D. 22-394 and should be read in conjunction therewith.

Held: Appeal refused. (1) In all the circumstances, the features relied upon referred to by the trial judge presented a highly compelling picture indicative of a course of conduct systematically pursued by L. (2) The trial judge did not require to identify for the jury the specific elements of the evidence which might make the case sufficiently compelling: it was made clear to the jury that they were looking for evidence which allowed them to conclude that the incidents were bound together as parts of a single course of criminal conduct systematically pursued by L and in that regard, they were advised that the doctrine required to be applied with caution, that a general disposition was not sufficient and their attention was specifically drawn to the gap in time and no more was required.

L v HM ADVOCATE *sub nom.* JL v HM ADVOCATE, [2016] HCJAC 61, 2016 S.C.L. 715, The Lord Justice Clerk (Lady Dorrian), Lord Bracadale, Lady Clark of Calton, HCJ.

2499 Corroboration–Moorov doctrine–Time gap between offences–Course of criminal conduct

[Criminal Law (Consolidation) (Scotland) Act 1995 (c.39) s.5; Criminal Procedure (Scotland) Act 1995 (c.46) s.97]

M, convicted of using lewd, indecent and libidinous behaviour and practices towards a child (B) on various occasions between July 1978 and July 1984 (charge 1), using lewd, indecent and libidinous behaviour and practices towards B, then aged above 12 and under 16, contrary to the Criminal Law (Consolidation) (Scotland) Act 1995 s.5, on various occasions between July 1984 and July 1986 (charge 3), assaulting and raping a child (C) between July 1997 and July 1999 (charge 4) and using lewd, indecent and libidinous behaviour and practices towards C's younger sister (D) between March 1996 and July 1999 (charge 5), appealed against the trial judge's refusal of his submission of no case to answer. M submitted that there was insufficient evidence to prove the charges 4 and 5, given the significant differences in the conduct libeled, *esto* the *Moorov* doctrine applied in respect of charges 4 and 5, there was a considerable gap in time between charges 1 and 3 and charges 4 and 5, the conduct in charges 1 and 3 was significantly different where it had involved repeated behaviour over a long period of time, and it could not be said that the offences were instances of a single course of criminal conduct.

Held: Appeal refused. (1) When considering a submission in terms of the Criminal Procedure (Scotland) Act 1995 s.97, the judge required to take the evidence at its highest, and it could not be said that the Moorov doctrine was not applicable to charges 4 and 5 where those charges were both serious and had involved penetration; digital penetration was corroborative of penile penetration and vice versa, *HM Advocate v P* [2015] HCJ 62, 2015 S.L.T. 485, [2015] C.L.Y. 2935 was distinguishable where the supporting evidence therein had been a single instance of conduct of a much less serious nature than in the present case, and any dissimilarities in the conduct proved to have occurred had been for the jury to assess, having been addressed by both Crown and M, and properly directed by the judge, *AP, distinguished*, *A v HM Advocate* [2014] HCJAC 41, 2015 J.C. 27, [2015] C.L.Y. 2936 and *S v HM Advocate* [2006] HCJAC 1, 2006 S.C.C.R. 70, [2006] C.L.Y. 5166, *considered*. (2) The key issue was whether there were "similarities in time, place and circumstances in the behaviour proved ... such as demonstrate that the individual incidents are component parts of one course of criminal conduct persistently pursued by the accused"; the evidence summarised in the judge's report and charge had satisfied that test, accordingly, the judge had not erred in repelling M's s.97 submission and leaving the evidence to the jury to assess the questions of fact and degree arising, to decide whether to apply the *Moorov* doctrine, and to reach the verdict that they had, in any event, in light of the evidence, no miscarriage of justice had occurred, *R v HM Advocate* [2013] HCJAC 8, 2013 J.C. 212, [2013] C.L.Y. 3573, *considered*.

MCCRAKEN (JAMES) v HM ADVOCATE, [2016] HCJAC 28, 2016 S.C.L. 485, Lady Paton, Lord Drummond Young, Lady Clark of Calton, HCJ.

2500 Corroboration–Rape–Evidence of incident occurring in foreign jurisdiction–Jury's verdicts inconsistent with judge's directions on corroboration

[Sexual Offences (Scotland) Act 2009 (asp 9) s.1]

C appealed against conviction and sentence for raping his partner (X) contrary to the Sexual Offences (Scotland) Act 2009 s.1 on the basis that the finding of guilt had been inconsistent with the other verdicts of acquittal of rape returned by the jury on charges involving two other former partners (collectively Y). C had been acquitted of charges of repeated assault and rape in relation to Y during the periods 2003-2004 and 2006-2009, in respect of Y's testimonies there was evidence, supported by a docket to the indictment, that Y had been raped by C in Paris during the course of holidays in 2003 and 2009. In relation to X, C was convicted of rape which had occurred in 2013 (charge 11) and of a rape which had occurred in 2014 (charge 16). The trial judge had given directions on corroboration and had stressed that there was no charge on the indictment relating to the events in Paris. The advocate depute submitted that evidence of an incident occurring in a foreign jurisdiction was available for the jury's consideration and evidence of charges upon which an accused had been acquitted had a similar status in that they remained available to prove the remaining charges, and the evidence relating to the rape charges upon which C was acquitted and those relative to Paris had been available as potential corroboration of the rape in charge 16.

Held: Conviction quashed. (1) The judge had directed the jury that, for mutual corroboration to apply, they had to accept the evidence of at least two of the complainers on the individual charges, had the jury followed the directions, they could only have convicted on charge 16 had they accepted the evidence of at least one of Y relating to the rape charges, and the inconsistency of the jury's verdicts in the context of the trial judge's directions had led to a miscarriage of justice on charge 16; the evidence of the Parisian episodes had not been presented to the jury as capable of providing corroboration of any charge, and in those circumstances, the jury's verdict on charge 16 had to be regarded as inconsistent with the directions. (2) Having regard to the trial judge's reasoning, C's significant criminal record and his high risk of further violent, sexual offending, the custodial element in the extended sentence of eight years would be quashed and seven years substituted therefor.

CLIMENT (ALAIN) v HM ADVOCATE, [2015] HCJAC 92, 2015 S.C.L. 965, The Lord Justice Clerk (Carloway), Lord Bracadale, Lord Matthews, HCJ.

2501 Corroboration–Responses–Lorry driver's response to police officer's inquiry under s.172 Road Traffic Act 1988–Use of response as corroborative evidence identifying driver for purposes of offensive behaviour charge

[Criminal Justice and Licensing (Scotland) Act 2010 (asp 13) s.38(1); Road Traffic Act 1988 (c.52) s.172, s.2]

A lorry driver (H) appealed by stated case against conviction for behaving in a threatening or abusive manner likely to cause a reasonable person to suffer fear or alarm, whereby he approached another driver (D), behaved aggressively and kicked the side of D's vehicle, contrary to the Criminal Justice and Licensing (Scotland) Act 2010 s.38(1) (charge 2). H had also been convicted of a contravention of the Road Traffic Act 1988 s.2 (charge 1) where, immediately prior to the aforementioned conduct, he had driven too close to D's car and attempted a dangerous overtaking manouevre. The Crown had relied for both charges on evidence that H had, in response to a police officer carrying out an inquiry in terms of s.172 of the 1988 Act, identified himself as the driver of the lorry in question. H submitted that the sheriff had erred in repelling his submission of no case to answer in relation to charge 2 where he had ruled the s.172 response to be admissible evidence on that charge; s.172 applied to road traffic offences only and it was not a legitimate purpose to use the reply given to a s.172 inquiry in order to corroborate an accused's identity in respect of a non-road traffic related matter.

Held: Appeal refused. H's response to the s.172 requirement was available as evidence in respect of both charges 1 and 2: the response had been lawfully obtained in terms of s.172 and was then available as evidence to the Crown for any offence related to the relevant vehicle at the time and place to which the s.172 inquiry was directed; it would be illogical and unprincipled if the s.172 response could not to be used as corroborative evidence identifying the driver in such a related offence, and in the present case, there was a sequence of events involving road traffic matters and also H's alleged behaviour in breach of s.38 of the 2010 Act, *Brown v Stott* [2003] 1 A.C. 681, [2001] C.L.Y. 6319, *considered.*

HOWE v HARVIE, [2016] HCJAC 9, 2016 S.L.T. 233, Lady Paton, Lord Menzies, Lord Matthews, HCJ.

2502 Corroboration–Sexual offences–Two charges of sexual assault–Doctrine of mutual corroboration

[Sexual Offences (Scotland) Act 2009 (asp 9) s.3]

L appealed against conviction and sentence for sexually assaulting his partner's niece (F), contrary to the Sexual Offences (Scotland) Act 2009 s.3, on an occasion between 1 May 2012 and 30 June 2013, by placing his hands inside her clothing and attempting to handle her genital area (charge 3) on the basis that no reasonable jury could have returned a guilty verdict given the sheriff's directions on the issue of corroboration. L had also been convicted of sexually assaulting F's twin sister (K), contrary to s.3 of the 2009 Act, on various occasions between 1 March 2013 and 31 August 2013, by repeatedly kissing her on the mouth, cuddling her, exposing his penis to her and compelling her to handle his penis (charge 1). F had given evidence that she had witnessed certain of L's conduct towards K. The trial judge had directed the jury that corroboration for charge 1 could be found in F's evidence in relation to charge 3 on the basis of mutual corroboration, and that should they disbelieve F in relation to charge 3, corroboration could be found in F's eyewitness testimony. The jury had returned a verdict of guilty on charge 1, subject to deletion of the events which F had not witnessed, and a verdict of guilty as libelled in respect of charge 3. L submitted that where the jury had elected not to apply the doctrine of mutual corroboration in relation to charge 1, that doctrine was not available for use in isolation in respect of charge 3.

Held: Appeal refused. (1) In addressing charge 1, the jury had been entitled to ask whether K's evidence was accepted and, if so, to what extent corroboration was available in F's eyewitness testimony, that approach would have entitled the jury to return the verdict which they had on charge 1 without considering the question of the doctrine of mutual corroboration, however, when considering the evidence in relation to charge 3, the jury had been well aware, from the trial judge's clear directions, that a conviction could only be returned on that charge were they satisfied that it was appropriate to apply the doctrine of mutual corroboration as between the evidence of K and F, and there was no basis in law or logic for the contention that had the jury not been required to address that issue in relation to charge 1, they were prevented from considering its application at a later or different stage. Accordingly, the court was satisfied that there remained a legitimate method by which the jury could have concluded that the Crown had established its case on charge 3 in addition, and it could not be said that no reasonable jury, properly directed, could have returned those verdicts. (2) L's appeal against sentence would be refused where his conviction in respect of charge 3 had been upheld.

L v HM ADVOCATE, [2015] HCJAC 117, 2016 S.C.L. 146, Lady Paton, Lord Bracadale, Lord Turnbull, HCJ.

2503 Corroboration–Sufficiency of evidence–Historic offence of attempted rape–Witness corroborating victim's evidence

B appealed against conviction for the attempted rape of X, then aged 13, between April 1979 and April 1980 while in the presence of a witness (S), then aged 12, on the grounds that the trial judge had erred in rejecting his no case to answer submission. X gave evidence that she had stayed overnight at S's home and had been in a double bed which she shared with S when B, then aged 26, had entered the room, had removed his trousers and shirt, had got into the bed beside X and had committed the aforementioned offence. X had not told anyone about the incident and had thereafter lost contact with S, only reuniting with her in 2009 via the internet. S gave evidence that B had come into the room on numerous occasions and had been asked to leave, and that when he was in bed she had heard noises from him which, as an adult, were reminiscent of sexual intercourse. B submitted that (1) the lack of conjunction of testimony, notably the discrepancies between X and S's accounts had been such that it could not be said that corroboration of X's account existed; (2) the verdict was one which no reasonable jury, properly directed, could have reached.

Held: Appeal refused. (1) The totality of X and S's evidence provided the sufficiency in relation to the facts in the libel. (2) There was no evidence to contradict X and S and thus no evidential support for the contention not only that the evidence could not be relied upon as credible or reliable, but also that X and S had joined together to tell lies about the incident. (3) The main line of S's cross examination had been that, after little or no contact with X for some decades, she had deliberately lied in order to support a fictitious account given by X, however, there was no obvious reason for S to have done so. (4) There was a corroborated case and the jury's verdict could not be described as unreasonable.

BYRNE (THOMAS) v HM ADVOCATE, [2015] HCJAC 108, 2016 S.C.L. 114, The Lord Justice Clerk (Carloway), Lord Malcolm, Lord Jones, HCJ.

2504 Defences–Alibis–Gamekeeper charged with killing buzzard–Adequacy of sheriff's reasons for rejecting alibi

[Wildlife and Countryside Act 1981 (c.69) s.1(1)(a), s.1(2)(a)]

A gamekeeper (D) appealed by stated case against conviction for killing a buzzard (B), contrary to the Wildlife and Countryside Act 1981 s.1(1)(a), and having a wild bird in his possession or control, contrary to s.1(2)(a), on the basis that the sheriff had given inadequate reasons for rejecting his defence of alibi. A couple (C), tenants on the estate on which D worked and who had been known to him, had been walking their dogs between 4.40 and 5 pm when they had heard a gunshot and had then witnessed D throwing stones at B, which had been hopping on the ground and unable to fly, deliberately stamping on B, and after B had stopped moving, wrapping it in a coat and driving away with it in a vehicle, waving to C as he did so. C had reported the matter and both of C had identified D as the perpetrator to the police. D lodged a special defence of alibi, maintaining that he and the head gamekeeper (H) had been on a course until 3 pm at a location from which the journey back to the estate was two hours and 40 minutes. The sheriff had accepted C's evidence of D's identification as credible and reliable, and had rejected D's testimony in relation to the journey time between the course and the estate, finding that there had been evidence that the normal journey time was 20 minutes shorter, that D had accepted that he had been carrying out pest control on the estate on the relevant date, albeit later in the day, that he drove a vehicle of the type described by C and had known C, that he had not accepted that B had been attacked, despite the evidence, and he had minimised the risk posed to pheasant chicks from buzzards. The sheriff had also rejected H's evidence where he had not mentioned the course when initially interviewed four weeks after the incident but had done so a year later during police investigations into D's alibi, and found there had been no reliable evidence of D's presence at the course at the relevant time.

Held: Appeal refused. (Lord Menzies, *dissenting*), that (1) the sheriff's rejection of D's alibi was not based solely upon an analysis of the evidence given in its support but upon an overall assessment of the evidence including the identification by C set against the background circumstances. (2) The sheriff had accepted the reliability of C's identification because of the manner in which they had given their evidence but partly also because of certain other features, it was in the knowledge of a resident sheriff in a rural area that buzzards were a significant threat to pheasant chicks and the sheriff had adequately explained his reason for accepting C's identifications. (3) The sheriff had explained in detail why he had not accepted the defence of alibi and had adequately explained his reason for rejecting it. (4) The sheriff's comments on D's testimony had been merited; he had been entitled to the view that it was odd for a gamekeeper to express the view that buzzards were not a significant problem and that D was being unreasonable in denying that B had been killed despite the evidence. (5) The issue in the case had been one of fact for the sheriff to resolve, which he had done satisfactorily. Per Lord Menzies, *dissenting,* that (1) there had been no evidence to contradict D's evidence that buzzards were not a particular problem and to suggest that the risk to pheasant chicks was greater than stated by D, further, D had merely stated that he had known nothing about an attack on a buzzard on the estate on the day in question, and neither of those factors, which appeared to have influenced the sheriff's assessment of D's credibility and reliability, could properly be regarded as factors affecting that assessment. (2) The evidence regarding D and H's estimates of the journey time between the course and the estate was an insufficient reason to describe their evidence as lacking in credibility. (3) There was no suggestion that anyone had asked H where he and D had been on the day of the incident until H had given his second statement a year thereafter. (4) The sheriff appeared to suggest that D had not attended the course at all, however, there had been no dispute at trial that he had indeed attended it, which had been supported by evidence, and the sheriff had not been entitled to make such a suggestion. (5) The sheriff had fallen into error in preferring the evidence of a flier, which stated an end time for the course of 2 pm, to that of the course organiser, who had given evidence of a target end time of 5 pm and that the earliest anyone had left had been 2.30 pm, and the evidence of course attendees who gave differing accounts of the end time, all later than 2 pm, and the evidence led by the Crown had not been that the course had finished at 2 pm. (6) The reasons given by the sheriff for rejecting the alibi evidence were insufficient to support his conclusion and the appeal ought to be allowed.

DICK v HARVIE *sub nom.* DICK v GIBSON, [2016] HCJAC 62, 2016 S.C.L. 696, Lord Justice General (Carloway), Lord Menzies, Lord Bracadale, HCJ.

2505 DNA evidence–Circumstantial evidence–Appeal against conviction for murder–Compelling circumstantial case despite deficiencies in DNA evidence

D appealed against conviction for the murder of a 16 year old girl (E) in terms of the Criminal Procedure (Scotland) Act 1995 s.106(3)(b) on the basis that the jury had returned a verdict which no reasonable jury, properly instructed, could have returned. D also appealed as excessive the imposition of a sentence of life imprisonment with a punishment part of 21 years. In 1986, E had been strangled after spending an evening at a club where D had also been at the same time. A forensic scientist took tapings from E's body and clothing which were kept in a sealed state, however, when they had examined the crime scene and E's body, investigators had worn gloves but no other protective clothing and a police blanket had been placed over E's body prior to the tapings. A sample of DNA taken from D in 2012 matched DNA found on the tapings taken in 1986. A witness (B) gave evidence that he had seen a girl being followed by a male near to where E's body had been found, and although he did not originally think the girl was E based on a photograph which had been shown by the media, when he was shown more recent photographs he identified the girl as E. In 2012, B was shown photographs of young males taken in the 1980s and said that the one of D was more like the male he had seen. A taxi driver gave evidence that he had seen a male with a similar description to D near the locus, and there was evidence that D had taken an interest in, and knew more than might be expected about, E's murder. D had joined the army in 1987 and had not been in any trouble until he was convicted of E's murder in 2014. D submitted that (1) the crime scene had been contaminated, his DNA could have transferred to E while they were near each other in the club, and B's evidence was unreliable; (2) he should have been sentenced in accordance with the practice at the time of the offence.

Held: Appeal refused. (1) D had not met the test for review of a jury's verdict: although there were significant deficiencies, applying modern standards, in the manner in which the crime scene and recoveries were preserved, that did not detract from the central finding that D's DNA was on the tapings, no other DNA other than that of investigators and E's family was found thereon, there was no plausible explanation as to how D's DNA could have found its way onto the tapings, other than if he had been the killer and had deposited DNA onto E when he had strangled her, and that evidence alone would have entitled the jury to convict him. (2) The DNA evidence did not exist in isolation, B's testimony amounted at least to an identification of E in her final moments, in a general sense D resembled the man seen by B and the jury was entitled to take that into account in looking at the DNA findings, and there were other adminicles that the jury would have been entitled to regard as incriminating and to take into account in assessing the DNA match, which remained the most important incriminating material, and in all the circumstances there was a compelling circumstantial case. (3) E's murder had been a crime of rare callousness and brutality, although D was in his early twenties when he committed the crime, a significant punishment part was inevitable notwithstanding his unblemished record since joining the army, to which the judge had had due regard, and although had he been sentenced in 1986 no punishment part would have been imposed, where there had been a change in penalty after the commission of a crime, it was incumbent upon a judge to sentence in accordance with the current sentencing practice, and in those circumstances the punishment part imposed was not excessive.

DOCHERTY (JOHN) v HM ADVOCATE, [2016] HCJAC 49, 2016 S.C.L. 627, Lord Justice General (Carloway), Lady Dorrian, Lord Bracadale, HCJ.

2506 DNA evidence–Sufficiency of evidence–Evidence from single source–Submission of no case to answer repelled

R, convicted of housebreaking and theft, appealed against the decision of the sheriff repelling his submission of no case to answer on the basis of insufficient evidence. A cigarette butt containing R's DNA, with a match of one in one billion, had been recovered by police from the scene. The sheriff, in repelling R's submission, had found that there was sufficient evidence from which to infer that the person who had smoked the cigarette had been the perpetrator of the crime, the butt had been found close to the point of entry and exit of the property, it had not been there when the householder (X) had left the house, and it had been in a reasonable condition, suggesting that it had not been brought into the house on a shoe. R submitted that (1) the evidence was from a single source, in *Dunbar (David) v HM Advocate* [2015] HCJAC 22, 2015 S.C.L. 465, [2015] C.L.Y. 2945, it had been determined that, where the only evidence was a DNA match of one in four million, that was insufficient; the statistical strength of the DNA finding did not provide a corroborated circumstantial case that R had been the perpetrator and there was a lack of evidence on how, why, when and where the cellular material containing the appellant's DNA had come to be on the butt, and it was speculation to say that he had smoked the cigarette; (2) the sheriff had not properly directed the jury on where corroborated evidence of R's participation in the housebreaking could be found.

Held: Appeal refused. (1) X had given clear and unchallenged evidence that her house had been broken into, searched and certain items taken, and evidence from a scene of crimes officer that the house had been ransacked conveyed the idea of search for the purpose of theft, and his independent evidence provided confirmation or support for X's testimony that the items had been stolen in the course of a housebreaking, *Fox (Richard John) v HM Advocate* 1998 J.C. 94, [1998] C.L.Y. 5564, *applied*. (2) Where the likelihood of the DNA in the present case coming from someone other than R was one in one billion, the jury had been entitled to hold that it had been his DNA on the cigarette butt, and it could be inferred therefrom that R had been smoking the cigarette and had dropped it in the course of the housebreaking, and absent any other explanation from R, the sheriff had been bound to refuse his submission of no case to answer, moreover, where R's ultimately tendered explanation for the presence of the DNA had been rejected by the jury, the sheriff had not required to give any "special route to verdict" instructions. Observed, that there remained a question in relation to the required statistic for proof beyond reasonable doubt which matter might require to be revisited by a larger court which might also attempt to review differing judicial views on what were matters for a jury and for a judge, *Dunbar* and *McGartland (Peter) v HM Advocate* [2015] HCJAC 23, 2015 S.C.L. 471, [2015] C.L.Y. 3004, *considered*. Per Lord Bracadale, that the approach to the statistical evidence in *Dunbar* required to be considered with a degree of caution where it had not reflected the local nature of that case. Per Lady Clark of Calton, that the issue regarding the corroboration that items had been stolen during the ransack of the house had not been raised by R and was not part of the appeal and ought not to be entertained, and the advocate depute had raised the matter but the court had not been fully addressed thereon, which might have more general implications.

REID (COLIN) v HM ADVOCATE, [2016] HCJAC 41, 2016 S.L.T. 797, Lord Justice General (Carloway), Lord Bracadale, Lady Clark of Calton, HCJ.

2507 Expert evidence–Police officers–Supply of drugs–Police officer's opinion evidence

[Misuse of Drugs Act 1971 (c.38) s.4(3)(b)]

J appealed against conviction and sentence for being concerned in the supply of amphetamine (charge 1) and of phenazepam (charge 2), contrary to the Misuse of Drugs Act 1971 s.4(3)(b). Prior to the trial, J had lodged a minute challenging the admissibility of certain opinion evidence to be given by a police officer (P) on the basis that P was not entitled to be treated as an expert. The trial judge had repelled the objection and P had given opinion evidence in relation to the items recovered at J's house and certain texts in her mobile telephone, which supported J's contention that she had been supplying a terminally ill friend with the phenazepam. The community justice social work report had found that J was suitable for a community based disposal, however, J had been sentenced to three months' imprisonment on charge 1 and 18 months' imprisonment on charge 2. J submitted that (1) P had not had the necessary qualifications, expertise and experience to give opinion evidence; (2) the sentence imposed on charge 2 was excessive.

Held: Appeal against conviction refused, appeal against sentence on charge 2 allowed, sentence of 18 months quashed and nine months substituted. (1) P's evidence was of a similar nature to that given by the police officers in *White (Yvonne) v HM Advocate* 1986 S.C.C.R. 224, [1986] C.L.Y. 3768 and *Ul-Haq (Anwar) v HM Advocate* 1987 S.C.C.R. 433, [1988] C.L.Y. 3896, the fact that members of the statement of opinion unit regularly gave such evidence did not mean that an officer with appropriate experience who was not a member of that unit was not able to give such evidence and, having regard to P's experience, the sheriff had been entitled to repel J's objection thereto, *White* and *Ul-Haq*, *considered*. (2) J was a woman of mature years who had raised her grandson and had carried out drug support work in the community, the circumstances of charge 2 were unusual and while the sheriff had been entitled to take the view that a custodial sentence was the only appropriate disposal, in the particular circumstances of the present case the sentence on charge 2 was excessive and would be quashed and nine months' imprisonment substituted.

JOHNSTON (JACQUELINE) v HM ADVOCATE, [2015] HCJAC 118, 2016 S.L.T. 42, Lady Paton, Lord Bracadale, Lord Malcolm, HCJ.

2508 Findings of fact–Offensive behaviour–Whether findings of fact sufficient to satisfy objective test of causing fear or alarm

[Criminal Justice and Licensing (Scotland) Act 2010 (asp 13) s.38(1)]

B appealed by stated case against conviction for behaving in a threatening or abusive manner, contrary to the Criminal Justice and Licensing (Scotland) Act 2010 s.38(1). B and his brother (C) had had an encounter with two parking attendants (P) after P had issued B with a penalty charge notice, whereupon B had approached P, had been aggressive, confrontational and verbally abusive and had followed them as they attempted to leave the incident. The sheriff found inter alia that B's conduct had been likely to cause a reasonable person to suffer fear or alarm, P had been fearful of, and alarmed by, his behaviour, B had intended his behaviour to cause P fear or alarm, or was at least reckless as to whether his behaviour would have that effect, and his behaviour had not been reasonable. The sheriff asked whether she had been entitled to convict B on the facts stated and whether B's behaviour had been such that even if it could have been considered threatening or abusive, it had been likely to cause a reasonable person to suffer either fear or alarm. B submitted that the findings in fact had been insufficient to satisfy the objective test of causing fear or alarm.

Held: Appeal refused. Section 38(1)(a) and (b) were questions of fact and the sheriff's findings thereon were to be accorded considerable respect where she had heard all the evidence, having had the benefit of hearing and seeing the witnesses and also viewing a video recording of B's behaviour; the findings in fact had entitled the sheriff to conclude that B had, as a matter of fact, behaved in a threatening or abusive manner, that objectively, his behaviour had been likely to cause a reasonable person to suffer fear or alarm, that P had in fact been fearful of, and alarmed by, B's behaviour, that B had intended his behaviour to cause P fear or alarm, or had at least been reckless as to whether it would have that effect, and to conclude that the necessary s.38(1) prerequisites for the offence had been established, and the questions would be answered in the affirmative, *Paterson v Harvie* [2014] HCJAC 87, 2015 J.C. 118, [2014] C.L.Y. 3410, *applied*.

BAIG v HARVIE, [2015] HCJAC 109, 2016 S.L.T. 67, Lady Paton, Lord Drummond Young, Lady Clark of Calton, HCJ.

2509 Food Standards Scotland–Authorisations–Covert human intelligence sources

THE REGULATION OF INVESTIGATORY POWERS (PRESCRIPTION OF RANKS AND POSITIONS) (SCOTLAND) ORDER 2016, SSI 2016/56; made under the Regulation of Investigatory Powers (Scotland) Act 2000 s.8(1). In force: 7 March 2016.

This order prescribes Food Standards Scotland (FSS) and more specifically the rank or position of staff within FSS, who are entitled to grant authorisations for directed surveillance and covert human intelligence sources, under the 2000 Act, to help combat food fraud and other food crime in Scotland.

2510 Hearsay evidence–Witnesses–Child refusing to give live link evidence–Admissibility of police statement under s.259 Criminal Procedure (Scotland) Act 1995

[Criminal Procedure (Scotland) Act 1995 (c.46) s.259, s.259(2)(e)(i)]

S appealed by stated case against conviction for assaulting his partner's mother (X) on the basis that his right to a fair trial had been breached. The assault had been witnessed by S's 10 year old daughter (D) who was to have been a witness at trial, appearing via video link. Due to D's distress and refusal to enter the video room on the day of the trial, as communicated to the court by staff at D's location and the fiscal depute, the sheriff did not compel her to appear. He allowed a Crown motion in terms of the Criminal Procedure (Scotland) Act 1995 s.259(2)(e)(i) to lead hearsay evidence of D's police statement, in which she described the assault as libelled. S submitted that the sheriff had erroneously proceeded under s.259(2)(e)(i) where D could not be held to have refused to answer questions or to accept the admonition to tell the truth as required by the statute, and D's evidence had been decisive.

Held: Appeal refused. (1) The sheriff was entitled to be satisfied that the witness had refused to be admonished to tell the truth such that the evidence of her statement was admissible under s.259 of the 1995 Act, *Cowie (Colin Alexander) v HM Advocate* [2009] HCJAC 76, 2010 J.C. 51, [2010] C.L.Y. 4059, *followed*, and *Macdonald (Robert Grant) v HM Advocate* 1999 S.L.T. 533, [1999] C.L.Y. 5803, *considered*. (2) There was direct evidence from X and other sources of corroboration apart from the hearsay evidence but even had D's evidence been decisive, that would not necessarily render the trial unfair, *Al-Khawaja v United Kingdom (26766/05)* [2012] 2 Costs L.O. 139, [2012] C.L.Y. 657, *considered*.

S v MURPHY, [2016] SAC (Crim) 3, 2016 S.L.T. (Sh Ct) 81, Sheriff Principal C A L Scott, QC, Sheriff Beckett, QC, Sheriff Principal B A Lockhart , SAC.

2511 Identification–Corroboration–Reliance on second eyewitness's police statement to corroborate first eyewitness's identification–Sufficiency of evidence

[Criminal Justice and Licensing (Scotland) Act 2010 (asp 13) s.38(1); Criminal Law (Consolidation) (Scotland) Act 1995 (c.39); Criminal Procedure (Scotland) Act 1995 (c.46) s.259]

O appealed against conviction for contravening the Criminal Justice and Licensing (Scotland) Act 2010 s.38(1) (charge 1) and the Criminal Law (Consolidation) (Scotland) Act 1995 s. 36(1) (charge 2) on the basis that the sheriff had erred in repelling his submission of no case to answer. An eyewitness (R) had identified O as the perpetrator and had given evidence that she had identified O on a photo board in the course of the police investigation, which was confirmed by police officers. Another eyewitness (M) had been unfit to give oral evidence at trial but his police statement had been admitted in evidence under the Criminal Procedure (Scotland) Act 1995 s.259. M's description of the perpetrator had included a bald patch on the left side of the head, rugged and slim built with dark skin. Two police officers (P) gave evidence that when they had interviewed O on the day after the incident, he had had a bald patch on the left side of his head. O submitted *inter alia* that (1) M's evidence was insufficient to corroborate R's identification where he had not made any positive identification and had neither attended an identification parade nor made an identification from a photo board; (2) R had not mentioned a bald patch in her evidence and in the absence of consistency as to the bald patch, M's description was too vague to provide sufficient corroboration.

Held: Appeal refused. The sheriff had concluded that R's clear and emphatic eyewitness identification was capable of being supported by M's account, and since M was an eyewitness, his account of O having a bald patch on the left side of his head was evidence capable of being commented on by others who seen O at the time of the offence and had commented on his having such a bald patch, P had been able to do that and the sheriff had been correct to repel the submission of no case to answer where M's description of the perpetrator related to his apparent age, build, complexion and height and his account thereof accorded with the description given by R, and her eyewitness identification.

ALUKO (OLU) v HM ADVOCATE, [2016] HCJAC 76, 2016 S.C.L. 846, The Lord Justice Clerk (Lady Dorrian), Lord Drummond Young, Lady Clark of Calton, HCJ.

2512 Recordings–Police interviews–Recordings of police and social work joint investigative interviews of child complainers–Inspection by defence

[Sexual Offences (Scotland) Act 2009 (asp 9) s.18, s.20, s.21; Criminal Justice and Licensing (Scotland) Act 2010 (asp 13) s.160(3), s.164; European Convention on Human Rights 1950 art.6(3); Criminal Procedure (Scotland) Act 1995 (c.46) s.68(2)]

The Crown appealed against a decision of a judge ordering disclosure of evidence, namely recordings of police and social work joint investigative interviews of two young boys (X), the complainers in the prosecution of two youths (M) accused of offences under the Sexual Offences (Scotland) Act 2009 ss.18, 20 and 21, by delivery to M's agents. The Lord Advocate had issued a code of practice in terms of the Criminal Justice and Licensing (Scotland) Act 2010 s.164, which provided *inter alia* that copies of visual and audio recordings of children were not given to the defence. The transcripts and recordings of X's interviews had been listed as productions in the lists attached to the indictment and had remained in the custody of the Crown, who had refused to provide M's agents with copies thereof in accordance with its code of practice and had elected to disclose the evidence by access in terms of s.160(3) of the 2010 Act. M sought to have the evidence viewed by a forensic psychologist and lodged preliminary and compatibility issue minutes relating thereto. In relation to the preliminary minutes, M had averred inter alia oppression, based on the limited means of access to the discs and inaccuracies in the transcriptions provided by the Crown, and the compatibility minutes had complained of a breach of ECHR art.6(3)(b), namely that the mode of access to the discs had not afforded M adequate time and facilities for the preparation of their defence. The judge had found that the Crown had adopted an illegitimate blanket policy which had left no element of discretion and offended M's right to a fair trial, and had ordered the Crown to provide copies of the discs to M's agents in a format which allowed their computers to read but not copy them.

Held: Appeals refused. (1) The disclosure regime was concerned with information which would (i) materially weaken or undermine the evidence likely to be led by the prosecution, (ii) materially strengthen the defence case, (iii) be likely to form part of the prosecution evidence, and whilst the joint investigative interviews might provide powerful information, they were also label productions and, as such, their inspection by the defence was regulated by a different regime and no issue of disclosure *per se* arose in those circumstances. (2) M was entitled to see the labels in terms of s.68(2) of the 1995 Act, those labels ought to have been lodged with the Justiciary Office along with the record copy indictment and whilst the modern practice might be for the Crown to retain those labels until the diet of trial, that was subject to any order of the court, and an accused was entitled to apply to the trial court to remove any production from the custody of the court or Crown for the purposes of copying or inspection by an expert and the court would thereafter decide, as a matter for its discretion but having regard to the principles of fairness, including equality of arms, whether it was in the interests of justice to grant the application, *Davies (William Turner), Petitioner* 1973 S.L.T. (Notes) 36, [1973] C.L.Y. 3595, *considered.* (3) It was difficult to conceive of a situation in which the court would refuse applications such as the present, given that the labels were to be used as evidence in chief.

HM ADVOCATE v M, [2016] HCJAC 34, 2016 S.L.T. 556, The Lord Justice Clerk (Carloway), Lady Smith, Lady Clark of Calton, HCJ.

2513 Sufficiency of evidence–Causing children to engage in sexual activity–Rejection of submission of no case to answer–Corroboration

[Sexual Offences (Scotland) Act 2009 (asp 9) s.31]

G, convicted of *inter alia* causing a child (X), aged between 13 and 16, to participate in a sexual activity, contrary to the Sexual Offences (Scotland) Act 2009 s.31 (charge 5), appealed against the sheriff's decision rejecting his submission of no case to answer. G had also pleaded guilty to a charge of taking, or permitting to be taken or making indecent photographs or pseudo-photographs of children, and the indictment had contained three charges of lewd and libidinous behaviour or sexual assault towards X and a charge of sexual assault on a further child (Y), aged between 13 and 16, which had been found not proven by the jury. A further charge of a contravention of s.31 of the 2009 Act in respect of Y (charge 6) had been withdrawn prior to the closing of the Crown case. X had given evidence that G had asked her for, and she had sent him, pictures of her vagina using her mobile phone, and that she had sent also him such pictures of Y, and that G had paid them £40 therefor. G submitted that X's evidence was not corroborated; Y's evidence having been considered insufficient to establish charge 6, could not corroborate X's evidence as to charge 5.

Held: Appeal refused. X's evidence was that she had been asked to, and had sent, photographs of her vagina to G and that similar photographs had been sent of Y, and there was additional evidence that Y had taken such a photograph of herself on a mobile phone which she understood X to have sent to G, she had received money from G therefor, there was an image of female genitalia on G's laptop which had come from a mobile phone and had been titled with Y's first name, and there was evidence of G's sexual interest in underage females, and that, taken together with X's evidence, created a sufficiency in relation to charge 5.

G (P) v HM ADVOCATE, [2016] HCJAC 72, 2016 S.C.L. 770, The Lord Justice Clerk (Lady Dorrian), Lord Menzies, Lord Brodie, HCJ Appeal.

2514 Sufficiency of evidence–Circumstantial evidence–Setting fire to caravans–Corroboration in totality of evidence

[Criminal Procedure (Scotland) Act 1995 (c.46) s.97]

M appealed against conviction for breach of the peace by, on 14 August and 22 October 2013, setting fire to caravans belonging to him (charges 2 and 3), wilful fire raising by setting fire to an armchair located in a stairwell (charge 4), wilful fire raising by, on 24 April and 15 July 2014, setting fire to caravans (charges 5 and 7) and theft (charge 6). M also appealed against a sentence of four years' imprisonment. Evidence was led at trial inter alia that all of the offences had involved property which M either occupied, lived adjacent to or cared for, and that M had been in possession of property stolen from the caravan that was set on fire on 15 July 2014. The sheriff had rejected M's submission of no case to answer on the basis that, applying *Howden (John) v HM Advocate* 1994 S.C.C.R. 19, [1994] C.L.Y. 5531, there was an adequate weight of circumstantial evidence to implicate M in respect of all charges.

Held: Appeal refused. (1) The evidence in support of charge 5 was wholly circumstantial, however, when taken together, it provided a corroborated case identifying M as having set fire to the caravan in that charge and it had been open to the jury to infer therefrom that M had set fire to the neighbouring caravan, and corroboration was found in the totality of the evidence. (2) There had been insufficient evidence to allow charges 2, 3, 4 and 7, when looked at individually, to go to the jury, however, it had been open to them to look to the circumstantial evidence to examine whether it was proved beyond reasonable doubt that it was the same person who had committed the proved offence and one or more other offences in respect of which there was insufficient evidence; charges 2, 3 and 7 had involved the catching fire of caravans in two laybys on the same road within a mile of each other, those events had occurred between August 2013 and July 2014, none of the offences had had any apparent motive and all had featured M's presence and while the fire in charge 4 had occurred in a building, it had happened very soon after the offence in charge 3, had occurred in the same general vicinity and very soon after M had been rehoused in that building, and there was further some circumstantial evidence capable of pointing towards M as being the perpetrator in relation to charge 4; in relation to charge 6, at the stage of the Criminal Procedure (Scotland) Act 1995 s.97 submission, there was at least sufficient evidence to found a charge of reset of the stolen property and that was sufficient to allow the sheriff to repel M's submission, and he had not erred in doing so. (3) The sheriff had had before him a report dated, 6 November 2014, by the psychiatrist responsible for M's care during the assessment period, that there was no clear evidence that M had ever suffered from a psychotic illness or had been suffering from a mental illness at the time of the alleged offences and that he did not have a mental disorder, and had further had a psychiatric report, dated 6 January 2015, that there was no evidence of mental disorder in M, and, having regard to M's past failures to engage with community support, his failure to cooperate with the court psychologist and the fact that significant psychiatric or psychology support would be available in prison, the sheriff had been entitled to conclude that only a custodial sentence would be appropriate. (4) M had been convicted of a course of conduct involving setting fire to caravans and premises, charge 4 was a particularly serious charge given that the lives of other persons in the building, including a family, had been endangered and in those circumstances, it could not be said that the length of the sentence was excessive.

MARTIN (MATTHEW) v HM ADVOCATE, [2016] HCJAC 42, 2016 S.C.L. 524, Lord Brodie, Lord Bracadale, Lady Clark of Calton, HCJ.

2515 Sufficiency of evidence–Corroboration–No corroboration of complainer's account of sexual assault

[Sexual Offences (Scotland) Act 2009 (asp 9) s.3]

M appealed by stated case against conviction for sexually assaulting X, contrary to the Sexual Offences (Scotland) Act 2009 s.3, by handling her private parts. X had spoken to the libel and the sheriff had found her to be a credible and reliable witness. There had also been evidence of M having apologised to X, X having been seen to be upset after the incident, M having put his arm around X's shoulder, and text messages between X and a witness (K) soon after the incident from which the sheriff had inferred that something untoward had happened to X. At trial, M had given evidence that the only physical contact between himself and X had involved him putting his arm around her neck and shoulder, his apology to her had been in the context of expressing sympathy for her ill grandmother and he had denied the libel. The sheriff asked whether the Crown had established a sufficiency of evidence against M at trial.

Held: Question answered in the negative and conviction quashed. The physical contact spoken to by K was a discrete form of physical contact from that which the Crown had set out to prove under reference to the libel, and a statutory libel required corroborated evidence of a sexual assault; it was not open to the Crown on the one hand to found upon K's testimony as corroboration of the sexual assault libelled and on the other hand to accept that the actual conduct specified by K amounted only to an arm around X's shoulder, in an attempt to establish corroboration for a sexual assault upon X, accordingly, the case was insufficient to support a conviction as there was no corroboration of X's account.

MCBRIDE v MCPHERSON, [2016] SAC (Crim) 20, 2016 S.L.T. (Sh Ct) 422, Sheriff Principal C A L Scott, QC, Sheriff S Murphy, QC, Sheriff Principal B A Lockhart , SAC.

2516 Sufficiency of evidence–Culpable homicide–Art and part liability

C appealed against conviction for the culpable homicide of X where the jury found him art and part guilty along with the principal actor (M), who was convicted of murder. At trial, the Crown led evidence of text messages sent by C after the event which spoke to having stabbed X and having engaged in an attack on him with M. C had further spoken in his police statement to M having taken a knife from the kitchen and having left the house with him as M wanted to dispose of it. It was agreed that M had delivered the fatal stab wound. C submitted that (1) there was insufficient evidence against him where the alleged admissions in the text messages were demonstrably wrong and could not be corroborated; (2) was there a sufficiency of evidence, the verdict was one which no reasonable jury could have returned; the admission could not properly have been used as a starting point as it was untrue, no reasonable jury could have found corroboration in the remaining evidence, and it was notable that the trial judge had expressed surprise at the verdict; (3) the trial judge had erred in directing the jury to regard the admission as a self corroborating confession.

Held: Appeal refused. (1) There was sufficient evidence that C had been aware of the potential use of lethal force, and sufficient support for the contention that he had engaged in a joint attack with M. (2) While the trial judge had expressed surprise at the verdict, he had not regarded it as an unreasonable one; there was a clear admission of involvement in the fatal attack and proof *aliunde* thereof, and a submission of unreasonableness could not be sustained. (3) The trial judge had specifically directed the jury that the contents of the texts and C's reference to the knife would not alone be enough, it was that evidence, coupled with the testimony of other witnesses speaking to C's actions, which had provided a sufficiency whereby the combination could be taken as demonstrating that the admissions of involvement were true and such a direction could not be described as erroneous. Observed, that there appeared to be an illogicality in the law as it stood where a person could be art and part guilty of culpable homicide when the victim was found to have been murdered, and a further review by the court or Parliament might be required.

CAREY (ALLAN MICHAEL) v HM ADVOCATE, [2016] HCJAC 10, 2016 S.L.T. 377, The Lord Justice Clerk (Carloway), Lady Dorrian, Lord Bracadale, HCJ.

2517 Sufficiency of evidence–Embezzlement–Evidence of dishonest intent

A sales executive (M) appealed by stated case against conviction for embezzling £8,334.80 from his employer (S). M had been provided by S with a credit card for expenses in connection with his employment and was the card used without prior approval, M was required to submit appropriate vouchers. Evidence was led that at a meeting relating to unauthorised expenditure by M, he had informed S's human resources manager and a commercial director that he had been blackmailed and had used company money to pay, for which no receipts were available. At the conclusion of the Crown case, M had made a submission of no case to answer, which had been repelled by the sheriff, who also made certain findings in fact having convicted M in terms of the libel, which did not include a specific finding in fact in relation to the dishonest appropriation of the funds, however, he stated in his note to the stated case that dishonest intent could have been inferred from M's actings. The sheriff asked (1) whether he had been correct in repelling the no case to answer submission; (2) whether he had been entitled, on the findings in fact, to find the charge proved.

Held: Questions answered in the affirmative and appeal refused. (1) There had been sufficient evidence before the sheriff to demonstrate that there had been charges to, and withdrawals from, M's credit card account which had gone beyond the scope of his employment; there was evidence of M's appropriation of relatively significant sums and an inability or refusal by him to account therefor and of M's reckless use of the credit card, and in the circumstances, that had been sufficient to infer the necessary intent. (2) There ought to have been a finding in fact dealing with dishonest intention, however, it was clear from the sheriff's note that he had made an inference of fact of dishonest appropriation, which the court was entitled to take into account in supplying the deficiency in his findings in fact, *Walton v Crowe* 1993 S.C.C.R. 885, [1993] C.L.Y. 5752, *applied.*

MCCRAW v MURPHY, [2016] HCJAC 20, 2016 S.C.L. 383, Lord Justice General (Carloway), Lord Brodie, Lord Drummond Young, HCJ.

2518 Sufficiency of evidence–Identification–Identification of perpetrator of two separate offences–Whether sufficient

W appealed against conviction for two charges of extortion and attempted extortion on the basis of insufficient evidence. W and a co-accused (C) had been charged with, between January and March 2013, sending an anonymous threatening letter to T demanding £60,000, making anonymous phone calls to T pretending that the letter had been sent by dangerous criminals and instructing him where and when to deposit the money (charge 1) and between April and May 2014, sending further threatening letters to T demanding £375,000, instructing him to give the letters to C for DNA analysis and thereafter where to deposit the money (charge 2). C's DNA had been found on the letters sent to T in 2014 and at interview he had admitted the charges, claiming that it had been W's idea, and at interview, W had admitted to knowing C. At trial, T's son had spoken to the threatening letters in 2013 and 2014 and T's withdrawal of money in March 2013, and the Crown led evidence of phone calls between T and W and W and C on 26 April 2014, when T had contacted the police. W submitted *inter alia* that there was no direct identification of him as the perpetrator in relation to charge 1 and there were insufficient similarities between the two charges to allow the application of *Howden (John) v HM Advocate* 1994 S.C.C.R. 19, [1994] C.L.Y. 5531.

Held: Appeal refused. There had been sources of evidence other than T's in relation to charge 2 which had pointed to W and in such circumstances there was no requirement for *Howden*, while there had been no other evidence specific to identification on charge 1, given the improbability of a different person being involved in charge 1, that gap had been filled by the circumstantial identification evidence on charge 2, and given the overall circumstances, the time gap between the two offences had neither disentitled the jury from reaching the verdicts which they had nor resulted in an insufficiency of evidence on charge 1, *Howden, considered*.

WILSON (JAMES) v HM ADVOCATE, [2016] HCJAC 70, 2016 S.C.L. 785, Lord Justice General (Carloway), Lady Paton, Lord Malcolm, HCJ.

2519 Sufficiency of evidence–Murder–Attempted murder by setting fire to former partner's property–Strong circumstantial case

H, convicted of the attempted murder of his former partner (X) and her male friend (Y) by placing a mattress against the door of Y's flat (F) and setting fire thereto, using an accelerant or similar substance, in the knowledge that X and Y were within F, appealed against a decision of the trial judge, repelling his submission of no case to answer. Evidence was led *inter alia* that H and X's relationship had broken down, that H knew Y and lived in close proximity to him, having visited him at his home, in the hours prior to the fireraising H had sent several text messages to X in an ill tempered exchange, approximately seven minutes after the fire had been started, H had called the emergency services, stating that he had seen a man light a fire in the front garden of a property in approximately the location of F, and that on arrival, the fire brigade had found a mattress on fire at F's door and the smell of white spirit. In a police interview later that day, H had inter alia claimed that he had been at his home, had no mobile telephone and had not sent any text messages to X, had no knowledge of the fire and had not set it, and that he vaguely knew Y and had visited F. H submitted that there was insufficient corroborated evidence to identify him as the perpetrator of the fireraising.

Held: Appeal refused. There was sufficient evidence entitling the jury to conclude that H had been the perpetrator; the evidence, if accepted by the jury, provided a strong circumstantial case against H, thus the trial judge had not erred in repelling H's submission and no miscarriage of justice had occurred.

HILL (WILLIAM THOMAS) v HM ADVOCATE, [2016] HCJAC 35, 2016 S.C.L. 516, Lady Paton, Lord Menzies, Lord Brodie, HCJ.

2520 Sufficiency of evidence–Murder–Cause of death–Evidence of asphyxiation

S appealed against conviction for the murder of X who had been found lying on a first floor landing outside S's flat, with blood on his face and in the surrounding area, and with his scarf tied very tightly around his neck. The central issue at trial was whether X had been killed by asphyxia as a result of pressure or blows to the neck as distinct from an alternative cause of death. S argued that (1) there had been insufficient evidence to prove that he had asphyxiated X: the cause given by a consultant forensic pathologist (T) in her post mortem report had not been stated to be asphyxia and a professor of neuropathology (P) had told the court that any restriction of the flow of blood or oxygen to the brain would have left signs thereon when there had been none; there had been other potential causes of death including hypothermia, cocaine, and cocaine combined with alcohol and buprenorphine; (2) the trial judge had failed to adequately direct the jury about the Crown case, in particular that the Crown required to establish that the cause of death had been asphyxiation caused by pressure or blows struck by S; (3) if the jury had been given proper directions, they would have come to the view that murder had not been made out, although they could have convicted of culpable homicide.

Held: Appeal refused. (1) There had been sufficient evidence from which the jury could conclude that asphyxia was an operative or significant cause of death, notwithstanding that, from a scientific view, no definitive opinion could be expressed: the jury had the evidence that, at or about the time of death, there had been an assault on X, a scarf had been tied very tightly around his neck such that markings could be seen and S had admitted to a neighbour shortly after the incident that he had killed X, and along with T's evidence that the medical findings were consistent with asphyxiation, the jury had been entitled to hold that asphyxia was the cause of death and that it had been brought about by S. (2) P's statement that there could be signs that asphyxia had occurred but that they were not present on X, was of little moment when he was not asked whether such signs were always present: there was no evidence that the axonal damage referred to had to have been caused in the course of the assault by S but could have resulted from almost any kind of minor trauma nor was there evidence that the damage occurred at the time of any incident involving S as distinct from an episode occurring hours or even days beforehand; there was no evidence of how the timing of axonal damage might gel with that of ischaemic injury in the context of the case where the precise mechanism of the asphyxia, and the onset of consequent death, was unclear and the reality of the situation was that the non-medical evidence, when coupled with its consistency with a pathology of asphyxia, overrode the significance of any uncertainty caused by this aspect of the proof. Further, the jury was entitled to exclude hypothermia as an operative cause of death of a relatively young man who was clothed and situated in a close, even in winter time; and the jury was entitled to reject the idea of a combination of alcohol and particular drugs given the quantities involved.

SMITH (GEORGE DONALD) v HM ADVOCATE, [2016] HCJAC 67, 2016 S.C.L. 773, Lord Justice General (Carloway), Lady Paton, Lord Malcolm, HCJ Appeal.

2521 Sufficiency of evidence–Offensive behaviour–Circumstantial sufficiency of evidence

[Criminal Justice and Licensing (Scotland) Act 2010 (asp 13) s.38(1)]

L appealed against conviction for *inter alia* striking the front door of a flat (F) with a machete, kicking it and breaking a window, contrary to the Criminal Justice and Licensing (Scotland) Act 2010 s.38(1) on the basis that the sheriff had erred in repelling his submission of no case to answer. None of F's occupants had positively identified the assailant, although they had broadly testified that it had been a male in his twenties, tall and slim with a Scottish accent. Blood had been found *inter alia* on a piece of broken glass outside the window which had matched L's DNA to a degree of probability that the likelihood of it coming from an unrelated male was one in one billion. At L's police interview, two days after the incident, he had three recent lacerations to his fingers which he explained had occurred when he had been struck by a bottle, and had stated that he did not know anyone at the street where F was located and had not been there for two years, although he knew the householder. The descriptions by F's occupants had coincided with the police's description of L at interview. The sheriff had been satisfied that there had been a circumstantial sufficiency of evidence.

Held: Appeal refused. The blood on the broken glass had permitted the inference that L had been present when the window had been broken and had therefore been the perpetrator, corroborated by evidence of L's recent hand injuries, the coincidences in general appearance between L and the descriptions of the perpetrator by eyewitnesses and that the householder was known to L, and in the circumstances, there had been a sufficiency to enable the jury to conclude that L had been the perpetrator.

LAING (BRIAN) v HM ADVOCATE, [2016] HCJAC 33, 2016 S.C.L. 474, Lord Justice General (Carloway), Lady Paton, Lord Bracadale, HCJ.

2522 Sufficiency of evidence–Rape–DNA evidence from victim's duvet cover

P appealed against conviction for raping his partner's daughter (X) on the basis that the trial judge had erred in failing to sustain the submission of insufficient evidence. After the alleged rape of X by P in X's bedroom, X had stayed with a neighbour before being placed into foster care. During a police search of the property a duvet cover was recovered from X's bedroom. A forensic scientist (F) identified semen traces with DNA matching P's profile on the duvet cover, the sample contained mixed profile DNA with the two major contributors being P and X. The conclusion in F's report was that one possible explanation for her findings was that sexual activity had taken place as alleged by X. P submitted that (1) evidence about whether the duvet cover had been on the bed at the relevant time had been equivocal, and the scientific evidence had been insufficient to corroborate X's testimony that penetration had occurred; (2) the test to be applied was that in *Munro (John Roberts) v HM Advocate* [2014] HCJAC 40, 2015 J.C. 1, [2014] C.L.Y. 3397 but also *HM Advocate v Donaghy*, High Court of Judiciary, 23 May 2014, unreported, in which the Crown had relied on forensic evidence recovered from a duvet on which there was mixed profile involving DNA of the accused and the complainer but it was determined that the evidence had been insufficient.

Held: Appeal refused. (1) There was sufficient evidence from which the jury could infer that the duvet cover had been on X's bed at the time when the incident was alleged to have occurred, that inference could be drawn from the finding of the cover there at the time of the search, which was distinguishable from *Donaghy* where there had been no evidence about which bed the duvet had been recovered from, *Donaghy, distinguished.* (2) The finding of P's semen, mixed with X's DNA, was indicative that there had been sexual activity involving ejaculation by P on that bed which provided sufficient support or confirmation of X's evidence that penetration had taken place.

PALMER (ARCHIBALD) v HM ADVOCATE, [2015] HCJAC 126, 2016 S.C.L. 193, The Lord Justice Clerk (Carloway), Lady Smith, Lord Bracadale, HCJ.

2523 Sufficiency of evidence–Rape–Evidence as to lack of reasonable belief regarding consent

P, convicted of raping X, contrary to the Sexual Offences (Scotland) Act 2009 s.1, appealed against a decision of the trial judge repelling his submission of no case to answer. P, X and two other friends (J and S) had returned to a flat following a lengthy period of drinking. X gave evidence that P had been overfamiliar with her, touching her and trying to kiss her and she had moved away, that she had had no sexual interest in him and had given him no indication that that was the case, and that she had been 21 at the time and had understood him to be substantially older. X had been tired and S had allowed her to go and sleep in his bed, which she had done for approximately a couple of hours before returning to sit with P, J and S, thereafter, she had felt unwell and had returned to S's bed fully clothed, whereupon P had entered the room and had raped her, during which she had not physically resisted or reacted, giving evidence that she had been frozen and had thought that if she pretended to be asleep he would be dissuaded. J and S gave evidence that X had shown no interest in being intimate with P, and J gave evidence that the first time X had gone to bed, she had warned P to stay out of the room in which X was sleeping, which P had acknowledged. The trial judge, in repelling P's submission, found that there was a body of evidence from more than one source which permitted the inference that P had lacked the reasonable belief that X was consenting to sexual activity with him. P submitted that there was an insufficiency of evidence which would have allowed for a jury to consider by way of corroborated evidence that P had had no reasonable belief that X had been consenting.

Held: Appeal refused. There was ample evidence to enable the trial judge to reach his conclusion and there was neither any error in his reasoning, nor in his subsequent charge to the jury; there was sufficient evidence to enable the jury to conclude that P had had no reasonable belief that X was consenting.

PARKER (CRAIG) v HM ADVOCATE, [2016] HCJAC 40, 2016 S.C.L. 520, Lord Menzies, Lady Dorrian, Lady Clark of Calton, HCJ.

2524 Sufficiency of evidence–Rape–Rape as opposed to attempted rape–Evidence of penetration

[Sexual Offences (Scotland) Act 2009 (asp 9) s.1]

D appealed against conviction for raping X, contrary to the Sexual Offences (Scotland) Act 2009 s.1, on the ground that there had been a miscarriage of justice. X had had consensual intercourse with another man (T) at the flat of a third party and had fallen asleep. She had later awoken, T had left the bedroom and D had approached her, had ignored her refusal to have intercourse with him, had climbed on top of her, had restrained her and had attempted to penetrate her, although X was unable to confirm whether he had succeeded. X had struggled, D had eventually stopped and X had left the property. Evidence had been led *inter alia* from two witnesses who had seen X walking home after the incident, looking dishevelled and appearing distressed and of text messages exchanged in the following days by X and T in relation to the incident. Evidence had also been led from a forensic scientist (F) who had given evidence that D's semen had been found on X's underwear and T's DNA had been found on penile swabs taken from D. D submitted that (1) the trial judge had erred in repelling his submission to the effect that there was insufficient evidence to prove rape as distinct from attempted rape; X had been unable to confirm that there had been penetration, and there had been various methods established in cross examination explaining the presence of T's DNA on D's penis; (2) the trial judge had misdirected the jury in relation to the exchange of text messages between X and T in directing them to ignore them as incompetent evidence.

Held: Appeal refused. (1) That T's DNA had been found on D's penis some hours after the incident was sufficient to enable the jury to draw an inference that D's penis had been in contact with X's vagina and thus that penetration had occurred. (2) The text messages had occurred some considerable time after the incident, none of what had been said therein by X could have been regarded as inconsistent with her testimony in court, at no point had there been any inconsistency as to whether she had or had not been raped, and there was no basis for leading the evidence and the trial judge had been correct in viewing it as inadmissible, in any event, there had remained the substantial accounts given by the witnesses in relation to X's state immediately after leaving the house, and in all the circumstances, no miscarriage of justice had occurred.

DIBA (TAYLOR) v HM ADVOCATE, [2015] HCJAC 123, 2016 S.C.L. 186, The Lord Justice Clerk (Carloway), Lady Smith, Lord Bracadale, HCJ.

CRIMINAL LAW

2525 Abusive Behaviour and Sexual Harm (Scotland) Act 2016 (asp 22)

An Act of the Scottish Parliament to make provision about abusive behaviour; and to make provision about sexual harm including provision about directions to be given to juries in sexual offence cases and provision about orders to prevent future sexual harm.

2526 Air weapons–Sale of air weapons–Licensing

THE AIR WEAPONS LICENSING (SCOTLAND) REGULATIONS 2016, SSI 2016/188; made under the Air Weapons and Licensing (Scotland) Act 2015 s.35(1), s.36(1), s.86. In force: 1 July 2016.

These Regulations make provision for the purposes of the Air Weapons and Licensing (Scotland) Act 2015 Pt 1, which relates to the licensing and regulation of air weapons.

2527 Human Trafficking and Exploitation (Scotland) Act 2015 (asp 12)–Commencement No.2 and Transitional Provisions Regulations

THE HUMAN TRAFFICKING AND EXPLOITATION (SCOTLAND) ACT 2015 (COMMENCEMENT NO.2 AND TRANSITIONAL PROVISIONS) REGULATIONS 2016, SSI 2016/385; made under the Human Trafficking and Exploitation (Scotland) Act 2015 s.45(2)(4). Commencement details: bringing into operation varous provisions of the 2015 Act 17 December 2016.

These Regulations bring into force the schedule of the Human Trafficking and Exploitation (Scotland) Act 2015 paras 2, 4 and 5 on 17 December 2016. Those paragraphs repeal offences under the Criminal Justice (Scotland) Act 2003 s.22 (traffic in prostitution etc.), the Asylum and Immigration (Treatment of Claimants, etc.) Act 2004 s.4 (trafficking people for exploitation) and the Criminal Justice and Licensing (Scotland) Act 2010 s.47 (slavery, servitude and forced or compulsory labour) which are replaced by offences under ss.1 and 4 of the Act.

2528 Offensive behaviour–Racially aggravated offences–Whether sheriff entitled to repel no case to answer submission

[Criminal Justice and Licensing (Scotland) Act 2010 (asp 13) s.38(1); Crime and Disorder Act 1998 (c.37) s.96]

M appealed by stated case against conviction for behaving in a threatening or abusive manner, contrary to the Criminal Justice and Licensing (Scotland) Act 2010 s.38(1), with a racial aggravation in terms of the Crime and Disorder Act 1998 s.96. While attending as an inpatient at a hospital alcohol detoxification unit M had made racist remarks to a consultant physician, he had refused to desist and had been asked to leave. As he had left, he continued to repeat the remarks in an increasingly raised voice. The sheriff asked whether he had been entitled to repel the no case to answer submission, and, if so, whether he had been entitled to convict M of the offence under s.38(1) of the 2010 Act and to find that it had been racially aggravated.

Held: Appeal refused. The issue of the likely effect of proved conduct was primarily one for the court of first instance to determine, having heard all of the circumstances; the sheriff had been entitled on the witness evidence to take the view that M's conduct had been likely to cause alarm on the part of those in the vicinity, and with regard to the interrelationship of s.38(1) of the 2010 Act and s.96 of the 1998 Act, the remarks libelled as made in a manner which was abusive and likely to cause alarm also involved a racial element.

MACK v DUNN, [2015] HCJAC 113, 2016 S.C.L. 125, The Lord Justice Clerk (Carloway), Lord Brodie, Lord Drummond Young, HCJ.

2529 Offensive behaviour–Reasonableness–Making statements on chatline promoting and encouraging sexual abuse of children–Whether conduct private and anonymous

[Criminal Justice and Licensing (Scotland) Act 2010 (asp 13) s.38(1), s.38(2)]

P appealed against conviction for behaving in a threatening or abusive manner by making statements on a chatline (C) in which he swore and promoted and encouraged the rape and other sexual abuse of children, contrary to the Criminal Justice and Licensing (Scotland) Act 2010 s.38(1). P had been a subscriber to C which enabled access to *inter alia* adult content. Introductory messages were recorded and moderated by C's employees who rejected any messages in breach of the guidelines, and were they not rejected, all subsequent calls and introductory messages were recorded, of which callers were made aware at the start of each call. P knew of a technical fault which meant that on occasion a caller would come across a wrong message or find himself participating in a conversation he had not intended to join. At trial, P had contended that his behaviour could be construed as reasonable where it had been private and anonymous and that the defence in s.38(2) of the 2010 Act had been made out, which the sheriff had rejected. P's appeal had been restricted, following sift, to the issue raised by the sheriff in question 4 of the stated case in relation to whether he had been entitled to convict P on the basis of the facts stated.

Held: Question 4 answered in the affirmative. (1) P's knowledge of the fault, the moderation of introductory messages and the recording of calls undermined his approach to C's use as being an entirely private matter. (2) There was nothing in the particular circumstances which might show that P's behaviour had been reasonable; the statements had been made in circumstances where P's actual and potential audience had not been, as he had known, restricted to the caller that had chosen to talk to him, the content had been abhorrent and shocking and any reasonable person would have been bound to have been alarmed thereby.

PRESTON v MURPHY, [2015] HCJAC 94, 2015 S.L.T. 870, Lady Smith, Lord Bracadale, Lady Clark of Calton, HCJ.

2530 Offensive behaviour–Self-defence–Behaving in threatening or abusive manner towards police–Directions on self-defence and burden of proof

[Criminal Justice and Licensing (Scotland) Act 2010 (asp 13) s.38(1)]

U appealed against conviction for behaving in a threatening or abusive manner by shouting, swearing and brandishing a sword at two police officers (D and B), contrary to the Criminal Justice and Licensing (Scotland) Act 2010 s.38(1) (charge 2), on the basis that the sheriff had misdirected the jury. U had also been convicted of assaulting a police officer (O) and striking him on the leg with the sword (charge 1). Police officers, including D and B, had attended at U's home address to enforce a warrant and in attempting to force open the front door, had cut a hole in it, through which U had thrust the sword on a number of occasions, striking O on the leg. Meanwhile, D, who had been in uniform, and another officer had entered U's home through the back entrance and had moved through the house, repeatedly shouting "police", eventually coming upon U, who had brandished the sword and shouted and sworn constantly. At trial, U had claimed that he had not known who had been at the door and had thought that a break in or robbery was imminent and had lodged a special defence of self defence. The trial judge had directed the jury that they could only consider the special defence of self defence in relation to charge 1 and it played no part in relation to charge 2. Regarding charge 2, he directed them that in general terms there was no burden of proof on an accused person but there was an exception in the present case in that U had to satisfy them on a balance of probabilities that his behaviour had been reasonable at the time he had so acted.

Held: Appeal refused. (1) It was clear from the structure of s.38(1) that the crime had three distinct elements: (i) the accused behaved in a threatening or abusive manner, (ii) his conduct would cause a reasonable person to suffer fear and alarm, (iii) he intended his conduct to cause fear and alarm or was reckless as to whether or not it would do so, and the special defence of self defence could not have any relevance thereto; were a person to conduct themselves in a manner which accorded with the descriptions in parts (i) and (ii) and the reason for them doing so was that they were acting in self defence, they were bound to have intended to cause fear and/or alarm to their assailant, and however cogent the case of self defence might be, it could not, accordingly, prevent part (iii) being established. (2) The defence afforded by s.38(2) was sufficiently wide to cover anything that an accused person might wish to advance to the effect that he had been acting in self defence, further, when doing so, it would not be necessary for the accused to meet all the requirements of self defence that applied when pled as a special defence, and the sheriff had not misdirected the jury. (3) The language of s.38(2) supported the conclusion that the burden was but an evidential one; the nature of the offence created by the section did not obviously support the imposition of a legal burden, and the defence thereto did not fall into the category of defences which related to matters likely to be so closely conditioned by the accused's own knowledge or state of mind at the time such that to require him to prove to them on a balance of probabilities did not infringe the presumption of innocence beyond reasonable limits and that the Crown was likely to encounter difficulties which could only be overcome by the imposition on the accused of a legal burden; the assessment of reasonableness was an objective matter and not, of itself, amenable to proof, and the defence might be asserted without the introduction of any evidence that was independent of the Crown case, moreover, the maximum sentence of five years in the present case did not support the contention that a legal burden was imposed, and the sheriff had misdirected the jury in that regard, *Adam (Derek) v HM Advocate* [2013] HCJAC 14, 2013 J.C. 221, [2013] C.L.Y. 3596, *applied* and *Sheldrake v DPP* [2004] UKHL 43, [2005] 1 A.C. 264, [2004] C.L.Y. 707, *considered.* (4) Where D and B's evidence had to have been accepted and looking at matters objectively, U's behaviour could not, on any view, be characterised as having been reasonable; he could not reasonably have thought that he had been dealing with intruders or had otherwise been required to defend himself, thus nothwithstanding the sheriff's misdirection there had been no miscarriage of justice.

URQUHART (ROBERT) v HM ADVOCATE, [2015] HCJAC 101, 2015 S.L.T. 853, Lady Smith, Lord Bracadale, Lady Clark of Calton, HCJ.

2531 Rape–Attempts–Jury returning verdict of attempting to commit rape under s.1 Sexual Offences (Scotland) Act 2009–Application of s.294 Criminal Procedure (Scotland) Act 1995 to statutory and common law offences

[Sexual Offences (Scotland) Act 2009 (asp 9) s.1, s.3; Criminal Procedure (Scotland) Act 1995 (c.46) Sch.3 para.10(1), s.294]

R appealed as incompetent his conviction for attempting to rape X, contrary to the Sexual Offences (Scotland) Act 2009 ss.1 and 3. R had gone to trial on an indictment containing the charge that he had penetrated and raped X, however, at the close of the Crown case, the trial judge had allowed the Crown's motion to amend the charge to narrate an attempt to penetrate and to rape X. R submitted that the amendments to the narrative of the charge ought also to have involved the deletion of the reference to s.1 of the 2009 Act where actual penetration was an essential element for any charge under that section, therefore it ought only to have been open to the jury to convict him of attempting to commit a s.1 offence and the terms of that section did not include attempted rape.

Held: Appeal refused. (1) The Criminal Procedure (Scotland) Act 1995 s.294 applied equally to statutory and common law offences, it was competent for a jury to return a verdict of an attempt to commit any indictable offence, which included an offence under s.1 of the 2009 Act and the fact that the completed offence required penetration did not prevent the libelling and proving of an attempt to commit a s.1 offence where penetration had been attempted but had failed, and the fact that the terms of the 2009 Act did not separately provide for attempt to rape or attempt to penetrate and that Sch.3 made no reference thereto at all was powerful support for the argument that such provision was unnecessary because the matter was covered by s.294 of the 1995 Act, *HM Advocate v K* [2015] HCJAC 114, 2016 S.L.T. 142, [2016] 2820, *considered.* (2) The fact that a statutory provision creating an offence made no reference to attempt was irrelevant, even if other provisions of the same statute made such reference and it might be that the emphasis placed on s.294 of the 1995 Act had been at the expense of full consideration of Sch.3 para.10(1) thereof which provided that under an indictment or complaint which charged a completed offence, the accused might lawfully be convicted of an attempt to commit the offence. (3) An attempt to commit the offence of rape under s.1 of the 2009 Act was not another form of offence of the kind referred to in s.3; the *mens rea* was the same as that required for the completed act, even though the *actus reus* was different, thus the advocate depute at trial had been correct not to delete reference to s.1. *Observed*, that with regard to R's concern that a contravention of s.1 *simpliciter* would appear on his record with no indication that his conviction had been for attempted rape, it ought not to be difficult administratively to indicate that his conviction was for an attempt and it would be desirable for that to happen.

B v HM ADVOCATE *sub nom.* RCB v HM ADVOCATE, [2016] HCJAC 63, 2016 S.L.T. 899, The Lord Justice Clerk (Lady Dorrian), Lord Bracadale, Lady Clark of Calton, HCJ.

2532 Road traffic offences–Careless driving–Appeal by stated case

[Road Traffic Act 1988 (c.52) s.3]

F appealed by stated case against conviction for driving without due care and attention, contrary to the Road Traffic Act 1988 s.3. A school patrol officer (E) had been working at a primary school on 16 December 2013. A mother (W) and her child (C) had been waiting to cross the road on the opposite side to where E had been standing. E had moved into the middle of the road with her lollipop stick erected in order to allow W and C to cross when F's vehicle came from the parking bays on her left and passed her along the side of the road where W and C were waiting to cross, failing to comply with E's requirement to stop and impeding W and C from crossing. The justice of the peace asked whether he had been entitled (1) to find that F's driving had fallen below the standard required of the reasonable, competent and prudent driver; (2) to convict F of the charge. F submitted that (1) the findings in fact had been insufficient to support a conviction in terms of s.3 of the 1988 Act and the justice had failed to identify what it was about F's driving that had amounted to carelessness; (2) it had been unreasonable for the justice to reject the evidence of the road traffic expert (X) and the reasons given therefor had been wholly inadequate.

Held: Appeal refused. (1) Neither of the questions in the stated case entitled F to argue that no reasonable justice could have rejected X's evidence, and it was too late in the appeal process to consider new proposed findings in fact not proposed to the justice, therefore the appeal would not be entertained in so far as it was based on those submissions. In any event, the justice had heard eye witness evidence, which he had preferred, he had accepted the eyewitness evidence as credible and reliable, and he had been entitled to be influenced by the fact that X had, in his report, gone beyond his expertise in giving views about legal matters. (2) Taking account of the busy location opposite a school, that E had been acting in accordance with her training, and with regard to the circumstances of the incident, the justice had been entitled to convict F of the charge; the second question focused the live issues in the case and superseded the first question, and the second question would be answered in the affirmative.

FITZPATRICK v HARVIE, [2015] HCJAC 127, 2016 S.C.L. 268, Lady Paton, Lord Drummond Young, Lady Clark of Calton, HCJ.

2533 Road traffic offences–Dangerous driving–Driver falling asleep–Whether sheriff entitled to convict of dangerous driving

[Road Traffic Act 1988 (c.52) s.2, s.3]

H appealed by stated case against a conviction for dangerous driving, contrary to the Road Traffic Act 1988 s.2. H had fallen asleep while driving, had crossed the central reservation and had collided with an oncoming car. The sheriff had found that H had been lethargic and lacking energy as a result of menopausal symptoms and had made a specific finding that by falling asleep, H's driving had fallen far below what would have been expected of a competent and careful driver. At the outset of the trial, H had offered to plead guilty to the lesser offence of careless driving in terms of s.3 of the 1988 Act but that had not been accepted by the procurator fiscal. The sheriff asked whether he had been entitled to convict H of dangerous driving by reason of her falling asleep.

Held: Appeal refused. (1) The test for what constituted dangerous driving was objective, and it was no defence for a driver to assert that he had not intended to drive in a dangerous manner or to fall asleep. (2) The act of driving, which was deemed to be dangerous, required to be voluntary, involuntary actions could not form the basis for a conviction, once a driver was asleep, his actions could not be said to be voluntary, however, the act of falling asleep, in the absence of special circumstances, was a voluntary act and when it occurred in the context of driving, would usually be regarded as dangerous; a jury was entitled to infer from the fact that a driver had fallen asleep that prior thereto, he had been aware of doing so and had ignored its obvious dangers. (3) There might be special circumstances which made falling asleep involuntary, including medical conditions, however, a driver who knew of his medical condition and could foresee that he might fall asleep, would be precluded from relying thereon. (4) The court had had regard to *Jiminez v The Queen* (1992) 173 C.L.R. 572, however, that decision was based upon a recognition that a driver might have no warning of the onset of sleep, and there was no basis for such a possibility in the present case, and the question had to be answered in the affirmative, *Jiminez, considered*.

ALEXANDER v DUNN, [2016] HCJAC 3, 2016 S.L.T. 337, The Lord Justice Clerk (Carloway), Lord Brodie, Lord Drummond Young, HCJ.

2534 Road traffic offences–Driving–Driver allowed girlfriend to sit on his lap in driver's seat and control vehicle–Meaning of "driving" in s.1 Road Traffic Act 1988

[Road Traffic Act 1988 (c.52) s.1]

In the course of the trial of a driver (C), charged with causing death by dangerous driving, contrary to the Road Traffic Act 1988 s.1, the judge directed the jury in relation to the meaning of "driving" within s.1. The charge alleged that C had allowed his girlfriend (G), who had also pleaded guilty to causing death by dangerous driving, to sit on his lap while he was sitting in the driver's seat of a vehicle (V) and to operate V while in that position. C averred that he had done that so that, should V go out of control, he would be able to control its direction and speed but that at the material time, he had been unable to do so. C submitted *inter alia* that he had abdicated his role as driver in G's favour and had not been driving within the meaning of the 1988 Act.

Held: Opinion issued. *Observed*, that driving normally meant controlling the movement, the speed and the direction of a vehicle through being in the driving seat and actually working the controls, however, the ways in which the movement, speed and direction of a vehicle might be controlled were infinite and included sitting in the driving seat of a towed vehicle and using the steering wheel and the brakes, coasting in a vehicle without power with the engine off and the steering locked, pushing a vehicle which had run out of fuel while standing outside it and leaning in with one hand on the steering wheel, furthermore, a vehicle could have more than one driver at the same time, driving involved the intention to control the movement, direction and speed of the vehicle and thus someone who had intended to drive might be a driver even where they had simply released the hand brake and let the car coast, however, grabbing the steering wheel from the passenger seat in an unintentional reflex action or operating the controls by accident was not driving because there was no intention to drive; whether or not someone was driving or was the driver was a question of fact and degree and in cases where a vehicle went out of control, the question for the jury was not so much about who had operated the controls as who had failed to operate them and where a person who was in the driver's seat of a moving vehicle with the intention of having or taking control thereof had put it beyond the driver's power to actually control that vehicle, that did not necessarily prevent them from being classed as a driver, *R. v MacDonagh (Brian)* [1974] Q.B. 448, [1974] C.L.Y. 3384, *R. (on the application of Traves) v DPP* [2005] EWHC 1482 (Admin), (2005) 169 J.P. 421, [2005] C.L.Y. 817, *McArthur (Duncan Milne) v Valentine* 1990 J.C. 146, [1990] C.L.Y. 5752, *Ames (Gerald Joseph) v MacLeod* 1969 J.C. 1, [1971] C.L.Y. 14161, *Langman v Valentine* [1952] 2 All E.R. 803, [1952] C.L.Y. 3105, *Tyler v Whatmore* [1976] R.T.R. 83, [1976] C.L.Y. 2374, *Burgoyne v Phillips* (1983) 147 J.P. 375, [1983] C.L.Y. 3255, *Jones v Pratt* [1983] R.T.R. 54, [1983] C.L.Y. 3285 and *Blayney v Knight* (1974) 60 Cr. App. R. 269, [1975] C.L.Y. 3006, *considered.*

HM ADVOCATE v COOPER (NATHANIEL DAVID), [2016] HCJ 47, 2016 S.L.T. 774, Lord Stewart, HCJ.

CRIMINAL PROCEDURE

2535 12 month rule–Extensions of time–Justification

[Criminal Procedure (Scotland) Act 1995 (c.46) s.65(3)]

P, charged with theft by housebreaking, appealed against the sheriff's decision to grant the Crown's motion to extend the 12 month time limit in terms of the Criminal Procedure (Scotland) Act 1995 s.65(3). The procurator fiscal depute had made the motion on the basis that he had identified a serious omission in the case whereby evidence which could have been led was unavailable, and although steps had been taken to recover it, further time was required. P's agent had opposed the motion on the basis *inter alia* that the case had been extended five times previously. The sheriff held that the reason for the extension had been an erroneous decision taken by a junior member of the procurator fiscal's staff, the extension would not cause prejudice to P, and where the prior extensions had been to accommodate P or other court business, the request ought not to be refused on that basis alone. At the appeal hearing, the Crown advised the court that the evidence had been omitted due to poor communication between regional offices and a consequent failure to obtain a warrant, and a decision had been made to proceed on the available evidence.

Held: Appeal allowed. (1) The full information in relation to the present matter, which had not been before the sheriff, indicated that there had been a complete and sustained breakdown within the procurator fiscal service, that error could have been readily avoided and detected, furthermore, it was clear that the procurator fiscal had decided to proceed without the evidence and had told the court on more than one occasion that the Crown were ready for trial; P's motions to adjourn the trial diets had been driven by late disclosure of the DNA report and the telephone analysis and the sheriff's observation had been made upon an incomplete understanding of the reasons for those motions, *Early (Gerald Patrick) v HM Advocate* [2006] HCJAC 65, 2007 J.C. 50, [2006] C.L.Y. 5205, *considered.* (2) It was unsurprising that, on the basis of the information which was placed before him, the sheriff had come to the conclusion that he had, however, in all the circumstances, the Crown had failed to advance sufficient reason to justify an extension.

POTTS (DONNIE DANIEL) v HM ADVOCATE, [2015] HCJAC 124, 2016 S.L.T. 121, Lord Brodie, Lord Bracadale, Lord Drummond Young, HCJ.

2536 12 month rule–Extensions of time–Lewd and libidinous conduct–Interests of justice

M, charged with two charges of lewd and libidinous conduct against two girls, aged between 6 and 8, appealed against a decision of the sheriff extending the 11 and 12 month time limits. The first charge had libelled conduct on dates between 1997 and 1999, and the second on a date in 2006. M had appeared on petition in respect of the charges in January 2007 and the police had thereafter identified evidential difficulties, namely the time gap between the offences relative to the application of mutual corroboration, and while there had been evidence from a third complainer (N) which had addressed that issue, N had refused to testify in court. Thereafter, no formal steps had been taken in respect of the charges against M until an application by the Crown in September 2013 for an extension of time in respect of the first petition on the basis that N's evidence had become available and was reflected in a second petition, which contained six charges of lewd and libidinous conduct, assault and rape involving N between 1996-2003 and two other complainers, neither of whom had featured in the first petition, in 2000 and 2009. M was fully committed, and released on bail, on 26 September 2013. The sheriff had granted the Crown's application and had observed that no criticism had been made of its decision to indict M in 2007 but rather of its alleged failure to obtain N's evidence at that time, and he had been satisfied that no fault had attached to the Crown in failing to do so.

Held: Appeal refused. (1) The delay had derived from the unavailability of corroborative evidence in 2007, no fault could be attributed to the Crown in that regard and in circumstances where new, potentially decisive, corroborative evidence had emerged, the first stage of the test had been met and the sheriff's exercise of discretion in favour of granting the extension could not be criticised where he had taken all relevant circumstances into account, including the length of time involved. (2) It was in the interests of accused persons, complainers, witnesses and the wider public that cases were tried within a reasonable time, however, the broader interests of justice required that serious allegations might be tried at a late stage rather than remain unprosecuted, subject to the overriding requirement of fairness, and in the present case, it was particularly compelling that without N's evidence there would be no mechanism by which the new serious allegations of child abuse made against M could be successfully prosecuted; it was in the interests of justice that those charges be allowed to proceed and the sheriff's discretionary decision in respect of the second element of the test could not be faulted, *Mejka v HM Advocate* 1993 S.L.T. 1321, [1993] C.L.Y. 4934 and *HM Advocate v McPhee (David William)* 2007 S.C.C.R. 91, [2007] C.L.Y. 5068, *considered.*

MCL v HM ADVOCATE, [2015] HCJAC 97, 2016 S.C.L. 15, The Lord Justice Clerk (Carloway), Lord Bracadale, Lady Clark of Calton, HCJ.

2537 12 month rule–Extensions of time–Sheriff's decision to adjourn trial diet and extend time limit–Witness unavailable to give evidence

[Criminal Procedure (Scotland) Act 1995 (c.46) s.65, s.65(8)]

X, indicted on three bogus workmen charges, lodged a bill of advocation challenging the decision of the sheriff to grant the Crown's motion to ajourn the trial diet and extend the time limit. X had been served with the indictment in November 2013, with a first diet on 23 November 2013 and a trial diet on 9 December. The initial trial diet had been postponed until 14 April 2014 on X's unopposed motion and the 12 month time limit had been extended unopposed until 1 May 2014. Thereafter, the sheriff had granted various adjournments until 12 November and had extended the time limit until 12 December. On 9 December, the Crown again moved to adjourn the trial diet and extend the time limit on the basis of the unavailability of the complainer (Y) in the first charge due to him being medically unfit to attend the court, with a medical certificate dated 3 December said to have been received by the Crown on 8 December, which X opposed on the basis of the multiple applications previously granted. The sheriff granted the motion on the basis that it was in the interests of justice to do so having regard to the serious nature of the charges, the elderly complainers involved, and that the Crown had not been at fault in relation to Y's unavailability.

Held: Bill refused. (1) The bill sought to appeal the decision of the sheriff to extend the time limit in terms of the Criminal Procedure (Scotland) Act 1995 s.65, such an application by bill was incompetent, standing the availability of an appeal under s.65(8) of the Act, moreover, it contained no basis upon which the sheriff's decision could validly be challenged where no specific ground of challenge had been advanced. (2) Cases involving decisions to adjourn or postpone trial diets were fact sensitive and it had been primarily for the court of first instance to determine where the interests of justice lay; the sheriff had been presented with a medical certificate stating that an essential witness had been unavailable to give evidence, which had provided a sound reason to adjourn the trial diet, and the court was unable to fault the sheriff's approach.

AYRES (JAMES) v HM ADVOCATE, [2015] HCJAC 98, 2016 S.C.L. 22, The Lord Justice Clerk (Carloway), Lady Smith, Lord Drummond Young, HCJ.

2538 Appeals against conviction–Amendments–Application to amend note of appeal–Note tendering new ground of appeal

[Civic Government (Scotland) Act 1982 (c.45) s.52(1)(a), s.52A(1)]

B, convicted of two charges of taking indecent photographs of children, contrary to the Civic Government (Scotland) Act 1982 s.52(1)(a), and having such photographs in his possession, contrary to s.52A(1), made an application to amend his note of appeal against conviction. The libel in each charge had not specified the devices on which the photographs were held and B had lodged a preliminary issue minute challenging the relevancy the charges, which he had then withdrawn at the first diet on the basis of an alleged undertaking by the procurator fiscal depute that the charges would be amended in due course to reflect the number of devices. The trial had proceeded and the issue had only been re-raised at the close of the Crown case, and there had been no amendment to the libel. B had lodged a note of appeal against conviction, which had contained no reference to the matter of amendment and had proceeded on the basis of insufficiency of evidence, and leave to appeal had been refused at first sift. B made an application for review of that decision, tendering a new ground of appeal that the Crown had acted oppressively.

Held: Application to amend refused. No sufficient reason had been advanced for the matter of oppression being raised at such a late stage, had it been of substance, it could have been included in the original note of appeal, on the narrative of events, there had been no oppression by the Crown, and in the absence of material supporting the assertion of any undertaking by the Crown, there was no arguable case set out in the new ground of appeal.

BAISLEY (ANDREW) v HM ADVOCATE, [2016] HCJAC 82, 2016 S.C.L. 854, Lord Justice General (Carloway), Lady Paton, Lord Menzies, HCJ.

2539 Appeals against conviction–Grounds for appeal–Resurrection of rejected ground for appeal

[Criminal Procedure (Scotland) Act 1995 (c.46) s.107, s.107(8)]

M, convicted of 13 charges of physical and sexual violence against former partners, applied under the Criminal Procedure (Scotland) Act 1995 s.107(8) to found upon a ground of appeal for which leave had not been granted. M had applied for leave to appeal against conviction on the basis of defective representation and had been refused at the first and second sifts. M submitted that the judges at the second sift had applied the test for defective representation in *Grant (William Gavin) v HM Advocate* [2006] HCJAC 42, 2006 J.C. 205, [2006] C.L.Y. 5192 too rigidly.

Held: Application refused. (1) M's application was not to be seen as a form of appeal against the decisions on leave to appeal made at sift; those decisions were final at that stage of the proceedings and M would have to demonstrate good reason, beyond mere arguability, to justify resurrection of the rejected grounds, such as a patent error or misunderstanding by the sifting judges, or circumstances where a ground was so important that it would be contrary to the interests of justice to exclude it. (2) The test set out in *Birnie (Josh) v HM Advocate* [2015] HCJAC 54, 2015 J.C. 314, [2015] C.L.Y. 2990 and *Beggs (William Frederick) v HM Advocate (Leave to Appeal)* 2006 S.C.C.R. 25, [2006] C.L.Y. 5223 had not been met where there had been no misapplication of the test in *Grant* and M was simply challenging the sifting judges' decision as erroneous, *Grant*, *Birnie* and *Beggs*, *applied.*

TUPPER (MICHAEL) v HM ADVOCATE, [2016] HCJAC 21, 2016 S.C.L. 441, Lord Justice General (Carloway), Lord Menzies, Lady Clark of Calton, HCJ Appeal.

2540 Appeals against sentence–Remittal–Sheriff Appeal Court remitting appeal against sentence to sheriff–Whether competent

[Road Traffic Act 1988 (c.52) s.2; Criminal Procedure (Scotland) Act 1995 (c.46) s.167(8), s.189, s.194ZB, s.299, s.299(4)(b)]

X, convicted of dangerous driving, contrary to the Road Traffic Act 1988 s.2, appealed under the Criminal Procedure (Scotland) Act 1995 s.194ZB against a decision of the sheriff appeal court remitting X's appeal to the sheriff. The sheriff had imposed *inter alia* 20 months' disqualification from driving, without discount, against which X had appealed. The sifting sheriff had refused leave to appeal that ground but had noted that the sheriff ought to have imposed a mandatory requirement to sit the extended driving test and had purported to grant leave to appeal only to allow the sheriff appeal court to remit the proceedings under s.299 of the 1995 Act to the sheriff court in order for the entry to be corrected, or otherwise to alter the sentence in terms of s.167(8) or to substitute an entirely competent sentence, including the appropriate order to sit the extended test. X had made an application seeking to be allowed to argue the ground which had been disallowed and the court had refused to allow the ground to be reinstated. The sheriff appeal court, noting that there were no other grounds of appeal other than that inserted by the sifting sheriff, had purported to exercise its s.299(4)(b) power to remit to the sheriff to amend the entry in the record of proceedings or to alter the sentence in terms of s.167 or to substitute an otherwise competent sentence, including the requirement to sit the extended test.

Held: Sentence of 20 months' disqualification quashed and 15 months' disqualification and order to sit extended test substituted. (1) The terms of s.299 of the 1995 Act had not been designed for a situation in which a sheriff had failed to pass the sentence which he ought to have passed, even when that sentence was mandatory, or to alter or modify any sentence which had been passed; s.299 might operate where it was clear that the record of proceedings or extract did not reflect the sentence passed, however, the present was not a case of an erroneous or incomplete record, and in purporting to act under the s.299(4) power, the sheriff appeal court had acted incompetently. (2) Section 167(8) of the 1995 Act allowed the sentencing court, at any time before imprisonment had followed on a sentence, to alter or modify the sentence, as long as it did not pass a higher sentence, more significantly however, s.167 conferred no power to an appeal court to remit the case to the sentencing court for such modification or alteration. (3) The sheriff appeal court had no power to remit to the sheriff to substitute a competent sentence, its powers regarding disposal of summary appeals were statutory, and in respect of an appeal against sentence, were contained in s.189 of the 1995 Act and were restricted to affirming the sentence or substituting a different sentence. (4) The whole matter of sentence was open to the court; that the sentencing sheriff had not specifically referred to the public protection in explaining the sentence which he had selected did not mean he had left it out of account altogether, the sheriff had been best placed to determine the extent of the public protection element in the sentence which he had imposed, given that he had considered that he ought to have discounted the disqualification to a period of 15 months, it appeared that he had not considered that a period in excess thereof was required for public protection, further, he had failed to realise that he had been required to make an order to sit the extended test, which was a factor designed for public protection and would have been a relevant factor in determining whether, and to what extent, to allow a discount to the period of disqualification, thus the sentence of disqualification would be quashed and 15 months substituted, *McGill (James) v HM Advocate* [2013] HCJAC 150, 2014 S.L.T. 238, [2014] C.L.Y. 3768, *considered*.

IQBAL v HARVIE, [2016] HCJAC 38, 2016 S.L.T. 633, Lady Smith, Lady Dorrian, Lord Bracadale, HCJ.

2541 Assisted suicide–Decisions to prosecute–Policy in relation to prosecution for homicide–Whether interference with rights under ECHR art.8 in accordance with law

[European Convention on Human Rights 1950 art.8(1), art.8(2); Suicide Act 1961 (c.60) s.2]

A disabled person (R) reclaimed against an interlocutor of the Lord Ordinary dismissing his petition for judicial review of the Lord Advocate's failure to promulgate a policy identifying the facts and circumstances which he would take into account in deciding whether or not to prosecute a person who had assisted another to commit suicide (*Ross v Lord Advocate* [2015] CSOH 123, 2015 S.L.T. 617, [2015] C.L.Y. 2986). R had claimed that the crown office and procurator fiscal service prosecution code failed to satisfy the Convention requirements of foreseeability and accessibility, therefore, the interference with his rights under ECHR art.8(1) was not in accordance with the law as required by art.8(2). The Lord Ordinary found *inter alia* that the prosecution policy was sufficiently accessible and foreseeable, that the absence of any divergence between law and practice demonstrated that any decision to prosecute would not turn on unpublished factors, and that there was no basis to conclude that the policy was inaccessible, unclear or not in accordance with the law.

Held: Reclaiming motion refused. (1) It was not a crime in Scotland to assist another to commit suicide, however, where a person had done something which he knew would cause the death of another, he was guilty of homicide where his act had been the immediate and direct cause of that person's death; in relation to a death caused by the ingestion of a lethal substance, the administration of such a substance might amount to homicide and supplying a lethal substance for immediate use might fall into that category, nevertheless, the voluntary ingestion of a drug normally broke the causal chain: when an adult with full capacity freely and voluntarily consumed a drug with the intention of ending his life, it was that act which had been the immediate and direct cause of death and had thus broken the causal link between any act of supply and the death; other acts which did not amount to an immediate and direct cause, including taking persons to places where they might commit, or seek assistance to commit, suicide, were not criminal where they had not, in a legal sense, caused the death, even had that death been predicted as the likely outcome of the visit; those concepts were well understood and there was no requirement for L to set those concepts out in offence specific guidelines. (2) The circumstances in which *R. (on the application of Purdy) v DPP* [2009] UKHL 45, [2010] 1 A.C. 345, [2009] C.L.Y. 2046 arose were materially different from the present case in three respects: (i) the underlying substantive criminal law in Scotland was different from that in England and Wales, there was no equivalent of the Suicide Act 1961 s.2 in Scotland and the conduct anticipated in *R (Purdy)* would not be criminal were it prosecuted in Scotland; (ii) the director of public prosecutions had consistently chosen not to prosecute those who had committed an offence under s.2 of the 1961 Act and there was a gulf between law and practice which was not apparent in Scotland where L had had only two instances of assisted suicide reported to him and in both cases there had been insufficient evidence of any crime having been committed; (iii) the code contained general guidance to allow the relevant issues to be taken into account, and L had further stated that, where there was a sufficiency of evidence that a homicide had been committed, there would be a prosecution in the absence of exceptional circumstances, and L had not attempted to distance himself from the code, *R (Purdy), considered*. (3) There was no evidence that L had applied the law in an arbitrary manner where he had expressed his policy clearly, namely that cases which amount to homicide would be prosecuted in the absence of exceptional circumstances, it could not be said that L had exercised his discretion in a way which was arbitrary and had not satisfied the requirements of legality, and the interference with R's rights was in accordance with the law in terms of art.8(2) of the Convention.

ROSS v LORD ADVOCATE, [2016] CSIH 12, 2016 S.C.C.R. 176, The Lord Justice Clerk (Carloway), Lady Dorrian, Lord Drummond Young, IH (2 Div).

2542 Bail–High Court of Justiciary–Accused indicted to preliminary hearing in High Court–Accused purporting to appeal sheriff's refusal to grant bail at full committal to Sheriff Appeal Court

X, charged with rape, appealed against a decision of the sheriff appeal court dismissing his appeal against a decision of the sheriff to refuse him bail at full committal. X had appeared on petition and was committed for further examination, with bail being refused at that stage. At full committal, the sheriff again refused bail. No appeals were taken against the decisions at the relevant time and X was indicted to a preliminary hearing in the High Court. Thereafter, X purported to appeal the sheriff's refusal to grant bail at full committal to the sheriff appeal court, which was unsuccessful. He then lodged a petition for bail to the High Court, and presented a note of appeal against the decision of the sheriff appeal court.

Held: Opinion issued. Where an accused had been indicted to a preliminary hearing in the High Court, once that diet had called, the High Court was the appropriate court to decide any applications for bail as it was inevitable that it would be apprised of all the information relative to the progress of the case; accordingly, it was not appropriate to revert to the sheriff once the case had called in the High Court and it followed that the procedure to appeal the original sheriff's decision on bail, after the calling of the preliminary hearing, was inappropriate, as was the procedure which had followed thereon.

A v HM ADVOCATE, [2016] HCJAC 17, 2016 S.C.L. 380, Lord Justice General (Carloway), Lord Brodie, Lord Drummond Young, HCJ.

2543 Bail conditions–Variation–Right to respect for private and family life–Compatibility of special bail conditions

[Criminal Procedure (Scotland) Act 1995 (c.46) s.288ZB; European Convention on Human Rights 1950 art.8; Criminal Justice and Licensing (Scotland) Act 2010 (asp 13) s.38(1); Act of Adjournal (Criminal Procedure Rules) 1996 Sch.2 para.40.12]

A bail judge made a reference to a bench of three judges in terms of the Criminal Procedure (Scotland) Act 1995 s.288ZB in light of a proposition advanced on behalf of an accused (P) that a refusal to grant variation of special bail conditions breached his rights under the ECHR art.8 and those of his partner (X). On 2 February 2015, P had appeared from custody charged with assaulting X at her address and damaging property, contrary to the Criminal Justice and Licensing (Scotland) Act 2010 s.38(1), whilst subject to two bail orders. P had pleaded not guilty and had been admitted to bail with additional conditions that he should neither enter the street (S) where X lived nor approach, contact or attempt to contact her. On 14 April, P appeared on summary complaint charged with being in S and having a knife without reasonable excuse, behaving in a threatening and abusive manner by shouting and brandishing a knife, contrary to s.38 of the 2010 Act, and breaching the 2 February bail conditions. P had pleaded not guilty to the first two charges but had pleaded guilty to the third, which had not been accepted and he had been refused bail. On 18 April, P had been granted bail upon the standard conditions and the two special conditions and bail had been continued on 8 June. On 23 June, the sheriff had refused P's application for variation of the bail conditions on the basis that it was not in the public interest to do so, noting that X's view was only one matter which had to be considered, and having regard to the seriousness of the allegations whilst on bail and breaching special conditions of bail previously imposed, to P's prior record, consisting of a breach of s.38 of the 2010 Act and assault to injury in September 2014, assault to severe injury in December 2014 and breach of a community payback order in February 2015, and to the fact that a relatively early trial diet had been set. P appealed and in the course thereof presented a compatibility minute averring that X did not wish P to be subject to the special conditions and that the Crown, in requesting the additional conditions and subsequently opposing the application for removal thereof, had acted in an incompatible manner with P and X's art.8 rights. On 10 July, the bail judge considered it appropriate to make the reference in light of P's proposition that given the particular facts and circumstances pertaining to both bail appeals, there was no basis upon which the refusal to grant variation of the special conditions would not breach P and X's art.8 rights. Having heard submissions, the court concluded that it would be appropriate to hear X, subject to all questions of competency. The issues referred to the High Court were: (i) was P's art.8 right engaged in relation to determining whether a bail condition preventing contact or communication with X should be imposed when bail was granted and, thereafter, in determining whether it should be removed; (ii) was X's art.8 right engaged in relation to determining whether a bail condition upon P preventing contact or communication with X should be imposed when bail was granted and, thereafter, in determining whether it should be removed; (iii) *esto* X's art.8 right was engaged, had she a right to be heard and to make effective representation to the court in relation to the determination thereof; (iv) *esto* X's art.8 was engaged, had she a right to access the court to review its determination; (v) *esto* X had a right to be heard and to make effective representation to the court, had she the right to legal representation, with such representation being funded by the state if necessary? P and X submitted *inter alia* that the Crown's adoption of a blanket policy of seeking to impose conditions such as the present ones in cases of domestic abuse amounted to an incompatible act. X further submitted inter alia that (1) the Crown had failed properly to take account of, or to represent, her interests; when the Crown had sought the imposition of the bail conditions, X had become the victim of an unlawful act and was entitled to rely upon her Convention rights in the proceedings; (2) the terms of the Act of Adjournal (Criminal Procedure Rules) 1996 Sch.2 para.40.12 would enable her to be represented during the hearing of a reference on a compatibility issue.

Held: Questions answered. (1) P's formulation of the alleged incompatibility related solely to the actings of the Crown, it was apparent that the sheriff had carried out an appropriate balancing exercise, and X's views had clearly been taken into account; the ultimate decision on bail was one for the court, carrying out the careful exercise of balancing all the relevant factors, in which neither the attitude of the Crown nor the views of a complainer would be be determinative, and it was difficult to see how the Crown's attitude or the arguments advanced on its behalf could give rise to an incompatibility issue; the bail conditions had been imposed because the court considered them to be necessary and appropriate, moreover, P had no locus to assert X's rights or interests, therefore, no compatibility issue arose on P's arguments, moreover, X's argument that the Crown's adoption of a blanket policy created an incompatibility fell to be discarded for the same reasons. (2) The Crown's policy provided for the gathering of detailed information as to a complainer's views in a case such as the present, the court was frequently presented with a letter from a complainer making their views known to the Crown or the defence, and in any event, the absence of any formal mechanism to place the views of a complainer before the court did not create any incompatibility with Convention rights; X's views might be a relevant factor in the bail decision but she did not thereby obtain any entitlement to seek to vindicate any rights or interest which she might have in the criminal process. (3) The fact that the proceedings had been intimated to X did not make her a party; it was clear from the interlocutor and the relevant legislation that the only parties anticipated, or indeed competent, under a reference were the Crown, the defence, and in certain circumstances the Advocate General, and X's attempt to rely on r.40.12.1 could not succeed where that rule operated only once a reference had been made and the parties determined, and X was unable to identify any authority to suggest that the Scottish practice that victims could not directly participate in criminal proceedings was other than Convention compatible, *Scottish Criminal Cases Review Commission v Swire* [2015] HCJAC 76, 2015 S.L.T. 556, [2015] C.L.Y. 2973, *considered.* (4) In circumstances where X had indicated that she did not wish bail conditions to be imposed, or would rather they were removed, the court had to consider the situation in the context of obligations in relation to the protection of victims of domestic violence, and such victims were of a particular vulnerability. (5) In all the circumstances, there was no merit in either P or X's submissions and no basis for considering, under either domestic law or European jurisprudence, that it was necessary to grant a right of audience to a complainer in the circumstances of a case such as the present, accordingly, with regard to the questions in the reference: (i) and (ii) X had art.8 rights which were sufficiently engaged but they had not been infringed; the existing procedures in relation to bail applications of the present kind were Convention compliant; (iii) X had no right to be represented in court or to address the court in the circumstances desiderated; (iv) X had no right to access the court to review its determination; (v) *esto* X had a right to be heard and to make effective representation to the court, she had no right to legal representation. Observed, that in making the reference, the bail judge appeared to have heard no significant debate and not to have considered determining the matter himself, deciding simply to refer the matter in light of the P's proposition, and it might be preferable to continue the case to a further hearing so that a full debate might take place, *O'Leary (Thomas) v HM Advocate* [2014] HCJAC 45, 2014 S.L.T. 711, [2014] C.L.Y. 3708, *considered.*

HM ADVOCATE v PORCH (ROSS) *sub nom.* DUNN v PORCH, [2015] HCJAC 111, 2016 S.L.T. 149, Lady Paton, Lady Dorrian, Lord Drummond Young, HCJ.

2544 Contempt of court–Failure to attend–Witness failing to attend due to son being in hospital–Sheriff having insufficient information about circumstances

[Criminal Procedure (Scotland) Act 1995 (c.46) s.155(2), s.299(4)]

S lodged a bill of suspension following the sheriff's finding that he was in contempt of court. S had been cited to attend court on 1 June 2015 as a witness to give evidence at the trial of his alleged assailant in an assault but had failed to attend where the night before, his eight year old son (X), who suffered from attention deficit hyperactivity disorder, had had an accident requiring surgery and two days in hospital, with a later readmission for further treatment. The sheriff had accepted that explanation but had relied on S's failure to communicate with the court on the morning of the trial diet. S submitted that (1) the minute of proceedings was inaccurate and where there had been no compliance with the Criminal Procedure (Scotland) Act 1995 s.155(2), the finding of contempt ought to be quashed; (2) the sheriff had failed to take up the invitation to hear evidence before making any finding of contempt; had further inquiry been made, fuller information could have been provided; (3) with reference to *Chappell v Friel* 1997 S.L.T. 1325, [1998] C.L.Y. 5398, S's failure to attend had not been wilful.

Held: Bill passed. (1) There was no dispute that the minute was inaccurate, however, the court would adopt the procedure in s.299(4) of the 1995 Act and continue to consider and determine the matter as if the minute were corrected. (2) Although the sheriff had accepted S's explanation, a hearing of evidence might have cast further light on his failure to contact the court. (3) The circumstances of the present case were different from those in *Chappell* due to the unexpectedness of the accident, its serious consequences, the fact that both S and his partner had required to be with X in hospital, and the stress and anxiety suffered, such that what had occurred had not amounted to a wilful defiance of a court order; the sheriff had had insufficient information about the circumstances in which no contact had been made on the morning of the diet to form a view, the high test for contempt had not been met and the finding of contempt would be quashed, *Chappell*, *considered*.

STRATHERN v HARVIE, [2015] HCJAC 107, 2016 S.L.T. 70, Lady Paton, Lord Bracadale, Lord Turnbull, HCJ.

2545 Criminal appeals–Competence–Minute proceeding as objection to criminal charge and admissibility of evidence, and purporting to raise preliminary issue objecting to admissibility of evidence–Whether preliminary plea objecting to competency or relevancy of summary complaint

[Police and Fire Reform (Scotland) Act 2012 (asp 8) s.90(2)(a); Criminal Justice and Licensing (Scotland) Act 2010 (asp 13) s.38(1); Criminal Procedure (Scotland) Act 1995 (c.46) s.174]

W, charged with resisting, obstructing or hindering police officers (P) in the execution of their duty, contrary to the Police and Fire Reform (Scotland) Act 2012 s.90(2)(a) (charge 1), behaving in a threatening or abusive manner likely to cause a reasonable person to suffer fear or alarm, contrary to the Criminal Justice and Licensing (Scotland) Act 2010 s.38(1) (charge 2) and possession of cannabis (charge 3), appealed under the Criminal Procedure (Scotland) Act 1995 s.174 against the sheriff's decision repelling his minute objecting to the lawfulness of P's actings in taking hold of him at the locus in charge 1. W claimed that P had acted unlawfully in taking hold of him as he had committed no offence and had had no reason or justification to arrest or detain him, accordingly, he had been assaulted by P who had not been acting in the course of their duty, thus he had been entitled to resist and could not have contravened s.90 of the 2012 Act. P had attended at the locus late at night in response to a call from the householder (H) requesting assistance in removing W, who was intoxicated, from outside their property, P had given W opportunities to leave voluntarily and he had refused, being verbally aggressive towards P. The sheriff found that it was plain that P had attended at the locus in the execution of their duty as police officers and that the evidence clearly described that, in laying hands on W's arms, they had not been seeking to either detain or arrest him but that the decision to do so had been an expedient one designed to assist an intoxicated, and unwanted, presence from the property.

Held: Appeal refused. (1) W's minute proceeded as an objection to charge 1 and the admissibility of evidence in support thereof, and purported to raise a preliminary issue objecting to the admissibility of evidence following his arrest and events thereafter, said arrest being unlawful, which was not a preliminary plea objecting to the competency or relevancy of the summary complaint or the proceedings thereon; any objection to the admissibility of evidence was to be taken at trial, accordingly the minute could not be the subject of an appeal under s.174(1) of the 1995 Act and the appeal fell to be refused as incompetent. (2) The minute was misconceived; looking at the facts and circumstances in their entirety, it was unnecessary that there be any complaint by a member of the public in order for there to be a breach of the peace or a contravention of s.38(1) of the 2010 Act, W's behaviour had been capable of causing a reasonable person to suffer fear and alarm, that being the objective test in terms of the statutory charge, the facts and circumstances as narrated in the sheriff's report were capable of constituting a breach of the peace or its statutory equivalent, however, the sheriff had decided the matter on the basis that P had clearly been acting in the course of their duties as police officers, the reasonable inference which could be drawn from the evidence was that P had been seeking to defuse the situation and avoid having to detain or arrest W, the sheriff had been entitled to reach the conclusion that P had been acting in the course of their duties having responded to H's complaint regarding W's presence at her property, therefore, there had been no error in the sheriff's approach to the minute, accordingly, the appeal would be refused as both lacking in competence and merit and the matter would be remitted to the sheriff to conclude the trial, *Craig v Normand* 1997 S.L.T. 919, [1997] C.L.Y. 5774, *considered* and *Twycross v Farrell* 1973 S.L.T. (Notes) 85, [1973] C.L.Y. 3576 and *Cardle v Murray* 1993 S.L.T. 525, [1993] C.L.Y. 5059, *distinguished*.

WARWICK v HARVIE, [2016] SAC (Crim) 13, 2016 S.C.L. 676, Sheriff Principal M M Stephen, QC, Sheriff Principal M Lewis, Sheriff P J Braid, SAC.

2546 Criminal procedure–Serious crime prevention orders

ACT OF ADJOURNAL (CRIMINAL PROCEDURE RULES 1996 AMENDMENT) (NO.2) (SERIOUS CRIME PREVENTION ORDERS) 2016, SSI 2016/137; made under the Criminal Procedure (Scotland) Act 1995 s.305. In force: 17 March 2016.

This Act of Adjournal inserts a new Chapter 63 (serious crime prevention orders) into the Criminal Procedure Rules 1996 in consequence of the amendments made to the Serious Crime Act 2007 by the Serious Crime Act 2015. Those amendments extend the availability of serious crime prevention orders so that they may be made in Scotland.

2547 Criminal proceedings–High Court of Justiciary–Legal representation

ACT OF ADJOURNAL (CRIMINAL PROCEDURE RULES 1996 AMENDMENT) (NO.3) (INSTRUCTION OF REPRESENTATION IN THE HIGH COURT) 2016, SSI 2016/201; made under the Criminal Procedure (Scotland) Act 1995 s.305. In force: 3 October 2016.

This Act of Adjournal sets out the steps which solicitors are to take in order that they can confirm to the court that an accused has been informed of his or her options regarding representation in the High Court of Justiciary. It inserts a new rule 9A.3A into the Act of Adjournal (Criminal Procedure Rules) 1996 and inserts new forms.

2548 Defence case–Legal representation–Conduct of defence–Whether defective

B appealed against conviction for assaulting and abducting a customer (X) within a shop (S), and, along with a co-accused (C), assaulting and robbing S's employee (Y), on the ground of defective representation, and against the imposition of nine years' imprisonment. C had pleaded guilty to the second charge at a preliminary hearing and had been sentenced to five years and seven months' imprisonment, discounted from eight for the early plea. CCTV images showed two men entering S, one carrying a metal pole and the other a knife, assaulting X and Y and robbing Y, then leaving S and entering another shop (T), with T's CCTV showing a man with a knife entering T and apparently disposing of a hat and the knife therein. At trial, Y had been unable to identify B but had identified the knife recovered from T as that used in the robbery and had identified the hat as resembling the one worn by the man who had assaulted him. On examination, both the knife and the hat had contained inter alia B's DNA. A police officer had identified B as the person shown in T's CCTV images. B submitted *inter alia* that (1) his facial features did not match those of the person in S's CCTV images and his representatives had failed to carry out his instruction for an analysis of T and S's CCTV images, which would have established that the male in T's CCTV, namely B, was not the robber; (2) B's representatives had failed, despite his express instructions, to obtain an independent DNA report; (3) B had wished to call C as a witness and no steps had been taken to precognose C; (4) B had sought to dispense with the services of his trial representatives and had been asked to sign a disclaimer, which he had refused to do; (5) B had not received a fair trial and a miscarriage of justice had occurred; (6) in relation to sentence, the advocate depute had misled the court by stating that B had a conviction in the sheriff court in 2005 for theft by housebreaking in which he had assaulted the 90 year old homeowner.

Held: Appeal against conviction refused, sentence of nine years' imprisonment quashed and seven years substituted. (1) There was no objective support for B's allegations, there was no material upon which to base the assertion that CCTV analysis would have established that the facial features of the man in the images from S were different from those in T's CCTV, B had made no attempt to place before the court evidence of any analysis having taken place and the differences involved having been established, and trial counsel had not focused upon the images for tactical reasons, similarly, there was no basis upon which it could be said that any further DNA analysis would have differed from that produced by the Crown, B had accepted in discussions with his legal representatives that the hat found in T, had belonged to him, the decision not to call C had been tactical and had been fully justified on the basis that if called, he would incriminate B, and as B's grounds of appeal did not contain any merit, the appeal against conviction fell to be refused, *Grant (William Gavin) v HM Advocate* [2006] HCJAC 42, 2006 J.C. 205, [2006] C.L.Y. 5192, *considered*. (2) B's conviction had in fact been in the High Court in 2007 and had only been for theft by housebreaking, the former libel in the indictment of violence having been deleted, and where the trial judge had taken into account B's previous convictions and the narrative which had been given by the advocate depute, it had to be assumed that not only had he had regard to the terms of the previous convictions but also the account given of the assault on the householder, moreover the trial judge had stated that the sentence imposed on B included a bail aggravation but B had neither been charged therewith nor convicted thereof, nevertheless, the present was an armed robbery against a background of offending and with regard to the sentence imposed on C, a sentence of seven years' imprisonment would be substituted.

BOATH (PETER) v HM ADVOCATE, [2016] HCJAC 81, 2016 S.C.L. 857, Lord Justice General (Carloway), Lady Paton, Lord Menzies, HCJ.

2549 Double jeopardy–Admissions–Crown seeking authority to bring fresh prosecution–Whether new evidence admissible

[Double Jeopardy (Scotland) Act 2011 (asp 16) s.3, s.3(3), s.3(3)(a)(i), s.3(4), s.3(4)(a), s.3(4)(b), s.3(4)(c); Telecommunications Act 1984 (c.12) s.43(1)]

The Crown made an application under the Double Jeopardy (Scotland) Act 2011 s.3 seeking that X's acquittal of murder in 1992, on the basis of a not proven verdict, be set aside and authority to bring a fresh prosecution. The victim (W) had last been seen in X's company and at trial, X had claimed to have left X in the company of another man. Character evidence had been led to support X's claim that he could not have committed such a crime. The Crown brought the application on the basis of several alleged admissions, made or becoming known of, after the date of his acquittal to four of X's friends (B, C, D and E, collectively F) and a prison officer (P). B alleged that X had stated that he had left W with another man and that he was "too cute" to be imprisoned for her murder. C alleged that she had asked X if he had murdered W and he had responded "that's something naebody will ever know", X had made remarks which had implied that he had murdered W, and C and D alleged that X had admitted to W's murder in threatening phone calls to them, which had resulted in his conviction under the Telecommunications Act 1984 s.43(1). E claimed that X had made remarks to him implying that he had murdered W. P claimed that, between 8 and 15 June 1992, when X had been remanded for further examination, they had a conversation in which X had implied that he had done something to W. The Crown submitted *inter alia* that (1) X's statements were to be construed as admissions where he had not denied responsibility but had appeared to accept his involvement; (2) P's conversation with X had not been in pursuance of a criminal investigation but in the ordinary course of his duties, and was therefore admissible; (3) E and P's evidence could not with reasonable diligence have become known earlier where there had been no basis for interviewing them at the time of the original trial; (4) the admissions mitigated the evidential weaknesses in the original trial and portrayed X's character in a different light; (5) the admissions increased the evidential and persuasive effect of the existing evidence and were likely to be believed by a jury; (6) it was in the interests of justice to set aside the acquittal where the crime was of the utmost seriousness and the admissions were compelling, and it could not be said that the passage of time would result in an unfair trial where copies and photographs were available of any missing evidence.

Held: Application refused. (1) It could not be said that any statement susceptible to being regarded as incriminating would necessarily qualify within the terms of s.3(3) of the 2011 Act, any statement relied upon required to be such as could fairly and reasonably be construed as an admission that the individual had committed the offence and the context in which the statement had been made was a vital consideration: X's response to C's confrontation could not be construed as an admission and none of the remaining statements had involved confronting X with the allegations; X had made an exculpatory statement to B and it was not possible to attribute the character of an admission of murder thereto, while it was a reasonable inference that X had made the telephone calls to C and D, in the circumstances those calls could not reasonably or fairly be taken to amount to an admission of murder, and the same reasoning applied to the incident with E; having regard to the whole circumstances in which the statements were made, they could not reasonably and fairly be construed as admissions, however, X's comments to P might be construed as an admission where the charge upon which he had been remanded had been specifically referred to, *Mackenzie (Lewis Wylie) v HM Advocate* 1983 J.C. 13, [1983] C.L.Y. 4162, *Moran (Joseph) v HM Advocate* 1990 J.C. 196, [1990] C.L.Y. 4903, *Greenshields (George) v HM Advocate* 1989 S.C.C.R. 637, [1990] C.L.Y. 4866 and *Stirling v McFadyen* 2000 S.C.C.R. 239, [2000] C.L.Y. 6005, *considered.* (2) The context of X's conversation with P robbed X's statement of any voluntary character, P had initiated the conversation to elicit a response, it was obvious that any response would be likely to relate to the charge against X, and where P had gone straight to the charge facing X, X's response was not voluntary or spontaneous, and was inadmissible, *Fraser (Kevin John) v HM Advocate* 1989 S.C.C.R. 82, [1989] C.L.Y. 3993 and *Van Lierop v McLeod* 2000 S.L.T. 291, [1999] C.L.Y. 5808, *considered.* (3) X's statements to F failed to meet the terms of s.3(3)(a)(i), and while his statement to P was capable of being construed as an admission, it was not admissible in evidence and therefore could not be said to strengthen the case against X, and was incapable of having any effect on a jury, and the remaining conditions of s.3(4)(b) and (c) had not been met. (4) The court required to look at the evidence upon which the application was based, and the evidence led at the trial, it could not be swayed by evidence which had not formed the basis of an application and it was a matter of concern that such evidence had been referred to in C's application when a decision had been taken that that material did not support a new evidence application under s.4 and required to be left out of account, it was not helpful for such material gratuitously to be included in applications such as the present where the law was clear that it was only in the interests of justice to set aside an acquittal where all the conditions imposed by Parliament had been met, those conditions had not been met and the application failed. *Opinion*, (1) that had the statements in question been admissible, the reasonable diligence test in s.3(4)(a) had been met; (2) that had the question of the interests of justice arisen, the court would have had to be cognisant of the fact that the vast majority of label productions had been destroyed, and could not now be subjected to any enhanced DNA analysis. *Observed*, that a prison officer dealing with a remand prisoner, especially a young person, required to think carefully about the subject matter upon which he opened conversation.

HM ADVOCATE v AULD (FRANCIS DAVID) *sub nom.* AULD (FRANCIS DAVID) v HM ADVOCATE, [2016] HCJAC 18, 2016 S.L.T. 636, Lord Justice General (Carloway), Lady Dorrian, Lord Bracadale, HCJ.

2550 Double jeopardy–Sexual offences–Crown accepting not guilty plea to previous charge libelling lewd, indecent and libidinous practices–Later charge involving act of sodomy not previously libelled

[Double Jeopardy (Scotland) Act 2011 (asp 16) s.7; Criminal Procedure (Scotland) Act 1995 (c.46) s.74]

K, charged with *inter alia* having an unnatural carnal connection with a child (P), then aged 11, on an occasion between 1 and 15 July 1998, appealed against a judge's decision repelling his plea in bar of trial founding upon the Double Jeopardy (Scotland) Act 2011 s.7. Attached to the indictment was a docket describing the occasion on which K was alleged to have used lewd, indecent and libidinous practices towards P by removing his clothing, handling his testicles, rubbing his buttocks, penetrating his anus with his fingers and pressing his erect penis against his body. In 2009, a plea of not guilty had been accepted from K in respect of an offence that, on various occasions between the same dates and at the same place, he had used lewd, indecent and libidinous practices towards P by touching him on the body and handling his private member. The judge at first instance had repelled K's plea in bar of trial on the basis that the crime charged was not the same act as had been previously libelled. The advocate depute submitted that (1) the allegation of sodomy had not been made prior to the acceptance of the plea on the earlier indictment; (2) the offences had arisen out of different acts.

Held: Appeal refused. (1) The two offences were not the same, K could not have been convicted of sodomy on the original indictment, sodomy was not an aggravation of lewd behaviour but was a separate and different crime, it had not been argued that the Crown's actions were oppressive and the only issue was whether, in terms of s.7 of the 2011 Act, the new libel offended the broader principle of being a re-prosecution of an offence arising out of the same, or largely the same, acts. (2) The statutory test was whether the act now charged, namely sodomy, arose out of the same, or largely the same, acts as those lewd practices originally libelled, and it had not, it had arisen out of a quite separate act, being that of penile penetration of P's anus, that act had not been previously libelled, and the single occasion act of sodomy was not inextricably linked to the various acts of touching libelled in the earlier indictment.

KERR (ALAN) v HM ADVOCATE *sub nom.* KERR (ALLAN) v HM ADVOCATE, [2015] HCJAC 96, 2015 S.L.T. 837, The Lord Justice Clerk (Carloway), Lord Bracadale, Lord Malcolm, HCJ.

2551 Extradition–Permission to appeal

ACT OF ADJOURNAL (CRIMINAL PROCEDURE RULES 1996 AMENDMENT) (MISCELLANEOUS) 2016, SSI 2016/103; made under the Criminal Procedure (Scotland) Act 1995 s.305. In force: 1 March 2016.

This Act of Adjournal amends Criminal Procedure Rules 1996 c.34 in consequence of amendments made to the Extradition Act 2003 by the Anti-social Behaviour, Crime and Policing Act 2014 s.160 which introduced a requirement to obtain leave to appeal in extradition cases.

2552 Interpreters–Prejudice–Interpreter knowing victim well–Risk of prejudice to accused

[Criminal Justice and Licensing (Scotland) Act 2010 (asp 13) s.38]

M, convicted of behaving in a threatening or abusive manner, contrary to the Criminal Justice and Licensing (Scotland) Act 2010 s.38, of assaulting X to his severe injury and permanent disfigurement, and of attempting to pervert the course of justice, appealed against the sheriff's dismissal of her compatibility minute. X had been deaf since birth and had no speech and only basic sign language skills, and prior to the trial, M had lodged a compatibility minute contending that there was a real risk of prejudice where X was to give evidence at trial with the assistance of a specialist interpreter (R) who was trained and qualified in minimal sign language and who knew X well, having assisted and supported him for 17 years, and had interpreted and translated X's complaint during his police statement. The sheriff was not satisfied that there was a real risk of prejudice to M, R was the best person to properly interpret X's evidence, any issue regarding the fact that she had interpreted for X during his police interview could be dealt with in the course of the trial, R had not taken any notes at the police interview, M's point regarding putting a prior inconsistent statement to X and the fact that if R acted as interpreter she could not be called as a witness in that connection, was not substantive, and the interviewing police officers would be the best persons to call in relation to the content of the interview.

Held: Appeal allowed. (1) There had been a viable alternative to R's instruction, namely instructing another interpreter and enabling them to spend time with X to gain familiarity with his particular form of communication in advance of the trial, and all the circumstances pointed to the presence of a significant risk of partiality; the nature of the association between R and X and R's knowledge of the content of X's police interview made it impossible to rule out the risk of her interpretation being affected by sympathy for him, and such a risk had not required to be run in the circumstances. Moreover, the police witnesses present at the interview could not have given evidence about the accuracy of R's interpretation, and the sheriff ought to have regarded that as adding weight to the inappropriateness of using R as interpreter; it could not be concluded that a risk of prejudice to M had been eliminated, the minute should not have been repelled and a miscarriage of justice had occurred, *R. (on the application of Bozkurt) v Thames Magistrates Court* [2001] EWHC Admin 400, [2002] R.T.R. 15, [2001] C.L.Y. 1141, *considered*. (2) The Crown's motion for authority for a fresh prosecution would be refused where the Crown had not been without fault in the matter, and given the time that M had already spent in custody, it would not be in the interests of justice to grant it. Observed, that unless proficient in the language being interpreted or otherwise independently advised as to the competency of ongoing interpretation, judges were not in a position to assess its quality, rather, the court trusted the interpreter not to lose sight of their role as being limited to that of an independent and impartial bilingual mouthpiece, which in turn elevated the importance of taking all reasonable steps to ensure that the accuracy and objectivity of interpretation could not be impugned.

MCDOUGALL (LOUISE) v HM ADVOCATE, [2015] HCJAC 88, 2015 S.L.T. 804, Lord Eassie, Lady Smith, Lord Drummond Young, HCJ.

2553 Jurors–Contempt of court–Juror disobeying instruction not to make any inquiries in relation to case–Juror using social media to make inquiries

A jury member (H) petitioned the nobile officium challenging a decision of the sheriff finding her in contempt of court by reason of wilfully defying a court order by using social media to make her own inquiries regarding a witness (M) during the trial. H submitted that she had checked the Facebook profile of M's sister to confirm whether or not M was known to her and she had made no inquiry into the nature of the charge or any matters surrounding the allegations in the indictment.

Held: Petition dismissed. In general terms and in more specific terms in relation to the internet and Facebook the sheriff had given the jury a clear instruction not to make any inquiries in relation to the case which H had disobeyed and had accordingly been in contempt of court.

HOWDEN, PETITONER *sub nom.* HOWDEN (ELIZABETH) v HM ADVOCATE, [2015] HCJAC 91, 2015 S.C.L. 960, Lord Brodie, Lord Bracadale, Lord Matthews, HCJ.

2554 Jury directions–Abuse of position of trust–Misdirection as to implication of lack of consent–Corroboration

[Sexual Offences (Scotland) Act 2009 (asp 9) s.3, s.42]

W appealed against conviction for the indecent assault of J while he was asleep and intoxicated, over two separate periods, contrary to the Sexual Offences (Scotland) Act 2009 s.3 (charges 1 and 2). W had pleaded guilty to a contravention of s.42 of the 2009 Act in relation to another complainer, D (charge 5), namely sexual abuse of trust. J had been in care and been introduced to W as a befriender through the social work department when he was aged 16 or 17; J gave evidence that he had consented to sexual conduct with W on a number of occasions but to which he had not consented when he was drunk or asleep. In relation to charge 5, W had been D's teacher, and his age during the period of the libel was from just before his 15th birthday for some six months. The central issue was whether the jury was entitled to treat D's undisputed evidence as corroborative of J's evidence; there was a related issue concerning an alleged misdirection of the jury based on an erroneous understanding as to s.42. W argued that the Crown had to prove that, to his knowledge, the sexual activity had taken place without J's consent; charge 5 was a breach of s.42 in respect of which the issue of consent had no relevance thus D's evidence could not provide the corroboration necessary for a guilty verdict on charges 1 and 2. The Crown submitted that the underlying rationale for an offence under s.42 was not crucial because there were sufficient similarities between the respective accounts for the rule in *Moorov* to be applied by the jury: in respect of both complainers, W had been in a position of trust; the complainers were of a similar age; the offences had occurred in W's home; alcohol had been involved; and the nature of the sexual conduct had been much the same. Any misdirection of the jury had not led to a miscarriage of justice because, even without an implied absence of consent approach to s.42, the necessary corroboration could be found in D's evidence.

Held: Appeal allowed. (1) The sheriff had erred in concluding that lack of consent was to be implied in a charge under s.42 where the focus therein was on the factual conditions required for proof of the offence, those being that the complainer was under the age of 18 and that, in relation to that person, the accused was in a position of trust, as defined in s.43; the question of consent was immaterial and any consent was effectively invalidated if the conditions in s.42 applied. (2) The question whether evidence in respect of a charge where consent, or absence thereof, was not relevant might properly be used to corroborate evidence of another complainer in respect of a charge where the absence of consent was a critical issue could be answered in the affirmative: the search was for evidence indicative of an underlying similarity between the circumstances of the offences such as to enable the conclusion to be drawn that there was a course of conduct which was being persisted in by W; the sheriff was correct to say that the Crown were relying on D's evidence to corroborate J's account which simply meant that if the evidence of similarity was sufficient for the application of the doctrine, D's different account of what happened to him would suffice to corroborate J's account, and so allow the several charges to be proved by the evidence of one witness to each; in such circumstances where the offence was one, such as a s.3 offence, which had certain essential elements for its commission, the account of the complainer speaking to that charge would require to provide evidence from which all three elements could be established and, in the present case, J had spoken to all three elements and it was not suggested that the similarities in the evidence were not otherwise sufficient for the *Moorov* doctrine to apply, *McMahon (Daniel Bowie) v HM Advocate* 1996 S.L.T. 1139, [1996] C.L.Y. 6721, *considered.* (3) The sheriff had erred in taking a compartmentalised approach to the issue of corroboration and while he was correct to advise the jury as to the three elements of which proof was required to establish charges 1 and 2, he was in error in saying that where each of those elements had been spoken to by the complainer, they required individually to be corroborated: the jury were effectively given the impression that an element of evidence of which it was critical for J to be believed was corroborated which impacted upon the central issues in dispute in the trial, constituted a material misdirection and a miscarriage of justice. Per Lord Malcolm, that in *Moorov (Samuel) v HM Advocate* 1930 J.C. 68, it was stated that the rule requiring corroboration guarded against the twin dangers of (a) that the crime might not have been committed, and (b) that had it been, it was not committed by the accused; the problem was that, as yet, the law had not developed a sufficiently clear and certain test for distinguishing between a case of "a general disposition to commit a particular kind of offence" and the "underlying unity of purpose"; the sheriff had erred in adopting an approach based upon a statutory implied absence of consent on D's part which W could be taken to have appreciated.

W v HM ADVOCATE *sub nom.* CW v HM ADVOCATE, [2016] HCJAC 44, 2016 S.L.T. 709, Lady Dorrian, Lord Bracadale, Lord Malcolm, HCJ.

2555 Jury directions–Concert–Directions on concert and causation

[Sexual Offences (Scotland) Act 2009 (asp 9) s.19, s.20]

A senior sea cadet (G), aged 16 at the time of the offence, appealed against conviction for sexual assault on a young child (X), aged 12, and sexual assault on X by penetration, by removing X from his bed, removing his clothing, recording the incident on his mobile phone and showing it to others, and thereby causing a younger cadet (C) to sexually penetrate X's anus with his finger, contrary to the the Sexual Offences (Scotland) Act 2009 ss.19 and 20, on the ground that the sheriff had misdirected the jury such that there had been a miscarriage of justice. A charge against G of instructing C and another cadet to rape X and insert a finger into his anus had been deleted by the jury. G had been placed in charge of a dormitory containing seven other cadets, including his brother (B), X and C. It was alleged that after the cadets had gone to bed, G had roused C and B (collectively Y) and, with their assistance, had removed X from his bed, placed him in the centre of the room and removed his clothes. C had thereafter touched X and simulated sexual acts with him, and had digitally penetrated his anus while being filmed by G, who had taken no steps to prevent the incidents, had recorded it on his mobile phone, laughing throughout, and had thereafter displayed the video to other cadets. Evidence was led that C had educational special needs, was vulnerable and easily led, and that X had encouraged his actions. The sheriff had given the jury the standard directions on concert and in relation to their power to delete parts of the charge. In the course of their deliberations, the jury asked whether their deletion impacted on the statement "cause" in the charge, which the sheriff answered in the negative. The following day, the sheriff repeated her answer to the jury's question and further directed the jury that causation was a matter for them on the facts. The jury returned a verdict of guilty subject to the deletion. G submitted that in answering the jury's question, the sheriff's had misdirected herself by focusing on causation rather than concert, thus negating her previous adequate directions on spontaneous concert.

Held: Appeal refused. (1) The sheriff's answer to the jury's question could not be criticised; while it was likely that the Crown had framed the indictment on the basis that *inter alia* an express instruction had been given to Y to penetrate X's anus with a finger, that was simply one element in a case which was properly categorised as spontaneous concert, such concert might comprise not only words uttered but also acts carried out and attitudes adopted by those involved and the sheriff's charge had warned the jury that a participant who had not known what another participant was about to do in escalation of an assault would not be responsible unless he continued with his involvement in the knowledge of the escalation, thus demonstrating that the escalation of the crime was part of the joint criminal purpose. (2) On the basis of the evidence, and armed with the sheriff's directions about *inter alia* concert and the ability to delete parts of the charge, the jury were entitled to conclude that they were not satisfied on the evidence that any express instruction had been given, but nevertheless to form the view that the evidence established an atmosphere of encouragement, hilarity, and approbation, on the part of the participants including G, together with an absence of any instruction to cease assaulting X or any threat of disciplinary measures were the assault to continue, further, the jury were entitled to conclude that the evidence established that the atmosphere had caused or induced one of Y to escalate his activities and to carry out the act of sexual penetration which he had, that G was the senior participant and the leader of the group, were *a fortiori* entitled to view G's behaviour as causing or inducing a more junior member of the group to carry out the acts he had, and were further entitled to conclude that G's failure to prevent the more serious assault, together with his laughing as he filmed the incident involving C touching X in a sexual fashion up to and including the anal penetration, his behaviour and words towards X after the incident, and his subsequent showing of the video to another person, amounted to his active association with the escalated level of criminality of the spontaneous common criminal purpose of the group. In those circumstances, the sheriff had not misdirected the jury, however, even had there had been a misdirection in answering the jury's question, there had been ample evidence of words and behaviour on G's part, the senior member and in effect the leader of the group, to entitle the jury to reach the verdict they had.

GAY (JEROME) v HM ADVOCATE, [2015] HCJAC 125, 2016 S.C.L. 258, Lady Paton, Lord Bracadale, Lord Turnbull, HCJ.

2556 Jury directions–Corroboration–Adequacy of directions on corroboration in relation to assault, abduction and sexual assault

[Sexual Offences (Scotland) Act 2009 (asp 9) s.2, s.3; Criminal Procedure (Scotland) Act 1995 (c.46) s.27(1)(b)]

M appealed against conviction for assaulting a former partner (P) on various occasions between 1 January 1998 and 29 October 1999 (charge 1), assaulting another partner (K) on various occasions between 30 October 1999 and 16 July 2013 (charge 6), raping K on various occasions between 1 January 2002 and 31 December 2004 (charge 7), assaulting and raping K on one occasion between 1 January 2002 and 31 December 2004 (charge 8), assaulting, abducting and sexually assaulting K on

9 May 2011, contrary to the Sexual Offences (Scotland) Act 2009 s.2 and 3 (charge 9), and breaching bail conditions by sending K messages on a social networking site, contrary to the Criminal Procedure (Scotland) Act 1995 s.27(1)(b) on the basis that the trial judge had misdirected the jury in relation to corroboration. M had been sentenced to six months' imprisonment on charge 1, an extended sentence of 10 years with a custodial element of eight years had been imposed in respect of charges 6, 7 and 8, and a *cumulo* sentence of three years' imprisonment had been imposed on charged 9 and 10, to run consecutively to the sentence on charges 6, 7 and 8, against which M also appealed. The trial judge had given the jury the standard directions on corroboration, in particular in line with the jury manual regarding the rape charges, and had given them directions on the definition of rape under s.1 of the 2009 Act for the purposes of charge 9, directing them that the three requirements were intentional or reckless penile penetration, lack of consent by the complainer and the absence of reasonable belief by the accused that the complainer consented, all of which had to be proved by corroborated evidence, and that the other elements in the charge were descriptive only and did not require corroboration. In relation to consent, the trial judge directed the jury that belief on the part of the accused that there was consent was a defence if it was a reasonable belief, an honest belief was insufficient so far as the statutory contravention was concerned. The trial judge also directed the jury that in relation to the penetrative sexual assault elements in charge 9, intentional or reckless penetration, as well as the absence of reasonable belief in consent, all had to be proved by corroborated evidence, the other elements being descriptive only and not requiring corroboration.

Held: Charge 9 amended, sentence in respect of charges 9 and 10 quashed and 12 months' imprisonment substituted for each. (1) The trial judge's directions, read as a whole, had been adequate, the jury could not have doubted that penetration required to be corroborated, the jury had to have accepted the testimony of the two witnesses who had been in the bedroom at the time when the rapes were alleged to have occurred in order to convict on charges 7 or 8 and having done so, had been entitled to find that there had been corroboration of penetration, further, the direction on honest, as distinct from reasonable, belief had been in M's favour, no miscarriage of justice could have occurred, and in any event, no direction thereon had been required standing the contrasting accounts from K and M. (2) Corroboration of the physical aspects on charge 9 had been adequately provided by M's admission that he had physically assaulted K and where it was conceded by the Crown that the sexual elements on charge 9 could not have been corroborated where M had been acquitted on a charge of raping P (charge 2), and there was no corroboration of an abduction and also an anomaly in respect that the conviction related to events on one day whereas the narrative referred to a period of days, certain words would be deleted from the charge such as to leave a conviction for common law assault. (3) In light of the deletions to charge 9, the sentence would be reduced to 12 months' imprisonment for that charge, and as the offence had been part of a single course of conduct, that sentence ought to be concurrent with the extended sentence on charges 6-8. (4) Where the trial judge had originally imposed a cumulative sentence exceeding the statutory minimum of 12 months in respect of charge 10, the court would substitute a sentence of 12 months, to run consecutively to the other custodial periods.

MILLER (ANDREW JOHN) v HM ADVOCATE, [2016] HCJAC 68, 2016 S.C.L. 762, Lord Justice General (Carloway), Lady Paton, Lady Clark of Calton, HCJ Appeal.

2557 Jury directions–Corroboration–Directions on mutual corroboration–Directions as to sufficiency of evidence

[Asylum and Immigration (Treatment of Claimants, etc.) Act 2004 (c.19) s.4(1)(a), s.4(2)(a)]

S appealed against conviction for four charges of arranging or facilitating the arrival into the United Kingdom of four Bangladeshi men (M) with intent to exploit them, contrary to the Asylum and Immigration (Treatment of Claimants, etc.) Act 2004 s.4(1)(a) and four charges of arranging or facilitating M's travel within the UK with the same intention, contrary to s.4(2)(a), and against the imposition of a three year custodial sentence. S had recruited M over the course of 2008 to work at his hotel and their written offers of employment had been conditional on an initial payment to S of approximately £5,000 but S had demanded further sums after M had secured their visas, with three paying approximately £18,000 and the fourth £15,000. On M's arrival at S's hotel, they had been informed that S could not afford the amount due under the contract but instead they would be paid £100 per week, with the balance provided later. M had thereafter been paid less than £100 per week and arrears had built up in terms of the arrangement, although those had been eventually paid off when M had left the hotel. The shortfall on the contractual entitlements had never been paid, and the deposits had been retained. The sheriff had introduced and explained the principle of mutual corroboration to the jury and had directed on three occasions that it was for them to be satisfied whether, on the evidence, the offences libelled were so closely linked in time, character and circumstances as to allow mutual corroboration to apply. The sheriff had further directed them that there was sufficient evidence in law that the trafficking crimes alleged had been sufficiently close in time, character, place of commission and circumstances for the rule to apply but just because there was evidence from different sources they might not accept that evidence, and that it was up to them to decide whether they ought to use the evidence and if the evidence in each case was credible and reliable, if the necessary link in time, character and circumstances had been established and if the rule ought to be applied. S submitted that (1) the sheriff had misdirected the jury in relation to mutual corroboration by directing them that there was a legal sufficiency and thus failing to leave it to the jury to decide whether mutual corroboration ought to apply; (2) the sheriff's use of "rule" when describing mutual corroboration had amounted to a misdirection because of the definite character of that particular description; (3) with regard to sentence, the sheriff had failed to give sufficient weight to the circumstances of the offences themselves, S's personal circumstances and the delay between the original investigation by the Home Office in 2010 and the conviction approximately five years later, and in the circumstances, a community disposal might have been imposed, alternatively, the sentence was excessive.

Held: Appeal refused. (1) Reading the charge as a whole, the overall tenor of the sheriff's directions was to the effect that it was open to the jury to apply mutual corroboration but that it was for them to decide whether the necessary link had been established, the decision on whether to apply the doctrine had been left for the jury; it was often important to inform a jury that there was a sufficiency of evidence in law and of the component parts of that sufficiency which would enable them to return an appropriate verdict, particularly one of acquittal, if an essential element of proof was rejected, *Sinclair v HM Advocate* 1990 S.C.C.R. 412, *distinguished* and *McPhee (William McAllister) v HM Advocate* [2009] HCJAC 54, 2009 J.C. 308, [2010] C.L.Y. 4103, *considered.* (2) Although the sheriff had referred to mutual corroboration as a rule, as distinct from a doctrine or principle, the overall effect of the direction had been that it was for the jury to decide whether to apply it or not, and reading the charge as a whole, the use of "rule" had not resulted in a miscarriage of justice. (3) The offences had been callous, deliberate and planned for the purposes of gain and M had suffered considerable hardship as a result, and in the circumstances of the case, only a custodial sentence could have been regarded as appropriate; the sheriff's selection of three years' imprisonment was not excessive, and he had taken into account the period of delay which had occurred and the strictures placed on S as a result of the special conditions of bail.

AREFIN (SHAMSUL) v HM ADVOCATE, [2016] HCJAC 32, 2016 S.C.L. 464, Lord Justice General (Carloway), Lord Menzies, Lady Cosgrove, HCJ.

2558 Jury directions–Corroboration–Directions on mutual corroboration, hearsay and res gestae

[Criminal Procedure (Scotland) Act 1995 (c.46) s.259]

L appealed against conviction for assaulting X in 1998, 2006 and 2007 (charges 2, 3 and 4) and assaulting G in 2012. L had been acquitted in respect of three other charges involving G (charges 5, 6 and 7) and a further charge involving a third complainer. G had passed away by the time of the trial and in terms of the Criminal Procedure (Scotland) Act 1995 s.259, the Crown had relied upon hearsay evidence concerning a 999 recording in which G had made certain complaints against L and G's subsequent signed written statement which contained more detailed allegations of her assault by L. As part of the evidence on charges 6 and 7, there had been testimony in the nature of *res gestae* about G shouting and indicating that certain things had happened to her at another location, which differed from those in the other charges. The sheriff had given the jury the standard directions on the application of mutual corroboration in relation to X's evidence and G's hearsay evidence and had given them particular directions on the care to be taken in relation to hearsay evidence. L submitted that (1) the hearsay evidence was insufficient to supply mutual corroboration; (2) the sheriff had misdirected the jury in respect of the evidence of *res gestae* on charges 6 and 7; as she had stated that the jury could use that evidence, they might have used it to prove the different charges on which L had eventually been convicted.

Held: Appeal refused. (1) There was no requirement that the evidence required for the doctrine of mutual corroboration to apply be direct testimony from eyewitnesses; once deemed admissible, the hearsay evidence became the equivalent of the testimony of the speaker and could be used as proof of fact and thus corroboration. (2) It was entirely speculative to suggest that the jury would have used the evidence of the *res gestae* relative to different charges with a different locus to show that L had committed unrelated offences on the indictment.

LEES (SEAN) v HM ADVOCATE, [2016] HCJAC 16, 2016 S.C.L. 377, Lord Justice General (Carloway), Lady Paton, Lord Drummond Young, HCJ Appeal.

2559 Jury directions–Corroboration–Rape–Adequacy of directions on mutual corroboration

C appealed against conviction for the rape of his former partner (B) on the basis that the trial judge had materially misdirected the jury such that there had been a miscarriage of justice. C had been found guilty of two charges of raping B (charges 10 and 11) in the course of a car journey on 2 January 2014. Three further charges alleging B's rape and the rape of another former partner (G) (charges 5, 8 and 9) had been found not proven by the jury. It was common ground that charges 5, 8 and 9 could be proved only by finding mutual corroboration in both B and G's evidence. In respect of charges 10 and 11 there was other evidence allowing the charges to be proved independently, namely, DNA evidence which was supportive of the fact that sexual intercourse had occured between C and B, and evidence from B's mother and her work colleague which was supportive of the absence of reasonable belief on C's part that B had been consenting to sexual intercourse. C submitted that (1) the trial judge's directions on the availability of distress for corroboration were in conflict with the earlier, repeated directions on mutual corroboration and the result had been a failure to provide clear instructions to the jury as to how they should understand and apply the law to the evidence; (2) the trial judge had not been sufficiently clear in explaining to the jury the precise route to the verdict and the nature of the directions had been such that the jury were bound to have been confused by them.

Held: Appeal refused. (1) The elaborate structure adopted by the trial judge in her charge had led her to give repeated directions on the requirements of mutual corroboration and the need to accept B and G's evidence and as a result, the directions would have been likely to have led the jury to understand that without the application of the doctrine none of the charges could be proved. (2) It would have been desirable for the trial judge to have given clearer directions to the effect that charges 10 and 11 could be proved independently, however, the trial judge had given directions to the effect that in respect of each of the three essential elements of the offence of rape it was open to the jury to find charges 10 and 11 proved without the application of the doctrine of mutual corroboration. (3) The independent observer, having considered the charge as a whole, would have concluded from their verdict that the jury had decided against the application of the doctrine of mutual corroboration and had then considered whether they were satisfied beyond reasonable doubt that charges 10 and 11 were proved by another route; the jury returned a verdict of not proven in respect of charge 5 as well as charges 8 and 9 which demonstrated that having considered and rejected the application of mutual corroboration, the jury had acquitted C of all the charges that required mutual corroboration for proof but had convicted him of the two charges which were capable of proof by another route; the jury were not confused and the judge's charge had provided sufficient directions in law

H v HM ADVOCATE *sub nom.* CH v HM ADVOCATE, [2016] HCJAC 4, 2016 S.C.L. 288, Lady Paton, Lord Bracadale, Lord Malcolm, HCJ.

2560 Jury directions–Corroboration–Rape–Misdirection

W, appealed against conviction for *inter alia* raping X, on the basis that the trial judge had materially misdirected the jury. W had stopped at secluded locations on two different occasions during a car journey with X and had raped her. That night she recorded the events in a diary. X's father testified that X had appeared distraught on her return home and looked as if she had been crying. The following day X attended her general practitioner (D) who spoke to her being upset and distressed whilst reporting that she had been raped. The Crown relied on a series of text messages sent by W to X the day after the incident in which *inter alia* he apologised for the previous night. The trial judge gave the jury the standard directions on the requirement for corroboration of lack of consent and also directed them that the content of X's diary and anything that she had said, could not provide corroboration of her account, however, the diary could provide evidence of her state of mind when she wrote it and could provide evidence that she was distressed, which could confirm that she had suffered a distressing event and that could provide corroboration of lack of consent. It was accepted that the trial judge's directions on the use of the diary as proof of distress, and thus corroboration of X's account of lack of consent, amounted to a misdirection.

Held: Appeal refused. Evidence that X had been distressed after the event, in particular when she returned home and when she saw D, was not disputed, therefore, the misdirection in relation to the diary had not been material, in any event the text messages were compelling and provided a powerful and general source of corroboration of X's account and having regard thereto, in conjunction with the accepted distress, it could not be said that a miscarriage of justice had occurred.

WALKER (IAN) v HM ADVOCATE, [2015] HCJAC 122, 2016 S.C.L. 190, The Lord Justice Clerk (Carloway), Lady Smith, Lord Bracadale, HCJ Appeal.

2561 Jury directions–Corroboration–Sexual offences–Mutual corroboration

M appealed against conviction for nine of 17 charges of repeatedly assaulting, indecently assaulting and raping two former partners (P). M had been acquitted of the assault and indecent assault of another former partner (R), who had given evidence *inter alia* that M had had sex with her whilst she had been asleep, which had not been libelled. Evidence had also been led from M's current partner (C) that there was neither physical nor sexual violence in their relationship. The trial judge had refused M's motion to desert the trial *pro loco et tempore* following R's statement and had directed the jury inter alia that R's evidence was not capable of corroborating P's evidence of rape and indecent assault, and that C's evidence was of limited significance. The trial judge also repelled M's submission of no case to answer due to lack of corroboration.

Held: Appeal refused. (1) The trial judge had given a direction regarding the lack of testimony from R which could corroborate P's allegations of sexual conduct and had deliberately not highlighted the answer given by R, it was not possible to fault his exercise of discretion and the manner in which he had addressed that issue in his directions had been one which he was entitled to take. (2) There was a sufficiency on each charge as a consequence of the application of mutual corroboration and the trial judge was correct to repel M's no case to answer submissions. (3) The trial judge's directions on the application of mutual corroboration could not be faulted where he had provided the overall option of a single course of criminal conduct, explained to the jury that it was a matter for them to determine whether and how to apply mutual corroboration, and had thereafter offered an alternative of separating the conduct into three different courses of rape, indecent assault and physical assault, both approaches were legitimate and the jury had been advised to exercise caution, especially in relation to the time gaps, none of which might legitimately be criticised. (4) C's evidence had been led without objection and it was open to the judge to give the jury some indication of its potential value, even where he was not bound to do so, that value had been limited and the trial judge's comment was legitimate where he had also made it clear that the weight of C's evidence had remained for the jury to assess.

MCASKILL (ANGUS) v HM ADVOCATE, [2016] HCJAC 64, 2016 S.C.L. 748, Lord Justice General (Carloway), Lady Paton, Lord Malcolm, HCJ.

2562 Jury directions–Murder–Trial judge's charge–Whether misdirection

H appealed against conviction for the murder of his wife (W) on the basis that the trial judge had materially misdirected the jury and a miscarriage of justice had occurred. There had been six other charges on the indictment, including four charges of assault against W, one of threatening behaviour, and one of malicious damage of clothing, which were withdrawn in advance of the jury's deliberations. H did not give evidence, however testimony was adduced regarding H's previous threats and assaults to W. Two of his acquaintances (collectively B) gave evidence that the day after W's death, H had said that he thought he had killed her. In the course of a lengthy police interview, H had generally made no comment. The trial judge's directions were given over two days, and she explained that her references to the evidence were to put her directions about the law into context, and she stressed that no adverse inference could be taken from H's lack of evidence at trial or lack of comment during interview and that witnesses might have conceded on cross examination that alternative suggestions were possible but that was not evidence that the possibility had actually occurred. She dealt with several aspects of the law of hearsay, including in relation to B's and W's hearsay evidence and stated that intention might be inferred from acts which were proved or from previous threats to kill, and that wicked recklessness had to be assessed objectively. As H's approach was that culpable homicide was a verdict open to the jury, she defined that crime and advised that although H had not addressed evidence that marks found on W's face had a similar spacing to the pattern of H's boots, the jury could still have regard thereto. She noted that although H had not provided contradictory expert evidence, it was for the jury to decide whether the Crown's expert evidence was strong and its case proved beyond reasonable doubt. She provided a summary of the Crown's evidence and H's criticisms of the Crown's case.

Held: Appeal refused. The charge was not unbalanced but was a studied charge in which the trial judge was careful to deal with each and every aspect of the case and the evidence heard at trial; on several occasions, she had stressed the entitlement of an accused to say nothing and that no adverse inference could be drawn therefrom, she had made the general point that her comments on the evidence were only to explain the application of the law to the facts, which necessitated referencing some of the testimony, thus she had explained, as she ought to have done, that the evidence of previous threats on the withdrawn charges was relevant to a consideration of the murder, her references to the relevance of a witness accepting something was possible, her treatment of the different types of hearsay, her caution about approaching such secondary evidence and her comments about H's lack of responsiveness at interview were merited, she had given standard directions on intention and recklessness, her directions on culpable homicide were prompted by H's speech, it was appropriate to have told the jury that they needed to examine the footprint evidence in order to gauge its significance, and her reference to the absence of evidence contradicting that of the experts was justified. After a lengthy trial the judge decided that she should provide a short summary of the evidence, and although that was all in the context of the Crown case, she balanced that by outlining the salient points of H's criticism and her approach was faultless.

HUMPHREY (ALAN PETER) v HM ADVOCATE, [2016] HCJAC 5, 2016 S.C.L. 275, The Lord Justice Clerk (Carloway), Lady Dorrian, Lord Bracadale, HCJ.

2563 Jury directions–Previous inconsistent statements–Failure to direct jury on limited use to which prior inconsistent statements could be put–Miscarriage of justice

[Sexual Offences (Scotland) Act 2009 (asp 9) s.3, s.30]

A founder and spiritual leader (M) of a church appealed against conviction for sexually assaulting a member of his church (G) (charge 3) and engaging in sexual activity with or towards an older child (P) (charge 4), contrary to the Sexual Offences (Scotland) Act 2009 ss. 3 and 30 respectively on the basis that *inter alia* the sheriff had misdirected the jury. M had originally appeared on five charges, however, the first charge involving another complainer (T) had been withdrawn by the Crown at the first diet and two other charges (charges 1 and 2) involving a further church member (X) had been withdrawn during the course of the trial. X, who was adduced in support of charges 1 and 2, denied that anything untoward had happened, however, she accepted that she had made a detailed statement to the police containing the allegations in the original libel which involved being induced to massage M when she was under 13 and later when she was under 16. T also spoke to having made certain allegations about being induced to massage M, which she had withdrawn, and had denied the truth of the allegations in evidence. The sheriff gave the jury a number of standard directions in relation to credibility and reliability and directed them that where the Crown was no longer seeking a conviction on charges 1 and 2, those were no longer before them for consideration and could be forgotten about, however, T and X's evidence remained available to them as part of the evidence in the case. The sheriff further directed the jury that before accepting evidence from a witness, they had to be satisfied that it was honest and reliable and that they could compare what one witness stated with other evidence in the case, and that in the context of mutual corroboration, for a conviction to follow, the jury had to accept both G and P as credible and reliable. The Crown conceded that a misdirection by omission had occurred, however, it had not been material.

Held: Appeal allowed. (1) The sheriff had not required to select certain aspects of the case and to repeat those contentions in his directions, it would have been obvious to the jury that the case involved a consideration of G and P's credibility, the sheriff had given them a clear direction that, for a conviction to follow, they required to accept both G and P as credible and reliable in their essentials, and he had not required to revisit those matters. (2) The contents of certain post incident emails between G and M, in which she had stated that she loved him and that she had misinterpreted his actions as abuse, had not amounted to prior inconsistent statements; she accepted the truth of what she had said therein as representing her views or feelings at the relevant time, and no directions beyond the general were required. (3) There had been a misdirection by omission in failing to direct the jury on the limited use to which the prior inconsistent statements, namely T and X's allegations, could be put; that evidence was hearsay and it was incumbent upon the sheriff to direct the jury as to its value, in particular, that those statements could not be used as proof of fact where T and X had denied their truth. (4) The sheriff had given contradictory directions to the effect that the evidence of charges 1 and 2 remained for the jury's consideration and, subsequently, that they were entitled to compare what one witness had said with other evidence in the case, which would have included T and X's prior inconsistent statements, and a miscarriage of justice had occurred where in the absence of the required direction, the jury were left in a position whereby they would have been able to accept the content of the original allegations made by T and X as having been true and to take them into account in assessing G and P's evidence, and the convictions would be quashed.

MASOCHA (WALTER) v HM ADVOCATE, [2016] HCJAC 15, 2016 S.C.L. 369, Lord Justice General (Carloway), Lady Paton, Lord Drummond Young, HCJ Appeal.

2564 Jury directions–Previous inconsistent statements–Leading evidence of prior extra-judicial consistent statements in order to bolster witness's evidence–Material misdirection

C appealed against conviction for raping X, and raping and assaulting Y, on the basis that the jury had been misdirected, resulting in a miscarriage of justice. At trial, an element of C's challenge to the credibility and reliability of Y's testimony was the inconsistency between that testimony and a detailed statement made to police (P) shortly after her alleged rape by C, in which she made no allegations of any sexual assault by him. The trial judge directed the jury that (1) they could compare and contrast a witness's testimony with what the witness said at the time, and any coincidences could bolster that witness's evidence; (2) Y's statement was a prose narrative of what P had understood her to be saying, and a police statement had limitations, whereby it was not taken under oath or subject to cross examination, in comparison to court testimony.

Held: Appeal allowed. (1) The trial judge had not entirely correctly stated the law to the jury: although a witness might be cross examined as to credit in respect of a prior inconsistent statement, it was not admissible to lead evidence of prior extra judicial consistent statements in order to bolster the witness's evidence, and while exceptions to that rule could no doubt be found in the case of a *de recenti* statement to the first natural confidant, or in a consistent utterance forming part of the *res gestae*, the relevant statements were not of that nature. (2) Y's statement was not a mixed statement but was a prior hearsay account by her which was inconsistent in material respects with her testimony on oath, and the prior statement's inconsistent content could not substitute for that testimony. (3) Neither the fact that a prior inconsistent statement was evidence of a statement not made on oath, nor that it was not subject to any cross examination, was relevant to, or represented a limitation on, the forensic value of a prior inconsistent statement as a means of questioning the credibility or reliability of the witness's testimony. (4) The trial judge's description of Y's statement as a prose narrative might have conveyed to the jury the notion of an inaccurate rendering of what she had said to P and his directions were not suitable or appropriate where what had been required were normal directions on hearsay evidence of a prior inconsistent statement by a witness. (5) The jury had been materially misdirected on a matter which was central to C's position at trial and it could not be said that no miscarriage of justice might have occurred.

CLARK (ALAN) v HM ADVOCATE, [2016] HCJAC 11, 2016 S.L.T. 307, Lord Eassie, Lady Smith, Lady Clark of Calton, HCJ.

2565 Jury directions–Provocation–Sheriff failing to give relevant direction on provocation–Conviction quashed and conviction in identical terms with rider "under provocation" substituted

F appealed against conviction and sentence for assault to severe injury and permanent disfigurement by repeatedly striking R on the face and body with a knife or similar implement and struggling with him, on the ground that the sheriff had erred in failing to direct the jury in relation to provocation resulting in a miscarriage of justice. Other than a joint minute, the evidence had been limited to that given by R and F, whose accounts of the events immediately preceding the stabbing had been entirely at odds where R had spoken to an unprovoked attack by F after he had knocked on F's lower ground floor flat window, and F spoke to having felt threatened on R's appearance, having heard R shouting and banging on his windows. F submitted that (1) on his evidence, in the event of the jury finding that there had not been self defence, it would have been open to them to find that F had been acting under provocation as a matter of law, accordingly, the sheriff had been obliged to direct the jury to consider the option of finding F guilty of assault but subject to the rider of the assault having been committed under provocation. The Crown submitted that there was no evidential basis for finding that F had been acting under provocation.

Held: Appeal allowed, conviction quashed and conviction in identical terms with rider "under provocation" substituted, and sentence of five years' imprisonment quashed and four years and six months substituted. (1) Although the circumstances were different from those in *Ferguson (Derek Charles) v HM Advocate* [2008] HCJAC 71, 2009 S.L.T. 67, [2009] C.L.Y. 4828 the rationale of the contention that there had been a miscarriage of justice was the same *Ferguson, applied*. (2) The sheriff might have been entitled to exclude provocation but he had failed to explain why, on the most favourable possible view of F's evidence, he had considered that he had been so entitled, therefore, it was possible that because he had failed to give the relevant direction, F had been convicted in terms that had been more adverse than might otherwise have been the case, and had that been what had occurred, that amounted to a miscarriage of justice.

FERGUSON (SHAUN DARROCH) v HM ADVOCATE, [2015] HCJAC 89, 2015 S.C.L. 972, Lord Brodie, Lord Bracadale, Lord Drummond Young, HCJ.

2566 Jury directions–Rape–Directions on consent–Mentally disordered persons

[Sexual Offences (Scotland) Act 2009 (asp 9) s.17(2)]

W appealed against conviction for raping a mentally disordered person (X) who was incapable of consenting in terms of the Sexual Offences (Scotland) Act 2009 s.17(2), on the basis that the trial judge had misdirected the jury. W's position at trial had been that he had reasonably believed that X had been consenting and his counsel had suggested in his speech to the jury that in a case such as the present the Crown also required to exclude that W had had an honest belief that X had been capable of consenting. The trial judge directed the jury that that was incorrect and that the Crown required to establish that there had been no reasonable belief on W's part that X had been consenting and, in the present instance, incapable of consent, it was only if W's belief that X had consented or was capable of consent was reasonable that his actions would not amount to rape and that they had to be satisfied that the Crown had shown that W had not had a reasonable belief.

Held: Appeal refused. (1) The effect of s.17 of the 2009 Act was that where the requirements thereof had been met, the Crown did not require to prove lack of consent. (2) The law in relation to rape and other sexual offences had been completely redrawn by the 2009 Act, and the terms of ss.1-9 did not provide for a defence of reasonable belief in consent, which would raise an evidential burden on the defence, but provided that an absence of reasonable belief in consent was an essential part of the offence to be proved by the Crown. (3) The trial judge had correctly directed the jury as to the factors which might be relevant to the question before them, such as the history of W and X's interaction and what objectively W had to have known as to X's condition, the trial judge had not directed the jury that there was an additional requirement over and above absence of reasonable belief in consent, rather than that the issue of reasonable belief in consent carried with it an implication of reasonable belief in capacity, and was it possible to read her directions in that manner, it would in any event be a misdirection favourable to W, *Flynn v HM Advocate*, 8 November 2013, unreported, *considered*. (4) The nature of X's condition, and its apparent presentation, were relevant factors to the question of whether an absence of reasonable belief in consent had been established and to introduce the concept of honest but unreasonable belief in the manner suggested by W was inconsistent with the 2009 Act.

WINTON (STEWART) v HM ADVOCATE, [2016] HCJAC 19, 2016 S.L.T. 393, Lady Dorrian, Lady Clark of Calton, Lord Malcolm, HCJ Appeal.

2567 Jury directions–Reasonable excuse

[Criminal Law (Consolidation) (Scotland) Act 1995 (c.39) s.47(1)]

L appealed against conviction for being in possession of an offensive weapon in a public place without a reasonable excuse or lawful authority, namely a broken glass bottle, contrary to the Criminal Law (Consolidation) (Scotland) Act 1995 s.47(1) (charge 4) on the basis that the sheriff had misdirected the jury. M claimed that she had had a reasonable excuse for having the broken bottle, having picked it up during a confrontation with several men, in which L and her female companion (F) had been physically attacked, having brandished it in F's defence. In speeches to the jury, the procurator fiscal had invited the jury to reject M's defence but had not elaborated in the interplay between charge 4 and a charge of assaulting one of the men by attempting to injure him with the broken bottle (charge 3), in particular, between the special defence of self defence lodged in respect of charge 3 and reasonable excuse in respect of charge 4. The sheriff, following the guidelines in the jury manual, had directed the jury that fear of attack was not a reasonable excuse for possession of an offensive weapon. The Crown conceded that had the matter been focused appropriately, the sheriff would have given appropriate guidelines, and the appeal was well founded.

Held: Appeal allowed and conviction quashed. (1) The Crown's position was that taking possession of an offensive weapon in anticipation of, or fear of, future violence would not constitute a reasonable excuse, however, matters would be different where a person took possession of a weapon during an incident where he or she was under attack for the purpose of preventing or discouraging further violence. (2) The jury manual was based more on the circumstances in *Grieve (William) v Macleod* 1967 J.C. 32, [1967] C.L.Y. 852, whereas in the circumstances of the present case a more flexible approach was necessary as it was for the jury to decide whom to believe and whom to disbelieve, and at least one of the versions of events which had been put before the jury in the course of the trial suggested that M, when under attack and *in extremis*, had come into possession of the bottle and used it solely to attempt to prevent further attack, *Grieve* and *Donnelly (Stephen) v HM Advocate* 2009 S.C.C.R. 512, [2009] C.L.Y. 4766, *considered*. (3) There had been a misdirection, the jury had not been able to form their own view about the evidence which they had heard, and a miscarriage of justice might have occurred. *Observed*, that the jury manual might require further refinement.

LUNN (LAURA) v HM ADVOCATE, [2015] HCJAC 103, 2016 S.L.T. 98, Lady Paton, Lord Bracadale, Lord Malcolm, HCJ.

2568 Jury directions–Robbery–Incident approached as single event–Directions as to available verdicts

B appealed against conviction for assaulting a beggar (X) by repeatedly punching and kicking him on the head and body and robbing him. CCTV images had shown B and a co-accused (P) approaching X and attacking him, searching his sleeping bag and rucksack, throwing them onto the road and thereafter removing certain items from the road and leaving the scene. In respect of B, the jury had returned a verdict of guilty to assault and theft, the sheriff had directed them that that verdict was not open to them, the options being either assault and robbery, assault, or theft, and they had thereafter returned a verdict of guilty of assault and robbery in respect of both B and P. B submitted that (1) the sheriff had erred in repelling his submission of no case to answer in respect of robbery where the incident had required to be approached in three phases, namely the assault, the robbery by P, and B's recovery of the money and the jury had not been entitled to infer that B had assaulted X with the intention of robbing him; (2) the jury had been incorrectly directed that it had not been open to them to return a verdict of guilty to assault and theft.

Held: Appeal refused. (1) B and P had both been shown assaulting X at the same time, P had been seen searching X's sleeping bag during the course of that joint assault, both had walked away before both returning to X's possessions, P had picked up X's cup and rucksack and B had subsequently removed items from the road; in those circumstances, it was open to the jury to hold that the assault had been linked with the search and removal of the items, they were entitled to consider that B had been engaged in a common criminal purpose with P to achieve that removal and the sheriff had been correct to repel B's submission relative to the robbery, and was entitled to approach the CCTV images, and the libel, as involving a single incident of violence and removal of property. (2) The sheriff had approached the matter correctly, namely that the event as libelled was a single episode, thus there were only the three guilty verdicts open on what was one charge, namely assault only, assault and robbery, and theft only; in those circumstances, the sheriff's directions had been correct.

BLACKWOOD (DAVID) v HM ADVOCATE, [2016] HCJAC 23, 2016 S.C.L. 430, Lord Justice General (Carloway), Lady Paton, Lord Drummond Young, HCJ Appeal.

2569 Jury directions–Weapons offences–Sheriff's description of knives as weapons–Whether misdirection

[Criminal Law (Consolidation) (Scotland) Act 1995 (c.39) s.47(1)]

C appealed against conviction for having an offensive weapon, namely two knives, in a public place, contrary to the Criminal Law (Consolidation) (Scotland) Act 1995 s.47(1). Two witnesses had spoken to observing C brandishing two large kitchen knives in the course of a fight that had occurred outside their home at 3 am. In his directions to the jury, the sheriff had referred to those knives as weapons. C submitted *inter alia* that the sheriff had misdirected the jury where the question of whether a particular article was an offensive weapon was for the jury to determine.

Held: Appeal refused. The sheriff had made it clear that, for a conviction to follow, the jury required to be satisfied that C had had the weapon with him with the intention of using it to cause personal injury to someone, the use of the noun "weapon" had been entirely appropriate in the context of the case and the sole issue for the jury had been to determine whether C had intended to use the knives to cause injury to a person in those circumstance, and no misdirection had occurred.

CHALMERS (PAUL) v HM ADVOCATE, [2016] HCJAC 27, 2016 S.C.L. 470, Lord Justice General (Carloway), Lady Paton, Lord Bracadale, HCJ.

2570 Misdirections–Hearsay evidence–Adequacy of directions on effect of hearsay evidence

W appealed against conviction for three historic charges of lewd, indecent and libidinous practices and behaviour towards two children (B and E), aged between 4 and 7, and the rape of E and of another child (G), aged between 9 and 10, on the basis that the trial judge had misdirected the jury. The incidents had occurred between August 1987 and April 1999. In the course of the trial evidence had been led from three witnesses in relation to hearsay statements made on prior occasions by B and from two witnesses in relation to hearsay statements made on earlier occasions by G, which had been agreed as admissible primary hearsay relevant to explaining the gap between the offences and the complaint to the police and to allegations of fabrication. The judge had directed the jury that evidence was anything that had been said by a witness and such evidence was for them to use as they saw fit, and, had thereafter directed that corroboration in the case required to be found by the application of *Moorov*. W submitted that the trial judge had not directed the jury on the effect of the hearsay evidence or the use to which it might be put, the jury might have used that evidence to either corroborate B or G's evidence or to enhance their credibility and the lack of directions constituted a material misdirection.

Held: Appeal refused. (1) The trial judge made it clear that he was dealing with generalities as to what constituted evidence and how it might be used, having moved to specifics relating to the trial in question, he gave very clear directions on the issue of corroboration, which had made it clear to the jury that in relation to each of the charges there was one source of evidence, namely the complainer herself, and that the only way in which corroboration might be found for the individual complainers was in the application of the *Moorov* doctrine, and while it might have been preferable for the trial judge to have directed the jury that the evidence in question could not be used as proof of fact or for the purposes of corroboration, in light of those clear directions there had been no risk that the jury might have been misled into thinking that the hearsay evidence might be used as corroboration. (2) The hearsay evidence might competently have been used to enhance G's credibility, and had been relevant to B's evidence for a similar purpose given the agreement that the evidence was relevant for the purpose of explaining the gap in time between the incidents alleged and the complaint to the police, and to counter any allegation or suspicion of fabrication on that account; the absence of a direction on that point was not material.

W (PR) v HM ADVOCATE, [2016] HCJAC 71, 2016 S.C.L. 791, The Lord Justice Clerk (Lady Dorrian), Lady Paton, Lady Clark of Calton, HCJ Appeal.

2571 Misdirections–Murder–Three co-accused–Alleged misdirections on concert and self-defence

Three co-accused (G, J and P, collectively C) appealed against conviction for X's murder by repeatedly striking, kicking and jumping on, his head and body, inflicting blunt force trauma to his head and body, and striking him with a garden fork, knife or other instrument, on the basis that the trial judge had misdirected the jury such that there had been a miscarriage of justice. C also appealed against the imposition of 20 year punishment parts in relation to their sentences of life imprisonment. C and X had been at a pub where G had had a confrontation with X. X had left the premises and G had followed, with J and P following shortly thereafter. X had entered his nearby house and had re-emerged with a garden fork and a knife but had thereafter come to be disarmed and lying in the road, whereupon C had assaulted and murdered him. After the incident, C had gone to the home of P's girlfriend (N), in whose presence P had explained that G and X had had a fight but it had gone too far and G had jumped on X's head, to which G had displayed no reaction. An eyewitness (W) had stated in an initial police statement that X had been lying on his back motionless and three men had been kicking him repeatedly with great force, and had given a police statement later that morning in which he had stated that the taller of the three men, namely G, had just been standing. During police interview, J had claimed to have attempted to stop the attack, and P had admitted to being at the locus but had denied involvement, blaming G, and claimed to have run away when G had started attacking X. G submitted that (1) the trial judge's directions on concert had been inadequate; (2) the trial judge had not properly addressed W's evidence. J submitted that the trial judge had misdirected the jury on his special defence of self defence. P submitted that (1) the statement made in N's presence had been a mixed statement and the trial judge ought to have directed the jury to consider its truth in so far as it exculpated him; (2) the trial judge had erred in directing the jury that they could draw certain inferences regarding the number of persons involved from the short time span over which the incident had occurred and the number of injuries sustained; (3) the trial judge's repeated reference to sufficiency was a misdirection in so far as it was unnecessary and apt to confuse the jury; (4) the trial judge's criticism of the meaning of self defence had adversely affected P's position where P had relied on J's position.

Held: Appeals refused. (1) The trial judge's directions on concert had been to the effect that, were the jury not to find concert established, they could only convict on the basis of individual responsibility, for concert to be proved against a particular accused, they had to be satisfied that it had been proved that the accused was a party to a common criminal purpose to commit the crime, in the case of the use of a weapon, they had to be satisfied that the accused knew that a weapon was being used, his directions had been sound and had explained to the jury in a few straightforward, readily understood sentences the requirement for concert to be established, he had given the jury examples of factors which they could take into account when assessing, not concert in general but participation in the use of the fork, including proximity, however, he had made it clear that that was insufficient on its own, and there had been no misdirection. (2) The trial judge had correctly described W's testimony, the differences in W's account between his initial and second police statements and that in examination in chief and cross examination had been focused in the speeches and would have been at the forefront of the jury's thinking, and there was no basis for G's contention that they had forgotten about them. (3) The trial judge's directions on P's statement regarding G's involvement in assaulting X had been correct where he had directed the jury that G's lack of reaction upon being accused of being involved in the attack could be used as evidence against him in the context of what, as a matter of law, they could make of that statement, and there was nothing implicit therein that the jury required to accept that the statement and non-reaction had been established, which was a matter for them. (4) There had been no evidence to support J's special defence of self defence, it ought to have been withdrawn from the jury's consideration and the trial judge's caution in allowing it to be considered had weighed heavily in J's favour. (5) The statement allegedly made by P regarding G's involvement had not contained any incriminatory material which would have rendered it mixed, however, were it classed as mixed, its significance so far as P's involvement was concerned was so minor that it was impossible to assert that a direction that it could be used as proof of fact in the case against him could have had any material bearing on the outcome of the trial. (6) P's remaining criticisms were attacks on selective pieces of the charge which, reading the trial judge's directions in context, had no substance. (7) All of C had criminal records, and although G's was not as significant as J and P's, he had started fighting with X in the pub and thereafter outside before participating in the murder itself, perpetrated when X lay helpless on the ground, and the judge had been entitled not to distinguish between C in selecting the appropriate punishment parts, and although the punishment parts selected had been severe, that had been justified having regard to the violence used, and they were not excessive.

SIM (GARY WILLIAM) v HM ADVOCATE; WATSON (JAMES EDWARD) v HM ADVOCATE; WATSON (PAUL JOHN) v HM ADVOCATE, [2016] HCJAC 48, 2016 S.C.L. 612, Lord Justice General (Carloway), Lord Menzies, Lord Malcolm, HCJ.

2572 Misdirections–Stalking–Direction as to whether actual fear and alarm had been caused–Jury's finding clear from verdict

[Criminal Justice and Licensing (Scotland) Act 2010 (asp 13) s.38, s.39]

M appealed against conviction for two charges of breach of the peace (charges 1 and 2) and two charges of stalking, contrary to the Criminal Justice and Licensing (Scotland) Act 2010 s.39 (charges 3 and 4) on the ground that the sheriff had misdirected the jury. The sheriff had come to be under the misapprehension that charge 3, which followed on from charge 2 and involved the same complainer (X), had alleged a contravention of s.38 of the 2010 Act and had not directed the jury on the requirement under s.39 for there to be actual fear or alarm, provided that it could reasonably have been anticipated, directing the jury that to establish the offence in charge 3, the Crown required to prove that M had behaved in a threatening or abusive manner, that his behaviour would have been likely to have caused a reasonable person to suffer fear or alarm and that M had intended that his behaviour would cause fear or alarm or had been reckless as to whether it would have that result. In relation to charge 4, which he had correctly noted was a breach of s.39 of the 2010 Act, the sheriff had directed the jury that to establish the offence of stalking, the conduct required to cause the victim to suffer fear and alarm and the Crown required to establish that M had engaged in the course of conduct set out in the charge, that the course of conduct had caused the complainer in that charge to suffer fear or alarm and that M had engaged in the course of conduct with the intention of causing her to suffer fear or alarm or alternatively, he had known or ought to have known in all the circumstances that engaging in the course of conduct would have been likely to have caused her to suffer fear or alarm. M submitted that following the sheriff's error in relation to charge 3, the jury would have understood that they had not required to find that there had been actual fear or alarm in respect of a breach of s.39 of the 2010 Act, provided that they had found that it was anticipated that a reasonable person would suffer fear and alarm as a result of the conduct, whereas the offence under s.39 was only committed if the conduct caused actual fear or alarm, which had been a material misdirection and had amounted to a miscarriage of justice.

Held: Appeal refused. There had been a misdirection in relation to charge 3 in that the sheriff had not directed the jury that they required to find it proved that actual fear and alarm had been caused, however, from their verdict, it had been clear that the jury had found that M's conduct had caused X fear or alarm, those words had remained in the charge upon the return of that verdict, and in addition, the jury had found that X had suffered actual fear and alarm in respect of charge 2, following the sheriff's directions in that regard, the difference between it and charge 3 being simply the use of the 2010 Act for conduct post dating its introduction, in those circumstances, there had been no material misdirection which could have resulted in a miscarriage of justice. *Observed*, that the sheriff's charge had involved a patent error which had to have been obvious to the legal representatives present and it would have been of assistance to the administration of justice had the error simply been drawn to the sheriff's attention at the end of his charge and before the jury had returned with their verdict; the court would have expected the procurator fiscal depute to have noticed the error and acted accordingly.

MCBRIDE (EDWARD STEPHEN) v HM ADVOCATE, [2016] HCJAC 66, 2016 S.C.L. 758, Lord Justice General (Carloway), Lady Paton, Lady Clark of Calton, HCJ Appeal.

2573 Permission to appeal–Miscarriage of justice–Refusal of leave to appeal to Supreme Court–No factual basis for assertion of miscarriage of justice

[European Convention on Human Rights 1950 art.6]

M, convicted of assault with intent to rape, sought leave to appeal to the Supreme Court on the basis that the sift judges had erred in determining a compatibility issue by refusing leave to appeal. M had appealed his conviction on the grounds that that there had been defective representation in the preparation, and therefore presentation, of his defence, and that he had been denied a fair trial because the Lord Advocate (L) had restrained his funds. Leave to appeal was refused at the first and second sift on the basis that the material presented had not amounted to an arguable case that a miscarriage of justice had occurred. M submitted that a compatibility issue had been raised in the sheriff court regarding the restraint of his funds by L.

Held: Leave to appeal refused. L had not presented any petition for a restraint order and could neither restrain M's property nor prevent the court from releasing his funds by opposing the motion: an order had been made by the Court of Session, which had also declined M's periodic motions to release funds, and in those circumstances, there had been no act by L which might have raised a compatibility issue in the form of a breach of ECHR art.6 had there been such a breach, M required to raise the matter in his note of appeal before the first trial, or to raise it anew before the second trial, and there was no indication that a compatibility issue had been raised and decided in the sheriff court. (2) There was no vouching for M's proposition that the prohibitory order had captured the totality of his assets and, in any event, had he had his funds available, it would have made no practical difference to the efficacy of his defence; there was no basis in fact for M's assertion that the existence of additional funds would have made any difference to the evidence led or the verdict returned and, in that regard, that any miscarriage of justice had occurred. *Observed*, that notwithstanding *Cadder (Peter) v HM Advocate* [2010] UKSC 43, [2010] 1 W.L.R. 2601, [2010] C.L.Y. 1733, it would only be in exceptional circumstances that leave to appeal to the Supreme Court would be granted where the court had already decided at first and second sifts that there were no arguable grounds of appeal which would have permitted the case proceeding to a hearing on its merits, *Cadder*, *considered*.

MIRZA (JOHAR JAVEED) v HM ADVOCATE, [2015] HCJAC 87, 2015 S.C.L. 947, The Lord Justice Clerk (Carloway), Lady Smith, Lady Clark of Calton, HCJ.

2574 Permission to appeal–Sheriff Appeal Court–Sheriff Appeal Court refusing application for leave to appeal–Whether decision appealable

[Criminal Procedure (Scotland) Act 1995 (c.46) s.175, s.186, s.187, s.194ZB]

A disqualified driver (M) made an application seeking leave to appeal from the High Court of Justiciary against a decision of the Sheriff Appeal Court refusing to grant him leave to appeal against sentence, and interim suspension of a sheriff's decision to disqualify him from holding a driving licence for eight months. M had challenged the sheriff's decision and his refusal to discount M's disqualification and had been granted interim suspension thereof, however, he had been refused leave to appeal at the first and second sift and the interim suspension had been recalled.

Held: Note of appeal refused. The Sheriff Appeal Court was entitled to take notice of questions of competency on the lodging of any appeal in terms of the Criminal Procedure (Scotland) Act 1995 s.194ZB and when considering interim suspension, and M's application for interim suspension could not be entertained where the note of appeal on which it depended was incompetent. M was not, and had not been, a party to any appeal before the court, and where an appeal required leave, there was no appeal before the court unless and until leave was granted. The right of appeal under ss.175 and 186 of the 1995 Act was subject to the requirement of leave which, in an appeal against sentence in summary criminal jurisdiction, was regulated by s.187. A note of appeal which was refused leave was of no effect and was incompetent, and a decision of the present court to grant or refuse leave was not appealable, in any event, no other court or authority had the statutory power to consider leave to appeal or to review the Sheriff Appeal Court's decisions on leave to appeal.

MACKAY v MURPHY, [2015] SAC (Crim) 2, 2016 S.L.T. (Sh Ct) 86, Sheriff Principal M M Stephen, QC, Sheriff Principal D C W Pyle, Sheriff Principal M Lewis, SAC.

2575 Prosecution disclosure–Criminal investigations–Disclosure about police operation–Fairness

[Criminal Justice and Licensing (Scotland) Act 2010 (asp 13) s.119(2), s.121(3), s.128; Regulation of Investigatory Powers (Scotland) Act 2000 (asp 11); European Convention on Human Rights 1950 art.6(3)]

Two accused persons (H and S, collectively X) and S's company (Y), who pleaded not guilty to 16 charges including contraventions of road traffic and regulatory legislation relevant to dealing in motor vehicles and attempting to pervert the course of justice by providing false insurance information in relation to a particular motor vehicle, made applications under the Criminal Justice and Licensing (Scotland) Act 2010 s.128 for a ruling on whether s.121(3) applied to certain information held by the prosecutor. H explained that two police officers (F and C, collectively P) were the most significant witnesses in relation to all of the charges, and had been tasked as part of a police operation (O) with targeting those whom they believed to be members of an organised crime group for road traffic offences, which had included H, neither O's existence nor any of that detail had been mentioned in the disclosure received in connection with the summary complaint, and information about O would bear upon P's reliability and would weaken or undermine the case against H. H's application sought an order instructing the Crown to disclose copies of any Regulation of Investigatory Powers (Scotland) Act 2000 authorities in respect of any surveillance carried out on *inter alia* H, any directions given to officers, including P, as to how disruption tactics were to be carried out, the identities of all officers involved in O and the officer heading O and thereby issuing the instructions, all reports, memoranda, surveillance logs or observations made in writing by P to O's reporting or collating officer, detailing their involvement with H in each of the charges on the complaint. S explained that the witness statements had not disclosed that he had been the subject of a surveillance operation, there was nothing therein to suggest that P had been involved in an operation targeting him, they had been carrying out surveillance of S and had been instructed to adopt disruption tactics in relation to Y, which information had been withheld, and the disclosure at an intermediate diet on 20 November of a redacted copy of a single authorisation for directed surveillance of S had been the first indication that he had been the subject of any surveillance, there had been deliberate omissions from the statements disclosed, giving rise to a reasonable apprehension that P had exceeded the bounds of any authorisation granted and that evidence had been obtained unfairly, and there were Crown statements in existence which had not been disclosed. S asked the court to hold that s.121(3) of the 2010 Act applied to all statements pertaining to S's surveillance, directed or otherwise, together with all surveillance logs, Regulation of Investigatory Powers (Scotland) Act 2000 certificates and all other material relevant to the surveillance and disruption tactics adopted by the police in relation to S, including surveillance authorisations and logs, directions to P including search warrants for Y, and also disclosure of statements apparently missing from the disclosure. The procurator fiscal opposed the applications on the basis that P had not been involved in surveillance and certain of the offences had not been detected by surveillance, O had been an investigation into a serious organised crime group and surveillance had been deployed in relation to S but P had not been involved, P had been provided regularly with intelligence about persons linked to O by an unknown source, certain of the charges had been detected as a result of an intelligence led patrol, not surveillance, and certain others when P had received intelligence that H had been driving whilst using a mobile phone, although the source of that intelligence was unknown, the co-ordinated visit to Y had been at the police's instigations, other than the DVLA, it was not known what agencies had been involved and the basis for any search was unknown, and the tactics employed and the manner of their employment was not disclosable because the police considered that this information was not material to the charges, there had been no surveillance in relation to the charges and the Crown had disclosed all of the statements which they had received.

Held: Applications continued. (1) On the basis of the limited information, the defence were entitled to think that the police activity leading to the complaint faced by X and Y had been part of, or closely related to, a larger operation involving surveillance requiring authorisation under the 2002 Act, and that P had been involved in co-ordinated action designed to disrupt X and Y's activities and it was possible that it had been their task to co-ordinate that action. (2) X and Y suspected that the multi-agency visit to Y's premises had been co-ordinated by the police in pursuance of the policy of disruption as a fishing expedition, therefore, the Crown would require to lead evidence that it had been lawful and had it not been, to lead evidence in support of the submission that any irregularity ought to be excused, thus, information on those matters was likely to form part of the evidence to be led by the prosecutor in the proceedings against X and Y and was, therefore, within s.121(3)(c) of the 2010 Act, and s.121(3) applied to: a full account of the aim of the visit and of briefing and instructions given to all who participated; a full account of the co-ordination of the visit, including the identities of those who proposed the visit and the content of their communications in relation thereto; the identities of all the agencies which had participated; the identities of all persons who had been present at Y's premises as part of the multi-agency visit; the positions held by each of those persons in their organisations; the addresses at which each of them could be contacted without going through the police; the powers which each had exercised, had purported to exercise or on the basis of which they had to be present; the content of all statements given by each of them in connection with the visit; the content of all reports made by each of them in relation to the visit both internally within their own agencies and to the police; a full list of items seized, including the identities of those who carried out each seizure and the nature of the power which they had purported to exercise in making those seizures. (3) It appeared that there was much that the police had not told the procurator fiscal on the basis that it was not material to the charges but the duty in s.119(2) of the 2010 Act was to inform the prosecutor of all the information that might be relevant to the case for, or against, the accused; the police might have applied the wrong test, materiality to the charge was not a criterion in s.121(3), and as the procurator fiscal had invoked that concept in opposing the applications, the Crown might also have applied the wrong test, further it appeared that the decisions taken about disclosure, by both the police and the Crown, might have been informed by the making of misguided distinctions. (4) The prosecution had been isolated from the context of O in a manner which was so artificial as to be misleading and which, by denying to the defence any real information about that context, placed the defence at a significant disadvantage vis a vis the Crown, and a fair trial and compliance with ECHR art.6.3(b) required disclosure of: the purpose of the operation on which P had been engaged so far as it related to X; the identity or identities of the officer or officers who had directed that operation; the identities of all officers who had participated therein; all instructions given to those officers; the activities engaged in by them officers in pursuance thereof, including, without prejudice to that generality, in relation to X; and the content of all reports made by them in relation thereto. (5) With regard to statements of witnesses on the list which formed part of an indictment, other than those made by those who had been present at Y's premises, there were none to which s.121(3) applied, further, the court could not make an order for disclosure of various documents such as search warrants, authorisations and surveillance logs, in any event, the Crown was likely to have to rely thereon at trial, thus the procurator fiscal would no doubt conclude that they ought to be disclosed. (6) Consideration of the applications would be continued to a further intermediate diet, in advance of which the ruling would be issued in order to allow parties to consider their positions and submissions as to future procedure in light thereof. Opinion, that had the procurator fiscal been able to give better information or even assurances about compliance with the disclosure regime, the conclusions reached by the court might have been different.

MURPHY v WTH, 2016 S.C.C.R. 135, Sheriff A N Brown, Sh Ct (Tayside) (Dundee).

2576 Prosecution disclosure–Incrimination–Information relating to whereabouts of alleged incriminee

[Criminal Procedure (Scotland) Act 1995 (c.46) s.70A(9)(e); Criminal Justice and Licensing (Scotland) Act 2010 (asp 13) s.124]

S appealed against his conviction for drugs offences on the basis that the Crown had failed in its duty to disclose information relating to the whereabouts of an alleged incriminee (X). The issue was whether, where an accused had lodged an incrimination of a named person, whose address was said to be "meantime unknown", the Crown were thereby under an obligation to investigate that incrimination and to disclose the address of the incriminee, if known to the police, to the defence.

Held: Appeal refused. There was no failure to disclose any information which had any effect on the conduct of the trial: the fundamental flaw was the assertion that S, or his agent, wanted to ascertain X's address and that, had they found it, they would have cited him, and either called him as a witness or used him as part of the cross examination on identification; it was clear that the defence had decided not to locate X and had they attempted to do so, it was clear that there would have been little difficulty in locating him; and had there been any difficulty, it could have been resolved by a simple request to the Crown. *Opinion*, (1) that was the address of an incriminee "information" in terms of the definition in the Criminal Procedure (Scotland) Act 1995 s.70A(9)(e), introduced by the Criminal Justice and Licensing (Scotland) Act 2010 s.124, and had S wanted to know what it was, it was open to him to include that in a defence statement where he could have asked the court for an order to disclose said information but that stage was never reached and it could not be said there was any unfairness in the trial proceedings; (2) that while the lodging of the special defence of incrimination might have prompted the Crown to review the case and disclose any material relevant thereto, there was no evidence to support the incrimination and had there been a breach of any statutory obligation of disclosure or of any right to a fair trial which the legislation was designed to secure, there was nothing to demonstrate that the use of any material now known could have had any effect on the jury.

SINCLAIR (JAMES) v HM ADVOCATE, [2016] HCJAC 26, 2016 S.L.T. 444, Lord Justice General (Carloway), Lord Bracadale, Lady Clark of Calton, HCJ.

2577 Reasons–Witnesses–Judge's failure to give adequate explanation for accepting evidence of two Crown witnesses–Entitlement to convict

[Criminal Justice and Licensing (Scotland) Act 2010 (asp 13) s.38(1); Criminal Law (Consolidation) (Scotland) Act 1995 (c.39) s.47(1); Criminal Procedure (Scotland) Act 1995 (c.46) s.259]

M appealed by stated case against conviction for behaving in a threatening or abusive manner, contrary to the Criminal Justice and Licensing (Scotland) Act 2010 s.38(1) and for having an offensive weapon, contrary to the Criminal Law (Consolidation) (Scotland) Act 1995 s.47(1). The former partner (X) of M's sister (S) had attended at S's house to collect the parties' child for contact. Following a disagreement about when contact was to start, X had gone to wait in his car with his partner (P), during which time there had been a telephone call between S's house and M, and M had driven to S's house. On the evidence, the sheriff had found *inter alia* that after arriving at S's house, M had shouted, sworn and uttered threats of violence towards X, had taken a metal pole from his van and had repeatedly struck X's car, principally on the windscreen but had made no finding of fact that there had been damage thereto. The sheriff had found X and P to be credible and reliable and that the statement of M's mother (Z), admitted in evidence under the Criminal Procedure (Scotland) Act 1995 s.259, was largely consistent with X and P's accounts, that it supported the Crown case that M had gone to S's house to sort X out, and further that M's evidence did not sit well with the other evidence, in particular, that in Z's statement. The sheriff asked *inter alia* whether she had been entitled to convict M.

Held: Question answered in the negative and conviction quashed. (1) The sheriff had not set out the relevant evidence of each witness and had referred to but had not set out all evidence in explaining why a witness's evidence was consistent or inconsistent with other evidence or why M was not credible, and had failed to set out the inconsistencies said to be found in the witness's evidence, *Cartner v Watson* [2012] HCJAC 67, 2013 J.C. 251, [2013] C.L.Y. 3612, *considered.* (2) The sheriff had erred in approaching the issue of damage to X's car from the point of view of whether the evidence was that there was no damage rather than considering whether there was evidence of damage, of which she had conceded that there was none and had made no finding of damage, the sheriff had thus been led into considering that it was presupposed that damage would be caused if M acted in the manner spoken to by X and P and had gone on to consider what would be in judicial knowledge regarding whether a windscreen might not be damaged by being struck but had not dealt with the issue of why, given that there was no damage, X and P should nonetheless be believed. (3) The court could look behind the sheriff's assessment of the Crown witnesses; having regard to the absence of evidence of damage, and Z's s.259 statement, there was no adequate explanation given by the sheriff for accepting X and P's evidence. *Observed*, that it was important for judges at first instance to give a full account of the evidence led and to make discrete findings in fact to cover the relevant evidence on which the decision was based and the reasons for making those findings in fact.

AIEN v DUNN *sub nom.* AIEN v RICHARDSON, [2016] SAC (Crim) 18, 2016 S.C.L. 690, Sheriff Principal C A L Scott, QC, Sheriff Principal M Lewis, Sheriff N M P Morrison, QC, SAC.

2578 Search warrants–Bills of suspension–Relevancy of averments

[Misuse of Drugs Act 1971 (c.38) s.23(3), s.4(3)(b)]

M, charged with being concerned in the supply of controlled drugs contrary to the Misuse of Drugs Act 1971 s.4(3)(b), lodged a bill of suspension seeking suspension of a search warrant. A detective constable had indicated to the justice of the peace that she had reasonable grounds for suspecting that a quantity of controlled drugs were to be found in a person's possession at M's property (P) on the basis of ongoing police surveillance and current intelligence that M and two others (X) were frequently involved in the use and distribution of controlled drugs, and that they had been observed by police witnesses apparently moving cocaine and money between P and one of X's nearby properties. M claimed inter alia that the information provided to the justice of the peace had not provided a comprehensive position such that a proper consideration of all the information could inform the justice of the peace's decision; the decision to grant the warrant had been based on an incomplete understanding of the evidence, and in the circumstances a sheriff or judge ought to preside over an evidential hearing, to establish whether the information provided had been correct, to provide an assessment on the behaviour of the police, and the court could have the opportunity to consider whether the grant of warrant in those circumstances ought to stand.

Held: Bill refused. (1) M's averments set out no relevant basis on which the court might be persuaded to suspend the search warrant; the justice of the peace had been entitled to form the requisite suspicion on the basis of the information presented to him on oath by D, it could not be said that the police had acted in bad faith and presented information which they knew to be false or clearly unreliable, the justice of the peace had followed the proper procedure, he had understood that he was carrying out a judicial function, the present case was not one in which it would be appropriate for matters to be remitted to an evidential hearing in order that a single judge or sheriff could hear the relevant evidence and report back; the bill did no more than present difficult or tenative criticisms of the quality of the information presented to the justice of the peace and did not claim that the justice had not been entitled to decide as he had on the basis of the information put before him, and he had been entitled to proceed on D's hearsay information. The bill contained no averments to the effect that no justice could reasonably have granted a warrant on the basis of the information provided, such that it was irrelevant and therefore could not be passed. (2) M, at best, was asking the court to embark on a hearing with a view to acquiring information which might allow him to plead a relevant basis for setting aside the warrant, moreover, the court had no power to evaluate, in the light of all available information, the quality and completeness of what had been put before the justice, with a view to revisiting the decision to grant a warrant, which the bill appeared to suggest. Observed, (1) that Scottish criminal procedure did not, and ought not to, provide for second guessing of the decision by a justice of the peace, magistrate or sheriff to grant a search warrant, in exercise of the power conferred by s.23(3) of the 1971 Act; the statutory scheme was to confer the jurisdiction to grant the warrant to the justice of the peace and with it the jurisdiction to consider whether the statutory criterion for granting the warrant had been met, which was no higher than the justice's satisfaction that there was reasonable ground for suspecting and, consistent with the frequent need for expedition, hearsay might be sufficient to supply the justice with the necessary information; (2) that a s.23(3) warrant could be suspended by the court if the justice's decision had proceeded on the basis of no, or very clearly insufficient, information, or the justice's decision had been vitiated by the police knowingly having supplied him with erroneous information.

STEWART v HARVIE, [2015] HCJAC 13, 2016 S.C.L. 93, Lord Brodie, Lord Drummond Young, Temporary Judge M M Stephen, QC, HCJ.

2579 Trials–Adjournment–Degree of prejudice–Exercise of discretion

[Criminal Procedure (Scotland) Act 1995 (c.46) s.283]

A police officer (W) lodged a bill of advocation challenging the adjournment of his trial by the justice of the peace. W had been charged with assault on 16 October 2013 but had only been cited to appear on 17 September 2014. The diet had been adjourned without plea until 15 October and again until 12 November. A trial diet fixed for 14 May 2015 had been postponed and a new trial diet had been fixed for 31 August, when W's case had been called in the morning but the necessary certificate under the Criminal Procedure (Scotland) Act 1995 s.283 had not been served and the procurator fiscal had commenced another trial pending recovery thereof. The case had been recalled in the afternoon, the procurator fiscal's motion to adjourn *ex proprio motu* had been refused and the trial had commenced at 5 pm but the justice of the peace had adjourned it almost immediately until 28 September 2015, having regard to the prejudice to W, the procurator fiscal and the public interest, taking into account the length of time the case had taken since the alleged offence and bearing in mind that the adjourned diet would take place only a few weeks later, limiting the degree of prejudice and that there was a public interest element stemming from W's position as a police officer and in that context, the allegation was not minor. W submitted that (1) the justice of the peace had failed to give sufficient weight to a number of factors, namely, the procedural history, the impact of the proceedings on W, the relatively minor nature of the charge, and the justice of the peace's failure to properly prepare the case relative to the certificate; (2) in adjourning the case, the justice of the peace had allowed the procurator fiscal to cure what would have been a fatal flaw, and had taken a decision which no reasonable justice of the peace could have reached, and in doing so had failed to apply herself to the test which she had enunciated relative to the earlier adjournment decision.

Held: Bill refused. (1) A decision on whether a trial diet ought to be adjourned was primarily one for the court of first instance, having regard to the circumstances of the particular case and the trial court in general, and the court would only intervene therewith had the court at first instance either misdirected itself or reached a decision which no reasonable court could have reached, which was a high test; the matters complained of, as averred in the bill, were solely matters to which it had been claimed that the justice of the peace had given insufficient weight, there was no averment of general unreasonableness or any reason for the decision to be categorised in that manner, and the averments were irrelevant. (2) The justice of the peace had addressed the prejudice to the prosecutor, to W and the public interest, there was no reason to suppose that she had forgotten those factors between her two decisions, it was clear, by the reference to the proposed new trial diet, that she had not, and there was no basis for the contention that she had erred in the exercise of her discretion, *Paterson (Scott) v McPherson* [2012] HCJAC 61, 2012 G.W.D. 19-384, *applied*, and *Tudhope v Lawrie (Henry)* 1979 J.C. 44, [1979] C.L.Y. 2937, *Christensen v Harvie* [2015] HCJAC 39, 2015 J.C. 277, [2015] C.L.Y. 2988 and *Bowden v Harvie* [2015] HCJAC 11, 2015 S.C.L. 325, [2015] C.L.Y. 3017, *considered*. Observed, that *Hunter v Cottam* 2011 S.C.C.R. 130, [2011] C.L.Y. 4186 was of limited relevance when assessing the exercise of a discretion by a court of first instance which had set out and applied the correct test, *Hunter*, *considered*.

WALKER v DUNN, [2015] HCJAC 119, 2016 S.L.T. 116, The Lord Justice Clerk (Carloway), Lord Brodie, Lord Drummond Young, HCJ.

2580 Trials–Adjournment–Prejudice–Balancing exercise

[Criminal Justice and Licensing (Scotland) Act 2010 (asp 13) s.38(1)]

The Crown lodged a bill of advocation challenging a decision of the sheriff refusing to grant an adjournment in T's trial for assaulting his wife (W) and 10 year old son (S), and contravening the Criminal Justice and Licensing (Scotland) Act 2010 s.38(1), resulting in T being acquitted of all charges. W had concluded her testimony before the presiding sheriff and the trial had been adjourned to allow further evidence to be led before the same sheriff. The trial was adjourned twice due to the trial sheriff not being in attendance at the sheriff court. The same situation arose at the next trial diet and the sheriff refused to grant a further adjournment on the basis that it would give rise to a fifth trial diet in a summary prosecution, a child witness would be required to attend court again, and the same circumstances had prevailed prior to the previous adjournment.

Held: Bill passed and case remitted to trial sheriff. (1) The sheriff had failed to have proper and accurate regard to the three clear and distinct interests involved, namely prejudice to the Crown, to T and to the public interest; her approach was confused in considering the matter to be a question of fairness and the balance of T's interests against the public interest in prosecuting the case to its conclusion. (2) The sheriff had misdirected herself or erred when balancing the prejudice likely to result from adjourning the trial: she had attached significance to T's special bail conditions which were a marginal feature where the proposed new trial date was two weeks later, and the requirement for S to give evidence should not have attracted the weight given thereto, and did not prejudice T. (3) The sheriff had failed to give consideration to the fact that W's evidence implicated T and a refusal to adjourn materially prejudiced the Crown by denying the use of that evidence, and she had failed to recognise that the public interest would be prejudiced where serious allegations of assaults upon a child would be wholly undermined by a refusal to adjourn where all the evidence thus far led served to confirm those allegations. (4) The overall procedural passage of time was proportionate for summary proceedings and the passage of time since the events libelled was not necessarily excessive, accordingly, the short continuation period should have weighed heavily with the sheriff. (5) The sheriff's balancing exercise had been flawed where the circumstances facing the court at the relevant time suggested that the prejudice to be suffered by the Crown and by the public interest far outweighed any prejudice affecting T.

MURPHY v TARIQ, [2016] SAC (Crim) 4, 2016 S.L.T. (Sh Ct) 89, Sheriff Principal C A L Scott, QC, Sheriff Beckett, QC, Sheriff Principal B A Lockhart , SAC.

2581 Trials–Adjournment–Prejudice–Whether sheriff addressed correct test

[Criminal Justice and Licensing (Scotland) Act 2010 (asp 13) s.38(1); Criminal Procedure (Scotland) Act 1995 (c.46) s.13(1), s.13(6)(a)(i); Police and Fire Reform (Scotland) Act 2012 (asp 8) s.90(2)(a)]

X, charged with behaving in a threatening or abusive manner likely to cause a reasonable person to suffer fear or alarm, contrary to the Criminal Justice and Licensing (Scotland) Act 2010 s.38(1), failing to provide his name and address, contrary to the Criminal Procedure (Scotland) Act 1995 ss.13(1) and 13(6)(a)(i), and resisting, obstructing or hindering the police in the execution of their duty and struggling violently with them, contrary to the Police and Fire Reform (Scotland) Act 2012 s.90(2)(a), all committed while on bail, lodged a bill of advocation challenging the sheriff's decision to adjourn his trial as erroneous and oppressive. Trial diets on 7 August 2015 and 7 January 2016 had been adjourned on Crown motion due to witness difficulties. The third trial diet on 25 May 2016 had been adjourned by the sheriff due to lack of court time on the basis that the case had called after 4 pm.

Held: Bill passed. (1) The decision whether a trial diet ought to be adjourned was primarily a matter for the court of first instance having regard to the circumstances of the particular case and of the court in general, and the appeal court would only intervene if it could be shown that the court at first instance had either misdirected itself in law or reached a decision which no reasonable court could have reached. (2) The sheriff had given scant information as to his approach to the test he required to apply when considering whether to grant or refuse an adjournment, his report failed to enunciate the test which he had applied when considering the Crown motion to adjourn, accordingly, the court had little confidence that the sheriff had addressed the correct test and had had regard to the three elements of prejudice set out in *Tudhope v Lawrie (Henry)* 1979 J.C. 44, [1979] C.L.Y. 2937, accordingly, it was for the court to assess prejudice, *Tudhope* and *Paterson (Scott) v McPherson* [2012] HCJAC 61, 2012 G.W.D. 19-384, *considered.* (3) The Crown had itself contributed to the difficulties in the procedural history, and as the charges were not the most serious, the consequences for the Crown of not being able to proceed with the complaint lost some significance in the balancing exercise; the bill would be passed and the complaint deserted *simpliciter.*

ARCHER v HARVIE, [2016] SAC (Crim) 23, 2016 S.C.L. 832, Sheriff Principal M M Stephen, QC, Sheriff Principal M Lewis, Sheriff P J Braid, SAC.

2582 Trials–Adjournment–Refusal of Crown's motion for adjournment–Failure to weigh up prejudice to Crown

The Crown raised a bill of advocation seeking recall of the justice of the peace's decision to refuse its motion for adjournment of a trial diet in respect of S, charged with assault, leading to desertion *simpliciter*, and remit to the justice of the peace for further diets to be fixed. S had pleaded not guilty and at the intermediate diet on 20 January 2016, the case had been continued to the trial diet on 11 February, at which the complainer (X) had attended, however, another witness, necessary for corroboration of the charge had not, and inquiries made after the intermediate diet had disclosed that W had moved to London and had no intention of returning to give evidence. The justice of the peace had refused the Crown's motion for a witness warrant and to adjourn the trial, noting that the offence had allegedly taken place almost one year previously, and taking into account that there had been no reference at intermediate diet stage to any difficulty in citing witnesses, that it would not be cost effective to bring W from London in custody, that there were doubts as to whether he would reappear for trial given his reluctance so far, and the public interest in having summary justice dealt with expeditiously.

Held: Bill passed. The justice of the peace had failed to properly weigh up the prejudice to the Crown, to S and to the public interest in general, had he done so he ought to have recognised the seriousness of the charge, that it was in the public interest that X be afforded the opportunity of bringing evidence to prove it, no fault, error or carelessness could be attributed to X in his preparation for trial, the justice appeared to have misdirected himself in his assessment of the extent of the prejudice to X, who by the justice's decision was prevented from proceeding with the prosecution, he had erred in ignoring or discounting the public interest that those charged with violent conduct were brought to justice, in the circumstances of the present case, the legitimate aim of speedy justice yielded to those other considerations, no specific prejudice had been advanced on S's behalf other than the time which had passed between the incident and the date of the first trial diet, the procedural history indicated that the case had proceeded to trial without delay, and in refusing X's motion for a witness warrant, the justice had misdirected himself by placing weight on an irrelevant factor namely the cost effectiveness of bringing W from London, which was a matter for the prosecutor not the court; in refusing the Crown adjournment in the absence of any real prejudice to S and in the face of significant prejudice to the Crown, the justice had reached a decision which no reasonable justice could have reached, *Tudhope v Lawrie (Henry)* 1979 J.C. 44, [1979] C.L.Y. 2937, *applied.*

HARVIE v SHAAN *sub nom.* MCPHERSON v SHAAN, [2016] SAC (Crim) 12, 2016 S.C.L. 683, Sheriff Principal M M Stephen, QC, Sheriff Principal D L Murray, Sheriff K M Maciver, QC, SAC.

2583 Trials–Delay–Oppression–Whether fairness of trial prejudiced

[Criminal Procedure (Scotland) Act 1995 (c.46) s.288ZA(2); European Convention on Human Rights 1950 art.6]

P, charged with housebreaking and theft, appealed against the sheriff's decisions to refuse his plea in bar of trial and his compatibility minute in terms of the Criminal Procedure (Scotland) Act 1995 s.288ZA(2). The evidence in support of the charge had consisted of DNA evidence, telephone records and bank records. P had appeared on petition on 1 August 2013 and had been released on bail pending service of the indictment, which had occurred on 29 March 2014. The case had subsequently been adjourned three times and the time bar extended to 21 June 2015, and on 18 June, the Crown had sought a further adjournment to obtain a warrant for the bank records. The sheriff had granted the motion and had adjourned the trial to 21 September and extended the time bar to 2 October. P had successfully appealed that decision (*Potts (Donnie Daniel) v HM Advocate* [2015] HCJAC 124, 2016 S.L.T. 121, [2016] 2535). In January 2016, the Crown had served a summary complaint on P in identical terms to the charges on the indictment and a trial had been set for 19 October 2016. P had lodged pleas in bar of trial on the basis that his continued prosecution was oppressive and, or alternatively, an abuse of process, and that it was a breach of his ECHR art.6 rights, which the sheriff had refused on the basis *inter alia* that the delay had ended and the art.6 violation had not been continuing, and any unfairness to P could be dealt with via lower sentencing.

Held: Appeal refused. (1) When considering a plea in bar of trial where oppression was alleged due to delay, the court required to consider that delay and the cause thereof as relevant factors when addressing the real test, namely whether the risk of prejudice from that delay was so grave that the sheriff could not be expected to put that prejudice out of his mind and reach a fair verdict on the evidence; in the present case, the evidence to be led was largely circumstantial and founded mainly on scientific and other documentary evidence, and P was unable to identify any material prejudice to the trial, and the lack of prejudice to the fairness of the trial and the granting of the charge outweighed the other relevant factors, and the test in *McFadyen (Donald) v Annan* 1992 J.C. 53, [1992] C.L.Y. 5466 had not been met, *McFadyen, considered.* (2) A plea in bar of trial on the ground of oppression was the proper vehicle for P to bring to the attention of the court his complaints in respect of the Crown's conduct, accordingly, in the circumstances of the present case, the plea of abuse of process was a plea which was neither separate nor distinct from the plea of oppression. (3) A trial had been fixed, the two prior debate discharges had not indicated carelessness on the part of the Crown, and the Crown had made full disclosure and was ready to proceed to trial; in those circumstances, the sheriff had been correct to conclude that the period of unreasonable delay had apparently ended, and having regard to all factors, there was no obvious continuing breach, P would be able to have a fair trial and the appeal in respect of the compatibility minute would be refused.

POTTS v GIBSON, [2016] SAC (Crim) 25, 2016 S.C.L. 819, Sheriff Principal M M Stephen, QC, Sheriff Principal M Lewis, Sheriff S Murphy, QC, SAC.

2584 Trials–Interpreters–Standard of full simultaneous interpretation in Korean–Fairness of trial

[Sexual Offences (Scotland) Act 2009 (asp 9) s.1]

L appealed against conviction for raping X while she was intoxicated and incapable of giving consent, contrary to the Sexual Offences (Scotland) Act 2009 s.1. L had come to England from Korea aged 14 and had spent two years at school in England, and there had been an interpreter (N) at the trial, however, during the reading of the joint minute, L had requested that N cease interpreting as the translation was distracting and he was able to follow the English used. The trial judge had endorsed L's agent's view that the status quo of full simultaneous interpretation ought to continue until later that day when the position could be reconsidered, and had directed N accordingly, however, the matter had not been revisited during the trial. X gave evidence that she had become separated from her friends in a nightclub, she had no memory of meeting L but the following morning had found herself in a van with L, who had suggested to her that they had had sexual intercourse. The trial judge had directed the jury that there could be no consent if a complainer was incapable of consenting because of the effects of alcohol, and that it was for the Crown to prove that L had had no reasonable belief that X had consented. The trial judge had thereafter returned to the issue of consent, directing the jury *inter alia* that the Crown's position was that there was a considerable crossover in the evidence relative to lack of consent and lack of reasonable belief that X had consented, or had been capable of giving her free agreement and consent. The trial judge had again directed the jury that the Crown's position was that L had had no reasonable basis for believing that X had consented or had been capable thereof, and if they decided that L had had a reasonable belief that X had not been incapable by reason of intoxication and L had had a reasonable belief that X had not been so incapable, they had to decide whether they were satisfied that he could not reasonably have held that belief, and in that eventuality, they would be entitled to have regard to the same chapters of evidence as related to the second element, and that if they accepted that L had believed that X had been capable of consenting and that that was reasonable, they required to acquit, as well as if they had a reasonable doubt about that matter. L submitted that (1) he had not had a fair trial because the interpretation had impeded his ability to understand the case against him, N had not been properly qualified and the standard of his interpretation had fallen below acceptable standards; (2) the trial judge had materially misdirected the jury in directing them to apply a further test, once reasonable belief had been established and in directing them that, in determining reasonable belief, they could have regard to the same features as they had considered relative to consent.

Held: Appeal refused. (1) L was proficient in English, however, the court had complied with his request for translation, L had not identified anything specific that he had either not followed or had been unable to deal with, he had elected not to give evidence in advance of trial, thus no issue arose in relation to his ability to present his account adequately to the jury, there had been no material language difficulty at trial, L had had no difficulty in understanding the case against him or in communicating the nature of his defence to his representatives, there had been no technical material requiring special translation, the fact that, occasionally, it had not been possible or practicable to translate everything word for word because of the speed of diction was not *per se* indicative of substantial unfairness, there was no evidence that N had not possessed the necessary skills and qualifications or had been other than efficient and professional, there was no substantial indication that L had suffered prejudice, and had there been continuing difficulty with N, L could have drawn that to the court's attention and in the absence of any further complaint, the trial judge had been entitled to assume that there was no ongoing difficulty. (2) There had been an error in the trial judge's use of "reasonable" in the impugned direction, which had clearly been a linguistic slip, however, the tenor of the charge would have been clear to the jury, and a more significant misdirection, where the trial judge had directed the jury that had L reasonably believed that X had been capable of consenting they ought to acquit, had favoured L and no miscarriage of justice had occurred, moreover, the trial judge's reference to using the material relative to the issue of consent when considering reasonable belief might not be strictly correct in legal theory, however, the general meaning was clear, and it ought not to be assumed that the jury would have taken X's memory loss into account in relation to L's belief at the time.

LEE (SAN) v HM ADVOCATE, [2016] HCJAC 39, 2016 S.C.L. 504, Lord Justice General (Carloway), Lord Menzies, Lord Bracadale, HCJ.

2585 Trials–Right to examine witnesses–Joint investigative interviews with child complainers–Equality of arms

[European Convention on Human Rights 1950 art.6(3)(d); Criminal Procedure (Scotland) Act 1995 (c.46) s.271I, s.271M]

M appealed against conviction for two charges of statutory sexual offences against children on the basis that his right under ECHR art.6(3)(d) to examine or have examined witnesses against him, and to obtain the attendance and examination of witnesses on his behalf under the same conditions as witnesses against him, had been breached. Joint investigative interviews (JIIs) had taken place with several child complainers (C) in June and July 2013, which had been sent to a psychologist (P), who recommended that C's evidence be taken on commission. M was indicted in March 2014 and the Crown lodged an unopposed motion for the JIIs to be treated as C's evidence in chief and for C to be cross examined and re-examined on commission in terms of the Criminal Procedure (Scotland) Act 1995 s.271M and s.271I. The commissions took place in July 2014, at which M's senior counsel cross examined C. M submitted that (1) there had been unjustified delay in initiating the commission process, and although he had been given the opportunity to cross examine C, the process had been inherently unfair where C's memories had been severely affected by the passage of time; (2) there had been no equality of arms in terms of the Crown's reliance on the JIIs as contemporaneous cross examination had not been possible.

Held: Appeal refused. (1) In determining whether a criminal trial had been art.6 compliant, it had to be ascertained whether the proceedings in their entirety, including the manner in which the evidence was taken, were fair, *Asch v Austria (A/203A)* (1993) 15 E.H.R.R. 597, [1993] C.L.Y. 2140, and *SN v Sweden (34209/96)* (2004) 39 E.H.R.R. 13, [2005] C.L.Y. 2083, *considered.* (2) M had had a full opportunity to cross examine, in a domestic sense, C, and had been able at trial to challenge the reliability of C's accounts at the JIIs having regard both to the content of the JIIs and the answers obtained at commission. (3) M had not objected to the JIIs being treated as C's evidence in chief and his right to a fair trial had been protected by other aspects of the system including the fact that JIIs were electronically recorded and capable of scrutiny by the jury in light of the cross examination at commission, and the trial judge's directions on the care required when analysing that type of evidence. Opinion, (1) that there was an obvious concern about the delay between the JIIs and the commission and the government might want to consider, in the shorter term, introducing into the 1995 Act a provision permitting the evidence of young children to be taken on commission at any time after the accused's appearance on petition, and in the longer term, allowing defence involvement soon after, or at, the JII; (2) that given the extensive material now available to lawyers on what constituted a fair interview of a young child, the assessment of fairness was for them, and ultimately the judge, to determine, and not for expert opinion from a psychologist. Observed, that there could be little force in a general objection which sought to prevent a recorded interview taken in the initial stages of a police investigation being used as proof of fact in the case of a very young child complainer where that material was likely to be the most accurate account of events, at least if the questioning was such that did not suggest the answers.

MACLENNAN (MARK WILLIAM PATRICK) v HM ADVOCATE, [2015] HCJAC 128, 2016 S.L.T. 339, The Lord Justice Clerk (Carloway), Lord Brodie, Lord Drummond Young, HCJ.

2586 Upper Tribunal for Scotland–Scottish Tribunals–Offences in relation to proceedings

THE SCOTTISH TRIBUNALS (OFFENCES IN RELATION TO PROCEEDINGS) REGULATIONS 2016, SSI 2016/342; made under the Tribunals (Scotland) Act 2014 s.67(1). In force: 1 December 2016.

These Regulations: create offences in relation to proceedings before the Scottish Tribunals, grounds of defence and associated maximum penalties; and provide for the circumstances in which a person need not give evidence or produce something to the Scottish Tribunals, which include when evidence or material is privileged.

2587 Verdicts–Indecent photographs of children–Inconsistency–Acquittal on one count

[Civic Government (Scotland) Act 1982 (c.45) s.52(1)(a), s.52A(1)]

S, appealed against conviction for having in his possession indecent photographs or pseudo-photographs of children, contrary to the Civic Government (Scotland) Act 1982 s.52A(1) on the ground that the verdict was one which no reasonable jury, properly directed, could have returned. He also appealed against sentence. S had been acquitted of a second charge alleging a breach of s.52(1)(a) of the 1982 Act, in respect of the same period, by taking or making the photographs or pseudo-photographs. S had sought to incriminate his flat mate (C), who gave evidence that he had had access in the past to S's computer with his permission but the computer had been protected by a password, unknown to him, and he had only been able to gain access to the computer with S's co-operation. A forensic analyst (F), who had examined the computer, had recovered 224 images and one video, the images all having been deleted, and had also found data erasure software. The sheriff had had regard to *HM Advocate v Graham (David William)* [2010] HCJAC 50, 2011 J.C. 1, [2010] C.L.Y. 4523, to the fact that S had been assessed as at a high risk of re-offending, that he had previous conviction for lewd, indecent and libidinous behaviour, and that he was not suitable for a community payback order, and had sentenced S to 18 months' imprisonment and made him subject to a sexual offences prevention order. S submitted that (1) the jury's verdict of not proven in respect of the second charge was inconsistent with the guilty verdict on the first charge; (2) the custodial term selected was excessive.

Held: Appeal refused. (1) There was no inconsistency in the jury's verdicts; possession was a legitimate inference for the jury to make from the circumstances of S's unique access to the computer, using a password, and the existence of recently deleted images using software installed on the hard drive, *Harrison (John) v HM Advocate* 2000 S.L.T. 2, [2000] C.L.Y. 6118, *considered*. (2) The sheriff had not erred in selecting imprisonment as the only appropriate disposal or in imposing a custodial term which was at the high end of the guideline range as it was justified by virtue of S's record.

SIMPSON (KEITH) v HM ADVOCATE, [2015] HCJAC 120, 2016 S.C.L. 182, The Lord Justice Clerk (Carloway), Lady Smith, Lord Bracadale, HCJ.

2588 Warrants–Fingerprints–Sheriff granting warrant to take accused's fingerprints during summary proceedings–Special circumstances

[Courts Reform (Scotland) Act 2014 (asp 18) s.118]

K, accused of theft, lodged a bill of suspension against a warrant to take his fingerprints granted by the sheriff while summary proceedings were in progress. K and his co-accused (C) had lived in a house of multiple occupancy and had been its only occupants in September 2014 when a theft from a locked office therein had occurred. The police had obtained a warrant to search K and C's rooms and had discovered certain of the missing items hidden in K's room. K's fingerprints had not been taken on his arrest and at the stage of marking the case for prosecution, there had been no reference to fingerprint evidence against him and the Crown had been prepared to proceed to trial on the basis of the existing evidence. In August 2015, it had emerged that fingerprint evidence pointing to K as a perpetrator was available, the crime examiner having submitted it directly to the laboratory rather than the normal practice of through the forensic science gateway but the Crown had considered that it was too late to act with regard thereto and would proceed to trial without it. The trial had thereafter been adjourned due to C's arrest and in light thereof, the Crown sought the warrant, which the sheriff had granted on the basis that (i) the taking of the fingerprints was a non-invasive procedure, (ii) the information relevant to the warrant application had come to light after the prosecution had commenced and the measure sought was not merely to correct an earlier failure on the part of police officers, (iii) there was no prejudice to K. A preliminary question arose as to whether it was competent for the High Court to hear the bill or whether it was subject to the jurisdiction of the sheriff appeal court.

Held: Bill refused. (1) The decision to grant a warrant to take samples or to search was an administrative act, in granting such a warrant the sheriff was not sitting as a court and a bill to suspend such a warrant did not constitute an appeal from a court of summary jurisdiction, thus, a bill to suspend a warrant of the type granted in the present case did not come within the ambit of the Courts Reform (Scotland) Act 2014 s.118 and was not included in the transfer of powers to the sheriff appeal court and such bills remained subject to the supervisory jurisdiction of the High Court. (2) Where a warrant to take fingerprints was sought after proceedings had commenced it would only be granted where the circumstances were special and in exercising his discretion the sheriff required to have regard to the whole circumstances, weighing the public interest in the investigation and suppression of crime against the interest of the accused person; the Crown had considered that it had a sufficiency of evidence to prosecute K in the absence of fingerprint evidence where property removed from the office had been recovered in his room soon after the theft in circumstances in which they had apparently been concealed, the existence of the fingerprint evidence had only come to the procurator fiscal's attention in August 2015 against a background where K's fingerprints had not been taken when he had been detained, had the procurator fiscal consulted the forensic science gateway it would not have informed him in relation to the submission of the fingerprints for comparison because the scenes of crime officer had adopted an irregular approach by submitting them directly to the laboratory, and the sheriff had been entitled to regard those circumstances as special, had exercised his discretion taking into account considerations such as the non-invasive nature of the procedure and the absence of prejudice to K, and he had been entitled to exercise his discretion in the manner in which he had.

MCWILLIAM v HARVIE, [2016] HCJAC 29, 2016 S.L.T. 648, Lady Dorrian, Lord Bracadale, Lord Malcolm, HCJ.

DAMAGES

2589 Loss of society–Title to sue–Biological siblings of deceased adopted person–Title to sue for damages for inter alia loss of society and guidance

[Damages (Scotland) Act 2011 (asp 7) s.14, s.4(3); European Convention on Human Rights 1950 art.14, art.8; Adoption and Children (Scotland) Act 2007 (asp 4); Human Rights Act 1998 (c.42)]

In an action of damages, raised by various family members of a deceased (F), including his adoptive parents, for *inter alia loss* of society and guidance under the Damages (Scotland) Act 2011 s.4(3), a question arose as to whether F's biological half brother (X) and his biological father (Y), as guardian on behalf of F's biological half sister (Z), had title to sue. X and Y submitted that (1) X, and Y as Z's guardian, qualified as F's immediate family members as they fell within s.14 of the 2011 Act, which did not distinguish between the biological and the non-biological; (2) the 2011 Act extinguished the claim of biological parents but did not affect biological siblings; (3) to deny X and Z title to sue but to allow non-biological siblings the right to do so would be discriminatory and incompatible with ECHR art.14 when read with art.8, and the court required to read down and give effect to legislation in a manner compatible with Convention rights.

Held: Action dismissed in so far as relating to Y and Z. (1) In terms of the Adoption and Children (Scotland) Act 2007, for all, or at least most, purposes relating to succession to the deceased person, an adopted person was to be treated as a child of the adopter and not of any other person, the right to sue under the 2011 Act was restricted to the deceased's immediate family, and it was not absurd or unjust that the 2011 Act gave no entitlement to sue to biological members of the family of a deceased who had been adopted, which was consistent with the underlying philosophy of adoption legislation. (2) The Scottish Parliament had clearly been aware of the all embracing effect of the adoption legislation when passing the 2011 Act, the law of adoption was Convention compliant, and Parliament had chosen not to interfere therewith, and the notion that the Human Rights Act 1998 was in play was unsound; accepting X and Y's submission would involve amending, and going against the grain of, the legislation.

FOREMAN v ADVOCATE GENERAL FOR SCOTLAND, [2016] CSOH 94, 2016 S.L.T. 962, J Gordon Reid QC, OH.

EDUCATION

2590 **Additional support needs–Age–Child with autistic spectrum disorder and dyspraxia reaching age of 18–Funding for additional year at independent private school–Reasonable adjustment**

[Equality Act 2010 (c.15) s.6; Education (Additional Support for Learning) (Scotland) Act 2004 (asp 4)]

A local education authority (F) appealed against a sheriff's decision finding that a disabled person (D) within the meaning of the Equality Act 2010 s.6 by reason of autistic spectrum disorder and dyspraxia, was entitled to receive funding for an additional year at an independent private school despite having attained the age of 18, and granting decree of payment in respect thereof (*M v Fife Council* 2014 S.L.T. (Sh Ct) 147, [2014] C.L.Y. 3476). By letter dated 16 April 2013, D's mother (M) had requested a further year of funding for the academic year 2013-2014 on account of D's difficulties with transition. F had refused the request on 23 May, advising that their statutory obligation under the Education (Additional Support for Learning) (Scotland) Act 2004 to provide education for a child came to an end when the child attained 18 years of age. Before the sheriff, D averred that F's decision constituted unlawful discrimination against him contrary to the 2010 Act. The sheriff granted decree for payment to D of £45,910 and £2,500 for the school fees and compensation for injured feelings respectively, finding *inter alia* that F's decision of 23 May was based solely on D's age, F had relied upon a policy, criterion or practice (PCP) in making their decision, it would have been a reasonable adjustment for F to pay the fees, F had failed to take D's disability into account, in implementing the PCP, F had failed to take account of D's disability, and D had accordingly been discriminated against.

Held: Appeal allowed in part. The sheriff was entitled to find that F had discriminated against D but the claim in respect of the payment of the fees had to fail: the central issue was D's transition from school to further education or training and in that respect, F had certain duties, particularly under s.12(5), (6) and (13) of the 2004 Act which the sheriff was entitled to find had not been fulfilled but that, in itself, would not have given rise to a cause for an action for damages in respect of discrimination, it would have been necessary to rely on one or more sections of the 2010 Act; the sheriff had found that it would have been a reasonable adjustment for F to pay D's fees and the duty to make such adjustments was provided in ss.20, 21 and 22 of the 2010 Act and, in relation to a person, such as F, exercising a public function, Sch.2; in D's case, it would be necessary to identify the class of disabled persons to which he belonged and in respect of whom a reasonable adjustment would be the payment of school fees but, on the material before the court, it was not possible to identify such a class of persons in respect of whom it could be said that the payment of fees by way of bursary would be a reasonable adjustment and it was highly unlikely that payment of such fees would ever be capable of applying as a reasonable adjustment in a generic way; the sheriff had treated the requirement to make reasonable adjustment under s.20 as one tailored to D's specific circumstances which left out of account the provisions of Sch.2, and while there had been a breach of duty by F to make reasonable adjustments, that breach would not have given rise to a requirement to pay the fees for a further year; the award in respect of the claim based on compensation for injured feelings would accordingly be affirmed but that in respect of the payment of fees would be quashed. Per Lady Paton, that there was unlawful discrimination against D arising from his disability contrary to s.19 of the 2010 Act, with a failure to make reasonable adjustments contrary to s.20 and while her Ladyship was initially of the view that the sheriff was entitled to make the awards he had, she was persuaded by the reasoning of their Lordships that it was not open to make the award for the school fees payable for the year 2013-2014. *Opinion* per Lords Bracadale and McGhie, that had F dealt with everything properly in May 2013 and treated M's letter as an application for a bursary, a decision that D should not receive one would not have been open to challenge. *Opinion*, per Lord McGhie, that the general approach of the tribunal in *Noor v Foreign and Commonwealth Office* [2011] I.C.R. 695, [2011] C.L.Y. 1059 might be misleading if relied on as a guide to the proper application of the duty to make reasonable adjustments in the context of the 2010 Act, *Noor, considered.*

M v FIFE COUNCIL *sub nom.* DM v FIFE COUNCIL, [2016] CSIH 17, 2016 S.L.T. 489, Lady Paton, Lord Bracadale, Lord McGhie, IH (Ex Div).

2591 Education (Scotland) Act 2016 (asp 15)–Commencement No.2 Regulations

THE EDUCATION (SCOTLAND) ACT 2016 (COMMENCEMENT NO.2) REGULATIONS 2016, SSI 2016/386; made under the Education (Scotland) Act 2016 s.33(2)(3). Commencement details: bringing into operation various provisions of the 2016 Act on 1 January 2017.

These Regulations bring into force the following provisions of the Education (Scotland) Act 2016 for all purposes, unless otherwise stated. Section 7 (assessment requests), in so far as it is not already in force, and ss.8 to 13 (assessments: primary education) are commenced on 1 February 2017. These sections set out the assessment process to be followed by an education authority upon receipt of a parental request under s.7(1) to assess the need for Gaelic medium primary education.

2592 Education (Scotland) Act 2016 (asp 8)

An Act to impose duties in relation to reducing pupils' inequalities of outcome; to modify the Education (Additional Support for Learning) (Scotland) Act 2004 and s.70 of the Education (Scotland) Act 1980; to make provision about Gaelic medium education, about the provision of school meals, for appointing Chief Education Officers and in relation to the registration of independent schools and teachers in grant-aided schools; to extend the duty to provide early learning and childcare to certain children; and for connected purposes.

2593 Education (Scotland) Act 2016 (asp 8)–Commencement No.1 Regulations

THE EDUCATION (SCOTLAND) ACT 2016 (COMMENCEMENT NO.1) REGULATIONS 2016, SSI 2016/192; made under the Education (Scotland) Act 2016 s.32(2)(3). Commencement details: bringing into operation various provisions of the 2016 Act on 15 July 2016.

These Regulations bring into force the following provisions of the Education (Scotland) Act 2016 for all purposes, unless otherwise stated. Section 16 of the 2016 Act, which amends the provision about guidance on Gaelic education in the Gaelic Language (Scotland) Act 2005 s.9, is commenced on 15 July 2016. Section 17 of the 2016 Act, which amends the definition of "Gaelic education" in s.10 of the 2005 Act and which also amends the definition of "Gaelic medium education" in the Schools (Consultation) (Scotland) Act 2010 Sch.1 para 12, is also commenced on 15 July 2016.

2594 Higher Education Governance (Scotland) Act 2016 (asp 15)

An Act of the Scottish Parliament to make provision about the composition of and appointment to the governing bodies and academic boards of higher education institutions; and to revise provision about the academic freedom of various persons carrying out activities at higher education and certain other institutions.

2595 Higher Education Governance (Scotland) Act 2016 (asp 15)–Commencement, Transitory, Transitional and Savings Provisions Regulations

THE HIGHER EDUCATION GOVERNANCE (SCOTLAND) ACT 2016 (COMMENCEMENT, TRANSITORY, TRANSITIONAL AND SAVINGS PROVISIONS) REGULATIONS 2016, SSI 2016/382; made under the Higher Education Governance (Scotland) Act 2016 s.26(2)(3). Commencement details: bringing into operation various provisions of the 2016 Act on 30 December 2016.

These Regulations bring into force for all purposes ss.1, 2, 10 to 25 and the schedule of the Higher Education Governance (Scotland) Act 2016 on 30 December 2016. Sections 3 to 9 of the 2016 Act are commenced by these Regulations on 30 June 2017. These Regulations, therefore, fully commence the 2016 Act.

2596 Placing requests–Additional support needs–Refusal of placing request for child with additional support needs–Ease of transition from nursery to school

[Education (Scotland) Act 1980 (c.44) s.28A(3)(a), s.28D, s.28F, s.28F(6), s.28F(7); Education (Additional Support for Learning) (Scotland) Act 2004 (asp 4) Sch.2, Sch.2 para.7; Convention on the Rights of the Child (United Nations) 1989 art.3(1)]

The parents (P) of a child (J) appealed against a decision of the local education authority (D) refusing their placing request in respect of J. P had sought a place at a primary school (S) where one of their older children was currently educated and which was situated near to the secondary school where their other child (Y) was educated. D had refused M's placing request on the grounds that it would require to employ an additional teacher in terms of the Education (Scotland) Act 1980 s.28A(3)(a)(i) where J's inclusion would take the class size above the limit recommended in Scottish Executive guidance, that accommodating the request would have been likely to give rise to significant expenditure on extending or otherwise altering S in terms of s.28A(3)(a)(ii), and would have been likely to be seriously detrimental to the educational wellbeing of other pupils in terms of s.28A(3)(a)(v). Evidence was led that J had additional support needs and received speech and language therapy, and that should the appeal be allowed, there were 24 other cases which D would come under a duty to review. P sought to amend the basis of their appeal from s.28F of the 1980 Act to an appeal in terms of the Education (Additional Support for Learning) (Scotland) Act 2004 Sch.2.

Held: Appeal allowed. (1) The exceptions in s.28A(3)(a) of the 1980 Act put forward by D had applied and while it was open to the court to allow P's appeal under s.28F of the 1980 Act, there would require to be compelling or exceptional circumstances to justify such a course being taken, and in light of the fact that there were places available for J at another school (X) located 0.1 miles from the family home, and P's logistical argument was not sufficiently compelling as Y could get a bus to school and J could be dropped off at the breakfast club, such circumstances had not been established, however, in an appeal under Sch.2 of the 2004 Act, the review procedure in s.28F(6) and (7) of the 1980 Act did not apply and in those circumstances, the exceptions in s.28A(3)(a)(i), (ii) and (v) had not been established because only J would require to be admitted to S. In any event, it was not appropriate to confirm D's decision on the basis of J's speech and language therapy difficulties, and where J's interests were a primary consideration, it was in his interests to attend S rather than X because he was reserved and had difficulty communicating; in those circumstances, J's transition from nursery to primary school was likely to be easier for him at S rather than X. (2) On the evidence, J was likely to be unable to benefit from school education directed to the development of his personality, talents, and mental and physical abilities to their fullest potential without additional support in the form of speech and language therapy; P's appeal was properly under Sch.2 to the 2004 Act and the amendment would be allowed. (3) Appeal committees set up by an education authority under s.28D of the 1980 Act considered placing request appeals under both the 1980 Act and Sch.2 to the 2004 Act, and regardless of the route by which the appeal might come to the sheriff, his decision on the appeal was final, he was not bound by what had occurred before, and having regard to the court's duty under the Convention on the Rights of the Child 1989 (United Nations) art.3(1), the amendment was competent and any prejudice to D had been adequately dealt with by not finding P entitled to expenses. (4) There had been good cause for P's late appeal under Sch.2 to the 2004 Act where they had not initially understood the significance of J's additional support needs to the potential success of their appeal, they had not engaged a solicitor until appearing before the sheriff, J's interests were a primary consideration under art.3(1) of the 1989 Convention, and the relevant legislation was overly complicated and untested. *Observed*, (1) that legal representatives ought to consider the question of additional support needs at the outset of their clients making a placing request to the education authority; (2) that in cases where there was doubt or dispute that the child had additional support needs, a single appeal by summary application could be made to the sheriff on alternate bases under s.28F(1) of the 1980 Act and para.7(1) of Sch.2 to the 2004 Act.

J'S PARENTS v DUMFRIES AND GALLOWAY COUNCIL, 2015 S.L.T. (Sh Ct) 253, Sheriff G Jamieson, Sh Ct (South Strathclyde) (Dumfries).

2597 School exclusions–Disability discrimination–Boarding school pupil with ADHD excluded for having sexual intercourse with another pupil–Whether tribunal erred in finding pupil not disabled

[Equality Act 2010 (c.15) s.15, s.19, s.20; Additional Support Needs Tribunals for Scotland (Disability Claims Procedure) Rules 2011 (SSI 2011/104)]

The mother (C) of a student (M) who had been excluded from a boarding school (G) after having been found having sexual intercourse with another student on school premises when she was 16 years old, appealed against a decision of the Additional Support Needs Tribunal for Scotland that M was not disabled and thus no question of unlawful discrimination by G arose. M had attention deficit hyperactivity disorder (ADHD) and the claim was presented under the Equality Act 2010. C sought a statement that G had discriminated against M, a written apology and training of school staff and alterations to the school's discipline policy to ensure that no similar incident occurred in future. C submitted that the tribunal had erred in concluding that M was not disabled, they had been too restrictive in their approach, had failed to have regard to both the expert evidence as well as that of C all of which demonstrated that M had a significant problem which had a substantial adverse effect on her day to day functioning, had failed to have regard to appropriate guidance, and had failed to provide a proper analysis together with adequate reasons.

Held: Appeal refused. (1) Not every person with a mental impairment was disabled for the purposes of the 2010 Act, it had to be established that the impairment was at a level which amounted to a substantial and long term adverse effect on normal day to day activities and the onus of so establishing lay firmly on the person claiming, the tribunal was not obliged to make its own inquiries. (2) The tribunal had correctly concluded that it could not take into account the effect of medication where it had no evidence about the likely effect on M of the particular medication in the particular dose prescribed when she was at school and had M a case to make about the effect of the medical treatment, it was for her to do so; further, the tribunal was entitled to prefer the evidence of the deputy principal about M's ability to perform normal day to day activities. (3) There was no proper basis for submitting that the tribunal failed to provide adequate reasons for the conclusion that M was not disabled: the reasons were shortly stated which, in the circumstances, was commendable; the reasons were not incomprehensible but should be considered in context; further, the tribunal was one where, under the Additional Support Needs Tribunals for Scotland (Disability Claims Procedure) Rules 2011, the emphasis was on informality and flexibility where the norm was that decisions were to be issued promptly without elaborate reasons and there was a duty, in terms of the overriding objective as stated in the rules, to deal with cases which were proportionate. *Opinion*, (1) that the tribunal had given cogent reasons for concluding that causation between M having sexual intercourse on the particular occasion and her having ADHD was not established, and it could not be said that, in reaching that conclusion, it had failed to correctly apply the provisions of s.15 of the 2010 Act; (2) that in concluding that expulsion was a proportionate response, the tribunal had identified a legitimate aim, namely the maintenance of standards of discipline and the health, safety and welfare of pupils and whilst they referred to expulsion being the punishment for all pupils found having sex in school, that was not by way of carrying out a comparator exercise but rather it was to emphasise the seriousness with which G regarded such conduct; in any event, proportionality did not require the tribunal to ask whether expulsion could be a proportionate response to the conduct in question, it required to focus on the likely impact on the disabled claimant of the sanction, in respect of which there was no evidence; (3) that it was difficult to understand how the tribunal would have been inclined to find that indirect discrimination had taken place had it been satisfied that M was disabled given that the school's code of conduct was discriminatory in terms of s.19 because its terms did not expressly allow for the impact that disability might have on a pupil's behaviour but there was no evidence that all young people with ADHD found it more difficult to comply with the rule about sexual relationships than those without, further, the code did not state the sanction of expulsion for breach of the rule in express terms; (4) that any finding that there was a duty to make a reasonable adjustment required the provisions of s.20 to be met and required particularity and it could not be said, on the evidence, that a s.20 duty arose; and the tribunal was correct to refrain from finding that the communication to housemates about M's exclusion amounted to unlawful detriment.

C v GORDONSTOUN SCHOOLS LTD, [2016] CSIH 32, 2016 S.L.T. 587, Lady Smith, Lord Brodie, Lord Malcolm, IH (Ex Div).

2598 **Schools–Closure–Proposed closure of four rural schools–Whether local education authority gave special regard to rural factors**

[Schools (Consultation) (Scotland) Act 2010 (asp 2) Sch.1 para.1, s.12(3), s.15(4), s.17B, s.2(1)]

A local education authority (H) appealed against a decision of the school closure review panel (S) refusing to consent to H's proposal to close four rural primary schools and replace them with a single purpose-built school. H had formally advised the Scottish Ministers (M) of its proposal, and M subsequently issued a call-in notice and referred the proposal for review and a decision by S under the Schools (Consultation) (Scotland) Act 2010 s.17B. S held that H had, in terms of s.17B(1), failed in a significant regard to comply with the statutory requirements by failing to have, in terms of s.12(2), special regard to the rural factors set out in s.12(3). H submitted that S had failed to apply the legislation correctly and had exceeded its jurisdiction by assuming to itself the weighing exercise entrusted by statute to H.

Held: Appeal refused. (1) For regard to be special, it had to go further than the norm, and, however it was qualified, it had to involve a conscious directing of the mind to the obligations; in the context of the 2010 Act, the words had only to be given that ordinary meaning to make sense, and the words "significant regard" meant in an important way, *Comhairle Nan Eilean Siar v Scottish Ministers* [2013] CSIH 45, 2013 S.C. 548, [2013] C.L.Y. 3670, 2013 S.L.T. 687, *followed.* (2) S was both entitled and obliged to investigate, weigh and assess the evidence and the particular facts relating to the rural factors in order to determine whether there had been compliance with the statutory requirement, otherwise it could not discharge its statutory function in relation to a proposed rural school closure, *Comhairle Nan Eilean Siar v Scottish Ministers* [2013] CSIH 6, 2013 S.C. 286, [2013] C.L.Y. 3673, 2013 S.L.T. 269, *considered.* (3) S knew the statutory tests it had to apply, and the terms of its decision demonstrated that it had applied them correctly throughout. (4) Given the terms of s.15(4) of the 2010 Act, it was Parliament's intention that S could take into account representations made in the statutory three week period. (5) The proposals to establish the new school and to combine the catchment area of the four existing schools, separately and together, constituted an arrangement of the sort mentioned in para.1(5) of Sch.1 to the 2010 Act, para.1(4) also applied and by virtue of para.1(6), those proposals fell within the scope of para.1(1) to Sch.1 only, and for the purposes of s.2(1) of the 2010 Act each became a closure proposal, and S had accordingly correctly given special regard to viable alternatives thereto. (6) There was no documentary evidence that H had at any relevant time applied any form of regard to the rural factors when considering viable alternatives to closure, which supported S's view that it had not complied with its statutory duty. (7) S had considered all of the issues pertaining to whether H had given special regard to the likely effect on the local community and that caused by different travel arrangements and had been entitled to determine that it had not done so, in breach of its duties under s.12 of the 2010 Act. (8) S's finding that the failures were significant and struck at the heart of the whole consultation process was not challengeable on the facts, and there was no error of law in its decision that the failures were so significant that they could not be resolved by imposing conditions or remitting the case back to H for a fresh decision. *Opinion*, that S had erred in law in finding that H had been required to conduct an explicitly recognisable consultation in respect of nursery closures in furtherance of the closure proposal, and its findings on that matter would be excluded from consideration in their entirety. *Observed*, (1) that the appropriate stage for representations to be made in respect of a closure proposal was during the period after the decision to implement the proposal was taken, in terms of s.15(4) of the 2010 Act; (2) that the s.12(2) requirement for the education authority to have special regard to the rural factors was not confined solely to the consultation period but applied until a decision was taken to implement the closure proposal in full or in part, or it was so implemented.

HIGHLAND COUNCIL v SCHOOL CLOSURE REVIEW PANEL, 2016 S.L.T. (Sh Ct) 207, Sheriff J K Tierney, Sh Ct (Grampian) (Portree).

2599 Student loans–Age discrimination–Age limit in reg.3(2)(b)(ii) Education (Student Loans) (Scotland) Regulations 2007–Compatibility with art.14 ECHR read with Protocol 1 art.2

[Education (Student Loans) (Scotland) Regulations 2007 (SSI 2007/154) reg.3, reg.3(2)(b)(ii); European Convention on Human Rights 1950 Protocol 1 art.1, Protocol 1 art.2, art.14; Equality Act 2010 (c.15) s.149; Scotland Act 1998 (c.46) s.100(1), s.102(2); Education (Fees, Awards and Student Support) (Miscellaneous Amendments) (Scotland) Regulations 2012 (SSI 2012/72)]

A student (H), aged 56, petitioned for judicial review of the refusal of the Student Awards Agency for Scotland (S) of her application for a student loan under the Education (Student Loans) (Scotland) Regulations 2007 on the basis that such loans were restricted to persons aged under 55 in terms of reg.3(2)(b)(ii). H claimed that the decision, and the regulations, unlawfully discriminated against her in violation of ECHR art.14 along with either Protocol 1 art.1 or Protocol 1 art.2, and that the Scottish Ministers (M) had failed to assess the discriminatory effects of the 2007 Regulations as regarded age and had thereby acted in breach of the duty imposed by the Equality Act 2010 s.149. H sought the loan to fund her living expenses while she undertook a year long HNC course, having been in receipt of a college bursary in relation college courses undertaken between 2011 and 2014, which had assisted with, but had not covered, her living and travelling expenses.

Held: Case put out by order. (1) The purpose of Protocol 1 art.1 was to protect the right to property and to have the use of possessions, and although given a broad interpretation, it did not extend to a right to acquire something someone did not already have, regardless of the interest of the individual in doing so; whilst H had an interest in obtaining the loan, and but for the disputed condition she was eligible, she was only otherwise qualified to apply therefor, it was not a welfare benefit as of right, she had no enforceable claim thereto, and her application therefor did not amount to a substantive interest or possession protected by, and therefore within the ambit of, Protocol 1 art.1, *Stec v United Kingdom (Admissibility) (65731/01)* (2005) 41 E.H.R.R. SE18, *considered*. (2) Protocol 1 art.2 conveyed express and direct protection to education, the 2007 Regulations had been made to encourage greater access to higher education, primarily for those wishing to improve their skills and qualifications, and the provision made for the loan was designed to further that purpose, which provided a clear link to the ambit of Protocol 1 art.2; there was clear authority that the requirement to pay tuition fees fell within the ambit of Protocol 1 art.2, there was no distinction to be drawn between student loans which supported payment of fees and those which paid living expenses as the purpose of both was to secure practical and effective access to the education provided, the absence of living support would render the right to education illusory, the requirement for that support was recognised in the 2007 Regulations, which reg.3(2) intended to address, and the student loan fell within the ambit of Protocol 1 art.2. (3) The test for justification of infringement of an ECHR right of "manifestly without foundation" derived from decisions where the European Court of

Human Rights had considered that a wide margin of appreciation ought to be allowed to Member States in relation to general measures of political, economic or social strategy, and the same test had been applied domestically but confined to cases concerning welfare benefits and national security policy, however, education was different in that it enjoyed direct protection under the Convention, and in the context of the significance of right to education, at the stage of justification, the question of proportionality had to be a straightforward question of law for the court, *Ponomaryov v Bulgaria (5335/05)* (2014) 59 E.H.R.R. 20 and *R. (on the application of Tigere) v Secretary of State for Business, Innovation and Skills* [2015] UKSC 57, [2015] 1 W.L.R. 3820, [2015] C.L.Y. 758, *considered.* (4) The primary purpose of student loans, namely to encourage greater access to higher education, was a legitimate aim, however, an aim of the 2007 Regulations to seek to encourage younger people to enter the workforce, which was a legitimate objective and in which context a cut off age of 55 was rationally connected thereto, was not the agreed primary purpose, where the state pension age had been raised to 67, it could not be assumed, absent objective support, that a person aged 55, with 12 years' working life, had much less opportunity for employment or that any such employment was liable to be so short as to significantly reduce the prospects of repayment of the loan, the regulations provided protection for finite resources elsewhere, which weakened the requirement for the age limit, and there was not a sufficiently clear and rational connection between the age limit in reg.3(2)(b)(ii) and the primary aim of encouraging access to education, and reviewing the relevant regulations in the round, it could not be said that there was no less intrusive measure which could be employed, and a fair balance had not been achieved, accordingly, reg.3(2) was not proportionate and the decision made in applying it to H had been in violation of her art.14 right, *Bank Mellat v HM Treasury* [2013] UKSC 38, [2014] A.C. 700, [2014] C.L.Y. 48, *applied.* (5) Even with the strong interpretative duty under the Scotland Act 1998 s.100(1), it would not be possible to read reg.3(2)(b) in a manner other than that those aged 55 or over were not eligible for a maintenance loan, thus it was incompatible with art.14 and as such was *ultra vires*, and, acceding to S's request, the court would suspend the effect of its findings and order a further hearing to address the court's powers under s.102(2) of the 1998 Act and the orders, if any, that the court should make to deal with the consequences. (6) There were grounds to believe that issues had arisen which triggered the duty under s.149 of the 2010 Act, in particular the implementation in 2012 of amendments to the 2007 Regulations by the Education (Fees, Awards and Student Support) (Miscellaneous Amendments) (Scotland) Regulations 2012, particularly to reg.3 of the 2007 Regulations disapplying the age limits in relation to eligibility for tuition fee loans of students of certain vocational courses, and declarator of said failure fell to be pronounced, *R. (on the application of Bapio Action Ltd) v Royal College of General Practitioners* [2014] EWHC 1416 (Admin), [2014] Eq. L.R. 409, [2014] C.L.Y. 1509, *considered.*

HUNTER v STUDENT AWARDS AGENCY FOR SCOTLAND, [2016] CSOH 71, 2016 S.L.T. 653, Lady Scott, OH.

ELECTORAL PROCESS

2600 **Absent voting–Local government elections**

THE REPRESENTATION OF THE PEOPLE (ABSENT VOTING AT LOCAL GOVERNMENT ELECTIONS) (SCOTLAND) AMENDMENT (NO.2) REGULATIONS 2016, SSI 2016/264; made under the Local Electoral Administration and Registration Services (Scotland) Act 2006 s.33, s.61(2). In force: 1 December 2016.

These Regulations amend the Representation of the People (Absent Voting at Local Government Elections) (Scotland) Regulations 2007 ("the 2007 Regulations"). Regulation 3 makes provision in relation to additional requirements for a proxy vote at a particular election. Regulation 4 inserts into the 2007 Regulations new regulations dealing with notification of a rejected postal voting statement and a requirement to provide fresh signatures following rejection of such a statement.

2601 Election candidates–False statements–Whether false statement in relation to personal character or conduct

[Representation of the People Act 1983 (c.2) s.106]

Constituents (M) of Orkney and Shetland petitioned the election court seeking to have a Liberal Democrat candidate (C), the then Secretary of Scotland, who had won the vote in their constituency at the 2015 general election, proved to have committed an illegal practice in terms of the Representation of the People Act 1983 s.106, that the court should determine that C was not duly elected and that his election was void (2015 S.L.T. 675). The petition alleged that during a general election, in which C was a candidate, he had been directly involved in the leak of a memorandum from the Scotland Office to the press, and having deliberately told untruths in that regard and concealed his role in the leak, had made an admittedly false statement of fact in relation to his personal character as a candidate in terms of s.106(1). After a preliminary legal debate, the court put the case out by order and ordered that evidence be led to assist in the resolution of the two remaining issues, namely, (i) whether the words complained of in the petition amounted to "false statements of fact ... in relation to the personal character or conduct" of C within the meaning of s.106 and, (ii) whether the words complained of were uttered "for the purpose of affecting the return of any candidate at the election". At a by order hearing counsel agreed that the onus of proof lay upon M, and that the standard of proof to be applied was the criminal standard of beyond reasonable doubt.

Held: Petition dismissed. (1) It was a crucial part of the offence in terms of s.106 that the false statement be "in relation to ... personal character or conduct" and, on this matter, the court was left with a reasonable doubt and in so far as the issue was a legal one, or rather a question of mixed fact and law, the court was not persuaded that the false statement proved to have been made was in relation to anything other than C's awareness, or lack thereof, of a political machination; even if the court were to apply a lesser standard of proof the court would not be satisfied that C had been proved to have made a false statement of fact in relation to his personal character or conduct in the course of an interview bearing in mind the desirability of a strict interpretation of s.106, *R. (on the application of Woolas) v Parliamentary Election Court* [2010] EWHC 3169 (Admin), [2012] Q.B. 1, [2011] C.L.Y. 59 [2012] Q.B. 1, *considered.* (2) The court was satisfied that the false statement of fact was made for the purpose of positively affecting C's return as a Liberal Democrat in the constituency of Orkney and Shetland and the evidence further established that there was another purpose underlying the false statement, namely a desire not to be identified as being involved in the leak. (3) M was entitled to explore C's response to the Cabinet Office inquiry, despite the lack of detailed averments thereon, given that it was a matter peculiarly within C's knowledge and M had no way of discovering, prior to the court hearing, the details which emerged during evidence and further, the proceedings in an election petition and answers were sui generis and as an election petition had to be presented to the Court of Session, it was necessary to have some rules of court governing procedure but those rules did not result in the imposition of the strict rules of relevancy and specification applicable to ordinary actions raised in the Court of Session or sheriff court. The relevant evidence demonstrated that C's role in, and response to, the inquiry were unimpressive and his approach was at best disingenuous and at worst, evasive and self serving, although that did not alter the conclusion that s.106 did not, on a proper application of the law to the facts proved, apply.

MORRISON v CARMICHAEL, 2016 S.L.T. 163, Lady Paton, Lord Matthews, IH.

2602 Local elections–Boundaries–Aberdeen

THE ABERDEEN CITY (ELECTORAL ARRANGEMENTS) ORDER 2016, SSI 2016/265; made under the Local Government (Scotland) Act 1973 s.17(2). In force: 30 September 2016.

This Order gives effect to proposals made by the Local Government Boundary Commission for Scotland for the future electoral arrangements for the area of Aberdeen City Council.

2603 **Local elections–Boundaries–Aberdeenshire**

THE ABERDEENSHIRE (ELECTORAL ARRANGEMENTS) ORDER 2016, SSI 2016/266; made under the Local Government (Scotland) Act 1973 s.17(2). In force: 30 September 2016.

This Order gives effect to proposals made by the Local Government Boundary Commission for Scotland for the future electoral arrangements for the area of Aberdeenshire Council.

2604 **Local elections–Boundaries–Angus**

THE ANGUS (ELECTORAL ARRANGEMENTS) ORDER 2016, SSI 2016/267; made under the Local Government (Scotland) Act 1973 s.17(2). In force: 30 September 2016.

This Order gives effect to proposals made by the Local Government Boundary Commission for Scotland for the future electoral arrangements for the area of Angus Council.

2605 **Local elections–Boundaries–Clackmannanshire**

THE CLACKMANNANSHIRE (ELECTORAL ARRANGEMENTS) ORDER 2016, SSI 2016/268; made under the Local Government (Scotland) Act 1973 s.17(2). In force: 30 September 2016.

This Order gives effect to proposals made by the Local Government Boundary Commission for Scotland for the future electoral arrangements for the area of Clackmannanshire Council.

2606 **Local elections–Boundaries–Dumfries and Galloway**

THE DUMFRIES AND GALLOWAY (ELECTORAL ARRANGEMENTS) ORDER 2016, SSI 2016/269; made under the Local Government (Scotland) Act 1973 s.17(2). In force: 30 September 2016.

This Order gives effect to proposals made by the Local Government Boundary Commission for Scotland for the future electoral arrangements for the area of Dumfries and Galloway Council.

2607 **Local elections–Boundaries–East Ayrshire**

THE EAST AYRSHIRE (ELECTORAL ARRANGEMENTS) ORDER 2016, SSI 2016/271; made under the Local Government (Scotland) Act 1973 s.17(2). In force: 30 September 2016.

This Order gives effect to proposals made by the Local Government Boundary Commission for Scotland for the future electoral arrangements for the area of East Ayrshire Council.

2608 **Local elections–Boundaries–East Dunbartonshire**

THE EAST DUNBARTONSHIRE (ELECTORAL ARRANGEMENTS) ORDER 2016, SSI 2016/272; made under the Local Government (Scotland) Act 1973 s.17(2). In force: 30 September 2016.

This Order gives effect to proposals made by the Local Government Boundary Commission for Scotland for the future electoral arrangements for the area of East Dunbartonshire Council.

2609 **Local elections–Boundaries–East Lothian**

THE EAST LOTHIAN (ELECTORAL ARRANGEMENTS) ORDER 2016, SSI 2016/273; made under the Local Government (Scotland) Act 1973 s.17(2). In force: 30 September 2016.

This Order gives effect to proposals made by the Local Government Boundary Commission for Scotland for the future electoral arrangements for the area of East Lothian Council.

2610 Local elections–Boundaries–East Renfrewshire

THE EAST RENFREWSHIRE (ELECTORAL ARRANGEMENTS) ORDER 2016, SSI 2016/274; made under the Local Government (Scotland) Act 1973 s.17(2). In force: 30 September 2016.

This Order gives effect to proposals made by the Local Government Boundary Commission for Scotland for the future electoral arrangements for the area of East Renfrewshire Council.

2611 Local elections–Boundaries–Edinburgh

THE CITY OF EDINBURGH (ELECTORAL ARRANGEMENTS) ORDER 2016, SSI 2016/270; made under the Local Government (Scotland) Act 1973 s.17(2). In force: 30 September 2016.

This Order gives effect to proposals made by the Local Government Boundary Commission for Scotland for the future electoral arrangements for the area of City of Edinburgh Council.

2612 Local elections–Boundaries–Falkirk

THE FALKIRK (ELECTORAL ARRANGEMENTS) ORDER 2016, SSI 2016/275; made under the Local Government (Scotland) Act 1973 s.17(2). In force: 30 September 2016.

This Order gives effect to proposals made by the Local Government Boundary Commission for Scotland for the future electoral arrangements for the area of Falkirk Council.

2613 Local elections–Boundaries–Fife

THE FIFE (ELECTORAL ARRANGEMENTS) ORDER 2016, SSI 2016/276; made under the Local Government (Scotland) Act 1973 s.17(2). In force: 30 September 2016.

This Order gives effect to proposals made by the Local Government Boundary Commission for Scotland for the future electoral arrangements for the area of Fife Council.

2614 Local elections–Boundaries–Glasgow

THE GLASGOW CITY (ELECTORAL ARRANGEMENTS) ORDER 2016, SSI 2016/277; made under the Local Government (Scotland) Act 1973 s.17(2). In force: 30 September 2016.

This Order gives effect to proposals made by the Local Government Boundary Commission for Scotland for the future electoral arrangements for the area of Glasgow City Council.

2615 Local elections–Boundaries–Inverclyde

THE INVERCLYDE (ELECTORAL ARRANGEMENTS) ORDER 2016, SSI 2016/279; made under the Local Government (Scotland) Act 1973 s.17(2). In force: 30 September 2016.

This Order gives effect to proposals made by the Local Government Boundary Commission for Scotland for the future electoral arrangements for the area of Inverclyde Council.

2616 Local elections–Boundaries–Local Government Boundary Commission for Scotland

THE HIGHLAND (ELECTORAL ARRANGEMENTS) ORDER 2016, SSI 2016/278; made under the Local Government (Scotland) Act 1973 s.17(2). In force: 30 September 2016.

This Order gives effect to proposals made by the Local Government Boundary Commission for Scotland for the future electoral arrangements for the area of Highland Council.

2617 **Local elections–Boundaries–Midlothian**

THE MIDLOTHIAN (ELECTORAL ARRANGEMENTS) ORDER 2016, SSI 2016/280; made under the Local Government (Scotland) Act 1973 s.17(2). In force: 30 September 2016.

This Order gives effect to proposals made by the Local Government Boundary Commission for Scotland for the future electoral arrangements for the area of Midlothian Council.

2618 **Local elections–Campaign expenditure**

THE REPRESENTATION OF THE PEOPLE (VARIATION OF LIMIT OF CANDIDATES' LOCAL GOVERNMENT ELECTION EXPENSES) (SCOTLAND) ORDER 2016, SSI 2016/263; made under the Representation of the People Act 1983 s.76A(1). In force: 1 November 2016.

This Order increases the maximum amount of candidates' election expenses at local government elections. The maximum amount of a candidate's election expenses is made up of a fixed amount (currently £705) plus the sum of 6p for each entry in the register of electors. This Order increases the fixed amount so that it will now be £740.

2619 **Local elections–Campaign expenditure–Exemptions**

THE SCOTTISH LOCAL GOVERNMENT ELECTIONS AMENDMENT (NO.2) ORDER 2016, SSI 2016/354; made under the Local Governance (Scotland) Act 2004 s.3(1), s.16(2)(3). In force: 8 November 2016.

Articles 3 to 5 of this Order make various amendments to the Scottish Local Government Elections Order 2011. Article 6 inserts into s.76 of the Representation of the People Act 1983 a new subsection (5A) so that certain personal expenses of a candidate at a local government election do not require to be included for the purposes of the maximum amount specified in that section. The changes made by this Order apply in relation to the local government elections due to be held on 4 May 2017 and subsequent elections.

2620 **Local elections–Electoral arrangements–South Lanarkshire**

THE SOUTH LANARKSHIRE (ELECTORAL ARRANGEMENTS) ORDER 2016, SSI 2016/287; made under the Local Government (Scotland) Act 1973 s.17(2). In force: 30 September 2016.

This Order gives effect to proposals made by the Local Government Boundary Commission for Scotland for the future electoral arrangements for the area of South Lanarkshire Council.

2621 **Local elections–Local government elections–Postal voting**

THE REPRESENTATION OF THE PEOPLE (POSTAL VOTING FOR LOCAL GOVERNMENT ELECTIONS) (SCOTLAND) AMENDMENT REGULATIONS 2016, SSI 2016/353; made under the Representation of the People Act 1983 s.53(1)(c)(3), Sch.2. In force: 8 November 2016.

These Regulations make various amendments to the Representation of the People (Postal Voting for Local Government Elections) (Scotland) Regulations 2007 which apply in relation to the local government elections due to be held on 4 May 2017 and subsequent elections.

EMPLOYMENT

2622 **Part-time workers–Less favourable treatment–Part-time clerk to general commissioners of income tax–Pension provision**

[Taxes Management Act 1970 (c.9) s.3(3); Part-time Workers (Prevention of Less Favourable Treatment) Regulations 2000 (SI 2000/1551) reg.1, reg.2, reg.2(1), reg.5, reg.8(8); Directive 75/117 on the application of the principle of equal pay for men and women 1975]

The Advocate General (S), representing the Secretary of State for Scotland, the Ministry of Justice (M) and Her Majesty's Courts and Tribunals Service, appealed against a decision of the employment appeal tribunal (T) finding that a part time clerk to the general commissioners of income tax (B) had been treated less favourably than a comparable full time clerk (H) regarding pension provision. H had worked for three and a half days per week, he had retired in November 2001 and had received a pension on the basis that he had devoted substantially the whole of his time to the duties of the office, in terms of the Taxes Management Act 1970 s.3(3), and that his predecessor had received a pension on a similar workload. B had worked for four hours per week and in 2008, he had applied for a pension, relying on *inter alia* the Part-time Workers (Prevention of Less Favourable Treatment) Regulations 2000 and Directive 75/117. His application had been refused on the basis that he could not be classed as full time within the meaning of s.3(3) of the 1970 Act where *inter alia* he had failed to identify a full time comparator. M subsequently published a policy document, which was agreed to have been the policy applied when B's application had been refused, prescribing the method for determining clerks' pension entitlement which provided *inter alia* that the threshold of 70% used in previous claims would be retained and only claims which had passed that threshold would move to stage two. T thereafter upheld B's appeal on the basis that, having regard to the Directive and the 2000 Regulations and applying *Marleasing SA v La Comercial Internacional de Alimentacion SA (C-106/89)* EU:C:1990:395, [1990] E.C.R. I-4135, offering a pension to a full time worker but denying such to a part time worker was discriminatory and the 1970 Act required to be read down by omitting the words "full time", B had been treated unfairly when M's policy had been decided, H had been employed at that time and he was therefore a valid comparator, and B had been unlawfully treated less favourably than a full time comparator in a manner that fell within reg.5(1)(b). The case was remitted to the employment tribunal (E) to consider a remedy. S submitted *inter alia* that (1) before the *Marleasing* principle was applied, the whole terms of the relevant parent directive had to be considered and in the present case that showed that the possibility of the less favourable treatment being justified and lawful was central to both it and the 2000 Regulations; (2) even were the *Marleasing* principle applicable, references to "full time" did not require to be removed from s.3(3) of the 1970 Act where to do so would be outwith appropriate limits, go against the grain of the legislation and distort the domestic law; (3) T had been wrong to remit the case to E for a hearing only on remedy where that had deprived S of the opportunity to show that B's treatment had been fair; (4) B had been refused a pension because he had not been a full time worker within the meaning of s.3(3) of the 1970 Act and not because he had been part time; (5) H was not a valid comparator where his employment had terminated prior to B's application.

Held: Appeal upheld. (1) B had failed to establish that H was a full time worker where he had relied solely on the fact that H had passed stage one in M's policy and had been treated for the purposes of s.3(3) of the 1970 Act as a full time clerk, that had not demonstrated that H was identifiable as a full time worker in terms of reg.2(1) of the 2000 Regulations, his part time worker status was unaffected by the policy and by the implementation of the policy in his favour and the sole issue had been whether B could bring himself within the terms of s.3(3) of the 1970 Act. (2) Section 3(3) did not provide for different treatment to be afforded to full time and part time workers, it solely concerned clerks, T's proposed redraft of the statutory provisions wholly undermined the clear intention of Parliament and the rewriting involved therein was so fundamental and distorted the primary domestic legislation such that it was not an appropriate application of the *Marleasing* principle, *Marleasing, considered.* (3) Had H been a valid comparator, B's claim would have been limited to the period between the coming into force of the 2000 Regulations and his retiral in 2009 and restricted to the value of employers' contributions that would have been paid during that period, had he been entitled to a pension, where, on a proper interpretation of regs 1(2) and 2(4) of the 2000 Regulations, H would have ceased to be a relevant comparator on retiral and comparability depended on relevant contemporaneous employment, and even had H been a valid comparator, the remit to T ought not to have been restricted to remedy or on the basis that reg.8(8) applied; the issues of whether or not B had received less favourable treatment on the ground that he was a part time worker, what that less favourable treatment amounted to and whether any such treatment was justified on objective grounds, had remained to be determined and ought not to have been prejudged. *Observed*, that there were limits to what the court might do to amend the expressed will of Parliament as set out in its legislation and care had to be taken to ensure that the court did not legislate under the guise of reading down, *Department of Constitutional Affairs v O'Brien* [2013] UKSC 6, [2013] 1 W.L.R. 522, [2013] C.L.Y. 998, *considered*.

BARTON v SECRETARY OF STATE FOR SCOTLAND *sub nom.* ADVOCATE GENERAL FOR SCOTLAND v BARTON; ADVOCATE GENERAL FOR SCOTLAND, APPELLANT, [2015] CSIH 92, 2016 S.L.T. 449, Lady Smith, Lord Drummond Young, Lady Clark of Calton, IH (Ex Div).

ENVIRONMENT

2623 Climate Change–Greenhouse gas emissions–Annual targets

THE CLIMATE CHANGE (ANNUAL TARGETS) (SCOTLAND) ORDER 2016, SSI 2016/328; made under the Climate Change (Scotland) Act 2009 s.4(1). In force: 28 October 2016.

For the purposes of Pt.1 of the Climate Change (Scotland) Act 2009, this Order sets annual emission reduction targets for each year in the period 2028-2032. The Scottish Ministers make the following Order in exercise of the powers conferred by s.4(1) of the Climate Change (Scotland) Act 2009(1) and all other powers enabling them to do so.

2624 Environment–Conservation–Salmon conservation

THE TWEED REGULATION (SALMON CONSERVATION) (NO.2) ORDER 2016, SSI 2016/391; made under the Scotland Act 1998 (River Tweed) Order 2006 (SI 2006 2913) art.54(1)(6)(c) , Sch.2 para.5(b), Sch.2 para.12(1). In force: 1 April 2017.

This Order makes provision to regulate the taking of salmon in the Tweed district. The Tweed district is defined in the Scotland Act 1998 (River Tweed) Order 2006 art.2. This Order places the Scottish Ministers under a duty to make, or make arrangements for, an assessment of the conservation status of salmon in the areas within the district described in art.2(1). Article 4 provides that the Scottish Ministers may agree a conservation plan with the River Tweed Commission.

2625 Environment–Financial assistance–Scottish Ministers

THE FINANCIAL ASSISTANCE FOR ENVIRONMENTAL PURPOSES (SCOTLAND) ORDER 2016, SSI 2016/406; made under the Environmental Protection Act 1990 s.153(4). In force: 1 February 2017.

This Order varies the Environmental Protection Act 1990 s.153(1) to add any programme of measures to achieve, in relation to a body of water, environmental objectives of the kind that may be set under the Water Environment and Water Services (Scotland) Act 2003 Pt 1 or the Water Environment (Water Framework Directive) (Solway Tweed River Basin District) Regulations 2004 Sch.1. This will enable the Scottish Ministers to give financial assistance for the purposes of any such programme of measures.

2626 Environmental protection–Contaminated land

THE WATER ENVIRONMENT (AMENDMENT OF PART IIA OF THE ENVIRONMENTAL PROTECTION ACT 1990: CONTAMINATED LAND) (SCOTLAND) REGULATIONS 2016, SSI 2016/99; made under the Water Environment and Water Services (Scotland) Act 2003 s.20, s.36(2)(3). In force: 8 March 2016.

These Regulations amend the Environmental Protection Act 1990 s78YB by substituting a new subsection (1A) into that provision. This new subsection sets out the circumstances in which a remediation notice under Part IIA of that Act (contaminated land) may not be served where the Water Environment (Controlled Activities) (Scotland) Regulations 2011 apply.

2627 Greenhouse gas emissions–Climate change–Limit on use of carbon units

THE CLIMATE CHANGE (LIMIT ON USE OF CARBON UNITS) (SCOTLAND) ORDER 2016, SSI 2016/330; made under the Climate Change (Scotland) Act 2009 s.21(1)(4). In force: 28 October 2016.

For the purposes of the Climate Change (Scotland) Act 2009 Pt 1, this Order sets a limit of zero on the net amount of carbon units that may be credited to net Scottish emissions accounts during the period 2018-2022. It also provides that carbon units credited to or debited from the net Scottish emissions account as a result of the operation of the European Union emission trading scheme in accordance with the Carbon Accounting Scheme (Scotland) Regulations 2010 do not count towards that zero limit.

2628 Marine conservation orders–Marine protected areas–Special Protection Areas

THE LOCH SUNART TO THE SOUND OF JURA MARINE CONSERVATION ORDER 2016, SSI 2016/90; made under the Marine (Scotland) Act 2010 s.85(1)(a)(d)(2)(4), s.86(1)(3), s.92(1)(5); Inshore Fishing (Scotland) Act 1984 s.1 , s.2A. In force: 23 March 2016.

This Order furthers the stated conservation objectives for the Loch Sunart to the Sound of Jura Marine Protected Areas insofar as they relate to common skate and protects the Firth of Lorn Special Area of Conservation in respect of reefs.

2629 Marine conservation orders–Wester Ross Marine Protected Areas

THE WESTER ROSS MARINE CONSERVATION ORDER 2016, SSI 2016/88; made under the Inshore Fishing (Scotland) Act 1984 s.1, s.2A; Marine (Scotland) Act 2010 s.85(1)(a)(2)(4), s.86(1)(3), s.88(1)(2), s.92(1)(5). In force: 23 March 2016.

This Order furthers the stated conservation objectives for the Wester Ross Marine Protected Areas insofar as they relate to burrowed mud, circalittoral muddy sand communities, flame shell beds, kelp and seaweed communities on sublittoral sediment, maerl beds, maerl or coarse shell gravel with burrowing sea cucumbers and northern feather star aggregations on mixed substrata.

2630 Smoke control areas–Authorised fuels–Revocation

THE SMOKE CONTROL AREAS (AUTHORISED FUELS) (SCOTLAND) REVOCATION REGULATIONS 2016, SSI 2016/293; made under the Clean Air Act 1993 s.20(6). In force: 31 October 2016.

These Regulations revoke the Smoke Control Areas (Authorised Fuels) (Scotland) Regulations 2014 which declared specified fuels to be authorised fuels for the purposes of the Clean Air Act 1993 Pt III.

2631 Smoke control areas–Prohibition–Exemptions

THE SMOKE CONTROL AREAS (EXEMPTED FIREPLACES) (SCOTLAND) REVOCATION ORDER 2016, SSI 2016/292; made under the Clean Air Act 1993 s.21(5). In force: 31 October 2016.

This Order revokes the Smoke Control Areas (Exempted Fireplaces) (Scotland) Order 2014 which made provision for certain fireplaces to be exempted from the prohibition, under the Clean Air Act 1993 s.20, of the emission of smoke in smoke control areas.

ENVIRONMENTAL HEALTH

2632 Burial and Cremation (Scotland) Act 2016 (asp 20)

An Act of the Scottish Parliament to restate and amend the law relating to burial and cremation; to make provision about exhumation of human remains; to make provision in relation to the inspection and licensing of funeral directors; and for connected purposes.

EXTRADITION

2633 **European arrest warrants–Right to respect for private and family life–Mother convicted of drug trafficking in Germany–Child suffering from acute lymphoblastic leukemia–Interference with art.8 rights**

[European Convention on Human Rights 1950 art.8]

The Lord Advocate made an application for M's extradition to Germany in compliance with a European arrest warrant issued by the German authorities following M's conviction for drug trafficking there. On 7 October 2005, M had been sentenced to 40 months' imprisonment by a German District Court for drug trafficking, and had been summoned to prison in early 2006 but had failed to appear. A domestic German arrest warrant was issued in April 2006 but M could not be traced and on 7 August, a European arrest warrant was issued. M and her German citizen husband (P) had fled with their two children to the United Kingdom in 2006. M and H were physically estranged but lived together with their now five children (C), aged between three and 17, the oldest of whom (O) had self harmed in the past, and the second youngest of whom (J), aged six, suffered from acute lymphoblastic leukemia, diagnosed in May 2014 and with treatment to continue until October 2017. Evidence was led *inter alia* that P had minimal involvement in C's care, which he left almost entirely to M, O had difficulties relating to P, J required constant monitoring and home treatment as well as frequent hospital visits, and had no understanding of his condition, M had been taught by the hospital how to administer his medications and was able to deal with the side effects they caused in J, and M and J had developed an intense physical dependency and an emotional bond, P had little or no understanding or appreciation of J's condition, he had been assessed by the hospital as unable to, and incapable of, providing the high level of care J required, neither M nor P had a kinship network in Scotland, and were M absent, J would require to be taken into care, which would have a profound, negative and possibly irrepairable, effect on him.

Held: European arrest warrant discharged. (1) In respect of P, O, and the three other children, no exceptionally compelling feature had been established on the facts which would justify the court holding that their right to a family life, either taken alone or in conjunction with each other, was capable of outweighing the strong public interest in returning a convicted criminal to serve a lawful sentence; the necessary interference with their ECHR art.8 rights which M's extradition would cause was proportionate given the strong public interest engaged. (2) There was an exceptionally compelling feature established from the facts in respect of J; M and J's rights were inextricably intertwined and J was deeply emotionally and psychologically bonded with M, and taking account of J's present need and best interests, they weighed significantly in the balance against the UK public interest in being seen to honour reciprocal treaty obligations; were M removed it would have devastating psychological consequences for J, it would constitute a radical and serious alteration of his treatment plan by the removal of a significant care provider and emotional support to whom he was deeply bonded, resulting in damaging, and possibly irrepairable, psychological consequences, and it would amount to a significant interference with his art.8 rights. (3) M's criminality, although not insignificant, had been amateur and on only one occasion, and where M was core to, if not entirely, J's family life, on balance, M's extradition to Germany to serve her sentence of imprisonment would constitute an unjustified and disproportionate interference with M and J's right to a family life together and would accordingly be incompatible with their art.8 rights, *Norris v United States* [2010] UKSC 9, [2010] 2 A.C. 487, [2010] C.L.Y. 1266, *R. (on the application of HH) v Westminster City Magistrates' Court* [2012] UKSC 25, [2013] 1 A.C. 338, [2012] C.L.Y. 1293, *Poland v Celinski* [2015] EWHC 1274 (Admin), [2016] 1 W.L.R. 551, [2016] 797, *considered* and *H v Lord Advocate* [2012] UKSC 24, [2013] 1 A.C. 413, [2012] C.L.Y. 1289, *applied*. Opinion, that extraditees and those representing them ought to be mindful of the rare and exceptional circumstances uniquely demonstrated in the present case.

LORD ADVOCATE v M, 2016 S.L.T. (Sh Ct) 129, Sheriff T Welsh, QC, Sh Ct (Lothian) (Edinburgh).

2634 Extradition orders–Inhuman or degrading treatment or punishment–Prison conditions in Taiwan

[Extradition Act 2003 (c.41) s.103, s.108; European Convention on Human Rights 1950 art.3]

An appeal by a British citizen (D) under the Extradition Act 2003 ss.103 and 108 against a decision of the Scottish Ministers (S) ordering his extradition to Taiwan, came before the Appeal Court of three judges for an evidential hearing in relation to whether the conditions in which D would be held in Taipei prison (P) were compliant with ECHR art.3. In 2011, D had been convicted in Taiwan of drink driving, negligent manslaughter and leaving the scene of an accident and had been sentenced to four years' imprisonment. He had thereafter absconded to Scotland. D referred to various Taiwanese and British, articles, reports, reviews and news items regarding prison conditions in Taiwan and gave evidence that there were systemic problems within P, including overcrowding, understaffing, bullying, sexual abuse and violence and insufficient medical facilities, as well as D's notoriety where his story had been widely publicised in Taiwan and in which he had been portrayed in an extremely negative light. A memorandum of understanding had been entered into between the Home Office and the judicial authorities of Taiwan and the Taiwanese authorities had given undertakings *inter alia* that D's safety in P would be assured by pre-screening inmates to select non-violent ones and to remove those with ill intent towards him, managing his care as a special case and if necessary separating him, providing additional prison staff and surveillance equipment, and that he would not be housed in P's main detention building but would share a special cell with one other prisoner in a different building with a bed and shower and toilet facilities and would be afforded an hour of solitary open air exercise per day. S led evidence from two expert witnesses *inter alia* that Taiwan had adopted the principle set out in art.3 of the ECHR and was attempting to conform to international human rights standards, and that the conditions in which D would be held in P would be safe and art.3 compliant.

Held: Appeal allowed and extradition order quashed (Lord Drummond Young, dissenting). (1) Little was known in the UK about prison conditions in Taiwan and there was no established UK or international system whereby those conditions were monitored; the evidence would be considered on the hypothesis that every effort would be made by the Taiwanese authorities and their prison staff to fulfil all assurances given. (2) It was beyond reasonable doubt, with regard to the corroborated evidence, that the main detention building in P suffered from gross overcrowding, significant understaffing, problems of unchecked and uncontrolled abuse and bullying, inadequate ventilation and toilet facilities and inadequate opportunities for prisoners to exercise in the open air, and further that D and his past offending behaviour had received such widespread adverse publicity in Taiwan that he was at particular risk of being the focus of hostility from prisoners within P, therefore, were he to be housed in the standard conditions in P's main detention building, substantial grounds had been shown for believing that there was a real risk of treatment incompatible with art.3. (3) Special arrangements for D in P would be viewed by its prison community and by the Taiwanese public as wholly exceptional and his being so favoured by the authorities would cause significant animosity amongst other prisoners, which would be highly disadvantageous for D given that he was already notorious and unpopular in Taiwan, it was obvious that the special cell and conditions had been tailored for D and provoked, and would continue to provoke, considerable anger and resentment. (4) The exceptional arrangements would not remove the real risk of D's treatment in a manner incompatible with art.3; P was grossly overcrowded and significantly understaffed and it was highly doubtful that even with well trained and motivated staff, P would be able to provide sufficient protection for D in the context of the large numbers of prisoners who required supervision; it was generally accepted that solitary confinement was very harmful to a prisoner's mental and physical health, on the other hand, were D to leave his cell, he would be at significant risk of attack, even with a personal escort or guard, which there was no evidence could be effectively provided; there were insufficient medical staff and services available for the prisoners, including D; it was of considerable concern that conditions in P were unmonitored and no route to remedial action could be pursued; and there was no established route with the Taiwanese courts whereby a prisoner could seek a remedy in respect of prison conditions; with regard to the aforementioned, and even taking into account the guidance in *Ahmad v United Kingdom (24027/07)* (2013) 56 E.H.R.R. 1, [2013] C.L.Y. 1184, substantial grounds has been made out for believing that, were all the undertakings and special conditions fulfilled, there remained a real risk of treatment of D incompatible with his art.3 rights, *Ahmad*, *considered*. (5) The appeal under s.103 of the 2003 Act would be allowed as the evidence, which had not been available at the extradition hearing before the sheriff, would have resulted in the sheriff deciding the art.3 question differently such that he would have been required to order D's discharge, and the extradition order would be quashed, and it would be unnecessary to issue an opinion in terms of s.108 or to decide the devolution issue minutes. Per Lord Drummond Young, *dissenting*, that (1) the undertakings by the Taiwanese authorities had to be accepted as having been made in good faith, and, if implemented, ought to secure D's safety in so far as practicable, and in light of the undertakings, which it had to be assumed would be observed in good faith, nothing in the proposed conditions in P amounted to a breach of art.3; (2) sufficient of the criteria in *Othman v United Kingdom (8139/09)* (2012) 55 E.H.R.R. 1, [2012] C.L.Y. 1664 had been satisfied for the court to accept the assurances given by the Taiwanese Ministry of Justice, *Othman*, *considered*; (3) although there were serious deficiencies in the prison system in Taiwan, they were irrelevant to D's position in view of the assurances given by the Taiwanese authorities as to the conditions in which he would be kept, the emphasis placed on the hostility of other prisoners had been exaggerated, no evidence had been produced to support the contention of a lack of medical services, and assurances had been given that consular services would be available to D, which was the standard manner in which assurances given in an international undertaking or assurance would be enforced; (4) solitary confinement was designed to secure D's safety and was used in that manner in the UK and was Convention compliant; (5) D had failed to establish that there was a real risk of his being subject to treatment which would infringe art.3 and the appeal would have been refused.

DEAN (ZAIN TAJ) v LORD ADVOCATE, [2016] HCJAC 83, 2016 S.L.T. 1105, Lady Paton, Lord Drummond Young, Lady Clark of Calton, HCJ.

2635 Extradition orders–Right to fair trial–Delay in prosecuting appellant–Risk of unfair trial

[Extradition Act 2003 (c.41) s.14, s.26(4); European Convention on Human Rights 1950 art.5, art.6]

A Polish national (P) made an application for leave to appeal under the Extradition Act 2003 s.26(4) against a decision of the sheriff ordering his extradition to Poland in terms of a European arrest warrant on the basis that his extradition was unjust or incompatible with ECHR arts 5 and 6 where there had been a significant delay in prosecuting him. P claimed that he had been in custody in Poland between 2004 and 2006 and between 2007 and 2009, and had thereafter remained in Poland until 2013 but the charges had not been resolved. Before the sheriff, P had not mentioned his detention between 2007 and 2009 and had relied solely on s.14 of the 2003 Act, and in the appeal he had sought to adduce evidence which related to charges other than the present ones and which he claimed supported his remand history.

Held: Appeal refused. (1) The evidence relating to P's remand history had been available before the sheriff but had not been placed before him and P was thus unable to advance his art.5 point. (2) There was no evidential basis for P's assertions of fact upon which the appeal was based where the sheriff had accepted only that P had been remanded between 2004 and 2006 and had concluded that the requirement to commence, end and thereafter re-raise criminal proceedings had been due to P's non-engagement. (3) The test to be applied in determining whether a person's ECHR art.6 rights would be infringed were he to be extradited to another Council of Europe state was whether he risked suffering a flagrant denial of justice in that state, which involved a high test, namely whether there might be a breach of art.6 which was so fundamental as to amount to a nullification, or destruction of the very essence, of the right guaranteed thereby; a Council of Europe country was presumed to be capable of protecting accused persons from an unfair trial and it was for P to adduce clear, cogent and compelling evidence capable of proving that there were substantial grounds for believing that such a risk existed, he had not done so and had not advanced arguable grounds of appeal against the sheriff's decision.

POFELSKI (JAROSLAW) v HM ADVOCATE, [2016] HCJAC 77, 2016 S.C.L. 850, The Lord Justice Clerk (Lady Dorrian), Lord Brodie, Lord Drummond Young, HCJ.

2636 Extradition proceedings–Oppression–No error in sheriff's reasoning

[Extradition Act 2003 (c.41); European Convention on Human Rights 1950 art.6]

C sought leave to appeal against an order for his extradition to Spain in terms of the Extradition Act 2003. C had been detained by Spanish police in February 2010, shortly after allegedly handing another person (X) drugs. C submitted that (1) the sheriff had been wrong in deciding that it would not be unjust to order extradition despite the passage of time, further, X was unavailable and untraceable; (2) the sheriff had erred in holding that it would not be oppressive to extradite; C had no expectation that proceedings would be raised where he had travelled to Spain on four occasions since his detention without hinderance; (3) in considering his ECHR art.6 rights, the sheriff had erred in law, having regard to X's absence.

Held: Appeal refused. (1) The court was unable to identify any error in the sheriff's reasoning, in particular, the absence of a witness did not constitute in itself injustice or oppression. (2) Council of Europe countries, of which Spain was one, were assumed to be capable of applying Convention jurisprudence and was there a substantial argument based upon delay, the absence of a witness or any other consideration which would have affected C's art.6 rights, the appropriate court to hear the submission was the Spanish court, *Lagunionek (Slawomir) v Lord Advocate* [2015] HCJAC 53, 2015 J.C. 300, [2015] C.L.Y. 3061, *considered.*

CAMERON (ROBERT) v HM ADVOCATE, [2016] HCJAC 13, 2016 S.C.L. 355, Lord Justice General (Carloway), Lady Dorrian, Lord Bracadale, HCJ.

2637 Extradition requests–United States–Pakistani national–Whether automatic return to Pakistan–Alleged breach of human rights

[European Convention on Human Rights 1950 art.2, art.3, art.5, art.6; Extradition Act 2003 (c.41) s.87(3); UN Convention Against Torture and other Cruel, Inhuman or Degrading Treatment or Punishment 1984]

A Pakistani national (M) opposed an application by the Lord Advocate (L) for his extradition to the United States for prosecution on nine serious fraud charges allegedly committed in Virginia. M had been born into a Muslim family but claimed to have converted to Judaism. M had been convicted in the sheriff court of an assault with attempt to rape and was sentenced to three years custody. As a result of a proceeds of crime investigation by the Scottish Ministers, he was made the subject of a disclosure order and during an interview referred to dollar transactions which he was concerned might be used against him during any US prosecution for fraud. L relied on evidence contained in affidavits of a US prosecutor setting out sentencing options if M were extradited and convicted and of a US Government attorney explaining the rules, procedure and law relating to the processing and removal of criminal aliens extradited to the US. During M's cross examination, he objected to late productions for L implying that he had lied to his employer about his whereabouts while he was on trial for the sexual assault, and that while employed he had improperly accessed some business files concerning a relative, however, the sheriff allowed the evidence. M submitted that (1) the sheriff should have recused himself in deciding a live issue of M's credibility on the basis that a prior inappropriate or dishonest act was revealed which was adverse to his credibility; (2) as the US operated a mandatory immigration policy to return illegal aliens to their country of origin, if returned to Pakistan after extradition to the US his life would be in danger due to his conversion to Judaism, in contravention of his ECHR arts 2 and 3 rights, and if not returned to Pakistan he would be indefinitely detained in the US in contravention of his art.5 rights, and in those circumstances he had to be discharged in terms of the Extradition Act 2003 s.87(3); (3) he would be exposed to a real risk of flagrant denial of justice in the US because information from the proceeds of crime interview could be used against him during any US fraud trial in breach of his art.6 rights.

Held: Application granted. (1) The sheriff was merely exercising a necessary judicial function to decide if productions tendered late should be received for proof, he considered himself able to attach such weight to its contents as was necessary and appropriate to determine M's credibility, and none of the documents precluded him from reaching a fair and balanced view; a fair minded and informed observer would not have concluded that any real possibility of judicial bias existed just because the sheriff had seen the contents of the documents and heard M questioned about them, accordingly, M's motion that the sheriff recuse himself would be refused. (2) Accepting the evidence contained in the affidavits, the extradition petition and supporting documents, the US Government did not operate a mandatory policy of return of criminal aliens to their country of origin after due process following extradition, it had in place a Convention compliant legal system with return protection under the UN Convention Against Torture and other Cruel, Inhuman or Degrading Treatment or Punishment 1984 for deportable aliens and *personae non gratae*, and on that basis M would not automatically be sent to Pakistan should extradition take place. There was no basis for holding breach of rights under the ECHR, arts 2, 3 and 5 arising from removal to Pakistan as no evidence was led to establish what the conditions would be for M and there was no real possibility that M would be detained indefinitely if extradited to the US. M's religion was neither relevant nor material to his extradition, he had led no expert evidence as to the fate of Muslims in Pakistan who converted to Judaism, and in so far as his religion related to any future post extradition ejection of M from the requesting state, it was too remote from the instant issue, and M's case fell far short of satisfying the onerous burden in *R. (on the application of Ullah) v Special Adjudicator* [2004] UKHL 26, [2004] 2 A.C. 323, [2004] C.L.Y. 2009, *Kapri (Fatjon) v HM Advocate* [2014] HCJAC 33, 2015 J.C. 30, [2014] C.L.Y. 3521, *applied*. (3) The fact that M made possible incriminating remarks during an investigative interview in Scotland did not *ipso facto* mean that he could not receive a fair trial in the US or that he would be the victim of a flagrant denial of justice there; there was no evidence that the US prosecutor was aware of the transcript or that he intended to use it, and even if he did M would have the right to challenge its admissibility, under the doctrine of specialty, M could not be prosecuted for offences other than those he was extradited to face, thus the statements could not found new charges against him in the US without further recourse to the UK Government, the legal process in the US could not be described as a flagrant denial of justice, against the background of the *prima facie* case directed at M by the US authorities, the exacting test in *Ullah* had not been satisfied in respect of M's art.6 argument, the question posed by s.87 of the 2003 Act could be answered in the affirmative and the case would be sent to the Scottish Ministers for their final decision on whether M was to be extradited, *Ullah, considered*.

LORD ADVOCATE v MIRZA, 2016 S.C.L. 212, Sheriff T Welsh, QC, Sh Ct (Lothian) (Edinburgh).

FAMILY LAW

2638 **Adoption–Permanence orders–Adequacy of sheriff's reasoning–Child's welfare**

[Adoption and Children (Scotland) Act 2007 (asp 4) s.83(2)(d), s.83(3)(b), s.83(3)(c), s.84, s.84(5)(c)(ii); European Convention on Human Rights 1950 art.8]

The father (F) of a child (E), aged three, appealed against a decision of the sheriff making a permanence order in respect of her and granting authority for her to be adopted following an application therefor by the local authority. While in the care of her mother (M), E had been assessed as being at risk of physical neglect and emotional abuse, a child protection order was granted and she was placed with a foster carer (X) when she was eight weeks old. For a period after E's placement, M had had direct contact with her, however matters deteriorated and M's engagement with social workers became almost non-existent. M suffered from mental health difficulties and on 10 occasions failed to attend for contact. When E was 11 months old, the children's hearing made a condition that there be no contact between M and E. Indirect contact with M and F was allowed by a children's hearing when E was 21 months old, however

M had never asked social workers for contact to resume, and F had had no contact with E from the age of eight weeks. F had a record of criminal offences but was in a relationship and had a child with his new partner, he had not been assessed as a potential carer for E and he was resentful towards the social work department. E and X had an extremely close relationship and E became distressed at the thought of separation from X, who was approved as a prospective adopter. Before the sheriff, M and F sought direct contact with E, with the view of E being returned to their separate care. The sheriff concluded *inter alia* that (1) because of the substantial lasting distress that removal from X would have caused to E, residence with either M or F would have been seriously detrimental to E's welfare; (2) the conditions of the Adoption and Children (Scotland) Act 2007 s.84 had been fully met and grounds for making a permanence order had been established; (3) M was unable satisfactorily to discharge her responsibilities or exercise her rights and was likely to continue to be unable to do so, the requirements of subs.83(3)(b) and (c) had been satisfied and her consent to the making of an adoption order ought to have been dispensed with; (4) F's failure to seek contact was motivated by his pique at not being allowed direct contact and his distrust of the social work department, and although s.83(3)(b) had been satisfied in relation to F, significant improvements in F's lifestyle meant that the requirements of s.83(3)(c) had not been met; (5) in considering whether in terms of s.83(2)(d) E's welfare otherwise required that F's consent be dispensed with, the "last resort" test had been met, the word "requires" in s.83(2)(d) implied necessity, and E's welfare would not have been safeguarded by returning her to either M's or F's care. F submitted that (1) the sheriff had erred in his approach to the welfare tests in ss.84(5)(c)(ii) and 83(2)(d), welfare had to be approached in a manner consistent with ECHR art.8, and he should have decided the question of serious detriment by taking account of F's capacity to look after E; (2) the sheriff had dispensed with F's consent to adoption without applying the high test of necessity and proportionality inherent in a proper interpretation of s.83(2)(d), his analysis had not met the stringency of reasoning required by *B-S (Children) (Adoption: Leave to Oppose), Re* [2013] EWCA Civ 1146, [2014] 1 W.L.R. 563, [2014] C.L.Y. 1245, and he had failed to make any reference to *S v L* [2012] UKSC 30, 2013 S.C. (U.K.S.C.) 20, [2012] C.L.Y. 1297 or art.8. M submitted that (1) distress on separation from X was not of itself sufficient to conclude that E's residence with M was likely to be seriously detrimental to her welfare; (2) there was no supportable basis for the sheriff's conclusion that M was likely to continue to be unable satisfactorily to discharge her parental rights and responsibilities.

Held: Appeal refused. (1) The sheriff had been entitled on the factual material before him to conclude that residence with M or F would have been likely to be seriously detrimental to E's welfare; there was uncertainty as to when, if ever, E could have lived with either M or F, the question of their capacity to look after her had to be considered in light thereof, he had not failed to have regard to F's capacity to look after E, and he had been entitled to take into account the long term security and stability provided by the arrangement with X. Having found that the requirement of s.84(5)(c)(ii) was met, the sheriff had given cogent reasons why it was better to make the order than not, and he had been entitled to make the permanence order. (2) The sheriff had not erred in concluding that M was unable satisfactorily to discharge her parental responsibilities and rights and was likely to continue to be unable to do so, that was a matter on which he had had to make an evaluative judgment assessing the facts, he had been entitled to conclude that M's consent to the making of an order granting authority for adoption should be dispensed with, and as the incapacity test was met, it had not been necessary for the sheriff to have considered the welfare test in s.83(2)(d) in respect of M. (3) The requirements of *B-S (Children)* had been met where the sheriff had been entitled to make the permanence order, there had been sufficient evidence before him to allow him to make the appropriate evaluative judgment and his reasoning had been adequate. The sheriff had recognised the requirement for an approach based on necessity, and although he made no reference to *S v L*, he had referred to *B (A Child) (Care Proceedings: Appeal), Re* [2013] UKSC 33, [2013] 1 W.L.R. 1911, [2013] C.L.Y. 1213 and *P (Children) (Placement Orders: Parental Consent), Re* [2008] EWCA Civ 535, [2009] P.T.S.R. 150, [2008] C.L.Y. 1575 and had identified and applied the last resort test. Although the sheriff had not specifically addressed art.8, it was clear from his analysis that "requires" denoted necessity and his recognition of the test in *B (A*

Child) indicated that he had taken account of the requirements of art.8, *B-S (Children), applied* and *S v L, B (A Child)* and *P (Children), considered*.

FIFE COUNCIL, APPLICANTS *sub nom.* FIFE COUNCIL, PETITIONER, [2015] CSIH 74, 2015 Fam. L.R. 159, Lord Menzies, Lord Bracadale, Lord Drummond Young, IH (Ex Div).

2639 Children and Young People (Scotland) Act 2014 (asp 8)–Commencement No.11 Order

THE CHILDREN AND YOUNG PEOPLE (SCOTLAND) ACT 2014 (COMMENCEMENT NO.11) ORDER 2016, SSI 2016/60; made under the Children and Young People (Scotland) Act 2014 s.102(3). Commencement details: bringing into operation various provisions of the 2014 Act on 31 August 2016.

This Order brings into force provisions of the Children and Young People (Scotland) Act 2014.

2640 Children and Young People (Scotland) Act 2014 (asp 8)–Commencement No.11 Partial Revocation Order

THE CHILDREN AND YOUNG PEOPLE (SCOTLAND) ACT 2014 (COMMENCEMENT NO.11) PARTIAL REVOCATION ORDER 2016, SSI 2016/233; made under the Children and Young People (Scotland) Act 2014 s.102(3). In force: 30 August 2016.

This Order amends the Children and Young People (Scotland) Act 2014 (Commencement No.11) Order 2016 ("Commencement No.11 Order") by revoking arts.2(a)(i) and (iii) of that Order. Commencement No. 11 Order now only provides for the commencement on 31 August 2016 of the Children and Young People (Scotland) Act 2014 s.68, so far as not already in force, and section 95 of that Act, for all purposes.

2641 Children's hearings–Safeguarders panel–Removal

THE CHILDREN'S HEARINGS (SCOTLAND) ACT 2011 (SAFEGUARDERS PANEL) AMENDMENT REGULATIONS 2016, SSI 2016/61; made under the Children's Hearings (Scotland) Act 2011 s.32(2), s.195(2). In force: 25 April 2016.

These regulations amend The Children's Hearings (Scotland) Act 2011 (Safeguarders Panel) Regulations 2012. They amends provisions in the 2012 Regulations regarding reappointment to and removal from the Safeguarders Panel. A member of the Panel may only be reappointed by Scottish Ministers if they are satisfied that the person is fit to be a member of the Panel.

2642 Children's services–Young persons–Children's welfare

THE CHILDREN AND YOUNG PEOPLE (SCOTLAND) ACT 2014 (MODIFICATION OF SCHEDULES 2 AND 3) ORDER 2016, SSI 2016/151; made under the Children and Young People (Scotland) Act 2014 s.31(2)(a), s.44(2)(a). In force: 16 March 2016.

This Order modifies the list of persons who are specified as relevant authorities in the Children and Young People (Scotland) Act 2014 Sch.2, and the list of persons who are specified as listed authorities in Sch.3 to that Act to add the Principal Reporter to each.

2643 Compulsory supervision orders–Procedural irregularity–Continuation of supervision requirement

[Children (Scotland) Act 1995 (c.36) s.51(5); Children's Hearings (Scotland) Act 2011 (asp 1) s.156(3)(a); Children's Hearings (Scotland) Act 2011 (Consequential and Transitional Provisions and Savings) Order 2013 (SI 2013/1465) art.7]

The children's reporter (C) appealed by stated case against a decision of the sheriff that a decision of the children's hearing (H) was not justified in all the circumstances as it had considered the issue of compulsory measures of care for a child (X) in terms of the Children (Scotland) Act 1995 rather than the Children's Hearings (Scotland) Act 2011. On 28 August 2013, H had made a supervision requirement under the 1995 Act, which had been appealed to the sheriff. On 21 October, C had conceded that the appeal ought to be allowed, and the sheriff had remitted the case to H for reconsideration. On 23 January 2014, H had made a supervision requirement under the 1995 Act, with the language of the decision giving rise to an inference that both the 1995 Act and the 2011 Act had been held under consideration, each of which was separately appealed. On 6 March, C had again conceded that the appeals ought to be allowed, with the interlocutor referring to the 2011 Act. On 19 December, H had continued the supervision requirement for a year in terms of the 1995 Act. C submitted that (1) the appeal required to meet the test in *C v Miller* 2003 S.L.T. 1379, [2004] C.L.Y. 4746, and the sheriff had been incorrect in holding that the existing supervision requirement made in August 2013 had fallen to be treated as if it were a compulsory supervision order under and in terms of the 2011 Act, having regard to the effect of the Children's Hearings (Scotland) Act 2011 (Consequential and Transitional Provisions and Savings) Order 2013 art.7, and the allowance of the appeal by the sheriff on 21 October 2013 under s.51(5) of the 1995 Act did not equate to the conclusion of relevant proceedings; whilst the appeal might have been allowed by the sheriff, following a remit to H under s.51(5)(c)(i), it did not come to an end until H had reconsidered its decision; (2) had there been a conclusion of the relevant proceedings, it remained open to the court to hold that the sheriff had erred in allowing the appeal.

Held: (1) The plain and intuitive construction to be placed upon an appeal being allowed by the sheriff under s.51(5) of the 1995 Act was that the appeal was thereby rendered at an end; the hearing of the appeal and deciding it were part of a judicial process, whereas reconsideration of a decision by H was not, and could never be. (2) The sheriff had proceeded on the basis that the supervision requirement had become a compulsory supervision order as at 21 October 2013, via art.7 of the 2013 Order, in the event, and well before hearing on 23 January 2014, a transition to 2011 Act procedure had been effected, moreover, in terms of art.8, the compulsory supervision order fell to be treated as if it had been made on 28 August 2013, being the date upon which the supervision requirement had been imposed under the 1995 Act. (3) Where H's December 2014 disposal had erroneously made reference to a 1995 supervision requirement instead of the 2011 Act compulsory supervision order, that had amounted to a procedural irregularity. (4) H's disposal of 23 January 2014 had made no explicit reference to either the 1995 Act or the 2011 Act, it had been open to the sheriff to conclude that H had directed itself towards continuing a compulsory supervision order at that hearing, and it was difficult to accept the sheriff's view that whilst H's decision of 23 January 2014 had amounted to a valid continuation of a compulsory supervision order, its December decision had not, the latter being vitiated by incorporation of the 1995 Act terminology: the issues to which H required to direct itself in making a compulsory supervision order were broadly the same as those involved in the making of a supervision requirement, and it was not suggested that H had materially misdirected itself as to the factual matrix before it; H's December 2014 decision was justified in all the circumstances, and it could not be said that the irregularity had been damaging to the justice of the proceedings, *C v Miller, applied.* (5) On the available evidence, there was no justification for the conclusion that it was not appropriate for X to be, or to remain, subject to compulsory measures of supervision, and H's decision of 19 December ought to be sustained subject to what had been purportedly described as the supervision requirement being treated as if it were the compulsory supervision order from 23 January 2014 being continued. Opinion, (1) that the interlocutor of 6 March 2014 had specifically proceeded under, and in terms of, s.156(3)(a) of the 2011 Act, and given C's subsequent stance on procedure, had that interlocutor been viewed as being incorrect, it ought to have been the subject of immediate challenge; the terms of that interlocutor were in direct conflict with C's apparent approach to the hearing on 19 December 2014; (2) that had H's decision not been justified, the sheriff would have been found to have erred in discharging X from any further hearings or proceedings in relation to the grounds that had given rise to that decision, where the sheriff's approach had largely been informed by *Kennedy v A (A Child)* 1986 S.L.T. 358, [1986] C.L.Y. 3639, which was readily capable of being distinguished from the present case, *Kennedy, distinguished.*

CHILDREN'S REPORTER v N *sub nom.* PRINCIPAL REPORTER v IN, 2016 S.L.T. (Sh Ct) 23, Sheriff Principal C A L Scott, QC, Sh Ct (Glasgow).

2644 Compulsory supervision orders–Variation–Refusal to defer decision on varying order until receipt of child psychologist's report on mother

[Children's Hearings (Scotland) Act 2011 (asp 1) Sch.1, s.138(2), s.154, s.67(2)(b)]

The mother (M) of a child (C), aged two, appealed in terms of the Children's Hearings (Scotland) Act 2011 s.154 against a decision of the children's hearing (H) varying a compulsory supervision order in respect of C. On 10 July 2015, it had been established that in terms of s.67(2)(b) of the 2011 Act, a Sch.1 offence had been committed in respect of C, who had been subjected to an assault while in the care of either, or both, M and M's then partner, and H had made a compulsory supervision order with an expiry date of 30 July 2016, in terms of which C resided with either of her grandmothers (G), with M having extensive contact supervised by G or by M's grandmother. On 12 April 2016, H had been reconvened at the behest of the implementation authority in terms of s.138(2) of the 2011 Act and M had requested that H consider a rehabilitation plan to return C to her care and defer making its decision until a subsequent hearing to allow receipt and consideration of an assessment by a child psychologist (P) of M, carried out some months previously. H had declined the request and had varied the compulsory supervision order with regard to C's residence and issues of contact.

Held: Appeal allowed. (1) When reviewing a compulsory supervision order, H ought not to restrict itself to a consideration of the issue raised by the party seeking the review but ought to consider all issues pertinent to the order reasonably raised by all parties, to do otherwise could have a significantly detrimental impact on the ability and the right of those parties to have the order reviewed because on conclusion of a review, they were precluded from requiring any further review for three months, whereas the implementation authority could require a review at any time. (2) Given the passage of time since the order had been made, that C had always been cared for within the birth family, and that M had exercised extensive contact with C throughout, her request had been reasonable. (3) Where there had been an awareness of the existence of P's report, and such a report would be highly relevant to the issue of a rehabilitation plan, no reasonable children's hearing would have concluded the review of the order without seeking to consider it. (4) The issue of potential criminal charges against M regarding the assault on C had not been an irrelevant consideration where that matter was a stumbling block to consideration of a rehabilitation plan and given the passage of time and the importance of the matter, any reasonable children's hearing would have wished to have further information thereon. (5) H had the power to take a proactive approach and could, and ought to have, deferred its decision and have required the children's reporter (R) to obtain reports from P with regard to M's assessment and from the police and/or the procurator fiscal regarding the issue of criminal charges, and not to have done so had been unfair to M and had amounted to a procedural irregularity. (6) H could have varied the order on an interim basis if it had considered that there was an urgent requirement to do so. (7) The only appropriate step was to require R to arrange a children's hearing to consider M's request for a rehabilitation plan.

P v CHILDREN'S REPORTER, 2016 S.L.T. (Sh Ct) 339, Sheriff P Mann, Sh Ct (Grampian) (Lerwick).

2645 Financial provision–Cohabitation–Cohabitee benefiting from payments made by former partner–Economic advantage

[Family Law (Scotland) Act 2006 (asp 2) s.28, s.28(3)(a), s.28(3)(b), s.28(4)]

A cohabitee (C) appealed against a decision of the sheriff principal finding her liable to pay her cohabitant (M) £29,515, following the breakdown of their relationship, on the basis that C had benefited from payments made by M, and awarding interest thereon at 8% per annum from the date of citation in 2008. C and M had cohabited for approximately 15 years and had lived in several houses which had been registered in C's name and funded by mortgages taken out in C's name, the last house being bought as a family home in November 2005 for £192,951. Following separation, M had sought payment in terms of the Family Law (Scotland) Act 2006 s.28 and had craved interest from the date of decree. The sheriff had treated M's claim in terms of s.28(3)(a) and (b) and had found *inter alia* that C could not have maintained the mortgage on her own where her annual earnings were approximately £17,000, on the evidence, the only available source of finance had been M and C had derived an economic advantage while M had suffered economic disadvantage, however, she had declined to make a capital award on the basis that M had not intended to benefit C, and having regard to *Gow v Grant* [2011] CSIH 25, 2011 S.C. 618, [2011] C.L.Y. 4289, she could not make any award under s.28. The sheriff principal had amended finding in fact 19 by deleting "input of some kind" and substituting "contribution" and had allowed M's appeal on the basis that it was not necessary for the purposes of s.28(3)(b) to find that M's economic disadvantage had been suffered in a manner intended to benefit C; having regard to *Gow v Grant* [2012] UKSC 29, 2013 S.C. (U.K.S.C.) 1, [2012] C.L.Y. 1441, there required to be fair compensation for contributions made or economic disadvantages suffered in the interests of the relationship on a broad assessment. C submitted *inter alia* that (1) the award of interest was regulated by the common law where s.28 made no provision therefor, and it could only run from the date of final affirmation of any award on appeal; (2) the sheriff principal had erred by amending finding in fact 19 without reference to the shorthand notes; (3) the sheriff's findings had been made in the light of the Inner House decision in *Gow* and the sheriff principal had erred in relying thereon; (4) the sheriff principal had erred in failing to carry out an offsetting exercise in terms of s.28(4); (5) the sheriff principal had refined his reasoning in *Smith-Milne v Langler* 2013 Fam. L.R. 58, [2013] C.L.Y. 3725 and had erred in not allowing parties to make further submissions in light thereof.

Held: Appeal refused subject to amendments. (1) It was appropriate in a family case such as the present that interest ran from the date of the sheriff principals' award, namely 16 May 2014, that was the norm and in so far as *Roger v JP Cochrane & Co (No.2)* 1910 S.C. 1 might be thought to suggest otherwise, it related to practice in reparation actions over a century ago and was, in any event, *obiter*, *Roger*, *considered*. (2) There were cases in which an appellate court was not entitled to alter a finding in fact without having identified a specific basis in the evidence either within the terms of a transcript or within the terms of parties' agreement as to the terms of the relevant evidence, however, the present was not such a case; the amendment had not effected any material alteration to the finding in fact and its meaning and import had not changed. (3) The issue for the sheriff principal was whether, contrary to the sheriff's decision, s.28 of the 2006 Act entitled the court to make an award of capital in M's favour and, if so, to what extent, findings in fact 17 and 19 provided a sound basis for concluding that s.28(3)(a) applied and that such an award ought to be made and where the important facts inherent in those findings had not been challenged, a transcript was not required. (4) The terms of s.28(4) were directory but it was incumbent on a party seeking the benefit of such offsetting to demonstrate through the written pleadings and in evidence and submission that they sought to have the court do so; absent that, there was no requirement for the court to spell out in its judgment that it had had regard to those subsections but since no case for offsetting was before it, no offsetting was being effected, and the task for the court was to resolve the issues raised and not to embark on an inevitably sterile or academic exercise. (5) The present case did not fall into the category where a judge ought, in the interests of justice, to give parties the opportunity to make further submissions, the sheriff principal's views had continued to be that there required to be "a causal link" between the contributions and the economic advantage, all he had added was that some links were closer than others, and there was no injustice in his refraining from issuing an invitation to parties to make further submissions. (6) C had not contended that, was the sheriff principal entitled to make an award of capital, he was not entitled to award the sum of £29,515. (7) The error in the sheriff principal's interlocutor which had deleted the sheriff's second finding in law, namely that C had achieved an economic advantage as a result of the parties' cohabitation, was inconsistent with his judgment and required to be reinstated, and his interlocutor would further be amended to provide for interest to run from the date of that interlocutor.

MELVIN v CHRISTIE, [2016] CSIH 43, 2016 Fam. L.R. 116, The Lord President (Carloway), Lady Smith, Lord Brodie, IH (1 Div).

2646 Financial provision–Cohabitation–Financial provision following separation–Economic disadvantage

[Family Law (Scotland) Act 2006 (asp 2) s.25, s.28; Family Law (Scotland) Act 1985 (c.37)]

A cohabitee (M) appealed against a decision of the sheriff finding him liable to pay his cohabitant (W) £46,214 on the basis that M had benefited from payments made by W. The sheriff had found that prior to commencing cohabitation the parties had been in a relationship since mid-2009 and had resided together one or two nights per week. M had been working in London in temporary employment and had returned to Scotland in May 2011 and had cohabited with W until February 2012 and the parties had been cohabitants in terms of the Family Law (Scotland) Act 2006 s.25 for that period. M claimed that the sheriff had erred in law (1) in finding that M had derived an economic advantage standing his financial position at the start of the period of cohabitation compared with that at the end thereof; (2) in finding that W had suffered an economic disadvantage having regard to the fact there had been no crave to that effect and having upheld M's objection to such evidence being led; (3) in making finding of fact and law number 4 in respect that there was neither any record for, nor evidence of, W having suffered a loss of income of any sum, particularly £11,214; (4) in holding as admissible, and in allowing reference to, a report lodged by W in respect that there was no record for it and M had made an objection; (5) in holding that the payments made by W to M totalling £1,500 in March and April 2011, outwith the period of cohabitation, were recoverable in terms of s.28 of the 2006 Act; (6) in taking into account the potential value of M's property once completed rather than at the time cohabitation had ended; (7) by not taking account of the cost of completion of the works at M's property in calculating in the economic advantage or disadvantage to M; (8) by not holding that M had suffered an economic disadvantage.

Held: Appeal dismissed. (1) Standing the provisions of s.28 of the 2006 Act, the sheriff had been entitled to make an award in W's favour; the sheriff had correctly applied a holistic approach and sought to achieve fairness between the parties and had reached the conclusion that there had been a disadvantage to W which had been reflected in some advantage to M; monies contributed by W and utilised towards the renovation works had contributed to an increase in the value of the property, resulting in economic advantage to M, and the first and second grounds of appeal would be dismissed. (2) It would have been preferable had the sheriff been able to make a finding in fact of the value of the property at the date when cohabitation had ceased, however, that was not fatal to her reasoning given that she had found the value to be in excess of the pre-renovation valuation and the cost paid towards the renovations, which were found to be £50,000 by M and £35,000 by W, which she had been entitled to find on the evidence, therefore, there was no substance to the sixth and seventh grounds of appeal. (3) W conceded that the sheriff had not been entitled to find that £11,214 had been paid from income, however, the terms of the joint minute made clear that sums were paid by W and the sheriff had accepted that £46,214 had been paid by W to M's benefit and that W had suffered economic disadvantage in that sum by which M had benefited; to accurately reflect the position finding in fact and law 4 would be adjusted to delete "has lost capital of £35,000 and income of £11,214 in the interests of the defender" and substitute "paid over £46,214 to the benefit of the defender", otherwise, there was no basis to interfere with the sheriff's discretion in assessing that disadvantage and consequent advantage at £46,214 and ground of appeal 3 would be rejected. (4) Standing W's averments and the joint minute, there was no substance in M's argument that W had not shown there to be economic advantage to him and there was no proper basis to suggest that the sheriff had seen merit in M's suggestion of a lack of pleading for economic disadvantage to W in the sums she had contributed to M. (5) M had had adequate notice of W's position that there had been an increase in the value of the property, and the court agreed with the sheriff's decision to allow the report and ground of appeal 4 would be dismissed, *Eadie Cairns v Programmed Maintenance Painting Ltd* 1987 S.L.T. 777, [1987] C.L.Y. 4892, *distinguished*. (6) The legislation did not specifically prescribe whether payments made and received prior to cohabitation resulting in economic disadvantage or advantage ought to be taken into account, no interpretive assistance could be drawn from the specific reference to contributions prior to marriage or civil partnership in the Family Law (Scotland) Act 1985 and there was an absence of any equivalent provision in the 2006 Act, and the question of taking account of sums contributed immediately prior to cohabitation was a matter not formally considered by the Supreme Court in *Gow v Grant* [2012] UKSC 29, 2013 S.C. (U.K.S.C.) 1, [2012] C.L.Y. 1441, however, where a fair outcome was seen as a key policy aim of the 2006 Act, the terms thereof did not exclude payments made prior to cohabitation commencing being taken into account, and it was appropriate that discretion should rest with the court in determining economic advantage and disadvantage and the relevance of payments or transactions towards that economic advantage and disadvantage, accordingly, the sheriff had been entitled to have regard to the £1,500 and, in the exercise of her discretion and in seeking to achieve fairness between the parties, to take account thereof in making her award to W, and there was no basis on which to interfere therewith, particularly where it was looked upon as part of the sheriff's overall assessment of economic advantage and disadvantage in terms of s.28 of the 2006 Act, *Gow, considered.* (7) Ground of appeal 8 was without foundation; the sheriff had been entitled to make the findings in fact and had demonstrated a cogent basis therefor.

W v M, 2016 S.L.T. (Sh Ct) 14, Sheriff Principal D L Murray, Sh Ct (North Strathclyde) (Paisley).

2647 **Foster carers–Registration–Couple deregistered as respite foster carers after alleged sexual misconduct by husband–Consideration of wife's position separately and distinctly**

[Looked After Children (Scotland) Regulations 2009 (SSI 2009/210) reg.25(3)(a), reg.26(9)(a); Interpretation Act 1978 (c.30) s.11, s.6]

A foster carer (W) petitioned for judicial review of a decision of the local authority (C) to deregister her and her husband (H) as respite carers. W and H had been jointly registered as respite foster carers. A child in their care had made an allegation of sexual contact by H and, pending a police and social work investigation, a hold was put on any further placements with W and H. No allegations of misconduct were made against W, and although no further action was taken by police, a review carried out for C recommended that W and H be removed from the list of approved carers. W instructed a solicitor (S) who acted on her behalf both at a hearing before the fostering panel, which supported the recommendation to deregister W and H as respite carers, and at a hearing before the appeal panel, which upheld the fostering panel's decision. At those hearings, neither the possibility of variation of the joint approval in terms of the Looked After Children (Scotland) Regulations 2009 regs 25(3)(a) and 26(9)(a) was raised, nor was it suggested that fostering would occur in a home in which H did not reside. W submitted that (1) C had erred in treating her and H's positions together; (2) C should have employed the powers of variation in the 2009 Regulations, which referred to foster carer in the singular; (3) although W could have made a fresh application as an individual for approval as a foster carer, that would not remove the stigma attached to her if the decisions were allowed to stand.

Held: Petition dismissed. (1) The rule of interpretation under the Interpretation Act 1978 ss.6 and 11 was that where the singular appeared in statutory language it should be held to embrace the plural unless the contrary was indicated, and there was nothing in the language of the 2009 Regulations to indicate that the normal rule of construction did not apply. (2) W was registered as a joint carer along with H and it was that registration which had to be considered by C in light of the allegation, W had not until recently sought to have matters addressed any differently, she was represented at all material times by S who at no time argued that W's position should be considered separately and distinctly from H, C was not invited to vary the registration at any point in the hearings before it, and although a discretionary power existed in the 2009 Regulations, that did not mean that the non-exercise of that power by a decision maker rendered the decision invalid. (3) Without W's suitability to carry on activities as a carer being investigated and ascertained, in particular how she would carry them out in the absence of H, reduction was wholly inappropriate: C's primary duty was to provide that the safety and welfare of the children in question were protected and promoted, and it had had in mind that overarching consideration when it had reached its decision.

W v HIGHLAND COUNCIL, [2016] CSOH 56, 2016 S.L.T. 751, Lord Clarke, OH.

2648 Guardians ad litem–Fees–Whether local authority liable in expenses for curator ad litem's fees

[Curators ad Litem and Reporting Officers (Panels) (Scotland) Regulations 2001 (SSI 2001/477) reg.10(1A), reg.4]

A local authority (E) appealed against a sheriff's decision to grant an opposed motion by a curator *ad litem* (P) under the Sheriff Court Adoption Rules 2009 r.2(a) for a finding that she was entitled to recover from E such fees, outlays and expenses which she had incurred as curator *ad litem* in the proceedings relating to an application for a permanence order, for which she had been appointed in July 2013, from 29 January 2015. An associated appeal was also heard by the court ([2016 CSIH 47; 2016 GWD 21-XX); in each case the curator was a member of the panel of curators established by the local authority for the relevant area, operating under the Curators ad Litem and Reporting Officers (Panels) (Scotland) Regulations 2001 reg.4. The sheriff had concluded that she was bound by *Scottish Borders Council, Petitioners* 2014 S.L.T. (Sh Ct) 140, [2014] C.L.Y. 3532, which could not be distinguished from the present case. E submitted that *Scottish Borders Council* was wrongly decided and the fee payable to a curator *ad litem* appointed under the 2001 Regulations was reserved to the discretion of the local authority: it had not been the legislature's intention to provide two separate sources of payment in respect of the work covered by curator *ad litem*; in each case the curator had accepted appointment as a member of the panel appointed under the 2001 Regulations and had accepted that remuneration would be determined under reg.10(1A) and were personally barred from seeking a judicial award of expenses against the authority; and if a member were dissatisfied with the fee proferred, recourse lay in a petition for judicial review, not an application under r.2.

Held: Case put out by order. (1) There was neither a conflict between reg.10(1A) and r.2, nor a reason that they could not be read together where the former was concerned with a local authority's duty to maintain a panel of curators *ad litem* and reporting officers, and the responsibilities associated therewith, and the latter concerned the court's power to award and allocate judicial expenses in a litigation; notwithstanding reg.10(1A), the court retained to make such award as it saw fit, which accorded with the traditional approach to expenses and there was no basis for discriminating between panel and non-panel members. On the aforementioned interpretation, the court retained a degree of control to ensure that the work of curators *ad litem* and reporting officers was done properly and independently, and that those appointed by the court were properly paid, *Scottish Borders Council*, *approved* and *Dundee City Council v D* 2007 Fam. L.R. 157, [2008] C.L.Y. 4788, *disapproved*. (2) The appeal would be refused, however, the case would be put out by order for further determination on expenses.

CITY OF EDINBURGH COUNCIL v O'S CURATOR AD LITEM *sub nom.* CITY OF EDINBURGH COUNCIL v PRINGLE; CITY OF EDINBURGH COUNCIL, PETITIONERS, [2016] CSIH 46, 2016 S.L.T. 1075, The Lord Justice Clerk (Lady Dorrian), Lady Clark of Calton, Lord Malcolm, IH (2 Div).

2649 Guardians ad litem–Fees–Whether local authority liable in expenses to curator ad litem

[Curators ad Litem and Reporting Officers (Panels) (Scotland) Regulations 2001 (SSI 2001/477) reg.10(1A), reg.4]

A local authority (C) appealed against a sheriff's finding that it was liable to a curator *ad litem* (D) in expenses as taxed by the auditor of court. D had been appointed in connection with an application for a permanence order and his motion for expenses in terms of the Sheriff Court Adoption Rules 2009 r.2(a), had been opposed on the basis that any fees required to be restricted in terms of the Curators ad Litem and Reporting Officers (Panels) (Scotland) Regulations 2001 reg.10(1A). An associated appeal was also heard by the court ([2016 CSIH 46; 2016 GWD 21-XX); in each case the curator was a member of the panel of curators established by the local authority for the relevant area, operating under reg.4 of the 2001 Regulations. The sheriff considered that the effect of the two sets of regulations was a creation of a binary arrangement for the remuneration of reporting officers and curators, and while the local authority had the discretion to set fees and allowances to be paid to members of its panel in terms of reg.10(1A), the overall authority in relation to expenses in an application under the 2009 Rules rested with the sheriff in terms of r.2. C submitted that *Scottish Borders Council, Petitioners* 2014 S.L.T. (Sh Ct) 140, [2014] C.L.Y. 3532 was wrongly decided and the fee payable to a curator *ad litem* appointed under the 2001 Regulations was reserved to the discretion of the local authority: it had not been the legislature's intention to provide two separate sources of payment in respect of the work covered by curator *ad litem*; in each case the curator had accepted appointment as a member of the panel appointed under the 2001 Regulations and had accepted that remuneration would be determined under reg.10(1A) and were personally barred from seeking a judicial award of expenses against the authority; and if a member were dissatisfied with the fee proferred, recourse lay in a petition for judicial review, not an application under r.2.

Held: Case put out by order. (1) There was neither a conflict between reg.10(1A) and r.2, nor a reason that they could not be read together where the former was concerned with a local authority's duty to maintain a panel of curators *ad litem* and reporting officers, and the responsibilities associated therewith, and the latter concerned the court's power to award and allocate judicial expenses in a litigation; notwithstanding reg.10(1A), the court retained power to make such award as it saw fit which accorded with the traditional approach to expenses and there was no basis for discriminating between panel and non-panel members. On the aforementioned interpretation, the court retained a degree of control to ensure that the work of curators *ad litem* and reporting officers was done properly and independently, and that those appointed by the court were properly paid, *Scottish Borders Council*, *approved* and *Dundee City Council v D* 2007 Fam. L.R. 157, [2008] C.L.Y. 4788, *disapproved*. (2) The appeal would be refused, however, the case would be put out by order for further determination on expenses.

CLACKMANNANSHIRE COUNCIL v K'S CURATOR AD LITEM *sub nom.* CLACKMANNANSHIRE COUNCIL v DUNBAR; CLACKMANNANSHIRE COUNCIL, PETITIONERS, [2016] CSIH 47, 2016 S.L.T. 1071, The Lord Justice Clerk (Lady Dorrian), Lady Clark of Calton, Lord Malcolm, IH (2 Div).

2650 Parental contact–Best interests–Need for separate test of necessity as basis for refusing contact

[Children (Scotland) Act 1995 (c.36) s.11]

A father (F) appealed a decision of the sheriff principal upholding a sheriff's decision refusing to grant a contact order in respect of his daughter (D). F and D's mother (M) had separated in March 2010, five days after D's birth. In November 2010, F had sought contact with D in terms of the Children (Scotland) Act 1995 s.11 and had obtained interim contact commencing with supervised contact and progressing to residential contact. In January 2014, D became the subject of a police and social work investigation following allegations of sexual abuse by F and in February, contact was suspended, although F was not charged and D was not referred to a children's hearing. At the proof, F alleged that M had falsely accused him, however, the sheriff found that M had had reasonable grounds to suspect that D had been the subject of sexual abuse while in F's care, and while he had declined to make a finding that F had sexually abused D, he had concluded that in light of hostilities between M and F and their respective families the restoration of contact would lead to further and increasing problems and would not be in the best interests of D's welfare. F submitted that the sheriff had erred in that (1) a separate test of necessity required to be undertaken before contact might be refused, having regard to *M v K* [2015] CSIH 54, 2015 S.L.T. 469, [2015] C.L.Y. 3088; (2) in the absence of a finding of abuse, there was nothing of sufficient weight to overcome the benefit to D of continuing to see F.

Held: Appeal refused. (1) *M v K* had not required a separate test of necessity as a basis for refusing contact, *M, considered* and *HTJH v FM,* 1 December 2015, unreported, *approved.* (2) The sheriff had not erred in his overall approach to the decision making process, a test of necessity added nothing to a sensible application of the statutory test to applications of the present nature, and the sheriff had carried out a careful balancing exercise and identified factors which made the refusal to make a contact order necessary and justified in the best interests of D's welfare, he had correctly articulated the statutory test, and had regarded D's welfare as the paramount consideration. (3) A parent ought not to be given a veto over contact, however, the present was not a case in which a parent who, with no reasonable basis, implacably opposed contact and sought to frustrate the court's orders, F had failed to consider the implications of his hostile relationship with M and the consequent effects thereof on D in respect of contact, those factors had been influential in the sheriff's decision and he had concluded that any contact would be against D's best interests, which was the paramount consideration; given the sheriff's unchallenged findings in fact, his decision could not be categorised as unreasonable, inexplicable, unjustifiable, and unnecessary, it fell within the generous ambit given to the sheriff, his decision was not plainly wrong and there was no good reason to interfere therewith.

J v M, [2016] CSIH 52, 2016 Fam. L.R. 124, Lady Smith, Lord Brodie, Lord Malcolm, IH.

2651 Parental contact–Indirect contact–Father's previous failure to attend for contact–Child's best interests

A father (C) sought a contact order in respect of his daughter (T), aged eight. C and T's mother (W) had separated when T was three weeks old, C had regular contact with T in W's home until T was six months old, and thereafter exercised intermittent contact for the next five years. After a period of 18 months with no contact, C again began exercising regular contact with T mainly at W's home for two hours weekly, however the quality thereof was poor and his interaction with T was limited. Nine months later, W informed T that C was her father, shortly thereafter he ceased contact and he did not attempt to re-engage contact for another year, when he instructed a solicitor to write letters requesting contact and raised the instant action, however, T had not had any further contact with C for approximately two years. C suffered from physical and mental health issues but did not comply with his recommended treatment, and he was a regular drug user. T had expressed a wish not to see C, and W opposed an order for direct contact due to concerns that C would fail to attend reliably for contact over a sustained period. A bar report did not consider that a contact order was in T's best interests.

Held: Order granted. (1) Although there was sufficient material to form the view that it would be in T's best interests for a contact order to be granted, the combination of the absence of any *de facto* relationship between C and T, T's expressed views and W's attitude to contact would have made the reintroduction of contact a challenge; many of the factors which had led to C's failure to attend for contact or to demonstrate any reliable commitment to T remained, and he was not sufficiently committed to T to recognise that taking steps to address his drug use and properly address his mental health issues were an important part of being able to form a positive and committed relationship with her; there was a very high likelihood that C would not commit to a sustained pattern of contact with T and even if he had a genuine intention to do so, the other issues in his life would impact upon that and ultimately he would fail to attend for contact reliably, it would be very emotionally damaging to T to introduce contact with C only to have him abandon her again, and it was not in T's best interests for an order for direct contact to be made, *White v White* 2001 S.C. 689, [2001] C.L.Y. 6510 and *H v M*, 1 December 2015, unreported, *considered.* (2) There was a benefit to T in having a link with C as her father, and it was in T's best interest for her to receive a present on her birthday and at Christmas from C and for him to have the option to write to her either by card, letter or email once a month, and he should also be given copies of her school reports and a photograph at least one a year, therefore an order for indirect contact would be made and, in order to ensure its frequency and regularity, it was better for T that such an order be made than that no order be made.

C v W *sub nom.* C v N, 2016 Fam. L.R. 85, Sheriff W Sheehan, Sh Ct (Lothian) (Edinburgh).

2652 Parental contact–Relocation–Specific issue order allowing mother to relocate with child to Cornwall–Meaningful ongoing contact with father

A father (J) sought a contact order in respect of his daughter (X), aged four, and X's mother (G) sought a specific issue order to allow her to relocate to Cornwall with X. J and G's relationship had broken down, they had separated in September 2013 and in

December 2013, G had moved with X to a nearby rented property, and J had exercised residential contact every alternate weekend and non-residential contact one evening per week. J had sought to increase contact with X, at times attending at G's property uninvited, the parties' relationship had become strained, and G had moved with X to rented accommodation over 100 miles away, and J had exercised alternate weekend residential contact since but midweek contact had ceased in November 2014 due to the long journey time for X. In October 2014, G had met a new partner (P) who lived in Cornwall and had three children (C), care of two of whom he shared equally with his ex-wife and could thus not relocate to Scotland. G and C had a strong genuine affection for each other and were committed to living together and developing their relationship, they had frequently visited each other throughout 2015, they had developed good relationships with C and X, who had also developed good relationships between themselves, and with each other's extended families, from whom there was clear and unqualified support for the relationship. G had no family or friends in the area in which she and X now resided, her present employment was pursuant to a fixed term contract which would not be renewed in January 2016, she had developed relationships with some of P's circle of friends, with X developing friendships with their children, including one who attended the school in the village in which P owned a home. G had no wish to remain in her current location and were G and X to remain in Scotland, there was uncertainty as to future location, accommodation, employment, and X's schooling. Were G and X to relocate to Cornwall, X's contact with J would be residential contact for half of the school holidays, amounting to six periods of contact per year, a total of five and a half weeks. It was also possible for J to exercise weekend contact with X, the travel time by plane from Cornwall to his home being similar to the current travel time from G and X's current residence.

Held: Orders granted. (1) Given the uncertainty in relation to G's rented accommodation, and where G's relationship with P was likely to endure for the foreseeable future, P's privately owned family home, which was available and suitable for, and familiar to, X, would provide stable long term accommodation for her, which was in her best interests. (2) Were the order for relocation granted, X would live with G, P and C as part of a stable, welcoming and more traditional family unit, with whom she had good relationships, she would enjoy and benefit from living and growing up in such a household and it was in her best interests to do so. (3) G 's financial means and resources to maintain X would be no better or worse if an order for relocation were made, however, were it to be made, P was willing and financially able to support X at an appropriate level pending G finding suitable employment in Cornwall, further, G's parents were willing and financially able to provide such support, therefore, the means and resources available to G to financially support X would be greater and more secure were the order for relocation made, which would be in X's best interests. (4) X's future education was currently uncertain where G would shortly be moving to a location as yet unknown, and there would be no continuity between her present nursery and any primary school, in the event that G were to relocate to Cornwall, X could and would attend the infant school in the village where P and C lived, it was located very close to P's house, X had already visited it and had started making friends with at least one pupil there, and she would have no significant difficulty in making the transition; X would likely enjoy attending the school and would benefit therefrom, and it would be in her best interests to do so. (5) X had no significant social life, friends or social activities outwith nursery, were an order for relocation refused, X would move to a different part of Scotland with G, and would continue to travel to visit J every alternate weekend and with G to Cornwall and elsewhere on the other weekends, therefore it was unlikely that the quality of her social life would significantly increase, however, were an order for relocation made, X would have greater opportunities to develop her social life, in particular through P and his family and friends, she would also no longer be travelling as much as presently and would therefore have a greater chance to develop a social life, which would be in her best interests. (6) Were an order for relocation made, X would continue to have regular residential contact with J in Scotland and in the Bristol or Cornwall areas, the total period of such contact would likely be less than at present overall but it would still be sufficient to enable X to maintain positive and meaningful contact with J, which would be in her best interests. (7) Were no order for relocation to be made, X would continue to have contact with the parties' extended families much as at present, however, were an order made, and a contact with J made in the terms aforementioned, X would continue to have contact with J's extended family when she had residential contact with him, which would be less than at present but would not be so reduced that regular and meaningful contact between them and X would not continue, X would continue to have contact with G's extended family, and contact between X and G's parents might be less than at present but not so reduced as to prevent regular and meaningful ongoing contact. (9) Were the order for relocation refused, G would be significantly and adversely emotionally affected, X's interests and welfare were strongly linked to G's, and X would be likely to experience an adverse indirect emotional impact, on the other hand, were the order for relocation granted, G would be happy, from which X would gain some indirect emotional benefit, and although J would be upset, any indirect emotional impact on X therefrom would be less significant for her than that which she would suffer were an order for relocation to be refused, therefore, making the order was in X's best interests. (10) Both J and G were to some extent pursuing their own interests, however, G's proposed relocation was more reasonable from her perspective than J's objections thereto from his, and G's motives were more rooted in the reality of the parties' situation than J's. (11) It was in X's best interests that a specific issue order and a contact order be made and it would be better for such orders to be made than not; X would have a comfortable and more secure future in Cornwall, although the contact order amounted to a reduction in the annual residential contact, significant continuing contact would be secured thereby, and the overall advantages to X of a move to Cornwall were clear by comparison with the available alternative.

M v F, 2016 Fam. L.R. 70, Sheriff S G Collins, QC, Sh Ct (Tayside) (Perth).

2653 Permanence orders–Children's welfare–Sheriff's error in approach to threshold test

[Adoption and Children (Scotland) Act 2007 (asp 4) s.83, s.83(2), s.83(3), s.84(5)(c)(ii); Children's Hearings (Scotland) Act 2011 (asp 1) Sch.1; European Convention on Human Rights 1950 art.8]

The mother (R) of a child (C), aged six, appealed against a decision of the sheriff, granting a permanence order in respect of C and also authority for adoption, and dispensing with R's parental consent in terms of the Adoption and Children (Scotland) Act 2007 s.83, and ordering indirect contact between R and C. Following C's birth, concerns had been raised regarding R's relationships with a convicted sex offender and a violent offender, and following a report in June 2012 from C's grandmother (G) that she had noted bruises on C's face and head, a child protection investigation had been undertaken in which R had given different explanations to social workers and a police officer for C's bruising than that earlier given to G, and following which she had failed to seek medical attention for C. On 21 June, a child protection order had been granted and C had been accommodated with foster carers (F) with whom he remained, with R exercising regular contact. On 21 December, grounds of referral were established on the basis of lack of parental care and R's relationship with a Children's Hearings (Scotland) Act 2011 Sch.1 offender. On 12 April, a children's hearing had reduced contact between R and C from twice to once per week. In 2013, R formed a relationship with a registered sex offender (L), with whom she had a child in June 2014, who was accommodated through a child protection order from birth. Thereafter, contact between C and R had been reduced and since February 2014, had been once every six weeks. The sheriff found that C was happy and settled with F, there were concerns about his behaviour before and after contact with R, R had consistently failed to engage with professionals who had attempted to offer parenting assistance, she remained in a relationship with L, who had been physically abusive towards her, and her domestic circumstances were such that C's rehabilitation with her would not be conducive to his welfare. The sheriff made findings in fact and law *inter alia* that it would be better for C that a permanence order be made than not, C's residence with R was likely to be detrimental to his welfare, and that R was unable satisfactorily to discharge her parental responsibilities or exercise her parental rights in relation to C and was likely to continue to be unable to do so. R submitted that (1) in making the permanence order, the sheriff had failed to the critical test for the making thereof in s.84(5)(c)(ii) of the 2007 Act; (2) the facts found by the sheriff were insufficient to satisfy the s.84(5)(c)(ii) test, if properly interpreted; (3) the grounds for dispensing with parental consent under s.83(2) and (3) had not been satisfied.

Held: Appeal refused. (1) The requirements of s.84(5)(c)(ii) set a threshold test and unless that test was satisfied, no permanence order could be made and any further consideration of s.84 was irrelevant, *W v Aberdeenshire Council* [2012] CSIH 37, 2013 S.C. 108, [2013] C.L.Y. 3710, *applied.* (2) The sheriff's findings in fact and law had failed to address the strict criterion in s.84(5)(c)(ii) that C's residence with R was, or was likely to be, seriously detrimental to his welfare, mere detriment was insufficient, serious detriment was required, and the sheriff had been in error in the reasoning whereby he had concluded that a permanence order ought to be granted. (3) The court required to consider whether the s.84(5)(c)(ii) test had been satisfied on the basis of the sheriff's findings in fact and the other material accepted by him; the sheriff had found in fact that to return C to R's care would be seriously detrimental to his welfare, which although different from the statutory test, was similar, moreover, the sheriff had expressly accepted the reasons for the s.84(5)(c)(ii) test being met as advanced by the local children's authority (S), which involved serious allegations, thus it was inevitable that he would be required to hold that residence with R was, or would be likely to be, seriously detrimental to C's welfare and the threshold test was met, and the challenge to his making of the permanence order had to fail, notwithstanding the sheriff's error in his method of reaching that conclusion. (4) The sheriff had been justified in dispensing with R's consent to placing C for adoption; the sheriff had expressly addressed the s.83(3) test and on the basis of the evidence, he had been entitled to reach the conclusion he had. (5) The sheriff had addressed the test of necessity; his findings that C's welfare required that parental consent be dispensed with, and that R was unable satisfactorily to discharge her parental responsibilities, both involved a test of necessity, and on the evidence and the sheriff's findings, that test had been satisfied, moreover, where that was so, there should be no contravention of human rights, *S v L* [2012] UKSC 30, 2013 S.C. (U.K.S.C.) 20, [2012] C.L.Y. 1297, *followed.* (6) The sheriff had been entitled to make the findings regarding contact and there was no basis for interfering with his decision, and his findings had been sufficient to ensure compatibility with ECHR art.8. *Observed*, that in s.84 of the 2007 Act, the fundamental threshold test came at the end, after the provisions dealing with the welfare of the child, there was an obvious risk that there would be a failure to appreciate the fundamental importance of the criterion in s.84(5), and any court considering whether or not to impose a permanence order had to have regard to the fact that the test in s.84(5) was a threshold test and required to be satisfied before the other provisions of s.84 became relevant.

R v STIRLING COUNCIL *sub nom.* KR v STIRLING COUNCIL, [2016] CSIH 36, 2016 S.L.T. 689, Lady Paton, Lord Drummond Young, Lord McGhie, IH (Ex Div).

2654 Permanence orders–Parental contact–Contact four times per year between child and natural father–Sheriff's exercise of discretion

A local authority (D) appealed against a decision of the sheriff granting contact four times per annum between a child (C) and his father (F) as part of a permanence order in respect of C. Parties had agreed that post adoption contact between F and C was in C's best interests and ought to continue, however, F had sought to have contact continued at the same frequency, namely once per month, while D had sought to limit contact to two times per annum and had led evidence from C's social worker that contact above that level would be detrimental to C's welfare. D claimed that as a result of the sheriff's decision on contact, C's prospective adoptive placement had been withdrawn.

Held: Appeal refused. The sheriff had displayed a careful and balanced approach to the issue of post adoption contact between F and C and there was no basis on which the exercise of her discretion in that regard might be interfered with, the reasons for withdrawal of C's placement were not properly known to the court and even had they been, they could not form a sound basis for a challenge to the sheriff's exercise of her discretion where the withdrawal had occurred after the court's decision had been taken and was not a feature which might *ex post facto* be utilised to criticise that decision, and the appeal was entirely without merit. *Observed*, that it was the court's duty in cases such as the present to place the evidence led before it under close and critical analysis before arriving at its decision as to the best interests of the child, and a court of first instance had not indulged in an improper exercise of its discretion where it had merely disagreed with the evidence of a particular witness.

DUNDEE CITY COUNCIL, APPELLANTS, [2016] SAC (Civ) 1, 2016 Fam. L.R. 128, Sheriff Principal C A L Scott, QC, Sheriff Principal M Lewis, Sheriff A L MacFadyen, SAC.

2655 Social care–Children–Local authorities' powers and duties

THE CONTINUING CARE (SCOTLAND) AMENDMENT ORDER 2016, SSI 2016/92; made under the Children (Scotland) Act 1995 s.26A(2)(b). In force: 1 April 2016.

This Order amends the Continuing Care (Scotland) Order 2015 art.2 with the effect that the higher age limit for "eligible persons" specified for the purposes of the Children (Scotland) Act 1995 s.26A(2)(b) is 18 years of age (increased from 17).

2656 Vocational training–Qualifications–Young persons

THE NAMED PERSONS (TRAINING, QUALIFICATIONS, EXPERIENCE AND POSITION) AND THE CHILD'S PLAN (SCOTLAND) REVOCATION ORDER 2016, SSI 2016/234; made under the Children and Young People (Scotland) Act 2014 s.19(3)(b), s.34(4), s.35(8)(9), s.39(6), s.99(1)(a)(b). In force: 30 August 2016.

This Order revokes the Named Persons (Training, Qualifications, Experience and Position) (Scotland) Order 2016 and the Child's Plan (Scotland) Order 2016.

FOOD

2657 EU law–Fitness for human consumption–Caseins and caseinates intended for human consumption

THE CASEINS AND CASEINATES (SCOTLAND) REGULATIONS 2016, SSI 2016/383; made under the Food Safety Act 1990 s.6(4), s.16(1), s.17(1), s.26(1)(3), s.31(1), s.48(1); European Communities Act 1972 s.2(2), Sch.2 para.1A. In force: 22 December 2016.

These Regulations make provision to implement in Scotland certain provisions of Directive (EU) 2015/2203 of the European Parliament and of the Council on the approximation of the laws of the Member States relating to caseins and caseinates intended for human consumption and repealing Council Directive. Regulation 4 provides for the restrictions in use and marketing of edible caseins and caseinates and reg.5 provides for labelling requirements.

2658 EU law–Food safety–Enforcement

THE FOOD INFORMATION (SCOTLAND) AMENDMENT REGULATIONS 2016, SSI 2016/191; made under the Food Safety Act 1990 s.6(4), s.16(1), s.17, s.18, s.26, s.48(1), Sch.1 para.1; European Communities Act 1972 s.2(2), Sch.2 para.1A. In force: 20 July 2016.

These Regulations make provision to enforce in Scotland the requirements of Regulation 828/2014 on the requirements for the provision of information to consumers on the absence or reduced presence of gluten in food. Reg.2 makes amendments to the Food Information (Scotland) Regulations 2014 to ensure that arts 3(1) and 4 of Regulation 828/2014 can be enforced. In particular, they have the effect of making it an offence to fail to comply with those articles and they ensure that powers of entry are available under s.32 of the Food Safety Act 1990 for the purposes of enforcing those articles. Reg.3 revokes the Foodstuffs Suitable for People Intolerant to Gluten (Scotland) Regulations 2010.

2659 EU law–Food safety–Food composition

THE FOODS FOR SPECIFIC GROUPS (SCOTLAND) REGULATIONS 2016, SSI 2016/190; made under the Food Safety Act 1990 s.6(4), s.16(1), s.17(1), s.26(1)(3), s.31(1), s.48(1); European Communities Act 1972 s.2(2), Sch.2 para.1A. In force: 20 July 2016.

These Regulations make provision to enforce in Scotland certain provisions of Regulation 609/2013 on food intended for infants and young children, food for special medical purposes, and total diet replacement for weight control and repealing Directives 92/52, 96/8, 1999/21, 2006/125, 2006/141 and 2009/39 and Regulations 41/2009 and 953/2009, which repeals and replaces a regime regulating (mostly, but not exclusively, compositional and labelling requirements) which must be met by certain groups of food before such food may be marketed in the Member States. Reg.3 provides for the execution and enforcement of these Regulations by local authorities. Reg.4 provides for offences and penalties. Reg.5 modifies certain provisions of the Food Safety Act 1990 for enforcement purposes. Reg.6 amends the Foods Intended for Use in Energy Restricted Diets for Weight Reduction Regulations 1997. Reg.7 provides for revocation of subordinate legislation.

2660 **Food composition–Food safety–Products containing meat**

THE PRODUCTS CONTAINING MEAT ETC. (SCOTLAND) AMENDMENT REGULATIONS 2016, SSI 2016/24; made under the Food Safety Act 1990 s.6(4), s.16(1)(a)(e)(f), s.26(1)(a)(3), s.48(1). In force: 25 February 2016.

These Regulations amend the Products Containing Meat etc. (Scotland) Regulations 2014. Regulation 2 of these Regulations amends reg.7 of the 2014 Regulations by inserting a reference to the Food Safety Act 1990 s.22 (defence of publication in the course of business).

GOVERNMENT ADMINISTRATION

2661 **Public Services Reform (Scotland) Act 2010 (asp 8)–Commencement No.7 Order**

THE PUBLIC SERVICES REFORM (SCOTLAND) ACT 2010 (COMMENCEMENT NO.7) ORDER 2016, SSI 2016/22; made under the Public Services Reform (Scotland) Act 2010 s.134(7). Commencement details: bringing into operation various provisions of the 2010 Act on 1 April 2016 and 1 April 2017.

This Order brings the Public Services Reform (Scotland) Act 2010 ss.108 to 110 further into force with certain exceptions. Sections 108 to 110 relate to health care: scrutiny and improvement and have already been commenced as regards Healthcare Improvement Scotland's functions in relation to independent hospitals and private psychiatric hospitals.

2662 **Registrar General–Research–Fees payable to Registrar General for internet searches**

THE REGISTRATION SERVICES (FEES, ETC.) (SCOTLAND) AMENDMENT REGULATIONS 2016, SSI 2016/64; made under the Registration of Births, Deaths and Marriages (Scotland) Act 1965 s.28A(4), s.38(2)(3), s.47, s.54(1); Civil Partnership Act 2004 s.122(4); Local Electoral Administration and Registration Services (Scotland) Act 2006 s.55(6), s.58(5). In force: 1 September 2016.

These Regulations amend fees payable to the Registrar General for internet searches under the Registration Services (Fees, etc.) (Scotland) Regulations 2006 and the Book of Scottish Connections Regulations 2008.

2663 **Scottish Fire and Rescue Service–Appointments**

THE SCOTTISH FIRE AND RESCUE SERVICE (APPOINTMENT OF CHIEF INSPECTOR) ORDER 2016, SSI 2016/96; made under the Fire (Scotland) Act 2005 s.43A(1)(a). In force: 26 February 2016.

This Order appoints Martyn Anthony Emberson QFSM as the Chief Inspector of the Scottish Fire and Rescue Service.

HEALTH

2664 **Health (Tobacco, Nicotine etc. and Care) (Scotland) Act 2016 (asp 14)**

An Act to make provision about tobacco, nicotine and related products, in particular to make provision about retailing, to amend the prohibition on smoking in certain areas and to control advertising and promotion; to make provision about a duty of candour following serious incidents in the course of providing care; to make provision about offences applying to ill-treatment or neglect where care is provided; and for connected purposes.

2665 **Health care–Healthcare Improvement Scotland–Registration**

THE HEALTHCARE IMPROVEMENT SCOTLAND (FEES) REGULATIONS 2016, SSI 2016/26; made under the National Health Service (Scotland) Act 1978 s.10Z5. In force: 1 April 2016.

These Regulations prescribe the maximum fees which may be imposed by Healthcare Improvement Scotland in respect of applications for registration or for cancellation of registration of independent health care services, the annual continuation of any such registration, and applications for the variation or removal of a condition of registration under the National Health Service (Scotland) Act 1978.

2666 **NHS–Compensation–Fees**

THE PERSONAL INJURIES (NHS CHARGES) (AMOUNTS) (SCOTLAND) AMENDMENT REGULATIONS 2016, SSI 2016/59; made under the Health and Social Care (Community Health and Standards) Act 2003 s.153(2)(5), s.168, s.195(1)(2). In force: 1 April 2016.

These Regulations amend the Personal Injuries (NHS Charges) (Amounts) (Scotland) Regulations 2006, which make provision in relation to the amount of NHS charges which a person (who pays compensation to an injured person) is liable to pay, where that injured person has received National Health Service treatment or ambulance services.

2667 **NHS–Patients' rights–Complaints procedure**

THE PATIENT RIGHTS (COMPLAINTS PROCEDURE AND CONSEQUENTIAL PROVISIONS) (SCOTLAND) AMENDMENT REGULATIONS 2016, SSI 2016/401; made under the Patient Rights (Scotland) Act 2011 s.15(4), s.25(1). In force: 1 April 2017.

These Regulations make changes to the requirements as to how relevant NHS bodies (Health Boards, Special Health Boards and the Common Services Agency) and service providers to the NHS are to deal with complaints received from, or on behalf of, patients or service users.

2668 **NHS–Prescription charges**

THE NATIONAL HEALTH SERVICE (FREE PRESCRIPTIONS AND CHARGES FOR DRUGS AND APPLIANCES) (SCOTLAND) AMENDMENT REGULATIONS 2016, SSI 2016/195; made under the National Health Service (Scotland) Act 1978 s.69, s.105(7). In force: 16 September 2016.

These Regulations amend the National Health Service (Free Prescriptions and Charges for Drugs and Appliances) (Scotland) Regulations 2011, which provide that where a person provides pharmaceutical services to a patient who presents an English prescription form, that person must make and recover from the patient the charges specified in the National Health Service (Charges for Drugs and Appliances) Regulations 2015 as at a specified date, unless certain exemptions apply. The amendments made by reg.2 ensure that the charge to be made will reflect the rate applicable under those Regulations, as amended by amended by SI 2016 325, as at 1 April 2016, specifically: £8.40 per item, or £16.80 per pair, in relation to the supply of elastic hosiery; £8.40 in relation to the supply of any other appliance; and £8.40 in relation to the supply of each quantity of a drug.

2669 Nursing and Midwifery Council–References–Decision to refer midwife to conduct and competence committee–Whether irrational

[Nursing and Midwifery Council (Fitness to Practise) Rules Order of Council 2004 (SI 2004/1761); Nursing and Midwifery Order (2001) 2002 (SI 2002/253)]

A registered midwife (S) raised a petition for judicial review seeking reduction of a decision of the investigating committee (C) of the Nursing and Midwifery Council (N) to refer her to N's conduct and competence committee (X), and to interdict N from taking any steps to convene a conduct hearing pursuant thereto. On 17 March 2010, S had been suspended from her employment following allegations of professional negligence. The matter was referred to N, which, in April 2010, suspended S from registration *ad interim*. The Nursing and Midwifery Council (Fitness to Practise) Rules Order of Council 2004 art.26 provided that C was responsible for investigating any allegation referred to it and was *inter alia* to take such steps as were reasonably practicable to obtain as much information as possible. Article 31 empowered the suspension of a registrant against whom allegations had been made, with approval from the court required to obtain an extension of the suspension after the expiry of 18 months. N sought several extensions between 2010 and 2014 to allow it *inter alia* to obtain expert opinions from a specialist obstetrician and a medical statistician. N's application for a further extension on 7 July 2014 was refused and on 24 July, C referred the matter to X for determination, having decided to present the case without obtaining expert medical opinions. S submitted *inter alia* that N had failed to supply the further information sought and had thereby failed in its duty to take all reasonable practicable steps to obtain as much information as possible.

Held: Petition dismissed. (1) Although the delay from 2010 until 2015 was not satisfactory, it was not such as to require reduction of C's decision to send the case to X and it could not be said that S had been prejudiced and would be unable to have a fair trial. (2) The Nursing and Midwifery Order (2001) 2002 and the 2004 Rules provided that N was to obtain as much information as was reasonably practicable, however, the decision as to whether to pursue a particular line of investigation was an exercise of professional judgment; in the present case, C had information which had enabled it to make a decision that there was a case to answer which could not be described as irrational, it was a decision that C was entitled to make, there were no grounds before the court to show the decision to be irrational and there were thus no grounds of reduction. *Opinion*, that while S's actions had caused some delay, the majority of the time had been taken by N.

STEWART, PETITIONER, [2015] CSOH 85, 2016 S.C.L.R. 166, Lady Stacey, OH.

2670 Public health–Smoking-related offences–Children in Motor Vehicles

THE SMOKING PROHIBITION (CHILDREN IN MOTOR VEHICLES) (SCOTLAND) ACT 2016 (FIXED PENALTY NOTICES) REGULATIONS 2016, SSI 2016/403; made under the Smoking Prohibition (Children in Motor Vehicles) (Scotland) Act 2016 Sch.1 para.2, Sch.1 para.11. In force: 5 December 2016.

These Regulations make provision in relation to the fixed penalty notice regime under the Smoking Prohibition (Children in Motor Vehicles) (Scotland) Act 2016 s.2.

HEALTH AND SAFETY AT WORK

2671 Prohibition notices–Offshore installations–Health and safety inspector's assessment of risk–Availability of appeal on facts

[Health and Safety at Work etc. Act 1974 (c.37) s.24]

An inspector of Health and Safety (H) appealed against a decision of the employment tribunal cancelling a prohibition notice which had been served on the operators (C) of an offshore installation. The main mode of access to, and egress from, the installation was by helicopter and the only access to the helipad was by three stairways which led to staging running around the perimeter of the helipad and one metre below it. The staging was constructed of steel grates and the stairways of steel treads. Two of the stairways were used as the main access to, and egress from, the helipad, the third was used as an evacuation route. H had visited the installation on 23 April 2013 for the purposes of carrying out a planned inspection which identified significant areas of what was thought to be corrosion in the stairway treads on all three stairways, as well as on the grates on the staging. H considered the stairways and staging unsafe and served a prohibition notice which stated that the use thereof would involve a risk of serious personal injury by reason of persons falling through them. At the time of the notice, H was aware that remedial works had commenced on the port side stairway, and the installation manager had offered an undertaking that the remedial work would be undertaken immediately, and that the staging and stairways would not be used until it was completed; by the time H departed on 25 April, all the remedial work had been carried out other than to the forward stairway. Following the inspection, C arranged for the stairways and staging to be removed and transported to the lab of Exova for testing. The testing took place in November which revealed that all of the pieces met the British Standard requirement apart from the panel which had been sheared by a fire axe during H's testing, the strength of which could not thereafter be determined. C appealed the issue of the notice under the Health and Safety at Work etc. Act 1974 s.24 and as a consequence of H's objection to the admission of evidence of the Exova testing, the tribunal considered (i) how it would determine the appeal without the evidence: and, given the willingness to immediately remedy the problem and the presence of H on the installation until 25 April, rendering him in effective control of the situation, the use of the stairway and staging was not likely to be carried on, there was no risk of serious personal injury and service of the notice had been unnecessary and unreasonable; when H left the installation, work had not yet commenced on the forward access stairway in respect of which H would have been justified in serving a notice confined thereto, and (ii) that evidence which had come into existence after the notice could be taken into account, as long as it shed light on what the situation had been at the time of the notice, the condition of the metal in November was circumstantial evidence from which an inference could be drawn about its state at the time of the notice and concluded that at said time, the condition of the stairways and staging, although visibly corroded, was not such as to pose a risk of serious personal injury.

Held: Appeal refused. An appeal under s.24 of the 1974 Act was not confined to points of law, an appeal on the facts was equally open and bearing in mind the effect a prohibition notice might have on an operator's business, it would be strange if an operator could not mount a successful appeal based upon the simple contention that, whatever the inspector thought at the time based on the information before him, it was now known, based on more complete or additional information, that the risk founded upon did not, in fact, exist; there was no sound basis for restricting appeals under s.24 to what would in essence be a form of judicial review of the inspector's opinion, an appeal on the facts was a much wider concept and it thus followed that the tribunal were entitled to have regard to the Exova report and conclude that the condition of the gratings and stairs, albeit plainly affected by considerable corrosion, did not in fact involve a risk of serious personal injury, *Rotary Yorkshire Ltd v Hague (Health and Safety Inspector)* [2014] EWHC 2126 (Admin), *not followed*, and *Railtrack Plc v Smallwood* [2001] EWHC Admin 78, [2001] I.C.R. 714, [2001] C.L.Y. 3317, *considered*. *Opinion*, (1) that on the first issue which presupposed the exclusion of the Exova results, the tribunal was entitled to reach the view it had having taken into account the temporary measures which had been put in place to prevent the use of stairways and staging, the remedial steps which were underway, the undertakings given by the installation manager, the fact that the stairways and staging would not be used until the remedial steps were completed, and the continued presence of H; (2) that while the tribunal might have erred in going on to consider what might have been appropriate two days after the notice, that had not affected the decision on the issue of risk at the time the notice was served. *Observed*, that the aforementioned analysis had no bearing upon an inspector's ability to act, in the interests of health and safety, where he formed the opinion that a risk existed and the emergence of new material to negate said risk did not, of itself, invalidate the notice or its effect at the time.

HM INSPECTOR OF HEALTH & SAFETY v CHEVRON NORTH SEA LTD, [2016] CSIH 29, 2016 S.L.T. 561, The Lord President (Carloway), Lord Menzies, Lord Bracadale, IH (1 Div).

HERITABLE PROPERTY

2672 Acquisition of land–Compensation–Land partly permanently acquired and partly temporarily entered and possessed–Amount of compensation for loss or disturbance of person's enjoyment of land

[Land Compensation (Scotland) Act 1963 (c.51) s.12, s.25, s.26, s.29, s.30(2); Forth Crossing Act 2011 (asp 2) Pt 4, s.37, s.54(2), s.54(3), s.54(4); Tribunal Procedure (Amendment) Rules 2010 (SI 2010/43)]

The owners (S) of land (L) appealed under the Land Compensation (Scotland) Act 1963 s.29 against a decision of the Scottish Ministers (M) upholding in part an appeal by Transport Scotland (T) against a decision of the local planning authority (F) issuing a certificate of appropriate alternative development (C) to S in respect of L, partly permanently acquired and partly temporarily entered and possessed by M in relation to the construction works for the new bridge over the Firth of Forth. The Forth Crossing Act 2011 s.54(2) provided that any dispute about the amount of compensation payable for any loss arising from the entry into and temporary possession of land was to be determined by the Lands Tribunal for Scotland, s.54(3) provided that where temporary possession was taken under s.37, such a dispute was to be determined in accordance with the 1963 Act as if it were a question of disputed compensation for the compulsory acquisition of land, and ss.25-30 of the 1963 Act, comprising Pt IV thereof, made provision for an application to the relevant planning authority for a certificate stating its opinion as to what planning permission would be appropriate for the land in question. T had appealed F's decision under s.26 of the 1963 Act and M had appointed a reporter (R), who had identified that he could not make a determination on the legal arguments as to the applicability of Pt IV of the 1963 Act to the assessment of compensation for entry and temporary possession of land and therefore the competency of the application but had not found T's argument in support of the proposition that the Pt IV procedure did not apply to the assessment of compensation for temporary possession to be persuasive, however, M had not adopted his conclusion on C's validity, had not accepted his recommendations to vary C, and, in accordance with s.26(2), upheld the appeal in so far as it related to C's validity and cancelled C, finding that the exercise of a power under under s.37, to enter and take temporary possession of land, did not amount, within the meaning of s.30(2) of the 1963 Act, and therefore, for the purposes of s.25, to a proposal to acquire an interest in land by an authority possessing compulsory purchase powers, and those provisions of the 1963 Act were not modified by s.54 of the 2011 Act. S argued that M had failed properly to apply s.54 of the 2011 Act such that they had failed to apply the provisions of the 1963 Act, particularly Pt IV, had erred in law and acted unreasonably in not granting a certificate in relation to the permanently acquired part of L, and had failed to set out proper and adequate reasons, accordingly they had erred in law and had acted unreasonably, and asked the court whether M (i) had erred in law in cancelling C and not granting a certificate, (ii) had erred in law and acted unreasonably in not granting a certificate in relation to the permanently acquired part of L, (iii) had failed to give proper and adequate reasons.

Held: Matter remitted to M. (1) The court would approach the question whether or not Pt IV of the 1963 Act had been applied by virtue of s.54(3) of the 2011 Act for the purpose of compensation for temporary loss of possession, on the understanding that irrespective of which construction was considered to be correct, it remained open to S to argue that compensation for the taking of possession of the temporarily acquired part of L ought to be assessed by reference to the likelihood of a grant of planning permission in particular terms. (2) The manner in which a dispute about the entitlement to, or computation of, the amount of compensation for loss or disturbance of a person's enjoyment of land as a result of M's entry and temporary possession thereof in terms of s.37, was to be determined, in terms of s.54(3), might be contrasted with the manner in which such compensation might be calculated, as addressed in s.54(4), suggesting that s.54(3) dealt only with matters of procedure, which obtained some support from the passage "so far as applicable and subject to the necessary modifications" in parenthesis, and all the words in a statute were to be assumed to have been included in order to assist in making Parliament's intention clear; the manner in which s.54(3) was formulated suggested that in enacting it, the Scottish Parliament had considered that the provisions which were applicable in the event of a dispute were accordingly the specified sections of the 1963 Act, what appeared in parenthesis was of the nature of a more specific restatement of what appeared outside them, and it could not be suggested that the plain meaning of the words outside parenthesis was to incorporate all the provisions of the 1963 Act subject only to such modifications as might be necessary. (3) That s.54(3) was to be interpreted as having a more limited effect received support from the references to "dispute" and "disputed" in s.54(3) and s.54(2), and the facility of application for a certificate ought not to be limited to a situation where there was a dispute to be determined. (4) The inclusion of s.12 of the 1963 Act in the parenthesis in s.54(3) of the 2011 Act meant that in any dispute about compensation for temporary possession of land it was not only the provisions of the 1963 Act relating to procedure before the lands tribunal which were to have effect, at least some of the provisions of Pt VI had also to apply, however, there could be no application of any of the provisions of Pt IV of the 1963 Act to a dispute over compensation for temporary possession; while Pt III referred to Pt IV, it did not incorporate it and its operation was not dependent thereupon; Pt IV presumed the acquisition of an interest in land, and on a proper construction of the 2011 Act it was not competent to apply for a certificate in respect of land which was not to be compulsorily acquired but was only to be temporarily possessed. (5) A dispute as to entitlement to, or assessment of, the amount of compensation for temporary possession was to be determined in accordance with the 1963 Act as if it were a question of disputed compensation for compulsory acquisition, with the specified sections having effect so far as applicable, thus, there were two different sorts of claim arising from the exercise of different sorts of power, which the 2011 Act recognised; it was clear that the facility of applying for a s.25 certificate arose in the context of the valuation of an interest in land which was to be compulsorily acquired, and in the event of an exercise of the s.37 powers of the 2011 Act, there was no interest proposed to be acquired by an authority possessing compulsory purchase powers, as that was defined in s.30(2) of the 1963 Act. (6) Nothing in the 2011 Act applied s.25 or any of the other provisions of Pt IV of the 1963 Act for the purposes of a claim for, or dispute over, compensation for temporary possession. (7) M's decision was within the powers of the 1963 Act in so far as it related to the temporarily acquired land, however, as M had erred in relation to the permanently acquired land, the decision would be quashed and the matter remitted to them with a view to confirming C in so far as the permanently acquired part of L was concerned and thereafter proceeding in terms of the 1963 Act. Observed, that *BPP (Farringdon Road) Ltd v Crossrail Ltd* [2015] UKUT 356 (LC), [2016] R.V.R. 117, [2016] 1805 concerned the proper interpretation of the Tribunal Procedure (Amendment) Rules 2010, in that context, the broad approach taken by the tribunal to the terms thereof was wholly understandable, however, s.54 of the 2011 Act required to be interpreted with regard to its own terms, purpose and background, in any event, there was no equivalent policy justification for a liberal approach, moreover, the Upper Tribunal had been influenced by the otherwise arbitrary effect of the competing submission, which did not apply in the present case, *Crossrail*, *considered*.

SCARBOROUGH MUIR GROUP LTD v SCOTTISH MINISTERS, [2016] CSIH 5, 2016 S.L.T. 409, Lord Brodie, Lady Clark of Calton, Lord Malcolm, IH (Ex Div).

2673 **Community bodies–Community relations–Savings**

THE COMMUNITY EMPOWERMENT (SCOTLAND) ACT 2015 (CONSEQUENTIAL MODIFICATIONS AND SAVINGS) ORDER 2016, SSI 2016/28; made under the Community Empowerment (Scotland) Act 2015 s.143. In force: 15 April 2016.

This Order makes provision in consequence of the Community Empowerment (Scotland) Act 2015. It makes provision modifying the Land Reform (Scotland) Act 2003. Modifications provided for in this Order are in consequence of the provision in the 2015 Act amending the 2003 Act in relation to the definition of community bodies.

2674 Compensation–Wayleaves–Overhead electricity cable running over private land–Date from which compensation payable

[Electricity Act 1989 (c.29) Sch.4 para.6, Sch.4 para.7; European Convention on Human Rights 1950 Protocol 1 art.1, art.14]

A recycling waste management company (W) sought compensation from the electricity transmission network (S) in respect of an overhead electricity cable running over its land (L) in relation to which a necessary wayleave was granted by the Scottish Ministers (M). The cable had been in situ since W had taken possession of L. In 1991, a predecessor in title to L had granted a voluntary wayleave in respect thereof in favour of the then proprietor, which had come to an end on W's occupation of L in 1998. During 2005, S had sought, and W had refused to grant, a voluntary wayleave, and on 8 December 2010, W had issued a notice of removal. On 3 March 2011, S had applied to M for a necessary wayleave pursuant to the Electricity Act 1989 Sch.4 para.6. In 2014, W had signed an agreement with S in terms of which W had consented to the continued presence of the apparatus over L for two years for the sole purpose of facilitating its removal and the diversion of the network route away from L, and to M granting a necessary wayleave in those terms. In August, M had granted S's application, specifying that it was to be in force from the date it had been signed because there was nothing in Sch.4 to the 1989 Act which allowed M to grant a wayleave which had effect from earlier than that date. W argued that compensation ought to be awarded as from the date of its notice to remove, or, at the latest, from the date of S's application for a necessary wayleave. W submitted that (1) Sch.4 para.6(3) of the 1989 Act permitted M to grant a wayleave subject to such terms and conditions as they thought fit, which was in the widest possible language and included the power to make the grant of the wayleave retrospective to backdate it to the time of the application or of the notice to remove, or require compensation to be awarded for that period; (2) with regard to ECHR Protocol 1 art.1, M's decision to grant the necessary wayleave from the date of signature rather than the date of notice to remove or the date of the application did not strike a fair balance between the general interests of the community under the 1989 Act and the protection of W's right to peaceful enjoyment its possessions; (3) art.14 of the ECHR was also engaged where M's decision to grant the wayleave only from the date of signature was that the owner or occupier of the land subjected to a *de facto* wayleave was treated differently, and less favourably, than an owner or occupier in respect of whose land a necessary wayleave had been granted which afforded W sufficient "other status" for the purposes of art.14.

Held: Petition refused. (1) On the plain meaning of the words used in Sch.4 para.7 of the 1989 Act, it was clear that para.7(1) made provision for compensation to be granted only when a wayleave was granted under para.6, and compensation could only be recovered in respect thereof, it made no provision for compensation for the presence of an electricity line otherwise than pursuant to the grant of a necessary wayleave, were an application for a wayleave refused, no compensation was recoverable, and the clear link between the grant of the wayleave and the right to compensation was also found in para.7(2) where the provision for compensation in respect of damage caused to land in the exercise of any right conferred by the wayleave did not cover such damage caused in circumstances where the line was on the site otherwise than in accordance with the wayleave, and that construction was consistent with the authorities in so far as they were of the view that the statutory provisions only provided for compensation from the date of the grant of the wayleave, *Welford v EDF Energy Networks (LPN) Plc* [2007] EWCA Civ 293, [2007] 2 P. & C.R. 15, [2007] C.L.Y. 3385, *Arnold White Estates Ltd v National Grid Electricity Transmission Plc* [2014] EWCA Civ 216, [2014] Ch. 385, [2014] C.L.Y. 2527, *Patersons of Greenoakhill Ltd v SP Transmission Ltd* [2009] CSOH 155, 2010 S.L.T. 115, [2010] C.L.Y. 4309 and *William Tracey Ltd v SP Transmission Plc* [2016] CSOH 14, 2016 S.L.T. 678, [2016] 2676, *considered.* (2) The legislative aim of the 1989 Act was legitimate and necessarily involved some interference with the enjoyment of land over which it was necessary to run power lines, provision was made for compensation, the period between an application for a necessary wayleave and its grant or refusal was likely to be a period of weeks or months, which was insignificant when measured against the likely 40 year duration of the necessary wayleave, moreover, compensation might be awarded in whole or in part on the basis of diminution in the value of the land, therefore W's posited position of interference with peaceful enjoyment of land without compensation for considerable periods was exaggerated and the scheme under Sch.4 of the 1989 Act did not result in interference in the use and enjoyment of the land without compensation; there was a statutory scheme for compensation which was appropriate in most, if not all, reasonably foreseeable circumstances, and the argument based on art.1 protocol 1 would be rejected. (3) The argument on discrimination contrary to art.14 would also be rejected where the situation of an owner or occupier of land before the grant of a necessary wayleave did not give him any particular status as compared with that which he enjoyed after the necessary wayleave had been granted, further, did he enjoy a separate status, a finding that an owner or occupier of land before the grant of a wayleave ought to be treated in terms of compensation in the same manner as the owner or occupier of land after the grant thereof gave rise to a discrimination in that he would be treated better than an owner or occupier of land where the application for a necessary wayleave was ultimately refused.

WILLIAM TRACEY LTD v SCOTTISH MINISTERS, [2016] CSOH 131, 2016 S.L.T. 1049, Lord Glennie, OH.

2675 Disposition of property–Forgery–Forged disposition conveying heritable property–Wholly void rather than merely voidable

C reclaimed against a decision of the Lord Ordinary refusing to grant decree of reduction of a forged disposition which had conveyed heritable property (P) to her son (S) (*Chalmers v Chalmers* [2014] CSOH 161, 2015 S.C.L.R. 299, [2015] 8 C.L. 321). C's husband (H) had instructed P's purchase in 1998 and the title had been registered in C's name without her knowledge or consent. In 2002, P had been conveyed to S via a disposition purportedly signed by C, who had subsequently discovered the disposition prior to commencing divorce proceedings against H in 2012. C and H had agreed a final financial settlement in 2013 by minute of agreement which *inter alia* had provided for C's resignation from their property letting partnership (R) and the transfer of C's rights and interests in R's assets, capital accounts and partnership income to H. C thereafter raised the action of reduction and interdict against S. The Lord Ordinary held that P had never operated as part of R's portfolio and C could not have held it in trust for R, it had never been intended for C to have any beneficial interest in P, she had deliberately delayed in raising the action beyond the signing of the minute of agreement, and S had not participated in any fraud on C.

Held: Case put out by order. (1) A forged disposition was a nullity, and was wholly void, not merely voidable, and only in exceptional circumstances, namely where the person whose signature had been forged expressly or impliedly authorised or adopted the forged signature as his or her own might a forged disposition have any effect, furthermore, the Scottish land registration system could be subverted if it were possible to forge a signature on a disposition which was duly registered, and then put forward equitable circumstances supporting a contention that the forged disposition ought not to be reduced, with the ultimate result depending upon the discretion of the court. There was no evidence that C had expressly or impliedly authorised or adopted the forged signature as her own, therefore, the Lord Ordinary had erred by adopting the approach of an exercise of discretion; the deed was null and of no effect, and C was entitled to decree of reduction. (2) The reclaiming motion would be allowed, decree of reduction would be granted and the case would be continued to a by order hearing to address the question of interdict and expenses. Opinion, (1) that on the assumption that the court had had a discretion to decide whether or not to reduce the deed, the Lord Ordinary had taken three inaccurate, and thus irrelevant, factors into account, namely that C had had no interest in P, that she had deliberately decided to delay raising the action until after the divorce and that the purpose underlying C's actions was so that she could gain advantage over H and not have to add P to the matrimonial property, where that was contradicted by the findings, and the Lord Ordinary's discretion had been substantially affected thereby and the court would have interfered with his discretion; (2) that had the matter been at large for the court to reconsider, with regard *inter alia* to the fact that C had been unaware of, and had not been a participant in, the forging of her signature on the disposition, that the Lord Ordinary had found H to be an incredible and unreliable witness, had not accepted parts of S's evidence, in particular, that C had known about P, had preferred C's evidence whenever S's evidence had differed from hers, and that C had been open about her discovery of P and the forged signature, and bearing in mind the general proposition that a forger had to bear the consequences of his own actions, the proper exercise of the court's discretion would have resulted in the granting of decree of reduction.

CHALMERS v CHALMERS *sub nom.* MCAULEY v CHALMERS, [2015] CSIH 75, 2015 S.L.T. 793, Lady Paton, Lady Smith, Lord Drummond Young, IH (Ex Div).

2676 Encroachment–Electricity lines–Wayleaves–Relevancy and specification of averments

[Electricity Act 1989 (c.29) Sch.4 para.6, Sch.4 para.8, Sch.4 para.8(1)(c), Sch.4 para.8(2), Sch.8 para.8(1), Sch.8 para.8(2), Sch.8 para.8(3)]

A recycling waste management company (W) raised an action of damages against the owner and operator of the electricity transmission network in central and southern Scotland (S) for unlawful encroachment. S sought dismissal of the action on ground that the circumstances disclosed by W's averments had not amounted to encroachment. Since 1997, W had possessed an area of land (L), initially as a tenant and since 2006 as heritable proprietor, over which ran overhead electricity cables supported by a tower (collectively E) located close to L's boundary, which had been *in situ* since W had taken possession of L. In 1991, a predecessor in title to L had granted a voluntary wayleave in S's favour in respect of E. In approximately 2005, W had refused to grant S a voluntary wayleave, and on 8 December 2010, had issued to S a notice of removal in accordance with the Electricity Act 1989 Sch.4 para.8, requiring E's removal within three months. On 3 March 2011, S applied to the Scottish Ministers (M) for a necessary wayleave pursuant to Sch.4 para.6. On 17 February 2014, W signed an agreement with S in terms of which W consented to E's continued presence over L for two years for the sole purpose of facilitating E's removal and the diversion of the network route away from L, and to M granting a necessary wayleave in those terms. On 13 August, following a reporter's recommendations, M granted S's application. W claimed that the necessary wayleave granted on 13 August was of prospective effect only, and where the consent had been personal to H, on change of ownership, E's presence had no longer been consented to, thus from 1997 until August 2014, no wayleave or consent had been in place therefore E's presence had constituted an unlawful encroachment on L, with consequential damage assessed at £4,686,727.66 and £1,419,365.27.

Held: Action dismissed. (1) As a matter of common law, installing and keeping installed electric lines and associated equipment on the land of another was an encroachment and, in the absence of consent, actionable accordingly, however, the common law position had been altered by the 1989 Act, although the statutory regime was superimposed upon but did not completely supersede the underlying common law, as reflected by Sch.4 para.8(1)(c) and (2), thus there appeared to be no reason in Scots law why the landowner who could show consequential loss should not be able to sue for damages in respect of encroachment. (2) On W's approach, as soon as consent to wayleave fell on change of ownership of the land occurred, and independent of whether the landowner had requested removal or made any other complaint, the transmission licence holder was guilty of encroachment and liable for damages, with the only manner in which that licence holder could bring that situation to an end entirely at its own hand being to remove the line and redirect it, which might not be practicable, having regard to the licence holder's duty to develop and maintain an efficient, co-ordinated and economical system of electrical distribution, and in that circumstance, was W's interpretation of the applicable law correct, a licence holder might find itself unavoidably guilty of delict. (3) The purpose of para.8(1) of the 1989 Act was to identify comprehensively the various events whereby a landowner's consent or deemed consent might become no longer effective, para.8(2) superseded the common law to the extent of replacing the common law remedy of an order for removal with the statutory remedy of giving notice to remove, to which the licence holder might respond by making an application to the Scottish Ministers for the grant of a necessary wayleave, and para.8(3), (4) and (5), which dealt with the consequences thereof, provided a remedy, and by necessary implication, that was the only remedy, thus superseding the common law remedy of damages; there could be said to be a lacuna in the absence of provision for compensation in respect of the interim period between the giving of notice and the Scottish Ministers' decision but with that exception the intention of Parliament seemed to have been to provide a comprehensive solution to the problem of a line having been installed by virtue of a consent which thereafter came to an end or otherwise became ineffective. (4) Where the landowner had given notice to remove, the process in para.8(2) and the succeeding subparagraphs was triggered, and unless and until the licence holder failed to remove, such that there might be scope for an action of damages, para.8(2) expressly provided that the licence holder would not be obliged to comply with the notice to remove; W's construction of para.8 was untenable where it required the presence of an electric line to be held to be wrongful in circumstances not only where it might be necessary for the maintenance of the public electricity supply but where statute expressly permitted the line to continue to be installed, *Patersons of Greenoakhill Ltd v SP Transmission Ltd* [2009] CSOH 155, 2010 S.L.T. 115, [2010] C.L.Y. 4309, *applied.* (5) The crossheading of para.8, "Temporary continuation of wayleaves", was consistent with a construction of para.8(2) as meaning that consent was continued by statute temporarily, and it would be appropriate to describe the effect of para.8 as the temporary continuation of a wayleave where a notice to remove had not yet been given, and also as where notice had been given but M had not yet decided on an application for a necessary wayleave. (6) Giving effect to the proper construction of para.8, W's claim, relying on the proposition that on a pre-existing wayleave ceasing to be binding on a change of ownership the presence of an electric line on land became an encroachment and thus actionable in damages, was irrelevant, both in respect of the pre- and post notice periods. Opinion, that had it been necessary to consider S's argument that the claim in respect of when W had been a tenant of L was irrelevant would have been rejected where W's averments sufficiently instructed its title to sue.

WILLIAM TRACEY LTD v SP TRANSMISSION PLC, [2016] CSOH 14, 2016 S.L.T. 678, Lord Brodie, OH.

2677 Heritable property–Valuation for rating–Lands and heritages in Scotland

THE VALUATION FOR RATING (DECAPITALISATION RATE) (SCOTLAND) REGULATIONS 2016, SSI 2016/402; made under the Valuation and Rating (Scotland) Act 1956 s.6(8A)(8B). In force: 1 March 2016.

These Regulations prescribe the decapitalisation rate to be applied when valuing lands and heritages in Scotland in accordance with the contractor's basis for the purposes of any valuation roll which comes into force on or after 1 April 2017. The contractor's basis is the method of ascertaining the net annual value of lands and heritages by reference to their cost of construction or provision or to their capital value.

2678 Land management–Land reform–Scottish Land Commission

THE LAND REFORM (SCOTLAND) ACT 2016 (CONSEQUENTIAL AND SAVING PROVISIONS) AMENDMENT REGULATIONS 2016, SSI 2016/389; made under the Land Reform (Scotland) Act 2016 s.127(1). In force: 23 December 2016.

These Regulations make corrections to the saving provision of the Land Reform (Scotland) Act 2016 (Consequential and Saving Provisions) Regulations 2016. Regulation 2(2) substitutes a new reg.3 (saving) for reg.3 of the principal Regulations. The effect of the amendment made by these Regulations is to clarify the application of the saving provision contained in reg.3 of the principal Regulations in circumstances where the estate of a deceased person contains more than one lease of an agricultural holding or relevant lease.

2679 Repossession–Sale of property–Creditor's duty to obtain best price for property–Misleading advertisement

[Conveyancing and Feudal Reform (Scotland) Act 1970 (c.35) s.25]

The heritable proprietors (P) of a hotel (H) raised an action against lenders (B) in whose favour P had granted a standard security over H. P had purchased H in 2005 for £202,000, with a loan of £147,000 provided by B. H had been unsuccessful, P had fallen into arrears and in August 2007, B had served calling up notices and had thereafter raised repossession and repayment proceedings. P and B had reached agreement for repayment of the arrears, however, P had failed to maintain payments at an acceptable level, H's alcohol licence had expired in August 2009, and B had repossessed H in October 2009, and had instructed chartered surveyors, who had valued H at £135,000. Between August 2007 and October 2009, P had marketed and advertised H for offers over £250,000 but two interested parties had not pursued its purchase. Following repossession, B had advertised H for sale, comprising only a single advertisement in the commercial property classified section of a Scottish newspaper, from which no buyer had been found. Meanwhile, a local businessman (M) had expressed an interest in acquiring H and had reached an agreement with B enabling him to restore H as a business. He had resumed trading in H in late 2009, had carried out certain restoration and refurbishment and on 25 February 2010, B had sold H for £135,000 to M's business partners. P asserted *inter alia* that B's advertising of H was inaccurate and inadequate, B had ignored their obligations to advertise H and obtain the best price, and consequently they had been prepared to sell H at below market value simply to clear P's debt.

Held: B assoilzied. (1) Neither X nor Y had made an offer, P had led no expert or other evidence to demonstrate a valuation of H at £250,000, thus it could not be concluded that that price ought to have been achieved, and H's value, with regard to evidence from two expert valuers, was, at most, £135,000. (2) B's advertisement of H fell short of the requirement under the Conveyancing and Feudal Reform (Scotland) Act 1970 s.25 as it had not correctly identified H as a hotel, had misleadingly described it as a public house, had inaccurately described H's condition and had not sought to attract interest in H, and B had failed to advertise H elsewhere, in particular, in recommended trade publications. (3) P and B's advertising of H for sale in 2009 had occurred during very difficult market conditions, which had had an effect on H's valuation and the availability of finance for any interested party, there was no evidence that buyers were paying more than valuation price for hotels in that particular market at that time, and there was no evidence that anything further done by B would have been likely to have generated any other offers, competing bids, a closing date or a higher sale price, accordingly, had B more fully marketed and advertised H, it was not likely that a higher price than £135,000 would have been achieved, thus B had complied with the second part of their obligation under s.25 of the 1970 Act, *Bank of Credit v Thomson*, Airdrie sheriff court, 11 February 1987, unreported (1987 G.W.D. 10-341), *Dick v Clydesdale Bank Plc* 1991 S.C. 365, [1991] C.L.Y. 5111, *Wilson v Dunbar Bank Plc* [2006] CSOH 105, 2006 S.L.T. 775, [2006] C.L.Y. 5497 and *Wilson v Dunbar Bank Plc* [2008] CSIH 27, 2008 S.C. 457, [2008] C.L.Y. 4703, *considered*.

PETERS v BELHAVEN FINANCE LTD, 2016 S.L.T. (Sh Ct) 156, Sheriff B A Mohan, Sh Ct (South Strathclyde) (Dumfries).

HOUSING

2680 Homelessness–Intentional homelessness–Local housing authority finding claimant intentionally made herself homeless–Reasonableness of decision

W petitioned for judicial review of a review decision of the local housing authority (S) upholding its decision that W was intentionally homeless. W had been a tenant of a private rental property (P) until decree for recovery of possession had been granted following service of a notice to quit where W had failed to pay the shortfall between the amount of housing benefit she received and the rent for P for two months such that rent arrears had accrued. W had a history of mental health difficulties, and a community practice nurse, in a letter dated 19 November 2014, had noted *inter alia* that W's illnesses significantly affected her ability to function and reduced her level of responsibility, W being unaware of her day to day responsibilities. On 28 October, S had found that W was intentionally homeless. W had appealed on the basis that there were significant mental health issues which if taken into account would mean that W had not made herself intentionally homeless. S refused the appeal on 4 February 2015, finding that while W had been known to S's mental health services for some years and had suffered periods of significant mental health difficulties, the duration thereof had not been for her entire tenancy, additionally, she had been assessed as being competent and having the capacity to manage her financial affairs and had had sole responsibility for doing so, which was demonstrated on the evidence, she had had sufficient income to meet her rent payments, had understood her responsibilities to pay rent and keep her benefits up to date, she had demonstrated the ability to do this, and had been provided with a significant amount of housing support in order to assist her to maintain the tenancy, and her tenancy had ultimately failed because of her own choices and actions. W submitted that (1) there was no proper basis in fact to support S's determination; (2) S's decision had failed to properly and reasonably take into account W's significant psychiatric history and ongoing treatment; (3) S's decision was *Wednesbury* unreasonable.

Held: Petition refused. (1) W's case was not one of total or complete incapacity, there was no medical assessment that would evidence her suffering from mental illness at the material time, it was not suggested that W had been incapable at the time she had assumed the tenancy of P, and in light of the fact that S had addressed the relevant question, it could neither be said that S had had no basis of fact from which the requisite intentionality could be found nor that the decision was one that no reasonable decision taker, properly directing itself as to its task and on the basis of the material before it, could have reached. (2) W's second ground amounted to no more than a complaint that S had not given certain factors the weight that W would have wished, which was not a permissible ground of judicial review of administrative decision taking; once there was relevant material before a decision taker, the weight to attach to it was a matter for it to assess, and it could not be said that S had misapprehended a potentially decisive element of the evidence on material before it. (3) As there had been material before S on the basis of which a finding of fact of intentionality could be made, it could not be said that its decision had been *Wednesbury* unreasonable or perverse.

W v STIRLING COUNCIL, [2015] CSOH 162, 2016 S.L.T. 35, Lady Wolffe, OH.

2681 Homelessness–Intentional homelessness–Settled residence

C petitioned for judicial review of a decision by a local housing authority (S) that she was intentionally homeless and they were thus not obliged to secure permanent accommodation for her. C had applied to S for accommodation as a homeless person on 22 June 2015 and on 23 June, she had been provided with temporary accommodation. C had previously held a tenancy of subjects (B) but had been served an eviction notice for breach of tenancy on or around 30 April. C averred that she left B to live with her boyfriend where she intended to reside long term until she discovered he had resumed drug taking. In the course of their inquiries, S had ascertained *inter alia* that C had been charged with possession of heroin at B on 29 April, that she had made an application for housing benefit and council tax relief in respect of B on 22 May, which she listed as her only address, and that S's housing department had C recorded as living at B until 31 May. S thus considered that C had decided to leave her tenancy to move in with her boyfriend because she was aware that the landlord would be seeking to terminate the tenancy due to her behaviour but she did not terminate her tenancy correctly and her actions were not suggestive of the move to her boyfriend's as intended to be long term thus her last settled accommodation was B. C argued that S should have concluded that she had acquired settled accommodation at her boyfriend's flat at the time she made her application for accommodation, which had broken the chain of causation between her state of homelessness, caused by her abandoning her tenancy at B, and her position as at the date of making her application to S.

Held: Petition dismissed. S had approached the legal question which they had to ascertain correctly and exercised their judgment in relation to a matter which was one of fact and degree in a way which was entirely legitimate: S had sufficient information to determine the issue of settled residence in the way they had given the evidence to suggest C's residence at her boyfriend's flat was anything but settled including the short period of time, namely, less than two months, during said time C was making representations in support of an application for housing benefit that her residence continued to be B, and C herself had informed S that she had left her boyfriend's flat because he had resumed drug taking.

C v STIRLING COUNCIL , [2016] CSOH 55, 2016 Hous. L.R. 58, Lord Clarke, OH.

HUMAN RIGHTS

2682 Freedom of assembly and association–Freedom of expression–Interference with rights by granting orders to remove protesters–Proportionality

[Court of Session Act 1988 (c.36) s.46; European Convention on Human Rights 1950 art.10]

In the course of a petition by the Scottish Parliamentary Corporate Body (S) for an order under the Court of Session Act 1988 s.46 for the removal of a pro-independence group (G) camped within the grounds of the Scottish Parliament, the Lord Ordinary held a hearing on the question whether the admitted interference with G's rights in granting the order sought, namely the rights to freedom of expression and freedom of assembly as enshrined in the ECHR art.10 and art.11 respectively, would be lawful, necessary and proportionate (*Scottish Parliamentary Corporate Body v Sovereign Indigenous Peoples of Scotland* [2016] CSOH 65, 2016 S.L.T. 761, [2016] 2470).

Held: Petition granted. (1) For the purposes of examining the proportionality of granting the order sought, it made no difference whether the camp was referred to as a protest or a vigil, in any event, the continuous nature of the camp was neither of the essence of the protest being made nor had the protest or presence of the camp acquired a symbolic force allowing it to sit above the comings and goings of particular individuals, and S had taken active steps to remove the camp from its very commencement, *R. (on the application of Barda) v Mayor of London* [2015] EWHC 3584 (Admin), [2016] 4 W.L.R. 20, [2016] 1046 and *Tabernacle v Secretary of State for Defence* [2008] EWHC 416 (Admin), Times, April 9, 2008, [2008] C.L.Y. 1884, *considered.* (2) The order sought would operate as a restriction on the art.10 and art.11 rights of those at the camp but said restriction would not go to the essence of their right of freedom of expression, or to protest: it was plain that protest was possible both in the vicinity of the Scottish Parliament and on the grounds owned by S and S remained willing to discuss facilitating G's right to freedom of expression or protest in line with its code of conduct and their right to engage in whatever protest it was they wished to state remained available; individuals did not have the absolute freedom to choose the manner of the expression of their rights under arts 10 and 11 to the detriment of others and G had been in exclusive possession of an area of the grounds of the Scottish Parliament for many months and as such were interfering with the rights of others to use the grounds openly, they had caused damage to the grounds themselves, their presence was incompatible with the nature of the Parliament's grounds which were unsuitable for use as a campsite and had acted as a precedent for other impermissible use thereof; in the whole circumstances, S had now established that G's activities on its property were interfering with its own rights and duties and with the rights of the public, and that the order sought met a pressing social need and the balance which had to be struck in light of all the foregoing circumstances came down firmly in favour of holding that the interference caused by granting the orders sought was proportionate.

SCOTTISH PARLIAMENTARY CORPORATE BODY v SOVEREIGN INDIGENOUS PEOPLES OF SCOTLAND, [2016] CSOH 113, 2016 S.L.T. 862, Lord Turnbull, OH.

IMMIGRATION

2683 Indefinite leave to remain–Residence–Application by Pakistani national for no time limit endorsement on passport–Secretary of state wrongly placing onus on applicant to show no lapse of leave

[Immigration Act 1971 (c.77) s.1(2); Immigration (Leave to Enter and Remain) Order 2000 (SI 2000/1161) art.13(4)]

A Pakistani citizen (M) petitioned for judicial review of a decision of the Secretary of State for the Home Department refusing to grant him a no time limit endorsement. M had come to the United Kingdom with his family in 1967 aged eight, he had moved to

Scotland aged 17, and had married a British citizen and had had five children, and claimed to only have left the UK on two occasions, once in 1981 for approximately six weeks and once in 1995 for approximately 12 days. M had been granted indefinite leave to remain, his Pakistani passport having been endorsed with those words after 1 January 1973 but he had not obtained citizenship. M had lost his passport in early 2012 and had been issued with a replacement by the Pakistani embassy. His requests to issue a replacement stamp vouching indefinite leave to remain had been refused by the Home Office, which had also informed him that he was liable to be removed from the UK, on the basis that he was unable to demonstrate that he had been continuously resident in the UK since 1988, although M had submitted documentation and other information. S accepted that by virtue of the Immigration Act 1971 s.1(2), M fell to be treated as having acquired indefinite leave to remain as from the commencement of that Act. M submitted that (1) the criteria which determined whether an endorsement would or would not be granted were to be seen as being in the nature of rules to be followed in the administration of the 1971 Act, and with regard to *R. (on the application of Alvi) v Secretary of State for the Home Department* [2012] UKSC 33, [2012] 1 W.L.R. 2208, [2012] C.L.Y. 1755, that was unlawful; (2) the policy guidance made it plain that only documentary evidence was to be considered in demonstrating continuous residency. S submitted that in the context of M's application, the onus was on him to establish that he was entitled to the endorsement.

Held: Decree of reduction granted. (1) A proper understanding of S's policy guidance made it clear that S had not adopted anything in the nature of a rule as to the practice to be followed in determining whether or not to grant a no time limit endorsement; the question of whether or not an applicant's indefinite leave to remain had lapsed had to be decided according to the test in the Immigration (Leave to Enter and Remain) Order 2000, which had Parliamentary approval, and S had not introduced a rule to the effect that only documentary evidence could be considered in support of an application such as M's, thus the requirement in *Alvi* had no application in the present circumstances and S had not unlawfully fettered her discretion, *Alvi, considered.* (2) With regard to the terms of art.13(4) of the 2000 Order, M had already acquired a particular status, namely leave which remained in force indefinitely, he was neither seeking a status nor to establish an exemption, there was nothing in the language of the order suggesting the existence of a burden on the beneficiary of leave to establish that his leave had not lapsed, and taking account of other guidance, requiring M to provide evidence of continuous residence over many years was to pass the whole burden onto him and not to focus on the correct question of whether it could be decided that leave had in fact lapsed, and as M had already acquired indefinite leave to remain, it was doubtful whether onus of proof, in the strict and ordinary sense, was a particularly helpful manner of deciding whether leave had in fact lapsed; S's rigid focus on what was required of M was misplaced and had led to a clouding of the correct decision making process, *R. (on the application of Diary Rafiq Qadir) v Secretary of State for the Home Department, considered.* (3) The relevant continuum with regard to the 2000 Order was absence from the UK rather than residence; S had applied a test of continuous residence to M's application, S's obligation was to assess the information provided by M in light of the correct test, S had never sought to assess whether the documentation which established M's presence in the UK cast any light on the question of whether she could conclude that he had in fact been absent for a continuous period in excess of two years either before or after the vouched periods of presence, she had not considered whether or not to view M's account of continuous presence in a more favourable light in view of his ability to demonstrate certain periods of presence, and she had not taken stock of the combined import of the information provided by M in light of her recent appreciation that she had no record in the landing card system of M's entry into the UK at any point in the last 20 years. (4) S had been wrong to assert that the onus was on M to vouch that his leave had not lapsed and had not considered the proper question at any stage and had not weighed what the preponderance of M's information tended to establish regarding his absence from the UK for any continuous period of two years; S's decision had been unlawful and would be reduced, consequently, S would be required to remake the decision.

ZM (PAKISTAN) v SECRETARY OF STATE FOR THE HOME DEPARTMENT, [2016] CSOH 73, 2016 S.L.T. 848, Lord Turnbull, OH.

2684 Leave to enter–Adopted children–Application by adopted children from Democratic Republic of Congo–Whether application made under Immigration Rule 352D

[Nationality, Immigration and Asylum Act 2002 (c.41) s.82; European Convention on Human Rights 1950 art.14, art.8; Immigration and Nationality (Fees) Regulations 2013 (SI 2013/749) Sch.2]

The adopted daughters (X and Y, collectively Z) of a refugee (F) petitioned for judicial review, seeking reduction of a decision of the Secretary of State for the Home Department (S) refusing to consider Z's application for leave to enter as F's children in terms of the Immigration Rules r.352D, and/or declarator that their application had been made thereunder. F had lawfully adopted Z in the Democratic Republic of Congo in 2008, and in 2011, had fled to the United Kingdom and had been granted refugee status. On 17 February 2014, Z had applied for entry clearance in order to join F in the UK. S had rejected Z's application without considering its merits on the basis that the application had not properly been made under r.352D of the Immigration Rules, which did not apply to family members who were neither biological children of the refugee nor adopted children as defined therein, namely children either adopted in Hague Adoption Convention countries, to which the Democratic Republic of Congo was not a signatory, or adopted *de facto* in terms of r.309A, consequently, no immigration decision had been made capable of being appealed to the First-tier and Upper Tribunals under the Nationality, Immigration and Asylum Act 2002 s.82, which would have been entitled to consider whether Z were entitled to succeed under para.352D but also whether the refusal of entry was a breach of ECHR art.8 and/or art.14. The matter at issue was whether F's application had been made under r.352D, and therefore in terms of the Immigration and Nationality (Fees) Regulations 2013 Sch.2, table 5.2, and was thus fee exempt and ought to have been considered on its merits.

Held: Petition granted. (1) It was for the applicant in the first instance to decide which paragraph applied to his or her case and, having done so, to make the application thereunder, that application had to be considered on its merits, were the criteria laid down therein not satisfied, the application might be refused, subject to S's wider obligations in terms of ECHR art.8, which would give rise to a right of appeal to the appropriate tribunal, which would consider whether the application fell within the terms of the paragraph under which it was made but also whether in refusing it, S had acted consistently with her obligations, and that approach would not enable any applicant to avoid paying the fee applicable to his case under the 2013 Regulations simply by choosing to make his or her application under a fee exempt paragraph. (2) As a matter of construction the 2013 Regulations ought not to be interpreted in a manner which gave the applicant carte blanche as to whether or not to pay a fee but the tribunal's consideration of the applicant's art.8 rights and the corresponding duty on S to consider the application having regard to her art.8 obligations was not carried out without regard to the whole circumstances of the application, including the paragraph of the Immigration Rules under which the application was made, and was that paragraph clearly inappropriate and it appeared that the applicant had deliberately chosen an inapplicable paragraph in order to avoid payment of a fee, that would be a factor weighing with the tribunal, which provided the necessary and sufficient control to prevent an abuse of the system; the alternative approach would lead to a highly unsatisfactory scheme of immigration control in terms of which S had the right not to consider an application which she considered did not fall within the paragraph under which it was presented, thus there was no refusal of the application and therefore no right of appeal to the tribunal, which was contrary to the Parliamentary intention to bring the immigration and asylum process under review by an independent tribunal system. (3) There was no other paragraph which more closely met Z's circumstances but even if there was, that would go into the balance when, after S's refusal of the application, the matter came on appeal before the tribunal. (4) The prayer of the petition would be granted to the extent of reducing S's decision that Z's application did not fall to be considered under r.352D of the Immigration Rules and granting declarator that F's application for leave to enter had been made thereunder. Observed, that it was of some concern that the problems with r.309A of the Immigration Rules as identified by Lord Carnwath in *AA (Somalia) v Entry Clearance Officer, Addis Ababa* [2013] UKSC 81,

[2014] 1 W.L.R. 43, [2014] C.L.Y. 1684 had not yet been resolved, *AA (Somalia), considered.*

EMM (DEMOCRATIC REPUBLIC OF CONGO) v SECRETARY OF STATE FOR THE HOME DEPARTMENT, [2016] CSOH 51, 2016 S.L.T. 931, Lord Glennie, OH.

2685 Leave to remain–Former spouses–Immigration Rules Appendix FM s.E-DVILR.1.2–Non-national spouses and former spouses of persons with refugee leave treated less favourably

[European Convention on Human Rights 1950 art.14]

A Ugandan national (X) reclaimed against a decision of the Lord Ordinary refusing her petition for judicial review of the refusal of Secretary of State for the Home Department (S) to grant her indefinite leave to remain in the United Kingdom, and declarator that the Immigration Rules Appendix FM s.E-DVILR.1.2 was *ultra vires* on the ground that it excluded from its scope spouses and former spouses of refugees, thus contravening ECHR art.14 (*A (Uganda) v Secretary of State for the Home Department* [2015] CSOH 62, 2015 S.L.T. 407, [2015] C.L.Y. 3159). X's husband (H), also a Ugandan national, had been granted refugee status and five years' leave to remain in the UK in 2009. On 20 September 2010, X and three of the couple's children (C) had entered the UK on a family visa. On 6 October 2011, following H's assault of X, the couple had separated. On 21 November, X had claimed asylum on the basis of imputed political opinion as a result of H's political involvement in Uganda and threat to her life from H's family there as a result of her separation from him, which had been refused but X and C had been granted three years' discretionary leave to remain on the basis of family life. On 20 January 2014, X had submitted an application for indefinite leave to remain under s.E-DVILR of Appendix FM of the Immigration Rules, which had been refused on 17 February 2014 on the basis that X was not the spouse of a British citizen or individual settled in the UK but X and C had been granted further discretionary leave to remain until February 2017 on the basis of private and family life. The Lord Ordinary found that while under s.E-DVILR.1.2 non-national spouses of persons with refugee leave were treated less favourably than the spouses of British citizens and persons with settled status, the state was entitled to pursue the aim of regulating immigration for the maintenance of economic and social order, and to determine where the line should be drawn, and that drawn by s.E-DVILR was not without objective or reasonable justification; a policy which granted a concession to those who already had a right but denied it to those who had not was comprehensible and not irrational, the provisions of the section were not disproportionate, therefore there was no room for the intervention of the court on the very limited basis available to it.

Held: Reclaiming motion allowed and S's decision reduced. (1) The aim of the measure was that the spouses of those settled in the UK should be treated differently from the spouses of those without that status, the rationale being that the former were likely to have a reasonable expectation of settlement in the UK and thus to have cut or loosened their ties with their country of origin, whereas the latter could have no such expectation and would be less likely to have done so, however, S's equiparation of the position of refugees with those granted work or study leave in asserting that rationale, was unsound; a person admitted as a student, or for work, was admitted on a limited and temporary basis, entirely at the discretion of the state but the status of refugee was declaratory, once it had been determined to exist, the state had no discretion in terms of its international and humanitarian obligations but had to grant asylum, accordingly, whilst it was not reasonable for the spouses of students or workers to have any reasonable expectation of having their future and a permanent home in the UK it could not be accepted to apply equally to the spouses of refugees; a refugee was not in the UK by choice and that the spouse of such a person might be any less likely from the outset to loosen or cut their ties with their country of origin was fanciful, and that approach ignored several aspects of the reality of the position of a refugee. (2) Approximately 95% of refugees granted five year limited leave to remain were granted indefinite leave to remain thereafter; the grounds upon which refugee status might be lost, or a refugee expelled, were significantly limited, accordingly, a refugee could reasonably expect to proceed to indefinite leave to remain, which indicated that the position of a refugee was not to be equiparated with that of a student or worker, and the spouse of a refugee corresponded more closely to the spouse of a British citizen or person settled in the UK, and the Lord Ordinary had misdirected himself in that regard. (3) In none of the authorities had the term "precarious" been applied to the immigration status of a refugee with five year limited leave to remain; family life established by a refugee pre-flight and which lawfully subsisted post flight could not be compared to family life established post flight and in the full knowledge that one of the parties had no right to remain, and the fact that the position of a refugee might come under review might introduce a degree of uncertainty, but that did not mean that his position therefore had to be considered precarious, and in so far as the Lord Ordinary appeared to have considered that H's immigration status had been precarious, he had been in error. (4) The difference in treatment had arisen as a consequence of the introduction in 2005 of a policy granting in the first place a five year limited leave to refugees, and on 25 August 2005 a guidance note issued by the Immigration and Nationality Appeals Directorate indicated that those who had been granted leave as a refugee would be subject to review of their claims if, during their initial leave, ministers were satisfied that there had been a significant and non-temporary change in the conditions in their country and that leave would also be reviewed or curtailed where the refugee had brought himself within the cessation provisions, had acquired his status by fraud, or had committed a serious crime; there was neither an indication that at the time of those changes any consideration had been given to the effect on the spouses of refugees who might otherwise have been able to avail themselves of the domestic violence concession, nor had a considered reason been advanced for their exclusion from the operation thereof. (5) The present was not a case in which a policy choice on the critical question had been made with due consideration of the issues, looked at in the light of the government policy both in relation to refugees and domestic violence, and in the absence thereof, or any reasonable basis upon which a refugee could be equiparated to a worker or student, or the reasonable expectations of their spouses being as limited as those of the spouses of students or workers, and having regard to the effect on the spouses of refugees, as well as the underlying aim of the domestic violence concession, the difference in treatment was not proportionate. (6) Even allowing full weight to the element of discretion to be accorded to the executive, the line had been drawn effectively by oversight, and the justification advanced was weak to the extent of being unjustifiable. (7) It was unnecessary to grant the declaratory sought.

A (UGANDA) v SECRETARY OF STATE FOR THE HOME DEPARTMENT, [2016] CSIH 38, 2016 S.L.T. 611, Lady Paton, Lady Dorrian, Lord Drummond Young, IH (Ex Div).

2686 Leave to remain–Points-based system–Whether compliance by entrepreneur migrant with points-based system requirements

A Pakistani national (N) appealed against a decision of the Upper Tribunal (U) refusing her appeal against the refusal by the First-tier Tribunal (F) of her appeal against a decision of the Secretary of State for the Home Department (S) refusing her application for leave to remain. N had sought leave to remain as a tier 1 entrepreneur migrant, and her husband (H) and their three children (C) had applied as her dependents. On 16 March 2013, S had refused the application on the basis that N had not complied with the requirement under the Immigration Rules Pt 6A to show that she had access to at least £200,000 for the purpose of investing in a business in the United Kingdom in order to gain sufficient points under the applicable points based system. S had found that a letter from H's bank (L) confirming that he had had a balance of £202,000, and a witnessed third party declaration signed by H on solicitors' headed notepaper and addressed to the UK Borders Agency *inter alia* giving his full consent to the application to use his funds in the UK and declaring that N had his full authority to access the sum upon request for use in the UK for the purposes of investing in her business, had not complied with the requirement in para.41-SD9(a)(i)(9) of the Immigration Rules that L's letter confirmed the amount provided to N from any third party, thus S had been unable to accept H's funds relied upon by N. F upheld that decision and found *inter alia* that para.245AA of the rules had no application where the specified document had not been submitted and there had been no obligation on S to request the missing information. U had found that F had not erred in law and had commented that it was a matter for S whether the fact that H was N's husband and co-applicant justified discretion outside the rules being exercised in N's favour.

Held: (1) Were N, H and C to receive relief, it could only be based on S's general duty to act fairly and rationally, the policy in force at the time, the original para.245AA was of no relevance to the present circumstances; as a general rule there was no unfairness in refusing an application under the points based system when the application was not accompanied by all the specified documentation, an applicant was expected to be appraised of the relevant requirements and to comply therewith at the outset by lodging the appropriate supporting documents, and if he did not, he was responsible for an adverse decision, even if the underlying facts demonstrated a mistake or unfortunate omission, however, that general rule could be overcome when such was justified after a consideration of the particular circumstances of the case, such as if S carried a degree of responsibility for the problem or where the decision could be described as perverse or in defiance of common sense, *R. (on the application of Forrester) v Secretary of State for the Home Department* [2008] EWHC 2307 (Admin) and *Mandalia v Secretary of State for the Home Department* [2015] UKSC 59, [2015] 1 W.L.R. 4546, [2015] C.L.Y. 1359, *considered.* (2) The necessary letter from L could not have been submitted until H had, in the context of N's investment in the UK business, made the money available to her for that purpose and L was in a position to confirm that state of affairs, however, in the circumstances, all L could vouch was the balance in H's bank account as at the date of the letter, and the Immigration Rules did not allow a positive decision simply because a person who was in a position to do so, promised to make the monies available at the time of the proposed investment. (3) The necessary letter had been missing, there was no suggestion that H had placed the funds under N's control and in those circumstances, it could not be said that a different approach from that taken by S had been required; it ought to have been obvious to N, H and C, who had had the benefit of legal advice, that unless the financial arrangements allowed the required letter from L to be written and submitted, it was more than likely that the application would be refused, it had never been explained why the necessary steps had not been taken at the time of the application, there was nothing to suggest that that had been anything other than a deliberate decision, and any unfair outcome was one for which N and H had to bear responsibility, *Alam v Secretary of State for the Home Department* [2012] EWCA Civ 960, [2012] Imm. A.R. 974, [2013] C.L.Y. 1619 and *EK (Ivory Coast) v Secretary of State for the Home Department* [2014] EWCA Civ 1517, [2015] Imm. A.R. 367, [2015] C.L.Y. 1365, *considered.*

N, APPELLANTS *sub nom.* ISN (PAKISTAN), APPELLANT, [2016] CSIH 6, 2016 S.L.T. 396, The Lord Justice Clerk (Carloway), Lord Bracadale, Lord Malcolm, IH (2 Div).

2687 Leave to remain–Withdrawal–Permission to proceed with claim for judicial review–Test of real prospect of success

[Act of Sederunt (Rules of the Court of Session 1994) 1994 Sch.2; Immigration and Asylum Act 1999 (c.33) s.10; Immigration Act 2014 (c.22)]

A Nigerian citizen (O) made an application under the Act of Sederunt (Rules of the Court of Session 1994) 1994 Sch.2 Ch.58 for permission to proceed with a petition for judicial review of a decision of the Secretary of State for the Home Department (S) to curtail O's conditional leave to remain on the basis that he had breached one of the conditions. O had been granted leave to remain until September 2017 as a entrepreneur and had set up a business (B), with the conditions that he was not limited from working in activities for B but he was prevented from inter alia undertaking employment other than for businesses he was establishing, joining or taking over. On 13 October 2015, O had been found working as a security guard for another company (C), in breach of his conditions. O contended that he had never been employed by C but rather had been working for B on a self employed basis trading under B's name thus the work had not been undertaken as C's employee. O submitted inter alia that (1) the test for permission to proceed was to be a low hurdle that he required to surmount in establishing a real prospect of success in showing that S had not established that he had worked in breach of his conditions; (2) S had to establish the precedent fact that O had been working in breach of one of his conditions of leave, and where such a breach constituted a criminal offence and carried the risk of imprisonment, the court ought not to be satisfied with anything less than "probability to a high degree", and S had had an insufficient evidential basis for her decision. S submitted inter alia that (1) the language in the Court of Session Act 1988 s.27B(2) was clear, the meaning of real prospect of success was well established and was the test set by the court in *Hoseini v Secretary of State for the Home Department* 2005 S.L.T. 550, [2005] C.L.Y. 5437; (2) having regard to the amendment to the Immigration and Asylum Act 1999 s.10 by the Immigration Act 2014, on a correct analysis, the precedent fact was whether or not O required leave but did not have it, and as that had been the precedent fact of S's decision, there had been no error as contended for by O; was there an error arising from the factual material considered, that had been taken at interview stage and was not justifiable, therefore, there would be no reason to enter into an inquiry as to the correctness of the precedent fact, at best, O sought to show that the anterior determination, to withdraw leave by reason of O's breach of the conditions thereof, was wrong, however, that was insufficient to establish a relevant case.

Held: Permission granted. (1) The test of real prospect of success was one which ought to be flexible in its application, having regard to all of the relevant factors, *Carroll v Scottish Borders Council* [2014] CSOH 30, 2014 S.L.T. 659, [2014] C.L.Y. 3338, *Hoseini* and *Swain v Hillman* [2001] 1 All E.R. 91, [1999] C.L.Y. 561, *considered.* (2) S's stance in cases of the present kind appeared to have shifted as a consequence of the amendment to s.10 of the 1999 Act, however, S's argument that that might lead to decisions to withdraw leave becoming impregnable had not yet been litigated, and upon a consideration of the arguments presented to the court, O had demonstrated a case with a real prospect of success. Observed, that it might be worth bearing in mind the principles applied by the Report on the Scottish Civil Courts Review as governing a reformed civil procedure when considering the application of the reformed procedures for judicial review in Ch.58 of the Rules.

JOO (NIGERIA) v SECRETARY OF STATE FOR THE HOME DEPARTMENT *sub nom.* O v SECRETARY OF STATE FOR THE HOME DEPARTMENT, [2016] CSOH 20, 2016 S.L.T. 545, Lady Wolffe, OH.

2688 Nationality–Citizenship–Scope of s.4C British Nationality Act 1981

[British Nationality Act 1981 (c.61) s.4C; Borders, Citizenship and Immigration Act 2009 (c.11)]

R reclaimed against a decision of the Lord Ordinary upholding the refusal of her application for registration as a British citizen pursuant to the British Nationality Act 1981 s.4C, as amended by the Borders, Citizenship and Immigration Act 2009 (*Romein v Advocate General for Scotland* [2014] CSOH 174, 2015 S.L.T. 32, [2015] C.L.Y. 3150). R, born in the United States on 16 June 1978, claimed British citizenship through descent from her mother (M). M was born in South Africa and was a British citizen by virtue of her father having been born in the United Kingdom. M had inquired at the British consulate in South Africa during her pregnancy with R about the possibility of securing citizenship for R where she had been informed that nationality could only be passed through the male line as a consequence of which M had not registered R's birth with the British consulate. R argued that, on a proper construction of s.4C, she was entitled to be registered as a British citizen.

Held: Case put out by order. (1) There was no good reason to limit the scope of s.4C(3) as first enacted in 2002, and it was inherently unlikely that the revised version in 2009 was intended to reintroduce aspects of gender discrimination which had been previously discarded: on a proper construction of s.4C(3), R was entitled to be registered as a British citizen if she could prove that she would have become a citizen of the United Kingdom and Colonies by virtue of s.5 of the British Nationality Act 1948, if the assumption in s.4C(3A) had applied at the relevant time, *R. (on the application of Navarro) v Secretary of State for the Home Department* [2014] EWHC 907 (Admin), *considered.* (2) The reclaiming motion would be allowed and R's application remitted for reconsideration, however, the case would meantime be put out by order for discussion as to the appropriate terms of the court's interlocutor.

ROMEIN v ADVOCATE GENERAL FOR SCOTLAND, [2016] CSIH 24, 2016 S.L.T. 459, Lord Brodie, Lady Dorrian, Lord Malcolm, IH (Ex Div).

2689 Points-based system–Sponsor licences–Application by Indian restaurant owners for tier two general and tier two (ICT) sponsor licence–Error in secretary of state's approach to application

Indian restaurant owners (V) petitioned for judicial review seeking reduction of a decision by the Secretary of State for the Home Department (S) refusing to grant V's application for a tier two general and a tier two (ICT) sponsor licence. V had sought to bring over from India a managing director for training purposes under the intra company transfer rules and to recruit a specialist chef under the general rules, and had relied upon a joint venture agreement document (J) in support thereof, however, J had contained a typographical error in the registration date, which V had drawn to S's attention three days after the original application had been made. S had refused V's application on the basis that J had not demonstrated that a *bona fide* joint venture for ICT purposes existed, and in her decision letter had referred to a business development manager, had purported to consider V's general application as an ICT application, had referred to a skill level of NQF 6 as necessary for the employment of a skilled chef, who of necessity had to be identified at the time of the application, and a requirement that V's connected business in India had to supply that chef.

Held: Petition granted. (1) The errors in S's decision letter were not merely errors in terminology but errors which went to the core of the decision, and exhibited a careless approach by S to the application and a complete failure to examine the application properly, to understand the basis upon which it was made and to understand the legal framework in terms of which the decision was being made; the errors had demonstrated a failure to separate the two parts of V's application and to consider those separate parts in terms of the correct legal framework, and those errors amounted to a material error of law which justified the reduction of the decision letter. (2) S had not been entitled to reach the conclusion that J had not constituted evidence of a *bona fide* joint venture, there was no basis for that conclusion and there was nothing within S's decision letter to show that she had considered V's explanation, there was neither any reason why that explanation was not found to be acceptable nor any proper basis for the inference that J was a fraudulent document, for S to properly make such an inference, there would require to be more than a mere error in the date, particularly where a tenable explanation had been proffered before S had noted the error, and S's position regarding J was one which she was not entitled to reach, was perverse and clearly amounted to a material error in law. (3) The description supplied by V matched the criteria in the code in all material respects, S's decision letter was riddled with errors and the reasoning contained therein had not entitled S to reach the decision she had; S had misdirected herself in material respects with reference to her own guidance and codes and the decision would be reduced.

VIKRAM FOODS GLASGOW LTD v SECRETARY OF STATE FOR THE HOME DEPARTMENT , [2016] CSOH 77, 2016 S.L.T. 902, Lord Bannatyne, OH.

2690 Rights of entry and residence–Certificates–Failure to renew certificate of application

[Immigration (European Economic Area) Regulations 2006 (SI 2006/1003) reg.17, reg.17(1), reg.9; Directive 2004/38 on the right of citizens of the Union and their family members to move and reside freely within the territory of the Member States amending Regulation (EEC) No 1612/68 and repealing Directives 64/221/EEC, 68/360/EEC, 72/194/EEC, 73/148/EEC, 75/34/EEC, 75/35/EEC, 90/364/EEC, 90/365/ 2004 art.10]

A Nigerian national (N) petitioned for judicial review of a decision of the Secretary of State for the Home Department (S) refusing to issue N a certificate of application, and sought damages. In August 2010, following the imposition of two consecutive sentences of six month's imprisonment, N had been deported to Nigeria in January 2011 in exchange for commuting his sentence. In March 2011, while in Nigeria, N had married a British national (X), and in 2012, they had moved to Germany, where X had found intermittent employment for a short period. In early 2013, N and X had returned to the United Kingdom and N had applied for entry clearance, which had been refused in March 2013 on the basis that he had not provided evidence that he was a family member of a person working or self employed in another Member State prior to entering the UK, and as he was the subject of a deportation order. On 14 May 2013, N had made an application for a residence card on the basis of his marriage to X, in terms of the Immigration (European Economic Area) Regulations 2006 reg.17(1) and had been issued with a six month certificate of application, which *inter alia* stated that N was entitled to accept offers of employment in the UK whilst his application was under consideration. N's application had been refused on 17 December, he had appealed unsuccessfully to the First-tier Tribunal (F) and thereafter successfully to the Upper Tribunal (U), which had remitted the matter to S for a new decision. On 8 December 2014, no fresh decision having been forthcoming, N had lodged his petition. On 12 January 2015, S had again refused N's application and he had again appealed unsuccessfully to F and successfully to U, which had again remitted the matter to S, with no decision having yet been made. In the course of the appeals, both F and U had found that the deportation order ought to be revoked. N averred that in October 2014, he had been offered temporary employment subject to proof of his right to work in the UK but his application to S for renewal of his certificate had been refused, thus he had been unable to take up the employment and had lost earnings. S submitted that (1) was N entitled to a certificate immediately upon applying for a residence card, he was not entitled to a replacement or renewal thereof once it had lapsed, even though the final decision on the residence card had not yet been made; (2) had she a duty to issue a second certificate, N was an illegal entrant, thus had committed a criminal offence and was thereby removable, therefore S had been entitled to take the view that on grounds of public policy she was not required to issue N with a certificate; (3) whether N was entitled to a certificate could not be detemined until the application for a residence card had been determined in terms of reg.9 of the 2006 Regulations; (4) as a matter of law any breach either of Directive 2004/38 or of the 2006 Regulations was not of the type which justified the award of damages; (5) there was no requirement either in Directive 2004/38 or in terms of the 2006 Regulations for the certificate to make a statement in relation to the right to work; (6) N had no basis to claim that he would necessarily have got the job, in particular, with regard to his previous convictions.

Held: Case put out by order. (1) There was nothing in the 2004 Directive equivalent to reg.9 of the 2006 Regulations giving rise to an argument that the obligation in art.10 of the Directive to issue a certificate immediately upon receipt of an application for a residence card was qualified by a consideration of whether that person was ultimately found to be entitled to a residence card and it was plain that no such qualification was intended, the residence card regime was intended to facilitate entry by non-Union family members in order to facilitate the free movement of Union citizens across the Union, and although it was recognised that it might take time to verify a person's entitlement to a residence card, while that investigation was being undertaken the applicant ought to be given a certificate as a temporary measure, therefore, was there no obligation to issue a certificate unless and until it was determined that the applicant met the conditions set out in reg.9(2), that would be an obstacle to free movement, which was not permitted by the directive. (2) Both reg.17(3) of the 2006 Regulations and art.10 of the Directive specifically required the residence card to be issued within six months of the application, and neither specified its duration, however, it was clearly intended that the certificate should remain in force until the application for a residence card was determined, and the UK practice for a certificate to state that it could be relied upon by employers only for a period of six months after its issue could not be elevated into a principle that six months was the maximum duration of a certificate and, if the application for a residence card was not determined within that period, the certificate would lapse and not be renewed. (3) The deportation order had not been lawfully made and had it not yet been revoked, it ought to be, thus removing that obstacle to the issue of a duplicate certificate; S could not legitimately fail to carry out F and U's unappealed findings and use the existence of the unlawful deportation order to block N's right to a certificate. Further, in terms of art.27, measures taken on grounds of public policy required to comply with the principle of proportionality, such measures were to be based exclusively on the personal conduct of the individual concerned and previous criminal convictions would not, in themselves, constitute grounds for taking such measures; there had been no assessment of whether N's own personal conduct represented a genuine, present and sufficiently serious threat to one of the fundamental interests of society, although N's conduct leading to conviction had been both serious and reprehensible, those offences had been committed over five years ago, and it could not be said that N posed a serious threat to one of the fundamental interests of society, that N still presented a threat of that gravity and that exclusion from the UK and the refusal to grant a residence card was a proportionate response, thus neither art.27 nor regs 19-21 could be relied upon as a justification for not issuing N a certificate, in any event, S had not made a decision that she was entitled to invoke the public policy exception therein, entitling her to refuse N's application for a residence card, and while the application was extant, she required to issue a certificate; S could not claim to have made a decision on that point so as to justify the refusal to issue a renewed certificate, not having yet determined the public policy point in the context of considering the application for a residence card. (4) S's breach of the 2006 Regulations had been sufficiently serious to justify, in principle, an award of damages; the terms of Directive 2004/38 left no room for doubt that the certificate had to be issued immediately on the application for a residence card being made, the wording of art.10 and reg.17(3) was clear; a certificate required to be issued immediately on receipt of an application for a residence card and had to remain in force or be renewed or replaced so as to cover the whole period until the application for a residence card was finally determined, the infringement of that rule was inexcusable, and in those circumstances, N was in principle entitled to damages. (5) As a matter of practice, S issued certificates in a form which stated on their face that the holder had the right to work in the UK, in any event, it was clear from the scheme of Directive 2004/38 that the certificate was intended to be a temporary document putting the holder temporarily in the position that he would be in were a residence card subsequently granted, neither the residence card nor the certificate created rights but simply evidenced the existence of rights conferred by Union law, and was a certificate issued in such circumstances without any recognition of the right to work in the UK pending determination of the application for a residence card, and the right to work was in practice impeded by the absence of some appropriate wording on the certificate, that would be contrary to EU law. (6) N accepted that he would not have been able to take up the employment offer where, contrary to his assumption, his conviction was not yet spent, however, that did not mean that he would have been unable to obtain any employment but the matter of his success in that regard had not been fully explored and it was appropriate to put the case out by order to ascertain whether the damages claim was pursued and if so on what factual basis and for the court to obtain further assistance on the question whether, even could no pecuniary loss be shown on the balance of probabilities, there was scope for damages to be awarded for disappointment, frustration and anxiety by analogy with the approach in human rights cases. Opinion, (1) that was S correct in claiming that it was not possible yet to say whether N was entitled to a certificate, the test in reg.9(2) of the 2006 Regulations was fully satisfied in the present case; X had been residing in Germany as a worker or self-employed person before returning to the UK, N was her spouse and they had been living together in Germany before they had returned to the UK, and nothing more was required, and it was difficult to see any basis from which N would not be entitled to a residence card under the regulations, therefore, there was no basis for refusing to issue the certificate; (2) that although S had been found to be in breach of obligations under EU law, she could equally have been found to be in breach of statutory duty in terms of the 2006 Regulations. Observed, that S appeared to follow a practice of issuing duplicate certificates where the original one had expired while the application for a residence card was outstanding or there was an appeal against the refusal, which was clearly a sensible policy and did not appear to reflect S's argument that there was no obligation to issue a replacement or duplicate certificate in such circumstances.

AA (NIGERIA) v SECRETARY OF STATE FOR THE HOME DEPARTMENT *sub nom.* A v SECRETARY OF STATE FOR THE HOME DEPARTMENT, [2015] CSOH 158, 2016 S.L.T. 182, Lord Glennie, OH.

2691 Rights of entry and residence–Spouses

[Directive 2004/38 on the right of citizens of the Union and their family members to move and reside freely within the territory of the Member States amending Regulation (EEC) No 1612/68 and repealing Directives 64/221/EEC, 68/360/EEC, 72/194/EEC, 73/148/EEC, 75/34/EEC, 75/35/EEC, 90/364/EEC, 90/365/ 2004 art.35; Immigration

(European Economic Area) Regulations 2006 (SI 2006/1003) reg.2(a), reg.26, reg.27, reg.29(3)]

An Albanian citizen (P) petitioned for judicial review of a decision of the Secretary of State for the Home Department (S) refusing his application for a European Economic Area residence card. P had arrived in the United Kingdom clandestinely and had been served removal papers in 2011, and his two applications in 2013 for a residence card had been refused. On 17 February 2014, P had married a Lithuanian national and had made another application for a residence card on the basis of his right to reside as the spouse of an EU national. S had refused P's application on the basis that the marriage was one of convenience, and P's appeal against that decision was ongoing. P submitted that (1) upon a proper reading of Directive 2004/38 which underpinned the Immigration (European Economic Area) Regulations 2006, his appeal afforded him a right to remain in the UK whilst it was pending such that his removal would be unlawful; (2) P qualified for protection under Directive 2004/38 and fell to be treated as a person under the Immigration (European Economic Area) Regulations 2006 reg.29(3) because the regulations did not exlude bringing an appeal in the UK, thus the appeal was not excluded under reg.27 and the right of an in country appeal and the consequential effect of removal were such that the sensible reading of the regulations would be to apply a suspensive effect.

Held: Petition refused. It was clear from reg.2(a) that persons in a marriage of convenience did not qualify as spouses for the purposes of the 2006 Regulations, the patent purpose was to prevent the abuse of parties to a marriage of convenience taking advantage of the Directive, and there was no conflict because art.35(4) of the Directive specifically allowed for such a restriction of safeguards in their domestic application, in any event, reg.29 only provided for suspensive effect of refusal of admission or removal, and the omission was deliberate and carried through the intention that an appeal against refusal of a residence card did not have suspensive effect. Moreover, simply because an appeal against an EEA decision to refuse a residence card was not listed as an appeal which required to be made “out of country” under reg.26 did not mean that it became a right of appeal to be exercised in country, there was no principle of law which conferred the right to remain in a jurisdiction to pursue such an appeal, and further, the decision to refuse an EEA card simply resulted in the applicant having no basis to remain, removal was a separate and further step and it neither necessarily followed, nor could be conflated with, a decision to refuse a residence card, nor did removal render the appeal redundant, *R. (on the application of Ahmed) v Secretary of State for the Home Department* [2015] UKUT 436 (IAC), [2015] Imm. A.R. 1320, [2016] 1148, *considered.*

DP (ALBANIA) v SECRETARY OF STATE FOR THE HOME DEPARTMENT *sub nom.* P v SECRETARY OF STATE FOR THE HOME DEPARTMENT, [2016] CSOH 16, 2016 S.L.T. 523, Lady Scott, OH.

INSOLVENCY

2692 Accountant in Bankruptcy–Sequestration–Creditors

THE BANKRUPTCY (SCOTLAND) REGULATIONS 2016, SSI 2016/397; made under the Bankruptcy (Scotland) Act 2016 s.2(2)(a)(ii)(f), s.3(1), s.4(1)(d)(2)(b), s.6(8), s.8(3)(a), s.9(4)(b), s.19(1), s.46(2)(a)(6), s.48(1)(a), s.51(14), s.54(4), s.141(2)(a)(c), s.142(2)(5), s.200(1)(c)(8), s.221, s.224(1)(, s.225(2), s.228(1), s.234(2)(b), Sch.1 para2(5)(a); Debt Arrangement and Attachment (Scotland) Act 2002 s.7(2)(bd). In force: 30 November 2016.

These Regulations prescribe matters which fall to be prescribed by the Scottish Ministers under the Bankruptcy (Scotland) Act 2016 which consolidates Scottish bankruptcy legislation. They apply from 30 November 2016 to sequestrations where the creditor petition for sequestration is presented, or the debtor application for sequestration is received by the Accountant in Bankruptcy on or after that date.

2693 Accountant in Bankruptcy–Writs of sequestration–Applications and decisions

THE BANKRUPTCY (APPLICATIONS AND DECISIONS) (SCOTLAND) REGULATIONS 2016, SSI 2016/295; made under the Bankruptcy (Scotland) Act 2016 s.224, s.225(2), s.227. In force: 30 November 2016.

These Regulations set out the procedure for the making of applications to, and decisions by, the Accountant in Bankruptcy ("AiB") under the Bankruptcy (Scotland) Act 2016. They apply to sequestrations as regards which a petition for sequestration is presented, or an application is made, on or after 30 November 2016 (and trust deeds for the benefit of creditors executed on or after that date). They replace and update the Bankruptcy (Applications and Decisions) (Scotland) Regulations 2014 for those sequestrations. They prescribe forms to be used in relation to applications to AiB under the Act.

2694 Balancing of accounts–Set-off–Post-insolvency settlement amounts against pre-insolvency debt

[Prescription and Limitation (Scotland) Act 1973 (c.52) Sch.1 para.2(a); Financial Services and Markets Act 2000 (c.8)]

D sought payment of sums allegedly due in settlement of three claims against a bank (B) concerning the misselling of payment protection insurance (PPI). Between 1997 and 2003, D borrowed sums of money from B and in connection therewith was allegedly missold PPI. On 29 August 2006, D executed a trust deed in favour of her creditors, which became a protected trust deed two months later. In December 2013, D was discharged from the trust deed and B received payment from the trustee of a dividend in respect of its claims on the trust estate. In 2014, D and B concluded three agreements whereby B offered to pay, and D accepted sums in full and final settlement of, all and any PPI claims relating to the loans. B's offer letters forming part of the first and second agreements recorded that it would uphold D's complaints, the third agreement narrated the deficiencies in B's conduct, and the agreements referred to compensation in line with Financial Ombudsman Service (FOS) and Financial Conduct Authority guidance, and to a decision by B that it was susceptible to review by the FOS. B subsequently paid part of the sum to D but averred that it had been paid in error. B sought to withhold payment of the sums and set them off against the greater alleged indebtedness due by D to it under the earlier loan contracts. D submitted *inter alia* that (1) the principle of balancing of accounts in bankruptcy had no application because she was no longer insolvent and had been discharged from the trust deed at the dates of the PPI agreement; (2) the effect of that discharge was to extinguish any pre-insolvency liability to B; (3) any obligation to B under the loan contracts was extinguished by operation of prescription, where any claim by B in the trust deed was a single event and not a continuing claim for the purposes of the Prescription and Limitation (Scotland) Act 1973; (4) B's debt under the PPI agreements was a post insolvency debt and could not be set off against the pre-insolvency obligations founded upon by B under the loan agreements; (5) if the sum sought fell within D's insolvent estate, the appropriate remedy was for B to seek reappointment of the trustee to ingather the asset. B submitted *inter alia* that the PPI payments were *ex gratia* in nature and made without admission of liability.

Held: Case management conference assigned. (1) D's obligation to repay each loan was in existence by virtue of each contractual relationship of loan that existed between the parties as at the date of her insolvency, and her discharge from the trust deed did not extinguish any obligation owed by her to B to pay the unsatisfied balance due under the pre-insolvency contracts of loan; the trust subsisted unless a discharge on composition was entered into or creditors' claims were satisfied in full, and she was not reinvested in any part of the insolvent estate merely upon the occurrence of her discharge. (2) The effect of B submitting a claim to a trustee under a relevant trust deed for implement of D's obligation was continuously to interrupt the running of the five year prescription period in respect of that obligation, for as long as the claim subsisted before the trustee and up to the final adjudication of the claims; upon the formal adjudication and acceptance by D's trustee of B's claims, the five year prescriptive period ceased to be applicable by virtue of Sch.1, para.2(a) of the 1973 Act because a new and different obligation to recognise or obtemper the order of the trustee as an authority exercising jurisdiction was engaged, and instead at that point the 20 year prescriptive period became applicable, and B's plea and averments anent prescription were irrelevant. (3) The obligations which D sought to enforce found their source in a binding statutory regulatory scheme prescribed by the Financial Services and Markets Act 2000 that was in existence prior to the date of her insolvency, and although they were not enforceable as at the date of insolvency, they were in existence by virtue of that statutory regime, albeit contingent in nature and unascertained; the scheme imposed obligations upon B, including the obligation to comply with adjudications by the FOS upon customer complaints and to handle, process and determine such customer complaints in accordance with the Financial Services Authority Handbook, which imposed a continent liability upon B to pay compensation to a customer, and the conclusion of the PPI agreements merely had the effect of ascertaining the present value of B's previously unascertained contingent liability, thus the obligation was properly characterised as a pre-insolvency obligation and D's right to enforce that obligation constituted an asset that formed part of her insolvent estate, *Liquidator of Ben Line Steamers Ltd, Noter* [2010] CSOH 174, 2011 S.L.T. 535, [2011] C.L.Y. 4396 and *Bloom v Pensions Regulator* [2013] UKSC 52, [2014] A.C. 209, [2013] C.L.Y. 2138, *applied*; *R. (on the application of British Bankers Association) v Financial Services Authority* [2011] EWHC 999 (Admin), [2011] Bus. L.R. 1531, [2012] C.L.Y. 1465, *considered*. (4) Although it was not necessary for B to admit PPI misselling, upon an ordinary construction of the PPI agreements it had admitted the misselling to D, and the payments were not *ex gratia* in nature or entered into without admission of liability: there was no doubt that in offering and concluding the PPI agreements, B was acting pursuant to its regulatory obligation to determine customer complaints, and its obligation to pay compensation was the fruition of its pre-insolvency contingent obligation; the agreements had neither been expressly stated to be without prejudice, without admission of liability or otherwise *ex gratia*, nor was there any basis upon which such a qualification could properly be implied, and in offering the sums referred to in the agreements without qualification, B admitted the pre-insolvency breach by it of regulatory obligations owed to D. (5) Since B's obligations to D arising under the PPI sales were in existence as at the date of D's insolvency, D's correlative rights against B were likewise in existence at that date, and accordingly vested in the trust estate for the benefit of her creditors; it did not matter that D or the trustee might have been discharged, and D was not thereby reinvested in any part of the insolvent estate. (6) B was entitled to plead set off and D's averments anent the alleged non-application of the principle of the balancing of accounts in bankruptcy were irrelevant: the entitlement to plead the balancing of accounts in bankruptcy arose from the fact of D's insolvency and not from the identity of the person against whom it was asserted; D sued *qua* constructive trustee for the benefit of her creditors, if the trustee had sued for payment he would have been met with a competent plea of set off, and D could be in no better position that the trustee would have been under the trust deed; it was plain as a matter of practical common sense that the whole rights and pleas that were available to B as a creditor in insolvency ought to remain exigible by it and there was no persuasive justification to compel the interposition of the trustee as claimant; substantial justice was achieved by allowing an unsatisfied creditor to invoke the principle of the balancing of accounts in bankruptcy in answer to a claim by a discharged debtor for payment of a pre-insolvency debt; the bankruptcy process continued until creditors' claims were satisfied in full or there was a discharge on composition, *MS Fashions Ltd v Bank of Credit and Commerce International SA (In Liquidation)* [1993] Ch. 425, [1993] C.L.Y. 2391, *applied*. (7) Dismissal was not appropriate because a material factual issue as to the amount of the subsisting loan balance owed by D to B had to be determined at proof, B's preliminary plea to the effect of finding the foregoing discrete parts of B's pleadings as irrelevant would be sustained, and a case management conference would be assigned to hear submissions on the precise averments that fell to be excluded from probation.

DONNELLY v ROYAL BANK OF SCOTLAND PLC, 2016 S.L.T. (Sh Ct) 307, Sheriff S Reid, Sh Ct (Glasgow).

2695 Bankruptcy (Scotland) Act 2016 (asp 21)–Commencement Regulations

THE BANKRUPTCY (SCOTLAND) ACT 2016 (COMMENCEMENT) REGULATIONS 2016, SSI 2016/294; made under the Bankruptcy (Scotland) Act 2016 s.237(2). Commencement details: bringing into operation various provisions of the 2016 Act on 31 November 2016.

These Regulations bring into force the Bankruptcy (Scotland) Act 2016 on 30 November 2016.

2696 Disposition of property–Gratuitous alienations–Whether alleged consideration was artificial construct

[Insolvency Act 1986 (c.45) s.242(1)]

A company director (D) reclaimed against a decision of the Lord Ordinary finding that no consideration had been paid in respect of alienations challenged by the joint administrators (J) of a company (O) and other associated companies (L, Q, S and H) under the Insolvency Act 1986 s.242(1) (*Joint Administrators of Oceancrown Ltd v Stonegale Ltd* [2013] CSOH 189, 2014 G.W.D. 2-47). D had negotiated a deal with a company (C) for the sale and purchase of a commercial property (P) owned by O. The bank (B) which held security over P considered that its sale was part of property transfers involving four other properties (E, F, G and Y) over which B also held standard securities. On 10 November 2010, O disponed P to S for £762,000 and on the same day S disponed P to C for £2,100,000 plus £367,500 VAT. Subsequently, L disponed E to H, O disponed F and G to H and Q disponed Y to D's son, with the purported sale price totaling £2.4 million. Three separate commercial actions by J seeking decree of reduction in respect of the alienations made by O, L and Q came before the Lord Ordinary for proof. D submitted *inter alia* that the Lord Ordinary had erred in finding that no consideration had been paid in respect of the alienations under challenge, where B had received payment of £2.4 million in return for the discharge of the standard securities.

Held: Reclaiming motions refused. (1) What was meant by consideration in the current case was not controversial; although the question of whether adequate consideration had been given was one of mixed fact and law, it was also a question that was informed by primary findings of fact and the finding that no party gave the sellers anything in return for the conveyances under challenge came very close to determining the matter, *MacFadyen's Trustee v MacFadyen* 1994 S.C. 416, [1994] C.L.Y. 5400, *considered*. (2) D's basis for a passing of consideration for the challenged alienations was an artificial construct which had not reflected the controlling mind of the companies; O might be taken to have received £2.4 million but, in disponing P, it had conveyed a property which D had agreed to sell at that price prior to the conveyance, and in the absence of further evidence, O would be regarded as having received adequate consideration for P, but as having received nothing at all for F or G, and L and Q similarly received nothing. (3) The transactions under consideration were devices for the diversion of assets from creditors, they were not commercial transactions, and if, despite their non-commercial nature, they were said to have had the result that adequate consideration had passed, that required to be proven and D had failed to do so.

JOINT ADMINISTRATORS OF OCEANCROWN LTD v STONEGALE LTD; JOINT ADMINISTRATORS OF LOANWELL LTD v STONEGALE LTD; JOINT ADMINISTRATORS OF QUESTWAY LTD v PELOSI *sub nom.* BROWN v OCEANCROWN LTD; BROWN v STONEGALE LTD; BROWN v PELOSI, [2015] CSIH 12, 2015 S.C.L.R. 619, Lord Menzies, Lord Brodie, Lord McGhie, IH (Ex Div).

2697 Inhibitions–Floating charges–Prior floating charge–Whether priority with regard to debt incurred after registration of inhibition

[Insolvency Act 1986 (c.45) s.55(3)(a), s.60, s.60(1)(b); Companies (Floating Charges and Receivers) (Scotland) Act 1972 (c.67) s.15(2)(a), s.20(1)(b); Companies Act 1985 (c.6) s.471, s.476; Bankruptcy and Diligence etc. (Scotland) Act 2007 (asp 3) s.154]

A heritable proprietor (M) sought decree that an inhibition served on a property development company (T) was an effectually executed diligence in terms of the Insolvency Act 1986 s.60 and on the sale of T's assets he was entitled to payment prior to a floating charge holder (B), or alternatively that a receiver (R) was obliged to distribute the sale proceeds first to B in respect of pre-inhibition debt, second to M, and third to B in respect of post inhibition debt. In 2000, T granted the floating charge in B's favour. In 2005, M purchased a plot of land from T and entered into a contract with it for the construction of a house. Following entry to the house, M discovered defects in its construction and raised proceedings against T in the sheriff court for breach of contract. Warrant to inhibit on the dependence was granted and served on T, and a notice of letters of inhibition was registered on 25 September 2006. Thereafter, T entered into a series of facility agreements with B. On 30 November 2010, decree by default was granted against T for payment of a sum of £333,993.42 to M. T's principal assets were two houses in the same development as M's house, and B appointed R under the floating charge on 18 February 2011. The Companies (Floating Charges and Receivers) (Scotland) Act 1972 s.15(2)(a) had provided that a receiver's powers were exercisable subject to the rights of any person who had effectually executed diligence on all or any part of the company's property prior to the receiver's appointment, and s.20(1)(b) had provided that a floating charge holder ranked behind all persons who had effectually executed such diligence on any part of the property which was subject to the charge. Those provisions were repealed and respectively re-enacted by the consolidating Companies Act 1985 s.471(2)(a) and s.476(1)(b), which were in turn repealed and re-enacted by ss.55(3)(a) and s.60(1)(b) of the 1986 Act. The Bankruptcy and Diligence etc. (Scotland) Act 2007 s.154 removed an inhibitor's common law preference over debts contracted by a debtor after the date of the inhibition. M submitted *inter alia* that the inhibition registered in his favour was an effectually executed diligence and the court should decline to follow *Lord Advocate v Royal Bank of Scotland Ltd* 1977 S.C. 155, [1978] C.L.Y. 3157, where the Inner House held that an arresting creditor, who had not raised an action of forthcoming before a receiver's appointment, had not effectually executed diligence on a debtor's property so as to obtain a ranking in preference to the charge holder in terms of s.20(1) of the 1972 Act, as that case had been wrongly decided and its reasoning was fundamentally at odds with the approach taken by the House of Lords in *Sharp v Thomson* 1997 S.C. (H.L.) 66, [1997] C.L.Y. 6156 to the interpretation of the legislative scheme relating to floating charges. T submitted *inter alia* that preferences among creditors were determined entirely by the ranking provisions in s.60 of the 1986 Act, the omission from s.60(1) of any express reference to an inhibiting creditor was because diligence of all kinds was dealt with by s.60(1)(b), and as M did not fall into the category of persons who had effectually executed diligence he did not rank in preference to T in respect of any part of the debt secured by the floating charge.

Held: Case put out by order. (1) The provisions at issue in *Lord Advocate* had undergone two re-enactments both of which were consolidations, on neither occasion was there an opportunity for Parliament to make substantive amendments to the law except in so far as necessitated by the consolidation process, and the distinction between the judicial interpretations of the corresponding provisions of the 1972 Act and the 1986 Act were so fine as to amount to little more than a technicality. The persuasive force of *Lord Advocate* was practically indistinguishable from binding authority and it was not open to the instant court to decline to follow it on the ground that it was wrongly decided; *Sharp* was not concerned with any issue of competition between a floating charge holder and a creditor who had executed diligence, *Lord Advocate* was concerned with interpretation of a different section of legislation and the meaning of the phrase "effectually executed diligence", and nothing in *Sharp* suggested that the approach in *Lord Advocate* was misconceived, *Lord Advocate, followed, Barras v Aberdeen Steam Trawling & Fishing Co Ltd* [1933] A.C. 402 and *Sharp, considered.* (2) Categorisation of inhibition as an effectually executed diligence on a debtor's property did not of itself entitle the inhibiting creditor to preference over a creditor whose floating charge was registered before the inhibition but crystallised after it; inhibition struck at future voluntary acts of the inhibitee, however crystallisation of the floating charge was not a voluntary act of the debtor company but was carried out by the charge holder; M's plea in terms that he had an effectually executed diligence on T's properties and was entitled to decree that R was obliged to pay the sum due in terms of the sheriff court decree to M before making payment to B as floating charge holder had to be repelled, regardless of whether the inhibition fell properly to be categorised as an effectually executed diligence. (3) Diligence could be effective against the holder of a floating charge otherwise than by falling within s.60(1)(b) of the 1986 Act, there was no reason to distinguish between arrestment and inhibition, and although the relevant effect of inhibition was to render the inhibitee's heritable property litigious and that did not give M a general preference over B when the charge crystallised, it did give preference over post inhibition advances because it conferred priority on M as inhibiting creditor over such advances; the fact that they were secured by a floating charge did not prevent the operation of the common law of inhibition to M's benefit, *Iona Hotels Ltd (In Receivership), Petitioners* 1990 S.C. 330, [1990] C.L.Y. 4772, *considered.* (4) M was entitled to have a plea sustained that all debts incurred by T on or after 25 September 2006 were subject to the inhibition in M's favour and he was entitled to decree as second concluded for, however the case would be put out by order to discuss the precise terms.

MACMILLAN v T LEITH DEVELOPMENTS LTD (IN RECEIVERSHIP AND IN LIQUIDATION), [2016] CSOH 19, 2016 S.L.T. 477, Lord Tyre, OH.

2698 Protected trust deeds–Creditors–Debtors

THE PROTECTED TRUST DEEDS (SCOTLAND) AMENDMENT REGULATIONS 2016, SSI 2016/399; made under the Bankruptcy (Scotland) Act 1985 s.72(1A), Sch.5 para.5. In force: 30 November 2016.

These Regulations amend Forms 4, 5, 6 and 7 used in relation to protected voluntary trust deeds entered into by debtors for the benefit of their creditors which were executed on or after 28 November 2013 but before 30 November 2016 prescribed in the Protected Trust Deeds (Scotland) Regulations 2013.

2699 Protected trust deeds–Prescribed forms

THE PROTECTED TRUST DEEDS (FORMS) (SCOTLAND) REGULATIONS 2016, SSI 2016/398; made under the Bankruptcy (Scotland) Act 2016 s.166(2)(b)(c), s.169, s.170(1)(b)(e), s.174(2)(3), s.175(1), s.182, s.183(1)(a)(b), s.184(1)(b)(2)(a), s.186(3)(9), s.194(1)(3), s.225(2). In force: 30 November 2016.

These Regulations set out the forms to be used in relation to protected voluntary trust deeds entered into by debtors for the benefit of their creditors governed by the Bankruptcy (Scotland) Act 2016 Pt 14.

2700 Sequestration–Standard securities–Sequestrated individual granting standard securities and dispositions of properties–Whether voidable

[Bankruptcy (Scotland) Act 1985 (c.66) s.14(1), s.14(2), s.14(3)(b), s.14(4), s.31, s.32(8), s.39A, s.44(4), s.63]

Two companies (M and C, collectively X) reclaimed against interlocutors of the Lord Ordinary granting decree *de plano* to the trustee (T) on the sequestrated estate of an individual (F) in her action seeking production and reduction of certain standard securities and dispositions granted by F in X's favour (*Fortune's Trustee v Medwin Investments Ltd* [2015] CSOH 139, 2015 G.W.D. 34-552, *Fortune's Trustee v Cooper Watson Ltd* [2015] CSOH 140, 2015 G.W.D. 34-553). T had been appointed on 7 February 2011 but the certified copy of the sheriff's order granting warrant to cite F, dated 24 December 2010, had not been recorded in the register of inhibitions and adjudications before 29 April 2014, pursuant to the Bankruptcy (Scotland) Act 1985 s.14(1). T had sought relief in terms of s.63 and on 6 February 2014, the sheriff had pronounced an interlocutor allowing the warrant to cite to be amended and ordaining the sheriff clerk to intimate to the keeper of the register of inhibitions and adjudications a certified copy of the interlocutors, dated 24 December 2011 and 6 February 2014, reserving to pronounce further, which the keeper had recorded on 11 February 2014. In March and April 2014, F had granted the aforementioned dispositions and heritable securities, all of which had been registered after the expiry of three years from the date of sequestration. In May, the sheriff had authorised the keeper to record the certified copy of the order of 24 December 2010 and had ordained the sheriff clerk to send to the keeper a memorandum in terms of s.14(4) of the 1985 Act for recording and the keeper to record it, notwithstanding the expiry of the three year period in s.14(3)(b). The Lord Ordinary found *inter alia* that the s.14 prohibitory effect could not take effect unless and until the certified copy had been recorded, the prohibitory effect of the recording of the certified copy had expired when the impugned deeds had been recorded in March and April 2014, three years having elapsed since the sequestration, that where X had been aware of F's sequestration and that T had continued to have a prior right to the subjects, the s.44(4)(c) protection had not applied but that the challenge open to T was not on the ground of sequestration but that X had acquired their rights in bad faith and the rule against offside goals was engaged, and had made the order on that basis.

Held: Reclaiming motions refused and C's case remitted to Lord Ordinary. (1) Where a trustee had not completed title and the title remained in the debtor's name, the effect of s.14(2) of the 1985 Act was to put the world on notice of the sequestration and thus of the impediment that the trustee in sequestration had a personal right to the property in question, and an individual with such knowledge was no longer entitled in safety to rely on the face of the register, the knowledge was effectively deemed by operation of statue, as a consequence of sequestration, once the effect of s.14(2) had expired, such individuals were no longer deemed to have that knowledge and transactions with them could not be challenged merely on the basis of the sequestration, however, that the effect of s.14(2) had expired did not affect individuals who had knowledge of the trustee's prior personal right, such an individual was not entitled to rely the expiry of public notification of the sequestration to transact with the debtor to the trustee and creditors' prejudice; s.44(4) did not entitle such a person to transact with the debtor in relation to the sequestrated estate in a manner which deprived the trustee of his rights, rather, the provisions of s.32(8) remained operative, and s.44(4)(c) did not impose a temporal restriction on s.32(8). (2) It could not have been Parliament's intention under s.44 to grant immunity to a deed which was in favour of a party who had actual knowledge of the fact of sequestration and the vesting of the estate on the trustee for the benefit of the creditors to the debtor, which would be absurd in the context of bankruptcy law as a whole and would be a statutorily sanctioned fraud on the creditors. (3) The reclaiming motions would be refused but C's action would be remitted to the Lord Ordinary to deal with the outstanding issue that the property to which the deed related might qualify as F's family home under s.39A of the 1985 Act. *Opinion*, that in any event, the Lord Ordinary had been correct to conclude that the matter came within the scope of the offside goals rule and to treat T as being in a position equivalent to that of a bona fide purchaser for value.

FORTUNE'S TRUSTEE v MEDWIN INVESTMENTS LTD, [2016] CSIH 49, 2016 S.L.T. 923, The Lord Justice Clerk (Lady Dorrian), Lord Bracadale, Lord Malcolm, IH (2 Div).

INSURANCE

2701 Insurance policies–Payments–Payment from life insurance company to deceased trustee's personal representative–Title or capacity to receive payment

[Revenue Act 1884 (c.62) s.11]

Two trustees (Y and Z, collectively T) raised an action seeking payment from a life insurance company (P) of a sum representing the value of two life assurance policies (X), issued in 1985 and held in two trusts, the first of which had been created by a husband (G) and the second by his wife (B), on the basis that an attorney (Q) had had no title to receive the sums paid. The sums assured under X had become payable on the second death, being G's in November 2010. P had made payment thereunder, amounting to £305,998.57 to Q, who had been the personal representative of G and his second late wife (C) in Florida, where G had latterly resided and had died. Over the lifetime of G's trust, a number of assumptions and resignations of trustees had taken place, including Y's, and B had died in April 2002. At the time of G's death, he had remained the sole trustee of his own trust. Following B's death, X had been treated as if they were held in G's trust until the true situation had come to light in February 2015 after the action had been raised, and in March 2015, Z had been assumed as a trustee and T had sought, and had been granted, leave to amend the summons to add a designation to the effect that they also sued as trustees of B's trust.

Held: Case put out by order. (1) Q had had no title, in any capacity, to receive the proceeds of the policy settled in G's trust. The Revenue Act 1884 s.11 had no application to trust property, the reference therein to "the personal estate and effects of any deceased person" had to be read as referring to moveable property forming part of the deceased's private patrimony, not to property to which he held title in a fiduciary capacity, and ought not to be construed as extending to property held in a lapsed trust of which the deceased had been a sole trustee, as that would put a foreign personal representative in a favourable position compared to that of an executor resident in Scotland and appointed by a Scottish domiciled testator, and s.11 did not assist Q as regarded title to receive the policy proceeds held in trust, and was equally of no assistance to P in responding to T's claim regarding G's trust. Moreover, Q had had no title in any capacity to receive the proceeds of B's policy; on G's death, B's policy had had two surviving trustees in whom the trust property had vested by survivorship. (2) It was clear from *Mrs Ann Yule or Neilson v The Mossend Iron Company and Others* (1885) 12 R. 499 that Y had no title to raise the action on his own, nor, at that time, had Z contributed anything to title, as she was not then a trustee, accordingly, when the present action had been raised, no competent claim was made in respect of the proceeds of the policy settled by B, however, the present action was not incompetent as regarded the claim for the proceeds of the policy settled by G; T were the whole trustees of B's trust, they had title to sue for payment of the policy proceeds, they had sought, and had been granted, leave to amend the grounds of their action against P by adding to their existing competent claim for payment of the proceeds of G's policy a new competent claim for payment of the proceeds of B's policy, and the two claims were so closely linked with regard to both factual background and legal analysis that it is appropriate for them to proceed together in a single action, *Neilson*, *considered*. (3) The case would be put out by order for the court to be addressed on the terms of any interlocutor to be pronounced and on further procedure. Opinion, that it would had been irrelevant to examine the capacity in which Q had purported to claim and receive payment, whether as G's or as C's legal representative; from P's perspective as debtor under the policy, Q was a single, indivisible, legal person, and had he purported to claim payment in the wrong capacity, P would still have paid the correct person and their liability would have been extinguished.

SHENKEN v PHOENIX LIFE LTD, [2015] CSOH 96, [2015] W.T.L.R. 1833, Lord Tyre, OH.

LANDLORD AND TENANT

2702 Agricultural holdings–Notices–Tenant sending notice to director of corporate landlord–Validity of notice under s.72(6) Agricultural Holdings (Scotland) Act 2003

[Agricultural Holdings (Scotland) Act 2003 (asp 11) s.72(6), s.88]

A company (B), the landlord of an agricultural holding (X), appealed against a decision of the Land Court under the Agricultural Holdings (Scotland) Act 2003 s.88, assoilzieing the tenant (H) from the craves of B's application for declarator that a letter sent by H's agents was not a valid notice under, and in terms of, s.72(6) of the 2003 Act, and was therefore not effective to continue the tenancy, and an order for removal. The letter had been addressed to a director (M) of B and the issue was whether a letter addressed to someone who was not the landlord of an agricultural holding might, in the circumstances of the case, nevertheless constitute the giving of notice for the purposes of s.72(6). H had been the general partner in a limited partnership which was X's tenant and the partnership was originally between H and M. The partnership was also tenant in the lease of a separate agricultural holding (Y) which was farmed by H, the landlord of which was M. On dissolution of the partnership by notice served by B and M, both leases terminated, and thereafter H's agents purported to give notice under s.72(6) in respect of X. At about the same time as M received the notice about X, he received a notice in identical terms in respect of Y. The Land Court inferred that the addressing of the letter to M was simply a mistake and M admitted that he was in no doubt as to what the notice intended to mean, namely that H had intended to become tenant of X in his own right. The Land Court considered the terms of s.72(6), and that the lack of requirement for writing meant that it was not so tightly bound to the terms of the notice which was given as the court was in *Ben Cleuch Estates Ltd v Scottish Enterprise* [2008] CSIH 1, 2008 S.C. 252, [2009] C.L.Y. 5033, as relied upon by B; and that the correct question was not whether the letter was a valid notice but whether the general partner had given notice to the landlord of his intention to become tenant under the tenancy in his own right. The questions of law for the court were (1) had the Land Court erroneously conclude that the letter should be construed as a notice to B on the basis that M happened to be the controlling mind of the company, and (2) had the Land Court erred in failing to acknowledge that the letter was, as a matter of fact, a notice given to another person and was not a notice to the landlord.

Held: Appeal allowed. (1) The Land Court's conclusion was wrong: it had failed to address the point that, in order to be valid, a s.72(6) notice had to be given to the landlord; as the Land Court found, what H had relied upon as a notice, namely the letter, was given to someone other than the landlord and any doubt in relation thereto could be resolved by reference to *Ben Cleuch*; and H's response that the contents of the letter nevertheless came to the attention of someone who, for practical purposes, could be regarded as the equivalent of B, as its directing mind and will, which while shifting the emphasis away from a juristic act by the general partner to something done by, or on behalf of, the landlord, the matter was again addressed by *Ben Cleuch*, *Ben Cleuch, considered.* (2) Both questions of law would be answered in the affirmative and the court was minded to grant decree in the terms proposed by B and grant declarator that the letter was not a valid notice under, and in terms of, s.72(6) and that the tenancy of X had come to an end as a result of the termination and dissolution of the tenant, and that H had not become tenant under that tenancy under his own right under s.72. *Observed*, that in the present area of law there was a need for certainty to the extent that it was possible and the law had to therefore provide a bright line test.

BALGRAY LTD v WILLIAM HODGSON, [2016] CSIH 55, 2016 S.L.T. 839, Lord Brodie, Lady Clark of Calton, Lord Tyre, IH.

2703 Assured Tenancies–Landlords' duties–Tenant information packs

THE TENANT INFORMATION PACKS (ASSURED TENANCIES) (SCOTLAND) AMENDMENT ORDER 2016, SSI 2016/334; made under the Housing (Scotland) Act 1988 s.30B(1). In force: 1 December 2016.

This Order substitutes a new schedule in the Tenant Information Packs (Assured Tenancies) (Scotland) Order 2013. It sets out a Tenant Information Pack that persons who are to be landlords under assured tenancies are to provide to persons who are to be their tenants. The changes are all concerned with reflecting that the responsibility for certain matters passes to the First-tier Tribunal for Scotland Housing and Property Chamber with effect from 1 December 2016.

2704 Business tenancies–Repair covenants–Construction of lease clauses

Landlords (L) reclaimed against decisions of the Lord Ordinary in relation to the construction of certain clauses of a commercial lease regarding the repair and maintenance obligations of L's tenants (T). T had leased an office block together with its car parking area and common parts (collectively P) from L between 1988 and 2012 and L averred that at the termination of the lease, P had not been in good and substantial repair. Clause 3(a) of the lease had provided *inter alia* that T was obliged to accept P in the condition they were in at the commencement of the lease, to keep them in good and substantial repair and maintained at their own cost, all to L's satisfaction, and to replace or renew or rebuild P in at least as good condition as they had been accepted by T, regardless of the age or state of the dilapidation thereof. Clause 3(b) had provided that T was to keep all lighting, heating, ventilation, security and drainage systems, water supply, gas and other installations, fire fighting equipment and all other machinery in or serving P in good working order, repair or condition, and, from time to time, when requisite or when reasonably required by L, to replace them by suitable articles or equipment of similar and modern kind, all to L's satisfaction. Clause 7 had provided *inter alia* that at the expiry of the lease, T would, subject to carrying out all restoration works called for by L to their satisfaction, surrender P together with all improvements made thereto, and conferred upon L an express option to serve notice on T requiring payment of a sum equal to the amount required to put P in good and substantial repair, in lieu of requiring T to carry out the work. T averred that they were not liable for material improvements to P over and above their state at the date of entry under the lease, beyond the repairing obligations thereof and that the sum sued for by L, which purported to be the cost of putting P into good and substantial repair in accordance with T's obligations under the lease, greatly exceeded such sum as might properly be due. In relation to cl.3(a), the Lord Ordinary found that an obligation to keep P in good and substantial repair did not necessarily import an obligation to put them into that condition and construed cl.3(a) as meaning that L's claim, in so far as based upon an obligation at termination to put P into a condition better than they had been in at commencement, had not been relevantly stated, and deleted the words "put and" from a sentence in an article of condescendence which, had read "The Defenders were obliged to effect all repairs, maintenance and renewal necessary to put and keep the Premises in good and substantial repair and maintained in at least as good a condition as they were accepted by them". The Lord Ordinary approached his consideration of cl.7 bearing in mind certain observations in *Grove Investments Ltd v Cape Building Products Ltd* [2014] CSIH 43, 2014 Hous. L.R. 35, [2014] C.L.Y. 3630, the circumstances of which were indistinguishable from those in the present case, and found that the words "a sum equal to the amount required to put the leased subjects into good and substantial repair" were amenable to two possible constructions and that the payment obligation was activated only if L intended to carry out the work required to put P into the condition in which they ought to have been left at termination of the lease, as that construction best accorded with commercial common sense, and that the proviso in cl.7 did not preclude T from offering to prove that the appropriate measure of L's loss was something other than the cost of repair.

Held: Case put out by order. (1) The Lord Ordinary's approach had involved a forensic analysis of the type that might be appropriate to statutory construction but redolent of that warned against in *Arnold v Britton* [2015] UKSC 36, [2015] A.C. 1619, [2015] C.L.Y. 1606, and whatever drafting deficiencies there might be in cl.3(a), they were not such as to entitle the court readily to depart from its natural meaning. (2) T's construction of cl.3(a), accepted by the Lord Ordinary, involved a substantial and unjustified departure from the natural meaning of its language, and it was clear that the parties' intention was that the repairing standard was to be that of "good and substantial repair" but if at the commencement of the lease P's condition was better than that, the standard to which it had to be maintained was that condition, however, had that not been the condition at the commencement of the lease, T had to perform its obligation to repair and keep in good and substantial repair in a manner which achieved that standard; the obligation to repair was, of itself, indicative thereof but were there any doubt, the balance of authority supported the conclusion that an obligation to keep subjects in good and substantial repair carried an obligation to put them into that state of repair, *Credit Suisse v Beegas Nominees Ltd* [1994] 4 All E.R. 803, [1995] C.L.Y. 2982, *Taylor Woodrow Properties Ltd v Strathclyde Regional Council*, 15 December 1995, unreported, *Lowe v Quayle Munro Ltd* 1997 S.C. 346, [1997] C.L.Y. 6179 and *L Batley Pet Products Ltd v North Lanarkshire Council* [2014] UKSC 27, [2014] 3 All E.R. 64, [2014] C.L.Y. 1978, *considered*. (3) Clause 3(b) could be regarded as standing alone and thereby not inconsistent with the Lord Ordinary's construction of cl.3(a), however, the more natural meaning was to read cl.3(a) and (b) together, and reference in cl.7, to T's obligation as being to put the leased subjects into good and substantial repair also supported L's construction of cl.3(a); had parties intended that the repairing standard could be less, the reference to good and substantial repair would have made no sense, and further, the Lord Ordinary's construction of cl.3(a) did not accord with commercial common sense where the clause bore the hallmarks of a full repairing lease and his construction involved such a departure therefrom that the parties would have been expected to make it clear, had that been their intention, *McCall's Entertainments (Ayr) Ltd v South Ayrshire Council (No.2)* 1998 S.L.T. 1421, [1999] C.L.Y. 6327, *distinguished*. (4) The only natural and ordinary meaning to be given to cl.7 was that the sum due was the repair costs, and questions of whether, and to what extent, P was worth less in capital terms was irrelevant, to do otherwise would produce an incomprehensible result which would fly in the face of common sense so as to exclude it from the possibility of being an alternative construction; it was clear from the wording of cl.7 that parties intended that was P not, at termination, in the condition in which it would have been had T complied with their repairing obligations, L was to be entitled to payment of a sum equal to the cost of bringing P up to that standard. (5) The language used in cl.7 connoted no alternative to assessing loss, there was no potential for importing into the words "a sum equal to the amount required" a meaning to the effect that L had to intend to use the money to carry out the works, failing which repair costs became wholly irrelevant and actual capital loss suffered became the only matter of relevance, the reference to the call for payment of the repair costs being in lieu of requiring the tenant to carry out the work accurately reflected the context which was that prior to termination L had the option of a different remedy but in the event that they were outstanding at termination, that option disappeared. (6) The reclaiming motion would be allowed and the Lord Ordinary's interlocutor reversed and in due course, the matter would be remitted to the Lord Ordinary to proceed as accords but meanwhile the case would be put out by order to deal with any outstanding matters. Observed, that the general observations in *Grove* ought not to be taken as indicating that the considerations of co-operation and mutuality applied across the board, care had to be taken to avoid reading anything said in *Grove* as being to the effect that the court could correct a bad bargain or even an unfair one, the observations in *Grove* predated the guidance provided by the Supreme Court in *Arnold* and accordingly had to be regarded with an appropriate degree of caution, and it was important to note that *Grove* did not lay down any general rule to the effect that the landlord in a commercial lease was, at termination, if repairs were outstanding only, entitled to be compensated for capital loss actually suffered, *Grove, distinguished* and *Arnold, considered.*

@SIPP PENSION TRUSTEES v INSIGHT TRAVEL SERVICES LTD, [2015] CSIH 91, 2016 S.L.T. 131, Lord Menzies, Lady Smith, Lady Clark of Calton, IH.

2705 Crofts–Landlords–Meaning of "landlord" in s.20 Crofters (Scotland) Act 1993–Owner of common grazing land

[Crofters (Scotland) Act 1993 (c.44) s.20, s.20(1), s.3(4), s.61]

A special case was stated by the Scottish Land Court for the opinion of the Inner House at the request of a grazing shareholder (K) on a question of law relating to the competency of an application to the Land Court by the owner of a cottage (S) under the Crofters (Scotland) Act 1993 s.20(1) for authority for resumption of a piece of ground behind her property which formed part of the common grazings, which K had opposed (*Sorbie v Kennedy* 2015 S.L.T. (Land Ct) 17, [2015] C.L.Y. 2866). Before the Land Court, K had submitted that S was not a landlord of the common grazing land such that the resumption was outwith the scope of s.20, with reference to s.61; all that could be resumed was croft land, defined in s.3(4). The Land Court authorised resumption, proceeding on the basis of S's concession that she did not fall within the definition of landlord in s.61, and found that in using "landlord" in s.20 Parliament meant the owner of the grazing land and that the right to resume was to resume the land and not simply the grazing rights held over the land. The Land Court asked whether it had erred in holding that the reference to "landlord" in s.20 of the 1993 Act applied to all owners of common grazing land and not only to those who meet the statutory definition of "landlord" in s.61 thereof. The court allowed S to withdraw her concession regarding s.61 as it was on a point of law and the court did not wish its consideration of the question of law to be constrained by a concession as to the effect of the relevant statute.

Held: Case put out by order. (1) A crofter's right of grazing in common, such as that which S sought to resume, was incorporeal and ancillary, it was a pertinent of the croft, thus, a crofter was not to be regarded as a tenant of the land over which the right was exercised, and equally, the crofter's landlord need not be owner of the land over which the tenant had a right of grazing in common; it was clear that when s.20(1) spoke of the application of the landlord that meant the landlord of that part of croft which was the subject of the application for authority to resume, in the present case, the right of grazing on the resumption subjects, being one right in the bundle of rights comprising

K's holding, which was a burden or restriction on what would otherwise be S's entitlement, as proprietor of the resumption subjects, to enjoy exclusive possession thereof; as proprietor, S was a person with title and interest, and indeed the only person with title and interest, to extinguish the restriction by resumption of the right, S was in right of something which was trenched upon or restricted by rights which truly constituted pertinents of the croft and which belonged to the tenant of the croft as such, and once those rights were left out of account, as owner, S was the person entitled to take possession of the croft and accordingly, by virtue of s.61, the landlord, and the application was competent. (2) The Land Court had given unequivocal, and what would be taken by the court as authoritative, statements that it had been the clear understanding of all those with an interest, that s.20 and its predecessors had been intended to cover an application by the owner of common grazings, that that understanding was well established and that it had never previously been challenged, therefore, the position was that from the time of the institution of crofting tenure, the relevant statutes had been consistently interpreted as comprehending the owner of common grazings within the expression "landlord", giving rise to an established practice in terms of which such owners had been able to apply to the Land Court for authority to resume the grazings or parts thereof, which was strong reinforcement for the court's construction of the relevant provision. (3) In answer to the Land Court's question, the meaning of "landlord" where it appeared in s.20 of the 1993 Act was provided by the definition in s.61 of the Act; having regard thereto, the Land Court had not erred in holding that the reference to "landlord" in s.20 applied to all owners of common grazing land and, in particular, S. (4) The case would be put out by order to allow the parties to address the court on the orders to be pronounced.

SORBIE v KENNEDY, [2015] CSIH 94, 2016 S.L.T. 239, Lord Menzies, Lord Brodie, Lady Dorrian, IH (Ex Div).

2706 **Private Housing (Tenancies) (Scotland) Act 2016 (asp 19)–Commencement No.1 Regulations**

THE PRIVATE HOUSING (TENANCIES) (SCOTLAND) ACT 2016 (COMMENCEMENT NO.1) REGULATIONS 2016, SSI 2016/298; made under the Private Housing (Tenancies) (Scotland) Act 2016 s.79(2). Commencement details: bringing into operation various provisions of the 2016 Act on 31 October 2016.

These Regulations bring into force the Private Housing (Tenancies) (Scotland) Act 2016 ss 7, 17(3), 22(2), 24(3)(4), 43(1), 61(3) and 62(1) for the limited purpose of making regulations, and ss 8, 11, 12 and 34(2) and Sch.2 for all purposes.

2707 **Rent reviews–Notice–Letter of rent review containing several errors–Whether valid notice**

Landlords (L) appealed against a decision of the sheriff granting decree of absolvitor in L's action seeking declarator that they had invoked the power to demand an increase in rental in terms of a lease. The lease had been entered into between L's predecessors and "William Thompson and Son (Dumbarton) Ltd", L's tenants (T), in 1973 and was to expire on 11 November 2031. Clause second provided *inter alia* that L had the power to demand increases in rent on 11 November 1991 and 2011 on giving T not less than six months' written notice. On 17 March 2011, L had written a letter of rent review to T, addressed to "Wm Thompson & Sons Ltd", and on 11 November 2011, in a further letter addressed to the same party, L had stated that they intended to revise the rent to £13,800 per annum. On 8 October 2012, T had written to L stating *inter alia* that the 17 March 2011 letter had not been a valid notice and the rent review had not been validly instigated in terms of the lease, and L had raised the action of declarator. The sheriff found that the 17 March 2011 letter had not been addressed to T in accordance with the requirements of the lease such that it did not constitute a valid notice in terms of cl.second thereof.

Held: Appeal refused. (1) There was no error in the sheriff's approach to the issue of the formal validity of the notice, and on the authorities, there was a clear distinction between errors which went to the fundamental validity of a notice by failing to meet the requirements of the empowering document and errors in the content of the notice. (2) The 17 March 2011 letter contained several errors, the most serious being the omission of "(Dumbarton)" from the designation, and that, together with the use of "Sons" rather than "Son" and the abbreviations, went beyond the obvious misspelling of a name; the letter did not constitute a valid notice to T for the purposes of cl.second of the lease, the notice had not been given to T as T were defined in the lease and had not been duly addressed to T in terms of the lease, it could not be said that for an error to invalidate such a notice, there required to be something in the error which might mislead the other party, and the notice was not a notice for the purposes of the lease sufficient to trigger the rent review provisions thereof, *Ben Cleuch Estates Ltd v Scottish Enterprise* [2008] CSIH 1, 2008 S.C. 252, [2009] C.L.Y. 5033 and *Batt Cables Plc v Spencer Business Parks Ltd* [2010] CSOH 81, 2010 S.L.T. 860, [2010] C.L.Y. 4356, *applied* and *Mannai Investment Co Ltd v Eagle Star Life Assurance Co Ltd* [1997] A.C. 749, [1997] C.L.Y. 3256, *considered*.

WEST DUNBARTONSHIRE COUNCIL v WILLIAM THOMPSON AND SON (DUMBARTON) LTD, [2015] CSIH 93, 2016 S.L.T. 125, Lord Menzies, Lady Smith, Lady Clark of Calton, IH (Ex Div).

2708 Secure tenancies–Repossession–Existence of further contractual tenancy

[Housing (Scotland) Act 2001 (asp 10) s.36, s.36(3)]

A local authority (C) sought recovery of possession of a property (P) let to S and decree for payment of arrears of rent. C averred that on 6 May 2010, it had agreed to let P to S in terms of a short secure tenancy agreement with an initial period of six months, renewed thereafter on a month to month basis. A notice to quit was delivered to S by one of C's managing agents requiring him to remove by 11 February 2015, and a notice of intention to raise proceedings for possession was served in terms of the Housing (Scotland) Act 2001 s.36(3). The summons was served upon S and when the case called, C advised the court that it had reached an agreement with S whereby he would remain in occupation of P upon payment of an agreed sum including payment of arrears of rent, and it moved to adjourn the case to a later date. C submitted *inter alia* that no further contractual tenancy was in existence that would have rendered the proceedings incompetent, and it was giving S an opportunity to comply with his obligations under the lease before seeking decree.

Held: Action dismissed. Provided a landlord complied with the provisions of s.36 and the three criteria, namely that the tenancy had reached its ish, tacit relocation was not operating and no further contractual tenancy was in existence, were met, the court had no discretion regarding the granting of an order for recovery of possession and was not required to consider the reasonableness of the landlord's crave: C had entered into an agreement with S for continued occupation, three of the essential clauses for a lease had been agreed, namely the parties, the subjects and the rent, and at common law the duration of the lease would have been implied to be one year, accordingly even if the short secure tenancy had come to its ish and tacit relocation was not operating, a further contractual tenancy was in existence and an order for recovery of possession could not be granted. *Opinion*, that where the short secure tenancy agreement was entered into on 6 May 2010 for an initial period of six months, the ish appeared to be 6 November 2010, thus the notice to quit was defective in that it specified a date other than the ish and would not have prevented tacit relocation, and the notice to quit had been served by hand delivery by C's managing agents whereas only sheriff officers had authority to serve such a notice personally, therefore, it appeared that the notice to quit had not been validly served and the other criteria, namely that the tenancy had reached its ish and that tacit relocation was not operating, might not have been met. *Observed*, that had Parliament intended that actions brought under s.36 were capable of being adjourned for various reasons, then a provision similar to that in s.16(1), whereby the court could adjourn upon certain specified grounds, could have been made; the nature of a short secure tenancy, the right given to landlords by s.36, the limited security of tenure given to tenants, and the absence of any provision whereby proceedings might be adjourned all pointed to an expectation that if proceedings were raised in terms of that section and the criteria appeared to be met, then, as provided in s.35(5), the court had to make an order for recovery of possession and not adjourn the proceedings.

CITY OF EDINBURGH COUNCIL v SMITH, 2016 S.L.T. (Sh Ct) 343, Sheriff K E C Mackie, Sh Ct (Lothian) (Edinburgh).

2709 Subtenancies–Tenants' rights–Right of severance in respect of chalet built on leased land–Removal of chalet consistent with terms of sublease

The heritable proprietor (L) of an estate (B), which included the solum upon which a chalet (C) was built, sought declarator that she was C's heritable proprietor and interdict against the subtenant (G) from dismantling or removing C. In April and May 1969, B's then heritable proprietor had granted a lease of a portion of B, including the solum on which C was built, to a company (F) from 1 March 1969 to 1 March 2000, which provided that F was to erect houses on the subjects and was entitled to sell the properties to third parties as holiday residences without granting title to the land on which they stood, and that all buildings would be removed by F at the termination of the lease. In December 1970, F had sublet the solum to G's father (X), who had built C thereon. In 1982, F had assigned its rights in the head lease and a number of subleases, including that in X's favour, to L and her husband, and in 1988, they had assigned the head lease together with their whole rights as immediate landlords in the subleases to themselves as partners of, and trustees for, a firm, which remained the head tenant until the termination of the head lease in March 2000. G had acquired the subtenant's interest in the sublease by virtue of an assignation in his favour in 1997 following X's death. On termination of the sublease, G had intimated to L that he was entitled to remove C and intended to do so. It was agreed that C had acceded to B by operation of law. L submitted that (1) as F had not been B's heritable proprietor, it had had no right to grant a severance of C in X's favour, accordingly, it had not been open to it to agree, as it had purported to do in the sublease, that C would remain X's property; (2) had any right of severance been granted to X, in terms of the lease, it had not transmitted to his successors or assignees; (3) while the sublease provided that any assignee of the subtenant would be bound by the provisions of the sublease, no corresponding obligation was placed on the head tenant's assignees.

Held: L's pleas repelled. (1) C's value could be assumed to be a small fraction of B's value, C was capable of being removed without destruction, erections such as C were foreign to the traditional use of estates and a future tenant wishing to put such an estate to its traditional use would be unlikely to wish them to remain, they were not intended to be permanent, and the circumstances of the present case were analogous to those in *Mrs Maggie Brack Ferguson and Others v Andrew Paul* (1885) 12 R. 1222 to the extent that C was capable of being endowed with the attributes of a trade fixture, *Bain v Brand* (1876) 1 App. Cas. 762, *considered.* (2) The lease drew a distinction between X's relationship to the solum and to C, and the head landlord's intention was that the subtenant should receive a right of property in the building, in doing so, he abandoned any right of property in the building but also stipulated for its removal at the end of the head lease, thus he had no right to prevent G, as subtenant and owner, removing the property, which was consistent with the terms of the sublease; the entire arrangement had been designed to circumvent C's accession to B beyond the termination of the lease and *Ferguson* showed that in appropriate circumstances, accession could be circumvented by parties to a lease agreeing to treat non-trade fixtures in the same manner as trade fixtures, or otherwise agreeing to a right of severance, moreover, standing the law of accession, the head landlord intended that the subtenant should have the right to occupy C during the currency of the lease, should retain ownership of the materials in the structure, and should be obliged to retain C, and so retain ownership of the materials, at the termination of the lease, *Ferguson, followed.* (3) L's predecessor in title, as B's proprietor, had abandoned any claim of property in C, thus L could not now revive it to prevent G, the valid assignee of the right of property in C, removing it; having regard to the length of the lease the landlord must have had in contemplation that the obligation to build would require to extend to the successors of the original tenants and subtenants, and the right of severance was part of the right of property in C conferred on G, and that right had been made real by G's occupation of C without challenge, and he could not now be denied the right of severance as his right of property did not fall to be equiparated to a personal right of occupancy, *Stodart v Dalzell* (1876) 4 R. 236 and *Wallace v Simmers* 1960 S.C. 255, [1961] C.L.Y. 10283, *considered.* (4) From the history of B's ownership and of the occupants of the head tenancy, and given that in one capacity or another, L had been a proprietor of B since 1988 and joint head tenant since 1982, L had to be taken to have been aware of the provisions of both the head lease and sublease. (5) G had a right of severance of C.

VAN LYNDEN v GILCHRIST, [2015] CSOH 147, 2015 S.L.T. 864, Lord Philip, OH.

2710 Tenancy deposit schemes–Non-compliance–Failure to pay deposit into approved scheme–Appropriate sanction

[Tenancy Deposit Schemes (Scotland) Regulations 2011 (SSI 2011/176) reg.10, reg.3; Housing (Scotland) Act 1988 (c.43)]

A tenant (C) applied to the sheriff for a sanction following the failure by his landlord (M) to pay the tenancy deposit of £550 into an approved scheme in contravention of the Tenancy Deposit Schemes (Scotland) Regulations 2011 reg.3. The action came to proof before the sheriff whereby C sought the maximum sanction in terms of reg.10 namely, three times the deposit amount. M argued that the tenancy was neither covered by the Housing (Scotland) Act 1988 nor the 2011 Regulations where the property was not used by C as his principal home; the original tenancy between June 2013 and June 2014 was not continued by operation of tacit relocation but a new tenancy had been created which did not have a deposit, thus the application was time barred; C should be disbelieved on account of his alleged dishonesty and fraud and he could therefore not apply to the court for sanction on the basis of the principle of *ex turpi causa*; and if the sheriff found in C's favour, any sanction should be at the lower end of the scale where M was an amateur landlord, unfamiliar with the regulations.

Held: £1,050 awarded. M would be ordered to pay C double the deposit, less £50 representing the estimated damage to a table, by way of sanction for flagrant and wilful disregard of the terms and purpose of the regulations: landlords who were in such blatant breach could never mitigate their own conduct and failing by reference to the character or conduct of the tenant, and even if it could be considered relevant to the assessment of the sanction, there was no conclusive basis upon which the allegations made against C could be held to be substantiated; M had to have known of the tenancy deposit scheme where it was mentioned in the tenancy agreement, even though ignorance was not an excuse, and the fact remained that the deposit was held by M, unprotected by the regulations, for two years, as a result of which C had been deprived of his right to invoke the dispute resolution service provided under Pt 6 of the regulations to settle issues about dilapidations at the end of the tenancy; further, the regulations did not recognise the status of amateur landlord but were applicable to all landlords regardless of the scale in which they operated.

COOPER v MARRIOT, 2016 S.L.T. (Sh Ct) 99, Sheriff T Welsh, QC, Sh Ct (Lothian) (Edinburgh).

LEGAL ADVICE AND FUNDING

2711 Civil legal aid–Fees

THE CIVIL LEGAL AID (SCOTLAND) (FEES) AMENDMENT REGULATIONS 2016, SSI 2016/290; made under the Legal Aid (Scotland) Act 1986 s.33(2)(a)(3). In force: 28 November 2016.

These Regulations amend the Civil Legal Aid (Scotland) (Fees) Regulations 1989 to provide for the fees of solicitors in simple procedure cases within the meaning of the Courts Reform (Scotland) Act 2014 s.72(3).

2712 Criminal legal aid–Advice and assistance–Contributions

THE ADVICE AND ASSISTANCE AND CIVIL LEGAL AID (FINANCIAL CONDITIONS AND CONTRIBUTIONS) (SCOTLAND) AMENDMENT REGULATIONS 2016, SSI 2016/136; made under the Legal Aid (Scotland) Act 1986 s.8A(1)(1A). In force: 1 April 2016.

Section 11(2) of the Legal Aid (Scotland) Act 1986 makes clients liable to pay financial contributions towards the cost of advice and assistance. These Regulations amend the principal Regulations to provide that s.11(2) is not to apply to advice and assistance made available in the circumstances referred to reg.8 of those regulations (which provides for the automatic availability of advice and assistance to a person who has a right of access to a solicitor in terms of the Criminal Procedure (Scotland) Act 1995 s.15A or the Criminal Law (Consolidation) (Scotland) Act 1995 s.25A or a person detained under s.26 of that Act).

2713 Legal aid–Commission and diligence–Accused petitioning for recovery of complainer's medical and psychiatric records–Complainer's right to be heard

[European Convention on Human Rights 1950 art.14, art.6, art.8; Criminal Procedure (Scotland) Act 1995 (c.46) s.301A; Legal Aid (Scotland) Act 1986 (c.47) s.4(2)(c)]

A complainer (F) in criminal proceedings petitioned for judicial review of a decision of the Scottish Ministers (S) refusing her application for legal aid to be represented at a hearing of a petition of the accused (X) for recovery of her medical records, and sought declarator that S's failure to promulgate legislation enabling her to be represented at the hearing breached her rights under ECHR art.6, art.8 and art.14. Charges of assault and domestic abuse were brought against X and he sought to recover all medical and psychiatric records relating to F. X's petition for commission and diligence brought in terms of the Criminal Procedure (Scotland) Act 1995 s.301A was intimated on *inter alia* F, who applied to S for legal aid in terms of the Legal Aid (Scotland) Act 1986 s.4(2)(c), and in support thereof submitted documentation that she suffered from recurrent depression, was vulnerable, lacked understanding of the legal process and how to assert her art.8 rights, and was unable to speak on her own behalf in a formal court setting. S refused her application on the basis that the decision-making process enabled her views to be taken into account sufficiently and her interest to be protected for the purposes of art.8, without the need for her to participate and be represented at the hearing.

Held: Petition granted in part. (1) The potential disclosure to any third party of medical records pertaining to F engaged her art.8 rights, and the requirement to take account of such rights had been recognised in Scotland in the context of an application by an accused for commission and diligence: the court would only grant an application for the recovery of documents if it was satisfied that their recovery would serve a proper purpose and was in the interests of justice, and a balancing exercise had to be carried out in every such case, which presupposed the possibility that the court, having decided that the documents were potentially relevant, could nonetheless refuse the application on grounds of the complainer's art.8 rights, *M v HM Advocate* [2015] HCJAC 4, 2015 S.C.L. 269, [2015] C.L.Y. 2989 *considered*. (2) Intimation to F and the provision of an opportunity to be heard before an order for recovery was made were required were her art.8 rights not to be breached, and it was not enough for the court to treat every case in the same way, balancing the accused's interest in obtaining the medical records against a typical complainer's art.8 privacy rights; although there was no express provision in any statute or rule requiring intimation to be made on F or requiring her to be given an opportunity to be heard, she had that right by virtue of art.8, the absence of any specific provision could not take that right away, and the lack of any specific provision had to be addressed by the appropriate rule making body, *Z v Finland (22009/93)* (1998) 25 E.H.R.R. 371, [1998] C.L.Y. 3104 and *R. (on the application of B) v Stafford Combined Court* [2006] EWHC 1645 (Admin), [2007] 1 W.L.R. 1524, [2006] C.L.Y. 990 *considered*, *Scottish Criminal Cases Review Commission v Swire* [2015] HCJAC 76, 2015 S.L.T. 556, [2015] C.L.Y. 2973 and *HM Advocate v Porch (Ross)* [2015] HCJAC 111, 2016 S.L.T. 149, [2016] 2543 *distinguished*. (3) The effect of s.301A of the 1995 Act was to allow the application for recovery of documents to be made in the sheriff court, and intimating those proceedings on the havers and on someone in F's position whose rights might be affected, and giving them the opportunity to be heard, did not make any substantial inroad into the general principle that the Scottish criminal justice system did not allow victims to be direct participants in criminal proceedings; in so far as the proceedings for commission and diligence were criminal proceedings, they were wholly separate from the substantive criminal proceedings against X and were focused entirely upon an issue in which F had a direct interest. (4) A haver and any person whose art.8 rights might be infringed by an order for recovery of medical records and other sensitive documents had to have the application for recovery intimated to them and had to be given the opportunity to be heard in opposition to the application before an order was made, or at least before the documents were handed over to the party seeking them, and it was a matter for the sheriff hearing the application to determine how best to ensure that a party seeking to vindicate his or her Convention rights was heard. (5) S's refusal to direct the grant of legal aid focused entirely on the question of whether F had a right to be heard and represented in the proceedings for recovery of her medical records, although material was presented to S concerning her means and her ability to represent herself, those matters were not addressed by S, and as its decision was founded on an error of law as to F's right to be heard, it would be reduced. (6) It was not necessary to make any declarator about the compatibility of the current rules, or lack thereof, regulating the ability of someone in F's position to be heard in defence of her Convention rights and to be granted legal aid for that purpose: there was a right to be heard and there was discretion as to whether to grant legal aid for representation at any such hearing, and the absence of rules did not make the current system incompatible with F's Convention rights. Opinion, (1) that F was entitled to have her Convention rights protected effectively, and if the grant of legal aid was necessary to make effective her right to be heard, that was a factor which had to be taken into account by S in arriving at a decision; (2) that S might wish to have regard to the approach set out in *R. (on the application of Gudanaviciene) v Director of Legal Aid Casework* [2014] EWCA Civ 1622, [2015] 1 W.L.R. 2247, [2015] C.L.Y. 1626, which had equal application in Scotland, whereby whether legal aid was required would depend on the particular facts and circumstances of each case, including *inter alia* the ability of the individual to represent themselves without legal assistance, having regard to age, mental capacity, vulnerability and continuing distress; if F was vulnerable and terrified by the whole court process so that she could not be expected to speak up for herself in court and present her arguments coherently and forcefully, that would be a strong reason for the application for legal aid to be favourably regarded, *Gudanaviciene considered.*

F v SCOTTISH MINISTERS, [2016] CSOH 27, 2016 S.L.T. 359, Lord Glennie, OH.

LEGAL PROFESSION

2714 Scottish Legal Complaints Commission–Appeals–Error in Commission's reasoning–Scotland

[Legal Profession and Legal Aid (Scotland) Act 2007 (asp 5) s.21]

An advocate (B) appealed under the Legal Profession and Legal Aid (Scotland) Act 2007 s.21 against a decision of the Scottish Legal Complaints Commission (C) upholding a complaint made against him by a client (H). B had acted as H's counsel in the Court of Session in respect of a debt for which H had obtained decree against the debtor (D) in 1992 but which had never been paid. H sought declarator of the expiry of the 10 year reversionary period and declarator that D's half share in a jointly owned house belonged to him, the value of which was greater than the accrued debt. Following the Lord Ordinary's indication on the first day of the hearing that he was not favourably disposed towards granting an unconditional decree, H instructed B that failing such a decree, his preferred option was to proceed to D's sequestration. On day three, H had not been in attendance at court, and the defender's counsel, contrary to his position in the written pleadings, sought a conditional decree. In reply, B had moved the court to grant an unconditional decree, failing which to dismiss the action or grant decree of absolvitor. The Lord Ordinary had found that he would only have been prepared to grant a conditional decree, thus, in accordance with B's position, he had dismissed the action (*Hull v Campbell* [2011] CSOH 24, 2011 S.L.T. 881, [2011] C.L.Y. 4019). H made a complaint to C, claiming that B had falsely stated during the hearing that it was his wish that the case be dismissed, despite having had no instructions to do so. C accepted the terms of the report by the investigator (X), in particular it agreed with X's conclusion that there was a substantial difference between the settlement proposals rejected by H and the likely terms of a conditional declarator and, on that basis, was of the view that B ought to have sought and obtained instructions from H, and as there was no evidence that he had tried to do so, the complaint should be upheld. C conceded that at least one of B's grounds of appeal was well founded and did not resist the appeal on its merits but invited the court to remit the complaint to C for a re-investigation and for it to be determined of new before a differently constituted committee, which B opposed, seeking for the court to rule on the substance of the complaint.

Held: Appeal upheld, C's decision quashed and court's determination substituted. (1) C's decision amounted to no more than an agreement with X's views, it did not address the material submitted after the circulation of the investigation report, such as the signed statement submitted by H's solicitor (S) which stated that H had made it clear that, failing an unconditional decree, he wished to preserve the option of sequestration, there was no indication that C had engaged with any of the detailed responses to X's report, C had not addressed the contemporaneous notes of the proceedings which indicated that the Lord Ordinary saw no difference between the outcome which he had raised as a possible way forward and that proposed by D on the last day of the hearing, C had made no reference to the detailed explanation as to why H would have preferred to sequestrate D, and it had also failed to address the fact that S had agreed with the course of action taken by B, which was because it coincided with S's instructions from H; C appeared simply to have agreed with X that an unqualified declarator plus undertaking was not the equivalent of the conditional declarator. (2) C had made at least one fundamental error, which went over and above the accepted inadequacy of reasons given for the decision, the error went to the heart of the reason given for upholding the complaint and was a matter of substance, and given that C had simply agreed with X, it followed that he had made the same error. (3) There was no distinction between the matter raised by the Lord Ordinary on day one, and the requirement for B to respond to D's conversion to a conditional declarator disposal on the last day; B had sensibly suggested a possible arrangment whereby the declarator could be granted but with H under an obligation to account to D for the balance, which H had rejected, it was clear that the conditional declarator at issue on the final day would have had the same unwelcome implications for H. (4) Two committees of the Faculty of Advocates had given affirmative responses as to whether the instructions given to B to the effect that sequestration was preferred to the suggested undertaking were applicable to events as they had unfolded, and the court endorsed that approach; there being no material difference between the consequences for H of, on the one hand, the proposed conditional declarator and, on the other, of the undertaking discussed and rejected earlier in the hearing, and given that B's understandable attempt to confirm his instructions afresh from H had been frustrated, his conduct was not open to reasonable criticism, on the contrary, any other course of action would have exposed him to serious questions for ignoring the clear implications of the instructions which he had received. (5) There was no good reason to remit the matter to C for a further investigation and a fresh adjudication by a new committee; given the history of the case, and that a further appeal by H was pending in respect of the proceedings in the Faculty, that would not be a reasonable or proportionate course of action, in any event, the court could, and ought to, substitute its own decision on the substance of the complaint: B's appeal would be upheld on the basis that H's complaint was without merit, C's decision would be quashed, and a determination that B had not provided an inadequate professional service to H would be substituted. Observed, (1) that C ought to be mindful that it had a statutory quasi-judicial function, adjudicating upon disputes, some of which previously would have been directed to the courts, and could make orders providing for financial compensation on questions of considerable importance, not just to complainers, but also to practitioners, whose careers might be prejudiced by an adverse finding; (2) that were the matter remitted to C, as with the first committee, the only qualified lawyer involved in the determination would have no experience of litigation in Scottish courts, and in its recruitment processes, C ought to bear in mind the requirement to ensure that the professionals involved had the appropriate background and standing.

BARTOS v SCOTTISH LEGAL COMPLAINTS COMMISSION, [2015] CSIH 50, 2015 S.C. 690, Lady Paton, Lady Clark of Calton, Lord Malcolm, IH (Ex Div).

2715 Scottish Legal Complaints Commission–Complaints–Categorisation of complaints as both services and conduct complaint–Power to investigate such complaints

[Legal Profession and Legal Aid (Scotland) Act 2007 (asp 5) Pt 1, s.21, s.5(1)(a), s.5(1)(b)]

A solicitors' firm (S) appealed under the Legal Profession and Legal Aid (Scotland) Act 2007 s.21 against decisions of the Scottish Legal Complaints Commission (C) categorising three complaints against them by a client (W) as hybrid complaints, namely as both services and conduct complaints under s.5(1)(a) and (b). S submitted *inter alia* that (1) with regard to the concerns expressed in *Bartos v Scottish Legal Complaints Commission* [2015] CSIH 50, 2015 S.C. 690, [2016] 2714, the statutory regime did not contemplate a practitioner having to defend both a services and a conduct complaint on the same factual narrative, and the hybrid categorisation of the complaints was erroneous in law and ought to be quashed; (2) a hybrid complaint did not exist, the first two complaints were time barred regarding any conduct element and no conduct element could be attributed to the third. C submitted *inter alia* that s.5 of the 2007 Act provided for a complaint to be classified as both a services and a conduct complaint, which classification had previously been used by the Law Society of Scotland, and it had been recognised in *Bartos* that many conduct complaints could be viewed as raising inadequate professional services issues.

Held: Order made. (1) The 2007 Act did not give C the power to investigate and determine a complaint which had been categorised as a matter of professional conduct, the expectation was that once C had decided that a complaint suggested that the practitioner was guilty of either professional misconduct or unsatisfactory professional conduct, it would remit the complaint to the professional body, the terms of the Act made no mention of a hybrid complaint, and while it was recognised that a complaint might consist of separate parts or elements, some of which might raise conduct issues and some services concerns, it was envisaged that such a complaint could be subdivided and dealt with according to the proper classification of its constituent parts, which differed materially from the hybrid complaint as categorised in *Bartos*; if a complaint, or part thereof, suggested a failure in proper professional conduct, a view taken by C that it also raised a services issue did not justify the course taken in *Bartos*, rather C had to decide whether to classify it as a conduct or services complaint, which was consistent with the Parliamentary intention to limit C's decision making jurisdiction to services complaints and was also in line with the rules in Pt 1 of the 2007 Act, which made no mention of hybrid complaints and had different time bar tests for the two types of complaint, *Bartos*, *considered*. (2) C's categorisation of the complaints as hybrid complaints would be quashed, the time bar concerns did not apply to the third complaint where it raised what was, on any view, a conduct matter, and did not arise in respect of the first two complaints where they suggested no more than concerns as to the level of service provided, and the court would pronounce an order to the effect that the first two issues were services complaints and the third was a conduct complaint.

ANDERSON STRATHERN LLP v SCOTTISH LEGAL COMPLAINTS COMMISSION, [2016] CSIH 71, 2016 S.L.T. 967, The Lord Justice Clerk (Lady Dorrian), Lady Clark of Calton, Lord Malcolm, IH (2 Div).

2716 Scottish Solicitors Discipline Tribunal–Penalties–Professional misconduct by settling claim without authority–Appropriate level of penalty

A solicitor (R) appealed against a decision of the Scottish Solicitors' Discipline Tribunal finding him guilty of professional misconduct by settling a claim without authority to do so, censuring him, restricting his practising certificate and ordaining payment of compensation to his client (X). X had been a serving prisoner and had instructed R to claim against the Scottish Ministers for breaching his human rights by virtue of the practice of slopping out. The Scottish Ministers subsequently accepted that slopping out conditions were a breach of prisoners' human rights and, with a view to settlement, offered £2,100 for doubled up slopping out where prisoners shared a cell with another, and £500 for single cell conditions. X was offered the latter sum which R had accepted without checking any file for instructions, and despite the fact that by the time of offer, X was being represented by a different firm of solicitors with whom R had been in correspondence.

Held: Appeal allowed in part. (1) The evidence before the tribunal, as contained in its findings in fact, was sufficient to support the finding that R was guilty of professional misconduct. (2) While accepting that the court should be slow to interfere with a penalty imposed by a specialist disciplinary tribunal, the tribunal had gone plainly wrong by simply awarding the difference between the two sums of £500 and £2,100 for single cell and doubled up slopping out respectively, with an additional £200 to reflect inconvenience, the aforementioned approach failed to take account of the fact that any loss sustained by X was merely a loss of an opportunity to pursue a claim for the larger sum, and a total sum of £350 should be substituted; the restriction of R's practising certificate for an aggregate period of two years was similarly wrong and unjustified where R's failings, while serious, did not concern dishonesty and the maintenance of the reputation of the solicitors' profession and the sustaining of public confidence in the integrity thereof did not require such a restriction and its associated consequences, the seriousness of the misconduct would be more appropriately marked by the imposition of a fine of £3,000.

ROBERTSON v COUNCIL OF THE LAW SOCIETY OF SCOTLAND, [2015] CSIH 95, 2016 S.L.T. 103, Lord Menzies, Lord Brodie, Lady Dorrian, IH (Ex Div).

2717 Solicitors–Complaints–Dismissal of firm's complaint against solicitor–Whether Scottish Legal Complaints Commission erred in law

[Legal Profession and Legal Aid (Scotland) Act 2007 (asp 5) s.2(4)]

A solicitors' firm (M) appealed against a decision of the Scottish Legal Complaints Commission (C) dismissing its complaint against a solicitor (J) as totally without merit in terms of the Legal Profession and Legal Aid (Scotland) Act 2007 s.2(4). As a result of C's conclusion, M's complaint had been ruled ineligible and had not been referred to the Law Society of Scotland (L). M had acted for a client (W) who had died and whose estate had been wound up by M on the basis of intestacy in accordance with a deed of variation. In March 2014, M, another solicitors' firm and W's chartered accountant had received letters, dated 5 March, from J, acting for one of W's children and his former cohabitee (collectively Z), claiming *inter alia* that when the deed of variation had been signed, M had been aware of the existence of an earlier will by W and that it appeared that the deed had been a fraud. J had sent a further letter to M, dated 24 March, *inter alia* making further allegations of fraud in relation to the deed of variation and stating that there appeared to have been collusion in perpetrating it. C had treated M's complaint as restricted to the contents of the letters of 5 March, had noted that two of them had concluded that J's clients might be misinformed or that there might be a geniune and legal explanation or reason, which M was to provide as soon as possible, referred to J's response, dated 7 March, in which *inter alia* he had confirmed that the letters had been sent on the basis of Z's instruction, noted that there was no suggestion that the letters had been sent other than in accordance with Z's instrucions or that the factual assertions had been based on anything other than the version of events provided by Z, and concluded that a solicitor did not warrant the truth of the allegations and that provided he had information to support the allegations, there was no duty to conduct further investigation before writing such a letter.

Held: Appeal allowed, C's decision quashed and matter remitted to C to proceed as accords. (1) C had erred in law, its decision was not supported by the facts and was irrational, further, was its determination to be read as proceeding on the basis that the letters had not asserted fraud on M's part, that had been an error where it was impossible to read the letters as other than doing so and the assertions of fraudulent conduct in the subsequent correspondence appeared to be even clearer. (2) C had erred in considering that the observations in *Council of the Law Society of Scotland v Scottish Legal Complaints Commission* [2010] CSIH 79, 2011 S.C. 94, [2011] C.L.Y. 4432 regarding assertions of primary fact had equal validity in relation to inferences of fact or law; in relation to imputations of dishonesty a solicitor was not entitled to write letters of the type in the present case on the basis that his client claimed to have been cheated on the facts asserted by him, the solicitor had to be able to conclude that on a reasonable interpretation of the facts it would be reasonable to draw an inference of dishonesty, and in so far as C's decision had proceeded on the basis that a solicitor would be entitled to make any assertion in correspondence, so long as it was made on the instructions of his client, that was an error in law. (3) Z's information was insufficient to support, or to provide the basis for, the allegations of fraud on M's part, there was no appreciation that J had merely been shown a copy of the will, and not the original, and that the conclusion had involved the drawing of inferences from a chain of asserted facts in which there had been a clear gap; although a solicitor was entitled to apply a legal analysis to the facts presented by his clients and to write accordingly, applying a legal analysis to the facts presented would not lead to an inference of fraud; the factual information provided to J had not provided any reasonable basis for drawing the inferences that the will had to have remained in force at the time of W's death, of which M had been aware but had nevertheless wound up the estate according to intestacy, thus making itself a party to fraud, *Law Society of Scotland*, *considered*. (4) To enable a solicitor to carry out his duty to represent his client without fear or favour properly, his correspondence carried qualified privilege but allegations of fraud ought not to be lightly made or inferred even in the course of correspondence, the fact that two of the letters had contained a rider that Z might be under a misapprehension did not answer the matter because the allegations did not stem from primary facts provided by Z but from the unwarranted drawing by J of conclusions of fraud and only two of the letters had contained the rider. (5) On a fair reading of the complaint it was about the subsequent correspondence, not merely the letters of 5 March. (6) Rejection of the complaint at the sift stage implied that it would not be open to L to conclude that J's conduct had amounted even to unsatisfactory professional conduct, which decision had been vitiated as having been reached on the basis of errors in law and being in certain respects unsupported by the facts found to be established by C, and its decision was irrational in that it was not one which it might reasonably make. Observed, per Lord Drummond Young, that when a complaint was made about a letter written by a solicitor on behalf of a client, it was essential to consider the seriousness of the allegations therein, that the allegations made in a typical solicitor's letter were frequently not simple allegations of fact, and that a distinction existed between a letter containing allegations about a particular person that was sent to that person and a letter containing such allegations that was sent to a third party.

MCSPARRAN MCCORMICK v SCOTTISH LEGAL COMPLAINTS COMMISSION, [2016] CSIH 7, 2016 S.L.T. 510, Lady Dorrian, Lord Drummond Young, Lord Malcolm, IH (Ex Div).

2718 Solicitors–Fees–Action for payment of professional fees–Whether solicitors in breach of contract

A limited company (X) reclaimed against a Lord Ordinary's decision finding in favour of a solicitors' firm (M) in the latter's action for professional fees for acting on X's behalf in its action against another solicitors' firm (Y) (*MacRoberts LLP v McCrindle Group Ltd* [2014] CSOH 99, 2015 S.C.L.R. 67, [2015] C.L.Y. 3198; 2014 G.W.D. 21-409). Y had been instructed to act on X's behalf in arbitration proceedings against another company (H), and in May 2002, X transferred its instructions from Y to M. In 2005, X raised an action of damages for professional negligence against Y, for failing to raise court proceedings to protect X's right to pre-decree interest in the arbitration proceedings and thereafter failing to advise it that it had no entitlement to recover pre-decree interest from H as any obligation to pay had prescribed. X's action against Y was sisted from 2006 until 2011 but came to proof in November 2012 on issues of causation and quantification of loss, as by that time Y had admitted that they had been negligent and in breach of contract. In September 2012, X withdrew its instructions from M, and subsequently M sued for professional fees for acting on X's behalf in its action against Y. X contended that no fees were due to M as they were in material breach of contract and counterclaimed for damages consisting of expense incurred as a consequence of having had to engage a new firm of solicitors shortly before the proof in the action against Y, and for fees paid to M for work that would not have been required had the breach of contract not occurred. X submitted that M were in material breach of contract as (1) they had destroyed manuscript notes taken by one of its partners (B) during a critical meeting on 29 May 2003 regarding X's litigation against Y, which had prejudiced the prosecution and quantification of its claims against Y, and accordingly created an actual or potential conflict of interest between M and X, so that X had no alternative but to withdraw its instructions; (2) M had failed to act in accordance with the instructions it had received from X in respect that B, without authority, conducted settlement negotiations with agents (D) acting on behalf of Y's indemnity insurers and further had failed to inform X that such discussions had taken place. The issues were whether the Lord Ordinary had erred in law in failing to hold that M had materially breached their contract by placing themselves in a position in which their interests conflicted or might conflict with those of X, and whether, in the event the Lord Ordinary had erred in that respect, the Inner House should hold in consequence that M were disabled from seeking to enforce the obligation which would otherwise have been incumbent on them to pay M their fees.

Held: Reclaiming motion refused. X's case was entirely dependent upon breach of the proposed term in their contract with X, namely that M would not, in their conduct of the litigation on X's behalf, place themselves in a position where there was a real and sensible possibility of their interests conflicting with those of X, which X contended was implied into the contract for the provision of professional services but the Lord Ordinary had held that what had been pled as the breach of contract, namely the destruction of the only notes of critical discussions in or around May 2003, had not occurred because no notes had been made and he was fully entitled to approach his decision making in such a way where he had cut straight to a factual issue capable of resolving the case. Opinion, (1) that had it been necessary to consider whether the proposed term had been implied into the contract as a matter of general law, no speciality having been pled, it would have been rejected as both unwarranted by authority and unnecessary, *Boardman v Phipps* [1967] 2 A.C. 46, [1966] C.L.Y. 11052, *considered*; (2) that the proposed term was modelled on, or was otherwise derived from, the duty of a fiduciary not to put himself in a position where his interest and duty conflicted but that which X had argued for, as a usual incident of every contract for a solicitor's service in the conduct of litigation, went beyond the ambit of the equivalent fiduciary duty, which was illogical; further, was the proposed term taken as being implied into all such contracts, it would render superfluous the duty to exercise the ordinary skill and care of a competent solicitor professing expertise in the conduct of litigation.

MACROBERTS LLP v MCCRINDLE GROUP LTD, [2016] CSIH 27, [2016] P.N.L.R. 28, Lord Brodie, Lady Clark of Calton, Lord McGhie, IH (Ex Div).

2719 Solicitors–Inadequate professional services–Correct advice given–Inadequate rendering of advice

[Legal Profession and Legal Aid (Scotland) Act 2007 (asp 5) s.21]

A solicitor (S) appealed against a decision of the Scottish Legal Complaints Commission (C) that he had provided an inadequate professional service to clients (X). X had instructed S in the purchase of a property (P). Damage to P's roof was incurred prior to settlement and on 19 January 2012, S agreed with the seller's agent (Y) that part of the purchase price would be retained until the damage had been repaired and advised X accordingly. The transaction settled on 20 January and on 1 February, S advised Y that no repairs had been carried out and had they not been by 5 February, X would instruct tradesmen and would use the retained funds therefor; Y replied *inter alia* that his clients did not consent to the use of the retained funds for repairs. On 27 March, S advised X to have the repairs carried out using the retained funds, however, on 2 April, Y advised S that the repairs had been carried out, his clients did not consent to the use of the retained funds for repairs, and that if S were to uplift the retained funds without consent he would be reported to the Law Society of Scotland. On 3 April, S retracted his earlier advice and informed X that the retained funds could not be used to pay for the repairs. X's complaint, that S had changed his advice, was accepted by C and determined to be a services complaint, however, after investigation, C concluded that the issue had been caused by S's failure to ensure that the terms of the retention were adequate.

Held: Appeal refused. (1) A service might be inadequate without being negligent and without having caused loss and it was within the statutory intent that a service consisting of the rendering of advice might be inadequate even though the advice provided was correct, depending on the particular facts and circumstances; the assessment as to whether the service provided was inadequate was a matter for C and its assessment might only be impugned where it was based on one of the errors specified in the Legal Profession and Legal Aid (Scotland) Act 2007 s.21, and there had been no such error. (2) The retention agreement had been limited in effect, it had neither included a provision whereby X would become entitled to use the retention money to carry out the repairs themselves, nor provisions whereby failure on the seller's part could be pinpointed, S had not attempted to have such provisions incorporated and no regard was had to the guidance provided by the Law Society of Scotland; in the circumstances, C had not erred. (3) Where it had neither been correct for S to advise X that they were entitled to use to retention money for repairs nor was there any indication that he had explained to X the limitations to their rights under the retention agreement, it had been open to C to hold that X had not received an adequate professional service; C did not require to prescribe what ought to have been in the agreement or what S ought to have sought to have included in it, particularly where the Law Society had provided guidance therefor. *Observed*, that allowances required to be made for the fact that applications to C were made by lay persons who might not be aware of the service failure to which they had been subjected.

SNEDDON v SCOTTISH LEGAL COMPLAINTS COMMISSION, [2015] CSIH 62, 2016 S.C. 36, Lady Smith, Lord Bracadale, Lord Philip, IH (Ex Div).

LIBRARIES

2720 Libraries–Ownership–Librarian seeking to establish ownership of library collection–Abandonment

[Civic Government (Scotland) Act 1982 (c.45)]

A librarian (C) sought sought transfer to her of a library collection (L) from a university (U). An unincorporated political association (D) also claimed ownership of L. L had been gifted to the Communist Party of Great Britain (X) in 1968 by one of its late founding members. In 1979, L was relocated to X's premises and C came to act as a part time volunteer librarian with the full knowledge and consent of X's Scottish committee (S), with sole responsibility for L's care, control, management and promotion. In 1987, L had required to be moved from X's premises and C had, under her own initiative, arranged suitable alternative accommodation therefor, had been authorised by X to move L thereto, and had continued, with S's knowledge and acquiescence, her role as L's sole librarian. In late 1991, X was dissolved and its whole rights, property and assets were assigned to an unincorporated political association (Y). In early 1997, C had been advised that L's present accommodation would no longer be available and, under her own initiative, had made an agreement for L to be housed in U's premises, had arranged L's relocation thereto and had continued her role as L's librarian, with U expressly agreeing to assume no role in, or responsibility for, L's management and not to remove any part thereof without C's permission. In mid-1998, D had been established as distinct from, and independent of, Y, and in 1999, Y had been dissolved and its whole rights, property and assets had been assigned to another unincorporated political association (N). Thereafter, D received a financial settlement from N and judicial sanction had been obtained by D for the transfer to its trustees of title to heritable property, which, at that time, had remained formally vested in X's trustees. In May 2013, the issue of C's retirement having been raised, a dispute arose between C and D as to L's ownership, and, pending resolution, U had excluded C therefrom and closed L to the public. C submitted that (1) her ownership of L came from its abandonment, as governed by the Civic Government (Scotland) Act 1982; L had been abandoned to her by X in 1987 and she had become the *de facto* owner; (2) *esto* the court was not satisfied that C was L's owner, her claim should be preferred over D's. D submitted *inter alia* that its ownership of L had been established as X's successor with regard to consecutive assignations from X to Y and from Y to D.

Held: Decree granted. (1) C's claim so far as founded upon abandonment failed: (i) had L's former owner abandoned it, as a matter of law, its ownership would have vested in the Crown, not C, further, there was no evidence that the 1982 Act procedure had ever been instigated or considered by C, accordingly, she could not avail herself thereof; (ii) on the evidence, as a matter of fact, X had not abandoned L in 1987 or subsequently; given the revered standing of the benefactor and the cherished status of the collection, X had never had any intention of doing so; and (iii) to the extent that C's use of the term "abandonment" was understood to mean a direct assignation or voluntary transfer of ownership to her, that had not occurred, on the evidence, S had had no power or authority to transfer L's ownership, which was vested in X's executive committee based in London, moreover, C could not found on the doctrine of reputed ownership where she had never had the necessary possession of L in the strict legal sense thereof, having held it not for herself but for its true owner. (2) D's evidence in support of its claim of ownership was unreliable and fell to be rejected; little weight could be attached to the evidence of any of its witnesses and to the extent that its claim rested upon a clause of Y's constitution, that claim was misconceived where *inter alia* the constitution was a political document which was never intended to be read as a disposition or an instrument of legal transfer, its terms were not habile to operate as a conveyance or assignation of Y's assets, and there was little evidence as to how D was said to have constituted itself as a national organisation thereunder, in any event, D formed part of Y and operated within its federal structure and constitution and an association such as D had no legal capacity as such, thus D had failed to establish ownership of L. (3) No conclusion could be reached on the evidence as to L's rightful owner. (4) C had established a lesser right as depositary to the custody, control and management of the fund *in medio* and, in order to discharge her duty to L's owner to keep and safeguard L, she had the right in that capacity to have custody, control and management of L, and to that extent she was entitled to be ranked and preferred upon the fund *in medio*. (5) Further procedure to attempt to identify L's true owner would not be appropriate; L had been closed for two years, C and D had expended considerable effort and expense and were entitled to adjudication of their competing claims without further delay, and it was appropriate to conclude the action by granting transfer of L to C.

CANNING v GLASGOW CALEDONIAN UNIVERSITY, 2016 S.L.T. (Sh Ct) 56, Sheriff S Reid, Sh Ct (Glasgow).

LICENSING

2721 **Licences–Taxis–Refusal to renew taxi operator's licence–Operator's failure to provide evidence or information to rebut police objections**

[Civic Government (Scotland) Act 1982 (c.45) Sch.1 para.5(3)(a)(ii), s.21, s.21(2); Companies Act 2006 (c.46) s.106(2)]

A licensing authority (G) appealed against the sheriff's decision allowing an appeal by a taxi operator (B) against G's refusal to renew his licence to operate a taxi booking office. On 19 June 2014, B had applied to G for renewal of his licence and the police (P) had lodged a letter of objections based on B's conduct in another licensing area, namely that B was the director of a company (T) licensed to operate in that area which had (i) breached the Civic Government (Scotland) Act 1982 s.21, (ii) continued to operate as a taxi business after 19 October 2010, when T had been dissolved and removed from the companies register, and after the licensing authority had sent a letter requiring it to cease trading with immediate effect. The licensing committee (C) had *inter alia* considered P's evidence and had found *inter alia* that T's restoration to the companies register had not altered the fact that B had operated a booking office without a licence for approximately two years and nine months and he had done so knowingly and willingly, he had permitted his drivers to contravene s.21 of the 1982 Act and had failed to establish an exception in terms thereof, and had refused B's application in terms of Sch.1 para.5(3)(a)(ii) of the 1982 Act. On appeal, the sheriff criticised C's approach to T's dissolution on the basis that (i) there was no evidence that B had knowingly traded without a licence, (ii) C had not addressed P's submission that T had continued to trade after being told to stop, and had not asked questions relating thereto, (iii) C's decision on the dissolution and licence issue was erroneous in law, (iv) C's decision on that issue represented an unreasonable exercise of its discretion, and allowed B's appeal.

Held: Sheriff's decision reduced and C's decision restored. (1) There were no provisions limiting or defining the bases upon which a licensing authority might conclude that an applicant was not a fit and proper person to hold a licence, an authority had a broad discretion when exercising its judgment and it was entitled to place weight on the nature and cumulative impression of a series of circumstances; it was also entitled to expect an applicant to provide information, explanations, or evidence in exculpation or mitigation of any alleged conduct or event which might suggest that he was not a fit and proper person, therefore, it had been for B to provide C with information, and if necessary evidence, in response to P's objections and the sheriff had erred in law in that he had failed to take into account the practical onus on B, and further in that, despite the evidence before C, he had decided that C was not entitled, on the basis thereof, to exercise its judgment as it had, those errors were reflected in two central issues which were before C, namely T's dissolution and breaches of s.21, *Coyle v Glasgow City Council* [2012] CSIH 33, 2012 S.L.T. 1018, [2013] C.L.Y. 3773,*McKay v Banff and Buchan Western Division Licensing Board* 1991 S.L.T. 20, [1990] C.L.Y. 5345, *Hughes v Hamilton DC* 1991 S.C. 251, [1991] C.L.Y. 5248, *McAllister v East Dunbartonshire Licensing Board* 1998 S.C. 748, [1998] C.L.Y. 6068 and *Calderwood v Renfrewshire Council* 2004 S.C. 691, [2004] C.L.Y. 5024, *considered.* (2) *Prima facie*, continuing to trade on the basis of a licence granted to a company which no longer existed, having been struck off the register, was conduct which C was entitled to regard as irresponsible and without regard to the law and it was for B to provide an explanation in exculpation for that *prima facie* failure, supported by evidence if necessary, B had not done so and in those circumstances, the sheriff had erred in law by adopting the speculative and exculpatory approach that he had, *Chief Constable of Strathclyde v North Lanarkshire Licensing Board* 2004 S.C. 304, [2003] C.L.Y. 5793, *considered.* (3) It had been for B to provide any exculpatory or mitigatory information and/or evidence in relation to P's evidence and the sheriff had erred in law by approaching the matter as if, despite that evidence, no onus had rested on B. (4) The sheriff had erred in concluding that C's decision was erroneous in law: while the restoration of a struck off company to the register might engage the Companies Act 2006 s.106(2), and might result in a licence held by that company being deemed not to have lapsed by virtue of the dissolution, it did not follow that C were unable to take into account the fact that B had carried on trading during the period of two years and nine months when T, which had held the licence, was no longer on the register, failure to notice that T had been struck off during such a long period indicated an approach to business that was at least careless and, on the evidence before it, C was entitled to take such conduct into account when considering whether B was a fit and proper person to be the holder of a licence, and thus to reach the conclusion it had. (5) The sheriff erred in law in holding that C's decision represented an unreasonable exercise of its discretion, on the evidence, it could not be said that no licensing authority acting reasonably could have reached the conclusion C had reached and C had been fully entitled to reach the view that B's conduct constituted significant non-compliance with the law, and to conclude that he was not a fit and proper person to be the holder of a licence. (6) It was clear from the evidence that C had not relied upon local knowledge but had relied upon P's evidence, B had failed to provide C with any information or evidence which established an exception in terms of s.21(2) of the 1982 Act, and the sheriff had erred in concluding that C had relied upon local knowledge and had not identified what local knowledge it had used, and had also erred in concluding that C had exercised its judgment unreasonably.

GLASGOW CITY COUNCIL v BIMENDI, [2016] CSIH 41, 2016 S.L.T. 1063, Lady Paton, Lord Drummond Young, Lord McGhie, IH (Ex Div).

2722 Licensing authorities–Street trading licences–Condition imposed by local licensing authority prohibiting street trade licence holders from trading near schools during school hours–Ultra vires

[Civic Government (Scotland) Act 1982 (c.45) Sch.1 para.10, Sch.1 para.18]

Street trade licence holders (collectively X) raised summary applications seeking to reverse a decision of a local licensing authority (N) imposing a condition in terms of the Civic Government (Scotland) Act 1982 Sch.1 para.18(1) prohibiting trading within a distance of 250m from all secondary schools between 08.00 and 17.00 on any school day during term time. The intention behind the condition was the promotion of healthy eating among children although there had neither been analysis of the nutritional value of the food sold by X, nor had there been any consultation or consideration of the financial impact thereon.

Held: Decision reversed. (1) The only power given to a licensing authority to attach conditions to an existing street trader's licence was that under Sch.1 para.10 of the 1982 Act, the extent of which was dependent on a close analysis of the condition, the effect thereof, and an examination of the scope of the power which the Act gave the authority. (2) In the case of one of X (M) who operated from a snack van on a designated static site which was situated on an industrial estate and was within 250m of a local academy, the time period covered by the condition would mean that she would be unable to trade with anyone for 75% of the calendar year, which would force her to cease trading all together, M's licence was location-specific and N had not offered an alternative site, 90% of her turnover came from workers or visitors to the industrial estate; the condition had the effect of seeking to control what M might sell from her snack van to her customers and affected the contract between them and M was effectively being ordered to meet nutritional standards with regard to the food she sold, no matter who bought it, since it was considered unhealthy in comparison to that which was available in schools, in respect of which no guidance had been issued, but if the standard was not met, M could not trade for the majority of the year and any attempt to do so would be a criminal offence. (3) The condition imposed by N was *ultra vires*: the quality of the food that consumers bought was covered by legislation to be found elsewhere and had Parliament intended to provide for the protection of consumers by means of conditions under the licensing system, that would have been set out in the 1982 Act with regard to street traders and attempts to insert conditions might have effects for the customer which were entirely arbitrary; child obesity was not a licensing purpose and neither was the promotion of school meals nor a ban on trading for the majority of the calendar year; Parliament could not have intended local licensing authorities to have the implied power to attach a condition with such a significant effect on the commercial contracts of street traders, regardless of the aim of the condition.

MCCLUSKEY v NORTH LANARKSHIRE COUNCIL, 2016 S.L.T. (Sh Ct) 31, Sheriff V Smith, Sh Ct (South Strathclyde) (Hamilton).

LOCAL GOVERNMENT

2723 Community asset transfers–Community empowerment–Community bodies

THE COMMUNITY EMPOWERMENT (SCOTLAND) ACT 2015 (COMMENCEMENT NO.5) ORDER 2016, SSI 2016/395; made under the Community Empowerment (Scotland) Act 2015 s.145(2). Commencement details: bringing into operation various provisions of the 2015 Act on 16 December 2016.

This Order brings into force certain provisions of the Community Empowerment (Scotland) Act 2015. Article 2 appoints 16 December 2016 for the coming into force of the provisions of the Act set out in the table in the schedule, for limited purposes where specified. The provisions relate to Ministerial powers to make subordinate legislation.

2724 Community Empowerment (Scotland) Act 2015 (asp 6)–Commencement No.6 Order

THE COMMUNITY EMPOWERMENT (SCOTLAND) ACT 2015 (COMMENCEMENT NO.6) ORDER 2016, SSI 2016/410; made under the Community Empowerment (Scotland) Act 2015 s.145(2). Commencement details: bringing into operation various provisions of the 2015 Act on 20 December 2016.

This Order appoints 20 December 2016 for the coming into force of the certain provisions of the Community Empowerment (Scotland) Act 2015. The provisions make amendments and repeals consequential to the commencement of the Act Pt 2 (community planning) on that date.

2725 Local government finance–Non-domestic rates–Revenue support grant

THE LOCAL GOVERNMENT FINANCE (SCOTLAND) ORDER 2016, SSI 2016/135; made under the Local Government Finance Act 1992 Sch.12 para.1, Sch.12 para.9(4). In force: 2 March 2016.

This Order: determines the amount of the revenue support grant payable to each local authority in Scotland in respect of the financial year 2016-2017; determines the amount of non-domestic rate income to be distributed to each local authority in respect of that year; redetermines the amount of the revenue support grant payable to each local authority in respect of the financial year 2015-2016; and makes consequential revocations in the Local Government Finance (Scotland) Order 2015.

2726 Rateable value–Houses–Flats entered in valuation roll as show houses–Whether flats were dwellings

[Local Government Finance Act 1992 (c.14) s.72(2)]

Proprietors (G) of a former hotel, converted into 26 flatted dwellings, appealed against a decision of the valuation appeal committee (V) refusing G's appeal against the entry in the valuation roll of two of the flats (X) as a showhouse. V found that G had decorated and furnished X to give potential purchasers a good impression of the apartments for sale and a realistic impression of what properties might look like once the purchaser had moved in, and X were occupied and used by G as a showhouse for the purpose of marketing and sale of all the apartments. G submitted that V had erred in law in determining that X were not dwellings in terms of the Local Government Finance Act 1992 s.72(2); X had at all material times been dwellinghouses and therefore dwellings, and the use made of subjects was irrelevant to the question of whether the subjects were a dwelling within the meaning of s.72(2).

Held: Appeal refused. Section 72(2) did not state that the existing use of subjects was to be irrelevant to the issue whether the subjects were a dwellinghouse, it did not provide that the only relevant consideration was to be the physical characteristics of the subjects, G's suggested construction was not the natural and ordinary reading of the provision and would produce absurd results, there was nothing further advanced by G to suggest that their interpretation of s.72(2) was correct, and on the facts found, there had been no real scope for V to have reached any other conclusion; at all material times, G had been in rateable occupation of X and the showhouse use was the only use to which X had been put.

OLD COURSE LTD v FIFE COUNCIL ASSESSOR, [2016] CSIH 40, 2016 S.L.T. 833, The Lord Justice Clerk (Lady Dorrian), Lord Malcolm, Lord Doherty, LVAC.

2727 Rateable value–Valuation–Valuation of retail unit–Appropriate comparators

[Valuation and Rating (Scotland) Act 1956 (c.60) s.6(8)]

An assessor (X) appealed against a decision of the valuation appeal committee (V) allowing an appeal by a retailer (B) against X's valuation of B's retail unit (R). R was adjacent to a supermarket (S) and part of a mixed use estate (E), with several other commercial enterprises nearby. In terms of its lease, B was prohibited from using R as a supermarket but allocated approximately 30 per cent of its floorspace to convenience items, of which 20 per cent were food products. X had entered R in the valuation roll as a new entry with effect from 21 February 2013 and classified it as a supermarket with a net annual value/rateable value of £168,000, basing it on a direct comparison with S, which had a net annual value/rateable value of £137,000 based upon an overall rate of £120 per square metre, and comparison evidence in relation to other supermarkets in the local area. B appealed, contending that R ought to have been classified as a retail warehouse with a valuation of £140,000, based on an overall rate of £95 per square metre, in line with valuations at another retail park (L), a 10 minute drive from R, which was the most appropriate comparator, and that as a result of greater demand at tone date for supermarkets, retail warehouses would generally be valued at a lower rate than supermarkets in the same vicinity, thus R's valution ought to be based on a figure less than that applied to S. X argued that were R to be classified as a retail warehouse, the valuation ought to be based upon an overall rate of £141 per square metre based on a comparison with retail warehouses at a purpose built retail park (G) which was approximately a five minute drive from R, and L was not an apt comparator as it was insufficiently local. V held that R ought to be classified as a retail warehouse, that the valuation ought to be based on local rental evidence, rejecting X's contention that L ought not to be considered, as retail warehouses in the local area within a short driving distance of R constituted appropriate comparators, that R was most appropriately compared with L which was of mixed use and gave a clear indication of the relative values between supermarkets and retail warehouses in the area, and that B ought to be valued at a lower rate than S, and found in favour of B's revaluation. X submitted that (1) V had adopted a valuation based on relative values for a retail warehouse and supermarket in L and in so doing had erred in law; (2) V had erred in determining R's value by reference to S's value rather than to local retail warehouse values at G and in assuming that any relativity in L would apply equally at E; (3) V had erred in taking account of the restriction on use as a supermarket, which was not a relevant consideration to the valuation of subjects as a retail warehouse.

Held: Appeal refused. (1) X's argument, that the reasons for preferring L over G were based on an invalid consideration of supermarket valuations and any alleged relativity between those and the valuations of retail warehouses, relied on an incomplete reading of V's conclusions; V had not based its valuation solely on comparative values for supermarkets against retail warehouses but had considered the whole evidence and having done so had accepted B's calculations, which were based on a rate of £90 per square metre, which derived principally from a comparison of retail warehouses, and in particular those at L; the revaluation of the adjacent supermarket at L as a retail warehouse at £95 per square metre was consistent with the valuations of retail warehouses at L, it did not reflect an assumption by V that the relativity at R would be the same as that which applied at L; V had determined as a matter of fact that R's value, classified as a retail warehouse, ought to be lower than S but V's determination of R's value was not by reference to S's value. (2) There was a clear route to the figure of £90 per square metre without any error of law being disclosed. (3) V had been entitled to take into account the restriction in the lease; in order to value R, it had been required to assume the statutory hypothesis in the Valuation and Valuation and Rating (Scotland) Act 1956 s.6(8), as part of which it had had to consider that R's potential for another use would be relevant to the extent that it would influence the rent at which R would be let, therefore the restriction was a relevant factor, *Happy Feet Nursery and Out of School Club Ltd v Assessor for Lanarkshire* [2014] CSIH 87, 2014 S.L.T. 1066, [2015] C.L.Y. 3206, *considered*. Observed, per Lord Malcolm, that the court would not interfere with V's view of the evidence when there was ample evidence to support it, it was for V to assess the evidence and reach a decision on disputed issues of valuation, including the assessment of comparisons, there was a wealth of information which could justify the decision reached, not least the evidence as to the assessed value of retail warehouses L, and the court could only interfere if an error of law had been demonstrated, *British Railways Board v Assessor for Glasgow* 1968 S.L.T. (Notes) 46, [1968] C.L.Y. 4654, *considered*.

FIFE COUNCIL ASSESSOR v B&M RETAIL LTD, [2015] CSIH 79, [2016] R.A. 106, Lady Dorrian, Lord Malcolm, Lord Woolman, LVAC.

2728 Valuation–Plant and machinery–Valuation of six hydro-electric schemes–Whether excepted plant and machinery

[Valuation for Rating (Plant and Machinery) (Scotland) Regulations 2000 (SSI 2000/58) Sch.1; Valuation for Rating (Plant and Machinery) (England) Regulations 2000 (SI 2000/540)]

An assessor (X) appealed against decisions of the valuation committee (V) valuing six hydroelectric schemes (H) on a comparative basis at the revaluation. V had proceeded on the basis that the most appropriate method of valuation, where suitable evidence was available, was the comparative basis rather than the receipts and expenditure basis. V had interpreted the Valuation for Rating (Plant and Machinery) (Scotland) Regulations 2000 to mean that, in general, the plant and machinery was not rateable where it accepted that H's plant and machinery were properly and fully covered under class 1 of the four classes set out in Sch.1 of the 2000 Regulations and constituted excepted plant and machinery for the purposes of valuation for rating, and further concluded that where an exception under one class applied it was unnecessary to consider the other classes, and therefore had not proceeded to consider whether any of the plant and machinery might nevertheless be rateable for the purposes of classes 2, 3 or 4.

Held: Appeals allowed. (1) V's interpretation was mistaken; the consumer exception for plant and machinery in class 1 was introduced by the words "in this class" thereby limiting its effect to that class, further, were that exception to cover all the other classes, repetition elsewhere would not be required; where items of plant and machinery fell within a class 1 exception it was still necessary to go on to consider whether they fell to be treated as rateable under any of the other classes, which approach did not create an internal conflict within the regulations, and they ought to be viewed as a whole. (2) The English courts, in *Union Cold Storage Co Ltd v Assessment Committee for Metropolitan Borough of Suffolk* and *BP Refinery (Kent) Ltd v Walker (Valuation Officer)* [1957] 2 Q.B. 305, [1957] C.L.Y. 2957, had followed a sequential approach in relation to earlier versions of the Valuation for Rating (Plant and Machinery) (England) Regulations 2000, which similarly categorised plant and machinery into separate classes, and the same interpretation ought to be given to the 2000 Regulations in Scotland as had been given to the English ones, accordingly, the appeals would be allowed, the valuations quashed and the matter remitted to V for reconsideration, *Union Cold Storage Co Ltd* and *BP Refinery (Kent) Ltd, considered.* Opinion, (1) that the nature and value of the comparative material was for V, however, once the 2000 regulations were approached in the correct manner, it might be necessary for V to have more detail upon, and make more specific findings as to, any comparators relied upon, including as to the implications, if any, of the involvement of connected parties in the lease agreements, and also to make more specific findings as to the facts in respect of each of H; (2) that when reconsidering the rateability of plant and machinery in light of the proper approach to the regulations, V might wish to elaborate upon its reasoning in respect of "penstock" and other relevant items. Observed, that the point at issue was dealt with in express terms in the English Regulations.

ASSESSOR FOR TAYSIDE VALUATION JOINT BOARD v OLD FASKALLY FARMING CO *sub nom.* TAYSIDE VALUATION JOINT BOARD ASSESSOR v OLD FASKALLY FARMING CO, [2016] CSIH 8, 2016 S.L.T. 333, Lady Dorrian, Lord Malcolm, Lord Woolman, LVAC.

MENTAL HEALTH

2729 Persons lacking capacity–Guardians–Solicitor's application seeking appointment of financial guardian for client–Whether sufficient interest to bring application

[Adults with Incapacity (Scotland) Act 2000 (asp 4) s.87(1)]

A solicitor (J) made an application under the Adults with Incapacity (Scotland) Act 2000 seeking the appointment of a financial guardian to her client (F) aged 87. J claimed a close relationship with F since having been instructed to act for her in June 2014, she had exclusive information about F's affairs, and claimed sufficient interest in terms of s.87(1) of the Act to entitle her to make the application. It was not disputed that anybody else had, or was able to claim an interest in, F's property and financial affairs, F's brother having no interest in bringing an application.

Held: Application refused. The interest expressed by J was not sufficient to entitle her to bring the application and she was not, in terms of the 2000 Act, a person claiming an interest: the averments of having formed a close relationship with F and those of moral duty to bring the application might have entitled J to claim an interest in F's personal welfare, having regard to the duty of a solicitor to society and bearing in mind that interest did not need to be patrimonial in nature in all contexts but interest in relation to the property and financial affairs of an adult did have to denote some form of patrimonial interest and J was neither a potential beneficiary, nor an attorney, nor did she hold any of said property; simply acting as F's solicitor did not import sufficient interest, nor were the averments of a special relationship sufficient given the length of time she had acted for F, having regard to F's age and time of life. *Opinion*, (1) that the local authority still had the power, and the duty, to bring an application; (2) that even if J had an interest, the fact that she sought the appointment of partners in the firm in which she was employed as guardian and substitute guardian to F, would have presented a clear conflict of interest.

J, APPLICANT, 2016 S.L.T. (Sh Ct) 119, Sheriff P J Braid, Sh Ct (Lothian) (Edinburgh).

NEGLIGENCE

2730 Breach of duty of care–Employment references–Social worker subject of disciplinary proceedings–Reference given to potential employer true, fair and accurate

An action of damages raised by a social worker (M) against her former employer (D) relating to the provision of an employment reference came before the sheriff for debate on liability. While employed by D, M's department had been undergoing investigation following the death of a child assigned to their supervision. Following the appointment of a new line manager (B) on 1 June 2008, M had become the subject of disciplinary proceedings, she applied for a social work position with a local authority (C) and on 8 August 2008, had been offered the job. In her application to C, M had used her previous line manager as a referee and had not disclosed that she was the subject of ongoing disciplinary proceedings. In a letter to C dated 1 September, which provided additional information to supplement the reference already received by C from D, B stated that she had noted significant concerns regarding M's practice, that M had postponed an investigatory meeting scheduled in terms of D's disciplinary procedures and had thereafter failed to attend the rescheduled meeting, and that where M had now resigned, the investigation had not been concluded and D could not advise on the outcome thereof. On 5 September 2008, D advised the Scottish Social Services Council (S) of M's outstanding disciplinary investigation and S commenced an investigation, advising M in December 2009 that it was of the view that her conduct had not called into question her suitability for registration and that it would take no further action. In December 2008 or January 2009, C had withdrawn their offer of employment, citing the lack of an outcome to S's investigation.

Held: D assoilzied. (1) M had resigned in circumstances where, but for her resignation, D would have considered dismissal on the grounds of misconduct and D had been required to notify S of M's resignation and to provide it with an account of the circumstances in which it had taken place; the evidence was that C would not progress M's appointment once it had become aware of the disciplinary proceedings and S's inquiry, and it had been that inquiry and not the terms of the reference that had caused M's loss. (2) The letter of 1 September had not been unfair to M where she had attempted to avoid B's involvement by seeking a reference from her former line manager and had failed to disclose the disciplinary proceedings against her where, standing the nature of the job she had and was applying for, it had been incumbent on her to disclose the disciplinary proceedings, and it had been legitimate of D, on learning that someone other than B had given her a reference, to take steps to inform S of the disciplinary proceedings; in those circumstances, the reference given by D to C was true, fair and accurate and had been given within a reasonable time, and D had not been in breach of their duty of care to M, *Spring v Guardian Assurance Plc* [1995] 2 A.C. 296, [1994] C.L.Y. 1918, *considered*. *Opinion*, that B's attitude had been the immediate cause of M's resignation, S's inquiry had demonstrated that M's failings were not such as to render her unfit for employment as a social worker and while it was understandable that the death of a child and the consequential investigations of the department ought to prompt a stricter attitude to record keeping and home visits than previously, it did not follow that M's failings therein were incapable of resolution, and a more moderate approach by D to M might have resulted in retaining her services.

MCDONALD v DUNDEE CITY COUNCIL, 2016 S.L.T. (Sh Ct) 122, Sheriff M Bovey, QC, Sh Ct (Tayside) (Dundee).

2731 Clinical negligence–Radiographers–Cannulation–Failure to detect arterial puncture

[Law Reform (Miscellaneous Provisions) (Scotland) Act 1940 (c.42) s.3]

A patient (B) raised an action of damages against a medical services provider (M), a radiographer (N) and the local health board (H) for injuries sustained through N's allegedly negligent cannulation of B's arm. Quantum of £700,000 was agreed and the proof restricted to liability. B had been referred for an MRI scan which required the injection of gadolinium through insertion of a cannula into a vein in the antecubital fossa. B gave evidence that on 26 January 2009, she attended at hospital for the scan and N had inserted the cannula into her left arm, which had caused her discomfort, and when it had been removed, there had been a spurt of blood, which N had ignored. B had visited her general practitioner (G) on several occasions in February and March 2009 with increasing arm pain, reduced grip and power in her left hand, swelling, and a cold left arm. B was ultimately referred to hospital and was found to have a blockage in the brachial artery and ischemia in the index finger of her left hand, which required surgery. B claimed that the spurt of blood was indicative of arterial puncture and N should have sought medical assistance immediately. Parties agreed that B had developed ischemia in her left arm caused by an occlusion in the brachial artery, and on the basis of a consensus of expert evidence, that had been caused by the cannulation. M, N and H denied that there had been a spurt of blood on removal of the cannula. M claimed that any liability on their part had been occasioned by N's breach of contract and that they were entitled to be indemnified by her against any consequential liability to make payment to B. Were they not to be indemnified, on the hypothesis that they were found liable to B, they were joint wrongdoers in terms of the Law Reform (Miscellaneous Provisions) (Scotland) Act 1940 s.3 and were entitled to a contribution towards payment from N. N denied liability and that M were entitled to be indemnified by her, however, if they were so entitled, or if she was found liable as a joint wrongdoer, she was entitled to a contribution from H, which H denied.

Held: Case put out by order. (1) On the evidence as a whole, on a balance of probability, there had been a spurt of blood on removal of the cannula, which had been ignored by N, and it was inconceivable that N had been unaware of it; from the medical records, B's account to the hospital medical staff on admission, at which point she had no reason to know that she had sustained a breach of the artery during the MRI scan, denoted excessive or inordinate bleeding which would not normally have occurred, and on the expert evidence, there were several aspects of her account that a member of the public would have found difficult to fabricate. (2) The expert witness for M, N and H had based his opinion on B's severe onset of pain, however, pain was only one of the signs sought when observing a patient who had suffered an arterial breach and it was unlikely that the other signs would not have been detected, and had the occlusion been detected, G would have been notified thereof and would have been able to act upon it; B had proved on a balance of probability that there was a causal link between the failure to detect the brachial artery puncture and the injury sustained by her, *Bolam v Friern Hospital Management Committee* [1957] 1 W.L.R. 582, [1957] C.L.Y. 2431 and *Bolitho (Deceased) v City and Hackney HA* [1998] A.C. 232, [1997] C.L.Y. 3789, *considered*. (3) N had been in breach of her duty of care to B, which had caused injury to B, and M, as N's employers, were liable therefor. (4) The *ratio* in *Lister v Romford Ice and Cold Storage Co Ltd* [1957] A.C. 555, [1957] C.L.Y. 1272 remained the law and M were entitled to look to N for indemnification, *Lister*, *applied*. (5) H owed a non-delegable duty of care to B, however, it would be wrong in principal to allow N to rely on her own negligence to secure a contribution from H, and no order would be made under the 1940 Act against H, *Woodland v Swimming Teachers Association* [2013] UKSC 66, [2014] A.C. 537, [2014] C.L.Y. 2200, *considered*. (6) The case would be put out by order to discuss the form of the interlocutor.

BELL v ALLIANCE MEDICAL LTD, [2015] CSOH 34, 2015 S.C.L.R. 676, Lord Boyd of Duncansby, OH.

2732 Duty of care–Fire services–Firefighters failing to extinguish fire–Duty of care owed to heritable proprietor

A fire service (S) reclaimed against a decision of the Lord Ordinary allowing a proof before answer in an action of damages raised against S by the the heritable proprietors (H) of a farmhouse (F) for damages on the basis of S's alleged negligence in extinguishing a fire at F (*A J Allan (Blairnyle) Ltd v Strathclyde Fire Board* [2014] CSOH 135, 2014 G.W.D. 29-568). On 31 October 2008, S had extinguished a fire at F and had left the scene at approximately 3 pm. H averred that rotten timbers in the roof space had continued to smoulder such that the fire had reignited in the early hours of the morning on 1 November and F had burned down, and that once the fire had appeared to be extinguished, S ought to have used thermal imaging to locate any questionable areas and further ought to have maintained a regular check on F to ensure that the fire had truly been extinguished.

Held: Reclaiming motion allowed. (1) Recent authorities from the House of Lords and Supreme Court had emphasised the requirement for a careful approach to the liability of public authorities to private individuals, the circumstances of the third case in *Capital and Counties Plc v Hampshire CC* [1997] Q.B. 1004, [1997] C.L.Y. 3778 were very similar to the circumstances in the present case, and the Court of Appeal's conclusion, that the fire brigade was not liable, had been specifically approved by the House of Lords in *Gorringe v Calderdale MBC* [2004] UKHL 15, [2004] 1 W.L.R. 1057, [2004] C.L.Y. 2752 and had not been criticised by the Supreme Court in *Michael v Chief Constable of South Wales* [2015] UKSC 2, [2015] A.C. 1732, [2015] C.L.Y. 2062, and the carefully developed, policy based, more restrictive approach, approved and adopted by the Supreme Court, had to be followed by the Scottish courts, contrary to the views expressed in *Duff v Highlands and Islands Fire Board* 1995 S.L.T. 1362, [1995] C.L.Y. 6156, *Gibson v Orr* 1999 S.C. 420, [1999] C.L.Y. 6370 and *Burnett v Grampian Fire and Rescue Service* [2007] CSOH 3, 2007 S.L.T. 61, [2007] C.L.Y. 5423 but in keeping with *Mackay v Scottish Fire & Rescue Service* [2015] CSOH 55, 2015 S.L.T. 342, [2015] C.L.Y. 3224; (i) the fire service ought not to be regarded as having undertaken an assumption of responsibility, in the sense defined in the authorities, on the basis of answering a 999 call, attending the scene of a fire or taking steps to extinguish a fire or to save lives or property, as those actions represented them carrying out their statutory functions and public duty; (ii) general policy considerations required be taken into account; (iii) while analogies might be drawn with the provision of medical services, or the ambulance service, they were of limited assistance, (iv) there was no general duty to rescue, the fire service had been held not to be liable if they failed to attend a fire, therefore, it seemed unprincipled to suggest that a fire service which did attend a fire and sought to extinguish it could be held liable for their actions, other than in circumstances where they negligently inflicted fresh injury; and (v) the line of English authority relevant to the liability of public bodies including fire services was well established and of considerable authority and it would be unfortunate to adopt a different approach in Scotland, *East Suffolk Rivers Catchment Board v Kent* [1941] A.C. 74, *Capital & Counties Plc*, *Gorringe*, *Mitchell v Glasgow City Council* [2009] UKHL 11, [2009] 1 A.C. 874, [2009] C.L.Y. 2848 and *Michael*, *considered*, *Duff*, *Gibson* and *Burnett*, *disapproved* and *Mackay*, *approved*. (2) In the present case, S owed a duty of care to the general public, including H but that duty was to take care not to negligently inflict a fresh injury; there were neither averments that S had made matters worse or that they had inflicted a fresh injury when they had arrived at, and dealt with, the fire, nor of circumstances which could properly be categorised as an assumption of responsibility giving rise to a common law duty to exercise reasonable care, and further, it would not be fair, just or reasonable to impose a duty of care of the scope contended for by H on S, thus H's case would necessarily fail even were all their averments proved, and the case as pled was irrelevant. *Observed*, per Lord Drummond Young, (1) that a distinction might properly be drawn between injury to the person and damage to property, consequently, it was hoped that in an appropriate case the law might develop in such a way that, at least in clear cases where action could be taken without danger to the rescuer, the officers of a public service such as the fire service or the police were obliged to take action to rescue persons in danger; (2) that the law had moved in the direction of attaching greater significance to the more traditional categorisation of distinct and recognisable situations as guides to the existence, scope and limits of the varied duties of care which the law imposed but rules derived from existing case law ought not to be applied mechanically to new situations, instead it should be asked whether, as a matter of policy directed to the specific situation under consideration, a new analysis was required, which would result in a law of negligence that was less unified than in the past but which dealt more fairly with individual cases.

A J ALLAN (BLAIRNYLE) LTD v STRATHCLYDE FIRE BOARD, [2016] CSIH 3, 2016 S.L.T. 253, Lady Paton, Lady Dorrian, Lord Drummond Young, IH (Ex Div).

2733 Duty of care–Highway authorities' powers and duties–Metal strips on road causing cyclist to lose control

A cyclist (R) sought damages from a roads authority (S) for injuries sustained when he lost control of his bicycle and fell to the ground while crossing a bridge. Quantum was agreed and the action restricted to liability. R's accident had allegedly occurred because of the presence of an approximately four metre long metal strip and grooves set into, and positioned at an acute angle across, the road surface. R argued that the state of the road presented a hazard to persons using it for which S were liable.

Held: Case put out by order. (1) The metal strips did pose a hazard to road users by reason of *inter alia* the nature of the material and the longitudinal position of the strips posed a risk of a destabilising slip to two wheeled vehicles, the gap between them could potentially catch a sufficiently thin bike wheel and the leading edge of the larger strip, in combination with the degradation of the surrounding road surface, was capable of deflecting a bike wheel, and it was irrelevant that R was unable to say precisely which of the aforementioned features caused him to lose control. (2) There was no case of contributory negligence against R but any suggestion that he was not riding with due skill and care had to be rejected, there was no foundation in the evidence to suggest that R should have seen the strips, or appreciated the hazard posed thereby, before he had, and the state of the road surface at the bridge, and in particular the presence and position of the metal strips, posed a hazard in the relevant sense. (3) The hazard posed would have been apparent to a roads authority of ordinary competence using reasonable care given that it appeared that S had never actively considered whether the strips were a hazard posing a significant risk of an accident to road users, having been designed into the bridge by an engineer when it was widened in 1990; and a competent roads authority would have corrected the hazard after identifying it, the remedial work having already been done for £1,000, *MacDonald v Aberdeenshire Council* [2012] CSOH 101, 2012 S.L.T. 863, [2012] C.L.Y. 4257, *applied.* (4) Decree would be granted in the agreed sum but before doing so, the court would put the case out by order to deal with expenses and ancillary matters.

ROBINSON v SCOTTISH BORDERS COUNCIL, [2016] CSOH 47, 2016 S.L.T. 435, Lady Wolffe, OH.

2734 Duty of care–Proximity–Clubhouse damaged by electrical fire from golf trolley–Whether fair just and reasonable to impose duty of care

[Consumer Protection Act 1987 (c.43) s.5(3)]

An action of damages raised by a golf club (R) against an electric golf trolley supplier (M) for damages sustained to R's club house when a golf trolley (T), owned by one of R's members (X) and supplied by M, caught fire, came before the Lord Ordinary on the procedure roll for debate on M's preliminary plea to the relevancy. X had purchased T approximately three years previously and had replaced the original battery. He had stored T in the locker room overnight and after the fire, T's power switch had been found to be in the "on" position. R claimed that T's battery connection had not had a fuse, which had existed on later models, the power switch had been in a location and operated such that it could be inadvertently activated, T had had no over temperature cut off, no short circuit protection and had been a fire risk. M sought dismissal of the action and submitted *inter alia* that (1) it was not liable under the Consumer Protection Act 1987 where the property damaged was used for economic activity; (2) R's common law case was irrelevant where it had failed to aver sufficient proximity or foreseeability. R submitted *inter alia* that its club house constituted private property where it was owned by R's members and intended for their own private use and occupation, and therefore fell within the ambit of the 1987 Act.

Held: Decree of dismissal granted. (1) It could not be said that the use made of the clubhouse was private in terms of s.5(3) of the 1987 Act simply because it was owned by the members of a club, the actual use to which it was put required to be examined and in light of the facts, it was clear that the clubhouse was used for a material amount of economic or commercial activity, moreover, Parliament had not intended that such a building, which was available to 700 members as well as others, could be described as being subject only to private use and in those circumstances, the clubhouse was not property ordinarily intended for private use or occupation. (2) There were a large number of factors leading to the fire over which M had had no control, the precise mechanics of the cause of the fire were uncertain and it was not averred that T's wires were actually damaged prior to the fire, merely that they could have been, M had no control over T's maintenance, or its use in the three years since it came into X's possession, X had changed the battery and the capacity of the previous one was not averred, M had no control over the place where T was left and G had failed to aver from whom X had obtained T; there was a great distance between M's alleged failure and the fire and in those circumstances, G had failed to aver sufficient proximity, and it would not be fair, just and reasonable to impose a duty of care on M.

RENFREW GOLF CLUB v MOTOCADDY LTD, [2015] CSOH 173, 2016 S.L.T. 345, Lord Philip, OH.

2735 Duty of care–Proximity–Golf trolley catching fire and causing damage to clubhouse–Action of damages against trolley supplier

[Consumer Protection Act 1987 (c.43) s.2(2)(b), s.2(2)(c)]

A golf club (R) reclaimed against the Lord Ordinary's decision dismissing its action of damages against a supplier of golf trollies (M) as irrelevant (*Renfrew Golf Club v Motocaddy Ltd* [2015] CSOH 173, 2016 S.L.T. 345, [2016] 2734). R had raised the action in respect of loss sustained from extensive damage to their club house when a golf trolley, owned by a golf club member and supplied by M, caught fire while being stored there. R sought a proof before action, averring that M were liable under the Consumer Protection Act 1987 s.2(2)(b) and (c), and at common law. The Lord Ordinary sustained M's plea to the relevancy having found inter alia that Parliament had not intended that a club house, used by in excess of 700 members and others, be classified as ordinarily intended for private use and, in relation to the common law case, there was insufficient proximity between the parties and, in the whole circumstances, it was not fair just and reasonable to impose a duty of care on M.

Held: Reclaiming motion refused. (1) The case under the 1987 Act had to be regarded as irrelevant: by the use of a double negative, s.5(3) restricted the recovery of damages caused by a defective product to property which was "ordinarily intended for private use, occupation or consumption" and "intended ... mainly for ... own private use, occupation or consumption" by the person suffering loss; on the issue whether R's club house fell to be regarded objectively as so intended, as the Lord Ordinary had recognised, the use of the word "private" was important and applying its ordinary meaning, "private" as applied to the "use" made of an object meant use by a person in his private life as distinct from in the context of his public persona; a golf club house was not ordinarily intended for private use, such as that of an individual or family, it was for the communal use, based upon financial conditions, of a large number of members of the public who had either paid a subscription, tendered a green fee, happened to be a guest or were simply present for a function; similarly, a club house was not intended for a persons's "own" private use but the use of many persons. (2) The fundamental problem with R's case, in terms of the reasoning in *Caparo Industries Plc v Dickman* [1990] 2 A.C. 605, [1990] C.L.Y. 3266, was that there was no category of known liability into which its circumstances might be placed and in the absence of analogous authority it was not possible to conclude that, at common law, there was a proximate relationship between the supplier of a golf trolley and the owner of a clubhouse, in which the trolley happened to be, three years after the supply and over which the supplier had no control; and it was certainly foreseeable that the trolley might be in transit in all sorts of public places to each of which it might cause indeterminate damage were it to go on fire, *Caparo, considered*. *Opinion*, that there was little room for the common law to be extended where the legislature had declined to do so and were it necessary to enter into the abstract world of fairness, justice and reasonableness, observing that it would have been difficult for M to obtain limitless product liability as opposed to the reasonable ease for R to insure the clubhouse premises given the ability to value the potential extent of any damage *ab ante*, the present would not have been a case in which to impose liability.

RENFREW GOLF CLUB v MOTOCADDY LTD, [2016] CSIH 57, 2016 S.L.T. 781, The Lord President (Carloway), Lady Smith, Lord Brodie, IH (1 Div).

2736 Duty of care–Reasonable care–Police officer sustaining eye injury during training manoeuvre

[Personal Protective Equipment at Work Regulations 1992 (SI 1992/2966) reg.4, reg.6]

A police officer (M) raised an action of damages against the Chief Constable of Police Scotland (C) for an eye injury sustained during the course of his employment. Quantum of £7,000 was agreed and the proof restricted to liability. S had been injured while assisting a police training officer (S) in demonstrating a headlock escape technique. M gave evidence that he had been holding S in a loose headlock and while looking at the ground, S had held both of his hands in front of him before raising them quickly upwards, contrary to the technique he had described, and his fingernail had struck M's eye. The training coordinator (F) gave evidence that a risk assessment had been in place which had covered the entire training course and not each manoeuvre individually and one of the measures used to control risk was a demonstration at a slow to medium pace, and had conceded that there was a risk of injury to the eye, however, he maintained that the use of goggles would have *inter alia* increased the risk of other injury.

Held: Decree for £7,000 granted. (1) In demonstrating the manoeuvre, S had been under a duty to take reasonable care for M's safety, specifically to avoid striking M in the eye and not to carry out the manoeuvre at a speed which took M by surprise or gave him insufficient time to react, and while M's understanding of the technique being demonstrated had been mistaken, his account of how the accident had occurred was otherwise accepted; S had carried out the manoeuvre at a pace which had given M insufficient time to react, he had not demonstrated the paradigm version of the technique and he had used excessive force in as much as his hand had moved at a speed which had given M insufficient time to either close his eyes or move his head and it was foreseeable that, were the manoeuvre carried out with S's fingers pointing upwards and his hand moving towards M's face without S being able to see what he was doing, there was a danger of M being struck in the eye; S had carried out the manoeuvre without sufficient regard for M's safety, his actions had been negligent and the accident had been wholly caused thereby. (2) A residual risk had existed such that the Personal Protective Equipment at Work Regulations 1992 reg.4 had been engaged and, given F's concession, it could not be said that the risk of occurrence had been so slight as to be *de minimis*, or that the nature of the harm had been so trivial that it ought to be ignored; F's risk assessment had been insufficient to comply with reg.6 of the 1992 Regulations and his approach to that assessment had wrongly involved an application of the common law test rather than the stringent requirements of regs 4 and 6, however, on the evidence the provision of goggles would not have been effective to prevent further injury without increasing overall risk, and separately, the provision of such goggles at a training session would not be appropriate given the requirement for realism and it would be disproportionate to require them to be worn to guard against the possibility of a finger entering the eye; M's case, in so far as it was based upon a breach of the 1992 Regulations by reason of the non-provision of goggles had to fail. (3) The provision of gloves was not appropriate and would have been disproportionate in the present case, particularly where the regulations required equipment to be provided to the person who was likely to be injured rather than anyone else, and M's case in so far as it was based upon the non-provision of gloves to S had to fail.

MAJID v CHIEF CONSTABLE OF SCOTLAND, 2016 S.L.T. (Sh Ct) 1, Sheriff P J Braid, Sh Ct (Lothian) (Edinburgh).

2737 Duty of care–Street lighting–Liability of local roads authority for injuries sustained by pedestrian–Policy of switching lights off between 00:00 and 07:00

[Roads (Scotland) Act 1984 (c.54) s.35, s.35(1)]

A pedestrian (M) raised an action of damages against the local roads authority (C) for injuries sustained as a result of C's decision to switch off street lighting between midnight and 7 am. Damages were agreed and the proof was restricted to liability. On 27 November 2011 at approximately 2 am, M had tripped on a kerb while walking home and had broken his ankle. M averred that he had lost his footing because he had been unable to see where he had been placing his feet, that in terms of the Roads (Scotland) Act 1984, C required to provide and maintain road lighting in the village (L) and prior to November 2011, C had introduced a practice of switching off the lighting in L between midnight and 7 am, which had been negligent and had contravened their common law duty to provide lighting. C averred that it had been acting under permissive powers in terms of the Roads (Scotland) Act 1984 s.35(1), no review of its decision that L had not required to be lit had been sought and as it had been acting under permissive powers, it was not liable for accidents arising from a failure to light. M gave evidence that the lighting had previously been on all night and the policy had been implemented without consultation or notice, and led supporting evidence from other residents. Two of C's employees (X) gave evidence that C's decision to switch the lighting off at midnight had been taken in February 2011 following a period of consultation and advertisement and implemented on 1 November, and that prior to 2011 the lighting had switched off at 1 am.

Held: C assoilzied. X's evidence that the lights had been switched off at midnight from 1 November 2011 was unchallenged and that policy had been agreed by C in February 2011 following a period of consultation and advertisement. While notices of the meetings had not been placed in L, and not everyone in L had been aware either of the consultation process, the making of the decision or the date of its implementation, prior to the implementation of that policy the lights had switched off at 1 am and it had not been established that prior to M's accident the lights had remained on any later than 1.15 am, in any event, even had there been a lack of consultation and notice, where the lights had not previously been on later that 1.15 am, neither C's policy itself nor its implementation could have caused an accident after 2 am. *Opinion*, (1) that s.35 of the 1984 Act invested C with a discretion rather than a duty to provide lighting and there appeared to be no common law duty to provide lighting; (2) that care ought to be taken in looking to English authorities in the area of the responsibility of local authorities where Scots law was more generous to pursuers in that regard; (3) that local authorities might incur common law liability had they switched off lights where it was averred and proved that a pursuer had come to rely on the lighting and that it had been switched off negligently, namely without taking reasonable care that those whom the authority knew, or ought to have known, relied on the light were made aware that it was to be switched off; (4) that while C had not erected posters or notices, the issue was whether the steps which it had taken were reasonable in the circumstances, not whether it might have taken other steps, and the steps taken by C had been reasonable; (5) that the relationship between M and C had been sufficiently proximate and it would have been fair, just and reasonable to impose a duty of care, *Caparo Industries Plc v Dickman* [1990] 2 A.C. 605, [1990] C.L.Y. 3266, *considered;* (6) that where M had not known that the lights were going to be switched off, he would not have been found contributorily negligent.

MACDONALD v COMHAIRLE NAN EILEAN SIAR, [2015] CSOH 132, 2016 Rep. L.R. 10, Lord Matthews, OH.

2738 Employers' liability–Safe systems of work–Employee using boiler to fill bucket where sink taps not working–Breach of common law and statutory duties

[Work at Height Regulations 2005 (SI 2005/735) reg.10(2); Provision and Use of Work Equipment Regulations 1998 (SI 1998/2306) reg.20]

A cleaner (M) raised an action of damages against her employer (E) for injuries sustained during the course of her employment. Quantum was agreed and the proof restricted to liability. While cleaning, M had required to fill a bucket with hot water from a sink in an equipment cupboard. M gave evidence that she had obtained the water from a boiler located next to the sink as the sink taps had never worked, that the boiler required to be refilled, which took approximately four minutes, and that while she had been waiting for the refill, she had wedged the bucket underneath the boiler on a flat surface adjacent to the sink to allow her to continue with her cleaning duties. The bucket had thereafter fallen and had splashed M's legs with boiling water. M's supervisor gave evidence that she had not been aware of any fault with the taps, and that she had not told the staff to use the boiler, nor had she told them not to use it. M submitted that there had been no proper system in place to maintain the sink taps in working order and ensure a safe supply of hot water required to carry out the cleaning job, and E had been in breach of the Work at Height Regulations 2005 reg.10(2) and the Provision and Use of Work Equipment Regulations 1998 reg.20. E submitted that the accident had been caused by M's actions in placing the bucket underneath the boiler and leaving it there, and she ought to have placed the bucket in the sink.

Held: E found liable to M. (1) Whilst the bucket had not fallen while being filled, that process had required a period where the boiler was refilled and the bucket, partially full of boiling water, had to be placed somewhere and while it might have been safer to place it in the sink, that too was inherently risky; the sink taps had not worked and but for that failure, M would not have used the boiler and would not have been placed in the position where she required to place or secure the bucket during the refill process. (2) A system of maintenance of equipment which relied entirely upon reporting by the worker using the equipment was not adequate or proper and where the hot water supply from the taps was inadequate, the use of the boiler had been expected by E and was in any event the obvious step to take; the risks inherent to the use of the boiler were clearly foreseeable and extended to consideration of the careless cleaner under pressure to complete her tasks and had E not wanted the boiler to be used, it ought to have given instructions or put up a sign to that effect; had it intended the use of the boiler, it ought to have taken steps to guard against the risk of the bucket containing hot water from falling or splashing, and E's liability was established, both at common law and in relation to the statutory case in respect of the 1998 and 2005 Regulations. (3) Having regard to E's breach of statutory duties, that the use of the boiler was an obvious step to take, was probably intended by E, and M's placing of the bucket had not been surprising in the circumstances, M's contributory negligence would be assessed at 20 per cent.

MCLELLAN v MITIE GROUP PLC, [2015] CSOH 151, 2015 S.L.T. 861, Lady Scott, OH.

2739 Professional negligence–Solicitors–Commercial lender sustaining loss in reliance on statements made by solicitor–Solicitor's assumption of responsibility for misstatements

A commercial lender (N), which held a standard security over three properties owned by a borrower (H), reclaimed against a Lord Ordinary's decision to pronounce decree of absolvitor in an action of damages against H's solicitor (S) and her firm in respect of loss and damage sustained in reliance on statements made by her (*NRAM Plc v Steel* [2014] CSOH 172, [2015] P.N.L.R. 16, [2015] C.L.Y. 3229). In 1997, H had purchased a business park comprised of four units, N had advanced H part of the purchase price and H had granted N an all sums standard security over the property. In May 2005, H had sold unit 3 and N had released the unit from the standard security in return for a partial redemption payment, and S had acted as H's solicitor in relation to conveyancing aspects thereof. In May 2006, H had entered into an agreement for the sale of unit 1 and N had required a capital repayment of £495,000 in return for the release of that unit from the standard security. The loan outstanding at that time was £1,221,850. It had been agreed that the transaction would settle on 23 March 2007 and on 22 March, S had sent an email to N attaching discharges of the standard security for N's signature and stating that the whole loan was being repaid. On 27 March, N had received payment of £495,000 from S and on 29 March, S had forwarded the discharges of the entire security to the solicitor for unit 1's purchaser, and they had been registered shortly thereafter. In 2010, H had become insolvent and an interim liquidator was appointed. In July 2014, H's liquidator made a payment to N of £50,000, and the outstanding balance of the loan was £458,723.99. N's primary case was that S owed it a duty to take reasonable care that the statements she made in the email were accurate and that they were negligent misstatements upon which it had relied, and as a result it had been misled into discharging a security over three properties owned by H when only unit 1 ought to have been released from the security. The Lord Ordinary concluded inter alia that it was not reasonable for a bank in N's position to rely on the misstatement information without checking its accuracy, and that a solicitor in S's position would not foresee that such a bank would reasonably rely on that information without carrying out such a check. The issues before the Inner House were whether the Lord Ordinary erred in law in holding that S owed no duty of care to N when she made the erroneous statements that led to the discharge of their entire security and whether the Lord Ordinary erred in law in assessing damages on the basis of assuming that N would recover £70,351.50 from H's liquidator.

Held: Reclaiming motion allowed. (Lord Brodie *dissenting in part*) (1) It was not disputed that N had relied on the email and that it caused not only the issue of a letter of non-crystallisation but, critically, the execution and return of two discharges, the effect of which was to leave a substantial debt unsecured and the facts simply could not support the proposition that no reasonable solicitor would have foreseen reliance by N on the misstatements and that, accordingly, an outcome whereby the discharges were signed and returned was also reasonably foreseeable, as a result of which, it could only be concluded that the question whether, in law, S was to be taken as having assumed responsibility for her misstatements had to be answered in the affirmative; as a consequence of the Lord Ordinary's approach, he did not go on to consider whether the imposition of a duty of care would be fair, just and reasonable but in the context of a background of inter alia S, while acting outwith her mandate and instructions, had started a series of events which caused the bank to suffer significant loss and the fact that such loss could have been avoided had the bank checked its file, did not render the imposition of a duty of care unfair nor did it demonstrate that S should be relieved of liability; indeed it might be thought invidious to suggest that a solicitor could abrogate responsibility for a serious error because the recipients of her communication might have checked rather than relying on what she, as a hitherto trustworthy professional, told them particularly when she took no action to correct the error when it was within her power to do so. (2) The Lord Ordinary could not be considered as having erred in his approach to damages in what he correctly saw as being a matter of wielding a broad axe. Per Lord Brodie, *dissenting in part*, that the Lord Ordinary's decisions on the key issues of reasonable foresight and reasonable reliance could not be considered plainly and obviously wrong: the Lord Ordinary was the primary decision maker; the function of the Inner House when hearing a reclaiming motion after proof was to review the Lord Ordinary's decision and to reverse it, and substitute their own, only if the decision could be found to be wrong in some sense; what the Lord Ordinary had to decide, namely whether S owed a duty of care, fell to be determined by reference to one or more vague standards through a process of weighing up a variety of competing considerations and he had heard all the evidence, which the appellate court had not, and was likely to have gained an impression of the case which could legitimately have informed his decision making.

NRAM PLC v STEEL *sub nom.* NRAM PLC v BELL & SCOTT LLP, [2016] CSIH 11, 2016 S.L.T. 285, Lady Smith, Lord Brodie, Lady Clark of Calton, IH (Ex Div).

2740 Road traffic accidents–Contributory negligence–Motorcyclist colliding with reversing tanker–Degree of motorcyclist's contributory negligence

A dairy company (C) reclaimed against a decision of the Lord Ordinary finding them liable for injuries sustained by a motorcyclist (W) in a road traffic accident involving one of their employees (G) and assessing W's contributory negligence at 40%. W reclaimed against the Lord Ordinary's decision to assoilzie G (*Wagner v Grant* [2015] CSOH 51, 2015 G.W.D. 15-272). W had been riding his motorcycle at approximately 11 pm, accompanied by his uncle (U), and had collided with a tanker driven by G, which had been reversing into a farm road on W's left. The tanker had consisted of a cab and trailer, the cab had been facing east in the eastbound lane with its headlights on towards the direction from which W was travelling and the trailer had been angled across the westbound lane, blocking it, and W had struck the rear thereof. U had given evidence that he had seen headlights on the opposite carriageway with a set of small lights above, that he knew it was a wagon of some description, that it was facing towards W and U and that he had been certain that it was on the other carriageway and not on his own. The Lord Ordinary had found that W and U had been misled into thinking that the tanker presented no danger to them, the nature of the manoeuvre had rendered it dangerous and C had been negligent, however, applying *Cronie v Messenger*, Outer House, 21 October 2005, unreported, he had found W 40% contributorily negligent.

Held: Case put out by order. (1) The key to the Lord Ordinary's reasoning had been that W and U had been misled into thinking that the tanker was in the other lane and presented no danger to them and it was not until W's headlights had lit the trailer across the road that he had perceived the danger, the feature which had caused W and U to be misled was the fact that the operation was being carried out by an articulated lorry, not a rigid lorry, with the consequence that although the trailer unit was diagonally across the westbound carriageway and blocking it, the headlights on the cab unit were still directed down the eastbound carriageway in a broadly easterly direction, causing W and U to believe that the vehicle was on its own carriageway and posed no danger to them, C accepted that a rigid vehicle might have been used, had that been done the risk of confusion to oncoming drivers would be reduced or eliminated, it was that risk which had been central to the Lord Ordinary's conclusion regarding fault and there was no basis to interfere with his decision that C had been at fault, in the absence of any error of the kind described in *Thomas v Thomas* [1947] A.C. 484, [1947-51] C.L.Y. 7496, and it could not be said that the Lord Ordinary had been plainly wrong, *Thomas, considered*, and *S v S* [2015] CSIH 14, 2015 S.C. 513, [2015] C.L.Y. 3076, *applied*. (2) In the circumstances of the case the Lord Ordinary had been entitled to conclude that the manoeuvre was dangerous and to reach the view that the accident had been caused by C, he had not erred in so doing, and to that extent the reclaiming motion would be refused. (3) The Lord Ordinary had given no indication that he had carried out any assessment of the causative potency or the blameworthiness of W's actions, had he done so, he had given no explanation for reaching the figure of 40%, except that that was the figure adopted in *Cronie*; there were material factual differences between *Cronie* and the present case and it was seldom appropriate to choose a figure for contributory negligence as between two vehicles in a road traffic accident solely by reference to an assessment in another case, even where similarities existed since in most such cases there would be points of difference, and while it might be helpful to refer to another case by way of yardstick or as a point of reference, it was necessary for a judge to state why he or she considerd that the same award ought to be made and to give express consideration to the causative potency and blameworthiness of the present pursuer's actions; the Lord Ordinary had not set out his reasoning thereon and in all the circumstances of the case, he had manifestly and to a substantial degree gone wrong; despite the misleading effect of the articulated lorry's headlights, the degree of blame attributable to W in failing to keep a proper lookout when the tanker trailer was lit up and he had had between 18 and 13 seconds to see it and slow down or stop was significantly greater than 40%, and a just and equitable figure was 60%. (4) The case would be put out by order for further procedure.

WAGNER v GRANT, [2016] CSIH 34, 2016 S.L.T. 699, Lord Menzies, Lady Smith, Lord Drummond Young, IH (Ex Div).

2741 Road traffic accidents–Dogs–Cyclist colliding with dog–Cyclist's contributory negligence

A cyclist (S) sought damages in respect of injuries sustained following a collision between the bicycle on which she was riding and a dog (D) owned by C. S and another cyclist were cycling along a single track public country road and approached a blind bend at a speed of 18-20 mph. C's fishing companion had parked a van in a recess within the bend. D and another dog had been allowed out of the van without leads and had crossed the road. As S was approaching the bend, C called D back to him without checking that the road was clear, it began to cross the road and collided with S's bicycle. S landed in the road and suffered a broken jaw, a gash in her chin, five broken teeth and her shoulder was broken in five places, which damaged her axillary nerve and led to a full shoulder replacement. C submitted that had S not rounded the bend at excessive speed, the collision would not have occurred.

Held: Case put out by order. (1) S had established negligence on C's part: he was parked in a layby adjacent to a public road, he allowed D to cross the road, he should have been aware of the possibility of other road users, particularly in the vicinity of a blind corner, and having taken no steps to ensure that the road was clear, he called D in the full knowledge that it would require to cross the public road; while there was a duty on all road users to take reasonable care for their own safety and to use roads at a safe speed, it was not an absolute duty against all potential hazards; S was not travelling at an unsafe speed with any degree of recklessness and had she seen D she would have been able to avoid the collision; had C moved to the blind corner to see round it he would have seen S approach, had D not been on a public road and had he not called for it, then the collision with S would not have occurred, and his carelessness amounted to negligence, *Welsh v Brady* [2008] CSOH 45, 2008 S.L.T. 363, [2008] C.L.Y. 4977, *considered.* (2) It was S's responsibility to take reasonable care for her own safety in avoiding any potential hazards that might have lain around the bend, given that the bicycle was under her sole control, on a quiet country road animals had to have been one of the potential hazards, and it was just and equitable that her contributory liability be assessed at 30%. (3) The case would be put out by order to determine further procedure.

SANDISON v COOPE, 2016 Rep. L.R. 70, Sheriff W M Wood, Sh Ct (Tayside) (Perth).

2742 Tripping and slipping–Employers' liability

[Workplace (Health, Safety and Welfare) Regulations 1992 (SI 1992/3004) reg.12(1), reg.12(2), reg.12(3)]

A sales manager (S) raised an action of damages against his employer (M) for injuries sustained during the course of his employment. Solatium was agreed and the proof restricted to liability and alleged loss of bonuses and wages. On 4 June 2013, S had been carrying a small, lightweight box through a doorway and into a hallway at M's premises when he had fallen, as a result of which he had suffered a soft tissue injury to his lower back. S had been unfit for work between 4 June 2013 and 30 September 2014, by which date his symptoms and injury had resolved, with no ongoing consequences, and he had undergone extensive physiotherapy. S averred that his foot had caught on the edge of a chip in the floor, causing his fall, and that M had breached the Workplace (Health, Safety and Welfare) Regulations 1992 regs 12(1), (2) and (3).

Held: Decree of absolvitor granted. (1) The evidence of M's expert, that it was only possible to catch a shoe in the chip if it was presented at an angle that would not arise from normal walking from any direction, and that its dimensions posed no trip hazard, fell to be preferred; other than S's own perception based on his memory of events three years ago, there was no other evidence to support his position that the dimensions of the chip posed a trip or other risk to health and safety. (2) The accepted evidence that a risk to health and safety would only begin to arise with a minimum depth of approximately 3 mm was fatal to S's case; on the evidence, the chip had been too shallow to pose any relevant risk to S's health and safety, its presence had neither given rise to a risk of a person tripping and falling when walking, nor rendered the floor unsuitable, and S had failed to prove a breach of either reg.12(1) or (2) of the 1992 Regulations. (3) Having regard to its features, the chip was not an obstruction and S's case under reg.12(3) also failed. *Opinion*, (1) that had it been necessary to consider causation, S had failed to prove that the chip had caused him to trip; (2) that had M been found liable, S would have been found to have been at least two thirds contributorily negligent where his own conduct had contributed substantially to the accident; S was not expected to move boxes himself, there had been no pressing requirement to do so, S had admittedly failed to follow his recent health and safety training advice, and had failed to look where he had been placing his feet; (3) that had M been found liable, no legal basis had been offered for S's claim for an extra month's salary and he had failed to prove a claim for loss of bonus in either 2013 or 2014, and no award would have been made in respect of either bonus.

SHACKLETON v M-I DRILLING FLUIDS UK LTD, [2016] CSOH 82, 2016 Rep. L.R. 96, Lady Wolffe, OH.

2743 Tripping and slipping–Footpaths–Child falling in national park–Mechanics of accident not proven

L reclaimed against a decision of the Lord Ordinary assoilzieing a park authority (N) from L's action of damages for injuries sustained in 2006, when aged 12, after he fell in a national park (*Leonard v Loch Lomond and the Trossachs National Park Authority* [2014] CSOH 38, 2014 Rep. L.R. 46, [2014] C.L.Y. 3700). L had been walking on a pathway ahead of his other family members (X), out of their view, and they had found him unconscious lying at the foot of a steep bank to the side of a set of steps. X had not witnessed the accident, and L had no memory thereof. L sought to attribute his accident to the physical condition of the pathway, namely that at, or above, the point where it turned sharply on its final descent to a road, L had tripped or lost his footing and fallen. The Lord Ordinary found that the mechanics of the accident had not been proved; there was no direct evidence in relation thereto and L's action had to fail. He further opined that had the alleged circumstances of the accident been proved, no liability accrued to N.

Held: Reclaiming motion refused. L's leading contention, that the Lord Ordinary had ignored or misstated relevant chapters of evidence was without substance, the Lord Ordinary had properly addressed himself to what was relevant material and in doing so had not omitted evidence of any relevant fact. The Lord Ordinary had been well justified in concluding that such primary facts as had been established in the evidence did not enable him properly to draw the crucial inference that the event precipitating L's injuries was that he had tripped or lost his footing on the path, and even had the facts allowed the necessary inference to be drawn, they did not compel that inference, accordingly, the primary issue in respect of the mechanics of the accident had to fail. Opinion, that the Lord Ordinary had not erred in holding that had L tripped or lost his footing on the path, no liability accrued to N; he had been fully entitled to hold that the path in question had been constructed to, and met, accepted standards for that particular type of path, and he had correctly concluded from the relevant authorities that the law was to the effect that there was no duty on the occupier of land to warn or fence against obvious dangers.

LEONARD v LOCH LOMOND AND THE TROSSACHS NATIONAL PARK AUTHORITY, [2015] CSIH 44, 2016 S.C.L.R. 102, Lord Eassie, Lady Smith, Lady Clark of Calton, IH (Ex Div).

PEERAGES AND DIGNITIES

2744 Peerage claims–Legitimacy–Baronetcy–Rebuttal of presumption as to legitimacy by DNA evidence

[Judicial Committee Act 1833 (c.41) s.4; Data Protection Act 1998 (c.29) Sch.2, Sch.3, s.2, s.4(4); Law Reform (Parent and Child) (Scotland) Act 1986 (c.9) s.5(4); Prescription and Limitation (Scotland) Act 1973 (c.52) Sch.3]

In a reference under the Judicial Committee Act 1833 s.4, the board was required to advise Her Majesty as to who was entitled to be entered onto the Official Roll of the Baronetage as the Baronet of Pringle of Stichill and whether DNA evidence was admissible to determine the question. The baronetcy, which was governed by Scots law, was granted in 1683 to Robert Pringle and the "male heirs of his body". There was evidence that in the late twentieth century the younger brother of the 9th baronet told two family members that he believed the baronet to be illegitimate. The title passed without open dispute until the latter years of the 10th baronet, whose son was the presumed heir. The son's cousin, who, it was agreed, knew nothing of any suggestion of illegitimacy, began a project to trace the line of the clan chief who died without an heir in 1738. Family members, including the 10th baronet provided mouth swabs for DNA testing. The tests showed that the 10th baronet had a separate lineage to that of the other family members whose Y-chromosome DNA haplotype test results were all identical. The cousin said he would act to restore the rightful lineage. After the 10th baronet's death, his son and the cousin registered their claims to inherit the baronetcy.

Expert interpretation of the DNA test results concluded that the 10th baronet and the core group of family members could not have had a common male ancestor in the previous 1,000 years. The cousin asserted that the 9th baronet had not been the son of the 8th baronet, whose second son, the cousin's father, had been the true heir. The son submitted that, although he did not dispute the DNA test results, the evidence should not be admitted as (1) under the Scots law of prescription the cousin's claim had been extinguished by the passage of time; (2) the claim was barred by the defence of mora, taciturnity and acquiescence; (3) the cousin had breached confidentiality or misused the DNA information to further his claim; (4) in so doing he had been in breach of the Data Protection Act 1998 s.4(4).

Held: Reference allowed. (1) The central issue was not one of legitimacy but of paternity, which was a question of fact, and unless the DNA evidence fell to be excluded on the basis of prescription or another ground of delay, it was of sufficient cogency, namely reaching the criminal standard of proof, to rebut an evidential presumption of legitimacy under either Scots or English law (see para.25 of judgment). The Scots common law presumption of paternity had required proof beyond reasonable doubt to rebut it, but proof on a balance of probabilities had become enough by virtue of the Law Reform (Parent and Child) (Scotland) Act 1986 s.5(4) (paras 30-31). The pre-1973 law of prescription did not protect the 9th or 10th baronets or their heirs so the claim of the cousin's father had not been extinguished before the Prescription and Limitation (Scotland) Act 1973. Under sch.3 para(h) of the 1973 Act the right to succeed to a title of honour survived the passage of time and thus the Act was not a bar to the cousin's claim or a basis for exclusion of the DNA evidence (paras 43-58, 61). (2) The claim was not barred by the defence of mora, taciturnity and acquiescence. The bar was personal and the inaction of the cousin's father, despite his belief that the 9th baronet was illegitimate, was irrelevant to the claim of the cousin, who in any case had been unaware of the issue until the DNA results (paras 62-64). (3) There was no breach of confidentiality or misuse of information. The 10th baronet's claim to be clan chief depended on his status as senior member of the family branch entitled to the baronetcy. He was aware that he was contributing to a genealogical record and had consented (paras 67-68). (4) Although DNA was sensitive personal data under s.2 of the 1998 Act so that explicit consent was required under sch2 and sch3, the cousin could not have stated a purpose which he did not have at the time, although he did have it later. However, even if he had acted in breach of statutory duty it was not enough to exclude the DNA evidence. That would be disproportionate, as it was central to the issue and it was not unfair to admit it, *Duke of Argyll v Duchess of Argyll (No.3)* 1963 S.L.T. (Notes) 42, [1963] C.L.Y. 4110, *Martin v McGuiness* 2003 S.L.T. 1424, [2003] C.L.Y. 5271 applied. (5) The evidential presumption that the 9th baronet was the legitimate son of the 8th was capable of rebuttal by evidence showing on the balance of probabilities that he was not. The DNA evidence demonstrated that to a high degree of probability. The board concluded that the claimant cousin was the grandson of the 8th baronet and thus the heir male of the 1st baronet (paras 81-82). (6) DNA evidence was capable of reopening family succession many generations into the past. Whether legal measures were needed to protect past property transactions, the rights of the perceived beneficiary of a trust of property and the long-established expectations of a family were questions for others to consider (para.85).

BARONETCY OF PRINGLE OF STICHILL, RE, [2016] UKPC 16, [2016] 1 W.L.R. 2870, Lord Neuberger, Lady Hale, Lord Mance, Lord Clarke, Lord Reed, Lord Hughes, Lord Hodge, PC (Sc).

PENOLOGY AND CRIMINOLOGY

2745 Disclosure–Protecting Vulnerable Groups Scheme–Vetting

THE PROTECTION OF VULNERABLE GROUPS (SCOTLAND) ACT 2007 (PRESCRIBED PURPOSES FOR CONSIDERATION OF SUITABILITY) REGULATIONS 2016, SSI 2016/27; made under the Protection of Vulnerable Groups (Scotland) Act 2007 s.73(g). In force: 1 April 2016.

These Regulations prescribe certain purposes in terms of the Protection of Vulnerable Groups (Scotland) Act 2007 s.73(g). This section provides a power to prescribe further purposes in relation to references in Pt.2 (vetting and disclosure) of the 2007 Act to a person considering an individual's suitability to do, or to be offered or supplied for, any type of regulated work.

2746 Electronic monitoring–Restriction of liberty orders

THE RESTRICTION OF LIBERTY ORDER ETC. (SCOTLAND) AMENDMENT REGULATIONS 2016, SSI 2016/89; made under the Criminal Procedure (Scotland) Act 1995 s.245C(3). In force: 13 March 2016.

These Regulations amend the Restriction of Liberty Order etc. (Scotland) Regulations 2013 (the Principal Regulations) by adding to reg.5 of the Principal Regulations a further purpose for which the devices specified in Sch.2 of the Principal Regulations may be used.

2747 Offenders–Spent convictions–Rehabilitation of offenders

THE REHABILITATION OF OFFENDERS ACT 1974 (EXCLUSIONS AND EXCEPTIONS) (SCOTLAND) AMENDMENT ORDER 2016, SSI 2016/91; made under the Rehabilitation of Offenders Act 1974 s.4(4), 7(4), 10(1). In force: 8 February 2016.

This Order amends the Rehabilitation of Offenders Act 1974 (Exclusions and Exceptions) (Scotland) Order 2013 (the 2013 Order). The 2013 Order disapplies specified provisions of the Rehabilitation of Offenders Act 1974 which would otherwise prevent a person from having to disclose a spent conviction and protect that person from being prejudiced by that conviction or any failure to disclose it.

2748 Prisoners–Handcuffing–Double handcuffing during hospital appointments–Whether contrary to art.3 and art.8 ECHR

[European Convention on Human Rights 1950 art.3, art.8]

An action raised by a prisoner (M), serving a nine year sentence for attempted murder in a secure prison, against a custodial and detention services company (G) seeking declarator that his double handcuffing and restraint by G on three occasions while he was being taken to attend hospital appointments and during said appointments was incompatible with his rights under ECHR arts 3 and 8, and damages, came before the sheriff for a hearing on evidence. The case had previously been discussed at debate and declarator had been granted (*McDowall v G4S Care and Justice Services (UK) Ltd* 2015 S.L.T. (Sh Ct) 129, [2015] C.L.Y. 3245). G had successfully appealed and the matter had been remitted for a proof before answer (*McDowall v G4S Care and Justice Services (UK) Ltd* 2016 S.L.T. (Sh Ct) 107, [2016] 2749). M gave evidence inter alia that he had felt affronted and uncomfortable, that members of the public had stared at him, that there had been no requirement for the cuffs, that he had expected single handcuffing and had felt humiliated at his double handcuffing, and he criticised the system of prisoner escort. G led evidence inter alia that the terms of its instructions for its employees provided that unless a risk assessment deemed otherwise, double handcuffs would be applied in an insecure area, such as a public area, that having regard to the prison risk assessment, the appropriate response had been to double handcuff M, and the risks associated with escorting M could only be properly controlled by double cuffing.

Held: G assoilzied. (1) M's unsupported evidence was not sufficiently credible or reliable to found a basis for his claim and was in any event insufficient; he had failed to state why single cuffing would have prevented people staring at him, he had given no evidence regarding the visibility of the double cuffing or the manner in which single cuffing would have been an improvement, he had failed to address his status as a prisoner with a marked record for violence, there was almost no evidence regarding causation, and his evidence was so deficient that it could not found any credible case. (2) M's evidence was thin, unspecific, and highlighted his inability to view the matter objectively, on the other hand, G had produced contemporary and accurate documentation which contradicted M's evidence, his evidence was undermined on a number of specific issues and was incredible and unreliable. (3) M's claim of affront or humiliation failed due to lack of credibility and reliability, in any event, were it to be accepted that he had felt affronted, humiliated or degraded, there was no clear causal connection with double handcuffing. (4) G's judgment that it was necessary to double cuff M, who was being taken from a secure environment to an insecure one, was reasonable and also necessary; there was no credible scenario where a prisoner such as M, with a significant record of violence, health problems and drug taking, could be treated on a non-cuff basis, single cuffing was insufficient due to the difficulty of controlling the prisoner and the corresponding requirement to escort more closely with additional staff which was likely to create a risk of injury due to responding to a situation, and double cuffing was reasonable and proportionate and M had failed to prove that its use was inhumane. (5) M's claim that an individual risk assessment had not been carried out on each occasion that M was transported to, and attended, each hospital appointment, was neither accurate nor a material factor; had an individualised risk assessment been carried out on each occasion, a prisoner with M's characteristics would have required the use of double handcuffs, in any event, risk assessments had been made on each occasion, and had led to the standard and appropriate precaution of double cuffing, which on the evidence was the only, minimum form of precaution and additional assessment would not have led to a lessening of that level of restraint. (6) It was inevitable that wearing handcuffs and being escorted would attract attention and there was no suggestion that M's treatment had been intended to cause adverse feelings in him, the exposure had been no more than necessary, no force had been used, M had been in lawful detention and being escorted in an insecure public area, the practical outcome had been just and proportionate, and M's art.3 rights had not been infringed, *Mouisel v France (67263/01)* (2004) 38 E.H.R.R. 34, [2004] C.L.Y. 1928, *considered*. (7) The use of double cuffing had been directly related to, and dictated by, the risks arising and no lesser restraint would have achieved the same or similar levels of safety in any less intrusive or embarrassing way, an individual risk assessment would not have changed matters and in any event, had at least been matched by G's dynamic risk assessment carried out on every escort as a matter of course, and M's art.8 rights had not been breached, *Bank Mellat v HM Treasury* [2013] UKSC 39, [2014] A.C. 700, [2013] C.L.Y. 194, *considered. Opinion*, (1) that had M proved that G's actings were unlawful, it would not have been just and appropriate to award any damages; M had a significant history of violence which would have, in itself, justified double handcuffing, his discomfiture had been minor and short lived and there was no evidence of any short or long term consequences, there was no just satisfaction to be had and had there been, no award of damages would have been required; (2) that had damages been appropriate, £100 would have been awared.

MCDOWALL v G4S CARE AND JUSTICE SERVICES (UK) LTD, 2016 S.L.T. (Sh Ct) 371, Sheriff N A Ross, Sh Ct (Lothian) (Edinburgh).

2749 Prisoners–Handcuffing–Prisoner double-handcuffed during hospital appointments–Sheriff granting summary decree and allowing proof before quantum on claim under art.3 and art.8 ECHR

[European Convention on Human Rights 1950 art.3, art.8]

A custodial and detention services company (G) appealed against a decision of the sheriff granting decree and reserving the quantum of damages for a proof as to just satisfaction in an action against G by a prisoner (M), seeking declarator that his double handcuffing on three occasions while he was being taken to attend hospital appointments and during said appointments was incompatible with his rights under the ECHR art.3 and art.8, and damages of £10,000 (*McDowall v G4S Care and Justice Services (UK) Ltd* 2015 S.L.T. (Sh Ct) 129, [2015] C.L.Y. 3245). The sheriff had found *inter alia* that it ought to have been possible for M to have been single handcuffed to one officer and tightly flanked by the others when moving about the hospital and in the waiting areas, and had such steps been taken the whole exercise would have been less obvious to the public and less intrusive for him, while retaining a necessary level of security, and that no risk assessment had been carried out as to the nature and level of security required for each of M's hospital visits. G contended that the sheriff had gone too far too fast in denying it proof of its averments on all craves. M argued that G had adopted a blanket policy which it had been mandated to implement in terms of the standard operating procedure governing the movement of prisoners to and from hospital as part of the contract between G and the Scottish prison service, accordingly, the disputed averments had been of no assistance to G as they had been essentially self-contradictory given that it had sought *ex post facto* to justify that blanket policy with reference to the facts of the case. The sheriff was therefore correct to ignore the disputed averments and find that G had been unable to succeed in resisting declarator standing its averments which failed to state in what manner the interference with M's art.8 rights was proportionate to the risk. The sheriff had pronounced no interlocutor giving effect to his decision and the parties were content to treat his decision as one which granted summary decree and allowing a proof before quantum. The parties were also agreed that whatever the outcome of the appeal, a proof at large was required on just satisfaction and, if appropriate, the quantum of damages.

Held: Appeal allowed and matter remitted for proof before answer. (1) To fall within the scope of art.3, the treatment had to attain a minimum level of severity, the assessment of which usually depended on all the circumstances of the case, although in considering an interference with art.8, there was no such requirement, and decisions of the European Court of Human Rights and the English authorities repeatedly emphasised the requirement to have regard to the facts and circumstances of each application, *Kudla v Poland (30210/96)* (2002) 35 E.H.R.R. 11, [2001] C.L.Y. 3543, *Mouisel v France (67263/01)* (2004) 38 E.H.R.R. 34, [2004] C.L.Y. 1928, *R. (on the application of Faizovas) v Secretary of State for Justice* [2009] EWCA Civ 373, [2009] U.K.H.R.R. 1093, [2009] C.L.Y. 2762 and *R. (on the application of Begum) v Denbigh High School Governors* [2006] UKHL 15, [2007] 1 A.C. 100, [2006] C.L.Y. 1145, *considered*. (2) G had offered justification for the use of handcuffs and it was necessary to allow it an opportunity of demonstrating that the use of handcuffs as a form of restraint when M attended outpatient appointments had been justified, in order to address whether the practical outcome had been justified and appropriate, accordingly, the sheriff had fallen into error by accepting that the lack of an individualised risk assessment had been fatal to G's case and by failing to notice that the case law relating to art.3 clearly emphasised that ill treatment had to attain a minimum level of severity if it was to fall within the scope of art.3. (3) The present case raised important questions of law which could not properly or adequately be dealt with without proof of the facts and circumstances; the absence of a risk assessment was not fatal to G's case, it could not be said at the present stage that the court had to find that G had violated M's art.3 rights or had interfered unnecessarily and disproportionately with his art.8 rights, there required to be an inquiry for that purpose and there ought to be a proof before answer, moreover, the sheriff had given no reason why certain of G's averments could be ignored and it appeared that certain of its averments offered to prove that the approach to M's restraint was not rigid but related to medical requirements. Observed, that an interlocutor was necessary to give effect to the sheriff's decision but also for the purpose of appeal and certainty and ought to record which pleas in law had been sustained or repelled and provide a clear audit trail of the orders made by the court and the nature of the restricted proof allowed.

MCDOWALL v G4S CARE AND JUSTICE SERVICES (UK) LTD, 2016 S.L.T. (Sh Ct) 107, Sheriff Principal M M Stephen, QC, Sh Pr.

2750 Prisoners–Rehabilitation–Existence of duty owed by local authority–Local authority having no role in detention and release of prisoner

[European Convention on Human Rights 1950 art.5; Social Work (Scotland) Act 1968 (c.49); Housing (Scotland) Act 1987 (c.26)]

A serving life prisoner (P), currently detained in the open estate, petitioned for judicial review of the failure by the local authority (C) to provide him with a reasonable opportunity of rehabilitation, in breach of his rights under ECHR art.5. P averred that C had an important role in the rehabilitation process, being involved with the supervision and monitoring of prisoners released on licence and providing them with advice, guidance and assistance outwith prison, and in so far as it had such a role, it owed a duty to P under art.5, in light of *R. (on the application of Kaiyam) v Secretary of State for Justice* [2014] UKSC 66, [2015] A.C. 1344, [2015] C.L.Y. 1811, and it had failed to provide him with a reasonable opportunity to rehabilitate himself and to demonstrate that he no longer presented an unacceptable danger to the public where on P's release into the community in the past C had subjected him to such stringent conditions that he had not been effectively tested, it had identified no home leave address for him, the licence conditions likely to be imposed on him and the likely conditions of any temporary release were so strict that he would inevitably fail to comply therewith and frustrated the purpose of testing him in conditions of greater freedom. P further averred that in order for the *Kaiyam* duty to be effective it ought to be interpreted to apply to C, as well as the Scottish Ministers.

Held: Case put out by order. (1) C owed no *Kaiyam* duty to P; that duty was not a freestanding one arising out of art.5 but was imposed on the state in circumstances where the state had detained the prisoner and relied upon the justification in art.5(1)(a), and where part of the purpose of the sentence was rehabilitation, it was implicit in art.5 that the state, which was responsible for detention, had to provide the prisoner with a reasonable opportunity to rehabilitate himself and to demonstrate that he no longer presented an unacceptable danger to the public, however, C was in an entirely different position as it had no role in P's detention or release, its only role was to provide assistance in some parts of the rehabilitation process, both before and after release, and as C was not in the position of having to justify P's detention, there was no reason to impose on it the duty associated therewith. (2) That C was under certain duties under particular statutes, such as the Social Work (Scotland) Act 1968 and the Housing (Scotland) Act 1987, was of no assistance; in so far as duties were owed under those particular Acts, and there was any breach thereof, P would have grounds for complaint which he could vindicate in court, and those duties required no assistance and gained nothing from any more general duty imported from *Kaiyam*, moreover, there were no averments indicating any breaches of specific duties under those statutes, *Kaiyam, considered*. (3) The petition would be refused and the case would be put out by order to determine further procedure.

ANSARI v ABERDEEN CITY COUNCIL, [2015] CSOH 168, 2016 S.L.T. 73, Lord Glennie, OH.

2751 Prisoners–Rehabilitation–Prioritising of prisoners' access to rehabilitative coursework–Whether adequate protection against arbitrariness in detention of life prisoners

[European Convention on Human Rights 1950 art.14, art.5]

A prisoner (Q) serving a sentence of life imprisonment for murder petitioned for judicial review of an alleged failure by the Scottish Ministers (M) to provide him with rehabilitation and of M's prioritisation policy for rehabilitative courses. Q would have become eligible to apply for release on licence from May 2019. Q was assessed as requiring various coursework, including a self change programme and a substance related offending behaviour programme. The Scottish Prison Service issued a guidance notice to prison governors and managers which stated that spaces on programmes were allocated according to critical dates based upon earliest possible release dates, and that no prisoner type was prioritised over another. Q submitted that (1) delays at all stages of progression through the prison system were such that life prisoners were unlikely to be in a position to demonstrate to the Parole Board for Scotland (P), at tariff expiry date, that the risk of release had reduced sufficiently that their detention was no longer necessary, indeterminate sentence prisoners had not been provided with reasonable opportunities for rehabilitation, and although they had been assessed as requiring rehabilitative coursework, they had not been provided timeously with the chance to undertake it; (2) M had behaved irrationally in not providing him timeously with the required coursework and were in breach of their public law duty to provide him with a reasonable opportunity to demonstrate at tariff expiry that he no longer required to be detained; (3) M's compliance with Q's rights under the ECHR had to be determined under reference to the duty, implicit in the scheme of ECHR art.5 and enunciated in *R. (on the application of Kaiyam) v Secretary of State for Justice* [2014] UKSC 66, [2015] A.C. 1344, [2015] C.L.Y. 1811, and such rights existed regardless of whether the failure occurred before or after the tariff expiry date; (4) it was not rational to prioritise access to rehabilitative coursework by reference to earliest possible release date, which discriminated irrationally against certain categories of prisoner; (5) M's prioritisation policy did not provide adequate protection against arbitrariness in the detention of life prisoners and as such was in breach of art.5, and the policy was unfair because it failed to take account of different categories of prisoner; (6) the prioritisation policy was in the ambit of art.5 so as to bring the art.14 duty of non-discrimination into play, differences between prisoner categories amounted to "other status" for the purposes thereof, and the policy discriminated between different categories of prisoners to the detriment of life prisoners.

Held: Petition put out by order. (1) Q had not provided a relevant basis for his averment that M had failed to provide him and other indeterminate sentence prisoners with reasonable opportunities for rehabilitation, and no relevant case had been made that there was systemic failure by M to enable life prisoners generally to demonstrate to P by the end of their punishment part that it was no longer necessary to detain them for public protection, and the petition would be dismissed to that extent. (2) The public law duty acknowledged in *R. (on the application of Wells) v Parole Board for England and Wales* [2009] UKHL 22, [2010] 1 A.C. 553, [2009] C.L.Y. 3407 was to make reasonable provision to enable indeterminate sentence prisoners to demonstrate their safety for release and the same duty applied with regard to a life prisoner. Q was not entitled, as a matter of law, to either an order in terms that M had acted unlawfully in failing to provide him with means to demonstrate to P by the end of his punishment part that it was no longer necessary for the protection of the public that he continued to be detained, or a proof on the question whether M were in breach of a duty formulated in such terms, where the terms thereof omitted any reference to reasonable provision of systems and resources. Q had sufficient averments to entitle him to proof as to whether M were in breach of such duty, and if the orders sought were framed in satisfactory terms, the court would fix a proof before answer on Q's complaints both under domestic law and the ECHR regarding his own treatment, *R (on the application of Wells), considered.* (3) The fact that it might not be possible to state with certainty that Q's art.5 right would have been breached at the time of his tariff expiry did not prevent him from raising the matter prior to expiry. It was appropriate for the court to have regard to the various matters listed in *Kaiyam*, and the possibility that Q might satisfy the court that there had been a failure to provide him with such an opportunity should not have been ruled out without enquiry. (4) Where Q had sought an order that M provide him with a reasonable opportunity for rehabilitation and to demonstrate to P that he no longer presented an unacceptable danger to the public by expiry of his punishment part, it was not competent to grant an order *ad factum praestandum* in such vague and unspecific terms as it afforded M no indication as to how to comply therewith. (5) The test of irrationality was a high one, the discretion afforded to M and to those tasked with administration of the prison service was a broad one with which the court should be slow to interfere, and the prioritisation policy could not be said to lie outwith the range reasonably open to M. Q had failed to make a relevant case under domestic law that he was entitled to any order with regard to the prioritisation policy, or that the court should make an order reducing the notice to prison governors and managers. (6) It was clear from the Strasbourg case law discussed in *Kaiyam* that arbitrariness had a more confined meaning than a general notion of unfairness. If unfairness meant a failure to take account of different categories of prisoner, then the argument effectively became one of discrimination and Q's argument based on art.5 alone had to be rejected, *Kaiyam, considered.* (7) Q had a personal interest in being afforded the opportunity to undertake the coursework, which was sufficiently close to the core of his art.5 right to fall within the ambit of art.5, and therefore the non-discrimination duty under art.14 was engaged. (8) The fact that some prisoners had determinate sentences and some had indeterminate sentences was neither a relevant difference nor an inequality which required correction, nor did it render their situations significantly different so as to require differential treatment in order to avoid a breach of the Convention right of any particular category, and Q's argument founded upon arts 5 and 14 together would be rejected, and his petition would be dismissed to that extent. (9) The petition would be put out by order for the court to be addressed on Q's amendment, if so advised, of the terms of the orders sought, if appropriate, the fixing and scope of a second hearing, and any other matters.

QUINN v SCOTTISH MINISTERS, [2015] CSOH 110, 2015 Rep. L.R. 133, Lord Tyre, OH.

2752 Prisoners–Rehabilitation–Scottish Ministers' prioritisation policy for coursework

[European Convention on Human Rights 1950 art.14, art.5]

A prisoner (D), subject to an order for lifelong restriction, petitioned for judicial review of a failure by the Scottish Ministers (S) to provide him with a reasonable opportunity to rehabilitate himself and demonstrate to the parole board at the expiry of the punishment part of his sentence that he no longer presented an unacceptable danger to the public. Prisoners' progression through the prison estate was based on their behaviour and level of continuing risk and before transferring to the open estate they had to complete outstanding coursework. The punishment part of D's sentence was due to end in approximately two years, he was assessed as requiring specific coursework which was a rolling programme and he was 152nd on the waiting list therefor. Under S's prioritisation policy, coursework was allocated to prisoners chronologically by reference to the first occasion when a prisoner might be released. D averred that (1) it would take 12 months to complete the rolling programme, eight months thereafter for transfer to conditions of lesser security and at least nine months spent on the open estate, totalling 29 months from the time he started coursework until he was ready to be assessed by the parole board, which was at least four months after the expiry of the punishment part of his sentence and thus breached his rights under the ECHR art.5 and at common law; (2) S's policy of allocating coursework by reference to earliest release date was irrational, discriminated between different categories of prisoners, and breached his rights under arts 5 and 14 of the Convention and at common law.

Held: Petition refused. (1) D's petition provided no basis for his assertions that the programme took 12 months to complete and that eight months would pass before transfer into the open estate, and there was no adequate basis for D's averment that it was already unlikely that he would have completed the relevant stages in time to be assessed by the parole board at the time of his earliest release date. D's averments regarding where he was on the waiting list at any particular time provided no sufficient basis for a conclusion that he would not be given a place on the programme in time to move to the open estate and thereafter be assessed by the parole board at the time of his earliest release date, and he had not made any proper averments to justify sending his case to proof. (2) D's arguments concerning S's prioritisation policy were identical to those advanced by the petitioner in *Quinn v Scottish Ministers* [2015] CSOH 110, 2015 Rep. L.R. 133, [2016] 2751, the court's reasoning set forth in *Quinn* would be adopted and that part of D's case refused for the same reasons, without prejudice to his right to argue the point should the matter go further, *Quinn, applied.*

DALY v SCOTTISH MINISTERS, [2015] CSOH 166, 2016 Rep. L.R. 38, Lord Glennie, OH.

2753 **Prisoners' rights–Right to respect for private and family life–Failure to deliver unopened prisoner's privileged mail–Appropriateness of award of damages**

[European Convention on Human Rights 1950 art.8]

Following a finding that the Scottish Prison Service (S) had breached the ECHR art.8 rights of a prisoner (B) by failing to deliver to him, unopened, mail which they ought to have regarded as privileged, the matter came before the Lord Ordinary for a hearing on the appropriate remedy (*Beggs v Scottish Ministers* [2015] CSOH 98, 2015 S.L.T. 487, [2015] C.L.Y. 3246).

Held: Opinion issued. Just satisfaction was constituted by the finding of breaches of B's art.8 rights and no award of damages was necessitated: the breaches had not involved any reading of confidential mail, apologies had been made following complaints made by B and investigated by S, the system for the recognition of privileged mail had been altered as a result of B's complaints and actions, and although B had been annoyed, he had not suffered distress of the severity in *R. (on the application of Greenfield) v Secretary of State for the Home Department* [2005] UKHL 14, [2005] 1 W.L.R. 673, [2005] C.L.Y. 2066, *Greenfield, considered.*

BEGGS v SCOTTISH MINISTERS, [2016] CSOH 80, 2016 S.L.T. 789, Lady Stacey, OH.

2754 **Prisoners' rights–Visitors–Same-sex couple in different prisons–Lawfulness of r.63(8) Prisons and Young Offenders Institutions (Scotland) Rules 2011**

[Prisons and Young Offenders Institutions (Scotland) Rules 2011 (SSI 2011/331) r.63(8), r.77, r.78; European Convention on Human Rights 1950 art.8]

Following the refusal of a petition by two male co-offenders (P), serving life sentences in different prisons for murder and concurrent sentences for sex offences against young males, for judicial review of the refusal of the Scottish Prison Service (S) to grant them inter-prison visits, the Lord Ordinary issued a supplementary opinion addressing P's claim that the Prisons and Young Offenders Institutions (Scotland) Rules 2011 r.63(8) was *ultra vires* of the Scottish Ministers (M) (*O'Neill v Scottish Ministers* [2015] CSOH 93, 2015 S.L.T. 811, [2016] 2755). P claimed to have been in a same sex relationship since prior to their incarceration and S had permitted them unlimited correspondence and fortnightly telephone calls, however, P sought face to face meetings, claiming that they were necessary to satisfy a family life purpose that could not be met by the correspondence and telephone calls. Rule 63(8) provided that a prisoner was entitled to receive a visit from another prisoner only in exceptional circumstances and where the prison governor gave consent, and in the event consent was refused, the prisoner had to be informed of the reasons therefor. P submitted that the exceptional circumstances entitlement itself was unlawful because it was incompatible with human rights *et separatim* lacked legal certainty. M submitted that an exceptional circumstances proviso lawfully allowed local managers to exercise discretion in complex and infinitely varied situations.

Held: Opinion given. (1) A provision that, generally speaking, did not allow inter-prison visits was not *per se* incompatible with ECHR art.8: with regard to the jurisprudence, visits were legitimately subject to a general limitation with certain exceptions because even ordinary visits imposed a heavy administrative and security burden, and as a legitimate public interest was involved, that increased burden might be sufficient justification for the general non-entitlement, moreover, the rationale of prison visits, namely to allow prisoners to maintain contact with the outside world and to foster rehabilitation and reintegration in society on release, did not on the face of it apply, or applied with reduced force, to visitations *inter se* by convicts, thus the imperative for inter-prison visits on human rights grounds was absent, all of which amounted to a legitimate presumption against inter-prison visits, *X v United Kingdom (9054/80)* (1983) 5 E.H.R.R. 260 and *R. v Secretary of State for the Home Department Ex p. Wynne* [1993] 1 W.L.R. 115, [1993] C.L.Y. 3369, *considered*. (2) "Exceptional circumstances" or similar figured repeatedly in art.8 case law, thus it could not *per se* be said to be a Convention incompatible formula; where there was a legitimate presumption in favour of interfering with private and family life, an exceptional circumstance qualification served the purpose of preserving scope in appropriate cases for a proportionality assessment in accordance with art.8.2, the Strasbourg case law acknowledged that there could be legitimate public interest presumptions against the enjoyment of private and family life where only exceptional circumstances would tip the proportionality balance in the individual's favour, and part of the implication of the key paragraphs of *MF (Nigeria) v Secretary of State for the Home Department* [2013] EWCA Civ 1192, [2014] 1 W.L.R. 544, [2014] C.L.Y. 1669 was that "exceptional circumstances" in and of itself, signalled that in striking the proportionality balance, decisive weight ought normally to be given to the general rule, therefore, the exceptional circumstances qualification in r.63(8) was not *per se* art.8 incompatible, *Dickson v United Kingdom (44362/04)* [2008] 1 F.L.R. 1315, [2008] C.L.Y. 1991 and *MF (Nigeria)*, *considered*. (3) With regard to the requirements of accessibility and foreseeability; as a matter of law, the "exceptional circumstances" provision in r.63(8) was not necessarily incompatible with the general principles of discretionary administrative decision making, however the context was not sufficiently informative; the prisoners and even prison staff could not know what kind of circumstance would support a successful inter-prison visit request, and the inter-prison visiting regime as a whole, rather than r.63(8) itself, was thus unlawful. Opinion, that had P's claim been otherwise well founded, S's reasons for refusing them inter-prison visits would have been held to have been inadequate and unlawful where the reasons for refusal tended to be uninformative and inadequate and there appeared to have been non-compliance with the r.63(8) requirement for the governor or governors to inform both prisoners of the reasons for refusal. Observed, that the following four suggestions would assist in giving effect to the intendment of r.63(8): "entitlement" should not be confined to "family life" reasons, though "family life" reasons demanded to be the main subject of the guidelines; a "near relative" connection should be treated as a relevant factor but not by itself sufficient to constitute "exceptional circumstances"; visits should be authorised only where "family life" could not be adequately maintained by correspondence, telephone calls and video linking; and other factors of relevance might include the extent to which visits were likely to promote socially useful objectives such as rehabilitation and re-integration in the community and might also include the conduct of the prisoners concerned, disciplinary and security issues, and in the latter context, it could be useful to remind prisoners of governors' powers in terms of rr.77 and 78 to prohibit or terminate visits by particular individuals and to order visits to take place in closed facilities.

O'NEILL v SCOTTISH MINISTERS, [2015] CSOH 144, 2015 S.L.T. 820, Lord Stewart, OH.

2755 Prisoners' rights–Visitors–Two male co-offenders in same sex relationship seeking inter-prison visits–Concept of family life within art.8 ECHR

[European Convention on Human Rights 1950 art.8; Prisons and Young Offenders Institutions (Scotland) Rules 2011 (SSI 2011/331) r.63(8)]

Two male co-offenders (O and L, collectively P), serving life sentences in different prisons for murder and concurrent sentences for sex offences against young males, petitioned for judicial review of the refusal by the Scottish Prison Service (S) to arrange inter-prison visits for them on the ground that it was contrary to their rights under ECHR art.8 and sought damages. P averred that they had been in a same sex relationship since before they had been taken into custody in 2008 and were treated less favourably by S than heterosexual couples. P had been charged in 1998 with sexually abusing males aged from eight to 17 years between March 1993 and January 1998 and drug offences and had been imprisoned. L had been released in January 2002 and O in May 2003 and they had moved to Spain, in breach of their licences, where they had been arrested and returned to prison in mid-2004, having been charged with jointly sexually assaulting two young men in Spain. P had been released by November 2006 and returned to Spain before returning to the United Kingdom in November 2007, and following police surveillance, they were charged with sexually assaulting a 17 year old youth, arranging to meet a six year old boy with the intention of engaging in unlawful sexual activity with him and using lewd, indecent and libidinous practices against him, as well as possessing indecent images of children over the whole period from 2003 to 2008. In 2010, P had been convicted of the aforementioned murder and sex offences.

Held: Petition refused. (1) Family life could refer to two different but overlapping matters, namely the type of relationship and the quality of the relations between, or among, those concerned: there was no exhaustive definition of the relationships which attracted the protection and support of art.8 but it seemed to include, potentially, near relatives of the full blood and of the half blood, near relatives by fostering or adoption and near relatives by affinity namely partners and the near relatives of partners; as to the quality of relations, living under the same roof would be an indicator, unique or strong bonds of affection, confidence and financial, social and emotional dependence, or the potential for such bonds, on the understanding, which might be displaced in particular cases, that positive value was to be attributed to those relations from an individual and a societal point of view. (2) During the period from September 1997 to November 2014, P had been simultaneously at liberty for only approximately 32 months, which was a relevant factor, however, more weight would be given to the fact that in their relatively brief periods of simultaneous liberty by far the most powerful evidence of P's togetherness had been their complicity in sexual offending against young males. (3) P's entire lives had, for many years, been focused on finding victims to groom and sexually abuse, the quality of their life together was sufficiently evidenced by the offences of which they had been convicted; P's life together when at liberty since 1993 had been so negative that it could not be family life as that concept ought to be understood, and P's relationship and relations between each other did not engage, attract the support of, or merit the protection of, the art.8 family life provisions; alternatively, P had failed to demonstrate that they had a life together of a type and quality that engaged art.8. (4) On the evidence, including the information, or lack thereof, available to S at the time with regard to P's supposed relationship and S's stated non-discrimination policies, there was insufficient evidence to show a difference of treatment capable of shifting the burden of proof to S, moreover, with regard to domestic law, something more than a difference in status coupled with a difference in treatment was required to raise a *prima facie* case of discrimination in a situation like the present. (5) S could justifiably claim ignorance or uncertainty until at least late 2013 because of equivocation and non-co-operation on P's part as to whether they had a family life together prior to imprisonment. (6) S had not acted unlawfully towards P, in particular, S had not failed to respect their private and family life in terms of art.8 of the ECHR and had not discriminated against them, accordingly, they were not entitled to damages or just satisfaction. Opinion, that had P demonstrated, on the available material, family life within the meaning of art.8.1, limited weight would have attached thereto for the purpose of assessing the proportionality of restrictions imposed by the prisons regime in terms of art.8.2; the European Prison Rules (2006), r.24.4 presupposed a degree of normality in the family relationships which were to be maintained and developed. Observed, that with regard to the issue of whether the Prisons and Young Offenders Institutions (Scotland) Rules 2011 r.63(8) was *ultra vires* of the Scottish Ministers, raised by P in the joint petition, the rule was not in itself *ultra vires* but was, without explanatory context, not fully intelligible and potentially unlawful, and the matter would be dealt with in a supplementary opinion (*O'Neill v Scottish Ministers* [2015] CSOH 144, 2015 S.L.T. 820, [2016] 2754).

O'NEILL v SCOTTISH MINISTERS, [2015] CSOH 93, 2015 S.L.T. 811, Lord Stewart, OH.

2756 Prisons–Smoking–Detention of life prisoner in prison conditions involving exposure to environmental tobacco smoke–Reasonableness and lawfulness

[Prisons and Young Offenders Institutions (Scotland) Rules 2011 (SSI 2011/331) r.36]

A serving life prisoner (G) petitioned for judicial review seeking declarator that it was unreasonable and therefore unlawful for the Scottish Ministers (S) to detain him in conditions in which he was exposed to environmental tobacco smoke. The Prisons and Young Offenders Institutions (Scotland) Rules 2011 r.36 provided that prisoners might only smoke in: a cell or room in which a single prisoner was accommodated; a cell or room in which two or more prisoners were accommodated and had not been designated as a non-smoking one; the open air in a place specified in a direction by S. G gave evidence that the majority of prisoners in the prison (P) in which he was detained were smokers and when prisoners smoked in their cells the cell doors were often open, allowing the smoke to enter and collect in the communal areas of the hall and also G's cell, exposing him thereto. Evidence was led *inter alia* of S's policy documents in relation to smoking in prisons dating from 31 July 2003 to February 2010 by which S sought to minimise the effect of passive smoking, and a document from February 2014 which introduced United Kingdom government proposals to implement a smoking ban in prisons in England and Wales.

Held: Petition refused. (1) The appropriate approach by which to determine whether or not the exercise of S's powers to detain G under the conditions currently existing in P was unreasonable and therefore unlawful was to review it by reference to *Wednesbury* principles, applied without rigidity, *R. (on the application of Khatun) v Newham LBC* [2004] EWCA Civ 55, [2005] Q.B. 37, [2004] C.L.Y. 1907, *Pham v Secretary of State for the Home Department* [2015] UKSC 19, [2015] 1 W.L.R. 1591, [2015] C.L.Y. 1316, *Shahid v Scottish Ministers* [2015] UKSC 58, [2016] A.C. 429, [2015] C.L.Y. 1817 and *R. (on the application of King) v Secretary of State for Justice* [2015] UKSC 54, [2016] A.C. 384, [2015] C.L.Y. 1819, *considered.* (2) Taking into account the extent of the prison estate, the internal design of individual establishments, the requirement to maintain order and discipline, the benefit of proximity of a prison to a prisoner's home area, the particular category of the prisoner concerned, the particular requirements of long term prisoners and the extent of the facilities available to address their needs and the requirement to consider not just G's individual situation but that of all others held in custody within the prison service, the Scottish government had a stated policy designed to achieve the objective of a smoke free prison service as part of a change in culture in relation to smoking in Scottish society generally, which was apparent from the content of primary legislation, published policy documents and, specifically in relation to prisons in Scotland, from measures put in place in order to reduce the harmful impact of environmental tabacco smoke; the relevant authorities in Scotland were alive to the issue raised by G and were seeking proactively to address it, *Napier v Scottish Ministers* 2005 1 S.C. 229, [2004] C.L.Y. 4955, *distinguished*. (3) The manner of the development and ongoing implementation of government policy had necessarily been informed by the requirement to have regard to the relevant considerations involved in the proper management of prisoners; although there might be a number of means of executing the Scottish government's stated policy, all of varying efficacy, the benefit of a measured approach was consistent with the requirement to have regard to all material considerations; while it was clear that S were alive to G's concerns, the appropriate means of addressing them necessarily required consideration of the likely consequential greater impact on the entire prison service, and in particular the likely effect on the whole prison population and the management of the prison estate. (4) Having regard to the criteria of *Wednesbury* reasonableness, and allowing for the impact of the whole relevant context, the exercise of S's powers to detain G in the circumstances in which he found himself, although unfortunate and undesirable, was neither unreasonable and therefore unlawful nor was it being implemented on a basis which could be said to be otherwise irrational. Opinion, that had it been necessary to determine the legitimacy of S's decision by reference to the proportionality principle or alternatively, by reference to the requirement for cogent justification to be established, the same decision would have been reached.

GAGE v SCOTTISH MINISTERS, [2015] CSOH 174, 2016 S.L.T. 424, Lord Armstrong, OH.

2757 **Sex offenders–Notification requirements**

THE SEXUAL OFFENCES ACT 2003 (PRESCRIBED POLICE STATIONS) (SCOTLAND) AMENDMENT REGULATIONS 2016, SSI 2016/187; made under the Sexual Offences Act 2003 s.87(1)(a). In force: 1 July 2016.

These Regulations amend the Sexual Offences Act 2003 (Prescribed Police Stations) (Scotland) Regulations 2014 Sch.1.

PENSIONS

2758 **Occupational pensions–Firefighters–Remarriage or forming of civil partnership**

THE FIREMEN'S PENSION SCHEME (AMENDMENT) (SCOTLAND) ORDER 2016, SSI 2016/79; made under the Superannuation Act 1972 s.12 , s.16; Fire Services Act 1947 s.26(1)(2)(2A)(3)(4)(5). In force: 1 April 2016.

This Order amends the Firefighters' Pension Scheme, as set out in the Firemen's Pension Scheme Order 1992 Sch.2. It allows a person entitled to a pension under the 1992 Order and also to a pension under the Firefighters' Compensation Scheme (Scotland) Order 2006 to retain the former pension following remarriage or the forming of a civil partnership. Pensions which have been withdrawn due to existing legislation in this connection are reinstated with effect from 1 October 2015.

2759 **Occupational pensions–NHS**

THE NATIONAL HEALTH SERVICE PENSION SCHEME (SCOTLAND) AMENDMENT REGULATIONS 2016, SSI 2016/97; made under the Public Service Pensions Act 2013 s.1(1)(2)(e), Sch.2 para.5(b). In force: 1 April 2016.

These Regulations amend the National Health Service Pension Scheme (Scotland) Regulations 2015: they include provision inserting new employee contributions tables which reflect the NHS pay uplift from 1 April 2015.

2760 **Occupational pensions–Pension contributions–Superannuation**

THE TEACHERS' SUPERANNUATION AND PENSION SCHEME (SCOTLAND) AMENDMENT REGULATIONS 2016, SSI 2016/62; made under the Superannuation

Act 1972 s.9, s.12, Sch.3; Public Service Pensions Act 2013 s.1(1)(2)(d), Sch.2 para.4(b). In force: 1 April 2016.

These Regulations amend the Teachers' Superannuation (Scotland) Regulations 2005 and the Teachers' Pension Scheme (Scotland) (No.2) Regulations 2014. The majority of the provisions have retrospective effect from 1 April 2015. They amend the 2005 Regulations so that an employee pays contributions by reference to actual annual salary (rather than full-time equivalent annual salary).

PERSONAL INJURY

2761 Measure of damages–Ankle–Soft tissue ankle injury resolving after three months–Damages for personal services

A local authority councillor (H), aged 63 at proof, sought damages for a soft tissue ankle injury sustained when he fell in a supermarket owned by a retailer (R). Liability was admitted and the proof restricted to quantum. Following the accident, H had been housebound for 12 days, he had required to use a walking stick for one month, had been unable to drive, had had difficulty walking and standing and had been unable to attend to his duties as a councillor for approximately two weeks, although he had lost no remuneration. H's partner (P), who had been employed full time, had undertaken the household chores normally performed by H prior to the accident. A medical report prepared by a doctor (D) had indicated that H's symptoms had resolved within three months of the date of the accident.

Held: Decree for £3,018 granted. (1) The effects of injury were most serious at the outset and an arithmetical approach of dividing the top end figure to reflect the proportion the recovery period bore to one year was inappropriate and unreasonable, however, it was reasonable for H's injury to be assessed at a figure significantly less than the top end of the Judicial College Guidelines where the duration of the symptoms had been much shorter than the period envisaged there and the solatium awarded in *Upadhyaya v Hodgekiss*, 9 May 2014, Perth sheriff court, unreported, was not far from what would be reasonable in the present case; in all the circumstances, and having regard to the various authorities, a reasonable level of compensation for H's injury was £2,500, with interest thereon at the rate of 4% per annum from the date of the accident until the date of decree, and 8% per annum thereafter until payment. (2) It was inappropriate to assess P's services by reference to an estimate of the number of hours over which she was engaged multiplied by the minimum wage where P was in employment and had had to rearrange a number of aspects of her life over a period to assist H, the impact upon her was greater than the impact on the pursuer's husband in *Upadhyaya*, in which £350 had been awarded, and £500 was reasonable compensation for those services, with interest thereon at the rate of 4% from the date of the accident until decree, and 8% per annum thereafter until payment, *Upadhyaya, considered.* (3) Parties had agreed out of pocket expenses at £18 and interest would be awarded thereon at the rate of 8% per annum from the date of the accident until payment.

HEER v ASDA STORES LTD, 2016 Rep. L.R. 112, Sheriff A G D Thornton, Sh Ct (Tayside) (Kirkcaldy).

2762 Measure of damages–Pleural thickening–Approach to take at proof on quantum in full and final settlement of claim for bilateral calcified pleural plaques–Future risk of lung cancer and mesothelioma

[Administration of Justice Act 1982 (c.53) s.8]

A former boiler maker (H), aged 70, raised an action of damages against the Advocate General for Scotland, representing the Ministry of Defence (M), following his exposure to asbestos dust and fibres during his employment, and consequent development of bilateral calcified pleural plaques. Liability was admitted and the proof restricted to quantum. H sought £15,233 in full and final settlement of his claim. The agreed evidence was that he had an increased risk of developing pleural mesothelioma of 5% and a 0.2% risk of developing asbestos related lung cancer in the course of his lifetime. It was submitted that the correct approach was thus to look at the value of the claim if it were settled on the basis of an award of provisional damages and add a sum equal to 5.2% of the value of the claim were he to go on to develop pleural mesothelioma or asbestos related lung cancer: parties were agreed that if an award were made today in respect of either pleural mesothelioma or lung cancer, solatium would be valued at £66,000 thus an award of solatium in respect of future risks should be £3,432, representing 5.2% thereof; the range of award for solatium for the development of bilateral calcified pleural plaques was between £5,500 and £9,000, from which £7,500 was appropriate; for a 70 year old male, the mulitiplier for pecuniary loss for life was 17.32 which it would be appropriate to round down to 17, the midpoint of which was 8.5 years which was a term certain, the appropriate multiplier for which was 2.5%. M disputed the necessity of the two stage approach with reference to *Grieves v FT Everard & Sons Ltd* [2006] EWCA Civ 27, [2006] 4 All E.R. 1161, [2006] C.L.Y. 2877, and moved for decree in the sum of £8,996; further, the estimate of a seven year reduction in life expectancy was a gross overestimate.

Held: Case put out by order to agree final calculations. The appropriate approach was to take the approximate full value for each of the two conditions, namely mesothelioma and lung cancer, which the parties agreed would be £66,000 for solatium in respect of both conditions, and apply the appropriate percentage risk to the full value of each condition, namely 5.2%, which was not overly precise in the context of the use of the Ogden Tables: an appropriate award for provisional damages would have been £7,500 with interest at the rate of 4% per annum on half that sum from 8 January 2013 to the date of decree, to which 5.2% of £66,000 should be added; on the issue of financial loss, it was not suggested that there was any reduction in life expectancy and H was entitled to rest on the presumption of normal lifespan, taken as 17.32 rounded down to 17, and while this approach potentially overcompensated because it did not take account of accelerated receipt, the resulting calculation was itself discounted to 5.2% of the calculated sum of future risk; parties were agreed on the pension figures as well as services provided in terms of the Administration of Justice Act 1982 s.8 in respect of which H's calculations could be adopted, *W v Advocate General for Scotland* [2015] CSOH 111, 2015 S.L.T. 537, [2015] C.L.Y. 3255, *applied* and *Grieves, considered.*

HARRIS v ADVOCATE GENERAL FOR SCOTLAND, [2016] CSOH 49, 2016 S.L.T. 572, Lord Boyd of Duncansby, OH.

PLANNING

2763 **Compulsory purchase–Compensation–Planning permission in principle for caravan park–Valuation process**

A property and development business (C) made an application to the lands tribunal for determination of appropriate compensation in respect of the compulsory purchase, for the purpose of a bypass works scheme, of its area of land (D) and servitude right over another area (L) belonging to the Scottish Ministers (S), and determination of the value of another area of land (X) retained by S which, along with L, was subject to a claim by C for injurious affection. D comprised 1.77 acres, L 0.2 acres and X 13.45 acres, totalling 15.42 acres. L protruded into X and parts of the site were sloped. C was owned by G, who also owned a business which owned caravan parks, and prior to the scheme D was in agricultural use as a nursery associated with a garden centre owned by G's brother. After the scheme's completion D could no longer be efficiently used in association with the garden centre. A certificate of appropriate alternative development granted by the local authority permitted holiday accommodation on an area (Y) identified in an appendix, which included D and L. In C's proposal for a holiday park before the reporter, the southeast corner of Y consisting of 3.94 acres had been left as amenity open space due to visibility concerns and a 2.15 acre wooded area to the northeast had not been included. The reporter's view was that part of Y was suitable for holiday park development, and he noted that under the local planning policy, development itself would not be permitted within 70 metres of the existing carriageway.

It was agreed that the residual value of X in the with scheme world was £68,500 and that L had no residual value. C also claimed for the cost of remedying deficiencies in an agreed package of accommodation works, including the reinstatement and tarring of field tracks and construction of service ducts, with an alternative claim for diminution in land value. C submitted that the no scheme valuation for D, L and X was £200,000 per acre, resulting in a claim in excess of £3 million, on the basis that there would have been planning permission for a caravan park, including on X, and a strong market for such use, based on a total of 231 units with development costs of £950 per pitch, an annual pitch fee of £1,800 each, with profits per resale of caravans of £11,200. S submitted that the no scheme world total valuation of D, L and X was between £676,000 and £900,000, based on an average density of 13-15 caravans per acre, development costs of £8,750 per pitch, and profits per resale of caravans of £4,500, with only two resales per year.

Held: Determination made. (1) Planning permission in principle was available for the larger part of Y, and therefore X, subject only to the restriction on development within 70 metres of the carriageway, and although built development or caravan pitches would not have been permitted on the northeast and southeast corners, those areas would for the purposes of valuation have been given permission for amenity use associated with holiday park use; a prospective purchaser would not have reasonably expected detailed planning permission for the construction of lodges or caravan pitches within those areas but would have made the assumption of approval for amenity use in an offer. (2) Given the sensitivities of the site, the fact that it was sloping and therefore more difficult to develop, and the need to comply with relevant planning policies, a prospective purchaser would have been more likely to assume the lowest average density of approximately 13 pitches per acre which, with 9.33 developable acres for pitches, would have resulted in an assumption of about 120 single pitches. (3) There was no good comparable transaction evidence for the value of an undeveloped caravan park in Scotland, however there was merit in attempting a valuation which relied upon a fair maintainable operating profit and was sensitive to appropriate development costs and potential operating profits: S's estimate of development costs was more reliable as the costs were akin to those which a potential purchaser would have been advised and a better indicator of how the market would assess the costs; given market conditions and because the features and outlook of the site would not attract premium prices and the potential for resale of caravans would be affected by the quality of the park's settings, S's more conservative estimate of continuing income from caravan sales commissions would be taken. (4) A two step approach to valuation would be adopted: the first step valued the first two acres comprising D and L, assuming 26 pitches, management costs deducted from pitch fees, resale income deferred for four years and discounted to present value, resulting in a valuation of £270,000 or £10,400 per pitch; the second step assumed that the remaining 94 pitches would be developed in stages and let at a rate of 13 per annum, accounted for years' purchase and discounted to present value, and resulted in a valuation in the no scheme world of approximately £725,000, and since X was subject to an injurious affection claim, its agreed residual value of £68,500 had to be deducted, therefore, the sum to be awarded was £656,000. (5) C had to establish that the accommodation works had to be carried out in order reasonably to mitigate loss, or that the land had been devalued further by the absence of the works; there was no evidence which allowed quantification of such diminution in value, C did not give evidence that it intended to do the works itself as a practical necessity, it could not be inferred from the evidence that the works were reasonably required to mitigate losses, and there was no disturbance element capable of quantification.

CHRISTIE'S OF SCOTLAND LTD v SCOTTISH MINISTERS *sub nom.* CHRISTIES OF SCOTLAND LTD v SCOTTISH MINISTERS, [2016] R.V.R. 265, Lord Minginish, R A Smith, QC, A Oswald, FRICS, Lands Tr (Scot).

2764 Compulsory purchase–Compensation–Plot in development site acquired by local authority for Edinburgh tram project–Appropriate comparator developments

Property developers (B) made an application to the lands tribunal for determination of disputed compensation in respect of a plot (P), part of a development site (D). A preliminary evidential hearing was held to establish the appropriate comparator developments in the scheme world and in the no scheme world. The local authority (E) had acquired P under statutory powers for the Edinburgh tram project. On 27 March 2007, a general vesting declaration had been made, in terms of which P had vested in E on 24 April, which was the valuation date. B had acquired D in April 2006 with planning permission for two large office buildings, with one having a net floorspace of 37,500 square feet and 33 parking spaces, and with a ten metre strip reserved, which became P. In 2006, B secured a new planning consent for an increased office building on D of 46,826 square feet, retaining 33 parking spaces and avoiding development on P. B submitted that (1) the with scheme world land valuation ought to reflect an appraisal based upon the design under the 2006 consent, namely a four storey building of approximately 46,826 square feet and 33 parking spaces, and the appropriate comparator for the no scheme world ought to reflect a larger building with the majority of the parking placed upon P, namely a four storey building of approximately 66,805 square feet plus parking spaces, an option denied on account of the tram scheme; (2) alternatively, the appropriate comparators ought to be a building of 66,478 square feet with 36-37 parking spaces, failing which 64,418 square feet with 36-37 spaces. E submitted that (1) the with scheme world comparator ought to be a four storey building of 64,418 square feet plus 15 parking spaces and the appropriate comparator for the no scheme world was the same building but with 36-37 parking spaces, the majority of which made use of P; (2) a building of 66,805 square feet would have raised planning issues, however, in the scheme world, a building of 64,418 square feet with 15 parking spaces would have been likely to have been granted planning permission.

Held: Decision issued. (1) At the time when P had been taken by E, B had already been constructing their development being the subject of the 2006 permission, they had acquired D and had assessed their project on the understanding that P ought to be left for the tram project, there was no suggestion that they had thought about using P other than in the short term, or that they had been required to make new plans in the shadow period because the scheme had gone ahead, equally, had there been no tram scheme and had P become available, B would have reappraised D with a view to adding value and would have proceeded accordingly. (2) In the scheme world, E's comparator would have been a riskier proposition, it might have taken longer to fully let with less parking and would most likely have been less attractive to the market in competition with alternatives, B's project was supported by firm evidence of viability, in that it was self evident, and taking E's position at its highest, there was insufficient evidence that a project with limited parking would have been likely to have been at least as successful as that actually built on D, accordingly, all that remained tending to objective market value was the comparator of the as built development, thus that was the appropriate comparator in the scheme world. (3) In the no scheme world, there was a baseline whereby the appropriate comparator was of not less than a building of 46,418 square feet with 36-37 parking spaces, and it could be concluded from the evidence that the planning authority would have had issues with any proposed larger building, in particular in relation to significant issues of privacy, shadowing and daylighting. (4) The appropriate comparator development for the scheme world was the as built project, namely a building of approximately 46,826 square feet and 33 car parking spaces and that for the no scheme world was a building of 64,418 square feet with 36-37 parking spaces.

BAM PROPERTIES LTD v CITY OF EDINBURGH COUNCIL *sub nom.* BAM PROPERTIES LTD v EDINBURGH CITY COUNCIL, 2015 S.L.T. (Lands Tr) 207, R A Smith, QC, A Oswald, FRICS, Lands Tr (Scot).

2765 Planning permission–Fish farms–Development of 10-cage rainbow trout farm

[Town and Country Planning (Marine Fish Farms Permitted Development) (Scotland) Order 2011 (SSI 2011/144) art.3; Town and Country Planning (Scotland) Act 1997 (c.8) s.26(1), s.26(6), s.75; Town and Country Planning (General Permitted Development) (Fish Farming) (Scotland) Amendment Order 2012 (SSI 2012/131)]

A charitable organisation (F) sought judicial review of a decision of the local planning authority (B) granting a company (D) planning permission for the development of a 10 cage rainbow trout farm on a loch (L). D already operated five farms on the loch under planning permission granted by the Town and Country Planning (Marine Fish Farms Permitted Development) (Scotland) Order 2011 art.3. The deemed planning permission under the 2011 Order was granted when the placing of such fish farm equipment began to constitute development in terms of the Town and Country Planning (Scotland) Act 1997 s.26(1), for which planning permission required to be sought. In seeking planning permission for the development of a sixth site, D had agreed under s.75 of the 1997 Act to permanent removal of its fish farm equipment from the first site, and the removal of the fish farm equipment from the fifth site. B's planning, protective services and licensing committee considered that that achieved the necessary degree of consolidation and rationalisation of farming activity on the loch to ensure compliance with the development plan and other material considerations. F submitted that (1) permanent planning permission existed for the development of fish farms at sites one and five, thus the removal of the equipment therefrom would not achieve rationalisation as the equipment could be replaced under the 2011 Order or the Town and Country Planning (General Permitted Development) (Fish Farming) (Scotland) Amendment Order 2012; (2) the s.75 agreement was not habile to achieve the permanent removal of sites one and five as it was personal to D and did not prevent future leases over the sites being granted; (3) the decision was unlawful, *ultra vires* and unreasonable because (i) to achieve B's objectives in granting permission for site six, any future application for permission to establish a fish farm at sites one and five would have to be refused and B was not permitted to bind itself that way; (ii) the s.75 agreement purported unilaterally to take away valuable rights of third parties in sites one and five and B had no power to do so without compensation; (4) the s.75 agreement sought to use a condition in the agreement to restrain the transfer of controlled activities regulations licences granted in respect of sites one and five, which was not a proper planning function.

Held: Petition dismissed. (1) Once D complied with the s.75 agreement, no fish farm equipment would exist at sites one and five and that would bring the deemed permission under the 2011 and 2012 Orders to an end; any future placing or assembly of equipment at those sites would constitute development under s.26(6) of the 1997 Act requiring the grant of planning permission, *Schwerzerhof v Wilkins* [1898] 1 Q.B. 640, *distinguished.* (2) Without planning permission, no lease over sites one and five would empower a leaseholder to place fish farming equipment at the sites. (3) Could a fish farm be said to exist after removal of all the equipment in place, another operator would not be permitted, under the 2012 Order, to replace the anchors and chains which secured the fish pens or barges to the sea bed where the 2012 Order was limited in its scope as to what items could be replaced, and the placing of anchors and chains would constitute development under s.26(6). (4) B had merely required the removal of the existing equipment belonging to D, and its decision did not have the effect that no permission could ever be granted for fish farms on the sites. (5) The local plan policy provided support for the consolidation and reorganisation of existing sites. (6) The clause in the agreement relating to controlled activities regulations licences could not be relied upon but its unenforceability did not affect the remainder of the agreement. (7) Could the lapse of planning permission in respect of the relevant sites be said to have adverse consequences on third parties, that did not render the grant of planning permission for another site or the operative terms of any s.75 agreement open to review in the present court; that consequence flowed from a proper exercise of the discretionary powers of the planning authority under the planning regime.

FRIENDS OF LOCH ETIVE v ARGYLL AND BUTE COUNCIL, [2015] CSOH 61, 2016 S.C.L.R. 52, Lord Burns, OH.

2766 Planning permission–Local planning authorities–Permission for erection of new secondary school on green belt land–Local authority acting as both education and planning authority

An environmental organisation (S) reclaimed against the decision of the Lord Ordinary dismissing its petition for judicial review of a decision by a local authority (L) granting planning permission for the erection of a new secondary school on green belt land (X) (*St Andrews Environmental Protection Association Ltd, Petitioner* [2015] CSOH 27, 2015 S.C.L.R. 535, [2015] C.L.Y. 3269). L's planning officer had considered a split site (Z) for the school but found that it was too small for future development and the requirement for a single site had rendered it unsuitable. L, as education authority, applied for planning permission to build the school on X. The local planning committee recommended that the application be refused as there was insufficient evidence that no other site was available, the proposal was contrary to local plan policies and no material considerations justified setting them aside. L's full council granted planning permission, and although it noted that the proposed development was contrary to the development plan, significant weight was placed on the need for the school and the lack of an alternative site, and only X was suitable. The Lord Ordinary held *inter alia* that L, as planning authority, had not overlooked Z, the planning officer's report showed that Z had not been ruled out only on the basis that it was a split site, and the weight attached to the disadvantage of Z being split and too small for future development were for L's judgment as planning authority.

Held: Reclaiming motion allowed. (1) A judgment had to be made by the planning authority and could not be delegated to the applicant, even where the applicant was L itself as education authority, and L, as planning authority, had to apply its own mind to the question of alternative sites and had to do so having regard to planning considerations, the question was not whether Z met L's requirements as education authority but whether its existence meant that a proposal in the green belt contrary to the development plan ought to have been refused. If the split site issue could have been addressed by a bridge or underpass, L had to assess whether it was proper to rule out Z on the grounds that it was not a single site and whether that rendered it unsuitable in the sense intended by national planning policy; "unsuitable" had to be construed as a site which could not reasonably be expected to be developed for the new school and did not mean inconsistent with L's wishes, and when judging whether other possible locations should have resulted in refusal of a proposal contrary to the development plan, the developer's criteria could not be given the decisive weight plainly afforded to them in the planning report and by L as planning authority. (2) L had adopted an erroneous approach in that it had been diverted from the planning judgment it had to carry out, the full council had effectively been told that it should ignore the issue of whether the green belt could be protected by using an alternative site because L had already considered the matter and its decision was determinative, thus the councillors were put in the position that if they wanted the new school that had to sanction development at X. The planning report had led L into a failure to discharge its duty, and it followed that the Lord Ordinary's decision would be quashed as unlawful and the whole matter remitted for reconsideration, *R. (on the application of Langley Park School for Girls Governors) v Bromley LBC* [2009] EWCA Civ 734, [2010] 1 P. & C.R. 10, [2010] C.L.Y. 2611 and *Tesco Stores Ltd v Dundee City Council* [2012] UKSC 13, [2012] P.T.S.R. 983, [2012] C.L.Y. 2595, *considered. Observed*, that when a local authority was both applicant and planning authority, it was not always easy for planning officers, councillors and others to safeguard its planning jurisdiction from its interest in the proposed development, and although the court was not suggesting that any conscious decision was taken to give priority to L's decision as education authority to build at X, the importance of constant vigilance against the obvious risks inherent in a local authority adjudicating upon its own application had to be emphasised.

ST ANDREWS ENVIRONMENTAL PROTECTION ASSOCIATION LTD, PETITIONER *sub nom.* ST ANDREW'S ENVIRONMENTAL PROTECTION ASSOCIATION LTD v FIFE COUNCIL, [2016] CSIH 22, 2016 S.L.T. 979, Lord Drummond Young, Lady Clark of Calton, Lord Malcolm, IH (Ex Div).

POLICE

2767 **Criminal Justice (Scotland) Act 2016 (asp 1)**

An Act of the Scottish Parliament to make provision about criminal justice including as to police powers and rights of suspects and as to criminal evidence, procedure and sentencing; to establish the Police Negotiating Board for Scotland; and for connected purposes.

2768 Criminal Justice (Scotland) Act 2016 (asp 1)–Commencement No.2 Order

THE CRIMINAL JUSTICE (SCOTLAND) ACT 2016 (COMMENCEMENT NO.2) ORDER 2016, SSI 2016/199; made under the Criminal Justice (Scotland) Act 2016 117(2). Commencement details: bringing into operation various provisions of the 2016 Act on 1 July 2016.

This Order brings into force the Criminal Justice (Scotland) Act 2016 s.112 on 1 July 2016. Section 112 inserts a definition of staff officer of the Police Investigations and Review Commissioner into the Police Act 1997 s.108, making it clear that all staff of the Commissioner who conduct investigations may be authorised to interfere with property under Pt 3 of the 1997 Act.

PRESCRIPTION

2769 Personal injury claims–Limitations–Former resident of children's care home–Whether equitable to allow action to proceed

[Prescription and Limitation (Scotland) Act 1973 (c.52) s.19A]

An action by a former resident (F) of a care home (H) against its operators (Q) in respect of injuries allegedly sustained by him between 1965 and 1971 while resident at H came before the Lord Ordinary for a preliminary proof on whether it was equitable in terms of the Prescription and Limitation (Scotland) Act 1973 s.19A to allow F to bring the action. F gave evidence that he had been physically, mentally and emotionally abused by the house parent (D) while he was resident in a particular house in H resulting in long term psychological damage. F claimed that on leaving H in 1971, aged 13, he had ceased to have any memories of the abuse as a result of dissociative amnesia until 2003 when he had watched a television programme about Q which had prompted him to obtain his records therefrom, and on reading them, the memories of the abuse had returned to him. F's action was signetted on 17 December 2004 against Q.

Held: Action dismissed. The equitable factors in favour of the exercise of the court's discretion in F's favour were far outweighed by the significant prejudice to Q were the action to proceed as Q could not be given a fair trial: D had died in January 1980, thus Q were denied the evidence of what would have been their most important witness and they would not be able to properly defend themselves, it was also clear that it would be extremely difficult to find other witnesses who had been present in the house with F at the material time, as well as it being inappropriate for Q to make unsolicited approaches to such persons, moreover, other staff members working in other parts of H would not be in a position to give any real insight into what might have happened at the material time; the events which were the subject of the action dated from more than 40 years ago and ended 33 years before the action was raised, there would be entire loss of evidence and a decline in the quality of the available evidence and the delay in bringing the action caused further prejudice; Q's position had been significantly prejudiced by the change in the law effected by *Lister v Hesley Hall Ltd* [2001] UKHL 22, [2002] 1 A.C. 215, [2001] C.L.Y. 5359; and the litigation would be costly for Q and as F was legally aided, any award in their favour would not be recoverable, *B v Murray (No.2)* [2008] UKHL 32, 2008 S.C. (H.L.) 146, [2008] C.L.Y. 4585, *followed* and *Lister*, *considered*. Opinion, that had the action proceeded, the objective evidence showed that F had had had some memory of certain of the events at H prior to 2003, which was inconsistent with his suffering from dissociative amnesia until that date, his position that he specifically remembered the point at which he had forgotten the abuse made no sense, could not possibly be correct and fundamentally undermined the acceptability of his evidence, moreover, his evidence was unreliable and contradictory, and where the medical records showed that he had a pre-existing history of mental health difficulties, there was a clear alternative explanation for his breakdown in 2003; it could not be concluded that F suffered from dissociative amnesia until 2003 and that as a result the proceedings had been delayed until December 2004.

F v QUARRIERS *sub nom.* SF v QUARRIERS, [2015] CSOH 82, 2016 S.C.L.R. 111, Lord Bannatyne, OH.

PUBLIC PROCUREMENT

2770 **EU law–Concession agreements–Contract award procedures**

THE CONCESSION CONTRACTS (SCOTLAND) REGULATIONS 2016, SSI 2016/65; made under the European Communities Act 1972 s.2(2), Sch.2 para.1A. In force: In accordance with reg.1.

These Regulations implement, for Scotland, Directive 2014/23/EU of the European Parliament and Council of 26 February 2014 on the award of concession contracts. They impose obligations and specify procedures in respect of the award of a concession contract by contracting entities, which term normally includes contracting authorities and utilities.

2771 **Public contracts–Declarations of ineffectiveness–Contract awarded to company not party to framework agreement**

[Public Contracts (Scotland) Regulations 2012 (SSI 2012/88) reg.19(3), reg.49]

A street lighting provider (L) raised an action against a local authority (C) seeking an ineffectiveness order under the Public Contracts (Scotland) Regulations 2012 reg.49(5) in respect of C's decision to award a contract for street lighting services to another company (X), part of a group of companies (Y), on the ground that the award was unlawful where X had not been a party to the framework agreement. In 2013, C had awarded a contract for street lighting services to X, following a competition held in terms of a framework agreement. L and X had not been listed as potential suppliers and had been unable to participate in the competition, however, another member of Y (Z) had been listed as a potential supplier. In 2015, C had held a second mini competition under the framework agreement and had thereafter awarded the contract to X. L submitted *inter alia* that the award of the contract to X in 2015 had been an unlawful direct award made without advertisement or prior intimation and had breached reg.19(3) of the 2012 Regulations. C accepted that the award of the contract to X had been an error, however, submitted *inter alia* that Z had been a party to the framework agreement and had been entitled to be awarded the contract, and where the same offer would have been made to Z as had been erroneously made to X, the error was capable of rectification by novation by X to Z.

Held: Ineffectiveness order granted. (1) The principle of proportionality was not applicable to the circumstances of the present case where that principle was concerned with the imposition of onerous conditions or requirements by a public authority, which encompassed a contracting authority conducting a procurement exercise and it could not be turned around and relied upon by a contracting authority which had failed to act within its statutory powers. (2) C's error was not one of misdesignation but had consisted of proceeding on the mistaken basis that X was a company within Y, which was a party to the framework agreement, the entity selected as the supplier was not a matter of indifference or irrelevance and it was readily apparent that C had intended to award the contract to Z; in those circumstances, there was no issue raised by C which could be resolved only at proof, C had no defence to L's challenge based on reg.19(3) and the test in *Henderson v 3052775 Nova Scotia Ltd* [2006] UKHL 21, 2006 S.C. (H.L.) 85, [2006] C.L.Y. 5134 had been met, *Henderson, applied*.

LIGHTWAYS (CONTRACTORS) LTD v INVERCLYDE COUNCIL, [2015] CSOH 169, 2016 S.L.T. 177, Lord Tyre, OH.

2772 **Public procurement–Dynamic purchasing systems–General duties and specific duties**

THE PROCUREMENT (SCOTLAND) REGULATIONS 2016, SSI 2016/145; made under the Procurement Reform (Scotland) Act 2014 s.5(2), s.7(1), s.12(3), s.14(1), 23(3), s.27, s.28, s.30, s.44(1). In force: 18 April 2016.

These Regulations make further provision about regulated contracts, dynamic purchasing systems, general duties and specific duties under the Procurement Reform (Scotland) Act 2014.

2773 **Public procurement procedures–Public contracts–Scottish Ministers procuring de-icing salt without publishing either contract notice or contract award notice–Basis for interfering with Lord Ordinary's findings**

[Public Contracts (Scotland) Regulations 2006 (SSI 2006/1) reg.14(1)(a)(iv); Directive 2004/18 on the coordination of procedures for the award of public works contracts, public supply contracts and public service contracts 2004; Directive 89/665 on the application of review procedures to the award of public supply and public works contracts 1989]

A salt supplier (S) reclaimed against a decision of Lord Ordinary assoilzieing the Scottish Ministers (M) in S's action alleging a breach by M of the Public Contracts (Scotland) Regulations 2006 by procuring de-icing salt without publishing either a contract notice or a contract award notice in relation to two winters of severe weather of 2009-2010 and 2010-2011 (winters 1 and 2), seeking declarator that contracts awarded to six different companies breached the 2006 Regulations, and damages. M cross appealed against the Lord Ordinary's finding that the extreme urgency in winter 2 had been created by them. M admitted that the failure to publish a contract award notice had been a breach of the regulations but maintained that it had been justified because of the extreme urgency of the situation. The Lord Ordinary found that the situation in winter 1 had been one of extreme urgency, brought about by unexpected and unforeseeable climate conditions, the lack of salt had not been attributable to M, and the use of the negotiated procedure had been strictly necessary but in relation to winter 2, although the situation had also been one of extreme urgency caused by unforeseen events, those had been brought about by M who had been aware that the salt supply arrangements had been fragile and ought to have acted sooner and arranged matters in a manner such as to be able to hold a tender exercise if necessary. In relation to damages, he found that S would not have made a bid in any tendering process in winters 1 and 2 and had it done so, any tender would have been unsuccessful, and as there was no evidence upon which to conclude that S would have tendered at a particular price, there was no basis for calculating any loss of profit, and any loss of a chance had not been established given that S would not have tendered at all. S submitted that (1) its case had to be decided consistently with the relevant principles of EU law and the jurisprudence of the European Court of Justice; reg.14(1)(a)(iv) of the 2006 Regulations had to be interpreted strictly, if one of the conditions for its application were not satisfied, the contracting authority could not derogate, and the evidence did not support any finding that the derogation had been made out for winter 1; (2) S had a right, as a matter of EU law, to an effective judicial remedy; S's only available remedy was one of damages, and the Lord Ordinary had given no explanation for his refusal to grant declarator; (3) a breach of the rules *per se*, without establishing fault, was sufficient to found a right to damages, S required only to prove that it had had a quantifiable chance of winning the contract and its losses should be assessed on the assumption that it would have won the contract, and then discounted by applying the probability/percentage chance of having done so, moreover, the Lord Ordinary had misdirected himself in holding that S had failed to prove loss in the absence of evidence of the price at which it would have tendered; (4) a significant breach of the regulations ought to be recognised in expenses; the litigation had been brought in the public interest, as well as in S's private commercial interests and the established breach was neither minor nor technical, nor had it been an isolated incident.

Held: Reclaiming motion and cross appeal refused. (1) S's attempts to divert attention away from the 2006 Regulations and onto the EU Directives were misconceived, it was not suggested that the regulations failed to implement the EU Directives fully or correctly, thus there was no scope for giving any underlying directive direct effect, especially where that would involve circumventing the plain terms of the implementing legislation, accordingly, the court would not attempt to decide the case under reference to the terms of Directive 2004/18 or Directive 89/665 but in terms of the 2006 Regulations. (2) The Lord Ordinary had heard the evidence and it had been for him to make appropriate findings in fact based thereupon; he had adequately, and succinctly explained the rationale for his findings based on the evidence, S's submissions to the contrary amounted simply to a disagreement therewith, and there was no basis, applying the proper test for the review of fact, to interfere with his findings. (3) S was a private limited company, its existence was purely commercial, it could not reasonably be maintained that it was seeking to vindicate a public right, a bare declarator, were it competent, would not provide it with an effective remedy, the effective, and only competent, remedy available under the 2006 Regulations, where contracts had already been entered into, was one of damages. (4) In terms of reg.47(5), a breach of duty owed under the 2006 Regulations was actionable only where the economic operator suffered loss or damage and it was for the operator to bring himself within the provision; the only evidence to support S's position had come from its commercial director, whom the Lord Ordinary had regarded as incredible and unreliable, which had effectively ended S's case on damages in its entirety, the Lord Ordinary's finding that S would not have tendered in relation to either winter 1 or 2 was adequately explained and justified, as was his conclusion that S would have failed in any bid, and there was no scope for any revaluation of the evidence. (5) Expenses generally fell upon the party who had caused the litigation, S had failed in its action, and there was no basis for interfering with the Lord Ordinary's decision.

SALT INTERNATIONAL LTD v SCOTTISH MINISTERS, [2015] CSIH 85, 2016 S.L.T. 82, The Lord Justice Clerk (Carloway), Lady Paton, Lord Menzies, IH (2 Div).

REAL PROPERTY

2774 Land Reform (Scotland) Act 2016 (asp 18)–Commencement No.1 and Transitional Provision Regulations

THE LAND REFORM (SCOTLAND) ACT 2016 (COMMENCEMENT NO.1 AND TRANSITIONAL PROVISION) REGULATIONS 2016, SSI 2016/193; made under the Land Reform (Scotland) Act 2016 s.130(2)(3)(4). Commencement details: bringing into operation various provisions of the 2016 Act on 28 June 2016.

These Regulations make provision in relation to bringing into force particular sections of the Land Reform (Scotland) Act 2016.

ROAD TRAFFIC

2775 Disabled persons' badges–Badges for motor vehicles

THE DISABLED PERSONS (BADGES FOR MOTOR VEHICLES) (SCOTLAND) AMENDMENT REGULATIONS 2016, SSI 2016/72; made under the Chronically Sick and Disabled Persons Act 1970 s.21. In force: 1 April 2016.

These Regulations amend the Disabled Persons (Badges for Motor Vehicles) (Scotland) Regulations 2000. Those Regulations deal with what is known as the "blue badge" scheme.

SENTENCING

2776 Assault–Custodial sentences–Assault of three year old child in public–Non-custodial alternative

W, who pleaded guilty to assaulting his three year old child, in public, appealed against the imposition of five months' imprisonment.

Held: Appeal allowed, sentence of five months' imprisonment quashed and two year community payback order substituted. Balancing the fact that the present was a deeply unpleasant assault on a three year old child, which breached W's position of trust as a parent, his apparent indifference to C's predicament in the aftermath and the suggestion in the background report that W had, to some degree, minimised his actions and was reluctant to accept responsibility, against the fact that he was 26, had no previous convictions and no outstanding cases, was married with two dependent children and that C had suffered no injury, it was clear that an alternative to custody was available and the court was bound to take account of the fact that W had served the equivalent of a two month sentence, therefore, the sentence imposed would be quashed and a two year community payback order, subject to supervision and containing an element of 100 hours' unpaid work, substituted.

W v HARVIE, [2016] SAC (Crim) 11, 2016 S.C.L. 671, Sheriff Principal M M Stephen, QC, Sheriff M G O'Grady, QC, SAC.

2777 Assault–Custodial sentences–First-time offender of good character–Non-custodial alternative

[Criminal Procedure (Scotland) Act 1995 (c.46) s.204]

G, convicted of brandishing a knife and punching a 17 year old, appealed against the imposition of a custodial sentence.

Held: Appeal allowed. Certain mitigating circumstances ought to have been given greater weight; at the time of sentencing, G had never before served a prison sentence, he had served in the Royal Navy for 20 years, holding a number of responsible positions, from which he had received a positive character reference, which would be given considerable weight, and G qualified for the protection afforded by the Criminal Procedure (Scotland) Act 1995 s.204; viewing the whole circumstances, including G's pro-social work and family orientated life, that he had the support of his family and that he would be likely to co-operate with any community disposal, an non-custodial alternative was available, despite the gravity of the offences, which ought to have been selected, and taking into account that G had spent some time in custody and that he would be willing to participate in community based work, the custodial sentence would be quashed, and a one year community payback order, with the conditions of unpaid work of 100 hours to be completed within a year and an undertaking to participate in such anger management or dispute resolution programme as ordered by G's supervising officer, would be substituted.

GOLDIE (SCOTT) v HM ADVOCATE, [2016] HCJAC 69, 2016 S.C.L. 796, Lady Paton, Lady Clark of Calton, HCJ Appeal.

2778 Assault to severe injury–Babies–Offender shaking and throwing baby on to sofa–Comparative justice

D, who pleaded guilty to assaulting his six week old daughter (X) by seizing hold of her, shaking her and throwing her against a surface, all to her severe injury, permanent impairment and to the danger of her life, appealed as excessive a custodial sentence of seven and a half years, discounted from nine due to his guilty plea. The sentencing judge had recognised in mitigation that there had been no history of abuse or neglect on D's part and no history of violence. D had shaken X and had thrown her down onto a couch, it had been a momentary loss of control and a one off event, D had not intended to cause serious harm and there had been no wickedness in his actions, however, it had been a deliberate and violent assault using a degree of force which was likely to cause serious harm to X and which had very significantly reduced the quality, and probably the length, of X's life. D submitted that (1) the sentencing judge's characterisation of what he had done as being likely to cause serious harm was inaccurate and that it would not have been apparent to a layman that such serious harm would be caused by the degree of force used; (2) the current case was indistinguishable from that of *S v HM Advocate* [2015] HCJAC 63, 2015 S.L.T. 531, [2015] C.L.Y. 3294 where the Appeal Court had selected seven years' imprisonment as appropriate prior to allowing a discount in respect of the guilty plea.

Held: Appeal allowed, sentence of seven and a half years quashed and six years and nine months substituted. (1) The consequences of the assault had been unintended, however, it could not be said that the risk of some degree of serious harm to a young baby consequent upon a single incident of shaking was not such as to be obvious to a layman. (2) The sentencing judge had been correct to approach the case as one involving a significant degree of culpability as well as a catastrophic result and had been entitled to take the view that only a significant custodial sentence was appropriate, however, she had not been addressed on comparative justice and *HM Advocate v IWKM* 2003 S.C.C.R. 499 and *RB v HM Advocate* 2004 S.C.C.R. 443, [2005] C.L.Y. 5650, and had passed sentence prior to *S*, and a starting point of nine years was inconsistent with what had been held to be appropriate in those cases. (3) There were parallels to be drawn with *S*, however, the current case was more serious where the evidence pointed to an act of real aggression on D's part and that had to be reflected in the sentence imposed, *IWKM*, *RB* and *S*, *considered*. (4) The substitute sentence would be calculated by taking a starting point of eight years and discounting it by a similar percentage to that adopted by the sentencing judge.

D v HM ADVOCATE, [2015] HCJAC 83, 2015 S.L.T. 808, Lord Brodie, Lord Drummond Young, HCJ.

2779 Assault to severe injury–Guilty pleas–10% discount–Value of plea

[Criminal Procedure (Scotland) Act 1995 (c.46) s.196(1)]

F, who along with a co-accused (C), pleaded guilty to assaulting S by repeatedly punching and kicking him on the head and body, appealed against the imposition of a sentence of 30 months' imprisonment, discounted by 10% on account of his plea in terms of the Criminal Procedure (Scotland) Act 1995 s.196(1). F, C and S had been part of a group of young people who had been drinking in a park, when S had fallen into C. F and C had chased S and after he had fallen to the ground, C had repeatedly punched and kicked him and F had approached S and kicked him on the head. On 9 November 2015, F's plea of guilty to assault by a single kick to S's head had been rejected, and on 17 November, his plea of guilty to assault by a single kick to S's head had also been rejected. At trial on 8 December, pleas of not guilty had been accepted from two other co-accused. F submitted that (1) the decision to restrict the discount to his sentence to 10% had been a miscarriage of justice; he had acknowledged his actions and a 10% discount for early acknowledgment of his actions had fallen short of the appropriate recognition for the utilitarian value of the plea; (2) an accused was not required to tender a detailed explanation for the basis of the plea being offered, to require him to determine whether there was a sufficient common purpose to justify his pleadings to a greater degree of the libel would be to set the bar too high.

Held: Appeal refused. (1) F had been in no different a position to an individual who delayed his plea until the position of the co-accused had been determined; the correlation between the plea originally offered and that tendered had been limited, it had not been obvious that F had not intended to proceed to trial, and in the absence of explanation for its terms, the pleas tendered would have been equally consistent with an intention to proceed to trial seeking to restrict his responsibility to that of actor. (2) F knew what he had done, and had known the actions he had participated in and even had he been in doubt thereof, he had received full disclosure of the Crown case and therefore had been able to identify that there had been sufficient common purpose to justify his pleading guilty to actions in which he was art and part. (3) The sheriff had given cogent reasons for restricting the discount and it was clear that F's plea had had very little utilitarian value, *Gemmell (James Kelly) v HM Advocate* [2011] HCJAC 129, 2012 J.C. 223, [2012] C.L.Y. 4277, *considered*.

FINDLAY (ERNEST) v HM ADVOCATE, [2016] HCJAC 59, 2016 S.C.L. 731, The Lord Justice Clerk (Lady Dorrian), Lord Bracadale, Lady Clark of Calton, HCJ.

2780 Causing death by dangerous driving–Sentence length–Aggravating factors

M, convicted of causing death by dangerous driving, contrary to the Road Traffic Act 1988 s.1, appealed as excessive his sentence of six years' imprisonment and disqualification from driving for eight years and until he passed the extended test of competence to drive. M submitted that he had not been speeding or driving whilst under the influence of drink or drugs, he had no analogous previous convictions and there were no aggravating factors; the sentencing judge had erred in categorising the offence as falling into the second level of seriousness in the English sentencing guidelines and it ought properly to have been categorised as falling within level 3.

Held: Appeal refused. (1) There had been some aggravating factors as those were identified in the guidelines including serious injury to one or more victims in addition to the death and disregard for warnings. (2) The trial judge had had the benefit of having heard all of the evidence and had been in a better position to assess the appropriate sentence having heard all of the evidence.

MILLIGAN (IAN) v HM ADVOCATE, [2015] HCJAC 84, 2015 S.C.L. 984, Lord Menzies, Lady Dorrian, HCJ.

2781 Causing death by dangerous driving–Undue leniency–Driver's blood alcohol content only aggravating factor

[Road Traffic Act 1988 (c.52) s.1; Criminal Procedure (Scotland) Act 1995 (c.46) s.76]

The Crown appealed as unduly lenient a sentence of four years' imprisonment, discounted from six years, imposed on M, who pleaded guilty to causing death by dangerous driving, contrary to the Road Traffic Act 1988 s.1. M had caused the death of another motorist (X) and seriously injured X's passenger (T) when he crossed the centre line of the road into the path of X's car, colliding therewith. A specimen of blood obtained from M six hours thereafter had revealed an alcohol count of 226 milligrams of alcohol per 100 millilitres of blood. The sentencing judge had had regard to the causing of death by driving guideline, issued by the Sentencing Guidelines Council in England in July 2008, had assessed M's driving as having created a substantial risk of danger, had taken into account M's intoxication and his awareness thereof, his previous convictions and the severe injuries suffered by T.

Held: Appeal refused. (1) The level of alcohol in M's blood had been high, however, there had been no indication of excessive speed or of M having embarked on a dangerous manoeuvre such as inappropriate overtaking or of gross impairment, which, taken along with the level of alcohol, would have placed the offence within level 1 of the guideline and indicated a significantly higher headline sentence; having regard to the absence of driving of that nature and the concession by the advocate depute that the sentencing judge had taken all relevant circumstances into account and had appropriately selected level 2 of the guideline as applicable, the sentencing judge's selection of a headline sentence of six years' imprisonment could not be said to have been outwith the range of disposals open to him. (2) The level of discount to be allowed in respect of the plea in the present case was primarily a matter for the discretion of the sentencing judge; having regard to the explanation of the history of the procedure under the Criminal Procedure (Scotland) Act 1995 s.76, it could not be said that the sentencing judge had erred in selecting the level of discount which he had, even were it open to criticism as being generous in light of the delay between M's appearance on petition and his tendering of a letter at the sentencing diet expressing his remorse, it could not be said that that had resulted in an unduly lenient sentence. *Observed*, that while it was appropriate in cases involving charges of causing death by dangerous driving or careless driving for sentencers in Scotland to have regard to the causing of death by driving guideline, too rigid or mechanistic an adherence to the guidelines was to be avoided, and sentencers ought to also have regard to existing Scottish precedent *Geddes (Murray Albert) v HM Advocate* [2015] HCJAC 43, 2015 S.L.T. 415, [2015] C.L.Y. 3295 and *Neill (James) v HM Advocate* [2014] HCJAC 67, 2014 G.W.D. 24-466, *considered*.

HM ADVOCATE v MCKEEVER (RUSSELL), [2016] HCJAC 43, 2016 S.C.L. 564, Lady Smith, Lady Dorrian, Lord Bracadale, HCJ.

2782 Communications offences–Notification requirements–Grossly offensive remarks made on social media about death of child and sexual remarks about children–Whether significant sexual element to offence

[Communications Act 2003 (c.21) s.127(1)(a); Sexual Offences Act 2003 (c.42) Sch.3 para.60]

R, who pleaded guilty to a contravention of the Communications Act 2003 s.127(1)(a) by sending messages on social media which were grossly offensive or of an indecent or obscene or menacing character in that they did contain grossly offensive remarks about the death of a child and sexual remarks about children, appealed against sentence. Despite submissions from R and the Crown that the requirements of the Sexual Offences Act 2003 para.60 had not been met, the sheriff found that there was a significant sexual aspect to R's behaviour, any reasonable person seeing the comments and postings between R and his co-accused would have observed that they were wholly associated with sexual abuse of children, making light thereof and turning it into a series of sick jokes, and the essence of the communications was sexual in nature and there was a sexual aspect to R's behaviour. The sheriff considered that the sharing of such material on the internet could be said to be analogous to the conduct involved in the sharing of indecent images of children, and it was irrelevant that R had derived no sexual pleasure or satisfaction therefrom.

Held: Appeal allowed. With regard to the guidance in *Hay (Ian Morris) v HM Advocate* [2012] HCJAC 28, 2014 J.C. 19, [2012] C.L.Y. 4271, examining R's behaviour in the light of the purpose and effects of registration, it could not be said that it contained a significant sexual element and the sheriff had erred in finding that it had; R had exchanged sick jokes in the worst possible taste, however, they had clearly been jokes and it had not been open to the sheriff to conclude that R constituted a continuing danger to others such that registration was required to protect the public; testing the matter as suggested in *Hay*, by considering whether the sexual aspect was important enough to merit attention as indicating an underlying sexual disorder or deviance from which society was entitled to be protected, R's behaviour did not fall into that category, thus the sheriff's order certifying R as being subject to the notification requirements of the 2003 Act would be quashed, *Hay, applied*.

RODGERSON v DUNN, [2016] HCJAC 12, 2016 S.L.T. 315, Lord Bracadale, Lord Drummond Young, HCJ.

2783 Community payback orders–Undue leniency–Theft and assault committed by offender with significant history of mental illness–Three-year community payback order with supervision and mental health treatment requirements

The Crown appealed as unduly lenient the imposition of a community payback order for a period of three years and also three-year supervision and mental health treatment requirements in respect of G, who pleaded guilty to charges of theft and assault of a shop assistant, by repeatedly striking her on the body with a knife to her severe injury and permanent disfigurement. G had a significant history of mental illness, had been admitted as an inpatient to psychiatric wards on several occasions, had been diagnosed as suffering from paranoid schizophrenia, a mixed personality disorder, and substance misuse, and had had a significant history of the use of psychoactive substances, having misused such a substance prior to the commission of the offences. The sentencing judge had considered that a custodial sentence was not appropriate where any such sentence would have required to be backdated and restricted in light of G's early guilty plea, G would have required to be imprisoned for a number of years in order to permit him to undergo programmed interventions, which would not have been conducive to good management of his mental health and that G had already spent the equivalent, after discount of 25%, of two and a half years' imprisonment, thus a period of punishment, in the sense of deprivation of liberty, had already been imposed, and that a sentence of that length would not have been an adequate disposal. The sentencing judge also considered that the imposition of an extended sentence, which, after discount, would have resulted in a custodial term of four years' imprisonment, would have been excessive and inappropriate in the whole circumstances, that the maximum period of 12 months' supervision for a supervised release order would have been insufficient to provide for rehabilitation and adequate public protection, and had concluded that a non-custodial sentence with an element of supervision would provide public protection and rehabilitation for G. The Crown averred that the sentence imposed failed to satisfy the requirement for retribution and deterrence and the sentencing judge had placed undue weight on G's rehabilitation.

Held: Appeal refused. The offence had been serious, G had a number of analogous and relevant previous convictions, and the circumstances gave rise to the strong likelihood of the imposition of a custodial sentence, from which position the sentencing judge had expressly started, however, G had had a history of serious mental illness and there had been significant improvement of his mental health over a period of months under the treatment order; the sentencing judge had put in place a robust package of supervision and mental health treatment designed to protect the public and provide a framework for G's rehabilitation, which had been imposed against a background where G had been either in custody or subject to a treatment order for a significant period of time prior to sentence, a scheme for regular review had been put in place, the report in respect of the first review after three months had been positive, was there a breach of the order it would be open to the court to impose a custodial sentence, and in the particular circumstances of the case, the sentence was not unduly lenient.

HM ADVOCATE v GRAYDON (KENNETH), [2016] HCJAC 14, 2016 S.C.L. 418, Lord Justice General (Carloway), Lady Dorrian, Lord Bracadale, HCJ.

2784 Community payback orders–Variation–Non-compliance with unpaid work requirement–Sheriff extending time limit for performance

[Misuse of Drugs Act 1971 (c.38) s.5(2); Criminal Procedure (Scotland) Act 1995 (c.46) s.227A(2), s.227L, s.227L(2), s.227Y, s.227Z, s.227Z(5), s.227ZA]

S lodged a bill of suspension seeking to suspend two orders of the sheriff, dated 6 May 2015 and 24 June 2015, extending the time limit for performance of his community payback order (CPO). On 19 January 2015, S had been sentenced for a contravention of the Misuse of Drugs Act 1971 s.5(2) by the imposition of the CPO, which required him to undertake 60 hours of unpaid work within three months. S had failed to do so and on 29 April 2015, a criminal justice officer (C) applied for a three month extension of the time period, leading to the order of 6 May. S subsequently received a further custodial sentence and C made a further application for an extension, resulting in the order of 24 June deferring sentence. S submitted *inter alia* that any variation in terms of the Criminal Procedure (Scotland) Act 1995 s.227Z(5) required to be made before the previous time limit expired, and where the CPO had expired on 18 April, the orders of 6 May and 24 June were incompetent.

Held: Bill refused. (1) In terms of s.227A(2) of the 1995 Act, a CPO was an order which imposed one or more requirements and in the present case, it was a requirement of the CPO that S perform 60 hours of unpaid work. The time limit within which that work was to be performed was ancillary to the requirement to perform the work where the provisions were in a separate part of the 1995 Act, namely s.227L, and the court had the power to depart from the statutory default periods in s.227L(2), which often required to yield for pragmatic reasons. (2) Sections 227Y and 227Z of the 1995 Act conferred wide powers in respect of variation on the court, in terms of s.227Z(5), the court might extend any time limit specified as part of an existing requirement and where the Act was silent as to the timing of any application to extend the time limit, there was no basis on which it could be concluded that the power to extend a time limit specified in a requirement was limited to those cases where the time limit had not expired before the date on which the application was presented. (3) Section 227ZA applied only where a court had varied a CPO by adding to its existing requirements, which was to be contrasted with s.227Z(5), which applied to variations of a requirement and it was clear from those provisions that s.227ZA only applied where the offender might, for the first time, be facing the imposition of one of the requirements listed in s.227A(2). Section 227ZA ensured that the same procedure was applied as would have been the case had the requirement been included when the CPO was originally imposed. *Observed*, that nowhere was it provided that failure to complete the required hours of unpaid work within the time limit provided by the court would bring an end to the CPO.

STEWART v DUNN, [2015] HCJAC 93, 2015 S.L.T. 872, Lady Smith, Lord Bracadale, Lady Clark of Calton, HCJ.

2785 Consecutive sentences–Delay–First-time offender guilty of lewd, indecent and libidinous behaviour and practices–Cumulative effect of delay and consecutive sentences

[Criminal Law (Consolidation) (Scotland) Act 1995 (c.39) s.6]

X, convicted of using lewd, indecent and libidinous behaviour and practices towards his daughter (S), then aged above 12 and under 16, contrary to the Criminal Law (Consolidation) (Scotland) Act 1995 s.6 (charge 1), raping S (charge 2), using lewd, indecent and libidinous behaviour and practices towards his work colleague's daughter (L), then aged above 12 and under 16, contrary to s.6 of the 1995 Act (charge 3) and raping L (charge 4), appealed as excessive a sentence of 16 years' imprisonment. X had no previous convictions and had been charged with the offences in 2010, with the trial only taking place in March 2015. The criminal justice social work report had assessed X as likely to reoffend and he had continued to deny the offences. The sentencing judge had considered that X was calculating and predatory and had sexually abused two vulnerable teenaged girls with troubled upbringings, one of whom was his daughter, over an extended period of time, and had sentenced him to five years' imprisonment on charge 1 and 10 years' imprisonment on charge 2, the sentences being ordered to run concurrently, and five years' imprisonment on charge 3 and six years' imprisonment on charge 4, the sentences being ordered to run concurrently with each other and consecutively to those imposed in respect of charges 1 and 2. At the appeal hearing, the crown had *inter alia* prepared a timeline of the preparation of the case which had not been available at the trial.

Held: Sentence in respect of charges 2, 3 and 4 quashed and eight years' imprisonment and concurrent sentences of four years' imprisonment substituted respectively. Although the sentencing judge had explained that she had taken into account the fact that X had been at risk of prosecution since September 2010 and had had to deal with the stress of having the allegations hanging over him for more than four and a half years, she had not had before her the detail in relation to the significant and unexplained delay which had emerged in the timeline made available to the court and she had not taken sufficient account thereof, moreover, the cumulative effect of the consecutive sentences had produced an overall sentence which was excessive, particularly in the case of a first offender; the sentence of 10 years' imprisonment on charge 2 would be quashed and eight years substituted, and in relation to charges 3 and 4, the sentences would be quashed and concurrent sentences of four years' imprisonment on each charge substituted, resulting in an overall sentence of 12 years' imprisonment.

A v HM ADVOCATE *sub nom.* WA v HM ADVOCATE, [2015] HCJAC 105, 2016 S.L.T. 26, The Lord Justice Clerk (Carloway), Lord Bracadale, Lord Matthews, HCJ.

2786 Criminal Justice (Scotland) Act 2016 (asp 1)–Commencement No.1 and Saving Provision Order

THE CRIMINAL JUSTICE (SCOTLAND) ACT 2016 (COMMENCEMENT NO.1 AND SAVING PROVISION) ORDER 2016, SSI 2016/95; made under the Criminal Justice (Scotland) Act 2016 s.117(2)(3). Commencement details: bringing into operation various provisions of the 2016 Act on 10 March 2016.

This Order brings into force the Criminal Justice (Scotland) Act 2016 s.84 on 10 March 2016, increasing the maximum custodial term available to the Court when sentencing a person on indictment for offences committed under section 47 (prohibition of the carrying of offensive weapons), 49 (offence of having in public place article with blade or point), 49A (offence of having a blade or point (or offensive weapon) on school premises) or 49C (offence of having article with offensive weapon etc. in prison) of the Criminal Law Consolidation (Scotland) Act 1995.

2787 Disqualification from driving–Drink driving offences–Evaluation of risk posed by offender–First time offender

[Road Traffic Act 1988 (c.52) s.5(1)(a)]

D, aged 18 and convicted of drink driving, contrary to the Road Traffic Act 1988 s.5(1)(a), appealed as excessive his disqualification from driving for two years. D's vehicle had been stopped by police officers and he had immediately admitted to them to having had a few drinks and having driven. At the police station, D was found to have 44 mg of alcohol in 100 ml of breath. Since committing the offence, D had voluntarily withdrawn himself from driving lessons and had not driven since, and he had also saved money to pay his fine in full.

Held: Two years' disqualification quashed and 12 months substituted. (1) The sheriff appeared to have fallen into the same error as that in *Jenkins v Harvie* [2016] SAC (Crim) 14, 2016 S.L.T. (Sh Ct) 205, [2016] 2810; the sheriff had plainly placed considerable weight upon the fact that D had been two times over the legal limit, and care had to be taken when evaluating the risk posed by an offender, in deciding upon a period of disqualification to be imposed in the context of drink driving offences involving the lower prescribed limit, under reference to the alcohol reading, and where the sheriff had misdirected himself, the assessment of the period of disqualification was at large for the court to determine, *Jenkins*, *applied*. (2) D fell to be sentenced for a first drink driving offence and was a first offender, the level of alcohol in his breath and other factors would be taken into account, including relatively significant financial penalties, and standing his guilty plea at the intermediate diet, the two year disqualification would be quashed and a headline period of 16 months, discounted to 12, substituted.

DOCHERTY v MCPHERSON, [2016] SAC (Crim) 21, 2016 S.L.T. (Sh Ct) 397, Sheriff Principal C A L Scott, QC, Sheriff M G O'Grady, QC, SAC.

2788 Disqualification from driving–Drink driving offences–First time offender severely intoxicated–Disqualification for six years and fine of £1,000

[Road Traffic Act 1988 (c.52) s.5(1)(a)]

S, aged 56, who pleaded guilty to drink driving, contrary to the Road Traffic Act 1988 s.5(1)(a), appealed as excessive his disqualification from driving for six years and a fine of £1,000. S had been drinking at home throughout the day and at approximately 4 pm, had driven to a town centre to buy alcohol but had been refused a sale due to his intoxication. S had immediately returned to his vehicle and the shop assistant had telephoned the police who had attended at S's home and he had been found to have 153 microgrammes of alcohol per 100 millilitres of breath. S had been a first time offender but the sheriff had considered that a substantial period of disqualification was required to mark the high level of culpability and alcohol in S's breath and also for public protection, given that S had chosen to drive in a severely intoxicated state in a small town centre just after the end of the school day.

Held: Six years' disqualification quashed and three years substituted. (1) S had no previous road traffic convictions and had driven throughout his adult life without apparent incident, and although the sheriff had been correct to consider a lengthy period of disqualification, it appeared she might have selected six years in order to encourage S to address the serious problems she believed he had with alcohol, which approach was flawed where other than the consumption of alcohol on the day in question, there was no further information to suggest that S had an alcohol abuse problem and it was wrong, in imposing a period of disqualification, to advert to the statutory provision which enabled a disqualified driver to apply for removal of the disqualification, and the correct approach was to impose the period of disqualification appropriate for the offence; looked at objectively, the areas of concern, including public protection, could properly be met by the imposition of a shorter period of disqualification, therefore the six year disqualification would be quashed and three years substituted. (2) S was currently in receipt of sick pay of approximately £800 a month, he required to meet mortgage payments and his employment was affected by his disqualification, however, the court would not interfere with the sheriff's assessment of the appropriate financial penalty as the offence had been serious and had called for a high fine.

STEVENSON v HARVIE *sub nom.* STEVENSON v MCPHERSON, [2016] SAC (Crim) 24, 2016 S.L.T. (Sh Ct) 421, Sheriff Principal M M Stephen, QC, Sheriff P J Braid, SAC.

2789 Disqualification from driving–Extended driving tests–Sheriff intended to make order requiring offender to resit ordinary driving test–No evidence of inexperience, incompetence or infirmity

[Road Traffic Act 1988 (c.52) s.5(1)(a); Road Traffic Offenders Act 1988 (c.53) s.34A(5), s.36(5)]

M, who pleaded guilty to a contravention of the Road Traffic Act 1988 s.5(1)(a), appealed against the imposition of three years' disqualification and a fine of £480, and an order to pass the extended driving test. M claimed that he ought not to have been required to undertake the extended driving test, and that the sheriff had failed to make an order allowing him to undertake a course which would lessen the period of disqualification in terms of the Road Traffic Offenders Act 1988 s.34A(5). In his report, the sheriff explained that he had intended to make an order requiring M to resit the ordinary driving test, however, that order had not been competent in terms of the Road Traffic Offenders Act 1988 s.36(5) and had he appreciated that at the time, he would not have made the order, particularly where the Magistrates Court Sentencing Guidelines applicable in England and Wales, recommended that the discretion to order a resit ought to be exercised where there was evidence of inexperience, incompetence or infirmity, or where the disqualification was lengthy, and those factors had not applied. The sheriff further explained that the Magistrates Court Guidelines required the courts to consider the imposition of an order of the type sought by M where there were good reasons for doing so, and he had not been given any reasons therefor.

Held: Appeal allowed to extent of quashing requirement to undertake extended driving test. (1) An order to pass a driving test, or the extended test, ought only to be made, unless mandatory, where the offence had resulted from inexperience, incompetence or infirmity, or where the disqualification period was a lengthy one, and given that the sheriff accepted that the order which he had intended to impose had been incompetent, and that he would not have imposed an obligation to pass the extended test, the relative order would be quashed and the appeal allowed to that extent, *Sweeney v Cardle (Sentencing)* 1982 S.L.T. 312, [1982] C.L.Y. 4294 and *Tariq v Carmichael (Sentencing)* 1982 S.C.C.R. 488, [1983] C.L.Y. 4890, *applied*. (2) While it would have been appropriate for the sheriff to make an order allowing M to attend a course, before he could do so he required to be either aware of, or supplied with, sufficient information to enable the order to be competently made, and where M was not present, the court could not make such an order without explaining certain things to him and the appeal would be refused to that extent, *Anderson v HM Advocate*, High Court of Justiciary, 5 February 2009, unreported, *Hayes v Harvie, Glasgow*, High Court of Justiciary, 6 July 2011, unreported, and *Birell v Dunn*, High Court of Justiciary, 8 October 2010, unreported, *considered*.

MCDOUGALL v MURPHY, [2015] HCJAC 112, 2016 S.L.T. 65, The Lord Justice Clerk (Carloway), Lord Brodie, Lord Matthews, HCJ.

2790 Disqualification from driving–Hardship–Exceptional hardship established–Discretionary period of disqualification imposed

H, who pleaded guilty inter alia to driving without insurance, appealed against the imposition of six months' disqualification from driving. An exceptional hardship proof had been assigned and in the course of H's plea in mitigation, that the court confine its sentence to monetary penalties coupled with endorsement of H's licence with appropriate penalty points on the basis that the requirement for disqualification had been avoided due to the finding of exceptional hardship, analogous offences had been disclosed, namely using a motor vehicle without insurance, which had clearly influenced the magistrate's approach to sentencing.

Held: Six month's disqualification quashed and eight penalty points substituted. The allowance of an exceptional hardship proof carried with it a clear implication that the court was restricting its consideration of the issue of whether a mandatory disqualification by manner of the totting up procedure might be avoided, moreover, where exceptional hardship was held established, the court could not then cast that aside and reintroduce a disposal already ruled out, therefore the magistrate's approach had been illegitimate as he had not been entitled to consider and impose a discretionary period of disqualification.

HAMAND v HARVIE *sub nom.* HAMAND v PROCURATOR FISCAL, GLASGOW, [2016] SAC (Crim) 15, 2016 S.L.T. (Sh Ct) 147, Sheriff Principal C A L Scott, QC, Sheriff J Morris, QC, SAC.

2791 Disqualification from driving–Hardship–Small business owner disqualified–Business unlikely to survive

[Road Traffic Offenders Act 1988 (c.53) s.35]

W, who pleaded guilty to driving while using a mobile telephone, appealed against his disqualification from driving for six months. The justice of the peace had imposed three penalty points which had resulted in the consideration of a period of disqualification as a result of the Road Traffic Offenders Act 1988 s.35. At an exceptional hardship proof, W and his wife (X) gave evidence that W owned a small business (B) with approximately 10 employees, X acted as B's accountant, W and X lived in a relatively remote location in Scotland, B's factory premises were located in England, with the nearest railway station some 30 miles away, W used his car to transport heavy items and travelled 1,500-2,500 miles per week, thus public transport would be of extremely limited value for the operation of the business, further, a quote had been tendered for a driver at £4,000 per week, with additional costs, and B would be placed in serious jeopardy by W's disqualification, access to the family home was difficult, and were B to fail, W and X would lose their livelihood and would experience difficulty in meeting their mortgage commitments of £700 per month. The justice considered that exceptional hardship had not been established where W was not employed as a driver, he did not require a driving licence to do his job, it was not essential that he drive himself to client meetings, a combination of public transport, taxis and the services of a driver, combined with overnight stays as necessary would enable him to attend many, if not all, of the meetings and no consideration had been given to the possibility of B""s employees taking it in turns to drive W, and with an effective system in place, it might be that no public transport would be required, further the justice was not satisfied that there were no other drivers who could perform the function for cheaper albeit at a significant cost to W and B, concluding that B would have the resources to invest to protect the contribution of a vital employee such as W, the justice being aware of his obligation to consider public safety as well as the hardship to be caused to W and others.

Held: Six months' disqualification quashed. The justice's conclusion was irreconcilable with the unchallenged evidence to the effect that B was unlikely to survive which would result in the loss of employment not just for W but for 10 staff members and the existence of exceptional hardship ought to have been held established and the six months' disqualification would be quashed.

WAINE v HARVIE, [2016] SAC (Crim) 19, 2016 S.L.T. (Sh Ct) 169, Sheriff Principal C A L Scott, QC, Sheriff S Murphy, QC, SAC.

2792 **Disqualification from driving–Mitigation–Offender's apprenticeship and integral role in keeping family farm business going by working at nights and at weekends**

[Road Traffic Act 1988 (c.52) s.2]

L, who pleaded guilty to *inter alia* dangerous driving, contrary to the Road Traffic Act 1988 s.2, appealed as excessive his disqualification from driving for 24 months. L had been seen by police officers (P) driving a tractor the wrong way down a one way road as he had negotiated a blind bend, and P having alerted L to their presence, the tractor had continued at its top speed of 30 mph, at times mounting the verge of the narrow carriageway and bouncing back onto the road. The sheriff found that L's driving had been a serious contravention of s.2 of the 1988 Act, there had been significant potential for harm to other road users, L could not be said to be an experienced driver and he had driven at speed, given the tractor's capacity, and the gravity of the offence merited the disqualification period. Nothing had been advanced before the sheriff in mitigation to incline her to the view that a more limited period of disqualification was appropriate, in particular, the sheriff had not been addressed on any impact on L's apprenticeship.

Held: Two years' disqualification quashed and 12 months' disqualification and order to sit extended driving test substituted. Had the mitigatory material regarding L's apprenticeship and his integral role in keeping the family farm business going by working at nights and at weekends been known to the sheriff, she most likely would have reflected those factors when it came to the period of disqualification imposed, moreover, in the whole circumstances of the case, the imposition of two years' disqualification was excessive, accordingly, the disqualification imposed by the sheriff would be quashed and disqualification for the minimum period, namely 12 months, substituted, and L would also be ordered to successfully complete the extended test of driving competency. *Opinion*, that the sheriff ought to have allowed a discount in regard to the disqualification period but that had in any event been taken into account in terms of the court's overall disposal.

LAMONT v HARVIE, [2016] SAC (Crim) 17, 2016 S.L.T. (Sh Ct) 365, Sheriff Principal C A L Scott, QC, Sheriff S Murphy, QC, SAC.

2793 Disqualification from driving–Police officers–Dangerous driving by police officer who activated flashing lights but not siren–Whether special reasons established

[Road Traffic Act 1988 (c.52) s.2]

A police officer (W), who pleaded guilty to dangerous driving, contrary to the Road Traffic Act 1988 s.2, appealed against her disqualification from driving. W had been driving a police vehicle and had received a distress call from colleagues, and in responding thereto, W had only activated the police vehicle's blue flashing lights and had inadvertently failed to active its siren, and a collision had occurred when she had driven through a red light at a junction. W and her colleague had been the only officers asked to attend to provide assistance and in mitigation, the sheriff had been informed that the distress of the officer making the call had been such that W had heard a scream. Evidence was also led that W had approached the junction at 15 mph and had slowed to 10 mph as she had passed through the red light. The sheriff had *inter alia* rejected the proposition that special reasons existed for W not to be subjected to the mandatory minimum 12 month disqualification period.

Held: Disqualification quashed and five penalty points substituted. (1) The sheriff's view that it was not inexpedient to punish W had not been a useful approach to the issue of whether special reasons had been established in all the circumstances of the case, the sheriff had placed too much weight on the fact that W was not an accredited emergency driver, which was an irrelevant factor, that W had pleaded guilty and that dangerous driving was a serious offence was also a neutral feature in the consideration of the establishment or otherwise of special reasons, and the sheriff had been wrong to distinguish *Husband (Brian) v Russell* 1998 S.L.T. 377, [1997] C.L.Y. 6398 and *R. v Lundt-Smith* [1964] 2 Q.B. 167, [1964] C.L.Y. 3194 owing to W's lack of emergency driver accreditation where W's manoeuvre had been embarked upon and executed because she had been involved in an emergency journey, *Husband* and *Lundt-Smith*, *considered*. (2) The sheriff's approach could not be supported; the extenuating circumstances generated by the emergency had been unquestionably connected to the commission of the offence, it had been created by a momentary failing on W's part, it had been unfortunate that W had overlooked to activate the siren but in driving as she had, she had had the safety of other road users in mind, having activated the lights and significantly reduced the vehicle's speed, and special reasons ought to have been found established by the sheriff and the disqualification would be quashed. (3) Where W was a new driver and would lose her licence were anything more than six penalty points imposed and a letter from her employers explained that her commute on public transport would be time consuming, she was a valued employee and her employment might be compromised were she not able to drive to her place of work, W's licence would be endorsed with five penalty points.

WATT v MURPHY, [2016] SAC (Crim) 16, 2016 S.L.T. (Sh Ct) 247, Sheriff Principal C A L Scott, QC, Sheriff J C Morris, QC, SAC.

2794 Drug offences–Comparative justice–Being concerned in production and supply of controlled drugs–Appropriate starting point

[Misuse of Drugs Act 1971 (c.38) s.4(3)(b); Road Traffic Act 1988 (c.52) s.2]

M, convicted of *inter alia* being concerned in the production and supply of controlled drugs, contrary to the Misuse of Drugs Act 1971 s.4(3)(b), appealed as excessive the imposition of four years and eight months' imprisonment discounted from six years and six months to reflect an early guilty plea. M had been convicted of several charges of contraventions of the 1971 Act, a charge of a contravention of the Road Traffic Act 1988 s.2 and two firearms charges, and had been sentenced to a total of seven years and 10 months' imprisonment in respect thereof, discounted to reflect the early guilty plea. M submitted that the sentence complained of had not taken account of the earlier sentence imposed on him which comprised part of the offending in charge 1 and had had a starting point of four years which had been discounted to three years to reflect the early plea, and adding the two starting points together, he had received a starting point sentence of ten and a half years, which fell to be compared with his two co-accused, whose involvement in the offences had been significantly greater, who had been sentenced to 12 years and 10 years respectively.

Held: Appeal allowed, sentence of four years and eight months' imprisonment quashed and three years and four months substituted. In terms of the principles of comparative justice, the sentence was unfair on M; the starting point ought to be a total of eight and a half years for his involvement in all the charge 1 matters, which included six months for the bail aggravation, from which the starting point of four years for the earlier sentence ought to be deducted, resulting in a starting point of four and a half years, including the bail aggravation of six months, to which a 25% discount ought to be applied to reflect the early guilty plea, resulting in a sentence of three years and four months' imprisonment, which would include four months for the bail aggravation, thus the total period of imprisonment would be six years and six months because of the reduction in the period applicable to charge 1; those charges that the sentencing judge had made concurrent would remain so, the sentences which he had made consecutive would remain so, and they all started from the same starting point.

MCMAHON (JOHN) v HM ADVOCATE, [2016] HCJAC 45, 2016 S.C.L. 570, Lord Menzies, Lord Malcolm, HCJ.

2795 Extended sentences–Child offenders–Offender convicted of serious sexual offences–Need to have regard to offender's welfare and need for rehabilitation

[Sexual Offences Act 2003 (c.42)]

M, convicted when aged 17 of serious sexual offences against two boys (X) aged between seven and 11, committed when he was aged between 14 and 15, appealed as excessive the imposition of a six year custodial sentence. The sentencing judge had considered that an adult offender could have had a sentence of nine years imposed for the offences, which was consistent with the eight to 13 years discussed in the Sentencing Guidelines for England and Wales, from which a substantial reduction had been required to reflect M's age and immaturity, and that no extended sentence had been required where M constituted a medium risk of reoffending, had a supportive family, would be released under licence in due course and would be subject to the Sexual Offences Act 2003 notification requirements.

Held: Sentence of six years' detention quashed and five years' detention with three year extension period substituted. (1) In sentencing a child, it was not illegitimate to consider the sentence which an adult offender might have attracted but the court ought to take careful regard of the observations in *H v HM Advocate* [2010] HCJAC 111, 2011 J.C. 149, [2011] C.L.Y. 4585; in selecting the sentence for a child, the court had to have regard to that child's best interests as a primary factor, in which a factor would be the desirability of that child's reintegration into society, *H*, *Greig (Paul William) v HM Advocate* [2012] HCJAC 127, 2013 J.C. 115, [2013] C.L.Y. 3993, and *R. (on the application of Smith) v Secretary of State for the Home Department* [2005] UKHL 51, [2006] 1 A.C. 159, [2005] C.L.Y. 2923, *applied*. (2) It was not clear that the sentencing judge had had any of the aforementioned important factors in mind other than that M's youth made him less blameworthy than an adult, thus she had erred. (3) The sentencing judge had erred in concluding that an extended sentence was unnecessary; the criminal justice social work report had highlighted M's denial of the offences as a considerable concern and one which limited the scope of offence focused work which could reduce risk, which was a significant factor in determining the extent to which an extended sentence might be necessary to protect the public from serious harm, persistent denial in those circumstances required the assessment of risk as moderate to be viewed with caution, M's lack of insight into his behaviour was troubling, and with regard to the terms of the report allied to the very serious nature of the offences committed by one so young, it could not be said that an extended sentence was unnecessary for the protection of the public. (4) Having regard to the fact that the extension period was designed to reduce risk, an appropriate sentence would be an extended sentence consisting of a five year custodial term with a three year extension period.

MCCORMICK (ADAM) v HM ADVOCATE, [2016] HCJAC 50, 2016 S.L.T. 793, Lady Dorrian, Lady Clark of Calton, HCJ.

2796 Fraud–Parental rights–Fraudulent scheme to falsely obtain parental rights and responsibilities–Appropriate sentence length

V and G (collectively X) appealed as excessive custodial sentences of three years' imprisonment for forming a fraudulent scheme by which V falsely obtained parental rights and responsibilities as the father of a child (C) to whom G was mother. The sentencing sheriff determined that X had given no consideration to the potential impact on C, had been wickedly indifferent as to the consequences of their actions, and had continued their deceit and obstructed investigations when civil proceedings were raised by C's true father (F). He considered that some assistance could be found in child abduction cases, and took into account the complexity, persistence and widespread nature of the fraud involving a child.

Held: Appeal refused. (1) The offence comprised a carefully planned scheme which involved a web of deceit and the telling of many lies, not only to F but to X's acquaintances and the authorities; the impact upon F and the potential impact on C had been significant, and the sheriff had been entitled to conclude that custodial sentences were the only appropriate disposals. (2) While the sheriff had found some parallels in child abduction cases, he recognised that they were of limited assistance and had clearly considered the case on its own merits, and having regard to the callous, complex and sustained nature of the fraud, the sentences imposed could not be said to be excessive.

G v HM ADVOCATE; Y v HM ADVOCATE *sub nom.* VG v HM ADVOCATE; CY v HM ADVOCATE, [2016] HCJAC 1, 2016 S.L.T. 282, Lady Dorrian, Lord Bracadale, HCJ.

2797 Fraud–Shoplifting–Attempted fraud and shoplifting–Consecutive sentences

J, who pleaded guilty to fraud and attempted fraud, and shoplifting, appealed against the imposition of consecutive sentences of 15 months' imprisonment, discounted from 18 months, and six months' imprisonment respectively. In relation to the first offence, J had, on three occasions, successfully fraudulently obtained a total of £18,000 from a bank and had unsuccessfully attempted to fraudulently obtain £11,000 on two other occasions. In relation to the second offence, J, having just been released from court, had taken cosmetics from a store to the value of £448 without paying therefor. The money and the items had never been recovered.

Held: Appeals refused. J's actions had been premeditated, carefully planned and sophisticated, her involvement had been sustained and determined, the sums involved had been considerable and were unrecovered, the offences had been committed while J was on bail, she had a significant record for dishonesty, having appeared in court on 27 occasions, 25 of which for dishonesty and nine while on bail, the nature, number and distribution of previous convictions suggested that she was a professional thief, and having regard thereto, the sheriff had not erred in the imposition of each of the sentences or in making them consecutive.

JACKSON v DUNN, [2016] SAC (Crim) 10, 2016 S.C.L. 673, Sheriff Principal M M Stephen, QC, Sheriff M G O'Grady, QC, SAC.

2798 Life imprisonment–Murder–Co-accused's punishment part reduced–Comparative justice

The Scottish Criminal Cases Review Commission referred the case of B, who pleaded guilty to X's murder and was sentenced to life imprisonment with a punishment part of 20 years, on the basis that there might have been a miscarriage of justice. B and his co-accused (M) had carried out a concerted and premeditated attack on X with knives, having forced their way into his home, pursuant to their decision that he ought to be punished following the death of M's friend after taking ecstasy supplied by X. In passing sentence, the trial judge had noted that both B and M had expressed remorse and that M had been suffering from a serious reaction to his friend's death but had not differentiated between B and M. B and M thereafter separately appealed against sentence. B's appeal had been refused but M's had been allowed, the court considering that the sentencing judge had erred in failing to differentiate between B and M on the basis of M's grief reaction and had reduced M's punishment part to 17 years.

Held: Sentence reduced and punishment part of 17 years substituted. An unsatisfactory situation had arisen due to the two appeals not being heard together and had they been, there would have been no distinction between B and M, and the requirement to ensure comparative justice dictated that B's punishment part ought also to be reduced.

BROWN (ANDREW) v HM ADVOCATE, [2016] HCJAC 31, 2016 S.C.L. 554, Lord Justice General (Carloway), Lord Brodie, Lord Bracadale, HCJ.

2799 Life imprisonment–Murder–Murder of two girls–Previous conviction for culpable homicide–Length of punishment part of sentence

[Double Jeopardy (Scotland) Act 2011 (asp 16); Criminal Procedure (Scotland) Act 1995 (c.46) s.101, s.101A]

S, convicted of the rape and murder of two 17 year old girls in 1977, appealed against the 37 year punishment part of his sentence of life imprisonment. S had previously been tried and acquitted of the murders in 2007, and was retried on Crown application following the passing of the Double Jeopardy (Scotland) Act 2011. S submitted that the punishment part was excessive (1) where the trial judge had selected the punishment part principally as it reflected the length of time between the murders and his conviction, which was irrelevant; (2) where the trial judge failed to take sufficient account of comparable sentences and of what sentence might have been recommended had he been convicted in 1977; (3) having regard to his criminal record as available in terms of the Criminal Procedure (Scotland) Act 1995 ss.101 and 101A; the sentencing judge had erred in having regard to previous convictions for sexual offences and murder which post dated the murders but pre-dated 28 March 2011, that being the commencement date of s.101A.

Held: Appeal refused. (1) The judge had assessed the case's gravity at the outset and had concluded that a punishment part in the high thirties should be imposed, and it was coincidental that the figure selected mirrored the passage of time since the offences. (2) An experienced sentencing judge who had presided over the trial and heard the evidence was best placed to decide the punishment part appropriate to the circumstances of the case, and an appeal court should be slow to alter such an assessment, *a fortiori* as other punishment parts might have been imposed in different circumstances and in a different sentencing era. (3) The offences were horrific and S's previous conviction for the culpable homicide of a young girl was a major aggravating factor, and the sentencing judge was entitled, exercising his discretion in the context of retribution and deterrence, to select a punishment part at the top of the range. (4) The common law, as developed in the context of modern sentencing practice, clearly envisaged that a sentencing judge should have an overall view of the accused's life in order to be able to sentence him appropriately, and that might properly be obtained from oral submissions, medical reports, psychiatric reports, social inquiry and criminal justice social work reports, and/or the production of extract convictions with certified extracts of the indictments; S's previous convictions for murder and sexual offences were therefore proper and relevant matters for the sentencing judge to take into consideration. (5) Section 101A of the 1995 Act merely reflected the current common law position and did not detract from or limit existing common law sentencing powers, and it also provided a procedural route for giving appropriate notice to the court and the accused. (6) The sentencing judge was not obliged to carry out a retrospective assessment of what a judge in 1977 might have recommended, S's sentencing should not be based on such a hypothetical, theoretical or speculative exercise but was a matter to be assessed at the time of his conviction, when all the relevant circumstances could be taken into account.

SINCLAIR (ANGUS) v HM ADVOCATE, [2016] HCJAC 24, 2016 S.L.T. 600, Lady Paton, Lady Clark of Calton, Lord Malcolm, HCJ.

2800 Life imprisonment–Murder–Wife murdering husband by assault–15-year punishment part

B, convicted of murdering her husband (H) by assaulting him, repeatedly scratching him with her fingernails, kicking, stamping and jumping on his head and body and inflicting blunt force injuries to his head and body, appealed as excessive the 15 year punishment part of her sentence of life imprisonment. B and H had been together for 20 years, they had habitually drunk heavily and there had been a history of some domestic violence directed by each towards the other. B and H had spent the day drinking in bed and B gave evidence that her next recollection was of waking the next morning to find H on the floor next to the bed unresponsive and cold to the touch and she had contacted emergency services. On arrival they had found B in a state of distress and continued intoxication, and she had accepted responsibility for H's death in due course, although she had no recollection of what had occurred. The pathology revealed that H had suffered numerous injuries, said to be equivalent to those occurring in a road traffic accident or a fall from a considerable height. The sentencing judge had had regard to B's lack of criminal history, her employment record, that she was 61, and that as a result of her actions she had lost her husband but also that she had been convicted of a murderous assault in circumstances where H appeared to have been unable to defend himself.

Held: Appeal refused. In the present case, there had been mitigatory factors, notably the absence of any criminal record, B's good work record and the age at which she found herself convicted of the murder of her life partner, however, there had also been aggravating features, notably the nature of the attack and the absence of a call for assistance for some hours after what must have been a sustained attack, in all those circumstance the selection of 15 years as a punishment part was not excessive and did not fall outwith the appropriate range of punishment parts, *HM Advocate v Boyle (Brian Robert)* [2009] HCJAC 89, 2010 J.C. 66, [2010] C.L.Y. 4531, *Jakovlev (Vladimir) v HM Advocate* [2011] HCJAC 90, 2012 J.C. 120, [2012] C.L.Y. 4266, *Cameron (Alan) v HM Advocate* [2011] HCJAC 29, 2011 S.C.L. 633, [2011] C.L.Y. 4084 and *HM Advocate v Callander (Darrin Alexander)* [2013] HCJAC 159, 2014 S.C.L. 206, [2014] C.L.Y. 3777, *considered.*

BRUCE (SANDRA ELIZABETH) v HM ADVOCATE, [2016] HCJAC 25, 2016 S.C.L. 492, Lord Justice General (Carloway), Lady Paton, Lady Clark of Calton, HCJ.

2801 Murder–Sentence length–Mitigating circumstances–Length of punishment part of life sentence

H, who pleaded guilty to murdering X, appealed as excessive the punishment part of 19 years of his life sentence, discounted from 22 years to reflect his guilty plea. H had sublet a property (P) from X and the evidence suggested that in the two months prior to X's murder, H and X had had an escalating dispute. On 14 May 2015, X had attended at P and had sent a text to a friend stating that she had been having an argument with X, he had assaulted her and had threatened to kill her by cutting her throat. H had then stabbed X 27 times and shortly thereafter, he had telephoned emergency services. H had minor previous convictions for road traffic offences, had not suffered from mental health problems and had expressed some remorse.

Held: Appeal allowed, punishment part of 19 years quashed, and 16 years substituted. The present case had involved a frenzied attack of a brutal nature, which had required the imposition of a substantial punishment part attached to the life sentence, however, H had no significant criminal record, the murder had neither been premeditated nor had it involved taking a weapon into the public arena, H had made no attempt to conceal the crime, he had telephoned the police shortly after the incident, there had been no other offences involved and H had expressed a degree of remorse; having regard to *HM Advocate v Boyle (Brian Robert)* [2009] HCJAC 89, 2010 J.C. 66, [2010] C.L.Y. 4531, the headline sentence of 22 years was excessive and would be quashed and 19 years substituted, discounted to 16 years, *Boyle, applied.*

HAUGEN (JOHN RICHARD) v HM ADVOCATE, [2015] HCJAC 121, 2016 S.L.T. 80, The Lord Justice Clerk (Carloway), Lord Bracadale, Lord Malcolm, HCJ.

2802 Offensive behaviour–Assault–Consecutive sentences–Sentence length

[Criminal Justice and Licensing (Scotland) Act 2010 (asp 13) s.38(1); Criminal Procedure (Scotland) Act 1995 (c.46) s.210]

R, convicted of behaving in a threatening or abusive manner and acting in an aggressive manner towards his ex-partner (X) at her home, contrary to the Criminal Justice and Licensing (Scotland) Act 2010 s.38(1), while subject to two bail orders, and convicted at a later date of assaulting X and a visitor (V) at X's home, while subject to three bail orders, appealed as excessive the imposition of custodial sentences of 119 days and 235 days respectively, to be served consecutively. In relation to the first complaint, the sheriff had selected a period of six months' imprisonment and had applied a 20 per cent discount to reflect the plea at the intermediate diet, resulting in 145 days, 45 of which represented the bail aggravations, and had deducted the 26 days of R's remand therefrom. Regarding the second complaint. the sheriff had determined that six months' imprisonment on each charge was appropriate, she had attributed 36 days on each charge to the bail aggravations and had applied a 25 per cent discount for the plea at the intermediate diet and reduced the period of imprisonment by 37 days to reflect the period of remand.

Held: Appeals refused. (1) It had been particularly important to consider R's record of offending against X and his record of offending with particular reference to crimes of violence, and in that context, a headline sentence of six months for an assault whilst on bail with complete disregard for the consequences, was not excessive. (2) The sheriff had allowed a generous discount on both complaints, and the discount allowed on the first could be said to be over generous as R had prolonged and interrupted the proceedings by his failure to attend at an intermediate diet, resulting in a trial diet being discharged and consequent delay; the consecutive sentences were not excessive, the sheriff had considered all relevant issues, she had been careful to discount the sentences and had had regard to the periods on remand as required by the Criminal Procedure (Scotland) Act 1995 s.210 and had given full credit therefor by reducing the overall sentences in the manner sought by R's agent, which had in fact exceeded the periods of remand, and looking at the sentence and the sheriff's sentencing process in the round, the sheriff had had regard to the period of remand even though the period was not precisely doubled, therefore, no miscarriage of justice had arisen, *Martin (Ronald O'Neill) v HM Advocate* [2006] HCJAC 86, 2007 J.C. 70, [2007] C.L.Y. 5518, *applied.*

ROBERTSON v DUNN, [2015] SAC (Crim) 1, 2016 S.L.T. (Sh Ct) 51, Sheriff Principal M M Stephen, QC, Sheriff Principal C A L Scott, QC, SAC.

2803 Orders for lifelong restriction–Risk–Physical and sexual abuse of five former partners–Criteria for order for lifelong restriction

L, convicted of the physical and sexual abuse of five former partners, two of whom had been under 16, over an 18 year period, appealed against the imposition of an order for lifelong restriction on the ground that it was inappropriate and excessive. A risk assessment report (R) had assessed L at medium risk. The trial judge had considered three other reports by three psychiatric consultants, of which two had classified L as medium risk and one had classified him as high risk.

Held: Appeal refused. (1) The sentencing judge had found that the criteria for an order for lifelong restriction had been met and that L's behaviour would remain wholly unpredictable and require constant supervision for the remainder of his life; where there had been no previous conviction, the sentencing judge required to make his own assessment as to whether the criteria had been met and whether it was likely that any treatment or other rehabilitative programme was likely to be successful. (2) The court was unable to detect any flaw in the reasoning of the sentencing judge, the present case had involving repeated serious violent and sexual offending against five vulnerable women, and the sentencing judge had been entitled to take the view that the criteria for an order for lifelong restriction had been met, notwithstanding that R had assessed the risk posed by L as medium; that in itself was not a bar to a judge holding that the criteria had been met and there had been good reason to consider that R had underestimated the risk posed and that the conclusion that L fitted into the high risk category was accurate.

LAIRD (THOMAS) v HM ADVOCATE, [2015] HCJAC 90, 2016 S.C.L. 62, The Lord Justice Clerk (Carloway), Lord Bracadale, Lord Malcolm, HCJ.

2804 Orders for lifelong restriction–Risk–Sufficiency of link between offence and risk posed

[Criminal Procedure (Scotland) Act 1995 (c.46)]

Prisoners (K and Q, collectively P) who pleaded guilty to threatening and abducting another prisoner (X) and holding him hostage for approximately five hours, appealed against the imposition of lifelong restriction orders with punishment parts of two years and six months and three years and four months respectively. While holding X hostage, P had demanded food, tobacco and transport to another prison, their motivation being a transfer to the west coast of Scotland, and the incident had resolved peacefully after six hours. Both of P's risk assessment reports had assessed them as high risk, which the sentencing judge had accepted.

Held: Orders for lifelong restriction quashed and extended sentences substituted. (1) The language of the Criminal Procedure (Scotland) Act 1995 was clear in requiring not only that there be a serious risk posed by the offender but also a link between the offence and that risk, and in the present appeals, there was no sufficient link between the offence and the risk; the offence had taken place during P's incarceration, the circumstances had been specific to that incarceration, the incident, whilst serious in terms of prison discipline, had involved neither injury nor any attempt to injure X, and looking at the matter in isolation, it was of limited nature and could not be said to demonstrate a likelihood that either K or Q would seriously endanger the lives or physical or psychological wellbeing of members of the public. (2) P's risks of repeat offending did not flow from the offence but from their general recidivist tendencies; whilst P had significant records, it was not possible to fit the offence into a pattern of behaviour within the scope of the risk criteria; although K had accumulated a record for possessing weapons, he appeared to have only one limited conviction for using one, and Q had a serious record involving violence but that was limited and linked to domestic circumstances, not to the incident in prison. In the circumstances, the risk criteria were not satisfied and the statutory test for the imposition of an order for lifelong restriction had not been met. (3) The orders for lifelong restriction would be substituted with extended sentences of six years with a custodial term of four years and an extension period of two years in respect of K, and eight years and four months with a custodial term of five years and four months and an extension period of three years in respect of Q. *Opinion*, that the absence of any reference to Q's education, social work and medical records called into question the issue of whether the statutory requirements for a risk assessment report had been met.

KINLOCH (ANDREW) v HM ADVOCATE; QUINN (JAMES) v HM ADVOCATE, [2015] HCJAC 102, 2015 S.L.T. 876, The Lord Justice Clerk (Carloway), Lord Drummond Young, Lord Eassie, HCJ.

2805 Rape–Sentence length–Seven years' imprisonment

X, convicted of rape, appealed as excessive a seven year custodial sentence. X had been 23 at the date of the offence, had no analgous previous convictions, and the sentencing judge had acknowledged that he had had a disturbed background, being an asylum seeker originally from Afghanistan. Before the court, H relied on two unreported cases which had broadly similar circumstances and had carried a four year custodial sentence, with the sentencing judge in one of the cases having stated that rapes of that type had to be taken seriously and the lowest possible sentence was four years' imprisonment.

Held: Sentence quashed and extended sentence of five years with two year extension period substituted. Having regard to the cirumstances of the case, a custodial sentence of seven years' imprisonment was excessive; the criminal justice social work report had assessed X as likely to reoffend in a similar nature and had suggested post custodial supervision, and the sentencing judge had been addressed on the question of extended sentence but appeard not to have given further consideration thereto in his reasoning.

AHMADI (IBRAHIM) v HM ADVOCATE, [2016] HCJAC 7, 2016 S.C.L. 329, Lord Menzies, Lady Smith, HCJ.

2806 Rape–Young persons–Oral rape of 14-year-old–Undue leniency

[Sexual Offences (Scotland) Act 2009 (asp 9) s.1]

The Crown appealed as unduly lenient the imposition of three years' imprisonment in respect of B, aged 31, convicted of assaulting and raping D, aged 14, by threatening her with violence and penetrating her mouth with his penis, contrary to the Sexual Offences (Scotland) Act 2009 s.1. B had been D's mother's partner at the time of the offence, which had occurred in the family home. The criminal justice social work report had concluded that B had no insight into the offence or the harm caused and had not accepted responsibility therefor, denying the commission thereof, and had assessed B as at a medium risk of re-offending. The sentencing judge had found that custody was the only appropriate disposal, had acknowledged that B had been in a position of trust, had taken into account the lack of analogous offending, the absence of penile penetration or other activity that had damaged D's physical integrity and that the violence had been limited to a single threat, and had not considered that there required to be a minimum period of imprisonment because of the *nomen criminis*.

Held: Sentence of three years quashed and five years substituted. (1) Parliament had recategorised penile penetration of the mouth as rape in the 2009 Act and the court required to sentence upon that basis, moreover, it had to be recognised that an act of oral rape might be as abhorrent, demeaning and traumatising as vaginal rape, and at common law the sentences available in Scotland in respect of rape and indecent assault were unrestricted. (2) Whether an act of oral rape attracted a higher sentence than a vaginal rape or vice versa was always a question of facts and circumstances, including the level of violence used, the offender and victim's relationship, the victim's age or other vulnerability, the degree of psychological as well as physical harm caused, the offender's age, previous convictions and character and any degree of remorse. (3) The sentencing judge appeared to have had no information on the psychological effects of the offence on D, however, she had been aware that this was a rape of a 14 year old child by a 31 year old adult who had been in a position of trust over her, although B was otherwise of reasonably good character and had been in steady employment, he had shown no remorse and remained in a state of denial, and in all these circumstances, the sentence of three years was unduly lenient as falling outwith the range reasonably open to the trial judge, and five years would be substituted.

HM ADVOCATE v B *sub nom.* HM ADVOCATE v AB, [2015] HCJAC 106, 2015 S.L.T. 841, The Lord Justice Clerk (Carloway), Lord Bracadale, Lord Matthews, HCJ.

2807 Risk of sexual harm orders–Interim orders–Gymnastics coach suspended from employment–Error in sheriff's approach to risk posed

[Protection of Children and Prevention of Sexual Offences (Scotland) Act 2005 (asp 9) s.5, s.5(4)(b); Communications Act 2003 (c.21) s.127]

The Chief Constable of the Police Service Scotland (C) appealed against the refusal by the sheriff of his motion for an interim risk of sexual harm order under the Protection of Children and Prevention of Sexual Offences (Scotland) Act 2005 s.5 against a gymnastics coach (M). The sheriff had not been satisfied that it was just to make the interim order. He had observed that M's alleged sexual activity involving children had arisen from the opportunities presented to him as a children's gymnastics coach, however, he had been suspended from his post, pending the outcome of a criminal investigation, from which the sheriff had concluded that there had been a material diminution in the *prima facie* risk of sexual harm presented by M in the interim period, and where the materiality of that risk was a relevant factor in deciding whether it was just to make an interim order, the sheriff had balanced the perceived diminished *prima facie* risk against the nature and extent of the interference with the M's rights were the interim order to be granted and had taken account of the fact that the proceedings against M were summary in nature and were likely, or at least ought to, proceed to a final hearing with relative expedition.

Held: Appeal allowed. (1) There appeared to be no mention within the statutory provisions of any *prima facie* risk of sexual conduct or activity towards children, the *prima facie* test under s.5(4)(b) of the 2005 Act was directed towards whether proscribed acts, at least two in number, had been perpetrated by the person in respect of whom the order was being sought, however, with regard to the titular nomenclature of the orders provided for under ss.2 and 5 and to the terms of s.2(6) of the 2005 Act it was plain that the legislation was directed towards protecting children generally or any child from harm emanating from the individual against whom the order was sought, therefore, risk of sexual harm orders and interim orders might properly be invoked in circumstances where a colourable risk of sexual harm existed to children generally or to any particular child, and the application of ss.2 and 5 was not necessarily context specific. (2) The sheriff had overlooked the significance of certain of C's averments relating to M's conviction in 2013 for a contravention of the Communications Act 2003 s.127 in relation to a 15 year old girl, which had occurred independent of his role as a gymnastics coach, which would give rise to the inference that M posed a risk of sexual harm towards children, who thus might require protection from his behaviour; the sheriff had placed undue focus upon M's role as a gymnastics coach and had confused the question of risk with that of opportunity; whilst one particular avenue of opportunity had been closed to M, it could not be said, particularly having regard to C's averments, that the wider risk of sexual harm presented by M had truly been diminished to any material extent, therefore, the basis for the sheriff's conclusion was flawed. (3) The sheriff ought to have given due weight to the more general risk posed by M rather than to certain, particular circumstances in which the risk might have happened to manifest itself, and had the sheriff given weight thereto, there would have been no basis for not finding that the the making of an interim order was just. (4) The making of an interim order was now at large for the court where in making such an order, the court was putting in place what ought to have been the decision of the court at first instance, on the basis of all the material presented to it, the manner in which the appeal had been conducted suggested that, should the appeal be allowed, an interim order would follow, and the legislative provisions existed for the protection of children and it could be absurd and potentially unsafe were the court to be precluded from making such an order should it consider it just to do so and that without any further delay, accordingly, the sheriff's interlocutor would be recalled and the interim order made instead.

CHIEF CONSTABLE OF POLICE SCOTLAND v M, 2016 S.L.T. (Sh Ct) 148, Sheriff Principal C A L Scott, QC, Sh Ct (Glasgow).

2808 Road traffic offences–Careless driving–Eight penalty points

[Road Traffic Act 1988 (c.52) s.3]

M, who pleaded guilty to driving without due care and attention, contrary to the Road Traffic Act 1988 s.3, by driving too close to the vehicle ahead of him on a motorway, appealed as excessive the imposition of eight penalty points, without discount. M submitted that (1) in the absence of other aggravating factors, he had been travelling at the same speed as other motorway traffic, albeit too close to the car ahead, which was at the lower end of the range of careless driving and which had not merited a starting point or headline sentence of eight penalty points, with the minimum three points being the appropriate penalty; (2) *esto* the penalty points imposed had been appropriate, discount ought to have been afforded such that a lower number of points would have been imposed.

Held: Appeal refused. (1) A driver who drove in a manner such as M deliberately courted danger, there was a high degree of culpability and a clear likelihood that a serious collision might occur and the sheriff had been fully justified in categorising it as being as the upper end of careless driving; the court would have been entitled to impose a period of disqualification for that type of aggressive driving and having categorised M's driving to be at the top end of the careless scale, the sentence imposed was lenient. (2) The question of discount was for the judgment or discretion of the sentencing court, M's guilty plea had been tendered at the trial diet, the utilitarian benefit thereof had been marginal, and the sheriff had given cogent reasons for not discounting the penalty points; the sheriff had properly and fairly set out his reasoning having given due regard to the nature of the driving, *Gemmell (James Kelly) v HM Advocate* [2011] HCJAC 129, 2012 J.C. 223, [2012] C.L.Y. 4277, *applied* and *Watt v Dunn* [2016] SAC (Crim) 2, 2016 S.L.T. (Sh Ct) 104, [2016] 2813, *considered*. (3) A period of disqualification would have been justified on the facts of the present case, and the sheriff had afforded M a generously discounted penalty by declining to disqualify and by restricting the penalty points imposed for reasons unduly in M's favour.

MCINALLY v DUNN, [2016] SAC (Crim) 5, 2016 S.C.C.R. 243, Sheriff Principal M M Stephen, QC, Sheriff P A Arthurson, QC, SAC.

2809 Road traffic offences–Drink driving offences–Imposition of vehicle forfeiture order–Previous analogous conviction

[Road Traffic Act 1988 (c.52) s.7(6); Road Traffic Offenders Act 1988 (c.53) s.33A]

D, who pleaded guilty to failing to provide a specimen of breath, contrary to the Road Traffic Act 1988 s.7(6) appealed as excessive the sheriff's imposition of an order for forfeiture of his vehicle in terms of the Road Traffic Offenders Act 1988 s.33A. D had a directly analogous conviction from February 2009 and a schedule of previous convictions including a High Court conviction under a sea fishing conservation order and offences of disorder. The sheriff had imposed no fine but had disqualified D from driving for four years.

Held: Appeal refused. The offence of failing to provide breath specimens when required was serious and D's previous analogous conviction was a significant aggravating factor; the sheriff, when considering forfeiture in terms of s.33A, required to consider the particular facts and circumstances of the offence and the offender with a view to determining the overall penalty to be imposed, in relation to which factors such as public safety and protection and deterrence would be relevant, and in the present case, it was the second occasion on which D had failed to provide a breath specimen in a jurisdiction in which drink driving was prevalent, which the sheriff had been entitled to take into account, no other financial penalty had been imposed, and the circumstances of the present case disclosed specific factors which supported the sheriff's decision to order forfeiture, accordingly, it was not excessive.

DUNCAN v MURPHY, [2016] SAC (Crim) 9, 2016 S.C.L. 573, Sheriff Principal M M Stephen, QC, Sheriff S Murphy, QC, SAC.

2810 Road traffic offences–Drink driving offences–Length of disqualification period–Misdirection

J, who pleaded guilty at the trial diet to a contravention of the Road Traffic Act 1988 s. 5(1)(a), appealed as excessive the imposition of 34 months' disqualification from driving, reduced from three years, and a fine of £1,400, reduced from £1,500. J had had a breath alcohol level of 87 mg in 100 ml at the time of the offence and had no previous convictions for drink driving offences but had other road traffic convictions. In determining sentence, the sheriff had applied a multiplier, being the ratio of 1 to 1.59, namely the difference between the Scottish prescribed limit and the applicable limit in England and Wales, had equated J's alcohol reading with 138 mg in England and had thereby determined a headline sentence of 36 months, having regard to the magistrates court sentencing guidelines for England and Wales.

Held: Appeal allowed, sentence quashed and 22 months' disqualification and £900 fine substituted. (1) The sheriff's approach was erroneous: the gravity of a drink driving offence ought to be measured in objective, absolute terms rather than by considering the number of times by which a driver exceeded the limit, the proper approach to sentence in a drink driving offence was to consider the alcohol reading together with any aggravating and mitigating circumstances relating to the offence, such as the quality of the driving, and the offender, which had to include consideration of his record or lack thereof; the significance of the lower prescribed limit in Scotland related not to the level of risk posed by the offender but that it was now an offence to drive a motor vehicle after consuming lower levels of alcohol, the offence threshold was thereby lowered in Scotland and drivers who breached that limit faced an obligatory one year disqualification. (2) J fell to be sentenced for a first drink driving offence, the alcohol level in his breath was relatively high and the sheriff had been correct to consider a period of disqualification above the minimum, however, the sheriff had misdirected himself by applying a formulaic calculation thereof based on the ratio of the alcohol reading above the prescribed limit rather than making an objective assessment of the alcohol reading and other factors, accordingly, the assessment of the period of disqualification was one which the court ought to determine on the facts and submissions, an appropriate period of disqualification was two years, which would be reduced to 22 months to reflect J's guilty plea, negotiated prior to but tendered at the trial diet. (3) The sheriff had misdirected himself as to the level of culpability and risk presented by J, the fine imposed was excessive and would be quashed and £1,000, reduced to £900, substituted.

JENKINS v HARVIE, [2016] SAC (Crim) 14, 2016 S.L.T. (Sh Ct) 205, Sheriff Principal M M Stephen, QC, Sheriff P J Braid, SAC.

2811 Road traffic offences–Fines–Offender's means–Fine to be paid in instalments over 92 weeks

[Criminal Procedure (Scotland) Act 1995 (c.46) s.211(7)]

X who pleaded guilty to driving without a licence (charge 2) and without insurance (charge 3), with both charges being subject to a bail aggravation, appealed as excessive the fines imposed by the justice of the peace. On charge 2 the justice had fined X £120, discounted from £180, which had included £20 for the bail aggravation, and on charge 3, £340, discounted from £510, including £40 for the bail aggravation. The justice had been aware that X was unemployed and in receipt of benefits but had considered it appropriate to impose fines comparable to fixed penalties, allowing them to be paid in instalments of £10 per fortnight, accordingly, it would have taken 92 weeks for the fines to be paid. Both on passing sentence and in his report to the court the justice had suggested that if X could find employment, he could clear the fines more quickly.

Held: Appeal allowed. (1) The justice had some discretion as to the level of fines to impose and the time within which they were to be paid, however, he was bound by the Criminal Procedure (Scotland) Act 1995 s.211(7) to have regard to X's means so far as known to the court and had not been entitled to proceed upon the basis of possible future developments which had no foundation in the information before him. (2) A fine ought to be capable of being paid in appoximately one year and in *Paterson (Derek) v McGlennan (Sentencing)* 1995 S.C.C.R. 42, [1995] C.L.Y. 5772 the court had considered that as the fines would have taken 90 weeks to be paid, and it was not satisfactory in view of the appellant's income to increase the instalments, they were excessive, *Paterson*, *considered*. (3) In the present case it was not appropriate to increase the instalments and the period of 92 weeks confirmed that the fines were excessive and amounted to a miscarriage of justice. A fine of £60, reduced from £90 for the guilty plea, would be imposed on charge 2, and £165, discounted from £250 on charge 3, with the total to be paid at £10 per fortnight.

JACKSON v MURPHY, [2016] SAC (Crim) 1, 2016 S.L.T. (Sh Ct) 55, Sheriff Principal C A L Scott, QC, Sheriff Beckett QC, SAC.

2812 Road traffic offences–Forfeiture orders–Forfeiture of vehicle–Whether proportionate

[Road Traffic Act 1988 (c.52) s.5, s.5(1)(a), s.7, s.7(6)]

L, who pleaded guilty to contraventions of the Road Traffic Act 1988 ss.5(1)(a) and 7(6) at an intermediate diet, appealed the sheriff's order for forfeiture of her vehicle (V), worth £15,000. In relation to the s.5 offence, L had been nearly three times over the limit and had been obstructive and unco-operative in relation to the s.7 offence, which had occurred just over a week later, and V had been used in the commission of both offences. The sheriff had found, with regard to the requirement for public protection, that L's attitude had been cavalier, irresponsible and dangerous, and had imposed fines and three years' disqualification as well as the forfeiture order.

Held: Appeal refused. (1) The sheriff had been of the view that L met the criteria in Wheatley, *Road Traffic Law in Scotland* (5th edn) para.8.11.5, p.317, had concluded that the forfeiture order imposed would tailor a sentence to achieve public protection, and had had regard to L's disregard of his bail undertaking, that the offences had occurred in close proximity and that the second offence had been an escalation in L's offending, she had concluded that forfeiture of V was a reasonable measure to prevent re-offending and against that background, and standing the scope of the argument presented on appeal, there was no basis upon which the sheriff had erred or misdirected herself. (2) On the information provided to the sheriff, there had been no basis upon which she might have concluded that forfeiture of V was disproportionate, she had had regard to the risk to the public posed by the nature of L's offending, it had been entirely legitimate for her to consider a forfeiture order and her consideration and imposition thereof were beyond criticism. (3) Whilst a forfeiture order could not constitute an absolute safeguard in respect of protection of the public, its use was not restricted where there were compelling circumstances suggesting that an offender's conduct had been redolent of an exceptional disregard for the consequences of his behaviour; L's conduct was sufficient to meet that test.

LI v DUNN, [2016] SAC (Crim) 7, 2016 S.L.T. (Sh Ct) 153, Sheriff Principal C A L Scott, QC, Sheriff A L MacFadyen, SAC.

2813 Road traffic offences–Penalty points–Justice of peace declining to discount four penalty points for public protection reasons

W, who pleaded guilty to speeding, appealed as excessive the imposition of four penalty points. W had been offered a fixed penalty notice with a fine of £100 and three penalty points but had been unable to pay, proceedings had been raised, and a discounted fine and the penalty points imposed, the justice of the peace applying no discount to the penalty points because of the risk to public safety presented by W's driving. W submitted that he would have paid the fixed penalty if he could have done so but he had been unemployed and therefore he ought to have been dealt with on the same basis as the fixed penalty.

Held: Appeal refused. (1) Penalty points were susceptible to discount in the same way as any other penalty and the consideration of public protection did not justify declining to discount for an early guilty plea, *Gemmell (James Kelly) v HM Advocate* [2011] HCJAC 129, 2012 J.C. 223, [2012] C.L.Y. 4277, *followed.* (2) The justice had erred in considering that public protection provided a valid reason for declining to discount the four penalty points, however, given the speed at which W had been travelling, the imposition of penalty points had not been excessive or inappropriate so as to represent a miscarriage of justice.

WATT v DUNN, [2016] SAC (Crim) 2, 2016 S.L.T. (Sh Ct) 104, Sheriff Principal C A L Scott, QC, Sheriff Beckett QC, SAC.

2814 Scottish Sentencing Council–Business plans–Time limits

THE SCOTTISH SENTENCING COUNCIL (SUBMISSION OF BUSINESS PLAN) ORDER 2016, SSI 2016/55; made under the Criminal Justice and Licensing (Scotland) Act 2010 s.12(2). In force: 7 March 2016.

This Order specifies the day before which the Scottish Sentencing Council must prepare and submit, to Scottish Ministers, its first business plan, setting out how it proposes to carry out its functions, in accordance with the Criminal Justice and Licensing (Scotland) Act 2010 s.12.

2815 Sexual offences–Child sex offences–Offender central player in conspiracy–Comparative justice

The Scottish Criminal Cases Review Commission referred the case of M, convicted of *inter alia* conspiring with others to commit sexual offences against a child, on the basis that a miscarriage of justice might have arisen. The charge contained 17 subheads of which M was convicted of 11. He was sentenced to an extended sentence of 12 years, with a custodial element of 10 years. The Crown conceded that there was insufficient evidence to convict M on various subheads within the charge, that the trial judge had failed to direct the jury that they required to restrict any verdict of guilty to those co-accused (X) with whom M was shown to have had direct contact, and to those subheads directly involving him, and that part of the conviction had been incompetent.

Held: Conviction quashed and amended conviction substituted, and custodial element of sentence quashed and seven years substituted. (1) The Crown concession was correct and the court would quash the verdict and substitute therefor an amended conviction. (2) The subheads of which M remained convicted were significant, he had been a central player in the conspiracy, and attempting to carry out an exercise of comparative justice in relation to the sentences imposed on X, the custodial element of the sentence would be quashed and seven years substituted.

MILLIGAN (JOHN) v HM ADVOCATE, [2016] HCJAC 22, 2016 S.C.L. 444, Lord Justice General (Carloway), Lord Bracadale, Lady Clark of Calton, HCJ.

2816 Sexual offences–Extended sentences–Rape and sexual abuse of daughter–Length of custodial period

M, convicted of various charges, including the sexual abuse of his daughter (X) between the ages of five and 15, raping her on one occasion and attempting to rape her on another, appealed against the imposition of a 16 year extended sentence, with a custodial part of 13 years and an extension period of three years. M had seriously sexually abused X throughout most of her childhood on a regular basis, and had also raped his niece. The trial judge had considered that in view of the persistence and gravity of the abuse, X's vulnerability and M's gross breach of trust, the case was exceptionally serious. M submitted that the 13 year custodial term was severe and excessive in the circumstances and sought reduction thereof to enable a longer extension period.

Held: Appeal refused. The court could not disagree with the trial judge's categorisation of M's persistent course of offending, the offences were very serious, and it could not be said that the sentence was excessive or that the trial judge had fallen into error in the makeup as between the custodial and extension periods.

M v HM ADVOCATE, [2016] HCJAC 80, 2016 S.C.L. 920, Lord Menzies, Lord Drummond Young, HCJ.

2817 **Sexual offences–Extended sentences–Two separate sets of offences–Sentence length**

E, convicted of installing a covert camera in his bathroom to film children's genitals, sexually assaulting a child, and a charge relating to indecent images (charges 1, 4, 5 and 6) and of using the covert camera to record adults using his bathroom (charges 7-11), appealed as excessive the concurrent custodial sentences imposed. E was 42, had no previous convictions and had been drinking heavily at the time of the offences, and realised that his offending behaviour required to be addressed. Immediately after arrest he had attended counselling and he had been considered suitable for offence focused work. The sheriff had considered it alarming that E could not offer any explanation for his behaviour and had emphasised the degree of planning and repetition. The sheriff imposed extended sentences and discounted the custodial term in respect of the plea, she selected a headline sentence of six years in relation to the first tranche of offences and the maximum available five years in relation to the second.

Held: Sentences quashed and 32 months' imprisonment with a concurrent two year extension in respect of each tranche of offences substituted. The sentences selected by the sheriff had been excessive, moreover, E's participation in a three year counselling programme might be started in prison and continued at liberty; the offences, although unpleasant and particularly disturbing where they involved children, did not merit a custodial term of the length of the headline sentences selected by the sheriff, and they were excessive and would be quashed and substituted with an extended sentence of 32 months' imprisonment with a two year extension in respect of each tranche of offences.

E v HM ADVOCATE, [2016] HCJAC 36, 2016 S.C.L. 557, Lady Dorrian, Lord Bracadale, HCJ.

2818 **Sexual offences–Notification requirements–Deliberate and voyeuristic conduct–Whether sexual aspect to conduct**

[Criminal Justice and Licensing (Scotland) Act 2010 (asp 13) s.38(1); Sexual Offences Act 2003 (c.42) Sch.3 para.60]

M, who pleaded guilty to behaving in a threatening or abusive manner, contrary to the Criminal Justice and Licensing (Scotland) Act 2010 s.38(1), by exhibiting to a third party (X) an image displaying C in a state of undress and with her private parts exposed, placing C in a state of fear and alarm, appealed against the sheriff's determination that there was a significant sexual aspect to the offence in terms of the Sexual Offences (Scotland) Act 2003 Sch.3 para.60 and making him subject to the notification requirements. C had permitted M to use her mobile telephone from which he had taken a screenshot of the image and had shared it electronically with X. The sheriff had found that M's motivation had been almost entirely of a sexual nature, the nature of his conduct had been deliberate and inherently voyeuristic, and where M's social enquiry report had recorded that he presented a risk of inappropriate sexual behaviour towards adult females and was in a high risk category relative to other adult male sex offenders the protective purpose of the notification requirement applied to him.

Held: Appeal refused. The offence had involved obtaining clandestine access to an intimate photograph on C's mobile telephone showing her private parts and transmitting it electronically to a third party; there had been a sexual aspect to that conduct and it had been both deliberate and voyeuristic, and the sheriff had been entitled to regard that as significant.

MCHUGH v HARVIE, [2015] HCJAC 86, 2015 S.C.L. 987, The Lord Justice Clerk (Carloway), Lord Bracadale, Lord Matthews, HCJ.

2819 Sexual offences–Orders for lifelong restriction–Four charges of sexual offences, including against a child–Level of risk requiring order for lifelong restriction

[Criminal Justice (Scotland) Act 2003 (Commencement No.9) Order 2006 (SSI 2006/332)]

M, convicted of the sexual assault and attempted rape of a nine-year-old girl on repeated occasions between December 1996 and December 1997 (charge 1), raping his partner on an occasion between 1 January 1998 and 31 December 2001 (charge 2), sexual assault and rape of a partner (charge 6), and raping a partner on various occasions between 1 November 2002 and 31 December 2004 (charge 9), appealed against the imposition of a sentence of life imprisonment with a 10-year punishment part. The trial judge had believed that it was not competent for him to impose an order for lifelong restriction and had selected the punishment part on the basis that had he imposed a determinate sentence, it would have been of 20 years' imprisonment, in doing so, overlooking the terms of the Criminal Justice (Scotland) Act 2003 (Commencement No. 9) Order 2006, in terms of which a lifelong restriction order was competent in relation to charges 2, 6 and 9. The appeal court had ordered the preparation of a criminal justice social work report (CJSWR) which had concluded that M presented a high level of risk, noting that he had been recalled to custody during a previous sentence imposed for sexual offences for failing to comply with licence conditions, his sexual offending spanned 11 years, his deviant sexual behaviour remained unaddressed due to his denials of guilt and despite a lengthy period in prison, and had indicated that the court might give consideration to the imposition of a lifelong restriction order. On the basis thereof, the appeal court had ordered a risk assessment, which had concluded that M presented a high risk to public safety, that there were few protective factors and long term risk management was required, that he had a narcissistic personality disorder with a sense of entitlement and there was partial evidence of some psychopathic traits. A second risk assessment report had been obtained following criticisms of certain aspects of the first one by M, which had made a similar assessment to the first. M submitted that (1) an extended sentence, which would have been available in respect of charges 6 and 9, would have provided adequate protection of the public, and met the requirements of punishment and deterrence; (2) *esto* a discretionary life sentence was appropriate, calculating the punishment part by reference to a determinate sentence of 20 years was excessive.

Held: Sentence quashed and order for lifelong restriction with seven year punishment part in relation to charges 2, 6 and 9, and nine years' imprisonment on charge 1, substituted. (1) The risk presented by M could not adequately be managed by an extended sentence and an order for lifelong restriction was required; both reports were clear that M presented a significant and enduring risk to the public in circumstances where there was little or no prospect of him properly engaging in work designed to reduce it, M was resistant to engagement with rehabilitative programmes, failing to acknowledge either any requirement for change on his part or guilt for any of his offences, the conclusions of the second risk assessment report indicated that the overall risk classification was high, that the nature, seriousness and pattern of M's behaviour indicated an enduring propensity to seriously endanger the physical and psychological wellbeing of the public, yet the potential for change appeared to be significantly limited, there were few protective factors to counterbalance the concerning characteristics, in the absence of concerted long term measures to manage the risk, including restriction, monitoring and supervision, he was likely to continue to seriously endanger the public, which accorded with the conclusions of the original report that there were few protective factors, a lack of motivation to change, and a family which colluded in his denials, the original report had noted that in his previous seven year prison sentence M had not participated in any offence specific programmes as he continued to deny his offending, and there was no evidence that his attitude thereto had changed or was likely to change in future. (2) An order for lifelong restriction would be made and in fixing the punishment part, the previous convictions and also the seriousness of the offences, or of the offence combined with other offences of which M had been convicted on the same indictment, would be taken into account; it had to be recognised that M had along with charges 2, 6, and 9 been convicted of charge 1, and in light thereof, the calculation ought to be commenced by reference to a determinate period of 20 years, of which six would be stripped out for the element of public protection, leaving 14 years for the purposes of punishment and deterrence, and the resulting punishment part would therefore be seven years, and a determinate sentence of nine years would be imposed in respect of charge 1.

MACINTOSH (JOHN DAVID) v HM ADVOCATE, [2016] HCJAC 75, 2016 S.C.L. 923, The Lord Justice Clerk (Lady Dorrian), Lord Menzies, Lord Drummond Young, HCJ.

2820 Sexual offences–Undue leniency–Multiple offences against former partners and their children–Appropriate length of extended sentence

[Criminal Law (Consolidation) (Scotland) Act 1995 (c.39) s.6; Sexual Offences (Scotland) Act 2009 (asp 9) s.1]

The Crown appealed as unduly lenient an extended sentence of seven years with two years' supervision imposed on K following his conviction for seven charges involving sexual offences against two of his former partners (G and W, collectively P) and their children (S and D, collectively C). The charges were using lewd practices against S, a boy aged between nine and 10, in 2007-2008 (charge 1), indecently assaulting S during the same period (charge 2), using lewd practices, in 2008-2010, against D, a girl aged between 12 and 14, contrary to the Criminal Law (Consolidation) (Scotland) Act 1995 s.6 (charge 7), indecently assaulting G in 2008 to 2010 in the form of continued anal penetration after the withdrawal of consent (charge 13) and of anal penetration on various occasions (charge 15), the anal rape of G on various occasions, contrary to the Sexual Offences (Scotland) Act 2009 s.1 (charge 18), and anally raping W on one occasion in 2013, contrary to s.1 of the 2009 Act (charge 19). K had continued to deny any sexual involvement with S or D and a criminal justice social work report had assessed him at medium risk of reoffending. In relation to P, the main thrust of K's plea in mitigation had been the impact of the offences against P and K's background of general sexual promiscuity. The sentencing judge had discounted any element of breach of trust in relation to C as no such aggravation had been libeled, and had considered that the rapes of P had been at the lower end of the seriousness scale, although he had not regarded K's relationships with P as mitigatory *per se*.

Held: Appeal allowed, sentence quashed and 12 years' extended sentence with four years' supervision substituted. (1) The conduct libeled in charges 1 and 2 had included the repeated oral penetration and attempted sodomy of a 9 or 10 year old boy over whom K had been in a position of trust, a matter which had not constituted a formal aggravation of the offence requiring a separate libel, and the behaviour had gone on for a considerable period of time, that type of abuse was particularly serious even had S coped with it in later years and although the conduct in relation to D had been more limited, it was still serious and significant, particularly when seen in light of the offending against S; those offences could be seen as a course of conduct which might be disposed of by a cumulative penalty, and a custodial sentence of at least four years would be appropriate for such lewd practices, *HM Advocate v Malley (Sentencing)* 2005 G.W.D. 12-207 and *HM Advocate v Briody (Sentencing)* 2000 G.W.D. 29-1138, *considered*. (2) The trial judge had afforded too much weight to P's past sexual experience and to the existence of both prior and continuing sexual relationships. Had the offences in charges 13, 15, 18 and 19 stood alone, a sentence of six years might have been regarded as appropriate, however, since it was appropriate that those offences ought to attract a consecutive sentence to that imposed for the lewd conduct against C, regard had to be had to their cumulative effect, and a consecutive period of four years was appropriate, to produce an overall custodial element of eight years, *HM Advocate v Cooperwhite (Stephen)* [2013] HCJAC 88, 2013 S.L.T. 975, [2013] C.L.Y. 3989 and *R v AM* [2010] 2 NZLR 750, *considered*, *Ramage (Stuart Robert) v HM Advocate* 1999 S.C.C.R. 592, [1999] C.L.Y. 5953 and *Petrie (James) v HM Advocate* [2011] HCJAC 1, 2012 J.C. 1, [2011] C.L.Y. 4598, *doubted*. *Opinion*, that whatever a judge's own views, he had to sentence on the basis of the crimes of which the accused had been convicted, albeit in the contexts in which those crimes had been committed, in light of current Scottish sentencing principles and practice, and while he was entitled to have regard to sentencing guidelines in other jurisdictions, especially in neighbouring countries such as England and Wales, such comparators ought not to be applied too rigidly, *HM Advocate v B* [2015] HCJAC 106, 2015 S.L.T. 841, [2016] 2806, *considered*.

HM ADVOCATE v K *sub nom.* HM ADVOCATE v SSK, [2015] HCJAC 114, 2016 S.L.T. 142, The Lord Justice Clerk (Carloway), Lord Bracadale, Lord Matthews, HCJ.

2821 Supervised release orders–Sentence length–Consideration of test of necessity–Discounting of order

[Criminal Procedure (Scotland) Act 1995 (c.46) s.196, s.209]

X, who pleaded guilty to assaulting his partner (P) on 22 September 2015, appealed against the imposition of a 12 month supervised release order. X had previously been convicted of two separate charges of assault against P in 2014 and had been sentenced to six months' imprisonment. The criminal justice social work report had recommended a 12 month action plan to help X overcome his aggression and avoid further offending, and the sheriff had considered that, having regard to that recommendation and to X's propensity for violence, a 12 months' supervised release order was required. X submitted that (1) the sheriff had not been entitled to conclude that the imposition of an supervised release order was necessary to protect the public from serious harm on X's release and he had failed to direct his mind to the question of whether or not the order was necessary for public protection; (2) the sheriff had erred in failing to discount the supervised release order, having regard to *Gemmell (James Kelly) v HM Advocate* [2011] HCJAC 129, 2012 J.C. 223, [2012] C.L.Y. 4277.

Held: Appeal refused. (1) In all the circumstances, the sheriff was plainly entitled to conclude that the order was necessary for protection of the public and it could not be said that he had failed to have regard to the test of necessity where his explanation for imposing the order was redolent of him concluding that that test had been met. (2) Such distinctions and differences as existed between supervised release orders and extended sentences were not indicative of the length of a supervised release order being amenable to a discount in terms of the Criminal Procedure (Scotland) Act 1995 s.196, on the contrary, they both fell into the category of sentences imposed for the purpose of protecting the public; once the headline sentence had been discounted to 18 months, the s.209(7)(b) cap had applied, had the supervised release order remained at 10 months, its length would have exceeded the date by which the entire term of imprisonment specified in X's sentence had elapsed, taking account of the relevant early release provisions meant that the supervised release order required to terminate after nine months, and the reduction was wholly explained by s.209(7)(b), *Gemmell*, *considered*.

O'NEIL (JASON THOMAS) v HM ADVOCATE, [2016] HCJAC 56, 2016 S.C.L. 657, Lady Smith, Lord Brodie, Lord Malcolm, HCJ.

2822 Supply of drugs–Sentence length–Usefulness of Definitive Guidelines from the Sentencing Council of England and Wales

[Misuse of Drugs Act 1971 (c.38) s.4(3)(b)]

S, who pleaded guilty to being concerned in the supply of a controlled drug, contrary to the Misuse of Drugs Act 1971 s.4(3)(b), appealed as excessive a sentence of 13 and a half years' imprisonment, discounted from 18 years to reflect his guilty plea. S had been the director of an organised criminal gang which was concerned in the acquisition, adulteration and onward supply of heroin, and the unadulterated drug had been sourced in Scotland. S had previously received a custodial sentence of 42 months for concern in the supply of drugs, part of which had remained unexpired at the date of the offending. In mitigation, S had relied *inter alia* on his extensive criminal background and the low profit he had received from the enterprise. S submitted that the starting point of 18 years was too high where the Sentencing Council of England and Wales recommended 12-16 years for the most serious offences, and the judge had erred in placing the present case in that category and in considering that there were aggravating factors justifying a greater headline sentence.

Held: Appeal refused. (1) The sentencing judge had been aware that there was no charge of importation of heroin, the drug had nevertheless been in a state permitting substantial re-bulking and, given the quantities and nature of the operation involved, any difference between the judge's description of the facts as and the position advanced as the reality at the appeal hearing would have had a minimal effect in terms of sentencing; any error made by the judge in relation to the volume of dealing fell into the *de minimis* category when the overall amounts were realised. (2) The sentence imposed was one which was in line with those considered by the High Court, sitting in its appellate capacity, as appropriate for persons directing large scale heroin supply networks in Scotland, and while the Definitive Guidelines from the Sentencing Council of England and Wales often provided a useful cross check for sentences in Scotland, especially where the offences were regulated by a United Kingdom statute and there were identical sentencing *maxima*, they ought not to be applied in Scotland in a rigid or mechanistic fashion, given the differences in sentencing purposes, practices and regimes between the two jurisdictions; had S been sentenced in England, in terms of the definitive guideline, it was likely that he would have received a longer custodial term, *Wright v HM Advocate* 2006 G.W.D. 27-604 and *Hamill v HM Advocate (Sentencing)* 2000 G.W.D. 13-480, *applied* and *R. v O'Neill (Joseph)* [2015] EWCA Crim 1438, *Attorney General's Reference (Nos 82 and 90 of 2014)* [2014] EWCA Crim 2884, [2015] 2 Cr. App. R. (S.) 1, [2015] C.L.Y. 2205, *R. v Tourh (Hussein)* [2009] EWCA Crim 874 and *R. v Welsh (Christopher Mark)* [2014] EWCA Crim 1027, *considered*. (3) It was the overall sentence which the court required to consider and in the present case, the discount was generous, and the final sentence arrived at was a reasonable one in all the circumstances. *Observed*, (1) that when using comparators, not only was the offender's role important but also the street value of the drug; it was that value which was the prime indicator of the damage caused to society thereby and the dealer's profit, whilst relevant, was far less significant for sentencing purposes; (2) that amongst the Class A drugs, heroin had a particularly dangerous part to play in societal terms, it was unique and care ought to be taken when using precedents involving other drugs, even those in the same classification; (3) that the effect of coming from a criminally oriented family might be seen as reducing moral culpability, however, that was a factor outweighed by the need to discourage endemic criminality.

SUTHERLAND (ALEXANDER) v HM ADVOCATE, [2015] HCJAC 115, 2016 S.L.T. 93, The Lord Justice Clerk (Carloway), Lord Brodie, Lord Matthews, HCJ.

2823 Supply of drugs–Young offenders–18-year-old first-time offender–Appropriateness of custodial sentence

S, aged 18, who pleaded guilty to being concerned in the supply of heroin, appealed as excessive the imposition of a 27 month custodial sentence, reduced from three years on account of his plea. The criminal justice social work report (CJSWR) had reported that S had only been looking after the drugs for a friend, he had not stood to gain financially therefrom, his behaviour appeared largely to have resulted from naivety and poor judgment, he had recognised that he had made a mistake which could have repercussions for his future life prospects, he had given up the tenancy of the property where the offence had occurred and he had taken steps to limit the possibility of reoffending and had returned to live with his grandparents, since which time he had not involved himself in offending, that he would be suitable for a non-custodial disposal with a supervision requirement to enable offence focused work, and that a placement for unpaid work would also be appropriate. The sheriff had considered that the report had been unrealistic on the basis that the writer appeared to be unaware that the courts had consistently expressed the view that those involved in supplying class A drugs could expect to receive significant custodial sentences in all but the most exceptional circumstances and S had failed to offer any substantive mitigation where he had not elaborated or explained the suggestion that he had been influenced by others, it had not been stated in mitigation that the plea had been tendered on the basis that S had been due to return the drugs to an acquaintance, and although S was a first offender and thus entitled to the protection of the Criminal Procedure (Scotland) Act 1995 s.204, the appeal court's position was not that first offenders ought not to be imprisoned for involving themselves in the supply of class A drugs.

Held: Appeal allowed, sentence quashed, and three year community payback order with supervision requirement and requirement to carry out 300 hours' unpaid work substituted. (1) The CJSWR had made it clear that S's position had been that he had been holding the drugs for another to whom they were to have been returned, there was no doubt that the fact that S had made no financial gain from his involvement in the offence had formed part of the plea in mitigation, and the report had indicated that S had recognised that he required to avoid certain individuals in the community and his decision to distance himself from his peers, the sheriff had made no reference to S's youth, s.204 of the 1995 Act dealt with first offenders who were unrepresented or over the age of 21, the sheriff had made no reference to s.207 which gave protection to S *inter alia* because of his youth, furthermore, the effect of S's youth, the bearing it might have on his offending or decision making, or the life opportunities available to him had not been addressed by the sheriff and appeared not to have featured in his thinking in relation to the appropriate sentence, and although the sheriff had made reference to the court's view that those involved in the present type of offence could expect to receive custodial sentences, it was always necessary to consider the individual context, in which the offenders youth would be an important consideration. (2) S had had an unsettled childhood, his decision to move away from the location of the offending to live with supportive family, the absence of any offending since doing so and the support of his family had all been described as protective factors in the CJSWR, S's recognition that he required to take steps himself to address his future and his steps in that respect were positive, and it was wrong to suggest that no method other than a custodial disposal was appropriate, *Kane (Michael) v HM Advocate* 2003 S.C.C.R. 749, [2004] C.L.Y. 5119, *applied.* (3) A three year community payback order would be substituted, with a supervision requirement that S was to follow his supervising officer's recommendations, additionally, S would be required to carry out 300 hours' unpaid work in the community for 12 months.

SMART (JORDAN THOMAS) v HM ADVOCATE, [2016] HCJAC 73, 2016 S.L.T. 1035, The Lord Justice Clerk (Lady Dorrian), Lord Brodie, HCJ.

SOCIAL WELFARE

2824 Community care–Needs assessments–Local authority's duty under s.12A Social Work (Scotland) Act 1968–Needs adequately met by care plan

[Adults with Incapacity (Scotland) Act 2000 (asp 4) Pt 6; Social Work (Scotland) Act 1968 (c.49) s.12A, s.12B]

The guardian (S) in property and financial matters under the Adults with Incapacity (Scotland) Act 2000 Pt 6, of L, who had been struck by a motor vehicle in 2002 and sustained serious head injuries, petitioned for judicial review of the alleged failure by a local authority (F) to carry out its statutory duty under the Social Work (Scotland) Act 1968 s.12A in respect of L's care in the community. L subsequently died in 2015. S had raised an action against the driver of the vehicle which had been settled for £5.1 million. F had intimated to S that, following an assessment of L's needs, there was no element of unmet need relating to her and that there was no requirement for the provision of services from F; further, L's needs were being adequately met, that the means were available to provide for her care for the foreseeable future and in those circumstances, no payment was appropriate in terms of s.12B. S submitted that F had failed to carry out an assessment of L's needs, as required to do in terms of s.12A(1); had it carried out such an assessment, it had taken into account an irrelevant consideration; further, F had failed to comply with s.12B which required it to determine the reasonably estimated cost of the community care services that L's needs called for and, in the absence of a means test, F ought to have offered to pay such cost. F argued that, on a proper construction of s.12A(1), it had done what was required by the legislation which did not extend to applying its mind to the provisions of s.12B; in any event, S had failed to exhaust an alternative statutory remedy, namely F's complaints procedure, and the petition was thus incompetent.

Held: Petition dismissed. (1) On the information provided to the court, the application could not be said to be incompetent on the basis that S had had an effective alternative remedy available to him which he had not exhausted. (2) S's challenge to each of F's decisions had to fail: it was clear that F had assessed L's needs on two separate occasions and that L's needs called for the provision of services, which were being adequately met by her care plan; F then had regard to s.12B as they had a duty to do whereby it was determined that it was appropriate to make no payment in respect of L's securing the provision of the service; what operated to permit F to make no payment in terms of s.12B(1) where the person was assessed as able to pay in full was the provision that the authority was to pay only "such amount" as they determined to be appropriate.

SMART'S GUARDIAN v FIFE COUNCIL, [2015] CSOH 183, 2016 S.L.T. 384, Lord Jones, OH.

2825 Residential accommodation–Care costs–Alleged gratuitous alienation of dwelling house to avoid accommodation charges–Local authority seeking to recover costs from transferee of dwelling house

[Health and Social Services and Social Security Adjudications Act 1983 (c.41) s.21; National Assistance Act 1948 (c.29) s.22; National Assistance (Assessment of Resources) Regulations 1992 (SI 1992/2977) reg.25]

A local authority (B) raised an action under the Health and Social Services and Social Security Adjudications Act 1983 s.21 seeking to recover £42,750 from G in respect of the provision of care accommodation to X, since deceased. A gratuitous alienation of a dwelling house had been made by X to G which B averred was made knowingly with the intention of avoiding the accommodation charges. B submitted that it had fixed the rate to be paid by X in the exercise of a statutory function, s.21 of the 1983 Act, the National Assistance Act 1948 s.22 and the National Assistance (Assessment of Resources) Regulations 1992 all formed part of a single scheme and once B had determined that the heritable property had been disponed of for the purpose, and with the intention of avoiding or decreasing the amount that X might be liable to pay for her accommodation, that was effectively the end of the matter, and that determination could only be challenged by way of judicial review in the Court of Session. Further, three points could be taken from s.22 of the 1948 Act, namely, the rates to be charged were to be fixed by the authority managing the premises, the local authority had the power to determine ability to pay in order to fix a rate lower than the fixed rate, and the local authority had to give effect to any regulations made for the purpose of assessing ability to pay, and taking all the provisions together, an authority when presented with information which might suggest deprivation of an asset might make a determination as to what the intention of the service user was, following which, there was no statutory mechanism for any form of appeal.

Held: Proof allowed. (1) There was nothing about the language used in s.21, when viewed in isolation and applying the normal principles of statutory construction, to suggest that a local authority was entrusted with a jurisdiction to make a determination as to whether or not a person to whom an asset had been transferred was liable to make payment thereto; the section set out three conditions which, if satisfied, rendered such a person liable and limited the amount to the value of the asset and a local authority could request payment from the transferee but, in the event of a denial, it was open to the local authority to address the courts in the usual way. (2) The statutory provisions relied upon by B, while all relevant to a local authority's ability to recover charges, were not all part of a unitary regime: s.22 of the 1948 Act specifically conferred the power to determine the amount to be paid by a service user for the provision of accommodation, in the course of which the local authority was empowered by reg.25 of the 1992 Regulations to treat a resident as possessing actual capital of which he had deprived himself for the purpose of decreasing the amount that he might be liable to pay for the accommodation; it could easily be seen that any determination under s.22 was challengeable only by judicial review since a local authority was exercising a function conferred upon it by the 1948 Act, but the charging regime applied only in a question between the local authority and the service user; further, s.21 liability only arose where the transfer had been made while the service user was residing in the accommodation whereas there was no such limitation in respect of reg.25, the issues raised by the provisions were simply not the same. (3) It was not anomalous that a local authority should be able to make a decision which was binding *quoad* the service user but not binding *quoad* the transferee where the aforementioned provisions were not part of one unitary scheme, different tests fell to be applied and the court ought to be the arbiter in relation to a third party's liability to pay for costs incurred by a service user; in any event, any anomaly was for Parliament to resolve. (4) The language used in B's decision letter to G strongly pointed to that decision being one under s.22 of the 1948 Act and amounted to no more than an intention to proceed in terms of s.21: there was no decision which G could have challenged by means of judicial review and she was entitled to defend the action on the basis that the conditions in s.21 had not been satisfied and she had no liability thereunder, *Yule v South Lanarkshire Council (No.2)* 2001 S.C. 203, [2000] C.L.Y. 6693, *distinguished*.

ARGYLL AND BUTE COUNCIL v GORDON, 2016 S.L.T. (Sh Ct) 196, Sheriff P J Braid, Sh Ct (Lothian) (Edinburgh).

2826 Residential accommodation–Means testing–Assessment of resources

THE NATIONAL ASSISTANCE (ASSESSMENT OF RESOURCES) AMENDMENT (SCOTLAND) REGULATIONS 2016, SSI 2016/25; made under the National Assistance Act 1948 s.22(5). In force: 4 April 2016.

These Regulations amend the National Assistance (Assessment of Resources) Regulations 1992 ("the principal Regulations"). The principal Regulations concern the assessment of a person's liability to pay for accommodation provided under the Social Work (Scotland) Act 1968.

2827 Residential accommodation–Ordinary residence–Person lacking capacity–Whether ordinary residence had changed

[Social Work (Scotland) Act 1968 (c.49) s.12, s.86(1); National Assistance Act 1948 (c.29) s.21]

An English local authority (M) petitioned for judicial review of a decision of the Scottish Ministers (S) that a care home patient (R) remained ordinarily resident in M's local authority area. R had formerly lived in her own home in M's local authority area but had been diagnosed with dementia in 2005 and admitted to a care centre (W) in late 2008, and in January 2009, M's finance manager (X) had been appointed as deputy for R's property and affairs. R had been assessed as lacking the capacity to decide where she should live. R's daughter (T), resident in Scotland, had decided that R should live close to her and had identified a local care home (C) as suitable, with M advising her to approach her local authority (E), an interested party in M's petition, in relation to funding. On 29 February 2009, R had been discharged from W and moved into C, where she had lived ever since. On 2 June 2009, T had been appointed deputy for R's property and affairs, replacing X. On 10 July, E had assessed R's needs in accordance with the Social Work (Scotland) Act 1968 s.12 and had concluded that she required residential accommodation with nursing care and had assumed responsibility as authority of the moment for the funding of R's placement, and E had made payments to C since July 2009, with R's home in England being sold in 2010. On 26 March 2015, S had decided, with regard to *R. v Barnet LBC Ex p. Shah* [1983] 2 A.C. 309, [1983] C.L.Y. 1157 and Scottish Government Guidance Circular 3/2010, that notwithstanding that R was living in C, there had been no change of her ordinary residence for the purposes of the s.86(1) of the 1968 Act, accordingly, she remained ordinarily resident in M's local authority area. M submitted that (1) S had applied the wrong legal test in deciding that, in circumstances where the person concerned lacked the requisite capacity, ordinary residence could only change where there had been appointed a welfare guardian or attorney who gave legal authority for a change; all that was required was an assessment of the characteristics of the residence, with its stability being of importance rather than its duration; (2) S had failed to consider the correct periods of residence and had wrongly disregarded the period between 2009 and 2015; (3) S had erred in in their consideration of what constituted a voluntary act by relying on the government circular, which misstated the correct legal position as to the circumstances which ought to be taken into account in that assessment; (4) S had reached a perverse decision where they had failed to give proper weight to factors recognised by them as relevant to the issue of whether R's period of residence in C had been sufficiently settled as to amount to ordinary residence; (5) S's decision had been *ultra vires* where they had considered matters arising from the National Assistance Act 1948 s.21, in respect of which S had no jurisdiction.

Held: Petition refused. (1) The *dictum* of Lord Scarman in *Shah*, remained the leading modern authority on the correct meaning of "ordinary residence", it had neither been overruled nor undermined by the *dicta* in *R. (on the application of Cornwall Council) v Secretary of State for Health* [2015] UKSC 46, [2016] A.C. 137, [2015] C.L.Y. 2394, which concluded that the two tests identified in *R. v Waltham Forest LBC Ex p. Vale* Times, February 25, 1985, [1985] C.L.Y. 2165, were not separable but complimentary approaches to the test in *Shah*; the determination of whether there had been a change in ordinary residence necessarily had to involve an assessment of the extent to which any adoption of a particular abode had been voluntary and such an assessment necessarily involved a consideration of the nature of such legal authority as there was in place, which was consistent with the legal framework in place in Scotland to protect the interests of those lacking full capacity, therefore, the Scottish Government Circular set out a correct statement of the law in that regard, and it had been appropriate for S to follow its guidance. In such circumstances, the issues surrounding what constituted the correct test and what constituted voluntary actings, were closely connected, and to a considerable extent intertwined, and S had applied the correct test in reaching their decision. (2) Given R's lack of mental capacity, the absence of T's legal authority to make decisions regarding R's personal welfare was fatal to any prospect of a finding that, notwithstanding the duration of R's presence in Scotland, there had been a change of her ordinary residence from M's local authority area to E's. (3) S had been correct in their consideration of whether R's actings had had the necessary voluntary character; the *Shah* test could never be met as the result of the failure to meet the requirement for voluntary adoption of a different abode, any question as to which period of residence ought to have been taken into account for the purposes of determining whether the nature of R's presence in E's local authority area had the relevant attributes of residence, was consequentially immaterial to the decision; S's determination, having proceeded on a correct basis and according to law, could not be said to be perverse in the legal sense, *Shah*, *Cornwall* and *Vale*, *considered*. (4) The relevant parts of S's determination addressing s.21 of the 1948 Act were *obiter*, in any event, where S had applied the correct test and the lack of appropriate legal authority was determinative, that issue was immaterial. (5) S's determination was legitimate, transparent, consistent with the guidance of the Scottish government as set out in the circular, and made according to law, and was not inconsistent with legal authority, perverse or unreasonable, S had not acted *ultra vires*, had taken into account all material considerations, and had not taken into account immaterial considerations.

MILTON KEYNES COUNCIL v SCOTTISH MINISTERS, [2015] CSOH 156, 2015 S.L.T. 843, Lord Armstrong, OH.

2828 **Residential accommodation–Social work–Fees**

THE NATIONAL ASSISTANCE (SUMS FOR PERSONAL REQUIREMENTS) (SCOTLAND) REGULATIONS 2016, SSI 2016/23; made under the National Assistance Act 1948 s.22(4). In force: 4 April 2016.

These Regulations prescribe the sum for accommodation provided under the Social Work (Scotland) Act 1968 as £25.80 per week from 4 April 2016.

TAX

2829 Income tax–Employee benefit trusts–Payments by taxpayer companies to employees under remuneration trust–Liability to income tax and national insurance contributions

[Income Tax (Earnings and Pensions) Act 2003 (c.1) s.6, s.62; Act of Sederunt (Rules of the Court of Session 1994) 1994 Sch.2 Pt 3 para.41.57; Tribunals, Courts and Enforcement Act 2007 (c.15) s.13]

The Advocate General for Scotland (S), representing Her Majesty's Revenue and Customs (H), appealed against a decision of the Upper Tribunal (U) refusing an appeal against a majority decision of the First-tier Tribunal (F) to uphold an appeal by a group of companies (M) against assessments by H to income tax under the PAYE system and corresponding National Insurance contributions (NICs). The fifth respondents (R) were the only party opposing the appeal, the other respondents being in liquidation, and it was agreed that any decision on the income tax issue would be equally applicable to NICs. One of M had set up a principal trust to which another company in the group, who wished to benefit one of its employees, made a cash payment in respect of that employee. The paying company recommended the trustee of the principal trust to resettle the sum on to a subtrust, and would ask that the income and capital thereof be applied in accordance with the employee's wishes. The employee would be appointed protector of the subtrust and the trustee of the subtrust would lend the employee the money that had been advanced to the subtrust from, ultimately, his employer. F held that the trustee of the principal trust had a genuine discretion as to how to apply the funds advanced to it, and the settlement on to the subtrust merely represented the exercise thereof thus the benefit enjoyed by the employee resulted from the exercise of a discretionary power by the trustee of the subtrust and such a payment was not a payment of emolument or earnings, and was therefore not subject to income tax. S argued that the cash payment made by the employing company to the trustee of the principal trust was in consideration of services by the employee and had thus been earned by the latter, and even if that employee had instructed payment to another, he was still obliged to pay income tax and NICs thereon where the monies had simply been misdirected; alternatively, the employee as protector could exercise his powers in such a way that the whole of the funds in his subtrust were paid to him, bringing the principle in *WT Ramsay Ltd v Inland Revenue Commissioners* [1982] A.C. 300, [1981] C.L.Y. 1385 into operation with the result that the amount paid into the subtrust was treated as at the absolute disposal of the employee and hence part of his emoluments or earnings.

Held: Appeal allowed. (1) The scheme involving payments to the various trusts and the application of the monies so paid amounted to a mere redirection of earnings which did not remove the liability of employees to income tax: the charge to income tax under the Income Tax (Earnings and Pensions) Act 2003 s.6, was a tax on earnings from employment, as defined by s.62, and the critical feature of an emolument and of earnings so defined was that it represented the product of the employee's work, namely, his personal exertion in the course of his employment: the fundamental principle that emerged from the authorities was that if income was derived from an employee's services *qua* employer, it was an emolument or earnings, and was thus assessable to income tax even if the employee requested, or agreed, that it be redirected to a third party; the principle was ultimately simple and straightforward which could easily be overlooked where elaborate trusts or analogous relationships were set up such as in the present case. (2) In assessing the liability of a transaction to taxation, it was imperative to determine the true nature of the transaction, viewed realistically, and in the present case, it was thus essential to have regard to the true nature of the individual transactions involving the principal trust, particular employees and the subtrusts set up in respect of each employee: (i) in relation to employees other than footballers, the critical element was that bonuses were paid on the basis of the work performance of the employee in question, *qua* employee, and the profitability of his employing company and the bonus amount was determined by reference to the employee's employment activity and while they were discretionary, they were obviously derived from, and based on, the work done by the particular employee on which basis the sums received by the trustee of the principal trust and, in due course by the trustees of the subtrusts, amounted to a redirection of income and thus constituted emoluments or earnings of the employees in question; (ii) in relation to footballers, where a contract of employment was concluded, an additional side letter provided for a discretionary trust payment and it appeared self evident that the obligations contained therein were part of the employee's employment package and provided him with additional remuneration, the amount of any bonus was typically negotiated with the footballer's agent which fact was itself decisive in so far as, once it was accepted that the bonus payments represented consideration for a footballer's services *qua* employee, it inevitably followed that said payments represented emoluments or earnings. (3) The redirection of earnings occurred at the point where the employer paid a sum to the trustee of the principal trust, what happened to the monies thereafter had no bearing on the liability that arose in consequence thereof; whatever happened, the sums paid to the trustees were redirected from income which was sufficient to render them liable to income tax in the ordinary way; the critical point when it could be said that an emolument or earnings had been paid was when the employer made a payment either directly to the employee or in a manner which had been requested, or acquiesced in, by the employee which, in the present case, was at the time of payment to the trustee of the principal trust with the result that the obligation to deduct tax under the PAYE system fell to the employer who made such a payment, *Hadlee and Sydney Bridge Nominees v Inland Revenue Commissioners* [1993] A.C. 524, [1993] C.L.Y. 3018, *applied*. (4) On S's alternative argument, the critical question was whether each employee had practical control over the disposal of the funds placed either in the principal trust or in the relevant subtrusts, the test was not one of absolute right, and it was critical to S's argument that an employee *qua* protector should have control over the disposal of funds held in trust, so that he could determine how they should be applied and, if necessary, alter the trust purposes so that he was the sole beneficiary: in the present case, the duties of a protector would be fiduciary in every case where there was no express declaration to the contrary and to the extent that the position of the protector was fiduciary, removing the existing beneficiaries and appointing himself in their place would amount to a clear breach of fiduciary duty; in any event, such an appointment would be subject to limitations on the power of the protector to amend the trust deed, which prevented the alteration of the fundamental declaration of trust, including the definition of the beneficiaries in that declaration; and the general defences which were available to a breach of fiduciary duty, namely consent by the beneficiaries of the fiduciary relationships and the appointment of the protector was in such terms as to override all fiduciary duties, did not apply, with the result that the argument had to fail. *Observed*, (1) that in a statutory appeal of the present nature, it was competent for the court to entertain a ground of appeal that had not been argued before F or U although it should be slow to do so where additional findings of fact were required, and should not do so if unfairness resulted; (2) that in accordance with the Act of Sederunt (Rules of the Court of Session 1994) 1994 Sch.2 Pt 3 para.41.57, leave to appeal would only be given in a case which raised an important point of principle or practice or where there was some other compelling reason for the court to hear an appeal and the redirection of earnings principle was of wide potential application and the circumstances in which it might apply required to be determined; (3) that the present appeal proceeded under the Tribunals, Courts and Enforcement Act 2007 s.13: the right of appeal was on a point of law and did not extend to the facts; F's findings were generally binding; (4) that an appeal on a point of law covered four different categories of cases, namely appeals on the general law, appeals on the application of the law as to the facts as found by F, appeals where the tribunal had made a finding for which there was no evidence or which was inconsistent with the evidence and contradictory of it, and cases where the tribunal had made a fundamental error in its approach to the case; the issues in the present case were the scope of the redirection of earnings principle and its application to the particular facts of the case, and the application of the *Ramsay* principle by reference to the powers of a protector of a trust, said issues raised clear questions of law and to the extent that legal principles had been misapplied, the court could, and had to, interfere with F's decision, *WT Ramsey Ltd*, *considered*; (5)

that proceedings had been initiated before F and an appeal heard before U, both of which had UK wide jurisdiction and had judicial knowledge of English law and the Court of Session had to be taken to have the same knowledge.

MURRAY GROUP HOLDINGS LTD v REVENUE AND CUSTOMS COMMISSIONERS *sub nom.* REVENUE AND CUSTOMS COMMISSIONERS v MURRAY GROUP HOLDINGS LTD; ADVOCATE GENERAL FOR SCOTLAND v MURRAY GROUP HOLDINGS LTD, [2015] CSIH 77, [2016] S.T.C. 468, The Lord Justice Clerk (Carloway), Lord Menzies, Lord Drummond Young, IH (2 Div).

2830 Scottish Fiscal Commission Act 2016 (asp 17)

An Act of the Scottish Parliament to establish the Scottish Fiscal Commission and to provide for its functions.

2831 Scottish Fiscal Commission Act 2016 (asp 17)–Commencement and Transitory Provision Regulations

THE SCOTTISH FISCAL COMMISSION ACT 2016 (COMMENCEMENT AND TRANSITORY PROVISION) REGULATIONS 2016, SSI 2016/326; made under the Scottish Fiscal Commission Act 2016 s.31(2)(3). Commencement details: bringing into operation various provisions of the Scottish Fiscal Commission Act 2016 on 9 November 2016.

These Regulations commence provisions of the Scottish Fiscal Commission Act 2016. In terms of reg.2 of the Regulations, s.8 of the Act is commenced on 9 November 2016 with the remaining provisions insofar as not yet in force commenced on 1 April 2017. Regulation 3 is a transitory provision allowing the Scottish Ministers' duty to consult the Scottish Fiscal Commission on making regulations to amend the Act to be discharged until 1 April 2017 by the Scottish Ministers consulting the non-statutory Scottish Fiscal Commission.

TORTS

2832 Tortious liability–Health and safety offences–Leisure operator convicted of health and safety offence–Victim's family seeking summary decree in action of damages

[Health and Safety at Work etc. Act 1974 (c.37) s.3; Law Reform (Miscellaneous Provisions) (Scotland) Act 1968 (c.70) s.10(1), s.10(2)]

The family (F) of a deceased child (X) moved for summary decree in their action of damages against the operators (R) of the Highland Show. X had been killed when a bollard within R's car park had fallen and struck him on the head. Following the incident, R had been convicted of a breach of the Health and Safety at Work etc. Act 1974 and F sought summary decree on the basis that the danger posed by the bollards had been obvious, and, as a fall back, R's conviction under s.3 of the 1974 Act, with reference to the Law Reform (Miscellaneous Provisions) (Scotland) Act 1968 s.10(1), notwithstanding that they had neither made reference to R's conviction in their pleadings nor intended to do so. R averred *inter alia* that should F choose to rely on s.10(1), it intended to rely on s.10(2), and further that the bollards had been used for many years and there had not been any issue or prior problem such as to instruct any knowledge on its part or from which any obvious danger might be inferred.

Held: Motion refused. (1) In light of R's averments regarding the use of the bollards without incident for many years, and in the absence of any other information, the characterisation of the risk they posed as obvious fell to be rejected for the purpose of F's motion. (2) The requisite identity of issues as between R's conviction and the bases of liability in the current proceedings had not been established, and was there an identity of issue such as to bring s.10(1) into play, R intended to invoke s.10(2) to demonstrate that it had not committed the offence. (3) Section 10(1) of the 1968 Act allowed parties to rely to advantage on a conviction as it reversed the onus onto the convicted party and, absent that onus being discharged, the subject of that conviction was taken as proved, however, there was a concomitant right afforded to the convicted party to attempt to rebut that onus and the scope thereof ought to be commensurate with the whole subject matter of the conviction, and s.10(2) had no qualification directed thereto. (4) R had raised certain issues in its pleadings which, if proved, would afford it a defence to the current action, which was sufficient for the purposes of meeting a motion for summary decree.

HALL-CRAGGS v ROYAL HIGHLAND AND AGRICULTURAL SOCIETY OF SCOTLAND, [2016] CSOH 8, 2016 S.L.T. 311, Lady Wolffe, OH.

TRUSTS

2833 Deeds–Rectification–Rectification of deed of appointment to delay its effect–Deed validly created legal right intended

[Law Reform (Miscellaneous Provisions) (Scotland) Act 1985 (c.73) s.8, s.8(1)(b); Inheritance Tax Act 1984 (c.51); Finance Act 2008 (c.9)]

Trustees (T) of a nil rate band discretionary trust (X) created in terms of a will by the wife (W) of one of T (H) petitioned for rectification of a deed of appointment in terms of the Law Reform (Miscellaneous Provisions) (Scotland) Act 1985 s.8. X had been created to use up W's nil rate band tax allowance on her death, thereby reducing the impact of inheritance tax on her estate. Following the changes to the Inheritance Inheritance Tax Act 1984 by the Finance Act 2008, it became possible to transfer unused tax allowance to a surviving spouse and following W's death on 2 September 2012, on 20 and 25 October 2012, T granted the deed of appointment to dismantle X, however, following *Frankland v Inland Revenue Commissioners* [1997] S.T.C. 1450, [1998] C.L.Y. 4687, X had required to be dismantled within a period commencing no earlier than three months after W's death to obtain the benefit of s.144 of the 1984 Act, accordingly, W's nil rate band would only be available to H's estate where the deed of appointment had taken effect no earlier than three months after her death. T sought addition of the words "such appointment to come into effect only on 5 December 2012 (and not before then)".

Held: Petition refused. (1) T's intention had been to wind up X in such a manner as would permit W's executors to take advantage of any unused portion of her nil rate band and had T been aware of *Frankland*, they would have allowed a period of three months from W's death to elapse before signing the deed. (2) The deed of appointment had as its purpose the appointment of the trust fund to H, and had intended to create a right in his favour, therefore, the deed was a unilateral deed, not an agreement, and the relevant provision for the purposes of the application was s.8(1)(b) of the 1985 Act, *Bank of Scotland v Graham's Trustee* 1992 S.C. 79, [1993] C.L.Y. 5364, *considered.* (3) The deed of appointment had been utilised to achieve a wider purpose for which X had required to be wound up, that legal result had been achieved by the deed of appointment but the wider purpose had not been achieved due to the application of a different legal rule, and s.8(1)(b) did not permit the court to change a deed of appointment which had validly created the legal right intended so as to delay its effect to take account of an entirely separate legal rule; the deed of appointment had accurately expressed T's intention when it was executed, and the fact that in bringing about their intended legal result T had fallen into the *Frankland* trap, and had failed to achieve their underlying purpose, was a different matter and not within the scope of rectification, *Frankland, considered.*

NICKSON'S TRUSTEES, PETITIONERS, [2016] CSOH 119, 2016 S.L.T. 1039, Lord Turnbull, OH.

VAT

2834 VAT groups–Repayments–Claim made by wholly owned subsidiary of representative member of VAT group

[Value Added Tax Act 1994 (c.23) s.43, s.80]

A trading company (T) appealed against a decision of the Upper Tribunal (Tax and Chancery Chamber) (U) rejecting its appeal against a decision of the First-tier Tribunal (F) rejecting its appeal against assessments by the Commissioners for Her Majesty's Revenue and Customs (H) on T for the repayment of VAT and interest (*Taylor Clark Leisure Plc v Revenue and Customs Commissioners* [2014] UKUT 396 (TCC), [2015] S.T.C. 223, [2014] C.L.Y. 3097). T and its subsidiaries were members of a VAT group (V). In 1990, T transferred certain of its businesses and assets to a wholly owned subsidiary (C) with effect from 1 April 1990. C was a member of V between 1990 and 1998, and between 1973 and 2009, T was the representative member of V. On 16 November 2007, C had submitted four claims to H in respect of VAT allegedly overpaid from 1973 to 1998, which H had rejected and C had appealed to F. On 27 April 2009, H had sent T a notice of voluntary disclosure stating that it was due £667,069 in respect of overpaid VAT and that the foregoing sum and interest of £663,300 was to be repaid to it. On 7 July, H had made assessments on T for repayment of the VAT and interest that had been repaid to it. On 14 September, T had sought review thereof and on 4 May 2010, had sought repayment of the VAT that had formed the subject of C's claims, all of T's claims being made after the expiry of the time limit on 31 March 2009. H had rejected T's claims on 23 September 2010, reversing its earlier decision and confirming that of 7 July 2009, which T had appealed to F on 28 February 2011. On 14 April, T had asserted that it was entitled to repayment of the claims, which H had rejected on 4 May and T had appealed to F. On 19 December 2012, F had rejected both of T's appeals, by which time C had withdrawn its appeals, and T had appealed F's decision to U, which had been rejected on 8 September 2014. The issue that arose, where the only timeous claim for repayment had been made by C, not by T itself, was whether V, embodied in T as representative member, could rely on those claims for the repayment of VAT overpaid by V where the claims had been made timeously but by a member other than T.

Held: Appeal allowed. (1) With regard to the Value Added Tax Act 1994 s.43, all rights, obligations, powers and liabilities in relation to VAT were, as far as H was concerned, those of the representative member and no other, subject to the joint and several liability imposed by the final part of s.43(1) for any VAT due from the representative member. (2) C's claims had to be construed as having been made on behalf of V, embodied in T as the representative member; reading s.80 of the 1994 Act together with s.43 *et seq*, in the case of a VAT group, "person" in s.80 was the representative member of that group, moreover, under the scheme of s.43, the representative member alone had the interest in making a VAT claim, nevertheless, the claim did not require to be advanced by the representative member itself, for VAT purposes, the VAT group was treated as a quasi-persona and the representative member was merely the embodiment thereof, having a personality in domestic law, thus the agent was acting for a principal that had a form of legal personality for VAT purposes, to hold that the person acting for the VAT group was not itself a member of that group other than the representative member would involve unwarranted formalism, further, s.80 made no suggestion that an individual member could not make a claim on behalf of the group as embodied in its representative member. (3) In the context of s.43, a claim for repayment or crediting of tax by an individual member of a VAT group had normally to be construed as a claim made on behalf of the representative member as embodying the group, otherwise the claim would have no meaning; s.43 made clear that the claim could not be made by the individual member in its own right and repayment could not be made thereto, consequently, a literal interpretation of such a claim was inconsistent with the scheme of the legislation and the claim required to be construed purposively; it was clearly designed to secure repayment of VAT paid as a result of the trading activities of a member of a VAT group and the obvious import was that the claim ought to proceed in the name of the representative member of the VAT group. (4) C's claims had to be regarded as having been made on behalf of, or as agent for, T as representative member of V; C had been a member of V for a substantial part of the period to which the claim related, it had had no independent existence for VAT purposes during that period, and its actions were attributed, for VAT purposes, to T as representative member of V, thus it could not make a claim on its own behalf but only on T's behalf as V's representative. (5) Although the claims extended to periods before C had been incorporated and had joined V, that did not matter provided that V existed at the relevant time as the claim was properly made on V's behalf. (6) The identity of a claimant was not a straightforward issue of fact, the identity of a claimant for the purposes of s.80 of the 1994 Act involved the application of a legal test to the facts, which type of exercise was properly the subject of reconsideration by an appellate court. (7) The concept of the single taxable person had no application beyond the incidence of VAT as between H and the taxpayer, nevertheless, the concept required to be applied consistently in relation to the incidence of VAT, and in interpreting a s.80 claim, regard had to be had to the existence of the VAT group as a single taxable person and the representative member as embodying the group, and H would not face any insuperable difficulties in the court's analysis. (8) C's claims had to properly be regarded as claims made by T as V's representative member, thus T's claims were not out of time.

TAYLOR CLARK LEISURE PLC v REVENUE AND CUSTOMS COMMISSIONERS, [2016] CSIH 54, 2016 S.L.T. 873, Lord Menzies, Lady Smith, Lord Drummond Young, IH (Ex Div).

WATER LAW

2835 Water Resources (Scotland) Act 2013 (asp 5)–Commencement No.4 Order

THE WATER RESOURCES (SCOTLAND) ACT 2013 (COMMENCEMENT NO.4) ORDER 2016, SSI 2016/327; made under the Water Resources (Scotland) Act 2013 s.56(2). Commencement details: bringing into operation various provisions of the Water Resources (Scotland) Act 2013 on 1 January 2017.

This Order brings into force, on 1 January 2017, s.33 (which makes provision in relation to notification of occupancy) of the Water Resources (Scotland) Act 2013. The Bill for the Act received Royal Assent on 9 April 2013. Section 56 of the Act brought into force Pt. 8 (except s.53 and sch.4) on the day after Royal Assent.

WORDS AND PHRASES JUDICIALLY CONSIDERED

The table below is a cumulative guide to words and phrases judicially considered in 2016

(N) denotes an entry in the Northern Ireland section and (S) denotes an entry in the Scottish section.

INDEX

"NI" denotes an entry in the Northern Ireland section and "S" denotes an entry in the Scottish section.